A Concordance to

The English Poetry of Richard Crashaw

For Gil

A Concordance to

The English Poetry of Richard Crashaw

compiled by

Robert M. Cooper

Computer Programs by

Sundaram Swetharanyam

The Whitston Publishing Company
Troy, New York
1981

Copyright 1980
Robert M. Cooper

Library of Congress Catalog Card Number 80-51219

ISBN 0-87875-188-2

Printed in the United States of America

Acknowledgments

*The Poems, English, Latin, and Greek, of Richard Crashaw*, edited by L. C. Martin (Oxford English Texts: 2nd ed. © Oxford University Press, 1957) is used by permission of Oxford University Press. *The Complete Poetry of Richard Crashaw*, edited by George Walton Williams (copyright © 1970 by Doubleday & Company, Inc.) is used by permission of Doubleday & Company, Inc. We are grateful to McNeese State University for the funding that made this project possible.

## Preface

The following concordance to the English poetry of Richard Crashaw is based on the second Oxford edition of L. C. Martin, but is also cross-referenced in order to include the Anchor edition by George Walton Williams (and the New York University Press and Norton Reprints of that text). The order of presentation is as follows: key word, complete line, title or short title, line number, date of the poem in Martin, page number in Martin, the page number in Williams.

The poems by Cowley and Car have been omitted, as have those labeled as probably spurious by Martin and subsequently omitted by Williams. Poems printed twice in Martin are included twice in the concordance. No footnote variants found in Martin are included. Refrains have been printed only once. Some obvious minor misprints have been corrected. "Which" has been substituted for "wch" in all cases. The prose portions of "Office of the Holy Cross" have been omitted. All poems have been assigned line counts. The IBM 1130 punctuates in period and comma form. Therefore, periods are used for all punctuation except commas.

An effort has been made to aid the reader in cross-checking variant spellings and in locating hyphenated words: the concordance was programmed twice to produce its final form, once to put the words in alphabetical order and once to group variant spellings and to cross-reference hyphenated words. Where two or more spellings occur, they are listed under the modern form; where no modern form occurs among variant spellings, alphabetical order is maintained.

**Contents**

v    Preface

vii    Words Omitted

ix    Words Included

1    Concordance Analysis

## WORDS OMITTED

| | | |
|---|---|---|
| a | each | my |
| about | erst | no |
| above | etc. | nor |
| after | for | not |
| again | from | now |
| against | get | o |
| ah | getting | of |
| alike | got | off |
| almost | had | oh |
| along | has | on |
| although | hast | or |
| among | hath | our |
| am | have | ours |
| and | having | out |
| an | he | over |
| are | her | shall |
| as | here | she |
| at | hereafter | should |
| be | him | so |
| because | himself | such |
| been | his | that |
| before | hither | the |
| but | how | thee |
| by | howsoe're | their |
| can | if | them |
| cannot | in | themselves |
| cause | into | then |
| could | is | there |
| did | it | therefore |
| do | its | therein |
| does | itself | these |
| done | may | they |
| doth | mr. | this |
| | | those |

| | | |
|---|---|---|
| though | we | whither |
| thou | well | will (verb) |
| thus | were | withall |
| thy | what | who |
| tis | whatever | whom |
| tither | when | whose |
| to | whence | why |
| too | where | with |
| under | wherever | would |
| until | wherein | yet |
| unto | whereof | ye |
| upon | wheresoever | you |
| up | which | your |
| us | while | yours |
| was | | |

## WORDS INCLUDED

abased
abash
abashed
abhorred
abode
aboad
abominable
abortive
abroad
th'absence
absent
absolute
abstinence
abundance
well-abused
abysse
accents
accord
account
acknowledg'd
acknowledging
acquaintance
acquainted
action
active
activ'st
actor
adamant
adamantine
adds
addes
adieu
adeiu
adoe

admirable
admire
admired
adore
adored
all-adored
adoring
adorne
adorning
adulterates
adulterous
adult'rous
advance
advis'd
aeacus
aelia
aeol
aeolus
aeriall
aiereall
aery
aiery
affect
afford
affords
affright
affrighted
afraid
africk-brood
age
aged
ages
agree
air

aire
th'aire
ayre
aires
ayres
alablaster
alarmes
alas
alcaeus
alecto
alecto's
alexis
alexis'
alive
all
world—all
all-adored
all-chearing
all-circling
all-composing
all-daring
all-embracing
all-imbracing
all-idolizing
all-obedient
all-soveraign
all-unblemish't
all-unwrinkled
all's
al
allay
alleage
allow
allow'd

allowes
allude
almes
almighty
allmighty
aloft
alone
aloofe
aloud
already
allready
altar
altar-stall'd
altars
alternate
amaine
amazed
amaz'd
amazement
th'amazing
amber-weeping
ambition
ambitious
ambrosiall
ambush
amidst
amorous
amorouse
ample
ampliate
amply
angell
angell-blinding
angell-imps
angels
angells
anger
angry
annals
annext
annihilations
anon

another
answer
answered
answer'd
answering
ant
anthem
anthems
anthony
antidote
antidotes
anvills
any
apart
ape
apes
apollo
vice-apollo
apollo's
appollo
appollo's
apology
appeal
appeale
appear
appear'd
appeare
appeares
appearance
soul-appeasing
appetites
applaud
applause
apply
apply'd
approach
aprobation
april
april-autumne
april's
aprils
apron

arabia
arabias
archerie
arches
architects
architecture
areopagite
argus
arise
arme
armefull
arm-full
arm'd
armes
armory
armour
arrive
arrow
arrowes
art (noun)
th'art
arts
artists
arteries
arteryes
artfull
artificer
artificiall
artillery
asham'd
ashes
aside
ask
askt
aske
asks
askes
asleep
asleepe
aspect
aspects
aspire
assay

## Words Included

| | | |
|---|---|---|
| asse | baalams | bargain |
| assist | babe | bargain'd |
| assumption | babe's | barke |
| assures | babes | barren |
| assyrian | babels | barres |
| th'astonish'd | back | barrs |
| astonisht | backe | base |
| th'astonisht | backs | basely |
| astray | bad | bashfull |
| astrology | badg | bate |
| astronomie | bait | bath |
| athens | baited | bath'd |
| atlas | baite | baths |
| atome | bak't | bathes |
| atreus | ballance | bathing |
| attempts | balles | bayes |
| attend | balm | bead |
| attended | balme | beam |
| attending | balmy | broad-beam'd |
| the'attending | baulmy | beame |
| attention | balsame | beames |
| augment | balsame-sweating | bear |
| aurora | balsom-sweating | beare |
| aurora's | balsom | beares |
| auroras | balsome | day-bearing |
| auspicious | band | beard |
| auspitious | bands | beast |
| auster | bandied | beasts |
| authority | banishment | beat |
| autumn | banish't | beate |
| april-autumne | bankes | beaten |
| avant | banne | beats |
| ave | banquett | beates |
| awake | baptism | beauteous |
| awak't | baptisme | beauteously |
| awakes | baptis'd | beauties |
| away | barbabbas | beautifull |
| awe | barbarous | beauty |
| awfull | barborous | beauty's |
| awry | barbill | beautyes |
| ayme | bare | becken'd |
| high-aym'd | barennesse | become |
| azure | | |

| | | |
|---|---|---|
| bed | bequeath | bind |
| marriage-bed | bereave | binding |
| bedd | beseem | bird |
| beds | beseeming | birds |
| bedds | well-beseeming | birth |
| sweat-bedewed | beseige | birthe |
| bedrid | beseig'd | births |
| beere | heav'n-besieged | virgin-births |
| bees | besett | birthright |
| began | besides | bitt |
| begin | bespeake | bitter |
| beginne | best | black |
| beguile | bestow | black-fac'd |
| beguilest | bethlem | coleblack |
| beguil'd | beth'lem | blacke |
| beguil | betimes | blackest |
| beguiles | betray'd | blank |
| beguiling | betraid | blanke |
| begun | betrai'd | blast |
| beheld | betroth | blasted |
| behind | better | blaze |
| behold | betwixt | blaz'd |
| beholden | twixt | blazing |
| beholders | 'twixt | bled |
| being | 'twist | bleed |
| beeing | twixt's | bleeding |
| belches | t'wixt | blended |
| belch'd | beyond | blends |
| believing | be-spilt | blesse |
| beleeving | bid | blessed |
| beleeve | bids | blesses |
| beleeves | biddes | blessings |
| beleive | bidds | blest |
| bellow'd | bide | well-bles't |
| belong | biding | blew |
| belongs | big | blew-ey'd |
| beloved | big-nam'd | blind |
| bend | bigg | blind-fold |
| bending | bigg-named | blinded |
| beneath | bigge | blinding |
| benign | bill | angell-blinding |
| bent | bills | blindnes |

## Words Included

| | | |
|---|---|---|
| blindnesse | blushes | borrowed |
| blisfull | blushing | borow'd |
| blissefull | ever-blushing | borrowes |
| blissfull | blusht | borrowing |
| blisse | board | bosome |
| blisses | bord | bosome's |
| blith | boast | bosom'd |
| blood | boasts | bosom |
| heart-blood | bodies | bosomes |
| blood-revolving | bodyes | both |
| blood-shot | body | bottles |
| bloodshott | body's | botome |
| blood-swolne | boile | bottomles |
| blood's | boyles | bottomlesse |
| bloud | boyl'd | bough |
| bloods | bold | bought |
| bloody | bolder | dear-bought |
| bloomes | boldly | overbought |
| full-bloom'd | bolts | bound |
| new-bloom'd | magick-bolts | frost-bount |
| blooming | bones | bounds |
| bloomy | book | boundles |
| blossom | booke | boundlesse |
| blossom'd | fortune-booke | bounteous |
| blossome | books | bounty |
| blossoms | bookes | bountyes |
| blossomes | bootes | bountyfull |
| maiden-blossomes | bore | bow |
| blot | borean | bow'd |
| blott | born | bowes |
| blots | first-born | bowels |
| blow | highborn | bowells |
| blowes | high-born | bowles |
| blown | new-born | bower |
| blowne | borne | bowers |
| bloune | first-borne | boxe |
| blubber'd | heav'ne-borne | boy |
| blubb'ring | high-borne | boyes |
| blunt | new-borne | boysterous |
| blurre | sun-borne | bracelet |
| blush | borrow | brag |
| blush'd | borrowd | bragge |

brags
brain
braine
braines
braynes
branch
branches
brand
brands
brandishing
ever-brandisht
brasen
brasse
brave
bravely
braver
braves
bravery
breach
bread
break
day-break
breake
breaks
breakes
breakfast
breast
brest
breasted
flaming-brested
breasts
brests
brest's
breath
sulphur-breathed
breath'd
sweet-breath'd
breath's
breaths
breathes
breathing
life-breathing

th'heart-bred
bredd
breed
bridall
bride
brides
bridegroom
bridegroom's
bridegrome
bridegroome
briefe
bright
too-bright
brighter
brightest
brightnesse
brim
brim-fill'd
brims
bring
brings
bringing
brisk
briske
brittaine
broach
broad-beam'd
broke
broken
brood
africk-brood
broodeth
brooding
brooke
brother
yonger-brother
brothers
brought
broughtst
brow
browes
brush

bubbles
bubling
ever-bubling
bud
buds
budds
build
builds
built
high-built
bulke
burden
burthen
heaven-burthen'd
buried
buryed
burye'd
burn
burne
burnes
burning
burnt
sun-burnt
sun-burn't
burnish
burnisht
burst
busy
busie
businesse
busynes
busiris
buxome
buy
buzzing
cabinet
cabinets
cadence
caelestiall
caesar
caesar's
cesar

## Words Included xv

caesars
cages
calculate
caldron-prison'd
call
called
calld
call'd
cal'd
calls't
calls
calm
came
cams't
campanion
cancell'd
candid
candidates
canopy
capacious
capacity
capacitye
capers
capring
captive
captiv'd
captivity
self-captivity
selfe-captivity
carcasse
care
care's
cares
carelesly
carelesse
carry
carryed
carv'd
carves
casements
caskets
cast

casts
cataracts
catch
catche
cates
caucasus
caught
cauldron
causes
caution
cavernes
caves
cease
cecilia
cell
cells
cellars
center
centring
cerberus
certain
certaine
certainty
chaine
challenge
challenges
chambers
chance
change
changd
chang'd
much-chang'd
channell
channels
channells
chant
chaunt
chaos
chappell
character
characters
charge

charg'd
charges
chariclia
chariot
charitie
charities
charles
charme
charmes
chase
chases
chaste
chast
chastest
chastis'd
chastity
chatting
chatt'ring
cheap
cheape
cheat
cheated
cheat'st
cheating
cheek
cheekt
fair-cheek't
cheeke
cheeks
cheekes
cheere
chear
all-chearing
cheerfull
cheerefull
cheerefullnesse
cheerfully
cherish
cherisht
cherry
cherryes
cherub

| | | |
|---|---|---|
| chest | circling | cloudes |
| chide | all-circling | clowds |
| chidde | circular | cloudy |
| chid | circumcising | clowdy |
| chidd | clad | clouts |
| chides | claim | cloying |
| chiefly | clapt | clusters |
| child | clasp't | coates |
| childe | clause | coheirs |
| childrens | clawes | colchos |
| children's | clay | cold |
| chill | clay-cottage | coleblack |
| chills | clean | colors |
| chirps | cleane | colours |
| choake | cleanly | high-colour'd |
| choakt | clear | combine |
| choak't | cleere | combin'd |
| choice | cleare | come |
| choise | clearer | come—into |
| choyce | climb | com'st |
| choicer | climbe | comes |
| choicest | clombe | comming |
| choycest | climbs | comet |
| choose | climbes | comets |
| chuse | clime | comfort |
| chusing | cling | comforts |
| chorister | clings | comly |
| chorus | cloath | command |
| christ | cloth | commanding |
| christ's | cloathed | commands |
| christs | well-cloth'd | commend |
| christian | clothes | commerce |
| chronologie | cloathes | common |
| church | close | common-people |
| th'church | closely | compacted |
| churches | closer | company |
| churlish | closes | comparison |
| chymick | closet | comparrison |
| cinnamon | clotted | compell |
| circe | cloud | compell'd |
| circle | clowd | compendious |
| circled | clouds | compile |

## Words Included

complain
complin
complaine
complayne
complaines
complaining
composes
all-composing
composition
composure
composures
computes
conceal'd
conceited
conceive
conceptions
concerning
concurrences
condensed
condition
conduct
joy-conducted
confederate
confederat
confess't
confes't
confesse
confesses
confessing
confessours
confidently
confines
confluence
confound
confusion
confute
confuting
conquer
conquering
conquests
conscience
conscious

consecrate
consecrated
consent
conserved
consider
consistent
consort
conspicuous
conspiracy
conspire
conspir'd
conspiring
constancy
constant
constellation
consult
consults
consume
consumption
contempt
contend
contending
content
contented
contentfull
contest
contract
contracts
contrarietyes
contrary
contrite
control'd
controll
controul
controules
controwlls
controverted
controverting
convenant
convene
converts
convey'd

convictors
coole
cools
cooles
cooperates
copy
coppy
coppie
corall
corrallize
cordiall
corner
corners
correspondent
cost
coste
costly
costlyer
clay-cottage
couch
couch'd
coucht
couch't
couches
cough
cought
counsaile
counsell
counsails
counsellours
counted
countenance
counter
counterfeit
countershine
countries
country-man
courage
course
court
court-fed
courted

courts
courteous
covenant
cover
cover'd
covers
covert
cow
cowardise
cowardly
coy
coyly
coynesse
crack
cradle
cradle-torments
craft
crafty
crave
crav'd
crawled
crawles
crawling
cream
creame
creation
creator
creature
creatures
credit
creep
creepe
creeps
crest
crested
crime
crimson
crisped
crooked
crop
croppe
crosse

crost
crowd
crown
crown-land
crown-lands
crownd
crown'd
love-crowned
silver-crowned
crowne
crowns
crownes
olive-crownes
crucifix
crucify
cruell
cruelty
crueltie
crumbled
crumme
crush
crusht
crush't
cry
cryd'st
cry'd
cryes
crying
crystall
christall
chrystall
cup
cure
curious
curld
curl'd
curle
curles
currents
curse
cursed
curst

curtains
curtain'd
curtaines
curteous
curtesy
short-cut
cuts
cutts
cyclopses
cymballs
cynthia
cynthia's
cypresse
cytherea
daintiest
dainty
dallying
damp't
damps
dance
dancing
dandle
danger
dangers
dangled
dare
dar'st
dares
daring
all-daring
dareing
dark
darke
darkness
darknes
darkenes
darknesse
darkenesse
darkest
darling
darlings
dart

## Words Included

darts
dash
dasht
dash't
date
daughter
david
david's
dawn
dawn'd
dawne
dawnes
dawning
day
day-bearing
day-break
day-starre
mid-day
day's
daye's
dayes
daies
dayly
dayly-dying
dazeling
dazle
dead
deadly
deafen'd
deafnes
deale
dealt
dear
dear-bought
deare
deare's
deere
dearer
dearest
dearly
death
death—to

death-full
death-like
death-seal'd
death's
deathles
deathlesse
deaths
debase
debt
deceased
deceive
deceived
deceivd
deceives
december
decent
decently
decide
decisive
deck
decke
declare
decree
dedicate
deedes
deep
deep-digg'd
deepe
deeper
deepest
deep'st
defects
defence
defend
deferr
defiance
defies
defyes
define
defined
definition
definitions

deflower
deflour
deflowers
degenerous
deigne
deign'd
deignes
deities
deityes
deity
delay
delegated
delicately
delicious
delight
delighted
delights
delightfull
deliquium
deliver
deliverance
delivery
deluge
den
denne
dens
denies
denyes
deny
deny'd
deny'de
deny't
denye
departing
deplore
deposed
descant
descry
descryer
deserve
desev'd
well-deserving

design
heavn-designed
desire
desires
desolation
despair
despair'd
despaire
desperate
desperately
despight
destiny
destinyes
destruction
detain
detect
determine
devills
devill's
divell
divells
devise
devising
devotion
devotions
devoure
devour'd
devoutest
dew
deaw
dewy
diadem
diademms
diadems
diamond
diamonds
mother-diamonds
diapason
dictate
die
dy
dye

died
di'd
dy'd
dyes
diet
difference
different
diffuse
digest
digested
digge
digg'd
deep-digg'd
dig'd
dight
dilemma
diligent
dim
dimme
diminutives
dining
dinne
diomed's
dipt
dipp't
dip't
dips
dire
direction
dirge
dir'ges
disappeares
disaster
disband
discerne
discerning
discharge
discharges
discipline
discloses
discord
discourse

discourses
discover
disdain
disdaines
disdaining
disdainefull
disdainfull
disease
disfigure
disgrace
disguises
disinheritt
dislodg'd
dismall
dismay'd
disolving
displace
displaces
display
displai'd
dispos'd
dispute
disputing
disrobed
dissipate
dissolve
distance
distant
distill
distill'd
distil'd
distills
distinctly
distinguish'd
distributed
ditty
divers
diversities
dives
divide
divided
dividend

## Words Included

| | | |
|---|---|---|
| dividers | dowr | drugg |
| divine | dowry | drunk |
| devine | drag | drunke |
| divinest | dragging | dry |
| divining | dragons | due |
| divinity | drake | dull |
| divisions | draught | duly |
| divorce | draughts | dumbe |
| doat | draw | dunghills |
| doats | drawn | durst |
| doating | drawne | durty |
| doting | dread | dusky |
| doctor's | dreadfull | dust |
| doctors | dream | dusty |
| doffs | dreame | duteous |
| dogs | dreampt | duty |
| dogges | dream't | dwell |
| dolefull | dresse | dwell't |
| domestick | dresses | dwelt |
| dominations | dressing | dwelling |
| doom | dressings | dying |
| doome | drest | dayly-dying |
| doomes | drew | never-dying |
| door | drink | eagle |
| dore | drinke | eagles |
| doore | drinks | eare |
| doors | driven | ears |
| doores | drop | eares |
| double | drop's | earlier |
| double-gilt | dropp | earlyer |
| double-guilded | drops | early |
| doubt | silver-drops | earth |
| doubtles | dropping | earth-laboring |
| doubtlesse | honey-dropping | earth-nurst |
| doubts | drove | earth's |
| dove | droves | earths |
| turtle-dove | drown | earthly |
| dove's | drowned | earthquake |
| doves | drown'd | ease |
| down (noun) | drowne | easily |
| downe | droune | east |
| doune | drowsinesse | th'east |
| downy | | |

| | | |
|---|---|---|
| easte | emperours | envy |
| eastern | empire | epiphany |
| easterne | empires | epitaph |
| easy | emptinesse | epitome |
| easie | emptynes | epode |
| eat | empty | equall |
| eate | empyraeum | aequall |
| eates | enacted | ere |
| eccho's | encloses | erinnys |
| eclipse | end | erisi-cthon |
| love-eclipse | ends | err |
| eclipsed | endlesse | error |
| eclips'd | endowments | errour |
| edom | endure | espied |
| effect | indure | espies |
| effects | indur'd | essence |
| effectuall | enemy | esteem |
| aegypt | enfold | esteemed |
| egyptian | engaddi | esteeme |
| aegyptian | engender | eternall |
| th'aegyptian | engines | aeternall |
| either | english | eternally |
| elaborate | enjoy | aeternally |
| elect | to'injoy | eternity |
| elegy | enobled | eternity—but |
| elgie | enough | aeternity |
| elfe | enow | ethiopian |
| elme | enquire | aethiope |
| eloquence | enraged | euphrates |
| else | enter | eve |
| embers | entertain | even |
| emblemes | entertaine | ev'en |
| embosom'd | enthusiast | ev'n |
| embrace | enthusiasticke | th'even |
| t'embrace | entice | evening |
| embrac't | tice | evening's |
| embraces | entity | ev'nsong |
| embracing | entombe | evenings |
| all-embracing | entombed | evenly |
| all-imbracing | entomb'd | events |
| embrave | envied | ever |
| embraves | envious | ever-blushing |

## Words Included

| | | |
|---|---|---|
| ever-brandisht | extasy | fair-cheek't |
| ever-bubling | extasies | fair-ey'd |
| ever-falling | extract | faire |
| ever-wakefull | extracted | fayre |
| ever-watry | eye | fairer |
| ever-youthfull | eye-lids | fairest |
| everlasting | eye-lidds | fair'st |
| e're | ey | fairly |
| every | ey's | fairely |
| exalations | eyliddes | faith |
| exalt | eyn | faith's |
| exalted | eyne | faithfull |
| examples | eyed | faithlesse |
| exceeding | blew-ey'd | fall |
| excellence | fair-ey'd | falls |
| except | red-ey'd | falling |
| excuse | right-ey'd | ever-falling |
| execution | eyes | fallacy |
| executioners | eyes' | false |
| exercise | ezelinus | fame |
| exhalation | fable | well-fam'd |
| exhalations | face | fames |
| exhale | faced | familiar |
| exhal'd | black-fac'd | family |
| exile | full-fac't | famine |
| expatiate | palefac't | fan |
| expect | pale-fac't | fan'd |
| expected | faces | fanning |
| expecting | fade | fancy |
| expectation | fading | fancy-framed |
| expence | never-fading | fancyes |
| th'expence | fail | fantastick |
| expenses | faile | far |
| experience | failes | farr |
| expire | failing | farre |
| expostulate | fayling | fare |
| expound | faine | farewell |
| expounds | fain'd | farwell |
| expresse | faint | farewel |
| exprest | fainted | farther |
| expression | faintly | farthest |
| extasie | fair | fashion |

fast
fastening
fastings
fatall
fate
fates
father
father's
fathers
fatt
fault
faults
fawning
fear
fear's
feared
fear'd
feare
feares
fearfull
fearfully
fearing
feast
feasts
feasting
feather
feathered
featherd
feature
features
fed
court-fed
fedd
feeble
feed
feed'st
feeds
feeding
life-feeding
feel
feele
feels

feeles
feeling
feet
feets
feign'd
feirce
feircest
felicity
fell
fellow
female
femal
fence
fenc'd
fertile
fetch
fetch't
fetcheth
fetter'd
fetters
fever
feaver
feav'rous
few
fictions
field
field's
feild
feild's
fields
feilds
fierce
fiercely
fiery
fift
fight
fighting
figures
fill
fill'd
brim-fill'd
fills

finall
find
find'st
finde
finds
finder
fine
finger
rosie-fingerd
fingers
fire
fire-works
firebrand
fired
fires
firm
firm-pointed
firme
firmly
firmament
first
first-born
first-borne
first-fruits
fit
fitt
fitt-tun'd
fitter
fix
fixed
fixt
fix't
fixe
flagrant
flairing
flame
falmes
flaming
flaming-brested
flash
flashing
flat

## Words Included

| | | |
|---|---|---|
| flatter'd | flowing | sylver-footed |
| flattering | high-floune | footsteps |
| flattery | flower | footsteppes |
| flatteryes | flowre | forbear |
| fled | flowers | forbeare |
| fleed | flowres | forbid |
| flee | flowrs | forbidden |
| fledg'd | flowry | force |
| fleece | floury | forc't |
| fleeces | fluent | forcing |
| fleecy | flushing | ford |
| fleeting | flutter | silver-forded |
| flesh | fluttering | fore |
| flies | fly | forepast |
| flyes | flie | forfeit |
| flight | flye | forfeited |
| flights | flying | forfeiture |
| flings | foams | forge |
| flints | foames | forget |
| flinty | foaming | forgett |
| float | foamy | forgive |
| floates | foe | forgot |
| flotes | foes | forgott |
| flock | fogs | forehead |
| flocke | fold | forehead's |
| flocks | blind-fold | fore-head |
| flockes | folded | forhead |
| flood | folds | forlorne |
| flood's | follow | form |
| floodgate | follow'd | formes |
| flood-gate | following | formidable |
| floud | fond | forrage |
| floods | fondly | forsake |
| flouds | food | forsaken |
| floud's | life-food | forsooth |
| floore | food-preparing | forswearing |
| flora's | fool's | fort |
| flourish | foole | forth |
| flourisht | foolish | forthwith |
| flow | foot | fortify |
| flow'd | light-foot | fortifie |
| flowes | silver-footed | fortresse |

| | | |
|---|---|---|
| fortunate | friend | full-grown |
| fortune | freind | full-mouth |
| fortune's | friends | fully |
| fortune-booke | freinds | fulnesse |
| fortunes | freindly | funerall |
| forward | frendly | furies |
| froward | fright | furnish |
| fought | frighted | furnisht |
| foul | friske | furnish't |
| foule | frisking | furrowed |
| foule-mouth'd | frizled | further |
| fowler | fro | fury |
| found | frolick | future |
| founded | front | gad |
| fount | fronts | gadde |
| founts | frost | gain |
| fonts | frost-bount | gain'd |
| fountain | frosts | gaind'st |
| fountaine | frosty | gaine |
| fountains | froth | gainer |
| fountaines | frown | gainfull |
| foure | frown'd | gales |
| fourth | frowne | galilean |
| fowles | frowns | gall |
| foyle | frownes | gallant |
| fragrancy | frozen | gallantry |
| fragrant | frugall | games |
| frail | fruit | gaping |
| fraile | fruits | garb |
| frame | first-fruits | garden |
| fancy-framed | fruites | gardens |
| frames | fruitfull | garland |
| frankincense | fruitles | garment |
| frankincence | fruitlesse | garments |
| fraud | fry | gasp |
| fraught | fryes | gaspes |
| free | fugitive | gastly |
| freely | full | gate |
| frequent | arm-full | gates |
| fresh | death-full | gather |
| fret | full-bloom'd | gaudy |
| frets | full-fac't | gave |

## Words Included

| | | |
|---|---|---|
| gay | glad | gold |
| gaze | gladd | golden |
| gaz'd | gladding | golden-headed |
| gemme | gladly | golden-winged |
| gems | gladnesse | gone |
| gemmes | glance | good |
| gemms | glances | goodly |
| generall | glasse | goodnesse |
| gen'rall | hour-glasse | goods |
| generation | hower-glasses | goose |
| generous | glassy | gore |
| genii | glimmering | gorgeous |
| genius | glimpse | gorgon |
| gentle | glistering | grace |
| gentler | glistring | graces |
| gentlest | glittering | gracious |
| gently | globe | graft |
| genuine | gloomy | grand |
| geryon | glories | grandsires |
| ghost | gloryes | grant |
| ghost's | glorious | grants |
| ghostly | glory | grape |
| giant | glory's | graspe |
| giddy | glosse | gratious |
| gift | glosses | gratitude |
| guift | glow | grave |
| gifts | glowing | grave's |
| double-gilt | glutt | graves |
| double-guilded | gnash | graver |
| guild | gnaw'd | great |
| guilded | go | greater |
| guilds | goest | greatnesse |
| gingle | goe | greedy |
| girt | goes | greene |
| give | going | greet |
| givest | he-goat | greisly |
| giv'st | goates | greived |
| gives | God | greiv'd |
| given | God's | greivous |
| giver | Gods | grew |
| giving | goddesse | grief |
| life-giving | godles | greif |

greif's
greife
griefe
griefs
griefes
greifes
grieves
grieving
grim
grimme
gripes
groan
groane
grone
groanes
groaning
grosse
grossest
ground
grounds
ground-worke
grove
groves
grow
grows
growes
growing
grown
full-grown
growne
groune
growth
grouth
grudge
grumbling
grutch
guard
guardian
guesse
guest
guests
guide

guilt
guilty
gust
hags
hail
haile
hair
haire
haires
half
half-sphear
halfe
hall
halls
hallow
hallowed
hallow'd
halters
hammers
hand
right-hand
hands
handfull
handling
handmaid
hand-maid
handmaids
handsome
hang
hangs
hanging
hangings
hanselld
happines
happy
happyer
hard
too-hard-tempted
hardest
hardly
hardnesse
hardy

hark
harke
harm
harme
harmes
harmlesse
harmonious
th'harmonious
harmony
harnessing
harp
harps
harpes
harpyes
harsh
harvest
haste
hasted
hasts
hasty
hatch
hatch'd
hatcht
hatchets
hate
hated
hatefull
hating
hatred
head
heads
th'heads
headed
golden-headed
hundred-headed
headlong
heal
heale
healing
health
healthfull
heap

## Words Included

heape
heap't
hear
hears't
heare
heard
heares
hearken
hearkened
hearkens
heart
heart-blood
th'heart-bred
heart's
hart
hart's
hearts
harts
hartlesse
harty
heat
heats
heates
heaven
th'heaven
heaven-burthen'd
heavenn
heavn
heavn-designed
heavn-instructed
heavn-saluting
heav'n
heav'n-besieged
heav'n-intreated
heav'n-rebuked
heav'ne-borne
heavenly
heavnly
heav'nly
heavens
heavns
heavn's

heav'ns
heavn'n's
heav'd
heaves
heaviest
heavy
heavyer
hebe's
hebrew
**he**brewes
hedge-quiristers
hedg'd
heed
heele
height
heir
heyre
heire
heirs
heyres
held
helicon
helicons
hell
hell's
hells
hels
hellish
help
helpe
hemisphaeare
hence
henceforth
hence-forth
hennes
henry
herald
heralds
herbe
herbes
herberts
hercules

herds
herod
herods
heroes
heroick
herse
hers'd
hesperides
hewe
hew'n
heyfer
hid
hid'st
hidd
hidde
hidden
hide
hides
hiding
hied
hy'd
hies
high
highborn
hibh-born
high-borne
high-aym'd
high-built
high-colour'd
high-floune
high-prech't
higher
highest
high'st
hill
hills
hinders
hire
hir'd
hisse
hisses
hist

history
historie
hitt
hive
hoarce
hoard
hoary
hoasts
hold
holding
holds
holinesse
hollow
holy
h[oly]
holyday
holyer
holyest
homage
home
homely
home-spun
honest
honesties
honey
honey-dropping
hony
hony-sweating
honied
honors
honour
honour'd
hookes
hope
hope-nurst
hope's
hopes
hopefull
horace
horn
horn'd
horne

hornes
horribly
horrid
horrizon
orizons
horror
horror's
horrors
horrour
horrours
horses
hospitality
host
hot
hott
hound
hour
hour's
hour-glasse
hower-glasses
houre
hower
houres
howers
howres
hourly
house
house-keeper
houses
houshold
hover
hovers
hover's
hovering
howl'd
huge
humane
humble
humblest
humbly
humility
humors

humours
humourous
hundred
hundred-headed
hung
hunger
hungers
hungry
hunter
huntresse
hurl'd
hurries
hurt
hurts
hurtes
hurting
husband
husbandman
husks
huswifes
hybla's
hydraes
hydra's
hymen
hyperbole's
hyperbolized
hyperion
hypocrisy
hypocrite
hipocrit
I
I'am
I'd
I'de
I'le
I'me
I've
th'icy
idaea
idle
idol
idols

## Words Included

all-idolizing
idolatrous
idolatry
ignoble
ile
ill
ill-nurtur'd
ills
illustrious
imagin'd
imitation
immediately
immodest
immortalities
immortall
th'immortall
impartiall
impatient
th'impatient
impenetrable
imperfect
imperiall
imperious
impes
angell-imps
impetuous
impiety
impossible
improve
inauspicious
incampt
incamp't
incarnate
incendiary
incense
incomparable
increase
encrease
t'encrease
increasing
increast
incurr

indeed
indefinite
index
indifferent
indulgence
industry
inebriated
inebriating
inexorable
infant
infant's
infants
inferior
inferiour
infernall
infinite
infinitely
influence
informes
th'inglorious
th'ingratefull (see un-)
inhabitant
inhabite
inheritance
to'inherit
inheritt
inhumane
injury
inke
inlarge
inmost
innocence
inquiring
inrich't
inscription
insinuation
instile
instinct
instructed
heavn-instructed
instrument
instruments
intangles

intelectuall
intellectuall
intelligences
intelligentiall
intent
intents
intentions
intercepted
intercourse
interiour
interpret
interpreters
intire
intolerable
intollerable
intreat
heav'n-intreated
inundation
invade
t'invest
inviolate
invitation
invited
h'invoke
involving
ire
iron-pointed
iron-sceptred
irresolute
isaacks
isack
island
isle
isles
issue
ite
ivory
james
jarres
jaylor
jealous
jealousie

| | | |
|---|---|---|
| jerusalem | keepe | knocke |
| jest | kept | knot |
| jesu | keep't | knott |
| jett | keeps | knotty |
| jetty | keepes | know |
| jewell | keeping | know'st |
| jewels | keeper | knowes |
| jewells | key | knowing |
| jezabell | keyes | known |
| jolly | kick | knowne |
| jordan | kickt | labor |
| joseph | kicks | laboring |
| jove | kickes | earth-laboring |
| jove's | kill | heav'n-labouring |
| joves | kill'd | labour |
| joy | sweetly-killing | labour'd |
| joy-conducted | kin | laboureth |
| joy'd | kind | labours |
| joye | kinder | lab'ring |
| joyes | kindest | lace |
| virgin-joyes | kindly | laces |
| joye's | kindnesse | lack |
| joyfull | kindle | lacke |
| joyne | kindled | lad |
| joynt | kindred | laden |
| jucy | kinred | lading |
| judahs | king | lady |
| judge | king's | ladyes |
| judg'd | kings | laid |
| judgement | kingdom | lakes |
| judgment-seat | kingdome | lamb |
| judgements | kingdoms | lamb's |
| june | kingdomes | lambe |
| juryes | kisse | lambes |
| just | kisses | lambent |
| juster | kissing | lamp |
| justice | kist | lampe |
| justle | kis't | lamps |
| justly | knee | lampes |
| keel | knew | land |
| keele | knife | crown-land |
| keep | knight | lands |

## Words Included

xxxiii

crown-lands
language
languish
languishing
languishments
laothsom
lap
lappe
large
large-look't
larg
larg-look't
larger
larkes
lash
lashes
last
lasting
late
latest
laugh
laught
laughing
laurell
law
laws
lawes
lawlesse
lawn
lawne
lawrels
lay
lay'd
lay't
laies
layes
lazarus
lazy
lazie
lead
leaden
leads

leafe
lean
leane
leap
leapt
leapes
leaping
learn
learn'd
learnt
learn't
learne
learned
learning
learnings
least
leave
leaves
leaving
leavy
led
miss-ledde
left
legacy
legacie
legible
leige
lend
lend'st
lends
lending
length
lengthened
lent
lesse
lesser
lesson
lest
lestrigonians
let
lett
lets

lett'st
letts
lethaean
lethargy
lethe
letter
letters
libanus
liberall
liberty
libian
licke
lickes
lids
eye-lids
liddes
eylidde s
lidds
eye-lidds
lie
ly
lye
ly'd
lies
lyes
ly'n
life
life-breathing
life-feeding
life-food
life-giving
life-meaning
life-speaking
life's
lifes
lift
lift'st
lifts
light
light-foot
light's
lighted

| | | |
|---|---|---|
| lights | listen | look |
| lighting | listned | lookt |
| lightly | listing | look't |
| lightnesse | listning | large-look't |
| lightning | lists | larg-look't |
| lightning-winged | little | looke |
| like | litle | looks |
| death-like | live | lookes |
| meteor-like | live's | looking |
| phoenix-like | lived | loose |
| swan-like | liv'd | lop |
| lik'st | long-liv'd | lord |
| likes | lives | lord's |
| lilly | living | lords |
| lilly's | lively | lose |
| lillies | livery | looses |
| limb | liverie | loosing |
| limbe | lo | losse |
| limme | loe | lost |
| well-lim'd | load | lottery |
| limbs | loaden | loud |
| limbes | loane | lowd |
| limmes | loathsome | lowder |
| limits | loath'd | lowdnesse |
| linage | lock | love |
| line | lock'd | love-crowned |
| lines | lockt | love-eclipse |
| linger | lock't | love-sick |
| lingring | locks | love-slain |
| linx | lockes | love-spun |
| lions | lodge | love-tost |
| lip | lodg'd | love's |
| sweet-lip't | lodging | loved |
| lipp | lodgings | lov'd |
| sweet-lipp'd | lofty | loves |
| sweet-lipp't | loftyer | lov'es |
| lips | loftyest | lovely |
| lippes | long | lover |
| lipps | long-liv'd | lovers |
| liquid | long-spun | loving |
| liquor | longer | low |
| lisp | longing | lowe |

## Words Included

lower
lowest
low'st
lowly
lownesse
lowre
lowres
loyall
loytering
lubricke
lucifer
lugges
lull
luminous
lump
lumpe
lumpes
lumpish
lungs
lurke
lurking
lust
lustre
lusty
lute
lutes
lutes-master
lycaon
lyons
lyre
lyres
mad
madnes
madnesse
madnesses
made
mad'st
maeanders
magazins
magdalene
magi
magick

magick-bolts
maid
hand-maid
handmaid
mother-maid
miads
maiden
maidenhead
maydenhead
maiden-blossomes
maine
maintain
maintaine
maintaining
maja's
majesty
majestie
make
mak'st
makes
making
maker
malice
malignant
man
country-man
man's
mans
manger
mankind
mankinds
manly
manna
mansion
mantle
mantles
mantletts
many
mapp
mappe
marble
marbles

march
marched
maria
mariner
mark
marke
markt
markes
marres
marriage
marriage-bed
married
marryed
marrow
mars
martyr
martyr'd
martyrdom
martyrdome
martyrdomes
mary
mary's
masculine
mask
maske
masse
master
lutes-master
master's
masters
mastring
o're-mastring
mastery
master-peece
matcht
mate
mates
matines
mattens
matter
maturest
maturity

maturitie
maugre
maxim
maxime
maybe
me
mee
meads
meades
meadowes
meddowes
meagre
meager
meal
meale
mean
mean'st
mean't
meane
means
meanes
meaning
life-mening
well-meaning
meant
meant'st
measure
measur'd
measures
meat
meate
medaea
mediate
meditate
meditates
medusa's
med'cinable
med'cinall
meek
meeke
meet
meets

meetes
meeting
meetings
melancholy
melody
melodie
melt
melted
melts
melting
memoriall
memory
memorye
men
mens
mend
merchandise
merchant
merchants
mercilesse
mercury
mercy
mercyes
mercyfull
mercylesse
meridian
merit
merits
merry
messengers
met
mett
metalls
metamorphosis
meteor
meteor-like
methinks
mezentius
midnight
midst
midwiferie
mid-day

might
mighty
mild
milde
milder
milk
virgin-milk
milke
milky
th'milky
milkey
mind
minds
mindfull
mine
mines
minions
ministers
minority
minoritie
minotaures
mint
minute
minutes
miracle
miracles
mirth
mirthe
mischeife
mischeife's
mischiefe
mischifes
miserable
miseries
miseryes
misery
misplac't
miss-ledde
misse
misses
missing

## Words Included

mist
mists
mistes
mistake
mystake
mistaken
mistresse
mistris
mites
mithra
mix
mixt
mixture
mock
mocke
mocks
mockes
moderatour
modest
modesty
moist
moisture
mold
moment
momentary
moments
monarchs
monster
monstrous
moneth
months
monthes
monumentall
mood
moon
moone
moores
more
morn
morne
morning
mourning

morning-sons
morning's
mornings
morpheus
morrow
morrow's
mortality
mortalitie
mortall
mortalls
most
mother
mother-diamonds
mother-maid
mother's
mothers
motion
motions
mount
mounted
mounts
mountaine
mountains
mountaines
mourn
mourn'd
mourne
mournfull
mouth
foule-mouth'd
full-mouth
mouths
mouthes
move
mov'd
moves
much
much-chang'd
much-wrong'd
muddy
mufling
multiply

multitude
multitudes
murther
murdred
murd'ring
murmur
murmure
murmurs
murmures
murmuring
murmurings
muse
muses
musicall
musically
musick
musick's
musicke
musicks
musitians
must
muster
mute
mutuall
myrrh
mirrh
mysteries
mysterious
mysteryes
mystick
mistick
misticke
mysticall
misticall
naile
nail'd
nailes
naked
naked'st
nak't
nakednesse
name

| | | |
|---|---|---|
| name's | neglected | nimblest |
| names | negligent | ninth |
| nameth | negligently | niobe |
| nam'd | negotiate | nip |
| big-nam'd | neighbour | nippe |
| bigg-named | neighbourhood | noble |
| nanus | neighbour-hood | nobler |
| narcissus | neighbouring | noblest |
| narrow | neither | nobly |
| narrower | nepturne | nod |
| nation | neptune's | nods |
| nation's | neptunes | nodding |
| nations | nero | noise |
| native | nerve | noyse |
| nativity | nest | nonage |
| nativitie | nests | none |
| nativitye | neasts | nooke |
| naturall | net | noon |
| nature | nets | noone |
| nature's | never | noons |
| natur's | never-dying | noones |
| natures | never-fading | north |
| nay | nere | northerne |
| near | ne're | nostrills |
| neare | n'ere | note |
| neerer | new | noat |
| neat | new-bloom'd | noate |
| neate | new-born | noted |
| neck | new-borne | notes |
| neck'd | new-saluted | nothing |
| necke | new-strung | nothing's |
| necks | newly | nothyng |
| nectar | next | nought |
| nectareall | nigh | nowhere |
| need | night | numbred |
| need'st | night's | numbers |
| needs | nights | numbring |
| needes | nightingale | numerous |
| needfull | nightingales | numerouse |
| needfully | nile | nunnery |
| negative | nilus | nurse |
| neglect | nimble | earth-nurst |

## Words Included

| | | |
|---|---|---|
| hope-nurst | oft | other |
| ill-nurtur'd | often | th'other |
| nuzzel'd | ointment | other's |
| nymph | old | others |
| nimph | th'old | ought |
| nymphs | olive-crownes | outragious |
| oake | olympian | outrunne |
| oakes | olympick | out-stare |
| oares | olympus | out-stares |
| oathes | omen | outstares |
| obedience | omnipotence | overbought |
| obedient | once | overflow |
| all-obedient | one | overflow'd |
| obey | th'one | o'reflow'd |
| t'obey | ones | o'reflowd |
| object | only | o'reflowing |
| objects | onely | o'relook |
| oblique | open | o'relooke |
| obscure | ope | orelooks |
| obscured | opes | overlaid |
| obscurely | opening | o're-mastring |
| obsequie | operation | oversee |
| obsequious | opportunity | overshadow |
| th'obsequious | oppresse | o'retakes |
| obtain | self-oppressed | owe |
| obtains | opprest | ow'st |
| occasions | oprest | ow |
| ocean | oppression | owes |
| oceans | oraculous | own |
| ochus | th'oraculous | owne |
| odoriferous | orbs | ox |
| ods | orbes | oxe |
| offence | ore | oyl'd |
| offend | organs | pace |
| offer | orient | padled |
| offers | orientall | paid |
| offerings | originall | payd |
| offring | orion | pay'd |
| offrings | ornament | payed'st |
| officers | ornaments | pain |
| officious | orphan | paine |
| th'officious | osyris | pains |
| the'officious | | |

| | | |
|---|---|---|
| paines | part | payments |
| painfull | part's | peace |
| paint | parted | peacefull |
| painted | parts | peacocks |
| painter | parting | peale |
| painters | partake | pearle |
| painting | parthenope | pearles |
| pair | parthian | pearle-tipt |
| paire | parthians | pearly |
| payre | particulars | peculiar |
| palace | partner | pedigree |
| palaces | pascha | peep |
| palates | paschal | peept |
| pale | passage | peep't |
| palefac't | passe | peepe |
| pal-fac't | passed | peeps |
| palestine | passest | peeping |
| palfreys | that-passest | peevish |
| pallace | passes | peirce |
| pallas | passenger | peirced |
| pallats | passing | well-peirc't |
| palsie | passive | peircing |
| panegyris | passives | soul-peircing |
| pangs | past | pelican |
| panting | pasture | pelops |
| pants | pastures | pen |
| paper | path | pens |
| papers | paths | pennes |
| pappe | pathes | penance |
| paradice | patience | pencil |
| paradises | patient | penitent |
| paragon | patron | common-people |
| parallel | patronage | peoples |
| paralell | pattern | perceiv'd |
| paramours | patterne | perch |
| paraphrase | pause | high-perch't |
| parcae | pauses | pertch't |
| pardon | pave | perching |
| parent | star-pav'd | perfect |
| parents | pavements | perfection |
| parentage | pay | perfidious |
| parlour-sermons | payes | perfune |

## Words Included

xli

| | | |
|---|---|---|
| perfumed | pile | plow'd |
| perfum'd | pillow | plough'd |
| perfumes | pills | pluck |
| perfuming | pilot | pluckt |
| perhaps | pilat | plume |
| period | pinions | plumes |
| perish't | pineons | plump |
| perjury | pipe | plumpe |
| persecutions | pipes | pluto's |
| persian | pitch | plyant |
| personate | pitchy | poasting |
| perspicill | pitty | poesy |
| persuasive | pitty's | poesie |
| perverse | pitties | point |
| pestiferouse | place | pointed |
| peter | place's | firm-pointed |
| phaethon | placed | iron-pointed |
| phaeton | plac't | well-pointed |
| phalaris | well-plac't | points |
| pharian | places | poynts |
| pharisees | plague | pointing |
| phasis | plain | poise |
| phereus | playne | well-pois'd |
| phlegeton | plaines | poyson |
| phoebus | plaints | poysons |
| phaebus | planet | pois'nous |
| phoenix | plant | poles |
| phoenix-like | plants | pomona |
| phoenix' | plat | pompe |
| phaenix | play | pompous |
| phaenix' | plea | pondrous |
| phoenixes | plead | poor |
| physick | pleads | poor-spirited |
| phisick | pleasant | poore |
| phisicke | pleasent | pope |
| physitian | please | poppy |
| picture | pleasing | porch |
| piece | pleasure | pores |
| peece | pleasures | portable |
| master-peece | pledge | portalls |
| peice | plenty | portend |
| piety | seed-plot | portents |

portion
ports
posed
pos'd
poseth
posies
possession
possest
posteritie
posture
pour
pour'd
poure
pouring
pourtraicted
powder'd
power
powe'r
powr
powr'd
powre
powers
powres
powrs
powerfull
powrfull
practice
practise
praeludium
praepar'd
praerogative
praesage
praesag'd
praescribed
praescription
praesume
praise
prayse
prayses
pratling
prattling
pray

prayer
praire
prayers
prayrs
prayres
praires
praie'rs
prai'rs
preachers
preach'd
precious
predictions
preferre
preferr'd
pregnant
prejudge
prejudicate
praejudicate
food-preparing
presence
present
praesent
presently
presse
wine-presse
prest
presume
pretence
pretences
pretends
pretious
pretty
prevent
prevents
prey
preys
price
prick
pride
priestesse
priests
prime

primrose's
primroses
prince
prince's
princes
princely
princesse
principall
prison
caldron-prison'd
selfe-prison'd
pris'ner
prisoners
private
prize
prise
pri'thee
prethee
proclaim
proclaime
proclayme
procrustes
prodigal
prodigall
prodigies
prodigious
profane
prophane
proffer
proficiencie
profound
progne
progressions
projects
prometheus
promise
pronounc'd
proof
proofe
prophecy
prophesy
prophecies

## Words Included

prophesies
prophetick
prophets
propitiate
propitious
prospective
prosp'rous
protection
protestant
proud
proudest
proudly
proudly-reposed
prove
prov'd
proves
proving
provinces
provoke
provok'st
provokes
psalm
publick
publicke
puddles
puft
pulpits
pulse
punish
purchas'd
pure
purer
purest
purple
th'purple
purpling
put
putt
putting
pyramids
pythons
quaffe

quakes
quak'st
qualifies
quarrell
qurrells
quarters
quavering
queen
queene
queens
quell'd
quel'd
quench
quench't
quenchlesse
quick
quicke
quickly
quicksands
quiet
quill
quintessence
quire
hedge-quiristers
quite
quiver
quivers
rabid
race
rackes
radiant
rage
ragged
rags
rain
rain-swoln
raine
raine-swolne
raise
rais'd
ram
ramme

rampant
ran
ranging
rank
well-rank'd
ranke
ranck'd
rankes
ransom'd
rape
rapes
rapsodyes
rapture
rare
rarefy'd
rarifyed
rarely-temper'd
rarest
rarity
raritie
rash
rate
rather
reather
ratling
raves
ravish
ravisht
ravish't
ravishers
ravishing
ray
raies
rayes
reach
reaches
reaching
read
reade
reader
reader's
readers

reading
readily
ready
reall
reap
reare
rear'd
reares
reason
rebellious
rebells
rebell-word
rebound
rebounding
rebuke
heav'n-rebuked
rebuk't
rebukes
receiving
reciprocally
reckon
reckons
reckoning
reckning
recline
reconciled
reconciles
recovers
rectifies
rectify
red
red-ey'd
redd
redeem
redeem'd
redeeme
redeeming
reel'd
referr
refine
refined
reflection

reflexion
reflex
refraine
reft
refus'd
regardles
regent
regions
reign
raigne
reigne
reignes
reine
raines
reinthron'd
rejoice
rejoyc't
rejoycing
relating
release
relent
relentlesse
reliefe
releife
religion
religious
reliques
rellish
remain'd
remaines
remedie
remember
self-remembring
remove
remov'd
rend
renders
renew
renoune
repaid
repaird
repaire

repeated
repent
reply'd
report
repose
proudly-reposed
reprive
repuls'd
repulst
request
requires
requitall
reserve
resolved
resolv'd
resolving
resort
respiration
rest
restlesse
resume
retired
retyr'd
return
returned
return'd
returns
returnes
returning
still-returning
reveale
reveald
reveal'd
revels
revenge
reverence
reverend
reverent
reverendly
rev'rently
revive
revived

| | | |
|---|---|---|
| reviving | robbery | royalle |
| revolution | robbing | royally |
| revolutions | robe | rub |
| revolves | robes | ruby |
| blood-revolving | roabes | ruby-teares |
| rhetoricall | rocke | rubies |
| rehtoricks | rocks | ruddy |
| rich | rockes | rude |
| riche | rod | rudenes |
| richer | roman | rugged |
| richest | rome | ruin |
| richly | rome's | ruine |
| riddle | roof | ruines |
| riddles | roofe | rule |
| ride | sylver-roofe | rul'd |
| rides | roofes | run |
| rife | room | runne |
| rifle | roome | runs |
| right | roomes | runnes |
| right-ey'd | root | rung |
| right-hand | rootes | rurall |
| rigour | rose | rush |
| rigourous | rose's | rustic |
| rills | roses | ru'th |
| ring | roseall | sable |
| rings | rosy | sack |
| riotous | rosie | sackcloth |
| ripe | rosie-fingerd | sacred |
| ripen | rough | sacrifice |
| ripend | roughly | sacrilegious |
| riper | roule | sad |
| rise | rowling | saddest |
| rises | round | sadly |
| rising | rounds | sadnes |
| rites | rouse | sadnesse |
| rivall | rouze | sadocus |
| rivall'd | rowz'd | safe |
| river | rowsing | safely |
| rivers | rowzing | sages |
| roaring | row | said |
| roaving | rowes | sailes |
| rob | royall | saint |

| | | |
|---|---|---|
| saints | schemes | seed-time's |
| sake | schinis | seek |
| sale | scholler | seekst |
| sally | schooles | seek'st |
| salomon | scorching | seeke |
| salt | score | seekes |
| heavn-saluting | scorn | seeking |
| new-saluted | scorn'd | seem |
| same | scorne | seem'd |
| self-same | scornes | seeme |
| sanctuaries | scoule | seems |
| sands | scouts | seemes |
| sans | scripture | seeming |
| sappho | scull | seemly |
| sate | sculls | seen |
| satisfied | scylla | seene |
| saucy | scyron | seethe |
| sawcy | scythian | seige |
| sauc't | sea | seege |
| save | seas | siege |
| sav'd | sister-seas | seize |
| saving | seald | seiz'd |
| saviour | seal'd | seldome |
| saw | death-seal'd | selected |
| say | sealing | self |
| saies | search | self-captivity |
| scale | searches | self-oppressed |
| scarce | season | self-remembring |
| scarse | seasonable | self-same |
| scare | seasonably | self-shutt |
| scarlet | seat | self-wounding |
| scar'd | judgment-seat | self's |
| scarres | second | selfe |
| scarrs | secure | selfe-captivity |
| scarus | see | selfe-prison'd |
| scattered | see'st | selfe-tormenting |
| scatter'd | see't | selfe-wise |
| sceane | sees | selves |
| scepter | seeing | send |
| iron-sceptred | seed | sends |
| scepters | seed-plot | sending's |
| | seed-time | sense |

## Words Included

| | | |
|---|---|---|
| sence | shaft | shipwrack |
| senses | shafts | shipwracks |
| sent | shaggy | shipwrack't |
| sentence | shake | shoale |
| sententious | shame | shoales |
| seraphicall | sham'd | shocke |
| seraphick | shames | shone |
| seraphim | shameth | shook |
| seraphims | shamefac't | shooke |
| series | shape | shoot |
| serious | shapes | shoots |
| sermons | share | shootes |
| parlour-sermons | shar'd | shoo-ty |
| serpent | shares | shop |
| servant | sharp | shops |
| serve | sharpe | shore |
| serv'd | sharply | shoar |
| serves | sheathed | shoure |
| service | sheath'd | shoures |
| services | shed | shores |
| set | shead | short |
| sett | shedd | short-cut |
| sets | sheep | shorter |
| setts | sheepe | shot |
| setting | winding-sheet | blood-shot |
| settle | sheets | shott |
| sever | sheetes | bloodshott |
| severall | shelter | shoulders |
| severe | shephard | show |
| severely | shepheard | show'd |
| severer | shepheards | shew |
| severest | sheild | shew'd |
| sev'n | silver-sheilded | shewd |
| seaven | shields | shewed |
| seav'n | sheilds | shewes |
| shackled | shifting | showes |
| shade | shine | showne |
| shades | countershine | shower |
| shady | shin'd | showr |
| shadow | shines | showre |
| shaddow | shining | showers |
| shadowes | ship | showres |

| | | |
|---|---|---|
| showrs | sylk | siren |
| shredds | silken | syren |
| shreeke | sylken | syrens |
| shrill | silkewormes | sirian |
| shrillest | silver | sister |
| shrine | silver-crowned | sister-seas |
| shrin'd | silver-drops | sisters |
| shrink | silver-footed | sit |
| shrinke | silver-forded | sith |
| shrinkes | silver-sheilded | sitt |
| shrowd | silver-sweating | sits |
| shrunke | silver-tipt | sitts |
| shut | sylver | sitting |
| shutt | sylver-footed | six |
| self-shutt | sylver-roofe | sixe |
| shuts | similes | size |
| shutting | simpering | skies |
| sibills | simple | skyes |
| sybyll | simplest | skill |
| sick | simplicity | skillfull |
| love-sick | sin | skin |
| sicknes | sin's | skip |
| sicknesse | sinne | skipps |
| side | sins | skirmishes |
| sides | since | sky |
| sifting | sing | slain |
| sigh | sings | love-slain |
| sigh'd | singing | slaine |
| sighs | single | slakt |
| sighes | sink | salkes |
| sight | sinke | slaughter |
| sighted | sinks | slaves |
| sights | sinkes | slayest |
| sign | sinner's | sleeke |
| signe | sinnes | sleep |
| signes | sion | sleep'st |
| silence | sions | sleepe |
| silenc't | sippe | sleeps |
| silent | sips | sleepes |
| silk | sippes | sleeper |
| silke | sir | sleeping |
| | sire | sleepy |

## Words Included

| | | |
|---|---|---|
| slept | soile | sorry |
| slender | soyle | sought |
| slew | sol | soul |
| slide | solace | soul-appeasing |
| slippery | sold | soul-peircing |
| slipt | soldjer | soul's |
| slow | souldier | soule |
| slowly | souldier's | souls |
| slownesse | soldiers | soules |
| sluggish | souldiers | sound |
| slumbers | sole | sounds |
| sluttish | solemn | soundeth |
| sluttishnesse | solemne | sourse |
| sly | solemnity | southwest-wind |
| small | solid | soveraign |
| smart | solitary | all-soveraign |
| smell | solliciters | soveraigne |
| smells | some | soverain |
| smile | something | sow'st |
| smil'd | somthing | sower |
| smiles | sometimes | sown |
| smiling | somewhat | sowne |
| smooth | son | sowrest |
| smother | sonne | spain |
| smutches | sons | spains |
| snake | morning-sons | spaine |
| snakes | sonnes | spake |
| snares | sonns | spak'st |
| snatch | song | span |
| snatch'd | songs | spangles |
| snatcht | soon | spaniards |
| snatch't | soone | spanish |
| snatches | sooner | spare |
| snow | sooty | spark |
| snowy | sutty | sparke |
| soare | sordid | sparkes |
| sober | sordidly | sparkling |
| sobs | sore | sparkeling |
| soft | sorrow | sparrowes |
| soft's | sorrow's | spatious |
| softer | sorrows | speak |
| softly | sorrowes | speak'st |

| | | |
|---|---|---|
| speake | spitefully | staggers |
| speaks | spittle | staggering |
| speakes | spleene | stain |
| speaking | splendor | staine |
| life-speaking | spoild | stained |
| spear | spoyle | staind |
| speare | spoyled | staines |
| speare's | spoiles | stale |
| spears | spoke | altar-stall'd |
| speares | sport | stallions |
| speciall | sporting | stamped |
| species | sports | stand |
| specious | spotlesse | stands |
| speed | spottlesse | star |
| speedily | spotted | star-pav'd |
| spell | spousall | starr |
| spend | spouse | starre |
| spending | spouse's | day-starre |
| spend-thrift | spowse | out-stare |
| spent | spowses | stars |
| sphear | sprang | starres |
| half-sphear | spread | outstares |
| spheare | wide-spread | out-stares |
| sphaere | spred | starrs |
| sphears | spreads | staring |
| sphaeares | spreading | starry |
| sphaeres | sprightly | start |
| spheares | spring | starts |
| sphinxes | springs | started |
| spices | springing | startle |
| spicy | sprucely | starv'd |
| spide | sprung | sterved |
| spill | home-spun | state |
| spilt | long-spun | states |
| be-spilt | love-spun | stately |
| spirit | spurn'd | stations |
| poor-spirited | spurns | statues |
| spirits | spy | stature |
| spirituall | spyes | stay |
| spite | stable | stay'd |
| spight | staffe | well-stay'd |
| spitefull | stagger | stayes |

## Words Included

| | | |
|---|---|---|
| stead | stomack | stretch |
| steady | stomacks | stretch'st |
| steal | stone | stretch't |
| steal'st | stones | strife |
| steale | stony | strike |
| steales | stood | striking |
| stealing | stoope | string |
| stealth | stooped | strings |
| steames | stoops | stringes |
| stedfast | stoopes | strive |
| steeds | stop | striv'd |
| steel | stopp | strives |
| steele | stopt | striving |
| steely | store | stroke |
| stemme | stories | stroake |
| stemms | storme | stroakt |
| stench | stormes | stroak't |
| steps | stormy | strokes |
| stepps | story | strong |
| steppes | stout | stronger |
| stepping | straight | strove |
| stept | streight | strow |
| sterne | streightway | strowes |
| steward | streightwais | struck |
| stiffe | straine | strooke |
| stif'led | straines | strucke |
| still | strynes | struggle |
| still-returning | strange | strugling |
| still-surviving | strangely | strung |
| still'd | stranger | new-strung |
| stil | strangers | stubborn |
| sting | stratagem | stubborne |
| stings | straw | stuck |
| stinke | stray'd | study |
| stirr | strayes | studied |
| stirre | stream | study'd |
| stitch | streame | studies |
| stock | streams | studyes |
| stocke | streames | stuffe |
| stole | streaming | stuft |
| stolne | strength | stumble'on |
| well-stoln | strengths | stumbling |

| | | |
|---|---|---|
| sturdy | sommer | suspicions |
| stygian | summers | sustaine |
| style | summon'd | swaid |
| stile | summons | swallowes |
| stiles | sun | swan |
| subject | sun-borne | swan-like |
| sublunary | sun-burnt | swarm |
| submit | sun-burn't | swear |
| substantiall | sun's | sweare |
| subtle | sunne | sweat |
| subtile | suns | sweat-bedewed |
| subtil | sunnes | sweating |
| subtlest | sunder | balsom-sweating |
| subt'lest | sung | balsame-sweating |
| successive | sunshine | hony-sweating |
| successour | sunneshine | silver-sweating |
| succour | sup | sweeping |
| suck | superficiall | sweet |
| suckt | superfluous | sweet-breath'd |
| suck't | superiour | sweet-lipp'd |
| suddenly | supernaturall | sweet-lipp't |
| sue | supple | sweet-lip't |
| suffered | suppliant | sweets |
| suffred | supplies | sweetes |
| suffring | supply | sweeter |
| sufferings | suppose | sweetest |
| suffrings | suppresse | sweetly |
| suffice | supprest | sweetly-killing |
| sugar | sure | sweetnes |
| sugred | surely | sweetnesse |
| suite | surer | swell |
| sute | surest | swells |
| suitours | surfets | swelling |
| suters | surfett | swept |
| sullen | surges | swift |
| sullied | surly | swill |
| sulphureous | surmises | swim |
| sulphur-breathed | surplisses | swim'st |
| sulph'ry | survive | swimme |
| summe | surviving | swims |
| summer | still-surviving | swine |
| summer's | suspect | swinging |

swolne
blood-swolne
raine-swolne
rain-swoln
sword
swords
swore
sworne
swound
sydnoean
sylla
syllable
sympathize
symptomes
synod
syth
table
tabled
tables
taffata
tagus
taint
take
taken
tane
ta'ne
takes
taking
talk
talke
talkes
tall
tame
tam'd
tames
tangled
tantalus
tapers
tardy
task
taske
taste

tast
tastes
tasts
taster
tastfull
tatling
taught
tayle
tayles
teach
teaches
teaching
tear
teare's
teare
tears
teares
ruby-teares
teat
teates
tediously
teeme
teeming
teeth
tell
tells
temper
temper'd
rarely-temper'd
tempest
temple
temples
too-hard-tempted
ten
tend
tender
tenement
tenor
teresa
teresia
terme
tearme

termes
terrestriall
territories
terror
terrors
text
than
thanke
thanklesse
thaw
thaw'd
thawes
thawing
thebes
thefts
theife
theme
theame
thence
therewithall
therodamas
thick
thicke
thickest
thin
thinne
thinner
thine
thing
thinge
things
thinges
think
thinke
thinks
thinkes
thinking
third
thirst
thirsts
thirsty
thomas

| | | |
|---|---|---|
| thorne | thundring | tones |
| thornes | thunderer | tongue |
| thrones | thyrsis | tongu'd |
| thought | thyselfe | tongues |
| thoughts | tiber | toungs |
| thousand | tickled | took |
| thousands | tide | took'st |
| thrall | ties | tooke |
| thread | ty | tooles |
| threads | tye | top |
| threds | ty'd | topp |
| threats | till | toppe |
| threat'st | time | tops |
| threaten | seed-time | torch |
| threatning | time's | torches |
| three | seed-time's | tore |
| threefold | timed-bee | torment |
| threw | times | tormented |
| thrice | timely | torments |
| spend-thrift | timerous | cradle-torments |
| thrills | timourous | selfe-tormenting |
| thrive | tinct | torn |
| thriv'd | tincture | torne |
| throat | tipt | torrent |
| throte | pearle-tipt | torrents |
| throate | silver-tipt | torrid |
| throats | tiptoe | torture |
| throates | tiptoes | tortur'd |
| throes | tire | tosse |
| throne | tires | tost |
| thron'd | tissew | love-tost |
| throng | tityrus | totall |
| thronging | together | totterer |
| throw | toile | touch |
| throws | toyle | toucht |
| throwes | toyles | touch't |
| throwne | toiling | touchstone |
| throune | tokens | towardnesse |
| thrust | told | towers |
| thrusts | tomb | towne |
| thunder | tombe | toyes |
| thunders | tone | trace |

## Words Included

| | | |
|---|---|---|
| trac'd | tribute | tumults |
| trade | trick | tumultuous |
| traffique | trim | tumultuouse |
| trafick | trim'st | tune |
| tragaedy | trip | tuned |
| tragicke | tripp | tun'd |
| traine | tripps | fitt-tun'd |
| traiterous | tript | tunefull |
| trance | triton | turn |
| trances | triumph | turn'd |
| transcendent | triumphs | turn'st |
| transcrib'd | triumphes | turne |
| transfer'd | triumphing | turnes |
| transfused | triumphant | turning |
| transfus'd | triumphantly | turtle |
| transpire | trod | turtle-dove |
| transpose | trophie | turtles |
| transsum'd | trophee | twelve |
| travail | trophies | twenty |
| traveld | troth | twice |
| travell | troubled | twig |
| traverse | troublesom | twinckling |
| trayles | truants | twine |
| tread | true | twin'd |
| treads | truly | twines |
| treason | truely | twinne |
| treasure | truest | twinnes |
| treasures | trump | twisted |
| treasurie | trumpe | two |
| tresury | trumpets | tympanie |
| treble | trunke | types |
| trebles | trust | tyranny |
| tree | truth | tyrant |
| tree's | truth's | tyrants |
| trees | truthes | tyrian |
| tremble | try | tyrrhene |
| trembled | tryd | ugly |
| trembles | try'd | unbent |
| trembling | try'de | unblemisht |
| tresses | tryes | all-unblemish't |
| tribunall | tugg | unblest |
| trigutary | tugge | unbounded |

| | | |
|---|---|---|
| unbroken | unluckily | urne |
| uncase | unmated | urns |
| uncharitable | unmeasur'd | use |
| uncloath | unmixed | us'd |
| uncomb'd | unmixt | uselesse |
| unconsum'd | unmov'd | usher |
| uncontrouled | unnatural | usuall |
| undanted | unnaturall | usurp't |
| undefil'd | unpartiall | vain |
| understand | unpearcht | vaine |
| understood | unpeer'd | vayne |
| undertook | unpittying | vainly |
| undertooke | th'unpolish't | vainely |
| undoe | unquiet | valerian |
| undone | unrest | valley |
| undresse | unruly | vanish |
| undresses | unseal'd | vanisht |
| unfeign'd | unsearcht | vanquish't |
| unfaign'd | unseasonable | variety |
| unfill'd | unseene | various |
| unfledg'd | unshorn | varnish |
| unfold | unspotted | vary |
| unforc't | unstained | vast |
| ungentle | unstain'd | vaults |
| th'ingratefull | unstrung | veil |
| unhappy | untaught | veile |
| union | untie | vail |
| united | untimely | vail'd |
| well-united | untouch't | vaile |
| universal | untroden | veyle |
| universall | untun'd | vailes |
| universe | untwin'd | veine |
| unkind | unity | veiw |
| unkindly | unvalued | vengeance |
| unknown | unwellcome | venging |
| unknowne | unwounded | venture |
| unlesse | unwrinckled | venus |
| unlesse't | all-unwrinkled | verdant |
| unload | upheld | vermillion |
| unlock | th'upright | vernall |
| unlockt | upwards | verse |
| unlook't | urge | vertue |

*Words Included*

| | | |
|---|---|---|
| vertues | volleyes | wanders |
| very | volume | wandring |
| vessells | volumes | wand'rer |
| vestments | voluntary | want |
| vex | vote | wanting |
| vext | votery | wanton |
| vex't | vouchsafe | wanton'st |
| vice-apollo | vouchsafes | wantonnesse |
| victim | vow | warbles |
| victime | vow'd | warbling |
| victory | vowes | wardrobe |
| victorie | vulgar | warm |
| victories | wades | warme |
| victorious | wage | warmed |
| victors | wages | well-warm'd |
| vie | wagge | warmes |
| vye | wait | warmest |
| vigorous | waite | warn |
| vigour | waited | warr |
| vile | waiteth | warr's |
| villanie | waits | warre |
| vindicate | waites | wars |
| vine | waiting | warres |
| violet's | waiward | warrs |
| violett | wake | wary |
| violets | wakt | wash |
| violls | wak't | washed |
| viperous | waken | washt |
| vipers | wakes | wash't |
| virgin | waking | washing |
| virgin-births | wakefull | wasted |
| virgin-joyes | ever-wakefull | watch |
| virgin-milk | walk | watches |
| virgin's | walke | watching |
| virgins | walks | water |
| virginity | walkes | water'd |
| virtues | walking | water't |
| visages | walls | waters |
| vitall | walles | watry |
| vocall | wallowed | ever-watry |
| voice | wan | wat'ry |
| voyce | wander'd | wave |

wav'd
waves
waveletts
wax
waxen
way
wayes
waies
weak
weake
weaknes
weaknesse
wealth
wealth's
wealthy
weapon
weapons
wear
weare
wears
weares
weary
wearynesse
weather
weave
wed
wedded
wedding
weeds
weekes
weep
weepest
weepe
weeps
weepes
weeping
amber-weeping
weepers
weighed'st
weighd
weigh'd
way'd

weighes
weigh's
weight
weighty
welcome
wellcome
welcomes
wellcomes
wells
went
wept
west
western
westward
wet
wett
wheels
whether
whips
whirle-wind
whisper
whisper'd
whispers
wispers
whit
white
whitest
whole
wholsome
wholsom
wide
wide-spread
wider
widow
widdow
wield
wife
wild
wildfire
wiles
willfull
willowes

win
wind
southwest-wind
whirle-wind
winds
winding-sheet
window
windows
windowes
wine
wine-presse
wing
winged
golden-winged
lightning-winged
wing'd
wings
winges
winter
winter's
winters
wipe
wip'd
wipt
wisdom
wisdome
wisdomes
wise
selfe-wise
wish
wish—no
wish'd
wisht
wishes
wit
witt
witch
wither'd
withheld
within
without
witnesse

## Words Included

| | | |
|---|---|---|
| witnest | working | writt |
| wittnes | world | well-writt |
| wittnesse | world—all | writes |
| wittnesses | world's | wrong |
| woe | worlds | wronged |
| woes | worm | wrong'd |
| wofull | worme | much-wrong'd |
| wolf | wormes | wrongs |
| wolvish | worn | well-wrought |
| woman | worne | yea |
| womb | worse | year |
| wombe | worser | yeare |
| wombes | worship | yeere |
| women | worship't | yeares |
| woemen | worst | yearly |
| won | worth | yee |
| wone | worthier | yell |
| wonne | worthlesse | yes |
| wonder | worthy | yield |
| wonders | wound | yeeld |
| wondering | wounded | yeild |
| wondring | wounds | yeelds |
| wont | wounding | yeilds |
| woo | self-wounding | yeilding |
| woo'd | wrack | yoke |
| wo'ed | wrangles | yoake |
| wooe | wrangling | yonder |
| wood | wrapt | young |
| woods | wrath | yonge |
| word | wrathfull | younger |
| rebell-word | wreath | yonger-brother |
| word's | wrest | youth |
| words | wrested | youth's |
| wordes | wretch | youths |
| wore | wretched | youthfull |
| work | wretches | ever-youthfull |
| worke | wrinckles | zeale |
| ground-worke | wrist | zephires |
| fire-works | write | zephirus |
| workes | writ | zone |

```
                    C O N C U R D A N C E   A N A L Y S I S                 PAGE    1
                    ---------------------------------------

KEYWORD         POEM LINE                              POEM TITLE                          LINE  YR  MAR  WIL
-------         ---------                              ----------                          ----------------

ABASED

        NOW BY ABASED LIDDES SHALL LEARN TO BE         IN GLORIOUS EPIPHANIE                231  52  253   39

ABASH

        ABASH THE PUREST BEAUTIES OF THE DAY.          UPON KINGS CORONATION                 26  MS  389  454

ABASHED

        THE DAYES ABASHED GLORIES, AND IN FACE         UPON YORKE HIS BIRTH                  75  46  176  500

ABHORRED

        THE FOULE QUEENS MOST ABHORRED MAIDS OF HONOUR SOSPETTO D'HERODE                    337  46  109  216

ABODE

        LEAVING HER CHAST ABODE.                       ON A PRAYER BOOKE                     43  46  126  139
        OH, WOULD'ST THOU HEERE STILL FIXE THY FAIRE ABODE,  LUKE 2.  QUAERIT JESUM          47  MS  379   11

ABOAD

        LEAVING HER CHAST ABOAD                        PRAYER TO GENTLE-WOMAN                49  52  328  139

ABOMINABLE

        THE WALLS, (ABOMINABLE ORNAMENTS.)             SOSPETTO D'HERODE                    322  46  109  216

ABORTIVE

        ALL HER BIRTHS ABORTIVE PROVE.                 UPON DEATH OF DESIRED HERRYS          74  46  168  467
        THE LIGHT'S FAIRE FACE, BUT STILL ABORTIVE BEE. UPON GUNPOWDER TREASON               58  MS  386  460

ABROAD

        TO GAD ABROAD.                                 ON A PRAYER BOOKE                     44  46  126  139
        AND POWRE ABROAD                               ON A PRAYER BOOKE                     87  46  126  139
        TO GADDE ABROAD                                PRAYER TO GENTLE-WOMAN                50  52  328  139
        AND POURE ABROAD                               PRAYER TO GENTLE-WOMAN                93  52  328  139

TH'ABSENCE

        YET LONG BY TH'ABSENCE OF THE DAY.             WISHES SUPPOSED MISTRESSE             64  46  195  479

ABSENT

        OUR ABSENT PRESENCE, AND OUR FUTURE NOW.       ON HOPE                               80  46  143   71
        AND BEE YEE CALL'D MY ABSENT KISSES.           WISHES SUPPOSED MISTRESSE             15  46  195  479
        OUR ABSENT PRESENCE, AND OUR FUTURE NOW.       (ON) HOPE                             40  52  345   71

ABSOLUTE

        BOUNDLESSE AND ABSOLUTE. HELL IS THINE OWNE.   SOSPETTO D'HERODE                    272  46  109  216
        LOVE THOU ART ABSOLUTE, SOLE LORD              IN MEMORY OF LADY MADRE TERESA         1  46  131   52
        LOVE, THOU ART ABSOLUTE SOLE LORD              TERESA                                 1  52  315   52

ABSTINENCE

        TWICE TWENTY DAYES PURE ABSTINENCE, TO FEED    OUT OF GROTIUS                        59  MS  398  198

ABUNDANCE

        CROWN'D ABUNDANCE SPREADS MY BORD.             PSALME 23                             50  46  102    5

WELL-ABUSED

        OF A MOST WISE & WELL-ABUSED NIGHT             IN GLORIOUS EPIPHANIE                210  52  253   39

ABYSSE

        BELOW THE BOTOME OF THE GREAT ABYSSE.          SOSPETTO D'HERODE                     33  46  109  216

ACCENTS

        WITH TENDER ACCENTS, AND SEVERELY JOYNT IT     MUSICKS DUELL                         40  46  149  535
        IN SHRILL TONGU'D ACCENTS, STRIVING TO BEE SINGLE. MUSICKS DUELL                    130  46  149  535
        OF HIS TUN'D ACCENTS. BUT IF ONCE              OUT OF GREEKE CUPID'S CRYER           28  46  159  519

ACCORD

        AND CRY WITH ONE ACCORD                        OFFICE H. CROSS COMPLINE              24  52  274  105

ACCOUNT

        AS KEEP ACCOUNT OF THE LAMBES WARRES           IN MEMORY OF LADY MADRE TERESA       155  46  131   52
        TAKE BOTH TO THINE ACCOUNT, THAT I & MINE      OFFICE H. CROSS RECOMMENDATION         3  52  276  106
        AS KEEP ACCOUNT OF THE LAMB'S WARRES.          TERESA                               154  52  315   52
```

## ACKNOWLEDG'D

| | | | | |
|---|---|---|---|---|
| A RIDDLE. (FATHER) STILL ACKNOWLEDG'D THINE | OUT OF GROTIUS | 35 | MS | 398 198 |

## ACKNOWLEDGING

| | | | | |
|---|---|---|---|---|
| TAKE THEM, AND ME IN THEM ACKNOWLEDGING. | UPON TWO GREENE APRICOCKES | 33 | 48 | 220 494 |

## ACQUAINTANCE

| | | | | |
|---|---|---|---|---|
| TO TAKE ACQUAINTANCE OF THE SPHEARE. | ON MR. G. HERBERTS BOOKE | 13 | 46 | 130 68 |
| TAKE ACQUAINTANCE OF THIS STONE, | HIS EPITAPH (HERRYS) | 3 | 46 | 172 471 |
| ACQUAINTANCE WITH THE SUNNE. WHAT SECOND MORNE | UPON YORKE HIS BIRTH | 69 | 46 | 176 500 |
| WILL TAKE ACQUAINTANCE OF MY WOES, & SAY | ALEXIAS FIRST ELEGIE | 28 | 52 | 334 204 |
| ACQUAINTANCE WITH THE USHER OF THE MORNE. | UPON KINGS CORONATION | 32 | MS | 389 454 |

## ACQUAINTED

| | | | | |
|---|---|---|---|---|
| NO MORE ACQUAINTED WITH MY HEART, | PSALME 137 | 22 | 46 | 104 7 |
| IF EVER PITTY WERE ACQUAINTED | ANOTHER ON HERRYS | 1 | 46 | 170 469 |

## ACTION

| | | | | |
|---|---|---|---|---|
| VERTUE TO ACTION, THAT LIFE-FEEDING FLAME | ON A TREATISE OF CHARITY | 51 | 46 | 137 69 |

## ACTIVE

| | | | | |
|---|---|---|---|---|
| WELL PETER DOST THOU WIELD THY ACTIVE SWORD. | ON ST. PETER CUTTING MALCHUS | 1 | 46 | 97 22 |

## ACTIV'ST

| | | | | |
|---|---|---|---|---|
| LOVE'S PASSIVES ARE HIS ACTIV'ST PART. | FLAMING HEART | 73 | 52 | 324 61 |

## ACTOR

| | | | | |
|---|---|---|---|---|
| MIGHT BE AN ACTOR IN THIS TRAGAEDY. | UPON GUNPOWDER TREASON | 34 | MS | 386 460 |

## ADAMANT

| | | | | |
|---|---|---|---|---|
| OF STURDY ADAMANT IS HIS STRONG CHAINE. | SOSPETTO D'HERODE | 144 | 46 | 109 216 |

## ADAMANTINE

| | | | | |
|---|---|---|---|---|
| HIS ADAMANTINE FETTERS FALL. GREENE VIGOUR | SOSPETTO D'HERODE | 107 | 46 | 109 216 |
| THE ADAMANTINE DOORS, FOR EVER STAND | SOSPETTO D'HERODE | 307 | 46 | 109 216 |
| OF AN ADAMANTINE RIGOUR. | ANOTHER ON HERRYS | 4 | 46 | 170 469 |

## ADDS

| | | | | |
|---|---|---|---|---|
| ADDS SWEETNESSE TO HIS SWEETEST LIPS. | THE WEEPER | 28 | 46 | 79 120 |

## ADDES

| | | | | |
|---|---|---|---|---|
| ADDES SWEETNES TO HIS SWEETEST LIPPES. | WEEPER | 28 | 52 | 307 120 |

## ADIEU

| | | | | |
|---|---|---|---|---|
| FAREWEL THEN, ALL THE WORLD. ADIEU. | TERESA | 57 | 52 | 315 52 |

## ADEIU

| | | | | |
|---|---|---|---|---|
| FAREWELL THEN ALL THE WORLD, ADEIU. | IN MEMORY OF LADY MADRE TERESA | 57 | 46 | 131 52 |

## ADOE

| | | | | |
|---|---|---|---|---|
| ALL TORNE. WITH MUCH ADOE YET ERE HE DYES, | HIGH MOUNTED ON AN ANT | 4 | 46 | 161 523 |

## ADMIRABLE

| | | | | |
|---|---|---|---|---|
| THEIR NEW & ADMIRABLE LIGHT. | IN GLORIOUS EPIPHANIE | 173 | 52 | 253 39 |

## ADMIRE

| | | | | |
|---|---|---|---|---|
| MAKE NOT TOO MUCH HAST TO' ADMIRE | FLAMING HEART | 3 | 52 | 324 61 |

## ADMIRED

| | | | | |
|---|---|---|---|---|
| TO SHADDOW FORTH TH' ADMIRED PARAGON. | UPON BIRTH PRINCESSE E | 42 | MS | 391 456 |

## ADORE

| | | | | |
|---|---|---|---|---|
| ADORE HER PRINCES BIRTH, FLAT ON HER BREST. | SOSPETTO D'HERODE | 124 | 46 | 109 216 |
| WILL NOT ADORE THEE, | TO THE NAME OF JESUS | 237 | 52 | 239 30 |
| SHALL ANY DAY BUT THINE ADORE. | IN GLORIOUS EPIPHANIE | 86 | 52 | 253 39 |
| LO, WE ADORE THEE, | OFFICE H. CROSS MATINES | 24 | 52 | 265 86 |
| LO WE ADORE THEE | OFFICE H. CROSS PRIME | 17 | 52 | 267 91 |
| LO WE ADORE THEE | OFFICE H. CROSS THIRD | 16 | 52 | 268 93 |
| LO WE ADORE THEE | OFFICE H. CROSS SIXT | 21 | 52 | 270 97 |
| LO WE ADORE THEE | OFFICE H. CROSS NINTH | 13 | 52 | 271 99 |
| LO WE ADORE THEE | OFFICE H. CROSS EVENSONG | 26 | 52 | 273 101 |
| STILL THRONES & DOMINATIONS WOULD ADORE THEE | CHARITAS NIMIA | 24 | 52 | 280 48 |
| A HEART BURNING IN LOVE. ALL DID ADORE | UPON KINGS CORONATION | 37 | MS | 390 453 |

ADORED

AND LEAVE THE LONG ADORED SUNNE.                    AN HIMNE FOR CIRCUMCISION        32    46 141   37
AT THY ADORED FEET, THUS, HE LAYES DOWN             IN GLORIOUS EPIPHANIE           240    52 253   39

ALL-ADORED

WELLCOME DEAR, ALL-ADORED NAME.                     TO THE NAME OF JESUS            225    52 239   30

ADORING

THE CONDUCT OF ADORING SPIRITS, THAT THRONG         TO THE NAME OF JESUS            152    52 239   30

ADORNE

SEAV'N CRESTED HYDRA'S HORRIBLY ADORNE.             SOSPETTO D'HERODE                46    46 109  216

ADORNING

WITH THINE OWNE BLUSH THY CHEEKES ADORNING,         AN HIMNE FOR CIRCUMCISION         3    46 141   37
WITH BLUSH OF THINE OWN BLOOD THY DAY ADORNING,     TO THE NAME OF JESUS            222    52 239   30
WITH THINE OWN BLUSH THY CHEEKS ADORNING            NEW YEAR'S DAY                    3    52 251   37

ADULTERATES

ADULTERATES THE VIRGIN AIRE, WITH DEATH             ON GUNPOWDER-TREASON             18    MS 384  458

ADULTEROUS

OF ADULTEROUS GODLES DUST                           IN GLORIOUS EPIPHANIE           102    52 253   39

ADULT'ROUS

A RAPE UPON'T. TILL THY ADULT'ROUS TOUCH            TO PONTIUS WASHING HANDS          3    46  94   23

ADVANCE

PORTENTS BEFORE MINE EYES THEIR POWERS ADVANCE.     SOSPETTO D'HERODE               202    46 109  216
ADVANCE OUR CLAIM                                   OFFICE H. CROSS COMPLINE         23    52 274  105

ADVIS'D

BUT STREIGHT HIS EYES ADVIS'D HIS CHEEKE.           A HYMNE OF THE NATIVITY          49    46 106   76

AEACUS

AND AEACUS ON HIS TRIBUNALL TOO,                    HORATIJ ILLE & NEFASTO           35    MS 382  530

AELIA

THIS LAST COUGH AELIA, COUGHT OUT ALL THY FEARE,    OUT OF MARTIALL                   5    46 168  527

AEOL

AEOL KEPT IN HIS WRANGLING SONNES, LEAST THEY       UPON GUNPOWDER TREASON           29    MS 366  460

AEOLUS

THY INFANTS, AEOLUS, WILL NOT SUFFICE.              ON GUNPOWDER-TREASON             38    MS 384  458

AERIALL

A THINNE, AERIALL VEIL, IS DRAWN                    TEMPERANCE                       26    52 342  510

AIEREALL

A THINNE AIEREALL VAILE IS DRAWNE                   IN PRAISE OF LESSIUS             28    46 156  510

AERY

EACH HOLDING FORTH TO LIGHT THE AERY BRAND,         UPON GUNPOWDER TREASON           14    MS 387  461
EACH AERY SIREN NOW HATH GOTT HER SONG,             UPON KINGS CORONATION            25    MS 390  453

AIERY

THE AIERY SHOP OF SOUL-APPEASING SOUND.             TO THE NAME OF JESUS             34    52 239   30
THE AIERY NATION OF NEAT DOVES,                     AGAINST IRRESOLUTION AND DELAY   45    52 347  146

AFFECT

AFFECT MORE COMLY BANDS                             PRAYER TO GENTLE-WOMAN            6    52 328  139

AFFORD

THOU DIDST AFFORD THE FAITHFULL THEIFE.             ADORO TE                         16    52 291  172

AFFORDS

FAITH IS MY FORCE. FAITH STRENGTH AFFORDS           ADORO TE                         13    52 291  172

## AFFRIGHT

| | | | | |
|---|---|---|---|---|
| ALL HIS TERRORS TO AFFRIGHT MEE. | OUT OF THE ITALIAN (1) | 45 | 46 188 | 545 |
| AFFRIGHT TH' AMAZED AIRE, & DANCE A ROUND | UPON KINGS CORONATION | 22 | MS 390 | 453 |

## AFFRIGHTED

| | | | | |
|---|---|---|---|---|
| WHILE THEIR AFFRIGHTED SOULES, NOW WING'D FOR FLIGHT | THE BEGINNING OF HELIODORUS | 19 | 46 158 | 517 |
| AFFRIGHTED PHAEBUS WOULD HAVE LOST HIS WAY, | UPON GUNPOWDER TREASON | 19 | MS 386 | 460 |
| BUT REST, AFFRIGHTED MUSE, THY SILVER WINGS | UPON GUNPOWDER TREASON | 27 | MS 387 | 461 |

## AFRAID

| | | | | |
|---|---|---|---|---|
| AND MAKE DARKNESSE SELFE AFRAID. | PSALME 23 | 42 | 46 102 | 5 |
| FEARE IS AFRAID TO TAST OF. ONLY THIS, | UPON GUNPOWDER TREASON | 45 | MS 387 | 461 |

## AFRICK-BROOD

| | | | | |
|---|---|---|---|---|
| OR CHOICEST HENNES OF AFRICK-BROOD. | PETRONIJ ALES PHASIACIS PETITA | 2 | MS 382 | 526 |

## AGE

| | | | | |
|---|---|---|---|---|
| AGE, WOULDST SEE DECEMBER SMILE. | IN PRAISE OF LESSIUS | 40 | 46 156 | 510 |
| AND TILL MY RIPER WOES TO AGE ARE COME, | OUR LORD IN HIS CIRCUMCISION | 17 | 46 98 | 9 |
| OF AGE AND BARENNESSE, AND HER BABE PREVENT | SOSPETTO D'HERODE | 102 | 46 109 | 216 |
| THE GENEROUS WINE WITH AGE GROWES STRONG, NOT SOWER. | ON HOPE | 53 | 46 143 | 71 |
| HIDE HIS HOT BEAMES IN SHADE OF SILVER AGE. | UPON DEATH OF HERRYS | 31 | 46 167 | 466 |
| WHEN AGE AND DEATH CALL'D FOR THE SCORE, | AN EPITAPH UPON ASHTON | 25 | 46 192 | 464 |
| AGE, WOULDST SEE DECEMBER SMILE. | TEMPERANCE | 36 | 52 342 | 510 |
| THY GENEROUS WINE WITH AGE GROWES STRONG, NOT SOWER. | (ON) HOPE | 23 | 52 345 | 71 |
| AND CRUELL RAVISHING OF FROSTY AGE, | UPON GUNPOWDER TREASON | 44 | MS 387 | 461 |
| A PRECIOUS SEASON, & A GOLDEN AGE. | UPON KINGS CORONATION | 18 | MS 389 | 454 |
| LONG TIME TO QUAVERING AGE YOU GIVE, | UPON DEATH OF A FREIND | 11 | MS 393 | 477 |
| AND TOO UNGENTLE NIPPE OF FROSTY AGE. | AN ELEGY MR STANNINOW | 34 | MS 394 | 473 |
| WAS NOT YETT FULL, (A TIME THAT TO MY AGE | OUT OF GROTIUS | 23 | MS 398 | 198 |

## AGED

| | | | | |
|---|---|---|---|---|
| THE AGED HONORS OF THIS DAY STILL NEW. | TO THE QUEEN'S MAJESTY | 24 | 52 261 | 47 |
| THE AGED PASCHA PLEADS NOT YEARES | LAUDA SION SALVATOREM | 21 | 52 294 | 178 |
| LET THEN THE AGED WORLD BE WISE, & ALL | O GLORIOSA DOMINA | 23 | 52 302 | 194 |
| HATH AGED WINTER, FLEDG'D WITH FEATHERED RAINE, | AN ELEGY MR STANNINOW | 1 | MS 394 | 473 |

## AGES

| | | | | |
|---|---|---|---|---|
| MEASURE THEIR AGES, THOU BY TEARES. | THE WEEPER | 120 | 46 79 | 120 |
| THE HEAV'N EXPECTING AGES, HOPE TO SEE | SOSPETTO D'HERODE | 158 | 46 109 | 216 |
| EACH ONE AN AGES LABOUR, THAT THY DAYES | UPON YORKE HIS BIRTH | 11 | 46 176 | 500 |
| MEASURE THEIR AGES, THOU, BY TEARES. | WEEPER | 156 | 52 307 | 120 |

## AGREE

| | | | | |
|---|---|---|---|---|
| AGREE. | UPON OUR SAVIOURS TOMBE | 2 | 46 93 | 25 |
| AGREE. | TO OUR B. LORD | 2 | 52 279 | 25 |
| CAN SO GREAT FLAMES AGREE | WEEPER | 99 | 52 307 | 120 |

## AIR

| | | | | |
|---|---|---|---|---|
| DOES THY SONG LULL THE AIR. | WEEPER | 139 | 52 307 | 120 |

## AIRE

| | | | | |
|---|---|---|---|---|
| WHOSE FLOURISH (METEOR-LIKE) DOTH CURLE THE AIRE | MUSICKS DUELL | 137 | 46 149 | 535 |
| WILL I FIND A PURER AIRE | PSALME 23 | 68 | 46 102 | 5 |
| AIRE, WITH A DISMALL SHADE, BUT ALL IN VAINE, | SOSPETTO D'HERODE | 143 | 46 109 | 216 |
| TO FLUTTER IN THE BALMY AIRE. | ON MR. G. HERBERTS BOOKE | 9 | 46 130 | 68 |
| OF FAITH, A MOUNTAINE WORD, MADE UP OF AIRE, | ON A TREATISE OF CHARITY | 53 | 46 137 | 69 |
| AS EVER WHISPER'D TO THE MORNING AIRE | UPON DEATH OF HERRYS | 2 | 46 167 | 466 |
| WHY RAN THE STARTED AIRE TREMBLING AWAY. | UPON YORKE HIS BIRTH | 67 | 46 176 | 500 |
| THE AIRE DOES WOOE THEE, | OUT OF THE ITALIAN (1) | 14 | 46 188 | 545 |
| ADULTERATES THE VIRGIN AIRE. WITH DEATH | ON GUNPOWDER-TREASON | 18 | MS 384 | 458 |
| TO TOSSE POORE MEN LIKE DUST INTO THE AIRE. | ON GUNPOWDER-TREASON | 40 | MS 384 | 458 |
| AND GREISLY VISAGES DOE FRIGHT THE AIRE. | UPON GUNPOWDER TREASON | 10 | MS 387 | 461 |
| AFFRIGHT TH' AMAZED AIRE, & DANCE A ROUND | UPON KINGS CORONATION | 22 | MS 390 | 453 |

## TH'AIRE

| | | | | |
|---|---|---|---|---|
| PALE PROOFE OF HER FELL PRESENCE, TH'AIRE TOO WELL | SOSPETTO D'HERODE | 374 | 46 109 | 216 |

## AYRE

| | | | | |
|---|---|---|---|---|
| DOES THY SONG LULL THE AYRE. | THE WEEPER | 103 | 46 79 | 120 |
| STARTLE THE DULL AYRE WITH A DISMALL RED. | SOSPETTO D'HERODE | 50 | 46 109 | 216 |
| FROM DEATH'S SAD SHADES, TO THE LIFE-BREATHING AYRE, | SOSPETTO D'HERODE | 81 | 46 109 | 216 |
| IN FREE AYRE, | OUT OF THE ITALIAN (1) | 7 | 46 188 | 545 |

## AIRES

| | | | | |
|---|---|---|---|---|
| A SWEET LUTES-MASTER, IN WHOSE GENTLE AIRES | MUSICKS DUELL | 5 | 46 149 | 535 |
| SHARPE AIRES, AND STAGGERS IN A WARBLING DOUBT | MUSICKS DUELL | 58 | 46 149 | 535 |
| MUSICKS BEST SEED-PLOT, WHENCE IN RIPEND AIRES | MUSICKS DUELL | 69 | 46 149 | 535 |
| OF FLASHING AIRES. SHEE QUALIFIES THEIR ZEALE | MUSICKS DUELL | 98 | 46 149 | 535 |
| WHOSE TREMBLING MURMURS MELTING IN WILD AIRES | MUSICKS DUELL | 141 | 46 149 | 535 |

| | | | | |
|---|---|---|---|---|
| THOSE SWEET AIRES THAT OFTEN SLEW MEE. | OUT OF THE ITALIAN (1) | 51 | 46 188 | 545 |
| OFT HAVE I WRAPT THY SLUMBERS IN SOFT AIRES, | LUKE 2. QUAERIT JESUM | 31 | MS 379 | 11 |

AYRES

| | | | | |
|---|---|---|---|---|
| ARE FAN'D AND FRIZLED, IN THE WANTON AYRES | MUSICKS DUELL | 116 | 46 149 | 535 |

ALABLASTER

| | | | | |
|---|---|---|---|---|
| FROM THE SAME SNOWY ALABLASTER ROCKE | UPON YORKE HIS BIRTH | 45 | 46 176 | 500 |

ALARMES

| | | | | |
|---|---|---|---|---|
| QUENCH HIS CURL'D FIRES, WEE'L WAKE WITH OUR ALARMES | SOSPETTO D'HERODE | 276 | 46 109 | 216 |
| AMAZED TRITON WITH HIS SHRILL ALARMES | UPON GUNPOWDER TREASON | 31 | MS 386 | 460 |

ALAS

| | | | | |
|---|---|---|---|---|
| ALAS. IN VAINE. FOR WHILE (SWEET SOULE) SHEE TRYES | MUSICKS DUELL | 161 | 46 149 | 535 |
| WAS THROWNE ALAS, AND GOT A DEADLY FALL. | HIGH MOUNTED ON AN ANT | 2 | 46 161 | 523 |
| THEY SWIM, ALAS. IN THEIR OWNE FLOOD. | ON BLEEDING WOUNDS OF LORD | 8 | 46 101 | 110 |
| SO MUCH. RUDE SHEPHEARDS. WHAT HIS STEEDS. ALAS | SOSPETTO D'HERODE | 527 | 46 109 | 216 |
| FORTUNE ALAS ABOVE THE WORLDS LAW WARRES. | ON HOPE | 71 | 46 143 | 71 |
| BUT HE, ALAS. EVEN HEE IS DEAD | ANOTHER ON HERRYS | 55 | 46 170 | 469 |
| FOR NOW (ALAS) NOT IN THIS STONE | HIS EPITAPH (HERRYS) | 50 | 46 172 | 471 |
| (ALAS) WILL NEVER DOE. | TO THE NAME OF JESUS | 25 | 52 239 | 30 |
| LITTLE, ALAS, THOUGHT THEY | TO THE NAME OF JESUS | 207 | 52 239 | 30 |
| ALAS WHAT WILL THEY DOE | TO THE NAME OF JESUS | 229 | 52 239 | 30 |
| ALAS WITH HOW MUCH HEAVYER SHADE | IN GLORIOUS EPIPHANIE | 117 | 52 253 | 39 |
| ALAS, SWEET LORD, WHAT WER'T TO THEE | CHARITAS NIMIA | 9 | 52 280 | 48 |
| NAME TO BE KNOWN, ALAS, BUT SORROW'S MOTHER. | SANCTA MARIA DOLORUM | 4 | 52 283 | 162 |
| THEY SWIMME, ALAS, IN THEIR OWN FLOOD. | UPON BLEEDING CRUCIFIX | 12 | 52 288 | 110 |
| NOT FOR MY SELF ALAS, BUT FOR MY DEARER LORD. | TO SAME CONCERNING CHOISE | 7 | 52 331 | 66 |
| LO HERE AM LEFT (ALAS), FOR MY LOST MATE | ALEXIAS FIRST ELEGIE | 3 | 52 334 | 204 |
| AH THOU THY SELF, ALAS, HAST TAUGHT ME HOW. | ALEXIAS FIRST ELEGIE | 16 | 52 334 | 204 |
| FOR HIM, ALAS, N'ERE SHALL I NEED TO BE | ALEXIAS SECONDE ELEGIE | 11 | 52 335 | 207 |
| MY TREASURES, RICH, ALAS, BY ROBBING MEE. | ALEXIAS THIRD ELEGIE | 2 | 52 336 | 209 |
| HALF TRUE, HALF FALSE, PROVES THAT POOR LINE. | ALEXIAS THIRD ELEGIE | 57 | 52 336 | 209 |
| FORTUNE, ALAS, ABOVE THE WORLD'S LOW WARRES | (ON) HOPE | 31 | 52 345 | 71 |
| ALAS. AND HAS THE YEAR NO SPRING FOR YOU. | AGAINST IRRESOLUTION AND DELAY | 36 | 52 347 | 146 |
| OFT HAVE THESE ARMES (ALAS.) SHOW'D TO THESE EYES | LUKE 2. QUAERIT JESUM | 43 | MS 379 | 11 |
| ALAS, THE EARTH, QUITE DRUNKE WITH TEARES, HAD REEL'D | UPON KINGS CORONATION | 9 | MS 390 | 453 |
| BUT THEN, ALAS, MY HEART. OH HOW SHALL I | UPON BIRTH PRINCESSE E | 11 | MS 391 | 456 |

ALCAEUS

| | | | | |
|---|---|---|---|---|
| RUNNES MURMURING ON THE STRINGS. ALCAEUS THERE | HORATIJ ILLE & NEFASTO | 41 | MS 382 | 530 |

ALECTO

| | | | | |
|---|---|---|---|---|
| WHAT THY ALECTO, WHAT THESE HANDS CAN DOE. | SOSPETTO D'HERODE | 265 | 46 109 | 216 |

ALECTO'S

| | | | | |
|---|---|---|---|---|
| OF CERBERUS, OR ALECTO'S VIPEROUS BROOD. | UPON GUNPOWDER TREASON | 4 | MS 386 | 460 |

ALEXIS

| | | | | |
|---|---|---|---|---|
| BUT HOW SHALL I STEAL HENCE. ALEXIS THOU | ALEXIAS FIRST ELEGIE | 15 | 52 334 | 204 |
| MY POOR ALEXIS, THEN IN PEACEFULL LIFE. | ALEXIAS THIRD ELEGIE | 13 | 52 336 | 209 |
| ALEXIS, HE ALONE IS MINE (SAID I) | ALEXIAS THIRD ELEGIE | 56 | 52 336 | 209 |
| ALEXIS IS ALONE. BUT IS NOT MINE. | ALEXIAS THIRD ELEGIE | 58 | 52 336 | 209 |

ALEXIS'

| | | | | |
|---|---|---|---|---|
| ALEXIS' WIDDOW NOW IS SORROW'S WIFE. | ALEXIAS SECONDE ELEGIE | 5 | 52 335 | 207 |

ALIVE

| | | | | |
|---|---|---|---|---|
| HIS LIFE STILL KEPT ALIVE IN THEE. | AN EPITAPH UPON ASHTON | 36 | 46 192 | 464 |
| AS SERVES TO KEEP ALIVE HER DEATH. | SANCTA MARIA DOLORUM | 40 | 52 283 | 162 |
| STILL ALIVE. AND STILL FOR ME. | DIES IRAE | 52 | 52 298 | 186 |
| AND KEEP'T ALIVE WITH LASTING SONGS. | O GLORIOSA DOMINA | 30 | 52 302 | 194 |

ALL

| | | | | |
|---|---|---|---|---|
| BLENDS ALL TOGETHER. THEN DISTINCTLY TRIPPS | MUSICKS DUELL | 31 | 46 149 | 535 |
| AND CLOSES THE SWEET QUARRELL, ROWSING ALL | MUSICKS DUELL | 53 | 46 149 | 535 |
| FEELES MUSICKS PULSE IN ALL HER ARTERYES, | MUSICKS DUELL | 120 | 46 149 | 535 |
| SWEETNESSE BY ALL HER NAMES. THUS, BRAVELY THUS | MUSICKS DUELL | 133 | 46 149 | 535 |
| BY A STRONG EXTASY) THROUGH ALL THE SPHAEARES | MUSICKS DUELL | 148 | 46 149 | 535 |
| OF ALL THE STRINGS, STILL BREATHING THE BEST LIFE | MUSICKS DUELL | 152 | 46 149 | 535 |
| A FULL-MOUTH DIAPASON SWALLOWES ALL. | MUSICKS DUELL | 156 | 46 149 | 535 |
| YET SUMMONS ALL HER SWEET POWERS FOR A NOATE | MUSICKS DUELL | 160 | 46 149 | 535 |
| TO MEASURE ALL THOSE WILD DIVERSITIES | MUSICKS DUELL | 162 | 46 149 | 535 |
| ALL TREES, ALL LEAVY GROVES CONFESSE THE SPRING | OUT OF VIRGIL | 1 | 46 155 | 529 |
| ALL TREES, ALL LEAVY GROVES CONFESSE THE SPRING | OUT OF VIRGIL | 1 | 46 155 | 529 |
| EACH BODY'S PLUMP AND JUCY, ALL THINGS FULL | OUT OF VIRGIL | 15 | 46 155 | 529 |
| WOULDST SEE A MAN ALL, IN HIS OWNE WEALTH, | IN PRAISE OF LESSIUS | 17 | 46 156 | 510 |
| THROUGH WHICH ALL HER BRIGHT FEATURES SHINE. | IN PRAISE OF LESSIUS | 26 | 46 156 | 510 |
| A HAPPY SOULE THAT ALL THE WAY, | IN PRAISE OF LESSIUS | 33 | 46 156 | 510 |
| LIFES LATE FORSAKEN HOUSES ALL LAY DROWN'D | THE BEGINNING OF HELIODORUS | 16 | 46 158 | 517 |
| AND COMMING LATE HAD EAT UP GUESTS AND ALL, | THE BEGINNING OF HELIODORUS | 27 | 46 158 | 517 |
| HEE IS ALL CRUELL, CRUELL ALL. | OUT OF GREEKE CUPID'S CRYER | 53 | 46 159 | 519 |

| | | | | |
|---|---|---|---|---|
| HEE IS ALL CRUELL, CRUELL ALL, | OUT OF GREEKE CUPID'S CRYER | 53 | 46 159 519 | |
| I'LE GIVE THEE ALL, TAKE ALL, TAKE HEED | OUT OF GREEKE CUPID'S CRYER | 71 | 46 159 519 | |
| I'LE GIVE THEE ALL, TAKE ALL, TAKE HEED | OUT OF GREEKE CUPID'S CRYER | 71 | 46 159 519 | |
| ALL ONE GREAT EYE, ALL DROWN'D IN ONE GREAT TEARE, | UPON BISHOP ANDREWES PICTURE | 4 | 46 163 490 | |
| ALL ONE GREAT EYE, ALL DROWN'D IN ONE GREAT TEARE, | UPON BISHOP ANDREWES PICTURE | 4 | 46 163 490 | |
| OF ALL THY WATRY ELOQUENCE, | UPON THE DEATH OF A GENTLEMAN | 32 | 46 166 472 | |
| ALL TORNE, WITH MUCH ADOE YET ERE HE DYES, | HIGH MOUNTED ON AN ANT | 4 | 46 161 523 | |
| BUT WEE ARE DECEIVED ALL, | THE WEEPER | 13 | 46 79 120 | |
| TASTES OF THIS BREAKFAST ALL DAY LONG, | THE WEEPER | 30 | 46 79 120 | |
| SADNESSE ALL THE WHILE | THE WEEPER | 61 | 46 79 120 | |
| THERE IS NO NEED AT ALL | THE WEEPER | 67 | 46 79 120 | |
| STILL THE FOUNTAINE WEEPS FOR ALL, | THE WEEPER | 112 | 46 79 120 | |
| TWO MITES, TWO DROPS, (YET ALL HER HOUSE AND LAND) | WIDOWES MITES | 1 | 46 86 21 | |
| WHAT ALL THY WEALTH IN COUNSAILE, ALL THY STATE, | ON THE PRODIGALL | 3 | 46 86 17 | |
| WHAT ALL THY WEALTH IN COUNSAILE, ALL THY STATE, | ON THE PRODIGALL | 3 | 46 86 17 | |
| MILKE ALL THE WAY, | TO INFANT MARTYRS | 6 | 46 88 10 | |
| NOTHING, WEE OWE ALL THINGS THAT BEE, | AND HE ANSWERED NOTHING | 2 | 46 91 22 | |
| GOD SPAKE ONCE WHEN HEE ALL THINGS MADE, | AND HE ANSWERED NOTHING | 3 | 46 91 22 | |
| HEE SAV'D ALL WHEN HEE NOTHING SAID, | AND HE ANSWERED NOTHING | 4 | 46 91 22 | |
| MIDST ALL THE DARKE AND KNOTTY SNARES, | NEITHER DURST MAN ASKE | 1 | 46 92 20 | |
| WHILE THEY SPEAKE NOTHING, THEY SPEAKE ALL | NEITHER DURST MAN ASKE | 21 | 46 92 20 | |
| TO HOLD THEIR PEACE IS ALL THE WAIES, | NEITHER DURST MAN ASKE | 25 | 46 92 20 | |
| ALL, AND EVERY WHIT OF ME, | IT IS BETTER TO GO WITH EYE | 6 | 46 93 16 | |
| ALL HYBLA'S HONEY, ALL THAT SWEETNESSE CAN | UPON OUR LORDS LAST DISCOURSE | 1 | 46 95 21 | |
| ALL HYBLA'S HONEY, ALL THAT SWEETNESSE CAN | UPON OUR LORDS LAST DISCOURSE | 1 | 46 95 21 | |
| ALL WE HAVE IS GOD'S, AND YET | GIVE TO CAESAR AND TO GOD | 1 | 46 96 20 | |
| ALL IS GOD'S, AND YET 'TIS TRUE | GIVE TO CAESAR AND TO GOD | 5 | 46 96 20 | |
| ALL WEE HAVE IS CAESAR'S TOO, | GIVE TO CAESAR AND TO GOD | 6 | 46 96 20 | |
| ALL IS CAESAR'S, AND WHAT ODS | GIVE TO CAESAR AND TO GOD | 7 | 46 96 20 | |
| TO CAST THY NETS ON ALL OCCASIONS WELL, | ON ST. PETER CASTING NETS | 2 | 46 98 13 | |
| NOW THOU SHAL'T HAVE ALL REPAID, | ON WOUNDS OF CRUCIFIED LORD | 11 | 46 99 24 | |
| OF ALL THE GLORYES MAKE NOONE GAY | EASTER DAY | 7 | 46 100 26 | |
| ALL CREATURES HAVE, | EASTER DAY | 14 | 46 100 26 | |
| ALL THY PURPLE RIVERS MEET, | ON BLEEDING WOUNDS OF LORD | 4 | 46 101 110 | |
| ALL THE RIVERS NAM'D BEFORE, | ON BLEEDING WOUNDS OF LORD | 30 | 46 101 110 | |
| BUT O THAT ONE IS ONE ALL O'RE, | ON BLEEDING WOUNDS OF LORD | 32 | 46 101 110 | |
| THREATNING ALL TO OVERFLOW, | ON BLEEDING WOUNDS OF LORD | 34 | 46 101 110 | |
| ALL THE YEARE DOTH SIT AND SING, | PSALME 23 | 6 | 46 102 5 | |
| CRAFT IN ALL HER KNOTTY WILES, | PSALME 23 | 26 | 46 102 5 | |
| COME NOW ALL YEE TERRORS, SALLY | PSALME 23 | 35 | 46 102 5 | |
| THE HEAD OF ALL MY HOPE-NURST JOYES, | PSALME 137 | 26 | 46 104 7 | |
| THE TYRRHENE SEAS, AND SHORES SOUND ALL THE SAME, | SOSPETTO D'HERODE | 31 | 46 109 216 | |
| THERE WHERE ONE CENTER RECONCILES ALL THINGS, | SOSPETTO D'HERODE | 34 | 46 109 216 | |
| THEE ALL THE BEAUTIES OF THY ONCE BRIGHT EYES, | SOSPETTO D'HERODE | 74 | 46 109 216 | |
| NARCISSUS, FOOLISH PHAETON, WHO FOR ALL | SOSPETTO D'HERODE | 79 | 46 109 216 | |
| HEE SAW THE FALLING IDOLS, ALL CONFESSE | SOSPETTO D'HERODE | 125 | 46 109 216 | |
| AIRE, WITH A DISMALL SHADE, BUT ALL IN VAINE, | SOSPETTO D'HERODE | 143 | 46 109 216 | |
| TO DRAW A LONG-LIV'D DEATH, WHERE ALL MY CHEERE | SOSPETTO D'HERODE | 214 | 46 109 216 | |
| WITH HIS FAIRE TRIUMPHS FILL ALL FUTURE STORIES, | SOSPETTO D'HERODE | 230 | 46 109 216 | |
| AND ALL THE POWERS OF HELL IN FULL APPLAUSE | SOSPETTO D'HERODE | 259 | 46 109 216 | |
| IF ALL FAILE WEE'L PUT ON OUR PROUDEST ARMES, | SOSPETTO D'HERODE | 276 | 46 109 216 | |
| I THANKE YOU ALL, BUT ONE MUST SINGLE OUT, | SOSPETTO D'HERODE | 287 | 46 109 216 | |
| OR RATHER ALL THE OTHER THREE IN ONE, | SOSPETTO D'HERODE | 290 | 46 109 216 | |
| MONGST ALL THE PALACES IN HELLS COMMAND, | SOSPETTO D'HERODE | 305 | 46 109 216 | |
| FOR HANGINGS AND FOR CURTAINES, ALL ALONG | SOSPETTO D'HERODE | 321 | 46 109 216 | |
| SWORDS, SPEARS, WITH ALL THE FATALL INSTRUMENTS | SOSPETTO D'HERODE | 326 | 46 109 216 | |
| HERE ARE THEY ALL, HERE ALL THE SWORDS OR FLAMES | SOSPETTO D'HERODE | 365 | 46 109 216 | |
| HERE ARE THEY ALL, HERE ALL THE SWORDS OR FLAMES | SOSPETTO D'HERODE | 365 | 46 109 216 | |
| WHERE ALL THE BUSIE DAY SHEE CLOSE DOTH LY, | SOSPETTO D'HERODE | 386 | 46 109 216 | |
| OF ALL THEIR CARES, TAM'D THE REBELLIOUS EYE | SOSPETTO D'HERODE | 390 | 46 109 216 | |
| SEALING ALL BRESTS IN A LETHAEAN BAND, | SOSPETTO D'HERODE | 392 | 46 109 216 | |
| POYSONS TO SPEED THEE, YET THROUGH ALL THE LAND | SOSPETTO D'HERODE | 445 | 46 109 216 | |
| ALL POINTED IN HIS HEART SEEM'D TO HUNTER HIM, | SOSPETTO D'HERODE | 476 | 46 109 216 | |
| WHENCE ALL HIS HIGH SPIRITS, AND HOT COURAGE CAME, | SOSPETTO D'HERODE | 488 | 46 109 216 | |
| BUT ALL HIS COUNSELLOURS MUST SUMMON'D BEE, | SOSPETTO D'HERODE | 507 | 46 109 216 | |
| IT IS IN ONE RICH HANDFULL, HEAVEN AND ALL | ON A PRAYER BOOKE | 5 | 46 126 139 | |
| OF ALL THIS HIDDEN STORE | ON A PRAYER BOOKE | 81 | 46 126 139 | |
| ALL FRESH AND FRAGRANT AS HEE RISES, | ON A PRAYER BOOKE | 102 | 46 126 139 | |
| AND ALL THE SMOOTH FACED KINDRED THERE, | ON MR. G. HERBERTS BOOKE | 14 | 46 130 68 | |
| WEE NEED TO GOE TO NONE OF ALL | IN MEMORY OF LADY MADRE TERESA | 3 | 46 131 52 | |
| GOOD REASON FOR SHEE BREATHS ALL FIRE, | IN MEMORY OF LADY MADRE TERESA | 39 | 46 131 52 | |
| FAREWELL THEN ALL THE WORLD, ADEIU, | IN MEMORY OF LADY MADRE TERESA | 57 | 46 131 52 | |
| FAREWELL ALL PLEASURES, SPORTS AND JOYES, | IN MEMORY OF LADY MADRE TERESA | 59 | 46 131 52 | |
| SHALL ALL AT LAST DYE INTO ONE, | IN MEMORY OF LADY MADRE TERESA | 112 | 46 131 52 | |
| ALL THY GOOD WORKES WHICH WENT BEFORE, | IN MEMORY OF LADY MADRE TERESA | 140 | 46 131 52 | |
| SHALL OWNE THEE THERE, AND ALL IN ONE | IN MEMORY OF LADY MADRE TERESA | 142 | 46 131 52 | |
| ALL THY OLD WOES SHALL NOW SMILE ON THEE, | IN MEMORY OF LADY MADRE TERESA | 146 | 46 131 52 | |
| ALL THY SORROWS HERE SHALL SHINE, | IN MEMORY OF LADY MADRE TERESA | 148 | 46 131 52 | |
| AND WITH THEM ALL ABOUT THEE, BOW | IN MEMORY OF LADY MADRE TERESA | 171 | 46 131 52 | |
| (BY ALL THY MYSTERIES THAT THERE LYE HID,) | AN APOLOGIE FOR HYMNE (TERESA) | 12 | 46 136 59 | |
| OF BAPTISME, BLENDS THEM ALL INTO ONE BLOOD, | AN APOLOGIE FOR HYMNE (TERESA) | 16 | 46 136 59 | |
| CHRISTS FAITH MAKES BUT ONE BODY OF ALL SOULES, | AN APOLOGIE FOR HYMNE (TERESA) | 17 | 46 136 59 | |
| DRINKE UP ALL SPAINE IN SACK, LET MY SOULE SWELL | AN APOLOGIE FOR HYMNE (TERESA) | 30 | 46 136 59 | |
| BUT HIM, WHO TROD THE WINE-PRESSE ALL ALONE, | AN APOLOGIE FOR HYMNE (TERESA) | 40 | 46 136 59 | |
| GIRT ALL THY GLORIES TO-THEE, THEN SIT DOWN, | ON A TREATISE OF CHARITY | 11 | 46 137 69 | |
| WHERE THOU SHALT REACH ALL HEARTS, COMMAND EACH EYE, | ON A TREATISE OF CHARITY | 16 | 46 137 69 | |
| ALL THE SWEETEST SHOWERS, | ON THE ASSUMPTION | 47 | 46 139 114 | |
| ALL THE PURPLE PRIDE OF LACES, | AN HIMNE FOR CIRCUMCISION | 5 | 46 141 37 | |
| OF ALL THE FAIRE CHEEKT FLOWERS THAT FILL THEE, | AN HIMNE FOR CIRCUMCISION | 9 | 46 141 37 | |
| PUT ALL HIS RED EYED RUBIES ON, | AN HIMNE FOR CIRCUMCISION | 15 | 46 141 37 | |
| WHEN HE HATH DONE ALL HE MAY, | AN HIMNE FOR CIRCUMCISION | 25 | 46 141 37 | |
| ALL WILL BE DARKNESS, TO THE DAY | AN HIMNE FOR CIRCUMCISION | 27 | 46 141 37 | |
| OF ALL HIS EASTERNE PARAMOURS, | AN HIMNE FOR CIRCUMCISION | 34 | 46 141 37 | |
| HIS PERSIAN LOVERS ALL SHALL LEAVE HIM, | AN HIMNE FOR CIRCUMCISION | 35 | 46 141 37 | |

| | | | | | |
|---|---|---|---|---|---|
| HIS FUGITIVE GOLD THROUGH ALL HER FACES, | ON HOPE | 86 | 46 | 143 | 71 |
| ONE FACE MORE FUGITIVE THEN ALL THEY, | ON HOPE | 88 | 46 | 143 | 71 |
| OF A MAD STORME THESE BLOOMY JOYES ALL TORE, | UPON DEATH OF HERRYS | 33 | 46 | 167 | 466 |
| ALL HIS LEAVES, SO FRESH, SO SWEET, | UPON DEATH OF DESIRED HERRYS | 45 | 46 | 168 | 467 |
| ALL HER BIRTHS ABORTIVE PROVE. | UPON DEATH OF DESIRED HERRYS | 74 | 46 | 168 | 467 |
| ALL THE STREAMES OF ALL HER SPRINGS. | ANOTHER ON HERRYS | 10 | 46 | 170 | 469 |
| ALL THE STREAMES OF ALL HER SPRINGS. | ANOTHER ON HERRYS | 10 | 46 | 170 | 469 |
| IN ALL THE GIFTS THAT BLESSE A CREATURE. | ANOTHER ON HERRYS | 12 | 46 | 170 | 469 |
| NOW ALL THEIR STEELY OPERATION, | ANOTHER ON HERRYS | 23 | 46 | 170 | 469 |
| IN ALL THE BOOKE IF ANY WHERE | ANOTHER ON HERRYS | 47 | 46 | 170 | 469 |
| ALL THE TEARES THAT GRIEFE CAN LEND. | ANOTHER ON HERRYS | 58 | 46 | 170 | 469 |
| IN HIS ASHES ALL HER PRIDE. | ANOTHER ON HERRYS | 60 | 46 | 170 | 469 |
| ALL HOPE OF NEVER DYING, HERE LYES DEAD. | ANOTHER ON HERRYS | 62 | 46 | 170 | 469 |
| FOR ALL PERSUASIVE GRACES THENCE | HIS EPITAPH (HERRYS) | 33 | 46 | 172 | 471 |
| POINTED HIM OUT IN ALL HIS WAYES. | HIS EPITAPH (HERRYS) | 39 | 46 | 172 | 471 |
| THAT TO HIS SWEETNESSE, ALL MENS EYES | HIS EPITAPH (HERRYS) | 41 | 46 | 172 | 471 |
| COME THEN YOUTH, BEAUTY, AND BLOOD, ALL YE SOFT POWERS. | UPON STANINOUGH'S DEATH | 7 | 46 | 175 | 473 |
| ALL THY WILD CIRCLE TO A POINT. O SINKE | UPON STANINOUGH'S DEATH | 14 | 46 | 175 | 473 |
| (THROUGH ALL YOUR PAINTING) SHOWES YOU YOUR OWN FACE. | UPON STANINOUGH'S DEATH | 22 | 46 | 175 | 473 |
| OF ALL INTERPRETERS READ NATURE TRUE. | UPON STANINOUGH'S DEATH | 30 | 46 | 175 | 473 |
| THE CORALL OF THY LIPS. THOU ART OF ALL | UPON YORKE HIS BIRTH | 47 | 46 | 176 | 500 |
| BUT THOU AT NOONE DOST SHINE, AND ART ALL DAY, | UPON YORKE HIS BIRTH | 78 | 46 | 176 | 500 |
| THAT NEST OF HEROES, ALL OUR HOPES FINDE ROOME. | UPON YORKE HIS BIRTH | 81 | 46 | 176 | 500 |
| O MAYST THOU THUS MAKE ALL THE YEARE THINE OWNE, | UPON YORKE HIS BIRTH | 96 | 46 | 176 | 500 |
| FOR SEE APOLLO ALL THIS WHILE STANDS MUTE, | UPON YORKE HIS BIRTH | 114 | 46 | 176 | 500 |
| NOW AFTER ALL HER TOYLES BY SEA AND LAND, | UPON FAIRE ETHIOPIAN | 3 | 46 | 183 | 493 |
| AND TRACE ETERNITY--BUT ALL IS DEAD. | TO THE MORNING | 29 | 46 | 183 | 497 |
| ALL THESE DELICIOUS HOPES ARE BURIED. | TO THE MORNING | 30 | 46 | 183 | 497 |
| ALL MISCHIEFE COMES AFTER ALL HALLOW. | UPON POWDER DAY | 2 | 46 | 185 | 74 |
| ALL MISCHIEFE COMES AFTER ALL HALLOW. | UPON POWDER DAY | 2 | 46 | 185 | 74 |
| TO PAVE HIS PATHES WITH ALL THE GOOD | LOVES HOROSCOPE | 29 | 46 | 185 | 483 |
| THIS LAST COUGH AELIA, COUGHT OUT ALL THY FEARE, | OUT OF MARTIALL | 5 | 46 | 188 | 527 |
| ALL THE FLOWERS THAT NATURE NAMETH. | OUT OF THE ITALIAN (1) | 6 | 46 | 188 | 545 |
| ALL THE GRACES | OUT OF THE ITALIAN (1) | 22 | 46 | 188 | 545 |
| ALL HIS TERRORS TO AFFRIGHT MEE. | OUT OF THE ITALIAN (1) | 45 | 46 | 188 | 545 |
| NOW ALL OBSCURED LYES | OUT OF THE ITALIAN (2) | 8 | 46 | 190 | 547 |
| SO MUCH O'RE-MASTRING ALL HIS MIGHT, | OUT OF THE ITALIAN (3) | 6 | 46 | 190 | 549 |
| TO THAT ONE SENSE, MADE ALL ELSE THRALL, | OUT OF THE ITALIAN (3) | 7 | 46 | 190 | 549 |
| AND SO HE LOST HIS CLOTHES, EYES, HEART AND ALL. | OUT OF THE ITALIAN (3) | 8 | 46 | 190 | 549 |
| HONOUR ALL PREACHERS. HEARE THEIR OWNE. | AN EPITAPH UPON ASHTON | 8 | 46 | 192 | 464 |
| THAT OWES NOT ALL HIS DUTY | WISHES SUPPOSED MISTRESSE | 17 | 46 | 195 | 479 |
| LIPPS, WHERE ALL DAY | WISHES SUPPOSED MISTRESSE | 37 | 46 | 195 | 479 |
| OF A CLEERE MIND ARE DAY ALL NIGHT. | WISHES SUPPOSED MISTRESSE | 81 | 46 | 195 | 479 |
| BOVE ALL. NOTHING WITHIN THAT LOWRES. | WISHES SUPPOSED MISTRESSE | 93 | 46 | 195 | 479 |
| HAVE NATURE ALL THE NAME, | WISHES SUPPOSED MISTRESSE | 98 | 46 | 195 | 479 |
| COULD SHE IN ALL HER BIRTHS BUT COPPIE THEE, | UPON TWO GREENE APRICOCKES | 23 | 48 | 220 | 494 |
| SPITE OF ALL THE MAIDEN SNOW | THOUGH NOW 'TIS NEITHER | 7 | MS | 397 | 492 |
| THERE ALL THE YEARE IS LOVES LONG SPRING. | THOUGH NOW 'TIS NEITHER | 29 | MS | 397 | 492 |
| THERE ALL THE YEARE LOVES NIGHTINGALES | THOUGH NOW 'TIS NEITHER | 30 | MS | 397 | 492 |
| KNOWES ALL THE CORNERS OF'T, & CAN CONTROUL | TO COUNTESSE OF DENBIGH | 35 | 52 | 236 | 146 |
| THAT SO, IN SPITE OF ALL THIS PEEVISH STRENGTH | TO COUNTESSE OF DENBIGH | 41 | 52 | 236 | 146 |
| THE NAME OF ALL OUR LIVES & LOVES. | TO THE NAME OF JESUS | 5 | 52 | 239 | 30 |
| ALL YE WISE SOULES, WHO IN THE WEALTHY BREST | TO THE NAME OF JESUS | 11 | 52 | 239 | 30 |
| AND THAT FAIR WORD AT ALL REFERR TO THEE) | TO THE NAME OF JESUS | 14 | 52 | 239 | 30 |
| AND BE ALL WING. | TO THE NAME OF JESUS | 16 | 52 | 239 | 30 |
| OF HIM WHO NEVER SLEEPS, ALL THINGS THAT ARE, | TO THE NAME OF JESUS | 56 | 52 | 239 | 30 |
| BRING ALL YOUR HOUSHOLD STUFFE OF HEAVN ON EARTH. | TO THE NAME OF JESUS | 63 | 52 | 239 | 30 |
| BRING ALL THE STORE | TO THE NAME OF JESUS | 66 | 52 | 239 | 30 |
| BRING ALL THE POWRES OF PRAISE | TO THE NAME OF JESUS | 72 | 52 | 239 | 30 |
| BRING ALL YOUR LUTES & HARPS OF HEAVN & EARTH. | TO THE NAME OF JESUS | 74 | 52 | 239 | 30 |
| AND WHEN YOU'ARE COME, WITH ALL | TO THE NAME OF JESUS | 80 | 52 | 239 | 30 |
| MIX ALL YOUR MANY WORLDS, ABOVE, | TO THE NAME OF JESUS | 86 | 52 | 239 | 30 |
| TO ALL THE DEAR-BOUGHT NATIONS THIS REDEEMING NAME, | TO THE NAME OF JESUS | 94 | 52 | 239 | 30 |
| LEAVE ALL THY NATIVE GLORIES IN THEIR GORGEOUS NEST. | TO THE NAME OF JESUS | 119 | 52 | 239 | 30 |
| ALL HEAVEN BY THEE, | TO THE NAME OF JESUS | 133 | 52 | 239 | 30 |
| OF ALL THIS PRETIOUS PATIENCE. | TO THE NAME OF JESUS | 140 | 52 | 239 | 30 |
| (LOVE'S EASTERN WINDOWES) ALL WIDE OPE | TO THE NAME OF JESUS | 146 | 52 | 239 | 30 |
| WHERE ALL THEIR HOARD OF HONY LYES. | TO THE NAME OF JESUS | 158 | 52 | 239 | 30 |
| ALL FORCE OF SO PROPHANE A FALLACY | TO THE NAME OF JESUS | 171 | 52 | 239 | 30 |
| AN UNIVERSALL SYNOD OF ALL SWEETS. | TO THE NAME OF JESUS | 176 | 52 | 239 | 30 |
| WHEN THY OLD FREINDS OF FIRE, ALL FULL OF THEE, | TO THE NAME OF JESUS | 198 | 52 | 239 | 30 |
| OF WRATH, & MADE THEE WAY THROUGH ALL THOSE WOUNDS. | TO THE NAME OF JESUS | 224 | 52 | 239 | 30 |
| TO ALL OUR WORLD OF WELL-STOLN JOY | IN HOLY NATIVITY | 5 | 52 | 246 | 76 |
| WELLCOME, ALL WONDERS IN ONE SIGHT. | IN HOLY NATIVITY | 79 | 52 | 246 | 76 |
| ALL THE PURPLE PRIDE THAT LACES | NEW YEAR'S DAY | 5 | 52 | 251 | 37 |
| OF ALL THE FAIR-CHEEK'T FLOWRS THAT FILL THEE | NEW YEAR'S DAY | 9 | 52 | 251 | 37 |
| PUT ALL HIS RED-EY'D RUBIES ON. | NEW YEAR'S DAY | 15 | 52 | 251 | 37 |
| WHEN HE HATH DONE ALL HE MAY | NEW YEAR'S DAY | 25 | 52 | 251 | 37 |
| ALL WILL BE DARKNES TO THE DAY | NEW YEAR'S DAY | 27 | 52 | 251 | 37 |
| OF ALL HIS EASTERN PARAMOURS. | NEW YEAR'S DAY | 34 | 52 | 251 | 37 |
| HIS PERSIAN LOVERS ALL SHALL LEAVE HIM. | NEW YEAR'S DAY | 35 | 52 | 251 | 37 |
| ALL-CIRCLING POINT. ALL CENTRING SPHEAR. | IN GLORIOUS EPIPHANIE | 26 | 52 | 253 | 39 |
| O LITTLE ALL. IN THY EMBRACE | IN GLORIOUS EPIPHANIE | 36 | 52 | 253 | 39 |
| THE DEATHLES HEIR OF ALL THY FATHER'S DAY. | IN GLORIOUS EPIPHANIE | 64 | 52 | 253 | 39 |
| THEN ALL THOSE HE SUFFERED. | IN GLORIOUS EPIPHANIE | 120 | 52 | 253 | 39 |
| LONG MADE TH'HARMONIOUS ORBES ALL MUTE TO US | IN GLORIOUS EPIPHANIE | 132 | 52 | 253 | 39 |
| ALL THE IDOLATROUS THEFTS DONE BY THIS NIGHT OF DAY. | IN GLORIOUS EPIPHANIE | 150 | 52 | 253 | 39 |
| THUS WE, WHO WHEN WITH ALL THE NOBLE POWRES | IN GLORIOUS EPIPHANIE | 219 | 52 | 253 | 39 |
| SWELLS HIGH, FAIR CONFLUENCE OF ALL HIGHBORN BLOUD. | TO THE QUEEN'S MAJESTY | 16 | 52 | 261 | 47 |
| WHILE ALL THE YEAR IS YOUR EPIPHANY, | TO THE QUEEN'S MAJESTY | 26 | 52 | 261 | 47 |
| ALL HAIL, FAIR TREE. | OFFICE H. CROSS MATINES | 18 | 52 | 265 | 66 |
| THREW ALL THE LOSSE. | OFFICE H. CROSS THIRD | 13 | 52 | 268 | 93 |
| ALL WOES INTO ONE CRUCIFIX. | OFFICE H. CROSS SIXT | 8 | 52 | 270 | 97 |

| | | | | |
|---|---|---|---|---|
| OF SOME MORE PAINFULL THING THEN ALL HIS PAINES. | OFFICE H. CROSS NINTH | 4 | 52 271 | 99 |
| OF ALL THE RANSOM'D WORLD, THOU HADST THE POWER | OFFICE H. CROSS EVENSONG | 16 | 52 273 | 101 |
| O'RELOCK ALL LIBANUS. THY LOFTY CROWN | OFFICE H. CROSS EVENSONG | 22 | 52 273 | 101 |
| RUN, MARY, RUN. BRING HITHER ALL THE BLEST | OFFICE H. CROSS COMPLINE | 5 | 52 274 | 105 |
| WHO LEND'ST TO ALL THINGS ALL THE LIFE THEY HAVE. | OFFICE H. CROSS COMPLINE | 10 | 52 274 | 105 |
| WHO LEND'ST TO ALL THINGS ALL THE LIFE THEY HAVE. | OFFICE H. CROSS COMPLINE | 10 | 52 274 | 105 |
| IN THAT HOUR, & IN THESE, MAY BE ALL THINE. | OFFICE H. CROSS RECOMMENDATION | 4 | 52 276 | 106 |
| BURN ALL AS BRIGHT, | CHARITAS NIMIA | 22 | 52 280 | 48 |
| HANGING ALL TORN SHE SEES. AND IN HIS WOES | SANCTA MARIA DOLORUM | 7 | 52 283 | 162 |
| ALL, MORE AT HOME IN HER OWNE HEART. | SANCTA MARIA DOLORUM | 10 | 52 283 | 162 |
| ME TOO MY TEARES. WHO, THOUGH ALL STONE, | SANCTA MARIA DOLORUM | 59 | 52 283 | 162 |
| OF GREIFES HIS PORTION, WHO (HAD ALL THEIR DUE) | SANCTA MARIA DOLORUM | 79 | 52 283 | 162 |
| BY ALL THOSE STINGS | SANCTA MARIA DOLORUM | 95 | 52 283 | 162 |
| ALL THE PURPLE RIVERS MEET. | UPON BLEEDING CRUCIFIX | 4 | 52 288 | 110 |
| ALL THE RIVERS NAM'D BEFORE. | UPON BLEEDING CRUCIFIX | 26 | 52 288 | 110 |
| BUT O THAT ONE IS ONE ALL ORE. | UPON BLEEDING CRUCIFIX | 28 | 52 288 | 110 |
| BENT ALL TO DROWN & OVERFLOW. | UPON BLEEDING CRUCIFIX | 30 | 52 288 | 110 |
| WITH ALL THE POWRES MY POOR HEART HATH | ADORO TE | 1 | 52 291 | 172 |
| YOUR PORTS ARE ALL SUPERFLUOUS HERE. | ADORO TE | 9 | 52 291 | 172 |
| STRETCH ALL THY POWRES. CALL IF YOU CAN | LAUDA SION SALVATOREM | 3 | 52 294 | 178 |
| BEARES HOME NO LESSE. ALL THEY NO MORE, | LAUDA SION SALVATOREM | 47 | 52 294 | 178 |
| BE ALL THE SAME TO EVERY GUEST, | LAUDA SION SALVATOREM | 50 | 52 294 | 178 |
| ON WHICH ALL FIGURES FIX'T THEIR EYES. | LAUDA SION SALVATOREM | 66 | 52 294 | 178 |
| COHEIRS OF SAINTS. THAT SO ALL MAY | LAUDA SION SALVATOREM | 77 | 52 294 | 178 |
| SHALL CRY WE COME, WE COME & ALL | DIES IRAE | 15 | 52 298 | 186 |
| SHALL ALL THAT LABOUR, ALL THAT COST | DIES IRAE | 33 | 52 298 | 186 |
| SHALL ALL THAT LABOUR, ALL THAT COST | DIES IRAE | 33 | 52 298 | 186 |
| THEN ALL THAT WAY, AND WEARYNESSE. | DIES IRAE | 36 | 52 298 | 186 |
| AND ALL THY LOST SHEEP FOUND SHALL BE, | DIES IRAE | 59 | 52 298 | 186 |
| O HEAR A SUPPLIANT HEART. ALL CRUSH'T | DIES IRAE | 65 | 52 298 | 186 |
| HE THAT MADE ALL THINGS, HAD NOT DONE | O GLORIOSA DOMINA | 5 | 52 302 | 194 |
| THE FEAST OF ALL THINGS FEEDS ON THEE. | O GLORIOSA DOMINA | 10 | 52 302 | 194 |
| E'RE SHE BORE ANY ONE, SLEW ALL. | O GLORIOSA DOMINA | 12 | 52 302 | 194 |
| WHICH RENDERS ALL THE STARRES SHE STOLE AWAY. | O GLORIOSA DOMINA | 22 | 52 302 | 194 |
| LET THEN THE AGED WORLD BE WISE, & ALL | O GLORIOSA DOMINA | 23 | 52 302 | 194 |
| (ALL YOU TO WHOM THIS LOVE BELONGS) | O GLORIOSA DOMINA | 29 | 52 302 | 194 |
| ALL THE SWEETEST SHOWRES | IN GLORIOUS ASSUMPTION B. LADY | 52 | 52 304 | 114 |
| BUT WE'ARE DECEIVED ALL. | WEEPER | 13 | 52 307 | 120 |
| TASTS OF THIS BREAKFAST ALL DAY LONG. | WEEPER | 30 | 52 307 | 120 |
| THERE'S NO NEED AT ALL | WEEPER | 49 | 52 307 | 120 |
| (MERCILESSE LOVE.) IS ALL. | WEEPER | 129 | 52 307 | 120 |
| ALL PLACES, TIMES, & OBJECTS BE | WEEPER | 131 | 52 307 | 120 |
| STILL THE FOUNTAIN WEEPS FOR ALL. | WEEPER | 136 | 52 307 | 120 |
| WEE'L NOW APPEAL TO NONE OF ALL | TERESA | 3 | 52 315 | 52 |
| GOOD REASON. FOR SHE BREATHES ALL FIRE. | TERESA | 39 | 52 315 | 52 |
| FAREWEL THEN, ALL THE WORLD. ADIEU. | TERESA | 57 | 52 315 | 52 |
| FAREWELL, ALL PLEASURES, SPORTS, & JOYES. | TERESA | 59 | 52 315 | 52 |
| SHALL ALL AT LAST DY INTO ONE, | TERESA | 111 | 52 315 | 52 |
| ALL THY GOOD WORKES WHICH WENT BEFORE | TERESA | 139 | 52 315 | 52 |
| SHALL OWN THEE THERE. AND ALL IN ONE | TERESA | 141 | 52 315 | 52 |
| ALL THY OLD WOES SHALL NOW SMILE ON THEE | TERESA | 145 | 52 315 | 52 |
| ALL THY SORROWS HERE SHALL SHINE, | TERESA | 147 | 52 315 | 52 |
| ALL THY SUFFRINGS BE DIVINE. | TERESA | 148 | 52 315 | 52 |
| AND WITH THEM ALL ABOUT THEE BOW | TERESA | 170 | 52 315 | 52 |
| (BY ALL THY MYSTERYES THAT HERE LY HIDDE) | AN APOLOGIE FOR (TERESA) HYMNE | 12 | 52 322 | 59 |
| OF BAPTISM BLENDS THEM ALL INTO A BLOOD. | AN APOLOGIE FOR (TERESA) HYMNE | 16 | 52 322 | 59 |
| CHRIST'S FAITH MAKES BUT ONE BODY OF ALL SOULES | AN APOLOGIE FOR (TERESA) HYMNE | 17 | 52 322 | 59 |
| BUT HIM WHO TROD THE WINE-PRESSE ALL ALONE | AN APOLOGIE FOR (TERESA) HYMNE | 40 | 52 322 | 59 |
| THOU WOULDST ON HER HAVE HEAP'T UP ALL | FLAMING HEART | 29 | 52 324 | 61 |
| ALL THOSE FAIR & FLAGRANT THINGS, | FLAMING HEART | 34 | 52 324 | 61 |
| BUT BEFORE ALL, THAT FIERY DART | FLAMING HEART | 35 | 52 324 | 61 |
| SAY, ALL YE WISE & WELL-PEIRC'T HEARTS | FLAMING HEART | 49 | 52 324 | 61 |
| FOR ALL THE GALLANTRY OF HIM, | FLAMING HEART | 63 | 52 324 | 61 |
| HIS BE THE BRAVERY OF ALL THOSE BRIGHT THINGS, | FLAMING HEART | 65 | 52 324 | 61 |
| LIVE IN THESE CONQUERING LEAVES. LIVE ALL THE SAME. | FLAMING HEART | 77 | 52 324 | 61 |
| AND WALK THROUGH ALL TONGUES ONE TRIUMPHANT FLAME | FLAMING HEART | 78 | 52 324 | 61 |
| LET ALL THY SCATTER'D SHAFTS OF LIGHT, THAT PLAY | FLAMING HEART | 87 | 52 324 | 61 |
| BY ALL THY DOWR OF LIGHTS & FIRES. | FLAMING HEART | 94 | 52 324 | 61 |
| BY ALL THE EAGLE IN THEE, ALL THE DOVE. | FLAMING HEART | 95 | 52 324 | 61 |
| BY ALL THE EAGLE IN THEE, ALL THE DOVE. | FLAMING HEART | 95 | 52 324 | 61 |
| BY ALL THY LIVES & DEATHS OF LOVE. | FLAMING HEART | 96 | 52 324 | 61 |
| BY ALL THY BRIM-FILL'D BOWLES OF FEIRCE DESIRE | FLAMING HEART | 99 | 52 324 | 61 |
| BY ALL THE HEAV'NS THOU HAST IN HIM | FLAMING HEART | 103 | 52 324 | 61 |
| BY ALL OF HIM WE HAVE IN THEE. | FLAMING HEART | 105 | 52 324 | 61 |
| UNTO ALL LIFE OF MINE MAY DY. | FLAMING HEART | 108 | 52 324 | 61 |
| IT IS, IN ONE CHOISE HANDFULL, HEAVENN, & ALL | PRAYER TO GENTLE-WOMAN | 11 | 52 328 | 139 |
| OF ALL THIS STORE | PRAYER TO GENTLE-WOMAN | 87 | 52 328 | 139 |
| ALL FRESH & FRAGRANT AS HE RISES | PRAYER TO GENTLE-WOMAN | 108 | 52 328 | 139 |
| THOUGH ALL THE JOYES I HAD FLEED HENCE WITH THEE | ALEXIAS SECONDE ELEGIE | 1 | 52 335 | 207 |
| HAVE STUDY'D OVER ALL ASTROLOGY. | ALEXIAS SECONDE ELEGIE | 22 | 52 335 | 207 |
| STANDS ARM'D, TO SHEILD ME FROM ALL WANTON WRONG. | ALEXIAS THIRD ELEGIE | 36 | 52 336 | 209 |
| ALL YE SOFT POWRES, | DEATH'S LECTURE | 8 | 52 340 | 475 |
| ALL THY WILD CIRCLE TO A POINT. O SINK | DEATH'S LECTURE | 15 | 52 340 | 475 |
| OF ALL INTERPRETERS READ NATURE TRUE. | DEATH'S LECTURE | 32 | 52 340 | 475 |
| WILT' SEE A MAN, ALL HIS OWN WEALTH, | TEMPERANCE | 15 | 52 342 | 510 |
| THROUGH WHICH ALL HER BRIGHT FEATURES SHINE. | TEMPERANCE | 24 | 52 342 | 510 |
| A HAPPY SOUL, THAT ALL THE WAY | TEMPERANCE | 31 | 52 342 | 510 |
| HIS FUGITIVE GOLD THROUGH ALL HER FACES. | (ON) HOPE | 46 | 52 345 | 71 |
| ONE FACE MORE FUGITIVE THEN ALL THEY. | (ON) HOPE | 48 | 52 345 | 71 |
| SEED-TIME'S NOT ALL. THERE SHOULD BE HARVEST TOO. | AGAINST IRRESOLUTION AND DELAY | 37 | 52 347 | 146 |
| ALL HATING TO BE LEFT BEHIND. | AGAINST IRRESOLUTION AND DELAY | 42 | 52 347 | 146 |
| ALL THINGS SWEAR FRIENDS TO FAIR AND GOOD, | AGAINST IRRESOLUTION AND DELAY | 57 | 52 347 | 146 |
| AND BREAKES THROUGH ALL TEN HEAV'NS TO OUR EMBRACE. | AGAINST IRRESOLUTION AND DELAY | 78 | 52 347 | 146 |
| PEACE, HEART. THE HEAVENS ARE ANGRY. ALL THEIR SPHAERES | LUKE 2. QUAERIT JESUM | 19 | MS 379 | 11 |

|     |     |     |     |     |
| --- | --- | --- | --- | --- |
| WITHOUT RELIGIOUS SILENCE. ABOVE ALL | HORATIJ ILLE & NEFASTO | 47 | MS 382 | 530 |
| ALL THIS IT THREATS, & MORE HORROR, THAT FLIES | ON GUNPOWDER-TREASON | 45 | MS 384 | 458 |
| TO TH' EMPYRAEUM OF ALL MISERIES. | ON GUNPOWDER-TREASON | 46 | MS 384 | 458 |
| ALL THIS IT ONLY THREATS. THE METEOR LY'D. | ON GUNPOWDER-TREASON | 49 | MS 384 | 458 |
| THE FALL OF ALL THINGS IT PRAESAG'D, ITS OWNE | ON GUNPOWDER-TREASON | 52 | MS 384 | 458 |
| THE STAGGERING LUMPE. EACH EYE SPENT ALL ITS STORE, | UPON KINGS CORONATION | 11 | MS 390 | 453 |
| A HEART BURNING IN LOVE. ALL DID ADORE | UPON KINGS CORONATION | 37 | MS 390 | 453 |
| ALL MELANCHOLY CLOWDS VANISHT AWAY. | UPON KINGS CORONATION | 40 | MS 390 | 453 |
| THEY SHALL PROCLAIME TO ALL, THAT THEY ARE THINE. | UPON BIRTH PRINCESSE E | 8 | MS 391 | 456 |
| THAT HAND OF MILKY DOUNE. ALL THESE ARE BASE. | UPON BIRTH PRINCESSE E | 52 | MS 391 | 456 |
| OF HEAVEN, & EARTH, & OF ALL RARITIE. | UPON BIRTH PRINCESSE E | 58 | MS 391 | 456 |
| AND ALL THEIR FELLOW DEITIES WILL BOW | EX EUPHORMIONE | 6 | MS 392 | 525 |
| GONE BE ALL CONSORT, SINCE ALONE | UPON DEATH OF A FREIND | 17 | MS 393 | 477 |
| OF ALL OUR GLORIOUS HOPES SHOULD FADE. | AN ELEGY MR STANNINOW | 43 | MS 394 | 473 |
| SEE ALL IN MOURNING NOW. THE WALLES ARE JETT, | AN ELEGIE ON DR PORTER | 7 | MS 395 | 476 |
| OF ALL PROUD NEPTUNES SILVER-SHEILDED GUARD. | AN ELEGIE ON DR PORTER | 34 | MS 395 | 476 |
| FEARE NOT TO DY WITH GREIFE. ALL BUBLING EYES | AN ELEGIE ON DR PORTER | 43 | MS 395 | 476 |
| AND STREIGHT OF ALL THIS APPROBATION GATE | OUT OF GROTIUS | 55 | MS 398 | 198 |
| GOOD WINE IN ALL POYNTS. BUT THE EASY RATE. | OUT OF GROTIUS | 56 | MS 398 | 198 |
| THE PEOPLES HUNGER, AND WHEN ALL WERE FULL | OUT OF GROTIUS | 63 | MS 398 | 198 |
| THE WIND IN ALL HIS ROARING BRAGS STOOD STILL | OUT OF GROTIUS | 65 | MS 398 | 198 |
| IN DEATH-FULL DESPERATE ILLS WHERE ART AND ALL | OUT OF GROTIUS | 69 | MS 398 | 198 |
| YETT HERE'S NOT ALL. NOR WAS'T ENOUGH FOR MEE | OUT OF GROTIUS | 81 | MS 398 | 198 |

WORLD--ALL

|     |     |     |     |     |
| --- | --- | --- | --- | --- |
| THE WORLD--ALL DARING DUST AND ASHES. ONELY YOU | UPON STANINOUGH'S DEATH | 29 | 46 175 | 475 |

ALL-ADORED

|     |     |     |     |     |
| --- | --- | --- | --- | --- |
| WELLCOME DEAR, ALL-ADORED NAME. | TO THE NAME OF JESUS | 225 | 52 239 | 30 |

ALL-CHEARING

|     |     |     |     |     |
| --- | --- | --- | --- | --- |
| THE BLISSFULL SPRINGS OF JOY, FROM WHOSE ALL-CHEARING | OFFICE H. CROSS PRIME | 7 | 52 267 | 91 |

ALL-CIRCLING

|     |     |     |     |     |
| --- | --- | --- | --- | --- |
| ALL-CIRCLING POINT. ALL CENTRING SPHEAR. | IN GLORIOUS EPIPHANIE | 26 | 52 253 | 39 |

ALL-COMPOSING

|     |     |     |     |     |
| --- | --- | --- | --- | --- |
| HATE THE SWEET PEACE OF ALL-COMPOSING NIGHT. | SOSPETTO D'HERODE | 496 | 46 109 | 216 |

ALL-DARING

|     |     |     |     |     |
| --- | --- | --- | --- | --- |
| THE WORLD. ALL-DARING DUST & ASHES. ONLY YOU | DEATH'S LECTURE | 31 | 52 340 | 475 |
| OF LOVES ALL-DARING HAND, THAT MAKES ME BURNE, | EX EUPHORMIONE | 5 | MS 392 | 525 |

ALL-EMBRACING

|     |     |     |     |     |
| --- | --- | --- | --- | --- |
| GREAT LITTLE ONE. WHOSE ALL-EMBRACING BIRTH | IN HOLY NATIVITY | 83 | 52 246 | 76 |

ALL-IMBRACING

|     |     |     |     |     |
| --- | --- | --- | --- | --- |
| OF THIS UNBOUNDED ALL-IMBRACING SONG. | TO THE NAME OF JESUS | 91 | 52 239 | 30 |

ALL-IDOLIZING

|     |     |     |     |     |
| --- | --- | --- | --- | --- |
| ALL-IDOLIZING WORMES. THAT THUS COULD CROWD | IN GLORIOUS EPIPHANIE | 113 | 52 253 | 39 |

ALL-OBEDIENT

|     |     |     |     |     |
| --- | --- | --- | --- | --- |
| THEN BOWES HIS ALL-OBEDIENT HEAD, & DYES | OFFICE H. CROSS NINTH | 5 | 52 271 | 99 |

ALL-SOVERAIGN

|     |     |     |     |     |
| --- | --- | --- | --- | --- |
| ALL-SOVERAIGN NAME | TO THE NAME OF JESUS | 36 | 52 239 | 30 |

ALL-UNBLEMISH'T

|     |     |     |     |     |
| --- | --- | --- | --- | --- |
| THE BLUSHES OF THY ALL-UNBLEMISH'T MOTHER. | IN GLORIOUS EPIPHANIE | 67 | 52 253 | 39 |

ALL-UNWRINKLED

|     |     |     |     |     |
| --- | --- | --- | --- | --- |
| WHOSE FULL & ALL-UNWRINKLED FACE | IN GLORIOUS EPIPHANIE | 28 | 52 253 | 39 |

ALL'S

|     |     |     |     |     |
| --- | --- | --- | --- | --- |
| BUT WHEN INDEED ALL'S OVERFLOW'D | ON BLEEDING WOUNDS OF LORD | 35 | 46 101 | 110 |
| BUT WHEN INDEED ALL'S OVERFLOW'D | UPON BLEEDING CRUCIFIX | 31 | 52 288 | 110 |
| IF ALL'S PRAESCRIPTION. & PROUD WRONG | FLAMING HEART | 61 | 52 324 | 61 |

AL

|     |     |     |     |     |
| --- | --- | --- | --- | --- |
| DRINK UP AL SPAIN IN SACK. LET MY SOUL SWELL | AN'APOLOGIE FOR (TERESA) HYMNE | 30 | 52 322 | 59 |

ALLAY

|     |     |     |     |     |
| --- | --- | --- | --- | --- |
| SUBSTANTIALL SHADE. WHOSE SWEET ALLAY | (ON) HOPE | 5 | 52 345 | 71 |

ALLEAGE

| | | | | | |
|---|---|---|---|---|---|
| PLEAD FOR ME, LOVE. ALLEAGE & SHOW | ADORO TE | 19 | 52 | 291 | 172 |

ALLOW

| | | | | | |
|---|---|---|---|---|---|
| TO TH'CHURCH HEE DID ALLOW HER DRESSE. | AN EPITAPH UPON ASHTON | 21 | 46 | 192 | 464 |

ALLOW'D

| | | | | | |
|---|---|---|---|---|---|
| THOUGH ALLOW'D NOR HAND NOR EYE | ADORO TE | 28 | 52 | 291 | 172 |

ALLOWES

| | | | | | |
|---|---|---|---|---|---|
| AND SO ALLOWES WHAT IT DENIES. | TO THE QUEEN | 8 | 48 | 215 | 501 |
| WHICH LIVES STILL, & ALLOWES US BREATH. | ADORO TE | 38 | 52 | 291 | 172 |

ALLUDE

| | | | | | |
|---|---|---|---|---|---|
| THINGS THAT IN HARDNESSE MORE ALLUDE TO THEE. | ALEXIAS SECONDE ELEGIE | 16 | 52 | 335 | 207 |

ALMES

| | | | | | |
|---|---|---|---|---|---|
| AT LEAST AN ALMES OF GREIF | SANCTA MARIA DOLORUM | 92 | 52 | 283 | 162 |

ALMIGHTY

| | | | | | |
|---|---|---|---|---|---|
| TO GENERATION. HEAVENS ALMIGHTY SIRE | OUT OF VIRGIL | 4 | 46 | 155 | 529 |
| UPP TO TH' ALMIGHTY THUNDERER THEY HIED. | UPON GUNPOWDER TREASON | 54 | MS | 386 | 460 |

ALLMIGHTY

| | | | | | |
|---|---|---|---|---|---|
| ALLMIGHTY LOVE. END THIS LONG WARR. | TO COUNTESSE OF DENBIGH | 29 | 52 | 236 | 146 |

ALOFT

| | | | | | |
|---|---|---|---|---|---|
| LO, WHERE ALOFT IT COMES. IT COMES, AMONG | TO THE NAME OF JESUS | 151 | 52 | 239 | 30 |
| ALOFT. AND FILL THE NATIONS WITH THY NOBLE FRUIT. | VEXILLA REGIS | 38 | 52 | 277 | 156 |

ALONE

| | | | | | |
|---|---|---|---|---|---|
| MARKES OF A FIGHT ALONE, BUT FEASTING TOO. | THE BEGINNING OF HELIODORUS | 24 | 46 | 158 | 517 |
| THOU, THOU (DEARE LORD) EVEN THOU ALONE. | VERILY YE SHALL WEEP | 5 | 46 | 95 | 22 |
| NO,NO,THY GOOD, SION, ALONE MUST CROWNE | PSALME 137 | 25 | 46 | 104 | 7 |
| DISDAINES TO THINKE THAT HEAV'N THUNDERS ALONE. | SOSPETTO D'HERODE | 56 | 46 | 109 | 216 |
| WITH HIM BELOW. HERE THOU ART LORD ALONE | SOSPETTO D'HERODE | 271 | 46 | 109 | 216 |
| CRUELTY, SHE ALONE SHALL CURE MY DOUBT. | SOSPETTO D'HERODE | 288 | 46 | 109 | 216 |
| LET PRAYER ALONE TO PLAY HIS PART. | ON A PRAYER BOOKE | 28 | 46 | 126 | 139 |
| STORE UP THEMSELVES FOR HIM, WHO IS ALONE | ON A PRAYER BOOKE | 39 | 46 | 126 | 139 |
| BUT HIM, WHO TROD THE WINE-PRESSE ALL ALONE. | AN APOLOGIE FOR HYMNE (TERESA) | 40 | 46 | 136 | 59 |
| HIS HEAD IN CLOUDES, AS IF IN HIM ALONE | UPON DEATH OF HERRYS | 5 | 46 | 167 | 466 |
| ALONE, LIGHT SUCH ANOTHER STARRE, AND TWINE | UPON YORKE HIS BIRTH | 56 | 46 | 176 | 500 |
| THE FIRST BLAST OF THY COUGH LEFT TWO ALONE, | OUT OF MARTIALL | 3 | 46 | 188 | 527 |
| AND CAN ALONE COMMEND THE REST. | WISHES SUPPOSED MISTRESSE | 27 | 46 | 195 | 479 |
| WITH THEE ALONE HE WEARES NO BEARD, THY BRAINE | UPON TWO GREENE APRICOCKES | 17 | 48 | 220 | 494 |
| THOU THAT ALONE CANST THAW THIS COLD, | TO COUNTESSE OF DENBIGH | 27 | 52 | 236 | 146 |
| BUT SUCH ALONE WHOSE SACRED PEDIGREE | TO THE NAME OF JESUS | 181 | 52 | 239 | 30 |
| AND LET THE MIGHTY BABE ALONE. | IN HOLY NATIVITY | 45 | 52 | 246 | 76 |
| HAIL, OUR ALONE HOPE. LET THY FAIR HEAD SHOOT | VEXILLA REGIS | 37 | 52 | 277 | 156 |
| THINK MUCH THAT THOU SHOULDST MOURN ALONE. | SANCTA MARIA DOLORUM | 60 | 52 | 283 | 162 |
| WHOSE VITALL GUST ALONE CAN GIVE | ADORO TE | 41 | 52 | 291 | 172 |
| BUT HIM WHO TROD THE WINE-PRESSE ALL ALONE | AN APOLOGIE FOR (TERESA) HYMNE | 40 | 52 | 322 | 59 |
| LEAVE HER ALONE THE FLAMING HEART. | FLAMING HEART | 68 | 52 | 324 | 61 |
| LET PRAYER ALONE TO PLAY HIS PART. | PRAYER TO GENTLE-WOMAN | 34 | 52 | 328 | 139 |
| STORE UP THEMSELVES FOR HIM, WHO IS ALONE | PRAYER TO GENTLE-WOMAN | 45 | 52 | 328 | 139 |
| NOR COULDST THOU, CRUELL, LEAVE ME QUITE ALONE. | ALEXIAS SECONDE ELEGIE | 4 | 52 | 335 | 207 |
| ALEXIS, HE ALONE IS MINE (SAID I) | ALEXIAS THIRD ELEGIE | 56 | 52 | 336 | 209 |
| ALEXIS IS ALONE. BUT IS NOT MINE. | ALEXIAS THIRD ELEGIE | 58 | 52 | 336 | 209 |
| IN YOU ALONE HATH LOST HIS WINGS. | AGAINST IRRESOLUTION AND DELAY | 28 | 52 | 347 | 146 |
| YEA SUITOURS. MAN ALONE IS WO'ED. | AGAINST IRRESOLUTION AND DELAY | 58 | 52 | 347 | 146 |
| ALONE MUST LY. | LUKE 2. QUAERIT JESUM | 12 | MS | 379 | 11 |
| GONE BE ALL CONSORT, SINCE ALONE | UPON DEATH OF A FREIND | 17 | MS | 393 | 477 |

ALOOFE

| | | | | | |
|---|---|---|---|---|---|
| THY HUMBLE FAITH AND FEARE KEEPES HIM ALOOFE. | I AM NOT WORTHY | 2 | 46 | 90 | 13 |

ALOUD

| | | | | | |
|---|---|---|---|---|---|
| THEIR SILENCE SPEAKES ALOUD, AND IS | NEITHER DURST MAN ASKE | 19 | 46 | 92 | 20 |
| WINTER CHIDDE ALOUD. & SENT | IN HOLY NATIVITY | 24 | 52 | 246 | 76 |

ALREADY

| | | | | | |
|---|---|---|---|---|---|
| BEASTS AND BASE STRAW. ALREADY IS THE STREAME | SOSPETTO D'HERODE | 437 | 46 | 109 | 216 |
| ALREADY IN THEIR BOSOMES, AND THEIR HAND | SOSPETTO D'HERODE | 443 | 46 | 109 | 216 |
| ALREADY REACHES AT A SWORD. THEY HIRE | SOSPETTO D'HERODE | 444 | 46 | 109 | 216 |
| FIXT IN DELIGHT, AS IF ALREADY THERE | UPON DEATH OF HERRYS | 27 | 46 | 167 | 466 |

ALLREADY

| | | | | | |
|---|---|---|---|---|---|
| YOU'AVE SEEN ALLREADY, IN THIS LOWER SPHEAR | TO SAME CONCERNING CHOISE | 8 | 52 | 331 | 66 |

ALTAR

ONE NEERER TO GODS ALTAR TROD,                                  TWO WENT TO PRAY                    5   46   89   18
BUSIRIS HA'S HIS BLOODY ALTAR HERE,                             SOSPETTO D'HERODE                 355   46  109  216
NOR ON GODS ALTAR CAST TWO SCORCHING EYES                       ON A TREATISE OF CHARITY           43   46  137   69
NO MORE MY PILLOW SHALL THINE ALTAR BE,                         TO THE MORNING                     49   46  183  497

ALTAR-STALL'D

THE ALTAR-STALL'D OX, FATT OSYRIS NOW                           IN GLORIOUS EPIPHANIE              96   52  253   39

ALTARS

THE OTHER TO THE ALTARS GOD.                                    TWO WENT TO PRAY                    6   46   89   18
GIRT ROUND THY AWFULL ALTARS, WITH BRIGHT WINGS                 ON A TREATISE OF CHARITY           22   46  137   69
BUT GODS ARE GRATIOUS. AND THEIR ALTARS, MAKE                   UPON YORKE HIS BIRTH              116   46  176  500
PRETIOUS THEIR OFFERINGS THAT THEIR ALTARS TAKE.                UPON YORKE HIS BIRTH              117   46  176  500

ALTERNATE

NOR BY ALTERNATE SHREDDS OF LIGHT                               IN GLORIOUS EPIPHANIE              34   52  253   39
DISCOURSE ALTERNATE WOUNDS TO ONE ANOTHER.                      SANCTA MARIA DOLORUM               24   52  283  162

AMAINE

THIS DONE, HOME TO HER HELL SHEE HY'D AMAINE.                   SOSPETTO D'HERODE                 472   46  109  216
AND WEPT AMAINE. THEN REAR'D A COSTLY TOMBE,                    UPON GUNPOWDER TREASON             50   MS  386  460

AMAZED

WITH HER SWEET SELFE SHEE WRANGLES. HEE AMAZED                  MUSICKS DUELL                      43   46  149  535
AMAZED TRITON WITH HIS SHRILL ALARMES                           UPON GUNPOWDER TREASON             31   MS  386  460
AMAZED SOL THROWES OF HIS MOURNFULL WEEDS,                      UPON KINGS CORONATION              15   MS  390  453
AFFRIGHT TH' AMAZED AIRE, & DANCE A ROUND                       UPON KINGS CORONATION              22   MS  390  453

AMAZ'D

AMAZ'D THE MIDNIGHT WORLD, AND MADE A DAY                       SOSPETTO D'HERODE                 116   46  109  216
GRIM DESTRUCTION HERE AMAZ'D                                    ANOTHER ON HERRYS                  31   46  170  469
POORE MEAGRE HORROR STREIGHTWAIS WAS AMAZ'D,                    UPON GUNPOWDER TREASON             47   MS  387  461

AMAZEMENT

STONY AMAZEMENT MAKES THEM STAND                                NEITHER DURST MAN ASKE              9   46   92   20

TH'AMAZING

SO MIGHTY WERE TH'AMAZING CHARACTERS                            SOSPETTO D'HERODE                 477   46  109  216

AMBER-WEEPING

STEALES FROM THE AMBER-WEEPING TREE,                            THE WEEPER                         44   46   79  120

AMBITION

HIS BEST AMBITION NOW, IS BUT TO BE                             IN GLORIOUS EPIPHANIE             248   52  253   39
THE BEST AMBITION OF THY LOVE.                                  LAUDA SION SALVATOREM               6   52  294  178

AMBITIOUS

BUT MORE AMBITIOUS LOSSE, AT LEST OF BRAIN.                     IN GLORIOUS EPIPHANIE             230   52  253   39
WOULD BE AMBITIOUS OF ASTRONOMIE.                               UPON KINGS CORONATION              34   MS  389  454

AMBROSIALL

THE BRIGHT AMBROSIALL NEST,                                     TO SAME CONCERNING CHOISE          52   52  331   66

AMBUSH

'TIS HEAVEN THAT LIES IN AMBUSH THERE, AND BREAKES              AN APOLOGIE FOR HYMNE (TERESA)     24   46  136   59
BY THE OBLIQUE AMBUSH OF THIS CLOSE NIGHT                       IN GLORIOUS EPIPHANIE             169   52  253   39
'TIS HEAV'N THAT LYES IN AMBUSH THERE, & BREAKS                 AN APOLOGIE FOR (TERESA) HYMNE     24   52  322   59

AMIDST

THAT LIVE & DY AMIDST HER DARTS,                                FLAMING HEART                      50   52  324   61

AMOROUS

AMOROUS LANGUISHMENTS, LUMINOUS TRANCES,                        ON A PRAYER BOOKE                  63   46  126  139
CAST AMOROUS GLANCES ON HIS BIRTH,                              LOVES HOROSCOPE                    27   46  185  483
THEN LET AMOROUS KISSES DWELL                                   OUT OF CATULLUS                     9   46  194  523
THE AMOROUS SPYES                                               IN GLORIOUS EPIPHANIE             224   52  253   39
FLOW IN AN AMOROUS FLOUD                                        VEXILLA REGIS                       9   52  277  156
AND STREIGHT HIS AMOROUS SYTH (GREEDY OF BLISSE)                AN ELEGY MR STANNINOW              47   MS  394  473

AMOROUSE

AMOROUSE LANGUISHMENTS, LUMINOUS TRANCES.                       PRAYER TO GENTLE-WOMAN             69   52  328  139
THERE AMOROUSE SAPPHO PLAINES UPON HER LUTE                     HORATIJ ILLE & NEFASTO             39   MS  382  530
CAST BACK SOME AMOROUSE GLANCES ON THE CATES,                   UPON GUNPOWDER TREASON             29   MS  387  461

AMPLE

   FOR EARTH, 'T HAD BEENE AN AMPLE PORTION.      UPON BIRTH PRINCESSE E        28   MS 391 456

AMPLIATE

   THOSE BEAMES THAT AMPLIATE MORTALITIE,       UPON YORKE HIS BIRTH         22   46 176 500

AMPLY

   NOW THAT TIME'S EMPIRE MIGHT BE AMPLY FILL'D,   ON FRONTISPIECE ISAACSONS    15   46 191 491

ANGELL

   WHERE NEVER WING OF ANGELL YET MADE WAY      SOSPETTO D'HERODE           222  46 109 216
   THINKE YOU HAVE AN ANGELL BY TH' WINGS.       ON MR. G. HERBERTS BOOKE     6   46 130  68

ANGELL-BLINDING

   THAT THE GREAT ANGELL-BLINDING LIGHT SHOULD SHRINKE  SOSPETTO D'HERODE         169  46 109 216

ANGELL-IMPS

   OF SWEET-LIPP'D ANGELL-IMPS, THAT SWILL THEIR THROATS  MUSICKS DUELL           76   46 149 535

ANGELS

   ANGELS WITH THEIR BOTTLES COME.             THE WEEPER                34   46  79 120
   STUFT WITH DOWNE OF ANGELS WING.             THE TEARE                 36   46  84  50
   I SAW TH'OFFICIOUS ANGELS BRING,            A HYMNE OF THE NATIVITY     41   46 106  76
   HOW BRIGHT A DAWNE OF ANGELS WITH NEW LIGHT    SOSPETTO D'HERODE         115  46 109 216
   AND TURNE NOT BEASTS, BUT ANGELS. LET THE KING,  AN APOLOGIE FOR HYMNE (TERESA)  37   46 136  59
   MARY, MEN AND ANGELS SING.                ON THE ASSUMPTION           53   46 139 114
   SWEET ANGELS COME, AND SING THE REST.        ON THE ASSUMPTION           64   46 139 114
   TO BE A SHADE FOR ANGELS WHILE THEY SING,     UPON DEATH OF HERRYS        40   46 167 466
   MARIA, MEN & ANGELS SING                 IN GLORIOUS ASSUMPTION B. LADY  58   52 304 114
   SWEET ANGELS COME, AND SING THE REST.        IN GLORIOUS ASSUMPTION B. LADY  69   52 304 114
   ANGELS WITH CRYSTALL VIOLLS COME             WEEPER                    70   52 307 120
   ANGELS, THY OLD FREINDS, THERE SHALL GREET THEE  TERESA                   137  52 315  52
   AND TURN NOT BEASTS, BUT ANGELS. LET THE KING   AN APOLOGIE FOR (TERESA) HYMNE 37   52 322  59
   TEN THOUSAND ANGELS IN ONE POINT CAN DWELL.    PRAYER TO GENTLE-WOMAN     14   52 328 139
   THE QUEEN OF ANGELS, (AND MEN CHAST AS YOU)    ALEXIAS THIRD ELEGIE        29   52 336 209

ANGELLS

   A THOUSAND ANGELLS IN ONE POINT CAN DWELL.     ON A PRAYER BOOKE            8   46 126 139
   ANGELLS CANNOT TELL, SUFFICE,                IN MEMORY OF LADY MADRE TERESA 120  46 131  52
   ANGELLS THY OLD FRIENDS THERE SHALL GREET THEE,  IN MEMORY OF LADY MADRE TERESA 138  46 131  52
   LO THE LIFE-FOOD OF ANGELLS THEN             LAUDA SION SALVATOREM        61   52 294 178
   ANGELLS CANNOT TELL, SUFFICE,                TERESA                    119  52 315  52
   OF SUCH BRIGHT ANGELLS, THAT YOU GIVE US MORE.   UPON BIRTH PRINCESSE E        26   MS 391 456

ANGER

   SHAME NOW AND ANGER MIXT A DOUBLE STAINE      MUSICKS DUELL             105  46 149 535
   HIS ANGER KINDLE, PRESENTLY                  OUT OF GREEKE CUPID'S CRYER   29   46 159 519
   HATH ONELY ANGER AN OMNIPOTENCE             UPON ASSE THAT BORE SAVIOUR   1   46  90  19
   ANGER, AND LOVE, BEST HOOKES OF HUMANE BLOOD.    SOSPETTO D'HERODE         275  46 109 216
   WILL KILL HIS ANGER, AND REVIVE MY BLISSE.      TO THE MORNING             38   46 183 497

ANGRY

   THE WIND HAD NEED BE ANGRY, AND THE WATER BLACK, WHY ARE YEE AFRAID           7   46  88  15
   THE ANGRY NORTH TO WAGE HIS WARRES.          A HYMNE OF THE NATIVITY     24   46 106  76
   IN THE DEEPE WRINCKLES OF HIS ANGRY BROW,     TO THE MORNING             31   46 183 497
   O MEET THE ANGRY GOD. INVADE HIS EYES,        TO THE MORNING             36   46 183 497
   THE ANGRY NORTH TO WAGE HIS WARRES.          IN HOLY NATIVITY            25   52 246  76
   O THOSE EYES. WHOSE ANGRY LIGHT              DIES IRAE                   7   52 298 186
   PEACE, HEART. THE HEAVENS ARE ANGRY. ALL THEIR  LUKE 2. QUAERIT JESUM        19   MS 379  11
                                         SPHAERES

   (ROWZ'D IN AN ANGRY TEMPEST). OH THE SEA.     HORATIJ ILLE & NEFASTO        21   MS 382 530
   AND IN FELL HATRED BURNING, ANGRY DY.         UPON GUNPOWDER TREASON       16   MS 387 461

ANNALS

   IN JOYES WHITE ANNALS LIVE THIS HOURE,        EASTER DAY                  10   46 100  26

ANNEXT

   OR CLOSE UNTO HIS NAME ANNEXT.               ANOTHER ON HERRYS            51   46 170 469

ANNIHILATIONS

   OF SOULE. DEARE, AND DIVINE ANNIHILATIONS.     ON A PRAYER BOOKE           72   46 126 139
   OF SOUL. DEAR & DIVINE ANNIHILATIONS.        PRAYER TO GENTLE-WOMAN     78   52 328 139

ANON

   DANCING IN LOFTY MEASURES, AND ANON          MUSICKS DUELL             139  46 149 535

## ANOTHER

| | | | | |
|---|---|---|---|---|
| ARE IN ANOTHER SENCE | ON MARKES OF SAVIOURS WOUNDS | 3 | 46 86 | 25 |
| HAD NERE ANOTHER WORD TO SAY, | NEITHER DURST MAN ASKE | 16 | 46 92 | 20 |
| ANOTHER DAY OF DIADEMS. | AN HIMNE FOR CIRCUMCISION | 24 | 46 141 | 37 |
| TO BE AT CHARGE OF SUCH ANOTHER. | UPON DEATH OF DESIRED HERRYS | 24 | 46 168 | 467 |
| MAKE SUCH ANOTHER SWEET COMPARISON. | UPON YORKE HIS BIRTH | 52 | 46 176 | 500 |
| TO SHEW HER TO HER SELFE IN SUCH ANOTHER. | UPON YORKE HIS BIRTH | 54 | 46 176 | 500 |
| ALONE, LIGHT SUCH ANOTHER STARRE, AND TWINE | UPON YORKE HIS BIRTH | 56 | 46 176 | 500 |
| REPEATED, AND THAT SON STILL IN ANOTHER, | UPON YORKE HIS BIRTH | 100 | 46 176 | 500 |
| TILL ANOTHER THOUSAND SMOTHER | OUT OF CATULLUS | 13 | 46 194 | 523 |
| THAT, AND THAT WIPE OF ANOTHER. | OUT OF CATULLUS | 14 | 46 194 | 523 |
| ANOTHER DAY OF DIADEMS. | NEW YEAR'S DAY | 24 | 52 251 | 37 |
| DISCOURSE ALTERNATE WOUNDS TO ONE ANOTHER. | SANCTA MARIA DOLORUM | 24 | 52 283 | 162 |
| WHILE FROM ANOTHER (UNSEENE) CORNER BLOWES | HORATIJ ILLE & NEFASTO | 23 | MS 382 | 530 |
| GOE ON THEN, HEAVEN, & LIMBE FORTH SUCH ANOTHER, | UPON BIRTH PRINCESSE E | 55 | MS 391 | 456 |

## ANSWER

| | | | | |
|---|---|---|---|---|
| IN ANSWER TO HER FORMIDABLE NAME. | SOSPETTO D'HERODE | 304 | 46 109 | 216 |
| OR ANSWER ARTFULL TOUCH, | TO THE NAME OF JESUS | 40 | 52 239 | 30 |
| ANSWER MY CALL | TO THE NAME OF JESUS | 59 | 52 239 | 30 |
| THE CAVES OF NIGHT ANSWER ONE CALL. | DIES IRAE | 16 | 52 298 | 186 |
| HIS ANSWER IS, WHY SHE DOES SO. | IN GLORIOUS ASSUMPTION B. LADY | 25 | 52 304 | 114 |
| AND ANSWER TOO FOR THEM IN TEARES AGAIN. | ALEXIAS SECONDE ELEGIE | 18 | 52 335 | 207 |
| MARK WITH WHAT FAITH FRUITS ANSWER FLOWERS, | AGAINST IRRESOLUTION AND DELAY | 33 | 52 347 | 146 |

## ANSWERED

| | | | | |
|---|---|---|---|---|
| OF DEEPEST SILENCE ANSWERED MY COMMAND. | OUT OF GROTIUS | 84 | MS 398 | 198 |

## ANSWER'D

| | | | | |
|---|---|---|---|---|
| WHENCE THE FOURTH FURY, ANSWER'D PLUTO'S CALL. | SOSPETTO D'HERODE | 368 | 46 109 | 216 |

## ANSWERING

| | | | | |
|---|---|---|---|---|
| OF CONFESSOURS, WHOSE THROATES ANSWERING HIS SWORDS, | SOSPETTO D'HERODE | 7 | 46 109 | 216 |

## ANT

| | | | | |
|---|---|---|---|---|
| HIGH MOUNTED ON AN ANT NANUS THE TALL | HIGH MOUNTED ON AN ANT | 1 | 46 161 | 523 |

## ANTHEM

| | | | | |
|---|---|---|---|---|
| AN ANTHEM AT THE DAYES NATIVITIE. | TO THE MORNING | 44 | 46 183 | 497 |

## ANTHEMS

| | | | | |
|---|---|---|---|---|
| PREFERRE SOFT ANTHEMS TO THE EARES OF MEN, | MUSICKS DUELL | 78 | 46 149 | 535 |

## ANTHONY

| | | | | |
|---|---|---|---|---|
| GREAT ANTHONY, SPAINS WELL-BESEEMING PRIDE, | SOSPETTO D'HERODE | 9 | 46 109 | 216 |

## ANTIDOTE

| | | | | |
|---|---|---|---|---|
| TOUCHT WITH THE WORLDS TRUE ANTIDOTE TO BURST. | SOSPETTO D'HERODE | 128 | 46 109 | 216 |
| FEARES ANTIDOTE. A WISE, AND WELL STAY'D FIRE | ON HOPE | 82 | 46 143 | 71 |
| FEAR'S ANTIDOTE. A WISE & WELL-STAY'D FIRE. | (ON) HOPE | 42 | 52 345 | 71 |

## ANTIDOTES

| | | | | |
|---|---|---|---|---|
| AS ANTIDOTES & POYSONS ARE. | OFFICE H. CROSS SIXT | 16 | 52 270 | 97 |

## ANVILLS

| | | | | |
|---|---|---|---|---|
| ARE TOOLES OF WRATH, ANVILLS OF TORMENTS HUNG. | SOSPETTO D'HERODE | 323 | 46 109 | 216 |

## ANY

| | | | | |
|---|---|---|---|---|
| O YES, IF ANY HAPPY EYE, | OUT OF GREEKE CUPID'S CRYER | 5 | 46 159 | 519 |
| THE FLOOD, IF ANY CAN, THAT CAN SUFFICE, | TO PONTIUS WASHING HANDS | 3 | 46 88 | 22 |
| (IF ANY CAN BE SOFT TO TYRANNY | SOSPETTO D'HERODE | 411 | 46 109 | 216 |
| WHAT SOULE SOEVER IN ANY LANGUAGE CAN | AN APOLOGIE FOR HYMNE (TERESA) | 21 | 46 136 | 59 |
| IN ALL THE BOOKE IF ANY WHERE | ANOTHER ON HERRYS | 47 | 46 170 | 469 |
| IN BRIEFE, IF ANY ONE WERE FREE, | ANOTHER ON HERRYS | 53 | 46 170 | 469 |
| TO GLAD THE SPHEARE OF ANY NATION. | UPON YORKE HIS BIRTH | 14 | 46 176 | 500 |
| NOR WILL I OFFER ANY MORE TO THEE | TO THE MORNING | 50 | 46 183 | 497 |
| WOULD ANY ONE THE TRUE CAUSE FIND | OUT OF THE ITALIAN (3) | 1 | 46 190 | 549 |
| AS LEFT NO TIME TO PRACTISE ANY. | AN EPITAPH UPON ASHTON | 10 | 46 192 | 464 |
| SHALL ANY DAY BUT THINE ADORE. | IN GLORIOUS EPIPHANIE | 86 | 52 253 | 39 |
| COULD LEND THEM ANY CRUELTY. | OFFICE H. CROSS PRIME | 4 | 52 267 | 91 |
| E'RE SHE BORE ANY ONE, SLEW ALL. | O GLORIOSA DOMINA | 12 | 52 302 | 194 |
| WHAT SOUL SO E'RE, IN ANY LANGUAGE, CAN | AN APOLOGIE FOR (TERESA) HYMNE | 21 | 52 322 | 59 |
| YOUR SOUL TO ANY SON OF DUST. | TO SAME CONCERNING CHOISE | 19 | 52 331 | 66 |
| WHO STILES IT ANY THINGE, KNOWES NOT THE SAME. | ON GUNPOWDER-TREASON | 2 | MS 384 | 458 |

## APART

| | | | | |
|---|---|---|---|---|
| THEE THEREFORE FROM THE REST APART SHE HURL'D, | UPON YORKE HIS BIRTH | 27 | 46 176 | 500 |

## APE

OF RAM, HE-GOAT, OR REVEREND APE.                     IN GLORIOUS EPIPHANIE              90  52 253  39

## APES

PEACOCKS & APES.                                       TO SAME CONCERNING CHOISE         12  52 331  66

## APOLLO

APOLLO GOLDEN THOUGH THOU BEE.                         UPON DEATH OF DESIRED HERRYS      13  46 168 467
MY OWNE APOLLO, TRY IF I CAN MAKE                      TO THE MORNING                    16  46 183 497
WHERE APOLLO                                           OUT OF THE ITALIAN (1)            16  46 188 545
DOTH BLITH APOLLO CLOATH THE HEAVENS WITH JOYE,        AN ELEGY MR STANNINOW             11  MS 394 473

## VICE-APOLLO

HIM THEY CALL THEIR VICE-APOLLO.                       UPON DEATH OF DESIRED HERRYS      12  46 168 467

## APOLLO'S

FOUNDED TO TH' NAME OF GREAT APOLLO'S LYRE.            MUSICKS DUELL                     74  46 149 535
A PRAESENT WORTHY OF APOLLO'S LOVE.                    UPON BIRTH PRINCESSE E            20  MS 391 456

## APPOLLO

CAUGHT IN A NET WHICH THERE APPOLLO SPREADS,           MUSICKS DUELL                    121  46 149 535
FOR SEE APPOLLO ALL THIS WHILE STANDS MUTE.            UPON YORKE HIS BIRTH             114  46 176 500

## APPOLLO'S

TREMBLING AS WHEN APPOLLO'S GOLDEN HAIRES              MUSICKS DUELL                    115  46 149 535

## APOLOGY

UNLESSE THE MUSE SING MY APOLOGY.                      TO THE MORNING                     4  46 183 497

## APPEAL

WEE'L NOW APPEAL TO NONE OF ALL                        TERESA                             3  52 315  52

## APPEALE

HER EYE A STRONG APPEALE CAN GIVE.                     LOVES HOROSCOPE                   39  46 185 483
FARRE FROM DARKE HORRORS HOME APPEALE TO REST.         HORATIJ ILLE & NEFASTO            38  MS 382 530

## APPEAR

AND SOON THIS SWEET TRUTH SHALL APPEAR                 NEW YEAR'S DAY                    29  52 251  37
THE SPRING IS COME, THE FLOWRS APPEAR                  IN GLORIOUS ASSUMPTION B. LADY    11  52 304 114
THE FLOWRS APPEAR.                                     IN GLORIOUS ASSUMPTION B. LADY    17  52 304 114
SO SOON AS THOU SHALT FIRST APPEAR.                    TERESA                           122  52 315  52

## APPEAR'D

APPEAR'D WITH OTHER LADING, FOR HER BREST              THE BEGINNING OF HELIODORUS       12  46 158 517

## APPEARE

MY LOVE, OR FEIGN'D OR PAINTED SHOULD APPEARE.         WITH A PICTURE TO A FRIEND         8  46 156 494
HERE DIOMED'S HORSES, PHEREUS DOGS APPEARE.            SOSPETTO D'HERODE                353  46 109 216
SO SOONE AS THOU SHALT FIRST APPEARE.                  IN MEMORY OF LADY MADRE TERESA   123  46 131  52
THE SPRING IS COME, THE FLOWERS APPEARE.               ON THE ASSUMPTION                 11  46 139 114
AND SOONE THE SWEET TRUTH SHALL APPEARE.               AN HIMNE FOR CIRCUMCISION         29  46 141  37
UNFOLD THY FAIRE FRONT, AND THERE SHALL APPEARE        ON A FOULE MORNING                 7  46 181 495
SHEE SHALL APPEARE TRUE ETHIOPIAN.                     UPON FAIRE ETHIOPIAN               6  46 183 493
OR PEARLE THAT DARE APPEARE,                           WISHES SUPPOSED MISTRESSE         53  46 195 479
WHERE YOUR EYES SHINE HIS SUNS APPEARE.                THOUGH NOW 'TIS NEITHER           28  MS 397 492
COME, LOVELY NAME. APPEARE FROM FORTH THE BRIGHT       TO THE NAME OF JESUS             115  52 239  30
STREIGHT FROM THIS SEA OF TEARES THERE DOES APPEARE    UPON KINGS CORONATION             13  MS 390 453

## APPEARES

SEE HOW SHE WEEPS, AND WEEPS, THAT SHE APPEARES        TO PONTIUS WASHING HANDS           9  46  94  23
THE DIFFERENCE ONELY THIS APPEARES,                    ON WOUNDS OF CRUCIFIED LORD       17  46  99  24
THAT CROWNES HIS HATED HEAD ON HIGH APPEARES.          SOSPETTO D'HERODE                 45  46 109 216
THE TOTALL SUMME OF MAN APPEARES,                      ANOTHER ON HERRYS                 44  46 170 469

## APPEARANCE

INTO THIS LESSE APPEARANCE. IF YOU THINKE,             UPON BISHOP ANDREWES PICTURE      14  46 163 490

## SOUL-APPEASING

THE AIERY SHOP OF SOUL-APPEASING SOUND.                TO THE NAME OF JESUS              34  52 239  30

## APPETITES

THEIR APPETITES WERE GONE AT TH' VERY SIGHT.           UPON GUNPOWDER TREASON            49  MS 387 461

APPLAUD
   APPLAUD YOUR HAPPY SELVES IN HER,            O GLORIOSA DOMINA            28  52 302 194

APPLAUSE
   AND ALL THE POWERS OF HELL IN FULL APPLAUSE    SOSPETTO D'HERODE          259  46 109 216

APPLY
   WHOSE MERIT DARE APPLY IT,                 WISHES SUPPOSED MISTRESSE    119  46 195 479

APPLY'D
   THE FOAMY LIPS OF CERBERUS) SHEE APPLY'D      SOSPETTO D'HERODE          468  46 109 216

APPROACH
   THE LUSTY BRIDEGROOM MADE APPROACH. YOUNG MAN,    ALEXIAS THIRD ELEGIE        33  52 336 209

APPROBATION
   AND STREIGHT OF ALL THIS APPROBATION GATE      OUT OF GROTIUS             55  MS 398 198

APRIL
   THE APRIL IN THINE EYES,                    THE WEEPER                   87  46  79 120
   NO APRIL E'RE LENT SOFTER SHOWRES,            THE WEEPER                   89  46  79 120
   THE APRIL IN THINE EYES.                    WEEPER                     81  52 307 120
   NO APRIL ERE LENT KINDER SHOWRES,             WEEPER                     83  52 307 120

APRIL-AUTUMNE
   HOW DOES THY APRIL-AUTUMNE MOCKE THESE COLD     UPON TWO GREENE APRICOCKES   15  48 220 494

APRIL'S
   YET WHEN YOUNG APRIL'S HUSBAND SHOWRS         IN HOLY NATIVITY            97  52 246  76

APRILS
   YET WHEN YOUNG APRILS HUSBAND SHOWRES,        A HYMNE OF THE NATIVITY     77  46 106  76

APRON
   IS TH' EARTH DISROBED OF HER APRON WHITE,      AN ELEGY MR STANNINOW       5  MS 394 473

ARABIA
   ARABIA, THERE TO BUILD HER VIRGIN NEST,        UPON DEATH OF HERRYS       14  46 167 466
   ARABIA, FOR THY ROYALL PHOENIX' NEST.          OFFICE H. CROSS COMPLINE      6  52 274 105

ARABIAS
   A THOUSAND BLEST ARABIAS DWELL.               TO THE NAME OF JESUS      164  52 239  30

ARCHERIE
   TO EXERCISE THEIR ARCHERIE.                   IN MEMORY OF LADY MADRE TERESA  96  46 131  52
   TO EXERCISE THEIR ARCHERIE.                   TERESA                     96  52 315  52

ARCHES
   OF HEAVENS HIGH'ST ARCHES TO FALL NARROW.      OUT OF GREEKE CUPID'S CRYER  48  46 159 519

ARCHITECTS
   OR YOU, MORE NOBLE ARCHITECTS OF INTELLECTUALL NOISE,  TO THE NAME OF JESUS       77  52 239  30

ARCHITECTURE
   LOVE'S ARCHITECTURE IS HIS OWN.                IN HOLY NATIVITY            47  52 246  76

AREOPAGITE
   THE RIGHT-EY'D AREOPAGITE                    IN GLORIOUS EPIPHANIE     191  52 253  39

ARGUS
   OF EYES THAT HAS BUT ARGUS STORE,             IT IS BETTER TO GO WITH EYE   3  46  93  16

ARISE
   DOES THE NIGHT ARISE.                         THE WEEPER                 109  46  79 120

ARME
   HEE THROWES HIS ARME, AND WITH A LONG DRAWNE DASH   MUSICKS DUELL              30  46 149 535
   A SHADY ARME ABOVE MY HEAD,                   PSALME 23                   60  46 102   5
   THE GRAVE, AND HOLD UP AN EXALTED ARME         TO THE MORNING                26  46 183 497

ARMEFULL

| | | | | | |
|---|---|---|---|---|---|
| HER HEAVENLY ARMEFULL, SHEE SHALL TAST | ON A PRAYER BOOKE | 106 | 46 | 126 | 139 |

ARM-FULL

| | | | | | |
|---|---|---|---|---|---|
| HER HEAVNLY ARM-FULL, SHE SHALL TAST | PRAYER TO GENTLE-WOMAN | 112 | 52 | 328 | 139 |

ARM'D

| | | | | | |
|---|---|---|---|---|---|
| WHY ART THOU ARM'D SO DESPERATELY TO DAY. | UPON VENUS PUTTING ARMES | 2 | 46 | 161 | 523 |
| PALLAS SAW VENUS ARM'D AND STREIGHT SHE CRY'D, | UPON THE SAME (VENUS ARMES) | 1 | 46 | 161 | 523 |
| THEIR HANDS WITH LASHES ARM'D, THEIR TOUNGS WITH LYES, | OFFICE H. CROSS PRIME | 5 | 52 | 267 | 91 |
| STANDS ARM'D, TO SHEILD ME FROM ALL WANTON WRONG. | ALEXIAS THIRD ELEGIE | 36 | 52 | 336 | 209 |

ARMES

| | | | | | |
|---|---|---|---|---|---|
| THAT THE SOUTHWEST-WIND HURRIES IN HIS ARMES, | OUT OF VIRGIL | 20 | 46 | 155 | 529 |
| A BAND OF MEN, ROUGH AS THE ARMES THEY WORE | THE BEGINNING OF HELIODORUS | 7 | 46 | 158 | 517 |
| WHAT NEED'ST THOU PUT ON ARMES AGAINST POORE MEN. | UPON VENUS PUTTING ARMES | 4 | 46 | 161 | 523 |
| THEN COULD I SHOW THESE ARMES OF MINE, AND SAY | COME SEE WHERE THE LORD LAY | 5 | 46 | 87 | 27 |
| WARME INTO THE ARMES OF DEATH. | PSALME 23 | 72 | 46 | 102 | 5 |
| MUST THE BRIGHT ARMES OF HEAV'N, REBUKE THESE EYES. | SOSPETTO D'HERODE | 231 | 46 | 109 | 216 |
| IF ALL FAILE WEE'L PUT ON OUR PROUDEST ARMES, | SOSPETTO D'HERODE | 276 | 46 | 109 | 216 |
| IN ARMES, WHEN LESSER CAUSE WAS TO COMPLAINE. | SOSPETTO D'HERODE | 454 | 46 | 109 | 216 |
| IN RAGE, MY ARMES, GIVE ME MY ARMES, HEE CRYES. | SOSPETTO D'HERODE | 480 | 46 | 109 | 216 |
| IN RAGE, MY ARMES, GIVE ME MY ARMES, HEE CRYES. | SOSPETTO D'HERODE | 480 | 46 | 109 | 216 |
| WITH STRONG ARMES THEIR TRIUMPHANT CROWNE. | IN MEMORY OF LADY MADRE TERESA | 6 | 46 | 131 | 52 |
| MOTHERS ARMES, OR FATHERS KNEE. | IN MEMORY OF LADY MADRE TERESA | 62 | 46 | 131 | 52 |
| MEET IT WITH WIDE-SPREAD ARMES. & SEE | TO COUNTESSE OF DENBIGH | 55 | 52 | 236 | 146 |
| THINE ARMES, AND WITH THY BRIGHT & BLISFULL HEAD | OFFICE H. CROSS EVENSONG | 21 | 52 | 273 | 101 |
| WITH STRONG ARMES, THEIR TRIUMPHANT CROWN, | TERESA | 6 | 52 | 315 | 52 |
| MOTHER'S ARMES OR FATHER'S KNEE | TERESA | 62 | 52 | 315 | 52 |
| INTO LOVE'S ARMES THOU SHALT LET FALL | TERESA | 77 | 52 | 315 | 52 |
| WHAT MAGAZINS OF IMMORTALL ARMES THERE SHINE. | FLAMING HEART | 55 | 52 | 324 | 61 |
| PALLAS BEARES ARMES, FORSOOTH, AND SHOULD THERE BE | ALEXIAS THIRD ELEGIE | 39 | 52 | 336 | 209 |
| AND IS HE GONE, WHOM THESE ARMES HELD BUT NOW. | LUKE 2. QUAERIT JESUM | 1 | MS | 379 | 11 |
| OFT HAVE THESE ARMES THY CRADLE ENVIED, | LUKE 2. QUAERIT JESUM | 27 | MS | 379 | 11 |
| OFT HAVE THESE ARMES (ALAS.) SHOW'D TO THESE EYES | LUKE 2. QUAERIT JESUM | 43 | MS | 379 | 11 |
| BY THY KIND ARMES TO A KIND WORLD UNKNOWNE. | ON GUNPOWDER-TREASON | 8 | MS | 384 | 458 |
| BAD SPORTING NEPTUNE TO PLUCK IN HIS ARMES, | UPON GUNPOWDER TREASON | 32 | MS | 386 | 460 |

ARMORY

| | | | | | |
|---|---|---|---|---|---|
| IT IS THE ARMORY OF LIGHT, | ON A PRAYER BOOKE | 15 | 46 | 126 | 139 |
| IT IS AN ARMORY OF LIGHT | PRAYER TO GENTLE-WOMAN | 21 | 52 | 328 | 139 |

ARMOUR

| | | | | | |
|---|---|---|---|---|---|
| WHAT ARMOUR DOES HE WEARE. A FEW THIN CLOUTS. | SOSPETTO D'HERODE | 525 | 46 | 109 | 216 |

ARRIVE

| | | | | | |
|---|---|---|---|---|---|
| O MAY SHE BUT ARRIVE AT YOUR WHITE HAND, | UPON FAIRE ETHIOPIAN | 4 | 46 | 183 | 493 |

ARROW

| | | | | | |
|---|---|---|---|---|---|
| NE'RE SUFFRED, YET HIS LITTLE ARROW, | OUT OF GREEKE CUPID'S CRYER | 47 | 46 | 159 | 519 |
| O DART OF LOVE. ARROW OF LIGHT. | TO COUNTESSE OF DENBIGH | 49 | 52 | 236 | 146 |

ARROWES

| | | | | | |
|---|---|---|---|---|---|
| FROM THY EYES HE SHOOTS HIS ARROWES, | OUT OF THE ITALIAN (1) | 15 | 46 | 186 | 545 |
| YET PAY LESSE ARROWES THEN THEY OWE. | WISHES SUPPOSED MISTRESSE | 60 | 46 | 195 | 479 |

ART

| | | | | | |
|---|---|---|---|---|---|
| THE MAN PERCEIV'D HIS RIVALL, AND HER ART, | MUSICKS DUELL | 15 | 46 | 149 | 535 |
| MEETS ART WITH ART. SOMETIMES AS IF IN DOUBT | MUSICKS DUELL | 35 | 46 | 149 | 535 |
| MEETS ART WITH ART. SOMETIMES AS IF IN DOUBT | MUSICKS DUELL | 35 | 46 | 149 | 535 |
| STRAINES HIGHER YET, THAT TICKLED WITH RARE ART | MUSICKS DUELL | 47 | 46 | 149 | 535 |
| TIS BUT A DEAD FACE, ART DOTH HERE BEQUEATH. | UPON BISHOP ANDREWES PICTURE | 15 | 46 | 163 | 490 |
| AND NOW TH'ART SET WIDE OPE, THE SPEARE'S SAD ART, | I AM THE DOORE | 1 | 46 | 90 | 17 |
| THOU HAST THE ART ON'T PETER, AND CANST TELL | ON ST. PETER CASTING NETS | 1 | 46 | 98 | 13 |
| LOSE THIS SAME BUSIE SPEAKING ART | PSALME 137 | 20 | 46 | 104 | 7 |
| HEE KNOWES (BUT KNOWES NOT HOW, OR BY WHAT ART) | SOSPETTO D'HERODE | 157 | 46 | 109 | 216 |
| WHAT HE BY NATURE WAS, IS SHE BY ART. | SOSPETTO D'HERODE | 420 | 46 | 109 | 216 |
| THAT STUDYES THIS HIGH ART, | ON A PRAYER BOOKE | 30 | 46 | 126 | 139 |
| JOY OF GOODNESSE, LOVE OF ART, | UPON DEATH OF DESIRED HERRYS | 9 | 46 | 168 | 467 |
| THOU CHEAT'ST US FORD, MAK'ST ONE SEEME TWO BY ART. | UPON FORD'S TRAGEDYES | 1 | 46 | 181 | 495 |
| ART AND ORNAMENT THE SHAME. | WISHES SUPPOSED MISTRESSE | 99 | 46 | 195 | 479 |
| OF NIMBLE ART, & TRAVERSE ROUND | TO THE NAME OF JESUS | 33 | 52 | 239 | 30 |
| NATURE & ART. | TO THE NAME OF JESUS | 69 | 52 | 239 | 30 |
| HAPPY HE WHO HAS THE ART | TO THE NAME OF JESUS | 193 | 52 | 239 | 30 |
| O TEACH MINE TOO THE ART | SANCTA MARIA DOLORUM | 98 | 52 | 283 | 162 |
| REDEEM THIS INJURY OF THY ART. | FLAMING HEART | 41 | 52 | 324 | 61 |
| O SWEET INCENDIARY. SHEW HERE THY ART, | FLAMING HEART | 85 | 52 | 324 | 61 |
| THAT STUDYES THIS HIGH ART | PRAYER TO GENTLE-WOMAN | 36 | 52 | 328 | 139 |
| THE HIDDEN ART | TO SAME CONCERNING CHOISE | 43 | 52 | 331 | 66 |
| IT WAS HIS HEAVNLY ART | TO SAME CONCERNING CHOISE | 45 | 52 | 331 | 66 |
| OF WHICH DOTH SHOW THE QUINTESSENCE OF ART. | UPON BIRTH PRINCESSE E | 38 | MS | 391 | 456 |
| WHAT MORE THAN WINTER HATH THAT DIRE ART FOUND, | AN ELEGY MR STANNINOW | 21 | MS | 394 | 473 |
| IN DEATH-FULL DESPERATE ILLS WHERE ART AND ALL | OUT OF GROTIUS | 69 | MS | 398 | 198 |

TH'ART

| | | | | | |
|---|---|---|---|---|---|
| AND NOW TH'ART SET WIDE OPE, THE SPEARE'S SAD ART, | I AM THE DOORE | 1 | 46 | 90 | 17 |
| TH'ART NOT FAIRER THEN IS HEE. | UPON DEATH OF DESIRED HERRYS | 14 | 46 | 168 | 467 |

ARTS

| | | | | | |
|---|---|---|---|---|---|
| THY FOE TO CROSSE THE SWEET ARTS OF THY REIGNE | TO LORD UPON WATER MADE WINE | 2 | 46 | 91 | 12 |
| THAT USE NO VARNISH, NO OYL'D ARTS, | A HYMNE OF THE NATIVITY | 75 | 46 | 106 | 76 |

ARTISTS

| | | | | | |
|---|---|---|---|---|---|
| BABELS BOLD ARTISTS STRIVE (BELOW) TO BUILD | ON FRONTISPIECE ISAACSONS | 16 | 46 | 191 | 491 |

ARTERIES

| | | | | | |
|---|---|---|---|---|---|
| UNPEARCHT, HER VOCALL ARTERIES UNSTRUNG, | PSALME 137 | 21 | 46 | 104 | 7 |

ARTERYES

| | | | | | |
|---|---|---|---|---|---|
| FEELES MUSICKS PULSE IN ALL HER ARTERYES, | MUSICKS DUELL | 120 | 46 | 149 | 535 |

ARTFULL

| | | | | | |
|---|---|---|---|---|---|
| OR ANSWER ARTFULL TOUCH, | TO THE NAME OF JESUS | 40 | 52 | 239 | 30 |

ARTIFICER

| | | | | | |
|---|---|---|---|---|---|
| SPEAKES THE GREAT WISDOME OF TH' ARTIFICER. | UPON BIRTH PRINCESSE E | 40 | MS | 391 | 456 |

ARTIFICIALL

| | | | | | |
|---|---|---|---|---|---|
| THE BREATH OF ARTIFICIALL LUNGS EMBRAVES. | SOSPETTO D'HERODE | 482 | 46 | 109 | 216 |

ARTILLERY

| | | | | | |
|---|---|---|---|---|---|
| IT IS LOVES GREAT ARTILLERY, | ON A PRAYER BOOKE | 9 | 46 | 126 | 139 |
| HEAVN'S GREAT ARTILLERY IN EACH LOVE-SPUN LINE. | FLAMING HEART | 56 | 52 | 324 | 61 |
| IT IS LOVE'S GREAT ARTILLERY | PRAYER TO GENTLE-WOMAN | 15 | 52 | 328 | 139 |
| MIGHTY LOVE'S ARTILLERY. | IN CICATRICES DOMINI JESU | 2 | MS | 381 | 27 |

ASHAM'D

| | | | | | |
|---|---|---|---|---|---|
| AND HAVE BEEN ASHAM'D TO SPOYLE | ANOTHER ON HERRYS | 38 | 46 | 170 | 469 |
| ASHAM'D THAT OUR WORLD, NOW, CAN SHOW | FLAMING HEART | 45 | 52 | 324 | 61 |
| HEAVEN WAS ASHAM'D, TO SEE OUR MOTHER EARTH | UPON GUNPOWDER TREASON | 11 | MS | 386 | 460 |

ASHES

| | | | | | |
|---|---|---|---|---|---|
| (DISDAINFULL DUST AND ASHES) BEND THY BROW. | ON A TREATISE OF CHARITY | 42 | 46 | 137 | 69 |
| IN HIS ASHES ALL HER PRIDE. | ANOTHER ON HERRYS | 60 | 46 | 170 | 469 |
| THE WORLD--ALL DARING DUST AND ASHES. ONELY YOU | UPON STANINOUGH'S DEATH | 29 | 46 | 175 | 475 |
| THE WORLD, ALL-DARING DUST & ASHES, ONLY YOU | DEATH'S LECTURE | 31 | 52 | 340 | 475 |
| AND ROUZE THE SLEEPY ASHES OF THE DEAD. | ON GUNPOWDER-TREASON | 29 | MS | 384 | 458 |

ASIDE

| | | | | | |
|---|---|---|---|---|---|
| HER SELFE A WHILE SHE LAYES ASIDE, AND MAKES | SOSPETTO D'HERODE | 417 | 46 | 109 | 216 |
| AND LEAST THY BLOODSHOTT EYES SHOULD LEAD ASIDE | UPON GUNPOWDER TREASON | 7 | MS | 387 | 461 |

ASK

| | | | | | |
|---|---|---|---|---|---|
| SO GOES THE VOTE (NOR ASK THEM, WHY.) | OFFICE H. CROSS THIRD | 3 | 52 | 266 | 93 |
| O WHAT. ASK NOT THE TONGUES OF MEN. | TERESA | 118 | 52 | 315 | 52 |
| TO ASK THE WINDOWS LEAVE TO PASSE THAT WAY. | PRAYER TO GENTLE-WOMAN | 76 | 52 | 328 | 139 |

ASKT

| | | | | | |
|---|---|---|---|---|---|
| (NOR ASKT LEAVE OF THE SUN) BY DAY AS NIGHT. | SOSPETTO D'HERODE | 133 | 46 | 109 | 216 |

ASKE

| | | | | | |
|---|---|---|---|---|---|
| TO ASKE THE WINDOWES LEAVE, TO PASSE THAT WAY. | ON A PRAYER BOOKE | 70 | 46 | 126 | 139 |
| O WHAT. ASKE NOT THE TONGUES OF MEN. | IN MEMORY OF LADY MADRE TERESA | 119 | 46 | 131 | 52 |

ASKS

| | | | | | |
|---|---|---|---|---|---|
| SHEE ASKS EACH STARRE THAT THEN STOOD BY, | LOVES HOROSCOPE | 7 | 46 | 185 | 483 |

ASKES

| | | | | | |
|---|---|---|---|---|---|
| SHEE ASKES IF SAD, OR SAVING POWERS, | LOVES HOROSCOPE | 5 | 46 | 185 | 483 |

ASLEEP

| | | | | | |
|---|---|---|---|---|---|
| PEACE, THE LOVERS ARE ASLEEP. | AN EPITAPH UPON MARRIED COUPLE | 8 | 52 | 339 | 478 |

ASLEEPE

| | | | | | |
|---|---|---|---|---|---|
| SHEE SINGS THY TEARES ASLEEPE, AND DIPS | A HYMNE OF THE NATIVITY | 65 | 46 | 106 | 76 |
| PEACE, THE LOVERS ARE ASLEEPE. | AN EPITAPH HUSBAND AND WIFE | 8 | 46 | 174 | 478 |
| SAD SHADES AND SING DULL NIGHT ASLEEPE. | THOUGH NOW 'TIS NEITHER | 20 | MS | 397 | 492 |

## ASPECT

| | | | | | |
|---|---|---|---|---|---|
| AND NOW THAT GRAVE ASPECT HATH DEIGN'D TO SHRINKE | UPON BISHOP ANDREWES PICTURE | 13 | 46 | 163 | 490 |

## ASPECTS

| | | | | | |
|---|---|---|---|---|---|
| THOUGH THEIR BEST ASPECTS TWIN'D UPON | LOVES HOROSCOPE | 25 | 46 | 185 | 483 |

## ASPIRE

| | | | | | |
|---|---|---|---|---|---|
| WHERE SEAV'N TALL HORNES (HIS EMPIRES PRIDE) ASPIRE. | SOSPETTO D'HERODE | 46 | 46 | 109 | 216 |
| WHO WOULD NOT BE A PHAENIX, & ASPIRE | UPON KINGS CORONATION | 35 | MS | 389 | 454 |

## ASSAY

| | | | | | |
|---|---|---|---|---|---|
| AND LOVES MORE FIERCE, MORE FRUITLESSE FIRES ASSAY | ON HOPE | 87 | 46 | 143 | 71 |
| THOUGH LOVE'S MORE FEIRCE, MORE FRUITLESSE, FIRES ASSAY | (ON) HOPE | 47 | 52 | 345 | 71 |

## ASSE

| | | | | | |
|---|---|---|---|---|---|
| WHY ELSE HAD BAALAMS ASSE A TONGUE TO CHIDE | UPON ASSE THAT BORE SAVIOUR | 5 | 46 | 90 | 19 |
| POORE BEASTS. A SLOW OXE, AND A SIMPLE ASSE. | SOSPETTO D'HERODE | 528 | 46 | 109 | 216 |

## ASSIST

| | | | | | |
|---|---|---|---|---|---|
| WITH EARTHS LARGE MASSE, DOTH CHERISH AND ASSIST | OUT OF VIRGIL | 8 | 46 | 155 | 529 |
| ASSIST THE THRONE OF TH' IRON-SCEPTRED KING. | SOSPETTO D'HERODE | 66 | 46 | 109 | 216 |
| AND STILL ASSIST THE EXECUTION. | SOSPETTO D'HERODE | 292 | 46 | 109 | 216 |

## ASSUMPTION

| | | | | | |
|---|---|---|---|---|---|
| AND NO ASSUMPTION SHALL DENY US. | ON THE ASSUMPTION | 46 | 46 | 139 | 114 |
| AND NO ASSUMPTION SHALL DENY US. | IN GLORIOUS ASSUMPTION B. LADY | 51 | 52 | 304 | 114 |

## ASSURES

| | | | | | |
|---|---|---|---|---|---|
| (VENUS ASSURES HIM) THEN A KISSE. | OUT OF GREEKE CUPID'S CRYER | 16 | 46 | 159 | 519 |

## ASSYRIAN

| | | | | | |
|---|---|---|---|---|---|
| ASSYRIAN TYRANTS, OR EGYPTIAN KNEW. | SOSPETTO D'HERODE | 366 | 46 | 109 | 216 |

## TH'ASTONISH'D

| | | | | | |
|---|---|---|---|---|---|
| TH'ASTONISH'D NYMPHS THEIR FLOUD'S STRANGE FATE DEPLORE, | AGAINST IRRESOLUTION AND DELAY | 25 | 52 | 347 | 146 |

## ASTONISHT

| | | | | | |
|---|---|---|---|---|---|
| THE' ASTONISHT NYMPHS THEIR FLOOD'S STRANGE FATE DEPLORE, | TO COUNTESSE OF DENBIGH | 25 | 52 | 236 | 146 |

## TH'ASTONISHT

| | | | | | |
|---|---|---|---|---|---|
| SHOT THEE LIKE LIGHTNING, TO TH'ASTONISHT EARTH. | ON A TREATISE OF CHARITY | 6 | 46 | 137 | 69 |

## ASTRAY

| | | | | | |
|---|---|---|---|---|---|
| WE, WHO STRANGELY WENT ASTRAY, | IN GLORIOUS EPIPHANIE | 15 | 52 | 253 | 39 |

## ASTROLOGY

| | | | | | |
|---|---|---|---|---|---|
| HAVE TAUGHT THEE NEW ASTROLOGY. | LOVES HOROSCOPE | 16 | 46 | 185 | 483 |
| HAVE STUDY'D OVER ALL ASTROLOGY. | ALEXIAS SECONDE ELEGIE | 22 | 52 | 335 | 207 |

## ASTRONOMIE

| | | | | | |
|---|---|---|---|---|---|
| WOULD BE AMBITIOUS OF ASTRONOMIE. | UPON KINGS CORONATION | 34 | MS | 389 | 454 |

## ATHENS

| | | | | | |
|---|---|---|---|---|---|
| THAT NEITHER ROME, NOR ATHENS CAN BRING FORTH | SOSPETTO D'HERODE | 27 | 46 | 109 | 216 |

## ATLAS

| | | | | | |
|---|---|---|---|---|---|
| OF TH'ICY NORTH, FROM FROST-BOUNT ATLAS HANDS | SOSPETTO D'HERODE | 106 | 46 | 109 | 216 |
| ATLAS SHALL BE THIPT UPP, JOVE'S GATE SHALL FEELE | ON GUNPOWDER-TREASON | 43 | MS | 384 | 458 |
| WITH NIMBLE CAPERS, & FORCE ATLAS TREAD | UPON KINGS CORONATION | 3 | MS | 389 | 454 |

## ATOME

| | | | | | |
|---|---|---|---|---|---|
| SEE. NOTHING'S VULGAR, EVERY ATOME HEERE | UPON BIRTH PRINCESSE E | 39 | MS | 391 | 456 |

## ATREUS

| | | | | | |
|---|---|---|---|---|---|
| TANTALUS, ATREUS, PROGNE, HERE ARE GUESTS. | SOSPETTO D'HERODE | 333 | 46 | 109 | 216 |

## ATTEMPTS

| | | | | | |
|---|---|---|---|---|---|
| CAN HIS ATTEMPTS ABOVE STILL PROSP'ROUS BE, | SOSPETTO D'HERODE | 207 | 46 | 109 | 216 |

## ATTEND

| | | | | | |
|---|---|---|---|---|---|
| WHOM FAINT, & PALEFAC'T FEARE DOTH STILL ATTEND. | UPON GUNPOWDER TREASON | 18 | MS | 387 | 461 |

## ATTENDED

| | | | | | |
|---|---|---|---|---|---|
| MISTRESSE ATTENDED BY SUCH BRIGHT | IN MEMORY OF LADY MADRE TERESA | 125 | 46 | 131 | 52 |
| MISTRESSE, ATTENDED BY SUCH BRIGHT | TERESA | 124 | 52 | 315 | 52 |

## ATTENDING

| | | | | | |
|---|---|---|---|---|---|
| OF BLEST VARIETY ATTENDING ON | MUSICKS DUELL | 153 | 46 | 149 | 535 |

## THE'ATTENDING

| | | | | | |
|---|---|---|---|---|---|
| THE'ATTENDING WORLD, TO WAIT THY RISE. | TO THE NAME OF JESUS | 135 | 52 | 239 | 30 |

## ATTENTION

| | | | | | |
|---|---|---|---|---|---|
| WHICH TAUGHT ATTENTION EV'N TO ROCKS & STONES. | OFFICE H. CROSS NINTH | 2 | 52 | 271 | 99 |

## AUGMENT

| | | | | | |
|---|---|---|---|---|---|
| THE WEEPING MARINER WILL AUGMENT THE WAVES. | ALEXIAS FIRST ELEGIE | 26 | 52 | 334 | 204 |

## AURORA

| | | | | | |
|---|---|---|---|---|---|
| WHAT HOPE AURORA TO PROPITIATE THEE, | TO THE MORNING | 3 | 46 | 183 | 497 |
| AURORA SHALL SETT OPE | IN GLORIOUS EPIPHANIE | 69 | 52 | 253 | 39 |

## AURORA'S

| | | | | | |
|---|---|---|---|---|---|
| THE DARLINGS OF AURORA'S BED, | THE WEEPER | 134 | 46 | 79 | 120 |
| (SLIPT FROM AURORA'S DEWY BREST) | THE TEARE | 20 | 46 | 84 | 50 |

## AURORAS

| | | | | | |
|---|---|---|---|---|---|
| THE DARLINGS OF AURORAS BED. | WEEPER | 176 | 52 | 307 | 120 |

## AUSPICIOUS

| | | | | | |
|---|---|---|---|---|---|
| AUSPICIOUS STILL, IN SPIGHT OF HELL AND ME. | SOSPETTO D'HERODE | 208 | 46 | 109 | 216 |

## AUSPITIOUS

| | | | | | |
|---|---|---|---|---|---|
| THEREFORE TO THEE & THINE AUSPITIOUS RAY | IN GLORIOUS EPIPHANIE | 233 | 52 | 253 | 39 |

## AUSTER

| | | | | | |
|---|---|---|---|---|---|
| THAT FEARES THE FOULE-MOUTH'D AUSTER, OR THOSE STORMES | OUT OF VIRGIL | 19 | 46 | 155 | 529 |
| HIS SWELLING GLORYES, AUSTER SPIDE HIM, | UPON DEATH OF DESIRED HERRYS | 41 | 46 | 168 | 467 |
| CRUELL AUSTER THITHER HY'D HIM, | UPON DEATH OF DESIRED HERRYS | 42 | 46 | 168 | 467 |

## AUTHORITY

| | | | | | |
|---|---|---|---|---|---|
| I HAVE AUTHORITY IN LOVE'S NAME TO TAKE YOU | TO THE NAME OF JESUS | 53 | 52 | 239 | 30 |

## AUTUMN

| | | | | | |
|---|---|---|---|---|---|
| 'TIS CHANG'D INDEED, DID AUTUMN E'RE SUCH BEAUTIES BRING | UPON THORNES FROM LORDS HEAD | 3 | 46 | 96 | 23 |

## APRIL-AUTUMNE

| | | | | | |
|---|---|---|---|---|---|
| HOW DOES THY APRIL-AUTUMNE MOCKE THESE COLD | UPON TWO GREENE APRICOCKES | 15 | 48 | 220 | 494 |

## AVANT

| | | | | | |
|---|---|---|---|---|---|
| VAIN LOVES AVANT. BOLD HANDS FORBEARE. | WEEPER | 107 | 52 | 307 | 120 |

## AVE

| | | | | | |
|---|---|---|---|---|---|
| WHAT WOULD THEY MORE. TH' AVE SEENE WHEN AT MY NOD | OUT OF GROTIUS | 49 | MS | 398 | 198 |

## AWAKE

| | | | | | |
|---|---|---|---|---|---|
| TILL THE SINGING ORBES AWAKE THEE, | THE TEARE | 41 | 46 | 84 | 50 |
| TO DRAW THE CURTAINES, AND AWAKE THE SUN. | TO THE MORNING | 10 | 46 | 183 | 497 |
| AWAKE, MY GLORY. SOUL, (IF SUCH THOU BE, | TO THE NAME OF JESUS | 13 | 52 | 239 | 30 |
| AWAKE & SING | TO THE NAME OF JESUS | 15 | 52 | 239 | 30 |
| TO AWAKE THEM, | TO THE NAME OF JESUS | 194 | 52 | 239 | 30 |
| CROWN'D WOES AWAKE. AS THINGS TOO WISE FOR SLEEP. | DESCRIPTION RELIGIOUS HOUSE | 29 | 52 | 338 | 213 |
| IF FLORA'S DARLINGS NOW AWAKE FROM SLEEPE, | AN ELEGY MR STANNINOW | 25 | MS | 394 | 473 |

## AWAK'T

| | | | | | |
|---|---|---|---|---|---|
| THE CAPTIVE WORLD AWAK'T, & FOUND | OFFICE H. CROSS THIRD | 14 | 52 | 268 | 93 |

## AWAKES

| | | | | | |
|---|---|---|---|---|---|
| AWAKES HIS LUTE, AND 'GAINST THE FIGHT TO COME | MUSICKS DUELL | 17 | 46 | 149 | 535 |

AWAY

| | | | | | |
|---|---|---|---|---|---|
| BOTH WHICH AWAY, I SHOULD NOT NEED TO FEARE, | WITH A PICTURE TO A FRIEND | 7 | 46 | 156 | 494 |
| WHITHER AWAY SO FAST. | THE WEEPER | 127 | 46 | 79 | 120 |
| WHY YEE TRIP SO FAST AWAY. | THE WEEPER | 132 | 46 | 79 | 120 |
| THE OTHER CAST AWAY, SHE ONELY GAVE. | WIDOWES MITES | 4 | 46 | 86 | 21 |
| WHITHER AWAY SO FROLICK. WHY SO GLAD. | ON THE PRODIGALL | 2 | 46 | 86 | 17 |
| TO CAST THEM WELL'S TO CAST THEM QUITE AWAY. | ON ST. PETER CASTING NETS | 4 | 46 | 98 | 13 |
| AND CHASE THE TREMBLING SHADES AWAY. | A HYMNE OF THE NATIVITY | 32 | 46 | 106 | 76 |
| THE HEAV'N-REBUKED SHADES MADE HAST AWAY. | SOSPETTO D'HERODE | 114 | 46 | 109 | 216 |
| BUT VERTUE HEARD IT, AND AWAY SHEE HY'D. | SOSPETTO D'HERODE | 470 | 46 | 109 | 216 |
| UPON THY CROWNE, WHO GIVES HIS OWNE AWAY. | SOSPETTO D'HERODE | 520 | 46 | 109 | 216 |
| FROM TH' DAWN OF THY FAIRE EYE-LIDS WIPE AWAY | ON A TREATISE OF CHARITY | 7 | 46 | 137 | 69 |
| COME AWAY MY LOVE. | ON THE ASSUMPTION | 13 | 46 | 139 | 114 |
| COME AWAY MY DOVE | ON THE ASSUMPTION | 14 | 46 | 139 | 114 |
| COME AWAY, COME AWAY. | ON THE ASSUMPTION | 18 | 46 | 139 | 114 |
| COME AWAY, COME AWAY. | ON THE ASSUMPTION | 18 | 46 | 139 | 114 |
| HEAV'N CALLS HER, AND SHE MUST AWAY. | ON THE ASSUMPTION | 21 | 46 | 139 | 114 |
| IT FALLS, AND DYES. OH NO, IT MELTS AWAY | ON HOPE | 57 | 46 | 143 | 71 |
| TO MORROW TO BE SNATCHT AWAY. | UPON DEATH OF DESIRED HERRYS | 30 | 46 | 168 | 467 |
| WHY RAN THE STARTED AIRE TREMBLING AWAY. | UPON YORKE HIS BIRTH | 67 | 46 | 176 | 500 |
| FLY, FLY PROPHANE FOGS, FARRE HENCE FLY AWAY, | ON A FOULE MORNING | 31 | 46 | 181 | 495 |
| YET CARRY NOTHING THENCE AWAY. | WISHES SUPPOSED MISTRESSE | 39 | 46 | 195 | 479 |
| THAT THEY CONVENE & COME AWAY | TO THE NAME OF JESUS | 41 | 52 | 239 | 30 |
| DEAREST SWEET, & COME AWAY. | TO THE NAME OF JESUS | 128 | 52 | 239 | 30 |
| O COME AWAY | TO THE NAME OF JESUS | 141 | 52 | 239 | 30 |
| TAKE THINE OWN WINGS, & COME AWAY. | TO THE NAME OF JESUS | 150 | 52 | 239 | 30 |
| AND CHASE THE TREMBLING SHADES AWAY. | IN HOLY NATIVITY | 34 | 52 | 246 | 76 |
| AND CHASE THE TREMBLING SHADES AWAY. | IN HOLY NATIVITY | 75 | 52 | 246 | 76 |
| FOR WHICH I LANGUISH, COME AWAY. | ADORO TE | 52 | 52 | 291 | 172 |
| SHALL HENCE FOR EVER BEAR AWAY. | LAUDA SION SALVATOREM | 18 | 52 | 294 | 178 |
| TYPES YEILD TO TRUTHES. SHADES SHRINK AWAY. | LAUDA SION SALVATOREM | 23 | 52 | 294 | 178 |
| THE WORLD IN FLAMES SHALL FLY AWAY. | DIES IRAE | 4 | 52 | 298 | 186 |
| WHICH RENDERS ALL THE STARRES SHE STOLE AWAY. | O GLORIOSA DOMINA | 22 | 52 | 302 | 194 |
| COME AWAY, MY LOVE. | IN GLORIOUS ASSUMPTION B. LADY | 13 | 52 | 304 | 114 |
| COME AWAY, MY DOVE. CAST OFF DELAY, | IN GLORIOUS ASSUMPTION B. LADY | 14 | 52 | 304 | 114 |
| TO WAIT UPON THEE HOME. COME COME AWAY. | IN GLORIOUS ASSUMPTION B. LADY | 16 | 52 | 304 | 114 |
| COME AWAY, COME AWAY. | IN GLORIOUS ASSUMPTION B. LADY | 27 | 52 | 304 | 114 |
| COME AWAY, COME AWAY. | IN GLORIOUS ASSUMPTION B. LADY | 27 | 52 | 304 | 114 |
| COME AWAY, MY LOVE. | IN GLORIOUS ASSUMPTION B. LADY | 31 | 52 | 304 | 114 |
| COME AWAY, MY DOVE. | IN GLORIOUS ASSUMPTION B. LADY | 32 | 52 | 304 | 114 |
| HEAVN CALLS HER, & SHE MUST AWAY. | IN GLORIOUS ASSUMPTION B. LADY | 35 | 52 | 304 | 114 |
| WHITHER AWAY SO FAST. | WEEPER | 169 | 52 | 307 | 120 |
| WHY YOU TRIP SO FAST AWAY. | WEEPER | 174 | 52 | 307 | 120 |
| AND TAKE AWAY FROM ME MY SELF & SIN, | FLAMING HEART | 90 | 52 | 324 | 61 |
| A KISSE, A SIGH, AND SO AWAY. | TEMPERANCE | 50 | 52 | 342 | 510 |
| IT FALLS, AND DYES. O NO, IT MELTS AWAY | (ON) HOPE | 27 | 52 | 345 | 71 |
| (THE DUST OF WARRE CLEANE WIP'D AWAY) | IN CICATRICES DOMINI JESU | 18 | MS | 381 | 27 |
| WITH THIS GRAND BLAST SHOULD HAVE BIN BLOUNE AWAY. | UPON GUNPOWDER TREASON | 30 | MS | 366 | 460 |
| AND SNATCH'D AWAY THE BANQUETT. EVERY ONE | UPON GUNPOWDER TREASON | 54 | MS | 387 | 461 |
| ALL MELANCHOLY CLOWDS VANISH AWAY. | UPON KINGS CORONATION | 40 | MS | 390 | 453 |
| AND WITH A GOLDEN WAVE WASH CLEANE AWAY | AN ELEGY MR STANNINOW | 12 | MS | 394 | 473 |
| MAKE THEIR SCAR'D SOULES TAKE WING, & FLY AWAY. | AN ELEGIE ON DR PORTER | 30 | MS | 395 | 476 |

AWE

| | | | | | |
|---|---|---|---|---|---|
| HOW LOW THE BRIGHT YOUTH BOW'D, AND WITH WHAT AWE | SOSPETTO D'HERODE | 99 | 46 | 109 | 216 |

AWFULL

| | | | | | |
|---|---|---|---|---|---|
| GIRT ROUND THY AWFULL ALTARS, WITH BRIGHT WINGS | ON A TREATISE OF CHARITY | 22 | 46 | 137 | 69 |
| 'TIS SHEE, 'TIS SHEE. HER AWFULL BEAUTIES CHASE | UPON YORKE HIS BIRTH | 74 | 46 | 176 | 500 |
| BRIGHT BABE. WHOSE AWFULL BEAUTYES MAKE | IN GLORIOUS EPIPHANIE | 1 | 52 | 253 | 39 |
| THE NINTH WITH AWFULL HORROR HEARKENED TO THOSE GROANES | OFFICE H. CROSS NINTH | 1 | 52 | 271 | 99 |
| WHY SHOULD THOU BOW THY AWFULL BREST TO SEE | CHARITAS NIMIA | 33 | 52 | 280 | 48 |

AWRY

| | | | | | |
|---|---|---|---|---|---|
| DRAGGING HIS CROOKED BURTHEN, LOOK'T AWRY, | AN ELEGY MR STANNINOW | 46 | MS | 394 | 473 |

AYME

| | | | | | |
|---|---|---|---|---|---|
| A BLOUD DRUNKE ERROUR SPILT THE COSTLY AYME | OUT OF GROTIUS | 29 | MS | 398 | 198 |

HIGH-AYM'D

| | | | | | |
|---|---|---|---|---|---|
| THY HIGH-AYM'D HOPES, GAIND'ST BUT A FLAMING FALL. | SOSPETTO D'HERODE | 80 | 46 | 109 | 216 |

AZURE

| | | | | | |
|---|---|---|---|---|---|
| AND BRUSH HER AZURE MANTLE, WHICH SHALL SWIM | ON A FOULE MORNING | 24 | 46 | 181 | 495 |
| OR ON HEAVN'S AZURE FOREHEAD HIGH TO STAND | IN GLORIOUS EPIPHANIE | 250 | 52 | 253 | 39 |
| IN AZURE CHANNELLS WARME THROUGH MOUNTS OF SNOW. | UPON GUNPOWDER TREASON | 42 | MS | 387 | 461 |

BAALAMS

| | | | | | |
|---|---|---|---|---|---|
| WHY ELSE HAD BAALAMS ASSE A TONGUE TO CHIDE | UPON ASSE THAT BORE SAVIOUR | 5 | 46 | 90 | 19 |

BABE

| | | | | | |
|---|---|---|---|---|---|
| THE BABE LOOKT UP, AND SHEW'D HIS FACE, | A HYMNE OF THE NATIVITY | 19 | 46 | 106 | 76 |
| THE BABE NO SOONER 'GAN TO SEEKE. | A HYMNE OF THE NATIVITY | 47 | 46 | 106 | 76 |

|   |   |   |   |   |   |
|---|---|---|---|---|---|
| OF AGE AND BARENNESSE, AND HER BABE PREVENT | SOSPETTO D'HERODE | 102 | 46 | 109 | 216 |
| THEIR SIMPLE TRIBUTE TO THE BABE, WHOSE BIRTH | SOSPETTO D'HERODE | 119 | 46 | 109 | 216 |
| A MIGHTY BABE, WHOSE PURE, UNSPOTTED BIRTH, | SOSPETTO D'HERODE | 159 | 46 | 109 | 216 |
| A MOST STRANGE BABE, WHO HERE CONCEAL'D BY THEM | SOSPETTO D'HERODE | 435 | 46 | 109 | 216 |
| DEARE BABE E'RE MANY DAYES BE DONE. | AN HIMNE FOR CIRCUMCISION | 30 | 46 | 141 | 37 |
| THE BABE LOOK'T UP & SHEW'D HIS FACE. | IN HOLY NATIVITY | 19 | 52 | 246 | 76 |
| AND LET THE MIGHTY BABE ALONE. | IN HOLY NATIVITY | 45 | 52 | 246 | 76 |
| THE BABE WHOSE BIRTH EMBRACES THIS MORN. | IN HOLY NATIVITY | 48 | 52 | 246 | 76 |
| DEAR BABE, ERE MANY DAYES BE DONE, | NEW YEAR'S DAY | 30 | 52 | 251 | 37 |
| BRIGHT BABE. WHOSE AWFULL BEAUTYES MAKE | IN GLORIOUS EPIPHANIE | 1 | 52 | 253 | 39 |
| LOOK UP, SWEET BABE, LOOK UP & SEE | IN GLORIOUS EPIPHANIE | 10 | 52 | 253 | 39 |

BABE'S

|   |   |   |   |   |   |
|---|---|---|---|---|---|
| AND SMIL'D I'TH' BABE'S BRIGHT FACE. THE PURPLING BUD | TO THE QUEEN'S MAJESTY | 5 | 52 | 261 | 47 |

BABES

|   |   |   |   |   |   |
|---|---|---|---|---|---|
| A THOUSAND SWEET BABES FROM THEIR MOTHERS BREST. | SOSPETTO D'HERODE | 4 | 46 | 109 | 216 |

BABELS

|   |   |   |   |   |   |
|---|---|---|---|---|---|
| DOST LAUGH. PROUD BABELS DAUGHTER. DO, LAUGH ON, | PSALME 137 | 31 | 46 | 104 | 7 |
| BABELS BOLD ARTISTS STRIVE (BELOW) TO BUILD | ON FRONTISPIECE ISAACSONS | 16 | 46 | 191 | 491 |

BACK

|   |   |   |   |   |   |
|---|---|---|---|---|---|
| AH WRETCH. WHAT BOOTES THEE TO CAST BACK THY EYES, | SOSPETTO D'HERODE | 241 | 46 | 109 | 216 |
| CALLS THEE BACK, AND BIDS THEE COME, | IN MEMORY OF LADY MADRE TERESA | 67 | 46 | 131 | 52 |
| THUS HAVE I BACK AGAINE TO THY BRIGHT NAME | AN APOLOGIE FOR HYMNE (TERESA) | 1 | 46 | 136 | 59 |
| HOW AT THE SIGHT DID'ST THOU DRAW BACK THINE EYES, | TO THE MORNING | 7 | 46 | 183 | 497 |
| OF BEAMES TO DAY, PAY BACK AGAINE TO MORROW, | UPON TWO GREENE APRICOCKES | 28 | 48 | 220 | 494 |
| AND SEND IT BACK TO YOU AGAINE. | TO THE NAME OF JESUS | 114 | 52 | 239 | 30 |
| SOFT BACK. AND BRINGS A BOSOM BIG WITH LOVES. | TO THE NAME OF JESUS | 160 | 52 | 239 | 30 |
| BADG OF THY FAITH CALLS BACK THY CARE, | VEXILLA REGIS | 2 | 52 | 277 | 156 |
| PAID BACK THE FLESH HE TOOK FOR THEE. | VEXILLA REGIS | 6 | 52 | 277 | 156 |
| PAYES BACK, WITH MORE THEN THEIR OWN SMART | SANCTA MARIA DOLORUM | 28 | 52 | 283 | 162 |
| CALLS THEE BACK, & BIDDS THEE COME | TERESA | 67 | 52 | 315 | 52 |
| THUS HAVE I BACK AGAIN TO THY BRIGHT NAME | AN APOLOGIE FOR (TERESA) HYMNE | 1 | 52 | 322 | 59 |
| CAST BACK SOME AMOROUSE GLANCES ON THE GATES, | UPON GUNPOWDER TREASON | 29 | MS | 387 | 461 |

BACKE

|   |   |   |   |   |   |
|---|---|---|---|---|---|
| SHEE GIVES HIM BACKE. HER SUPPLE BREST THRILLS OUT | MUSICKS DUELL | 57 | 46 | 149 | 535 |
| ON THE WAV'D BACKE OF EVERY SWELLING STRAINE, | MUSICKS DUELL | 95 | 46 | 149 | 535 |
| AND SO TURNES WINE TO WATER BACKE AGAINE. | TO LORD UPON WATER MADE WINE | 4 | 46 | 91 | 12 |

BACKS

|   |   |   |   |   |   |
|---|---|---|---|---|---|
| THEIR GREENE BACKS WERE HIS LIVERIE. | PSALME 23 | 8 | 46 | 102 | 5 |

BAD

|   |   |   |   |   |   |
|---|---|---|---|---|---|
| BAD SPORTING NEPTUNE TO PLUCK IN HIS ARMES, | UPON GUNPOWDER TREASON | 32 | MS | 386 | 460 |
| HIS WAY THROUGH BAD, TO MY SUCCESSIVE HURT. | OUT OF GROTIUS | 13 | MS | 398 | 198 |

BADG

|   |   |   |   |   |   |
|---|---|---|---|---|---|
| BADG OF THY FAITH CALLS BACK THY CARE, | VEXILLA REGIS | 2 | 52 | 277 | 156 |

BAIT

|   |   |   |   |   |   |
|---|---|---|---|---|---|
| BAIT THY DISEASE, AND WHILST THEY TUGGE, | TEMPERANCE | 2 | 52 | 342 | 510 |

BAITED

|   |   |   |   |   |   |
|---|---|---|---|---|---|
| WITH BAITED SMILES IF HE DISPLAY | OUT OF GREEKE CUPID'S CRYER | 63 | 46 | 159 | 519 |

BAITE

|   |   |   |   |   |   |
|---|---|---|---|---|---|
| BAITE THY DISEASE, AND WHILE THEY TUGG | IN PRAISE OF LESSIUS | 2 | 46 | 156 | 510 |

BAK'T

|   |   |   |   |   |   |
|---|---|---|---|---|---|
| BAK'T IN HOT SCORN, FOR A BURNT SACRIFICE. | ON A TREATISE OF CHARITY | 44 | 46 | 137 | 69 |

BALLANCE

|   |   |   |   |   |   |
|---|---|---|---|---|---|
| EVEN BALLANCE OF BOTH WORLDS. OUR WORLD OF SIN, | VEXILLA REGIS | 31 | 52 | 277 | 156 |

BALLES

|   |   |   |   |   |   |
|---|---|---|---|---|---|
| LIKE BANDIED BALLES, INTO THE FIRMAMENT. | ON GUNPOWDER-TREASON | 42 | MS | 384 | 458 |

BALM

|   |   |   |   |   |   |
|---|---|---|---|---|---|
| WITH MANNA, MILK, AND BALM, NEW BROACH THE MOUNTAINES. | SOSPETTO D'HERODE | 112 | 46 | 109 | 216 |
| WHOSE BREST WEEPES BALM FOR WOUNDED MAN. | ADORO TE | 46 | 52 | 291 | 172 |

BALME

|   |   |   |   |   |   |
|---|---|---|---|---|---|
| BALME AND NECTAR IN MY CUP, | PSALME 23 | 70 | 46 | 102 | 5 |

## BALMY

| | | | |
|---|---|---|---|
| WE SAW THEE IN THY BALMY NEST, | A HYMNE OF THE NATIVITY | 29 | 46 106 76 |
| DROPPING WITH A BALMY SHOWRE | ON A PRAYER BOOKE | 103 | 46 126 139 |
| TO FLUTTER IN THE BALMY AIRE, | ON MR. G. HERBERTS BOOKE | 9 | 46 130 68 |
| THE BALMY ZEPHIRUS GOT SO SWEET A BREATH | UPON DEATH OF HERRYS | 20 | 46 167 466 |
| WITH WANTON GALES. HIS BALMY BREATH SHALL LICKE | ON A FOULE MORNING | 13 | 46 181 495 |
| IN BALMY SHOWRS. | TO THE NAME OF JESUS | 169 | 52 239 30 |
| EXTRACTED HAVE A BALMY ELOQUENCE. | UPON BIRTH PRINCESSE E | 10 | MS 391 456 |
| HIS BALMY TREASURES TO THE BEDD OF DEATH. | AN ELEGY MR STANNINOW | 30 | MS 394 473 |

## BAULMY

| | | | |
|---|---|---|---|
| WE SAW THEE IN THY BAULMY NEST, | IN HOLY NATIVITY | 31 | 52 246 76 |
| WE SAW THEE IN THY BAULMY NEST, | IN HOLY NATIVITY | 72 | 52 246 76 |
| DROPPING WITH A BAULMY SHOWR | PRAYER TO GENTLE-WOMAN | 109 | 52 328 139 |

## BALSAME

| | | | |
|---|---|---|---|
| MAY BALSAME BEE FOR THEIR OWN GRIEF. | THE WEEPER | 78 | 46 79 120 |

## BALSAME-SWEATING

| | | | |
|---|---|---|---|
| THAT THE BALSAME-SWEATING BOUGH | THE WEEPER | 68 | 46 79 120 |

## BALSOM-SWEATING

| | | | |
|---|---|---|---|
| THAT THE BALSOM-SWEATING BOUGH | WEEPER | 50 | 52 307 120 |

## BALSOM

| | | | |
|---|---|---|---|
| BALSOM MAYBE, FOR THEIR OWN GREIFE. | WEEPER | 60 | 52 307 120 |
| BALSOM TO HEAL THEMSELVES WITH. THUS | TERESA | 109 | 52 315 52 |

## BALSOME

| | | | |
|---|---|---|---|
| BALSUME FOR MINE. | ON MARKES OF SAVIOURS WOUNDS | 10 | 46 86 28 |
| BALSOME, TO HEALE THEMSELVES WITH | IN MEMORY OF LADY MADRE TERESA | 109 | 46 131 52 |

## BAND

| | | | |
|---|---|---|---|
| A BAND OF MEN, ROUGH AS THE ARMES THEY WORE | THE BEGINNING OF HELIODORUS | 7 | 46 158 517 |
| SEALING ALL BRESTS IN A LETHAEAN BAND. | SOSPETTO D'HERODE | 392 | 46 109 216 |
| TO TH'HEADS AND OFFICERS OF EVERY BAND. | SOSPETTO D'HERODE | 511 | 46 109 216 |

## BANDS

| | | | |
|---|---|---|---|
| COME DEATH, COME BANDS, NOR DO YOU SHRINK, MY EARS, | I AM READY NOT ONELY BOUND | 1 | 46 98 29 |
| SAVE THOSE OF FEARE, NO OTHER BANDS FEARE I. | I AM READY NOT ONELY BOUND | 3 | 46 98 29 |
| WHAT FATALL, YET FANTASTICK, BANDS | TO COUNTESSE OF DENBIGH | 19 | 52 236 146 |
| AFFECT MORE COMLY BANDS | PRAYER TO GENTLE-WOMAN | 6 | 52 328 139 |
| WHAT FATALL, YET FANTASTICK, BANDS | AGAINST IRRESOLUTION AND DELAY | 13 | 52 347 146 |

## BANDIED

| | | | |
|---|---|---|---|
| LIKE BANDIED BALLES, INTO THE FIRMAMENT. | ON GUNPOWDER-TREASON | 42 | MS 384 458 |

## BANISHMENT

| | | | |
|---|---|---|---|
| HOW HARD BY SEA, BY WARRE, BY BANISHMENT. | HORATIJ ILLE & NEFASTO | 44 | MS 382 530 |

## BANISH'T

| | | | |
|---|---|---|---|
| E'RE BORNE WAS BANISH'T. BORNE WAS GLAD T'EMBRACE | OUT OF GROTIUS | 15 | MS 398 198 |

## BANKES

| | | | |
|---|---|---|---|
| ON THE PROUD BANKES OF GREAT EUPHRATES FLOOD, | PSALME 137 | 1 | 46 104 7 |
| THUNDRING UPON THE BANKES OF THOSE BLACK LAKES | SOSPETTO D'HERODE | 298 | 46 109 216 |
| WHOSE BANKES THE MUSES DWELT UPON. | AN EPITAPH DOCTOR BROOKE | 3 | 46 175 465 |
| MEANE WHILE HIS LOVED BANKES NOW DRY. | AN EPITAPH DOCTOR BROOKE | 7 | 46 175 465 |
| ON THOSE DELICIOUS BANKES DISTILL'D AGAINE | ON A FOULE MORNING | 16 | 46 181 495 |
| THAT ON THY BANKES SITTS IN A VERDANT BOWER, | AN ELEGIE ON DR PORTER | 22 | MS 395 476 |

## BANNE

| | | | |
|---|---|---|---|
| THEY BANNE THE BLAZE, & CURSE ITS CURTESY. | ON GUNPOWDER-TREASON | 59 | MS 384 458 |

## BANQUETT

| | | | |
|---|---|---|---|
| A COMMON BANQUETT. NOE, HEERE'S PRINCELY FARE | UPON GUNPOWDER TREASON | 6 | MS 387 461 |
| HE HUMBLY CRAV'D TO BANQUETT ON A KISSE. | UPON GUNPOWDER TREASON | 46 | MS 387 461 |
| AND SNATCH'D AWAY THE BANQUETT. EVERY ONE | UPON GUNPOWDER TREASON | 54 | MS 387 461 |

## BAPTISM

| | | | |
|---|---|---|---|
| OF BAPTISM BLENDS THEM ALL INTO A BLOOD. | AN APOLOGIE FOR (TERESA) HYMNE | 16 | 52 322 59 |

## BAPTISME

| | | | |
|---|---|---|---|
| OF BAPTISME, BLENDS THEM ALL INTO ONE BLOOD. | AN APOLOGIE FOR HYMNE (TERESA) | 16 | 46 136 59 |

BAPTIS'D

| | | | | |
|---|---|---|---|---|
| HE YEILDS, AND STRAIGHT BAPTIS'D, OBTAINS THE GRACE | ALEXIAS THIRD ELEGIE | 45 | 52 336 | 209 |

BARABBAS

| | | | | |
|---|---|---|---|---|
| LIVE BARABBAS, & LET GOD DY. | OFFICE H. CROSS THIRD | 4 | 52 268 | 93 |

BARBAROUS

| | | | | |
|---|---|---|---|---|
| SHOULD BLEED UPON A BARBAROUS KNIFE. | IN MEMORY OF LADY MADRE TERESA | 70 | 46 131 | 52 |
| FROM HIS OLD FATHER, THAT MANS BARBAROUS KNIFE | HORATIJ ILLE & NEFASTO | 8 | MS 382 | 530 |

BARBOROUS

| | | | | |
|---|---|---|---|---|
| SHOULD BLEED UPON A BARBOROUS KNIFE. | TERESA | 70 | 52 315 | 52 |

BARBILL

| | | | | |
|---|---|---|---|---|
| THE PRETIOUS BARBILL, NOW GROUNE RIFE, | PETRONIJ ALES PHASIACIS PETITA | 15 | MS 382 | 526 |

BARE

| | | | | |
|---|---|---|---|---|
| THOUGH BARE HIS SKIN, HIS MIND HEE COVERS, | OUT OF GREEKE CUPID'S CRYER | 39 | 46 159 | 519 |

BARENNESSE

| | | | | |
|---|---|---|---|---|
| OF AGE AND BARENNESSE, AND HER BABE PREVENT | SOSPETTO D'HERODE | 102 | 46 109 | 216 |

BARGAIN

| | | | | |
|---|---|---|---|---|
| SHEEL BARGAIN WITH THEM, AND WILL GIVE | IN MEMORY OF LADY MADRE TERESA | 51 | 46 131 | 52 |
| SH'EL BARGAIN WITH THEM, & WILL GIVE | TERESA | 51 | 52 315 | 52 |
| AS IF THE BARGAIN HAD BEEN DRIVEN | AGAINST IRRESOLUTION AND DELAY | 61 | 52 347 | 146 |

BARGAIN'D

| | | | | |
|---|---|---|---|---|
| BARGAIN'D WITH DEATH & WELL-BESEEMING DUST | CHARITAS NIMIA | 56 | 52 280 | 48 |

BARKE

| | | | | |
|---|---|---|---|---|
| SO SLEEPS A PILOT, WHOSE POORE BARKE IS PREST | SOSPETTO D'HERODE | 425 | 46 109 | 216 |

BARREN

| | | | | |
|---|---|---|---|---|
| O SEE, SO MANY WORLDS OF BARREN YEARES | TO THE NAME OF JESUS | 143 | 52 239 | 30 |

BARRES

| | | | | |
|---|---|---|---|---|
| WHAT MAGICK BOLTS, WHAT MYSTICK BARRES | TO COUNTESSE OF DENBIGH | 17 | 52 236 | 146 |
| WITH ROCKS. NOR BOLD HANDS STRUCK THE WORLD'S STRONG BARRES. | ALEXIAS THIRD ELEGIE | 10 | 52 336 | 209 |

BARRS

| | | | | |
|---|---|---|---|---|
| WHAT MAGICK-BOLTS, WHAT MYSTICK BARRS | AGAINST IRRESOLUTION AND DELAY | 11 | 52 347 | 146 |

BASE

| | | | | |
|---|---|---|---|---|
| MOST KINDLY DOE FALL OUT. THE GRUMBLING BASE | MUSICKS DUELL | 49 | 46 149 | 535 |
| HEE STRAINES THESE WORDS. BASE ENVY, DOE, LAUGH ON. | HIGH MOUNTED ON AN ANT | 5 | 46 161 | 523 |
| BEASTS AND BASE STRAW. ALREADY IS THE STREAME | SOSPETTO D'HERODE | 437 | 46 109 | 216 |
| OR SOME BASE HAND HAVE POWER TO RACE, | IN MEMORY OF LADY MADRE TERESA | 71 | 46 131 | 52 |
| ON THESE SHE LIFTS THE WORLD, AND ON THEIR BASE | ON FRONTISPIECE ISAACSONS | 21 | 46 191 | 491 |
| IF MY BASE LUST, | CHARITAS NIMIA | 55 | 52 280 | 48 |
| OR SOME BASE HAND HAVE POWER TO RACE | TERESA | 71 | 52 315 | 52 |
| THAT HAND OF MILKY DOUNE. ALL THESE ARE BASE. | UPON BIRTH PRINCESSE E | 52 | MS 391 | 456 |

BASELY

| | | | | |
|---|---|---|---|---|
| HER KINDRED WITH THE STARRS. NOT BASELY HOVERS | DESCRIPTION RELIGIOUS HOUSE | 37 | 52 338 | 213 |
| BASELY DEGENEROUS. AGAINST MEE FLOCKE | OUT OF GROTIUS | 41 | MS 398 | 198 |

BASHFULL

| | | | | |
|---|---|---|---|---|
| THEIR BASHFULL CHEEKES TOGETHER, NEWLY THEY | UPON YORKE HIS BIRTH | 61 | 46 176 | 500 |
| OF DUST, WHERE IN THE BASHFULL SHADES OF NIGHT | TO THE NAME OF JESUS | 233 | 52 239 | 30 |
| THY RISING TOPP FIRST STAIND THE BASHFULL LIGHT. | HORATIJ ILLE & NEFASTO | 6 | MS 382 | 530 |

BATE

| | | | | |
|---|---|---|---|---|
| NOR SHOULD'ST THOU BATE IN PRIDE, BECAUSE THAT NOW, | SOSPETTO D'HERODE | 267 | 46 109 | 216 |

BATH

| | | | | |
|---|---|---|---|---|
| AND IN SOFT SLUMBERS BATH THY WOE. | THE TEARE | 40 | 46 84 | 50 |
| NOR LET THE MILKY FONTS THAT BATH YOUR THIRST, | TO INFANT MARTYRS | 3 | 46 88 | 10 |
| OF EVERLASTING JOYES BATH THY WHITE BREST. | ON THE ASSUMPTION | 58 | 46 139 | 114 |
| OF EVERLASTING JOYES BATH THY WHITE BREST. | IN GLORIOUS ASSUMPTION B. LADY | 63 | 52 304 | 114 |

BATH'D

| | | | |
|---|---|---|---|
| SHEW'D, THAT STERNE WARRE HAD NEWLY BATH'D HIM THERE | THE BEGINNING OF HELIODORUS | 22 | 46 158 517 |
| INTO THY BOSOME, BATH'D WITH LIQUID LIGHT. | ON A FOULE MORNING | 30 | 46 181 495 |

BATHS

| | | | |
|---|---|---|---|
| TWO WALKING BATHS. TWO WEEPING MOTIONS. | WEEPER | 113 | 52 307 120 |

BATHES

| | | | |
|---|---|---|---|
| BATHES HIM IN A GENUINE FLOOD. | IN PRAISE OF LESSIUS | 36 | 46 156 510 |
| BATHES IN TEARES OF EVERY EYE. | ANOTHER ON HERRYS | 8 | 46 170 469 |
| BATHES HIM IN A GENUINE FLOOD. | TEMPERANCE | 34 | 52 342 510 |

BATHING

| | | | |
|---|---|---|---|
| BATHING IN STREAMES OF LIQUID MELODIE. | MUSICKS DUELL | 68 | 46 149 535 |
| BATHING THEIR HOT LIMBS IN LIFE'S PRETIOUS FLOOD. | SOSPETTO D'HERODE | 316 | 46 109 216 |

BAYES

| | | | |
|---|---|---|---|
| HER WHOSE JUST BAYES, | WISHES SUPPOSED MISTRESSE | 109 | 46 195 479 |

BEAD

| | | | |
|---|---|---|---|
| A BEAD, THAT IS A TEARE DOTH DROP. | THE WEEPER | 108 | 46 79 120 |
| A BEAD, THAT IS, A TEAR, DOES DROP. | WEEPER | 144 | 52 307 120 |

BEAM

| | | | |
|---|---|---|---|
| WHOSE ROSY BEAM SHALL POINT MY SUN TO ME. | ALEXIAS SECONDE ELEGIE | 26 | 52 335 207 |

BROAD-BEAM'D

| | | | |
|---|---|---|---|
| OUT-STARE THE BROAD-BEAM'D DAYES MERIDIAN) | ON FRONTISPIECE ISAACSONS | 10 | 46 191 491 |

BEAME

| | | | |
|---|---|---|---|
| BRIGHT EVER WITH A BEAME THAT FALLS | PSALME 23 | 64 | 46 102 5 |
| THE GOLDEN EYES OF NIGHT. WHOSE BEAME MADE BRIGHT | SOSPETTO D'HERODE | 131 | 46 109 216 |
| WHERE DAWNING HOPE NO BEAME OF COMFORT SHOWES. | SOSPETTO D'HERODE | 242 | 46 109 216 |
| TO THEM SHEE GAVE THE FIRST AND FAIREST BEAME | UPON DEATH OF HERRYS | 17 | 46 167 466 |
| WHOSE EACH DIVIDED BEAME WOULD BE A SUN. | UPON YORKE HIS BIRTH | 13 | 46 176 500 |
| EACH LITTLE BEAME OF WHICH WOULD MAKE A SUNNE. | UPON KINGS CORONATION | 30 | MS 389 454 |

BEAMES

| | | | |
|---|---|---|---|
| NOW WESTWARD SOL HAD SPENT THE RICHEST BEAMES | MUSICKS DUELL | 1 | 46 149 535 |
| A SOULE WHOSE INTELECTUALL BEAMES | IN PRAISE OF LESSIUS | 31 | 46 156 510 |
| THIS FLAME THUS QUENCH'T HATH BRIGHTER BEAMES. | SHE BEGAN TO WASH HIS FEET | 3 | 46 97 13 |
| MAKE HIGH NOONE FORGET HIS BEAMES. | PSALME 23 | 16 | 46 102 5 |
| GUILDED I'TH' BEAMES OF EARTHLY KINGS | A HYMNE OF THE NATIVITY | 72 | 46 106 76 |
| AND THINE OWNE BEAMES ABOUT THEE. BRING THE BEST | ON A TREATISE OF CHARITY | 9 | 46 137 69 |
| BURNISHT IN HIS GLORIOUS BEAMES. | AN HIMNE FOR CIRCUMCISION | 14 | 46 141 37 |
| HIDE HIS HOT BEAMES IN SHADE OF SILVER AGE. | UPON DEATH OF HERRYS | 31 | 46 167 466 |
| THOSE BEAMES THAT AMPLIATE MORTALITIE, | UPON YORKE HIS BIRTH | 22 | 46 176 500 |
| THE BEAMES THAT DANCE IN THOSE FULL STARRES OF THINE. | UPON YORKE HIS BIRTH | 44 | 46 176 500 |
| THEIR ROSIE BEAMES, SO THAT THE MORNE FOR ONE | UPON YORKE HIS BIRTH | 57 | 46 176 500 |
| POINT HERE THY BEAMES. O GLANCE ON YONDER FLOCKES. | ON A FOULE MORNING | 5 | 46 181 495 |
| HEIRE OF THE SUNS FIRST BEAMES. WHY THREAT'ST THOU SO. | TO THE MORNING | 53 | 46 183 497 |
| ARE THESE THE BEAMES THAT RULE THY DAY. | LOVES HOROSCOPE | 10 | 46 185 483 |
| (DREST IN THOSE BEAMES) START FORTH | OUT OF THE ITALIAN (2) | 9 | 46 190 547 |
| OF BEAMES TO DAY, PAY BACK AGAINE TO MORROW. | UPON TWO GREENE APRICOCKES | 28 | 48 220 494 |
| GUILDED ITH' BEAMES OF EARTHLY KINGS. | IN HOLY NATIVITY | 92 | 52 246 76 |
| BURNISH IN HIS BEST BEAMES RISE. | NEW YEAR'S DAY | 14 | 52 251 37 |
| HIS SUPERFICIALL BEAMES SUN-BURN'T OUR SKIN. | IN GLORIOUS EPIPHANIE | 75 | 52 253 39 |
| A SOUL, WHOSE INTELLECTUALL BEAMES | TEMPERANCE | 29 | 52 342 510 |
| WHOSE BLAZING BEAMES, MAUGRE THE BLACKEST NIGHT, | UPON KINGS CORONATION | 15 | MS 389 454 |
| MAY DRAW THEIR FIRST BREATH FROM THY STARRY BEAMES. | EX EUPHORMIONE | 14 | MS 392 525 |

BEAR

| | | | |
|---|---|---|---|
| BEARES THAT HUGE TREE WHICH MUST BEAR HIM. | OFFICE H. CROSS SIXT | 4 | 52 270 97 |
| WHAT NEED THY FAIR HEAD BEAR A PART | UPON BLEEDING CRUCIFIX | 5 | 52 288 110 |
| SHALL HENCE FOR EVER BEAR AWAY. | LAUDA SION SALVATOREM | 18 | 52 294 178 |
| SAY & BEAR WITNES. SENDS SHE NOT | FLAMING HEART | 53 | 52 324 61 |
| TO BEAR ME HARMLESSE THROUGH THE HARDEST THINGS. | ALEXIAS FIRST ELEGIE | 18 | 52 334 204 |

BEARE

| | | | |
|---|---|---|---|
| WHAT NEED THY FAIRE HEAD BEARE A PART | ON BLEEDING WOUNDS OF LORD | 17 | 46 101 110 |
| AND RADIANT SCEPTER THIS BOLD HAND SHOULD BEARE. | SOSPETTO D'HERODE | 210 | 46 109 216 |
| OR HAD EVER LEARNT TO BEARE, | ANOTHER ON HERRYS | 19 | 46 170 469 |
| NOW THAT HIS ROOT SUCH FRUIT AGAINE MAY BEARE, | AN ELEGY MR STANNINOW | 55 | MS 394 473 |
| I SHRINKE NOT. BUT THUS READY STAND TO BEARE | OUT OF GROTIUS | 7 | MS 398 198 |
| AND 'GAINST RELIGION HER OWNE COLOURS BEARE. | OUT OF GROTIUS | 44 | MS 398 198 |

BEARES

| | | | |
|---|---|---|---|
| BEARES THAT HUGE TREE WHICH MUST BEAR HIM. | OFFICE H. CROSS SIXT | 4 | 52 270 97 |
| BEARES HOME NO LESSE, ALL THEY NO MORE. | LAUDA SION SALVATOREM | 47 | 52 294 178 |

|  |  |  |  |  |  |
|---|---|---|---|---|---|
| PALLAS BEARES ARMES, FORSOOTH, AND SHOULD THERE BE | ALEXIAS THIRD ELEGIE | 39 | 52 | 336 | 209 |

### DAY-BEARING

|  |  |  |  |  |  |
|---|---|---|---|---|---|
| HEE SAW HOW IN THAT BLEST DAY-BEARING NIGHT, | SOSPETTO D'HERODE | 113 | 46 | 109 | 216 |

### BEARD

|  |  |  |  |  |  |
|---|---|---|---|---|---|
| WITH THEE ALONE HE WEARES NO BEARD, THY BRAINE | UPON TWO GREENE APRICOCKES | 17 | 48 | 220 | 494 |

### BEAST

|  |  |  |  |  |  |
|---|---|---|---|---|---|
| AND THOU (HEAVEN-BURTHEN'D BEAST) HAST NE'RE A WORD | UPON ASSE THAT BORE SAVIOUR | 7 | 46 | 90 | 19 |
| WHAT WONDER, WHEN THE HUNDRED-HEADED BEAST | HORATIJ ILLE & NEFASTO | 50 | MS | 382 | 530 |

### BEASTS

|  |  |  |  |  |  |
|---|---|---|---|---|---|
| WHEN LIFES SWEET LIGHT FIRST SHONE ON BEASTS, AND WHEN | OUT OF VIRGIL | 29 | 46 | 155 | 529 |
| WHEN BEASTS TOOKE UP THEIR LODGING IN THE WOOD, | OUT OF VIRGIL | 31 | 46 | 155 | 529 |
| UNDER TH' UNRULY BEASTS PROUD FEET HE LIES | HIGH MOUNTED ON AN ANT | 3 | .46 | 161 | 523 |
| BEASTS AND BASE STRAW. ALREADY IS THE STREAME | SOSPETTO D'HERODE | 437 | 46 | 109 | 216 |
| POORE BEASTS. A SLOW OXE, AND A SIMPLE ASSE. | SOSPETTO D'HERODE | 528 | 46 | 109 | 216 |
| MY SOULE, SOME DRINKE FROM MEN TO BEASTS. O THEN, | AN APOLOGIE FOR HYMNE (TERESA) | 35 | 46 | 136 | 59 |
| AND TURNE NOT BEASTS, BUT ANGELS. LET THE KING, | AN APOLOGIE FOR HYMNE (TERESA) | 37 | 46 | 136 | 59 |
| (MY SOUL,) SOME DRINK FROM MEN TO BEASTS. O THEN | AN APOLOGIE FOR (TERESA) HYMNE | 35 | 52 | 322 | 59 |
| AND TURN NOT BEASTS, BUT ANGELS. LET THE KING | AN APOLOGIE FOR (TERESA) HYMNE | 37 | 52 | 322 | 59 |

### BEAT

|  |  |  |  |  |  |
|---|---|---|---|---|---|
| AND SERVES MY PURER SIGHT, ONELY TO BEAT | SOSPETTO D'HERODE | 203 | 46 | 109 | 216 |
| AND BEAT THE HOT BRASSE WITH REBELLIOUS WAVES. | SOSPETTO D'HERODE | 484 | 46 | 109 | 216 |
| AND BEAT A SUMMONS IN THE SAME | TO THE NAME OF JESUS | 35 | 52 | 239 | 30 |

### BEATE

|  |  |  |  |  |  |
|---|---|---|---|---|---|
| SHOULD BEATE HER HEADLONG FROM HER JETTY THRONE. | UPON GUNPOWDER TREASON | 26 | MS | 386 | 460 |

### BEATEN

|  |  |  |  |  |  |
|---|---|---|---|---|---|
| MARS THOU HAST BEATEN NAKED, AND O THEN | UPON VENUS PUTTING ARMES | 3 | 46 | 161 | 523 |

### BEATS

|  |  |  |  |  |  |
|---|---|---|---|---|---|
| LOVE TOUCHT HER HEART, AND LOE IT BEATS | IN MEMORY OF LADY MADRE TERESA | 35 | 46 | 131 | 52 |
| BEATS BRIGHT UPON THE BURNING FACES | IN MEMORY OF LADY MADRE TERESA | 85 | 46 | 131 | 52 |

### BEATES

|  |  |  |  |  |  |
|---|---|---|---|---|---|
| LOVE TOUCH'T HER HEART, & LO IT BEATES | TERESA | 35 | 52 | 315 | 52 |
| BEATES BRIGHT UPON THE BURNING FACES | TERESA | 85 | 52 | 315 | 52 |

### BEAUTEOUS

|  |  |  |  |  |  |
|---|---|---|---|---|---|
| THOSE BEAUTEOUS RAVISHERS OPPREST SO SORE | IN GLORIOUS EPIPHANIE | 91 | 52 | 253 | 39 |
| REVENGE THY BOUNTYES IN THEIR BEAUTEOUS SHAPES. | IN GLORIOUS EPIPHANIE | 106 | 52 | 253 | 39 |
| AND LAOTHSOM SPITTLE, BLOTT THOSE BEAUTEOUS EYES, | OFFICE H. CROSS PRIME | 6 | 52 | 267 | 91 |
| STILL WOULD THOSE BEAUTEOUS MINISTERS OF LIGHT | CHARITAS NIMIA | 21 | 52 | 280 | 48 |
| THUS VEX THE EARTH & TEARE THE BEAUTEOUS SKYES. | ALEXIAS SECONDE ELEGIE | 10 | 52 | 335 | 207 |

### BEAUTEOUSLY

|  |  |  |  |  |  |
|---|---|---|---|---|---|
| WHOSE BLUSH THE MOON BEAUTEOUSLY MARRES | O GLORIOSA DOMINA | 3 | 52 | 302 | 194 |

### BEAUTIES

|  |  |  |  |  |  |
|---|---|---|---|---|---|
| O'RE BEAUTIES FACE, SEEMING TO HIDE | IN PRAISE OF LESSIUS | 29 | 46 | 156 | 510 |
| 'TIS CHANG'D INDEED, DID AUTUMN E'RE SUCH BEAUTIES BRING | UPON THORNES FROM LORDS HEAD | 3 | 46 | 96 | 23 |
| THE BEAUTIES OF WHOSE DAWNE WHAT EYE MAY BIDE, | SOSPETTO D'HERODE | 11 | 46 | 109 | 216 |
| OTHER THEN WHAT THEIR OWNE BLEST BEAUTIES BRING. | SOSPETTO D'HERODE | 16 | 46 | 109 | 216 |
| THEE ALL THE BEAUTIES OF THY ONCE BRIGHT EYES. | SOSPETTO D'HERODE | 74 | 46 | 109 | 216 |
| BE WHAT THY BEAUTIES, NOT OUR BLOTS, HAVE MADE THEE, | ON A TREATISE OF CHARITY | 3 | 46 | 137 | 69 |
| 'TIS SHEE, 'TIS SHEE, HER AWFULL BEAUTIES CHASE | UPON YORKE HIS BIRTH | 74 | 46 | 176 | 500 |
| BUT SUCH WHOSE SUN-BORNE BEAUTIES WHAT THEY BORROW | UPON TWO GREENE APRICOCKES | 27 | 48 | 220 | 494 |
| ABASH THE PUREST BEAUTIES OF THE DAY. | UPON KINGS CORONATION | 26 | MS | 389 | 454 |
| HIGH BEAUTIES SOVERAIGNE, THAT MY FUNERALL FLAMES | EX EUPHORMIONE | 13 | MS | 392 | 525 |
| THEIR WRONGED BEAUTIES SPEAKE A TRAGAEDY, | AN ELEGIE ON DR PORTER | 11 | MS | 395 | 476 |

### BEAUTIFULL

|  |  |  |  |  |  |
|---|---|---|---|---|---|
| TO BECOME BEAUTIFULL IN HUMANE BLOOD. | SOSPETTO D'HERODE | 84 | 46 | 109 | 216 |

### BEAUTY

|  |  |  |  |  |  |
|---|---|---|---|---|---|
| THY NOBLER BEAUTY SHALL BEREAVE HIM. | AN HIMNE FOR CIRCUMCISION | 33 | 46 | 141 | 37 |
| COME THEN YOUTH, BEAUTY, AND BLOOD, ALL YE SOFT POWERS, | UPON STANINOUGH'S DEATH | 7 | 46 | 175 | 475 |
| BEAUTY LAYES OPE LOVES FORTUNE-BOOKE. | LOVES HOROSCOPE | 12 | 46 | 185 | 483 |
| BEAUTY FROWNES, AND LOVE MUST DYE. | LOVES HOROSCOPE | 32 | 46 | 185 | 483 |
| BEAUTY SMILES AND LOVE SHALL LIVE. | LOVES HOROSCOPE | 40 | 46 | 185 | 483 |
| YET THY BEAUTY | OUT OF THE ITALIAN (1) | 40 | 46 | 188 | 545 |
| TRUE BEAUTY, TO TRUE HOLINESSE. | AN EPITAPH UPON ASHTON | 22 | 46 | 192 | 464 |
| I WISH HER BEAUTY, | WISHES SUPPOSED MISTRESSE | 16 | 46 | 195 | 479 |
| BY ITS OWNE BEAUTY DREST, | WISHES SUPPOSED MISTRESSE | 26 | 46 | 195 | 479 |

|   |   |   |   |   |
|---|---|---|---|---|
| IT WAS THEIR WEAKNES WOO'D HIS BEAUTY. | IN GLORIOUS EPIPHANIE | 183 | 52 253 | 39 |
| THY BURTHEN, TOO MUCH BEAUTY. | VEXILLA REGIS | 28 | 52 277 | 156 |
| COME THEN, YOUTH, BEAUTY, & BLOOD. | DEATH'S LECTURE | 7 | 52 340 | 475 |
| WITTNESSE THIS MAPP OF BEAUTY. EVERY PART | UPON BIRTH PRINCESSE E | 37 | MS 391 | 456 |

BEAUTY'S

|   |   |   |   |   |
|---|---|---|---|---|
| OR'E BEAUTY'S FACE. SEEMING TO HIDE | TEMPERANCE | 27 | 52 342 | 510 |

BEAUTYES

|   |   |   |   |   |
|---|---|---|---|---|
| HERE ARE BEAUTYES SHALL BEREAVE HIM | NEW YEAR'S DAY | 33 | 52 251 | 37 |
| BRIGHT BABE, WHOSE AWFULL BEAUTYES MAKE | IN GLORIOUS EPIPHANIE | 1 | 52 253 | 39 |
| USE IT TO SPELL THY BEAUTYES BETTER. | IN GLORIOUS EPIPHANIE | 187 | 52 253 | 39 |

BECKEN'D

|   |   |   |   |   |
|---|---|---|---|---|
| BECKEN'D FROM FARR | IN GLORIOUS EPIPHANIE | 19 | 52 253 | 39 |

BECOME

|   |   |   |   |   |
|---|---|---|---|---|
| TO BECOME BEAUTIFULL IN HUMANE BLOOD. | SOSPETTO D'HERODE | 84 | 46 109 | 216 |
| THY SELFE INTO A SHAPE THAT MAY BECOME THEE. | SOSPETTO D'HERODE | 462 | 46 109 | 216 |
| TO HAVE A GOD BECOME HER LOVER. | ON A PRAYER BOOKE | 118 | 46 126 | 139 |
| OUR SELVES BECOME OUR OWN BEST SACRIFICE. | IN HOLY NATIVITY | 108 | 52 246 | 76 |
| WOUNDS. AND BECOME ONE CRUCIFIX. | SANCTA MARIA DOLORUM | 100 | 52 283 | 162 |
| TO HAVE HER GOD BECOME HER LOVER. | PRAYER TO GENTLE-WOMAN | 124 | 52 328 | 139 |
| EACH STONE HAD STREIGHT A NIOBE BECOME, | UPON GUNPOWDER TREASON | 49 | MS 386 | 460 |

BED

|   |   |   |   |   |
|---|---|---|---|---|
| IN A BED OF REVEREND SNOW. | IN PRAISE OF LESSIUS | 42 | 46 156 | 510 |
| A DURTY PILLOW IN DEATH'S BED. | UPON THE DEATH OF A GENTLEMAN | 12 | 46 166 | 472 |
| THE DARLINGS OF AURORA'S BED. | THE WEEPER | 134 | 46 79 | 120 |
| SWEATING IN TOO WARME A BED. | THE TEARE | 24 | 46 84 | 50 |
| THE DUST SHALL NEVER BEE THY BED. | THE TEARE | 34 | 46 84 | 50 |
| TO FURNISH THE FAIRE INFANTS BED. | A HYMNE OF THE NATIVITY | 38 | 46 106 | 76 |
| 'TWIXT MOTHERS BRESTS TO GOE TO BED. | A HYMNE OF THE NATIVITY | 50 | 46 106 | 76 |
| SHALL BLESSE THE FRUITFULL MAJA'S BED. | A HYMNE OF THE NATIVITY | 78 | 46 106 | 76 |
| THAT A VILE MANGER HIS LOW BED SHOULD PROVE. | SOSPETTO D'HERODE | 175 | 46 109 | 216 |
| HERE STRONG PROCRUSTES PLANTS HIS BED OF BRASSE. | SOSPETTO D'HERODE | 358 | 46 109 | 216 |
| AND SELFE-TORMENTING SIN) HAD A SOFT BED. | SOSPETTO D'HERODE | 412 | 46 109 | 216 |
| HIS SWEAT-BEDEWED BED HAD NOW BETRAI'D HIM. | SOSPETTO D'HERODE | 474 | 46 109 | 216 |
| THE CRIMSON CURTAINES OF THY BED. | AN HIMNE FOR CIRCUMCISION | 6 | 46 141 | 37 |
| THAT FLAMING IN THEIR FAIRE BED SLEEP. | AN HIMNE FOR CIRCUMCISION | 20 | 46 141 | 37 |
| COME LESSE UNBROKEN TO OUR BED. | ON HOPE | 36 | 46 143 | 71 |
| BLUSHING FROM THINE EASTERNE BED. | UPON DEATH OF DESIRED HERRYS | 16 | 46 168 | 467 |
| AND WIND THY SELFE UP CLOSE IN THY COLD BED. | UPON STANINOUGH'S DEATH | 4 | 46 175 | 475 |
| THAT WARMES THE BED OF YOUTH AND BLOOD) | LOVES HOROSCOPE | 30 | 46 185 | 483 |
| IN YOUR WHITE BOSOME HER CHAST BED. | THOUGH NOW 'TIS NEITHER | 6 | MS 397 | 492 |
| TO FITT A BED FOR THIS HUGE BIRTHE. | IN HOLY NATIVITY | 42 | 52 246 | 76 |
| MADE HIS OWN BED E'RE HE WAS BORN. | IN HOLY NATIVITY | 49 | 52 246 | 76 |
| TO FURNISH THE FAIR INFANT'S BED | IN HOLY NATIVITY | 54 | 52 246 | 76 |
| TWIXT'S MOTHER'S BRESTS IS GONE TO BED. | IN HOLY NATIVITY | 68 | 52 246 | 76 |
| SHALL BLESSE THE FRUITFULL MAJA'S BED | IN HOLY NATIVITY | 98 | 52 246 | 76 |
| THE CRIMSON CURTAINS OF THY BED. | NEW YEAR'S DAY | 6 | 52 251 | 37 |
| BUT MUST THY BED, LORD, BE A BOROW'D GRAVE | OFFICE H. CROSS COMPLINE | 9 | 52 274 | 105 |
| OR E'RE THE SOONER SEEK HIS WESTERN BED. | CHARITAS NIMIA | 42 | 52 280 | 48 |
| SWEATING IN A TOO WARM BED. | WEEPER | 162 | 52 307 | 120 |
| THE DARLINGS OF AURORAS BED, | WEEPER | 176 | 52 307 | 120 |
| BOTH MIXT AT LAST THEIR BLOOD IN ONE RICH BED | ALEXIAS THIRD ELEGIE | 47 | 52 336 | 209 |
| LOVE MADE THE BED. THEY'L TAKE NO HARM | AN EPITAPH UPON MARRIED COUPLE | 14 | 52 339 | 478 |
| AND WIND THY SELF UP CLOSE IN THY COLD BED. | DEATH'S LECTURE | 4 | 52 340 | 475 |
| IN A BED OF REVEREND SNOW. | TEMPERANCE | 40 | 52 342 | 510 |
| COME LESSE UNBROKEN TO OUR BED. | (ON) HOPE | 16 | 52 345 | 71 |
| THEN SPOUSALL RITES PREJUDGE THE MARRIAGE BED. | (ON) HOPE | 20 | 52 345 | 71 |
| BEGUIL'D THY BED. | LUKE 2. QUAERIT JESUM | 28 | MS 379 | 11 |
| MAKING THEM SKIP OUT OF THEIR DUSTY BED. | ON GUNPOWDER-TREASON | 30 | MS 384 | 458 |
| OR CALL HER CHEEKE A BED OF NEW BLOWNE ROSES. | UPON BIRTH PRINCESSE E | 45 | MS 391 | 456 |
| THY MAIDEN STREAMES SOE SOONE TO NEPTUNES BED. | AN ELEGIE ON DR PORTER | 2 | MS 395 | 476 |

MARRIAGE-BED

|   |   |   |   |   |
|---|---|---|---|---|
| THEN SPOUSALL RITES PREJUDGE THE MARRIAGE-BED. | ON HOPE | 40 | 46 143 | 71 |
| THIS GRAVE'S THE SECOND MARRIAGE-BED. | AN EPITAPH HUSBAND AND WIFE | 2 | 46 174 | 478 |
| THIS GRAVE'S THEIR SECOND MARRIAGE-BED. | AN EPITAPH UPON MARRIED COUPLE | 2 | 52 339 | 478 |

BEDD

|   |   |   |   |   |
|---|---|---|---|---|
| HIS BALMY TREASURES TO THE BEDD OF DEATH. | AN ELEGY MR STANNINOW | 30 | MS 394 | 473 |
| AND PLANTS IT IN A PRECIOUS PERFUM'D BEDD, | AN ELEGY MR STANNINOW | 51 | MS 394 | 473 |

BEDS

|   |   |   |   |   |
|---|---|---|---|---|
| TO WOO THEM FROM THEIR BEDS, STILL MURMURING | MUSICKS DUELL | 79 | 46 149 | 535 |
| THEIR LOCKES ARE BEDS OF UNCOMB'D SNAKES THAT WIND | SOSPETTO D'HERODE | 69 | 46 109 | 216 |
| TWO EVER BLUSHING BEDS OF NEW-BORNE ROSES. | ON A FOULE MORNING | 18 | 46 181 | 495 |
| MOUNTAINS OF MYRRH, & BEDS OF SPICES. | TO THE NAME OF JESUS | 186 | 52 239 | 30 |
| TO SEEK FOR HUMBLE BEDS | TO THE NAME OF JESUS | 232 | 52 239 | 30 |
| THAT FLAMING IN THEIR FAIR BEDS SLEEP. | NEW YEAR'S DAY | 20 | 52 251 | 37 |

## BEDDS

| | | | |
|---|---|---|---|
| O CHEEKS. BEDDS OF CHAST LOVES | WEEPER | 85 | 52 307 120 |

## SWEAT-BEDEWED

| | | | |
|---|---|---|---|
| HIS SWEAT-BEDEWED BED HAD NOW BETRAI'D HIM. | SOSPETTO D'HERODE | 474 | 46 109 216 |

## BEDRID

| | | | |
|---|---|---|---|
| HIS BEDRID LIMMES, WRAPT IN A FLEECY CLOWD. | AN ELEGY MR STANNINOW | 4 | MS 394 473 |

## BEERE

| | | | |
|---|---|---|---|
| TO MAKE HIS COSTLY CRADLE OF THY BEERE. | UPON YORKE HIS BIRTH | 95 | 46 176 500 |

## BEES

| | | | |
|---|---|---|---|
| THE WORKING BEES SOFT MELTING GOLD, | OUT OF GREEKE CUPID'S CRYER | 25 | 46 159 519 |
| FROM WHENCE HEAV'N-LABOURING BEES WITH BUSIE WING, | SOSPETTO D'HERODE | 22 | 46 109 216 |
| LIKE DILIGENT BEES, AND SWARM ABOUT IT. | TO THE NAME OF JESUS | 153 | 52 239 30 |

## BEGAN

| | | | |
|---|---|---|---|
| HIS BIRTH, BY HIS DEVOTION, WHO BEGAN | SOSPETTO D'HERODE | 103 | 46 109 216 |

## BEGIN

| | | | |
|---|---|---|---|
| OF CLOSER STRAINES, AND ERE THE WARRE BEGIN, | MUSICKS DUELL | 19 | 46 149 535 |
| THEIR GENTLEST FRIEND, THEN, THEN THE LANDS BEGIN | OUT OF VIRGIL | 2 | 46 155 529 |
| LESSER AND LESSER YET, TILL THOU BEGIN | UPON STANINOUGH'S DEATH | 17 | 46 175 475 |
| ON OUR LIPS, BEGIN AND TELL | OUT OF CATULLUS | 10 | 46 194 523 |
| LESSER & LESSER YET. TILL THOU BEGIN | DEATH'S LECTURE | 18 | 52 340 475 |

## BEGINNE

| | | | |
|---|---|---|---|
| DOTH SHE BEGINNE TO DANDLE IN HER LAPPE | AN ELEGY MR STANNINOW | 7 | MS 394 473 |

## BEGUILE

| | | | |
|---|---|---|---|
| WOULDST SEE BLITH LOOKES, FRESH CHEEKS BEGUILE | IN PRAISE OF LESSIUS | 39 | 46 156 510 |
| DEATH'S BUSIE SEARCH I'LE EASILY BEGUILE. | SICKE IMPLORE SHADOW | 2 | 46 87 28 |

## BEGUILEST

| | | | |
|---|---|---|---|
| IN OUR BEST HOPES BEGUILEST US. | UPON THE DEATH OF A GENTLEMAN | 4 | 46 166 472 |

## BEGUIL'D

| | | | |
|---|---|---|---|
| BEGUIL'D THY BED. | LUKE 2. QUAERIT JESUM | 28 | MS 379 11 |

## BEGUIL

| | | | |
|---|---|---|---|
| WOULDST' SEE BLITH LOOKES, FRESH CHEEKES BEGUIL | TEMPERANCE | 37 | 52 342 510 |

## BEGUILES

| | | | |
|---|---|---|---|
| AND BEHIND ME, HE BEGUILES | PSALME 23 | 25 | 46 102 5 |

## BEGUILING

| | | | |
|---|---|---|---|
| BUT BEGUILING | ON A PRAYER BOOKE | 49 | 46 126 139 |
| BUT BEGUILING | PRAYER TO GENTLE-WOMAN | 55 | 52 328 139 |

## BEGUN

| | | | |
|---|---|---|---|
| BY OFTEN KISSING THEM, AND NOW BEGUN | UPON DEATH OF HERRYS | 21 | 46 167 466 |

## BEHELD

| | | | |
|---|---|---|---|
| WHEN NIGHT BEHELD THEM, SHAME DID ALMOST TURNE | UPON GUNPOWDER TREASON | 11 | MS 387 461 |

## BEHIND

| | | | |
|---|---|---|---|
| AND BEHIND ME, HE BEGUILES | PSALME 23 | 25 | 46 102 5 |
| THREE RIGOUROUS VIRGINS WAITING STILL BEHIND. | SOSPETTO D'HERODE | 65 | 46 109 216 |
| LEFT HIS YEARES SO MUCH BEHIND, | HIS EPITAPH (HERRYS) | 8 | 46 172 471 |
| ALL HATING TO BE LEFT BEHIND. | AGAINST IRRESOLUTION AND DELAY | 42 | 52 347 146 |
| DETAIN HIM, BUT HE LEAVES BEHIND | AGAINST IRRESOLUTION AND DELAY | 75 | 52 347 146 |

## BEHOLD

| | | | |
|---|---|---|---|
| BLUSHING, TO BEHOLD THE RAY | UPON DEATH OF DESIRED HERRYS | 33 | 46 168 467 |
| STILL MAY BEHOLD, THOUGH STILL I DY. | A SONG | 8 | 52 327 65 |
| THE LAUGHING MEADES, AS JOYFULL TO BEHOLD | UPON KINGS CORONATION | 27 | MS 390 453 |

## BEHOLDEN

| | | | |
|---|---|---|---|
| BEE BEHOLDEN | OUT OF THE ITALIAN (1) | 10 | 46 188 545 |

BEHOLDERS

  BEHOLDERS LOST IN SWEET DELIGHT                 ON THE ASSUMPTION           33  46 139 114

BEING

  BY SHORT DIMINUTIVES, THAT BEING REAR'D       MUSICKS DUELL               41  46 149 535
    THAT BEING NAK'T, THOU KNOW'ST COULD CONQUER THEE.  UPON THE SAME (VENUS ARMES)    4  46 161 523
  A BORROWED BEING, MAKE THY BOLD DEFENCE.      SOSPETTO D'HERODE          252  46 109 216
  SUBT'LEST, BUT SUREST BEING. THOU BY WHOM      ON HOPE                   13  46 143  71
  TO WHAT HIS BOWELS BIRTH AND BEING GAVE.       ON FRONTISPIECE ISAACSONS      2  46 191 491
  WHICH TO NO BOXE HIS BEING OWES.               WISHES SUPPOSED MISTRESSE     36  46 195 479
  GUILTY OF BEING MUCH FOR THEM TOO GOOD.        IN GLORIOUS EPIPHANIE       108  52 253  39
  KEPT THEM FROM BEING SO UNKINDLY KIS'T.        IN GLORIOUS EPIPHANIE       124  52 253  39
  BY BEING SCHOLLER FIRST OF THAT NEW NIGHT.     IN GLORIOUS EPIPHANIE       206  52 253  39
  FOR BEING SHOW'D BY THIS DAY'S LIGHT, HOW FARR   IN GLORIOUS EPIPHANIE       246  52 253  39

BEEING

  SUBTLEST, BUT SUREST BEEING. THOU BY WHOM      (ON) HOPE                  3  52 345  71

BELCHES

  EVEN HEE THAT BELCHES OUT A FOAMING FLOOD      OUT OF GROTIUS              75  MS 398 198

BELCH'D

  BELCH'D FROM THE SULPH'RY LUNGS OF PHLEGETON.    ON GUNPOWDER-TREASON        16  MS 384 458

BELIEVING

  AND BELIEVING WHAT THEY TOLD.                 HIS EPITAPH (HERRYS)        11  46 172 471

BELEEVING

  TO THE BELEEVING WORLD FAME BOLDLY SINGS.      SOSPETTO D'HERODE          14  46 109 216

BELEEVE

  NOW LORD, OR NEVER, THEY'L BELEEVE ON THEE.    ON MIRACLE OF LOAVES         1  46  88  16
  BELEEVE MEE, READER CAN SAY MORE              AN EPITAPH UPON ASHTON      2  46 192 464

BELEEVES

  NOR BELEEVES SHEE SADNESSE IS.                THE WEEPER                64  46  79 120
  FANNING THY FAIRE LOCKS (WHICH THE WORLD BELEEVES ON A TREATISE OF CHARITY      23  46 137  69

BELEIVE

  FAITH IS MY SKILL. FAITH CAN BELEIVE          ADORO TE                 11  52 291 172
  BOTH YET BELEIVE. AND WITTNESSE THEE          ADORO TE                 31  52 291 172
  BOLD FAITH TAKES HEART, & DARES BELEIVE.       LAUDA SION SALVATOREM       38  52 294 178

BELLOW'D

  OH MEE. (THUS BELLOW'D HEE) OH MEE. WHAT GREAT  SOSPETTO D'HERODE         201  46 109 216

BELONG

  THE HEIRS ELECT OF LOVE. WHOSE NAMES BELONG   TO THE NAME OF JESUS         9  52 239  30

BELONGS

  (ALL YOU TO WHOM THIS LOVE BELONGS)          O GLORIOSA DOMINA          29  52 302 194

BELOVED

  TRUST HIS BELOVED BOSOME TO THE SUN           OUT OF VIRGIL              17  46 155 529

BEND

  WHILE OTHERS BEND THEIR KNEE, NO MORE SHALT THOU ON A TREATISE OF CHARITY      41  46 137  69
  (DISDAINFULL DUST AND ASHES) BEND THY BROW.    ON A TREATISE OF CHARITY      42  46 137  69
  WITH YOUR BRIGHT HEAD WHOLE GROVES OF SCEPTERS BEND TO THE QUEEN'S MAJESTY     17  52 261  47
  AH THIS WAY BEND THY BENIGN FLOOD              ADORO TE                 47  52 291 172

BENDING

  BENDING HER BLESSED EYES ON THEE              IN MEMORY OF LADY MADRE TERESA 135  46 131  52
  BENDING HER BLESSED EYES ON THEE              TERESA                   134  52 315  52

BENEATH

  (HIS SHOP OF FLAMES) HEE FRYES HIMSELFE, BENEATH SOSPETTO D'HERODE          62  46 109 216
  THIS STONE WILL TELL THEE THAT BENEATH,        HIS EPITAPH (HERRYS)         5  46 172 471
  FOLD UP MY LIFE IN LOVE, AND LAY'T BENEATH    SANCTA MARIA DOLORUM       107  52 283 162
  WHEN A DEEP GROAN FROM BENEATH               DIES IRAE                14  52 298 186

BENIGN

  AH THIS WAY BEND THY BENIGN FLOOD              ADORO TE                 47  52 291 172

PAGE 28

## BENT

| | | | | | |
|---|---|---|---|---|---|
| BENT ALL TO DROWN & OVERFLOW. | UPON BLEEDING CRUCIFIX | 30 | 52 | 288 | 110 |

## BEQUEATH

| | | | | | |
|---|---|---|---|---|---|
| TIS BUT A DEAD FACE, ART DOTH HERE BEQUEATH. | UPON BISHOP ANDREWES PICTURE | 15 | 46 | 163 | 490 |
| THOU TRIM'ST A PROPHETS TOMBE, AND DOST BEQUEATH | YEE BUILD SEPULCHRES | 1 | 46 | 95 | 21 |
| (FOR WHAT ELSE IS MY LIFE.) LO I BEQUEATH. | OUR LORD IN HIS CIRCUMCISION | 2 | 46 | 98 | 9 |
| SO WHILE THESE LINES CAN BUT BEQUEATH | AN EPITAPH UPON ASHTON | 33 | 46 | 192 | 464 |
| TO HIDE HIS BLOOMING GLORIES, & BEQUEATH | AN ELEGY MR STANNINOW | 29 | MS | 394 | 473 |

## BEREAVE

| | | | | | |
|---|---|---|---|---|---|
| THY NOBLER BEAUTY SHALL BEREAVE HIM, | AN HIMNE FOR CIRCUMCISION | 33 | 46 | 141 | 37 |
| HERE ARE BEAUTYES SHALL BEREAVE HIM | NEW YEAR'S DAY | 33 | 52 | 251 | 37 |

## BESEEM

| | | | | | |
|---|---|---|---|---|---|
| A MAJESTIE THAT MAY BESEEM THY THRONE. | ON A TREATISE OF CHARITY | 20 | 46 | 137 | 69 |

## BESEEMING

| | | | | | |
|---|---|---|---|---|---|
| FOR A BESEEMING BRACELET SHEE HAD TY'D | SOSPETTO D'HERODE | 466 | 46 | 109 | 216 |

## WELL-BESEEMING

| | | | | | |
|---|---|---|---|---|---|
| GREAT ANTHONY. SPAINS WELL-BESEEMING PRIDE. | SOSPETTO D'HERODE | 9 | 46 | 109 | 216 |
| BARGAIN'D WITH DEATH & WELL-BESEEMING DUST | CHARITAS NIMIA | 56 | 52 | 280 | 48 |

## BESEIGE

| | | | | | |
|---|---|---|---|---|---|
| OF SUTERS THAT BESEIGE YOUR MAIDEN BREST. | TO SAME CONCERNING CHOISE | 3 | 52 | 331 | 66 |

## BESEIG'D

| | | | | | |
|---|---|---|---|---|---|
| BY HIS WORST FOES (BECAUSE HE WOULD) BESEIG'D & TAKEN. | OFFICE H. CROSS MATINES | 17 | 52 | 265 | 86 |

## HEAV'N-BESIEGED

| | | | | | |
|---|---|---|---|---|---|
| WHAT HEAV'N-BESIEGED HEART IS THIS | AGAINST IRRESOLUTION AND DELAY | 1 | 52 | 347 | 146 |

## BESETT

| | | | | | |
|---|---|---|---|---|---|
| WITH PEARLY PAPERS CARELESLY BESETT. | AN ELEGIE ON DR PORTER | 8 | MS | 395 | 476 |

## BESIDES

| | | | | | |
|---|---|---|---|---|---|
| BESIDES THIS FEARE OF DANGER, THERE'S NO DANGER HERE | WHY ARE YEE AFRAID | 15 | 46 | 88 | 15 |

## BESPEAKE

| | | | | | |
|---|---|---|---|---|---|
| BESPEAKE HER TO MY BLISSES. | WISHES SUPPOSED MISTRESSE | 14 | 46 | 195 | 479 |

## BEST

| | | | | | |
|---|---|---|---|---|---|
| MUSICKS BEST SEED-PLOT, WHENCE IN RIPEND AIRES | MUSICKS DUELL | 69 | 46 | 149 | 535 |
| OF ALL THE STRINGS, STILL BREATHING THE BEST LIFE | MUSICKS DUELL | 152 | 46 | 149 | 535 |
| IN OUR BEST HOPES BEGUILEST US. | UPON THE DEATH OF A GENTLEMAN | 4 | 46 | 166 | 472 |
| SORROWES BEST JEWELS LYE IN THESE | THE WEEPER | 47 | 46 | 79 | 120 |
| WEE'L BURNE, OUR OWNE BEST SACRIFICE. | A HYMNE OF THE NATIVITY | 88 | 46 | 106 | 76 |
| OF LANGUAGE TO MY INFANT LIPS, YEE BEST | SOSPETTO D'HERODE | 6 | 46 | 109 | 216 |
| ANGER, AND LOVE, BEST HOOKES OF HUMANE BLOOD. | SOSPETTO D'HERODE | 275 | 46 | 109 | 216 |
| BUT HER BEST HUSWIFES ARE THE PARCAE, WHICH | SOSPETTO D'HERODE | 340 | 46 | 109 | 216 |
| AND THINE OWNE BEAMES ABOUT THEE. BRING THE BEST | ON A TREATISE OF CHARITY | 9 | 46 | 137 | 69 |
| EMBRACE THY RADIANT BROWES, O MAY THE BEST | ON THE ASSUMPTION | 57 | 46 | 139 | 114 |
| OUR WEAK DESIRES HAVE DONE THEIR BEST. | ON THE ASSUMPTION | 63 | 46 | 139 | 114 |
| EARTH HER BEST PERFECTION, | UPON DEATH OF DESIRED HERRYS | 27 | 46 | 166 | 467 |
| HIS MOUTH WAS RHETORICKS BEST MOLD. | HIS EPITAPH (HERRYS) | 29 | 46 | 172 | 471 |
| AS SITS ABOVE THY BEST CAPACITYE. | UPON YORKE HIS BIRTH | 8 | 46 | 176 | 500 |
| THOUGH THEIR BEST ASPECTS TWIN'D UPON | LOVES HOROSCOPE | 25 | 46 | 185 | 483 |
| THAT NO MORE SUMMERS BEST DRESSES, | OUT OF THE ITALIAN (1) | 9 | 46 | 188 | 545 |
| A FACE THATS BEST | WISHES SUPPOSED MISTRESSE | 25 | 46 | 195 | 479 |
| YET ARE SCARCE RIPE ENOUGH AT BEST TO SHOW | UPON TWO GREENE APRICOCKES | 5 | 48 | 220 | 494 |
| AND DID HIS BEST TO HAVE DENY'D. | TO COUNTESSE OF DENBIGH | 16 | 52 | 236 | 146 |
| IS THIS THE BEST THOU CANST BESTOW. | IN HOLY NATIVITY | 39 | 52 | 246 | 76 |
| OUR SELVES BECOME OUR OWN BEST SACRIFICE. | IN HOLY NATIVITY | 108 | 52 | 246 | 76 |
| RISE, THOU BEST & BRIGHTEST MORNING. | NEW YEAR'S DAY | 1 | 52 | 251 | 37 |
| BURNISHT IN HIS BEST BEAMES RISE, | NEW YEAR'S DAY | 14 | 52 | 251 | 37 |
| AND PUNISH BEST THINGS WORST. BECAUSE THEY STOOD | IN GLORIOUS EPIPHANIE | 107 | 52 | 253 | 39 |
| AND THEIR BEST USE OF HIM THEY WORSHIP'T BE | IN GLORIOUS EPIPHANIE | 161 | 52 | 253 | 39 |
| HIS BEST AMBITION NOW, IS BUT TO BE | IN GLORIOUS EPIPHANIE | 248 | 52 | 253 | 39 |
| OF HIS BEST FRIENDS (YEA OF HIMSELF) FORSAKEN, | OFFICE H. CROSS MATINES | 16 | 52 | 265 | 86 |
| O YOU, YOUR OWN BEST DARTS | SANCTA MARIA DOLORUM | 71 | 52 | 283 | 162 |
| THE BEST AMBITION OF THY LOVE. | LAUDA SION SALVATOREM | 6 | 52 | 294 | 178 |
| EMBRACE THY RADIANT BROWES, O MAY THE BEST | IN GLORIOUS ASSUMPTION B. LADY | 62 | 52 | 304 | 114 |
| OUR WEAK DESIRES HAVE DONE THEIR BEST, | IN GLORIOUS ASSUMPTION B. LADY | 68 | 52 | 304 | 114 |
| WE' ARE TAUGHT BEST BY THY TEARES & THEE. | WEEPER | 24 | 52 | 307 | 120 |
| AND MY BEST FORTUNES SUCH FAIR SPOILES OF ME. | FLAMING HEART | 92 | 52 | 324 | 61 |
| THAT NIP THE BOSOME OF THE WORLDS BEST THINGS, | DESCRIPTION RELIGIOUS HOUSE | 26 | 52 | 338 | 213 |
| AND DID HIS BEST TO HAVE DENY'DE. | AGAINST IRRESOLUTION AND DELAY | 10 | 52 | 347 | 146 |
| HE, THAT ONCE BORE THE BEST PART'S GONE. | UPON DEATH OF A FREIND | 18 | MS | 393 | 477 |
| THE BEST MY CRADLE AND MY BIRTH COULD FIND. | OUT OF GROTIUS | 18 | MS | 398 | 198 |

BESTOW

| BESTOW THY POPPY UPON WAKEFULL WOE. | TO THE MORNING | 55 | 46 | 183 | 497 |
| EYES, THAT BESTOW | WISHES SUPPOSED MISTRESSE | 58 | 46 | 195 | 479 |
| IS THIS THE BEST THOU CANST BESTOW. | IN HOLY NATIVITY | 39 | 52 | 246 | 76 |
| THEIR ROSY FLEECE OF FIRE BESTOW. | IN HOLY NATIVITY | 59 | 52 | 246 | 76 |
| OUR PURCHAS'D SELVES TOO SOON BESTOW | AGAINST IRRESOLUTION AND DELAY | 65 | 52 | 347 | 146 |
| OR THAT THE DYING LILLY DID BESTOW | UPON BIRTH PRINCESSE E | 49 | MS | 391 | 456 |

BETHLEM

| AND CAME TO BETHLEM, WHERE THE CRUELL KING | SOSPETTO D'HERODE | 394 | 46 | 109 | 216 |

BETH'LEM

| THE WAY TO BETH'LEM, AND AS BOLDLY BLAZ'D, | SOSPETTO D'HERODE | 132 | 46 | 109 | 216 |

BETIMES

| BETIMES TO BE A SAINT, BEFORE A MAN. | SOSPETTO D'HERODE | 104 | 46 | 109 | 216 |

BETRAY'D

| SUCH AS (E'RE OUR DARK SINNES TO DUST BETRAY'D THEE) | ON A TREATISE OF CHARITY | 4 | 46 | 137 | 69 |

BETRAID

| MAN, FOR MAN, BY MAN'S BETRAID. | OFFICE H. CROSS MATINES | 13 | 52 | 265 | 86 |

BETRAI'D

| HIS SWEAT-BEDEWED BED HAD NOW BETRAI'D HIM, | SOSPETTO D'HERODE | 474 | 46 | 109 | 216 |

BETROTH

| A JOSEPH DID BETROTH | UPON OUR SAVIOURS TOMBE | 5 | 46 | 93 | 25 |
| A JOSEPH DID BETROTH | TO OUR B. LORD | 5 | 52 | 279 | 25 |

BETTER

| NOW, (WHAT IS BETTER) | ON MARKES OF SAVIOURS WOUNDS | 9 | 46 | 86 | 28 |
| BUT GIVE THEE A BETTER WITH HIMSELFE ABOVE. | SOSPETTO D'HERODE | 518 | 46 | 109 | 216 |
| HIS BETTER EPITAPH SHALL BEE. | AN EPITAPH UPON ASHTON | 35 | 46 | 192 | 464 |
| USE IT TO SPELL THY BEAUTYES BETTER. | IN GLORIOUS EPIPHANIE | 187 | 52 | 253 | 39 |
| HAD NOT A BETTER FRUIT FORBIDDEN IT. | O GLORIOSA DOMINA | 17 | 52 | 302 | 194 |
| SWEET MISTRIS SOUNDS A GREAT DEALE BETTER. | PETRONIJ ALES PHASIACIS PETITA | 18 | MS | 382 | 526 |

BETWIXT

| WE TWO BETWIXT US HAVE DIVIDED IT. | OUT OF THE ITALIAN (2) | 2 | 46 | 190 | 547 |
| SO HARDLY BETWIXT EARTH AND HEAVEN. | AGAINST IRRESOLUTION AND DELAY | 62 | 52 | 347 | 146 |

TWIXT

| TWIXT LIFE & DEATH, TWIXT IN & OUT. | TO COUNTESSE OF DENBIGH | 6 | 52 | 236 | 146 |
| TWIXT LIFE & DEATH, TWIXT IN & OUT. | TO COUNTESSE OF DENBIGH | 6 | 52 | 236 | 146 |
| TEMPER TWIXT CHILL DESPAIR, & TORRID JOY. | (ON) HOPE | 43 | 52 | 345 | 71 |

'TWIXT

| 'TWIXT MOTHERS BRESTS TO GOE TO BED. | A HYMNE OF THE NATIVITY | 50 | 46 | 106 | 76 |
| TEMPER'D 'TWIXT COLD DESPAIRE, AND TORRID JOY. | ON HOPE | 83 | 46 | 143 | 71 |
| 'TWIXT SOULE AND BODY A DIVORCE. | AN EPITAPH HUSBAND AND WIFE | 4 | 46 | 174 | 478 |
| TO MEDIATE 'TWIXT YOUR SELF AND YOU. | TO THE QUEEN | 10 | 48 | 215 | 501 |
| PROGRESSIONS 'TWIXT WHOSE TERMES POOR TIME GROWS OLD. | UPON TWO GREENE APRICOCKES | 16 | 46 | 220 | 494 |
| 'TWIXT SPRING & FROST. | IN GLORIOUS EPIPHANIE | 33 | 52 | 253 | 39 |
| 'TWIXT SUN & SHADE. | IN GLORIOUS EPIPHANIE | 216 | 52 | 253 | 39 |
| SO FAST 'TWIXT HIM & THEE. | SANCTA MARIA DOLORUM | 68 | 52 | 283 | 162 |
| 'TWIXT SOUL & BODY A DIVORCE. | AN EPITAPH UPON MARRIED COUPLE | 4 | 52 | 339 | 478 |
| 'TWIXT LIFE AND DEATH, 'TWIXT IN AND OUT. | AGAINST IRRESOLUTION AND DELAY | 6 | 52 | 347 | 146 |
| 'TWIXT LIFE AND DEATH, 'TWIXT IN AND OUT. | AGAINST IRRESOLUTION AND DELAY | 6 | 52 | 347 | 146 |

'TWIST

| 'TWIST DEATH'S & LOVE'S FARR DIFFERENT FRUIT. | OFFICE H. CROSS SIXT | 14 | 52 | 270 | 97 |

TWIXT'S

| TWIXT'S MOTHER'S BRESTS IS GONE TO BED. | IN HOLY NATIVITY | 68 | 52 | 246 | 76 |

T'WIXT

| MAINTAINING T'WIXT THY WORLD & OURS | IN GLORIOUS EPIPHANIE | 213 | 52 | 253 | 39 |

BEYOND

| BEYOND THY SELFE. FOR LO. THE GODS, THE GODS | UPON YORKE HIS BIRTH | 5 | 46 | 176 | 500 |
| BEYOND THE KINGDOMES OF CONTENTFULL CELLS. | DESCRIPTION RELIGIOUS HOUSE | 35 | 52 | 338 | 213 |
| I SING IMPIETY BEYOND A NAME. | ON GUNPOWDER-TREASON | 1 | MS | 384 | 458 |
| SHOULD HAVE HIS SOULE FRIGHTED BEYOND THE SPHAERES. | UPON GUNPOWDER TREASON | 10 | MS | 386 | 460 |

BE-SPILT

| | | | |
|---|---|---|---|
| THY BROTHERS BLOOD BE-SPILT LIFE SPENT IN VAINE. | SOSPETTO D'HERODE | 452 | 46 109 216 |

BID

| | | | |
|---|---|---|---|
| BID THE GOLDEN GOD THE SUNNE, | AN HIMNE FOR CIRCUMCISION | 13 | 46 141 37 |
| POINTS OF DEATH BID LOVE BE GONE | LOVES HOROSCOPE | 22 | 46 185 483 |
| BID THY GOLDEN GOD, THE SUN, | NEW YEAR'S DAY | 13 | 52 251 37 |
| BUT LEST THAT DY TOO, WE ARE BID | LAUDA SION SALVATOREM | 25 | 52 294 178 |

BIDS

| | | | |
|---|---|---|---|
| CHRIST BIDS THE DUMBE TONGUE SPEAKE, IT SPEAKES, THE SOUND | THE DUMBE HEALED | 1 | 46 87 16 |
| HARKE HOW SHE BIDS HER FRIGHTED DROPS MAKE HAST, | TO PONTIUS WASHING HANDS | 13 | 46 94 23 |
| CALLS THEE BACK, AND BIDS THEE COME, | IN MEMORY OF LADY MADRE TERESA | 67 | 46 131 52 |
| WHEN HEAVEN BIDS COME, WHO CAN SAY NO. | ON THE ASSUMPTION | 20 | 46 139 114 |
| AND POINTING TO DULL MORPHEUS, BIDS ME TAKE | TO THE MORNING | 15 | 46 183 497 |
| THY BLOOD BIDS US BE BOLD. | OFFICE H. CROSS COMPLINE | 19 | 52 274 105 |

BIDDES

| | | | |
|---|---|---|---|
| AND BIDDES THEE NE'RE FORGET | VEXILLA REGIS | 3 | 52 277 156 |
| TRUTH BIDDES ME SAY, 'TIS TIME YOU CEASE TO TRUST | TO SAME CONCERNING CHOISE | 18 | 52 331 66 |
| AND BIDDES YOU COME | TO SAME CONCERNING CHOISE | 23 | 52 331 66 |

BIDDS

| | | | |
|---|---|---|---|
| WHEN HEAVN BIDDS COME, WHO CAN SAY NO. | IN GLORIOUS ASSUMPTION B. LADY | 34 | 52 304 114 |
| CALLS THEE BACK, & BIDDS THEE COME | TERESA | 67 | 52 315 52 |

BIDE

| | | | |
|---|---|---|---|
| THE BEAUTIES OF WHOSE DAWNE WHAT EYE MAY BIDE, | SOSPETTO D'HERODE | 11 | 46 109 216 |
| THE QUIVER, THAT HE BORE, DID BIDE | IN CICATRICES DOMINI JESU | 7 | MS 381 27 |

BIDING

| | | | |
|---|---|---|---|
| AND SOFT OBEDIENCE, FIND SWEET BIDING HERE. | DESCRIPTION RELIGIOUS HOUSE | 31 | 52 338 213 |

BIG

| | | | |
|---|---|---|---|
| SOFT BACK, AND BRINGS A BOSOM BIG WITH LOVES. | TO THE NAME OF JESUS | 160 | 52 239 30 |

BIG-NAM'D

| | | | |
|---|---|---|---|
| SOME BIG-NAM'D COMPOSITION. | TEMPERANCE | 6 | 52 342 510 |

BIGG

| | | | |
|---|---|---|---|
| FOR THIS HE LOOK'T SO BIGG. & EVERY MORN | IN GLORIOUS EPIPHANIE | 121 | 52 253 39 |

BIGG-NAMED

| | | | |
|---|---|---|---|
| SOME BIGG-NAMED COMPOSITION. | IN PRAISE OF LESSIUS | 6 | 46 156 510 |

BIGGE

| | | | |
|---|---|---|---|
| BIGGE ALIKE WITH WOUNDS & DARTS. | FLAMING HEART | 76 | 52 324 61 |
| MAKE BIGGE THY BREST WITH IMMORTALL FIRE, | ALEXIAS THIRD ELEGIE | 22 | 52 336 209 |
| EACH BIGGE WITH BUSINESSE THRUSTS THE OTHER. | AGAINST IRRESOLUTION AND DELAY | 43 | 52 347 146 |

BILL

| | | | |
|---|---|---|---|
| AND FOLDS IN WAV'D NOTES WITH A TREMBLING BILL, | MUSICKS DUELL | 60 | 46 149 535 |

BILLS

| | | | |
|---|---|---|---|
| THE ORACULOUS DOCTORS MISTICK BILLS. | IN PRAISE OF LESSIUS | 7 | 46 156 510 |
| TH'ORACULOUS DOCTOR'S MYSTICK BILLS. | TEMPERANCE | 7 | 52 342 510 |

BIND

| | | | |
|---|---|---|---|
| CEASE HIM, BRING HIM, (BUT FIRST BIND HIM) | OUT OF GREEKE CUPID'S CRYER | 58 | 46 159 519 |
| ETERNALLY BIND EACH REBELLIOUS LIMBE. | SOSPETTO D'HERODE | 140 | 46 109 216 |

BINDING

| | | | |
|---|---|---|---|
| OF A RICH BINDING IN YOUR BREST. | PRAYER TO GENTLE-WOMAN | 10 | 52 328 139 |

BIRD

| | | | |
|---|---|---|---|
| WOULD REACH THE BRASEN VOYCE OF WARR'S HOARCE BIRD. | MUSICKS DUELL | 101 | 46 149 535 |
| AND LIKE A SAUCY BIRD HE HOVERS | OUT OF GREEKE CUPID'S CRYER | 40 | 46 159 519 |
| THE BIRD, THAT'S FETCH'T FROM PHASIS FLOUD, | PETRONIJ ALES PHASIACIS PETITA | 1 | MS 382 526 |

BIRDS

| | | | |
|---|---|---|---|
| WITH CHATTING BIRDS DELICIOUS MURMURINGS. | OUT OF VIRGIL | 10 | 46 155 529 |
| THE MORNING MUSES PERCH LIKE BIRDS, AND SING | UPON DEATH OF HERRYS | 11 | 46 167 466 |
| NOR LETT HER KINRED BIRDS COMPLAYNE | THOUGH NOW 'TIS NEITHER | 15 | MS 397 492 |

BIRTH

| | | | | |
|---|---|---|---|---|
| THEIR PREGNANT BOSOMES IN A FRAGRANT BIRTH. | OUT OF VIRGIL | 14 | 46 155 | 529 |
| NOR DOES THE DUST DESERVE YOUR BIRTH. | THE WEEPER | 130 | 46 79 | 120 |
| GREAT LITLE ONE, WHOSE GLORIOUS BIRTH. | A HYMNE OF THE NATIVITY | 57 | 46 106 | 76 |
| HIS BIRTH, BY HIS DEVOTION, WHO BEGAN | SOSPETTO D'HERODE | 103 | 46 109 | 216 |
| THEIR SIMPLE TRIBUTE TO THE BABE, WHOSE BIRTH | SOSPETTO D'HERODE | 119 | 46 109 | 216 |
| ADORE HER PRINCES BIRTH, FLAT ON HER BREST. | SOSPETTO D'HERODE | 124 | 46 109 | 216 |
| A MIGHTY BABE, WHOSE PURE, UNSPOTTED BIRTH. | SOSPETTO D'HERODE | 159 | 46 109 | 216 |
| HEAV'N SET THEE DOWN NEW DREST. WHEN THY BRIGHT BIRTH | ON A TREATISE OF CHARITY | 5 | 46 137 | 69 |
| THE PURE BIRTH OF EACH SPARKLING NEST, | AN HIMNE FOR CIRCUMCISION | 19 | 46 141 | 37 |
| THAT WAITED ON HER BIRTH. SHE GAVE TO THEM | UPON DEATH OF HERRYS | 18 | 46 167 | 466 |
| THE SPLENDOR OF HIS BIRTH AND BLOOD, | HIS EPITAPH (HERRYS) | 23 | 46 172 | 471 |
| NE'RE MAY A BIRTH OF THINE BE BOUGHT SO DEARE. | UPON YORKE HIS BIRTH | 94 | 46 176 | 500 |
| CAST AMOROUS GLANCES ON HIS BIRTH, | LOVES HOROSCOPE | 27 | 46 185 | 483 |
| TO WHAT HIS BOWELS BIRTH AND BEING GAVE. | ON FRONTISPIECE ISAACSONS | 2 | 46 191 | 491 |
| TILL THAT RIPE BIRTH | WISHES SUPPOSED MISTRESSE | 7 | 46 195 | 479 |
| SAY, LINGRING FAIR. WHY COMES THE BIRTH | TO COUNTESSE OF DENBIGH | 7 | 52 236 | 146 |
| LEAPES AT THY BIRTH. | TO THE NAME OF JESUS | 134 | 52 239 | 30 |
| THE BIRTH OF OUR BRIGHT JOYES. | TO THE NAME OF JESUS | 164 | 52 239 | 30 |
| THE BABE WHOSE BIRTH EMBRAVES THIS MORN, | IN HOLY NATIVITY | 48 | 52 246 | 76 |
| GREAT LITLE ONE, WHOSE ALL-EMBRACING BIRTH | IN HOLY NATIVITY | 83 | 52 246 | 76 |
| NOR DOES THE DUST DESERVE YOUR BIRTH. | WEEPER | 172 | 52 307 | 120 |
| SAY, LINGRING FAIR, WHY COMES THE BIRTH | AGAINST IRRESOLUTION AND DELAY | 15 | 52 347 | 146 |
| WHAT, BUT THE FAIREST HEAVEN, COULD OWNE THE BIRTH | LUKE 2. QUAERIT JESUM | 23 | MS 379 | 11 |
| ENGENDER WITH THE NIGHT, & TEEME A BIRTH | UPON GUNPOWDER TREASON | 12 | MS 386 | 460 |
| OF PEARLY DROPS, & SENT HER NUMEROUSE BIRTH | UPON KINGS CORONATION | 7 | MS 390 | 453 |
| AS IS THY BIRTH. YET FROM THY FLAMING EYE | UPON BIRTH PRINCESSE E | 18 | MS 391 | 456 |
| THE BEST MY CRADLE AND MY BIRTH COULD FIND. | OUT OF GROTIUS | 18 | MS 398 | 198 |

BIRTHE

| | | | | |
|---|---|---|---|---|
| TO FITT A BED FOR THIS HUGE BIRTHE. | IN HOLY NATIVITY | 42 | 52 246 | 76 |

BIRTHS

| | | | | |
|---|---|---|---|---|
| THE VIRGIN BIRTHS WITH WHICH THY SPOWSE | IN MEMORY OF LADY MADRE TERESA | 169 | 46 131 | 52 |
| ALL HER BIRTHS ABORTIVE PROVE. | UPON DEATH OF DESIRED HERRYS | 74 | 46 168 | 467 |
| COULD SHE IN ALL HER BIRTHS BUT COPPIE THEE. | UPON TWO GREENE APRICOCKES | 23 | 48 220 | 494 |
| ROB THE RICH BIRTHS OF EACH BRIGHT NEST | NEW YEAR'S DAY | 19 | 52 251 | 37 |

VIRGIN-BIRTHS

| | | | | |
|---|---|---|---|---|
| THE VIRGIN-BIRTHS WITH WHICH THY SOVEREIGN SPOUSE | TERESA | 168 | 52 315 | 52 |

BIRTHRIGHT

| | | | | |
|---|---|---|---|---|
| TO MORE THEN CAESARS BIRTHRIGHT IS. | A HYMNE OF THE NATIVITY | 60 | 46 106 | 76 |
| TO MORE THEN CAESAR'S BIRTHRIGHT IS. | IN HOLY NATIVITY | 86 | 52 246 | 76 |

BITT

| | | | | |
|---|---|---|---|---|
| OF ONE FORBIDDEN BITT. | O GLORIOSA DOMINA | 16 | 52 302 | 194 |

BITTER

| | | | | |
|---|---|---|---|---|
| WITH BITTER SHAFTS 'TIS SAUC'T TOO WELL. | OUT OF GREEKE CUPID'S CRYER | 52 | 46 159 | 519 |
| GALL, & MORE BITTER MOCKS, SHALL MAKE IT UP. | OFFICE H. CROSS SIXT | 10 | 52 270 | 97 |
| OF LOVE, SWEET BITTER THINGS, | SANCTA MARIA DOLORUM | 96 | 52 283 | 162 |

BLACK

| | | | | |
|---|---|---|---|---|
| THE WIND HAD NEED BE ANGRY, AND THE WATER BLACK. | WHY ARE YEE AFRAID | 7 | 46 88 | 15 |
| FROM HIS BLACK NOSTRILLS, AND BLEW LIPS, IN SPIGHT | SOSPETTO D'HERODE | 53 | 46 109 | 216 |
| AND WHILE THE BLACK SOULES BOILE IN THEIR OWNE GORE, | SOSPETTO D'HERODE | 295 | 46 109 | 216 |
| THUNDRING UPON THE BANKES OF THOSE BLACK LAKES | SOSPETTO D'HERODE | 298 | 46 109 | 216 |
| THE HOUSE IS HERS'D ABOUT WITH A BLACK WOOD. | SOSPETTO D'HERODE | 345 | 46 109 | 216 |
| BY A BLACK FOUNT, WHICH WEEPS INTO A FLOOD. | SOSPETTO D'HERODE | 349 | 46 109 | 216 |
| WHEN THE ERINNYS HER BLACK PINEONS SPREAD, | SOSPETTO D'HERODE | 393 | 46 109 | 216 |
| BRIGHT IDOL. BLACK IDOLATRY. | IN GLORIOUS EPIPHANIE | 51 | 52 253 | 39 |
| THEIR BLACK, BUT FAITHFULL PROSPECTIVE OF THEE. | IN GLORIOUS EPIPHANIE | 171 | 52 253 | 39 |
| TO'INJOY HIS BLOTT. & AS A LARGE BLACK LETTER | IN GLORIOUS EPIPHANIE | 186 | 52 253 | 39 |
| BY CONFEDERAT BLACK & WHITE | IN GLORIOUS EPIPHANIE | 217 | 52 253 | 39 |
| MAKES MANY A MOURNING PAPER PUT ON BLACK. | DEATH'S LECTURE | 2 | 52 340 | 475 |
| BLACK, AS THE DAY WAS DISMALL, IN WHOSE SIGHT | HORATIJ ILLE & NEFASTO | 5 | MS 382 | 530 |
| AND WHATSOE'RE WILD SINNES BLACK THOUGHTS DOE FEED, | HORATIJ ILLE & NEFASTO | 12 | MS 382 | 530 |
| HANGS HIS BLACK LUGGES, STROAKT WITH THOSE HEAVENLY LINES. | HORATIJ ILLE & NEFASTO | 51 | MS 382 | 530 |
| BLACK DISMALL HORROR, COME. MAKE PERFECT NOW | UPON GUNPOWDER TREASON | 20 | MS 387 | 461 |
| WITH A BLACK MASKE. THE CLOUDS WITH CHILD BY GREIFE | UPON KINGS CORONATION | 3 | MS 390 | 453 |

BLACK-FAC'D

| | | | | |
|---|---|---|---|---|
| A BLACK-FAC'D HOUSE WILL LOVE. | ON BAPTIZED AETHIOPIAN | 6 | 46 85 | 29 |

COLEBLACK

| | | | | |
|---|---|---|---|---|
| THREE COLEBLACK SISTERS, (WHOSE LONG SUTTY HAIRE, | UPON GUNPOWDER TREASON | 9 | MS 387 | 461 |

BLACKE

| | | | | |
|---|---|---|---|---|
| BLACKE WIT OR MALICE CAN OR DARES. | NEITHER DURST MAN ASKE | 2 | 46 92 | 20 |
| HOW HATH ONE BLACKE ECLIPSE CANCELL'D, AND CROST | SOSPETTO D'HERODE | 75 | 46 109 | 216 |

```
                                                                              PAGE  33


  MAKES MANY A MOURNING PAPER PUT ON BLACKE.       UPON STANINOUGH'S DEATH              2  46 175 475
  LAY BLACKE ON LOVES NATIVITYE.                   LOVES HOROSCOPE                     36  46 185 483

BLACKEST

  THY GREISLY MAJESTY, HELL'S BLACKEST QUEENE.     HORATIJ ILLE & NEFASTO              34  MS 382 530
  WHOSE BLAZING BEAMES, MAUGRE THE BLACKEST NIGHT, UPON KINGS CORONATION               15  MS 389 454

BLANK

  FORTUNE'S WHOLE LOTTERY IS ONE BLANK TO HER.     (ON) HOPE                           34  52 345  71

BLANKE

  AND FATES WHOLE LOTTERY IS ONE BLANKE TO HER.    ON HOPE                             74  46 143  71

BLAST

  IN A CLAY-COTTAGE, BY EACH BLAST CONTROL'D.      SOSPETTO D'HERODE                  182  46 109 216
  AND WITH THE RUSH OF ONE RUDE BLAST.             UPON DEATH OF DESIRED HERRYS        43  46 168 467
  THE FIRST BLAST OF THY COUGH LEFT TWO ALONE.     OUT OF MARTIALL                      3  46 188 527
  O THAT TRUMP, WHOSE BLAST SHALL RUN              DIES IRAE                            9  52 298 186
  WITH THIS GRAND BLAST SHOULD HAVE BIN BLOUNE AWAY. UPON GUNPOWDER TREASON            30  MS 386 460
  O TELL ME THEN, WHAT RUDE OUTRAGIOUS BLAST       AN ELEGY MR STANNINOW               27  MS 394 473

BLASTED

  THE FRESH FACE OF THE MORNE HAD BLASTED BEENE.   UPON GUNPOWDER TREASON              14  MS 386 460

BLAZE

  HIS BLAZE, TO SHINE IN A POORE SHEPHEARDS EYE.   SOSPETTO D'HERODE                  170  46 109 216
  THEY BANNE THE BLAZE, & CURSE ITS CURTESY.       ON GUNPOWDER-TREASON                59  MS 384 458

BLAZ'D

  THE WAY TO BETH'LEM, AND AS BOLDLY BLAZ'D,       SOSPETTO D'HERODE                  132  46 109 216

BLAZING

  WHOSE BLAZING BEAMES, MAUGRE THE BLACKEST NIGHT, UPON KINGS CORONATION               15  MS 389 454

BLED

  SOME PANTING IN THEIR YET WARME RUINES BLED.     THE BEGINNING OF HELIODORUS         18  46 158 517

BLEED

  LEST HIS KINDNESSE MAKE THEE BLEED.              OUT OF GREEKE CUPID'S CRYER         72  46 159 519
  SHOULD BLEED IN HIS OWNE LAWES OBEDIENCE.        SOSPETTO D'HERODE                  186  46 109 216
  SHOULD BLEED UPON A BARBAROUS KNIFE.             IN MEMORY OF LADY MADRE TERESA      70  46 131  52
  WHEN ON THE CROSSE MY KING DID BLEED.            OFFICE H. CROSS NINTH               11  52 271  99
  WHEN THE WOLF SINS, HIMSELF TO BLEED.            CHARITAS NIMIA                      54  52 280  48
  HER EYES BLEED TEARES, HIS WOUNDS WEEP BLOOD.    SANCTA MARIA DOLORUM                20  52 283 162
  O TEACH THOSE WOUNDS TO BLEED                    SANCTA MARIA DOLORUM                51  52 283 162
  TO BLEED WITH HIM, FAIL NOT TO WEEP WITH HER.    SANCTA MARIA DOLORUM                90  52 283 162
  SHOULD BLEED UPON A BARBOROUS KNIFE.             TERESA                              70  52 315  52
  AND BLEED & WOUND. AND YEILD & CONQUER STILL.    FLAMING HEART                       80  52 324  61
  IN WHAT STRANGE PATH MY LORD'S FOOTSTEPPES BLEED. ALEXIAS FIRST ELEGIE                8  52 334 204

BLEEDING

  EACH BLEEDING PART SOME ONE SUPPLIES.            ON WOUNDS OF CRUCIFIED LORD          4  46  99  24
  LAUGH, TILL THY CHILDRENS BLEEDING BONES         PSALME 137                          35  46 104   7
  THEY PRICK A BLEEDING HEART AT EVERY STITCH.     SOSPETTO D'HERODE                  342  46 109 216
  TO'A BLEEDING HEART THAT GASPES FOR BLOOD.       ADORO TE                            48  52 291 172
  WITH BLUSHING CHEEK & BLEEDING EY,               DIES IRAE                           42  52 298 186

BLENDED

  TO SEE BOTH BLENDED IN ONE FLOOD                 UPON INFANT MARTYRS                  1  46  95  10

BLENDS

  BLENDS ALL TOGETHER. THEN DISTINCTLY TRIPPS      MUSICKS DUELL                       31  46 149 535
  OF BAPTISME, BLENDS THEM ALL INTO ONE BLOOD.     AN APOLOGIE FOR HYMNE (TERESA)      16  46 136  59
  OF BAPTISM BLENDS THEM ALL INTO A BLOOD.         AN APOLOGIE FOR (TERESA) HYMNE      16  52 322  59
  BLENDS BOTH THE NOONES OF NIGHT & DAY.           (ON) HOPE                            6  52 345  71

BLESSE

  SHALL BLESSE THE FRUITFULL MAJA'S BED.           A HYMNE OF THE NATIVITY             78  46 106  76
  FROM A CHAST VIRGIN WOMBE, SHOULD BLESSE THE EARTH. SOSPETTO D'HERODE               160  46 109 216
  IN ALL THE GIFTS THAT BLESSE A CREATURE.         ANOTHER ON HERRYS                   12  46 170 469
  WHOSE FRUIT AND BLOSSOMS BOTH BLESSE THE SAME BOUGH. UPON TWO GREENE APRICOCKES      20  48 220 494
  SHALL BLESSE THE FRUITFULL MAJA'S BED            IN HOLY NATIVITY                    98  52 246  76

BLESSED

  THAT THE UNBLEMISHT LAMBE, BLESSED FOR EVER.     SOSPETTO D'HERODE                  189  46 109 216
  BENDING HER BLESSED EYES ON THEE                 IN MEMORY OF LADY MADRE TERESA     135  46 131  52
  LET COME YE BLESSED THEN CALL ME.                DIES IRAE                           60  52 298 186
  BENDING HER BLESSED EYES ON THEE                 TERESA                             134  52 315  52
  THY BLESSED EYES BREED SUCH DESIRE.              A SONG                               3  52 327  65
```

| | | PAGE | 34 | | |
|---|---|---|---|---|---|
| BE STILL TRIUMPHANT, BLESSED EYES. | A SONG | 6 | 52 | 327 | 65 |

## BLESSES

| | | | | | |
|---|---|---|---|---|---|
| WITH A NEW LAMB BLESSES THE BOARD. | LAUDA SION SALVATOREM | 20 | 52 | 294 | 178 |

## BLESSINGS

| | | | | | |
|---|---|---|---|---|---|
| AND BRING HER BOSOME FULL OF BLESSINGS, | ON A PRAYER BOOKE | 35 | 46 | 126 | 139 |
| OF BLESSINGS, AND TEN THOUSAND MORE. | ON A PRAYER BOOKE | 82 | 46 | 126 | 139 |
| BODY OF BLESSINGS. SPIRIT OF SOULES EXTRACTED. | TO THE NAME OF JESUS | 166 | 52 | 239 | 30 |
| AND BRING HIS BOSOM FRAUGHT WITH BLESSINGS, | PRAYER TO GENTLE-WOMAN | 41 | 52 | 328 | 139 |
| OF BLESSINGS & TEN THOUSAND MORE | PRAYER TO GENTLE-WOMAN | 88 | 52 | 328 | 139 |

## BLEST

| | | | | | |
|---|---|---|---|---|---|
| THEIR MASTERS BLEST SOULE (SNATCHT OUT AT HIS EARES | MUSICKS DUELL | 147 | 46 | 149 | 535 |
| OF BLEST VARIETY ATTENDING ON | MUSICKS DUELL | 153 | 46 | 149 | 535 |
| EACH BLEST DROP, ON EACH BLEST LIMME, | ON WATER OF LORDS BAPTISME | 1 | 46 | 85 | 12 |
| EACH BLEST DROP, ON EACH BLEST LIMME, | ON WATER OF LORDS BAPTISME | 1 | 46 | 85 | 12 |
| THE THORNES THAT THY BLEST BROWES ENCLOSES | ON BLEEDING WOUNDS OF LORD | 22 | 46 | 101 | 110 |
| WEE SAW THEE (AND WEE BLEST THE SIGHT) | A HYMNE OF THE NATIVITY | 33 | 46 | 106 | 76 |
| OTHER THEN WHAT THEIR OWNE BLEST BEAUTIES BRING. | SOSPETTO D'HERODE | 18 | 46 | 109 | 216 |
| HEE SAW HOW IN THAT BLEST DAY-BEARING NIGHT, | SOSPETTO D'HERODE | 113 | 46 | 109 | 216 |
| IS WHAT IN SIGNE OF JOY AMONG THE BLEST | SOSPETTO D'HERODE | 197 | 46 | 109 | 216 |
| BLEST POWERS FORBID THY TENDER LIFE, | IN MEMORY OF LADY MADRE TERESA | 69 | 46 | 131 | 52 |
| BLEST SERAPHIMS SHALL LEAVE THEIR QUIRE. | IN MEMORY OF LADY MADRE TERESA | 94 | 46 | 131 | 52 |
| TO NONE BUT THE BLEST HEAVENS, WHOSE BRIGHT | ON THE ASSUMPTION | 32 | 46 | 139 | 114 |
| HIS OWNE DELICIOUS PHOENIX FROM THE BLEST | UPON DEATH OF HERRYS | 13 | 46 | 167 | 466 |
| WITH THINE OWNE GLORYES. AND ART STRANGELY BLEST | UPON YORKE HIS BIRTH | 4 | 46 | 176 | 500 |
| THOU BY THY SELFE MAIST SIT, (BLEST ISLE) AND SEE | UPON YORKE HIS BIRTH | 25 | 46 | 176 | 500 |
| BLOSSOMS, BUT OUR BLEST TAST CONFESSES FRUITS. | UPON TWO GREENE APRICOCKES | 14 | 48 | 220 | 494 |
| BLEST HEAVNS, TO YOU, & YOUR SUPERIOUR SONG, | TO THE NAME OF JESUS | 98 | 52 | 239 | 30 |
| A THOUSAND BLEST ARABIAS DWELL. | TO THE NAME OF JESUS | 184 | 52 | 239 | 30 |
| COME WE SHEPHEARDS WHOSE BLEST SIGHT | IN HOLY NATIVITY | 1 | 52 | 246 | 76 |
| WE SAW THEE. & WE BLEST THE SIGHT | IN HOLY NATIVITY | 35 | 52 | 246 | 76 |
| WE SAW THEE. & WE BLEST THE SIGHT. | IN HOLY NATIVITY | 76 | 52 | 246 | 76 |
| RUN, MARY, RUN. BRING HITHER ALL THE BLEST | OFFICE H. CROSS COMPLINE | 5 | 52 | 274 | 105 |
| WHEN THE BLEST SIGNES THOU BROKE SHALL SEE, | LAUDA SION SALVATOREM | 55 | 52 | 294 | 178 |
| BLEST POWRES FORBID, THY TENDER LIFE | TERESA | 69 | 52 | 315 | 52 |
| BLEST SERAPHIM, SHALL LEAVE THEIR QUIRE | TERESA | 94 | 52 | 315 | 52 |
| I, 'MONGST THE BLEST STARRES A NEW NAME SHALL BE. | ALEXIAS FIRST ELEGIE | 24 | 52 | 334 | 204 |
| WAS THY BLEST MOTHER. | LUKE 2. QUAERIT JESUM | 22 | MS | 379 | 11 |
| YOU EVER-BLUSHING MEADS, WHERE DOE THE BLEST | HORATIJ ILLE & NEFASTO | 37 | MS | 382 | 530 |
| IN THIS BLEST EARTH HEAVENS BRIGHT EPITOME, | UPON KINGS CORONATION | 12 | MS | 389 | 454 |
| HONESTIES NURSE, VERTUES BLEST GUARDIAN, | AN ELEGIE ON DR PORTER | 17 | MS | 395 | 476 |

## WELL-BLES'T

| | | | | | |
|---|---|---|---|---|---|
| WITH A WELL-BLES'T BREAD & WINE | LAUDA SION SALVATOREM | 29 | 52 | 294 | 178 |

## BLEW

| | | | | | |
|---|---|---|---|---|---|
| FROM HIS BLACK NOSTRILLS, AND BLEW LIPS, IN SPIGHT | SOSPETTO D'HERODE | 53 | 46 | 109 | 216 |

## BLEW-EY'D

| | | | | | |
|---|---|---|---|---|---|
| RISE THEN (FAIRE BLEW-EY'D MAID) RISE AND DISCOVER | ON A FOULE MORNING | 27 | 46 | 181 | 495 |

## BLIND

| | | | | | |
|---|---|---|---|---|---|
| THOU SPAK'ST AND STREIGHT THE BLIND MAN SAW. | THE BLIND CURED | 2 | 46 | 91 | 19 |
| TO SPEAKE AND MAKE THE BLIND MAN SEE. | THE BLIND CURED | 3 | 46 | 91 | 19 |
| HOW LOVE CAME NAK'T, A BOY, AND BLIND. | OUT OF THE ITALIAN (3) | 2 | 46 | 190 | 549 |
| WAS THEIR MORE BLIND IDOLATRY, | IN GLORIOUS EPIPHANIE | 169 | 52 | 253 | 39 |
| SHALL WITH ONE FLASH OF LIGHTING BE STRUCK BLIND. | ON GUNPOWDER-TREASON | 32 | MS | 384 | 458 |

## BLIND-FOLD

| | | | | | |
|---|---|---|---|---|---|
| WHERE ART THOU SOL, WHILE THUS THE BLIND-FOLD DAY | ON A FOULE MORNING | 1 | 46 | 181 | 495 |

## BLINDED

| | | | | | |
|---|---|---|---|---|---|
| THAT ROME'S BOLD EAGLES NOW WERE BLINDED QUITE, | UPON KINGS CORONATION | 34 | MS | 390 | 453 |

## BLINDING

| | | | | | |
|---|---|---|---|---|---|
| COULD NOT ONCE BLINDING ME,CRUELL,SUFFICE. | SAMPSON TO HIS DALILAH | 1 | 46 | 102 | 8 |

## ANGELL-BLINDING

| | | | | | |
|---|---|---|---|---|---|
| THAT THE GREAT ANGELL-BLINDING LIGHT SHOULD SHRINKE | SOSPETTO D'HERODE | 169 | 46 | 109 | 216 |

## BLINDNES

| | | | | | |
|---|---|---|---|---|---|
| THE BLINDNES OF THE WORLD DID CALL THE EYE. | IN GLORIOUS EPIPHANIE | 45 | 52 | 253 | 39 |
| SO HIS OFFICIOUS BLINDNES NOW SHALL BE | IN GLORIOUS EPIPHANIE | 170 | 52 | 253 | 39 |

## BLINDNESSE

| | | | | | |
|---|---|---|---|---|---|
| OLD CLOUDS OF THICKEST BLINDNESSE FLED MY SIGHT | OUT OF GROTIUS | 71 | MS | 398 | 198 |

BLISFULL

| | | | | | |
|---|---|---|---|---|---|
| THINE ARMES, AND WITH THY BRIGHT & BLISFULL HEAD | OFFICE H. CROSS EVENSONG | 21 | 52 | 273 | 101 |

BLISSEFULL

| | | | | | |
|---|---|---|---|---|---|
| CANDIDATES OF BLISSEFULL LIGHT, | TO THE NAME OF JESUS | 8 | 52 | 239 | 30 |

BLISSFULL

| | | | | | |
|---|---|---|---|---|---|
| IN STEAD OF BRINGING IN THE BLISSFULL PRIZE | IN GLORIOUS EPIPHANIE | 226 | 52 | 253 | 39 |
| THE BLISSFULL SPRINGS OF JOY, FROM WHOSE ALL-CHEARING | OFFICE H. CROSS PRIME | 7 | 52 | 267 | 91 |
| O LET THE BLISSFULL HEART HOLD FAST | PRAYER TO GENTLE-WOMAN | 111 | 52 | 328 | 139 |

BLISSE

| | | | | | |
|---|---|---|---|---|---|
| THAT POINTS ME TO THESE WAYES OF BLISSE. | PSALME 23 | 4 | 46 | 102 | 5 |
| WHAT JOY, WHAT BLISSE, | ON A PRAYER BOOKE | 116 | 46 | 126 | 139 |
| BECAUSE THAT FROM THE BRIDALL CHEEKE OF BLISSE, | ON HOPE | 37 | 46 | 143 | 71 |
| WILL KILL HIS ANGER, AND REVIVE MY BLISSE. | TO THE MORNING | 38 | 46 | 183 | 497 |
| STANDS TREMBLING AT THE GATE OF BLISSE. | TO COUNTESSE OF DENBIGH | 2 | 52 | 236 | 146 |
| OUR BLISSE. & SUPERNATURALL BLOOD. | TO THE NAME OF JESUS | 4 | 52 | 239 | 30 |
| IN BOSOM OF THY FATHER'S BLISSE. | O GLORIOSA DOMINA | 38 | 52 | 302 | 194 |
| WHAT JOY, WHAT BLISSE, | PRAYER TO GENTLE-WOMAN | 122 | 52 | 328 | 139 |
| BECAUSE THAT FROM THE BRIDAL CHEEK OF BLISSE | (ON) HOPE | 17 | 52 | 345 | 71 |
| STANDS TREMBLING AT THE GATE OF BLISSE. | AGAINST IRRESOLUTION AND DELAY | 2 | 52 | 347 | 146 |
| STUFT THEE SOE FULL WITH BLISSE, THOU CAN'ST NOT MOVE. | ON GUNPOWDER-TREASON | 6 | MS | 384 | 456 |
| OF BLISSE, DEBASE THEE. BUT WITH A JUST PRIDE | UPON KINGS CORONATION | 8 | MS | 389 | 454 |
| AND STREIGHT HIS AMOROUS SYTH (GREEDY OF BLISSE) | AN ELEGY MR STANNINOW | 47 | MS | 394 | 473 |

BLISSES

| | | | | | |
|---|---|---|---|---|---|
| BESPEAKE HER TO MY BLISSES, | WISHES SUPPOSED MISTRESSE | 14 | 46 | 195 | 479 |

BLITH

| | | | | | |
|---|---|---|---|---|---|
| WOULDST SEE BLITH LOOKES, FRESH CHEEKS BEGUILE | IN PRAISE OF LESSIUS | 39 | 46 | 156 | 510 |
| LIVES AGAINE AS BLITH TO MORROW, | OUT OF CATULLUS | 5 | 46 | 194 | 523 |
| WOULDST' SEE BLITH LOOKES, FRESH CHEEKES BEGUIL | TEMPERANCE | 37 | 52 | 342 | 510 |
| DOTH BLITH APOLLO CLOATH THE HEAVENS WITH JOYE, | AN ELEGY MR STANNINOW | 11 | MS | 394 | 473 |

BLOOD

| | | | | | |
|---|---|---|---|---|---|
| WOULD'ST THOU SEE A MAN WHOSE WELL WARMED BLOOD, | IN PRAISE OF LESSIUS | 35 | 46 | 156 | 510 |
| THE MOTHERS MILKE, THE CHILDRENS BLOOD, | UPON INFANT MARTYRS | 2 | 46 | 95 | 10 |
| FUR THEE TO WEARE, BUT THESE, OF THINE OWNE BLOOD. | ON CRUCIFIED LORD BLOODY | 6 | 46 | 100 | 24 |
| TO THIS RED SEA OF THY BLOOD, | ON BLEEDING WOUNDS OF LORD | 26 | 46 | 101 | 110 |
| GAVE FORTH YOUR BLOOD FOR BREATH, SPOKE SOULES FOR WORDS. | SOSPETTO D'HERODE | 8 | 46 | 109 | 216 |
| TO BECOME BEAUTIFULL IN HUMANE BLOOD. | SOSPETTO D'HERODE | 84 | 46 | 109 | 216 |
| ANGER, AND LOVE, BEST HOOKES OF HUMANE BLOOD. | SOSPETTO D'HERODE | 275 | 46 | 109 | 216 |
| WHOSE EVER-BRANDISHT SWORD IS SHEATH'D IN BLOOD. | SOSPETTO D'HERODE | 314 | 46 | 109 | 216 |
| OF BROTHERS MUTUALL BLOOD, AND FATHERS BRAINES. | SOSPETTO D'HERODE | 328 | 46 | 109 | 216 |
| WHICH MIXT WITH GALL & BLOOD THEY QUAFFE BRIM FULL. | SOSPETTO D'HERODE | 336 | 46 | 109 | 216 |
| WHAT EVER SCHEMES OF BLOOD, FANTASTICK FRAMES | SOSPETTO D'HERODE | 361 | 46 | 109 | 216 |
| WHY DID I SPEND MY LIFE, AND SPILL MY BLOOD, | SOSPETTO D'HERODE | 449 | 46 | 109 | 216 |
| THY BROTHERS BLOOD BE-SPILT LIFE SPENT IN VAINE. | SOSPETTO D'HERODE | 452 | 46 | 109 | 216 |
| NOT TO BE SLAKT BUT BY A SEA OF BLOOD. | SOSPETTO D'HERODE | 490 | 46 | 109 | 216 |
| WHY TO SHOW LOVE SHEE SHOULD SHED BLOOD. | IN MEMORY OF LADY MADRE TERESA | 22 | 46 | 131 | 52 |
| SCARCE HAD SHEE BLOOD ENOUGH, TO MAKE | IN MEMORY OF LADY MADRE TERESA | 25 | 46 | 131 | 52 |
| HER LORDS BLOOD, OR AT LEST HER OWNE. | IN MEMORY OF LADY MADRE TERESA | 56 | 46 | 131 | 52 |
| OF BAPTISME, BLENDS THEM ALL INTO ONE BLOOD. | AN APOLOGIE FOR HYMNE (TERESA) | 16 | 46 | 136 | 59 |
| BOWLES FULL OF RICHER BLOOD THEN BLUSH OF GRAPE | AN APOLOGIE FOR HYMNE (TERESA) | 33 | 46 | 136 | 59 |
| THE SPLENDOR OF HIS BIRTH AND BLOOD. | HIS EPITAPH (HERRYS) | 23 | 46 | 172 | 471 |
| COME THEN YOUTH, BEAUTY, AND BLOOD, ALL YE SOFT POWERS, | UPON STANINOUGH'S DEATH | 7 | 46 | 175 | 475 |
| THAT WARMES THE BED OF YOUTH AND BLOOD) | LOVES HOROSCOPE | 30 | 46 | 185 | 483 |
| AND BLOOD, WITH PEN OF TRUTH | WISHES SUPPOSED MISTRESSE | 32 | 46 | 195 | 479 |
| THE BLOOD, YET TEACH A CHARME, | WISHES SUPPOSED MISTRESSE | 62 | 46 | 195 | 479 |
| OUR BLISSE. & SUPERNATURALL BLOOD. | TO THE NAME OF JESUS | 4 | 52 | 239 | 30 |
| WITH BLUSH OF THINE OWN BLOOD THY DAY ADORNING, | TO THE NAME OF JESUS | 222 | 52 | 239 | 30 |
| AND ROSY DAWN OF THE RIGHT ROYALL BLOOD. | TO THE QUEEN'S MAJESTY | 6 | 52 | 261 | 47 |
| THY BLOOD BIDS US BE BOLD. | OFFICE H. CROSS COMPLINE | 19 | 52 | 274 | 105 |
| OF WATER WEDDING BLOOD. | VEXILLA REGIS | 10 | 52 | 277 | 156 |
| THY COSTLY EXCELLENCE WITH THY KING'S OWN BLOOD. | VEXILLA REGIS | 30 | 52 | 277 | 156 |
| WHAT WAS IT TO THY PRETIOUS BLOOD | CHARITAS NIMIA | 47 | 52 | 280 | 48 |
| HER EYES BLEED TEARS, HIS WOUNDS WEEP BLOOD. | SANCTA MARIA DOLORUM | 20 | 52 | 283 | 162 |
| TO THIS RED SEA OF THY BLOOD | UPON BLEEDING CRUCIFIX | 22 | 52 | 288 | 110 |
| FOR THEE TO WEAR, BUT THIS, OF THINE OWN BLOOD. | UPON BODY OF OUR LORD | 6 | 52 | 290 | 24 |
| TO'A BLEEDING HEART THAT GASPES FOR BLOOD. | ADORO TE | 48 | 52 | 291 | 172 |
| THAT BLOOD, WHOSE LEAST DROPS SOVERAIGN BE | ADORO TE | 49 | 52 | 291 | 172 |
| BY'A NOBLER BREAD, MORE NEEDFULL BLOOD. | LAUDA SION SALVATOREM | 36 | 52 | 294 | 178 |
| FOR LOVE AT LARG TO FILL. SPARE BLOOD & SWEAT. | TERESA | 11 | 52 | 315 | 52 |
| WHY TO SHOW LOVE, SHE SHOULD SHED BLOOD | TERESA | 22 | 52 | 315 | 52 |
| SCARSE HAS SHE BLOOD ENOUGH TO MAKE | TERESA | 25 | 52 | 315 | 52 |
| HER LORD'S BLOOD, OR AT LEST HER OWN. | TERESA | 56 | 52 | 315 | 52 |
| OF BAPTISM BLENDS THEM ALL INTO A BLOOD. | AN APOLOGIE FOR (TERESA) HYMNE | 16 | 52 | 322 | 59 |
| BOWLES FULL OF RICHER BLOOD THEN BLUSH OF GRAPE | AN APOLOGIE FOR (TERESA) HYMNE | 33 | 52 | 322 | 59 |
| CECILIA, GLORY OF HER NAME & BLOOD | ALEXIAS THIRD ELEGIE | 31 | 52 | 336 | 209 |
| BOTH MIXT AT LAST THEIR BLOOD IN ONE RICH BED | ALEXIAS THIRD ELEGIE | 47 | 52 | 336 | 209 |
| MIX THE MAD SONS OF MEN IN MUTUALL BLOOD. | DESCRIPTION RELIGIOUS HOUSE | 8 | 52 | 338 | 213 |
| COME THEN, YOUTH, BEAUTY, & BLOOD. | DEATH'S LECTURE | 7 | 52 | 340 | 475 |
| WOULDST' SEE A MAN, WHOSE WELL-WARM'D BLOOD | TEMPERANCE | 33 | 52 | 342 | 510 |

| | | | |
|---|---|---|---|
| THEN GLUTT THY DIRE LAMPE WITH THE WARMEST BLOOD, | ON GUNPOWDER-TREASON | 63 | MS 384 458 |
| DEATH TO THE LIFE. MY INKE SHALL BE THE BLOOD | UPON GUNPOWDER TREASON | 3 | MS 386 460 |

HEART-BLOOD

| | | | |
|---|---|---|---|
| MY BLUSHES WITH HIS OWN HEART-BLOOD. | CHARITAS NIMIA | 62 | 52 280 48 |

BLOOD-REVOLVING

| | | | |
|---|---|---|---|
| THY BLOOD-REVOLVING BREST TO RAGE DOTH MOVE. | SOSPETTO D'HERODE | 514 | 46 109 216 |

BLOOD-SHOT

| | | | |
|---|---|---|---|
| LO. A BLOOD-SHOT EYE. THAT WEEPES | ON WOUNDS OF CRUCIFIED LORD | 7 | 46 99 24 |

BLOODSHOTT

| | | | |
|---|---|---|---|
| AND LEAST THY BLOODSHOTT EYES SHOULD LEAD ASIDE | UPON GUNPOWDER TREASON | 7 | MS 387 461 |

BLOOD-SWOLNE

| | | | |
|---|---|---|---|
| SO BOYLES THE FIRED HERODS BLOOD-SWOLNE BREST, | SOSPETTO D'HERODE | 489 | 46 109 216 |

BLOOD'S

| | | | |
|---|---|---|---|
| THIS THY BLOOD'S DELUGE, A DIRE CHANCE | UPON BLEEDING CRUCIFIX | 33 | 52 288 110 |

BLOUD

| | | | |
|---|---|---|---|
| SWELLS HIGH, FAIR CONFLUENCE OF ALL HIGHBORN BLOUD. | TO THE QUEEN'S MAJESTY | 16 | 52 261 47 |
| A BLOUD DRUNKE ERROUR SPILT THE COSTLY AYME | OUT OF GROTIUS | 29 | MS 398 198 |
| THE BLOUD HOUND BROOD OF PRIESTS AGAINST MEE DRAW | OUT OF GROTIUS | 45 | MS 398 198 |

BLOODS

| | | | |
|---|---|---|---|
| IN THEIR OWNE BLOODS DEARE DELUGE, SOME NEW DEAD. | THE BEGINNING OF HELIODORUS | 17 | 46 158 517 |
| THIS THY BLOODS DELUGE (A DIRE CHANCE | ON BLEEDING WOUNDS OF LORD | 37 | 46 101 110 |

BLOODY

| | | | |
|---|---|---|---|
| HEE'L HAVE HIS TEAT E'RE LONG (A BLOODY ONE) | BLESSED BE THE PAPS | 3 | 46 94 14 |
| THEIR UGLY ORNAMENTS ARE THE BLOODY STAINES. | SOSPETTO D'HERODE | 311 | 46 109 216 |
| BUSIRIS HA'S HIS BLOODY ALTAR HERE. | SOSPETTO D'HERODE | 355 | 46 109 216 |
| HERE CRUELL SCYRON BOASTS HIS BLOODY ROCKES, | SOSPETTO D'HERODE | 359 | 46 109 216 |
| A BLOODY SIDE, & HAND, & HEART. | IN CICATRICES DOMINI JESU | 16 | MS 381 27 |
| (WHEREOF THE BLUSHING WALLES TOOKE BLOODY NOTE) | HORATIJ ILLE & NEFASTO | 10 | MS 382 530 |

BLOOMES

| | | | |
|---|---|---|---|
| THE BLOOMES OF MARTYRDOME. O BE A DORE | SOSPETTO D'HERODE | 5 | 46 109 216 |

FULL-BLOOM'D

| | | | |
|---|---|---|---|
| LO. A MOUTH, WHOSE FULL-BLOOM'D LIPS | ON WOUNDS OF CRUCIFIED LORD | 5 | 46 99 24 |

NEW-BLOOM'D

| | | | |
|---|---|---|---|
| SEE SEE. HOW SOON HIS NEW-BLOOM'D CHEEK | IN HOLY NATIVITY | 67 | 52 246 76 |

BLOOMING

| | | | |
|---|---|---|---|
| THESE PURPLE BUDS OF BLOOMING DEATH MAY BEE, | OUR LORD IN HIS CIRCUMCISION | 15 | 46 98 9 |
| TO HIDE HIS BLOOMING GLORIES, & BEQUEATH | AN ELEGY MR STANNINOW | 29 | MS 394 473 |

BLOOMY

| | | | |
|---|---|---|---|
| OF A MAD STORME THESE BLOOMY JOYES ALL TORE, | UPON DEATH OF HERRYS | 33 | 46 167 466 |

BLOSSOM

| | | | |
|---|---|---|---|
| THIS WATRY BLOSSOM OF THY EYN, | WEEPER | 65 | 52 307 120 |

BLOSSOM'D

| | | | |
|---|---|---|---|
| TO BLOT THE NEWLY BLOSSOM'D LIGHT. | UPON DEATH OF DESIRED HERRYS | 54 | 46 168 467 |

BLOSSOME

| | | | |
|---|---|---|---|
| THIS WATRY BLOSSOME OF THY EYNE | THE TEARE | 29 | 46 84 50 |
| HE SAW HEAV'N BLOSSOME WITH A NEW-BORNE LIGHT, | SOSPETTO D'HERODE | 129 | 46 109 216 |

BLOSSOMS

| | | | |
|---|---|---|---|
| RAVISHT THE MAIDEN BLOSSOMS, AND DOWNE BORE | UPON DEATH OF HERRYS | 34 | 46 167 466 |
| BLOSSOMS, BUT OUR BLEST TAST CONFESSES FRUITS. | UPON TWO GREENE APRICOCKES | 14 | 48 220 494 |
| WHOSE FRUIT AND BLOSSOMS BOTH BLESSE THE SAME BOUGH. | UPON TWO GREENE APRICOCKES | 20 | 48 220 494 |

BLOSSOMES

| | | | |
|---|---|---|---|
| BUT HASTS HER FORWARD BLOSSOMES, AND LAYES OUT | OUT OF VIRGIL | 21 | 46 155 529 |

```
MAIDEN-BLOSSOMES

  THE TIMOUROUS MAIDEN-BLOSSOMES ON EACH BOUGH,    UPON DEATH OF HERRYS                  23  46 167 466

BLOT

  TO BLOT THE NEWLY BLOSSOM'D LIGHT.               UPON DEATH OF DESIRED HERRYS         54  46 168 467

BLOTT

  TO'INJOY HIS BLOTT, & AS A LARGE BLACK LETTER    IN GLORIOUS EPIPHANIE                186  52 253  39
  AND LAOTHSOM SPITTLE, BLOTT THOSE BEAUTEOUS EYES, OFFICE H. CROSS PRIME                 6  52 267  91

BLOTS

  BE WHAT THY BEAUTIES, NOT OUR BLOTS, HAVE MADE THEE, ON A TREATISE OF CHARITY           3  46 137  69

BLOW

  NOW THOUGH THE BLOW THAT SNATCHT HIM HENCE,      UPON THE DEATH OF A GENTLEMAN        15  46 166 472
  TWO DEVILLS AT ONE BLOW THOU HAST LAID FLAT,     UPON DUMBE DEVILL CAST OUT            1  46  93  14
  WHAT THOUGH I MIST MY BLOW, YET I STROOKE HIGH,  SOSPETTO D'HERODE                   223  46 109 216
  DEATH, WHAT DOST. O HOLD THY BLOW,               UPON DEATH OF DESIRED HERRYS          1  46 168 467

BLOWES

  WHILE FROM ANOTHER (UNSEENE) CORNER BLOWES       HORATIJ ILLE & NEFASTO               23  MS 382 530

BLOWN

  BUT THE WORLD'S HOMAGE, SCARSE IN THESE WELL BLOWN, TO THE QUEEN'S MAJESTY             9  52 261  47

BLOWNE

  OR CALL HER CHEEKE A BED OF NEW BLOWNE ROSES.    UPON BIRTH PRINCESSE E               45  MS 391 456

BLOUNE

  WITH THIS GRAND BLAST SHOULD HAVE BIN BLOUNE AWAY. UPON GUNPOWDER TREASON             30  MS 386 460

BLUBBER'D

  TAUGHT HER THESE SULLIED CHEEKS THIS BLUBBER'D FACE, TO PONTIUS WASHING HANDS          4  46  94  23
  SO OFT WITH BLUBBER'D EYES.                      IN GLORIOUS EPIPHANIE               126  52 253  39

BLUBB'RING

  AT MY FEET THE BLUBB'RING MOUNTAINE              PSALME 23                            13  46 102   5

BLUNT

  FROM THEE THEIR THINNE DILEMMA WITH BLUNT HORNE  ON HOPE                              19  46 143  71
  ARE NAILES BLUNT PENS OF SUPERFICIALL SMART.     OFFICE H. CROSS SIXT                 11  52 270  97
  FROM THEE THEIR LEAN DILEMMA, WITH BLUNT HORN.   (ON) HOPE                             9  52 345  71

BLURRE

  AND I'LE NOT BLURRE IT WITH MY PARAPHRASE.       UPON BIRTH PRINCESSE E               60  MS 391 456

BLUSH

  NOR NEEDS MY MUSE A BLUSH, OR THESE BRIGHT FLOWERS SOSPETTO D'HERODE                  17  46 109 216
  A GUILTY SWORD BLUSH FOR HER SAKE.               IN MEMORY OF LADY MADRE TERESA       26  46 131  52
  THY WOUNDS SHALL BLUSH TO SUCH BRIGHT SCARRES,   IN MEMORY OF LADY MADRE TERESA      154  46 131  52
  BOWLES FULL OF RICHER BLOOD THEN BLUSH OF GRAPE  AN APOLOGIE FOR HYMNE (TERESA)       33  46 136  59
  WITH THINE OWNE BLUSH THY CHEEKES ADORNING,      AN HIMNE FOR CIRCUMCISION             3  46 141  37
  BUT WERE THE ROSES BLUSH SO RARE,                UPON DEATH OF DESIRED HERRYS         55  46 168 467
  THAT SWEET BLUSH OF THINE THAT SHAMETH           OUT OF THE ITALIAN (1)                3  46 188 545
  OR A BOUGHT BLUSH, OR A SET SMILE.               WISHES SUPPOSED MISTRESSE            24  46 195 479
  BEE ITS OWNE BLUSH, BEE ITS OWNE TEARE.          WISHES SUPPOSED MISTRESSE            54  46 195 479
  THE REDD, BUT OF THE BLUSH TO THEE THEY OW.      UPON TWO GREENE APRICOCKES            6  48 220 494
  WITH BLUSH OF THINE OWN BLOOD THY DAY ADORNING,  TO THE NAME OF JESUS                222  52 239  30
  WITH THINE OWN BLUSH THY CHEEKS ADORNING         NEW YEAR'S DAY                        3  52 251  37
  WHOSE BLUSH THE MOON BEAUTEOUSLY MARRES          O GLORIOSA DOMINA                     3  52 302 194
  A GUILTY SWORD BLUSH FOR HER SAKE.               TERESA                               26  52 315  52
  THY WOUNDS SHALL BLUSH TO SUCH BRIGHT SCARRES    TERESA                              153  52 315  52
  BOWLES FULL OF RICHER BLOOD THEN BLUSH OF GRAPE  AN APOLOGIE FOR (TERESA) HYMNE       33  52 322  59

BLUSH'D

  THE WATER BLUSH'D, AND STARTED INTO WINE.        OUT OF GROTIUS                       52  MS 398 198

BLUSHES

  AND BLUSHES ON THE MANLY SUN.                    THE TEARE                            28  46  84  50
  PEEPT FORTH FROM THEIR FIRST BLUSHES, SO THAT NOW UPON DEATH OF HERRYS                24  46 167 466
  TWICE DI'D IN THINE OWNE BLUSHES, AND DID'ST RUN TO THE MORNING                        9  46 183 497
  BLUSHES, THAT BIN                                WISHES SUPPOSED MISTRESSE            64  46 195 479
  THE BLUSHES OF THY ALL-UNBLEMISH'T MOTHER.       IN GLORIOUS EPIPHANIE                67  52 253  39
  THE EARLY PRIME BLUSHES TO SAY                   OFFICE H. CROSS PRIME                 1  52 267  91
  MY BLUSHES WITH HIS OWN HEART-BLOOD.             CHARITAS NIMIA                       62  52 280  48
  AND BLUSHES AT THE BRIDEGROOME SUN.              WEEPER                               64  52 307 120
  SINCE HIS THE BLUSHES BE, & HER'S THE FIRES,     FLAMING HEART                        38  52 324  61
```

| | | | |
|---|---|---|---|
| DY'D IN VERMILLION BLUSHES, AS BEFORE. | UPON GUNPOWDER TREASON | 16 | MS 386 460 |

BLUSHING

| | | | |
|---|---|---|---|
| PREVENTS THE EYE-LIDDS OF THE BLUSHING DAY. | MUSICKS DUELL | 82 | 46 149 535 |
| MORE SWEETLY SHOWES THE BLUSHING BRIDE. | IN PRAISE OF LESSIUS | 30 | 46 156 510 |
| DEATH'S PURPLE TRIUMPH, ON THE BLUSHING GROUND | THE BEGINNING OF HELIODORUS | 15 | 46 158 517 |
| HIS SKIN AS WITH A FIERY BLUSHING | OUT OF GREEKE CUPID'S CRYER | 19 | 46 159 519 |
| THAT IN THEIR BUDS YET BLUSHING LYE. | A HYMNE OF THE NATIVITY | 68 | 46 106 76 |
| THAT SELDOME LETT'ST A BLUSHING YOUTHFULL PRIME | UPON DEATH OF HERRYS | 30 | 46 167 466 |
| BLUSHING FROM THINE EASTERNE BED. | UPON DEATH OF DESIRED HERRYS | 16 | 46 168 467 |
| BLUSHING, TO BEHOLD THE RAY | UPON DEATH OF DESIRED HERRYS | 33 | 46 168 467 |
| TWO EVER BLUSHING BEDS OF NEW-BORNE ROSES. | ON A FOULE MORNING | 18 | 46 181 495 |
| WITH BLUSHING CHEEK & BLEEDING EY, | DIES IRAE | 42 | 52 298 186 |
| MORE SWEETLY SHOWES THE BLUSHING BRIDE. | TEMPERANCE | 28 | 52 342 510 |
| (WHEREOF THE BLUSHING WALLES TOOKE BLOODY NOTE) | HORATIJ ILLE & NEFASTO | 10 | MS 382 530 |
| HER SABLE CHEEKES INTO A BLUSHING MORNE. | UPON GUNPOWDER TREASON | 12 | MS 387 461 |

EVER-BLUSHING

| | | | |
|---|---|---|---|
| YOU EVER-BLUSHING MEADS, WHERE DOE THE BLEST | HORATIJ ILLE & NEFASTO | 37 | MS 382 530 |

BLUSHT

| | | | |
|---|---|---|---|
| BUT STAY, WHAT GLIMPSE WAS THAT. WHY BLUSHT THE DAY. | UPON YORKE HIS BIRTH | 66 | 46 176 500 |

BOARD

| | | | |
|---|---|---|---|
| WITH A NEW LAMB BLESSES THE BOARD. | LAUDA SION SALVATOREM | 20 | 52 294 178 |
| AND BOARD HIMSELF AT THY RICH BREST. | O GLORIOSA DOMINA | 8 | 52 302 194 |

BORD

| | | | |
|---|---|---|---|
| CROWN'D ABUNDANCE SPREADS MY BORD. | PSALME 23 | 50 | 46 102 5 |

BOAST

| | | | |
|---|---|---|---|
| COME TRY WHO DARES, HEAV'N, EARTH, WHAT ERE DOST BOAST, | SOSPETTO D'HERODE | 251 | 46 109 216 |
| AND WILT THOU, (O CRUELL BOAST.) | UPON DEATH OF DESIRED HERRYS | 21 | 46 168 467 |
| THAT THUS CAN BOAST TO BE | WEEPER | 123 | 52 307 120 |

BOASTS

| | | | |
|---|---|---|---|
| HERE CRUELL SCYRON BOASTS HIS BLOODY ROCKES, | SOSPETTO D'HERODE | 359 | 46 109 216 |
| TO THE LOWD BOASTS OF POOR MORTALITY | DEATH'S LECTURE | 26 | 52 340 475 |

BODIES

| | | | |
|---|---|---|---|
| AND LOVES THAT BODIES SOULE. NO LAW CONTROULES | AN APOLOGIE FOR HYMNE (TERESA) | 18 | 46 136 59 |

BODYES

| | | | |
|---|---|---|---|
| MY MINDS DEVOTION IN MY BODYES NEED. | OUT OF GROTIUS | 60 | MS 398 198 |

BODY

| | | | |
|---|---|---|---|
| CHRISTS FAITH MAKES BUT ONE BODY OF ALL SOULES, | AN APOLOGIE FOR HYMNE (TERESA) | 17 | 46 136 59 |
| 'TWIXT SOULE AND BODY A DIVORCE. | AN EPITAPH HUSBAND AND WIFE | 4 | 46 174 478 |
| BODY OF BLESSINGS. SPIRIT OF SOULES EXTRACTED. | TO THE NAME OF JESUS | 166 | 52 239 30 |
| THIS SWEETER BODY, SHALL INDEED BE SUCH. | OFFICE H. CROSS COMPLINE | 8 | 52 274 105 |
| CHRIST'S FAITH MAKES BUT ONE BODY OF ALL SOULES | AN APOLOGIE FOR (TERESA) HYMNE | 17 | 52 322 59 |
| 'TWIXT SOUL & BODY A DIVORCE, | AN EPITAPH UPON MARRIED COUPLE | 4 | 52 339 478 |
| SOUL & BODY PART LIKE FREINDS. | TEMPERANCE | 48 | 52 342 510 |

BODY'S

| | | | |
|---|---|---|---|
| EACH BODY'S PLUMP AND JUCY, ALL THINGS FULL | OUT OF VIRGIL | 15 | 46 155 529 |
| AND LOVE'S THAT BODY'S SOUL, NO LAW CONTROWLLS | AN APOLOGIE FOR (TERESA) HYMNE | 18 | 52 322 59 |

BOILE

| | | | |
|---|---|---|---|
| AND WHILE THE BLACK SOULES BOILE IN THEIR OWNE GORE, | SOSPETTO D'HERODE | 295 | 46 109 216 |

BOYLES

| | | | |
|---|---|---|---|
| IT BOYLES OUT INTO CRUELTY. | OUT OF GREEKE CUPID'S CRYER | 30 | 46 159 519 |
| SO BOYLES THE FIRED HERODS BLOOD-SWOLNE BREST, | SOSPETTO D'HERODE | 489 | 46 109 216 |

BOYL'D

| | | | |
|---|---|---|---|
| WHILE NEW THOUGHTS BOYL'D IN HIS ENRAGED BREST. | SOSPETTO D'HERODE | 193 | 46 109 216 |

BOLD

| | | | |
|---|---|---|---|
| FORBEARE (SAID I) BE NOT TOO BOLD. | A HYMNE OF THE NATIVITY | 39 | 46 106 76 |
| DISDAINEFULL WRETCH. HOW HATH ONE BOLD SINNE COST | SOSPETTO D'HERODE | 73 | 46 109 216 |
| AND RADIANT SCEPTER THIS BOLD HAND SHOULD BEARE. | SOSPETTO D'HERODE | 210 | 46 109 216 |
| A BORROWED BEING, MAKE THY BOLD DEFENCE. | SOSPETTO D'HERODE | 252 | 46 109 216 |
| THOU MAD'ST BOLD PROOFE UPON THE BROW OF HEAV'N, | SOSPETTO D'HERODE | 266 | 46 109 216 |
| HE MURMURES, AND REBUKES THEIR BOLD DESIRE. | SOSPETTO D'HERODE | 485 | 46 109 216 |
| BABELS BOLD ARTISTS STRIVE (BELOW) TO BUILD | ON FRONTISPIECE ISAACSONS | 16 | 46 191 491 |
| ON THEIR BOLD BRESTS ABOUT THE WORLD THEY BORE THEE | TO THE NAME OF JESUS | 203 | 52 239 30 |
| FORBEAR, SAID I. BE NOT TOO BOLD. | IN HOLY NATIVITY | 55 | 52 246 76 |

|                                                                                                                    |                                   |     |            |
|--------------------------------------------------------------------------------------------------------------------|-----------------------------------|-----|------------|
| THE WORLD'S PRICE SETT TO SALE, & BY THE BOLD                                                                      | OFFICE H. CROSS MATINES           | 14  | 52 265  86 |
| THY BLOOD BIDS US BE BOLD.                                                                                         | OFFICE H. CROSS COMPLINE          | 19  | 52 274 105 |
| BOLD PAINTERS HAVE PUTT OUT HIS EYES.                                                                              | CHARITAS NIMIA                    |  8  | 52 280  48 |
| BOLD FAITH TAKES HEART, & DARES BELEIVE.                                                                           | LAUDA SION SALVATOREM             | 38  | 52 294 178 |
| VAIN LOVES AVANT. BOLD HANDS FORBEAR.                                                                              | WEEPER                            | 107 | 52 307 120 |
| WITH ROCKS. NOR BOLD HANDS STRUCK THE WORLD'S STRONG BARRES.                                                       | ALEXIAS THIRD ELEGIE              | 10  | 52 336 209 |
| THAT ROME'S BOLD EAGLES NOW WERE BLINDED QUITE,                                                                    | UPON KINGS CORONATION             | 34  | MS 390 453 |

BOLDER

|                                                |                       |    |            |
|------------------------------------------------|-----------------------|----|------------|
| T'OBEY MY BOLDER TOUCH.                        | TO THE NAME OF JESUS  | 52 | 52 239  30 |

BOLDLY

|                                                |                       |     |            |
|------------------------------------------------|-----------------------|-----|------------|
| TO THE BELEEVING WORLD FAME BOLDLY SINGS.      | SOSPETTO D'HERODE     | 14  | 46 109 216 |
| THE WAY TO BETH'LEM, AND AS BOLDLY BLAZ'D,     | SOSPETTO D'HERODE     | 132 | 46 109 216 |

BOLTS

|                                                |                       |    |            |
|------------------------------------------------|-----------------------|----|------------|
| WHAT MAGICK BOLTS, WHAT MYSTICK BARRES         | TO COUNTESSE OF DENBIGH | 17 | 52 236 146 |

MAGICK-BOLTS

|                                                |                                   |    |            |
|------------------------------------------------|-----------------------------------|----|------------|
| WHAT MAGICK-BOLTS, WHAT MYSTICK BARRS          | AGAINST IRRESOLUTION AND DELAY    | 11 | 52 347 146 |

BONES

|                                                |                           |    |          |
|------------------------------------------------|---------------------------|----|----------|
| LAUGH,TILL THY CHILDRENS BLEEDING BONES        | PSALME 137                | 35 | 46 104  7 |
| LIE SCATTER'D LIKE THE BURNT AND MARTYR'D BONES | ON A TREATISE OF CHARITY | 32 | 46 137 69 |

BOOK

|                                                |                            |    |            |
|------------------------------------------------|----------------------------|----|------------|
| THIS BOOK OF LOVES, THUS WRIT                  | SANCTA MARIA DOLORUM       | 53 | 52 283 162 |
| O THAT BOOK. WHOSE LEAVES SO BRIGHT            | DIES IRAE                  | 17 | 52 298 186 |
| LO HERE A LITTLE VOLUME, BUT GREAT BOOK.       | PRAYER TO GENTLE-WOMAN     |  1 | 52 328 139 |
| HOLD BUT THIS BOOK BEFORE YOUR HEART           | PRAYER TO GENTLE-WOMAN     | 33 | 52 328 139 |

BOOKE

|                                                |                                 |    |            |
|------------------------------------------------|---------------------------------|----|------------|
| LOE HERE A LITTLE VOLUME, BUT LARGE BOOKE.     | ON A PRAYER BOOKE               |  1 | 46 126 139 |
| HOLD BUT THIS BOOKE BEFORE YOUR HEART,         | ON A PRAYER BOOKE               | 27 | 46 126 139 |
| DIVINEST LOVE LYES IN THIS BOOKE.              | ON MR. G. HERBERTS BOOKE        |  2 | 46 130  68 |
| OPEN THIS BOOKE, FAIRE QUEEN, AND TAKE THY CROWN. | ON A TREATISE OF CHARITY     | 12 | 46 137  69 |
| IN ALL THE BOOKE IF ANY WHERE                  | ANOTHER ON HERRYS               | 47 | 46 170 469 |
| FIRE FROM THE BURNING CHEEKS OF THAT BRIGHT BOOKE | FLAMING HEART                | 28 | 52 324  61 |

FORTUNE-BOOKE

|                                                |                       |    |            |
|------------------------------------------------|-----------------------|----|------------|
| BEAUTY LAYES OPE LOVES FORTUNE-BOOKE.          | LOVES HOROSCOPE       | 12 | 46 185 483 |

BOOKS

|                                                |                                   |    |            |
|------------------------------------------------|-----------------------------------|----|------------|
| THINE OWN DEARE BOOKS ARE GUILTY, FOR FROM THENCE | AN APOLOGIE FOR HYMNE (TERESA) |  7 | 46 136  59 |
| AMONG THE LEAVES OF THY LARG BOOKS OF DAY,     | FLAMING HEART                     | 86 | 52 324  61 |

BOOKES

|                                                |                                   |    |            |
|------------------------------------------------|-----------------------------------|----|------------|
| THINE OWN DEAR BOOKES ARE GUILTY. FOR FROM THENCE | AN APOLOGIE FOR (TERESA) HYMNE |  7 | 52 322  59 |

BOOTES

|                                                |                       |     |            |
|------------------------------------------------|-----------------------|-----|------------|
| AH WRETCH. WHAT BOOTES THEE TO CAST BACK THY EYES, | SOSPETTO D'HERODE  | 241 | 46 109 216 |

BORE

|                                                |                              |     |            |
|------------------------------------------------|------------------------------|-----|------------|
| RAVISHT THE MAIDEN BLOSSOMS, AND DOWNE BORE    | UPON DEATH OF HERRYS         | 34  | 46 167 466 |
| ON THEIR BOLD BRESTS ABOUT THE WORLD THEY BORE THEE | TO THE NAME OF JESUS    | 203 | 52 239  30 |
| E'RE SHE BORE ANY ONE, SLEW ALL.               | O GLORIOSA DOMINA            | 12  | 52 302 194 |
| THE QUIVER, THAT HE BORE, DID BIDE             | IN CICATRICES DOMINI JESU    |  7  | MS 381  27 |
| HE, THAT ONCE BORE THE BEST PART'S GONE.       | UPON DEATH OF A FREIND       | 18  | MS 393 477 |

BOREAN

|                                                |                       |    |            |
|------------------------------------------------|-----------------------|----|------------|
| NOR SIRIAN FLAME, NOR BOREAN FROST DEFLOWERS.  | SOSPETTO D'HERODE     | 21 | 46 109 216 |

BORN

|                                                |                          |     |            |
|------------------------------------------------|--------------------------|-----|------------|
| MADE HIS OWN BED E'RE HE WAS BORN.             | IN HOLY NATIVITY         | 49  | 52 246  76 |
| O THOU BORN KING OF LOVES,                     | IN GLORIOUS EPIPHANIE    |  7  | 52 253  39 |
| DECENTLY BORN.                                 | IN GLORIOUS EPIPHANIE    | 65  | 52 253  39 |
| YOU TO BE BORN. WHAT CAUSE CAN BORROW          | WEEPER                   | 167 | 52 307 120 |

FIRST-BORN

|                                                |                       |    |            |
|------------------------------------------------|-----------------------|----|------------|
| WE'L BRING THE FIRST-BORN OF HER FLOWRS        | IN HOLY NATIVITY      | 99 | 52 246  76 |
| THE FAIR'ST & FIRST-BORN SONS OF FIRE          | TERESA                | 93 | 52 315  52 |

HIGHBORN

|                                                |                           |    |            |
|------------------------------------------------|---------------------------|----|------------|
| SWELLS HIGH, FAIR CONFLUENCE OF ALL HIGHBORN BLOUD. | TO THE QUEEN'S MAJESTY | 16 | 52 261  47 |

HIGH-BORN

 THE HIGH-BORN BROOD OF DAY. YOU BRIGHT     TO THE NAME OF JESUS    7 52 239 30

NEW-BORN

 A NEST OF NEW-BORN SWEETS.     PRAYER TO GENTLE-WOMAN    2 52 328 139

BORNE

 YOU TO BE BORNE. WHAT IS'T CAN BORROW     THE WEEPER    125 46 79 120
 WHEN LIFE WAS BORNE,     EASTER DAY    11 46 100 26
 BY HEROD LEIGE TO CESAR NOW WAS BORNE     SOSPETTO D'HERODE    401 46 109 216
 THE FAIREST, AND THE FIRST BORNE SONS OF FIRE,     IN MEMORY OF LADY MADRE TERESA    93 46 131 52
 MY SELFE A MELTING SACRIFICE. I'ME BORNE     TO THE MORNING    51 46 183 497
 MY SOULE SHEE WAS SECURE. STILL HAVE I BORNE     OUT OF GROTIUS    11 MS 398 198
 E'RE BORNE WAS BANISH'T. BORNE WAS GLAD T'EMBRACE     OUT OF GROTIUS    15 MS 398 198
 E'RE BORNE WAS BANISH'T. BORNE WAS GLAD T'EMBRACE     OUT OF GROTIUS    15 MS 398 198

FIRST-BORNE

 WEE'L BRING THE FIRST-BORNE OF HER FLOWERS,     A HYMNE OF THE NATIVITY    79 46 106 76
 THE FAIREST, AND THE FIRST-BORNE SMILE OF HEAV'N.     SOSPETTO D'HERODE    236 46 109 216

HEAV'NE-BORNE

 MY WOMBES CHAST PRIDE IS GONE, MY HEAV'NE-BORNE BOY.     LUKE 2. QUAERIT JESUM    7 MS 379 11

HIGH-BORNE

 WITH FLASH OF HIGH-BORNE FANCYES. HERE AND THERE     MUSICKS DUELL    138 46 149 535

NEW-BORNE

 MY TEARES BUT TENDER AND MY DEATH NEW-BORNE.     OUR LORD IN HIS CIRCUMCISION    12 46 98 9
 HE SAW HEAV'N BLOSSOME WITH A NEW-BORNE LIGHT,     SOSPETTO D'HERODE    129 46 109 216
 HOVER O'RE THE NEW-BORNE DAY.     UPON DEATH OF DESIRED HERRYS    46 46 168 467
 TWO EVER BLUSHING BEDS OF NEW-BORNE ROSES.     ON A FOULE MORNING    18 46 181 495

SUN-BORNE

 BUT SUCH WHOSE SUN-BORNE BEAUTIES WHAT THEY BORROW     UPON TWO GREENE APRICOCKES    27 48 220 494

BORROW

 YOU TO BE BORNE. WHAT IS'T CAN BORROW     THE WEEPER    125 46 79 120
 SO DEARE GLORIES DARE NOT BORROW.     OUT OF THE ITALIAN (1)    39 46 188 545
 DAYES, THAT NEED BORROW,     WISHES SUPPOSED MISTRESSE    76 46 195 479
 BUT SUCH WHOSE SUN-BORNE BEAUTIES WHAT THEY BORROW     UPON TWO GREENE APRICOCKES    27 48 220 494
 A WHILE DARE BORROW     TO THE NAME OF JESUS    100 52 239 30
 THAT THESE DRY LIDDS MIGHT BORROW     SANCTA MARIA DOLORUM    43 52 283 162
 YOU TO BE BORN. WHAT CAUSE CAN BORROW     WEEPER    167 52 307 120

BORROWD

 OF BORROWD SINS. AND SWIMME     SANCTA MARIA DOLORUM    33 52 283 162

BORROWED

 A BORROWED BEING, MAKE THY BOLD DEFENCE.     SOSPETTO D'HERODE    252 46 109 216
 HAD NOW RETYR'D HIMSELFE, AND BORROWED     SOSPETTO D'HERODE    395 46 109 216

BOROW'D

 BUT MUST THY BED, LORD, BE A BOROW'D GRAVE     OFFICE H. CROSS COMPLINE    9 52 274 105

BORROWES

 SAVE THOSE DOMESTICK WHICH HE BORROWES     IN GLORIOUS EPIPHANIE    155 52 253 39

BORROWING

 BORROWING DAY & LENDING NIGHT.     IN GLORIOUS EPIPHANIE    218 52 253 39

BOSOME

 HEAVES HER SOFT BOSOME, WANDERS ROUND ABOUT.     MUSICKS DUELL    88 46 149 535
 MELTS ON THE BOSOME OF HIS LOVE, AND POWRES     OUT OF VIRGIL    5 46 155 529
 TRUST HIS BELOVED BOSOME TO THE SUN     OUT OF VIRGIL    17 46 155 529
 HEAVENS BOSOME DRINKS THE GENTLE STREAME.     THE WEEPER    20 46 79 120
 CLOSE COUCHT IN YOUR WHITE BOSOME, AND FROM THENCE     ON A PRAYER BOOKE    11 46 126 139
 AND BRING HER BOSOME FULL OF BLESSINGS.     ON A PRAYER BOOKE    35 46 126 139
 WHICH WITH A SWELLING BOSOME THERE SHEE MEETS,     ON A PRAYER BOOKE    111 46 126 139
 NONE SO FAIRE THY BOSOME STROWES.     AN HIMNE FOR CIRCUMCISION    10 46 141 37
 THY BOSOME AND MAKE ROOME. THOU ART OPPREST     UPON YORKE HIS BIRTH    3 46 176 500
 INTO THY BOSUME, BATH'D WITH LIQUID LIGHT.     ON A FOULE MORNING    30 46 181 495
 HIS HEAD IN THY FAIRE BOSOME, AND STILL HIDES     TO THE MORNING    13 46 183 497
 IN YOUR WHITE BOSOME HER CHAST BED,     THOUGH NOW 'TIS NEITHER    6 MS 397 492
 YOUR VIRGIN BOSOME. THEN WHAT E'RE     THOUGH NOW 'TIS NEITHER    23 MS 397 492
 HEAVN'S BOSOME DRINKS THE GENTLE STREAM.     WEEPER    20 52 307 120
 WHICH WITH A SWELLING BOSOME THERE SHEE MEETS     PRAYER TO GENTLE-WOMAN    117 52 328 139
 THAT NIP THE BOSOME OF THE WORLDS BEST THINGS,     DESCRIPTION RELIGIOUS HOUSE    26 52 338 213
 HEE'S GONE. THE FAIR'ST FLOWER, THAT E'RE BOSOME     LUKE 2. QUAERIT JESUM    5 MS 379 11
  DREST,

| | | | | | |
|---|---|---|---|---|---|
| MY BOSOME GOD. | LUKE 2. QUAERIT JESUM | 48 | MS | 379 | 11 |
| WHAT HINDERS, BUT MY BOSOME STILL MIGHT BE | LUKE 2. QUAERIT JESUM | 49 | MS | 379 | 11 |
| SLY, LURKING TREASON IS HIS BOSOME FREIND, | UPON GUNPOWDER TREASON | 17 | MS | 387 | 461 |
| AMONGST THOSE LILLIES, WHICH HIS BOSOME BREDD. | AN ELEGY MR STANNINOW | 52 | MS | 394 | 473 |
| SINKES INTO HORROURS BOSOME, GLAD TO HIDE | OUT OF GROTIUS | 78 | MS | 398 | 198 |

**BOSOME'S**

| | | | | | |
|---|---|---|---|---|---|
| MY BOSOME'S GUARD, A SPIRIT GREAT & STRONG, | ALEXIAS THIRD ELEGIE | 35 | 52 | 336 | 209 |

**BOSOM'D**

| | | | | | |
|---|---|---|---|---|---|
| WHICH LIKE TWO BOSOM'D SAILES EMBRACE THE DIMME | SOSPETTO D'HERODE | 142 | 46 | 109 | 216 |

**BOSOM**

| | | | | | |
|---|---|---|---|---|---|
| SOFT BACK. AND BRINGS A BOSOM BIG WITH LOVES. | TO THE NAME OF JESUS | 160 | 52 | 239 | 30 |
| NONE SO FAIR THY BOSOM STROWES, | NEW YEAR'S DAY | 10 | 52 | 251 | 37 |
| LAMB'S BOSOM WRITE | CHARITAS NIMIA | 58 | 52 | 280 | 48 |
| IN BOSOM OF THY FATHER'S BLISSE. | O GLORIOSA DOMINA | 38 | 52 | 302 | 194 |
| FREINDS WITH THE BOSOM FIRES THAT FILL THEE | WEEPER | 98 | 52 | 307 | 120 |
| CLOSE COUCH'T IN YOUR WHITE BOSOM. & FROM THENCE | PRAYER TO GENTLE-WOMAN | 17 | 52 | 328 | 139 |
| AND BRING HIS BOSOM FRAUGHT WITH BLESSINGS. | PRAYER TO GENTLE-WOMAN | 41 | 52 | 328 | 139 |

**BOSOMES**

| | | | | | |
|---|---|---|---|---|---|
| THEIR PREGNANT BOSOMES IN A FRAGRANT BIRTH. | OUT OF VIRGIL | 14 | 46 | 155 | 529 |
| HIS GLOOMY BOSOMES DARKEST CHARACTER. | SOSPETTO D'HERODE | 194 | 46 | 109 | 216 |
| ALREADY IN THEIR BOSOMES, AND THEIR HAND | SOSPETTO D'HERODE | 443 | 46 | 109 | 216 |
| THAT WOUNDED BOSOMES THEIR OWN WEAPONS BE. | SANCTA MARIA DOLORUM | 74 | 52 | 283 | 162 |
| OF THOSE WHOSE SPATIOUS BOSOMES SPREAD A THRONE | TERESA | 10 | 52 | 315 | 52 |

**BOTH**

| | | | | | |
|---|---|---|---|---|---|
| BOTH WHICH AWAY, I SHOULD NOT NEED TO FEARE. | WITH A PICTURE TO A FRIEND | 7 | 46 | 156 | 494 |
| AND LEAVE THEM BOTH TO BEE THY TEARE. | THE WEEPER | 42 | 46 | 79 | 120 |
| THEY, BOTH AT ONCE THY CONQUESTS BEE, | NEITHER DURST MAN ASKE | 7 | 46 | 92 | 20 |
| THEM BOTH. | UPON OUR SAVIOURS TOMBE | 6 | 46 | 93 | 25 |
| TO SEE BOTH BLENDED IN ONE FLOOD | UPON INFANT MARTYRS | 1 | 46 | 95 | 10 |
| THAT BREATHES AT ONCE BOTH MAID AND MOTHER. | A HYMNE OF THE NATIVITY | 63 | 46 | 106 | 76 |
| HIS SCEPTER AND HIMSELFE BOTH HE DISDAINES. | SOSPETTO D'HERODE | 72 | 46 | 109 | 216 |
| TO CROWNE THEIR PAST PREDICTIONS, BOTH HEE LAYES | SOSPETTO D'HERODE | 95 | 46 | 109 | 216 |
| TOGETHER, IN HIS PONDROUS MIND BOTH WEIGHES. | SOSPETTO D'HERODE | 96 | 46 | 109 | 216 |
| WAS THE GREAT BUSINESSE BOTH OF HEAV'N AND EARTH. | SOSPETTO D'HERODE | 120 | 46 | 109 | 216 |
| IN OUR GREAT PROJECTS, BOTH 'GAINST HEAV'N AND EARTH. | SOSPETTO D'HERODE | 286 | 46 | 109 | 216 |
| IMPENETRABLE, BOTH TO PRAI'RS AND TEARS, | SOSPETTO D'HERODE | 308 | 46 | 109 | 216 |
| BOTH FIRE TO US, AND FLAME TO THEE. | IN MEMORY OF LADY MADRE TERESA | 163 | 46 | 131 | 52 |
| FAIRE CLOUD OF FIRE, BOTH SHADE, AND LIGHT, | ON HOPE | 15 | 46 | 143 | 71 |
| BECAUSE THEY BOTH LIV'D BUT ONE LIFE. | AN EPITAPH HUSBAND AND WIFE | 6 | 46 | 174 | 478 |
| BOTH LAWRELS TWINE INTO ONE WREATH, AND WOOE | UPON YORKE HIS BIRTH | 38 | 46 | 176 | 500 |
| BOTH WILL BE GOOD FRIENDS TOGETHER. | OUT OF THE ITALIAN (1) | 30 | 46 | 188 | 545 |
| OF LOVE, BURNE BOTH TOGETHER. | OUT OF THE ITALIAN (2) | 14 | 46 | 190 | 547 |
| WHOSE FRUIT AND BLOSSOMS BOTH BLESSE THE SAME BOUGH. | UPON TWO GREENE APRICOCKES | 20 | 48 | 220 | 494 |
| THAT BREATHES AT ONCE BOTH MAID & MOTHER, | IN HOLY NATIVITY | 89 | 52 | 246 | 76 |
| KIST ON BOTH HIS CHEEKS BY THEE. | IN GLORIOUS EPIPHANIE | 39 | 52 | 253 | 39 |
| SHALL SWELL WITH BOTH FOR HIM. & MIX | OFFICE H. CROSS SIXT | 7 | 52 | 270 | 97 |
| BOTH LIFE & LIBERTY | OFFICE H. CROSS SIXT | 18 | 52 | 270 | 97 |
| BY THIS THEY BOTH LOOK UP, & LIVE AGAINE. | OFFICE H. CROSS SIXT | 20 | 52 | 270 | 97 |
| BOTH WEEP & SING IN SHADE OF THEE. | OFFICE H. CROSS EVENSONG | 11 | 52 | 273 | 101 |
| TAKE BOTH TO THINE ACCOUNT, THAT I & MINE | OFFICE H. CROSS RECOMMENDATION | 3 | 52 | 276 | 106 |
| EVEN BALLANCE OF BOTH WORLDS. OUR WORLD OF SIN, | VEXILLA REGIS | 31 | 52 | 277 | 156 |
| THEM BOTH. | TO OUR B. LORD | 6 | 52 | 279 | 25 |
| BOTH NIGHTS & DAYES, | CHARITAS NIMIA | 27 | 52 | 280 | 48 |
| BOTH OF LOVE'S FIRES & FLOUDS) MIGHT I RECLINE | SANCTA MARIA DOLORUM | 47 | 52 | 283 | 162 |
| BOTH YET BELEIVE. AND WITTNESSE THEE | ADORO TE | 31 | 52 | 291 | 172 |
| THE SAME LEAVE BOTH TO EAT & LIVE. | ADORO TE | 42 | 52 | 291 | 172 |
| BUT STILL IN BOTH ONE CHRIST HE IS. | LAUDA SION SALVATOREM | 42 | 52 | 294 | 178 |
| NOR LEAVE THEY BOTH LESSE THEN BEFORE. | LAUDA SION SALVATOREM | 48 | 52 | 294 | 178 |
| BOTH THE PSALM AND SYBYLL SINGS | DIES IRAE | 2 | 52 | 298 | 186 |
| THOUGH BOTH MY PRAYRES & TEARES COMBINE. | DIES IRAE | 53 | 52 | 298 | 186 |
| BOTH WORTHLESSE ARE. FOR THEY ARE MINE, | DIES IRAE | 54 | 52 | 298 | 186 |
| AND LEAVE THEM BOTH TO TREMBLE HERE. | WEEPER | 48 | 52 | 307 | 120 |
| BOTH FIRE TO US & FLAME TO THEE. | TERESA | 162 | 52 | 315 | 52 |
| (FAIR YOUTH) SHOOTES BOTH THY SHAFT & THEE | FLAMING HEART | 48 | 52 | 324 | 61 |
| O HEART. THE AEQUALL POISE OF LOV'ES BOTH PARTS | FLAMING HEART | 75 | 52 | 324 | 61 |
| BOTH MIXT AT LAST THEIR BLOOD IN ONE RICH BED | ALEXIAS THIRD ELEGIE | 47 | 52 | 336 | 209 |
| 'CAUSE THEY BOTH LIVED BUT ONE LIFE. | AN EPITAPH UPON MARRIED COUPLE | 6 | 52 | 339 | 478 |
| BLENDS BOTH THE NOONES OF NIGHT & DAY. | (ON) HOPE | 6 | 52 | 345 | 71 |
| BOTH WINDS AND WATERS URGE THEIR WAY. | AGAINST IRRESOLUTION AND DELAY | 39 | 52 | 347 | 146 |

**BOTTLES**

| | | | | | |
|---|---|---|---|---|---|
| ANGELS WITH THEIR BOTTLES COME. | THE WEEPER | 34 | 46 | 79 | 120 |

**BOTOME**

| | | | | | |
|---|---|---|---|---|---|
| BELOW THE BOTOME OF THE GREAT ABYSSE. | SOSPETTO D'HERODE | 33 | 46 | 109 | 216 |

**BOTTOMLES**

| | | | | | |
|---|---|---|---|---|---|
| BOTTOMLES TREASURES | PRAYER TO GENTLE-WOMAN | 119 | 52 | 328 | 139 |

BOTTOMLESSE

  BOTTOMLESSE TREASURES. ON A PRAYER BOOKE 113 46 126 139

BOUGH

  THAT THE BALSAME-SWEATING BOUGH THE WEEPER 68 46 79 120
  THE TIMOUROUS MAIDEN-BLOSSOMES ON EACH BOUGH. UPON DEATH OF HERRYS 23 46 167 466
  WHOSE FRUIT AND BLOSSOMS BOTH BLESSE THE SAME BOUGH. UPON TWO GREENE APRICOCKES 20 48 220 494
  THAT THE BALSOM-SWEATING BOUGH WEEPER 50 52 307 120

BOUGHT

  NE'RE MAY A BIRTH OF THINE BE BOUGHT SO DEARE. UPON YORKE HIS BIRTH 94 46 176 500
  OR A BOUGHT BLUSH, OR A SET SMILE. WISHES SUPPOSED MISTRESSE 24 46 195 479
  MERCHANTS OF DEATH & SIN, IS BOUGHT & SOLD. OFFICE H. CROSS MATINES 15 52 265 86
  IN FARTHEST CLIME. WHAT E'RE IS BOUGHT PETRONIJ ALES PHASIACIS PETITA 12 MS 382 526

DEAR-BOUGHT

  TO ALL THE DEAR-BOUGHT NATIONS THIS REDEEMING NAME, TO THE NAME OF JESUS 94 52 239 30

OVERBOUGHT

  LORD WHAT IS MAN. THAT THOU HAST OVERBOUGHT CHARITAS NIMIA 3 52 280 48

BOUND

  IT DROPS THOUGH BOUND, THOUGH BOUND 'TIS FREE. ON BLEEDING WOUNDS OF LORD 12 46 101 110
  IT DROPS THOUGH BOUND, THOUGH BOUND 'TIS FREE. ON BLEEDING WOUNDS OF LORD 12 46 101 110
  FAST BOUND, SINCE FIRST HE FORFEITED THE SKIES. SOSPETTO D'HERODE 40 46 109 216
  BOUND IN THE PERIOD OF DEATH, ANOTHER ON HERRYS 46 46 170 469
  THE PRISONERS LOOSE, THE JAYLOR BOUND. OFFICE H. CROSS THIRD 15 52 268 93
  IT GIVES THOUGH BOUND. THOUGH BOUND 'TIS FREE. UPON BLEEDING CRUCIFIX 16 52 288 110
  IT GIVES THOUGH BOUND. THOUGH BOUND 'TIS FREE. UPON BLEEDING CRUCIFIX 16 52 288 110

FROST-BOUNT

  OF TH'ICY NORTH, FROM FROST-BOUNT ATLAS HANDS SOSPETTO D'HERODE 106 46 109 216

BOUNDS

  IT WAS THE WITT OF LOVE O'REFLOWD THE BOUNDS TO THE NAME OF JESUS 223 52 239 30
  NOR LOST IN TOO LARG BOUNDS, OUR LITTLE ROME ALEXIAS THIRD ELEGIE 11 52 336 209

BOUNDLES

  O BOUNDLES HOSPITALITY. O GLORIOSA DOMINA 9 52 302 194
  BOUNDLES & INFINITE PRAYER TO GENTLE-WOMAN 118 52 328 139

BOUNDLESSE

  BOUNDLESSE AND ABSOLUTE. HELL IS THINE OWNE. SOSPETTO D'HERODE 272 46 109 216
  BOUNDLESSE AND INFINITE ON A PRAYER BOOKE 112 46 126 139

BOUNTEOUS

  BUT THOU THY BOUNTEOUS SELF STILL BE. DIES IRAE 55 52 298 186

BOUNTY

  THIS GRATIOUS ROBBERY SHALL THY BOUNTY BE. FLAMING HEART 91 52 324 61

BOUNTYES

  REVENGE THY BOUNTYES IN THEIR BEAUTEOUS SHAPES. IN GLORIOUS EPIPHANIE 106 52 253 39

BOUNTYFULL

  RICH, ROYALL FOOD. BOUNTYFULL BREAD. ADORO TE 39 52 291 172

BOW

  HIS WEAPON IS A LITTLE BOW, OUT OF GREEKE CUPID'S CRYER 45 46 159 519
  HERE'S MY QUIVER SHAFTS AND BOW, OUT OF GREEKE CUPID'S CRYER 70 46 159 519
  BOW OUR BRIGHT HEADS. BEFORE A KING OF CLAY. SOSPETTO D'HERODE 220 46 109 216
  AND WITH THEM ALL ABOUT THEE, BOW IN MEMORY OF LADY MADRE TERESA 171 46 131 52
  TAKE THINE OWNE MEASURE HERE, DOWNE, DOWNE, AND BOW UPON STANINOUGH'S DEATH 11 46 175 475
  FULL QUIVERS ON LOVES BOW. WISHES SUPPOSED MISTRESSE 59 46 195 479
  WHEN STUBBORN ROCKS SHALL BOW TO THE NAME OF JESUS 230 52 239 30
  SHALL THEN WITH JUST CONFUSION, BOW TO THE NAME OF JESUS 238 52 239 30
  DREAD LAMB. AND BOW THUS LOW BEFORE THEE. OFFICE H. CROSS MATINES 25 52 265 86
  DREAD LAMB. & BOW THUS LOW BEFORE THEE. OFFICE H. CROSS SIXT 22 52 270 97
  DREAD LAMB. & BOW THUS BEFORE THEE. OFFICE H. CROSS EVENSONG 29 52 273 101
  AND BOW THEIR FLAMING HEADS BEFORE THEE CHARITAS NIMIA 23 52 280 48
  WHY SHOULD THOU BOW THY AWFULL BREST TO SEE CHARITAS NIMIA 33 52 280 48
  BOW WITH A LOAD SANCTA MARIA DOLORUM 32 52 283 162
  THUS LOWE (MY HIDDEN LIFE.) I BOW TO THEE ADORO TE 3 52 291 172
  AND WITH THEM ALL ABOUT THEE BOW TERESA 170 52 315 52
  TAKE THINE OWN MEASURE HERE. DOWN, DOWN, & BOW DEATH'S LECTURE 12 52 340 475
  THERE SHINES HIS QUIVER, THERE HIS BOW. IN CICATRICES DOMINI JESU 4 MS 381 27
  FOR BOW HIS UNBENT HAND DID SERVE. IN CICATRICES DOMINI JESU 13 MS 381 27
  STRANGE THE QUIVER, BOW, & DART. IN CICATRICES DOMINI JESU 15 MS 381 27

| | | | |
|---|---|---|---|
| BY PARTHIANS BOW THE SOLDJER LOOKES TO DIE, | HORATIJ ILLE & NEFASTO | 25 | MS 382 530 |
| AND ALL THEIR FELLOW DEITIES WILL BOW | EX EUPHORMIONE | 8 | MS 392 525 |

BOW'D

| | | | |
|---|---|---|---|
| HOW LOW THE BRIGHT YOUTH BOW'D, AND WITH WHAT AWE | SOSPETTO D'HERODE | 99 | 46 109 216 |
| WHOM TOO MUCH LOVE HATH BOW'D MORE LOW FOR ME. | ADORO TE | 4 | 52 291 172 |
| BOW'D TO THE LOWLY MOUTHS OF MEN. | LAUDA SION SALVATOREM | 62 | 52 294 178 |

BOWES

| | | | |
|---|---|---|---|
| DEIGNE THOU TO WEARE THIS HUMBLE WREATH THAT BOWES, | SOSPETTO D'HERODE | 15 | 46 109 216 |
| THEN BOWES HIS ALL-OBEDIENT HEAD, & DYES | OFFICE H. CROSS NINTH | 5 | 52 271 99 |
| BOWES LOW'ST HIS HEAVY TOP, TO LOOK FOR THEE. | IN GLORIOUS ASSUMPTION B. LADY | 30 | 52 304 114 |

BOWELS

| | | | |
|---|---|---|---|
| LET HOARY TIME'S VAST BOWELS BE THE GRAVE | ON FRONTISPIECE ISAACSONS | 1 | 46 191 491 |
| TO WHAT HIS BOWELS BIRTH AND BEING GAVE. | ON FRONTISPIECE ISAACSONS | 2 | 46 191 491 |

BOWELLS

| | | | |
|---|---|---|---|
| O LET THINE OWN SOFT BOWELLS PAY | DIES IRAE | 45 | 52 298 186 |

BOWLES

| | | | |
|---|---|---|---|
| BOWLES FULL OF RICHER BLOOD THEN BLUSH OF GRAPE | AN APOLOGIE FOR HYMNE (TERESA) | 33 | 46 136 59 |
| BOWLES FULL OF RICHER BLOOD THEN BLUSH OF GRAPE | AN APOLOGIE FOR (TERESA) HYMNE | 33 | 52 322 59 |
| BY ALL THY BRIM-FILL'D BOWLES OF FEIRCE DESIRE | FLAMING HEART | 99 | 52 324 61 |

BOWER

| | | | |
|---|---|---|---|
| THAT ON THY BANKES SITTS IN A VERDANT BOWER, | AN ELEGIE ON DR PORTER | 22 | MS 395 476 |

BOWERS

| | | | |
|---|---|---|---|
| THEY WERE THE SMILING SONS OF THOSE SWEET BOWERS, | SOSPETTO D'HERODE | 19 | 46 109 216 |
| OPEN SUNNES. SHADY BOWERS, | WISHES SUPPOSED MISTRESSE | 92 | 46 195 479 |

BOXE

| | | | |
|---|---|---|---|
| WHICH TO NO BOXE HIS BEING OWES. | WISHES SUPPOSED MISTRESSE | 36 | 46 195 479 |

BOY

| | | | |
|---|---|---|---|
| TELL ME BRIGHT BOY, TELL ME MY GOLDEN LAD, | ON THE PRODIGALL | 1 | 46 86 17 |
| WHILE WE FOUND OUT THE FAIR-EY'D BOY. | A HYMNE OF THE NATIVITY | 7 | 46 106 76 |
| HOW LOVE CAME NAK'T, A BOY, AND BLIND. | OUT OF THE ITALIAN (3) | 2 | 46 190 549 |
| MY WOMBES CHAST PRIDE IS GONE, MY HEAV'NE-BORNE BOY. | LUKE 2. QUAERIT JESUM | 7 | MS 379 11 |
| OH COME, SWEET BOY. | LUKE 2. QUAERIT JESUM | 16 | MS 379 11 |

BOYES

| | | | |
|---|---|---|---|
| HALLS FULL OF FLATTERING MEN & FRISKING BOYES. | DESCRIPTION RELIGIOUS HOUSE | 6 | 52 338 213 |

BOYSTEROUS

| | | | |
|---|---|---|---|
| THE WEIGHTY RUDENES OF HIS BOYSTEROUS HEELE. | ON GUNPOWDER-TREASON | 44 | MS 384 458 |

BRACELET

| | | | |
|---|---|---|---|
| FOR A BESEEMING BRACELET SHEE HAD TY'D | SOSPETTO D'HERODE | 466 | 46 109 216 |

BRAG

| | | | |
|---|---|---|---|
| ONE WENT TO BRAG, TH'OTHER TO PRAY. | TWO WENT TO PRAY | 2 | 46 89 18 |
| JUSTLY, GREAT NATURE, MAY'ST THOU BRAG AND TELL | UPON YORKE HIS BIRTH | 49 | 46 176 500 |

BRAGGE

| | | | |
|---|---|---|---|
| THEN LET THE EASTERNE WORLD BRAGGE AND BE PROUD | UPON YORKE HIS BIRTH | 86 | 46 176 500 |

BRAGS

| | | | |
|---|---|---|---|
| THE WIND IN ALL HIS ROARING BRAGS STOOD STILL | OUT OF GROTIUS | 65 | MS 398 198 |

BRAIN

| | | | |
|---|---|---|---|
| BUT MORE AMBITIOUS LOSSE, AT LEST OF BRAIN. | IN GLORIOUS EPIPHANIE | 230 | 52 253 39 |

BRAINE

| | | | |
|---|---|---|---|
| WITH THEE ALONE HE WEARES NO BEARD, THY BRAINE | UPON TWO GREENE APRICOCKES | 17 | 48 220 494 |

BRAINES

| | | | |
|---|---|---|---|
| OF RAGGED LIMBS, TORNE SCULLS, & DASHT OUT BRAINES. | SOSPETTO D'HERODE | 312 | 46 109 216 |
| OF BROTHERS MUTUALL BLOOD, AND FATHERS BRAINES. | SOSPETTO D'HERODE | 328 | 46 109 216 |
| OF THY KIND MASTER'S WELL-DESERVING BRAINES. | HORATIJ ILLE & NEFASTO | 16 | MS 382 530 |

BRAYNES

| | | | |
|---|---|---|---|
| ON TIPTOE IN THEIR GIDDY BRAYNES. TH' HAVE FIRE | SOSPETTO D'HERODE | 442 | 46 109 216 |

BRANCH

| | | | | |
|---|---|---|---|---|
| THOU MIGHTY BRANCH OF EMPEROURS AND KINGS. | SOSPETTO D'HERODE | 10 | 46 109 | 216 |
| (THAT OLD DRY STOCKE) A DESPAIR'D BRANCH IS SPRUNG | SOSPETTO D'HERODE | 434 | 46 109 | 216 |

BRANCHES

| | | | | |
|---|---|---|---|---|
| AMONG HIS BRANCHES. YEA, AND VOW'D TO BRING | UPON DEATH OF HERRYS | 12 | 46 167 | 466 |

BRAND

| | | | | |
|---|---|---|---|---|
| EACH HOLDING FORTH TO LIGHT THE AERY BRAND, | UPON GUNPOWDER TREASON | 14 | MS 387 | 461 |

BRANDS

| | | | | |
|---|---|---|---|---|
| FLOURISHT THEIR SNAKES, AND TOST THEIR FLAMING BRANDS. | SOSPETTO D'HERODE | 260 | 46 109 | 216 |

BRANDISHING

| | | | | |
|---|---|---|---|---|
| HER SULPHUR-BREATHED TORCHES BRANDISHING, | SOSPETTO D'HERODE | 398 | 46 109 | 216 |

EVER-BRANDISHT

| | | | | |
|---|---|---|---|---|
| WHOSE EVER-BRANDISHT SWORD IS SHEATH'D IN BLOOD. | SOSPETTO D'HERODE | 314 | 46 109 | 216 |

BRASEN

| | | | | |
|---|---|---|---|---|
| WOULD REACH THE BRASEN VOYCE OF WARR'S HOARCE BIRD. | MUSICKS DUELL | 101 | 46 149 | 535 |

BRASSE

| | | | | |
|---|---|---|---|---|
| HERE STRONG PROCRUSTES PLANTS HIS BED OF BRASSE. | SOSPETTO D'HERODE | 358 | 46 109 | 216 |
| AND BEAT THE HOT BRASSE WITH REBELLIOUS WAVES. | SOSPETTO D'HERODE | 484 | 46 109 | 216 |
| HIS WEAPONS WERE NOR STEELE, NOR BRASSE. | IN CICATRICES DOMINI JESU | 11 | MS 381 | 27 |

BRAVE

| | | | | |
|---|---|---|---|---|
| THE OTHERS WANTON WEALTH FOAMS HIGH, AND BRAVE, | WIDOWES MITES | 3 | 46 86 | 21 |
| HEAV'N SAW US STRUGGLE ONCE, AS BRAVE A FIGHT | SOSPETTO D'HERODE | 255 | 46 109 | 216 |
| STAY OF MY STRONG HOPES, YOU OF WHOSE BRAVE WORTH, | SOSPETTO D'HERODE | 282 | 46 109 | 216 |
| WHY DOST THOU LET THY BRAVE SOULE LYE SUPPREST, | SOSPETTO D'HERODE | 429 | 46 109 | 216 |
| WHICH SPENT CAN BUY SO BRAVE A DEATH. | IN MEMORY OF LADY MADRE TERESA | 18 | 46 131 | 52 |
| HIGH, AND BURNES WITH SUCH BRAVE HEATS. | IN MEMORY OF LADY MADRE TERESA | 36 | 46 131 | 52 |
| THIS POSTURE IS THE BRAVE ONE. THIS THAT LYES | UPON STANINOUGH'S DEATH | 27 | 46 175 | 475 |
| LOVE, BRAVE VERTUES YOUNGER BROTHER, | LOVES HOROSCOPE | 1 | 46 185 | 483 |
| OF YOUR BRAVE SOUL SO SLOWLY FORTH. | TO COUNTESSE OF DENBIGH | 8 | 52 236 | 146 |
| OF DEATH & FEIRCEST DANGERS, DURST WITH BRAVE | TO THE NAME OF JESUS | 201 | 52 239 | 30 |
| WE VOW TO MAKE BRAVE WAY | IN GLORIOUS EPIPHANIE | 221 | 52 253 | 39 |
| WHICH SPENT CAN BUY SO BRAVE A DEATH. | TERESA | 18 | 52 315 | 52 |
| HIGH, & BURNES WITH SUCH BRAVE HEATES. | TERESA | 36 | 52 315 | 52 |
| THIS POSTURE IS THE BRAVE ONE THIS THAT LYES | DEATH'S LECTURE | 29 | 52 340 | 475 |
| OF YOUR BRAVE SOUL SO SLOWLY FORTH. | AGAINST IRRESOLUTION AND DELAY | 16 | 52 347 | 146 |
| COME, BRAVE SOLDIERS, COME, & SEE | IN CICATRICES DOMINI JESU | 1 | MS 381 | 27 |
| THERE THESE BRAVE SOULES DEALE TO EACH WONDRING EARE | HORATIJ ILLE & NEFASTO | 45 | MS 382 | 530 |
| THOSE PLUMPE SOFT RUBIES HAD BIN DREST SOE BRAVE. | UPON BIRTH PRINCESSE E | 48 | MS 391 | 456 |
| TO PAINT ITS PERFUM'D FACE WITH COLOURS BRAVE. | AN ELEGIE ON DR PORTER | 24 | MS 395 | 476 |

BRAVELY

| | | | | |
|---|---|---|---|---|
| SWEETNESSE BY ALL HER NAMES. THUS, BRAVELY THUS | MUSICKS DUELL | 133 | 46 149 | 535 |

BRAVER

| | | | | |
|---|---|---|---|---|
| THEN MANY A BRAVER MARBLE CAN. | AN EPITAPH UPON ASHTON | 3 | 46 192 | 464 |
| 'TIS TIME YOU LISTEN TO A BRAVER LOVE, | TO SAME CONCERNING CHOISE | 20 | 52 331 | 66 |

BRAVES

| | | | | |
|---|---|---|---|---|
| THAT BRAVES YOU OUT. | WHY ARE YEE AFRAID | 11 | 46 88 | 15 |

BRAVERY

| | | | | |
|---|---|---|---|---|
| HIS BE THE BRAVERY OF ALL THOSE BRIGHT THINGS, | FLAMING HEART | 65 | 52 324 | 61 |

BREACH

| | | | | |
|---|---|---|---|---|
| NOR WOUND NOR BREACH IN WHAT HE TAKES. | LAUDA SION SALVATOREM | 44 | 52 294 | 178 |

BREAD

| | | | | |
|---|---|---|---|---|
| A SUBTLE HARVEST OF UNBOUNDED BREAD, | ON MIRACLE OF LOAVES | 3 | 46 86 | 15 |
| SO THAT WITH THE SELF-SAME BREAD | PSALME 23 | 53 | 46 102 | 5 |
| RICH, ROYALL FOOD. BOUNTYFULL BREAD. | ADORO TE | 39 | 52 291 | 172 |
| LIVE EVER BREAD OF LOVES, & BE | ADORO TE | 43 | 52 291 | 172 |
| LO THE BREAD OF LIFE, THIS DAY'S | LAUDA SION SALVATOREM | 7 | 52 294 | 178 |
| THE LIVING & LIFE-GIVING BREAD, | LAUDA SION SALVATOREM | 9 | 52 294 | 178 |
| WITH A WELL-BLES'T BREAD & WINE | LAUDA SION SALVATOREM | 29 | 52 294 | 178 |
| BY'A NOBLER BREAD, MORE NEEDFULL BLOOD. | LAUDA SION SALVATOREM | 36 | 52 294 | 178 |
| YET ON THE SAME (LIFE-MEANING) BREAD | LAUDA SION SALVATOREM | 51 | 52 294 | 178 |
| THE CHILDREN'S BREAD. THE BRIDEGROOM'S WINE. | LAUDA SION SALVATOREM | 63 | 52 294 | 178 |

BREAK

| | | | | | |
|---|---|---|---|---|---|
| WEE SAW THINE EYES BREAK FROM THE EAST. | A HYMNE OF THE NATIVITY | 31 | 46 | 106 | 76 |
| (CLOWD OF CONDENSED SWEETS) & BREAK UPON US | TO THE NAME OF JESUS | 168 | 52 | 239 | 30 |
| AND BREAK BEFORE THEE. | TO THE NAME OF JESUS | 239 | 52 | 239 | 30 |
| WE SAW THINE EYES BREAK FROM THEIR EASTE | IN HOLY NATIVITY | 33 | 52 | 246 | 76 |
| WE SAW THINE EYES BREAK FROM THEIR EAST | IN HOLY NATIVITY | 74 | 52 | 246 | 76 |
| COMBIN'D AGAINST THIS BREST AT ONCE BREAK IN | FLAMING HEART | 89 | 52 | 324 | 61 |

DAY-BREAK

| | | | | | |
|---|---|---|---|---|---|
| TO CATCH THE DAY-BREAK OF THY DAWN, | TO THE NAME OF JESUS | 148 | 52 | 239 | 30 |
| THE DAY-BREAK OF THE NATIONS. THEIR FIRST RAY. | TO THE QUEEN'S MAJESTY | 3 | 52 | 261 | 47 |

BREAKE

| | | | | | |
|---|---|---|---|---|---|
| GOE SMILING SOULES, YOUR NEW BUILT CAGES BREAKE, | TO INFANT MARTYRS | 1 | 46 | 68 | 10 |
| HER PARDON OR HER SENTENCE. ONELY BREAKE | UPON YORKE HIS BIRTH | 109 | 46 | 176 | 500 |
| LEAST IT BREAKE FORTH, & BURNE THY SOOTY CELL. | ON GUNPOWDER-TREASON | 66 | MS | 384 | 458 |
| AND BREAKE UPON MEE. MY OWNE VIRTUES HEIGHT | OUT OF GROTIUS | 33 | MS | 398 | 198 |

BREAKS

| | | | | | |
|---|---|---|---|---|---|
| 'TIS HEAV'N THAT LYES IN AMBUSH THERE, & BREAKS | AN APOLOGIE FOR (TERESA) HYMNE | 24 | 52 | 322 | 59 |

BREAKES

| | | | | | |
|---|---|---|---|---|---|
| THY GLORIOUS WISDOME BREAKES THE NETS. | NEITHER DURST MAN ASKE | 3 | 46 | 92 | 20 |
| 'TIS HEAVEN THAT LIES IN AMBUSH THERE, AND BREAKES | AN APOLOGIE FOR HYMNE (TERESA) | 24 | 46 | 136 | 59 |
| THAT BREAKES FROM ONE OF THESE FAIRE EYES. | AN HIMNE FOR CIRCUMCISION | 28 | 46 | 141 | 37 |
| BECAUSE SHEE BREAKES THE YEARES OLD RAIGNE | THOUGH NOW 'TIS NEITHER | 16 | MS | 397 | 492 |
| THAT BREAKES FROM ONE OF THESE BRIGHT EYES. | NEW YEAR'S DAY | 28 | 52 | 251 | 37 |
| AND BREAKES THROUGH ALL TEN HEAV'NS TO OUR EMBRACE. | AGAINST IRRESOLUTION AND DELAY | 78 | 52 | 347 | 146 |
| MANS BREST (HIS TENEMENT) AND BREAKES UP HOUSE. | OUT OF GROTIUS | 80 | MS | 398 | 198 |

BREAKFAST

| | | | | | |
|---|---|---|---|---|---|
| TASTES OF THIS BREAKFAST ALL DAY LONG. | THE WEEPER | 30 | 46 | 79 | 120 |
| TASTS OF THIS BREAKFAST ALL DAY LONG. | WEEPER | 30 | 52 | 307 | 120 |

BREAST

| | | | | | |
|---|---|---|---|---|---|
| IN PANTING MURMURS, STILL'D OUT OF HER BREAST | MUSICKS DUELL | 65 | 46 | 149 | 535 |
| AND MAKES A PRETTY EARTHQUAKE IN HER BREAST, | MUSICKS DUELL | 89 | 46 | 149 | 535 |
| PLENTY WEARES ME AT HER BREAST, | PSALME 23 | 10 | 46 | 102 | 5 |
| HER WEAKE BREAST HEAVES WITH STRONG DESIRE, | IN MEMORY OF LADY MADRE TERESA | 40 | 46 | 131 | 52 |
| FROM THENCE INTO THE WONDRING READERS BREAST, | AN APOLOGIE FOR HYMNE (TERESA) | 25 | 46 | 136 | 59 |
| THOU ART THE MOTHER PHOENIX AND THY BREAST | UPON YORKE HIS BIRTH | 82 | 46 | 176 | 500 |
| O'TH PRETIOUS PHOENIX, WARME UPON HER BREAST. | ON A FOULE MORNING | 22 | 46 | 181 | 495 |
| IN HER BREATH, OR IN HER BREAST, | LOVES HOROSCOPE | 49 | 46 | 185 | 483 |
| OF LOVES, THY LORD'S TOO LIBERALL BREAST. | VEXILLA REGIS | 6 | 52 | 277 | 156 |
| OFT FROM THIS BREAST TO THINE MY LOVE-TOST HEART | LUKE 2. QUAERIT JESUM | 39 | MS | 379 | 11 |
| IN THY COLD BREAST, & YEARLY ON THIS DAY | ON GUNPOWDER-TREASON | 13 | MS | 384 | 458 |
| LETT THY SWOLNE BREAST DISCHARGE THY STRUGLING GROANES | AN ELEGIE ON DR PORTER | 31 | MS | 395 | 476 |

BREST

| | | | | | |
|---|---|---|---|---|---|
| SHEE GIVES HIM BACKE. HER SUPPLE BREST THRILLS OUT | MUSICKS DUELL | 57 | 46 | 149 | 535 |
| APPEAR'D WITH OTHER LADING, FOR HER BREST | THE BEGINNING OF HELIODORUS | 12 | 46 | 158 | 517 |
| IN THE CLOSET OF THEIR BREST. | OUT OF GREEKE CUPID'S CRYER | 44 | 46 | 159 | 519 |
| (SLIPT FROM AURORA'S DEWY BREST) | THE TEARE | 20 | 46 | 84 | 50 |
| THEY, THEY THAT SNATCHT US FROM OUR COUNTRIES BREST | PSALME 137 | 7 | 46 | 104 | 7 |
| A THOUSAND SWEET BABES FROM THEIR MOTHERS BREST. | SOSPETTO D'HERODE | 4 | 46 | 109 | 216 |
| ADORE HER PRINCES BIRTH, FLAT ON HER BREST. | SOSPETTO D'HERODE | 124 | 46 | 109 | 216 |
| THAT FROM HIS MOTHERS BREST HEE MILKE SHOULD DRINKE, | SOSPETTO D'HERODE | 173 | 46 | 109 | 216 |
| WHILE NEW THOUGHTS BOYL'D IN HIS ENRAGED BREST, | SOSPETTO D'HERODE | 193 | 46 | 109 | 216 |
| A DESPERATE, OH MEE, DREW FROM HIS DEEPE BREST. | SOSPETTO D'HERODE | 200 | 46 | 109 | 216 |
| AND RISING WITH RICH SPOILES UPON HIS BREST, | SOSPETTO D'HERODE | 229 | 46 | 109 | 216 |
| HIS BREST A WHILE FROM CARE'S UNQUIET STING. | SOSPETTO D'HERODE | 396 | 46 | 109 | 216 |
| AND BRING HOME ON THY BREST MORE THANKLESSE SCARRS. | SOSPETTO D'HERODE | 448 | 46 | 109 | 216 |
| SO BOYLES THE FIRED HERODS BLOOD-SWOLNE BREST, | SOSPETTO D'HERODE | 489 | 46 | 109 | 216 |
| HAD SOWNE OF OLD THESE DOUBTS IN HIS DEEPE BREST. | SOSPETTO D'HERODE | 498 | 46 | 109 | 216 |
| THY BLOOD-REVOLVING BREST TO RAGE DOTH MOVE. | SOSPETTO D'HERODE | 514 | 46 | 109 | 216 |
| OF EVERLASTING JOYES BATH THY WHITE BREST. | ON THE ASSUMPTION | 58 | 46 | 139 | 114 |
| THAT IN THE CENTER OF HIS BREST | HIS EPITAPH (HERRYS) | 17 | 46 | 172 | 471 |
| SO WARME IN THY SOFT BREST IT CANNOT DYE. | TO THE MORNING | 34 | 46 | 183 | 497 |
| IN HER BREST, OR IN HER BREATH, | LOVES HOROSCOPE | 43 | 46 | 185 | 483 |
| ALL YE WISE SOULES, WHO IN THE WEALTHY BREST | TO THE NAME OF JESUS | 11 | 52 | 239 | 30 |
| A CHOICER LESSON THEN THE JOYFULL BREST | TO THE NAME OF JESUS | 107 | 52 | 239 | 30 |
| WHY SHOULD THOU BOW THY AWFULL BREST TO SEE | CHARITAS NIMIA | 33 | 52 | 280 | 48 |
| WHY SHOULD HIS UNSTAINED BREST MAKE GOOD | CHARITAS NIMIA | 61 | 52 | 280 | 48 |
| SO FAST FOR ONE SOFT BREST. | SANCTA MARIA DOLORUM | 18 | 52 | 283 | 162 |
| O IN THAT BREST | SANCTA MARIA DOLORUM | 45 | 52 | 283 | 162 |
| MY BREST MAY CATCH THE KISSE OF SOME KIND DART, | SANCTA MARIA DOLORUM | 69 | 52 | 283 | 162 |
| WHOSE BREST WEEPES BALM FOR WOUNDED MAN. | ADORO TE | 46 | 52 | 291 | 172 |
| AND BOARD HIMSELF AT THY RICH BREST. | O GLORIOSA DOMINA | 8 | 52 | 302 | 194 |
| OF EVERLASTING JOYES BATH THY WHITE BREST. | IN GLORIOUS ASSUMPTION B. LADY | 63 | 52 | 304 | 114 |
| HER WEAKE BREST HEAVES WITH STRONG DESIRE | TERESA | 40 | 52 | 315 | 52 |
| FROM THENCE INTO THE WONDRING READER'S BREST. | AN APOLOGIE FOR (TERESA) HYMNE | 25 | 52 | 322 | 59 |
| COMBIN'D AGAINST THIS BREST AT ONCE BREAK IN | FLAMING HEART | 89 | 52 | 324 | 61 |
| OF A RICH BINDING IN YOUR BREST. | PRAYER TO GENTLE-WOMAN | 10 | 52 | 328 | 139 |
| OF SUTERS THAT BESEIGE YOUR MAIDEN BREST, | TO SAME CONCERNING CHOISE | 3 | 52 | 331 | 66 |
| HOME TO HIMSELF. TO HIDE IT IN HIS BREST | TO SAME CONCERNING CHOISE | 51 | 52 | 331 | 66 |

|                                                                  |                              | PAGE | 46           |
|------------------------------------------------------------------|------------------------------|------|--------------|
| MAKE BIGGE THY BREST WITH IMMORTALL FIRE,                        | ALEXIAS THIRD ELEGIE         | 22   | 52 336 209   |
| WAS IN THE MODEST NUNNERY OF HIS BREST.                          | AN ELEGY MR STANNINOW        | 36   | MS 394 473   |
| MANS BREST (HIS TENEMENT) AND BREAKES UP HOUSE.                  | OUT OF GROTIUS               | 80   | MS 398 198   |

BREASTED

| DEARE SILVER BREASTED DOVE | ON A PRAYER BOOKE | 92 | 46 126 139 |

FLAMING-BRESTED

| INLARGE THY FLAMING-BRESTED LOVERS | TO THE NAME OF JESUS | 212 | 52 239 30 |

BREASTS

| OF THOSE WHOSE LARGE BREASTS BUILT A THRONE      | IN MEMORY OF LADY MADRE TERESA | 10 | 46 131  52 |
| THY BREASTS CHAST CABINET, AND UNCASE            | IN MEMORY OF LADY MADRE TERESA | 72 | 46 131  52 |
| AND FRUITFULL CHARITIES FULL BREASTS (OF OLD)    | ON A TREATISE OF CHARITY       | 55 | 46 137  69 |
| BUT DARES DESTRUCTION EATE THESE CANDID BREASTS. | UPON GUNPOWDER TREASON         | 37 | MS 387 461 |

BRESTS

| THE DOWNE THAT THEIR SOFT BRESTS DID STROW,      | A HYMNE OF THE NATIVITY   |  42 | 46 106  76 |
| 'TWIXT MOTHERS BRESTS TO GOE TO BED.             | A HYMNE OF THE NATIVITY   |  50 | 46 106  76 |
| SEALING ALL BRESTS IN A LETHAEAN BAND.           | SOSPETTO D'HERODE         | 392 | 46 109 216 |
| ON THEIR BOLD BRESTS ABOUT THE WORLD THEY BORE THEE | TO THE NAME OF JESUS   | 203 | 52 239  30 |
| WHO TORE THE FAIR BRESTS OF THY FREINDS.         | TO THE NAME OF JESUS      | 208 | 52 239  30 |
| TWIXT'S MOTHER'S BRESTS IS GONE TO BED.          | IN HOLY NATIVITY          |  68 | 52 246  76 |
| WHEN A WILD SWORD EV'N FROM THEIR BRESTS, DID LOP | OUT OF GROTIUS           |  25 | MS 398 198 |

BREST'S

| THY BREST'S CHAST CABINET, & UNCASE | TERESA | 72 | 52 315 52 |

BREATH

| HIS HONEY-DROPPING TOPS, PLOW'D BY HER BREATH          | MUSICKS DUELL                      |  71 | 46 149 535 |
| OF HIS OWNE BREATH. WHICH MARRYED TO HIS LYRE          | MUSICKS DUELL                      | 117 | 46 149 535 |
| (QUICK WITH WARME ZEPHIRES LIVELY BREATH) LAY FORTH    | OUT OF VIRGIL                      |  13 | 46 155 529 |
| LED ROUND IN HIS GREAT CIRCLE. NO WINDS BREATH         | OUT OF VIRGIL                      |  27 | 46 155 529 |
| LOOKE ON THE FOLLOWING LEAVES, AND SEE HIM BREATH.     | UPON BISHOP ANDREWES PICTURE       |  16 | 46 163 490 |
| NOT US'D TO SPEAKE BUT IN HIS BREATH,                  | UPON THE DEATH OF A GENTLEMAN      |  18 | 46 166 472 |
| AS IF THEY ONELY MEANT TO BREATH,                      | NEITHER DURST MAN ASKE             |  13 | 46  92  20 |
| WHEN MY WAIWARD BREATH IS FLYING,                      | PSALME 23                          |  17 | 46 102   5 |
| LET THE DAMPS OF THY DULL BREATH                       | PSALME 23                          |  40 | 46 102   5 |
| AND THENCE MY RIPE SOULE WILL I BREATH                 | PSALME 23                          |  71 | 46 102   5 |
| GAVE FORTH YOUR BLOOD FOR BREATH, SPOKE SOULES FOR WORDS. | SOSPETTO D'HERODE                |   8 | 46 109 216 |
| HIS BREATH HELLS LIGHTNING IS. AND EACH DEEPE GRONE    | SOSPETTO D'HERODE                  |  55 | 46 109 216 |
| UNTO A DREADFULL PILE GIVES FIERY BREATH.              | SOSPETTO D'HERODE                  |  58 | 46 109 216 |
| WITH ENDLESSE BUSINESSE ALMOST OUT OF BREATH.          | SOSPETTO D'HERODE                  | 320 | 46 109 216 |
| THE BREATH OF ARTIFICIALL LUNGS EMBRAVES.              | SOSPETTO D'HERODE                  | 482 | 46 109 216 |
| SUCH AS COULD WITH LUSTY BREATH                        | IN MEMORY OF LADY MADRE TERESA     |   7 | 46 131  52 |
| LIFE SHOULD SO LONG PLAY WITH THAT BREATH,             | IN MEMORY OF LADY MADRE TERESA     |  17 | 46 131  52 |
| SHEE OFFERS THEM HER DEAREST BREATH,                   | IN MEMORY OF LADY MADRE TERESA     |  49 | 46 131  52 |
| WHOSE STROAKE SHALL TASTE THY HALLOWED BREATH.         | IN MEMORY OF LADY MADRE TERESA     |  80 | 46 131  52 |
| THE BALMY ZEPHIRUS GOT SO SWEET A BREATH               | UPON DEATH OF HERRYS               |  20 | 46 167 466 |
| AND THE SHORT CLAUSE OF MORTALL BREATH.                | ANOTHER ON HERRYS                  |  45 | 46 170 469 |
| WHAT WORD SO E'RE HIS BREATH KEPT WARME,               | HIS EPITAPH (HERRYS)               |  31 | 46 172 471 |
| WITH WANTON GALES. HIS BALMY BREATH SHALL LICKE        | ON A FOULE MORNING                 |  13 | 46 181 495 |
| A FRAGRANT BREATH SUCKT FROM THE SPICY NEST            | ON A FOULE MORNING                 |  21 | 46 181 495 |
| IN HER BREST, OR IN HER BREATH,                        | LOVES HOROSCOPE                    |  43 | 46 185 483 |
| IN HER BREATH, OR IN HER BREAST,                       | LOVES HOROSCOPE                    |  49 | 46 185 483 |
| REVIVED NATURE TAKE A SECOND BREATH.                   | ON FRONTISPIECE ISAACSONS          |   4 | 46 191 491 |
| THAT AS I DEDICATE MY DEVOUTEST BREATH                 | OFFICE H. CROSS RECOMMENDATION     |   5 | 52 276 106 |
| MY DYING LIFE MAY DRAW A NEW, & NEVER FLEETING BREATH. | OFFICE H. CROSS RECOMMENDATION     |   8 | 52 276 106 |
| LEAVING HER ONLY SO MUCH BREATH                        | SANCTA MARIA DOLORUM               |  39 | 52 283 162 |
| LO, HEART, THY HOPE'S WHOLE PLEA. HER PRETIOUS BREATH  | SANCTA MARIA DOLORUM               | 109 | 52 283 162 |
| WHICH LIVES STILL, & ALLOWES US BREATH.                | ADORO TE                           |  38 | 52 291 172 |
| AND BY A MINDFULLL, MYSTICK BREATH                     | LAUDA SION SALVATOREM              |  27 | 52 294 178 |
| SUCH AS COULD WITH LUSTY BREATH                        | TERESA                             |   7 | 52 315  52 |
| LIFE SHOULD SO LONG PLAY WITH THAT BREATH              | TERESA                             |  17 | 52 315  52 |
| SHE'L OFFER THEM HER DEAREST BREATH,                   | TERESA                             |  49 | 52 315  52 |
| WHOSE STROKE SHALL TAST THY HALLOW'D BREATH.           | TERESA                             |  80 | 52 315  52 |
| SO GAINFULL IS SUCH LOSSE OF BREATH,                   | A SONG                             |  11 | 52 327  65 |
| LETT NOT MY SUPPLIANT BREATH RAISE A RUDE STORME       | ON GUNPOWDER-TREASON               |  11 | MS 384 458 |
| A LIVING COMET, WHOSE PESTIFEROUSE BREATH              | ON GUNPOWDER-TREASON               |  17 | MS 384 458 |
| EACH SOULE IN SIGHES HAD SPENT ITS DEAREST BREATH,     | UPON GUNPOWDER TREASON             |  41 | MS 386 460 |
| MAY DRAW THEIR FIRST BREATH FROM THY STARRY BEAMES.    | EX EUPHORMIONE                     |  14 | MS 392 525 |

SULPHUR-BREATHED

| HER SULPHUR-BREATHED TORCHES BRANDISHING. | SOSPETTO D'HERODE | 398 | 46 109 216 |

BREATH'D

| DOES THY SWEET BREATH'D PRAYER | THE WEEPER | 105 | 46 79 120 |

SWEET-BREATH'D

| DOES THY SWEET-BREATH'D PRAIRE | WEEPER | 141 | 52 307 120 |

| | | | |
|---|---|---|---|
| BREATH'S | | | |
| AND SHEE ALTHOUGH HER BREATH'S LATE EXERCISE | MUSICKS DUELL | 158 | 46 149 535 |
| BREATHS | | | |
| GOOD REASON FOR SHEE BREATHS ALL FIRE, | IN MEMORY OF LADY MADRE TERESA | 39 | 46 131 52 |
| A LONG & DAYLY-DYING LIFE, WHICH BREATHS | DESCRIPTION RELIGIOUS HOUSE | 23 | 52 338 213 |
| BREATHES | | | |
| THAT BREATHES AT ONCE BOTH MAID AND MOTHER, | A HYMNE OF THE NATIVITY | 63 | 46 106 76 |
| THAT BREATHES AT ONCE BOTH MAID & MOTHER, | IN HOLY NATIVITY | 89 | 52 246 76 |
| GOOD REASON, FOR SHE BREATHES ALL FIRE, | TERESA | 39 | 52 315 52 |
| BREATHING | | | |
| THE TATLING STRINGS (EACH BREATHING IN HIS PART) | MUSICKS DUELL | 48 | 46 149 535 |
| OF ALL THE STRINGS, STILL BREATHING THE BEST LIFE | MUSICKS DUELL | 152 | 46 149 535 |
| LIFE-BREATHING | | | |
| FROM DEATH'S SAD SHADES, TO THE LIFE-BREATHING AYRE, | SOSPETTO D'HERODE | 81 | 46 109 216 |
| TH'HEART-BRED | | | |
| AND TH'HEART-BRED LUSTRE OF HIS WORTH, | HIS EPITAPH (HERRYS) | 37 | 46 172 471 |
| BREDD | | | |
| AMONGST THOSE LILLIES, WHICH HIS BOSOME BREDD. | AN ELEGY MR STANNINOW | 52 | MS 394 473 |
| BREED | | | |
| THY BLESSED EYES BREED SUCH DESIRE, | A SONG | 3 | 52 327 65 |
| NOR CAN I TELL (AND THIS NEW TEARES DOTH BREED) | ALEXIAS FIRST ELEGIE | 7 | 52 334 204 |
| HUGE HIGH-FLOUNE POYSONS, EV'N OF COLCHOS BREED, | HORATIJ ILLE & NEFASTO | 11 | MS 382 530 |
| BRIDALL | | | |
| BECAUSE THAT FROM THE BRIDALL CHEEKE OF BLISSE, | ON HOPE | 37 | 46 143 71 |
| BECAUSE THAT FROM THE BRIDALL CHEEK OF BLISSE | (ON) HOPE | 17 | 52 345 71 |
| BRIDE | | | |
| MORE SWEETLY SHOWES THE BLUSHING BRIDE. | IN PRAISE OF LESSIUS | 30 | 46 156 510 |
| BRITTAINE, THE MIGHTY OCEANS LOVELY BRIDE, | UPON YORKE HIS BIRTH | 1 | 46 176 500 |
| NOR DOE EMBRACES ONELY MAKE A BRIDE. | ALEXIAS THIRD ELEGIE | 28 | 52 336 209 |
| MORE SWEETLY SHOWES THE BLUSHING BRIDE. | TEMPERANCE | 28 | 52 342 510 |
| BRIDES | | | |
| AS THE COY BRIDES, WHEN NIGHT | WISHES SUPPOSED MISTRESSE | 71 | 46 195 479 |
| BRIDEGROOM | | | |
| BUT IF THE NOBLE BRIDEGROOM, WHEN HE COME, | PRAYER TO GENTLE-WOMAN | 47 | 52 328 139 |
| THE LUSTY BRIDEGROOM MADE APPROACH. YOUNG MAN, | ALEXIAS THIRD ELEGIE | 33 | 52 336 209 |
| BRIDEGROOM'S | | | |
| THE CHILDREN'S BREAD. THE BRIDEGROOM'S WINE. | LAUDA SION SALVATOREM | 63 | 52 294 178 |
| BRIDEGROME | | | |
| BUT IF THE NOBLE BRIDEGROME WHEN HEE COMES | ON A PRAYER BOOKE | 41 | 46 126 139 |
| BRIDEGROOME | | | |
| AND BLUSHES AT THE BRIDEGROOME SUN. | WEEPER | 64 | 52 307 120 |
| BRIEFE | | | |
| IN BRIEFE, IF ANY ONE WERE FREE, | ANOTHER ON HERRYS | 53 | 46 170 469 |
| BRIGHT | | | |
| THROUGH WHICH ALL HER BRIGHT FEATURES SHINE. | IN PRAISE OF LESSIUS | 26 | 46 156 510 |
| SNATCH'T HER SELF HENCE, TO HEAVEN. FILL'D A BRIGHT PLACE, | UPON BISHOP ANDREWES PICTURE | 9 | 46 163 490 |
| WHEN SOME NEW BRIGHT GUEST | THE WEEPER | 31 | 46 79 120 |
| WHAT BRIGHT SOFT THING IS THIS. | THE TEARE | 1 | 46 84 50 |
| AND ONE OF THEIR BRIGHT CHORUS MAKE THEE. | THE TEARE | 42 | 46 84 50 |
| TELL ME BRIGHT BOY, TELL ME MY GOLDEN LAD, | ON THE PRODIGALL | 1 | 46 86 17 |
| SHOW ME HIMSELFE, HIMSELFE (BRIGHT SIR) O SHOW | COME SEE WHERE THE LORD LAY | 1 | 46 87 27 |
| BRIGHT EVER WITH A BEAME THAT FALLS | PSALME 23 | 64 | 46 102 5 |
| BRIGHT DAWNE OF OUR ETERNALL DAY. | A HYMNE OF THE NATIVITY | 30 | 46 106 76 |
| NOR NEEDS MY MUSE A BLUSH, OR THESE BRIGHT FLOWERS | SOSPETTO D'HERODE | 17 | 46 109 216 |
| THEE ALL THE BEAUTIES OF THY ONCE BRIGHT EYES. | SOSPETTO D'HERODE | 74 | 46 109 216 |
| HOW LOW THE BRIGHT YOUTH BOW'D, AND WITH WHAT AWE | SOSPETTO D'HERODE | 99 | 46 109 216 |
| HOW BRIGHT A DAWNE OF ANGELS WITH NEW LIGHT | SOSPETTO D'HERODE | 115 | 46 109 216 |
| THE GOLDEN EYES OF NIGHT. WHOSE BEAME MADE BRIGHT | SOSPETTO D'HERODE | 131 | 46 109 216 |
| HEE HAS MY HEAVEN (WHAT WOULD HE MORE.) WHOSE BRIGHT | SOSPETTO D'HERODE | 209 | 46 109 216 |

PAGE 47

| | | | | |
|---|---|---|---|---|
| BOW OUR BRIGHT HEADS, BEFORE A KING OF CLAY. | SOSPETTO D'HERODE | 220 | 46 109 | 216 |
| MUST THE BRIGHT ARMES OF HEAV'N, REBUKE THESE EYES. | SOSPETTO D'HERODE | 231 | 46 109 | 216 |
| AND NOW HIS DREAM (HELS FIREBRAND) STIL MORE BRIGHT, | SOSPETTO D'HERODE | 503 | 46 109 | 216 |
| LET CONSTANT USE BUT KEEP IT BRIGHT, | ON A PRAYER BOOKE | 16 | 46 126 | 139 |
| BEATS BRIGHT UPON THE BURNING FACES | IN MEMORY OF LADY MADRE TERESA | 85 | 46 131 | 52 |
| MISTRESSE ATTENDED BY SUCH BRIGHT | IN MEMORY OF LADY MADRE TERESA | 125 | 46 131 | 52 |
| AND THY PAINS SET BRIGHT UPON THEE. | IN MEMORY OF LADY MADRE TERESA | 147 | 46 131 | 52 |
| THY WOUNDS SHALL BLUSH TO SUCH BRIGHT SCARRES, | IN MEMORY OF LADY MADRE TERESA | 154 | 46 131 | 52 |
| WHOSE LIGHT SHALL LIVE BRIGHT, IN THY FACE | IN MEMORY OF LADY MADRE TERESA | 164 | 46 131 | 52 |
| HEAVEN KEEPS UPON THY SCORE (THY BRIGHT | IN MEMORY OF LADY MADRE TERESA | 176 | 46 131 | 52 |
| THUS HAVE I BACK AGAINE TO THY BRIGHT NAME | AN APOLOGIE FOR HYMNE (TERESA) | 1 | 46 136 | 59 |
| HEAV'N SET THEE DOWN NEW DREST. WHEN THY BRIGHT BIRTH | ON A TREATISE OF CHARITY | 5 | 46 137 | 69 |
| GIRT ROUND THY AWFULL ALTARS, WITH BRIGHT WINGS | ON A TREATISE OF CHARITY | 22 | 46 137 | 69 |
| OF THE BRIGHT YOUTH OF HEAVEN, THAT SINGS | ON THE ASSUMPTION | 24 | 46 139 | 114 |
| TO NONE BUT THE BLEST HEAVENS, WHOSE BRIGHT | ON THE ASSUMPTION | 32 | 46 139 | 114 |
| LIVE RAREST PRINCESSE, AND MAY THE BRIGHT | ON THE ASSUMPTION | 55 | 46 139 | 114 |
| LET HIM EMBRACE HIS OWNE BRIGHT TRESSES, | AN HIMNE FOR CIRCUMCISION | 21 | 46 141 | 37 |
| WITH ROSIE WINGS SO RICHLY BRIGHT, | UPON DEATH OF DESIRED HERRYS | 49 | 46 168 | 467 |
| OF NOONE WEARE THEIR OWNE SUNSHINE. O THOU BRIGHT | UPON YORKE HIS BIRTH | 76 | 46 176 | 500 |
| PARDON (BRIGHT EXCELLENCE) AN UNTUN'D STRING. | UPON YORKE HIS BIRTH | 106 | 46 176 | 500 |
| HEE'L FAN HER BRIGHT LOCKS TEACHING THEM TO FLOW, | ON A FOULE MORNING | 19 | 46 181 | 495 |
| BRIGHT CLOUDS LIKE GOLDEN FLEECES SHALL BE SPREAD. | ON A FOULE MORNING | 26 | 46 181 | 495 |
| BRIGHT LADY OF THE MORNE, PITTY DOTH LYE | TO THE MORNING | 33 | 46 183 | 497 |
| ONE BRIGHT SMILE TO CLEERE THE WEATHER. | OUT OF THE ITALIAN (1) | 27 | 46 188 | 545 |
| BURNE IN THY IMITATION BRIGHT. | AN EPITAPH UPON ASHTON | 32 | 46 192 | 464 |
| OF GEMS, THAT IN THEIR BRIGHT SHADES PLAY. | WISHES SUPPOSED MISTRESSE | 51 | 46 195 | 479 |
| CAN MAKE DAYES FOREHEAD BRIGHT. | WISHES SUPPOSED MISTRESSE | 95 | 46 195 | 479 |
| THE HIGH-BORN BROOD OF DAY. YOU BRIGHT | TO THE NAME OF JESUS | 7 | 52 239 | 30 |
| THE SAME BRIGHT BUSYNES (YE THIRD HEAVENS) WITH YOU. | TO THE NAME OF JESUS | 110 | 52 239 | 30 |
| COME, LOVELY NAME. APPEAR FROM FORTH THE BRIGHT | TO THE NAME OF JESUS | 115 | 52 239 | 30 |
| THE BIRTH OF OUR BRIGHT JOYES. | TO THE NAME OF JESUS | 164 | 52 239 | 30 |
| BRIGHT DAWN OF OUR AETERNALL DAY. | IN HOLY NATIVITY | 73 | 52 246 | 76 |
| ROB THE RICH BIRTHS OF EACH BRIGHT NEST | NEW YEAR'S DAY | 19 | 52 251 | 37 |
| LET HIM EMBRACE HIS OWN BRIGHT TRESSES | NEW YEAR'S DAY | 21 | 52 251 | 37 |
| THAT BREAKES FROM ONE OF THESE BRIGHT EYES. | NEW YEAR'S DAY | 28 | 52 251 | 37 |
| BRIGHT BABE. WHOSE AWFULL BEAUTYES MAKE | IN GLORIOUS EPIPHANIE | 1 | 52 253 | 39 |
| LOST IN A BRIGHT | IN GLORIOUS EPIPHANIE | 16 | 52 253 | 39 |
| BRIGHT IDOL. BLACK IDOLATRY. | IN GLORIOUS EPIPHANIE | 51 | 52 253 | 39 |
| MORE DESPERATELY DARK, BECAUSE MORE BRIGHT. | IN GLORIOUS EPIPHANIE | 59 | 52 253 | 39 |
| AND SMIL'D I'TH' BABE'S BRIGHT FACE. THE PURPLING BUD | TO THE QUEEN'S MAJESTY | 5 | 52 261 | 47 |
| WITH YOUR BRIGHT HEAD WHOLE GROVES OF SCEPTERS BEND | TO THE QUEEN'S MAJESTY | 17 | 52 261 | 47 |
| THINE ARMES. AND WITH THY BRIGHT & BLISFULL HEAD | OFFICE H. CROSS EVENSONG | 21 | 52 273 | 101 |
| BURN ALL AS BRIGHT, | CHARITAS NIMIA | 22 | 52 280 | 48 |
| WHICH ON HIS WHITE BROWES THIS BRIGHT DAY | LAUDA SION SALVATOREM | 17 | 52 294 | 178 |
| O THAT BOOK. WHOSE LEAVES SO BRIGHT | DIES IRAE | 17 | 52 298 | 186 |
| OF THE BRIGHT YOUTH OF HEAVN, THAT SINGS | IN GLORIOUS ASSUMPTION B. LADY | 39 | 52 304 | 114 |
| LIVE, ROSY PRINCESSE, LIVE. AND MAY THE BRIGHT | IN GLORIOUS ASSUMPTION B. LADY | 60 | 52 304 | 114 |
| WHEN SOME NEW BRIGHT GUEST | WEEPER | 67 | 52 307 | 120 |
| SAY, YE BRIGHT BROTHERS, | WEEPER | 163 | 52 307 | 120 |
| BEATES BRIGHT UPON THE BURNING FACES | TERESA | 85 | 52 315 | 52 |
| MISTRESSE, ATTENDED BY SUCH BRIGHT | TERESA | 124 | 52 315 | 52 |
| AND THY PAINES SITT BRIGHT UPON THEE | TERESA | 146 | 52 315 | 52 |
| THY WOUNDS SHALL BLUSH TO SUCH BRIGHT SCARRES | TERESA | 153 | 52 315 | 52 |
| WHOSE LIGHT SHALL LIVE BRIGHT IN THY FACE | TERESA | 163 | 52 315 | 52 |
| HEAV'N KEEPS UPON THY SCORE. (THY BRIGHT | TERESA | 175 | 52 315 | 52 |
| THUS HAVE I BACK AGAIN TO THY BRIGHT NAME | AN APOLOGIE FOR (TERESA) HYMNE | 1 | 52 322 | 59 |
| FIRE FROM THE BURNING CHEEKS OF THAT BRIGHT BOOKE | FLAMING HEART | 28 | 52 324 | 61 |
| HIS BE THE BRAVERY OF ALL THOSE BRIGHT THINGS, | FLAMING HEART | 65 | 52 324 | 61 |
| LET CONSTANT USE BUT KEEP IT BRIGHT, | PRAYER TO GENTLE-WOMAN | 22 | 52 328 | 139 |
| THE BRIGHT AMBROSIALL NEST. | TO SAME CONCERNING CHOISE | 52 | 52 331 | 66 |
| O BURN OUR HYMEN BRIGHT IN SUCH HIGH FLAME. | ALEXIAS THIRD ELEGIE | 49 | 52 336 | 209 |
| THROUGH WHICH ALL HER BRIGHT FEATURES SHINE. | TEMPERANCE | 24 | 52 342 | 510 |
| SHALL HANG THE ROOME, & FOR YOUR TAPERS BRIGHT, | UPON GUNPOWDER TREASON | 25 | MS 387 | 461 |
| IN THIS BLEST EARTH HEAVENS BRIGHT EPITOME, | UPON KINGS CORONATION | 12 | MS 389 | 454 |
| THE LUSTRE OF HIS FACE DID SHINE SOE BRIGHT, | UPON KINGS CORONATION | 33 | MS 390 | 453 |
| BRIGHT STARRE OF MAJESTY, OH SHEDD ON MEE | UPON BIRTH PRINCESSE E | 1 | MS 391 | 456 |
| OF SUCH BRIGHT ANGELLS, THAT GIVE US MORE. | UPON BIRTH PRINCESSE E | 26 | MS 391 | 456 |
| BRIGHT GODDESSE, (WHETHER JOVE THY FATHER BE, | EX EUPHORMIONE | 1 | MS 392 | 525 |
| WHICH THEIR BRIGHT FATHER IN A PRETIOUS SHOWRE | AN ELEGY MR STANNINOW | 9 | MS 394 | 473 |
| IN A BRIGHT CHRISTALL TIDE, TO THEE THEY TEND, | AN ELEGIE ON DR PORTER | 40 | MS 395 | 476 |

TOO-BRIGHT

| | | | | |
|---|---|---|---|---|
| AND AS BEFORE HIS TOO-BRIGHT EYE | IN GLORIOUS EPIPHANIE | 168 | 52 253 | 39 |

BRIGHTER

| | | | | |
|---|---|---|---|---|
| THIS FLAME THUS QUENCH'T HATH BRIGHTER BEAMES. | SHE BEGAN TO WASH HIS FEET | 3 | 46 97 | 13 |
| A PEECE OF HEAVENLY LIGHT PURER AND BRIGHTER | ON THE ASSUMPTION | 3 | 46 139 | 114 |
| BRIGHTER HOPES THEN HE CAN SHEW. | UPON DEATH OF DESIRED HERRYS | 18 | 46 168 | 467 |
| SOMTHING A BRIGHTER SHADOW (SWEET) OF THEE. | IN GLORIOUS EPIPHANIE | 249 | 52 253 | 39 |
| A PIECE OF HEAV'NLY EARTH. PURER & BRIGHTER | IN GLORIOUS ASSUMPTION B. LADY | 3 | 52 304 | 114 |

BRIGHTEST

| | | | | |
|---|---|---|---|---|
| IN HER BRIGHTEST MAJESTY, | THE WEEPER | 50 | 46 79 | 120 |
| BRIGHTEST SOL THAT DYES TO DAY | OUT OF CATULLUS | 4 | 46 194 | 523 |
| RISE, THOU BEST & BRIGHTEST MORNING. | NEW YEAR'S DAY | 1 | 52 251 | 37 |
| IN HER BRIGHTEST MAJESTY | WEEPER | 38 | 52 307 | 120 |

BRIGHTNESSE

| | | | | |
|---|---|---|---|---|
| SUCH WAS THE BRIGHTNESSE OF THIS NORTHERNE STARRE, | UPON KINGS CORONATION | 29 | MS 390 | 453 |

## BRIM

| | | | |
|---|---|---|---|
| WHICH MIXT WITH GALL & BLOOD THEY QUAFFE BRIM FULL. | SOSPETTO D'HERODE | 336 | 46 109 216 |

## BRIM-FILL'D

| | | | |
|---|---|---|---|
| BY ALL THY BRIM-FILL'D BOWLES OF FEIRCE DESIRE | FLAMING HEART | 99 | 52 324 61 |

## BRIMS

| | | | |
|---|---|---|---|
| HOW MY CUP ORELOOKS HER BRIMS. | PSALME 23 | 56 | 46 102 5 |

## BRING

| | | | |
|---|---|---|---|
| CEASE HIM, BRING HIM, (BUT FIRST BIND HIM) | OUT OF GREEKE CUPID'S CRYER | 58 | 46 159 519 |
| A PILLOW FOR THEE WILL I BRING. | THE TEARE | 35 | 46 84 50 |
| 'TIS CHANG'D INDEED, DID AUTUMN E'RE SUCH BEAUTIES BRING | UPON THORNES FROM LORDS HEAD | 3 | 46 96 23 |
| WATER'D BY THE SHOWRES THEY BRING. | ON BLEEDING WOUNDS OF LORD | 21 | 46 101 110 |
| I SAW TH'OFFICIOUS ANGELS BRING. | A HYMNE OF THE NATIVITY | 41 | 46 106 76 |
| WEE'L BRING THE FIRST-BORNE OF HER FLOWERS. | A HYMNE OF THE NATIVITY | 79 | 46 106 76 |
| EACH OF US HIS LAMB WILL BRING, | A HYMNE OF THE NATIVITY | 85 | 46 106 76 |
| OTHER THEN WHAT THEIR OWNE BLEST BEAUTIES BRING. | SOSPETTO D'HERODE | 18 | 46 109 216 |
| THAT NEITHER ROME, NOR ATHENS CAN BRING FORTH | SOSPETTO D'HERODE | 27 | 46 109 216 |
| SHEE ROSE, AND WITH HER TO OUR WORLD DID BRING, | SOSPETTO D'HERODE | 373 | 46 109 216 |
| AND BRING HOME ON THY BREST MORE THANKLESSE SCARRS. | SOSPETTO D'HERODE | 448 | 46 109 216 |
| AND BRING HER BOSOME FULL OF BLESSINGS. | ON A PRAYER BOOKE | 35 | 46 126 139 |
| OF THE DEARE SPOWSE OF SPIRITS WITH THEM WILL BRING. | ON A PRAYER BOOKE | 78 | 46 126 139 |
| MEE EVER INTO THESE HIS CELLARS BRING. | AN APOLOGIE FOR HYMNE (TERESA) | 38 | 46 136 59 |
| AND THINE OWNE BEAMES ABOUT THEE. BRING THE BEST | ON A TREATISE OF CHARITY | 9 | 46 137 69 |
| TO BRING A PAIRE OF MEEK AND HUMBLE EYES. | ON A TREATISE OF CHARITY | 48 | 46 137 69 |
| AMONG HIS BRANCHES. YEA, AND VOW'D TO BRING | UPON DEATH OF HERRYS | 12 | 46 167 466 |
| BRING THEIR HEAVEN WITH THEM, THEIR GREAT FOOTSTEPS PLACE | UPON YORKE HIS BIRTH | 19 | 46 176 500 |
| HER HAND TO BRING HIM TO HIS END. | AN EPITAPH UPON ASHTON | 24 | 46 192 464 |
| BRING HITHER THY WHOLE SELF, & LET ME SEE | TO THE NAME OF JESUS | 17 | 52 239 30 |
| SHALL WE DARE THIS, MY SOUL. WE'L DOE'T AND BRING | TO THE NAME OF JESUS | 44 | 52 239 30 |
| BRING ALL YOUR HOUSHOLD STUFFE OF HEAVN ON EARTH, | TO THE NAME OF JESUS | 63 | 52 239 30 |
| BRING ALL THE STORE | TO THE NAME OF JESUS | 66 | 52 239 30 |
| BRING ALL THE POWRES OF PRAISE | TO THE NAME OF JESUS | 72 | 52 239 30 |
| BRING ALL YOUR LUTES & HARPS OF HEAVN & EARTH. | TO THE NAME OF JESUS | 74 | 52 239 30 |
| THAT YOU CAN BRING OR WE CAN CALL. | TO THE NAME OF JESUS | 81 | 52 239 30 |
| WE'L BRING THE FIRST-BORN OF HER FLOWRS | IN HOLY NATIVITY | 99 | 52 246 76 |
| EACH OF US HIS LAMB WILL BRING | IN HOLY NATIVITY | 105 | 52 246 76 |
| RUN, MARY, RUN. BRING HITHER ALL THE BLEST | OFFICE H. CROSS COMPLINE | 5 | 52 274 105 |
| AND URGE THE MURMURING GRAVES TO BRING | DIES IRAE | 11 | 52 298 186 |
| ME EVER INTO THESE HIS CELLARS BRING | AN APOLOGIE FOR (TERESA) HYMNE | 38 | 52 322 59 |
| AND BRING HIS BOSOM FRAUGHT WITH BLESSINGS, | PRAYER TO GENTLE-WOMAN | 41 | 52 328 139 |
| OF THE DEARE SPOUSE OF SPIRITS WITH THEM WILL BRING | PRAYER TO GENTLE-WOMAN | 84 | 52 328 139 |
| SUCH AS THE SACRED LIGHT THAT ERST DID BRING | ALEXIAS SECONDE ELEGIE | 27 | 52 335 207 |
| OH COME THEN. BRING THY MOTHER HER LOST JOY. | LUKE 2. QUAERIT JESUM | 15 | MS 379 11 |

## BRINGS

| | | | |
|---|---|---|---|
| THAT BRINGS HIM TO MEE, HEE SHALL SWIM | OUT OF GREEKE CUPID'S CRYER | 14 | 46 159 519 |
| OUR CROWN-LANDS LYE ABOVE, YET EACH MEALE BRINGS | ON HOPE | 33 | 46 143 71 |
| HEE TO WHOM OUR SORROW BRINGS, | ANOTHER ON HERRYS | 9 | 46 170 469 |
| NO NIMBLE RAPTURE STARTS TO HEAVEN AND BRINGS | TO THE MORNING | 20 | 46 183 497 |
| FAIR ONE, IT IS YOUR FATE. AND BRINGS | TO COUNTESSE OF DENBIGH | 53 | 52 236 146 |
| SOFT BACK. AND BRINGS A BOSOM BIG WITH LOVES. | TO THE NAME OF JESUS | 160 | 52 239 30 |
| WHILE YOUR EACH DAY'S DEVOTION DULY BRINGS | TO THE QUEEN'S MAJESTY | 27 | 52 261 47 |
| HIMSELF TO ME MY SAVIOVR BRINGS. | LAUDA SION SALVATOREM | 40 | 52 294 178 |
| OUR CROWN-LAND LYES ABOVE YET EACH MEAL BRINGS | (ON) HOPE | 13 | 52 345 71 |
| BROODETH THIS SACRED PLACE. HITHER PEACE BRINGS | UPON KINGS CORONATION | 22 | MS 389 454 |

## BRINGING

| | | | |
|---|---|---|---|
| BRINGING HIM NOTHING BUT NEW FEARES FROM TH'EAST, | SOSPETTO D'HERODE | 500 | 46 109 216 |
| IN STEAD OF BRINGING IN THE BLISSFULL PRIZE | IN GLORIOUS EPIPHANIE | 226 | 52 253 39 |

## BRISK

| | | | |
|---|---|---|---|
| A BRISK CHERUB SOMTHING SIPPES | WEEPER | 26 | 52 307 120 |

## BRISKE

| | | | |
|---|---|---|---|
| A BRISKE CHERUB SOMETHING SIPS | THE WEEPER | 26 | 46 79 120 |

## BRITTAINE

| | | | |
|---|---|---|---|
| BRITTAINE, THE MIGHTY OCEANS LOVELY BRIDE, | UPON YORKE HIS BIRTH | 1 | 46 176 500 |
| TH'AST NEED O BRITTAINE TO BE TRULY GREAT. | UPON YORKE HIS BIRTH | 16 | 46 176 500 |

## BROACH

| | | | |
|---|---|---|---|
| WITH MANNA, MILK, AND BALM, NEW BROACH THE MOUNTAINES. | SOSPETTO D'HERODE | 112 | 46 109 216 |

## BROAD-BEAM'D

| | | | |
|---|---|---|---|
| OUT-STARE THE BROAD-BEAM'D DAYES MERIDIAN) | ON FRONTISPIECE ISAACSONS | 10 | 46 191 491 |

```
                                                                                    PAGE   50


    BROKE

       WHEN THE BLEST SIGNES THOU BROKE SHALL SEE.         LAUDA SION SALVATOREM             55   52 294 178

    BROKEN

       WHAT IS LOVES SACRIFICE, BUT THE BROKEN HEART.      UPON FORD'S TRAGEDYES               2   46 181 495
       IN BROKEN FORMES A STABLE FAITH                     LAUDA SION SALVATOREM              59   52 294 178
       WELL STRUNG WITH MANY A BROKEN NERVE.               IN CICATRICES DOMINI JESU          14   MS 381  27
       THE BROKEN MEATE WAS MUCH MORE THEN THE WHOLE.      OUT OF GROTIUS                     64   MS 398 198

    BROOD

       AND THERE, AS MASTER OF THIS MURD'RING BROOD,       SOSPETTO D'HERODE                 318   46 109 216
       OF ONE COY PHOENIX, WHILE WE HAVE A BROOD           UPON YORKE HIS BIRTH               87   46 176 500
       A BROOD OF PHOENIXES.  WHILE WE HAVE BROTHER        UPON YORKE HIS BIRTH               88   46 176 500
       THE HIGH-BORN BROOD OF DAY.  YOU BRIGHT             TO THE NAME OF JESUS                7   52 239  30
       OF CERBERUS, OR ALECTO'S VIPEROUS BROOD.            UPON GUNPOWDER TREASON              4   MS 386 460
       THE BLOUD HOUND BROOD OF PRIESTS AGAINST MEE DRAW   OUT OF GROTIUS                     45   MS 398 198

    AFRICK-BROOD

       OR CHOICEST HENNES OF AFRICK-BROOD.                 PETRONIJ ALES PHASIACIS PETITA      2   MS 382 526

    BROODETH

       BROODETH THIS SACRED PLACE. HITHER PEACE BRINGS     UPON KINGS CORONATION              22   MS 389 454

    BROODING

       BROODING HORROR. COME THOU DEATH.                   PSALME 23                          39   46 102   5

    BROOKE

       A BROOKE WHOSE STREAME SO GREAT, SO GOOD,           AN EPITAPH DOCTOR BROOKE            1   46 175 465

    BROTHER

       HOW GODS ETERNALL SONNE SHOULD BE MANS BROTHER,     SOSPETTO D'HERODE                 165   46 109 216
       SEE, SEE THY REALL SHADOW. SEE THY BROTHER,         UPON YORKE HIS BIRTH               42   46 176 500
       A BROOD OF PHOENIXES.  WHILE WE HAVE BROTHER        UPON YORKE HIS BIRTH               88   46 176 500
       LOVE, BRAVE VERTUES YOUNGER BROTHER,                LOVES HOROSCOPE                     1   46 185 483
       BROTHER PEARLES, AND SISTER ROSES.                  OUT OF THE ITALIAN (1)             24   46 188 545
       AND SEEMS TO SAY, MAKE HASTE, MY BROTHER.           AGAINST IRRESOLUTION AND DELAY     44   52 347 146
       DRAW TO THIS SISTER MIRACLE A BROTHER.              UPON BIRTH PRINCESSE E             56   MS 391 456

    YONGER-BRUTHER

       NOR GRUDGE A YONGER-BRUTHER                         SANCTA MARIA DOLORUM               78   52 283 162

    BROTHERS

       SAY WATRY BROTHERS                                  THE WEEPER                        121   46  79 120
       OF BROTHERS MUTUALL BLOOD, AND FATHERS BRAINES.     SOSPETTO D'HERODE                 328   46 109 216
       JOSEPH THE KINGS DEAD BROTHERS SHAPE SHE TAKES,     SOSPETTO D'HERODE                 419   46 109 216
       THY BROTHERS BLOOD BE-SPILT LIFE SPENT IN VAINE.    SOSPETTO D'HERODE                 452   46 109 216
       'GAINST THY OWNE SONS AND BROTHERS THOU HAST STOOD  SOSPETTO D'HERODE                 453   46 109 216
       SAY, YE BRIGHT BROTHERS,                            WEEPER                            163   52 307 120

    BROUGHT

       LIFE, BROUGHT THEM FIRST TO KISSE THE LIGHT         IN MEMORY OF LADY MADRE TERESA    177   46 131  52
       LIFE BROUGHT THEM FIRST TO KISSE THE LIGHT          TERESA                            176   52 315  52
       AS TO REFRAINE) BROUGHT FORTH A COSTLY SHOWER       UPON KINGS CORONATION               6   MS 390 453

    BROUGHTST

       WHO BROUGHTST TO LIGHT                              OFFICE H. CROSS MATINES            22   52 265  86

    BROW

       WHEN ON A HILL (WHOSE HIGH IMPERIOUS BROW           THE BEGINNING OF HELIODORUS         3   46 158 517
       WITH HIS FOULE CLAWES HEE FENC'D HIS FURROWED BROW, SOSPETTO D'HERODE                 149   46 109 216
       THOU MAD'ST BOLD PROOFE UPON THE BROW OF HEAV'N,    SOSPETTO D'HERODE                 266   46 109 216
       (DISDAINFULL DUST AND ASHES) BEND THY BROW.         ON A TREATISE OF CHARITY           42   46 137  69
       OF PEACE AND WARRE.  THOU FOR WHOSE MANLY BROW      UPON YORKE HIS BIRTH               37   46 176 500
       THE BROW OF EVERY MONETH.  AND WHEN THAT'S DONE     UPON YORKE HIS BIRTH               98   46 176 500
       THY SILVER BROW, AND MEET THY GOLDEN LOVER.         ON A FOULE MORNING                 28   46 181 495
       TO SIT AND SCOULE UPON NIGHTS HEAVY BROW.           ON A FOULE MORNING                 34   46 181 495
       IN THE DEEPE WRINCKLES OF HIS ANGRY BROW.           TO THE MORNING                     31   46 183 497
       WRITE THESE LINES, READER, IN THY BROW.             AN EPITAPH UPON ASHTON             30   46 192 464
       AND SITT TRIUMPHING IN EACH CHEERFULL BROW.         UPON KINGS CORONATION              20   MS 389 454
       THE SULLEN HEAVEN HAD VAIL'D ITS MOURNFULL BROW     UPON KINGS CORONATION               2   MS 390 453

    BROWES

       THE THORNES THAT THY BLEST BROWES ENCLOSES          ON BLEEDING WOUNDS OF LORD         22   46 101 110
       TO BE THE SACRED HONOUR OF THY BROWES.              SOSPETTO D'HERODE                  16   46 109 216
       ABOUT THEIR SHADY BROWES IN WANTON RINGS.           SOSPETTO D'HERODE                  70   46 109 216
       WITH HER SOFT WING, WIPT FROM THE BROWES OF MEN     SOSPETTO D'HERODE                 387   46 109 216
       SHALL BUILD UP THY TRIUMPHANT BROWES.               IN MEMORY OF LADY MADRE TERESA    145   46 131  52
       SHALL FLOURISH ON THY BROWES.  AND BEE              IN MEMORY OF LADY MADRE TERESA    162   46 131  52
       EMBRACE THY RADIANT BROWES, O MAY THE BEST          ON THE ASSUMPTION                  57   46 139 114
```

|  |  |  |  |  |  |
|---|---|---|---|---|---|
| THAT HER WHOSE RADIANT BROWES, | WISHES SUPPOSED MISTRESSE | 107 | 46 | 195 | 479 |
| WHICH ON HIS WHITE BROWES THIS BRIGHT DAY | LAUDA SION SALVATOREM | 17 | 52 | 294 | 178 |
| EMBRACE THY RADIANT BROWES. O MAY THE BEST | IN GLORIOUS ASSUMPTION B. LADY | 62 | 52 | 304 | 114 |
| SHALL BUILD UP THY TRIUMPHANT BROWES. | TERESA | 144 | 52 | 315 | 52 |
| SHALL FLOURISH ON THY BROWES. & BE | TERESA | 161 | 52 | 315 | 52 |

BRUSH

|  |  |  |  |  |  |
|---|---|---|---|---|---|
| AND BRUSH HER AZURE MANTLE, WHICH SHALL SWIM | ON A FOULE MORNING | 24 | 46 | 181 | 495 |

BUBBLES

|  |  |  |  |  |  |
|---|---|---|---|---|---|
| OF FROTH & BUBBLES. WHAT TO LOOK FOR HERE. | TO SAME CONCERNING CHOISE | 9 | 52 | 331 | 66 |

BUBLING

|  |  |  |  |  |  |
|---|---|---|---|---|---|
| EVER BUBLING THINGS. | THE WEEPER | 3 | 46 | 79 | 120 |
| EVER BUBLING THINGS. | WEEPER | 3 | 52 | 307 | 120 |
| FEARE NOT TO DY WITH GREIFE. ALL BUBLING EYES | AN ELEGIE ON DR PORTER | 43 | MS | 395 | 476 |

EVER-BUBLING

|  |  |  |  |  |  |
|---|---|---|---|---|---|
| THAT EVER-BUBLING SPRING. THE SUGRED NEST | MUSICKS DUELL | 66 | 46 | 149 | 535 |

BUD

|  |  |  |  |  |  |
|---|---|---|---|---|---|
| A THOUSAND RUDDY HOPES SMIL'D IN EACH BUD. | UPON DEATH OF HERRYS | 25 | 46 | 167 | 466 |
| I'VE SEEN INDEED THE HOPEFULL BUD, | UPON DEATH OF DESIRED HERRYS | 31 | 46 | 168 | 467 |
| AND SMIL'D I'TH' BABE'S BRIGHT FACE. THE PURPLING BUD | TO THE QUEEN'S MAJESTY | 5 | 52 | 261 | 47 |
| THE HOPE AND PROMISE OF HIS BUD. | AGAINST IRRESOLUTION AND DELAY | 36 | 52 | 347 | 146 |

BUDS

|  |  |  |  |  |  |
|---|---|---|---|---|---|
| THE ROSE BUDS SWEET LIP KISSES. | THE TEARE | 21 | 46 | 84 | 50 |
| THESE PURPLE BUDS OF BLOOMING DEATH MAY BEE, | OUR LORD IN HIS CIRCUMCISION | 15 | 46 | 98 | 9 |
| THIS ROCKE BUDS FORTH THE FOUNTAINE OF THE STREAMES OF DAY. | EASTER DAY | 9 | 46 | 100 | 26 |
| THAT IN THEIR BUDS YET BLUSHING LYE. | A HYMNE OF THE NATIVITY | 68 | 46 | 106 | 76 |
| PEEP'T FROM THEIR BUDS, SHEW'D LIKE THE GARDENS EYES | UPON YORKE HIS BIRTH | 62 | 46 | 176 | 500 |

BUDDS

|  |  |  |  |  |  |
|---|---|---|---|---|---|
| AS WHEN THE ROSIE MORNE BUDDS INTO DAY. | ON FRONTISPIECE ISAACSONS | 14 | 46 | 191 | 491 |

BUILD

|  |  |  |  |  |  |
|---|---|---|---|---|---|
| SHALL BUILD UP THY TRIUMPHANT BROWES. | IN MEMORY OF LADY MADRE TERESA | 145 | 46 | 131 | 52 |
| ARABIA, THERE TO BUILD HER VIRGIN NEST. | UPON DEATH OF HERRYS | 14 | 46 | 167 | 466 |
| SHALL I BUILD HIS FUNERALL NEST. | LOVES HOROSCOPE | 50 | 46 | 185 | 483 |
| BABELS BOLD ARTISTS STRIVE (BELOW) TO BUILD | ON FRONTISPIECE ISAACSONS | 16 | 46 | 191 | 491 |
| OF THIS UNBOUNDED NAME BUILD YOUR WARM NEST. | TO THE NAME OF JESUS | 12 | 52 | 239 | 30 |
| SHALL BUILD UP THY TRIUMPHANT BROWES. | TERESA | 144 | 52 | 315 | 52 |

BUILDS

|  |  |  |  |  |  |
|---|---|---|---|---|---|
| THE PHAENIX BUILDS THE PHAENIX' NEST. | IN HOLY NATIVITY | 46 | 52 | 246 | 76 |

BUILT

|  |  |  |  |  |  |
|---|---|---|---|---|---|
| GOE SMILING SOULES, YOUR NEW BUILT CAGES BREAKE, | TO INFANT MARTYRS | 1 | 46 | 88 | 10 |
| OF THOSE WHOSE LARGE BREASTS BUILT A THRONE | IN MEMORY OF LADY MADRE TERESA | 10 | 46 | 131 | 52 |
| NO FORTRESSE BUILT FOR TRUE VIRGINITY. | ALEXIAS THIRD ELEGIE | 40 | 52 | 336 | 209 |

HIGH-BUILT

|  |  |  |  |  |  |
|---|---|---|---|---|---|
| IN HIGH-BUILT NUMBERS WAKES HIS GOLDEN LYRE. | HORATIJ ILLE & NEFASTO | 42 | MS | 382 | 530 |

BULKE

|  |  |  |  |  |  |
|---|---|---|---|---|---|
| HUGE EMPTINESSE CONTRACT THY BULKE, AND SHRINKE | UPON STANINOUGH'S DEATH | 13 | 46 | 175 | 475 |

BURDEN

|  |  |  |  |  |  |
|---|---|---|---|---|---|
| UNDER SO SWEET A BURDEN. GOE. | ON THE ASSUMPTION | 25 | 46 | 139 | 114 |
| A STILL INCREASING BURDEN. WORSE HATH TORNE | OUT OF GROTIUS | 12 | MS | 398 | 198 |

BURTHEN

|  |  |  |  |  |  |
|---|---|---|---|---|---|
| THY BURTHEN, TOO MUCH BEAUTY. | VEXILLA REGIS | 28 | 52 | 277 | 156 |
| UNDER SO SWEET A BURTHEN GOE. | IN GLORIOUS ASSUMPTION B. LADY | 40 | 52 | 304 | 114 |
| SHALL KISSE HIS GOLDEN BURTHEN. THOU, GLAD ISLE, | UPON KINGS CORONATION | 5 | MS | 389 | 454 |
| DRAGGING HIS CROOKED BURTHEN, LOOK'T AWRY, | AN ELEGY MR STANNINOW | 46 | MS | 394 | 473 |

HEAVEN-BURTHEN'D

|  |  |  |  |  |  |
|---|---|---|---|---|---|
| AND THOU (HEAVEN-BURTHEN'D BEAST) HAST NE'RE A WORD | UPON ASSE THAT BORE SAVIOUR | 7 | 46 | 90 | 19 |

BURIED

|  |  |  |  |  |  |
|---|---|---|---|---|---|
| NOW THE GRAVE LIES BURIED. | UPON SEPULCHRE OF OUR LORD | 2 | 46 | 86 | 26 |
| ALL THESE DELICIOUS HOPES ARE BURIED. | TO THE MORNING | 30 | 46 | 183 | 497 |

BURYED

  NOW THE GRAVE LYES BURYED.                        UPON THE H. SEPULCHER        2  52 277  26

BURYE'D

  QUICK BURYE'D IN THE WANTON TOMB             O GLORIOSA DOMINA           15  52 302 194

BURN

  BURN ALL AS BRIGHT,                               CHARITAS NIMIA             22  52 280  48
  O BURN OUR HYMEN BRIGHT IN SUCH HIGH FLAME.    ALEXIAS THIRD ELEGIE       49  52 336 209

BURNE

  WEE'L BURNE, OUR OWNE BEST SACRIFICE.         A HYMNE OF THE NATIVITY     88  46 106  76
  OF LOVE, BURNE BOTH TOGETHER.                 OUT OF THE ITALIAN (2)      14  46 190 547
  BURNE IN THY IMITATION BRIGHT.                AN EPITAPH UPON ASHTON     32  46 192 464
  LEAST IT BREAKE FORTH, & BURNE THY SOOTY CELL.  ON GUNPOWDER-TREASON       66  MS 384 458
  OF LOVES ALL-DARING HAND, THAT MAKES ME BURNE,  EX EUPHORMIONE             5  MS 392 525
  THE PHAENIX SELFE SHALL NOT MORE PROUDLY BURNE. EX EUPHORMIONE            15  MS 392 525
  AND MADE IT BURNE IN LOVE. 'TWAS NOT THE RAGE.  AN ELEGY MR STANNINOW      33  MS 394 473

BURNES

  HIGH, AND BURNES WITH SUCH BRAVE HEATS.       IN MEMORY OF LADY MADRE TERESA 36  46 131  52
  HIGH, & BURNES WITH SUCH BRAVE HEATES.        TERESA                         36  52 315  52

BURNING

  BEATS BRIGHT UPON THE BURNING FACES          IN MEMORY OF LADY MADRE TERESA 85  46 131  52
  BURNING, ONELY IN HIS LOVE.                  ANOTHER ON HERRYS          28  46 170 469
  BEATES BRIGHT UPON THE BURNING FACES         TERESA                         85  52 315  52
  FIRE FROM THE BURNING CHEEKS OF THAT BRIGHT BOOKE FLAMING HEART             28  52 324  61
  IN FLAMES, & OF A BURNING FEVER DY.          ON GUNPOWDER-TREASON       26  MS 384 458
  AND IN FELL HATRED BURNING, ANGRY DY.        UPON GUNPOWDER TREASON     16  MS 387 461
  A HEART BURNING IN LOVE. ALL DID ADORE        UPON KINGS CORONATION      37  MS 390 453

BURNT

  LIE SCATTER'D LIKE THE BURNT AND MARTYR'D BONES ON A TREATISE OF CHARITY    32  46 137  69
  BAK'T IN HOT SCORN, FOR A BURNT SACRIFICE.     ON A TREATISE OF CHARITY    44  46 137  69
  TILL BURNT AT LAST IN FIRE OF THY FAIR EYES,   IN HOLY NATIVITY         107  52 246  76

SUN-BURNT

  WORSE THEN SUN-BURNT IN HIS FIRE.            OUT OF GREEKE CUPID'S CRYER   56  46 159 519

SUN-BURN'T

  HIS SUPERFICIALL BEAMES SUN-BURN'T OUR SKIN.    IN GLORIOUS EPIPHANIE      75  52 253  39

BURNISH

  THE BURNISH OF NO SIN,                        WISHES SUPPOSED MISTRESSE    65  46 195 479

BURNISHT

  HEE FILLS A BURNISHT THRONE OF QUENCHLESSE FIRE. SOSPETTO D'HERODE         42  46 109 216
  BURNISHT IN HIS GLORIOUS BEAMES.             AN HIMNE FOR CIRCUMCISION    14  46 141  37
  BURNISHT IN HIS BEST BEAMES RISE.            NEW YEAR'S DAY              14  52 251  37

BURST

  TOUCHT WITH THE WORLDS TRUE ANTIDOTE TO BURST.  SOSPETTO D'HERODE        128  46 109 216

BUSY

  WHAT BUSY MOTIONS, WHAT WILD ENGINES STAND     SOSPETTO D'HERODE        441  46 109 216

BUSIE

  DEATH'S BUSIE SEARCH I'LE EASILY BEGUILE.      SICKE IMPLORE SHADOW        2  46  87  28
  LOSE THIS SAME BUSIE SPEAKING ART            PSALME 137                    20  46 104   7
  FROM WHENCE HEAV'N-LABOURING BEES WITH BUSIE WING, SOSPETTO D'HERODE        22  46 109 216
  WHERE ALL THE BUSIE DAY SHEE CLOSE DOTH LY.    SOSPETTO D'HERODE       386  46 109 216

BUSINESSE

  WAS THE GREAT BUSINESSE BOTH OF HEAV'N AND EARTH. SOSPETTO D'HERODE        120  46 109 216
  WITH ENDLESSE BUSINESSE ALMOST OUT OF BREATH.   SOSPETTO D'HERODE        320  46 109 216
  TH'HAST LEFT THE THIRD COUGH NOW NO BUSINESSE HERE. OUT OF MARTIALL          6  46 188 527
  EACH BIGGE WITH BUSINESSE THRUSTS THE OTHER,    AGAINST IRRESOLUTION AND DELAY 43  52 347 146

BUSYNES

  THEN THIS GREAT MORNINGS MIGHTY BUSYNES.       TO THE NAME OF JESUS       23  52 239  30
  THE SAME BRIGHT BUSYNES (YE THIRD HEAVENS) WITH YOU. TO THE NAME OF JESUS     110  52 239  30

BUSIRIS

  BUSIRIS HA'S HIS BLOODY ALTAR HERE,           SOSPETTO D'HERODE        355  46 109 216

## BUXOME

| | | | | | |
|---|---|---|---|---|---|
| AGAINE A FRESH CHILD OF THE BUXOME MORNE, | TO THE MORNING | 52 | 46 | 183 | 497 |

## BUY

| | | | | | |
|---|---|---|---|---|---|
| WHICH SPENT CAN BUY SO BRAVE A DEATH. | IN MEMORY OF LADY MADRE TERESA | 18 | 46 | 131 | 52 |
| WHICH SPENT CAN BUY SO BRAVE A DEATH. | TERESA | 18 | 52 | 315 | 52 |

## BUZZING

| | | | | | |
|---|---|---|---|---|---|
| AND MURMUR IN A BUZZING DINNE, THEN GINGLE | MUSICKS DUELL | 129 | 46 | 149 | 535 |

## CABINET

| | | | | | |
|---|---|---|---|---|---|
| THY BREASTS CHAST CABINET, AND UNCASE | IN MEMORY OF LADY MADRE TERESA | 72 | 46 | 131 | 52 |
| THE SELF-SHUTT CABINET OF AN UNSEARCHT SOUL. | TO COUNTESSE OF DENBIGH | 36 | 52 | 236 | 146 |
| UNLOCK THY CABINET OF DAY | TO THE NAME OF JESUS | 127 | 52 | 239 | 30 |
| THY, BREST'S CHAST CABINET, & UNCASE | TERESA | 72 | 52 | 315 | 52 |

## CABINETS

| | | | | | |
|---|---|---|---|---|---|
| ROB THE RICH STORE HER CABINETS KEEP, | AN HIMNE FOR CIRCUMCISION | 18 | 46 | 141 | 37 |
| SEARCH WHAT THE WORLD'S CLOSE CABINETS KEEP. | NEW YEAR'S DAY | 18 | 52 | 251 | 37 |

## CADENCE

| | | | | | |
|---|---|---|---|---|---|
| THEIR CADENCE IS RHETORICALL. | UPON THE DEATH OF A GENTLEMAN | 30 | 46 | 166 | 472 |
| THY TEARES JUST CADENCE STILL KEEPS TIME. | THE WEEPER | 104 | 46 | 79 | 120 |

## CAELESTIALL

| | | | | | |
|---|---|---|---|---|---|
| SOUND FORTH, CAELESTIALL ORGANS, LETT HEAVNS QUIRE | UPON KINGS CORONATION | 1 | MS | 389 | 454 |
| BUT SUCH IS THE CAELESTIALL EXCELLENCE, | UPON BIRTH PRINCESSE E | 33 | MS | 391 | 456 |

## CAESAR

| | | | | | |
|---|---|---|---|---|---|
| CAESAR CHALLENGES A DEBT. | GIVE TO CAESAR AND TO GOD | 2 | 46 | 96 | 20 |

## CAESAR'S

| | | | | | |
|---|---|---|---|---|---|
| WHAT EVER CAESAR'S PAYMENTS ARE. | GIVE TO CAESAR AND TO GOD | 4 | 46 | 96 | 20 |
| ALL WEE HAVE IS CAESAR'S TOO. | GIVE TO CAESAR AND TO GOD | 6 | 46 | 96 | 20 |
| ALL IS CAESAR'S. AND WHAT ODS | GIVE TO CAESAR AND TO GOD | 7 | 46 | 96 | 20 |
| SO LONG AS CAESAR'S SELFE IS GODS. | GIVE TO CAESAR AND TO GOD | 8 | 46 | 96 | 20 |
| TO MORE THEN CAESAR'S BIRTHRIGHT IS. | IN HOLY NATIVITY | 86 | 52 | 246 | 76 |

## CESAR

| | | | | | |
|---|---|---|---|---|---|
| BY HEROD LEIGE TO CESAR NOW WAS BORNE | SOSPETTO D'HERODE | 401 | 46 | 109 | 216 |

## CAESARS

| | | | | | |
|---|---|---|---|---|---|
| TO MORE THEN CAESARS BIRTHRIGHT IS. | A HYMNE OF THE NATIVITY | 60 | 46 | 106 | 76 |

## CAGES

| | | | | | |
|---|---|---|---|---|---|
| GOE SMILING SOULES, YOUR NEW BUILT CAGES BREAKE, | TO INFANT MARTYRS | 1 | 46 | 88 | 10 |

## CALCULATE

| | | | | | |
|---|---|---|---|---|---|
| TO CALCULATE HER YOUNG SONS YEARES. | LOVES HOROSCOPE | 4 | 46 | 185 | 483 |

## CALDRON-PRISON'D

| | | | | | |
|---|---|---|---|---|---|
| THE CALDRON-PRISON'D WATERS STREIGHT CONSPIRE, | SOSPETTO D'HERODE | 483 | 46 | 109 | 216 |

## CALL

| | | | | | |
|---|---|---|---|---|---|
| HORACE, SHRILL, AT ONCE, AS WHEN THE TRUMPETS CALL | MUSICKS DUELL | 54 | 46 | 149 | 535 |
| WHENCE THE FOURTH FURY, ANSWER'D PLUTO'S CALL. | SOSPETTO D'HERODE | 368 | 46 | 109 | 216 |
| O CALL THY SELFE HOME TO THY SELFE, WAKE, WAKE, | SOSPETTO D'HERODE | 459 | 46 | 109 | 216 |
| HIM THEY CALL THEIR VICE-APOLLO. | UPON DEATH OF DESIRED HERRYS | 12 | 46 | 168 | 467 |
| STAY BUT A LITTLE WHILE, UNTILL I CALL | UPON STANINOUGH'S DEATH | 5 | 46 | 175 | 475 |
| CALL HEAVEN TO LOOKE ON THEE WITH NARROW EYES. | UPON STANINOUGH'S DEATH | 16 | 46 | 175 | 475 |
| ANSWER MY CALL | TO THE NAME OF JESUS | 59 | 52 | 239 | 30 |
| THAT YOU CAN BRING OR WE CAN CALL. | TO THE NAME OF JESUS | 81 | 52 | 239 | 30 |
| THE BLINDNES OF THE WORLD DID CALL THE EYE. | IN GLORIOUS EPIPHANIE | 45 | 52 | 253 | 39 |
| THE COMPLIN HOUR COMES LAST, TO CALL | OFFICE H. CROSS COMPLINE | 1 | 52 | 274 | 105 |
| STRETCH ALL THY POWRES. CALL IF YOU CAN | LAUDA SION SALVATOREM | 3 | 52 | 294 | 178 |
| THE CAVES OF NIGHT ANSWER ONE CALL. | DIES IRAE | 16 | 52 | 298 | 186 |
| LET COME YE BLESSED THEN CALL ME. | DIES IRAE | 60 | 52 | 298 | 186 |
| AND CALL THE MAIDEN EVE THEIR MOTHER. | O GLORIOSA DOMINA | 26 | 52 | 302 | 194 |
| AND CALL THE SAINT THE SERAPHIM. | FLAMING HEART | 12 | 52 | 324 | 61 |
| STAY BUT A LITTLE WHILE, UNTILL I CALL | DEATH'S LECTURE | 5 | 52 | 340 | 475 |
| CALL HEAVN TO LOOK ON THEE WITH NARROW EYES. | DEATH'S LECTURE | 17 | 52 | 340 | 475 |
| AND KNOW THE CALL OF HEAV'N'S KIND SHOWERS. | AGAINST IRRESOLUTION AND DELAY | 34 | 52 | 347 | 146 |
| OR CALL HER CHEEKE A BED OF NEW BLOWNE ROSES. | UPON BIRTH PRINCESSE E | 45 | MS | 391 | 456 |
| WEE MUST THAT DISCORD SURELY CALL. | UPON DEATH OF A FREIND | 3 | MS | 393 | 477 |

## CALLED

| | | | | | |
|---|---|---|---|---|---|
| HARKE SHEE IS CALLED, THE PARTING HOURE IS COME, | ON THE ASSUMPTION | 1 | 46 | 139 | 114 |

## CALLD

| | | | | | |
|---|---|---|---|---|---|
| SHE'S CALLD. HARK, HOW THE DEAR IMMORTALL DOVE | IN GLORIOUS ASSUMPTION B. LADY | 7 | 52 | 304 | 114 |

## CALL'D

| | | | | | |
|---|---|---|---|---|---|
| SHEE'S CALL'D AGAINE, HARKE HOW TH'IMMORTALL DOVE | ON THE ASSUMPTION | 7 | 46 | 139 | 114 |
| SHEE'S CALL'D AGAINE, AND WILL SHEE GOE. | ON THE ASSUMPTION | 19 | 46 | 139 | 114 |
| CALL'D FOR AN UNTIMELY NIGHT, | UPON DEATH OF DESIRED HERRYS | 53 | 46 | 168 | 467 |
| WHEN AGE AND DEATH CALL'D FOR THE SCORE, | AN EPITAPH UPON ASHTON | 25 | 46 | 192 | 464 |
| AND BEE YEE CALL'D MY ABSENT KISSES. | WISHES SUPPOSED MISTRESSE | 15 | 46 | 195 | 479 |
| BUT CALL'D IT DEAW. | IN GLORIOUS EPIPHANIE | 128 | 52 | 253 | 39 |
| ONCE CALL'D A SUN. | IN GLORIOUS EPIPHANIE | 201 | 52 | 253 | 39 |
| THAT (AT THY COST) ARE CALL'D, NOT VAINLY, OURS | IN GLORIOUS EPIPHANIE | 220 | 52 | 253 | 39 |
| CALL'D PILAT UP, TO TRY IF HE | OFFICE H. CROSS PRIME | 3 | 52 | 267 | 91 |
| IF MY FOUL HEART CALL'D FOR A FLOUD. | CHARITAS NIMIA | 48 | 52 | 280 | 48 |
| HARK. SHE IS CALL'D, THE PARTING HOURE IS COME. | IN GLORIOUS ASSUMPTION B. LADY | 1 | 52 | 304 | 114 |
| SHE'S CALL'D AGAIN. AND WILL SHE GOE. | IN GLORIOUS ASSUMPTION B. LADY | 33 | 52 | 304 | 114 |
| WHO CALLS'T HIS CROWN TO BE CALL'D THINE, | WEEPER | 122 | 52 | 307 | 120 |
| WHEN LOVE OF US CALL'D HIM TO SEE | AGAINST IRRESOLUTION AND DELAY | 67 | 52 | 347 | 146 |
| WAS ONCE CALL'D THINE. | LUKE 2. QUAERIT JESUM | 26 | MS | 379 | 11 |

## CAL'D

| | | | | | |
|---|---|---|---|---|---|
| I CAL'D A HUNDRED MIRACLES TO TELL | OUT OF GROTIUS | 31 | MS | 398 | 198 |

## CALLS'T

| | | | | | |
|---|---|---|---|---|---|
| WHO CALLS'T HIS CROWN TO BE CALL'D THINE, | WEEPER | 122 | 52 | 307 | 120 |

## CALLS

| | | | | | |
|---|---|---|---|---|---|
| THE PLACE THAT CALLS YOU HENCE, IS AT THE WORST | TO INFANT MARTYRS | 5 | 46 | 88 | 10 |
| AT THOSE HARD WORDS MANS COWARDISE CALLS FEARES. | I AM READY NOT ONELY BOUND | 2 | 46 | 98 | 29 |
| WHEN CHRIST CALLS, AND THY NETS WOULD HAVE THEE STAY. | ON ST. PETER CASTING NETS | 3 | 46 | 98 | 13 |
| HEE CALLS HOME MY SOULE FROM DYING, | PSALME 23 | 18 | 46 | 102 | 5 |
| HE CALLS TO MIND TH'OLD QUARRELL, AND WHAT SPARKE | SOSPETTO D'HERODE | 89 | 46 | 109 | 216 |
| CALLS THEE BACK, AND BIDS THEE COME. | IN MEMORY OF LADY MADRE TERESA | 67 | 46 | 131 | 52 |
| HEAV'N CALLS HER, AND SHE MUST AWAY, | ON THE ASSUMPTION | 21 | 46 | 139 | 114 |
| BADG OF THY FAITH CALLS BACK THY CARE, | VEXILLA REGIS | 2 | 52 | 277 | 156 |
| HEAVN CALLS HER, & SHE MUST AWAY. | IN GLORIOUS ASSUMPTION B. LADY | 35 | 52 | 304 | 114 |
| CALLS THEE BACK, & BIDDS THEE COME | TERESA | 67 | 52 | 315 | 52 |
| CALLS YOU UP HIGHER | TO SAME CONCERNING CHOISE | 22 | 52 | 331 | 66 |

## CALM

| | | | | | |
|---|---|---|---|---|---|
| THE CALM THAT COOLS THINE EYE DOES SHIPWRACK MINE, FOR O. | AND A CERTAINE PRIEST PASSED | 3 | 46 | 94 | 17 |

## CAME

| | | | | | |
|---|---|---|---|---|---|
| REBOUNDING, THROUGH HELLS INMOST CAVERNES CAME, | SOSPETTO D'HERODE | 303 | 46 | 109 | 216 |
| AND CAME TO BETHLEM, WHERE THE CRUELL KING | SOSPETTO D'HERODE | 394 | 46 | 109 | 216 |
| WHENCE ALL HIS HIGH SPIRITS, AND HOT COURAGE CAME. | SOSPETTO D'HERODE | 488 | 46 | 109 | 216 |
| AND NOW OF LATE CAME TRIBUTARY KINGS, | SOSPETTO D'HERODE | 499 | 46 | 109 | 216 |
| WHO ROWZING HIS ILLUSTRIOUS TRESSES CAME, | TO THE MORNING | 11 | 46 | 183 | 497 |
| HOW LOVE CAME NAK'T, A BOY, AND BLIND. | OUT OF THE ITALIAN (3) | 2 | 46 | 190 | 549 |
| HE LEFT HIS FATHER'S COURT, AND CAME | AGAINST IRRESOLUTION AND DELAY | 69 | 52 | 347 | 146 |
| EACH VERTUE FOR A PART CAME IN. | UPON DEATH OF A FREIND | 20 | MS | 393 | 477 |
| STAY, SILVER-FOOTED CAME, STRIVE NOT TO WED | AN ELEGIE ON DR PORTER | 1 | MS | 395 | 476 |
| (FOR ELSE WHY CAME I.) EV'N WHAT E'RE I FEARE. | OUT OF GROTIUS | 8 | MS | 398 | 198 |

## CAMS'T

| | | | | | |
|---|---|---|---|---|---|
| WHO WAS THE CAUSE THOU CAMS'T THIS WAY. | DIES IRAE | 30 | 52 | 298 | 186 |

## CAMPANION

| | | | | | |
|---|---|---|---|---|---|
| NOW HAD THE NIGHT'S CAMPANION FROM HER DEN. | SOSPETTO D'HERODE | 385 | 46 | 109 | 216 |

## CANCELL'D

| | | | | | |
|---|---|---|---|---|---|
| HOW HATH ONE BLACKE ECLIPSE CANCELL'D, AND CROST | SOSPETTO D'HERODE | 75 | 46 | 109 | 216 |

## CANDID

| | | | | | |
|---|---|---|---|---|---|
| BUT DARES DESTRUCTION EATE THESE CANDID BREASTS, | UPON GUNPOWDER TREASON | 37 | MS | 387 | 461 |

## CANDIDATES

| | | | | | |
|---|---|---|---|---|---|
| CANDIDATES OF BLISSEFULL LIGHT, | TO THE NAME OF JESUS | 8 | 52 | 239 | 30 |

## CANOPY

| | | | | | |
|---|---|---|---|---|---|
| BE' A GLOOMY CANOPY TO PLUTO'S MINIONS. | UPON GUNPOWDER TREASON | 22 | MS | 387 | 461 |

CAPACIOUS

| | | | | | |
|---|---|---|---|---|---|
| WHERE HELLS CAPACIOUS CAULDRON IS SET ON. | SOSPETTO D'HERODE | 294 | 46 | 109 | 216 |

CAPACITY

| | | | | | |
|---|---|---|---|---|---|
| FATES CANNOT FIND OUT A CAPACITY | ON HOPE | 17 | 46 | 143 | 71 |
| FATES CANNOT FIND OUT A CAPACITY | (ON) HOPE | 7 | 52 | 345 | 71 |

CAPACITYE

| | | | | | |
|---|---|---|---|---|---|
| AS SITS ABOVE THY BEST CAPACITYE. | UPON YORKE HIS BIRTH | 8 | 46 | 176 | 500 |

CAPERS

| | | | | | |
|---|---|---|---|---|---|
| WITH NIMBLE CAPERS, & FORCE ATLAS TREAD | UPON KINGS CORONATION | 3 | MS | 389 | 454 |

CAPRING

| | | | | | |
|---|---|---|---|---|---|
| A CAPRING CHEEREFULLNESSE. AND MADE THEM SING | MUSICKS DUELL | 28 | 46 | 149 | 535 |

CAPTIVE

| | | | | | |
|---|---|---|---|---|---|
| THE CAPTIVE WORLD AWAK'T, & FOUND | OFFICE H. CROSS THIRD | 14 | 52 | 268 | 93 |
| AND OUR CAPTIVITY HIS CAPTIVE TA'NE. | OFFICE H. CROSS EVENSONG | 27 | 52 | 273 | 101 |

CAPTIV'D

| | | | | | |
|---|---|---|---|---|---|
| WHILE UNHAPPY CAPTIV'D WEE | PSALME 137 | 5 | 46 | 104 | 7 |

CAPTIVITY

| | | | | | |
|---|---|---|---|---|---|
| LAY FOLDED UP IN SLEEPES CAPTIVITY. | TO THE MORNING | 6 | 46 | 183 | 497 |
| AND OUR CAPTIVITY HIS CAPTIVE TA'NE. | OFFICE H. CROSS EVENSONG | 27 | 52 | 273 | 101 |
| OF HIS CAPTIVITY RINGS IN HIS EARES. | HORATIJ ILLE & NEFASTO | 29 | MS | 382 | 530 |

SELF-CAPTIVITY

| | | | | | |
|---|---|---|---|---|---|
| IN A COLD SELF-CAPTIVITY. | AGAINST IRRESOLUTION AND DELAY | 24 | 52 | 347 | 146 |

SELFE-CAPTIVITY

| | | | | | |
|---|---|---|---|---|---|
| IN A SAD SELFE-CAPTIVITY. | TO COUNTESSE OF DENBIGH | 24 | 52 | 236 | 146 |

CARCASSE

| | | | | | |
|---|---|---|---|---|---|
| UPON THIS CARCASSE OF A HARD, COLD, HART. | FLAMING HEART | 86 | 52 | 324 | 61 |

CARE

| | | | | | |
|---|---|---|---|---|---|
| LIFTS HIS MALIGNANT EYES, WASTED WITH CARE. | SOSPETTO D'HERODE | 83 | 46 | 109 | 216 |
| THOSE STINGS OF CARE THAT HIS STRONG HEART OPPREST. | SOSPETTO D'HERODE | 199 | 46 | 109 | 216 |
| (I CARE NOT WHITHER) | OUT OF THE ITALIAN (2) | 12 | 46 | 190 | 547 |
| WE WILL HAVE CARE | TO THE NAME OF JESUS | 112 | 52 | 239 | 30 |
| BADG OF THY FAITH CALLS BACK THY CARE. | VEXILLA REGIS | 2 | 52 | 277 | 156 |
| WITH HOLY CARE WILL KEEP IT BY US. | IN GLORIOUS ASSUMPTION B. LADY | 46 | 52 | 304 | 114 |
| MANS DAINTIEST CARE, & CAUTION CANNOT SPY | HORATIJ ILLE & NEFASTO | 17 | MS | 382 | 530 |

CARE'S

| | | | | | |
|---|---|---|---|---|---|
| HIS BREST A WHILE FROM CARE'S UNQUIET STING. | SOSPETTO D'HERODE | 396 | 46 | 109 | 216 |

CARES

| | | | | | |
|---|---|---|---|---|---|
| HEE LOST THE DAYES HEAT, AND HIS OWNE HOT CARES. | MUSICKS DUELL | 6 | 46 | 149 | 535 |
| RUNS TO AND FRO, COMPLAINING HIS SWEET CARES | MUSICKS DUELL | 142 | 46 | 149 | 535 |
| OF ALL THEIR CARES, TAM'D THE REBELLIOUS EYE | SOSPETTO D'HERODE | 390 | 46 | 109 | 216 |
| WITH WHICH HIS FEAV'ROUS CARES THEIR COLD INCREAST. | SOSPETTO D'HERODE | 502 | 46 | 109 | 216 |
| WITH HOLY CARES WILL KEEPE IT BY US. | ON THE ASSUMPTION | 43 | 46 | 139 | 114 |
| IN THE AETERNITY OF THY OLD CARES. | CHARITAS NIMIA | 32 | 52 | 280 | 48 |
| WITH LOYALL CARES. | SANCTA MARIA DOLORUM | 55 | 52 | 283 | 162 |
| NO CRUELL GUARD OF DILIGENT CARES, THAT KEEP | DESCRIPTION RELIGIOUS HOUSE | 28 | 52 | 338 | 213 |
| NOR CAN THE CARES OF HIS WHOLE CROWN | AGAINST IRRESOLUTION AND DELAY | 73 | 52 | 347 | 146 |
| AND STROAK'T THY CARES. | LUKE 2. QUAERIT JESUM | 32 | MS | 379 | 11 |

CARELESLY

| | | | | | |
|---|---|---|---|---|---|
| WITH PEARLY PAPERS CARELESLY BESETT. | AN ELEGIE ON DR PORTER | 6 | MS | 395 | 476 |

CARELESSE

| | | | | | |
|---|---|---|---|---|---|
| CAN'ST THOU BE CARELESSE NOW. NOW CAN'ST THOU SLEEP. | SOSPETTO D'HERODE | 456 | 46 | 109 | 216 |

CARRY

| | | | | | |
|---|---|---|---|---|---|
| EACH STRING HIS NOTE, AS IF THEY MEANT TO CARRY | MUSICKS DUELL | 146 | 46 | 149 | 535 |
| YET CARRY NOTHING THENCE AWAY. | WISHES SUPPOSED MISTRESSE | 39 | 46 | 195 | 479 |

CARRYED

| | | | | | |
|---|---|---|---|---|---|
| THUS CARRYED UP ON HIGH, | THE TEARE | 37 | 46 | 84 | 50 |

CARV'D
  WOULD HAVE A SONG CARV'D TO THEIR EARES            PSALME 137                          8   46 104    7
CARVES
  CARVES OUT HER DAINTY VOYCE AS READILY,            MUSICKS DUELL                      22   46 149  535
CASEMENTS
  HER RUBY CASEMENTS, OR HEREAFTER HOPE              IN GLORIOUS EPIPHANIE              70   52 253   39
  OFT HATH THIS HAND THOSE SILKEN CASEMENTS KEPT,    LUKE 2. QUAERIT JESUM              33   MS 379   11
CASKETS
  CASKETS, OF WHICH HEAVEN KEEPS THE KEYES.          THE WEEPER                         48   46  79  120
CAST
  THIS REVEREND SHADOW CAST THAT SETTING SUN,        UPON BISHOP ANDREWES PICTURE        1   46 163  490
  THE OTHER CAST AWAY, SHE ONELY GAVE.               WIDOWES MITES                       4   46  86   21
  TO CAST THY NETS ON ALL OCCASIONS WELL.            ON ST. PETER CASTING NETS           2   46  98   13
  TO CAST THEM WELL'S TO CAST THEM QUITE AWAY.       ON ST. PETER CASTING NETS           4   46  98   13
  TO CAST THEM WELL'S TO CAST THEM QUITE AWAY.       ON ST. PETER CASTING NETS           4   46  98   13
  AH WRETCH. WHAT BOOTES THEE TO CAST BACK THY EYES, SOSPETTO D'HERODE                 241   46 109  216
  NOR ON GODS ALTAR CAST TWO SCORCHING EYES          ON A TREATISE OF CHARITY           43   46 137   69
  CAST OFF DELAY.                                    ON THE ASSUMPTION                  15   46 139  114
  CAST AMOROUS GLANCES ON HIS BIRTH,                 LOVES HOROSCOPE                    27   46 185  483
  NOT TO BE CAST TO DOGGES, OR SWINE.                LAUDA SION SALVATOREM              64   52 294  178
  COME AWAY, MY DOVE. CAST OFF DELAY.                IN GLORIOUS ASSUMPTION B. LADY     14   52 304  114
  CAST BACK SOME AMOROUSE GLANCES ON THE CATES,      UPON GUNPOWDER TREASON             29   MS 387  461
CASTS
  THAT ON HER LAP SHE CASTS HER HUMBLE EYE.          ON VIRGINS BASHFULNESSE             1   46  89    9
CATARACTS
  THESE CATARACTS OF GREIFE, THAT DARE EV'N VIE      AN ELEGY MR STANNINOW              17   MS 394  473
CATCH
  TO CATCH THE DAY-BREAK OF THY DAWN,                TO THE NAME OF JESUS              148   52 239   30
  MY BREST MAY CATCH THE KISSE OF SOME KIND DART,    SANCTA MARIA DOLORUM               69   52 283  162
  AND CATCH THE PRETIOUS NAME THIS PEICE PRETENDS.   FLAMING HEART                       2   52 324   61
CATCHE
  AND CATCHE THY QUICK REFLEX, AND SHARPLY SEE       IN GLORIOUS EPIPHANIE             193   52 253   39
CATES
  CAST BACK SOME AMOROUSE GLANCES ON THE CATES,      UPON GUNPOWDER TREASON             29   MS 387  461
CAUCASUS
  TO FROZEN CAUCASUS HIS FLIGHT NOW TANE.            AN ELEGY MR STANNINOW               2   MS 394  473
CAUGHT
  CAUGHT IN A NET WHICH THERE APPOLLO SPREADS,       MUSICKS DUELL                     121   46 149  535
CAULDRON
  WHERE HELLS CAPACIOUS CAULDRON IS SET ON.          SOSPETTO D'HERODE                 294   46 109  216
CAUSES
  LOOKE HOW BELOW THY FEARES THEIR CAUSES ARE.       SOSPETTO D'HERODE                 522   46 109  216
CAUTION
  MANS DAINTIEST CARE, & CAUTION CANNOT SPY          HORATIJ ILLE & NEFASTO             17   MS 382  530
CAVERNES
  REBOUNDING, THROUGH HELLS INMOST CAVERNES CAME,    SOSPETTO D'HERODE                 303   46 109  216
CAVES
  THRICE HOWL'D THE CAVES OF NIGHT, AND THRICE THE   SOSPETTO D'HERODE                 297   46 109  216
                                           SOUND.
  THE CAVES OF NIGHT ANSWER ONE CALL.                DIES IRAE                          16   52 298  186
CEASE
  CEASE HIM, BRING HIM, (BUT FIRST BIND HIM)         OUT OF GREEKE CUPID'S CRYER        58   46 159  519
  PROUD WORLD, SAID I. CEASE YOUR CONTEST            IN HOLY NATIVITY                   44   52 246   76
  TRUTH BIDDES ME SAY, 'TIS TIME YOU CEASE TO TRUST  TO SAME CONCERNING CHOISE          18   52 331   66

## CECILIA

| | | | | | |
|---|---|---|---|---|---|
| CECILIA, GLORY OF HER NAME & BLOOD | ALEXIAS THIRD ELEGIE | 31 | 52 | 336 | 209 |

## CELL

| | | | | | |
|---|---|---|---|---|---|
| LEAST IT BREAKE FORTH, & BURNE THY SOOTY CELL. | ON GUNPOWDER-TREASON | 66 | MS | 384 | 458 |

## CELLS

| | | | | | |
|---|---|---|---|---|---|
| BEYOND THE KINGDOMES OF CONTENTFULL CELLS. | DESCRIPTION RELIGIOUS HOUSE | 35 | 52 | 338 | 213 |

## CELLARS

| | | | | | |
|---|---|---|---|---|---|
| MEE EVER INTO THESE HIS CELLARS BRING. | AN APOLOGIE FOR HYMNE (TERESA) | 38 | 46 | 136 | 59 |
| ME EVER INTO THESE HIS CELLARS BRING | AN APOLOGIE FOR (TERESA) HYMNE | 38 | 52 | 322 | 59 |

## CENTER

| | | | | | |
|---|---|---|---|---|---|
| THE FAIRE CENTER OF MY MIND | PSALME 23 | 62 | 46 | 102 | 5 |
| THERE WHERE ONE CENTER RECONCILES ALL THINGS. | SOSPETTO D'HERODE | 34 | 46 | 109 | 216 |
| THAT IN THE CENTER OF HIS BREST | HIS EPITAPH (HERRYS) | 17 | 46 | 172 | 471 |
| CENTER OF THOSE THY GRANDSIRES, SHALL I SAY | UPON YORKE HIS BIRTH | 30 | 46 | 176 | 500 |
| IT'S SEAT YOUR SOUL'S JUST CENTER BE. | TO COUNTESSE OF DENBIGH | 56 | 52 | 236 | 146 |
| IN CENTER OF THEIR INMOST SOULES THEY WORE THEE. | TO THE NAME OF JESUS | 205 | 52 | 239 | 30 |
| THE CENTER SHOOK. HER USELESSE VEIL TH'INGLORIOUS TEMPLE TORE. | OFFICE H. CROSS NINTH | 8 | 52 | 271 | 99 |
| AND START FROM OFF THY CENTER. HATH HEAVENS LOVE | ON GUNPOWDER-TREASON | 5 | MS | 384 | 458 |
| FROM OF HER CENTER, HAD NOT JOVE UPHELD | UPON KINGS CORONATION | 10 | MS | 390 | 453 |

## CENTRING

| | | | | | |
|---|---|---|---|---|---|
| ALL-CIRCLING POINT. ALL CENTRING SPHEAR. | IN GLORIOUS EPIPHANIE | 26 | 52 | 253 | 39 |

## CERBERUS

| | | | | | |
|---|---|---|---|---|---|
| THE FOAMY LIPS OF CERBERUS) SHEE APPLY'D | SOSPETTO D'HERODE | 468 | 46 | 109 | 216 |
| OF CERBERUS, OR ALECTO'S VIPEROUS BROOD. | UPON GUNPOWDER TREASON | 4 | MS | 386 | 460 |

## CERTAIN

| | | | | | |
|---|---|---|---|---|---|
| CERTAIN HARD WORDS MADE INTO PILLS. | IN PRAISE OF LESSIUS | 8 | 46 | 156 | 510 |
| O YOU, MY SOUL'S MOST CERTAIN WINGS. | TO THE NAME OF JESUS | 64 | 52 | 239 | 30 |
| THOU'HAST SAV'D THE WORLD FROM CERTAIN LOSSE. | OFFICE H. CROSS SIXT | 24 | 52 | 270 | 97 |
| THOU'HAST SAV'D THE WORLD FROM CERTAIN LOSSE. | OFFICE H. CROSS EVENSONG | 31 | 52 | 273 | 101 |
| CERTAIN HARD WORDS MADE INTO PILLS, | TEMPERANCE | 8 | 52 | 342 | 510 |

## CERTAINE

| | | | | | |
|---|---|---|---|---|---|
| THY SOFTER YET MORE CERTAINE DARTS | IN GLORIOUS EPIPHANIE | 78 | 52 | 253 | 39 |

## CERTAINTY

| | | | | | |
|---|---|---|---|---|---|
| SOME SOLACE IN MY SORROW'S CEPTAINTY | ALEXIAS FIRST ELEGIE | 10 | 52 | 334 | 204 |

## CHAINE

| | | | | | |
|---|---|---|---|---|---|
| OF STURDY ADAMANT IS HIS STRONG CHAINE. | SOSPETTO D'HERODE | 144 | 46 | 109 | 216 |
| FLEDG'D WITH HER EAGLES WING. THE VERY CHAINE | HORATIJ ILLE & NEFASTO | 28 | MS | 382 | 530 |

## CHALLENGE

| | | | | | |
|---|---|---|---|---|---|
| A CHALLENGE TO HIS END. | WISHES SUPPOSED MISTRESSE | 86 | 46 | 195 | 479 |

## CHALLENGES

| | | | | | |
|---|---|---|---|---|---|
| CAESAR CHALLENGES A DEBT. | GIVE TO CAESAR AND TO GOD | 2 | 46 | 96 | 20 |

## CHAMBERS

| | | | | | |
|---|---|---|---|---|---|
| STARRES IN THEIR HIGHER CHAMBERS. NEVER COU'D | OUT OF VIRGIL | 32 | 46 | 155 | 529 |

## CHANCE

| | | | | | |
|---|---|---|---|---|---|
| WHERESOE'RE YOU CHANCE TO FIND HIM | OUT OF GREEKE CUPID'S CRYER | 57 | 46 | 159 | 519 |
| THIS THY BLOODS DELUGE (A DIRE CHANCE | ON BLEEDING WOUNDS OF LORD | 37 | 46 | 101 | 110 |
| THIS THY BLOOD'S DELUGE, A DIRE CHANCE | UPON BLEEDING CRUCIFIX | 33 | 52 | 288 | 110 |
| OF FUTURE CHANCE. THE WORLD'S GRAND SIRE. AND MINE | OUT OF GROTIUS | 3 | MS | 398 | 198 |

## CHANGE

| | | | | | |
|---|---|---|---|---|---|
| OF SUCH A CHANGE, BUT THAT THE HEAV'NS INDULGENCE | OUT OF VIRGIL | 34 | 46 | 155 | 529 |
| (NOR CAN THE CHANGE OFFEND) | ON WOUNDS OF CRUCIFIED LORD | 18 | 46 | 99 | 24 |
| TO CHANGE HER FACES STILE SHE DOTH DEVISE, | SOSPETTO D'HERODE | 415 | 46 | 109 | 216 |
| WITH CHRISTS NAME INT IN CHANGE FOR DEATH. | IN MEMORY OF LADY MADRE TERESA | 50 | 46 | 131 | 52 |
| WAS EVER GUILTY OF, CHANGE WEE OUR SHAPE, | AN APOLOGIE FOR HYMNE (TERESA) | 34 | 46 | 136 | 59 |
| NOR CHANGE THE PASTURE, BUT THE PLACE | LAUDA SION SALVATOREM | 79 | 52 | 294 | 178 |
| WITH CHRIST'S NAME IN'T, IN CHANGE FOR DEATH. | TERESA | 50 | 52 | 315 | 52 |
| WAS EVER GUILTY OF, CHANGE WE TOO 'OUR SHAPE | AN APOLOGIE FOR (TERESA) HYMNE | 34 | 52 | 322 | 59 |
| THE NOTED SEA SHALL CHANGE HIS NAME WITH ME. | ALEXIAS FIRST ELEGIE | 23 | 52 | 334 | 204 |
| SOE SOONE CHANGE PART. | LUKE 2. QUAERIT JESUM | 4 | MS | 379 | 11 |
| THE SEA SHALL CHANGE HIS YOUTHFULL GREENE, & SLIDE | ON GUNPOWDER-TREASON | 33 | MS | 384 | 458 |

## CHANGD

| | | | | | |
|---|---|---|---|---|---|
| THEIR HATED LOVES CHANGD INTO WHOLSOM FEARES. | IN GLORIOUS EPIPHANIE | 161 | 52 | 253 | 39 |

## CHANG'D

| | | | | | |
|---|---|---|---|---|---|
| KNOW'ST THOU THIS, SOULDIER. 'TIS A MUCH CHANG'D PLANT, WHICH YE T | UPON THORNES FROM LORDS HEAD | 1 | 46 | 96 | 23 |
| 'TIS CHANG'D INDEED, DID AUTUMN E'RE SUCH BEAUTIES BRING | UPON THORNES FROM LORDS HEAD | 3 | 46 | 96 | 23 |
| WITH A CHANG'D COUNTENANCE WITNEST THE SIGHT, | SOSPETTO D'HERODE | 375 | 46 | 109 | 216 |
| AND CHANG'D HIS FALSE CROWN FOR THY CROSSE. | IN GLORIOUS EPIPHANIE | 142 | 52 | 253 | 39 |
| THEIR USE IS CHANG'D, NOT LOST. AND NOW THEY MOVE | VEXILLA REGIS | 17 | 52 | 277 | 156 |

## MUCH-CHANG'D

| | | | | | |
|---|---|---|---|---|---|
| KNOW'ST THOU THIS, SOULDIER. 'TIS A MUCH-CHANG'D PLANT WHICH YET | UPON CROWNE OF THORNS | 1 | 52 | 290 | 23 |

## CHANNELL

| | | | | | |
|---|---|---|---|---|---|
| THAT FROM SO SMALL A CHANNELL SHOULD BE RAIS'D | MUSICKS DUELL | 44 | 46 | 149 | 535 |

## CHANNELS

| | | | | | |
|---|---|---|---|---|---|
| THEIR LITTLE CHANNELS CAN DELIVER | ON BLEEDING WOUNDS OF LORD | 27 | 46 | 101 | 110 |

## CHANNELLS

| | | | | | |
|---|---|---|---|---|---|
| THEIR LITTLE CHANNELLS CAN DELIVER | UPON BLEEDING CRUCIFIX | 23 | 52 | 288 | 110 |
| IN AZURE CHANNELLS WARME THROUGH MOUNTS OF SNOW. | UPON GUNPOWDER TREASON | 42 | MS | 387 | 461 |

## CHANT

| | | | | | |
|---|---|---|---|---|---|
| CHANT TO MY SELFE WITH RUSTIC MELODIE. | UPON BIRTH PRINCESSE E | 24 | MS | 391 | 456 |
| THEIR SHACKLED TONGUES TO CHANT AN ELGIE. | AN ELEGIE ON DR PORTER | 36 | MS | 395 | 476 |

## CHAUNT

| | | | | | |
|---|---|---|---|---|---|
| TO CHAUNT MY PRAYSES IN A NEW-STRUNG SONG. | OUT OF GROTIUS | 74 | MS | 398 | 198 |

## CHAOS

| | | | | | |
|---|---|---|---|---|---|
| BUT WHEN THE WORLD FIRST OUT OF CHAOS SPRANG | OUT OF VIRGIL | 23 | 46 | 155 | 529 |
| READY TO DROPP INTO A CHAOS, ROUND | ON GUNPOWDER-TREASON | 20 | MS | 384 | 458 |

## CHAPPELL

| | | | | | |
|---|---|---|---|---|---|
| THE HOLY CHAPPELL OF CHAST LOVE | THOUGH NOW 'TIS NEITHER | 22 | MS | 397 | 492 |

## CHARACTER

| | | | | | |
|---|---|---|---|---|---|
| HIS GLOOMY BOSOMES DARKEST CHARACTER, | SOSPETTO D'HERODE | 194 | 46 | 109 | 216 |
| MY WISHES CLOUDY CHARACTER. | WISHES SUPPOSED MISTRESSE | 117 | 46 | 195 | 479 |
| DEFECTS I DRAW MINE OWNE DULL CHARACTER. | UPON TWO GREENE APRICOCKES | 32 | 48 | 220 | 494 |

## CHARACTERS

| | | | | | |
|---|---|---|---|---|---|
| SO MIGHTY WERE TH'AMAZING CHARACTERS | SOSPETTO D'HERODE | 477 | 46 | 109 | 216 |

## CHARGE

| | | | | | |
|---|---|---|---|---|---|
| OF STARS, THAT GUILD THE MORNE IN CHARGE WERE GIVEN. | SOSPETTO D'HERODE | 234 | 46 | 109 | 216 |
| TO BE AT CHARGE OF SUCH ANOTHER. | UPON DEATH OF DESIRED HERRYS | 24 | 46 | 168 | 467 |
| TAKE CHARGE OF ME, & OF MY END. | DIES IRAE | 68 | 52 | 298 | 186 |

## CHARG'D

| | | | | | |
|---|---|---|---|---|---|
| CHARG'D WITH A FLYING TOUCH, AND STREIGHTWAY SHEE | MUSICKS DUELL | 21 | 46 | 149 | 535 |
| CHARG'D TO LOOK ON, & WITH A STEDFAST EY | SANCTA MARIA DOLORUM | 37 | 52 | 283 | 162 |

## CHARGES

| | | | | | |
|---|---|---|---|---|---|
| HEE CHARGES TO BE QUIET, IT RUNS ROUND. | THE DUMBE HEALED | 2 | 46 | 87 | 16 |
| WHATSOE'RE THY CHARGES WERE. | ON WOUNDS OF CRUCIFIED LORD | 12 | 46 | 99 | 24 |

## CHARICLIA

| | | | | | |
|---|---|---|---|---|---|
| LO HERE THE FAIRE CHARICLIA, IN WHOM STROVE | UPON FAIRE ETHIOPIAN | 1 | 46 | 183 | 493 |

## CHARIOT

| | | | | | |
|---|---|---|---|---|---|
| THAT DRAW THE CHARIOT OF CHAST LOVES, | AGAINST IRRESOLUTION AND DELAY | 46 | 52 | 347 | 146 |

## CHARITIE

| | | | | | |
|---|---|---|---|---|---|
| THY HOLYEST, HUMBLEST, HANDMAID CHARITIE. | ON A TREATISE OF CHARITY | 14 | 46 | 137 | 69 |
| UNCHARITABLE EV'N TO CHARITIE. | ON A TREATISE OF CHARITY | 58 | 46 | 137 | 69 |

## CHARITIES

| | | | | | |
|---|---|---|---|---|---|
| AND FRUITFULL CHARITIES FULL BREASTS (OF OLD) | ON A TREATISE OF CHARITY | 55 | 46 | 137 | 69 |

## CHARLES

| | | | | | |
|---|---|---|---|---|---|
| GREAT CHARLES, THOU SWEET DAWNE OF A GLORIOUS DAY, | UPON YORKE HIS BIRTH | 29 | 46 | 176 | 500 |

## CHARME

| | | | | | |
|---|---|---|---|---|---|
| WAS NO WORD NOW BUT A CHARME. | HIS EPITAPH (HERRYS) | 32 | 46 | 172 | 471 |
| THE BLOOD, YET TEACH A CHARME. | WISHES SUPPOSED MISTRESSE | 62 | 46 | 195 | 479 |

## CHARMES

| | | | | | |
|---|---|---|---|---|---|
| VERTUES OF STONES, NOR HERBES, USE STRONGER CHARMES. | SOSPETTO D'HERODE | 274 | 46 | 109 | 216 |

## CHASE

| | | | | | |
|---|---|---|---|---|---|
| AND CHASE THE TREMBLING SHADES AWAY. | A HYMNE OF THE NATIVITY | 32 | 46 | 106 | 76 |
| TRUE HOPE'S A GLORIOUS HUNTRESSE, AND HER CHASE | ON HOPE | 89 | 46 | 143 | 71 |
| 'TIS SHEE, 'TIS SHEE. HER AWFULL BEAUTIES CHASE | UPON YORKE HIS BIRTH | 74 | 46 | 176 | 500 |
| FOUGHT AGAINST FROWNS WITH SMILES.  GAVE GLORIOUS CHASE | TO THE NAME OF JESUS | 199 | 52 | 239 | 30 |
| AND CHASE THE TREMBLING SHADES AWAY. | IN HOLY NATIVITY | 34 | 52 | 246 | 76 |
| AND CHASE THE TREMBLING SHADES AWAY. | IN HOLY NATIVITY | 75 | 52 | 246 | 76 |
| O PRIZE OF THE RICH SPIRIT.  WITH WHAT FEIRCE CHASE | IN GLORIOUS EPIPHANIE | 196 | 52 | 253 | 39 |
| WHEN GLORY'S SUN FAITH'S SHADES SHALL CHASE, | ADORO TE | 55 | 52 | 291 | 172 |
| TRUE HOPE'S A GLORIOUS HUNTER & HER CHASE. | (ON) HOPE | 49 | 52 | 345 | 71 |

## CHASES

| | | | | | |
|---|---|---|---|---|---|
| THOUGH THE VEXT CHYMICK VAINLY CHASES | ON HOPE | 85 | 46 | 143 | 71 |
| THOUGH THE VEXT CHYMICK VAINLY CHASES | (ON) HOPE | 45 | 52 | 345 | 71 |

## CHASTE

| | | | | | |
|---|---|---|---|---|---|
| LIVE OUR CHASTE LOVE, THE HOLY MIRTH | ON THE ASSUMPTION | 59 | 46 | 139 | 114 |
| HOPES CHASTE KISSE WRONGS NO MORE JOYES MAIDENHEAD, | ON HOPE | 39 | 46 | 143 | 71 |

## CHAST

| | | | | | |
|---|---|---|---|---|---|
| FROM A CHAST VIRGIN WOMBE, SHOULD BLESSE THE EARTH. | SOSPETTO D'HERODE | 160 | 46 | 109 | 216 |
| AND FORTIFIE THE HOLD OF YOUR CHAST HEART. | ON A PRAYER BOOKE | 14 | 46 | 126 | 139 |
| THOSE OF TURTLES, CHAST, AND TRUE. | ON A PRAYER BOOKE | 24 | 46 | 126 | 139 |
| LEAVING HER CHAST ABODE, | ON A PRAYER BOOKE | 43 | 46 | 126 | 139 |
| THY BREASTS CHAST CABINET, AND UNCASE | IN MEMORY OF LADY MADRE TERESA | 72 | 46 | 131 | 52 |
| THEN THE CHAST STARS, WHOSE CHOICE LAMPS COME TO LIGHT HER. | ON THE ASSUMPTION | 4 | 46 | 139 | 114 |
| CHAST AS THAT VIRGIN HONOUR OF THE EAST, | UPON YORKE HIS BIRTH | 83 | 46 | 176 | 500 |
| IN YOUR WHITE BOSOME HER CHAST BED. | THOUGH NOW 'TIS NEITHER | 6 | MS | 397 | 492 |
| THE HOLY CHAPPELL OF CHAST LOVE | THOUGH NOW 'TIS NEITHER | 22 | MS | 397 | 492 |
| WE GUILD THE HUMBLE CHEEK OF THIS CHAST PLACE. | IN GLORIOUS EPIPHANIE | 83 | 52 | 253 | 39 |
| AND IN THESE CHAST WARRES WHILE THE WING'D WOUNDS FLEE | SANCTA MARIA DOLORUM | 67 | 52 | 283 | 162 |
| SO LONG OF THIS CHAST VINE | SANCTA MARIA DOLORUM | 102 | 52 | 283 | 162 |
| THEN THE CHAST STARRES, WHOSE CHOISE LAMPS COME TO LIGHT HER | IN GLORIOUS ASSUMPTION B. LADY | 4 | 52 | 304 | 114 |
| LIVE, OUR CHAST LOVE, THE HOLY MIRTH | IN GLORIOUS ASSUMPTION B. LADY | 64 | 52 | 304 | 114 |
| O CHEEKS, BEDDS OF CHAST LOVES | WEEPER | 85 | 52 | 307 | 120 |
| THY BREST'S CHAST CABINET, & UNCASE | TERESA | 72 | 52 | 315 | 52 |
| AND FORTIFY THE HOLD OF YOUR CHAST HEART. | PRAYER TO GENTLE-WOMAN | 20 | 52 | 328 | 139 |
| THOSE OF TURTLES, CHAST & TRUE. | PRAYER TO GENTLE-WOMAN | 30 | 52 | 328 | 139 |
| LEAVING HER CHAST ABOAD | PRAYER TO GENTLE-WOMAN | 49 | 52 | 328 | 139 |
| WITTNESSE, CHAST HEAVNS, NO HAPPYER VOWES I KNOW | ALEXIAS THIRD ELEGIE | 25 | 52 | 336 | 209 |
| THE QUEEN OF ANGELS, (AND MEN CHAST AS YOU) | ALEXIAS THIRD ELEGIE | 29 | 52 | 336 | 209 |
| THAT CHAST & CHEAP, AS THE FEW CLOTHES WE WEARE. | DESCRIPTION RELIGIOUS HOUSE | 12 | 52 | 338 | 213 |
| HOPE'S CHAST STEALTH HARMES NO MORE JOYE'S MAIDENHEAD | (ON) HOPE | 19 | 52 | 345 | 71 |
| THAT DRAW THE CHARIOT OF CHAST LOVES, | AGAINST IRRESOLUTION AND DELAY | 46 | 52 | 347 | 146 |
| MY WOMBES CHAST PRIDE IS GONE, MY HEAV'NE-BORNE BOY. | LUKE 2. QUAERIT JESUM | 7 | MS | 379 | 11 |
| 'TWAS NOT THE CHAST, & PURER SNOW, WHOSE NEST | AN ELEGY MR STANNINOW | 35 | MS | 394 | 473 |

## CHASTEST

| | | | | | |
|---|---|---|---|---|---|
| A PHAENIX, & IN CHASTEST FLAMES OF LOVE | UPON GUNPOWDER TREASON | 34 | MS | 387 | 461 |

## CHASTIS'D

| | | | | | |
|---|---|---|---|---|---|
| TO BE CHASTIS'D (SWEET FRIEND) AND CHIDD BY THEE. | UPON TWO GREENE APRICOCKES | 2 | 48 | 220 | 494 |

## CHASTITY

| | | | | | |
|---|---|---|---|---|---|
| THAT CHASTITY SHALL TAKE NO HARME. | WISHES SUPPOSED MISTRESSE | 63 | 46 | 195 | 479 |
| MY CHASTITY IS SACRED, & MY SLEEP | ALEXIAS THIRD ELEGIE | 37 | 52 | 336 | 209 |

## CHATTING

| | | | | | |
|---|---|---|---|---|---|
| WITH CHATTING BIRDS DELICIOUS MURMURINGS. | OUT OF VIRGIL | 10 | 46 | 155 | 529 |

## CHATT'RING

| | | | | | |
|---|---|---|---|---|---|
| OF CHATT'RING STRINGES, BY THE SMALL SIZE OF ONE | MUSICKS DUELL | 163 | 46 | 149 | 535 |

## CHEAP

| | | | | | |
|---|---|---|---|---|---|
| FOR CHEAP AEGYPTIAN DEITYES. | IN GLORIOUS EPIPHANIE | 88 | 52 | 253 | 39 |
| THAT CHAST & CHEAP, AS THE FEW CLOTHES WE WEARE. | DESCRIPTION RELIGIOUS HOUSE | 12 | 52 | 338 | 213 |

CHEAPE

    IS MURTHER NO SIN. OR A SIN SO CHEAPE,    TO PONTIUS WASHING HANDS    1  46  94  23

CHEAT

    SWEET HOPE. KIND CHEAT. FAIRE FALLACY. BY THEE    ON HOPE    77  46 143  71
    SWEET HOPE. KIND CHEAT. FAIR FALLACY BY THEE    (ON) HOPE    37  52 345  71

CHEATED

    ARE CHEATED OF THEIR PAINES. ORION THINKES    HORATIJ ILLE & NEFASTO    55  MS 382 530

CHEAT'ST

    THOU CHEAT'ST US FORD, MAK'ST ONE SEEME TWO BY ART.    UPON FORD'S TRAGEDYES    1  46 181 495

CHEATING

    AND SWEET OPPRESSION. KINDLY CHEATING THEM    SOSPETTO D'HERODE    389  46 109 216

CHEEK

    SEE SEE, HOW SOON HIS NEW-BLOOM'D CHEEK    IN HOLY NATIVITY    67  52 246  76
    WE GUILD THE HUMBLE CHEEK OF THIS CHAST PLACE.    IN GLORIOUS EPIPHANIE    83  52 253  39
    WITH BLUSHING CHEEK & BLEEDING EY.    DIES IRAE    42  52 298 186
    THE PRIMROSE'S PALE CHEEK TO DECK.    WEEPER    44  52 307 120
    THE ROSE'S MODEST CHEEK    WEEPER    177  52 307 120
    GLOWING CHEEK, & GLISTERING WINGS.    FLAMING HEART    33  52 324  61
    BECAUSE THAT FROM THE BRIDALL CHEEK OF BLISSE    (ON) HOPE    17  52 345  71

CHEEKT

    OF ALL THE FAIRE CHEEKT FLOWERS THAT FILL THEE.    AN HIMNE FOR CIRCUMCISION    9  46 141  37

FAIR-CHEEK'T

    OF ALL THE FAIR-CHEEK'T FLOWRS THAT FILL THEE    NEW YEAR'S DAY    9  52 251  37
    THAT FAIR-CHEEK'T FALLACY OF FIRE.    FLAMING HEART    4  52 324  61

CHEEKE

    THE PRIMROSES PALE CHEEKE TO DECKE.    THE WEEPER    38  46  79 120
    THE ROSES MODEST CHEEKE    THE WEEPER    135  46  79 120
    BUT STREIGHT HIS EYES ADVIS'D HIS CHEEKE.    A HYMNE OF THE NATIVITY    49  46 106  76
    BECAUSE THAT FROM THE BRIDALL CHEEKE OF BLISSE.    ON HOPE    37  46 143  71
    THE TENDER DROPS WHICH TREMBLE ON HER CHEEKE.    ON A FOULE MORNING    14  46 181 495
    A CHEEKE WHERE YOUTH,    WISHES SUPPOSED MISTRESSE    31  46 195 479
    A CHEEKE WHERE GROWES    WISHES SUPPOSED MISTRESSE    34  46 195 479
    ON THY SOFT CHEEKE.    LUKE 2. QUAERIT JESUM    42  MS 379  11
    OR CALL HER CHEEKE A BED OF NEW BLOWNE ROSES.    UPON BIRTH PRINCESSE E    45  MS 391 456

CHEEKS

    WOULDST SEE BLITH LOOKES, FRESH CHEEKS BEGUILE    IN PRAISE OF LESSIUS    39  46 156 510
    HIS FAWNING CHEEKS, LOOKE NOT THAT WAY    OUT OF GREEKE CUPID'S CRYER    64  46 159 519
    TAUGHT HER THESE SULLIED CHEEKS THIS BLUBBER'D FACE,    TO PONTIUS WASHING HANDS    4  46  94  23
    WITH THINE OWN BLUSH THY CHEEKS ADORNING    NEW YEAR'S DAY    3  52 251  37
    KIST ON BOTH HIS CHEEKS BY THEE.    IN GLORIOUS EPIPHANIE    39  52 253  39
    OR HIDING HIS VEX'T CHEEKS IN A HIR'D MIST    IN GLORIOUS EPIPHANIE    123  52 253  39
    SMILING IN THY CHEEKS, CONFESSE    WEEPER    80  52 307 120
    O CHEEKS. BEDDS OF CHAST LOVES    WEEPER    85  52 307 120
    FIRE FROM THE BURNING CHEEKS OF THAT BRIGHT BOOKE    FLAMING HEART    28  52 324  61
    THE RED CHEEKS OF A RIVALL'D LOVER.    FLAMING HEART    44  52 324  61

CHEEKES

    SMILING IN THY CHEEKES, CONFESSE.    THE WEEPER    86  46  79 120
    HIS CORRESPONDENT CHEEKES. THESE LOATHSOME STRINGS    SOSPETTO D'HERODE    38  46 109 216
    WITH THINE OWNE BLUSH THY CHEEKES ADORNING,    AN HIMNE FOR CIRCUMCISION    3  46 141  37
    HIS SMOOTH CHEEKES, WITH A DOWNY SHADE.    HIS EPITAPH (HERRYS)    46  46 172 471
    THEIR BASHFULL CHEEKES TOGETHER. NEWLY THEY    UPON YORKE HIS BIRTH    61  46 176 500
    NOT ON THE FRESH CHEEKES OF THE VIRGIN MORNE.    ON A FOULE MORNING    35  46 181 495
    AND STROAKE HIS RADIANT CHEEKES. ONE TIMELY KISSE    TO THE MORNING    37  46 183 497
    PALE SONS OF OUR POMONA. WHOSE WAN CHEEKES    UPON TWO GREENE APRICOCKES    3  48 220 494
    WHILE RAIN & SUNSHINE, CHEEKES & EYES    WEEPER    95  52 307 120
    THE GLOWING CHEEKES. THE GLISTERING WINGS.    FLAMING HEART    66  52 324  61
    WOULDST' SEE BLITH LOOKES, FRESH CHEEKES BEGUIL    TEMPERANCE    37  52 342 510
    HER ROSY CHEEKES YOU SHOULD HAVE SEENE NOE MORE    UPON GUNPOWDER TREASON    15  MS 386 460
    HER SABLE CHEEKES INTO A BLUSHING MORNE,    UPON GUNPOWDER TREASON    12  MS 387 461
    WHOSE SNOWY CHEEKES, LEAST JOY SHOULD BE EXPREST,    AN ELEGIE ON DR PORTER    9  MS 395 476

CHEERE

    TO DRAW A LONG-LIV'D DEATH, WHERE ALL MY CHEERE    SOSPETTO D'HERODE    214  46 109 216

CHEAR

    CHEAR THEE MY HEART.    TO THE NAME OF JESUS    88  52 239  30

PAGE 61

ALL-CHEARING

THE BLISSFULL SPRINGS OF JOY, FROM WHOSE ALL-CHEARING    OFFICE H. CROSS PRIME           7   52 267  91

CHEERFULL

AND SITT TRIUMPHING IN EACH CHEERFULL BROW.             UPON KINGS CORONATION         20   MS 389 454

CHEEREFULL

ON WHOSE PASTURES CHEEREFULL SPRING,                    PSALME 23                      5   46 102   5

CHEEREFULLNESSE

A CAPRING CHEEREFULLNESSE. AND MADE THEM SING           MUSICKS DUELL                 28   46 149 535

CHEERFULLY

TO START FROM TIME, AND CHEERFULLY TO FLY               UPON DEATH OF HERRYS           7   46 167 466

CHERISH

WITH EARTHS LARGE MASSE, DOTH CHERISH AND ASSIST        OUT OF VIRGIL                  8   46 155 529

CHERISHT

CHERISHT IN HIS GOLDEN PRIME.                           HIS EPITAPH (HERRYS)          44   46 172 471

CHERRY

DARES HUNGRY DEATH SNATCH OF ONE CHERRY LIPP.           UPON GUNPOWDER TREASON        39   MS 387 461

CHERRYES

THESE HANDS AND THINE WERE HEW'N, THESE CHERRYES MOCKE  UPON YORKE HIS BIRTH          46   46 176 500

CHERUB

A BRISKE CHERUB SOMETHING SIPS                          THE WEEPER                    26   46  79 120
A BRISK CHERUB SOMTHING SIPPES                          WEEPER                        26   52 307 120

CHEST

GREAT NATURE FOR THE KEY OF HER HUGE CHEST              TO THE NAME OF JESUS          29   52 239  30

CHIDE

WHY ELSE HAD BAALAMS ASSE A TONGUE TO CHIDE             UPON ASSE THAT BORE SAVIOUR    5   46  90  19
LET HEAV'NS LORD CHIDE ABOVE LOWDER THEN THOU           SOSPETTO D'HERODE            269   46 109 216
FAINE WOULD I CHIDE THEIR SLOWNESSE, BUT IN THEIR       UPON TWO GREENE APRICOCKES    31   48 220 494
THY SORROWS CHIDE OUR SHAME.                            OFFICE H. CROSS COMPLINE      21   52 274 105
THE SHRILL WINDS CHIDE, THE WATERS WEEP THY STAY.       IN GLORIOUS ASSUMPTION B. LADY 28  52 304 114
CHIDE YOUR DELAY. YEA THOSE DULL THINGS,                AGAINST IRRESOLUTION AND DELAY 47  52 347 146
FATHER AND HEYRE OF DARKENESSE, WHEN I CHIDE            OUT OF GROTIUS                77   MS 398 198

CHIDDE

WINTER CHIDDE ALOUD. & SENT                             IN HOLY NATIVITY              24   52 246  76

CHID

WINTER CHID THE WORLD, AND SENT                         A HYMNE OF THE NATIVITY       23   46 106  76

CHIDD

TO BE CHASTIS'D (SWEET FRIEND) AND CHIDD BY THEE.       UPON TWO GREENE APRICOCKES     2   48 220 494

CHIDES

THE HIGH-PERCH'T TREBLE CHIRPS AT THIS, AND CHIDES      MUSICKS DUELL                 51   46 149 535
AND WITH SAD MURMURS, CHIDES THE HANDS THAT STAIN HER.  TO PONTIUS WASHING HANDS      14   46  94  23
MEE FROM HIS PATRONAGE. I PRAY, HE CHIDES.              TO THE MORNING                14   46 183 497

CHIEFLY

BUT CHIEFLY THERE DO'S SHEE DELIGHT TO BE.              SOSPETTO D'HERODE            293   46 109 216

CHILD

ETERNALL WORD SHOULD BEE A CHILD, AND WEEPE.            SUSPETTO D'HERODE            179   46 109 216
AND SO IN EACH CHILD OFTEN PROVE A MOTHER.              UPON YORKE HIS BIRTH         101   46 176 500
AGAINE A FRESH CHILD OF THE BUXOME MORNE,               TO THE MORNING                52   46 183 497
THUS SHALL THAT REVEREND CHILD OF LIGHT,                IN GLORIOUS EPIPHANIE        205   52 253  39
THE CHILD OF DEATH EATES HIMSELF DEAD.                  LAUDA SION SALVATUREM         52   52 294 178
AND MILKY SOUL OF A SOFT CHILD.                         TERESA                        14   52 315  52
WITH A BLACK MASKE. THE CLOUDS WITH CHILD BY GREIFE     UPON KINGS CORONATION          3   MS 390 453
A WEAKE A WRETCHED CHILD. EV'N THEN WAS I               OUT OF GROTIUS                20   MS 398 198
THE SEARCH OF ONE CHILD (CRUELL INDUSTRY.)              OUT OF GROTIUS                27   MS 398 198

CHILDE

AND MILKY SOULE OF A SOFT CHILDE.                       IN MEMORY OF LADY MADRE TERESA 14  46 131  52

CHILDRENS

    THE MOTHERS MILKE, THE CHILDRENS BLOOD,    UPON INFANT MARTYRS    2  46  95  10
    LAUGH,TILL THY CHILDRENS BLEEDING BONES    PSALME 137    35  46  104  7

CHILDREN'S

    THE CHILDREN'S BREAD.  THE BRIDEGROOM'S WINE.    LAUDA SION SALVATOREM    63  52  294  178

CHILL

    THE CHILL LUMP WOULD RELENT, & PROVE    SANCTA MARIA DOLORUM    49  52  283  162
    TEMPER TWIXT CHILL DESPAIR, & TORRID JOY.    (ON) HOPE    43  52  345  71

CHILLS

    HIS SPIRITS, THE SPARKES OF LIFE, AND CHILLS HIS    SOSPETTO D'HERODE    422  46  109  216
        HEART.

CHIRPS

    THE HIGH-PERCH'T TREBLE CHIRPS AT THIS, AND CHIDES    MUSICKS DUELL    51  46  149  535

CHOAKE

    AND LET NO DULL MISTS CHOAKE THE LIGHTS FAIRE GROWTH.    ON A FOULE MORNING    4  46  181  495
    SHALL CHOAKE THE GAPING EARTH, WHICH THEN SHALL FRY    ON GUNPOWDER-TREASON    25  MS  384  458

CHOAKT

    NOR CHOAKT WITH WHAT SHEE SHOULD BEE DREST.    IN PRAISE OF LESSIUS    24  46  156  510

CHOAK'T

    NOR CHOAK'T WITH WHAT SHE SHOULD BE DREST.    TEMPERANCE    22  52  342  510

CHOICE

    UPON WHOSE CHOICE POINT SHALL BE SPENT,    IN MEMORY OF LADY MADRE TERESA    90  46  131  52
    THEN THE CHAST STARS, WHOSE CHOICE LAMPS COME TO    ON THE ASSUMPTION    4  46  139  114
        LIGHT HER.
    UPON WHOSE CHOICE POINT SHALL BE SENT    TERESA    90  52  315  52
    SOME RARE CHOICE TORTURE. NOW 'TIS HELL INDEED.    ON GUNPOWDER-TREASON    62  MS  384  458

CHOISE

    SWEET CHOISE (SAID I) NO WAY BUT SO,    A HYMNE OF THE NATIVITY    51  46  106  76
    SWEET CHOISE, SAID WE. NO WAY BUT SO    IN HOLY NATIVITY    69  52  246  76
    THEN THE CHAST STARRES, WHOSE CHOISE LAMPS COME TO    IN GLORIOUS ASSUMPTION B. LADY    4  52  304  114
        LIGHT HER
    IT IS, IN ONE CHOISE HANDFULL, HEAVENN. & ALL    PRAYER TO GENTLE-WOMAN    11  52  328  139

CHOYCE

    YOUR FIRST CHOYCE FAILES, O WHEN YOU CHOOSE AGEN    TO SAME CONCERNING CHOISE    58  52  331  66
    UNTO A CHUYCE, AND CURIOUS EARE.    UPON DEATH OF A FREIND    2  MS  393  477

CHOICER

    A CHOICER LESSON THEN THE JOYFULL BREST    TO THE NAME OF JESUS    107  52  239  30

CHOICEST

    OR CHOICEST HENNES OF AFRICK-BROOD.    PETRONIJ ALES PHASIACIS PETITA    2  MS  382  526
    THE CHOICEST OF HER OLIVE-CROWNES, & PRAISE    UPON KINGS CORONATION    23  MS  389  454

CHOYCEST

    THIS IS NATURES CHOYCEST JEWELL.    UPON DEATH OF DESIRED HERRYS    4  46  168  467

CHOOSE

    IN WEAKNES, WHY YOU CHOOSE SO LONG    TO COUNTESSE OF DENBIGH    10  52  236  146
    CHOOSE OUT THAT SURE DECISIVE DART    TO COUNTESSE OF DENBIGH    33  52  236  146
    AND CHOOSE YOUR ROOME    TO SAME CONCERNING CHOISE    24  52  331  66
    YOUR FIRST CHOYCE FAILES, O WHEN YOU CHOOSE AGEN    TO SAME CONCERNING CHOISE    58  52  331  66

CHUSE

    COULD NOT CHUSE BUT SHINE WITHOUT.    HIS EPITAPH (HERRYS)    36  46  172  471
    WHOSE FEET CAN WALKE THE MILKY WAY, AND CHUSE    TO THE MORNING    24  46  183  497
    AND TO WHAT PATRON CHUSE TO PRAY.    DIES IRAE    22  52  298  186
    IN WEAKNESSE) WHY YOU CHUSE SO LONG    AGAINST IRRESOLUTION AND DELAY    18  52  347  146

CHUSING

    LOVE MAY BEE LONG CHUSING A DART.    WISHES SUPPOSED MISTRESSE    57  46  195  479

CHORISTER

    EACH WINGED CHORISTER WOULD SWAN-LIKE SING    UPON GUNPOWDER TREASON    43  MS  386  460

## CHORUS

| | | | | | |
|---|---|---|---|---|---|
| AND ONE OF THEIR BRIGHT CHORUS MAKE THEE. | THE TEARE | 42 | 46 | 84 | 50 |

## CHRIST

| | | | | | |
|---|---|---|---|---|---|
| CHRIST BIDS THE DUMBE TONGUE SPEAKE. IT SPEAKES, THE SOUND | THE DUMBE HEALED | 1 | 46 | 87 | 16 |
| WHEN CHRIST CALLS, AND THY NETS WOULD HAVE THEE STAY. | ON ST. PETER CASTING NETS | 3 | 46 | 98 | 13 |
| CHRIST WHEN HE DY'D | OFFICE H. CROSS THIRD | 10 | 52 | 268 | 93 |
| BUT STILL IN BOTH ONE CHRIST HE IS. | LAUDA SION SALVATOREM | 42 | 52 | 294 | 178 |
| LESSE THEN WHOLE CHRIST IN EVERY CRUMME. | LAUDA SION SALVATOREM | 58 | 52 | 294 | 178 |
| I'AM YOURS. O WERE MY GOD, MY CHRIST SO TOO. | ALEXIAS THIRD ELEGIE | 43 | 52 | 336 | 209 |

## CHRIST'S

| | | | | | |
|---|---|---|---|---|---|
| WITH CHRIST'S NAME IN'T, IN CHANGE FOR DEATH. | TERESA | 50 | 52 | 315 | 52 |
| CHRIST'S FAITH MAKES BUT ONE BODY OF ALL SOULES | AN APOLOGIE FOR (TERESA) HYMNE | 17 | 52 | 322 | 59 |

## CHRISTS

| | | | | | |
|---|---|---|---|---|---|
| WITH CHRISTS NAME INT IN CHANGE FOR DEATH. | IN MEMORY OF LADY MADRE TERESA | 50 | 46 | 131 | 52 |
| CHRISTS FAITH MAKES BUT ONE BODY OF ALL SOULES, | AN APOLOGIE FOR HYMNE (TERESA) | 17 | 46 | 136 | 59 |

## CHRISTIAN

| | | | | | |
|---|---|---|---|---|---|
| WHEN THE DARK WORLD DAWN'D INTO CHRISTIAN DAY | TO THE QUEEN'S MAJESTY | 4 | 52 | 261 | 47 |

## CHRONOLOGIE

| | | | | | |
|---|---|---|---|---|---|
| NE'RE SO FARRE DISTANT, YET CHRONOLOGIE | ON FRONTISPIECE ISAACSONS | 8 | 46 | 191 | 491 |

## CHURCH

| | | | | | |
|---|---|---|---|---|---|
| THAT TROUBLED NEITHER CHURCH NOR KING. | AN EPITAPH UPON ASHTON | 6 | 46 | 192 | 464 |

## TH'CHURCH

| | | | | | |
|---|---|---|---|---|---|
| TO TH'CHURCH HEE DID ALLOW HER DRESSE. | AN EPITAPH UPON ASHTON | 21 | 46 | 192 | 464 |

## CHURCHES

| | | | | | |
|---|---|---|---|---|---|
| NO LONGER SHALL OUR CHURCHES FRIGHTED STONES | ON A TREATISE OF CHARITY | 31 | 46 | 137 | 69 |

## CHURLISH

| | | | | | |
|---|---|---|---|---|---|
| WHERE NO CHURLISH RUB SAIES NAY | PSALME 23 | 30 | 46 | 102 | 5 |
| RICH, CHURLISH LAND. THAT HID'ST SO LONG IN THEE, | ALEXIAS THIRD ELEGIE | 1 | 52 | 336 | 209 |
| TO TH' CHURLISH ROCKS. & TEACH THE STUBBORNE STONES | AN ELEGIE ON DR PORTER | 32 | MS | 395 | 476 |

## CHYMICK

| | | | | | |
|---|---|---|---|---|---|
| THOUGH THE VEXT CHYMICK VAINLY CHASES | ON HOPE | 85 | 46 | 143 | 71 |
| THOUGH THE VEXT CHYMICK VAINLY CHASES | (ON) HOPE | 45 | 52 | 345 | 71 |

## CINNAMON

| | | | | | |
|---|---|---|---|---|---|
| ROSE QUAKES AT NAME OF CINNAMON. | PETRONIJ ALES PHASIACIS PETITA | 19 | MS | 382 | 526 |

## CIRCE

| | | | | | |
|---|---|---|---|---|---|
| WITH CIRCE, SCYLLA, STAND TO WAIT UPON HER. | SOSPETTO D'HERODE | 339 | 46 | 109 | 216 |

## CIRCLE

| | | | | | |
|---|---|---|---|---|---|
| LED ROUND IN HIS GREAT CIRCLE. NO WINDS BREATH | OUT OF VIRGIL | 27 | 46 | 155 | 529 |
| ALL THY WILD CIRCLE TO A POINT. O SINKE | UPON STANINOUGH'S DEATH | 14 | 46 | 175 | 475 |
| ALL THY WILD CIRCLE TO A POINT. O SINK | DEATH'S LECTURE | 15 | 52 | 340 | 475 |
| HIS FEARE. THE CIRCLE OF A YEARES ROUND GROWTH | OUT OF GROTIUS | 22 | MS | 398 | 198 |

## CIRCLED

| | | | | | |
|---|---|---|---|---|---|
| REV'RENTLY CIRCLED BY THE LESSER SEAVEN, | SOSPETTO D'HERODE | 238 | 46 | 109 | 216 |
| CIRCLED ROUND IN HIS OWNE RAYES. | HIS EPITAPH (HERRYS) | 40 | 46 | 172 | 471 |
| WHO'S THIS THAT COMES CIRCLED IN RAYES, THAT SCORNE | UPON YORKE HIS BIRTH | 68 | 46 | 176 | 500 |
| CIRCLED WITH PURE REFINED GLORY. HEERE | UPON KINGS CORONATION | 13 | MS | 389 | 454 |

## CIRCLING

| | | | | | |
|---|---|---|---|---|---|
| AN EVEN ROUND WITH THE CIRCLING SUN. | DIES IRAE | 10 | 52 | 298 | 166 |

## ALL-CIRCLING

| | | | | | |
|---|---|---|---|---|---|
| ALL-CIRCLING POINT. ALL CENTRING SPHEAR. | IN GLORIOUS EPIPHANIE | 26 | 52 | 253 | 39 |

## CIRCULAR

| | | | | | |
|---|---|---|---|---|---|
| INTO ETERNITY, AND CIRCULAR JOYES | UPON DEATH OF HERRYS | 37 | 46 | 167 | 466 |

## CIRCUMCISING

| | | | | | |
|---|---|---|---|---|---|
| AND TO THE CIRCUMCISING KNIFE DELIVER | SOSPETTO D'HERODE | 187 | 46 | 109 | 216 |

## CLAD

| | | | | |
|---|---|---|---|---|
| THEE WITH THY SELFE THEY HAVE TOO RICHLY CLAD, | ON CRUCIFIED LORD BLOODY | 3 | 46 | 100 | 24 |
| THEE WITH THY SELF THEY HAVE TOO RICHLY CLAD. | UPON BODY OF OUR LORD | 3 | 52 | 290 | 24 |
| WHO, HOWSOE'RE CLAD, CANNOT COME | LAUDA SION SALVATOREM | 57 | 52 | 294 | 178 |

## CLAIM

| | | | | |
|---|---|---|---|---|
| ADVANCE OUR CLAIM | OFFICE H. CROSS COMPLINE | 23 | 52 | 274 | 105 |
| O LET ME, HERE, CLAIM SHARES. | SANCTA MARIA DOLORUM | 56 | 52 | 283 | 162 |

## CLAPT

| | | | | |
|---|---|---|---|---|
| HIS FOULE HAGS RAIS'D THEIR HEADS, & CLAPT THEIR HANDS. | SOSPETTO D'HERODE | 258 | 46 | 109 | 216 |

## CLASP'T

| | | | | |
|---|---|---|---|---|
| AND WITH CLASP'T WINGES PROCLAYME A SPRING | THOUGH NOW 'TIS NEITHER | 11 | MS | 397 | 492 |

## CLAUSE

| | | | | |
|---|---|---|---|---|
| AND THE SHORT CLAUSE OF MORTALL BREATH. | ANOTHER ON HERRYS | 45 | 46 | 170 | 469 |

## CLAWES

| | | | | |
|---|---|---|---|---|
| WITH HIS FOULE CLAWES HEE FENC'D HIS FURROWED BROW. | SOSPETTO D'HERODE | 149 | 46 | 109 | 216 |

## CLAY

| | | | | |
|---|---|---|---|---|
| BOW OUR BRIGHT HEADS, BEFORE A KING OF CLAY. | SOSPETTO D'HERODE | 220 | 46 | 109 | 216 |
| WHY SHOULD A PIECE OF PEEVISH CLAY PLEAD SHARES | CHARITAS NIMIA | 31 | 52 | 280 | 48 |

## CLAY-COTTAGE

| | | | | |
|---|---|---|---|---|
| IN A CLAY-COTTAGE, BY EACH BLAST CONTROL'D. | SOSPETTO D'HERODE | 182 | 46 | 109 | 216 |

## CLEAN

| | | | | |
|---|---|---|---|---|
| BUT LIFT CLEAN HANDS FULL OF CLEARE HEARTS. | A HYMNE OF THE NATIVITY | 76 | 46 | 106 | 76 |

## CLEANE

| | | | | |
|---|---|---|---|---|
| (THE DUST OF WARRE CLEANE WIP'D AWAY) | IN CICATRICES DOMINI JESU | 18 | MS | 381 | 27 |
| AND WITH A GOLDEN WAVE WASH CLEANE AWAY | AN ELEGY MR STANNINOW | 12 | MS | 394 | 473 |
| WAS NOT SO MUCH AS CLEANE. A STABLE KIND. | OUT OF GROTIUS | 17 | MS | 398 | 198 |

## CLEANLY

| | | | | |
|---|---|---|---|---|
| A COLD, AND NOT TOO CLEANLY, MANGER. | IN HOLY NATIVITY | 40 | 52 | 246 | 76 |

## CLEAR

| | | | | |
|---|---|---|---|---|
| THAT DARK DAY'S CLEAR DOOM SHALL DEFINE | IN GLORIOUS EPIPHANIE | 143 | 52 | 253 | 39 |

## CLEERE

| | | | | |
|---|---|---|---|---|
| ONE BRIGHT SMILE TO CLEERE THE WEATHER. | OUT OF THE ITALIAN (1) | 27 | 46 | 188 | 545 |
| OF A CLEERE MIND ARE DAY ALL NIGHT. | WISHES SUPPOSED MISTRESSE | 81 | 46 | 195 | 479 |

## CLEARE

| | | | | |
|---|---|---|---|---|
| A CLEARE UNWRINCKLED SONG, THEN DOTH SHEE POINT IT | MUSICKS DUELL | 39 | 46 | 149 | 535 |
| SPREADS A PATH CLEARE AS THE DAY, | PSALME 23 | 29 | 46 | 102 | 5 |
| BUT LIFT CLEAN HANDS FULL OF CLEARE HEARTS. | A HYMNE OF THE NATIVITY | 76 | 46 | 106 | 76 |
| LO I UNCLOATH AND CLEARE, | WISHES SUPPOSED MISTRESSE | 116 | 46 | 195 | 479 |
| AND FOULE THE CLEARE TEXT WITH A MUDDY GLOSSE. | UPON BIRTH PRINCESSE E | 54 | MS | 391 | 456 |

## CLEARER

| | | | | |
|---|---|---|---|---|
| WHILE THROUGH THE CHRISTALL ORBS CLEARER THEN THEY | ON THE ASSUMPTION | 5 | 46 | 139 | 114 |
| WHILE THROUGH THE CRYSTALL ORBES, CLEARER THEN THEY | IN GLORIOUS ASSUMPTION B. LADY | 5 | 52 | 304 | 114 |

## CLIMB

| | | | | |
|---|---|---|---|---|
| UP IN CLOUDS OF INCENSE CLIMB. | WEEPER | 142 | 52 | 307 | 120 |

## CLIMBE

| | | | | |
|---|---|---|---|---|
| UP IN CLOUDS OF INCENSE CLIMBE. | THE WEEPER | 106 | 46 | 79 | 120 |
| TO LIFT ME FROM MY LAZY URNE, TO CLIMBE | TO THE MORNING | 27 | 46 | 183 | 497 |
| IT DOES PRAESAGE, THAT A GREAT PRINCE SHALL CLIMBE, | ON GUNPOWDER-TREASON | 35 | MS | 384 | 458 |

## CLOMBE

| | | | | |
|---|---|---|---|---|
| IT SHALL NOT BE, SAID I, AND CLOMBE THE NORTH, | SOSPETTO D'HERODE | 221 | 46 | 109 | 216 |

## CLIMBS

| | | | | |
|---|---|---|---|---|
| SHE CLIMBS, AND MAKES A FARRE MORE MILKEY WAY. | IN GLORIOUS ASSUMPTION B. LADY | 6 | 52 | 304 | 114 |

## CLIMBES

| | | | | |
|---|---|---|---|---|
| SHEE CLIMBES, AND MAKES A FARRE MORE MILKY WAY. | ON THE ASSUMPTION | 6 | 46 139 | 114 |

## CLIME

| | | | | |
|---|---|---|---|---|
| IN FARTHEST CLIME. WHAT E'RE IS BOUGHT | PETRONIJ ALES PHASIACIS PETITA | 12 | MS 382 | 526 |

## CLING

| | | | | |
|---|---|---|---|---|
| WINDS CLING TO THEE. | OUT OF THE ITALIAN (1) | 32 | 46 188 | 545 |

## CLINGS

| | | | | |
|---|---|---|---|---|
| MISCHIFES OLD MASTER, CLOSE ABOUT HIM CLINGS | SOSPETTO D'HERODE | 36 | 46 109 | 216 |

## CLOATH

| | | | | |
|---|---|---|---|---|
| THEY FEED OUR SOULES, SHALL CLOATH THINE THERE. | IN MEMORY OF LADY MADRE TERESA | 159 | 46 131 | 52 |
| GLADNESSE SHALL CLOATH THE EARTH, WE WILL INSTILE | ON A FOULE MORNING | 9 | 46 181 | 495 |
| AND CLOATH THEIR SIMPLEST NAKEDNESSE. | WISHES SUPPOSED MISTRESSE | 42 | 46 195 | 479 |
| DOTH BLITH APOLLO CLOATH THE HEAVENS WITH JOYE, | AN ELEGY MR STANNINOW | 11 | MS 394 | 473 |

## CLOTH

| | | | | |
|---|---|---|---|---|
| THEY FEED OUR SOULES, SHALL CLOTH THINE THERE. | TERESA | 158 | 52 315 | 52 |
| WHETHER THE MUSE THEY CLOTH SHALL LIVE OR DIE. | AT TH' IVORY TRIBUNALL | 4 | MS 397 | 492 |

## CLOATHED

| | | | | |
|---|---|---|---|---|
| A WELL CLOATHED SOULE THATS NOT OPPREST. | IN PRAISE OF LESSIUS | 23 | 46 156 | 510 |

## WELL-CLOTH'D

| | | | | |
|---|---|---|---|---|
| A WELL-CLOTH'D SOUL. THAT'S NOT OPPREST | TEMPERANCE | 21 | 52 342 | 510 |

## CLOTHES

| | | | | |
|---|---|---|---|---|
| AND SO HE LOST HIS CLOTHES, EYES, HEART AND ALL. | OUT OF THE ITALIAN (3) | 8 | 46 190 | 549 |
| THAT CHAST & CHEAP, AS THE FEW CLOTHES WE WEARE. | DESCRIPTION RELIGIOUS HOUSE | 12 | 52 338 | 213 |

## CLOATHES

| | | | | |
|---|---|---|---|---|
| HER CRUELL CLOATHES OF COSTLY THREDS THEY WEAVE, | SOSPETTO D'HERODE | 343 | 46 109 | 216 |

## CLOSE

| | | | | |
|---|---|---|---|---|
| CLOSE IN THE COVERT OF THE LEAVES THERE STOOD | MUSICKS DUELL | 7 | 46 149 | 535 |
| IN THE CLOSE MURMUR OF A SPARKLING NOYSE. | MUSICKS DUELL | 84 | 46 149 | 535 |
| AS GARMENTS SHOULD DOE CLOSE AND FIT. | IN PRAISE OF LESSIUS | 22 | 46 156 | 510 |
| ONE STANDS UP CLOSE AND TREADS ON HIGH. | TWO WENT TO PRAY | 3 | 46 89 | 18 |
| MISCHIFES OLD MASTER, CLOSE ABOUT HIM CLINGS | SOSPETTO D'HERODE | 36 | 46 109 | 216 |
| WHERE ALL THE BUSIE DAY SHEE CLOSE DOTH LY, | SOSPETTO D'HERODE | 386 | 46 109 | 216 |
| CLOSE COUCHT IN YOUR WHITE BOSOME, AND FROM THENCE | ON A PRAYER BOOKE | 11 | 46 126 | 139 |
| AND CLOSE WITH HIS IMMORTALL KISSES. | ON A PRAYER BOOKE | 97 | 46 126 | 139 |
| AND CLOSE IN HIS EMBRACES KEEP. | IN MEMORY OF LADY MADRE TERESA | 107 | 46 131 | 52 |
| OR CLOSE UNTO HIS NAME ANNEXT, | ANOTHER ON HERRYS | 51 | 46 170 | 469 |
| AND WIND THY SELFE UP CLOSE IN THY COLD BED. | UPON STANINOUGH'S DEATH | 4 | 46 175 | 475 |
| WHICH HAS THE KEY OF THIS CLOSE HEART, | TO COUNTESSE OF DENBIGH | 34 | 52 236 | 146 |
| SEARCH WHAT THE WORLD'S CLOSE CABINETS KEEP, | NEW YEAR'S DAY | 18 | 52 251 | 37 |
| BY THE OBLIQUE AMBUSH OF THIS CLOSE NIGHT | IN GLORIOUS EPIPHANIE | 189 | 52 253 | 39 |
| AND TEACH OBSCURE MANKIND A MORE CLOSE WAY | IN GLORIOUS EPIPHANIE | 208 | 52 253 | 39 |
| KEEP CLOSE, MY SOUL'S INQUIRING EY. | ADORO TE | 6 | 52 291 | 172 |
| CLOSE IN KIND CONTRARIETYES. | WEEPER | 96 | 52 307 | 120 |
| DOES DAY CLOSE HIS EYES. | WEEPER | 135 | 52 307 | 120 |
| AND CLOSE IN HIS EMBRACES KEEP | TERESA | 107 | 52 315 | 52 |
| CLOSE COUCH'T IN YOUR WHITE BOSOM. & FROM THENCE | PRAYER TO GENTLE-WOMAN | 17 | 52 328 | 139 |
| AND CLOSE WITH HIS IMMORTALL KISSES. | PRAYER TO GENTLE-WOMAN | 103 | 52 328 | 139 |
| KIND LOVES KEEP HOUSE, LY CLOSE, AND MAKE NO NOISE, | DESCRIPTION RELIGIOUS HOUSE | 33 | 52 338 | 213 |
| AND WIND THY SELF UP CLOSE IN THY COLD BED. | DEATH'S LECTURE | 4 | 52 340 | 475 |
| AS GARMENTS SHOULD DOE, CLOSE & FITT. | TEMPERANCE | 20 | 52 342 | 510 |
| IN THIS INFERNALL MAJESTY CLOSE SHROWD | UPON GUNPOWDER TREASON | 23 | MS 387 | 461 |
| TO THE CLOSE CLOSET OF AETERNITY. | UPON GUNPOWDER TREASON | 56 | MS 387 | 461 |

## CLOSELY

| | | | | |
|---|---|---|---|---|
| DOTH HEE IN DOWNY SNOW THERE CLOSELY SHROWD | AN ELEGY MR STANNINOW | 3 | MS 394 | 473 |

## CLOSER

| | | | | |
|---|---|---|---|---|
| OF CLOSER STRAINES, AND ERE THE WARRE BEGIN. | MUSICKS DUELL | 19 | 46 149 | 535 |

## CLOSES

| | | | | |
|---|---|---|---|---|
| AND CLOSES THE SWEET QUARRELL, ROWSING ALL | MUSICKS DUELL | 53 | 46 149 | 535 |

## CLOSET

| | | | | |
|---|---|---|---|---|
| IN THE CLOSET OF THEIR BREST. | OUT OF GREEKE CUPID'S CRYER | 44 | 46 159 | 519 |
| TO THE CLOSE CLOSET OF AETERNITY. | UPON GUNPOWDER TREASON | 56 | MS 387 | 461 |

CLOTTED

    THE THRONGING CLOTTED MULTITUDE DOTH FEAST.    HORATIJ ILLE & NEFASTO    49    MS 382 530

CLOUD

    HIS NEEDS A CLOUD    WHY ARE YEE AFRAID    3    46  88  15
    NO CLOUD SCOULE ON HIS RADIANT LIDS NO TEMPEST LOWRE.    EASTER DAY    12    46 100  26
    FAIRE CLOUD OF FIRE, BOTH SHADE, AND LIGHT,    ON HOPE    15    46 143  71
    AS IS HE, NOR CLOUD, NOR WIND    UPON DEATH OF DESIRED HERRYS    57    46 168 467
    AND URGE THEIR SUN INTO THY CLOUD.    IN GLORIOUS EPIPHANIE    114    52 253  39
    FROM THIS OBSEQUIOUS CLOUD.    IN GLORIOUS EPIPHANIE    200    52 253  39

CLOWD

    (CLOWD OF CONDENSED SWEETS) & BREAK UPON US    TO THE NAME OF JESUS    168    52 239  30
    YOUR SELVES, YOU STYGIAN STATES. A PITCHY CLOWD    UPON GUNPOWDER TREASON    24    MS 387 461
    HIS BEDRID LIMMES, WRAPT IN A FLEECY CLOWD.    AN ELEGY MR STANNINOW    4    MS 394 473

CLOUDS

    UP IN CLOUDS OF INCENSE CLIMBE.    THE WEEPER    106    46  79 120
    THROUGH CLOUDS OF INFANT FLESH. THAT HEE THE OLD    SOSPETTO D'HERODE    178    46 109 216
    DULL MISTS AND MELANCHOLY CLOUDS. TAKE DAY    ON A TREATISE OF CHARITY    8    46 137  69
    BRIGHT CLOUDS LIKE GOLDEN FLEECES SHALL BE SPREAD.    ON A FOULE MORNING    26    46 181 495
    TO HIM, WHO BY THESE MORTALL CLOUDS HAST MADE    IN GLORIOUS EPIPHANIE    46    52 253  39
    SHALL KICK THE CLOUDS NO MORE. BUT LEAN & TAME,    IN GLORIOUS EPIPHANIE    98    52 253  39
    UP IN CLOUDS OF INCENSE CLIMB.    WEEPER    142    52 307 120
    INTO PERFUMING CLOUDS, SO FAST    TERESA    115    52 315  52
    BUT IN A VAILE OF CLOUDS MUFLING HER HEAD    UPON GUNPOWDER TREASON    17    MS 386 460
    WITH A BLACK MASKE. THE CLOUDS WITH CHILD BY GREIFE    UPON KINGS CORONATION    3    MS 390 453
    OLD CLOUDS OF THICKEST BLINDNESSE FLED MY SIGHT    OUT OF GROTIUS    71    MS 398 198

CLOUDES

    INTO PERFUMING CLOUDES. SO FAST    IN MEMORY OF LADY MADRE TERESA    116    46 131  52
    HIS HEAD IN CLOUDES, AS IF IN HIM ALONE    UPON DEATH OF HERRYS    5    46 167 466

CLOWDS

    ALL MELANCHOLY CLOWDS VANISHT AWAY.    UPON KINGS CORONATION    40    MS 390 453
    WITH TH' RICHEST CLOWDS THEIR PEARLY TREASURIE.    AN ELEGY MR STANNINOW    18    MS 394 473

CLOUDY

    MY WISHES CLOUDY CHARACTER.    WISHES SUPPOSED MISTRESSE    117    46 195 479

CLOWDY

    NAY. STOPP THY CLOWDY EYES. IT IS NOT GOOD.    UPON GUNPOWDER TREASON    31    MS 387 461

CLOUTS

    WHAT ARMOUR DOES HE WEARE. A FEW THIN CLOUTS.    SOSPETTO D'HERODE    525    46 109 216

CLOYING

    IS CLOYING MEAT. HOW STALE IS WIFE.    PETRONIJ ALES PHASIACIS PETITA    16    MS 382 526

CLUSTERS

    LONG MAYEST THOU LADEN WITH SUCH CLUSTERS LEANE    UPON YORKE HIS BIRTH    102    46 176 500

COATES

    FOR JOYE OF THIER NEATE COATES. BUT WOULD HAVE TORE    UPON GUNPOWDER TREASON    46    MS 386 460
    THEIR WINTER COATES COVER'D WITH FLAMING GOLD.    UPON KINGS CORONATION    28    MS 390 453

COHEIRS

    COHEIRS OF SAINTS. THAT SO ALL MAY    LAUDA SION SALVATOREM    77    52 294 178

COLCHOS

    HUGE HIGH-FLOUNE POYSONS, EV'N OF COLCHOS BREED.    HORATIJ ILLE & NEFASTO    11    MS 382 530

COLD

    A SWEETLY TEMPER'D MEANE, NOR HOT NOR COLD.    OUT OF VIRGIL    36    46 155 529
    YOUR FLEECE IS WHITE, BUT 'TIS TOO COLD.    A HYMNE OF THE NATIVITY    40    46 106  76
    NOT TO LYE COLD, YET SLEEPE IN SNOW.    A HYMNE OF THE NATIVITY    52    46 106  76
    THAT HEE WHO MADE THE FIRE, SHOULD FEARE THE COLD.    SOSPETTO D'HERODE    180    46 109 216
    SHE COMES TOTH' KING AND WITH HER COLD HAND SLAKES    SOSPETTO D'HERODE    421    46 109 216
    WITH WHICH HIS FEAV'ROUS CARES THEIR COLD INCREASE.    SOSPETTO D'HERODE    502    46 109 216
    A THOUSAND COLD DEATHS IN ONE CUP.    IN MEMORY OF LADY MADRE TERESA    38    46 131  52
    A MELANCHOLY MANSION IN THOSE COLD    ON A TREATISE OF CHARITY    35    46 137  69
    TURNING HER OUT TO TREMBLE IN THE COLD.    ON A TREATISE OF CHARITY    56    46 137  69
    TEMPER'D 'TWIXT COLD DESPAIRE, AND TORRID JOY.    ON HOPE    83    46 143  71
    AND WIND THY SELFE UP CLOSE IN THY COLD BED.    UPON STANINOUGH'S DEATH    4    46 175 475
    KINDLED ON THEIR COLD LIPS. O HAD MY WISHES    UPON TWO GREENE APRICOCKES    10    48 220 494
    HOW DOES THY APRIL-AUTUMNE MOCKE THESE COLD    UPON TWO GREENE APRICOCKES    15    48 220 494
    SO WHEN THE YEAR TAKES COLD, WE SEE    TO COUNTESSE OF DENBIGH    21    52 236 146
    THOU THAT ALONE CANST THAW THIS COLD.    TO COUNTESSE OF DENBIGH    27    52 236 146

| Entry / Line | Source | | | | |
|---|---|---|---|---|---|
| A COLD, AND NOT TOO CLEANLY, MANGER. | IN HOLY NATIVITY | 40 | 52 | 246 | 76 |
| YOUR FLEECE IS WHITE BUT T'IS TOO COLD. | IN HOLY NATIVITY | 56 | 52 | 246 | 76 |
| NOT TO LY COLD, YET SLEEP IN SNOW. | IN HOLY NATIVITY | 70 | 52 | 246 | 76 |
| 'CAUSE, THOUGH A HARD & COLD ONE, YET IT IS THINE OWNE. | OFFICE H. CROSS COMPLINE | 12 | 52 | 274 | 105 |
| IS THAT COLD MAN | SANCTA MARIA DOLORUM | 12 | 52 | 283 | 162 |
| THIS HARD, COLD, HEART OF MINE. | SANCTA MARIA DOLORUM | 48 | 52 | 283 | 162 |
| A THOUSAND COLD DEATHS IN ONE CUP. | TERESA | 38 | 52 | 315 | 52 |
| HAD THY COLD PENCIL KIST HER PEN | FLAMING HEART | 20 | 52 | 324 | 61 |
| UPON THIS CARCASSE OF A HARD, COLD, HART, | FLAMING HEART | 66 | 52 | 324 | 61 |
| AND WIND THY SELF UP CLOSE IN THY COLD BED. | DEATH'S LECTURE | 4 | 52 | 340 | 475 |
| SO WHEN THE YEAR TAKES COLD WE SEE | AGAINST IRRESOLUTION AND DELAY | 21 | 52 | 347 | 146 |
| IN A COLD SELF-CAPTIVITY. | AGAINST IRRESOLUTION AND DELAY | 24 | 52 | 347 | 146 |
| AND STRETCH THEIR COLD LIMBES IN A PLEASING FIRE. | HORATIJ ILLE & NEFASTO | 53 | MS | 382 | 530 |
| GRIPES THY COLD LIMBES SOE FAST, THOU CANST NOT FLY, | ON GUNPOWDER-TREASON | 4 | MS | 384 | 458 |
| IN THY COLD BREAST, & YEARLY ON THIS DAY | ON GUNPOWDER-TREASON | 13 | MS | 384 | 458 |
| IF WINTER'S GONE, WHENCE THIS UNTIMELY COLD, | AN ELEGY MR STANNINOW | 19 | MS | 394 | 473 |

COLEBLACK

| | | | | | |
|---|---|---|---|---|---|
| THREE COLEBLACK SISTERS, (WHOSE LONG SUTTY HAIRE, | UPON GUNPOWDER TREASON | 9 | MS | 387 | 461 |

COLORS

| | | | | | |
|---|---|---|---|---|---|
| THE CONSCIOUS COLORS OF MY SIN | DIES IRAE | 43 | 52 | 298 | 186 |

COLOURS

| | | | | | |
|---|---|---|---|---|---|
| TO PAINT ITS PERFUM'D FACE WITH COLOURS BRAVE. | AN ELEGIE ON DR PORTER | 24 | MS | 395 | 476 |
| AND 'GAINST RELIGION HER OWNE COLOURS BEARE. | OUT OF GROTIUS | 44 | MS | 398 | 198 |

HIGH-COLOUR'D

| | | | | | |
|---|---|---|---|---|---|
| HIGH-COLOUR'D IS, HIS EYES STILL FLUSHING | OUT OF GREEKE CUPID'S CRYER | 20 | 46 | 159 | 519 |

COMBINE

| | | | | | |
|---|---|---|---|---|---|
| THOUGH BOTH MY PRAYRES & TEARES COMBINE, | DIES IRAE | 53 | 52 | 298 | 186 |

COMBIN'D

| | | | | | |
|---|---|---|---|---|---|
| COMBIN'D AGAINST THIS BREST AT ONCE BREAK IN | FLAMING HEART | 69 | 52 | 324 | 61 |

COME

| | | | | | |
|---|---|---|---|---|---|
| A NIGHTINGALE, COME FROM THE NEIGHBOURING WOOD. | MUSICKS DUELL | 8 | 46 | 149 | 535 |
| AWAKES HIS LUTE, AND 'GAINST THE FIGHT TO COME | MUSICKS DUELL | 17 | 46 | 149 | 535 |
| (MISTRESSE) I COME, NOW REACH A STRAINE MY LUTE | MUSICKS DUELL | 107 | 46 | 149 | 535 |
| COME IF THOU DAR'ST, THUS, THUS LET US BE TRY'D. | UPON THE SAME (VENUS ARMES) | 2 | 46 | 161 | 523 |
| AS TO SPEAKE NOTHING, COME THEN TELL | UPON THE DEATH OF A GENTLEMAN | 24 | 46 | 166 | 472 |
| ANGELS WITH THEIR BOTTLES COME. | THE WEEPER | 34 | 46 | 79 | 120 |
| COME DEATH, COME BANDS, NOR DO YOU SHRINK, MY EARS, | I AM READY NOT ONELY BOUND | 1 | 46 | 98 | 29 |
| COME DEATH, COME BANDS, NOR DO YOU SHRINK, MY EARS, | I AM READY NOT ONELY BOUND | 1 | 46 | 98 | 29 |
| ARE YET BUT IN THEIR HOPES, NOT COME TO YEARES. | OUR LORD IN HIS CIRCUMCISION | 10 | 46 | 98 | 9 |
| AND TILL MY RIPER WOES TO AGE ARE COME, | OUR LORD IN HIS CIRCUMCISION | 17 | 46 | 98 | 9 |
| COME NOW ALL YEE TERRORS, SALLY | PSALME 23 | 35 | 46 | 102 | 5 |
| BROODING HORROR, COME THOU DEATH, | PSALME 23 | 39 | 46 | 102 | 5 |
| COME, THEY CRY'D, COME SING AND PLAY | PSALME 137 | 11 | 46 | 104 | 7 |
| COME, THEY CRY'D, COME SING AND PLAY | PSALME 137 | 11 | 46 | 104 | 7 |
| COME WEE SHEPHEARDS WHO HAVE SEENE | A HYMNE OF THE NATIVITY | 1 | 46 | 106 | 76 |
| COME LIFT WE UP OUR LOFTY SONG, | A HYMNE OF THE NATIVITY | 3 | 46 | 106 | 76 |
| COME HOVERING O'RE THE PLACES HEAD. | A HYMNE OF THE NATIVITY | 36 | 46 | 106 | 76 |
| COME TRY WHO DARES, HEAV'N, EARTH, WHAT ERE DOST BOAST, | SOSPETTO D'HERODE | 251 | 46 | 109 | 216 |
| COME THY CREATOR TOO, WHAT THOUGH IT COST | SOSPETTO D'HERODE | 253 | 46 | 109 | 216 |
| MERCY WILL COME ERE LONG. | ON A PRAYER BOOKE | 34 | 46 | 126 | 139 |
| IF WHEN HEE COME | ON A PRAYER BOOKE | 83 | 46 | 126 | 139 |
| CALLS THEE BACK, AND BIDS THEE COME. | IN MEMORY OF LADY MADRE TERESA | 67 | 46 | 131 | 52 |
| SOULES AS THY SHINING SELFE, SHALL COME, | IN MEMORY OF LADY MADRE TERESA | 126 | 46 | 131 | 52 |
| HARKE SHEE IS CALLED, THE PARTING HOURE IS COME. | ON THE ASSUMPTION | 1 | 46 | 139 | 114 |
| THEN THE CHAST STARS, WHOSE CHOICE LAMPS COME TO LIGHT HER. | ON THE ASSUMPTION | 4 | 46 | 139 | 114 |
| THE SPRING IS COME, THE FLOWERS APPEARE, | ON THE ASSUMPTION | 11 | 46 | 139 | 114 |
| COME AWAY MY LOVE, | ON THE ASSUMPTION | 13 | 46 | 139 | 114 |
| COME AWAY MY DOVE | ON THE ASSUMPTION | 14 | 46 | 139 | 114 |
| THE COURT OF HEAV'N IS COME, | ON THE ASSUMPTION | 16 | 46 | 139 | 114 |
| COME AWAY, COME AWAY. | ON THE ASSUMPTION | 18 | 46 | 139 | 114 |
| COME AWAY, COME AWAY. | ON THE ASSUMPTION | 18 | 46 | 139 | 114 |
| WHEN HEAVEN BIDS COME, WHO CAN SAY NO. | ON THE ASSUMPTION | 20 | 46 | 139 | 114 |
| SWEET ANGELS COME, AND SING THE REST. | ON THE ASSUMPTION | 64 | 46 | 139 | 114 |
| THE MOONE SHALL COME TO MEET THEE HERE. | AN HIMNE FOR CIRCUMCISION | 31 | 46 | 141 | 37 |
| COME LESSE UNBROKEN TO OUR BED. | ON HOPE | 36 | 46 | 143 | 71 |
| COME THEN YOUTH, BEAUTY, AND BLOOD, ALL YE SOFT POWERS. | UPON STANINOUGH'S DEATH | 7 | 46 | 175 | 475 |
| INTO A FALSE ETERNITY, COME MAN, | UPON STANINOUGH'S DEATH | 9 | 46 | 175 | 475 |
| COME FAST UPON THEE, AND THOSE GLORIOUS ODS, | UPON YORKE HIS BIRTH | 6 | 46 | 176 | 500 |
| COME AND LET US LIVE MY DEARE, | OUT OF CATULLUS | 1 | 46 | 194 | 523 |
| COME ONCE THE CONQUERING WAY, NOT TO CONFUTE | TO COUNTESSE OF DENBIGH | 39 | 52 | 236 | 146 |
| THAT THEY CONVENE & COME AWAY | TO THE NAME OF JESUS | 41 | 52 | 239 | 30 |
| AND COME ALONG. | TO THE NAME OF JESUS | 60 | 52 | 239 | 30 |
| COME, YE SOFT MINISTERS OF SWEET SAD MIRTH, | TO THE NAME OF JESUS | 62 | 52 | 239 | 30 |
| COME, NERE TO PART, | TO THE NAME OF JESUS | 68 | 52 | 239 | 30 |
| COME, & COME STRONG, | TO THE NAME OF JESUS | 70 | 52 | 239 | 30 |
| COME, & COME STRONG, | TO THE NAME OF JESUS | 70 | 52 | 239 | 30 |

| | | | | |
|---|---|---|---|---|
| AND WHEN YOU'ARE COME, WITH ALL | TO THE NAME OF JESUS | 80 | 52 239 | 30 |
| COME, LOVELY NAME. APPEARE FROM FORTH THE BRIGHT | TO THE NAME OF JESUS | 115 | 52 239 | 30 |
| FAIR KING OF NAMES, & COME. | TO THE NAME OF JESUS | 118 | 52 239 | 30 |
| COME, LOVELY NAME. LIFE OF OUR HOPE. | TO THE NAME OF JESUS | 125 | 52 239 | 30 |
| DEAREST SWEET, & COME AWAY. | TO THE NAME OF JESUS | 128 | 52 239 | 30 |
| COME ROYALL NAME, & PAY THE EXPENCE | TO THE NAME OF JESUS | 139 | 52 239 | 30 |
| O COME AWAY | TO THE NAME OF JESUS | 141 | 52 239 | 30 |
| TAKE THINE OWN WINGS, & COME AWAY. | TO THE NAME OF JESUS | 150 | 52 239 | 30 |
| COME WE SHEPHEARDS WHOSE BLEST SIGHT | IN HOLY NATIVITY | 1 | 52 246 | 76 |
| COME LIFT WE UP OUR LOFTYER SONG | IN HOLY NATIVITY | 3 | 52 246 | 76 |
| COME HOVERING O'RE THE PLACE'S HEAD. | IN HOLY NATIVITY | 52 | 52 246 | 76 |
| THE MORN SHALL COME TO MEET THEE HERE, | NEW YEAR'S DAY | 31 | 52 251 | 37 |
| THE EAST IS COME | IN GLORIOUS EPIPHANIE | 13 | 52 253 | 39 |
| COME FORTH GREAT MASTER OF THE MYSTICK DAY. | IN GLORIOUS EPIPHANIE | 207 | 52 253 | 39 |
| AND GATHER, AS THEY COME & GOE. | SANCTA MARIA DOLORUM | 26 | 52 283 | 162 |
| TURN SPEARES, & STRAIGHT COME HOME AGAIN. | SANCTA MARIA DOLORUM | 30 | 52 283 | 162 |
| COME WOUNDS. COME DARTS. | SANCTA MARIA DOLORUM | 75 | 52 283 | 162 |
| COME WOUNDS. COME DARTS. | SANCTA MARIA DOLORUM | 75 | 52 283 | 162 |
| COME YOUR WHOLE SELVES, SORROW'S GREAT SON & MOTHER. | SANCTA MARIA DOLORUM | 77 | 52 283 | 162 |
| COME LOVE. COME LORD. & THAT LONG DAY | ADORO TE | 51 | 52 291 | 172 |
| COME LOVE. COME LORD. & THAT LONG DAY | ADORO TE | 51 | 52 291 | 172 |
| FOR WHICH I LANGUISH, COME AWAY. | ADORO TE | 52 | 52 291 | 172 |
| COME, LOVE. & LET US WORK A SONG | LAUDA SION SALVATOREM | 13 | 52 294 | 178 |
| WHO, HOWSOE'RE CLAD, CANNOT COME | LAUDA SION SALVATOREM | 57 | 52 294 | 178 |
| SHALL CRY WE COME, WE COME & ALL | DIES IRAE | 15 | 52 298 | 186 |
| SHALL CRY WE COME, WE COME & ALL | DIES IRAE | 15 | 52 298 | 186 |
| LET OUR TEARE YE BLESSED THEN CALL ME. | DIES IRAE | 60 | 52 298 | 186 |
| HARK, SHE IS CALL'D, THE PARTING HOURE IS COME. | IN GLORIOUS ASSUMPTION B. LADY | 1 | 52 304 | 114 |
| THEN THE CHAST STARRES, WHOSE CHOISE LAMPS COME TO LIGHT HER | IN GLORIOUS ASSUMPTION B. LADY | 4 | 52 304 | 114 |
| THE SPRING IS COME, THE FLOWRS APPEAR | IN GLORIOUS ASSUMPTION B. LADY | 11 | 52 304 | 114 |
| COME AWAY, MY LOVE. | IN GLORIOUS ASSUMPTION B. LADY | 13 | 52 304 | 114 |
| COME AWAY, MY DOVE. CAST OFF DELAY. | IN GLORIOUS ASSUMPTION B. LADY | 14 | 52 304 | 114 |
| THE COURT OF HEAV'N IS COME | IN GLORIOUS ASSUMPTION B. LADY | 15 | 52 304 | 114 |
| TO WAIT UPON THEE HOME. COME COME AWAY. | IN GLORIOUS ASSUMPTION B. LADY | 16 | 52 304 | 114 |
| TO WAIT UPON THEE HOME. COME COME AWAY. | IN GLORIOUS ASSUMPTION B. LADY | 16 | 52 304 | 114 |
| THE SPRING IS COME, OR IF IT STAY. | IN GLORIOUS ASSUMPTION B. LADY | 19 | 52 304 | 114 |
| IF SOMMER COME NOT, HOW CAN WINTER GOE. | IN GLORIOUS ASSUMPTION B. LADY | 26 | 52 304 | 114 |
| COME AWAY, COME AWAY. | IN GLORIOUS ASSUMPTION B. LADY | 27 | 52 304 | 114 |
| COME AWAY, COME AWAY. | IN GLORIOUS ASSUMPTION B. LADY | 27 | 52 304 | 114 |
| COME AWAY, MY LOVE. | IN GLORIOUS ASSUMPTION B. LADY | 31 | 52 304 | 114 |
| COME AWAY, MY DOVE. | IN GLORIOUS ASSUMPTION B. LADY | 32 | 52 304 | 114 |
| WHEN HEAVN BIDDS COME, WHO CAN SAY NO. | IN GLORIOUS ASSUMPTION B. LADY | 34 | 52 304 | 114 |
| SWEET ANGELS COME, AND SING THE REST. | IN GLORIOUS ASSUMPTION B. LADY | 69 | 52 307 | 120 |
| ANGELS WITH CRYSTALL VIOLLS COME | WEEPER | 70 | 52 307 | 120 |
| CALLS THEE BACK, & BIDDS THEE COME | TERESA | 67 | 52 315 | 52 |
| SOULES AS THY SHINING SELF, SHALL COME | TERESA | 125 | 52 315 | 52 |
| PEACE, SURE, WITH PIETY, THOUGH IT COME FROM SPAIN. | AN APOLOGIE FOR (TERESA) HYMNE | 20 | 52 322 | 59 |
| WELL MEANING READERS. YOU THAT COME AS FREINDS | FLAMING HEART | 1 | 52 324 | 61 |
| MERCY WILL COME E'RE LONG | PRAYER TO GENTLE-WOMAN | 40 | 52 328 | 139 |
| BUT IF THE NOBLE BRIDEGROOM, WHEN HE COME, | PRAYER TO GENTLE-WOMAN | 47 | 52 328 | 139 |
| (IF WHEN HE COME | PRAYER TO GENTLE-WOMAN | 89 | 52 328 | 139 |
| AND BIDDES YOU COME | TO SAME CONCERNING CHOISE | 23 | 52 331 | 66 |
| COME THEN, YOUTH, BEAUTY, & BLOOD. | DEATH'S LECTURE | 7 | 52 340 | 475 |
| INTO A FALSE AETERNITY. COME MAN. | DEATH'S LECTURE | 10 | 52 340 | 475 |
| COME LESSE UNBROKEN TO OUR BED, | (ON) HOPE | 16 | 52 345 | 71 |
| HEE'S GONE. NOT LEAVING WITH ME, TILL HE COME. | LUKE 2. QUAERIT JESUM | 13 | MS 379 | 11 |
| OH COME THEN. BRING THY MOTHER HER LOST JOY. | LUKE 2. QUAERIT JESUM | 15 | MS 379 | 11 |
| OH COME, SWEET BOY. | LUKE 2. QUAERIT JESUM | 16 | MS 379 | 11 |
| MAKE HAST, & COME, OR E'RE MY GREIFE, & I | LUKE 2. QUAERIT JESUM | 17 | MS 379 | 11 |
| COME, BRAVE SOLDIERS, COME, & SEE | IN CICATRICES DOMINI JESU | 1 | MS 381 | 27 |
| COME, BRAVE SOLDIERS, COME, & SEE | IN CICATRICES DOMINI JESU | 1 | MS 381 | 27 |
| MISCHIEFE, THAT SCORNES EXPRESSION SHOULD COME NIGH IT. | ON GUNPOWDER-TREASON | 48 | MS 384 | 458 |
| COME GRIMME DESTRUCTION, & IN PURPLE GORE | UPON GUNPOWDER TREASON | 3 | MS 387 | 461 |
| BLACK DISMALL HORROR, COME, MAKE PERFECT NOW | UPON GUNPOWDER TREASON | 20 | MS 387 | 461 |
| IT MADE THE VIRGIN PHOENIX COME FARRE | UPON KINGS CORONATION | 30 | MS 390 | 453 |

COME--INTO

| | | | | |
|---|---|---|---|---|
| HEE'L COME--INTO THY HOUSE. NO, INTO THEE. | I AM NOT WORTHY | 4 | 46 90 | 13 |

COM'ST

| | | | | |
|---|---|---|---|---|
| SAY TO THE SULLEN MORNE, THOU COM'ST TO COURT HER. | ON A FOULE MORNING | 11 | 46 181 | 495 |

COMES

| | | | | |
|---|---|---|---|---|
| SUCH TO THE FRIGHTED PALACE NOW SHEE COMES, | SOSPETTO D'HERODE | 399 | 46 109 | 216 |
| SHE COMES TOTH' KING AND WITH HER COLD HAND SLAKES | SOSPETTO D'HERODE | 421 | 46 109 | 216 |
| WHAT ONE COMES TO REVEALE WHAT THEY CONSPIRE. | SOSPETTO D'HERODE | 446 | 46 109 | 216 |
| COMES NOT TO RULE IN WRATH, BUT SERVE IN LOVE. | SOSPETTO D'HERODE | 516 | 46 109 | 216 |
| WHICH HERE CONTRACTS IT SELFE AND COMES TO LYE | ON A PRAYER BOOKE | 10 | 46 126 | 139 |
| BUT IF THE NOBLE BRIDEGROME WHEN HEE COMES | ON A PRAYER BOOKE | 41 | 46 126 | 139 |
| WHO'S THIS THAT COMES CIRCLED IN RAYES, THAT SCORNE | UPON YORKE HIS BIRTH | 68 | 46 176 | 500 |
| ALL MISCHIEFE COMES AFTER ALL HALLOW. | UPON POWDER DAY | 2 | 46 185 | 74 |
| AND WHEN IT COMES SAY WELCOME FRIEND. | WISHES SUPPOSED MISTRESSE | 87 | 46 195 | 479 |
| SAY, LINGRING FAIR. WHY COMES THE BIRTH | TO COUNTESSE OF DENBIGH | 7 | 52 236 | 146 |
| LO, WHERE ALOFT IT COMES. IT COMES. AMONG | TO THE NAME OF JESUS | 151 | 52 239 | 30 |
| LO, WHERE ALOFT IT COMES. IT COMES. AMONG | TO THE NAME OF JESUS | 151 | 52 239 | 30 |
| LO WHERE IT COMES, UPON THE SNOWY DOVE'S | TO THE NAME OF JESUS | 159 | 52 239 | 30 |
| THE COMPLIN HOUR COMES LAST, TO CALL | OFFICE H. CROSS COMPLINE | 1 | 52 274 | 105 |
| HER HAPPY FIRE-WORKS, HERE, COMES DOWN TO SEE. | FLAMING HEART | 18 | 52 324 | 61 |
| LET THIS IMMORTALL LIFE WHERERE IT COMES | FLAMING HEART | 81 | 52 324 | 61 |

|  |  |  |  |  |  |
|---|---|---|---|---|---|
| WHICH HERE CONTRACTS IT SELF, & COMES TO LY | PRAYER TO GENTLE-WOMAN | 16 | 52 | 328 | 139 |
| SAY, LINGRING FAIR, WHY COMES THE BIRTH | AGAINST IRRESOLUTION AND DELAY | 15 | 52 | 347 | 146 |

COMMING

|  |  |  |  |  |  |
|---|---|---|---|---|---|
| AND COMMING LATE HAD EAT UP GUESTS AND ALL, | THE BEGINNING OF HELIODORUS | 27 | 46 | 158 | 517 |
| A COMMING DEITY. HEE SAW THE NEST | SOSPETTO D'HERODE | 126 | 46 | 109 | 216 |

COMET

|  |  |  |  |  |  |
|---|---|---|---|---|---|
| A LIVING COMET, WHOSE PESTIFEROUSE BREATH | ON GUNPOWDER-TREASON | 17 | MS | 384 | 458 |

COMETS

|  |  |  |  |  |  |
|---|---|---|---|---|---|
| OF STARING COMETS, THAT LOOKE KINGDOMES DEAD. | SOSPETTO D'HERODE | 52 | 46 | 109 | 216 |

COMFORT

|  |  |  |  |  |  |
|---|---|---|---|---|---|
| WHERE DAWNING HOPE NO BEAME OF COMFORT SHOWES. | SOSPETTO D'HERODE | 242 | 46 | 109 | 216 |
| TEARES SHALL TAKE COMFORT, AND TURNE GEMS. | IN MEMORY OF LADY MADRE TERESA | 150 | 46 | 131 | 52 |
| TEARES SHALL TAKE COMFORT, & TURN GEMMS | TERESA | 149 | 52 | 315 | 52 |

COMFORTS

|  |  |  |  |  |  |
|---|---|---|---|---|---|
| OF COMFORTS, WHICH THOU HAST IN KEEPING. | TO THE NAME OF JESUS | 190 | 52 | 239 | 30 |

COMLY

|  |  |  |  |  |  |
|---|---|---|---|---|---|
| AFFECT MORE COMLY BANDS | PRAYER TO GENTLE-WOMAN | 6 | 52 | 328 | 139 |

COMMAND

|  |  |  |  |  |  |
|---|---|---|---|---|---|
| MONGST ALL THE PALACES IN HELLS COMMAND, | SOSPETTO D'HERODE | 305 | 46 | 109 | 216 |
| DECLARE WHO SENDS, AND WHAT IS HIS COMMAND. | SOSPETTO D'HERODE | 512 | 46 | 109 | 216 |
| WHERE THOU SHALT REACH ALL HEARTS, COMMAND EACH EYE. | ON A TREATISE OF CHARITY | 16 | 46 | 137 | 69 |
| AND WILT COMMAND PROUD ZEPHIRUS TO SPORT HER | ON A FOULE MORNING | 12 | 46 | 181 | 495 |
| THAT SHALL COMMAND MY HEART AND MEE. | WISHES SUPPOSED MISTRESSE | 3 | 46 | 195 | 479 |
| AH HARD COMMAND | SANCTA MARIA DOLORUM | 35 | 52 | 283 | 162 |
| LET THOSE LIFE-SPEAKING LIPPS COMMAND | DIES IRAE | 63 | 52 | 298 | 186 |
| YET SHALL MY LOYALL TONGUE KEEPE THIS COMMAND. | UPON BIRTH PRINCESSE E | 15 | MS | 391 | 456 |
| OF DEEPEST SILENCE ANSWERED MY COMMAND. | OUT OF GROTIUS | 84 | MS | 398 | 198 |

COMMANDING

|  |  |  |  |  |  |
|---|---|---|---|---|---|
| THE HEAT COMMANDING IN MY HEART DOTH SIT. | OUT OF THE ITALIAN (2) | 4 | 46 | 190 | 547 |

COMMANDS

|  |  |  |  |  |  |
|---|---|---|---|---|---|
| TH'OBSEQUIOUS HANDMAIDS OF THY HIGH COMMANDS. | SOSPETTO D'HERODE | 262 | 46 | 109 | 216 |
| ON US THY DREAD COMMANDS, OURS TO OBEY. | SOSPETTO D'HERODE | 264 | 46 | 109 | 216 |

COMMEND

|  |  |  |  |  |  |
|---|---|---|---|---|---|
| AND CAN ALONE COMMEND THE REST. | WISHES SUPPOSED MISTRESSE | 27 | 46 | 195 | 479 |
| INTO THY HANDS, AND HART, LORD, I COMMEND. | OFFICE H. CROSS RECOMMENDATION | 2 | 52 | 276 | 106 |

COMMERCE

|  |  |  |  |  |  |
|---|---|---|---|---|---|
| A COMMERCE OF CONTRARY POWRES, | IN GLORIOUS EPIPHANIE | 214 | 52 | 253 | 39 |

COMMON

|  |  |  |  |  |  |
|---|---|---|---|---|---|
| O 'TWILL UNDOE OUR COMMON MOTHER, | UPON DEATH OF DESIRED HERRYS | 23 | 46 | 168 | 467 |
| COMMON CREATURES, | OUT OF THE ITALIAN (1) | 38 | 46 | 188 | 545 |
| WHAT E'RE COOPERATES TO THE COMMON MIRTHE | TO THE NAME OF JESUS | 75 | 52 | 239 | 30 |
| A COMMON BANQUETT. NOE, HEERE'S PRINCELY FARE | UPON GUNPOWDER TREASON | 6 | MS | 387 | 461 |

COMMON-PEOPLE

|  |  |  |  |  |  |
|---|---|---|---|---|---|
| OPREST THE COMMON-PEOPLE OF THE SKYES. | SOSPETTO D'HERODE | 240 | 46 | 109 | 216 |

COMPACTED

|  |  |  |  |  |  |
|---|---|---|---|---|---|
| O THOU COMPACTED | TO THE NAME OF JESUS | 165 | 52 | 239 | 30 |

COMPANY

|  |  |  |  |  |  |
|---|---|---|---|---|---|
| NOR KEEP SUCH NOBLE SORROWES COMPANY. | SANCTA MARIA DOLORUM | 14 | 52 | 283 | 162 |
| IF WEE'D VOUCHSAFE HIS COMPANY, | AGAINST IRRESOLUTION AND DELAY | 68 | 52 | 347 | 146 |

COMPARISON

|  |  |  |  |  |  |
|---|---|---|---|---|---|
| MAKE SUCH ANOTHER SWEET COMPARISON. | UPON YORKE HIS BIRTH | 52 | 46 | 176 | 500 |

COMPARRISON

|  |  |  |  |  |  |
|---|---|---|---|---|---|
| BY THE COMPARRISON THEY SHALL PUT ON | UPON TWO GREENE APRICOCKES | 7 | 48 | 220 | 494 |

COMPELL

|  |  |  |  |  |  |
|---|---|---|---|---|---|
| PROUD SONS OF DEATH, THAT DURST COMPELL | IN GLORIOUS EPIPHANIE | 109 | 52 | 253 | 39 |

COMPELL'D
  WHOM THEY COMPELL'D BEFORE TO BE THEIR SIN)        IN GLORIOUS EPIPHANIE            177  52 253  39
COMPENDIOUS
  PORTABLE, & COMPENDIOUS OCEANS.                    WEEPER                           114  52 307 120
COMPILE
  COMPILE A FIFT GLORIOUS EPITOME                    UPON BIRTH PRINCESSE E            57  MS 391 456
COMPLAIN
  GENTLE SPIRITS, DOE NOT COMPLAIN.                  TO THE NAME OF JESUS             111  52 239  30
  O HOW OFT SHALT THOU COMPLAIN                      TERESA                            97  52 315  52
COMPLIN
  THE COMPLIN HOUR COMES LAST, TO CALL               OFFICE H. CROSS COMPLINE           1  52 274 105
COMPLAINE
  HARKE HOW AT EVERY TOUCH SHE DOES COMPLAINE HER.   TO PONTIUS WASHING HANDS          12  46  94  23
  IN ARMES, WHEN LESSER CAUSE WAS TO COMPLAINE.      SOSPETTO D'HERODE                454  46 109 216
  O HOW OFT SHALT THOU COMPLAINE                     IN MEMORY OF LADY MADRE TERESA    97  46 131  52
COMPLAYNE
  NOR LETT HER KINRED BIRDS COMPLAYNE                THOUGH NOW 'TIS NEITHER           15  MS 397 492
COMPLAINES
  HEAR, FATHER, HEAR, THY LAMB (AT LAST) COMPLAINES. OFFICE H. CROSS NINTH              3  52 271  99
COMPLAINING
  RUNS TO AND FRO, COMPLAINING HIS SWEET CARES       MUSICKS DUELL                    142  46 149 535/
  COMPLAINING PIPES, & PRATTLING STRINGS,            TO THE NAME OF JESUS              65  52 239  30
  TO LY THUS FOLDED, & COMPLAINING                   PRAYER TO GENTLE-WOMAN             4  52 328 139
COMPOSES
  AND SAY THAT IVORY HER FRONT COMPOSES.             UPON BIRTH PRINCESSE E            46  MS 391 456
ALL-COMPOSING
  HATE THE SWEET PEACE OF ALL-COMPOSING NIGHT.       SOSPETTO D'HERODE                496  46 109 216
COMPOSITION
  SOME BIGG-NAMED COMPOSITION,                       IN PRAISE OF LESSIUS               6  46 156 510
  SOME BIG-NAM'D COMPOSITION.                        TEMPERANCE                         6  52 342 510
COMPOSURE
  IN COMPOSURE OF HIS FACE.                          HIS EPITAPH (HERRYS)              27  46 172 471
COMPOSURES
  RIPE AS THOSE RICH COMPOSURES TIME COMPUTES        UPON TWO GREENE APRICOCKES        13  48 220 494
COMPUTES
  RIPE AS THOSE RICH COMPOSURES TIME COMPUTES        UPON TWO GREENE APRICOCKES        13  48 220 494
CONCEAL'D
  A MOST STRANGE BABE. WHO HERE CONCEAL'D BY THEM    SOSPETTO D'HERODE                435  46 109 216
CONCEITED
  THOUGH HIS WINGS CONCEITED HEWE                    PETRONIJ ALES PHASIACIS PETITA     7  MS 382 526
CONCEIVE
  CONCEIVE PROUD HOPES OF PROVING ROSES.             ON BLEEDING WOUNDS OF LORD        24  46 101 110
CONCEPTIONS
  HER WEAKE CONCEPTIONS. NO LOANE SHADE, BUT RINGS   OUT OF VIRGIL                      9  46 155 529
  UNFOLD THY FAIR CONCEPTIONS. AND DISPLAY           TO THE NAME OF JESUS             163  52 239  30
CONCERNING
  WE COURT THY MORE CONCERNING SMILES.               IN GLORIOUS EPIPHANIE             81  52 253  39

| | | | | |
|---|---|---|---|---|
| CONCURRENCES | | | | |
| STRUCKE WITH THESE GREAT CONCURRENCES OF THINGS, | SOSPETTO D'HERODE | 137 | 46 109 | 216 |
| CONDENSED | | | | |
| (CLOWD OF CONDENSED SWEETS) & BREAK UPON US | TO THE NAME OF JESUS | 168 | 52 239 | 30 |
| CONDITION | | | | |
| DEATH WILL ON THIS CONDITION BE CONTENT TO DY. | EASTER DAY | 18 | 46 100 | 26 |
| CONDUCT | | | | |
| THE CONDUCT OF ADORING SPIRITS, THAT THRONG | TO THE NAME OF JESUS | 152 | 52 239 | 30 |
| JOY-CONDUCTED | | | | |
| TO MY JOY-CONDUCTED FEET, | PSALME 23 | 31 | 46 102 | 5 |
| CONFEDERATE | | | | |
| AND WHISPER'D THE CONFEDERATE EARTH | LOVES HOROSCOPE | 28 | 46 185 | 483 |
| CONFEDERAT | | | | |
| BY CONFEDERAT BLACK & WHITE | IN GLORIOUS EPIPHANIE | 217 | 52 253 | 39 |
| CONFESS'T | | | | |
| MAKES ME CONFESS'T. OH, DOE NOT THOU WITH SCORNE. | EX EUPHORMIONE | 6 | MS 392 | 525 |
| CONFES'T | | | | |
| WITH A RED FACE CONFES'T THIS SCORN. | IN GLORIOUS EPIPHANIE | 122 | 52 253 | 39 |
| OR WHO THY CROSSE CONFES'T & CROWN'D. | DIES IRAE | 50 | 52 298 | 186 |
| CONFESSE | | | | |
| ALL TREES, ALL LEAVY GROVES CONFESSE THE SPRING | OUT OF VIRGIL | 1 | 46 155 | 529 |
| SMILING IN THY CHEEKES, CONFESSE, | THE WEEPER | 86 | 46 79 | 120 |
| HEE SAW THE FALLING IDOLS, ALL CONFESSE | SOSPETTO D'HERODE | 125 | 46 109 | 216 |
| BECAUSE HE'S STIFFE, AND WILL CONFESSE NO KNEE. | ON A TREATISE OF CHARITY | 40 | 46 137 | 69 |
| TO SHOW A FACE, FIT TO CONFESSE THY KIN | UPON STANINOUGH'S DEATH | 18 | 46 175 | 475 |
| JOYES, THAT CONFESSE, | WISHES SUPPOSED MISTRESSE | 67 | 46 195 | 479 |
| SMILING IN THY CHEEKS, CONFESSE | WEEPER | 80 | 52 307 | 120 |
| TO SHOW A FACE, FITT TO CONFESSE THY KIN, | DEATH'S LECTURE | 19 | 52 340 | 475 |
| CONFESSES | | | | |
| NO HOME FOR HER CONFESSES SHEE, | IN MEMORY OF LADY MADRE TERESA | 45 | 46 131 | 52 |
| BLOSSOMS, BUT OUR BLEST TAST CONFESSES FRUITS. | UPON TWO GREENE APRICOCKES | 14 | 48 220 | 494 |
| NO HOME FOR HERS CONFESSES SHE | TERESA | 45 | 52 315 | 52 |
| CONFESSING | | | | |
| CONFESSING THEE. OR (IF TOO LONG I STAY) | UPON YORKE HIS BIRTH | 112 | 46 176 | 500 |
| CONFESSOURS | | | | |
| OF CONFESSOURS, WHOSE THROATES ANSWERING HIS SWORDS, | SOSPETTO D'HERODE | 7 | 46 109 | 216 |
| CONFIDENTLY | | | | |
| AND CONFIDENTLY LOOK | PRAYER TO GENTLE-WOMAN | 8 | 52 328 | 139 |
| CONFINES | | | | |
| MY FAIRE INHERITANCE, HEE CONFINES ME HERE, | SOSPETTO D'HERODE | 212 | 46 109 | 216 |
| CONFLUENCE | | | | |
| SWELLS HIGH, FAIR CONFLUENCE OF ALL HIGHBORN BLOUD. | TO THE QUEEN'S MAJESTY | 16 | 52 261 | 47 |
| CONFOUND | | | | |
| WEE'L CONFOUND THE RECKONING QUITE, | OUT OF CATULLUS | 17 | 46 194 | 523 |
| CONFUSION | | | | |
| SHALL THEN WITH JUST CONFUSION, BOW | TO THE NAME OF JESUS | 238 | 52 239 | 30 |
| CONFUTE | | | | |
| COME ONCE THE CONQUERING WAY. NOT TO CONFUTE | TO COUNTESSE OF DENBIGH | 39 | 52 236 | 146 |
| CONFUTING | | | | |
| EACH OTHER KISSING & CONFUTING. | WEEPER | 94 | 52 307 | 120 |

CONQUER

| | | | | | |
|---|---|---|---|---|---|
| THAT BEING NAK'T, THOU KNOW'ST COULD CONQUER THEE. | UPON THE SAME (VENUS ARMES) | 4 | 46 | 161 | 523 |
| AND BLEED & WOUND, AND YEILD & CONQUER STILL. | FLAMING HEART | 80 | 52 | 324 | 61 |

CONQUERING

| | | | | | |
|---|---|---|---|---|---|
| COME ONCE THE CONQUERING WAY. NOT TO CONFUTE | TO COUNTESSE OF DENBIGH | 39 | 52 | 236 | 146 |
| WHERE YEILDING & YET CONQUERING HE | OFFICE H. CROSS EVENSONG | 24 | 52 | 273 | 101 |
| LIVE IN THESE CONQUERING LEAVES, LIVE ALL THE SAME. | FLAMING HEART | 77 | 52 | 324 | 61 |
| THIS WAS THE CONQUERING DART, & LOE | IN CICATRICES DOMINI JESU | 3 | MS | 381 | 27 |

CONQUESTS

| | | | | | |
|---|---|---|---|---|---|
| THEY, BOTH AT ONCE THY CONQUESTS BEE, | NEITHER DURST MAN ASKE | 7 | 46 | 92 | 20 |
| AND THY CONQUESTS MEMORYE. | NEITHER DURST MAN ASKE | 8 | 46 | 92 | 20 |

CONSCIENCE

| | | | | | |
|---|---|---|---|---|---|
| ONE WHOSE CONSCIENCE WAS A THING. | AN EPITAPH UPON ASHTON | 5 | 46 | 192 | 464 |

CONSCIOUS

| | | | | | |
|---|---|---|---|---|---|
| SHEE CONSULTS THE CONSCIOUS SPHEARES, | LOVES HOROSCOPE | 3 | 46 | 185 | 483 |
| COUCH'T IN THAT CONSCIOUS SHADE | IN GLORIOUS EPIPHANIE | 190 | 52 | 253 | 39 |
| THE CONSCIOUS COLORS OF MY SIN | DIES IRAE | 43 | 52 | 298 | 186 |

CONSECRATE

| | | | | | |
|---|---|---|---|---|---|
| NOW SEEM THEY TEMPLES CONSECRATE TO NONE, | ON A TREATISE OF CHARITY | 37 | 46 | 137 | 69 |

CONSECRATED

| | | | | | |
|---|---|---|---|---|---|
| HEAP UP THY CONSECRATED KISSES. | IN MEMORY OF LADY MADRE TERESA | 133 | 46 | 131 | 52 |
| HEAP UP THY CONSECRATED KISSES. | TERESA | 132 | 52 | 315 | 52 |
| BEE CONSECRATED TO THIS WORKE, WHILE I | UPON BIRTH PRINCESSE E | 23 | MS | 391 | 456 |

CONSENT

| | | | | | |
|---|---|---|---|---|---|
| AND LATE CONSENT WAS A LONG NO, | TO COUNTESSE OF DENBIGH | 14 | 52 | 236 | 146 |
| AND LATE CONSENT WAS A LONG NO. | AGAINST IRRESOLUTION AND DELAY | 8 | 52 | 347 | 146 |

CONSERVED

| | | | | | |
|---|---|---|---|---|---|
| THE ROSES FRESH, CONSERVED FROM THE RAGE. | UPON GUNPOWDER TREASON | 43 | MS | 387 | 461 |

CONSIDER

| | | | | | |
|---|---|---|---|---|---|
| SWEET, CONSIDER THEN, THAT I | ADORO TE | 27 | 52 | 291 | 172 |

CONSISTENT

| | | | | | |
|---|---|---|---|---|---|
| IS ONE CONSISTENT SOLID SMILE. | IN GLORIOUS EPIPHANIE | 31 | 52 | 253 | 39 |

CONSORT

| | | | | | |
|---|---|---|---|---|---|
| THAT JARRES, AND SPOILES SWEET CONSORT SOE. | UPON DEATH OF A FREIND | 8 | MS | 393 | 477 |
| GONE BE ALL CONSORT, SINCE ALONE | UPON DEATH OF A FREIND | 17 | MS | 393 | 477 |

CONSPICUOUS

| | | | | | |
|---|---|---|---|---|---|
| IF NOT MORE GLORIOUS, MORE CONSPICUOUS THO. | ON A TREATISE OF CHARITY | 26 | 46 | 137 | 69 |
| HIS PENANCE, AS OUR FAULT, CONSPICUOUS. | IN GLORIOUS EPIPHANIE | 158 | 52 | 253 | 39 |

CONSPIRACY

| | | | | | |
|---|---|---|---|---|---|
| THE FATES RIPE, IN THEIR GREAT CONSPIRACY. | SOSPETTO D'HERODE | 432 | 46 | 109 | 216 |
| TO THE CONSPIRACY OF OUR SPATIOUS SONG. | TO THE NAME OF JESUS | 71 | 52 | 239 | 30 |

CONSPIRE

| | | | | | |
|---|---|---|---|---|---|
| HOW MANY PRESENT PRODIGIES CONSPIRE, | SOSPETTO D'HERODE | 94 | 46 | 109 | 216 |
| WHAT ONE COMES TO REVEALE WHAT THEY CONSPIRE. | SOSPETTO D'HERODE | 446 | 46 | 109 | 216 |
| THE CALDRON-PRISON'D WATERS STREIGHT CONSPIRE. | SOSPETTO D'HERODE | 483 | 46 | 109 | 216 |

CONSPIR'D

| | | | | | |
|---|---|---|---|---|---|
| CONSPIR'D WITH DARKNES 'GAINST THE STRANGERS THROATE. | HORATIJ ILLE & NEFASTO | 9 | MS | 382 | 530 |

CONSPIRING

| | | | | | |
|---|---|---|---|---|---|
| HOPE KICKS THE CURL'D HEADS OF CONSPIRING STARRES. | ON HOPE | 72 | 46 | 143 | 71 |
| HOPE WALKS, & KICKES THE CURLD HEADS OF CONSPIRING STARRES. | (ON) HOPE | 32 | 52 | 345 | 71 |

CONSTANCY

| | | | | | |
|---|---|---|---|---|---|
| THE TOO FRAIL LIFE OF FEMAL CONSTANCY. | ALEXIAS FIRST ELEGIE | 34 | 52 | 334 | 204 |

CONSTANT

| | | | | | |
|---|---|---|---|---|---|
| LET CONSTANT USE BUT KEEP IT BRIGHT. | ON A PRAYER BOOKE | 16 | 46 | 126 | 139 |
| LET CONSTANT USE BUT KEEP IT BRIGHT. | PRAYER TO GENTLE-WOMAN | 22 | 52 | 328 | 139 |

## CONSTELLATION

| | | | | | |
|---|---|---|---|---|---|
| AT LAST A CONSTANT LOVE THAT LEAVES ME NOT. | ALEXIAS SECONDE ELEGIE | 8 | 52 | 335 | 207 |

## CONSTELLATION

| | | | | | |
|---|---|---|---|---|---|
| WEAVE A CONSTELLATION | IN MEMORY OF LADY MADRE TERESA | 143 | 46 | 131 | 52 |
| VENUS, MAY HAVE A CONSTELLATION. | UPON YORKE HIS BIRTH | 58 | 46 | 176 | 500 |
| THE KINDEST CONSTELLATION, | LOVES HOROSCOPE | 26 | 46 | 185 | 483 |
| WEAVE A CONSTELLATION | TERESA | 142 | 52 | 315 | 52 |
| DOE I NOT SEE A CONSTELLATION. | UPON KINGS CORONATION | 29 | MS | 389 | 454 |

## CONSULT

| | | | | | |
|---|---|---|---|---|---|
| TWO SILKEN SISTER FLOWERS CONSULT, AND LAY | UPON YORKE HIS BIRTH | 60 | 46 | 176 | 500 |

## CONSULTS

| | | | | | |
|---|---|---|---|---|---|
| SHEE CONSULTS THE CONSCIOUS SPHEARES. | LOVES HOROSCOPE | 3 | 46 | 185 | 483 |

## CONSUME

| | | | | | |
|---|---|---|---|---|---|
| THAT THOUGH IT SHINES, 'TIS FIRE AND WILL CONSUME. | OUT OF GREEKE CUPID'S CRYER | 74 | 46 | 159 | 519 |

## CONSUMPTION

| | | | | | |
|---|---|---|---|---|---|
| WHOSE UNCONSUM'D CONSUMPTION PREYS UPON | SOSPETTO D'HERODE | 59 | 46 | 109 | 216 |

## CONTEMPT

| | | | | | |
|---|---|---|---|---|---|
| CONTEMPT & SCORN CAN SEND WOUNDS TO SEARCH THE INMOST | OFFICE H. CROSS SIXT | 12 | 52 | 270 | 97 |

## CONTEND

| | | | | | |
|---|---|---|---|---|---|
| CONTEND, YE POWRES OF HEAV'N & EARTH. | IN HOLY NATIVITY | 41 | 52 | 246 | 76 |
| THEIR WEALTHY TOPS. & FOR THESE FEET CONTEND. | TO THE QUEEN'S MAJESTY | 18 | 52 | 261 | 47 |

## CONTENDING

| | | | | | |
|---|---|---|---|---|---|
| SET THE CONTENDING SONS OF HEAV'N ON FIRE. | SOSPETTO D'HERODE | 90 | 46 | 109 | 216 |

## CONTENT

| | | | | | |
|---|---|---|---|---|---|
| CONTENT AND QUIET WOULD HE GOE, | THE WEEPER | 82 | 46 | 79 | 120 |
| DEATH WILL ON THIS CONDITION BE CONTENT TO DY. | EASTER DAY | 18 | 46 | 100 | 26 |
| CONTENT & QUIET HE WOULD GOE. | WEEPER | 76 | 52 | 307 | 120 |

## CONTENTED

| | | | | | |
|---|---|---|---|---|---|
| WEE ARE CONTENTED. FOR THEN THIS | UPON THE DEATH OF A GENTLEMAN | 21 | 46 | 166 | 472 |

## CONTENTFULL

| | | | | | |
|---|---|---|---|---|---|
| BEYOND THE KINGDOMES OF CONTENTFULL CELLS. | DESCRIPTION RELIGIOUS HOUSE | 35 | 52 | 338 | 213 |

## CONTEST

| | | | | | |
|---|---|---|---|---|---|
| FOR WHOM (AS DEAD) THE WRATHFULL WINDS CONTEST, | SOSPETTO D'HERODE | 427 | 46 | 109 | 216 |
| PROUD WORLD, SAID I. CEASE YOUR CONTEST | IN HOLY NATIVITY | 44 | 52 | 246 | 76 |
| TO SEE SO MANY UNKIND SWORDS CONTEST | SANCTA MARIA DOLORUM | 17 | 52 | 283 | 162 |
| O SWEET CONTEST. OF WOES | WEEPER | 91 | 52 | 307 | 120 |

## CONTRACT

| | | | | | |
|---|---|---|---|---|---|
| HUGE EMPTINESSE CONTRACT THY BULKE, AND SHRINKE | UPON STANINOUGH'S DEATH | 13 | 46 | 175 | 475 |
| HUGE EMPTYNES. CONTRACT THY SELF. & SHRINKE | DEATH'S LECTURE | 14 | 52 | 340 | 475 |

## CONTRACTS

| | | | | | |
|---|---|---|---|---|---|
| WHICH HERE CONTRACTS IT SELFE AND COMES TO LYE | ON A PRAYER BOOKE | 10 | 46 | 126 | 139 |
| WHICH HERE CONTRACTS IT SELF, & COMES TO LY | PRAYER TO GENTLE-WOMAN | 16 | 52 | 328 | 139 |

## CONTRARIETYES

| | | | | | |
|---|---|---|---|---|---|
| CLOSE IN KIND CONTRARIETYES. | WEEPER | 96 | 52 | 307 | 120 |

## CONTRARY

| | | | | | |
|---|---|---|---|---|---|
| A COMMERCE OF CONTRARY POWRES, | IN GLORIOUS EPIPHANIE | 214 | 52 | 253 | 39 |

## CONTRITE

| | | | | | |
|---|---|---|---|---|---|
| AND CRUMBLED INTO CONTRITE DUST. | DIES IRAE | 66 | 52 | 298 | 186 |

## CONTROL'D

| | | | | | |
|---|---|---|---|---|---|
| IN A CLAY-COTTAGE, BY EACH BLAST CONTROL'D. | SOSPETTO D'HERODE | 182 | 46 | 109 | 216 |

## CONTROLL

| | | | | | |
|---|---|---|---|---|---|
| AND BY THEIR LOVE CONTROLL THEIR FATE. | AGAINST IRRESOLUTION AND DELAY | 50 | 52 | 347 | 146 |

## CONTROUL

| | | | | | |
|---|---|---|---|---|---|
| KNOWES ALL THE CORNERS OF'T, & CAN CONTROUL | TO COUNTESSE OF DENBIGH | 35 | 52 | 236 | 146 |

CONTROULES

   AND LOVES THAT BODIES SOULE. NO LAW CONTROULES     AN APOLOGIE FOR HYMNE (TERESA)    18   46 136   59

CONTROWLLS

   AND LOVE'S THAT BODY'S SOUL, NO LAW CONTROWLLS     AN APOLOGIE FOR (TERESA) HYMNE    18   52 322   59

CONTROVERTED

   OF CONTROVERTED LIGHT,     IN GLORIOUS EPIPHANIE    147   52 253   39

CONTROVERTING

   IN CONTROVERTING WARBLES EVENLY SHAR'D.     MUSICKS DUELL    42   46 149 535

CONVENANT

   'CAUSE BY THE CONVENANT OF THY CROSSE     OFFICE H. CROSS PRIME    20   52 267   91
   'CAUSE BY THE CONVENANT OF THY CROSSE,     OFFICE H. CROSS THIRD    19   52 268   93
   'CAUSE BY THE CONVENANT OF THY CROSSE.     OFFICE H. CROSS SIXT    23   52 270   97
   'CAUSE BY THE CONVENANT OF THY CROSSE     OFFICE H. CROSS NINTH    16   52 271   99
   'CAUSE BY THE CONVENANT OF THY CROSSE.     OFFICE H. CROSS EVENSONG    30   52 273 101

CONVENE

   THAT THEY CONVENE & COME AWAY     TO THE NAME OF JESUS    41   52 239   30

CONVERTS

   (THE HAPPY CONVERTS NOW OF HIM     IN GLORIOUS EPIPHANIE    176   52 253   39

CONVEY'D

   CONVEY'D HIS SWEET DELICIOUS TRESURY     UPON GUNPOWDER TREASON    55   MS 387 461

CONVICTORS

   CONVICTORS OF THINE OWN FULL CUP,     LAUDA SION SALVATOREM    76   52 294 178

COOLE

   WITH THE COOLE EPODE OF A GRAVER NOAT,     MUSICKS DUELL    99   46 149 535
   SHOULD COOLE HIS FIERY WHEELS, & NEVER SINKE     UPON GUNPOWDER TREASON    39   MS 386 460

COOLS

   THE CALM THAT COOLS THINE EYE DOES SHIPWRACK MINE,     AND A CERTAINE PRIEST PASSED    3   46   94   17
       FOR O.

COOLES

   WARMES IN THE ONE, COOLES IN THE OTHER.     A HYMNE OF THE NATIVITY    64   46 106   76
   WARMES IN THE ONE, COOLES IN THE OTHER.     IN HOLY NATIVITY    90   52 246   76

COOPERATES

   WHAT E'RE COOPERATES TO THE COMMON MIRTHE     TO THE NAME OF JESUS    75   52 239   30

COPY

   THIS WELL-WROUGHT COPY THE FAIRE PRINCIPALL.     UPON YORKE HIS BIRTH    48   46 176 500

COPPY

   IN LINES OF DEATH, MY LIFE MAY COPPY IT     SANCTA MARIA DOLORUM    54   52 283 162
   HAD YOU BUT DRAWNE ONE LIVELY COPPY FORTH,     UPON BIRTH PRINCESSE E    29   MS 391 456

COPPIE

   COULD SHE IN ALL HER BIRTHS BUT COPPIE THEE,     UPON TWO GREENE APRICOCKES    23   48 220 494

CORALL

   THE CORALL OF THY LIPS. THOU ART OF ALL     UPON YORKE HIS BIRTH    47   46 176 500

CORRALLIZE

   TO CORRALLIZE, WHICH SOFTLY WONT TO SLIDE     AN ELEGY MR STANNINOW    23   MS 394 473

CORDIALL

   BUT WITH ONE CORDIALL SMILE. FOR (LOE) THAT POWER     EX EUPHORMIONE    4   MS 392 525

CORNER

   AT EACH CORNER PEEPING FORTH,     HIS EPITAPH (HERRYS)    38   46 172 471
   WHILE FROM ANOTHER (UNSEENE) CORNER BLOWES     HORATIJ ILLE & NEFASTO    23   MS 382 530

CORNERS

   AND CRUSH THE WORLD TILL HIS WIDE CORNERS MEET.     SOSPETTO D'HERODE    280   46 109 216
   KNOWES ALL THE CORNERS OF'T, & CAN CONTROUL     TO COUNTESSE OF DENBIGH    35   52 236 146

## CORRESPONDENT

| | | | | | |
|---|---|---|---|---|---|
| HIS CORRESPONDENT CHEEKES. THESE LOATHSOME STRINGS | SOSPETTO D'HERODE | 38 | 46 | 109 | 216 |

## COST

| | | | | | |
|---|---|---|---|---|---|
| DISDAINEFULL WRETCH. HOW HATH ONE BOLD SINNE COST | SOSPETTO D'HERODE | 73 | 46 | 109 | 216 |
| COME THY CREATOR TOO, WHAT THOUGH IT COST | SOSPETTO D'HERODE | 253 | 46 | 109 | 216 |
| PUT POORE NATURE TO SUCH COST. | UPON DEATH OF DESIRED HERRYS | 22 | 46 | 168 | 467 |
| THAT (AT THY COST) ARE CALL'D, NOT VAINLY, OURS | IN GLORIOUS EPIPHANIE | 220 | 52 | 253 | 39 |
| SHALL ALL THAT LABOUR, ALL THAT COST | DIES IRAE | 33 | 52 | 298 | 166 |
| 'EVN FOR HIM WITH WHOM NOR COST. | TO SAME CONCERNING CHOISE | 38 | 52 | 331 | 66 |
| O HAD HE NERE BEEN AT THAT CRUELL COST | ALEXIAS THIRD ELEGIE | 5 | 52 | 336 | 209 |

## COSTE

| | | | | | |
|---|---|---|---|---|---|
| LORD, WHAT IS MAN, WHY SHOULD HE COSTE THEE | CHARITAS NIMIA | 1 | 52 | 280 | 48 |

## COSTLY

| | | | | | |
|---|---|---|---|---|---|
| (A CRUELL AND A COSTLY SPRING) | ON BLEEDING WOUNDS OF LORD | 23 | 46 | 101 | 110 |
| HER CRUELL CLOATHES OF COSTLY THREDS THEY WEAVE, | SOSPETTO D'HERODE | 343 | 46 | 109 | 216 |
| TO MAKE HIS COSTLY CRADLE OF THY BEERE. | UPON YORKE HIS BIRTH | 95 | 46 | 176 | 500 |
| THY COSTLY EXCELLENCE WITH THY KING'S OWN BLOOD. | VEXILLA REGIS | 30 | 52 | 277 | 156 |
| O COSTLY INTERCOURSE | SANCTA MARIA DOLORUM | 21 | 52 | 283 | 162 |
| AND WEPT AMAINE. THEN REAR'D A COSTLY TOMBE, | UPON GUNPOWDER TREASON | 50 | MS | 366 | 460 |
| AS TO REFRAINE) BROUGHT FORTH A COSTLY SHOWER | UPON KINGS CORONATION | 6 | MS | 390 | 453 |
| A BLOUD DRUNKE ERROUR SPILT THE COSTLY AYME | OUT OF GROTIUS | 29 | MS | 398 | 198 |

## COSTLYER

| | | | | | |
|---|---|---|---|---|---|
| ONELY A COSTLYER DISEASE. | IN PRAISE OF LESSIUS | 10 | 46 | 156 | 510 |
| NOR IVORY COUCHES COSTLYER SLUMBERS KEEPING. | DESCRIPTION RELIGIOUS HOUSE | 4 | 52 | 338 | 213 |
| ONLY A COSTLYER DISEASE. | TEMPERANCE | 10 | 52 | 342 | 510 |

## CLAY-COTTAGE

| | | | | | |
|---|---|---|---|---|---|
| IN A CLAY-COTTAGE, BY EACH BLAST CONTROL'D. | SOSPETTO D'HERODE | 182 | 46 | 109 | 216 |

## COUCH

| | | | | | |
|---|---|---|---|---|---|
| AND COUCH BEFORE THE DAZELING LIGHT OF THY DREAD MAJESTY. | TO THE NAME OF JESUS | 235 | 52 | 239 | 30 |

## COUCH'D

| | | | | | |
|---|---|---|---|---|---|
| THE WILD WAVES COUCH'D. THE SEA FORGOTT TO SWEAT | OUT OF GROTIUS | 67 | MS | 398 | 198 |

## COUCHT

| | | | | | |
|---|---|---|---|---|---|
| CLOSE COUCHT IN YOUR WHITE BOSOME, AND FROM THENCE | ON A PRAYER BOOKE | 11 | 46 | 126 | 139 |

## COUCH'T

| | | | | | |
|---|---|---|---|---|---|
| COUCH'T IN THAT CONSCIOUS SHADE | IN GLORIOUS EPIPHANIE | 190 | 52 | 253 | 39 |
| CLOSE COUCH'T IN YOUR WHITE BOSOM. & FROM THENCE | PRAYER TO GENTLE-WOMAN | 17 | 52 | 328 | 139 |

## COUCHES

| | | | | | |
|---|---|---|---|---|---|
| NOR IVORY COUCHES COSTLYER SLUMBERS KEEPING. | DESCRIPTION RELIGIOUS HOUSE | 4 | 52 | 338 | 213 |

## COUGH

| | | | | | |
|---|---|---|---|---|---|
| THE FIRST BLAST OF THY COUGH LEFT TWO ALONE, | OUT OF MARTIALL | 3 | 46 | 188 | 527 |
| THIS LAST COUGH AELIA, COUGHT OUT ALL THY FEARE, | OUT OF MARTIALL | 5 | 46 | 188 | 527 |
| TH'HAST LEFT THE THIRD COUGH NOW NO BUSINESSE HERE. | OUT OF MARTIALL | 6 | 46 | 188 | 527 |

## COUGHT

| | | | | | |
|---|---|---|---|---|---|
| THIS LAST COUGH AELIA, COUGHT OUT ALL THY FEARE, | OUT OF MARTIALL | 5 | 46 | 188 | 527 |

## COUNSAILE

| | | | | | |
|---|---|---|---|---|---|
| WHAT ALL THY WEALTH IN COUNSAILE. ALL THY STATE. | ON THE PRODIGALL | 3 | 46 | 86 | 17 |

## COUNSELL

| | | | | | |
|---|---|---|---|---|---|
| (THOUGH THE HEAVENS IN COUNSELL SATE, | LOVES HOROSCOPE | 23 | 46 | 185 | 483 |
| HER COUNSELL HER OWNE VERTUE BEE. | WISHES SUPPOSED MISTRESSE | 102 | 46 | 195 | 479 |

## COUNSAILS

| | | | | | |
|---|---|---|---|---|---|
| WHILE THUS HEAV'NS HIGHEST COUNSAILS, BY THE LOW | SOSPETTO D'HERODE | 145 | 46 | 109 | 216 |

## COUNSELLOURS

| | | | | | |
|---|---|---|---|---|---|
| BUT ALL HIS COUNSELLOURS MUST SUMMON'D BEE, | SOSPETTO D'HERODE | 507 | 46 | 109 | 216 |

## COUNTED

| | | | | | |
|---|---|---|---|---|---|
| I COUNTED WRONG. THERE IS BUT ONE, | ON BLEEDING WOUNDS OF LORD | 31 | 46 | 101 | 110 |
| I COUNTED WRONG. THERE IS BUT ONE. | UPON BLEEDING CRUCIFIX | 27 | 52 | 288 | 110 |

## COUNTENANCE

| | | | | |
|---|---|---|---|---|
| WITH A CHANG'D COUNTENANCE WITNEST THE SIGHT. | SOSPETTO D'HERODE | 375 | 46 109 | 216 |

## COUNTER

| | | | | |
|---|---|---|---|---|
| PROMISE THE EARTH TO COUNTER SHINE | WEEPER | 11 | 52 307 | 120 |

## COUNTERFEIT

| | | | | |
|---|---|---|---|---|
| THEY'R COUNTERFEIT, AND WILL UNDOE THEE. | OUT OF GREEKE CUPID'S CRYER | 62 | 46 159 | 519 |

## COUNTERSHINE

| | | | | |
|---|---|---|---|---|
| PROMISE THE EARTH. TO COUNTERSHINE | THE WEEPER | 11 | 46 79 | 120 |

## COUNTRIES

| | | | | |
|---|---|---|---|---|
| THEY, THEY THAT SNATCHT US FROM OUR COUNTRIES BREST | PSALME 137 | 7 | 46 104 | 7 |

## COUNTRY-MAN

| | | | | |
|---|---|---|---|---|
| SPEAKE HEAVEN LIKE HERS, IS MY SOULES COUNTRY-MAN. | AN APOLOGIE FOR HYMNE (TERESA) | 22 | 46 136 | 59 |
| SPEAK HEAV'N LIKE HER'S IS MY SOULS COUNTRY-MAN. | AN APOLOGIE FOR (TERESA) HYMNE | 22 | 52 322 | 59 |

## COURAGE

| | | | | |
|---|---|---|---|---|
| WHENCE ALL HIS HIGH SPIRITS, AND HOT COURAGE CAME. | SOSPETTO D'HERODE | 488 | 46 109 | 216 |
| AND WANT OF COURAGE NOT TO YEILD. | TO COUNTESSE OF DENBIGH | 62 | 52 236 | 146 |
| AND WANT OF COURAGE NOT TO YEILD. | AGAINST IRRESOLUTION AND DELAY | 84 | 52 347 | 146 |

## COURSE

| | | | | |
|---|---|---|---|---|
| WHOSE GLORIOUS COURSE THROUGH OUR HORRIZON RUN, | UPON BISHOP ANDREWES PICTURE | 2 | 46 163 | 490 |
| THOSE, COURSE & NEGLIGENT, AS THE NATURALL LOCKES | DESCRIPTION RELIGIOUS HOUSE | 13 | 52 338 | 213 |

## COURT

| | | | | |
|---|---|---|---|---|
| THAT HEAV'NS HIGH MAJESTY HIS COURT SHOULD KEEPE | SOSPETTO D'HERODE | 181 | 46 109 | 216 |
| THE COURT OF HEAV'N IS COME. | ON THE ASSUMPTION | 16 | 46 139 | 114 |
| SAY TO THE SULLEN MORNE, THOU COM'ST TO COURT HER. | ON A FOULE MORNING | 11 | 46 181 | 495 |
| WE COURT THY MORE CONCERNING SMILES. | IN GLORIOUS EPIPHANIE | 81 | 52 253 | 39 |
| CROWNES, & THE HEADS THEY KISSE, MUST COURT THESE FEET. | TO THE QUEEN'S MAJESTY | 20 | 52 261 | 47 |
| THE COURT OF HEAV'N IS COME | IN GLORIOUS ASSUMPTION B. LADY | 15 | 52 304 | 114 |
| HE LEFT HIS FATHER'S COURT, AND CAME | AGAINST IRRESOLUTION AND DELAY | 69 | 52 347 | 146 |
| THINKING HER FATHER HAD REMOV'D HIS COURT. | UPON KINGS CORONATION | 32 | MS 390 | 453 |
| I LEFT MY GLORIOUS FATHERS STAR-PAV'D COURT | OUT OF GROTIUS | 14 | MS 398 | 198 |

## COURT-FED

| | | | | |
|---|---|---|---|---|
| HIS COURT-FED IMPES AGAINST THIS HATED HEAD. | OUT OF GROTIUS | 48 | MS 398 | 198 |

## COURTED

| | | | | |
|---|---|---|---|---|
| AND COURTED IN THE POMPOUS MASK OF A MORE SPECIOUS MIST. | IN GLORIOUS EPIPHANIE | 53 | 52 253 | 39 |
| WHOM THEY SO LONG COURTED AS GOD. | IN GLORIOUS EPIPHANIE | 180 | 52 253 | 39 |

## COURTS

| | | | | |
|---|---|---|---|---|
| JUSTLE DOWN MOUNTAINS. KINGS COURTS SHALL BE SENT. | ON GUNPOWDER-TREASON | 41 | MS 384 | 458 |

## COURTEOUS

| | | | | |
|---|---|---|---|---|
| BUT WOULD BE COURTEOUS, WOULD BE KIND. | UPON DEATH OF DESIRED HERRYS | 58 | 46 168 | 467 |
| TO HAVE THEM GUILDED WITH HIS COURTEOUS RAIES. | UPON KINGS CORONATION | 24 | MS 389 | 454 |
| LET EACH EYE WATER'T WITH A COURTEOUS TEARE. | AN ELEGY MR STANNINOW | 56 | MS 394 | 473 |

## COVENANT

| | | | | |
|---|---|---|---|---|
| 'CAUSE, BY THE COVENANT OF THY CROSSE, | OFFICE H. CROSS MATINES | 26 | 52 265 | 86 |

## COVER

| | | | | |
|---|---|---|---|---|
| AND THAT TOO WAS THY SELF WHICH THEE DID COVER, | ADORO TE | 25 | 52 291 | 172 |
| GIVE HIM THE VAIL. THAT HE MAY COVER | FLAMING HEART | 43 | 52 324 | 61 |

## COVER'D

| | | | | |
|---|---|---|---|---|
| THEIR WINTER COATES COVER'D WITH FLAMING GOLD. | UPON KINGS CORONATION | 28 | MS 390 | 453 |

## COVERS

| | | | | |
|---|---|---|---|---|
| THOUGH BARE HIS SKIN, HIS MIND HEE COVERS. | OUT OF GREEKE CUPID'S CRYER | 39 | 46 159 | 519 |
| WITH A SABLE WING, THAT COVERS | PSALME 23 | 38 | 46 102 | 5 |
| THE HEART THAT HIDES THEE HARDLY COVERS. | TO THE NAME OF JESUS | 215 | 52 239 | 30 |

## COVERT

| | | | | |
|---|---|---|---|---|
| CLOSE IN THE COVERT OF THE LEAVES THERE STOOD | MUSICKS DUELL | 7 | 46 149 | 535 |

## COW

| | | | | | |
|---|---|---|---|---|---|
| WITH HIS FAIR SISTER COW. | IN GLORIOUS EPIPHANIE | 97 | 52 | 253 | 39 |

## COWARDISE

| | | | | | |
|---|---|---|---|---|---|
| OF YOUR OWNE COWARDISE | WHY ARE YEE AFRAID | 10 | 46 | 88 | 15 |
| AT THOSE HARD WORDS MANS COWARDISE CALLS FEARES. | I AM READY NOT ONELY BOUND | 2 | 46 | 98 | 29 |
| 'TIS COWARDISE THAT KEEPS THIS FEILD | TO COUNTESSE OF DENBIGH | 61 | 52 | 236 | 146 |
| 'TIS COWARDISE THAT KEEPS THIS FIELD. | AGAINST IRRESOLUTION AND DELAY | 83 | 52 | 347 | 146 |

## COWARDLY

| | | | | | |
|---|---|---|---|---|---|
| WHERE ART THOU MAN. WHAT COWARDLY MISTAKE | SOSPETTO D'HERODE | 457 | 46 | 109 | 216 |

## COY

| | | | | | |
|---|---|---|---|---|---|
| OF SUPPLE MOISTURE. NO COY TWIG BUT WILL | OUT OF VIRGIL | 16 | 46 | 155 | 529 |
| OF ONE COY PHOENIX, WHILE WE HAVE A BROOD | UPON YORKE HIS BIRTH | 87 | 46 | 176 | 500 |
| AS THE COY BRIDES, WHEN NIGHT | WISHES SUPPOSED MISTRESSE | 71 | 46 | 195 | 479 |
| THE SUBTILE POINT OF HIS COY DESTINY. | HORATIJ ILLE & NEFASTO | 18 | MS | 382 | 530 |

## COYLY

| | | | | | |
|---|---|---|---|---|---|
| SO COYLY SHOULD LET FALL, | THE WEEPER | 69 | 46 | 79 | 120 |
| SO COYLY SHOULD LET FALL | WEEPER | 51 | 52 | 307 | 120 |

## COYNESSE

| | | | | | |
|---|---|---|---|---|---|
| AND WITH A QUAVERING COYNESSE TASTS THE STRINGS. | MUSICKS DUELL | 112 | 46 | 149 | 535 |

## CRACK

| | | | | | |
|---|---|---|---|---|---|
| AND CRACK THE CHRISTALL GLOBE. THE MILKY STREAME | ON GUNPOWDER-TREASON | 23 | MS | 384 | 458 |
| THAT GREIFE MAY CRACK THAT STRING, & NOW UNTIE | AN ELEGIE ON DR PORTER | 35 | MS | 395 | 476 |

## CRADLE

| | | | | | |
|---|---|---|---|---|---|
| AND KIST THE CRADLE OF OUR KING. | A HYMNE OF THE NATIVITY | 8 | 46 | 106 | 76 |
| TO MAKE HIS COSTLY CRADLE OF THY BEERE. | UPON YORKE HIS BIRTH | 95 | 46 | 176 | 500 |
| AND KIS'T THE CRADLE OF OUR KING. | IN HOLY NATIVITY | 8 | 52 | 246 | 76 |
| OFT HAVE THESE ARMES THY CRADLE ENVIED, | LUKE 2. QUAERIT JESUM | 27 | MS | 379 | 11 |
| THE BEST MY CRADLE AND MY BIRTH COULD FIND. | OUT OF GROTIUS | 16 | MS | 398 | 198 |

## CRADLE-TORMENTS

| | | | | | |
|---|---|---|---|---|---|
| THESE CRADLE-TORMENTS HAVE THEIR TOWARDNESSE. | OUR LORD IN HIS CIRCUMCISION | 14 | 46 | 98 | 9 |

## CRAFT

| | | | | | |
|---|---|---|---|---|---|
| CRAFT IN ALL HER KNOTTY WILES. | PSALME 23 | 26 | 46 | 102 | 5 |

## CRAFTY

| | | | | | |
|---|---|---|---|---|---|
| THOUGH THOU SEE THE CRAFTY ELFE. | OUT OF GREEKE CUPID'S CRYER | 60 | 46 | 159 | 519 |

## CRAVE

| | | | | | |
|---|---|---|---|---|---|
| IN DEATH-LIKE SLUMBERS. WHILE THY DANGERS CRAVE | SOSPETTO D'HERODE | 430 | 46 | 109 | 216 |

## CRAV'D

| | | | | | |
|---|---|---|---|---|---|
| HE HUMBLY CRAV'D TO BANQUETT ON A KISSE. | UPON GUNPOWDER TREASON | | 46 | MS 387 | 461 |

## CRAWLED

| | | | | | |
|---|---|---|---|---|---|
| THOSE YET FRESH STREAMES WHICH CRAWLED EVERY WHERE | THE BEGINNING OF HELIODORUS | 21 | 46 | 158 | 517 |

## CRAWLES

| | | | | | |
|---|---|---|---|---|---|
| THINE CRAWLES ABOVE AND IS THE CREAME. | THE WEEPER | 22 | 46 | 79 | 120 |

## CRAWLING

| | | | | | |
|---|---|---|---|---|---|
| THY LAZY CRAWLING STREAMES, PRI'THEE BE GONE. | AN ELEGIE ON DR PORTER | 20 | MS | 395 | 476 |

## CREAM

| | | | | | |
|---|---|---|---|---|---|
| THINE FLOATES ABOVE. & IS THE CREAM. | WEEPER | 22 | 52 | 307 | 120 |

## CREAME

| | | | | | |
|---|---|---|---|---|---|
| IN CREAME OF MORNING HELICON, AND THEN | MUSICKS DUELL | 77 | 46 | 149 | 535 |
| THINE CRAWLES ABOVE AND IS THE CREAME. | THE WEEPER | 22 | 46 | 79 | 120 |
| SHALL IN A SILVER RAINE RUNNE OUT, WHOSE CREAME | ON GUNPOWDER-TREASON | 24 | MS | 384 | 458 |

## CREATION

| | | | | | |
|---|---|---|---|---|---|
| THAT, THE CREATION IS. THE JUDGEMENT, THIS. | ON FRONTISPIECE ISAACSONS | 23 | 46 | 191 | 491 |

## CREATOR

| | | | | | |
|---|---|---|---|---|---|
| COME THY CREATOR TOO, WHAT THOUGH IT COST | SOSPETTO D'HERODE | 253 | 46 | 109 | 216 |

## CREATURE

| | | | | | |
|---|---|---|---|---|---|
| THE PATTERNE OF A PERFECT CREATURE. | UPON DEATH OF DESIRED HERRYS | 8 | 46 | 168 | 467 |
| IN ALL THE GIFTS THAT BLESSE A CREATURE. | ANOTHER ON HERRYS | 12 | 46 | 170 | 469 |

## CREATURES

| | | | | | |
|---|---|---|---|---|---|
| ALL CREATURES HAVE. | EASTER DAY | 14 | 46 | 100 | 26 |
| COMMON CREATURES, | OUT OF THE ITALIAN (1) | 38 | 46 | 188 | 545 |

## CREDIT

| | | | | | |
|---|---|---|---|---|---|
| WHO WILL EVER CREDIT THEE. | UPON THE DEATH OF A GENTLEMAN | 2 | 46 | 166 | 472 |

## CREEP

| | | | | | |
|---|---|---|---|---|---|
| WHERE TH'MILKY RIVERS CREEP, | WEEPER | 21 | 52 | 307 | 120 |
| SOFTLY LET THEM CREEP, | WEEPER | 57 | 52 | 307 | 120 |

## CREEPE

| | | | | | |
|---|---|---|---|---|---|
| SOFTLY LET THEM CREEPE | THE WEEPER | 75 | 46 | 79 | 120 |

## CREEPS

| | | | | | |
|---|---|---|---|---|---|
| CREEPS ON THE SOFT TOUCH OF A TENDER TONE. | MUSICKS DUELL | 140 | 46 | 149 | 535 |

## CREST

| | | | | | |
|---|---|---|---|---|---|
| HIS FAITHLESSE CROWNE HE FEELES LOOSE ON HIS CREST, | SOSPETTO D'HERODE | 491 | 46 | 109 | 216 |

## CRESTED

| | | | | | |
|---|---|---|---|---|---|
| SEAV'N CRESTED HYDRA'S HORRIBLY ADORNE. | SOSPETTO D'HERODE | 48 | 46 | 109 | 216 |

## CRIME

| | | | | | |
|---|---|---|---|---|---|
| IS ENTOMB'D THE CRIME OF DEATH. | HIS EPITAPH (HERRYS) | 6 | 46 | 172 | 471 |
| THY CRIME IS TOO MUCH DUTY. | VEXILLA REGIS | 27 | 52 | 277 | 156 |
| AND I, WHAT IS MY CRIME I CANNOT TELL. | ALEXIAS THIRD ELEGIE | 19 | 52 | 336 | 209 |
| UNLESSE IT BE A CRIME TO'HAVE LOV'D TOO WELL. | ALEXIAS THIRD ELEGIE | 20 | 52 | 336 | 209 |

## CRIMSON

| | | | | | |
|---|---|---|---|---|---|
| THE CRIMSON CURTAINES OF THY BED. | AN HIMNE FOR CIRCUMCISION | 6 | 46 | 141 | 37 |
| SCARCE WAKT. LIKE WAS THE CRIMSON OF THEIR JOYES, | UPON YORKE HIS BIRTH | 63 | 46 | 176 | 500 |
| THE CRIMSON CURTAINS OF THY BED, | NEW YEAR'S DAY | 6 | 52 | 251 | 37 |
| IN CRIMSON WAVELETTS, & IN SCARLET TIDE. | AN ELEGY MR STANNINOW | 24 | MS | 394 | 473 |

## CRISPED

| | | | | | |
|---|---|---|---|---|---|
| NOR SHOULD WEE NEED THY CRISPED WAVES, FOR WEE | UPON GUNPOWDER TREASON | 35 | MS | 386 | 460 |

## CROOKED

| | | | | | |
|---|---|---|---|---|---|
| DRAGGING HIS CROOKED BURTHEN, LOOK'T AWRY, | AN ELEGY MR STANNINOW | 46 | MS | 394 | 473 |

## CROP

| | | | | | |
|---|---|---|---|---|---|
| THE MOTHERS JOYES IN AN UNTIMELY CROP. | OUT OF GROTIUS | 26 | MS | 398 | 198 |

## CROPPE

| | | | | | |
|---|---|---|---|---|---|
| DOES RISE A RADIANT CROPPE OF ROYALLE STEMMS. | TO THE QUEEN'S MAJESTY | 12 | 52 | 261 | 47 |

## CROSSE

| | | | | | |
|---|---|---|---|---|---|
| THY FOE TO CROSSE THE SWEET ARTS OF THY REIGNE | TO LORD UPON WATER MADE WINE | 2 | 46 | 91 | 12 |
| AND NOW CROSSE FATES A WATCH ABOUT THEE KEEPE, | SOSPETTO D'HERODE | 455 | 46 | 109 | 216 |
| AND CHANG'D HIS FALSE CROWN FOR THY CROSSE. | IN GLORIOUS EPIPHANIE | 142 | 52 | 253 | 39 |
| 'CAUSE, BY THE COVENANT OF THY CROSSE, | OFFICE H. CROSS MATINES | 26 | 52 | 265 | 86 |
| 'CAUSE BY THE COVENANT OF THY CROSSE | OFFICE H. CROSS PRIME | 20 | 52 | 267 | 91 |
| DECEIVD THE CROSSE. | OFFICE H. CROSS THIRD | 11 | 52 | 268 | 93 |
| 'CAUSE BY THE COVENANT OF THY CROSSE, | OFFICE H. CROSS THIRD | 19 | 52 | 268 | 93 |
| 'CAUSE BY THE COVENANT OF THY CROSSE. | OFFICE H. CROSS SIXT | 23 | 52 | 270 | 97 |
| WHEN ON THE CROSSE MY KING DID BLEED, | OFFICE H. CROSS NINTH | 11 | 52 | 271 | 99 |
| 'CAUSE BY THE COVENANT OF THY CROSSE | OFFICE H. CROSS NINTH | 16 | 52 | 271 | 99 |
| 'CAUSE BY THE COVENANT OF THY CROSSE. | OFFICE H. CROSS EVENSONG | 30 | 52 | 273 | 101 |
| THY CROSSE, THY NATURE, & THY NAME | OFFICE H. CROSS COMPLINE | 22 | 52 | 274 | 105 |
| THAT KINGDOM WHICH THIS CROSSE DID MERIT. | VEXILLA REGIS | 46 | 52 | 277 | 156 |
| OR WHO THY CROSSE CONFES'T & CROWN'D. | DIES IRAE | 50 | 52 | 298 | 186 |
| KINDLY TO CROSSE YOU | TO SAME CONCERNING CHOISE | 46 | 52 | 331 | 66 |
| HER LOVES CROSSE FORTUNE, THAT THE SAD DISPUTE | HORATIJ ILLE & NEFASTO | 40 | MS | 382 | 530 |

## CROST

| | | | | | |
|---|---|---|---|---|---|
| HOW HATH ONE BLACKE ECLIPSE CANCELL'D, AND CROST | SOSPETTO D'HERODE | 75 | 46 | 109 | 216 |

## CROWD

| | | | | |
|---|---|---|---|---|
| ALL-IDOLIZING WORMES. THAT THUS COULD CROWD | IN GLORIOUS EPIPHANIE | 113 | 52 253 | 39 |
| AND CROWD FOR KISSES FROM THE LAMB'S WHITE FEET. | TO THE QUEEN'S MAJESTY | 14 | 52 261 | 47 |
| WALK IN A CROWD OF LOVES & MARTYRDOMES. | FLAMING HEART | 82 | 52 324 | 61 |
| ENOUGH IS SAID. NOW, IF THOU CANST CROWD ON | AN ELEGIE ON DR PORTER | 19 | MS 395 | 476 |

## CROWN

| | | | | |
|---|---|---|---|---|
| NOR WOULD HE THIS THY FEAR'D CROWN FROM THEE TEARE, | SOSPETTO D'HERODE | 517 | 46 109 | 216 |
| OPEN THIS BOOKE, FAIRE QUEEN, AND TAKE THY CROWN. | ON A TREATISE OF CHARITY | 12 | 46 137 | 69 |
| CROWN OF AN INCOMPARABLE LIGHT | ON THE ASSUMPTION | 56 | 46 139 | 114 |
| TO KISSE THY FEET & CROWN THY HEAD. | IN HOLY NATIVITY | 100 | 52 246 | 76 |
| AND CHANG'D HIS FALSE CROWN FOR THY CROSSE. | IN GLORIOUS EPIPHANIE | 142 | 52 253 | 39 |
| HIS GLITTERING ROBE, HIS SPARKLING CROWN. | IN GLORIOUS EPIPHANIE | 243 | 52 253 | 39 |
| FOR WHILE IN SPORT HE WEARES A SPITEFULL CROWN, | OFFICE H. CROSS THIRD | 7 | 52 268 | 93 |
| O'RELOOK ALL LIBANUS. THY LOFTY CROWN | OFFICE H. CROSS EVENSONG | 22 | 52 273 | 101 |
| CROWN OF A MOST INCOMPARABLE LIGHT | IN GLORIOUS ASSUMPTION B. LADY | 61 | 52 304 | 114 |
| LIVE, CROWN OF WOEMEN. QUEEN OF MEN. | IN GLORIOUS ASSUMPTION B. LADY | 66 | 52 304 | 114 |
| WHO CALLS'T HIS CROWN TO BE CALL'D THINE. | WEEPER | 122 | 52 307 | 120 |
| WITH STRONG ARMES, THEIR TRIUMPHANT CROWN, | TERESA | 6 | 52 315 | 52 |
| THEMSELVES THY CROWN. SONS OF THY VOWES | TERESA | 167 | 52 315 | 52 |
| FIRM IN THY CROWN, AS HERE FAST IN THY LOVE. | ALEXIAS FIRST ELEGIE | 36 | 52 334 | 204 |
| NOR CAN THE CARES OF HIS WHOLE CROWN | AGAINST IRRESOLUTION AND DELAY | 73 | 52 347 | 146 |

## CROWN-LAND

| | | | | |
|---|---|---|---|---|
| OUR CROWN-LAND LYES ABOVE YET EACH MEAL BRINGS | (ON) HOPE | 13 | 52 345 | 71 |

## CROWN-LANDS

| | | | | |
|---|---|---|---|---|
| OUR CROWN-LANDS LYE ABOVE, YET EACH MEALE BRINGS | ON HOPE | 33 | 46 143 | 71 |

## CROWND

| | | | | |
|---|---|---|---|---|
| THOUSANDS OF CROWND SOULES, THRONG TO BEE | IN MEMORY OF LADY MADRE TERESA | 167 | 46 131 | 52 |

## CROWN'D

| | | | | |
|---|---|---|---|---|
| IS CROWN'D ABOUT. BUT O WHAT PLACE, | OUT OF GREEKE CUPID'S CRYER | 34 | 46 159 | 519 |
| CROWN'D ABUNDANCE SPREADS MY BORD. | PSALME 23 | 50 | 46 102 | 5 |
| HER HOPES ARE CROWN'D, ONELY SHE FEARES THAT THAN. | UPON FAIRE ETHIOPIAN | 5 | 46 183 | 493 |
| A GOLDEN HARVEST OF CROWN'D HEADS, THAT MEET | TO THE QUEEN'S MAJESTY | 13 | 52 261 | 47 |
| OR WHO THY CROSSE CONFES'T & CROWN'D, | DIES IRAE | 50 | 52 298 | 186 |
| CROWN'D HEADS ARE TOYES. WE GOE TO MEET | WEEPER | 185 | 52 307 | 120 |
| THOUSANDS OF CROWN'D SOULES THRONG TO BE | TERESA | 166 | 52 315 | 52 |
| CROWN'D WOES AWAKE. AS THINGS TOO WISE FOR SLEEP. | DESCRIPTION RELIGIOUS HOUSE | 29 | 52 338 | 213 |

## LOVE-CROWNED

| | | | | |
|---|---|---|---|---|
| TO WAIT AT THE LOVE-CROWNED DOORES OF | TO THE NAME OF JESUS | 42 | 52 239 | 30 |

## SILVER-CROWNED

| | | | | |
|---|---|---|---|---|
| FOR A SILVER-CROWNED HEAD. | UPON THE DEATH OF A GENTLEMAN | 11 | 46 166 | 472 |

## CROWNE

| | | | | |
|---|---|---|---|---|
| NO,NO,THY GOOD, SION, ALONE MUST CROWNE | PSALME 137 | 25 | 46 104 | 7 |
| TO KISSE THY FEET, AND CROWNE THY HEAD. | A HYMNE OF THE NATIVITY | 80 | 46 106 | 76 |
| TO CROWNE THEIR PAST PREDICTIONS, BOTH HEE LAYES | SOSPETTO D'HERODE | 95 | 46 109 | 216 |
| THE CROWNE, FOR WHICH UPON THEIR NECKS HE LAID | SOSPETTO D'HERODE | 406 | 46 109 | 216 |
| HIS FAITHLESSE CROWNE HE FEELES LOOSE ON HIS CREST. | SOSPETTO D'HERODE | 491 | 46 109 | 216 |
| UPON THY CROWNE, WHO GIVES HIS OWNE AWAY. | SOSPETTO D'HERODE | 520 | 46 109 | 216 |
| WITH STRONG ARMES THEIR TRIUMPHANT CROWNE. | IN MEMORY OF LADY MADRE TERESA | 6 | 46 131 | 52 |
| THEMSELVES THY CROWNE. SONNES OF THY VOWES. | IN MEMORY OF LADY MADRE TERESA | 168 | 46 131 | 52 |
| LIVE CROWNE OF WOMEN, QUEEN OF MEN. | ON THE ASSUMPTION | 61 | 46 139 | 114 |
| HIS CROWNE EXPECTED. WHEN (O FATE, O TIME | UPON DEATH OF HERRYS | 29 | 46 167 | 466 |
| TO CROWNE AN UNCONTROULED FATE, | LOVES HOROSCOPE | 24 | 46 185 | 483 |
| THOUGH EVERY DIAMOND IN JOVES CROWNE | LOVES HOROSCOPE | 37 | 46 185 | 483 |
| CAN CROWNE OLD WINTERS HEAD WITH FLOWERS. | WISHES SUPPOSED MISTRESSE | 90 | 46 195 | 479 |
| OH CROWNE THESE PRAIE'RS (MOV'D IN A HAPPY HOWER) | EX EUPHORMIONE | 3 | MS 392 | 525 |

## CROWNS

| | | | | |
|---|---|---|---|---|
| OF CROWNS, WITH WHICH THE KING THY SPOUSE | TERESA | 143 | 52 315 | 52 |

## CROWNES

| | | | | |
|---|---|---|---|---|
| THAT CROWNES HIS HATED HEAD ON HIGH APPEARES. | SOSPETTO D'HERODE | 45 | 46 109 | 216 |
| REPLY'D THE PROUD KING, O MY CROWNES DEFENCE. | SOSPETTO D'HERODE | 281 | 46 109 | 216 |
| OF CROWNES, WITH WHICH THE KING THY SPOUSE. | IN MEMORY OF LADY MADRE TERESA | 144 | 46 131 | 52 |
| 'MONGST THOSE LONG ROWES OF CROWNES THAT GUILD YOUR RACE. | TO THE QUEEN'S MAJESTY | 1 | 52 261 | 47 |
| CROWNES, & THE HEADS THEY KISSE, MUST COURT THESE FEET. | TO THE QUEEN'S MAJESTY | 20 | 52 261 | 47 |
| TO REAP NEW CROWNES & KINGDOMS FROM THAT KISSE. | TO THE QUEEN'S MAJESTY | 22 | 52 261 | 47 |

## OLIVE-CROWNES

| | | | | |
|---|---|---|---|---|
| THE CHOICEST OF HER OLIVE-CROWNES, & PRAISE | UPON KINGS CORONATION | 23 | MS 389 | 454 |

## CRUCIFIX

| | | | | | |
|---|---|---|---|---|---|
| ALL WOES INTO ONE CRUCIFIX. | OFFICE H. CROSS SIXT | 8 | 52 | 270 | 97 |
| WOUNDS. AND BECOME ONE CRUCIFIX. | SANCTA MARIA DOLORUM | 100 | 52 | 283 | 162 |

## CRUCIFY

| | | | | | |
|---|---|---|---|---|---|
| OF CRUCIFY HIM, CRUCIFY. | OFFICE H. CROSS THIRD | 2 | 52 | 268 | 93 |
| OF CRUCIFY HIM, CRUCIFY. | OFFICE H. CROSS THIRD | 2 | 52 | 268 | 93 |
| A HAIL MORE CRUELL THEN THEIR CRUCIFY. | OFFICE H. CROSS THIRD | 6 | 52 | 268 | 93 |

## CRUELL

| | | | | | |
|---|---|---|---|---|---|
| THOU TO MAINTAIN THEIR CRUELL STRIFE. | IN PRAISE OF LESSIUS | 3 | 46 | 156 | 510 |
| THE OBJECTS OF HIS CRUELL SPORTS. | OUT OF GREEKE CUPID'S CRYER | 32 | 46 | 159 | 519 |
| HEE IS ALL CRUELL, CRUELL ALL. | OUT OF GREEKE CUPID'S CRYER | 53 | 46 | 159 | 519 |
| HEE IS ALL CRUELL, CRUELL ALL. | OUT OF GREEKE CUPID'S CRYER | 53 | 46 | 159 | 519 |
| AND MANY A CRUELL TEARE DISCLOSES. | ON WOUNDS OF CRUCIFIED LORD | 8 | 46 | 99 | 24 |
| (A CRUELL AND A COSTLY SPRING) | ON BLEEDING WOUNDS OF LORD | 23 | 46 | 101 | 110 |
| COULD NOT ONCE BLINDING ME, CRUELL, SUFFICE. | SAMPSON TO HIS DALILAH | 1 | 46 | 102 | 8 |
| IN HEBREW NUMBERS, THEN (O CRUELL JEST.) | PSALME 137 | 1 | 46 | 104 | 7 |
| BUT EDOM CRUELL THOU. THOU CRYD'ST DOWNE, DOWNE | PSALME 137 | 9 | 46 | 104 | 7 |
| HER CRUELL CLOATHES OF COSTLY THREDS THEY WEAVE, | SOSPETTO D'HERODE | 27 | 46 | 104 | 7 |
| HERE CRUELL SCYRON BOASTS HIS BLOODY ROCKES. | SOSPETTO D'HERODE | 343 | 46 | 109 | 216 |
| AND CAME TO BETHLEM, WHERE THE CRUELL KING | SOSPETTO D'HERODE | 359 | 46 | 109 | 216 |
| DEATH THOU MUST NOT HERE BE CRUELL, | UPON DEATH OF DESIRED HERRYS | 394 | 46 | 109 | 216 |
| AND WILT THOU, (O CRUELL BOAST.) | UPON DEATH OF DESIRED HERRYS | 3 | 46 | 168 | 467 |
| CRUELL AUSTER THITHER HY'D HIM, | UPON DEATH OF DESIRED HERRYS | 21 | 46 | 168 | 467 |
| OR FORGOT THE CRUELL VIGOUR, | ANOTHER ON HERRYS | 42 | 46 | 168 | 467 |
| WOULD QUITE HAVE LOST THE CRUELL FASHION. | ANOTHER ON HERRYS | 3 | 46 | 170 | 469 |
| OF A CRUELL STOP ILL PLAC'T. | ANOTHER ON HERRYS | 24 | 46 | 170 | 469 |
| A HAIL MORE CRUELL THEN THEIR CRUCIFY. | OFFICE H. CROSS THIRD | 40 | 46 | 170 | 469 |
| NOR COULDST THOU, CRUELL, LEAVE ME QUITE ALONE. | ALEXIAS SECONDE ELEGIE | 6 | 52 | 268 | 93 |
| O HAD HE NERE BEEN AT THAT CRUELL COST | ALEXIAS THIRD ELEGIE | 4 | 52 | 335 | 207 |
| CRUELL RETURN. OR TELL THE REASON WHY | ALEXIAS THIRD ELEGIE | 5 | 52 | 336 | 209 |
| NO CRUELL GUARD OF DILIGENT CARES, THAT KEEP | DESCRIPTION RELIGIOUS HOUSE | 17 | 52 | 336 | 209 |
| AND CRUELL RAVISHING OF FROSTY AGE, | UPON GUNPOWDER TREASON | 28 | 52 | 338 | 213 |
| THE SEARCH OF ONE CHILD (CRUELL INDUSTRY.) | OUT OF GROTIUS | 44 | MS | 387 | 461 |
| | | 27 | MS | 398 | 198 |

## CRUELTY

| | | | | | |
|---|---|---|---|---|---|
| IT BOYLES OUT INTO CRUELTY, | OUT OF GREEKE CUPID'S CRYER | 30 | 46 | 159 | 519 |
| CRUELTY, SHE ALONE SHALL CURE MY DOUBT. | SOSPETTO D'HERODE | 288 | 46 | 109 | 216 |
| COULD LEND THEM ANY CRUELTY. | OFFICE H. CROSS PRIME | 4 | 52 | 267 | 91 |
| THIS MASSE OF CRUELTY, TO BE THY GUIDE | UPON GUNPOWDER TREASON | 8 | MS | 387 | 461 |
| PURE, & UNMIXED CRUELTY THEY TELL, | AN ELEGIE ON DR PORTER | 13 | MS | 395 | 476 |

## CRUELTIE

| | | | | | |
|---|---|---|---|---|---|
| WHAT EVER STORY OF THEIR CRUELTIE. | ON MARKES OF SAVIOURS WOUNDS | 1 | 46 | 86 | 28 |

## CRUMBLED

| | | | | | |
|---|---|---|---|---|---|
| AND CRUMBLED INTO CONTRITE DUST. | DIES IRAE | 66 | 52 | 298 | 186 |

## CRUMME

| | | | | | |
|---|---|---|---|---|---|
| LESSE THEN WHOLE CHRIST IN EVERY CRUMME. | LAUDA SION SALVATOREM | 58 | 52 | 294 | 178 |

## CRUSH

| | | | | | |
|---|---|---|---|---|---|
| AND CRUSH THE WORLD TILL HIS WIDE CORNERS MEET. | SOSPETTO D'HERODE | 280 | 46 | 109 | 216 |

## CRUSHT

| | | | | | |
|---|---|---|---|---|---|
| THE MONSTER CRUSHT, MAUGRE THEIR MIDWIFERIE. | UPON GUNPOWDER TREASON | 56 | MS | 386 | 460 |

## CRUSH'T

| | | | | | |
|---|---|---|---|---|---|
| O HEAR A SUPPLIANT HEART. ALL CRUSH'T | DIES IRAE | 65 | 52 | 298 | 186 |

## CRY

| | | | | | |
|---|---|---|---|---|---|
| THE THIRD HOUR'S DEAFEN'D WITH THE CRY | OFFICE H. CROSS THIRD | 1 | 52 | 268 | 93 |
| AND CRY WITH ONE ACCORD | OFFICE H. CROSS COMPLINE | 24 | 52 | 274 | 105 |
| SHALL CRY WE COME, WE COME & ALL | DIES IRAE | 15 | 52 | 298 | 186 |
| MERCY (MY JUDGE) MERCY I CRY | DIES IRAE | 41 | 52 | 298 | 186 |

## CRYD'ST

| | | | | | |
|---|---|---|---|---|---|
| BUT EDOM CRUELL THOU. THOU CRYD'ST DOWNE, DOWNE | PSALME 137 | 27 | 46 | 104 | 7 |

## CRY'D

| | | | | | |
|---|---|---|---|---|---|
| PALLAS SAW VENUS ARM'D AND STREIGHT SHE CRY'D, | UPON THE SAME (VENUS ARMES) | 1 | 46 | 161 | 523 |
| COME, THEY CRY'D, COME SING AND PLAY | PSALME 137 | 11 | 46 | 104 | 7 |

## CRYES

| | | | | | |
|---|---|---|---|---|---|
| LOVE IS LOST. AND THUS SHEE CRYES HIM. | OUT OF GREEKE CUPID'S CRYER | 4 | 46 | 159 | 519 |
| IN RAGE, MY ARMES, GIVE ME MY ARMES, HEE CRYES. | SOSPETTO D'HERODE | 480 | 46 | 109 | 216 |
| HIS TRUMPETS. TENDER CRYES, HIS MEN TO DARE | SOSPETTO D'HERODE | 526 | 46 | 109 | 216 |
| FIRM HE, AS THOU ART FALSE, NOR NEED MY CRYES | ALEXIAS SECONDE ELEGIE | 9 | 52 | 335 | 207 |

CRYING

| WOOE, INTREAT, AND CRYING SAY | OUT OF GREEKE CUPID'S CRYER | 68 | 46 159 519 |

CRYSTALL

| WHILE THROUGH THE CRYSTAL ORBES, CLEARER THEN THEY | IN GLORIOUS ASSUMPTION B. LADY | 5 | 52 304 114 |
| THAWING CRYSTALL. SNOWY HILLS. | WEEPER | 4 | 52 307 120 |
| ANGELS WITH CRYSTALL VIOLLS COME | WEEPER | 70 | 52 307 120 |

CHRISTALL

| A SOULE SHEATHED IN A CHRISTALL SHRINE, | IN PRAISE OF LESSIUS | 25 | 46 156 510 |
| THAWING CHRISTALL. SNOWY HILLS. | THE WEEPER | 4 | 46 79 120 |
| HEAVEN THE CHRISTALL OCEAN IS. | THE WEEPER | 24 | 46 79 120 |
| WHILE THROUGH THE CHRISTALL ORBS CLEARER THEN THEY | ON THE ASSUMPTION | 5 | 46 139 114 |
| A SOUL SHEATH'D IN A CHRISTALL SHRINE. | TEMPERANCE | 23 | 52 342 510 |
| AND CRACK THE CHRISTALL GLOBE. THE MILKY STREAME | ON GUNPOWDER-TREASON | 23 | MS 384 458 |
| IN A BRIGHT CHRISTALL TIDE, TO THEE THEY TEND. | AN ELEGIE ON DR PORTER | 40 | MS 395 476 |

CHRYSTALL

| WHERE JORDAN MELTS HIS CHRYSTALL, TO MAKE FAIRE | SOSPETTO D'HERODE | 85 | 46 109 216 |
| OF CHRYSTALL FLESH, THROUGH WHICH TO SHINE. | WISHES SUPPOSED MISTRESSE | 12 | 46 195 479 |

CUP

| SOFTER THEN THAT WHICH PANTS IN HEBE'S CUP. | MUSICKS DUELL | 126 | 46 149 535 |
| HOW MY CUP ORELOOKS HER BRIMS. | PSALME 23 | 56 | 46 102 5 |
| BALME AND NECTAR IN MY CUP. | PSALME 23 | 70 | 46 102 5 |
| THE CUP THEY DRINKE IN IS MEDUSA'S SCULL, | SOSPETTO D'HERODE | 335 | 46 109 216 |
| A THOUSAND COLD DEATHS IN ONE CUP. | IN MEMORY OF LADY MADRE TERESA | 38 | 46 131 52 |
| IS TORTUR'D THIRST, IT SELFE, TOO SWEET A CUP. | OFFICE H. CROSS SIXT | 9 | 52 270 97 |
| CONVICTORS OF THINE OWN FULL CUP, | LAUDA SION SALVATOREM | 76 | 52 294 178 |
| A THOUSAND COLD DEATHS IN ONE CUP. | TERESA | 38 | 52 315 52 |

CURE

| CRUELTY, SHE ALONE SHALL CURE MY DOUBT. | SOSPETTO D'HERODE | 288 | 46 109 216 |
| CURE THEE OF THY DELIGHTFULL TYMPANIE. | UPON BIRTH PRINCESSE E | 12 | MS 391 456 |

CURIOUS

| HIS CURIOUS FINGERS LENT, HER VOYCE MADE GOOD. | MUSICKS DUELL | 14 | 46 149 535 |
| UNTO A CHOYCE, AND CURIOUS EARE. | UPON DEATH OF A FREIND | 2 | MS 393 477 |

CURLD

| HOPE WALKS, & KICKS THE CURLD HEADS OF CONSPIRING STARRES. | (ON) HOPE | 32 | 52 345 71 |

CURL'D

| I SAW THE CURL'D DROPS, SOFT AND SLOW | A HYMNE OF THE NATIVITY | 35 | 46 106 76 |
| A CURL'D KNOT OF EMBRACING SNAKES, THAT KISSE | SOSPETTO D'HERODE | 37 | 46 109 216 |
| QUENCH HIS CURL'D FIRES, WEE'L WAKE WITH OUR ALARMES | SOSPETTO D'HERODE | 278 | 46 109 216 |
| HOPE KICKS THE CURL'D HEADS OF CONSPIRING STARRES. | ON HOPE | 72 | 46 143 71 |
| AND FRISKE IN CURL'D MAEANDERS. HEE WILL THROW | ON A FOULE MORNING | 20 | 46 181 495 |
| I SAW THE CURL'D DROPS, SOFT & SLOW. | IN HOLY NATIVITY | 51 | 52 246 76 |
| MARK HOW THE CURL'D WAVES WORK AND WIND, | AGAINST IRRESOLUTION AND DELAY | 41 | 52 347 146 |
| THE FURIES CURL'D SNAKES MEET IN GENTLE TWINES, | HORATIJ ILLE & NEFASTO | 52 | MS 382 530 |

CURLE

| WHOSE FLOURISH (METEOR-LIKE) DOTH CURLE THE AIRE | MUSICKS DUELL | 137 | 46 149 535 |

CURLES

| WITH DAINTY CURLES HIS FROWARD FACE | OUT OF GREEKE CUPID'S CRYER | 33 | 46 159 519 |

CURRENTS

| THESE PURPLE CURRENTS HEDG'D WITH VIOLETS ROUND | AN ELEGY MR STANNINOW | 22 | MS 394 473 |

CURSE

| THEY BANNE THE BLAZE, & CURSE ITS CURTESY, | ON GUNPOWDER-TREASON | 59 | MS 384 458 |

CURSED

| FOURTH OF THE CURSED KNOT OF HAGS IS SHEE, | SOSPETTO D'HERODE | 289 | 46 109 216 |
| THE TABLES FURNISHT WITH A CURSED FEAST, | SOSPETTO D'HERODE | 329 | 46 109 216 |

CURST

| BE NE'RE SO CURST, HIS TONGUE IS KIND. | OUT OF GREEKE CUPID'S CRYER | 22 | 46 159 519 |

CURTAINS

| WITH CURTAINS DRAWN, | TO THE NAME OF JESUS | 147 | 52 239 30 |
| THE CRIMSON CURTAINS OF THY BED, | NEW YEAR'S DAY | 6 | 52 251 37 |

## CURTAIN'D

| | | | |
|---|---|---|---|
| THESE CURTAIN'D WINDOWES, THIS SELFE-PRISON'D EYE, | UPON STANINOUGH'S DEATH | 25 | 46 175 475 |
| THESE CURTAIN'D WINDOWS, THIS RETIRED EYE | DEATH'S LECTURE | 27 | 52 340 475 |

## CURTAINES

| | | | |
|---|---|---|---|
| FOR HANGINGS AND FOR CURTAINES, ALL ALONG | SOSPETTO D'HERODE | 321 | 46 109 216 |
| THE CRIMSON CURTAINES OF THY BED. | AN HIMNE FOR CIRCUMCISION | 6 | 46 141 37 |
| THEN THE CURTAINES WILL BEE DRAWNE, | AN EPITAPH HUSBAND AND WIFE | 14 | 46 174 478 |
| TO DRAW THE CURTAINES, AND AWAKE THE SUN. | TO THE MORNING | 10 | 46 183 497 |
| THEN THE CURTAINES WILL BE DRAWN | AN EPITAPH UPON MARRIED COUPLE | 18 | 52 339 478 |

## CURTEOUS

| | | | |
|---|---|---|---|
| THEN WONDRING STARTS, & HAD THE CURTEOUS NIGHT | UPON KINGS CORONATION | 19 | MS 390 453 |
| WHISPER THY PLAINTS TO TH' OCEANS CURTEOUS EARES, | AN ELEGIE ON DR PORTER | 37 | MS 395 476 |

## CURTESY

| | | | |
|---|---|---|---|
| THEY BANNE THE BLAZE, & CURSE ITS CURTESY, | ON GUNPOWDER-TREASON | 59 | MS 384 458 |

## SHORT-CUT

| | | | |
|---|---|---|---|
| WHICH SHORT-CUT LIVES OF MURDRED INFANTS LEAVE. | SOSPETTO D'HERODE | 344 | 46 109 216 |

## CUTS

| | | | |
|---|---|---|---|
| HER KEELE CUTS NOT THE WAVES, WHERE OUR WINDS STIRRE, | ON HOPE | 73 | 46 143 71 |

## CUTTS

| | | | |
|---|---|---|---|
| HER KEEL CUTTS NOT THE WAVES WHERE THESE WINDS STIRR | (ON) HOPE | 33 | 52 345 71 |

## CYCLOPSES

| | | | |
|---|---|---|---|
| MINOTAURES, CYCLOPSES, WITH A DARKE DROVE | SOSPETTO D'HERODE | 351 | 46 109 216 |

## CYMBALLS

| | | | |
|---|---|---|---|
| CYMBALLS OF HEAV'N, OR HUMANE SPHEARS, | TO THE NAME OF JESUS | 78 | 52 239 30 |

## CYNTHIA

| | | | |
|---|---|---|---|
| (NOR DOES THE SUNNE DENY'T) OUR CYNTHIA, | UPON YORKE HIS BIRTH | 79 | 46 176 500 |
| DOE I NOT SEE A CYNTHIA, WHO MAY | UPON KINGS CORONATION | 25 | MS 389 454 |

## CYNTHIA'S

| | | | |
|---|---|---|---|
| MISTRESSE OF WONDERS. CYNTHIA'S IS THE NIGHT, | UPON YORKE HIS BIRTH | 77 | 46 176 500 |
| THAT MIGHT INTERPRET OUR FAIRE CYNTHIA'S WORTH, | UPON BIRTH PRINCESSE E | 30 | MS 391 456 |

## CYPRESSE

| | | | |
|---|---|---|---|
| THE SULLEN CYPRESSE O'RE HIS HERSE. | UPON THE DEATH OF A GENTLEMAN | 10 | 46 166 472 |

## CYTHEREA

| | | | |
|---|---|---|---|
| WHAT. MARS HIS SWORD. FAIRE CYTHEREA SAY, | UPON VENUS PUTTING ARMES | 1 | 46 161 523 |

## DAINTIEST

| | | | |
|---|---|---|---|
| OFT HAVE I SPOILD MY KISSES DAINTIEST DIET, | LUKE 2. QUAERIT JESUM | 37 | MS 379 11 |
| MANS DAINTIEST CARE, & CAUTION CANNOT SPY | HORATIJ ILLE & NEFASTO | 17 | MS 382 530 |

## DAINTY

| | | | |
|---|---|---|---|
| CARVES OUT HER DAINTY VOYCE AS READILY, | MUSICKS DUELL | 22 | 46 149 535 |
| WITH DAINTY CURLES HIS FROWARD FACE | OUT OF GREEKE CUPID'S CRYER | 33 | 46 159 519 |
| OF MUSICKS DAINTY TOUCH, THEN I | PSALME 137 | 17 | 46 104 7 |
| HEE WITH A DAINTY AND SOFT HAND, WILL TRIM | ON A FOULE MORNING | 23 | 46 181 495 |
| BUT THE DAINTY SCARUS, SOUGHT | PETRONIJ ALES PHASIACIS PETITA | 11 | MS 382 526 |

## DALLYING

| | | | |
|---|---|---|---|
| OF DALLYING SWEETNESSE, HOVERS ORE HER SKILL, | MUSICKS DUELL | 59 | 46 149 535 |

## DAMP'T

| | | | |
|---|---|---|---|
| SILENC'T THE MORNING-SONS, & DAMP'T THEIR SONG | IN GLORIOUS EPIPHANIE | 130 | 52 253 39 |

## DAMPS

| | | | |
|---|---|---|---|
| LET THE DAMPS OF THY DULL BREATH | PSALME 23 | 40 | 46 102 5 |

## DANCE

| | | | |
|---|---|---|---|
| TO THEIR OWNE DANCE. NOW NEGLIGENTLY RASH | MUSICKS DUELL | 29 | 46 149 535 |
| AND THE GAY STARRS LEAD ON THEIR GOLDEN DANCE. | SOSPETTO D'HERODE | 206 | 46 109 216 |
| TO DANCE IN THE SUNNESHINE OF SOME SMILING | ON A PRAYER BOOKE | 48 | 46 126 139 |
| DANCE IN AN ENDLESSE ROUND, AGAINE SHALL RISE | UPON DEATH OF HERRYS | 38 | 46 167 466 |
| THE BEAMES THAT DANCE IN THOSE FULL STARRES OF THINE. | UPON YORKE HIS BIRTH | 44 | 46 176 500 |
| AND DANCE BEFORE YOUR EYES. | OUT OF THE ITALIAN (2) | 10 | 46 190 547 |

|   |   |   |   |   |   |
|---|---|---|---|---|---|
| TO DANCE ITH' SUNSHINE OF SOME SMILING | PRAYER TO GENTLE-WOMAN | 54 | 52 | 328 | 139 |
| AFFRIGHT TH' AMAZED AIRE, & DANCE A ROUND | UPON KINGS CORONATION | 22 | MS | 390 | 453 |
| DANCE, LIKE THE NIMBLE SPHAERES, A JOYFULL ROUND. | UPON BIRTH PRINCESSE E | 32 | MS | 391 | 456 |

DANCING

|   |   |   |   |   |   |
|---|---|---|---|---|---|
| DANCING IN LOFTY MEASURES, AND ANON | MUSICKS DUELL | 139 | 46 | 149 | 535 |
| RAVISH THE DANCING ORBES, MAKE THEM MOUNT HIGHER | UPON KINGS CORONATION | 2 | MS | 389 | 454 |

DANDLE

|   |   |   |   |   |   |
|---|---|---|---|---|---|
| DOTH SHE BEGINNE TO DANDLE IN HER LAPPE | AN ELEGY MR STANNINOW | 7 | MS | 394 | 473 |

DANGER

|   |   |   |   |   |   |
|---|---|---|---|---|---|
| BESIDES THIS FEARE OF DANGER, THERE'S NO DANGER HERE | WHY ARE YEE AFRAID | 15 | 46 | 88 | 15 |
| BESIDES THIS FEARE OF DANGER, THERE'S NO DANGER HERE | WHY ARE YEE AFRAID | 15 | 46 | 88 | 15 |
| AND HE THAT HERE FEARES DANGER, DOES DESERVE HIS FEARE. | WHY ARE YEE AFRAID | 16 | 46 | 88 | 15 |

DANGERS

|   |   |   |   |   |   |
|---|---|---|---|---|---|
| IN DEATH-LIKE SLUMBERS. WHILE THY DANGERS CRAVE | SOSPETTO D'HERODE | 430 | 46 | 109 | 216 |
| OF DEATH & FEIRCEST DANGERS, DURST WITH BRAVE | TO THE NAME OF JESUS | 201 | 52 | 239 | 30 |
| WHAT DANGERS CAN THERE BE DARE SAY ME NAY. | ALEXIAS FIRST ELEGIE | 20 | 52 | 334 | 204 |

DANGLED

|   |   |   |   |   |   |
|---|---|---|---|---|---|
| THOSE RARE FRUITS DANGLED, WHENCE THE GOLDEN YEARE | UPON DEATH OF HERRYS | 28 | 46 | 167 | 466 |

DARE

|   |   |   |   |   |   |
|---|---|---|---|---|---|
| IN MUSICK'S RAVISH'T SOULE HEE DARE NOT TELL, | MUSICKS DUELL | 144 | 46 | 149 | 535 |
| THAT TO THE MIGHTY NEPTUNE'S SELF DARE THREATEN WRACK. | WHY ARE YEE AFRAID | 8 | 46 | 88 | 15 |
| AND TO DARE SOMETHING, IS SOME VICTORY. | SOSPETTO D'HERODE | 224 | 46 | 109 | 216 |
| HIS TRUMPETS. TENDER CRYES, HIS MEN TO DARE | SOSPETTO D'HERODE | 526 | 46 | 109 | 216 |
| SUCH THIRST TO DYE, AS DARE DRINKE UP, | IN MEMORY OF LADY MADRE TERESA | 37 | 46 | 131 | 52 |
| SCARCE DAWNES, O PARDON, IF I DARE TO SAY | AN APOLOGIE FOR HYMNE (TERESA) | 6 | 46 | 136 | 59 |
| THESE DEATH-SEAL'D LIPPS ARE THEY DARE GIVE THE LYE. | UPON STANINOUGH'S DEATH | 23 | 46 | 175 | 475 |
| SO DEARE GLORIES DARE NOT BORROW. | OUT OF THE ITALIAN (1) | 39 | 46 | 188 | 545 |
| OR PEARLE THAT DARE APPEARE, | WISHES SUPPOSED MISTRESSE | 53 | 46 | 195 | 479 |
| WHOSE MERIT DARE APPLY IT, | WISHES SUPPOSED MISTRESSE | 119 | 46 | 195 | 479 |
| SHALL WE DARE THIS, MY SOUL. WE'L DOE'T AND BRING | TO THE NAME OF JESUS | 44 | 52 | 239 | 30 |
| A WHILE DARE BORROW | TO THE NAME OF JESUS | 100 | 52 | 239 | 30 |
| SCARSE DAWNES. O PARDON IF I DARE TO SAY | AN APOLOGIE FOR (TERESA) HYMNE | 6 | 52 | 322 | 59 |
| WHAT DANGERS CAN THERE BE DARE SAY ME NAY. | ALEXIAS FIRST ELEGIE | 20 | 52 | 334 | 204 |
| THESE DEATH-SEAL'D LIPPES ARE THEY DARE GIVE THE LY | DEATH'S LECTURE | 25 | 52 | 340 | 475 |
| AND MISTS OF GREIFE, DARE FORCE A JOYFULL LIGHT. | UPON KINGS CORONATION | 16 | MS | 389 | 454 |
| LETT NONE DARE SPEAKE OF THEE, BUT SUCH AS THENCE | UPON BIRTH PRINCESSE E | 9 | MS | 391 | 456 |
| THESE CATARACTS OF GREIFE, THAT DARE EV'N VIE | AN ELEGY MR STANNINOW | 17 | MS | 394 | 473 |
| AND OUT OF THEIR GREENE MANTLETTS DARE TO PEEPE. | AN ELEGY MR STANNINOW | 26 | MS | 394 | 473 |

DAR'ST

|   |   |   |   |   |   |
|---|---|---|---|---|---|
| COME IF THOU DAR'ST, THUS, THUS LET US BE TRY'D. | UPON THE SAME (VENUS ARMES) | 2 | 46 | 161 | 523 |

DARES

|   |   |   |   |   |   |
|---|---|---|---|---|---|
| AND STARS THOU SOW'ST WHOSE HARVEST DARES | THE WEEPER | 10 | 46 | 79 | 120 |
| WHERE TH'OTHER DARES NOT SEND HIS EYE. | TWO WENT TO PRAY | 4 | 46 | 89 | 18 |
| BLACKE WIT OR MALICE CAN OR DARES, | NEITHER DURST MAN ASKE | 2 | 46 | 92 | 20 |
| HAND (O WHAT DARES NOT JEALOUS GREATNESSE.) TORE | SOSPETTO D'HERODE | 3 | 46 | 109 | 216 |
| COME TRY WHO DARES, HEAV'N, EARTH, WHAT ERE DOST BOAST, | SOSPETTO D'HERODE | 251 | 46 | 109 | 216 |
| YET HAS SHEE A HEART DARES HOPE TO PROVE, | IN MEMORY OF LADY MADRE TERESA | 27 | 46 | 131 | 52 |
| THIS RURALL WREATH DARES BE THY SACRIFICE. | UPON YORKE HIS BIRTH | 119 | 46 | 176 | 500 |
| LIFE, THAT DARES SEND | WISHES SUPPOSED MISTRESSE | 65 | 46 | 195 | 479 |
| HER THAT DARES BEE, | WISHES SUPPOSED MISTRESSE | 112 | 46 | 195 | 479 |
| BUT MODESTY DARES STILL DENY IT. | WISHES SUPPOSED MISTRESSE | 120 | 46 | 195 | 479 |
| HOLDS FAST THE DOOR, YET DARES NOT VENTURE | TO COUNTESSE OF DENBIGH | 3 | 52 | 236 | 146 |
| BOLD FAITH TAKES HEART, & DARES BELEIVE. | LAUDA SION SALVATOREM | 38 | 52 | 294 | 178 |
| AND STARRES THOU SOW'ST, WHOSE HARVEST DARES | WEEPER | 10 | 52 | 307 | 120 |
| YET HAS SHE'A HEART DARES HOPE TO PROVE | TERESA | 27 | 52 | 315 | 52 |
| SUCH THIRSTS TO DY, AS DARES DRINK UP, | TERESA | 37 | 52 | 315 | 52 |
| HOLDS FAST THE DOOR, YET DARES NOT VENTURE | AGAINST IRRESOLUTION AND DELAY | 3 | 52 | 347 | 146 |
| BUT DARES DESTRUCTION EATE THESE CANDID BREASTS, | UPON GUNPOWDER TREASON | 37 | MS | 387 | 461 |
| DARES HUNGRY DEATH SNATCH OF ONE CHERRY LIPP. | UPON GUNPOWDER TREASON | 39 | MS | 387 | 461 |

DARING

|   |   |   |   |   |   |
|---|---|---|---|---|---|
| THE WORLD--ALL DARING DUST AND ASHES. ONELY YOU | UPON STANINOUGH'S DEATH | 29 | 46 | 175 | 475 |
| NOR DARING QUITE TO LIVE NOR DY. | TO COUNTESSE OF DENBIGH | 12 | 52 | 236 | 146 |
| GOE NOW, AND WITH SOME DARING DRUGG | TEMPERANCE | 1 | 52 | 342 | 510 |
| NOT DARING QUITE TO LIVE NOR DIE. | AGAINST IRRESOLUTION AND DELAY | 20 | 52 | 347 | 146 |
| NOT DARING TO PEEPE FORTH, LEAST THAT A STONE | UPON GUNPOWDER TREASON | 25 | MS | 366 | 460 |

ALL-DARING

|   |   |   |   |   |   |
|---|---|---|---|---|---|
| THE WORLD, ALL-DARING DUST & ASHES. ONLY YOU | DEATH'S LECTURE | 31 | 52 | 340 | 475 |
| OF LOVES ALL-DARING HAND, THAT MAKES ME BURNE, | EX EUPHORMIONE | 5 | MS | 392 | 525 |

## DAREING

| | | | | | |
|---|---|---|---|---|---|
| GOE NOW WITH SOME DAREING DRUGG. | IN PRAISE OF LESSIUS | 1 | 46 | 156 | 510 |

## DARK

| | | | | | |
|---|---|---|---|---|---|
| SUCH AS (E'RE OUR DARK SINNES TO DUST BETRAY'D THEE) | ON A TREATISE OF CHARITY | 4 | 46 | 137 | 69 |
| AND, THROUGH THE NIGHT OF ERROR AND DARK DOUBT, | ON FRONTISPIECE ISAACSONS | 12 | 46 | 191 | 491 |
| THAT WE, DARK SONS OF DUST & SORROW. | TO THE NAME OF JESUS | 99 | 52 | 239 | 30 |
| WELCOME TO OUR DARK WORLD, THOU | TO THE NAME OF JESUS | 161 | 52 | 239 | 30 |
| MORE DESPERATELY DARK, BECAUSE MORE BRIGHT. | IN GLORIOUS EPIPHANIE | 59 | 52 | 253 | 39 |
| THAT DARK DAY'S CLEAR DOOM SHALL DEFINE | IN GLORIOUS EPIPHANIE | 143 | 52 | 253 | 39 |
| ON THIS DARK GROUND | IN GLORIOUS EPIPHANIE | 194 | 52 | 253 | 39 |
| WHEN THE DARK WORLD DAWN'D INTO CHRISTIAN DAY | TO THE QUEEN'S MAJESTY | 4 | 52 | 261 | 47 |

## DARKE

| | | | | | |
|---|---|---|---|---|---|
| MIDST ALL THE DARKE AND KNOTTY SNARES, | NEITHER DURST MAN ASKE | 1 | 46 | 92 | 20 |
| THE DAY OF MY DARKE WOES IS YET BUT MORNE, | OUR LORD IN HIS CIRCUMCISION | 11 | 46 | 98 | 9 |
| A GLOOMY MANTLE OF DARKE FLAMES, THE TIRE | SOSPETTO D'HERODE | 44 | 46 | 109 | 216 |
| OFT IN HIS DEEPE THOUGHT HE REVOLVES THE DARKE | SOSPETTO D'HERODE | 91 | 46 | 109 | 216 |
| THESE ARE THE KNOTTY RIDDLES, WHOSE DARKE DOUBT | SOSPETTO D'HERODE | 191 | 46 | 109 | 216 |
| TO THIS DARKE HOUSE OF SHADES, HORROUR, AND NIGHT, | SOSPETTO D'HERODE | 213 | 46 | 109 | 216 |
| DARKE, DUSTY MAN, HE NEEDS WOULD SINGLE FORTH, | SOSPETTO D'HERODE | 217 | 46 | 109 | 216 |
| MOCKE ME, AND DAZLE MY DARKE MYSTERIES. | SOSPETTO D'HERODE | 232 | 46 | 109 | 216 |
| MINOTAURES, CYCLOPSES, WITH A DARKE DROVE | SOSPETTO D'HERODE | 351 | 46 | 109 | 216 |
| AND OUR DARKE WORLD NO MORE SHALL SEE. | ON THE ASSUMPTION | 36 | 46 | 139 | 114 |
| SAFE, THOU DARKE HOME OF THE DEAD, | UPON DEATH OF DESIRED HERRYS | 69 | 46 | 168 | 467 |
| IN THE DARKE VOLUME OF OUR FATE, | ANOTHER ON HERRYS | 41 | 46 | 170 | 469 |
| BUT IF WE DARKE SONS OF SORROW | OUT OF CATULLUS | 6 | 46 | 194 | 523 |
| FARRE FROM DARKE HORRORS HOME APPEALE TO REST. | HORATIJ ILLE & NEFASTO | 38 | MS | 382 | 530 |
| SITTING SOE LONG AT EASE IN HER DARKE DENNE. | UPON GUNPOWDER TREASON | 24 | MS | 386 | 460 |
| AND TO MY TOUCH DARKE EYES DID OWE THE LIGHT. | OUT OF GROTIUS | 72 | MS | 398 | 198 |

## DARKNESS

| | | | | | |
|---|---|---|---|---|---|
| ALL WILL BE DARKNESS, TO THE DAY | AN HIMNE FOR CIRCUMCISION | 27 | 46 | 141 | 37 |

## DARKNES

| | | | | | |
|---|---|---|---|---|---|
| IN SPITE OF DARKNES, IT WAS DAY. | IN HOLY NATIVITY | 20 | 52 | 246 | 76 |
| ALL WILL BE DARKNES TO THE DAY | NEW YEAR'S DAY | 27 | 52 | 251 | 37 |
| THE DIRE FACE OF INFERIOR DARKNES, KIS'T | IN GLORIOUS EPIPHANIE | 52 | 52 | 253 | 39 |
| AND MAKE OUR DARKNES SERVE THY DAY. | IN GLORIOUS EPIPHANIE | 212 | 52 | 253 | 39 |
| CONSPIR'D WITH DARKNES 'GAINST THE STRANGERS THROATE. | HORATIJ ILLE & NEFASTO | 9 | MS | 382 | 530 |

## DARKENES

| | | | | | |
|---|---|---|---|---|---|
| A DARKENES MADE OF TOO MUCH DAY, | IN GLORIOUS EPIPHANIE | 18 | 52 | 253 | 39 |

## DARKNESSE

| | | | | | |
|---|---|---|---|---|---|
| THE WORLD WILL LOVE ITS DARKNESSE STILL. | BUT MEN LOVED DARKNESSE | 2 | 46 | 97 | 13 |
| IT WILL NOT LOVE ITS DARKNESSE HALFE SO WELL. | BUT MEN LOVED DARKNESSE | 4 | 46 | 97 | 13 |
| WHERE TRIUMPHANT DARKNESSE HOVERS | PSALME 23 | 37 | 46 | 102 | 5 |
| AND MAKE DARKNESSE SELFE AFRAID. | PSALME 23 | 42 | 46 | 102 | 5 |
| IN SPIGHT OF DARKNESSE IT WAS DAY. | A HYMNE OF THE NATIVITY | 20 | 46 | 106 | 76 |

## DARKENESSE

| | | | | | |
|---|---|---|---|---|---|
| OF DARKENESSE, BY THE LIGHT | WISHES SUPPOSED MISTRESSE | 80 | 46 | 195 | 479 |
| FATHER AND HEYRE OF DARKENESSE, WHEN I CHIDE | OUT OF GROTIUS | 77 | MS | 398 | 198 |

## DARKEST

| | | | | | |
|---|---|---|---|---|---|
| HIS GLOOMY BOSOMES DARKEST CHARACTER. | SOSPETTO D'HERODE | 194 | 46 | 109 | 216 |

## DARLING

| | | | | | |
|---|---|---|---|---|---|
| TO GLUTT THE STOMACK OF HIS DARLING FLOWER. | UPON BIRTH PRINCESSE E | 6 | MS | 391 | 456 |

## DARLINGS

| | | | | | |
|---|---|---|---|---|---|
| THE DARLINGS OF AURORA'S BED. | THE WEEPER | 134 | 46 | 79 | 120 |
| THE DARLINGS OF AURORAS BED, | WEEPER | 176 | 52 | 307 | 120 |
| IF FLORA'S DARLINGS NOW AWAKE FROM SLEEPE, | AN ELEGY MR STANNINOW | 25 | MS | 394 | 473 |

## DART

| | | | | | |
|---|---|---|---|---|---|
| HIS IS THE DART MUST MAKE THE DEATH | IN MEMORY OF LADY MADRE TERESA | 79 | 46 | 131 | 52 |
| A DART THRICE DIPT IN THAT RICH FLAME. | IN MEMORY OF LADY MADRE TERESA | 81 | 46 | 131 | 52 |
| KISSE THE SWEETLY-KILLING DART. | IN MEMORY OF LADY MADRE TERESA | 106 | 46 | 131 | 52 |
| THOSE SECOND SMILES OF HEAVEN SHALL DART, | IN MEMORY OF LADY MADRE TERESA | 136 | 46 | 131 | 52 |
| NEW STRUCK BY LOVE, STILL TREMBLING ON HIS DART. | ON A TREATISE OF CHARITY | 46 | 46 | 137 | 69 |
| LOVE MAY BEE LONG CHUSING A DART. | WISHES SUPPOSED MISTRESSE | 57 | 46 | 195 | 479 |
| CHOOSE OUT THAT SURE DECISIVE DART | TO COUNTESSE OF DENBIGH | 33 | 52 | 236 | 146 |
| AND HAST TO DRINK THE WHOLSOME DART. | TO COUNTESSE OF DENBIGH | 46 | 52 | 236 | 146 |
| O DART OF LOVE. ARROW OF LIGHT. | TO COUNTESSE OF DENBIGH | 49 | 52 | 236 | 146 |
| MY BREST MAY CATCH THE KISSE OF SOME KIND DART. | SANCTA MARIA DOLORUM | 69 | 52 | 283 | 162 |
| TWAS HIS WELL-POINTED DART | WEEPER | 103 | 52 | 307 | 120 |
| HIS IS THE DART MUST MAKE THE DEATH | TERESA | 79 | 52 | 315 | 52 |
| A DART THRICE DIP'T IN THAT RICH FLAME | TERESA | 81 | 52 | 315 | 52 |
| KISSE THE SWEETLY-KILLING DART. | TERESA | 106 | 52 | 315 | 52 |

|   |   |   |   |   |   |
|---|---|---|---|---|---|
| (THOSE SECOND SMILES OF HEAV'N) SHALL DART | TERESA | 135 | 52 | 315 | 52 |
| TO PUT HER DART INTO HIS HAND. | FLAMING HEART | 14 | 52 | 324 | 61 |
| BUT BEFORE ALL, THAT FIERY DART | FLAMING HEART | 35 | 52 | 324 | 61 |
| GIVE HIM THE VAIL, GIVE HER THE DART. | FLAMING HEART | 42 | 52 | 324 | 61 |
| GIVE HER THE DART FOR IT IS SHE | FLAMING HEART | 47 | 52 | 324 | 61 |
| GIVE THEN THE DART TO HER WHO GIVES THE FLAME. | FLAMING HEART | 57 | 52 | 324 | 61 |
| THE ROSY HAND, THE RADIANT DART. | FLAMING HEART | 67 | 52 | 324 | 61 |
| THIS WAS THE CONQUERING DART. & LOE | IN CICATRICES DOMINI JESU | 3 | MS | 381 | 27 |
| IN IT THERE SATE BUT ONE SOLE DART. | IN CICATRICES DOMINI JESU | 9 | MS | 381 | 27 |
| STRANGE THE QUIVER, BOW, & DART. | IN CICATRICES DOMINI JESU | 15 | MS | 381 | 27 |

DARTS

|   |   |   |   |   |   |
|---|---|---|---|---|---|
| THEN SINNE HATH SNARES, OR HELL HATH DARTS. | ON A PRAYER BOOKE | 20 | 46 | 126 | 139 |
| THY SOFTER YET MORE CERTAINE DARTS | IN GLORIOUS EPIPHANIE | 78 | 52 | 253 | 39 |
| O YOU, YOUR OWN BEST DARTS | SANCTA MARIA DOLORUM | 71 | 52 | 283 | 162 |
| COME WOUNDS, COME DARTS. | SANCTA MARIA DOLORUM | 75 | 52 | 283 | 162 |
| THAT LIVE & DY AMIDST HER DARTS, | FLAMING HEART | 50 | 52 | 324 | 61 |
| BIGGE ALIKE WITH WOUNDS & DARTS. | FLAMING HEART | 76 | 52 | 324 | 61 |
| THEN SIN HATH SNARES, OR HELL HATH DARTS. | PRAYER TO GENTLE-WOMAN | 26 | 52 | 328 | 139 |
| THE RADIANT DARTS, SHOTT FROM HIS SPARKLING EYES, | UPON KINGS CORONATION | 35 | MS | 390 | 453 |

DASH

|   |   |   |   |   |   |
|---|---|---|---|---|---|
| HEE THROWES HIS ARME, AND WITH A LONG DRAWNE DASH | MUSICKS DUELL | 30 | 46 | 149 | 535 |
| AND HASTE TO DASH HER INTO DUST. | PSALME 137 | 30 | 46 | 104 | 7 |
| THE SWEET DASH OF A SHOWER NOW SHEAD. | UPON DEATH OF DESIRED HERRYS | 36 | 46 | 168 | 467 |

DASHT

|   |   |   |   |   |   |
|---|---|---|---|---|---|
| OF RAGGED LIMBS, TORNE SCULLS, & DASHT OUT BRAINES. | SOSPETTO D'HERODE | 312 | 46 | 109 | 216 |

DASH'T

|   |   |   |   |   |   |
|---|---|---|---|---|---|
| BY YOUR OWN SHOWRES SEASONABLY DASH'T | WEEPER | 86 | 52 | 307 | 120 |

DATE

|   |   |   |   |   |   |
|---|---|---|---|---|---|
| THUS MUST WE DATE THY MEMORY. | THE WEEPER | 118 | 46 | 79 | 120 |
| WHENCE EACH LEAFE OF LIFE HATH DATE, | ANOTHER ON HERRYS | 42 | 46 | 170 | 469 |
| THUS MUST WE DATE THY MEMORY. | WEEPER | 154 | 52 | 307 | 120 |

DAUGHTER

|   |   |   |   |   |   |
|---|---|---|---|---|---|
| THE DAUGHTER OF A FAIRE AND WELL-FAM'D FOUNTAINE | TO PONTIUS WASHING HANDS | 7 | 46 | 94 | 23 |
| DOST LAUGH, PROUD BABELS DAUGHTER, DO, LAUGH ON, | PSALME 137 | 31 | 46 | 104 | 7 |
| O THOU UNDANTED DAUGHTER OF DESIRES. | FLAMING HEART | 93 | 52 | 324 | 61 |

DAVID

|   |   |   |   |   |   |
|---|---|---|---|---|---|
| THE SCEPTER, WHICH OF OLD GREAT DAVID SWAID. | SOSPETTO D'HERODE | 402 | 46 | 109 | 216 |

DAVID'S

|   |   |   |   |   |   |
|---|---|---|---|---|---|
| WHOSE RIGHT BY DAVID'S LINAGE SO LONG WORNE, | SOSPETTO D'HERODE | 403 | 46 | 109 | 216 |

DAWN

|   |   |   |   |   |   |
|---|---|---|---|---|---|
| FROM TH' DAWN OF THY FAIRE EYE-LIDS WIPE AWAY | ON A TREATISE OF CHARITY | 7 | 46 | 137 | 69 |
| TO CATCH THE DAY-BREAK OF THY DAWN, | TO THE NAME OF JESUS | 148 | 52 | 239 | 30 |
| O DAWN, AT LAST, LONG LOOK'T FOR DAY. | TO THE NAME OF JESUS | 149 | 52 | 239 | 30 |
| YOUNG DAWN OF OUR AETERNALL DAY. | IN HOLY NATIVITY | 32 | 52 | 246 | 76 |
| BRIGHT DAWN OF OUR AETERNALL DAY. | IN HOLY NATIVITY | 73 | 52 | 246 | 76 |
| THE SUPERNATURALL DAWN OF THY PURE DAY. | IN GLORIOUS EPIPHANIE | 174 | 52 | 253 | 39 |
| AND ROSY DAWN OF THE RIGHT ROYALL BLOOD. | TO THE QUEEN'S MAJESTY | 6 | 52 | 261 | 47 |
| BUT SPYES LOVE'S DAWN, & DISAPPEARES. | LAUDA SION SALVATOREM | 22 | 52 | 294 | 178 |
| THINE WAS THE ROSY DAWN THAT SPRUNG THE DAY | O GLORIOSA DOMINA | 21 | 52 | 302 | 194 |
| TILL TH' AETERNALL MORROW DAWN | AN EPITAPH UPON MARRIED COUPLE | 17 | 52 | 339 | 478 |
| AS DOES THE DAWN INTO THE DAY. | (ON) HOPE | 28 | 52 | 345 | 71 |

DAWN'D

|   |   |   |   |   |   |
|---|---|---|---|---|---|
| WHEN THE DARK WORLD DAWN'D INTO CHRISTIAN DAY | TO THE QUEEN'S MAJESTY | 4 | 52 | 261 | 47 |

DAWNE

|   |   |   |   |   |   |
|---|---|---|---|---|---|
| BRIGHT DAWNE OF OUR ETERNALL DAY. | A HYMNE OF THE NATIVITY | 30 | 46 | 106 | 76 |
| THE BEAUTIES OF WHOSE DAWNE WHAT EYE MAY BIDE, | SOSPETTO D'HERODE | 11 | 46 | 109 | 216 |
| HOW BRIGHT A DAWNE OF ANGELS WITH NEW LIGHT | SOSPETTO D'HERODE | 115 | 46 | 109 | 216 |
| AS DOTH THE DAWNE INTO THE DAY. | ON HOPE | 58 | 46 | 143 | 71 |
| AND TH' ETERNALL MORROW DAWNE, | AN EPITAPH HUSBAND AND WIFE | 13 | 46 | 174 | 478 |
| GREAT CHARLES, THOU SWEET DAWNE OF A GLORIOUS DAY, | UPON YORKE HIS BIRTH | 29 | 46 | 176 | 500 |
| DISCERNE THE DAWNE OF TRUTH'S ETERNALL RAY, | ON FRONTISPIECE ISAACSONS | 13 | 46 | 191 | 491 |
| DAWNE THEN TO ME, THOU MORNE OF MINE OWNE DAY, | LUKE 2. QUAERIT JESUM | 45 | MS | 379 | 11 |

DAWNES

|   |   |   |   |   |   |
|---|---|---|---|---|---|
| SCARCE DAWNES, O PARDON, IF I DARE TO SAY | AN APOLOGIE FOR HYMNE (TERESA) | 6 | 46 | 136 | 59 |
| SCARSE DAWNES. O PARDON IF I DARE TO SAY | AN APOLOGIE FOR (TERESA) HYMNE | 6 | 52 | 322 | 59 |

DAWNING

|   |   |   |   |   |   |
|---|---|---|---|---|---|
| WHERE DAWNING HOPE NO BEAME OF COMFORT SHOWES. | SOSPETTO D'HERODE | 242 | 46 | 109 | 216 |

DAY

PREVENTS THE EYE-LIDDS OF THE BLUSHING DAY.
TO HEAVEN, HATH A SUMMERS DAY.
THE SMILING MORNE HAD NEWLY WAK'T THE DAY,
WHY ART THOU ARM'D SO DESPERATELY TO DAY.
TASTES OF THIS BREAKFAST ALL DAY LONG.
LET NIGHT OR DAY DOE WHAT THEY WILL
THE DAY OF MY DARKE WOES IS YET BUT MORNE.
THIS ROCKE BUDS FORTH THE FOUNTAINE OF THE STREAMES
                                              OF DAY.
SPREADS A PATH CLEARE AS THE DAY,
ONE OF SIONS SONGS TO DAY.
IN SPIGHT OF DARKNESSE IT WAS DAY.
IT WAS THY DAY, SWEET, AND DID RISE,
BRIGHT DAWNE OF OUR ETERNALL DAY.
SUMMER IN WINTER. DAY IN NIGHT.
PROUD MORNING OF A PERVERSE DAY. HOW LOST
AMAZ'D THE MIDNIGHT WORLD, AND MADE A DAY
(NOR ASKT LEAVE OF THE SUN) BY DAY AS NIGHT.
WHERE ALL THE BUSIE DAY SHEE CLOSE DOTH LY,
(NIGHT HANGS YET HEAVY ON THE LIDS OF DAY)
AND KEEP THE DIVELLS HOLY DAY.
AND EVERY DAY,
WHICH EVERY DAY TO HEAVEN WILL SEND YOU.
THOU HERE ART SET TO SHINE, WHERE THY FULL DAY
DULL MISTS AND MELANCHOLY CLOUDS. TAKE DAY
AND THE DEARE DROPS THIS DAY WERE SHED.
ANOTHER DAY OF DIADEMS.
ALL WILL BE DARKNESS, TO THE DAY
OUR LIFE IN DEATH, OUR DAY IN NIGHT.
AS DOTH THE DAWNE INTO THE DAY.
TO HATCH HER SELFE IN, 'MONGST HIS LEAVES THE DAY
THEREFORE ONELY GIVE TO DAY,
OF THE NEW-SALUTED DAY.
HOVER O'RE THE NEW-BORNE DAY.
WHOSE DAY SHALL NEVER SLEEPE IN NIGHT.
GREAT CHARLES. THOU SWEET DAWNE OF A GLORIOUS DAY,
BUT STAY, WHAT GLIMPSE WAS THAT. WHY BLUSHT THE DAY.
BUT THOU AT NOONE DOST SHINE, AND ART ALL DAY,
WHERE ART THOU SOL, WHILE THUS THE BLIND-FOLD DAY
TAINT NOT THE PURE STREAMES OF THE SPRINGING DAY.
LET IT SUFFICE, SHEE'L WEARE NO MASKE TO DAY.
ARE THESE THE BEAMES THAT RULE THY DAY.
'TIS THIS. LISTNING ONE DAY TOO LONG.
AS WHEN THE ROSIE MORNE BUDDS INTO DAY.
BRIGHTEST SOL THAT DYES TO DAY
LIPPS, WHERE ALL DAY
CAN TAME THE WANTON DAY
OF A CLEERE MIND ARE DAY ALL NIGHT.
YET LONG BY TH'ABSENCE OF THE DAY.
OF BEAMES TO DAY, PAY BACK AGAINE TO MORROW,
DISBAND DULL FEARES. GIVE FAITH THE DAY.
THE HIGH-BORN BROOD OF DAY. YOU BRIGHT
THIS ILLUSTRIOUS DAY.
UNLOCK THY CABINET OF DAY
O DAWN, AT LAST, LONG LOOK'T FOR DAY.
WOMB OF DAY.
WITH BLUSH OF THINE OWN BLOOD THY DAY ADORNING,
IN SPITE OF DARKNES, IT WAS DAY.
IT WAS THY DAY, SWEET, & DID RISE
YOUNG DAWN OF OUR AETERNALL DAY.
BRIGHT DAWN OF OUR AETERNALL DAY.
SOMMER IN WINTER. DAY IN NIGHT.
AND THE DEAR DROPS THIS DAY WERE SHED.
ANOTHER DAY OF DIADEMS.
ALL WILL BE DARKNES TO THE DAY
THE DAY, & PLANT IT FAIRER IN THY FACE.
A DARKENES MADE OF TOO MUCH DAY.
TO THEE, THOU DAY OF NIGHT. THOU EAST OF WEST.
THE GENERALL & INDIFFERENT DAY.
AND DOUBLE-GUILDED AS THE DOORES OF DAY.
THE DEATHLES HEIR OF ALL THY FATHER'S DAY.
SHALL ANY DAY BUT THINE ADORE.
IT WAS FOR THIS THE DAY DID RISE
TIME HAS A DAY IN STORE
ALL THE IDOLATROUS THEFTS DONE BY THIS NIGHT OF DAY.
AS BY A FAIR-EY'D FALLACY OF DAY
THE SUPERNATURALL DAWN OF THY PURE DAY.
COME FORTH GREAT MASTER OF THE MYSTICK DAY.
AND MAKE OUR DARKNES SERVE THY DAY.
BORROWING DAY & LENDING NIGHT.
THE DELEGATED EYE OF DAY
WHEN THE DARK WORLD DAWN'D INTO CHRISTIAN DAY
THE AGED HONORS OF THIS DAY STILL NEW.
LIFE OUT OF DEATH, DAY OUT OF NIGHT.
THE FAIR STARRS FILL THEIR WAKEFULL FIRES THE SUN
                                    HIMSELFE DRINKS
                                                DAY.
COME LOVE. COME LORD. & THAT LONG DAY
WHICH ON HIS WHITE BROWES THIS BRIGHT DAY
AND THEIR NIGHT DYES INTO OUR DAY.
MUST BE THE DAY OF THAT DREAD NIGHT.
DEAR, REMEMBER IN THAT DAY

| Title | | | | |
|---|---|---|---|---|
| MUSICKS DUELL | 82 | 46 | 149 | 535 |
| IN PRAISE OF LESSIUS | 34 | 46 | 156 | 510 |
| THE BEGINNING OF HELIODORUS | 1 | 46 | 158 | 517 |
| UPON VENUS PUTTING ARMES | 2 | 46 | 161 | 523 |
| THE WEEPER | 30 | 46 | 79 | 120 |
| THE WEEPER | 113 | 46 | 79 | 120 |
| OUR LORD IN HIS CIRCUMCISION | 11 | 46 | 98 | 9 |
| EASTER DAY | 9 | 46 | 100 | 26 |
| PSALME 23 | 29 | 46 | 102 | 5 |
| PSALME 137 | 12 | 46 | 104 | 7 |
| A HYMNE OF THE NATIVITY | 20 | 46 | 106 | 76 |
| A HYMNE OF THE NATIVITY | 21 | 46 | 106 | 76 |
| A HYMNE OF THE NATIVITY | 30 | 46 | 106 | 76 |
| A HYMNE OF THE NATIVITY | 55 | 46 | 106 | 76 |
| SOSPETTO D'HERODE | 77 | 46 | 109 | 216 |
| SOSPETTO D'HERODE | 116 | 46 | 109 | 216 |
| SOSPETTO D'HERODE | 133 | 46 | 109 | 216 |
| SOSPETTO D'HERODE | 386 | 46 | 109 | 216 |
| SOSPETTO D'HERODE | 506 | 46 | 109 | 216 |
| ON A PRAYER BOOKE | 47 | 46 | 126 | 139 |
| ON A PRAYER BOOKE | 100 | 46 | 126 | 139 |
| ON MR. G. HERBERTS BOOKE | 12 | 46 | 130 | 68 |
| AN APOLOGIE FOR HYMNE (TERESA) | 5 | 46 | 136 | 59 |
| ON A TREATISE OF CHARITY | 8 | 46 | 137 | 69 |
| AN HIMNE FOR CIRCUMCISION | 4 | 46 | 141 | 37 |
| AN HIMNE FOR CIRCUMCISION | 24 | 46 | 141 | 37 |
| AN HIMNE FOR CIRCUMCISION | 27 | 46 | 141 | 37 |
| ON HOPE | 16 | 46 | 143 | 71 |
| ON HOPE | 58 | 46 | 143 | 71 |
| UPON DEATH OF HERRYS | 15 | 46 | 167 | 466 |
| UPON DEATH OF DESIRED HERRYS | 29 | 46 | 168 | 467 |
| UPON DEATH OF DESIRED HERRYS | 34 | 46 | 168 | 467 |
| UPON DEATH OF DESIRED HERRYS | 48 | 46 | 168 | 467 |
| AN EPITAPH HUSBAND AND WIFE | 16 | 46 | 174 | 478 |
| UPON YORKE HIS BIRTH | 29 | 46 | 176 | 500 |
| UPON YORKE HIS BIRTH | 66 | 46 | 176 | 500 |
| UPON YORKE HIS BIRTH | 78 | 46 | 176 | 500 |
| ON A FOULE MORNING | 1 | 46 | 181 | 495 |
| ON A FOULE MORNING | 32 | 46 | 181 | 495 |
| ON A FOULE MORNING | 38 | 46 | 181 | 495 |
| LOVES HOROSCOPE | 10 | 46 | 185 | 483 |
| OUT OF THE ITALIAN (3) | 3 | 46 | 190 | 549 |
| ON FRONTISPIECE ISAACSONS | 14 | 46 | 191 | 491 |
| OUT OF CATULLUS | 4 | 46 | 194 | 523 |
| WISHES SUPPOSED MISTRESSE | 37 | 46 | 195 | 479 |
| WISHES SUPPOSED MISTRESSE | 50 | 46 | 195 | 479 |
| WISHES SUPPOSED MISTRESSE | 81 | 46 | 195 | 479 |
| WISHES SUPPOSED MISTRESSE | 84 | 46 | 195 | 479 |
| UPON TWO GREENE APRICOCKES | 28 | 48 | 220 | 494 |
| TO COUNTESSE OF DENBIGH | 57 | 52 | 236 | 146 |
| TO THE NAME OF JESUS | 7 | 52 | 239 | 30 |
| TO THE NAME OF JESUS | 43 | 52 | 239 | 30 |
| TO THE NAME OF JESUS | 127 | 52 | 239 | 30 |
| TO THE NAME OF JESUS | 149 | 52 | 239 | 30 |
| TO THE NAME OF JESUS | 162 | 52 | 239 | 30 |
| TO THE NAME OF JESUS | 222 | 52 | 239 | 30 |
| IN HOLY NATIVITY | 20 | 52 | 246 | 76 |
| IN HOLY NATIVITY | 21 | 52 | 246 | 76 |
| IN HOLY NATIVITY | 32 | 52 | 246 | 76 |
| IN HOLY NATIVITY | 73 | 52 | 246 | 76 |
| IN HOLY NATIVITY | 81 | 52 | 246 | 76 |
| NEW YEAR'S DAY | 2 | 52 | 251 | 37 |
| NEW YEAR'S DAY | 24 | 52 | 251 | 37 |
| NEW YEAR'S DAY | 27 | 52 | 251 | 37 |
| IN GLORIOUS EPIPHANIE | 6 | 52 | 253 | 39 |
| IN GLORIOUS EPIPHANIE | 18 | 52 | 253 | 39 |
| IN GLORIOUS EPIPHANIE | 22 | 52 | 253 | 39 |
| IN GLORIOUS EPIPHANIE | 25 | 52 | 253 | 39 |
| IN GLORIOUS EPIPHANIE | 57 | 52 | 253 | 39 |
| IN GLORIOUS EPIPHANIE | 64 | 52 | 253 | 39 |
| IN GLORIOUS EPIPHANIE | 86 | 52 | 253 | 39 |
| IN GLORIOUS EPIPHANIE | 125 | 52 | 253 | 39 |
| IN GLORIOUS EPIPHANIE | 133 | 52 | 253 | 39 |
| IN GLORIOUS EPIPHANIE | 150 | 52 | 253 | 39 |
| IN GLORIOUS EPIPHANIE | 163 | 52 | 253 | 39 |
| IN GLORIOUS EPIPHANIE | 174 | 52 | 253 | 39 |
| IN GLORIOUS EPIPHANIE | 207 | 52 | 253 | 39 |
| IN GLORIOUS EPIPHANIE | 212 | 52 | 253 | 39 |
| IN GLORIOUS EPIPHANIE | 218 | 52 | 253 | 39 |
| IN GLORIOUS EPIPHANIE | 236 | 52 | 253 | 39 |
| TO THE QUEEN'S MAJESTY | 4 | 52 | 261 | 47 |
| TO THE QUEEN'S MAJESTY | 24 | 52 | 261 | 47 |
| OFFICE H. CROSS MATINES | 23 | 52 | 265 | 86 |
| OFFICE H. CROSS PRIME | 8 | 52 | 267 | 91 |
| ADORO TE | 51 | 52 | 291 | 172 |
| LAUDA SION SALVATOREM | 1 | 52 | 294 | 178 |
| LAUDA SION SALVATOREM | 24 | 52 | 294 | 178 |
| DIES IRAE | 8 | 52 | 298 | 186 |
| DIES IRAE | 29 | 52 | 298 | 186 |

| | | | | |
|---|---|---|---|---|
| THY SELF, AND SO DISCHARGE THAT DAY. | DIES IRAE | 46 | 52 298 | 186 |
| THINE WAS THE ROSY DAWN THAT SPRUNG THE DAY | O GLORIOSA DOMINA | 21 | 52 302 | 194 |
| HAIL, DOOR OF LIFE, & SOURSE OF DAY. | O GLORIOSA DOMINA | 32 | 52 302 | 194 |
| THE DOOR WAS SHUTT, YET LET IN DAY, | O GLORIOSA DOMINA | 35 | 52 302 | 194 |
| TASTS OF THIS BREAKFAST ALL DAY LONG. | WEEPER | 30 | 52 307 | 120 |
| DOES DAY CLOSE HIS EYES. | WEEPER | 135 | 52 307 | 120 |
| LET NIGHT OR DAY DOE WHAT THEY WILL, | WEEPER | 137 | 52 307 | 120 |
| THOU HERE ART SETT TO SHINE WHERE THY FULL DAY | AN APOLOGIE FOR (TERESA) HYMNE | 5 | 52 322 | 59 |
| AMONG THE LEAVES OF THY LARG BOOKS OF DAY, | FLAMING HEART | 88 | 52 324 | 61 |
| BY THY LARG DRAUGHTS OF INTELLECTUALL DAY, | FLAMING HEART | 97 | 52 324 | 61 |
| AND EVERY DAY | PRAYER TO GENTLE-WOMAN | 106 | 52 328 | 139 |
| HOME TO THE ORIGINALL SOURSE OF LIGHT & INTELLECTUALL | DESCRIPTION RELIGIOUS HOUSE | 39 | 52 338 | 213 |
| WHOSE DAY SHALL NEVER DY IN NIGHT. | AN EPITAPH UPON MARRIED COUPLE | 20 | 52 339 | 478 |
| TO HEAVN RIDES IN A SUMMER'S DAY. | TEMPERANCE | 32 | 52 342 | 510 |
| BLENDS BOTH THE NOONES OF NIGHT & DAY. | (ON) HOPE | 6 | 52 345 | 71 |
| AS DOES THE DAWN INTO THE DAY. | (ON) HOPE | 28 | 52 345 | 71 |
| DISBAND DULL FEARES, GIVE FAITH THE DAY. | AGAINST IRRESOLUTION AND DELAY | 81 | 52 347 | 146 |
| DAWNE THEN TO ME,THOU MORNE OF MINE OWNE DAY, | LUKE 2. QUAERIT JESUM | 45 | MS 379 | 11 |
| BLACK, AS THE DAY WAS DISMALL, IN WHOSE SIGHT | HORATIJ ILLE & NEFASTO | 5 | MS 382 | 530 |
| LETT HER SURVIVE THIS DAY, ONCE MOCK HER FATE, | ON GUNPOWDER-TREASON | 9 | MS 384 | 458 |
| IN THY COLD BREAST, & YEARLY ON THIS DAY | ON GUNPOWDER-TREASON | 13 | MS 384 | 458 |
| ABASH THE PUREST BEAUTIES OF THE DAY. | UPON KINGS CORONATION | 26 | MS 389 | 454 |
| BUT SMILES, & RUDDY JOYES, & AT THIS DAY | UPON KINGS CORONATION | 39 | MS 390 | 453 |
| THAT THERE INHABITE, THOU ON EVERY DAY | AN ELEGIE ON DR PORTER | 5 | MS 395 | 476 |
| OF MY SAD LABOURS. NO DAY YETT COULD TELL | OUT OF GROTIUS | 10 | MS 398 | 198 |

AY-BEARING

| | | | | |
|---|---|---|---|---|
| HEE SAW HOW IN THAT BLEST DAY-BEARING NIGHT, | SOSPETTO D'HERODE | 113 | 46 109 | 216 |

Y-BREAK

| | | | | |
|---|---|---|---|---|
| TO CATCH THE DAY-BREAK OF THY DAWN. | TO THE NAME OF JESUS | 148 | 52 239 | 30 |
| THE DAY-BREAK OF THE NATIONS. THEIR FIRST RAY. | TO THE QUEEN'S MAJESTY | 3 | 52 261 | 47 |

DAY-STARRE

| | | | | |
|---|---|---|---|---|
| DOES THE DAY-STARRE RISE. | WEEPER | 133 | 52 307 | 120 |

MID-DAY

| | | | | |
|---|---|---|---|---|
| AT MID-DAY OPES A PRESENCE WHICH HEAVENS EYE | UPON YORKE HIS BIRTH | 70 | 46 176 | 500 |

DAY'S

| | | | | |
|---|---|---|---|---|
| DAY'S SWEAT, AND BY A GENTLE TYRANNY, | SOSPETTO D'HERODE | 386 | 46 109 | 216 |
| THAT DARK DAY'S CLEAR DOOM SHALL DEFINE | IN GLORIOUS EPIPHANIE | 143 | 52 253 | 39 |
| FOR BEING SHOW'D BY THIS DAY'S LIGHT, HOW FARR | IN GLORIOUS EPIPHANIE | 246 | 52 253 | 39 |
| FOR FROM THIS DAY'S RICH SEED OF DIADEMS | TO THE QUEEN'S MAJESTY | 11 | 52 261 | 47 |
| WHILE YOUR EACH DAY'S DEVOTION DULY BRINGS | TO THE QUEEN'S MAJESTY | 27 | 52 261 | 47 |
| THREE KINGDOMES TO SUPPLY THIS DAY'S THREE KINGS. | TO THE QUEEN'S MAJESTY | 28 | 52 261 | 47 |
| LO THE BREAD OF LIFE, THIS DAY'S | LAUDA SION SALVATOREM | 7 | 52 294 | 178 |

DAYE'S

| | | | | |
|---|---|---|---|---|
| NEW DROPS, WASH OFF THE SWEAT OF THIS DAYE'S SORROWS. | DESCRIPTION RELIGIOUS HOUSE | 22 | 52 338 | 213 |

DAYES

| | | | | |
|---|---|---|---|---|
| HEE LOST THE DAYES HEAT, AND HIS OWNE HOT CARES. | MUSICKS DUELL | 6 | 46 149 | 535 |
| SO SMIL'D THE DAYES, AND SO THE TENOR RAN | OUT OF VIRGIL | 24 | 46 155 | 529 |
| OTHERS BY DAYES, BY MONTHES, BY YEARES | THE WEEPER | 119 | 46 79 | 120 |
| DEATH ONELY BY THIS DAYES JUST DOOME IS FORC'T TO DYE. | EASTER DAY | 15 | 46 100 | 26 |
| DAYES KING DEPOSED BY NIGHTS QUEENE. | A HYMNE OF THE NATIVITY | 2 | 46 106 | 76 |
| DEARE BABE E'RE MANY DAYES BE DONE. | AN HIMNE FOR CIRCUMCISION | 30 | 46 141 | 37 |
| DEATH LOST THE RECKONING OF HIS DAYES. | HIS EPITAPH (HERRYS) | 10 | 46 172 | 471 |
| EACH ONE AN AGES LABOUR, THAT THY DAYES | UPON YORKE HIS BIRTH | 11 | 46 176 | 500 |
| THE DAYES ABASHED GLORIES, AND IN FACE | UPON YORKE HIS BIRTH | 75 | 46 176 | 500 |
| AN ANTHEM AT THE DAYES NATIVITIE. | TO THE MORNING | 44 | 46 183 | 497 |
| OUT-STARE THE BROAD-BEAM'D DAYES MERIDIAN) | ON FRONTISPIECE ISAACSONS | 10 | 46 191 | 491 |
| DAYES, THAT NEED BORROW, | WISHES SUPPOSED MISTRESSE | 76 | 46 195 | 479 |
| DAYES, THAT IN SPIGHT | WISHES SUPPOSED MISTRESSE | 79 | 46 195 | 479 |
| CAN MAKE DAYES FOREHEAD BRIGHT. | WISHES SUPPOSED MISTRESSE | 95 | 46 195 | 479 |
| DEAR BABE, ERE MANY DAYES BE DONE, | NEW YEAR'S DAY | 30 | 52 251 | 37 |
| BOTH NIGHTS & DAYES, | CHARITAS NIMIA | 27 | 52 280 | 48 |
| DISSOLVE MY DAYES & HOWRES. | SANCTA MARIA DOLORUM | 68 | 52 283 | 162 |
| GIVE LOVE FOR LIFE. NOR LET MY DAYES | ADORO TE | 35 | 52 291 | 172 |
| WHOLE DAYES & SUNS DEVOUR'D WITH ENDLESSE DINING. | DESCRIPTION RELIGIOUS HOUSE | 2 | 52 338 | 213 |
| TWICE TWENTY DAYES PURE ABSTINENCE, TO FEED | OUT OF GROTIUS | 59 | MS 398 | 198 |

DAIES

| | | | | |
|---|---|---|---|---|
| BY THREE DAIES LOSSE AETERNALLY TO SAVE. | MATH. 16. 25. WHOSOEVER SHALL | 4 | MS 381 | 16 |

DAYLY

| | | | | |
|---|---|---|---|---|
| THIS DAYLY WRONG | IN GLORIOUS EPIPHANIE | 129 | 52 253 | 39 |

DAYLY-DYING

| | | | | |
|---|---|---|---|---|
| A LONG & DAYLY-DYING LIFE, WHICH BREATHS | DESCRIPTION RELIGIOUS HOUSE | 23 | 52 338 | 213 |

## DAZELING

| | | | | | |
|---|---|---|---|---|---|
| AND COUCH BEFORE THE DAZELING LIGHT OF THY DREAD MAJESTY. | TO THE NAME OF JESUS | 235 | 52 | 239 | 30 |

## DAZLE

| | | | | | |
|---|---|---|---|---|---|
| MOCKE ME, AND DAZLE MY DARKE MYSTERIES. | SOSPETTO D'HERODE | 232 | 46 | 109 | 216 |

## DEAD

| | | | | | |
|---|---|---|---|---|---|
| (THAT LIV'D SO SWEETLY) DEAD, SO SWEET A GRAVE. | MUSICKS DUELL | 168 | 46 | 149 | 535 |
| IN THEIR OWNE BLOODS DEARE DELUGE, SOME NEW DEAD. | THE BEGINNING OF HELIODORUS | 17 | 46 | 158 | 517 |
| TIS BUT A DEAD FACE, ART DOTH HERE BEQUEATH. | UPON BISHOP ANDREWES PICTURE | 15 | 46 | 163 | 490 |
| A LINE OR TWO, TO SPEAKE HIM DEAD. | UPON THE DEATH OF A GENTLEMAN | 8 | 46 | 166 | 472 |
| THUS MUCH, HEE'S DEAD, AND WEEPE THE REST. | UPON THE DEATH OF A GENTLEMAN | 34 | 46 | 166 | 472 |
| OF STARING COMETS, THAT LOOKE KINGDOMES DEAD. | SOSPETTO D'HERODE | 52 | 46 | 109 | 216 |
| JOSEPH THE KINGS DEAD BROTHERS SHAPE SHE TAKES, | SOSPETTO D'HERODE | 419 | 46 | 109 | 216 |
| FOR WHOM (AS DEAD) THE WRATHFULL WINDS CONTEST, | SOSPETTO D'HERODE | 427 | 46 | 109 | 216 |
| OF DEAD DEVOTION. NOR FAINT MARBLES WEEP | ON A TREATISE OF CHARITY | 33 | 46 | 137 | 69 |
| SAFE, THOU DARKE HOME OF THE DEAD, | UPON DEATH OF DESIRED HERRYS | 69 | 46 | 168 | 467 |
| BUT HE, ALAS. EVEN HEE IS DEAD | ANOTHER ON HERRYS | 55 | 46 | 170 | 469 |
| ALL HOPE OF NEVER DYING, HERE LYES DEAD. | ANOTHER ON HERRYS | 62 | 46 | 170 | 469 |
| AND TRACE ETERNITY--BUT ALL IS DEAD. | TO THE MORNING | 29 | 46 | 183 | 497 |
| AND LIVES IN HIM THAT HERE LYES DEAD. | OFFICE H. CROSS COMPLINE | 4 | 52 | 274 | 105 |
| WHOSE USE DENYES US TO THE DEAD. | ADORO TE | 40 | 52 | 291 | 172 |
| THE CHILD OF DEATH EATES HIMSELF DEAD. | LAUDA SION SALVATOREM | 52 | 52 | 294 | 178 |
| DEAD TO MY SELFE, I LIVE IN THEE. | A SONG | 16 | 52 | 327 | 65 |
| AND THOUGH THEY LY AS THEY WERE DEAD, | AN EPITAPH UPON MARRIED COUPLE | 11 | 52 | 339 | 478 |
| AND ROUZE THE SLEEPY ASHES OF THE DEAD, | ON GUNPOWDER-TREASON | 29 | MS | 384 | 458 |
| HEE'S DEAD. OH WHAT HARSH MUSICKS THERE | UPON DEATH OF A FREIND | 1 | MS | 393 | 477 |
| PEACE IS AN ORPHAN NOW. HER FATHER'S DEAD. | AN ELEGIE ON DR PORTER | 16 | MS | 395 | 476 |

## DEADLY

| | | | | | |
|---|---|---|---|---|---|
| WAS THROWNE ALAS, AND GOT A DEADLY FALL. | HIGH MOUNTED ON AN ANT | 2 | 46 | 161 | 523 |
| SYMPTOMES SO DEADLY, UNTO DEATH AND HIM. | SOSPETTO D'HERODE | 138 | 46 | 109 | 216 |
| MORE DEEPE SUSPICIONS, AND MORE DEADLY STINGS, | SOSPETTO D'HERODE | 501 | 46 | 109 | 216 |
| THEIR DEADLY HATE LIVES STILL, & HATH | OFFICE H. CROSS EVENSONG | 3 | 52 | 273 | 101 |

## DEAFEN'D

| | | | | | |
|---|---|---|---|---|---|
| THE THIRD HOUR'S DEAFEN'D WITH THE CRY | OFFICE H. CROSS THIRD | 1 | 52 | 268 | 93 |

## DEAFNES

| | | | | | |
|---|---|---|---|---|---|
| NOR WAS'T OUR DEAFNES, BUT OUR SINS, THAT THUS | IN GLORIOUS EPIPHANIE | 131 | 52 | 253 | 39 |

## DEALE

| | | | | | |
|---|---|---|---|---|---|
| SWEET MISTRIS SOUNDS A GREAT DEALE BETTER. | PETRONIJ ALES PHASIACIS PETITA | 18 | MS | 382 | 526 |
| THERE THESE BRAVE SOULES DEALE TO EACH WONDRING EARE | HORATIJ ILLE & NEFASTO | 45 | MS | 382 | 530 |

## DEALT

| | | | | | |
|---|---|---|---|---|---|
| HAD DEALT TOO ROUGHLY WITH HER TENDER THROATE, | MUSICKS DUELL | 159 | 46 | 149 | 535 |

## DEAR

| | | | | | |
|---|---|---|---|---|---|
| WELLCOME DEAR, ALL-ADORED NAME. | TO THE NAME OF JESUS | 225 | 52 | 239 | 30 |
| AND THE DEAR DROPS THIS DAY WERE SHED. | NEW YEAR'S DAY | 4 | 52 | 251 | 37 |
| DEAR BABE, ERE MANY DAYES BE DONE, | NEW YEAR'S DAY | 30 | 52 | 251 | 37 |
| WHEN THE DEAR NAILES DID LOCK | OFFICE H. CROSS EVENSONG | 12 | 52 | 273 | 101 |
| SO DEAR. WHAT HAD HIS RUIN LOST THEE. | CHARITAS NIMIA | 2 | 52 | 280 | 48 |
| DEAR, DOLEFULL HEARTS. | SANCTA MARIA DOLORUM | 72 | 52 | 283 | 162 |
| (DEAR WOUNDS) & ONELY NOW | SANCTA MARIA DOLORUM | 83 | 52 | 283 | 162 |
| TILL DRUNK OF THE DEAR WOUNDS, I BE | SANCTA MARIA DOLORUM | 103 | 52 | 283 | 162 |
| MY DEAR LORD'S VITALL DEATH. | SANCTA MARIA DOLORUM | 108 | 52 | 283 | 162 |
| DEAR LORD TO THEE, TO US IS FOUND | UPON BLEEDING CRUCIFIX | 34 | 52 | 288 | 110 |
| O DEAR MEMORIALL OF THAT DEATH | ADORO TE | 37 | 52 | 291 | 172 |
| DEAR, REMEMBER IN THAT DAY | DIES IRAE | 29 | 52 | 298 | 186 |
| SHE'S CALLD. HARK, HOW THE DEAR IMMORTALL DOVE | IN GLORIOUS ASSUMPTION B. LADY | 7 | 52 | 304 | 114 |
| THINE OWN DEAR BOOKES ARE GUILTY. FOR FROM THENCE | AN APOLOGIE FOR (TERESA) HYMNE | 7 | 52 | 322 | 59 |
| DEAR SOUL, BE STRONG. | PRAYER TO GENTLE-WOMAN | 39 | 52 | 328 | 139 |
| OF SOUL, DEAR & DIVINE ANNIHILATIONS. | PRAYER TO GENTLE-WOMAN | 78 | 52 | 328 | 139 |
| O FAIR, O FORTUNATE, O RICHE, O DEAR. | PRAYER TO GENTLE-WOMAN | 96 | 52 | 328 | 139 |
| DEAR, HEAVN-DESIGNED SOUL. | TO SAME CONCERNING CHOISE | 1 | 52 | 331 | 66 |
| WAKEFULL. HER DEAR VOWES UNDEFIL'D TO KEEP. | ALEXIAS THIRD ELEGIE | 38 | 52 | 336 | 209 |
| DEAR RELIQUES OF A DISLODG'D SOUL, WHOSE LACK | DEATH'S LECTURE | 1 | 52 | 340 | 475 |
| SPEND THE DEAR TREASURES OF THY LIFE. | TEMPERANCE | 4 | 52 | 342 | 510 |
| DEAR HOPE, EARTH'S DOWRY, & HEAVN'S DEBT. | (ON) HOPE | 1 | 52 | 345 | 71 |

## DEAR-BOUGHT

| | | | | | |
|---|---|---|---|---|---|
| TO ALL THE DEAR-BOUGHT NATIONS THIS REDEEMING NAME, | TO THE NAME OF JESUS | 94 | 52 | 239 | 30 |

## DEARE

| | | | | | |
|---|---|---|---|---|---|
| SPEND THE DEARE TREASURE OF THY LIFE. | IN PRAISE OF LESSIUS | 4 | 46 | 156 | 510 |
| IN THEIR OWNE BLOODS DEARE DELUGE, SOME NEW DEAD. | THE BEGINNING OF HELIODORUS | 17 | 46 | 158 | 517 |
| FOR SO DEARE, SO DEEP A TRUST. | UPON THE DEATH OF A GENTLEMAN | 13 | 46 | 166 | 472 |
| EACH DROP LEAVING A PLACE SO DEARE, | THE TEARE | 17 | 46 | 84 | 50 |
| ARE HUSKS SO DEARE. TROTH 'TIS A MIGHTY RATE. | ON THE PRODIGALL | 4 | 46 | 86 | 17 |

```
THOU, THOU (DEARE LORD) EVEN THOU ALONE,        VERILY YE SHALL WEEP                 5  46  95 22
AT TOO DEARE A RATE ARE ROSES.                  ON WOUNDS OF CRUCIFIED LORD          6  46  99 24
DEARE LORD TO THEE) TO US IS FOUND              ON BLEEDING WOUNDS OF LORD          38  46 101 110
BY THE LINE OF THY DEARE LOVE.                  PSALME 23                           58  46 102   5
DEARE SOULE BEE STRONG,                         ON A PRAYER BOOKE                   33  46 126 139
OF SOULE. DEARE, AND DIVINE ANNIHILATIONS.      ON A PRAYER BOOKE                   72  46 126 139
OF THE DEARE SPOWSE OF SPIRITS WITH THEM WILL BRING. ON A PRAYER BOOKE              78  46 126 139
O FAIRE. O FORTUNATE. O RICH. O DEARE.          ON A PRAYER BOOKE                   90  46 126 139
DEARE SILVER BREASTED DOVE                      ON A PRAYER BOOKE                   92  46 126 139
FAREWELL WHAT EVER DEARE MAY BEE,               IN MEMORY OF LADY MADRE TERESA      61  46 131  52
THINE OWN DEARE BOOKS ARE GUILTY, FOR FROM THENCE AN APOLOGIE FOR HYMNE (TERESA)     7  46 136  59
WITH THOSE DEARE SPOILES THAT WONT TO DRESSE THE FAIRE ON A TREATISE OF CHARITY     54  46 137  69
AND THE DEARE DROPS THIS DAY WERE SHED.         AN HIMNE FOR CIRCUMCISION            4  46 141  37
DEARE BABE E'RE MANY DAYES BE DONE.             AN HIMNE FOR CIRCUMCISION           30  46 141  37
DEARE HOPE. EARTHS DOWRY, AND HEAVENS DEBT,     ON HOPE                             11  46 143  71
DEARE RELIQUES OF A DISLODG'D SOULE, WHOSE LACKE UPON STANINOUGH'S DEATH             1  46 175 475
NE'RE MAY A BIRTH OF THINE BE BOUGHT SO DEARE,  UPON YORKE HIS BIRTH                94  46 176 500
SO DEARE GLORIES DARE NOT BORROW.               OUT OF THE ITALIAN (1)              39  46 188 545
COME AND LET US LIVE MY DEARE,                  OUT OF CATULLUS                      1  46 194 523
AND THE DEARE MERITS OF YOUR MUSE, THEIR DUE,   UPON TWO GREENE APRICOCKES          11  48 220 494
O DEARE & SWEET DISPUTE                         OFFICE H. CROSS SIXT                13  52 270  97
FAREWELL WHAT EVER DEARE MAY BEE,               TERESA                              61  52 315  52
OF THE DEARE SPOUSE OF SPIRITS WITH THEM WILL BRING PRAYER TO GENTLE-WOMAN          84  52 326 139
DEARE WIFE HATH NE'RE A HANDSOME LETTER,        PETRONIJ ALES PHASIACIS PETITA      17  MS 382 526

DEARE'S

WELCOME MY GRIEFE, MY JOY, HOW DEARE'S          VERILY YE SHALL WEEP                 1  46  95  22

DEERE

DEERE, DISCOVER                                 OUT OF THE ITALIAN (1)               2  46 188 545
THOSE DEERE LIPS WHOSE DOORE ENCLOSES           OUT OF THE ITALIAN (1)              21  46 188 545

DEARER

NOT FOR MY SELF ALAS, BUT FOR MY DEARER LORD.   TO SAME CONCERNING CHOISE            7  52 331  66

DEAREST

SHEE OFFERS THEM HER DEAREST BREATH,            IN MEMORY OF LADY MADRE TERESA      49  46 131  52
AND THOUGH MY DEAREST LOOKS MUST NOW BE LIGHT   ON THE ASSUMPTION                   31  46 139 114
DEAREST SWEET, & COME AWAY.                     TO THE NAME OF JESUS               128  52 239  30
SHE'L OFFER THEM HER DEAREST BREATH,            TERESA                              49  52 315  52
THY DEAREST PARENTS HAVE DESERV'D TO DY.        ALEXIAS THIRD ELEGIE                18  52 336 209
EACH SOULE IN SIGHES HAD SPENT ITS DEAREST BREATH, UPON GUNPOWDER TREASON           41  MS 386 460

DEARLY

TILL DEARLY THUS UNDONE,                        IN GLORIOUS EPIPHANIE              202  52 253  39
HOW DEARLY THOU HAST PAYD FOR ME                CHARITAS NIMIA                      64  52 280  48

DEATH

AS THEN DID SMELL OF WINTER, OR OF DEATH.       OUT OF VIRGIL                       28  46 155 529
THOUGH SHEE BE DUMBE E'RE SINCE HIS DEATH,      UPON THE DEATH OF A GENTLEMAN       17  46 166 472
TO BEE THE LIFE OF THEIR OWNE DEATH.            NEITHER DURST MAN ASKE              14  46  92  20
HOW LIFE AND DEATH IN THEE                      UPON OUR SAVIOURS TOMBE              1  46  93  25
THE LIFE THOU TOOK'ST FROM HIM UNTO HIS DEATH.  YEE BUILD SEPULCHRES                 2  46  95  21
COME DEATH, COME BANDS, NOR DO YOU SHRINK, MY EARS, I AM READY NOT ONELY BOUND      1  46  98  29
NOR OTHER DEATH THEN THIS. THE FEARE TO DYE.    I AM READY NOT ONELY BOUND           4  46  98  29
TO THEE THESE FIRST FRUITS OF MY GROWING DEATH  OUR LORD IN HIS CIRCUMCISION         1  46  98   9
MY TEARES BUT TENDER AND MY DEATH NEW-BORNE.    OUR LORD IN HIS CIRCUMCISION        12  46  98   9
THESE PURPLE BUDS OF BLOOMING DEATH MAY BEE,    OUR LORD IN HIS CIRCUMCISION        15  46  98   9
DEATH ONELY BY THIS DAYES JUST DOOME IS FORC'T TO DYE. EASTER DAY                   15  46 100  26
NOR IS DEATH FORC'T. FOR MAY HEE LY             EASTER DAY                          16  46 100  26
DEATH WILL ON THIS CONDITION BE CONTENT TO DY.  EASTER DAY                          18  46 100  26
BROODING HORROR. COME THOU DEATH,               PSALME 23                           39  46 102   5
WARME INTO THE ARMES OF DEATH.                  PSALME 23                           72  46 102   5
HIS EYES, THE SULLEN DENS OF DEATH AND NIGHT,   SOSPETTO D'HERODE                   49  46 109 216
THE NEVER-DYING LIFE, OF A LONG DEATH.          SOSPETTO D'HERODE                   60  46 109 216
SYMPTOMES SO DEADLY, UNTO DEATH AND HIM.        SOSPETTO D'HERODE                  138  46 109 216
TO DRAW A LONG-LIV'D DEATH, WHERE ALL MY CHEERE SOSPETTO D'HERODE                  214  46 109 216
SWINGING A HUGE SITH STANDS IMPARTIALL DEATH,   SOSPETTO D'HERODE                  319  46 109 216
OF SIN, AND DEATH, TWICE DIPT IN THE DIRE STAINES SOSPETTO D'HERODE                327  46 109 216
OF DEATH MEZENTIUS, OR GERYON DREW.             SOSPETTO D'HERODE                  362  46 109 216
SPEAKE LOWD UNTO THE FACE OF DEATH              IN MEMORY OF LADY MADRE TERESA       8  46 131  52
WHICH SPENT CAN BUY SO BRAVE A DEATH.           IN MEMORY OF LADY MADRE TERESA      18  46 131  52
WHAT DEATH WITH LOVE SHOULD HAVE TO DOE         IN MEMORY OF LADY MADRE TERESA      20  46 131  52
HOW MUCH LESSE STRONG IS DEATH THEN LOVE.       IN MEMORY OF LADY MADRE TERESA      28  46 131  52
WITH CHRISTS NAME INT IN CHANGE FOR DEATH.      IN MEMORY OF LADY MADRE TERESA      50  46 131  52
A DEATH MORE MISTICALL AND HIGH.                IN MEMORY OF LADY MADRE TERESA      76  46 131  52
HIS IS THE DART MUST MAKE THE DEATH             IN MEMORY OF LADY MADRE TERESA      79  46 131  52
OF A DEATH IN WHICH WHO DYES                    IN MEMORY OF LADY MADRE TERESA     100  46 131  52
LOVES HIS DEATH, AND DYES AGAINE,               IN MEMORY OF LADY MADRE TERESA     101  46 131  52
WHICH WHO IN DEATH WOULD LIVE TO SEE.           IN MEMORY OF LADY MADRE TERESA     182  46 131  52
OUR LIFE IN DEATH, OUR DAY IN NIGHT.            ON HOPE                             16  46 143  71
THE PUREST PEARLES, THAT WEPT HER EVENING DEATH, UPON DEATH OF HERRYS               19  46 167 466
DEATH, WHAT DOST. O HOLD THY BLOW.              UPON DEATH OF DESIRED HERRYS         1  46 168 467
DEATH THOU MUST NOT HERE BE CRUELL.             UPON DEATH OF DESIRED HERRYS         3  46 168 467
SPARE HIM DEATH, O SPARE HIM THEN,              UPON DEATH OF DESIRED HERRYS        59  46 168 467
WITH STERNE DEATH, IF E'RE HE FAINTED,          ANOTHER ON HERRYS                    2  46 170 469
BOUND IN THE PERIOD OF DEATH,                   ANOTHER ON HERRYS                   46  46 170 469
IS ENTOMB'D THE CRIME OF DEATH.                 HIS EPITAPH (HERRYS)                 6  46 172 471
```

| | | | | |
|---|---|---|---|---|
| DEATH LOST THE RECKONING OF HIS DAYES. | HIS EPITAPH (HERRYS) | 10 | 46 172 | 471 |
| TO THESE, WHOM DEATH AGAIN DID WED. | AN EPITAPH HUSBAND AND WIFE | 1 | 46 174 | 478 |
| POINTS OF DEATH BID LOVE BE GONE | LOVES HOROSCOPE | 22 | 46 185 | 483 |
| SHALL I HIDE POORE LOVE FROM DEATH. | LOVES HOROSCOPE | 44 | 46 185 | 483 |
| DEATH SHALL SEND MEE | OUT OF THE ITALIAN (1) | 44 | 46 188 | 545 |
| LET NATURE DIE, IF (PHOENIX-LIKE) FROM DEATH | ON FRONTISPIECE ISAACSONS | 3 | 46 191 | 491 |
| WHEN AGE AND DEATH CALL'D FOR THE SCORE, | AN EPITAPH UPON ASHTON | 25 | 46 192 | 464 |
| DEATH TORE NOT (THEREFORE) BUT SANS STRIFE | AN EPITAPH UPON ASHTON | 27 | 46 192 | 464 |
| A LIFE PERHAPS UNTO HIS DEATH. | AN EPITAPH UPON ASHTON | 34 | 46 192 | 464 |
| TWIXT LIFE & DEATH, TWIXT IN & OUT. | TO COUNTESSE OF DENBIGH | 6 | 52 236 | 146 |
| AND KILL THE DEATH OF THIS DELAY. | TO THE NAME OF JESUS | 142 | 52 239 | 30 |
| OF DEATH & FEIRCEST DANGERS, DURST WITH BRAVE | TO THE NAME OF JESUS | 201 | 52 239 | 30 |
| THE DEEP HYPOCRISY OF DEATH & NIGHT | IN GLORIOUS EPIPHANIE | 58 | 52 253 | 39 |
| THE NIGHT & WINTER STILL OF DEATH & SIN. | IN GLORIOUS EPIPHANIE | 77 | 52 253 | 39 |
| PROUD SONS OF DEATH. THAT DURST COMPELL | IN GLORIOUS EPIPHANIE | 109 | 52 253 | 39 |
| MERCHANTS OF DEATH & SIN, IS BOUGHT & SOLD. | OFFICE H. CROSS MATINES | 15 | 52 265 | 86 |
| LIFE OUT OF DEATH, DAY OUT OF NIGHT. | OFFICE H. CROSS MATINES | 23 | 52 265 | 86 |
| OF OPEN DEATH & HIDDEN LIFE. | OFFICE H. CROSS NINTH | 10 | 52 271 | 99 |
| LIFE SEEM'D TO DY, DEATH DY'D INDEED. | OFFICE H. CROSS NINTH | 12 | 52 271 | 99 |
| WHEN WONDERING DEATH BY DEATH WAS SLAIN. | OFFICE H. CROSS EVENSONG | 26 | 52 273 | 101 |
| WHEN WONDERING DEATH BY DEATH WAS SLAIN. | OFFICE H. CROSS EVENSONG | 26 | 52 273 | 101 |
| TO MAKE A KIND OF LIFE FOR MY LORD'S DEATH, | OFFICE H. CROSS RECOMMENDATION | 6 | 52 276 | 106 |
| SO FROM HIS LIVING, & LIFE-GIVING DEATH. | OFFICE H. CROSS RECOMMENDATION | 7 | 52 276 | 106 |
| HOW MUCH DEATH WEIGH'D MORE LIGHT THEN LOVE. | VEXILLA REGIS | 36 | 52 277 | 156 |
| HOW LIFE & DEATH IN THEE | TO OUR B. LORD | 1 | 52 279 | 25 |
| BARGAIN'D WITH DEATH & WELL-BESEEMING DUST | CHARITAS NIMIA | 56 | 52 280 | 48 |
| AS THEN IN DEATH, SO NOW IN LOVE. | CHARITAS NIMIA | 66 | 52 280 | 48 |
| AS SERVES TO KEEP ALIVE HER DEATH. | SANCTA MARIA DOLORUM | 40 | 52 283 | 162 |
| IN LINES OF DEATH, MY LIFE MAY COPPY IT | SANCTA MARIA DOLORUM | 54 | 52 283 | 162 |
| MY DEAR LORD'S VITALL DEATH. | SANCTA MARIA DOLORUM | 108 | 52 283 | 162 |
| POWR'D OUT IN PRAYRS FOR THEE. THY LORD'S IN DEATH. | SANCTA MARIA DOLORUM | 110 | 52 283 | 162 |
| O DEAR MEMORIALL OF THAT DEATH | ADORO TE | 37 | 52 291 | 172 |
| THAT WE MAY LIVE, REVIVE HIS DEATH. | LAUDA SION SALVATOREM | 26 | 52 294 | 178 |
| THE CHILD OF DEATH EATES HIMSELF DEAD. | LAUDA SION SALVATOREM | 52 | 52 294 | 178 |
| THAT THUS FROM LIFE CAN DEATH DISTILL. | LAUDA SION SALVATOREM | 54 | 52 294 | 178 |
| HORROR OF NATURE, HELL & DEATH. | DIES IRAE | 13 | 52 298 | 186 |
| THOSE LIMBS OF DEATH FROM THY LEFT SIDE. | DIES IRAE | 62 | 52 298 | 186 |
| OF LIFE & DEATH. TO PROVE THE WORD. | TERESA | 2 | 52 315 | 52 |
| SPEAK LOWD INTO THE FACE OF DEATH | TERESA | 8 | 52 315 | 52 |
| WHICH SPENT CAN BUY SO BRAVE A DEATH. | TERESA | 18 | 52 315 | 52 |
| WHAT DEATH WITH LOVE SHOULD HAVE TO DOE. | TERESA | 20 | 52 315 | 52 |
| HOW MUCH LESSE STRONG IS DEATH THEN LOVE. | TERESA | 28 | 52 315 | 52 |
| WITH CHRIST'S NAME IN'T, IN CHANGE FOR DEATH. | TERESA | 50 | 52 315 | 52 |
| A DEATH MORE MYSTICALL & HIGH. | TERESA | 76 | 52 315 | 52 |
| HIS IS THE DART MUST MAKE THE DEATH | TERESA | 79 | 52 315 | 52 |
| OF A DEATH, IN WHICH WHO DYES | TERESA | 100 | 52 315 | 52 |
| LOVES HIS DEATH, AND DYES AGAIN. | TERESA | 101 | 52 315 | 52 |
| WHICH WHO IN DEATH WOULD LIVE TO SEE. | TERESA | 181 | 52 315 | 52 |
| I DY EVEN IN DESIRE OF DEATH. | A SONG | 12 | 52 327 | 65 |
| OF LIVING DEATH & DYING LIFE. | A SONG | 14 | 52 327 | 65 |
| IF DROWN'D. SWEET IS THE DEATH INDUR'D FOR HIM, | ALEXIAS FIRST ELEGIE | 22 | 52 334 | 204 |
| TO THESE, WHOM DEATH AGAIN DID WED. | AN EPITAPH UPON MARRIED COUPLE | 1 | 52 339 | 478 |
| 'TWIXT LIFE AND DEATH, 'TWIXT IN AND OUT. | AGAINST IRRESOLUTION AND DELAY | 6 | 52 347 | 146 |
| SOE I MAY GAINE THY DEATH, MY LIFE I'LE GIVE. | MATH. 16. 25. WHOSOEVER SHALL | 1 | MS 381 | 16 |
| (MY LIFE'S THY DEATH, & IN THY DEATH I LIVE.) | MATH. 16. 25. WHOSOEVER SHALL | 2 | MS 381 | 16 |
| (MY LIFE'S THY DEATH, & IN THY DEATH I LIVE.) | MATH. 16. 25. WHOSOEVER SHALL | 2 | MS 381 | 16 |
| ADULTERATES THE VIRGIN AIRE. WITH DEATH | ON GUNPOWDER-TREASON | 18 | MS 384 | 458 |
| DEATH TO THE LIFE. MY INKE SHALL BE THE BLOOD | UPON GUNPOWDER TREASON | 3 | MS 386 | 460 |
| AS GLAD TO WAITE UPON THEIR KING IN DEATH. | UPON GUNPOWDER TREASON | 42 | MS 386 | 460 |
| GROW PLUMPE, LEANE DEATH. HIS HOLINESSE A FEAST | UPON GUNPOWDER TREASON | 1 | MS 387 | 461 |
| DARES HUNGRY DEATH SNATCH OF ONE CHERRY LIPP. | UPON GUNPOWDER TREASON | 39 | MS 387 | 461 |
| O DEATH, 'TIS THOU. YOU FALSE TIME KEEPE. | UPON DEATH OF A FREIND | 9 | MS 393 | 477 |
| HIS BALMY TREASURES TO THE BEDD OF DEATH. | AN ELEGY MR STANNINOW | 30 | MS 394 | 473 |
| NOE. 'TWAS OLD DOTING DEATH, WHO, STEALING BY, | AN ELEGY MR STANNINOW | 45 | MS 394 | 473 |
| TO FREIND THE LIVING WORLD EVEN DEATH DID SEE | OUT OF GROTIUS | 82 | MS 398 | 198 |

DEATH--TO

| | | | | |
|---|---|---|---|---|
| OF LIFE AND DEATH--TO PROVE THE WORD, | IN MEMORY OF LADY MADRE TERESA | 2 | 46 131 | 52 |

DEATH-FULL

| | | | | |
|---|---|---|---|---|
| IN DEATH-FULL DESPERATE ILLS WHERE ART AND ALL | OUT OF GROTIUS | 69 | MS 398 | 198 |

DEATH-LIKE

| | | | | |
|---|---|---|---|---|
| IN DEATH-LIKE SLUMBERS. WHILE THY DANGERS CRAVE | SOSPETTO D'HERODE | 430 | 46 109 | 216 |

DEATH-SEAL'D

| | | | | |
|---|---|---|---|---|
| THESE DEATH-SEAL'D LIPPS ARE THEY DARE GIVE THE LYE, | UPON STANINOUGH'S DEATH | 23 | 46 175 | 475 |
| THESE DEATH-SEAL'D LIPPES ARE THEY DARE GIVE THE LY | DEATH'S LECTURE | 25 | 52 340 | 475 |

DEATH'S

| | | | | |
|---|---|---|---|---|
| DEATH'S PURPLE TRIUMPH, ON THE BLUSHING GROUND | THE BEGINNING OF HELIODORUS | 15 | 46 158 | 517 |
| A DURTY PILLOW IN DEATH'S BED. | UPON THE DEATH OF A GENTLEMAN | 12 | 46 166 | 472 |
| DEATH'S BUSIE SEARCH I'LE EASILY BEGUILE. | SICKE IMPLORE SHADOW | 2 | 46 87 | 26 |
| FROM DEATH'S SAD SHADES, TO THE LIFE-BREATHING AYRE, | SOSPETTO D'HERODE | 81 | 46 109 | 216 |
| THE RUSH OF DEATH'S UNRULY WAVE, | HIS EPITAPH (HERRYS) | 47 | 46 172 | 471 |
| DEATH'S PREY, BEFORE THE PRIZE OF LOVE. | TO COUNTESSE OF DENBIGH | 66 | 52 236 | 146 |
| AND ON DEATH'S SIDE | OFFICE H. CROSS THIRD | 12 | 52 268 | 93 |
| 'TWIST DEATH'S & LOVE'S FARR DIFFERENT FRUIT. | OFFICE H. CROSS SIXT | 14 | 52 270 | 97 |
| IN SHADE OF DEATH'S SAD TREE | SANCTA MARIA DOLORUM | 1 | 52 283 | 162 |

## DEATH'S

| | | | | |
|---|---|---|---|---|
| DEATH'S PREY, BEFORE THE PRIZE OF LOVE. | AGAINST IRRESOLUTION AND DELAY | 88 | 52 347 | 146 |
| IS HER LIFES WING, OR HER DEATH'S WINDING-SHEET. | AT TH' IVORY TRIBUNALL | 6 | MS 397 | 492 |

## DEATHLES

| | | | | |
|---|---|---|---|---|
| THE DEATHLES HEIR OF ALL THY FATHER'S DAY. | IN GLORIOUS EPIPHANIE | 64 | 52 253 | 39 |

## DEATHLESSE

| | | | | |
|---|---|---|---|---|
| THAT DRINKE THE DEAW OF LIFE, WHOSE DEATHLESSE SPRING, | SOSPETTO D'HERODE | 20 | 46 109 | 216 |
| AND EVERLASTING SERIES OF A DEATHLESSE SONG. | TO THE NAME OF JESUS | 85 | 52 239 | 30 |

## DEATHS

| | | | | |
|---|---|---|---|---|
| HOT MARS TO TH' HARVEST OF DEATHS FIELD, AND WOO | MUSICKS DUELL | 55 | 46 149 | 535 |
| AND LIFE SELFE IT WEARE DEATHS FRAILE LIVERY. | SOSPETTO D'HERODE | 168 | 46 109 | 216 |
| DELICIOUS DEATHS, SOFT EXHALATIONS | ON A PRAYER BOOKE | 71 | 46 126 | 139 |
| A THOUSAND COLD DEATHS IN ONE CUP. | IN MEMORY OF LADY MADRE TERESA | 38 | 46 131 | 52 |
| WHEN THESE THY DEATHS SO NUMEROUS, | IN MEMORY OF LADY MADRE TERESA | 111 | 46 131 | 52 |
| EVEN THY DEATHS SHALL LIVE, AND NEW | IN MEMORY OF LADY MADRE TERESA | 152 | 46 131 | 52 |
| WINE OF YOUTHS LIFE, AND THE SWEET DEATHS OF LOVE, | AN APOLOGIE FOR HYMNE (TERESA) | 41 | 46 136 | 59 |
| AND TO MANY DEATHS RENEW MEE. | OUT OF THE ITALIAN (1) | 54 | 46 188 | 545 |
| WILL LOOK NO WOUNDS BE LOST, NO DEATHS SHALL DY. | OFFICE H. CROSS EVENSONG | 6 | 52 273 | 101 |
| OF DEATHS, & WORSE, | SANCTA MARIA DOLORUM | 22 | 52 283 | 162 |
| QUICK DEATHS THAT GROW | SANCTA MARIA DOLORUM | 25 | 52 283 | 162 |
| A THOUSAND COLD DEATHS IN ONE CUP. | TERESA | 38 | 52 315 | 52 |
| WHEN THESE THY DEATHS, SO NUMEROUS, | TERESA | 110 | 52 315 | 52 |
| EV'N THY DEATHS SHALL LIVE. & NEW | TERESA | 151 | 52 315 | 52 |
| WINE OF YOUTH, LIFE, & THE SWEET DEATHS OF LOVE. | AN APOLOGIE FOR (TERESA) HYMNE | 41 | 52 322 | 59 |
| LET MYSTICK DEATHS WAIT ON'T. & WISE SOULES BE | FLAMING HEART | 83 | 52 324 | 61 |
| BY ALL THY LIVES & DEATHS OF LOVE. | FLAMING HEART | 96 | 52 324 | 61 |
| DELICIOUS DEATHS. SOFT EXALATIONS | PRAYER TO GENTLE-WOMAN | 77 | 52 328 | 139 |
| A RESPIRATION OF REVIVING DEATHS. | DESCRIPTION RELIGIOUS HOUSE | 24 | 52 338 | 213 |

## DEBASE

| | | | | |
|---|---|---|---|---|
| OF BLISSE, DEBASE THEE. BUT WITH A JUST PRIDE | UPON KINGS CORONATION | 8 | MS 369 | 454 |

## DEBT

| | | | | |
|---|---|---|---|---|
| CAESAR CHALLENGES A DEBT, | GIVE TO CAESAR AND TO GOD | 2 | 46 96 | 20 |
| THE DEBT IS PAID IN RUBY-TEARES, | ON WOUNDS OF CRUCIFIED LORD | 19 | 46 99 | 24 |
| DEARE HOPE. EARTHS DOWRY, AND HEAVENS DEBT, | ON HOPE | 11 | 46 143 | 71 |
| THY LIFE IS ONE LONG DEBT | VEXILLA REGIS | 4 | 52 277 | 156 |
| DEAR HOPE. EARTH'S DOWRY, & HEAVN'S DEBT. | (ON) HOPE | 1 | 52 345 | 71 |

## DECEASED

| | | | | |
|---|---|---|---|---|
| A MOURNFULL DIRGE TO THEIR DECEASED KING. | UPON GUNPOWDER TREASON | 44 | MS 386 | 460 |

## DECEIVE

| | | | | |
|---|---|---|---|---|
| HIM WHO NEVER WILL DECEIVE YE. | TO SAME CONCERNING CHOISE | 40 | 52 331 | 66 |
| DOE NOT DECEIVE MEE, EYES. DOE I NOT SEE | UPON KINGS CORONATION | 11 | MS 389 | 454 |

## DECEIVED

| | | | | |
|---|---|---|---|---|
| BUT WEE ARE DECEIVED ALL, | THE WEEPER | 13 | 46 79 | 120 |
| BUT WE'ARE DECEIVED ALL. | WEEPER | 13 | 52 307 | 120 |

## DECEIVD

| | | | | |
|---|---|---|---|---|
| DECEIVD THE CROSSE. | OFFICE H. CROSS THIRD | 11 | 52 268 | 93 |

## DECEIVES

| | | | | |
|---|---|---|---|---|
| DECEIVES MENS FEARES WITH FLATTERING WILES. | OUT OF GREEKE CUPID'S CRYER | 50 | 46 159 | 519 |

## DECEMBER

| | | | | |
|---|---|---|---|---|
| AGE, WOULDST SEE DECEMBER SMILE, | IN PRAISE OF LESSIUS | 40 | 46 156 | 510 |
| AGE, WOULDST SEE DECEMBER SMILE, | TEMPERANCE | 38 | 52 342 | 510 |

## DECENT

| | | | | |
|---|---|---|---|---|
| THESE ROYALL SAGES SUE FOR DECENT PLACE. | TO THE QUEEN'S MAJESTY | 2 | 52 261 | 47 |
| THE SERIOUS SHOWRES ALONG HIS DECENT | OFFICE H. CROSS THIRD | 8 | 52 268 | 93 |
| FLOW, TARDY FOUNTS, & INTO DECENT SHOWRES | SANCTA MARIA DOLORUM | 87 | 52 283 | 162 |

## DECENTLY

| | | | | |
|---|---|---|---|---|
| DECENTLY BORN. | IN GLORIOUS EPIPHANIE | 65 | 52 253 | 39 |
| IN YOUR OWN WELLS DECENTLY WASHT, | WEEPER | 88 | 52 307 | 120 |

## DECIDE

| | | | | |
|---|---|---|---|---|
| DECIDE & SETTLE THE GREAT CAUSE | IN GLORIOUS EPIPHANIE | 146 | 52 253 | 39 |

## DECISIVE

| | | | | |
|---|---|---|---|---|
| CHOOSE OUT THAT SURE DECISIVE DART | TO COUNTESSE OF DENBIGH | 33 | 52 236 | 146 |

DECK

  THE PRIMROSE'S PALE CHEEK TO DECK,                    WEEPER                              44    52  307  120

DECKE

  THE PRIMROSES PALE CHEEKE TO DECKE,                   THE WEEPER                          38    46   79  120

DECLARE

  DECLARE WHO SENDS, AND WHAT IS HIS COMMAND.           SOSPETTO D'HERODE                  512    46  109  216
  JEWELLS, BUT TO DECLARE                               WISHES SUPPOSED MISTRESSE           47    46  195  479

DECREE

  LEAVE, LEAVE, FOR SHAME, OR ELSE (GOOD JUDGE) DECREE, TO PONTIUS WASHING HANDS            15    46   94   23

DEDICATE

  THAT AS I DEDICATE MY DEVOUTEST BREATH                OFFICE H. CROSS RECOMMENDATION       5    52  276  106

DEEDES

  A NAME IN NOBLE DEEDES RIVALL TO THEE.                SOSPETTO D'HERODE                   28    46  109  216
  AN AEQUALL PACE THUS FARRE, THY WORD MY DEEDES        OUT OF GROTIUS                       5    MS  398  198

DEEP

  DEEP IN THE GROANING WATERS WALLOWED                  THE BEGINNING OF HELIODORUS         13    46  158  517
  FOR SO DEARE, SO DEEP A TRUST,                        UPON THE DEATH OF A GENTLEMAN       13    46  166  472
  THERE ARE ENOW WHOSE DRAUGHTS AS DEEP AS HELL         AN APOLOGIE FOR HYMNE (TERESA)      29    46  136   59
  THE DEEP HYPOCRISY OF DEATH & NIGHT                   IN GLORIOUS EPIPHANIE               58    52  253   39
  IN THE DEEP HELL,                                     CHARITAS NIMIA                      13    52  280   48
  SO DEEP A SHARE                                       SANCTA MARIA DOLORUM                82    52  283  162
  WHEN A DEEP GROAN FROM BENEATH                        DIES IRAE                           14    52  298  186
  THERE ARE ENOW, WHOSE DRAUGHTS (AS DEEP AS HELL)      AN APOLOGIE FOR (TERESA) HYMNE      29    52  322   59
  AND DEEP DISGUISES,                                   TO SAME CONCERNING CHOISE           16    52  331   66

DEEP-DIGG'D

  BUT O THY SIDE, THEY DEEP-DIGG'D SIDE.                UPON BLEEDING CRUCIFIX              17    52  288  110

DEEPE

  BUT O THY SIDE, THY DEEPE DIG'D SIDE                  ON BLEEDING WOUNDS OF LORD          13    46  101  110
  HIS BREATH HELLS LIGHTNING IS, AND EACH DEEPE GRONE   SOSPETTO D'HERODE                   55    46  109  216
  OFT IN HIS DEEPE THOUGHT HE REVOLVES THE DARKE        SOSPETTO D'HERODE                   91    46  109  216
  A DESPERATE, OH MEE, DREW FROM HIS DEEPE BREST.       SOSPETTO D'HERODE                  200    46  109  216
  HAD SOWNE OF OLD THESE DOUBTS IN HIS DEEPE BREST.     SOSPETTO D'HERODE                  498    46  109  216
  MORE DEEPE SUSPICIONS, AND MORE DEADLY STINGS,        SOSPETTO D'HERODE                  501    46  109  216
  TEARES WOULD NOW HAVE FLOW'D SO DEEPE,                ANOTHER ON HERRYS                   21    46  170  469
  IN THE DEEPE WRINCKLES OF HIS ANGRY BROW,             TO THE MORNING                      31    46  183  497
  IS PLOUGH'D AS DEEPE, AS IS THE SEA WITH WIND,        HORATIJ ILLE & NEFASTO              20    MS  382  530
  THAT SWIM'ST AS DEEPE IN JOY, AS SEAS, NOW SMILE      UPON KINGS CORONATION                6    MS  389  454
  AND STRETCH'ST THY DISMALL VOICE TOO DEEPE.           UPON DEATH OF A FREIND              10    MS  393  477

DEEPER

  DYE SEV'N TIMES DEEPER THAN THEY WERE BEFORE          UPON GUNPOWDER TREASON               4    MS  367  461

DEEPEST

  OF DEEPEST SILENCE ANSWERED MY COMMAND.               OUT OF GROTIUS                      84    MS  398  198

DEEP'ST

  WHICH OF THEM DEEP'ST SHALL DIGGE HER WATRY GRAVE.    SOSPETTO D'HERODE                  428    46  109  216

DEFECTS

  DEFECTS I DRAW MINE OWNE DULL CHARACTER.              UPON TWO GREENE APRICOCKES          32    48  220  494

DEFENCE

  GIVES DIRECTION, GIVES DEFENCE.                       PSALME 23                           48    46  102    5
  A BORROWED BEING, MAKE THY BOLD DEFENCE.              SOSPETTO D'HERODE                  252    46  109  216
  REPLY'D THE PROUD KING, O MY CROWNES DEFENCE.         SOSPETTO D'HERODE                  281    46  109  216
  AS FROM A SNOWY FORTRESSE OF DEFENCE                  ON A PRAYER BOOKE                   12    46  126  139
  AS FROM A SNOWY FORTRESSE OF DEFENCE,                 PRAYER TO GENTLE-WOMAN              18    52  328  139

DEFEND

  DEFEND US FROM OUR FOES & THINE.                      OFFICE H. CROSS MATINES              2    52  265   86

DEFERR

  AND IF THOU YET (FAINT SOUL.) DEFERR                  SANCTA MARIA DOLORUM                89    52  283  162

DEFIANCE

  OF HOT DEFIANCE 'GAINST WHAT E'RE IS GOOD             OUT OF GROTIUS                      76    MS  398  198

DEFIES

| | | | |
|---|---|---|---|
| HEE HIS OWNE FANCY-FRAMED FOES DEFIES. | SOSPETTO D'HERODE | 479 | 46 109 216 |
| THUS LOW, STANDS UP (ME THINKES,) THUS & DEFIES | DEATH'S LECTURE | 30 | 52 340 475 |

DEFYES

| | | | |
|---|---|---|---|
| THUS LOW STANDS UP (ME THINKES) THUS, AND DEFYES | UPON STANINOUGH'S DEATH | 28 | 46 175 475 |

DEFINE

| | | | |
|---|---|---|---|
| THAT DARK DAY'S CLEAR DOOM SHALL DEFINE | IN GLORIOUS EPIPHANIE | 143 | 52 253 39 |

DEFINED

| | | | |
|---|---|---|---|
| BY WHOM IT IS DEFINED THUS | TO THE NAME OF JESUS | 177 | 52 239 30 |

DEFINITION

| | | | |
|---|---|---|---|
| OOR NOTHING HATH A DEFINITION. | ON HOPE | 14 | 46 143 71 |
| WHOSE DEFINITION IS A DOUBT | TO COUNTESSE OF DENBIGH | 5 | 52 236 146 |
| OUR NOTHING HAS A DEFINITION. | (ON) HOPE | 4 | 52 345 71 |

DEFINITIONS

| | | | |
|---|---|---|---|
| WHOSE DEFINITIONS IS, A DOUBT | AGAINST IRRESOLUTION AND DELAY | 5 | 52 347 146 |

DEFLOWER

| | | | |
|---|---|---|---|
| TO RIFLE AND DEFLOWER, | ON A PRAYER BOOKE | 109 | 46 126 139 |

DEFLOUR

| | | | |
|---|---|---|---|
| TO RIFLE & DEFLOUR | PRAYER TO GENTLE-WOMAN | 115 | 52 328 139 |

DEFLOWERS

| | | | |
|---|---|---|---|
| NOR SIRIAN FLAME, NOR BOREAN FROST DEFLOWERS. | SOSPETTO D'HERODE | 21 | 46 109 216 |

DEGENEROUS

| | | | |
|---|---|---|---|
| BASELY DEGENEROUS. AGAINST MEE FLOCKE | OUT OF GROTIUS | 41 | MS 398 198 |

DEIGNE

| | | | |
|---|---|---|---|
| DEIGNE THOU TO WEARE THIS HUMBLE WREATH THAT BOWES, | SOSPETTO D'HERODE | 15 | 46 109 216 |
| TO MAJESTY, AND FULNESSE, DEIGNE TO DWELL. | UPON YORKE HIS BIRTH | 24 | 46 176 500 |

DEIGN'D

| | | | |
|---|---|---|---|
| AND NOW THAT GRAVE ASPECT HATH DEIGN'D TO SHRINKE | UPON BISHOP ANDREWES PICTURE | 13 | 46 163 490 |

DEIGNES

| | | | |
|---|---|---|---|
| STEPT FROM HER THRONE OF STARRES DEIGNES TO BE SEENE. | UPON YORKE HIS BIRTH | 72 | 46 176 500 |

DEITIES

| | | | |
|---|---|---|---|
| TO QUENCH THE RAGE OF HELLISH DEITIES. | UPON GUNPOWDER TREASON | 36 | MS 387 461 |
| AND ALL THEIR FELLOW DEITIES WILL BOW | EX EUPHORMIONE | 8 | MS 392 525 |

DEITYES

| | | | |
|---|---|---|---|
| FOR CHEAP AEGYPTIAN DEITYES. | IN GLORIOUS EPIPHANIE | 88 | 52 253 39 |

DEITY

| | | | |
|---|---|---|---|
| THOU TO THEIR TEETH HAST PROV'D THY DEITY. | ON MIRACLE OF LOAVES | 2 | 46 88 16 |
| A COMMING DEITY. HEE SAW THE NEST | SOSPETTO D'HERODE | 126 | 46 109 216 |
| STANDS OFF AND POINTS AT. IS'T SOME DEITY | UPON YORKE HIS BIRTH | 71 | 46 176 500 |
| IS IT SOME DEITY, OR IS'T OUR QUEENE. | UPON YORKE HIS BIRTH | 73 | 46 176 500 |
| DENY TO MIGHTY LOVE A DEITY. | UPON YORKE HIS BIRTH | 85 | 46 176 500 |
| SHINE FORTH,YE FLAMING SPARKES OF DEITY, | UPON KINGS CORONATION | 37 | MS 389 454 |

DELAY

| | | | |
|---|---|---|---|
| BEE YOUR DELAY. | TO INFANT MARTYRS | 4 | 46 88 10 |
| TO MEET THEIR TROUBLED LORD WITHOUT DELAY. | SOSPETTO D'HERODE | 508 | 46 109 216 |
| CAST OFF DELAY. | ON THE ASSUMPTION | 15 | 46 139 114 |
| TO SAVE YOUR LIFE, KILL YOUR DELAY | TO COUNTESSE OF DENBIGH | 58 | 52 236 146 |
| AND KILL THE DEATH OF THIS DELAY. | TO THE NAME OF JESUS | 142 | 52 239 30 |
| COME AWAY, MY DOVE. CAST OFF DELAY, | IN GLORIOUS ASSUMPTION B. LADY | 14 | 52 304 114 |
| 'TIS TO KEEP TIME WITH THY DELAY. | IN GLORIOUS ASSUMPTION B. LADY | 20 | 52 304 114 |
| NO QURRELLS, MURMURS, NO DELAY. | TEMPERANCE | 49 | 52 342 510 |
| CHIDE YOUR DELAY. YEA THOSE DULL THINGS, | AGAINST IRRESOLUTION AND DELAY | 47 | 52 347 146 |
| TO SAVE YOUR LIFE, KILL YOUR DELAY. | AGAINST IRRESOLUTION AND DELAY | 82 | 52 347 146 |

DELEGATED

| | | | |
|---|---|---|---|
| THE DELEGATED EYE OF DAY | IN GLORIOUS EPIPHANIE | 236 | 52 253 39 |

DELICATELY

  DELICATELY TO DISPLACE                                    IN GLORIOUS EPIPHANIE              5   52 253  39

DELICIOUS

  OF HER DELICIOUS SOULE, THAT THERE DOES LYE             MUSICKS DUELL                      67   46 149 535
  EVERY SMOOTH TURNE, EVERY DELICIOUS STROAKE             MUSICKS DUELL                     131   46 149 535
  WITH CHATTING BIRDS DELICIOUS MURMURINGS.               OUT OF VIRGIL                      10   46 155 529
  DELICIOUS DEATHS, SOFT EXHALATIONS                      ON A PRAYER BOOKE                  71   46 126 139
  A DELICIOUS DEW OF SPICES.                              ON A PRAYER BOOKE                 104   46 126 139
  THOSE DELICIOUS WOUNDS THAT WEEP                        IN MEMORY OF LADY MADRE TERESA    108   46 131  52
  HIS OWNE DELICIOUS PHOENIX FROM THE BLEST               UPON DEATH OF HERRYS               13   46 167 466
  ON THOSE DELICIOUS BANKES DISTILL'D AGAINE              ON A FOULE MORNING                 16   46 181 495
  ALL THESE DELICIOUS HOPES ARE BURIED,                   TO THE MORNING                     30   46 183 497
  THOSE DELICIOUS WOUNDS, THAT WEEP                       TERESA                            108   52 315  52
  I DY IN LOVE'S DELICIOUS FIRE.                          A SONG                              4   52 327  65
  DELICIOUS DEATHS. SOFT EXALATIONS                       PRAYER TO GENTLE-WOMAN             77   52 328 139
  A DELICIOUS DEW OF SPICES.                              PRAYER TO GENTLE-WOMAN            110   52 328 139
  CONVEY'D HIS SWEET DELICIOUS TRESURY                    UPON GUNPOWDER TREASON             55   MS 387 461
    THE JOYFULL SPHAERES WITH A DELICIOUS SOUND         UPON KINGS CORONATION              21   MS 390 453

DELIGHT

  BUT CHIEFLY THERE DO'S SHEE DELIGHT TO BE,              SOSPETTO D'HERODE                 293   46 109 216
  O WHAT DELIGHT WHEN SHEE SHALL STAND,                   IN MEMORY OF LADY MADRE TERESA    130   46 131  52
  BEHOLDERS LOST IN SWEET DELIGHT                         ON THE ASSUMPTION                  33   46 139 114
  FIXT IN DELIGHT, AS IF ALREADY THERE                    UPON DEATH OF HERRYS               27   46 167 466
  AND THOSE TERRORS SHALL DELIGHT MEE.                    OUT OF THE ITALIAN (1)             48   46 188 545
  THE EXTASIE OF A DELIGHT                                OUT OF THE ITALIAN (3)              5   46 190 549
  AND LOSE OUR SELVES IN WILD DELIGHT.                    OUT OF CATULLUS                    18   46 194 523
  WHAT ERE DELIGHT                                        WISHES SUPPOSED MISTRESSE          94   46 195 479
  O WHAT DELIGHT, WHEN REVEAL'D LIFE SHALL STAND          TERESA                            129   52 315  52
  AND THE DRAKE YEELD NOE DELIGHT,                        PETRONIJ ALES PHASIACIS PETITA      6   MS 382 526
  BUT YET THEIR EYES SURFETT WITH SWEET DELIGHT.          UPON GUNPOWDER TREASON             50   MS 387 461

DELIGHTED

  SINGING THEIR FEARES ARE FEARFULLY DELIGHTED.           MUSICKS DUELL                     114   46 149 535

DELIGHTS

  OF JOYES, AND RARIFYED DELIGHTS.                        ON A PRAYER BOOKE                  74   46 126 139
  THE NAME OF YOUR DELIGHTS & OUR DESIRES,                TO THE NAME OF JESUS              101   52 239  30
  OF JOYES & RAREFY'D DELIGHTS.                           PRAYER TO GENTLE-WOMAN             80   52 328 139

DELIGHTFULL

  CURE THEE OF THY DELIGHTFULL TYMPANIE.                  UPON BIRTH PRINCESSE E             12   MS 391 456

DELIQUIUM

  A LONG DELIQUIUM TO THE LIGHT OF THEE.                  IN GLORIOUS EPIPHANIE             116   52 253  39

DELIVER

  THEIR LITTLE CHANNELS CAN DELIVER                       ON BLEEDING WOUNDS OF LORD         27   46 101 110
  AND TO THE CIRCUMCISING KNIFE DELIVER                   SOSPETTO D'HERODE                 187   46 109 216
  O DELIVER                                               OUT OF THE ITALIAN (1)             13   46 188 545
  THEIR LITTLE CHANNELLS CAN DELIVER                      UPON BLEEDING CRUCIFIX             23   52 288 110

DELIVERANCE

  A DELUGE OF DELIVERANCE,                                ON BLEEDING WOUNDS OF LORD         39   46 101 110
  A DELUGE OF DELIVERANCE.                                UPON BLEEDING CRUCIFIX             35   52 288 110

DELIVERY

  HAD DIED JUST IN HER DELIVERY.                          UPON GUNPOWDER TREASON             52   MS 386 460

DELUGE

  IN THEIR OWNE BLOODS DEARE DELUGE, SOME NEW DEAD,       THE BEGINNING OF HELIODORUS        17   46 158 517
  THIS THY BLOODS DELUGE (A DIRE CHANCE                   ON BLEEDING WOUNDS OF LORD         37   46 101 110
  A DELUGE OF DELIVERANCE,                                ON BLEEDING WOUNDS OF LORD         39   46 101 110
  A DELUGE LEAST WE SHOULD BE DROWN'D.                    ON BLEEDING WOUNDS OF LORD         40   46 101 110
  THIS THY BLOOD'S DELUGE, A DIRE CHANCE                  UPON BLEEDING CRUCIFIX             33   52 288 110
  A DELUGE OF DELIVERANCE.                                UPON BLEEDING CRUCIFIX             35   52 288 110
  A DELUGE LEAST WE SHOULD BE DROWN'D.                    UPON BLEEDING CRUCIFIX             36   52 288 110
  AND RAISE A DELUGE, WHERE THE FLAMING SUNNE             UPON GUNPOWDER TREASON             38   MS 386 460

DEN

  NOW HAD THE NIGHT'S CAMPANION FROM HER DEN.             SOSPETTO D'HERODE                 385   46 109 216

DENNE

  SITTING SOE LONG AT EASE IN HER DARKE DENNE,            UPON GUNPOWDER TREASON             24   MS 386 460

DENS

  HIS EYES, THE SULLEN DENS OF DEATH AND NIGHT.           SOSPETTO D'HERODE                  49   46 109 216

## DENIES

| | | | | |
|---|---|---|---|---|
| AND SO ALLOWES WHAT IT DENIES. | TO THE QUEEN | 8 | 48 215 | 501 |

## DENYES

| | | | | |
|---|---|---|---|---|
| YET IF AT LEAST SHEE NOT DENYES, | UPON THE DEATH OF A GENTLEMAN | 19 | 46 166 | 472 |
| WHOSE USE DENYES US TO THE DEAD. | ADORO TE | 40 | 52 291 | 172 |

## DENY

| | | | | |
|---|---|---|---|---|
| AND NO ASSUMPTION SHALL DENY US. | ON THE ASSUMPTION | 46 | 46 139 | 114 |
| DENY TO MIGHTY LOVE A DEITY. | UPON YORKE HIS BIRTH | 85 | 46 176 | 500 |
| BUT MODESTY DARES STILL DENY IT. | WISHES SUPPOSED MISTRESSE | 120 | 46 195 | 479 |
| AND NO ASSUMPTION SHALL DENY US. | IN GLORIOUS ASSUMPTION B. LADY | 51 | 52 304 | 114 |
| IN HIM, OR, IF THEY THIS DENY, | TERESA | 53 | 52 315 | 52 |

## DENY'D

| | | | | |
|---|---|---|---|---|
| THE SHORE THAT SHEWED THEM WHAT THE SEA DENY'D, | THE BEGINNING OF HELIODORUS | 9 | 46 158 | 517 |
| THIS GARMENT TOO I WOULD THEY HAD DENY'D. | ON CRUCIFIED LORD BLOODY | 2 | 46 100 | 24 |
| AND DID HIS BEST TO HAVE DENY'D. | TO COUNTESSE OF DENBIGH | 16 | 52 236 | 146 |
| THIS GARMENT TOO I WOULD THEY HAD DENY'D. | UPON BODY OF OUR LORD | 2 | 52 290 | 24 |

## DENY'DE

| | | | | |
|---|---|---|---|---|
| AND DID HIS BEST TO HAVE DENY'DE. | AGAINST IRRESOLUTION AND DELAY | 10 | 52 347 | 146 |

## DENY'T

| | | | | |
|---|---|---|---|---|
| (NOR DOES THE SUNNE DENY'T) OUR CYNTHIA, | UPON YORKE HIS BIRTH | 79 | 46 176 | 500 |

## DENYE

| | | | | |
|---|---|---|---|---|
| IN HIM, OR IF THEY THIS DENYE, | IN MEMORY OF LADY MADRE TERESA | 53 | 46 131 | 52 |

## DEPARTING

| | | | | |
|---|---|---|---|---|
| AS IF THE OFT DEPARTING SUNNE HAD DY'D. | AN ELEGIE ON DR PORTER | 26 | MS 395 | 476 |

## DEPLORE

| | | | | |
|---|---|---|---|---|
| THE' ASTONISHT NYMPHS THEIR FLOOD'S STRANGE FATE DEPLORE, | TO COUNTESSE OF DENBIGH | 25 | 52 236 | 146 |
| TH'ASTONISH'D NYMPHS THEIR FLOUD'S STRANGE FATE DEPLORE, | AGAINST IRRESOLUTION AND DELAY | 25 | 52 347 | 146 |

## DEPOSED

| | | | | |
|---|---|---|---|---|
| DAYES KING DEPOSED BY NIGHTS QUEENE. | A HYMNE OF THE NATIVITY | 2 | 46 106 | 76 |

## DESCANT

| | | | | |
|---|---|---|---|---|
| TO DESCANT THEE. | IN GLORIOUS EPIPHANIE | 195 | 52 253 | 39 |

## DESCRY

| | | | | |
|---|---|---|---|---|
| THIS ROAVING WANTON SHALL DESCRY. | OUT OF GREEKE CUPID'S CRYER | 6 | 46 159 | 519 |
| MOST TALL HYPERBOLE'S CANNOT DESCRY IT. | ON GUNPOWDER-TREASON | 47 | MS 384 | 458 |

## DESCRYER

| | | | | |
|---|---|---|---|---|
| THE GLAD DESCRYER SHALL NOT MISSE, | OUT OF GREEKE CUPID'S CRYER | 11 | 46 159 | 519 |

## DESERVE

| | | | | |
|---|---|---|---|---|
| NOR DOES THE DUST DESERVE YOUR BIRTH. | THE WEEPER | 130 | 46 79 | 120 |
| AND HE THAT HERE FEARES DANGER, DOES DESERVE HIS FEARE. | WHY ARE YEE AFRAID | 16 | 46 88 | 15 |
| NOR DOES THE DUST DESERVE YOUR BIRTH. | WEEPER | 172 | 52 307 | 120 |

## DESERV'D

| | | | | |
|---|---|---|---|---|
| THY DEAREST PARENTS HAVE DESERV'D TO DY. | ALEXIAS THIRD ELEGIE | 18 | 52 336 | 209 |

## WELL-DESERVING

| | | | | |
|---|---|---|---|---|
| OF THY KIND MASTER'S WELL-DESERVING BRAINES. | HORATIJ ILLE & NEFASTO | 16 | MS 382 | 530 |

## DESIGN

| | | | | |
|---|---|---|---|---|
| RESUME & RECTIFY THY RUDE DESIGN. | FLAMING HEART | 39 | 52 324 | 61 |

## HEAVN-DESIGNED

| | | | | |
|---|---|---|---|---|
| DEAR, HEAVN-DESIGNED SOUL. | TO SAME CONCERNING CHOISE | 1 | 52 331 | 66 |

## DESIRE

| | | | | |
|---|---|---|---|---|
| TO SWELL WITH FORWARD PRIDE, AND SEED DESIRE | OUT OF VIRGIL | 3 | 46 155 | 529 |
| HE MURMURES, AND REBUKES THEIR BOLD DESIRE. | SOSPETTO D'HERODE | 485 | 46 109 | 216 |
| AND MELTS IT DOWNE IN SWEET DESIRE. | ON A PRAYER BOOKE | 68 | 46 126 | 139 |
| HER WEAKE BREAST HEAVES WITH STRONG DESIRE, | IN MEMORY OF LADY MADRE TERESA | 40 | 46 131 | 52 |

|   |   |   |
|---|---|---|
| FAITH'S SISTER. NURSE OF FAIRE DESIRE. | ON HOPE | 81  46 143  71 |
| HER WEAKE BREST HEAVES WITH STRONG DESIRE | TERESA | 40  52 315  52 |
| BY ALL THY BRIM-FILL'D BOWLES OF FEIRCE DESIRE | FLAMING HEART | 99  52 324  61 |
| THY BLESSED EYES BREED SUCH DESIRE. | A SONG | 3  52 327  65 |
| I DY EVEN IN DESIRE OF DEATH. | A SONG | 12  52 327  65 |
| AND MELTS IT DOWN IN SWEET DESIRE | PRAYER TO GENTLE-WOMAN | 74  52 328 139 |
| IF HEATES OF HOLYER LOVE & HIGH DESIRE | ALEXIAS THIRD ELEGIE | 21  52 336 209 |
| FAITH'S SISTER. NURSE OF FAIR DESIRE. | (ON) HOPE | 41  52 345  71 |

DESIRES

|   |   |   |
|---|---|---|
| OUR WEAK DESIRES HAVE DONE THEIR BEST. | ON THE ASSUMPTION | 63  46 139 114 |
| THE NAME OF YOUR DELIGHTS & OUR DESIRES, | TO THE NAME OF JESUS | 101  52 239  30 |
| OUR WEAK DESIRES HAVE DONE THEIR BEST. | IN GLORIOUS ASSUMPTION B. LADY | 68  52 304 114 |
| O THOU UNDANTED DAUGHTER OF DESIRES. | FLAMING HEART | 93  52 324  61 |

DESOLATION

|   |   |   |
|---|---|---|
| OR TO A NEW GOD DESOLATION. | ON A TREATISE OF CHARITY | 38  46 137  69 |

DESPAIR

|   |   |   |
|---|---|---|
| TEMPER TWIXT CHILL DESPAIR, & TORRID JOY. | (ON) HOPE | 43  52 345  71 |

DESPAIR'D

|   |   |   |
|---|---|---|
| (THAT OLD DRY STOCKE) A DESPAIR'D BRANCH IS SPRUNG | SOSPETTO D'HERODE | 434  46 109 216 |

DESPAIRE

|   |   |   |
|---|---|---|
| TEMPER'D 'TWIXT COLD DESPAIRE, AND TORRID JOY. | ON HOPE | 83  46 143  71 |

DESPERATE

|   |   |   |
|---|---|---|
| A DESPERATE, OH MEE, DREW FROM HIS DEEPE BREST. | SOSPETTO D'HERODE | 200  46 109 216 |
| BECAUSE SOME DESPERATE FOOL'S UNDONE. | CHARITAS NIMIA | 36  52 280  48 |
| IN DEATH-FULL DESPERATE ILLS WHERE ART AND ALL | OUT OF GROTIUS | 69  MS 398 198 |

DESPERATELY

|   |   |   |
|---|---|---|
| WHY ART THOU ARM'D SO DESPERATELY TO DAY. | UPON VENUS PUTTING ARMES | 2  46 161 523 |
| MORE DESPERATELY DARK, BECAUSE MORE BRIGHT. | IN GLORIOUS EPIPHANIE | 59  52 253  39 |

DESPIGHT

|   |   |   |
|---|---|---|
| (O MY DESPIGHT.) WITH HIS DIVINEST GLORIES. | SOSPETTO D'HERODE | 228  46 109 216 |
| NOT ONELY IN DESPIGHT OF ROME. | AN EPITAPH UPON ASHTON | 18  46 192 464 |
| UNMATED MALICE. OH UNPEER'D DESPIGHT. | UPON GUNPOWDER TREASON | 5  MS 386 460 |

DESTINY

|   |   |   |
|---|---|---|
| IN SHADY LEAVES OF DESTINY. | WISHES SUPPOSED MISTRESSE | 6  46 195 479 |
| THE SUBTILE POINT OF HIS COY DESTINY, | HORATIJ ILLE & NEFASTO | 18  MS 382 530 |
| OH, THAT'S HIS FEARE. THERE FLOTES HIS DESTINY. | HORATIJ ILLE & NEFASTO | 22  MS 382 530 |

DESTINYES

|   |   |   |
|---|---|---|
| OF THE FLINTY DESTINYES. | ANOTHER ON HERRYS | 36  46 170 469 |

DESTRUCTION

|   |   |   |
|---|---|---|
| IN THIS SAD HOUSE OF SLOW DESTRUCTION. | SOSPETTO D'HERODE | 61  46 109 216 |
| GRIM DESTRUCTION HERE AMAZ'D | ANOTHER ON HERRYS | 31  46 170 469 |
| COME GRIMME DESTRUCTION, & IN PURPLE GORE | UPON GUNPOWDER TREASON | 3  MS 387 461 |
| BUT DARES DESTRUCTION EATE THESE CANDID BREASTS. | UPON GUNPOWDER TREASON | 37  MS 387 461 |

DETAIN

|   |   |   |
|---|---|---|
| DETAIN IN NEEDFULL TEARES TO WEEP THE WANT OF THEE. | IN GLORIOUS ASSUMPTION B. LADY | 22  52 304 114 |
| DETAIN HIM, BUT HE LEAVES BEHIND | AGAINST IRRESOLUTION AND DELAY | 75  52 347 146 |

DETECT

|   |   |   |
|---|---|---|
| THERE DOES HE FIX HIS EYES, AND THERE DETECT | SOSPETTO D'HERODE | 87  46 109 216 |

DETERMINE

|   |   |   |
|---|---|---|
| AND DETERMINE THEM TO KISSES. | WISHES SUPPOSED MISTRESSE | 123  46 195 479 |

DEVILLS

|   |   |   |
|---|---|---|
| TWO DEVILLS AT ONE BLOW THOU HAST LAID FLAT. | UPON DUMBE DEVILL CAST OUT | 1  46  93  14 |

DEVILL'S

|   |   |   |
|---|---|---|
| AND KEEP THE DEVILL'S HOLYDAY. | PRAYER TO GENTLE-WOMAN | 53  52 328 139 |

DIVELL

|   |   |   |
|---|---|---|
| A SPEAKING DIVELL THIS, A DUMBE ONE THAT. | UPON DUMBE DEVILL CAST OUT | 2  46  93  14 |

DIVELLS

AND KEEP THE DIVELLS HOLY DAY.                        ON A PRAYER BOOKE              47  46 126 139

DEVISE

WHAT FORCE CANNOT EFFECT, FRAUD SHALL DEVISE.         SOSPETTO D'HERODE             248  46 109 216
TO CHANGE HER FACES STILE SHE DOTH DEVISE,            SOSPETTO D'HERODE             415  46 109 216
FOR WHOM THE OFFICIOUS HEAVNS DEVISE                  IN GLORIOUS EPIPHANIE           3  52 253  39

DEVISING

FOR THEE, FAIR, PURPLE DOORES, OF LOVE'S DEVISING.    TO THE NAME OF JESUS          217  52 239  30

DEVOTION

HIS BIRTH, BY HIS DEVOTION, WHO BEGAN                 SOSPETTO D'HERODE             103  46 109 216
OF DEAD DEVOTION. NOR FAINT MARBLES WEEP              ON A TREATISE OF CHARITY       33  46 137  69
WHILE YOUR EACH DAY'S DEVOTION DULY BRINGS            TO THE QUEEN'S MAJESTY         27  52 261  47
MY MINDS DEVOTION IN MY BODYES NEED.                  OUT OF GROTIUS                 60  MS 398 198

DEVOTIONS

THESE DEVOTIONS, FAIREST, KNOW                        ON MR. G. HERBERTS BOOKE       16  46 130  68

DEVOURE

AND REASON (FOR WHAT'S FAITH TO HIM.) DEVOURE.        SOSPETTO D'HERODE             162  46 109 216

DEVOUR'D

WHOLE DAYES & SUNS DEVOUR'D WITH ENDLESSE DINING.     DESCRIPTION RELIGIOUS HOUSE     2  52 338 213

DEVOUTEST

THAT AS I DEDICATE MY DEVOUTEST BREATH                OFFICE H. CROSS RECOMMENDATION  5  52 276 106

DEW

THE DEW NO MORE WILL WEEPE,                           THE WEEPER                     37  46  79 120
NATURE HATH LEARN'T T' EXTRACT A DEW,                 THE WEEPER                     71  46  79 120
A DELICIOUS DEW OF SPICES.                            ON A PRAYER BOOKE             104  46 126 139
A DELICIOUS DEW OF SPICES.                            PRAYER TO GENTLE-WOMAN        110  52 328 139

DEAW

THE DEAW NO MORE WILL SLEEPE,                         THE WEEPER                     39  46  79 120
THAT DRINKE THE DEAW OF LIFE, WHOSE DEATHLESSE SPRING, SOSPETTO D'HERODE             20  46 109 216
SO TO THE TREASURE OF THY PEARLY DEAW,                TO THE MORNING                 39  46 183 497
BUT CALL'D IT DEAW.                                   IN GLORIOUS EPIPHANIE         128  52 253  39
THE DEAW NO MORE WILL WEEP                            WEEPER                         43  52 307 120
THE DEAW NO MORE WILL SLEEP                           WEEPER                         45  52 307 120
NATURE HATH LEARN'T TO EXTRACT A DEAW                 WEEPER                         53  52 307 120

DEWY

(SLIPT FROM AURORA'S DEWY BREST)                      THE TEARE                      20  46  84  50

DIADEM

FOR THIS UNVALUED DIADEM,                             IN MEMORY OF LADY MADRE TERESA 48  46 131  52
FOR THIS UNVALUED DIADEM.                             TERESA                         48  52 315  52

DIADEMMS

AND WRONGS REPENT TO DIADEMMS.                        TERESA                        150  52 315  52

DIADEMS

AND WRONGS REPENT TO DIADEMS.                         IN MEMORY OF LADY MADRE TERESA 151  46 131  52
ANOTHER DAY OF DIADEMS.                               AN HIMNE FOR CIRCUMCISION      24  46 141  37
ANOTHER DAY OF DIADEMS.                               NEW YEAR'S DAY                 24  52 251  37
FOR FROM THIS DAY'S RICH SEED OF DIADEMS              TO THE QUEEN'S MAJESTY         11  52 261  47
OR PERTCH'T UPON FEAR'D DIADEMS.                      WEEPER                        184  52 307 120

DIAMOND

A WATRY DIAMOND. FROM WHENCE                          THE TEARE                       4  46  84  50
THE WATER OF A DIAMOND.                               THE TEARE                       6  46  84  50
THOUGH EVERY DIAMOND IN JOVES CROWNE                  LOVES HOROSCOPE                37  46 185 483
THE NEIGHBOUR DIAMOND, AND OUT FACES                  WISHES SUPPOSED MISTRESSE      44  46 195 479

DIAMONDS

RICH DIAMONDS, SETT IN A PURE SILVER FOYLE.           UPON BIRTH PRINCESSE E         44  MS 391 456

MOTHER-DIAMONDS

SHEE 'GAINST THOSE MOTHER-DIAMONDS TRYES              A HYMNE OF THE NATIVITY        69  46 106  76

```
DIAPASON

  A FULL-MOUTH DIAPASON SWALLOWES ALL.           MUSICKS DUELL                        156   46 149 535

DICTATE

  THEY THAT BY LOVE'S MILD DICTATE NOW           TO THE NAME OF JESUS                 236   52 239  30
  HERE A HOLY DICTATE HATH                       LAUDA SION SALVATOREM                 32   52 294 178

DIE

  LET NATURE DIE, IF (PHOENIX-LIKE) FROM DEATH   ON FRONTISPIECE ISAACSONS              3   46 191 491
  NOT DARING QUITE TO LIVE NOR DIE.              AGAINST IRRESOLUTION AND DELAY        20   52 347 146
  BY PARTHIANS BOW THE SOLDJER LOOKES TO DIE.    HORATIJ ILLE & NEFASTO                25   MS 382 530
  BY THEE, BY THEE YET LETT ME DIE. THIS GIVE,   EX EUPHORMIONE                        12   MS 392 525
  WHETHER THE MUSE THEY CLOTH SHALL LIVE OR DIE. AT TH' IVORY TRIBUNALL                 4   MS 397 492

DY

  DEATH WILL ON THIS CONDITION BE CONTENT TO DY. EASTER DAY                            18   46 100  26
  TO LIVE, BUT THAT HE STILL MAY DY.             IN MEMORY OF LADY MADRE TERESA       104   46 131  52
  MAY DRINKE IT SELFE UP, AND FORGET TO DY.      AN APOLOGIE FOR HYMNE (TERESA)        46   46 136  59
  IF POORE LOVE SHALL LIVE OR DY.                LOVES HOROSCOPE                        8   46 185 483
  NOR DARING QUITE TO LIVE NOR DY.               TO COUNTESSE OF DENBIGH               12   52 236 146
  SEE HIS HORN'D FACE, & DY FOR SHAME.           IN GLORIOUS EPIPHANIE                 99   52 253  39
  LIVE BARABBAS, & LET GOD DY.                   OFFICE H. CROSS THIRD                  4   52 268  93
  LIFE SEEM'D TO DY, DEATH DY'D INDEED.          OFFICE H. CROSS NINTH                 12   52 271  99
  WILL LOOK NO WOUNDS BE LOST, NO DEATHS SHALL DY. OFFICE H. CROSS EVENSONG             6   52 273 101
  GROWES WANTON, & WILL DY.                      CHARITAS NIMIA                        44   52 280  48
  WHAT DID THE LAMB, THAT HE SHOULD DY.          CHARITAS NIMIA                        52   52 280  48
  SEE HER LIFE DY.                               SANCTA MARIA DOLORUM                  38   52 283 162
  DOWN DOWN, PROUD SENSE, DISCOURSES DY.         ADORO TE                               5   52 291 172
  WHEN LIFE, HIMSELF, AT POINT TO DY             LAUDA SION SALVATOREM                 11   52 294 178
  BUT LEST THAT DY TOO, WE ARE BID               LAUDA SION SALVATOREM                 25   52 294 178
  SHE CAN LOVE, & SHE CAN DY.                    TERESA                                24   52 315  52
  SUCH THIRSTS TO DY, AS DARES DRINK UP,         TERESA                                37   52 315  52
  FOR HIM SHE'L TEACH THEM HOW TO DY.            TERESA                                54   52 315  52
  THOU ART LOVE'S VICTIM, & MUST DY              TERESA                                75   52 315  52
  TO LIVE, BUT THAT HE THUS MAY NEVER LEAVE TO DY. TERESA                             104   52 315  52
  SHALL ALL AT LAST DY INTO ONE,                 TERESA                               111   52 315  52
  MUST LEARN IN LIFE TO DY LIKE THEE.            TERESA                               182   52 315  52
  FLIGHTS SCORN THE LAZY DUST, & THINGS THAT DY. AN APOLOGIE FOR (TERESA) HYMNE        28   52 322  59
  MAY DRINK IT SELF UP, AND FORGET TO DY.        AN APOLOGIE FOR (TERESA) HYMNE        46   52 322  59
  THAT LIVE & DY AMIDST HER DARTS,               FLAMING HEART                         50   52 324  61
  LIVE HERE, GREAT HEART, & LOVE AND DY & KILL.  FLAMING HEART                         79   52 324  61
  UNTO ALL LIFE OF MINE MAY DY.                  FLAMING HEART                        108   52 324  61
  I DY IN LOVE'S DELICIOUS FIRE.                 A SONG                                 4   52 327  65
  STILL MAY BEHOLD, THOUGH STILL I DY.           A SONG                                 8   52 327  65
  THOUGH STILL I DY, I LIVE AGAIN.               A SONG                                 9   52 327  65
  I DY EVEN IN DESIRE OF DEATH.                  A SONG                                12   52 327  65
  THY DEAREST PARENTS HAVE DESERV'D TO DY.       ALEXIAS THIRD ELEGIE                  18   52 336 209
  WHOSE DAY SHALL NEVER DY IN NIGHT.             AN EPITAPH UPON MARRIED COUPLE        20   52 339 478
  MAKE HAST, & DY.                               LUKE 2. QUAERIT JESUM                 18   MS 379  11
  IN FLAMES, & OF A BURNING FEVER DY.            ON GUNPOWDER-TREASON                  26   MS 384 458
  AND IN FELL HATRED BURNING, ANGRY DY.          UPON GUNPOWDER TREASON                16   MS 387 461
  FEARE NOT TO DY WITH GREIFE, ALL BUBLING EYES  AN ELEGIE ON DR PORTER                43   MS 395 476

DYE

  KEEPE BUT THE SCORE OF THEM THAT MADE HIM DYE. YEE BUILD SEPULCHRES                   4   46  95  21
  NOR OTHER DEATH THEN THIS, THE FEARE TO DYE.   I AM READY NOT ONELY BOUND             4   46  98  29
  DEATH ONELY BY THIS DAYES JUST DOOME IS FORC'T TO DYE. EASTER DAY                    15   46 100  26
  SHEE CAN LOVE AND SHEE CAN DYE.                IN MEMORY OF LADY MADRE TERESA        24   46 131  52
  SUCH THIRST TO DYE, AS DARE DRINKE UP,         IN MEMORY OF LADY MADRE TERESA        37   46 131  52
  FOR HIM SHEEL TEACH THEM HOW TO DYE.           IN MEMORY OF LADY MADRE TERESA        54   46 131  52
  THOU ART LOVES VICTIM, AND MUST DYE            IN MEMORY OF LADY MADRE TERESA        75   46 131  52
  SHALL ALL AT LAST DYE INTO ONE,                IN MEMORY OF LADY MADRE TERESA       112   46 131  52
  MUST LEARNE IN LIFE TO DYE LIKE THEE.          IN MEMORY OF LADY MADRE TERESA       183   46 131  52
  FLIGHTS SCORNE THE LAZIE DUST, AND THINGS THAT DYE. AN APOLOGIE FOR HYMNE (TERESA)   28   46 136  59
  SO WARME IN THY SOFT BREST IT CANNOT DYE.      TO THE MORNING                        34   46 183 497
  IF POORE LOVE SHALL LIVE OR DYE.               LOVES HOROSCOPE                       20   46 185 483
  BEAUTY FROWNES, AND LOVE MUST DYE.             LOVES HOROSCOPE                       32   46 185 483
  LOVE SHALL DYE ALTHOUGH HE LIVE.               LOVES HOROSCOPE                       46   46 185 483
  OR IF LOVE SHALL DYE, O WHERE,                 LOVES HOROSCOPE                       47   46 185 483
  LOVE SHALL LIVE, ALTHOUGH HE DYE.              LOVES HOROSCOPE                       52   46 185 483
  (THAT WE DYE NOT)                              OUT OF THE ITALIAN (1)                20   46 188 545
  DYE SEV'N TIMES DEEPER THAN THEY WERE BEFORE   UPON GUNPOWDER TREASON                 4   MS 387 461
  LIVE SHEE, OR DYE TO FAME, EACH LEAFE YOU MEET AT TH' IVORY TRIBUNALL                 5   MS 397 492

DIED

  HAD DIED JUST IN HER DELIVERY.                 UPON GUNPOWDER TREASON                52   MS 386 460

DI'D

  TWICE DI'D IN THINE OWNE BLUSHES, AND DID'ST RUN TO THE MORNING                       9   46 183 497

DY'D

  CHRIST WHEN HE DY'D                            OFFICE H. CROSS THIRD                 10   52 268  93
  LIFE SEEM'D TO DY, DEATH DY'D INDEED.          OFFICE H. CROSS NINTH                 12   52 271  99
  IT WAS EXHAL'D, A WHILE IT HUNG, & DY'D.       ON GUNPOWDER-TREASON                  50   MS 384 458
  DY'D IN VERMILLION BLUSHES, AS BEFORE.         UPON GUNPOWDER TREASON                16   MS 386 460
```

| | | | |
|---|---|---|---|
| AS IF THE OFT DEPARTING SUNNE HAD DY'D. | AN ELEGIE ON DR PORTER | 26 | MS 395 476 |

## DYES

| | | | |
|---|---|---|---|
| SHEE FAILES, AND FAILING GRIEVES, AND GRIEVING DYES. | MUSICKS DUELL | 165 | 46 149 535 |
| SHEE DYES, AND LEAVES HER LIFE THE VICTORS PRISE. | MUSICKS DUELL | 166 | 46 149 535 |
| ALL TORNE, WITH MUCH ADOE YET ERE HE DYES, | HIGH MOUNTED ON AN ANT | 4 | 46 161 523 |
| FOR THE SUN THAT DYES, | THE WEEPER | 57 | 46  79 120 |
| OF A DEATH IN WHICH WHO DYES | IN MEMORY OF LADY MADRE TERESA | 100 | 46 131  52 |
| LOVES HIS DEATH, AND DYES AGAINE, | IN MEMORY OF LADY MADRE TERESA | 101 | 46 131  52 |
| AND LIVES AND DYES, AND KNOWES NOT WHY | IN MEMORY OF LADY MADRE TERESA | 103 | 46 131  52 |
| IT FALLS, AND DYES.  OH NO, IT MELTS AWAY | ON HOPE | 57 | 46 143  71 |
| BRIGHTEST SOL THAT DYES TO DAY | OUT OF CATULLUS | 4 | 46 194 523 |
| THEN BOWES HIS ALL-OBEDIENT HEAD, & DYES | OFFICE H. CROSS NINTH | 5 | 52 271  99 |
| WEEP FOR EVERY WORM THAT DYES. | CHARITAS NIMIA | 38 | 52 280  48 |
| AND THEIR NIGHT DYES INTO OUR DAY. | LAUDA SION SALVATOREM | 24 | 52 294 178 |
| FOR THE SUN THAT DYES. | WEEPER | 33 | 52 307 120 |
| OF A DEATH, IN WHICH WHO DYES | TERESA | 100 | 52 315  52 |
| LOVES HIS DEATH, AND DYES AGAIN. | TERESA | 101 | 52 315  52 |
| AND LIVES, & DYES.  AND KNOWES NOT WHY | TERESA | 103 | 52 315  52 |
| IT FALLS, AND DYES. O NO, IT MELTS AWAY | (ON) HOPE | 27 | 52 345  71 |

## DIET

| | | | |
|---|---|---|---|
| OFT HAVE I SPOILD MY KISSES DAINTIEST DIET. | LUKE 2.  QUAERIT JESUM | 37 | MS 379  11 |

## DIFFERENCE

| | | | |
|---|---|---|---|
| SWEET IS THE DIFFERENCE. | ON MARKES OF SAVIOURS WOUNDS | 5 | 46  86  28 |
| THE DIFFERENCE ONELY THIS APPEARES. | ON WOUNDS OF CRUCIFIED LORD | 17 | 46  99  24 |

## DIFFERENT

| | | | |
|---|---|---|---|
| 'TWIST DEATH'S & LOVE'S FARR DIFFERENT FRUIT. | OFFICE H. CROSS SIXT | 14 | 52 270  97 |
| DIFFERENT AS FARR | OFFICE H. CROSS SIXT | 15 | 52 270  97 |
| IN DIFFERENT SPECIES, NAMES NOT THINGS. | LAUDA SION SALVATOREM | 39 | 52 294 178 |

## DIFFUSE

| | | | |
|---|---|---|---|
| DIRE FLAMES DIFFUSE THEMSELVES THROUGH EVERY VEINE, | SOSPETTO D'HERODE | 471 | 46 109 216 |

## DIGEST

| | | | |
|---|---|---|---|
| IT CAN DIGEST. THEN WATCH THE WILDFIRE WELL. | ON GUNPOWDER-TREASON | 65 | MS 384 458 |

## DIGESTED

| | | | |
|---|---|---|---|
| SUCK HIDDEN SWEETS, WHICH WELL DIGESTED PROVES | SOSPETTO D'HERODE | 23 | 46 109 216 |

## DIGGE

| | | | |
|---|---|---|---|
| WHICH OF THEM DEEP'ST SHALL DIGGE HER WATRY GRAVE. | SOSPETTO D'HERODE | 428 | 46 109 216 |

## DIGG'D

| | | | |
|---|---|---|---|
| THAT DIGG'D THESE WELLS, & DREST THIS VINE. | WEEPER | 104 | 52 307 120 |

## DEEP-DIGG'D

| | | | |
|---|---|---|---|
| BUT O THY SIDE, THEY DEEP-DIGG'D SIDE. | UPON BLEEDING CRUCIFIX | 17 | 52 288 110 |

## DIG'D

| | | | |
|---|---|---|---|
| BUT O THY SIDE, THY DEEPE DIG'D SIDE | ON BLEEDING WOUNDS OF LORD | 13 | 46 101 110 |

## DIGHT

| | | | |
|---|---|---|---|
| KIND WINTER'S GUIFT, & IN A GREENE ONE DIGHT. | AN ELEGY MR STANNINOW | 6 | MS 394 473 |
| GOE LEARNE THAT FATALL QUIRE, SOE SPRUCELY DIGHT | AN ELEGIE ON DR PORTER | 27 | MS 395 476 |

## DILEMMA

| | | | |
|---|---|---|---|
| FROM THEE THEIR THINNE DILEMMA WITH BLUNT HORNE | ON HOPE | 19 | 46 143  71 |
| FROM THEE THEIR LEAN DILEMMA, WITH BLUNT HORN. | (ON) HOPE | 9 | 52 345  71 |

## DILIGENT

| | | | |
|---|---|---|---|
| LIKE DILIGENT BEES, AND SWARM ABOUT IT. | TO THE NAME OF JESUS | 153 | 52 239  30 |
| NO CRUELL GUARD OF DILIGENT CARES, THAT KEEP | DESCRIPTION RELIGIOUS HOUSE | 28 | 52 338 213 |

## DIM

| | | | |
|---|---|---|---|
| OR, 'CAUSE HEAVENS FACE IS DIM, | WHY ARE YEE AFRAID | 2 | 46  88  15 |

## DIMME

| | | | |
|---|---|---|---|
| LEFT THE DIMME FACE OF THIS DULL HEMISPHAEARE, | UPON BISHOP ANDREWES PICTURE | 3 | 46 163 490 |
| WHICH LIKE TWO BOSOM'D SAILES EMBRACE THE DIMME | SOSPETTO D'HERODE | 142 | 46 109 216 |
| HER GLORIES I SHOULD DIMME WITH THINGS SOE GROSSE, | UPON BIRTH PRINCESSE E | 53 | MS 391 456 |

## DIMINUTIVES

| | | | |
|---|---|---|---|
| BY SHORT DIMINUTIVES, THAT BEING REAR'D | MUSICKS DUELL | 41 | 46 149 535 |

DINING

  WHOLE DAYES & SUNS DEVOUR'D WITH ENDLESSE DINING.    DESCRIPTION RELIGIOUS HOUSE    2  52 338 213

DINNE

  AND MURMUR IN A BUZZING DINNE, THEN GINGLE    MUSICKS DUELL    129  46 149 535

DIOMED'S

  HERE DIOMED'S HORSES, PHEREUS DOGS APPEARE,    SOSPETTO D'HERODE    353  46 109 216

DIPT

  OF SIN, AND DEATH, TWICE DIPT IN THE DIRE STAINES    SOSPETTO D'HERODE    327  46 109 216
  A DART THRICE DIPT IN THAT RICH FLAME,    IN MEMORY OF LADY MADRE TERESA    81  46 131 52

DIPP'T

  THE LAMB HATH DIPP'T HIS WHITE FOOT HERE.    WEEPER    108  52 307 120

DIP'T

  A DART THRICE DIP'T IN THAT RICH FLAME    TERESA    81  52 315 52

DIPS

  SHEE SINGS THY TEARES ASLEEPE, AND DIPS    A HYMNE OF THE NATIVITY    65  46 106 76

DIRE

  THIS THY BLOODS DELUGE (A DIRE CHANCE    ON BLEEDING WOUNDS OF LORD    37  46 101 110
  HIS FLAMING EYES DIRE EXHALATION,    SOSPETTO D'HERODE    57  46 109 216
  OF SIN, AND DEATH, TWICE DIPT IN THE DIRE STAINES    SOSPETTO D'HERODE    327  46 109 216
  THE FACE OF THINGS, FROM HER DIRE EYES HAD RUN,    SOSPETTO D'HERODE    363  46 109 216
  SUCH AS AT THEBES DIRE FEAST SHEE SHEW'D HER HEAD,    SOSPETTO D'HERODE    397  46 109 216
  DIRE FLAMES DIFFUSE THEMSELVES THROUGH EVERY VEINE,    SOSPETTO D'HERODE    471  46 109 216
  SO RARE IS HOARY VERTUE) THE DIRE RAGE    UPON DEATH OF HERRYS    32  46 167 466
  THE DIRE FACE OF INFERIOR DARKNES, KIS'T    IN GLORIOUS EPIPHANIE    52  52 253 39
  THIS THY BLOOD'S DELUGE, A DIRE CHANCE    UPON BLEEDING CRUCIFIX    33  52 288 110
  NOR IS'T LOVE'S FAULT, BUT SIN'S DIRE SKILL    LAUDA SION SALVATOREM    53  52 294 178
  THEN GLUTT THY DIRE LAMPE WITH THE WARMEST BLOOD,    ON GUNPOWDER-TREASON    63  MS 384 458
  INTO DIRE SABLE WEEDS, & SATE, & MOURN'D.    UPON GUNPOWDER TREASON    48  MS 386 460
  WHAT MORE THAN WINTER HATH THAT DIRE ART FOUND.    AN ELEGY MR STANNINOW    21  MS 394 473

DIRECTION

  GIVES DIRECTION, GIVES DEFENCE.    PSALME 23    48  46 102 5

DIRGE

  A MOURNFULL DIRGE TO THEIR DECEASED KING.    UPON GUNPOWDER TREASON    44  MS 386 460

DIR'GES

  TO SING THEIR SADDEST DIR'GES, SUCH AS MAY    AN ELEGIE ON DR PORTER    29  MS 395 476

DISAPPEARES

  BUT SPYES LOVE'S DAWN, & DISAPPEARES.    LAUDA SION SALVATOREM    22  52 294 178

DISASTER

  NOR DID THE FACE OF THIS DISASTER SHOW    THE BEGINNING OF HELIODORUS    23  46 158 517

DISBAND

  DISBAND DULL FEARES. GIVE FAITH THE DAY.    TO COUNTESSE OF DENBIGH    57  52 236 146
  DISBAND DULL FEARES, GIVE FAITH THE DAY.    AGAINST IRRESOLUTION AND DELAY    81  52 347 146

DISCERNE

  DISCERNE THE DAWNE OF TRUTH'S ETERNALL RAY,    ON FRONTISPIECE ISAACSONS    13  46 191 491

DISCERNING

  BUT LEAST YOUR EYE DISCERNING SLIDE    OUT OF GREEKE CUPID'S CRYER    17  46 159 519

DISCHARGE

  THY SELF. AND SO DISCHARGE THAT DAY.    DIES IRAE    46  52 298 186
  LETT THY SWOLNE BREAST DISCHARGE THY STRUGLING GROANES  AN ELEGIE ON DR PORTER    31  MS 395 476

DISCHARGES

  AND WHILE SHEE THUS DISCHARGES A SHRILL PEALE    MUSICKS DUELL    97  46 149 535

DISCIPLINE

  BUT REVERENT DISCIPLINE, & RELIGIOUS FEAR,    DESCRIPTION RELIGIOUS HOUSE    30  52 338 213

## DISCLOSES

| | | | | | |
|---|---|---|---|---|---|
| AND MANY A CRUELL TEARE DISCLOSES. | ON WOUNDS OF CRUCIFIED LORD | 8 | 46 | 99 | 24 |
| SHALL RISE IN A SWEET HARVEST. WHICH DISCLOSES | ON A FOULE MORNING | 17 | 46 | 181 | 495 |
| IT DISCLOSES) | OUT OF THE ITALIAN (1) | 5 | 46 | 188 | 545 |

## DISCORD

| | | | | | |
|---|---|---|---|---|---|
| WEE MUST THAT DISCORD SURELY CALL, | UPON DEATH OF A FREIND | 3 | MS | 393 | 477 |

## DISCOURSE

| | | | | | |
|---|---|---|---|---|---|
| OF SWEET DISCOURSE, WHOSE POWERS | WISHES SUPPOSED MISTRESSE | 89 | 46 | 195 | 479 |
| DISCOURSE ALTERNATE WOUNDS TO ONE ANOTHER. | SANCTA MARIA DOLORUM | 24 | 52 | 283 | 162 |

## DISCOURSES

| | | | | | |
|---|---|---|---|---|---|
| DOWN DOWN, PROUD SENSE. DISCOURSES DY. | ADORO TE | 5 | 52 | 291 | 172 |

## DISCOVER

| | | | | | |
|---|---|---|---|---|---|
| HER LITTLE FUGITIVE DISCOVER. | OUT OF GREEKE CUPID'S CRYER | 2 | 46 | 159 | 519 |
| HAPPY SOULE SHEE SHALL DISCOVER, | ON A PRAYER BOOKE | 115 | 46 | 126 | 139 |
| RISE THEN (FAIRE BLEW-EY'D MAID) RISE AND DISCOVER | ON A FOULE MORNING | 27 | 46 | 181 | 495 |
| DEERE, DISCOVER | OUT OF THE ITALIAN (1) | 2 | 46 | 188 | 545 |
| HAPPY PROOF. SHE SHAL DISCOVER | PRAYER TO GENTLE-WOMAN | 121 | 52 | 328 | 139 |
| OF SOULES, DISDAIN THAT I DISCOVER | TO SAME CONCERNING CHOISE | 42 | 52 | 331 | 66 |

## DISDAIN

| | | | | | |
|---|---|---|---|---|---|
| OF SOULES, DISDAIN THAT I DISCOVER | TO SAME CONCERNING CHOISE | 42 | 52 | 331 | 66 |

## DISDAINES

| | | | | | |
|---|---|---|---|---|---|
| IN SURLY GROANES DISDAINES THE TREBLES GRACE. | MUSICKS DUELL | 50 | 46 | 149 | 535 |
| DISDAINES TO THINKE THAT HEAV'N THUNDERS ALONE. | SOSPETTO D'HERODE | 56 | 46 | 109 | 216 |
| HIS SCEPTER AND HIMSELFE BOTH HE DISDAINES. | SOSPETTO D'HERODE | 72 | 46 | 109 | 216 |

## DISDAINING

| | | | | | |
|---|---|---|---|---|---|
| WHOSE NATIVE FIRES DISDAINING | PRAYER TO GENTLE-WOMAN | 3 | 52 | 328 | 139 |

## DISDAINEFULL

| | | | | | |
|---|---|---|---|---|---|
| DISDAINEFULL WRETCH. HOW HATH ONE BOLD SINNE COST | SOSPETTO D'HERODE | 73 | 46 | 109 | 216 |

## DISDAINFULL

| | | | | | |
|---|---|---|---|---|---|
| (DISDAINFULL DUST AND ASHES) BEND THY BROW. | ON A TREATISE OF CHARITY | 42 | 46 | 137 | 69 |

## DISEASE

| | | | | | |
|---|---|---|---|---|---|
| BAITE THY DISEASE, AND WHILE THEY TUGG | IN PRAISE OF LESSIUS | 2 | 46 | 156 | 510 |
| ONELY A COSTLYER DISEASE. | IN PRAISE OF LESSIUS | 10 | 46 | 156 | 510 |
| BAIT THY DISEASE. AND WHILST THEY TUGGE, | TEMPERANCE | 2 | 52 | 342 | 510 |
| ONLY A COSTLYER DISEASE. | TEMPERANCE | 10 | 52 | 342 | 510 |

## DISFIGURE

| | | | | | |
|---|---|---|---|---|---|
| HEE SAW A VERNALL SMILE, SWEETLY DISFIGURE | SOSPETTO D'HERODE | 109 | 46 | 109 | 216 |

## DISGRACE

| | | | | | |
|---|---|---|---|---|---|
| THERFORE WITH HIS DISGRACE | IN GLORIOUS EPIPHANIE | 82 | 52 | 253 | 39 |

## DISGUISES

| | | | | | |
|---|---|---|---|---|---|
| AND DEEP DISGUISES. | TO SAME CONCERNING CHOISE | 16 | 52 | 331 | 66 |

## DISINHERITT

| | | | | | |
|---|---|---|---|---|---|
| TO DISINHERITT THE SUN'S RISE. | IN GLORIOUS EPIPHANIE | 4 | 52 | 253 | 39 |

## DISLODG'D

| | | | | | |
|---|---|---|---|---|---|
| DEARE RELIQUES OF A DISLODG'D SOULE, WHOSE LACKE | UPON STANINOUGH'S DEATH | 1 | 46 | 175 | 475 |
| DEAR RELIQUES OF A DISLODG'D SOUL, WHOSE LACK | DEATH'S LECTURE | 1 | 52 | 340 | 475 |

## DISMALL

| | | | | | |
|---|---|---|---|---|---|
| STARTLE THE DULL AYRE WITH A DISMALL RED. | SOSPETTO D'HERODE | 50 | 46 | 109 | 216 |
| AIRE, WITH A DISMALL SHADE, BUT ALL IN VAINE. | SOSPETTO D'HERODE | 143 | 46 | 109 | 216 |
| E'RE PROVE THE DISMALL MORNING OF THY NIGHT. | UPON YORKE HIS BIRTH | 93 | 46 | 176 | 500 |
| BLACK, AS THE DAY WAS DISMALL, IN WHOSE SIGHT | HORATIJ ILLE & NEFASTO | 5 | MS | 382 | 530 |
| BLACK DISMALL HORROR. COME. MAKE PERFECT NOW | UPON GUNPOWDER TREASON | 20 | MS | 387 | 461 |
| AND STRETCH'ST THY DISMALL VOICE TOO DEEPE. | UPON DEATH OF A FREIND | 10 | MS | 393 | 477 |

## DISMAY'D

| | | | | | |
|---|---|---|---|---|---|
| WITH WHICH HIS FEELING DREAME HAD THUS DISMAY'D HIM. | SOSPETTO D'HERODE | 478 | 46 | 109 | 216 |

DISOLVING
 IN A DISOLVING SIGH, AND THEN  IN MEMORY OF LADY MADRE TERESA 118 46 131 52

DISPLACE
 DELICATELY TO DISPLACE  IN GLORIOUS EPIPHANIE 5 52 253 39

DISPLACES
 EYES, THAT DISPLACES  WISHES SUPPOSED MISTRESSE 43 46 195 479

DISPLAY
 WITH BAITED SMILES IF HE DISPLAY  OUT OF GREEKE CUPID'S CRYER 63 46 159 519
 UNFOLD THY FAIR CONCEPTIONS. AND DISPLAY  TO THE NAME OF JESUS 163 52 239 30

DISPLAI'D
 ABOUT HORROR'S DISPLAI'D. IT DOTH PORTEND,  ON GUNPOWDER-TREASON 21 MS 384 458

DISPOS'D
 DISPOS'D TO GIVE THE LIGHT-FOOT LADY SPORT  MUSICKS DUELL 16 46 149 535

DISPUTE
 O DEARE & SWEET DISPUTE  OFFICE H. CROSS SIXT 13 52 270 97
 HER LOVES CROSSE FORTUNE, THAT THE SAD DISPUTE  HORATIJ ILLE & NEFASTO 40 MS 382 530

DISPUTING
 WITH LOVES, OF TEARS WITH SMILES DISPUTING.  WEEPER 92 52 307 120

DISROBED
 IS TH' EARTH DISROBED OF HER APRON WHITE.  AN ELEGY MR STANNINOW 5 MS 394 473

DISSIPATE
 O DISSIPATE THY SPICY POWRES  TO THE NAME OF JESUS 167 52 239 30

DISSOLVE
 DISSOLVE MY DAYES & HOWRES.  SANCTA MARIA DOLORUM 88 52 283 162

DISTANCE
 KEEPE SUCH DISTANCE FROM THINE EARES.  UPON DEATH OF DESIRED HERRYS 62 46 168 467

DISTANT
 THOU THUS STEAL'ST DOWNE A DISTANT KISSE.  ON HOPE 38 46 143 71
 NE'RE SO FARRE DISTANT, YET CHRONOLOGIE  ON FRONTISPIECE ISAACSONS 8 46 191 491
 THOU STEAL'ST US DOWN A DISTANT KISSE.  (ON) HOPE 18 52 345 71
 FARRE DISTANT FROM OUR FATES. OUR FATES, THAT MOCKE  HORATIJ ILLE & NEFASTO 31 MS 382 530

DISTILL
 THAT THUS FROM LIFE CAN DEATH DISTILL.  LAUDA SION SALVATOREM 54 52 294 178
 AETERNALL TEARES SHOULD THUS DISTILL THEE.  WEEPER 100 52 307 120

DISTILL'D
 ON THOSE DELICIOUS BANKES DISTILL'D AGAINE  ON A FOULE MORNING 16 46 181 495

DISTIL'D
 AS THE DROPS DISTIL'D FROM THEE.  THE WEEPER 46 46 79 120

DISTILLS
 DISTILLS FROM THENCE THE TEARES OF WRATH AND STRIFE.  TO LORD UPON WATER MADE WINE 3 46 91 12

DISTINCTLY
 BLENDS ALL TOGETHER. THEN DISTINCTLY TRIPPS  MUSICKS DUELL 31 46 149 535

DISTINGUISH'D
 INTO A THOUSAND SWEET DISTINGUISH'D TONES.  MUSICKS DUELL 23 46 149 535

DISTRIBUTED
 TO THE GREAT TWELVE DISTRIBUTED  LAUDA SION SALVATOREM 10 52 294 178

DITTY
 TRAYLES HER PLAYNE DITTY IN ONE LONG-SPUN NOTE,  MUSICKS DUELL 37 46 149 535

DIVERS

| | | | | | |
|---|---|---|---|---|---|
| ARE MARS AND PHOEBUS UNDER DIVERS NAMES. | UPON YORKE HIS BIRTH | 34 | 46 | 176 | 500 |

DIVERSITIES

| | | | | | |
|---|---|---|---|---|---|
| TO MEASURE ALL THOSE WILD DIVERSITIES | MUSICKS DUELL | 162 | 46 | 149 | 535 |

DIVES

| | | | | | |
|---|---|---|---|---|---|
| THEN DIVES IN THE ROABES HE WEARES. | UPON LAZARUS HIS TEARES | 2 | 46 | 89 | 18 |
| SPARE THIS ONE JEWELL. I'LE BE DIVES STILL. | DIVES ASKING A DROP | 4 | 46 | 96 | 18 |

DIVIDE

| | | | | | |
|---|---|---|---|---|---|
| POORE LAWES DIVIDE THE PUBLICKE YEARE, | THOUGH NOW 'TIS NEITHER | 24 | MS | 397 | 492 |
| WHEN THE DREAD ITE SHALL DIVIDE | DIES IRAE | 61 | 52 | 298 | 186 |

DIVIDED

| | | | | | |
|---|---|---|---|---|---|
| WHOSE EACH DIVIDED BEAME WOULD BE A SUN. | UPON YORKE HIS BIRTH | 13 | 46 | 176 | 500 |
| WE TWO BETWIXT US HAVE DIVIDED IT. | OUT OF THE ITALIAN (2) | 2 | 46 | 190 | 547 |
| DIVIDED LOVES. WHILE SON & MOTHER | SANCTA MARIA DOLORUM | 23 | 52 | 283 | 162 |

DIVIDEND

| | | | | | |
|---|---|---|---|---|---|
| IN SORROWS DRAW NO DIVIDEND WITH YOU. | SANCTA MARIA DOLORUM | 84 | 52 | 283 | 162 |

DIVIDERS

| | | | | | |
|---|---|---|---|---|---|
| HERE DIVIDERS, SINGLE HE | LAUDA SION SALVATOREM | 46 | 52 | 294 | 178 |

DIVINE

| | | | | | |
|---|---|---|---|---|---|
| (MOST DIVINE SERVICE) WHOSE SO EARLY LAY, | MUSICKS DUELL | 81 | 46 | 149 | 535 |
| OF SOULE. DEARE. AND DIVINE ANNIHILATIONS. | ON A PRAYER BOOKE | 72 | 46 | 126 | 139 |
| WHICH THE DIVINE EMBRACES | ON A PRAYER BOOKE | 77 | 46 | 126 | 139 |
| TILL THAT DIVINE | WISHES SUPPOSED MISTRESSE | 10 | 46 | 195 | 479 |
| TRANSSUM'D, & TAUGHT TO TURN DIVINE. | LAUDA SION SALVATOREM | 30 | 52 | 294 | 178 |
| ALL THY SUFFRINGS BE DIVINE. | TERESA | 148 | 52 | 315 | 52 |
| OF SOUL. DEAR & DIVINE ANNIHILATIONS. | PRAYER TO GENTLE-WOMAN | 78 | 52 | 328 | 139 |
| WHICH THE DIVINE EMBRACES | PRAYER TO GENTLE-WOMAN | 83 | 52 | 328 | 139 |

DEVINE

| | | | | | |
|---|---|---|---|---|---|
| AND THY SUFFERINGS BEE DEVINE. | IN MEMORY OF LADY MADRE TERESA | 149 | 46 | 131 | 52 |

DIVINEST

| | | | | | |
|---|---|---|---|---|---|
| (O MY DESPIGHT.) WITH HIS DIVINEST GLORIES. | SOSPETTO D'HERODE | 228 | 46 | 109 | 216 |
| DIVINEST LOVE LYES IN THIS BOOKE. | ON MR. G. HERBERTS BOOKE | 2 | 46 | 130 | 68 |
| WITH THOSE DIVINEST EYES, WHICH WEE | ON THE ASSUMPTION | 35 | 46 | 139 | 114 |

DIVINING

| | | | | | |
|---|---|---|---|---|---|
| SIBILLS DIVINING LEAVES. HEE DOES ENQUIRE | SOSPETTO D'HERODE | 92 | 46 | 109 | 216 |

DIVINITY

| | | | | | |
|---|---|---|---|---|---|
| THERE STILL TO READ TRUE PURE DIVINITY. | UPON BISHOP ANDREWES PICTURE | 12 | 46 | 163 | 490 |
| YEE PERFECT EMBLEMES OF DIVINITY. | UPON KINGS CORONATION | 38 | MS | 389 | 454 |

DIVISIONS

| | | | | | |
|---|---|---|---|---|---|
| AND RECKONS UP IN SOFT DIVISIONS, | MUSICKS DUELL | 24 | 46 | 149 | 535 |

DIVORCE

| | | | | | |
|---|---|---|---|---|---|
| 'TWIXT SOULE AND BODY A DIVORCE. | AN EPITAPH HUSBAND AND WIFE | 4 | 46 | 174 | 478 |
| 'TWIXT SOUL & BODY A DIVORCE, | AN EPITAPH UPON MARRIED COUPLE | 4 | 52 | 339 | 478 |

DOAT

| | | | | | |
|---|---|---|---|---|---|
| GOE TAKE PHISICKE, DOAT UPON | IN PRAISE OF LESSIUS | 5 | 46 | 156 | 510 |
| GOE, TAKE PHYSICK DOAT UPON | TEMPERANCE | 5 | 52 | 342 | 510 |

DOATS

| | | | | | |
|---|---|---|---|---|---|
| HOW THY GREAT MOTHER NATURE DOATS ON THEE. | UPON YORKE HIS BIRTH | 26 | 46 | 176 | 500 |

DOATING

| | | | | | |
|---|---|---|---|---|---|
| THE DOATING NATIONS NOW NO MORE | IN GLORIOUS EPIPHANIE | 85 | 52 | 253 | 39 |

DOTING

| | | | | | |
|---|---|---|---|---|---|
| NOE. 'TWAS OLD DOTING DEATH, WHO, STEALING BY, | AN ELEGY MR STANNINOW | 45 | MS | 394 | 473 |

DOCTOR'S

| | | | | | |
|---|---|---|---|---|---|
| TH'ORACULOUS DOCTOR'S MYSTICK BILLS. | TEMPERANCE | 7 | 52 | 342 | 510 |

DOCTORS

  THE ORACULOUS DOCTORS MISTICK BILLS,    IN PRAISE OF LESSIUS    7  46 156 510

DOFFS

  HEAVENS KING, WHO DOFFS HIMSELFE WEAKE FLESH TO WEARE,  SOSPETTO D'HERODE    515  46 109 216

DOGS

  HERE DIOMED'S HORSES, PHEREUS DOGS APPEARE,    SOSPETTO D'HERODE    353  46 109 216

DOGGES

  NOT TO BE CAST TO DOGGES, OR SWINE.    LAUDA SION SALVATOREM    64  52 294 178

DOLEFULL

  STOOD DOLEFULL SHEE.    SANCTA MARIA DOLORUM    2  52 283 162
  DEAR, DOLEFULL HEARTS.    SANCTA MARIA DOLORUM    72  52 283 162

DOMESTICK

  SAVE THOSE DOMESTICK WHICH HE BORROWES    IN GLORIOUS EPIPHANIE    155  52 253 39

DOMINATIONS

  STILL THRONES & DOMINATIONS WOULD ADORE THEE    CHARITAS NIMIA    24  52 280 48

DOOM

  THAT DARK DAY'S CLEAR DOOM SHALL DEFINE    IN GLORIOUS EPIPHANIE    143  52 253 39

DOOME

  DEATH ONELY BY THIS DAYES JUST DOOME IS FORC'T TO DYE.  EASTER DAY    15  46 100 26
  KNOWING 'TIS IN THE DOOME OF YOUR SWEET EYE    AT TH' IVORY TRIBUNALL    3  MS 397 492

DOOMES

  THAT NOTES THE TRAGICKE DOOMES OF MEN    ANOTHER ON HERRYS    34  46 170 469

DOOR

  HOLDS FAST THE DOOR, YET DARES NOT VENTURE    TO COUNTESSE OF DENBIGH    3  52 236 146
  HAIL, DOOR OF LIFE, & SOURSE OF DAY.    O GLORIOSA DOMINA    32  52 302 194
  THE DOOR WAS SHUTT, THE FOUNTAIN SEAL'D.    O GLORIOSA DOMINA    33  52 302 194
  THE DOOR WAS SHUTT, YET LET IN DAY,    O GLORIOSA DOMINA    35  52 302 194
  AND WAITED FOR THEE, AT THE DOOR,    TERESA    140  52 315 52
  HOLDS FAST THE DOOR, YET DARES NOT VENTURE    AGAINST IRRESOLUTION AND DELAY    3  52 347 146

DORE

  THE BLOOMES OF MARTYRDOME, O BE A DORE    SOSPETTO D'HERODE    5  46 109 216
  BUT EACH SITT STILL IN HIS OWN DORE.    ADORO TE    8  52 291 172

DOORE

  AND WAITED FOR THEE AT THE DOORE.    IN MEMORY OF LADY MADRE TERESA    141  46 131 52
  THOSE DEERE LIPS WHOSE DOORE ENCLOSES    OUT OF THE ITALIAN (1)    21  46 188 545

DOORS

  THE ADAMANTINE DOORS, FOR EVER STAND    SOSPETTO D'HERODE    307  46 109 216

DOORES

  HATH SHUT THESE DOORES OF HEAVEN, THAT DURST    I AM THE DOORE    5  46 90 17
  TO WAIT AT THE LOVE-CROWNED DOORES OF    TO THE NAME OF JESUS    42  52 239 30
  WHAT DID THEIR WEAPONS BUT SETT WIDE THE DOORES    TO THE NAME OF JESUS    216  52 239 30
  FOR THEE, FAIR, PURPLE DOORES, OF LOVE'S DEVISING.    TO THE NAME OF JESUS    217  52 239 30
  AND DOUBLE-GUILDED AS THE DOORES OF DAY.    IN GLORIOUS EPIPHANIE    57  52 253 39
  THAT WATCHES AT HIS PALACE DOORES    TO SAME CONCERNING CHOISE    28  52 331 66

DOUBLE

  SHAME NOW AND ANGER MIXT A DOUBLE STAINE    MUSICKS DUELL    105  46 149 535
  THAT HATH A DOUBLE NILUS GOING,    ON BLEEDING WOUNDS OF LORD    14  46 101 110
  RENDERS THEE DOUBLE TO THY PRESENT WOES.    SOSPETTO D'HERODE    244  46 109 216
  ROSIE WITH A DOUBLE RED.    AN HIMNE FOR CIRCUMCISION    2  46 141 37
  ROSY WITH A DOUBLE RED.    NEW YEAR'S DAY    2  52 251 37
  THAT HATH A DOUBLE NILUS GOING.    UPON BLEEDING CRUCIFIX    18  52 288 110

DOUBLE-GILT

  NOR NEED BE DOUBLE-GILT. HOW THEN MUST THESE,    UPON TWO GREENE APRICOCKES    29  48 220 494

DOUBLE-GUILDED

  AND DOUBLE-GUILDED AS THE DOORES OF DAY.    IN GLORIOUS EPIPHANIE    57  52 253 39

## DOUBT

| | | | | | |
|---|---|---|---|---|---|
| MEETS ART WITH ART. SOMETIMES AS IF IN DOUBT | MUSICKS DUELL | 35 | 46 | 149 | 535 |
| SHARPE AIRES, AND STAGGERS IN A WARBLING DOUBT | MUSICKS DUELL | 58 | 46 | 149 | 535 |
| FREELY LAYES OUT HER LEAVES. NOR DOE I DOUBT | OUT OF VIRGIL | 22 | 46 | 155 | 529 |
| YET I DOUBT OF THEE, | THE TEARE | 45 | 46 | 84 | 50 |
| AND NOW, I DOUBT NOT, THE ETERNALL DOVE, | ON BAPTIZED AETHIOPIAN | 5 | 46 | 85 | 29 |
| OF YOUR OWNE DOUBT. | WHY ARE YEE AFRAID | 14 | 46 | 88 | 15 |
| MAKES ME DOUBT IF HEAVEN WILL GATHER, | UPON INFANT MARTYRS | 3 | 46 | 95 | 10 |
| I DOUBT THOUGH WHEN THE WORLD'S IN HELL, | BUT MEN LOVED DARKNESSE | 3 | 46 | 97 | 13 |
| THESE ARE THE KNOTTY RIDDLES, WHOSE DARKE DOUBT | SOSPETTO D'HERODE | 191 | 46 | 109 | 216 |
| CRUELTY, SHE ALONE SHALL CURE MY DOUBT. | SOSPETTO D'HERODE | 288 | 46 | 109 | 216 |
| AND, THROUGH THE NIGHT OF ERROR AND DARK DOUBT, | ON FRONTISPIECE ISAACSONS | 12 | 46 | 191 | 491 |
| WHOSE DEFINITION IS A DOUBT | TO COUNTESSE OF DENBIGH | 5 | 52 | 236 | 146 |
| WHOSE DEFINITIONS IS, A DOUBT | AGAINST IRRESOLUTION AND DELAY | 5 | 52 | 347 | 146 |

## DOUBTLES

| | | | | | |
|---|---|---|---|---|---|
| DOUBTLES SOME OTHER HEART | ON A PRAYER BOOKE | 54 | 46 | 126 | 139 |
| DOUBTLES HEE WILL UNLOAD | ON A PRAYER BOOKE | 85 | 46 | 126 | 139 |

## DOUBTLESSE

| | | | | | |
|---|---|---|---|---|---|
| DOUBTLESSE SOME OTHER HEART | PRAYER TO GENTLE-WOMAN | 60 | 52 | 328 | 139 |
| DOUBTLESSE HE WILL UNLOAD | PRAYER TO GENTLE-WOMAN | 91 | 52 | 328 | 139 |

## DOUBTS

| | | | | | |
|---|---|---|---|---|---|
| HAD SOWNE OF OLD THESE DOUBTS IN HIS DEEPE BREST. | SOSPETTO D'HERODE | 498 | 46 | 109 | 216 |
| MAKE TO THY REASON MAN, AND MOCKE THY DOUBTS. | SOSPETTO D'HERODE | 521 | 46 | 109 | 216 |

## DOVE

| | | | | | |
|---|---|---|---|---|---|
| AND NOW, I DOUBT NOT, THE ETERNALL DOVE. | ON BAPTIZED AETHIOPIAN | 5 | 46 | 85 | 29 |
| DEARE SILVER BREASTED DOVE | ON A PRAYER BOOKE | 92 | 46 | 126 | 139 |
| SHEE'S CALL'D AGAINE. HARKE HOW TH'IMMORTALL DOVE | ON THE ASSUMPTION | 7 | 46 | 139 | 114 |
| COME AWAY MY DOVE | ON THE ASSUMPTION | 14 | 46 | 139 | 114 |
| AND WITH THE WINGS OF THINE OWN DOVE | DIES IRAE | 27 | 52 | 298 | 166 |
| SHE'S CALLD. HARK, HOW THE DEAR IMMORTALL DOVE | IN GLORIOUS ASSUMPTION B. LADY | 7 | 52 | 304 | 114 |
| COME AWAY, MY DOVE. CAST OFF DELAY, | IN GLORIOUS ASSUMPTION B. LADY | 14 | 52 | 304 | 114 |
| COME AWAY, MY DOVE. | IN GLORIOUS ASSUMPTION B. LADY | 32 | 52 | 304 | 114 |
| BY ALL THE EAGLE IN THEE, ALL THE DOVE. | FLAMING HEART | 95 | 52 | 324 | 61 |
| SELECTED DOVE | PRAYER TO GENTLE-WOMAN | 98 | 52 | 328 | 139 |

## TURTLE-DOVE

| | | | | | |
|---|---|---|---|---|---|
| OF A POOR PANTING TURTLE-DOVE. | TO THE NAME OF JESUS | 108 | 52 | 239 | 30 |
| O MOTHER TURTLE-DOVE. | SANCTA MARIA DOLORUM | 41 | 52 | 283 | 162 |

## DOVE'S

| | | | | | |
|---|---|---|---|---|---|
| LO WHERE IT COMES, UPON THE SNOWY DOVE'S | TO THE NAME OF JESUS | 159 | 52 | 239 | 30 |

## DOVES

| | | | | | |
|---|---|---|---|---|---|
| EACH HIS PAYRE OF SILVER DOVES. | A HYMNE OF THE NATIVITY | 86 | 46 | 106 | 76 |
| OR (FOR TWO TURTLE DOVES) IT SHALL SUFFICE | ON A TREATISE OF CHARITY | 47 | 46 | 137 | 69 |
| HEARKEN, AND HELP, YE HOLY DOVES. | TO THE NAME OF JESUS | 6 | 52 | 239 | 30 |
| EACH HIS PAIR OF SYLVER DOVES. | IN HOLY NATIVITY | 106 | 52 | 246 | 76 |
| EYES, NESTS OF MILKY DOVES | WEEPER | 87 | 52 | 307 | 120 |
| THE AIERY NATION OF NEAT DOVES, | AGAINST IRRESOLUTION AND DELAY | 45 | 52 | 347 | 146 |
| BY TH'EVEN WINGS OF HIS OWN DOVES, | AGAINST IRRESOLUTION AND DELAY | 54 | 52 | 347 | 146 |

## DOWN

| | | | | | |
|---|---|---|---|---|---|
| YOUR DOWN SO WARM, WILL PASSE FOR PURE. | IN HOLY NATIVITY | 63 | 52 | 246 | 76 |

## DOWNE

| | | | | | |
|---|---|---|---|---|---|
| LOOKES DOWNE, AND SEES THE HUMBLE NILE BELOW | THE BEGINNING OF HELIODORUS | 4 | 46 | 158 | 517 |
| STUFT WITH DOWNE OF ANGELS WING. | THE TEARE | 36 | 46 | 84 | 50 |
| 'TWAS ONCE LOOKE UP, 'TIS NOW LOOKE DOWNE TO HEAVEN. | ON VIRGINS BASHFULNESSE | 8 | 46 | 89 | 9 |
| BUT EDOM CRUELL THOU. THOU CRYD'ST DOWNE, DOWNE | PSALME 137 | 27 | 46 | 104 | 7 |
| BUT EDOM CRUELL THOU. THOU CRYD'ST DOWNE, DOWNE | PSALME 137 | 27 | 46 | 104 | 7 |
| SINKE SION, DOWNE AND NEVER RISE, | PSALME 137 | 28 | 46 | 104 | 7 |
| THE DOWNE THAT THEIR SOFT BRESTS DID STROW. | A HYMNE OF THE NATIVITY | 42 | 46 | 106 | 76 |
| THY DOWNE THOUGH SOFT'S NOT SOFT ENOUGH. | A HYMNE OF THE NATIVITY | 46 | 46 | 106 | 76 |
| DOWNE MY PROUD THOUGHT, AND LEAVE IT IN A TRANCE. | SOSPETTO D'HERODE | 204 | 46 | 109 | 216 |
| AND MELTS IT DOWNE IN SWEET DESIRE. | ON A PRAYER BOOKE | 68 | 46 | 126 | 139 |
| RIPE AND FULL GROWNE, THAT COULD REACH DOWNE. | IN MEMORY OF LADY MADRE TERESA | 5 | 46 | 131 | 52 |
| THOU THUS STEAL'ST DOWNE A DISTANT KISSE, | ON HOPE | 38 | 46 | 143 | 71 |
| THY GOLDEN HEAD NEVER HANGS DOWNE. | ON HOPE | 55 | 46 | 143 | 71 |
| RAVISHT THE MAIDEN BLOSSOMS, AND DOWNE BORE | UPON DEATH OF HERRYS | 34 | 46 | 167 | 466 |
| TAKE THINE OWNE MEASURE HERE, DOWNE, DOWNE, AND BOW | UPON STANINOUGH'S DEATH | 11 | 46 | 175 | 475 |
| TAKE THINE OWNE MEASURE HERE, DOWNE, DOWNE, AND BOW | UPON STANINOUGH'S DEATH | 11 | 46 | 175 | 475 |
| OR GIVE DOWNE TO THE WINGS OF NIGHT. | WISHES SUPPOSED MISTRESSE | 96 | 46 | 195 | 479 |
| DROP DOWNE ONE SPARKE OF GLORY, & THEY'L PROVE | UPON BIRTH PRINCESSE E | 19 | MS | 391 | 456 |

## DOUNE

| | | | | | |
|---|---|---|---|---|---|
| HEAVEN KICKT THE MONSTER DOUNE. DOUNE IT WAS THROUNE, | ON GUNPOWDER-TREASON | 51 | MS | 384 | 458 |
| HEAVEN KICKT THE MONSTER DOUNE. DOUNE IT WAS THROUNE, | ON GUNPOWDER-TREASON | 51 | MS | 384 | 458 |
| THAT HAND OF MILKY DOUNE. ALL THESE ARE BASE. | UPON BIRTH PRINCESSE E | 52 | MS | 391 | 456 |

DOWNY

| | | | | | |
|---|---|---|---|---|---|
| OF SORROW, WITH A SOFT AND DOWNY HAND, | SOSPETTO D'HERODE | 391 | 46 | 109 | 216 |
| HIS SMOOTH CHEEKES, WITH A DOWNY SHADE. | HIS EPITAPH (HERRYS) | 46 | 46 | 172 | 471 |
| THY DOWNY FINGER, DWELL UPON THEIR EYES, | TO THE MORNING | 57 | 46 | 183 | 497 |
| DOTH HEE IN DOWNY SNOW THERE CLOSELY SHROWD | AN ELEGY MR STANNINOW | 3 | MS | 394 | 473 |
| IN DOWNY SURPLISSES, & VESTMENTS WHITE, | AN ELEGIE ON DR PORTER | 28 | MS | 395 | 476 |

DOWR

| | | | | | |
|---|---|---|---|---|---|
| BY ALL THY DOWR OF LIGHTS & FIRES. | FLAMING HEART | 94 | 52 | 324 | 61 |

DOWRY

| | | | | | |
|---|---|---|---|---|---|
| DEARE HOPE. EARTHS DOWRY, AND HEAVENS DEBT, | ON HOPE | 11 | 46 | 143 | 71 |
| DEAR HOPE. EARTH'S DOWRY, & HEAVN'S DEBT. | (ON) HOPE | 1 | 52 | 345 | 71 |

DRAG

| | | | | | |
|---|---|---|---|---|---|
| DRAW HIM, DRAG HIM, THOUGH HEE PRAY | OUT OF GREEKE CUPID'S CRYER | 67 | 46 | 159 | 519 |

DRAGGING

| | | | | | |
|---|---|---|---|---|---|
| DRAGGING HIS CROOKED BURTHEN, LOOK'T AWRY. | AN ELEGY MR STANNINOW | 46 | MS | 394 | 473 |

DRAGONS

| | | | | | |
|---|---|---|---|---|---|
| OF DRAGONS, HYDRAES, SPHINXES, FILL THE GROVE. | SOSPETTO D'HERODE | 352 | 46 | 109 | 216 |

DRAKE

| | | | | | |
|---|---|---|---|---|---|
| AND THE DRAKE YEELD NOE DELIGHT, | PETRONIJ ALES PHASIACIS PETITA | 6 | MS | 382 | 526 |

DRAUGHT

| | | | | | |
|---|---|---|---|---|---|
| OUR DUST, THAT IN ONE DRAUGHT, MORTALITY | AN APOLOGIE FOR HYMNE (TERESA) | 45 | 46 | 136 | 59 |
| OUR DUST, THAT AT ONE DRAUGHT, MORTALITY | AN APOLOGIE FOR (TERESA) HYMNE | 45 | 52 | 322 | 59 |
| BY THY LAST MORNING'S DRAUGHT OF LIQUID FIRE. | FLAMING HEART | 100 | 52 | 324 | 61 |

DRAUGHTS

| | | | | | |
|---|---|---|---|---|---|
| THERE ARE ENOW WHOSE DRAUGHTS AS DEEP AS HELL | AN APOLOGIE FOR HYMNE (TERESA) | 29 | 46 | 136 | 59 |
| THERE ARE ENOW, WHOSE DRAUGHTS (AS DEEP AS HELL) | AN APOLOGIE FOR (TERESA) HYMNE | 29 | 52 | 322 | 59 |
| BY THY LARG DRAUGHTS OF INTELLECTUALL DAY, | FLAMING HEART | 97 | 52 | 324 | 61 |

DRAW

| | | | | | |
|---|---|---|---|---|---|
| DRAW HIM, DRAG HIM, THOUGH HEE PRAY | OUT OF GREEKE CUPID'S CRYER | 67 | 46 | 159 | 519 |
| AND DRAW FROM THESE FULL EYES OF THINE. | THE WEEPER | 35 | 46 | 79 | 120 |
| TO DRAW A LONG-LIV'D DEATH, WHERE ALL MY CHEERE | SOSPETTO D'HERODE | 214 | 46 | 109 | 216 |
| O STAY A WHILE E'RE THOU DRAW IN THY HEAD, | UPON STANINOUGH'S DEATH | 3 | 46 | 175 | 475 |
| HOW AT THE SIGHT DID'ST THOU DRAW BACK THINE EYES, | TO THE MORNING | 7 | 46 | 183 | 497 |
| TO DRAW THE CURTAINES, AND AWAKE THE SUN. | TO THE MORNING | 10 | 46 | 183 | 497 |
| DEFECTS I DRAW MINE OWNE DULL CHARACTER. | UPON TWO GREENE APRICOCKES | 32 | 48 | 220 | 494 |
| MY DYING LIFE MAY DRAW A NEW, & NEVER FLEETING BREATH. | OFFICE H. CROSS RECOMMENDATION | 8 | 52 | 276 | 106 |
| IN SORROWS DRAW NO DIVIDEND WITH YOU. | SANCTA MARIA DOLORUM | 84 | 52 | 283 | 162 |
| AND DRAW FROM THESE FULL EYES OF THINE | WEEPER | 71 | 52 | 307 | 120 |
| O STAY A WHILE, ERE THOU DRAW IN THY HEAD | DEATH'S LECTURE | 3 | 52 | 340 | 475 |
| THAT DRAW THE CHARIOT OF CHAST LOVES, | AGAINST IRRESOLUTION AND DELAY | 46 | 52 | 347 | 146 |
| DRAW TO THIS SISTER MIRACLE A BROTHER. | UPON BIRTH PRINCESSE E | 56 | MS | 391 | 456 |
| MAY DRAW THEIR FIRST BREATH FROM THY STARRY BEAMES. | EX EUPHORMIONE | 14 | MS | 392 | 525 |
| THE BLOUD HOUND BROOD OF PRIESTS AGAINST MEE DRAW | OUT OF GROTIUS | 45 | MS | 398 | 198 |

DRAWN

| | | | | | |
|---|---|---|---|---|---|
| WITH CURTAINS DRAWN, | TO THE NAME OF JESUS | 147 | 52 | 239 | 30 |
| THEN THE CURTAINES WILL BE DRAWN | AN EPITAPH UPON MARRIED COUPLE | 18 | 52 | 339 | 478 |
| A THINNE, AERIALL VEIL, IS DRAWN | TEMPERANCE | 26 | 52 | 342 | 510 |

DRAWNE

| | | | | | |
|---|---|---|---|---|---|
| HEE THROWES HIS ARME, AND WITH A LONG DRAWNE DASH | MUSICKS DUELL | 30 | 46 | 149 | 535 |
| A THINNE AIEREALL VAILE IS DRAWNE | IN PRAISE OF LESSIUS | 28 | 46 | 156 | 510 |
| THEN THE CURTAINES WILL BEE DRAWNE, | AN EPITAPH HUSBAND AND WIFE | 14 | 46 | 174 | 478 |
| HOW EVEN TH'AST DRAWNE THIS FAITHFULL PARALELL. | UPON YORKE HIS BIRTH | 50 | 46 | 176 | 500 |
| HAD YOU BUT DRAWNE ONE LIVELY COPPY FORTH, | UPON BIRTH PRINCESSE E | 29 | MS | 391 | 456 |

DREAD

| | | | | | |
|---|---|---|---|---|---|
| TO THEE (DREAD LAMBE) WHOSE LOVE MUST KEEPE | A HYMNE OF THE NATIVITY | 81 | 46 | 106 | 76 |
| ON US THY DREAD COMMANDS, OURS TO OBEY. | SOSPETTO D'HERODE | 264 | 46 | 109 | 216 |
| MIGHTY IN MISCHIEFE, WITH DREAD NERO TOO, | SOSPETTO D'HERODE | 364 | 46 | 109 | 216 |
| AS IT IS SEENE BY HELL, AND SEENE WITH DREAD. | SOSPETTO D'HERODE | 414 | 46 | 109 | 216 |
| SAY THEN DREAD QUEEN, HOW MAY WE DOE | TO THE QUEEN | 9 | 48 | 215 | 501 |
| AND COUCH BEFORE THE DAZELING LIGHT OF THY DREAD MAJESTY. | TO THE NAME OF JESUS | 235 | 52 | 239 | 30 |
| TO THEE, DREAD LAMB, WHOSE LOVE MUST KEEP | IN HOLY NATIVITY | 101 | 52 | 246 | 76 |
| (DREAD SWEET.) LO THUS | IN GLORIOUS EPIPHANIE | 234 | 52 | 253 | 39 |
| SO SWORE THE LAMB'S DREAD SIRE. AND SO WE SEE'T. | TO THE QUEEN'S MAJESTY | 19 | 52 | 261 | 47 |
| DREAD LAMB. AND BOW THUS LOW BEFORE THEE, | OFFICE H. CROSS MATINES | 25 | 52 | 265 | 86 |
| DREAD LAMB. AND FALL | OFFICE H. CROSS PRIME | 18 | 52 | 267 | 91 |
| DREAD LAMB, & FALL | OFFICE H. CROSS THIRD | 17 | 52 | 268 | 93 |
| DREAD LAMB, & BOW THUS LOW BEFORE THEE. | OFFICE H. CROSS SIXT | 22 | 52 | 270 | 97 |

| | | | |
|---|---|---|---|
| DREAD LAMB, AND FALL | OFFICE H. CROSS NINTH | 14 | 52 271 99 |
| DREAD LAMB, & BOW THUS BEFORE THEE. | OFFICE H. CROSS EVENSONG | 29 | 52 273 101 |
| MUST BE THE DAY OF THAT DREAD NIGHT. | DIES IRAE | 8 | 52 298 186 |
| BUT THOU GIV'ST LEAVE (DREAD LORD) THAT WE | DIES IRAE | 25 | 52 298 186 |
| WHEN THE DREAD ITE SHALL DIVIDE | DIES IRAE | 61 | 52 298 186 |
| SINCE THY DREAD SON WILL HAVE IT SO. | IN GLORIOUS ASSUMPTION B. LADY | 41 | 52 304 114 |

DREADFULL

| | | | |
|---|---|---|---|
| UNTO A DREADFULL PILE GIVES FIERY BREATH. | SOSPETTO D'HERODE | 58 | 46 109 216 |

DREAM

| | | | |
|---|---|---|---|
| AND NOW HIS DREAM (HELS FIREBRAND) STIL MORE BRIGHT, | SOSPETTO D'HERODE | 503 | 46 109 216 |

DREAME

| | | | |
|---|---|---|---|
| WITH WHICH HIS FEELING DREAME HAD THUS DISMAY'D HIM, | SOSPETTO D'HERODE | 478 | 46 109 216 |

DREAMPT

| | | | |
|---|---|---|---|
| SLEPT, AND DREAMPT OF NO SUCH THING | A HYMNE OF THE NATIVITY | 6 | 46 106 76 |

DREAM'T

| | | | |
|---|---|---|---|
| HE SLEPT, AND DREAM'T OF NO SUCH THING. | IN HOLY NATIVITY | 6 | 52 246 76 |

DRESSE

| | | | |
|---|---|---|---|
| DRESSE THE SOULE, WHICH LATE THEY SLEW. | IN MEMORY OF LADY MADRE TERESA | 153 | 46 131 52 |
| SH'L DRESSE THEE LIKE THY SELFE, SET THEE ON HIGH | ON A TREATISE OF CHARITY | 15 | 46 137 69 |
| WITH THOSE DEARE SPOILES THAT WONT TO DRESSE THE FAIRE | ON A TREATISE OF CHARITY | 54 | 46 137 69 |
| SO HAVE I SEENE (TO DRESSE THEIR MISTRESSE MAY) | UPON YORKE HIS BIRTH | 59 | 46 176 500 |
| TO TH'CHURCH HEE DID ALLOW HER DRESSE, | AN EPITAPH UPON ASHTON | 21 | 46 192 464 |
| THEIR RICHEST TIRES BUT DRESSE | WISHES SUPPOSED MISTRESSE | 41 | 46 195 479 |
| AND HAVE NO OTHER HEAD TO DRESSE. | WISHES SUPPOSED MISTRESSE | 69 | 46 195 479 |
| DRESSE THE SOUL THAT ERST THEY SLEW. | TERESA | 152 | 52 315 52 |

DRESSES

| | | | |
|---|---|---|---|
| AND WEARE IN THEM HIS WEALTHY DRESSES, | AN HIMNE FOR CIRCUMCISION | 23 | 46 141 37 |
| THAT NO MORE SUMMERS BEST DRESSES, | OUT OF THE ITALIAN (1) | 9 | 46 188 545 |
| AND WEAR, IN THOSE HIS WEALTHY DRESSES, | NEW YEAR'S DAY | 23 | 52 251 37 |

DRESSING

| | | | |
|---|---|---|---|
| THAT HEERE ARE DRESSING BY THE HASTY FATES. | UPON GUNPOWDER TREASON | 30 | MS 387 461 |

DRESSINGS

| | | | |
|---|---|---|---|
| TO MAKE IMMORTALL DRESSINGS | ON A PRAYER BOOKE | 37 | 46 126 139 |
| TO MAKE IMMORTALL DRESSINGS | PRAYER TO GENTLE-WOMAN | 43 | 52 328 139 |

DREST

| | | | |
|---|---|---|---|
| NOR CHOAKT WITH WHAT SHEE SHOULD BEE DREST. | IN PRAISE OF LESSIUS | 24 | 46 156 510 |
| THEN IS SHEE DREST BY NONE BUT THEE. | THE WEEPER | 52 | 46 79 120 |
| HEAV'N SET THEE DOWN NEW DREST. WHEN THY BRIGHT BIRTH | ON A TREATISE OF CHARITY | 5 | 46 137 69 |
| DREST IN THE GLORIOUS MADNESSE OF A MUSE, | TO THE MORNING | 23 | 46 183 497 |
| (DREST IN THOSE BEAMES) START FORTH | OUT OF THE ITALIAN (2) | 9 | 46 190 547 |
| BY ITS OWNE BEAUTY DREST, | WISHES SUPPOSED MISTRESSE | 26 | 46 195 479 |
| THEN IS SHE DREST BY NONE BUT THEE. | WEEPER | 40 | 52 307 120 |
| THAT DIGG'D THESE WELLS, & DREST THIS VINE. | WEEPER | 104 | 52 307 120 |
| NOR CHOAK'T WITH WHAT SHE SHOULD BE DREST. | TEMPERANCE | 22 | 52 342 510 |
| HEE'S GONE. THE FAIR'ST FLOWER, THAT E'RE BOSOME DREST. | LUKE 2. QUAERIT JESUM | 5 | MS 379 11 |
| THOSE PLUMPE SOFT RUBIES HAD BIN DREST SOE BRAVE. | UPON BIRTH PRINCESSE E | 48 | MS 391 456 |
| THE WEEPING PEN WITH SABLE TEARES HATH DREST. | AN ELEGIE ON DR PORTER | 10 | MS 395 476 |

DREW

| | | | |
|---|---|---|---|
| A DESPERATE, OH MEE, DREW FROM HIS DEEPE BREST. | SOSPETTO D'HERODE | 200 | 46 109 216 |
| OF DEATH MEZENTIUS, OR GERYON DREW. | SOSPETTO D'HERODE | 362 | 46 109 216 |

DRINK

| | | | |
|---|---|---|---|
| AND HAST TO DRINK THE WHOLSOME DART. | TO COUNTESSE OF DENBIGH | 46 | 52 236 146 |
| AND DRINK THE UNSEAL'D SOURSE OF THEE. | ADORO TE | 54 | 52 291 172 |
| AS MEAT IN THAT, AS DRINK IN THIS, | LAUDA SION SALVATOREM | 41 | 52 294 178 |
| DRINK THE SAME WINE. AND THE SAME WAY. | LAUDA SION SALVATOREM | 78 | 52 294 178 |
| SUCH THIRSTS TO DY, AS DARES DRINK UP, | TERESA | 37 | 52 315 52 |
| DRINK UP AL SPAIN IN SACK. LET MY SOUL SWELL | AN APOLOGIE FOR (TERESA) HYMNE | 30 | 52 322 59 |
| (MY SOUL,) SOME DRINK FROM MEN TO BEASTS, O THEN | AN APOLOGIE FOR (TERESA) HYMNE | 35 | 52 322 59 |
| DRINK WE TILL WE PROVE MORE, NOT LESSE, THEN MEN, | AN APOLOGIE FOR (TERESA) HYMNE | 36 | 52 322 59 |
| MAY DRINK IT SELF UP, AND FORGET TO DY. | AN APOLOGIE FOR (TERESA) HYMNE | 46 | 52 322 59 |

DRINKE

| | | | |
|---|---|---|---|
| HERE'S A THEAME WILL DRINKE TH'EXPENCE. | UPON THE DEATH OF A GENTLEMAN | 31 | 46 166 472 |
| THEN LET HIM DRINKE, AND DRINKE, AND DOE HIS WORST, | OUR LORD IN HIS CIRCUMCISION | 7 | 46 98 9 |
| THEN LET HIM DRINKE, AND DRINKE, AND DOE HIS WORST, | OUR LORD IN HIS CIRCUMCISION | 7 | 46 98 9 |
| THAT DRINKE THE DEAW OF LIFE, WHOSE DEATHLESSE SPRING, | SOSPETTO D'HERODE | 20 | 46 109 216 |
| THAT FROM HIS MOTHERS BREST HEE MILKE SHOULD DRINKE, | SOSPETTO D'HERODE | 173 | 46 109 216 |
| THE CUP THEY DRINKE IN IS MEDUSA'S SCULL, | SOSPETTO D'HERODE | 335 | 46 109 216 |

```
                                                                              PAGE 108

          SUCH THIRST TO DYE, AS DARE DRINKE UP,            IN MEMORY OF LADY MADRE TERESA       37   46 131  52
          DRINKE UP ALL SPAINE IN SACK, LET MY SOULE SWELL  AN APOLOGIE FOR HYMNE (TERESA)       30   46 136  59
          MY SOULE, SOME DRINKE FROM MEN TO BEASTS.  O THEN,AN APOLOGIE FOR HYMNE (TERESA)       35   46 136  59
          DRINKE WEE TILL WE PROVE MORE, NOT LESSE THEN MEN. AN APOLOGIE FOR HYMNE (TERESA)      36   46 136  59
          MAY DRINKE IT SELFE UP, AND FORGET TO DY.         AN APOLOGIE FOR HYMNE (TERESA)       46   46 136  59
          SOE LOW TO GIVE HIS THIRSTY STALLIONS DRINKE.     UPON GUNPOWDER TREASON               40   MS 386 460
          DRINKE FAYLING THERE WHERE I A GUEST DID SHINE    OUT OF GROTIUS                       51   MS 398 198

DRINKS

          HEAVENS BOSOME DRINKS THE GENTLE STREAME.         THE WEEPER                           20   46  79 120
          THE FAIR STARRS FILL THEIR WAKEFULL FIRES THE SUN OFFICE H. CROSS PRIME                 8   52 267  91
                                       HIMSELFE DRINKS
                                       DAY.
          HEAVN'S BOSOME DRINKS THE GENTLE STREAM.          WEEPER                               20   52 307 120

DRIVEN

          TO THESE THY SOOTY KINGDOMES THOU ART DRIVEN.     SOSPETTO D'HERODE                   268   46 109 216
          AS IF THE BARGAIN HAD BEEN DRIVEN                 AGAINST IRRESOLUTION AND DELAY       61   52 347 146

DROP

          THOSE PARTS OF SWEETNESSE WHICH WITH NECTAR DROP, MUSICKS DUELL                       125   46 149 535
          A BEAD, THAT IS A TEARE DOTH DROP.                THE WEEPER                          108   46  79 120
          'TIS A STARRE ABOUT TO DROP                       THE TEARE                             8   46  84  50
          EACH DROP LEAVING A PLACE SO DEARE,               THE TEARE                            17   46  84  50
          FAIRE DROP, WHY QUAK'ST THOU SO.                  THE TEARE                            31   46  84  50
          EACH BLEST DROP, ON EACH BLEST LIMME,             ON WATER OF LORDS BAPTISME            1   46  85  12
          A DROP, ONE DROP, HOW SWEETLY ONE FAIRE DROP      DIVES ASKING A DROP                   1   46  96  18
          A DROP, ONE DROP, HOW SWEETLY ONE FAIRE DROP      DIVES ASKING A DROP                   1   46  96  18
          A DROP, ONE DROP, HOW SWEETLY ONE FAIRE DROP      DIVES ASKING A DROP                   1   46  96  18
          A BEAD, THAT IS, A TEAR, DOES DROP.               WEEPER                              144   52 307 120
          DROP DOWNE ONE SPARKE OF GLORY, & THEY'L PROVE    UPON BIRTH PRINCESSE E               19   MS 391 456

DROP'S

          EACH DROP'S A TEARE THAT WEEPS FOR HER OWN WAST.  TO PONTIUS WASHING HANDS             11   46  94  23

DROPP

          READY TO DROPP INTO A CHAOS, ROUND                ON GUNPOWDER-TREASON                 20   MS 384 458
          ONE DROPP OF THIS PURE NECTAR, WHICH DOTH FLOW    UPON GUNPOWDER TREASON               41   MS 387 461

DROPS

          AS THE DROPS DISTIL'D FROM THEE.                  THE WEEPER                           46   46  79 120
          YET LET THE POORE DROPS WEEPE,                    THE WEEPER                           73   46  79 120
          TWO MITES, TWO DROPS, (YET ALL HER HOUSE AND LAND) WIDDOWES MITES                       1   46  86  21
          HARKE HOW SHE BIDS HER FRIGHTED DROPS MAKE HAST,  TO PONTIUS WASHING HANDS             13   46  94  23
          IT DROPS THOUGH BOUND, THOUGH BOUND 'TIS FREE.    ON BLEEDING WOUNDS OF LORD           12   46 101 110
          I SAW THE CURL'D DROPS,SOFT AND SLOW              A HYMNE OF THE NATIVITY              35   46 106  76
          AND THE DEARE DROPS THIS DAY WERE SHED.           AN HIMNE FOR CIRCUMCISION             4   46 141  37
          THE TENDER DROPS WHICH TREMBLE ON HER CHEEKE.     ON A FOULE MORNING                   14   46 181 495
          I SAW THE CURL'D DROPS, SOFT & SLOW,              IN HOLY NATIVITY                     51   52 246  76
          AND THE DEAR DROPS THIS DAY WERE SHED.            NEW YEAR'S DAY                        4   52 251  37
          (MY FLINTS) SOME DROPS ARE DUE                    SANCTA MARIA DOLORUM                 16   52 283 162
          THAT BLOOD, WHOSE LEAST DROPS SOVERAIGN BE        ADORO TE                             49   52 291 172
          YET LET THE POORE DROPS WEEP                      WEEPER                               55   52 307 120
          NEW DROPS, WASH OFF THE SWEAT OF THIS DAYE'S SORROWS. DESCRIPTION RELIGIOUS HOUSE      22   52 338 213
          OF PEARLY DROPS, & SENT HER NUMEROUSE BIRTH       UPON KINGS CORONATION                 7   MS 390 453
          TO MELT IN GENTLE DROPS, LETT THEM BE HEARD       AN ELEGIE ON DR PORTER               33   MS 395 476

SILVER-DROPS

          TELL DOWN HIS SILVER-DROPS UNTO THEE,             OUT OF GREEKE CUPID'S CRYER          61   46 159 519

DROPPING

          DROPPING WITH A BALMY SHOWRE                      ON A PRAYER BOOKE                   103   46 126 139
          DROPPING WITH A BAULMY SHOWR                      PRAYER TO GENTLE-WOMAN              109   52 328 139

HONEY-DROPPING

          HIS HONEY-DROPPING TOPS, PLOW'D BY HER BREATH     MUSICKS DUELL                        71   46 149 535

DROVE

          MINOTAURES, CYCLOPSES, WITH A DARKE DROVE         SOSPETTO D'HERODE                   351   46 109 216

DROVES

          ART THOU NOT LUCIFER. HEE TO WHOM THE DROVES      SOSPETTO D'HERODE                   233   46 109 216

DROWN

          WHAT NEED THEY HELP TO DROWN THY HEART.           UPON BLEEDING CRUCIFIX                7   52 288 110
          BENT ALL TO DROWN & OVERFLOW.                     UPON BLEEDING CRUCIFIX               30   52 288 110

DROWNED

          THEY THEMSELVES ARE DROWNED TOO.                  ON BLEEDING WOUNDS OF LORD           36   46 101 110
          THEY THEMSELVES ARE DROWNED TOO.                  UPON BLEEDING CRUCIFIX               32   52 288 110
          AN OCEAN COULD HAVE MADE T' HAVE DROWNED THEE.    UPON GUNPOWDER TREASON               36   MS 386 460
```

## DROWN'D

| | | | | |
|---|---|---|---|---|
| LIFES LATE FORSAKEN HOUSES ALL LAY DROWN'D | THE BEGINNING OF HELIODORUS | 16 | 46 158 | 517 |
| ALL ONE GREAT EYE, ALL DROWN'D IN ONE GREAT TEARE. | UPON BISHOP ANDREWES PICTURE | 4 | 46 163 | 490 |
| A DELUGE LEAST WE SHOULD BE DROWN'D. | ON BLEEDING WOUNDS OF LORD | 40 | 46 101 | 110 |
| WHEN HARPES AND HEARTS WERE DROWN'D IN TEARES. | PSALME 137 | 10 | 46 104 | 7 |
| A DELUGE LEAST WE SHOULD BE DROWN'D. | UPON BLEEDING CRUCIFIX | 36 | 52 288 | 110 |
| IF DROWN'D, SWEET IS THE DEATH INDUR'D FOR HIM, | ALEXIAS FIRST ELEGIE | 22 | 52 334 | 204 |

## DROWNE

| | | | | |
|---|---|---|---|---|
| TO DROWNE THE WANTONNESSE OF HIS WILD THIRST. | OUR LORD IN HIS CIRCUMCISION | 8 | 46 98 | 9 |
| WHAT NEED THEY HELPE TO DROWNE THINE HEART, | ON BLEEDING WOUNDS OF LORD | 19 | 46 101 | 110 |

## DROUNE

| | | | | |
|---|---|---|---|---|
| TO DROUNE THY SELFE IN THIS PURE PEARLY FLOOD. | UPON GUNPOWDER TREASON | 32 | MS 387 | 461 |

## DROWSINESSE

| | | | | |
|---|---|---|---|---|
| WHOSE DROWSINESSE HATH WRONG'D THE MUSES FRIEND. | TO THE MORNING | 2 | 46 183 | 497 |

## DRUGG

| | | | | |
|---|---|---|---|---|
| GOE NOW WITH SOME DAREING DRUGG, | IN PRAISE OF LESSIUS | 1 | 46 156 | 510 |
| GOE NOW, AND WITH SOME DARING DRUGG | TEMPERANCE | 1 | 52 342 | 510 |

## DRUNK

| | | | | |
|---|---|---|---|---|
| TILL DRUNK UP THE DEAR WOUNDS, I BE | SANCTA MARIA DOLORUM | 103 | 52 283 | 162 |

## DRUNKE

| | | | | |
|---|---|---|---|---|
| ALAS, THE EARTH, QUITE DRUNKE WITH TEARES, HAD REEL'D | UPON KINGS CORONATION | 9 | MS 390 | 453 |
| A BLOUD DRUNKE ERROUR SPILT THE COSTLY AYME | OUT OF GROTIUS | 29 | MS 398 | 198 |

## DRY

| | | | | |
|---|---|---|---|---|
| ON MY DRY PALLATS ROOFE TO REST | PSALME 137 | 23 | 46 104 | 7 |
| (THAT OLD DRY STOCKE) A DESPAIR'D BRANCH IS SPRUNG | SOSPETTO D'HERODE | 434 | 46 109 | 216 |
| MEANE WHILE HIS LOVED BANKES NOW DRY, | AN EPITAPH DOCTOR BROOKE | 7 | 46 175 | 465 |
| NOT MARK THE DRY REGARDLES DUST. | TO COUNTESSE OF DENBIGH | 52 | 52 236 | 146 |
| THAT THESE DRY LIDDS MIGHT BORROW | SANCTA MARIA DOLORUM | 43 | 52 283 | 162 |
| WHEN THIS DRY SOUL THOSE EYES SHALL SEE, | ADORO TE | 53 | 52 291 | 172 |

## DUE

| | | | | |
|---|---|---|---|---|
| AND THE DEARE MERITS OF YOUR MUSE, THEIR DUE, | UPON TWO GREENE APRICOCKES | 11 | 48 220 | 494 |
| (MY FLINTS) SOME DROPS ARE DUE | SANCTA MARIA DOLORUM | 16 | 52 283 | 162 |
| OF GREIFES HIS PORTION, WHO (HAD ALL THEIR DUE) | SANCTA MARIA DOLORUM | 79 | 52 283 | 162 |
| COULD PROVE THE WHOLE SUMME (TOO SURE) DUE TO HIM. | SANCTA MARIA DOLORUM | 94 | 52 283 | 162 |

## DULL

| | | | | |
|---|---|---|---|---|
| LEFT THE DIMME FACE OF THIS DULL HEMISPHAEARE, | UPON BISHOP ANDREWES PICTURE | 3 | 46 163 | 490 |
| LET THE DAMPS OF THY DULL BREATH | PSALME 23 | 40 | 46 102 | 5 |
| STARTLE THE DULL AYRE WITH A DISMALL RED. | SOSPETTO D'HERODE | 50 | 46 109 | 216 |
| THAT DULL MORTALITY MUST NOT KNOW A NAME. | ON A PRAYER BOOKE | 80 | 46 126 | 139 |
| DULL MISTS AND MELANCHOLY CLOUDS, TAKE DAY | ON A TREATISE OF CHARITY | 8 | 46 137 | 69 |
| AND LET NO DULL MISTS CHOAKE THE LIGHTS FAIRE GROWTH. | ON A FOULE MORNING | 4 | 46 181 | 495 |
| WITH YOUR DULL INFLUENCE, IT IS FOR YOU. | ON A FOULE MORNING | 33 | 46 181 | 495 |
| AND POINTING TO DULL MORPHEUS, BIDS ME TAKE | TO THE MORNING | 15 | 46 183 | 497 |
| DEFECTS I DRAW MINE OWNE DULL CHARACTER. | UPON TWO GREENE APRICOCKES | 32 | 48 220 | 494 |
| SAD SHADES AND SING DULL NIGHT ASLEEPE. | THOUGH NOW 'TIS NEITHER | 20 | MS 397 | 492 |
| DISBAND DULL FEARES. GIVE FAITH THE DAY. | TO COUNTESSE OF DENBIGH | 57 | 52 236 | 146 |
| (WHICH DULL MORTALITY MORE FEELES THEN HEARES) | TO THE NAME OF JESUS | 31 | 52 239 | 30 |
| THAT DULL MORTALITY MUST NOT KNOW A NAME. | PRAYER TO GENTLE-WOMAN | 86 | 52 328 | 139 |
| CHIDE YOUR DELAY. YEA THOSE DULL THINGS, | AGAINST IRRESOLUTION AND DELAY | 47 | 52 347 | 146 |
| DISBAND DULL FEARES; GIVE FAITH THE DAY. | AGAINST IRRESOLUTION AND DELAY | 81 | 52 347 | 146 |
| DULL SLUGGISH ILE. WHAT MORE THAN LETHARGY | ON GUNPOWDER-TREASON | 3 | MS 384 | 458 |

## DULY

| | | | | |
|---|---|---|---|---|
| AT TH' ORIENTALL GATES. AND DULY MOCKE | TO THE MORNING | 42 | 46 183 | 497 |
| WHILE YOUR EACH DAY'S DEVOTION DULY BRINGS | TO THE QUEEN'S MAJESTY | 27 | 52 261 | 47 |

## DUMBE

| | | | | |
|---|---|---|---|---|
| THOUGH SHEE BE DUMBE E'RE SINCE HIS DEATH, | UPON THE DEATH OF A GENTLEMAN | 17 | 46 166 | 472 |
| CHRIST BIDS THE DUMBE TONGUE SPEAKE. IT SPEAKES, THE SOUND | THE DUMBE HEALED | 1 | 46 87 | 16 |
| A SPEAKING DIVELL THIS, A DUMBE ONE THAT. | UPON DUMBE DEVILL CAST OUT | 2 | 46 93 | 14 |

## DUNGHILLS

| | | | | |
|---|---|---|---|---|
| GUILDED DUNGHILLS, GLORIOUS LYES, | TO SAME CONCERNING CHOISE | 14 | 52 331 | 66 |

## DURST

| | | | | |
|---|---|---|---|---|
| HATH SHUT THESE DOORES OF HEAVEN, THAT DURST | I AM THE DOORE | 5 | 46 90 | 17 |
| OF DEATH & FEIRCEST DANGERS, DURST WITH BRAVE | TO THE NAME OF JESUS | 201 | 52 239 | 30 |
| PROUD SONS OF DEATH. THAT DURST COMPELL | IN GLORIOUS EPIPHANIE | 109 | 52 253 | 39 |
| AND DURST NOT TOUCH IT. HEERE IT MADE NOE STAY. | ON GUNPOWDER-TREASON | 54 | MS 384 | 458 |

```
             NEVER DURST HATCH BEFORE. EXTRACTED SEE            UPON GUNPOWDER TREASON              7   MS 386 460

DURTY

             A DURTY PILLOW IN DEATH'S BED.                     UPON THE DEATH OF A GENTLEMAN      12   46 166 472
             THOSE DURTY SMUTCHES, WHICH THEIR FAIRE FRONTS WORE, AN ELEGY MR STANNINOW            13   MS 394 473

DUSKY

             MAY NOT ROW NEERER TO THESE DUSKY KINGS.           UPON GUNPOWDER TREASON             28   MS 387 461

DUST

             SAD REQUITALL, THUS MUCH DUST.                     UPON THE DEATH OF A GENTLEMAN      14   46 166 472
             NOR DOES THE DUST DESERVE YOUR BIRTH.              THE WEEPER                        130   46  79 120
             IN THE DUST. O NO.                                 THE TEARE                          33   46  84  50
             THE DUST SHALL NEVER BEE THY BED.                  THE TEARE                          34   46  84  50
             AND HASTE TO DASH HER INTO DUST.                   PSALME 137                         30   46 104   7
             FLIGHTS SCORNE THE LAZIE DUST, AND THINGS THAT DYE. AN APOLOGIE FOR HYMNE (TERESA)    28   46 136  59
             OUR DUST, THAT IN ONE DRAUGHT, MORTALITY           AN APOLOGIE FOR HYMNE (TERESA)     45   46 136  59
             SUCH AS (E'RE OUR DARK SINNES TO DUST BETRAY'D THEE) ON A TREATISE OF CHARITY          4   46 137  69
             FROM THE PALE DUST OF THAT STRANGE SACRIFICE       ON A TREATISE OF CHARITY           18   46 137  69
             (DISDAINFULL DUST AND ASHES) BEND THY BROW.        ON A TREATISE OF CHARITY           42   46 137  69
             IN THE DUST. PITTY NOW SPEND                       ANOTHER ON HERRYS                  57   46 170 469
             THE WORLD--ALL DARING DUST AND ASHES. ONELY YOU    UPON STANINOUGH'S DEATH            29   46 175 475
             NOT MARK THE DRY REGARDLES DUST.                   TO COUNTESSE OF DENBIGH            52   52 236 146
             THAT WE, DARK SONS OF DUST & SORROW,               TO THE NAME OF JESUS               99   52 239  30
             OF DUST, WHERE IN THE BASHFULL SHADES OF NIGHT     TO THE NAME OF JESUS              233   52 239  30
             OF ADULTEROUS GODLES DUST                          IN GLORIOUS EPIPHANIE             102   52 253  39
             LET FROWARD DUST THEN DOE IT'S KIND.               CHARITAS NIMIA                     29   52 280  48
             BARGAIN'D WITH DEATH & WELL-BESEEMING DUST         CHARITAS NIMIA                     56   52 280  48
             AND CRUMBLED INTO CONTRITE DUST.                   DIES IRAE                          66   52 298 186
             NOR DOES THE DUST DESERVE YOUR BIRTH.              WEEPER                            172   52 307 120
             FLIGHTS SCORN THE LAZY DUST, & THINGS THAT DY.     AN APOLOGIE FOR (TERESA) HYMNE     28   52 322  59
             OUR DUST, THAT AT ONE DRAUGHT, MORTALITY           AN APOLOGIE FOR (TERESA) HYMNE     45   52 322  59
             YOUR SOUL TO ANY SON OF DUST.                      TO SAME CONCERNING CHOISE          19   52 331  66
             THE WORLD. ALL-DARING DUST & ASHES. ONLY YOU       DEATH'S LECTURE                    31   52 340 475
             (THE DUST OF WARRE CLEANE WIP'D AWAY)              IN CICATRICES DOMINI JESU          18   MS 381  27
             TO TOSSE POORE MEN LIKE DUST INTO THE AIRE.        ON GUNPOWDER-TREASON               40   MS 384 458
             IN VAILES OF DUST THEIR SILKEN HEADS THEY'LE HIDE. AN ELEGIE ON DR PORTER             25   MS 395 476

DUSTY

             DARKE, DUSTY MAN, HE NEEDS WOULD SINGLE FORTH,     SOSPETTO D'HERODE                 217   46 109 216
             MAKING THEM SKIP OUT OF THEIR DUSTY BED.           ON GUNPOWDER-TREASON               30   MS 384 458

DUTEOUS

             THY GOLDEN INDEX. WITH A DUTEOUS HAND              IN GLORIOUS EPIPHANIE             251   52 253  39
             THIS IS THE MISTRESSE FLAME. & DUTEOUS HE          FLAMING HEART                      17   52 324  61

DUTY

             OWES A DUTY.                                       OUT OF THE ITALIAN (1)             41   46 188 545
             THAT OWES NOT ALL HIS DUTY                         WISHES SUPPOSED MISTRESSE          17   46 195 479
             THEIR WISDOME NOW, AS WELL AS DUTY,                IN GLORIOUS EPIPHANIE             185   52 253  39
             THY CRIME IS TOO MUCH DUTY.                        VEXILLA REGIS                      27   52 277 156

DWELL

             BECAUSE THOSE PRETIOUS MYSTERYES THAT DWELL,       MUSICKS DUELL                     143   46 149 535
             WITHIN THE LIPS OF LOVE AND JOY DOTH DWELL         UPON ASSE THAT BORE SAVIOUR         3   46  90  19
             THERE I'LE DWELL FOR EVER, THERE                   PSALME 23                          67   46 102   5
             A THOUSAND ANGELLS IN ONE POINT CAN DWELL.         ON A PRAYER BOOKE                   8   46 126 139
             PEACE SURE WITH PIETY, THOUGH IT DWELL IN SPAINE.  AN APOLOGIE FOR HYMNE (TERESA)     20   46 136  59
             TO MAJESTY, AND FULNESSE, DEIGNE TO DWELL,         UPON YORKE HIS BIRTH               24   46 176 500
             AND NAME DWELL SWEET IN SOME ETERNALL STORY.       UPON YORKE HIS BIRTH              105   46 176 500
             THY DOWNY FINGER, DWELL UPON THEIR EYES,           TO THE MORNING                     57   46 183 497
             THEN LET AMOROUS KISSES DWELL                      OUT OF CATULLUS                     9   46 194 523
             A THOUSAND BLEST ARABIAS DWELL.                    TO THE NAME OF JESUS              184   52 239  30
             SHOULD MANKIND DWELL                               CHARITAS NIMIA                     12   52 280  48
             TEN THOUSAND ANGELS IN ONE POINT CAN DWELL.        PRAYER TO GENTLE-WOMAN             14   52 328 139
             YETT O WHAT END. WHERE DOES THE PERIOD DWELL       OUT OF GROTIUS                      9   MS 398 198

DWELL'T

             FULL SWEETLY WITH IT SELFE HAD DWELL'T AT HOME.    ALEXIAS THIRD ELEGIE               12   52 336 209

DWELT

             WHOSE BANKES THE MUSES DWELT UPON.                 AN EPITAPH DOCTOR BROOKE            3   46 175 465

DWELLING

             THY TRAITEROUS ROOT A DWELLING IN MY GROUND.       HORATIJ ILLE & NEFASTO             14   MS 382 530

DYING

             FLOWES IN THY SONG (O FAIRE, O DYING SWAN.)        UPON OUR LORDS LAST DISCOURSE       2   46  95  21
             HEE CALLS HOME MY SOULE FROM DYING.                PSALME 23                          18   46 102   5
             ALL HOPE OF NEVER DYING, HERE LYES DEAD.           ANOTHER ON HERRYS                  62   46 170 469
             THAT SHUTS NIGHTS DYING EYES, SHALL OPEN MINE.     TO THE MORNING                     46   46 183 497
             WHEN MY DYING                                      OUT OF THE ITALIAN (1)             49   46 188 545
             FOR A DYING MAYDENHEAD.                            WISHES SUPPOSED MISTRESSE          75   46 195 479
```

| | | | | | |
|---|---|---|---|---|---|
| MY DYING LIFE MAY DRAW A NEW, & NEVER FLEETING BREATH. | OFFICE H. CROSS RECOMMENDATION | 8 | 52 | 276 | 106 |
| OF LIVING DEATH & DYING LIFE. | A SONG | 14 | 52 | 327 | 65 |
| OR THAT THE DYING LILLY DID BESTOW | UPON BIRTH PRINCESSE E | 49 | MS | 391 | 456 |

DAYLY-DYING

| | | | | | |
|---|---|---|---|---|---|
| A LONG & DAYLY-DYING LIFE, WHICH BREATHS | DESCRIPTION RELIGIOUS HOUSE | 23 | 52 | 338 | 213 |

NEVER-DYING

| | | | | | |
|---|---|---|---|---|---|
| THE NEVER-DYING LIFE, OF A LONG DEATH. | SOSPETTO D'HERODE | 60 | 46 | 109 | 216 |

EAGLE

| | | | | | |
|---|---|---|---|---|---|
| BY ALL THE EAGLE IN THEE, ALL THE DOVE. | FLAMING HEART | 95 | 52 | 324 | 61 |

EAGLES

| | | | | | |
|---|---|---|---|---|---|
| THE POINTS OF HER YOUNG EAGLES EYES. | A HYMNE OF THE NATIVITY | 70 | 46 | 106 | 76 |
| OF LITTLE EAGLES, AND YOUNG LOVES, WHOSE HIGH | AN APOLOGIE FOR HYMNE (TERESA) | 27 | 46 | 136 | 59 |
| (SHARPE SIGHTED AS THE EAGLES EYE, THAT CAN | ON FRONTISPIECE ISAACSONS | 9 | 46 | 191 | 491 |
| EAGLES, AND SHUTT OUR EYES THAT WE MAY SEE. | IN GLORIOUS EPIPHANIE | 232 | 52 | 253 | 39 |
| OF LITTLE EAGLES & YOUNG LOVES, WHOSE HIGH | AN APOLOGIE FOR (TERESA) HYMNE | 27 | 52 | 322 | 59 |
| FLEDG'D WITH HER EAGLES WING. THE VERY CHAINE | HORATIJ ILLE & NEFASTO | 26 | MS | 382 | 530 |
| THAT ROME'S BOLD EAGLES NOW WERE BLINDED QUITE, | UPON KINGS CORONATION | 34 | MS | 390 | 453 |

EARE

| | | | | | |
|---|---|---|---|---|---|
| THIS THINE EYES JEWELL IN HER EARE. | THE TEARE | 12 | 46 | 84 | 50 |
| NOT TO HIS EARE, BUT TO HIS EYE. | THE BLIND CURED | 6 | 46 | 91 | 19 |
| BUT IN HER EYE, OR IN HER EARE, | LOVES HOROSCOPE | 42 | 46 | 185 | 483 |
| BUT IN HER EYE, OR IN HER EARE. | LOVES HOROSCOPE | 48 | 46 | 185 | 483 |
| THOSE TO THE EYE, THEN TO THE EARE. | AN EPITAPH UPON ASHTON | 14 | 46 | 192 | 464 |
| SAVE THAT WHICH LETS IN FAITH, THE EARE. | ADORO TE | 10 | 52 | 291 | 172 |
| THERE THESE BRAVE SOULES DEALE TO EACH WONDRING EARE | HORATIJ ILLE & NEFASTO | 45 | MS | 382 | 530 |
| UNTO A CHOYCE, AND CURIOUS EARE. | UPON DEATH OF A FREIND | 2 | MS | 393 | 477 |

EARS

| | | | | | |
|---|---|---|---|---|---|
| COME DEATH, COME BANDS, NOR DO YOU SHRINK, MY EARS, | I AM READY NOT ONELY BOUND | 1 | 46 | 98 | 29 |

EARES

| | | | | | |
|---|---|---|---|---|---|
| PREFERRE SOFT ANTHEMS TO THE EARES OF MEN, | MUSICKS DUELL | 78 | 46 | 149 | 535 |
| THEIR MASTERS BLEST SOULE (SNATCHT OUT AT HIS EARES | MUSICKS DUELL | 147 | 46 | 149 | 535 |
| TO STRIKE AT EARES, IS TO TAKE HEED THERE BEE | ON ST. PETER CUTTING MALCHUS | 3 | 46 | 97 | 22 |
| WOULD HAVE A SONG CARV'D TO THEIR EARES | PSALME 137 | 8 | 46 | 104 | 7 |
| AT LAST HER LISTING EARES THE NOISE O'RETAKES, | SOSPETTO D'HERODE | 300 | 46 | 109 | 216 |
| WORDS WHICH ARE NOT HEARD WITH EARES. | ON A PRAYER BOOKE | 59 | 46 | 126 | 139 |
| KEEPE SUCH DISTANCE FROM THINE EARES. | UPON DEATH OF DESIRED HERRYS | 62 | 46 | 166 | 467 |
| THAT IN THY EARES THUS KEEPS A MURMURING. | UPON YORKE HIS BIRTH | 107 | 46 | 176 | 500 |
| SOLLICITERS OF SOULES OR EARES. | TO THE NAME OF JESUS | 79 | 52 | 239 | 30 |
| OF WARBLING SERAPHIM TO THE EARES OF LOVE, | TO THE NAME OF JESUS | 106 | 52 | 239 | 30 |
| WORDS WHICH ARE NOT HEARD WITH EARES | PRAYER TO GENTLE-WOMAN | 65 | 52 | 328 | 139 |
| OFT TO THY EASY EARES HATH THIS SHRILL TONGUE | LUKE 2. QUAERIT JESUM | 29 | MS | 379 | 11 |
| OF HIS CAPTIVITY RINGS IN HIS EARES. | HORATIJ ILLE & NEFASTO | 29 | MS | 382 | 530 |
| WHISPER THY PLAINTS TO TH' OCEANS CURTEOUS EARES, | AN ELEGIE ON DR PORTER | 37 | MS | 395 | 476 |

EARLIER

| | | | | | |
|---|---|---|---|---|---|
| FAIRE HOPE. OUR EARLIER HEAVEN. BY THEE | ON HOPE | 51 | 46 | 143 | 71 |

EARLYER

| | | | | | |
|---|---|---|---|---|---|
| FAIR HOPE. OUR EARLYER HEAV'N BY THEE | (ON) HOPE | 21 | 52 | 345 | 71 |

EARLY

| | | | | | |
|---|---|---|---|---|---|
| (MOST DIVINE SERVICE) WHOSE SO EARLY LAY, | MUSICKS DUELL | 81 | 46 | 149 | 535 |
| WHOSE EARLY LOVE | ON A PRAYER BOOKE | 94 | 46 | 126 | 139 |
| THE EARLY LARKES SHRILL ORIZONS TO BE | TO THE MORNING | 43 | 46 | 183 | 497 |
| THE YEARE HAD FOUND SOME FRUIT EARLY AS YOU. | UPON TWO GREENE APRICOCKES | 12 | 48 | 220 | 494 |
| THE EARLY PRIME BLUSHES TO SAY | OFFICE H. CROSS PRIME | 1 | 52 | 267 | 91 |
| WHOSE EARLY LOVE | PRAYER TO GENTLE-WOMAN | 100 | 52 | 328 | 139 |
| SURE IN MY EARLY WOES STARRES WERE AT STRIFE. | ALEXIAS FIRST ELEGIE | 5 | 52 | 334 | 204 |
| TOO EARLY RISE. | LUKE 2. QUAERIT JESUM | 36 | MS | 379 | 11 |

EARTH

| | | | | | |
|---|---|---|---|---|---|
| FROM THEIR HARD MOTHER EARTH, SPRANG HARDY MEN. | OUT OF VIRGIL | 30 | 46 | 155 | 529 |
| PROMISE THE EARTH. TO COUNTERSHINE | THE WEEPER | 11 | 46 | 79 | 120 |
| IT IS NOT FOR OUR EARTH AND US, | THE WEEPER | 17 | 46 | 79 | 120 |
| O WHITHER. FOR THE SLUTTISH EARTH | THE WEEPER | 128 | 46 | 79 | 120 |
| HEAVEN IN EARTH. AND GOD IN MAN. | A HYMNE OF THE NATIVITY | 56 | 46 | 106 | 76 |
| LIFTS EARTH TO HEAVEN, STOOPS HEAVEN TO EARTH. | A HYMNE OF THE NATIVITY | 58 | 46 | 106 | 76 |
| LIFTS EARTH TO HEAVEN, STOOPS HEAVEN TO EARTH. | A HYMNE OF THE NATIVITY | 58 | 46 | 106 | 76 |
| THY FAMES FULL NOISE, MAKES PROUD THE PATIENT EARTH. | SOSPETTO D'HERODE | 29 | 46 | 109 | 216 |
| WAS THE GREAT BUSINESSE BOTH OF HEAV'N AND EARTH. | SOSPETTO D'HERODE | 120 | 46 | 109 | 216 |
| FROM A CHAST VIRGIN WOMBE, SHOULD BLESSE THE EARTH. | SOSPETTO D'HERODE | 160 | 46 | 109 | 216 |
| COME TRY WHO DARES, HEAV'N, EARTH, WHAT ERE DOST BOAST. | SOSPETTO D'HERODE | 251 | 46 | 109 | 216 |
| EARTH NOW SHOULD SEE, AND TREMBLE AT THE SIGHT. | SOSPETTO D'HERODE | 256 | 46 | 109 | 216 |
| IN OUR GREAT PROJECTS, BOTH 'GAINST HEAV'N AND EARTH. | SOSPETTO D'HERODE | 286 | 46 | 109 | 216 |
| THAT CAN EXALT WEAK EARTH, AND SO REFINE | AN APOLOGIE FOR HYMNE (TERESA) | 44 | 46 | 136 | 59 |

| | | | | | |
|---|---|---|---|---|---|
| SHOT THEE LIKE LIGHTNING, TO TH'ASTONISHT EARTH. | ON A TREATISE OF CHARITY | 6 | 46 | 137 | 69 |
| OF HEAVEN, AND HUMBLE PRIDE OF EARTH. | ON THE ASSUMPTION | 60 | 46 | 139 | 114 |
| EARTH HER BEST PERFECTION. | UPON DEATH OF DESIRED HERRYS | 27 | 46 | 168 | 467 |
| OF THE GLAD EARTH THEY TREAD ON. WHILE WITH THEE | UPON YORKE HIS BIRTH | 21 | 46 | 176 | 500 |
| GLADNESSE SHALL CLOATH THE EARTH, WE WILL INSTILE | ON A FOULE MORNING | 9 | 46 | 181 | 495 |
| AND WHISPER'D THE CONFEDERATE EARTH | LOVES HOROSCOPE | 28 | 46 | 185 | 483 |
| EARTH AND HEAVEN | OUT OF THE ITALIAN (1) | 28 | 46 | 188 | 545 |
| AND TEACH HER FAIRE STEPS TO OUR EARTH. | WISHES SUPPOSED MISTRESSE | 9 | 46 | 195 | 479 |
| BRING ALL YOUR HOUSHOLD STUFFE OF HEAVN ON EARTH, | TO THE NAME OF JESUS | 63 | 52 | 239 | 30 |
| BRING ALL YOUR LUTES & HARPS OF HEAVN & EARTH. | TO THE NAME OF JESUS | 74 | 52 | 239 | 30 |
| LO HOW THE LABORING EARTH | TO THE NAME OF JESUS | 131 | 52 | 239 | 30 |
| CONTEND, YE POWRES OF HEAV'N & EARTH. | IN HOLY NATIVITY | 41 | 52 | 246 | 76 |
| HEAVEN IN EARTH, & GOD IN MAN. | IN HOLY NATIVITY | 82 | 52 | 246 | 76 |
| LIFTS EARTH TO HEAVEN, STOOPES HEAV'N TO EARTH. | IN HOLY NATIVITY | 84 | 52 | 246 | 76 |
| LIFTS EARTH TO HEAVEN, STOOPES HEAV'N TO EARTH. | IN HOLY NATIVITY | 84 | 52 | 246 | 76 |
| HEAVN & EARTH SHALL FIND NO PLACE. | DIES IRAE | 6 | 52 | 298 | 186 |
| A PIECE OF HEAV'NLY EARTH. PURER & BRIGHTER | IN GLORIOUS ASSUMPTION B. LADY | 3 | 52 | 304 | 114 |
| OF HEAVN. THE HUMBLE PRIDE OF EARTH. | IN GLORIOUS ASSUMPTION B. LADY | 65 | 52 | 304 | 114 |
| PROMISE THE EARTH TO COUNTER SHINE | WEEPER | 11 | 52 | 307 | 120 |
| IT IS NOT FOR OUR EARTH & US | WEEPER | 17 | 52 | 307 | 120 |
| FOR SURE THE SORDID EARTH | WEEPER | 170 | 52 | 307 | 120 |
| THAT CAN EXALT WEAK EARTH. & SO REFINE | AN APOLOGIE FOR (TERESA) HYMNE | 44 | 52 | 322 | 59 |
| THUS VEX THE EARTH & TEARE THE BEAUTEOUS SKYES. | ALEXIAS SECONDE ELEGIE | 10 | 52 | 335 | 207 |
| I'D KNOW NO NAME OF LOVE ON EARTH BUT YOU. | ALEXIAS THIRD ELEGIE | 44 | 52 | 336 | 209 |
| SO HARDLY BETWIXT EARTH AND HEAVEN. | AGAINST IRRESOLUTION AND DELAY | 62 | 52 | 347 | 146 |
| OF SOE FAIRE EARTH. | LUKE 2. QUAERIT JESUM | 24 | MS | 379 | 11 |
| THAT EARTH A SHOURE OF STONES TO HEAVEN SHALL SEND, | ON GUNPOWDER-TREASON | 22 | MS | 384 | 458 |
| SHALL CHOAKE THE GAPING EARTH, WHICH THEN SHALL FRY | ON GUNPOWDER-TREASON | 25 | MS | 384 | 458 |
| IT QUITE FORGOTT. THE FEARFULL EARTH GAVE WAY. | ON GUNPOWDER-TREASON | 53 | MS | 384 | 458 |
| HEAVEN WAS ASHAM'D, TO SEE OUR MOTHER EARTH | UPON GUNPOWDER TREASON | 11 | MS | 386 | 460 |
| T' ENTOMBE THE LAB'RING EARTH. FOR SURELY SHEE | UPON GUNPOWDER TREASON | 51 | MS | 386 | 460 |
| IN THIS BLEST EARTH HEAVENS BRIGHT EPITOME, | UPON KINGS CORONATION | 12 | MS | 389 | 454 |
| (AS TOKENS OF HER GREIFE) UNTO THE EARTH. | UPON KINGS CORONATION | 8 | MS | 390 | 453 |
| ALAS, THE EARTH, QUITE DRUNKE WITH TEARES, HAD REEL'D | UPON KINGS CORONATION | 9 | MS | 390 | 453 |
| FOR EARTH, 'T HAD BEENE AN AMPLE PORTION. | UPON BIRTH PRINCESSE E | 28 | MS | 391 | 456 |
| POORE EARTH HATH NOT ENOUGH PERFECTION. | UPON BIRTH PRINCESSE E | 41 | MS | 391 | 456 |
| OF HEAVEN, & EARTH, & OF ALL RARITIE. | UPON BIRTH PRINCESSE E | 58 | MS | 391 | 456 |
| IS TH' EARTH DISROBED OF HER APRON WHITE, | AN ELEGY MR STANNINOW | 5 | MS | 394 | 473 |
| HEAV'N, EARTH, AND SEA, MY TRIUMPHS. WHAT REMAIN'D | OUT OF GROTIUS | 85 | MS | 398 | 198 |

EARTH-LABORING

| | | | | | |
|---|---|---|---|---|---|
| AND LASH EARTH-LABORING SOULS. | DESCRIPTION RELIGIOUS HOUSE | 27 | 52 | 338 | 213 |

EARTH-NURST

| | | | | | |
|---|---|---|---|---|---|
| OF POIS'NOUS AND UNNATURALL LOVES. EARTH-NURST. | SOSPETTO D'HERODE | 127 | 46 | 109 | 216 |

EARTH'S

| | | | | | |
|---|---|---|---|---|---|
| THRIV'D IN THESE HAPPY GROUNDS, THE EARTH'S JUST PRIDE. | UPON DEATH OF HERRYS | 3 | 46 | 167 | 466 |
| DEAR HOPE. EARTH'S DOWRY, & HEAVN'S DEBT. | (ON) HOPE | 1 | 52 | 345 | 71 |
| MURDRED THE EARTH'S JUST PRIDE WITH A RUDE KISSE. | AN ELEGY MR STANNINOW | 48 | MS | 394 | 473 |

EARTHS

| | | | | | |
|---|---|---|---|---|---|
| WITH EARTHS LARGE MASSE, DOTH CHERISH AND ASSIST | OUT OF VIRGIL | 8 | 46 | 155 | 529 |
| DEARE HOPE. EARTHS DOWRY, AND HEAVENS DEBT. | ON HOPE | 11 | 46 | 143 | 71 |

EARTHLY

| | | | | | |
|---|---|---|---|---|---|
| GUILDED I'TH' BEAMES OF EARTHLY KINGS | A HYMNE OF THE NATIVITY | 72 | 46 | 106 | 76 |
| GUILDED ITH' BEAMES OF EARTHLY KINGS. | IN HOLY NATIVITY | 92 | 52 | 246 | 76 |

EARTHQUAKE

| | | | | | |
|---|---|---|---|---|---|
| AND MAKES A PRETTY EARTHQUAKE IN HER BREAST. | MUSICKS DUELL | 89 | 46 | 149 | 535 |

EASE

| | | | | | |
|---|---|---|---|---|---|
| WEEPING IS THE EASE OF WOE, | THE WEEPER | 74 | 46 | 79 | 120 |
| (WEEPING IS THE EASE OF WOE) | WEEPER | 56 | 52 | 307 | 120 |
| SITTING SOE LONG AT EASE IN HER DARKE DENNE. | UPON GUNPOWDER TREASON | 24 | MS | 386 | 460 |
| BUT GIVE ME LEAVE TO EASE IT WITH MY HAND. | UPON BIRTH PRINCESSE E | 16 | MS | 391 | 456 |

EASILY

| | | | | | |
|---|---|---|---|---|---|
| DEATH'S BUSIE SEARCH I'LE EASILY BEGUILE. | SICKE IMPLORE SHADOW | 2 | 46 | 87 | 28 |
| NATURE (METHINKS) MIGHT EASILY MEND HER GROWTH. | UPON TWO GREENE APRICOCKES | 22 | 48 | 220 | 494 |

EAST

| | | | | | |
|---|---|---|---|---|---|
| THY TOMBE, THE UNIVERSALL EAST, | EASTER DAY | 4 | 46 | 100 | 26 |
| NOT FROM THE EAST, BUT FROM THY EYES. | A HYMNE OF THE NATIVITY | 22 | 46 | 106 | 76 |
| WEE SAW THINE EYES BREAK FROM THE EAST, | A HYMNE OF THE NATIVITY | 31 | 46 | 106 | 76 |
| MAKE PROUD THE RUBY PORTALLS OF THE EAST. | SOSPETTO D'HERODE | 122 | 46 | 109 | 216 |
| LET HIM MAKE POORE THE PURPLE EAST. | AN HIMNE FOR CIRCUMCISION | 17 | 46 | 141 | 37 |
| FRESH FROM THE ROSIE EAST REJOYC'T TO PLAY. | UPON DEATH OF HERRYS | 16 | 46 | 167 | 466 |
| CHAST AS THAT VIRGIN HONOUR OF THE EAST, | UPON YORKE HIS BIRTH | 83 | 46 | 176 | 500 |
| STAGGERS OUT OF THE EAST, LOOSES HER WAY | ON A FOULE MORNING | 2 | 46 | 181 | 495 |
| THE RUBY WINDOWES WHICH INRICH'T THE EAST | TO THE NAME OF JESUS | 218 | 52 | 239 | 30 |
| NOT FROM THE EAST, BUT FROM THINE EYES. | IN HOLY NATIVITY | 22 | 52 | 246 | 76 |
| WE SAW THINE EYES BREAK FROM THEIR EAST | IN HOLY NATIVITY | 74 | 52 | 246 | 76 |

|  |  |  |  |  |  |
|---|---|---|---|---|---|
| LET HIM MAKE POOR THE PURPLE EAST. | NEW YEAR'S DAY | 17 | 52 | 251 | 37 |
| THE EAST IS COME | IN GLORIOUS EPIPHANIE | 13 | 52 | 253 | 39 |
| TO THEE, THOU DAY OF NIGHT. THOU EAST OF WEST. | IN GLORIOUS EPIPHANIE | 22 | 52 | 253 | 39 |
| TO THEE, THE WORLD'S GREAT UNIVERSAL EAST. | IN GLORIOUS EPIPHANIE | 24 | 52 | 253 | 39 |
| FROM THIS WORLD'S EAST THE OTHER'S WEST. | IN GLORIOUS EPIPHANIE | 112 | 52 | 253 | 39 |

## TH'EAST

|  |  |  |  |  |  |
|---|---|---|---|---|---|
| BRINGING HIM NOTHING BUT NEW FEARES FROM TH'EAST, | SOSPETTO D'HERODE | 500 | 46 | 109 | 216 |

## EASTE

|  |  |  |  |  |  |
|---|---|---|---|---|---|
| WE SAW THINE EYES BREAK FROM THEIR EASTE | IN HOLY NATIVITY | 33 | 52 | 246 | 76 |

## EASTERN

|  |  |  |  |  |  |
|---|---|---|---|---|---|
| OF WHATSOE'RE PERFUM'D THY EASTERN NEST. | ON A TREATISE OF CHARITY | 10 | 46 | 137 | 69 |
| (LOVE'S EASTERN WINDOWES) ALL WIDE OPE | TO THE NAME OF JESUS | 146 | 52 | 239 | 30 |
| OF ALL HIS EASTERN PARAMOURS. | NEW YEAR'S DAY | 34 | 52 | 251 | 37 |
| THE WORLD'S NEW EASTERN WINDOW BIN | O GLORIOSA DOMINA | 19 | 52 | 302 | 194 |
| THE EASTERN PRINCES TO THEIR INFANT KING. | ALEXIAS SECONDE ELEGIE | 28 | 52 | 335 | 207 |

## EASTERNE

|  |  |  |  |  |  |
|---|---|---|---|---|---|
| OF ALL HIS EASTERNE PARAMOURS. | AN HIMNE FOR CIRCUMCISION | 34 | 46 | 141 | 37 |
| BLUSHING FROM THINE EASTERNE BED. | UPON DEATH OF DESIRED HERRYS | 16 | 46 | 168 | 467 |
| THEN LET THE EASTERNE WORLD BRAGGE AND BE PROUD | UPON YORKE HIS BIRTH | 86 | 46 | 176 | 500 |

## EASY

|  |  |  |  |  |  |
|---|---|---|---|---|---|
| OFT TO THY EASY FARES HATH THIS SHRILL TONGUE | LUKE 2. QUAERIT JESUM | 29 | MS | 379 | 11 |
| GOOD WINE IN ALL POYNTS. BUT THE EASY RATE. | OUT OF GROTIUS | 56 | MS | 398 | 198 |

## EASIE

|  |  |  |  |  |  |
|---|---|---|---|---|---|
| SEE HERE AN EASIE FEAST THAT KNOWES NO WOUND, | ON MIRACLE OF LOAVES | 1 | 46 | 86 | 15 |

## EAT

|  |  |  |  |  |  |
|---|---|---|---|---|---|
| AND COMMING LATE HAD EAT UP GUESTS AND ALL, | THE BEGINNING OF HELIODORUS | 27 | 46 | 158 | 517 |
| THE SAME LEAVE BOTH TO EAT & LIVE. | ADORO TE | 42 | 52 | 291 | 172 |

## EATE

|  |  |  |  |  |  |
|---|---|---|---|---|---|
| BUT DARES DESTRUCTION EATE THESE CANDID BREASTS, | UPON GUNPOWDER TREASON | 37 | MS | 387 | 461 |

## EATES

|  |  |  |  |  |  |
|---|---|---|---|---|---|
| THY HUNGER FEELES NOT WHAT HE EATES. | BLESSED BE THE PAPS | 2 | 46 | 94 | 14 |
| THE CHILD OF DEATH EATES HIMSELF DEAD. | LAUDA SION SALVATOREM | 52 | 52 | 294 | 178 |

## ECCHO'S

|  |  |  |  |  |  |
|---|---|---|---|---|---|
| WING'D WITH THEIR OWNE WILD ECCHO'S PRATLING FLY. | MUSICKS DUELL | 92 | 46 | 149 | 535 |

## ECLIPSE

|  |  |  |  |  |  |
|---|---|---|---|---|---|
| HOW HATH ONE BLACKE ECLIPSE CANCELL'D, AND CROST | SOSPETTO D'HERODE | 75 | 46 | 109 | 216 |
| FOR THAT ONE ECLIPSE HE MADE | IN GLORIOUS EPIPHANIE | 119 | 52 | 253 | 39 |

## LOVE-ECLIPSE

|  |  |  |  |  |  |
|---|---|---|---|---|---|
| WITH AN ELABORATE LOVE-ECLIPSE | IN GLORIOUS EPIPHANIE | 152 | 52 | 253 | 39 |

## ECLIPSED

|  |  |  |  |  |  |
|---|---|---|---|---|---|
| AND BE ECLIPSED WITH AN ENVIOUS SHADE. | AN ELEGY MR STANNINOW | 44 | MS | 394 | 473 |

## ECLIPS'D

|  |  |  |  |  |  |
|---|---|---|---|---|---|
| FORCING HIS SOMETIMES ECLIPS'D FACE TO BE | IN GLORIOUS EPIPHANIE | 115 | 52 | 253 | 39 |

## EDOM

|  |  |  |  |  |  |
|---|---|---|---|---|---|
| BUT EDOM CRUELL THOU. THOU CRYD'ST DOWNE, DOWNE | PSALME 137 | 27 | 46 | 104 | 7 |

## EFFECT

|  |  |  |  |  |  |
|---|---|---|---|---|---|
| WHAT FORCE CANNOT EFFECT, FRAUD SHALL DEVISE. | SOSPETTO D'HERODE | 248 | 46 | 109 | 216 |

## EFFECTS

|  |  |  |  |  |  |
|---|---|---|---|---|---|
| FOOTSTEPS OF THEIR EFFECTS, HEE TRAC'D TOO WELL, | SOSPETTO D'HERODE | 146 | 46 | 109 | 216 |

## EFFECTUALL

|  |  |  |  |  |  |
|---|---|---|---|---|---|
| EFFECTUALL WHISPERS WHOSE STILL VOYCE, | ON A PRAYER BOOKE | 61 | 46 | 126 | 139 |
| EFFECTUALL WISPERS, WHOSE STILL VOICE | PRAYER TO GENTLE-WOMAN | 67 | 52 | 328 | 139 |

## AEGYPT

|  |  |  |  |  |  |
|---|---|---|---|---|---|
| AEGYPT. A LONG FAREWELL TO THEE | IN GLORIOUS EPIPHANIE | 50 | 52 | 253 | 39 |

EGYPTIAN

    ASSYRIAN TYRANTS, OR EGYPTIAN KNEW.              SOSPETTO D'HERODE             366  46 109 216
    TH' EGYPTIAN PYRAMIDS THEMSELVES MUST LIVE.)    ON FRONTISPIECE ISAACSONS    20  46 191 491

AEGYPTIAN

    FOR CHEAP AEGYPTIAN DEITYES.                     IN GLORIOUS EPIPHANIE        88  52 253  39

TH'AEGYPTIAN

    THEN WERE TH'AEGYPTIAN (BY THE LIFE, THESE GIVE,  ON FRONTISPIECE ISAACSONS    19  46 191 491

EITHER

    THOUGH AS AT SECOND HAND, FROM EITHER HEART.     SANCTA MARIA DOLORUM        70  52 283 162

ELABORATE

    WITH AN ELABORATE LOVE-ECLIPSE                IN GLORIOUS EPIPHANIE       152  52 253  39

ELECT

    THE HEIRS ELECT OF LOVE. WHOSE NAMES BELONG     TO THE NAME OF JESUS         9  52 239  30

ELEGY

    SOMEWHAT MORE HORRID THAN AN ELEGY.            AN ELEGIE ON DR PORTER     12  MS 395 476

ELGIE

    THEIR SHACKLED TONGUES TO CHANT AN ELGIE.      AN ELEGIE ON DR PORTER     36  MS 395 476

ELFE

    THOUGH THOU SEE THE CRAFTY ELFE,              OUT OF GREEKE CUPID'S CRYER  60  46 159 519

ELME

    UPON THY ROYALL ELME (FAIRE VINE) AND WHEN     UPON YORKE HIS BIRTH       103  46 176 500

ELOQUENCE

    STOPT THE MOUTH OF ELOQUENCE,                 UPON THE DEATH OF A GENTLEMAN  16  46 166 472
    OF ALL THY WATRY ELOQUENCE.                  UPON THE DEATH OF A GENTLEMAN  32  46 166 472
    IN ELOQUENCE.                                  UPON ASSE THAT BORE SAVIOUR    2  46  90  19
    I LEARNT TO KNOW THAT LOVE IS ELOQUENCE.       AN APOLOGIE FOR HYMNE (TERESA)  8  46 136  59
    I LEARN'T TO KNOW THAT LOVE IS ELOQUENCE       AN APOLOGIE FOR (TERESA) HYMNE  8  52 322  59
    EXTRACTED HAVE A BALMY ELOQUENCE.             UPON BIRTH PRINCESSE E     10  MS 391 456

ELSE

    WHY ELSE HAD BAALAMS ASSE A TONGUE TO CHIDE    UPON ASSE THAT BORE SAVIOUR    5  46  90  19
    LEAVE, LEAVE, FOR SHAME, OR ELSE (GOOD JUDGE) DECREE,  TO PONTIUS WASHING HANDS    15  46  94  23
    (FOR WHAT ELSE IS MY LIFE.) LO I BEQUEATH.     OUR LORD IN HIS CIRCUMCISION    2  46  98   9
    FOR IN THE LIFE OUGHT ELSE CAN GIVE,          LOVES HOROSCOPE              45  46 185 483
    OR ELSE PARTAKE MY FLAMES                    OUT OF THE ITALIAN (2)     11  46 190 547
    TO THAT ONE SENSE, MADE ALL ELSE THRALL,       OUT OF THE ITALIAN (3)      7  46 190 549
    AND FULL OF NOTHING ELSE BUT EMPTY ME.         TO THE NAME OF JESUS        21  52 239  30
    OR ELSE, MY LIFE, I'LE HIDE THEE IN HIS GRAVE,   MATH. 16. 25. WHOSOEVER SHALL  3  MS 381  16
    (FOR ELSE WHY CAME I.) EV'N WHAT E'RE I FEARE.   OUT OF GROTIUS               8  MS 398 198

EMBERS

    HEE TOST HIS TROUBLED EYES, EMBERS THAT GLOW    SOSPETTO D'HERODE            147  46 109 216

EMBLEMES

    YEE PERFECT EMBLEMES OF DIVINITY.              UPON KINGS CORONATION      38  MS 389 454

EMBOSOM'D

    EMBOSOM'D IN A MUCH MORE ROSY MORN.            IN GLORIOUS EPIPHANIE       66  52 253  39

EMBRACE

    WHICH LIKE TWO BOSOM'D SAILES EMBRACE THE DIMME  SOSPETTO D'HERODE           142  46 109 216
    EMBRACE THY RADIANT BROWES, O MAY THE BEST     ON THE ASSUMPTION            57  46 139 114
    LET HIM EMBRACE HIS OWNE BRIGHT TRESSES,       AN HIMNE FOR CIRCUMCISION    21  46 141  37
    O LITTLE ALL. IN THY EMBRACE                  IN GLORIOUS EPIPHANIE       36  52 253  39
    EMBRACE THY RADIANT BROWES. O MAY THE BEST     IN GLORIOUS ASSUMPTION B. LADY 72  52 304 114
    AND BREAKES THROUGH ALL TEN HEAV'NS TO OUR EMBRACE. AGAINST IRRESOLUTION AND DELAY 78  52 347 146

T'EMBRACE

    T'EMBRACE A MILDER MARTYRDOME.                IN MEMORY OF LADY MADRE TERESA 68  46 131  52
    T'EMBRACE A MILDER MARTYRDOM.                 TERESA                           68  52 315  52
    T'EMBRACE MY TEARES, & KISSE AN UNKIND FATE.    ALEXIAS FIRST ELEGIE        4  52 334 204
    E'RE BORNE WAS BANISH'T. BORNE WAS GLAD T'EMBRACE OUT OF GROTIUS              15  MS 398 198

EMBRAC'T

| | | | | | |
|---|---|---|---|---|---|
| GLOOMY NIGHT EMBRAC'T THE PLACE | A HYMNE OF THE NATIVITY | 17 | 46 | 106 | 76 |
| GLOOMY NIGHT EMBRAC'T THE PLACE | IN HOLY NATIVITY | 17 | 52 | 246 | 76 |

EMBRACES

| | | | | | |
|---|---|---|---|---|---|
| FOR WORTHY SOULS WHOSE WISE EMBRACES | ON A PRAYER BOOKE | 38 | 46 | 126 | 139 |
| WHICH THE DIVINE EMBRACES | ON A PRAYER BOOKE | 77 | 46 | 126 | 139 |
| AND CLOSE IN HIS EMBRACES KEEP, | IN MEMORY OF LADY MADRE TERESA | 107 | 46 | 131 | 52 |
| AND CLOSE IN HIS EMBRACES KEEP | TERESA | 107 | 52 | 315 | 52 |
| FOR WORTHY SOULES, WHOSE WISE EMBRACES | PRAYER TO GENTLE-WOMAN | 44 | 52 | 328 | 139 |
| WHICH THE DIVINE EMBRACES | PRAYER TO GENTLE-WOMAN | 83 | 52 | 328 | 139 |
| NOR DOE EMBRACES ONELY MAKE A BRIDE. | ALEXIAS THIRD ELEGIE | 28 | 52 | 336 | 209 |

EMBRACING

| | | | | | |
|---|---|---|---|---|---|
| A CURL'D KNOT OF EMBRACING SNAKES, THAT KISSE | SOSPETTO D'HERODE | 37 | 46 | 109 | 216 |
| AND LEAVE EMBRACING OF THE ISLES, LEAST HEE | UPON GUNPOWDER TREASON | 33 | MS | 386 | 460 |

ALL-EMBRACING

| | | | | | |
|---|---|---|---|---|---|
| GREAT LITTLE ONE. WHOSE ALL-EMBRACING BIRTH | IN HOLY NATIVITY | 63 | 52 | 246 | 76 |

ALL-IMBRACING

| | | | | | |
|---|---|---|---|---|---|
| OF THIS UNBOUNDED ALL-IMBRACING SONG. | TO THE NAME OF JESUS | 91 | 52 | 239 | 30 |

EMBRAVE

| | | | | | |
|---|---|---|---|---|---|
| LET HIM EMBRAVE HIS OWN BRIGHT TRESSES | NEW YEAR'S DAY | 21 | 52 | 251 | 37 |

EMBRAVES

| | | | | | |
|---|---|---|---|---|---|
| THE BREATH OF ARTIFICIALL LUNGS EMBRAVES, | SOSPETTO D'HERODE | 482 | 46 | 109 | 216 |
| THE BABE WHOSE BIRTH EMBRAVES THIS MORN, | IN HOLY NATIVITY | 48 | 52 | 246 | 76 |

EMPEROURS

| | | | | | |
|---|---|---|---|---|---|
| THOU MIGHTY BRANCH OF EMPEROURS AND KINGS. | SOSPETTO D'HERODE | 10 | 46 | 109 | 216 |

EMPIRE

| | | | | | |
|---|---|---|---|---|---|
| NOW THAT TIME'S EMPIRE MIGHT BE AMPLY FILL'D, | ON FRONTISPIECE ISAACSONS | 15 | 46 | 191 | 491 |

EMPIRES

| | | | | | |
|---|---|---|---|---|---|
| WHERE SEAV'N TALL HORNES (HIS EMPIRES PRIDE) ASPIRE. | SOSPETTO D'HERODE | 46 | 46 | 109 | 216 |

EMPTINESSE

| | | | | | |
|---|---|---|---|---|---|
| HUGE EMPTINESSE CONTRACT THY BULKE, AND SHRINKE | UPON STANINOUGH'S DEATH | 13 | 46 | 175 | 475 |

EMPTYNES

| | | | | | |
|---|---|---|---|---|---|
| HUGE EMPTYNES. CONTRACT THY SELF. & SHRINKE | DEATH'S LECTURE | 14 | 52 | 340 | 475 |

EMPTY

| | | | | | |
|---|---|---|---|---|---|
| IF, FROM THE SEED OF EMPTY RUINE, SHE | ON FRONTISPIECE ISAACSONS | 6 | 46 | 191 | 491 |
| AND FULL OF NOTHING ELSE BUT EMPTY ME. | TO THE NAME OF JESUS | 21 | 52 | 239 | 30 |

EMPYRAEUM

| | | | | | |
|---|---|---|---|---|---|
| IN TH' EMPYRAEUM OF PURE HARMONY. | MUSICKS DUELL | 150 | 46 | 149 | 535 |
| TO TH' EMPYRAEUM OF ALL MISERIES. | ON GUNPOWDER-TREASON | 46 | MS | 384 | 458 |

ENACTED

| | | | | | |
|---|---|---|---|---|---|
| BE IT ENACTED THEN | ON A TREATISE OF CHARITY | 27 | 46 | 137 | 69 |

ENCLOSES

| | | | | | |
|---|---|---|---|---|---|
| THE THORNES THAT THY BLEST BROWES ENCLOSES | ON BLEEDING WOUNDS OF LORD | 22 | 46 | 101 | 110 |
| THOSE DEERE LIPS WHOSE DOORE ENCLOSES | OUT OF THE ITALIAN (1) | 21 | 46 | 188 | 545 |

END

| | | | | | |
|---|---|---|---|---|---|
| WHAT. THINKE WE TO NO OTHER END, | UPON DEATH OF DESIRED HERRYS | 25 | 46 | 168 | 467 |
| WHEN TO END MEE | OUT OF THE ITALIAN (1) | 43 | 46 | 188 | 545 |
| HER HAND TO BRING HIM TO HIS END. | AN EPITAPH UPON ASHTON | 24 | 46 | 192 | 464 |
| A CHALLENGE TO HIS END. | WISHES SUPPOSED MISTRESSE | 86 | 46 | 195 | 479 |
| ALLMIGHTY LOVE. END THIS LONG WARR, | TO COUNTESSE OF DENBIGH | 29 | 52 | 236 | 146 |
| THESE HOURES, & THAT WHICH HOVER'S O'RE MY END, | OFFICE H. CROSS RECOMMENDATION | 1 | 52 | 276 | 106 |
| OF ME & OF MY END. | SANCTA MARIA DOLORUM | 106 | 52 | 283 | 162 |
| TAKE CHARGE OF ME, & OF MY END. | DIES IRAE | 68 | 52 | 298 | 186 |
| YETT O WHAT END. WHERE DOES THE PERIOD DWELL | OUT OF GROTIUS | 9 | MS | 398 | 198 |

ENDS

| | | | | | |
|---|---|---|---|---|---|
| FOR THEE. AND SERV'D THEREIN THY GLORIOUS ENDS. | TO THE NAME OF JESUS | 210 | 52 | 239 | 30 |
| AND WHEN LIFE'S SWEET FABLE ENDS, | TEMPERANCE | 47 | 52 | 342 | 510 |

## ENDLESSE

| | | | |
|---|---|---|---|
| WITH ENDLESSE BUSINESSE ALMOST OUT OF BREATH. | SOSPETTO D'HERODE | 320 | 46 109 216 |
| DANCE IN AN ENDLESSE ROUND, AGAINE SHALL RISE | UPON DEATH OF HERRYS | 38 | 46 167 466 |
| WHOLE DAYES & SUNS DEVOUR'D WITH ENDLESSE DINING. | DESCRIPTION RELIGIOUS HOUSE | 2 | 52 338 213 |

## ENDOWMENTS

| | | | |
|---|---|---|---|
| THE RIPE ENDOWMENTS OF WHOSE MIND, | HIS EPITAPH (HERRYS) | 7 | 46 172 471 |

## ENDURE

| | | | |
|---|---|---|---|
| THE TENDER GROWTH OF THINGS ENDURE THE SENCE | OUT OF VIRGIL | 33 | 46 155 529 |

## INDURE

| | | | |
|---|---|---|---|
| NONE CAN INDURE. YET NONE CAN FLY. | DIES IRAE | 20 | 52 298 186 |

## INDUR'D

| | | | |
|---|---|---|---|
| IF DROWN'D. SWEET IS THE DEATH INDUR'D FOR HIM, | ALEXIAS FIRST ELEGIE | 22 | 52 334 204 |

## ENEMY

| | | | |
|---|---|---|---|
| THIS MORTALL ENEMY TO MANKINDS GOOD, | SOSPETTO D'HERODE | 82 | 46 109 216 |
| FOR JURYES KING AN ENEMY, EVEN WORTH | OUT OF GROTIUS | 21 | MS 398 198 |

## ENFOLD

| | | | |
|---|---|---|---|
| THAT WHICH THEIR WAXEN MINES ENFOLD, | OUT OF GREEKE CUPID'S CRYER | 26 | 46 159 519 |

## ENGADDI

| | | | |
|---|---|---|---|
| OF FAIRE ENGADDI HONY-SWEATING FOUNTAINES | SOSPETTO D'HERODE | 111 | 46 109 216 |

## ENGENDER

| | | | |
|---|---|---|---|
| ENGENDER WITH THE NIGHT, & TEEME A BIRTH | UPON GUNPOWDER TREASON | 12 | MS 386 460 |

## ENGINES

| | | | |
|---|---|---|---|
| WHAT BUSY MOTIONS, WHAT WILD ENGINES STAND | SOSPETTO D'HERODE | 441 | 46 109 216 |

## ENGLISH

| | | | |
|---|---|---|---|
| THY PRAISE MIGHT NOT SPEAK ENGLISH TOO, FORBID | AN APOLOGIE FOR HYMNE (TERESA) | 11 | 46 136 59 |
| THY PRAISE MIGHT NOT SPEAK ENGLISH TOO. FORBID | AN APOLOGIE FOR (TERESA) HYMNE | 11 | 52 322 59 |

## ENJOY

| | | | |
|---|---|---|---|
| MAY SHEE ENJOY IT, | WISHES SUPPOSED MISTRESSE | 118 | 46 195 479 |

## TO'INJOY

| | | | |
|---|---|---|---|
| TO'INJOY HIS BLOTT. & AS A LARGE BLACK LETTER | IN GLORIOUS EPIPHANIE | 186 | 52 253 39 |

## ENOBLED

| | | | |
|---|---|---|---|
| BY THINE EYES TINCT ENOBLED THUS | THE WEEPER | 95 | 46 79 120 |
| BY THINE EY'S TINCT ENOBLED THUS | WEEPER | 149 | 52 307 120 |

## ENOUGH

| | | | |
|---|---|---|---|
| WERE IT ENOUGH TO SHOW THE PLACE, AND SAY, | COME SEE WHERE THE LORD LAY | 3 | 46 87 27 |
| THY DOWNE THOUGH SOFT'S NOT SOFT ENOUGH. | A HYMNE OF THE NATIVITY | 46 | 46 106 76 |
| SCARCE HAD SHEE BLOOD ENOUGH, TO MAKE | IN MEMORY OF LADY MADRE TERESA | 25 | 46 131 52 |
| ENOUGH, NOW (IF THOU CANST) PASSE ON, | HIS EPITAPH (HERRYS) | 49 | 46 172 471 |
| YET ARE SCARCE RIPE ENOUGH AT BEST TO SHOW | UPON TWO GREENE APRICOCKES | 5 | 48 220 494 |
| HE IS FROM SUN ENOUGH TO MAKE THY STARR, | IN GLORIOUS EPIPHANIE | 247 | 52 253 39 |
| SCARSE HAS SHE BLOOD ENOUGH TO MAKE | TERESA | 25 | 52 315 52 |
| AND ROOM ENOUGH FOR MONARCHS, WHILE NONE SWELLS | DESCRIPTION RELIGIOUS HOUSE | 34 | 52 338 213 |
| Y' HAD DONE ENOUGH TO MAKE THE LAZY GROUND | UPON BIRTH PRINCESSE E | 31 | MS 391 456 |
| POORE EARTH HATH NOT ENOUGH PERFECTION, | UPON BIRTH PRINCESSE E | 41 | MS 391 456 |
| ENOUGH IS SAID. NOW, IF THOU CANST CROWD ON | AN ELEGIE ON DR PORTER | 19 | MS 395 476 |
| YETT HERE'S NOT ALL. NOR WAS'T ENOUGH FOR MEE | OUT OF GROTIUS | 61 | MS 398 198 |

## ENOW

| | | | |
|---|---|---|---|
| THERE ARE ENOW WHOSE DRAUGHTS AS DEEP AS HELL | AN APOLOGIE FOR HYMNE (TERESA) | 29 | 46 136 59 |
| THERE ARE ENOW, WHOSE DRAUGHTS (AS DEEP AS HELL) | AN APOLOGIE FOR (TERESA) HYMNE | 29 | 52 322 59 |

## ENQUIRE

| | | | |
|---|---|---|---|
| SIBILLS DIVINING LEAVES. HEE DOES ENQUIRE | SOSPETTO D'HERODE | 92 | 46 109 216 |

## ENRAGED

| | | | |
|---|---|---|---|
| WHILE NEW THOUGHTS BOYL'D IN HIS ENRAGED BREST, | SOSPETTO D'HERODE | 193 | 46 109 216 |

## ENTER

| | | | |
|---|---|---|---|
| FAIRLY TO OPEN IT, AND ENTER. | TO COUNTESSE OF DENBIGH | 4 | 52 236 146 |
| FAIRLY TO OPEN AND TO ENTER. | AGAINST IRRESOLUTION AND DELAY | 4 | 52 347 146 |

ENTERTAIN

   TO ENTERTAIN THIS STARRY STRANGER.          IN HOLY NATIVITY            38   52  246   76

ENTERTAINE

   THERE STOOD SHE LISTNING, AND DID ENTERTAINE     MUSICKS DUELL              11   46  149  535

ENTHUSIAST

   ABOVE HER SELFE, MUSICKS ENTHUSIAST.           MUSICKS DUELL             104  46  149  535

ENTHUSIASTICKE

   ENTHUSIASTICKE FLAMES, SUCH AS CAN GIVE        TO THE MORNING           21   46  183  497

ENTICE

   WHAT HATH OUR WORLD THAT CAN ENTICE            THE WEEPER              124  46   79  120

TICE

   WHAT MAKE YOU HERE. WHAT HOPES CAN TICE        WEEPER                  166  52  307  120

ENTITY

   THE ENTITY OF THINGS THAT ARE NOT YET.         ON HOPE                   12   46  143   71
   THE ENTITY OF THOSE THAT ARE NOT YET.         (ON) HOPE                 2   52  345   71

ENTOMBE

   T' ENTOMBE THE LAB'RING EARTH. FOR SURELY SHEE   UPON GUNPOWDER TREASON    51   MS  386  460

ENTOMBED

   WHILE LOVE SHALL THUS ENTOMBED LYE,            LOVES HOROSCOPE           51   46  185  483

ENTOMB'D

   IS ENTOMB'D THE CRIME OF DEATH.                HIS EPITAPH (HERRYS)      6   46  172  471
   IS HE ENTOMB'D, BUT IN THY HEART.              HIS EPITAPH (HERRYS)     52   46  172  471

ENVIED

   OFT HAVE THESE ARMES THY CRADLE ENVIED,        LUKE 2.  QUAERIT JESUM    27   MS  379   11

ENVIOUS

   AS SHALL MOCKE THE ENVIOUS EYE.                OUT OF CATULLUS           20   46  194  523
   AND BE ECLIPSED WITH AN ENVIOUS SHADE.         AN ELEGY MR STANNINOW    44   MS  394  473

ENVY

   HEE STRAINES THESE WORDS. BASE ENVY, DOE, LAUGH ON.  HIGH MOUNTED ON AN ANT    5   46  161  523
   THE WORME OF JEALOUS ENVY AND UNREST,          SOSPETTO D'HERODE        493  46  109  216
   O ENVY NOT                                       OUT OF THE ITALIAN (1)    19   46  188  545
   THE WORLD MY FATHER.  THEN DOES ENVY SWELL     OUT OF GROTIUS            32   MS  398  198

EPIPHANY

   WHILE ALL THE YEAR IS YOUR EPIPHANY,            TO THE QUEEN'S MAJESTY    26   52  261   47

EPITAPH

   HIS BETTER EPITAPH SHALL BEE,                  AN EPITAPH UPON ASHTON    35   46  192  464

EPITOME

   TH' EPITOME OF HELL. OH LETT THY PINIONS       UPON GUNPOWDER TREASON    21   MS  387  461
   IN THIS BLEST EARTH HEAVENS BRIGHT EPITOME,     UPON KINGS CORONATION     12   MS  389  454
   COMPILE A FIFT GLORIOUS EPITOME                UPON BIRTH PRINCESSE E    57   MS  391  456

EPODE

   WITH THE COOLE EPODE OF A GRAVER NOAT,         MUSICKS DUELL              99   46  149  535

EQUALL

   WHICH WITH THE SUN HIMSELFE WEIGH'S EQUALL WINGS.  SOSPETTO D'HERODE        12   46  109  216
   DOE THEN AS EQUALL RIGHT REQUIRES,              FLAMING HEART              37   52  324   61

AEQUALL

   O HEART. THE AEQUALL POISE OF LOV'ES BOTH PARTS   FLAMING HEART              75   52  324   61
   AN AEQUALL PACE THUS FARRE. THY WORD MY DEEDES    OUT OF GROTIUS             5   MS  398  198

ERE

   OF CLOSER STRAINES, AND ERE THE WARRE BEGIN,    MUSICKS DUELL              19   46  149  535
   ALL TORNE. WITH MUCH ADOE YET ERE HE DYES,     HIGH MOUNTED ON AN ANT     4   46  161  523
   IN HEAV'N YOU'L LEARNE TO SING ERE HERE TO SPEAKE, TO INFANT MARTYRS         2   46   88   10
   COME TRY WHO DARES. HEAV'N, EARTH, WHAT ERE DOST  SOSPETTO D'HERODE       251  46  109  216
                                           BOAST,

|  |  |  |  |  |  |
|---|---|---|---|---|---|
| MERCY WILL COME ERE LONG. | ON A PRAYER BOOKE | 34 | 46 | 126 | 139 |
| WHO ERE SHE BEE, | ON A PRAYER BOOKE | 93 | 46 | 126 | 139 |
| NOR HATH SHEE ERE YET UNDERSTOOD | IN MEMORY OF LADY MADRE TERESA | 21 | 46 | 131 | 52 |
| WHO ERE SHEE BEE. | WISHES SUPPOSED MISTRESSE | 1 | 46 | 195 | 479 |
| WHERE ERE SHEE LYE. | WISHES SUPPOSED MISTRESSE | 4 | 46 | 195 | 479 |
| WHAT ERE DELIGHT | WISHES SUPPOSED MISTRESSE | 94 | 46 | 195 | 479 |
| THAN ERE THE FRUITFULL PHOEBUS FLAMING KISSES | UPON TWO GREENE APRICOCKES | 9 | 48 | 220 | 494 |
| DEAR BABE, ERE MANY DAYES BE DONE, | NEW YEAR'S DAY | 30 | 52 | 251 | 37 |
| NO APRIL ERE LENT KINDER SHOWRES, | WEEPER | 83 | 52 | 307 | 120 |
| WHO ERE SHE BE, | PRAYER TO GENTLE-WOMAN | 99 | 52 | 328 | 139 |
| AND TRY'D TO MAKE A WIDOW ERE A WIFE. | ALEXIAS FIRST ELEGIE | 6 | 52 | 334 | 204 |
| O STAY A WHILE, ERE THOU DRAW IN THY HEAD | DEATH'S LECTURE | 3 | 52 | 340 | 475 |

ERINNYS

|  |  |  |  |  |  |
|---|---|---|---|---|---|
| WHEN THE ERINNYS HER BLACK PINEONS SPREAD. | SOSPETTO D'HERODE | 393 | 46 | 109 | 216 |

ERISI-CTHON

|  |  |  |  |  |  |
|---|---|---|---|---|---|
| INHUMANE ERISI-CTHON TOO MAKES ONE. | SOSPETTO D'HERODE | 332 | 46 | 109 | 216 |

ERR

|  |  |  |  |  |  |
|---|---|---|---|---|---|
| THOU COULDST NOT SO UNKINDLY ERR | FLAMING HEART | 21 | 52 | 324 | 61 |

ERROR

|  |  |  |  |  |  |
|---|---|---|---|---|---|
| AND, THROUGH THE NIGHT OF ERROR AND DARK DOUBT, | ON FRONTISPIECE ISAACSONS | 12 | 46 | 191 | 491 |

ERROUR

|  |  |  |  |  |  |
|---|---|---|---|---|---|
| A BLOUD DRUNKE ERROUR SPILT THE COSTLY AYME | OUT OF GROTIUS | 29 | MS | 398 | 198 |

ESPIED

|  |  |  |  |  |  |
|---|---|---|---|---|---|
| BUT WHEN JOVES WINGED HERALDS THIS ESPIED. | UPON GUNPOWDER TREASON | 53 | MS | 386 | 460 |

ESPIES

|  |  |  |  |  |  |
|---|---|---|---|---|---|
| FROM WHENCE HIS GLORIOUS RIVALL HEE ESPIES. | UPON KINGS CORONATION | 18 | MS | 390 | 453 |

ESSENCE

|  |  |  |  |  |  |
|---|---|---|---|---|---|
| THEIR SUBTILE ESSENCE WITH THE SOULE OF WINE. | ON HOPE | 60 | 46 | 143 | 71 |
| THEIR SUPPLE ESSENCE WITH THE SOUL OF WINE. | (ON) HOPE | 30 | 52 | 345 | 71 |

ESTEEM

|  |  |  |  |  |  |
|---|---|---|---|---|---|
| SO MUCH MORE RICH WOULD HE ESTEEM | WEEPER | 77 | 52 | 307 | 120 |

ESTEEMED

|  |  |  |  |  |  |
|---|---|---|---|---|---|
| NEVER TILL NOW ESTEEMED TOYES. | IN MEMORY OF LADY MADRE TERESA | 60 | 46 | 131 | 52 |
| (NEVER TILL NOW ESTEEMED TOYES) | TERESA | 60 | 52 | 315 | 52 |

ESTEEME

|  |  |  |  |  |  |
|---|---|---|---|---|---|
| RICHER FAR DOES HE ESTEEME | THE WEEPER | 83 | 46 | 79 | 120 |

ETERNALL

|  |  |  |  |  |  |
|---|---|---|---|---|---|
| AND NOW, I DOUBT NOT, THE ETERNALL DOVE, | ON BAPTIZED AETHIOPIAN | 5 | 46 | 85 | 29 |
| FOR US AND OUR ETERNALL GOOD | ON BLEEDING WOUNDS OF LORD | 6 | 46 | 101 | 110 |
| BRIGHT DAWNE OF OUR ETERNALL DAY. | A HYMNE OF THE NATIVITY | 30 | 46 | 106 | 76 |
| HOLD THE PERVERSE PRINCE IN ETERNALL TIES | SOSPETTO D'HERODE | 39 | 46 | 109 | 216 |
| HOW GODS ETERNALL SONNE SHOULD BE MANS BROTHER, | SOSPETTO D'HERODE | 165 | 46 | 109 | 216 |
| ETERNALL WORD SHOULD BEE A CHILD, AND WEEPE. | SOSPETTO D'HERODE | 179 | 46 | 109 | 216 |
| AND FURTHER,THAT THE LAWES ETERNALL GIVER, | SOSPETTO D'HERODE | 165 | 46 | 109 | 216 |
| AND TH' ETERNALL MORROW DAWNE, | AN EPITAPH HUSBAND AND WIFE | 13 | 46 | 174 | 478 |
| AND NAME DWELL SWEET IN SOME ETERNALL STORY. | UPON YORKE HIS BIRTH | 105 | 46 | 176 | 500 |
| DISCERNE THE DAWNE OF TRUTH'S ETERNALL RAY, | ON FRONTISPIECE ISAACSONS | 13 | 46 | 191 | 491 |
| OF THIS FAIR TREE TAKE OUR ETERNALL ROOT. | SANCTA MARIA DOLORUM | 64 | 52 | 283 | 162 |
| FOR US & OUR ETERNALL GOOD. | UPON BLEEDING CRUCIFIX | 10 | 52 | 288 | 110 |

AETERNALL

|  |  |  |  |  |  |
|---|---|---|---|---|---|
| AETERNALL WORLDS UPON IT'S WINGS. | TO COUNTESSE OF DENBIGH | 54 | 52 | 236 | 146 |
| YOUNG DAWN OF OUR AETERNALL DAY. | IN HOLY NATIVITY | 32 | 52 | 246 | 76 |
| BRIGHT DAWN OF OUR AETERNALL DAY. | IN HOLY NATIVITY | 73 | 52 | 246 | 76 |
| THE WORLD'S ONE. ROUND, AETERNALL YEAR. | IN GLORIOUS EPIPHANIE | 27 | 52 | 253 | 39 |
| AETERNALL TEARES SHOULD THUS DISTILL THEE. | WEEPER | 100 | 52 | 307 | 120 |
| TILL THE' AETERNALL MORROW DAWN | AN EPITAPH UPON MARRIED COUPLE | 17 | 52 | 339 | 478 |
| AETERNALL LOVE. WHAT 'TIS TO LOVE THEE WELL, | IN AMOREM DIVINUM | 1 | MS | 381 | 212 |
| SULPHUREOUS FLAMES, SNATCH'D FROM AETERNALL NIGHT. | UPON GUNPOWDER TREASON | 26 | MS | 387 | 461 |
| A GOLDEN SUMMER, AN AETERNALL SPRING. | AN ELEGY MR STANNINOW | 54 | MS | 394 | 473 |

ETERNALLY

|  |  |  |  |  |  |
|---|---|---|---|---|---|
| ETERNALLY BIND EACH REBELLIOUS LIMBE. | SOSPETTO D'HERODE | 140 | 46 | 109 | 216 |

AETERNALLY

|  |  |  |  |  |  |
|---|---|---|---|---|---|
| BY THREE DAIES LOSSE AETERNALLY TO SAVE. | MATH. 16. 25. WHOSOEVER SHALL | 4 | MS | 381 | 16 |

ETERNITY

| | | | | | |
|---|---|---|---|---|---|
| RISE, HEIRE OF FRESH ETERNITY, | EASTER DAY | 1 | 46 | 100 | 26 |
| LIGHTING TO ETERNITY. | PSALME 23 | 66 | 46 | 102 | 5 |
| ETERNITY SHUT IN A SPAN. | A HYMNE OF THE NATIVITY | 54 | 46 | 106 | 76 |
| AND FREE ETERNITY, SUBMIT TO YEARES. | SOSPETTO D'HERODE | 184 | 46 | 109 | 216 |
| YOUNG TIME IS TASTER TO ETERNITY. | ON HOPE | 52 | 46 | 143 | 71 |
| INTO ETERNITY, AND CIRCULAR JOYES | UPON DEATH OF HERRYS | 37 | 46 | 167 | 466 |
| INTO A FALSE ETERNITY, COME MAN, | UPON STANINOUGH'S DEATH | 9 | 46 | 175 | 475 |
| YOUNG TIME IS TASTER TO ETERNITY | (ON) HOPE | 22 | 52 | 345 | 71 |

ETERNITY--BUT

| | | | | | |
|---|---|---|---|---|---|
| AND TRACE ETERNITY--BUT ALL IS DEAD, | TO THE MORNING | 29 | 46 | 183 | 497 |

AETERNITY

| | | | | | |
|---|---|---|---|---|---|
| AETERNITY SHUTT IN A SPAN. | IN HOLY NATIVITY | 80 | 52 | 246 | 76 |
| IN THE AETERNITY OF THY OLD CARES. | CHARITAS NIMIA | 32 | 52 | 280 | 48 |
| INTO A FALSE AETERNITY, COME MAN. | DEATH'S LECTURE | 10 | 52 | 340 | 475 |
| TO THE CLOSE CLOSET OF AETERNITY. | UPON GUNPOWDER TREASON | 56 | MS | 387 | 461 |

ETHIOPIAN

| | | | | | |
|---|---|---|---|---|---|
| SHEE SHALL APPEAR TRUE ETHIOPIAN. | UPON FAIRE ETHIOPIAN | 6 | 46 | 183 | 493 |

AETHIOPE

| | | | | | |
|---|---|---|---|---|---|
| TO WASH AN AETHIOPE. | ON BAPTIZED AETHIOPIAN | 2 | 46 | 85 | 29 |

EUPHRATES

| | | | | | |
|---|---|---|---|---|---|
| ON THE PROUD BANKES OF GREAT EUPHRATES FLOOD, | PSALME 137 | 1 | 46 | 104 | 7 |

EVE

| | | | | | |
|---|---|---|---|---|---|
| THE FIRST EVE, MOTHER OF OUR FALL, | O GLORIOSA DOMINA | 11 | 52 | 302 | 194 |
| AND CALL THE MAIDEN EVE THEIR MOTHER. | O GLORIOSA DOMINA | 26 | 52 | 302 | 194 |

EVEN

| | | | | | |
|---|---|---|---|---|---|
| THOU, THOU (DEARE LORD) EVEN THOU ALONE, | VERILY YE SHALL WEEP | 5 | 46 | 95 | 22 |
| GIV'ST JOY, EVEN WHEN THOU GIVEST NONE. | VERILY YE SHALL WEEP | 6 | 46 | 95 | 22 |
| EVEN MY GOD, EVEN HE IT IS, | PSALME 23 | 3 | 46 | 102 | 5 |
| EVEN MY GOD, EVEN HE IT IS, | PSALME 23 | 3 | 46 | 102 | 5 |
| OVERSHADOW EVEN THE SHADE, | PSALME 23 | 41 | 46 | 102 | 5 |
| THERE MY FEET, EVEN THERE SHALL FIND | PSALME 23 | 43 | 46 | 102 | 5 |
| SO, EVEN SO STILL MAY I MOVE | PSALME 23 | 57 | 46 | 102 | 5 |
| EVEN SUCH AS THESE, LAUGH, TILL A VENGING THRONG | PSALME 137 | 33 | 46 | 104 | 7 |
| IN LANGUAGE OF HIS THUNDER, THOU ART EVEN | SOSPETTO D'HERODE | 270 | 46 | 109 | 216 |
| EVEN THY DEATHS SHALL LIVE, AND NEW | IN MEMORY OF LADY MADRE TERESA | 152 | 46 | 131 | 52 |
| EVEN THE IRON-POINTED PEN, | ANOTHER ON HERRYS | 33 | 46 | 170 | 469 |
| BUT HE, ALAS. EVEN HEE IS DEAD | ANOTHER ON HERRYS | 55 | 46 | 170 | 469 |
| MADE SO REVEREND, EVEN IN YOUTH, | HIS EPITAPH (HERRYS) | 16 | 46 | 172 | 471 |
| HOW EVEN TH'AST DRAWNE THIS FAITHFULL PARALELL, | UPON YORKE HIS BIRTH | 50 | 46 | 176 | 500 |
| THUS MADE EVEN, | OUT OF THE ITALIAN (1) | 29 | 46 | 188 | 545 |
| EVEN BALLANCE OF BOTH WORLDS. OUR WORLD OF SIN, | VEXILLA REGIS | 31 | 52 | 277 | 156 |
| AN EVEN ROUND WITH THE CIRCLING SUN. | DIES IRAE | 10 | 52 | 298 | 186 |
| EVEN LOST THY SELF IN SEEKING ME. | DIES IRAE | 32 | 52 | 298 | 186 |
| EVEN WHEN HE SHOW'D MOST POOR, | WEEPER | 117 | 52 | 307 | 120 |
| EVEN TO THE LAST PEARLE IN THY TREASURE. | WEEPER | 130 | 52 | 307 | 120 |
| SEE, EVEN THE YEARES & SIZE OF HIM | FLAMING HEART | 15 | 52 | 324 | 61 |
| I DY EVEN IN DESIRE OF DEATH. | A SONG | 12 | 52 | 327 | 65 |
| FOR JURYES KING AN ENEMY, EVEN WORTH | OUT OF GROTIUS | 21 | MS | 398 | 198 |
| EVEN HEE THAT BELCHES OUT A FOAMING FLOOD | OUT OF GROTIUS | 75 | MS | 398 | 198 |
| TO FREIND THE LIVING WORLD EVEN DEATH DID SEE | OUT OF GROTIUS | 82 | MS | 398 | 198 |

EV'EN

| | | | | | |
|---|---|---|---|---|---|
| SURE EV'EN FROM YOU | SANCTA MARIA DOLORUM | 15 | 52 | 283 | 162 |
| EV'EN TO THE NAKED'ST VOWES. THOU ART MY FATE. | EX EUPHORMIONE | 9 | MS | 392 | 525 |

EV'N

| | | | | | |
|---|---|---|---|---|---|
| UNCHARITABLE EV'N TO CHARITIE. | ON A TREATISE OF CHARITY | 58 | 46 | 137 | 69 |
| YET THINKS IT SO. BUT EV'N THAT TOO | TO THE QUEEN | 5 | 48 | 215 | 501 |
| WHICH TAUGHT ATTENTION EV'N TO ROCKS & STONES. | OFFICE H. CROSS NINTH | 2 | 52 | 271 | 99 |
| BUT HERE EV'N THAT'S HID TOO WHICH HIDES THE OTHER, | ADORO TE | 26 | 52 | 291 | 172 |
| OF LOVE, AND EV'N THAT LOSSE, BE LOST. | DIES IRAE | 34 | 52 | 298 | 186 |
| EV'N THY DEATHS SHALL LIVE, & NEW | TERESA | 151 | 52 | 315 | 52 |
| HUGE HIGH-FLOUNE POYSONS, EV'N OF COLCHOS BREED, | HORATIJ ILLE & NEFASTO | 11 | MS | 382 | 530 |
| THOSE TWINCKLING EYES OF HEAVEN, WHICH EV'N NOW SHIN'D, | ON GUNPOWDER-TREASON | 31 | MS | 384 | 458 |
| THESE CATARACTS OF GREIFE, THAT DARE EV'N VIE | AN ELEGY MR STANNINOW | 17 | MS | 394 | 473 |
| (FOR ELSE WHY CAME I.) EV'N WHAT E'RE I FEARE. | OUT OF GROTIUS | 8 | MS | 398 | 198 |
| A WEAKE A WRETCHED CHILD. EV'N THEN WAS I | OUT OF GROTIUS | 20 | MS | 398 | 198 |
| WHEN A WILD SWORD EV'N FROM THEIR BRESTS, DID LOP | OUT OF GROTIUS | 25 | MS | 398 | 198 |

TH'EVEN

| | | | | | |
|---|---|---|---|---|---|
| BY TH'EVEN WINGS OF HIS OWN DOVES, | AGAINST IRRESOLUTION AND DELAY | 54 | 52 | 347 | 146 |

EVENING

| | | | | | |
|---|---|---|---|---|---|
| THE PUREST PEARLES, THAT WEPT HER EVENING DEATH, | UPON DEATH OF HERRYS | 19 | 46 | 167 | 466 |
| FOR THIS THE EVENING WEPT, AND WE NE'RE KNEW | IN GLORIOUS EPIPHANIE | 127 | 52 | 253 | 39 |

EVENING'S

| | | | | | |
|---|---|---|---|---|---|
| NOT IN THE EVENING'S EYES | WEEPER | 31 | 52 | 307 | 120 |

EV'NSONG

| | | | | | |
|---|---|---|---|---|---|
| THEN SITT THEE DOWN, & SING THINE EV'NSONG IN THE SAD | OFFICE H. CROSS EVENSONG | 8 | 52 | 273 | 101 |

EVENINGS

| | | | | | |
|---|---|---|---|---|---|
| NOT IN THE EVENINGS EYES | THE WEEPER | 55 | 46 | 79 | 120 |

EVENLY

| | | | | | |
|---|---|---|---|---|---|
| IN CONTROVERTING WARBLES EVENLY SHAR'D, | MUSICKS DUELL | 42 | 46 | 149 | 535 |

EVENTS

| | | | | | |
|---|---|---|---|---|---|
| DOTH GRASPE THE FATE OF THINGES, AND SHARE TH' EVENTS | OUT OF GROTIUS | 2 | MS | 398 | 198 |

EVER

| | | | | | |
|---|---|---|---|---|---|
| IN HER OWNE MURMURES, THAT WHAT EVER MOOD | MUSICKS DUELL | 13 | 46 | 149 | 535 |
| ABOVE HER MOCKE, OR BEE FOR EVER MUTE. | MUSICKS DUELL | 108 | 46 | 149 | 535 |
| WHO WILL EVER CREDIT THEE, | UPON THE DEATH OF A GENTLEMAN | 2 | 46 | 166 | 472 |
| EVER BUBLING THINGS. | THE WEEPER | 3 | 46 | 79 | 120 |
| WHAT EVER MAKES HEAVENS FORE-HEAD FINE. | THE WEEPER | 12 | 46 | 79 | 120 |
| NOWHERE BUT HEERE DID EVER MEET | THE WEEPER | 59 | 46 | 79 | 120 |
| WHAT EVER STORY OF THEIR CRUELTIE, | ON MARKES OF SAVIOURS WOUNDS | 1 | 46 | 86 | 28 |
| WAS EVER FROWARD WIND | WHY ARE YEE AFRAID | 4 | 46 | 88 | 15 |
| AS EVER SILVER-TIPT, THE SIDE OF SHADY MOUNTAINE. | TO PONTIUS WASHING HANDS | 8 | 46 | 94 | 23 |
| WHAT EVER CAESAR'S PAYMENTS ARE. | GIVE TO CAESAR AND TO GOD | 4 | 46 | 96 | 20 |
| O. WHO SO HARD AN HUSBANDMAN COULD EVER FIND | UPON THORNES FROM LORDS HEAD | 5 | 46 | 96 | 23 |
| NOR EVER WAS THE PHARIAN TIDE | ON BLEEDING WOUNDS OF LORD | 15 | 46 | 101 | 110 |
| BRIGHT EVER WITH A BEAME THAT FALLS | PSALME 23 | 64 | 46 | 102 | 5 |
| THERE I'LE DWELL FOR EVER, THERE | PSALME 23 | 67 | 46 | 102 | 5 |
| THAT THE UNBLEMISHT LAMBE, BLESSED FOR EVER, | SOSPETTO D'HERODE | 189 | 46 | 109 | 216 |
| THE ADAMANTINE DOORS, FOR EVER STAND | SOSPETTO D'HERODE | 307 | 46 | 109 | 216 |
| UNFILL'D FOR EVER. HERE AMONG THE REST, | SOSPETTO D'HERODE | 331 | 46 | 109 | 216 |
| WHAT EVER SCHEMES OF BLOOD, FANTASTICK FRAMES | SOSPETTO D'HERODE | 361 | 46 | 109 | 216 |
| BUT SHUT THEIR FLOWRY LIDS FOR EVER. NIGHT, | SOSPETTO D'HERODE | 379 | 46 | 109 | 216 |
| THAT THY FIRME HAND FOR EVER MIGHT SUSTAINE | SOSPETTO D'HERODE | 450 | 46 | 109 | 216 |
| (A SPECIALL WORME IT WAS AS EVER KIST | SOSPETTO D'HERODE | 467 | 46 | 109 | 216 |
| FAREWELL WHAT EVER DEARE MAY BEE. | IN MEMORY OF LADY MADRE TERESA | 61 | 46 | 131 | 52 |
| AND WOULD FOR EVER SO BE SLAINE. | IN MEMORY OF LADY MADRE TERESA | 102 | 46 | 131 | 52 |
| AND HOLD THEM FAST FOR EVER. THERE, | IN MEMORY OF LADY MADRE TERESA | 122 | 46 | 131 | 52 |
| WAS EVER GUILTY OF, CHANGE WEE OUR SHAPE, | AN APOLOGIE FOR HYMNE (TERESA) | 34 | 46 | 136 | 59 |
| MEE EVER INTO THESE HIS CELLARS BRING. | AN APOLOGIE FOR HYMNE (TERESA) | 38 | 46 | 136 | 59 |
| FEED FOR EVER THEIR FAIRE SIGHT | ON THE ASSUMPTION | 34 | 46 | 139 | 114 |
| AS EVER WHISPER'D TO THE MORNING AIRE | UPON DEATH OF HERRYS | 2 | 46 | 167 | 466 |
| IF EVER PITTY WERE ACQUAINTED | ANOTHER ON HERRYS | 1 | 46 | 170 | 469 |
| OR HAD EVER LEARNT TO BEARE, | ANOTHER ON HERRYS | 19 | 46 | 170 | 469 |
| TWO EVER BLUSHING BEDS OF NEW-BORNE ROSES. | ON A FOULE MORNING | 18 | 46 | 181 | 495 |
| WAS EVER KNOWNE TO BE THY VOTERY. | TO THE MORNING | 48 | 46 | 183 | 497 |
| WHAT EVER STARRY SYNOD MET, | LOVES HOROSCOPE | 18 | 46 | 185 | 483 |
| O. THAT POORE LOVE BE NOT FOR EVER SPOYLED, | OUT OF THE ITALIAN (2) | 5 | 46 | 190 | 547 |
| FOR EVER HERE, & MIX | TO THE NAME OF JESUS | 83 | 52 | 239 | 30 |
| FOR EVER SHALL PRESUME | TO THE NAME OF JESUS | 179 | 52 | 239 | 30 |
| LIVE, O FOR EVER LIVE & REIGN | VEXILLA REGIS | 43 | 52 | 277 | 156 |
| AS THEY WERE EVER WONT. WHAT THOUGH. | UPON BLEEDING CRUCIFIX | 11 | 52 | 288 | 110 |
| NOR EVER WAS THE PHARIAN TIDE | UPON BLEEDING CRUCIFIX | 19 | 52 | 288 | 110 |
| O WHO SO HARD A HUSBANDMAN DID EVER FIND | UPON CROWNE OF THORNS | 3 | 52 | 290 | 23 |
| LIVE EVER BREAD OF LOVES, & BE | ADORO TE | 43 | 52 | 291 | 172 |
| SHALL HENCE FOR EVER BEAR AWAY. | LAUDA SION SALVATOREM | 18 | 52 | 294 | 178 |
| EVER TO DOE WHAT HE ONCE DID. | LAUDA SION SALVATOREM | 26 | 52 | 294 | 178 |
| AS EVER SHALL BE, WAS, & IS. | O GLORIOSA DOMINA | 40 | 52 | 302 | 194 |
| EVER BUBLING THINGS. | WEEPER | 3 | 52 | 307 | 120 |
| NO WHERE BUT HERE DID EVER MEET | WEEPER | 35 | 52 | 307 | 120 |
| FAREWELL WHAT EVER DEARE MAY BEE. | TERESA | 61 | 52 | 315 | 52 |
| AND WOULD FOR EVER SO BE SLAIN. | TERESA | 102 | 52 | 315 | 52 |
| AND HOLD THEM FAST FOR EVER. THERE | TERESA | 121 | 52 | 315 | 52 |
| WAS EVER GUILTY OF, CHANGE WE TOO 'OUR SHAPE | AN APOLOGIE FOR (TERESA) HYMNE | 34 | 52 | 322 | 59 |
| ME EVER INTO THESE HIS CELLARS BRING | AN APOLOGIE FOR (TERESA) HYMNE | 38 | 52 | 322 | 59 |
| BE HAPPY. AND FOR EVER HOLD HIM FAST. | ALEXIAS FIRST ELEGIE | 38 | 52 | 334 | 204 |
| DID EVER GREIFE, & JOY IN ONE POORE HEART | LUKE 2. QUAERIT JESUM | 3 | MS | 379 | 11 |

EVER-BLUSHING

| | | | | | |
|---|---|---|---|---|---|
| YOU EVER-BLUSHING MEADS, WHERE DOE THE BLEST | HORATIJ ILLE & NEFASTO | 37 | MS | 382 | 530 |

EVER-BRANDISHT

| | | | | | |
|---|---|---|---|---|---|
| WHOSE EVER-BRANDISHT SWORD IS SHEATH'D IN BLOOD. | SOSPETTO D'HERODE | 314 | 46 | 109 | 216 |

EVER-BUBLING

| | | | | | |
|---|---|---|---|---|---|
| THAT EVER-BUBLING SPRING. THE SUGRED NEST | MUSICKS DUELL | 66 | 46 | 149 | 535 |

## EVER-FALLING

| | | | | | |
|---|---|---|---|---|---|
| HEAVENS OF EVER-FALLING STARS, | THE WEEPER | 8 | 46 | 79 | 120 |
| HEAVENS OF EVER-FALLING STARRES. | WEEPER | 8 | 52 | 307 | 120 |

## EVER-WAKEFULL

| | | | | | |
|---|---|---|---|---|---|
| STILL WOULD THOSE EVER-WAKEFULL SONS OF FIRE | CHARITAS NIMIA | 25 | 52 | 280 | 48 |

## EVER-WATRY

| | | | | | |
|---|---|---|---|---|---|
| MAKES THY EVER-WATRY EYES | THE WEEPER | 98 | 46 | 79 | 120 |

## EVER-YOUTHFULL

| | | | | | |
|---|---|---|---|---|---|
| THE FAIRE SON OF AN EVER-YOUTHFULL SPRING, | UPON DEATH OF HERRYS | 39 | 46 | 167 | 466 |

## EVERLASTING

| | | | | | |
|---|---|---|---|---|---|
| AN EVERLASTING SPRING, THE JOLLY YEARE | OUT OF VIRGIL | 26 | 46 | 155 | 529 |
| FIND EVERLASTING SMILES. SO RARE, | IN MEMORY OF LADY MADRE TERESA | 87 | 46 | 131 | 52 |
| OF EVERLASTING JOYES BATH THY WHITE BREST. | ON THE ASSUMPTION | 58 | 46 | 139 | 114 |
| AN EVERLASTING SMILE UPON THE FACE, | UPON YORKE HIS BIRTH | 20 | 46 | 176 | 500 |
| UNTO THE EVERLASTING LIFE OF SONG. | TO THE NAME OF JESUS | 10 | 52 | 239 | 30 |
| AND EVERLASTING SERIES OF A DEATHLESSE SONG. | TO THE NAME OF JESUS | 85 | 52 | 239 | 30 |
| OF EVERLASTING JOYES BATH THY WHITE BREST. | IN GLORIOUS ASSUMPTION B. LADY | 63 | 52 | 304 | 114 |
| FIND EVERLASTING SMILES. SO RARE, | TERESA | 87 | 52 | 315 | 52 |
| OF LOVE, OF LIFE, & EVERLASTING REST. | TO SAME CONCERNING CHOISE | 53 | 52 | 331 | 66 |

## E'RE

| | | | | | |
|---|---|---|---|---|---|
| WHAT E'RE IT BE LOVE OFFERS, STILL PRESUME | OUT OF GREEKE CUPID'S CRYER | 73 | 46 | 159 | 519 |
| THOUGH SHEE BE DUMBE E'RE SINCE HIS DEATH, | UPON THE DEATH OF A GENTLEMAN | 17 | 46 | 166 | 472 |
| THY MIND IN TEARES WHO E'RE THOU BE, | UPON THE DEATH OF A GENTLEMAN | 25 | 46 | 166 | 472 |
| NO APRIL E'RE LENT SOFTER SHOWRES, | THE WEEPER | 89 | 46 | 79 | 120 |
| HOW SAD SO E'RE | THE TEARE | 15 | 46 | 84 | 50 |
| HEE'L HAVE HIS TEAT E'RE LONG (A BLOODY ONE) | BLESSED BE THE PAPS | 3 | 46 | 94 | 14 |
| 'TIS CHANG'D INDEED, DID AUTUMN E'RE SUCH BEAUTIES BRING | UPON THORNES FROM LORDS HEAD | 3 | 46 | 96 | 23 |
| THY WRATH THAT WADES HEERE NOW, E'RE LONG SHALL SWIM | OUR LORD IN HIS CIRCUMCISION | 5 | 46 | 98 | 9 |
| THEN HEE E'RE SHEWD TO MORTALL SIGHT, | A HYMNE OF THE NATIVITY | 12 | 46 | 106 | 76 |
| THEN HEE HIMSELFE E'RE SAW BEFORE, | A HYMNE OF THE NATIVITY | 13 | 46 | 106 | 76 |
| RUINE, WHERE E'RE SHE SLEEPES AT NATURES FEET. | SOSPETTO D'HERODE | 279 | 46 | 109 | 216 |
| AND WHERE SO E'RE HEE SITTS HIS WHITE | IN MEMORY OF LADY MADRE TERESA | 180 | 46 | 131 | 52 |
| SUCH AS (E'RE OUR DARK SINNES TO DUST BETRAY'D THEE) | ON A TREATISE OF CHARITY | 4 | 46 | 137 | 69 |
| DEARE BABE E'RE MANY DAYES BE DONE. | AN HIMNE FOR CIRCUMCISION | 30 | 46 | 141 | 37 |
| MEANE WHILE WHO E'RE THOU ART THAT PASSEST HERE, | UPON DEATH OF HERRYS | 41 | 46 | 167 | 466 |
| WHY THEN SHOULD IT E'RE BE SEENE, | UPON DEATH OF DESIRED HERRYS | 19 | 46 | 168 | 467 |
| WITH STERNE DEATH, IF E'RE HE FAINTED, | ANOTHER ON HERRYS | 2 | 46 | 170 | 469 |
| PASSENGER WHO E'RE THOU ART, | HIS EPITAPH (HERRYS) | 1 | 46 | 172 | 471 |
| WHAT WORD SO E'RE HIS BREATH KEPT WARME. | HIS EPITAPH (HERRYS) | 31 | 46 | 172 | 471 |
| E'RE HEBE'S HAND HAD OVERLAID | HIS EPITAPH (HERRYS) | 45 | 46 | 172 | 471 |
| (PASSENGER WHO E'RE THOU ART) | HIS EPITAPH (HERRYS) | 51 | 46 | 172 | 471 |
| O STAY A WHILE E'RE THOU DRAW IN THY HEAD, | UPON STANINOUGH'S DEATH | 3 | 46 | 175 | 475 |
| THEY ARE THY GREATNESSE. GODS WHERE E'RE THEY GO | UPON YORKE HIS BIRTH | 18 | 46 | 176 | 500 |
| E'RE PROVE THE DISMALL MORNING OF THY NIGHT. | UPON YORKE HIS BIRTH | 93 | 46 | 176 | 500 |
| HOW E'RE LOVES NATIVE HOURES WERE SET. | LOVES HOROSCOPE | 17 | 46 | 185 | 483 |
| YOUR VIRGIN BOSOME. THEN WHAT E'RE | THOUGH NOW 'TIS NEITHER | 23 | MS | 397 | 492 |
| WHAT E'RE COOPERATES TO THE COMMON MIRTHE | TO THE NAME OF JESUS | 75 | 52 | 239 | 30 |
| THEN HE E'RE SHOW'D TO MORTALL SIGHT. | IN HOLY NATIVITY | 12 | 52 | 246 | 76 |
| THEN HE HIMSELFE E'RE SAW BEFORE. | IN HOLY NATIVITY | 13 | 52 | 246 | 76 |
| MADE HIS OWN BED E'RE HE WAS BORN. | IN HOLY NATIVITY | 49 | 52 | 246 | 76 |
| E'RE THE LESSE GLORIOUS RUN. | CHARITAS NIMIA | 40 | 52 | 280 | 48 |
| OR E'RE THE SOONER SEEK HIS WESTERN BED, | CHARITAS NIMIA | 42 | 52 | 280 | 48 |
| E'RE SHE BORE ANY ONE, SLEW ALL. | O GLORIOSA DOMINA | 12 | 52 | 302 | 194 |
| WHAT PRINCE'S WANTON'ST PRIDE E'RE COULD | WEEPER | 119 | 52 | 307 | 120 |
| NOR HAS SHE E'RE YET UNDERSTOOD | TERESA | 21 | 52 | 315 | 52 |
| WHAT SOUL SO E'RE, IN ANY LANGUAGE, CAN | AN APOLOGIE FOR (TERESA) HYMNE | 21 | 52 | 322 | 59 |
| WHAT E'RE THIS YOUTH OF FIRE WEARES FAIR, | FLAMING HEART | 31 | 52 | 324 | 61 |
| MERCY WILL COME E'RE LONG | PRAYER TO GENTLE-WOMAN | 40 | 52 | 328 | 139 |
| WHO E'RE HE BE WAS THE FIRST WANDRING KNIGHT. | ALEXIAS THIRD ELEGIE | 4 | 52 | 336 | 209 |
| WHAT E'RE LOVE'S MATTER BE, HE MOVES | AGAINST IRRESOLUTION AND DELAY | 53 | 52 | 347 | 146 |
| HEE'S GONE. THE FAIR'ST FLOWER, THAT E'RE BOSOME DREST, | LUKE 2. QUAERIT JESUM | 5 | MS | 379 | 11 |
| MAKE HAST, & COME, OR E'RE MY GREIFE, & I | LUKE 2. QUAERIT JESUM | 17 | MS | 379 | 11 |
| IN FARTHEST CLIME. WHAT E'RE IS BOUGHT | PETRONIJ ALES PHASIACIS PETITA | 12 | MS | 382 | 526 |
| THAT HAND. (WHAT E'RE IT WERE) THAT WAS THY NURSE | HORATIJ ILLE & NEFASTO | 3 | MS | 382 | 530 |
| UPON HIS TIPTOES, E'RE HIS SILVER HEAD | UPON KINGS CORONATION | 4 | MS | 389 | 454 |
| (FOR ELSE WHY CAME I.) EV'N WHAT E'RE I FEARE. | OUT OF GROTIUS | 8 | MS | 398 | 198 |
| E'RE BORNE WAS BANISH'T. BORNE WAS GLAD T'EMBRACE | OUT OF GROTIUS | 15 | MS | 398 | 198 |
| OF HOT DEFIANCE 'GAINST WHAT E'RE IS GOOD | OUT OF GROTIUS | 76 | MS | 398 | 198 |

## EVERY

| | | | | | |
|---|---|---|---|---|---|
| HEE LIGHTLY SKIRMISHES ON EVERY STRING | MUSICKS DUELL | 20 | 46 | 149 | 535 |
| SHEE MEASURES EVERY MEASURE, EVERY WHERE | MUSICKS DUELL | 34 | 46 | 149 | 535 |
| SHEE MEASURES EVERY MEASURE, EVERY WHERE | MUSICKS DUELL | 34 | 46 | 149 | 535 |
| ON THE WAV'D BACKE OF EVERY SWELLING STRAINE, | MUSICKS DUELL | 95 | 46 | 149 | 535 |
| EVERY SMOOTH TURNE, EVERY DELICIOUS STROAKE | MUSICKS DUELL | 131 | 46 | 149 | 535 |
| EVERY SMOOTH TURNE, EVERY DELICIOUS STROAKE | MUSICKS DUELL | 131 | 46 | 149 | 535 |
| THOSE YET FRESH STREAMES WHICH CRAWLED EVERY WHERE | THE BEGINNING OF HELIODORUS | 21 | 46 | 158 | 517 |
| EVERY MORNE FROM HENCE, | THE WEEPER | 25 | 46 | 79 | 120 |
| EVERY RED LETTER | ON MARKES OF SAVIOURS WOUNDS | 7 | 46 | 86 | 28 |

PAGE 122

| | | | | |
|---|---|---|---|---|
| ALL, AND EVERY WHIT OF ME. | IT IS BETTER TO GO WITH EYE | 6 | 46 | 93 | 16 |
| HARKE HOW AT EVERY TOUCH SHE DOES COMPLAINE HER. | TO PONTIUS WASHING HANDS | 12 | 46 | 94 | 23 |
| AND FEELE THE PULSE OF EVERY PROPHECY. | SOSPETTO D'HERODE | 156 | 46 | 109 | 216 |
| THEY PRICK A BLEEDING HEART AT EVERY STITCH. | SOSPETTO D'HERODE | 342 | 46 | 109 | 216 |
| DIRE FLAMES DIFFUSE THEMSELVES THROUGH EVERY VEINE, | SOSPETTO D'HERODE | 471 | 46 | 109 | 216 |
| ARE SENT ABOUT, WHO POASTING EVERY WAY | SOSPETTO D'HERODE | 510 | 46 | 109 | 216 |
| TO TH'HEADS AND OFFICERS OF EVERY BAND. | SOSPETTO D'HERODE | 511 | 46 | 109 | 216 |
| AND EVERY DAY, | ON A PRAYER BOOKE | 100 | 46 | 126 | 139 |
| WHICH EVERY DAY TO HEAVEN WILL SEND YOU. | ON MR. G. HERBERTS BOOKE | 12 | 46 | 130 | 68 |
| AND FLATTER'D EVERY GREEDY EYE THAT STOOD | UPON DEATH OF HERRYS | 26 | 46 | 167 | 466 |
| BATHES IN TEARES OF EVERY EYE. | ANOTHER ON HERRYS | 8 | 46 | 170 | 469 |
| EVERY RECONCILED GRACE, | HIS EPITAPH (HERRYS) | 19 | 46 | 172 | 471 |
| THE BROW OF EVERY MONETH. AND WHEN THAT'S DONE | UPON YORKE HIS BIRTH | 98 | 46 | 176 | 500 |
| MAYEST IN A SUN OF HIS FIND EVERY SON | UPON YORKE HIS BIRTH | 99 | 46 | 176 | 500 |
| THOUGH EVERY DIAMOND IN JOVES CROWNE | LUVES HOROSCOPE | 37 | 46 | 185 | 483 |
| AND EVERY SWEET-LIPP'T THING | TO THE NAME OF JESUS | 47 | 52 | 239 | 30 |
| BUT EVERY WHERE & EVERY WHILE | IN GLORIOUS EPIPHANIE | 30 | 52 | 253 | 39 |
| BUT EVERY WHERE & EVERY WHILE | IN GLORIOUS EPIPHANIE | 30 | 52 | 253 | 39 |
| FOR THIS HE LOOK'T SO BIGG. & EVERY MORN | IN GLORIOUS EPIPHANIE | 121 | 52 | 253 | 39 |
| WEEP FOR EVERY WORM THAT DYES. | CHARITAS NIMIA | 38 | 52 | 280 | 48 |
| EACH WOUND OF HIS, FROM EVERY PART, | SANCTA MARIA DOLORUM | 9 | 52 | 283 | 162 |
| BE ALL THE SAME TO EVERY GUEST, | LAUDA SION SALVATOREM | 50 | 52 | 294 | 178 |
| LESSE THEN WHOLE CHRIST IN EVERY CRUMME. | LAUDA SION SALVATOREM | 58 | 52 | 294 | 178 |
| EVERY MORN FROM HENCE | WEEPER | 25 | 52 | 307 | 120 |
| A SERAPHIM AT EVERY SHOTT. | FLAMING HEART | 54 | 52 | 324 | 61 |
| AND EVERY DAY | PRAYER TO GENTLE-WOMAN | 106 | 52 | 328 | 139 |
| I'AM PERFECT IN HEAVN'S STATE, WITH EVERY STARR | ALEXIAS SECONDE ELEGIE | 23 | 52 | 335 | 207 |
| AND SNATCH'D AWAY THE BANQUETT. EVERY ONE | UPON GUNPOWDER TREASON | 54 | MS | 387 | 461 |
| MADE EVERY MORTALL GLADLY SACRIFICE | UPON KINGS CORONATION | 36 | MS | 390 | 453 |
| WITTNESSE THIS MAPP OF BEAUTY. EVERY PART | UPON BIRTH PRINCESSE E | 37 | MS | 391 | 456 |
| SEE. NOTHING'S VULGAR, EVERY ATOME HEERE | UPON BIRTH PRINCESSE E | 39 | MS | 391 | 456 |
| THAT THERE INHABITE, THOU ON EVERY DAY | AN ELEGIE ON DR PORTER | 5 | MS | 395 | 476 |
| AND MURMUR FORTH THY WOES TO EVERY FLOWER. | AN ELEGIE ON DR PORTER | 21 | MS | 395 | 476 |

EXALATIONS

| | | | | |
|---|---|---|---|---|
| DELICIOUS DEATHS. SOFT EXALATIONS | PRAYER TO GENTLE-WOMAN | 77 | 52 | 328 | 139 |

EXALT

| | | | | |
|---|---|---|---|---|
| THAT CAN EXALT WEAK EARTH, AND SO REFINE | AN APOLOGIE FOR HYMNE (TERESA) | 44 | 46 | 136 | 59 |
| THAT CAN EXALT WEAK EARTH. & SO REFINE | AN APOLOGIE FOR (TERESA) HYMNE | 44 | 52 | 322 | 59 |

EXALTED

| | | | | |
|---|---|---|---|---|
| THE GRAVE, AND HOLD UP AN EXALTED ARME | TO THE MORNING | 26 | 46 | 183 | 497 |

EXAMPLES

| | | | | |
|---|---|---|---|---|
| AND BY HIS FAIRE EXAMPLES LIGHT, | AN EPITAPH UPON ASHTON | 31 | 46 | 192 | 464 |

EXCEEDING

| | | | | |
|---|---|---|---|---|
| IMAGIN'D HIM EXCEEDING OLD. | HIS EPITAPH (HERRYS) | 12 | 46 | 172 | 471 |

EXCELLENCE

| | | | | |
|---|---|---|---|---|
| PARDON (BRIGHT EXCELLENCE) AN UNTUN'D STRING, | UPON YORKE HIS BIRTH | 106 | 46 | 176 | 500 |
| THY COSTLY EXCELLENCE WITH THY KING'S OWN BLOOD. | VEXILLA REGIS | 30 | 52 | 277 | 156 |
| BUT SUCH IS THE CAELESTIALL EXCELLENCE, | UPON BIRTH PRINCESSE E | 33 | MS | 391 | 456 |

EXCEPT

| | | | | |
|---|---|---|---|---|
| THE RAIN IS GONE, EXCEPT SO MUCH AS WE | IN GLORIOUS ASSUMPTION B. LADY | 21 | 52 | 304 | 114 |

EXCUSE

| | | | | |
|---|---|---|---|---|
| THAT MADE IT LONG EXCUSE THE LENGTH. | TO THE QUEEN | 14 | 48 | 215 | 501 |
| WHERE CAN YOU FIX, TO FIND EXCUSE | AGAINST IRRESOLUTION AND DELAY | 31 | 52 | 347 | 146 |

EXECUTION

| | | | | |
|---|---|---|---|---|
| AND STILL ASSIST THE EXECUTION. | SOSPETTO D'HERODE | 292 | 46 | 109 | 216 |

EXECUTIONERS

| | | | | |
|---|---|---|---|---|
| FELL EXECUTIONERS OF FOULE INTENTS, | SOSPETTO D'HERODE | 324 | 46 | 109 | 216 |
| FIT EXECUTIONERS FOR THEE. | IN MEMORY OF LADY MADRE TERESA | 92 | 46 | 131 | 52 |
| FITT EXECUTIONERS FOR THEE, | TERESA | 92 | 52 | 315 | 52 |

EXERCISE

| | | | | |
|---|---|---|---|---|
| AND SHEE ALTHOUGH HER BREATH'S LATE EXERCISE | MUSICKS DUELL | 158 | 46 | 149 | 535 |
| TO EXERCISE THEIR ARCHERIE. | IN MEMORY OF LADY MADRE TERESA | 96 | 46 | 131 | 52 |
| TO EXERCISE THEIR ARCHERIE. | TERESA | 96 | 52 | 315 | 52 |

EXHALATION

| | | | | |
|---|---|---|---|---|
| HIS FLAMING EYES DIRE EXHALATION, | SOSPETTO D'HERODE | 57 | 46 | 109 | 216 |
| DO'ST THOU NOT SEE AN EXHALATION | ON GUNPOWDER-TREASON | 15 | MS | 384 | 458 |

EXHALATIONS

  DELICIOUS DEATHS, SOFT EXHALATIONS         ON A PRAYER BOOKE              71  46 126 139

EXHALE

  SHALT THOU EXHALE TO HEAVEN AT LAST,      IN MEMORY OF LADY MADRE TERESA  117  46 131  52
  SHALT THOU EXHALE TO HEAVN AT LAST        TERESA                               116  52 315  52

EXHAL'D

  IT WAS EXHAL'D, A WHILE IT HUNG, & DY'D.    ON GUNPOWDER-TREASON          50  MS 384 458

EXILE

  HE FLYES, & INTO WILLFULL EXILE GOES.      ALEXIAS THIRD ELEGIE          16  52 336 209

EXPATIATE

  AND TEACH IT TO EXPATIATE, AND SWELL       UPON YORKE HIS BIRTH          23  46 176 500

EXPECT

  EXPECT A SEA, MY HEART SHALL MAKE IT GOOD.   OUR LORD IN HIS CIRCUMCISION    4  46  98   9

EXPECTED

  HIS CROWNE EXPECTED, WHEN (O FATE, O TIME   UPON DEATH OF HERRYS          29  46 167 466

EXPECTING

  THE HEAV'N EXPECTING AGES, HOPE TO SEE     SOSPETTO D'HERODE           158  46 109 216
  EXPECTING FIRE FROM YOUR EYES,             ON MR. G. HERBERTS BOOKE       3  46 130  68
  EXPECTING BY THY VOYCE TO TUNE HIS LUTE.    UPON YORKE HIS BIRTH         115  46 176 500
  HAVE SPENT THE PATIENCE OF EXPECTING WEEKES, UPON TWO GREENE APRICOCKES     4  48 220 494

EXPECTATION

  GLAD TIME TO RIPEN EXPECTATION.            UPON DEATH OF HERRYS          22  46 167 466

EXPENCE

  SWEET MARY THY FAIRE EYES EXPENCE.         THE TEARE                     2  46  84  50
  STILL YOU ARE PRODIGAL OF YOUR LOVE'S EXPENCE SOSPETTO D'HERODE           285  46 109 216
  COME ROYALL NAME, & PAY THE EXPENCE        TO THE NAME OF JESUS         139  52 239  30

TH'EXPENCE

  HERE'S A THEAME WILL DRINKE TH'EXPENCE.    UPON THE DEATH OF A GENTLEMAN  31  46 166 472

EXPENSES

  IN THY SO RICH & RARE EXPENSES,            WEEPER                       116  52 307 120

EXPERIENCE

  THE FRIGHTED STARS TOOKE FAINT EXPERIENCE,  SOSPETTO D'HERODE           283  46 109 216

EXPIRE

  SO DOE PERFUMES EXPIRE.                    WEEPER                       157  52 307 120

EXPOSTULATE

  EXPOSTULATE MY WOES & MUCH-WRONG'D LOVES.   ALEXIAS SECONDE ELEGIE       14  52 335 207

EXPOUND

  THE HUMOUROUS STRINGS EXPOUND HIS LEARNED TOUCH, MUSICKS DUELL             127  46 149 535

EXPOUNDS

  HEE EXPOUNDS THE GIDDY WONDER              PSALME 23                    27  46 102   5

EXPRESSE

  MUTUALL SWEETNESSE THEY EXPRESSE.          THE WEEPER                    68  46  79 120
  MUTUALL SWEETNESSE THEY EXPRESSE.          WEEPER                       82  52 307 120

EXPREST

  WEEPE THEN, ONELY BE EXPREST               UPON THE DEATH OF A GENTLEMAN  33  46 166 472
  WAS IN HIS SHADY FOREHEAD SEEN EXPREST.    SOSPETTO D'HERODE           195  46 109 216
  WHOSE SNOWY CHEEKES, LEAST JOY SHOULD BE EXPREST, AN ELEGIE ON DR PORTER     9  MS 395 476

EXPRESSION

  THE FOREHEAD'S SHADE IN GRIEFES EXPRESSION THERE, SOSPETTO D'HERODE           196  46 109 216
  MISCHEIFE, THAT SCORNES EXPRESSION SHOULD COME NIGH ON GUNPOWDER-TREASON        48  MS 384 458
                           IT.

EXTASIE

| | | | | | |
|---|---|---|---|---|---|
| THE EXTASIE OF A DELIGHT | OUT OF THE ITALIAN (3) | 5 | 46 | 190 | 549 |

EXTASY

| | | | | | |
|---|---|---|---|---|---|
| BY A STRONG EXTASY) THROUGH ALL THE SPHAEARES | MUSICKS DUELL | 148 | 46 | 149 | 535 |
| A SWEET INEBRIATED EXTASY. | OUT OF GROTIUS | 54 | MS | 398 | 198 |

EXTASIES

| | | | | | |
|---|---|---|---|---|---|
| INTO LOOSE EXTASIES, THAT SHEE IS PLAC'T | MUSICKS DUELL | 103 | 46 | 149 | 535 |

EXTRACT

| | | | | | |
|---|---|---|---|---|---|
| NATURE HATH LEARN'T T' EXTRACT A DEW, | THE WEEPER | 71 | 46 | 79 | 120 |
| NATURE HATH LEARN'T TO EXTRACT A DEAW | WEEPER | 53 | 52 | 307 | 120 |

EXTRACTED

| | | | | | |
|---|---|---|---|---|---|
| BODY OF BLESSINGS. SPIRIT OF SOULES EXTRACTED. | TO THE NAME OF JESUS | 166 | 52 | 239 | 30 |
| NEVER DURST HATCH BEFORE. EXTRACTED SEE | UPON GUNPOWDER TREASON | 7 | MS | 386 | 460 |
| EXTRACTED HAVE A BALMY ELOQUENCE. | UPON BIRTH PRINCESSE E | 10 | MS | 391 | 456 |

EYE

| | | | | | |
|---|---|---|---|---|---|
| O YES. IF ANY HAPPY EYE, | OUT OF GREEKE CUPID'S CRYER | 5 | 46 | 159 | 519 |
| BUT LEAST YOUR EYE DISCERNING SLIDE | OUT OF GREEKE CUPID'S CRYER | 17 | 46 | 159 | 519 |
| ALL ONE GREAT EYE, ALL DROWN'D IN ONE GREAT TEARE. | UPON BISHOP ANDREWES PICTURE | 4 | 46 | 163 | 490 |
| OF HER GREAT MAKER FIXT HER FLAMING EYE, | UPON BISHOP ANDREWES PICTURE | 11 | 46 | 163 | 490 |
| FROM THINE EYE ITS SPHEARE. | THE TEARE | 9 | 46 | 84 | 50 |
| AN EYE, BUT NOT A WEEPING ONE, | THE TEARE | 44 | 46 | 84 | 50 |
| AN EYE OF HEAVEN. OR STILL SHINE HERE | THE TEARE | 47 | 46 | 84 | 50 |
| IN TH'HEAVEN OF MARY'S EYE, A TEARE. | THE TEARE | 48 | 46 | 84 | 50 |
| THAT ON HER LAP SHE CASTS HER HUMBLE EYE. | ON VIRGINS BASHFULNESSE | 1 | 46 | 89 | 9 |
| WHERE TH'OTHER DARES NOT SEND HIS EYE. | TWO WENT TO PRAY | 4 | 46 | 89 | 18 |
| NOT TO HIS EARE, BUT TO HIS EYE. | THE BLIND CURED | 6 | 46 | 91 | 19 |
| ONE EYE. A THOUSAND RATHER, AND A THOUSAND MORE | IT IS BETTER TO GO WITH EYE | 1 | 46 | 93 | 16 |
| YET IF THOU'LT FILL ONE POORE EYE, WITH THY HEAVEN AND THEE, | IT IS BETTER TO GO WITH EYE | 4 | 46 | 93 | 16 |
| O GRANT (SWEET GOODNESSE) THAT ONE EYE MAY BE | IT IS BETTER TO GO WITH EYE | 5 | 46 | 93 | 16 |
| HANDLING & TURNING THEM WITH AN UNWOUNDED EYE. | AND A CERTAINE PRIEST PASSED | 2 | 46 | 94 | 17 |
| THE CALM THAT COOLS THINE EYE DOES SHIPWRACK MINE, FOR O. | AND A CERTAINE PRIEST PASSED | 3 | 46 | 94 | 17 |
| LO. A BLOOD-SHOT EYE. THAT WEEPES | ON WOUNDS OF CRUCIFIED LORD | 7 | 46 | 99 | 24 |
| TO PAY THY TEARES, AN EYE THAT WEEPS | ON WOUNDS OF CRUCIFIED LORD | 15 | 46 | 99 | 24 |
| FRESH FROM THE PURE GLANCE OF THINE EYE. | PSALME 23 | 65 | 46 | 102 | 5 |
| HER KISSES IN THY WEEPING EYE. | A HYMNE OF THE NATIVITY | 66 | 46 | 106 | 76 |
| THE BEAUTIES OF WHOSE DAWNE WHAT EYE MAY BIDE, | SOSPETTO D'HERODE | 11 | 46 | 109 | 216 |
| HIS BLAZE, TO SHINE IN A POORE SHEPHEARDS EYE. | SOSPETTO D'HERODE | 170 | 46 | 109 | 216 |
| OF ALL THEIR CARES, TAM'D THE REBELLIOUS EYE | SOSPETTO D'HERODE | 390 | 46 | 109 | 216 |
| A WAKING EYE AND HAND. LOOKE UP AND SEE | SOSPETTO D'HERODE | 431 | 46 | 109 | 216 |
| WHERE THOU SHALT REACH ALL HEARTS, COMMAND EACH EYE. | ON A TREATISE OF CHARITY | 16 | 46 | 137 | 69 |
| AND FLATTER'D EVERY GREEDY EYE THAT STOOD | UPON DEATH OF HERRYS | 26 | 46 | 167 | 466 |
| BATHES IN TEARES OF EVERY EYE. | ANOTHER ON HERRYS | 8 | 46 | 170 | 469 |
| THESE CURTAIN'D WINDOWES, THIS SELFE-PRISON'D EYE, | UPON STANINGHS'S DEATH | 25 | 46 | 175 | 475 |
| AT MID-DAY OPES A PRESENCE WHICH HEAVENS EYE | UPON YORKE HIS BIRTH | 70 | 46 | 176 | 500 |
| 'TIS IN THE MERCY OF HER EYE, | LOVES HOROSCOPE | 19 | 46 | 185 | 483 |
| LOVE HA'S NO PLEA AGAINST HER EYE | LOVES HOROSCOPE | 31 | 46 | 185 | 483 |
| (THOUGH HEAVENS INAUSPICIOUS EYE | LOVES HOROSCOPE | 35 | 46 | 185 | 483 |
| HER EYE A STRONG APPEALE CAN GIVE. | LOVES HOROSCOPE | 39 | 46 | 185 | 483 |
| BUT IN HER EYE, OR IN HER EARE, | LOVES HOROSCOPE | 42 | 46 | 185 | 483 |
| BUT IN HER EYE, OR IN HER EARE, | LOVES HOROSCOPE | 48 | 46 | 185 | 483 |
| (SHARPE SIGHTED AS THE EAGLES EYE, THAT CAN | ON FRONTISPIECE ISAACSONS | 9 | 46 | 191 | 491 |
| THOSE TO THE EYE, THEN TO THE EARE. | AN EPITAPH UPON ASHTON | 14 | 46 | 192 | 464 |
| AS SHALL MOCKE THE ENVIOUS EYE. | OUT OF CATULLUS | 20 | 46 | 194 | 523 |
| LOCK'T UP FROM MORTALL EYE, | WISHES SUPPOSED MISTRESSE | 5 | 46 | 195 | 479 |
| THE BLINDNES OF THE WORLD DID CALL THE EYE. | IN GLORIOUS EPIPHANIE | 45 | 52 | 253 | 39 |
| THE SHUTTING OF HIS EYE SHALL OPEN THEIRS. | IN GLORIOUS EPIPHANIE | 162 | 52 | 253 | 39 |
| AND AS BEFORE HIS TOO-BRIGHT EYE | IN GLORIOUS EPIPHANIE | 168 | 52 | 253 | 39 |
| THE DELEGATED EYE OF DAY | IN GLORIOUS EPIPHANIE | 236 | 52 | 253 | 39 |
| THOUGH ALLOW'D NOR HAND NOR EYE | ADORO TE | 28 | 52 | 291 | 172 |
| O THAT JUDGE. WHOSE HAND, WHOSE EYE | DIES IRAE | 19 | 52 | 298 | 186 |
| THESE CURTAIN'D WINDOWS, THIS RETIRED EYE | DEATH'S LECTURE | 27 | 52 | 340 | 475 |
| TO GAZE UPON SUCH STARRES EACH HUMBLE EYE | UPON KINGS CORONATION | 33 | MS | 389 | 454 |
| THE STAGGERING LUMPE. EACH EYE SPENT ALL ITS STORE, | UPON KINGS CORONATION | 11 | MS | 390 | 453 |
| AS IS THY BIRTH. YET FROM THY FLAMING EYE | UPON BIRTH PRINCESSE E | 18 | MS | 391 | 456 |
| SHOTT FROM HIS FLAMING EYE, HAD THAW'D IT'S IRE. | AN ELEGY MR STANNINOW | 32 | MS | 394 | 473 |
| LET EACH EYE WATER'T WITH A COURTEOUS TEARE. | AN ELEGY MR STANNINOW | 56 | MS | 394 | 473 |
| KNOWING 'TIS IN THE DOOME OF YOUR SWEET EYE | AT TH' IVORY TRIBUNALL | 3 | MS | 397 | 492 |

EYE-LIDS

| | | | | | |
|---|---|---|---|---|---|
| FROM TH' DAWN OF THY FAIRE EYE-LIDS WIPE AWAY | ON A TREATISE OF CHARITY | 7 | 46 | 137 | 69 |
| NOR MAY THE LIGHT THAT GIVES THEIR EYE-LIDS LIGHT, | UPON YORKE HIS BIRTH | 92 | 46 | 176 | 500 |

EYE-LIDDS

| | | | | | |
|---|---|---|---|---|---|
| PREVENTS THE EYE-LIDDS OF THE BLUSHING DAY. | MUSICKS DUELL | 82 | 46 | 149 | 535 |

## EY

| | | | | | |
|---|---|---|---|---|---|
| WHILE WE FOUND OUT HEAVN'S FAIRER EY | IN HOLY NATIVITY | 7 | 52 | 246 | 76 |
| CHARG'D TO LOOK ON, & WITH A STEDFAST EY | SANCTA MARIA DOLORUM | 37 | 52 | 283 | 162 |
| KEEP CLOSE, MY SOUL'S INQUIRING EY. | ADORO TE | 6 | 52 | 291 | 172 |
| WITH BLUSHING CHEEK & BLEEDING EY. | DIES IRAE | 42 | 52 | 298 | 186 |

## EY'S

| | | | | | |
|---|---|---|---|---|---|
| BY THINE EY'S TINCT ENOBLED THUS | WEEPER | 149 | 52 | 307 | 120 |

## EYLIDDES

| | | | | | |
|---|---|---|---|---|---|
| PROUD LOOKES, & LOFTY EYLIDDES, HERE PUTT ON | DEATH'S LECTURE | 21 | 52 | 340 | 475 |

## EYN

| | | | | | |
|---|---|---|---|---|---|
| THIS WATRY BLOSSOM OF THY EYN, | WEEPER | 65 | 52 | 307 | 120 |
| THE WAY INTO THESE WEEPING EYN. | WEEPER | 106 | 52 | 307 | 120 |

## EYNE

| | | | | | |
|---|---|---|---|---|---|
| TOO TRUE A TEARE. FOR NO SAD EYNE, | THE TEARE | 14 | 46 | 84 | 50 |
| THIS WATRY BLOSSOME OF THY EYNE | THE TEARE | 29 | 46 | 84 | 50 |
| BE THEY MOUTHES, OR BE THEY EYNE, | ON WOUNDS OF CRUCIFIED LORD | 3 | 46 | 99 | 24 |
| THY LITTLE SELFE IN LESSE, READ IN THESE EYNE | UPON YORKE HIS BIRTH | 43 | 46 | 176 | 500 |

## EYED

| | | | | | |
|---|---|---|---|---|---|
| PUT ALL HIS RED EYED RUBIES ON, | AN HIMNE FOR CIRCUMCISION | 15 | 46 | 141 | 37 |

## BLEW-EY'D

| | | | | | |
|---|---|---|---|---|---|
| RISE THEN (FAIRE BLEW-EY'D MAID) RISE AND DISCOVER | ON A FOULE MORNING | 27 | 46 | 181 | 495 |

## FAIR-EY'D

| | | | | | |
|---|---|---|---|---|---|
| WHILE WE FOUND OUT THE FAIR-EY'D BOY. | A HYMNE OF THE NATIVITY | 7 | 46 | 106 | 76 |
| AS BY A FAIR-EY'D FALLACY OF DAY | IN GLORIOUS EPIPHANIE | 163 | 52 | 253 | 39 |

## RED-EY'D

| | | | | | |
|---|---|---|---|---|---|
| PUT ALL HIS RED-EY'D RUBIES ON. | NEW YEAR'S DAY | 15 | 52 | 251 | 37 |

## RIGHT-EY'D

| | | | | | |
|---|---|---|---|---|---|
| THE RIGHT-EY'D AREOPAGITE | IN GLORIOUS EPIPHANIE | 191 | 52 | 253 | 39 |

## EYES

| | | | | | |
|---|---|---|---|---|---|
| HIGH-COLOUR'D IS. HIS EYES STILL FLUSHING | OUT OF GREEKE CUPID'S CRYER | 20 | 46 | 159 | 519 |
| THE SAD LANGUAGE OF OUR EYES, | UPON THE DEATH OF A GENTLEMAN | 20 | 46 | 166 | 472 |
| EYES ARE VOCALL, TEARES HAVE TONGUES, | UPON THE DEATH OF A GENTLEMAN | 27 | 46 | 166 | 472 |
| THY FAIRE EYES SWEET MAGDALENE. | THE WEEPER | 6 | 46 | 79 | 120 |
| HEAVENS THY FAIRE EYES BEE. | THE WEEPER | 7 | 46 | 79 | 120 |
| AND DRAW FROM THESE FULL EYES OF THINE, | THE WEEPER | 35 | 46 | 79 | 120 |
| NOT IN THE EVENINGS EYES | THE WEEPER | 55 | 46 | 79 | 120 |
| THE APRIL IN THINE EYES, | THE WEEPER | 87 | 46 | 79 | 120 |
| BY THINE EYES TINCT ENOBLED THUS | THE WEEPER | 95 | 46 | 79 | 120 |
| MAKES THY EVER-WATRY EYES | THE WEEPER | 98 | 46 | 79 | 120 |
| DOES NIGHT LOOSE HER EYES. | THE WEEPER | 111 | 46 | 79 | 120 |
| YEE SIMPERING SONS OF THOSE FAIRE EYES, | THE WEEPER | 122 | 46 | 79 | 120 |
| YOU FROM HER EYES SWOLNE WOMBES OF SORROW. | THE WEEPER | 126 | 46 | 79 | 120 |
| SWEET MARY THY FAIRE EYES EXPENCE. | THE TEARE | 2 | 46 | 84 | 50 |
| THIS THINE EYES JEWELL IN HER EARE. | THE TEARE | 12 | 46 | 84 | 50 |
| MUST HAVE ITS FOUNTAINE IN THINE EYES. | TO PONTIUS WASHING HANDS | 4 | 46 | 88 | 22 |
| SHE CAN SEE HEAVEN, AND NE'RE LIFT UP HER EYES. | ON VIRGINS BASHFULNESSE | 6 | 46 | 89 | 9 |
| THIS NEW GUEST TO HER EYES NEW LAWES HATH GIVEN, | ON VIRGINS BASHFULNESSE | 7 | 46 | 89 | 9 |
| OF EYES THAT HAS BUT ARGUS STORE, | IT IS BETTER TO GO WITH EYE | 3 | 46 | 93 | 16 |
| HER EYES FLOOD LICKES HIS FEETS FAIRE STAINE, | SHE BEGAN TO WASH HIS FEET | 1 | 46 | 97 | 13 |
| ARE THEY MOUTHES, OR ARE THEY EYES. | ON WOUNDS OF CRUCIFIED LORD | 2 | 46 | 99 | 24 |
| IN TEARS. AS IF THINE EYES HAD NONE. | ON BLEEDING WOUNDS OF LORD | 18 | 46 | 101 | 110 |
| WHEN FIRST I LOOK'T ON THEE, I LOST MINE EYES. | SAMPSON TO HIS DALILAH | 2 | 46 | 102 | 8 |
| NOT FROM THE EAST, BUT FROM THY EYES. | A HYMNE OF THE NATIVITY | 22 | 46 | 106 | 76 |
| BY THOSE SWEET EYES PERSUASIVE POWERS. | A HYMNE OF THE NATIVITY | 27 | 46 | 106 | 76 |
| WEE SAW THINE EYES BREAK FROM THE EAST. | A HYMNE OF THE NATIVITY | 31 | 46 | 106 | 76 |
| BUT STREIGHT HIS EYES ADVIS'D HIS CHEEKE. | A HYMNE OF THE NATIVITY | 49 | 46 | 106 | 76 |
| THE POINTS OF HER YOUNG EAGLES EYES. | A HYMNE OF THE NATIVITY | 70 | 46 | 106 | 76 |
| SLIPPERY SOULES IN SMILING EYES) | A HYMNE OF THE NATIVITY | 73 | 46 | 106 | 76 |
| AT LAST, IN FIRE OF THY FAIRE EYES. | A HYMNE OF THE NATIVITY | 87 | 46 | 106 | 76 |
| HIS EYES, THE SULLEN DENS OF DEATH AND NIGHT. | SOSPETTO D'HERODE | 49 | 46 | 109 | 216 |
| HIS FLAMING EYES DIRE EXHALATION, | SOSPETTO D'HERODE | 57 | 46 | 109 | 216 |
| THEE ALL THE BEAUTIES OF THY ONCE BRIGHT EYES. | SOSPETTO D'HERODE | 74 | 46 | 109 | 216 |
| LIFTS HIS MALIGNANT EYES, WASTED WITH CARE, | SOSPETTO D'HERODE | 83 | 46 | 109 | 216 |
| THERE DOES HE FIXE HIS EYES, AND THERE DETECT | SOSPETTO D'HERODE | 87 | 46 | 109 | 216 |
| THE GOLDEN EYES OF NIGHT, WHOSE BEAME MADE BRIGHT | SOSPETTO D'HERODE | 131 | 46 | 109 | 216 |
| HEE TOST HIS TROUBLED EYES, EMBERS THAT GLOW | SOSPETTO D'HERODE | 147 | 46 | 109 | 216 |
| PORTENTS BEFORE MINE EYES THEIR POWERS ADVANCE. | SOSPETTO D'HERODE | 202 | 46 | 109 | 216 |
| MUST THE BRIGHT ARMES OF HEAV'N, REBUKE THESE EYES. | SOSPETTO D'HERODE | 231 | 46 | 109 | 216 |
| SUCH, AND SO RICH, THE FLAMES THAT FROM THINE EYES. | SOSPETTO D'HERODE | 239 | 46 | 109 | 216 |
| AH WRETCH. WHAT BOOTES THEE TO CAST BACK THY EYES, | SOSPETTO D'HERODE | 241 | 46 | 109 | 216 |
| THE FIELD'S FAIRE EYES SAW HER, AND SAW NO MORE, | SOSPETTO D'HERODE | 378 | 46 | 109 | 216 |
| THE FACE OF THINGS, FROM HER DIRE EYES HAD RUN, | SOSPETTO D'HERODE | 383 | 46 | 109 | 216 |

| | | | | |
|---|---|---|---|---|
| AND IN A PALE GHOST'S SHAPE TO SPARE HIS EYES. | SOSPETTO D'HERODE | 416 | 46 109 | 216 |
| THAT HOLD THESE WEAPONS AND THE EYES | ON A PRAYER BOOKE | 23 | 46 126 | 139 |
| FLATTERING BUT FORSWEARING EYES | ON A PRAYER BOOKE | 53 | 46 126 | 139 |
| SIGHTS WHICH ARE NOT SEEN WITH EYES, | ON A PRAYER BOOKE | 64 | 46 126 | 139 |
| EXPECTING FIRE FROM YOUR EYES, | ON MR. G. HERBERTS BOOKE | 3 | 46 130 | 68 |
| BENDING HER BLESSED EYES ON THEE | IN MEMORY OF LADY MADRE TERESA | 135 | 46 131 | 52 |
| PUT ON THY SELFE IN THINE OWN LOOKS. T' OUR EYES | ON A TREATISE OF CHARITY | 2 | 46 137 | 69 |
| NOR ON GODS ALTAR CAST TWO SCORCHING EYES | ON A TREATISE OF CHARITY | 43 | 46 137 | 69 |
| TO BRING A PAIRE OF MEEK AND HUMBLE EYES. | ON A TREATISE OF CHARITY | 48 | 46 137 | 69 |
| WITH THOSE DIVINEST EYES, WHICH WEE | ON THE ASSUMPTION | 35 | 46 139 | 114 |
| THESE RUBIES SHALL PUT OUT HIS EYES. | AN HIMNE FOR CIRCUMCISION | 16 | 46 141 | 37 |
| THAT BREAKES FROM ONE OF THESE FAIRE EYES. | AN HIMNE FOR CIRCUMCISION | 28 | 46 141 | 37 |
| BUT IN THY FAIREST EYES FIND TWO FOR ONE. | AN HIMNE FOR CIRCUMCISION | 38 | 46 141 | 37 |
| WET WITH TEARES STILL'D FROM THE EYES, | ANOTHER ON HERRYS | 35 | 46 170 | 469 |
| THAT TO HIS SWEETNESSE, ALL MENS EYES | HIS EPITAPH (HERRYS) | 41 | 46 172 | 471 |
| CALL HEAVEN TO LOOKE ON THEE WITH NARROW EYES. | UPON STANINOUGH'S DEATH | 16 | 46 175 | 475 |
| PEEP'T FROM THEIR BUDS, SHEW'D LIKE THE GARDENS EYES | UPON YORKE HIS BIRTH | 62 | 46 176 | 500 |
| GIVE THEN THIS RURALL WREATH FREE FRUM THINE EYES. | UPON YORKE HIS BIRTH | 118 | 46 176 | 500 |
| HOW AT THE SIGHT DID'ST THOU DRAW BACK THINE EYES, | TO THE MORNING | 7 | 46 183 | 497 |
| O MEET THE ANGRY GOD, INVADE HIS EYES. | TO THE MORNING | 36 | 46 183 | 497 |
| THAT SHUTS NIGHTS DYING EYES, SHALL OPEN MINE. | TO THE MORNING | 46 | 46 183 | 497 |
| THY DOWNY FINGER, DWELL UPON THEIR EYES, | TO THE MORNING | 57 | 46 183 | 497 |
| AH MY HEART, HER EYES AND SHEE, | LOVES HOROSCOPE | 15 | 46 185 | 483 |
| FROM THY EYES HE SHOOTS HIS ARROWES. | OUT OF THE ITALIAN (1) | 15 | 46 188 | 545 |
| THINE EYES GRACES, | OUT OF THE ITALIAN (1) | 46 | 46 188 | 545 |
| YOUR EYES THE LIGHT HATH REFT HIM. | OUT OF THE ITALIAN (2) | 3 | 46 190 | 547 |
| AND DANCE BEFORE YOUR EYES. | OUT OF THE ITALIAN (2) | 10 | 46 190 | 547 |
| AND SO HE LOST HIS CLOTHES, EYES, HEART AND ALL. | OUT OF THE ITALIAN (3) | 8 | 46 190 | 549 |
| SHUTS THE EYES OF OUR SHORT LIGHT. | OUT OF CATULLUS | 8 | 46 194 | 523 |
| EYES, THAT DISPLACES | WISHES SUPPOSED MISTRESSE | 43 | 46 195 | 479 |
| EYES, THAT BESTOW | WISHES SUPPOSED MISTRESSE | 58 | 46 195 | 479 |
| (SWORNE SERVANT TO YOUR SWEETEST EYES) | THOUGH NOW 'TIS NEITHER | 4 | MS 397 | 492 |
| TAKING FRESH LIFE FROM YOUR FAYRE EYES. | THOUGH NOW 'TIS NEITHER | 10 | MS 397 | 492 |
| WHERE THY EYES SHINE HIS SUNS APPEARE. | THOUGH NOW 'TIS NEITHER | 28 | MS 397 | 492 |
| FIRST TURN'D TO EYES. | TO THE NAME OF JESUS | 136 | 52 239 | 30 |
| NOT FROM THE EAST, BUT FROM THINE EYES. | IN HOLY NATIVITY | 22 | 52 246 | 76 |
| WE SAW THINE EYES BREAK FROM THEIR EASTE | IN HOLY NATIVITY | 33 | 52 246 | 76 |
| WE SAW THINE EYES BREAK FROM THEIR EAST | IN HOLY NATIVITY | 74 | 52 246 | 76 |
| SLIPPERY SOULES IN SMILING EYES. | IN HOLY NATIVITY | 93 | 52 246 | 76 |
| TILL BURNT AT LAST IN FIRE OF THY FAIR EYES, | IN HOLY NATIVITY | 107 | 52 246 | 76 |
| THESE RUBIES SHALL PUTT OUT THEIR EYES. | NEW YEAR'S DAY | 16 | 52 251 | 37 |
| THAT BREAKES FROM ONE OF THESE BRIGHT EYES. | NEW YEAR'S DAY | 28 | 52 251 | 37 |
| TO SEEK HER SELF IN THY SWEET EYES | IN GLORIOUS EPIPHANIE | 14 | 52 253 | 39 |
| FROM MORTALL EYES | IN GLORIOUS EPIPHANIE | 71 | 52 253 | 39 |
| SPARE OUR EYES, BUT PEIRCE OUR HARTS. | IN GLORIOUS EPIPHANIE | 79 | 52 253 | 39 |
| NOR (MUCH LESSE) SHALL THEY LEAVE THESE EYES | IN GLORIOUS EPIPHANIE | 87 | 52 253 | 39 |
| SO OFT WITH BLUBBER'D EYES, | IN GLORIOUS EPIPHANIE | 126 | 52 253 | 39 |
| AND FASTENING ON THINE EYES, | IN GLORIOUS EPIPHANIE | 227 | 52 253 | 39 |
| EAGLES. AND SHUTT OUR EYES THAT WE MAY SEE. | IN GLORIOUS EPIPHANIE | 232 | 52 253 | 39 |
| AND LAOTHSOM SPITTLE, BLOTT THOSE BEAUTEOUS EYES. | OFFICE H. CROSS PRIME | 6 | 52 267 | 91 |
| BOLD PAINTERS HAVE PUTT OUT HIS EYES. | CHARITAS NIMIA | 8 | 52 280 | 48 |
| OR WILL THE WORLD'S ILLUSTRIOUS EYES. | CHARITAS NIMIA | 37 | 52 280 | 48 |
| BEFORE HER EYES | SANCTA MARIA DOLORUM | 5 | 52 283 | 162 |
| HER EYES BLEED TEARES, HIS WOUNDS WEEP BLOOD. | SANCTA MARIA DOLORUM | 20 | 52 283 | 162 |
| IF NOT MORE SOFT, MINE EYES. | SANCTA MARIA DOLORUM | 86 | 52 283 | 162 |
| IN SHOWRES, AS IF THINE EYES HAD NONE. | UPON BLEEDING CRUCIFIX | 6 | 52 288 | 110 |
| WHEN THIS DRY SOUL THOSE EYES SHALL SEE, | ADORO TE | 53 | 52 291 | 172 |
| ON WHICH ALL FIGURES FIX'T THEIR EYES. | LAUDA SION SALVATOREM | 66 | 52 294 | 178 |
| O THOSE EYES. WHOSE ANGRY LIGHT | DIES IRAE | 7 | 52 298 | 186 |
| THY FAIR EYES, SWEET MAGDALENE. | WEEPER | 6 | 52 307 | 120 |
| HEAVENS THY FAIR EYES BE, | WEEPER | 7 | 52 307 | 120 |
| NOT IN THE EVENING'S EYES | WEEPER | 31 | 52 307 | 120 |
| AND DRAW FROM THESE FULL EYES OF THINE | WEEPER | 71 | 52 307 | 120 |
| THE APRIL IN THINE EYES. | WEEPER | 81 | 52 307 | 120 |
| EYES, NESTS OF MILKY DOVES | WEEPER | 87 | 52 307 | 120 |
| WHILE RAIN & SUNSHINE, CHEEKES & EYES | WEEPER | 95 | 52 307 | 120 |
| DOES DAY CLOSE HIS EYES. | WEEPER | 135 | 52 307 | 120 |
| THE FUGITIVE SONS OF THOSE FAIR EYES | WEEPER | 164 | 52 307 | 120 |
| THOUGH THE FEILD'S EYES TOO WEEPERS BE | WEEPER | 179 | 52 307 | 120 |
| BENDING HER BLESSED EYES ON THEE | TERESA | 134 | 52 315 | 52 |
| THY BLESSED EYES BREED SUCH DESIRE. | A SONG | 3 | 52 327 | 65 |
| BE STILL TRIUMPHANT, BLESSED EYES. | A SONG | 6 | 52 327 | 65 |
| THAT HOLD THESE WEAPONS. & THE EYES | PRAYER TO GENTLE-WOMAN | 29 | 52 328 | 139 |
| FLATTERING BUT FORSWEARING EYES. | PRAYER TO GENTLE-WOMAN | 59 | 52 328 | 139 |
| SIGHTS WHICH ARE NOT SEEN WITH EYES. | PRAYER TO GENTLE-WOMAN | 70 | 52 328 | 139 |
| CALL HEAVN TO LOOK ON THEE WITH NARROW EYES. | DEATH'S LECTURE | 17 | 52 340 | 475 |
| OFT HAVE MY HUNGRY KISSES MADE THINE EYES | LUKE 2. QUAERIT JESUM | 35 | MS 379 | 11 |
| OFT HAVE THESE ARMES (ALAS.) SHOW'D TO THESE EYES | LUKE 2. QUAERIT JESUM | 43 | MS 379 | 11 |
| MINE EYES A TRIBUTARY STREAME SHALL PAY. | ON GUNPOWDER-TREASON | 14 | MS 384 | 458 |
| THOSE TWINCKLING EYES OF HEAVEN, WHICH EV'N NOW SHIN'D, | ON GUNPOWDER-TREASON | 31 | MS 384 | 458 |
| TORRENTS OF SALT TEARES FROM OUR EYES SHOULD RUNNE, | UPON GUNPOWDER TREASON | 37 | MS 386 | 460 |
| AND LEAST THY BLOODSHOTT EYES SHOULD LEAD ASIDE | UPON GUNPOWDER TREASON | 7 | MS 387 | 461 |
| NAY, STOPP THY CLOWDY EYES. IT IS NOT GOOD. | UPON GUNPOWDER TREASON | 31 | MS 387 | 461 |
| BUT YET THEIR EYES SURFETT WITH SWEET DELIGHT. | UPON GUNPOWDER TREASON | 50 | MS 387 | 461 |
| DOE NOT DECEIVE MEE, EYES. DOE I NOT SEE | UPON KINGS CORONATION | 11 | MS 389 | 454 |
| THE RADIANT DARTS, SHOTT FROM HIS SPARKLING EYES. | UPON KINGS CORONATION | 35 | MS 390 | 453 |
| FIXE HEERE THY WAT'RY EYES UPON THESE TOWERS. | AN ELEGIE ON DR PORTER | 3 | MS 395 | 476 |
| FEARE NOT TO DY WITH GREIFE. ALL BUBLING EYES | AN ELEGIE ON DR PORTER | 43 | MS 395 | 476 |
| AND TO MY TOUCH DARKE EYES DID OWE THE LIGHT. | OUT OF GROTIUS | 72 | MS 398 | 198 |

## EYES'

| | | | | | |
|---|---|---|---|---|---|
| BY THOSE SWEET EYES' PERSUASIVE POWRS | IN HOLY NATIVITY | 28 | 52 | 246 | 76 |

## EZELINUS

| | | | | | |
|---|---|---|---|---|---|
| PHALARIS, OCHUS, EZELINUS, NAMES | SOSPETTO D'HERODE | 363 | 46 | 109 | 216 |

## FABLE

| | | | | | |
|---|---|---|---|---|---|
| AND WHEN LIFE'S SWEET FABLE ENDS, | TEMPERANCE | 47 | 52 | 342 | 510 |

## FACE

| | | | | | |
|---|---|---|---|---|---|
| IN THE MUSITIANS FACE, YET ONCE AGAINE | MUSICKS DUELL | 106 | 46 | 149 | 535 |
| O'RE BEAUTIES FACE, SEEMING TO HIDE | IN PRAISE OF LESSIUS | 29 | 46 | 156 | 510 |
| NOR DID THE FACE OF THIS DISASTER SHOW | THE BEGINNING OF HELIODORUS | 23 | 46 | 158 | 517 |
| WITH DAINTY CURLES HIS FROWARD FACE | OUT OF GREEKE CUPID'S CRYER | 33 | 46 | 159 | 519 |
| LEFT THE DIMME FACE OF THIS DULL HEMISPHAEARE, | UPON BISHOP ANDREWES PICTURE | 3 | 46 | 163 | 490 |
| MONGST THOSE IMMORTALL FIRES, AND ON THE FACE | UPON BISHOP ANDREWES PICTURE | 10 | 46 | 163 | 490 |
| TIS BUT A DEAD FACE, ART DOTH HERE BEQUEATH. | UPON BISHOP ANDREWES PICTURE | 15 | 46 | 163 | 490 |
| SITS SORROW WITH A FACE SO FAIRE. | THE WEEPER | 58 | 46 | 79 | 120 |
| OR, 'CAUSE HEAVENS FACE IS DIM, | WHY ARE YEE AFRAID | 2 | 46 | 88 | 15 |
| TAUGHT HER THESE SULLIED CHEEKS THIS BLUBBER'D FACE, | TO PONTIUS WASHING HANDS | 4 | 46 | 94 | 23 |
| THE BABE LOOKT UP, AND SHEW'D HIS FACE. | A HYMNE OF THE NATIVITY | 19 | 46 | 106 | 76 |
| WINTERS SAD FACE, AND THROUGH THE FLOWRY LANDS | SOSPETTO D'HERODE | 110 | 46 | 109 | 216 |
| AND POURING ON HEAV'NS FACE THE SEAS HUGE FLOOD | SOSPETTO D'HERODE | 277 | 46 | 109 | 216 |
| THE FACE OF THINGS, FROM HER DIRE EYES HAD RUN, | SOSPETTO D'HERODE | 383 | 46 | 109 | 216 |
| SHE THINKES NOT FIT SUCH HE HER FACE SHOULD SEE. | SOSPETTO D'HERODE | 413 | 46 | 109 | 216 |
| SPEAKE LOWD UNTO THE FACE OF DEATH | IN MEMORY OF LADY MADRE TERESA | 8 | 46 | 131 | 52 |
| WHOSE LIGHT SHALL LIVE BRIGHT, IN THY FACE | IN MEMORY OF LADY MADRE TERESA | 164 | 46 | 131 | 52 |
| ONE FACE MORE FUGITIVE THEN ALL THEY, | ON HOPE | 88 | 46 | 143 | 71 |
| MADE HEAVENS RADIANT FACE LOOKE FOULE. | UPON DEATH OF DESIRED HERRYS | 52 | 46 | 168 | 467 |
| IN COMPOSURE OF HIS FACE, | HIS EPITAPH (HERRYS) | 27 | 46 | 172 | 471 |
| TO SHOW A FACE, FIT TO CONFESSE THY KIN | UPON STANINOUGH'S DEATH | 18 | 46 | 175 | 475 |
| (THROUGH ALL YOUR PAINTING) SHOWES YOU YOUR OWN FACE. | UPON STANINOUGH'S DEATH | 22 | 46 | 175 | 475 |
| AN EVERLASTING SMILE UPON THE FACE, | UPON YORKE HIS BIRTH | 20 | 46 | 176 | 500 |
| THE DAYES ABASHED GLORIES, AND IN FACE | UPON YORKE HIS BIRTH | 75 | 46 | 176 | 500 |
| THE FACE OF THINGS, AN UNIVERSALL SMILE. | ON A FOULE MORNING | 10 | 46 | 181 | 495 |
| THOU KNOW'ST A FACE IN WHOSE EACH LOOKE, | LOVES HOROSCOPE | 11 | 46 | 185 | 483 |
| A FACE THATS BEST | WISHES SUPPOSED MISTRESSE | 25 | 46 | 195 | 479 |
| A FACE MADE UP | WISHES SUPPOSED MISTRESSE | 28 | 46 | 195 | 479 |
| NO FRUIT SHOULD HAVE THE FACE TO SMILE ON THEE | UPON TWO GREENE APRICOCKES | 25 | 48 | 220 | 494 |
| TO PERSECUTIONS. AND AGAINST THE FACE | TO THE NAME OF JESUS | 200 | 52 | 239 | 30 |
| THE BABE LOOK'T UP & SHEW'D HIS FACE. | IN HOLY NATIVITY | 19 | 52 | 246 | 76 |
| THE DAY, & PLANT IT FAIRER IN THY FACE. | IN GLORIOUS EPIPHANIE | 6 | 52 | 253 | 39 |
| WHOSE FULL & ALL-UNWRINKLED FACE | IN GLORIOUS EPIPHANIE | 28 | 52 | 253 | 39 |
| THE DIRE FACE OF INFERIOR DARKNES, KIS'T | IN GLORIOUS EPIPHANIE | 52 | 52 | 253 | 39 |
| AND AT THY FEET POWR FORTH HIS FACE. | IN GLORIOUS EPIPHANIE | 64 | 52 | 253 | 39 |
| SEE HIS HORN'D FACE, & DY FOR SHAME. | IN GLORIOUS EPIPHANIE | 99 | 52 | 253 | 39 |
| FLY IN THE FACE OF HEAV'N. AS IF IT WERE | IN GLORIOUS EPIPHANIE | 103 | 52 | 253 | 39 |
| FORCING HIS SOMETIMES ECLIPS'D FACE TO BE | IN GLORIOUS EPIPHANIE | 115 | 52 | 253 | 39 |
| WITH A RED FACE CONFES'T THIS SCORN. | IN GLORIOUS EPIPHANIE | 122 | 52 | 253 | 39 |
| LEAP AT THY LOFTY FACE, | IN GLORIOUS EPIPHANIE | 196 | 52 | 253 | 39 |
| AND SMIL'D I'TH' BABE'S BRIGHT FACE, THE PURPLING BUD | TO THE QUEEN'S MAJESTY | 5 | 52 | 261 | 47 |
| FACE RUN SADLY DOWN. | OFFICE H. CROSS THIRD | 9 | 52 | 268 | 93 |
| TO REACH AT THY LOV'D FACE. NOR CAN | ADORO TE | 29 | 52 | 291 | 172 |
| AND FOR THY VEIL GIVE MY THY FACE. | ADORO TE | 56 | 52 | 291 | 172 |
| THAT THEY BUT LEND THEIR FORM & FACE, | LAUDA SION SALVATOREM | 33 | 52 | 294 | 178 |
| TO FEED OF THEE IN THINE OWN FACE. | LAUDA SION SALVATOREM | 80 | 52 | 294 | 178 |
| O THAT FIRE, BEFORE WHOSE FACE | DIES IRAE | 5 | 52 | 298 | 186 |
| SITTS SORROW WITH A FACE SO FAIR. | WEEPER | 34 | 52 | 307 | 120 |
| FOUNTAIN & GARDEN IN ONE FACE. | WEEPER | 90 | 52 | 307 | 120 |
| PREFERR'D TO SOME PROUD FACE | WEEPER | 183 | 52 | 307 | 120 |
| SPEAK LOWD INTO THE FACE OF DEATH | TERESA | 8 | 52 | 315 | 52 |
| WHOSE LIGHT SHALL LIVE BRIGHT IN THY FACE | TERESA | 163 | 52 | 315 | 52 |
| SENDS UP MY SOUL TO SEEK THY FACE. | A SONG | 2 | 52 | 327 | 65 |
| TO GAZE ON THE FAIR SOULDIER'S GLORIOUS FACE. | ALEXIAS THIRD ELEGIE | 46 | 52 | 336 | 209 |
| TO SHOW A FACE, FITT TO CONFESSE THY KIN, | DEATH'S LECTURE | 19 | 52 | 340 | 475 |
| (THOUGH YOU BE PAINTED) SHOWES YOU YOUR TRUE FACE. | DEATH'S LECTURE | 24 | 52 | 340 | 475 |
| OR'E BEAUTY'S FACE, SEEMING TO HIDE | TEMPERANCE | 27 | 52 | 342 | 510 |
| ONE FACE MORE FUGITIVE THEN ALL THEY. | (ON) HOPE | 48 | 52 | 345 | 71 |
| LOOK ROUND AND READE THE WORLD'S WIDE FACE. | AGAINST IRRESOLUTION AND DELAY | 29 | 52 | 347 | 146 |
| THE FRESH FACE OF THE MORNE HAD BLASTED BEENE. | UPON GUNPOWDER TREASON | 14 | MS | 386 | 460 |
| THE LIGHT'S FAIRE FACE, BUT STILL ABORTIVE BEE. | UPON GUNPOWDER TREASON | 58 | MS | 386 | 460 |
| THE LUSTRE OF HIS FACE DID SHINE SOE BRIGHT, | UPON KINGS CORONATION | 33 | MS | 390 | 453 |
| WHICH, WHILE THEY SMILING SATE UPON HIS FACE, | AN ELEGY MR STANNINOW | 39 | MS | 394 | 473 |
| TO PAINT ITS PERFUM'D FACE WITH COLOURS BRAVE. | AN ELEGIE ON DR PORTER | 24 | MS | 395 | 476 |

## FACED

| | | | | | |
|---|---|---|---|---|---|
| AND ALL THE SMOOTH FACED KINDRED THERE. | ON MR. G. HERBERTS BOOKE | 14 | 46 | 130 | 68 |

## BLACK-FAC'D

| | | | | | |
|---|---|---|---|---|---|
| A BLACK-FAC'D HOUSE WILL LOVE. | ON BAPTIZED AETHIOPIAN | 6 | 46 | 85 | 29 |

## FULL-FAC'T

| | | | | | |
|---|---|---|---|---|---|
| TO FIX THOSE FULL-FAC'T GLORIES, O HE'S POORE | IT IS BETTER TO GO WITH EYE | 2 | 46 | 93 | 16 |

```
PALEFAC'T

  WHOM FAINT, & PALEFAC'T FEARE DOTH STILL ATTEND.     UPON GUNPOWDER TREASON           18   MS 387 461
PALE-FAC'T

  BUT HAD THY PALE-FAC'T PURPLE TOOK                   FLAMING HEART                    27   52 324  61
FACES

  THE FACES LIGHTNING, OR A SMILE IS HERE.             SOSPETTO D'HERODE               198   46 109 216
  TO CHANGE HER FACES STILE SHE DOTH DEVISE,           SOSPETTO D'HERODE               415   46 109 216
  BEATS BRIGHT UPON THE BURNING FACES                  IN MEMORY OF LADY MADRE TERESA   85   46 131  52
  HIS FUGITIVE GOLD THROUGH ALL HER FACES,             ON HOPE                          86   46 143  71
  GUILD THEIR FACES,                                   OUT OF THE ITALIAN (1)           47   46 188 545
  THE NEIGHBOUR DIAMOND, AND OUT FACES                 WISHES SUPPOSED MISTRESSE        44   46 195 479
  BEATES BRIGHT UPON THE BURNING FACES                 TERESA                           85   52 315  52
  HIS FUGITIVE GOLD THROUGH ALL HER FACES.             (ON) HOPE                        46   52 345  71
  THIS RISING SUNNE, THEIR FACES NOTHING WORE,         UPON KINGS CORONATION            38   MS 390 453
FADE

  THAT HIS SHOULD FADE, WHILE THINE IS GREENE.         UPON DEATH OF DESIRED HERRYS     20   46 168 467
  OF ALL OUR GLORIOUS HOPES SHOULD FADE,               AN ELEGY MR STANNINOW            43   MS 394 473
FADING

  FLOWERS OF NEVER FADING GRACES.                      ON A PRAYER BOOKE                36   46 126 139
  FLOWERS OF NEVER FADING GRACES                       PRAYER TO GENTLE-WOMAN           42   52 328 139
NEVER-FADING

  AND FOR THE NEVER-FADING FIELDS OF LIGHT             SOSPETTO D'HERODE               211   46 109 216
FAIL

  NOR DOES HIS FULL GLOBE FAIL TO BE                   IN GLORIOUS EPIPHANIE            38   52 253  39
  TO BLEED WITH HIM, FAIL NOT TO WEEP WITH HER.        SANCTA MARIA DOLORUM             90   52 283 162
FAILE

  IF ALL FAILE WEE'L PUT ON OUR PROUDEST ARMES,        SOSPETTO D'HERODE               276   46 109 216
FAILES

  SHEE FAILES, AND FAILING GRIEVES, AND GRIEVING DYES. MUSICKS DUELL                   165   46 149 535
  YOUR FIRST CHOYCE FAILES, O WHEN YOU CHOOSE AGEN     TO SAME CONCERNING CHOISE        58   52 331  66
FAILING

  SHEE FAILES, AND FAILING GRIEVES, AND GRIEVING DYES. MUSICKS DUELL                   165   46 149 535
FAYLING

  DRINKE FAYLING THERE WHERE I A GUEST DID SHINE       OUT OF GROTIUS                   51   MS 398 198
FAINE

  FAINE WOULD HEE HAVE FORGOT WHAT FATALL STRINGS,     SOSPETTO D'HERODE               139   46 109 216
  YET ON THE OTHER SIDE, FAINE WOULD HE START          SOSPETTO D'HERODE               153   46 109 216
  FAINE WOULD I CHIDE THEIR SLOWNESSE, BUT IN THEIR    UPON TWO GREENE APRICOCKES       31   48 220 494
FAIN'D

  LIFES FORGE. FAIN'D IS HER VOICE, AND FALSE TOO, BE  SOSPETTO D'HERODE               423   46 109 216
FAINT

  THE FRIGHTED STARS TOOKE FAINT EXPERIENCE,           SOSPETTO D'HERODE               283   46 109 216
  OF DEAD DEVOTION. NOR FAINT MARBLES WEEP             ON A TREATISE OF CHARITY         33   46 137  69
  BUT THOU, FAINT GOD OF SLEEPE, FORGET THAT I         TO THE MORNING                   47   46 183 497
  LO THE FAINT LAMB, WITH WEARY LIMB                   OFFICE H. CROSS SIXT              3   52 270  97
  AND IF THOU YET (FAINT SOUL.) DEFERR                 SANCTA MARIA DOLORUM             89   52 283 162
  TO SHOW US THIS FAINT SHADE FOR HER                  FLAMING HEART                    22   52 324  61
  WHOM FAINT, & PALEFAC'T FEARE DOTH STILL ATTEND.     UPON GUNPOWDER TREASON           18   MS 387 461
FAINTED

  WITH STERNE DEATH, IF E'RE HE FAINTED,               ANOTHER ON HERRYS                 2   46 170 469
FAINTLY

  THAT HEE WHOM THE SUN SERVES, SHOULD FAINTLY PEEPE   SOSPETTO D'HERODE               177   46 109 216
FAIR

  SAY, LINGRING FAIR. WHY COMES THE BIRTH              TO COUNTESSE OF DENBIGH           7   52 236 146
  O FIX THIS FAIR INDEFINITE.                          TO COUNTESSE OF DENBIGH          31   52 236 146
  UNFOLD AT LENGTH, UNFOLD FAIR FLOWRE                 TO COUNTESSE OF DENBIGH          43   52 236 146
  FAIR ONE, IT IS YOUR FATE.  AND BRINGS               TO COUNTESSE OF DENBIGH          53   52 236 146
  THIS FORT OF YOUR FAIR SELFE, IF'T BE NOT WON,       TO COUNTESSE OF DENBIGH          67   52 236 146
  AND THAT FAIR WORD AT ALL REFERR TO THEE)            TO THE NAME OF JESUS             14   52 239  30
  TO KEEP IT FAIR,                                     TO THE NAME OF JESUS            113   52 239  30
```

```
FAIR KING OF NAMES, & COME.                              TO THE NAME OF JESUS             118   52 239   30
UNFOLD THY FAIR CONCEPTIONS. AND DISPLAY                 TO THE NAME OF JESUS             163   52 239   30
FAIR, FLOWRY NAME, IN NONE BUT THEE                      TO THE NAME OF JESUS             173   52 239   30
WHO TORE THE FAIR BRESTS OF THY FREINDS,                 TO THE NAME OF JESUS             208   52 239   30
FOR THEE, FAIR, PURPLE DOORES, OF LOVE'S DEVISING.       TO THE NAME OF JESUS             217   52 239   30
TO FURNISH THE FAIR INFANT'S BED                         IN HOLY NATIVITY                  54   52 246   76
TILL BURNT AT LAST IN FIRE OF THY FAIR EYES,             IN HOLY NATIVITY                 107   52 246   76
NONE SO FAIR THY BOSOM STROWES,                          NEW YEAR'S DAY                    10   52 251   37
THAT FLAMING IN THEIR FAIR BEDS SLEEP,                   NEW YEAR'S DAY                    20   52 251   37
BY THY FAIR STARR,                                       IN GLORIOUS EPIPHANIE             20   52 253   39
WITH HIS FAIR SISTER COW,                                IN GLORIOUS EPIPHANIE             97   52 253   39
THE POOR WORLD'S FAULT THAT HE IS FAIR.                  IN GLORIOUS EPIPHANIE            104   52 253   39
FAIR FIRST-FRUITS OF THE LAMB. SURE KINGS IN THIS.       TO THE QUEEN'S MAJESTY             7   52 261   47
SWELLS HIGH, FAIR CONFLUENCE OF ALL HIGHBORN BLOUD.      TO THE QUEEN'S MAJESTY            16   52 261   47
FIX HERE, FAIR MAJESTY. MAY YOUR HEART NE'RE MISSE       TO THE QUEEN'S MAJESTY            21   52 261   47
ALL HAIL, FAIR TREE.                                     OFFICE H. CROSS MATINES           18   52 265   86
THE FAIR STARRS FILL THEIR WAKEFULL FIRES THE SUN        OFFICE H. CROSS PRIME              8   52 267   91
                         HIMSELFE DRINKS
                              DAY.
THY WOUNDS GIVE US FAIR HOLD.                            OFFICE H. CROSS COMPLINE          20   52 274  105
LOOK UP, LANGUISHING SOUL. LO WHERE THE FAIR             VEXILLA REGIS                      1   52 277  156
HAIL, OUR ALONE HOPE. LET THY FAIR HEAD SHOOT            VEXILLA REGIS                     37   52 277  156
GROW THOU & THEY. AND BE THY FAIR INCREASE               VEXILLA REGIS                     41   52 277  156
OF THIS FAIR TREE TAKE OUR ETERNALL ROOT.                SANCTA MARIA DOLORUM              64   52 283  162
WHAT NEED THY FAIR HEAD BEAR A PART                      UPON BLEEDING CRUCIFIX             5   52 288  110
RISE UP, MY FAIR, MY SPOTTLESSE ONE.                     IN GLORIOUS ASSUMPTION B. LADY     9   52 304  114
THY FAIR EYES, SWEET MAGDALENE.                          WEEPER                             6   52 307  120
HEAVENS THY FAIR EYES BE.                                WEEPER                             7   52 307  120
SITTS SORROW WITH A FACE SO FAIR.                        WEEPER                            34   52 307  120
O FAIR, & FRFINDLY FOES,                                 WEEPER                            93   52 307  120
BUT CAN THESE FAIR FLOUDS BE                             WEEPER                            97   52 307  120
O THOU, THY LORD'S FAIR STORE.                           WEEPER                           115   52 307  120
FAIR SPEND-THRIFT OF THY SELF, THY MEASURE               WEEPER                           128   52 307  120
THE FUGITIVE SONS OF THOSE FAIR EYES                     WEEPER                           164   52 307  120
SWEET, NOT SO FAST. LO THY FAIR SPOUSE                   TERESA                            65   52 315   52
SO SPIRITUALL, PURE, & FAIR                              TERESA                            88   52 315   52
MADE FRUITFULL THY FAIR SOUL, GOE NOW                    TERESA                           169   52 315   52
(FAIR FLOUD OF HOLY FIRES.) TRANSFUS'D THE FLAME         AN APOLOGIE FOR (TERESA) HYMNE     2   52 322   59
WHAT E'RE THIS YOUTH OF FIRE WEARES FAIR,                FLAMING HEART                     31   52 324   61
ALL THOSE FAIR & FLAGRANT THINGS,                        FLAMING HEART                     34   52 324   61
(FAIR YOUTH) SHOOTES BOTH THY SHAFT & THEE               FLAMING HEART                     46   52 324   61
AND MY BEST FORTUNES SUCH FAIR SPOILES OF ME.            FLAMING HEART                     92   52 324   61
(FAIR SISTER OF THE SERAPHIM.)                           FLAMING HEART                    104   52 324   61
STILL SHINE ON ME, FAIR SUNS, THAT I                     A SONG                             7   52 327   65
(FAIR ONE) FROM THY KIND HANDS                           PRAYER TO GENTLE-WOMAN             7   52 328  139
OF FALSE, PERHAPS AS FAIR,                               PRAYER TO GENTLE-WOMAN            58   52 328  139
ON THE FAIR SOUL WHOM FIRST HE MEETS.                    PRAYER TO GENTLE-WOMAN            95   52 328  139
O FAIR, O FORTUNATE, O RICHE, O DEAR.                    PRAYER TO GENTLE-WOMAN            96   52 328  139
AMONG HIS OWN FAIR SONNES OF FIRE,                       TO SAME CONCERNING CHOISE         25   52 331   66
AND FOLLOW THOSE FAIR STARRES OF YOURS.                  TO SAME CONCERNING CHOISE         30   52 331   66
STARRS MUCH TOO FAIR & PURE TO WAIT UPON                 TO SAME CONCERNING CHOISE         31   52 331   66
FAREWELL. & SHINE, FAIR SOUL, SHINE THERE ABOVE          ALEXIAS FIRST ELEGIE              35   52 334  204
TO GAZE ON THE FAIR SOULDIER'S GLORIOUS FACE.            ALEXIAS THIRD ELEGIE              46   52 336  209
FAIR HOPE. OUR EARLYER HEAV'N BY THEE                    (ON) HOPE                         21   52 345   71
SWEET HOPE, KIND CHEAT, FAIR FALLACY BY THEE             (ON) HOPE                         37   52 345   71
FAITH'S SISTER, NURSE OF FAIR DESIRE.                    (ON) HOPE                         41   52 345   71
SAY, LINGRING FAIR, WHY COMES THE BIRTH                  AGAINST IRRESOLUTION AND DELAY    15   52 347  146
ALL THINGS SWEAR FRIENDS TO FAIR AND GOOD,               AGAINST IRRESOLUTION AND DELAY    57   52 347  146
THIS FORT OF YOUR FAIR SELF IF'T BE NOT WONE,            AGAINST IRRESOLUTION AND DELAY    89   52 347  146

FAIR-CHEEK'T

OF ALL THE FAIR-CHEEK'T FLOWRS THAT FILL THEE            NEW YEAR'S DAY                     9   52 251   37
THAT FAIR-CHEEK'T FALLACY OF FIRE.                       FLAMING HEART                      4   52 324   61

FAIR-EY'D

WHILE WE FOUND OUT THE FAIR-EY'D BOY,                    A HYMNE OF THE NATIVITY            7   46 106   76
AS BY A FAIR-EY'D FALLACY OF DAY                         IN GLORIOUS EPIPHANIE            163   52 253   39

FAIRE

WHAT, MARS HIS SWORD, FAIRE CYTHEREA SAY,                UPON VENUS PUTTING ARMES           1   46 161  523
WHOSE FAIRE ILLUSTRIOUS SOULE, LED HIS FREE THOUGHT      UPON BISHOP ANDREWES PICTURE       5   46 163  490
THY FAIRE EYES SWEET MAGDALENE.                          THE WEEPER                         6   46  79  120
HEAVENS THY FAIRE EYES BEE,                              THE WEEPER                         7   46  79  120
HEAVEN, OF SUCH FAIRE FLOODS AS THIS,                    THE WEEPER                        23   46  79  120
SITS SORROW WITH A FACE SO FAIRE.                        THE WEEPER                        58   46  79  120
YEE SIMPERING SONS OF THOSE FAIRE EYES,                  THE WEEPER                       122   46  79  120
SWEET MARY THY FAIRE EYES EXPENCE.                       THE TEARE                          2   46  84   50
FAIRE DROP, WHY QUAK'ST THOU SO.                         THE TEARE                         31   46  84   50
THE FAIRE STARRE IS WELL FIXT, FOR WHERE, O WHERE        ON VIRGINS BASHFULNESSE            3   46  89    9
THOU WATER TURN'ST TO WINE (FAIRE FRIEND OF LIFE)        TO LORD UPON WATER MADE WINE       1   46  91   12
THE DAUGHTER OF A FAIRE AND WELL-FAM'D FOUNTAINE         TO PONTIUS WASHING HANDS           7   46  94   23
FLOWES IN THY SONG (O FAIRE, O DYING SWAN.)              UPON OUR LORDS LAST DISCOURSE      2   46  95   21
A DROP, ONE DROP, HOW SWEETLY ONE FAIRE DROP             DIVES ASKING A DROP                1   46  96   18
HER EYES FLOOD LICKES HIS FEETS FAIRE STAINE,            SHE BEGAN TO WASH HIS FEET         1   46  97   13
THY TOMBE, FAIRE IMMORTALITIES PERFUMED NEST.            EASTER DAY                         6   46 100   26
WHAT NEED THY FAIRE HEAD BEARE A PART                    ON BLEEDING WOUNDS OF LORD        17   46 101  110
THE FAIRE CENTER OF MY MIND                              PSALME 23                         62   46 102    5
TO FURNISH THE FAIRE INFANTS BED.                        A HYMNE OF THE NATIVITY           38   46 106   76
FAIRE YOUTH (SAID I) BE NOT TOO ROUGH.                   A HYMNE OF THE NATIVITY           45   46 106   76
AT LAST, IN FIRE OF THY FAIRE EYES,                      A HYMNE OF THE NATIVITY           87   46 106   76
HOLDS HIGH THE REINE OF FAIRE PARTHENOPE,                SOSPETTO D'HERODE                 26   46 109  216
AND FOR HIS OLD FAIRE ROABES OF LIGHT, HEE WEARES        SOSPETTO D'HERODE                 43   46 109  216
```

PAGE 130

```
WHERE JORDAN MELTS HIS CHRYSTALL, TO MAKE FAIRE       SOSPETTO D'HERODE                 85  46 109 216
IMMORTALL FLOWERS TO HER FAIRE HAND PRESENT.          SOSPETTO D'HERODE                100  46 109 216
OF FAIRE ENGADDI HONY-SWEATING FOUNTAINES             SOSPETTO D'HERODE                111  46 109 216
WHO FEEDS WITH NECTAR HEAV'NS FAIRE FAMILY.           SOSPETTO D'HERODE                174  46 109 216
MY FAIRE INHERITANCE, HEE CONFINES ME HERE,           SOSPETTO D'HERODE                212  46 109 216
WITH HIS FAIRE TRIUMPHS FILL ALL FUTURE STORIES.      SOSPETTO D'HERODE                230  46 109 216
THE FIELD'S FAIRE EYES SAW HER, AND SAW NO MORE.      SOSPETTO D'HERODE                378  46 109 216
OF FALSE PERHAPS AS FAIRE                             ON A PRAYER BOOKE                 52  46 126 139
ON THE FAIRE SOULE WHOM FIRST HEE MEETS.              ON A PRAYER BOOKE                 89  46 126 139
O FAIRE. O FORTUNATE. O RICH. O DEARE.                ON A PRAYER BOOKE                 90  46 126 139
KNOW YOU FAIRE, ON WHAT YOU LOOKE.                    ON MR. G. HERBERTS BOOKE           1  46 130  68
SWEET NOT SO FAST, LOE THY FAIRE SPOUSE,              IN MEMORY OF LADY MADRE TERESA    65  46 131  52
SO SPIRITUALL, PURE AND FAIRE,                        IN MEMORY OF LADY MADRE TERESA    88  46 131  52
MADE FRUITFULL THY FAIRE SOULE. GOE NOW               IN MEMORY OF LADY MADRE TERESA   170  46 131  52
FAIRE SEA OF HOLY FIRES TRANSFUSED THE FLAME          AN APOLOGIE FOR HYMNE (TERESA)     2  46 136  59
FROM TH' DAWN OF THY FAIRE EYE-LIDS WIPE AWAY         ON A TREATISE OF CHARITY           7  46 137  69
OPEN THIS BOOKE, FAIRE QUEEN, AND TAKE THY CROWN.     ON A TREATISE OF CHARITY          12  46 137  69
FANNING THY FAIRE LOCKS (WHICH THE WORLD BELEEVES     ON A TREATISE OF CHARITY          23  46 137  69
BY THE FAIRE LAWES OF THY FIRM-POINTED PEN.           ON A TREATISE OF CHARITY          28  46 137  69
WITH THOSE DEARE SPOILES THAT WONT TO DRESSE THE FAIRE ON A TREATISE OF CHARITY         54  46 137  69
RISE UP MY FAIRE, MY SPOTLESSE ONE.                   ON THE ASSUMPTION                  9  46 139 114
FEED FOR EVER THEIR FAIRE SIGHT                       ON THE ASSUMPTION                 34  46 139 114
OF ALL THE FAIRE CHEEKT FLOWERS THAT FILL THEE.       AN HIMNE FOR CIRCUMCISION          9  46 141  37
NONE SO FAIRE THY BOSOME STROWES.                     AN HIMNE FOR CIRCUMCISION         10  46 141  37
THAT FLAMING IN THEIR FAIRE BED SLEEP.                AN HIMNE FOR CIRCUMCISION         20  46 141  37
THAT BREAKES FROM ONE OF THESE FAIRE EYES.            AN HIMNE FOR CIRCUMCISION         28  46 141  37
FAIRE CLOUD OF FIRE, BOTH SHADE, AND LIGHT,           ON HOPE                           15  46 143  71
FAIRE HOPE. OUR EARLIER HEAVEN. BY THEE               ON HOPE                           51  46 143  71
SWEET HOPE. KIND CHEAT. FAIRE FALLACY. BY THEE        ON HOPE                           77  46 143  71
FAITH'S SISTER. NURSE OF FAIRE DESIRE.                ON HOPE                           81  46 143  71
A PLANT OF NOBLE STEMME, FORWARD AND FAIRE,           UPON DEATH OF HERRYS               1  46 167 466
THE FAIRE SON OF AN EVER-YOUTHFULL SPRING,            UPON DEATH OF HERRYS              39  46 167 466
WERE THE MORNINGS SMILE SO FAIRE                      UPON DEATH OF DESIRED HERRYS      56  46 168 467
FLOURISHT IN SO FAIRE A GROWTH.                       ANOTHER ON HERRYS                 14  46 170 469
THE FAIRE GLOSSE OF A FAIRER TEXT.                    ANOTHER ON HERRYS                 52  46 170 469
AND OUR HOPES FAIRE HARVEST SPREAD                    ANOTHER ON HERRYS                 56  46 170 469
LIV'D A FAIRE, BUT MANLY GRACE.                       HIS EPITAPH (HERRYS)              28  46 172 471
NOW STRETCH THY SELF (FAIRE ILE) AND GROW, SPREAD WIDE UPON YORKE HIS BIRTH              2  46 176 500
THIS WELL-WROUGHT COPY THE FAIRE PRINCIPALL.          UPON YORKE HIS BIRTH              48  46 176 500
UPON THY ROYALL ELME (FAIRE VINE) AND WHEN            UPON YORKE HIS BIRTH             103  46 176 500
AND LET NO DULL MISTS CHOAKE THE LIGHTS FAIRE GROWTH. ON A FOULE MORNING                 4  46 181 495
UNFOLD THY FAIRE FRONT, AND THERE SHALL APPEARE       ON A FOULE MORNING                 7  46 181 495
RISE THEN (FAIRE BLEW-EY'D MAID) RISE AND DISCOVER    ON A FOULE MORNING                27  46 181 495
LO HERE THE FAIRE CHARICLIA. IN WHOM STROVE           UPON FAIRE ETHIOPIAN               1  46 183 493
HIS HEAD IN THY FAIRE BOSOME, AND STILL HIDES         TO THE MORNING                    13  46 183 497
ON WHOSE FAIRE REVOLUTIONS WAIT                       LOVES HOROSCOPE                   13  46 185 483
IF ON TIMES RIGHT HAND, SIT FAIRE HISTORIE.           ON FRONTISPIECE ISAACSONS          5  46 191 491
CAN RAISE SO FAIRE AN HARVEST. LET HER BE             ON FRONTISPIECE ISAACSONS          7  46 191 491
AND BY HIS FAIRE EXAMPLES LIGHT,                      AN EPITAPH UPON ASHTON            31  46 192 464
AND TEACH HER FAIRE STEPS TO OUR EARTH.               WISHES SUPPOSED MISTRESSE          9  46 195 479
YETT IN THESE LEAVES (FAIRE ONE) THERE LYES           THOUGH NOW 'TIS NEITHER            3  MS 397 492
I WAS MISTAKEN. SOME FAIRE SPHAERE, OR OTHER          LUKE 2.   QUAERIT JESUM           21  MS 379  11
OF SOE FAIRE EARTH.                                   LUKE 2.   QUAERIT JESUM           24  MS 379  11
OH, WOULD'ST THOU HEERE STILL FIXE THY FAIRE ABODE,   LUKE 2.   QUAERIT JESUM           47  MS 379  11
THE LIGHT'S FAIRE FACE, BUT STILL ABORTIVE BEE.       UPON GUNPOWDER TREASON            58  MS 386 460
THAT MIGHT INTERPRET OUR FAIRE CYNTHIA'S WORTH.       UPON BIRTH PRINCESSE E             30  MS 391 456
THOSE DURTY SMUTCHES, WHICH THEIR FAIRE FRONTS WORE,  AN ELEGY MR STANNINOW             13  MS 394 473
(FAIRE ONE) THESE TENDER LEAVES DOE TREMBLING STAND.  AT TH' IVORY TRIBUNALL             2  MS 397 492
```

FAYRE

```
TAKING FRESH LIFE FROM YOUR FAYRE EYES.               THOUGH NOW 'TIS NEITHER           10  MS 397 492
```

FAIRER

```
NOR MAY RETURNED FAIRER FLOWERS.                      THE WEEPER                        90  46  79 120
COULD SHE HAVE FIXT IT ON A FAIRER SPEARE.            ON VIRGINS BASHFULNESSE            4  46  89   9
WA'ST THY FULL VICTORIES FAIRER INCREASE.             UPON DUMBE DEVILL CAST OUT         3  46  93  14
THIS FLOOD THUS STAINED FAIRER STREAMES.              SHE BEGAN TO WASH HIS FEET         4  46  97  13
TH'ART NOT FAIRER THEN IS HEE.                        UPON DEATH OF DESIRED HERRYS      14  46 168 467
THE FAIRE GLOSSE OF A FAIRER TEXT.                    ANOTHER ON HERRYS                 52  46 170 469
WHILE WE FOUND OUT HEAVN'S FAIRER EY                  IN HOLY NATIVITY                   7  52 246  76
THE DAY, & PLANT IT FAIRER IN THY FACE.               IN GLORIOUS EPIPHANIE              6  52 253  39
```

FAIREST

```
HIS FINGERS FAIREST REVOLUTION                        MUSICKS DUELL                    154  46 149 535
THE FAIREST, AND THE FIRST-BORNE SMILE OF HEAV'N.     SOSPETTO D'HERODE                236  46 109 216
THESE DEVOTIONS, FAIREST. KNOW                        ON MR. G. HERBERTS BOOKE          16  46 130  68
THE FAIREST, AND THE FIRST BORNE SONS OF FIRE.        IN MEMORY OF LADY MADRE TERESA    93  46 131  52
OF OUR FAIREST FLOWERS,                               ON THE ASSUMPTION                 48  46 139 114
RISE THOU FIRST AND FAIREST MORNING.                  AN HIMNE FOR CIRCUMCISION          1  46 141  37
BUT IN THY FAIREST EYES FIND TWO FOR ONE.             AN HIMNE FOR CIRCUMCISION         38  46 141  37
TO THEM SHEE GAVE THE FIRST AND FAIREST BEAME         UPON DEATH OF HERRYS              17  46 167 466
OF OUR FAIREST FLOWRES                                IN GLORIOUS ASSUMPTION B. LADY    53  52 304 114
RISE, FAIREST OF THOSE FIRES. WHATE'RE THOU BE        ALEXIAS SECONDE ELEGIE            25  52 335 207
WHAT, BUT THE FAIREST HEAVEN, COULD OWNE THE BIRTH    LUKE 2.   QUAERIT JESUM           23  MS 379  11
```

FAIR'ST

```
THE FAIR'ST & FIRST-BORN SONS OF FIRE                 TERESA                            93  52 315  52
HEE'S GONE. THE FAIR'ST FLOWER, THAT E'RE BOSOME      LUKE 2.   QUAERIT JESUM            5  MS 379  11
                                        DREST.
```

FAIRLY

| | | | | | |
|---|---|---|---|---|---|
| FAIRLY TO OPEN IT, AND ENTER. | TO COUNTESSE OF DENBIGH | 4 | 52 | 236 | 146 |
| FAIRLY TO OPEN AND TO ENTER. | AGAINST IRRESOLUTION AND DELAY | 4 | 52 | 347 | 146 |

FAIRELY

| | | | | | |
|---|---|---|---|---|---|
| A GOLDEN-HEADED HARVEST FAIRELY REARES | MUSICKS DUELL | 70 | 46 | 149 | 535 |

FAITH

| | | | | | |
|---|---|---|---|---|---|
| THY HUMBLE FAITH AND FEARE KEEPES HIM ALOOFE. | I AM NOT WORTHY | 2 | 46 | 90 | 13 |
| AND REASON (FOR WHAT'S FAITH TO HIM.) DEVOURE. | SOSPETTO D'HERODE | 162 | 46 | 109 | 216 |
| CHRISTS FAITH MAKES BUT ONE BODY OF ALL SOULES, | AN APOLOGIE FOR HYMNE (TERESA) | 17 | 46 | 136 | 59 |
| OF FAITH, A MOUNTAINE WORD, MADE UP OF AIRE, | ON A TREATISE OF CHARITY | 53 | 46 | 137 | 69 |
| AND SWEARE FAITH TO THY SWEETER POWERS. | AN HIMNE FOR CIRCUMCISION | 36 | 46 | 141 | 37 |
| OF FAITH. THE STEWARD OF OUR GROWING STOCKE. | ON HOPE | 32 | 46 | 143 | 71 |
| DISBAND DULL FEARES. GIVE FAITH THE DAY. | TO COUNTESSE OF DENBIGH | 57 | 52 | 236 | 146 |
| AND SWEAR FAITH TO THY SWEETER POWRES. | NEW YEAR'S DAY | 36 | 52 | 251 | 37 |
| BADG OF THY FAITH CALLS BACK THY CARE, | VEXILLA REGIS | 2 | 52 | 277 | 156 |
| OF HUMBLE LOVE & LOYALL FAITH, | ADORO TE | 2 | 52 | 291 | 172 |
| SAVE THAT WHICH LETS IN FAITH, THE EARE. | ADORO TE | 10 | 52 | 291 | 172 |
| FAITH IS MY SKILL. FAITH CAN BELEIVE | ADORO TE | 11 | 52 | 291 | 172 |
| FAITH IS MY SKILL. FAITH CAN BELEIVE | ADORO TE | 11 | 52 | 291 | 172 |
| FAITH IS MY FORCE. FAITH STRENGTH AFFORDS | ADORO TE | 13 | 52 | 291 | 172 |
| FAITH IS MY FORCE. FAITH STRENGTH AFFORDS | ADORO TE | 13 | 52 | 291 | 172 |
| THAT FAITH HAS FARTHER, HERE TO GOE | ADORO TE | 20 | 52 | 291 | 172 |
| HELP LORD, MY FAITH, MY HOPE INCREASE. | ADORO TE | 33 | 52 | 291 | 172 |
| THE HEAVN-INSTRUCTED HOUSE OF FAITH | LAUDA SION SALVATOREM | 31 | 52 | 294 | 178 |
| BOLD FAITH TAKES HEART, & DARES BELEIVE. | LAUDA SION SALVATOREM | 38 | 52 | 294 | 178 |
| HOLD BUT THY FAITH INTIRE AS HE | LAUDA SION SALVATOREM | 56 | 52 | 294 | 178 |
| IN BROKEN FORMES A STABLE FAITH | LAUDA SION SALVATOREM | 59 | 52 | 294 | 178 |
| THY FALLING TEARES KEEP FAITH FULL TIME. | WEEPER | 140 | 52 | 307 | 120 |
| CHRIST'S FAITH MAKES BUT ONE BODY OF ALL SOULES | AN APOLOGIE FOR (TERESA) HYMNE | 17 | 52 | 322 | 59 |
| OF FAITH. STILL SPENDING, & STILL GROWING STOCK. | (ON) HOPE | 12 | 52 | 345 | 71 |
| MARK WITH WHAT FAITH FRUITS ANSWER FLOWERS, | AGAINST IRRESOLUTION AND DELAY | 33 | 52 | 347 | 146 |
| DISBAND DULL FEARES, GIVE FAITH THE DAY. | AGAINST IRRESOLUTION AND DELAY | 81 | 52 | 347 | 146 |

FAITH'S

| | | | | | |
|---|---|---|---|---|---|
| FAITH'S SISTER. NURSE OF FAIRE DESIRE. | ON HOPE | 81 | 46 | 143 | 71 |
| WHEN GLORY'S SUN FAITH'S SHADES SHALL CHASE, | ADORO TE | 55 | 52 | 291 | 172 |
| FAITH'S SISTER. NURSE OF FAIR DESIRE. | (ON) HOPE | 41 | 52 | 345 | 71 |

FAITHFULL

| | | | | | |
|---|---|---|---|---|---|
| HOW EVEN TH'AST DRAWNE THIS FAITHFULL PARALELL, | UPON YORKE HIS BIRTH | 50 | 46 | 176 | 500 |
| ILLUSTRIOUS SWEETNESSE. IN THY FAITHFULL WOMBE, | UPON YORKE HIS BIRTH | 80 | 46 | 176 | 500 |
| THEIR BLACK, BUT FAITHFULL PROSPECTIVE OF THEE. | IN GLORIOUS EPIPHANIE | 171 | 52 | 253 | 39 |
| STRUCK LOWD HIS FAITHFULL STRING. | VEXILLA REGIS | 22 | 52 | 277 | 156 |
| NOR SPHEARES LET FALL THEIR FAITHFULL ROUNDS. | CHARITAS NIMIA | 18 | 52 | 280 | 48 |
| WHILE WITH A FAITHFULL, MUTUALL, FLOUD | SANCTA MARIA DOLORUM | 19 | 52 | 283 | 162 |
| O FAITHFULL FREIND | SANCTA MARIA DOLORUM | 105 | 52 | 283 | 162 |
| THOU DIDST AFFORD THE FAITHFULL THEIFE. | ADORO TE | 18 | 52 | 291 | 172 |
| OUR FOOD, & FAITHFULL SHEPHARD TOO. | LAUDA SION SALVATOREM | 70 | 52 | 294 | 178 |
| NOR MAY RETURN'D MORE FAITHFULL FLOWRES. | WEEPER | 84 | 52 | 307 | 120 |
| HE'S FOLLOW'D BY TWO FAITHFULL FOUNTAINES. | WEEPER | 112 | 52 | 307 | 120 |

FAITHLESSE

| | | | | | |
|---|---|---|---|---|---|
| FAITHLESSE AND FOND MORTALITY, | UPON THE DEATH OF A GENTLEMAN | 1 | 46 | 166 | 472 |
| FOND AND FAITHLESSE THING. THAT THUS, | UPON THE DEATH OF A GENTLEMAN | 3 | 46 | 166 | 472 |
| HIS FAITHLESSE CROWNE HE FEELES LOOSE ON HIS CREST, | SOSPETTO D'HERODE | 491 | 46 | 109 | 216 |
| WHAT IF MY FAITHLESSE SOUL & I | CHARITAS NIMIA | 49 | 52 | 280 | 48 |

FALL

| | | | | | |
|---|---|---|---|---|---|
| MOST KINDLY DOE FALL OUT. THE GRUMBLING BASE | MUSICKS DUELL | 49 | 46 | 149 | 535 |
| IN MANY A SWEET RISE, MANY AS SWEET A FALL) | MUSICKS DUELL | 155 | 46 | 149 | 535 |
| OF HEAVENS HIGH'ST ARCHES TO FALL NARROW. | OUT OF GREEKE CUPID'S CRYER | 48 | 46 | 159 | 519 |
| SENTENTIOUS SHOWERS, O LET THEM FALL | UPON THE DEATH OF A GENTLEMAN | 29 | 46 | 166 | 472 |
| WAS THROWNE ALAS, AND GOT A DEADLY FALL. | HIGH MOUNTED ON AN ANT | 2 | 46 | 161 | 523 |
| THUS DID I FALL, AND THUS FELL PHAETHON. | HIGH MOUNTED ON AN ANT | 6 | 46 | 161 | 523 |
| FOR THEY BUT SEEME TO FALL | THE WEEPER | 15 | 46 | 79 | 120 |
| SO COYLY SHOULD LET FALL. | THE WEEPER | 69 | 46 | 79 | 120 |
| STILL THY TEARES DOE FALL, AND FALL. | THE WEEPER | 110 | 46 | 79 | 120 |
| STILL THY TEARES DOE FALL, AND FALL. | THE WEEPER | 110 | 46 | 79 | 120 |
| THY HIGH-AYM'D HOPES, GAIND'ST BUT A FLAMING FALL. | SOSPETTO D'HERODE | 80 | 46 | 109 | 216 |
| HIS ADAMANTINE FETTERS FALL. GREENE VIGOUR | SOSPETTO D'HERODE | 107 | 46 | 109 | 216 |
| MEE YET A SECOND FALL. WEE'D TRY OUR STRENGTHS. | SOSPETTO D'HERODE | 254 | 46 | 109 | 216 |
| INTO LOVES HAND THOU SHALT LET FALL, | IN MEMORY OF LADY MADRE TERESA | 77 | 46 | 131 | 52 |
| RUINE A TEMPLE. ON WHOSE FRUITFULL FALL | ON FRONTISPIECE ISAACSONS | 17 | 46 | 191 | 491 |
| IT MUST NOT FALL IN VAIN, IT MUST | TO COUNTESSE OF DENBIGH | 51 | 52 | 236 | 146 |
| DREAD LAMB. AND FALL | OFFICE H. CROSS PRIME | 16 | 52 | 267 | 91 |
| DREAD LAMB, & FALL | OFFICE H. CROSS THIRD | 17 | 52 | 268 | 93 |
| DREAD LAMB, AND FALL | OFFICE H. CROSS NINTH | 14 | 52 | 271 | 99 |
| NOR SPHEARES LET FALL THEIR FAITHFULL ROUNDS. | CHARITAS NIMIA | 18 | 52 | 280 | 48 |
| WOULD NEEDS FALL IN | CHARITAS NIMIA | 50 | 52 | 280 | 48 |
| THE FIRST EVE, MOTHER OF OUR FALL, | O GLORIOSA DOMINA | 11 | 52 | 302 | 194 |
| FOR THEY SEEM TO FALL, | WEEPER | 15 | 52 | 307 | 120 |
| SO COYLY SHOULD LET FALL | WEEPER | 51 | 52 | 307 | 120 |
| STILL THY STARRES DOE FALL & FALL | WEEPER | 134 | 52 | 307 | 120 |
| STILL THY STARRES DOE FALL & FALL | WEEPER | 134 | 52 | 307 | 120 |

```
INTO LOVE'S ARMES THOU SHALT LET FALL            TERESA                           77   52 315   52
FALL WITH SOFT WINGS, STUCK WITH SOFT FLOWRES.   TEMPERANCE                       46   52 342  510
WARRES RATLING TUMULTS, OR SOME TYRANTS FALL.    HORATIJ ILLE & NEFASTO           48   MS 382  530
THE FALL OF ALL THINGS IT PRAESAG'D, ITS OWNE    ON GUNPOWDER-TREASON             52   MS 384  458
THAT WITH EACH WORD, MY LOADEN PEN LETTS FALL.   UPON BIRTH PRINCESSE E            3   MS 391  456
SINCE SIGHS DOE RISE, AND TEARES DOE FALL.       UPON DEATH OF A FREIND            4   MS 393  477
TEARES FALL TOO LOW, SIGHES RISE TOO HIGH,       UPON DEATH OF A FREIND            5   MS 393  477
SINCE YOUTH MUST FALL, WHEN IT SHOULD RISE.      UPON DEATH OF A FREIND           16   MS 393  477

FALLS

WHILE IT FALLS HENCE 'TIS A TEARE.               ON WATER OF LORDS BAPTISME        4   46  85   12
FALLS FROM A STEADY HEART, THOUGH TREMBLING HAND. WIDOWES MITES                    2   46  86   21
BRIGHT EVER WITH A BEAME THAT FALLS              PSALME 23                        64   46 102    5
IT FALLS, AND DYES.  OH NO, IT MELTS AWAY        ON HOPE                          57   46 143   71
IT FALLS, AND DYES. O NO, IT MELTS AWAY          (ON) HOPE                        27   52 345   71

FALLING

RISING AND FALLING IN A POMPOUS TRAINE.          MUSICKS DUELL                    96   46 149  535
FALLING UPON HIS LUTE. O FIT TO HAVE             MUSICKS DUELL                   167   46 149  535
HER FALLING THOU DID'ST URGE AND THRUST,         PSALME 137                       29   46 104    7
HEE SAW THE FALLING IDOLS, ALL CONFESSE          SOSPETTO D'HERODE               125   46 109  216
THY FALLING TEARES KEEP FAITH FULL TIME.         WEEPER                          140   52 307  120
SNATCH'T UPP THE FALLING STARRE, SOE RICHLY GAY, AN ELEGY MR STANNINOW            50   MS 394  473

EVER-FALLING

HEAVENS OF EVER-FALLING STARS,                   THE WEEPER                        8   46  79  120
HEAVENS OF EVER-FALLING STARRES.                 WEEPER                            8   52 307  120

FALLACY

SWEET HOPE. KIND CHEAT. FAIRE FALLACY. BY THEE   ON HOPE                          77   46 143   71
ALL FORCE OF SO PROPHANE A FALLACY               TO THE NAME OF JESUS            171   52 239   30
AS BY A FAIR-EY'D FALLACY OF DAY                 IN GLORIOUS EPIPHANIE           163   52 253   39
THAT FAIR-CHEEK'T FALLACY OF FIRE.               FLAMING HEART                     4   52 324   61
SWEET HOPE. KIND CHEAT. FAIR FALLACY BY THEE     (ON) HOPE                        37   52 345   71

FALSE

LIFES FORGE. FAIN'D IS HER VOICE, AND FALSE TOO, BE SOSPETTO D'HERODE            423   46 109  216
WHICH ON FALSE TYRANTS HEAD NE'RE FIRMLY STOOD.  SOSPETTO D'HERODE               492   46 109  216
OF FALSE PERHAPS AS FAIRE                        ON A PRAYER BOOKE                52   46 126  139
INTO A FALSE ETERNITY, COME MAN,                 UPON STANINOUGH'S DEATH           9   46 175  475
SO FALSE A FORTUNE, AND SO TRUE A LOVE.          UPON FAIRE ETHIOPIAN              2   46 183  493
FAREWELL, THE WORLD'S FALSE LIGHT.               IN GLORIOUS EPIPHANIE            48   52 253   39
AND CHANG'D HIS FALSE CROWN FOR THY CROSSE.      IN GLORIOUS EPIPHANIE           142   52 253   39
OF FALSE, PERHAPS AS FAIR,                       PRAYER TO GENTLE-WOMAN           58   52 328  139
THE FALSE SMILES OF A SUBLUNARY SUN.             TO SAME CONCERNING CHOISE        32   52 331   66
FIRM HE, AS THOU ART FALSE, NOR NEED MY CRYES    ALEXIAS SECONDE ELEGIE            9   52 335  207
HALF TRUE, ALAS, HALF FALSE, PROVES THAT POOR LINE. ALEXIAS THIRD ELEGIE          57   52 336  209
FALSE LIGHTS OF FLAIRING GEMMES. TUMULTUOUS JOYES. DESCRIPTION RELIGIOUS HOUSE     5   52 338  213
WHATE'RE FALSE SHOWES OF SHORT & SLIPPERY GOOD   DESCRIPTION RELIGIOUS HOUSE       7   52 338  213
INTO A FALSE AETERNITY. COME MAN.                DEATH'S LECTURE                  10   52 340  475
O DEATH, 'TIS THOU. YOU FALSE TIME KEEPE,        UPON DEATH OF A FREIND            9   MS 393  477

FAME

LIKE STATUES FIXED TO THE FAME                   NEITHER DURST MAN ASKE           11   46  92   20
THEE, WITH THE SHRILLEST TRUMPE OF FAME.         NEITHER DURST MAN ASKE           24   46  92   20
TO THE BELEEVING WORLD FAME BOLDLY SINGS.        SOSPETTO D'HERODE                14   46 109  216
MASTER (WITH VOYCE FREE AS THE TRUMPE OF FAME)   SOSPETTO D'HERODE               439   46 109  216
THAT FATALL PLANT, SO GREAT OF FAME              OFFICE H. CROSS SIXT              5   52 270   97
LIVE SHEE, OR DYE TO FAME. EACH LEAFE YOU MEET   AT TH' IVORY TRIBUNALL            5   MS 397  492

WELL-FAM'D

THE DAUGHTER OF A FAIRE AND WELL-FAM'D FOUNTAINE TO PONTIUS WASHING HANDS          7   46  94   23

FAMES

THY FAMES FULL NOISE, MAKES PROUD THE PATIENT EARTH. SOSPETTO D'HERODE            29   46 109  216

FAMILIAR

MY SKILLFULL GREIFE IS GROWN FAMILIAR.           ALEXIAS SECONDE ELEGIE           24   52 335  207

FAMILY

WHO FEEDS WITH NECTAR HEAV'NS FAIRE FAMILY.      SOSPETTO D'HERODE               174   46 109  216
WHERE WANDER'D HER SNOWY FAMILY,                 IN MEMORY OF LADY MADRE TERESA  128   46 131   52
THE HOUSE AND FAMILY OF PHOENIXES.               UPON YORKE HIS BIRTH             91   46 176  500
WHERE 'MONGST HER SNOWY FAMILY                   TERESA                          127   52 315   52

FAMINE

WHICH HARPYES, WITH LEANE FAMINE FEED UPON,      SOSPETTO D'HERODE               330   46 109  216

FAN

HEE'L FAN HER BRIGHT LOCKS TEACHING THEM TO FLOW, ON A FOULE MORNING              19   46 181  495
OR RAMPANT FEATHER, OR RICH FAN.                 WISHES SUPPOSED MISTRESSE        21   46 195  479
```

FAN'D

| | | | | | |
|---|---|---|---|---|---|
| ARE FAN'D AND FRIZLED, IN THE WANTON AYRES | MUSICKS DUELL | 116 | 46 | 149 | 535 |

FANNING

| | | | | | |
|---|---|---|---|---|---|
| FANNING THY FAIRE LOCKS (WHICH THE WORLD BELEEVES | ON A TREATISE OF CHARITY | 23 | 46 | 137 | 69 |

FANCY

| | | | | | |
|---|---|---|---|---|---|
| HENCE 'TIS MY HUMBLE FANCY FINDS NO WINGS, | TO THE MORNING | 19 | 46 | 183 | 497 |

FANCY-FRAMED

| | | | | | |
|---|---|---|---|---|---|
| HEE HIS OWNE FANCY-FRAMED FOES DEFIES. | SOSPETTO D'HERODE | 479 | 46 | 109 | 216 |

FANCYES

| | | | | | |
|---|---|---|---|---|---|
| WITH FLASH OF HIGH-BORNE FANCYES, HERE AND THERE | MUSICKS DUELL | 138 | 46 | 149 | 535 |
| MY FANCYES, FLY BEFORE YEE, | WISHES SUPPOSED MISTRESSE | 125 | 46 | 195 | 479 |

FANTASTICK

| | | | | | |
|---|---|---|---|---|---|
| WHAT EVER SCHEMES OF BLOOD, FANTASTICK FRAMES | SOSPETTO D'HERODE | 361 | 46 | 109 | 216 |
| WHAT FATALL, YET FANTASTICK, BANDS | TO COUNTESSE OF DENBIGH | 19 | 52 | 236 | 146 |
| WHAT FATALL, YET FANTASTICK, BANDS | AGAINST IRRESOLUTION AND DELAY | 13 | 52 | 347 | 146 |

FAR

| | | | | | |
|---|---|---|---|---|---|
| RICHER FAR DOES HE ESTEEME | THE WEEPER | 83 | 46 | 79 | 120 |
| HURTES MEE FAR WORSE THEN HERODS HIGHEST SPITE. | OUT OF GROTIUS | 34 | MS | 398 | 198 |

FARR

| | | | | | |
|---|---|---|---|---|---|
| AND FITT IT TO SO FARR INFERIOR LYRES. | TO THE NAME OF JESUS | 102 | 52 | 239 | 30 |
| THUS FARR FROM HOME | IN GLORIOUS EPIPHANIE | 12 | 52 | 253 | 39 |
| BECKEN'D FROM FARR | IN GLORIOUS EPIPHANIE | 19 | 52 | 253 | 39 |
| FOR BEING SHOW'D BY THIS DAY'S LIGHT, HOW FARR | IN GLORIOUS EPIPHANIE | 246 | 52 | 253 | 39 |
| 'TWIST DEATH'S & LOVE'S FARR DIFFERENT FRUIT. | OFFICE H. CROSS SIXT | 14 | 52 | 270 | 97 |
| DIFFERENT AS FARR | OFFICE H. CROSS SIXT | 15 | 52 | 270 | 97 |
| O RATHER USE THIS HEART, THUS FARR A FITTER STONE. | OFFICE H. CROSS COMPLINE | 11 | 52 | 274 | 105 |
| YEE REDEEM'D NATIONS FARR & NEAR, | O GLORIOSA DOMINA | 27 | 52 | 302 | 194 |
| OF NAMES & WORDES, SO FARR PRAEJUDICATE. | AN APOLOGIE FOR (TERESA) HYMNE | 14 | 52 | 322 | 59 |

FARRE

| | | | | | |
|---|---|---|---|---|---|
| BUT O ME THINKES 'TIS A FARRE GREATER ONE | UPON ASSE THAT BORE SAVIOUR | 11 | 46 | 90 | 19 |
| MAPPE OF HEROICK WORTH, WHOM FARRE AND WIDE | SOSPETTO D'HERODE | 13 | 46 | 109 | 216 |
| FARRE MORE THEN MATTER FOR MY MUSE AND MEE. | SOSPETTO D'HERODE | 30 | 46 | 109 | 216 |
| OF NAMES AND WORDS SO FARRE PREJUDICATE. | AN APOLOGIE FOR HYMNE (TERESA) | 14 | 46 | 136 | 59 |
| SHEE CLIMBES, AND MAKES A FARRE MORE MILKY WAY. | ON THE ASSUMPTION | 6 | 46 | 139 | 114 |
| HER SHAFTS, AND SHEE FLY FARRE ABOVE, | ON HOPE | 75 | 46 | 143 | 71 |
| FLY, FLY PROPHANE FOGS, FARRE HENCE FLY AWAY, | ON A FOULE MORNING | 31 | 46 | 181 | 495 |
| NE'RE SO FARRE DISTANT, YET CHRONOLOGIE | ON FRONTISPIECE ISAACSONS | 8 | 46 | 191 | 491 |
| SHE CLIMBES, AND MAKES A FARRE MORE MILKEY WAY. | IN GLORIOUS ASSUMPTION B. LADY | 6 | 52 | 304 | 114 |
| AND MEANES THEM FOR A FARRE MORE WORTHY SPOUSE | TO SAME CONCERNING CHOISE | 36 | 52 | 331 | 60 |
| HER SHAFTS, AND SHEE FLY FARRE ABOVE, | (ON) HOPE | 35 | 52 | 345 | 71 |
| FARRE DISTANT FROM OUR FATES, THAT MOCKE | HORATIJ ILLE & NEFASTO | 31 | MS | 382 | 530 |
| FARRE FROM DARKE HORRORS HOME APPEALE TO REST. | HORATIJ ILLE & NEFASTO | 38 | MS | 382 | 530 |
| IF SOE, OH NEPTUNE, MAY SHE FARRE BE THROUNE | ON GUNPOWDER-TREASON | 7 | MS | 384 | 458 |
| IT MADE THE VIRGIN PHOENIX COME FARRE | UPON KINGS CORONATION | 30 | MS | 390 | 453 |
| AN AEQUALL PACE THUS FARRE. THY WORD MY DEEDES | OUT OF GROTIUS | 5 | MS | 398 | 198 |

FARE

| | | | | | |
|---|---|---|---|---|---|
| OUR LODGINGS HARD & HOMELY AS OUR FARE. | DESCRIPTION RELIGIOUS HOUSE | 11 | 52 | 338 | 213 |
| A COMMON BANQUETT. NOE, HEERE'S PRINCELY FARE | UPON GUNPOWDER TREASON | 6 | MS | 367 | 461 |

FAREWELL

| | | | | | |
|---|---|---|---|---|---|
| FAREWELL THEN ALL THE WORLD, ADEIU, | IN MEMORY OF LADY MADRE TERESA | 57 | 46 | 131 | 52 |
| FAREWELL ALL PLEASURES, SPORTS AND JOYES, | IN MEMORY OF LADY MADRE TERESA | 59 | 46 | 131 | 52 |
| FAREWELL WHAT EVER DEARE MAY BEE, | IN MEMORY OF LADY MADRE TERESA | 61 | 46 | 131 | 52 |
| FAREWELL HOUSE, AND FAREWELL HOME. | IN MEMORY OF LADY MADRE TERESA | 63 | 46 | 131 | 52 |
| FAREWELL, THE WORLD'S FALSE LIGHT. | IN GLORIOUS EPIPHANIE | 48 | 52 | 253 | 39 |
| FAREWELL, THE WHITE | IN GLORIOUS EPIPHANIE | 49 | 52 | 253 | 39 |
| AEGYPT. A LONG FAREWELL TO THEE | IN GLORIOUS EPIPHANIE | 50 | 52 | 253 | 39 |
| FAREWELL, FAREWELL | IN GLORIOUS EPIPHANIE | 54 | 52 | 253 | 39 |
| FAREWELL, FAREWELL | IN GLORIOUS EPIPHANIE | 54 | 52 | 253 | 39 |
| TAKE THY FAREWELL, POOR WORLD. HEAVN MUST GOE HOME. | IN GLORIOUS ASSUMPTION B. LADY | 2 | 52 | 304 | 114 |
| FAREWELL, ALL PLEASURES, SPORTS, & JOYES, | TERESA | 59 | 52 | 315 | 52 |
| FAREWELL WHAT EVER DEARE MAY BEE, | TERESA | 61 | 52 | 315 | 52 |
| FAREWELL HOUSE, & FAREWELL HOME. | TERESA | 63 | 52 | 315 | 52 |
| FAREWELL HOUSE, & FAREWELL HOME. | TERESA | 63 | 52 | 315 | 52 |
| FAREWELL, & SHINE, FAIR SOUL, SHINE THERE ABOVE | ALEXIAS FIRST ELEGIE | 35 | 52 | 334 | 204 |

FARWELL

| | | | | | |
|---|---|---|---|---|---|
| FARWELL HOUSE, AND FARWELL HOME. | IN MEMORY OF LADY MADRE TERESA | 63 | 46 | 131 | 52 |

## FAREWEL

| | | | |
|---|---|---|---|
| TAKE THY FAREWEL POORE WORLD, HEAVEN MUST GO HOME. | ON THE ASSUMPTION | 2 | 46 139 114 |
| FAREWEL THEN, ALL THE WORLD.  ADIEU. | TERESA | 57 | 52 315  52 |

## FARTHER

| | | | |
|---|---|---|---|
| THAT FAITH HAS FARTHER, HERE TO GOE | ADORO TE | 20 | 52 291 172 |

## FARTHEST

| | | | |
|---|---|---|---|
| WHAT FARTHEST NOOKE OF LOWEST HELL | OUT OF GREEKE CUPID'S CRYER | 35 | 46 159 519 |
| IN FARTHEST CLIME, WHAT E'RE IS BOUGHT | PETRONIJ ALES PHASIACIS PETITA | 12 | MS 382 526 |

## FASHION

| | | | |
|---|---|---|---|
| WOULD QUITE HAVE LOST THE CRUELL FASHION. | ANOTHER ON HERRYS | 24 | 46 170 469 |
| THAT WONDERS MAY IN FASHION BE, NOT RARE, | ON GUNPOWDER-TREASON | 27 | MS 384 458 |

## FAST

| | | | |
|---|---|---|---|
| WHITHER AWAY SO FAST. | THE WEEPER | 127 | 46  79 120 |
| WHY YEE TRIP SO FAST AWAY. | THE WEEPER | 132 | 46  79 120 |
| FAST BOUND, SINCE FIRST HE FORFEITED THE SKIES. | SOSPETTO D'HERODE | 40 | 46 109 216 |
| O LET THAT HAPPY SOULE HOLD FAST | ON A PRAYER BOOKE | 105 | 46 126 139 |
| SWEET NOT SO FAST, LOE THY FAIRE SPOUSE, | IN MEMORY OF LADY MADRE TERESA | 65 | 46 131  52 |
| INTO PERFUMING CLOUDES.  SO FAST | IN MEMORY OF LADY MADRE TERESA | 116 | 46 131  52 |
| AND HOLD THEM FAST FOR EVER.  THERE, | IN MEMORY OF LADY MADRE TERESA | 122 | 46 131  52 |
| OUR LOVING SONG SHALL HOLD IT FAST. | ON THE ASSUMPTION | 40 | 46 139 114 |
| WILL HOLD IT FAST, | ON THE ASSUMPTION | 45 | 46 139 114 |
| COME FAST UPON THEE, AND THOSE GLORIOUS ODS. | UPON YORKE HIS BIRTH | 6 | 46 176 500 |
| HOLDS FAST THE DOOR, YET DARES NOT VENTURE | TO COUNTESSE OF DENBIGH | 3 | 52 236 146 |
| FETTER'D. & LOCKT UP FAST THEY LY | TO COUNTESSE OF DENBIGH | 23 | 52 236 146 |
| SO FAST FOR ONE SOFT BREST. | SANCTA MARIA DOLORUM | 18 | 52 283 162 |
| SO FAST 'TWIXT HIM & THEE, | SANCTA MARIA DOLORUM | 68 | 52 283 162 |
| AS FAST AS LOVE NEW LAWES CAN GIVE. | ADORO TE | 12 | 52 291 172 |
| WILL HOLD IT FAST | IN GLORIOUS ASSUMPTION B. LADY | 50 | 52 304 114 |
| WHITHER AWAY SO FAST. | WEEPER | 169 | 52 307 120 |
| WHY YOU TRIP SO FAST AWAY. | WEEPER | 174 | 52 307 120 |
| SWEET, NOT SO FAST.  LO THY FAIR SPOUSE | TERESA | 65 | 52 315  52 |
| INTO PERFUMING CLOUDS, SO FAST | TERESA | 115 | 52 315  52 |
| AND HOLD THEM FAST FOR EVER.  THERE | TERESA | 121 | 52 315  52 |
| O LET THE BLISSFULL HEART HOLD FAST | PRAYER TO GENTLE-WOMAN | 111 | 52 328 139 |
| FIRM IN THY CROWN, AS HERE FAST IN THY LOVE. | ALEXIAS FIRST ELEGIE | 36 | 52 334 204 |
| BE HAPPY. AND FOR EVER HOLD HIM FAST. | ALEXIAS FIRST ELEGIE | 38 | 52 334 204 |
| HOLDS FAST THE DOOR, YET DARES NOT VENTURE | AGAINST IRRESOLUTION AND DELAY | 3 | 52 347 146 |
| FETTER'D AND LOCK'D UP FAST THEY LIE | AGAINST IRRESOLUTION AND DELAY | 23 | 52 347 146 |
| OUR GOD WOULD THRIVE TOO FAST, AND BE | AGAINST IRRESOLUTION AND DELAY | 63 | 52 347 146 |
| GRIPES THY COLD LIMBES SOE FAST, THOU CANST NOT FLY. | ON GUNPOWDER-TREASON | 4 | MS 384 458 |

## FASTENING

| | | | |
|---|---|---|---|
| AND FASTENING ON THINE EYES. | IN GLORIOUS EPIPHANIE | 227 | 52 253  39 |

## FASTINGS

| | | | |
|---|---|---|---|
| MINE OWNE WITH STRANGER FASTINGS, WHEN I HELD | OUT OF GROTIUS | 58 | MS 398 198 |

## FATALL

| | | | |
|---|---|---|---|
| ERST THE FULL STATURE OF A FATALL TREE. | OUR LORD IN HIS CIRCUMCISION | 16 | 46  98   9 |
| SUCH HIS FELL GLANCES AS THE FATALL LIGHT | SOSPETTO D'HERODE | 51 | 46 109 216 |
| FAINE WOULD HEE HAVE FORGOT WHAT FATALL STRINGS, | SOSPETTO D'HERODE | 139 | 46 109 216 |
| SWORDS, SPEARS, WITH ALL THE FATALL INSTRUMENTS | SOSPETTO D'HERODE | 326 | 46 109 216 |
| WHAT FATALL, YET FANTASTICK, BANDS | TO COUNTESSE OF DENBIGH | 19 | 52 236 146 |
| THAT FATALL PLANT, SO GREAT OF FAME | OFFICE H. CROSS SIXT | 5 | 52 270  97 |
| BY THAT FIRST FATALL TREE | OFFICE H. CROSS SIXT | 17 | 52 270  97 |
| WHAT FATALL, YET FANTASTICK, BANDS | AGAINST IRRESOLUTION AND DELAY | 13 | 52 347 146 |
| GOE LEARNE THAT FATALL QUIRE, SOE SPRUCELY DIGHT | AN ELEGIE ON DR PORTER | 27 | MS 395 476 |

## FATE

| | | | |
|---|---|---|---|
| YET MAY THESE UNFLEDG'D GRIEFES GIVE FATE SOME GUESSE. | OUR LORD IN HIS CIRCUMCISION | 13 | 46  98   9 |
| HIS CROWNE EXPECTED, WHEN (O FATE, O TIME | UPON DEATH OF HERRYS | 29 | 46 167 466 |
| IN THE DARKE VOLUME OF OUR FATE, | ANOTHER ON HERRYS | 41 | 46 170 469 |
| FOR THOUGH THE HAND OF FATE COULD FORCE, | AN EPITAPH HUSBAND AND WIFE | 3 | 46 174 478 |
| THE OBSEQUIOUS MOTIONS OF LOVES FATE. | LOVES HOROSCOPE | 14 | 46 185 483 |
| TO CROWNE AN UNCONTROULED FATE, | LOVES HOROSCOPE | 24 | 46 185 483 |
| OF STUDIED FATE STAND FORTH, | WISHES SUPPOSED MISTRESSE | 8 | 46 195 479 |
| THE' ASTONISHT NYMPHS THEIR FLOOD'S STRANGE FATE DEPLORE, | TO COUNTESSE OF DENBIGH | 25 | 52 236 146 |
| FAIR ONE, IT IS YOUR FATE. AND BRINGS | TO COUNTESSE OF DENBIGH | 53 | 52 236 146 |
| BUT IF IT BE THE FREQUENT FATE | FLAMING HEART | 59 | 52 324  61 |
| T'EMBRACE MY TEARES, & KISSE AN UNKIND FATE. | ALEXIAS FIRST ELEGIE | 4 | 52 334 204 |
| HERE'T WAS THE ROMAN MAID FOUND A HARD FATE | ALEXIAS FIRST ELEGIE | 29 | 52 334 204 |
| FOR THOUGH THE HAND OF FATE COULD FORCE | AN EPITAPH UPON MARRIED COUPLE | 3 | 52 339 478 |
| TH'ASTONISH'D NYMPHS THEIR FLOUD'S STRANGE FATE DEPLORE, | AGAINST IRRESOLUTION AND DELAY | 25 | 52 347 146 |
| AND BY THEIR LOVE CONTROLL THEIR FATE. | AGAINST IRRESOLUTION AND DELAY | 50 | 52 347 146 |
| THE STORME OF FATE, TO WHICH HIS LIFE HE OWES. | HORATIJ ILLE & NEFASTO | 24 | MS 382 530 |
| LETT HER SURVIVE THIS DAY, ONCE MOCK HER FATE, | ON GUNPOWDER-TREASON | 9 | MS 384 458 |
| EV'EN TO THE NAKED'ST VOWES. THOU ART MY FATE. | EX EUPHORMIONE | 9 | MS 392 525 |
| DOTH GRASPE THE FATE OF THINGES, AND SHARE TH' EVENTS | OUT OF GROTIUS | 2 | MS 398 198 |

## FATES

| | | | | |
|---|---|---|---|---|
| THE FATES RIPE, IN THEIR GREAT CONSPIRACY. | SOSPETTO D'HERODE | 432 | 46 109 | 216 |
| AND NOW CROSSE FATES A WATCH ABOUT THEE KEEPE. | SOSPETTO D'HERODE | 455 | 46 109 | 216 |
| FATES CANNOT FIND OUT A CAPACITY | ON HOPE | 17 | 46 143 | 71 |
| AND FATES WHOLE LOTTERY IS ONE BLANKE TO HER. | ON HOPE | 74 | 46 143 | 71 |
| AND THE FATES WILL HAVE IT SO, | UPON DEATH OF DESIRED HERRYS | 66 | 46 168 | 467 |
| THAT COULD THE FATES KNOW TO RELENT. | ANOTHER ON HERRYS | 17 | 46 170 | 469 |
| FATES CANNOT FIND OUT A CAPACITY | (ON) HOPE | 7 | 52 345 | 71 |
| FARRE DISTANT FROM OUR FATES. OUR FATES, THAT MOCKE | HORATIJ ILLE & NEFASTO | 31 | MS 382 | 530 |
| FARRE DISTANT FROM OUR FATES. OUR FATES, THAT MOCKE | HORATIJ ILLE & NEFASTO | 31 | MS 382 | 530 |
| THAT HEERE ARE DRESSING BY THE HASTY FATES. | UPON GUNPOWDER TREASON | 30 | MS 387 | 461 |

## FATHER

| | | | | |
|---|---|---|---|---|
| IF THIS WERE WISDOMES GOD, THAT WARS STERNE FATHER, | UPON YORKE HIS BIRTH | 32 | 46 176 | 500 |
| HEE LOV'D HIS FATHER. YET HIS ZEALE | AN EPITAPH UPON ASHTON | 19 | 46 192 | 464 |
| GLORY BE TO THE FATHER, | OFFICE H. CROSS MATINES | 7 | 52 265 | 86 |
| HEAR, FATHER, HEAR. THY LAMB (AT LAST) COMPLAINES. | OFFICE H. CROSS NINTH | 3 | 52 271 | 99 |
| FROM HIS OLD FATHER. THAT MANS BARBAROUS KNIFE | HORATIJ ILLE & NEFASTO | 8 | MS 382 | 530 |
| THINKING HER FATHER HAD REMOV'D HIS COURT. | UPON KINGS CORONATION | 32 | MS 390 | 453 |
| BRIGHT GODDESSE, (WHETHER JOVE THY FATHER BE, | EX EUPHORMIONE | 1 | MS 392 | 525 |
| OR JOVE A FATHER WILL BE MADE BY THEE) | EX EUPHORMIONE | 2 | MS 392 | 525 |
| WHICH THEIR BRIGHT FATHER IN A PRETIOUS SHOWRE | AN ELEGY MR STANNINOW | 9 | MS 394 | 473 |
| THE WORLD MY FATHER. THEN DOES ENVY SWELL | OUT OF GROTIUS | 32 | MS 398 | 198 |
| A RIDDLE. (FATHER) STILL ACKNOWLEDG'D THINE | OUT OF GROTIUS | 35 | MS 398 | 198 |
| FATHER AND HEYRE OF DARKENESSE, WHEN I CHIDE | OUT OF GROTIUS | 77 | MS 398 | 198 |

## FATHER'S

| | | | | |
|---|---|---|---|---|
| THE DEATHLES HEIR OF ALL THY FATHER'S DAY. | IN GLORIOUS EPIPHANIE | 64 | 52 253 | 39 |
| THE FATHER'S WORD & WISDOM, MADE | OFFICE H. CROSS MATINES | 12 | 52 265 | 86 |
| IN BOSOM OF THY FATHER'S BLISSE. | O GLORIOSA DOMINA | 38 | 52 302 | 194 |
| MOTHER'S ARMES OR FATHER'S KNEE | TERESA | 62 | 52 315 | 52 |
| HE LEFT HIS FATHER'S COURT, AND CAME | AGAINST IRRESOLUTION AND DELAY | 69 | 52 347 | 146 |
| PEACE IS AN ORPHAN NOW. HER FATHER'S DEAD. | AN ELEGIE ON DR PORTER | 16 | MS 395 | 476 |

## FATHERS

| | | | | |
|---|---|---|---|---|
| OF BROTHERS MUTUALL BLOOD, AND FATHERS BRAINES. | SOSPETTO D'HERODE | 328 | 46 109 | 216 |
| MOTHERS ARMES, OR FATHERS KNEE. | IN MEMORY OF LADY MADRE TERESA | 62 | 46 131 | 52 |
| WHAT THE SOWREST FATHERS SAY. | OUT OF CATULLUS | 3 | 46 194 | 523 |
| I LEFT MY GLORIOUS FATHERS STAR-PAV'D COURT | OUT OF GROTIUS | 14 | MS 398 | 198 |

## FATT

| | | | | |
|---|---|---|---|---|
| THE ALTAR-STALL'D OX, FATT OSYRIS NOW | IN GLORIOUS EPIPHANIE | 96 | 52 253 | 39 |

## FAULT

| | | | | |
|---|---|---|---|---|
| THE POOR WORLD'S FAULT THAT HE IS FAIR. | IN GLORIOUS EPIPHANIE | 104 | 52 253 | 39 |
| HIS PENANCE, AS OUR FAULT, CONSPICUOUS. | IN GLORIOUS EPIPHANIE | 156 | 52 253 | 39 |
| NOR IS'T LOVE'S FAULT, BUT SIN'S DIRE SKILL | LAUDA SION SALVATOREM | 53 | 52 294 | 178 |

## FAULTS

| | | | | |
|---|---|---|---|---|
| OF WORST FAULTS TO BE FORTUNATE. | FLAMING HEART | 60 | 52 324 | 61 |

## FAWNING

| | | | | |
|---|---|---|---|---|
| HIS FAWNING CHEEKS, LOOKE NOT THAT WAY | OUT OF GREEKE CUPID'S CRYER | 64 | 46 159 | 519 |

## FEAR

| | | | | |
|---|---|---|---|---|
| TURN'D THE STEEL POINT OF FEAR, | VEXILLA REGIS | 16 | 52 277 | 156 |
| MY HOPE, MY FEAR. MY JUDGE, MY FREIND. | DIES IRAE | 67 | 52 298 | 186 |
| BUT REVERENT DISCIPLINE, & RELIGIOUS FEAR, | DESCRIPTION RELIGIOUS HOUSE | 30 | 52 338 | 213 |

## FEAR'S

| | | | | |
|---|---|---|---|---|
| FEAR'S ANTIDOTE. A WISE & WELL-STAY'D FIRE. | (ON) HOPE | 42 | 52 345 | 71 |

## FEARED

| | | | | |
|---|---|---|---|---|
| AND HATEFULL SCHINIS HIS SO FEARED OAKES. | SOSPETTO D'HERODE | 360 | 46 109 | 216 |

## FEAR'D

| | | | | |
|---|---|---|---|---|
| NOR WOULD HE THIS THY FEAR'D CROWN FROM THEE TEARE, | SOSPETTO D'HERODE | 517 | 46 109 | 216 |
| SEE HOW HEE'S FURNISH'T FOR SO FEAR'D A WARRE. | SOSPETTO D'HERODE | 524 | 46 109 | 216 |
| OR PERTCH'T UPON FEAR'D DIADEMS. | WEEPER | 184 | 52 307 | 120 |

## FEARE

| | | | | |
|---|---|---|---|---|
| BOTH WHICH AWAY, I SHOULD NOT NEED TO FEARE, | WITH A PICTURE TO A FRIEND | 7 | 46 156 | 494 |
| PITTY NOT HIM, BUT FEARE THY SELFE | OUT OF GREEKE CUPID'S CRYER | 59 | 46 159 | 519 |
| BESIDES THIS FEARE OF DANGER, THERE'S NO DANGER HERE | WHY ARE YEE AFRAID | 15 | 46 88 | 15 |
| AND HE THAT HERE FEARES DANGER, DOES DESERVE HIS FEARE. | WHY ARE YEE AFRAID | 16 | 46 88 | 15 |
| THY HUMBLE FAITH AND FEARE KEEPES HIM ALOOFE. | I AM NOT WORTHY | 2 | 46 90 | 13 |
| HEE TO HIMSELFE (I FEARE THE WORST) | I AM THE DOORE | 3 | 46 90 | 17 |
| SAVE THOSE OF FEARE, NO OTHER BANDS FEARE I. | I AM READY NOT ONELY BOUND | 3 | 46 98 | 29 |
| SAVE THOSE OF FEARE, NO OTHER BANDS FEARE I. | I AM READY NOT ONELY BOUND | 3 | 46 98 | 29 |

| | | | | | |
|---|---|---|---|---|---|
| NOR OTHER DEATH THEN THIS. THE FEARE TO DYE. | I AM READY NOT ONELY BOUND | 4 | 46 | 98 | 29 |
| THAT HEE WHO MADE THE FIRE, SHOULD FEARE THE COLD. | SOSPETTO D'HERODE | 180 | 46 | 109 | 216 |
| AND YET WHOSE FORCE FEARE I, HAVE I SO LOST | SOSPETTO D'HERODE | 249 | 46 | 109 | 216 |
| WHY ART THOU TROUBLED HEROD. WHAT VAINE FEARE | SOSPETTO D'HERODE | 513 | 46 | 109 | 216 |
| (FEARE IT NOT, SWEET. | ON A PRAYER BOOKE | 2 | 46 | 126 | 139 |
| THIS LAST COUGH AELIA, COUGHT OUT ALL THY FEARE, | OUT OF MARTIALL | 5 | 46 | 188 | 527 |
| LET US LOVE AND NEVER FEARE. | OUT OF CATULLUS | 2 | 46 | 194 | 523 |
| WHICH WAY IT THREATS, WITH FEARE THE MERCHANTS MIND | HORATIJ ILLE & NEFASTO | 19 | MS | 382 | 530 |
| OH. THAT'S HIS FEARE. THERE FLOTES HIS DESTINY. | HORATIJ ILLE & NEFASTO | 22 | MS | 382 | 530 |
| I FEARE TO NAME IT. LEAST THAT HE. WHICH HEARES. | UPON GUNPOWDER TREASON | 9 | MS | 386 | 460 |
| WHOM FAINT, & PALEFAC'T FEARE DOTH STILL ATTEND. | UPON GUNPOWDER TREASON | 18 | MS | 387 | 461 |
| FEARE IS AFRAID TO TAST OF. ONLY THIS, | UPON GUNPOWDER TREASON | 45 | MS | 387 | 461 |
| FOR IF YOU SETT, WHO MAY NOT JUSTLY FEARE, | UPON KINGS CORONATION | 41 | MS | 389 | 454 |
| FEARE NOT TO DY WITH GREIFE. ALL BUBLING EYES | AN ELEGIE ON DR PORTER | 43 | MS | 395 | 476 |
| (FOR ELSE WHY CAME I.) EV'N WHAT E'RE I FEARE. | OUT OF GROTIUS | 8 | MS | 398 | 198 |
| HIS FEARE. THE CIRCLE OF A YEARES ROUND GROWTH | OUT OF GROTIUS | 22 | MS | 398 | 198 |

FEARES

| | | | | | |
|---|---|---|---|---|---|
| SINGING THEIR FEARES ARE FEARFULLY DELIGHTED. | MUSICKS DUELL | 114 | 46 | 149 | 535 |
| THAT FEARES THE FOULE-MOUTH'D AUSTER, OR THOSE STORMES | OUT OF VIRGIL | 19 | 46 | 155 | 529 |
| DECEIVES MENS FEARES WITH FLATTERING WILES. | OUT OF GREEKE CUPID'S CRYER | 50 | 46 | 159 | 519 |
| AND HE THAT HERE FEARES DANGER, DOES DESERVE HIS FEARE. | WHY ARE YEE AFRAID | 16 | 46 | 88 | 15 |
| AT THOSE HARD WORDS MANS COWARDISE CALLS FEARES. | I AM READY NOT ONELY BOUND | 2 | 46 | 98 | 29 |
| NOW'S BUT THE NONAGE OF MY PAINES, MY FEARES | OUR LORD IN HIS CIRCUMCISION | 9 | 46 | 98 | 9 |
| OF WOES, TOO LATE DOE ROUZE THY FEARES. | PSALME 137 | 34 | 46 | 104 | 7 |
| ABOVE HIS FEARES, AND THINKE IT CANNOT BE. | SOSPETTO D'HERODE | 154 | 46 | 109 | 216 |
| THAT GLORIES SELFE SHOULD SERVE OUR GRIEFS, & FEARES. | SOSPETTO D'HERODE | 183 | 46 | 109 | 216 |
| OF TIME, OR TEETH OF HUNGRY RUINE FEARES. | SOSPETTO D'HERODE | 310 | 46 | 109 | 216 |
| HEE WAKES, AND WITH HIM (NE'RE TO SLEEPE) NEW FEARES. | SOSPETTO D'HERODE | 473 | 46 | 109 | 216 |
| BRINGING HIM NOTHING BUT NEW FEARES FROM TH'EAST, | SOSPETTO D'HERODE | 500 | 46 | 109 | 216 |
| SHEW'D HIM HIS FEARES, AND KILL'D HIM WITH THE SIGHT. | SOSPETTO D'HERODE | 504 | 46 | 109 | 216 |
| LOOKE HOW BELOW THY FEARES THEIR CAUSES ARE. | SOSPETTO D'HERODE | 522 | 46 | 109 | 216 |
| BEE POSED WITH THE MATUREST FEARES | IN MEMORY OF LADY MADRE TERESA | 30 | 46 | 131 | 52 |
| FEARES ANTIDOTE. A WISE, AND WELL STAY'D FIRE | ON HOPE | 82 | 46 | 143 | 71 |
| HER HOPES ARE CROWN'D, ONELY SHE FEARES THAT THAN, | UPON FAIRE ETHIOPIAN | 5 | 46 | 183 | 493 |
| FEARES, FOND AND FLIGHT. | WISHES SUPPOSED MISTRESSE | 70 | 46 | 195 | 479 |
| DISBAND DULL FEARES. GIVE FAITH THE DAY. | TO COUNTESSE OF DENBIGH | 57 | 52 | 236 | 146 |
| THEIR HATED LOVES CHANG'D INTO WHOLSOM FEARES, | IN GLORIOUS EPIPHANIE | 161 | 52 | 253 | 39 |
| BE POS'D WITH THE MATUREST FEARES | TERESA | 30 | 52 | 315 | 52 |
| DISBAND DULL FEARES. GIVE FAITH THE DAY. | AGAINST IRRESOLUTION AND DELAY | 81 | 52 | 347 | 146 |
| THUS, O THUS FONDLY DOE WEE PITCH OUR FEARES | HORATIJ ILLE & NEFASTO | 30 | MS | 382 | 530 |
| OUR GIDDY FEARES WITH AN UNLOOK'T FOR SHOCKE. | HORATIJ ILLE & NEFASTO | 32 | MS | 382 | 530 |

FEARFULL

| | | | | | |
|---|---|---|---|---|---|
| IT QUITE FORGOTT. THE FEARFULL EARTH GAVE WAY, | ON GUNPOWDER-TREASON | 53 | MS | 384 | 458 |

FEARFULLY

| | | | | | |
|---|---|---|---|---|---|
| SINGING THEIR FEARES ARE FEARFULLY DELIGHTED. | MUSICKS DUELL | 114 | 46 | 149 | 535 |

FEARING

| | | | | | |
|---|---|---|---|---|---|
| NOT PERFECT YET, AND FEARING TO BEE OUT | MUSICKS DUELL | 36 | 46 | 149 | 535 |

FEAST

| | | | | | |
|---|---|---|---|---|---|
| A MISERABLE AND A MONSTROUS FEAST. | THE BEGINNING OF HELIODORUS | 25 | 46 | 158 | 517 |
| WHO PROV'D THE FEAST TO THEIR OWNE FUNERALL. | THE BEGINNING OF HELIODORUS | 28 | 46 | 158 | 517 |
| AND HEAVEN WILL MAKE A FEAST. | THE WEEPER | 33 | 46 | 79 | 120 |
| SEE HERE AN EASIE FEAST THAT KNOWES NO WOUND. | ON MIRACLE OF LOAVES | 1 | 46 | 86 | 15 |
| WHILE I FEAST, MY FOES DOE FEED | PSALME 23 | 51 | 46 | 102 | 5 |
| THE TABLES FURNISHT WITH A CURSED FEAST, | SOSPETTO D'HERODE | 329 | 46 | 109 | 216 |
| SUCH AS AT THEBES DIRE FEAST SHEE SHEW'D HER HEAD. | SOSPETTO D'HERODE | 397 | 46 | 109 | 216 |
| THOUGH IN IT SELF THIS SOVERAIN FEAST | LAUDA SION SALVATOREM | 49 | 52 | 294 | 178 |
| THE FEAST OF ALL THINGS FEEDS ON THEE. | O GLORIOSA DOMINA | 10 | 52 | 302 | 194 |
| AND HEAVN WILL MAKE A FEAST, | WEEPER | 69 | 52 | 307 | 120 |
| THE THRONGING CLOTTED MULTITUDE DOTH FEAST. | HORATIJ ILLE & NEFASTO | 49 | MS | 382 | 530 |
| GROW PLUMPE, LEANE DEATH. HIS HOLINESSE A FEAST | UPON GUNPOWDER TREASON | 1 | MS | 387 | 461 |

FEASTS

| | | | | | |
|---|---|---|---|---|---|
| HOW FIT OUR WELL-RANK'D FEASTS DOE FOLLOW. | UPON POWDER DAY | 1 | 46 | 185 | 74 |
| OTHER MENS HUNGER WITH STRANGE FEASTS I QUELL'D | OUT OF GROTIUS | 57 | MS | 398 | 198 |

FEASTING

| | | | | | |
|---|---|---|---|---|---|
| MARKES OF A FIGHT ALONE, BUT FEASTING TOO, | THE BEGINNING OF HELIODORUS | 24 | 46 | 158 | 517 |

FEATHER

| | | | | | |
|---|---|---|---|---|---|
| OR RAMPANT FEATHER, OR RICH FAN. | WISHES SUPPOSED MISTRESSE | 21 | 46 | 195 | 479 |
| PAINT EACH FEATHER, AS IF NEW. | PETRONIJ ALES PHASIACIS PETITA | 8 | MS | 382 | 526 |

FEATHERED

| | | | | | |
|---|---|---|---|---|---|
| HATH AGED WINTER, FLEDG'D WITH FEATHERED RAINE. | AN ELEGY MR STANNINOW | 1 | MS | 394 | 473 |

FEATHERD

| | | | | | |
|---|---|---|---|---|---|
| FEATHERD WITH HIS MOTHERS SPARROWES. | OUT OF THE ITALIAN (1) | 18 | 46 | 188 | 545 |

FEATURE

AND MEANT TO LEAVE HIS PRETIOUS FEATURE,        UPON DEATH OF DESIRED HERRYS        7    46 168 467

FEATURES

THROUGH WHICH ALL HER BRIGHT FEATURES SHINE.    IN PRAISE OF LESSIUS                26    46 156 510
THROUGH WHICH ALL HER BRIGHT FEATURES SHINE.    TEMPERANCE                          24    52 342 510

FED

WHAT WOULD YE MORE. HERE FOOD IT SELFE IS FED.  ON MIRACLE OF LOAVES                 4    46  86  15
THEY ARE STARV'D, AND I AM FED.                 PSALME 23                           54    46 102   5

COURT-FED

HIS COURT-FED IMPES AGAINST THIS HATED HEAD.    OUT OF GROTIUS                      48    MS 398 198

FEDD

HER PAINTED INFANTS, FEDD WITH PLEASENT PAPPE,  AN ELEGY MR STANNINOW                8    MS 394 473

FEEBLE

THAT MAN (I THINKE) WRESTED THE FEEBLE LIFE     HORATIJ ILLE & NEFASTO               7    MS 382 530

FEED

WHILE I FEAST, MY FOES DOE FEED                 PSALME 23                           51    46 102   5
TO FEED MY LIFE WITH, THERE I'LE SUP            PSALME 23                           69    46 102   5
THE SHEPHEARDS, WHILE THEY FEED THEIR SHEEPE.   A HYMNE OF THE NATIVITY             82    46 106  76
WHICH HARPYES, WITH LEANE FAMINE FEED UPON,     SOSPETTO D'HERODE                  330    46 109 216
THEY FEED OUR SOULES, SHALL CLOATH THINE THERE. IN MEMORY OF LADY MADRE TERESA     159    46 131  52
FEED FOR EVER THEIR FAIRE SIGHT                 ON THE ASSUMPTION                   34    46 139 114
TO FEED OF THEE IN THINE OWN FACE.              LAUDA SION SALVATOREM               80    52 294 178
THEY FEED OUR SOULES, SHALL CLOTH THINE THERE.  TERESA                             158    52 315  52
AND WHATSOE'RE WILD SINNES BLACK THOUGHTS DOE FEED, HORATIJ ILLE & NEFASTO         12    MS 382 530
TWICE TWENTY DAYES PURE ABSTINENCE, TO FEED     OUT OF GROTIUS                      59    MS 398 198

FEED'ST

AS WITH THY SELFE THOU FEED'ST THY SHEEP.       LAUDA SION SALVATOREM               72    52 294 178

FEEDS

WHO FEEDS WITH NECTAR HEAV'NS FAIRE FAMILY.     SOSPETTO D'HERODE                  174    46 109 216
THE FEAST OF ALL THINGS FEEDS ON THEE.          O GLORIOSA DOMINA                   10    52 302 194

FEEDING

AND IN THE STEAD OF FEEDING STOOD, & GAZ'D.     UPON GUNPOWDER TREASON              48    MS 387 461

LIFE-FEEDING

VERTUE TO ACTION, THAT LIFE-FEEDING FLAME       ON A TREATISE OF CHARITY            51    46 137  69

FEEL

THY SELFE SHALT FEEL THINE OWNE FULL JOYES.     IN MEMORY OF LADY MADRE TERESA     121    46 131  52
THY SELFE SHALL FEEL THINE OWN FULL JOYES       TERESA                             120    52 315  52

FEELE

AND FEELE THE PULSE OF EVERY PROPHECY.          SOSPETTO D'HERODE                  156    46 109 216
ATLAS SHALL BE TRIPT UPP, JOVE'S GATE SHALL FEELE ON GUNPOWDER-TREASON             43    MS 384 458

FEELS

WHO FEELS HIS WARM HEART HATCH'D INTO A NEST    AN APOLOGIE FOR (TERESA) HYMNE      26    52 322  59
THE SOUL IT SELFE MORE FEELS THEN HEARES.       PRAYER TO GENTLE-WOMAN              68    52 328 139

FEELES

FEELES MUSICKS PULSE IN ALL HER ARTERYES.       MUSICKS DUELL                      120    46 149 535
FEELES NOT THE STRENGTH, THE REACHING SPELL     OUT OF GREEKE CUPID'S CRYER         36    46 159 519
THY HUNGER FEELES NOT WHAT HE EATES.            BLESSED BE THE PAPS                  2    46  94  14
HIS FAITHLESSE CROWNE HE FEELES LOOSE ON HIS CREST, SOSPETTO D'HERODE             491    46 109 216
THE SOULE IT SELFE MORE FEELES THEN HEARES.     ON A PRAYER BOOKE                   62    46 126 139
(WHICH DULL MORTALITY MORE FEELES THEN HEARES)  TO THE NAME OF JESUS                31    52 239  30
NONE, BUT HIMSELFE, WHO FEELES IT, NONE CAN TELL. IN AMOREM DIVINUM                 2    MS 381 212
NONE, NOT HIMSELFE, WHO FEELES IT, NONE CAN TELL. IN AMOREM DIVINUM                 4    MS 381 212

FEELING

WITH WHICH HIS FEELING DREAME HAD THUS DISMAY'D HIM, SOSPETTO D'HERODE            478    46 109 216

FEET

LICKE HIS PROUD FEET, AND HAST INTO THE SEAS    THE BEGINNING OF HELIODORUS          5    46 158 517
UNDER TH' UNRULY BEASTS PROUD FEET HE LIES      HIGH MOUNTED ON AN ANT               3    46 161 523
A WORTHIER OBJECT, OUR LORDS FEET.              THE WEEPER                         138    46  79 120
FROM THY HANDS AND FROM THY FEET,               ON BLEEDING WOUNDS OF LORD           2    46 101 110
THY RESTLESSE FEET THEY CANNOT GOE.             ON BLEEDING WOUNDS OF LORD           5    46 101 110

```
AT MY FEET THE BLUBB'RING MOUNTAINE          PSALME 23                         13   46 102    5
TO MY JOY-CONDUCTED FEET.                    PSALME 23                         31   46 102    5
THERE MY FEET. EVEN THERE SHALL FIND         PSALME 23                         43   46 102    5
TO KISSE THY FEET, AND CROWNE THY HEAD.      A HYMNE OF THE NATIVITY           80   46 106   76
RUINE, WHERE E'RE SHE SLEEPES AT NATURES FEET. SOSPETTO D'HERODE              279   46 109  216
AND WITH SOFT FEET SEARCHES THE SILENT ROOMES. SOSPETTO D'HERODE              400   46 109  216
AND LAY THEM TREMBLING AT HIS FEET.          UPON DEATH OF DESIRED HERRYS      46   46 168  467
WHOSE FEET CAN WALKE THE MILKY WAY, AND CHUSE TO THE MORNING                   24   46 183  497
TO KISSE THY FEET & CROWN THY HEAD.          IN HOLY NATIVITY                 100   52 246   76
AND AT THY FEET POWR FORTH HIS FACE.         IN GLORIOUS EPIPHANIE             84   52 253   39
AT THY ADORED FEET, THUS, HE LAYES DOWN      IN GLORIOUS EPIPHANIE            240   52 253   39
AND CROWD FOR KISSES FROM THE LAMB'S WHITE FEET. TO THE QUEEN'S MAJESTY        14   52 261   47
THEIR WEALTHY TOPS. & FOR THESE FEET CONTEND. TO THE QUEEN'S MAJESTY           18   52 261   47
CROWNES, & THE HEADS THEY KISSE, MUST COURT THESE TO THE QUEEN'S MAJESTY       20   52 261   47
                                       FEET.

FROM THY HEAD & FROM THY FEET.               UPON BLEEDING CRUCIFIX             2   52 288  110
THY RESTLESSE FEET NOW CANNOT GOE            UPON BLEEDING CRUCIFIX             9   52 288  110
A WORTHY OBJECT, OUR LORD'S FEET.            WEEPER                           186   52 307  120
(WHOSE HANDS ARE FIGHTING, WHILE THEIR FEET DOE FLIE.) HORATIJ ILLE & NEFASTO  26   MS 382  530
UNTO WHOSE FEET IN REVERENCE OF THE POWERS,  AN ELEGIE ON DR PORTER             4   MS 395  476
OF MY WEAKE FEET THE PERSIAN MAGI LAY        OUT OF GROTIUS                    37   MS 398  198
UNDER MY FEET, THE WATERS TO BEE WETT.       OUT OF GROTIUS                    68   MS 398  198

FEETS

HER EYES FLOOD LICKES HIS FEETS FAIRE STAINE. SHE BEGAN TO WASH HIS FEET        1   46  97   13

FEIGN'D

MY LOVE, OR FEIGN'D OR PAINTED SHOULD APPEARE. WITH A PICTURE TO A FRIEND       8   46 156  494

FEIRCE

THE NORTH FORGOTT HIS FEIRCE INTENT.         IN HOLY NATIVITY                  26   52 246   76
O PRIZE OF THE RICH SPIRIT. WITH WHAT FEIRCE CHASE IN GLORIOUS EPIPHANIE      196   52 253   39
BY ALL THE BRIM-FILL'D BOWLES OF FEIRCE DESIRE FLAMING HEART                   99   52 324   61
THOUGH LOVE'S MORE FEIRCE, MORE FRUITLESSE, FIRES (ON) HOPE                    47   52 345   71
                                      ASSAY

FEIRCEST

OF DEATH & FEIRCEST DANGERS, DURST WITH BRAVE TO THE NAME OF JESUS            201   52 239   30

FELICITY

OF THEIR FELICITY. A SPRING WAS THERE,       OUT OF VIRGIL                     25   46 155  529
UNMIXT FELICITY WITH SILVER WINGS            UPON KINGS CORONATION             21   MS 389  454

FELL

THUS DID I FALL, AND THUS FELL PHAETHON.     HIGH MOUNTED ON AN ANT             6   46 161  523
SUCH HIS FELL GLANCES AS THE FATALL LIGHT    SOSPETTO D'HERODE                 51   46 109  216
FELL EXECUTIONERS OF FOULE INTENTS,          SOSPETTO D'HERODE                324   46 109  216
PALE PROOFE OF HER FELL PRESENCE. TH'AIRE TOO WELL SOSPETTO D'HERODE          374   46 109  216
AND IN FELL HATRED BURNING, ANGRY DY.        UPON GUNPOWDER TREASON            16   MS 387  461

FELLOW

FELLOW THIS WONDER TOO, NOR LET HER SHINE    UPON YORKE HIS BIRTH              55   46 176  500
AND ALL THEIR FELLOW DEITIES WILL BOW        EX EUPHORMIONE                     8   MS 392  525

FEMALE

AND MOCKES WITH FEMALE FROST LOVE'S MANLY FLAME. FLAMING HEART                 24   52 324   61

FEMAL

THE TOO FRAIL LIFE OF FEMAL CONSTANCY.       ALEXIAS FIRST ELEGIE              34   52 334  204

FENCE

AND FENCE THE HANGING SWORD HEAV'N THROWS UPON THEE. SOSPETTO D'HERODE        460   46 109  216

FENC'D

WITH HIS FOULE CLAWES HEE FENC'D HIS FURROWED BROW. SOSPETTO D'HERODE         149   46 109  216

FERTILE

YOUR FERTILE MOTHERS.                        THE WEEPER                       123   46  79  120

FETCH

AND FETCH THE HEART FROM IT'S STRONG HOLD.   TO COUNTESSE OF DENBIGH           28   52 236  146

FETCH'T

THE BIRD, THAT'S FETCH'T FROM PHASIS FLOUD,  PETRONIJ ALES PHASIACIS PETITA     1   MS 382  526

FETCHETH

THAT FETCHETH FRESH LIFE FROM HER FRUITFULL URNE. EX EUPHORMIONE               16   MS 392  525
```

FETTER'D

  FETTER'D, & LOCKT UP FAST THEY LY                TO COUNTESSE OF DENBIGH      23  52 236 146
  FETTER'D AND LOCK'D UP FAST THEY LIE          AGAINST IRRESOLUTION AND DELAY  23  52 347 146

FETTERS

  HIS ADAMANTINE FETTERS FALL. GREENE VIGOUR     SOSPETTO D'HERODE             107  46 109 216

FEVER

  IN FLAMES, & OF A BURNING FEVER DY.            ON GUNPOWDER-TREASON         26  MS 384 456

FEAVER

  AND HIS FEAVER WISH'D TO PROVE               ANOTHER ON HERRYS            27  46 170 469

FEAV'ROUS

  WITH WHICH HIS FEAV'ROUS CARES THEIR COLD INCREAST.  SOSPETTO D'HERODE             502  46 109 216

FEW

  AS PRIS'NER IN A FEW POORE RAGS TO LYE.        SOSPETTO D'HERODE             172  46 109 216
  WHAT ARMOUR DOES HE WEARE.  A FEW THIN CLOUTS.    SOSPETTO D'HERODE             525  46 109 216
  WHOSE SILKEN FLATTERYES SWELL A FEW FOND HOURES   UPON STANINOUGH'S DEATH        8  46 175 475
  ONE OF THOSE FEW THAT IN THIS TOWNE.           AN EPITAPH UPON ASHTON         7  46 192 464
  THAT CHAST & CHEAP, AS THE FEW CLOTHES WE WEARE.  DESCRIPTION RELIGIOUS HOUSE    12  52 338 213
  WHOSE SYLKEN FLATTERYES SWELL A FEW FOND HOWRES  DEATH'S LECTURE                9  52 340 475

FICTIONS

  BEE YE MY FICTIONS.  BUT HER STORY.            WISHES SUPPOSED MISTRESSE    126  46 195 479

FIELD

  HOT MARS TO TH' HARVEST OF DEATHS FIELD, AND WOO  MUSICKS DUELL                 55  46 149 535
  TO A VAST FIELD OF THORNES, TEN THOUSAND SPEARES  SOSPETTO D'HERODE             475  46 109 216
  THE GOD OF NATURE IN THE FIELD OF GRACE.       ON HOPE                       90  46 143  71
  'TIS COWARDISE THAT KEEPS THIS FIELD.           AGAINST IRRESOLUTION AND DELAY  83  52 347 146

FIELD'S

  THE FIELD'S FAIRE EYES SAW HER, AND SAW NO MORE,  SOSPETTO D'HERODE             378  46 109 216

FEILD

  'TIS COWARDISE THAT KEEPS THIS FEILD           TO COUNTESSE OF DENBIGH      61  52 236 146
  FOR IN LOVE'S FEILD WAS NEVER FOUND            FLAMING HEART                 71  52 324  61
  THE FEILD OF NATURE OR OF GRACE.              AGAINST IRRESOLUTION AND DELAY  30  52 347 146
  BUT NOW THE FEILD IS WONNE, & THEY             IN CICATRICES DOMINI JESU     17  MS 381  27

FEILD'S

  THOUGH THE FEILD'S EYES TOO WEEPERS BE         WEEPER                         179  52 307 120

FIELDS

  THE HERDS TO KINDLY MEETINGS, THEN THE FIELDS    OUT OF VIRGIL                 12  46 155 529
  THE FIELDS OF PALESTINE, WITH SO PURE A FLOOD,   SOSPETTO D'HERODE             86  46 109 216
  AND FOR THE NEVER-FADING FIELDS OF LIGHT       SOSPETTO D'HERODE            211  46 109 216
  AND FORRAGE IN THE FIELDS OF LIGHT, AND LOVE.    ON HOPE                       76  46 143  71
  AND FORRAGE IN THE FIELDS OF LIGHT AND LOVE.     (ON) HOPE                     36  52 345  71

FEILDS

  THE GOD OF NATURE IN THE FEILDS OF GRACE.      (ON) HOPE                     50  52 345  71

FIERCE

  THE NORTH FORGOT HIS FIERCE INTENT,             A HYMNE OF THE NATIVITY      25  46 106  76
  WITH THE FIERCE LYONS OF THERODAMAS.            SOSPETTO D'HERODE             354  46 109 216
  AND LOVES MORE FIERCE, MORE FRUITLESSE FIRES ASSAY ON HOPE                       87  46 143  71

FIERCELY

  PROFANE SADOCUS TOO DOES FIERCELY LEAD         OUT OF GROTIUS                  47  MS 398 198

FIERY

  HIS SKIN AS WITH A FIERY BLUSHING              OUT OF GREEKE CUPID'S CRYER   19  46 159 519
  UNTO A DREADFULL PILE GIVES FIERY BREATH.      SOSPETTO D'HERODE             56  46 109 216
  BUT BEFORE ALL, THAT FIERY DART                FLAMING HEART                 35  52 324  61
  SHOULD COOLE HIS FIERY WHEELS, & NEVER SINKE     UPON GUNPOWDER TREASON       39  MS 386 460
  SPEEDILY HARNESSING HIS FIERY STEEDS,           UPON KINGS CORONATION        16  MS 390 453

FIFT

  COMPILE A FIFT GLORIOUS EPITOME                 UPON BIRTH PRINCESSE E        57  MS 391 456

FIGHT

| | | | | | |
|---|---|---|---|---|---|
| AWAKES HIS LUTE, AND 'GAINST THE FIGHT TO COME | MUSICKS DUELL | 17 | 46 | 149 | 535 |
| MARKES OF A FIGHT ALONE, BUT FEASTING TOO. | THE BEGINNING OF HELIODORUS | 24 | 46 | 158 | 517 |
| HEAV'N SAW US STRUGGLE ONCE, AS BRAVE A FIGHT | SOSPETTO D'HERODE | 255 | 46 | 109 | 216 |
| HERE IS A FRIEND SHALL FIGHT FOR YOU, | ON A PRAYER BOOKE | 26 | 46 | 126 | 139 |
| HERE IS A FREIND SHALL FIGHT FOR YOU, | PRAYER TO GENTLE-WOMAN | 32 | 52 | 328 | 139 |

FIGHTING

| | | | | | |
|---|---|---|---|---|---|
| (WHOSE HANDS ARE FIGHTING, WHILE THEIR FEET DOE FLIE.) | HORATIJ ILLE & NEFASTO | 26 | MS | 382 | 530 |

FIGURES

| | | | | | |
|---|---|---|---|---|---|
| ON WHICH ALL FIGURES FIX'T THEIR EYES. | LAUDA SION SALVATOREM | 66 | 52 | 294 | 178 |

FILL

| | | | | | |
|---|---|---|---|---|---|
| YET IF THOU'LT FILL ONE POORE EYE, WITH THY HEAVEN AND THEE, | IT IS BETTER TO GO WITH EYE | 4 | 46 | 93 | 16 |
| WITH HIS FAIRE TRIUMPHS FILL ALL FUTURE STORIES. | SOSPETTO D'HERODE | 230 | 46 | 109 | 216 |
| OF DRAGONS, HYDRAES, SPHINXES, FILL THE GROVE. | SOSPETTO D'HERODE | 352 | 46 | 109 | 216 |
| OF ALL THE FAIRE CHEEKT FLOWERS THAT FILL THEE. | AN HIMNE FOR CIRCUMCISION | 9 | 46 | 141 | 37 |
| O FILL OUR SENSES, AND TAKE FROM US | TO THE NAME OF JESUS | 170 | 52 | 239 | 30 |
| OF ALL THE FAIR-CHEEK'T FLOWRS THAT FILL THEE | NEW YEAR'S DAY | 9 | 52 | 251 | 37 |
| THE FAIR STARRS FILL THEIR WAKEFULL FIRES THE SUN HIMSELFE DRINKS DAY. | OFFICE H. CROSS PRIME | 8 | 52 | 267 | 91 |
| ALOFT, AND FILL THE NATIONS WITH THY NOBLE FRUIT. | VEXILLA REGIS | 38 | 52 | 277 | 156 |
| AND FILL MY PORTION IN THY PEACE. | ADORO TE | 34 | 52 | 291 | 172 |
| FREINDS WITH THE BOSOM FIRES THAT FILL THEE | WEEPER | 98 | 52 | 307 | 120 |
| FOR LOVE AT LARG TO FILL, SPARE BLOOD & SWEAT. | TERESA | 11 | 52 | 315 | 52 |

FILL'D

| | | | | | |
|---|---|---|---|---|---|
| SNATCH'T HER SELF HENCE, TO HEAVEN, FILL'D A BRIGHT PLACE, | UPON BISHOP ANDREWES PICTURE | 9 | 46 | 163 | 490 |
| NOW THAT TIME'S EMPIRE MIGHT BE AMPLY FILL'D. | ON FRONTISPIECE ISAACSONS | 15 | 46 | 191 | 491 |
| HAD FILL'D THE HAND OF THIS GREAT HEART. | FLAMING HEART | 36 | 52 | 324 | 61 |

BRIM-FILL'D

| | | | | | |
|---|---|---|---|---|---|
| BY ALL THY BRIM-FILL'D BOWLES OF FEIRCE DESIRE | FLAMING HEART | 99 | 52 | 324 | 61 |

FILLS

| | | | | | |
|---|---|---|---|---|---|
| HEE FILLS A BURNISHT THRONE OF QUENCHLESSE FIRE. | SOSPETTO D'HERODE | 42 | 46 | 109 | 216 |

FINALL

| | | | | | |
|---|---|---|---|---|---|
| LO, THE FULL, FINALL, SACRIFICE | LAUDA SION SALVATOREM | 65 | 52 | 294 | 178 |
| BY THE FULL KINGDOME OF THAT FINALL KISSE | FLAMING HEART | 101 | 52 | 324 | 61 |

FIND

| | | | | | |
|---|---|---|---|---|---|
| WHERESOE'RE YOU CHANCE TO FIND HIM | OUT OF GREEKE CUPID'S CRYER | 57 | 46 | 159 | 519 |
| THAT HE SHOULD FIND A TONGUE AND VOCALL THUNDER, | UPON ASSE THAT BORE SAVIOUR | 9 | 46 | 90 | 19 |
| O, WHO SO HARD AN HUSBANDMAN COULD EVER FIND | UPON THORNES FROM LORDS HEAD | 5 | 46 | 96 | 23 |
| THERE MY FEET, EVEN THERE SHALL FIND | PSALME 23 | 43 | 46 | 102 | 5 |
| ABOUT MY PATHS, SO SHALL I FIND | PSALME 23 | 61 | 46 | 102 | 5 |
| WILL I FIND A PURER AIRE | PSALME 23 | 68 | 46 | 102 | 5 |
| WESTWARD TO FIND THE WORLDS TRUE ORIENT. | SOSPETTO D'HERODE | 136 | 46 | 109 | 216 |
| YOUL FIND IT YEELDS | ON A PRAYER BOOKE | 17 | 46 | 126 | 139 |
| SHALL FIND THE WANDRING HEART FROM HOME. | ON A PRAYER BOOKE | 42 | 46 | 126 | 139 |
| HEE FIND THE HEART FROM HOME. | ON A PRAYER BOOKE | 84 | 46 | 126 | 139 |
| MAN TREMBLES AT, WEE STRAIGHT SHALL FIND | IN MEMORY OF LADY MADRE TERESA | 31 | 46 | 131 | 52 |
| FIND EVERLASTING SMILES. SO RARE, | IN MEMORY OF LADY MADRE TERESA | 87 | 46 | 131 | 52 |
| BUT IN THY FAIREST EYES FIND TWO FOR ONE. | AN HIMNE FOR CIRCUMCISION | 38 | 46 | 141 | 37 |
| FATES CANNOT FIND OUT A CAPACITY | ON HOPE | 17 | 46 | 143 | 71 |
| O IF FOR THESE THOU MEAN'ST TO FIND A SEAT, | UPON YORKE HIS BIRTH | 15 | 46 | 176 | 500 |
| MAYEST IN A SON OF HIS FIND EVERY SON | UPON YORKE HIS BIRTH | 99 | 46 | 176 | 500 |
| WHERE MERCY CANNOT FIND THEM, BUT O THOU | TO THE MORNING | 32 | 46 | 183 | 497 |
| WOULD ANY ONE THE TRUE CAUSE FIND | OUT OF THE ITALIAN (3) | 1 | 46 | 190 | 549 |
| WILL HAVE A PERSPICILL TO FIND HER OUT, | ON FRONTISPIECE ISAACSONS | 11 | 46 | 191 | 491 |
| OF HUMBLE SOULES, THAT SEEK TO FIND | TO THE NAME OF JESUS | 121 | 52 | 239 | 30 |
| HEAV'N IT SELF TO FIND THEM HELL. | IN GLORIOUS EPIPHANIE | 110 | 52 | 253 | 39 |
| O WHO SO HARD A HUSBANDMAN DID EVER FIND | UPON CROWNE OF THORNS | 3 | 52 | 290 | 23 |
| O LET THY WRETCH FIND THAT RELEIFE | ADORO TE | 17 | 52 | 291 | 172 |
| HEAVN & EARTH SHALL FIND NO PLACE. | DIES IRAE | 6 | 52 | 298 | 186 |
| MAN TREMBLES AT, YOU STRAIGHT SHALL FIND | TERESA | 31 | 52 | 315 | 52 |
| FIND EVERLASTING SMILES, SO RARE. | TERESA | 87 | 52 | 315 | 52 |
| TO FIND THE REST | PRAYER TO GENTLE-WOMAN | 9 | 52 | 328 | 139 |
| YOU'L FIND IT YEILDS | PRAYER TO GENTLE-WOMAN | 23 | 52 | 328 | 139 |
| SHALL FIND THE LOYTERING HEART FROM HOME. | PRAYER TO GENTLE-WOMAN | 48 | 52 | 328 | 139 |
| HE FIND THE HEART FROM HOME) | PRAYER TO GENTLE-WOMAN | 90 | 52 | 328 | 139 |
| SAY, GENTLE SOUL, WHAT CAN YOU FIND | TO SAME CONCERNING CHOISE | 10 | 52 | 331 | 66 |
| THAT WEARY LOVE AT LAST MAY FIND HIS WAY. | ALEXIAS SECONDE ELEGIE | 30 | 52 | 335 | 207 |
| OF YOUR LEARN'D LYES, HERE YOU'L FIND NO SUCH JEST. | ALEXIAS THIRD ELEGIE | 42 | 52 | 336 | 209 |
| AND SOFT OBEDIENCE, FIND SWEET BIDING HERE. | DESCRIPTION RELIGIOUS HOUSE | 31 | 52 | 338 | 213 |
| FATES CANNOT FIND OUT A CAPACITY | (ON) HOPE | 7 | 52 | 345 | 71 |
| TO FIND THEMSELVES THEIR OWN SEVERER SHOAR. | AGAINST IRRESOLUTION AND DELAY | 26 | 52 | 347 | 146 |
| WHERE CAN YOU FIX, TO FIND EXCUSE | AGAINST IRRESOLUTION AND DELAY | 31 | 52 | 347 | 146 |
| ONLY THE POPE A STOMACK STILL COULD FIND. | UPON GUNPOWDER TREASON | 51 | MS | 387 | 461 |
| TRAVELD TH' OLYMPIAN PLAINES TO FIND RELEIFE. | UPON KINGS CORONATION | 4 | MS | 390 | 453 |

```
THE BEST MY CRADLE AND MY BIRTH COULD FIND.        OUT OF GROTIUS                         18  MS 398 198

FIND'ST

THAT THOU FIND'ST NONE.                            UPON ASSE THAT BORE SAVIOUR            12  46  90  19

FINDE

THAT NEST OF HEROES, ALL OUR HOPES FINDE ROOME.    UPON YORKE HIS BIRTH                   81  46 176 500

FINDS

WHO FINDS HIS WARME HEART, HATCHT INTO A NEST      AN APOLOGIE FOR HYMNE (TERESA)         26  46 136  59
HENCE 'TIS MY HUMBLE FANCY FINDS NO WINGS,         TO THE MORNING                         19  46 183 497
HEE THAT NE'RE HEARD NOW SPEAKES, AND FINDS A TONGUE  OUT OF GROTIUS                      73  MS 398 198

FINDER

LET THE FINDER SURELY KNOW                         OUT OF GREEKE CUPID'S CRYER             7  46 159 519

FINE

WHAT EVER MAKES HEAVENS FORE-HEAD FINE.            THE WEEPER                             12  46  79 120
WHATEVER MAKES HEAVN'S FORHEAD FINE.               WEEPER                                 12  52 307 120
WITH SUCH A SUGRED LIVERY MADE FINE.               UPON BIRTH PRINCESSE E                  7  MS 391 456

FINGER

UNTILL HIS FINGER(MODERATOUR)HIDES                 MUSICKS DUELL                          52  46 149 535
THY DOWNY FINGER, DWELL UPON THEIR EYES,           TO THE MORNING                         57  46 183 497

ROSIE-FINGERD

AND THE SAME ROSIE-FINGERD HAND OF THINE,          TO THE MORNING                         45  46 183 497

FINGERS

HIS CURIOUS FINGERS LENT, HER VOYCE MADE GOOD.     MUSICKS DUELL                          14  46 149 535
HIS FINGERS STRUGGLE WITH THE VOCALL THREADS.      MUSICKS DUELL                         122  46 149 535
HIS FINGERS FAIREST REVOLUTION                     MUSICKS DUELL                         154  46 149 535
IF IN THE FIRST HE US'D HIS FINGERS TOUCH.         THE DUMBE HEALED                        3  46  87  16
WOULD TREMBLE ON MY PEARLE-TIPT FINGERS TOP.       DIVES ASKING A DROP                     2  46  96  18
ROSY FINGERS, RADIANT HAIR,                        FLAMING HEART                          32  52 324  61
SPRANG IN THE SPENDING FINGERS, AND O'REFLOW'D     OUT OF GROTIUS                         62  MS 398 198

FIRE

SO SAID, HIS HANDS SPRIGHTLY AS FIRE HEE FLINGS,   MUSICKS DUELL                         111  46 149 535
WORSE THEN SUN-BURNT IN HIS FIRE.                  OUT OF GREEKE CUPID'S CRYER            56  46 159 519
THAT THOUGH IT SHINES, 'TIS FIRE AND WILL CONSUME. OUT OF GREEKE CUPID'S CRYER            74  46 159 519
AT LAST, IN FIRE OF THY FAIRE EYES.                A HYMNE OF THE NATIVITY                87  46 106  76
HEE FILLS A BURNISHT THRONE OF QUENCHLESSE FIRE.   SOSPETTO D'HERODE                      42  46 109 216
SET THE CONTENDING SONS OF HEAV'N ON FIRE.         SOSPETTO D'HERODE                      90  46 109 216
THAT HEE WHO MADE THE FIRE, SHOULD FEARE THE COLD. SOSPETTO D'HERODE                     180  46 109 216
ON TIPTOE IN THEIR GIDDY BRAYNES. TH' HAVE FIRE    SOSPETTO D'HERODE                     442  46 109 216
AS WHEN A PILE OF FOOD-PREPARING FIRE,             SOSPETTO D'HERODE                     481  46 109 216
HOME TO THE HEART, AND SETTS THE HOUSE ON FIRE.    ON A PRAYER BOOKE                      67  46 126 139
EXPECTING FIRE FROM YOUR EYES.                     ON MR. G. HERBERTS BOOKE                3  46 130  68
GOOD REASON FOR SHEE BREATHS ALL FIRE,             IN MEMORY OF LADY MADRE TERESA         39  46 131  52
THE FAIREST, AND THE FIRST BORNE SONS OF FIRE.     IN MEMORY OF LADY MADRE TERESA         93  46 131  52
BY TOO HOT A FIRE, AND WASTED,                     IN MEMORY OF LADY MADRE TERESA        115  46 131  52
OUR HARD HEARTS SHALL STRIKE FIRE, THE SAME        IN MEMORY OF LADY MADRE TERESA        161  46 131  52
BOTH FIRE TO US, AND FLAME TO THEE.                IN MEMORY OF LADY MADRE TERESA        163  46 131  52
FAIRE CLOUD OF FIRE, BOTH SHADE, AND LIGHT,        ON HOPE                                15  46 143  71
FEARES ANTIDOTE. A WISE, AND WELL STAY'D FIRE      ON HOPE                                82  46 143  71
GIVE THEN THIS RURALL WREATH FIRE FROM THINE EYES. UPON YORKE HIS BIRTH                  118  46 176 500
LOVE NOW NO FIRE HATH LEFT HIM,                    OUT OF THE ITALIAN (2)                  1  46 190 547
WHEN THY OLD FREINDS OF FIRE, ALL FULL OF THEE,    TO THE NAME OF JESUS                  198  52 239  30
THAT IMPATIENT FIRE;                               TO THE NAME OF JESUS                  214  52 239  30
THEIR ROSY FLEECE OF FIRE BESTOW.                  IN HOLY NATIVITY                       59  52 246  76
TILL BURNT AT LAST IN FIRE OF THY FAIR EYES.       IN HOLY NATIVITY                      107  52 246  76
WHOSE IS THE MASTER FIRE, WHICH SUN SHOULD SHINE.  IN GLORIOUS EPIPHANIE                 144  52 253  39
OF FLAME & FIRE,                                   IN GLORIOUS EPIPHANIE                 242  52 253  39
STILL WOULD THOSE EVER-WAKEFULL SONS OF FIRE       CHARITAS NIMIA                         25  52 280  48
O THAT FIRE. BEFORE WHOSE FACE                     DIES IRAE                               5  52 298 186
WITH PROUD UNPITTYING FIRE.                        WEEPER                                159  52 307 120
GOOD REASON. FOR SHE BREATHES ALL FIRE.            TERESA                                 39  52 315  52
THE FAIR'ST & FIRST-BORN SONS OF FIRE              TERESA                                 93  52 315  52
BY TOO HOTT A FIRE, & WASTED                       TERESA                                114  52 315  52
OUR HARD HEARTS SHALL STRIKE FIRE, THE SAME        TERESA                                160  52 315  52
BOTH FIRE TO US & FLAME TO THEE.                   TERESA                                162  52 315  52
THAT FAIR-CHEEK'T FALLACY OF FIRE.                 FLAMING HEART                           4  52 324  61
FIRE FROM THE BURNING CHEEKS OF THAT BRIGHT BOOKE  FLAMING HEART                          28  52 324  61
WHAT E'RE THIS YOUTH OF FIRE WEARES FAIR,          FLAMING HEART                          31  52 324  61
BY THY LAST MORNING'S DRAUGHT OF LIQUID FIRE.      FLAMING HEART                         100  52 324  61
I DY IN LOVE'S DELICIOUS FIRE.                     A SONG                                  4  52 327  65
HOME TO THE HEART, & SETTS THE HOUSE ON FIRE       PRAYER TO GENTLE-WOMAN                 73  52 328 139
AMONG HIS OWN FAIR SONNES OF FIRE.                 TO SAME CONCERNING CHOISE              25  52 331  66
MAKE BIGGE THY BREST WITH IMMORTALL FIRE,          ALEXIAS THIRD ELEGIE                   22  52 336 209
FEAR'S ANTIDOTE. A WISE & WELL-STAY'D FIRE.        (ON) HOPE                              42  52 345  71
AND STRETCH THEIR COLD LIMBES IN A PLEASING FIRE.  HORATIJ ILLE & NEFASTO                 53  MS 382 530
BUT SINCE THEY ARE FIRE WORKES, RATHER PROVE       UPON GUNPOWDER TREASON                 33  MS 387 461
TO SACRIFICE HIMSELFE IN SUCH SWEET FIRE.          UPON KINGS CORONATION                  36  MS 369 454
'TWAS NOT THE FROZEN ZONE. ONE SPARKE OF FIRE.     AN ELEGY MR STANNINOW                  31  MS 394 473
```

PAGE 142

## FIRE-WORKS

| | | | | |
|---|---|---|---|---|
| HER HAPPY FIRE-WORKS, HERE, COMES DOWN TO SEE. | FLAMING HEART | 18 | 52 324 | 61 |

## FIREBRAND

| | | | | |
|---|---|---|---|---|
| AND NOW HIS DREAM (HELS FIREBRAND) STIL MORE BRIGHT. | SOSPETTO D'HERODE | 503 | 46 109 | 216 |

## FIRED

| | | | | |
|---|---|---|---|---|
| SO BOYLES THE FIRED HERODS BLOOD-SWOLNE BREST. | SOSPETTO D'HERODE | 489 | 46 109 | 216 |

## FIRES

| | | | | |
|---|---|---|---|---|
| MONGST THOSE IMMORTALL FIRES, AND ON THE FACE | UPON BISHOP ANDREWES PICTURE | 10 | 46 163 | 490 |
| QUENCH HIS CURL'D FIRES, WEE'L WAKE WITH OUR ALARMES | SOSPETTO D'HERODE | 278 | 46 109 | 216 |
| FAIRE SEA OF HOLY FIRES TRANSFUSED THE FLAME | AN APOLOGIE FOR HYMNE (TERESA) | 2 | 46 136 | 59 |
| AND LOVES MORE FIERCE, MORE FRUITLESSE FIRES ASSAY | ON HOPE | 87 | 46 143 | 71 |
| THE FAIR STARRS FILL THEIR WAKEFULL FIRES THE SUN HIMSELFE DRINKS DAY. | OFFICE H. CROSS PRIME | 8 | 52 267 | 91 |
| BOTH OF LOVE'S FIRES & FLOUDS) MIGHT I RECLINE | SANCTA MARIA DOLORUM | 47 | 52 283 | 162 |
| FREINDS WITH THE BOSOM FIRES THAT FILL THEE | WEEPER | 98 | 52 307 | 120 |
| O FLOUDS, O FIRES. O SUNS O SHOWRES. | WEEPER | 101 | 52 307 | 120 |
| (FAIR FLOUD OF HOLY FIRES.) TRANSFUS'D THE FLAME | AN APOLOGIE FOR (TERESA) HYMNE | 2 | 52 322 | 59 |
| SINCE HIS THE BLUSHES BE, & HER'S THE FIRES. | FLAMING HEART | 38 | 52 324 | 61 |
| BY ALL THY DOW OF LIGHTS & FIRES. | FLAMING HEART | 94 | 52 324 | 61 |
| WHOSE NATIVE FIRES DISDAINING | PRAYER TO GENTLE-WOMAN | 3 | 52 328 | 139 |
| RISE, FAIREST OF THOSE FIRES. WHATE'RE THOU BE | ALEXIAS SECONDE ELEGIE | 25 | 52 335 | 207 |
| WHEN HOLY FIRES MAINTAIN LOVE'S HEAVNLY LIFE. | ALEXIAS THIRD ELEGIE | 52 | 52 336 | 209 |
| THOUGH LOVE'S MORE FEIRCE, MORE FRUITLESSE, FIRES ASSAY | (ON) HOPE | 47 | 52 345 | 71 |

## FIRM

| | | | | |
|---|---|---|---|---|
| THE MOST FIRM FOOT NO MORE THEN STAND. | DIES IRAE | 24 | 52 298 | 186 |
| FIRM IN THY CROWN, AS HERE FAST IN THY LOVE. | ALEXIAS FIRST ELEGIE | 36 | 52 334 | 204 |
| FIRM HE. AS THOU ART FALSE, NOR NEED MY CRYES | ALEXIAS SECONDE ELEGIE | 9 | 52 335 | 207 |

## FIRM-POINTED

| | | | | |
|---|---|---|---|---|
| BY THE FAIRE LAWES OF THY FIRM-POINTED PEN, | ON A TREATISE OF CHARITY | 28 | 46 137 | 69 |

## FIRME

| | | | | |
|---|---|---|---|---|
| THAT THY FIRME HAND FOR EVER MIGHT SUSTAINE | SOSPETTO D'HERODE | 450 | 46 109 | 216 |

## FIRMLY

| | | | | |
|---|---|---|---|---|
| WHICH ON FALSE TYRANTS HEAD NE'RE FIRMLY STOOD. | SOSPETTO D'HERODE | 492 | 46 109 | 216 |

## FIRMAMENT

| | | | | |
|---|---|---|---|---|
| LIKE BANDIED BALLES, INTO THE FIRMAMENT. | ON GUNPOWDER-TREASON | 42 | MS 384 | 458 |

## FIRST

| | | | | |
|---|---|---|---|---|
| BUT WHEN THE WORLD FIRST OUT OF CHAOS SPRANG | OUT OF VIRGIL | 23 | 46 155 | 529 |
| WHEN LIFES SWEET LIGHT FIRST SHONE ON BEASTS, AND WHEN | OUT OF VIRGIL | 29 | 46 155 | 529 |
| LOOK'T ROUND, FIRST TO THE SEA, THEN TO THE SHORE. | THE BEGINNING OF HELIODORUS | 8 | 46 158 | 517 |
| CEASE HIM, BRING HIM. (BUT FIRST BIND HIM) | OUT OF GREEKE CUPID'S CRYER | 58 | 46 159 | 519 |
| IF IN THE FIRST HE US'D HIS FINGERS TOUCH. | THE DUMBE HEALED | 3 | 46 87 | 16 |
| TO THEE THESE FIRST FRUITS OF MY GROWING DEATH | OUR LORD IN HIS CIRCUMCISION | 1 | 46 98 | 9 |
| WHEN FIRST I LOOK'T ON THEE, I LOST MINE EYES. | SAMPSON TO HIS DALILAH | 2 | 46 102 | 8 |
| FAST BOUND, SINCE FIRST HE FORFEITED THE SKIES, | SOSPETTO D'HERODE | 40 | 46 109 | 216 |
| ON THE FAIRE SOULE WHOM FIRST HEE MEETS. | ON A PRAYER BOOKE | 89 | 46 126 | 139 |
| THE FAIREST, AND THE FIRST BORNE SONS OF FIRE, | IN MEMORY OF LADY MADRE TERESA | 93 | 46 131 | 52 |
| SO SOONE AS THOU SHALT FIRST APPEARE, | IN MEMORY OF LADY MADRE TERESA | 123 | 46 131 | 52 |
| AND IN HER FIRST RANKES MAKE THEE ROOME. | IN MEMORY OF LADY MADRE TERESA | 127 | 46 131 | 52 |
| LIFE, BROUGHT THEM FIRST TO KISSE THE LIGHT | IN MEMORY OF LADY MADRE TERESA | 177 | 46 131 | 52 |
| RISE THOU FIRST AND FAIREST MORNING, | AN HIMNE FOR CIRCUMCISION | 1 | 46 141 | 37 |
| TO THEM SHEE GAVE THE FIRST AND FAIREST BEAME | UPON DEATH OF HERRYS | 17 | 46 167 | 466 |
| PEEPT FORTH FROM THEIR FIRST BLUSHES. SO THAT NOW | UPON DEATH OF HERRYS | 24 | 46 167 | 466 |
| HEIRE OF THE SUNS FIRST BEAMES. WHY THREAT'ST THOU SO. | TO THE MORNING | 53 | 46 183 | 497 |
| THE FIRST BLAST OF THY COUGH LEFT TWO ALONE, | OUT OF MARTIALL | 3 | 46 188 | 527 |
| FIRST DOES THE LONGING LOVER RIGHT. | WISHES SUPPOSED MISTRESSE | 72 | 46 195 | 479 |
| FIRST TURN'D TO EYES. | TO THE NAME OF JESUS | 136 | 52 239 | 30 |
| BY BEING SCHOLLER FIRST OF THAT NEW NIGHT. | IN GLORIOUS EPIPHANIE | 206 | 52 253 | 39 |
| DOES FIRST HIS SCEPTER, THEN HIMSELF IN SOLEMNE TRIBUTE PAY. | IN GLORIOUS EPIPHANIE | 237 | 52 253 | 39 |
| THE DAY-BREAK OF THE NATIONS. THEIR FIRST RAY. | TO THE QUEEN'S MAJESTY | 3 | 52 261 | 47 |
| BY THAT FIRST FATALL TREE | OFFICE H. CROSS SIXT | 17 | 52 270 | 97 |
| 'TWAS PAY'D AT FIRST WITH TOO MUCH PAIN. | DIES IRAE | 39 | 52 298 | 186 |
| THE FIRST EVE, MOTHER OF OUR FALL. | O GLORIOSA DOMINA | 11 | 52 302 | 194 |
| SO SOONE AS THOU SHALT FIRST APPEAR, | TERESA | 122 | 52 315 | 52 |
| AND IN HER FIRST RANKES MAKE THEE ROOM | TERESA | 126 | 52 315 | 52 |
| LIFE BROUGHT THEM FIRST TO KISSE THE LIGHT | TERESA | 176 | 52 315 | 52 |
| ON THE FAIR SOUL WHOM FIRST HE MEETS. | PRAYER TO GENTLE-WOMAN | 95 | 52 328 | 139 |
| YOUR FIRST CHOYCE FAILES, O WHEN YOU CHOOSE AGEN | TO SAME CONCERNING CHOISE | 58 | 52 331 | 66 |
| WHO E'RE HE BE WAS THE FIRST WANDRING KNIGHT. | ALEXIAS THIRD ELEGIE | 4 | 52 336 | 209 |
| LEARN'D FIRST HIS LIGHTNESSE BY HIS LOVE. | AGAINST IRRESOLUTION AND DELAY | 52 | 52 347 | 146 |
| THY RISING TOPP FIRST STAIND THE BASHFULL LIGHT. | HORATIJ ILLE & NEFASTO | 6 | MS 382 | 530 |
| MAY DRAW THEIR FIRST BREATH FROM THY STARRY BEAMES. | EX EUPHORMIONE | 14 | MS 392 | 525 |

FIRST-BORN

| | | | | | |
|---|---|---|---|---|---|
| WE'L BRING THE FIRST-BORN OF HER FLOWRS | IN HOLY NATIVITY | 99 | 52 | 246 | 76 |
| THE FAIR'ST & FIRST-BORN SONS OF FIRE | TERESA | 93 | 52 | 315 | 52 |

FIRST-BORNE

| | | | | | |
|---|---|---|---|---|---|
| WEE'L BRING THE FIRST-BORNE OF HER FLOWERS, | A HYMNE OF THE NATIVITY | 79 | 46 | 106 | 76 |
| THE FAIREST, AND THE FIRST-BORNE SMILE OF HEAV'N. | SOSPETTO D'HERODE | 236 | 46 | 109 | 216 |

FIRST-FRUITS

| | | | | | |
|---|---|---|---|---|---|
| FAIR FIRST-FRUITS OF THE LAMB. SURE KINGS IN THIS. | TO THE QUEEN'S MAJESTY | 7 | 52 | 261 | 47 |

FIT

| | | | | | |
|---|---|---|---|---|---|
| FALLING UPON HIS LUTE. O FIT TO HAVE | MUSICKS DUELL | 167 | 46 | 149 | 535 |
| AS GARMENTS SHOULD DOE CLOSE AND FIT. | IN PRAISE OF LESSIUS | 22 | 46 | 156 | 510 |
| SHE THINKES NOT FIT SUCH HE HER FACE SHOULD SEE, | SOSPETTO D'HERODE | 413 | 46 | 109 | 216 |
| FIT EXECUTIONERS FOR THEE, | IN MEMORY OF LADY MADRE TERESA | 92 | 46 | 131 | 52 |
| TO SHOW A FACE, FIT TO CONFESSE THY KIN | UPON STANINOUGH'S DEATH | 18 | 46 | 175 | 475 |
| HOW FIT OUR WELL-RANK'D FEASTS DOE FOLLOW, | UPON POWDER DAY | 1 | 46 | 185 | 74 |

FITT

| | | | | | |
|---|---|---|---|---|---|
| AND FITT IT TO SO FARR INFERIOR LYRES. | TO THE NAME OF JESUS | 102 | 52 | 239 | 30 |
| TO FITT A BED FOR THIS HUGE BIRTHE. | IN HOLY NATIVITY | 42 | 52 | 246 | 76 |
| FITT EXECUTIONERS FOR THEE, | TERESA | 92 | 52 | 315 | 52 |
| TO SHOW A FACE, FITT TO CONFESSE THY KIN, | DEATH'S LECTURE | 19 | 52 | 340 | 475 |
| AS GARMENTS SHOULD DOE, CLOSE & FITT. | TEMPERANCE | 20 | 52 | 342 | 510 |

FITT-TUN'D

| | | | | | |
|---|---|---|---|---|---|
| INTO A HASTY FITT-TUN'D HARMONY. | TO THE NAME OF JESUS | 50 | 52 | 239 | 30 |

FITTER

| | | | | | |
|---|---|---|---|---|---|
| O RATHER USE THIS HEART, THUS FARR A FITTER STONE, | OFFICE H. CROSS COMPLINE | 11 | 52 | 274 | 105 |

FIX

| | | | | | |
|---|---|---|---|---|---|
| TO FIX THOSE FULL-FAC'T GLORIES. O HE'S POORE | IT IS BETTER TO GO WITH EYE | 2 | 46 | 93 | 16 |
| O FIX THIS FAIR INDEFINITE. | TO COUNTESSE OF DENBIGH | 31 | 52 | 236 | 146 |
| O MAY YOU FIX | TO THE NAME OF JESUS | 82 | 52 | 239 | 30 |
| FIX HERE, FAIR MAJESTY. MAY YOUR HEART NE'RE MISSE | TO THE QUEEN'S MAJESTY | 21 | 52 | 261 | 47 |
| FIX HERE WITH THEE. | SANCTA MARIA DOLORUM | 62 | 52 | 283 | 162 |
| WHERE CAN YOU FIX, TO FIND EXCUSE | AGAINST IRRESOLUTION AND DELAY | 31 | 52 | 347 | 146 |

FIXED

| | | | | | |
|---|---|---|---|---|---|
| LIKE STATUES FIXED TO THE FAME | NEITHER DURST MAN ASKE | 11 | 46 | 92 | 20 |

FIXT

| | | | | | |
|---|---|---|---|---|---|
| OF HER GREAT MAKER FIXT HER FLAMING EYE, | UPON BISHOP ANDREWES PICTURE | 11 | 46 | 163 | 490 |
| THE FAIRE STARRE IS WELL FIXT, FOR WHERE, O WHERE | ON VIRGINS BASHFULNESSE | 3 | 46 | 89 | 9 |
| COULD SHE HAVE FIXT IT ON A FAIRER SPEARE. | ON VIRGINS BASHFULNESSE | 4 | 46 | 89 | 9 |
| FIXT IN DELIGHT, AS IF ALREADY THERE | UPON DEATH OF HERRYS | 27 | 46 | 167 | 466 |
| FIXT HIS FOREHEAD TO A FROWNE,) | LOVES HOROSCOPE | 38 | 46 | 185 | 483 |
| FIXT IN YOUR SPHAERES OF GLORY, SHED FROM THENCE | UPON KINGS CORONATION | 39 | MS | 389 | 454 |

FIX'T

| | | | | | |
|---|---|---|---|---|---|
| ON WHICH ALL FIGURES FIX'T THEIR EYES. | LAUDA SION SALVATOREM | 66 | 52 | 294 | 178 |

FIXE

| | | | | | |
|---|---|---|---|---|---|
| THERE DOES HE FIXE HIS EYES. AND THERE DETECT | SOSPETTO D'HERODE | 87 | 46 | 109 | 216 |
| SHALL FIXE MY FLYING WISHES, | WISHES SUPPOSED MISTRESSE | 122 | 46 | 195 | 479 |
| OH, WOULD'ST THOU HEERE STILL FIXE THY FAIRE ABODE, | LUKE 2. QUAERIT JESUM | 47 | MS | 379 | 11 |
| FIXE HEERE THY WAT'RY EYES UPON THESE TOWERS, | AN ELEGIE ON DR PORTER | 3 | MS | 395 | 476 |

FLAGRANT

| | | | | | |
|---|---|---|---|---|---|
| ALL THOSE FAIR & FLAGRANT THINGS, | FLAMING HEART | 34 | 52 | 324 | 61 |

FLAIRING

| | | | | | |
|---|---|---|---|---|---|
| FALSE LIGHTS OF FLAIRING GEMMES. TUMULTUOUS JOYES. | DESCRIPTION RELIGIOUS HOUSE | 5 | 52 | 338 | 213 |

FLAME

| | | | | | |
|---|---|---|---|---|---|
| HER HAIRES FLAME LICKES UP THAT AGAINE. | SHE BEGAN TO WASH HIS FEET | 2 | 46 | 97 | 13 |
| THIS FLAME THUS QUENCH'T HATH BRIGHTER BEAMES. | SHE BEGAN TO WASH HIS FEET | 3 | 46 | 97 | 13 |
| NOR SIRIAN FLAME, NOR BOREAN FROST DEFLOWERS. | SOSPETTO D'HERODE | 21 | 46 | 109 | 216 |
| TILL HIS O'REFLOWING PRIDE SUPPRESSE THE FLAME, | SOSPETTO D'HERODE | 487 | 46 | 109 | 216 |
| A DART THRICE DIPT IN THAT RICH FLAME, | IN MEMORY OF LADY MADRE TERESA | 81 | 46 | 131 | 52 |
| EACH HEAVENLY WORD, BY WHOSE HID FLAME | IN MEMORY OF LADY MADRE TERESA | 160 | 46 | 131 | 52 |
| BOTH FIRE TO US, AND FLAME TO THEE. | IN MEMORY OF LADY MADRE TERESA | 163 | 46 | 131 | 52 |
| FAIRE SEA OF HOLY FIRES TRANSFUSED THE FLAME | AN APOLOGIE FOR HYMNE (TERESA) | 2 | 46 | 136 | 59 |
| VERTUE TO ACTION, THAT LIFE-FEEDING FLAME | ON A TREATISE OF CHARITY | 51 | 46 | 137 | 69 |
| OF FLAME & FIRE, | IN GLORIOUS EPIPHANIE | 242 | 52 | 253 | 39 |
| THE FLOCKS OF GOATES TO FOLDS OF FLAME. | DIES IRAE | 58 | 52 | 298 | 186 |

| | | | | |
|---|---|---|---|---|
| A DART THRICE DIP'T IN THAT RICH FLAME | TERESA | 81 | 52 315 | 52 |
| EACH HEAVNLY WORD BY WHOSE HID FLAME | TERESA | 159 | 52 315 | 52 |
| BOTH FIRE TO US & FLAME TO THEE. | TERESA | 162 | 52 315 | 52 |
| (FAIR FLOUD OF HOLY FIRES.) TRANSFUS'D THE FLAME | AN APOLOGIE FOR (TERESA) HYMNE | 2 | 52 322 | 59 |
| THIS IS THE MISTRESSE FLAME. & DUTEOUS HE | FLAMING HEART | 17 | 52 324 | 61 |
| AND MOCKES WITH FEMALE FROST LOVE'S MANLY FLAME. | FLAMING HEART | 24 | 52 324 | 61 |
| GIVE THEN THE DART TO HER WHO GIVES THE FLAME. | FLAMING HEART | 57 | 52 324 | 61 |
| AND WALK THROUGH ALL TONGUES ONE TRIUMPHANT FLAME | FLAMING HEART | 78 | 52 324 | 61 |
| O BURN OUR HYMEN BRIGHT IN SUCH HIGH FLAME. | ALEXIAS THIRD ELEGIE | 49 | 52 336 | 209 |
| LIGHTLY AS A LAMBENT FLAME, | AGAINST IRRESOLUTION AND DELAY | 70 | 52 347 | 146 |

FLAMES

| | | | | |
|---|---|---|---|---|
| WITH NIMBLE FLAMES, AND THOUGH HIS MIND | OUT OF GREEKE CUPID'S CRYER | 21 | 46 159 | 519 |
| MAKES THE SUNNE (OF FLAMES THE SIRE) | OUT OF GREEKE CUPID'S CRYER | 55 | 46 159 | 519 |
| WITH UNGENTLE FLAMES, DOES SHED, | THE TEARE | 23 | 46 84 | 50 |
| A GLOOMY MANTLE OF DARKE FLAMES, THE TIRE | SOSPETTO D'HERODE | 44 | 46 109 | 216 |
| (HIS SHOP OF FLAMES) HEE FRYES HIMSELFE, BENEATH | SOSPETTO D'HERODE | 62 | 46 109 | 216 |
| SUCH, AND SO RICH, THE FLAMES THAT FROM THINE EYES, | SOSPETTO D'HERODE | 239 | 46 109 | 216 |
| HERE ARE THEY ALL, HERE ALL THE SWORDS OR FLAMES | SOSPETTO D'HERODE | 365 | 46 109 | 216 |
| DIRE FLAMES DIFFUSE THEMSELVES THROUGH EVERY VEINE. | SOSPETTO D'HERODE | 471 | 46 109 | 216 |
| SPARKELING WITH THE SACRED FLAMES, | IN MEMORY OF LADY MADRE TERESA | 174 | 46 131 | 52 |
| ENTHUSIASTICKE FLAMES, SUCH AS CAN GIVE | TO THE MORNING | 21 | 46 183 | 497 |
| SO SHALL THESE FLAMES, WHOSE WORTH | OUT OF THE ITALIAN (2) | 7 | 46 190 | 547 |
| OR ELSE PARTAKE MY FLAMES | OUT OF THE ITALIAN (2) | 11 | 46 190 | 547 |
| NOR FLAMES OF OUGHT TOO HOT WITHIN. | WISHES SUPPOSED MISTRESSE | 66 | 46 195 | 479 |
| THE WORLD IN FLAMES SHALL FLY AWAY. | DIES IRAE | 4 | 52 298 | 186 |
| CAN SO GREAT FLAMES AGREE | WEEPER | 99 | 52 307 | 120 |
| WITH UNGENTLE FLAMES DOES SHED, | WEEPER | 161 | 52 307 | 120 |
| SPARKLING WITH THE SACRED FLAMES | TERESA | 173 | 52 315 | 52 |
| IN FLAMES, & OF A BURNING FEVER DY. | ON GUNPOWDER-TREASON | 26 | MS 384 | 458 |
| WHOSE PURER FLAMES TREMBLE TO BE SOE NIGH, | UPON GUNPOWDER TREASON | 15 | MS 387 | 461 |
| SULPHUREOUS FLAMES, SNATCH'D FROM AETERNALL NIGHT. | UPON GUNPOWDER TREASON | 26 | MS 387 | 461 |
| A PHAENIX, IN CHASTEST FLAMES OF LOVE | UPON GUNPOWDER TREASON | 34 | MS 387 | 461 |
| THE GOLD, IN WHICH HE FLAMES, DOES WELL PRAESAGE | UPON KINGS CORONATION | 17 | MS 389 | 454 |
| HIGH BEAUTIES SOVERAIGNE, THAT MY FUNERALL FLAMES | EX EUPHORMIONE | 13 | MS 392 | 525 |

FLAMING

| | | | | |
|---|---|---|---|---|
| OF HER GREAT MAKER FIXT HER FLAMING EYE. | UPON BISHOP ANDREWES PICTURE | 11 | 46 163 | 490 |
| HIS FLAMING EYES DIRE EXHALATION, | SOSPETTO D'HERODE | 57 | 46 109 | 216 |
| THY HIGH-AYM'D HOPES, GAIND'ST BUT A FLAMING FALL. | SOSPETTO D'HERODE | 80 | 46 109 | 216 |
| FLOURISH THEIR SNAKES, AND TOST THEIR FLAMING BRANDS. | SOSPETTO D'HERODE | 260 | 46 109 | 216 |
| THAT FLAMING IN THEIR FAIRE BED SLEEP. | AN HIMNE FOR CIRCUMCISION | 20 | 46 141 | 37 |
| WERE VOW'D LOVES FLAMING SACRIFICE. | HIS EPITAPH (HERRYS) | 42 | 46 172 | 471 |
| FULL GLORY, FLAMING IN HER OWNE FREE SPHEARE. | ON A FOULE MORNING | 8 | 46 181 | 495 |
| LOCKES. THORNS FLAMING TRESSES. | OUT OF THE ITALIAN (1) | 12 | 46 188 | 545 |
| THAN ERE THE FRUITFULL PHOEBUS FLAMING KISSES | UPON TWO GREENE APRICOCKES | 9 | 48 220 | 494 |
| THAT FLAMING IN THEIR FAIR BEDS SLEEP. | NEW YEAR'S DAY | 20 | 52 251 | 37 |
| AND BOW THEIR FLAMING HEADS BEFORE THEE | CHARITAS NIMIA | 23 | 52 280 | 48 |
| LEAVE HER ALONE THE FLAMING HEART. | FLAMING HEART | 68 | 52 324 | 61 |
| REACH ME A QUILL, PLUCKT FROM THE FLAMING WING | UPON GUNPOWDER TREASON | 1 | MS 386 | 460 |
| AND RAISE A DELUGE, WHERE THE FLAMING SUNNE | UPON GUNPOWDER TREASON | 38 | MS 386 | 460 |
| SHINE FORTH,YE FLAMING SPARKES OF DEITY, | UPON KINGS CORONATION | 37 | MS 389 | 454 |
| FULL GLORY FLAMING IN HER OWNE FREE SPHEARE. | UPON KINGS CORONATION | 14 | MS 390 | 453 |
| THEIR WINTER COATES COVER'D WITH FLAMING GOLD. | UPON KINGS CORONATION | 28 | MS 390 | 453 |
| AS IS THY BIRTH. YET FROM THY FLAMING EYE | UPON BIRTH PRINCESSE E | 18 | MS 391 | 456 |
| SHOTT FROM HIS FLAMING EYE, HAD THAW'D IT'S IRE, | AN ELEGY MR STANNINOW | 32 | MS 394 | 473 |

FLAMING-BRESTED

| | | | | |
|---|---|---|---|---|
| INLARGE THY FLAMING-BRESTED LOVERS | TO THE NAME OF JESUS | 212 | 52 239 | 30 |

FLASH

| | | | | |
|---|---|---|---|---|
| WITH FLASH OF HIGH-BORNE FANCYES. HERE AND THERE | MUSICKS DUELL | 138 | 46 149 | 535 |
| LENT THEM THE LAST FLASH OF HER GLIMMERING LIGHT. | THE BEGINNING OF HELIODORUS | 20 | 46 158 | 517 |
| AND SEIZE THE SWIFT FLASH, IN REBOUND | IN GLORIOUS EPIPHANIE | 199 | 52 253 | 39 |
| SHALL WITH ONE FLASH OF LIGHTING BE STRUCK BLIND. | ON GUNPOWDER-TREASON | 32 | MS 384 | 458 |

FLASHING

| | | | | |
|---|---|---|---|---|
| OF FLASHING AIRES. SHEE QUALIFIES THEIR ZEALE | MUSICKS DUELL | 98 | 46 149 | 535 |

FLAT

| | | | | |
|---|---|---|---|---|
| TWO DEVILLS AT ONE BLOW THOU HAST LAID FLAT, | UPON DUMBE DEVILL CAST OUT | 1 | 46 93 | 14 |
| ADORE HER PRINCES BIRTH, FLAT ON HER BREST. | SOSPETTO D'HERODE | 124 | 46 109 | 216 |

FLATTER'D

| | | | | |
|---|---|---|---|---|
| AND FLATTER'D EVERY GREEDY EYE THAT STOOD | UPON DEATH OF HERRYS | 26 | 46 167 | 466 |

FLATTERING

| | | | | |
|---|---|---|---|---|
| WARME THOUGHTS FREE SPIRITS, FLATTERING | IN PRAISE OF LESSIUS | 43 | 46 156 | 510 |
| DECEIVES MENS FEARES WITH FLATTERING WILES. | OUT OF GREEKE CUPID'S CRYER | 50 | 46 159 | 519 |
| FLATTERING BUT FORSWEARING EYES | ON A PRAYER BOOKE | 53 | 46 126 | 139 |
| FLATTERING BUT FORSWEARING EYES | PRAYER TO GENTLE-WOMAN | 59 | 52 328 | 139 |
| HALLS FULL OF FLATTERING MEN & FRISKING BOYES. | DESCRIPTION RELIGIOUS HOUSE | 6 | 52 338 | 213 |
| WARM THOUGHTS, FREE SPIRITS FLATTERING | TEMPERANCE | 41 | 52 342 | 510 |

## FLATTERY

| | | | | |
|---|---|---|---|---|
| HER FLATTERY. | WISHES SUPPOSED MISTRESSE | 100 | 46 195 | 479 |

## FLATTERYES

| | | | | |
|---|---|---|---|---|
| WHOSE SILKEN FLATTERYES SWELL A FEW FOND HOURES | UPON STANINOUGH'S DEATH | 8 | 46 175 | 475 |
| WHOSE SYLKEN FLATTERYES SWELL A FEW FOND HOWRES | DEATH'S LECTURE | 9 | 52 340 | 475 |

## FLED

| | | | | |
|---|---|---|---|---|
| TEARES, QUICKLY FLED, | WISHES SUPPOSED MISTRESSE | 73 | 46 195 | 479 |
| OLD CLOUDS OF THICKEST BLINDNESSE FLED MY SIGHT | OUT OF GROTIUS | 71 | MS 398 | 198 |

## FLEED

| | | | | |
|---|---|---|---|---|
| THOUGH ALL THE JOYES I HAD FLEED HENCE WITH THEE | ALEXIAS SECONDE ELEGIE | 1 | 52 335 | 207 |

## FLEE

| | | | | |
|---|---|---|---|---|
| FROM HIM WE FLEE | IN GLORIOUS EPIPHANIE | 43 | 52 253 | 39 |
| FROM THEM & FROM HIMSELF SHALL FLEE | IN GLORIOUS EPIPHANIE | 139 | 52 253 | 39 |
| AND IN THESE CHAST WARRES WHILE THE WING'D WOUNDS FLEE | SANCTA MARIA DOLORUM | 67 | 52 283 | 162 |

## FLEDG'D

| | | | | |
|---|---|---|---|---|
| TILL THE FLEDG'D NOTES AT LENGTH FORSAKE THEIR NEST. | MUSICKS DUELL | 90 | 46 149 | 535 |
| FLEDG'D WITH HER EAGLES WING. THE VERY CHAINE | HORATIJ ILLE & NEFASTO | 28 | MS 382 | 530 |
| HATH AGED WINTER. FLEDG'D WITH FEATHERED RAINE. | AN ELEGY MR STANNINOW | 1 | MS 394 | 473 |

## FLEECE

| | | | | |
|---|---|---|---|---|
| YOUR FLEECE IS WHITE, BUT 'TIS TOO COLD. | A HYMNE OF THE NATIVITY | 40 | 46 106 | 76 |
| YOUR FLEECE IS WHITE BUT T'IS TOO COLD. | IN HOLY NATIVITY | 56 | 52 246 | 76 |
| THEIR ROSY FLEECE OF FIRE BESTOW. | IN HOLY NATIVITY | 59 | 52 246 | 76 |

## FLEECES

| | | | | |
|---|---|---|---|---|
| AND MAKE THEIR FLEECES GOLDEN AS THY LOCKES. | ON A FOULE MORNING | 6 | 46 181 | 495 |
| BRIGHT CLOUDS LIKE GOLDEN FLEECES SHALL BE SPREAD. | ON A FOULE MORNING | 26 | 46 181 | 495 |

## FLEECY

| | | | | |
|---|---|---|---|---|
| HIS BEDRID LIMMES, WRAPT IN A FLEECY CLOWD. | AN ELEGY MR STANNINOW | 4 | MS 394 | 473 |

## FLEETING

| | | | | |
|---|---|---|---|---|
| MY DYING LIFE MAY DRAW A NEW, & NEVER FLEETING BREATH. | OFFICE H. CROSS RECOMMENDATION | 8 | 52 276 | 106 |

## FLESH

| | | | | |
|---|---|---|---|---|
| THROUGH CLOUDS OF INFANT FLESH. THAT HEE THE OLD | SOSPETTO D'HERODE | 178 | 46 109 | 216 |
| HEAVENS KING, WHO DOFFS HIMSELFE WEAKE FLESH TO WEARE, | SOSPETTO D'HERODE | 515 | 46 109 | 216 |
| OF CHRYSTALL FLESH, THROUGH WHICH TO SHINE. | WISHES SUPPOSED MISTRESSE | 12 | 46 195 | 479 |
| PAID BACK THE FLESH HE TOOK FOR THEE. | VEXILLA REGIS | 6 | 52 277 | 156 |

## FLIES

| | | | | |
|---|---|---|---|---|
| WHOSE PURE AND SUBTLE LIGHTNING, FLIES | ON A PRAYER BOOKE | 66 | 46 126 | 139 |
| ALL THIS IT THREATS, & MORE HORROR, THAT FLIES | ON GUNPOWDER-TREASON | 45 | MS 384 | 458 |

## FLYES

| | | | | |
|---|---|---|---|---|
| FROM THIS TO THAT, FROM THAT TO THIS HEE FLYES | MUSICKS DUELL | 119 | 46 149 | 535 |
| WELCOME, (THOUGH NOT TO THOSE GAY FLYES | A HYMNE OF THE NATIVITY | 71 | 46 106 | 76 |
| AMONGST THE GAY MATES OF THE GOD OF FLYES. | ON A PRAYER BOOKE | 45 | 46 126 | 139 |
| WELCOME, THOUGH NOT TO THOSE GAY FLYES. | IN HOLY NATIVITY | 91 | 52 246 | 76 |
| AMONG THE GAY MATES OF THE GOD OF FLYES. | PRAYER TO GENTLE-WOMAN | 51 | 52 328 | 139 |
| WHOSE PURE & SUBTIL LIGHTNING FLYES | PRAYER TO GENTLE-WOMAN | 72 | 52 328 | 139 |
| ILLUSTRIOUS FLYES. | TO SAME CONCERNING CHOISE | 13 | 52 331 | 66 |
| HE FLYES. & INTO WILLFULL EXILE GOES. | ALEXIAS THIRD ELEGIE | 16 | 52 336 | 209 |

## FLIGHT

| | | | | |
|---|---|---|---|---|
| WHILE THEIR AFFRIGHTED SOULES, NOW WING'D FOR FLIGHT | THE BEGINNING OF HELIODORUS | 19 | 46 158 | 517 |
| AND POORE FOWLES INTERCEPTED IN THEIR FLIGHT. | SOSPETTO D'HERODE | 376 | 46 109 | 216 |
| SEE HOW HEE RUNS, WITH WHAT A HASTY FLIGHT | ON A FOULE MORNING | 29 | 46 181 | 495 |
| FEARES, FOND AND FLIGHT, | WISHES SUPPOSED MISTRESSE | 70 | 46 195 | 479 |
| TO FROZEN CAUCASUS HIS FLIGHT NOW TANE. | AN ELEGY MR STANNINOW | 2 | MS 394 | 473 |

## FLIGHTS

| | | | | |
|---|---|---|---|---|
| FLIGHTS SCORNE THE LAZIE DUST, AND THINGS THAT DYE. | AN APOLOGIE FOR HYMNE (TERESA) | 28 | 46 136 | 59 |
| FLIGHTS SCORN THE LAZY DUST, & THINGS THAT DY. | AN APOLOGIE FOR (TERESA) HYMNE | 28 | 52 322 | 59 |

## FLINGS

| | | | | |
|---|---|---|---|---|
| SO SAID, HIS HANDS SPRIGHTLY AS FIRE HEE FLINGS, | MUSICKS DUELL | 111 | 46 149 | 535 |

## FLINTS

| | | | | |
|---|---|---|---|---|
| (MY FLINTS) SOME DROPS ARE DUE | SANCTA MARIA DOLORUM | 16 | 52 283 | 162 |

## FLINTY

| | | | | | |
|---|---|---|---|---|---|
| OF THE FLINTY DESTINYES. | ANOTHER ON HERRYS | 36 | 46 | 170 | 469 |

## FLOAT

| | | | | | |
|---|---|---|---|---|---|
| OF SHORT THICKE SOBS, WHOSE THUNDRING VOLLEYES FLOAT, | MUSICKS DUELL | 63 | 46 | 149 | 535 |

## FLOATES

| | | | | | |
|---|---|---|---|---|---|
| THINE FLOATES ABOVE, & IS THE CREAM. | WEEPER | 22 | 52 | 307 | 120 |

## FLOTES

| | | | | | |
|---|---|---|---|---|---|
| OH. THAT'S HIS FEARE. THERE FLOTES HIS DESTINY. | HORATIJ ILLE & NEFASTO | 22 | MS | 382 | 530 |

## FLOCK

| | | | | | |
|---|---|---|---|---|---|
| WHOSE WEALTH'S THEIR FLOCK, WHOSE WITT, TO BE | IN HOLY NATIVITY | 95 | 52 | 246 | 76 |

## FLOCKE

| | | | | | |
|---|---|---|---|---|---|
| BASELY DEGENEROUS. AGAINST MEE FLOCKE | OUT OF GROTIUS | 41 | MS | 398 | 198 |

## FLOCKS

| | | | | | |
|---|---|---|---|---|---|
| THE FLOCKS OF GOATES TO FOLDS OF FLAME. | DIES IRAE | 58 | 52 | 298 | 186 |

## FLOCKES

| | | | | | |
|---|---|---|---|---|---|
| POINT HERE THY BEAMES. O GLANCE ON YONDER FLOCKES, | ON A FOULE MORNING | 5 | 46 | 181 | 495 |

## FLOOD

| | | | | | |
|---|---|---|---|---|---|
| BATHES HIM IN A GENUINE FLOOD. | IN PRAISE OF LESSIUS | 36 | 46 | 156 | 510 |
| THE FLOOD, IF ANY CAN, THAT CAN SUFFICE, | TO PONTIUS WASHING HANDS | 3 | 46 | 88 | 22 |
| TO SEE BOTH BLENDED IN ONE FLOOD | UPON INFANT MARTYRS | 1 | 46 | 95 | 10 |
| HER EYES FLOOD LICKES HIS FEETS FAIRE STAINE, | SHE BEGAN TO WASH HIS FEET | 1 | 46 | 97 | 13 |
| THIS FLOOD THUS STAINED FAIRER STREAMES. | SHE BEGAN TO WASH HIS FEET | 4 | 46 | 97 | 13 |
| TAST THIS, AND AS THOU LIK'ST THIS LESSER FLOOD | OUR LORD IN HIS CIRCUMCISION | 3 | 46 | 98 | 9 |
| THEY SWIM, ALAS, IN THEIR OWNE FLOOD. | ON BLEEDING WOUNDS OF LORD | 8 | 46 | 101 | 110 |
| SOMETHING TO THE GENERALL FLOOD. | ON BLEEDING WOUNDS OF LORD | 28 | 46 | 101 | 110 |
| ON THE PROUD BANKES OF GREAT EUPHRATES FLOOD, | PSALME 137 | 1 | 46 | 104 | 7 |
| THE FIELDS OF PALESTINE, WITH SO PURE A FLOOD, | SOSPETTO D'HERODE | 86 | 46 | 109 | 216 |
| AND POURING ON HEAV'NS FACE THE SEAS HUGE FLOOD | SOSPETTO D'HERODE | 277 | 46 | 109 | 216 |
| BATHING THEIR HOT LIMBS IN LIFE'S PRETIOUS FLOOD. | SOSPETTO D'HERODE | 316 | 46 | 109 | 216 |
| BY A BLACK FOUNT, WHICH WEEPS INTO A FLOOD. | SOSPETTO D'HERODE | 349 | 46 | 109 | 216 |
| SOULES ARE NOT SPANIARDS TOO, ONE FRENDLY FLOOD | AN APOLOGIE FOR HYMNE (TERESA) | 15 | 46 | 136 | 59 |
| WAS LOV'D AS HONOUR'D AS A FLOOD. | AN EPITAPH DOCTOR BROOKE | 2 | 46 | 175 | 465 |
| BATHES HIM IN A GENUINE FLOOD. | TEMPERANCE | 34 | 52 | 342 | 510 |
| TO DROUNE THY SELFE IN THIS PURE PEARLY FLOOD. | UPON GUNPOWDER TREASON | 32 | MS | 387 | 461 |
| EVEN HEE THAT BELCHES OUT A FOAMING FLOOD | OUT OF GROTIUS | 75 | MS | 398 | 198 |

## FLOOD'S

| | | | | | |
|---|---|---|---|---|---|
| THE' ASTONISHT NYMPHS THEIR FLOOD'S STRANGE FATE DEPLORE, | TO COUNTESSE OF DENBIGH | 25 | 52 | 236 | 146 |

## FLOODGATE

| | | | | | |
|---|---|---|---|---|---|
| SHEE OPES THE FLOODGATE, AND LETS LOOSE A TIDE | MUSICKS DUELL | 93 | 46 | 149 | 535 |

## FLOOD-GATE

| | | | | | |
|---|---|---|---|---|---|
| THE FLOOD-GATE SHALL BE SET WIDE OPE FOR HIM. | OUR LORD IN HIS CIRCUMCISION | 6 | 46 | 98 | 9 |

## FLOUD

| | | | | | |
|---|---|---|---|---|---|
| IN THIS ILLUSTRIOUS THRONG, YOUR LOFTY FLOUD | TO THE QUEEN'S MAJESTY | 15 | 52 | 261 | 47 |
| FLOW IN AN AMOROUS FLOUD | VEXILLA REGIS | 9 | 52 | 277 | 156 |
| IF MY FOUL HEART CALL'D FOR A FLOUD. | CHARITAS NIMIA | 48 | 52 | 280 | 48 |
| WHILE WITH A FAITHFULL, MUTUALL, FLOUD | SANCTA MARIA DOLORUM | 19 | 52 | 283 | 162 |
| THEY SWIMME, ALAS, IN THEIR OWN FLOUD. | UPON BLEEDING CRUCIFIX | 12 | 52 | 288 | 110 |
| SOMTHING TO THE GENERALL FLOUD. | UPON BLEEDING CRUCIFIX | 24 | 52 | 288 | 110 |
| AH THIS WAY BEND THY BENIGN FLOUD | ADORO TE | 47 | 52 | 291 | 172 |
| (FAIR FLOUD OF HOLY FIRES,) TRANSFUS'D THE FLAME | AN APOLOGIE FOR (TERESA) HYMNE | 2 | 52 | 322 | 59 |
| SOULS ARE NOT SPANIARDS TOO, ONE FREINDLY FLOUD | AN APOLOGIE FOR (TERESA) HYMNE | 15 | 52 | 322 | 59 |
| THE BIRD, THAT'S FETCH'T FROM PHASIS FLOUD, | PETRONIJ ALES PHASIACIS PETITA | 1 | MS | 382 | 526 |

## FLOODS

| | | | | | |
|---|---|---|---|---|---|
| HEAVEN, OF SUCH FAIRE FLOODS AS THIS. | THE WEEPER | 23 | 46 | 79 | 120 |

## FLOUDS

| | | | | | |
|---|---|---|---|---|---|
| BOTH OF LOVE'S FIRES & FLOUDS) MIGHT I RECLINE | SANCTA MARIA DOLORUM | 47 | 52 | 283 | 162 |
| BUT CAN THESE FAIR FLOUDS BE | WEEPER | 97 | 52 | 307 | 120 |
| O FLOUDS, O FIRES, O SUNS O SHOWRES. | WEEPER | 101 | 52 | 307 | 120 |

## FLOUD'S

| | | | | | |
|---|---|---|---|---|---|
| TH'ASTONISH'D NYMPHS THEIR FLOUD'S STRANGE FATE DEPLORE, | AGAINST IRRESOLUTION AND DELAY | 25 | 52 | 347 | 146 |

FLOORE

| | | | |
|---|---|---|---|
| THE MODEST FRONT OF THIS SMALL FLOORE | AN EPITAPH UPON ASHTON | 1 | 46 192 464 |

FLORA'S

| | | | |
|---|---|---|---|
| IF FLORA'S DARLINGS NOW AWAKE FROM SLEEPE, | AN ELEGY MR STANNINOW | 25 | MS 394 473 |

FLOURISH

| | | | |
|---|---|---|---|
| WHOSE FLOURISH (METEOR-LIKE) DOTH CURLE THE AIRE | MUSICKS DUELL | 137 | 46 149 535 |
| SHALL FLOURISH ON THY BROWES. AND BEE | IN MEMORY OF LADY MADRE TERESA | 162 | 46 131 52 |
| THE FLOURISH OF HIS SOBER YOUTH, | HIS EPITAPH (HERRYS) | 25 | 46 172 471 |
| SHALL FLOURISH ON THY BROWES. & BE | TERESA | 161 | 52 315 52 |

FLOURISHT

| | | | |
|---|---|---|---|
| FLOURISHT THEIR SNAKES, AND TOST THEIR FLAMING BRANDS. | SOSPETTO D'HERODE | 260 | 46 109 216 |
| FLOURISHT IN SO FAIRE A GROUTH. | ANOTHER ON HERRYS | 14 | 46 170 469 |

FLOW

| | | | |
|---|---|---|---|
| FLOW NOT SO SWEET AS DOE THE TONES | OUT OF GREEKE CUPID'S CRYER | 27 | 46 159 519 |
| MIGHT HEE FLOW FROM THEE | THE WEEPER | 81 | 46 79 120 |
| HEE'L FAN HER BRIGHT LOCKS TEACHING THEM TO FLOW, | ON A FOULE MORNING | 19 | 46 181 495 |
| FLOW THY HAIRE. | OUT OF THE ITALIAN (1) | 8 | 46 188 545 |
| FLOW IN AN AMOROUS FLOUD | VEXILLA REGIS | 9 | 52 277 156 |
| FLOW, TARDY FOUNTS, & INTO DECENT SHOWRES | SANCTA MARIA DOLORUM | 87 | 52 283 162 |
| ONE DROPP OF THIS PURE NECTAR, WHICH DOTH FLOW | UPON GUNPOWDER TREASON | 41 | MS 387 461 |

FLOW'D

| | | | |
|---|---|---|---|
| TEARES WOULD NOW HAVE FLOW'D SO DEEPE, | ANOTHER ON HERRYS | 21 | 46 170 469 |
| HAVE FLOW'D TOGETHER. IF OUGHT FURTHER NEEDES | OUT OF GROTIUS | 6 | MS 398 198 |

FLOWES

| | | | |
|---|---|---|---|
| FLOWES IN THY SONG (O FAIRE, O DYING SWAN.) | UPON OUR LORDS LAST DISCOURSE | 2 | 46 95 21 |
| WHERE FLOWES SUCH WINE AS WE CAN HAVE OF NONE | AN APOLOGIE FOR HYMNE (TERESA) | 39 | 46 136 59 |
| WHERE FLOWES SUCH WINE AS WE CAN HAVE OF NONE | AN APOLOGIE FOR (TERESA) HYMNE | 39 | 52 322 59 |

FLOWING

| | | | |
|---|---|---|---|
| HALFE SO FRUITFULL, HALFE SO FLOWING. | ON BLEEDING WOUNDS OF LORD | 16 | 46 101 110 |
| HALF SO FRUITFULL, HALF SO FLOWING. | UPON BLEEDING CRUCIFIX | 20 | 52 288 110 |

HIGH-FLOUNE

| | | | |
|---|---|---|---|
| HUGE HIGH-FLOUNE POYSONS, EV'N OF COLCHOS BREED, | HORATIJ ILLE & NEFASTO | 11 | MS 382 530 |

FLOWER

| | | | |
|---|---|---|---|
| YET KEEPE INVIOLATE HER VIRGIN FLOWER. | SOSPETTO D'HERODE | 164 | 46 109 216 |
| NOR NEED WEE KILL THY FRUIT TO SMELL THY FLOWER. | ON HOPE | 54 | 46 143 71 |
| OF HIS FORWARD FLOWER, WHEN LO | UPON DEATH OF DESIRED HERRYS | 39 | 46 168 467 |
| HEE'S GONE. THE FAIR'ST FLOWER, THAT E'RE BOSOME DREST, | LUKE 2. QUAERIT JESUM | 5 | MS 379 11 |
| TO GLUTT THE STOMACK OF HIS DARLING FLOWER. | UPON BIRTH PRINCESSE E | 6 | MS 391 456 |
| AND MURMUR FORTH THY WOES TO EVERY FLOWER, | AN ELEGIE ON DR PORTER | 21 | MS 395 476 |

FLOWRE

| | | | |
|---|---|---|---|
| UNFOLD AT LENGTH, UNFOLD FAIR FLOWRE | TO COUNTESSE OF DENBIGH | 43 | 52 236 146 |
| NOR DOES IT KILL THY FRUIT, TO SMELL THY FLOWRE. | (ON) HOPE | 24 | 52 345 71 |
| FORC'T THIS PRIME FLOWRE OF YOUTH TO MAKE SUCH HAST | AN ELEGY MR STANNINOW | 28 | MS 394 473 |

FLOWERS

| | | | |
|---|---|---|---|
| NOR MAY RETURNED FAIRER FLOWERS. | THE WEEPER | 90 | 46 79 120 |
| WHERE HE MEANT FROSTS, HE SCATTERED FLOWERS. | A HYMNE OF THE NATIVITY | 28 | 46 106 76 |
| WEE'L BRING THE FIRST-BORNE OF HER FLOWERS. | A HYMNE OF THE NATIVITY | 79 | 46 106 76 |
| NOR NEEDS MY MUSE A BLUSH, OR THESE BRIGHT FLOWERS | SOSPETTO D'HERODE | 17 | 46 109 216 |
| IMMORTALL FLOWERS TO HER FAIRE HAND PRESENT. | SOSPETTO D'HERODE | 100 | 46 109 216 |
| EACH FLOWERS A PREGNANT POYSON, TRY'D AND GOOD, | SOSPETTO D'HERODE | 347 | 46 109 216 |
| FLOWERS OF NEVER FADING GRACES. | ON A PRAYER BOOKE | 36 | 46 126 139 |
| THE SPRING IS COME, THE FLOWERS APPEARE, | ON THE ASSUMPTION | 11 | 46 139 114 |
| OF OUR FAIREST FLOWERS, | ON THE ASSUMPTION | 48 | 46 139 114 |
| OF ALL THE FAIRE CHEEKT FLOWERS THAT FILL THEE, | AN HIMNE FOR CIRCUMCISION | 9 | 46 141 37 |
| TWO SILKEN SISTER FLOWERS CONSULT, AND LAY | UPON YORKE HIS BIRTH | 60 | 46 176 500 |
| ALL THE FLOWERS THAT NATURE NAMETH. | OUT OF THE ITALIAN (1) | 6 | 46 188 545 |
| CAN CROWNE OLD WINTERS' HEAD WITH FLOWERS. | WISHES SUPPOSED MISTRESSE | 90 | 46 195 479 |
| FLOWERS OF NEVER FADING GRACES | PRAYER TO GENTLE-WOMAN | 42 | 52 328 139 |
| MARK WITH WHAT FAITH FRUITS ANSWER FLOWERS. | AGAINST IRRESOLUTION AND DELAY | 33 | 52 347 146 |

FLOWRES

| | | | |
|---|---|---|---|
| OF OUR FAIREST FLOWRES | IN GLORIOUS ASSUMPTION B. LADY | 53 | 52 304 114 |
| NOR MAY RETURN'D MORE FAITHFULL FLOWRES. | WEEPER | 84 | 52 307 120 |
| FALL WITH SOFT WINGS, STUCK WITH SOFT FLOWRES. | TEMPERANCE | 46 | 52 342 510 |

FLOWRS

| | | | | | |
|---|---|---|---|---|---|
| WHERE HE MEAN'T FROST, HE SCATTER'D FLOWRS. | IN HOLY NATIVITY | 29 | 52 | 246 | 76 |
| WE'L BRING THE FIRST-BORN OF HER FLOWRS | IN HOLY NATIVITY | 99 | 52 | 246 | 76 |
| OF ALL THE FAIR-CHEEK'T FLOWRS THAT FILL THEE | NEW YEAR'S DAY | 9 | 52 | 251 | 37 |
| THE SPRING IS COME, THE FLOWRS APPEAR | IN GLORIOUS ASSUMPTION B. LADY | 11 | 52 | 304 | 114 |
| THE FLOWRS APPEAR. | IN GLORIOUS ASSUMPTION B. LADY | 17 | 52 | 304 | 114 |

FLOWRY

| | | | | | |
|---|---|---|---|---|---|
| WINTERS SAD FACE, AND THROUGH THE FLOWRY LANDS | SOSPETTO D'HERODE | 110 | 46 | 109 | 216 |
| BUT SHUT THEIR FLOWRY LIDS FOR EVER. NIGHT, | SOSPETTO D'HERODE | 379 | 46 | 109 | 216 |
| FAIR, FLOWRY NAME. IN NONE BUT THEE | TO THE NAME OF JESUS | 173 | 52 | 239 | 30 |

FLOURY

| | | | | | |
|---|---|---|---|---|---|
| THEIR SHAGGY LOCKS, THEIR FLOURY MANTLES TURN'D | UPON GUNPOWDER TREASON | 47 | MS | 386 | 460 |

FLUENT

| | | | | | |
|---|---|---|---|---|---|
| LANGUAGE NONE MORE FLUENT IS. | UPON THE DEATH OF A GENTLEMAN | 22 | 46 | 166 | 472 |

FLUSHING

| | | | | | |
|---|---|---|---|---|---|
| HIGH-COLOUR'D IS. HIS EYES STILL FLUSHING | OUT OF GREEKE CUPID'S CRYER | 20 | 46 | 159 | 519 |

FLUTTER

| | | | | | |
|---|---|---|---|---|---|
| TO FLUTTER IN THE BALMY AIRE, | ON MR. G. HERBERTS BOOKE | 9 | 46 | 130 | 68 |

FLUTTERING

| | | | | | |
|---|---|---|---|---|---|
| FLUTTERING IN WANTON SHOALES, AND TO THE SKY | MUSICKS DUELL | 91 | 46 | 149 | 535 |

FLY

| | | | | | |
|---|---|---|---|---|---|
| WING'D WITH THEIR OWNE WILD ECCHO'S PRATLING FLY. | MUSICKS DUELL | 92 | 46 | 149 | 535 |
| HER SHAFTS, AND SHEE FLY FARRE ABOVE. | ON HOPE | 75 | 46 | 143 | 71 |
| TO START FROM TIME, AND CHEERFULLY TO FLY | UPON DEATH OF HERRYS | 7 | 46 | 167 | 466 |
| FLY, FLY PROPHANE FOGS, FARRE HENCE FLY AWAY. | ON A FOULE MORNING | 31 | 46 | 181 | 495 |
| FLY, FLY PROPHANE FOGS, FARRE HENCE FLY AWAY. | ON A FOULE MORNING | 31 | 46 | 181 | 495 |
| FLY, FLY PROPHANE FOGS, FARRE HENCE FLY AWAY. | ON A FOULE MORNING | 31 | 46 | 181 | 495 |
| FLY THEN, AND DOE NOT THINKE WITH HER TO STAY. | ON A FOULE MORNING | 37 | 46 | 181 | 495 |
| MY FANCYES, FLY BEFORE YEE. | WISHES SUPPOSED MISTRESSE | 125 | 46 | 195 | 479 |
| FLY IN THE FACE OF HEAV'N. AS IF IT WERE | IN GLORIOUS EPIPHANIE | 103 | 52 | 253 | 39 |
| BECAUSE SOME FOOLISH FLY | CHARITAS NIMIA | 43 | 52 | 280 | 48 |
| THE WORLD IN FLAMES SHALL FLY AWAY. | DIES IRAE | 4 | 52 | 298 | 186 |
| NONE CAN INDURE. YET NONE CAN FLY. | DIES IRAE | 20 | 52 | 298 | 186 |
| FLY TO THY SCEPTER OF SOFT LOVE. | DIES IRAE | 26 | 52 | 298 | 186 |
| SENDING'S TOO SLOW A WORD, MY SELFE WOULD FLY. | ALEXIAS FIRST ELEGIE | 13 | 52 | 334 | 204 |
| WHAT NEEDES MY VIRGIN LORD FLY THUS FROM ME, | ALEXIAS THIRD ELEGIE | 23 | 52 | 336 | 209 |
| HER SHAFTS, AND SHEE FLY FARRE ABOVE, | (ON) HOPE | 35 | 52 | 345 | 71 |
| GRIPES THY COLD LIMBES SOE FAST, THOU CANST NOT FLY, | ON GUNPOWDER-TREASON | 4 | MS | 384 | 458 |
| MAKE THEIR SCAR'D SOULES TAKE WING, & FLY AWAY. | AN ELEGIE ON DR PORTER | 30 | MS | 395 | 476 |

FLIE

| | | | | | |
|---|---|---|---|---|---|
| (WHOSE HANDS ARE FIGHTING, WHILE THEIR FEET DOE FLIE.) | HORATIJ ILLE & NEFASTO | 26 | MS | 382 | 530 |

FLYE

| | | | | | |
|---|---|---|---|---|---|
| MIGHT A WORD ONCE FLYE FROM OUT THEE. | OUT OF THE ITALIAN (1) | 33 | 46 | 188 | 545 |

FLYING

| | | | | | |
|---|---|---|---|---|---|
| CHARG'D WITH A FLYING TOUCH. AND STREIGHTWAY SHEE | MUSICKS DUELL | 21 | 46 | 149 | 535 |
| WHEN MY WAIWARD BREATH IS FLYING, | PSALME 23 | 17 | 46 | 102 | 5 |
| LIFE IS FLYING. | OUT OF THE ITALIAN (1) | 50 | 46 | 188 | 545 |
| SHALL FIXE MY FLYING WISHES. | WISHES SUPPOSED MISTRESSE | 122 | 46 | 195 | 479 |

FOAMS

| | | | | | |
|---|---|---|---|---|---|
| THE OTHERS WANTON WEALTH FOAMS HIGH, AND BRAVE, | WIDOWES MITES | 3 | 46 | 86 | 21 |

FOAMES

| | | | | | |
|---|---|---|---|---|---|
| TH'IMPATIENT LIQUOR, FRETS, AND FOAMES, AND RAVES. | SOSPETTO D'HERODE | 486 | 46 | 109 | 216 |

FOAMING

| | | | | | |
|---|---|---|---|---|---|
| EVEN HEE THAT BELCHES OUT A FOAMING FLOOD | OUT OF GROTIUS | 75 | MS | 398 | 198 |

FOAMY

| | | | | | |
|---|---|---|---|---|---|
| THE FOAMY LIPS OF CERBERUS) SHEE APPLY'D | SOSPETTO D'HERODE | 468 | 46 | 109 | 216 |

FOE

| | | | | | |
|---|---|---|---|---|---|
| THY FOE TO CROSSE THE SWEET ARTS OF THY REIGNE | TO LORD UPON WATER MADE WINE | 2 | 46 | 91 | 12 |
| AGAINST THE GHOSTLY FOE TO TAKE YOUR PART. | ON A PRAYER BOOKE | 13 | 46 | 126 | 139 |

FOES

| | | | | | |
|---|---|---|---|---|---|
| THY QUEL'D FOES ARE NOT ONELY NOW | NEITHER DURST MAN ASKE | 5 | 46 | 92 | 20 |
| WHILE I FEAST, MY FOES DOE FEED | PSALME 23 | 51 | 46 | 102 | 5 |
| HEE HIS OWNE FANCY-FRAMED FOES DEFIES. | SOSPETTO D'HERODE | 479 | 46 | 109 | 216 |
| DEFEND US FROM OUR FOES & THINE. | OFFICE H. CROSS MATINES | 2 | 52 | 265 | 86 |
| BY HIS WORST FOES (BECAUSE HE WOULD) BESEIG'D & TAKEN. | OFFICE H. CROSS MATINES | 17 | 52 | 265 | 86 |
| O FAIR, & FREINDLY FOES, | WEEPER | 93 | 52 | 307 | 120 |
| AGAINST YOUR GHOSTLY FOES TO TAKE YOUR PART, | PRAYER TO GENTLE-WOMAN | 19 | 52 | 328 | 139 |
| BUT NOW, AH ME, FROM WHERE HE HAS NO FOES | ALEXIAS THIRD ELEGIE | 15 | 52 | 336 | 209 |

FOGS

| | | | | | |
|---|---|---|---|---|---|
| FLY, FLY PROPHANE FOGS, FARRE HENCE FLY AWAY, | ON A FOULE MORNING | 31 | 46 | 181 | 495 |

FOLD

| | | | | | |
|---|---|---|---|---|---|
| FOLD UP MY LIFE IN LOVE, AND LAY'T BENEATH | SANCTA MARIA DOLORUM | 107 | 52 | 283 | 162 |

BLIND-FOLD

| | | | | | |
|---|---|---|---|---|---|
| WHERE ART THOU SOL, WHILE THUS THE BLIND-FOLD DAY | ON A FOULE MORNING | 1 | 46 | 181 | 495 |

FOLDED

| | | | | | |
|---|---|---|---|---|---|
| THEY (SWEET TURTLES) FOLDED LYE, | AN EPITAPH HUSBAND AND WIFE | 9 | 46 | 174 | 478 |
| LAY FOLDED UP IN SLEEPES CAPTIVITY. | TO THE MORNING | 6 | 46 | 183 | 497 |
| TO LY THUS FOLDED, & COMPLAINING | PRAYER TO GENTLE-WOMAN | 4 | 52 | 328 | 139 |
| THEY, SWEET TURTLES, FOLDED LY | AN EPITAPH UPON MARRIED COUPLE | 9 | 52 | 339 | 478 |

FOLDS

| | | | | | |
|---|---|---|---|---|---|
| AND FOLDS IN WAV'D NOTES WITH A TREMBLING BILL, | MUSICKS DUELL | 60 | 46 | 149 | 535 |
| THE FLOCKS OF GOATES TO FOLDS OF FLAME. | DIES IRAE | 58 | 52 | 298 | 186 |

FOLLOW

| | | | | | |
|---|---|---|---|---|---|
| HIM THE MUSES LOVE TO FOLLOW, | UPON DEATH OF DESIRED HERRYS | 11 | 46 | 168 | 467 |
| HOW FIT OUR WELL-RANK'D FEASTS DOE FOLLOW, | UPON POWDER DAY | 1 | 46 | 185 | 74 |
| CANNOT FOLLOW. | OUT OF THE ITALIAN (1) | 17 | 46 | 188 | 545 |
| AND FOLLOW THOSE FAIR STARRES OF YOURS. | TO SAME CONCERNING CHOISE | 30 | 52 | 331 | 66 |

FOLLOW'D

| | | | | | |
|---|---|---|---|---|---|
| HE'S FOLLOW'D BY TWO FAITHFULL FOUNTAINES. | WEEPER | 112 | 52 | 307 | 120 |

FOLLOWING

| | | | | | |
|---|---|---|---|---|---|
| FOLLOWING THOSE LITTLE RILLS, HEE SINKES INTO | MUSICKS DUELL | 123 | 46 | 149 | 535 |
| LOOKE ON THE FOLLOWING LEAVES, AND SEE HIM BREATH. | UPON BISHOP ANDREWES PICTURE | 16 | 46 | 163 | 490 |

FOND

| | | | | | |
|---|---|---|---|---|---|
| FAITHLESSE AND FOND MORTALITY, | UPON THE DEATH OF A GENTLEMAN | 1 | 46 | 166 | 472 |
| FOND AND FAITHLESSE THING, THAT THUS, | UPON THE DEATH OF A GENTLEMAN | 3 | 46 | 166 | 472 |
| HER WORDS, SLEEP'ST THOU FOND MAN. SLEEP'ST THOU. (SAID SHE) | SOSPETTO D'HERODE | 424 | 46 | 109 | 216 |
| FORBID IT MIGHTY LOVE, LET NO FOND HATE | AN APOLOGIE FOR HYMNE (TERESA) | 13 | 46 | 136 | 59 |
| WHOSE SILKEN FLATTERYES SWELL A FEW FOND HOURES | UPON STANINOUGH'S DEATH | 8 | 46 | 175 | 475 |
| FEARES, FOND AND FLIGHT, | WISHES SUPPOSED MISTRESSE | 70 | 46 | 195 | 479 |
| FORBID IT, MIGHTY LOVE. LET NO FOND HATE | AN APOLOGIE FOR (TERESA) HYMNE | 13 | 52 | 322 | 59 |
| WHOSE SYLKEN FLATTERYES SWELL A FEW FOND HOWRES | DEATH'S LECTURE | 9 | 52 | 340 | 475 |

FONDLY

| | | | | | |
|---|---|---|---|---|---|
| THUS, O THUS FONDLY DOE WEE PITCH OUR FEARES | HORATIJ ILLE & NEFASTO | 30 | MS | 382 | 530 |

FOOD

| | | | | | |
|---|---|---|---|---|---|
| WHAT WOULD YE MORE, HERE FOOD IT SELFE IS FED. | ON MIRACLE OF LOAVES | 4 | 46 | 86 | 15 |
| TO WHICH HIS GNAW'D HEART IS THE GROWING FOOD | SOSPETTO D'HERODE | 494 | 46 | 109 | 216 |
| RICH, ROYALL FOOD. BOUNTYFULL BREAD. | ADORO TE | 39 | 52 | 291 | 172 |
| OUR FOOD, & FAITHFULL SHEPHARD TOO. | LAUDA SION SALVATOREM | 70 | 52 | 294 | 178 |
| THAT RUNNES IN VIOLETT PIPES. NONE OTHER FOOD | ON GUNPOWDER-TREASON | 64 | MS | 384 | 458 |
| A SUBTLE INUNDATION OF QUICKE FOOD | OUT OF GROTIUS | 61 | MS | 398 | 198 |

LIFE-FOOD

| | | | | | |
|---|---|---|---|---|---|
| LO THE LIFE-FOOD OF ANGELLS THEN | LAUDA SION SALVATOREM | 61 | 52 | 294 | 178 |

FOOD-PREPARING

| | | | | | |
|---|---|---|---|---|---|
| AS WHEN A PILE OF FOOD-PREPARING FIRE. | SOSPETTO D'HERODE | 481 | 46 | 109 | 216 |

FOOL'S

| | | | | | |
|---|---|---|---|---|---|
| BECAUSE SOME DESPERATE FOOL'S UNDONE. | CHARITAS NIMIA | 36 | 52 | 280 | 48 |

FOOLE

| | | | | | |
|---|---|---|---|---|---|
| WHY FOOLE, SAIES VENUS, THUS PROVOK'ST THOU MEE, | UPON THE SAME (VENUS ARMES) | 3 | 46 | 161 | 523 |

FOOLISH

| | | | | | |
|---|---|---|---|---|---|
| NARCISSUS. FOOLISH PHAETON. WHO FOR ALL | SOSPETTO D'HERODE | 79 | 46 | 109 | 216 |
| BECAUSE SOME FOOLISH FLY | CHARITAS NIMIA | 43 | 52 | 280 | 48 |

FOOT

| | | | | | |
|---|---|---|---|---|---|
| O THOU THAT ON THIS FOOT HAST LAID | ON WOUNDS OF CRUCIFIED LORD | 9 | 46 | 99 | 24 |
| THIS FOOT HATH GOT A MOUTH AND LIPPES, | ON WOUNDS OF CRUCIFIED LORD | 13 | 46 | 99 | 24 |
| AND AT THE HUMBLE FOOT | SANCTA MARIA DOLORUM | 63 | 52 | 283 | 162 |
| THE MOST FIRM FOOT NO MORE THEN STAND. | DIES IRAE | 24 | 52 | 298 | 186 |
| THE LAMB HATH DIPP'T HIS WHITE FOOT HERE. | WEEPER | 108 | 52 | 307 | 120 |

LIGHT-FOOT

| | | | | | |
|---|---|---|---|---|---|
| DISPOS'D TO GIVE THE LIGHT-FOOT LADY SPORT | MUSICKS DUELL | 16 | 46 | 149 | 535 |

SILVER-FOOTED

| | | | | | |
|---|---|---|---|---|---|
| STAY, SILVER-FOOTED DAME, STRIVE NOT TO WED | AN ELEGIE ON DR PORTER | 1 | MS | 395 | 476 |

SYLVER-FOOTED

| | | | | | |
|---|---|---|---|---|---|
| PARENTS OF SYLVER-FOOTED RILLS. | WEEPER | 2 | 52 | 307 | 120 |

FOOTSTEPS

| | | | | | |
|---|---|---|---|---|---|
| FOOTSTEPS OF THEIR EFFECTS, HEE TRAC'D TOO WELL, | SOSPETTO D'HERODE | 146 | 46 | 109 | 216 |
| BRING THEIR HEAVEN WITH THEM. THEIR GREAT FOOTSTEPS PLACE | UPON YORKE HIS BIRTH | 19 | 46 | 176 | 500 |

FOOTSTEPPES

| | | | | | |
|---|---|---|---|---|---|
| IN WHAT STRANGE PATH MY LORD'S FOOTSTEPPES BLEED. | ALEXIAS FIRST ELEGIE | 8 | 52 | 334 | 204 |

FORBEAR

| | | | | | |
|---|---|---|---|---|---|
| FORBEAR, SAID I. BE NOT TOO BOLD. | IN HOLY NATIVITY | 55 | 52 | 246 | 76 |
| VAIN LOVES AVANT. BOLD HANDS FORBEAR. | WEEPER | 107 | 52 | 307 | 120 |

FORBEARE

| | | | | | |
|---|---|---|---|---|---|
| FORBEARE (SAID I) BE NOT TOO BOLD. | A HYMNE OF THE NATIVITY | 39 | 46 | 106 | 76 |

FORBID

| | | | | | |
|---|---|---|---|---|---|
| BLEST POWERS FORBID THY TENDER LIFE, | IN MEMORY OF LADY MADRE TERESA | 69 | 46 | 131 | 52 |
| THY PRAISE MIGHT NOT SPEAK ENGLISH TOO. FORBID | AN APOLOGIE FOR HYMNE (TERESA) | 11 | 46 | 136 | 59 |
| FORBID IT MIGHTY LOVE, LET NO FOND HATE | AN APOLOGIE FOR HYMNE (TERESA) | 13 | 46 | 136 | 59 |
| BLEST POWRES FORBID, THY TENDER LIFE | TERESA | 69 | 52 | 315 | 52 |
| THY PRAISE MIGHT NOT SPEAK ENGLISH TOO. FORBID | AN APOLOGIE FOR (TERESA) HYMNE | 11 | 52 | 322 | 59 |
| FORBID IT, MIGHTY LOVE. LET NO FOND HATE | AN APOLOGIE FOR (TERESA) HYMNE | 13 | 52 | 322 | 59 |

FORBIDDEN

| | | | | | |
|---|---|---|---|---|---|
| (TANGLED IN FORBIDDEN WAYES) | PSALME 23 | 22 | 46 | 102 | 5 |
| OF ONE FORBIDDEN BITT. | O GLORIOSA DOMINA | 16 | 52 | 302 | 194 |
| HAD NOT A BETTER FRUIT FORBIDDEN IT. | O GLORIOSA DOMINA | 17 | 52 | 302 | 194 |

FORCE

| | | | | | |
|---|---|---|---|---|---|
| WHAT FORCE CANNOT EFFECT, FRAUD SHALL DEVISE. | SOSPETTO D'HERODE | 248 | 46 | 109 | 216 |
| AND YET WHOSE FORCE FEARE I. HAVE I SO LOST | SOSPETTO D'HERODE | 249 | 46 | 109 | 216 |
| FOR THOUGH THE HAND OF FATE COULD FORCE, | AN EPITAPH HUSBAND AND WIFE | 3 | 46 | 174 | 478 |
| ALL FORCE OF SO PROPHANE A FALLACY | TO THE NAME OF JESUS | 171 | 52 | 239 | 30 |
| FAITH IS MY FORCE. FAITH STRENGTH AFFORDS | ADORO TE | 13 | 52 | 291 | 172 |
| FOR THOUGH THE HAND OF FATE COULD FORCE | AN EPITAPH UPON MARRIED COUPLE | 3 | 52 | 339 | 478 |
| WITH NIMBLE CAPERS, & FORCE ATLAS TREAD | UPON KINGS CORONATION | 3 | MS | 389 | 454 |
| AND MISTS OF GREIFE, DARE FORCE A JOYFULL LIGHT. | UPON KINGS CORONATION | 16 | MS | 389 | 454 |
| MUST HAVE A PASSAGE, OR 'TWILL FORCE A WAY. | UPON BIRTH PRINCESSE E | 14 | MS | 391 | 456 |
| THEY FORCE A LILLY PATH THROUGH ROSY MOUNTAINS. | AN ELEGIE ON DR PORTER | 42 | MS | 395 | 476 |

FORC'T

| | | | | | |
|---|---|---|---|---|---|
| DEATH ONELY BY THIS DAYES JUST DOOME IS FORC'T TO DYE. | EASTER DAY | 15 | 46 | 100 | 26 |
| NOR IS DEATH FORC'T. FOR MAY HEE LY | EASTER DAY | 16 | 46 | 100 | 26 |
| FORC'T THIS PRIME FLOWRE OF YOUTH TO MAKE SUCH HAST | AN ELEGY MR STANNINOW | 28 | MS | 394 | 473 |

FORCING

| | | | | | |
|---|---|---|---|---|---|
| FORCING HIS SOMETIMES ECLIPS'D FACE TO BE | IN GLORIOUS EPIPHANIE | 115 | 52 | 253 | 39 |

FORD

| | | | | | |
|---|---|---|---|---|---|
| THOU CHEAT'ST US FORD, MAK'ST ONE SEEME TWO BY ART. | UPON FORD'S TRAGEDYES | 1 | 46 | 181 | 495 |

SILVER-FORDED

| | | | | | |
|---|---|---|---|---|---|
| PARENTS OF SILVER-FORDED RILLS. | THE WEEPER | 2 | 46 | 79 | 120 |

FORE

| | | | | | |
|---|---|---|---|---|---|
| FROM A FORE SPENT NIGHT OF SORROW. | WISHES SUPPOSED MISTRESSE | 78 | 46 | 195 | 479 |

FOREPAST

| | | | | | |
|---|---|---|---|---|---|
| WHILE THE REFLECTION OF THY FOREPAST JOYES, | SOSPETTO D'HERODE | 243 | 46 | 109 | 216 |

FORFEIT

| | | | | | |
|---|---|---|---|---|---|
| HIMSELFE, THE FORFEIT OF HIS SLAVES OFFENCE. | SOSPETTO D'HERODE | 188 | 46 | 109 | 216 |
| FORFEIT OUR OWN | IN GLORIOUS EPIPHANIE | 228 | 52 | 253 | 39 |

FORFEITED

| | | | | | |
|---|---|---|---|---|---|
| FAST BOUND, SINCE FIRST HE FORFEITED THE SKIES, | SOSPETTO D'HERODE | 40 | 46 | 109 | 216 |
| WITHHELD HER VAILE, H' HAD FORFEITED HIS SIGHT. | UPON KINGS CORONATION | 20 | MS | 390 | 453 |

FORFEITURE

| | | | | | |
|---|---|---|---|---|---|
| THAT FORFEITURE OF NOON TO NIGHT SHALL PAY | IN GLORIOUS EPIPHANIE | 149 | 52 | 253 | 39 |

FORGE

| | | | | | |
|---|---|---|---|---|---|
| LIFES FORGE. FAIN'D IS HER VOICE, AND FALSE TOO, BE | SOSPETTO D'HERODE | 423 | 46 | 109 | 216 |

FORGET

| | | | | | |
|---|---|---|---|---|---|
| MAKE HIGH NOONE FORGET HIS BEAMES. | PSALME 23 | 16 | 46 | 102 | 5 |
| THIS HAND FORGET THE MASTERY | PSALME 137 | 16 | 46 | 104 | 7 |
| MAY DRINKE IT SELFE UP, AND FORGET TO DY. | AN APOLOGIE FOR HYMNE (TERESA) | 46 | 46 | 136 | 59 |
| BUT THOU, FAINT GOD OF SLEEPE, FORGET THAT I | TO THE MORNING | 47 | 46 | 183 | 497 |
| AND BIDDES THEE NE'RE FORGET | VEXILLA REGIS | 3 | 52 | 277 | 156 |
| MAY DRINK IT SELF UP, AND FORGET TO DY. | AN APOLOGIE FOR (TERESA) HYMNE | 46 | 52 | 322 | 59 |

FORGETT

| | | | | | |
|---|---|---|---|---|---|
| 'TIS GRATITUDE TO FORGETT THAT OTHER | O GLORIOSA DOMINA | 25 | 52 | 302 | 194 |

FORGIVE

| | | | | | |
|---|---|---|---|---|---|
| IF SIN CAN SIGH, LOVE CAN FORGIVE. | DIES IRAE | 47 | 52 | 298 | 186 |

FORGOT

| | | | | | |
|---|---|---|---|---|---|
| THE NORTH FORGOT HIS FIERCE INTENT, | A HYMNE OF THE NATIVITY | 25 | 46 | 106 | 76 |
| FAINE WOULD HEE HAVE FORGOT WHAT FATALL STRINGS, | SOSPETTO D'HERODE | 139 | 46 | 109 | 216 |
| OR FORGOT THE CRUELL VIGOUR, | ANOTHER ON HERRYS | 3 | 46 | 170 | 469 |
| IF HEAVEN HATH NOW FORGOT TO WEEPE. O THEN | AN ELEGY MR STANNINOW | 15 | MS | 394 | 473 |

FORGOTT

| | | | | | |
|---|---|---|---|---|---|
| THE NORTH FORGOTT HIS FEIRCE INTENT. | IN HOLY NATIVITY | 26 | 52 | 246 | 76 |
| IT QUITE FORGOTT. THE FEARFULL EARTH GAVE WAY, | ON GUNPOWDER-TREASON | 53 | MS | 384 | 456 |
| THE WILD WAVES COUCH'D. THE SEA FORGOTT TO SWEAT | OUT OF GROTIUS | 67 | MS | 398 | 198 |

FOREHEAD

| | | | | | |
|---|---|---|---|---|---|
| WAS IN HIS SHADY FOREHEAD SEEN EXPREST. | SOSPETTO D'HERODE | 195 | 46 | 109 | 216 |
| FIXT HIS FOREHEAD INTO A FROWNE,) | LOVES HOROSCOPE | 38 | 46 | 185 | 483 |
| CAN MAKE DAYES FOREHEAD BRIGHT. | WISHES SUPPOSED MISTRESSE | 95 | 46 | 195 | 479 |

FOREHEAD'S

| | | | | | |
|---|---|---|---|---|---|
| THE FOREHEAD'S SHADE IN GRIEFES EXPRESSION THERE, | SOSPETTO D'HERODE | 196 | 46 | 109 | 216 |

FORE-HEAD

| | | | | | |
|---|---|---|---|---|---|
| WHAT EVER MAKES HEAVENS FORE-HEAD FINE. | THE WEEPER | 12 | 46 | 79 | 120 |

FORHEAD

| | | | | | |
|---|---|---|---|---|---|
| OR ON HEAVN'S AZURE FORHEAD HIGH TO STAND | IN GLORIOUS EPIPHANIE | 250 | 52 | 253 | 39 |
| WHATEVER MAKES HEAVN'S FORHEAD FINE. | WEEPER | 12 | 52 | 307 | 120 |

FORLORNE

| | | | | | |
|---|---|---|---|---|---|
| LET IT NO LONGER BE A FORLORNE HOPE | ON BAPTIZED AETHIOPIAN | 1 | 46 | 85 | 29 |

FORM

| | | | | | |
|---|---|---|---|---|---|
| THAT THEY BUT LEND THEIR FORM & FACE, | LAUDA SION SALVATOREM | 33 | 52 | 294 | 178 |

FORMES

| | | | | | |
|---|---|---|---|---|---|
| IN BROKEN FORMES A STABLE FAITH | LAUDA SION SALVATOREM | 59 | 52 | 294 | 178 |

FORMIDABLE

| | | | | | |
|---|---|---|---|---|---|
| IN ANSWER TO HER FORMIDABLE NAME. | SOSPETTO D'HERODE | 304 | 46 | 109 | 216 |

## FORRAGE

| | | | | |
|---|---|---|---|---|
| AND FORRAGE IN THE FIELDS OF LIGHT, AND LOVE. | ON HOPE | 76 | 46 143 | 71 |
| AND FORRAGE IN THE FIELDS OF LIGHT AND LOVE. | (ON) HOPE | 36 | 52 345 | 71 |

## FORSAKE

| | | | | |
|---|---|---|---|---|
| TILL THE FLEDG'D NOTES AT LENGTH FORSAKE THEIR NEST. | MUSICKS DUELL | 90 | 46 149 | 535 |

## FORSAKEN

| | | | | |
|---|---|---|---|---|
| LIFES LATE FORSAKEN HOUSES ALL LAY DROWN'D | THE BEGINNING OF HELIODORUS | 16 | 46 158 | 517 |
| OF HIS BEST FRIENDS (YEA OF HIMSELF) FORSAKEN. | OFFICE H. CROSS MATINES | 16 | 52 265 | 86 |

## FORSOOTH

| | | | | |
|---|---|---|---|---|
| PALLAS BEARES ARMES, FORSOOTH, AND SHOULD THERE BE | ALEXIAS THIRD ELEGIE | 39 | 52 336 | 209 |

## FORSWEARING

| | | | | |
|---|---|---|---|---|
| FLATTERING BUT FORSWEARING EYES | ON A PRAYER BOOKE | 53 | 46 126 | 139 |
| FLATTERING BUT FORSWEARING EYES. | PRAYER TO GENTLE-WOMAN | 59 | 52 328 | 139 |

## FORT

| | | | | |
|---|---|---|---|---|
| THE FORT AT LAST, AND LET LIFE IN. | TO COUNTESSE OF DENBIGH | 64 | 52 236 | 146 |
| THIS FORT OF YOUR FAIR SELFE, IF'T BE NOT WON, | TO COUNTESSE OF DENBIGH | 67 | 52 236 | 146 |
| THE FORT AT LAST, AND LET LIFE IN. | AGAINST IRRESOLUTION AND DELAY | 86 | 52 347 | 146 |
| THIS FORT OF YOUR FAIR SELF IF'T BE NOT WONE. | AGAINST IRRESOLUTION AND DELAY | 89 | 52 347 | 146 |

## FORTH

| | | | | |
|---|---|---|---|---|
| (QUICK WITH WARME ZEPHIRES LIVELY BREATH) LAY FORTH | OUT OF VIRGIL | 13 | 46 155 | 529 |
| THIS ROCKE BUDS FORTH THE FOUNTAINE OF THE STREAMES OF DAY. | EASTER DAY | 9 | 46 100 | 26 |
| MUSTER FORTH INTO THE VALLEY, | PSALME 23 | 36 | 46 102 | 5 |
| GAVE FORTH YOUR BLOOD FOR BREATH, SPOKE SOULES FOR WORDS. | SOSPETTO D'HERODE | 8 | 46 109 | 216 |
| THAT NEITHER ROME, NOR ATHENS CAN BRING FORTH | SOSPETTO D'HERODE | 27 | 46 109 | 216 |
| DARKE, DUSTY MAN, HE NEEDS WOULD SINGLE FORTH. | SOSPETTO D'HERODE | 217 | 46 109 | 216 |
| WHEN 'GAINST THE THUNDERS MOUTH WEE MARCHED FORTH. | SOSPETTO D'HERODE | 284 | 46 109 | 216 |
| PEEPT FORTH FROM THEIR FIRST BLUSHES. SO THAT NOW | UPON DEATH OF HERRYS | 24 | 46 167 | 466 |
| IN HIM PERFECTION DID SET FORTH. | HIS EPITAPH (HERRYS) | 13 | 46 172 | 471 |
| AT EACH CURNER PEEPING FORTH, | HIS EPITAPH (HERRYS) | 38 | 46 172 | 471 |
| (DREST IN THOSE BEAMES) START FORTH | OUT OF THE ITALIAN (2) | 9 | 46 190 | 547 |
| OF STUDIED FATE STAND FORTH, | WISHES SUPPOSED MISTRESSE | 8 | 46 195 | 479 |
| OF YOUR BRAVE SOUL SO SLOWLY FORTH. | TO COUNTESSE OF DENBIGH | 8 | 52 236 | 146 |
| COME, LOVELY NAME. APPEARE FROM FORTH THE BRIGHT | TO THE NAME OF JESUS | 115 | 52 239 | 30 |
| AND AT THY FEET POWR FORTH HIS FACE. | IN GLORIOUS EPIPHANIE | 84 | 52 253 | 39 |
| COME FORTH GREAT MASTER OF THE MYSTICK DAY. | IN GLORIOUS EPIPHANIE | 207 | 52 253 | 39 |
| AND MY MOUTH SHALL SHEW FORTH THY PRAYSE. | OFFICE H. CROSS MATINES | 4 | 52 265 | 86 |
| PALE MANKIND FORTH TO MEET HIS KING. | DIES IRAE | 12 | 52 298 | 186 |
| OF YOUR BRAVE SOUL SO SLOWLY FORTH. | AGAINST IRRESOLUTION AND DELAY | 16 | 52 347 | 146 |
| LEAST IT BREAKE FORTH, & BURNE THY SOOTY CELL. | ON GUNPOWDER-TREASON | 66 | MS 384 | 458 |
| NOT DARING TO PEEPE FORTH, LEAST THAT A STONE | UPON GUNPOWDER TREASON | 25 | MS 386 | 460 |
| EACH HOLDING FORTH TO LIGHT THE AERY BRAND. | UPON GUNPOWDER TREASON | 14 | MS 387 | 461 |
| SOUND FORTH, CAELESTIALL ORGANS,LETT HEAVNS QUIRE | UPON KINGS CORONATION | 1 | MS 389 | 454 |
| SHINE FORTH,YE FLAMING SPARKES OF DEITY. | UPON KINGS CORONATION | 37 | MS 389 | 454 |
| AS TO REFRAINE) BROUGHT FORTH A COSTLY SHOWER | UPON KINGS CORONATION | 6 | MS 390 | 453 |
| HAD YOU BUT DRAWNE ONE LIVELY COPPY FORTH, | UPON BIRTH PRINCESSE E | 29 | MS 391 | 456 |
| TO SHADDOW FORTH TH' ADMIRED PARAGON. | UPON BIRTH PRINCESSE E | 42 | MS 391 | 456 |
| GOE ON THEN, HEAVEN, & LIMBE FORTH SUCH ANOTHER, | UPON BIRTH PRINCESSE E | 55 | MS 391 | 456 |
| AND SETT IT FORTH IN THE SAME HAPPY PLACE. | UPON BIRTH PRINCESSE E | 59 | MS 391 | 456 |
| AND MURMUR FORTH THY WOES TO EVERY FLOWER, | AN ELEGIE ON DR PORTER | 21 | MS 395 | 476 |

## FORTHWITH

| | | | | |
|---|---|---|---|---|
| FORTHWITH EACH GOD STEPT FROM HIS STARRY THRONE. | UPON GUNPOWDER TREASON | 53 | MS 387 | 461 |

## FORTIFY

| | | | | |
|---|---|---|---|---|
| AND FORTIFY THE HOLD OF YOUR CHAST HEART. | PRAYER TO GENTLE-WOMAN | 20 | 52 328 | 139 |

## FORTIFIE

| | | | | |
|---|---|---|---|---|
| AND FORTIFIE THE HOLD OF YOUR CHAST HEART. | ON A PRAYER BOOKE | 14 | 46 126 | 139 |

## FORTRESSE

| | | | | |
|---|---|---|---|---|
| AS FROM A SNOWY FORTRESSE OF DEFENCE | ON A PRAYER BOOKE | 12 | 46 126 | 139 |
| AS FROM A SNOWY FORTRESSE OF DEFENCE. | PRAYER TO GENTLE-WOMAN | 18 | 52 328 | 139 |
| NO FORTRESSE BUILT FOR TRUE VIRGINITY. | ALEXIAS THIRD ELEGIE | 40 | 52 336 | 209 |

## FORTUNATE

| | | | | |
|---|---|---|---|---|
| O FAIRE, O FORTUNATE, O RICH, O DEARE. | ON A PRAYER BOOKE | 90 | 46 126 | 139 |
| OF WORST FAULTS TO BE FORTUNATE. | FLAMING HEART | 60 | 52 324 | 61 |
| O FAIR, O FORTUNATE, O RICHE, O DEAR. | PRAYER TO GENTLE-WOMAN | 96 | 52 328 | 139 |
| AND SHEE'S AN ISLAND TRUELY FORTUNATE. | ON GUNPOWDER-TREASON | 10 | MS 384 | 458 |

## FORTUNE

| | | | | | |
|---|---|---|---|---|---|
| FORTUNE ALAS ABOVE THE WORLDS LAW WARRES. | ON HOPE | 71 | 46 | 143 | 71 |
| SO FALSE A FORTUNE, AND SO TRUE A LOVE. | UPON FAIRE ETHIOPIAN | 2 | 46 | 183 | 493 |
| THE FORTUNE OF INFERIOR GEMMES, | WEEPER | 182 | 52 | 307 | 120 |
| MY FORTUNE TRY | TO SAME CONCERNING CHOISE | 5 | 52 | 331 | 66 |
| FORTUNE, ALAS, ABOVE THE WORLD'S LOW WARRES | (ON) HOPE | 31 | 52 | 345 | 71 |
| HER LOVES CROSSE FORTUNE, THAT THE SAD DISPUTE | HORATIJ ILLE & NEFASTO | 40 | MS | 382 | 530 |

## FORTUNE'S

| | | | | | |
|---|---|---|---|---|---|
| FORTUNE'S WHOLE LOTTERY IS ONE BLANK TO HER. | (ON) HOPE | 34 | 52 | 345 | 71 |

## FORTUNE-BOOKE

| | | | | | |
|---|---|---|---|---|---|
| BEAUTY LAYES OPE LOVES FORTUNE-BOOKE. | LOVES HOROSCOPE | 12 | 46 | 185 | 483 |

## FORTUNES

| | | | | | |
|---|---|---|---|---|---|
| AND MY BEST FORTUNES SUCH FAIR SPOILES OF ME. | FLAMING HEART | 92 | 52 | 324 | 61 |

## FORWARD

| | | | | | |
|---|---|---|---|---|---|
| STILL KEEPING IN THE FORWARD STREAME, SO LONG | MUSICKS DUELL | 86 | 46 | 149 | 535 |
| TO SWELL WITH FORWARD PRIDE, AND SEED DESIRE | OUT OF VIRGIL | 3 | 46 | 155 | 529 |
| BUT HASTS HER FORWARD BLOSSOMES, AND LAYES OUT | OUT OF VIRGIL | 21 | 46 | 155 | 529 |
| A PLANT OF NOBLE STEMME, FORWARD AND FAIRE, | UPON DEATH OF HERRYS | 1 | 46 | 167 | 466 |
| OF HIS FORWARD FLOWER, WHEN LO | UPON DEATH OF DESIRED HERRYS | 39 | 46 | 168 | 467 |

## FROWARD

| | | | | | |
|---|---|---|---|---|---|
| WITH DAINTY CURLES HIS FROWARD FACE | OUT OF GREEKE CUPID'S CRYER | 33 | 46 | 159 | 519 |
| WAS EVER FROWARD WIND | WHY ARE YEE AFRAID | 4 | 46 | 88 | 15 |
| LET FROWARD DUST THEN DOE IT'S KIND. | CHARITAS NIMIA | 29 | 52 | 280 | 48 |

## FOUGHT

| | | | | | |
|---|---|---|---|---|---|
| FOUGHT AGAINST FROWNS WITH SMILES.   GAVE GLORIOUS CHASE | TO THE NAME OF JESUS | 199 | 52 | 239 | 30 |

## FOUL

| | | | | | |
|---|---|---|---|---|---|
| IF MY FOUL HEART CALL'D FOR A FLOUD. | CHARITAS NIMIA | 48 | 52 | 280 | 48 |

## FOULE

| | | | | | |
|---|---|---|---|---|---|
| WITH HIS FOULE CLAWES HEE FENC'D HIS FURROWED BROW, | SOSPETTO D'HERODE | 149 | 46 | 109 | 216 |
| HIS FOULE HAGS RAIS'D THEIR HEADS, & CLAPT THEIR HANDS. | SOSPETTO D'HERODE | 258 | 46 | 109 | 216 |
| FELL EXECUTIONERS OF FOULE INTENTS, | SOSPETTO D'HERODE | 324 | 46 | 109 | 216 |
| THE FOULE QUEENS MOST ABHORRED MAIDS OF HONOUR | SOSPETTO D'HERODE | 337 | 46 | 109 | 216 |
| MADE HEAVENS RADIANT FACE LOOKE FOULE. | UPON DEATH OF DESIRED HERRYS | 52 | 46 | 168 | 467 |
| SOE FOULE, ONE MINUTES LIGHT HAD IT BUT SEENE, | UPON GUNPOWDER TREASON | 13 | MS | 386 | 460 |
| AND FOULE THE CLEARE TEXT WITH A MUDDY GLOSSE. | UPON BIRTH PRINCESSE E | 54 | MS | 391 | 456 |

## FOULE-MOUTH'D

| | | | | | |
|---|---|---|---|---|---|
| THAT FEARES THE FOULE-MOUTH'D AUSTER, OR THOSE STORMES | OUT OF VIRGIL | 19 | 46 | 155 | 529 |

## FOWLER

| | | | | | |
|---|---|---|---|---|---|
| TO SEE SOME FOWLER THAN HERSELFE) THESE STAND, | UPON GUNPOWDER TREASON | 13 | MS | 387 | 461 |

## FOUND

| | | | | | |
|---|---|---|---|---|---|
| FOUND THE PURE ISSUE OF HIS THOUGHT. | OUT OF GREEKE CUPID'S CRYER | 24 | 46 | 159 | 519 |
| SHEE FOUND THE WAY HOME, WITH AN HOLY STRENGTH | UPON BISHOP ANDREWES PICTURE | 8 | 46 | 163 | 490 |
| THE VERY TERME, I THINK, WAS FOUND | THE TEARE | 5 | 46 | 84 | 50 |
| O NEVER COULD BEE FOUND GARMENTS TOO GOOD | ON CRUCIFIED LORD BLOODY | 46 | 46 | 100 | 24 |
| DEARE LORD TO THEE) TO US IS FOUND | ON BLEEDING WOUNDS OF LORD | 38 | 46 | 101 | 110 |
| WHILE WE FOUND OUT THE FAIR-EY'D BOY, | A HYMNE OF THE NATIVITY | 7 | 46 | 106 | 76 |
| COULD HAVE BEEN FOUND 'TWOULD HAVE BEEN READ, | ANOTHER ON HERRYS | 49 | 46 | 170 | 469 |
| HERE AT LENGTH, HATH GLADLY FOUND | AN EPITAPH DOCTOR BROOKE | 5 | 46 | 175 | 465 |
| THE YEARE HAD FOUND SOME FRUIT EARLY AS YOU. | UPON TWO GREENE APRICOCKES | 12 | 46 | 220 | 494 |
| WHILE WE FOUND OUT HEAVN'S FAIRER EY | IN HOLY NATIVITY | 7 | 52 | 246 | 76 |
| LO AT LAST HAVE FOUND OUR WAY. | IN GLORIOUS EPIPHANIE | 21 | 52 | 253 | 39 |
| LO WE AT LAST HAVE FOUND THE WAY. | IN GLORIOUS EPIPHANIE | 23 | 52 | 253 | 39 |
| THE CAPTIVE WORLD AWAK'T, & FOUND | OFFICE H. CROSS THIRD | 14 | 52 | 268 | 93 |
| DEAR LORD TO THEE, TO US IS FOUND | UPON BLEEDING CRUCIFIX | 34 | 52 | 288 | 110 |
| THOSE MERCYES WHICH THY MARY FOUND | DIES IRAE | 49 | 52 | 298 | 186 |
| AND ALL THY LOST SHEEP FOUND SHALL BE. | DIES IRAE | 59 | 52 | 298 | 186 |
| THE FOUNTAIN SEALD, YET LIFE FOUND WAY. | O GLORIOSA DOMINA | 36 | 52 | 302 | 194 |
| THAT COULD BE FOUND SERAPHICALL. | FLAMING HEART | 30 | 52 | 324 | 61 |
| FOR IN LOVE'S FEILD WAS NEVER FOUND | FLAMING HEART | 71 | 52 | 324 | 61 |
| HERE'T WAS THE ROMAN MAID FOUND A HARD FATE | ALEXIAS FIRST ELEGIE | 29 | 52 | 334 | 204 |
| THERE THY LOST FUGITIVE THOU'HAST FOUND AT LAST. | ALEXIAS FIRST ELEGIE | 37 | 52 | 334 | 204 |
| HIS HANDS HAVE PADLED IN. HIS HANDS, THAT FOUND | HORATIJ ILLE & NEFASTO | 13 | MS | 382 | 530 |
| WHAT MORE THAN WINTER HATH THAT DIRE ART FOUND, | AN ELEGY MR STANNINOW | 21 | MS | 394 | 473 |

## FOUNDED

| | | | | | |
|---|---|---|---|---|---|
| FOUNDED TO TH' NAME OF GREAT APOLLO'S LYRE. | MUSICKS DUELL | 74 | 46 | 149 | 535 |

FOUNT

| | | | | | |
|---|---|---|---|---|---|
| BY A BLACK FOUNT, WHICH WEEPS INTO A FLOOD. | SOSPETTO D'HERODE | 349 | 46 | 109 | 216 |

FOUNTS

| | | | | | |
|---|---|---|---|---|---|
| FLOW. TARDY FOUNTS. & INTO DECENT SHOWRES | SANCTA MARIA DOLORUM | 87 | 52 | 283 | 162 |

FONTS

| | | | | | |
|---|---|---|---|---|---|
| NOR LET THE MILKY FONTS THAT BATH YOUR THIRST, | TO INFANT MARTYRS | 3 | 46 | 88 | 10 |

FOUNTAIN

| | | | | | |
|---|---|---|---|---|---|
| THE DOOR WAS SHUTT, THE FOUNTAIN SEAL'D. | O GLORIOSA DOMINA | 33 | 52 | 302 | 194 |
| THE FOUNTAIN SEALD, YET LIFE FOUND WAY. | O GLORIOSA DOMINA | 36 | 52 | 302 | 194 |
| FOUNTAIN & GARDEN IN ONE FACE. | WEEPER | 90 | 52 | 307 | 120 |
| STILL THE FOUNTAIN WEEPS FOR ALL. | WEEPER | 136 | 52 | 307 | 120 |

FOUNTAINE

| | | | | | |
|---|---|---|---|---|---|
| STILL THE FOUNTAINE WEEPS FOR ALL. | THE WEEPER | 112 | 46 | 79 | 120 |
| MUST HAVE ITS FOUNTAINE IN THINE EYES. | TO PONTIUS WASHING HANDS | 4 | 46 | 88 | 22 |
| THE DAUGHTER OF A FAIRE AND WELL-FAM'D FOUNTAINE | TO PONTIUS WASHING HANDS | 7 | 46 | 94 | 23 |
| THIS ROCKE BUDS FORTH THE FOUNTAINE OF THE STREAMES OF DAY. | EASTER DAY | 9 | 46 | 100 | 26 |
| WEEPING, MELTS INTO A FOUNTAINE, | PSALME 23 | 14 | 46 | 102 | 5 |

FOUNTAINS

| | | | | | |
|---|---|---|---|---|---|
| THE FOUNTAINS MURMUR. & EACH LOFTYEST TREE | IN GLORIOUS ASSUMPTION B. LADY | 29 | 52 | 304 | 114 |

FOUNTAINES

| | | | | | |
|---|---|---|---|---|---|
| OF FAIRE ENGADDI HONY-SWEATING FOUNTAINES | SOSPETTO D'HERODE | 111 | 46 | 109 | 216 |
| HE'S FOLLOW'D BY TWO FAITHFULL FOUNTAINES. | WEEPER | 112 | 52 | 307 | 120 |
| LEAVING THOSE MINES OF NECTAR, THEIR SWEET FOUNTAINES, | AN ELEGIE ON DR PORTER | 41 | MS | 395 | 476 |

FOURE

| | | | | | |
|---|---|---|---|---|---|
| FOURE TEETH THOU HAD'ST THAT RANCK'D IN GOODLY STATE | OUT OF MARTIALL | 1 | 46 | 188 | 527 |

FOURTH

| | | | | | |
|---|---|---|---|---|---|
| FOURTH OF THE CURSED KNOT OF HAGS IS SHEE, | SOSPETTO D'HERODE | 289 | 46 | 109 | 216 |
| WHENCE THE FOURTH FURY, ANSWER'D PLUTO'S CALL. | SOSPETTO D'HERODE | 368 | 46 | 109 | 216 |

FOWLES

| | | | | | |
|---|---|---|---|---|---|
| AND POORE FOWLES INTERCEPTED IN THEIR FLIGHT. | SOSPETTO D'HERODE | 376 | 46 | 109 | 216 |

FOYLE

| | | | | | |
|---|---|---|---|---|---|
| RICH DIAMONDS, SETT IN A PURE SILVER FOYLE. | UPON BIRTH PRINCESSE E | 44 | MS | 391 | 456 |

FRAGRANCY

| | | | | | |
|---|---|---|---|---|---|
| AND THY NECTAREALL FRAGRANCY. | TO THE NAME OF JESUS | 174 | 52 | 239 | 30 |

FRAGRANT

| | | | | | |
|---|---|---|---|---|---|
| THEIR PREGNANT BOSOMES IN A FRAGRANT BIRTH. | OUT OF VIRGIL | 14 | 46 | 155 | 529 |
| ALL FRESH AND FRAGRANT AS HEE RISES. | ON A PRAYER BOOKE | 102 | 46 | 126 | 139 |
| HIM WHILE FRESH AND FRAGRANT TIME | HIS EPITAPH (HERRYS) | 43 | 46 | 172 | 471 |
| A FRAGRANT BREATH SUCKT FROM THE SPICY NEST | ON A FOULE MORNING | 21 | 46 | 181 | 495 |
| ALL FRESH & FRAGRANT AS HE RISES | PRAYER TO GENTLE-WOMAN | 108 | 52 | 328 | 139 |
| THE FRAGRANT SPRING MAY BE PERFUM'D WITHALL. | UPON BIRTH PRINCESSE E | 4 | MS | 391 | 456 |
| THE MUSES, & THE GRACES FRAGRANT POSIES. | AN ELEGY MR STANNINOW | 38 | MS | 394 | 473 |

FRAIL

| | | | | | |
|---|---|---|---|---|---|
| THE TOO FRAIL LIFE OF FEMAL CONSTANCY. | ALEXIAS FIRST ELEGIE | 34 | 52 | 334 | 204 |

FRAILE

| | | | | | |
|---|---|---|---|---|---|
| AND LIFE SELFE IT WEARE DEATHS FRAILE LIVERY. | SOSPETTO D'HERODE | 168 | 46 | 109 | 216 |

FRAME

| | | | | | |
|---|---|---|---|---|---|
| THIS IS HEE IN WHOSE RARE FRAME, | UPON DEATH OF DESIRED HERRYS | 5 | 46 | 168 | 467 |
| IN HER WHOLE FRAME. | WISHES SUPPOSED MISTRESSE | 97 | 46 | 195 | 479 |
| WHY MAN, THIS SPEAKES PURE MORTALL FRAME. | FLAMING HEART | 23 | 52 | 324 | 61 |

FANCY-FRAMED

| | | | | | |
|---|---|---|---|---|---|
| HEE HIS OWNE FANCY-FRAMED FOES DEFIES. | SOSPETTO D'HERODE | 479 | 46 | 109 | 216 |

FRAMES

| | | | | | |
|---|---|---|---|---|---|
| WHAT EVER SCHEMES OF BLOOD, FANTASTICK FRAMES | SOSPETTO D'HERODE | 361 | 46 | 109 | 216 |

## FRANKINCENSE

| | | | | |
|---|---|---|---|---|
| A THOUSAND HILLS OF FRANKINCENSE. | TO THE NAME OF JESUS | 185 | 52 239 | 30 |

## FRANKINCENCE

| | | | | |
|---|---|---|---|---|
| HIS GOLD, HIS MIRRH, HIS FRANKINCENCE. | IN GLORIOUS EPIPHANIE | 244 | 52 253 | 39 |

## FRAUD

| | | | | |
|---|---|---|---|---|
| AND FRAUD. HEE MAKES POORE MORTALLS HURTS, | OUT OF GREEKE CUPID'S CRYER | 31 | 46 159 | 519 |
| WHAT FORCE CANNOT EFFECT, FRAUD SHALL DEVISE. | SOSPETTO D'HERODE | 248 | 46 109 | 216 |

## FRAUGHT

| | | | | |
|---|---|---|---|---|
| (FRAUGHT WITH A FURY SO HARMONIOUS) | MUSICKS DUELL | 134 | 46 149 | 535 |
| AND BRING HIS BOSOM FRAUGHT WITH BLESSINGS, | PRAYER TO GENTLE-WOMAN | 41 | 52 328 | 139 |

## FREE

| | | | | |
|---|---|---|---|---|
| WARME THOUGHTS FREE SPIRITS, FLATTERING | IN PRAISE OF LESSIUS | 43 | 46 156 | 510 |
| WHOSE FAIRE ILLUSTRIOUS SOULE, LED HIS FREE THOUGHT | UPON BISHOP ANDREWES PICTURE | 5 | 46 163 | 490 |
| IT DROPS THOUGH BOUND, THOUGH BOUND 'TIS FREE. | ON BLEEDING WOUNDS OF LORD | 12 | 46 101 | 110 |
| AND FREE ETERNITY, SUBMIT TO YEARES. | SOSPETTO D'HERODE | 184 | 46 109 | 216 |
| MASTER (WITH VOYCE FREE AS THE TRUMPE OF FAME) | SOSPETTO D'HERODE | 439 | 46 109 | 216 |
| OUR FREE TRAFICK FOR HEAVEN, WE MAY MAINTAINE. | AN APOLOGIE FOR HYMNE (TERESA) | 19 | 46 136 | 59 |
| IN BRIEFE, IF ANY ONE WERE FREE. | ANOTHER ON HERRYS | 53 | 46 170 | 469 |
| FULL GLORY, FLAMING IN HER OWNE FREE SPHEARE. | ON A FOULE MORNING | 8 | 46 181 | 495 |
| IN FREE AYRE, | OUT OF THE ITALIAN (1) | 7 | 46 188 | 545 |
| KEEP THE FREE HEART FROM IT'S OWN HANDS. | TO COUNTESSE OF DENBIGH | 20 | 52 236 | 146 |
| IT GIVES THOUGH BOUND. THOUGH BOUND 'TIS FREE. | UPON BLEEDING CRUCIFIX | 16 | 52 288 | 110 |
| OUR FREE TRAFFIQUE FOR HEAV'N, WE MAY MAINTAINE | AN APOLOGIE FOR (TERESA) HYMNE | 19 | 52 322 | 59 |
| WARM THOUGHTS, FREE SPIRITS FLATTERING | TEMPERANCE | 41 | 52 342 | 510 |
| KEEP THE FREE HEART FROM HIS OWN HANDS. | AGAINST IRRESOLUTION AND DELAY | 14 | 52 347 | 146 |
| FULL GLORY FLAMING IN HER OWNE FREE SPHAERE. | UPON KINGS CORONATION | 14 | MS 390 | 453 |

## FREELY

| | | | | |
|---|---|---|---|---|
| FREELY LAYES OUT HER LEAVES. NOR DOE I DOUBT | OUT OF VIRGIL | 22 | 46 155 | 529 |
| MORE FREELY TO TRANSPIRE | TO THE NAME OF JESUS | 213 | 52 239 | 30 |

## FREQUENT

| | | | | |
|---|---|---|---|---|
| BUT IF IT BE THE FREQUENT FATE | FLAMING HEART | 59 | 52 324 | 61 |

## FRESH

| | | | | |
|---|---|---|---|---|
| WOULDST SEE BLITH LOOKES, FRESH CHEEKES BEGUILE | IN PRAISE OF LESSIUS | 39 | 46 156 | 510 |
| THOSE YET FRESH STREAMES WHICH CRAWLED EVERY WHERE | THE BEGINNING OF HELIODORUS | 21 | 46 156 | 517 |
| RISE, HEIRE OF FRESH ETERNITY, | EASTER DAY | 1 | 46 100 | 26 |
| FRESH FROM THE PURE GLANCE OF THINE EYE. | PSALME 23 | 65 | 46 102 | 5 |
| ALL FRESH AND FRAGRANT AS HEE RISES, | ON A PRAYER BOOKE | 102 | 46 126 | 139 |
| FRESH FROM THE ROSIE EAST REJOYC'T TO PLAY. | UPON DEATH OF HERRYS | 16 | 46 167 | 466 |
| ALL HIS LEAVES, SO FRESH, SO SWEET, | UPON DEATH OF DESIRED HERRYS | 45 | 46 168 | 467 |
| THE FRESH HOPES OF HIS LOVELY YOUTH, | ANOTHER ON HERRYS | 13 | 46 170 | 469 |
| HIM WHILE FRESH AND FRAGRANT TIME | HIS EPITAPH (HERRYS) | 43 | 46 172 | 471 |
| NOT ON THE FRESH CHEEKES OF THE VIRGIN MORNE, | ON A FOULE MORNING | 35 | 46 181 | 495 |
| AGAINE A FRESH CHILD OF THE BUXOME MORNE, | TO THE MORNING | 52 | 46 183 | 497 |
| GIVES HIM THE MORNING WORLDS FRESH GOLD AGAINE. | UPON TWO GREENE APRICOCKES | 18 | 48 220 | 494 |
| TAKING FRESH LIFE FROM YOUR FAYRE EYES. | THOUGH NOW 'TIS NEITHER | 10 | MS 397 | 492 |
| ALL FRESH & FRAGRANT AS HE RISES | PRAYER TO GENTLE-WOMAN | 108 | 52 328 | 139 |
| WOULDST' SEE BLITH LOOKES, FRESH CHEEKES BEGUIL | TEMPERANCE | 37 | 52 342 | 510 |
| THE FRESH FACE OF THE MORNE HAD BLASTED BEENE. | UPON GUNPOWDER TREASON | 14 | MS 386 | 460 |
| THE ROSES FRESH, CONSERVED FROM THE RAGE, | UPON GUNPOWDER TREASON | 43 | MS 387 | 461 |
| THAT FETCHETH FRESH LIFE FROM HER FRUITFULL URNE. | EX EUPHORMIONE | 16 | MS 392 | 525 |
| ARE TEEMING NOW WITH STORE OF FRESH SUPPLIES. | AN ELEGIE ON DR PORTER | 44 | MS 395 | 476 |

## FRET

| | | | | |
|---|---|---|---|---|
| THERE RUDE IMPETUOUS RAGE DO'S STORME, AND FRET. | SOSPETTO D'HERODE | 317 | 46 109 | 216 |

## FRETS

| | | | | |
|---|---|---|---|---|
| TH'IMPATIENT LIQUOR, FRETS, AND FOAMES, AND RAVES. | SOSPETTO D'HERODE | 486 | 46 109 | 216 |

## FRIEND

| | | | | |
|---|---|---|---|---|
| THEIR GENTLEST FRIEND, THEN, THEN THE LANDS BEGIN | OUT OF VIRGIL | 2 | 46 155 | 529 |
| THOU WATER TURN'ST TO WINE (FAIRE FRIEND OF LIFE) | TO LORD UPON WATER MADE WINE | 1 | 46 91 | 12 |
| HERE IS A FRIEND SHALL FIGHT FOR YOU, | ON A PRAYER BOOKE | 26 | 46 126 | 139 |
| WHOSE DROWSINESSE HATH WRONG'D THE MUSES FRIEND. | TO THE MORNING | 2 | 46 183 | 497 |
| AND WHEN IT COMES SAY WELCOME FRIEND. | WISHES SUPPOSED MISTRESSE | 87 | 46 195 | 479 |
| TO BE CHASTIS'D (SWEET FRIEND) AND CHIDD BY THEE. | UPON TWO GREENE APRICOCKES | 2 | 48 220 | 494 |

## FREIND

| | | | | |
|---|---|---|---|---|
| O FAITHFULL FREIND | SANCTA MARIA DOLORUM | 105 | 52 283 | 162 |
| MY HOPE, MY FEAR, MY JUDGE, MY FREIND. | DIES IRAE | 67 | 52 296 | 186 |
| HERE IS A FREIND SHALL FIGHT FOR YOU. | PRAYER TO GENTLE-WOMAN | 32 | 52 328 | 139 |
| SLY, LURKING TREASON IS HIS BOSOME FREIND. | UPON GUNPOWDER TREASON | 17 | MS 387 | 461 |
| TO FREIND THE LIVING WORLD EVEN DEATH DID SEE | OUT OF GROTIUS | 82 | MS 398 | 198 |

## FRIENDS

| | | | | |
|---|---|---|---|---|
| ANGELLS THY OLD FRIENDS THERE SHALL GREET THEE, | IN MEMORY OF LADY MADRE TERESA | 138 | 46 131 | 52 |
| BOTH WILL BE GOOD FRIENDS TOGETHER. | OUT OF THE ITALIAN (1) | 30 | 46 188 | 545 |
| OF HIS BEST FRIENDS (YEA OF HIMSELF) FORSAKEN, | OFFICE H. CROSS MATINES | 16 | 52 265 | 86 |
| MIXT & MADE FRIENDS BY LOVE'S SWEET POWRES. | WEEPER | 102 | 52 307 | 120 |
| ALL THINGS SWEAR FRIENDS TO FAIR AND GOOD. | AGAINST IRRESOLUTION AND DELAY | 57 | 52 347 | 146 |

## FREINDS

| | | | | |
|---|---|---|---|---|
| WHEN THY OLD FREINDS OF FIRE, ALL FULL OF THEE, | TO THE NAME OF JESUS | 198 | 52 239 | 30 |
| WHO TORE THE FAIR BRESTS OF THY FREINDS. | TO THE NAME OF JESUS | 208 | 52 239 | 30 |
| FREINDS WITH THE BOSOM FIRES THAT FILL THEE | WEEPER | 98 | 52 307 | 120 |
| ANGELS, THY OLD FREINDS, THERE SHALL GREET THEE | TERESA | 137 | 52 315 | 52 |
| WELL MEANING READERS. YOU THAT COME AS FREINDS | FLAMING HEART | 1 | 52 324 | 61 |
| SOUL & BODY PART LIKE FREINDS. | TEMPERANCE | 48 | 52 342 | 510 |

## FREINDLY

| | | | | |
|---|---|---|---|---|
| O FAIR, & FREINDLY FOES, | WEEPER | 93 | 52 307 | 120 |
| SOULS ARE NOT SPANIARDS TOO, ONE FREINDLY FLOUD | AN APOLOGIE FOR (TERESA) HYMNE | 15 | 52 322 | 59 |

## FRENDLY

| | | | | |
|---|---|---|---|---|
| SOULES ARE NOT SPANIARDS TOO, ONE FRENDLY FLOOD | AN APOLOGIE FOR HYMNE (TERESA) | 15 | 46 136 | 59 |

## FRIGHT

| | | | | |
|---|---|---|---|---|
| IS SHEE TO NATURE, THAT A GENERALL FRIGHT, | SOSPETTO D'HERODE | 381 | 46 109 | 216 |
| SO SHALL THEY, BY THE SEASONABLE FRIGHT | IN GLORIOUS EPIPHANIE | 165 | 52 253 | 39 |
| AND GREISLY VISAGES DOE FRIGHT THE AIRE. | UPON GUNPOWDER TREASON | 10 | MS 387 | 461 |

## FRIGHTED

| | | | | |
|---|---|---|---|---|
| THE SWEET-LIP'T SISTERS MUSICALLY FRIGHTED, | MUSICKS DUELL | 113 | 46 149 | 535 |
| HARKE HOW SHE BIDS HER FRIGHTED DROPS MAKE HAST, | TO PONTIUS WASHING HANDS | 13 | 46 94 | 23 |
| THE FRIGHTED STARS TOOKE FAINT EXPERIENCE, | SOSPETTO D'HERODE | 283 | 46 109 | 216 |
| SUCH TO THE FRIGHTED PALACE NOW SHEE COMES. | SOSPETTO D'HERODE | 399 | 46 109 | 216 |
| NO LONGER SHALL OUR CHURCHES FRIGHTED STONES | ON A TREATISE OF CHARITY | 31 | 46 137 | 69 |
| SHOULD HAVE HIS SOULE FRIGHTED BEYOND THE SPHAERES. | UPON GUNPOWDER TREASON | 10 | MS 386 | 460 |

## FRISKE

| | | | | |
|---|---|---|---|---|
| AND FRISKE IN CURL'D MAEANDERS. HEE WILL THROW | ON A FOULE MORNING | 20 | 46 181 | 495 |

## FRISKING

| | | | | |
|---|---|---|---|---|
| HALLS FULL OF FLATTERING MEN & FRISKING BOYES. | DESCRIPTION RELIGIOUS HOUSE | 6 | 52 338 | 213 |

## FRIZLED

| | | | | |
|---|---|---|---|---|
| ARE FAN'D AND FRIZLED, IN THE WANTON AYRES | MUSICKS DUELL | 116 | 46 149 | 535 |

## FRO

| | | | | |
|---|---|---|---|---|
| RUNS TO AND FRO, COMPLAINING HIS SWEET CARES | MUSICKS DUELL | 142 | 46 149 | 535 |

## FROLICK

| | | | | |
|---|---|---|---|---|
| WHITHER AWAY SO FROLICK. WHY SO GLAD. | ON THE PRODIGALL | 2 | 46 86 | 17 |

## FRONT

| | | | | |
|---|---|---|---|---|
| UNFOLD THY FAIRE FRONT, AND THERE SHALL APPEARE | ON A FOULE MORNING | 7 | 46 181 | 495 |
| THE MODEST FRONT OF THIS SMALL FLOORE | AN EPITAPH UPON ASHTON | 1 | 46 192 | 464 |
| AND SAY THAT IVORY HER FRONT COMPOSES. | UPON BIRTH PRINCESSE E | 46 | MS 391 | 456 |

## FRONTS

| | | | | |
|---|---|---|---|---|
| THOSE DURTY SMUTCHES, WHICH THEIR FAIRE FRONTS WORE, | AN ELEGY MR STANNINOW | 13 | MS 394 | 473 |

## FROST

| | | | | |
|---|---|---|---|---|
| NOR SIRIAN FLAME, NOR BOREAN FROST DEFLOWERS. | SOSPETTO D'HERODE | 21 | 46 109 | 216 |
| WHERE HE MEAN'T FROST, HE SCATTER'D FLOWRS. | IN HOLY NATIVITY | 29 | 52 246 | 76 |
| 'TWIXT SPRING & FROST, | IN GLORIOUS EPIPHANIE | 33 | 52 253 | 39 |
| AND MOCKES WITH FEMALE FROST LOVE'S MANLY FLAME. | FLAMING HEART | 24 | 52 324 | 61 |

## FROST-BOUNT

| | | | | |
|---|---|---|---|---|
| OF TH'ICY NORTH, FROM FROST-BOUNT ATLAS HANDS | SOSPETTO D'HERODE | 106 | 46 109 | 216 |

## FROSTS

| | | | | |
|---|---|---|---|---|
| WHERE HE MEANT FROSTS, HE SCATTERED FLOWERS. | A HYMNE OF THE NATIVITY | 28 | 46 106 | 76 |

## FROSTY

| | | | | |
|---|---|---|---|---|
| AND CRUELL RAVISHING OF FROSTY AGE, | UPON GUNPOWDER TREASON | 44 | MS 387 | 461 |
| AND TOO UNGENTLE NIPPE OF FROSTY AGE. | AN ELEGY MR STANNINOW | 34 | MS 394 | 473 |

FROTH

OF FROTH & BUBBLES, WHAT TO LOOK FOR HERE.                TO SAME CONCERNING CHOISE           9   52  331   66

FROWN

O WHEN THY LAST FROWN SHALL PROCLAIM                       DIES IRAE                          57   52  298  186

FROWN'D

AND MAKE THEM LAUGH, WHICH FROWN'D, & WEPT BEFORE.         AN ELEGY MR STANNINOW              14   MS  394  473

FROWNE

FROWNE I. AND CAN GREAT NATURE KEEP HER SEAT.              SOSPETTO D'HERODE                 205   46  109  216
FIXT HIS FOREHEAD TO A FROWNE,)                            LOVES HOROSCOPE                    38   46  185  483

FROWNS

FOUGHT AGAINST FROWNS WITH SMILES.   GAVE GLORIOUS         TO THE NAME OF JESUS              199   52  239   30
                                     CHASE


FROWNES

BEAUTY FROWNES, AND LOVE MUST DYE.                         LOVES HOROSCOPE                    32   46  185  483

FROZEN

TO FROZEN CAUCASUS HIS FLIGHT NOW TANE.                    AN ELEGY MR STANNINOW               2   MS  394  473
'TWAS NOT THE FROZEN ZONE. ONE SPARKE OF FIRE.             AN ELEGY MR STANNINOW              31   MS  394  473

FRUGALL

BY THE FRUGALL NEGATIVE LIGHT                              IN GLORIOUS EPIPHANIE             209   52  253   39

FRUIT

NOR NEED WEE KILL THY FRUIT TO SMELL THY FLOWER.           ON HOPE                            54   46  143   71
THE YEARE HAD FOUND SOME FRUIT EARLY AS YOU.               UPON TWO GREENE APRICOCKES         12   48  220  494
WHOSE FRUIT AND BLOSSOMS BOTH BLESSE THE SAME BOUGH.       UPON TWO GREENE APRICOCKES         20   48  220  494
NO FRUIT SHOULD HAVE THE FACE TO SMILE ON THEE             UPON TWO GREENE APRICOCKES         25   48  220  494
WHOSE FRUIT WE BE.                                         OFFICE H. CROSS MATINES            19   52  265   86
FOR FRUIT OF SORROW & OF SHAME,                            OFFICE H. CROSS SIXT                6   52  270   97
'TWIST DEATH'S & LOVE'S FARR DIFFERENT FRUIT.              OFFICE H. CROSS SIXT               14   52  270   97
GATHER NOW THY GREIF'S RIPE FRUIT. GREAT MOTHER-MAID.      OFFICE H. CROSS EVENSONG            7   52  273  101
ALOFT. AND FILL THE NATIONS WITH THY NOBLE FRUIT.          VEXILLA REGIS                      38   52  277  156
HAD NOT A BETTER FRUIT FORBIDDEN IT.                       O GLORIOSA DOMINA                  17   52  302  194
NOR DOES IT KILL THY FRUIT, TO SMELL THY FLOWRE.           (ON) HOPE                          24   52  345   71
NOW THAT HIS ROOT SUCH FRUIT AGAINE MAY BEARE,             AN ELEGY MR STANNINOW              55   MS  394  473

FRUITS

TO THEE THESE FIRST FRUITS OF MY GROWING DEATH             OUR LORD IN HIS CIRCUMCISION        1   46   98    9
THOSE RARE FRUITS DANGLED, WHENCE THE GOLDEN YEARE         UPON DEATH OF HERRYS               28   46  167  466
BLOSSOMS. BUT OUR BLEST TAST CONFESSES FRUITS.             UPON TWO GREENE APRICOCKES         14   48  220  494
MARK WITH WHAT FAITH FRUITS ANSWER FLOWERS.                AGAINST IRRESOLUTION AND DELAY     33   52  347  146

FIRST-FRUITS

FAIR FIRST-FRUITS OF THE LAMB.  SURE KINGS IN THIS.        TO THE QUEEN'S MAJESTY              7   52  261   47

FRUITES

POORE FRUITES LOOKE PALE AT THY HESPERIDES.                UPON TWO GREENE APRICOCKES         30   48  220  494

FRUITFULL

HIMSELFE INTO HER LAP IN FRUITFULL SHOWERS.                OUT OF VIRGIL                       6   46  155  529
HALFE SO FRUITFULL, HALFE SO FLOWING.                      ON BLEEDING WOUNDS OF LORD         16   46  101  110
SHALL BLESSE THE FRUITFULL MAJA'S BED.                     A HYMNE OF THE NATIVITY            78   46  106   76
MADE FRUITFULL THY FAIRE SOULE. GOE NOW                    IN MEMORY OF LADY MADRE TERESA    170   46  131   52
AND FRUITFULL CHARITIES FULL BREASTS (OF OLD)              ON A TREATISE OF CHARITY           55   46  137   69
BUT MUCH MORE FRUITFULL IS.  NOR DOES, AS SHEE,            UPON YORKE HIS BIRTH               84   46  176  500
RUINE A TEMPLE.  ON WHOSE FRUITFULL FALL                   ON FRONTISPIECE ISAACSONS          17   46  191  491
THAN ERE THE FRUITFULL PHOEBUS FLAMING KISSES              UPON TWO GREENE APRICOCKES          9   48  220  494
SHALL BLESSE THE FRUITFULL MAJA'S BED                      IN HOLY NATIVITY                   98   52  246   76
HALF SO FRUITFULL, HALF SO FLOWING.                        UPON BLEEDING CRUCIFIX             20   52  288  110
YOUR FRUITFULL MOTHERS.                                    WEEPER                            165   52  307  120
MADE FRUITFULL THY FAIR SOUL, GOE NOW                      TERESA                            169   52  315   52
THAT FETCHETH FRESH LIFE FROM HER FRUITFULL URNE.          EX EUPHORMIONE                     16   MS  392  525

FRUITLES

OF WHAT SHE MAY WITH FRUITLES WISHES                       TERESA                             41   52  315   52

FRUITLESSE

OF WHAT SHEE MAY WITH FRUITLESSE WISHES                    IN MEMORY OF LADY MADRE TERESA     41   46  131   52
AND LOVES MORE FIERCE, MORE FRUITLESSE FIRES ASSAY         ON HOPE                            87   46  143   71
THOUGH LOVE'S MORE FEIRCE, MORE FRUITLESSE, FIRES          (ON) HOPE                          47   52  345   71
                                       ASSAY

FRY

| | | | | |
|---|---|---|---|---|
| SHALL CHOAKE THE GAPING EARTH, WHICH THEN SHALL FRY | ON GUNPOWDER-TREASON | 25 | MS 384 | 458 |

FRYES

| | | | | |
|---|---|---|---|---|
| (HIS SHOP OF FLAMES) HEE FRYES HIMSELFE, BENEATH | SOSPETTO D'HERODE | 62 | 46 109 | 216 |

FUGITIVE

| | | | | |
|---|---|---|---|---|
| HER LITTLE FUGITIVE DISCOVER. | OUT OF GREEKE CUPID'S CRYER | 2 | 46 159 | 519 |
| HIS FUGITIVE GOLD THROUGH ALL HER FACES. | ON HOPE | 86 | 46 143 | 71 |
| ONE FACE MORE FUGITIVE THEN ALL THEY. | ON HOPE | 88 | 46 143 | 71 |
| THE FUGITIVE SONS OF THOSE FAIR EYES | WEEPER | 164 | 52 307 | 120 |
| THERE THY LOST FUGITIVE THOU'HAST FOUND AT LAST. | ALEXIAS FIRST ELEGIE | 37 | 52 334 | 204 |
| HIS FUGITIVE GOLD THROUGH ALL HER FACES. | (ON) HOPE | 46 | 52 345 | 71 |
| ONE FACE MORE FUGITIVE THEN ALL THEY. | (ON) HOPE | 48 | 52 345 | 71 |

FULL

| | | | | |
|---|---|---|---|---|
| EACH BODY'S PLUMP AND JUCY, ALL THINGS FULL | OUT OF VIRGIL | 15 | 46 155 | 529 |
| AND DRAW FROM THESE FULL EYES OF THINE. | THE WEEPER | 35 | 46 79 | 120 |
| HE SCORNES THEM NOW, BUT O THEY'L SUTE FULL WELL | UPON LAZARUS HIS TEARES | 3 | 46 89 | 18 |
| THE FULL SOUND OF THY VICTORY. | NEITHER DURST MAN ASKE | 18 | 46 92 | 20 |
| WA'ST THY FULL VICTORIES FAIRER INCREASE, | UPON DUMBE DEVILL CAST OUT | 3 | 46 93 | 14 |
| ERST THY FULL STATURE OF A FATALL TREE. | OUR LORD IN HIS CIRCUMCISION | 16 | 46 98 | 9 |
| JESU, NO MORE, IT IS FULL TIDE | ON BLEEDING WOUNDS OF LORD | 1 | 46 101 | 110 |
| BUT LIFT CLEAN HANDS FULL OF CLEARE HEARTS. | A HYMNE OF THE NATIVITY | 76 | 46 106 | 76 |
| THY FAMES FULL NOISE, MAKES PROUD THE PATIENT EARTH, | SOSPETTO D'HERODE | 29 | 46 109 | 216 |
| AND ALL THE POWERS OF HELL IN FULL APPLAUSE | SOSPETTO D'HERODE | 259 | 46 109 | 216 |
| WHICH MIXT WITH GALL & BLOOD THEY QUAFFE BRIM FULL. | SOSPETTO D'HERODE | 336 | 46 109 | 216 |
| AND BRING HER BOSOME FULL OF BLESSINGS, | ON A PRAYER BOOKE | 35 | 46 126 | 139 |
| RIPE AND FULL GROWNE, THAT COULD REACH DOWNE, | IN MEMORY OF LADY MADRE TERESA | 5 | 46 131 | 52 |
| THY SELFE SHALT FEEL THINE OWNE FULL JOYES. | IN MEMORY OF LADY MADRE TERESA | 121 | 46 131 | 52 |
| THOU HERE ART SET TO SHINE, WHERE THY FULL DAY | AN APOLOGIE FOR HYMNE (TERESA) | 5 | 46 136 | 59 |
| BOWLES FULL OF RICHER BLOOD THEN BLUSH OF GRAPE | AN APOLOGIE FOR HYMNE (TERESA) | 33 | 46 136 | 59 |
| AND FRUITFULL CHARITIES FULL BREASTS (OF OLD) | ON A TREATISE OF CHARITY | 55 | 46 137 | 69 |
| TILL IN THE LAP OF LOVES FULL NOONE | ON HOPE | 56 | 46 143 | 71 |
| SWELL THY FULL GLORYES TO A PITCH SO HIGH, | UPON YORKE HIS BIRTH | 7 | 46 176 | 500 |
| O THOU FULL MIXTURE OF THOSE MIGHTY SOULES, | UPON YORKE HIS BIRTH | 35 | 46 176 | 500 |
| THE BEAMES THAT DANCE IN THOSE FULL STARRES OF THINE. | UPON YORKE HIS BIRTH | 44 | 46 176 | 500 |
| FULL GLORY, FLAMING IN HER OWNE FREE SPHEARE. | ON A FOULE MORNING | 8 | 46 181 | 495 |
| FULL QUIVERS ON LOVES BOW. | WISHES SUPPOSED MISTRESSE | 59 | 46 195 | 479 |
| LET HER FULL GLORY, | WISHES SUPPOSED MISTRESSE | 124 | 46 195 | 479 |
| AND FULL OF NOTHING ELSE BUT EMPTY ME. | TO THE NAME OF JESUS | 21 | 52 239 | 30 |
| WHEN THY OLD FREINDS OF FIRE, ALL FULL OF THEE, | TO THE NAME OF JESUS | 198 | 52 239 | 30 |
| WHOSE FULL & ALL-UNWRINKLED FACE | IN GLORIOUS EPIPHANIE | 28 | 52 253 | 39 |
| NOR DOES HIS FULL GLOBE FAIL TO BE | IN GLORIOUS EPIPHANIE | 38 | 52 253 | 39 |
| LO, HOW THE STREAMES OF LIFE, FROM THAT FULL NEST | VEXILLA REGIS | 7 | 52 277 | 156 |
| SOMTHING FROM THY FULL SEAS OF SORROW. | SANCTA MARIA DOLORUM | 44 | 52 283 | 162 |
| JESU, NO MORE. IT IS FULL TIDE. | UPON BLEEDING CRUCIFIX | 1 | 52 288 | 110 |
| LO, THE FULL, FINALL, SACRIFICE | LAUDA SION SALVATOREM | 65 | 52 294 | 178 |
| CONVICTORS OF THINE OWN FULL CUP. | LAUDA SION SALVATOREM | 76 | 52 294 | 178 |
| AND DRAW FROM THESE FULL EYES OF THINE | WEEPER | 71 | 52 307 | 120 |
| THY FALLING TEARES KEEP FAITH FULL TIME. | WEEPER | 140 | 52 307 | 120 |
| THY SELFE SHALL FEEL THINE OWN FULL JOYES | TERESA | 120 | 52 315 | 52 |
| THOU HERE ART SETT TO SHINE WHERE THY FULL DAY | AN APOLOGIE FOR (TERESA) HYMNE | 5 | 52 322 | 59 |
| BOWLES FULL OF RICHER BLOOD THEN BLUSH OF GRAPE | AN APOLOGIE FOR (TERESA) HYMNE | 33 | 52 322 | 59 |
| BY THE FULL KINGDOME OF THAT FINALL KISSE | FLAMING HEART | 101 | 52 324 | 61 |
| FULL SWEETLY WITH IT SELFE HAD DWELL'T AT HOME. | ALEXIAS THIRD ELEGIE | 12 | 52 336 | 209 |
| HALLS FULL OF FLATTERING MEN & FRISKING BOYES. | DESCRIPTION RELIGIOUS HOUSE | 6 | 52 338 | 213 |
| HANDS FULL OF HARTY LABOURS, PAINES THAT PAY | DESCRIPTION RELIGIOUS HOUSE | 19 | 52 338 | 213 |
| TILL IN THE LAPPE OF LOVES FULL NOONE | (ON) HOPE | 26 | 52 345 | 71 |
| STUFT THEE SOE FULL WITH BLISSE, THOU CAN'ST NOT MOVE. | ON GUNPOWDER-TREASON | 6 | MS 384 | 458 |
| LETT NOT THY WEIGHTY GLORIES, THIS FULL TIDE | UPON KINGS CORONATION | 7 | MS 389 | 454 |
| FULL GLORY FLAMING IN HER OWNE FREE SPHAERE. | UPON KINGS CORONATION | 14 | MS 390 | 453 |
| WAS NOT YETT FULL, (A TIME THAT TO MY AGE | OUT OF GROTIUS | 23 | MS 398 | 198 |
| FULL OF HIGH SPARKELING VIGOUR. TAUGHT BE MEE | OUT OF GROTIUS | 53 | MS 398 | 198 |
| THE PEOPLES HUNGER, AND WHEN ALL WERE FULL | OUT OF GROTIUS | 63 | MS 398 | 198 |

ARM-FULL

| | | | | |
|---|---|---|---|---|
| HER HEAVNLY ARM-FULL, SHE SHALL TAST | PRAYER TO GENTLE-WOMAN | 112 | 52 328 | 139 |

DEATH-FULL

| | | | | |
|---|---|---|---|---|
| IN DEATH-FULL DESPERATE ILLS WHERE ART AND ALL | OUT OF GROTIUS | 69 | MS 398 | 198 |

FULL-BLOOM'D

| | | | | |
|---|---|---|---|---|
| LO, A MOUTH, WHOSE FULL-BLOOM'D LIPS | ON WOUNDS OF CRUCIFIED LORD | 5 | 46 99 | 24 |

FULL-FAC'T

| | | | | |
|---|---|---|---|---|
| TO FIX THOSE FULL-FAC'T GLORIES, O HE'S POORE | IT IS BETTER TO GO WITH EYE | 2 | 46 93 | 16 |

FULL-GROWN

| | | | | |
|---|---|---|---|---|
| WE READ IN YOU (RARE QUEEN) RIPE & FULL-GROWN. | TO THE QUEEN'S MAJESTY | 10 | 52 261 | 47 |

## FULL-MOUTH

| | | | |
|---|---|---|---|
| A FULL-MOUTH DIAPASON SWALLOWES ALL. | MUSICKS DUELL | 156 | 46 149 535 |

## FULLY

| | | | |
|---|---|---|---|
| (HIS TENDER TOPPE NOT FULLY SPREAD) | UPON DEATH OF DESIRED HERRYS | 35 | 46 168 467 |

## FULNESSE

| | | | |
|---|---|---|---|
| TO MAJESTY, AND FULNESSE, DEIGNE TO DWELL. | UPON YORKE HIS BIRTH | 24 | 46 176 500 |

## FUNERALL

| | | | |
|---|---|---|---|
| WHO PROV'D THE FEAST TO THEIR OWNE FUNERALL. | THE BEGINNING OF HELIODORUS | 28 | 46 158 517 |
| A STILL SURVIVING FUNERALL. | IN MEMORY OF LADY MADRE TERESA | 78 | 46 131 52 |
| A SUMMONS, WORTHY OF THY FUNERALL. | UPON STANINOUGH'S DEATH | 6 | 46 175 475 |
| SHALL I BUILD HIS FUNERALL NEST. | LOVES HOROSCOPE | 50 | 46 185 463 |
| US TO OUR OWN LIVE'S FUNERALL. | OFFICE H. CROSS COMPLINE | 2 | 52 274 105 |
| A STILL-SURVIVING FUNERALL. | TERESA | 78 | 52 315 52 |
| A SUMMONS WORTHY OF THY FUNERALL. | DEATH'S LECTURE | 6 | 52 340 475 |
| HIGH BEAUTIES SOVERAIGNE, THAT MY FUNERALL FLAMES | EX EUPHORMIONE | 13 | MS 392 525 |

## FURIES

| | | | |
|---|---|---|---|
| THE FURIES CURL'D SNAKES MEET IN GENTLE TWINES, | HORATIJ ILLE & NEFASTO | 52 | MS 382 530 |

## FURNISH

| | | | |
|---|---|---|---|
| TO FURNISH THE FAIRE INFANTS BED. | A HYMNE OF THE NATIVITY | 38 | 46 106 76 |
| TO FURNISH THE FAIR INFANT'S BED | IN HOLY NATIVITY | 54 | 52 246 76 |

## FURNISHT

| | | | |
|---|---|---|---|
| THE TABLES FURNISHT WITH A CURSED FEAST, | SOSPETTO D'HERODE | 329 | 46 109 216 |
| SUCH WAS THE HOUSE, SO FURNISHT WAS THE HALL, | SOSPETTO D'HERODE | 367 | 46 109 216 |

## FURNISH'T

| | | | |
|---|---|---|---|
| SEE HOW HEE'S FURNISH'T FOR SO FEAR'D A WARRE. | SOSPETTO D'HERODE | 524 | 46 109 216 |

## FURROWED

| | | | |
|---|---|---|---|
| WITH HIS FOULE CLAWES HEE FENC'D HIS FURROWED BROW. | SOSPETTO D'HERODE | 149 | 46 109 216 |

## FURTHER

| | | | |
|---|---|---|---|
| AND FURTHER, THAT THE LAWES ETERNALL GIVER, | SOSPETTO D'HERODE | 185 | 46 109 216 |
| BEFORE THOU PASSEST FURTHER ON. | HIS EPITAPH (HERRYS) | 4 | 46 172 471 |
| I SEEKE NO FURTHER, IT IS SHEE. | WISHES SUPPOSED MISTRESSE | 114 | 46 195 479 |
| HAVE FLOW'D TOGETHER. IF OUGHT FURTHER NEEDES | OUT OF GROTIUS | 6 | MS 398 198 |

## FURY

| | | | |
|---|---|---|---|
| (FRAUGHT WITH A FURY SO HARMONIOUS) | MUSICKS DUELL | 134 | 46 149 535 |
| WHENCE THE FOURTH FURY, ANSWER'D PLUTO'S CALL. | SOSPETTO D'HERODE | 368 | 46 109 216 |
| THEIR FURY BUT MADE WAY | TO THE NAME OF JESUS | 209 | 52 239 30 |

## FUTURE

| | | | |
|---|---|---|---|
| WITH HIS FAIRE TRIUMPHS FILL ALL FUTURE STORIES. | SOSPETTO D'HERODE | 230 | 46 109 216 |
| OUR ABSENT PRESENCE, AND OUR FUTURE NOW. | ON HOPE | 80 | 46 143 71 |
| MY FUTURE HOPES CAN RAISE, | WISHES SUPPOSED MISTRESSE | 110 | 46 195 479 |
| OUR ABSENT PRESENCE, AND OUR FUTURE NOW. | (ON) HOPE | 40 | 52 345 71 |
| OF FUTURE CHANCE. THE WORLD'S GRAND SIRE. AND MINE | OUT OF GROTIUS | 3 | MS 398 198 |

## GAD

| | | | |
|---|---|---|---|
| TO GAD ABROAD. | ON A PRAYER BOOKE | 44 | 46 126 139 |

## GADDE

| | | | |
|---|---|---|---|
| TO GADDE ABROAD | PRAYER TO GENTLE-WOMAN | 50 | 52 328 139 |

## GAIN

| | | | |
|---|---|---|---|
| AND NOTHING GAIN | IN GLORIOUS EPIPHANIE | 229 | 52 253 39 |
| BUT THOUGH GREAT LOVE, GREEDY OF SUCH SAD GAIN | VEXILLA REGIS | 13 | 52 277 156 |
| WITH HAPPY GAIN HER MAIDEN VOWES MADE GOOD. | ALEXIAS THIRD ELEGIE | 32 | 52 336 209 |
| AND WHAT AT LAST SHALT' GAIN BY THESE. | TEMPERANCE | 9 | 52 342 510 |

## GAIN'D

| | | | |
|---|---|---|---|
| PROUD TO HAVE GAIN'D THIS PRETIOUS LOSSE | IN GLORIOUS EPIPHANIE | 141 | 52 253 39 |

## GAIND'ST

| | | | |
|---|---|---|---|
| THY HIGH-AYM'D HOPES, GAIND'ST BUT A FLAMING FALL. | SOSPETTO D'HERODE | 80 | 46 109 216 |

## GAINE

| | | | |
|---|---|---|---|
| SOE I MAY GAINE THY DEATH, MY LIFE I'LE GIVE. | MATH. 16. 25. WHOSOEVER SHALL | 1 | MS 381 16 |

GAINER

  TOO MUCH A GAINER BY'T, SHOULD WE     AGAINST IRRESOLUTION AND DELAY  64  52 347 146

GAINFULL

  SO GAINFULL IS SUCH LOSSE OF BREATH,     A SONG  11  52 327  65

GALES

  WITH WANTON GALES. HIS BALMY BREATH SHALL LICKE     ON A FOULE MORNING  13  46 181 495

GALILEAN

  TO A POORE GALILEAN VIRGIN SENT.     SOSPETTO D'HERODE  98  46 109 216
  AMONG THE GALILEAN MOUNTAINES,     WEEPER  110  52 307 120

GALL

  WHICH MIXT WITH GALL & BLOOD THEY QUAFFE BRIM FULL.     SOSPETTO D'HERODE  336  46 109 216
  GALL, & MORE BITTER MOCKS, SHALL MAKE IT UP.     OFFICE H. CROSS SIXT  10  52 270  97

GALLANT

  HERE GALLANT LADYES, THIS UNPARTIALL GLASSE     UPON STANINOUGH'S DEATH  21  46 175 475
  WILL THE GALLANT SUN     CHARITAS NIMIA  39  52 280  48
  HERE, GALLANT LADYES. THIS UNPARTIALL GLASSE     DEATH'S LECTURE  23  52 340 475

GALLANTRY

  FOR ALL THE GALLANTRY OF HIM,     FLAMING HEART  63  52 324  61

GAMES

  OLYMPICK GAMES IN TH' OLYMPIAN PLAINES.     UPON GUNPOWDER TREASON  21  MS 386 460

GAPING

  NO GAPING GORGON, THIS. NONE, LIKE THE REST     ALEXIAS THIRD ELEGIE  41  52 336 209
  SHALL CHOAKE THE GAPING EARTH, WHICH THEN SHALL FRY     ON GUNPOWDER-TREASON  25  MS 384 458

GARB

  TRICK THEIR TALL PLUMES, AND IN THAT GARB SHALL GO     ON A TREATISE OF CHARITY  25  46 137  69

GARDEN

  FOUNTAIN & GARDEN IN ONE FACE.     WEEPER  90  52 307 120

GARDENS

  PEEP'T FROM THEIR BUDS, SHEW'D LIKE THE GARDENS EYES     UPON YORKE HIS BIRTH  62  46 176 500

GARLAND

  TO BE THY GARLAND. SEE (SWEET PRINCE) O SEE     UPON YORKE HIS BIRTH  39  46 176 500
  WEAVE THEM A GARLAND OF MY VOWES.     WISHES SUPPOSED MISTRESSE  108  46 195 479
  A GARLAND, OR A GUILDED HORN.     IN GLORIOUS EPIPHANIE  95  52 253  39

GARMENT

  THIS GARMENT TOO I WOULD THEY HAD DENY'D.     ON CRUCIFIED LORD BLOODY  2  46 100  24
  THIS GARMENT TOO I WOULD THEY HAD DENY'D.     UPON BODY OF OUR LORD  2  52 290  24
  O NEVER COULD THERE BE GARMENT TOO GOOD     UPON BODY OF OUR LORD  5  52 290  24

GARMENTS

  HOW TO WEARE HER GARMENTS WELL.     IN PRAISE OF LESSIUS  20  46 156 510
  HER GARMENTS THAT UPON HER SIT,     IN PRAISE OF LESSIUS  21  46 156 510
  AS GARMENTS SHOULD DOE CLOSE AND FIT.     IN PRAISE OF LESSIUS  22  46 156 510
  O NEVER COULD BEE FOUND GARMENTS TOO GOOD     ON CRUCIFIED LORD BLOODY  5  46 100  24
  HOW TO WEAR HER GARMENTS WELL.     TEMPERANCE  18  52 342 510
  HER GARMENTS, THAT UPON HER SITT     TEMPERANCE  19  52 342 510
  AS GARMENTS SHOULD DOE, CLOSE & FITT.     TEMPERANCE  20  52 342 510

GASP

  GASP FOR THY GOLDEN SHOWRES. WITH LONG STRETCH'T HANDS     TO THE NAME OF JESUS  130  52 239  30

GASPES

  TO'A BLEEDING HEART THAT GASPES FOR BLOOD.     ADORO TE  48  52 291 172

GASTLY

  AND GAVE A GASTLY SHREEKE, WHOSE HORRID YELL     SOSPETTO D'HERODE  150  46 109 216

GATE

  KEPT THY MOUTHES GATE.     OUT OF MARTIALL  2  46 188 527
  STANDS TREMBLING AT THE GATE OF BLISSE.     TO COUNTESSE OF DENBIGH  2  52 236 146
  STANDS TREMBLING AT THE GATE OF BLISSE.     AGAINST IRRESOLUTION AND DELAY  2  52 347 146

PAGE 161

|   |   |   |   |
|---|---|---|---|
| ATLAS SHALL BE TRIPT UPP, JOVE'S GATE SHALL FEELE | ON GUNPOWDER-TREASON | 43 | MS 384 458 |
| AND STREIGHT OF ALL THIS APPROBATION GATE | OUT OF GROTIUS | 55 | MS 398 198 |

**GATES**

|   |   |   |   |
|---|---|---|---|
| AT TH' ORIENTALL GATES. AND DULY MOCKE | TO THE MORNING | 42 | 46 183 497 |
| THE PROUD & MISPLAC'T GATES OF HELL, | IN GLORIOUS EPIPHANIE | 55 | 52 253  39 |
| AT THESE THY WEEPING GATES. | WEEPER | 145 | 52 307 120 |

**GATHER**

|   |   |   |   |
|---|---|---|---|
| MAKES ME DOUBT IF HEAVEN WILL GATHER, | UPON INFANT MARTYRS | 3 | 46  95  10 |
| GATHER NOW THY GREIF'S RIPE FRUIT, GREAT MOTHER-MAID. | OFFICE H. CROSS EVENSONG | 7 | 52 273 101 |
| AND GATHER, AS THEY COME & GOE. | SANCTA MARIA DOLORUM | 26 | 52 283 162 |

**GAUDY**

|   |   |   |   |
|---|---|---|---|
| TO GAUDY TIRE, OR GLISTRING SHOO-TY. | WISHES SUPPOSED MISTRESSE | 18 | 46 195 479 |

**GAVE**

|   |   |   |   |
|---|---|---|---|
| THE OTHER CAST AWAY, SHE ONELY GAVE. | WIDOWES MITES | 4 | 46  86  21 |
| GAVE FORTH YOUR BLOOD FOR BREATH, SPOKE SOULES FOR WORDS. | SOSPETTO D'HERODE | 8 | 46 109 216 |
| AND GAVE A GASTLY SHREEKE, WHOSE HORRID YELL | SOSPETTO D'HERODE | 150 | 46 109 216 |
| THAT HEAVENLY MAXIM GAVE ME HEART TO TRY | AN APOLOGIE FOR HYMNE (TERESA) | 9 | 46 136  59 |
| TO THEM SHEE GAVE THE FIRST AND FAIREST BEAME | UPON DEATH OF HERRYS | 17 | 46 167 466 |
| THAT WAITED ON HER BIRTH. SHE GAVE TO THEM | UPON DEATH OF HERRYS | 18 | 46 167 466 |
| GAVE OMEN TO HIS INFANT HOWERS, | LOVES HOROSCOPE | 6 | 46 185 483 |
| TO WHAT HIS BOWELS BIRTH AND BEING GAVE. | ON FRONTISPIECE ISAACSONS | 2 | 46 191 491 |
| FOUGHT AGAINST FROWNS WITH SMILES.  GAVE GLORIOUS CHASE | TO THE NAME OF JESUS | 199 | 52 239  30 |
| THEY TOOK A KINGDOM WHILE THEY GAVE A KISSE. | TO THE QUEEN'S MAJESTY | 8 | 52 261  47 |
| THAT HOPEFULL MAXIME GAVE ME HART TO TRY | AN APOLOGIE FOR (TERESA) HYMNE | 9 | 52 322  59 |
| IT QUITE FORGOTT. THE FEARFULL EARTH GAVE WAY, | ON GUNPOWDER-TREASON | 53 | MS 384 458 |

**GAY**

|   |   |   |   |
|---|---|---|---|
| OF ALL THE GLORYES MAKE NOONE GAY | EASTER DAY | 7 | 46 100  26 |
| WELCOME, (THOUGH NOT TO THOSE GAY FLYES | A HYMNE OF THE NATIVITY | 71 | 46 106  76 |
| AND THE GAY STARRS LEAD ON THEIR GOLDEN DANCE. | SOSPETTO D'HERODE | 206 | 46 109 216 |
| AMONGST THE GAY MATES OF THE GOD OF FLYES, | ON A PRAYER BOOKE | 45 | 46 126 139 |
| WELCOME, THOUGH NOT TO THOSE GAY FLYES. | IN HOLY NATIVITY | 91 | 52 246  76 |
| AMONG THE GAY MATES OF THE GOD OF FLYES. | PRAYER TO GENTLE-WOMAN | 51 | 52 328 139 |
| SNATCH'T UPP THE FALLING STARRE, SOE RICHLY GAY, | AN ELEGY MR STANNINOW | 50 | MS 394 473 |

**GAZE**

|   |   |   |   |
|---|---|---|---|
| TO GAZE ON THE FAIR SOULDIER'S GLORIOUS FACE. | ALEXIAS THIRD ELEGIE | 46 | 52 336 209 |
| TO GAZE UPON SUCH STARRES EACH HUMBLE EYE | UPON KINGS CORONATION | 33 | MS 389 454 |

**GAZ'D**

|   |   |   |   |
|---|---|---|---|
| ON WHICH, AS ON A GLORIOUS STRANGER GAZ'D | SOSPETTO D'HERODE | 130 | 46 109 216 |
| IN STEAD OF STRIKING WOULD HAVE GAZ'D. | ANOTHER ON HERRYS | 32 | 46 170 469 |
| AND IN THE STEAD OF FEEDING STOOD, & GAZ'D. | UPON GUNPOWDER TREASON | 48 | MS 387 461 |

**GEMME**

|   |   |   |   |
|---|---|---|---|
| SUCH THE MAIDEN GEMME | THE TEARE | 25 | 46  84  50 |
| TIS A GEMME WHILE IT STAYES HERE, | ON WATER OF LORDS BAPTISME | 3 | 46  85  12 |
| SUCH THE MAIDEN GEMME | WEEPER | 61 | 52 307 120 |

**GEMS**

|   |   |   |   |
|---|---|---|---|
| RICH LAZARUS, RICHER IN THOSE GEMS, THY TEARS, | UPON LAZARUS HIS TEARES | 1 | 46  89  18 |
| IN STEAD OF TEARES SUCH GEMS AS THIS IS. | ON WOUNDS OF CRUCIFIED LORD | 16 | 46  99  24 |
| TEARES SHALL TAKE COMFORT, AND TURNE GEMS. | IN MEMORY OF LADY MADRE TERESA | 150 | 46 131  52 |
| WITH A NEW MORNING MADE OF GEMS. | AN HIMNE FOR CIRCUMCISION | 22 | 46 141  37 |
| OF GEMS, THAT IN THEIR BRIGHT SHADES PLAY. | WISHES SUPPOSED MISTRESSE | 51 | 46 195 479 |

**GEMMES**

|   |   |   |   |
|---|---|---|---|
| WITH A NEW MORNING MADE OF GEMMES. | NEW YEAR'S DAY | 22 | 52 251  37 |
| THE FORTUNE OF INFERIOR GEMMES, | WEEPER | 182 | 52 307 120 |
| FALSE LIGHTS OF FLAIRING GEMMES. TUMULTUOUS JOYES. | DESCRIPTION RELIGIOUS HOUSE | 5 | 52 338 213 |

**GEMMS**

|   |   |   |   |
|---|---|---|---|
| TEARES SHALL TAKE COMFORT, & TURN GEMMS | TERESA | 149 | 52 315  52 |

**GENERALL**

|   |   |   |   |
|---|---|---|---|
| SOMETHING TO THE GENERALL FLOOD. | ON BLEEDING WOUNDS OF LORD | 28 | 46 101 110 |
| HEE IN THIS OUR GENERALL JOY. | A HYMNE OF THE NATIVITY | 5 | 46 106  76 |
| IS SHEE TO NATURE, THAT A GENERALL FRIGHT, | SOSPETTO D'HERODE | 381 | 46 109 216 |
| HAD THEIR GENERALL MEETING PLACE. | HIS EPITAPH (HERRYS) | 20 | 46 172 471 |
| THE GENERALL & INDIFFERENT DAY. | IN GLORIOUS EPIPHANIE | 25 | 52 253  39 |
| SOMTHING TO THE GENERALL FLOUD. | UPON BLEEDING CRUCIFIX | 24 | 52 288 110 |

**GEN'RALL**

|   |   |   |   |
|---|---|---|---|
| A GEN'RALL HISSE, FROM THE WHOLE TIRE OF SNAKES | SOSPETTO D'HERODE | 302 | 46 109 216 |

## GENERATION

| | | | | | |
|---|---|---|---|---|---|
| TO GENERATION. HEAVENS ALMIGHTY SIRE | OUT OF VIRGIL | 4 | 46 | 155 | 529 |

## GENEROUS

| | | | | | |
|---|---|---|---|---|---|
| THE GENEROUS WINE WITH AGE GROWES STRONG, NOT SOWER. | ON HOPE | 53 | 46 | 143 | 71 |
| THY GENEROUS WINE WITH AGE GROWES STRONG, NOT SOWER. | (ON) HOPE | 23 | 52 | 345 | 71 |

## GENII

| | | | | | |
|---|---|---|---|---|---|
| THOSE MIGHTY GENII THRONG, WHICH WELL MIGHT BEE | UPON YORKE HIS BIRTH | 10 | 46 | 176 | 500 |

## GENIUS

| | | | | | |
|---|---|---|---|---|---|
| THE LUTES LIGHT GENIUS NOW DOES PROUDLY RISE. | MUSICKS DUELL | 135 | 46 | 149 | 535 |
| MARROW TO MY PLUMPE GENIUS, MAKE IT LIVE | TO THE MORNING | 22 | 46 | 183 | 497 |

## GENTLE

| | | | | | |
|---|---|---|---|---|---|
| A SWEET LUTES-MASTER. IN WHOSE GENTLE AIRES | MUSICKS DUELL | 5 | 46 | 149 | 535 |
| HEAVENS BOSOME DRINKS THE GENTLE STREAME. | THE WEEPER | 20 | 46 | 79 | 120 |
| DAY'S SWEAT, AND BY A GENTLE TYRANNY, | SOSPETTO D'HERODE | 388 | 46 | 109 | 216 |
| HOW KINDLY WILL THY GENTLE HEART, | IN MEMORY OF LADY MADRE TERESA | 105 | 46 | 131 | 52 |
| WHICH RARIFYED, AND IN A GENTLE RAINE | ON A FOULE MORNING | 15 | 46 | 181 | 495 |
| GENTLE SPIRITS. DOE NOT COMPLAIN. | TO THE NAME OF JESUS | 111 | 52 | 239 | 30 |
| HEAVN'S BOSOME DRINKS THE GENTLE STREAM. | WEEPER | 20 | 52 | 307 | 120 |
| HOW KINDLY WILL THY GENTLE HEART | TERESA | 105 | 52 | 315 | 52 |
| SAY, GENTLE SOUL, WHAT CAN YOU FIND | TO SAME CONCERNING CHOISE | 10 | 52 | 331 | 66 |
| THE FURIES CURL'D SNAKES MEET IN GENTLE TWINES, | HORATIJ ILLE & NEFASTO | 52 | MS | 382 | 530 |
| TO MELT IN GENTLE DROPS, LETT THEM BE HEARD | AN ELEGIE ON DR PORTER | 33 | MS | 395 | 476 |

## GENTLER

| | | | | | |
|---|---|---|---|---|---|
| A GENTLER MORN, A JUSTER SUN. | IN GLORIOUS EPIPHANIE | 74 | 52 | 253 | 39 |

## GENTLEST

| | | | | | |
|---|---|---|---|---|---|
| THEIR GENTLEST FRIEND, THEN, THEN THE LANDS BEGIN | OUT OF VIRGIL | 2 | 46 | 155 | 529 |

## GENTLY

| | | | | | |
|---|---|---|---|---|---|
| GENTLY UNTWIN'D HIS THREAD OF LIFE. | AN EPITAPH UPON ASHTON | 28 | 46 | 192 | 464 |
| FROM HEAVENS SWEET MILKY STREAME DOTH GENTLY POURE. | AN ELEGY MR STANNINOW | 10 | MS | 394 | 473 |

## GENUINE

| | | | | | |
|---|---|---|---|---|---|
| BATHES HIM IN A GENUINE FLOOD. | IN PRAISE OF LESSIUS | 36 | 46 | 156 | 510 |
| UNFORC'T & GENUINE. BUT NOT SHADY THO. | DESCRIPTION RELIGIOUS HOUSE | 10 | 52 | 338 | 213 |
| BATHES HIM IN A GENUINE FLOOD. | TEMPERANCE | 34 | 52 | 342 | 510 |

## GERYON

| | | | | | |
|---|---|---|---|---|---|
| OF DEATH MEZENTIUS, OR GERYON DREW. | SOSPETTO D'HERODE | 362 | 46 | 109 | 216 |

## GHOST

| | | | | | |
|---|---|---|---|---|---|
| AND TO THE H. GHOST. | OFFICE H. CROSS MATINES | 9 | 52 | 265 | 86 |

## GHOST'S

| | | | | | |
|---|---|---|---|---|---|
| AND IN A PALE GHOST'S SHAPE TO SPARE HIS EYES. | SOSPETTO D'HERODE | 416 | 46 | 109 | 216 |

## GHOSTLY

| | | | | | |
|---|---|---|---|---|---|
| AGAINST THE GHOSTLY FOE TO TAKE YOUR PART. | ON A PRAYER BOOKE | 13 | 46 | 126 | 139 |
| AGAINST YOUR GHOSTLY FOES TO TAKE YOUR PART, | PRAYER TO GENTLE-WOMAN | 19 | 52 | 326 | 139 |

## GIANT

| | | | | | |
|---|---|---|---|---|---|
| NOE, NOE, A GIANT WIND, THAT WILL NOT SPARE | ON GUNPOWDER-TREASON | 39 | MS | 384 | 458 |

## GIDDY

| | | | | | |
|---|---|---|---|---|---|
| HEE EXPOUNDS THE GIDDY WONDER | PSALME 23 | 27 | 46 | 102 | 5 |
| ON TIPTOE IN THEIR GIDDY BRAYNES. TH' HAVE FIRE | SOSPETTO D'HERODE | 442 | 46 | 109 | 216 |
| OUR GIDDY FEARES WITH AN UNLOOK'T FOR SHOCKE. | HORATIJ ILLE & NEFASTO | 32 | MS | 382 | 530 |

## GIFT

| | | | | | |
|---|---|---|---|---|---|
| IT GIVES BUT O. IT SELF'S THE GIFT. | UPON BLEEDING CRUCIFIX | 15 | 52 | 288 | 110 |
| OF HER UNKIND GIFT MIGHT WE HAVE | O GLORIOSA DOMINA | 13 | 52 | 302 | 194 |

## GUIFT

| | | | | | |
|---|---|---|---|---|---|
| IT GIVES, BUT O IT SELF'S THE GUIFT, | ON BLEEDING WOUNDS OF LORD | 11 | 46 | 101 | 110 |
| KIND WINTER'S GUIFT, & IN A GREENE ONE DIGHT. | AN ELEGY MR STANNINOW | 6 | MS | 394 | 473 |

## GIFTS

| | | | | | |
|---|---|---|---|---|---|
| IN ALL THE GIFTS THAT BLESSE A CREATURE. | ANOTHER ON HERRYS | 12 | 46 | 170 | 469 |

## DOUBLE-GILT

| | | | | | |
|---|---|---|---|---|---|
| NOR NEED BE DOUBLE-GILT. HOW THEN MUST THESE. | UPON TWO GREENE APRICOCKES | 29 | 48 | 220 | 494 |

## DOUBLE-GUILDED

| | | | | | |
|---|---|---|---|---|---|
| AND DOUBLE-GUILDED AS THE DOORES OF DAY. | IN GLORIOUS EPIPHANIE | 57 | 52 | 253 | 39 |

## GUILD

| | | | | | |
|---|---|---|---|---|---|
| THE GLORIES THAT DID GUILD THEE IN THY RISE. | SOSPETTO D'HERODE | 76 | 46 | 109 | 216 |
| OF STARS, THAT GUILD THE MORNE IN CHARGE WERE GIVEN. | SOSPETTO D'HERODE | 234 | 46 | 109 | 216 |
| GUILD THEE NOT WITH SO SWEET GRACES. | AN HIMNE FOR CIRCUMCISION | 7 | 46 | 141 | 37 |
| AND GUILD THE HOPES OF HUMBLE LOVE. | LOVES HOROSCOPE | 34 | 46 | 185 | 483 |
| GUILD THEIR FACES, | OUT OF THE ITALIAN (1) | 47 | 46 | 188 | 545 |
| WE GUILD THE HUMBLE CHEEK OF THIS CHAST PLACE. | IN GLORIOUS EPIPHANIE | 83 | 52 | 253 | 39 |
| 'MONGST THOSE LONG ROWES OF CROWNES THAT GUILD YOUR RACE, | TO THE QUEEN'S MAJESTY | 1 | 52 | 261 | 47 |

## GUILDED

| | | | | | |
|---|---|---|---|---|---|
| GUILDED I'TH' BEAMES OF EARTHLY KINGS | A HYMNE OF THE NATIVITY | 72 | 46 | 106 | 76 |
| ARE GUILDED WITH THE UNION OF THOSE RAYES. | UPON YORKE HIS BIRTH | 12 | 46 | 176 | 500 |
| GUILDED ITH' BEAMES OF EARTHLY KINGS. | IN HOLY NATIVITY | 92 | 52 | 246 | 76 |
| A GARLAND, OR A GUILDED HORN. | IN GLORIOUS EPIPHANIE | 95 | 52 | 253 | 39 |
| GUILDED DUNGHILLS, GLORIOUS LYES, | TO SAME CONCERNING CHOISE | 14 | 52 | 331 | 66 |
| TO HAVE THEM GUILDED WITH HIS COURTEOUS RAIES. | UPON KINGS CORONATION | 24 | MS | 389 | 454 |

## GUILDS

| | | | | | |
|---|---|---|---|---|---|
| GUILDS THEE NOT WITH SO SWEET GRACES | NEW YEAR'S DAY | 7 | 52 | 251 | 37 |

## GINGLE

| | | | | | |
|---|---|---|---|---|---|
| AND MURMUR IN A BUZZING DINNE, THEN GINGLE | MUSICKS DUELL | 129 | 46 | 149 | 535 |

## GIRT

| | | | | | |
|---|---|---|---|---|---|
| GIRT ALL THY GLORIES TO THEE. THEN SIT DOWN, | ON A TREATISE OF CHARITY | 11 | 46 | 137 | 69 |
| GIRT ROUND THY AWFULL ALTARS, WITH BRIGHT WINGS | ON A TREATISE OF CHARITY | 22 | 46 | 137 | 69 |

## GIVE

| | | | | | |
|---|---|---|---|---|---|
| DISPOS'D TO GIVE THE LIGHT-FOOT LADY SPORT | MUSICKS DUELL | 16 | 46 | 149 | 535 |
| I'LE GIVE THEE ALL, TAKE ALL, TAKE HEED | OUT OF GREEKE CUPID'S CRYER | 71 | 46 | 159 | 519 |
| YET MAY THESE UNFLEDG'D GRIEFES GIVE FATE SOME GUESSE, | OUR LORD IN HIS CIRCUMCISION | 13 | 46 | 98 | 9 |
| THY HAND TO GIVE THOU CANST NOT LIFT. | ON BLEEDING WUUNDS OF LORD | 9 | 46 | 101 | 110 |
| IN RAGE, MY ARMES, GIVE ME MY ARMES, HEE CRYES. | SOSPETTO D'HERODE | 480 | 46 | 109 | 216 |
| BUT GIVE THEE A BETTER WITH HIMSELFE ABOVE. | SOSPETTO D'HERODE | 518 | 46 | 109 | 216 |
| SHEEL BARGAIN WITH THEM, AND WILL GIVE | IN MEMORY OF LADY MADRE TERESA | 51 | 46 | 131 | 52 |
| THEREFORE ONELY GIVE TO DAY, | UPON DEATH OF DESIRED HERRYS | 29 | 46 | 168 | 467 |
| THESE DEATH-SEAL'D LIPPS ARE THEY DARE GIVE THE LYE. | UPON STANINOUGH'S DEATH | 23 | 46 | 175 | 475 |
| GIVE THEM THIS RURALL WREATH FIRE FROM THINE EYES. | UPON YORKE HIS BIRTH | 118 | 46 | 176 | 500 |
| ENTHUSIASTICKE FLAMES, SUCH AS CAN GIVE | TO THE MORNING | 21 | 46 | 183 | 497 |
| HER EYE A STRONG APPEALE CAN GIVE | LOVES HOROSCOPE | 39 | 46 | 185 | 483 |
| FOR IN THE LIFE OUGHT ELSE CAN GIVE, | LOVES HOROSCOPE | 45 | 46 | 185 | 483 |
| THEN WERE TH'AEGYPTIAN (BY THE LIFE, THESE GIVE, | ON FRONTISPIECE ISAACSONS | 19 | 46 | 191 | 491 |
| OR GIVE DOWNE TO THE WINGS OF NIGHT. | WISHES SUPPOSED MISTRESSE | 96 | 46 | 195 | 479 |
| DISBAND DULL FEARES. GIVE FAITH THE DAY. | TO COUNTESSE OF DENBIGH | 57 | 52 | 236 | 146 |
| AND GIVE THY SELF A WHILE THE GRACIOUS GUEST | TO THE NAME OF JESUS | 120 | 52 | 239 | 30 |
| THY WOUNDS GIVE US FAIR HOLD. | OFFICE H. CROSS COMPLINE | 20 | 52 | 274 | 105 |
| AND GIVE IT SELF FOR SPORT TO THE PROUD WIND. | CHARITAS NIMIA | 30 | 52 | 280 | 48 |
| (GREAT QUEEN OF GREIFES) & GIVE | SANCTA MARIA DOLORUM | 58 | 52 | 283 | 162 |
| THY HANDS TO GIVE, THOU CANST NOT LIFT. | UPON BLEEDING CRUCIFIX | 13 | 52 | 288 | 110 |
| AS FAST AS LOVE NEW LAWES CAN GIVE, | ADORO TE | 12 | 52 | 291 | 172 |
| GIVE LOVE FOR LIFE. NOR LET MY DAYES | ADORO TE | 35 | 52 | 291 | 172 |
| WHOSE VITALL GUST ALONE CAN GIVE | ADORO TE | 41 | 52 | 291 | 172 |
| AND FOR THY VEIL GIVE MY THY FACE. | ADORO TE | 56 | 52 | 291 | 172 |
| WHERE NATURE'S LAWES NO LEAVE WILL GIVE, | LAUDA SION SALVATOREM | 37 | 52 | 294 | 178 |
| SH'EL BARGAIN WITH THEM. & WILL GIVE | TERESA | 51 | 52 | 315 | 52 |
| GIVE HIM THE VAIL, GIVE HER THE DART. | FLAMING HEART | 42 | 52 | 324 | 61 |
| GIVE HIM THE VAIL, GIVE HER THE DART. | FLAMING HEART | 42 | 52 | 324 | 61 |
| GIVE HIM THE VAIL. THAT HE MAY COVER | FLAMING HEART | 43 | 52 | 324 | 61 |
| GIVE HER THE DART FOR IT IS SHE | FLAMING HEART | 47 | 52 | 324 | 61 |
| GIVE THEN THE DART TO HER WHO GIVES THE FLAME. | FLAMING HEART | 57 | 52 | 324 | 61 |
| GIVE HIM THE VEIL, WHO KINDLY TAKES THE SHAME. | FLAMING HEART | 58 | 52 | 324 | 61 |
| GIVE ME THE SUFFRING SERAPHIM. | FLAMING HEART | 64 | 52 | 324 | 61 |
| THEN THIS WORLD OF LYES CAN GIVE ME | TO SAME CONCERNING CHOISE | 37 | 52 | 331 | 66 |
| THESE DEATH-SEAL'D LIPPES ARE THEY DARE GIVE THE LY | DEATH'S LECTURE | 25 | 52 | 340 | 475 |
| DISBAND DULL FEARES, GIVE FAITH THE DAY. | AGAINST IRRESOLUTION AND DELAY | 81 | 52 | 347 | 146 |
| SOE I MAY GAINE THY DEATH, MY LIFE I'LE GIVE. | MATH. 16. 25. WHOSOEVER SHALL | 1 | MS | 381 | 16 |
| SOE LOW TO GIVE HIS THIRSTY STALLIONS DRINKE. | UPON GUNPOWDER TREASON | 40 | MS | 386 | 460 |
| BUT GIVE ME LEAVE TO EASE IT WITH MY HAND. | UPON BIRTH PRINCESSE E | 16 | MS | 391 | 456 |
| OF SUCH BRIGHT ANGELLS, THAT YOU GIVE US MORE. | UPON BIRTH PRINCESSE E | 26 | MS | 391 | 456 |
| BY THEE, BY THEE YET LETT ME DIE. THIS GIVE, | EX EUPHORMIONE | 12 | MS | 392 | 525 |
| LONG TIME TO QUAVERING AGE YOU GIVE, | UPON DEATH OF A FREIND | 11 | MS | 393 | 477 |

## GIVEST

| | | | | | |
|---|---|---|---|---|---|
| GIV'ST JOY, EVEN WHEN THOU GIVEST NONE. | VERILY YE SHALL WEEP | 6 | 46 | 95 | 22 |

## GIV'ST

| | | | | |
|---|---|---|---|---|
| GIV'ST JOY, EVEN WHEN THOU GIVEST NONE. | VERILY YE SHALL WEEP | 6 | 46 | 95 22 |
| BUT THOU GIV'ST LEAVE (DREAD LORD) THAT WE | DIES IRAE | 25 | 52 | 298 186 |

## GIVES

| | | | | |
|---|---|---|---|---|
| SHEE GIVES HIM BACKE. HER SUPPLE BREST THRILLS OUT | MUSICKS DUELL | 57 | 46 | 149 535 |
| GIVES LIFE TO SOME NEW GRACE. THUS DOTH H'INVOKE | MUSICKS DUELL | 132 | 46 | 149 535 |
| IT GIVES, BUT O IT SELF'S THE GUIFT. | ON BLEEDING WOUNDS OF LORD | 11 | 46 | 101 110 |
| GIVES DIRECTION. GIVES DEFENCE. | PSALME 23 | 48 | 46 | 102 5 |
| GIVES DIRECTION. GIVES DEFENCE. | PSALME 23 | 48 | 46 | 102 5 |
| UNTO A DREADFULL PILE GIVES FIERY BREATH. | SOSPETTO D'HERODE | 58 | 46 | 109 216 |
| UPON THY CROWNE, WHO GIVES HIS OWNE AWAY. | SOSPETTO D'HERODE | 520 | 46 | 109 216 |
| NOR MAY THE LIGHT THAT GIVES THEIR EYE-LIDS LIGHT, | UPON YORKE HIS BIRTH | 92 | 46 | 176 500 |
| GIVES HIM THE MORNING WORLDS FRESH GOLD AGAINE. | UPON TWO GREENE APRICOCKES | 18 | 48 | 220 494 |
| IT GIVES BUT O, IT SELF'S THE GIFT. | UPON BLEEDING CRUCIFIX | 15 | 52 | 288 110 |
| IT GIVES THOUGH BOUND. THOUGH BOUND 'TIS FREE. | UPON BLEEDING CRUCIFIX | 16 | 52 | 288 110 |
| GIVE THEN THE DART TO HER WHO GIVES THE FLAME. | FLAMING HEART | 57 | 52 | 324 61 |
| NOW TO THOSE TOILING SOULES IT GIVES ITS LIGHT, | ON GUNPOWDER-TREASON | 57 | MS | 384 458 |

## GIVEN

| | | | | |
|---|---|---|---|---|
| THIS NEW GUEST TO HER EYES NEW LAWES HATH GIVEN. | ON VIRGINS BASHFULNESSE | 7 | 46 | 89 9 |
| OF STARS, THAT GUILD THE MORNE IN CHARGE WERE GIVEN. | SOSPETTO D'HERODE | 234 | 46 | 109 216 |
| AND GIVEN US HEAV'N AGAIN, IN GIVING HIM. | O GLORIOSA DOMINA | 20 | 52 | 302 194 |
| TO THEE THE PARCAE HAVE GIVEN UP OF LATE | EX EUPHORMIONE | 10 | MS | 392 525 |

## GIVER

| | | | | |
|---|---|---|---|---|
| AND FURTHER, THAT THE LAWES ETERNALL GIVER, | SOSPETTO D'HERODE | 185 | 46 | 109 216 |

## GIVING

| | | | | |
|---|---|---|---|---|
| YET WILL THY HAND STILL GIVING BEE. | ON BLEEDING WOUNDS OF LORD | 10 | 46 | 101 110 |
| YET WILL THY HAND STILL GIVING BE. | UPON BLEEDING CRUCIFIX | 14 | 52 | 288 110 |
| AND GIVEN US HEAV'N AGAIN, IN GIVING HIM. | O GLORIOSA DOMINA | 20 | 52 | 302 194 |
| GIVING HIS WANTON PALFREYS LEAVE TO PLAY | UPON GUNPOWDER TREASON | 20 | MS | 386 460 |

## LIFE-GIVING

| | | | | |
|---|---|---|---|---|
| SO FROM HIS LIVING, & LIFE-GIVING DEATH, | OFFICE H. CROSS RECOMMENDATION | 7 | 52 | 276 106 |
| THE LIVING & LIFE-GIVING BREAD, | LAUDA SION SALVATOREM | 9 | 52 | 294 178 |

## GLAD

| | | | | |
|---|---|---|---|---|
| (THE SWEET INHABITANT OF EACH GLAD TREE, | MUSICKS DUELL | 9 | 46 | 149 535 |
| THE GLAD DESCRYER SHALL NOT MISSE. | OUT OF GREEKE CUPID'S CRYER | 11 | 46 | 159 519 |
| GLADNESSE IT SELFE WOULD BEE MORE GLAD | THE WEEPER | 65 | 46 | 79 120 |
| WHITHER AWAY SO FROLICK. WHY SO GLAD. | ON THE PRODIGALL | 2 | 46 | 86 17 |
| GLAD AT THEIR OWNE HOME NOW TO MEET THEE. | IN MEMORY OF LADY MADRE TERESA | 139 | 46 | 131 52 |
| GLAD TIME TO RIPEN EXPECTATION. | UPON DEATH OF HERRYS | 22 | 46 | 167 466 |
| TO GLAD THE SPHEARE OF ANY NATION. | UPON YORKE HIS BIRTH | 14 | 46 | 176 500 |
| OF THE GLAD EARTH THEY TREAD ON. WHILE WITH THEE | UPON YORKE HIS BIRTH | 21 | 46 | 176 500 |
| GLAD AT THEIR OWN HOME NOW TO MEET THEE. | TERESA | 138 | 52 | 315 52 |
| OFT MY SOULE HAVE I BIN GLAD TO SEEKE | LUKE 2. QUAERIT JESUM | 41 | MS | 379 11 |
| AS GLAD TO WAITE UPON THEIR KING IN DEATH. | UPON GUNPOWDER TREASON | 42 | MS | 386 460 |
| SHALL KISSE HIS GOLDEN BURTHEN. THOU, GLAD ISLE, | UPON KINGS CORONATION | 5 | MS | 389 454 |
| E'RE BORNE WAS BANISH'T. BORNE WAS GLAD T'EMBRACE | OUT OF GROTIUS | 15 | MS | 398 198 |
| SINKES INTO HORROURS BOSOME, GLAD TO HIDE | OUT OF GROTIUS | 78 | MS | 398 198 |

## GLADD

| | | | | |
|---|---|---|---|---|
| A WINGED HERALD, GLADD OF SOE SWEET A PREY, | AN ELEGY MR STANNINOW | 49 | MS | 394 473 |

## GLADDING

| | | | | |
|---|---|---|---|---|
| GLADDING THE SCYTHIAN ROCKS, AND LIBIAN SANDS. | SOSPETTO D'HERODE | 108 | 46 | 109 216 |

## GLADLY

| | | | | |
|---|---|---|---|---|
| WHIL'ST THEY GLADLY GOE TO MEET | PSALME 23 | 32 | 46 | 102 5 |
| ONE THAT GLADLY WILL BEE NIGH, | ON MR. G. HERBERTS BOOKE | 7 | 46 | 130 68 |
| SICKNESSE WOULD HAVE GLADLY BEEN, | ANOTHER ON HERRYS | 25 | 46 | 170 469 |
| HERE AT LENGTH, HATH GLADLY FOUND | AN EPITAPH DOCTOR BROOKE | 5 | 46 | 175 465 |
| MADE EVERY MORTALL GLADLY SACRIFICE | UPON KINGS CORONATION | 36 | MS | 390 453 |

## GLADNESSE

| | | | | |
|---|---|---|---|---|
| GLADNESSE IT SELFE WOULD BEE MORE GLAD | THE WEEPER | 65 | 46 | 79 120 |
| GLADNESSE SHALL CLOATH THE EARTH, WE WILL INSTILE | ON A FOULE MORNING | 9 | 46 | 181 495 |

## GLANCE

| | | | | |
|---|---|---|---|---|
| FRESH FROM THE PURE GLANCE OF THINE EYE. | PSALME 23 | 65 | 46 | 102 5 |
| POINT HERE THY BEAMES. O GLANCE ON YONDER FLOCKES, | ON A FOULE MORNING | 5 | 46 | 181 495 |

## GLANCES

| | | | | |
|---|---|---|---|---|
| SUCH HIS FELL GLANCES AS THE FATALL LIGHT | SOSPETTO D'HERODE | 51 | 46 | 109 216 |
| SPIRITUALL AND SOULE PEIRCING GLANCES. | ON A PRAYER BOOKE | 65 | 46 | 126 139 |
| CAST AMOROUS GLANCES ON HIS BIRTH, | LOVES HOROSCOPE | 27 | 46 | 185 483 |
| SPIRITUALL & SOUL-PEIRCING GLANCES | PRAYER TO GENTLE-WOMAN | 71 | 52 | 328 139 |

|   |   |   |   |   |
|---|---|---|---|---|
| CAST BACK SOME AMOROUSE GLANCES ON THE CATES, | UPON GUNPOWDER TREASON | 29 | MS 387 | 461 |

## GLASSE

|   |   |   |   |   |
|---|---|---|---|---|
| HERE GALLANT LADYES, THIS UNPARTIALL GLASSE | UPON STANINOUGH'S DEATH | 21 | 46 175 | 475 |
| HERE, GALLANT LADYES, THIS UNPARTIALL GLASSE | DEATH'S LECTURE | 23 | 52 340 | 475 |

## HOUR-GLASSE

|   |   |   |   |   |
|---|---|---|---|---|
| MY WATRY HOUR-GLASSE HATH OLD TIMES OUTRUNNE. | ALEXIAS SECONDE ELEGIE | 20 | 52 335 | 207 |

## HOWER-GLASSES

|   |   |   |   |   |
|---|---|---|---|---|
| HIS HOWER-GLASSES. | THE WEEPER | 99 | 46 79 | 120 |

## GLASSY

|   |   |   |   |   |
|---|---|---|---|---|
| AND IS INSTRUCTED BY THY GLASSY WAVE | AN ELEGIE ON DR PORTER | 23 | MS 395 | 476 |

## GLIMMERING

|   |   |   |   |   |
|---|---|---|---|---|
| LENT THEM THE LAST FLASH OF HER GLIMMERING LIGHT. | THE BEGINNING OF HELIODORUS | 20 | 46 158 | 517 |

## GLIMPSE

|   |   |   |   |   |
|---|---|---|---|---|
| BUT STAY, WHAT GLIMPSE WAS THAT. WHY BLUSHT THE DAY. | UPON YORKE HIS BIRTH | 66 | 46 176 | 500 |

## GLISTERING

|   |   |   |   |   |
|---|---|---|---|---|
| GLOWING CHEEK, & GLISTERING WINGS, | FLAMING HEART | 33 | 52 324 | 61 |
| THE GLOWING CHEEKES, THE GLISTERING WINGS. | FLAMING HEART | 66 | 52 324 | 61 |

## GLISTRING

|   |   |   |   |   |
|---|---|---|---|---|
| TO GAUDY TIRE, OR GLISTRING SHOO-TY. | WISHES SUPPOSED MISTRESSE | 18 | 46 195 | 479 |

## GLITTERING

|   |   |   |   |   |
|---|---|---|---|---|
| HIS GLITTERING ROBE, HIS SPARKLING CROWN, | IN GLORIOUS EPIPHANIE | 243 | 52 253 | 39 |

## GLOBE

|   |   |   |   |   |
|---|---|---|---|---|
| NOR DOES HIS FULL GLOBE FAIL TO BE | IN GLORIOUS EPIPHANIE | 38 | 52 253 | 39 |
| AND CRACK THE CHRISTALL GLOBE, THE MILKY STREAME | ON GUNPOWDER-TREASON | 23 | MS 384 | 458 |

## GLOOMY

|   |   |   |   |   |
|---|---|---|---|---|
| HE'S WASHT, HIS GLOOMY SKIN A PEACEFULL SHADE | ON BAPTIZED AETHIOPIAN | 3 | 46 85 | 29 |
| GLOOMY NIGHT EMBRAC'T THE PLACE | A HYMNE OF THE NATIVITY | 17 | 46 106 | 76 |
| A GLOOMY MANTLE OF DARKE FLAMES, THE TIRE | SOSPETTO D'HERODE | 44 | 46 109 | 216 |
| HIS GLOOMY BOSOMES DARKEST CHARACTER, | SOSPETTO D'HERODE | 194 | 46 109 | 216 |
| GLOOMY NIGHT EMBRAC'T THE PLACE | IN HOLY NATIVITY | 17 | 52 246 | 76 |
| AT LAST IT STOPT AT PLUTO'S GLOOMY PORCH. | ON GUNPOWDER-TREASON | 55 | MS 384 | 458 |
| BE' A GLOOMY CANOPY TO PLUTO'S MINIONS. | UPON GUNPOWDER TREASON | 22 | MS 387 | 461 |

## GLORIES

|   |   |   |   |   |
|---|---|---|---|---|
| TO FIX THOSE FULL-FAC'T GLORIES, O HE'S POORE | IT IS BETTER TO GO WITH EYE | 2 | 46 93 | 16 |
| THE GLORIES THAT DID GUILD THEE IN THY RISE. | SOSPETTO D'HERODE | 76 | 46 109 | 216 |
| THAT GLORIES SELFE SHOULD SERVE OUR GRIEFS, & FEARES. | SOSPETTO D'HERODE | 183 | 46 109 | 216 |
| (O MY DESPIGHT,) WITH HIS DIVINEST GLORIES. | SOSPETTO D'HERODE | 228 | 46 109 | 216 |
| GIRT ALL THY GLORIES TO THEE. THEN SIT DOWN, | ON A TREATISE OF CHARITY | 11 | 46 137 | 69 |
| WHOSE RISING GLORIES MADE SUCH HASTE TO HIDE | UPON DEATH OF HERRYS | 4 | 46 167 | 466 |
| THE DAYES ABASHED GLORIES, AND IN FACE | UPON YORKE HIS BIRTH | 75 | 46 176 | 500 |
| SO DEARE GLORIES DARE NOT BORROW. | OUT OF THE ITALIAN (1) | 39 | 46 188 | 545 |
| LEAVE ALL THY NATIVE GLORIES IN THEIR GORGEOUS NEST, | TO THE NAME OF JESUS | 119 | 52 239 | 30 |
| A HUNDRED THOUSAND GOODS, GLORIES, & GRACES, | PRAYER TO GENTLE-WOMAN | 81 | 52 328 | 139 |
| LETT NOT THY WEIGHTY GLORIES, THIS FULL TIDE | UPON KINGS CORONATION | 7 | MS 369 | 454 |
| HER GLORIES I SHOULD DIMME WITH THINGS SOE GROSSE, | UPON BIRTH PRINCESSE E | 53 | MS 391 | 456 |
| TO HIDE HIS BLOOMING GLORIES, & BEQUEATH | AN ELEGY MR STANNINOW | 29 | MS 394 | 473 |

## GLORYES

|   |   |   |   |   |
|---|---|---|---|---|
| OF ALL THE GLORYES MAKE NOONE GAY | EASTER DAY | 7 | 46 100 | 26 |
| THE GLORYES OF THY YOUTH NE'RE KNEW, | UPON DEATH OF DESIRED HERRYS | 17 | 46 168 | 467 |
| HIS SWELLING GLORYES, AUSTER SPIDE HIM, | UPON DEATH OF DESIRED HERRYS | 41 | 46 168 | 467 |
| WITH THINE OWNE GLORYES. AND ART STRANGELY BLEST | UPON YORKE HIS BIRTH | 4 | 46 176 | 500 |
| SWELL THY FULL GLORYES TO A PITCH SO HIGH, | UPON YORKE HIS BIRTH | 7 | 46 176 | 500 |

## GLORIOUS

|   |   |   |   |   |
|---|---|---|---|---|
| WHOSE GLORIOUS COURSE THROUGH OUR HORRIZON RUN, | UPON BISHOP ANDREWES PICTURE | 2 | 46 163 | 490 |
| THY GLORIOUS WISDOME BREAKES THE NETS, | NEITHER DURST MAN ASKE | 3 | 46 92 | 20 |
| GREAT LITLE ONE, WHOSE GLORIOUS BIRTH, | A HYMNE OF THE NATIVITY | 57 | 46 106 | 76 |
| ON WHICH, AS ON A GLORIOUS STRANGER GAZ'D | SOSPETTO D'HERODE | 130 | 46 109 | 216 |
| THEIR GREAT LORDS GLORIOUS NAME, TO NONE | IN MEMORY OF LADY MADRE TERESA | 9 | 46 131 | 52 |
| FOR LOVE THEIR LORD, GLORIOUS AND GREAT, | IN MEMORY OF LADY MADRE TERESA | 11 | 46 131 | 52 |
| IF NOT MORE GLORIOUS, MORE CONSPICUOUS THO. | ON A TREATISE OF CHARITY | 26 | 46 137 | 69 |
| GOE THEN, GOE (GLORIOUS) ON THE GOLDEN WINGS | ON THE ASSUMPTION | 23 | 46 139 | 114 |
| BURNISHT IN HIS GLORIOUS BEAMES. | AN HIMNE FOR CIRCUMCISION | 14 | 46 141 | 37 |
| TRUE HOPE'S A GLORIOUS HUNTRESSE, AND HER CHASE | ON. HOPE | 89 | 46 143 | 71 |
| COME FAST UPON THEE, AND THOSE GLORIOUS ODS, | UPON YORKE HIS BIRTH | 6 | 46 176 | 500 |
| ARE THEY NOT ODS, AND GLORIOUS, THAT TO THEE | UPON YORKE HIS BIRTH | 9 | 46 176 | 500 |
| GREAT CHARLES, THOU SWEET DAWNE OF A GLORIOUS DAY, | UPON YORKE HIS BIRTH | 29 | 46 176 | 500 |

|   |   |   |   |   |   |
|---|---|---|---|---|---|
| DREST IN THE GLORIOUS MADNESSE OF A MUSE, | TO THE MORNING | 23 | 46 | 183 | 497 |
| FOUGHT AGAINST FROWNS WITH SMILES. GAVE GLORIOUS CHASE | TO THE NAME OF JESUS | 199 | 52 | 239 | 30 |
| FOR THEE. AND SERV'D THEREIN THY GLORIOUS ENDS. | TO THE NAME OF JESUS | 210 | 52 | 239 | 30 |
| WEARY OF THIS GLORIOUS WRONG | IN GLORIOUS EPIPHANIE | 138 | 52 | 253 | 39 |
| GLORIOUS, OR GREIVOUS MORE. THUS TO MAKE GOOD | VEXILLA REGIS | 29 | 52 | 277 | 156 |
| E'RE THE LESSE GLORIOUS RUN. | CHARITAS NIMIA | 40 | 52 | 280 | 48 |
| GOE THEN. GOE GLORIOUS. | IN GLORIOUS ASSUMPTION B. LADY | 37 | 52 | 304 | 114 |
| THEIR GREAT LORD'S GLORIOUS NAME, TO NONE | TERESA | 9 | 52 | 315 | 52 |
| GUILDED DUNGHILLS, GLORIOUS LYES, | TO SAME CONCERNING CHOISE | 14 | 52 | 331 | 66 |
| TO GAZE ON THE FAIR SOULDIER'S GLORIOUS FACE. | ALEXIAS THIRD ELEGIE | 46 | 52 | 336 | 209 |
| TRUE HOPE'S A GLORIOUS HUNTER & HER CHASE. | (ON) HOPE | 49 | 52 | 345 | 71 |
| FROM WHENCE HIS GLORIOUS RIVALL HEE ESPIES. | UPON KINGS CORONATION | 18 | MS | 390 | 453 |
| THIS GLORIOUS PHAEBUS SETT) WILL QUIET BEE. | UPON KINGS CORONATION | 24 | MS | 390 | 453 |
| COMPILE A FIFT GLORIOUS EPITOME | UPON BIRTH PRINCESSE E | 57 | MS | 391 | 456 |
| OF ALL OUR GLORIOUS HOPES SHOULD FADE, | AN ELEGY MR STANNINOW | 43 | MS | 394 | 473 |
| I LEFT MY GLORIOUS FATHERS STAR-PAV'D COURT | OUT OF GROTIUS | 14 | MS | 398 | 198 |

GLORY

|   |   |   |   |   |   |
|---|---|---|---|---|---|
| OF NOONS HIGH GLORY, WHEN HARD BY THE STREAMS | MUSICKS DUELL | 2 | 46 | 149 | 535 |
| BY GLORY, IN OUT HEARTS BY GRACE. | IN MEMORY OF LADY MADRE TERESA | 165 | 46 | 131 | 52 |
| THE HEAVENS WILL STAY NO LONGER, MAY THY GLORY | UPON YORKE HIS BIRTH | 104 | 46 | 176 | 500 |
| FULL GLORY, FLAMING IN HER OWNE FREE SPHEARE. | ON A FOULE MORNING | 8 | 46 | 181 | 495 |
| LET HER FULL GLORY, | WISHES SUPPOSED MISTRESSE | 124 | 46 | 195 | 479 |
| AWAKE, MY GLORY. SOUL, (IF SUCH THOU BE, | TO THE NAME OF JESUS | 13 | 52 | 239 | 30 |
| GLORY BE TO THE FATHER, | OFFICE H. CROSS MATINES | 7 | 52 | 265 | 86 |
| GLORY TO THEE, GREAT VIRGIN'S SON | O GLORIOSA DOMINA | 37 | 52 | 302 | 194 |
| BY GLORY, IN OUR HEARTS BY GRACE. | TERESA | 164 | 52 | 315 | 52 |
| CECILIA, GLORY OF HER NAME & BLOOD | ALEXIAS THIRD ELEGIE | 31 | 52 | 336 | 209 |
| CIRCLED WITH PURE REFINED GLORY. HEERE | UPON KINGS CORONATION | 13 | MS | 389 | 454 |
| FIXT IN YOUR SPHAERES OF GLORY, SHED FROM THENCE | UPON KINGS CORONATION | 39 | MS | 389 | 454 |
| FULL GLORY FLAMING IN HER OWNE FREE SPHAERE. | UPON KINGS CORONATION | 14 | MS | 390 | 453 |
| DROP DOWNE ONE SPARKE OF GLORY, & THEY'L PROVE | UPON BIRTH PRINCESSE E | 19 | MS | 391 | 456 |

GLORY'S

|   |   |   |   |   |   |
|---|---|---|---|---|---|
| WHEN GLORY'S SUN FAITH'S SHADES SHALL CHASE. | ADORO TE | 55 | 52 | 291 | 172 |

GLOSSE

|   |   |   |   |   |   |
|---|---|---|---|---|---|
| THE FAIRE GLOSSE OF A FAIRER TEXT. | ANOTHER ON HERRYS | 52 | 46 | 170 | 469 |
| WAS BUT THE GLOSSE OF HIS OWNE GOOD. | HIS EPITAPH (HERRYS) | 24 | 46 | 172 | 471 |
| AND FOULE THE CLEARE TEXT WITH A MUDDY GLOSSE. | UPON BIRTH PRINCESSE E | 54 | MS | 391 | 456 |

GLOSSES

|   |   |   |   |   |   |
|---|---|---|---|---|---|
| BY VARIOUS GLOSSES. NOW THEY SEEME TO GRUTCH, | MUSICKS DUELL | 128 | 46 | 149 | 535 |

GLOW

|   |   |   |   |   |   |
|---|---|---|---|---|---|
| HEE TOST HIS TROUBLED EYES, EMBERS THAT GLOW | SOSPETTO D'HERODE | 147 | 46 | 109 | 216 |

GLOWING

|   |   |   |   |   |   |
|---|---|---|---|---|---|
| GLOWING CHEEK, & GLISTERING WINGS, | FLAMING HEART | 33 | 52 | 324 | 61 |
| THE GLOWING CHEEKES. THE GLISTERING WINGS. | FLAMING HEART | 66 | 52 | 324 | 61 |

GLUTT

|   |   |   |   |   |   |
|---|---|---|---|---|---|
| THEN GLUTT THY DIRE LAMPE WITH THE WARMEST BLOOD, | ON GUNPOWDER-TREASON | 63 | MS | 384 | 458 |
| TO GLUTT THE STOMACK OF HIS DARLING FLOWER. | UPON BIRTH PRINCESSE E | 6 | MS | 391 | 456 |

GNASH

|   |   |   |   |   |   |
|---|---|---|---|---|---|
| A MASSE OF WOES. HIS TEETH FOR TORMENT GNASH, | SOSPETTO D'HERODE | 63 | 46 | 109 | 216 |

GNAW'D

|   |   |   |   |   |   |
|---|---|---|---|---|---|
| THE WHILE HIS TWISTED TAYLE HEE GNAW'D FOR SPIGHT. | SOSPETTO D'HERODE | 152 | 46 | 109 | 216 |
| TO WHICH HIS GNAW'D HEART IS THE GROWING FOOD | SOSPETTO D'HERODE | 494 | 46 | 109 | 216 |

GO

|   |   |   |   |   |   |
|---|---|---|---|---|---|
| TRICK THEIR TALL PLUMES, AND IN THAT GARB SHALL GO | ON A TREATISE OF CHARITY | 25 | 46 | 137 | 69 |
| TAKE THY FAREWEL POORE WORLD. HEAVEN MUST GO HOME. | ON THE ASSUMPTION | 2 | 46 | 139 | 114 |
| THEREFORE IF HEE NEEDS MUST GO, | UPON DEATH OF DESIRED HERRYS | 65 | 46 | 168 | 467 |
| THEY ARE THY GREATNESSE. GODS WHERE E'RE THEY GO | UPON YORKE HIS BIRTH | 18 | 46 | 176 | 500 |
| AND MATCHT THY MASTER-PEECE. O THEN GO ON | UPON YORKE HIS BIRTH | 51 | 46 | 176 | 500 |

GOEST

|   |   |   |   |   |   |
|---|---|---|---|---|---|
| AND WHILE THOU GOEST, OUR SONG AND WEE, | ON THE ASSUMPTION | 27 | 46 | 139 | 114 |
| AND WHILE THOU GOEST, OUR SONG & WE | IN GLORIOUS ASSUMPTION B. LADY | 42 | 52 | 304 | 114 |

GOE

|   |   |   |   |   |   |
|---|---|---|---|---|---|
| A SEA OF HELICON. HIS HAND DOES GOE | MUSICKS DUELL | 124 | 46 | 149 | 535 |
| GOE NOW WITH SOME DAREING DRUGG, | IN PRAISE OF LESSIUS | 1 | 46 | 156 | 510 |
| GOE TAKE PHISICKE. DOAT UPON | IN PRAISE OF LESSIUS | 5 | 46 | 156 | 510 |
| GOE POORE MAN THINKE WHAT SHALL BEE, | IN PRAISE OF LESSIUS | 11 | 46 | 156 | 510 |
| PRETHEE, SWEET NOW LET ME GOE, | OUT OF GREEKE CUPID'S CRYER | 69 | 46 | 159 | 519 |
| CONTENT AND QUIET WOULD HE GOE, | THE WEEPER | 82 | 46 | 79 | 120 |
| WE GOE NOT TO SEEKE | THE WEEPER | 133 | 46 | 79 | 120 |

| | | | | | |
|---|---|---|---|---|---|
| NO SUCH THING. WE GOE TO MEET | THE WEEPER | 137 | 46 | 79 | 120 |
| (FOR TO HEAVEN THOU MUST GOE) | THE TEARE | 38 | 46 | 84 | 50 |
| WHICH WAY MY POORE TEARS TO HIMSELFE MAY GOE. | COME SEE WHERE THE LORD LAY | 2 | 46 | 87 | 27 |
| GOE SMILING SOULES, YOUR NEW BUILT CAGES BREAKE. | TO INFANT MARTYRS | 1 | 46 | 88 | 10 |
| MY WEALTH IS GONE, O GOE IT WHERE IT WILL. | DIVES ASKING A DROP | 3 | 46 | 96 | 18 |
| THY RESTLESSE FEET THEY CANNOT GOE. | ON BLEEDING WOUNDS OF LORD | 5 | 46 | 101 | 110 |
| WHIL'ST THEY GLADLY GOE TO MEET | PSALME 23 | 32 | 46 | 102 | 5 |
| 'TWIXT MOTHERS BRESTS TO GOE TO BED. | A HYMNE OF THE NATIVITY | 50 | 46 | 106 | 76 |
| GOE NOW, MAKE MUCH OF THESE. WAGE STILL THEIR WARS | SOSPETTO D'HERODE | 447 | 46 | 109 | 216 |
| WEE NEED TO GOE TO NONE OF ALL | IN MEMORY OF LADY MADRE TERESA | 3 | 46 | 131 | 52 |
| MADE FRUITFULL THY FAIRE SOULE. GOE NOW | IN MEMORY OF LADY MADRE TERESA | 170 | 46 | 131 | 52 |
| THOU WITH THE LAMBE THY LORD SHALL GOE. | IN MEMORY OF LADY MADRE TERESA | 179 | 46 | 131 | 52 |
| SHEE'S CALL'D AGAINE, AND WILL SHEE GOE. | ON THE ASSUMPTION | 19 | 46 | 139 | 114 |
| GOE THEN, GOE (GLORIOUS) ON THE GOLDEN WINGS | ON THE ASSUMPTION | 23 | 46 | 139 | 114 |
| GOE THEN, GOE (GLORIOUS) ON THE GOLDEN WINGS | ON THE ASSUMPTION | 23 | 46 | 139 | 114 |
| UNDER SO SWEET A BURDEN. GOE, | ON THE ASSUMPTION | 25 | 46 | 139 | 114 |
| YET SHALL OUR LIPS NEVER LET GOE | ON THE ASSUMPTION | 36 | 46 | 139 | 114 |
| WHY DOST THOU SHAKE THY LEADEN SCEPTER. GOE | TO THE MORNING | 54 | 46 | 183 | 497 |
| GOE, SOUL, OUT OF THY SELF, & SEEK FOR MORE. | TO THE NAME OF JESUS | 27 | 52 | 239 | 30 |
| GOE & REQUEST | TO THE NAME OF JESUS | 28 | 52 | 239 | 30 |
| LET HIM GOE WEEP | CHARITAS NIMIA | 15 | 52 | 280 | 48 |
| AND GATHER, AS THEY COME & GOE. | SANCTA MARIA DOLORUM | 26 | 52 | 283 | 162 |
| THY RESTLESSE FEET NOW CANNOT GOE | UPON BLEEDING CRUCIFIX | 9 | 52 | 288 | 110 |
| THAT FAITH HAS FARTHER, HERE TO GOE | ADORO TE | 20 | 52 | 291 | 172 |
| TAKE THY FAREWELL, POORE WORLD. HEAVN MUST GOE HOME. | IN GLORIOUS ASSUMPTION B. LADY | 2 | 52 | 304 | 114 |
| IF SUMMER COME NOT, HOW CAN WINTER GOE. | IN GLORIOUS ASSUMPTION B. LADY | 26 | 52 | 304 | 114 |
| SHE'S CALL'D AGAIN, AND WILL SHE GOE. | IN GLORIOUS ASSUMPTION B. LADY | 33 | 52 | 304 | 114 |
| GOE THEN, GOE GLORIOUS | IN GLORIOUS ASSUMPTION B. LADY | 37 | 52 | 304 | 114 |
| GOE THEN, GOE GLORIOUS. | IN GLORIOUS ASSUMPTION B. LADY | 37 | 52 | 304 | 114 |
| UNDER SO SWEET A BURTHEN GOE. | IN GLORIOUS ASSUMPTION B. LADY | 40 | 52 | 304 | 114 |
| CONTENT & QUIET HE WOULD GOE. | WEEPER | 76 | 52 | 307 | 120 |
| WE GOE NOT TO SEEK, | WEEPER | 175 | 52 | 307 | 120 |
| CROWN'D HEADS ARE TOYES. WE GOE TO MEET | WEEPER | 185 | 52 | 307 | 120 |
| MADE FRUITFULL THY FAIR SOUL, GOE NOW | TERESA | 169 | 52 | 315 | 52 |
| THOU WITH THE LAMB, THY LORD, SHALT GOE. | TERESA | 178 | 52 | 315 | 52 |
| THEN TO A VIRGIN GRAVE UNTOUCH'T TO GOE. | ALEXIAS THIRD ELEGIE | 26 | 52 | 336 | 209 |
| GOE NOW, AND WITH SOME DARING DRUGG | TEMPERANCE | 1 | 52 | 342 | 510 |
| GOE, TAKE PHYSICK DOAT UPON | TEMPERANCE | 5 | 52 | 342 | 510 |
| GOE ON THEN, HEAVEN, & LIMBE FORTH SUCH ANOTHER. | UPON BIRTH PRINCESSE E | 55 | MS | 391 | 456 |
| GOE LEARNE THAT FATALL QUIRE, SOE SPRUCELY DIGHT | AN ELEGIE ON DR PORTER | 27 | MS | 395 | 476 |

GOES

| | | | | | |
|---|---|---|---|---|---|
| SO GOES THE VOTE (NOR ASK THEM, WHY.) | OFFICE H. CROSS THIRD | 3 | 52 | 268 | 93 |
| WARM SYLVER SHOURES WHERE'RE HE GOES. | WEEPER | 126 | 52 | 307 | 120 |
| HE FLYES. & INTO WILLFULL EXILE GOES. | ALEXIAS THIRD ELEGIE | 16 | 52 | 336 | 209 |

GOING

| | | | | | |
|---|---|---|---|---|---|
| THAT HATH A DOUBLE NILUS GOING, | ON BLEEDING WOUNDS OF LORD | 14 | 46 | 101 | 110 |
| THAT HATH A DOUBLE NILUS GOING. | UPON BLEEDING CRUCIFIX | 18 | 52 | 288 | 110 |

HE-GOAT

| | | | | | |
|---|---|---|---|---|---|
| OF RAM, HE-GOAT, OR REVEREND APE. | IN GLORIOUS EPIPHANIE | 90 | 52 | 253 | 39 |

GOATES

| | | | | | |
|---|---|---|---|---|---|
| THE FLOCKS OF GOATES TO FOLDS OF FLAME, | DIES IRAE | 58 | 52 | 298 | 166 |

GOD

| | | | | | |
|---|---|---|---|---|---|
| 'TIS HEAV'N 'TIS HEAVEN SHE SEES, HEAVENS GOD THERE LYES | ON VIRGINS BASHFULNESSE | 5 | 46 | 89 | 9 |
| THE OTHER TO THE ALTARS GOD. | TWO WENT TO PRAY | 6 | 46 | 89 | 18 |
| THY GOD WAS MAKING HAST INTO THY ROOFE, | I AM NOT WORTHY | 1 | 46 | 90 | 13 |
| GOD SPAKE ONCE WHEN HEE ALL THINGS MADE, | AND HE ANSWERED NOTHING | 3 | 46 | 91 | 22 |
| NOR HATH GOD A THINNER SHARE, | GIVE TO CAESAR AND TO GOD | 3 | 46 | 96 | 20 |
| WHOM MY GOD VOUCHSAFES TO KEEPE | PSALME 23 | 2 | 46 | 102 | 5 |
| EVEN MY GOD, EVEN HE IS, | PSALME 23 | 3 | 46 | 102 | 5 |
| STILL MY SHEPHEARD, STILL MY GOD | PSALME 23 | 45 | 46 | 102 | 5 |
| HEAVEN IN EARTH, AND GOD IN MAN. | A HYMNE OF THE NATIVITY | 56 | 46 | 106 | 76 |
| THAT THE UNMEASUR'D GOD SO LOW SHOULD SINKE, | SOSPETTO D'HERODE | 171 | 46 | 109 | 216 |
| AMONGST THE GAY MATES OF THE GOD OF FLYES, | ON A PRAYER BOOKE | 45 | 46 | 126 | 139 |
| TO HAVE A GOD BECOME HER LOVER. | ON A PRAYER BOOKE | 118 | 46 | 126 | 139 |
| THEM GOD, AND TEACH THEM HOW TO LIVE | IN MEMORY OF LADY MADRE TERESA | 52 | 46 | 131 | 52 |
| OR TO A NEW GOD DESOLATION. | ON A TREATISE OF CHARITY | 38 | 46 | 137 | 69 |
| BID THE GOLDEN GOD THE SUNNE, | AN HIMNE FOR CIRCUMCISION | 13 | 46 | 141 | 37 |
| THE GOD OF NATURE IN THE FIELD OF GRACE. | ON HOPE | 90 | 46 | 143 | 71 |
| IF THIS WERE WISDOMES GOD, THAT WARS STERNE FATHER, | UPON YORKE HIS BIRTH | 32 | 46 | 176 | 500 |
| O MEET THE ANGRY GOD, INVADE HIS EYES. | TO THE MORNING | 36 | 46 | 183 | 497 |
| BUT THOU, FAINT GOD OF SLEEPE, FORGET THAT I | TO THE MORNING | 47 | 46 | 183 | 497 |
| HEAVEN IN EARTH, & GOD IN MAN. | IN HOLY NATIVITY | 82 | 52 | 246 | 76 |
| BID THY GOLDEN GOD, THE SUN. | NEW YEAR'S DAY | 13 | 52 | 251 | 37 |
| WHOM THEY SO LONG COURTED AS GOD, | IN GLORIOUS EPIPHANIE | 180 | 52 | 253 | 39 |
| O GOD MAKE SPEED TO SAVE ME. | OFFICE H. CROSS MATINES | 5 | 52 | 265 | 86 |
| LIVE BARABBAS, & LET GOD DY. | OFFICE H. CROSS THIRD | 4 | 52 | 268 | 93 |
| SHE SEES HER SON, HER GOD, | SANCTA MARIA DOLORUM | 31 | 52 | 283 | 162 |
| THOUGH HIDD AS GOD, WOUNDS WRITT THEE MAN, | ADORO TE | 22 | 52 | 291 | 172 |
| TAST THEE GOD, OR TOUCH THEE MAN | ADORO TE | 30 | 52 | 291 | 172 |
| MY LORD TOO & MY GOD, AS LOWD AS HE. | ADORO TE | 32 | 52 | 291 | 172 |
| THEM GOD. TEACH THEM HOW TO LIVE | TERESA | 52 | 52 | 315 | 52 |
| AMONG THE GAY MATES OF THE GOD OF FLYES. | PRAYER TO GENTLE-WOMAN | 51 | 52 | 328 | 139 |
| TO HAVE HER GOD BECOME HER LOVER. | PRAYER TO GENTLE-WOMAN | 124 | 52 | 328 | 139 |

```
                                                                        PAGE   168


     I'AM YOURS, O WERE MY GOD, MY CHRIST SO TOO,    ALEXIAS THIRD ELEGIE         43   52 336 209
     THE GOD OF NATURE IN THE FEILDS OF GRACE.       (ON) HOPE                    50   52 345  71
     OUR GOD WOULD THRIVE TOO FAST, AND BE           AGAINST IRRESOLUTION AND DELAY  63  52 347 146
     MY BOSOME GOD.                                  LUKE 2.  QUAERIT JESUM        48   MS 379  11
     FORTHWITH EACH GOD STEPT FROM HIS STARRY THRONE, UPON GUNPOWDER TREASON       53   MS 387 461
     GREAT NATURES SELFE HATH SHRUNKE AND SPOKE MEE GOD. OUT OF GROTIUS            50   MS 398 198

GOD'S

     ALL WE HAVE IS GOD'S, AND YET                   GIVE TO CAESAR AND TO GOD      1   46  96  20
     ALL IS GOD'S. AND YET 'TIS TRUE                 GIVE TO CAESAR AND TO GOD      5   46  96  20

GODS

     ONE NEERER TO GODS ALTAR TROD.                  TWO WENT TO PRAY               5   46  89  18
     SO LONG AS CAESAR'S SELFE IS GODS.              GIVE TO CAESAR AND TO GOD      8   46  96  20
     HOW GODS ETERNALL SONNE SHOULD BE MANS BROTHER, SOSPETTO D'HERODE            165   46 109 216
     GODS SERVICES NO LONGER SHALL PUT ON            ON A TREATISE OF CHARITY      29   46 137  69
     URNS.  LIKE GODS SANCTUARIES THEY LOOKT OF OLD. ON A TREATISE OF CHARITY      36   46 137  69
     NOR ON GODS ALTAR CAST TWO SCORCHING EYES       ON A TREATISE OF CHARITY      43   46 137  69
     BEYOND THY SELFE.  FOR LO. THE GODS, THE GODS   UPON YORKE HIS BIRTH           5   46 176 500
     BEYOND THY SELFE.  FOR LO. THE GODS, THE GODS   UPON YORKE HIS BIRTH           5   46 176 500
     THEY ARE THY GREATNESSE.  GODS WHERE E'RE THEY GO UPON YORKE HIS BIRTH        18   46 176 500
     BUT GODS ARE GRATIOUS.  AND THEIR ALTARS, MAKE  UPON YORKE HIS BIRTH         116   46 176 500

GODDESSE

     BRIGHT GODDESSE, (WHETHER JOVE THY FATHER BE.   EX EUPHORMIONE                 1   MS 392 525

GODLES

     OF ADULTEROUS GODLES DUST                       IN GLORIOUS EPIPHANIE        102   52 253  39

GOLD

     THE WORKING BEES SOFT MELTING GOLD,             OUT OF GREEKE CUPID'S CRYER   25   46 159 519
     THE GOLD THAT ON HIS QUIVER SMILES,             OUT OF GREEKE CUPID'S CRYER   49   46 159 519
     NOT THE SOFT GOLD WHICH                         THE WEEPER                    43   46  79 120
     WELCOME, THOUGH NOT TO GOLD, NOR SILKE.         A HYMNE OF THE NATIVITY       59   46 106  76
     HIS FUGITIVE GOLD THROUGH ALL HER FACES.        ON HOPE                       86   46 143  71
     HIS TONGUE THE TOUCHSTONE OF HER GOLD.          HIS EPITAPH (HERRYS)          30   46 172 471
     GIVES HIM THE MORNING WORLDS FRESH GOLD AGAINE. UPON TWO GREENE APRICOCKES    18   48 220 494
     WELLCOME.  THOUGH NOR TO GOLD NOR SILK.         IN HOLY NATIVITY              85   52 246  76
     HIS GOLD, HIS MIRRH, HIS FRANKINCENCE,          IN GLORIOUS EPIPHANIE        244   52 253  39
     WASH WITH SYLVER, WIPE WITH GOLD.               WEEPER                       120   52 307 120
     NO ROOFES OF GOLD O'RE RIOTOUS TABLES SHINING   DESCRIPTION RELIGIOUS HOUSE    1   52 338 213
     HIS FUGITIVE GOLD THROUGH ALL HER FACES.        (ON) HOPE                     46   52 345  71
     IN GROSSEST METALLS HIS OWN GOLD.               AGAINST IRRESOLUTION AND DELAY 56  52 347 146
     THE GOLD, IN WHICH HE FLAMES, DOES WELL PRAESAGE UPON KINGS CORONATION        17   MS 389 454
     THEIR WINTER COATES COVER'D WITH FLAMING GOLD.  UPON KINGS CORONATION         28   MS 390 453

GOLDEN

     TREMBLING AS WHEN APPOLLO'S GOLDEN HAIRES       MUSICKS DUELL                115   46 149 535
     GOLDEN THOUGH HEE BEE,                          THE WEEPER                    79   46  79 120
     GOLDEN TAGUS MURMURS THOUGH,                    THE WEEPER                    80   46  79 120
     THY SILVER, THEN HIS GOLDEN STREAME.            THE WEEPER                    84   46  79 120
     TELL ME BRIGHT BOY, TELL ME MY GOLDEN LAD.      ON THE PRODIGALL               1   46  86  17
     THE GOLDEN EYES OF NIGHT. WHOSE BEAME MADE BRIGHT SOSPETTO D'HERODE          131   46 109 216
     AND THE GAY STARRS LEAD ON THEIR GOLDEN DANCE.  SOSPETTO D'HERODE            206   46 109 216
     THE HOLY YOUTH OF HEAV'N, WHOSE GOLDEN RINGS    ON A TREATISE OF CHARITY      21   46 137  69
     GOE THEN, GOE (GLORIOUS) ON THE GOLDEN WINGS    ON THE ASSUMPTION             23   46 139 114
     BID THE GOLDEN GOD THE SUNNE,                   AN HIMNE FOR CIRCUMCISION     13   46 141  37
     THY GOLDEN HEAD NEVER HANGS DOWNE,              ON HOPE                       55   46 143  71
     THOSE RARE FRUITS DANGLED, WHENCE THE GOLDEN YEARE UPON DEATH OF HERRYS      28   46 167 466
     APOLLO GOLDEN THOUGH THOU BEE,                  UPON DEATH OF DESIRED HERRYS  13   46 168 467
     CHERISHT IN HIS GOLDEN PRIME.                   HIS EPITAPH (HERRYS)          44   46 172 471
     AND MAKE THEIR FLEECES GOLDEN AS THY LOCKES.    ON A FOULE MORNING             6   46 181 495
     BRIGHT CLOUDS LIKE GOLDEN FLEECES SHALL BE SPREAD. ON A FOULE MORNING        26   46 181 495
     THY SILVER BROW, AND MEET THY GOLDEN LOVER.     ON A FOULE MORNING            28   46 181 495
     FOR THEIR GOLDEN                                OUT OF THE ITALIAN (1)        11   46 188 545
     GASP FOR THY GOLDEN SHOWRES.  WITH LONG STRETCH'T TO THE NAME OF JESUS      130   52 239  30
                                          HANDS

     BID THY GOLDEN GOD, THE SUN,                    NEW YEAR'S DAY                13   52 251  37
     THY GOLDEN INDEX.  WITH A DUTEOUS HAND          IN GLORIOUS EPIPHANIE        251   52 253  39
     A GOLDEN HARVEST OF CROWN'D HEADS, THAT MEET    TO THE QUEEN'S MAJESTY        13   52 261  47
     WILL HE HANG DOWN HIS GOLDEN HEAD               CHARITAS NIMIA                41   52 280  48
     ON THE GOLDEN WINGS                             IN GLORIOUS ASSUMPTION B. LADY 38  52 304 114
     GOLDEN THOUGH HE BE,                            WEEPER                        73   52 307 120
     GOLDEN TAGUS MURMURES THO.                      WEEPER                        74   52 307 120
     THY SYLVER, THEN HIS GOLDEN STREAM.             WEEPER                        78   52 307 120
     THE GOLDEN THRONG                               TO SAME CONCERNING CHOISE     27   52 331  66
     O RISE, PURE LAMP, & LEND THY GOLDEN RAY        ALEXIAS SECONDE ELEGIE        29   52 335 207
     THY GOLDEN, GROWING HEAD NEVER HANGS DOWN       (ON) HOPE                     25   52 345  71
     IN HIGH-BUILT NUMBERS WAKES HIS GOLDEN LYRE,    HORATIJ ILLE & NEFASTO        42   MS 382 530
     HIS TREMBLING HANDS LOOSING THE GOLDEN RAINES.  UPON GUNPOWDER TREASON        22   MS 386 460
     SHALL KISSE HIS GOLDEN BURTHEN. THOU, GLAD ISLE, UPON KINGS CORONATION         5   MS 389 454
     A PRECIOUS SEASON, & A GOLDEN AGE.              UPON KINGS CORONATION         18   MS 389 454
     AND WITH A GOLDEN WAVE WASH CLEANE AWAY         AN ELEGY MR STANNINOW         12   MS 394 473
     THE GOLDEN HARVEST OF OUR JOYES, THE NOONE      AN ELEGY MR STANNINOW         42   MS 394 473
     A GOLDEN SUMMER, AN AETERNALL SPRING.           AN ELEGY MR STANNINOW         54   MS 394 473
```

## GOLDEN-HEADED

| | | | | |
|---|---|---|---|---|
| A GOLDEN-HEADED HARVEST FAIRELY REARES | MUSICKS DUELL | 70 | 46 149 | 535 |

## GOLDEN-WINGED

| | | | | |
|---|---|---|---|---|
| HEAVENS GOLDEN-WINGED HERALD, LATE HEE SAW | SOSPETTO D'HERODE | 97 | 46 109 | 216 |

## GONE

| | | | | |
|---|---|---|---|---|
| MAY THINKE HIS LABOUR VAINELY GONE, | OUT OF GREEKE CUPID'S CRYER | 10 | 46 159 | 519 |
| TAKES HIS TEARE AND GETS HIM GONE. | THE WEEPER | 94 | 46 79 | 120 |
| MY WEALTH IS GONE, O GOE IT WHERE IT WILL, | DIVES ASKING A DROP | 3 | 46 96 | 18 |
| THE WINTER'S PAST, THE RAINE IS GONE. | ON THE ASSUMPTION | 10 | 46 139 | 114 |
| BUT TO VANISH AND BE GONE. | UPON DEATH OF DESIRED HERRYS | 28 | 46 168 | 467 |
| TILL THIS STORMY NIGHT BE GONE. | AN EPITAPH HUSBAND AND WIFE | 12 | 46 174 | 478 |
| POINTS OF DEATH BID LOVE BE GONE | LOVES HOROSCOPE | 22 | 46 185 | 483 |
| TWIXT'S MOTHER'S BRESTS IS GONE TO BED. | IN HOLY NATIVITY | 68 | 52 246 | 76 |
| THE WINTER'S PAST, THE RAIN IS GONE. | IN GLORIOUS ASSUMPTION B. LADY | 10 | 52 304 | 114 |
| THE RAIN IS GONE, EXCEPT SO MUCH AS WE | IN GLORIOUS ASSUMPTION B. LADY | 21 | 52 304 | 114 |
| TAKES HIS TEAR, & GETS HIM GONE. | WEEPER | 148 | 52 307 | 120 |
| I'AM WEDDED ORE AGAIN SINCE THOU ART GONE. | ALEXIAS SECONDE ELEGIE | 3 | 52 335 | 207 |
| TILL THIS STORMY NIGHT BE GONE, | AN EPITAPH UPON MARRIED COUPLE | 16 | 52 339 | 478 |
| AND IS HE GONE, WHOM THESE ARMES HELD BUT NOW. | LUKE 2. QUAERIT JESUM | 1 | MS 379 | 11 |
| HEE'S GONE. THE FAIR'ST FLOWER, THAT E'RE BOSOME DREST, | LUKE 2. QUAERIT JESUM | 5 | MS 379 | 11 |
| MY WOMBES CHAST PRIDE IS GONE, MY HEAV'NE-BORNE BOY. | LUKE 2. QUAERIT JESUM | 7 | MS 379 | 11 |
| HEE'S GONE. & HIS LOV'D STEPPES TO WAIT UPON, | LUKE 2. QUAERIT JESUM | 9 | MS 379 | 11 |
| MY JOY IS GONE. | LUKE 2. QUAERIT JESUM | 10 | MS 379 | 11 |
| MY JOYES, & HEE ARE GONE. MY GREIFE, & I | LUKE 2. QUAERIT JESUM | 11 | MS 379 | 11 |
| HEE'S GONE. NOT LEAVING WITH ME, TILL HE COME, | LUKE 2. QUAERIT JESUM | 13 | MS 379 | 11 |
| THEIR APPETITES WERE GONE AT TH' VERY SIGHT. | UPON GUNPOWDER TREASON | 49 | MS 387 | 461 |
| GONE BE ALL CONSORT, SINCE ALONE | UPON DEATH OF A FREIND | 17 | MS 393 | 477 |
| HE, THAT ONCE BORE THE BEST PART'S GONE. | UPON DEATH OF A FREIND | 18 | MS 393 | 477 |
| IF WINTER'S GONE, WHENCE THIS UNTIMELY COLD, | AN ELEGY MR STANNINOW | 19 | MS 394 | 473 |
| THY LAZY CRAWLING STREAMES, PRI'THEE BE GONE, | AN ELEGIE ON DR PORTER | 20 | MS 395 | 476 |

## GOOD

| | | | | |
|---|---|---|---|---|
| HIS CURIOUS FINGERS LENT, HER VOYCE MADE GOOD. | MUSICKS DUELL | 14 | 46 149 | 535 |
| PAINTED AGAINE BY SOME GOOD POESIE. | WITH A PICTURE TO A FRIEND | 2 | 46 156 | 494 |
| LEAVE, LEAVE, FOR SHAME, OR ELSE (GOOD JUDGE) DECREE, | TO PONTIUS WASHING HANDS | 15 | 46 94 | 23 |
| EXPECT A SEA, MY HEART SHALL MAKE IT GOOD. | OUR LORD IN HIS CIRCUMCISION | 4 | 46 98 | 9 |
| O NEVER COULD BEE FOUND GARMENTS TOO GOOD | ON CRUCIFIED LORD BLOODY | 5 | 46 100 | 24 |
| FOR US AND OUR ETERNALL GOOD | ON BLEEDING WOUNDS OF LORD | 6 | 46 101 | 110 |
| NO,NO,THY GOOD. SION, ALONE MUST CROWNE | PSALME 137 | 25 | 46 104 | 7 |
| THIS MORTALL ENEMY TO MANKINDS GOOD, | SOSPETTO D'HERODE | 82 | 46 109 | 216 |
| NEW MATTER, TO MAKE GOOD HIS GREAT SUSPECT. | SOSPETTO D'HERODE | 88 | 46 109 | 216 |
| IF USUALL WIT, AND STRENGTH WILL DOE NO GOOD, | SOSPETTO D'HERODE | 273 | 46 109 | 216 |
| EACH FLOWERS A PREGNANT POYSON, TRY'D AND GOOD, | SOSPETTO D'HERODE | 347 | 46 109 | 216 |
| A WELL-POIS'D SCEPTER. DOES IT NOW SEEME GOOD | SOSPETTO D'HERODE | 451 | 46 109 | 216 |
| GOOD REASON FOR SHEE BREATHS ALL FIRE, | IN MEMORY OF LADY MADRE TERESA | 39 | 46 131 | 52 |
| ALL THY GOOD WORKES WHICH WENT BEFORE, | IN MEMORY OF LADY MADRE TERESA | 140 | 46 131 | 52 |
| WAS BUT THE GLOSSE OF HIS OWNE GOOD. | HIS EPITAPH (HERRYS) | 24 | 46 172 | 471 |
| PEACE, GOOD READER, DOE NOT WEEPE. | AN EPITAPH HUSBAND AND WIFE | 7 | 46 174 | 478 |
| A BROOKE WHOSE STREAME SO GREAT, SO GOOD. | AN EPITAPH DOCTOR BROOKE | 1 | 46 175 | 465 |
| TO PAVE HIS PATHES WITH ALL THE GOOD | LOVES HOROSCOPE | 29 | 46 185 | 483 |
| BOTH WILL BE GOOD FRIENDS TOGETHER. | OUT OF THE ITALIAN (1) | 30 | 46 188 | 545 |
| NO PART OF THEIR GOOD MORROW. | WISHES SUPPOSED MISTRESSE | 77 | 46 195 | 479 |
| THE NAME OF OUR NEW PEACE. OUR GOOD. | TO THE NAME OF JESUS | 3 | 52 239 | 30 |
| GUILTY OF BEING MUCH FOR THEM TOO GOOD. | IN GLORIOUS EPIPHANIE | 108 | 52 253 | 39 |
| TALL TREE OF LIFE. THY TRUTH MAKES GOOD | VEXILLA REGIS | 19 | 52 277 | 156 |
| GLORIOUS, OR GREIVOUS MORE. THUS TO MAKE GOOD | VEXILLA REGIS | 29 | 52 277 | 156 |
| WHY SHOULD HIS UNSTAINED BREST MAKE GOOD | CHARITAS NIMIA | 61 | 52 280 | 48 |
| FOR US & OUR ETERNALL GOOD, | UPON BLEEDING CRUCIFIX | 10 | 52 288 | 110 |
| O NEVER COULD THERE BE GARMENT TOO GOOD | UPON BODY OF OUR LORD | 5 | 52 290 | 24 |
| NATURE, & NAME, TO BE MADE GOOD | LAUDA SION SALVATOREM | 35 | 52 294 | 178 |
| GOOD REASON. FOR SHE BREATHES ALL FIRE. | TERESA | 39 | 52 315 | 52 |
| ALL THY GOOD WORKES WHICH WENT BEFORE | TERESA | 139 | 52 315 | 52 |
| AND VENTURE TO SPEAK ONE GOOD WORD | TO SAME CONCERNING CHOISE | 6 | 52 331 | 66 |
| WITH HAPPY GAIN HER MAIDEN VOWES MADE GOOD. | ALEXIAS THIRD ELEGIE | 32 | 52 336 | 209 |
| WHATE'RE FALSE SHOWES OF SHORT & SLIPPERY GOOD | DESCRIPTION RELIGIOUS HOUSE | 7 | 52 33e | 213 |
| PEACE, GOOD READER. DOE NOT WEEP. | AN EPITAPH UPON MARRIED COUPLE | 7 | 52 339 | 478 |
| EACH MINDFULL PLANT HASTS TO MAKE GOOD | AGAINST IRRESOLUTION AND DELAY | 35 | 52 347 | 146 |
| ALL THINGS SWEAR FRIENDS TO FAIR AND GOOD, | AGAINST IRRESOLUTION AND DELAY | 57 | 52 347 | 146 |
| NAY. STOPP THY CLOWDY EYES. IT IS NOT GOOD, | UPON GUNPOWDER TREASON | 31 | MS 387 | 461 |
| GOOD WINE IN ALL POYNTS. BUT THE EASY RATE. | OUT OF GROTIUS | 56 | MS 398 | 198 |
| OF HOT DEFIANCE 'GAINST WHAT E'RE IS GOOD | OUT OF GROTIUS | 76 | MS 398 | 198 |

## GOODLY

| | | | | |
|---|---|---|---|---|
| FOURE TEETH THOU HAD'ST THAT RANCK'D IN GOODLY STATE | OUT OF MARTIALL | 1 | 46 188 | 527 |
| GOODLY SURMISES | TO SAME CONCERNING CHOISE | 15 | 52 331 | 66 |
| WHIL'ST THE GOOSE SOE GOODLY WHITE, | PETRONIJ ALES PHASIACIS PETITA | 5 | MS 382 | 526 |

## GOODNESSE

| | | | | |
|---|---|---|---|---|
| O GRANT (SWEET GOODNESSE) THAT ONE EYE MAY BE | IT IS BETTER TO GO WITH EYE | 5 | 46 93 | 16 |
| JOY OF GOODNESSE, LOVE OF ART, | UPON DEATH OF DESIRED HERRYS | 9 | 46 168 | 467 |
| IN HIM GOODNESSE JOY'D TO SEE | HIS EPITAPH (HERRYS) | 21 | 46 172 | 471 |
| OF THY OLD GOODNESSE, KNOW THEE NOT FOR THEIRES. | OUT OF GROTIUS | 40 | MS 398 | 198 |
| SOUND GOODNESSE WITH HER SHADOW WHICH THEY WEARE. | OUT OF GROTIUS | 43 | MS 398 | 198 |

## GOODS

| | | | | | |
|---|---|---|---|---|---|
| A HUNDRED THOUSAND GOODS, GLORIES, & GRACES. | PRAYER TO GENTLE-WOMAN | 81 | 52 | 328 | 139 |

## GOOSE

| | | | | | |
|---|---|---|---|---|---|
| WHIL'ST THE GOOSE SOE GOODLY WHITE, | PETRONIJ ALES PHASIACIS PETITA | 5 | MS | 382 | 526 |

## GORE

| | | | | | |
|---|---|---|---|---|---|
| AND WHILE THE BLACK SOULES BOILE IN THEIR OWNE GORE, | SOSPETTO D'HERODE | 295 | 46 | 109 | 216 |
| COME GRIMME DESTRUCTION, & IN PURPLE GORE | UPON GUNPOWDER TREASON | 3 | MS | 387 | 461 |

## GORGEOUS

| | | | | | |
|---|---|---|---|---|---|
| LEAVE ALL THY NATIVE GLORIES IN THEIR GORGEOUS NEST, | TO THE NAME OF JESUS | 119 | 52 | 239 | 30 |
| HIS GORGEOUS TIRE | IN GLORIOUS EPIPHANIE | 241 | 52 | 253 | 39 |

## GORGON

| | | | | | |
|---|---|---|---|---|---|
| NO GAPING GORGON, THIS. NONE, LIKE THE REST | ALEXIAS THIRD ELEGIE | 41 | 52 | 336 | 209 |

## GRACE

| | | | | | |
|---|---|---|---|---|---|
| IN SURLY GROANES DISDAINES THE TREBLES GRACE. | MUSICKS DUELL | 50 | 46 | 149 | 535 |
| GIVES LIFE TO SOME NEW GRACE. THUS DOTH H'INVOKE | MUSICKS DUELL | 132 | 46 | 149 | 535 |
| GRACE AND PEACE, TO MEET NEW LAIES | PSALME 23 | 33 | 46 | 102 | 5 |
| BY GLORY, IN OUT HEARTS BY GRACE. | IN MEMORY OF LADY MADRE TERESA | 165 | 46 | 131 | 52 |
| THE GOD OF NATURE IN THE FIELD OF GRACE. | ON HOPE | 90 | 46 | 143 | 71 |
| WAS SO RICH IN GRACE AND NATURE, | ANOTHER ON HERRYS | 11 | 46 | 170 | 469 |
| EVERY RECONCILED GRACE, | HIS EPITAPH (HERRYS) | 19 | 46 | 172 | 471 |
| LIV'D A FAIRE, BUT MANLY GRACE. | HIS EPITAPH (HERRYS) | 28 | 46 | 172 | 471 |
| AND THAT OF GRACE HEAVN WAY'D IN HIM, | VEXILLA REGIS | 32 | 52 | 277 | 156 |
| BY GLORY, IN OUR HEARTS BY GRACE. | TERESA | 164 | 52 | 315 | 52 |
| LORD, WHEN THE SENSE OF THY SWEET GRACE | A SONG | 1 | 52 | 327 | 65 |
| HE YEILDS, AND STRAIGHT BAPTIS'D, OBTAINS THE GRACE | ALEXIAS THIRD ELEGIE | 45 | 52 | 336 | 209 |
| THE GOD OF NATURE IN THE FEILDS OF GRACE. | (ON) HOPE | 50 | 52 | 345 | 71 |
| THE FEILD OF NATURE OR OF GRACE. | AGAINST IRRESOLUTION AND DELAY | 30 | 52 | 347 | 146 |

## GRACES

| | | | | | |
|---|---|---|---|---|---|
| OF SIMPLE GRACES, AND SWEET LOVES, | A HYMNE OF THE NATIVITY | 84 | 46 | 106 | 76 |
| FLOWERS OF NEVER FADING GRACES. | ON A PRAYER BOOKE | 36 | 46 | 126 | 139 |
| AN HUNDRED THOUSAND LOVES AND GRACES, | ON A PRAYER BOOKE | 75 | 46 | 126 | 139 |
| OF SOULES, WHICH IN THAT NAMES SWEET GRACES. | IN MEMORY OF LADY MADRE TERESA | 86 | 46 | 131 | 52 |
| GUILD THEE NOT WITH SO SWEET GRACES. | AN HIMNE FOR CIRCUMCISION | 7 | 46 | 141 | 37 |
| FOR ALL PERSUASIVE GRACES THENCE | HIS EPITAPH (HERRYS) | 33 | 46 | 172 | 471 |
| ALL THE GRACES | OUT OF THE ITALIAN (1) | 22 | 46 | 188 | 545 |
| THINE EYES GRACES, | OUT OF THE ITALIAN (1) | 46 | 46 | 188 | 545 |
| THAT SUNSHINE BY THEIR OWNE SWEET GRACES. | WISHES SUPPOSED MISTRESSE | 45 | 46 | 195 | 479 |
| OF SIMPLE GRACES & SWEET LOVES. | IN HOLY NATIVITY | 104 | 52 | 246 | 76 |
| GUILDS THEE NOT WITH SO SWEET GRACES | NEW YEAR'S DAY | 7 | 52 | 251 | 37 |
| OF SOULES WHICH IN THAT NAME'S SWEET GRACES | TERESA | 86 | 52 | 315 | 52 |
| FLOWERS OF NEVER FADING GRACES | PRAYER TO GENTLE-WOMAN | 42 | 52 | 328 | 139 |
| A HUNDRED THOUSAND GOODS, GLORIES, & GRACES. | PRAYER TO GENTLE-WOMAN | 81 | 52 | 328 | 139 |
| THE MUSES, & THE GRACES SUGRED NEASTS. | UPON GUNPOWDER TREASON | 38 | MS | 387 | 461 |
| THE MUSES, & THE GRACES FRAGRANT POSIES. | AN ELEGY MR STANNINOW | 38 | MS | 394 | 473 |

## GRACIOUS

| | | | | | |
|---|---|---|---|---|---|
| THY GRACIOUS NAME, BUT TO THE LAST, | ON THE ASSUMPTION | 39 | 46 | 139 | 114 |
| GRACIOUS HEAVENS DO USE TO SEND | UPON DEATH OF DESIRED HERRYS | 26 | 46 | 168 | 467 |
| AND GIVE THY SELF A WHILE THE GRACIOUS GUEST | TO THE NAME OF JESUS | 120 | 52 | 239 | 30 |
| AND GRAFT INTO THY GRACIOUS STOCK | OFFICE H. CROSS EVENSONG | 13 | 52 | 273 | 101 |

## GRAFT

| | | | | | |
|---|---|---|---|---|---|
| AND GRAFT INTO THY GRACIOUS STOCK | OFFICE H. CROSS EVENSONG | 13 | 52 | 273 | 101 |
| THUS GRAFT OUR SELVES ON THEE. | VEXILLA REGIS | 40 | 52 | 277 | 156 |

## GRAND

| | | | | | |
|---|---|---|---|---|---|
| WITH THIS GRAND BLAST SHOULD HAVE BIN BLOUNE AWAY. | UPON GUNPOWDER TREASON | 30 | MS | 386 | 460 |
| OF FUTURE CHANCE. THE WORLD'S GRAND SIRE. AND MINE | OUT OF GROTIUS | 3 | MS | 398 | 198 |

## GRANDSIRES

| | | | | | |
|---|---|---|---|---|---|
| CENTER OF THOSE THY GRANDSIRES, SHALL I SAY | UPON YORKE HIS BIRTH | 30 | 46 | 176 | 500 |

## GRANT

| | | | | | |
|---|---|---|---|---|---|
| O GRANT (SWEET GOODNESSE) THAT ONE EYE MAY BE | IT IS BETTER TO GO WITH EYE | 5 | 46 | 93 | 16 |

## GRANTS

| | | | | | |
|---|---|---|---|---|---|
| WHO GRANTS AT LAST, LONG TIME TRYD | TO COUNTESSE OF DENBIGH | 15 | 52 | 236 | 146 |
| WHO GRANTS AT LAST, A GREAT TRY'DE. | AGAINST IRRESOLUTION AND DELAY | 9 | 52 | 347 | 146 |

## GRAPE

| | | | | | |
|---|---|---|---|---|---|
| BOWLES FULL OF RICHER BLOOD THEN BLUSH OF GRAPE | AN APOLOGIE FOR HYMNE (TERESA) | 33 | 46 | 136 | 59 |
| BOWLES FULL OF RICHER BLOOD THEN BLUSH OF GRAPE | AN APOLOGIE FOR (TERESA) HYMNE | 33 | 52 | 322 | 59 |

## GRASPE

| | | | |
|---|---|---|---|
| DOTH GRASPE THE FATE OF THINGES, AND SHARE TH' EVENTS | OUT OF GROTIUS | 2 | MS 398 198 |

## GRATIOUS

| | | | |
|---|---|---|---|
| THUS GREW THIS GRATIOUS PLANT, IN WHOSE SWEET SHADE | UPON DEATH OF HERRYS | 9 | 46 167 466 |
| BUT GODS ARE GRATIOUS. AND THEIR ALTARS, MAKE | UPON YORKE HIS BIRTH | 116 | 46 176 500 |
| THIS GRATIOUS ROBBERY SHALL THY BOUNTY BE. | FLAMING HEART | 91 | 52 324 61 |

## GRATITUDE

| | | | |
|---|---|---|---|
| 'TIS GRATITUDE TO FORGETT THAT OTHER | O GLORIOSA DOMINA | 25 | 52 302 194 |

## GRAVE

| | | | |
|---|---|---|---|
| (THAT LIV'D SO SWEETLY) DEAD, SO SWEET A GRAVE. | MUSICKS DUELL | 168 | 46 149 535 |
| AND NOW THAT GRAVE ASPECT HATH DEIGN'D TO SHRINKE | UPON BISHOP ANDREWES PICTURE | 13 | 46 163 490 |
| NOW THE GRAVE LIES BURIED. | UPON SEPULCHRE OF OUR LORD | 2 | 46 86 26 |
| THRON'D IN THY GRAVE. | EASTER DAY | 17 | 46 100 26 |
| WHICH OF THEM DEEP'ST SHALL DIGGE HER WATRY GRAVE. | SOSPETTO D'HERODE | 428 | 46 109 216 |
| SWEPT HIM OFF INTO HIS GRAVE. | HIS EPITAPH (HERRYS) | 48 | 46 172 471 |
| THE GRAVE, AND HOLD UP AN EXALTED ARME | TO THE MORNING | 26 | 46 183 497 |
| LET HOARY TIME'S VAST BOWELS BE THE GRAVE | ON FRONTISPIECE ISAACSONS | 1 | 46 191 491 |
| AND SOBER PACE MARCH ON TO MEET A GRAVE. | TO THE NAME OF JESUS | 202 | 52 239 30 |
| BUT MUST THY BED, LORD, BE A BOROW'D GRAVE | OFFICE H. CROSS COMPLINE | 9 | 52 274 105 |
| NOW THE GRAVE LYES BURYED. | UPON THE H. SEPULCHER | 2 | 52 277 26 |
| THE INHERITANCE OF A HASTY GRAVE. | O GLORIOSA DOMINA | 14 | 52 302 194 |
| THEN TO A VIRGIN GRAVE UNTOUCH'T TO GOE. | ALEXIAS THIRD ELEGIE | 26 | 52 336 209 |
| OR ELSE, MY LIFE, I'LE HIDE THEE IN HIS GRAVE, | MATH. 16. 25. WHOSOEVER SHALL | 3 | MS 381 16 |
| ALONG THE SHORE IN A GRAVE PURPLE TIDE. | ON GUNPOWDER-TREASON | 34 | MS 384 458 |
| NOW BUT THE GRAVE. THE GRAVE IT SELFE I TAM'D. | OUT OF GROTIUS | 86 | MS 398 198 |
| NOW BUT THE GRAVE. THE GRAVE IT SELFE I TAM'D. | OUT OF GROTIUS | 86 | MS 398 198 |

## GRAVE'S

| | | | |
|---|---|---|---|
| THIS GRAVE'S THE SECOND MARRIAGE-BED. | AN EPITAPH HUSBAND AND WIFE | 2 | 46 174 478 |
| THIS GRAVE'S THEIR SECOND MARRIAGE-BED. | AN EPITAPH UPON MARRIED COUPLE | 2 | 52 339 478 |

## GRAVES

| | | | |
|---|---|---|---|
| AND URGE THE MURMURING GRAVES TO BRING | DIES IRAE | 11 | 52 298 186 |
| AND SURE WHERE LOVERS MAKE THEIR WATRY GRAVES | ALEXIAS FIRST ELEGIE | 25 | 52 334 204 |

## GRAVER

| | | | |
|---|---|---|---|
| WITH THE COOLE EPODE OF A GRAVER NOAT, | MUSICKS DUELL | 99 | 46 149 535 |

## GREAT

| | | | |
|---|---|---|---|
| FOUNDED TO TH' NAME OF GREAT APOLLO'S LYRE. | MUSICKS DUELL | 74 | 46 149 535 |
| LED ROUND IN HIS GREAT CIRCLE. NO WINDS BREATH | OUT OF VIRGIL | 27 | 46 155 529 |
| THROUGH THE GREAT MOUTH THATS NAM'D FROM HERCULES) | THE BEGINNING OF HELIODORUS | 6 | 46 158 517 |
| ALL ONE GREAT EYE, ALL DROWN'D IN ONE GREAT TEARE. | UPON BISHOP ANDREWES PICTURE | 4 | 46 163 490 |
| ALL ONE GREAT EYE, ALL DROWN'D IN ONE GREAT TEARE. | UPON BISHOP ANDREWES PICTURE | 4 | 46 163 490 |
| OF HER GREAT MAKER FIXT HER FLAMING EYE, | UPON BISHOP ANDREWES PICTURE | 11 | 46 163 490 |
| WAS A GREAT WONDER. | UPON ASSE THAT BORE SAVIOUR | 10 | 46 90 19 |
| TUN'D TO MY GREAT SHEPHEARDS PRAISE. | PSALME 23 | 34 | 46 102 5 |
| ON THE PROUD BANKES OF GREAT EUPHRATES FLOOD, | PSALME 137 | 1 | 46 104 7 |
| GREAT LITLE ONE, WHOSE GLORIOUS BIRTH, | A HYMNE OF THE NATIVITY | 57 | 46 106 76 |
| GREAT ANTHONY. SPAINS WELL-BESEEMING PRIDE. | SOSPETTO D'HERODE | 9 | 46 109 216 |
| BELOW THE BOTOME OF THE GREAT ABYSSE, | SOSPETTO D'HERODE | 33 | 46 109 216 |
| NEW MATTER, TO MAKE GOOD HIS GREAT SUSPECT. | SOSPETTO D'HERODE | 88 | 46 109 216 |
| WAS THE GREAT BUSINESSE BOTH OF HEAV'N AND EARTH. | SOSPETTO D'HERODE | 120 | 46 109 216 |
| STRUCKE WITH THESE GREAT CONCURRENCES OF THINGS. | SOSPETTO D'HERODE | 137 | 46 109 216 |
| THAT THE GREAT ANGELL-BLINDING LIGHT SHOULD SHRINKE | SOSPETTO D'HERODE | 169 | 46 109 216 |
| OH MEE. (THUS BELLOW'D HEE) OH MEE, WHAT GREAT | SOSPETTO D'HERODE | 201 | 46 109 216 |
| FROWNE I. AND CAN GREAT NATURE KEEP HER SEAT. | SOSPETTO D'HERODE | 205 | 46 109 216 |
| IN OUR GREAT PROJECTS, BOTH 'GAINST HEAV'N AND EARTH. | SOSPETTO D'HERODE | 286 | 46 109 216 |
| THE SCEPTER, WHICH OF OLD GREAT DAVID SWAID. | SOSPETTO D'HERODE | 402 | 46 109 216 |
| THE FATES RIPE, IN THEIR GREAT CONSPIRACY. | SOSPETTO D'HERODE | 432 | 46 109 216 |
| OF THY GREAT SELFE, HATH STOLNE KING HEROD FROM THEE. | SOSPETTO D'HERODE | 458 | 46 109 216 |
| IMMORTALL STINGS TO THY GREAT THOUGHTS, AND THEE. | SOSPETTO D'HERODE | 464 | 46 109 216 |
| IT IS LOVES GREAT ARTILLERY, | ON A PRAYER BOOKE | 9 | 46 126 139 |
| THEIR GREAT LORDS GLORIOUS NAME, TO NONE | IN MEMORY OF LADY MADRE TERESA | 9 | 46 131 52 |
| FOR LOVE THEIR LORD, GLORIOUS AND GREAT, | IN MEMORY OF LADY MADRE TERESA | 11 | 46 131 52 |
| SINCE THY GREAT SONNE WILL HAVE IT SO. | ON THE ASSUMPTION | 26 | 46 139 114 |
| A BROOKE WHOSE STREAMES SO GREAT, SO GOOD, | AN EPITAPH DOCTOR BROOKE | 1 | 46 175 465 |
| TH'AST NEED O BRITTAINE TO BE TRULY GREAT. | UPON YORKE HIS BIRTH | 16 | 46 176 500 |
| BRING THEIR HEAVEN WITH THEM, THEIR GREAT FOOTSTEPS PLACE | UPON YORKE HIS BIRTH | 19 | 46 176 500 |
| HOW THY GREAT MOTHER NATURE DOATS ON THEE. | UPON YORKE HIS BIRTH | 26 | 46 176 500 |
| GREAT CHARLES. THOU SWEET DAWNE OF A GLORIOUS DAY. | UPON YORKE HIS BIRTH | 29 | 46 176 500 |
| ARE TA'NE OUT AND TRANSCRIB'D BY THY GREAT MOTHER, | UPON YORKE HIS BIRTH | 41 | 46 176 500 |
| JUSTLY, GREAT NATURE, MAY'ST THOU BRAG AND TELL | UPON YORKE HIS BIRTH | 49 | 46 176 500 |
| THEN THIS GREAT MORNINGS MIGHTY BUSYNES. | TO THE NAME OF JESUS | 23 | 52 239 30 |
| GREAT NATURE FOR THE KEY OF HER HUGE CHEST | TO THE NAME OF JESUS | 29 | 52 239 30 |
| AND PLACE IN THE GREAT THRONG | TO THE NAME OF JESUS | 90 | 52 239 30 |
| GREAT LITTLE ONE, WHOSE ALL-EMBRACING BIRTH | IN HOLY NATIVITY | 83 | 52 246 76 |
| TO THEE, THE WORLD'S GREAT UNIVERSAL EAST. | IN GLORIOUS EPIPHANIE | 24 | 52 253 39 |
| DECIDE & SETTLE THE GREAT CAUSE | IN GLORIOUS EPIPHANIE | 146 | 52 253 39 |
| AND THE GREAT PENITENT PRESSE HIS OWN PALE LIPPS | IN GLORIOUS EPIPHANIE | 151 | 52 253 39 |
| COME FORTH GREAT MASTER OF THE MYSTICK DAY. | IN GLORIOUS EPIPHANIE | 207 | 52 253 39 |

| | | | | | |
|---|---|---|---|---|---|
| MAY THE GREAT TIME, IN YOU, STILL GREATER BE | TO THE QUEEN'S MAJESTY | 25 | 52 | 261 | 47 |
| THAT FATALL PLANT, SO GREAT OF FAME | OFFICE H. CROSS SIXT | 5 | 52 | 270 | 97 |
| HIS OWN LOVE'S, & OUR SIN'S GREAT SACRIFICE. | OFFICE H. CROSS NINTH | 6 | 52 | 271 | 99 |
| GATHER NOW THY GREIF'S RIPE FRUIT. GREAT MOTHER-MAID. | OFFICE H. CROSS EVENSONG | 7 | 52 | 273 | 101 |
| BUT THOUGH GREAT LOVE, GREEDY OF SUCH SAD GAIN | VEXILLA REGIS | 13 | 52 | 277 | 156 |
| (GREAT QUEEN OF GREIFES) & GIVE | SANCTA MARIA DOLORUM | 58 | 52 | 283 | 162 |
| COME YOUR WHOLE SELVES, SORROW'S GREAT SON & MOTHER. | SANCTA MARIA DOLORUM | 77 | 52 | 283 | 162 |
| TO THE GREAT TWELVE DISTRIBUTED | LAUDA SION SALVATOREM | 10 | 52 | 294 | 178 |
| GLORY TO THEE, GREAT VIRGIN'S SON | O GLORIOSA DOMINA | 37 | 52 | 302 | 194 |
| CAN SO GREAT FLAMES AGREE | WEEPER | 99 | 52 | 307 | 120 |
| THOSE THY OLD SOULDIERS, GREAT & TALL, | TERESA | 4 | 52 | 315 | 52 |
| THEIR GREAT LORD'S GLORIOUS NAME, TO NONE | TERESA | 9 | 52 | 315 | 52 |
| AND THIS THE GREAT TERESIA. | FLAMING HEART | 6 | 52 | 324 | 61 |
| HAD FILL'D THE HAND OF THIS GREAT HEART. | FLAMING HEART | 36 | 52 | 324 | 61 |
| HEAVN'S GREAT ARTILLERY IN EACH LOVE-SPUN LINE. | FLAMING HEART | 56 | 52 | 324 | 61 |
| LIVE HERE, GREAT HEART, & LOVE AND DY & KILL. | FLAMING HEART | 79 | 52 | 324 | 61 |
| LO HERE A LITTLE VOLUME, BUT GREAT BOOK. | PRAYER TO GENTLE-WOMAN | 1 | 52 | 328 | 139 |
| IT IS LOVE'S GREAT ARTILLERY | PRAYER TO GENTLE-WOMAN | 15 | 52 | 328 | 139 |
| MY BOSOME'S GUARD, A SPIRIT GREAT & STRONG. | ALEXIAS THIRD ELEGIE | 35 | 52 | 336 | 209 |
| WHO GRANTS AT LAST, A GREAT TRY'DE. | AGAINST IRRESOLUTION AND DELAY | 9 | 52 | 347 | 146 |
| THAT MADE GREAT LOVE A MAN OF WARRE. | IN CICATRICES DOMINI JESU | 6 | MS | 381 | 27 |
| SWEET MISTRIS SOUNDS A GREAT DEALE BETTER. | PETRONIJ ALES PHASIACIS PETITA | 18 | MS | 382 | 526 |
| IT DOES PRAESAGE, THAT A GREAT PRINCE SHALL CLIMBE, | ON GUNPOWDER-TREASON | 35 | MS | 384 | 458 |
| I MEANE THOSE THREE GREAT STARRES, WHO WELL MAY SCORNE | UPON KINGS CORONATION | 31 | MS | 389 | 454 |
| THE WORLD WILL BE ONE OCEAN, ONE GREAT TEARE. | UPON KINGS CORONATION | 42 | MS | 389 | 454 |
| HAD YOU, LIKE OUR GREAT SUNNE, STAMPED BUT ONE | UPON BIRTH PRINCESSE E | 27 | MS | 391 | 456 |
| SPEAKES THE GREAT WISDOME OF TH' ARTIFICER. | UPON BIRTH PRINCESSE E | 40 | MS | 391 | 456 |
| GREAT NYMPH, O'RELOOKE MY LOWNESSE. HEAV'N YOU KNOW, | EX EUPHORMIONE | 7 | MS | 392 | 525 |
| OF THEIR MAD SIN. (HOW GREAT. AND YETT HOW VAYNE.) | OUT OF GROTIUS | 30 | MS | 398 | 198 |
| GREAT NATURES SELFE HATH SHRUNKE AND SPOKE MEE GOD. | OUT OF GROTIUS | 50 | MS | 398 | 198 |

GREATER

| | | | | | |
|---|---|---|---|---|---|
| BUT O ME THINKES 'TIS A FARRE GREATER ONE | UPON ASSE THAT BORE SAVIOUR | 11 | 46 | 90 | 19 |
| MAY THE GREAT TIME, IN YOU, STILL GREATER BE | TO THE QUEEN'S MAJESTY | 25 | 52 | 261 | 47 |

GREATNESSE

| | | | | | |
|---|---|---|---|---|---|
| HAND (O WHAT DARES NOT JEALOUS GREATNESSE.) TORE | SOSPETTO D'HERODE | 3 | 46 | 109 | 216 |
| THEY ARE THY GREATNESSE. GODS WHERE E'RE THEY GO | UPON YORKE HIS BIRTH | 18 | 46 | 176 | 500 |

GREEDY

| | | | | | |
|---|---|---|---|---|---|
| AND FLATTER'D EVERY GREEDY EYE THAT STOOD | UPON DEATH OF HERRYS | 26 | 46 | 167 | 466 |
| BUT THOUGH GREAT LOVE, GREEDY OF SUCH SAD GAIN | VEXILLA REGIS | 13 | 52 | 277 | 156 |
| AND STREIGHT HIS AMOROUS SYTH (GREEDY OF BLISSE) | AN ELEGY MR STANNINOW | 47 | MS | 394 | 473 |

GREENE

| | | | | | |
|---|---|---|---|---|---|
| OF TIBER, ON THE SCEANE OF A GREENE PLAT, | MUSICKS DUELL | 3 | 46 | 149 | 535 |
| THEIR GREENE BACKS WERE HIS LIVERIE. | PSALME 23 | 8 | 46 | 102 | 5 |
| HIS ADAMANTINE FETTERS FALL. GREENE VIGOUR | SOSPETTO D'HERODE | 107 | 46 | 109 | 216 |
| THAT HIS SHOULD FADE, WHILE THINE IS GREENE. | UPON DEATH OF DESIRED HERRYS | 20 | 46 | 168 | 467 |
| THE SEA SHALL CHANGE HIS YOUTHFULL GREENE, & SLIDE | ON GUNPOWDER-TREASON | 33 | MS | 384 | 458 |
| THE QUEENE OF NIGHT GOTT THE GREENE SICKNES THEN, | UPON GUNPOWDER TREASON | 23 | MS | 386 | 460 |
| KIND WINTER'S GUIFT, & IN A GREENE ONE DIGHT. | AN ELEGY MR STANNINOW | 6 | MS | 394 | 473 |
| AND OUT OF THEIR GREENE MANTLETTS DARE TO PEEPE. | AN ELEGY MR STANNINOW | 26 | MS | 394 | 473 |

GREET

| | | | | | |
|---|---|---|---|---|---|
| ANGELLS THY OLD FRIENDS THERE SHALL GREET THEE, | IN MEMORY OF LADY MADRE TERESA | 138 | 46 | 131 | 52 |
| ANGELS, THY OLD FREINDS, THERE SHALL GREET THEE | TERESA | 137 | 52 | 315 | 52 |

GREISLY

| | | | | | |
|---|---|---|---|---|---|
| THY GREISLY MAJESTY, HELL'S BLACKEST QUEENE. | HORATIJ ILLE & NEFASTO | 34 | MS | 382 | 530 |
| AND GREISLY VISAGES DOE FRIGHT THE AIRE. | UPON GUNPOWDER TREASON | 10 | MS | 387 | 461 |

GREIVED

| | | | | | |
|---|---|---|---|---|---|
| BUT, SO LONG SHE GREIVED, | WEEPER | 153 | 52 | 307 | 120 |

GREIV'D

| | | | | | |
|---|---|---|---|---|---|
| BUT SO LONG SHE GREIV'D, | THE WEEPER | 117 | 46 | 79 | 120 |

GREIVOUS

| | | | | | |
|---|---|---|---|---|---|
| GLORIOUS, OR GREIVOUS MORE. THUS TO MAKE GOOD | VEXILLA REGIS | 29 | 52 | 277 | 156 |

GREW

| | | | | | |
|---|---|---|---|---|---|
| THUS GREW THIS GRATIOUS PLANT, IN WHOSE SWEET SHADE | UPON DEATH OF HERRYS | 9 | 46 | 167 | 466 |

GRIEF

| | | | | | |
|---|---|---|---|---|---|
| MAY BALSAME BEE FOR THEIR OWN GRIEF. | THE WEEPER | 78 | 46 | 79 | 120 |

GREIF

| | | | | | |
|---|---|---|---|---|---|
| AT LEAST AN ALMES OF GREIF | SANCTA MARIA DOLORUM | 92 | 52 | 283 | 162 |

## GREIF'S

| | | | |
|---|---|---|---|
| GATHER NOW THY GREIF'S RIPE FRUIT. GREAT MOTHER-MAID. | OFFICE H. CROSS EVENSONG | 7 | 52 273 101 |

## GREIFE

| | | | |
|---|---|---|---|
| BALSOM MAYBE, FOR THEIR OWN GREIFE. | WEEPER | 60 | 52 307 120 |
| MY SKILLFULL GREIFE IS GROWN FAMILIAR. | ALEXIAS SECONDE ELEGIE | 24 | 52 335 207 |
| DID EVER GREIFE, & JOY IN ONE POORE HEART | LUKE 2. QUAERIT JESUM | 3 | MS 379 11 |
| MY JOYES, & HEE ARE GONE. MY GREIFE, & I | LUKE 2. QUAERIT JESUM | 11 | MS 379 11 |
| MAKE HAST, & COME, OR E'RE MY GREIFE, & I | LUKE 2. QUAERIT JESUM | 17 | MS 379 11 |
| AND MISTS OF GREIFE, DARE FORCE A JOYFULL LIGHT. | UPON KINGS CORONATION | 16 | MS 389 454 |
| WITH A BLACK MASKE. THE CLOUDS WITH CHILD BY GREIFE | UPON KINGS CORONATION | 3 | MS 390 453 |
| (AS TOKENS OF HER GREIFE) UNTO THE EARTH. | UPON KINGS CORONATION | 8 | MS 390 453 |
| THESE CATARACTS OF GREIFE, THAT DARE EV'N VIE | AN ELEGY MR STANNINOW | 17 | MS 394 473 |
| THAT GREIFE MAY CRACK THAT STRING, & NOW UNTIE | AN ELEGIE ON DR PORTER | 35 | MS 395 476 |
| FEARE NOT TO DY WITH GREIFE. ALL BUBLING EYES | AN ELEGIE ON DR PORTER | 43 | MS 395 476 |

## GRIEFE

| | | | |
|---|---|---|---|
| NOTHING SPEAKES OUR GRIEFE SO WELL | UPON THE DEATH OF A GENTLEMAN | 23 | 46 166 472 |
| WELCOME MY GRIEFE, MY JOY. HOW DEARE'S | VERILY YE SHALL WEEP | 1 | 46 95 22 |
| STROKES AND TAMES MY RABID GRIEFE, | PSALME 23 | 19 | 46 102 5 |
| LEST FOR GRIEFE HIS LOSSE MAY MOVE. | UPON DEATH OF DESIRED HERRYS | 73 | 46 168 467 |
| AS MIGHT HAVE TAUGHT GRIEFE HOW TO WEEPE. | ANOTHER ON HERRYS | 22 | 46 170 469 |
| ALL THE TEARES THAT GRIEFE CAN LEND. | ANOTHER ON HERRYS | 58 | 46 170 469 |
| MY GRIEFE IS. SO MY WAKEFULL LAY SHALL KNOCKE | TO THE MORNING | 41 | 46 183 497 |

## GRIEFS

| | | | |
|---|---|---|---|
| THAT GLORIES SELFE SHOULD SERVE OUR GRIEFS, & FEARES. | SOSPETTO D'HERODE | 183 | 46 109 216 |

## GRIEFES

| | | | |
|---|---|---|---|
| YET MAY THESE UNFLEDG'D GRIEFES GIVE FATE SOME GUESSE. | OUR LORD IN HIS CIRCUMCISION | 13 | 46 98 9 |
| THE FOREHEAD'S SHADE IN GRIEFES EXPRESSION THERE. | SOSPETTO D'HERODE | 196 | 46 109 216 |

## GREIFES

| | | | |
|---|---|---|---|
| (GREAT QUEEN OF GREIFES) & GIVE | SANCTA MARIA DOLORUM | 58 | 52 283 162 |
| OF GREIFES HIS PORTION. WHO (HAD ALL THEIR DUE) | SANCTA MARIA DOLORUM | 79 | 52 283 162 |

## GRIEVES

| | | | |
|---|---|---|---|
| SHEE FAILES, AND FAILING GRIEVES, AND GRIEVING DYES. | MUSICKS DUELL | 165 | 46 149 535 |

## GRIEVING

| | | | |
|---|---|---|---|
| SHEE FAILES, AND FAILING GRIEVES, AND GRIEVING DYES. | MUSICKS DUELL | 165 | 46 149 535 |

## GRIM

| | | | |
|---|---|---|---|
| GRIM DESTRUCTION HERE AMAZ'D | ANOTHER ON HERRYS | 31 | 46 170 469 |

## GRIMME

| | | | |
|---|---|---|---|
| COME GRIMME DESTRUCTION, & IN PURPLE GORE | UPON GUNPOWDER TREASON | 3 | MS 387 461 |

## GRIPES

| | | | |
|---|---|---|---|
| GRIPES THY COLD LIMBES SOE FAST, THOU CANST NOT FLY, | ON GUNPOWDER-TREASON | 4 | MS 384 458 |

## GROAN

| | | | |
|---|---|---|---|
| WHEN A DEEP GROAN FROM BENEATH | DIES IRAE | 14 | 52 298 186 |

## GROANE

| | | | |
|---|---|---|---|
| A WINTERS THUNDER WITH A GROANE SHALL SCARE. | ON GUNPOWDER-TREASON | 28 | MS 384 458 |

## GRONE

| | | | |
|---|---|---|---|
| HIS BREATH HELLS LIGHTNING IS, AND EACH DEEPE GRONE | SOSPETTO D'HERODE | 55 | 46 109 216 |

## GROANES

| | | | |
|---|---|---|---|
| IN SURLY GROANES DISDAINES THE TREBLES GRACE. | MUSICKS DUELL | 50 | 46 149 535 |
| THE NINTH WITH AWFULL HORROR HEARKENED TO THOSE GROANES | OFFICE H. CROSS NINTH | 1 | 52 271 99 |
| LETT THY SWOLNE BREAST DISCHARGE THY STRUGLING GROANES | AN ELEGIE ON DR PORTER | 31 | MS 395 476 |

## GROANING

| | | | |
|---|---|---|---|
| DEEP IN THE GROANING WATERS WALLOWED | THE BEGINNING OF HELIODORUS | 13 | 46 158 517 |

## GROSSE

| | | | |
|---|---|---|---|
| HER GLORIES I SHOULD DIMME WITH THINGS SOE GROSSE. | UPON BIRTH PRINCESSE E | 53 | MS 391 456 |

## GROSSEST

| | | | |
|---|---|---|---|
| IN GROSSEST METALLS HIS OWN GOLD. | AGAINST IRRESOLUTION AND DELAY | 56 | 52 347 146 |

## GROUND

| | | | | |
|---|---|---|---|---|
| DEATH'S PURPLE TRIUMPH, ON THE BLUSHING GROUND | THE BEGINNING OF HELIODORUS | 15 | 46 158 | 517 |
| THE TRUNKE.  YET IN THIS GROUND HIS PRETIOUS ROOT | UPON DEATH OF HERRYS | 35 | 46 167 | 466 |
| A QUIET PASSAGE UNDER GROUND. | AN EPITAPH DOCTOR BROOKE | 6 | 46 175 | 465 |
| ON THIS DARK GROUND | IN GLORIOUS EPIPHANIE | 194 | 52 253 | 39 |
| THY TRAITEROUS ROOT A DWELLING IN MY GROUND. | HORATIJ ILLE & NEFASTO | 14 | MS 382 | 530 |
| Y' HAD DONE ENOUGH TO MAKE THE LAZY GROUND | UPON BIRTH PRINCESSE E | 31 | MS 391 | 456 |

## GROUNDS

| | | | | |
|---|---|---|---|---|
| THRIV'D IN THESE HAPPY GROUNDS, THE EARTH'S JUST PRIDE, | UPON DEATH OF HERRYS | 3 | 46 167 | 466 |

## GROUND-WORKE

| | | | | |
|---|---|---|---|---|
| AND LAY THE GROUND-WORKE OF HER HOPEFULL SONG. | MUSICKS DUELL | 85 | 46 149 | 535 |

## GROVE

| | | | | |
|---|---|---|---|---|
| OF DRAGONS, HYDRAES, SPHINXES, FILL THE GROVE. | SOSPETTO D'HERODE | 352 | 46 109 | 216 |
| NO SHEE'S A PRIESTESSE OF THAT GROVE | THOUGH NOW 'TIS NEITHER | 21 | MS 397 | 492 |

## GROVES

| | | | | |
|---|---|---|---|---|
| ALL TREES, ALL LEAVY GROVES CONFESSE THE SPRING | OUT OF VIRGIL | 1 | 46 155 | 529 |
| WITH YOUR BRIGHT HEAD WHOLE GROVES OF SCEPTERS BEND | TO THE QUEEN'S MAJESTY | 17 | 52 261 | 47 |
| FOR THEE I TALK TO TREES, WITH SILENT GROVES | ALEXIAS SECONDE ELEGIE | 13 | 52 335 | 207 |
| OF THESE LOOSE GROVES, ROUGH AS TH'UNPOLISH'T ROCKES. | DESCRIPTION RELIGIOUS HOUSE | 14 | 52 336 | 213 |

## GROW

| | | | | |
|---|---|---|---|---|
| WOULDST SEE A NEST OF ROSES GROW | IN PRAISE OF LESSIUS | 41 | 46 156 | 510 |
| NOW STRETCH THY SELF (FAIRE ILE) AND GROW, SPREAD WIDE | UPON YORKE HIS BIRTH | 2 | 46 176 | 500 |
| GROW THOU & THEY, AND BE THY FAIR INCREASE | VEXILLA REGIS | 41 | 52 277 | 156 |
| QUICK DEATHS THAT GROW | SANCTA MARIA DOLORUM | 25 | 52 283 | 162 |
| GROW, BUT IN NEW POWRES TO THY NAME & PRAISE. | ADORO TE | 36 | 52 291 | 172 |
| WOULDST' SEE NESTS OF NEW ROSES GROW | TEMPERANCE | 39 | 52 342 | 510 |
| GROW PLUMPE, LEANE DEATH. HIS HOLINESSE A FEAST | UPON GUNPOWDER TREASON | 1 | MS 387 | 461 |

## GROWS

| | | | | |
|---|---|---|---|---|
| PROGRESSIONS 'TWIXT WHOSE TERMES POOR TIME GROWS OLD. | UPON TWO GREENE APRICOCKES | 16 | 48 220 | 494 |

## GROWES

| | | | | |
|---|---|---|---|---|
| AND MEET THE MISCHIEFE THAT UPON THEE GROWES. | SOSPETTO D'HERODE | 246 | 46 109 | 216 |
| THE GENEROUS WINE WITH AGE GROWES STRONG, NOT SOWER. | ON HOPE | 53 | 46 143 | 71 |
| A CHEEKE WHERE GROWES | WISHES SUPPOSED MISTRESSE | 34 | 46 195 | 479 |
| GROWES WANTON, & WILL DY. | CHARITAS NIMIA | 44 | 52 280 | 48 |
| THY GENEROUS WINE WITH AGE GROWES STRONG, NOT SOWER. | (ON) HOPE | 23 | 52 345 | 71 |

## GROWING

| | | | | |
|---|---|---|---|---|
| TO THEE THESE FIRST FRUITS OF MY GROWING DEATH | OUR LORD IN HIS CIRCUMCISION | 1 | 46 98 | 9 |
| TO WHICH HIS GNAW'D HEART IS THE GROWING FOOD | SOSPETTO D'HERODE | 494 | 46 109 | 216 |
| OF FAITH.  THE STEWARD OF OUR GROWING STOCKE. | ON HOPE | 32 | 46 143 | 71 |
| HER SWORDS, STILL GROWING WITH HIS PAIN. | SANCTA MARIA DOLORUM | 29 | 52 283 | 162 |
| OF FAITH. STILL SPENDING, & STILL GROWING STOCK. | (ON) HOPE | 12 | 52 345 | 71 |
| THY GOLDEN, GROWING HEAD NEVER HANGS DOWN | (ON) HOPE | 25 | 52 345 | 71 |

## GROWN

| | | | | |
|---|---|---|---|---|
| O I AM LEARNED GROWN, POOR LOVE & I | ALEXIAS SECONDE ELEGIE | 21 | 52 335 | 207 |
| MY SKILLFULL GREIFE IS GROWN FAMILIAR. | ALEXIAS SECONDE ELEGIE | 24 | 52 335 | 207 |

## FULL-GROWN

| | | | | |
|---|---|---|---|---|
| WE READ IN YOU (RARE QUEEN) RIPE & FULL-GROWN. | TO THE QUEEN'S MAJESTY | 10 | 52 261 | 47 |

## GROWNE

| | | | | |
|---|---|---|---|---|
| (GROWNE LUSTY NOW.) NO VINE SO WEAKE AND YOUNG | OUT OF VIRGIL | 18 | 46 155 | 529 |
| RIPE AND FULL GROWNE, THAT COULD REACH DOWNE, | IN MEMORY OF LADY MADRE TERESA | 5 | 46 131 | 52 |

## GROUNE

| | | | | |
|---|---|---|---|---|
| THE PRETIOUS BARBILL, NOW GROUNE RIFE, | PETRONIJ ALES PHASIACIS PETITA | 15 | MS 382 | 526 |

## GROWTH

| | | | | |
|---|---|---|---|---|
| THE TENDER GROWTH OF THINGS ENDURE THE SENCE | OUT OF VIRGIL | 33 | 46 155 | 529 |
| HIM HIS WISDOMES PREGNANT GROWTH | HIS EPITAPH (HERRYS) | 15 | 46 172 | 471 |
| AND LET NO DULL MISTS CHOAKE THE LIGHTS FAIRE GROWTH. | ON A FOULE MORNING | 4 | 46 181 | 495 |
| NATURE (METHINKS) MIGHT EASILY MEND HER GROWTH. | UPON TWO GREENE APRICOCKES | 22 | 48 220 | 494 |
| HIS FEARE.  THE CIRCLE OF A YEARES ROUND GROWTH | OUT OF GROTIUS | 22 | MS 398 | 198 |

## GROUTH

| | | | | |
|---|---|---|---|---|
| FLOURISHT IN SO FAIRE A GROUTH. | ANOTHER ON HERRYS | 14 | 46 170 | 469 |

## GRUDGE

| | | | |
|---|---|---|---|
| NOR GRUDGE A YONGER-BROTHER | SANCTA MARIA DOLORUM | 78 | 52 283 162 |

## GRUMBLING

| | | | |
|---|---|---|---|
| MOST KINDLY DOE FALL OUT. THE GRUMBLING BASE | MUSICKS DUELL | 49 | 46 149 535 |

## GRUTCH

| | | | |
|---|---|---|---|
| BY VARIOUS GLOSSES. NOW THEY SEEME TO GRUTCH, | MUSICKS DUELL | 128 | 46 149 535 |

## GUARD

| | | | |
|---|---|---|---|
| MY BOSOME'S GUARD, A SPIRIT GREAT & STRONG, | ALEXIAS THIRD ELEGIE | 35 | 52 336 209 |
| NO CRUELL GUARD OF DILIGENT CARES, THAT KEEP | DESCRIPTION RELIGIOUS HOUSE | 28 | 52 336 213 |
| OF ALL PROUD NEPTUNES SILVER-SHEILDED GUARD. | AN ELEGIE ON DR PORTER | 34 | MS 395 476 |

## GUARDIAN

| | | | |
|---|---|---|---|
| HONESTIES NURSE, VERTUES BLEST GUARDIAN, | AN ELEGIE ON DR PORTER | 17 | MS 395 476 |

## GUESSE

| | | | |
|---|---|---|---|
| YET MAY THESE UNFLEDG'D GRIEFES GIVE FATE SOME GUESSE, | OUR LORD IN HIS CIRCUMCISION | 13 | 46 98 9 |
| SHALL WITH A VIGOROUS GUESSE INVADE | IN GLORIOUS EPIPHANIE | 192 | 52 253 39 |

## GUEST

| | | | |
|---|---|---|---|
| WHERE HUNGRY WARRE HAD MADE HIMSELF A GUEST. | THE BEGINNING OF HELIODORUS | 26 | 46 158 517 |
| WHEN SOME NEW BRIGHT GUEST | THE WEEPER | 31 | 46 79 120 |
| THIS NEW GUEST TO HER EYES NEW LAWES HATH GIVEN, | ON VIRGINS BASHFULNESSE | 7 | 46 89 9 |
| HEE'L BE THY GUEST, BECAUSE HE MAY NOT BE, | I AM NOT WORTHY | 3 | 46 90 13 |
| A WITHER'D LEAFE, AN IDLE GUEST. | PSALME 137 | 24 | 46 104 7 |
| AND GIVE THY SELF A WHILE THE GRACIOUS GUEST | TO THE NAME OF JESUS | 120 | 52 239 30 |
| BE ALL THE SAME TO EVERY GUEST, | LAUDA SION SALVATOREM | 50 | 52 294 178 |
| THE WHOLE WORLD'S HOST WOULD BE THY GUEST | O GLORIOSA DOMINA | 7 | 52 302 194 |
| WHEN SOME NEW BRIGHT GUEST | WEEPER | 67 | 52 307 120 |
| HATH NOW PRAEPAR'D, & YOU MUST BE HIS GUEST. | UPON GUNPOWDER TREASON | 2 | MS 387 461 |
| DRINKE FAYLING THERE WHERE I A GUEST DID SHINE | OUT OF GROTIUS | 51 | MS 398 198 |

## GUESTS

| | | | |
|---|---|---|---|
| AND COMMING LATE HAD EAT UP GUESTS AND ALL, | THE BEGINNING OF HELIODORUS | 27 | 46 158 517 |
| TANTALUS, ATREUS, PROGNE, HERE ARE GUESTS. | SOSPETTO D'HERODE | 333 | 46 109 216 |

## GUIDE

| | | | |
|---|---|---|---|
| THESE MARKES MAY BEE YOUR JUDGEMENTS GUIDE. | OUT OF GREEKE CUPID'S CRYER | 18 | 46 159 519 |
| HEE (MY SHEPHEARD) IS MY GUIDE, | PSALME 23 | 23 | 46 102 5 |
| THIS MASSE OF CRUELTY, TO BE THY GUIDE | UPON GUNPOWDER TREASON | 8 | MS 387 461 |

## GUILT

| | | | |
|---|---|---|---|
| THAT LABOUR'D TO HAVE WASHT THY GUILT. | TO PONTIUS WASHING HANDS | 2 | 46 88 22 |
| WITH GUILT & SIN, | CHARITAS NIMIA | 51 | 52 280 48 |
| SIFTING THE SOULES OF GUILT. & YOU, (OH YOU.) | HORATIJ ILLE & NEFASTO | 36 | MS 382 530 |

## GUILTY

| | | | |
|---|---|---|---|
| A GUILTY SWORD BLUSH FOR HER SAKE. | IN MEMORY OF LADY MADRE TERESA | 26 | 46 131 52 |
| THINE OWN DEARE BOOKS ARE GUILTY, FOR FROM THENCE | AN APOLOGIE FOR HYMNE (TERESA) | 7 | 46 136 59 |
| WAS EVER GUILTY OF, CHANGE WEE OUR SHAPE, | AN APOLOGIE FOR HYMNE (TERESA) | 34 | 46 136 59 |
| GUILTY OF BEING MUCH FOR THEM TOO GOOD. | IN GLORIOUS EPIPHANIE | 108 | 52 253 39 |
| A GUILTY SWORD BLUSH FOR HER SAKE. | TERESA | 26 | 52 315 52 |
| THINE OWN DEAR BOOKES ARE GUILTY, FOR FROM THENCE | AN APOLOGIE FOR (TERESA) HYMNE | 7 | 52 322 59 |
| WAS EVER GUILTY OF, CHANGE WE TOO 'OUR SHAPE | AN APOLOGIE FOR (TERESA) HYMNE | 34 | 52 322 59 |

## GUST

| | | | |
|---|---|---|---|
| WHOSE VITALL GUST ALONE CAN GIVE | ADORO TE | 41 | 52 291 172 |

## HAGS

| | | | |
|---|---|---|---|
| HIS FOULE HAGS RAIS'D THEIR HEADS, & CLAPT THEIR HANDS. | SOSPETTO D'HERODE | 258 | 46 109 216 |
| FOURTH OF THE CURSED KNOT OF HAGS IS SHEE, | SOSPETTO D'HERODE | 289 | 46 109 216 |

## HAIL

| | | | |
|---|---|---|---|
| ALL HAIL, FAIR TREE. | OFFICE H. CROSS MATINES | 18 | 52 265 86 |
| A HAIL MORE CRUELL THEN THEIR CRUCIFY. | OFFICE H. CROSS THIRD | 6 | 52 268 93 |
| HAIL, OUR ALONE HOPE. LET THY FAIR HEAD SHOOT | VEXILLA REGIS | 37 | 52 277 156 |
| HAIL. & STRIKE HOME & MAKE ME SEE | SANCTA MARIA DOLORUM | 73 | 52 283 162 |
| HAIL, MOST HIGH, MOST HUMBLE ONE. | O GLORIOSA DOMINA | 1 | 52 302 194 |
| HAIL, DOOR OF LIFE, & SOURSE OF DAY. | O GLORIOSA DOMINA | 32 | 52 302 194 |
| HAIL, HOLY QUEEN OF HUMBLE HEARTS. | IN GLORIOUS ASSUMPTION B. LADY | 44 | 52 304 114 |
| HAIL, SISTER SPRINGS. | WEEPER | 1 | 52 307 120 |

## HAILE

| | | | |
|---|---|---|---|
| HAILE SISTER SPRINGS, | THE WEEPER | 1 | 46 79 120 |
| HAILE HOLY QUEEN OF HUMBLE HEARTS. | ON THE ASSUMPTION | 29 | 46 139 114 |

HAIR

| | | | | | |
|---|---|---|---|---|---|
| NO HAIR SO SMALL, BUT PAYES HIS RIVER | UPON BLEEDING CRUCIFIX | 21 | 52 | 288 | 110 |
| ROSY FINGERS, RADIANT HAIR, | FLAMING HEART | 32 | 52 | 324 | 61 |

HAIRE

| | | | | | |
|---|---|---|---|---|---|
| NOT A HAIRE BUT PAYES HIS RIVER | ON BLEEDING WOUNDS OF LORD | 25 | 46 | 101 | 110 |
| FLOW THY HAIRE. | OUT OF THE ITALIAN (1) | 8 | 46 | 188 | 545 |
| THREE COLEBLACK SISTERS, (WHOSE LONG SUTTY HAIRE, | UPON GUNPOWDER TREASON | 9 | MS | 387 | 461 |

HAIRES

| | | | | | |
|---|---|---|---|---|---|
| TREMBLING AS WHEN APPOLLO'S GOLDEN HAIRES | MUSICKS DUELL | 115 | 46 | 149 | 535 |
| HER HAIRES FLAME LICKES UP THAT AGAINE. | SHE BEGAN TO WASH HIS FEET | 2 | 46 | 97 | 13 |

HALF

| | | | | | |
|---|---|---|---|---|---|
| HALF SO FRUITFULL, HALF SO FLOWING. | UPON BLEEDING CRUCIFIX | 20 | 52 | 288 | 110 |
| HALF SO FRUITFULL, HALF SO FLOWING. | UPON BLEEDING CRUCIFIX | 20 | 52 | 288 | 110 |
| HALF TRUE, ALAS, HALF FALSE, PROVES THAT POOR LINE. | ALEXIAS THIRD ELEGIE | 57 | 52 | 336 | 209 |
| HALF TRUE, ALAS, HALF FALSE, PROVES THAT POOR LINE. | ALEXIAS THIRD ELEGIE | 57 | 52 | 336 | 209 |

HALF-SPHEAR

| | | | | | |
|---|---|---|---|---|---|
| NOR MAKES THE WHOLE WORLD THY HALF-SPHEAR. | IN GLORIOUS EPIPHANIE | 41 | 52 | 253 | 39 |

HALFE

| | | | | | |
|---|---|---|---|---|---|
| MAKES SORROW HALFE SO RICH, | THE WEEPER | 45 | 46 | 79 | 120 |
| IT WILL NOT LOVE ITS DARKNESSE HALFE SO WELL. | BUT MEN LOVED DARKNESSE | 4 | 46 | 97 | 13 |
| HALFE SO FRUITFULL, HALFE SO FLOWING. | ON BLEEDING WOUNDS OF LORD | 16 | 46 | 101 | 110 |
| HALFE SO FRUITFULL, HALFE SO FLOWING. | ON BLEEDING WOUNDS OF LORD | 16 | 46 | 101 | 110 |

HALL

| | | | | | |
|---|---|---|---|---|---|
| SUCH WAS THE HOUSE, SO FURNISHT WAS THE HALL, | SOSPETTO D'HERODE | 367 | 46 | 109 | 216 |

HALLS

| | | | | | |
|---|---|---|---|---|---|
| HALLS FULL OF FLATTERING MEN & FRISKING BOYES. | DESCRIPTION RELIGIOUS HOUSE | 6 | 52 | 338 | 213 |

HALLOW

| | | | | | |
|---|---|---|---|---|---|
| ALL MISCHIEFE COMES AFTER ALL HALLOW. | UPON POWDER DAY | 2 | 46 | 185 | 74 |

HALLOWED

| | | | | | |
|---|---|---|---|---|---|
| WHOSE STROAKE SHALL TASTE THY HALLOWED BREATH. | IN MEMORY OF LADY MADRE TERESA | 80 | 46 | 131 | 52 |
| LETT TH' HALLOWED PLUME OF A SERAPHICK WING | UPON BIRTH PRINCESSE E | 22 | MS | 391 | 456 |

HALLOW'D

| | | | | | |
|---|---|---|---|---|---|
| WHOSE STROKE SHALL TAST THY HALLOW'D BREATH. | TERESA | 80 | 52 | 315 | 52 |

HALTERS

| | | | | | |
|---|---|---|---|---|---|
| NAILES, HAMMERS, HATCHETS SHARPE, AND HALTERS STRONG, | SOSPETTO D'HERODE | 325 | 46 | 109 | 216 |

HAMMERS

| | | | | | |
|---|---|---|---|---|---|
| NAILES, HAMMERS, HATCHETS SHARPE, AND HALTERS STRONG, | SOSPETTO D'HERODE | 325 | 46 | 109 | 216 |

HAND

| | | | | | |
|---|---|---|---|---|---|
| A SEA OF HELICON. HIS HAND DOES GOE | MUSICKS DUELL | 124 | 46 | 149 | 535 |
| OF HIS SMALL HAND, YET NOT SO SMALL | OUT OF GREEKE CUPID'S CRYER | 37 | 46 | 159 | 519 |
| FALLS FROM A STEADY HEART, THOUGH TREMBLING HAND. | WIDOWES MITES | 2 | 46 | 86 | 21 |
| WAITING ON THY VICTORIOUS HAND, | NEITHER DURST MAN ASKE | 10 | 46 | 92 | 20 |
| THY HAND TO GIVE THOU CANST NOT LIFT. | ON BLEEDING WOUNDS OF LORD | 9 | 46 | 101 | 110 |
| YET WILL THY HAND STILL GIVING BEE. | ON BLEEDING WOUNDS OF LORD | 10 | 46 | 101 | 110 |
| THIS HAND FORGET THE MASTERY | PSALME 137 | 16 | 46 | 104 | 7 |
| HAND (O WHAT DARES NOT JEALOUS GREATNESSE.) TORE | SOSPETTO D'HERODE | 3 | 46 | 109 | 216 |
| THOU, WHOSE STRONG HAND WITH SO TRANSCENDENT WORTH, | SOSPETTO D'HERODE | 25 | 46 | 109 | 216 |
| IMMORTALL FLOWERS TO HER FAIRE HAND PRESENT. | SOSPETTO D'HERODE | 100 | 46 | 109 | 216 |
| AND RADIANT SCEPTER THIS BOLD HAND SHOULD BEARE. | SOSPETTO D'HERODE | 210 | 46 | 109 | 216 |
| THE WALLS INEXORABLE STEELE, NO HAND | SOSPETTO D'HERODE | 309 | 46 | 109 | 216 |
| OF SORROW, WITH A SOFT AND DOWNY HAND, | SOSPETTO D'HERODE | 391 | 46 | 109 | 216 |
| SHE COMES TOTH' KING AND WITH HER COLD HAND SLAKES | SOSPETTO D'HERODE | 421 | 46 | 109 | 216 |
| A WAKING EYE AND HAND. LOOKE UP AND SEE | SOSPETTO D'HERODE | 431 | 46 | 109 | 216 |
| ALREADY IN THEIR BOSOMES, AND THEIR HAND | SOSPETTO D'HERODE | 443 | 46 | 109 | 216 |
| THAT THY FIRME HAND FOR EVER MIGHT SUSTAINE | SOSPETTO D'HERODE | 450 | 46 | 109 | 216 |
| OF YOUR WHITE HAND, THEY ARE MINE. | ON MR. G. HERBERTS BOOKE | 18 | 46 | 130 | 68 |
| OR SOME BASE HAND HAVE POWER TO RACE, | IN MEMORY OF LADY MADRE TERESA | 71 | 46 | 131 | 52 |
| INTO LOVES HAND THOU SHALT LET FALL, | IN MEMORY OF LADY MADRE TERESA | 77 | 46 | 131 | 52 |
| AND TEACH THY LIPPS HEAVEN, WITH HER HAND, | IN MEMORY OF LADY MADRE TERESA | 131 | 46 | 131 | 52 |
| E'RE HEBE'S HAND HAD OVERLAID | HIS EPITAPH (HERRYS) | 45 | 46 | 172 | 471 |
| FOR THOUGH THE HAND OF FATE COULD FORCE, | AN EPITAPH HUSBAND AND WIFE | 3 | 46 | 174 | 478 |
| HEE WITH A DAINTY AND SOFT HAND, WILL TRIM | ON A FOULE MORNING | 23 | 46 | 181 | 495 |
| O MAY SHE BUT ARRIVE AT YOUR WHITE HAND, | UPON FAIRE ETHIOPIAN | 4 | 46 | 183 | 493 |
| AND THE SAME ROSIE-FINGERD HAND OF THINE, | TO THE MORNING | 45 | 46 | 183 | 497 |
| IF ON TIMES RIGHT HAND, SIT FAIRE HISTORIE. | ON FRONTISPIECE ISAACSONS | 5 | 46 | 191 | 491 |
| HER HAND TO BRING HIM TO HIS END. | AN EPITAPH UPON ASHTON | 24 | 46 | 192 | 464 |

| | | | | |
|---|---|---|---|---|
| THEN WHAT NATURES WHITE HAND SETS OPE. | WISHES SUPPOSED MISTRESSE | 30 | 46 195 | 479 |
| THY GOLDEN INDEX. WITH A DUTEOUS HAND | IN GLORIOUS EPIPHANIE | 251 | 52 253 | 39 |
| THOUGH AS AT SECOND HAND, FROM EITHER HEART. | SANCTA MARIA DOLORUM | 70 | 52 283 | 162 |
| YET WILL THY HAND STILL GIVING BE. | UPON BLEEDING CRUCIFIX | 14 | 52 288 | 110 |
| THOUGH ALLOW'D NOR HAND NOR EYE | ADORO TE | 28 | 52 291 | 172 |
| O THAT JUDGE. WHOSE HAND, WHOSE EYE | DIES IRAE | 19 | 52 298 | 186 |
| THAT I INHERITT THY RIGHT HAND. | DIES IRAE | 64 | 52 298 | 186 |
| OR SOME BASE HAND HAVE POWER TO RACE | TERESA | 71 | 52 315 | 52 |
| AND TEACH THY LIPPS HEAV'N WITH HIS HAND. | TERESA | 130 | 52 315 | 52 |
| TO PUT HER DART INTO HIS HAND. | FLAMING HEART | 14 | 52 324 | 61 |
| HAD FILL'D THE HAND OF THIS GREAT HEART. | FLAMING HEART | 36 | 52 324 | 61 |
| THE ROSY HAND, THE RADIANT DART. | FLAMING HEART | 67 | 52 324 | 61 |
| FOR THOUGH THE HAND OF FATE COULD FORCE | AN EPITAPH UPON MARRIED COUPLE | 3 | 52 339 | 478 |
| OFT HATH THIS HAND THOSE SILKEN CASEMENTS KEPT. | LUKE 2. QUAERIT JESUM | 33 | MS 379 | 11 |
| FOR BOW HIS UNBENT HAND DID SERVE. | IN CICATRICES DOMINI JESU | 13 | MS 381 | 27 |
| A BLOODY SIDE, & HAND, & HEART. | IN CICATRICES DOMINI JESU | 16 | MS 381 | 27 |
| THAT HAND, (WHAT E'RE IT WERE) THAT WAS THY NURSE | HORATIJ ILLE & NEFASTO | 3 | MS 382 | 530 |
| BUT GIVE ME LEAVE TO EASE IT WITH MY HAND. | UPON BIRTH PRINCESSE E | 16 | MS 391 | 456 |
| THAT HAND OF MILKY DOUNE. ALL THESE ARE BASE. | UPON BIRTH PRINCESSE E | 52 | MS 391 | 456 |
| OF LOVES ALL-DARING HAND, THAT MAKES ME BURNE, | EX EUPHORMIONE | 5 | MS 392 | 525 |
| JUSTICE HATH LOST HER HAND, THE LAW HER HEAD. | AN ELEGIE ON DR PORTER | 15 | MS 395 | 476 |
| AT TH' IVORY TRIBUNALL OF YOUR HAND | AT TH' IVORY TRIBUNALL | 1 | MS 397 | 492 |

RIGHT-HAND

| | | | | |
|---|---|---|---|---|
| SOON AS THE RIGHT-HAND SCALE REJOYC'T TO PROVE | VEXILLA REGIS | 35 | 52 277 | 156 |

HANDS

| | | | | |
|---|---|---|---|---|
| HIS NIMBLE HANDS INSTINCT THEN TAUGHT EACH STRING | MUSICKS DUELL | 27 | 46 149 | 535 |
| MENS HEARTS INTO THEIR HANDS. THIS LESSON TOO | MUSICKS DUELL | 56 | 46 149 | 535 |
| SO SAID, HIS HANDS SPRIGHTLY AS FIRE HEE FLINGS, | MUSICKS DUELL | 111 | 46 149 | 535 |
| HIS HANDS WHOLE STRENGTH HERE, COULD NOT BE TOO MUCH. | THE DUMBE HEALED | 4 | 46 87 | 16 |
| THY HANDS ARE WASHT, BUT O THE WATERS SPILT, | TO PONTIUS WASHING HANDS | 1 | 46 88 | 22 |
| AND WITH SAD MURMURS, CHIDES THE HANDS THAT STAIN HER. | TO PONTIUS WASHING HANDS | 14 | 46 94 | 23 |
| FROM THY HANDS AND FROM THY FEET, | ON BLEEDING WOUNDS OF LORD | 2 | 46 101 | 110 |
| BUT LIFT CLEAN HANDS FULL OF CLEARE HEARTS. | A HYMNE OF THE NATIVITY | 76 | 46 106 | 76 |
| OF TH'ICY NORTH, FROM FROST-BOUND ATLAS HANDS | SOSPETTO D'HERODE | 106 | 46 109 | 216 |
| HIS FOULE HAGS RAIS'D THEIR HEADS, & CLAPT THEIR HANDS. | SOSPETTO D'HERODE | 258 | 46 109 | 216 |
| WHAT THY ALECTO, WHAT THESE HANDS CAN DOE, | SOSPETTO D'HERODE | 265 | 46 109 | 216 |
| TO HOLY HANDS, AND HUMBLE HEARTS, | ON A PRAYER BOOKE | 18 | 46 126 | 139 |
| THE HANDS BEE PURE. | ON A PRAYER BOOKE | 22 | 46 126 | 139 |
| WHEN YOUR HANDS UNTY THESE STRINGS, | ON MR. G. HERBERTS BOOKE | 5 | 46 130 | 68 |
| THESE HANDS AND THINE WERE HEW'N, THESE CHERRYES MOCKE | UPON YORKE HIS BIRTH | 46 | 46 176 | 500 |
| KEEP THE FREE HEART FROM IT'S OWN HANDS. | TO COUNTESSE OF DENBIGH | 20 | 52 236 | 146 |
| GASP FOR THY GOLDEN SHOWRES. WITH LONG STRETCH'T HANDS | TO THE NAME OF JESUS | 130 | 52 239 | 30 |
| SORDIDLY SHIFTING HANDS WITH SHADES & NIGHT. | IN GLORIOUS EPIPHANIE | 35 | 52 253 | 39 |
| THEIR HANDS WITH LASHES ARM'D, THEIR TOUNGS WITH LYES, | OFFICE H. CROSS PRIME | 5 | 52 267 | 91 |
| INTO THY HANDS, AND HART, LORD, I COMMEND. | OFFICE H. CROSS RECOMMENDATION | 2 | 52 276 | 106 |
| NAIL'D HANDS, & PEIRCED HEARTS. | SANCTA MARIA DOLORUM | 76 | 52 283 | 162 |
| WHICH THESE TORN HANDS TRANSCRIB'D ON THY TRUE HEART | SANCTA MARIA DOLORUM | 97 | 52 283 | 162 |
| FROM THY HANDS & FROM THY SIDE | UPON BLEEDING CRUCIFIX | 3 | 52 288 | 110 |
| THY HANDS TO GIVE, THOU CANST NOT LIFT. | UPON BLEEDING CRUCIFIX | 13 | 52 288 | 110 |
| HARPES OF HEAVN TO HANDS OF MAN. | LAUDA SION SALVATOREM | 4 | 52 294 | 178 |
| VAIN LOVES AVANT. BOLD HANDS FORBEAR. | WEEPER | 107 | 52 307 | 120 |
| (FAIR ONE) FROM THY KIND HANDS | PRAYER TO GENTLE-WOMAN | 7 | 52 328 | 139 |
| TO HOLY HANDS & HUMBLE HEARTS | PRAYER TO GENTLE-WOMAN | 24 | 52 328 | 139 |
| THE HANDS BE PURE | PRAYER TO GENTLE-WOMAN | 28 | 52 328 | 139 |
| WITH ROCKS. NOR BOLD HANDS STRUCK THE WORLD'S STRONG BARRES. | ALEXIAS THIRD ELEGIE | 10 | 52 336 | 209 |
| HANDS FULL OF HARTY LABOURS. PAINES THAT PAY | DESCRIPTION RELIGIOUS HOUSE | 19 | 52 338 | 213 |
| KEEP THE FREE HEART FROM HIS OWN HANDS. | AGAINST IRRESOLUTION AND DELAY | 14 | 52 347 | 146 |
| HIS HANDS HAVE PADLED IN. HIS HANDS, THAT FOUND | HORATIJ ILLE & NEFASTO | 13 | MS 382 | 530 |
| HIS HANDS HAVE PADLED IN. HIS HANDS, THAT FOUND | HORATIJ ILLE & NEFASTO | 13 | MS 382 | 530 |
| (WHOSE HANDS ARE FIGHTING, WHILE THEIR FEET DOE FLIE.) | HORATIJ ILLE & NEFASTO | 26 | MS 382 | 530 |
| HIS TREMBLING HANDS LOOSING THE GOLDEN RAINES. | UPON GUNPOWDER TREASON | 22 | MS 386 | 460 |

HANDFULL

| | | | | |
|---|---|---|---|---|
| IT IS IN ONE RICH HANDFULL, HEAVEN AND ALL | ON A PRAYER BOOKE | 6 | 46 126 | 139 |
| IT IS, IN ONE CHOISE HANDFULL, HEAVENN, & ALL | PRAYER TO GENTLE-WOMAN | 11 | 52 328 | 139 |

HANDLING

| | | | | |
|---|---|---|---|---|
| HANDLING & TURNING THEM WITH AN UNWOUNDED EYE. | AND A CERTAINE PRIEST PASSED | 2 | 46 94 | 17 |

HANDMAID

| | | | | |
|---|---|---|---|---|
| THY HOLYEST, HUMBLEST, HANDMAID CHARITIE. | ON A TREATISE OF CHARITY | 14 | 46 137 | 69 |

HAND-MAID

| | | | | |
|---|---|---|---|---|
| BY WHOM (AS HEAV'NS ILLUSTRIOUS HAND-MAID) RAIS'D | SOSPETTO D'HERODE | 134 | 46 109 | 216 |

HANDMAIDS

| | | | | |
|---|---|---|---|---|
| TH'OBSEQUIOUS HANDMAIDS OF THY HIGH COMMANDS. | SOSPETTO D'HERODE | 262 | 46 109 | 216 |

HANDSOME

| | | | | |
|---|---|---|---|---|
| DEARE WIFE HATH NE'RE A HANDSOME LETTER, | PETRONIJ ALES PHASIACIS PETITA | 17 | MS 382 | 526 |

HANG

| | | | | |
|---|---|---|---|---|
| AND HILLS HANG DOWN THEIR HEAVN-SALUTING HEADS | TO THE NAME OF JESUS | 231 | 52 239 | 30 |
| WILL HE HANG DOWN HIS GOLDEN HEAD | CHARITAS NIMIA | 41 | 52 280 | 48 |
| SHALL HANG THE ROOME, & FOR YOUR TAPERS BRIGHT, | UPON GUNPOWDER TREASON | 25 | MS 387 | 461 |

HANGS

| | | | | |
|---|---|---|---|---|
| (NIGHT HANGS YET HEAVY ON THE LIDS OF DAY) | SOSPETTO D'HERODE | 506 | 46 109 | 216 |
| THY GOLDEN HEAD NEVER HANGS DOWNE, | ON HOPE | 55 | 46 143 | 71 |
| THY GOLDEN, GROWING HEAD NEVER HANGS DOWN | (ON) HOPE | 25 | 52 345 | 71 |
| HANGS HIS BLACK LUGGES, STROAKT WITH THOSE HEAVENLY LINES. | HORATIJ ILLE & NEFASTO | 51 | MS 382 | 530 |

HANGING

| | | | | |
|---|---|---|---|---|
| AND FENCE THE HANGING SWORD HEAV'N THROWS UPON THEE. | SOSPETTO D'HERODE | 460 | 46 109 | 216 |
| HANGING ALL TORN SHE SEES, AND IN HIS WOES | SANCTA MARIA DOLORUM | 7 | 52 283 | 162 |

HANGINGS

| | | | | |
|---|---|---|---|---|
| FOR HANGINGS AND FOR CURTAINES, ALL ALONG | SOSPETTO D'HERODE | 321 | 46 109 | 216 |

HANSELLD

| | | | | |
|---|---|---|---|---|
| 'CAUSE THE QUICKSANDS HANSELLD IT. | PETRONIJ ALES PHASIACIS PETITA | 14 | MS 382 | 526 |

HAPPINES

| | | | | |
|---|---|---|---|---|
| WHICH HAD THE HAPPINES TO WORKE I'TH' NIGHT. | ON GUNPOWDER-TREASON | 58 | MS 384 | 458 |

HAPPY

| | | | | |
|---|---|---|---|---|
| A HAPPY SOULE THAT ALL THE WAY, | IN PRAISE OF LESSIUS | 33 | 46 156 | 510 |
| O YES, IF ANY HAPPY EYE, | OUT OF GREEKE CUPID'S CRYER | 5 | 46 159 | 519 |
| HAPPY ME, O HAPPY SHEEPE. | PSALME 23 | 1 | 46 102 | 5 |
| HAPPY ME, O HAPPY SHEEPE. | PSALME 23 | 1 | 46 102 | 5 |
| O HAPPY AND THRICE HAPPY SHEE | ON A PRAYER BOOKE | 91 | 46 126 | 139 |
| O HAPPY AND THRICE HAPPY SHEE | ON A PRAYER BOOKE | 91 | 46 126 | 139 |
| HAPPY SOULE WHO NEVER MISSES, | ON A PRAYER BOOKE | 98 | 46 126 | 139 |
| O LET THAT HAPPY SOULE HOLD FAST | ON A PRAYER BOOKE | 105 | 46 126 | 139 |
| HAPPY SOULE SHEE SHAL DISCOVER, | ON A PRAYER BOOKE | 115 | 46 126 | 139 |
| OF THOUSAND SOULES WHOSE HAPPY NAMES, | IN MEMORY OF LADY MADRE TERESA | 175 | 46 131 | 52 |
| THRIV'D IN THESE HAPPY GROUNDS, THE EARTH'S JUST PRIDE, | UPON DEATH OF HERRYS | 3 | 46 167 | 466 |
| O HAPPY YOU, IF IT HITT RIGHT, | TO COUNTESSE OF DENBIGH | 50 | 52 236 | 146 |
| HAPPY HE WHO HAS THE ART | TO THE NAME OF JESUS | 193 | 52 239 | 30 |
| (THE HAPPY CONVERTS NOW OF HIM | IN GLORIOUS EPIPHANIE | 176 | 52 253 | 39 |
| APPLAUD YOUR HAPPY SELVES IN HER, | O GLORIOSA DOMINA | 28 | 52 302 | 194 |
| OF THOUSAND SOULES, WHOSE HAPPY NAMES | TERESA | 174 | 52 315 | 52 |
| HER HAPPY FIRE-WORKS, HERE, COMES DOWN TO SEE. | FLAMING HEART | 18 | 52 324 | 61 |
| O HAPPY & THRICE HAPPY SHE | PRAYER TO GENTLE-WOMAN | 97 | 52 328 | 139 |
| O HAPPY & THRICE HAPPY SHE | PRAYER TO GENTLE-WOMAN | 97 | 52 328 | 139 |
| HAPPY INDEED, WHO NEVER MISSES | PRAYER TO GENTLE-WOMAN | 104 | 52 328 | 139 |
| HAPPY PROOF. SHE SHAL DISCOVER | PRAYER TO GENTLE-WOMAN | 121 | 52 328 | 139 |
| HAPPY MYSTAKE. | TO SAME CONCERNING CHOISE | 54 | 52 331 | 66 |
| BE HAPPY, AND FOR EVER HOLD HIM FAST. | ALEXIAS FIRST ELEGIE | 38 | 52 334 | 204 |
| WITH HAPPY GAIN HER MAIDEN VOWES MADE GOOD. | ALEXIAS THIRD ELEGIE | 32 | 52 336 | 209 |
| A HAPPY SOUL, THAT ALL THE WAY | TEMPERANCE | 31 | 52 342 | 510 |
| AND SETT IT FORTH IN THE SAME HAPPY PLACE, | UPON BIRTH PRINCESSE E | 59 | MS 391 | 456 |
| OH CROWNE THESE PRAIE'RS (MOV'D IN A HAPPY HOWER) | EX EUPHORMIONE | 3 | MS 392 | 525 |

HAPPYER

| | | | | |
|---|---|---|---|---|
| WITTNESSE, CHAST HEAVNS. NO HAPPYER VOWES I KNOW | ALEXIAS THIRD ELEGIE | 25 | 52 336 | 209 |

HARD

| | | | | |
|---|---|---|---|---|
| OF NOONS HIGH GLORY, WHEN HARD BY THE STREAMS | MUSICKS DUELL | 2 | 46 149 | 535 |
| FROM THEIR HARD MOTHER EARTH, SPRANG HARDY MEN, | OUT OF VIRGIL | 30 | 46 155 | 529 |
| CERTAIN HARD WORDS MADE INTO PILLS, | IN PRAISE OF LESSIUS | 8 | 46 156 | 510 |
| O, WHO SO HARD AN HUSBANDMAN COULD EVER FIND | UPON THORNES FROM LORDS HEAD | 5 | 46 96 | 23 |
| AT THOSE HARD WORDS MANS COWARDISE CALLS FEARES. | I AM READY NOT ONELY BOUND | 2 | 46 98 | 29 |
| OUR HARD HEARTS SHALL STRIKE FIRE, THE SAME | IN MEMORY OF LADY MADRE TERESA | 161 | 46 131 | 52 |
| 'CAUSE, THOUGH A HARD & COLD ONE, YET IT IS THINE OWNE. | OFFICE H. CROSS COMPLINE | 12 | 52 274 | 105 |
| AH HARD COMMAND | SANCTA MARIA DOLORUM | 35 | 52 283 | 162 |
| THIS HARD, COLD, HEART OF MINE. | SANCTA MARIA DOLORUM | 40 | 52 283 | 162 |
| O WHO SO HARD A HUSBANDMAN DID EVER FIND | UPON CROWNE OF THORNS | 3 | 52 290 | 23 |
| OUR HARD HEARTS SHALL STRIKE FIRE, THE SAME | TERESA | 160 | 52 315 | 52 |
| UPON THIS CARCASSE OF A HARD, COLD, HART, | FLAMING HEART | 86 | 52 324 | 61 |
| FOR WHO SO HARD, BUT PASSING BY THAT WAY | ALEXIAS FIRST ELEGIE | 27 | 52 334 | 204 |
| HERE'T WAS THE ROMAN MAID FOUND A HARD FATE | ALEXIAS FIRST ELEGIE | 29 | 52 334 | 204 |
| OUR LODGINGS HARD & HOMELY AS OUR FARE. | DESCRIPTION RELIGIOUS HOUSE | 11 | 52 338 | 213 |
| (PILLOW HARD, & SHEETES NOT WARM) | AN EPITAPH UPON MARRIED COUPLE | 13 | 52 339 | 478 |
| CERTAIN HARD WORDS MADE INTO PILLS, | TEMPERANCE | 8 | 52 342 | 510 |
| TO TELL THE WORLD, HOW HARD THE MATTER WENT, | HORATIJ ILLE & NEFASTO | 43 | MS 382 | 530 |
| HOW HARD BY SEA, BY WARRE, BY BANISHMENT. | HORATIJ ILLE & NEFASTO | 44 | MS 382 | 530 |

TOO-HARD-TEMPTED

| | | | | |
|---|---|---|---|---|
| THE TOO-HARD-TEMPTED NATIONS. | IN GLORIOUS EPIPHANIE | 92 | 52 253 | 39 |

HARDEST

TO BEAR ME HARMLESSE THROUGH THE HARDEST THINGS.        ALEXIAS FIRST ELEGIE                18    52 334 204

HARDLY

THE HEART THAT HIDES THEE HARDLY COVERS.               TO THE NAME OF JESUS              215    52 239  30
TEDIOUSLY WO'ED, AND HARDLY WONE.                      AGAINST IRRESOLUTION AND DELAY     59    52 347 146
SO HARDLY BETWIXT EARTH AND HEAVEN.                    AGAINST IRRESOLUTION AND DELAY     62    52 347 146

HARDNESSE

THINGS THAT IN HARDNESSE MORE ALLUDE TO THEE.          ALEXIAS SECONDE ELEGIE             16    52 335 207

HARDY

FROM THEIR HARD MOTHER EARTH, SPRANG HARDY MEN,        OUT OF VIRGIL                      30    46 155 529

HARK

HARK. SHE IS CALL'D, THE PARTING HOURE IS COME.        IN GLORIOUS ASSUMPTION B. LADY      1    52 304 114
SHE'S CALLD. HARK, HOW THE DEAR IMMORTALL DOVE         IN GLORIOUS ASSUMPTION B. LADY      7    52 304 114
HARK HITHER, READER, WILT THOU SEE                     TEMPERANCE                         13    52 342 510
HARK HITHER, AND THY SELF BE HE.                       TEMPERANCE                         52    52 342 510

HARKE

HARKE HETHER, READER, WOULDST THOU SEE                 IN PRAISE OF LESSIUS               15    46 156 510
HARKE HOW AT EVERY TOUCH SHE DOES COMPLAINE HER.       TO PONTIUS WASHING HANDS           12    46  94  23
HARKE HOW SHE BIDS HER FRIGHTED DROPS MAKE HAST,       TO PONTIUS WASHING HANDS           13    46  94  23
HARKE SHEE IS CALLED, THE PARTING HOURE IS COME,       ON THE ASSUMPTION                   1    46 139 114
SHEE'S CALL'D AGAINE, HARKE HOW TH'IMMORTALL DOVE      ON THE ASSUMPTION                   7    46 139 114

HARM

LOVE MADE THE BED. THEY'L TAKE NO HARM                 AN EPITAPH UPON MARRIED COUPLE     14    52 339 478

HARME

THAT CHASTITY SHALL TAKE NO HARME.                     WISHES SUPPOSED MISTRESSE          63    46 195 479

HARMES

HOPE'S CHAST STEALTH HARMES NO MORE JOYE'S MAIDENHEAD  (ON) HOPE                          19    52 345  71

HARMLESSE

THEIR MUSE, THEIR SYREN, HARMLESSE SYREN SHEE)         MUSICKS DUELL                      10    46 149 535
TO BEAR ME HARMLESSE THROUGH THE HARDEST THINGS.       ALEXIAS FIRST ELEGIE               18    52 334 204

HARMONIOUS

(FRAUGHT WITH A FURY SO HARMONIOUS)                    MUSICKS DUELL                     134    46 149 535

TH'HARMONIOUS

LONG MADE TH'HARMONIOUS ORBES ALL MUTE TO US           IN GLORIOUS EPIPHANIE             132    52 253  39

HARMONY

IN TH' EMPYRAEUM OF PURE HARMONY.                      MUSICKS DUELL                     150    46 149 535
A SET OF RAREST HARMONY.                               IN PRAISE OF LESSIUS               38    46 156 510
INTO A HASTY FITT-TUN'D HARMONY.                       TO THE NAME OF JESUS               50    52 239  30
A SET OF RAREST HARMONY.                               TEMPERANCE                         36    52 342 510
HOW THEN CAN THERE BE HARMONY.                         UPON DEATH OF A FREIND              6    MS 393 477

HARNESSING

SPEEDILY HARNESSING HIS FIERY STEEDS,                  UPON KINGS CORONATION              16    MS 390 453

HARP

WAKE LUTE & HARP                                       TO THE NAME OF JESUS               46    52 239  30

HARPS

BRING ALL YOUR LUTES & HARPS OF HEAVN & EARTH.         TO THE NAME OF JESUS               74    52 239  30

HARPES

OUR HARPES THAT NOW NO MUSICKE UNDERSTOOD,             PSALME 137                          3    46 104   7
WHEN HARPES AND HEARTS WERE DROWN'D IN TEARES.         PSALME 137                         10    46 104   7
HARPES OF HEAVN TO HANDS OF MAN.                       LAUDA SION SALVATOREM               4    52 294 178

HARPYES

WHICH HARPYES, WITH LEANE FAMINE FEED UPON,            SOSPETTO D'HERODE                 330    46 109 216

HARSH

HEE'S DEAD. OH WHAT HARSH MUSICKS THERE                UPON DEATH OF A FREIND              1    MS 393 477

```
HARVEST

  HOT MARS TO TH' HARVEST OF DEATHS FIELD, AND WOO    MUSICKS DUELL                    55   46 149 535
  A GOLDEN-HEADED HARVEST FAIRELY REARES              MUSICKS DUELL                    70   46 149 535
  AND STARS THOU SOW'ST WHOSE HARVEST DARES           THE WEEPER                       10   46  79 120
  A SUBTLE HARVEST OF UNBOUNDED BREAD.                ON MIRACLE OF LOAVES              3   46  86  15
  AND OUR HOPES FAIRE HARVEST SPREAD                  ANOTHER ON HERRYS                56   46 170 469
  SHALL RISE IN A SWEET HARVEST. WHICH DISCLOSES      ON A FOULE MORNING               17   46 181 495
  CAN RAISE SO FAIRE AN HARVEST. LET HER BE           ON FRONTISPIECE ISAACSONS         7   46 191 491
  A GOLDEN HARVEST OF CROWN'D HEADS, THAT MEET        TO THE QUEEN'S MAJESTY           13   52 261  47
  AND STARRES THOU SOW'ST, WHOSE HARVEST DARES        WEEPER                           10   52 307 120
  SEED-TIME'S NOT ALL. THERE SHOULD BE HARVEST TOO.   AGAINST IRRESOLUTION AND DELAY   37   52 347 146
  THE GOLDEN HARVEST OF OUR JOYES, THE NOONE          AN ELEGY MR STANNINOW            42   MS 394 473

HASTE

  AND HASTE TO DASH HER INTO DUST.                    PSALME 137                       30   46 104   7
  MAKES HASTE TO MEET HER MORNING SPOWSE.             ON A PRAYER BOOKE                96   46 126 139
  WHOSE RISING GLORIES MADE SUCH HASTE TO HIDE        UPON DEATH OF HERRYS              4   46 167 466
  HASTE HATH NEVER TIME TO HEARE.                     UPON DEATH OF DESIRED HERRYS     64   46 168 467
  LOVE, THAT LENDS HASTE TO HEAVIEST THINGS,          AGAINST IRRESOLUTION AND DELAY   27   52 347 146
  AND SEEMS TO SAY, MAKE HASTE, MY BROTHER.           AGAINST IRRESOLUTION AND DELAY   44   52 347 146

HASTED

  LIKE A SOFT LUMPE OF INCENSE, HASTED                IN MEMORY OF LADY MADRE TERESA  114   46 131  52
  LIKE A SOFT LUMP OF INCENSE, HASTED                 TERESA                          113   52 315  52

HASTS

  BUT HASTS HER FORWARD BLOSSOMES, AND LAYES OUT      OUT OF VIRGIL                    21   46 155 529
  EACH MINDFULL PLANT HASTS TO MAKE GOOD              AGAINST IRRESOLUTION AND DELAY   35   52 347 146

HASTY

  SEE HOW HEE RUNS, WITH WHAT A HASTY FLIGHT          ON A FOULE MORNING               29   46 181 495
  INTO A HASTY FITT-TUN'D HARMONY.                    TO THE NAME OF JESUS             50   52 239  30
  THE INHERITANCE OF A HASTY GRAVE.                   O GLORIOSA DOMINA                14   52 302 194
  A HASTY PORTION OF PRAESCRIBED SLEEP.               DESCRIPTION RELIGIOUS HOUSE      15   52 338 213
  THAT HEERE ARE DRESSING BY THE HASTY FATES.         UPON GUNPOWDER TREASON           30   MS 387 461

HATCH

  TO HATCH HER SELFE IN, 'MONGST HIS LEAVES THE DAY   UPON DEATH OF HERRYS             15   46 167 466
  NEVER DURST HATCH BEFORE. EXTRACTED SEE             UPON GUNPOWDER TREASON            7   MS 386 460

HATCH'D

  WHO FEELS HIS WARM HEART HATCH'D INTO A NEST        AN APOLOGIE FOR (TERESA) HYMNE   26   52 322  59

HATCHT

  WHO FINDS HIS WARME HEART, HATCHT INTO A NEST       AN APOLOGIE FOR HYMNE (TERESA)   26   46 136  59

HATCHETS

  NAILES, HAMMERS, HATCHETS SHARPE, AND HALTERS STRONG,  SOSPETTO D'HERODE            325   46 109 216

HATE

  WHO SAW OUGHT IN THEE, THAT THEIR HATE COULD MOVE.  BUT NOW THEY HAVE SEEN            4   46  96  21
  HATE IS THY THEAME, AND HEROD, WHOSE UNBLEST        SOSPETTO D'HERODE                 2   46 109 216
  ABOUT HER HATE, WRATH, WARRE, AND SLAUGHTER SWEAT.  SOSPETTO D'HERODE               315   46 109 216
  HATE THE SWEET PEACE OF ALL-COMPOSING NIGHT.        SOSPETTO D'HERODE               496   46 109 216
  FORBID IT MIGHTY LOVE, LET NO FOND HATE             AN APOLOGIE FOR HYMNE (TERESA)   13   46 136  59
  THEIR DEADLY HATE LIVES STILL. & HATH               OFFICE H. CROSS EVENSONG          3   52 273 101
  FORBID IT, MIGHTY LOVE. LET NO FOND HATE            AN APOLOGIE FOR (TERESA) HYMNE   13   52 322  59

HATED

  SEENE. AND YET HATED THEE. THEY DID NOT SEE,        BUT NOW THEY HAVE SEEN            1   46  96  21
  THEY SAW THEE NOT, THAT SAW AND HATED THEE.         BUT NOW THEY HAVE SEEN            2   46  96  21
  THAT CROWNES HIS HATED HEAD ON HIGH APPEARES.       SOSPETTO D'HERODE                45   46 109 216
  THEIR HATED LOVES CHANGD INTO WHOLSOM FEARES.       IN GLORIOUS EPIPHANIE           161   52 253  39
  HIS COURT-FED IMPES AGAINST THIS HATED HEAD.        OUT OF GROTIUS                   48   MS 398 198

HATEFULL

  AND HATEFULL SCHINIS HIS SO FEARED OAKES.           SOSPETTO D'HERODE               360   46 109 216

HATING

  ALL HATING TO BE LEFT BEHIND.                       AGAINST IRRESOLUTION AND DELAY   42   52 347 146

HATRED

  AND IN FELL HATRED BURNING, ANGRY DY.               UPON GUNPOWDER TREASON           16   MS 387 461

HEAD

  FOR A SILVER-CROWNED HEAD,                          UPON THE DEATH OF A GENTLEMAN    11   46 166 472
  NOR THE VIOLETS HUMBLE HEAD.                        THE WEEPER                      136   46  79 120
  'CAUSE THOU STREIGHT MUST LAY THY HEAD              THE TEARE                        32   46  84  50
```

| | | | | |
|---|---|---|---|---|
| HERE, WHERE OUR LORD ONCE LAID HIS HEAD, | UPON SEPULCHRE OF OUR LORD | 1 | 46 | 86 26 |
| FROM THY HEAD, AND FROM THY SIDE, | ON BLEEDING WOUNDS OF LORD | 3 | 46 | 101 110 |
| WHAT NEED THY FAIRE HEAD BEARE A PART | ON BLEEDING WOUNDS OF LORD | 17 | 46 | 101 110 |
| HOW MY HEAD IN OINTMENT SWIMS. | PSALME 23 | 55 | 46 | 102 5 |
| A SHADY ARME ABOVE MY HEAD, | PSALME 23 | 60 | 46 | 102 5 |
| THE HEAD OF ALL MY HOPE-NURST JOYES. | PSALME 137 | 26 | 46 | 104 7 |
| COME HOVERING O'RE THE PLACES HEAD, | A HYMNE OF THE NATIVITY | 36 | 46 | 106 76 |
| WHERE TO LAY HIS LOVELY HEAD, | A HYMNE OF THE NATIVITY | 48 | 46 | 106 76 |
| TO KISSE THY FEET, AND CROWNE THY HEAD. | A HYMNE OF THE NATIVITY | 80 | 46 | 106 76 |
| THAT CROWNES HIS HATED HEAD ON HIGH APPEARES. | SOSPETTO D'HERODE | 45 | 46 | 109 216 |
| SUCH AS AT THEBES DIRE FEAST SHEE SHEW'D HER HEAD, | SOSPETTO D'HERODE | 397 | 46 | 109 216 |
| AND FROM THE HEAD OF JUDAHS HOUSE QUITE TORNE | SOSPETTO D'HERODE | 405 | 46 | 109 216 |
| TO WHERE THE KINGS PROUDLY-REPOSED HEAD | SOSPETTO D'HERODE | 410 | 46 | 109 216 |
| WHICH ON FALSE TYRANTS HEAD NE'RE FIRMLY STOOD. | SOSPETTO D'HERODE | 492 | 46 | 109 216 |
| THY GOLDEN HEAD NEVER HANGS DOWNE, | ON HOPE | 55 | 46 | 143 71 |
| HIS HEAD IN CLOUDES, AS IF IN HIM ALONE | UPON DEATH OF HERRYS | 5 | 46 | 167 466 |
| NOR MORE LOVELY LIFT'ST THY HEAD, | UPON DEATH OF DESIRED HERRYS | 15 | 46 | 168 467 |
| SAFE O HIDE HIS LOVED HEAD. | UPON DEATH OF DESIRED HERRYS | 70 | 46 | 168 467 |
| WRIT IN WHITE LETTERS O'RE HIS HEAD. | ANOTHER ON HERRYS | 50 | 46 | 170 469 |
| WITH THIS INSCRIPTION O'RE HIS HEAD | ANOTHER ON HERRYS | 61 | 46 | 170 469 |
| O`STAY A WHILE, ERE THOU DRAW IN THY HEAD, | UPON STANINOUGH'S DEATH | 3 | 46 | 175 475 |
| HIS HEAD IN THY FAIRE BOSOME, AND STILL HIDES | TO THE MORNING | 13 | 46 | 183 497 |
| AND HAVE NO OTHER HEAD TO DRESSE. | WISHES SUPPOSED MISTRESSE | 69 | 46 | 195 479 |
| CAN CROWNE OLD WINTERS HEAD WITH FLOWERS, | WISHES SUPPOSED MISTRESSE | 90 | 46 | 195 479 |
| COME HOVERING O'RE THE PLACE'S HEAD. | IN HOLY NATIVITY | 52 | 52 | 246 76 |
| WHERE TO REPOSE HIS ROYALL HEAD | IN HOLY NATIVITY | 66 | 52 | 246 76 |
| TO KISSE THY FEET & CROWN THY HEAD. | IN HOLY NATIVITY | 100 | 52 | 246 76 |
| THE SHAMEFAC'T LAMP HUNG DOWN HIS HEAD | IN GLORIOUS EPIPHANIE | 118 | 52 | 253 39 |
| WITH YOUR BRIGHT HEAD WHOLE GROVES OF SCEPTERS BEND | TO THE QUEEN'S MAJESTY | 17 | 52 | 261 47 |
| THEN BOWES HIS ALL-OBEDIENT HEAD, & DYES | OFFICE H. CROSS NINTH | 5 | 52 | 271 99 |
| THINE ARMES, AND WITH THY BRIGHT & BLISFULL HEAD | OFFICE H. CROSS EVENSONG | 21 | 52 | 273 101 |
| AH HARTLESSE TASK. YET HOPE TAKES HEAD. | OFFICE H. CROSS COMPLINE | 3 | 52 | 274 105 |
| HERE WHERE OUR LORD ONCE LAY'D HIS HEAD, | UPON THE H. SEPULCHER | 1 | 52 | 277 26 |
| HAIL, OUR ALONE HOPE. LET THY FAIR HEAD SHOOT | VEXILLA REGIS | 37 | 52 | 277 156 |
| WILL HE HANG DOWN HIS GOLDEN HEAD | CHARITAS NIMIA | 41 | 52 | 280 48 |
| FROM THY HEAD & FROM THY FEET. | UPON BLEEDING CRUCIFIX | 2 | 52 | 288 110 |
| WHAT NEED THY FAIR HEAD BEAR A PART | UPON BLEEDING CRUCIFIX | 5 | 52 | 288 110 |
| NOR THE VIOLET'S HUMBLE HEAD. | WEEPER | 178 | 52 | 307 120 |
| O STAY A WHILE, ERE THOU DRAW IN THY HEAD | DEATH'S LECTURE | 3 | 52 | 340 475 |
| THY GOLDEN, GROWING HEAD NEVER HANGS DOWN | (ON) HOPE | 25 | 52 | 345 71 |
| BUT IN A VAILE OF CLOUDS MUFLING HER HEAD | UPON GUNPOWDER TREASON | 17 | MS | 386 460 |
| UPON HIS TIPTOES, E'RE HIS SILVER HEAD | UPON KINGS CORONATION | 4 | MS | 389 454 |
| JUSTICE HATH LOST HER HAND, THE LAW HER HEAD. | AN ELEGIE ON DR PORTER | 15 | MS | 395 476 |
| HIS COURT-FED IMPES AGAINST THIS HATED HEAD. | OUT OF GROTIUS | 48 | MS | 398 198 |

HEADS

| | | | | |
|---|---|---|---|---|
| BOW OUR BRIGHT HEADS, BEFORE A KING OF CLAY. | SOSPETTO D'HERODE | 220 | 46 | 109 216 |
| HIS FOULE HAGS RAIS'D THEIR HEADS, & CLAPT THEIR HANDS. | SOSPETTO D'HERODE | 258 | 46 | 109 216 |
| HOPE KICKS THE CURL'D HEADS OF CONSPIRING STARRES. | ON HOPE | 72 | 46 | 143 71 |
| AND HILLS HANG DOWN THEIR HEAVN-SALUTING HEADS | TO THE NAME OF JESUS | 231 | 52 | 239 30 |
| A GOLDEN HARVEST OF CROWN'D HEADS, THAT MEET | TO THE QUEEN'S MAJESTY | 13 | 52 | 261 47 |
| CROWNES, & THE HEADS THEY KISSE, MUST COURT THESE FEET. | TO THE QUEEN'S MAJESTY | 20 | 52 | 261 47 |
| AND BOW THEIR FLAMING HEADS BEFORE THEE | CHARITAS NIMIA | 23 | 52 | 280 48 |
| CROWN'D HEADS ARE TOYES. WE GOE TO MEET | WEEPER | 185 | 52 | 307 120 |
| HOPE WALKS, & KICKES THE CURLD HEADS OF CONSPIRING STARRES. | (ON) HOPE | 32 | 52 | 345 71 |
| IN VAILES OF DUST THEIR SILKEN HEADS THEY'LE HIDE. | AN ELEGIE ON DR PORTER | 25 | MS | 395 476 |

TH'HEADS

| | | | | |
|---|---|---|---|---|
| TO TH'HEADS AND OFFICERS OF EVERY BAND. | SOSPETTO D'HERODE | 511 | 46 | 109 216 |

HEADED

| | | | | |
|---|---|---|---|---|
| WHICH NODS WITH MANY A HEAVY HEADED TREE. | SOSPETTO D'HERODE | 346 | 46 | 109 216 |

GOLDEN-HEADED

| | | | | |
|---|---|---|---|---|
| A GOLDEN-HEADED HARVEST FAIRELY REARES | MUSICKS DUELL | 70 | 46 | 149 535 |

HUNDRED-HEADED

| | | | | |
|---|---|---|---|---|
| WHAT WONDER, WHEN THE HUNDRED-HEADED BEAST | HORATIJ ILLE & NEFASTO | 50 | MS | 382 530 |

HEADLONG

| | | | | |
|---|---|---|---|---|
| SHOULD BEATE HER HEADLONG FROM HER JETTY THRONE. | UPON GUNPOWDER TREASON | 26 | MS | 386 460 |

HEAL

| | | | | |
|---|---|---|---|---|
| BALSOM TO HEAL THEMSELVES WITH. THUS | TERESA | 109 | 52 | 315 52 |

HEALE

| | | | | |
|---|---|---|---|---|
| BALSOME, TO HEALE THEMSELVES WITH | IN MEMORY OF LADY MADRE TERESA | 109 | 46 | 131 52 |

HEALING

| | | | | |
|---|---|---|---|---|
| THAT HEALING SHAFT, WHICH HEAVN TILL NOW | TO COUNTESSE OF DENBIGH | 47 | 52 | 236 146 |

HEALTH

 HIS OWNE PHYSICK, HIS OWNE HEALTH.    IN PRAISE OF LESSIUS  18 46 156 510
 THE HOPE. THE HEALTH,         OFFICE H. CROSS EVENSONG 14 52 273 101
 HIS OWN MUSICK, HIS OWN HEALTH.    TEMPERANCE       16 52 342 510

HEALTHFULL

 HAD NOT THY HEALTHFULL WOMB      O GLORIOSA DOMINA    18 52 302 194

HEAP

 HEAP UP THY CONSECRATED KISSES.    IN MEMORY OF LADY MADRE TERESA 133 46 131 52
 HEAP UP THY CONSECRATED KISSES.    TERESA        132 52 315 52

HEAPE

 THAT THOU NEED'ST HEAPE        TO PONTIUS WASHING HANDS  2 46 94 23

HEAP'T

 THOU WOULDST ON HER HAVE HEAP'T UP ALL  FLAMING HEART       29 52 324 61

HEAR

 HEAR, FATHER, HEAR. THY LAMB (AT LAST) COMPLAINES. OFFICE H. CROSS NINTH  3 52 271 99
 HEAR, FATHER, HEAR. THY LAMB (AT LAST) COMPLAINES. OFFICE H. CROSS NINTH  3 52 271 99
 O HEAR A SUPPLIANT HEART. ALL CRUSH'T    DIES IRAE       65 52 298 186

HEARS'T

 HEARS'T THOU, MY SOUL, WHAT SERIOUS THINGS  DIES IRAE        1 52 298 186

HEARE

 THERE MIGHT YOU HEARE HER KINDLE HER SOFT VOYCE, MUSICKS DUELL      83 46 149 535
 HASTE HATH NEVER TIME TO HEARE.      UPON DEATH OF DESIRED HERRYS 64 46 168 467
 HONOUR ALL PREACHERS. HEARE THEIR OWNE.  AN EPITAPH UPON ASHTON   8 46 192 464

HEARD

 BUT VERTUE HEARD IT, AND AWAY SHEE HY'D,  SOSPETTO D'HERODE    470 46 109 216
 WORDS WHICH ARE NOT HEARD WITH EARES,   ON A PRAYER BOOKE     59 46 126 139
 SERMONS HE HEARD, YET NOT SO MANY,    AN EPITAPH UPON ASHTON   9 46 192 464
 HEE HEARD THEM REVERENDLY, AND THEN    AN EPITAPH UPON ASHTON   11 46 192 464
 WORDS WHICH ARE NOT HEARD WITH EARES    PRAYER TO GENTLE-WOMAN   65 52 328 139
 TO MELT IN GENTLE DROPS, LETT THEM BE HEARD AN ELEGIE ON DR PORTER   33 MS 395 476
 HEE THAT NE'RE HEARD NOW SPEAKES, AND FINDS A TONGUE OUT OF GROTIUS    73 MS 398 198

HEARES

 THE SOULE IT SELFE MORE FEELES THEN HEARES. ON A PRAYER BOOKE     62 46 126 139
 (WHICH DULL MORTALITY MORE FEELES THEN HEARES) TO THE NAME OF JESUS   31 52 239 30
 THE SOUL IT SELFE MORE FEELS THEN HEARES.  PRAYER TO GENTLE-WOMAN   68 52 328 139
 I FEARE TO NAME IT. LEAST THAT HE, WHICH HEARES, UPON GUNPOWDER TREASON   9 MS 386 460

HEARKEN

 HEARKEN, AND HELP, YE HOLY DOVES.     TO THE NAME OF JESUS    6 52 239 30

HEARKENED

 THE NINTH WITH AWFULL HORROR HEARKENED TO THOSE OFFICE H. CROSS NINTH   1 52 271 99
              GROANES

HEARKENS

 HEARKENS NOT TO AN HUMBLE SONG.      FLAMING HEART       62 52 324 61

HEART

 FALLS FROM A STEADY HEART, THOUGH TREMBLING HAND. WIDOWES MITES       2 46 86 21
 LO. HATH UNLOCKT THEE AT THE VERY HEART.  I AM THE DOORE        2 46 90 17
 EXPECT A SEA, MY HEART SHALL MAKE IT GOOD. OUR LORD IN HIS CIRCUMCISION  4 46 98 9
 WHAT NEED THEY HELPE TO DROWNE THINE HEART. ON BLEEDING WOUNDS OF LORD  19 46 101 110
 NO MORE ACQUAINTED WITH MY HEART,     PSALME 137         22 46 104 7
 THE WORLDS PROFOUND HEART PANTS. THERE PLACED IS SOSPETTO D'HERODE    35 46 109 216
 HEE STUDIES SCRIPTURE, STRIVES TO SOUND THE HEART, SOSPETTO D'HERODE    155 46 109 216
 THOSE STINGS OF CARE THAT HIS STRONG HEART OPPREST, SOSPETTO D'HERODE    199 46 109 216
 THEY PRICK A BLEEDING HEART AT EVERY STITCH. SOSPETTO D'HERODE    342 46 109 216
 HIS SPIRITS, THE SPARKES OF LIFE, AND CHILLS HIS SOSPETTO D'HERODE    422 46 109 216
              HEART,

 TO THE KINGS HEART, THE SNAKE NO SOONER HIST, SOSPETTO D'HERODE    469 46 109 216
 ALL POINTED IN HIS HEART SEEM'D TO INVADE HIM. SOSPETTO D'HERODE    476 46 109 216
 TO WHICH HIS GNAW'D HEART IS THE GROWING FOOD SOSPETTO D'HERODE    494 46 109 216
 AND FORTIFIE THE HOLD OF YOUR CHAST HEART. ON A PRAYER BOOKE     14 46 126 139
 HOLD BUT THIS BOOKE BEFORE YOUR HEART,   ON A PRAYER BOOKE     27 46 126 139
 BUT O', THE HEART            ON A PRAYER BOOKE     29 46 126 139
 SHALL FIND THE WANDRING HEART FROM HOME,  ON A PRAYER BOOKE     42 46 126 139
 DOUBTLES SOME OTHER HEART         ON A PRAYER BOOKE     54 46 126 139
 HOME TO THE HEART, AND SETTS THE HOUSE ON FIRE. ON A PRAYER BOOKE     67 46 126 139
 HEE FIND THE HEART FROM HOME,       ON A PRAYER BOOKE     84 46 126 139
 YET HAS SHEE A HEART DARES HOPE TO PROVE. IN MEMORY OF LADY MADRE TERESA 27 46 131 52

| | | | | |
|---|---|---|---|---|
| LOVE TOUCHT HER HEART, AND LOE IT BEATS | IN MEMORY OF LADY MADRE TERESA | 35 | 46 | 131 52 |
| HOW KINDLY WILL THY GENTLE HEART, | IN MEMORY OF LADY MADRE TERESA | 105 | 46 | 131 52 |
| HER MILD RAYES, THROUGH THY MELTING HEART. | IN MEMORY OF LADY MADRE TERESA | 137 | 46 | 131 52 |
| THAT HEAVENLY MAXIM GAVE ME HEART TO TRY | AN APOLOGIE FOR HYMNE (TERESA) | 9 | 46 | 136 59 |
| WHO FINDS HIS WARME HEART, HATCH'D INTO A NEST | AN APOLOGIE FOR HYMNE (TERESA) | 26 | 46 | 136 59 |
| BUT (FOR A LAMBE) THY TAME AND TENDER HEART | ON A TREATISE OF CHARITY | 45 | 46 | 137 69 |
| VERTUE WEARES HIM NEXT HER HEART. | UPON DEATH OF DESIRED HERRYS | 10 | 46 | 168 467 |
| STAY A WHILE, AND LET THY HEART | HIS EPITAPH (HERRYS) | 2 | 46 | 172 471 |
| IS HE ENTOMB'D, BUT IN THY HEART. | HIS EPITAPH (HERRYS) | 52 | 46 | 172 471 |
| WHAT IS LOVES SACRIFICE, BUT THE BROKEN HEART. | UPON FORD'S TRAGEDYES | 2 | 46 | 181 495 |
| ERST HATH MADE MY HEART A MOTHER, | LOVES HOROSCOPE | 2 | 46 | 185 483 |
| AH MY HEART, IS THAT THE WAY. | LOVES HOROSCOPE | 9 | 46 | 185 483 |
| AH MY HEART, HER EYES AND SHEE. | LOVES HOROSCOPE | 15 | 46 | 185 483 |
| THE HEAT COMMANDING IN MY HEART DOTH SIT, | OUT OF THE ITALIAN (2) | 4 | 46 | 190 547 |
| AND SO HE LOST HIS CLOTHES, EYES, HEART AND ALL. | OUT OF THE ITALIAN (3) | 8 | 46 | 190 549 |
| THAT SHALL COMMAND MY HEART AND MEE. | WISHES SUPPOSED MISTRESSE | 3 | 46 | 195 479 |
| A WELL TAM'D HEART, | WISHES SUPPOSED MISTRESSE | 55 | 46 | 195 479 |
| WHAT HEAV'N-INTREATED HEART IS THIS. | TO COUNTESSE OF DENBIGH | 1 | 52 | 236 146 |
| KEEP THE FREE HEART FROM IT'S OWN HANDS. | TO COUNTESSE OF DENBIGH | 20 | 52 | 236 146 |
| AND FETCH THE HEART FROM IT'S STRONG HOLD. | TO COUNTESSE OF DENBIGH | 28 | 52 | 236 146 |
| WHICH HAS THE KEY OF THIS CLOSE HEART, | TO COUNTESSE OF DENBIGH | 34 | 52 | 236 146 |
| MEET HIS WELL-MEANING WOUNDS, WISE HEART. | TO COUNTESSE OF DENBIGH | 45 | 52 | 236 146 |
| CHEAR THEE MY HEART. | TO THE NAME OF JESUS | 88 | 52 | 239 30 |
| WHICH MAN'S HEART MEETS | TO THE NAME OF JESUS | 123 | 52 | 239 30 |
| HOME, & LODGE THEM IN HIS HEART. | TO THE NAME OF JESUS | 196 | 52 | 239 30 |
| THE HEART THAT HIDES THEE HARDLY COVERS. | TO THE NAME OF JESUS | 215 | 52 | 239 30 |
| FIX HERE, FAIR MAJESTY. MAY YOUR HEART NE'RE MISSE | TO THE QUEEN'S MAJESTY | 21 | 52 | 261 47 |
| CONTEMPT & SCORN CAN SEND WOUNDS TO SEARCH THE INMOST | OFFICE H. CROSS SIXT | 12 | 52 | 270 97 |
| SUPERFLUOUS SPEAR. BUT THERE'S A HEART STANDS BY | OFFICE H. CROSS EVENSONG | 5 | 52 | 273 101 |
| O RATHER USE THIS HEART, THUS FARR A FITTER STONE, | OFFICE H. CROSS COMPLINE | 11 | 52 | 274 105 |
| AND TOOK IT HOME TO HIS OWN HEART. | VEXILLA REGIS | 12 | 52 | 277 156 |
| IF MY FOUL HEART CALL'D FOR A FLOOD. | CHARITAS NIMIA | 48 | 52 | 280 48 |
| ALL, MORE AT HOME IN HER OWNE HEART. | SANCTA MARIA DOLORUM | 10 | 52 | 283 162 |
| HIS NAILES WRITE SWORDS IN HER, WHICH SOON HER HEART | SANCTA MARIA DOLORUM | 27 | 52 | 283 162 |
| THIS HARD, COLD, HEART OF MINE. | SANCTA MARIA DOLORUM | 48 | 52 | 283 162 |
| THOUGH AS AT SECOND HAND, FROM EITHER HEART. | SANCTA MARIA DOLORUM | 70 | 52 | 283 162 |
| TO A HEART WHO BY SAD RIGHT OF SIN | SANCTA MARIA DOLORUM | 93 | 52 | 283 162 |
| WHICH THESE TORN HANDS TRANSCRIB'D ON THY TRUE HEART | SANCTA MARIA DOLORUM | 97 | 52 | 283 162 |
| LO, HEART, THY HOPE'S WHOLE PLEA. HER PRETIOUS BREATH | SANCTA MARIA DOLORUM | 109 | 52 | 283 162 |
| WHAT NEED THEY HELP TO DROWN THY HEART. | UPON BLEEDING CRUCIFIX | 7 | 52 | 288 110 |
| WITH ALL THE POWRES MY POOR HEART HATH | ADORO TE | 1 | 52 | 291 172 |
| TO A BLEEDING HEART THAT GASPES FOR BLOOD. | ADORO TE | 48 | 52 | 291 172 |
| BOLD FAITH TAKES HEART, & DARES BELEIVE. | LAUDA SION SALVATOREM | 38 | 52 | 294 178 |
| HOPE TELLS MY HEART, THE SAME LOVES BE | DIES IRAE | 51 | 52 | 298 186 |
| O HEAR A SUPPLIANT HEART. ALL CRUSH'T | DIES IRAE | 65 | 52 | 298 166 |
| AND TAUGHT THE WOUNDED HEART | WEEPER | 105 | 52 | 307 120 |
| YET HAS SHE'A HEART DARES HOPE TO PROVE | TERESA | 27 | 52 | 315 52 |
| LOVE TOUCH'T HER HEART, & LO IT BEATES | TERESA | 35 | 52 | 315 52 |
| HOW KINDLY WILL THY GENTLE HEART | TERESA | 105 | 52 | 315 52 |
| HER MILD RAYES THROUGH THY MELTING HEART. | TERESA | 136 | 52 | 315 52 |
| WHO FEELS HIS WARM HEART HATCH'D INTO A NEST | AN APOLOGIE FOR (TERESA) HYMNE | 26 | 52 | 322 59 |
| HAD FILL'D THE HAND OF THIS GREAT HEART. | FLAMING HEART | 36 | 52 | 324 61 |
| LEAVE HIM ALONE THE FLAMING HEART. | FLAMING HEART | 66 | 52 | 324 61 |
| THE WOUNDED IS THE WOUNDING HEART. | FLAMING HEART | 74 | 52 | 324 61 |
| O HEART, THE AEQUALL POISE OF LOV'ES BOTH PARTS | FLAMING HEART | 75 | 52 | 324 61 |
| LIVE HERE, GREAT HEART, & LOVE AND DY & KILL. | FLAMING HEART | 79 | 52 | 324 61 |
| AND FORTIFY THE HOLD OF YOUR CHAST HEART. | PRAYER TO GENTLE-WOMAN | 20 | 52 | 328 139 |
| HOLD BUT THIS BOOK BEFORE YOUR HEART | PRAYER TO GENTLE-WOMAN | 33 | 52 | 328 139 |
| BUT O THE HEART | PRAYER TO GENTLE-WOMAN | 35 | 52 | 328 139 |
| SHALL FIND THE LOYTERING HEART FROM HOME. | PRAYER TO GENTLE-WOMAN | 48 | 52 | 328 139 |
| DOUBTLESSE SOME OTHER HEART | PRAYER TO GENTLE-WOMAN | 60 | 52 | 328 139 |
| HOME TO THE HEART, & SETTS THE HOUSE ON FIRE | PRAYER TO GENTLE-WOMAN | 73 | 52 | 328 139 |
| HE FIND THE HEART FROM HOME) | PRAYER TO GENTLE-WOMAN | 90 | 52 | 328 139 |
| O LET THE BLISSFULL HEART HOLD FAST | PRAYER TO GENTLE-WOMAN | 111 | 52 | 328 139 |
| OF HIS HIGH STRATAGEM TO WIN YOUR HEART, | TO SAME CONCERNING CHOISE | 44 | 52 | 331 66 |
| AND STRIKE YOUR TROUBLED HEART | TO SAME CONCERNING CHOISE | 50 | 52 | 331 66 |
| HERE PERISH'T SHE, PUOR HEART, HEAVNS, BE MY VOWES | ALEXIAS FIRST ELEGIE | 31 | 52 | 334 204 |
| WHAT HEAV'N-BESIEGED HEART IS THIS | AGAINST IRRESOLUTION AND DELAY | 1 | 52 | 347 146 |
| KEEP THE FREE HEART FROM HIS OWN HANDS. | AGAINST IRRESOLUTION AND DELAY | 14 | 52 | 347 146 |
| DID EVER GREIFE, & JOY IN ONE POORE HEART | LUKE 2. QUAERIT JESUM | 3 | MS | 379 11 |
| PEACE, HEART. THE HEAVENS ARE ANGRY. ALL THEIR SPHAERES | LUKE 2. QUAERIT JESUM | 19 | MS | 379 11 |
| OFT FROM THIS BREAST TO THINE MY LOVE-TOST HEART | LUKE 2. QUAERIT JESUM | 39 | MS | 379 11 |
| A PEIRCING SIDE. HIS PEIRCED HEART. | IN CICATRICES DOMINI JESU | 10 | MS | 381 27 |
| A BLOODY SIDE, & HAND, & HEART. | IN CICATRICES DOMINI JESU | 16 | MS | 381 27 |
| A HEART BURNING IN LOVE. ALL DID ADORE | UPON KINGS CORONATION | 37 | MS | 390 453 |
| BUT THEN, ALAS, MY HEART. OH HOW SHALL I | UPON BIRTH PRINCESSE E | 11 | MS | 391 456 |

HEART-BLOOD

| | | | | |
|---|---|---|---|---|
| MY BLUSHES WITH HIS OWN HEART-BLOOD. | CHARITAS NIMIA | 62 | 52 | 280 48 |

TH'HEART-BRED

| | | | | |
|---|---|---|---|---|
| AND TH'HEART-BRED LUSTRE OF HIS WORTH. | HIS EPITAPH (HERRYS) | 37 | 46 | 172 471 |

HEART'S

| | | | | |
|---|---|---|---|---|
| WHO KNOWES MY OWN HEART'S WOES SO WELL AS I. | ALEXIAS FIRST ELEGIE | 14 | 52 | 334 204 |

HART

| | | | | |
|---|---|---|---|---|
| INTO THY HANDS, AND HART, LORD, I COMMEND. | OFFICE H. CROSS RECOMMENDATION | 2 | 52 | 276 106 |
| THAT HOPEFULL MAXIME GAVE ME HART TO TRY | AN APOLOGIE FOR (TERESA) HYMNE | 9 | 52 | 322 59 |

|     |     |     |     |     |     |
| --- | --- | --- | --- | --- | --- |
| UPON THIS CARCASSE OF A HARD, COLD, HART. | FLAMING HEART | 86 | 52 | 324 | 61 |

HART'S

| THY SOUL'S KIND SHEPHEARD, THY HART'S KING. | LAUDA SION SALVATOREM | 2 | 52 | 294 | 178 |
| --- | --- | --- | --- | --- | --- |

HEARTS

| MENS HEARTS INTO THEIR HANDS. THIS LESSON TOO | MUSICKS DUELL | 56 | 46 | 149 | 535 |
| --- | --- | --- | --- | --- | --- |
| WHEN HARPES AND HEARTS WERE DROWN'D IN TEARES. | PSALME 137 | 10 | 46 | 104 | 7 |
| BUT LIFT CLEAN HANDS FULL OF CLEARE HEARTS. | A HYMNE OF THE NATIVITY | 76 | 46 | 106 | 76 |
| TO HOLY HANDS, AND HUMBLE HEARTS, | ON A PRAYER BOOKE | 18 | 46 | 126 | 139 |
| OUR HARD HEARTS SHALL STRIKE FIRE, THE SAME | IN MEMORY OF LADY MADRE TERESA | 161 | 46 | 131 | 52 |
| BY GLORY, IN OUT HEARTS BY GRACE. | IN MEMORY OF LADY MADRE TERESA | 165 | 46 | 131 | 52 |
| WHERE THOU SHALT REACH ALL HEARTS, COMMAND EACH EYE. | ON A TREATISE OF CHARITY | 16 | 46 | 137 | 69 |
| HAILE HOLY QUEEN OF HUMBLE HEARTS, | ON THE ASSUMPTION | 29 | 46 | 139 | 114 |
| LO WE HOLD OUR HEARTS WIDE OPE. | TO THE NAME OF JESUS | 126 | 52 | 239 | 30 |
| LO, FOR THEIR OWN HEARTS, THEY REND HIS. | OFFICE H. CROSS EVENSONG | 2 | 52 | 273 | 101 |
| THE WHILE OUR HEARTS & WE | VEXILLA REGIS | 39 | 52 | 277 | 156 |
| DEAR, DOLEFULL HEARTS, | SANCTA MARIA DOLORUM | 72 | 52 | 283 | 162 |
| NAIL'D HANDS, & PEIRCED HEARTS. | SANCTA MARIA DOLORUM | 76 | 52 | 283 | 162 |
| LET LIPPES & HEARTS LIFT HIGH THE NOISE | LAUDA SION SALVATOREM | 15 | 52 | 294 | 178 |
| LET HEARTS & LIPPES SPEAK LOWD, AND SAY | O GLORIOSA DOMINA | 31 | 52 | 302 | 194 |
| HAIL, HOLY QUEEN OF HUMBLE HEARTS. | IN GLORIOUS ASSUMPTION B. LADY | 44 | 52 | 304 | 114 |
| OUR HARD HEARTS SHALL STRIKE FIRE, THE SAME | TERESA | 160 | 52 | 315 | 52 |
| BY GLORY, IN OUR HEARTS BY GRACE. | TERESA | 164 | 52 | 315 | 52 |
| SAY, ALL YE WISE & WELL-PEIRC'T HEARTS | FLAMING HEART | 49 | 52 | 324 | 61 |
| TO HOLY HANDS & HUMBLE HEARTS | PRAYER TO GENTLE-WOMAN | 24 | 52 | 328 | 139 |

HARTS

| SPARE OUR EYES, BUT PEIRCE OUR HARTS. | IN GLORIOUS EPIPHANIE | 79 | 52 | 253 | 39 |
| --- | --- | --- | --- | --- | --- |

HARTLESSE

| AH HARTLESSE TASK. YET HOPE TAKES HEAD. | OFFICE H. CROSS COMPLINE | 3 | 52 | 274 | 105 |
| --- | --- | --- | --- | --- | --- |

HARTY

| HANDS FULL OF HARTY LABOURS. PAINES THAT PAY | DESCRIPTION RELIGIOUS HOUSE | 19 | 52 | 338 | 213 |
| --- | --- | --- | --- | --- | --- |

HEAT

| HEE LOST THE DAYES HEAT, AND HIS OWNE HOT CARES. | MUSICKS DUELL | 6 | 46 | 149 | 535 |
| --- | --- | --- | --- | --- | --- |
| THE HEAT COMMANDING IN MY HEART DOTH SIT, | OUT OF THE ITALIAN (2) | 4 | 46 | 190 | 547 |
| LET MY HEAT TO YOUR LIGHT BE RECONCILED. | OUT OF THE ITALIAN (2) | 6 | 46 | 190 | 547 |

HEATS

| HIGH, AND BURNES WITH SUCH BRAVE HEATS. | IN MEMORY OF LADY MADRE TERESA | 36 | 46 | 131 | 52 |
| --- | --- | --- | --- | --- | --- |
| HER STARRY THRUNE. WHOSE HOLY HEATS CAN WARME | TO THE MORNING | 25 | 46 | 183 | 497 |

HEATES

| HIGH, & BURNES WITH SUCH BRAVE HEATES. | TERESA | 36 | 52 | 315 | 52 |
| --- | --- | --- | --- | --- | --- |
| IF HEATES OF HOLYER LOVE & HIGH DESIRE | ALEXIAS THIRD ELEGIE | 21 | 52 | 336 | 209 |

HEAVEN

| OF MUSICKS HEAVEN. AND SEAT IT THERE ON HIGH | MUSICKS DUELL | 149 | 46 | 149 | 535 |
| --- | --- | --- | --- | --- | --- |
| TO HEAVEN, HATH A SUMMERS DAY. | IN PRAISE OF LESSIUS | 34 | 46 | 156 | 510 |
| SNATCH'T HER SELF HENCE, TO HEAVEN. FILL'D A BRIGHT PLACE, | UPON BISHOP ANDREWES PICTURE | 9 | 46 | 163 | 490 |
| HEAVEN, OF SUCH FAIRE FLOODS AS THIS, | THE WEEPER | 23 | 46 | 79 | 120 |
| HEAVEN THE CHRISTALL OCEAN IS. | THE WEEPER | 24 | 46 | 79 | 120 |
| AND HEAVEN WILL MAKE A FEAST, | THE WEEPER | 33 | 46 | 79 | 120 |
| CASKETS, OF WHICH HEAVEN KEEPS THE KEYES. | THE WEEPER | 48 | 46 | 79 | 120 |
| (FOR TO HEAVEN THOU MUST GOE) | THE TEARE | 36 | 46 | 84 | 50 |
| AN EYE OF HEAVEN. OR STILL SHINE HERE | THE TEARE | 47 | 46 | 84 | 50 |
| 'TIS HEAV'N 'TIS HEAVEN SHE SEES, HEAVENS GOD THERE LYES | ON VIRGINS BASHFULNESSE | 5 | 46 | 89 | 9 |
| SHE CAN SEE HEAVEN, AND NE'RE LIFT UP HER EYES. | ON VIRGINS BASHFULNESSE | 6 | 46 | 89 | 9 |
| 'TWAS ONCE LOOKE UP, 'TIS NOW LOOKE DOWNE TO HEAVEN. | ON VIRGINS BASHFULNESSE | 8 | 46 | 89 | 9 |
| HATH SHUT THESE DOORES OF HEAVEN, THAT DURST | I AM THE DOORE | 5 | 46 | 90 | 17 |
| YET IF THOU'LT FILL ONE POORE EYE, WITH THY HEAVEN AND THEE, | IT IS BETTER TO GO WITH EYE | 4 | 46 | 93 | 16 |
| MAKES ME DOUBT IF HEAVEN WILL GATHER, | UPON INFANT MARTYRS | 3 | 46 | 95 | 10 |
| WHEN HEAVEN IT SELFE LYES HERE BELOW. | A HYMNE OF THE NATIVITY | 44 | 46 | 106 | 76 |
| HEAVEN IN EARTH, AND GOD IN MAN. | A HYMNE OF THE NATIVITY | 56 | 46 | 106 | 76 |
| LIFTS EARTH TO HEAVEN, STOOPS HEAVEN TO EARTH. | A HYMNE OF THE NATIVITY | 58 | 46 | 106 | 76 |
| LIFTS EARTH TO HEAVEN, STOOPS HEAVEN TO EARTH. | A HYMNE OF THE NATIVITY | 58 | 46 | 106 | 76 |
| HEE HAS MY HEAVEN (WHAT WOULD HE MORE.) WHOSE BRIGHT | SOSPETTO D'HERODE | 209 | 46 | 109 | 216 |
| IT IS IN ONE RICH HANDFULL, HEAVEN AND ALL | ON A PRAYER BOOKE | 5 | 46 | 126 | 139 |
| WHICH EVERY DAY TO HEAVEN WILL SEND YOU. | ON MR. G. HERBERTS BOOKE | 12 | 46 | 130 | 68 |
| WISE HEAVEN WILL NEVER HAVE IT SO. | IN MEMORY OF LADY MADRE TERESA | 74 | 46 | 131 | 52 |
| UPON THE ROOFE OF HEAVEN WHERE AY | IN MEMORY OF LADY MADRE TERESA | 83 | 46 | 131 | 52 |
| SHALT THOU EXHALE TO HEAVEN AT LAST, | IN MEMORY OF LADY MADRE TERESA | 117 | 46 | 131 | 52 |
| AND TEACH THY LIPPS HEAVEN, WITH HER HAND, | IN MEMORY OF LADY MADRE TERESA | 131 | 46 | 131 | 52 |
| THOSE SECOND SMILES OF HEAVEN SHALL DART, | IN MEMORY OF LADY MADRE TERESA | 136 | 46 | 131 | 52 |
| HEAVEN KEEPS UPON THY SCORE (THY BRIGHT | IN MEMORY OF LADY MADRE TERESA | 176 | 46 | 131 | 52 |
| OUR FREE TRAFICK FOR HEAVEN, WE MAY MAINTAINE. | AN APOLOGIE FOR HYMNE (TERESA) | 19 | 46 | 136 | 59 |
| SPEAKE HEAVEN LIKE HERS, IS MY SOULES COUNTRY-MAN. | AN APOLOGIE FOR HYMNE (TERESA) | 22 | 46 | 136 | 59 |
| O 'TIS NOT SPANISH, BUT 'TIS HEAVEN SHE SPEAKES, | AN APOLOGIE FOR HYMNE (TERESA) | 23 | 46 | 136 | 59 |
| 'TIS HEAVEN THAT LIES IN AMBUSH THERE, AND BREAKES | AN APOLOGIE FOR HYMNE (TERESA) | 24 | 46 | 136 | 59 |

| | | | | | |
|---|---|---|---|---|---|
| TAKE THY FAREWEL POORE WORLD, HEAVEN MUST GO HOME. | ON THE ASSUMPTION | 2 | 46 | 139 | 114 |
| WHEN HEAVEN BIDS COME, WHO CAN SAY NO. | ON THE ASSUMPTION | 20 | 46 | 139 | 114 |
| HEAVEN WILL NOT, AND SHE CANNOT STAY. | ON THE ASSUMPTION | 22 | 46 | 139 | 114 |
| OF THE BRIGHT YOUTH OF HEAVEN, THAT SINGS | ON THE ASSUMPTION | 24 | 46 | 139 | 114 |
| OF HEAVEN, AND HUMBLE PRIDE OF EARTH. | ON THE ASSUMPTION | 60 | 46 | 139 | 114 |
| FAIRE HOPE. OUR EARLIER HEAVEN. BY THEE | ON HOPE | 51 | 46 | 143 | 71 |
| CALL HEAVEN TO LOOKE ON THEE WITH NARROW EYES. | UPON STANINOUGH'S DEATH | 16 | 46 | 175 | 475 |
| BRING THEIR HEAVEN WITH THEM, THEIR GREAT FOOTSTEPS PLACE | UPON YORKE HIS BIRTH | 19 | 46 | 176 | 500 |
| NO NIMBLE RAPTURE STARTS TO HEAVEN AND BRINGS | TO THE MORNING | 20 | 46 | 183 | 497 |
| EARTH AND HEAVEN | OUT OF THE ITALIAN (1) | 28 | 46 | 188 | 545 |
| ALL HEAVEN BY THEE, | TO THE NAME OF JESUS | 133 | 52 | 239 | 30 |
| HEAVEN IN EARTH, & GOD IN MAN. | IN HOLY NATIVITY | 82 | 52 | 246 | 76 |
| LIFTS EARTH TO HEAVEN, STOOPES HEAV'N TO EARTH. | IN HOLY NATIVITY | 84 | 52 | 246 | 76 |
| SO HARDLY BETWIXT EARTH AND HEAVEN. | AGAINST IRRESOLUTION AND DELAY | 62 | 52 | 347 | 146 |
| WHAT, BUT THE FAIREST HEAVEN, COULD OWNE THE BIRTH | LUKE 2. QUAERIT JESUM | 23 | MS | 379 | 11 |
| AND LETT HEAVEN STAY. | LUKE 2. QUAERIT JESUM | 46 | MS | 379 | 11 |
| THY HEAVEN TO THEE. | LUKE 2. QUAERIT JESUM | 50 | MS | 379 | 11 |
| THAT EARTH A SHOURE OF STONES TO HEAVEN SHALL SEND, | ON GUNPOWDER-TREASON | 22 | MS | 384 | 458 |
| THOSE TWINCKLING EYES OF HEAVEN, WHICH EV'N NOW SHIN'D. | ON GUNPOWDER-TREASON | 31 | MS | 384 | 458 |
| HEAVEN KICKT THE MONSTER DOUNE. DOUNE IT WAS THROUNE, | ON GUNPOWDER-TREASON | 51 | MS | 384 | 458 |
| HEAVEN WAS ASHAM'D, TO SEE OUR MOTHER EARTH | UPON GUNPOWDER TREASON | 11 | MS | 386 | 460 |
| WITH HEAVEN ITSELF FOR STATELY MAJESTY. | UPON KINGS CORONATION | 10 | MS | 389 | 454 |
| THE SULLEN HEAVEN HAD VAIL'D ITS MOURNFULL BROW | UPON KINGS CORONATION | 2 | MS | 390 | 453 |
| RICH, LIBERALL HEAVEN, WHAT, HATH YOUR TREASURE STORE | UPON BIRTH PRINCESSE E | 25 | MS | 391 | 456 |
| TO RAVISH HEAVEN TO LIMBE THEM O'RE AGAINE. | UPON BIRTH PRINCESSE E | 36 | MS | 391 | 456 |
| GOE ON THEN, HEAVEN, & LIMBE FORTH SUCH ANOTHER, | UPON BIRTH PRINCESSE E | 55 | MS | 391 | 456 |
| OF HEAVEN, & EARTH, & OF ALL RARITIE. | UPON BIRTH PRINCESSE E | 58 | MS | 391 | 456 |
| IF HEAVEN HATH NOW FORGOT TO WEEPE. O THEN | AN ELEGY MR STANNINOW | 15 | MS | 394 | 473 |

TH'HEAVEN

| | | | | | |
|---|---|---|---|---|---|
| IN TH'HEAVEN OF MARY'S EYE, A TEARE. | THE TEARE | 48 | 46 | 84 | 50 |

HEAVEN-BURTHEN'D

| | | | | | |
|---|---|---|---|---|---|
| AND THOU (HEAVEN-BURTHEN'D BEAST) HAST NE'RE A WORD | UPON ASSE THAT BORE SAVIOUR | 7 | 46 | 90 | 19 |

HEAVENN

| | | | | | |
|---|---|---|---|---|---|
| IT IS, IN ONE CHOISE HANDFULL, HEAVENN. & ALL | PRAYER TO GENTLE-WOMAN | 11 | 52 | 328 | 139 |

HEAVN

| | | | | | |
|---|---|---|---|---|---|
| THAT HEALING SHAFT, WHICH HEAVN TILL NOW | TO COUNTESSE OF DENBIGH | 47 | 52 | 236 | 146 |
| WHAT OF THY PARENT HEAVN YET SPEAKES IN THEE. | TO THE NAME OF JESUS | 18 | 52 | 239 | 30 |
| BRING ALL YOUR HOUSHOLD STUFFE OF HEAVN ON EARTH, | TO THE NAME OF JESUS | 63 | 52 | 239 | 30 |
| BRING ALL YOUR LUTES & HARPS OF HEAVN & EARTH. | TO THE NAME OF JESUS | 74 | 52 | 239 | 30 |
| SINCE HEAVN ITSELF LYES HERE BELOW. | IN HOLY NATIVITY | 61 | 52 | 246 | 76 |
| AND THAT OF GRACE HEAVN WAY'D IN HIM, | VEXILLA REGIS | 32 | 52 | 277 | 156 |
| HEAV'N NE'RE THE LESSE STILL HEAVN WOULD BE, | CHARITAS NIMIA | 11 | 52 | 280 | 48 |
| WHAT WAS IT TO THY HEAVN & THEE. | CHARITAS NIMIA | 46 | 52 | 280 | 48 |
| HARPES OF HEAVN TO HANDS OF MAN. | LAUDA SION SALVATOREM | 4 | 52 | 294 | 178 |
| HEAVN & EARTH SHALL FIND NO PLACE. | DIES IRAE | 6 | 52 | 298 | 166 |
| TAKE THY FAREWELL, POOR WORLD, HEAVN MUST GOE HOME. | IN GLORIOUS ASSUMPTION B. LADY | 2 | 52 | 304 | 114 |
| WHEN HEAVN BIDDS COME, WHO CAN SAY NO. | IN GLORIOUS ASSUMPTION B. LADY | 34 | 52 | 304 | 114 |
| HEAVN CALLS HER, & SHE MUST AWAY. | IN GLORIOUS ASSUMPTION B. LADY | 35 | 52 | 304 | 114 |
| HEAVN WILL NOT, & SHE CANNOT STAY. | IN GLORIOUS ASSUMPTION B. LADY | 36 | 52 | 304 | 114 |
| OF THE BRIGHT YOUTH OF HEAVN, THAT SINGS | IN GLORIOUS ASSUMPTION B. LADY | 39 | 52 | 304 | 114 |
| OF HEAVN. THE HUMBLE PRIDE OF EARTH. | IN GLORIOUS ASSUMPTION B. LADY | 65 | 52 | 304 | 114 |
| AND HEAVN WILL MAKE A FEAST, | WEEPER | 69 | 52 | 307 | 120 |
| WISE HEAVN WILL NEVER HAVE IT SO | TERESA | 74 | 52 | 315 | 52 |
| SHALT THOU EXHALE TO HEAVN AT LAST | TERESA | 116 | 52 | 315 | 62 |
| BUT I, (SO HELP ME HEAVN MY HOPES TO SEE) | ALEXIAS THIRD ELEGIE | 53 | 52 | 336 | 209 |
| CALL HEAVN TO LOOK ON THEE WITH NARROW EYES. | DEATH'S LECTURE | 17 | 52 | 340 | 475 |
| TO HEAVN RIDES IN A SUMMER'S DAY. | TEMPERANCE | 32 | 52 | 342 | 510 |

HEAVN-DESIGNED

| | | | | | |
|---|---|---|---|---|---|
| DEAR, HEAVN-DESIGNED SOUL. | TO SAME CONCERNING CHOISE | 1 | 52 | 331 | 66 |

HEAVN-INSTRUCTED

| | | | | | |
|---|---|---|---|---|---|
| THE HEAVN-INSTRUCTED HOUSE OF FAITH | LAUDA SION SALVATOREM | 31 | 52 | 294 | 178 |

HEAVN-SALUTING

| | | | | | |
|---|---|---|---|---|---|
| AND HILLS HANG DOWN THEIR HEAVN-SALUTING HEADS | TO THE NAME OF JESUS | 231 | 52 | 239 | 30 |

HEAV'N

| | | | | | |
|---|---|---|---|---|---|
| IN HEAV'N YOU'L LEARNE TO SING ERE HERE TO SPEAKE, | TO INFANT MARTYRS | 2 | 46 | 88 | 10 |
| 'TIS HEAV'N 'TIS HEAVEN SHE SEES, HEAVENS GOD THERE LYES | ON VIRGINS BASHFULNESSE | 5 | 46 | 89 | 9 |
| DISDAINES TO THINKE THAT HEAV'N THUNDERS ALONE. | SOSPETTO D'HERODE | 56 | 46 | 109 | 216 |
| SET THE CONTENDING SONS OF HEAV'N ON FIRE. | SOSPETTO D'HERODE | 90 | 46 | 109 | 216 |
| WAS THE GREAT BUSINESSE BOTH OF HEAV'N AND EARTH. | SOSPETTO D'HERODE | 120 | 46 | 109 | 216 |
| HE SAW HEAV'N BLOSSOME WITH A NEW-BORNE LIGHT, | SOSPETTO D'HERODE | 129 | 46 | 109 | 216 |
| THE HEAV'N EXPECTING AGES, HOPE TO SEE | SOSPETTO D'HERODE | 156 | 46 | 109 | 216 |
| AND SHOULD WE POWERS OF HEAV'N, SPIRITS OF WORTH | SOSPETTO D'HERODE | 219 | 46 | 109 | 216 |
| MUST THE BRIGHT ARMES OF HEAV'N, REBUKE THESE EYES. | SOSPETTO D'HERODE | 231 | 46 | 109 | 216 |
| THE FAIREST, AND THE FIRST-BORNE SMILE OF HEAV'N. | SOSPETTO D'HERODE | 236 | 46 | 109 | 216 |
| IF HELL MUST MOURNE, HEAV'N SURE SHALL SYMPATHIZE | SOSPETTO D'HERODE | 247 | 46 | 109 | 216 |

| | | | | |
|---|---|---|---|---|
| COME TRY WHO DARES, HEAV'N, EARTH, WHAT ERE DOST BOAST, | SOSPETTO D'HERODE | 251 | 46 109 216 | |
| HEAV'N SAW US STRUGGLE ONCE, AS BRAVE A FIGHT | SOSPETTO D'HERODE | 255 | 46 109 216 | |
| THOU MAD'ST BOLD PROOFE UPON THE BROW OF HEAV'N, | SOSPETTO D'HERODE | 266 | 46 109 216 | |
| IN OUR GREAT PROJECTS, BOTH 'GAINST HEAV'N AND EARTH. | SOSPETTO D'HERODE | 286 | 46 109 216 | |
| HEAV'N SAW HER RISE, AND SAW HELL IN THE SIGHT. | SOSPETTO D'HERODE | 377 | 46 109 216 | |
| AND FENCE THE HANGING SWORD HEAV'N THROWS UPON THEE. | SOSPETTO D'HERODE | 460 | 46 109 216 | |
| HEAV'N SET DOWN NEW DREST.   WHEN THY BRIGHT BIRTH | ON A TREATISE OF CHARITY | 5 | 46 137 69 | |
| THE HOLY YOUTH OF HEAV'N, WHOSE GOLDEN RINGS | ON A TREATISE OF CHARITY | 21 | 46 137 69 | |
| THE COURT OF HEAV'N IS COME. | ON THE ASSUMPTION | 16 | 46 139 114 | |
| HEAV'N CALLS HER, AND SHE MUST AWAY. | ON THE ASSUMPTION | 21 | 46 139 114 | |
| CYMBALLS OF HEAV'N, OR HUMANE SPHEARS, | TO THE NAME OF JESUS | 78 | 52 239 30 | |
| CONTEND, YE POWRES OF HEAV'N & EARTH. | IN HOLY NATIVITY | 41 | 52 246 76 | |
| LIFTS EARTH TO HEAVEN, STOOPES HEAV'N TO EARTH. | IN HOLY NATIVITY | 84 | 52 246 76 | |
| FLY IN THE FACE OF HEAV'N. AS IF IT WERE | IN GLORIOUS EPIPHANIE | 103 | 52 253 39 | |
| HEAV'N IT SELF TO FIND THEM HELL. | IN GLORIOUS EPIPHANIE | 110 | 52 253 39 | |
| HEAV'N NE'RE THE LESSE STILL HEAVN WOULD BE, | CHARITAS NIMIA | 11 | 52 280 48 | |
| AND GIVEN US HEAV'N AGAIN, IN GIVING HIM. | O GLORIOSA DOMINA | 20 | 52 302 194 | |
| THE COURT OF HEAV'N IS COME | IN GLORIOUS ASSUMPTION B. LADY | 15 | 52 304 114 | |
| UPON THE ROOF OF HEAV'N. WHERE AY | TERESA | 83 | 52 315 52 | |
| AND TEACH THY LIPPS HEAV'N WITH HIS HAND. | TERESA | 130 | 52 315 52 | |
| (THOSE SECOND SMILES OF HEAV'N) SHALL DART | TERESA | 135 | 52 315 52 | |
| HEAV'N KEEPS UPON THY SCORE.  (THY BRIGHT | TERESA | 175 | 52 315 52 | |
| OUR FREE TRAFFIQUE FOR HEAV'N, WE MAY MAINTAINE | AN APOLOGIE FOR (TERESA) HYMNE | 19 | 52 322 59 | |
| SPEAK HEAV'N LIKE HER'S IS MY SOULS COUNTRY-MAN. | AN APOLOGIE FOR (TERESA) HYMNE | 22 | 52 322 59 | |
| O 'TIS NOT SPANISH, BUT 'TIS HEAV'N SHE SPEAKS. | AN APOLOGIE FOR (TERESA) HYMNE | 23 | 52 322 59 | |
| 'TIS HEAV'N THAT LYES IN AMBUSH THERE, & BREAKS | AN APOLOGIE FOR (TERESA) HYMNE | 24 | 52 322 59 | |
| FAIR HOPE. OUR EARLYER HEAV'N BY THEE | (ON) HOPE | 21 | 52 345 71 | |
| GREAT NYMPH, O'RELOOKE MY LOWNESSE. HEAV'N YOU KNOW, | EX EUPHORMIONE | 7 | MS 392 525 | |
| HEAV'N, EARTH, AND SEA, MY TRIUMPHS.   WHAT REMAIN'D | OUT OF GROTIUS | 85 | MS 398 198 | |

HEAV'N-BESIEGED

| | | | |
|---|---|---|---|
| WHAT HEAV'N-BESIEGED HEART IS THIS | AGAINST IRRESOLUTION AND DELAY | 1 | 52 347 146 |

HEAV'N-INTREATED

| | | | |
|---|---|---|---|
| WHAT HEAV'N-INTREATED HEART IS THIS. | TO COUNTESSE OF DENBIGH | 1 | 52 236 146 |

HEAV'N-REBUKED

| | | | |
|---|---|---|---|
| THE HEAV'N-REBUKED SHADES MADE HAST AWAY. | SOSPETTO D'HERODE | 114 | 46 109 216 |

HEAV'NE-BORNE

| | | | |
|---|---|---|---|
| MY WOMBES CHAST PRIDE IS GONE, MY HEAV'NE-BORNE BOY. | LUKE 2.  QUAERIT JESUM | 7 | MS 379 11 |

HEAVENLY

| | | | |
|---|---|---|---|
| HER HEAVENLY ARMEFULL, SHEE SHALL TAST | ON A PRAYER BOOKE | 106 | 46 126 139 |
| EACH HEAVENLY WORD, BY WHOSE HID FLAME | IN MEMORY OF LADY MADRE TERESA | 160 | 46 131 52 |
| THAT HEAVENLY MAXIM GAVE ME HEART TO TRY | AN APOLOGIE FOR HYMNE (TERESA) | 9 | 46 136 59 |
| A PEECE OF HEAVENLY LIGHT PURER AND BRIGHTER | ON THE ASSUMPTION | 3 | 46 139 114 |
| HANGS HIS BLACK LUGGES, STROAKT WITH THOSE HEAVENLY LINES. | HORATIJ ILLE & NEFASTO | 51 | MS 382 530 |
| THAT HEAVENLY MORTALL, THAT SERAPHICK MAN. | AN ELEGIE ON DR PORTER | 18 | MS 395 476 |

HEAVNLY

| | | | |
|---|---|---|---|
| EACH HEAVNLY WORD BY WHOSE HID FLAME | TERESA | 159 | 52 315 52 |
| HER HEAVNLY ARM-FULL, SHE SHALL TAST | PRAYER TO GENTLE-WOMAN | 112 | 52 328 139 |
| IT WAS HIS HEAVNLY ART | TO SAME CONCERNING CHOISE | 45 | 52 331 66 |
| WHEN HOLY FIRES MAINTAIN LOVE'S HEAVNLY LIFE. | ALEXIAS THIRD ELEGIE | 52 | 52 336 209 |

HEAV'NLY

| | | | |
|---|---|---|---|
| A PIECE OF HEAV'NLY EARTH. PURER & BRIGHTER | IN GLORIOUS ASSUMPTION B. LADY | 3 | 52 304 114 |

HEAVENS

| | | | |
|---|---|---|---|
| DOTH TUNE THE SPHAEARES, AND MAKE HEAVENS SELFE LOOKE | MUSICKS DUELL | 118 | 46 149 535 |
| TO GENERATION. HEAVENS ALMIGHTY SIRE | OUT OF VIRGIL | 4 | 46 155 529 |
| OF HEAVENS HIGH'ST ARCHES TO FALL NARROW. | OUT OF GREEKE CUPID'S CRYER | 48 | 46 159 519 |
| HEAVENS THY FAIRE EYES BEE. | THE WEEPER | 7 | 46 79 120 |
| HEAVENS OF EVER-FALLING STARS. | THE WEEPER | 8 | 46 79 120 |
| WHAT EVER MAKES HEAVENS FORE-HEAD FINE. | THE WEEPER | 12 | 46 79 120 |
| AS HEAVENS OTHER SPANGLES DOE. | THE WEEPER | 16 | 46 79 120 |
| HEAVENS BOSOME DRINKS THE GENTLE STREAME. | THE WEEPER | 20 | 46 79 120 |
| OR, 'CAUSE HEAVENS FACE IS DIM, | WHY ARE YEE AFRAID | 2 | 46 88 15 |
| 'TIS HEAV'N 'TIS HEAVEN SHE SEES, HEAVENS GOD THERE LYES | ON VIRGINS BASHFULNESSE | 5 | 46 89 9 |
| HEAVENS GOLDEN-WINGED HERALD, LATE HEE SAW | SOSPETTO D'HERODE | 97 | 46 109 216 |
| HEAVENS KING, WHO DOFFS HIMSELFE WEAKE FLESH TO WEARE. | SOSPETTO D'HERODE | 515 | 46 109 216 |
| HEAVENS ROYALL HOASTS INCAMPT, THUS SMALL. | ON A PRAYER BOOKE | 6 | 46 126 139 |
| HOW MANY HEAVENS AT ONCE IT IS, | ON A PRAYER BOOKE | 117 | 46 126 139 |
| TO NONE BUT THE BLEST HEAVENS, WHOSE BRIGHT | ON THE ASSUMPTION | 32 | 46 139 114 |
| DEARE HOPE.  EARTHS DOWRY, AND HEAVENS DEBT, | ON HOPE | 11 | 46 143 71 |
| GRACIOUS HEAVENS DO USE TO SEND | UPON DEATH OF DESIRED HERRYS | 26 | 46 168 467 |
| MADE HEAVENS RADIANT FACE LOOKE FOULE. | UPON DEATH OF DESIRED HERRYS | 52 | 46 168 467 |
| AT MID-DAY OPES A PRESENCE WHICH HEAVENS EYE | UPON YORKE HIS BIRTH | 70 | 46 176 500 |
| THE HEAVENS WILL STAY NO LONGER, MAY THY GLORY | UPON YORKE HIS BIRTH | 104 | 46 176 500 |
| (THOUGH THE HEAVENS IN COUNSELL SATE. | LOVES HOROSCOPE | 23 | 46 185 483 |
| (THOUGH HEAVENS INAUSPICIOUS EYE | LOVES HOROSCOPE | 35 | 46 185 483 |
| THE SAME BRIGHT BUSYNES (YE THIRD HEAVENS) WITH YOU. | TO THE NAME OF JESUS | 110 | 52 239 30 |

| | | | | |
|---|---|---|---|---|
| HEAVENS THY FAIR EYES BE, | WEEPER | 7 | 52 307 | 120 |
| HEAVENS OF EVER-FALLING STARRES. | WEEPER | 8 | 52 307 | 120 |
| PEACE, HEART. THE HEAVENS ARE ANGRY. ALL THEIR SPHAERES | LUKE 2. QUAERIT JESUM | 19 | MS 379 | 11 |
| AND START FROM OFF THY CENTER. HATH HEAVENS LOVE | ON GUNPOWDER-TREASON | 5 | MS 384 | 458 |
| IN THIS BLEST EARTH HEAVENS BRIGHT EPITOME, | UPON KINGS CORONATION | 12 | MS 389 | 454 |
| TO WHOM HEAVENS LAMPES OFTEN IN SILENT NIGHT | UPON KINGS CORONATION | 27 | MS 389 | 454 |
| FROM HEAVENS SWEET MILKY STREAME DOTH GENTLY POURE. | AN ELEGY MR STANNINOW | 10 | MS 394 | 473 |
| DOTH BLITH APOLLO CLOATH THE HEAVENS WITH JOYE, | AN ELEGY MR STANNINOW | 11 | MS 394 | 473 |

HEAVNS

| | | | | |
|---|---|---|---|---|
| OF HEAVNS, THE SELF INVOLVING SETT OF SPHEARS | TO THE NAME OF JESUS | 30 | 52 239 | 30 |
| BLEST HEAVNS, TO YOU, & YOUR SUPERIOUR SONG. | TO THE NAME OF JESUS | 98 | 52 239 | 30 |
| FOR WHOM THE'OFFICIOUS HEAVNS DEVISE | IN GLORIOUS EPIPHANIE | 3 | 52 253 | 39 |
| WATERS ABOVE TH' HEAVNS, WHAT THEY BE | WEEPER | 23 | 52 307 | 120 |
| HERE PERISH'T SHE, POOR HEART, HEAVNS, BE MY VOWES | ALEXIAS FIRST ELEGIE | 31 | 52 334 | 204 |
| WITTNESSE, CHAST HEAVNS. NO HAPPYER VOWES I KNOW | ALEXIAS THIRD ELEGIE | 25 | 52 336 | 209 |
| SOUND FORTH, CAELESTIALL ORGANS,LETT HEAVNS QUIRE | UPON KINGS CORONATION | 1 | MS 389 | 454 |

HEAVN'S

| | | | | |
|---|---|---|---|---|
| WHILE WE FOUND OUT HEAVN'S FAIRER EY | IN HOLY NATIVITY | 7 | 52 246 | 76 |
| HEAVN'S WHOLSOM RAY. | IN GLORIOUS EPIPHANIE | 61 | 52 253 | 39 |
| OR ON HEAVN'S AZURE FOREHEAD HIGH TO STAND | IN GLORIOUS EPIPHANIE | 250 | 52 253 | 39 |
| WHATEVER MAKES HEAVN'S FOREHEAD FINE. | WEEPER | 12 | 52 307 | 120 |
| AS HEAVN'S OTHER SPANGLES DOE. | WEEPER | 16 | 52 307 | 120 |
| HEAVN'S BOSOME DRINKS THE GENTLE STREAM. | WEEPER | 20 | 52 307 | 120 |
| HEAVN'S GREAT ARTILLERY IN EACH LOVE-SPUN LINE. | FLAMING HEART | 56 | 52 324 | 61 |
| HEAVN'S ROYALL HOST. INCAMP'T THUS SMALL | PRAYER TO GENTLE-WOMAN | 12 | 52 328 | 139 |
| I'AM PERFECT IN HEAVN'S STATE, WITH EVERY STARR | ALEXIAS SECONDE ELEGIE | 23 | 52 335 | 207 |
| DEAR HOPE. EARTH'S DOWRY, & HEAVN'S DEBT. | (ON) HOPE | 1 | 52 345 | 71 |

HEAV'NS

| | | | | |
|---|---|---|---|---|
| OF SUCH A CHANGE, BUT THAT THE HEAV'NS INDULGENCE | OUT OF VIRGIL | 34 | 46 155 | 529 |
| BY WHOM (AS HEAV'NS ILLUSTRIOUS HAND-MAID) RAIS'D | SOSPETTO D'HERODE | 134 | 46 109 | 216 |
| WHILE THUS HEAV'NS HIGHEST COUNSAILS, BY THE LOW | SOSPETTO D'HERODE | 145 | 46 109 | 216 |
| WHO FEEDS WITH NECTAR HEAV'NS FAIRE FAMILY. | SOSPETTO D'HERODE | 174 | 46 109 | 216 |
| THAT HEAV'NS HIGH MAJESTY HIS COURT SHOULD KEEPE | SOSPETTO D'HERODE | 181 | 46 109 | 216 |
| LET HEAV'NS LORD CHIDE ABOVE LOWDER THEN THOU | SOSPETTO D'HERODE | 269 | 46 109 | 216 |
| AND POURING ON HEAV'NS FACE THE SEAS HUGE FLOOD | SOSPETTO D'HERODE | 277 | 46 109 | 216 |
| BY ALL THE HEAV'NS THOU HAST IN HIM | FLAMING HEART | 103 | 52 324 | 61 |
| HOW MANY HEAV'NS AT ONCE IT IS | PRAYER TO GENTLE-WOMAN | 123 | 52 328 | 139 |
| AND BREAKES THROUGH ALL TEN HEAV'NS TO OUR EMBRACE. | AGAINST IRRESOLUTION AND DELAY | 78 | 52 347 | 146 |

HEAV'N'S

| | | | | |
|---|---|---|---|---|
| AND KNOW THE CALL OF HEAV'N'S KIND SHOWERS. | AGAINST IRRESOLUTION AND DELAY | 34 | 52 347 | 146 |

HEAV'D

| | | | | |
|---|---|---|---|---|
| HEAV'D ON THE SURGES OF SWOLNE RAPSODYES. | MUSICKS DUELL | 136 | 46 149 | 535 |

HEAVES

| | | | | |
|---|---|---|---|---|
| HEAVES HER SOFT·BOSOME, WANDERS ROUND ABOUT, | MUSICKS DUELL | 86 | 46 149 | 535 |
| HER WEAKE BREAST HEAVES WITH STRONG DESIRE, | IN MEMORY OF LADY MADRE TERESA | 40 | 46 131 | 52 |
| HER WEAKE BREST HEAVES WITH STRONG DESIRE | TERESA | 40 | 52 315 | 52 |

HEAVIEST

| | | | | |
|---|---|---|---|---|
| LOVE, THAT LENDS HASTE TO HEAVIEST THINGS. | AGAINST IRRESOLUTION AND DELAY | 27 | 52 347 | 146 |

HEAVY

| | | | | |
|---|---|---|---|---|
| WHICH NODS WITH MANY A HEAVY HEADED TREE. | SOSPETTO D'HERODE | 346 | 46 109 | 216 |
| (NIGHT HANGS YET HEAVY ON THE LIDS OF DAY) | SOSPETTO D'HERODE | 506 | 46 109 | 216 |
| TO SIT AND SCOULE UPON NIGHTS HEAVY BROW, | ON A FOULE MORNING | 34 | 46 181 | 495 |
| BOWES LOW'ST HIS HEAVY TOP, TO LOOK FOR THEE. | IN GLORIOUS ASSUMPTION B. LADY | 30 | 52 304 | 114 |

HEAVYER

| | | | | |
|---|---|---|---|---|
| ALAS WITH HOW MUCH HEAVYER SHADE | IN GLORIOUS EPIPHANIE | 117 | 52 253 | 39 |

HEBE'S

| | | | | |
|---|---|---|---|---|
| SOFTER THEN THAT WHICH PANTS IN HEBE'S CUP. | MUSICKS DUELL | 126 | 46 149 | 535 |
| E'RE HEBE'S HAND HAD OVERLAID | HIS EPITAPH (HERRYS) | 45 | 46 172 | 471 |

HEBREW

| | | | | |
|---|---|---|---|---|
| IN HEBREW NUMBERS, THEN (O CRUELL JEST.) | PSALME 137 | 9 | 46 104 | 7 |

HEBREWES

| | | | | |
|---|---|---|---|---|
| HEE SAW TH'OLD HEBREWES WOMBE, NEGLECT THE LAW | SOSPETTO D'HERODE | 101 | 46 109 | 216 |
| KNOW'ST THOU NOT HOW OF TH' HEBREWES ROYALL STEMME | SOSPETTO D'HERODE | 433 | 46 109 | 216 |

HEDGE-QUIRISTERS

| | | | | |
|---|---|---|---|---|
| HEDGE-QUIRISTERS WHOSE MUSICKE OWES | THOUGH NOW 'TIS NEITHER | 18 | MS 397 | 492 |

HEDG'D

   THESE PURPLE CURRENTS HEDG'D WITH VIOLETS ROUND     AN ELEGY MR STANNINOW     22   MS 394 473

HEED

   I'LE GIVE THEE ALL, TAKE ALL, TAKE HEED     OUT OF GREEKE CUPID'S CRYER    71   46 159 519
   TO STRIKE AT EARES, IS TO TAKE HEED THERE BEE    ON ST. PETER CUTTING MALCHUS   3   46  97  22
   TAKE HEED (SAID SHE) TAKE HEED, VALERIAN.     ALEXIAS THIRD ELEGIE      34   52 336 209
   TAKE HEED (SAID SHE) TAKE HEED, VALERIAN.     ALEXIAS THIRD ELEGIE      34   52 336 209

HEELE

                                                                 ON MR. G. HERBERTS BOOKE       11   46 130  68
   THE WEIGHTY RUDENES OF HIS BOYSTEROUS HEELE.    ON GUNPOWDER-TREASON       44   MS 384 458

HEIGHT

   SWELL. SWELL TO SUCH AN HEIGHT, THAT THOU MAIST VYE  UPON KINGS CORONATION      9   MS 389 454
   AND BREAKE UPON MEE. MY OWNE VIRTUES HEIGHT    OUT OF GROTIUS           33   MS 398 198

HEIR

   THE DEATHLES HEIR OF ALL THY FATHER'S DAY.     IN GLORIOUS EPIPHANIE      64   52 253  39

HEYRE

   FATHER AND HEYRE OF DARKENESSE, WHEN I CHIDE   OUT OF GROTIUS           77   MS 398 198

HEIRE

   RISE, HEIRE OF FRESH ETERNITY,               EASTER DAY                1   46 100  26
   HEIRE OF THE SUNS FIRST BEAMES.   WHY THREAT'ST THOU  TO THE MORNING           53   46 183 497
                                                    SO.

HEIRS

   THE HEIRS ELECT OF LOVE. WHOSE NAMES BELONG    TO THE NAME OF JESUS       9   52 239  30

HEYRES

   BUT ISAACKS ISSUE THE PECULIAR HEYRES,        OUT OF GROTIUS           39   MS 398 198

HELD

   THAT TH'ONE SPAKE, OR THAT TH'OTHER HELD HIS PEACE.  UPON DUMBE DEVILL CAST OUT   4   46  93  14
   AND IS HE GONE, WHOM THESE ARMES HELD BUT NOW.   LUKE 2. QUAERIT JESUM       1   MS 379  11
   MINE OWNE HELICON WITH STRANGER FASTINGS, WHEN I HELD OUT OF GROTIUS           58   MS 398 198

HELICON

   IN CREAME OF MORNING HELICON, AND THEN        MUSICKS DUELL            77   46 149 535
   A SEA OF HELICON. HIS HAND DOES GOE          MUSICKS DUELL            124   46 149 535
   MORE THEN THEIR OWNE HELICON.                AN EPITAPH DOCTOR BROOKE     4   46 175 465
   HIS LETHE BE MY HELICON. AND SEE            TO THE MORNING           17   46 183 497

HELICONS

   A THOUSAND HELICONS THE MUSES SEND           AN ELEGIE ON DR PORTER      39   MS 395 476

HELL

   WHAT FARTHEST NOOKE OF LOWEST HELL.           OUT OF GREEKE CUPID'S CRYER   35   46 159 519
   WITH TH'PURPLE HE MUST WEARE IN HELL.         UPON LAZARUS HIS TEARES      4   46  89  18
   I DOUBT THOUGH WHEN THE WORLD'S IN HELL,       BUT MEN LOVED DARKNESSE      3   46  97  13
   NOW WITH NEW RAGE, AND WAX TOO HOT FOR HELL.    SOSPETTO D'HERODE         148   46 109 216
   AUSPICIOUS STILL, IN SPIGHT OF HELL AND ME.     SOSPETTO D'HERODE         208   46 109 216
   HELL FROM ME TOO, AND SACK MY TERRITORIES.     SOSPETTO D'HERODE         226   46 109 216
   IF HELL MUST MOURNE, HEAV'N SURE SHALL SYMPATHIZE  SOSPETTO D'HERODE         247   46 109 216
   AND ALL THE POWERS OF HELL IN FULL APPLAUSE     SOSPETTO D'HERODE         259   46 109 216
   BOUNDLESSE AND ABSOLUTE. HELL IS THINE OWNE.     SOSPETTO D'HERODE         272   46 109 216
   RUNG, THROUGH THE HOLLOW VAULTS OF HELL PROFOUND.  SOSPETTO D'HERODE         299   46 109 216
   OF LIGHTNING, OR THE WORDS HE SPOKE) LEFT HELL.   SOSPETTO D'HERODE         372   46 109 216
   HEAV'N SAW HER RISE, AND SAW HELL IN THE SIGHT.   SOSPETTO D'HERODE         377   46 109 216
   AS IT IS SEENE BY HELL. AND SEENE WITH DREAD.    SOSPETTO D'HERODE         414   46 109 216
   THIS DONE, HOME TO HER HELL SHEE HY'D AMAINE.    SOSPETTO D'HERODE         472   46 109 216
   THEN SINNE HATH SNARES, OR HELL HATH DARTS.     ON A PRAYER BOOKE          20   46 126 139
   THERE ARE ENOW WHOSE DRAUGHTS AS DEEP AS HELL    AN APOLOGIE FOR HYMNE (TERESA) 29   46 136  59
   AND TO THE TEETH OF HELL STOOD UP TO TEACH THEE,  TO THE NAME OF JESUS     204   52 239  30
   THE PROUD & MISPLAC'T GATES OF HELL.          IN GLORIOUS EPIPHANIE      55   52 253  39
   HEAV'N IT SELF TO FIND THEM HELL.            IN GLORIOUS EPIPHANIE     110   52 253  39
   IN THE DEEP HELL.                                  CHARITAS NIMIA           13   52 280  48
   HORROR OF NATURE, HELL & DEATH.              DIES IRAE               13   52 298 186
   THERE ARE ENOW, WHOSE DRAUGHTS (AS DEEP AS HELL)  AN APOLOGIE FOR (TERESA) HYMNE 29   52 322  59
   THEN SIN HATH SNARES, OR HELL HATH DARTS.      PRAYER TO GENTLE-WOMAN     26   52 328 139
   TILL NOW HELL WAS IMPERFECT. IT DID NEED       ON GUNPOWDER-TREASON       61   MS 384 458
   SOME RARE CHOICE TORTURE. NOW 'TIS HELL INDEED.   ON GUNPOWDER-TREASON       62   MS 384 458
   TH' EPITOME OF HELL. OH LETT THY PINIONS       UPON GUNPOWDER TREASON     21   MS 387 461
   HIMSELFE IN HIS OWNE HELL. AND NOW LETS LOOSE    OUT OF GROTIUS           79   MS 398 198

## HELL'S

| | | | |
|---|---|---|---|
| THY GREISLY MAJESTY, HELL'S BLACKEST QUEENE. | HORATIJ ILLE & NEFASTO | 34 | MS 382 530 |

## HELLS

| | | | |
|---|---|---|---|
| AND TO MAKE UP HELLS MAJESTY, EACH HORNE | SOSPETTO D'HERODE | 47 | 46 109 216 |
| OF HELLS OWNE STINKE, A WORSER STENCH IS SPREAD. | SOSPETTO D'HERODE | 54 | 46 109 216 |
| HIS BREATH HELLS LIGHTNING IS, AND EACH DEEPE GRONE | SOSPETTO D'HERODE | 55 | 46 109 216 |
| BE IT THY PART, HELLS MIGHTY LORD, TO LAY | SOSPETTO D'HERODE | 263 | 46 109 216 |
| HELLS SHOP OF SLAUGHTER SHEE DO'S OVERSEE, | SOSPETTO D'HERODE | 291 | 46 109 216 |
| WHERE HELLS CAPACIOUS CAULDRON IS SET ON. | SOSPETTO D'HERODE | 294 | 46 109 216 |
| REBOUNDING, THROUGH HELLS INMOST CAVERNES CAME, | SOSPETTO D'HERODE | 303 | 46 109 216 |
| MONGST ALL THE PALACES IN HELLS COMMAND. | SOSPETTO D'HERODE | 305 | 46 109 216 |

## HELS

| | | | |
|---|---|---|---|
| AND NOW HIS DREAM (HELS FIREBRAND) STIL MORE BRIGHT, | SOSPETTO D'HERODE | 503 | 46 109 216 |

## HELLISH

| | | | |
|---|---|---|---|
| TO QUENCH THE RAGE OF HELLISH DEITIES. | UPON GUNPOWDER TREASON | 36 | MS 387 461 |

## HELP

| | | | |
|---|---|---|---|
| HEARKEN, AND HELP, YE HOLY DOVES. | TO THE NAME OF JESUS | 6 | 52 239 30 |
| HELP ME TO MEDITATE MINE IMMORTALL SONG. | TO THE NAME OF JESUS | 61 | 52 239 30 |
| O LORD MAKE HAST TO HELP ME. | OFFICE H. CROSS MATINES | 6 | 52 265 86 |
| WHAT NEED THEY HELP TO DROWN THY HEART. | UPON BLEEDING CRUCIFIX | 7 | 52 288 110 |
| HELP LORD, MY FAITH, MY HOPE INCREASE. | ADORO TE | 33 | 52 291 172 |
| BUT I, (SO HELP ME HEAVN MY HOPES TO SEE) | ALEXIAS THIRD ELEGIE | 53 | 52 336 209 |

## HELPE

| | | | |
|---|---|---|---|
| WHAT NEED THEY HELPE TO DROWNE THINE HEART, | ON BLEEDING WOUNDS OF LORD | 19 | 46 101 110 |

## HEMISPHAEARE

| | | | |
|---|---|---|---|
| LEFT THE DIMME FACE OF THIS DULL HEMISPHAEARE, | UPON BISHOP ANDREWES PICTURE | 3 | 46 163 490 |

## HENCE

| | | | |
|---|---|---|---|
| SNATCH'T HER SELF HENCE, TO HEAVEN. FILL'D A BRIGHT PLACE, | UPON BISHOP ANDREWES PICTURE | 9 | 46 163 490 |
| NOW THOUGH THE BLOW THAT SNATCHT HIM HENCE, | UPON THE DEATH OF A GENTLEMAN | 15 | 46 166 472 |
| EVERY MORNE FROM HENCE, | THE WEEPER | 25 | 46 79 120 |
| WHILE IT FALLS HENCE 'TIS A TEARE. | ON WATER OF LORDS BAPTISME | 4 | 46 85 12 |
| THE PLACE THAT CALLS YOU HENCE, IS AT THE WORST | TO INFANT MARTYRS | 5 | 46 88 10 |
| ROSES HENCE, OR LILLIES RATHER. | UPON INFANT MARTYRS | 4 | 46 95 10 |
| FLY, FLY PROPHANE FOGS, FARRE HENCE FLY AWAY, | ON A FOULE MORNING | 31 | 46 181 495 |
| HENCE 'TIS MY HUMBLE FANCY FINDS NO WINGS, | TO THE MORNING | 19 | 46 183 497 |
| SHALL HENCE FOR EVER BEAR AWAY. | LAUDA SION SALVATOREM | 18 | 52 294 178 |
| EVERY MORN FROM HENCE | WEEPER | 25 | 52 307 120 |
| BUT HOW SHALL I STEAL HENCE, ALEXIS THOU | ALEXIAS FIRST ELEGIE | 15 | 52 334 204 |
| THOUGH ALL THE JOYES I HAD FLEED HENCE WITH THEE | ALEXIAS SECONDE ELEGIE | 1 | 52 335 207 |

## HENCEFORTH

| | | | |
|---|---|---|---|
| SHALL HENCEFORTH SEE | IN GLORIOUS EPIPHANIE | 178 | 52 253 39 |

## HENCE-FORTH

| | | | |
|---|---|---|---|
| THIS SHALL FROM HENCE-FORTH BE THE MASCULINE THEME | ON A TREATISE OF CHARITY | 49 | 46 137 69 |

## HENNES

| | | | |
|---|---|---|---|
| OR CHOICEST HENNES OF AFRICK-BROOD. | PETRONIJ ALES PHASIACIS PETITA | 2 | MS 382 526 |

## HENRY

| | | | |
|---|---|---|---|
| HENRY AND JAMES, OR MARS AND PHOEBUS RATHER. | UPON YORKE HIS BIRTH | 31 | 46 176 500 |
| 'TIS BUT THE SAME IS SAID, HENRY AND JAMES | UPON YORKE HIS BIRTH | 33 | 46 176 500 |

## HERALD

| | | | |
|---|---|---|---|
| HEAVENS GOLDEN-WINGED HERALD, LATE HEE SAW | SOSPETTO D'HERODE | 97 | 46 109 216 |
| A WINGED HERALD, GLADD OF SOE SWEET A PREY, | AN ELEGY MR STANNINOW | 49 | MS 394 473 |

## HERALDS

| | | | |
|---|---|---|---|
| HERALDS AND MESSENGERS IMMEDIATELY | SOSPETTO D'HERODE | 509 | 46 109 216 |
| BUT WHEN JOVES WINGED HERALDS THIS ESPIED, | UPON GUNPOWDER TREASON | 53 | MS 386 460 |

## HERBE

| | | | |
|---|---|---|---|
| EACH HERBE A PLAGUE. THE WINDS SIGHES TIMED-BEE | SOSPETTO D'HERODE | 348 | 46 109 216 |

## HERBES

| | | | |
|---|---|---|---|
| VERTUES OF STONES, NOR HERBES, USE STRONGER CHARMES, | SOSPETTO D'HERODE | 274 | 46 109 216 |

HERBERTS

    AND THOUGH HERBERTS NAME DOE OWE  ON MR. G. HERBERTS BOOKE  15  46 130  68

HERCULES

    THROUGH THE GREAT MOUTH THATS NAM'D FROM HERCULES)  THE BEGINNING OF HELIODORUS  6  46 158 517

HERDS

    THE HERDS TO KINDLY MEETINGS, THEN THE FIELDS  OUT OF VIRGIL  12  46 155 529

HEROD

    HATE IS THY THEAME, AND HEROD, WHOSE UNBLEST  SOSPETTO D'HERODE  2  46 109 216
    BY HEROD LEIGE TO CESAR NOW WAS BORNE  SOSPETTO D'HERODE  401  46 109 216
    OF THY GREAT SELFE, HATH STOLNE KING HEROD FROM THEE.  SOSPETTO D'HERODE  458  46 109 216
    BE HEROD, AND THOU SHALT NOT MISSE FROM MEE  SOSPETTO D'HERODE  463  46 109 216
    WHY ART THOU TROUBLED HEROD. WHAT VAINE FEARE  SOSPETTO D'HERODE  513  46 109 216
    THOU ART A SOULDIER HEROD, SEND THY SCOUTS  SOSPETTO D'HERODE  523  46 109 216

HERODS

    SO BOYLES THE FIRED HERODS BLOOD-SWOLNE BREST,  SOSPETTO D'HERODE  489  46 109 216
    HURTES MEE FAR WORSE THEN HERODS HIGHEST SPITE.  OUT OF GROTIUS  34  MS 398 198

HEROES

    THAT NEST OF HEROES, ALL OUR HOPES FINDE ROOME.  UPON YORKE HIS BIRTH  81  46 176 500

HEROICK

    MAPPE OF HEROICK WORTH. WHOM FARRE AND WIDE  SOSPETTO D'HERODE  13  46 109 216

HERSE

    THE SULLEN CYPRESSE O'RE HIS HERSE.  UPON THE DEATH OF A GENTLEMAN  10  46 166 472

HERS'D

    THE HOUSE IS HERS'D ABOUT WITH A BLACK WOOD,  SOSPETTO D'HERODE  345  46 109 216

HESPERIDES

    POORE FRUITES LOOKE PALE AT THY HESPERIDES.  UPON TWO GREENE APRICOCKES  30  48 220 494

HEWE

    THOUGH HIS WINGS CONCEITED HEWE  PETRONIJ ALES PHASIACIS PETITA  7  MS 382 526

HEW'N

    THESE HANDS AND THINE WERE HEW'N, THESE CHERRYES MOCKE  UPON YORKE HIS BIRTH  46  46 176 500

HEYFER

    BY WANTON HEYFER SHALL BE WORN  IN GLORIOUS EPIPHANIE  94  52 253  39

HID

    HAD NOT HER THICK SNAKES HID THEM FROM THE SUN.  SOSPETTO D'HERODE  384  46 109 216
    EACH HEAVENLY WORD, BY WHOSE HID FLAME  IN MEMORY OF LADY MADRE TERESA  160  46 131  52
    (BY ALL THY MYSTERIES THAT THERE LYE HID.)  AN APOLOGIE FOR HYMNE (TERESA)  12  46 136  59
    AND SEEING THE LOATH'D OBJECT, HID FOR SHAME  TO THE MORNING  12  46 183 497
    HATH IN LOVE'S QUIVER HID FOR YOU.  TO COUNTESSE OF DENBIGH  48  52 236 146
    BUT HERE EV'N THAT'S HID TOO WHICH HIDES THE OTHER.  ADORO TE  26  52 291 172
    EACH HEAVNLY WORD BY WHOSE HID FLAME  TERESA  159  52 315  52

HID'ST

    RICH, CHURLISH LAND, THAT HID'ST SO LONG IN THEE,  ALEXIAS THIRD ELEGIE  1  52 336 209

HIDD

    THOUGH HIDD AS GOD, WOUNDS WRITT THEE MAN,  ADORO TE  22  52 291 172

HIDDE

    (BY ALL THY MYSTERYES THAT HERE LY HIDDE)  AN APOLOGIE FOR (TERESA) HYMNE  12  52 322  59

HIDDEN

    SUCK HIDDEN SWEETS, WHICH WELL DIGESTED PROVES  SOSPETTO D'HERODE  23  46 109 216
    OF HIDDEN SWEETS, AND HOLY JOYES,  ON A PRAYER BOOKE  58  46 126 139
    OF ALL THIS HIDDEN STORE  ON A PRAYER BOOKE  81  46 126 139
    THE HIDDEN SWEETS  TO THE NAME OF JESUS  122  52 239  30
    OF OPEN DEATH & HIDDEN LIFE.  OFFICE H. CROSS NINTH  10  52 271  99
    THUS LOWE (MY HIDDEN LIFE,) I BOW TO THEE  ADORO TE  3  52 291 172
    OF HIDDEN SWEETS & HOLY JOYES.  PRAYER TO GENTLE-WOMAN  64  52 328 139
    THE HIDDEN ART  TO SAME CONCERNING CHOISE  43  52 331  66

HIDE

| | | | | |
|---|---|---|---|---|
| O'RE BEAUTIES FACE, SEEMING TO HIDE | IN PRAISE OF LESSIUS | 29 | 46 156 | 510 |
| WHOSE RISING GLORIES MADE SUCH HASTE TO HIDE | UPON DEATH OF HERRYS | 4 | 46 167 | 466 |
| HIDE HIS HOT BEAMES IN SHADE OF SILVER AGE. | UPON DEATH OF HERRYS | 31 | 46 167 | 466 |
| INVITED HIM NO MORE TO HIDE | UPON DEATH OF DESIRED HERRYS | 37 | 46 168 | 467 |
| SAFE O HIDE HIS LOVED HEAD. | UPON DEATH OF DESIRED HERRYS | 70 | 46 168 | 467 |
| FOR PITTIES SAKE O HIDE HIM QUITE. | UPON DEATH OF DESIRED HERRYS | 71 | 46 168 | 467 |
| SAD MORTALITY MAY HIDE, | ANOTHER ON HERRYS | 59 | 46 170 | 469 |
| SHALL I HIDE POORE LOVE FROM DEATH. | LOVES HOROSCOPE | 44 | 46 185 | 483 |
| HOME TO HIMSELF, TO HIDE IT IN HIS BREST | TO SAME CONCERNING CHOISE | 51 | 52 331 | 66 |
| OR'E BEAUTY'S FACE, SEEMING TO HIDE | TEMPERANCE | 27 | 52 342 | 510 |
| OR ELSE, MY LIFE, I'LE HIDE THEE IN HIS GRAVE, | MATH. 16. 25. WHOSOEVER SHALL | 3 | MS 381 | 16 |
| TO HIDE HIS BLOOMING GLORIES, & BEQUEATH | AN ELEGY MR STANNINOW | 29 | MS 394 | 473 |
| IN VAILES OF DUST THEIR SILKEN HEADS THEY'LE HIDE, | AN ELEGIE ON DR PORTER | 25 | MS 395 | 476 |
| SINKES INTO HORROURS BOSOME, GLAD TO HIDE | OUT OF GROTIUS | 78 | MS 398 | 198 |

HIDES

| | | | | |
|---|---|---|---|---|
| UNTILL HIS FINGER(MODERATOUR)HIDES | MUSICKS DUELL | 52 | 46 149 | 535 |
| HIS HEAD IN THY FAIRE BOSOME, AND STILL HIDES | TO THE MORNING | 13 | 46 183 | 497 |
| THE HEART THAT HIDES THEE HARDLY COVERS. | TO THE NAME OF JESUS | 215 | 52 239 | 30 |
| BUT HERE EV'N THAT'S HID TOO WHICH HIDES THE OTHER. | ADORO TE | 26 | 52 291 | 172 |

HIDING

| | | | | |
|---|---|---|---|---|
| OR HIDING HIS VEX'T CHEEKS IN A HIR'D MIST | IN GLORIOUS EPIPHANIE | 123 | 52 253 | 39 |

HIED

| | | | | |
|---|---|---|---|---|
| UPP TO TH' ALMIGHTY THUNDERER THEY HIED, | UPON GUNPOWDER TREASON | 54 | MS 386 | 460 |

HY'D

| | | | | |
|---|---|---|---|---|
| BUT VERTUE HEARD IT, AND AWAY SHEE HY'D, | SOSPETTO D'HERODE | 470 | 46 109 | 216 |
| THIS DONE, HOME TO HER HELL SHEE HY'D AMAINE. | SOSPETTO D'HERODE | 472 | 46 109 | 216 |
| CRUELL AUSTER THITHER HY'D HIM, | UPON DEATH OF DESIRED HERRYS | 42 | 46 168 | 467 |

HIES

| | | | | |
|---|---|---|---|---|
| UP TO OLYMPUS STATELY TOPP HE HIES, | UPON KINGS CORONATION | 17 | MS 390 | 453 |

HIGH

| | | | | |
|---|---|---|---|---|
| OF NOONS HIGH GLORY, WHEN HARD BY THE STREAMS | MUSICKS DUELL | 2 | 46 149 | 535 |
| THUS HIGH, THUS LOW, AS IF HER SILVER THROAT | MUSICKS DUELL | 100 | 46 149 | 535 |
| OF MUSICKS HEAVEN, AND SEAT IT THERE ON HIGH | MUSICKS DUELL | 149 | 46 149 | 535 |
| WHEN ON A HILL (WHOSE HIGH IMPERIOUS BROW | THE BEGINNING OF HELIODORUS | 3 | 46 158 | 517 |
| HIGH MOUNTED ON AN ANT NANUS THE TALL | HIGH MOUNTED ON AN ANT | 1 | 46 161 | 523 |
| THUS CARRYED UP ON HIGH, | THE TEARE | 37 | 46 84 | 50 |
| THE OTHERS WANTON WEALTH FOAMS HIGH, AND BRAVE, | WIDOWES MITES | 3 | 46 86 | 21 |
| ONE STANDS UP CLOSE AND TREADS ON HIGH, | TWO WENT TO PRAY | 3 | 46 89 | 18 |
| MAKE HIGH NOONE FORGET HIS BEAMES. | PSALME 23 | 16 | 46 102 | 5 |
| HOLDS HIGH THE REINE OF FAIRE PARTHENOPE, | SOSPETTO D'HERODE | 26 | 46 109 | 216 |
| THAT CROWNES HIS MATED HEAD ON HIGH APPEARES. | SOSPETTO D'HERODE | 45 | 46 109 | 216 |
| THAT HEAV'NS HIGH MAJESTY HIS COURT SHOULD KEEPE | SOSPETTO D'HERODE | 181 | 46 109 | 216 |
| WHAT THOUGH I MIST MY BLOW. YET I STROOKE HIGH, | SOSPETTO D'HERODE | 223 | 46 109 | 216 |
| TH'OBSEQUIOUS HANDMAIDS OF THY HIGH COMMANDS. | SOSPETTO D'HERODE | 262 | 46 109 | 216 |
| WHENCE ALL HIS HIGH SPIRITS, AND HOT COURAGE CAME. | SOSPETTO D'HERODE | 483 | 46 109 | 216 |
| THAT STUDYES THIS HIGH ART, | ON A PRAYER BOOKE | 30 | 46 126 | 139 |
| HIGH, AND BURNES WITH SUCH BRAVE HEATS. | IN MEMORY OF LADY MADRE TERESA | 36 | 46 131 | 52 |
| A DEATH MORE MISTICALL AND HIGH. | IN MEMORY OF LADY MADRE TERESA | 76 | 46 131 | 52 |
| IF WHAT TO OTHER TONGUES IS TUN'D SO HIGH, | AN APOLOGIE FOR HYMNE (TERESA) | 10 | 46 136 | 59 |
| OF LITTLE EAGLES, AND YOUNG LOVES, WHOSE HIGH | AN APOLOGIE FOR HYMNE (TERESA) | 27 | 46 136 | 59 |
| SH'L DRESSE THEE LIKE THY SELFE, SET THEE ON HIGH | ON A TREATISE OF CHARITY | 15 | 46 137 | 69 |
| SWELL THY FULL GLORYES TO A PITCH SO HIGH, | UPON YORKE HIS BIRTH | 7 | 46 176 | 500 |
| OR ON HEAVN'S AZURE FORHEAD HIGH TO STAND | IN GLORIOUS EPIPHANIE | 250 | 52 253 | 39 |
| SWELLS HIGH, FAIR CONFLUENCE OF ALL HIGHBORN BLOUD. | TO THE QUEEN'S MAJESTY | 16 | 52 261 | 47 |
| HIGH IN HIS PATIENCE, AS THEIR SPITE. | OFFICE H. CROSS SIXT | 2 | 52 270 | 97 |
| LET LIPPES & HEARTS LIFT HIGH THE NOISE | LAUDA SION SALVATOREM | 15 | 52 294 | 178 |
| HAIL, MOST HIGH, MOST HUMBLE ONE. | O GLORIOSA DOMINA | 1 | 52 302 | 194 |
| HIGH, & BURNES WITH SUCH BRAVE HEATES. | TERESA | 36 | 52 315 | 52 |
| A DEATH MORE MYSTICALL & HIGH. | TERESA | 76 | 52 315 | 52 |
| IF, WHAT TO OTHER TONGUES IS TUN'D SO HIGH, | AN APOLOGIE FOR (TERESA) HYMNE | 10 | 52 322 | 59 |
| OF LITTLE EAGLES & YOUNG LOVES, WHOSE HIGH | AN APOLOGIE FOR (TERESA) HYMNE | 27 | 52 322 | 59 |
| THAT STUDYES THIS HIGH ART | PRAYER TO GENTLE-WOMAN | 36 | 52 328 | 139 |
| OF HIS HIGH STRATAGEM TO WIN YOUR HEART, | TO SAME CONCERNING CHOISE | 44 | 52 331 | 66 |
| IF HEATES OF HOLYER LOVE & HIGH DESIRE | ALEXIAS THIRD ELEGIE | 21 | 52 336 | 209 |
| O BURN OUR HYMEN BRIGHT IN SUCH HIGH FLAME. | ALEXIAS THIRD ELEGIE | 49 | 52 336 | 209 |
| AND THOUGH THESE HUMBLE LINES SOARE NOT SOE HIGH, | UPON BIRTH PRINCESSE E | 17 | MS 391 | 456 |
| HIGH BEAUTIES SOVERAIGNE, THAT MY FUNERALL FLAMES | EX EUPHORMIONE | 13 | MS 392 | 525 |
| TEARES FALL TOO LOW, SIGHES RISE TOO HIGH, | UPON DEATH OF A FREIND | 5 | MS 393 | 477 |
| FULL OF HIGH SPARKELING VIGOUR. TAUGHT BE MEE | OUT OF GROTIUS | 53 | MS 398 | 198 |

HIGHBORN

| | | | | |
|---|---|---|---|---|
| SWELLS HIGH, FAIR CONFLUENCE OF ALL HIGHBORN BLOUD. | TO THE QUEEN'S MAJESTY | 16 | 52 261 | 47 |

HIGH-BORN

| | | | | |
|---|---|---|---|---|
| THE HIGH-BORN BROOD OF DAY. YOU BRIGHT | TO THE NAME OF JESUS | 7 | 52 239 | 30 |

HIGH-BORNE

    WITH FLASH OF HIGH-BORNE FANCYES. HERE AND THERE    MUSICKS DUELL    138  46 149 535

HIGH-AYM'D

    THY HIGH-AYM'D HOPES, GAIND'ST BUT A FLAMING FALL.    SOSPETTO D'HERODE    80  46 109 216

HIGH-BUILT

    IN HIGH-BUILT NUMBERS WAKES HIS GOLDEN LYRE.    HORATIJ ILLE & NEFASTO    42  MS 382 530

HIGH-COLOUR'D

    HIGH-COLOUR'D IS. HIS EYES STILL FLUSHING    OUT OF GREEKE CUPID'S CRYER    20  46 159 519

HIGH-FLOUNE

    HUGE HIGH-FLOUNE POYSONS, EV'N OF COLCHOS BREED.    HORATIJ ILLE & NEFASTO    11  MS 382 530

HIGH-PERCH'T

    THE HIGH-PERCH'T TREBLE CHIRPS AT THIS, AND CHIDES    MUSICKS DUELL    51  46 149 535

HIGHER

    STRAINES HIGHER YET. THAT TICKLED WITH RARE ART    MUSICKS DUELL    47  46 149 535
    DOTH TUNE THE SPHAEARES, AND MAKE HEAVENS SELFE LOOKE    MUSICKS DUELL    118  46 149 535
    STARRES IN THEIR HIGHER CHAMBERS. NEVER COU'D    OUT OF VIRGIL    32  46 155 529
    CALLS YOU UP HIGHER    TO SAME CONCERNING CHOISE    22  52 331  66
    RAVISH THE DANCING ORBES, MAKE THEM MOUNT HIGHER    UPON KINGS CORONATION    2  MS 389 454

HIGHEST

    WHILE THUS HEAV'NS HIGHEST COUNSAILS, BY THE LOW    SOSPETTO D'HERODE    145  46 109 216
    HURTES MEE FAR WORSE THEN HERODS HIGHEST SPITE.    OUT OF GROTIUS    34  MS 398 198

HIGH'ST

    OF HEAVENS HIGH'ST ARCHES TO FALL NARROW.    OUT OF GREEKE CUPID'S CRYER    48  46 159 519

HILL

    WHEN ON A HILL (WHOSE HIGH IMPERIOUS BROW    THE BEGINNING OF HELIODORUS    3  46 158 517

HILLS

    THAWING CHRISTALL. SNOWY HILLS.    THE WEEPER    4  46  79 120
    A THOUSAND HILLS OF FRANKINCENSE.    TO THE NAME OF JESUS    185  52 239  30
    AND HILLS HANG DOWN THEIR HEAVN-SALUTING HEADS    TO THE NAME OF JESUS    231  52 239  30
    THAWING CRYSTALL. SNOWY HILLS,    WEEPER    4  52 307 120
    HILLS & RELENTLESSE ROCKES, OR IF THERE BE    ALEXIAS SECONDE ELEGIE    15  52 335 207
    LEAPING UPON THE HILLS, TO BE    AGAINST IRRESOLUTION AND DELAY    71  52 347 146

HINDERS

    WHAT HINDERS, BUT MY BOSOME STILL MIGHT BE    LUKE 2. QUAERIT JESUM    49  MS 379  11

HIRE

    ALREADY REACHES AT A SWORD. THEY HIRE    SOSPETTO D'HERODE    444  46 109 216

HIR'D

    OR HIDING HIS VEX'T CHEEKS IN A HIR'D MIST    IN GLORIOUS EPIPHANIE    123  52 253  39

HISSE

    A GEN'RALL HISSE, FROM THE WHOLE TIRE OF SNAKES    SOSPETTO D'HERODE    302  46 109 216

HISSES

    START, AND SAY, THE SERPENT HISSES.    OUT OF GREEKE CUPID'S CRYER    66  46 159 519

HIST

    TO THE KINGS HEART, THE SNAKE NO SOONER HIST.    SOSPETTO D'HERODE    469  46 109 216

HISTORY

    LOVES NOBLE HISTORY, WITH WITT    IN MEMORY OF LADY MADRE TERESA    157  46 131  52
    HISTORY REARES HER PYRAMIDS MORE TALL    ON FRONTISPIECE ISAACSONS    18  46 191 491
    LOVE'S NOBLE HISTORY, WITH WITT    TERESA    156  52 315  52

HISTORIE

    IF ON TIMES RIGHT HAND, SIT FAIRE HISTORIE.    ON FRONTISPIECE ISAACSONS    5  46 191 491

HITT

    O HAPPY YOU, IF IT HITT RIGHT.    TO COUNTESSE OF DENBIGH    50  52 236 146

## HIVE

| | | | | | |
|---|---|---|---|---|---|
| IMMORTALL HONY FOR THE HIVE OF LOVES. | SOSPETTO D'HERODE | 24 | 46 | 109 | 216 |
| IT IS THE HIVE, | TO THE NAME OF JESUS | 156 | 52 | 239 | 30 |

## HOARCE

| | | | | | |
|---|---|---|---|---|---|
| WOULD REACH THE BRASEN VOYCE OF WARR'S HOARCE BIRD. | MUSICKS DUELL | 101 | 46 | 149 | 535 |

## HOARD

| | | | | | |
|---|---|---|---|---|---|
| WHERE ALL THEIR HOARD OF HONY LYES. | TO THE NAME OF JESUS | 158 | 52 | 239 | 30 |

## HOARY

| | | | | | |
|---|---|---|---|---|---|
| SO RARE IS HOARY VERTUE) THE DIRE RAGE | UPON DEATH OF HERRYS | 32 | 46 | 167 | 466 |
| LET HOARY TIME'S VAST BOWELS BE THE GRAVE | ON FRONTISPIECE ISAACSONS | 1 | 46 | 191 | 491 |

## HOASTS

| | | | | | |
|---|---|---|---|---|---|
| HEAVENS ROYALL HOASTS INCAMPT, THUS SMALL. | ON A PRAYER BOOKE | 6 | 46 | 126 | 139 |

## HOLD

| | | | | | |
|---|---|---|---|---|---|
| 'TWAS TIME TO HOLD THEIR PEACE WHEN THEY, | NEITHER DURST MAN ASKE | 15 | 46 | 92 | 20 |
| TO HOLD THEIR PEACE IS ALL THE WAIES, | NEITHER DURST MAN ASKE | 25 | 46 | 92 | 20 |
| HOLD THE PERVERSE PRINCE IN ETERNALL TIES | SOSPETTO D'HERODE | 39 | 46 | 109 | 216 |
| TO HOLD THEM DOWN, AND LOOKE THAT NONE SEETHE O'RE. | SOSPETTO D'HERODE | 296 | 46 | 109 | 216 |
| AND FORTIFIE THE HOLD OF YOUR CHAST HEART. | ON A PRAYER BOOKE | 14 | 46 | 126 | 139 |
| THAT HOLD THESE WEAPONS AND THE EYES | ON A PRAYER BOOKE | 23 | 46 | 126 | 139 |
| HOLD BUT THIS BOOKE BEFORE YOUR HEART, | ON A PRAYER BOOKE | 27 | 46 | 126 | 139 |
| O LET THAT HAPPY SOULE HOLD FAST | ON A PRAYER BOOKE | 105 | 46 | 126 | 139 |
| AND HOLD THEM FAST FOR EVER. THERE, | IN MEMORY OF LADY MADRE TERESA | 122 | 46 | 131 | 52 |
| OUR LOVING SONG SHALL HOLD IT FAST. | ON THE ASSUMPTION | 40 | 46 | 139 | 114 |
| WILL HOLD IT FAST, | ON THE ASSUMPTION | 45 | 46 | 139 | 114 |
| DEATH, WHAT DOST. O HOLD THY BLOW, | UPON DEATH OF DESIRED HERRYS | 1 | 46 | 168 | 467 |
| THE GRAVE, AND HOLD UP AN EXALTED ARME | TO THE MORNING | 26 | 46 | 183 | 497 |
| AND FETCH THE HEART FROM IT'S STRONG HOLD. | TO COUNTESSE OF DENBIGH | 28 | 52 | 236 | 146 |
| LO WE HOLD OUR HEARTS WIDE OPE. | TO THE NAME OF JESUS | 126 | 52 | 239 | 30 |
| THY WOUNDS GIVE US FAIR HOLD. | OFFICE H. CROSS COMPLINE | 20 | 52 | 274 | 105 |
| HOLD BUT THY FAITH INTIRE AS HE | LAUDA SION SALVATOREM | 56 | 52 | 294 | 178 |
| WILL HOLD IT FAST | IN GLORIOUS ASSUMPTION B. LADY | 50 | 52 | 304 | 114 |
| AND HOLD THEM FAST FOR EVER. THERE | TERESA | 121 | 52 | 315 | 52 |
| AND FORTIFY THE HOLD OF YOUR CHAST HEART. | PRAYER TO GENTLE-WOMAN | 20 | 52 | 328 | 139 |
| THAT HOLD THESE WEAPONS. & THE EYES | PRAYER TO GENTLE-WOMAN | 29 | 52 | 328 | 139 |
| HOLD BUT THIS BOOK BEFORE YOUR HEART | PRAYER TO GENTLE-WOMAN | 33 | 52 | 328 | 139 |
| O LET THE BLISSFULL HEART HOLD FAST | PRAYER TO GENTLE-WOMAN | 111 | 52 | 328 | 139 |
| BE HAPPY. AND FOR EVER HOLD HIM FAST. | ALEXIAS FIRST ELEGIE | 38 | 52 | 334 | 204 |
| LIVES BY HIS OWN LAWS, AND DOES HOLD | AGAINST IRRESOLUTION AND DELAY | 55 | 52 | 347 | 146 |
| I CANNOT HOLD, SUCH A SPRING TIDE OF JOY | UPON BIRTH PRINCESSE E | 13 | MS | 391 | 456 |
| THAT ON THESE SNOWY LIMMES HATH LAID SUCH HOLD. | AN ELEGY MR STANNINOW | 20 | MS | 394 | 473 |

## HOLDING

| | | | | | |
|---|---|---|---|---|---|
| EACH HOLDING FORTH TO LIGHT THE AERY BRAND, | UPON GUNPOWDER TREASON | 14 | MS | 387 | 461 |

## HOLDS

| | | | | | |
|---|---|---|---|---|---|
| HOLDS HIGH THE REINE OF FAIRE PARTHENOPE, | SOSPETTO D'HERODE | 26 | 46 | 109 | 216 |
| HOLDS FAST THE DOOR, YET DARES NOT VENTURE | TO COUNTESSE OF DENBIGH | 3 | 52 | 236 | 146 |
| HOLDS FAST THE DOOR, YET DARES NOT VENTURE | AGAINST IRRESOLUTION AND DELAY | 3 | 52 | 347 | 146 |

## HOLINESSE

| | | | | | |
|---|---|---|---|---|---|
| TRUE BEAUTY, TO TRUE HOLINESSE. | AN EPITAPH UPON ASHTON | 22 | 46 | 192 | 464 |
| GROW PLUMPE, LEANE DEATH. HIS HOLINESSE A FEAST | UPON GUNPOWDER TREASON | 1 | MS | 387 | 461 |

## HOLLOW

| | | | | | |
|---|---|---|---|---|---|
| RAN TREMBLING THROUGH THE HOLLOW VAULTS OF NIGHT, | SOSPETTO D'HERODE | 151 | 46 | 109 | 216 |
| RUNG, THROUGH THE HOLLOW VAULTS OF HELL PROFOUND. | SOSPETTO D'HERODE | 299 | 46 | 109 | 216 |

## HOLY

| | | | | | |
|---|---|---|---|---|---|
| IN THAT SWEET SOYLE. IT SEEMES A HOLY QUIRE | MUSICKS DUELL | 73 | 46 | 149 | 535 |
| SHEE FOUND THE WAY HOME, WITH AN HOLY STRENGTH | UPON BISHOP ANDREWES PICTURE | 8 | 46 | 163 | 490 |
| TO HOLY HANDS, AND HUMBLE HEARTS, | ON A PRAYER BOOKE | 18 | 46 | 126 | 139 |
| AND KEEP THE DIVELLS HOLY DAY. | ON A PRAYER BOOKE | 47 | 46 | 126 | 139 |
| OF HIDDEN SWEETS, AND HOLY JOYES. | ON A PRAYER BOOKE | 58 | 46 | 126 | 139 |
| FAIRE SEA OF HOLY FIRES TRANSFUSED THE FLAME | AN APOLOGIE FOR HYMNE (TERESA) | 2 | 46 | 136 | 59 |
| THE HOLY YOUTH OF HEAV'N, WHOSE GOLDEN RINGS | ON A TREATISE OF CHARITY | 21 | 46 | 137 | 69 |
| HAILE HOLY QUEEN OF HUMBLE HEARTS | ON THE ASSUMPTION | 29 | 46 | 139 | 114 |
| WITH HOLY CARES WILL KEEPE IT BY US, | ON THE ASSUMPTION | 43 | 46 | 139 | 114 |
| LIVE OUR CHASTE LOVE, THE HOLY MIRTH | ON THE ASSUMPTION | 59 | 46 | 139 | 114 |
| HER STARRY THRONE. WHOSE HOLY HEATS CAN WARME | TO THE MORNING | 25 | 46 | 183 | 497 |
| THE HOLY CHAPPELL OF CHAST LOVE | THOUGH NOW 'TIS NEITHER | 22 | MS | 397 | 492 |
| HEARKEN, AND HELP, YE HOLY DOVES. | TO THE NAME OF JESUS | 6 | 52 | 239 | 30 |
| HERE A HOLY DICTATE HATH | LAUDA SION SALVATOREM | 32 | 52 | 294 | 178 |
| HAIL, HOLY QUEEN OF HUMBLE HEARTS. | IN GLORIOUS ASSUMPTION B. LADY | 44 | 52 | 304 | 114 |
| WITH HOLY CARE WILL KEEP IT BY US. | IN GLORIOUS ASSUMPTION B. LADY | 48 | 52 | 304 | 114 |
| LIVE, OUR CHAST LOVE, THE HOLY MIRTH | IN GLORIOUS ASSUMPTION B. LADY | 64 | 52 | 304 | 114 |
| (FAIR FLOUD OF HOLY FIRES.) TRANSFUS'D THE FLAME | AN APOLOGIE FOR (TERESA) HYMNE | 2 | 52 | 322 | 59 |
| TO HOLY HANDS & HUMBLE HEARTS | PRAYER TO GENTLE-WOMAN | 24 | 52 | 328 | 139 |

|  |  |  |  |  |  |
|---|---|---|---|---|---|
| OF HIDDEN SWEETS & HOLY JOYES. | PRAYER TO GENTLE-WOMAN | 64 | 52 | 328 | 139 |
| WHEN HOLY FIRES MAINTAIN LOVE'S HEAVNLY LIFE. | ALEXIAS THIRD ELEGIE | 52 | 52 | 336 | 209 |

H

|  |  |  |  |  |  |
|---|---|---|---|---|---|
| AND TO THE H. GHOST. | OFFICE H. CROSS MATINES | 9 | 52 | 265 | 86 |

HOLYDAY

|  |  |  |  |  |  |
|---|---|---|---|---|---|
| AND KEEP THE DEVILL'S HOLYDAY. | PRAYER TO GENTLE-WOMAN | 53 | 52 | 328 | 139 |

HOLYER

|  |  |  |  |  |  |
|---|---|---|---|---|---|
| IF HEATES OF HOLYER LOVE & HIGH DESIRE | ALEXIAS THIRD ELEGIE | 21 | 52 | 336 | 209 |

HOLYEST

|  |  |  |  |  |  |
|---|---|---|---|---|---|
| THY HOLYEST, HUMBLEST, HANDMAID CHARITIE. | ON A TREATISE OF CHARITY | 14 | 46 | 137 | 69 |

HOMAGE

|  |  |  |  |  |  |
|---|---|---|---|---|---|
| BUT THE WORLD'S HOMAGE, SCARSE IN THESE WELL BLOWN, | TO THE QUEEN'S MAJESTY | 9 | 52 | 261 | 47 |

HOME

|  |  |  |  |  |  |
|---|---|---|---|---|---|
| SHEE FOUND THE WAY HOME, WITH AN HOLY STRENGTH | UPON BISHOP ANDREWES PICTURE | 8 | 46 | 163 | 490 |
| HEE CALLS HOME MY SOULE FROM DYING, | PSALME 23 | 18 | 46 | 102 | 5 |
| AND BRING HOME ON THY BREST MORE THANKLESSE SCARRS. | SOSPETTO D'HERODE | 448 | 46 | 109 | 216 |
| O CALL THY SELFE HOME TO THY SELFE. WAKE, WAKE, | SOSPETTO D'HERODE | 459 | 46 | 109 | 216 |
| THIS DONE, HOME TO HER HELL SHEE HY'D AMAINE. | SOSPETTO D'HERODE | 472 | 46 | 109 | 216 |
| SHALL FIND THE WANDRING HEART FROM HOME, | ON A PRAYER BOOKE | 42 | 46 | 126 | 139 |
| HOME TO THE HEART, AND SETTS THE HOUSE ON FIRE. | ON A PRAYER BOOKE | 67 | 46 | 126 | 139 |
| HEE FIND THE HEART FROM HOME, | ON A PRAYER BOOKE | 84 | 46 | 126 | 139 |
| SINCE TIS NOT TO BEE HAD AT HOME, | IN MEMORY OF LADY MADRE TERESA | 43 | 46 | 131 | 52 |
| NO HOME FOR HER CONFESSES SHEE, | IN MEMORY OF LADY MADRE TERESA | 45 | 46 | 131 | 52 |
| FAREWELL HOUSE, AND FARWELL HOME. | IN MEMORY OF LADY MADRE TERESA | 63 | 46 | 131 | 52 |
| GLAD AT THEIR OWNE HOME NOW TO MEET THEE. | IN MEMORY OF LADY MADRE TERESA | 139 | 46 | 131 | 52 |
| TAKE THY FAREWEL POORE WORLD, HEAVEN MUST GO HOME. | ON THE ASSUMPTION | 2 | 46 | 139 | 114 |
| TO WAIT UPON THEE HOME. | ON THE ASSUMPTION | 17 | 46 | 139 | 114 |
| SAFE, THOU DARKE HOME OF THE DEAD. | UPON DEATH OF DESIRED HERRYS | 69 | 46 | 168 | 467 |
| HEE WAS A PROTESTANT AT HOME, | AN EPITAPH UPON ASHTON | 17 | 46 | 192 | 464 |
| LOOK FROM THINE OWN ILLUSTRIOUS HOME, | TO THE NAME OF JESUS | 117 | 52 | 239 | 30 |
| HOME, & LODGE THEM IN HIS HEART. | TO THE NAME OF JESUS | 196 | 52 | 239 | 30 |
| THUS FARR FROM HOME | IN GLORIOUS EPIPHANIE | 12 | 52 | 253 | 39 |
| POINTING US HOME TO OUR OWN SUN | IN GLORIOUS EPIPHANIE | 252 | 52 | 253 | 39 |
| AND TOOK IT HOME TO HIS OWN HEART. | VEXILLA REGIS | 12 | 52 | 277 | 156 |
| ALL, MORE AT HOME IN HER OWNE HEART. | SANCTA MARIA DOLORUM | 10 | 52 | 283 | 162 |
| TURN SPEARES, & STRAIGHT COME HOME AGAIN. | SANCTA MARIA DOLORUM | 30 | 52 | 283 | 162 |
| HAIL. & STRIKE HOME & MAKE ME SEE | SANCTA MARIA DOLORUM | 73 | 52 | 283 | 162 |
| BEARES HOME NO LESSE, ALL THEY NO MORE, | LAUDA SION SALVATOREM | 47 | 52 | 294 | 178 |
| TAKE THY FAREWELL, POOR WORLD. HEAVN MUST GOE HOME. | IN GLORIOUS ASSUMPTION B. LADY | 2 | 52 | 304 | 114 |
| TO WAIT UPON THEE HOME. COME COME AWAY. | IN GLORIOUS ASSUMPTION B. LADY | 16 | 52 | 304 | 114 |
| SINCE 'TIS NOT TO BE HAD AT HOME | TERESA | 43 | 52 | 315 | 52 |
| NO HOME FOR HERS CONFESSES SHE | TERESA | 45 | 52 | 315 | 52 |
| FAREWELL HOUSE, & FAREWELL HOME. | TERESA | 63 | 52 | 315 | 52 |
| GLAD AT THEIR OWN HOME NOW TO MEET THEE. | TERESA | 138 | 52 | 315 | 52 |
| SHALL FIND THE LOYTERING HEART FROM HOME. | PRAYER TO GENTLE-WOMAN | 48 | 52 | 328 | 139 |
| HOME TO THE HEART, & SETTS THE HOUSE ON FIRE | PRAYER TO GENTLE-WOMAN | 73 | 52 | 328 | 139 |
| HE FIND THE HEART FROM HOME) | PRAYER TO GENTLE-WOMAN | 90 | 52 | 328 | 139 |
| HOME TO HIMSELF. TO HIDE IT IN HIS BREST | TO SAME CONCERNING CHOISE | 51 | 52 | 331 | 66 |
| FULL SWEETLY WITH IT SELFE HAD DWELL'T AT HOME. | ALEXIAS THIRD ELEGIE | 12 | 52 | 336 | 209 |
| HOME TO THE ORIGINALL SOURSE OF LIGHT & INTELLECTUALL | DESCRIPTION RELIGIOUS HOUSE | 39 | 52 | 338 | 213 |
| ONE SMILE AT HOME. | LUKE 2. QUAERIT JESUM | 14 | MS | 379 | 11 |
| FARRE FROM DARKE HORRORS HOME APPEALE TO REST. | HORATIJ ILLE & NEFASTO | 38 | MS | 382 | 530 |

HOMELY

|  |  |  |  |  |  |
|---|---|---|---|---|---|
| OUR LODGINGS HARD & HOMELY AS OUR FARE. | DESCRIPTION RELIGIOUS HOUSE | 11 | 52 | 338 | 213 |

HOME-SPUN

|  |  |  |  |  |  |
|---|---|---|---|---|---|
| BUT TO POOR SHEPHEARDS, HOME-SPUN THINGS. | IN HOLY NATIVITY | 94 | 52 | 246 | 76 |

HONEST

|  |  |  |  |  |  |
|---|---|---|---|---|---|
| OF HONEST PARENTAGE OF UNSTAIN'D RACE, | TO PONTIUS WASHING HANDS | 6 | 46 | 94 | 23 |
| HERE LYES A TRULY HONEST MAN. | AN EPITAPH UPON ASHTON | 4 | 46 | 192 | 464 |

HONESTIES

|  |  |  |  |  |  |
|---|---|---|---|---|---|
| HONESTIES NURSE, VERTUES BLEST GUARDIAN, | AN ELEGIE ON DR PORTER | 17 | MS | 395 | 476 |

HONEY

|  |  |  |  |  |  |
|---|---|---|---|---|---|
| ALL HYBLA'S HONEY, ALL THAT SWEETNESSE CAN | UPON OUR LORDS LAST DISCOURSE | 1 | 46 | 95 | 21 |

HONEY-DROPPING

|  |  |  |  |  |  |
|---|---|---|---|---|---|
| HIS HONEY-DROPPING TOPS, PLOW'D BY HER BREATH | MUSICKS DUELL | 71 | 46 | 149 | 535 |

HONY

|  |  |  |  |  |  |
|---|---|---|---|---|---|
| IMMORTALL HONY FOR THE HIVE OF LOVES. | SOSPETTO D'HERODE | 24 | 46 | 109 | 216 |
| WHERE ALL THEIR HOARD OF HONY LYES. | TO THE NAME OF JESUS | 158 | 52 | 239 | 30 |

PAGE 194

## HONY-SWEATING

| | | | | |
|---|---|---|---|---|
| OF FAIRE ENGADDI HONY-SWEATING FOUNTAINES | SOSPETTO D'HERODE | 111 | 46 109 | 216 |

## HONIED

| | | | | |
|---|---|---|---|---|
| THAT SOL FROM THEM MAY SUCK AN HONIED SHOWER. | UPON BIRTH PRINCESSE E | 5 | MS 391 | 456 |

## HONORS

| | | | | |
|---|---|---|---|---|
| THE AGED HONORS OF THIS DAY STILL NEW. | TO THE QUEEN'S MAJESTY | 24 | 52 261 | 47 |

## HONOUR

| | | | | |
|---|---|---|---|---|
| TO BE THE SACRED HONOUR OF THY BROWES. | SOSPETTO D'HERODE | 16 | 46 109 | 216 |
| THE FOULE QUEENS MOST ABHORRED MAIDS OF HONOUR | SOSPETTO D'HERODE | 337 | 46 109 | 216 |
| CHAST AS THAT VIRGIN HONOUR OF THE EAST. | UPON YORKE HIS BIRTH | 83 | 46 176 | 500 |
| HONOUR ALL PREACHERS. HEARE THEIR OWNE. | AN EPITAPH UPON ASHTON | 8 | 46 192 | 464 |

## HONOUR'D

| | | | | |
|---|---|---|---|---|
| WAS LOV'D WAS HONOUR'D AS A FLOOD. | AN EPITAPH DOCTOR BROOKE | 2 | 46 175 | 465 |

## HOOKES

| | | | | |
|---|---|---|---|---|
| ANGER, AND LOVE, BEST HOOKES OF HUMANE BLOOD. | SOSPETTO D'HERODE | 275 | 46 109 | 216 |

## HOPE

| | | | | |
|---|---|---|---|---|
| HOPE OF A PREY. THERE TO THE MAINE LAND TY'D | THE BEGINNING OF HELIODORUS | 10 | 46 158 | 517 |
| LET IT NO LONGER BE A FORLORNE HOPE | ON BAPTIZED AETHIOPIAN | 1 | 46 65 | 29 |
| AND HIS OWNE HOPE | I AM THE DOORE | 4 | 46 90 | 17 |
| THE HEAV'N EXPECTING AGES, HOPE TO SEE | SOSPETTO D'HERODE | 158 | 46 109 | 216 |
| WHERE DAWNING HOPE NO BEAME OF COMFORT SHOWES. | SOSPETTO D'HERODE | 242 | 46 109 | 216 |
| YET HAS SHEE A HEART DARES HOPE TO PROVE, | IN MEMORY OF LADY MADRE TERESA | 27 | 46 131 | 52 |
| WHAT CAN THE POORE HOPE FROM US, WHEN WE BE | ON A TREATISE OF CHARITY | 57 | 46 137 | 69 |
| DEARE HOPE. EARTHS DOWRY, AND HEAVENS DEBT, | ON HOPE | 11 | 46 143 | 71 |
| FAIRE HOPE. OUR EARLIER HEAVEN. BY THEE | ON HOPE | 51 | 46 143 | 71 |
| HOPE KICKS THE CURL'D HEADS OF CONSPIRING STARRES. | ON HOPE | 72 | 46 143 | 71 |
| SWEET HOPE. KIND CHEAT. FAIRE FALLACY. BY THEE | ON HOPE | 77 | 46 143 | 71 |
| ALL HOPE OF NEVER DYING, HERE LYES DEAD. | ANOTHER ON HERRYS | 62 | 46 170 | 469 |
| WHAT SUCCOUR CAN I HOPE THE MUSE WILL SEND | TO THE MORNING | 1 | 46 183 | 497 |
| WHAT HOPE AURORA TO PROPITIATE THEE, | TO THE MORNING | 3 | 46 183 | 497 |
| COME, LOVELY NAME. LIFE OF OUR HOPE. | TO THE NAME OF JESUS | 125 | 52 239 | 30 |
| O SEE, THE WEARY LIDDES OF WAKEFULL HOPE | TO THE NAME OF JESUS | 145 | 52 239 | 30 |
| HER RUBY CASEMENTS, OR HEREAFTER HOPE | IN GLORIOUS EPIPHANIE | 70 | 52 253 | 39 |
| THE HOPE. THE HEALTH. | OFFICE H. CROSS EVENSONG | 14 | 52 273 | 101 |
| AH HARTLESSE TASK. YET HOPE TAKES HEAD. | OFFICE H. CROSS COMPLINE | 3 | 52 274 | 105 |
| HAIL, OUR ALONE HOPE. LET THY FAIR HEAD SHOOT | VEXILLA REGIS | 37 | 52 277 | 156 |
| HELP LORD, MY FAITH, MY HOPE INCREASE. | ADORO TE | 33 | 52 291 | 172 |
| HOPE TELLS MY HEART, THE SAME LOVES BE | DIES IRAE | 51 | 52 298 | 186 |
| MY HOPE, MY FEAR. MY JUDGE, MY FREIND. | DIES IRAE | 67 | 52 298 | 186 |
| YET HAS SHE'A HEART DARES HOPE TO PROVE | TERESA | 27 | 52 315 | 52 |
| DEAR HOPE. EARTH'S DOWRY, & HEAVN'S DEBT. | (ON) HOPE | 1 | 52 345 | 71 |
| RICH HOPE. LOVE'S LEGACY, UNDER LOCK | (ON) HOPE | 11 | 52 345 | 71 |
| FAIR HOPE. OUR EARLYER HEAV'N BY THEE | (ON) HOPE | 21 | 52 345 | 71 |
| HOPE WALKS. & KICKES THE CURLD HEADS OF CONSPIRING STARRES. | (ON) HOPE | 32 | 52 345 | 71 |
| SWEET HOPE. KIND CHEAT. FAIR FALLACY BY THEE | (ON) HOPE | 37 | 52 345 | 71 |
| THE HOPE AND PROMISE OF HIS BUD. | AGAINST IRRESOLUTION AND DELAY | 36 | 52 347 | 146 |
| THEIR HOPE, THEIR VOW. | LUKE 2. QUAERIT JESUM | 2 | MS 379 | 11 |

## HOPE-NURST

| | | | | |
|---|---|---|---|---|
| THE HEAD OF ALL MY HOPE-NURST JOYES. | PSALME 137 | 26 | 46 104 | 7 |

## HOPE'S

| | | | | |
|---|---|---|---|---|
| TRUE HOPE'S A GLORIOUS HUNTRESSE, AND HER CHASE | ON HOPE | 89 | 46 143 | 71 |
| LO, HEART, THY HOPE'S WHOLE PLEA. HER PRETIOUS BREATH | SANCTA MARIA DOLORUM | 109 | 52 283 | 162 |
| HOPE'S CHAST STEALTH HARMES NO MORE JOYE'S MAIDENHEAD | (ON) HOPE | 19 | 52 345 | 71 |
| TRUE HOPE'S A GLORIOUS HUNTER & HER CHASE. | (ON) HOPE | 49 | 52 345 | 71 |

## HOPES

| | | | | |
|---|---|---|---|---|
| IN OUR BEST HOPES BEGUILEST US. | UPON THE DEATH OF A GENTLEMAN | 4 | 46 166 | 472 |
| OF THE HOPES IN HIM WE LAID. | UPON THE DEATH OF A GENTLEMAN | 6 | 46 166 | 472 |
| ARE YET BUT IN THEIR HOPES, NOT COME TO YEARES. | OUR LORD IN HIS CIRCUMCISION | 10 | 46 98 | 9 |
| CONCEIVE PROUD HOPES OF PROVING ROSES. | ON BLEEDING WOUNDS OF LORD | 24 | 46 101 | 110 |
| THY HIGH-AYM'D HOPES, GAIND'ST BUT A FLAMING FALL. | SOSPETTO D'HERODE | 80 | 46 109 | 216 |
| STAY OF MY STRONG HOPES, YOU OF WHOSE BRAVE WORTH, | SOSPETTO D'HERODE | 282 | 46 109 | 216 |
| HOPES CHASTE KISSE WRONGS NO MORE JOYES MAIDENHEAD. | ON HOPE | 39 | 46 143 | 71 |
| A THOUSAND RUDDY HOPES SMIL'D IN EACH BUD, | UPON DEATH OF HERRYS | 25 | 46 167 | 466 |
| BRIGHTER HOPES THEN HE CAN SHEW. | UPON DEATH OF DESIRED HERRYS | 18 | 46 168 | 467 |
| THE FRESH HOPES OF HIS LOVELY YOUTH, | ANOTHER ON HERRYS | 13 | 46 170 | 469 |
| AND OUR HOPES FAIRE HARVEST SPREAD | ANOTHER ON HERRYS | 56 | 46 170 | 469 |
| TO THE PROUD HOPES OF POOR MORTALITY. | UPON STANINOUGH'S DEATH | 24 | 46 175 | 475 |
| THOU AND THE LOVELY HOPES THAT SMILE IN THEE | UPON YORKE HIS BIRTH | 40 | 46 176 | 500 |
| THAT NEST OF HEROES, ALL OUR HOPES FINDE ROOME. | UPON YORKE HIS BIRTH | 81 | 46 176 | 500 |
| HER HOPES ARE CROWN'D. ONELY SHE FEARES THAT THAN, | UPON FAIRE ETHIOPIAN | 5 | 46 183 | 493 |
| ALL THESE DELICIOUS HOPES ARE BURIED, | TO THE MORNING | 30 | 46 183 | 497 |
| AND GUILD THE HOPES OF HUMBLE LOVE. | LOVES HOROSCOPE | 34 | 46 185 | 483 |
| MY FUTURE HOPES CAN RAISE, | WISHES SUPPOSED MISTRESSE | 110 | 46 195 | 479 |

HOPES TO BE
| | | | | |
|---|---|---|---|---|
| THAT HOPES TO BE | TO THE NAME OF JESUS | 132 | 52 239 | 30 |
| WHAT MAKE YOU HERE, WHAT HOPES CAN TICE | WEEPER | 166 | 52 307 | 120 |
| BUT I, (SO HELP ME HEAVN MY HOPES TO SEE) | ALEXIAS THIRD ELEGIE | 53 | 52 336 | 209 |
| OF ALL OUR GLORIOUS HOPES SHOULD FADE. | AN ELEGY MR STANNINOW | 43 | MS 394 | 473 |

HOPEFULL
| | | | | |
|---|---|---|---|---|
| AND LAY THE GROUND-WORKE OF HER HOPEFULL SONG, | MUSICKS DUELL | 85 | 46 149 | 535 |
| I'VE SEEN INDEED THE HOPEFULL BUD, | UPON DEATH OF DESIRED HERRYS | 31 | 46 168 | 467 |
| THAT HOPEFULL MAXIME GAVE ME HART TO TRY | AN APOLOGIE FOR (TERESA) HYMNE | 9 | 52 322 | 59 |

HORACE
| | | | | |
|---|---|---|---|---|
| HORACE, SHRILL, AT ONCE. AS WHEN THE TRUMPETS CALL | MUSICKS DUELL | 54 | 46 149 | 535 |

HORN
| | | | | |
|---|---|---|---|---|
| A GARLAND, OR A GUILDED HORN. | IN GLORIOUS EPIPHANIE | 95 | 52 253 | 39 |
| FROM THEE THEIR LEAN DILEMMA, WITH BLUNT HORN, | (ON) HOPE | 9 | 52 345 | 71 |

HORN'D
| | | | | |
|---|---|---|---|---|
| SEE HIS HORN'D FACE, & DY FOR SHAME. | IN GLORIOUS EPIPHANIE | 99 | 52 253 | 39 |

HORNE
| | | | | |
|---|---|---|---|---|
| AND TO MAKE UP HELLS MAJESTY, EACH HORNE | SOSPETTO D'HERODE | 47 | 46 109 | 216 |
| FROM THEE THEIR THINNE DILEMMA WITH BLUNT HORNE | ON HOPE | 19 | 46 143 | 71 |

HORNES
| | | | | |
|---|---|---|---|---|
| WHERE SEAV'N TALL HORNES (HIS EMPIRES PRIDE) ASPIRE. | SOSPETTO D'HERODE | 46 | 46 109 | 216 |

HORRIBLY
| | | | | |
|---|---|---|---|---|
| SEAV'N CRESTED HYDRA'S HORRIBLY ADORNE. | SOSPETTO D'HERODE | 48 | 46 109 | 216 |

HORRID
| | | | | |
|---|---|---|---|---|
| AND GAVE A GASTLY SHREEKE, WHOSE HORRID YELL | SOSPETTO D'HERODE | 150 | 46 109 | 216 |
| WEE (SAID THE HORRID SISTERS) WAIT THY LAWES, | SOSPETTO D'HERODE | 261 | 46 109 | 216 |
| THE HORRID SUMME OF HIS INTENTIONS TELL. | SOSPETTO D'HERODE | 370 | 46 109 | 216 |
| SOMEWHAT MORE HORRID THAN AN ELEGY. | AN ELEGIE ON DR PORTER | 12 | MS 395 | 476 |

HORRIZON
| | | | | |
|---|---|---|---|---|
| WHOSE GLORIOUS COURSE THROUGH OUR HORRIZON RUN, | UPON BISHOP ANDREWES PICTURE | 2 | 46 163 | 490 |

ORIZONS
| | | | | |
|---|---|---|---|---|
| THE EARLY LARKES SHRILL ORIZONS TO BE | TO THE MORNING | 43 | 46 183 | 497 |

HORROR
| | | | | |
|---|---|---|---|---|
| BROODING HORROR, COME THOU DEATH, | PSALME 23 | 39 | 46 102 | 5 |
| THE NINTH WITH AWFULL HORROR HEARKENED TO THOSE GROANES | OFFICE H. CROSS NINTH | 1 | 52 271 | 99 |
| HORROR OF NATURE, HELL & DEATH. | DIES IRAE | 13 | 52 298 | 186 |
| ALL THIS IT THREATS, & MORE HORROR, THAT FLIES | ON GUNPOWDER-TREASON | 45 | MS 384 | 458 |
| BLACK DISMALL HORROR, COME, MAKE PERFECT NOW | UPON GUNPOWDER TREASON | 20 | MS 387 | 461 |
| POORE MEAGRE HORROR STREIGHTWAIS WAS AMAZ'D, | UPON GUNPOWDER TREASON | 47 | MS 387 | 461 |

HORROR'S
| | | | | |
|---|---|---|---|---|
| ABOUT HORROR'S DISPLAI'D. IT DOTH PORTEND. | ON GUNPOWDER-TREASON | 21 | MS 384 | 458 |

HORRORS
| | | | | |
|---|---|---|---|---|
| FARRE FROM DARKE HORRORS HOME APPEALE TO REST. | HORATIJ ILLE & NEFASTO | 38 | MS 382 | 530 |

HORROUR
| | | | | |
|---|---|---|---|---|
| TO THIS DARKE HOUSE OF SHADES, HORROUR, AND NIGHT, | SOSPETTO D'HERODE | 213 | 46 109 | 216 |

HORROURS
| | | | | |
|---|---|---|---|---|
| SINKES INTO HORROURS BOSOME, GLAD TO HIDE | OUT OF GROTIUS | 78 | MS 398 | 198 |

HORSES
| | | | | |
|---|---|---|---|---|
| HERE DIOMED'S HORSES, PHEREUS DOGS APPEARE, | SOSPETTO D'HERODE | 353 | 46 109 | 216 |

HOSPITALITY
| | | | | |
|---|---|---|---|---|
| O BOUNDLES HOSPITALITY. | O GLORIOSA DOMINA | 9 | 52 302 | 194 |

HOST
| | | | | |
|---|---|---|---|---|
| THE WHOLE WORLD'S HOST WOULD BE THY GUEST | O GLORIOSA DOMINA | 7 | 52 302 | 194 |
| HEAVN'S ROYALL HOST, INCAMP'T THUS SMALL | PRAYER TO GENTLE-WOMAN | 12 | 52 328 | 139 |

## HOT

| | | | | |
|---|---|---|---|---|
| HEE LOST THE DAYES HEAT, AND HIS OWNE HOT CARES. | MUSICKS DUELL | 6 | 46 149 | 535 |
| HOT MARS TO TH' HARVEST OF DEATHS FIELD, AND WOO | MUSICKS DUELL | 55 | 46 149 | 535 |
| A SWEETLY TEMPER'D MEANE, NOR HOT NOR COLD. | OUT OF VIRGIL | 36 | 46 155 | 529 |
| NOW WITH NEW RAGE, AND WAX TOO HOT FOR HELL. | SOSPETTO D'HERODE | 148 | 46 109 | 216 |
| BATHING THEIR HOT LIMBS IN LIFE'S PRETIOUS FLOOD. | SOSPETTO D'HERODE | 316 | 46 109 | 216 |
| AND BEAT THE HOT BRASSE WITH REBELLIOUS WAVES. | SOSPETTO D'HERODE | 484 | 46 109 | 216 |
| WHENCE ALL HIS HIGH SPIRITS, AND HOT COURAGE CAME. | SOSPETTO D'HERODE | 486 | 46 109 | 216 |
| BY TOO HOT A FIRE, AND WASTED, | IN MEMORY OF LADY MADRE TERESA | 115 | 46 131 | 52 |
| BAK'T IN HOT SCORN, FOR A BURNT SACRIFICE. | ON A TREATISE OF CHARITY | 44 | 46 137 | 69 |
| HIDE HIS HOT BEAMES IN SHADE OF SILVER AGE. | UPON DEATH OF HERRYS | 31 | 46 167 | 466 |
| NOR FLAMES OF OUGHT TOO HOT WITHIN. | WISHES SUPPOSED MISTRESSE | 66 | 46 195 | 479 |
| OF HOT DEFIANCE 'GAINST WHAT E'RE IS GOOD | OUT OF GROTIUS | 76 | MS 398 | 198 |

## HOTT

| | | | | |
|---|---|---|---|---|
| BY TOO HOTT A FIRE, & WASTED | TERESA | 114 | 52 315 | 52 |

## HOUND

| | | | | |
|---|---|---|---|---|
| THE BLOUD HOUND BROOD OF PRIESTS AGAINST MEE DRAW | OUT OF GROTIUS | 45 | MS 398 | 198 |

## HOUR

| | | | | |
|---|---|---|---|---|
| (IN THAT PROPITIOUS HOUR) | OFFICE H. CROSS EVENSONG | 17 | 52 273 | 101 |
| THE COMPLIN HOUR COMES LAST, TO CALL | OFFICE H. CROSS COMPLINE | 1 | 52 274 | 105 |
| IN THAT HOUR, & IN THESE, MAY BE ALL THINE. | OFFICE H. CROSS RECOMMENDATION | 4 | 52 276 | 106 |
| TO IMPROVE THAT PRETIOUS HOUR, | PRAYER TO GENTLE-WOMAN | 105 | 52 328 | 139 |

## HOUR'S

| | | | | |
|---|---|---|---|---|
| THREE SAD HOUR'S SACKCLOTH THEN SHALL SHOW TO US | IN GLORIOUS EPIPHANIE | 157 | 52 253 | 39 |
| THE THIRD HOUR'S DEAFEN'D WITH THE CRY | OFFICE H. CROSS THIRD | 1 | 52 268 | 93 |

## HOUR-GLASSE

| | | | | |
|---|---|---|---|---|
| MY WATRY HOUR-GLASSE HATH OLD TIMES OUTRUNNE. | ALEXIAS SECONDE ELEGIE | 20 | 52 335 | 207 |

## HOWER-GLASSES

| | | | | |
|---|---|---|---|---|
| HIS HOWER-GLASSES. | THE WEEPER | 99 | 46 79 | 120 |

## HOURE

| | | | | |
|---|---|---|---|---|
| IN JOYES WHITE ANNALS LIVE THIS HOURE, | EASTER DAY | 10 | 46 100 | 26 |
| TO IMPROVE THAT PRECIOUS HOURE. | ON A PRAYER BOOKE | 99 | 46 126 | 139 |
| HARKE SHEE IS CALLED, THE PARTING HOURE IS COME. | ON THE ASSUMPTION | 1 | 46 139 | 114 |
| O LET IT BE AT LAST, LOVE'S HOURE. | TO COUNTESSE OF DENBIGH | 37 | 52 236 | 146 |
| HARK, SHE IS CALL'D, THE PARTING HOURE IS COME. | IN GLORIOUS ASSUMPTION B. LADY | 1 | 52 304 | 114 |

## HOWER

| | | | | |
|---|---|---|---|---|
| OH CROWNE THESE PRAIE'RS (MOV'D IN A HAPPY HOWER) | EX EUPHORMIONE | 3 | MS 392 | 525 |

## HOURES

| | | | | |
|---|---|---|---|---|
| WHOSE SILKEN FLATTERYES SWELL A FEW FOND HOURES | UPON STANINOUGH'S DEATH | 8 | 46 175 | 475 |
| HOW E'RE LOVES NATIVE HOURES WERE SET, | LOVES HOROSCOPE | 17 | 46 185 | 483 |
| SOFT SILKEN HOURES, | WISHES SUPPOSED MISTRESSE | 91 | 46 195 | 479 |
| THESE HOURES, & THAT WHICH HOVER'S O'RE MY END, | OFFICE H. CROSS RECOMMENDATION | 1 | 52 276 | 106 |
| WHOSE LATEST & MOST LEADEN HOURES | TEMPERANCE | 45 | 52 342 | 510 |

## HOWERS

| | | | | |
|---|---|---|---|---|
| GAVE OMEN TO HIS INFANT HOWERS, | LOVES HOROSCOPE | 6 | 46 185 | 483 |

## HOWRES

| | | | | |
|---|---|---|---|---|
| DISSOLVE MY DAYES & HOWRES. | SANCTA MARIA DOLORUM | 88 | 52 283 | 162 |
| WHOSE SYLKEN FLATTERYES SWELL A FEW FOND HOWRES | DEATH'S LECTURE | 9 | 52 340 | 475 |

## HOURLY

| | | | | |
|---|---|---|---|---|
| HOURLY THERE MEETES | TO THE NAME OF JESUS | 175 | 52 239 | 30 |

## HOUSE

| | | | | |
|---|---|---|---|---|
| A BLACK-FAC'D HOUSE WILL LOVE. | ON BAPTIZED AETHIOPIAN | 6 | 46 85 | 29 |
| TWO MITES, TWO DROPS, (YET ALL HER HOUSE AND LAND) | WIDOWES MITES | 1 | 46 86 | 21 |
| HEE'L COME--INTO THY HOUSE. NO, INTO THEE. | I AM NOT WORTHY | 4 | 46 90 | 13 |
| IN THIS SAD HOUSE OF SLOW DESTRUCTION, | SOSPETTO D'HERODE | 61 | 46 109 | 216 |
| TO THIS DARKE HOUSE OF SHADES, HORROUR, AND NIGHT, | SOSPETTO D'HERODE | 213 | 46 109 | 216 |
| THE HOUSE IS HERS'D ABOUT WITH A BLACK WOOD, | SOSPETTO D'HERODE | 345 | 46 109 | 216 |
| SUCH WAS THE HOUSE, SO FURNISHT WAS THE HALL. | SOSPETTO D'HERODE | 367 | 46 109 | 216 |
| AND FROM THE HEAD OF JUDAHS HOUSE QUITE TORNE | SOSPETTO D'HERODE | 405 | 46 109 | 216 |
| MUST BEE A SURE HOUSE KEEPER, | ON A PRAYER BOOKE | 31 | 46 126 | 139 |
| HOME TO THE HEART, AND SETTS THE HOUSE ON FIRE. | ON A PRAYER BOOKE | 67 | 46 126 | 139 |
| FAREWELL HOUSE, AND FARWELL HOME. | IN MEMORY OF LADY MADRE TERESA | 63 | 46 131, | 52 |
| THE HOUSE AND FAMILY OF PHOENIXES. | UPON YORKE HIS BIRTH | 91 | 46 176 | 500 |
| THE HEAVN-INSTRUCTED HOUSE OF FAITH | LAUDA SION SALVATOREM | 31 | 52 294 | 178 |
| FAREWELL HOUSE, & FAREWELL HOME. | TERESA | 63 | 52 315 | 52 |
| HOME TO THE HEART, & SETTS THE HOUSE ON FIRE | PRAYER TO GENTLE-WOMAN | 73 | 52 328 | 139 |

|  |  |  |  |  |  |
|---|---|---|---|---|---|
| KIND LOVES KEEP HOUSE, LY CLOSE, AND MAKE NO NOISE, | DESCRIPTION RELIGIOUS HOUSE | 33 | 52 | 336 | 213 |
| MANS BREST (HIS TENEMENT) AND BREAKES UP HOUSE. | OUT OF GROTIUS | 80 | MS | 398 | 198 |

HOUSE-KEEPER

|  |  |  |  |  |  |
|---|---|---|---|---|---|
| MUST BE A SURE HOUSE-KEEPER. | PRAYER TO GENTLE-WOMAN | 37 | 52 | 328 | 139 |

HOUSES

|  |  |  |  |  |  |
|---|---|---|---|---|---|
| LIFES LATE FORSAKEN HOUSES ALL LAY DROWN'D | THE BEGINNING OF HELIODORUS | 16 | 46 | 158 | 517 |

HOUSHOLD

|  |  |  |  |  |  |
|---|---|---|---|---|---|
| BRING ALL YOUR HOUSHOLD STUFFE OF HEAVN ON EARTH. | TO THE NAME OF JESUS | 63 | 52 | 239 | 30 |

HOVER

|  |  |  |  |  |  |
|---|---|---|---|---|---|
| HOVER O'RE THE NEW-BORNE DAY. | UPON DEATH OF DESIRED HERRYS | 48 | 46 | 168 | 467 |

HOVERS

|  |  |  |  |  |  |
|---|---|---|---|---|---|
| OF DALLYING SWEETNESSE, HOVERS ORE HER SKILL, | MUSICKS DUELL | 59 | 46 | 149 | 535 |
| AND LIKE A SAUCY BIRD HE HOVERS | OUT OF GREEKE CUPID'S CRYER | 40 | 46 | 159 | 519 |
| WHERE TRIUMPHANT DARKNESSE HOVERS | PSALME 23 | 37 | 46 | 102 | 5 |
| HER KINDRED WITH THE STARRS. NOT BASELY HOVERS | DESCRIPTION RELIGIOUS HOUSE | 37 | 52 | 338 | 213 |
| WHERE ROUND ABOUT HOVERS WITH SILVER WING | AN ELEGY MR STANNINOW | 53 | MS | 394 | 473 |

HOVER'S

|  |  |  |  |  |  |
|---|---|---|---|---|---|
| THESE HOURES, & THAT WHICH HOVER'S O'RE MY END, | OFFICE H. CROSS RECOMMENDATION | 1 | 52 | 276 | 106 |

HOVERING

|  |  |  |  |  |  |
|---|---|---|---|---|---|
| COME HOVERING O'RE THE PLACES HEAD, | A HYMNE OF THE NATIVITY | 36 | 46 | 106 | 76 |
| COME HOVERING O'RE THE PLACE'S HEAD. | IN HOLY NATIVITY | 52 | 52 | 246 | 76 |

HOWL'D

|  |  |  |  |  |  |
|---|---|---|---|---|---|
| THRICE HOWL'D THE CAVES OF NIGHT, AND THRICE THE SOUND, | SOSPETTO D'HERODE | 297 | 46 | 109 | 216 |

HUGE

|  |  |  |  |  |  |
|---|---|---|---|---|---|
| AND POURING ON HEAV'NS FACE THE SEAS HUGE FLOOD | SOSPETTO D'HERODE | 277 | 46 | 109 | 216 |
| SWINGING A HUGE SITH STANDS IMPARTIALL DEATH, | SOSPETTO D'HERODE | 319 | 46 | 109 | 216 |
| HUGE EMPTINESSE CONTRACT THY BULKE, AND SHRINKE | UPON STANINOUGH'S DEATH | 13 | 46 | 175 | 475 |
| GREAT NATURE FOR THE KEY OF HER HUGE CHEST | TO THE NAME OF JESUS | 29 | 52 | 239 | 30 |
| TO FITT A BED FOR THIS HUGE BIRTHE. | IN HOLY NATIVITY | 42 | 52 | 246 | 76 |
| BEARES THAT HUGE TREE WHICH MUST BEAR HIM. | OFFICE H. CROSS SIXT | 4 | 52 | 270 | 97 |
| HUGE EMPTYNES. CONTRACT THY SELF. & SHRINKE | DEATH'S LECTURE | 14 | 52 | 340 | 475 |
| HUGE HIGH-FLOUNE POYSONS, EV'N OF COLCHOS BREED, | HORATIJ ILLE & NEFASTO | 11 | MS | 382 | 530 |

HUMANE

|  |  |  |  |  |  |
|---|---|---|---|---|---|
| TO BECOME BEAUTIFULL IN HUMANE BLOOD. | SOSPETTO D'HERODE | 84 | 46 | 109 | 216 |
| VILE HUMANE NATURE MEANS HE NOW T'INVEST | SOSPETTO D'HERODE | 227 | 46 | 109 | 216 |
| ANGER, AND LOVE, BEST HOOKES OF HUMANE BLOOD. | SOSPETTO D'HERODE | 275 | 46 | 109 | 216 |
| CYMBALLS OF HEAV'N, OR HUMANE SPHEARS, | TO THE NAME OF JESUS | 78 | 52 | 239 | 30 |

HUMBLE

|  |  |  |  |  |  |
|---|---|---|---|---|---|
| LOOKES DOWNE, AND SEES THE HUMBLE NILE BELOW | THE BEGINNING OF HELIODORUS | 4 | 46 | 158 | 517 |
| NOR THE VIOLETS HUMBLE HEAD. | THE WEEPER | 136 | 46 | 79 | 120 |
| THAT ON HER LAP SHE CASTS HER HUMBLE EYE. | ON VIRGINS BASHFULNESSE | 1 | 46 | 89 | 9 |
| THY HUMBLE FAITH AND FEARE KEEPES HIM ALOOFE. | I AM NOT WORTHY | 2 | 46 | 90 | 13 |
| DEIGNE THOU TO WEARE THIS HUMBLE WREATH THAT BOWES, | SOSPETTO D'HERODE | 15 | 46 | 109 | 216 |
| TO HOLY HANDS, AND HUMBLE HEARTS, | ON A PRAYER BOOKE | 18 | 46 | 126 | 139 |
| TO BRING A PAIRE OF MEEK AND HUMBLE EYES. | ON A TREATISE OF CHARITY | 48 | 46 | 137 | 69 |
| HAILE HOLY QUEEN OF HUMBLE HEARTS, | ON THE ASSUMPTION | 29 | 46 | 139 | 114 |
| OF HEAVEN, AND HUMBLE PRIDE OF EARTH. | ON THE ASSUMPTION | 60 | 46 | 139 | 114 |
| HENCE 'TIS MY HUMBLE FANCY FINDS NO WINGS, | TO THE MORNING | 19 | 46 | 183 | 497 |
| AND GUILD THE HOPES OF HUMBLE LOVE. | LOVES HOROSCOPE | 34 | 46 | 185 | 483 |
| OF HUMBLE SOULES, THAT SEEK TO FIND | TO THE NAME OF JESUS | 121 | 52 | 239 | 30 |
| TO SEEK FOR HUMBLE BEDS | TO THE NAME OF JESUS | 232 | 52 | 239 | 30 |
| WE GUILD THE HUMBLE CHEEK OF THIS CHAST PLACE. | IN GLORIOUS EPIPHANIE | 83 | 52 | 253 | 39 |
| THE KING HIMSELF IS. THOU HIS HUMBLE THRONE. | OFFICE H. CROSS EVENSONG | 23 | 52 | 273 | 101 |
| AND AT THE HUMBLE FOOT | SANCTA MARIA DOLORUM | 63 | 52 | 283 | 162 |
| OF HUMBLE LOVE & LOYALL FAITH, | ADORO TE | 2 | 52 | 291 | 172 |
| HAIL, HOLY QUEEN OF HUMBLE HEARTS. | IN GLORIOUS ASSUMPTION B. LADY | 44 | 52 | 304 | 114 |
| OF HEAVN. THE HUMBLE PRIDE OF EARTH. | IN GLORIOUS ASSUMPTION B. LADY | 65 | 52 | 304 | 114 |
| NOR THE VIOLET'S HUMBLE HEAD. | WEEPER | 178 | 52 | 307 | 120 |
| HEARKENS NOT TO AN HUMBLE SONG. | FLAMING HEART | 62 | 52 | 324 | 61 |
| TO HOLY HANDS & HUMBLE HEARTS | PRAYER TO GENTLE-WOMAN | 24 | 52 | 328 | 139 |
| THE HUMBLE KING OF YOU AND ME. | AGAINST IRRESOLUTION AND DELAY | 72 | 52 | 347 | 146 |
| TO GAZE UPON SUCH STARRES EACH HUMBLE EYE | UPON KINGS CORONATION | 33 | MS | 389 | 454 |
| AND THOUGH THESE HUMBLE LINES SOARE NOT SOE HIGH. | UPON BIRTH PRINCESSE E | 17 | MS | 391 | 456 |
| WITH TREMBLING LIPPES AN HUMBLE KISSE DO'ST PAY. | AN ELEGIE ON DR PORTER | 6 | MS | 395 | 476 |
| HAIL, MOST HIGH, MOST HUMBLE ONE. | O GLORIOSA DOMINA | 1 | 52 | 302 | 194 |

HUMBLEST

THY HOLYEST, HUMBLEST, HANDMAID CHARITIE.             ON A TREATISE OF CHARITY             14    46 137  69

HUMBLY

HE HUMBLY CRAV'D TO BANQUETT ON A KISSE.              UPON GUNPOWDER TREASON               46    MS 387 461

HUMILITY

'TIS THE SWEET PRIDE OF HER HUMILITY.                 ON VIRGINS BASHFULNESSE               2    46  89   9
LEARNING, LEARNE HUMILITY.                            HIS EPITAPH (HERRYS)                 22    46 172 471

HUMORS

A MAN, WHOSE TUNED HUMORS BE                          TEMPERANCE                           35    52 342 510

HUMOURS

A MAN WHOSE TUNED HUMOURS BEE.                        IN PRAISE OF LESSIUS                 37    46 156 510

HUMOUROUS

THE HUMOUROUS STRINGS EXPOUND HIS LEARNED TOUCH.      MUSICKS DUELL                       127    46 149 535

HUNDRED

AN HUNDRED THOUSAND LOVES AND GRACES,                 ON A PRAYER BOOKE                    75    46 126 139
A THOUSAND, AND A HUNDRED, SCORE                      OUT OF CATULLUS                      11    46 194 523
AN HUNDRED, AND A THOUSAND MORE,                      OUT OF CATULLUS                      12    46 194 523
MANY A THOUSAND, MANY A HUNDRED.                      OUT OF CATULLUS                      16    46 194 523
A HUNDRED THOUSAND GOODS, GLORIES, & GRACES.          PRAYER TO GENTLE-WOMAN               81    52 328 139
I CAL'D A HUNDRED MIRACLES TO TELL                    OUT OF GROTIUS                       31    MS 398 198

HUNDRED-HEADED

WHAT WONDER, WHEN THE HUNDRED-HEADED BEAST            HORATIJ ILLE & NEFASTO               50    MS 382 530

HUNG

ARE TOOLES OF WRATH, ANVILLS OF TORMENTS HUNG.        SOSPETTO D'HERODE                   323    46 109 216
THE SHAMEFAC'T LAMP HUNG DOWN HIS HEAD                IN GLORIOUS EPIPHANIE               118    52 253  39
IT WAS EXHAL'D, A WHILE IT HUNG, & DY'D.              ON GUNPOWDER-TREASON                 50    MS 384 458

HUNGER

THY HUNGER FEELES NOT WHAT HE EATES.                  BLESSED BE THE PAPS                   2    46  94  14
OTHER MENS HUNGER WITH STRANGE FEASTS I QUELL'D       OUT OF GROTIUS                       57    MS 398 198
THE PEOPLES HUNGER, AND WHEN ALL WERE FULL            OUT OF GROTIUS                       63    MS 398 198

HUNGERS

THAT UNDER HUNGERS TEETH WILL NEEDS BE SOUND.         ON MIRACLE OF LOAVES                  2    46  86  15

HUNGRY

WHERE HUNGRY WARRE HAD MADE HIMSELF A GUEST.          THE BEGINNING OF HELIODORUS          26    46 158 517
OF TIME, OR TEETH OF HUNGRY RUINE FEARES.             SOSPETTO D'HERODE                   310    46 109 216
OFT HAVE MY HUNGRY KISSES MADE THINE EYES             LUKE 2. QUAERIT JESUM                35    MS 379  11
CARES HUNGRY DEATH SNATCH OF ONE CHERRY LIPP.         UPON GUNPOWDER TREASON               39    MS 387 461

HUNTER

TRUE HOPE'S A GLORIOUS HUNTER & HER CHASE.            (ON) HOPE                            49    52 345  71

HUNTRESSE

TRUE HOPE'S A GLORIOUS HUNTRESSE, AND HER CHASE       ON HOPE                              89    46 143  71

HURL'D

THEE THEREFORE FROM THE REST APART SHE HURL'D,        UPON YORKE HIS BIRTH                 27    46 176 500
HAD BEENE PUFT OUT, & FROM THEIR STATIONS HURL'D.     UPON GUNPOWDER TREASON               28    MS 386 460

HURRIES

THAT THE SOUTHWEST-WIND HURRIES IN HIS ARMES,         OUT OF VIRGIL                        20    46 155 529

HURT

HIS WAY THROUGH BAD, TO MY SUCCESSIVE HURT.           OUT OF GROTIUS                       13    MS 398 198

HURTS

AND FRAUD, HEE MAKES POORE MORTALLS HURTS.            OUT OF GREEKE CUPID'S CRYER          31    46 159 519

HURTES

HURTES MEE FAR WORSE THEN HERODS HIGHEST SPITE.       OUT OF GROTIUS                       34    MS 398 198

HURTING
  OF HURTING THEE.                                        ON HOPE                              18  46 143  71
  OF HURTING THEE.                                        (ON) HOPE                             8  52 345  71

HUSBAND
  YET WHEN YOUNG APRILS HUSBAND SHOWRES,                  A HYMNE OF THE NATIVITY              77  46 106  76
  YET WHEN YOUNG APRIL'S HUSBAND SHOWRS                   IN HOLY NATIVITY                     97  52 246  76

HUSBANDMAN
  O, WHO SO HARD AN HUSBANDMAN COULD EVER FIND            UPON THORNES FROM LORDS HEAD          5  46  96  23
  O WHO SO HARD A HUSBANDMAN DID EVER FIND                UPON CROWNE OF THORNS                 3  52 290  23

HUSKS
  ARE HUSKS SO DEARE. TROTH 'TIS A MIGHTY RATE.           ON THE PRODIGALL                      4  46  86  17

HUSWIFES
  BUT HER BEST HUSWIFES ARE THE PARCAE, WHICH             SOSPETTO D'HERODE                   340  46 109 216

HYBLA'S
  ALL HYBLA'S HONEY, ALL THAT SWEETNESSE CAN              UPON OUR LORDS LAST DISCOURSE         1  46  95  21

HYDRAES
  OF DRAGONS, HYDRAES, SPHINXES, FILL THE GROVE.          SOSPETTO D'HERODE                   352  46 109 216

HYDRA'S
  SEAV'N CRESTED HYDRA'S HORRIBLY ADORNE.                 SOSPETTO D'HERODE                    48  46 109 216

HYMEN
  O BURN OUR HYMEN BRIGHT IN SUCH HIGH FLAME.             ALEXIAS THIRD ELEGIE                 49  52 336 209

HYPERBOLE'S
  MOST TALL HYPERBOLE'S CANNOT DESCRY IT.                 ON GUNPOWDER-TREASON                 47  MS 384 458

HYPERBOLIZED
  (HYPERBOLIZED NOTHING.) KNOW THY SPAN.                  UPON STANINOUGH'S DEATH              10  46 175 475
  HYPERBOLIZED NOTHING. KNOW THY SPAN.                    DEATH'S LECTURE                      11  52 340 475

HYPERION
  THE WORLD'S & HIS HYPERION.                             IN GLORIOUS EPIPHANIE               253  52 253  39

HYPOCRISY
  THE DEEP HYPOCRISY OF DEATH & NIGHT                     IN GLORIOUS EPIPHANIE                58  52 253  39

HYPOCRITE
  NO MORE THE HYPOCRITE SHALL TH'UPRIGHT BE               ON A TREATISE OF CHARITY             39  46 137  69

HIPOCRIT
  IT IS NOT HIPOCRIT)                                     ON A PRAYER BOOKE                     3  46 126 139

I
  (MISTRESSE) I COME. NOW REACH A STRAINE MY LUTE         MUSICKS DUELL                       107  46 149 535
  FREELY LAYES OUT HER LEAVES. NOR DOE I DOUBT            OUT OF VIRGIL                        22  46 155 529
  I PAINT SO ILL, MY PEECE HAD NEED TO BEE                WITH A PICTURE TO A FRIEND            1  46 156 494
  I WRITE SO ILL, MY SLENDER LINE IS SCARCE               WITH A PICTURE TO A FRIEND            3  46 156 494
  YET MAY THE LOVE I SEND BE TRUE, THOUGH I               WITH A PICTURE TO A FRIEND            5  46 156 494
  YET MAY THE LOVE I SEND BE TRUE, THOUGH I               WITH A PICTURE TO A FRIEND            5  46 156 494
  BOTH WHICH AWAY, I SHOULD NOT NEED TO FEARE,            WITH A PICTURE TO A FRIEND            7  46 156 494
  MINE IS THE WAGGE. TIS I THAT OWE                       OUT OF GREEKE CUPID'S CRYER           8  46 159 519
  THUS DID I FALL, AND THUS FELL PHAETHON.                HIGH MOUNTED ON AN ANT                6  46 161 523
  STILL SPENDING, NEVER SPENT. I MEANE                    THE WEEPER                            5  46  79 120
  HER RICHEST PEARLES, I MEANE THY TEARES.                THE WEEPER                           54  46  79 120
  THE VERY TERME, I THINK, WAS FOUND                      THE TEARE                             5  46  84  50
  A PILLOW FOR THEE WILL I BRING,                         THE TEARE                            35  46  84  50
  YET I DOUBT OF THEE,                                    THE TEARE                            45  46  84  50
  AND NOW, I DOUBT NOT, THE ETERNALL DOVE,                ON BAPTIZED AETHIOPIAN                5  46  85  29
  ONCE I DID SPELL                                        ON MARKES OF SAVIOURS WOUNDS          6  46  86  28
  UNDER THY SHADOW MAY I LURKE A WHILE,                   SICKE IMPLORE SHADOW                  1  46  87  28
  THEN COULD I SHOW THESE ARMES OF MINE, AND SAY          COME SEE WHERE THE LORD LAY           5  46  87  27
  HEE TO HIMSELFE (I FEARE THE WORST)                     I AM THE DOORE                        3  46  90  17
  TO SPEAKE THUS, WAS TO SPEAKE (SAY I)                   THE BLIND CURED                       5  46  91  19
  WEEPE, 'CAUSE I CAN WEEPE NO MORE.                      VERILY YE SHALL WEEP                  4  46  95  22
  YET IS THE JOY I TAKE IN'T SMALL OR NONE.               UPON OUR LORDS LAST DISCOURSE         3  46  95  21
  WELL FOR THY SELFE (I MEANE) NOT FOR THY LORD.          ON ST. PETER CUTTING MALCHUS          2  46  97  22
  I DOUBT THOUGH WHEN THE WORLD'S IN HELL.                BUT MEN LOVED DARKNESSE               3  46  97  13
  SAVE THOSE OF FEARE, NO OTHER BANDS FEARE I.            I AM READY NOT ONELY BOUND            3  46  98  29
  (FOR WHAT ELSE IS MY LIFE.) LO I BEQUEATH.              OUR LORD IN HIS CIRCUMCISION          2  46  98   9
  THIS GARMENT TOO I WOULD THEY HAD DENY'D.               ON CRUCIFIED LORD BLOODY              2  46 100  24

| | | | | |
|---|---|---|---|---|
| BUT WHILE I SPEAKE, WHITHER ARE RUN | ON BLEEDING WOUNDS OF LORD | 29 | 46 | 101 | 110 |
| I COUNTED WRONG. THERE IS BUT ONE, | ON BLEEDING WOUNDS OF LORD | 31 | 46 | 101 | 110 |
| WHEN FIRST I LOOK'T ON THEE, I LOST MINE EYES. | SAMPSON TO HIS DALILAH | 2 | 46 | 102 | 8 |
| WHEN FIRST I LOOK'T ON THEE, I LOST MINE EYES. | SAMPSON TO HIS DALILAH | 2 | 46 | 102 | 8 |
| WHILE I FEAST, MY FOES DOE FEED | PSALME 23 | 51 | 46 | 102 | 5 |
| THEY ARE STARV'D, AND I AM FED. | PSALME 23 | 54 | 46 | 102 | 5 |
| SO, EVEN SO STILL MAY I MOVE | PSALME 23 | 57 | 46 | 102 | 5 |
| ABOUT MY PATHS, SO SHALL I FIND | PSALME 23 | 61 | 46 | 102 | 5 |
| WILL I FIND A PURER AIRE | PSALME 23 | 68 | 46 | 102 | 5 |
| AND THENCE MY RIPE SOULE WILL I BREATH | PSALME 23 | 71 | 46 | 102 | 5 |
| OF MUSICKS DAINTY TOUCH, THEN I | PSALME 137 | 17 | 46 | 104 | 7 |
| WHICH WHEN I LOSE, O MAY AT ONCE MY TONGUE | PSALME 137 | 19 | 46 | 104 | 7 |
| I SAW THE CURL'D DROPS,SOFT AND SLOW | A HYMNE OF THE NATIVITY | 35 | 46 | 106 | 76 |
| FORBEARE (SAID I) BE NOT TOO BOLD, | A HYMNE OF THE NATIVITY | 39 | 46 | 106 | 76 |
| I SAW TH'OFFICIOUS ANGELS BRING, | A HYMNE OF THE NATIVITY | 41 | 46 | 106 | 76 |
| FAIRE YOUTH (SAID I) BE NOT TOO ROUGH, | A HYMNE OF THE NATIVITY | 45 | 46 | 106 | 76 |
| SWEET CHOISE (SAID I) NO WAY BUT SO, | A HYMNE OF THE NATIVITY | 51 | 46 | 106 | 76 |
| FROWNE I, AND CAN GREAT NATURE KEEP HER SEAT. | SOSPETTO D'HERODE | 205 | 46 | 109 | 216 |
| IT SHALL NOT BE, SAID I, AND CLOMBE THE NORTH, | SOSPETTO D'HERODE | 221 | 46 | 109 | 216 |
| WHAT THOUGH I MIST MY BLOW. YET I STROOKE HIGH, | SOSPETTO D'HERODE | 223 | 46 | 109 | 216 |
| WHAT THOUGH I MIST MY BLOW. YET I STROOKE HIGH, | SOSPETTO D'HERODE | 223 | 46 | 109 | 216 |
| AND YET WHOSE FORCE FEARE I, HAVE I SO LOST | SOSPETTO D'HERODE | 249 | 46 | 109 | 216 |
| AND YET WHOSE FORCE FEARE I, HAVE I SO LOST | SOSPETTO D'HERODE | 249 | 46 | 109 | 216 |
| I THANKE YOU ALL, BUT ONE MUST SINGLE OUT, | SOSPETTO D'HERODE | 287 | 46 | 109 | 216 |
| WHY DID I SPEND MY LIFE, AND SPILL MY BLOOD, | SOSPETTO D'HERODE | 449 | 46 | 109 | 216 |
| THAT WHILE I LAY THEM ON THE SHRINE | ON MR. G. HERBERTS BOOKE | 17 | 46 | 130 | 68 |
| THUS HAVE I BACK AGAINE TO THY BRIGHT NAME | AN APOLOGIE FOR HYMNE (TERESA) | 1 | 46 | 136 | 59 |
| I TOOKE FROM READING THEE. 'TIS TO THY WRONG | AN APOLOGIE FOR HYMNE (TERESA) | 3 | 46 | 136 | 59 |
| I KNOW THAT IN MY WEAK AND WORTHLESSE SONG | AN APOLOGIE FOR HYMNE (TERESA) | 4 | 46 | 136 | 59 |
| SCARCE DAWNES. O PARDON, IF I DARE TO SAY | AN APOLOGIE FOR HYMNE (TERESA) | 6 | 46 | 136 | 59 |
| I LEARNT TO KNOW THAT LOVE IS ELOQUENCE. | AN APOLOGIE FOR HYMNE (TERESA) | 8 | 46 | 136 | 59 |
| LO WHERE I SEE THY OFFRINGS WAKE, AND RISE | ON A TREATISE OF CHARITY | 17 | 46 | 137 | 69 |
| STAY BUT A LITTLE WHILE, UNTILL I CALL | UPON STANINOUGH'S DEATH | 5 | 46 | 175 | 475 |
| CENTER OF THOSE THY GRANDSIRES, SHALL I SAY | UPON YORKE HIS BIRTH | 30 | 46 | 176 | 500 |
| SO HAVE I SEENE (TO DRESSE THEIR MISTRESSE MAY) | UPON YORKE HIS BIRTH | 59 | 46 | 176 | 500 |
| CONFESSING THEE. OR (IF TOO LONG I STAY) | UPON YORKE HIS BIRTH | 112 | 46 | 176 | 500 |
| I WOULD BE MARRIED, BUT I'DE HAVE NO WIFE, | ON MARRIAGE | 1 | 46 | 183 | 485 |
| I WOULD BE MARRIED TO A SINGLE LIFE. | ON MARRIAGE | 2 | 46 | 183 | 485 |
| WHAT SUCCOUR CAN I HOPE THE MUSE WILL SEND | TO THE MORNING | 1 | 46 | 183 | 497 |
| O IN THAT MORNING OF MY SHAME. WHEN I | TO THE MORNING | 5 | 46 | 183 | 497 |
| MEE FROM HIS PATRONAGE. I PRAY, HE CHIDES. | TO THE MORNING | 14 | 46 | 183 | 497 |
| MY OWNE APOLLO, TRY IF I CAN MAKE | TO THE MORNING | 16 | 46 | 183 | 497 |
| THRICE WILL I PAY THREE TEARES, TO SHOW HOW TRUE | TO THE MORNING | 40 | 46 | 183 | 497 |
| BUT THOU, FAINT GOD OF SLEEPE, FORGET THAT I | TO THE MORNING | 47 | 46 | 183 | 497 |
| NOR WILL I OFFER ANY MORE TO THEE | TO THE MORNING | 50 | 46 | 183 | 497 |
| SHALL I HIDE POORE LOVE FROM DEATH. | LOVES HOROSCOPE | 44 | 46 | 185 | 483 |
| SHALL I BUILD HIS FUNERALL NEST. | LOVES HOROSCOPE | 50 | 46 | 185 | 483 |
| (I CARE NOT WHITHER) | OUT OF THE ITALIAN (2) | 12 | 46 | 190 | 547 |
| I WISH HER BEAUTY, | WISHES SUPPOSED MISTRESSE | 16 | 46 | 195 | 479 |
| I WISH, HER STORE | WISHES SUPPOSED MISTRESSE | 103 | 46 | 195 | 479 |
| OF WISHES. AND I WISH--NO MORE. | WISHES SUPPOSED MISTRESSE | 105 | 46 | 195 | 479 |
| I SEEKE NO FURTHER, IT IS SHEE. | WISHES SUPPOSED MISTRESSE | 114 | 46 | 195 | 479 |
| LO I UNCLOATH AND CLEARE, | WISHES SUPPOSED MISTRESSE | 116 | 46 | 195 | 479 |
| FAINE WOULD I CHIDE THEIR SLOWNESSE, BUT IN THEIR | UPON TWO GREENE APRICOCKES | 31 | 48 | 220 | 494 |
| DEFECTS I DRAW MINE OWNE DULL CHARACTER. | UPON TWO GREENE APRICOCKES | 32 | 48 | 220 | 494 |
| I SING THE NAME WHICH NONE CAN SAY | TO THE NAME OF JESUS | 1 | 52 | 239 | 30 |
| OF NOBLE POWRES, I SEE, | TO THE NAME OF JESUS | 20 | 52 | 239 | 30 |
| I HAVE AUTHORITY IN LOVE'S NAME TO TAKE YOU | TO THE NAME OF JESUS | 53 | 52 | 239 | 30 |
| POOR WORLD (SAID I.) WHAT WILT THOU DOE | IN HOLY NATIVITY | 37 | 52 | 246 | 76 |
| PROUD WORLD, SAID I. CEASE YOUR CONTEST | IN HOLY NATIVITY | 44 | 52 | 246 | 76 |
| I SAW THE CURL'D DROPS, SOFT & SLOW, | IN HOLY NATIVITY | 51 | 52 | 246 | 76 |
| FORBEAR, SAID I. BE NOT TOO BOLD. | IN HOLY NATIVITY | 55 | 52 | 246 | 76 |
| I SAW THE OBSEQUIOUS SERAPHIMS | IN HOLY NATIVITY | 58 | 52 | 246 | 76 |
| WELL DONE, SAID I. BUT ARE YOU SURE | IN HOLY NATIVITY | 62 | 52 | 246 | 76 |
| INTO THY HANDS, AND HART, LORD, I COMMEND. | OFFICE H. CROSS RECOMMENDATION | 2 | 52 | 276 | 106 |
| TAKE BOTH TO THINE ACCOUNT, THAT I & MINE | OFFICE H. CROSS RECOMMENDATION | 3 | 52 | 276 | 106 |
| THAT AS I DEDICATE MY DEVOUTEST BREATH | OFFICE H. CROSS RECOMMENDATION | 5 | 52 | 276 | 106 |
| LOVE IS TOO KIND, I SEE, & CAN | CHARITAS NIMIA | 5 | 52 | 280 | 48 |
| IF I WERE LOST IN MISERY, | CHARITAS NIMIA | 45 | 52 | 280 | 48 |
| WHAT IF MY FAITHLESSE SOUL & I | CHARITAS NIMIA | 49 | 52 | 280 | 48 |
| BOTH OF LOVE'S FIRES & FLOUDS) MIGHT I RECLINE | SANCTA MARIA DOLORUM | 47 | 52 | 283 | 162 |
| SHALL I, SETT THERE | SANCTA MARIA DOLORUM | 81 | 52 | 283 | 162 |
| TILL DRUNK OF THE DEAR WOUNDS, I BE | SANCTA MARIA DOLORUM | 103 | 52 | 283 | 162 |
| BUT WHILE I SPEAKE, WHITHER ARE RUN | UPON BLEEDING CRUCIFIX | 25 | 52 | 288 | 110 |
| I COUNTED WRONG. THERE IS BUT ONE. | UPON BLEEDING CRUCIFIX | 27 | 52 | 288 | 110 |
| THIS GARMENT TOO I WOULD THEY HAD DENY'D. | UPON BODY OF OUR LORD | 2 | 52 | 290 | 24 |
| THUS LOWE (MY HIDDEN LIFE.) I BOW TO THEE | ADORO TE | 3 | 52 | 291 | 172 |
| SWEET, CONSIDER THEN, THAT I | ADORO TE | 27 | 52 | 291 | 172 |
| FOR WHICH I LANGUISH, COME AWAY. | ADORO TE | 52 | 52 | 291 | 172 |
| MERCY (MY JUDGE) MERCY I CRY | DIES IRAE | 41 | 52 | 298 | 186 |
| THAT I INHERITT THY RIGHT HAND. | DIES IRAE | 64 | 52 | 298 | 186 |
| STILL SPENDING, NEVER SPENT. I MEAN | WEEPER | 5 | 52 | 307 | 120 |
| HER PROUDEST PEARLES. I MEAN THY TEARES. | WEEPER | 42 | 52 | 307 | 120 |
| THUS HAVE I BACK AGAIN TO THY BRIGHT NAME | AN APOLOGIE FOR (TERESA) HYMNE | 1 | 52 | 322 | 59 |
| I TOOK FROM READING THEE, TIS TO THY WRONG | AN APOLOGIE FOR (TERESA) HYMNE | 3 | 52 | 322 | 59 |
| I KNOW, THAT IN MY WEAK & WORTHLESSE SONG | AN APOLOGIE FOR (TERESA) HYMNE | 4 | 52 | 322 | 59 |
| SCARSE DAWNES. O PARDON IF I DARE TO SAY | AN APOLOGIE FOR (TERESA) HYMNE | 6 | 52 | 322 | 59 |
| I LEARN'T TO KNOW THAT LOVE IS ELOQUENCE | AN APOLOGIE FOR (TERESA) HYMNE | 8 | 52 | 322 | 59 |
| LET ME SO READ THY LIFE, THAT I | FLAMING HEART | 107 | 52 | 324 | 61 |
| I DY IN LOVE'S DELICIOUS FIRE. | A SONG | 4 | 52 | 327 | 65 |
| O LOVE, I AM THY SACRIFICE. | A SONG | 5 | 52 | 327 | 65 |
| STILL SHINE ON ME, FAIR SUNS, THAT I | A SONG | 7 | 52 | 327 | 65 |
| STILL MAY BEHOLD, THOUGH STILL I DY. | A SONG | 8 | 52 | 327 | 65 |
| THOUGH STILL I DY, I LIVE AGAIN. | A SONG | 9 | 52 | 327 | 65 |

| | | | | | |
|---|---|---|---|---|---|
| THOUGH STILL I DY, I LIVE AGAIN. | A SONG | 9 | 52 | 327 | 65 |
| I DY EVEN IN DESIRE OF DEATH. | A SONG | 12 | 52 | 327 | 65 |
| DEAD TO MY SELFE, I LIVE IN THEE. | A SONG | 16 | 52 | 327 | 65 |
| WHY MAY NOT I | TO SAME CONCERNING CHOISE | 4 | 52 | 331 | 66 |
| OF SOULES, DISDAIN THAT I DISCOVER | TO SAME CONCERNING CHOISE | 42 | 52 | 331 | 66 |
| I LATE THE ROMAN YOUTH'S LOV'D PRAYSE & PRIDE, | ALEXIAS FIRST ELEGIE | 1 | 52 | 334 | 204 |
| NOR CAN I TELL (AND THIS NEW TEARES DOTH BREED) | ALEXIAS FIRST ELEGIE | 7 | 52 | 334 | 204 |
| O KNEW I WHERE HE WANDER'D, I SHOULD SEE | ALEXIAS FIRST ELEGIE | 9 | 52 | 334 | 204 |
| O KNEW I WHERE HE WANDER'D, I SHOULD SEE | ALEXIAS FIRST ELEGIE | 9 | 52 | 334 | 204 |
| WHO KNOWES MY OWN HEART'S WOES SO WELL AS I. | ALEXIAS FIRST ELEGIE | 14 | 52 | 334 | 204 |
| BUT HOW SHALL I STEAL HENCE, ALEXIS THOU | ALEXIAS FIRST ELEGIE | 15 | 52 | 334 | 204 |
| IF I BE SHIPWRACK'T, LOVE SHALL TEACH TO SWIMME. | ALEXIAS FIRST ELEGIE | 21 | 52 | 334 | 204 |
| I, 'MONGST THE BLEST STARRES A NEW NAME SHALL BE. | ALEXIAS FIRST ELEGIE | 24 | 52 | 334 | 204 |
| THOUGH ALL THE JOYES I HAD FLEED HENCE WITH THEE | ALEXIAS SECONDE ELEGIE | 1 | 52 | 335 | 207 |
| WITH HIM SHALL I WEEP OUT MY WEARY LIFE. | ALEXIAS SECONDE ELEGIE | 6 | 52 | 335 | 207 |
| WELLCOME, MY SAD SWEET MATE. NOW HAVE I GOTT | ALEXIAS SECONDE ELEGIE | 7 | 52 | 335 | 207 |
| FOR HIM, ALAS, N'ERE SHALL I NEED TO BE | ALEXIAS SECONDE ELEGIE | 11 | 52 | 335 | 207 |
| FOR THEE I TALK TO TREES. WITH SILENT GROVES | ALEXIAS SECONDE ELEGIE | 13 | 52 | 335 | 207 |
| TO THESE I TALK IN TEARES, & TELL MY PAIN. | ALEXIAS SECONDE ELEGIE | 17 | 52 | 335 | 207 |
| HOW OFT HAVE I WEPT OUT THE WEARY SUN. | ALEXIAS SECONDE ELEGIE | 19 | 52 | 335 | 207 |
| O I AM LEARNED GROWN, POOR LOVE & I | ALEXIAS SECONDE ELEGIE | 21 | 52 | 335 | 207 |
| O I AM LEARNED GROWN, POOR LOVE & I | ALEXIAS SECONDE ELEGIE | 21 | 52 | 335 | 207 |
| AND I, WHAT IS MY CRIME I CANNOT TELL. | ALEXIAS THIRD ELEGIE | 19 | 52 | 336 | 209 |
| AND I, WHAT IS MY CRIME I CANNOT TELL. | ALEXIAS THIRD ELEGIE | 19 | 52 | 336 | 209 |
| WITTNESSE, CHAST HEAVNS, NO HAPPYER VOWES I KNOW | ALEXIAS THIRD ELEGIE | 25 | 52 | 336 | 209 |
| BUT I, (SO HELP ME HEAVN MY HOPES TO SEE) | ALEXIAS THIRD ELEGIE | 53 | 52 | 336 | 209 |
| ALEXIS, HE ALONE IS MINE (SAID I) | ALEXIAS THIRD ELEGIE | 56 | 52 | 336 | 209 |
| STAY BUT A LITTLE WHILE, UNTILL I CALL | DEATH'S LECTURE | 5 | 52 | 340 | 475 |
| MY JOYES, & HEE ARE GONE. MY GREIFE, & I | LUKE 2. QUAERIT JESUM | 11 | MS | 379 | 11 |
| MAKE HAST, & COME, OR E'RE MY GREIFE, & I | LUKE 2. QUAERIT JESUM | 17 | MS | 379 | 11 |
| I WAS MISTAKEN. SOME FAIRE SPHAERE, OR OTHER | LUKE 2. QUAERIT JESUM | 21 | MS | 379 | 11 |
| OFT HAVE I WRAPT THY SLUMBERS IN SOFT AIRES, | LUKE 2. QUAERIT JESUM | 31 | MS | 379 | 11 |
| OFT HAVE I SPOILD MY KISSES DAINTIEST DIET, | LUKE 2. QUAERIT JESUM | 37 | MS | 379 | 11 |
| OFT HAVE MY SOULE HAVE I BIN GLAD TO SEEKE | LUKE 2. QUAERIT JESUM | 41 | MS | 379 | 11 |
| SOE I MAY GAINE THY DEATH, MY LIFE I'LE GIVE. | MATH. 16. 25. WHOSOEVER SHALL | 1 | MS | 381 | 16 |
| (MY LIFE'S MERCURY, AND I, IN THY DEATH I LIVE.) | MATH. 16. 25. WHOSOEVER SHALL | 2 | MS | 381 | 16 |
| THAT MAN (I THINKE) WRESTED THE FEEBLE LIFE | HORATIJ ILLE & NEFASTO | 7 | MS | 382 | 530 |
| A LITTLE MORE, & I HAD SURELY SEENE | HORATIJ ILLE & NEFASTO | 33 | MS | 382 | 530 |
| I SING IMPIETY BEYOND A NAME. | ON GUNPOWDER-TREASON | 1 | MS | 384 | 458 |
| OF PLUTO'S MERCURY, THAT I MAY SING | UPON GUNPOWDER TREASON | 2 | MS | 386 | 460 |
| I FEARE TO NAME IT. LEAST THAT HE, WHICH HEARES, | UPON GUNPOWDER TREASON | 9 | MS | 386 | 460 |
| DOE NOT DECEIVE MEE. EYES. DOE I NOT SEE | UPON KINGS CORONATION | 11 | MS | 389 | 454 |
| I VEIW A RISING SUNNE IN THIS OUR SPHAERE. | UPON KINGS CORONATION | 14 | MS | 389 | 454 |
| DOE I NOT SEE JOY KEEPE HIS REVELS NOW. | UPON KINGS CORONATION | 19 | MS | 389 | 454 |
| DOE I NOT SEE A CYNTHIA, WHO MAY | UPON KINGS CORONATION | 25 | MS | 389 | 454 |
| DOE I NOT SEE A CONSTELLATION. | UPON KINGS CORONATION | 29 | MS | 389 | 454 |
| I MEANE THOSE THREE GREAT STARRES, WHO WELL MAY SCORNE | UPON KINGS CORONATION | 31 | MS | 389 | 454 |
| BUT THEN, ALAS, MY HEART. OH HOW SHALL I | UPON BIRTH PRINCESSE E | 11 | MS | 391 | 456 |
| I CANNOT HOLD. SUCH A SPRING TIDE OF JOY | UPON BIRTH PRINCESSE E | 13 | MS | 391 | 456 |
| BEE CONSECRATED TO THIS WORKE, WHILE I | UPON BIRTH PRINCESSE E | 23 | MS | 391 | 456 |
| THOSE SPARKLING TWINNES OF LIGHT SHOULD I NOW STILE | UPON BIRTH PRINCESSE E | 43 | MS | 391 | 456 |
| OR SHOULD I SAY, THAT WITH A SCARLET WAVE | UPON BIRTH PRINCESSE E | 47 | MS | 391 | 456 |
| HER GLORIES I SHOULD DIMME WITH THINGS SOE GROSSE. | UPON BIRTH PRINCESSE E | 53 | MS | 391 | 456 |
| MY THREDS OF LIFE. IF THEN I SHALL NOT LIVE | EX EUPHORMIONE | 11 | MS | 392 | 525 |
| BEFORE THE WORLD. OBEDIENT LO. I JOYNE | OUT OF GROTIUS | 4 | MS | 398 | 198 |
| I SHRINKE NOT. BUT THUS READY STAND TO BEARE | OUT OF GROTIUS | 7 | MS | 398 | 198 |
| (FOR ELSE WHY CAME I.) EV'N WHAT E'RE I FEARE. | OUT OF GROTIUS | 8 | MS | 398 | 198 |
| (FOR ELSE WHY CAME I.) EV'N WHAT E'RE I FEARE. | OUT OF GROTIUS | 8 | MS | 398 | 198 |
| MY SOULE SHEE WAS SECURE. STILL HAVE I BORNE | OUT OF GROTIUS | 11 | MS | 398 | 198 |
| I LEFT MY GLORIOUS FATHERS STAR-PAV'D COURT | OUT OF GROTIUS | 14 | MS | 398 | 198 |
| THEN WAS I KNOWNE, AND KNOWNE UNLUCKILY | OUT OF GROTIUS | 19 | MS | 398 | 198 |
| A WEAKE A WRETCHED CHILD. EV'N THEN WAS I | OUT OF GROTIUS | 20 | MS | 398 | 198 |
| I CAL'D A HUNDRED MIRACLES TO TELL | OUT OF GROTIUS | 31 | MS | 398 | 198 |
| DRINKE FAYLING THERE WHERE I A GUEST DID SHINE | OUT OF GROTIUS | 51 | MS | 398 | 198 |
| OTHER MENS HUNGER WITH STRANGE FEASTS I QUELL'D | OUT OF GROTIUS | 57 | MS | 398 | 198 |
| MINE OWNE WITH STRANGER FASTINGS, WHEN I HELD | OUT OF GROTIUS | 58 | MS | 398 | 198 |
| FATHER AND HEYRE OF DARKENESSE, WHEN I CHIDE | OUT OF GROTIUS | 77 | MS | 398 | 198 |
| NOW BUT THE GRAVE. THE GRAVE IT SELFE I TAM'D. | OUT OF GROTIUS | 86 | MS | 398 | 198 |

I'AM

| | | | | | |
|---|---|---|---|---|---|
| I'AM WEDDED ORE AGAIN SINCE THOU ART GONE. | ALEXIAS SECONDE ELEGIE | 3 | 52 | 335 | 207 |
| I'AM PERFECT IN HEAVN'S STATE, WITH EVERY STARR | ALEXIAS SECONDE ELEGIE | 23 | 52 | 335 | 207 |
| I'AM YOURS, O WERE MY GOD, MY CHRIST SO TOO, | ALEXIAS THIRD ELEGIE | 43 | 52 | 336 | 209 |

I'D

| | | | | | |
|---|---|---|---|---|---|
| I'D SEND MY WOES IN WORDS SHOULD WEEP FOR ME. | ALEXIAS FIRST ELEGIE | 11 | 52 | 334 | 204 |
| I'D KNOW NO NAME OF LOVE ON EARTH BUT YOU. | ALEXIAS THIRD ELEGIE | 44 | 52 | 336 | 209 |

I'DE

| | | | | | |
|---|---|---|---|---|---|
| I WOULD BE MARRIED, BUT I'DE HAVE NO WIFE, | ON MARRIAGE | 1 | 46 | 183 | 485 |

I'LE

| | | | | | |
|---|---|---|---|---|---|
| I'LE GIVE THEE ALL, TAKE ALL, TAKE HEED | OUT OF GREEKE CUPID'S CRYER | 71 | 46 | 159 | 519 |
| DEATH'S BUSIE SEARCH I'LE EASILY BEGUILE. | SICKE IMPLORE SHADOW | 2 | 46 | 87 | 28 |
| I'LE WEEPE, AND WEEPE, AND WILL THEREFORE | VERILY YE SHALL WEEP | 3 | 46 | 95 | 22 |
| SPARE THIS ONE JEWELL. I'LE BE DIVES STILL. | DIVES ASKING A DROP | 4 | 46 | 96 | 18 |
| THERE I'LE DWELL FOR EVER, THERE | PSALME 23 | 67 | 46 | 102 | 5 |
| TO FEED MY LIFE WITH, THERE I'LE SUP | PSALME 23 | 69 | 46 | 102 | 5 |
| SOE I MAY GAINE THY DEATH, MY LIFE I'LE GIVE. | MATH. 16. 25. WHOSOEVER SHALL | 1 | MS | 381 | 16 |
| OR ELSE, MY LIFE, I'LE HIDE THEE IN HIS GRAVE, | MATH. 16. 25. WHOSOEVER SHALL | 3 | MS | 381 | 16 |

| | | | |
|---|---|---|---|
| AND I'LE NOT BLURRE IT WITH MY PARAPHRASE. | UPON BIRTH PRINCESSE E | 60 | MS 391 456 |

**I'ME**

| | | | |
|---|---|---|---|
| MY SELFE A MELTING SACRIFICE. I'ME BORNE | TO THE MORNING | 51 | 46 183 497 |

**I'VE**

| | | | |
|---|---|---|---|
| I'VE SEEN INDEED THE HOPEFULL BUD, | UPON DEATH OF DESIRED HERRYS | 31 | 46 168 467 |
| I'VE SEENE THE MORNINGS LOVELY RAY, | UPON DEATH OF DESIRED HERRYS | 47 | 46 168 467 |

**TH'ICY**

| | | | |
|---|---|---|---|
| OF TH'ICY NORTH, FROM FROST-BOUND ATLAS HANDS | SOSPETTO D'HERODE | 106 | 46 109 216 |

**IDAEA**

| | | | |
|---|---|---|---|
| BEFORE THY SELFE IN THY IDAEA, THOU | UPON STANINOUGH'S DEATH | 12 | 46 175 475 |
| IDAEA, TAKE A SHRINE | WISHES SUPPOSED MISTRESSE | 11 | 46 195 479 |
| BEFORE THY SELF IN THINE IDAEA. THOU | DEATH'S LECTURE | 13 | 52 340 475 |

**IDLE**

| | | | |
|---|---|---|---|
| A WITHER'D LEAFE, AN IDLE GUEST. | PSALME 137 | 24 | 46 104 7 |

**IDOL**

| | | | |
|---|---|---|---|
| BRIGHT IDOL. BLACK IDOLATRY. | IN GLORIOUS EPIPHANIE | 51 | 52 253 39 |

**IDOLS**

| | | | |
|---|---|---|---|
| HEE SAW THE FALLING IDOLS, ALL CONFESSE | SOSPETTO D'HERODE | 125 | 46 109 216 |

**ALL-IDOLIZING**

| | | | |
|---|---|---|---|
| ALL-IDOLIZING WORMES. THAT THUS COULD CROWD | IN GLORIOUS EPIPHANIE | 113 | 52 253 39 |

**IDOLATROUS**

| | | | |
|---|---|---|---|
| ALL THE IDOLATROUS THEFTS DONE BY THIS NIGHT OF DAY. | IN GLORIOUS EPIPHANIE | 150 | 52 253 39 |

**IDOLATRY**

| | | | |
|---|---|---|---|
| BRIGHT IDOL. BLACK IDOLATRY. | IN GLORIOUS EPIPHANIE | 51 | 52 253 39 |
| WAS THEIR MORE BLIND IDOLATRY, | IN GLORIOUS EPIPHANIE | 169 | 52 253 39 |

**IGNOBLE**

| | | | |
|---|---|---|---|
| OF THESE IGNOBLE SHEETS, | PRAYER TO GENTLE-WOMAN | 5 | 52 328 139 |
| BUT NEITHER ARE THERE THOSE IGNOBLE STINGS | DESCRIPTION RELIGIOUS HOUSE | 25 | 52 338 213 |

**ILE**

| | | | |
|---|---|---|---|
| NOW STRETCH THY SELF (FAIRE ILE) AND GROW, SPREAD WIDE | UPON YORKE HIS BIRTH | 2 | 46 176 500 |
| DULL SLUGGISH ILE. WHAT MORE THAN LETHARGY | ON GUNPOWDER-TREASON | 3 | MS 384 458 |

**ILL**

| | | | |
|---|---|---|---|
| I PAINT SO ILL, MY PEECE HAD NEED TO BEE | WITH A PICTURE TO A FRIEND | 1 | 46 156 494 |
| I WRITE SO ILL, MY SLENDER LINE IS SCARCE | WITH A PICTURE TO A FRIEND | 3 | 46 156 494 |
| OF A CRUELL STOP ILL PLAC'T. | ANOTHER ON HERRYS | 40 | 46 170 469 |

**ILL-NURTUR'D**

| | | | |
|---|---|---|---|
| SHAME OF THY MOTHER SOYLE. ILL-NURTUR'D TREE. | HORATIJ ILLE & NEFASTO | 1 | MS 382 530 |

**ILLS**

| | | | |
|---|---|---|---|
| IN DEATH-FULL DESPERATE ILLS WHERE ART AND ALL | OUT OF GROTIUS | 69 | MS 398 198 |

**ILLUSTRIOUS**

| | | | |
|---|---|---|---|
| WHOSE FAIRE ILLUSTRIOUS SOULE, LED HIS FREE THOUGHT | UPON BISHOP ANDREWES PICTURE | 5 | 46 163 490 |
| BY WHOM (AS HEAV'NS ILLUSTRIOUS HAND-MAID) RAIS'D | SOSPETTO D'HERODE | 134 | 46 109 216 |
| ILLUSTRIOUS SWEETNESSE. IN THY FAITHFULL WOMBE, | UPON YORKE HIS BIRTH | 80 | 46 176 500 |
| STUMBLING ON NIGHT. ROUZE THEE ILLUSTRIOUS YOUTH, | ON A FOULE MORNING | 3 | 46 181 495 |
| WHO ROWZING HIS ILLUSTRIOUS TRESSES CAME, | TO THE MORNING | 11 | 46 183 497 |
| THIS ILLUSTRIOUS DAY. | TO THE NAME OF JESUS | 43 | 52 239 30 |
| LOOK FROM THINE OWN ILLUSTRIOUS HOME, | TO THE NAME OF JESUS | 117 | 52 239 30 |
| FROM HIM, WHOM BY A MORE ILLUSTRIOUS LY, | IN GLORIOUS EPIPHANIE | 44 | 52 253 39 |
| IN THIS ILLUSTRIOUS THRONG, YOUR LOFTY FLOUD | TO THE QUEEN'S MAJESTY | 15 | 52 261 47 |
| OR WILL THE WORLD'S ILLUSTRIOUS EYES. | CHARITAS NIMIA | 37 | 52 280 48 |
| ILLUSTRIOUS FLYES, | TO SAME CONCERNING CHOISE | 13 | 52 331 66 |

**IMAGIN'D**

| | | | |
|---|---|---|---|
| IMAGIN'D HIM EXCEEDING OLD. | HIS EPITAPH (HERRYS) | 12 | 46 172 471 |

**IMITATION**

| | | | |
|---|---|---|---|
| BURNE IN THY IMITATION BRIGHT. | AN EPITAPH UPON ASHTON | 32 | 46 192 464 |

IMMEDIATELY

  HERALDS AND MESSENGERS IMMEDIATELY                SOSPETTO D'HERODE                  509  46 109 216

IMMODEST

  NO LONGER SHALL THE IMMODEST LUST                 IN GLORIOUS EPIPHANIE              101  52 253  39

IMMORTALITIES

  THY TOMBE, FAIRE IMMORTALITIES PERFUMED NEST.     EASTER DAY                           6  46 100  26

IMMORTALL

  MONGST THOSE IMMORTALL FIRES, AND ON THE FACE     UPON BISHOP ANDREWES PICTURE        10  46 163 490
  IMMORTALL HONY FOR THE HIVE OF LOVES.             SOSPETTO D'HERODE                   24  46 109 216
  IMMORTALL FLOWERS TO HER FAIRE HAND PRESENT.      SOSPETTO D'HERODE                  100  46 109 216
  IMMORTALL STINGS TO THY GREAT THOUGHTS, AND THEE. SOSPETTO D'HERODE                  464  46 109 216
  TO MAKE IMMORTALL DRESSINGS                       ON A PRAYER BOOKE                   37  46 126 139
  AND CLOSE WITH HIS IMMORTALL KISSES.              ON A PRAYER BOOKE                   97  46 126 139
  MUST BE THE IMMORTALL INSTRUMENT,                 IN MEMORY OF LADY MADRE TERESA      89  46 131  52
  IMMORTALL WELLCOMES WAIT ON THEE.                 IN MEMORY OF LADY MADRE TERESA     129  46 131  52
  WINE OF IMMORTALL MIXTURE, WHICH CAN PROVE        AN APOLOGIE FOR HYMNE (TERESA)      42  46 136  59
  RISE THEN, IMMORTALL MAID.  RELIGION RISE.        ON A TREATISE OF CHARITY             1  46 137  69
  HELP ME TO MEDITATE MINE IMMORTALL SONG.          TO THE NAME OF JESUS                61  52 239  30
  SHE'S CALL'D. HARK, HOW THE DEAR IMMORTALL DOVE   IN GLORIOUS ASSUMPTION B. LADY       7  52 304 114
  IMMORTALL WELLCOMES WAIT FOR THEE.                TERESA                             128  52 315  52
  WINE OF IMMORTALL MIXTURE.  WHICH CAN PROVE       AN APOLOGIE FOR (TERESA) HYMNE      42  52 322  59
  WHAT MAGAZINS OF IMMORTALL ARMES THERE SHINE.     FLAMING HEART                       55  52 324  61
  LET THIS IMMORTALL LIFE WHERERE IT COMES          FLAMING HEART                       81  52 324  61
  TO MAKE IMMORTALL DRESSINGS                       PRAYER TO GENTLE-WOMAN              43  52 328 139
  AND CLOSE WITH HIS IMMORTALL KISSES.              PRAYER TO GENTLE-WOMAN             103  52 328 139
  MAKE BIGGE THY BREST WITH IMMORTALL FIRE,         ALEXIAS THIRD ELEGIE                22  52 336 209
  BELOW. BUT MEDITATES HER IMMORTALL WAY            DESCRIPTION RELIGIOUS HOUSE         38  52 338 213

TH'IMMORTALL

  SHEE'S CALL'D AGAINE. HARKE HOW TH'IMMORTALL DOVE ON THE ASSUMPTION                    7  46 139 114
  MUST BE TH'IMMORTALL INSTRUMENT                   TERESA                              89  52 315  52

IMPARTIALL

  SWINGING A HUGE SITH STANDS IMPARTIALL DEATH.     SOSPETTO D'HERODE                  319  46 109 216

IMPATIENT

  MAKES HIM IMPATIENT OF THE LINGRING LIGHT.        SOSPETTO D'HERODE                  495  46 109 216
  IMPATIENT NATURE HAD TAUGHT MOTION                UPON DEATH OF HERRYS                 6  46 167 466
  THAT IMPATIENT FIRE                               TO THE NAME OF JESUS               214  52 239  30

TH'IMPATIENT

  THUS SPOKE TH'IMPATIENT PRINCE, AND MADE A PAUSE. SOSPETTO D'HERODE                  257  46 109 216
  TH'IMPATIENT LIQUOR, FRETS, AND FOAMES, AND RAVES. SOSPETTO D'HERODE                 486  46 109 216

IMPENETRABLE

  IMPENETRABLE, BOTH TO PRAI'RS AND TEARS,          SOSPETTO D'HERODE                  308  46 109 216

IMPERFECT

  TILL NOW HELL WAS IMPERFECT. IT DID NEED          ON GUNPOWDER-TREASON                61  MS 384 458

IMPERIALL

  THE PARTHIAN STARTS AT ROME'S IMPERIALL NAME,     HORATIJ ILLE & NEFASTO              27  MS 382 530

IMPERIOUS

  WHEN ON A HILL (WHOSE HIGH IMPERIOUS BROW         THE BEGINNING OF HELIODORUS          3  46 158 517
  HIS TORCH IMPERIOUS THOUGH BUT SMALL              OUT OF GREEKE CUPID'S CRYER         54  46 159 519

IMPES

  HIS COURT-FED IMPES AGAINST THIS HATED HEAD.      OUT OF GROTIUS                      48  MS 398 198

ANGELL-IMPS

  OF SWEET-LIPP'D ANGELL-IMPS, THAT SWILL THEIR THROATS MUSICKS DUELL                   76  46 149 535

IMPETUOUS

  THERE RUDE IMPETUOUS RAGE DO'S STORME, AND FRET.  SOSPETTO D'HERODE                  317  46 109 216

IMPIETY

  I SING IMPIETY BEYOND A NAME.                     ON GUNPOWDER-TREASON                 1  MS 384 458

IMPOSSIBLE

  THAT NOT IMPOSSIBLE SHEE                          WISHES SUPPOSED MISTRESSE            2  46 195 479

## IMPROVE

| | | | | | |
|---|---|---|---|---|---|
| TO IMPROVE THAT PRECIOUS HOURE. | ON A PRAYER BOOKE | 99 | 46 | 126 | 139 |
| TO IMPROVE THAT PRETIOUS HOUR, | PRAYER TO GENTLE-WOMAN | 105 | 52 | 328 | 139 |

## INAUSPICIOUS

| | | | | | |
|---|---|---|---|---|---|
| (THOUGH HEAVENS INAUSPICIOUS EYE | LOVES HOROSCOPE | 35 | 46 | 185 | 483 |

## INCAMPT

| | | | | | |
|---|---|---|---|---|---|
| HEAVENS ROYALL HOASTS INCAMPT, THUS SMALL. | ON A PRAYER BOOKE | 6 | 46 | 126 | 139 |

## INCAMP'T

| | | | | | |
|---|---|---|---|---|---|
| HEAVN'S ROYALL HOST. INCAMP'T THUS SMALL | PRAYER TO GENTLE-WOMAN | 12 | 52 | 328 | 139 |

## INCARNATE

| | | | | | |
|---|---|---|---|---|---|
| HOW A PURE SPIRIT SHOULD INCARNATE BEE, | SOSPETTO D'HERODE | 167 | 46 | 109 | 216 |

## INCENDIARY

| | | | | | |
|---|---|---|---|---|---|
| O SWEET INCENDIARY. SHEW HERE THY ART, | FLAMING HEART | 85 | 52 | 324 | 61 |

## INCENSE

| | | | | | |
|---|---|---|---|---|---|
| UP IN CLOUDS OF INCENSE CLIMBE. | THE WEEPER | 106 | 46 | 79 | 120 |
| LIKE A SOFT LUMPE OF INCENSE, HASTED | IN MEMORY OF LADY MADRE TERESA | 114 | 46 | 131 | 52 |
| UP IN CLOUDS OF INCENSE CLIMB. | WEEPER | 142 | 52 | 307 | 120 |
| LIKE A SOFT LUMP OF INCENSE, HASTED | TERESA | 113 | 52 | 315 | 52 |

## INCOMPARABLE

| | | | | | |
|---|---|---|---|---|---|
| CROWN OF AN INCOMPARABLE LIGHT | ON THE ASSUMPTION | 56 | 46 | 139 | 114 |
| CROWN OF A MOST INCOMPARABLE LIGHT | IN GLORIOUS ASSUMPTION B. LADY | 61 | 52 | 304 | 114 |

## INCREASE

| | | | | | |
|---|---|---|---|---|---|
| WA'ST THY FULL VICTORIES FAIRER INCREASE, | UPON DUMBE DEVILL CAST OUT | 3 | 46 | 93 | 14 |
| GROW THOU & THEY. AND BE THY FAIR INCREASE | VEXILLA REGIS | 41 | 52 | 277 | 156 |
| HELP LORD, MY FAITH, MY HOPE INCREASE. | ADORO TE | 33 | 52 | 291 | 172 |

## ENCREASE

| | | | | | |
|---|---|---|---|---|---|
| HEE SAW A THREEFOLD SUN, WITH RICH ENCREASE, | SOSPETTO D'HERODE | 121 | 46 | 109 | 216 |

## T'ENCREASE

| | | | | | |
|---|---|---|---|---|---|
| AND MAY WE LONG. LONG MAY'ST THOU LIVE, T'ENCREASE | UPON YORKE HIS BIRTH | 90 | 46 | 176 | 500 |

## INCREASING

| | | | | | |
|---|---|---|---|---|---|
| A STILL INCREASING BURDEN. WORSE HATH TORNE | OUT OF GROTIUS | 12 | MS | 398 | 198 |

## INCREAST

| | | | | | |
|---|---|---|---|---|---|
| WITH WHICH HIS FEAV'ROUS CARES THEIR COLD INCREAST. | SOSPETTO D'HERODE | 502 | 46 | 109 | 216 |

## INCURR

| | | | | | |
|---|---|---|---|---|---|
| THE MORN INCURR A SWEET MISTAKE. | IN GLORIOUS EPIPHANIE | 2 | 52 | 253 | 39 |

## INDEED

| | | | | | |
|---|---|---|---|---|---|
| OF PHISICK THATS PHISICK INDEED. | IN PRAISE OF LESSIUS | 14 | 46 | 156 | 510 |
| STARS THEY ARE INDEED TOO TRUE, | THE WEEPER | 14 | 46 | 79 | 120 |
| 'TIS CHANG'D INDEED, DID AUTUMN E'RE SUCH BEAUTIES BRING | UPON THORNES FROM LORDS HEAD | 3 | 46 | 96 | 23 |
| BUT WHEN INDEED ALL'S OVERFLOW'D | ON BLEEDING WOUNDS OF LORD | 35 | 46 | 101 | 110 |
| I'VE SEEN INDEED THE HOPEFULL BUD, | UPON DEATH OF DESIRED HERRYS | 31 | 46 | 166 | 467 |
| HE IS REPULST INDEED. BUT YOU ARE UNDONE. | TO COUNTESSE OF DENBIGH | 68 | 52 | 236 | 146 |
| LIFE SEEM'D TO DY, DEATH DY'D INDEED. | OFFICE H. CROSS NINTH | 12 | 52 | 271 | 99 |
| THIS SWEETER BODY, SHALL INDEED BE SUCH. | OFFICE H. CROSS COMPLINE | 8 | 52 | 274 | 105 |
| BUT WHEN INDEED ALL'S OVERFLOW'D | UPON BLEEDING CRUCIFIX | 31 | 52 | 288 | 110 |
| STARRES INDEED THEY ARE TOO TRUE. | WEEPER | 14 | 52 | 307 | 120 |
| HAPPY INDEED, WHO NEVER MISSES | PRAYER TO GENTLE-WOMAN | 104 | 52 | 328 | 139 |
| OF PHYSICK, THAT'S PHYSICK INDEED. | TEMPERANCE | 12 | 52 | 342 | 510 |
| HE IS REPULS'D INDEED, BUT YOU'R UNDONE. | AGAINST IRRESOLUTION AND DELAY | 90 | 52 | 347 | 146 |
| SOME RARE CHOICE TORTURE. NOW 'TIS HELL INDEED. | ON GUNPOWDER-TREASON | 62 | MS | 384 | 458 |

## INDEFINITE

| | | | | | |
|---|---|---|---|---|---|
| O FIX THIS FAIR INDEFINITE. | TO COUNTESSE OF DENBIGH | 31 | 52 | 236 | 146 |

## INDEX

| | | | | | |
|---|---|---|---|---|---|
| THY GOLDEN INDEX. WITH A DUTEOUS HAND | IN GLORIOUS EPIPHANIE | 251 | 52 | 253 | 39 |

## INDIFFERENT

| | | | | | |
|---|---|---|---|---|---|
| THE GENERALL & INDIFFERENT DAY. | IN GLORIOUS EPIPHANIE | 25 | 52 | 253 | 39 |

## INDULGENCE

| | | | |
|---|---|---|---|
| OF SUCH A CHANGE, BUT THAT THE HEAV'NS INDULGENCE | OUT OF VIRGIL | 34 | 46 155 529 |

## INDUSTRY

| | | | |
|---|---|---|---|
| THE SEARCH OF ONE CHILD (CRUELL INDUSTRY.) | OUT OF GROTIUS | 27 | MS 398 198 |

## INEBRIATED

| | | | |
|---|---|---|---|
| A SWEET INEBRIATED EXTASY. | OUT OF GROTIUS | 54 | MS 398 198 |

## INEBRIATING

| | | | |
|---|---|---|---|
| OF PURE INEBRIATING PLEASURES, | ON A PRAYER BOOKE | 114 | 46 126 139 |
| OF PURE INEBRIATING PLEASURES. | PRAYER TO GENTLE-WOMAN | 120 | 52 328 139 |

## INEXORABLE

| | | | |
|---|---|---|---|
| THE WALLS INEXORABLE STEELE, NO HAND | SUSPETTO D'HERODE | 309 | 46 109 216 |

## INFANT

| | | | |
|---|---|---|---|
| WHERE THE NOBLE INFANT LAY. | A HYMNE OF THE NATIVITY | 18 | 46 106 76 |
| OF LANGUAGE TO MY INFANT LIPS, YEE BEST | SOSPETTO D'HERODE | 6 | 46 109 216 |
| THROUGH CLOUDS OF INFANT FLESH. THAT HEE THE OLD | SOSPETTO D'HERODE | 178 | 46 109 216 |
| GAVE OMEN TO HIS INFANT HOWERS, | LOVES HOROSCOPE | 6 | 46 185 483 |
| WHERE THE NOBLE INFANT LAY. | IN HOLY NATIVITY | 18 | 52 246 76 |
| THE EASTERN PRINCES TO THEIR INFANT KING. | ALEXIAS SECONDE ELEGIE | 28 | 52 335 207 |
| AM STILL REFUS'D. BEFORE THE INFANT SHRINE | OUT OF GROTIUS | 36 | MS 398 198 |

## INFANT'S

| | | | |
|---|---|---|---|
| TO FURNISH THE FAIR INFANT'S BED | IN HOLY NATIVITY | 54 | 52 246 76 |

## INFANTS

| | | | |
|---|---|---|---|
| TO FURNISH THE FAIRE INFANTS BED. | A HYMNE OF THE NATIVITY | 38 | 46 106 76 |
| WHICH SHORT-CUT LIVES OF MURDRED INFANTS LEAVE. | SOSPETTO D'HERODE | 344 | 46 109 216 |
| THY INFANTS, AEOLUS, WILL NOT SUFFICE. | ON GUNPOWDER-TREASON | 38 | MS 384 458 |
| HER PAINTED INFANTS, FEDD WITH PLEASENT PAPPE, | AN ELEGY MR STANNINOW | 8 | MS 394 473 |

## INFERIOR

| | | | |
|---|---|---|---|
| AND FITT IT TO SO FARR INFERIOR LYRES. | TO THE NAME OF JESUS | 102 | 52 239 30 |
| THE DIRE FACE OF INFERIOR DARKNES, KIS'T | IN GLORIOUS EPIPHANIE | 52 | 52 253 39 |
| THE FORTUNE OF INFERIOR GEMMES, | WEEPER | 182 | 52 307 120 |

## INFERIOUR

| | | | |
|---|---|---|---|
| SOME WEAK, INFERIOUR, WOMAN SAINT. | FLAMING HEART | 26 | 52 324 61 |

## INFERNALL

| | | | |
|---|---|---|---|
| IN THIS INFERNALL MAJESTY CLOSE SHROWD | UPON GUNPOWDER TREASON | 23 | MS 387 461 |

## INFINITE

| | | | |
|---|---|---|---|
| BOUNDLESSE AND INFINITE | ON A PRAYER BOOKE | 112 | 46 126 139 |
| (INFINITE, SINCE PART OF YOU) | TO THE QUEEN | 6 | 48 215 501 |
| BOUNDLES & INFINITE | PRAYER TO GENTLE-WOMAN | 118 | 52 328 139 |

## INFINITELY

| | | | |
|---|---|---|---|
| NARROW, & LOW, & INFINITELY LESSE | TO THE NAME OF JESUS | 22 | 52 239 30 |

## INFLUENCE

| | | | |
|---|---|---|---|
| WHOSE SOFT INFLUENCE | THE WEEPER | 27 | 46 79 120 |
| AND THY STAFFE, WHOSE INFLUENCE | PSALME 23 | 47 | 46 102 5 |
| SUCK'T THEIR SWEETEST INFLUENCE. | HIS EPITAPH (HERRYS) | 34 | 46 172 471 |
| NUMBERS, AND SWEETNESSE, AND AN INFLUENCE | UPON YORKE HIS BIRTH | 111 | 46 176 500 |
| WITH YOUR DULL INFLUENCE, IT IS FOR YOU. | ON A FOULE MORNING | 33 | 46 181 495 |
| BUT IF HER MILDER INFLUENCE MOVE. | LOVES HOROSCOPE | 33 | 46 185 483 |
| WHOSE SACRED INFLUENCE | WEEPER | 27 | 52 307 120 |
| THE TREASURES OF OUR LIVES, YOUR INFLUENCE. | UPON KINGS CORONATION | 40 | MS 389 454 |
| A PRECIOUS INFLUENCE, AS SWEET AS THEE. | UPON BIRTH PRINCESSE E | 2 | MS 391 456 |

## INFORMES

| | | | |
|---|---|---|---|
| INFORMES IT, IN A SWEET PRAELUDIUM | MUSICKS DUELL | 18 | 46 149 535 |

## TH'INGLORIOUS

| | | | |
|---|---|---|---|
| THE CENTER SHOOK. HER USELESSE VEIL TH'INGLORIOUS TEMPLE TORE. | OFFICE H. CROSS NINTH | 8 | 52 271 99 |

## INHABITANT

| | | | |
|---|---|---|---|
| (THE SWEET INHABITANT OF EACH GLAD TREE. | MUSICKS DUELL | 9 | 46 149 535 |

INHABITE

| THAT THERE INHABITE, THOU ON EVERY DAY | AN ELEGIE ON DR PORTER | 5 MS 395 476 |

INHERITANCE

| MY FAIRE INHERITANCE, HEE CONFINES ME HERE, | SOSPETTO D'HERODE | 212 46 109 216 |
| THE INHERITANCE OF A HASTY GRAVE. | O GLORIOSA DOMINA | 14 52 302 194 |

TO'INHERIT

| AND LET THY LOST SHEEP LIVE TO'INHERIT | VEXILLA REGIS | 45 52 277 156 |

INHERITT

| THAT I INHERITT THY RIGHT HAND. | DIES IRAE | 64 52 298 186 |

INHUMANE

| INHUMANE ERISI-CTHON TOO MAKES ONE. | SOSPETTO D'HERODE | 332 46 109 216 |

INJURY

| REDEEM THIS INJURY OF THY ART. | FLAMING HEART | 41 52 324 61 |

INKE

| DEATH TO THE LIFE, MY INKE SHALL BE THE BLOOD | UPON GUNPOWDER TREASON | 3 MS 386 460 |

INLARGE

| INLARGE THY FLAMING-BRESTED LOVERS | TO THE NAME OF JESUS | 212 52 239 30 |

INMOST

| REBOUNDING, THROUGH HELLS INMOST CAVERNES CAME, | SOSPETTO D'HERODE | 303 46 109 216 |
| IN CENTER OF THEIR INMOST SOULES THEY WORE THEE, | TO THE NAME OF JESUS | 205 52 239 30 |
| CONTEMPT & SCORN CAN SEND WOUNDS TO SEARCH THE INMOST | OFFICE H. CROSS SIXT | 12 52 270 97 |

INNOCENCE

| MY SELFE, MY STRENGTH TOO WITH MY INNOCENCE. | SOSPETTO D'HERODE | 250 46 109 216 |

INQUIRING

| KEEP CLOSE, MY SOUL'S INQUIRING EY. | ADORO TE | 6 52 291 172 |

INRICH'T

| THE RUBY WINDOWES WHICH INRICH'T THE EAST | TO THE NAME OF JESUS | 216 52 239 30 |

INSCRIPTION

| WITH THIS INSCRIPTION O'RE HIS HEAD | ANOTHER ON HERRYS | 61 46 170 469 |

INSINUATION

| AND BY A SOFT INSINUATION, MIXT | OUT OF VIRGIL | 7 46 155 529 |

INSTILE

| GLADNESSE SHALL CLOATH THE EARTH, WE WILL INSTILE | ON A FOULE MORNING | 9 46 181 495 |

INSTINCT

| HIS NIMBLE HANDS INSTINCT THEN TAUGHT EACH STRING | MUSICKS DUELL | 27 46 149 535 |
| THEN VENUS MILD INSTINCT (AT SET TIMES) YEILDS | OUT OF VIRGIL | 11 46 155 529 |

INSTRUCTED

| AND IS INSTRUCTED BY THY GLASSY WAVE | AN ELEGIE ON DR PORTER | 23 MS 395 476 |

HEAVN-INSTRUCTED

| THE HEAVN-INSTRUCTED HOUSE OF FAITH | LAUDA SION SALVATOREM | 31 52 294 178 |

INSTRUMENT

| MUST BE THE IMMORTALL INSTRUMENT, | IN MEMORY OF LADY MADRE TERESA | 89 46 131 52 |
| MUST BE TH'IMMORTALL INSTRUMENT | TERESA | 89 52 315 52 |

INSTRUMENTS

| SWORDS, SPEARS, WITH ALL THE FATALL INSTRUMENTS | SOSPETTO D'HERODE | 326 46 109 216 |

INTANGLES

| INTANGLES HIS LOST THOUGHTS, PAST GETTING OUT. | SOSPETTO D'HERODE | 192 46 109 216 |

INTELECTUALL

| A SOULE WHOSE INTELECTUALL BEAMES | IN PRAISE OF LESSIUS | 31 46 156 510 |

## INTELLECTUALL

| | | | | | |
|---|---|---|---|---|---|
| OR YOU, MORE NOBLE ARCHITECTS OF INTELLECTUALL NOISE, | TO THE NAME OF JESUS | 77 | 52 | 239 | 30 |
| BY THY LARG DRAUGHTS OF INTELLECTUALL DAY. | FLAMING HEART | 97 | 52 | 324 | 61 |
| HOME TO THE ORIGINALL SOURSE OF LIGHT & INTELLECTUALL | DESCRIPTION RELIGIOUS HOUSE | 39 | 52 | 338 | 213 |
| A SOUL, WHOSE INTELLECTUALL BEAMES | TEMPERANCE | 29 | 52 | 342 | 510 |
| POSETH HIS PROUDEST INTELLECTUALL POWER. | SOSPETTO D'HERODE | 166 | 46 | 109 | 216 |

## INTELLIGENCES

| | | | | | |
|---|---|---|---|---|---|
| WHOSE VAST INTELLIGENCES TUN'D THE POLES | UPON YORKE HIS BIRTH | 36 | 46 | 176 | 500 |

## INTELLIGENTIALL

| | | | | | |
|---|---|---|---|---|---|
| UPWARDS, & PRESSE ON FOR THE PURE INTELLIGENTIALL PREY. | IN GLORIOUS EPIPHANIE | 222 | 52 | 253 | 39 |

## INTENT

| | | | | | |
|---|---|---|---|---|---|
| THE NORTH FORGOT HIS FIERCE INTENT, | A HYMNE OF THE NATIVITY | 25 | 46 | 106 | 76 |
| THE NORTH FORGOTT HIS FEIRCE INTENT. | IN HOLY NATIVITY | 26 | 52 | 246 | 76 |

## INTENTS

| | | | | | |
|---|---|---|---|---|---|
| FELL EXECUTIONERS OF FOULE INTENTS, | SOSPETTO D'HERODE | 324 | 46 | 109 | 216 |

## INTENTIONS

| | | | | | |
|---|---|---|---|---|---|
| THE HORRID SUMME OF HIS INTENTIONS TELL. | SOSPETTO D'HERODE | 370 | 46 | 109 | 216 |

## INTERCEPTED

| | | | | | |
|---|---|---|---|---|---|
| AND POORE FOWLES INTERCEPTED IN THEIR FLIGHT. | SOSPETTO D'HERODE | 376 | 46 | 109 | 216 |

## INTERCOURSE

| | | | | | |
|---|---|---|---|---|---|
| O COSTLY INTERCOURSE | SANCTA MARIA DOLORUM | 21 | 52 | 283 | 162 |

## INTERIOUR

| | | | | | |
|---|---|---|---|---|---|
| BUT TOUCH'T WITH AN INTERIOUR RAY. | TO THE NAME OF JESUS | 2 | 52 | 239 | 30 |

## INTERPRET

| | | | | | |
|---|---|---|---|---|---|
| THAT MIGHT INTERPRET OUR FAIRE CYNTHIA'S WORTH, | UPON BIRTH PRINCESSE E | 30 | MS | 391 | 456 |

## INTERPRETERS

| | | | | | |
|---|---|---|---|---|---|
| OF ALL INTERPRETERS READ NATURE TRUE. | UPON STANINOUGH'S DEATH | 30 | 46 | 175 | 475 |
| OF ALL INTERPRETERS READ NATURE TRUE. | DEATH'S LECTURE | 32 | 52 | 340 | 475 |

## INTIRE

| | | | | | |
|---|---|---|---|---|---|
| HOLD BUT THY FAITH INTIRE AS HE | LAUDA SION SALVATOREM | 56 | 52 | 294 | 178 |

## INTOLERABLE

| | | | | | |
|---|---|---|---|---|---|
| OF INTOLERABLE JOYES. | TERESA | 99 | 52 | 315 | 52 |

## INTOLLERABLE

| | | | | | |
|---|---|---|---|---|---|
| OF INTOLLERABLE JOYES. | IN MEMORY OF LADY MADRE TERESA | 99 | 46 | 131 | 52 |

## INTREAT

| | | | | | |
|---|---|---|---|---|---|
| WOOE, INTREAT, AND CRYING SAY | OUT OF GREEKE CUPID'S CRYER | 68 | 46 | 159 | 519 |

## HEAV'N-INTREATED

| | | | | | |
|---|---|---|---|---|---|
| WHAT HEAV'N-INTREATED HEART IS THIS. | TO COUNTESSE OF DENBIGH | 1 | 52 | 236 | 146 |

## INUNDATION

| | | | | | |
|---|---|---|---|---|---|
| A SUBTLE INUNDATION OF QUICKE FOOD | OUT OF GROTIUS | 61 | MS | 398 | 198 |

## INVADE

| | | | | | |
|---|---|---|---|---|---|
| ALL POINTED IN HIS HEART SEEM'D TO INVADE HIM. | SOSPETTO D'HERODE | 476 | 46 | 109 | 216 |
| O MEET THE ANGRY GOD, INVADE HIS EYES, | TO THE MORNING | 36 | 46 | 183 | 497 |
| SHALL WITH A VIGOROUS GUESSE INVADE | IN GLORIOUS EPIPHANIE | 192 | 52 | 253 | 39 |

## T'INVEST

| | | | | | |
|---|---|---|---|---|---|
| VILE HUMANE NATURE MEANS HE NOW T'INVEST | SOSPETTO D'HERODE | 227 | 46 | 109 | 216 |

## INVIOLATE

| | | | | | |
|---|---|---|---|---|---|
| YET KEEPE INVIOLATE HER VIRGIN FLOWER. | SOSPETTO D'HERODE | 164 | 46 | 109 | 216 |

| | | | |
|---|---|---|---|
| INVITATION | | | |
| THESE NEED NOE INVITATION. ONELY THOU, | UPON GUNPOWDER TREASON | 19 | MS 387 461 |
| INVITED | | | |
| INVITED HIM NO MORE TO HIDE | UPON DEATH OF DESIRED HERRYS | 37 | 46 168 467 |
| H'INVOKE | | | |
| GIVES LIFE TO SOME NEW GRACE. THUS DOTH H'INVOKE | MUSICKS DUELL | 132 | 46 149 535 |
| INVOLVING | | | |
| OF HEAVNS, THE SELF INVOLVING SETT OF SPHEARS | TO THE NAME OF JESUS | 30 | 52 239 30 |
| IRE | | | |
| SHOTT FROM HIS FLAMING EYE, HAD THAW'D IT'S IRE, | AN ELEGY MR STANNINOW | 32 | MS 394 473 |
| IRON-POINTED | | | |
| EVEN THE IRON-POINTED PEN. | ANOTHER ON HERRYS | 33 | 46 170 469 |
| IRON-SCEPTRED | | | |
| ASSIST THE THRONE OF TH' IRON-SCEPTRED KING. | SOSPETTO D'HERODE | 66 | 46 109 216 |
| IRRESOLUTE | | | |
| BUT KILL THIS REBELL-WORD, IRRESOLUTE | TO COUNTESSE OF DENBIGH | 40 | 52 236 146 |
| ISAACKS | | | |
| BUT ISAACKS ISSUE THE PECULIAR HEYRES, | OUT OF GROTIUS | 39 | MS 398 198 |
| ISACK | | | |
| THE RANSOM'D ISACK, & HIS RAMME. | LAUDA SION SALVATOREM | 67 | 52 294 178 |
| ISLAND | | | |
| AND SHEE'S AN ISLAND TRUELY FORTUNATE. | ON GUNPOWDER-TREASON | 10 | MS 384 458 |
| ISLE | | | |
| THOU BY THY SELFE MAIST SIT, (BLEST ISLE) AND SEE | UPON YORKE HIS BIRTH | 25 | 46 176 500 |
| AND SEEM'D TO MAKE AN ISLE, BUT MADE A WORLD. | UPON YORKE HIS BIRTH | 28 | 46 176 500 |
| SHALL KISSE HIS GOLDEN BURTHEN. THOU, GLAD ISLE, | UPON KINGS CORONATION | 5 | MS 389 454 |
| ISLES | | | |
| AND LEAVE EMBRACING OF THE ISLES, LEAST HEE | UPON GUNPOWDER TREASON | 33 | MS 386 460 |
| ISSUE | | | |
| FOUND THE PURE ISSUE OF HIS THOUGHT. | OUT OF GREEKE CUPID'S CRYER | 24 | 46 159 519 |
| BUT ISAACKS ISSUE THE PECULIAR HEYRES, | OUT OF GROTIUS | 39 | MS 398 198 |
| ITE | | | |
| WHEN THE DREAD ITE SHALL DIVIDE | DIES IRAE | 61 | 52 298 186 |
| IVORY | | | |
| NOR IVORY COUCHES COSTLYER SLUMBERS KEEPING. | DESCRIPTION RELIGIOUS HOUSE | 4 | 52 338 213 |
| AND SAY THAT IVORY HER FRONT COMPOSES. | UPON BIRTH PRINCESSE E | 46 | MS 391 456 |
| AT TH' IVORY TRIBUNALL OF YOUR HAND | AT TH' IVORY TRIBUNALL | 1 | MS 397 492 |
| JAMES | | | |
| HENRY AND JAMES, OR MARS AND PHOEBUS RATHER. | UPON YORKE HIS BIRTH | 31 | 46 176 500 |
| 'TIS BUT THE SAME IS SAID, HENRY AND JAMES | UPON YORKE HIS BIRTH | 33 | 46 176 500 |
| JARRES | | | |
| THAT JARRES, AND SPOILES SWEET CONSORT SOE. | UPON DEATH OF A FREIND | 8 | MS 393 477 |
| JAYLOR | | | |
| THE PRISONERS LOOSE, THE JAYLOR BOUND. | OFFICE H. CROSS THIRD | 15 | 52 268 93 |
| JEALOUS | | | |
| HAND (O WHAT DARES NOT JEALOUS GREATNESSE.) TORE | SOSPETTO D'HERODE | 3 | 46 109 216 |
| THE WORME OF JEALOUS ENVY AND UNREST, | SOSPETTO D'HERODE | 493 | 46 109 216 |
| JEALOUSIE | | | |
| POORE JEALOUSIE. WHY SHOULD HE WISH TO PREY | SOSPETTO D'HERODE | 519 | 46 109 216 |

JERUSALEM

 IF NOT JERUSALEM TO THEE.         PSALME 137     14   46   104    7
 AH THEE JERUSALEM. AH SOONER MAY      PSALME 137     15   46   104    7

JEST

 IN HEBREW NUMBERS. THEN (O CRUELL JEST.)    PSALME 137      9   46   104    7
 OF YOUR LEARN'D LYES. HERE YOU'L FIND NO SUCH JEST.   ALEXIAS THIRD ELEGIE   42   52   336   209

JESU

 JESU, NO MORE, IT IS FULL TIDE        ON BLEEDING WOUNDS OF LORD   1   46   101   110
 JESU, NO MORE. IT IS FULL TIDE.        UPON BLEEDING CRUCIFIX    1   52   288   110
 JESU MASTER, JUST & TRUE.          LAUDA SION SALVATOREM    69   52   294   178

JETT

 SEE ALL IN MOURNING NOW. THE WALLES ARE JETT,   AN ELEGIE ON DR PORTER    7   MS   395   476

JETTY

 SHOULD BEATE HER HEADLONG FROM HER JETTY THRONE.   UPON GUNPOWDER TREASON   26   MS   386   460

JEWELL

 THIS THINE EYES JEWELL IN HER EARE.      THE TEARE        12   46    84    50
 SPARE THIS ONE JEWELL. I'LE BE DIVES STILL.    DIVES ASKING A DROP    4   46    96    18
 THIS IS NATURES CHOYCEST JEWELL.       UPON DEATH OF DESIRED HERRYS   4   46   168   467

JEWELS

 SORROWES BEST JEWELS LYE IN THESE       THE WEEPER       47   46    79   120

JEWELLS

 JEWELLS, BUT TO DECLARE          WISHES SUPPOSED MISTRESSE   47   46   195   479

JEZABELL

 MEDAEA, JEZABELL, MANY A MEAGER WITCH .     SOSPETTO D'HERODE     338   46   109   216

JOLLY

 AN EVERLASTING SPRING, THE JOLLY YEARE     OUT OF VIRGIL       26   46   155   529

JORDAN

 WHERE JORDAN MELTS HIS CHRYSTALL. TO MAKE FAIRE   SOSPETTO D'HERODE     85   46   109   216

JOSEPH

 A JOSEPH DID BETROTH           UPON OUR SAVIOURS TOMBE    5   46    93    25
 JOSEPH THE KINGS DEAD BROTHERS SHAPE SHE TAKES.   SOSPETTO D'HERODE    419   46   109   216
 A JOSEPH DID BETROTH           TO OUR B. LORD       5   52   279    25

JOVE

 YET SUCH A ONE AS (JOVE KNOWES HOW)      OUT OF GREEKE CUPID'S CRYER   46   46   159   519
 FROM OF HER CENTER, HAD NOT JOVE UPHELD     UPON KINGS CORONATION    10   MS   390   453
 BRIGHT GODDESSE. (WHETHER JOVE THY FATHER BE.   EX EUPHORMIONE       1   MS   392   525
 OR JOVE A FATHER WILL BE MADE BY THEE)      EX EUPHORMIONE       2   MS   392   525

JOVE'S

 ATLAS SHALL BE TRIPT UPP, JOVE'S GATE SHALL FEELE   ON GUNPOWDER-TREASON    43   MS   384   458

JOVES

 THOUGH EVERY DIAMOND IN JOVES CROWNE      LOVES HOROSCOPE       37   46   185   483
 JOVES TWINCKLING TAPERS, THAT DOE LIGHT THE WORLD.   UPON GUNPOWDER TREASON   27   MS   386   460
 BUT WHEN JOVES WINGED HERALDS THIS ESPIED,    UPON GUNPOWDER TREASON   53   MS   386   460

JOY

 WITHIN THE LIPS OF LOVE AND JOY DOTH DWELL    UPON ASSE THAT BORE SAVIOUR   3   46    90    19
 WELCOME MY GRIEFE, MY JOY. HOW DEARE'S      VERILY YE SHALL WEEP     1   46    95    22
 GIV'ST JOY, EVEN WHEN THOU GIVEST NONE.      VERILY YE SHALL WEEP     6   46    95    22
 YET IS THE JOY I TAKE IN'T SMALL OR NONE.     UPON OUR LORDS LAST DISCOURSE   3   46    95    21
 HEE IN THIS OUR GENERALL JOY,         A HYMNE OF THE NATIVITY    5   46   106    76
 IS WHAT IN SIGNE OF JOY AMONG THE BLEST     SOSPETTO D'HERODE    197   46   109   216
 WHAT JOY, WHAT BLISSE,            ON A PRAYER BOOKE     116   46   126   139
 WHAT JOY SHALL SEIZE THY SOULE WHEN SHEE     IN MEMORY OF LADY MADRE TERESA   134   46   131    52
 TEMPER'D 'TWIXT COLD DESPAIRE, AND TORRID JOY.   ON HOPE         83   46   143    71
 JOY OF GOODNESSE, LOVE OF ART,         UPON DEATH OF DESIRED HERRYS   9   46   168   467
 AND SEE SUCH NAMES OF JOY SIT WHITE UPON     UPON YORKE HIS BIRTH    97   46   176   500
 TO ALL OUR WORLD OF WELL-STOLN JOY       IN HOLY NATIVITY       5   52   246    76
 NOR MAY WE MISSE THE JOY TO MEET IN YOU     TO THE QUEEN'S MAJESTY    23   52   261    47
 THE BLISSFULL SPRINGS OF JOY, FROM WHOSE ALL-CHEARING   OFFICE H. CROSS PRIME   7   52   267    91
 WHAT JOY, WHAT BLISSE,            PRAYER TO GENTLE-WOMAN   122   52   328   139
 TEMPER TWIXT CHILL DESPAIR, & TORRID JOY.     (ON) HOPE         43   52   345    71
 DID EVER GREIFE, & JOY IN ONE POORE HEART     LUKE 2. QUAERIT JESUM    3   MS   379    11
 AND WHERE IS JOY.             LUKE 2. QUAERIT JESUM    6   MS   379    11

PAGE 210

| | | | | |
|---|---|---|---|---|
| MY JOY IS GONE. | LUKE 2. QUAERIT JESUM | 10 | MS 379 | 11 |
| OH COME THEN. BRING THY MOTHER HER LOST JOY. | LUKE 2. QUAERIT JESUM | 15 | MS 379 | 11 |
| THAT SWIM'ST AS DEEPE IN JOY, AS SEAS, NOW SMILE | UPON KINGS CORONATION | 6 | MS 389 | 454 |
| DOE I NOT SEE JOY KEEPE HIS REVELS NOW, | UPON KINGS CORONATION | 19 | MS 389 | 454 |
| I CANNOT HOLD, SUCH A SPRING TIDE OF JOY | UPON BIRTH PRINCESSE E | 13 | MS 391 | 456 |
| WHOSE SNOWY CHEEKES, LEAST JOY SHOULD BE EXPREST, | AN ELEGIE ON DR PORTER | 9 | MS 395 | 476 |

JOY-CONDUCTED

| | | | | |
|---|---|---|---|---|
| TO MY JOY-CONDUCTED FEET, | PSALME 23 | 31 | 46 102 | 5 |

JOY'D

| | | | | |
|---|---|---|---|---|
| IN HIM GOODNESSE JOY'D TO SEE | HIS EPITAPH (HERRYS) | 21 | 46 172 | 471 |

JOYE

| | | | | |
|---|---|---|---|---|
| FOR JOYE OF THIER NEATE COATES, BUT WOULD HAVE TORE | UPON GUNPOWDER TREASON | 46 | MS 386 | 460 |
| DOTH BLITH APOLLO CLOATH THE HEAVENS WITH JOYE, | AN ELEGY MR STANNINOW | 11 | MS 394 | 473 |

JOYES

| | | | | |
|---|---|---|---|---|
| IN RIPER JOYES, MORE SHALL BEE HIS | OUT OF GREEKE CUPID'S CRYER | 15 | 46 159 | 519 |
| IN JOYES WHITE ANNALS LIVE THIS HOURE, | EASTER DAY | 10 | 46 100 | 26 |
| THE HEAD OF ALL MY HOPE-NURST JOYES, | PSALME 137 | 26 | 46 104 | 7 |
| WHILE THE REFLECTION OF THY FOREPAST JOYES, | SOSPETTO D'HERODE | 243 | 46 109 | 216 |
| OF HIDDEN SWEETS, AND HOLY JOYES, | ON A PRAYER BOOKE | 58 | 46 126 | 139 |
| OF JOYES, AND RARIFYED DELIGHTS. | ON A PRAYER BOOKE | 74 | 46 126 | 139 |
| FAREWELL ALL PLEASURES, SPORTS AND JOYES, | IN MEMORY OF LADY MADRE TERESA | 59 | 46 131 | 52 |
| OF INTOLLERABLE JOYES. | IN MEMORY OF LADY MADRE TERESA | 99 | 46 131 | 52 |
| THY SELFE SHALT FEEL THINE OWNE FULL JOYES. | IN MEMORY OF LADY MADRE TERESA | 121 | 46 131 | 52 |
| THOUGH, OUR POORE JOYES ARE PARTED SO, | ON THE ASSUMPTION | 37 | 46 139 | 114 |
| OF EVERLASTING JOYES BATH THY WHITE BREST. | ON THE ASSUMPTION | 58 | 46 139 | 114 |
| HOPES CHASTE KISSE WRONGS NO MORE JOYES MAIDENHEAD | ON HOPE | 39 | 46 143 | 71 |
| OF A MAD STORME THESE BLOOMY JOYES ALL TORE, | UPON DEATH OF HERRYS | 33 | 46 167 | 466 |
| INTO ETERNITY, AND CIRCULAR JOYES | UPON DEATH OF HERRYS | 37 | 46 167 | 466 |
| SCARCE WAKT. LIKE WAS THE CRIMSON OF THEIR JOYES, | UPON YORKE HIS BIRTH | 63 | 46 176 | 500 |
| WHERE NOUGHT BUT SMILES, AND RUDDY JOYES ARE WORNE. | ON A FOULE MORNING | 36 | 46 181 | 495 |
| WHILE OUR JOYES SO MULTIPLY, | OUT OF CATULLUS | 19 | 46 194 | 523 |
| JOYES, THAT CONFESSE. | WISHES SUPPOSED MISTRESSE | 67 | 46 195 | 479 |
| VESSELLS OF VOCALL JOYES, | TO THE NAME OF JESUS | 76 | 52 239 | 30 |
| THE BIRTH OF OUR BRIGHT JOYES. | TO THE NAME OF JESUS | 164 | 52 239 | 30 |
| OF JOYES. | IN GLORIOUS EPIPHANIE | 9 | 52 253 | 39 |
| HER'S, & THE WHOLE WORLD'S JOYES, | SANCTA MARIA DOLORUM | 6 | 52 283 | 162 |
| OF SO JUST & SOLEMN JOYES, | LAUDA SION SALVATOREM | 16 | 52 294 | 178 |
| OF EVERLASTING JOYES BATH THY WHITE BREST. | IN GLORIOUS ASSUMPTION B. LADY | 63 | 52 304 | 114 |
| FAREWELL, ALL PLEASURES, SPORTS, & JOYES, | TERESA | 59 | 52 315 | 52 |
| OF INTOLERABLE JOYES. | TERESA | 99 | 52 315 | 52 |
| THY SELFE SHALL FEEL THINE OWN FULL JOYES | TERESA | 120 | 52 315 | 52 |
| WHAT JOYES SHALL SEIZE THY SOUL, WHEN SHE | TERESA | 133 | 52 315 | 52 |
| OF HIDDEN SWEETS & HOLY JOYES. | PRAYER TO GENTLE-WOMAN | 64 | 52 328 | 139 |
| OF JOYES & RAREFY'D DELIGHTS. | PRAYER TO GENTLE-WOMAN | 80 | 52 328 | 139 |
| THOUGH ALL THE JOYES I HAD FLEED HENCE WITH THEE | ALEXIAS SECONDE ELEGIE | 1 | 52 335 | 207 |
| FALSE LIGHTS OF FLAIRING GEMMES, TUMULTUOUS JOYES, | DESCRIPTION RELIGIOUS HOUSE | 5 | 52 338 | 213 |
| SILENCE, & SACRED REST, PEACE, & PURE JOYES. | DESCRIPTION RELIGIOUS HOUSE | 32 | 52 338 | 213 |
| NOR WILL THE VIRGIN JOYES WE WED | (ON) HOPE | 15 | 52 345 | 71 |
| MY JOYES, & HEE ARE GONE. MY GREIFE, & I | LUKE 2. QUAERIT JESUM | 11 | MS 379 | 11 |
| THEIR NOW LOST JOYES. | LUKE 2. QUAERIT JESUM | 44 | MS 379 | 11 |
| BUT SMILES, & RUDDY JOYES, & AT THIS DAY | UPON KINGS CORONATION | 39 | MS 390 | 453 |
| THE GOLDEN HARVEST OF OUR JOYES, THE NOONE | AN ELEGY MR STANNINOW | 42 | MS 394 | 473 |
| THE MOTHERS JOYES IN AN UNTIMELY CROP. | OUT OF GROTIUS | 26 | MS 398 | 198 |

VIRGIN-JOYES

| | | | | |
|---|---|---|---|---|
| NOR WILL THE VIRGIN-JOYES WEE WED | ON HOPE | 35 | 46 143 | 71 |

JOYE'S

| | | | | |
|---|---|---|---|---|
| HOPE'S CHAST STEALTH HARMES NO MORE JOYE'S MAIDENHEAD | (ON) HOPE | 19 | 52 345 | 71 |

JOYFULL

| | | | | |
|---|---|---|---|---|
| A CHOICER LESSON THEN THE JOYFULL BREST | TO THE NAME OF JESUS | 107 | 52 239 | 30 |
| WOFULL & JOYFULL WE | OFFICE H. CROSS EVENSONG | 10 | 52 273 | 101 |
| AND MISTS OF GREIFE, DARE FORCE A JOYFULL LIGHT. | UPON KINGS CORONATION | 16 | MS 389 | 454 |
| THE JOYFULL SPHAERES WITH A DELICIOUS SOUND | UPON KINGS CORONATION | 21 | MS 390 | 453 |
| THE LAUGHING MEADES, AS JOYFULL TO BEHOLD | UPON KINGS CORONATION | 27 | MS 390 | 453 |
| DANCE, LIKE THE NIMBLE SPHAERES, A JOYFULL ROUND. | UPON BIRTH PRINCESSE E | 32 | MS 391 | 456 |

JOYNE

| | | | | |
|---|---|---|---|---|
| BEFORE THE WORLD. OBEDIENT LO. I JOYNE | OUT OF GROTIUS | 4 | MS 398 | 198 |

JOYNT

| | | | | |
|---|---|---|---|---|
| WITH TENDER ACCENTS, AND SEVERELY JOYNT IT | MUSICKS DUELL | 40 | 46 149 | 535 |

JUCY

| | | | | |
|---|---|---|---|---|
| EACH BODY'S PLUMP AND JUCY, ALL THINGS FULL | OUT OF VIRGIL | 15 | 46 155 | 529 |

JUDAHS

| | | | | | |
|---|---|---|---|---|---|
| AND FROM THE HEAD OF JUDAHS HOUSE QUITE TORNE | SOSPETTO D'HERODE | 405 | 46 | 109 | 216 |

JUDGE

| | | | | | |
|---|---|---|---|---|---|
| LEAVE, LEAVE, FOR SHAME, OR ELSE (GOOD JUDGE) DECREE, | TO PONTIUS WASHING HANDS | 15 | 46 | 94 | 23 |
| THE JUDGE OF TORMENTS, AND THE KING OF TEARES. | SOSPETTO D'HERODE | 41 | 46 | 109 | 216 |
| OF A SURE JUDGE, FROM WHOSE SHARP RAY | DIES IRAE | 3 | 52 | 298 | 186 |
| O THAT JUDGE. WHOSE HAND, WHOSE EYE | DIES IRAE | 19 | 52 | 298 | 186 |
| MERCY (MY JUDGE) MERCY I CRY | DIES IRAE | 41 | 52 | 298 | 186 |
| MY HOPE, MY FEAR. MY JUDGE, MY FREIND. | DIES IRAE | 67 | 52 | 298 | 186 |

JUDG'D

| | | | | | |
|---|---|---|---|---|---|
| AND THIS LOV'D SOUL, JUDG'D WORTH NO LESSE | DIES IRAE | 35 | 52 | 298 | 186 |

JUDGEMENT

| | | | | | |
|---|---|---|---|---|---|
| THAT, THE CREATION IS. THE JUDGEMENT, THIS. | ON FRONTISPIECE ISAACSONS | 23 | 46 | 191 | 491 |

JUDGMENT-SEAT

| | | | | | |
|---|---|---|---|---|---|
| THAT SABLE JUDGMENT-SEAT SHALL BY NEW LAWES | IN GLORIOUS EPIPHANIE | 145 | 52 | 253 | 39 |

JUDGEMENTS

| | | | | | |
|---|---|---|---|---|---|
| THESE MARKES MAY BEE YOUR JUDGEMENTS GUIDE. | OUT OF GREEKE CUPID'S CRYER | 18 | 46 | 159 | 519 |

JUNE

| | | | | | |
|---|---|---|---|---|---|
| THOUGH NOW 'TIS NEITHER MAY NOR JUNE | THOUGH NOW 'TIS NEITHER | 1 | MS | 397 | 492 |

JURYES

| | | | | | |
|---|---|---|---|---|---|
| FOR JURYES KING AN ENEMY, EVEN WORTH | OUT OF GROTIUS | 21 | MS | 398 | 198 |

JUST

| | | | | | |
|---|---|---|---|---|---|
| THY TEARES JUST CADENCE STILL KEEPS TIME. | THE WEEPER | 104 | 46 | 79 | 120 |
| DEATH ONELY BY THIS DAYES JUST DOOME IS FORC'T TO DYE. | EASTER DAY | 15 | 46 | 100 | 26 |
| THRIV'D IN THESE HAPPY GROUNDS, THE EARTH'S JUST PRIDE, | UPON DEATH OF HERRYS | 3 | 46 | 167 | 466 |
| HER WHOSE JUST BAYES, | WISHES SUPPOSED MISTRESSE | 109 | 46 | 195 | 479 |
| IT'S SEAT YOUR SOUL'S JUST CENTER BE. | TO COUNTESSE OF DENBIGH | 56 | 52 | 236 | 146 |
| SHALL THEN WITH JUST CONFUSION, BOW | TO THE NAME OF JESUS | 238 | 52 | 239 | 30 |
| THE SINNER'S PARDON, & THE JUST MAN'S PEACE. | VEXILLA REGIS | 42 | 52 | 277 | 156 |
| OF SO JUST & SOLEMN JOYES, | LAUDA SION SALVATOREM | 16 | 52 | 294 | 178 |
| JESU MASTER, JUST & TRUE. | LAUDA SION SALVATOREM | 69 | 52 | 294 | 178 |
| JUST MERCY THEN, THY RECKNING BE | DIES IRAE | 37 | 52 | 298 | 186 |
| BUT WALKES & UNSHORN WOODS. AND SOULES, JUST SO | DESCRIPTION RELIGIOUS HOUSE | 9 | 52 | 338 | 213 |
| HAD DIED JUST IN HER DELIVERY. | UPON GUNPOWDER TREASON | 52 | MS | 386 | 460 |
| OF BLISSE, DEBASE THEE. BUT WITH A JUST PRIDE | UPON KINGS CORONATION | 8 | MS | 389 | 454 |
| MURDRED THE EARTH'S JUST PRIDE WITH A RUDE KISSE. | AN ELEGY MR STANNINOW | 48 | MS | 394 | 473 |

JUSTER

| | | | | | |
|---|---|---|---|---|---|
| A GENTLER MORN, A JUSTER SUN. | IN GLORIOUS EPIPHANIE | 74 | 52 | 253 | 39 |

JUSTICE

| | | | | | |
|---|---|---|---|---|---|
| JUSTICE HATH LOST HER HAND, THE LAW HER HEAD. | AN ELEGIE ON DR PORTER | 15 | MS | 395 | 476 |

JUSTLE

| | | | | | |
|---|---|---|---|---|---|
| JUSTLE DOWN MOUNTAINS. KINGS COURTS SHALL BE SENT, | ON GUNPOWDER-TREASON | 41 | MS | 384 | 458 |

JUSTLY

| | | | | | |
|---|---|---|---|---|---|
| JUSTLY, GREAT NATURE, MAY'ST THOU BRAG AND TELL | UPON YORKE HIS BIRTH | 49 | 46 | 176 | 500 |
| FOR IF YOU SETT, WHO MAY NOT JUSTLY FEARE, | UPON KINGS CORONATION | 41 | MS | 389 | 454 |

KEEL

| | | | | | |
|---|---|---|---|---|---|
| HER KEEL CUTTS NOT THE WAVES WHERE THESE WINDS STIRR | (ON) HOPE | 33 | 52 | 345 | 71 |

KEELE

| | | | | | |
|---|---|---|---|---|---|
| HER KEELE CUTS NOT THE WAVES, WHERE OUR WINDS STIRRE, | ON HOPE | 73 | 46 | 143 | 71 |

KEEP

| | | | | | |
|---|---|---|---|---|---|
| FROWNE I. AND CAN GREAT NATURE KEEP HER SEAT. | SOSPETTO D'HERODE | 205 | 46 | 109 | 216 |
| LET CONSTANT USE BUT KEEP IT BRIGHT, | ON A PRAYER BOOKE | 16 | 46 | 126 | 139 |
| AND KEEP THE DIVELLS HOLY DAY. | ON A PRAYER BOOKE | 47 | 46 | 126 | 139 |
| AND CLOSE IN HIS EMBRACES KEEP, | IN MEMORY OF LADY MADRE TERESA | 107 | 46 | 131 | 52 |
| AS KEEP ACCOUNT OF THE LAMBES WARRES | IN MEMORY OF LADY MADRE TERESA | 155 | 46 | 131 | 52 |
| IN THEIR SAD RUINES . NOR RELIGION KEEP | ON A TREATISE OF CHARITY | 34 | 46 | 137 | 69 |
| ROB THE RICH STORE HER CABINETS KEEP, | AN HIMNE FOR CIRCUMCISION | 18 | 46 | 141 | 37 |
| KEEP THE FREE HEART FROM IT'S OWN HANDS. | TO COUNTESSE OF DENBIGH | 20 | 52 | 236 | 146 |
| TO KEEP IT FAIR, | TO THE NAME OF JESUS | 113 | 52 | 239 | 30 |
| TO THEE, DREAD LAMB. WHOSE LOVE MUST KEEP | IN HOLY NATIVITY | 101 | 52 | 246 | 76 |
| SEARCH WHAT THE WORLD'S CLOSE CABINETS KEEP, | NEW YEAR'S DAY | 18 | 52 | 251 | 37 |

PAGE 212

## KEEP

| | | | | |
|---|---|---|---|---|
| KEEP WARM THY PRAYSE | CHARITAS NIMIA | 26 | 52 | 280 48 |
| NOR KEEP SUCH NOBLE SORROWES COMPANY. | SANCTA MARIA DOLORUM | 14 | 52 | 283 162 |
| AS SERVES TO KEEP ALIVE HER DEATH. | SANCTA MARIA DOLORUM | 40 | 52 | 283 162 |
| KEEP CLOSE, MY SOUL'S INQUIRING EY. | ADORO TE | 6 | 52 | 291 172 |
| TO KEEP PACE WITH THOSE POWRFULL WORDS. | ADORO TE | 14 | 52 | 291 172 |
| O BY THY SELF VOUCHSAFE TO KEEP, | LAUDA SION SALVATOREM | 71 | 52 | 294 178 |
| 'TIS TO KEEP TIME WITH THY DELAY. | IN GLORIOUS ASSUMPTION B. LADY | 20 | 52 | 304 114 |
| WITH HOLY CARE WILL KEEP IT BY US. | IN GLORIOUS ASSUMPTION B. LADY | 48 | 52 | 304 114 |
| THY FALLING TEARES FATES KEEP FAITH FULL TIME. | WEEPER | 140 | 52 | 307 120 |
| AND CLOSE IN HIS EMBRACES KEEP | TERESA | 107 | 52 | 315 52 |
| AS KEEP ACCOUNT OF THE LAMB'S WARRES. | TERESA | 154 | 52 | 315 52 |
| LET CONSTANT USE BUT KEEP IT BRIGHT, | PRAYER TO GENTLE-WOMAN | 22 | 52 | 328 139 |
| AND KEEP THE DEVILL'S HOLYDAY. | PRAYER TO GENTLE-WOMAN | 53 | 52 | 328 139 |
| WAKEFULL, HER DEAR VOWES UNDEFIL'D TO KEEP. | ALEXIAS THIRD ELEGIE | 38 | 52 | 336 209 |
| NO CRUELL GUARD OF DILIGENT CARES, THAT KEEP | DESCRIPTION RELIGIOUS HOUSE | 28 | 52 | 338 213 |
| KIND LOVES KEEP HOUSE, LY CLOSE, AND MAKE NO NOISE, | DESCRIPTION RELIGIOUS HOUSE | 33 | 52 | 338 213 |
| KEEP THE FREE HEART FROM HIS OWN HANDS. | AGAINST IRRESOLUTION AND DELAY | 14 | 52 | 347 146 |

## KEEPE

| | | | | |
|---|---|---|---|---|
| KEEPE BUT THE SCORE OF THEM THAT MADE HIM DYE. | YEE BUILD SEPULCHRES | 4 | 46 | 95 21 |
| WHOM MY GOD VOUCHSAFES TO KEEPE | PSALME 23 | 2 | 46 | 102 5 |
| TO THEE (DREAD LAMBE) WHOSE LOVE MUST KEEPE | A HYMNE OF THE NATIVITY | 81 | 46 | 106 76 |
| AND IN THEIR MURMURES KEEPE THY MIGHTY NAME. | SOSPETTO D'HERODE | 32 | 46 | 109 216 |
| YET KEEPE INVIOLATE HER VIRGIN FLOWER. | SOSPETTO D'HERODE | 164 | 46 | 109 216 |
| THAT HEAV'NS HIGH MAJESTY HIS COURT SHOULD KEEPE | SOSPETTO D'HERODE | 181 | 46 | 109 216 |
| AND NOW CROSSE FATES A WATCH ABOUT THEE KEEPE, | SOSPETTO D'HERODE | 455 | 46 | 109 216 |
| WITH HOLY CARES WILL KEEPE IT BY US. | ON THE ASSUMPTION | 43 | 46 | 139 114 |
| KEEPE SUCH DISTANCE FROM THINE EARES. | UPON DEATH OF DESIRED HERRYS | 62 | 46 | 168 467 |
| AND KEEPE SILENCE ROUND ABOUT THEE. | OUT OF THE ITALIAN (1) | 36 | 46 | 188 545 |
| ONELY SUCH STRYNES AS SERVE TO KEEPE | THOUGH NOW 'TIS NEITHER | 19 | MS | 397 492 |
| SHOULD NOT THE KING STILL KEEPE HIS THRONE | CHARITAS NIMIA | 35 | 52 | 280 48 |
| TO WRACK MY SUITE. OH KEEPE PITTY WARME | ON GUNPOWDER-TREASON | 12 | MS | 384 458 |
| WHERE THEY WILL SAFELY KEEPE IT, FROM THE RUDE, | UPON GUNPOWDER TREASON | 57 | MS | 387 461 |
| DUE I NOT SEE JOY KEEPE HIS REVELS NOW, | UPON KINGS CORONATION | 19 | MS | 389 454 |
| YET SHALL MY LOYALL TONGUE KEEPE THIS COMMAND. | UPON BIRTH PRINCESSE E | 15 | MS | 391 456 |
| O DEATH, 'TIS THOU, YOU FALSE TIME KEEPE, | UPON DEATH OF A FREIND | 9 | MS | 393 477 |

## KEPT

| | | | | |
|---|---|---|---|---|
| A SOULE KEPT THERE SO SWEET. O NO, | IN MEMORY OF LADY MADRE TERESA | 73 | 46 | 131 52 |
| WHAT WORD SO E'RE HIS BREATH KEPT WARME, | HIS EPITAPH (HERRYS) | 31 | 46 | 172 471 |
| KEPT THY MOUTHES GATE. | OUT OF MARTIALL | 2 | 46 | 188 527 |
| HIS LIFE STILL KEPT ALIVE IN THEE. | AN EPITAPH UPON ASHTON | 36 | 46 | 192 464 |
| KEPT THEM FROM BEING SO UNKINDLY KIS'T. | IN GLORIOUS EPIPHANIE | 124 | 52 | 253 39 |
| A SOUL KEPT THERE SO SWEET. O NO. | TERESA | 73 | 52 | 315 52 |
| OFT HATH THIS HAND THOSE SILKEN CASEMENTS KEPT, | LUKE 2. QUAERIT JESUM | 33 | MS | 379 11 |
| AEOL KEPT IN HIS WRANGLING SONNES, LEAST THEY | UPON GUNPOWDER TREASON | 29 | MS | 386 460 |

## KEEP'T

| | | | | |
|---|---|---|---|---|
| AND KEEP'T ALIVE WITH LASTING SONGS. | O GLORIOSA DOMINA | 30 | 52 | 302 194 |

## KEEPS

| | | | | |
|---|---|---|---|---|
| CASKETS, OF WHICH HEAVEN KEEPS THE KEYES. | THE WEEPER | 48 | 46 | 79 120 |
| THY TEARES JUST CADENCE STILL KEEPS TIME. | THE WEEPER | 104 | 46 | 79 120 |
| HEAVEN KEEPS UPON THY SCORE (THY BRIGHT | IN MEMORY OF LADY MADRE TERESA | 176 | 46 | 131 52 |
| THAT KEEPS RELIGION WARME. NOT SWELL A NAME | ON A TREATISE OF CHARITY | 52 | 46 | 137 69 |
| THAT IN THY EARES THUS KEEPS A MURMURING. | UPON YORKE HIS BIRTH | 107 | 46 | 176 500 |
| 'TIS COWARDISE THAT KEEPS THIS FEILD | TO COUNTESSE OF DENBIGH | 61 | 52 | 236 146 |
| HEAV'N KEEPS UPON THY SCORE. (THY BRIGHT | TERESA | 175 | 52 | 315 52 |
| 'TIS COWARDISE THAT KEEPS THIS FIELD. | AGAINST IRRESOLUTION AND DELAY | 83 | 52 | 347 146 |

## KEEPES

| | | | | |
|---|---|---|---|---|
| THY HUMBLE FAITH AND FEARE KEEPES HIM ALOOFE. | I AM NOT WORTHY | 2 | 46 | 90 13 |

## KEEPING

| | | | | |
|---|---|---|---|---|
| STILL KEEPING IN THE FORWARD STREAME, SO LONG | MUSICKS DUELL | 86 | 46 | 149 535 |
| OF COMFORTS, WHICH THOU HAST IN KEEPING. | TO THE NAME OF JESUS | 190 | 52 | 239 30 |
| NOR IVORY COUCHES COSTLYER SLUMBERS KEEPING. | DESCRIPTION RELIGIOUS HOUSE | 4 | 52 | 338 213 |

## KEEPER

| | | | | |
|---|---|---|---|---|
| MUST BEE A SURE HOUSE KEEPER, | ON A PRAYER BOOKE | 31 | 46 | 126 139 |

## KEY

| | | | | |
|---|---|---|---|---|
| WHICH HAS THE KEY OF THIS CLOSE HEART. | TO COUNTESSE OF DENBIGH | 34 | 52 | 236 146 |
| GREAT NATURE FOR THE KEY OF HER HUGE CHEST | TO THE NAME OF JESUS | 29 | 52 | 239 30 |

## KEYES

| | | | | |
|---|---|---|---|---|
| CASKETS, OF WHICH HEAVEN KEEPS THE KEYES. | THE WEEPER | 48 | 46 | 79 120 |

## KICK

| | | | | |
|---|---|---|---|---|
| SHALL KICK THE CLOUDS NO MORE. BUT LEAN & TAME, | IN GLORIOUS EPIPHANIE | 98 | 52 | 253 39 |

## KICKT

| | | | | |
|---|---|---|---|---|
| HEAVEN KICKT THE MONSTER DOUNE. DOUNE IT WAS THROUNE. | ON GUNPOWDER-TREASON | 51 | MS 384 | 458 |

## KICKS

| | | | | |
|---|---|---|---|---|
| HOPE KICKS THE CURL'D HEADS OF CONSPIRING STARRES. | ON HOPE | 72 | 46 143 | 71 |

## KICKES

| | | | | |
|---|---|---|---|---|
| HOPE WALKS, & KICKES THE CURLD HEADS OF CONSPIRING STARRES. | (ON) HOPE | 32 | 52 345 | 71 |

## KILL

| | | | | |
|---|---|---|---|---|
| NOR NEED WEE KILL THY FRUIT TO SMELL THY FLOWER. | ON HOPE | 54 | 46 143 | 71 |
| WILL KILL HIS ANGER, AND REVIVE MY BLISSE. | TO THE MORNING | 38 | 46 183 | 497 |
| BUT KILL THIS REBELL-WORD, IRRESOLUTE | TO COUNTESSE OF DENBIGH | 40 | 52 236 | 146 |
| TO SAVE YOUR LIFE, KILL YOUR DELAY | TO COUNTESSE OF DENBIGH | 58 | 52 236 | 146 |
| AND KILL THE DEATH OF THIS DELAY. | TO THE NAME OF JESUS | 142 | 52 239 | 30 |
| LIVE HERE, GREAT HEART, & LOVE AND DY & KILL. | FLAMING HEART | 79 | 52 324 | 61 |
| NOR DOES IT KILL THY FRUIT, TO SMELL THY FLOWRE. | (ON) HOPE | 24 | 52 345 | 71 |
| TO SAVE YOUR LIFE, KILL YOUR DELAY. | AGAINST IRRESOLUTION AND DELAY | 82 | 52 347 | 146 |

## KILL'D

| | | | | |
|---|---|---|---|---|
| SHEW'D HIM HIS FEARES, AND KILL'D HIM WITH THE SIGHT. | SOSPETTO D'HERODE | 504 | 46 109 | 216 |

## SWEETLY-KILLING

| | | | | |
|---|---|---|---|---|
| KISSE THE SWEETLY-KILLING DART. | IN MEMORY OF LADY MADRE TERESA | 106 | 46 131 | 52 |
| KISSE THE SWEETLY-KILLING DART. | TERESA | 106 | 52 315 | 52 |

## KIN

| | | | | |
|---|---|---|---|---|
| TO SHOW A FACE, FIT TO CONFESSE THY KIN | UPON STANINOUGH'S DEATH | 18 | 46 175 | 475 |
| CAN PROVE IT SELF SOME KIN (SWEET NAME) TO THEE. | TO THE NAME OF JESUS | 182 | 52 239 | 30 |
| TO SHOW A FACE, FITT TO CONFESSE THY KIN, | DEATH'S LECTURE | 19 | 52 340 | 475 |

## KIND

| | | | | |
|---|---|---|---|---|
| BE NE'RE SO CURST, HIS TONGUE IS KIND. | OUT OF GREEKE CUPID'S CRYER | 22 | 46 159 | 519 |
| A SOYLE SO KIND. | UPON THORNES FROM LORDS HEAD | 6 | 46 96 | 23 |
| IS NOT THE SOILE A KIND ONE (THINKE YE) THAT RETURNS | UPON THORNES FROM LORDS HEAD | 7 | 46 96 | 23 |
| SWEET HOPE. KIND CHEAT. FAIRE FALLACY. BY THEE | ON HOPE | 77 | 46 143 | 71 |
| O DOE THOU WATER IT WITH ONE KIND TEARE. | UPON DEATH OF HERRYS | 42 | 46 167 | 466 |
| BUT WOULD BE COURTEOUS, WOULD BE KIND. | UPON DEATH OF DESIRED HERRYS | 58 | 46 168 | 467 |
| SEEM'D BUT THE OTHERS KIND REFLECTION. | UPON YORKE HIS BIRTH | 65 | 46 176 | 500 |
| TO WARN EACH SEVERALL KIND | TO THE NAME OF JESUS | 37 | 52 239 | 30 |
| TO MAKE A KIND OF LIFE FOR MY LORD'S DEATH, | OFFICE H. CROSS RECOMMENDATION | 6 | 52 276 | 106 |
| LOVE IS TOO KIND, I SEE. & CAN | CHARITAS NIMIA | 5 | 52 280 | 48 |
| LET FROWARD DUST THEN DOE IT'S KIND. | CHARITAS NIMIA | 29 | 52 280 | 48 |
| WHAT KIND OF MARBLE THAN | SANCTA MARIA DOLORUM | 11 | 52 283 | 162 |
| MY BREST MAY CATCH THE KISSE OF SOME KIND DART, | SANCTA MARIA DOLORUM | 69 | 52 283 | 162 |
| A SOILE SO KIND. | UPON CROWNE OF THORNS | 4 | 52 290 | 23 |
| IS NOT THE SOILE A KIND ONE, WHICH RETURNES | UPON CROWNE OF THORNS | 5 | 52 290 | 23 |
| THY SOUL'S KIND SHEPHEARD, THY HART'S KING. | LAUDA SION SALVATOREM | 2 | 52 294 | 178 |
| CLOSE IN KIND CONTRARIETYES. | WEEPER | 96 | 52 307 | 120 |
| (FAIR ONE) FROM THY KIND HANDS | PRAYER TO GENTLE-WOMAN | 7 | 52 328 | 139 |
| KIND LOVES KEEP HOUSE, LY CLOSE, AND MAKE NO NOISE, | DESCRIPTION RELIGIOUS HOUSE | 33 | 52 338 | 213 |
| SWEET HOPE. KIND CHEAT. FAIR FALLACY BY THEE | (ON) HOPE | 37 | 52 345 | 71 |
| AND KNOW THE CALL OF HEAV'N'S KIND SHOWERS. | AGAINST IRRESOLUTION AND DELAY | 34 | 52 347 | 146 |
| OF THY KIND MASTER'S WELL-DESERVING BRAINES. | HORATIJ ILLE & NEFASTO | 16 | MS 382 | 530 |
| BY THY KIND ARMES TO A KIND WORLD UNKNOWNE. | ON GUNPOWDER-TREASON | 8 | MS 384 | 458 |
| BY THY KIND ARMES TO A KIND WORLD UNKNOWNE. | ON GUNPOWDER-TREASON | 8 | MS 384 | 458 |
| KIND WINTER'S GUIFT, & IN A GREENE ONE DIGHT. | AN ELEGY MR STANNINOW | 6 | MS 394 | 473 |
| WAS NOT SO MUCH AS CLEANE. A STABLE KIND. | OUT OF GROTIUS | 17 | MS 398 | 198 |

## KINDER

| | | | | |
|---|---|---|---|---|
| NO APRIL ERE LENT KINDER SHOWRES, | WEEPER | 83 | 52 307 | 120 |

## KINDEST

| | | | | |
|---|---|---|---|---|
| THE KINDEST CONSTELLATION, | LOVES HOROSCOPE | 26 | 46 185 | 483 |

## KINDLY

| | | | | |
|---|---|---|---|---|
| MOST KINDLY DOE FALL OUT. THE GRUMBLING BASE | MUSICKS DUELL | 49 | 46 149 | 535 |
| THE HERDS TO KINDLY MEETINGS, THEN THE FIELDS | OUT OF VIRGIL | 12 | 46 155 | 529 |
| KINDLY SUPPLIES SICK NATURE, AND DOTH MOLD | OUT OF VIRGIL | 35 | 46 155 | 529 |
| AND SWEET OPPRESSION, KINDLY CHEATING THEM | SOSPETTO D'HERODE | 389 | 46 109 | 216 |
| HOW KINDLY WILL THY GENTLE HEART, | IN MEMORY OF LADY MADRE TERESA | 105 | 46 131 | 52 |
| HOW KINDLY WILL THY GENTLE HEART | TERESA | 105 | 52 315 | 52 |
| GIVE HIM THE VEIL, WHO KINDLY TAKES THE SHAME. | FLAMING HEART | 58 | 52 324 | 61 |
| KINDLY TO CROSSE YOU | TO SAME CONCERNING CHOISE | 46 | 52 331 | 66 |

## KINDNESSE

| | | | | |
|---|---|---|---|---|
| LEST HIS KINDNESSE MAKE THEE BLEED. | OUT OF GREEKE CUPID'S CRYER | 72 | 46 159 | 519 |

PAGE 214

## KINDLE

| | | | | |
|---|---|---|---|---|
| THERE MIGHT YOU HEARE HER KINDLE HER SOFT VOYCE. | MUSICKS DUELL | 83 | 46 149 | 535 |
| HIS ANGER KINDLE, PRESENTLY | OUT OF GREEKE CUPID'S CRYER | 29 | 46 159 | 519 |
| TO KINDLE THIS HIS SACRIFICE. | ON MR. G. HERBERTS BOOKE | 4 | 46 130 | 68 |

## KINDLED

| | | | | |
|---|---|---|---|---|
| THAT KINDLED THEM TO STARRES,) AND SO | IN MEMORY OF LADY MADRE TERESA | 178 | 46 131 | 52 |
| KINDLED ON THEIR COLD LIPS. O HAD MY WISHES | UPON TWO GREENE APRICOCKES | 10 | 48 220 | 494 |
| THAT KINDLED THEM TO STARRS,) AND SO | TERESA | 177 | 52 315 | 52 |

## KINDRED

| | | | | |
|---|---|---|---|---|
| AND ALL THE SMOOTH FACED KINDRED THERE. | ON MR. G. HERBERTS BOOKE | 14 | 46 130 | 68 |
| HER KINDRED WITH THE STARRS. NOT BASELY HOVERS | DESCRIPTION RELIGIOUS HOUSE | 37 | 52 338 | 213 |

## KINRED

| | | | | |
|---|---|---|---|---|
| NOR LETT HER KINRED BIRDS COMPLAYNE | THOUGH NOW 'TIS NEITHER | 15 | MS 397 | 492 |

## KING

| | | | | |
|---|---|---|---|---|
| DAYES KING DEPOSED BY NIGHTS QUEENE. | A HYMNE OF THE NATIVITY | 2 | 46 106 | 76 |
| AND KIST THE CRADLE OF OUR KING. | A HYMNE OF THE NATIVITY | 8 | 46 106 | 76 |
| TO THEE MEEKE MAJESTY, SOFT KING | A HYMNE OF THE NATIVITY | 83 | 46 106 | 76 |
| THE JUDGE OF TORMENTS, AND THE KING OF TEARES. | SOSPETTO D'HERODE | 41 | 46 109 | 216 |
| ASSIST THE THRONE OF TH' IRON-SCEPTRED KING. | SOSPETTO D'HERODE | 66 | 46 109 | 216 |
| THUS REIGNES THE WRATHFULL KING, AND WHILE HE REIGNES | SOSPETTO D'HERODE | 71 | 46 109 | 216 |
| BOW OUR BRIGHT HEADS, BEFORE A KING OF CLAY. | SOSPETTO D'HERODE | 220 | 46 109 | 216 |
| REPLY'D THE PROUD KING, O MY CROWNES DEFENCE. | SOSPETTO D'HERODE | 281 | 46 109 | 216 |
| SCARCE TO THIS MONSTER COULD THE SHADY KING, | SOSPETTO D'HERODE | 369 | 46 109 | 216 |
| AND CAME TO BETHLEM, WHERE THE CRUELL KING | SOSPETTO D'HERODE | 394 | 46 109 | 216 |
| SHE COMES TOTH' KING AND WITH HER COLD HAND SLAKES | SOSPETTO D'HERODE | 421 | 46 109 | 216 |
| THEIR NEW KING, AND THY SUCCESSOUR PROCLAIME. | SOSPETTO D'HERODE | 440 | 46 109 | 216 |
| OF THY GREAT SELFE, HATH STOLNE KING HEROD FROM THEE. | SOSPETTO D'HERODE | 458 | 46 109 | 216 |
| HEAVENS KING, WHO DOFFS HIMSELFE WEAKE FLESH TO WEARE. | SOSPETTO D'HERODE | 515 | 46 109 | 216 |
| OF CROWNES, WITH WHICH THE KING THY SPOUSE, | IN MEMORY OF LADY MADRE TERESA | 144 | 46 131 | 52 |
| AND TURNE NOT BEASTS, BUT ANGELS. LET THE KING, | AN APOLOGIE FOR HYMNE (TERESA) | 37 | 46 136 | 59 |
| MARIA MOTHER OF OUR KING. | ON THE ASSUMPTION | 54 | 46 139 | 114 |
| THAT TROUBLED NEITHER CHURCH NOR KING. | AN EPITAPH UPON ASHTON | 6 | 46 192 | 464 |
| FAIR KING OF NAMES, & COME. | TO THE NAME OF JESUS | 118 | 52 239 | 30 |
| AND KIS'T THE CRADLE OF OUR KING. | IN HOLY NATIVITY | 8 | 52 246 | 76 |
| TO THEE, MEEK MAJESTY. SOFT KING | IN HOLY NATIVITY | 103 | 52 246 | 76 |
| O THOU BORN KING OF LOVES, | IN GLORIOUS EPIPHANIE | 7 | 52 253 | 39 |
| THE UNKNOWN SORROWS OF OUR KING, | OFFICE H. CROSS MATINES | 11 | 52 265 | 86 |
| WHEN ON THE CROSSE MY KING DID BLEED, | OFFICE H. CROSS NINTH | 11 | 52 271 | 99 |
| THE KING HIMSELF IS. THOU HIS HUMBLE THRONE. | OFFICE H. CROSS EVENSONG | 23 | 52 273 | 101 |
| MERCYFULL KING OF MEN. | OFFICE H. CROSS COMPLINE | 14 | 52 274 | 105 |
| THOUGH THE PROPHETICK KING | VEXILLA REGIS | 21 | 52 277 | 156 |
| SHOULD NOT THE KING STILL KEEPE HIS THRONE | CHARITAS NIMIA | 35 | 52 280 | 48 |
| THY SOUL'S KIND SHEPHEARD, THY HART'S KING. | LAUDA SION SALVATOREM | 2 | 52 294 | 178 |
| PALE MANKIND FORTH TO MEET HIS KING. | DIES IRAE | 12 | 52 298 | 186 |
| MARIA, MOTHER OF OUR KING. | IN GLORIOUS ASSUMPTION B. LADY | 59 | 52 304 | 114 |
| WHO IS THAT KING, BUT HE | WEEPER | 121 | 52 307 | 120 |
| OF CROWNS, WITH WHICH THE KING THY SPOUSE | TERESA | 143 | 52 315 | 52 |
| AND TURN NOT BEASTS, BUT ANGELS. LET THE KING | AN APOLOGIE FOR (TERESA) HYMNE | 37 | 52 322 | 59 |
| THE EASTERN PRINCES TO THEIR INFANT KING. | ALEXIAS SECONDE ELEGIE | 28 | 52 335 | 207 |
| THE HUMBLE KING OF YOU AND ME. | AGAINST IRRESOLUTION AND DELAY | 72 | 52 347 | 146 |
| AS GLAD TO WAITE UPON THEIR KING IN DEATH. | UPON GUNPOWDER TREASON | 42 | MS 386 | 460 |
| A MOURNFULL DIRGE TO THEIR DECEASED KING. | UPON GUNPOWDER TREASON | 44 | MS 386 | 460 |
| FOR JURYES KING AN ENEMY, EVEN WORTH | OUT OF GROTIUS | 21 | MS 398 | 198 |

## KING'S

| | | | | |
|---|---|---|---|---|
| NO NO. YOUR KING'S NOT YET TO SEEKE | IN HOLY NATIVITY | 65 | 52 246 | 76 |
| THY COSTLY EXCELLENCE WITH THY KING'S OWN BLOOD. | VEXILLA REGIS | 30 | 52 277 | 156 |

## KINGS

| | | | | |
|---|---|---|---|---|
| GUILDED I'TH' BEAMES OF EARTHLY KINGS | A HYMNE OF THE NATIVITY | 72 | 46 106 | 76 |
| THOU MIGHTY BRANCH OF EMPEROURS AND KINGS. | SOSPETTO D'HERODE | 10 | 46 109 | 216 |
| THREE KINGS (OR WHAT IS MORE) THREE WISE MEN WENT | SOSPETTO D'HERODE | 135 | 46 109 | 216 |
| TO WHERE THE KINGS PROUDLY-REPOSED HEAD | SOSPETTO D'HERODE | 410 | 46 109 | 216 |
| JOSEPH THE KINGS DEAD BROTHERS SHAPE SHE TAKES, | SOSPETTO D'HERODE | 419 | 46 109 | 216 |
| TO THE KINGS HEART, THE SNAKE NO SOONER HIST, | SOSPETTO D'HERODE | 469 | 46 109 | 216 |
| AND NOW OF LATE CAME TRIBUTARY KINGS, | SOSPETTO D'HERODE | 499 | 46 109 | 216 |
| A SEEMLY PORTION FOR THE SONS OF KINGS. | ON HOPE | 34 | 46 143 | 71 |
| GUILDED ITH' BEAMES OF EARTHLY KINGS. | IN HOLY NATIVITY | 92 | 52 246 | 76 |
| FAIR FIRST-FRUITS OF THE LAMB. SURE KINGS IN THIS. | TO THE QUEEN'S MAJESTY | 7 | 52 261 | 47 |
| THREE KINGDOMES TO SUPPLY THIS DAY'S THREE KINGS. | TO THE QUEEN'S MAJESTY | 28 | 52 261 | 47 |
| A SEEMLY PORTION FOR THE SONNES OF KINGS. | (ON) HOPE | 14 | 52 345 | 71 |
| JUSTLE DOWN MOUNTAINS. KINGS COURTS SHALL BE SENT, | ON GUNPOWDER-TREASON | 41 | MS 384 | 458 |
| MAY NOT ROW NEERER TO THESE DUSKY KINGS. | UPON GUNPOWDER TREASON | 28 | MS 387 | 461 |

## KINGDOM

| | | | | |
|---|---|---|---|---|
| THEY TOOK A KINGDOM WHILE THEY GAVE A KISSE. | TO THE QUEEN'S MAJESTY | 8 | 52 261 | 47 |
| THAT KINGDOM WHICH THIS CROSSE DID MERIT. | VEXILLA REGIS | 46 | 52 277 | 156 |

KINGDOME

 BY THE FULL KINGDOME OF THAT FINALL KISSE    FLAMING HEART    101   52   324   61

KINGDOMS

 TO REAP NEW CROWNES & KINGDOMS FROM THAT KISSE.    TO THE QUEEN'S MAJESTY    22   52   261   47

KINGDOMES

 OF STARING COMETS, THAT LOOKE KINGDOMES DEAD.    SOSPETTO D'HERODE    52   46   109   216
 TO THESE THY SOOTY KINGDOMS THOU ART DRIVEN.    SOSPETTO D'HERODE    268   46   109   216
 THREE KINGDOMES TO SUPPLY THIS DAY'S THREE KINGS.    TO THE QUEEN'S MAJESTY    28   52   261   47
 BEYOND THE KINGDOMES OF CONTENTFULL CELLS.    DESCRIPTION RELIGIOUS HOUSE    35   52   338   213

KISSE

 TO TAST THE NECTAR OF A KISSE    OUT OF GREEKE CUPID'S CRYER    12   46   159   519
 (VENUS ASSURES HIM) THEN A KISSE.    OUT OF GREEKE CUPID'S CRYER    16   46   159   519
 MANY A KISSE, AND MANY A TEARE,    ON WOUNDS OF CRUCIFIED LORD    10   46   99   24
 WITH MANY A RARELY-TEMPER'D KISSE,    A HYMNE OF THE NATIVITY    62   46   106   76
 TO KISSE THY FEET, AND CROWNE THY HEAD.    A HYMNE OF THE NATIVITY    80   46   106   76
 A CURL'D KNOT OF EMBRACING SNAKES, THAT KISSE    SOSPETTO D'HERODE    37   46   109   216
 KISSE THE SWEETLY-KILLING DART.    IN MEMORY OF LADY MADRE TERESA    106   46   131   52
 LIFE, BROUGHT THEM FIRST TO KISSE THE LIGHT    IN MEMORY OF LADY MADRE TERESA    177   46   131   52
 THOU THUS STEAL'ST DOWNE A DISTANT KISSE.    ON HOPE    38   46   143   71
 HOPES CHASTE KISSE WRONGS NO MORE JOYES MAIDENHEAD.    ON HOPE    39   46   143   71
 AND STROAKE HIS RADIANT CHEEKES. ONE TIMELY KISSE    TO THE MORNING    37   46   183   497
 A LOVERS KISSE MAY PLAY,    WISHES SUPPOSED MISTRESSE    38   46   195   479
 WITH MANY A RARELY-TEMPER'D KISSE    IN HOLY NATIVITY    88   52   246   76
 TO KISSE THY FEET & CROWN THY HEAD.    IN HOLY NATIVITY    100   52   246   76
 TO KISSE HIM ONLY AS THEIR ROD    IN GLORIOUS EPIPHANIE    179   52   253   39
 THEY TOOK A KINGDOM WHILE THEY GAVE A KISSE.    TO THE QUEEN'S MAJESTY    8   52   261   47
 CROWNES, & THE HEADS THEY KISSE, MUST COURT THESE    TO THE QUEEN'S MAJESTY    20   52   261   47
  FEET.
 TO REAP NEW CROWNES & KINGDOMS FROM THAT KISSE.    TO THE QUEEN'S MAJESTY    22   52   261   47
 MY BREST MAY CATCH THE KISSE OF SOME KIND DART,    SANCTA MARIA DOLORUM    69   52   283   162
 KISSE THE SWEETLY-KILLING DART.    TERESA    106   52   315   52
 LIFE BROUGHT THEM FIRST TO KISSE THE LIGHT    TERESA    176   52   315   52
 BY THE FULL KINGDOME OF THAT FINALL KISSE    FLAMING HEART    101   52   324   61
 T'EMBRACE MY TEARES, & KISSE AN UNKIND FATE.    ALEXIAS FIRST ELEGIE    4   52   334   204
 A KISSE, A SIGH, AND SO AWAY.    TEMPERANCE    50   52   342   510
 THOU STEAL'ST US DOWN A DISTANT KISSE.    (ON) HOPE    18   52   345   71
 HE HUMBLY CRAV'D TO BANQUETT ON A KISSE.    UPON GUNPOWDER TREASON    46   MS   387   461
 SHALL KISSE HIS GOLDEN BURTHEN. THOU, GLAD ISLE,    UPON KINGS CORONATION    5   MS   389   454
 MURDRED THE EARTH'S JUST PRIDE WITH A RUDE KISSE.    AN ELEGY MR STANNINOW    48   MS   394   473
 WITH TREMBLING LIPPES AN HUMBLE KISSE DO'ST PAY.    AN ELEGIE ON DR PORTER    6   MS   395   476

KISSES

 IF HEE OFFER SUGRED KISSES,    OUT OF GREEKE CUPID'S CRYER    65   46   159   519
 THE ROSE BUDS SWEET LIP KISSES.    THE TEARE    21   46   84   50
 TO PAY THE SWEET SUMME OF THY KISSES.    ON WOUNDS OF CRUCIFIED LORD    14   46   99   24
 HER KISSES IN THY WEEPING EYE,    A HYMNE OF THE NATIVITY    66   46   106   76
 AND CLOSE WITH HIS IMMORTALL KISSES.    ON A PRAYER BOOKE    97   46   126   139
 SEEKE FOR, AMONGST HER MOTHERS KISSES.    IN MEMORY OF LADY MADRE TERESA    42   46   131   52
 HEAP UP THY CONSECRATED KISSES.    IN MEMORY OF LADY MADRE TERESA    133   46   131   52
 THEN LET AMOROUS KISSES DWELL    OUT OF CATULLUS    9   46   194   523
 AND BEE YEE CALL'D MY ABSENT KISSES.    WISHES SUPPOSED MISTRESSE    15   46   195   479
 AND DETERMINE THEM TO KISSES.    WISHES SUPPOSED MISTRESSE    123   46   195   479
 THAN ERE THE FRUITFULL PHOEBUS FLAMING KISSES    UPON TWO GREENE APRICOCKES    9   48   220   494
 AND CROWD FOR KISSES FROM THE LAMB'S WHITE FEET.    TO THE QUEEN'S MAJESTY    14   52   261   47
 SEEK FOR AMONGST HER MOTHER'S KISSES,    TERESA    42   52   315   52
 HEAP UP THY CONSECRATED KISSES.    TERESA    132   52   315   52
 AND CLOSE WITH HIS IMMORTALL KISSES.    PRAYER TO GENTLE-WOMAN    103   52   328   139
 OFT HAVE MY HUNGRY KISSES MADE THINE EYES    LUKE 2. QUAERIT JESUM    35   MS   379   11
 OFT HAVE I SPOILD MY KISSES DAINTIEST DIET,    LUKE 2. QUAERIT JESUM    37   MS   379   11

KISSING

 BY OFTEN KISSING THEM, AND NOW BEGUN    UPON DEATH OF HERRYS    21   46   167   466
 EACH OTHER KISSING & CONFUTING.    WEEPER    94   52   307   120

KIST

 AND KIST THE CRADLE OF OUR KING.    A HYMNE OF THE NATIVITY    8   46   106   76
 (A SPECIALL WORME IT WAS AS EVER KIST    SOSPETTO D'HERODE    467   46   109   216
 KIST ON BOTH HIS CHEEKS BY THEE.    IN GLORIOUS EPIPHANIE    39   52   253   39
 HAD THY COLD PENCIL KIST HER PEN    FLAMING HEART    20   52   324   61
 THEY OFTEN KIST, & IN THE SUGRED PLACE    AN ELEGY MR STANNINOW    40   MS   394   473

KIS'T

 AND KIS'T THE CRADLE OF OUR KING.    IN HOLY NATIVITY    8   52   246   76
 THE DIRE FACE OF INFERIOR DARKNES, KIS'T    IN GLORIOUS EPIPHANIE    52   52   253   39
 KEPT THEM FROM BEING SO UNKINDLY KIS'T.    IN GLORIOUS EPIPHANIE    124   52   253   39

KNEE

 MOTHERS ARMES, OR FATHERS KNEE.    IN MEMORY OF LADY MADRE TERESA    62   46   131   52
 BECAUSE HE'S STIFFE, AND WILL CONFESSE NO KNEE.    ON A TREATISE OF CHARITY    40   46   137   69
 WHILE OTHERS BEND THEIR KNEE, NO MORE SHALT THOU    ON A TREATISE OF CHARITY    41   46   137   69
 FOR SURE THERE IS NO KNEE    TO THE NAME OF JESUS    226   52   239   30

|   |   |   |   |   |   |
|---|---|---|---|---|---|
| MOTHER'S ARMES OR FATHER'S KNEE | TERESA | 62 | 52 | 315 | 52 |

## KNEW

|   |   |   |   |   |   |
|---|---|---|---|---|---|
| SHE WAS A NIMPH, THE MEADOWES KNEW NONE SUCH. | TO PONTIUS WASHING HANDS | 5 | 46 | 94 | 23 |
| OF WHICH THE MORNING KNEW NOT. MAD WITH SPIGHT | SOSPETTO D'HERODE | 117 | 46 | 109 | 216 |
| ASSYRIAN TYRANTS, OR EGYPTIAN KNEW. | SOSPETTO D'HERODE | 366 | 46 | 109 | 216 |
| THE GLORYES OF THY YOUTH NE'RE KNEW. | UPON DEATH OF DESIRED HERRYS | 17 | 46 | 168 | 467 |
| FOR THIS THE EVENING WEPT. AND WE NE'RE KNEW | IN GLORIOUS EPIPHANIE | 127 | 52 | 253 | 39 |
| O KNEW I WHERE HE WANDER'D, I SHOULD SEE | ALEXIAS FIRST ELEGIE | 9 | 52 | 334 | 204 |

## KNIFE

|   |   |   |   |   |   |
|---|---|---|---|---|---|
| THIS KNIFE MAY BE THE SPEARES PRAELUDIUM. | OUR LORD IN HIS CIRCUMCISION | 18 | 46 | 98 | 9 |
| AND TO THE CIRCUMCISING KNIFE DELIVER | SOSPETTO D'HERODE | 187 | 46 | 109 | 216 |
| SHOULD BLEED UPON A BARBAROUS KNIFE. | IN MEMORY OF LADY MADRE TERESA | 70 | 46 | 131 | 52 |
| SHOULD BLEED UPON A BARBAROUS KNIFE. | TERESA | 70 | 52 | 315 | 52 |
| FROM HIS OLD FATHER. THAT MANS BARBAROUS KNIFE | HORATIJ ILLE & NEFASTO | 8 | MS | 362 | 530 |

## KNIGHT

|   |   |   |   |   |   |
|---|---|---|---|---|---|
| WHO E'RE HE BE WAS THE FIRST WANDRING KNIGHT. | ALEXIAS THIRD ELEGIE | 4 | 52 | 336 | 209 |

## KNOCKE

|   |   |   |   |   |   |
|---|---|---|---|---|---|
| MY GRIEFE IS. SO MY WAKEFULL LAY SHALL KNOCKE | TO THE MORNING | 41 | 46 | 183 | 497 |

## KNOT

|   |   |   |   |   |   |
|---|---|---|---|---|---|
| A CURL'D KNOT OF EMBRACING SNAKES, THAT KISSE | SOSPETTO D'HERODE | 37 | 46 | 109 | 216 |
| FOURTH OF THE CURSED KNOT OF HAGS IS SHEE. | SOSPETTO D'HERODE | 289 | 46 | 109 | 216 |
| IN THE LAST KNOT THAT LOVE COULD TYE. | AN EPITAPH HUSBAND AND WIFE | 10 | 46 | 174 | 478 |

## KNOTT

|   |   |   |   |   |   |
|---|---|---|---|---|---|
| LOVE'S TRUEST KNOTT BY VENUS IS NOT TY'D. | ALEXIAS THIRD ELEGIE | 27 | 52 | 336 | 209 |
| IN THE LAST KNOTT LOVE COULD TY. | AN EPITAPH UPON MARRIED COUPLE | 10 | 52 | 339 | 478 |

## KNOTTY

|   |   |   |   |   |   |
|---|---|---|---|---|---|
| MIDST ALL THE DARKE AND KNOTTY SNARES, | NEITHER DURST MAN ASKE | 1 | 46 | 92 | 20 |
| CRAFT IN ALL HER KNOTTY WILES. | PSALME 23 | 26 | 46 | 102 | 5 |
| WITH WHIPS OF THRONES AND KNOTTY VIPERS TWIN'D | SOSPETTO D'HERODE | 67 | 46 | 109 | 216 |
| THESE ARE THE KNOTTY RIDDLES, WHOSE DARKE DOUBT | SOSPETTO D'HERODE | 191 | 46 | 109 | 216 |

## KNOW

|   |   |   |   |   |   |
|---|---|---|---|---|---|
| QUICKE VOLUMES OF WILD NOTES, TO LET HIM KNOW | MUSICKS DUELL | 25 | 46 | 149 | 535 |
| LET THE FINDER SURELY KNOW | OUT OF GREEKE CUPID'S CRYER | 7 | 46 | 159 | 519 |
| THAT DULL MORTALITY MUST NOT KNOW A NAME. | ON A PRAYER BOOKE | 80 | 46 | 126 | 139 |
| KNOW YOU FAIRE, ON WHAT YOU LOOKE. | ON MR. G. HERBERTS BOOKE | 1 | 46 | 130 | 68 |
| THESE DEVOTIONS, FAIREST. KNOW | ON MR. G. HERBERTS BOOKE | 16 | 46 | 130 | 68 |
| SHEE NEVER UNDERTOOKE TO KNOW, | IN MEMORY OF LADY MADRE TERESA | 19 | 46 | 131 | 52 |
| I KNOW THAT IN MY WEAK AND WORTHLESSE SONG | AN APOLOGIE FOR HYMNE (TERESA) | 4 | 46 | 136 | 59 |
| I LEARNT TO KNOW THAT LOVE IS ELOQUENCE. | AN APOLOGIE FOR HYMNE (TERESA) | 8 | 46 | 136 | 59 |
| WHAT THOU DOST, THOU DOST NOT KNOW. | UPON DEATH OF DESIRED HERRYS | 2 | 46 | 168 | 467 |
| THAT COULD THE FATES KNOW TO RELENT. | ANOTHER ON HERRYS | 17 | 46 | 170 | 469 |
| COULD THEY KNOW WHAT MERCY MEANT. | ANOTHER ON HERRYS | 18 | 46 | 170 | 469 |
| (HYPERBOLIZED NOTHING.) KNOW THY SPAN. | UPON STANINOUGH'S DEATH | 10 | 46 | 175 | 475 |
| SICKNESSE, AND SORROW, WHOSE PALE LIDDS NE'RE KNOW | TO THE MORNING | 56 | 46 | 183 | 497 |
| FOR LETT THEM KNOW SHEE'S NONE OF THOSE | THOUGH NOW 'TIS NEITHER | 17 | MS | 397 | 492 |
| AND KNOW WHAT SWEETES ARE SUCK'T FROM OUT IT. | TO THE NAME OF JESUS | 155 | 52 | 239 | 30 |
| SHE NEVER UNDERTOOK TO KNOW | TERESA | 19 | 52 | 315 | 52 |
| I KNOW, THAT IN MY WEAK & WORTHLESSE SONG | AN APOLOGIE FOR (TERESA) HYMNE | 4 | 52 | 322 | 59 |
| I LEARN'T TO KNOW THAT LOVE IS ELOQUENCE | AN APOLOGIE FOR (TERESA) HYMNE | 8 | 52 | 322 | 59 |
| THAT DULL MORTALITY MUST NOT KNOW A NAME. | PRAYER TO GENTLE-WOMAN | 86 | 52 | 328 | 139 |
| WITTNESSE, CHAST HEAVNS. NO HAPPYER VOWES I KNOW | ALEXIAS THIRD ELEGIE | 25 | 52 | 336 | 209 |
| I'D KNOW NO NAME OF LOVE ON EARTH BUT YOU. | ALEXIAS THIRD ELEGIE | 44 | 52 | 336 | 209 |
| HYPERBOLIZED NOTHING. KNOW THY SPAN. | DEATH'S LECTURE | 11 | 52 | 340 | 475 |
| AND KNOW THE CALL OF HEAV'N'S KIND SHOWERS. | AGAINST IRRESOLUTION AND DELAY | 34 | 52 | 347 | 146 |
| GREAT NYMPH, O'RELOOKE MY LOWNESSE. HEAV'N YOU KNOW. | EX EUPHORMIONE | 7 | MS | 392 | 525 |
| BUT WHO IS HE. HIM MAY WEE KNOW, | UPON DEATH OF A FREIND | 7 | MS | 393 | 477 |
| OF THY OLD GOODNESSE, KNOW THEE NOT FOR THEIRES, | OUT OF GROTIUS | 40 | MS | 398 | 198 |

## KNOW'ST

|   |   |   |   |   |   |
|---|---|---|---|---|---|
| THAT BEING NAK'T, THOU KNOW'ST COULD CONQUER THEE. | UPON THE SAME (VENUS ARMES) | 4 | 46 | 161 | 523 |
| KNOW'ST THOU THIS, SOULDIER. 'TIS A MUCH CHANG'D PLANT, WHICH YE T | UPON THORNES FROM LORDS HEAD | 1 | 46 | 96 | 23 |
| KNOW'ST THOU NOT HOW OF TH' HEBREWES ROYALL STEMME | SOSPETTO D'HERODE | 433 | 46 | 109 | 216 |
| THOU KNOW'ST A FACE IN WHOSE EACH LOOKE, | LUVES HOROSCOPE | 11 | 46 | 185 | 483 |
| KNOW'ST THOU THIS, SOULDIER. 'TIS A MUCH-CHANG'D PLANT WHICH YET | UPON CROWNE OF THORNS | 1 | 52 | 290 | 23 |

## KNOWES

|   |   |   |   |   |   |
|---|---|---|---|---|---|
| YET SUCH A ONE AS (JOVE KNOWES HOW) | OUT OF GREEKE CUPID'S CRYER | 46 | 46 | 159 | 519 |
| SEE HERE AN EASIE FEAST THAT KNOWES NO WOUND, | ON MIRACLE OF LOAVES | 1 | 46 | 86 | 15 |
| HEE KNOWES (BUT KNOWES NOT HOW, OR BY WHAT ART) | SOSPETTO D'HERODE | 157 | 46 | 109 | 216 |
| HEE KNOWES (BUT KNOWES NOT HOW, OR BY WHAT ART) | SOSPETTO D'HERODE | 157 | 46 | 109 | 216 |
| LOVE KNOWES NO NONAGE, NOR THE MIND. | IN MEMORY OF LADY MADRE TERESA | 32 | 46 | 131 | 52 |
| AND LIVES AND DYES, AND KNOWES NOT WHY | IN MEMORY OF LADY MADRE TERESA | 103 | 46 | 131 | 52 |
| NOW IF TIME KNOWES | WISHES SUPPOSED MISTRESSE | 106 | 46 | 195 | 479 |
| KNOWES ALL THE CORNERS OF'T, & CAN CONTROUL | TO COUNTESSE OF DENBIGH | 35 | 52 | 236 | 146 |

```
                                                                    PAGE  218

  THAT KNOWES NOT THEE.                          TO THE NAME OF JESUS          227   52 239   30
  LOVE KNOWES NO NONAGE, NOR THE MIND.           TERESA                         32   52 315   52
  AND LIVES, & DYES.  AND KNOWES NOT WHY         TERESA                        103   52 315   52
  (WHO KNOWES HOW POWRFULL WELL-WRITT PRAIRES WOULD BE.)  ALEXIAS FIRST ELEGIE  12   52 334  204
  WHO KNOWES MY OWN HEART'S WOES SO WELL AS I.   ALEXIAS FIRST ELEGIE           14   52 334  204
  WHO STILES IT ANY THINGE, KNOWES NOT THE SAME. ON GUNPOWDER-TREASON            2   MS 384  458

KNOWING

  AND THEN, NOT KNOWING WHAT TO DOE.             TO THE NAME OF JESUS          137   52 239   30
  KNOWING 'TIS IN THE DOOME OF YOUR SWEET EYE    AT TH' IVORY TRIBUNALL          3   MS 397  492

KNOWN

  NAME TO BE KNOWN, ALAS, BUT SORROW'S MOTHER.   SANCTA MARIA DOLORUM            4   52 283  162

KNOWNE

  HERE, O HERE WE SHOULD HAVE KNOWNE IT,         ANOTHER ON HERRYS               5   46 170  469
  WAS EVER KNOWNE TO BE THY VOTERY.              TO THE MORNING                 48   46 183  497
  THEN WAS I KNOWNE.  AND KNOWNE UNLUCKILY       OUT OF GROTIUS                 19   MS 398  198
  THEN WAS I KNOWNE.  AND KNOWNE UNLUCKILY       OUT OF GROTIUS                 19   MS 398  198

LABOR

  IN LABOR OF YOUR SELFE TO LY.                  TO COUNTESSE OF DENBIGH        11   52 236  146

LABORING

  LO HOW THE LABORING EARTH                      TO THE NAME OF JESUS          131   52 239   30

EARTH-LABORING

  AND LASH EARTH-LABORING SOULS.                 DESCRIPTION RELIGIOUS HOUSE    27   52 338  213

HEAV'N-LABOURING

  FROM WHENCE HEAV'N-LABOURING BEES WITH BUSIE WING,  SOSPETTO D'HERODE         22   46 109  216

LABOUR

  MAY THINKE HIS LABOUR VAINELY GONE,            OUT OF GREEKE CUPID'S CRYER    10   46 159  519
  EACH ONE AN AGES LABOUR, THAT THY DAYES        UPON YORKE HIS BIRTH           11   46 176  500
  SHALL ALL THAT LABOUR, ALL THAT COST           DIES IRAE                      33   52 298  186
  NOR LOVE, NOR LABOUR CAN BE LOST.              TO SAME CONCERNING CHOISE      39   52 331   66
  IN LABOUR OF YOUR SELF TO LY.                  AGAINST IRRESOLUTION AND DELAY 19   52 347  146

LABOUR'D

  THAT LABOUR'D TO HAVE WASHT THY GUILT.         TO PONTIUS WASHING HANDS        2   46  88   22
  NATURE LABOUR'D FOR A NAME,                    UPON DEATH OF DESIRED HERRYS    6   46 168  467

LABOURETH

  WHICH THERE RECIPROCALLY LABOURETH             MUSICKS DUELL                  72   46 149  535

LABOURS

  HANDS FULL OF HARTY LABOURS. PAINES THAT PAY   DESCRIPTION RELIGIOUS HOUSE    19   52 338  213
  IT LABOURS. STIF'LED NATURE'S IN A SWOUND,     ON GUNPOWDER-TREASON           19   MS 384  458
  OF MY SAD LABOURS.  NO DAY YETT COULD TELL     OUT OF GROTIUS                 10   MS 398  198

LAB'RING

  T' ENTOMBE THE LAB'RING EARTH. FOR SURELY SHEE UPON GUNPOWDER TREASON         51   MS 386  460

LACE

  OR THAT THE PURPLE VIOLETS DID LACE            UPON BIRTH PRINCESSE E         51   MS 391  456

LACES

  ALL THE PURPLE PRIDE OF LACES,                 AN HIMNE FOR CIRCUMCISION       5   46 141   37
  ALL THE PURPLE PRIDE THAT LACES                NEW YEAR'S DAY                  5   52 251   37

LACK

  DEAR RELIQUES OF A DISLODG'D SOUL, WHOSE LACK  DEATH'S LECTURE                 1   52 340  475

LACKE

  DEARE RELIQUES OF A DISLODG'D SOULE, WHOSE LACKE  UPON STANINOUGH'S DEATH      1   46 175  475

LAD

  TELL ME BRIGHT BOY, TELL ME MY GOLDEN LAD,     ON THE PRODIGALL                1   46  86   17

LADEN

  LONG MAYEST THOU LADEN WITH SUCH CLUSTERS LEANE  UPON YORKE HIS BIRTH        102   46 176  500
```

## LADING

| | | | | | |
|---|---|---|---|---|---|
| APPEAR'D WITH OTHER LADING, FOR HER BREST | THE BEGINNING OF HELIODORUS | 12 | 46 | 158 | 517 |

## LADY

| | | | | | |
|---|---|---|---|---|---|
| DISPUS'D TO GIVE THE LIGHT-FOOT LADY SPORT | MUSICKS DUELL | 16 | 46 | 149 | 535 |
| BRIGHT LADY OF THE MORNE, PITTY DOTH LYE | TO THE MORNING | 33 | 46 | 183 | 497 |
| BEE YOU THE LADY OF LOVES YEERE. | THOUGH NOW 'TIS NEITHER | 27 | MS | 397 | 492 |

## LADYES

| | | | | | |
|---|---|---|---|---|---|
| HERE GALLANT LADYES, THIS UNPARTIALL GLASSE | UPON STANINOUGH'S DEATH | 21 | 46 | 175 | 475 |
| HERE, GALLANT LADYES, THIS UNPARTIALL GLASSE | DEATH'S LECTURE | 23 | 52 | 340 | 475 |

## LAID

| | | | | | |
|---|---|---|---|---|---|
| OF THE HOPES IN HIM WE LAID. | UPON THE DEATH OF A GENTLEMAN | 6 | 46 | 166 | 472 |
| HERE, WHERE OUR LORD ONCE LAID HIS HEAD, | UPON SEPULCHRE OF OUR LORD | 1 | 46 | 86 | 26 |
| TWO DEVILLS AT ONE BLOW THOU HAST LAID FLAT, | UPON DUMBE DEVILL CAST OUT | 1 | 46 | 93 | 14 |
| O THOU THAT ON THIS FOOT HAST LAID | ON WOUNDS OF CRUCIFIED LORD | 9 | 46 | 99 | 24 |
| THE CROWNE, FOR WHICH UPON THEIR NECKS HE LAID | SOSPETTO D'HERODE | 406 | 46 | 109 | 216 |
| THAT ON THESE SNOWY LIMMES HATH LAID SUCH HOLD. | AN ELEGY MR STANNINOW | 20 | MS | 394 | 473 |

## LAKES

| | | | | | |
|---|---|---|---|---|---|
| THUNDRING UPON THE BANKES OF THOSE BLACK LAKES | SOSPETTO D'HERODE | 298 | 46 | 109 | 216 |

## LAMB

| | | | | | |
|---|---|---|---|---|---|
| EACH OF US HIS LAMB WILL BRING, | A HYMNE OF THE NATIVITY | 85 | 46 | 106 | 76 |
| TO THEE, DREAD LAMB, WHOSE LOVE MUST KEEP | IN HOLY NATIVITY | 101 | 52 | 246 | 76 |
| EACH OF US HIS LAMB WILL BRING | IN HOLY NATIVITY | 105 | 52 | 246 | 76 |
| FAIR FIRST-FRUITS OF THE LAMB. SURE KINGS IN THIS. | TO THE QUEEN'S MAJESTY | 7 | 52 | 261 | 47 |
| DREAD LAMB, AND BOW THUS LOW BEFORE THEE, | OFFICE H. CROSS MATINES | 25 | 52 | 265 | 86 |
| DREAD LAMB, AND FALL | OFFICE H. CROSS PRIME | 18 | 52 | 267 | 91 |
| DREAD LAMB, & FALL | OFFICE H. CROSS THIRD | 17 | 52 | 268 | 93 |
| LO THE FAINT LAMB, WITH WEARY LIMB | OFFICE H. CROSS SIXT | 3 | 52 | 270 | 97 |
| DREAD LAMB, & BOW THUS LOW BEFORE THEE. | OFFICE H. CROSS SIXT | 22 | 52 | 270 | 97 |
| HEAR, FATHER, HEAR, THY LAMB (AT LAST) COMPLAINES. | OFFICE H. CROSS NINTH | 3 | 52 | 271 | 99 |
| DREAD LAMB, AND FALL | OFFICE H. CROSS NINTH | 14 | 52 | 271 | 99 |
| DREAD LAMB, & BOW THUS BEFORE THEE. | OFFICE H. CROSS EVENSONG | 29 | 52 | 273 | 101 |
| THE LAMB WHOM HIS OWN LOVE HATH SLAIN. | VEXILLA REGIS | 44 | 52 | 277 | 156 |
| WHAT DID THE LAMB, THAT HE SHOULD DY. | CHARITAS NIMIA | 52 | 52 | 280 | 48 |
| WHAT DID THE LAMB, THAT HE SHOULD NEED, | CHARITAS NIMIA | 53 | 52 | 280 | 48 |
| WITH A NEW LAMB BLESSES THE BOARD. | LAUDA SION SALVATOREM | 20 | 52 | 294 | 178 |
| THE MANNA, & THE PASCHAL LAMB. | LAUDA SION SALVATOREM | 68 | 52 | 294 | 178 |
| THE LAMB HATH DIPP'T HIS WHITE FOOT HERE. | WEEPER | 108 | 52 | 307 | 120 |
| THOU WITH THE LAMB, THY LORD, SHALT GOE. | TERESA | 178 | 52 | 315 | 52 |

## LAMB'S

| | | | | | |
|---|---|---|---|---|---|
| AND CROWD FOR KISSES FROM THE LAMB'S WHITE FEET. | TO THE QUEEN'S MAJESTY | 14 | 52 | 261 | 47 |
| SO SWORE THE LAMB'S DREAD SIRE. AND SO WE SEE'T. | TO THE QUEEN'S MAJESTY | 19 | 52 | 261 | 47 |
| LAMB'S BOSOM WRITE | CHARITAS NIMIA | 58 | 52 | 280 | 48 |
| AS KEEP ACCOUNT OF THE LAMB'S WARRES. | TERESA | 154 | 52 | 315 | 52 |

## LAMBE

| | | | | | |
|---|---|---|---|---|---|
| TO THEE (DREAD LAMBE) WHOSE LOVE MUST KEEPE | A HYMNE OF THE NATIVITY | 81 | 46 | 106 | 76 |
| THAT THE UNBLEMISHT LAMBE, BLESSED FOR EVER, | SOSPETTO D'HERODE | 189 | 46 | 109 | 216 |
| THOU WITH THE LAMBE THY LORD SHALL GOE. | IN MEMORY OF LADY MADRE TERESA | 179 | 46 | 131 | 52 |
| BUT (FOR A LAMBE) THY TAME AND TENDER HEART | ON A TREATISE OF CHARITY | 45 | 46 | 137 | 69 |

## LAMBES

| | | | | | |
|---|---|---|---|---|---|
| AS KEEP ACCOUNT OF THE LAMBES WARRES | IN MEMORY OF LADY MADRE TERESA | 155 | 46 | 131 | 52 |
| TO WHOM THE MERRY LAMBES DOE TRIPP ALONG | UPON KINGS CORONATION | 26 | MS | 390 | 453 |

## LAMBENT

| | | | | | |
|---|---|---|---|---|---|
| LIGHTLY AS A LAMBENT FLAME, | AGAINST IRRESOLUTION AND DELAY | 70 | 52 | 347 | 146 |

## LAMP

| | | | | | |
|---|---|---|---|---|---|
| THE SHAMEFAC'T LAMP HUNG DOWN HIS HEAD | IN GLORIOUS EPIPHANIE | 118 | 52 | 253 | 39 |
| O RISE, PURE LAMP, & LEND THY GOLDEN RAY | ALEXIAS SECONDE ELEGIE | 29 | 52 | 335 | 207 |

## LAMPE

| | | | | | |
|---|---|---|---|---|---|
| THEN GLUTT THY DIRE LAMPE WITH THE WARMEST BLOOD, | ON GUNPOWDER-TREASON | 63 | MS | 384 | 458 |

## LAMPS

| | | | | | |
|---|---|---|---|---|---|
| THEN THE CHAST STARS, WHOSE CHOICE LAMPS COME TO LIGHT HER. | ON THE ASSUMPTION | 4 | 46 | 139 | 114 |
| THEN THE CHAST STARRES, WHOSE CHOISE LAMPS COME TO LIGHT HER | IN GLORIOUS ASSUMPTION B. LADY | 4 | 52 | 304 | 114 |

## LAMPES

| | | | | | |
|---|---|---|---|---|---|
| SHEE LIFTS HER SOOTY LAMPES, AND LOOKING ROUND | SOSPETTO D'HERODE | 301 | 46 | 109 | 216 |
| TO WHOM HEAVENS LAMPES OFTEN IN SILENT NIGHT | UPON KINGS CORONATION | 27 | MS | 389 | 454 |

LAND

| | | | | | |
|---|---|---|---|---|---|
| HOPE OF A PREY. THERE TO THE MAINE LAND TY'D | THE BEGINNING OF HELIODORUS | 10 | 46 | 158 | 517 |
| TWO MITES, TWO DROPS, (YET ALL HER HOUSE AND LAND) | WIDOWES MITES | 1 | 46 | 86 | 21 |
| POYSONS TO SPEED THEE.  YET THROUGH ALL THE LAND | SOSPETTO D'HERODE | 445 | 46 | 109 | 216 |
| NOW AFTER ALL HER TOYLES BY SEA AND LAND, | UPON FAIRE ETHIOPIAN | 3 | 46 | 183 | 493 |
| INTO THE LAND OF LIGHT & LOVE. | OFFICE H. CROSS PRIME | 12 | 52 | 267 | 91 |
| RICH, CHURLISH LAND, THAT HID'ST SO LONG IN THEE, | ALEXIAS THIRD ELEGIE | 1 | 52 | 336 | 209 |
| MEE RANGING IN HIS QUARTERS.  AND THE LAND | OUT OF GROTIUS | 83 | MS | 398 | 198 |

CROWN-LAND

| | | | | | |
|---|---|---|---|---|---|
| OUR CROWN-LAND LYES ABOVE YET EACH MEAL BRINGS | (ON) HOPE | 13 | 52 | 345 | 71 |

LANDS

| | | | | | |
|---|---|---|---|---|---|
| THEIR GENTLEST FRIEND, THEN, THEN THE LANDS BEGIN | OUT OF VIRGIL | 2 | 46 | 155 | 529 |
| WINTERS SAD FACE, AND THROUGH THE FLOWRY LANDS | SOSPETTO D'HERODE | 110 | 46 | 109 | 216 |
| LO HOW THE THIRSTY LANDS | TO THE NAME OF JESUS | 129 | 52 | 239 | 30 |

CROWN-LANDS

| | | | | | |
|---|---|---|---|---|---|
| OUR CROWN-LANDS LYE ABOVE, YET EACH MEALE BRINGS | ON HOPE | 33 | 46 | 143 | 71 |

LANGUAGE

| | | | | | |
|---|---|---|---|---|---|
| THE SAD LANGUAGE OF OUR EYES, | UPON THE DEATH OF A GENTLEMAN | 20 | 46 | 166 | 472 |
| LANGUAGE NONE MORE FLUENT IS. | UPON THE DEATH OF A GENTLEMAN | 22 | 46 | 166 | 472 |
| OF LANGUAGE TO MY INFANT LIPS, YEE BEST | SOSPETTO D'HERODE | 6 | 46 | 109 | 216 |
| IN LANGUAGE OF HIS THUNDER, THOU ART EVEN | SOSPETTO D'HERODE | 270 | 46 | 109 | 216 |
| WHAT SOULE SOEVER IN ANY LANGUAGE CAN | AN APOLOGIE FOR HYMNE (TERESA) | 21 | 46 | 136 | 59 |
| WHAT SOUL SO E'RE, IN ANY LANGUAGE, CAN | AN APOLOGIE FOR (TERESA) HYMNE | 21 | 52 | 322 | 59 |

LANGUISH

| | | | | | |
|---|---|---|---|---|---|
| FOR WHICH I LANGUISH, COME AWAY. | ADORO TE | 52 | 52 | 291 | 172 |

LANGUISHING

| | | | | | |
|---|---|---|---|---|---|
| LOOK UP, LANGUISHING SOUL. LO WHERE THE FAIR | VEXILLA REGIS | 1 | 52 | 277 | 156 |

LANGUISHMENTS

| | | | | | |
|---|---|---|---|---|---|
| AMOROUS LANGUISHMENTS, LUMINOUS TRANCES, | ON A PRAYER BOOKE | 63 | 46 | 126 | 139 |
| AMOROUSE LANGUISHMENTS, LUMINOUS TRANCES. | PRAYER TO GENTLE-WOMAN | 69 | 52 | 328 | 139 |

LAOTHSOM

| | | | | | |
|---|---|---|---|---|---|
| AND LAOTHSOM SPITTLE, BLOTT THOSE BEAUTEOUS EYES, | OFFICE H. CROSS PRIME | 6 | 52 | 267 | 91 |

LAP

| | | | | | |
|---|---|---|---|---|---|
| HIMSELFE INTO HER LAP IN FRUITFULL SHOWERS. | OUT OF VIRGIL | 6 | 46 | 155 | 529 |
| THAT ON HER LAP SHE CASTS HER HUMBLE EYE. | ON VIRGINS BASHFULNESSE | 1 | 46 | 89 | 9 |
| TILL IN THE LAP OF LOVES FULL NOONE | ON HOPE | 56 | 46 | 143 | 71 |
| IN PITTY'S SOFT LAP LY A SLEEPING. | TO THE NAME OF JESUS | 192 | 52 | 239 | 30 |

LAPPE

| | | | | | |
|---|---|---|---|---|---|
| TILL IN THE LAPPE OF LOVES FULL NOONE | (ON) HOPE | 26 | 52 | 345 | 71 |
| DOTH SHE BEGINNE TO DANDLE IN HER LAPPE | AN ELEGY MR STANNINOW | 7 | MS | 394 | 473 |

LARGE

| | | | | | |
|---|---|---|---|---|---|
| WITH EARTHS LARGE MASSE, DOTH CHERISH AND ASSIST | OUT OF VIRGIL | 8 | 46 | 155 | 529 |
| LOE HERE A LITTLE VOLUME, BUT LARGE BOOKE, | ON A PRAYER BOOKE | 1 | 46 | 126 | 139 |
| OF THOSE WHOSE LARGE BREASTS BUILT A THRONE | IN MEMORY OF LADY MADRE TERESA | 10 | 46 | 131 | 52 |
| TO'INJOY HIS BLOTT. & AS A LARGE BLACK LETTER | IN GLORIOUS EPIPHANIE | 186 | 52 | 253 | 39 |
| AND BY THY THIRSTS OF LOVE MORE LARGE THEN THEY. | FLAMING HEART | 98 | 52 | 324 | 61 |
| BUT TO LARGE YOUTH SHORT TIME TO LIVE. | UPON DEATH OF A FREIND | 12 | MS | 393 | 477 |

LARGE-LOOK'T

| | | | | | |
|---|---|---|---|---|---|
| OUT-STARES THE LIDDES OF LARGE-LOOK'T TYRANNY. | UPON STANINOUGH'S DEATH | 26 | 46 | 175 | 475 |

LARG

| | | | | | |
|---|---|---|---|---|---|
| LARG THRONE OF LOVE. ROYALLY SPRED | VEXILLA REGIS | 25 | 52 | 277 | 156 |
| FOR LOVE AT LARG TO FILL. SPARE BLOOD & SWEAT. | TERESA | 11 | 52 | 315 | 52 |
| AMONG THE LEAVES OF THY LARG BOOKS OF DAY, | FLAMING HEART | 88 | 52 | 324 | 61 |
| BY THY LARG DRAUGHTS OF INTELLECTUALL DAY, | FLAMING HEART | 97 | 52 | 324 | 61 |
| NOR LOST IN TOO LARG BOUNDS, OUR LITTLE ROME | ALEXIAS THIRD ELEGIE | 11 | 52 | 336 | 209 |

LARG-LOOK'T

| | | | | | |
|---|---|---|---|---|---|
| OUTSTARES THE LIDDES OF LARG-LOOK'T TYRANNY. | DEATH'S LECTURE | 28 | 52 | 340 | 475 |

LARGER

| | | | | | |
|---|---|---|---|---|---|
| MUCH LARGER IN IT SELFE THEN IN ITS LOOKE. | ON A PRAYER BOOKE | 4 | 46 | 126 | 139 |

## LARKES

| | | | | | |
|---|---|---|---|---|---|
| THE EARLY LARKES SHRILL ORIZONS TO BE | TO THE MORNING | 43 | 46 | 183 | 497 |

## LASH

| | | | | | |
|---|---|---|---|---|---|
| WHILE HIS STEELE SIDES SOUND WITH HIS TAYLES STRONG LASH. | SOSPETTO D'HERODE | 64 | 46 | 109 | 216 |
| AND LASH EARTH-LABORING SOULS. | DESCRIPTION RELIGIOUS HOUSE | 27 | 52 | 336 | 213 |

## LASHES

| | | | | | |
|---|---|---|---|---|---|
| THEIR HANDS WITH LASHES ARM'D, THEIR TOUNGS WITH LYES, | OFFICE H. CROSS PRIME | 5 | 52 | 267 | 91 |

## LAST

| | | | | | |
|---|---|---|---|---|---|
| LENT THEM THE LAST FLASH OF HER GLIMMERING LIGHT. | THE BEGINNING OF HELIODORUS | 20 | 46 | 158 | 517 |
| AT LAST, IN FIRE OF THY FAIRE EYES, | A HYMNE OF THE NATIVITY | 87 | 46 | 106 | 76 |
| AT LAST HER LISTING EARES THE NOISE O'RETAKES. | SOSPETTO D'HERODE | 300 | 46 | 109 | 216 |
| SHALL ALL AT LAST DYE INTO ONE, | IN MEMORY OF LADY MADRE TERESA | 112 | 46 | 131 | 52 |
| SHALT THOU EXHALE TO HEAVEN AT LAST, | IN MEMORY OF LADY MADRE TERESA | 117 | 46 | 131 | 52 |
| THY GRACIOUS NAME, BUT TO THE LAST, | ON THE ASSUMPTION | 39 | 46 | 139 | 114 |
| WEE TO THE LAST, | ON THE ASSUMPTION | 44 | 46 | 139 | 114 |
| IN THE LAST KNOT THAT LOVE COULD TYE. | AN EPITAPH HUSBAND AND WIFE | 10 | 46 | 174 | 478 |
| THIS LAST COUGH AELIA, COUGHT OUT ALL THY FEARE. | OUT OF MARTIALL | 5 | 46 | 188 | 527 |
| THUS AT LAST WHEN WE HAVE NUMBRED | OUT OF CATULLUS | 15 | 46 | 194 | 523 |
| WHO GRANTS AT LAST, LONG TIME TRYD | TO COUNTESSE OF DENBIGH | 15 | 52 | 236 | 146 |
| O LET IT BE AT LAST, LOVE'S HOURE. | TO COUNTESSE OF DENBIGH | 37 | 52 | 236 | 146 |
| THE FORT AT LAST, AND LET LIFE IN. | TO COUNTESSE OF DENBIGH | 64 | 52 | 236 | 146 |
| O DAWN, AT LAST, LONG LOOK'T FOR DAY. | TO THE NAME OF JESUS | 149 | 52 | 239 | 30 |
| TILL BURNT AT LAST IN FIRE OF THY FAIR EYES. | IN HOLY NATIVITY | 107 | 52 | 246 | 76 |
| LO AT LAST HAVE FOUND OUR WAY. | IN GLORIOUS EPIPHANIE | 21 | 52 | 253 | 39 |
| LO WE AT LAST HAVE FOUND THE WAY. | IN GLORIOUS EPIPHANIE | 23 | 52 | 253 | 39 |
| HEAR, FATHER, HEAR. THY LAMB (AT LAST) COMPLAINES. | OFFICE H. CROSS NINTH | 3 | 52 | 271 | 99 |
| THE COMPLIN HOUR COMES LAST, TO CALL | OFFICE H. CROSS COMPLINE | 1 | 52 | 274 | 105 |
| O WHEN THY LAST FROWN SHALL PROCLAIM | DIES IRAE | 57 | 52 | 298 | 186 |
| WE TO THE LAST | IN GLORIOUS ASSUMPTION B. LADY | 49 | 52 | 304 | 114 |
| EVEN THE LAST PEARLE IN THY TREASURE. | WEEPER | 130 | 52 | 307 | 120 |
| SHALL ALL AT LAST DY INTO ONE, | TERESA | 111 | 52 | 315 | 52 |
| SHALT THOU EXHALE TO HEAVN AT LAST | TERESA | 116 | 52 | 315 | 52 |
| BY THY LAST MORNING'S DRAUGHT OF LIQUID FIRE. | FLAMING HEART | 100 | 52 | 324 | 61 |
| SWEET, LET ME PROPHESY THAT AT LAST T'WILL PROVE | TO SAME CONCERNING CHOISE | 33 | 52 | 331 | 66 |
| THERE THY LOST FUGITIVE THOU'HAST FOUND AT LAST. | ALEXIAS FIRST ELEGIE | 37 | 52 | 334 | 204 |
| AT LAST A CONSTANT LOVE THAT LEAVES ME NOT. | ALEXIAS SECONDE ELEGIE | 8 | 52 | 335 | 207 |
| THAT WEARY LOVE AT LAST MAY FIND HIS WAY. | ALEXIAS SECONDE ELEGIE | 30 | 52 | 335 | 207 |
| BOTH MIXT AT LAST THEIR BLOOD IN ONE RICH BED | ALEXIAS THIRD ELEGIE | 47 | 52 | 336 | 209 |
| IN THE LAST KNOTT LOVE COULD TY. | AN EPITAPH UPON MARRIED COUPLE | 10 | 52 | 339 | 478 |
| AND WHAT AT LAST SHALT' GAIN BY THESE. | TEMPERANCE | 9 | 52 | 342 | 510 |
| WHO GRANTS AT LAST, A GREAT TRY'DE, | AGAINST IRRESOLUTION AND DELAY | 9 | 52 | 347 | 146 |
| THE FORT AT LAST, AND LET LIFE IN. | AGAINST IRRESOLUTION AND DELAY | 86 | 52 | 347 | 146 |
| AT LAST IT STOPT AT PLUTO'S GLOOMY PORCH. | ON GUNPOWDER-TREASON | 55 | MS | 384 | 458 |
| BUT AT THE LAST (HAVING NOT SOE MUCH POWE'R | UPON KINGS CORONATION | 5 | MS | 390 | 453 |

## LASTING

| | | | | | |
|---|---|---|---|---|---|
| AND KEEP'T ALIVE WITH LASTING SONGS. | O GLORIOSA DOMINA | 30 | 52 | 302 | 194 |

## LATE

| | | | | | |
|---|---|---|---|---|---|
| AND SHEE ALTHOUGH HER BREATH'S LATE EXERCISE | MUSICKS DUELL | 158 | 46 | 149 | 535 |
| LIFES LATE FORSAKEN HOUSES ALL LAY DROWN'D | THE BEGINNING OF HELIODORUS | 16 | 46 | 158 | 517 |
| AND COMMING LATE HAD EAT UP GUESTS AND ALL, | THE BEGINNING OF HELIODORUS | 27 | 46 | 158 | 517 |
| OF WOES, TOO LATE DOE ROUZE THY FEARES. | PSALME 137 | 34 | 46 | 104 | 7 |
| TELL HIM HEE RISES NOW TOO LATE, | A HYMNE OF THE NATIVITY | 9 | 46 | 106 | 76 |
| HEAVENS GOLDEN-WINGED HERALD, LATE HEE SAW | SOSPETTO D'HERODE | 97 | 46 | 109 | 216 |
| AND NOW OF LATE CAME TRIBUTARY KINGS, | SOSPETTO D'HERODE | 499 | 46 | 109 | 216 |
| DRESSE THE SOULE, WHICH LATE THEY SLEW. | IN MEMORY OF LADY MADRE TERESA | 153 | 46 | 131 | 52 |
| AND LATE CONSENT WAS A LONG NO. | TO COUNTESSE OF DENBIGH | 14 | 52 | 236 | 146 |
| TELL HIM HE RISES NOW, TOO LATE | IN HOLY NATIVITY | 9 | 52 | 246 | 76 |
| I LATE THE ROMAN YOUTH'S LOV'D PRAYSE & PRIDE, | ALEXIAS FIRST ELEGIE | 1 | 52 | 334 | 204 |
| AND LATE CONSENT WAS A LONG NO. | AGAINST IRRESOLUTION AND DELAY | 8 | 52 | 347 | 146 |
| THE LATE WINGS OF THE LAZY WIND. | AGAINST IRRESOLUTION AND DELAY | 76 | 52 | 347 | 146 |
| TO THEE THE PARCAE HAVE GIVEN UP OF LATE | EX EUPHORMIONE | 10 | MS | 392 | 525 |

## LATEST

| | | | | | |
|---|---|---|---|---|---|
| WHOSE LATEST & MOST LEADEN HOURES | TEMPERANCE | 45 | 52 | 342 | 510 |

## LAUGH

| | | | | | |
|---|---|---|---|---|---|
| HEE STRAINES THESE WORDS. BASE ENVY, DOE, LAUGH ON. | HIGH MOUNTED ON AN ANT | 5 | 46 | 161 | 523 |
| DOST LAUGH. PROUD BABELS DAUGHTER. DO. LAUGH ON. | PSALME 137 | 31 | 46 | 104 | 7 |
| DOST LAUGH. PROUD BABELS DAUGHTER. DO. LAUGH ON. | PSALME 137 | 31 | 46 | 104 | 7 |
| EVEN SUCH AS THESE, LAUGH, TILL A VENGING THRONG | PSALME 137 | 33 | 46 | 104 | 7 |
| LAUGH,TILL THY CHILDRENS BLEEDING BONES | PSALME 137 | 35 | 46 | 104 | 7 |
| AND MAKE THEM LAUGH, WHICH FROWN'D, & WEPT BEFORE. | AN ELEGY MR STANNINOW | 14 | MS | 394 | 473 |

## LAUGHT

| | | | | | |
|---|---|---|---|---|---|
| THE PAINTED MEDDOWES WOULD HAVE LAUGHT NOE MORE | UPON GUNPOWDER TREASON | 45 | MS | 386 | 460 |

## LAUGHING

THE LAUGHING MEADES, AS JOYFULL TO BEHOLD          UPON KINGS CORONATION              27   MS 390 453

## LAURELL

FOR THE LAURELL IN HIS VERSE,                      UPON THE DEATH OF A GENTLEMAN       9   46 166 472

## LAW

THOU SPEAK'ST THE WORD (THY WORD'S A LAW)          THE BLIND CURED                     1   46  91  19
HEE SAW TH'OLD HEBREWES WOMBE, NEGLECT THE LAW     SOSPETTO D'HERODE                 101   46 109 216
AND LOVES THAT BODIES SOULE, NO LAW CONTROULES     AN APOLOGIE FOR HYMNE (TERESA)     18   46 136  59
FORTUNE ALAS ABOVE THE WORLDS LAW WARRES.          ON HOPE                            71   46 143  71
LO THE NEW LAW OF A NEW LORD                       LAUDA SION SALVATOREM              19   52 294 178
AND LOVE'S THAT BODY'S SOUL, NO LAW CONTROWLLS     AN APOLOGIE FOR (TERESA) HYMNE     18   52 322  59
JUSTICE HATH LOST HER HAND, THE LAW HER HEAD.      AN ELEGIE ON DR PORTER             15   MS 395 476
THOSE LAWLESS TYRANT MASTERS OF THE LAW.           OUT OF GROTIUS                     46   MS 398 198

## LAWS

LIVES BY HIS OWN LAWS, AND DOES HOLD               AGAINST IRRESOLUTION AND DELAY     55   52 347 146
SPURNS THE TAME LAWS OF TIME AND PLACE.            AGAINST IRRESOLUTION AND DELAY     77   52 347 146

## LAWES

THIS NEW GUEST TO HER EYES NEW LAWES HATH GIVEN,   ON VIRGINS BASHFULNESSE             7   46  89   9
AND FURTHER,THAT THE LAWES ETERNALL GIVER,         SOSPETTO D'HERODE                 185   46 109 216
SHOULD BLEED IN HIS OWNE LAWES OBEDIENCE.          SOSPETTO D'HERODE                 186   46 109 216
WEE (SAID THE HORRID SISTERS) WAIT THY LAWES,      SOSPETTO D'HERODE                 261   46 109 216
BY THE FAIRE LAWES OF THY FIRM-POINTED PEN,        ON A TREATISE OF CHARITY           28   46 137  69
POORE LAWES DIVIDE THE PUBLICKE YEARE.             THOUGH NOW 'TIS NEITHER            24   MS 397 492
THAT SABLE JUDGMENT-SEAT SHALL BY NEW LAWES        IN GLORIOUS EPIPHANIE             145   52 253  39
TO WHICH THE LOW WORLD'S LAWES                     IN GLORIOUS EPIPHANIE             153   52 253  39
AS FAST AS LOVE NEW LAWES CAN GIVE.                ADORO TE                           12   52 291 172
WHERE NATURE'S LAWES NO LEAVE WILL GIVE,           LAUDA SION SALVATOREM              37   52 294 178

## LAWLESSE

THOSE LAWLESSE TYRANT MASTERS OF THE LAW.          OUT OF GROTIUS                     46   MS 398 198

## LAWN

AS WHEN A PEICE OF WANTON LAWN                     TEMPERANCE                         25   52 342 510

## LAWNE

AS WHEN A PEECE OF WANTON LAWNE,                   IN PRAISE OF LESSIUS               27   46 156 510

## LAWRELS

BOTH LAWRELS TWINE INTO ONE WREATH, AND WOOE       UPON YORKE HIS BIRTH               38   46 176 500

## LAY

(MOST DIVINE SERVICE) WHOSE SO EARLY LAY,          MUSICKS DUELL                      81   46 149 535
AND LAY THE GROUND-WORKE OF HER HOPEFULL SONG.     MUSICKS DUELL                      85   46 149 535
(QUICK WITH WARME ZEPHIRES LIVELY BREATH) LAY FORTH OUT OF VIRGIL                     13   46 155 529
-IFES LATE FORSAKEN HOUSES ALL LAY DROWN'D         THE BEGINNING OF HELIODORUS        16   46 158 517
'CAUSE THOU STREIGHT MUST LAY THY HEAD             THE TEARE                          32   46  84  50
LOOKE, MARY, HERE SEE, WHERE THY LORD ONCE LAY,    COME SEE WHERE THE LORD LAY         4   46  87  27
LOOKE, MARY, HERE SEE, WHERE THY LORD ONCE LAY,    COME SEE WHERE THE LORD LAY         6   46  87  27
WHERE THE NOBLE INFANT LAY.                        A HYMNE OF THE NATIVITY            18   46 106  76
WHERE TO LAY HIS LOVELY HEAD,                      A HYMNE OF THE NATIVITY            48   46 106  76
BE IT THY PART, HELLS MIGHTY LORD, TO LAY          SOSPETTO D'HERODE                 263   46 109 216
THAT WHILE I LAY THEM ON THE SHRINE                ON MR. G. HERBERTS BOOKE           17   46 130  68
AND LAY THEM TREMBLING AT HIS FEET.                UPON DEATH OF DESIRED HERRYS       46   46 168 467
TWO SILKEN SISTER FLOWERS CONSULT, AND LAY         UPON YORKE HIS BIRTH               60   46 176 500
_AY FOLDED UP IN SLEEPES CAPTIVITY.                TO THE MORNING                      6   46 183 497
MY GRIEFE IS, SO MY WAKEFULL LAY SHALL KNOCKE      TO THE MORNING                     41   46 183 497
LAY BLACKE ON LOVES NATIVITYE.                     LOVES HOROSCOPE                    36   46 185 483
WHERE THE NOBLE INFANT LAY.                        IN HOLY NATIVITY                   18   52 246  76
OF MY WEAKE FEET THE PERSIAN MAGI LAY              OUT OF GROTIUS                     37   MS 398 198

## LAY'D

HERE WHERE OUR LORD ONCE LAY'D HIS HEAD,           UPON THE H. SEPULCHER               1   52 277  26

## LAY'T

FOLD UP MY LIFE IN LOVE, AND LAY'T BENEATH         SANCTA MARIA DOLORUM              107   52 283 162

## LAIES

GRACE AND PEACE, TO MEET NEW LAIES                 PSALME 23                          33   46 102   5

## LAYES

BUT HASTS HER FORWARD BLOSSOMES, AND LAYES OUT     OUT OF VIRGIL                      21   46 155 529
FREELY LAYES OUT HER LEAVES. NOR DOE I DOUBT       OUT OF VIRGIL                      22   46 155 529
TIME LAYES HIM UP. HE'S PRETIOUS.                  THE WEEPER                         96   46  79 120
TO CROWNE THEIR PAST PREDICTIONS, BOTH HEE LAYES   SOSPETTO D'HERODE                  95   46 109 216
HER SELFE A WHILE SHE LAYES ASIDE, AND MAKES       SOSPETTO D'HERODE                 417   46 109 216

|  |  |  |  |  |
|---|---|---|---|---|
| BEAUTY LAYES OPE LOVES FORTUNE-BOOKE, | LOVES HOROSCOPE | 12 | 46 185 | 483 |
| AT THY ADORED FEET, THUS, HE LAYES DOWN | IN GLORIOUS EPIPHANIE | 240 | 52 253 | 39 |
| TIME LAYES HIM UP. HE'S PRETIOUS. | WEEPER | 150 | 52 307 | 120 |
| LAYES UP HIS PURER & MORE PRETIOUS VOWES. | TO SAME CONCERNING CHOISE | 35 | 52 331 | 66 |

## LAZARUS

|  |  |  |  |  |
|---|---|---|---|---|
| RICH LAZARUS, RICHER IN THOSE GEMS, THY TEARS. | UPON LAZARUS HIS TEARES | 1 | 46 89 | 18 |

## LAZY

|  |  |  |  |  |
|---|---|---|---|---|
| NO MISTES DOE MASKE NO LAZY STEAMES. | IN PRAISE OF LESSIUS | 32 | 46 156 | 510 |
| TO LIFT ME FROM MY LAZY URNE, TO CLIMBE | TO THE MORNING | 27 | 46 183 | 497 |
| FLIGHTS SCORN THE LAZY DUST, & THINGS THAT DY. | AN APOLOGIE FOR (TERESA) HYMNE | 28 | 52 322 | 59 |
| NO MISTS DOE MASK, NO LAZY STEAMES. | TEMPERANCE | 30 | 52 342 | 510 |
| THE LATE WINGS OF THE LAZY WIND, | AGAINST IRRESOLUTION AND DELAY | 76 | 52 347 | 146 |
| Y' HAD DONE ENOUGH TO MAKE THE LAZY GROUND | UPON BIRTH PRINCESSE E | 31 | MS 391 | 456 |
| THY LAZY CRAWLING STREAMES, PRI'THEE BE GONE. | AN ELEGIE ON DR PORTER | 20 | MS 395 | 476 |

## LAZIE

|  |  |  |  |  |
|---|---|---|---|---|
| FLIGHTS SCORNE THE LAZIE DUST, AND THINGS THAT DYE. | AN APOLOGIE FOR HYMNE (TERESA) | 28 | 46 136 | 59 |

## LEAD

|  |  |  |  |  |
|---|---|---|---|---|
| AND THE GAY STARRS LEAD ON THEIR GOLDEN DANCE. | SOSPETTO D'HERODE | 206 | 46 109 | 216 |
| THEIR PILLOW STONE, THEIR SHEETES OF LEAD, | AN EPITAPH UPON MARRIED COUPLE | 12 | 52 339 | 478 |
| AND LEAST THY BLOODSHOTT EYES SHOULD LEAD ASIDE | UPON GUNPOWDER TREASON | 7 | MS 387 | 461 |
| PROFANE SADOCUS TOO DOES FIERCELY LEAD | OUT OF GROTIUS | 47 | MS 398 | 198 |

## LEADEN

|  |  |  |  |  |
|---|---|---|---|---|
| WHY DOST THOU SHAKE THY LEADEN SCEPTER. GOE | TO THE MORNING | 54 | 46 183 | 497 |
| WHOSE LATEST & MOST LEADEN HOURES | TEMPERANCE | 45 | 52 342 | 510 |

## LEADS

|  |  |  |  |  |
|---|---|---|---|---|
| LOVE TOO, THAT LEADS THE WAY, WOULD LEND THE WINGS | ALEXIAS FIRST ELEGIE | 17 | 52 334 | 204 |
| AND WHERE LOVE LENDS THE WING, & LEADS THE WAY. | ALEXIAS FIRST ELEGIE | 19 | 52 334 | 204 |

## LEAFE

|  |  |  |  |  |
|---|---|---|---|---|
| A WITHER'D LEAFE, AN IDLE GUEST. | PSALME 137 | 24 | 46 104 | 7 |
| WHENCE EACH LEAFE OF LIFE HATH DATE, | ANOTHER ON HERRYS | 42 | 46 170 | 469 |
| LIVE SHEE, OR DYE TO FAME. EACH LEAFE YOU MEET | AT TH' IVORY TRIBUNALL | 5 | MS 397 | 492 |

## LEAN

|  |  |  |  |  |
|---|---|---|---|---|
| SHALL KICK THE CLOUDS NO MORE. BUT LEAN & TAME, | IN GLORIOUS EPIPHANIE | 98 | 52 253 | 39 |
| AND LESSE TO LEAN ON. BECAUSE THAN | ADORO TE | 21 | 52 291 | 172 |
| LIFT OUR LEAN SOULES, & SETT US UP | LAUDA SION SALVATOREM | 75 | 52 294 | 178 |
| FROM THEE THEIR LEAN DILEMMA, WITH BLUNT HORN, | (ON) HOPE | 9 | 52 345 | 71 |

## LEANE

|  |  |  |  |  |
|---|---|---|---|---|
| WHICH HARPYES, WITH LEANE FAMINE FEED UPON, | SOSPETTO D'HERODE | 330 | 46 109 | 216 |
| LONG MAYEST THOU LADEN WITH SUCH CLUSTERS LEANE | UPON YORKE HIS BIRTH | 102 | 46 176 | 500 |
| LOWER & LOWER YET. TILL THY LEANE SIZE | DEATH'S LECTURE | 16 | 52 340 | 475 |
| GROW PLUMPE, LEANE DEATH. HIS HOLINESSE A FEAST | UPON GUNPOWDER TREASON | 1 | MS 387 | 461 |

## LEAP

|  |  |  |  |  |
|---|---|---|---|---|
| START INTO LIFE, AND LEAP WITH ME | TO THE NAME OF JESUS | 49 | 52 239 | 30 |
| LEAP AT THY LOFTY FACE. | IN GLORIOUS EPIPHANIE | 198 | 52 253 | 39 |

## LEAPT

|  |  |  |  |  |
|---|---|---|---|---|
| HATH LEAPT, TO PART. | LUKE 2. QUAERIT JESUM | 40 | MS 379 | 11 |

## LEAPES

|  |  |  |  |  |
|---|---|---|---|---|
| LEAPES AT THY BIRTH. | TO THE NAME OF JESUS | 134 | 52 239 | 30 |

## LEAPING

|  |  |  |  |  |
|---|---|---|---|---|
| LEAPING UPON THE HILLS, TO BE | AGAINST IRRESOLUTION AND DELAY | 71 | 52 347 | 146 |

## LEARN

|  |  |  |  |  |
|---|---|---|---|---|
| TO LEARN OF HIM AT LEST, TO WORSHIP THEE. | IN GLORIOUS EPIPHANIE | 182 | 52 253 | 39 |
| NOW BY ABASED LIDDES SHALL LEARN TO BE | IN GLORIOUS EPIPHANIE | 231 | 52 253 | 39 |
| MUST LEARN IN LIFE TO DY LIKE THEE. | TERESA | 182 | 52 315 | 52 |

## LEARN'D

|  |  |  |  |  |
|---|---|---|---|---|
| OF YOUR LEARN'D LYES. HERE YOU'L FIND NO SUCH JEST. | ALEXIAS THIRD ELEGIE | 42 | 52 336 | 209 |
| LEARN'D FIRST HIS LIGHTNESSE BY HIS LOVE. | AGAINST IRRESOLUTION AND DELAY | 52 | 52 347 | 146 |

## LEARNT

|  |  |  |  |  |
|---|---|---|---|---|
| SCARCE HAD SHEE LEARNT TO LISP A NAME | IN MEMORY OF LADY MADRE TERESA | 15 | 46 131 | 52 |
| I LEARNT TO KNOW THAT LOVE IS ELOQUENCE. | AN APOLOGIE FOR HYMNE (TERESA) | 8 | 46 136 | 59 |
| OR HAD EVER LEARNT TO BEARE, | ANOTHER ON HERRYS | 19 | 46 170 | 469 |

LEARN'T

| | | | | | |
|---|---|---|---|---|---|
| NATURE HATH LEARN'T T' EXTRACT A DEW, | THE WEEPER | 71 | 46 | 79 | 120 |
| WOULD HAVE LEARN'T A SOFTER STYLE, | ANOTHER ON HERRYS | 37 | 46 | 170 | 469 |
| NATURE HATH LEARN'T TO EXTRACT A DEAW | WEEPER | 53 | 52 | 307 | 120 |
| SCARSE HAS SHE LEARN'T TO LISP THE NAME | TERESA | 15 | 52 | 315 | 52 |
| I LEARN'T TO KNOW THAT LOVE IS ELOQUENCE | AN APOLOGIE FOR (TERESA) HYMNE | 8 | 52 | 322 | 59 |

LEARNE

| | | | | | |
|---|---|---|---|---|---|
| IN HEAV'N YOU'L LEARNE TO SING ERE HERE TO SPEAKE, | TO INFANT MARTYRS | 2 | 46 | 88 | 10 |
| MUST LEARNE IN LIFE TO DYE LIKE THEE. | IN MEMORY OF LADY MADRE TERESA | 183 | 46 | 131 | 52 |
| LEARNING, LEARNE HUMILITY. | HIS EPITAPH (HERRYS) | 22 | 46 | 172 | 471 |
| GOE LEARNE THAT FATALL QUIRE, SOE SPRUCELY DIGHT | AN ELEGIE ON DR PORTER | 27 | MS | 395 | 476 |

LEARNED

| | | | | | |
|---|---|---|---|---|---|
| THE HUMOUROUS STRINGS EXPOUND HIS LEARNED TOUCH, | MUSICKS DUELL | 127 | 46 | 149 | 535 |
| THESE LEARNED LEAVES SHALL VINDICATE TO THEE | ON A TREATISE OF CHARITY | 13 | 46 | 137 | 69 |
| O I AM LEARNED GROWN, POOR LOVE & I | ALEXIAS SECONDE ELEGIE | 21 | 52 | 335 | 207 |

LEARNING

| | | | | | |
|---|---|---|---|---|---|
| LEARNING, LEARNE HUMILITY. | HIS EPITAPH (HERRYS) | 22 | 46 | 172 | 471 |

LEARNINGS

| | | | | | |
|---|---|---|---|---|---|
| THROUGH LEARNINGS UNIVERSE, AND (VAINELY) SOUGHT | UPON BISHOP ANDREWES PICTURE | 6 | 46 | 163 | 490 |

LEAST

| | | | | | |
|---|---|---|---|---|---|
| BUT LEAST YOUR EYE DISCERNING SLIDE | OUT OF GREEKE CUPID'S CRYER | 17 | 46 | 159 | 519 |
| YET IF AT LEAST SHEE NOT DENYES, | UPON THE DEATH OF A GENTLEMAN | 19 | 46 | 166 | 472 |
| A DELUGE LEAST WE SHOULD BE DROWN'D. | ON BLEEDING WOUNDS OF LORD | 40 | 46 | 101 | 110 |
| AT LEAST BE IN LOVES WAY. | SANCTA MARIA DOLORUM | 66 | 52 | 283 | 162 |
| AT LEAST AN ALMES OF GREIF | SANCTA MARIA DOLORUM | 92 | 52 | 283 | 162 |
| A DELUGE LEAST WE SHOULD BE DROWN'D. | UPON BLEEDING CRUCIFIX | 36 | 52 | 288 | 110 |
| AT LEAST THE SUFFRING SIDE OF THEE. | ADORO TE | 24 | 52 | 291 | 172 |
| THAT BLOOD, WHOSE LEAST DROPS SOVERAIGN BE | ADORO TE | 49 | 52 | 291 | 172 |
| WHOSE WAYES HAVE LEAST TO DOE WITH WINGS. | AGAINST IRRESOLUTION AND DELAY | 48 | 52 | 347 | 146 |
| MAKE WINGS AT LEAST OF THEIR OWN WEIGHT. | AGAINST IRRESOLUTION AND DELAY | 49 | 52 | 347 | 146 |
| LEAST IT BREAKE FORTH, & BURNE THY SOOTY CELL. | ON GUNPOWDER-TREASON | 66 | MS | 384 | 458 |
| I FEARE TO NAME IT, LEAST THAT HE, WHICH HEARES, | UPON GUNPOWDER TREASON | 9 | MS | 386 | 460 |
| NOT DARING TO PEEPE FORTH, LEAST THAT A STONE | UPON GUNPOWDER TREASON | 25 | MS | 386 | 460 |
| AEOL KEPT IN HIS WRANGLING SONNES, LEAST THEY | UPON GUNPOWDER TREASON | 29 | MS | 386 | 460 |
| AND LEAVE EMBRACING OF THE ISLES, LEAST HEE | UPON GUNPOWDER TREASON | 33 | MS | 386 | 460 |
| AND LEAST THY BLOODSHOTT EYES SHOULD LEAD ASIDE | UPON GUNPOWDER TREASON | 7 | MS | 387 | 461 |
| WHOSE SNOWY CHEEKES, LEAST JOY SHOULD BE EXPREST, | AN ELEGIE ON DR PORTER | 9 | MS | 395 | 476 |

LEAVE

| | | | | | |
|---|---|---|---|---|---|
| AND LEAVE THEM BOTH TO BEE THY TEARE. | THE WEEPER | 42 | 46 | 79 | 120 |
| LEAVE, LEAVE, FOR SHAME, OR ELSE (GOOD JUDGE) DECREE, | TO PONTIUS WASHING HANDS | 15 | 46 | 94 | 23 |
| LEAVE, LEAVE, FOR SHAME, OR ELSE (GOOD JUDGE) DECREE, | TO PONTIUS WASHING HANDS | 15 | 46 | 94 | 23 |
| (NOR ASKT LEAVE OF THE SUN) BY DAY AS NIGHT. | SOSPETTO D'HERODE | 133 | 46 | 109 | 216 |
| DOWNE MY PROUD THOUGHT, AND LEAVE IT IN A TRANCE. | SOSPETTO D'HERODE | 204 | 46 | 109 | 216 |
| WHICH SHORT-CUT LIVES OF MURDRED INFANTS LEAVE. | SOSPETTO D'HERODE | 344 | 46 | 109 | 216 |
| TO ASKE THE WINDOWES LEAVE, TO PASSE THAT WAY. | ON A PRAYER BOOKE | 70 | 46 | 126 | 139 |
| SO SHALL SHEE LEAVE AMONGST THEM SOWNE. | IN MEMORY OF LADY MADRE TERESA | 55 | 46 | 131 | 52 |
| BLEST SERAPHIMS SHALL LEAVE THEIR QUIRE, | IN MEMORY OF LADY MADRE TERESA | 94 | 46 | 131 | 52 |
| THOSE RARE WORKES, WHERE THOU SHALT LEAVE WRIT. | IN MEMORY OF LADY MADRE TERESA | 156 | 46 | 131 | 52 |
| AND LEAVE THE LONG ADORED SUNNE. | AN HIMNE FOR CIRCUMCISION | 32 | 46 | 141 | 37 |
| HIS PERSIAN LOVERS ALL SHALL LEAVE HIM. | AN HIMNE FOR CIRCUMCISION | 35 | 46 | 141 | 37 |
| NOR WHILE THEY LEAVE HIM SHALL THEY LOOSE THE SUNNE. | AN HIMNE FOR CIRCUMCISION | 37 | 46 | 141 | 37 |
| AND MEANT TO LEAVE HIS PRETIOUS FEATURE, | UPON DEATH OF DESIRED HERRYS | 7 | 46 | 168 | 467 |
| OF WURTH, MAY LEAVE HER POORE | WISHES SUPPOSED MISTRESSE | 104 | 46 | 195 | 479 |
| AND WE, LOW WORMES HAVE LEAVE TO DOE | TO THE NAME OF JESUS | 109 | 52 | 239 | 30 |
| LEAVE ALL THY NATIVE GLORIES IN THEIR GORGEOUS NEST, | TO THE NAME OF JESUS | 119 | 52 | 239 | 30 |
| AND LEAVE HER OWN NEGLECTED SUN. | NEW YEAR'S DAY | 32 | 52 | 251 | 37 |
| HIS PERSIAN LOVERS ALL SHALL LEAVE HIM. | NEW YEAR'S DAY | 35 | 52 | 251 | 37 |
| NOR (MUCH LESSE) SHALL THEY LEAVE THESE EYES | IN GLORIOUS EPIPHANIE | 87 | 52 | 253 | 39 |
| THE SAME LEAVE BOTH TO EAT & LIVE. | ADORO TE | 42 | 52 | 291 | 172 |
| THEMSELVES WITH REVERENCE LEAVE THEIR PLACE | LAUDA SION SALVATOREM | 34 | 52 | 294 | 178 |
| WHERE NATURE'S LAWES NO LEAVE WILL GIVE, | LAUDA SION SALVATOREM | 37 | 52 | 294 | 178 |
| NOR LEAVE THEM BOTH LESSE THEN BEFORE. | LAUDA SION SALVATOREM | 48 | 52 | 294 | 178 |
| BUT THOU GIV'ST LEAVE (DREAD LORD) THAT WE | DIES IRAE | 25 | 52 | 298 | 186 |
| AND LEAVE THEM BOTH TO TREMBLE HERE. | WEEPER | 48 | 52 | 307 | 120 |
| SO SHALL SHE LEAVE AMONGST THEM SOWN | TERESA | 55 | 52 | 315 | 52 |
| BLEST SERAPHIM, SHALL LEAVE THEIR QUIRE | TERESA | 94 | 52 | 315 | 52 |
| TO LIVE, BUT THAT HE THUS MAY NEVER LEAVE TO DY. | TERESA | 104 | 52 | 315 | 52 |
| THOSE RARE WORKES WHERE THOU SHALT LEAVE WRITT. | TERESA | 155 | 52 | 315 | 52 |
| LEAVE HER ALONE THE FLAMING HEART. | FLAMING HEART | 68 | 52 | 324 | 61 |
| LEAVE HER THAT, & THOU SHALT LEAVE HER | FLAMING HEART | 69 | 52 | 324 | 61 |
| LEAVE HER THAT, & THOU SHALT LEAVE HER | FLAMING HEART | 69 | 52 | 324 | 61 |
| LEAVE NOTHING OF MY SELF IN ME. | FLAMING HEART | 106 | 52 | 324 | 61 |
| TO ASK THE WINDOWS LEAVE TO PASSE THAT WAY. | PRAYER TO GENTLE-WOMAN | 76 | 52 | 328 | 139 |
| NOR COULDST THOU, CRUELL, LEAVE ME QUITE ALONE. | ALEXIAS SECONDE ELEGIE | 4 | 52 | 335 | 207 |
| GIVING HIS WANTON PALFREYS LEAVE TO PLAY | UPON GUNPOWDER TREASON | 20 | MS | 386 | 460 |
| AND LEAVE EMBRACING OF THE ISLES, LEAST HEE | UPON GUNPOWDER TREASON | 33 | MS | 386 | 460 |
| BUT GIVE ME LEAVE TO EASE IT WITH MY HAND. | UPON BIRTH PRINCESSE E | 16 | MS | 391 | 456 |

## LEAVES

| | | | | |
|---|---|---|---|---|
| CLOSE IN THE COVERT OF THE LEAVES THERE STOOD | MUSICKS DUELL | 7 | 46 149 | 535 |
| SHEE DYES. AND LEAVES HER LIFE THE VICTORS PRISE. | MUSICKS DUELL | 166 | 46 149 | 535 |
| FREELY LAYES OUT HER LEAVES. NOR DOE I DOUBT | OUT OF VIRGIL | 22 | 46 155 | 529 |
| LOOKE ON THE FOLLOWING LEAVES, AND SEE HIM BREATH. | UPON BISHOP ANDREWES PICTURE | 16 | 46 163 | 490 |
| SHEE SPREADS THE RED LEAVES OF THY LIPS. | A HYMNE OF THE NATIVITY | 67 | 46 106 | 76 |
| SIBILLS DIVINING LEAVES. HEE DOES ENQUIRE | SOSPETTO D'HERODE | 92 | 46 109 | 216 |
| THESE LEARNED LEAVES SHALL VINDICATE TO THEE | ON A TREATISE OF CHARITY | 13 | 46 137 | 69 |
| AS MUCH AS SEES) SHALL WITH THESE SACRED LEAVES | ON A TREATISE OF CHARITY | 24 | 46 137 | 69 |
| TO HATCH HER SELFE IN, 'MONGST HIS LEAVES THE DAY | UPON DEATH OF HERRYS | 15 | 46 167 | 466 |
| ALL HIS LEAVES. SO FRESH, SO SWEET. | UPON DEATH OF DESIRED HERRYS | 45 | 46 168 | 467 |
| IN SHADY LEAVES OF DESTINY. | WISHES SUPPOSED MISTRESSE | 6 | 46 195 | 479 |
| YETT IN THESE LEAVES (FAIRE ONE) THERE LYES | THOUGH NOW 'TIS NEITHER | 3 | MS 397 | 492 |
| O THAT BOOK. WHOSE LEAVES SO BRIGHT | DIES IRAE | 17 | 52 298 | 186 |
| LIVE IN THESE CONQUERING LEAVES. LIVE ALL THE SAME. | FLAMING HEART | 77 | 52 324 | 61 |
| AMONG THE LEAVES OF THY LARG BOOKS OF DAY. | FLAMING HEART | 88 | 52 324 | 61 |
| AT LAST A CONSTANT LOVE THAT LEAVES ME NOT. | ALEXIAS SECONDE ELEGIE | 8 | 52 335 | 207 |
| DETAIN HIM, BUT HE LEAVES BEHIND | AGAINST IRRESOLUTION AND DELAY | 75 | 52 347 | 146 |
| (FAIRE ONE) THESE TENDER LEAVES DOE TREMBLING STAND. | AT TH' IVORY TRIBUNALL | 2 | MS 397 | 492 |

## LEAVING

| | | | | |
|---|---|---|---|---|
| EACH DROP LEAVING A PLACE SO DEARE. | THE TEARE | 17 | 46 84 | 50 |
| LEAVING HER CHAST ABODE. | ON A PRAYER BOOKE | 43 | 46 126 | 139 |
| LEAVING HER ONLY SO MUCH BREATH | SANCTA MARIA DOLORUM | 39 | 52 283 | 162 |
| LEAVING HER CHAST ABOAD | PRAYER TO GENTLE-WOMAN | 49 | 52 328 | 139 |
| HEE'S GONE. NOT LEAVING WITH ME, TILL HE COME, | LUKE 2. QUAERIT JESUM | 13 | MS 379 | 11 |
| LEAVING THOSE MINES OF NECTAR, THEIR SWEET FOUNTAINES. | AN ELEGIE ON DR PORTER | 41 | MS 395 | 476 |

## LEAVY

| | | | | |
|---|---|---|---|---|
| ALL TREES, ALL LEAVY GROVES CONFESSE THE SPRING | OUT OF VIRGIL | 1 | 46 155 | 529 |

## LED

| | | | | |
|---|---|---|---|---|
| LED ROUND IN HIS GREAT CIRCLE. NO WINDS BREATH | OUT OF VIRGIL | 27 | 46 155 | 529 |
| WHOSE FAIRE ILLUSTRIOUS SOULE, LED HIS FREE THOUGHT | UPON BISHOP ANDREWES PICTURE | 5 | 46 163 | 490 |
| A SOLITARY LIFE SHE WOULD HAVE LED. | UPON GUNPOWDER TREASON | 18 | MS 386 | 460 |

## MISS-LEDDE

| | | | | |
|---|---|---|---|---|
| MISS-LEDDE BEFORE THEY LOST THEIR WAY. | IN GLORIOUS EPIPHANIE | 164 | 52 253 | 39 |

## LEFT

| | | | | |
|---|---|---|---|---|
| LEFT THE DIMME FACE OF THIS DULL HEMISPHAEARE. | UPON BISHOP ANDREWES PICTURE | 3 | 46 163 | 490 |
| TH'HAVE LEFT THEE NAKED LORD, O THAT THEY HAD. | ON CRUCIFIED LORD BLOODY | 1 | 46 100 | 24 |
| AND LEFT PERFUMES, IN STEAD OF SCARRES. | A HYMNE OF THE NATIVITY | 26 | 46 106 | 76 |
| OF LIGHTNING, OR THE WORDS HE SPOKE) LEFT HELL. | SOSPETTO D'HERODE | 372 | 46 109 | 216 |
| LEFT HIS YEARES SO MUCH BEHIND. | HIS EPITAPH (HERRYS) | 8 | 46 172 | 471 |
| THE FIRST BLAST OF THY COUGH LEFT TWO ALONE, | OUT OF MARTIALL | 3 | 46 188 | 527 |
| TH'HAST LEFT THE THIRD COUGH NOW NO BUSINESSE HERE. | OUT OF MARTIALL | 6 | 46 188 | 527 |
| LOVE NOW NO FIRE HATH LEFT HIM. | OUT OF THE ITALIAN (2) | 1 | 46 190 | 547 |
| AS LEFT NO TIME TO PRACTISE ANY. | AN EPITAPH UPON ASHTON | 10 | 46 192 | 464 |
| AND LEFT PERFUMES IN STEAD OF SCARRES. | IN HOLY NATIVITY | 27 | 52 246 | 76 |
| BUT LEFT WITHIN | IN GLORIOUS EPIPHANIE | 76 | 52 253 | 39 |
| ONE SINGLE WOUND SHOULD NOT HAVE LEFT FOR YOU. | SANCTA MARIA DOLORUM | 80 | 52 283 | 162 |
| THEY 'HAVE LEFT THEE NAKED, LORD, O THAT THEY HAD. | UPON BODY OF OUR LORD | 1 | 52 290 | 24 |
| THOSE LIMBS OF DEATH FROM THY LEFT SIDE. | DIES IRAE | 62 | 52 298 | 186 |
| LO HERE AM LEFT (ALAS), FOR MY LOST MATE | ALEXIAS FIRST ELEGIE | 3 | 52 334 | 204 |
| ALL HATING TO BE LEFT BEHIND. | AGAINST IRRESOLUTION AND DELAY | 42 | 52 347 | 146 |
| HE LEFT HIS FATHER'S COURT, AND CAME | AGAINST IRRESOLUTION AND DELAY | 69 | 52 347 | 146 |
| LEFT MANY A STARRY TEARE, TO THINKE HOW SOONE | AN ELEGY MR STANNINOW | 41 | MS 394 | 473 |
| I LEFT MY GLORIOUS FATHERS STAR-PAV'D COURT | OUT OF GROTIUS | 14 | MS 398 | 198 |
| AND LEFT THEIR MITHRA FOR MY STAR. THIS THEY. | OUT OF GROTIUS | 38 | MS 398 | 198 |

## LEGACY

| | | | | |
|---|---|---|---|---|
| TO ME MY LEGACY OF TEARES. | VERILY YE SHALL WEEP | 2 | 46 95 | 22 |
| OF LOVE, WAS HIS OWN LEGACY. | LAUDA SION SALVATOREM | 12 | 52 294 | 178 |
| RICH HOPE. LOVE'S LEGACY, UNDER LOCK | (ON) HOPE | 11 | 52 345 | 71 |

## LEGACIE

| | | | | |
|---|---|---|---|---|
| THOU ART LOVES LEGACIE UNDER LOCK | ON HOPE | 31 | 46 143 | 71 |

## LEGIBLE

| | | | | |
|---|---|---|---|---|
| STILL LEGIBLE. | ON MARKES OF SAVIOURS WOUNDS | 4 | 46 86 | 26 |
| TO READ MORE LEGIBLE THINE ORIGINALL RAY. | IN GLORIOUS EPIPHANIE | 211 | 52 253 | 39 |

## LEIGE

| | | | | |
|---|---|---|---|---|
| BY HEROD LEIGE TO CESAR NOW WAS BORNE | SOSPETTO D'HERODE | 401 | 46 109 | 216 |

## LEND

| | | | | |
|---|---|---|---|---|
| WHICH THOU IN PEARLES DID'ST LEND. | ON WOUNDS OF CRUCIFIED LORD | 20 | 46 99 | 24 |
| THESE WHITE PLUMES OF HIS HEELE LEND YOU. | ON MR. G. HERBERTS BOOKE | 11 | 46 130 | 68 |
| ALL THE TEARES THAT GRIEFE CAN LEND. | ANOTHER ON HERRYS | 58 | 46 170 | 469 |
| PEACE, WHICH HEE LOV'D IN LIFE, DID LEND | AN EPITAPH UPON ASHTON | 23 | 46 192 | 464 |
| SHALL LEND NO CAUSE | IN GLORIOUS EPIPHANIE | 154 | 52 253 | 39 |

PAGE 226

## LEND

| | | | | |
|---|---|---|---|---|
| COULD LEND THEM ANY CRUELTY. | OFFICE H. CROSS PRIME | 4 | 52 | 267 | 91 |
| RICH QUEEN, LEND SOME RELEIFE. | SANCTA MARIA DOLORUM | 91 | 52 | 283 | 162 |
| THAT THEY BUT LEND THEIR FORM & FACE. | LAUDA SION SALVATOREM | 33 | 52 | 294 | 178 |
| LOVE TOO, THAT LEADS THE WAY, WOULD LEND THE WINGS | ALEXIAS FIRST ELEGIE | 17 | 52 | 334 | 204 |
| O RISE, PURE LAMP, & LEND THY GOLDEN RAY | ALEXIAS SECONDE ELEGIE | 29 | 52 | 335 | 207 |

## LEND'ST

| | | | | |
|---|---|---|---|---|
| WHO LEND'ST TO ALL THINGS ALL THE LIFE THEY HAVE. | OFFICE H. CROSS COMPLINE | 10 | 52 | 274 | 105 |

## LENDS

| | | | | |
|---|---|---|---|---|
| AND WHERE LOVE LENDS THE WING, & LEADS THE WAY, | ALEXIAS FIRST ELEGIE | 19 | 52 | 334 | 204 |
| LOVE, THAT LENDS HASTE TO HEAVIEST THINGS, | AGAINST IRRESOLUTION AND DELAY | 27 | 52 | 347 | 146 |

## LENDING

| | | | | |
|---|---|---|---|---|
| BORROWING DAY & LENDING NIGHT. | IN GLORIOUS EPIPHANIE | 218 | 52 | 253 | 39 |

## LENGTH

| | | | | |
|---|---|---|---|---|
| TILL THE FLEDG'D NOTES AT LENGTH FORSAKE THEIR NEST. | MUSICKS DUELL | 90 | 46 | 149 | 535 |
| AT LENGTH (AFTER SO LONG, SO LOUD A STRIFE | MUSICKS DUELL | 151 | 46 | 149 | 535 |
| AND WHAT AT LENGTH SHALT GET BY THESE. | IN PRAISE OF LESSIUS | 9 | 46 | 156 | 510 |
| TILL AT LENGTH HE PERCHING REST, | OUT OF GREEKE CUPID'S CRYER | 43 | 46 | 159 | 519 |
| ROOME FOR HER SPATIOUS SELFE, UNTILL AT LENGTH | UPON BISHOP ANDREWES PICTURE | 7 | 46 | 163 | 490 |
| HERE AT LENGTH, HATH GLADLY FOUND | AN EPITAPH DOCTOR BROOKE | 5 | 46 | 175 | 465 |
| NOT FROM THE LOWDNESSE, NOR THE LENGTH. | AN EPITAPH UPON ASHTON | 16 | 46 | 192 | 464 |
| THAT MADE IT LONG EXCUSE THE LENGTH. | TO THE QUEEN | 14 | 48 | 215 | 501 |
| OF WEAKNES, SHE MAY WRITE RESOLV'D AT LENGTH, | TO COUNTESSE OF DENBIGH | 42 | 52 | 236 | 146 |
| UNFOLD AT LENGTH, UNFOLD FAIR FLOWRE | TO COUNTESSE OF DENBIGH | 43 | 52 | 236 | 146 |

## LENGTHENED

| | | | | |
|---|---|---|---|---|
| FOR LIFE BY VOLUMES LENGTHENED, | UPON THE DEATH OF A GENTLEMAN | 7 | 46 | 166 | 472 |

## LENT

| | | | | |
|---|---|---|---|---|
| HIS CURIOUS FINGERS LENT, HER VOYCE MADE GOOD. | MUSICKS DUELL | 14 | 46 | 149 | 535 |
| LENT THEM THE LAST FLASH OF HER GLIMMERING LIGHT. | THE BEGINNING OF HELIODORUS | 20 | 46 | 158 | 517 |
| NO APRIL E'RE LENT SOFTER SHOWRES, | THE WEEPER | 89 | 46 | 79 | 145 |
| NO APRIL ERE LENT KINDER SHOWRES, | WEEPER | 83 | 52 | 307 | 120 |

## LESSE

| | | | | |
|---|---|---|---|---|
| INTO THIS LESSE APPEARANCE, IF YOU THINKE, | UPON BISHOP ANDREWES PICTURE | 14 | 46 | 163 | 490 |
| HOW MUCH LESSE STRONG IS DEATH THEN LOVE. | IN MEMORY OF LADY MADRE TERESA | 28 | 46 | 131 | 52 |
| DRINKE WEE TILL WE PROVE MORE, NOT LESSE THEN MEN. | AN APOLOGIE FOR HYMNE (TERESA) | 36 | 46 | 136 | 59 |
| COME LESSE UNBROKEN TO OUR BED, | ON HOPE | 36 | 46 | 143 | 71 |
| THY LITTLE SELFE IN LESSE, READ IN THESE EYNE | UPON YORKE HIS BIRTH | 43 | 46 | 176 | 500 |
| YET PAY LESSE ARROWES THEN THEY OWE. | WISHES SUPPOSED MISTRESSE | 60 | 46 | 195 | 479 |
| NARROW, & LOW, & INFINITELY LESSE | TO THE NAME OF JESUS | 22 | 52 | 239 | 30 |
| NOR (MUCH LESSE) SHALL THEY LEAVE THESE EYES | IN GLORIOUS EPIPHANIE | 87 | 52 | 253 | 39 |
| HEAV'N NE'RE THE LESSE STILL HEAVN WOULD BE. | CHARITAS NIMIA | 11 | 52 | 280 | 48 |
| E'RE THE LESSE GLORIOUS RUN. | CHARITAS NIMIA | 40 | 52 | 280 | 48 |
| AND LESSE TO LEAN ON. BECAUSE THAN | ADORO TE | 21 | 52 | 291 | 172 |
| BEARES HOME NO LESSE, ALL THEY NO MORE, | LAUDA SION SALVATOREM | 47 | 52 | 294 | 178 |
| NOR LEAVE THEY BOTH LESSE THEN BEFORE. | LAUDA SION SALVATOREM | 48 | 52 | 294 | 178 |
| LESSE THEN WHOLE CHRIST IN EVERY CRUMME. | LAUDA SION SALVATOREM | 58 | 52 | 294 | 178 |
| AND THIS LOV'D SOUL, JUDG'D WORTH NO LESSE | DIES IRAE | 35 | 52 | 298 | 186 |
| OR IF HE MAKE LESSE HAST, | IN GLORIOUS ASSUMPTION B. LADY | 24 | 52 | 304 | 114 |
| MUCH LESSE MEAN WE TO TRACE | WEEPER | 181 | 52 | 307 | 120 |
| HOW MUCH LESSE STRONG IS DEATH THEN LOVE. | TERESA | 28 | 52 | 315 | 52 |
| DRINK WE TILL WE PROVE MORE, NOT LESSE, THEN MEN, | AN APOLOGIE FOR (TERESA) HYMNE | 36 | 52 | 322 | 59 |
| COME LESSE UNBROKEN TO OUR BED, | (ON) HOPE | 16 | 52 | 345 | 71 |

## LESSER

| | | | | |
|---|---|---|---|---|
| TAST THIS, AND AS THOU LIK'ST THIS LESSER FLOOD | OUR LORD IN HIS CIRCUMCISION | 3 | 46 | 98 | 9 |
| REV'RENTLY CIRCLED BY THE LESSER SEAVEN, | SOSPETTO D'HERODE | 238 | 46 | 109 | 216 |
| IN ARMES, WHEN LESSER CAUSE WAS TO COMPLAINE. | SOSPETTO D'HERODE | 454 | 46 | 109 | 216 |
| LESSER AND LESSER YET, TILL THOU BEGIN | UPON STANINOUGH'S DEATH | 17 | 46 | 175 | 475 |
| LESSER & LESSER YET, TILL THOU BEGIN | UPON STANINOUGH'S DEATH | 17 | 46 | 175 | 475 |
| LESSER & LESSER YET, TILL THOU BEGIN | DEATH'S LECTURE | 18 | 52 | 340 | 475 |
| LESSER & LESSER YET, TILL THOU BEGIN | DEATH'S LECTURE | 18 | 52 | 340 | 475 |

## LESSON

| | | | | |
|---|---|---|---|---|
| MENS HEARTS INTO THEIR HANDS, THIS LESSON TOO | MUSICKS DUELL | 56 | 46 | 149 | 535 |
| A CHOICER LESSON THEN THE JOYFULL BREST | TO THE NAME OF JESUS | 107 | 52 | 239 | 30 |

## LEST

| | | | | |
|---|---|---|---|---|
| LEST HIS KINDNESSE MAKE THEE BLEED. | OUT OF GREEKE CUPID'S CRYER | 72 | 46 | 159 | 519 |
| HER LORDS BLOOD, OR AT LEST HER OWNE. | IN MEMORY OF LADY MADRE TERESA | 56 | 46 | 131 | 52 |
| LEST FOR GRIEFE HIS LOSSE MAY MOVE, | UPON DEATH OF DESIRED HERRYS | 73 | 46 | 168 | 467 |
| YEILD QUICKLY, LEST PERHAPS YOU PROVE | TO COUNTESSE OF DENBIGH | 65 | 52 | 236 | 146 |
| TO LEARN OF HIM AT LEST, TO WORSHIP THEE. | IN GLORIOUS EPIPHANIE | 182 | 52 | 253 | 39 |
| AT LEST TO PLAY | IN GLORIOUS EPIPHANIE | 223 | 52 | 253 | 39 |
| BUT MORE AMBITIOUS LOSSE, AT LEST OF BRAIN. | IN GLORIOUS EPIPHANIE | 230 | 52 | 253 | 39 |
| AT LEST BY US, | IN GLORIOUS EPIPHANIE | 235 | 52 | 253 | 39 |
| BUT LEST THAT DY TOO, WE ARE BID | LAUDA SION SALVATOREM | 25 | 52 | 294 | 178 |
| HER LORD'S BLOOD, OR AT LEST HER OWN. | TERESA | 56 | 52 | 315 | 52 |
| YIELD QUICKLY, LEST PERHAPS YOU PROVE | AGAINST IRRESOLUTION AND DELAY | 87 | 52 | 347 | 146 |

LESTRIGONIANS

THE LESTRIGONIANS HERE THEIR TABLE REARE.                    SOSPETTO D'HERODE                  357  46 109 216

LET

QUICKE VOLUMES OF WILD NOTES. TO LET HIM KNOW                MUSICKS DUELL                       25  46 149 535
LET THE FINDER SURELY KNOW                                   OUT OF GREEKE CUPID'S CRYER          7  46 159 519
PRETHEE, SWEET NOW LET ME GOE,                               OUT OF GREEKE CUPID'S CRYER         69  46 159 519
COME IF THOU DAR'ST. THUS, THUS LET US BE TRY'D.             UPON THE SAME (VENUS ARMES)          2  46 161 523
SENTENTIOUS SHOWERS. O LET THEM FALL,                        UPON THE DEATH OF A GENTLEMAN       29  46 166 472
SO COYLY SHOULD LET FALL,                                    THE WEEPER                          69  46  79 120
YET LET THE POORE DROPS WEEPE,                               THE WEEPER                          73  46  79 120
SOFTLY LET THEM CREEPE                                       THE WEEPER                          75  46  79 120
LET NIGHT OR DAY DOE WHAT THEY WILL                          THE WEEPER                         113  46  79 120
LET IT NO LONGER BE A FORLORNE HOPE                          ON BAPTIZED AETHIOPIAN               1  46  85  29
NOR LET THE MILKY FONTS THAT BATH YOUR THIRST,               TO INFANT MARTYRS                    3  46  88  10
THEN LET HIM DRINKE, AND DRINKE, AND DOE HIS WORST,          OUR LORD IN HIS CIRCUMCISION         7  46  98   9
LET THE DAMPS OF THY DULL BREATH                             PSALME 23                           40  46 102   5
LET HEAV'NS LORD CHIDE ABOVE LOWDER THEN THOU                SOSPETTO D'HERODE                  269  46 109 216
WHY DOST THOU LET THY BRAVE SOULE LYE SUPPREST,              SOSPETTO D'HERODE                  429  46 109 216
LET CONSTANT USE BUT KEEP IT BRIGHT,                         ON A PRAYER BOOKE                   16  46 126 139
LET PRAYER ALONE TO PLAY HIS PART.                           ON A PRAYER BOOKE                   28  46 126 139
O LET THAT HAPPY SOULE HOLD FAST                             ON A PRAYER BOOKE                  105  46 126 139
BEE LOVE BUT THERE, LET POORE SIXE YEARES,                   IN MEMORY OF LADY MADRE TERESA      29  46 131  52
INTO LOVES HAND THOU SHALT LET FALL,                         IN MEMORY OF LADY MADRE TERESA      77  46 131  52
FORBID IT MIGHTY LOVE, LET NO FOND HATE                      AN APOLOGIE FOR HYMNE (TERESA)      13  46 136  59
DRINKE UP ALL SPAINE IN SACK, LET MY SOULE SWELL             AN APOLOGIE FOR HYMNE (TERESA)      30  46 136  59
WITH THEE STRONG WINE OF LOVE, LET OTHERS SWIMME             AN APOLOGIE FOR HYMNE (TERESA)      31  46 136  59
AND TURNE NOT BEASTS, BUT ANGELS. LET THE KING,              AN APOLOGIE FOR HYMNE (TERESA)      37  46 136  59
YET SHALL OUR LIPS NEVER LET GOE                             ON THE ASSUMPTION                   38  46 139 114
LET HIM MAKE POORE THE PURPLE EAST,                          AN HIMNE FOR CIRCUMCISION           17  46 141  37
LET HIM EMBRACE HIS OWNE BRIGHT TRESSES,                     AN HIMNE FOR CIRCUMCISION           21  46 141  37
LET NOT PITTY WITH HER TEARES,                               UPON DEATH OF DESIRED HERRYS        61  46 168 467
STAY A WHILE, AND LET THY HEART                              HIS EPITAPH (HERRYS)                 2  46 172 471
LET THEM SLEEPE, LET THEM SLEEPE ON,                         AN EPITAPH HUSBAND AND WIFE         11  46 174 478
LET THEM SLEEPE, LET THEM SLEEPE ON,                         AN EPITAPH HUSBAND AND WIFE         11  46 174 478
FELLOW THE WONDER TOO, NOR LET HER SHINE                     UPON YORKE HIS BIRTH                55  46 176 500
THEN LET THE EASTERNE WORLD BRAGGE AND BE PROUD              UPON YORKE HIS BIRTH                86  46 176 500
AND LET NO DULL MISTS CHOAKE THE LIGHTS FAIRE GROWTH.        ON A FOULE MORNING                   4  46 181 495
LET IT SUFFICE, SHEE'L WEARE NO MASKE TO DAY.                ON A FOULE MORNING                  38  46 181 495
LET MY HEAT TO YOUR LIGHT BE RECONCILED.                     OUT OF THE ITALIAN (2)               6  46 190 547
LET HOARY TIME'S VAST BOWELS BE THE GRAVE                    ON FRONTISPIECE ISAACSONS            1  46 191 491
LET NATURE DIE, IF (PHOENIX-LIKE) FROM DEATH                 ON FRONTISPIECE ISAACSONS            3  46 191 491
CAN RAISE SO FAIRE AN HARVEST. LET HER BE                    ON FRONTISPIECE ISAACSONS            7  46 191 491
COME AND LET US LIVE MY DEARE,                               OUT OF CATULLUS                      1  46 194 523
LET US LOVE AND NEVER FEARE,                                 OUT OF CATULLUS                      2  46 194 523
THEN LET AMOROUS KISSES DWELL                                OUT OF CATULLUS                      9  46 194 523
LET HER FULL GLORY,                                          WISHES SUPPOSED MISTRESSE          124  46 195 479
O LET IT BE AT LAST, LOVE'S HOURE.                           TO COUNTESSE OF DENBIGH             37  52 236 146
THE FORT AT LAST, AND LET LIFE IN.                           TO COUNTESSE OF DENBIGH             64  52 236 146
BRING HITHER THY WHOLE SELF. & LET ME SEE                    TO THE NAME OF JESUS                17  52 239  30
AND LET THE MIGHTY BABE ALONE.                               IN HOLY NATIVITY                    45  52 246  76
LET HIM MAKE POOR THE PURPLE EAST,                           NEW YEAR'S DAY                      17  52 251  37
LET HIM EMBRAVE HIS OWN BRIGHT TRESSES                       NEW YEAR'S DAY                      21  52 251  37
O LET US TWINE                                               OFFICE H. CROSS PRIME               13  52 267  91
LIVE BARABBAS. & LET GOD DY.                                 OFFICE H. CROSS THIRD                4  52 268  93
HAIL, OUR ALONE HOPE. LET THY FAIR HEAD SHOOT                VEXILLA REGIS                       37  52 277 156
AND LET THY LOST SHEEP LIVE TO'INHERIT                       VEXILLA REGIS                       45  52 277 156
LET HIM GOE WEEP                                             CHARITAS NIMIA                      15  52 280  48
NOR SPHEARES LET FALL THEIR FAITHFULL ROUNDS.                CHARITAS NIMIA                      18  52 280  48
LET FROWARD DUST THEN DOE IT'S KIND.                         CHARITAS NIMIA                      29  52 280  48
O LET ME, HERE, CLAIM SHARES.                                SANCTA MARIA DOLORUM                56  52 283 162
YEA LET MY LIFE & ME                                         SANCTA MARIA DOLORUM                61  52 283 162
O LET ME SUCK THE WINE                                       SANCTA MARIA DOLORUM               101  52 283 162
O LET THY WRETCH FIND THAT RELEIFE                           ADORO TE                            17  52 291 172
GIVE LOVE FOR LIFE. NOR LET MY DAYES                         ADORO TE                            35  52 291 172
COME, LOVE. & LET US WORK A SONG                             LAUDA SION SALVATOREM               13  52 294 178
LET LIPPES & HEARTS LIFT HIGH THE NOISE                      LAUDA SION SALVATOREM               15  52 294 178
LET ONE, OR ONE THOUSAND BE                                  LAUDA SION SALVATOREM               45  52 294 178
O LET THAT LOVE WHICH THUS MAKES THEE                        LAUDA SION SALVATOREM               73  52 294 178
O LET THINE OWN SOFT BOWELLS PAY                             DIES IRAE                           45  52 298 186
LET COME YE BLESSED THEN CALL ME.                            DIES IRAE                           60  52 298 186
LET THOSE LIFE-SPEAKING LIPPS COMMAND                        DIES IRAE                           63  52 298 186
LET THEN THE AGED WORLD BE WISE, & ALL                       O GLORIOSA DOMINA                   23  52 302 194
LET HEARTS & LIPPES SPEAK LOWD. AND SAY                      O GLORIOSA DOMINA                   31  52 302 194
THE DOOR WAS SHUTT, YET LET IN DAY,                          O GLORIOSA DOMINA                   35  52 302 194
SO COYLY SHOULD LET FALL                                     WEEPER                              51  52 307 120
YET LET THE POORE DROPS WEEP                                 WEEPER                              55  52 307 120
SOFTLY LET THEM CREEP,                                       WEEPER                              57  52 307 120
LET NIGHT OR DAY DOE WHAT THEY WILL,                         WEEPER                             137  52 307 120
BE LOVE BUT THERE. LET POOR SIX YEARES                       TERESA                              29  52 315  52
INTO LOVE'S ARMES THOU SHALT LET FALL                        TERESA                              77  52 315  52
FORBID IT, MIGHTY LOVE. LET NO FOND HATE                     AN APOLOGIE FOR (TERESA) HYMNE      13  52 322  59
DRINK UP AL SPAIN IN SACK. LET MY SOUL SWELL                 AN APOLOGIE FOR (TERESA) HYMNE      30  52 322  59
WITH THEE, STRONG WINE OF LOVE. LET OTHERS SWIMME            AN APOLOGIE FOR (TERESA) HYMNE      31  52 322  59
AND TURN NOT BEASTS, BUT ANGELS. LET THE KING                AN APOLOGIE FOR (TERESA) HYMNE      37  52 322  59
LET THIS IMMORTALL LIFE WHERERE IT COMES                     FLAMING HEART                       81  52 324  61
LET MYSTICK DEATHS WAIT ON'T. & WISE SOULES BE               FLAMING HEART                       83  52 324  61
LET ALL THY SCATTER'D SHAFTS OF LIGHT, THAT PLAY             FLAMING HEART                       87  52 324  61
LET ME SO READ THY LIFE, THAT I                              FLAMING HEART                      107  52 324  61
LET CONSTANT USE BUT KEEP IT BRIGHT,                         PRAYER TO GENTLE-WOMAN              22  52 328 139
LET PRAYER ALONE TO PLAY HIS PART.                           PRAYER TO GENTLE-WOMAN              34  52 328 139

| | | | | |
|---|---|---|---|---|
| O LET THE BLISSFULL HEART HOLD FAST | PRAYER TO GENTLE-WOMAN | 111 | 52 328 | 139 |
| SWEET, LET ME PROPHESY THAT AT LAST T'WILL PROVE | TO SAME CONCERNING CHOISE | 33 | 52 331 | 66 |
| LET NOT MY LORD, THE MIGHTY LOVER | TO SAME CONCERNING CHOISE | 41 | 52 331 | 66 |
| AND WORK FOR WORK, NOT WAGES. LET TO MORROW'S | DESCRIPTION RELIGIOUS HOUSE | 21 | 52 338 | 213 |
| LET THEM SLEEP. LET THEM SLEEP ON. | AN EPITAPH UPON MARRIED COUPLE | 15 | 52 339 | 478 |
| LET THEM SLEEP. LET THEM SLEEP ON. | AN EPITAPH UPON MARRIED COUPLE | 15 | 52 339 | 478 |
| THE FORT AT LAST, AND LET LIFE IN. | AGAINST IRRESOLUTION AND DELAY | 86 | 52 347 | 146 |
| LET EACH EYE WATER'T WITH A COURTEOUS TEARE. | AN ELEGY MR STANNINOW | 56 | MS 394 | 473 |

LETT

| | | | | |
|---|---|---|---|---|
| NOR LETT HER KINRED BIRDS COMPLAYNE | THOUGH NOW 'TIS NEITHER | 15 | MS 397 | 492 |
| FOR LETT THEM KNOW SHEE'S NONE OF THOSE | THOUGH NOW 'TIS NEITHER | 17 | MS 397 | 492 |
| AND LETT HEAVEN STAY. | LUKE 2. QUAERIT JESUM | 46 | MS 379 | 11 |
| LETT HER SURVIVE THIS DAY, ONCE MOCK HER FATE. | ON GUNPOWDER-TREASON | 9 | MS 384 | 458 |
| LETT NOT MY SUPPLIANT BREATH RAISE A RUDE STORME | ON GUNPOWDER-TREASON | 11 | MS 384 | 458 |
| TH' EPITOME OF HELL. OH LETT THY PINIONS | UPON GUNPOWDER TREASON | 21 | MS 387 | 461 |
| SOUND FORTH, CAELESTIALL ORGANS,LETT HEAVNS QUIRE | UPON KINGS CORONATION | 1 | MS 389 | 454 |
| LETT NOT THY WEIGHTY GLORIES, THIS FULL TIDE | UPON KINGS CORONATION | 7 | MS 389 | 454 |
| LETT NONE DARE SPEAKE OF THEE, BUT SUCH AS THENCE | UPON BIRTH PRINCESSE E | 9 | MS 391 | 456 |
| LETT TH' HALLOWED PLUME OF A SERAPHICK WING | UPON BIRTH PRINCESSE E | 22 | MS 391 | 456 |
| BY THEE, BY THEE YET LETT ME DIE. THIS GIVE. | EX EUPHORMIONE | 12 | MS 392 | 525 |
| LETT THY SWOLNE BREAST DISCHARGE THY STRUGLING GROANES | AN ELEGIE ON DR PORTER | 31 | MS 395 | 476 |
| TO MELT IN GENTLE DROPS, LETT THEM BE HEARD | AN ELEGIE ON DR PORTER | 33 | MS 395 | 476 |

LETS

| | | | | |
|---|---|---|---|---|
| SHEE OPES THE FLOODGATE, AND LETS LOOSE A TIDE | MUSICKS DUELL | 93 | 46 149 | 535 |
| SAVE THAT WHICH LETS IN FAITH, THE EARE. | ADORO TE | 10 | 52 291 | 172 |
| HIMSELFE IN HIS OWNE HELL. AND NOW LETS LOOSE | OUT OF GROTIUS | 79 | MS 398 | 198 |

LETT'ST

| | | | | |
|---|---|---|---|---|
| THAT SELDOME LETT'ST A BLUSHING YOUTHFULL PRIME | UPON DEATH OF HERRYS | 30 | 46 167 | 466 |

LETTS

| | | | | |
|---|---|---|---|---|
| THAT WITH EACH WORD, MY LOADEN PEN LETTS FALL. | UPON BIRTH PRINCESSE E | 3 | MS 391 | 456 |

LETHAEAN

| | | | | |
|---|---|---|---|---|
| SEALING ALL BRESTS IN A LETHAEAN BAND. | SOSPETTO D'HERODE | 392 | 46 109 | 216 |

LETHARGY

| | | | | |
|---|---|---|---|---|
| DULL SLUGGISH ILE. WHAT MORE THAN LETHARGY | ON GUNPOWDER-TREASON | 3 | MS 384 | 458 |

LETHE

| | | | | |
|---|---|---|---|---|
| HIS LETHE BE MY HELICON. AND SEE | TO THE MORNING | 17 | 46 183 | 497 |

LETTER

| | | | | |
|---|---|---|---|---|
| EVERY RED LETTER | ON MARKES OF SAVIOURS WOUNDS | 7 | 46 86 | 28 |
| TO'INJOY HIS BLOTT. & AS A LARGE BLACK LETTER | IN GLORIOUS EPIPHANIE | 186 | 52 253 | 39 |
| DEARE WIFE HATH NE'RE A HANDSOME LETTER. | PETRONIJ ALES PHASIACIS PETITA | 17 | MS 382 | 526 |

LETTERS

| | | | | |
|---|---|---|---|---|
| WRIT IN WHITE LETTERS O'RE HIS HEAD. | ANOTHER ON HERRYS | 50 | 46 170 | 469 |

LIBANUS

| | | | | |
|---|---|---|---|---|
| O'RELOOK ALL LIBANUS. THY LOFTY CROWN | OFFICE H. CROSS EVENSONG | 22 | 52 273 | 101 |

LIBERALL

| | | | | |
|---|---|---|---|---|
| OF LOVES. THY LORD'S TOO LIBERALL BREAST. | VEXILLA REGIS | 8 | 52 277 | 156 |
| RICH, LIBERALL HEAVEN, WHAT, HATH YOUR TREASURE STORE | UPON BIRTH PRINCESSE E | 25 | MS 391 | 456 |

LIBERTY

| | | | | |
|---|---|---|---|---|
| BOTH LIFE & LIBERTY | OFFICE H. CROSS SIXT | 18 | 52 270 | 97 |

LIBIAN

| | | | | |
|---|---|---|---|---|
| GLADDING THE SCYTHIAN ROCKS, AND LIBIAN SANDS. | SOSPETTO D'HERODE | 108 | 46 109 | 216 |

LICKE

| | | | | |
|---|---|---|---|---|
| LICKE HIS PROUD FEET. AND HAST INTO THE SEAS | THE BEGINNING OF HELIODORUS | 5 | 46 158 | 517 |
| WITH WANTON GALES. HIS BALMY BREATH SHALL LICKE | ON A FOULE MORNING | 13 | 46 181 | 495 |

LICKES

| | | | | |
|---|---|---|---|---|
| HER EYES FLOOD LICKES HIS FEETS FAIRE STAINE. | SHE BEGAN TO WASH HIS FEET | 1 | 46 97 | 13 |
| HER HAIRES FLAME LICKES UP THAT AGAINE. | SHE BEGAN TO WASH HIS FEET | 2 | 46 97 | 13 |

LIDS

| | | | | |
|---|---|---|---|---|
| NO CLOUD SCOULE ON HIS RADIANT LIDS NO TEMPEST LOWRE. | EASTER DAY | 12 | 46 100 | 26 |
| BUT SHUT THEIR FLOWRY LIDS FOR EVER. NIGHT. | SOSPETTO D'HERODE | 379 | 46 109 | 216 |
| (NIGHT HANGS YET HEAVY ON THE LIDS OF DAY) | SOSPETTO D'HERODE | 506 | 46 109 | 216 |

## EYE-LIDS

| | | | | |
|---|---|---|---|---|
| FROM TH' DAWN OF THY FAIRE EYE-LIDS WIPE AWAY | ON A TREATISE OF CHARITY | 7 | 46 137 | 69 |
| NOR MAY THE LIGHT THAT GIVES THEIR EYE-LIDS LIGHT, | UPON YORKE HIS BIRTH | 92 | 46 176 | 500 |

## LIDDES

| | | | | |
|---|---|---|---|---|
| OUT-STARES THE LIDDES OF LARGE-LOOK'T TYRANNY. | UPON STANINOUGH'S DEATH | 26 | 46 175 | 475 |
| O SEE, THE WEARY LIDDES OF WAKEFULL HOPE | TO THE NAME OF JESUS | 145 | 52 239 | 30 |
| NOW BY ABASED LIDDES SHALL LEARN TO BE | IN GLORIOUS EPIPHANIE | 231 | 52 253 | 39 |
| OUTSTARES THE LIDDES OF LARG-LOOK'T TYRANNY. | DEATH'S LECTURE | 28 | 52 340 | 475 |

## EYLIDDES

| | | | | |
|---|---|---|---|---|
| PROUD LOOKES, & LOFTY EYLIDDES, HERE PUTT ON | DEATH'S LECTURE | 21 | 52 340 | 475 |

## LIDDS

| | | | | |
|---|---|---|---|---|
| SICKNESSE, AND SORROW, WHOSE PALE LIDDS NE'RE KNOW | TO THE MORNING | 56 | 46 183 | 497 |
| THAT THESE DRY LIDDS MIGHT BORROW | SANCTA MARIA DOLORUM | 43 | 52 283 | 162 |

## EYE-LIDDS

| | | | | |
|---|---|---|---|---|
| PREVENTS THE EYE-LIDDS OF THE BLUSHING DAY. | MUSICKS DUELL | 82 | 46 149 | 535 |

## LIE

| | | | | |
|---|---|---|---|---|
| LIE SCATTER'D LIKE THE BURNT AND MARTYR'D BONES | ON A TREATISE OF CHARITY | 32 | 46 137 | 69 |
| FETTER'D AND LOCK'D UP FAST THEY LIE | AGAINST IRRESOLUTION AND DELAY | 23 | 52 347 | 146 |

## LY

| | | | | |
|---|---|---|---|---|
| NOR IS DEATH FORC'T. FOR MAY HEE LY | EASTER DAY | 16 | 46 100 | 26 |
| WHERE ALL THE BUSIE DAY SHEE CLOSE DOTH LY, | SOSPETTO D'HERODE | 386 | 46 109 | 216 |
| IN LABOR OF YOUR SELFE TO LY, | TO COUNTESSE OF DENBIGH | 11 | 52 236 | 146 |
| FETTER'D, & LOCKT UP FAST THEY LY | TO COUNTESSE OF DENBIGH | 23 | 52 236 | 146 |
| IN PITTY'S SOFT LAP LY A SLEEPING. | TO THE NAME OF JESUS | 192 | 52 239 | 30 |
| NEXT TO THEIR OWN LOW NOTHING THEY MAY LY, | TO THE NAME OF JESUS | 234 | 52 239 | 30 |
| NOT TO LY COLD, YET SLEEP IN SNOW. | IN HOLY NATIVITY | 70 | 52 246 | 76 |
| FROM HIM, WHOM BY A MORE ILLUSTRIOUS LY, | IN GLORIOUS EPIPHANIE | 44 | 52 253 | 39 |
| (BY ALL THY MYSTERYES THAT HERE LY HIDDE) | AN APOLOGIE FOR (TERESA) HYMNE | 12 | 52 322 | 59 |
| TO LY THUS FOLDED, & COMPLAINING | PRAYER TO GENTLE-WOMAN | 4 | 52 328 | 139 |
| WHICH HERE CONTRACTS IT SELF, & COMES TO LY | PRAYER TO GENTLE-WOMAN | 16 | 52 328 | 139 |
| KIND LOVES KEEP HOUSE, LY CLOSE, AND MAKE NO NOISE, | DESCRIPTION RELIGIOUS HOUSE | 33 | 52 338 | 213 |
| THEY, SWEET TURTLES, FOLDED LY | AN EPITAPH UPON MARRIED COUPLE | 9 | 52 339 | 478 |
| AND THOUGH THEY LY AS THEY WERE DEAD, | AN EPITAPH UPON MARRIED COUPLE | 11 | 52 339 | 478 |
| THESE DEATH-SEAL'D LIPPES ARE THEY DARE GIVE THE LY | DEATH'S LECTURE | 25 | 52 340 | 475 |
| IN LABOUR OF YOUR SELF TO LY, | AGAINST IRRESOLUTION AND DELAY | 19 | 52 347 | 146 |
| ALONE MUST LY. | LUKE 2. QUAERIT JESUM | 12 | MS 379 | 11 |

## LYE

| | | | | |
|---|---|---|---|---|
| OF HER DELICIOUS SOULE, THAT THERE DOES LYE | MUSICKS DUELL | 67 | 46 149 | 535 |
| SORROWES BEST JEWELS LYE IN THESE | THE WEEPER | 47 | 46 79 | 120 |
| SWEETLY SHALT THOU LYE, | THE TEARE | 39 | 46 84 | 50 |
| VAINE MAN. THE STONES THAT ON HIS TOMBE DOE LYE, | YEE BUILD SEPULCHRES | 3 | 46 95 | 21 |
| NOT TO LYE COLD, YET SLEEPE IN SNOW. | A HYMNE OF THE NATIVITY | 52 | 46 106 | 76 |
| THAT IN THEIR BUDS YET BLUSHING LYE. | A HYMNE OF THE NATIVITY | 68 | 46 106 | 76 |
| AS PRIS'NER IN A FEW POORE RAGS TO LYE. | SOSPETTO D'HERODE | 172 | 46 109 | 216 |
| WHY DOST THOU LET THY BRAVE SOULE LYE SUPPREST, | SOSPETTO D'HERODE | 429 | 46 109 | 216 |
| WHICH HERE CONTRACTS IT SELFE AND COMES TO LYE | ON A PRAYER BOOKE | 10 | 46 126 | 139 |
| (BY ALL THY MYSTERIES THAT THERE LYE HID.) | AN APOLOGIE FOR HYMNE (TERESA) | 12 | 46 136 | 59 |
| OUR CROWN-LANDS LYE ABOVE, YET EACH MEALE BRINGS | ON HOPE | 33 | 46 143 | 71 |
| THEY (SWEET TURTLES) FOLDED LYE, | AN EPITAPH HUSBAND AND WIFE | 9 | 46 174 | 478 |
| THESE DEATH-SEAL'D LIPPS ARE THEY DARE GIVE THE LYE, | UPON STANINOUGH'S DEATH | 23 | 46 175 | 475 |
| BRIGHT LADY OF THE MORNE, PITTY DOTH LYE | TO THE MORNING | 33 | 46 183 | 497 |
| WHILE LOVE SHALL THUS ENTOMBED LYE, | LOVES HOROSCOPE | 51 | 46 185 | 483 |
| WHERE ERE SHEE LYE. | WISHES SUPPOSED MISTRESSE | 4 | 46 195 | 479 |

## LY'D

| | | | | |
|---|---|---|---|---|
| ALL THIS IT ONLY THREATS. THE METEOR LY'D. | ON GUNPOWDER-TREASON | 49 | MS 384 | 458 |

## LIES

| | | | | |
|---|---|---|---|---|
| UNDER TH' UNRULY BEASTS PROUD FEET HE LIES | HIGH MOUNTED ON AN ANT | 3 | 46 161 | 523 |
| NOW THE GRAVE LIES BURIED. | UPON SEPULCHRE OF OUR LORD | 2 | 46 86 | 26 |
| IN A NEGLECTED STABLE LIES, AMONG | SOSPETTO D'HERODE | 436 | 46 109 | 216 |
| SPHEARE OF SWEET, AND SUGRED LIES, | ON A PRAYER BOOKE | 50 | 46 126 | 139 |
| 'TIS HEAVEN THAT LIES IN AMBUSH THERE, AND BREAKES | AN APOLOGIE FOR HYMNE (TERESA) | 24 | 46 136 | 59 |
| HOW OUT OF TUNE THE WORLD NOW LIES, | UPON DEATH OF A FREIND | 15 | MS 393 | 477 |

## LYES

| | | | | |
|---|---|---|---|---|
| WELL DOES THE MAY THAT LYES | THE WEEPER | 65 | 46 79 | 120 |
| 'TIS HEAV'N 'TIS HEAVEN SHE SEES, HEAVENS GOD THERE LYES | ON VIRGINS BASHFULNESSE | 5 | 46 89 | 9 |
| WHEN HEAVEN IT SELFE LYES HERE BELOW. | A HYMNE OF THE NATIVITY | 44 | 46 106 | 76 |
| DIVINEST LOVE LYES IN THIS BOOKE. | ON MR. G. HERBERTS BOOKE | 2 | 46 130 | 68 |
| ALL HOPE OF NEVER DYING, HERE LYES DEAD. | ANOTHER ON HERRYS | 62 | 46 170 | 469 |
| THIS POSTURE IS THE BRAVE ONE. THIS THAT LYES | UPON STANINOUGH'S DEATH | 27 | 46 175 | 475 |
| NOW ALL OBSCURED LYES | OUT OF THE ITALIAN (2) | 8 | 46 190 | 547 |
| HERE LYES A TRULY HONEST MAN. | AN EPITAPH UPON ASHTON | 4 | 46 192 | 464 |

| | | | | | |
|---|---|---|---|---|---|
| YETT IN THESE LEAVES (FAIRE ONE) THERE LYES | THOUGH NOW 'TIS NEITHER | 3 | MS | 397 | 492 |
| WHERE ALL THEIR HOARD OF HONY LYES. | TO THE NAME OF JESUS | 158 | 52 | 239 | 30 |
| AND WAKE THE SUN THAT LYES TOO LONG. | IN HOLY NATIVITY | 4 | 52 | 246 | 76 |
| SINCE HEAVN ITSELF LYES HERE BELOW. | IN HOLY NATIVITY | 61 | 52 | 246 | 76 |
| THE WORLD LYES WARM, & LIKES HIS PLACE. | IN GLORIOUS EPIPHANIE | 37 | 52 | 253 | 39 |
| THEIR HANDS WITH LASHES ARM'D, THEIR TOUNGS WITH LYES. | OFFICE H. CROSS PRIME | 5 | 52 | 267 | 91 |
| AND LIVES IN HIM THAT HERE LYES DEAD. | OFFICE H. CROSS COMPLINE | 4 | 52 | 274 | 105 |
| NOW THE GRAVE LYES BURYED. | UPON THE H. SEPULCHER | 2 | 52 | 277 | 26 |
| WELL DOES THE MAY THAT LYES | WEEPER | 79 | 52 | 307 | 120 |
| 'TIS HEAV'N THAT LYES IN AMBUSH THERE, & BREAKS | AN APOLOGIE FOR (TERESA) HYMNE | 24 | 52 | 322 | 59 |
| SPHEARES OF SWEET & SUGRED LYES, | PRAYER TO GENTLE-WOMAN | 56 | 52 | 328 | 139 |
| GUILDED DUNGHILLS, GLORIOUS LYES, | TO SAME CONCERNING CHOISE | 14 | 52 | 331 | 66 |
| THEN THIS WORLD OF LYES CAN GIVE YE | TO SAME CONCERNING CHOISE | 37 | 52 | 331 | 66 |
| OF YOUR LEARN'D LYES. HERE YOU'L FIND NO SUCH JEST. | ALEXIAS THIRD ELEGIE | 42 | 52 | 336 | 209 |
| THIS POSTURE IS THE BRAVE ONE THIS THAT LYES | DEATH'S LECTURE | 29 | 52 | 340 | 475 |
| OUR CROWN-LAND LYES ABOVE YET EACH MEAL BRINGS | (ON) HOPE | 13 | 52 | 345 | 71 |

LY'N

| | | | | | |
|---|---|---|---|---|---|
| BUT LY'N LOCK'T UP SAFE IN THEIR SACRED SHORES. | ALEXIAS THIRD ELEGIE | 8 | 52 | 336 | 209 |

LIFE

| | | | | | |
|---|---|---|---|---|---|
| GIVES LIFE TO SOME NEW GRACE. THUS DOTH H'INVOKE | MUSICKS DUELL | 132 | 46 | 149 | 535 |
| OF ALL THE STRINGS, STILL BREATHING THE BEST LIFE | MUSICKS DUELL | 152 | 46 | 149 | 535 |
| SHEE DYES, AND LEAVES HER LIFE THE VICTORS PRISE, | MUSICKS DUELL | 166 | 46 | 149 | 535 |
| SPEND THE DEARE TREASURE OF THY LIFE. | IN PRAISE OF LESSIUS | 4 | 46 | 156 | 510 |
| FOR LIFE BY VOLUMES LENGTHENED, | UPON THE DEATH OF A GENTLEMAN | 7 | 46 | 166 | 472 |
| THOU WATER TURN'ST TO WINE (FAIRE FRIEND OF LIFE) | TO LORD UPON WATER MADE WINE | 1 | 46 | 91 | 12 |
| TO BEE THE LIFE OF THEIR OWNE DEATH. | NEITHER DURST MAN ASKE | 14 | 46 | 92 | 20 |
| HOW LIFE AND DEATH IN THEE | UPON OUR SAVIOURS TOMBE | 1 | 46 | 93 | 25 |
| THE LIFE THOU TOOK'ST FROM HIM UNTO HIS DEATH. | YEE BUILD SEPULCHRES | 2 | 46 | 95 | 21 |
| NO,NO, THEY SAW THE NOT, O LIFE, O LOVE, | BUT NOW THEY HAVE SEEN | 3 | 46 | 96 | 21 |
| (FOR WHAT ELSE IS MY LIFE.) LO I BEQUEATH. | OUR LORD IN HIS CIRCUMCISION | 2 | 46 | 98 | 9 |
| WHEN LIFE WAS BORNE, | EASTER DAY | 11 | 46 | 100 | 26 |
| LIFE, BY THIS LIGHT'S NATIVITY | EASTER DAY | 13 | 46 | 100 | 26 |
| AND DOES WOE ME INTO LIFE. | PSALME 23 | 20 | 46 | 102 | 5 |
| TO FEED MY LIFE WITH,THERE I'LE SUP | PSALME 23 | 69 | 46 | 102 | 5 |
| THAT DRINKE THE DEAW OF LIFE, WHOSE DEATHLESSE SPRING, | SOSPETTO D'HERODE | 20 | 46 | 109 | 216 |
| THE NEVER-DYING LIFE, OF A LONG DEATH. | SOSPETTO D'HERODE | 60 | 46 | 109 | 216 |
| AND LIFE SELFE IT WEARE DEATHS FRAILE LIVERY. | SOSPETTO D'HERODE | 168 | 46 | 109 | 216 |
| HIS SPIRITS, THE SPARKES OF LIFE, AND CHILLS HIS HEART. | SOSPETTO D'HERODE | 422 | 46 | 109 | 216 |
| WHY DID I SPEND MY LIFE, AND SPILL MY BLOOD, | SOSPETTO D'HERODE | 449 | 46 | 109 | 216 |
| THY BROTHERS BLOOD BE-SPILT LIFE SPENT IN VAINE. | SOSPETTO D'HERODE | 452 | 46 | 109 | 216 |
| OF LIFE AND DEATH--TO PROVE THE WORD. | IN MEMORY OF LADY MADRE TERESA | 2 | 46 | 131 | 52 |
| LIFE SHOULD SO LONG PLAY WITH THAT BREATH, | IN MEMORY OF LADY MADRE TERESA | 17 | 46 | 131 | 52 |
| BLEST POWERS FORBID THY TENDER LIFE. | IN MEMORY OF LADY MADRE TERESA | 69 | 46 | 131 | 52 |
| A LIFE SO LOVED, AND THAT THERE BEE | IN MEMORY OF LADY MADRE TERESA | 91 | 46 | 131 | 52 |
| LIFE, BROUGHT THEM FIRST TO KISSE THE LIGHT | IN MEMORY OF LADY MADRE TERESA | 177 | 46 | 131 | 52 |
| MUST LEARNE IN LIFE TO DYE LIKE THEE. | IN MEMORY OF LADY MADRE TERESA | 183 | 46 | 131 | 52 |
| WINE OF YOUTHS LIFE, AND THE SWEET DEATHS OF LOVE, | AN APOLOGIE FOR HYMNE (TERESA) | 41 | 46 | 136 | 59 |
| OUR LIFE IN DEATH, OUR DAY IN NIGHT. | ON HOPE | 16 | 46 | 143 | 71 |
| WHENCE EACH LEAFE OF LIFE HATH DATE, | ANOTHER ON HERRYS | 42 | 46 | 170 | 469 |
| BECAUSE THEY BOTH LIV'D BUT ONE LIFE. | AN EPITAPH HUSBAND AND WIFE | 6 | 46 | 174 | 473 |
| I WOULD BE MARRIED TO A SINGLE LIFE. | ON MARRIAGE | 2 | 46 | 183 | 485 |
| FOR IN THE LIFE OUGHT ELSE CAN GIVE, | LOVES HOROSCOPE | 45 | 46 | 185 | 483 |
| LIFE IS FLYING. | OUT OF THE ITALIAN (1) | 50 | 46 | 188 | 545 |
| THEN WERE TH'AEGYPTIAN (BY THE LIFE, THESE GIVE, | ON FRONTISPIECE ISAACSONS | 19 | 46 | 191 | 491 |
| PEACE, WHICH HEE LOV'D IN LIFE, DID LEND | AN EPITAPH UPON ASHTON | 23 | 46 | 192 | 464 |
| GENTLY UNTWIN'D HIS THREAD OF LIFE. | AN EPITAPH UPON ASHTON | 28 | 46 | 192 | 464 |
| A LIFE PERHAPS UNTO HIS DEATH. | AN EPITAPH UPON ASHTON | 34 | 46 | 192 | 464 |
| HIS LIFE STILL KEPT ALIVE IN THEE. | AN EPITAPH UPON ASHTON | 36 | 46 | 192 | 464 |
| LIFE, THAT DARES SEND | WISHES SUPPOSED MISTRESSE | 85 | 46 | 195 | 479 |
| TAKING FRESH LIFE FROM YOUR FAYRE EYES. | THOUGH NOW 'TIS NEITHER | 10 | MS | 397 | 492 |
| TWIXT LIFE & DEATH, TWIXT IN & OUT. | TO COUNTESSE OF DENBIGH | 6 | 52 | 236 | 146 |
| TO SAVE YOUR LIFE, KILL YOUR DELAY | TO COUNTESSE OF DENBIGH | 58 | 52 | 236 | 146 |
| THE FORT AT LAST, AND LET LIFE IN. | TO COUNTESSE OF DENBIGH | 64 | 52 | 236 | 146 |
| UNTO THE EVERLASTING LIFE OF SONG. | TO THE NAME OF JESUS | 10 | 52 | 239 | 30 |
| START INTO LIFE, AND LEAP WITH ME | TO THE NAME OF JESUS | 49 | 52 | 239 | 30 |
| COME, LOVELY NAME. LIFE OF OUR HOPE. | TO THE NAME OF JESUS | 125 | 52 | 239 | 30 |
| LIFE OUT OF DEATH, DAY OUT OF NIGHT. | OFFICE H. CROSS MATINES | 23 | 52 | 265 | 86 |
| BOTH LIFE & LIBERTY | OFFICE H. CROSS SIXT | 18 | 52 | 270 | 97 |
| OF OPEN DEATH & HIDDEN LIFE. | OFFICE H. CROSS NINTH | 10 | 52 | 271 | 99 |
| LIFE SEEM'D TO DY, DEATH DY'D INDEED. | OFFICE H. CROSS NINTH | 12 | 52 | 271 | 99 |
| WHO LEND'ST TO ALL THINGS ALL THE LIFE THEY HAVE. | OFFICE H. CROSS COMPLINE | 10 | 52 | 274 | 105 |
| TO MAKE A KIND OF LIFE FOR MY LORD'S DEATH. | OFFICE H. CROSS RECOMMENDATION | 6 | 52 | 276 | 106 |
| MY DYING LIFE MAY DRAW A NEW, & NEVER FLEETING BREATH. | OFFICE H. CROSS RECOMMENDATION | 8 | 52 | 276 | 106 |
| THY LIFE IS ONE LONG DEBT | VEXILLA REGIS | 4 | 52 | 277 | 156 |
| LO, HOW THE STREAMES OF LIFE, FROM THAT FULL NEST | VEXILLA REGIS | 7 | 52 | 277 | 156 |
| TALL TREE OF LIFE. THY TRUTH MAKES GOOD | VEXILLA REGIS | 19 | 52 | 277 | 156 |
| HOW LIFE & DEATH IN THEE | TO OUR B. LORD | 1 | 52 | 279 | 25 |
| THAT LOST AGAIN MY LIFE MAY PROVE | CHARITAS NIMIA | 65 | 52 | 280 | 48 |
| SEE HER LIFE DY. | SANCTA MARIA DOLORUM | 38 | 52 | 283 | 162 |
| IN LINES OF DEATH, MY LIFE MAY COPPY IT | SANCTA MARIA DOLORUM | 54 | 52 | 283 | 162 |
| YEA LET MY LIFE & ME | SANCTA MARIA DOLORUM | 61 | 52 | 283 | 162 |
| FOLD UP MY LIFE IN LOVE. AND LAY'T BENEATH | SANCTA MARIA DOLORUM | 107 | 52 | 283 | 162 |
| THUS LOWE (MY HIDDEN LIFE.) I BOW TO THEE | ADORO TE | 3 | 52 | 291 | 172 |
| GIVE LOVE FOR LIFE. NOR LET MY DAYES | ADORO TE | 35 | 52 | 291 | 172 |
| MY LIFE, MY SOUL, MY SURER SELFE TO MEE. | ADORO TE | 44 | 52 | 291 | 172 |
| O THE BREAD OF LIFE, THIS DAY'S | LAUDA SION SALVATOREM | 7 | 52 | 294 | 178 |
| WHEN LIFE, HIMSELF, AT POINT TO DY | LAUDA SION SALVATOREM | 11 | 52 | 294 | 178 |
| THAT THUS FROM LIFE CAN DEATH DISTILL. | LAUDA SION SALVATOREM | 54 | 52 | 294 | 178 |
| HAIL, DOOR OF LIFE, & SOURSE OF DAY. | O GLORIOSA DOMINA | 32 | 52 | 302 | 194 |

| | | | | |
|---|---|---|---|---|
| YET LIGHT WAS SEEN & LIFE REVEAL'D. | O GLORIOSA DOMINA | 34 | 52 302 | 194 |
| THE FOUNTAIN SEAL'D, YET LIFE FOUND WAY. | O GLORIOSA DOMINA | 36 | 52 302 | 194 |
| OF LIFE & DEATH. TO PROVE THE WORD, | TERESA | 2 | 52 315 | 52 |
| LIFE SHOULD SO LONG PLAY WITH THAT BREATH | TERESA | 17 | 52 315 | 52 |
| BLEST POWRES FORBID, THY TENDER LIFE | TERESA | 69 | 52 315 | 52 |
| A LIFE SO LOV'D. AND THAT THERE BE | TERESA | 91 | 52 315 | 52 |
| O WHAT DELIGHT, WHEN REVEAL'D LIFE SHALL STAND | TERESA | 129 | 52 315 | 52 |
| LIFE BROUGHT THEM FIRST TO KISSE THE LIGHT | TERESA | 176 | 52 315 | 52 |
| MUST LEARN IN LIFE TO DY LIKE THEE. | TERESA | 182 | 52 315 | 52 |
| WINE OF YOUTH, LIFE, & THE SWEET DEATHS OF LOVE. | AN APOLOGIE FOR (TERESA) HYMNE | 41 | 52 322 | 59 |
| IN THAT RARE LIFE OF HER, AND LOVE. | FLAMING HEART | 52 | 52 324 | 61 |
| LET THIS IMMORTALL LIFE WHERERE IT COMES | FLAMING HEART | 81 | 52 324 | 61 |
| THE LOVE-SLAIN WITTNESSES OF THIS LIFE OF THEE. | FLAMING HEART | 84 | 52 324 | 61 |
| LET ME SO READ THY LIFE, THAT I | FLAMING HEART | 107 | 52 324 | 61 |
| UNTO ALL LIFE OF MINE MAY DY. | FLAMING HEART | 108 | 52 324 | 61 |
| OF LIVING DEATH & DYING LIFE. | A SONG | 14 | 52 327 | 65 |
| OF LOVE, OF LIFE, & EVERLASTING REST. | TO SAME CONCERNING CHOISE | 53 | 52 331 | 66 |
| THE TOO FRAIL LIFE OF FEMAL CONSTANCY. | ALEXIAS FIRST ELEGIE | 34 | 52 334 | 204 |
| WITH HIM SHALL I WEEP OUT MY WEARY LIFE. | ALEXIAS SECONDE ELEGIE | 6 | 52 335 | 207 |
| MY POOR ALEXIS. THEN IN PEACEFULL LIFE, | ALEXIAS THIRD ELEGIE | 13 | 52 336 | 209 |
| WHEN HOLY FIRES MAINTAIN LOVE'S HEAVNLY LIFE. | ALEXIAS THIRD ELEGIE | 52 | 52 336 | 209 |
| A LONG & DAYLY-DYING LIFE, WHICH BREATHS | DESCRIPTION RELIGIOUS HOUSE | 23 | 52 338 | 213 |
| 'CAUSE THEY BOTH LIVED BUT ONE LIFE. | AN EPITAPH UPON MARRIED COUPLE | 6 | 52 339 | 478 |
| SPEND THE DEAR TREASURES OF THY LIFE. | TEMPERANCE | 4 | 52 342 | 510 |
| 'TWIXT LIFE AND DEATH, 'TWIXT IN AND OUT. | AGAINST IRRESOLUTION AND DELAY | 6 | 52 347 | 146 |
| TO SAVE YOUR LIFE, KILL YOUR DELAY. | AGAINST IRRESOLUTION AND DELAY | 82 | 52 347 | 146 |
| THE FORT AT LAST, AND LET LIFE IN. | AGAINST IRRESOLUTION AND DELAY | 86 | 52 347 | 146 |
| SOE I MAY GAINE THY DEATH, MY LIFE I'LE GIVE. | MATH. 16. 25. WHOSOEVER SHALL | 1 | MS 381 | 16 |
| OR ELSE, MY LIFE, I'LE HIDE THEE IN HIS GRAVE, | MATH. 16. 25. WHOSOEVER SHALL | 3 | MS 381 | 16 |
| THAT MAN (I THINKE) WRESTED THE FEEBLE LIFE | HORATIJ ILLE & NEFASTO | 7 | MS 382 | 530 |
| THE STORME OF FATE, TO WHICH HIS LIFE HE OWES. | HORATIJ ILLE & NEFASTO | 24 | MS 382 | 530 |
| DEATH TO THE LIFE. MY INKE SHALL BE THE BLOOD | UPON GUNPOWDER TREASON | 3 | MS 386 | 460 |
| A SOLITARY LIFE SHE WOULD HAVE LED. | UPON GUNPOWDER TREASON | 16 | MS 386 | 460 |
| MY THREDS OF LIFE. IF THEN I SHALL NOT LIVE | EX EUPHORMIONE | 11 | MS 392 | 525 |
| THAT FETCHETH FRESH LIFE FROM HER FRUITFULL URNE. | EX EUPHORMIONE | 16 | MS 392 | 525 |
| WHOSE WHOLE LIFE MUSICK WAS. WHEREIN | UPON DEATH OF A FREIND | 19 | MS 393 | 477 |
| AND THOUGH THAT MUSICK OF HIS LIFE BE STILL. | UPON DEATH OF A FREIND | 21 | MS 393 | 477 |

LIFE-BREATHING

| | | | | |
|---|---|---|---|---|
| FROM DEATH'S SAD SHADES, TO THE LIFE-BREATHING AYRE. | SOSPETTO D'HERODE | 81 | 46 109 | 216 |

LIFE-FEEDING

| | | | | |
|---|---|---|---|---|
| VERTUE TO ACTION, THAT LIFE-FEEDING FLAME | ON A TREATISE OF CHARITY | 51 | 46 137 | 69 |

LIFE-FOOD

| | | | | |
|---|---|---|---|---|
| LO THE LIFE-FOOD OF ANGELLS THEN | LAUDA SION SALVATOREM | 61 | 52 294 | 178 |

LIFE-GIVING

| | | | | |
|---|---|---|---|---|
| SO FROM HIS LIVING, & LIFE-GIVING DEATH. | OFFICE H. CROSS RECOMMENDATION | 7 | 52 276 | 106 |
| THE LIVING & LIFE-GIVING BREAD, | LAUDA SION SALVATOREM | 9 | 52 294 | 178 |

LIFE-MEANING

| | | | | |
|---|---|---|---|---|
| YET ON THE SAME (LIFE-MEANING) BREAD | LAUDA SION SALVATOREM | 51 | 52 294 | 178 |

LIFE-SPEAKING

| | | | | |
|---|---|---|---|---|
| LET THOSE LIFE-SPEAKING LIPPS COMMAND | DIES IRAE | 63 | 52 298 | 186 |

LIFE'S

| | | | | |
|---|---|---|---|---|
| BATHING THEIR HOT LIMBS IN LIFE'S PRETIOUS FLOOD. | SOSPETTO D'HERODE | 316 | 46 109 | 216 |
| AND WHEN LIFE'S SWEET FABLE ENDS. | TEMPERANCE | 47 | 52 342 | 510 |
| (MY LIFE'S THY DEATH, & IN THY DEATH I LIVE.) | MATH. 16. 25. WHOSOEVER SHALL | 2 | MS 381 | 16 |

LIFES

| | | | | |
|---|---|---|---|---|
| WHEN LIFES SWEET LIGHT FIRST SHONE ON BEASTS. AND WHEN | OUT OF VIRGIL | 29 | 46 155 | 529 |
| LIFES LATE FORSAKEN HOUSES ALL LAY DROWN'D | THE BEGINNING OF HELIODORUS | 16 | 46 158 | 517 |
| LIFES FORGE. FAIN'D IS HER VOICE, AND FALSE TOO. BE | SOSPETTO D'HERODE | 423 | 46 109 | 216 |
| IS HER LIFES WING, OR HER DEATH'S WINDING-SHEET. | AT TH' IVORY TRIBUNALL | 6 | MS 397 | 492 |

LIFT

| | | | | |
|---|---|---|---|---|
| SHE CAN SEE HEAVEN, AND NE'RE LIFT UP HER EYES. | ON VIRGINS BASHFULNESSE | 6 | 46 89 | 9 |
| THY HAND TO GIVE THOU CANST NOT LIFT. | ON BLEEDING WOUNDS OF LORD | 9 | 46 101 | 110 |
| COME LIFT WE UP OUR LOFTY SONG. | A HYMNE OF THE NATIVITY | 3 | 46 106 | 76 |
| BUT LIFT CLEAN HANDS FULL OF CLEARE HEARTS. | A HYMNE OF THE NATIVITY | 76 | 46 106 | 76 |
| TO LIFT ME FROM MY LAZY URNE, TO CLIMBE | TO THE MORNING | 27 | 46 183 | 497 |
| COME LIFT WE UP OUR LOFTYER SONG | IN HOLY NATIVITY | 3 | 52 246 | 76 |
| THY HANDS TO GIVE, THOU CANST NOT LIFT. | UPON BLEEDING CRUCIFIX | 13 | 52 288 | 110 |
| LET LIPPES & HEARTS LIFT HIGH THE NOISE | LAUDA SION SALVATOREM | 15 | 52 294 | 178 |
| LIFT OUR LEAN SOULES, & SETT US UP | LAUDA SION SALVATOREM | 75 | 52 294 | 178 |

LIFT'ST

| | | | | |
|---|---|---|---|---|
| NOR MORE LOVELY LIFT'ST THY HEAD. | UPON DEATH OF DESIRED HERRYS | 15 | 46 168 | 467 |

PAGE 232

LIFTS

| | | | | | |
|---|---|---|---|---|---|
| LIFTS EARTH TO HEAVEN, STOOPS HEAVEN TO EARTH. | A HYMNE OF THE NATIVITY | 58 | 46 | 106 | 76 |
| _IFTS HIS MALIGNANT EYES, WASTED WITH CARE, | SOSPETTO D'HERODE | 83 | 46 | 109 | 216 |
| SHEE LIFTS HER SOOTY LAMPES, AND LOOKING ROUND | SOSPETTO D'HERODE | 301 | 46 | 109 | 216 |
| ON THESE SHE LIFTS THE WORLD, AND ON THEIR BASE | ON FRONTISPIECE ISAACSONS | 21 | 46 | 191 | 491 |
| _IFTS EARTH TO HEAVEN, STOOPES HEAV'N TO EARTH. | IN HOLY NATIVITY | 84 | 52 | 246 | 76 |

LIGHT

| | | | | | |
|---|---|---|---|---|---|
| THE LUTES LIGHT GENIUS NOW DOES PROUDLY RISE, | MUSICKS DUELL | 135 | 46 | 149 | 535 |
| WHEN LIFES SWEET LIGHT FIRST SHONE ON BEASTS, AND WHEN | OUT OF VIRGIL | 29 | 46 | 155 | 529 |
| _ENT THEM THE LAST FLASH OF HER GLIMMERING LIGHT. | THE BEGINNING OF HELIODORUS | 20 | 46 | 158 | 517 |
| THE WORLDS LIGHT SHINES, SHINE AS IT WILL, | BUT MEN LOVED DARKNESSE | 1 | 46 | 97 | 13 |
| WHICH TO BE SEENE NEEDS NOT HIS LIGHT. | A HYMNE OF THE NATIVITY | 14 | 46 | 106 | 76 |
| WEE SAW THEE BY THINE OWNE SWEET LIGHT. | A HYMNE OF THE NATIVITY | 34 | 46 | 106 | 76 |
| AND FOR HIS OLD FAIRE ROABES OF LIGHT, HEE WEARES | SOSPETTO D'HERODE | 43 | 46 | 109 | 216 |
| SUCH HIS FELL GLANCES AS THE FATALL LIGHT | SOSPETTO D'HERODE | 51 | 46 | 109 | 216 |
| HOW BRIGHT A DAWNE OF ANGELS WITH NEW LIGHT | SOSPETTO D'HERODE | 115 | 46 | 109 | 216 |
| HE SAW HEAV'N BLOSSOME WITH A NEW-BORNE LIGHT, | SOSPETTO D'HERODE | 129 | 46 | 109 | 216 |
| THAT THE GREAT ANGELL-BLINDING LIGHT SHOULD SHRINKE | SOSPETTO D'HERODE | 169 | 46 | 109 | 216 |
| AND FOR THE NEVER-FADING FIELDS OF LIGHT | SOSPETTO D'HERODE | 211 | 46 | 109 | 216 |
| MAKES HIM IMPATIENT OF THE LINGRING LIGHT. | SOSPETTO D'HERODE | 495 | 46 | 109 | 216 |
| IT IS THE ARMORY OF LIGHT, | ON A PRAYER BOOKE | 15 | 46 | 126 | 139 |
| WHOSE LIGHT SHALL LIVE BRIGHT, IN THY FACE | IN MEMORY OF LADY MADRE TERESA | 164 | 46 | 131 | 52 |
| _IFE, BROUGHT THEM FIRST TO KISSE THE LIGHT | IN MEMORY OF LADY MADRE TERESA | 177 | 46 | 131 | 52 |
| STEPS, WALKE WITH HIM THOSE WAYES OF LIGHT. | IN MEMORY OF LADY MADRE TERESA | 181 | 46 | 131 | 52 |
| A PEECE OF HEAVENLY LIGHT PURER AND BRIGHTER | ON THE ASSUMPTION | 3 | 46 | 139 | 114 |
| THEN THE CHAST STARS, WHOSE CHOICE LAMPS COME TO LIGHT HER. | ON THE ASSUMPTION | 4 | 46 | 139 | 114 |
| AND THOUGH THY DEAREST LOOKS MUST NOW BE LIGHT | ON THE ASSUMPTION | 31 | 46 | 139 | 114 |
| CROWN OF AN INCOMPARABLE LIGHT | ON THE ASSUMPTION | 56 | 46 | 139 | 114 |
| FAIRE CLOUD OF FIRE, BOTH SHADE, AND LIGHT, | ON HOPE | 15 | 46 | 143 | 71 |
| AND FORRAGE IN THE FIELDS OF LIGHT, AND LOVE. | ON HOPE | 76 | 46 | 143 | 71 |
| TO BLOT THE NEWLY BLOSSOM'D LIGHT. | UPON DEATH OF DESIRED HERRYS | 54 | 46 | 168 | 467 |
| AND THEY WAKEN WITH THAT LIGHT, | AN EPITAPH HUSBAND AND WIFE | 15 | 46 | 174 | 478 |
| ALONE, LIGHT SUCH ANOTHER STARRE, AND TWINE | UPON YORKE HIS BIRTH | 56 | 46 | 176 | 500 |
| NOR MAY THE LIGHT THAT GIVES THEIR EYE-LIDS LIGHT, | UPON YORKE HIS BIRTH | 92 | 46 | 176 | 500 |
| NOR MAY THE LIGHT THAT GIVES THEIR EYE-LIDS LIGHT, | UPON YORKE HIS BIRTH | 92 | 46 | 176 | 500 |
| INTO THY BOSOME, BATH'D WITH LIQUID LIGHT. | ON A FOULE MORNING | 30 | 46 | 181 | 495 |
| YOUR EYES THE LIGHT HATH REFT HIM. | OUT OF THE ITALIAN (2) | 3 | 46 | 190 | 547 |
| LET MY HEAT TO YOUR LIGHT BE RECONCILED. | OUT OF THE ITALIAN (2) | 6 | 46 | 190 | 547 |
| AND BY HIS FAIRE EXAMPLES LIGHT, | AN EPITAPH UPON ASHTON | 31 | 46 | 192 | 464 |
| SHUTS THE EYES OF OUR SHORT LIGHT. | OUT OF CATULLUS | 8 | 46 | 194 | 523 |
| OF DARKENESSE, BY THE LIGHT | WISHES SUPPOSED MISTRESSE | 80 | 46 | 195 | 479 |
| AND 'MONGST THY SHAFTS OF SOVERAIGN LIGHT | TO COUNTESSE OF DENBIGH | 32 | 52 | 236 | 146 |
| O DART OF LOVE. ARROW OF LIGHT. | TO COUNTESSE OF DENBIGH | 49 | 52 | 236 | 146 |
| CANDIDATES OF BLISSEFULL LIGHT, | TO THE NAME OF JESUS | 8 | 52 | 239 | 30 |
| REGIONS OF PEACEFULL LIGHT | TO THE NAME OF JESUS | 116 | 52 | 239 | 30 |
| AND COUCH BEFORE THE DAZELING LIGHT OF THY DREAD MAJESTY. | TO THE NAME OF JESUS | 235 | 52 | 239 | 30 |
| WHICH TO BE SEEN NEEDES NOT HIS LIGHT. | IN HOLY NATIVITY | 14 | 52 | 246 | 76 |
| WE SAW THEE BY THINE OWN SWEET LIGHT. | IN HOLY NATIVITY | 36 | 52 | 246 | 76 |
| WE SAW THEE, BY THINE OWN SWEET LIGHT. | IN HOLY NATIVITY | 77 | 52 | 246 | 76 |
| NOR BY ALTERNATE SHREDDS OF LIGHT | IN GLORIOUS EPIPHANIE | 34 | 52 | 253 | 39 |
| FAREWELL, THE WORLD'S FALSE LIGHT. | IN GLORIOUS EPIPHANIE | 48 | 52 | 253 | 39 |
| A LONG DELIQUIUM TO THE LIGHT OF THEE. | IN GLORIOUS EPIPHANIE | 116 | 52 | 253 | 39 |
| OF CONTROVERTED LIGHT, | IN GLORIOUS EPIPHANIE | 147 | 52 | 253 | 39 |
| _OOSING IT ONCE AGAINE, STUMBLE'ON TRUE LIGHT | IN GLORIOUS EPIPHANIE | 167 | 52 | 253 | 39 |
| THEIR NEW & ADMIRABLE LIGHT. | IN GLORIOUS EPIPHANIE | 173 | 52 | 253 | 39 |
| THUS SHALL THAT REVEREND CHILD OF LIGHT. | IN GLORIOUS EPIPHANIE | 205 | 52 | 253 | 39 |
| BY THE FRUGALL NEGATIVE LIGHT | IN GLORIOUS EPIPHANIE | 209 | 52 | 253 | 39 |
| FOR BEING SHOW'D BY THIS DAY'S LIGHT, HOW FARR | IN GLORIOUS EPIPHANIE | 246 | 52 | 253 | 39 |
| WHO BROUGHTST TO LIGHT | OFFICE H. CROSS MATINES | 22 | 52 | 265 | 86 |
| INTO THE LAND OF LIGHT & LOVE. | OFFICE H. CROSS PRIME | 12 | 52 | 267 | 91 |
| AND PROVE HOW LIGHT THE WORLD WAS, WHEN IT WEIGHD WITH HIM. | OFFICE H. CROSS EVENSONG | 19 | 52 | 273 | 101 |
| HOW MUCH DEATH WEIGH'D MORE LIGHT THEN LOVE. | VEXILLA REGIS | 36 | 52 | 277 | 156 |
| STILL WOULD THOSE BEAUTEOUS MINISTERS OF LIGHT | CHARITAS NIMIA | 21 | 52 | 280 | 48 |
| O THOSE EYES. WHOSE ANGRY LIGHT | DIES IRAE | 7 | 52 | 298 | 186 |
| WILL SETT THE WORLD IN SEVERE LIGHT. | DIES IRAE | 18 | 52 | 298 | 186 |
| AND STAINES THE TIMEROUS LIGHT OF STARRES. | O GLORIOSA DOMINA | 4 | 52 | 302 | 194 |
| YET LIGHT WAS SEEN & LIFE REVEAL'D. | O GLORIOSA DOMINA | 34 | 52 | 302 | 194 |
| THEN THE CHAST STARRES, WHOSE CHOISE LAMPS COME TO LIGHT HER | IN GLORIOUS ASSUMPTION B. LADY | 4 | 52 | 304 | 114 |
| CROWN OF A MOST INCOMPARABLE LIGHT | IN GLORIOUS ASSUMPTION B. LADY | 61 | 52 | 304 | 114 |
| WHOSE LIGHT SHALL LIVE BRIGHT IN THY FACE | TERESA | 163 | 52 | 315 | 52 |
| _IFE BROUGHT THEM FIRST TO KISSE THE LIGHT | TERESA | 176 | 52 | 315 | 52 |
| STEPPS, WALK WITH HIM THOSE WAYES OF LIGHT | TERESA | 180 | 52 | 315 | 52 |
| _ET ALL THY SCATTER'D SHAFTS OF LIGHT, THAT PLAY | FLAMING HEART | 87 | 52 | 324 | 61 |
| IT IS AN ARMORY OF LIGHT | PRAYER TO GENTLE-WOMAN | 21 | 52 | 328 | 139 |
| SUCH AS THE SACRED LIGHT THAT ERST DID BRING | ALEXIAS SECONDE ELEGIE | 27 | 52 | 335 | 207 |
| HOME TO THE ORIGINALL SOURSE OF LIGHT & INTELLECTUALL | DESCRIPTION RELIGIOUS HOUSE | 39 | 52 | 338 | 213 |
| AND THEY WAKE INTO A LIGHT, | AN EPITAPH UPON MARRIED COUPLE | 19 | 52 | 339 | 478 |
| AND FORRAGE IN THE FIELDS OF LIGHT AND LOVE. | (ON) HOPE | 36 | 52 | 345 | 71 |
| THY RISING TOPP FIRST STAIND THE BASHFULL LIGHT. | HORATIJ ILLE & NEFASTO | 6 | MS | 382 | 530 |
| NOW TO THOSE TOILING SOULES IT GIVES ITS LIGHT, | ON GUNPOWDER-TREASON | 57 | MS | 384 | 458 |
| SOE FOULE, ONE MINUTES LIGHT HAD IT BUT SEENE, | UPON GUNPOWDER TREASON | 13 | MS | 386 | 460 |
| JOVES TWINCKLING TAPERS, THAT DOE LIGHT THE WORLD, | UPON GUNPOWDER TREASON | 27 | MS | 386 | 460 |
| EACH HOLDING FORTH TO LIGHT THE AERY BRAND, | UPON GUNPOWDER TREASON | 14 | MS | 387 | 461 |
| AND MISTS OF GREIFE, DARE FORCE A JOYFULL LIGHT. | UPON KINGS CORONATION | 16 | MS | 389 | 454 |
| STEALE FROM THEIR STATIONS TO REPAIRE THEIR LIGHT. | UPON KINGS CORONATION | 28 | MS | 389 | 454 |
| THOSE SPARKLING TWINNES OF LIGHT SHOULD I NOW STILE | UPON BIRTH PRINCESSE E | 43 | MS | 391 | 456 |

| | | | | |
|---|---|---|---|---|
| AND TO MY TOUCH DARKE EYES DID OWE THE LIGHT. | OUT OF GROTIUS | 72 | MS | 398 198 |

### LIGHT-FOOT

| | | | | |
|---|---|---|---|---|
| DISPOS'D TO GIVE THE LIGHT-FOOT LADY SPORT | MUSICKS DUELL | 16 | 46 | 149 535 |

### LIGHT'S

| | | | | |
|---|---|---|---|---|
| LIFE, BY THIS LIGHT'S NATIVITY | EASTER DAY | 13 | 46 | 100  26 |
| THE LIGHT'S FAIRE FACE, BUT STILL ABORTIVE BEE. | UPON GUNPOWDER TREASON | 58 | MS | 386 460 |

### LIGHTED

| | | | | |
|---|---|---|---|---|
| HE STREIGHTWAY LIGHTED UPP HIS PITCHY TORCH. | ON GUNPOWDER-TREASON | 56 | MS | 384 458 |

### LIGHTS

| | | | | |
|---|---|---|---|---|
| MY LIGHTS THY SHADOWES SHADOW, OR 'TIS DONE. | SICKE IMPLORE SHADOW | 4 | 46 | 87  28 |
| AND LET NO DULL MISTS CHOAKE THE LIGHTS FAIRE GROWTH. | ON A FOULE MORNING | 4 | 46 | 181 495 |
| OF LIGHTS, | IN GLORIOUS EPIPHANIE | 8 | 52 | 253  39 |
| BY ALL THY DOWR OF LIGHTS & FIRES. | FLAMING HEART | 94 | 52 | 324  61 |
| FALSE LIGHTS OF FLAIRING GEMMES. TUMULTUOUS JOYES. | DESCRIPTION RELIGIOUS HOUSE | 5 | 52 | 338 213 |

### LIGHTING

| | | | | |
|---|---|---|---|---|
| LIGHTING TO ETERNITY. | PSALME 23 | 66 | 46 | 102   5 |
| SHALL WITH ONE FLASH OF LIGHTING BE STRUCK BLIND. | ON GUNPOWDER-TREASON | 32 | MS | 384 458 |
| FOR LIGHTING THEM UNTO THEIR MISERY. | ON GUNPOWDER-TREASON | 60 | MS | 384 458 |

### LIGHTLY

| | | | | |
|---|---|---|---|---|
| HEE LIGHTLY SKIRMISHES ON EVERY STRING | MUSICKS DUELL | 20 | 46 | 149 535 |
| LIGHTLY AS A LAMBENT FLAME, | AGAINST IRRESOLUTION AND DELAY | 70 | 52 | 347 146 |

### LIGHTNESSE

| | | | | |
|---|---|---|---|---|
| LEARN'D FIRST HIS LIGHTNESSE BY HIS LOVE. | AGAINST IRRESOLUTION AND DELAY | 52 | 52 | 347 146 |

### LIGHTNING

| | | | | |
|---|---|---|---|---|
| HIS BREATH HELLS LIGHTNING IS. AND EACH DEEPE GRONE | SOSPETTO D'HERODE | 55 | 46 | 109 216 |
| THE FACES LIGHTNING, OR A SMILE IS HERE. | SOSPETTO D'HERODE | 198 | 46 | 109 216 |
| OF LIGHTNING, OR THE WORDS HE SPOKE) LEFT HELL. | SOSPETTO D'HERODE | 372 | 46 | 109 216 |
| WHOSE PURE AND SUBTLE LIGHTNING, FLIES | ON A PRAYER BOOKE | 66 | 46 | 126 139 |
| SHOT THEE LIKE LIGHTNING, TO TH'ASTONISHT EARTH. | ON A TREATISE OF CHARITY | 6 | 46 | 137  69 |
| WHOSE PURE & SUBTIL LIGHTNING FLYES | PRAYER TO GENTLE-WOMAN | 72 | 52 | 328 139 |

### LIGHTNING-WINGED

| | | | | |
|---|---|---|---|---|
| THE NIMBLEST OF THE LIGHTNING-WINGED LOVES. | SOSPETTO D'HERODE | 235 | 46 | 109 216 |

### LIKE

| | | | | |
|---|---|---|---|---|
| AND LIKE A SAUCY BIRD HE HOVERS | OUT OF GREEKE CUPID'S CRYER | 40 | 46 | 159 519 |
| WAS NEVER MAN LORD SPAKE LIKE THEE. | THE BLIND CURED | 4 | 46 | 91  19 |
| LIKE STATUES FIXED TO THE FAME | NEITHER DURST MAN ASKE | 11 | 46 | 92  20 |
| WHICH LIKE TWO BOSOM'D SAILES EMBRACE THE DIMME | SOSPETTO D'HERODE | 142 | 46 | 109 216 |
| LIKE A SOFT LUMPE OF INCENSE, HASTED | IN MEMORY OF LADY MADRE TERESA | 114 | 46 | 131  52 |
| MUST LEARNE IN LIFE TO DYE LIKE THEE. | IN MEMORY OF LADY MADRE TERESA | 183 | 46 | 131  52 |
| SPEAKE HEAVEN LIKE HERS, IS MY SOULES COUNTRY-MAN. | AN APOLOGIE FOR HYMNE (TERESA) | 22 | 46 | 136  59 |
| SHOT THEE LIKE LIGHTNING, TO TH'ASTONISHT EARTH. | ON A TREATISE OF CHARITY | 6 | 46 | 137  69 |
| SH'L DRESSE THEE LIKE THY SELFE, SET THEE ON HIGH | ON A TREATISE OF CHARITY | 15 | 46 | 137  69 |
| LIE SCATTER'D LIKE THE BURNT AND MARTYR'D BONES | ON A TREATISE OF CHARITY | 32 | 46 | 137  69 |
| URNS. LIKE GODS SANCTUARIES THEY LOOKT OF OLD. | ON A TREATISE OF CHARITY | 36 | 46 | 137  69 |
| SHRINKES, LIKE THE SICK MOONE AT THE WHOLSOME MORNE. | ON HOPE | 20 | 46 | 143  71 |
| THE MORNING MUSES PERCH LIKE BIRDS, AND SING | UPON DEATH OF HERRYS | 11 | 46 | 167 466 |
| PEEP'T FROM THEIR BUDS, SHEW'D LIKE THE GARDENS EYES | UPON YORKE HIS BIRTH | 62 | 46 | 176 500 |
| SCARCE WAKT. LIKE WAS THE CRIMSON OF THEIR JOYES, | UPON YORKE HIS BIRTH | 63 | 46 | 176 500 |
| LIKE WERE THE PEARLES THEY WEPT, SO LIKE THAT ONE | UPON YORKE HIS BIRTH | 64 | 46 | 176 500 |
| LIKE WERE THE PEARLES THEY WEPT, SO LIKE THAT ONE | UPON YORKE HIS BIRTH | 64 | 46 | 176 500 |
| BRIGHT CLOUDS LIKE GOLDEN FLEECES SHALL BE SPREAD. | ON A FOULE MORNING | 26 | 46 | 181 495 |
| LIKE DILIGENT BEES, AND SWARM ABOUT IT. | TO THE NAME OF JESUS | 153 | 52 | 239  30 |
| LIKE A SOFT LUMP OF INCENSE, HASTED | TERESA | 113 | 52 | 315  52 |
| MUST LEARN IN LIFE TO DY LIKE THEE. | TERESA | 182 | 52 | 315  52 |
| SPEAK HEAV'N LIKE HER'S IS MY SOULS COUNTRY-MAN. | AN APOLOGIE FOR (TERESA) HYMNE | 22 | 52 | 322  59 |
| NO GAPING GORGON, THIS. NONE, LIKE THE REST | ALEXIAS THIRD ELEGIE | 41 | 52 | 336 209 |
| SOUL & BODY PART LIKE FREINDS. | TEMPERANCE | 48 | 52 | 342 510 |
| TO TOSSE PUORE MEN LIKE DUST INTO THE AIRE. | ON GUNPOWDER-TREASON | 40 | MS | 384 458 |
| LIKE BANDIED BALLES, INTO THE FIRMAMENT. | ON GUNPOWDER-TREASON | 42 | MS | 384 458 |
| HAD YOU, LIKE OUR GREAT SUNNE, STAMPED BUT ONE | UPON BIRTH PRINCESSE E | 27 | MS | 391 456 |
| DANCE, LIKE THE NIMBLE SPHAERES, A JOYFULL ROUND. | UPON BIRTH PRINCESSE E | 32 | MS | 391 456 |

### DEATH-LIKE

| | | | | |
|---|---|---|---|---|
| IN DEATH-LIKE SLUMBERS. WHILE THY DANGERS CRAVE | SOSPETTO D'HERODE | 430 | 46 | 109 216 |

### METEOR-LIKE

| | | | | |
|---|---|---|---|---|
| WHOSE FLOURISH (METEOR-LIKE) DOTH CURLE THE AIRE | MUSICKS DUELL | 137 | 46 | 149 535 |

### PHOENIX-LIKE

| | | | | |
|---|---|---|---|---|
| LET NATURE DIE, IF (PHOENIX-LIKE) FROM DEATH | ON FRONTISPIECE ISAACSONS | 3 | 46 | 191 491 |

SWAN-LIKE

    EACH WINGED CHORISTER WOULD SWAN-LIKE SING      UPON GUNPOWDER TREASON      43   MS 386 460

LIK'ST

    TAST THIS, AND AS THOU LIK'ST THIS LESSER FLOOD    OUR LORD IN HIS CIRCUMCISION    3   46  98   9

LIKES

    THE WORLD LYES WARM, & LIKES HIS PLACE.      IN GLORIOUS EPIPHANIE      37   52 253  39

LILLY

    AS THIS MODEST MAIDEN LILLY,      AN HIMNE FOR CIRCUMCISION      11   46 141  37
    AS THIS MODEST MAIDEN LILLY      NEW YEAR'S DAY      11   52 251  37
    OR THAT THE DYING LILLY DID BESTOW      UPON BIRTH PRINCESSE E      49   MS 391 456
    THEY FORCE A LILLY PATH THROUGH ROSY MOUNTAINS.    AN ELEGIE ON DR PORTER      42   MS 395 476

LILLY'S

    NUZZEL'D IN THE LILLY'S NECK.      WEEPER      46   52 307 120

LILLIES

    NUZZEL'D IN THE LILLIES NECKE.      THE WEEPER      40   46  79 120
    ROSES HENCE, OR LILLIES RATHER.      UPON INFANT MARTYRS      4   46  95  10
    AMONGST THOSE LILLIES, WHICH HIS BOSOME BREDD.    AN ELEGY MR STANNINOW      52   MS 394 473

LIMB

    LO THE FAINT LAMB, WITH WEARY LIMB      OFFICE H. CROSS SIXT      3   52 270  97
    TO POISE EACH PRETIOUS LIMB.      OFFICE H. CROSS EVENSONG      18   52 273 101

LIMBE

    ETERNALLY BIND EACH REBELLIOUS LIMBE.      SOSPETTO D'HERODE      140   46 109 216
    TO RAVISH HEAVEN TO LIMBE THEM O'RE AGAINE.    UPON BIRTH PRINCESSE E      36   MS 391 456
    GOE ON THEN, HEAVEN, & LIMBE FORTH SUCH ANOTHER,    UPON BIRTH PRINCESSE E      55   MS 391 456

LIMME

    EACH BLEST DROP, ON EACH BLEST LIMME,      ON WATER OF LORDS BAPTISME      1   46  85  12

WELL-LIM'D

    SO MUCH AS TH' PICTURE OF A WELL-LIM'D VERSE.    WITH A PICTURE TO A FRIEND      4   46 156 494

LIMBS

    OF RAGGED LIMBS, TORNE SCULLS, & DASHT OUT BRAINES.    SOSPETTO D'HERODE      312   46 109 216
    BATHING THEIR HOT LIMBS IN LIFE'S PRETIOUS FLOOD.    SOSPETTO D'HERODE      316   46 109 216
    THOSE LIMBS OF DEATH FROM THY LEFT SIDE,      DIES IRAE      62   52 298 186
    'TIS LOVE, NOT YEARES OR LIMBS THAT CAN      TERESA      33   52 315  52

LIMBES

    TIS LOVE, NOT YEARES, OR LIMBES, THAT CAN    IN MEMORY OF LADY MADRE TERESA      33   46 131  52
    AND STRETCH THEIR COLD LIMBES IN A PLEASING FIRE.    HORATIJ ILLE & NEFASTO      53   MS 382 530
    GRIPES THY COLD LIMBES SOE FAST, THOU CANST NOT FLY,    ON GUNPOWDER-TREASON      4   MS 384 458

LIMMES

    HIS BEDRID LIMMES, WRAPT IN A FLEECY CLOWD.    AN ELEGY MR STANNINOW      4   MS 394 473
    THAT ON THESE SNOWY LIMMES HATH LAID SUCH HOLD.    AN ELEGY MR STANNINOW      20   MS 394 473

LIMITS

    SHEWES THE TWO TERMES AND LIMITS OF TIME'S RACE.    ON FRONTISPIECE ISAACSONS      22   46 191 491

LINAGE

    WHOSE RIGHT BY DAVID'S LINAGE SO LONG WORNE,    SOSPETTO D'HERODE      403   46 109 216

LINE

    I WRITE SO ILL, MY SLENDER LINE IS SCARCE    WITH A PICTURE TO A FRIEND      3   46 156 494
    A LINE OR TWO, TO SPEAKE HIM DEAD.      UPON THE DEATH OF A GENTLEMAN      8   46 166 472
    BY THE LINE OF THY DEARE LOVE.      PSALME 23      58   46 102   5
    HEAVN'S GREAT ARTILLERY IN EACH LOVE-SPUN LINE.    FLAMING HEART      56   52 324  61
    HALF TRUE, ALAS, HALF FALSE, PROVES THAT POOR LINE.    ALEXIAS THIRD ELEGIE      57   52 336 209

LINES

    WRITE THESE LINES, READER, IN THY BROW,    AN EPITAPH UPON ASHTON      30   46 192 464
    SO WHILE THESE LINES CAN BUT BEQUEATH    AN EPITAPH UPON ASHTON      33   46 192 464
    WHAT THESE LINES WISH TO SEE.    WISHES SUPPOSED MISTRESSE      113   46 195 479
    IN LINES OF DEATH, MY LIFE MAY COPPY IT    SANCTA MARIA DOLORUM      54   52 283 162
    HANGS HIS BLACK LUGGES, STROAKT WITH THOSE HEAVENLY    HORATIJ ILLE & NEFASTO      51   MS 382 530
        LINES.

    AND THOUGH THESE HUMBLE LINES SOARE NOT SOE HIGH,    UPON BIRTH PRINCESSE E      17   MS 391 456

LINGER

| | | | | | |
|---|---|---|---|---|---|
| AH LINGER NOT, LOV'D SOUL. A SLOW | TO COUNTESSE OF DENBIGH | 13 | 52 | 236 | 146 |
| AH, LINGER NOT, LOV'D SOUL. A SLOW | AGAINST IRRESOLUTION AND DELAY | 7 | 52 | 347 | 146 |

LINGRING

| | | | | | |
|---|---|---|---|---|---|
| MAKES HIM IMPATIENT OF THE LINGRING LIGHT. | SOSPETTO D'HERODE | 495 | 46 | 109 | 216 |
| TO MY LOVING, LINGRING SORROW. | OUT OF THE ITALIAN (1) | 42 | 46 | 188 | 545 |
| SAY, LINGRING FAIR. WHY COMES THE BIRTH | TO COUNTESSE OF DENBIGH | 7 | 52 | 236 | 146 |
| SAY, LINGRING FAIR, WHY COMES THE BIRTH | AGAINST IRRESOLUTION AND DELAY | 15 | 52 | 347 | 146 |

LINX

| | | | | | |
|---|---|---|---|---|---|
| OF LIONS NOW NOE MORE, OR SPOTTED LINX. | HORATIJ ILLE & NEFASTO | 56 | MS | 382 | 530 |

LIONS

| | | | | | |
|---|---|---|---|---|---|
| OF LIONS NOW NOE MORE, OR SPOTTED LINX. | HORATIJ ILLE & NEFASTO | 56 | MS | 382 | 530 |

LIP

| | | | | | |
|---|---|---|---|---|---|
| THE ROSE BUDS SWEET LIP KISSES. | THE TEARE | 21 | 46 | 84 | 50 |

SWEET-LIP'T

| | | | | | |
|---|---|---|---|---|---|
| THE SWEET-LIP'T SISTERS MUSICALLY FRIGHTED. | MUSICKS DUELL | 113 | 46 | 149 | 535 |

LIPP

| | | | | | |
|---|---|---|---|---|---|
| DARES HUNGRY DEATH SNATCH OF ONE CHERRY LIPP. | UPON GUNPOWDER TREASON | 39 | MS | 387 | 461 |

SWEET-LIPP'D

| | | | | | |
|---|---|---|---|---|---|
| OF SWEET-LIPP'D ANGELL-IMPS, THAT SWILL THEIR THROATS | MUSICKS DUELL | 76 | 46 | 149 | 535 |

SWEET-LIPP'T

| | | | | | |
|---|---|---|---|---|---|
| AND EVERY SWEET-LIPP'T THING | TO THE NAME OF JESUS | 47 | 52 | 239 | 30 |

LIPS

| | | | | | |
|---|---|---|---|---|---|
| ADDS SWEETNESSE TO HIS SWEETEST LIPS. | THE WEEPER | 28 | 46 | 79 | 120 |
| WITHIN THE LIPS OF LOVE AND JOY DOTH DWELL | UPON ASSE THAT BORE SAVIOUR | 3 | 46 | 90 | 19 |
| LO. A MOUTH, WHOSE FULL-BLOOM'D LIPS | ON WOUNDS OF CRUCIFIED LORD | 5 | 46 | 99 | 24 |
| SHEE SPREADS THE RED LEAVES OF THY LIPS, | A HYMNE OF THE NATIVITY | 67 | 46 | 106 | 76 |
| OF LANGUAGE TO MY INFANT LIPS, YEE BEST | SOSPETTO D'HERODE | 6 | 46 | 109 | 216 |
| FROM HIS BLACK NOSTRILLS, AND BLEW LIPS, IN SPIGHT | SOSPETTO D'HERODE | 53 | 46 | 109 | 216 |
| THE FOAMY LIPS OF CERBERUS) SHEE APPLY'D | SOSPETTO D'HERODE | 466 | 46 | 109 | 216 |
| YET SHALL OUR LIPS NEVER LET GOE | ON THE ASSUMPTION | 38 | 46 | 139 | 114 |
| THE CORALL OF THY LIPS. THOU ART OF ALL | UPON YORKE HIS BIRTH | 47 | 46 | 176 | 500 |
| THOSE DEERE LIPS WHOSE DOORE ENCLOSES | OUT OF THE ITALIAN (1) | 21 | 46 | 188 | 545 |
| ON OUR LIPS, BEGIN AND TELL | OUT OF CATULLUS | 10 | 46 | 194 | 523 |
| KINDLED ON THEIR COLD LIPS. O HAD MY WISHES | UPON TWO GREENE APRICOCKES | 10 | 48 | 220 | 494 |

LIPPES

| | | | | | |
|---|---|---|---|---|---|
| THIS FOOT HATH GOT A MOUTH AND LIPPES. | ON WOUNDS OF CRUCIFIED LORD | 13 | 46 | 99 | 24 |
| THOU SHALT OPEN MY LIPPES, O LORD. | OFFICE H. CROSS MATINES | 3 | 52 | 265 | 66 |
| LET LIPPES & HEARTS LIFT HIGH THE NOISE | LAUDA SION SALVATOREM | 15 | 52 | 294 | 178 |
| LET HEARTS & LIPPES SPEAK LOWD. AND SAY | O GLORIOSA DOMINA | 31 | 52 | 302 | 194 |
| ADDES SWEETNES TO HIS SWEETEST LIPPES. | WEEPER | 28 | 52 | 307 | 120 |
| THESE DEATH-SEAL'D LIPPES ARE THEY DARE GIVE THE LY | DEATH'S LECTURE | 25 | 52 | 340 | 475 |
| WITH TREMBLING LIPPES AN HUMBLE KISSE DO'ST PAY. | AN ELEGIE ON DR PORTER | 6 | MS | 395 | 476 |

LIPPS

| | | | | | |
|---|---|---|---|---|---|
| FROM VENUS LIPPS. BUT AS FOR HIM | OUT OF GREEKE CUPID'S CRYER | 13 | 46 | 159 | 519 |
| AND TEACH THY LIPPS HEAVEN, WITH HER HAND, | IN MEMORY OF LADY MADRE TERESA | 131 | 46 | 131 | 52 |
| THESE DEATH-SEAL'D LIPPS ARE THEY DARE GIVE THE LYE. | UPON STANINOUGH'S DEATH | 23 | 46 | 175 | 475 |
| LIPPS, WHERE ALL DAY | WISHES SUPPOSED MISTRESSE | 37 | 46 | 195 | 479 |
| AND THE GREAT PENITENT PRESSE HIS OWN PALE LIPPS | IN GLORIOUS EPIPHANIE | 151 | 52 | 253 | 39 |
| LET THOSE LIFE-SPEAKING LIPPS COMMAND | DIES IRAE | 63 | 52 | 298 | 166 |
| AND TEACH THY LIPPS HEAV'N WITH HIS HAND. | TERESA | 130 | 52 | 315 | 52 |

LIQUID

| | | | | | |
|---|---|---|---|---|---|
| BATHING IN STREAMES OF LIQUID MELODIE. | MUSICKS DUELL | 68 | 46 | 149 | 535 |
| INTO THY BOSOME, BATH'D WITH LIQUID LIGHT. | ON A FOULE MORNING | 30 | 46 | 181 | 495 |
| BY THY LAST MORNING'S DRAUGHT OF LIQUID FIRE. | FLAMING HEART | 100 | 52 | 324 | 61 |

LIQUOR

| | | | | | |
|---|---|---|---|---|---|
| TH'IMPATIENT LIQUOR, FRETS, AND FOAMES, AND RAVES. | SOSPETTO D'HERODE | 486 | 46 | 109 | 216 |

LISP

| | | | | | |
|---|---|---|---|---|---|
| SCARCE HAD SHEE LEARNT TO LISP A NAME | IN MEMORY OF LADY MADRE TERESA | 15 | 46 | 131 | 52 |
| SCARSE HAS SHE LEARN'T TO LISP THE NAME | TERESA | 15 | 52 | 315 | 52 |

LISTEN

'TIS TIME YOU LISTEN TO A BRAVER LOVE.        TO SAME CONCERNING CHOISE           20    52 331   66

LISTNED

AND LISTNED TO THE WHISPER OF MY WILL.        OUT OF GROTIUS                      66    MS 398  198

LISTING

AT LAST HER LISTING EARES THE NOISE O'RETAKES.  SOSPETTO D'HERODE               300    46 109  216

LISTNING

THERE STOOD SHE LISTNING, AND DID ENTERTAINE    MUSICKS DUELL                    11    46 149  535
'TIS THIS.  LISTNING ONE DAY TOO LONG.          OUT OF THE ITALIAN (3)            3    46 190  549

LISTS

THIS DONE, HEE LISTS WHAT SHEE WOULD SAY TO THIS.  MUSICKS DUELL              157    46 149  535

LITTLE

HER LITTLE SOULE IS RAVISHT. AND SO POUR'D       MUSICKS DUELL                  102    46 149  535
FOLLOWING THOSE LITTLE RILLS, HEE SINKES INTO    MUSICKS DUELL                  123    46 149  535
HER LITTLE FUGITIVE DISCOVER.                    OUT OF GREEKE CUPID'S CRYER      2    46 159  519
HIS WEAPON IS A LITTLE BOW,                      OUT OF GREEKE CUPID'S CRYER     45    46 159  519
WE'RE SUFFRED, YET HIS LITTLE ARROW.             OUT OF GREEKE CUPID'S CRYER     47    46 159  519
THEIR LITTLE CHANNELS CAN DELIVER                ON BLEEDING WOUNDS OF LORD      27    46 101  110
LOE HERE A LITTLE VOLUME, BUT LARGE BOOKE.       ON A PRAYER BOOKE                1    46 126  139
OF LITTLE EAGLES, AND YOUNG LOVES, WHOSE HIGH    AN APOLOGIE FOR HYMNE (TERESA)  27    46 136   59
STAY BUT A LITTLE WHILE, UNTILL I CALL           UPON STANINOUGH'S DEATH          5    46 175  475
THY LITTLE SELFE IN LESSE, READ IN THESE EYNE    UPON YORKE HIS BIRTH            43    46 176  500
ONE LITTLE WORLD OR TWO                          TO THE NAME OF JESUS            24    52 239   30
LITTLE, ALAS, THOUGHT THEY                       TO THE NAME OF JESUS           207    52 239   30
GREAT LITTLE ONE. WHOSE ALL-EMBRACING BIRTH      IN HOLY NATIVITY                83    52 246   76
O LITTLE ALL.  IN THY EMBRACE                    IN GLORIOUS EPIPHANIE           36    52 253   39
THEIR LITTLE CHANNELLS CAN DELIVER               UPON BLEEDING CRUCIFIX          23    52 288  110
OF LITTLE EAGLES & YOUNG LOVES, WHOSE HIGH       AN APOLOGIE FOR (TERESA) HYMNE  27    52 322   59
LO HERE A LITTLE VOLUME, BUT GREAT BOOK.         PRAYER TO GENTLE-WOMAN           1    52 328  139
NOR LOST IN TOO LARG BOUNDS, OUR LITTLE ROME     ALEXIAS THIRD ELEGIE            11    52 336  209
STAY BUT A LITTLE WHILE, UNTILL I CALL           DEATH'S LECTURE                  5    52 340  475
A LITTLE MORE, & I HAD SURELY SEENE              HORATIJ ILLE & NEFASTO          33    MS 382  530
EACH LITTLE BEAME OF WHICH WOULD MAKE A SUNNE.   UPON KINGS CORONATION           30    MS 389  454

LITLE

GREAT LITLE ONE, WHOSE GLORIOUS BIRTH.           A HYMNE OF THE NATIVITY         57    46 106   76
MADE LITLE, NOT A LITTLE TO HIS RAGE)            OUT OF GROTIUS                  24    MS 398  198
MADE LITLE, NOT A LITTLE TO HIS RAGE)            OUT OF GROTIUS                  24    MS 398  198

LIVE

LIVE TO BEE OLD AND STILL A MAN.                 IN PRAISE OF LESSIUS            46    46 156  510
IN JOYES WHITE ANNALS LIVE THIS HOURE,           EASTER DAY                      10    46 100   26
THEM GOD, AND TEACH THEM HOW TO LIVE             IN MEMORY OF LADY MADRE TERESA  52    46 131   52
TO LIVE, BUT THAT HE STILL MAY DY.               IN MEMORY OF LADY MADRE TERESA 104    46 131   52
EVEN THY DEATHS SHALL LIVE, AND NEW              IN MEMORY OF LADY MADRE TERESA 152    46 131   52
WHOSE LIGHT SHALL LIVE BRIGHT, IN THY FACE       IN MEMORY OF LADY MADRE TERESA 164    46 131   52
WHICH WHO IN DEATH WOULD LIVE TO SEE.            IN MEMORY OF LADY MADRE TERESA 182    46 131   52
LIVE RAREST PRINCESSE, AND MAY THE BRIGHT        ON THE ASSUMPTION               55    46 139  114
LIVE OUR CHASTE LOVE, THE HOLY MIRTH             ON THE ASSUMPTION               59    46 139  114
LIVE CROWNE OF WOMEN, QUEEN OF MEN.              ON THE ASSUMPTION               61    46 139  114
LIVE MISTRIS OF OUR SONG, AND WHEN               ON THE ASSUMPTION               62    46 139  114
AND MAY WE LONG.  LONG MAY'ST THOU LIVE, T'ENCREASE  UPON YORKE HIS BIRTH        90    46 176  500
MARROW TO MY PLUMPE GENIUS, MAKE IT LIVE         TO THE MORNING                  22    46 183  497
IF POORE LOVE SHALL LIVE OR CRY,                 LOVES HOROSCOPE                  8    46 185  483
IF POORE LOVE SHALL LIVE OR DYE.                 LOVES HOROSCOPE                 20    46 185  483
BEAUTY SMILES AND LOVE SHALL LIVE.               LOVES HOROSCOPE                 40    46 185  483
O IF LOVE SHALL LIVE, O WHERE                    LOVES HOROSCOPE                 41    46 185  483
LOVE SHALL DYE ALTHOUGH HE LIVE,                 LOVES HOROSCOPE                 46    46 185  483
LOVE SHALL LIVE, ALTHOUGH HE DYE.                LOVES HOROSCOPE                 52    46 185  483
TH' EGYPTIAN PYRAMIDS THEMSELVES MUST LIVE.)     ON FRONTISPIECE ISAACSONS       20    46 191  491
COME AND LET US LIVE MY DEARE,                   OUT OF CATULLUS                  1    46 194  523
NOR DARING QUITE TO LIVE NOR DY.                 TO COUNTESSE OF DENBIGH         12    52 236  146
LIVE BARABBAS, & LET GOD DY.                     OFFICE H. CROSS THIRD            4    52 268   93
BY THIS THEY BOTH LOOK UP, & LIVE AGAIN.         OFFICE H. CROSS SIXT            20    52 270   97
LIVE, O FOR EVER LIVE & REIGN                    VEXILLA REGIS                   43    52 277  156
LIVE, O FOR EVER LIVE & REIGN                    VEXILLA REGIS                   43    52 277  156
AND LET THY LOST SHEEP LIVE TO'INHERIT           VEXILLA REGIS                   45    52 277  156
THE SAME LEAVE BOTH TO EAT & LIVE.               ADORO TE                        42    52 291  172
LIVE EVER BREAD OF LOVES, & BE                   ADORO TE                        43    52 291  172
THAT WE MAY LIVE, REVIVE HIS DEATH.              LAUDA SION SALVATOREM           28    52 294  178
O SAY THE WORD MY SOUL SHALL LIVE.               DIES IRAE                       48    52 298  186
LIVE, ROSY PRINCESSE, LIVE. AND MAY THE BRIGHT   IN GLORIOUS ASSUMPTION B. LADY  60    52 304  114
LIVE, ROSY PRINCESSE, LIVE. AND MAY THE BRIGHT   IN GLORIOUS ASSUMPTION B. LADY  60    52 304  114
LIVE, OUR CHAST LOVE, THE HOLY MIRTH             IN GLORIOUS ASSUMPTION B. LADY  64    52 304  114
LIVE, CROWN OF WOEMEN. QUEEN OF MEN.             IN GLORIOUS ASSUMPTION B. LADY  66    52 304  114
LIVE MISTRESSE OF OUR SONG. AND WHEN             IN GLORIOUS ASSUMPTION B. LADY  67    52 304  114
THEM GOD.  TEACH THEM HOW TO LIVE                TERESA                          52    52 315   52
TO LIVE, BUT THAT HE THUS MAY NEVER LEAVE TO DY. TERESA                         104    52 315   52
EV'N THY DEATHS SHALL LIVE.  & NEW               TERESA                         151    52 315   52
WHOSE LIGHT SHALL LIVE BRIGHT IN THY FACE        TERESA                         163    52 315   52

```
                WHICH WHO IN DEATH WOULD LIVE TO SEE.        TERESA                                 181   52 315   52
                THAT LIVE & DY AMIDST HER DARTS.             FLAMING HEART                           50   52 324   61
                LIVE IN THESE CONQUERING LEAVES. LIVE ALL THE SAME.   FLAMING HEART                  77   52 324   61
                LIVE IN THESE CONQUERING LEAVES. LIVE ALL THE SAME.   FLAMING HEART                  77   52 324   61
                LIVE HERE, GREAT HEART. & LOVE AND DY & KILL.         FLAMING HEART                  79   52 324   61
                THOUGH STILL I DY, I LIVE AGAIN.             A SONG                                   9   52 327   65
                STILL LIVE IN ME THIS LOVING STRIFE          A SONG                                  13   52 327   65
                DEAD TO MY SELFE, I LIVE IN THEE.            A SONG                                  16   52 327   65
                O LIVE, SO RARE A LOVE. LIVE. & IN THEE      ALEXIAS FIRST ELEGIE                    33   52 334  204
                O LIVE, SO RARE A LOVE. LIVE. & IN THEE      ALEXIAS FIRST ELEGIE                    33   52 334  204
                LIVE TO BE OLD, AND STILL A MAN.             TEMPERANCE                              44   52 342  510
                NOT DARING QUITE TO LIVE NOR DIE.            AGAINST IRRESOLUTION AND DELAY          20   52 347  146
                (MY LIFE'S THY DEATH, & IN THY DEATH I LIVE.)   MATH. 16. 25. WHOSOEVER SHALL          2   MS 381   16
                AND MAY SUCH PYTHONS NEVER LIVE TO SEE       UPON GUNPOWDER TREASON                  57   MS 386  460
                MY THREDS OF LIFE. IF THEN I SHALL NOT LIVE  EX EUPHORMIONE                          11   MS 392  525
                BUT TO LARGE YOUTH SHORT TIME TO LIVE.       UPON DEATH OF A FREIND                  12   MS 393  477
                WHETHER THE MUSE THEY CLOTH SHALL LIVE OR DIE.   AT TH' IVORY TRIBUNALL               4   MS 397  492
                LIVE SHEE, OR DYE TO FAME. EACH LEAFE YOU MEET   AT TH' IVORY TRIBUNALL               5   MS 397  492

LIVE'S

                US TO OUR OWN LIVE'S FUNERALL.               OFFICE H. CROSS COMPLINE                 2   52 274  105

LIVED

                NOT, SO LONG SHE LIVED,                      WEEPER                                 151   52 307  120
                'CAUSE THEY BOTH LIVED BUT ONE LIFE.         AN EPITAPH UPON MARRIED COUPLE           6   52 339  478

LIV'D

                (THAT LIV'D SO SWEETLY) DEAD, SO SWEET A GRAVE.   MUSICKS DUELL                    168   46 149  535
                NOT, SO LONG SHE LIV'D,                      THE WEEPER                             115   46  79  120
                LIV'D A FAIRE, BUT MANLY GRACE.              HIS EPITAPH (HERRYS)                    28   46 172  471
                BECAUSE THEY BOTH LIV'D BUT ONE LIFE.        AN EPITAPH HUSBAND AND WIFE              6   46 174  478

LONG-LIV'D

                IT IS TOO SWEET TO BE A  LONG-LIV'D ONE.     UPON OUR LORDS LAST DISCOURSE            4   46  95   21
                TO DRAW A LONG-LIV'D DEATH, WHERE ALL MY CHEERE   SOSPETTO D'HERODE                 214   46 109  216

LIVES

                WHICH SHORT-CUT LIVES OF MURDRED INFANTS LEAVE.   SOSPETTO D'HERODE                 344   46 109  216
                AND LIVES AND DYES, AND KNOWES NOT WHY       IN MEMORY OF LADY MADRE TERESA         103   46 131   52
                STILL LIVES, WHICH WHEN WEAKE TIME SHALL BE POUR'D OUT   UPON DEATH OF HERRYS        36   46 167  466
                HIS LIVES SWEET STORY, BY THE HAST,          ANOTHER ON HERRYS                       39   46 170  469
                LIVES AGAINE AS BLITH TO MORROW,             OUT OF CATULLUS                          5   46 194  523
                THE NAME OF ALL OUR LIVES & LOVES.           TO THE NAME OF JESUS                     5   52 239   30
                THEIR DEADLY HATE LIVES STILL. & HATH        OFFICE H. CROSS EVENSONG                 3   52 273  101
                AND LIVES IN HIM THAT HERE LYES DEAD.        OFFICE H. CROSS COMPLINE                 4   52 274  105
                WHICH LIVES STILL, & ALLOWES US BREATH.      ADORO TE                                38   52 291  178
                AND LIVES, & DYES.  AND KNOWES NOT WHY       TERESA                                 103   52 315   52
                BY ALL THY LIVES & DEATHS OF LOVE.           FLAMING HEART                           96   52 324   61
                LIVES BY HIS OWN LAWS, AND DOES HOLD         AGAINST IRRESOLUTION AND DELAY          55   52 347  146
                THE TREASURES OF OUR LIVES, YOUR INFLUENCE.  UPON KINGS CORONATION                   40   MS 389  454

LIVING

                THE WELL OF LIVING WATERS, LORD, TILL NOW.   ON BLEEDING WOUNDS OF LORD              42   46 101  110
                SO FROM HIS LIVING, & LIFE-GIVING DEATH,     OFFICE H. CROSS RECOMMENDATION           7   52 276  106
                THE WELL OF LIVING WATERS, LORD, TILL NOW.   UPON BLEEDING CRUCIFIX                  38   52 288  110
                THE LIVING & LIFE-GIVING BREAD,              LAUDA SION SALVATOREM                    9   52 294  178
                OF LIVING DEATH & DYING LIFE.                A SONG                                  14   52 327   65
                A LIVING COMET, WHOSE PESTIFEROUSE BREATH    ON GUNPOWDER-TREASON                    17   MS 384  458
                TO FREIND THE LIVING WORLD EVEN DEATH DID SEE   OUT OF GROTIUS                      82   MS 398  198

LIVELY

                (QUICK WITH WARME ZEPHIRES LIVELY BREATH) LAY FORTH   OUT OF VIRGIL                  13   46 155  529
                HAD YOU BUT DRAWNE ONE LIVELY COPPY FORTH.   UPON BIRTH PRINCESSE E                  29   MS 391  456

LIVERY

                AND LIFE SELFE IT WEARE DEATHS FRAILE LIVERY.   SOSPETTO D'HERODE                  168   46 109  216
                WITH SUCH A SUGRED LIVERY MADE FINE.         UPON BIRTH PRINCESSE E                   7   MS 391  456

LIVERIE

                THEIR GREENE BACKS WERE HIS LIVERIE.         PSALME 23                                8   46 102    5

LO

                LO. HATH UNLOCKT THEE AT THE VERY HEART.     I AM THE DOORE                           2   46  90   17
                (FOR WHAT ELSE IS MY LIFE.) LO I BEQUEATH.   OUR LORD IN HIS CIRCUMCISION             2   46  98    9
                LO. A MOUTH, WHOSE FULL-BLOOM'D LIPS         ON WOUNDS OF CRUCIFIED LORD              5   46  99   24
                LO. A BLOOD-SHOT EYE. THAT WEEPES            ON WOUNDS OF CRUCIFIED LORD              7   46  99   24
                LO WHERE I SEE THY OFFRINGS WAKE, AND RISE   ON A TREATISE OF CHARITY                17   46 137   69
                OF HIS FORWARD FLOWER, WHEN LO               UPON DEATH OF DESIRED HERRYS            39   46 168  467
                BEYOND THY SELFE. FOR LO. THE GODS, THE GODS UPON YORKE HIS BIRTH                     5   46 176  500
                LO HERE THE FAIRE CHARICLIA. IN WHOM STROVE  UPON FAIRE ETHIOPIAN                     1   46 183  493
                LO I UNCLOATH AND CLEARE.                    WISHES SUPPOSED MISTRESSE              116   46 195  479
                LO WE HOLD OUR HEARTS WIDE OPE.              TO THE NAME OF JESUS                   126   52 239   30
                LO HOW THE THIRSTY LANDS                     TO THE NAME OF JESUS                   129   52 239   30
                LO HOW THE LABORING EARTH                    TO THE NAME OF JESUS                   131   52 239   30
```

| | | | | |
|---|---|---|---|---|
| LO, WHERE ALOFT IT COMES.  IT COMES, AMONG | TO THE NAME OF JESUS | 151 | 52 239 | 30 |
| LO WHERE IT COMES, UPON THE SNOWY DOVE'S | TO THE NAME OF JESUS | 159 | 52 239 | 30 |
| LO AT LAST HAVE FOUND OUR WAY. | IN GLORIOUS EPIPHANIE | 21 | 52 253 | 39 |
| LO WE AT LAST HAVE FOUND THE WAY. | IN GLORIOUS EPIPHANIE | 23 | 52 253 | 39 |
| (DREAD SWEET.)  LO THUS | IN GLORIOUS EPIPHANIE | 234 | 52 253 | 39 |
| LO, WE ADORE THEE, | OFFICE H. CROSS MATINES | 24 | 52 265 | 86 |
| LO WE ADORE THEE | OFFICE H. CROSS PRIME | 17 | 52 267 | 91 |
| LO WE ADORE THEE | OFFICE H. CROSS THIRD | 16 | 52 268 | 93 |
| LO THE FAINT LAMB, WITH WEARY LIMB | OFFICE H. CROSS SIXT | 3 | 52 270 | 97 |
| LO WE ADORE THEE | OFFICE H. CROSS SIXT | 21 | 52 270 | 97 |
| LO WE ADORE THEE | OFFICE H. CROSS NINTH | 13 | 52 271 | 99 |
| LO, FOR THEIR OWN HEARTS, THEY REND HIS. | OFFICE H. CROSS EVENSONG | 2 | 52 273 | 101 |
| LO WE ADORE THEE | OFFICE H. CROSS EVENSONG | 28 | 52 273 | 101 |
| LOOK UP, LANGUISHING SOUL.  LO WHERE THE FAIR | VEXILLA REGIS | 1 | 52 277 | 156 |
| LO, HOW THE STREAMES OF LIFE, FROM THAT FULL NEST | VEXILLA REGIS | 7 | 52 277 | 156 |
| LO, HEART, THY HOPE'S WHOLE PLEA.  HER PRETIOUS BREATH | SANCTA MARIA DOLORUM | 109 | 52 283 | 162 |
| LO THE BREAD OF LIFE, THIS DAY'S | LAUDA SION SALVATOREM | 7 | 52 294 | 178 |
| LO THE NEW LAW OF A NEW LORD | LAUDA SION SALVATOREM | 19 | 52 294 | 178 |
| LO THE LIFE-FOOD OF ANGELLS THEN | LAUDA SION SALVATOREM | 61 | 52 294 | 178 |
| LO, THE FULL, FINALL, SACRIFICE | LAUDA SION SALVATOREM | 65 | 52 294 | 178 |
| LOVE TOUCH'T HER HEART, & LO IT BEATES | TERESA | 35 | 52 315 | 52 |
| SWEET, NOT SO FAST.  LO THY FAIR SPOUSE | TERESA | 65 | 52 315 | 52 |
| LO HERE A LITTLE VOLUME, BUT GREAT BOOK. | PRAYER TO GENTLE-WOMAN | 1 | 52 328 | 139 |
| LO HERE AM LEFT (ALAS), FOR MY LOST MATE | ALEXIAS FIRST ELEGIE | 3 | 52 334 | 204 |
| BEFORE THE WORLD.  OBEDIENT LO.  I JOYNE | OUT OF GROTIUS | 4 | MS 398 | 198 |

LOE

| | | | | |
|---|---|---|---|---|
| LOE HERE A LITTLE VOLUME, BUT LARGE BOOKE, | ON A PRAYER BOOKE | 1 | 46 126 | 139 |
| LOVE TOUCHT HER HEART, AND LOE IT BEATS | IN MEMORY OF LADY MADRE TERESA | 35 | 46 131 | 52 |
| SWEET NOT SO FAST, LOE THY FAIRE SPOUSE, | IN MEMORY OF LADY MADRE TERESA | 65 | 46 131 | 52 |
| THIS WAS THE CONQUERING DART, & LOE | IN CICATRICES DOMINI JESU | 3 | MS 381 | 27 |
| BUT WITH ONE CORDIALL SMILE, FOR (LOE) THAT POWER | EX EUPHORMIONE | 4 | MS 392 | 525 |

LOAD

| | | | | |
|---|---|---|---|---|
| BOW WITH A LOAD | SANCTA MARIA DOLORUM | 32 | 52 283 | 162 |

LOADEN

| | | | | |
|---|---|---|---|---|
| THAT WITH EACH WORD, MY LOADEN PEN LETTS FALL. | UPON BIRTH PRINCESSE E | 3 | MS 391 | 456 |

LOANE

| | | | | |
|---|---|---|---|---|
| HER WEAKE CONCEPTIONS.  NO LOANE SHADE, BUT RINGS | OUT OF VIRGIL | 9 | 46 155 | 529 |

LOATHSOME

| | | | | |
|---|---|---|---|---|
| HIS CORRESPONDENT CHEEKES.  THESE LOATHSOME STRINGS | SOSPETTO D'HERODE | 38 | 46 109 | 216 |

LOATH'D

| | | | | |
|---|---|---|---|---|
| AND SEEING THE LOATH'D OBJECT, HID FOR SHAME | TO THE MORNING | 12 | 46 183 | 497 |

LOCK

| | | | | |
|---|---|---|---|---|
| THOU ART LOVES LEGACIE UNDER LOCK | ON HOPE | 31 | 46 143 | 71 |
| WHEN THE DEAR NAILES DID LOCK | OFFICE H. CROSS EVENSONG | 12 | 52 273 | 101 |
| RICH HOPE, LOVE'S LEGACY, UNDER LOCK | (ON) HOPE | 11 | 52 345 | 71 |

LOCK'D

| | | | | |
|---|---|---|---|---|
| FETTER'D AND LOCK'D UP FAST THEY LIE | AGAINST IRRESOLUTION AND DELAY | 23 | 52 347 | 146 |

LOCKT

| | | | | |
|---|---|---|---|---|
| FETTER'D, & LOCKT UP FAST THEY LY | TO COUNTESSE OF DENBIGH | 23 | 52 236 | 146 |

LOCK'T

| | | | | |
|---|---|---|---|---|
| LOCK'T UP FROM MORTALL EYE, | WISHES SUPPOSED MISTRESSE | 5 | 46 195 | 479 |
| BUT LY'N LOCK'T UP SAFE IN THEIR SACRED SHORES. | ALEXIAS THIRD ELEGIE | 8 | 52 336 | 209 |

LOCKS

| | | | | |
|---|---|---|---|---|
| FANNING THY FAIRE LOCKS (WHICH THE WORLD BELEEVES | ON A TREATISE OF CHARITY | 23 | 46 137 | 69 |
| HEE'L FAN HER BRIGHT LOCKS TEACHING THEM TO FLOW. | ON A FOULE MORNING | 19 | 46 181 | 495 |
| THEIR SHAGGY LOCKS, THEIR FLOURY MANTLES TURN'D | UPON GUNPOWDER TREASON | 47 | MS 386 | 460 |

LOCKES

| | | | | |
|---|---|---|---|---|
| THEIR LOCKES ARE BEDS OF UNCOMB'D SNAKES THAT WIND | SOSPETTO D'HERODE | 69 | 46 109 | 216 |
| AND MAKE THEIR FLEECES GOLDEN AS THY LOCKES. | ON A FOULE MORNING | 6 | 46 181 | 495 |
| LOCKES, TO PHOEBUS FLAMING TRESSES. | OUT OF THE ITALIAN (1) | 12 | 46 188 | 545 |
| THOSE, COURSE & NEGLIGENT, AS THE NATURALL LOCKES | DESCRIPTION RELIGIOUS HOUSE | 13 | 52 338 | 213 |

LODGE

| | | | | |
|---|---|---|---|---|
| HOME, & LODGE THEM IN HIS HEART. | TO THE NAME OF JESUS | 196 | 52 239 | 30 |
| YET SURE THOU DID'ST LODGE HEERE. THIS WOMBE OF MINE | LUKE 2.  QUAERIT JESUM | 25 | MS 379 | 11 |

LODG'D

| | | | | |
|---|---|---|---|---|
| FOR LODG'D SO NE'RE YOUR SWEETEST THROTE | THOUGH NOW 'TIS NEITHER | 13 | MS 397 | 492 |

LODGING

| | | | | |
|---|---|---|---|---|
| WHEN BEASTS TOOKE UP THEIR LODGING IN THE WOOD, | OUT OF VIRGIL | 31 | 46 155 | 529 |

LODGINGS

| | | | | |
|---|---|---|---|---|
| OUR LODGINGS HARD & HOMELY AS OUR FARE. | DESCRIPTION RELIGIOUS HOUSE | 11 | 52 338 | 213 |

LOFTY

| | | | | |
|---|---|---|---|---|
| DANCING IN LOFTY MEASURES, AND ANON | MUSICKS DUELL | 139 | 46 149 | 535 |
| COME LIFT WE UP OUR LOFTY SONG, | A HYMNE OF THE NATIVITY | 3 | 46 106 | 76 |
| LEAP AT THY LOFTY FACE, | IN GLORIOUS EPIPHANIE | 198 | 52 253 | 39 |
| IN THIS ILLUSTRIOUS THRONG, YOUR LOFTY FLOUD | TO THE QUEEN'S MAJESTY | 15 | 52 261 | 47 |
| O'RELOOK ALL LIBANUS, THY LOFTY CROWN | OFFICE H. CROSS EVENSONG | 22 | 52 273 | 101 |
| PROUD LOOKES, & LOFTY EYLIDDES, HERE PUTT ON | DEATH'S LECTURE | 21 | 52 340 | 475 |

LOFTYER

| | | | | |
|---|---|---|---|---|
| COME LIFT WE UP OUR LOFTYER SONG | IN HOLY NATIVITY | 3 | 52 246 | 76 |

LOFTYEST

| | | | | |
|---|---|---|---|---|
| THE FOUNTAINS MURMUR, & EACH LOFTYEST TREE | IN GLORIOUS ASSUMPTION B. LADY | 29 | 52 304 | 114 |

LONG

| | | | | |
|---|---|---|---|---|
| HEE THROWES HIS ARME, AND WITH A LONG DRAWNE DASH | MUSICKS DUELL | 30 | 46 149 | 535 |
| STILL KEEPING IN THE FORWARD STREAME, SO LONG | MUSICKS DUELL | 86 | 46 149 | 535 |
| AT LENGTH (AFTER SO LONG, SO LOUD A STRIFE | MUSICKS DUELL | 151 | 46 149 | 535 |
| TASTES OF THIS BREAKFAST ALL DAY LONG. | THE WEEPER | 30 | 46 79 | 120 |
| NOT, SO LONG SHE LIV'D, | THE WEEPER | 115 | 46 79 | 120 |
| BUT SO LONG SHE GREIV'D, | THE WEEPER | 117 | 46 79 | 120 |
| HEE'L HAVE HIS TEAT E'RE LONG (A BLOODY ONE) | BLESSED BE THE PAPS | 3 | 46 94 | 14 |
| SO LONG AS CAESAR'S SELFE IS GODS. | GIVE TO CAESAR AND TO GOD | 8 | 46 96 | 20 |
| THY WRATH THAT WADES HEERE NOW, E'RE LONG SHALL SWIM | OUR LORD IN HIS CIRCUMCISION | 5 | 46 98 | 9 |
| TO WAKE THE SUN THAT SLEEPS TOO LONG. | A HYMNE OF THE NATIVITY | 4 | 46 106 | 76 |
| THE NEVER-DYING LIFE, OF A LONG DEATH. | SOSPETTO D'HERODE | 60 | 46 109 | 216 |
| WHOSE RIGHT BY DAVID'S LINAGE SO LONG WORNE, | SOSPETTO D'HERODE | 403 | 46 109 | 216 |
| MERCY WILL COME ERE LONG, | ON A PRAYER BOOKE | 34 | 46 126 | 139 |
| LIFE SHOULD SO LONG PLAY WITH THAT BREATH, | IN MEMORY OF LADY MADRE TERESA | 17 | 46 131 | 52 |
| AND LEAVE THE LONG ADORED SUNNE. | AN HIMNE FOR CIRCUMCISION | 32 | 46 141 | 37 |
| AND MAY WE LONG. LONG MAY'ST THOU LIVE, T'ENCREASE | UPON YORKE HIS BIRTH | 90 | 46 176 | 500 |
| AND MAY WE LONG. LONG MAY'ST THOU LIVE, T'ENCREASE | UPON YORKE HIS BIRTH | 90 | 46 176 | 500 |
| LONG MAYEST THOU LADEN WITH SUCH CLUSTERS LEANE | UPON YORKE HIS BIRTH | 102 | 46 176 | 500 |
| CONFESSING THEE. OR (IF TOO LONG I STAY) | UPON YORKE HIS BIRTH | 112 | 46 176 | 500 |
| 'TIS THIS. LISTNING ONE DAY TOO LONG, | OUT OF THE ITALIAN (3) | 3 | 46 190 | 549 |
| SET. O THEN, HOW LONG A NIGHT | OUT OF CATULLUS | 7 | 46 194 | 523 |
| LOVE MAY BEE LONG CHUSING A DART. | WISHES SUPPOSED MISTRESSE | 57 | 46 195 | 479 |
| YET LONG BY TH'ABSENCE OF THE DAY. | WISHES SUPPOSED MISTRESSE | 84 | 46 195 | 479 |
| MIGHTY QUEEN, TO THINKE IT LONG, | TO THE QUEEN | 2 | 48 215 | 501 |
| NOR BE TO SHORT, NOR SEEME TO LONG. | TO THE QUEEN | 12 | 48 215 | 501 |
| THAT MADE IT LONG EXCUSE THE LENGTH. | TO THE QUEEN | 14 | 48 215 | 501 |
| THERE ALL THE YEARE IS LOVES LONG SPRING. | THOUGH NOW 'TIS NEITHER | 29 | MS 397 | 492 |
| IN WEAKNES, WHY YOU CHOSE SO LONG | TO COUNTESSE OF DENBIGH | 10 | 52 236 | 146 |
| AND LATE CONSENT WAS A LONG NO, | TO COUNTESSE OF DENBIGH | 14 | 52 236 | 146 |
| WHO GRANTS AT LAST, LONG TIME TRYD | TO COUNTESSE OF DENBIGH | 15 | 52 236 | 146 |
| ALLMIGHTY LOVE. END THIS LONG WARR, | TO COUNTESSE OF DENBIGH | 29 | 52 236 | 146 |
| YOUR SELVES INTO THE LONG | TO THE NAME OF JESUS | 64 | 52 239 | 30 |
| GASP FOR THY GOLDEN SHOWRES. WITH LONG STRETCH'T HANDS | TO THE NAME OF JESUS | 130 | 52 239 | 30 |
| O DAWN, AT LAST, LONG LOOK'T FOR DAY. | TO THE NAME OF JESUS | 149 | 52 239 | 30 |
| AND WAKE THE SUN THAT LYES TOO LONG, | IN HOLY NATIVITY | 4 | 52 246 | 76 |
| AEGYPT. A LONG FAREWELL TO THEE | IN GLORIOUS EPIPHANIE | 50 | 52 253 | 39 |
| A LONG DELIQUIUM TO THE LIGHT OF THEE. | IN GLORIOUS EPIPHANIE | 116 | 52 253 | 39 |
| LONG MADE TH'HARMONIOUS ORBES ALL MUTE TO US | IN GLORIOUS EPIPHANIE | 132 | 52 253 | 39 |
| AND SELF-OPPRESSED SPARK, THAT HAS SO LONG | IN GLORIOUS EPIPHANIE | 135 | 52 253 | 39 |
| WHOM THEY SO LONG COURTED AS GOD, | IN GLORIOUS EPIPHANIE | 180 | 52 253 | 39 |
| 'MONGST THOSE LONG ROWES OF CROWNES THAT GUILD YOUR RACE, | TO THE QUEEN'S MAJESTY | 1 | 52 261 | 47 |
| THY LIFE IS ONE LONG DEBT | VEXILLA REGIS | 4 | 52 277 | 156 |
| SO LONG OF THIS CHAST VINE | SANCTA MARIA DOLORUM | 102 | 52 283 | 162 |
| COME LOVE. COME LORD. & THAT LONG DAY | ADORO TE | 51 | 52 291 | 172 |
| LOWD & PLEASANT, SWEET & LONG. | LAUDA SION SALVATOREM | 14 | 52 294 | 176 |
| TASTES OF THIS BREAKFAST ALL DAY LONG. | WEEPER | 30 | 52 307 | 120 |
| NOT, SO LONG SHE LIVED, | WEEPER | 151 | 52 307 | 120 |
| BUT, SO LONG SHE GREIVED, | WEEPER | 153 | 52 307 | 120 |
| LIFE SHOULD SO LONG PLAY WITH THAT BREATH | TERESA | 17 | 52 315 | 52 |
| MERCY WILL COME E'RE LONG | PRAYER TO GENTLE-WOMAN | 40 | 52 328 | 139 |
| WHOM LONG NONE COULD OBTAIN, THOUGH THOUSANDS TRY'D, | ALEXIAS FIRST ELEGIE | 2 | 52 334 | 204 |
| RICH, CHURLISH LAND, THAT HID'ST SO LONG IN THEE, | ALEXIAS THIRD ELEGIE | 1 | 52 336 | 209 |
| A LONG & DAYLY-DYING LIFE, WHICH BREATHS | DESCRIPTION RELIGIOUS HOUSE | 23 | 52 338 | 213 |
| AND LATE CONSENT WAS A LONG NO. | AGAINST IRRESOLUTION AND DELAY | 8 | 52 347 | 146 |
| IN WEAKNESS) WHY YOU CHUSE SO LONG | AGAINST IRRESOLUTION AND DELAY | 18 | 52 347 | 146 |
| SITTING SOE LONG AT EASE IN HER DARKE DENNE. | UPON GUNPOWDER TREASON | 24 | MS 386 | 460 |
| THREE COLEBLACK SISTERS, (WHOSE LONG SUTTY HAIRE, | UPON GUNPOWDER TREASON | 9 | MS 387 | 461 |
| LONG TIME TO QUAVERING AGE YOU GIVE, | UPON DEATH OF A FREIND | 11 | MS 393 | 477 |

## LONG-LIV'D

| | | | | | |
|---|---|---|---|---|---|
| IT IS TOO SWEET TO BE A  LONG-LIV'D ONE. | UPON OUR LORDS LAST DISCOURSE | 4 | 46 | 95 | 21 |
| TO DRAW A LONG-LIV'D DEATH, WHERE ALL MY CHEERE | SOSPETTO D'HERODE | 214 | 46 | 109 | 216 |

## LONG-SPUN

| | | | | | |
|---|---|---|---|---|---|
| TRAYLES HER PLAYNE DITTY IN ONE LONG-SPUN NOTE. | MUSICKS DUELL | 37 | 46 | 149 | 535 |

## LONGER

| | | | | | |
|---|---|---|---|---|---|
| THE SANDS HE US'D NO LONGER PLEASE, | THE WEEPER | 101 | 46 | 79 | 120 |
| LET IT NO LONGER BE A FORLORNE HOPE | ON BAPTIZED AETHIOPIAN | 1 | 46 | 85 | 29 |
| GODS SERVICES NO LONGER SHALL PUT ON | ON A TREATISE OF CHARITY | 29 | 46 | 137 | 69 |
| NO LONGER SHALL OUR CHURCHES FRIGHTED STONES | ON A TREATISE OF CHARITY | 31 | 46 | 137 | 69 |
| THE HEAVENS WILL STAY NO LONGER, MAY THY GLORY | UPON YORKE HIS BIRTH | 104 | 46 | 176 | 500 |
| NO LONGER SHALL THE IMMODEST LUST | IN GLORIOUS EPIPHANIE | 101 | 52 | 253 | 39 |

## LONGING

| | | | | | |
|---|---|---|---|---|---|
| FIRST DOES THE LONGING LOVER RIGHT. | WISHES SUPPOSED MISTRESSE | 72 | 46 | 195 | 479 |
| STILL LONGING SO TO BE STILL SLAIN, | A SONG | 10 | 52 | 327 | 65 |
| PERFIDIOUS TOTTERER. LONGING FOR THE STAINES | HORATIJ ILLE & NEFASTO | 15 | MS | 382 | 530 |

## LOOK

| | | | | | |
|---|---|---|---|---|---|
| LOOK FROM THINE OWN ILLUSTRIOUS HOME, | TO THE NAME OF JESUS | 117 | 52 | 239 | 30 |
| LOOK UP, SWEET BABE, LOOK UP & SEE | IN GLORIOUS EPIPHANIE | 10 | 52 | 253 | 39 |
| LOOK UP, SWEET BABE, LOOK UP & SEE | IN GLORIOUS EPIPHANIE | 10 | 52 | 253 | 39 |
| BY THIS THEY BOTH LOOK UP, & LIVE AGAIN. | OFFICE H. CROSS SIXT | 20 | 52 | 270 | 97 |
| WILL LOOK NO WOUNDS BE LOST, NO DEATHS SHALL DY. | OFFICE H. CROSS EVENSONG | 6 | 52 | 273 | 101 |
| LOOK UP, LANGUISHING SOUL. LO WHERE THE FAIR | VEXILLA REGIS | 1 | 52 | 277 | 156 |
| WHO CAN LOOK ON & SEE. | SANCTA MARIA DOLORUM | 13 | 52 | 283 | 162 |
| CHARG'D TO LOOK ON, & WITH A STEDFAST EY | SANCTA MARIA DOLORUM | 37 | 52 | 283 | 162 |
| NOR TOUCH NOR TAST MUST LOOK FOR MORE | ADORO TE | 7 | 52 | 291 | 172 |
| BOWES LOW'ST HIS HEAVY TOP, TO LOOK FOR THEE. | IN GLORIOUS ASSUMPTION B. LADY | 30 | 52 | 304 | 114 |
| THOU SHALT LOOK ROUND ABOUT, & SEE | TERESA | 165 | 52 | 315 | 52 |
| AND CONFIDENTLY LOOK | PRAYER TO GENTLE-WOMAN | 8 | 52 | 328 | 139 |
| OF FROTH & BUBBLES, WHAT TO LOOK FOR HERE. | TO SAME CONCERNING CHOISE | 9 | 52 | 331 | 66 |
| CALL HEAVN TO LOOK ON THEE WITH NARROW EYES. | DEATH'S LECTURE | 17 | 52 | 340 | 475 |
| LOOK ROUND AND READE THE WORLD'S WIDE FACE. | AGAINST IRRESOLUTION AND DELAY | 29 | 52 | 347 | 146 |

## LOOKT

| | | | | | |
|---|---|---|---|---|---|
| THE BABE LOOKT UP, AND SHEW'D HIS FACE, | A HYMNE OF THE NATIVITY | 19 | 46 | 106 | 76 |
| URNS. LIKE GODS SANCTUARIES THEY LOOKT OF OLD. | ON A TREATISE OF CHARITY | 36 | 46 | 137 | 69 |

## LOOK'T

| | | | | | |
|---|---|---|---|---|---|
| LOOK'T ROUND, FIRST TO THE SEA, THEN TO THE SHORE. | THE BEGINNING OF HELIODORUS | 8 | 46 | 158 | 517 |
| WHEN FIRST I LOOK'T ON THEE, I LOST MINE EYES. | SAMPSON TO HIS DALILAH | 2 | 46 | 102 | 8 |
| O DAWN, AT LAST, LONG LOOK'T FOR DAY. | TO THE NAME OF JESUS | 149 | 52 | 239 | 30 |
| THE BABE LOOK'T UP & SHEW'D HIS FACE. | IN HOLY NATIVITY | 19 | 52 | 246 | 76 |
| FOR THIS HE LOOK'T SO BIGG. & EVERY MORN | IN GLORIOUS EPIPHANIE | 121 | 52 | 253 | 39 |
| DRAGGING HIS CROOKED BURTHEN, LOOK'T AWRY. | AN ELEGY MR STANNINOW | 46 | MS | 394 | 473 |

## LARGE-LOOK'T

| | | | | | |
|---|---|---|---|---|---|
| OUT-STARES THE LIDDES OF LARGE-LOOK'T TYRANNY. | UPON STANINOUGH'S DEATH | 26 | 46 | 175 | 475 |

## LARG-LOOK'T

| | | | | | |
|---|---|---|---|---|---|
| OUTSTARES THE LIDDES OF LARG-LOOK'T TYRANNY. | DEATH'S LECTURE | 28 | 52 | 340 | 475 |

## LOOKE

| | | | | | |
|---|---|---|---|---|---|
| DOTH TUNE THE SPHAEARES, AND MAKE HEAVENS SELFE LOOKE | MUSICKS DUELL | 118 | 46 | 149 | 535 |
| HIS FAWNING CHEEKS, LOOKE NOT THAT WAY | OUT OF GREEKE CUPID'S CRYER | 64 | 46 | 159 | 519 |
| LOOKE ON THE FOLLOWING LEAVES, AND SEE HIM BREATH. | UPON BISHOP ANDREWES PICTURE | 16 | 46 | 163 | 490 |
| LOOKE, MARY, HERE SEE, WHERE THY LORD ONCE LAY. | COME SEE WHERE THE LORD LAY | 4 | 46 | 87 | 27 |
| LOOKE, MARY, HERE SEE, WHERE THY LORD ONCE LAY. | COME SEE WHERE THE LORD LAY | 6 | 46 | 87 | 27 |
| 'TWAS ONCE LOOKE UP, 'TIS NOW LOOKE DOWNE TO HEAVEN. | ON VIRGINS BASHFULNESSE | 8 | 46 | 89 | 9 |
| 'TWAS ONCE LOOKE UP, 'TIS NOW LOOKE DOWNE TO HEAVEN. | ON VIRGINS BASHFULNESSE | 8 | 46 | 89 | 9 |
| OF STARING COMETS, THAT LOOKE KINGDOMES DEAD. | SOSPETTO D'HERODE | 52 | 46 | 109 | 216 |
| LOOKE IN WHAT POMPE THE MISTRESSE PLANET MOVES | SOSPETTO D'HERODE | 237 | 46 | 109 | 216 |
| TO HOLD THEM DOWN, AND LOOKE THAT NONE SEETHE O'RE. | SOSPETTO D'HERODE | 296 | 46 | 109 | 216 |
| A WAKING EYE AND HAND. LOOKE UP AND SEE | SOSPETTO D'HERODE | 431 | 46 | 109 | 216 |
| LOOKE HOW BELOW THY FEARES THEIR CAUSES ARE. | SOSPETTO D'HERODE | 522 | 46 | 109 | 216 |
| MUCH LARGER IN IT SELFE THEN IN ITS LOOKE. | ON A PRAYER BOOKE | 4 | 46 | 126 | 139 |
| KNOW YOU FAIRE, ON WHAT YOU LOOKE. | ON MR. G. HERBERTS BOOKE | 1 | 46 | 130 | 68 |
| THOU SHALT LOOKE ROUND ABOUT, AND SEE | IN MEMORY OF LADY MADRE TERESA | 166 | 46 | 131 | 52 |
| MADE HEAVENS RADIANT FACE LOOKE FOULE. | UPON DEATH OF DESIRED HERRYS | 52 | 46 | 168 | 467 |
| CALL HEAVEN TO LOOKE ON THEE WITH NARROW EYES. | UPON STANINOUGH'S DEATH | 16 | 46 | 175 | 475 |
| THOU KNOW'ST A FACE IN WHOSE EACH LOOKE, | LOVES HOROSCOPE | 11 | 46 | 185 | 483 |
| POORE FRUITES LOOKE PALE AT THY HESPERIDES. | UPON TWO GREENE APRICOCKES | 30 | 48 | 220 | 494 |

## LOOKS

| | | | | | |
|---|---|---|---|---|---|
| PUT ON THY SELFE IN THINE OWN LOOKS. T' OUR EYES | ON A TREATISE OF CHARITY | 2 | 46 | 137 | 69 |
| AND THOUGH THY DEAREST LOOKS MUST NOW BE LIGHT | ON THE ASSUMPTION | 31 | 46 | 139 | 114 |

LOOKES

| | | | | | |
|---|---|---|---|---|---|
| WOULDST SEE BLITH LOOKES, FRESH CHEEKS BEGUILE | IN PRAISE OF LESSIUS | 39 | 46 | 156 | 510 |
| LOOKES DOWNE, AND SEES THE HUMBLE NILE BELOW | THE BEGINNING OF HELIODORUS | 4 | 46 | 158 | 517 |
| LOOKES THAT OPPRESSE | WISHES SUPPOSED MISTRESSE | 40 | 46 | 195 | 479 |
| PROUD LOOKES, & LOFTY EYLIDDES, HERE PUTT ON | DEATH'S LECTURE | 21 | 52 | 340 | 475 |
| WOULDST' SEE BLITH LOOKES, FRESH CHEEKES BEGUIL | TEMPERANCE | 37 | 52 | 342 | 510 |
| BY PARTHIANS BOW THE SOLDJER LOOKES TO DIE. | HORATIJ ILLE & NEFASTO | 25 | MS | 382 | 530 |

LOOKING

| | | | | | |
|---|---|---|---|---|---|
| TO SHEW US OUGHT WORTH LOOKING AT. | A HYMNE OF THE NATIVITY | 10 | 46 | 106 | 76 |
| SHEE LIFTS HER SOOTY LAMPES, AND LOOKING ROUND | SOSPETTO D'HERODE | 301 | 46 | 109 | 216 |
| AND LOOKING ON THEIR LOST STATE SIGH'D AGAINE. | SOSPETTO D'HERODE | 408 | 46 | 109 | 216 |
| TO SHOW US OUGHT WORTH LOOKING AT. | IN HOLY NATIVITY | 10 | 52 | 246 | 76 |

LOOSE

| | | | | | |
|---|---|---|---|---|---|
| SHEE OPES THE FLOODGATE, AND LETS LOOSE A TIDE | MUSICKS DUELL | 93 | 46 | 149 | 535 |
| INTO LOOSE EXTASIES, THAT SHEE IS PLAC'T | MUSICKS DUELL | 103 | 46 | 149 | 535 |
| DOES NIGHT LOOSE HER EYES. | THE WEEPER | 111 | 46 | 79 | 120 |
| HIS FAITHLESSE CROWNE HE FEELES LOOSE ON HIS CREST. | SOSPETTO D'HERODE | 491 | 46 | 109 | 216 |
| NOR WHILE THEY LEAVE HIM SHALL THEY LOOSE THE SUNNE. | AN HIMNE FOR CIRCUMCISION | 37 | 46 | 141 | 37 |
| WHAT NIGHTINGALE CAN LOOSE HER NOATE. | THOUGH NOW 'TIS NEITHER | 14 | MS | 397 | 492 |
| AND LOOSE THEM INTO ONE OF LOVE. | TO THE NAME OF JESUS | 87 | 52 | 239 | 30 |
| THE PRISONERS LOOSE, THE JAYLOR BOUND. | OFFICE H. CROSS THIRD | 15 | 52 | 268 | 93 |
| NOT ONE LOOSE SHAFT BUT LOVE'S WHOLE QUIVER. | FLAMING HEART | 70 | 52 | 324 | 61 |
| OF THESE LOOSE GROVES, ROUGH AS TH'UNPOLISH'T ROCKES. | DESCRIPTION RELIGIOUS HOUSE | 14 | 52 | 338 | 213 |
| AS LUMPES OF SUGAR LOOSE THEMSELVES. AND TWINE | (ON) HOPE | 29 | 52 | 345 | 71 |
| HIMSELFE IN HIS OWNE HELL. AND NOW LETS LOOSE | OUT OF GROTIUS | 79 | MS | 398 | 198 |

LOP

| | | | | | |
|---|---|---|---|---|---|
| WHEN A WILD SWORD EV'N FROM THEIR BRESTS, DID LOP | OUT OF GROTIUS | 25 | MS | 398 | 198 |

LORD

| | | | | | |
|---|---|---|---|---|---|
| HERE, WHERE OUR LORD ONCE LAID HIS HEAD, | UPON SEPULCHRE OF OUR LORD | 1 | 46 | 86 | 26 |
| LOOKE, MARY, HERE SEE, WHERE THY LORD ONCE LAY. | COME SEE WHERE THE LORD LAY | 4 | 46 | 87 | 27 |
| LOOKE, MARY, HERE SEE, WHERE THY LORD ONCE LAY. | COME SEE WHERE THE LORD LAY | 6 | 46 | 87 | 27 |
| NOW LORD, OR NEVER, THEY'L BELEEVE ON THEE, | ON MIRACLE OF LOAVES | 1 | 46 | 88 | 16 |
| TO PRAISE THY LORD. | UPON ASSE THAT BORE SAVIOUR | 8 | 46 | 90 | 19 |
| WAS NEVER MAN LORD SPAKE LIKE THEE. | THE BLIND CURED | 4 | 46 | 91 | 19 |
| THOU, THOU (DEARE LORD) EVEN THOU ALONE, | VERILY YE SHALL WEEP | 5 | 46 | 95 | 22 |
| WELL FOR THY SELFE (I MEANE) NOT FOR THY LORD. | ON ST. PETER CUTTING MALCHUS | 2 | 46 | 97 | 22 |
| TH'HAVE LEFT THEE NAKED LORD, O THAT THEY HAD. | ON CRUCIFIED LORD BLOODY | 1 | 46 | 100 | 24 |
| DEARE LORD TO THEE) TO US IS FOUND | ON BLEEDING WOUNDS OF LORD | 38 | 46 | 101 | 110 |
| THE WELL OF LIVING WATERS, LORD, TILL NOW. | ON BLEEDING WOUNDS OF LORD | 42 | 46 | 101 | 110 |
| BE IT THY PART, HELLS MIGHTY LORD, TO LAY | SOSPETTO D'HERODE | 263 | 46 | 109 | 216 |
| LET HEAV'NS LORD CHIDE ABOVE LOWDER THEN THOU | SOSPETTO D'HERODE | 269 | 46 | 109 | 216 |
| WITH HIM BELOW. HERE THOU ART LORD ALONE | SOSPETTO D'HERODE | 271 | 46 | 109 | 216 |
| TO MEET THEIR TROUBLED LORD WITHOUT DELAY. | SOSPETTO D'HERODE | 508 | 46 | 109 | 216 |
| LOVE THOU ART ABSOLUTE, SOLE LORD | IN MEMORY OF LADY MADRE TERESA | 1 | 46 | 131 | 52 |
| FOR LOVE THEIR LORD, GLORIOUS AND GREAT, | IN MEMORY OF LADY MADRE TERESA | 11 | 46 | 131 | 52 |
| THOU WITH THE LAMBE THY LORD SHALL GOE. | IN MEMORY OF LADY MADRE TERESA | 179 | 46 | 131 | 52 |
| LORD, BY THY SWEET & SAVING SIGN, | OFFICE H. CROSS MATINES | 1 | 52 | 265 | 86 |
| THOU SHALT OPEN MY LIPPES, O LORD. | OFFICE H. CROSS MATINES | 3 | 52 | 265 | 86 |
| O LORD MAKE HAST TO HELP ME. | OFFICE H. CROSS MATINES | 6 | 52 | 265 | 86 |
| BUT MUST THY BED, LORD, BE A BOROW'D GRAVE | OFFICE H. CROSS COMPLINE | 9 | 52 | 274 | 105 |
| SAVE US, O SAVE US, LORD. | OFFICE H. CROSS COMPLINE | 17 | 52 | 274 | 105 |
| SAVE THEM, O SAVE THEM, LORD. | OFFICE H. CROSS COMPLINE | 25 | 52 | 274 | 105 |
| INTO THY HANDS, AND HART, LORD, I COMMEND. | OFFICE H. CROSS RECOMMENDATION | 2 | 52 | 276 | 106 |
| HERE WHERE OUR LORD ONCE LAY'D HIS HEAD. | UPON THE H. SEPULCHER | 1 | 52 | 277 | 26 |
| LORD, WHAT IS MAN. WHY SHOULD HE COSTE THEE | CHARITAS NIMIA | 1 | 52 | 280 | 48 |
| LORD WHAT IS MAN. THAT THOU HAST OVERBOUGHT | CHARITAS NIMIA | 3 | 52 | 280 | 48 |
| ALAS, SWEET LORD, WHAT WER'T TO THEE | CHARITAS NIMIA | 9 | 52 | 280 | 48 |
| DEAR LORD TO THEE, TO US IS FOUND | UPON BLEEDING CRUCIFIX | 34 | 52 | 288 | 110 |
| THE WELL OF LIVING WATERS, LORD, TILL NOW. | UPON BLEEDING CRUCIFIX | 38 | 52 | 288 | 110 |
| THEY 'HAVE LEFT THEE NAKED, LORD, O THAT THEY HAD. | UPON BODY OF OUR LORD | 1 | 52 | 290 | 24 |
| MY LORD TOO & MY GOD, AS LOWD AS HE. | ADORO TE | 32 | 52 | 291 | 172 |
| HELP LORD, MY FAITH, MY HOPE INCREASE. | ADORO TE | 33 | 52 | 291 | 172 |
| COME LOVE. COME LORD. & THAT LONG DAY | ADORO TE | 51 | 52 | 291 | 172 |
| LO THE NEW LAW OF A NEW LORD | LAUDA SION SALVATOREM | 19 | 52 | 294 | 178 |
| BUT MUST THOU GIV'ST LEAVE (DREAD LORD) THAT WE | DIES IRAE | 25 | 52 | 296 | 166 |
| LOVE, THOU ART ABSOLUTE SOLE LORD | TERESA | 1 | 52 | 315 | 52 |
| THOU WITH THE LAMB. THY LORD, SHALT GOE. | TERESA | 178 | 52 | 315 | 52 |
| LORD, WHEN THE SENSE OF THY SWEET GRACE | A SONG | 1 | 52 | 327 | 65 |
| NOT FOR MY SELF ALAS, BUT FOR MY DEARER LORD. | TO SAME CONCERNING CHOISE | 7 | 52 | 331 | 66 |
| LET NOT MY LORD, THE MIGHTY LOVER | TO SAME CONCERNING CHOISE | 41 | 52 | 331 | 66 |
| WHAT NEEDES MY VIRGIN LORD FLY THUS FROM ME. | ALEXIAS THIRD ELEGIE | 23 | 52 | 336 | 209 |

LORD'S

| | | | | | |
|---|---|---|---|---|---|
| TO MAKE A KIND OF LIFE FOR MY LORD'S DEATH. | OFFICE H. CROSS RECOMMENDATION | 6 | 52 | 276 | 106 |
| OF LOVES, THY LORD'S TOO LIBERALL BREAST, | VEXILLA REGIS | 8 | 52 | 277 | 156 |
| MY DEAR LORD'S VITALL DEATH. | SANCTA MARIA DOLORUM | 108 | 52 | 283 | 162 |
| POWR'D OUT IN PRAYRS FOR THEE. THY LORD'S IN DEATH. | SANCTA MARIA DOLORUM | 110 | 52 | 283 | 162 |
| O THOU, THY LORD'S FAIR STORE. | WEEPER | 115 | 52 | 307 | 120 |
| A WORTHY OBJECT, OUR LORD'S FEET. | WEEPER | 186 | 52 | 307 | 120 |
| THEIR GREAT LORD'S GLORIOUS NAME, TO NONE | TERESA | 9 | 52 | 315 | 52 |
| HER LORD'S BLOOD, OR AT LEST HER OWN. | TERESA | 56 | 52 | 315 | 52 |
| IN WHAT STRANGE PATH MY LORD'S FOOTSTEPPES BLEED. | ALEXIAS FIRST ELEGIE | 8 | 52 | 334 | 204 |

LORDS

| | | | | |
|---|---|---|---|---|
| A WORTHIER OBJECT, OUR LORDS FEET. | THE WEEPER | 138 | 46 | 79 120 |
| THEIR GREAT LORDS GLORIOUS NAME, TO NONE | IN MEMORY OF LADY MADRE TERESA | 9 | 46 | 131 52 |
| HER LORDS BLOOD, OR AT LEST HER OWNE. | IN MEMORY OF LADY MADRE TERESA | 56 | 46 | 131 52 |

LOSE

| | | | | |
|---|---|---|---|---|
| WHICH WHEN I LOSE, O MAY AT ONCE MY TONGUE | PSALME 137 | 19 | 46 | 104 7 |
| LOSE THIS SAME BUSIE SPEAKING ART | PSALME 137 | 20 | 46 | 104 7 |
| AS LUMPES OF SUGAR LOSE THEMSELVES, AND TWINE | ON HOPE | 59 | 46 | 143 71 |
| AND LOSE OUR SELVES IN WILD DELIGHT. | OUT OF CATULLUS | 18 | 46 | 194 523 |

LOOSES

| | | | | |
|---|---|---|---|---|
| STAGGERS OUT OF THE EAST, LOOSES HER WAY | ON A FOULE MORNING | 2 | 46 | 181 495 |

LOOSING

| | | | | |
|---|---|---|---|---|
| LOOSING IT ONCE AGAINE, STUMBLE'ON TRUE LIGHT | IN GLORIOUS EPIPHANIE | 167 | 52 | 253 39 |
| HIS TREMBLING HANDS LOOSING THE GOLDEN RAINES. | UPON GUNPOWDER TREASON | 22 | MS | 386 460 |

LOSSE

| | | | | |
|---|---|---|---|---|
| LEST FOR GRIEFE HIS LOSSE MAY MOVE, | UPON DEATH OF DESIRED HERRYS | 73 | 46 | 168 467 |
| PROUD TO HAVE GAIN'D THIS PRETIOUS LOSSE | IN GLORIOUS EPIPHANIE | 141 | 52 | 253 39 |
| BUT MORE AMBITIOUS LOSSE, AT LEST OF BRAIN. | IN GLORIOUS EPIPHANIE | 230 | 52 | 253 39 |
| THOU'HAST SAV'D AT ONCE THE WHOLE WORLD'S LOSSE. | OFFICE H. CROSS MATINES | 27 | 52 | 265 86 |
| THOU'HAST SAV'D AT ONCE THE WHOLE WORLD'S LOSSE. | OFFICE H. CROSS PRIME | 21 | 52 | 267 91 |
| THREW ALL THE LOSSE. | OFFICE H. CROSS THIRD | 13 | 52 | 268 93 |
| THOU'HAST SAV'D AT ONCE THE WHOLE WORLD'S LOSSE. | OFFICE H. CROSS THIRD | 20 | 52 | 268 93 |
| THOU'HAST SAV'D THE WORLD FROM CERTAIN LOSSE. | OFFICE H. CROSS SIXT | 24 | 52 | 270 97 |
| THOU'HAST SAV'D AT ONCE THE WHOLE WORLD'S LOSSE. | OFFICE H. CROSS NINTH | 17 | 52 | 271 99 |
| THOU'HAST SAV'D THE WORLD FROM CERTAIN LOSSE. | OFFICE H. CROSS EVENSONG | 31 | 52 | 273 101 |
| OF LOVE, AND EV'N THAT LOSSE, BE LOST. | DIES IRAE | 34 | 52 | 298 186 |
| SO GAINFULL IS SUCH LOSSE OF BREATH, | A SONG | 11 | 52 | 327 65 |
| BY THREE DAIES LOSSE AETERNALLY TO SAVE. | MATH. 16. 25. WHOSOEVER SHALL | 4 | MS | 381 16 |
| WAS LOSSE OF MULTITUDES. AND MISSING MEE | OUT OF GROTIUS | 28 | MS | 398 198 |

LOST

| | | | | |
|---|---|---|---|---|
| HEE LOST THE DAYES HEAT, AND HIS OWNE HOT CARES. | MUSICKS DUELL | 6 | 46 | 149 535 |
| LOVE IS LOST, NOR CAN HIS MOTHER | OUT OF GREEKE CUPID'S CRYER | 1 | 46 | 159 519 |
| LOVE IS LOST. AND THUS SHEE CRYES HIM. | OUT OF GREEKE CUPID'S CRYER | 4 | 46 | 159 519 |
| WHEN FIRST I LOOK'T ON THEE, I LOST MINE EYES. | SAMPSON TO HIS DALILAH | 2 | 46 | 102 8 |
| PROUD MORNING OF A PERVERSE DAY. HOW LOST | SOSPETTO D'HERODE | 77 | 46 | 109 216 |
| INTANGLES HIS LOST THOUGHTS. PAST GETTING OUT. | SOSPETTO D'HERODE | 192 | 46 | 109 216 |
| AND YET WHOSE FORCE FEARE I. HAVE I SO LOST | SOSPETTO D'HERODE | 249 | 46 | 109 216 |
| AND LOOKING ON THEIR LOST STATE SIGH'D AGAINE. | SOSPETTO D'HERODE | 408 | 46 | 109 216 |
| BEHOLDERS LOST IN SWEET DELIGHT | ON THE ASSUMPTION | 33 | 46 | 139 114 |
| WOULD QUITE HAVE LOST THE CRUELL FASHION. | ANOTHER ON HERRYS | 24 | 46 | 170 469 |
| WRATH ITS SELFE HAD LOST HIS SPLEENE. | ANOTHER ON HERRYS | 30 | 46 | 170 469 |
| DEATH LOST THE RECKONING OF HIS DAYES. | HIS EPITAPH (HERRYS) | 10 | 46 | 172 471 |
| AND SO HE LOST HIS CLOTHES, EYES, HEART AND ALL. | OUT OF THE ITALIAN (3) | 8 | 46 | 190 549 |
| LOST IN A BRIGHT | IN GLORIOUS EPIPHANIE | 16 | 52 | 253 39 |
| MISS-LEDDE BEFORE THEY LOST THEIR WAY. | IN GLORIOUS EPIPHANIE | 164 | 52 | 253 39 |
| WILL LOOK NO WOUNDS BE LOST, NO DEATHS SHALL DY. | OFFICE H. CROSS EVENSONG | 6 | 52 | 273 101 |
| THEIR USE IS CHANG'D, NOT LOST. AND NOW THEY MOVE | VEXILLA REGIS | 17 | 52 | 277 156 |
| AND LET THY LOST SHEEP LIVE TO'INHERIT | VEXILLA REGIS | 45 | 52 | 277 156 |
| SO DEAR. WHAT HAD HIS RUIN LOST THEE. | CHARITAS NIMIA | 2 | 52 | 280 48 |
| IF I WERE LOST IN MISERY, | CHARITAS NIMIA | 45 | 52 | 280 48 |
| THAT LOST AGAIN MY LIFE MAY PROVE | CHARITAS NIMIA | 65 | 52 | 280 48 |
| A LOST THING TO THE WORLD, AS IT TO ME. | SANCTA MARIA DOLORUM | 104 | 52 | 283 162 |
| EVEN LOST THY SELF IN SEEKING ME. | DIES IRAE | 32 | 52 | 298 186 |
| OF LOVE, AND EV'N THAT LOSSE, BE LOST. | DIES IRAE | 34 | 52 | 298 186 |
| AND ALL THY LOST SHEEP FOUND SHALL BE, | DIES IRAE | 59 | 52 | 298 186 |
| NOR LOVE, NOR LABOUR CAN BE LOST. | TO SAME CONCERNING CHOISE | 39 | 52 | 331 66 |
| LO HERE AM LEFT (ALAS), FOR MY LOST MATE | ALEXIAS FIRST ELEGIE | 3 | 52 | 334 204 |
| THERE THY LOST FUGITIVE THOU'HAST FOUND AT LAST. | ALEXIAS FIRST ELEGIE | 37 | 52 | 334 204 |
| NATURES VIRGINITY HAD NERE BEEN LOST. | ALEXIAS THIRD ELEGIE | 6 | 52 | 336 209 |
| NOR LOST IN TOO LARG BOUNDS, OUR LITTLE ROME | ALEXIAS THIRD ELEGIE | 11 | 52 | 336 209 |
| IN YOU ALONE HATH LOST HIS WINGS. | AGAINST IRRESOLUTION AND DELAY | 28 | 52 | 347 146 |
| OH COME THEN. BRING THY MOTHER HER LOST JOY. | LUKE 2. QUAERIT JESUM | 15 | MS | 379 11 |
| THEIR NOW LOST JOYES. | LUKE 2. QUAERIT JESUM | 44 | MS | 379 11 |
| AFFRIGHTED PHAEBUS WOULD HAVE LOST HIS WAY, | UPON GUNPOWDER TREASON | 19 | MS | 386 460 |
| JUSTICE HATH LOST HER HAND. THE LAW HER HEAD. | AN ELEGIE ON DR PORTER | 15 | MS | 395 476 |

LOTTERY

| | | | | |
|---|---|---|---|---|
| AND FATES WHOLE LOTTERY IS ONE BLANKE TO HER. | ON HOPE | 74 | 46 | 143 71 |
| FORTUNE'S WHOLE LOTTERY IS ONE BLANK TO HER. | (ON) HOPE | 34 | 52 | 345 71 |

LOUD

| | | | | |
|---|---|---|---|---|
| AT LENGTH (AFTER SO LONG, SO LOUD A STRIFE | MUSICKS DUELL | 151 | 46 | 149 535 |

LOWD

| | | | | |
|---|---|---|---|---|
| SPEAKE LOWD UNTO THE FACE OF DEATH | IN MEMORY OF LADY MADRE TERESA | 8 | 46 | 131 52 |
| AND SPEAKE LOWD | TO THE NAME OF JESUS | 93 | 52 | 239 30 |
| STRUCK LOWD HIS FAITHFULL STRING, | VEXILLA REGIS | 22 | 52 | 277 156 |
| MY LORD TOO & MY GOD, AS LOWD AS HE. | ADORO TE | 32 | 52 | 291 172 |
| LOWD & PLEASANT, SWEET & LONG. | LAUDA SION SALVATOREM | 14 | 52 | 294 178 |

| Line | Reference | | | | |
|---|---|---|---|---|---|
| LET HEARTS & LIPPES SPEAK LOWD, AND SAY | O GLORIOSA DOMINA | 31 | 52 | 302 | 194 |
| SPEAK LOWD INTO THE FACE OF DEATH | TERESA | 8 | 52 | 315 | 52 |
| TO THE LOWD BOASTS OF POOR MORTALITY | DEATH'S LECTURE | 26 | 52 | 340 | 475 |

LOWDER

| | | | | | |
|---|---|---|---|---|---|
| LET HEAV'NS LORD CHIDE ABOVE LOWDER THEN THOU | SOSPETTO D'HERODE | 269 | 46 | 109 | 216 |

LOWDNESSE

| | | | | | |
|---|---|---|---|---|---|
| NOT FROM THE LOWDNESSE, NOR THE LENGTH. | AN EPITAPH UPON ASHTON | 16 | 46 | 192 | 464 |

LOVE

| | | | | | |
|---|---|---|---|---|---|
| MELTS ON THE BOSOME OF HIS LOVE, AND POWRES | OUT OF VIRGIL | 5 | 46 | 155 | 529 |
| YET MAY THE LOVE I SEND BE TRUE, THOUGH I | WITH A PICTURE TO A FRIEND | 5 | 46 | 156 | 494 |
| MY LOVE, OR FEIGN'D OR PAINTED SHOULD APPEARE. | WITH A PICTURE TO A FRIEND | 8 | 46 | 156 | 494 |
| LOVE IS LOST, NOR CAN HIS MOTHER | OUT OF GREEKE CUPID'S CRYER | 1 | 46 | 159 | 519 |
| LOVE IS LOST, AND THUS SHEE CRYES HIM. | OUT OF GREEKE CUPID'S CRYER | 4 | 46 | 159 | 519 |
| WHAT E'RE IT BE LOVE OFFERS, STILL PRESUME | OUT OF GREEKE CUPID'S CRYER | 73 | 46 | 159 | 519 |
| A BLACK-FAC'D HOUSE WILL LOVE. | ON BAPTIZED AETHIOPIAN | 6 | 46 | 85 | 29 |
| WITHIN THE LIPS OF LOVE AND JOY DOTH DWELL | UPON ASSE THAT BORE SAVIOUR | 3 | 46 | 90 | 19 |
| NO,NO, THEY SAW THE NOT, O LIFE, O LOVE. | BUT NOW THEY HAVE SEEN | 3 | 46 | 96 | 21 |
| THE WORLD WILL LOVE ITS DARKNESSE STILL. | BUT MEN LOVED DARKNESSE | 2 | 46 | 97 | 13 |
| IT WILL NOT LOVE ITS DARKNESSE HALFE SO WELL. | BUT MEN LOVED DARKNESSE | 4 | 46 | 97 | 13 |
| BY THE LINE OF THY DEARE LOVE. | PSALME 23 | 56 | 46 | 102 | 5 |
| TO THEE (DREAD LAMBE) WHOSE LOVE MUST KEEPE | A HYMNE OF THE NATIVITY | 81 | 46 | 106 | 76 |
| ANGER, AND LOVE, BEST HOOKES OF HUMANE BLOOD. | SOSPETTO D'HERODE | 275 | 46 | 109 | 216 |
| COMES NOT TO RULE IN WRATH, BUT SERVE IN LOVE. | SOSPETTO D'HERODE | 516 | 46 | 109 | 216 |
| WHOSE EARLY LOVE | ON A PRAYER BOOKE | 94 | 46 | 126 | 139 |
| DIVINEST LOVE LYES IN THIS BOOKE. | ON MR. G. HERBERTS BOOKE | 2 | 46 | 130 | 68 |
| LOVE THOU ART ABSOLUTE, SOLE LORD | IN MEMORY OF LADY MADRE TERESA | 1 | 46 | 131 | 52 |
| FOR LOVE THEIR LORD, GLORIOUS AND GREAT, | IN MEMORY OF LADY MADRE TERESA | 11 | 46 | 131 | 52 |
| WHAT DEATH WITH LOVE SHOULD HAVE TO DOE | IN MEMORY OF LADY MADRE TERESA | 20 | 46 | 131 | 52 |
| WHY TO SHOW LOVE SHEE SHOULD SHED BLOOD. | IN MEMORY OF LADY MADRE TERESA | 22 | 46 | 131 | 52 |
| SHEE CAN LOVE AND SHEE CAN DYE. | IN MEMORY OF LADY MADRE TERESA | 24 | 46 | 131 | 52 |
| HOW MUCH LESSE STRONG IS DEATH THEN LOVE. | IN MEMORY OF LADY MADRE TERESA | 28 | 46 | 131 | 52 |
| BEE LOVE BUT THERE, LET POORE SIXE YEARES, | IN MEMORY OF LADY MADRE TERESA | 29 | 46 | 131 | 52 |
| LOVE KNOWES NO NONAGE, NOR THE MIND. | IN MEMORY OF LADY MADRE TERESA | 32 | 46 | 131 | 52 |
| TIS LOVE, NOT YEARES, OR LIMBES, THAT CAN | IN MEMORY OF LADY MADRE TERESA | 33 | 46 | 131 | 52 |
| LOVE TOUCHT HER HEART, AND LOE IT BEATS | IN MEMORY OF LADY MADRE TERESA | 35 | 46 | 131 | 52 |
| MY ROSY LOVE, THAT THY RICH ZONE. | IN MEMORY OF LADY MADRE TERESA | 173 | 46 | 131 | 52 |
| I LEARNT TO KNOW THAT LOVE IS ELOQUENCE. | AN APOLOGIE FOR HYMNE (TERESA) | 6 | 46 | 136 | 59 |
| FORBID IT MIGHTY LOVE, LET NO FOND HATE | AN APOLOGIE FOR HYMNE (TERESA) | 13 | 46 | 136 | 59 |
| WITH THE STRONG WINE OF LOVE, LET OTHERS SWIMME | AN APOLOGIE FOR HYMNE (TERESA) | 31 | 46 | 136 | 59 |
| WINE OF YOUTHS LIFE, AND THE SWEET DEATHS OF LOVE. | AN APOLOGIE FOR HYMNE (TERESA) | 41 | 46 | 136 | 59 |
| NEW STRUCK BY LOVE, STILL TREMBLING ON HIS DART. | ON A TREATISE OF CHARITY | 46 | 46 | 137 | 69 |
| SIGHS TO HIS SILVER MATE. RISE UP MY LOVE, | ON THE ASSUMPTION | 8 | 46 | 139 | 114 |
| CUME AWAY MY LOVE, | ON THE ASSUMPTION | 13 | 46 | 139 | 114 |
| LIVE OUR CHASTE LOVE, THE HOLY MIRTH | ON THE ASSUMPTION | 59 | 46 | 139 | 114 |
| AND FORRAGE IN THE FIELDS OF LIGHT, AND LOVE. | ON HOPE | 76 | 46 | 143 | 71 |
| JOY OF GOODNESSE, LOVE OF ART, | UPON DEATH OF DESIRED HERRYS | 9 | 46 | 168 | 467 |
| HIM THE MUSES LOVE TO FOLLOW, | UPON DEATH OF DESIRED HERRYS | 11 | 46 | 168 | 467 |
| BURNING, ONELY IN HIS LOVE. | ANOTHER ON HERRYS | 26 | 46 | 170 | 469 |
| IN THE LAST KNOT THAT LOVE COULD TYE. | AN EPITAPH HUSBAND AND WIFE | 10 | 46 | 174 | 478 |
| DENY TO MIGHTY LOVE A DEITY. | UPON YORKE HIS BIRTH | 85 | 46 | 176 | 500 |
| SO FALSE A FORTUNE, AND SO TRUE A LOVE. | UPON FAIRE ETHIOPIAN | 2 | 46 | 183 | 493 |
| LOVE, BRAVE VERTUES YOUNGER BROTHER, | LOVES HOROSCOPE | 1 | 46 | 185 | 483 |
| IF POORE LOVE SHALL LIVE OR DY. | LOVES HOROSCOPE | 8 | 46 | 185 | 483 |
| IF POORE LOVE SHALL LIVE OR DYE. | LOVES HOROSCOPE | 20 | 46 | 185 | 483 |
| POINTS OF DEATH BID LOVE BE GONE | LOVES HOROSCOPE | 22 | 46 | 185 | 483 |
| LOVE HA'S NO PLEA AGAINST HER EYE | LOVES HOROSCOPE | 31 | 46 | 185 | 483 |
| BEAUTY FROWNES, AND LOVE MUST DYE. | LOVES HOROSCOPE | 32 | 46 | 185 | 483 |
| AND GUILD THE HOPES OF HUMBLE LOVE. | LOVES HOROSCOPE | 34 | 46 | 185 | 483 |
| BEAUTY SMILES AND LOVE SHALL LIVE. | LOVES HOROSCOPE | 40 | 46 | 185 | 483 |
| O IF LOVE SHALL LIVE, O WHERE | LOVES HOROSCOPE | 41 | 46 | 185 | 483 |
| SHALL I HIDE POORE LOVE FROM DEATH. | LOVES HOROSCOPE | 44 | 46 | 185 | 483 |
| LOVE SHALL DYE ALTHOUGH HE LIVE. | LOVES HOROSCOPE | 46 | 46 | 185 | 483 |
| OR IF LOVE SHALL DYE, O WHERE, | LOVES HOROSCOPE | 47 | 46 | 185 | 483 |
| WHILE LOVE SHALL THUS ENTOMBED LYE, | LOVES HOROSCOPE | 51 | 46 | 185 | 483 |
| LOVE SHALL LIVE, ALTHOUGH HE DYE. | LOVES HOROSCOPE | 52 | 46 | 185 | 483 |
| LOVE HIS QUIVER, | OUT OF THE ITALIAN (1) | 14 | 46 | 188 | 545 |
| LOVE NOW NO FIRE HATH LEFT HIM, | OUT OF THE ITALIAN (2) | 1 | 46 | 190 | 547 |
| O, THAT POORE LOVE BE NOT FOR EVER SPOYLED. | OUT OF THE ITALIAN (2) | 5 | 46 | 190 | 547 |
| OF LOVE, BURNE BOTH TOGETHER. | OUT OF THE ITALIAN (2) | 14 | 46 | 190 | 547 |
| HOW LOVE CAME NAK'T, A BOY, AND BLIND. | OUT OF THE ITALIAN (3) | 2 | 46 | 190 | 549 |
| LET US LOVE AND NEVER FEARE, | OUT OF CATULLUS | 2 | 46 | 194 | 523 |
| LOVE MAY BEE LONG CHUSING A DART. | WISHES SUPPOSED MISTRESSE | 57 | 46 | 195 | 479 |
| WHERE LOVE AND SHEE SHALL SIT AND SING | THOUGH NOW 'TIS NEITHER | 12 | MS | 397 | 492 |
| THE HOLY CHAPPELL OF CHAST LOVE | THOUGH NOW 'TIS NEITHER | 22 | MS | 397 | 492 |
| ALLMIGHTY LOVE. END THIS LONG WARR, | TO COUNTESSE OF DENBIGH | 29 | 52 | 236 | 146 |
| O DART OF LOVE. ARROW OF LIGHT, | TO COUNTESSE OF DENBIGH | 49 | 52 | 236 | 146 |
| YEILD THEN, O YEILD, THAT LOVE MAY WIN | TO COUNTESSE OF DENBIGH | 63 | 52 | 236 | 146 |
| DEATH'S PREY, BEFORE THE PRIZE OF LOVE. | TO COUNTESSE OF DENBIGH | 66 | 52 | 236 | 146 |
| THE HEIRS ELECT OF LOVE, WHOSE NAMES BELONG | TO THE NAME OF JESUS | 9 | 52 | 239 | 30 |
| AND TO THE WORKE OF LOVE THIS MORNING WAKE YOU | TO THE NAME OF JESUS | 54 | 52 | 239 | 30 |
| AND LOOSE THEM INTO ONE OF LOVE. | TO THE NAME OF JESUS | 87 | 52 | 239 | 30 |
| OF WARBLING SERAPHIM TO THE EARES OF LOVE. | TO THE NAME OF JESUS | 106 | 52 | 239 | 30 |
| IT WAS THE WITT OF LOVE O'REFLOWD THE BOUNDS | TO THE NAME OF JESUS | 223 | 52 | 239 | 30 |
| TO THEE, DREAD LAMB, WHOSE LOVE MUST KEEP | IN HOLY NATIVITY | 101 | 52 | 246 | 76 |
| FOR LOVE OF THEE | IN GLORIOUS EPIPHANIE | 11 | 52 | 253 | 39 |
| THE NATION'S TERROR NOW THEN ERST THEIR LOVE. | IN GLORIOUS EPIPHANIE | 160 | 52 | 253 | 39 |
| INTO THE LAND OF LIGHT & LOVE. | OFFICE H. CROSS PRIME | 12 | 52 | 267 | 91 |
| OF LOVE TO HIM, WHO ON THIS PAINFULL TREE | VEXILLA REGIS | 5 | 52 | 277 | 156 |

| | | | | |
|---|---|---|---|---|
| BUT THOUGH GREAT LOVE, GREEDY OF SUCH SAD GAIN | VEXILLA REGIS | 13 | 52 277 | 156 |
| LARG THRONE OF LOVE, ROYALLY SPRED | VEXILLA REGIS | 25 | 52 277 | 156 |
| HOW MUCH DEATH WEIGH'D MORE LIGHT THEN LOVE, | VEXILLA REGIS | 36 | 52 277 | 156 |
| THE LAMB WHOM HIS OWN LOVE HATH SLAIN, | VEXILLA REGIS | 44 | 52 277 | 156 |
| LOVE IS TOO KIND, I SEE. & CAN | CHARITAS NIMIA | 5 | 52 280 | 48 |
| AS THEN IN DEATH, SO NOW IN LOVE, | CHARITAS NIMIA | 66 | 52 280 | 48 |
| OF LOVE. HERE MUST SHE STAND | SANCTA MARIA DOLORUM | 36 | 52 283 | 162 |
| SOFT SOURSE OF LOVE | SANCTA MARIA DOLORUM | 42 | 52 283 | 162 |
| SOFT SUBJECT FOR THE SEIGE OF LOVE. | SANCTA MARIA DOLORUM | 50 | 52 283 | 162 |
| OF LOVE, SWEET BITTER THINGS, | SANCTA MARIA DOLORUM | 96 | 52 283 | 162 |
| FOLD UP MY LIFE IN LOVE. AND LAY'T BENEATH | SANCTA MARIA DOLORUM | 107 | 52 283 | 162 |
| OF HUMBLE LOVE & LOYALL FAITH, | ADORO TE | 2 | 52 291 | 172 |
| WHOM TOO MUCH LOVE HATH BOW'D MORE LOW FOR ME. | ADORO TE | 4 | 52 291 | 172 |
| AS FAST AS LOVE NEW LAWES CAN GIVE. | ADORO TE | 12 | 52 291 | 172 |
| LOVE COULD NOT THINK, TRUTH COULD NOT SAY. | ADORO TE | 16 | 52 291 | 172 |
| PLEAD FOR ME, LOVE. ALLEAGE & SHOW | ADORO TE | 19 | 52 291 | 172 |
| GIVE LOVE FOR LIFE. NOR LET MY DAYES | ADORO TE | 35 | 52 291 | 172 |
| COME LOVE. COME LORD. & THAT LONG DAY | ADORO TE | 51 | 52 291 | 172 |
| THE BEST AMBITION OF THY LOVE. | LAUDA SION SALVATOREM | 6 | 52 294 | 178 |
| OF LOVE, WAS HIS OWN LEGACY. | LAUDA SION SALVATOREM | 12 | 52 294 | 178 |
| COME, LOVE. & LET US WORK A SONG | LAUDA SION SALVATOREM | 13 | 52 294 | 178 |
| O LET THAT LOVE WHICH THUS MAKES THEE | LAUDA SION SALVATOREM | 73 | 52 294 | 178 |
| FLY TO THY SCEPTER OF SOFT LOVE. | DIES IRAE | 28 | 52 298 | 186 |
| OF LOVE, AND EV'N THAT LOSSE, BE LOST. | DIES IRAE | 34 | 52 298 | 186 |
| IF SIN CAN SIGH, LOVE CAN FORGIVE. | DIES IRAE | 47 | 52 298 | 186 |
| (ALL YOU TO WHOM THIS LOVE BELONGS) | O GLORIOSA DOMINA | 29 | 52 302 | 194 |
| SIGHES TO HIS SYLVER MATE RISE UP, MY LOVE. | IN GLORIOUS ASSUMPTION B. LADY | 8 | 52 304 | 114 |
| COME AWAY, MY LOVE. | IN GLORIOUS ASSUMPTION B. LADY | 13 | 52 304 | 114 |
| COME AWAY, MY LOVE. | IN GLORIOUS ASSUMPTION B. LADY | 31 | 52 304 | 114 |
| LIVE, OUR CHAST LOVE, THE HOLY MIRTH | IN GLORIOUS ASSUMPTION B. LADY | 64 | 52 304 | 114 |
| O WIT OF LOVE. THAT THUS COULD PLACE | WEEPER | 89 | 52 307 | 120 |
| (MERCILESSE LOVE.) IS ALL. | WEEPER | 129 | 52 307 | 120 |
| LOVE, THOU ART ABSOLUTE SOLE LORD | TERESA | 1 | 52 315 | 52 |
| FOR LOVE AT LARG TO FILL. SPARE BLOOD & SWEAT. | TERESA | 11 | 52 315 | 52 |
| WHAT DEATH WITH LOVE SHOULD HAVE TO DOE. | TERESA | 20 | 52 315 | 52 |
| WHY TO SHOW LOVE, SHE SHOULD SHED BLOOD | TERESA | 22 | 52 315 | 52 |
| SHE CAN LOVE, & SHE CAN DY. | TERESA | 24 | 52 315 | 52 |
| HOW MUCH LESSE STRONG IS DEATH THEN LOVE. | TERESA | 28 | 52 315 | 52 |
| BE LOVE BUT THERE. LET POOR SIX YEARES | TERESA | 29 | 52 315 | 52 |
| LOVE KNOWES NO NONAGE, NOR THE MIND. | TERESA | 32 | 52 315 | 52 |
| 'TIS LOVE, NOT YEARES OR LIMBS THAT CAN | TERESA | 33 | 52 315 | 52 |
| LOVE TOUCH'T HER HEART, & LO IT BEATES | TERESA | 35 | 52 315 | 52 |
| (MY ROSY LOVE) THAT THY RICH ZONE | TERESA | 172 | 52 315 | 52 |
| I LEARN'T TO KNOW THAT LOVE IS ELOQUENCE | AN APOLOGIE FOR (TERESA) HYMNE | 8 | 52 322 | 59 |
| FORBID IT, MIGHTY LOVE. LET NO FOND HATE | AN APOLOGIE FOR (TERESA) HYMNE | 13 | 52 322 | 59 |
| WITH THEE, STRONG WINE OF LOVE. LET OTHERS SWIMME | AN APOLOGIE FOR (TERESA) HYMNE | 31 | 52 322 | 59 |
| WINE OF YOUTH, LIFE, & THE SWEET DEATHS OF LOVE. | AN APOLOGIE FOR (TERESA) HYMNE | 41 | 52 322 | 59 |
| IN THAT RARE LIFE OF HER, AND LOVE. | FLAMING HEART | 52 | 52 324 | 61 |
| LIVE HERE, GREAT HEART. & LOVE AND DY & KILL. | FLAMING HEART | 79 | 52 324 | 61 |
| BY ALL THY LIVES & DEATHS OF LOVE. | FLAMING HEART | 96 | 52 324 | 61 |
| AND BY THY THIRSTS OF LOVE MORE LARGE THEN THEY. | FLAMING HEART | 98 | 52 324 | 61 |
| O LOVE, I AM THY SACRIFICE. | A SONG | 5 | 52 327 | 65 |
| WHOSE EARLY LOVE | PRAYER TO GENTLE-WOMAN | 100 | 52 328 | 139 |
| 'TIS TIME YOU LISTEN TO A BRAVER LOVE, | TO SAME CONCERNING CHOISE | 20 | 52 331 | 66 |
| YOUR WARY LOVE | TO SAME CONCERNING CHOISE | 34 | 52 331 | 66 |
| NOR LOVE, NOR LABOUR CAN BE LOST. | TO SAME CONCERNING CHOISE | 39 | 52 331 | 66 |
| IN YOUR MISTAKEN LOVE, | TO SAME CONCERNING CHOISE | 47 | 52 331 | 66 |
| OF LOVE, OF LIFE, & EVERLASTING REST. | TO SAME CONCERNING CHOISE | 53 | 52 331 | 66 |
| NOW WITH A LOVE BELOW THE SUN. | TO SAME CONCERNING CHOISE | 57 | 52 331 | 66 |
| LOVE TOO, THAT LEADS THE WAY, WOULD LEND THE WINGS | ALEXIAS FIRST ELEGIE | 17 | 52 334 | 204 |
| AND WHERE LOVE LENDS THE WING, & LEADS THE WAY, | ALEXIAS FIRST ELEGIE | 19 | 52 334 | 204 |
| IF I BE SHIPWRACK'T, LOVE SHALL TEACH TO SWIMME | ALEXIAS FIRST ELEGIE | 21 | 52 334 | 204 |
| O LIVE, SO RARE A LOVE. LIVE. & IN THEE | ALEXIAS FIRST ELEGIE | 33 | 52 334 | 204 |
| FIRM IN THY CROWN, AS HERE FAST IN THY LOVE. | ALEXIAS FIRST ELEGIE | 36 | 52 334 | 204 |
| AT LAST A CONSTANT LOVE THAT LEAVES ME NOT. | ALEXIAS SECONDE ELEGIE | 8 | 52 335 | 207 |
| O I AM LEARNED GROWN, POOR LOVE & I | ALEXIAS SECONDE ELEGIE | 21 | 52 335 | 207 |
| THAT WEARY LOVE AT LAST MAY FIND HIS WAY. | ALEXIAS SECONDE ELEGIE | 30 | 52 335 | 207 |
| IF HEATES OF HOLYER LOVE & HIGH DESIRE | ALEXIAS THIRD ELEGIE | 21 | 52 336 | 209 |
| I'D KNOW NO NAME OF LOVE ON EARTH BUT YOU. | ALEXIAS THIRD ELEGIE | 44 | 52 336 | 209 |
| THY TORCH, TERRESTRIALL LOVE, HAVE HERE NO NAME. | ALEXIAS THIRD ELEGIE | 50 | 52 336 | 209 |
| WHEN THOUSANDS SOUGHT MY LOVE, LOV'D NONE BUT THEE. | ALEXIAS THIRD ELEGIE | 54 | 52 336 | 209 |
| IN THE LAST KNOTT LOVE COULD TY. | AN EPITAPH UPON MARRIED COUPLE | 10 | 52 339 | 478 |
| LOVE MADE THE BED. THEY'L TAKE NO HARM | AN EPITAPH UPON MARRIED COUPLE | 14 | 52 339 | 478 |
| AND FORRAGE IN THE FIELDS OF LIGHT AND LOVE. | (ON) HOPE | 36 | 52 345 | 71 |
| LOVE, THAT LENDS HASTE TO HEAVIEST THINGS, | AGAINST IRRESOLUTION AND DELAY | 27 | 52 347 | 146 |
| AND BY THEIR LOVE CONTROLL THEIR FATE. | AGAINST IRRESOLUTION AND DELAY | 50 | 52 347 | 146 |
| LEARN'D FIRST HIS LIGHTNESSE BY HIS LOVE. | AGAINST IRRESOLUTION AND DELAY | 52 | 52 347 | 146 |
| WHEN LOVE OF US CALL'D HIM TO SEE | AGAINST IRRESOLUTION AND DELAY | 67 | 52 347 | 146 |
| YIELD THEN, O YIELD, THAT LOVE MAY WIN | AGAINST IRRESOLUTION AND DELAY | 85 | 52 347 | 146 |
| DEATH'S PREY, BEFORE THE PRIZE OF LOVE. | AGAINST IRRESOLUTION AND DELAY | 88 | 52 347 | 146 |
| THAT MADE GREAT LOVE A MAN OF WARRE. | IN CICATRICES DOMINI JESU | 6 | MS 381 | 27 |
| AETERNALL LOVE. WHAT 'TIS TO LOVE THEE WELL, | IN AMOREM DIVINUM | 1 | MS 381 | 212 |
| AETERNALL LOVE. WHAT 'TIS TO LOVE THEE WELL, | IN AMOREM DIVINUM | 1 | MS 381 | 212 |
| AND START FROM OFF THY CENTER. HATH HEAVENS LOVE | ON GUNPOWDER-TREASON | 5 | MS 384 | 458 |
| A PHAENIX, & IN CHASTEST FLAMES OF LOVE | UPON GUNPOWDER TREASON | 34 | MS 387 | 461 |
| A HEART BURNING IN LOVE. ALL DID ADORE | UPON KINGS CORONATION | 37 | MS 390 | 453 |
| A PRAESENT WORTHY OF APOLLO'S LOVE. | UPON BIRTH PRINCESSE E | 20 | MS 391 | 456 |
| AND MADE IT BURNE IN LOVE. 'TWAS NOT THE RAGE. | AN ELEGY MR STANNINOW | 33 | MS 394 | 473 |
| NOT STINGS OF WRATH, BUT WOUNDS OF LOVE. | VEXILLA REGIS | 18 | 52 277 | 156 |

LOVE-CROWNED

  TO WAIT AT THE LOVE-CROWNED DOORES OF                  TO THE NAME OF JESUS          42  52 239  30

LOVE-ECLIPSE

  WITH AN ELABORATE LOVE-ECLIPSE                           IN GLORIOUS EPIPHANIE         152  52 253  39

LOVE-SICK

  BY THE LOVE-SICK WORLD BIN MADE                          IN GLORIOUS EPIPHANIE         136  52 253  39

LOVE-SLAIN

  THE LOVE-SLAIN WITTNESSES OF THIS LIFE OF THEE.      FLAMING HEART                  84  52 324  61

LOVE-SPUN

  HEAVN'S GREAT ARTILLERY IN EACH LOVE-SPUN LINE.     FLAMING HEART                  56  52 324  61

LOVE-TOST

  OFT FROM THIS BREAST TO THINE MY LOVE-TOST HEART    LUKE 2.  QUAERIT JESUM        39  MS 379  11

LOVE'S

  STILL YOU ARE PRODIGAL OF YOUR LOVE'S EXPENCE      SOSPETTO D'HERODE           285  46 109 216
  O LET IT BE AT LAST, LOVE'S HOURE.                    TO COUNTESSE OF DENBIGH     37  52 236 146
  AND USE THE SEASON OF LOVE'S SHOWRE.                TO COUNTESSE OF DENBIGH     44  52 236 146
  HATH IN LOVE'S QUIVER HID FOR YOU.                  TO COUNTESSE OF DENBIGH     48  52 236 146
  IT IS LOVE'S SEEGE.  AND SURE TO BE                   TO COUNTESSE OF DENBIGH     59  52 236 146
  I HAVE AUTHORITY IN LOVE'S NAME TO TAKE YOU        TO THE NAME OF JESUS        53  52 239  30
  (LOVE'S EASTERN WINDOWES) ALL WIDE OPE               TO THE NAME OF JESUS       146  52 239  30
  FOR FAIR, PURPLE DOORES, OF LOVE'S DEVISING.       TO THE NAME OF JESUS       217  52 239  30
  THEY THAT BY LOVE'S MILD DICTATE NOW                 TO THE NAME OF JESUS       236  52 239  30
  HATH METT LOVE'S NOON IN NATURE'S NIGHT.           IN HOLY NATIVITY            2  52 246  76
  LOVE'S ARCHITECTURE IS HIS OWN.                     IN HOLY NATIVITY          47  52 246  76
  'TWIST DEATH'S & LOVE'S FARR DIFFERENT FRUIT.       OFFICE H. CROSS SIXT        14  52 270  97
  HIS OWN LOVE'S, & OUR SIN'S GREAT SACRIFICE.        OFFICE H. CROSS NINTH       6  52 271  99
  BOTH OF LOVE'S FIRES & FLOODS) MIGHT I RECLINE     SANCTA MARIA DOLORUM        47  52 283 162
  BUT SPYES LOVE'S DAWN, & DISAPPEARES.               LAUDA SION SALVATOREM      22  52 294 178
  NOR IS'T LOVE'S FAULT, BUT SIN'S DIRE SKILL        LAUDA SION SALVATOREM      53  52 294 178
  MIXT & MADE FRIENDS BY LOVE'S SWEET POWRES.        WEEPER                    102  52 307 120
  THOU ART LOVE'S VICTIME.  & MUST DY                   TERESA                    75  52 315  52
  INTO LOVE'S ARMES THOU SHALT LET FALL                TERESA                    77  52 315  52
  AND TURN LOVE'S SOULDIERS, UPON THEE                 TERESA                    95  52 315  52
  LOVE'S NOBLE HISTORY, WITH WITT                     TERESA                   156  52 315  52
  AND LOVE'S THAT BODY'S SOUL, NO LAW CONTROWLLS     AN APOLOGIE FOR (TERESA) HYMNE  18  52 322  59
  AND MOCKES WITH FEMALE FROST LOVE'S MANLY FLAME.   FLAMING HEART                24  52 324  61
  NOT UNE LOOSE SHAFT BUT LOVE'S WHOLE QUIVER.       FLAMING HEART                70  52 324  61
  FOR IN LOVE'S FEILD WAS NEVER FOUND                  FLAMING HEART                71  52 324  61
  LOVE'S PASSIVES ARE HIS ACTIV'ST PART.               FLAMING HEART                73  52 324  61
  I DY IN LOVE'S DELICIOUS FIRE.                       A SONG                     4  52 327  65
  IT IS LOVE'S GREAT ARTILLERY                        PRAYER TO GENTLE-WOMAN      15  52 328 139
  LOVE'S TRUEST KNOTT BY VENUS IS NOT TY'D.           ALEXIAS THIRD ELEGIE       27  52 336 209
  WHEN HOLY FIRES MAINTAIN LOVE'S HEAVNLY LIFE.      ALEXIAS THIRD ELEGIE       52  52 336 209
  RICH HOPE. LOVE'S LEGACY, UNDER LOCK                (ON) HOPE                    11  52 345  71
  QUEEN REGENT IN YONGE LOVE'S MINORITY.              (ON) HOPE                    44  52 345  71
  THOUGH LOVE'S MORE FEIRCE, MORE FRUITLESSE, FIRES  (ON) HOPE                    47  52 345  71
                                              ASSAY
  WHAT E'RE LOVE'S MATTER BE, HE MOVES                 AGAINST IRRESOLUTION AND DELAY  53  52 347 146
  MIGHTY LOVE'S ARTILLERY.                              IN CICATRICES DOMINI JESU     2  MS 381  27

LOVED

  A LIFE SO LOVED, AND THAT THERE BEE                  IN MEMORY OF LADY MADRE TERESA  91  46 131  52
  SAFE O HIDE HIS LOVED HEAD.                          UPON DEATH OF DESIRED HERRYS    70  46 168 467
  MEANE WHILE HIS LOVED BANKES NOW DRY,               AN EPITAPH DOCTOR BROOKE      7  46 175 465

LOV'D

  WAS LOV'D WAS HONOUR'D AS A FLOOD.                  AN EPITAPH DOCTOR BROOKE      2  46 175 465
  HEE LOV'D HIS FATHER.  YET HIS ZEALE                 AN EPITAPH UPON ASHTON     19  46 192 464
  PEACE, WHICH HEE LOV'D IN LIFE, DID LEND            AN EPITAPH UPON ASHTON     23  46 192 464
  AH LINGER NOT, LOV'D SOUL. A SLOW                    TO COUNTESSE OF DENBIGH     13  52 236 146
  AND TEACH THY LOV'D NAME TO THEIR NOBLE LYRE.      CHARITAS NIMIA               28  52 280  48
  TO REACH AT THY LOV'D FACE.  NOR CAN                 ADORO TE                     29  52 291 172
  AND THIS LOV'D SOUL, JUDG'D WORTH NO LESSE          DIES IRAE                    35  52 298 186
  A LIFE SO LOV'D.  AND THAT THERE BE                  TERESA                    91  52 315  52
  I LATE THE ROMAN YOUTH'S LOV'D PRAYSE & PRIDE,     ALEXIAS FIRST ELEGIE        1  52 334 204
  HAD UNDER SOME LOW ROOFE LOV'D HIS PLAIN WIFE.     ALEXIAS THIRD ELEGIE       14  52 336 209
  UNLESSE IT BE A CRIME TO'HAVE LOV'D TOO WELL.      ALEXIAS THIRD ELEGIE       20  52 336 209
  WHEN THOUSANDS SOUGHT MY LOVE, LOV'D NONE BUT THEE.  ALEXIAS THIRD ELEGIE       54  52 336 209
  AH. LINGER NOT, LOV'D SOUL. A SLOW                   AGAINST IRRESOLUTION AND DELAY   7  52 347 146
  ON HIM, WHO HAS LOV'D US SO.                         AGAINST IRRESOLUTION AND DELAY  66  52 347 146
  HEE'S GONE. & HIS LOV'D STEPPES TO WAIT UPON,      LUKE 2.  QUAERIT JESUM        9  MS 379  11
  BUT OH, WHAT TO BE LOV'D OF THEE AS WELL.           IN AMOREM DIVINUM             3  MS 381 212

LOVES

  OF SIMPLE GRACES, AND SWEET LOVES.                  A HYMNE OF THE NATIVITY     84  46 106  76
  MUSE, NOW THE SERVANT OF SOFT LOVES NO MORE,       SOSPETTO D'HERODE            1  46 109 216
  IMMORTALL HONY FOR THE HIVE OF LOVES.               SOSPETTO D'HERODE           24  46 109 216

| Concordance Line | Title | | | |
|---|---|---|---|---|
| OF POIS'NOUS AND UNNATURALL LOVES. EARTH-NURST. | SOSPETTO D'HERODE | 127 | 46 109 | 216 |
| THE NIMBLEST OF THE LIGHTNING-WINGED LOVES. | SOSPETTO D'HERODE | 235 | 46 109 | 216 |
| IT IS LOVES GREAT ARTILLERY, | ON A PRAYER BOOKE | 9 | 46 126 | 139 |
| AN HUNDRED THOUSAND LOVES AND GRACES. | ON A PRAYER BOOKE | 75 | 46 126 | 139 |
| THOU ART LOVES VICTIM, AND MUST DYE | IN MEMORY OF LADY MADRE TERESA | 75 | 46 131 | 52 |
| INTO LOVES HAND THOU SHALT LET FALL, | IN MEMORY OF LADY MADRE TERESA | 77 | 46 131 | 52 |
| AND TURNE LOVES SOULDIERS, UPON THEE, | IN MEMORY OF LADY MADRE TERESA | 95 | 46 131 | 52 |
| LOVES HIS DEATH, AND DYES AGAINE, | IN MEMORY OF LADY MADRE TERESA | 101 | 46 131 | 52 |
| LOVES NOBLE HISTORY, WITH WITT | IN MEMORY OF LADY MADRE TERESA | 157 | 46 131 | 52 |
| AND LOVES THAT BODIES SOULE. NO LAW CONTROULES | AN APOLOGIE FOR HYMNE (TERESA) | 18 | 46 136 | 59 |
| OF LITTLE EAGLES, AND YOUNG LOVES, WHOSE HIGH | AN APOLOGIE FOR HYMNE (TERESA) | 27 | 46 136 | 59 |
| THOU ART LOVES LEGACIE UNDER LOCK | ON HOPE | 31 | 46 143 | 71 |
| TILL IN THE LAP OF LOVES FULL NOONE | ON HOPE | 56 | 46 143 | 71 |
| QUEEN REGENT IN YOUNG LOVES MINORITIE. | ON HOPE | 84 | 46 143 | 71 |
| AND LOVES MORE FIERCE, MORE FRUITLESSE FIRES ASSAY | ON HOPE | 87 | 46 143 | 71 |
| WERE VOW'D LOVES FLAMING SACRIFICE. | HIS EPITAPH (HERRYS) | 42 | 46 172 | 471 |
| WHAT IS LOVES SACRIFICE, BUT THE BROKEN HEART. | UPON FORD'S TRAGEDYES | 2 | 46 181 | 495 |
| BEAUTY LAYES OPE LOVES FORTUNE-BOOKE, | LOVES HOROSCOPE | 12 | 46 185 | 483 |
| THE OBSEQUIOUS MOTIONS OF LOVES FATE, | LOVES HOROSCOPE | 14 | 46 185 | 483 |
| HOW E'RE LOVES NATIVE HOURES WERE SET, | LOVES HOROSCOPE | 17 | 46 185 | 483 |
| LAY BLACKE ON LOVES NATIVITYE. | LOVES HOROSCOPE | 36 | 46 185 | 483 |
| FULL QUIVERS ON LOVES BOW. | WISHES SUPPOSED MISTRESSE | 59 | 46 195 | 479 |
| BEE YOU THE LADY OF LOVES YEERE. | THOUGH NOW 'TIS NEITHER | 27 | MS 397 | 492 |
| THERE ALL THE YEARE IS LOVES LONG SPRING. | THOUGH NOW 'TIS NEITHER | 29 | MS 397 | 492 |
| THERE ALL THE YEARE LOVES NIGHTINGALES | THOUGH NOW 'TIS NEITHER | 30 | MS 397 | 492 |
| THE NAME OF ALL OUR LIVES & LOVES. | TO THE NAME OF JESUS | 5 | 52 239 | 30 |
| SOFT BACK. AND BRINGS A BOSOM BIG WITH LOVES. | TO THE NAME OF JESUS | 160 | 52 239 | 30 |
| OF SIMPLE GRACES & SWEET LOVES. | IN HOLY NATIVITY | 104 | 52 246 | 76 |
| O THOU BORN KING OF LOVES, | IN GLORIOUS EPIPHANIE | 7 | 52 253 | 39 |
| NOR WITH PERVERSE LOVES & RELIGIOUS RAPES | IN GLORIOUS EPIPHANIE | 105 | 52 253 | 39 |
| THEIR HATED LOVES CHANGD INTO WHOLSOM FEARES. | IN GLORIOUS EPIPHANIE | 161 | 52 253 | 39 |
| OF LOVES, THY LORD'S TOO LIBERALL BREAST, | VEXILLA REGIS | 8 | 52 277 | 156 |
| DIVIDED LOVES. WHILE SON & MOTHER | SANCTA MARIA DOLORUM | 23 | 52 283 | 162 |
| THIS BOOK OF LOVES, THUS WRIT | SANCTA MARIA DOLORUM | 53 | 52 283 | 162 |
| AT LEAST BE IN LOVES WAY. | SANCTA MARIA DOLORUM | 66 | 52 283 | 162 |
| LIVE EVER BREAD OF LOVES, & BE | ADORO TE | 43 | 52 291 | 172 |
| HOPE TELLS MY HEART, THE SAME LOVES BE | DIES IRAE | 51 | 52 298 | 186 |
| O CHEEKS. BEDDS OF CHAST LOVES | WEEPER | 85 | 52 307 | 120 |
| WITH LOVES, OF TEARS WITH SMILES DISPUTING. | WEEPER | 92 | 52 307 | 120 |
| VAIN LOVES AVANT. BOLD HANDS FORBEAR. | WEEPER | 107 | 52 307 | 120 |
| LOVES HIS DEATH, AND DYES AGAIN. | TERESA | 101 | 52 315 | 52 |
| OF LITTLE EAGLES & YOUNG LOVES, WHOSE HIGH | AN APOLOGIE FOR (TERESA) HYMNE | 27 | 52 322 | 59 |
| WALK IN A CROWD OF LOVES & MARTYRDOMES. | FLAMING HEART | 82 | 52 324 | 61 |
| EXPOSTULATE MY WOES & MUCH-WRONG'D LOVES. | ALEXIAS SECONDE ELEGIE | 14 | 52 335 | 207 |
| KIND LOVES KEEP HOUSE, LY CLOSE, AND MAKE NO NOISE, | DESCRIPTION RELIGIOUS HOUSE | 33 | 52 338 | 213 |
| TILL IN THE LAPPE OF LOVES FULL NOONE | (ON) HOPE | 26 | 52 345 | 71 |
| THAT DRAW THE CHARIOT OF CHAST LOVES. | AGAINST IRRESOLUTION AND DELAY | 46 | 52 347 | 146 |
| HER LOVES CROSSE FORTUNE, THAT THE SAD DISPUTE | HORATIJ ILLE & NEFASTO | 40 | MS 382 | 530 |
| OF LOVES ALL-DARING HAND, THAT MAKES ME BURNE, | EX EUPHORMIONE | 5 | MS 392 | 525 |

LOV'ES

| | | | | |
|---|---|---|---|---|
| O HEART. THE AEQUALL POISE OF LOV'ES BOTH PARTS | FLAMING HEART | 75 | 52 324 | 61 |

LOVELY

| | | | | |
|---|---|---|---|---|
| THY TEMPLE, AND THOSE LOVELY WALLS | PSALME 23 | 63 | 46 102 | 5 |
| LOVELY SION THOUGHT ON THEE. | PSALME 137 | 6 | 46 104 | 7 |
| WHERE TO LAY HIS LOVELY HEAD, | A HYMNE OF THE NATIVITY | 48 | 46 106 | 76 |
| NOR MORE LOVELY LIFT'ST THY HEAD, | UPON DEATH OF DESIRED HERRYS | 15 | 46 168 | 467 |
| I'VE SEENE THE MORNINGS LOVELY RAY, | UPON DEATH OF DESIRED HERRYS | 47 | 46 168 | 467 |
| THE FRESH HOPES OF HIS LOVELY YOUTH, | ANOTHER ON HERRYS | 13 | 46 170 | 469 |
| BRITTAINE, THE MIGHTY OCEANS LOVELY BRIDE. | UPON YORKE HIS BIRTH | 1 | 46 176 | 500 |
| THOU AND THE LOVELY HOPES THAT SMILE IN THEE | UPON YORKE HIS BIRTH | 40 | 46 176 | 500 |
| COME, LOVELY NAME. APPEARE FROM FORTH THE BRIGHT | TO THE NAME OF JESUS | 115 | 52 239 | 30 |
| COME, LOVELY NAME. LIFE OF OUR HOPE. | TO THE NAME OF JESUS | 125 | 52 239 | 30 |

LOVER

| | | | | |
|---|---|---|---|---|
| TO HAVE A GOD BECOME HER LOVER. | ON A PRAYER BOOKE | 118 | 46 126 | 139 |
| THY SILVER BROW, AND MEET THY GOLDEN LOVER. | ON A FOULE MORNING | 28 | 46 181 | 495 |
| TO THY LOVER | OUT OF THE ITALIAN (1) | 1 | 46 188 | 545 |
| FIRST DOES THE LONGING LOVER RIGHT. | WISHES SUPPOSED MISTRESSE | 72 | 46 195 | 479 |
| THE RED CHEEKS OF A RIVALL'D LOVER. | FLAMING HEART | 44 | 52 324 | 61 |
| TO HAVE HER GOD BECOME HER LOVER. | PRAYER TO GENTLE-WOMAN | 124 | 52 328 | 139 |
| LET NOT MY LORD, THE MIGHTY LOVER | TO SAME CONCERNING CHOISE | 41 | 52 331 | 66 |

LOVERS

| | | | | |
|---|---|---|---|---|
| HIS PERSIAN LOVERS ALL SHALL LEAVE HIM. | AN HIMNE FOR CIRCUMCISION | 35 | 46 141 | 37 |
| PEACE, THE LOVERS ARE ASLEEPE. | AN EPITAPH HUSBAND AND WIFE | 8 | 46 174 | 478 |
| A LOVERS KISSE MAY PLAY. | WISHES SUPPOSED MISTRESSE | 38 | 46 195 | 479 |
| MADE SHORT BY LOVERS PLAY, | WISHES SUPPOSED MISTRESSE | 83 | 46 195 | 479 |
| INLARGE THY FLAMING-BRESTED LOVERS | TO THE NAME OF JESUS | 212 | 52 239 | 30 |
| HIS PERSIAN LOVERS ALL SHALL LEAVE HIM. | NEW YEAR'S DAY | 35 | 52 251 | 37 |
| AND SURE WHERE LOVERS MAKE THEIR WATRY GRAVES | ALEXIAS FIRST ELEGIE | 25 | 52 334 | 204 |
| PEACE, THE LOVERS ARE ASLEEP. | AN EPITAPH UPON MARRIED COUPLE | 8 | 52 339 | 478 |

LOVING

| | | | | |
|---|---|---|---|---|
| OUR LOVING SONG SHALL HOLD IT FAST. | ON THE ASSUMPTION | 40 | 46 139 | 114 |
| TO MY LOVING, LINGRING SORROW. | OUT OF THE ITALIAN (1) | 42 | 46 188 | 545 |
| STILL LIVE IN ME THIS LOVING STRIFE | A SONG | 13 | 52 327 | 65 |

```
LOW

  THUS HIGH, THUS LOW, AS IF HER SILVER THROAT        MUSICKS DUELL                    100  46 149 535
  HOW LOW THE BRIGHT YOUTH BOW'D, AND WITH WHAT AWE   SOSPETTO D'HERODE                 99  46 109 216
  WHILE THUS HEAV'NS HIGHEST COUNSAILS, BY THE LOW    SOSPETTO D'HERODE                145  46 109 216
  THAT THE UNMEASUR'D GOD SO LOW SHOULD SINKE,        SOSPETTO D'HERODE                171  46 109 216
  THAT A VILE MANGER HIS LOW BED SHOULD PROVE,        SOSPETTO D'HERODE                175  46 109 216
  THUS LOW STANDS UP (ME THINKES) THUS, AND DEFYES    UPON STANINOUGH'S DEATH           28  46 175 475
  NARROW, & LOW, & INFINITELY LESSE                   TO THE NAME OF JESUS              22  52 239  30
  AND WE, LOW WORMES HAVE LEAVE TO DOE                TO THE NAME OF JESUS             109  52 239  30
  NEXT TO THEIR OWN LOW NOTHING THEY MAY LY,          TO THE NAME OF JESUS             234  52 239  30
  TO WHICH THE LOW WORLD'S LAWES                      IN GLORIOUS EPIPHANIE            153  52 253  39
  DREAD LAMB, AND BOW THUS LOW BEFORE THEE,           OFFICE H. CROSS MATINES           25  52 265  86
  THUS LOW BEFORE THEE                                OFFICE H. CROSS PRIME             19  52 267  91
  THUS LOW BEFORE THEE                                OFFICE H. CROSS THIRD             18  52 268  93
  DREAD LAMB, & BOW THUS LOW BEFORE THEE.             OFFICE H. CROSS SIXT              22  52 270  97
  THUS LOW BEFORE THEE                                OFFICE H. CROSS NINTH             15  52 271  99
  WHOM TOO MUCH LOVE HATH BOW'D MORE LOW FOR ME.      ADORO TE                           4  52 291 172
  MIX WITH OUR LOW MORTALITY.                         LAUDA SION SALVATOREM             74  52 294 178
  HAD UNDER SOME LOW ROOFE LOV'D HIS PLAIN WIFE.      ALEXIAS THIRD ELEGIE              14  52 336 209
  THUS LOW, STANDS UP (ME THINKS,) THUS & DEFIES      DEATH'S LECTURE                   30  52 340 475
  FORTUNE. ALAS, ABOVE THE WORLD'S LOW WARRES         (ON) HOPE                         31  52 345  71
  SOE LOW TO GIVE HIS THIRSTY STALLIONS DRINKE.       UPON GUNPOWDER TREASON            40  MS 386 460
  TEARES FALL TOO LOW, SIGHES RISE TOO HIGH,          UPON DEATH OF A FREIND             5  MS 393 477

LOWE

  THUS LOWE (MY HIDDEN LIFE.) I BOW TO THEE           ADORO TE                           3  52 291 172

LOWER

  LOWER, AND LOWER YET. TILL THY SMALL SIZE,          UPON STANINOUGH'S DEATH           15  46 175 475
  LOWER, AND LOWER YET. TILL THY SMALL SIZE,          UPON STANINOUGH'S DEATH           15  46 175 475
  YOU'AVE SEEN ALLREADY, IN THIS LOWER SPHEAR         TO SAME CONCERNING CHOISE          8  52 331  66
  LOWER & LOWER YET. TILL THY LEANE SIZE              DEATH'S LECTURE                   16  52 340 475
  LOWER & LOWER YET. TILL THY LEANE SIZE              DEATH'S LECTURE                   16  52 340 475

LOWEST

  WHAT FARTHEST NOOKE OF LOWEST HELL                  OUT OF GREEKE CUPID'S CRYER       35  46 159 519

LOW'ST

  BOWES LOW'ST HIS HEAVY TOP, TO LOOK FOR THEE.       IN GLORIOUS ASSUMPTION B. LADY    30  52 304 114

LOWLY

  O SPEAKE A LOWLY MUSES PARDON.  SPEAKE              UPON YORKE HIS BIRTH             108  46 176 500
  BOW'D TO THE LOWLY MOUTHS OF MEN.                   LAUDA SION SALVATOREM             62  52 294 178

LOWNESSE

  GREAT NYMPH, O'RELOOKE MY LOWNESSE. HEAV'N YOU KNOW, EX EUPHORMIONE                    7  MS 392 525

LOWRE

  NO CLOUD SCOULE ON HIS RADIANT LIDS NO TEMPEST LOWRE. EASTER DAY                      12  46 100  26

LOWRES

  BOVE ALL. NOTHING WITHIN THAT LOWRES.               WISHES SUPPOSED MISTRESSE         93  46 195 479

LOYALL

  WITH LOYALL CARES.                                  SANCTA MARIA DOLORUM              55  52 283 162
  OF HUMBLE LOVE & LOYALL FAITH,                      ADORO TE                           2  52 291 172
  YET SHALL MY LOYALL TONGUE KEEPE THIS COMMAND.      UPON BIRTH PRINCESSE E            15  MS 391 456

LOYTERING

  SHALL FIND THE LOYTERING HEART FROM HOME.           PRAYER TO GENTLE-WOMAN            48  52 328 139

LUBRICKE

  AND ROULE THEMSELVES OVER HER LUBRICKE THROAT       MUSICKS DUELL                     64  46 149 535

LUCIFER

  ART THOU NOT LUCIFER. HEE TO WHOM THE DROVES        SOSPETTO D'HERODE                233  46 109 216

LUGGES

                                                                                        *
  HANGS HIS BLACK LUGGES, STROAKT WITH THOSE HEAVENLY  HORATIJ ILLE & NEFASTO           51  MS 382 530
                            LINES.

LULL

  DOES THY SONG LULL THE AYRE.                        THE WEEPER                       103  46  79 120
  DOES THY SONG LULL THE AIR.                         WEEPER                           139  52 307 120
```

## LUMINOUS

| | | | | | |
|---|---|---|---|---|---|
| AMOROUS LANGUISHMENTS, LUMINOUS TRANCES. | ON A PRAYER BOOKE | 63 | 46 | 126 | 139 |
| AMOROUSE LANGUISHMENTS, LUMINOUS TRANCES. | PRAYER TO GENTLE-WOMAN | 69 | 52 | 328 | 139 |

## LUMP

| | | | | | |
|---|---|---|---|---|---|
| THE CHILL LUMP WOULD RELENT, & PROVE | SANCTA MARIA DOLORUM | 49 | 52 | 283 | 162 |
| LIKE A SOFT LUMP OF INCENSE, HASTED | TERESA | 113 | 52 | 315 | 52 |

## LUMPE

| | | | | | |
|---|---|---|---|---|---|
| LIKE A SOFT LUMPE OF INCENSE, HASTED | IN MEMORY OF LADY MADRE TERESA | 114 | 46 | 131 | 52 |
| THE STAGGERING LUMPE. EACH EYE SPENT ALL ITS STORE, | UPON KINGS CORONATION | 11 | MS | 390 | 453 |

## LUMPES

| | | | | | |
|---|---|---|---|---|---|
| AS LUMPES OF SUGAR LOSE THEMSELVES, AND TWINE | ON HOPE | 59 | 46 | 143 | 71 |
| AS LUMPES OF SUGAR LOOSE THEMSELVES, AND TWINE | (ON) HOPE | 29 | 52 | 345 | 71 |

## LUMPISH

| | | | | | |
|---|---|---|---|---|---|
| SO LUMPISH STEEL, UNTAUGHT TO MOVE. | AGAINST IRRESOLUTION AND DELAY | 51 | 52 | 347 | 146 |

## LUNGS

| | | | | | |
|---|---|---|---|---|---|
| AND THERE BE WORDS NOT MADE WITH LUNGS. | UPON THE DEATH OF A GENTLEMAN | 28 | 46 | 166 | 472 |
| THE BREATH OF ARTIFICIALL LUNGS EMBRAVES, | SOSPETTO D'HERODE | 482 | 46 | 109 | 216 |
| BELCH'D FROM THE SULPH'RY LUNGS OF PHLEGETON. | ON GUNPOWDER-TREASON | 16 | MS | 384 | 458 |

## LURKE

| | | | | | |
|---|---|---|---|---|---|
| UNDER THY SHADOW MAY I LURKE A WHILE. | SICKE IMPLORE SHADOW | 1 | 46 | 87 | 28 |

## LURKING

| | | | | | |
|---|---|---|---|---|---|
| SLY, LURKING TREASON IS HIS BOSOME FREIND, | UPON GUNPOWDER TREASON | 17 | MS | 387 | 461 |

## LUST

| | | | | | |
|---|---|---|---|---|---|
| NO LONGER SHALL THE IMMODEST LUST | IN GLORIOUS EPIPHANIE | 101 | 52 | 253 | 39 |
| IF MY BASE LUST, | CHARITAS NIMIA | 55 | 52 | 280 | 48 |

## LUSTRE

| | | | | | |
|---|---|---|---|---|---|
| AND TH'HEART-BRED LUSTRE OF HIS WORTH, | HIS EPITAPH (HERRYS) | 37 | 46 | 172 | 471 |
| THE LUSTRE OF HIS FACE DID SHINE SOE BRIGHT, | UPON KINGS CORONATION | 33 | MS | 390 | 453 |

## LUSTY

| | | | | | |
|---|---|---|---|---|---|
| (GROWNE LUSTY NOW.) NO VINE SO WEAKE AND YOUNG | OUT OF VIRGIL | 18 | 46 | 155 | 529 |
| SUCH AS COULD WITH LUSTY BREATH | IN MEMORY OF LADY MADRE TERESA | 7 | 46 | 131 | 52 |
| SUCH AS COULD WITH LUSTY BREATH | TERESA | 7 | 52 | 315 | 52 |
| THE LUSTY BRIDEGROOM MADE APPROACH. YOUNG MAN, | ALEXIAS THIRD ELEGIE | 33 | 52 | 336 | 209 |

## LUTE

| | | | | | |
|---|---|---|---|---|---|
| AWAKES HIS LUTE, AND 'GAINST THE FIGHT TO COME | MUSICKS DUELL | 17 | 46 | 149 | 535 |
| (MISTRESSE) I COME. NOW REACH A STRAINE MY LUTE | MUSICKS DUELL | 107 | 46 | 149 | 535 |
| FALLING UPON HIS LUTE. O FIT TO HAVE | MUSICKS DUELL | 167 | 46 | 149 | 535 |
| EXPECTING BY THY VOYCE TO TUNE HIS LUTE. | UPON YORKE HIS BIRTH | 115 | 46 | 176 | 500 |
| WAKE LUTE & HARP | TO THE NAME OF JESUS | 46 | 52 | 239 | 30 |
| THERE AMOROUSE SAPPHO PLAINES UPON HER LUTE | HORATIJ ILLE & NEFASTO | 39 | MS | 382 | 530 |

## LUTES

| | | | | | |
|---|---|---|---|---|---|
| THE LUTES LIGHT GENIUS NOW DOES PROUDLY RISE, | MUSICKS DUELL | 135 | 46 | 149 | 535 |
| BRING ALL YOUR LUTES & HARPS OF HEAVN & EARTH. | TO THE NAME OF JESUS | 74 | 52 | 239 | 30 |

## LUTES-MASTER

| | | | | | |
|---|---|---|---|---|---|
| A SWEET LUTES-MASTER. IN WHOSE GENTLE AIRES | MUSICKS DUELL | 5 | 46 | 149 | 535 |

## LYCAON

| | | | | | |
|---|---|---|---|---|---|
| WOLVISH LYCAON HERE A PLACE HATH WON. | SOSPETTO D'HERODE | 334 | 46 | 109 | 216 |

## LYONS

| | | | | | |
|---|---|---|---|---|---|
| WITH THE FIERCE LYONS OF THERODAMAS. | SOSPETTO D'HERODE | 354 | 46 | 109 | 216 |

## LYRE

| | | | | | |
|---|---|---|---|---|---|
| FOUNDED TO TH' NAME OF GREAT APOLLO'S LYRE. | MUSICKS DUELL | 74 | 46 | 149 | 535 |
| OF HIS OWNE BREATH, WHICH MARRYED TO HIS LYRE | MUSICKS DUELL | 117 | 46 | 149 | 535 |
| AND TEACH THY LOV'D NAME TO THEIR NOBLE LYRE. | CHARITAS NIMIA | 28 | 52 | 280 | 48 |
| IN HIGH-BUILT NUMBERS WAKES HIS GOLDEN LYRE. | HORATIJ ILLE & NEFASTO | 42 | MS | 382 | 530 |

## LYRES

| | | | | | |
|---|---|---|---|---|---|
| AND FITT IT TO SO FARR INFERIOR LYRES. | TO THE NAME OF JESUS | 102 | 52 | 239 | 30 |

## MAD

| | | | | |
|---|---|---|---|---|
| OF WHICH THE MORNING KNEW NOT, MAD WITH SPIGHT | SOSPETTO D'HERODE | 117 | 46 109 | 216 |
| OF A MAD STORME THESE BLOOMY JOYES ALL TORE, | UPON DEATH OF HERRYS | 33 | 46 167 | 466 |
| MIX THE MAD SONS OF MEN IN MUTUALL BLOOD, | DESCRIPTION RELIGIOUS HOUSE | 8 | 52 338 | 213 |
| OF THEIR MAD SIN. (HOW GREAT, AND YETT HOW VAYNE.) | OUT OF GROTIUS | 30 | MS 398 | 198 |

## MADNES

| | | | | |
|---|---|---|---|---|
| AND BY STRANGE WITT OF MADNES WREST | IN GLORIOUS EPIPHANIE | 111 | 52 253 | 39 |

## MADNESSE

| | | | | |
|---|---|---|---|---|
| DREST IN THE GLORIOUS MADNESSE OF A MUSE, | TO THE MORNING | 23 | 46 183 | 497 |

## MADNESSES

| | | | | |
|---|---|---|---|---|
| WHAT MINE OWN MADNESSES HAVE DONE WITH ME, | CHARITAS NIMIA | 34 | 52 280 | 48 |

## MADE

| | | | | |
|---|---|---|---|---|
| HIS CURIOUS FINGERS LENT, HER VOYCE MADE GOOD, | MUSICKS DUELL | 14 | 46 149 | 535 |
| A CAPRING CHEEREFULLNESSE, AND MADE THEM SING | MUSICKS DUELL | 28 | 46 149 | 535 |
| CERTAIN HARD WORDS MADE INTO PILLS, | IN PRAISE OF LESSIUS | 8 | 46 156 | 510 |
| WHERE HUNGRY WARRE HAD MADE HIMSELF A GUEST, | THE BEGINNING OF HELIODORUS | 26 | 46 158 | 517 |
| WHAT A RECKONING HAST THOU MADE, | UPON THE DEATH OF A GENTLEMAN | 5 | 46 166 | 472 |
| AND THERE BE WORDS NOT MADE WITH LUNGS, | UPON THE DEATH OF A GENTLEMAN | 28 | 46 166 | 472 |
| TO BEE MADE SO SWEETLY SAD, | THE WEEPER | 66 | 46 79 | 120 |
| FOR HIS WHITE SOULE IS MADE, | ON BAPTIZED AETHIOPIAN | 4 | 46 65 | 29 |
| GOD SPAKE ONCE WHEN HEE ALL THINGS MADE, | AND HE ANSWERED NOTHING | 3 | 46 91 | 22 |
| THE WORLD WAS MADE OF NOTHING THEN, | AND HE ANSWERED NOTHING | 5 | 46 91 | 22 |
| 'TIS MADE BY NOTHYNG NOW AGAINE, | AND HE ANSWERED NOTHING | 6 | 46 91 | 22 |
| KEEPE BUT THE SCORE OF THEM THAT MADE HIM DYE, | YEE BUILD SEPULCHRES | 4 | 46 95 | 21 |
| THE HEAV'N-REBUKED SHADES MADE HAST AWAY, | SOSPETTO D'HERODE | 114 | 46 109 | 216 |
| AMAZ'D THE MIDNIGHT WORLD, AND MADE A DAY | SOSPETTO D'HERODE | 116 | 46 109 | 216 |
| THE GOLDEN EYES OF NIGHT, WHOSE BEAME MADE BRIGHT | SOSPETTO D'HERODE | 131 | 46 109 | 216 |
| THAT HEE WHO MADE THE FIRE, SHOULD FEARE THE COLD, | SOSPETTO D'HERODE | 180 | 46 109 | 216 |
| WHERE NEVER WING OF ANGELL YET MADE WAY | SOSPETTO D'HERODE | 222 | 46 109 | 216 |
| THUS SPOKE TH'IMPATIENT PRINCE, AND MADE A PAUSE, | SOSPETTO D'HERODE | 257 | 46 109 | 216 |
| HIMSELFE A STRANGER TO, HIS OWNE HAD MADE, | SOSPETTO D'HERODE | 404 | 46 109 | 216 |
| MADE FRUITFULL THY FAIRE SOULE, GOE NOW | IN MEMORY OF LADY MADRE TERESA | 170 | 46 131 | 52 |
| BE WHAT THY BEAUTIES, NOT OUR BLOTS, HAVE MADE THEE, | ON A TREATISE OF CHARITY | 3 | 46 137 | 69 |
| OF FAITH, A MOUNTAINE WORD, MADE UP OF AIRE, | ON A TREATISE OF CHARITY | 53 | 46 137 | 69 |
| WITH A NEW MORNING MADE OF GEMS, | AN HIMNE FOR CIRCUMCISION | 22 | 46 141 | 37 |
| WHOSE RISING GLORIES MADE SUCH HASTE TO HIDE | UPON DEATH OF HERRYS | 4 | 46 167 | 466 |
| THE SUNNE HIMSELFE OFT WISHT TO SIT, AND MADE | UPON DEATH OF HERRYS | 10 | 46 167 | 466 |
| MADE HEAVENS RADIANT FACE LOOKE FOULE, | UPON DEATH OF DESIRED HERRYS | 52 | 46 168 | 467 |
| MADE SO REVEREND, EVEN IN YOUTH, | HIS EPITAPH (HERRYS) | 16 | 46 172 | 471 |
| AND SEEM'D TO MAKE AN ISLE, BUT MADE A WORLD, | UPON YORKE HIS BIRTH | 28 | 46 176 | 500 |
| ERST HATH MADE MY HEART A MOTHER, | LOVES HOROSCOPE | 2 | 46 185 | 483 |
| THUS MADE EVEN, | OUT OF THE ITALIAN (1) | 29 | 46 188 | 545 |
| TO THAT ONE SENSE, MADE ALL ELSE THRALL, | OUT OF THE ITALIAN (3) | 7 | 46 190 | 549 |
| A FACE MADE UP | WISHES SUPPOSED MISTRESSE | 28 | 46 195 | 479 |
| MADE SHORT BY LOVERS PLAY, | WISHES SUPPOSED MISTRESSE | 83 | 46 195 | 479 |
| THAT MADE IT LONG EXCUSE THE LENGTH, | TO THE QUEEN | 14 | 48 215 | 501 |
| THEIR FURY BUT MADE WAY | TO THE NAME OF JESUS | 209 | 52 239 | 30 |
| OF WRATH, & MADE THEE WAY THROUGH ALL THOSE WOUNDS, | TO THE NAME OF JESUS | 224 | 52 239 | 30 |
| MADE HIS OWN BED E'RE HE WAS BORN, | IN HOLY NATIVITY | 49 | 52 246 | 76 |
| WITH A NEW MORNING MADE OF GEMMES, | NEW YEAR'S DAY | 22 | 52 251 | 37 |
| A DARKENES MADE OF TOO MUCH DAY, | IN GLORIOUS EPIPHANIE | 18 | 52 253 | 39 |
| TO HIM, WHO BY THESE MORTALL CLOUDS HAST MADE | IN GLORIOUS EPIPHANIE | 46 | 52 253 | 39 |
| FOR THAT ONE ECLIPSE HE MADE | IN GLORIOUS EPIPHANIE | 119 | 52 253 | 39 |
| LONG MADE TH'HARMONIOUS ORBES ALL MUTE TO US | IN GLORIOUS EPIPHANIE | 132 | 52 253 | 39 |
| BY THE LOVE-SICK WORLD BIN MADE | IN GLORIOUS EPIPHANIE | 136 | 52 253 | 39 |
| THE FATHER'S WORD & WISDOM, MADE | OFFICE H. CROSS MATINES | 12 | 52 265 | 66 |
| IN WOES THAT WERE NOT MADE FOR HIM, | SANCTA MARIA DOLORUM | 34 | 52 283 | 162 |
| NATURE, & NAME, TO BE MADE GOOD | LAUDA SION SALVATOREM | 35 | 52 294 | 178 |
| HE THAT MADE ALL THINGS, HAD NOT DONE | O GLORIOSA DOMINA | 5 | 52 302 | 194 |
| TILL HE HAD MADE HIMSELF THY SON | O GLORIOSA DOMINA | 6 | 52 302 | 194 |
| MIXT & MADE FRIENDS BY LOVE'S SWEET POWRES, | WEEPER | 102 | 52 307 | 120 |
| MADE FRUITFULL THY FAIR SOUL, GOE NOW | TERESA | 169 | 52 315 | 52 |
| MEN HAD NOT SPURN'D AT MOUNTAINES, NOR MADE WARRS | ALEXIAS THIRD ELEGIE | 9 | 52 336 | 209 |
| WITH HAPPY GAIN HER MAIDEN VOWES MADE GOOD, | ALEXIAS THIRD ELEGIE | 32 | 52 336 | 209 |
| THE LUSTY BRIDEGROOM MADE APPROACH, YOUNG MAN, | ALEXIAS THIRD ELEGIE | 33 | 52 336 | 209 |
| LOVE MADE THE BED, THEY'L TAKE NO HARM | AN EPITAPH UPON MARRIED COUPLE | 14 | 52 339 | 478 |
| CERTAIN HARD WORDS MADE INTO PILLS, | TEMPERANCE | 8 | 52 342 | 510 |
| OFT HAVE MY HUNGRY KISSES MADE THINE EYES | LUKE 2. QUAERIT JESUM | 35 | MS 379 | 11 |
| THAT MADE GREAT LOVE A MAN OF WARRE, | IN CICATRICES DOMINI JESU | 6 | MS 381 | 27 |
| AND DURST NOT TOUCH IT, HEERE IT MADE NOE STAY, | ON GUNPOWDER-TREASON | 54 | MS 384 | 458 |
| AN OCEAN COULD HAVE MADE T' HAVE DROWNED THEE, | UPON GUNPOWDER TREASON | 36 | MS 386 | 460 |
| IT MADE THE VIRGIN PHOENIX COME FARRE | UPON KINGS CORONATION | 30 | MS 390 | 453 |
| MADE EVERY MORTALL GLADLY SACRIFICE | UPON KINGS CORONATION | 36 | MS 390 | 453 |
| WITH SUCH A SUGRED LIVERY MADE FINE, | UPON BIRTH PRINCESSE E | 7 | MS 391 | 456 |
| OR JOVE A FATHER WILL BE MADE BY THEE) | EX EUPHORMIONE | 2 | MS 392 | 525 |
| AND MADE IT BURNE IN LOVE, 'TWAS NOT THE RAGE, | AN ELEGY MR STANNINOW | 33 | MS 394 | 473 |
| MADE LITLE, NOT A LITTLE TO HIS RAGE) | OUT OF GROTIUS | 24 | MS 398 | 198 |

## MAD'ST

| | | | | |
|---|---|---|---|---|
| THOU MAD'ST BOLD PROOFE UPON THE BROW OF HEAV'N, | SOSPETTO D'HERODE | 266 | 46 109 | 216 |

MAEANDERS

    AND FRISKE IN CURL'D MAEANDERS.  HEE WILL THROW    ON A FOULE MORNING    20  46 181 495

MAGAZINS

    WHAT MAGAZINS OF IMMORTALL ARMES THERE SHINE.    FLAMING HEART    55  52 324  61

MAGDALENE

    THY FAIRE EYES SWEET MAGDALENE.    THE WEEPER    6  46  79 120
    THY FAIR EYES, SWEET MAGDALENE.    WEEPER    6  52 307 120

MAGI

    OF MY WEAKE FEET THE PERSIAN MAGI LAY    OUT OF GROTIUS    37  MS 398 198

MAGICK

    WHAT MAGICK BOLTS, WHAT MYSTICK BARRES    TO COUNTESSE OF DENBIGH    17  52 236 146

MAGICK-BOLTS

    WHAT MAGICK-BOLTS, WHAT MYSTICK BARRS    AGAINST IRRESOLUTION AND DELAY    11  52 347 146

MAID

    THAT BREATHES AT ONCE BOTH MAID AND MOTHER.    A HYMNE OF THE NATIVITY    63  46 106  76
    HOW SHE THAT IS A MAID SHOULD PROVE A MOTHER.    SOSPETTO D'HERODE    163  46 109 216
    RISE THEN, IMMORTALL MAID.  RELIGION RISE.    ON A TREATISE OF CHARITY    1  46 137  69
    RISE THEN (FAIRE BLEW-EY'D MAID) RISE AND DISCOVER    ON A FOULE MORNING    27  46 181 495
    THAT BREATHES AT ONCE BOTH MAID & MOTHER,    IN HOLY NATIVITY    89  52 246  76
    HERE'T WAS THE ROMAN MAID FOUND A HARD FATE    ALEXIAS FIRST ELEGIE    29  52 334 204

HAND-MAID

    BY WHOM (AS HEAV'NS ILLUSTRIOUS HAND-MAID) RAIS'D    SOSPETTO D'HERODE    134  46 109 216

HANDMAID

    THY HOLYEST, HUMBLEST, HANDMAID CHARITIE.    ON A TREATISE OF CHARITY    14  46 137  69

MOTHER-MAID

    GATHER NOW THY GREIF'S RIPE FRUIT. GREAT MOTHER-MAID.    OFFICE H. CROSS EVENSONG    7  52 273 101

MAIDS

    THE FOULE QUEENS MOST ABHORRED MAIDS OF HONOUR    SOSPETTO D'HERODE    337  46 109 216

MAIDEN

    SUCH THE MAIDEN GEMME    THE TEARE    25  46  84  50
    THE MOONE OF MAIDEN STARRES.  THY WHITE    IN MEMORY OF LADY MADRE TERESA    124  46 131  52
    AS THIS MODEST MAIDEN LILLY.    AN HIMNE FOR CIRCUMCISION    11  46 141  37
    RAVISHT THE MAIDEN BLOSSOMS, AND DOWNE BORE    UPON DEATH OF HERRYS    34  46 167 466
    SPITE OF ALL THE MAIDEN SNOW    THOUGH NOW 'TIS NEITHER    7  MS 397 492
    AS THIS MODEST MAIDEN LILLY    NEW YEAR'S DAY    11  52 251  37
    AND CALL THE MAIDEN EVE THEIR MOTHER.    O GLORIOSA DOMINA    26  52 302 194
    SUCH THE MAIDEN GEMME    WEEPER    61  52 307 120
    THE MOON OF MAIDEN STARRS, THY WHITE    TERESA    123  52 315  52
    OF SUTERS THAT BESEIGE YOUR MAIDEN BREST,    TO SAME CONCERNING CHOISE    3  52 331  66
    WAS MAIDEN WIFE & MAIDEN MOTHER TOO.    ALEXIAS THIRD ELEGIE    30  52 336 209
    WAS MAIDEN WIFE & MAIDEN MOTHER TOO.    ALEXIAS THIRD ELEGIE    30  52 336 209
    WITH HAPPY GAIN HER MAIDEN VOWES MADE GOOD.    ALEXIAS THIRD ELEGIE    32  52 336 209
    THY MAIDEN STREAMES SOE SOONE TO NEPTUNES BED.    AN ELEGIE ON DR PORTER    2  MS 395 476

MAIDENHEAD

    HOPES CHASTE KISSE WRONGS NO MORE JOYES MAIDENHEAD,    ON HOPE    39  46 143  71
    HOPE'S CHAST STEALTH HARMES NO MORE JOYE'S MAIDENHEAD    (ON) HOPE    19  52 345  71

MAYDENHEAD

    FOR A DYING MAYDENHEAD.    WISHES SUPPOSED MISTRESSE    75  46 195 479

MAIDEN-BLOSSOMES

    THE TIMOUROUS MAIDEN-BLOSSOMES ON EACH BOUGH,    UPON DEATH OF HERRYS    23  46 167 466

MAINE

    HOPE OF A PREY. THERE TO THE MAINE LAND TY'D    THE BEGINNING OF HELIODORUS    10  46 158 517

MAINTAIN

    MAINTAIN THE WILL IN THESE STRANGE WARRES.    TO COUNTESSE OF DENBIGH    18  52 236 146
    WHEN HOLY FIRES MAINTAIN LOVE'S HEAVNLY LIFE.    ALEXIAS THIRD ELEGIE    52  52 336 209
    THOU TO MAINTAIN THEIR PRETIOUS STRIFE    TEMPERANCE    3  52 342 510
    MAINTAIN THE WILL IN THESE STRANGE WARRS.    AGAINST IRRESOLUTION AND DELAY    12  52 347 146

## MAINTAINE

| | | | | | |
|---|---|---|---|---|---|
| THOU TO MAINTAINE THEIR CRUELL STRIFE, | IN PRAISE OF LESSIUS | 3 | 46 | 156 | 510 |
| OUR FREE TRAFICK FOR HEAVEN, WE MAY MAINTAINE, | AN APOLOGIE FOR HYMNE (TERESA) | 19 | 46 | 136 | 59 |
| OUR FREE TRAFFIQUE FOR HEAV'N, WE MAY MAINTAINE | AN APOLOGIE FOR (TERESA) HYMNE | 19 | 52 | 322 | 59 |

## MAINTAINING

| | | | | | |
|---|---|---|---|---|---|
| MAINTAINING T'WIXT THY WORLD & OURS | IN GLORIOUS EPIPHANIE | 213 | 52 | 253 | 39 |

## MAJA'S

| | | | | | |
|---|---|---|---|---|---|
| SHALL BLESSE THE FRUITFULL MAJA'S BED, | A HYMNE OF THE NATIVITY | 78 | 46 | 106 | 76 |
| SHALL BLESSE THE FRUITFULL MAJA'S BED | IN HOLY NATIVITY | 98 | 52 | 246 | 76 |

## MAJESTY

| | | | | | |
|---|---|---|---|---|---|
| IN HER BRIGHTEST MAJESTY, | THE WEEPER | 50 | 46 | 79 | 120 |
| TO THEE MEEKE MAJESTY, SOFT KING | A HYMNE OF THE NATIVITY | 83 | 46 | 106 | 76 |
| AND TO MAKE UP HELLS MAJESTY, EACH HORNE | SOSPETTO D'HERODE | 47 | 46 | 109 | 216 |
| THAT HEAV'NS HIGH MAJESTY HIS COURT SHOULD KEEPE | SOSPETTO D'HERODE | 181 | 46 | 109 | 216 |
| TO MAJESTY, AND FULNESSE, DEIGNE TO DWELL. | UPON YORKE HIS BIRTH | 24 | 46 | 176 | 500 |
| WERE TREASON 'GAINST THAT MAJESTY | TO THE QUEEN | 3 | 48 | 215 | 501 |
| AND COUCH BEFORE THE DAZELING LIGHT OF THY DREAD MAJESTY. | TO THE NAME OF JESUS | 235 | 52 | 239 | 30 |
| TO THEE, MEEK MAJESTY. SOFT KING | IN HOLY NATIVITY | 103 | 52 | 246 | 76 |
| FIX HERE, FAIR MAJESTY. MAY YOUR HEART NE'RE MISSE | TO THE QUEEN'S MAJESTY | 21 | 52 | 261 | 47 |
| IN HER BRIGHTEST MAJESTY | WEEPER | 38 | 52 | 79 | 120 |
| THY GREISLY MAJESTY, HELL'S BLACKEST QUEENE. | HORATIJ ILLE & NEFASTO | 34 | MS | 362 | 530 |
| IN THIS INFERNALL MAJESTY CLOSE SHROWD | UPON GUNPOWDER TREASON | 23 | MS | 387 | 461 |
| WITH HEAVEN ITSELF FOR STATELY MAJESTY. | UPON KINGS CORONATION | 10 | MS | 389 | 454 |
| BRIGHT STARRE OF MAJESTY, OH SHEDD ON MEE | UPON BIRTH PRINCESSE E | 1 | MS | 391 | 456 |

## MAJESTIE

| | | | | | |
|---|---|---|---|---|---|
| A MAJESTIE THAT MAY BESEEM THY THRONE. | ON A TREATISE OF CHARITY | 20 | 46 | 137 | 69 |

## MAKE

| | | | | | |
|---|---|---|---|---|---|
| DOTH TUNE THE SPHAEARES, AND MAKE HEAVENS SELFE LOOKE | MUSICKS DUELL | 118 | 46 | 149 | 535 |
| LEST HIS KINDNESSE MAKE THEE BLEED. | OUT OF GREEKE CUPID'S CRYER | 72 | 46 | 159 | 519 |
| AND HEAVEN WILL MAKE A FEAST, | THE WEEPER | 33 | 46 | 79 | 120 |
| RIPE, WILL MAKE THE RICHER WINE. | THE TEARE | 30 | 46 | 84 | 50 |
| AND ONE OF THEIR BRIGHT CHORUS MAKE THEE. | THE TEARE | 42 | 46 | 84 | 50 |
| TO SPEAKE AND MAKE THE BLIND MAN SEE, | THE BLIND CURED | 3 | 46 | 91 | 19 |
| UNMOV'D TO SEE ONE WRETCHED, IS TO MAKE HIM SO. | AND A CERTAINE PRIEST PASSED | 4 | 46 | 94 | 17 |
| HARKE HOW SHE BIDS HER FRIGHTED DROPS MAKE HAST, | TO PONTIUS WASHING HANDS | 13 | 46 | 94 | 23 |
| EXPECT A SEA, MY HEART SHALL MAKE IT GOOD. | OUR LORD IN HIS CIRCUMCISION | 4 | 46 | 98 | 9 |
| OF ALL THE GLORYES MAKE NOONE GAY | EASTER DAY | 7 | 46 | 100 | 26 |
| MAKE HIGH NOONE FORGET HIS BEAMES. | PSALME 23 | 16 | 46 | 102 | 5 |
| AND MAKE DARKNESSE SELFE AFRAID. | PSALME 23 | 42 | 46 | 102 | 5 |
| AND TO MAKE UP HELLS MAJESTY, EACH HORNE | SOSPETTO D'HERODE | 47 | 46 | 109 | 216 |
| WHERE JORDAN MELTS HIS CHRYSTALL, TO MAKE FAIRE | SOSPETTO D'HERODE | 85 | 46 | 109 | 216 |
| NEW MATTER, TO MAKE GOOD HIS GREAT SUSPECT. | SOSPETTO D'HERODE | 88 | 46 | 109 | 216 |
| MAKE PROUD THE RUBY PORTALLS OF THE EAST. | SOSPETTO D'HERODE | 122 | 46 | 109 | 216 |
| TO MAKE THE PARTNER OF HIS OWNE PURE RAY. | SOSPETTO D'HERODE | 218 | 46 | 109 | 216 |
| RATHER MAKE UP TO THY NEW MISERIES. | SOSPETTO D'HERODE | 245 | 46 | 109 | 216 |
| A BORROWED BEING, MAKE THY BOLD DEFENCE. | SOSPETTO D'HERODE | 252 | 46 | 109 | 216 |
| GOE NOW, MAKE MUCH OF THESE. WAGE STILL THEIR WARS | SOSPETTO D'HERODE | 447 | 46 | 109 | 216 |
| MAKE TO THY REASON MAN, AND MOCKE THY DOUBTS. | SOSPETTO D'HERODE | 521 | 46 | 109 | 216 |
| TO MAKE IMMORTALL DRESSINGS | ON A PRAYER BOOKE | 37 | 46 | 126 | 139 |
| AND MAKE HIS MANSION IN THE MILDE | IN MEMORY OF LADY MADRE TERESA | 13 | 46 | 131 | 52 |
| SCARCE HAD SHEE BLOOD ENOUGH, TO MAKE | IN MEMORY OF LADY MADRE TERESA | 25 | 46 | 131 | 52 |
| MAKE THE MARTYR OR THE MAN. | IN MEMORY OF LADY MADRE TERESA | 34 | 46 | 131 | 52 |
| HIS IS THE DART MUST MAKE THE DEATH | IN MEMORY OF LADY MADRE TERESA | 79 | 46 | 131 | 52 |
| AND IN HER FIRST RANKES MAKE THEE ROOME. | IN MEMORY OF LADY MADRE TERESA | 127 | 46 | 131 | 52 |
| THOUGH OUR SWEETNESSE CANNOT MAKE | ON THE ASSUMPTION | 50 | 46 | 139 | 114 |
| LET HIM MAKE POORE THE PURPLE EAST, | AN HIMNE FOR CIRCUMCISION | 17 | 46 | 141 | 37 |
| TO MAKE HIMSELFE RICH IN HIS RISE, | AN HIMNE FOR CIRCUMCISION | 26 | 46 | 141 | 37 |
| THY BOSOME AND MAKE ROOME. THOU ART OPPREST | UPON YORKE HIS BIRTH | 3 | 46 | 176 | 500 |
| AND SEEM'D TO MAKE AN ISLE, BUT MADE A WORLD. | UPON YORKE HIS BIRTH | 28 | 46 | 176 | 500 |
| MAKE SUCH ANOTHER SWEET COMPARISON. | UPON YORKE HIS BIRTH | 52 | 46 | 176 | 500 |
| TO MAKE HIS COSTLY CRADLE OF THY BEERE. | UPON YORKE HIS BIRTH | 95 | 46 | 176 | 500 |
| O MAYST THOU THUS MAKE ALL THE YEARE THINE OWNE, | UPON YORKE HIS BIRTH | 96 | 46 | 176 | 500 |
| BUT GODS ARE GRATIOUS. AND THEIR ALTARS, MAKE | UPON YORKE HIS BIRTH | 116 | 46 | 176 | 500 |
| AND MAKE THEIR FLEECES GOLDEN AS THY LOCKES. | ON A FOULE MORNING | 6 | 46 | 181 | 495 |
| MY OWNE APOLLO, TRY IF I CAN MAKE | TO THE MORNING | 16 | 46 | 183 | 497 |
| MARROW TO MY PLUMPE GENIUS, MAKE IT LIVE | TO THE MORNING | 22 | 46 | 183 | 497 |
| CAN MAKE DAYES FOREHEAD BRIGHT. | WISHES SUPPOSED MISTRESSE | 95 | 46 | 195 | 479 |
| AND OF A METEOR MAKE A STARR. | TO COUNTESSE OF DENBIGH | 30 | 52 | 236 | 146 |
| LET HIM MAKE POOR THE PURPLE EAST, | NEW YEAR'S DAY | 17 | 52 | 251 | 37 |
| TO MAKE HIMSELFE RICH IN HIS RISE, | NEW YEAR'S DAY | 26 | 52 | 251 | 37 |
| BRIGHT BABE. WHOSE AWFULL BEAUTYES MAKE | IN GLORIOUS EPIPHANIE | 1 | 52 | 253 | 39 |
| AND MAKE THE NIGHT IT SELF THEIR TORCH TO THEE. | IN GLORIOUS EPIPHANIE | 188 | 52 | 253 | 39 |
| AND MAKE OUR DARKNES SERVE THY DAY. | IN GLORIOUS EPIPHANIE | 212 | 52 | 253 | 39 |
| WE VOW TO MAKE BRAVE WAY | IN GLORIOUS EPIPHANIE | 221 | 52 | 253 | 39 |
| HE IS FROM SUN ENOUGH TO MAKE THY STARR, | IN GLORIOUS EPIPHANIE | 247 | 52 | 253 | 39 |
| O GOD MAKE SPEED TO SAVE ME. | OFFICE H. CROSS MATINES | 5 | 52 | 265 | 86 |
| O LORD MAKE HAST TO HELP ME. | OFFICE H. CROSS MATINES | 6 | 52 | 265 | 86 |
| GALL, & MORE BITTER MOCKS, SHALL MAKE IT UP. | OFFICE H. CROSS SIXT | 10 | 52 | 270 | 97 |
| TO MAKE A KIND OF LIFE FOR MY LORD'S DEATH, | OFFICE H. CROSS RECOMMENDATION | 6 | 52 | 276 | 106 |
| IT WAS THY WOOD HE MEANT SHOULD MAKE THE THRONE | VEXILLA REGIS | 23 | 52 | 277 | 156 |
| GLORIOUS, OR GREIVOUS MORE. THUS TO MAKE GOOD | VEXILLA REGIS | 29 | 52 | 277 | 156 |

PAGE 252

```
                                                  MAKE BUT A SIMPLE MERCHANT MAN.                CHARITAS NIMIA                         6   52 280  48
                                                  WHY SHOULD HIS UNSTAINED BREST MAKE GOOD       CHARITAS NIMIA                        61   52 280  48
                                                  O MY SAVIOVR, MAKE ME SEE                      CHARITAS NIMIA                        63   52 280  48
                                                  HAIL. & STRIKE HOME & MAKE ME SEE              SANCTA MARIA DOLORUM                  73   52 263 162
                                                  OR IF HE MAKE LESSE HAST,                      IN GLORIOUS ASSUMPTION B. LADY        24   52 304 114
                                                  THOUGH OUR SWEET CANNOT MAKE                   IN GLORIOUS ASSUMPTION B. LADY        55   52 304 114
                                                  RIPE, WILL MAKE THE RICHER WINE.               WEEPER                                66   52 307 120
                                                  AND HEAVN WILL MAKE A FEAST.                   WEEPER                                69   52 307 120
                                                  WHAT MAKE YOU HERE. WHAT HOPES CAN TICE        WEEPER                               166   52 307 120
                                                  SCARSE HAS SHE BLOOD ENOUGH TO MAKE            TERESA                                25   52 315  52
                                                  MAKE THE MARTYR, OR THE MAN.                   TERESA                                34   52 315  52
                                                  HIS IS THE DART MUST MAKE THE DEATH            TERESA                                79   52 315  52
                                                  AND IN HER FIRST RANKES MAKE THEE ROOM         TERESA                               126   52 315  52
                                                  MAKE NOT TOO MUCH HAST TO' ADMIRE              FLAMING HEART                          3   52 324  61
                                                  READERS, BE RUL'D BY ME,  & MAKE               FLAMING HEART                          7   52 324  61
                                                  TO MAKE IMMORTALL DRESSINGS                    PRAYER TO GENTLE-WOMAN                43   52 328 139
                                                  AND TRY'D TO MAKE A WIDOW ERE A WIFE.          ALEXIAS FIRST ELEGIE                   6   52 334 204
                                                  AND SURE WHERE LOVERS MAKE THEIR WATRY GRAVES  ALEXIAS FIRST ELEGIE                  25   52 334 204
                                                  MAKE BIGGE THY BREST WITH IMMORTALL FIRE.      ALEXIAS THIRD ELEGIE                  22   52 336 209
                                                  NOR DOE EMBRACES ONELY MAKE A BRIDE.           ALEXIAS THIRD ELEGIE                  28   52 336 209
                                                  KIND LOVES KEEP HOUSE, LY CLOSE, AND MAKE NO NOISE.  DESCRIPTION RELIGIOUS HOUSE     33   52 338 213
                                                  EACH MINDFULL PLANT HASTS TO MAKE GOOD         AGAINST IRRESOLUTION AND DELAY        35   52 347 146
                                                  AND SEEMS TO SAY, MAKE HASTE, MY BROTHER.      AGAINST IRRESOLUTION AND DELAY        44   52 347 146
                                                  MAKE WINGS AT LEAST OF THEIR OWN WEIGHT,       AGAINST IRRESOLUTION AND DELAY        49   52 347 146
                                                  MAKE HAST, & COME, OR E'RE MY GREIFE, & I      LUKE 2. QUAERIT JESUM                 17   MS 379   11
                                                  MAKE HAST, & DY.                               LUKE 2. QUAERIT JESUM                 18   MS 379   11
                                                  BLACK DISMALL HORROR. COME. MAKE PERFECT NOW   UPON GUNPOWDER TREASON                20   MS 387 461
                                                  RAVISH THE DANCING ORBES. MAKE THEM MOUNT HIGHER  UPON KINGS CORONATION               2   MS 389 454
                                                  EACH LITTLE BEAME OF WHICH WOULD MAKE A SUNNE.  UPON KINGS CORONATION               30   MS 389 454
                                                  Y' HAD DONE ENOUGH TO MAKE THE LAZY GROUND     UPON BIRTH PRINCESSE E                31   MS 391 456
                                                  AND MAKE THEM LAUGH, WHICH FROWN'D, & WEPT BEFORE.  AN ELEGY MR STANNINOW            14   MS 394 473
                                                  FORC'T THIS PRIME FLOWRE OF YOUTH TO MAKE SUCH HAST  AN ELEGY MR STANNINOW           28   MS 394 473
                                                  MAKE THEIR SCAR'D SOULES TAKE WING, & FLY AWAY.  AN ELEGIE ON DR PORTER              30   MS 395 476

MAK'ST

                                                  THOU CHEAT'ST US FORD. MAK'ST ONE SEEME TWO BY ART.  UPON FORD'S TRAGEDYES            1   46 181 495

MAKES

                                                  AND MAKES A PRETTY EARTHQUAKE IN HER BREAST,   MUSICKS DUELL                         89   46 149 535
                                                  THAT WHICH MAKES US HAVE NO NEED               IN PRAISE OF LESSIUS                  13   46 156 510
                                                  AND FRAUD. HEE MAKES POORE MORTALLS HURTS,     OUT OF GREEKE CUPID'S CRYER           31   46 159 519
                                                  MAKES THE SUNNE (OF FLAMES THE SIRE)           OUT OF GREEKE CUPID'S CRYER           55   46 159 519
                                                  WHAT EVER MAKES HEAVENS FORE-HEAD FINE.        THE WEEPER                            12   46  79 120
                                                  MAKES SORROW HALFE SO RICH,                    THE WEEPER                            45   46  79 120
                                                  MAKES THY EVER-WATRY EYES                      THE WEEPER                            98   46  79 120
                                                  STONY AMAZEMENT MAKES THEM STAND               NEITHER DURST MAN ASKE                 9   46  92  20
                                                  MAKES ME DOUBT IF HEAVEN WILL GATHER.          UPON INFANT MARTYRS                    3   46  95  10
                                                  THY FAMES FULL NOISE, MAKES PROUD THE PATIENT EARTH,  SOSPETTO D'HERODE             29   46 109 216
                                                  INHUMANE ERISI-CTHON TOO MAKES ONE.            SOSPETTO D'HERODE                    332   46 109 216
                                                  HER SELFE A WHILE SHE LAYES ASIDE, AND MAKES   SOSPETTO D'HERODE                    417   46 109 216
                                                  MAKES HIM IMPATIENT OF THE LINGRING LIGHT.     SOSPETTO D'HERODE                    495   46 109 216
                                                  MAKES HASTE TO MEET HER MORNING SPOWSE.        ON A PRAYER BOOKE                     96   46 126 398
                                                  CHRISTS FAITH MAKES BUT ONE BODY OF ALL SOULES,  AN APOLOGIE FOR HYMNE (TERESA)      17   46 136  59
                                                  SHEE CLIMBES, AND MAKES A FARRE MORE MILKY WAY.  ON THE ASSUMPTION                    6   46 139 114
                                                  MAKES MANY A MOURNING PAPER PUT ON BLACKE.     UPON STANINOUGH'S DEATH                2   46 175 475
                                                  AND SO THOU ART, THEIR PRESENCE MAKES THEE SO,  UPON YORKE HIS BIRTH                 17   46 176 500
                                                  NOR MAKES THE WHOLE WORLD THY HALF-SPHEAR.     IN GLORIOUS EPIPHANIE                 41   52 253  39
                                                  TALL TREE OF LIFE. THY TRUTH MAKES GOOD        VEXILLA REGIS                         19   52 277 156
                                                  THE RECEIVING MOUTH HERE MAKES                 LAUDA SION SALVATOREM                 43   52 294 178
                                                  O LET THAT LOVE WHICH THUS MAKES THEE          LAUDA SION SALVATOREM                 73   52 294 178
                                                  SHE CLIMBS. AND MAKES A FARRE MORE MILKEY WAY.  IN GLORIOUS ASSUMPTION B. LADY        6   52 304 114
                                                  WHATEVER MAKES HEAVN'S FOREHEAD FINE.          WEEPER                                12   52 307 120
                                                  CHRIST'S FAITH MAKES BUT ONE BODY OF ALL SOULES  AN APOLOGIE FOR (TERESA) HYMNE      17   52 322  59
                                                  MAKES HAST TO MEET HER MORNING SPOUSE          PRAYER TO GENTLE-WOMAN               102   52 328 139
                                                  MAKES MANY A MOURNING PAPER PUT ON BLACK.      DEATH'S LECTURE                        2   52 340 475
                                                  THAT WHICH MAKES US HAVE NO NEED               TEMPERANCE                            11   52 342 510
                                                  OF LOVES ALL-DARING HAND, THAT MAKES ME BURNE.  EX EUPHORMIONE                        5   MS 392 525
                                                  MAKES ME CONFESS'T. OH, DOE NOT THOU WITH SCORNE,  EX EUPHORMIONE                     6   MS 392 525

MAKING

                                                  THY GOD WAS MAKING HAST INTO THY ROOFE,        I AM NOT WORTHY                        1   46  90  13
                                                  MAKING HIS MANSION IN THE MILD                 TERESA                                13   52 315  52
                                                  MAKING THEM SKIP OUT OF THEIR DUSTY BED.       ON GUNPOWDER-TREASON                  30   MS 384 458

MAKER

                                                  OF HER GREAT MAKER FIXT HER FLAMING EYE.       UPON BISHOP ANDREWES PICTURE          11   46 163 490

MALICE

                                                  BLACKE WIT OR MALICE CAN OR DARES,             NEITHER DURST MAN ASKE                 2   46  92  20
                                                  THEIR RANK MALICE NOT THEIR NEED.              PSALME 23                             52   46 102   5
                                                  UNMATED MALICE. OH UNPEER'D DESPIGHT.          UPON GUNPOWDER TREASON                 5   MS 386 460

MALIGNANT

                                                  LIFTS HIS MALIGNANT EYES, WASTED WITH CARE,    SOSPETTO D'HERODE                     83   46 109 216
```

## MAN

| | | | | | |
|---|---|---|---|---|---|
| THE MAN PERCEIV'D HIS RIVALL, AND HER ART, | MUSICKS DUELL | 15 | 46 | 149 | 535 |
| GOE POORE MAN THINKE WHAT SHALL BEE, | IN PRAISE OF LESSIUS | 11 | 46 | 156 | 510 |
| WOULDST SEE A MAN ALL, HIS OWNE WEALTH, | IN PRAISE OF LESSIUS | 17 | 46 | 156 | 510 |
| A MAN WHOSE SOBER SOULE CAN TELL, | IN PRAISE OF LESSIUS | 19 | 46 | 156 | 510 |
| WOULD'ST THOU SEE A MAN WHOSE WELL WARMED BLOOD, | IN PRAISE OF LESSIUS | 35 | 46 | 156 | 510 |
| A MAN WHOSE TUNED HUMOURS BEE, | IN PRAISE OF LESSIUS | 37 | 46 | 156 | 510 |
| IN SUMME, WOULDST SEE A MAN THAT CAN | IN PRAISE OF LESSIUS | 45 | 46 | 156 | 510 |
| LIVE TO BEE OLD AND STILL A MAN. | IN PRAISE OF LESSIUS | 46 | 46 | 156 | 510 |
| THOU SPAK'ST AND STREIGHT THE BLIND MAN SAW. | THE BLIND CURED | 2 | 46 | 91 | 19 |
| TO SPEAKE AND MAKE THE BLIND MAN SEE, | THE BLIND CURED | 3 | 46 | 91 | 19 |
| WAS NEVER MAN LORD SPAKE LIKE THEE. | THE BLIND CURED | 4 | 46 | 91 | 19 |
| VAINE MAN. THE STONES THAT ON HIS TOMBE DOE LYE, | YEE BUILD SEPULCHRES | 3 | 46 | 95 | 21 |
| RISE MIGHTY MAN OF WONDERS, AND THY WORLD WITH THEE | EASTER DAY | 3 | 46 | 100 | 26 |
| HEAVEN IN EARTH, AND GOD IN MAN. | A HYMNE OF THE NATIVITY | 56 | 46 | 106 | 76 |
| BETIMES TO BE A SAINT, BEFORE A MAN. | SOSPETTO D'HERODE | 104 | 46 | 109 | 216 |
| DARKE, DUSTY MAN, HE NEEDS WOULD SINGLE FORTH, | SOSPETTO D'HERODE | 217 | 46 | 109 | 216 |
| HER WORDS, SLEEP'ST THOU FOND MAN.   SLEEP'ST THOU. (SAID SHE) | SOSPETTO D'HERODE | 424 | 46 | 109 | 216 |
| WHERE ART THOU MAN. WHAT COWARDLY MISTAKE | SOSPETTO D'HERODE | 457 | 46 | 109 | 216 |
| MAKE TO THY REASON MAN, AND MOCKE THY DOUBTS, | SOSPETTO D'HERODE | 521 | 46 | 109 | 216 |
| MAN TREMBLES AT, WEE STRAIGHT SHALL FIND | IN MEMORY OF LADY MADRE TERESA | 31 | 46 | 131 | 52 |
| MAKE THE MARTYR OR THE MAN. | IN MEMORY OF LADY MADRE TERESA | 34 | 46 | 131 | 52 |
| THE TOTALL SUMME OF MAN APPEARES, | ANOTHER ON HERRYS | 44 | 46 | 170 | 469 |
| IT COULD NOT SEVER MAN AND WIFE, | AN EPITAPH HUSBAND AND WIFE | 5 | 46 | 174 | 478 |
| INTO A FALSE ETERNITY, COME MAN, | UPON STANINOUGH'S DEATH | 9 | 46 | 175 | 475 |
| HERE LYES A TRULY HONEST MAN. | AN EPITAPH UPON ASHTON | 4 | 46 | 192 | 464 |
| HEAVEN IN EARTH, & GOD IN MAN. | IN HOLY NATIVITY | 82 | 52 | 246 | 76 |
| MAN, FOR MAN, BY MAN'S BETRAID. | OFFICE H. CROSS MATINES | 13 | 52 | 265 | 86 |
| MAN, FOR MAN, BY MAN'S BETRAID. | OFFICE H. CROSS MATINES | 13 | 52 | 265 | 86 |
| LORD, WHAT IS MAN. WHY SHOULD HE COSTE THEE | CHARITAS NIMIA | 1 | 52 | 280 | 48 |
| LORD WHAT IS MAN. THAT THOU HAST OVERBOUGHT | CHARITAS NIMIA | 3 | 52 | 280 | 48 |
| MAKE BUT A SIMPLE MERCHANT MAN. | CHARITAS NIMIA | 6 | 52 | 280 | 48 |
| IS THAT COLD MAN | SANCTA MARIA DOLORUM | 12 | 52 | 283 | 162 |
| THOUGH HIDD AS GOD, WOUNDS WRITT THEE MAN, | ADORO TE | 22 | 52 | 291 | 172 |
| TAST THEE GOD, OR TOUCH THEE MAN | ADORO TE | 30 | 52 | 291 | 172 |
| WHOSE BREST WEEPES BALM FOR WOUNDED MAN. | ADORO TE | 46 | 52 | 291 | 172 |
| HARPES OF HEAVN TO HANDS OF MAN. | LAUDA SION SALVATOREM | 4 | 52 | 294 | 178 |
| MAN TREMBLES AT, YOU STRAIGHT SHALL FIND | TERESA | 31 | 52 | 315 | 52 |
| MAKE THE MARTYR, OR THE MAN. | TERESA | 34 | 52 | 315 | 52 |
| WHY MAN, THIS SPEAKES PURE MORTALL FRAME. | FLAMING HEART | 23 | 52 | 324 | 61 |
| NEEDS MUST MY MISERYES OWE THAT MAN A SPITE | ALEXIAS THIRD ELEGIE | 3 | 52 | 336 | 209 |
| THE LUSTY BRIDEGROOM MADE APPROACH. YOUNG MAN, | ALEXIAS THIRD ELEGIE | 33 | 52 | 336 | 209 |
| HOW SWEET THE MUTUALL YOKE OF MAN & WIFE, | ALEXIAS THIRD ELEGIE | 51 | 52 | 336 | 209 |
| IT COULD NOT SUNDER MAN & WIFE, | AN EPITAPH UPON MARRIED COUPLE | 5 | 52 | 339 | 478 |
| INTO A FALSE AETERNITY. COME MAN. | DEATH'S LECTURE | 10 | 52 | 340 | 475 |
| WILT' SEE A MAN, ALL HIS OWN WEALTH, | TEMPERANCE | 15 | 52 | 342 | 510 |
| A MAN WHOSE SOBER SOUL CAN TELL | TEMPERANCE | 17 | 52 | 342 | 510 |
| WOULDST' SEE A MAN, WHOSE WELL-WARM'D BLOOD | TEMPERANCE | 33 | 52 | 342 | 510 |
| A MAN, WHOSE TUNED HUMORS BE | TEMPERANCE | 35 | 52 | 342 | 510 |
| IN SUMME, WOULDST SEE A MAN THAT CAN | TEMPERANCE | 43 | 52 | 342 | 510 |
| LIVE TO BE OLD, AND STILL A MAN. | TEMPERANCE | 44 | 52 | 342 | 510 |
| YEA SUITOURS. MAN ALONE IS WO'ED, | AGAINST IRRESOLUTION AND DELAY | 58 | 52 | 347 | 146 |
| THAT MADE GREAT LOVE A MAN OF WARRE. | IN CICATRICES DOMINI JESU | 6 | MS | 381 | 27 |
| THAT MAN (I THINKE) WRESTED THE FEEBLE LIFE | HORATIJ ILLE & NEFASTO | 7 | MS | 382 | 530 |
| THAT HEAVENLY MORTALL, THAT SERAPHICK MAN. | AN ELEGIE ON DR PORTER | 18 | MS | 395 | 476 |

## COUNTRY-MAN

| | | | | | |
|---|---|---|---|---|---|
| SPEAKE HEAVEN LIKE HERS, IS MY SOULES COUNTRY-MAN. | AN APOLOGIE FOR HYMNE (TERESA) | 22 | 46 | 136 | 59 |
| SPEAK HEAV'N LIKE HER'S IS MY SOULS COUNTRY-MAN. | AN APOLOGIE FOR (TERESA) HYMNE | 22 | 52 | 322 | 59 |

## MAN'S

| | | | | | |
|---|---|---|---|---|---|
| WHICH MAN'S HEART MEETS | TO THE NAME OF JESUS | 123 | 52 | 239 | 30 |
| MAN, FOR MAN, BY MAN'S BETRAID. | OFFICE H. CROSS MATINES | 13 | 52 | 265 | 86 |
| THE SINNER'S PARDON & THE JUST MAN'S PEACE. | VEXILLA REGIS | 42 | 52 | 277 | 156 |

## MANS

| | | | | | |
|---|---|---|---|---|---|
| AT THOSE HARD WORDS MANS COWARDISE CALLS FEARES. | I AM READY NOT ONELY BOUND | 2 | 46 | 98 | 29 |
| HOW GODS ETERNALL SONNE SHOULD BE MANS BROTHER, | SOSPETTO D'HERODE | 165 | 46 | 109 | 216 |
| FROM HIS OLD FATHER. THAT MANS BARBAROUS KNIFE | HORATIJ ILLE & NEFASTO | 8 | MS | 382 | 530 |
| MANS DAINTIEST CARE, & CAUTION CANNOT SPY | HORATIJ ILLE & NEFASTO | 17 | MS | 382 | 530 |
| MANS BREST (HIS TENEMENT) AND BREAKES UP HOUSE. | OUT OF GROTIUS | 80 | MS | 398 | 198 |

## MANGER

| | | | | | |
|---|---|---|---|---|---|
| THAT A VILE MANGER HIS LOW BED SHOULD PROVE, | SOSPETTO D'HERODE | 175 | 46 | 109 | 216 |
| A COLD, AND NOT TOO CLEANLY, MANGER. | IN HOLY NATIVITY | 40 | 52 | 246 | 76 |

## MANKIND

| | | | | | |
|---|---|---|---|---|---|
| AND TEACH OBSCURE MANKIND A MORE CLOSE WAY | IN GLORIOUS EPIPHANIE | 208 | 52 | 253 | 39 |
| SHOULD MANKIND DWELL | CHARITAS NIMIA | 12 | 52 | 280 | 48 |
| PALE MANKIND FORTH TO MEET HIS KING. | DIES IRAE | 12 | 52 | 298 | 186 |

## MANKINDS

| | | | | | |
|---|---|---|---|---|---|
| THIS MORTALL ENEMY TO MANKINDS GOOD, | SOSPETTO D'HERODE | 82 | 46 | 109 | 216 |
| THAT MANKINDS TORMENT WAITS UPON MY TEARS. | SOSPETTO D'HERODE | 216 | 46 | 109 | 216 |

MANLY

| AND BLUSHES ON THE MANLY SUN. | THE TEARE | 28 | 46 | 84 | 50 |
| LIV'D A FAIRE, BUT MANLY GRACE. | HIS EPITAPH (HERRYS) | 28 | 46 | 172 | 471 |
| OF PEACE AND WARRE. THOU FOR WHOSE MANLY BROW | UPON YORKE HIS BIRTH | 37 | 46 | 176 | 500 |
| AND MOCKES WITH FEMALE FROST LOVE'S MANLY FLAME. | FLAMING HEART | 24 | 52 | 324 | 61 |

MANNA

| WITH MANNA, MILK, AND BALM, NEW BROACH THE MOUNTAINES. | SOSPETTO D'HERODE | 112 | 46 | 109 | 216 |
| THE MANNA, & THE PASCHAL LAMB. | LAUDA SION SALVATOREM | 68 | 52 | 294 | 178 |

MANSION

| AND MAKE HIS MANSION IN THE MILDE | IN MEMORY OF LADY MADRE TERESA | 13 | 46 | 131 | 52 |
| AND MELT THY SOULES SWEET MANSION. | IN MEMORY OF LADY MADRE TERESA | 113 | 46 | 131 | 52 |
| A MELANCHOLY MANSION IN THOSE COLD | ON A TREATISE OF CHARITY | 35 | 46 | 137 | 69 |
| MAKING HIS MANSION IN THE MILD | TERESA | 13 | 52 | 315 | 52 |
| AND MELT THY SOUL'S SWEET MANSION. | TERESA | 112 | 52 | 315 | 52 |

MANTLE

| A GLOOMY MANTLE OF DARKE FLAMES, THE TIRE | SOSPETTO D'HERODE | 44 | 46 | 109 | 216 |
| AND BRUSH HER AZURE MANTLE, WHICH SHALL SWIM | ON A FOULE MORNING | 24 | 46 | 181 | 495 |

MANTLES

| THEIR SHAGGY LOCKS, THEIR FLOURY MANTLES TURN'D | UPON GUNPOWDER TREASON | 47 | MS | 386 | 460 |

MANTLETTS

| AND OUT OF THEIR GREENE MANTLETTS DARE TO PEEPE. | AN ELEGY MR STANNINOW | 26 | MS | 394 | 473 |

MANY

| IN MANY A SWEET RISE, MANY AS SWEET A FALL) | MUSICKS DUELL | 155 | 46 | 149 | 535 |
| IN MANY A SWEET RISE, MANY AS SWEET A FALL) | MUSICKS DUELL | 155 | 46 | 149 | 535 |
| AND MANY A CRUELL TEARE DISCLOSES. | ON WOUNDS OF CRUCIFIED LORD | 8 | 46 | 99 | 24 |
| MANY A KISSE, AND MANY A TEARE, | ON WOUNDS OF CRUCIFIED LORD | 10 | 46 | 99 | 24 |
| MANY A KISSE, AND MANY A TEARE, | ON WOUNDS OF CRUCIFIED LORD | 10 | 46 | 99 | 24 |
| WITH MANY A RARELY-TEMPER'D KISSE, | A HYMNE OF THE NATIVITY | 62 | 46 | 106 | 76 |
| HOW MANY PRESENT PRODIGIES CONSPIRE. | SOSPETTO D'HERODE | 94 | 46 | 109 | 216 |
| MEDAEA, JEZABELL, MANY A MEAGER WITCH | SOSPETTO D'HERODE | 338 | 46 | 109 | 216 |
| WHICH NODS WITH MANY A HEAVY HEADED TREE. | SOSPETTO D'HERODE | 346 | 46 | 109 | 216 |
| WITH MANY A MERCYLESSE O'RE MASTRING WAVE. | SOSPETTO D'HERODE | 426 | 46 | 109 | 216 |
| AND MANY A MISTICKE THING, | ON A PRAYER BOOKE | 76 | 46 | 126 | 139 |
| HOW MANY HEAVENS AT ONCE IT IS, | ON A PRAYER BOOKE | 117 | 46 | 126 | 139 |
| DEARE BABE E'RE MANY DAYES BE DONE. | AN HIMNE FUR CIRCUMCISION | 30 | 46 | 141 | 37 |
| MAKES MANY A MOURNING PAPER PUT ON BLACKE. | UPON STANINOUGH'S DEATH | 2 | 46 | 175 | 475 |
| AND TO MANY DEATHS RENEW MEE. | OUT OF THE ITALIAN (1) | 54 | 46 | 188 | 545 |
| THEN MANY A BRAVER MARBLE CAN. | AN EPITAPH UPON ASHTON | 3 | 46 | 192 | 464 |
| SERMONS HE HEARD, YET NOT SO MANY, | AN EPITAPH UPON ASHTON | 9 | 46 | 192 | 464 |
| MANY A THOUSAND, MANY A HUNDRED. | OUT OF CATULLUS | 16 | 46 | 194 | 523 |
| MANY A THOUSAND, MANY A HUNDRED. | OUT OF CATULLUS | 16 | 46 | 194 | 523 |
| MIX ALL YOUR MANY WORLDS, ABOVE, | TO THE NAME OF JESUS | 86 | 52 | 239 | 30 |
| O SEE. SO MANY WORLDS OF BARREN YEARES | TO THE NAME OF JESUS | 143 | 52 | 239 | 30 |
| HOW MANY UNKNOWN WORLDS THERE ARE | TO THE NAME OF JESUS | 189 | 52 | 239 | 30 |
| HOW MANY THOUSAND MERCYES THERE | TO THE NAME OF JESUS | 191 | 52 | 239 | 30 |
| WITH MANY A RARELY-TEMPER'D KISSE | IN HOLY NATIVITY | 88 | 52 | 246 | 76 |
| DEAR BABE, ERE MANY DAYES BE DONE. | NEW YEAR'S DAY | 30 | 52 | 251 | 37 |
| TO SEE SO MANY UNKIND SWORDS CONTEST | SANCTA MARIA DOLORUM | 17 | 52 | 283 | 162 |
| AND MANY A MYSTICK THING | PRAYER TO GENTLE-WOMAN | 82 | 52 | 328 | 139 |
| HOW MANY HEAV'NS AT ONCE IT IS | PRAYER TO GENTLE-WOMAN | 123 | 52 | 328 | 139 |
| MAKES MANY A MOURNING PAPER PUT ON BLACK. | DEATH'S LECTURE | 2 | 52 | 340 | 475 |
| WELL STRUNG WITH MANY A BROKEN NERVE. | IN CICATRICES DOMINI JESU | 14 | MS | 381 | 27 |
| LEFT MANY A STARRY TEARE, TO THINKE HOW SOONE | AN ELEGY MR STANNINOW | 41 | MS | 394 | 473 |

MAPP

| WITTNESSE THIS MAPP OF BEAUTY. EVERY PART | UPON BIRTH PRINCESSE E | 37 | MS | 391 | 456 |

MAPPE

| MAPPE OF HEROICK WORTH. WHOM FARRE AND WIDE | SOSPETTO D'HERODE | 13 | 46 | 109 | 216 |

MARBLE

| THEN MANY A BRAVER MARBLE CAN. | AN EPITAPH UPON ASHTON | 3 | 46 | 192 | 464 |
| WHAT KIND OF MARBLE THAN | SANCTA MARIA DOLORUM | 11 | 52 | 283 | 162 |

MARBLES

| OF DEAD DEVOTION. NOR FAINT MARBLES WEEP | ON A TREATISE OF CHARITY | 33 | 46 | 137 | 69 |

MARCH

| AND SOBER PACE MARCH ON TO MEET A GRAVE. | TO THE NAME OF JESUS | 202 | 52 | 239 | 30 |

MARCHED

| WHEN 'GAINST THE THUNDERS MOUTH WEE MARCHED FORTH. | SOSPETTO D'HERODE | 284 | 46 | 109 | 216 |

## MARIA

| | | | |
|---|---|---|---|
| MARIA MOTHER OF OUR KING. | ON THE ASSUMPTION | 54 | 46 139 114 |
| MARIA, MEN & ANGELS SING | IN GLORIOUS ASSUMPTION B. LADY | 58 | 52 304 114 |
| MARIA, MOTHER OF OUR KING. | IN GLORIOUS ASSUMPTION B. LADY | 59 | 52 304 114 |

## MARINER

| | | | |
|---|---|---|---|
| THE WEEPING MARINER WILL AUGMENT THE WAVES. | ALEXIAS FIRST ELEGIE | 26 | 52 334 204 |

## MARK

| | | | |
|---|---|---|---|
| NOT MARK THE DRY REGARDLES DUST. | TO COUNTESSE OF DENBIGH | 52 | 52 236 146 |
| MARK WITH WHAT FAITH FRUITS ANSWER FLOWERS. | AGAINST IRRESOLUTION AND DELAY | 33 | 52 347 146 |
| MARK HOW THE CURL'D WAVES WORK AND WIND. | AGAINST IRRESOLUTION AND DELAY | 41 | 52 347 146 |

## MARKE

| | | | |
|---|---|---|---|
| INTO TH'OLD PROPHESIES, TREMBLING TO MARKE | SOSPETTO D'HERODE | 93 | 46 109 216 |
| SHOULD TAKE THE MARKE OF SIN, AND PAINE OF SENCE. | SOSPETTO D'HERODE | 190 | 46 109 216 |

## MARKT

| | | | |
|---|---|---|---|
| HEE MARKT HOW THE POORE SHEPHEARDS RAN TO PAY | SOSPETTO D'HERODE | 118 | 46 109 216 |

## MARKES

| | | | |
|---|---|---|---|
| MARKES OF A FIGHT ALONE, BUT FEASTING TOO. | THE BEGINNING OF HELIODORUS | 24 | 46 158 517 |
| THESE MARKES MAY BEE YOUR JUDGEMENTS GUIDE. | OUT OF GREEKE CUPID'S CRYER | 18 | 46 159 519 |

## MARRES

| | | | |
|---|---|---|---|
| WHOSE BLUSH THE MOON BEAUTEOUSLY MARRES | O GLORIOSA DOMINA | 3 | 52 302 194 |

## MARRIAGE

| | | | |
|---|---|---|---|
| THEN SPOUSALL RITES PREJUDGE THE MARRIAGE BED. | (ON) HOPE | 20 | 52 345 71 |

## MARRIAGE-BED

| | | | |
|---|---|---|---|
| THEN SPOUSALL RITES PREJUDGE THE MARRIAGE-BED. | ON HOPE | 40 | 46 143 71 |
| THIS GRAVE'S THE SECOND MARRIAGE-BED. | AN EPITAPH HUSBAND AND WIFE | 2 | 46 174 478 |
| THIS GRAVE'S THEIR SECOND MARRIAGE-BED. | AN EPITAPH UPON MARRIED COUPLE | 2 | 52 339 478 |

## MARRIED

| | | | |
|---|---|---|---|
| I WOULD BE MARRIED, BUT I'DE HAVE NO WIFE. | ON MARRIAGE | 1 | 46 183 485 |
| I WOULD BE MARRIED TO A SINGLE LIFE. | ON MARRIAGE | 2 | 46 183 485 |
| OF ROSY MARTYRDOME, TWICE MARRIED. | ALEXIAS THIRD ELEGIE | 48 | 52 336 209 |

## MARRYED

| | | | |
|---|---|---|---|
| OF HIS OWNE BREATH, WHICH MARRYED TO HIS LYRE | MUSICKS DUELL | 117 | 46 149 535 |

## MARROW

| | | | |
|---|---|---|---|
| MARROW TO MY PLUMPE GENIUS, MAKE IT LIVE | TO THE MORNING | 22 | 46 183 497 |

## MARS

| | | | |
|---|---|---|---|
| HOT MARS TO TH' HARVEST OF DEATHS FIELD, AND WOO | MUSICKS DUELL | 55 | 46 149 535 |
| WHAT, MARS HIS SWORD. FAIRE CYTHEREA SAY, | UPON VENUS PUTTING ARMES | 1 | 46 161 523 |
| MARS THOU HAST BEATEN NAKED, AND O THEN | UPON VENUS PUTTING ARMES | 3 | 46 161 523 |
| HENRY AND JAMES, OR MARS AND PHOEBUS RATHER. | UPON YORKE HIS BIRTH | 31 | 46 176 500 |
| ARE MARS AND PHOEBUS UNDER DIVERS NAMES. | UPON YORKE HIS BIRTH | 34 | 46 176 500 |

## MARTYR

| | | | |
|---|---|---|---|
| OF MARTYR, YET SHEE THINKES IT SHAME | IN MEMORY OF LADY MADRE TERESA | 16 | 46 131 52 |
| MAKE THE MARTYR OR THE MAN. | IN MEMORY OF LADY MADRE TERESA | 34 | 46 131 52 |
| BUT WHERE SHEE MAY A MARTYR BEE. | IN MEMORY OF LADY MADRE TERESA | 46 | 46 131 52 |
| OF MARTYR. YET SHE THINKS IT SHAME | TERESA | 16 | 52 315 52 |
| MAKE THE MARTYR, OR THE MAN. | TERESA | 34 | 52 315 52 |
| BUT WHERE SHE MAY A MARTYR BE. | TERESA | 46 | 52 315 52 |

## MARTYR'D

| | | | |
|---|---|---|---|
| LIE SCATTER'D LIKE THE BURNT AND MARTYR'D BONES | ON A TREATISE OF CHARITY | 32 | 46 137 69 |

## MARTYRDOM

| | | | |
|---|---|---|---|
| RIPE MEN OF MARTYRDOM, THAT COULD REACH DOWN | TERESA | 5 | 52 315 52 |
| SHE'L TRAVAIL TO A MARTYRDOM. | TERESA | 44 | 52 315 52 |
| SHE'S FOR THE MOORES, & MARTYRDOM. | TERESA | 64 | 52 315 52 |
| T'EMBRACE A MILDER MARTYRDOM. | TERESA | 68 | 52 315 52 |

## MARTYRDOME

| | | | |
|---|---|---|---|
| THE BLOOMES OF MARTYRDOME. O BE A DORE | SOSPETTO D'HERODE | 5 | 46 109 216 |
| SHEEL TRAVELL TO A MARTYRDOME. | IN MEMORY OF LADY MADRE TERESA | 44 | 46 131 52 |
| SHEES FOR THE MOORES AND MARTYRDOME. | IN MEMORY OF LADY MADRE TERESA | 64 | 46 131 52 |
| T'EMBRACE A MILDER MARTYRDOME. | IN MEMORY OF LADY MADRE TERESA | 68 | 46 131 52 |
| OF ROSY MARTYRDOME, TWICE MARRIED. | ALEXIAS THIRD ELEGIE | 48 | 52 336 209 |

MARTYRDOMES

    WALK IN A CROWD OF LOVES & MARTYRDOMES.          FLAMING HEART                    82  52 324  61

MARY

    SWEET MARY THY FAIRE EYES EXPENCE.                  THE TEARE                             2  46  84  50
    LOOKE, MARY, HERE SEE, WHERE THY LORD ONCE LAY.        COME SEE WHERE THE LORD LAY     4  46  87  27
    LOOKE, MARY, HERE SEE, WHERE THY LORD ONCE LAY.        COME SEE WHERE THE LORD LAY     6  46  87  27
    MARY, MEN AND ANGELS SING.                           ON THE ASSUMPTION                  53  46 139 114
    SEE'ST THOU THAT MARY THERE.  O TEACH HER MOTHER       UPON YORKE HIS BIRTH             53  46 176 500
    RUN, MARY, RUN. BRING HITHER ALL THE BLEST             OFFICE H. CROSS COMPLINE         5  52 274 105
    THOSE MERCYES WHICH THY MARY FOUND                     DIES IRAE                         49  52 298 186

MARY'S

    IN TH'HEAVEN OF MARY'S EYE, A TEARE.                   THE TEARE                         48  46  84  50

MASCULINE

    THIS SHALL FROM HENCE-FORTH BE THE MASCULINE THEME     ON A TREATISE OF CHARITY        49  46 137  69

MASK

    AND COURTED IN THE POMPOUS MASK OF A MORE SPECIOUS     IN GLORIOUS EPIPHANIE            53  52 253  39
                                          MIST.
    NO MISTS DOE MASK, NO LAZY STEAMES.                    TEMPERANCE                        30  52 342 510

MASKE

    NO MISTES DOE MASKE NO LAZY STEAMES.                 IN PRAISE OF LESSIUS             32  46 156 510
    LET IT SUFFICE, SHEE'L WEARE NO MASKE TO DAY.          ON A FOULE MORNING                 38  46 181 495
    WITH A BLACK MASKE, THE CLOUDS WITH CHILD BY GREIFE    UPON KINGS CORONATION           3  MS 390 453

MASSE

    WITH EARTHS LARGE MASSE, DOTH CHERISH AND ASSIST       OUT OF VIRGIL                        8  46 155 529
    A MASSE OF WOES, HIS TEETH FOR TORMENT GNASH,          SOSPETTO D'HERODE                  63  46 109 216
    THIS MASSE OF CRUELTY, TO BE THY GUIDE                  UPON GUNPOWDER TREASON           8  MS 387 461

MASTER

    MISCHIFES OLD MASTER, CLOSE ABOUT HIM CLINGS           SOSPETTO D'HERODE                  36  46 109 216
    AND THERE, AS MASTER OF THIS MURD'RING BROOD,          SOSPETTO D'HERODE                318  46 109 216
    MASTER (WITH VOYCE FREE AS THE TRUMPE OF FAME)          SOSPETTO D'HERODE                439  46 109 216
    (YOUNG MASTER OF THE WORLDS MATURITIE)                  UPON TWO GREENE APRICOCKES     26  48 220 494
    WHEN THOU ART MASTER OF THE MIND.                      TO THE NAME OF JESUS           124  52 239  30
    WHOSE IS THE MASTER FIRE, WHICH SUN SHOULD SHINE.      IN GLORIOUS EPIPHANIE          144  52 253  39
    COME FORTH GREAT MASTER OF THE MYSTICK DAY.            IN GLORIOUS EPIPHANIE          207  52 253  39
    JESU MASTER, JUST & TRUE.                            LAUDA SION SALVATOREM           69  52 294 178

LUTES-MASTER

    A SWEET LUTES-MASTER. IN WHOSE GENTLE AIRES            MUSICKS DUELL                        5  46 149 535

MASTER'S

    THEIR MASTER'S WATER. THEIR OWN WINE.                  WEEPER                             72  52 307 120
    OF THY KIND MASTER'S WELL-DESERVING BRAINES.            HORATIJ ILLE & NEFASTO          16  MS 382 530

MASTERS

    THEIR MASTERS BLEST SOULE (SNATCHT OUT AT HIS EARES   MUSICKS DUELL                   147  46 149 535
    THEIR MASTERS WATER, THEIR OWNE WINE.                  THE WEEPER                        36  46  79 120
    HIS MASTERS PRIDE.                                        UPON ASSE THAT BORE SAVIOUR    6  46  90  19
    THOSE LAWLESSE TYRANT MASTERS OF THE LAW.              OUT OF GROTIUS                      46  MS 398 198

MASTRING

    WITH MANY A MERCYLESSE O'RE MASTRING WAVE.            SOSPETTO D'HERODE                426  46 109 216

O'RE-MASTRING

    SO MUCH O'RE-MASTRING ALL HIS MIGHT,                    OUT OF THE ITALIAN (3)           6  46 190 549

MASTERY

    THIS HAND FORGET THE MASTERY                            PSALME 137                        16  46 104   7

MASTER-PEECE

    AND MATCHT THY MASTER-PEECE. O THEN GO ON              UPON YORKE HIS BIRTH            51  46 176 500

MATCHT

    AND MATCHT THY MASTER-PEECE. O THEN GO ON              UPON YORKE HIS BIRTH            51  46 176 500

MATE

    SIGHS TO HIS SILVER MATE. RISE UP MY LOVE,             ON THE ASSUMPTION                   8  46 139 114
    SIGHES TO HIS SYLVER MATE RISE UP, MY LOVE.             IN GLORIOUS ASSUMPTION B. LADY   8  52 304 114
    LO HERE AM LEFT (ALAS), FOR MY LOST MATE              ALEXIAS FIRST ELEGIE             3  52 334 204
    WHILE THROUGH THE WORLD SHE SOUGHT HER WANDRING MATE.  ALEXIAS FIRST ELEGIE           30  52 334 204

|  |  |  |  |  |
|---|---|---|---|---|
| WELLCOME, MY SAD SWEET MATE. NOW HAVE I GOTT | ALEXIAS SECONDE ELEGIE | 7 | 52 335 | 207 |

**MATES**

|  |  |  |  |  |
|---|---|---|---|---|
| AMONGST THE GAY MATES OF THE GOD OF FLYES, | ON A PRAYER BOOKE | 45 | 46 126 | 139 |
| AMONG THE GAY MATES OF THE GOD OF FLYES. | PRAYER TO GENTLE-WOMAN | 51 | 52 328 | 139 |

**MATINES**

|  |  |  |  |  |
|---|---|---|---|---|
| THE WAKEFULL MATINES HAST TO SING | OFFICE H. CROSS MATINES | 10 | 52 265 | 86 |

**MATTENS**

|  |  |  |  |  |
|---|---|---|---|---|
| THAT MEN CAN SLEEPE WHILE THEY THEIR MATTENS SING. | MUSICKS DUELL | 80 | 46 149 | 535 |

**MATTER**

|  |  |  |  |  |
|---|---|---|---|---|
| FARRE MORE THEN MATTER FOR MY MUSE AND MEE. | SOSPETTO D'HERODE | 30 | 46 109 | 216 |
| NEW MATTER, TO MAKE GOOD HIS GREAT SUSPECT. | SOSPETTO D'HERODE | 86 | 46 109 | 216 |
| NEW MATTER FOR OUR MUSE SUPPLIES. | TO THE QUEEN | 7 | 48 215 | 501 |
| WHAT E'RE LOVE'S MATTER BE, HE MOVES | AGAINST IRRESOLUTION AND DELAY | 53 | 52 347 | 146 |
| TO TELL THE WORLD, HOW HARD THE MATTER WENT. | HORATIJ ILLE & NEFASTO | 43 | MS 382 | 530 |

**MATUREST**

|  |  |  |  |  |
|---|---|---|---|---|
| BEE POSED WITH THE MATUREST FEARES | IN MEMORY OF LADY MADRE TERESA | 30 | 46 131 | 52 |
| BE POS'D WITH THE MATUREST FEARES | TERESA | 30 | 52 315 | 52 |

**MATURITY**

|  |  |  |  |  |
|---|---|---|---|---|
| BEFORE, AND SEIZE UPON MATURITY. | UPON DEATH OF HERRYS | 6 | 46 167 | 466 |

**MATURITIE**

|  |  |  |  |  |
|---|---|---|---|---|
| (YOUNG MASTER OF THE WORLDS MATURITIE) | UPON TWO GREENE APRICOCKES | 26 | 48 220 | 494 |

**MAUGRE**

|  |  |  |  |  |
|---|---|---|---|---|
| THE MONSTER CRUSHT, MAUGRE THEIR MIDWIFERIE. | UPON GUNPOWDER TREASON | 56 | MS 386 | 460 |
| WHOSE BLAZING BEAMES, MAUGRE THE BLACKEST NIGHT, | UPON KINGS CORONATION | 15 | MS 389 | 454 |

**MAXIM**

|  |  |  |  |  |
|---|---|---|---|---|
| THAT HEAVENLY MAXIM GAVE ME HEART TO TRY | AN APOLOGIE FOR HYMNE (TERESA) | 9 | 46 136 | 59 |

**MAXIME**

|  |  |  |  |  |
|---|---|---|---|---|
| THAT HOPEFULL MAXIME GAVE ME HART TO TRY | AN APOLOGIE FOR (TERESA) HYMNE | 9 | 52 322 | 59 |

**MAYBE**

|  |  |  |  |  |
|---|---|---|---|---|
| BALSOM MAYBE, FOR THEIR OWN GREIFE. | WEEPER | 60 | 52 307 | 120 |

**ME**

|  |  |  |  |  |
|---|---|---|---|---|
| PRETHEE, SWEET NOW LET ME GOE. | OUT OF GREEKE CUPID'S CRYER | 69 | 46 159 | 519 |
| TELL ME BRIGHT BOY, TELL ME MY GOLDEN LAD, | ON THE PRODIGALL | 1 | 46 86 | 17 |
| TELL ME BRIGHT BOY, TELL ME MY GOLDEN LAD, | ON THE PRODIGALL | 1 | 46 86 | 17 |
| THY SHADOW PETER, MUST SHEW ME THE SUN, | SICKE IMPLORE SHADOW | 3 | 46 87 | 26 |
| SHOW ME HIMSELFE, HIMSELFE (BRIGHT SIR) O SHOW | COME SEE WHERE THE LORD LAY | 1 | 46 87 | 27 |
| BUT O ME THINKES 'TIS A FARRE GREATER ONE | UPON ASSE THAT BORE SAVIOUR | 11 | 46 90 | 19 |
| ALL, AND EVERY WHIT OF ME. | IT IS BETTER TO GO WITH EYE | 6 | 46 93 | 16 |
| MAKES ME DOUBT IF HEAVEN WILL GATHER, | UPON INFANT MARTYRS | 3 | 46 95 | 10 |
| TO ME MY LEGACY OF TEARES. | VERILY YE SHALL WEEP | 2 | 46 95 | 22 |
| COULD NOT ONCE BLINDING ME,CRUELL,SUFFICE. | SAMPSON TO HIS DALILAH | 1 | 46 102 | 8 |
| HAPPY ME, O HAPPY SHEEPE. | PSALME 23 | 1 | 46 102 | 5 |
| THAT POINTS ME TO THESE WAYES OF BLISSE. | PSALME 23 | 4 | 46 102 | 5 |
| PLENTY WEARES ME AT HER BREAST, | PSALME 23 | 10 | 46 102 | 5 |
| WHOSE SWEET TEMPER TEACHES ME | PSALME 23 | 11 | 46 102 | 5 |
| AND DOES WOE ME INTO LIFE. | PSALME 23 | 20 | 46 102 | 5 |
| HEE'S BEFORE ME,ON MY SIDE, | PSALME 23 | 24 | 46 102 | 5 |
| AND BEHIND ME, HE BEGUILES | PSALME 23 | 25 | 46 102 | 5 |
| THOU ART WITH ME, STILL THY ROD, | PSALME 23 | 46 | 46 102 | 5 |
| AUSPICIOUS STILL, IN SPIGHT OF HELL AND ME. | SOSPETTO D'HERODE | 208 | 46 109 | 216 |
| MY FAIRE INHERITANCE, HEE CONFINES ME HERE, | SOSPETTO D'HERODE | 212 | 46 109 | 216 |
| HELL FROM ME TOO, AND SACK MY TERRITORIES. | SOSPETTO D'HERODE | 226 | 46 109 | 216 |
| MUCKE ME, AND DAZLE MY DARKE MYSTERIES. | SOSPETTO D'HERODE | 232 | 46 109 | 216 |
| IN RAGE, MY ARMES, GIVE ME MY ARMES, HEE CRYES. | SOSPETTO D'HERODE | 480 | 46 109 | 216 |
| THAT HEAVENLY MAXIM GAVE ME HEART TO TRY | AN APOLOGIE FOR HYMNE (TERESA) | 9 | 46 136 | 59 |
| THUS LOW STANDS UP (ME THINKES) THUS, AND DEFYES | UPON STANINOUGH'S DEATH | 28 | 46 175 | 475 |
| AND POINTING TO DULL MORPHEUS, BIDS ME TAKE | TO THE MORNING | 15 | 46 183 | 497 |
| TO LIFT ME FROM MY LAZY URNE, TO CLIMBE | TO THE MORNING | 27 | 46 183 | 497 |
| TAKE THESE, TIMES TARDY TRUANTS, SENT BY ME. | UPON TWO GREENE APRICOCKES | 1 | 48 220 | 494 |
| TAKE THEM, AND ME IN THEM ACKNOWLEGING. | UPON TWO GREENE APRICOCKES | 33 | 48 220 | 494 |
| BRING HITHER THY WHOLE SELF. & LET ME SEE | TO THE NAME OF JESUS | 17 | 52 239 | 30 |
| AND FULL OF NOTHING ELSE BUT EMPTY ME. | TO THE NAME OF JESUS | 21 | 52 239 | 30 |
| START INTO LIFE, AND LEAP WITH ME | TO THE NAME OF JESUS | 49 | 52 239 | 30 |
| HELP ME TO MEDITATE MINE IMMORTALL SONG. | TO THE NAME OF JESUS | 61 | 52 239 | 30 |
| O GOD MAKE SPEED TO SAVE ME. | OFFICE H. CROSS MATINES | 5 | 52 265 | 86 |
| O LORD MAKE HAST TO HELP ME. | OFFICE H. CROSS MATINES | 6 | 52 265 | 86 |
| WHAT MINE OWN MADNESSES HAVE DONE WITH ME. | CHARITAS NIMIA | 34 | 52 280 | 48 |
| O MY SAVIOVR, MAKE ME SEE | CHARITAS NIMIA | 63 | 52 280 | 48 |
| HOW DEARLY THOU HAST PAYD FOR ME | CHARITAS NIMIA | 64 | 52 280 | 48 |
| IN ME, ME, SO TO READ | SANCTA MARIA DOLORUM | 52 | 52 283 | 162 |

| | | | | |
|---|---|---|---|---|
| IN ME. ME, SO TO READ | SANCTA MARIA DOLORUM | 52 | 52 283 | 162 |
| O LET ME, HERE, CLAIM SHARES. | SANCTA MARIA DOLORUM | 56 | 52 283 | 162 |
| ME TOO MY TEARES. WHO, THOUGH ALL STONE, | SANCTA MARIA DOLORUM | 59 | 52 283 | 162 |
| YEA LET MY LIFE & ME | SANCTA MARIA DOLORUM | 61 | 52 283 | 162 |
| HAIL. & STRIKE HOME & MAKE ME SEE | SANCTA MARIA DOLORUM | 73 | 52 283 | 162 |
| O LET ME SUCK THE WINE | SANCTA MARIA DOLORUM | 101 | 52 283 | 162 |
| A LOST THING TO THE WORLD, AS IT TO ME. | SANCTA MARIA DOLORUM | 104 | 52 283 | 162 |
| OF ME & OF MY END. | SANCTA MARIA DOLORUM | 106 | 52 283 | 162 |
| WHOM TOO MUCH LOVE HATH BOW'D MORE LOW FOR ME. | ADORO TE | 4 | 52 291 | 172 |
| PLEAD FOR ME, LOVE. ALLEAGE & SHOW | ADORO TE | 19 | 52 291 | 172 |
| TO WASH MY WORLDS OF SINS FROM ME. | ADORO TE | 50 | 52 291 | 172 |
| HIMSELF TO ME MY SAVIOVR BRINGS, | LAUDA SION SALVATOREM | 40 | 52 294 | 178 |
| EVEN LOST THY SELF IN SEEKING ME. | DIES IRAE | 32 | 52 298 | 186 |
| WITH MY PRICE, & NOT WITH ME | DIES IRAE | 38 | 52 298 | 186 |
| STILL ALIVE. AND STILL FOR ME. | DIES IRAE | 52 | 52 298 | 186 |
| AND SHOW THOU ART, BY SAVING ME. | DIES IRAE | 56 | 52 298 | 186 |
| LET COME YE BLESSED THEN CALL ME. | DIES IRAE | 60 | 52 298 | 186 |
| TAKE CHARGE OF ME, & OF MY END. | DIES IRAE | 68 | 52 298 | 186 |
| THAT HOPEFULL MAXIME GAVE ME HART TO TRY | AN APOLOGIE FOR (TERESA) HYMNE | 9 | 52 322 | 59 |
| ME EVER INTO THESE HIS CELLARS BRING | AN APOLOGIE FOR (TERESA) HYMNE | 38 | 52 322 | 59 |
| READERS, BE RUL'D BY ME, & MAKE | FLAMING HEART | 7 | 52 324 | 61 |
| GIVE ME THE SUFFRING SERAPHIM. | FLAMING HEART | 64 | 52 324 | 61 |
| AND TAKE AWAY FROM ME MY SELF & SIN, | FLAMING HEART | 90 | 52 324 | 61 |
| AND MY BEST FORTUNES SUCH FAIR SPOILES OF ME. | FLAMING HEART | 92 | 52 324 | 61 |
| LEAVE NOTHING OF MY SELF IN ME. | FLAMING HEART | 106 | 52 324 | 61 |
| LET ME SO READ THY LIFE, THAT I | FLAMING HEART | 107 | 52 324 | 61 |
| STILL SHINE ON ME, FAIR SUNS. THAT I | A SONG | 7 | 52 327 | 65 |
| STILL LIVE IN ME THIS LOVING STRIFE | A SONG | 13 | 52 327 | 65 |
| FOR WHILE THOU SWEETLY SLAYEST ME | A SONG | 15 | 52 327 | 65 |
| TRUTH BIDDES ME SAY, 'TIS TIME YOU CEASE TO TRUST | TO SAME CONCERNING CHOISE | 18 | 52 331 | 66 |
| SWEET, LET ME PROPHESY THAT AT LAST T'WILL PROVE | TO SAME CONCERNING CHOISE | 33 | 52 331 | 66 |
| I'D SEND MY WOES IN WORDS SHOULD WEEP FOR ME. | ALEXIAS FIRST ELEGIE | 11 | 52 334 | 204 |
| AH THOU THY SELF, ALAS, HAST TAUGHT ME HOW. | ALEXIAS FIRST ELEGIE | 16 | 52 334 | 204 |
| TO BEAR ME HARMLESSE THROUGH THE HARDEST THINGS. | ALEXIAS FIRST ELEGIE | 18 | 52 334 | 204 |
| WHAT DANGERS CAN THERE BE DARE SAY ME NAY. | ALEXIAS FIRST ELEGIE | 20 | 52 334 | 204 |
| THE NOTED SEA SHALL CHANGE HIS NAME WITH ME. | ALEXIAS FIRST ELEGIE | 23 | 52 334 | 204 |
| AS TRUE TO ME, AS SHE WAS TO HER SPOUSE. | ALEXIAS FIRST ELEGIE | 32 | 52 334 | 204 |
| UNKIND. YET ARE MY TEARES STILL TRUE TO ME | ALEXIAS SECONDE ELEGIE | 2 | 52 335 | 207 |
| NOR COULDST THOU, CRUELL, LEAVE ME QUITE ALONE. | ALEXIAS SECONDE ELEGIE | 4 | 52 335 | 207 |
| AT LAST A CONSTANT LOVE THAT LEAVES ME NOT. | ALEXIAS SECONDE ELEGIE | 8 | 52 335 | 207 |
| WHOSE ROSY BEAM SHALL POINT MY SUN TO ME. | ALEXIAS SECONDE ELEGIE | 26 | 52 335 | 207 |
| BUT NOW, AH ME, FROM WHERE HE HAS NO FOES | ALEXIAS THIRD ELEGIE | 15 | 52 336 | 209 |
| WHAT NEEDES MY VIRGIN LORD FLY THUS FROM ME, | ALEXIAS THIRD ELEGIE | 23 | 52 336 | 209 |
| STANDS ARM'D, TO SHEILD ME FROM ALL WANTON WRONG. | ALEXIAS THIRD ELEGIE | 36 | 52 336 | 209 |
| BUT I, (SO HELP ME HEAVN MY HOPES TO SEE) | ALEXIAS THIRD ELEGIE | 53 | 52 336 | 209 |
| THUS LOW, STANDS UP (ME THINKES,) THUS & DEFIES | DEATH'S LECTURE | 30 | 52 340 | 475 |
| THE HUMBLE KING OF YOU AND ME. | AGAINST IRRESOLUTION AND DELAY | 72 | 52 347 | 146 |
| HEE'S GONE. NOT LEAVING WITH ME, TILL HE COME, | LUKE 2. QUAERIT JESUM | 13 | MS 379 | 11 |
| DAWNE THEN TO ME,THOU MORNE OF MINE OWNE DAY. | LUKE 2. QUAERIT JESUM | 45 | MS 379 | 11 |
| REACH ME A QUILL, PLUCKT FROM THE FLAMING WING | UPON GUNPOWDER TREASON | 1 | MS 386 | 460 |
| BUT GIVE ME LEAVE TO EASE IT WITH MY HAND. | UPON BIRTH PRINCESSE E | 16 | MS 391 | 456 |
| OF LOVES ALL-DARING HAND, THAT MAKES ME BURNE. | EX EUPHORMIONE | 5 | MS 392 | 525 |
| MAKES ME CONFESS'T. OH, DOE NOT THOU WITH SCORNE, | EX EUPHORMIONE | 6 | MS 392 | 525 |
| BY THEE. BY THEE YET LETT ME DIE. THIS GIVE, | EX EUPHORMIONE | 12 | MS 392 | 525 |
| O TELL ME THEN, WHAT RUDE OUTRAGIOUS BLAST | AN ELEGY MR STANNINOW | 27 | MS 394 | 473 |

MEE

| | | | | |
|---|---|---|---|---|
| OR TUNE A SONG OF VICTORY TO MEE, | MUSICKS DUELL | 109 | 46 149 | 535 |
| THAT BRINGS HIM TO MEE, HEE SHALL SWIM | OUT OF GREEKE CUPID'S CRYER | 14 | 46 159 | 519 |
| WHY FOOLE. SAIES VENUS, THUS PROVOK'ST THOU MEE, | UPON THE SAME (VENUS ARMES) | 3 | 46 161 | 523 |
| FARRE MORE THEN MATTER FOR MY MUSE AND MEE. | SOSPETTO D'HERODE | 30 | 46 109 | 216 |
| A DESPERATE, OH MEE, DREW FROM HIS DEEPE BREST. | SOSPETTO D'HERODE | 200 | 46 109 | 216 |
| OH MEE. (THUS BELLOW'D HEE) OH MEE. WHAT GREAT | SOSPETTO D'HERODE | 201 | 46 109 | 216 |
| OH MEE. (THUS BELLOW'D HEE) OH MEE. WHAT GREAT | SOSPETTO D'HERODE | 201 | 46 109 | 216 |
| MEE YET A SECOND FALL. WE'D TRY OUR STRENGTHS. | SOSPETTO D'HERODE | 254 | 46 109 | 216 |
| BE HEROD, AND THOU SHALT NOT MISSE FROM MEE | SOSPETTO D'HERODE | 463 | 46 109 | 216 |
| MEE EVER INTO THESE HIS CELLARS BRING. | AN APOLOGIE FOR HYMNE (TERESA) | 38 | 46 136 | 59 |
| MEE FROM HIS PATRONAGE. I PRAY, HE CHIDES. | TO THE MORNING | 14 | 46 183 | 497 |
| IF MORPHEUS HAVE A MUSE TO WAIT ON MEE. | TO THE MORNING | 18 | 46 183 | 497 |
| WHEN TO END MEE | OUT OF THE ITALIAN (1) | 43 | 46 188 | 545 |
| DEATH SHALL SEND MEE | OUT OF THE ITALIAN (1) | 44 | 46 188 | 545 |
| ALL HIS TERRORS TO AFFRIGHT MEE. | OUT OF THE ITALIAN (1) | 45 | 46 188 | 545 |
| AND THOSE TERRORS SHALL DELIGHT MEE. | OUT OF THE ITALIAN (1) | 48 | 46 188 | 545 |
| THOSE SWEET AIRES THAT OFTEN SLEW MEE. | OUT OF THE ITALIAN (1) | 51 | 46 188 | 545 |
| SHALL REVIVE MEE, | OUT OF THE ITALIAN (1) | 52 | 46 188 | 545 |
| OR REPRIVE MEE, | OUT OF THE ITALIAN (1) | 53 | 46 188 | 545 |
| AND TO MANY DEATHS RENEW MEE. | OUT OF THE ITALIAN (1) | 54 | 46 188 | 545 |
| BELEEVE MEE, READER CAN SAY MORE | AN EPITAPH UPON ASHTON | 2 | 46 192 | 464 |
| THAT SHALL COMMAND MY HEART AND MEE. | WISHES SUPPOSED MISTRESSE | 3 | 46 195 | 479 |
| MY LIFE, MY SOUL, MY SURER SELFE TO MEE. | ADORO TE | 44 | 52 291 | 172 |
| MY TREASURES, RICH, ALAS, BY ROBBING MEE. | ALEXIAS THIRD ELEGIE | 2 | 52 336 | 209 |
| DOE NOT DECEIVE MEE, EYES. DOE I NOT SEE | UPON KINGS CORONATION | 11 | MS 389 | 454 |
| BRIGHT STARRE OF MAJESTY, OH SHEDD ON MEE | UPON BIRTH PRINCESSE E | 1 | MS 391 | 456 |
| WAS LOSSE OF MULTITUDES. AND MISSING MEE | OUT OF GROTIUS | 28 | MS 398 | 198 |
| AND BREAKE UPON MEE. MY OWNE VIRTUES HEIGHT | OUT OF GROTIUS | 33 | MS 398 | 198 |
| HURTES MEE FAR WORSE THEN HERODS HIGHEST SPITE. | OUT OF GROTIUS | 34 | MS 398 | 198 |
| BASELY DEGENEROUS. AGAINST MEE FLOCKE | OUT OF GROTIUS | 41 | MS 398 | 198 |
| THE BLOUD HOUND BROOD OF PRIESTS AGAINST MEE DRAW | OUT OF GROTIUS | 45 | MS 398 | 198 |
| GREAT NATURES SELFE HATH SHRUNKE AND SPOKE MEE GOD. | OUT OF GROTIUS | 50 | MS 398 | 198 |
| FULL OF HIGH SPARKELING VIGOUR. TAUGHT MEE | OUT OF GROTIUS | 53 | MS 398 | 198 |
| YETT HERE'S NOT ALL. NOR WAS'T ENOUGH FOR MEE | OUT OF GROTIUS | 81 | MS 398 | 198 |
| MEE RANGING IN HIS QUARTERS. AND THE LAND | OUT OF GROTIUS | 83 | MS 398 | 198 |

MEADS

| YOU EVER-BLUSHING MEADS, WHERE DOE THE BLEST | HORATIJ ILLE & NEFASTO | 37 | MS | 382 | 530 |

MEADES

| THE LAUGHING MEADES, AS JOYFULL TO BEHOLD | UPON KINGS CORONATION | 27 | MS | 390 | 453 |

MEADOWES

| SHE WAS A NIMPH, THE MEADOWES KNEW NONE SUCH, | TO PONTIUS WASHING HANDS | 5 | 46 | 94 | 23 |

MEDDOWES

| THE PAINTED MEDDOWES WOULD HAVE LAUGHT NOE MORE | UPON GUNPOWDER TREASON | 45 | MS | 386 | 460 |

MEAGRE

| POORE MEAGRE HORROR STREIGHTWAIS WAS AMAZ'D, | UPON GUNPOWDER TREASON | 47 | MS | 387 | 461 |

MEAGER

| MEDAEA, JEZABELL, MANY A MEAGER WITCH | SOSPETTO D'HERODE | 336 | 46 | 109 | 216 |

MEAL

| OUR CROWN-LAND LYES ABOVE YET EACH MEAL BRINGS | (ON) HOPE | 13 | 52 | 345 | 71 |

MEALE

| OUR CROWN-LANDS LYE ABOVE, YET EACH MEALE BRINGS | ON HOPE | 33 | 46 | 143 | 71 |

MEAN

| STILL SPENDING, NEVER SPENT. I MEAN | WEEPER | 5 | 52 | 307 | 120 |
| HER PROUDEST PEARLES. I MEAN THY TEARES. | WEEPER | 42 | 52 | 307 | 120 |
| MUCH LESSE MEAN WE TO TRACE | WEEPER | 181 | 52 | 307 | 120 |
| MEAN WHILE, & STEPPING IN BEFORE | PRAYER TO GENTLE-WOMAN | 62 | 52 | 328 | 139 |

MEAN'ST

| O IF FOR THESE THOU MEAN'ST TO FIND A SEAT, | UPON YORKE HIS BIRTH | 15 | 46 | 176 | 500 |

MEAN'T

| WHERE HE MEAN'T FROST, HE SCATTER'D FLOWRS. | IN HOLY NATIVITY | 29 | 52 | 246 | 76 |

MEANE

| A SWEETLY TEMPER'D MEANE, NOR HOT NOR COLD. | OUT OF VIRGIL | 36 | 46 | 155 | 529 |
| STILL SPENDING, NEVER SPENT. I MEANE | THE WEEPER | 5 | 46 | 79 | 120 |
| HER RICHEST PEARLES, I MEANE THY TEARES. | THE WEEPER | 54 | 46 | 79 | 120 |
| WELL FOR THY SELFE (I MEANE) NOT FOR THY LORD. | ON ST. PETER CUTTING MALCHUS | 2 | 46 | 97 | 22 |
| MEANE WHILE WHO E'RE THOU ART THAT PASSEST HERE, | UPON DEATH OF HERRYS | 41 | 46 | 167 | 466 |
| MEANE WHILE HIS LOVED BANKES NOW DRY, | AN EPITAPH DOCTOR BROOKE | 7 | 46 | 175 | 465 |
| I MEANE THOSE THREE GREAT STARRES, WHO WELL MAY SCORNE | UPON KINGS CORONATION | 31 | MS | 389 | 454 |
| WHAT MEANE THESE SHOURES OF TEARES AMONGST US MEN. | AN ELEGY MR STANNINOW | 16 | MS | 394 | 473 |

MEANS

| VILE HUMANE NATURE MEANS HE NOW T'INVEST | SOSPETTO D'HERODE | 227 | 46 | 109 | 216 |

MEANES

| IS HEE NOT SATISFIED. MEANES HE TO WREST | SOSPETTO D'HERODE | 225 | 46 | 109 | 216 |
| AND MEANES THEM FOR A FARRE MORE WORTHY SPOUSE | TO SAME CONCERNING CHOISE | 36 | 52 | 331 | 66 |

MEANING

| WELL MEANING READERS. YOU THAT COME AS FREINDS | FLAMING HEART | 1 | 52 | 324 | 61 |

LIFE-MEANING

| YET ON THE SAME (LIFE-MEANING) BREAD | LAUDA SION SALVATOREM | 51 | 52 | 294 | 178 |

WELL-MEANING

| MEET HIS WELL-MEANING WOUNDS, WISE HEART. | TO COUNTESSE OF DENBIGH | 45 | 52 | 236 | 146 |

MEANT

| EACH STRING HIS NOTE, AS IF THEY MEANT TO CARRY | MUSICKS DUELL | 146 | 46 | 149 | 535 |
| AS IF THE STORME MEANT HIM. | WHY ARE YEE AFRAID | 1 | 46 | 88 | 15 |
| AS IF THEY ONELY MEANT TO BREATH, | NEITHER DURST MAN ASKE | 13 | 46 | 92 | 20 |
| WHERE HE MEANT FROSTS, HE SCATTERED FLOWERS. | A HYMNE OF THE NATIVITY | 28 | 46 | 106 | 76 |
| AND MEANT TO LEAVE HIS PRETIOUS FEATURE, | UPON DEATH OF DESIRED HERRYS | 7 | 46 | 168 | 467 |
| COULD THEY KNOW WHAT MERCY MEANT. | ANOTHER ON HERRYS | 18 | 46 | 170 | 469 |
| IT WAS THY WOOD HE MEANT SHOULD MAKE THE THRONE | VEXILLA REGIS | 23 | 52 | 277 | 156 |

MEANT'ST

| ONE WOULD SUSPECT THOU MEANT'ST TO PAINT | FLAMING HEART | 25 | 52 | 324 | 61 |

MEASURE

| | | | | | |
|---|---|---|---|---|---|
| SHEE MEASURES EVERY MEASURE, EVERY WHERE | MUSICKS DUELL | 34 | 46 | 149 | 535 |
| TO MEASURE ALL THOSE WILD DIVERSITIES | MUSICKS DUELL | 162 | 46 | 149 | 535 |
| MEASURE THEIR AGES, THOU BY TEARES. | THE WEEPER | 120 | 46 | 79 | 120 |
| TAKE THINE OWNE MEASURE HERE, DOWNE, DOWNE, AND BOW | UPON STANINOUGH'S DEATH | 11 | 46 | 175 | 475 |
| FAIR SPEND-THRIFT OF THY SELF. THY MEASURE | WEEPER | 128 | 52 | 307 | 120 |
| MEASURE THEIR AGES. THOU, BY TEARES. | WEEPER | 156 | 52 | 307 | 120 |
| TAKE THINE OWN MEASURE HERE. DOWN, DOWN, & BOW | DEATH'S LECTURE | 12 | 52 | 340 | 475 |

MEASUR'D

| | | | | | |
|---|---|---|---|---|---|
| MELTED & MEASUR'D OUT IN SEAS OF TEARES | TO THE NAME OF JESUS | 144 | 52 | 239 | 30 |

MEASURES

| | | | | | |
|---|---|---|---|---|---|
| SHEE MEASURES EVERY MEASURE, EVERY WHERE | MUSICKS DUELL | 34 | 46 | 149 | 535 |
| DANCING IN LOFTY MEASURES, AND ANON | MUSICKS DUELL | 139 | 46 | 149 | 535 |

MEAT

| | | | | | |
|---|---|---|---|---|---|
| AS MEAT IN THAT, AS DRINK IN THIS, | LAUDA SION SALVATOREM | 41 | 52 | 294 | 178 |
| IS CLOYING MEAT. HOW STALE IS WIFE. | PETRONIJ ALES PHASIACIS PETITA | 16 | MS | 382 | 526 |

MEATE

| | | | | | |
|---|---|---|---|---|---|
| THE BROKEN MEATE WAS MUCH MORE THEN THE WHOLE. | OUT OF GROTIUS | 64 | MS | 398 | 198 |

MEDAEA

| | | | | | |
|---|---|---|---|---|---|
| MEDAEA, JEZABELL, MANY A MEAGER WITCH | SOSPETTO D'HERODE | 338 | 46 | 109 | 216 |

MEDIATE

| | | | | | |
|---|---|---|---|---|---|
| TO MEDIATE 'TWIXT YOUR SELF AND YOU. | TO THE QUEEN | 10 | 48 | 215 | 501 |

MEDITATE

| | | | | | |
|---|---|---|---|---|---|
| HELP ME TO MEDITATE MINE IMMORTALL SONG. | TO THE NAME OF JESUS | 61 | 52 | 239 | 30 |

MEDITATES

| | | | | | |
|---|---|---|---|---|---|
| BELOW. BUT MEDITATES HER IMMORTALL WAY | DESCRIPTION RELIGIOUS HOUSE | 38 | 52 | 338 | 213 |

MEDUSA'S

| | | | | | |
|---|---|---|---|---|---|
| THE CUP THEY DRINKE IN IS MEDUSA'S SCULL, | SOSPETTO D'HERODE | 335 | 46 | 109 | 216 |

MED'CINABLE

| | | | | | |
|---|---|---|---|---|---|
| HIS MED'CINABLE TEARES. FOR NOW | THE WEEPER | 70 | 46 | 79 | 120 |
| HIS MED'CINABLE TEARES. FOR NOW | WEEPER | 52 | 52 | 307 | 120 |

MED'CINALL

| | | | | | |
|---|---|---|---|---|---|
| WAS NOTHING, THERE MY VOYCE WAS MED'CINALL. | OUT OF GROTIUS | 70 | MS | 398 | 198 |

MEEK

| | | | | | |
|---|---|---|---|---|---|
| TO BRING A PAIRE OF MEEK AND HUMBLE EYES. | ON A TREATISE OF CHARITY | 48 | 46 | 137 | 69 |
| TO THEE, MEEK MAJESTY. SOFT KING | IN HOLY NATIVITY | 103 | 52 | 246 | 76 |

MEEKE

| | | | | | |
|---|---|---|---|---|---|
| TO THEE MEEKE MAJESTY. SOFT KING | A HYMNE OF THE NATIVITY | 83 | 46 | 106 | 76 |

MEET

| | | | | | |
|---|---|---|---|---|---|
| WHERE TH' MILKY RIVERS MEET, | THE WEEPER | 21 | 46 | 79 | 120 |
| NOWHERE BUT HEERE DID EVER MEET | THE WEEPER | 59 | 46 | 79 | 120 |
| NO SUCH THING. WE GOE TO MEET | THE WEEPER | 137 | 46 | 79 | 120 |
| ALL THY PURPLE RIVERS MEET. | ON BLEEDING WOUNDS OF LORD | 4 | 46 | 101 | 110 |
| WHIL'ST THEY GLADLY GOE TO MEET | PSALME 23 | 32 | 46 | 102 | 5 |
| GRACE AND PEACE, TO MEET NEW LAIES | PSALME 23 | 33 | 46 | 102 | 5 |
| AND MEET THE MISCHIEFE THAT UPON THEE GROWES. | SOSPETTO D'HERODE | 246 | 46 | 109 | 216 |
| AND CRUSH THE WORLD TILL HIS WIDE CORNERS MEET. | SOSPETTO D'HERODE | 280 | 46 | 109 | 216 |
| TO MEET THEIR TROUBLED LORD WITHOUT DELAY. | SOSPETTO D'HERODE | 508 | 46 | 109 | 216 |
| MAKES HASTE TO MEET HER MORNING SPOWSE. | ON A PRAYER BOOKE | 96 | 46 | 126 | 139 |
| GLAD AT THEIR OWNE HOME NOW TO MEET THEE. | IN MEMORY OF LADY MADRE TERESA | 139 | 46 | 131 | 52 |
| THE MOONE SHALL COME TO MEET THEE HERE, | AN HIMNE FOR CIRCUMCISION | 31 | 46 | 141 | 37 |
| THY SILVER BROW, AND MEET THY GOLDEN LOVER. | ON A FOULE MORNING | 28 | 46 | 181 | 495 |
| O MEET THE ANGRY GOD, INVADE HIS EYES, | TO THE MORNING | 36 | 46 | 183 | 497 |
| MEET YOU HER MY WISHES, | WISHES SUPPOSED MISTRESSE | 13 | 46 | 195 | 479 |
| MEET HIS WELL-MEANING WOUNDS, WISE HEART. | TO COUNTESSE OF DENBIGH | 45 | 52 | 236 | 146 |
| MEET IT WITH WIDE-SPREAD ARMES. & SEE | TO COUNTESSE OF DENBIGH | 55 | 52 | 236 | 146 |
| AND SOBER PACE MARCH ON TO MEET A GRAVE. | TO THE NAME OF JESUS | 202 | 52 | 239 | 30 |
| THE MORN SHALL COME TO MEET THEE HERE, | NEW YEAR'S DAY | 31 | 52 | 251 | 37 |
| TO MEET RELIGIOUS WELCOMES AT HER RISE. | IN GLORIOUS EPIPHANIE | 72 | 52 | 253 | 39 |
| A GOLDEN HARVEST OF CROWN'D HEADS, THAT MEET | TO THE QUEEN'S MAJESTY | 13 | 52 | 261 | 47 |
| NOR MAY WE MISSE THE JOY TO MEET IN YOU | TO THE QUEEN'S MAJESTY | 23 | 52 | 261 | 47 |
| ALL THE PURPLE RIVERS MEET. | UPON BLEEDING CRUCIFIX | 4 | 52 | 288 | 110 |
| PALE MANKIND FORTH TO MEET HIS KING. | DIES IRAE | 12 | 52 | 298 | 186 |
| NO WHERE BUT HERE DID EVER MEET | WEEPER | 35 | 52 | 307 | 120 |

```
CROWN'D HEADS ARE TOYES. WE GOE TO MEET          WEEPER                             185  52 307 120
GLAD AT THEIR OWN HOME NOW TO MEET THEE.         TERESA                             138  52 315  52
MAKES HAST TO MEET HER MORNING SPOUSE            PRAYER TO GENTLE-WOMAN             102  52 328 139
AND MURMURE IF THEY MEET A STAY.                 AGAINST IRRESOLUTION AND DELAY      40  52 347 146
THE FURIES CURL'D SNAKES MEET IN GENTLE TWINES,  HORATIJ ILLE & NEFASTO              52  MS 382 530
LIVE SHEE, OR DYE TO FAME. EACH LEAFE YOU MEET   AT TH' IVORY TRIBUNALL               5  MS 397 492

MEETS

MEETS ART WITH ART. SOMETIMES AS IF IN DOUBT     MUSICKS DUELL                       35  46 149 535
ON THE FAIRE SOULE WHOM FIRST HEE MEETS.         ON A PRAYER BOOKE                   89  46 126 139
WHICH WITH A SWELLING BOSOME THERE SHEE MEETS.   ON A PRAYER BOOKE                  111  46 126 139
WHICH MAN'S HEART MEETS                          TO THE NAME OF JESUS               123  52 239  30
ON THE FAIR SOUL WHOM FIRST HE MEETS.            PRAYER TO GENTLE-WOMAN              95  52 328 139
WHICH WITH A SWELLING BOSOME THERE SHE MEETS     PRAYER TO GENTLE-WOMAN             117  52 328 139

MEETES

HOURLY THERE MEETES                              TO THE NAME OF JESUS               175  52 239  30

MEETING

HAD THEIR GENERALL MEETING PLACE.                HIS EPITAPH (HERRYS)                20  46 172 471

MEETINGS

THE HERDS TO KINDLY MEETINGS, THEN THE FIELDS    OUT OF VIRGIL                       12  46 155 529

MELANCHOLY

DULL MISTS AND MELANCHOLY CLOUDS. TAKE DAY       ON A TREATISE OF CHARITY             8  46 137  69
A MELANCHOLY MANSION IN THOSE COLD               ON A TREATISE OF CHARITY            35  46 137  69
ALL MELANCHOLY CLOWDS VANISHT AWAY.              UPON KINGS CORONATION               40  MS 390 453

MELODY

THE TORRENT OF A VOYCE, WHOSE MELODY             MUSICKS DUELL                       45  46 149 535

MELODIE

BATHING IN STREAMES OF LIQUID MELODIE.           MUSICKS DUELL                       68  46 149 535
CHANT TO MY SELFE WITH RUSTIC MELODIE.           UPON BIRTH PRINCESSE E               24  MS 391 456

MELT

COULD MELT INTO SUCH SWEET VARIETY               MUSICKS DUELL                       46  46 149 535
THUS DOST THOU MELT THE YEARE                    THE WEEPER                          91  46  79 120
AND MELT THY SOULES SWEET MANSION.               IN MEMORY OF LADY MADRE TERESA     113  46 131  52
AND MELT THY SOUL'S SWEET MANSION.               TERESA                             112  52 315  52
TO MELT IN GENTLE DROPS, LETT THEM BE HEARD      AN ELEGIE ON DR PORTER              33  MS 395 476

MELTED

MELTED & MEASUR'D OUT IN SEAS OF TEARES          TO THE NAME OF JESUS               144  52 239  30

MELTS

MELTS ON THE BOSOME OF HIS LOVE, AND POWRES      OUT OF VIRGIL                        5  46 155 529
WEEPING, MELTS INTO A FOUNTAINE,                 PSALME 23                           14  46 102   5
WHERE JORDAN MELTS HIS CHRYSTALL, TO MAKE FAIRE  SUSPETTO D'HERODE                   85  46 109 216
AND MELTS IT DOWNE IN SWEET DESIRE.              ON A PRAYER BOOKE                   68  46 126 139
IT FALLS, AND DYES. OH NO, IT MELTS AWAY         ON HOPE                             57  46 143  71
AND MELTS IT DOWN IN SWEET DESIRE                PRAYER TO GENTLE-WOMAN              74  52 328 139
IT FALLS. AND DYES. O NO. IT MELTS AWAY          (ON) HOPE                           27  52 345  71

MELTING

WHOSE TREMBLING MURMURS MELTING IN WILD AIRES    MUSICKS DUELL                      141  46 149 535
THE WORKING BEES SOFT MELTING GOLD.              OUT OF GREEKE CUPID'S CRYER         25  46 159 519
HER MILD RAYES, THROUGH THY MELTING HEART.       IN MEMORY OF LADY MADRE TERESA     137  46 131  52
MY SELFE A MELTING SACRIFICE. I'ME BORNE         TO THE MORNING                      51  46 183 497
HER MILD RAYES THROUGH THY MELTING HEART.        TERESA                             136  52 315  52

MEMORIALL

THEIR SHARE, IN THY MEMORIALL.                   NEITHER DURST MAN ASKE              22  46  92  20
O DEAR MEMORIALL OF THAT DEATH                   ADORO TE                            37  52 291 172

MEMORY

THUS MUST WE DATE THY MEMORY.                    THE WEEPER                         116  46  79 120
THE MUSICKE OF THY MEMORY.                       PSALME 137                          18  46 104   7
FOR HEE WHOSE PRETIUUS MEMORY,                   ANOTHER ON HERRYS                    7  46 170 469
THUS MUST WE DATE THY MEMORY.                    WEEPER                             154  52 307 120

MEMORYE

AND THY CONQUESTS MEMORYE.                       NEITHER DURST MAN ASKE               8  46  92  20

MEN

PREFERRE SOFT ANTHEMS TO THE EARES OF MEN,       MUSICKS DUELL                       78  46 149 535
THAT MEN CAN SLEEPE WHILE THEY THEIR MATTENS SING. MUSICKS DUELL                     80  46 149 535
FROM THEIR HARD MOTHER EARTH, SPRANG HARDY MEN,  OUT OF VIRGIL                       30  46 155 529
```

|   |   |   |   |   |   |
|---|---|---|---|---|---|
| A BAND OF MEN, ROUGH AS THE ARMES THEY WORE | THE BEGINNING OF HELIODORUS | 7 | 46 | 158 | 517 |
| A SHIP THEY SAW, NO MEN SHEE HAD. YET PREST | THE BEGINNING OF HELIODORUS | 11 | 46 | 158 | 517 |
| 'BOUT MEN AND WOMEN, NOR WILL SPARE | OUT OF GREEKE CUPID'S CRYER | 42 | 46 | 159 | 519 |
| WHAT NEED'ST THOU PUT ON ARMES AGAINST POORE MEN. | UPON VENUS PUTTING ARMES | 4 | 46 | 161 | 523 |
| THREE KINGS (OR WHAT IS MORE) THREE WISE MEN WENT | SOSPETTO D'HERODE | 135 | 46 | 109 | 216 |
| WITH HER SOFT WING, WIPT FROM THE BROWES OF MEN | SOSPETTO D'HERODE | 387 | 46 | 109 | 216 |
| HIS TRUMPETS, TENDER CRYES, HIS MEN TO DARE | SOSPETTO D'HERODE | 526 | 46 | 109 | 216 |
| O WHAT. ASKE NOT THE TONGUES OF MEN. | IN MEMORY OF LADY MADRE TERESA | 119 | 46 | 131 | 52 |
| MY SOULE, SOME DRINKE FROM MEN TO BEASTS. O THEN, | AN APOLOGIE FOR HYMNE (TERESA) | 35 | 46 | 136 | 59 |
| DRINKE WEE TILL WE PROVE MORE, NOT LESSE THEN MEN. | AN APOLOGIE FOR HYMNE (TERESA) | 36 | 46 | 136 | 59 |
| MARY, MEN AND ANGELS SING | ON THE ASSUMPTION | 53 | 46 | 139 | 114 |
| LIVE CROWNE OF WOMEN, QUEEN OF MEN. | ON THE ASSUMPTION | 61 | 46 | 139 | 114 |
| SPARE THE SWEETEST AMONG MEN. | UPON DEATH OF DESIRED HERRYS | 60 | 46 | 168 | 467 |
| THAT NOTES THE TRAGICKE DOOMES OF MEN | ANOTHER ON HERRYS | 34 | 46 | 170 | 469 |
| MERCYFULL KING OF MEN. | OFFICE H. CROSS COMPLINE | 14 | 52 | 274 | 105 |
| BOW'D TO THE LOWLY MOUTHS OF MEN. | LAUDA SION SALVATOREM | 62 | 52 | 294 | 178 |
| MARIA, MEN & ANGELS SING | IN GLORIOUS ASSUMPTION B. LADY | 58 | 52 | 304 | 114 |
| LIVE, CROWN OF WOEMEN, QUEEN OF MEN. | IN GLORIOUS ASSUMPTION B. LADY | 66 | 52 | 304 | 114 |
| RIPE MEN OF MARTYRDOM, THAT COULD REACH DOWN | TERESA | 5 | 52 | 315 | 52 |
| O WHAT. ASK NOT THE TONGUES OF MEN. | TERESA | 118 | 52 | 315 | 52 |
| (MY SOUL,) SOME DRINK FROM MEN TO BEASTS, O THEN | AN APOLOGIE FOR (TERESA) HYMNE | 35 | 52 | 322 | 59 |
| DRINK WE TILL WE PROVE MORE, NOT LESSE, THEN MEN, | AN APOLOGIE FOR (TERESA) HYMNE | 36 | 52 | 322 | 59 |
| O MOST POOR-SPIRITED OF MEN. | FLAMING HEART | 19 | 52 | 324 | 61 |
| MAY IT NOT BE AMONGST THE SONNES OF MEN. | TO SAME CONCERNING CHOISE | 59 | 52 | 331 | 66 |
| MEN HAD NOT SPURN'D AT MOUNTAINES, NOR MADE WARRS | ALEXIAS THIRD ELEGIE | 9 | 52 | 336 | 209 |
| THE QUEEN OF ANGELS, (AND MEN CHAST AS YOU) | ALEXIAS THIRD ELEGIE | 29 | 52 | 336 | 209 |
| HALLS FULL OF FLATTERING MEN & FRISKING BOYES. | DESCRIPTION RELIGIOUS HOUSE | 6 | 52 | 338 | 213 |
| MIX THE MAD SONS OF MEN IN MUTUALL BLOOD. | DESCRIPTION RELIGIOUS HOUSE | 8 | 52 | 338 | 213 |
| TO TOSSE POORE MEN LIKE DUST INTO THE AIRE. | ON GUNPOWDER-TREASON | 40 | MS | 384 | 458 |
| WHAT MEANE THESE SHOURES OF TEARES AMONGST US MEN. | AN ELEGY MR STANNINOW | 16 | MS | 394 | 473 |

MENS

|   |   |   |   |   |   |
|---|---|---|---|---|---|
| MENS HEARTS INTO THEIR HANDS. THIS LESSON TOO | MUSICKS DUELL | 56 | 46 | 149 | 535 |
| DECEIVES MENS FEARES WITH FLATTERING WILES. | OUT OF GREEKE CUPID'S CRYER | 50 | 46 | 159 | 519 |
| THAT TO HIS SWEETNESSE, ALL MENS EYES | HIS EPITAPH (HERRYS) | 41 | 46 | 172 | 471 |
| OTHER MENS HUNGER WITH STRANGE FEASTS I QUELL'D | OUT OF GROTIUS | 57 | MS | 398 | 198 |

MEND

|   |   |   |   |   |   |
|---|---|---|---|---|---|
| NATURE (METHINKS) MIGHT EASILY MEND HER GROWTH. | UPON TWO GREENE APRICOCKES | 22 | 48 | 220 | 494 |

MERCHANDISE

|   |   |   |   |   |   |
|---|---|---|---|---|---|
| 'TWAS FOR SUCH SORRY MERCHANDISE | CHARITAS NIMIA | 7 | 52 | 280 | 48 |

MERCHANT

|   |   |   |   |   |   |
|---|---|---|---|---|---|
| MAKE BUT A SIMPLE MERCHANT MAN. | CHARITAS NIMIA | 6 | 52 | 280 | 48 |

MERCHANTS

|   |   |   |   |   |   |
|---|---|---|---|---|---|
| MERCHANTS OF DEATH & SIN, IS BOUGHT & SOLD. | OFFICE H. CROSS MATINES | 15 | 52 | 265 | 86 |
| WHICH WAY IT THREATS, WITH FEARE THE MERCHANTS MIND | HORATIJ ILLE & NEFASTO | 19 | MS | 382 | 530 |

MERCILESSE

|   |   |   |   |   |   |
|---|---|---|---|---|---|
| NO ONE SO MERCILESSE AS THIS OF HERS. | SOSPETTO D'HERODE | 306 | 46 | 109 | 216 |
| (MERCILESSE LOVE.) IS ALL. | WEEPER | 129 | 52 | 307 | 120 |

MERCURY

|   |   |   |   |   |   |
|---|---|---|---|---|---|
| OF PLUTO'S MERCURY, THAT I MAY SING | UPON GUNPOWDER TREASON | 2 | MS | 386 | 460 |

MERCY

|   |   |   |   |   |   |
|---|---|---|---|---|---|
| STILL MAY THY SWEET MERCY SPREAD | PSALME 23 | 59 | 46 | 102 | 5 |
| MERCY WILL COME ERE LONG, | ON A PRAYER BOOKE | 34 | 46 | 126 | 139 |
| COULD THEY KNOW WHAT MERCY MEANT. | ANOTHER ON HERRYS | 18 | 46 | 170 | 469 |
| WHERE MERCY CANNOT FIND THEM. BUT O THOU | TO THE MORNING | 32 | 46 | 183 | 497 |
| HAVE MERCY THEN, AND WHEN HE NEXT SHALL RISE | TO THE MORNING | 35 | 46 | 183 | 497 |
| 'TIS IN THE MERCY OF HER EYE, | LOVES HOROSCOPE | 19 | 46 | 185 | 483 |
| JUST MERCY THEN, THY RECKNING BE | DIES IRAE | 37 | 52 | 298 | 186 |
| MERCY (MY JUDGE) MERCY I CRY | DIES IRAE | 41 | 52 | 298 | 186 |
| MERCY (MY JUDGE) MERCY I CRY | DIES IRAE | 41 | 52 | 298 | 186 |
| MERCY WILL COME E'RE LONG | PRAYER TO GENTLE-WOMAN | 40 | 52 | 328 | 139 |

MERCYES

|   |   |   |   |   |   |
|---|---|---|---|---|---|
| HOW MANY THOUSAND MERCYES THERE | TO THE NAME OF JESUS | 191 | 52 | 239 | 30 |
| THOSE MERCYES WHICH THY MARY FOUND | DIES IRAE | 49 | 52 | 298 | 186 |

MERCYFULL

|   |   |   |   |   |   |
|---|---|---|---|---|---|
| MERCYFULL KING OF MEN. | OFFICE H. CROSS COMPLINE | 14 | 52 | 274 | 105 |

MERCYLESSE

|   |   |   |   |   |   |
|---|---|---|---|---|---|
| WITH MANY A MERCYLESSE O'RE MASTRING WAVE. | SOSPETTO D'HERODE | 426 | 46 | 109 | 216 |

MERIDIAN

|   |   |   |   |   |   |
|---|---|---|---|---|---|
| OUT-STARE THE BROAD-BEAM'D DAYES MERIDIAN) | ON FRONTISPIECE ISAACSONS | 10 | 46 | 191 | 491 |
| MERIDIAN NIGHT, | IN GLORIOUS EPIPHANIE | 17 | 52 | 253 | 39 |

## MERIT

| | | | | |
|---|---|---|---|---|
| WHOSE MERIT DARE APPLY IT, | WISHES SUPPOSED MISTRESSE | 119 | 46 195 479 |
| THAT KINGDOM WHICH THIS CROSSE DID MERIT. | VEXILLA REGIS | | 46  52 277 156 |

## MERITS

AND THE DEARE MERITS OF YOUR MUSE, THEIR DUE,   UPON TWO GREENE APRICOCKES   11  48 220 494

## MERRY

TO WHOM THE MERRY LAMBES DOE TRIPP ALONG   UPON KINGS CORONATION   26  MS 390 453

## MESSENGERS

HERALDS AND MESSENGERS IMMEDIATELY   SOSPETTO D'HERODE   509  46 109 216

## MET

WHAT EVER STARRY SYNOD MET,   LOVES HOROSCOPE   18  46 185 483

## METT

HATH METT LOVE'S NOON IN NATURE'S NIGHT.   IN HOLY NATIVITY   2  52 246  76

## METALLS

IN GROSSEST METALLS HIS OWN GOLD.   AGAINST IRRESOLUTION AND DELAY   56  52 347 146

## METAMORPHOSIS

STRANGE METAMORPHOSIS. IT WAS BUT NOW   UPON KINGS CORONATION   1  MS 390 453

## METEOR

AND OF A METEOR MAKE A STARR.   TO COUNTESSE OF DENBIGH   30  52 236 146
ALL THIS IT ONLY THREATS. THE METEOR LY'D.   ON GUNPOWDER-TREASON   49  MS 384 458

## METEOR-LIKE

WHOSE FLOURISH (METEOR-LIKE) DOTH CURLE THE AIRE   MUSICKS DUELL   137  46 149 535

## METHINKS

NATURE (METHINKS) MIGHT EASILY MEND HER GROWTH.   UPON TWO GREENE APRICOCKES   22  48 220 494

## MEZENTIUS

OF DEATH MEZENTIUS, OR GERYON DREW.   SOSPETTO D'HERODE   362  46 109 216

## MIDNIGHT

AMAZ'D THE MIDNIGHT WORLD, AND MADE A DAY   SOSPETTO D'HERODE   116  46 109 216
THAT, THE WORLD'S MORNING, THIS HER MIDNIGHT IS.   ON FRONTISPIECE ISAACSONS   24  46 191 491

## MIDST

MIDST ALL THE DARKE AND KNOTTY SNARES,   NEITHER DURST MAN ASKE   1  46  92  20

## MIDWIFERIE

THE MONSTER CRUSHT, MAUGRE THEIR MIDWIFERIE.   UPON GUNPOWDER TREASON   56  MS 386 460

## MID-DAY

AT MID-DAY OPES A PRESENCE WHICH HEAVENS EYE   UPON YORKE HIS BIRTH   70  46 176 500

## MIGHT

| | | | |
|---|---|---|---|
| THERE MIGHT YOU HEARE HER KINDLE HER SOFT VOYCE, | MUSICKS DUELL | 83 | 46 149 535 |
| MIGHT HEE FLOW FROM THEE | THE WEEPER | 61 | 46  79 120 |
| THROUGH THE THICK SHADES OBSCURELY MIGHT YOU SEE | SOSPETTO D'HERODE | 350 | 46 109 216 |
| THAT THY FIRME HAND FOR EVER MIGHT SUSTAINE | SOSPETTO D'HERODE | 450 | 46 109 216 |
| THY PRAISE MIGHT NOT SPEAK ENGLISH TOO, FORBID | AN APOLOGIE FOR HYMNE (TERESA) | 11 | 46 136  59 |
| AS MIGHT HAVE TAUGHT GRIEFE HOW TO WEEPE. | ANOTHER ON HERRYS | 22 | 46 170 469 |
| THOSE MIGHTY GENII THRONG, WHICH WELL MIGHT BEE | UPON YORKE HIS BIRTH | 10 | 46 176 500 |
| MIGHT A WORD ONCE FLYE FROM OUT THEE. | OUT OF THE ITALIAN (1) | 33 | 46 188 545 |
| SO MUCH O'RE-MASTRING ALL HIS MIGHT, | OUT OF THE ITALIAN (3) | 6 | 46 190 549 |
| NOW THAT TIME'S EMPIRE MIGHT BE AMPLY FILL'D. | ON FRONTISPIECE ISAACSONS | 15 | 46 191 491 |
| NATURE (METHINKS) MIGHT EASILY MEND HER GROWTH. | UPON TWO GREENE APRICOCKES | 22 | 48 220 494 |
| THAT THESE DRY LIDDS MIGHT BORROW | SANCTA MARIA DOLORUM | 43 | 52 283 162 |
| BOTH OF LOVE'S FIRES & FLOUDS) MIGHT I RECLINE | SANCTA MARIA DOLORUM | 47 | 52 283 162 |
| THOMAS MIGHT TOUCH. NONE BUT MIGHT SEE | ADORO TE | 23 | 52 291 172 |
| THOMAS MIGHT TOUCH. NONE BUT MIGHT SEE | ADORO TE | 23 | 52 291 172 |
| OF HER UNKIND GIFT MIGHT WE HAVE | O GLORIOSA DOMINA | 13 | 52 302 194 |
| HE MIGHT PROVOKE THE WEALTH OF PRINCES. | WEEPER | 118 | 52 307 120 |
| THY PRAISE MIGHT NOT SPEAK ENGLISH TOO. FORBID | AN APOLOGIE FOR (TERESA) HYMNE | 11 | 52 322  59 |
| THENCE HE MIGHT TOSSE YOU | TO SAME CONCERNING CHOISE | 49 | 52 331  66 |
| WHAT HINDERS, BUT MY BOSOME STILL MIGHT BE | LUKE 2. QUAERIT JESUM | 49 | MS 379  11 |
| MIGHT BE AN ACTOR IN THIS TRAGAEDY. | UPON GUNPOWDER TREASON | 34 | MS 386 460 |
| THAT MIGHT INTERPRET OUR FAIRE CYNTHIA'S WORTH, | UPON BIRTH PRINCESSE E | 30 | MS 391 456 |

MIGHTY

```
ARE HUSKS SO DEARE. TROTH 'TIS A MIGHTY RATE.          ON THE PRODIGALL                    4   46  86  17
THAT TO THE MIGHTY NEPTUNE'S SELF DARE THREATEN WRACK. WHY ARE YEE AFRAID                  8   46  88  15
O MIGHTY NOTHING, UNTO THEE,                           AND HE ANSWERED NOTHING             1   46  91  22
RISE MIGHTY MAN OF WONDERS, AND THY WORLD WITH THEE    EASTER DAY                          3   46 100  26
THOU MIGHTY BRANCH OF EMPERORS AND KINGS.              SOSPETTO D'HERODE                  10   46 109 216
AND IN THEIR MURMURES KEEPE THY MIGHTY NAME.           SOSPETTO D'HERODE                  32   46 109 216
A MIGHTY BABE, WHOSE PURE, UNSPOTTED BIRTH,            SOSPETTO D'HERODE                 159   46 109 216
BE IT THY PART, HELLS MIGHTY LORD, TO LAY              SOSPETTO D'HERODE                 263   46 109 216
MIGHTY IN MISCHIEFE, WITH DREAD NERO TOO,              SOSPETTO D'HERODE                 364   46 109 216
SO MIGHTY WERE TH'AMAZING CHARACTERS                   SOSPETTO D'HERODE                 477   46 109 216
FORBID IT MIGHTY LOVE, LET NO FOND HATE                AN APOLOGIE FOR HYMNE (TERESA)     13   46 136  59
BRITTAINE, THE MIGHTY OCEANS LOVELY BRIDE.             UPON YORKE HIS BIRTH                1   46 176 500
THOSE MIGHTY GENII THRONG, WHICH WELL MIGHT BEE        UPON YORKE HIS BIRTH               10   46 176 500
O THOU FULL MIXTURE OF THOSE MIGHTY SOULES,            UPON YORKE HIS BIRTH               35   46 176 500
DENY TO MIGHTY LOVE A DEITY.                           UPON YORKE HIS BIRTH               85   46 176 500
MIGHTY QUEEN, TO THINKE IT LONG,                       TO THE QUEEN                        2   48 215 501
THEN THIS GREAT MORNINGS MIGHTY BUSYNES.               TO THE NAME OF JESUS               23   52 239  30
YE MIGHTY ORBES, AS WELL AS YOU.                       TO THE NAME OF JESUS              104   52 239  30
AND LET THE MIGHTY BABE ALONE.                         IN HOLY NATIVITY                   45   52 246  76
FORBID IT, MIGHTY LOVE. LET NO FOND HATE               AN APOLOGIE FOR (TERESA) HYMNE     13   52 322  59
LET NOT MY LORD, THE MIGHTY LOVER                      TO SAME CONCERNING CHOISE          41   52 331  66
MIGHTY LOVE'S ARTILLERY.                               IN CICATRICES DOMINI JESU           2   MS 381  27
```

MILD

```
THEN VENUS MILD INSTINCT (AT SET TIMES) YEILDS         OUT OF VIRGIL                      11   46 155 529
HER MILD RAYES, THROUGH THY MELTING HEART.             IN MEMORY OF LADY MADRE TERESA    137   46 131  52
THEY THAT BY LOVE'S MILD DICTATE NOW                   TO THE NAME OF JESUS              236   52 239  30
MAKING HIS MANSION IN THE MILD                         TERESA                             13   52 315  52
HER MILD RAYES THROUGH THY MELTING HEART.              TERESA                            136   52 315  52
```

MILDE

```
AND MAKE HIS MANSION IN THE MILDE                      IN MEMORY OF LADY MADRE TERESA     13   46 131  52
```

MILDER

```
T'EMBRACE A MILDER MARTYRDOME.                         IN MEMORY OF LADY MADRE TERESA     68   46 131  52
BUT IF HER MILDER INFLUENCE MOVE.                      LOVES HOROSCOPE                    33   46 185 483
T'EMBRACE A MILDER MARTYRDOM.                          TERESA                             68   52 315  52
```

MILK

```
WITH MANNA, MILK, AND BALM, NEW BROACH THE MOUNTAINES. SOSPETTO D'HERODE                 112   46 109 216
```

VIRGIN-MILK

```
TWO SISTER-SEAS OF VIRGIN-MILK,                        IN HOLY NATIVITY                   87   52 246  76
```

MILKE

```
MILKE ALL THE WAY.                                     TO INFANT MARTYRS                   6   46  88  10
  THE MOTHERS MILKE, THE CHILDRENS BLOOD,              UPON INFANT MARTYRS                 2   46  95  10
TWO SISTER-SEAS OF VIRGINS MILKE,                      A HYMNE OF THE NATIVITY            61   46 106  76
THAT FROM HIS MOTHERS BREST HEE MILKE SHOULD DRINKE.   SOSPETTO D'HERODE                 173   46 109 216
```

MILKY

```
WHERE TH' MILKY RIVERS MEET,                           THE WEEPER                         21   46  79 120
NOR LET THE MILKY FONTS THAT BATH YOUR THIRST,         TO INFANT MARTYRS                   3   46  88  10
AND MILKY SOULE OF A SOFT CHILDE.                      IN MEMORY OF LADY MADRE TERESA     14   46 131  52
SHEE CLIMBES, AND MAKES A FARRE MORE MILKY WAY.        ON THE ASSUMPTION                   6   46 139 114
WHOSE FEET CAN WALKE THE MILKY WAY, AND CHUSE          TO THE MORNING                     24   46 163 497
EYES, NESTS OF MILKY DOVES                             WEEPER                             87   52 307 120
AND MILKY SOUL OF A SOFT CHILD.                        TERESA                             14   52 315  52
AND CRACK THE CHRISTALL GLOBE. THE MILKY STREAME       ON GUNPOWDER-TREASON               23   MS 384 458
THAT HAND OF MILKY DOUNE. ALL THESE ARE BASE.          UPON BIRTH PRINCESSE E             52   46 391 456
FROM HEAVENS SWEET MILKY STREAME DOTH GENTLY POURE.    AN ELEGY MR STANNINOW              10   MS 394 473
```

TH'MILKY

```
WHERE TH'MILKY RIVERS CREEP,                           WEEPER                             21   52 307 120
```

MILKEY

```
SHE CLIMBS, AND MAKES A FARRE MORE MILKEY WAY.         IN GLORIOUS ASSUMPTION B. LADY      6   52 304 114
```

MIND

```
WITH NIMBLE FLAMES, AND THOUGH HIS MIND                OUT OF GREEKE CUPID'S CRYER        21   46 159 519
THOUGH BARE HIS SKIN, HIS MIND HEE COVERS,             OUT OF GREEKE CUPID'S CRYER        39   46 159 519
THY MIND IN TEARES WHO E'RE THOU BE,                   UPON THE DEATH OF A GENTLEMAN      25   46 166 472
WAY FOR A RESOLVED MIND.                               PSALME 23                          44   46 102   5
THE FAIRE CENTER OF MY MIND                            PSALME 23                          62   46 102   5
HE CALLS TO MIND TH'OLD QUARRELL, AND WHAT SPARKE      SOSPETTO D'HERODE                  89   46 109 216
TOGETHER, IN HIS PONDROUS MIND BOTH WEIGHES.           SOSPETTO D'HERODE                  96   46 109 216
LOVE KNOWES NO NONAGE, NOR THE MIND.                   IN MEMORY OF LADY MADRE TERESA     32   46 131  52
THE SACRED SWEETNESSE OF HIS MIND.                     ANOTHER ON HERRYS                  16   46 170 469
THE RIPE ENDOWMENTS OF WHOSE MIND,                     HIS EPITAPH (HERRYS)                7   46 172 471
OF A CLEERE MIND ARE DAY ALL NIGHT.                    WISHES SUPPOSED MISTRESSE          81   46 195 479
WHEN THOU ART MASTER OF THE MIND.                      TO THE NAME OF JESUS              124   52 239  30
```

PAGE 265

| | | | | | |
|---|---|---|---|---|---|
| LOVE KNOWES NO NONAGE, NOR THE MIND. | TERESA | 32 | 52 | 315 | 52 |
| WHICH WAY IT THREATS. WITH FEARE THE MERCHANTS MIND | HORATIJ ILLE & NEFASTO | 19 | MS | 382 | 530 |
| BUT YETT THEY WERE NOT POWDER'D TO HIS MIND. | UPON GUNPOWDER TREASON | 52 | MS | 387 | 461 |

MINDS

| | | | | | |
|---|---|---|---|---|---|
| MY MINDS DEVOTION IN MY BODYES NEED. | OUT OF GROTIUS | 60 | MS | 398 | 198 |

MINDFULL

| | | | | | |
|---|---|---|---|---|---|
| EACH MINDFULL PLANT HASTS TO MAKE GOOD | AGAINST IRRESOLUTION AND DELAY | 35 | 52 | 347 | 146 |
| AND BY A MINDFULL, MYSTICK BREATH | LAUDA SION SALVATOREM | 27 | 52 | 294 | 178 |

MINE

| | | | | | |
|---|---|---|---|---|---|
| MINE IS THE WAGGE. TIS I THAT OWE | OUT OF GREEKE CUPID'S CRYER | 8 | 46 | 159 | 519 |
| BALSOME FOR MINE. | ON MARKES OF SAVIOURS WOUNDS | 10 | 46 | 86 | 28 |
| THEN COULD I SHOW THESE ARMES OF MINE, AND SAY | COME SEE WHERE THE LORD LAY | 5 | 46 | 87 | 27 |
| THE CALM THAT COOLS THINE EYE DOES SHIPWRACK MINE, | AND A CERTAINE PRIEST PASSED | 3 | 46 | 94 | 17 |
| FOR O. | | | | | |
| WHEN FIRST I LOOK'T ON THEE, I LOST MINE EYES. | SAMPSON TO HIS DALILAH | 2 | 46 | 102 | 8 |
| PORTENTS BEFORE MINE EYES THEIR POWERS ADVANCE. | SOSPETTO D'HERODE | 202 | 46 | 109 | 216 |
| OF YOUR WHITE HAND, THEY ARE MINE. | ON MR. G. HERBERTS BOOKE | 18 | 46 | 130 | 68 |
| THAT SHUTS NIGHTS DYING EYES, SHALL OPEN MINE. | TO THE MORNING | 46 | 46 | 183 | 497 |
| DEFECTS I DRAW MINE OWNE DULL CHARACTER. | UPON TWO GREENE APRICOCKES | 32 | 48 | 220 | 494 |
| HELP ME TO MEDITATE MINE IMMORTALL SONG. | TO THE NAME OF JESUS | 61 | 52 | 239 | 30 |
| TAKE BOTH TO THINE ACCOUNT. THAT I & MINE | OFFICE H. CROSS RECOMMENDATION | 3 | 52 | 276 | 106 |
| WHAT MINE OWN MADNESSES HAVE DONE WITH ME. | CHARITAS NIMIA | 34 | 52 | 280 | 48 |
| THIS HARD, COLD, HEART OF MINE. | SANCTA MARIA DOLORUM | 48 | 52 | 283 | 162 |
| IF NOT MORE SOFT, MINE EYES. | SANCTA MARIA DOLORUM | 86 | 52 | 283 | 162 |
| O TEACH MINE TOO THE ART | SANCTA MARIA DOLORUM | 98 | 52 | 283 | 162 |
| BOTH WORTHLESSE ARE. FOR THEY ARE MINE, | DIES IRAE | 54 | 52 | 298 | 186 |
| WAITED ON BY A WANDRING MINE. | WEEPER | 124 | 52 | 307 | 120 |
| UNDRESSE THY SERAPHIM INTO MINE. | FLAMING HEART | 40 | 52 | 324 | 61 |
| UNTO ALL LIFE OF MINE MAY DY. | FLAMING HEART | 108 | 52 | 324 | 61 |
| ALEXIS, HE ALONE IS MINE (SAID I) | ALEXIAS THIRD ELEGIE | 56 | 52 | 336 | 209 |
| ALEXIS IS ALONE. BUT IS NOT MINE. | ALEXIAS THIRD ELEGIE | 58 | 52 | 336 | 209 |
| YET SURE THOU DID'ST LODGE HEERE. THIS WOMBE OF MINE | LUKE 2. QUAERIT JESUM | 25 | MS | 379 | 11 |
| DAWNE THEN TO ME,THOU MORNE OF MINE OWNE DAY, | LUKE 2. QUAERIT JESUM | 45 | MS | 379 | 11 |
| MINE EYES A TRIBUTARY STREAME SHALL PAY. | ON GUNPOWDER-TREASON | 14 | MS | 384 | 458 |
| OF FUTURE CHANCE. THE WORLD'S GRAND SIRE. AND MINE | OUT OF GROTIUS | 3 | MS | 398 | 198 |
| MINE OWNE WITH STRANGER FASTINGS, WHEN I HELD | OUT OF GROTIUS | 58 | MS | 398 | 198 |

MINES

| | | | | | |
|---|---|---|---|---|---|
| THAT WHICH THEIR WAXEN MINES ENFOLD, | OUT OF GREEKE CUPID'S CRYER | 26 | 46 | 159 | 519 |
| LEAVING THOSE MINES OF NECTAR, THEIR SWEET FOUNTAINES, | AN ELEGIE ON DR PORTER | 41 | MS | 395 | 476 |

MINIONS

| | | | | | |
|---|---|---|---|---|---|
| BE' A GLOOMY CANOPY TO PLUTO'S MINIONS. | UPON GUNPOWDER TREASON | 22 | MS | 387 | 461 |

MINISTERS

| | | | | | |
|---|---|---|---|---|---|
| COME, YE SOFT MINISTERS OF SWEET SAD MIRTH, | TO THE NAME OF JESUS | 62 | 52 | 239 | 30 |
| STILL WOULD THOSE BEAUTEOUS MINISTERS OF LIGHT | CHARITAS NIMIA | 21 | 52 | 280 | 48 |

MINORITY

| | | | | | |
|---|---|---|---|---|---|
| QUEEN REGENT IN YONGE LOVE'S MINORITY. | (ON) HOPE | 44 | 52 | 345 | 71 |

MINORITIE

| | | | | | |
|---|---|---|---|---|---|
| QUEEN REGENT IN YOUNG LOVES MINORITIE. | ON HOPE | 84 | 46 | 143 | 71 |

MINOTAURES

| | | | | | |
|---|---|---|---|---|---|
| MINOTAURES, CYCLOPSES, WITH A DARKE DROVE | SOSPETTO D'HERODE | 351 | 46 | 109 | 216 |

MINT

| | | | | | |
|---|---|---|---|---|---|
| A VOLUNTARY MINT, THAT STROWES | WEEPER | 125 | 52 | 307 | 120 |

MINUTE

| | | | | | |
|---|---|---|---|---|---|
| EACH MINUTE WAITETH HEERE. | THE WEEPER | 93 | 46 | 79 | 120 |

MINUTES

| | | | | | |
|---|---|---|---|---|---|
| SOE FOULE, ONE MINUTES LIGHT HAD IT BUT SEENE. | UPON GUNPOWDER TREASON | 13 | MS | 386 | 460 |

MIRACLE

| | | | | | |
|---|---|---|---|---|---|
| NO MIRACLE. | UPON ASSE THAT BORE SAVIOUR | 4 | 46 | 90 | 19 |
| DRAW TO THIS SISTER MIRACLE A BROTHER. | UPON BIRTH PRINCESSE E | 56 | MS | 391 | 456 |

MIRACLES

| | | | | | |
|---|---|---|---|---|---|
| I CAL'D A HUNDRED MIRACLES TO TELL | OUT OF GROTIUS | 31 | MS | 398 | 198 |

MIRTH

| | | | | |
|---|---|---|---|---|
| LIVE OUR CHASTE LOVE, THE HOLY MIRTH | ON THE ASSUMPTION | 59 | 46 139 | 114 |
| COME, YE SOFT MINISTERS OF SWEET SAD MIRTH, | TO THE NAME OF JESUS | 62 | 52 239 | 30 |
| LIVE, OUR CHAST LOVE, THE HOLY MIRTH | IN GLORIOUS ASSUMPTION B. LADY | 64 | 52 304 | 114 |

MIRTHE

| | | | | |
|---|---|---|---|---|
| WHAT E'RE COOPERATES TO THE COMMON MIRTHE | TO THE NAME OF JESUS | 75 | 52 239 | 30 |

MISCHEIFE

| | | | | |
|---|---|---|---|---|
| SETT TO THE MISCHEIFE OF POSTERITIE. | HORATIJ ILLE & NEFASTO | 2 | MS 382 | 530 |
| MISCHEIFE, THAT SCORNES EXPRESSION SHOULD COME NIGH IT. | ON GUNPOWDER-TREASON | 48 | MS 384 | 458 |

MISCHEIFE'S

| | | | | |
|---|---|---|---|---|
| WHICH POSETH MISCHEIFE'S SELFE TO PARALLEL. | AN ELEGIE ON DR PORTER | 14 | MS 395 | 476 |

MISCHIEFE

| | | | | |
|---|---|---|---|---|
| AND MEET THE MISCHIEFE THAT UPON THEE GROWES. | SOSPETTO D'HERODE | 246 | 46 109 | 216 |
| MIGHTY IN MISCHIEFE, WITH DREAD NERO TOO, | SOSPETTO D'HERODE | 364 | 46 109 | 216 |
| ALL MISCHIEFE COMES AFTER ALL HALLOW. | UPON POWDER DAY | 2 | 46 185 | 74 |

MISCHIFES

| | | | | |
|---|---|---|---|---|
| MISCHIFES OLD MASTER, CLOSE ABOUT HIM CLINGS | SOSPETTO D'HERODE | 36 | 46 109 | 216 |

MISERABLE

| | | | | |
|---|---|---|---|---|
| A MISERABLE AND A MONSTROUS FEAST, | THE BEGINNING OF HELIODORUS | 25 | 46 158 | 517 |

MISERIES

| | | | | |
|---|---|---|---|---|
| RATHER MAKE UP TO THY NEW MISERIES, | SOSPETTO D'HERODE | 245 | 46 109 | 216 |
| TO TH' EMPYRAEUM OF ALL MISERIES. | ON GUNPOWDER-TREASON | 46 | MS 384 | 458 |

MISERYES

| | | | | |
|---|---|---|---|---|
| SHUT IN THEIR TEARES. SHUT OUT THEIR MISERYES. | TO THE MORNING | 58 | 46 183 | 497 |
| NEEDS MUST MY MISERYES OWE THAT MAN A SPITE | ALEXIAS THIRD ELEGIE | 3 | 52 336 | 209 |

MISERY

| | | | | |
|---|---|---|---|---|
| THAT OW'ST A NAME TO MISERY. | UPON THE DEATH OF A GENTLEMAN | 26 | 46 166 | 472 |
| IF I WERE LOST IN MISERY, | CHARITAS NIMIA | 45 | 52 280 | 48 |
| FOR LIGHTING THEM UNTO THEIR MISERY. | ON GUNPOWDER-TREASON | 60 | MS 384 | 458 |

MISPLAC'T

| | | | | |
|---|---|---|---|---|
| THE PROUD & MISPLAC'T GATES OF HELL, | IN GLORIOUS EPIPHANIE | 55 | 52 253 | 39 |

MISS-LEDDE

| | | | | |
|---|---|---|---|---|
| MISS-LEDDE BEFORE THEY LOST THEIR WAY, | IN GLORIOUS EPIPHANIE | 164 | 52 253 | 39 |

MISSE

| | | | | |
|---|---|---|---|---|
| THE GLAD DESCRYER SHALL NOT MISSE, | OUT OF GREEKE CUPID'S CRYER | 11 | 46 159 | 519 |
| BE HEROD, AND THOU SHALT NOT MISSE FROM MEE | SOSPETTO D'HERODE | 463 | 46 109 | 216 |
| FIX HERE, FAIR MAJESTY. MAY YOUR HEART NE'RE MISSE | TO THE QUEEN'S MAJESTY | 21 | 52 261 | 47 |
| NOR MAY WE MISSE THE JOY TO MEET IN YOU | TO THE QUEEN'S MAJESTY | 23 | 52 261 | 47 |

MISSES

| | | | | |
|---|---|---|---|---|
| HAPPY SOULE WHO NEVER MISSES, | ON A PRAYER BOOKE | 98 | 46 126 | 139 |
| HAPPY INDEED, WHO NEVER MISSES | PRAYER TO GENTLE-WOMAN | 104 | 52 328 | 139 |

MISSING

| | | | | |
|---|---|---|---|---|
| WAS LOSSE OF MULTITUDES. AND MISSING MEE | OUT OF GROTIUS | 28 | MS 398 | 198 |

MIST

| | | | | |
|---|---|---|---|---|
| WHAT THOUGH I MIST MY BLOW. YET I STROOKE HIGH, | SOSPETTO D'HERODE | 223 | 46 109 | 216 |
| AND COURTED IN THE POMPOUS MASK OF A MORE SPECIOUS MIST. | IN GLORIOUS EPIPHANIE | 53 | 52 253 | 39 |
| OR HIDING HIS VEX'T CHEEKS IN A HIR'D MIST | IN GLORIOUS EPIPHANIE | 123 | 52 253 | 39 |

MISTS

| | | | | |
|---|---|---|---|---|
| DULL MISTS AND MELANCHOLY CLOUDS. TAKE DAY | ON A TREATISE OF CHARITY | 8 | 46 137 | 69 |
| AND LET NO DULL MISTS CHOAKE THE LIGHTS FAIRE GROWTH. | ON A FOULE MORNING | 4 | 46 181 | 495 |
| NO MISTS DOE MASK, NO LAZY STEAMES. | TEMPERANCE | 30 | 52 342 | 510 |
| AND MISTS OF GREIFE, DARE FORCE A JOYFULL LIGHT. | UPON KINGS CORONATION | 16 | MS 389 | 454 |

MISTES

| | | | | |
|---|---|---|---|---|
| NO MISTES DOE MASKE NO LAZY STEAMES. | IN PRAISE OF LESSIUS | 32 | 46 156 | 510 |

MISTAKE

| | | | | |
|---|---|---|---|---|
| WHERE ART THOU MAN. WHAT COWARDLY MISTAKE | SOSPETTO D'HERODE | 457 | 46 109 | 216 |
| THE MORN INCURR A SWEET MISTAKE. | IN GLORIOUS EPIPHANIE | 2 | 52 253 | 39 |
| HERE A WELL-PLAC'T & WISE MISTAKE | FLAMING HEART | 8 | 52 324 | 61 |

MYSTAKE

| | | | | |
|---|---|---|---|---|
| HAPPY MYSTAKE. | TO SAME CONCERNING CHOISE | 54 | 52 331 | 66 |

MISTAKEN

| | | | | |
|---|---|---|---|---|
| IN YOUR MISTAKEN LOVE, | TO SAME CONCERNING CHOISE | 47 | 52 331 | 66 |
| I WAS MISTAKEN. SOME FAIRE SPHAERE, OR OTHER | LUKE 2. QUAERIT JESUM | 21 | MS 379 | 11 |

MISTRESSE

| | | | | |
|---|---|---|---|---|
| (MISTRESSE) I COME. NOW REACH A STRAINE MY LUTE | MUSICKS DUELL | 107 | 46 149 | 535 |
| LOOKE IN WHAT POMPE THE MISTRESSE PLANET MOVES | SOSPETTO D'HERODE | 237 | 46 109 | 216 |
| MISTRESSE ATTENDED BY SUCH BRIGHT | IN MEMORY OF LADY MADRE TERESA | 125 | 46 131 | 52 |
| SO HAVE I SEENE (TO DRESSE THEIR MISTRESSE MAY) | UPON YORKE HIS BIRTH | 59 | 46 176 | 500 |
| MISTRESSE OF WONDERS. CYNTHIA'S IS THE NIGHT, | UPON YORKE HIS BIRTH | 77 | 46 176 | 500 |
| TO TH' SYRENS IN MY MISTRESSE SONG, | OUT OF THE ITALIAN (3) | 4 | 46 190 | 549 |
| VERTUE THEIR MISTRESSE, | WISHES SUPPOSED MISTRESSE | 68 | 46 195 | 479 |
| WHEN YOU ARE MISTRESSE OF THE SONG, | TO THE QUEEN | 1 | 48 215 | 501 |
| LIVE MISTRESSE OF OUR SONG. AND WHEN | IN GLORIOUS ASSUMPTION B. LADY | 67 | 52 304 | 114 |
| MISTRESSE, ATTENDED BY SUCH BRIGHT | TERESA | 124 | 52 315 | 52 |
| THIS IS THE MISTRESSE FLAME. & DUTEOUS HE | FLAMING HEART | 17 | 52 324 | 61 |

MISTRIS

| | | | | |
|---|---|---|---|---|
| LIVE MISTRIS OF OUR SONG, AND WHEN | ON THE ASSUMPTION | 62 | 46 139 | 114 |
| SWEET MISTRIS SOUNDS A GREAT DEALE BETTER. | PETRONIJ ALES PHASIACIS PETITA | 18 | MS 382 | 526 |

MITES

| | | | | |
|---|---|---|---|---|
| TWO MITES, TWO DROPS, (YET ALL HER HOUSE AND LAND) | WIDOWES MITES | 1 | 46 86 | 21 |

MITHRA

| | | | | |
|---|---|---|---|---|
| AND MITHRA NOW SHALL BE NO NAME. | IN GLORIOUS EPIPHANIE | 100 | 52 253 | 39 |
| AND LEFT THEIR MITHRA FOR MY STAR. THIS THEY. | OUT OF GROTIUS | 38 | MS 398 | 198 |

MIX

| | | | | |
|---|---|---|---|---|
| FOR EVER HERE, & MIX | TO THE NAME OF JESUS | 83 | 52 239 | 30 |
| MIX ALL YOUR MANY WORLDS, ABOVE, | TO THE NAME OF JESUS | 86 | 52 239 | 30 |
| SHALL SWELL WITH BOTH FOR HIM. & MIX | OFFICE H. CROSS SIXT | 7 | 52 270 | 97 |
| TO STUDY HIM SO, TILL WE MIX | SANCTA MARIA DOLORUM | 99 | 52 283 | 162 |
| MIX WITH OUR LOW MORTALITY, | LAUDA SION SALVATOREM | 74 | 52 294 | 178 |
| MIX THE MAD SONS OF MEN IN MUTUALL BLOOD. | DESCRIPTION RELIGIOUS HOUSE | 8 | 52 338 | 213 |

MIXT

| | | | | |
|---|---|---|---|---|
| SHAME NOW AND ANGER MIXT A DOUBLE STAINE | MUSICKS DUELL | 105 | 46 149 | 535 |
| AND BY A SOFT INSINUATION, MIXT | OUT OF VIRGIL | 7 | 46 155 | 529 |
| WHICH MIXT WITH GALL & BLOOD THEY QUAFFE BRIM FULL. | SOSPETTO D'HERODE | 336 | 46 109 | 216 |
| MIXT & MADE FRIENDS BY LOVE'S SWEET POWRES. | WEEPER | 102 | 52 307 | 120 |
| BOTH MIXT AT LAST THEIR BLOOD IN ONE RICH BED | ALEXIAS THIRD ELEGIE | 47 | 52 336 | 209 |

MIXTURE

| | | | | |
|---|---|---|---|---|
| WINE OF IMMORTALL MIXTURE, WHICH CAN PROVE | AN APOLOGIE FOR HYMNE (TERESA) | 42 | 46 136 | 59 |
| O THOU FULL MIXTURE OF THOSE MIGHTY SOULES, | UPON YORKE HIS BIRTH | 35 | 46 176 | 500 |
| WINE OF IMMORTALL MIXTURE. WHICH CAN PROVE | AN APOLOGIE FOR (TERESA) HYMNE | 42 | 52 322 | 59 |

MOCK

| | | | | |
|---|---|---|---|---|
| LETT HER SURVIVE THIS DAY, ONCE MOCK HER FATE, | ON GUNPOWDER-TREASON | 9 | MS 384 | 458 |

MOCKE

| | | | | |
|---|---|---|---|---|
| ABOVE HER MOCKE, OR BEE FOR EVER MUTE. | MUSICKS DUELL | 108 | 46 149 | 535 |
| MOCKE ME, AND DAZLE MY DARKE MYSTERIES. | SOSPETTO D'HERODE | 232 | 46 109 | 216 |
| MAKE TO THY REASON MAN, AND MOCKE THY DOUBTS, | SOSPETTO D'HERODE | 521 | 46 109 | 216 |
| THESE HANDS AND THINE WERE HEW'N, THESE CHERRYES MOCKE | UPON YORKE HIS BIRTH | 46 | 46 176 | 500 |
| AT TH' ORIENTALL GATES. AND DULY MOCKE | TO THE MORNING | 42 | 46 163 | 497 |
| AS SHALL MOCKE THE ENVIOUS EYE. | OUT OF CATULLUS | 20 | 46 134 | 523 |
| HOW DOES THY APRIL-AUTUMNE MOCKE THESE COLD | UPON TWO GREENE APRICOCKES | 15 | 48 220 | 494 |
| FARRE DISTANT FROM OUR FATES. OUR FATES, THAT MOCKE | HORATIJ ILLE & NEFASTO | 31 | MS 382 | 530 |
| THE STIFFE NECK'D PHARISEES THAT USE TO MOCKE | OUT OF GROTIUS | 42 | MS 398 | 198 |

MOCKS

| | | | | |
|---|---|---|---|---|
| YOU ARE THE STORME THAT MOCKS | WHY ARE YEE AFRAID | 12 | 46 88 | 15 |
| GALL, & MORE BITTER MOCKS, SHALL MAKE IT UP. | OFFICE H. CROSS SIXT | 10 | 52 270 | 97 |

MOCKES

| | | | | |
|---|---|---|---|---|
| AND MOCKES WITH FEMALE FROST LOVE'S MANLY FLAME. | FLAMING HEART | 24 | 52 324 | 61 |

MODERATOUR

| | | | | | |
|---|---|---|---|---|---|
| UNTILL HIS FINGER(MODERATOUR)HIDES | MUSICKS DUELL | 52 | 46 | 149 | 535 |

MODEST

| | | | | | |
|---|---|---|---|---|---|
| THE ROSES MODEST CHEEKE | THE WEEPER | 135 | 46 | 79 | 120 |
| AS THIS MODEST MAIDEN LILLY, | AN HIMNE FOR CIRCUMCISION | 11 | 46 | 141 | 37 |
| INTO THY MODEST VEYLE. HOW DID'ST THOU RISE | TO THE MORNING | 8 | 46 | 183 | 497 |
| THE MODEST FRONT OF THIS SMALL FLOORE | AN EPITAPH UPON ASHTON | 1 | 46 | 192 | 464 |
| AS THIS MODEST MAIDEN LILLY | NEW YEAR'S DAY | 11 | 52 | 251 | 37 |
| THE ROSE'S MODEST CHEEK | WEEPER | 177 | 52 | 307 | 120 |
| WAS IN THE MODEST NUNNERY OF HIS BREST. | AN ELEGY MR STANNINOW | 36 | | MS 394 | 473 |

MODESTY

| | | | | | |
|---|---|---|---|---|---|
| BUT MODESTY DARES STILL DENY IT. | WISHES SUPPOSED MISTRESSE | 120 | 46 | 195 | 479 |
| YOUR VERTUE WEARS. YOUR MODESTY | TO THE QUEEN | 4 | 48 | 215 | 501 |

MOIST

| | | | | | |
|---|---|---|---|---|---|
| A MOIST SPARKE IT IS, | THE TEARE | 3 | 46 | 84 | 50 |

MOISTURE

| | | | | | |
|---|---|---|---|---|---|
| OF SUPPLE MOISTURE. NO COY TWIG BUT WILL | OUT OF VIRGIL | 16 | 46 | 155 | 529 |

MOLD

| | | | | | |
|---|---|---|---|---|---|
| THE MUSICKS SOFT REPORT. AND MOLD THE SAME | MUSICKS DUELL | 12 | 46 | 149 | 535 |
| KINDLY SUPPLIES SICK NATURE. AND DOTH MOLD | OUT OF VIRGIL | 35 | 46 | 155 | 529 |
| HIS MOUTH WAS RHETORICKS BEST MOLD, | HIS EPITAPH (HERRYS) | 29 | 46 | 172 | 471 |

MOMENT

| | | | | | |
|---|---|---|---|---|---|
| EACH WINGED MOMENT WAITS, | WEEPER | 147 | 52 | 307 | 120 |

MOMENTARY

| | | | | | |
|---|---|---|---|---|---|
| BUT SHEE (SWIFT AS THE MOMENTARY WING | SOSPETTO D'HERODE | 371 | 46 | 109 | 216 |

MOMENTS

| | | | | | |
|---|---|---|---|---|---|
| OTHERS BY MOMENTS, MONTHS, & YEARES | WEEPER | 155 | 52 | 307 | 120 |

MONARCHS

| | | | | | |
|---|---|---|---|---|---|
| AND ROOM ENOUGH FOR MONARCHS, WHILE NONE SWELLS | DESCRIPTION RELIGIOUS HOUSE | 34 | 52 | 338 | 213 |

MONSTER

| | | | | | |
|---|---|---|---|---|---|
| SCARCE TO THIS MONSTER COULD THE SHADY KING, | SOSPETTO D'HERODE | 369 | 46 | 109 | 216 |
| HEAVEN KICKT THE MONSTER DOUNE. DOUNE IT WAS THROUNE, | ON GUNPOWDER-TREASON | 51 | | MS 384 | 458 |
| THE MONSTER CRUSHT, MAUGRE THEIR MIDWIFERIE. | UPON GUNPOWDER TREASON | 56 | | MS 386 | 460 |

MONSTROUS

| | | | | | |
|---|---|---|---|---|---|
| A MISERABLE AND A MONSTROUS FEAST, | THE BEGINNING OF HELIODORUS | 25 | 46 | 158 | 517 |

MONETH

| | | | | | |
|---|---|---|---|---|---|
| THE BROW OF EVERY MONETH. AND WHEN THAT'S DONE | UPON YORKE HIS BIRTH | 98 | 46 | 176 | 500 |

MONTHS

| | | | | | |
|---|---|---|---|---|---|
| OTHERS BY MOMENTS, MONTHS, & YEARES | WEEPER | 155 | 52 | 307 | 120 |

MONTHES

| | | | | | |
|---|---|---|---|---|---|
| OTHERS BY DAYES, BY MONTHES, BY YEARES | THE WEEPER | 119 | 46 | 79 | 120 |

MONUMENTALL

| | | | | | |
|---|---|---|---|---|---|
| OF HIS MONUMENTALL REST. | UPON DEATH OF DESIRED HERRYS | 68 | 46 | 168 | 467 |

MOOD

| | | | | | |
|---|---|---|---|---|---|
| IN HER OWNE MURMURES, THAT WHAT EVER MOOD | MUSICKS DUELL | 13 | 46 | 149 | 535 |

MOON

| | | | | | |
|---|---|---|---|---|---|
| WHOSE BLUSH THE MOON BEAUTEOUSLY MARRES | O GLORIOSA DOMINA | 3 | 52 | 302 | 194 |
| THE MOON OF MAIDEN STARRS, THY WHITE | TERESA | 123 | 52 | 315 | 52 |
| SHRINKES. AS THE SICK MOON FROM THE WHOLSOME MORN. | (ON) HOPE | 10 | 52 | 345 | 71 |

MOONE

| | | | | | |
|---|---|---|---|---|---|
| THE MOONE OF MAIDEN STARRES. THY WHITE | IN MEMORY OF LADY MADRE TERESA | 124 | 46 | 131 | 52 |
| THE MOONE SHALL COME TO MEET THEE HERE, | AN HIMNE FOR CIRCUMCISION | 31 | 46 | 141 | 37 |
| SHRINKES, LIKE THE SICK MOONE AT THE WHOLSOME MORNE. | ON HOPE | 20 | 46 | 143 | 71 |

## MOORES

| | | | | | |
|---|---|---|---|---|---|
| SHEEL TO THE MOORES, AND TRADE WITH THEM. | IN MEMORY OF LADY MADRE TERESA | 47 | 46 | 131 | 52 |
| SHEES FOR THE MOORES AND MARTYRDOME. | IN MEMORY OF LADY MADRE TERESA | 64 | 46 | 131 | 52 |
| SH'EL TO THE MOORES, AND TRADE WITH THEM, | TERESA | 47 | 52 | 315 | 52 |
| SHE'S FOR THE MOORES, & MARTYRDOM. | TERESA | 64 | 52 | 315 | 52 |

## MORE

| | | | | | |
|---|---|---|---|---|---|
| MORE SWEETLY SHOWES THE BLUSHING BRIDE. | IN PRAISE OF LESSIUS | 30 | 46 | 156 | 510 |
| IN RIPER JOYES, MORE SHALL BEE HIS | OUT OF GREEKE CUPID'S CRYER | 15 | 46 | 159 | 519 |
| LANGUAGE NONE MORE FLUENT IS. | UPON THE DEATH OF A GENTLEMAN | 22 | 46 | 166 | 472 |
| THE DEW NO MORE WILL WEEPE. | THE WEEPER | 37 | 46 | 79 | 120 |
| THE DEAW NO MORE WILL SLEEPE, | THE WEEPER | 39 | 46 | 79 | 120 |
| GLADNESSE IT SELFE WOULD BEE MORE GLAD | THE WEEPER | 65 | 46 | 79 | 120 |
| MORE SOVERAIGNE AND SWEET FROM YOU. | THE WEEPER | 72 | 46 | 79 | 120 |
| WHAT WOULD YE MORE. HERE FOOD IT SELFE IS FED. | ON MIRACLE OF LOAVES | 4 | 46 | 86 | 15 |
| ONE EYE, A THOUSAND RATHER, AND A THOUSAND MORE | IT IS BETTER TO GO WITH EYE | 1 | 46 | 93 | 16 |
| WEEPE, 'CAUSE I CAN WEEPE NO MORE. | VERILY YE SHALL WEEP | 4 | 46 | 95 | 22 |
| JESU, NO MORE, IT IS FULL TIDE | ON BLEEDING WOUNDS OF LORD | 1 | 46 | 101 | 110 |
| NO MORE ACQUAINTED WITH MY HEART, | PSALME 137 | 22 | 46 | 104 | 7 |
| TELL HIM WEE NOW CAN SHEW HIM MORE | A HYMNE OF THE NATIVITY | 11 | 46 | 106 | 76 |
| TO MORE THEN CAESARS BIRTHRIGHT IS. | A HYMNE OF THE NATIVITY | 60 | 46 | 106 | 76 |
| MUSE, NOW THE SERVANT OF SOFT LOVES NO MORE, | SOSPETTO D'HERODE | 1 | 46 | 109 | 216 |
| FARRE MORE THEN MATTER FOR MY MUSE AND MEE. | SOSPETTO D'HERODE | 30 | 46 | 109 | 216 |
| THREE KINGS (OR WHAT IS MORE) THREE WISE MEN WENT | SOSPETTO D'HERODE | 135 | 46 | 109 | 216 |
| HEE HAS MY HEAVEN (WHAT WOULD HE MORE.) WHOSE BRIGHT | SOSPETTO D'HERODE | 209 | 46 | 109 | 216 |
| THE FIELD'S FAIRE EYES SAW HER, AND SAW NO MORE, | SOSPETTO D'HERODE | 378 | 46 | 109 | 216 |
| AND BRING HOME ON THY BREST MORE THANKLESSE SCARRS. | SOSPETTO D'HERODE | 448 | 46 | 109 | 216 |
| MORE DEEPE SUSPICIONS, AND MORE DEADLY STINGS, | SOSPETTO D'HERODE | 501 | 46 | 109 | 216 |
| MORE DEEPE SUSPICIONS, AND MORE DEADLY STINGS, | SOSPETTO D'HERODE | 501 | 46 | 109 | 216 |
| AND NOW HIS DREAM (HELS FIREBRAND) STIL MORE BRIGHT, | SOSPETTO D'HERODE | 503 | 46 | 109 | 216 |
| MORE SWORDS AND SHIELDS | ON A PRAYER BOOKE | 19 | 46 | 126 | 139 |
| THE SOULE IT SELFE MORE FEELES THEN HEARES. | ON A PRAYER BOOKE | 62 | 46 | 126 | 139 |
| OF BLESSINGS, AND TEN THOUSAND MORE. | ON A PRAYER BOOKE | 82 | 46 | 126 | 139 |
| TERESA IS NO MORE FOR YOU. | IN MEMORY OF LADY MADRE TERESA | 58 | 46 | 131 | 52 |
| A DEATH MORE MISTICALL AND HIGH. | IN MEMORY OF LADY MADRE TERESA | 76 | 46 | 131 | 52 |
| DRINKE WEE TILL WE PROVE MORE, NOT LESSE THEN MEN. | AN APOLOGIE FOR HYMNE (TERESA) | 36 | 46 | 136 | 59 |
| IF NOT MORE GLORIOUS, MORE CONSPICUOUS THO. | ON A TREATISE OF CHARITY | 26 | 46 | 137 | 69 |
| IF NOT MORE GLORIOUS, MORE CONSPICUOUS THO. | ON A TREATISE OF CHARITY | 26 | 46 | 137 | 69 |
| NO MORE THE HYPOCRITE SHALL TH'UPRIGHT BE | ON A TREATISE OF CHARITY | 39 | 46 | 137 | 69 |
| WHILE OTHERS BEND THEIR KNEE, NO MORE SHALT THOU | ON A TREATISE OF CHARITY | 41 | 46 | 137 | 69 |
| SHEE CLIMBES, AND MAKES A FARRE MORE MILKY WAY. | ON THE ASSUMPTION | 6 | 46 | 139 | 114 |
| AND OUR DARKE WORLD NO MORE SHALL SEE. | ON THE ASSUMPTION | 36 | 46 | 139 | 114 |
| HOPES CHASTE KISSE WRONGS NO MORE JOYES MAIDENHEAD, | ON HOPE | 39 | 46 | 143 | 71 |
| AND LOVES MORE FIERCE, MORE FRUITLESSE FIRES ASSAY | ON HOPE | 87 | 46 | 143 | 71 |
| AND LOVES MORE FIERCE, MORE FRUITLESSE FIRES ASSAY | ON HOPE | 87 | 46 | 143 | 71 |
| ONE FACE MORE FUGITIVE THEN ALL THEY, | ON HOPE | 88 | 46 | 143 | 71 |
| NOR MORE LOVELY LIFT'ST THY HEAD, | UPON DEATH OF DESIRED HERRYS | 15 | 46 | 168 | 467 |
| INVITED HIM NO MORE TO HIDE | UPON DEATH OF DESIRED HERRYS | 37 | 46 | 168 | 467 |
| MORE THEN THEIR OWNE HELICON. | AN EPITAPH DOCTOR BROOKE | 4 | 46 | 175 | 465 |
| BUT MUCH MORE FRUITFULL IS. NOR DOES, AS SHEE, | UPON YORKE HIS BIRTH | 84 | 46 | 176 | 500 |
| NO MORE MY PILLOW SHALL THINE ALTAR BE, | TO THE MORNING | 49 | 46 | 183 | 497 |
| NOR WILL I OFFER ANY MORE TO THEE | TO THE MORNING | 50 | 46 | 183 | 497 |
| THAT NO MORE SUMMERS BEST DRESSES, | OUT OF THE ITALIAN (1) | 9 | 46 | 188 | 545 |
| HISTORY REARES HER PYRAMIDS MORE TALL | ON FRONTISPIECE ISAACSONS | 18 | 46 | 191 | 491 |
| BELEEVE MEE, READER CAN SAY MORE | AN EPITAPH UPON ASHTON | 2 | 46 | 192 | 464 |
| AN HUNDRED, AND A THOUSAND MORE, | OUT OF CATULLUS | 12 | 46 | 194 | 523 |
| SOMETHING MORE THAN | WISHES SUPPOSED MISTRESSE | 19 | 46 | 195 | 479 |
| MORE THEN THE SPOYLE | WISHES SUPPOSED MISTRESSE | 22 | 46 | 195 | 479 |
| MORE THEN A MORNING ROSE. | WISHES SUPPOSED MISTRESSE | 35 | 46 | 195 | 479 |
| HOW MUCH THEMSELVES MORE PRETIOUS ARE. | WISHES SUPPOSED MISTRESSE | 48 | 46 | 195 | 479 |
| FOR WHOSE MORE NOBLE SMART, | WISHES SUPPOSED MISTRESSE | 56 | 46 | 195 | 479 |
| OF WISHES. AND I WISH--NO MORE. | WISHES SUPPOSED MISTRESSE | 105 | 46 | 195 | 479 |
| MORE SUMMER IN THEIR SHAMES REFLECTION, | UPON TWO GREENE APRICOCKES | 8 | 48 | 220 | 494 |
| GOE, SOUL, OUT OF THY SELF, & SEEK FOR MORE. | TO THE NAME OF JESUS | 27 | 52 | 239 | 30 |
| (WHICH DULL MORTALITY MORE FEELES THEN HEARES) | TO THE NAME OF JESUS | 31 | 52 | 239 | 30 |
| OF SWEETS YOU HAVE. AND MURMUR THAT YOU HAVE NO MORE. | TO THE NAME OF JESUS | 67 | 52 | 239 | 30 |
| OR YOU, MORE NOBLE ARCHITECTS OF INTELLECTUALL NOISE, | TO THE NAME OF JESUS | 77 | 52 | 239 | 30 |
| MORE FREELY TO TRANSPIRE | TO THE NAME OF JESUS | 213 | 52 | 239 | 30 |
| TELL HIM WE NOW CAN SHOW HIM MORE | IN HOLY NATIVITY | 11 | 52 | 246 | 76 |
| TO MORE THEN CAESAR'S BIRTHRIGHT IS. | IN HOLY NATIVITY | 86 | 52 | 246 | 76 |
| THE SHEPHEARDS, MORE THEN THEY THE SHEEP. | IN HOLY NATIVITY | 102 | 52 | 246 | 76 |
| FROM HIM, WHOM BY A MORE ILLUSTRIOUS LY, | IN GLORIOUS EPIPHANIE | 44 | 52 | 253 | 39 |
| AND COURTED IN THE POMPOUS MASK OF A MORE SPECIOUS MIST. | IN GLORIOUS EPIPHANIE | 53 | 52 | 253 | 39 |
| MORE DESPERATELY DARK, BECAUSE MORE BRIGHT. | IN GLORIOUS EPIPHANIE | 59 | 52 | 253 | 39 |
| MORE DESPERATELY DARK, BECAUSE MORE BRIGHT. | IN GLORIOUS EPIPHANIE | 59 | 52 | 253 | 39 |
| EMBOSOM'D IN A MUCH MORE ROSY MORN, | IN GLORIOUS EPIPHANIE | 66 | 52 | 253 | 39 |
| NO MORE THAT OTHER | IN GLORIOUS EPIPHANIE | 68 | 52 | 253 | 39 |
| THY SOFTER YET MORE CERTAINE DARTS | IN GLORIOUS EPIPHANIE | 78 | 52 | 253 | 39 |
| WE COURT THY MORE CONCERNING SMILES. | IN GLORIOUS EPIPHANIE | 81 | 52 | 253 | 39 |
| THE DOATING NATIONS NOW NO MORE | IN GLORIOUS EPIPHANIE | 85 | 52 | 253 | 39 |
| IN WHATSOE'RE MORE SACRED SHAPE | IN GLORIOUS EPIPHANIE | 89 | 52 | 253 | 39 |
| NEVER MORE | IN GLORIOUS EPIPHANIE | 93 | 52 | 253 | 39 |
| SHALL KICK THE CLOUDS NO MORE. BUT LEAN & TAME, | IN GLORIOUS EPIPHANIE | 98 | 52 | 253 | 39 |
| AND HE MORE NEEDFULLY & NOBLE PROVE | IN GLORIOUS EPIPHANIE | 159 | 52 | 253 | 39 |
| WAS THEIR MORE BLIND IDOLATRY, | IN GLORIOUS EPIPHANIE | 169 | 52 | 253 | 39 |
| AND TEACH OBSCURE MANKIND A MORE CLOSE WAY | IN GLORIOUS EPIPHANIE | 208 | 52 | 253 | 39 |
| TO READ MORE LEGIBLE THINE ORIGINALL RAY. | IN GLORIOUS EPIPHANIE | 211 | 52 | 253 | 39 |
| BUT MORE AMBITIOUS LOSSE, AT LEST OF BRAIN. | IN GLORIOUS EPIPHANIE | 230 | 52 | 253 | 39 |
| A HAIL MORE CRUELL THEN THEIR CRUCIFY. | OFFICE H. CROSS THIRD | 6 | 52 | 268 | 93 |
| GALL, & MORE BITTER MOCKS, SHALL MAKE IT UP. | OFFICE H. CROSS SIXT | 10 | 52 | 270 | 97 |

PAGE 270

| | | | | |
|---|---|---|---|---|
| OF SOME MORE PAINFULL THING THEN ALL HIS PAINES. | OFFICE H. CROSS NINTH | 4 | 52 271 | 99 |
| THE SUN SAW THAT, AND WOULD HAVE SEEN NO MORE. | OFFICE H. CROSS NINTH | 7 | 52 271 | 99 |
| FOR A MORE THEN SALOMON. | VEXILLA REGIS | 24 | 52 277 | 156 |
| GLORIOUS, OR GREIVOUS MORE. THUS TO MAKE GOOD | VEXILLA REGIS | 29 | 52 277 | 156 |
| HOW MUCH DEATH WEIGH'D MORE LIGHT THEN LOVE. | VEXILLA REGIS | 36 | 52 277 | 156 |
| ALL, MORE AT HOME IN HER OWNE HEART, | SANCTA MARIA DOLORUM | 10 | 52 283 | 162 |
| PAYES BACK, WITH MORE THEN THEIR OWN SMART | SANCTA MARIA DOLORUM | 28 | 52 283 | 162 |
| O BE MORE WISE | SANCTA MARIA DOLORUM | 85 | 52 283 | 162 |
| IF NOT MORE SOFT, MINE EYES. | SANCTA MARIA DOLORUM | 86 | 52 283 | 162 |
| JESU, NO MORE. IT IS FULL TIDE. | UPON BLEEDING CRUCIFIX | 1 | 52 288 | 110 |
| WHOM TOO MUCH LOVE HATH BOW'D MORE LOW FOR ME. | ADORO TE | 4 | 52 291 | 172 |
| NOR TOUCH NOR TAST MUST LOOK FOR MORE | ADORO TE | 7 | 52 291 | 172 |
| AND WORDS MORE SURE, MORE SWEET, THEN THEY | ADORO TE | 15 | 52 291 | 172 |
| AND WORDS MORE SURE, MORE SWEET, THEN THEY | ADORO TE | 15 | 52 291 | 172 |
| BY A NOBLER BREAD, MORE NEEDFULL BLOOD. | LAUDA SION SALVATOREM | 36 | 52 294 | 178 |
| BEARES HOME NO LESSE, ALL THEY NO MORE. | LAUDA SION SALVATOREM | 47 | 52 294 | 178 |
| THE MOST FIRM FOOT NO MORE THEN STAND. | DIES IRAE | 24 | 52 298 | 186 |
| SHE CLIMBS. AND MAKES A FARRE MORE MILKEY WAY. | IN GLORIOUS ASSUMPTION B. LADY | 6 | 52 304 | 114 |
| THE DEAW NO MORE WILL WEEP | WEEPER | 43 | 52 307 | 120 |
| THE DEAW NO MORE WILL SLEEP | WEEPER | 45 | 52 307 | 120 |
| MORE SOVERAIGN & SWEET FROM YOU, | WEEPER | 54 | 52 307 | 120 |
| SO MUCH MORE RICH WOULD HE ESTEEM | WEEPER | 77 | 52 307 | 120 |
| NOR MAY RETURN'D MORE FAITHFULL FLOWRES, | WEEPER | 84 | 52 307 | 120 |
| OR MORE UNWELLCOME WAYES, | WEEPER | 111 | 52 307 | 120 |
| TERESA IS NO MORE FOR YOU, | TERESA | 58 | 52 315 | 52 |
| A DEATH MORE MYSTICALL & HIGH. | TERESA | 76 | 52 315 | 52 |
| DRINK WE TILL WE PROVE MORE, NOT LESSE, THEN MEN, | AN APOLOGIE FOR (TERESA) HYMNE | 36 | 52 322 | 59 |
| AND BY THY THIRSTS OF LOVE MORE LARGE THEN THEY. | FLAMING HEART | 98 | 52 324 | 61 |
| AFFECT MORE COMLY BANDS | PRAYER TO GENTLE-WOMAN | 6 | 52 328 | 139 |
| MORE SWORDS & SHEILDS | PRAYER TO GENTLE-WOMAN | 25 | 52 328 | 139 |
| THE SOUL IT SELFE MORE FEELS THEN HEARES. | PRAYER TO GENTLE-WOMAN | 68 | 52 328 | 139 |
| OF BLESSINGS & TEN THOUSAND MORE | PRAYER TO GENTLE-WOMAN | 88 | 52 328 | 139 |
| LAYES UP HIS PURER & MORE PRETIOUS VOWES, | TO SAME CONCERNING CHOISE | 35 | 52 331 | 66 |
| AND MEANES THEM FOR A FARRE MORE WORTHY SPOUSE | TO SAME CONCERNING CHOISE | 36 | 52 331 | 66 |
| THINGS THAT IN HARDNESSE MORE ALLUDE TO THEE. | ALEXIAS SECONDE ELEGIE | 16 | 52 335 | 207 |
| AND PRIZE THEMSELVES. DOE MUCH, THAT MORE THEY MAY, | DESCRIPTION RELIGIOUS HOUSE | 20 | 52 338 | 213 |
| MORE SWEETLY SHOWES THE BLUSHING BRIDE. | TEMPERANCE | 28 | 52 342 | 510 |
| HOPE'S CHAST STEALTH HARMES NO MORE JOYE'S MAIDENHEAD | (ON) HOPE | 19 | 52 345 | 71 |
| THOUGH LOVE'S MORE FEIRCE, MORE FRUITLESSE, FIRES ASSAY | (ON) HOPE | 47 | 52 345 | 71 |

| | | | | |
|---|---|---|---|---|
| THOUGH LOVE'S MORE FEIRCE, MORE FRUITLESSE, FIRES ASSAY | (ON) HOPE | 47 | 52 345 | 71 |

| | | | | |
|---|---|---|---|---|
| ONE FACE MORE FUGITIVE THEN ALL THEY. | (ON) HOPE | 48 | 52 345 | 71 |
| A LITTLE MORE, & I HAD SURELY SEENE | HORATIJ ILLE & NEFASTO | 33 | MS 382 | 530 |
| OF LIONS NOW NOE MORE, OR SPOTTED LINX. | HORATIJ ILLE & NEFASTO | 56 | MS 382 | 530 |
| DULL SLUGGISH ILE, WHAT MORE THAN LETHARGY | ON GUNPOWDER-TREASON | 3 | MS 384 | 458 |
| ALL THIS IT THREATS, & MORE HORROR, THAT FLIES | ON GUNPOWDER-TREASON | 45 | MS 384 | 458 |
| HER ROSY CHEEKES YOU SHOULD HAVE SEENE NOE MORE | UPON GUNPOWDER TREASON | 15 | MS 386 | 460 |
| THE PAINTED MEDDOWES WOULD HAVE LAUGHT NOE MORE | UPON GUNPOWDER TREASON | 45 | MS 386 | 460 |
| AS IF HEEREAFTER THEY WOULD WEEPE NOE MORE. | UPON KINGS CORONATION | 12 | MS 390 | 453 |
| OF SUCH BRIGHT ANGELLS, THAT YOU GIVE US MORE. | UPON BIRTH PRINCESSE E | 26 | MS 391 | 456 |
| THE PHOENIX SELFE SHALL NOT MORE PROUDLY BURNE, | EX EUPHORMIONE | 15 | MS 392 | 525 |
| WHAT MORE THAN WINTER HATH THAT DIRE ART FOUND, | AN ELEGY MR STANNINOW | 21 | MS 394 | 473 |
| SOMEWHAT MORE HORRID THAN AN ELEGY. | AN ELEGIE ON DR PORTER | 12 | MS 395 | 476 |
| WHAT WOULD THEY MORE. TH' AVE SEENE WHEN AT MY NOD | OUT OF GROTIUS | 49 | MS 398 | 198 |
| THE BROKEN MEATE WAS MUCH MORE THEN THE WHOLE. | OUT OF GROTIUS | 64 | MS 398 | 198 |

MORN

| | | | | |
|---|---|---|---|---|
| THE BABE WHOSE BIRTH EMBRAVES THIS MORN, | IN HOLY NATIVITY | 48 | 52 246 | 76 |
| THE MORN SHALL COME TO MEET THEE HERE, | NEW YEAR'S DAY | 31 | 52 251 | 37 |
| THE MORN INCURR A SWEET MISTAKE. | IN GLORIOUS EPIPHANIE | 2 | 52 253 | 39 |
| EMBOSOM'D IN A MUCH MORE ROSY MORN, | IN GLORIOUS EPIPHANIE | 66 | 52 253 | 39 |
| A GENTLER MORN, A JUSTER SUN. | IN GLORIOUS EPIPHANIE | 74 | 52 253 | 39 |
| FOR THIS HE LOOK'T SO BIGG, & EVERY MORN | IN GLORIOUS EPIPHANIE | 121 | 52 253 | 39 |
| EVERY MORN FROM HENCE | WEEPER | 25 | 52 307 | 120 |
| SHRINKES, AS THE SICK MOON FROM THE WHOLSOME MORN. | (ON) HOPE | 10 | 52 345 | 71 |

MORNE

| | | | | |
|---|---|---|---|---|
| THE SMILING MORNE HAD NEWLY WAK'T THE DAY, | THE BEGINNING OF HELIODORUS | 1 | 46 158 | 517 |
| EVERY MORNE FROM HENCE, | THE WEEPER | 25 | 46 79 | 120 |
| THE DAY OF MY DARKE WOES IS YET BUT MORNE, | OUR LORD IN HIS CIRCUMCISION | 11 | 46 98 | 9 |
| THIS IS THE MORNE. | EASTER DAY | 8 | 46 100 | 26 |
| OF STARS, THAT GUILD THE MORNE IN CHARGE WERE GIVEN. | SOSPETTO D'HERODE | 234 | 46 109 | 216 |
| SHRINKES, LIKE THE SICK MOONE AT THE WHOLSOME MORNE. | ON HOPE | 20 | 46 143 | 71 |
| THEIR ROSIE BEAMES, SO THAT THE MORNE FOR ONE | UPON YORKE HIS BIRTH | 57 | 46 176 | 500 |
| ACQUAINTANCE WITH THE SUNNE. WHAT SECOND MORNE | UPON YORKE HIS BIRTH | 69 | 46 176 | 500 |
| SAY TO THE SULLEN MORNE, THOU COM'ST TO COURT HER, | ON A FOULE MORNING | 11 | 46 181 | 495 |
| NOT ON THE FRESH CHEEKES OF THE VIRGIN MORNE, | ON A FOULE MORNING | 35 | 46 181 | 495 |
| BRIGHT LADY OF THE MORNE, PITTY DOTH LYE | TO THE MORNING | 33 | 46 183 | 497 |
| AGAINE A FRESH CHILD OF THE BUXOME MORNE, | TO THE MORNING | 52 | 46 183 | 497 |
| AS WHEN THE ROSIE MORNE BUDDS INTO DAY, | ON FRONTISPIECE ISAACSONS | 14 | 46 191 | 491 |
| DAWNE THEN TO ME, THOU MORNE OF MINE OWNE DAY, | LUKE 2. QUAERIT JESUM | 45 | MS 379 | 11 |
| THE FRESH FACE OF THE MORNE HAD BLASTED BEENE. | UPON GUNPOWDER TREASON | 14 | MS 386 | 460 |
| HER SABLE CHEEKES INTO A BLUSHING MORNE. | UPON GUNPOWDER TREASON | 12 | MS 387 | 461 |
| ACQUAINTANCE WITH THE USHER OF THE MORNE. | UPON KINGS CORONATION | 32 | MS 389 | 454 |

MORNING

| | | | | |
|---|---|---|---|---|
| IN CREAME OF MORNING HELICON, AND THEN | MUSICKS DUELL | 77 | 46 149 | 535 |
| PROUD MORNING OF A PERVERSE DAY. HOW LOST | SOSPETTO D'HERODE | 77 | 46 109 | 216 |
| OF WHICH THE MORNING KNEW NOT. MAD WITH SPIGHT | SOSPETTO D'HERODE | 117 | 46 109 | 216 |
| NO SOONER THEREFORE SHALL THE MORNING SEE | SOSPETTO D'HERODE | 505 | 46 109 | 216 |

| | | | | | |
|---|---|---|---|---|---|
| MAKES HASTE TO MEET HER MORNING SPOWSE. | ON A PRAYER BOOKE | 96 | 46 | 126 | 139 |
| TO WAIT UPON EACH MORNING SIGH. | ON MR. G. HERBERTS BOOKE | 8 | 46 | 130 | 68 |
| RISE THOU FIRST AND FAIREST MORNING, | AN HIMNE FOR CIRCUMCISION | 1 | 46 | 141 | 37 |
| WITH A NEW MORNING MADE OF GEMS. | AN HIMNE FOR CIRCUMCISION | 22 | 46 | 141 | 37 |
| AS EVER WHISPER'D TO THE MORNING AIRE | UPON DEATH OF HERRYS | 2 | 46 | 167 | 466 |
| THE MORNING MUSES PERCH LIKE BIRDS, AND SING | UPON DEATH OF HERRYS | 11 | 46 | 167 | 466 |
| E'RE PROVE THE DISMALL MORNING OF THY NIGHT. | UPON YORKE HIS BIRTH | 93 | 46 | 176 | 500 |
| O IN THAT MORNING OF MY SHAME, WHEN I | TO THE MORNING | 5 | 46 | 183 | 497 |
| THAT, THE WORLD'S MORNING, THIS HER MIDNIGHT IS. | ON FRONTISPIECE ISAACSONS | 24 | 46 | 191 | 491 |
| MORE THEN A MORNING ROSE. | WISHES SUPPOSED MISTRESSE | 35 | 46 | 195 | 479 |
| GIVES HIM THE MORNING WORLDS FRESH GOLD AGAINE. | UPON TWO GREENE APRICOCKES | 18 | 48 | 220 | 494 |
| AND TO THE WORKE OF LOVE THIS MORNING WAKE YOU | TO THE NAME OF JESUS | 54 | 52 | 239 | 30 |
| EACH WOUND OF THEIRS WAS THY NEW MORNING. | TO THE NAME OF JESUS | 220 | 52 | 239 | 30 |
| RISE, THOU BEST & BRIGHTEST MORNING. | NEW YEAR'S DAY | 1 | 52 | 251 | 37 |
| WITH A NEW MORNING MADE OF GEMMES. | NEW YEAR'S DAY | 22 | 52 | 251 | 37 |
| MAKES HAST TO MEET HER MORNING SPOUSE | PRAYER TO GENTLE-WOMAN | 102 | 52 | 328 | 139 |

MOURNING

| | | | | | |
|---|---|---|---|---|---|
| MAKES MANY A MOURNING PAPER PUT ON BLACKE. | UPON STANINOUGH'S DEATH | 2 | 46 | 175 | 475 |
| MAKES MANY A MOURNING PAPER PUT ON BLACK. | DEATH'S LECTURE | 2 | 52 | 340 | 475 |
| SEE ALL IN MOURNING NOW, THE WALLES ARE JETT, | AN ELEGIE ON DR PORTER | 7 | MS | 395 | 476 |

MORNING-SONS

| | | | | | |
|---|---|---|---|---|---|
| SILENC'T THE MORNING-SONS, & DAMP'T THEIR SONG | IN GLORIOUS EPIPHANIE | 130 | 52 | 253 | 39 |

MORNING'S

| | | | | | |
|---|---|---|---|---|---|
| PERCH'T IN THE MORNING'S WAY | IN GLORIOUS EPIPHANIE | 56 | 52 | 253 | 39 |
| BY THY LAST MORNING'S DRAUGHT OF LIQUID FIRE. | FLAMING HEART | 100 | 52 | 324 | 61 |

MORNINGS

| | | | | | |
|---|---|---|---|---|---|
| I'VE SEENE THE MORNINGS LOVELY RAY, | UPON DEATH OF DESIRED HERRYS | 47 | 46 | 168 | 467 |
| WERE THE MORNINGS SMILE SO FAIRE | UPON DEATH OF DESIRED HERRYS | 56 | 46 | 168 | 467 |
| THEN THIS GREAT MORNINGS MIGHTY BUSYNES. | TO THE NAME OF JESUS | 23 | 52 | 239 | 30 |

MORPHEUS

| | | | | | |
|---|---|---|---|---|---|
| AND POINTING TO DULL MORPHEUS, BIDS ME TAKE | TO THE MORNING | 15 | 46 | 183 | 497 |
| IF MORPHEUS HAVE A MUSE TO WAIT ON MEE. | TO THE MORNING | 18 | 46 | 183 | 497 |

MORROW

| | | | | | |
|---|---|---|---|---|---|
| TO MORROW TO BE SNATCHT AWAY. | UPON DEATH OF DESIRED HERRYS | 30 | 46 | 168 | 467 |
| AND TH' ETERNALL MORROW DAWNE, | AN EPITAPH HUSBAND AND WIFE | 13 | 46 | 174 | 478 |
| LIVES AGAINE AS BLITH TO MORROW, | OUT OF CATULLUS | 5 | 46 | 194 | 523 |
| NO PART OF THEIR GOOD MORROW. | WISHES SUPPOSED MISTRESSE | 77 | 46 | 195 | 479 |
| OF BEAMES TO DAY, PAY BACK AGAINE TO MORROW, | UPON TWO GREENE APRICOCKES | 28 | 48 | 220 | 494 |
| TILL THE' AETERNALL MORROW DAWN | AN EPITAPH UPON MARRIED COUPLE | 17 | 52 | 339 | 478 |

MORROW'S

| | | | | | |
|---|---|---|---|---|---|
| AND WORK FOR WORK, NOT WAGES. LET TO MORROW'S | DESCRIPTION RELIGIOUS HOUSE | 21 | 52 | 338 | 213 |

MORTALITY

| | | | | | |
|---|---|---|---|---|---|
| FAITHLESSE AND FOND MORTALITY. | UPON THE DEATH OF A GENTLEMAN | 1 | 46 | 166 | 472 |
| THAT DULL MORTALITY MUST NOT KNOW A NAME. | ON A PRAYER BOOKE | 80 | 46 | 126 | 139 |
| OUR DUST, THAT IN ONE DRAUGHT, MORTALITY | AN APOLOGIE FOR HYMNE (TERESA) | 45 | 46 | 136 | 59 |
| SAD MORTALITY MAY HIDE, | ANOTHER ON HERRYS | 59 | 46 | 170 | 469 |
| TO THE PROUD HOPES OF POOR MORTALITY. | UPON STANINOUGH'S DEATH | 24 | 46 | 175 | 475 |
| (WHICH DULL MORTALITY MORE FEELES THEN HEARES) | TO THE NAME OF JESUS | 31 | 52 | 239 | 30 |
| MIX WITH OUR LOW MORTALITY, | LAUDA SION SALVATOREM | 74 | 52 | 294 | 178 |
| OUR DUST, THAT AT ONE DRAUGHT, MORTALITY | AN APOLOGIE FOR (TERESA) HYMNE | 45 | 52 | 322 | 59 |
| THAT DULL MORTALITY MUST NOT KNOW A NAME. | PRAYER TO GENTLE-WOMAN | 66 | 52 | 328 | 139 |
| TO THE LOWD BLASTS OF POOR MORTALITY | DEATH'S LECTURE | 26 | 52 | 340 | 475 |

MORTALITIE

| | | | | | |
|---|---|---|---|---|---|
| THOSE BEAMES THAT AMPLIATE MORTALITIE, | UPON YORKE HIS BIRTH | 22 | 46 | 176 | 500 |

MORTALL

| | | | | | |
|---|---|---|---|---|---|
| THEN HEE E'RE SHEWD TO MORTALL SIGHT. | A HYMNE OF THE NATIVITY | 12 | 46 | 106 | 76 |
| THIS MORTALL ENEMY TO MANKINDS GOOD. | SOSPETTO D'HERODE | 82 | 46 | 109 | 216 |
| READY TO PERSONATE A MORTALL PART. | SOSPETTO D'HERODE | 418 | 46 | 109 | 216 |
| AND THE SHORT CLAUSE OF MORTALL BREATH. | ANOTHER ON HERRYS | 45 | 46 | 170 | 469 |
| LOCK'T UP FROM MORTALL EYE, | WISHES SUPPOSED MISTRESSE | 5 | 46 | 195 | 479 |
| THEN HE E'RE SHOW'D TO MORTALL SIGHT. | IN HOLY NATIVITY | 12 | 52 | 246 | 76 |
| TO HIM, WHO BY THESE MORTALL CLOUDS HAST MADE | IN GLORIOUS EPIPHANIE | 46 | 52 | 253 | 39 |
| FROM MORTALL EYES | IN GLORIOUS EPIPHANIE | 71 | 52 | 253 | 39 |
| WHY MAN, THIS SPEAKES PURE MORTALL FRAME. | FLAMING HEART | 23 | 52 | 324 | 61 |
| MADE EVERY MORTALL GLADLY SACRIFICE | UPON KINGS CORONATION | 36 | MS | 390 | 453 |
| THAT HEAVENLY MORTALL, THAT SERAPHICK MAN. | AN ELEGIE ON DR PORTER | 18 | MS | 395 | 476 |

MORTALLS

| | | | | | |
|---|---|---|---|---|---|
| AND FRAUD. HEE MAKES POORE MORTALLS HURTS, | OUT OF GREEKE CUPID'S CRYER | 31 | 46 | 139 | 519 |

## MOST

| | | | | | |
|---|---|---|---|---|---|
| MOST KINDLY DOE FALL OUT. THE GRUMBLING BASE | MUSICKS DUELL | 49 | 46 | 149 | 535 |
| (MOST DIVINE SERVICE) WHOSE SO EARLY LAY. | MUSICKS DUELL | 81 | 46 | 149 | 535 |
| THE FOULE QUEENS MOST ABHORRED MAIDS OF HONOUR | SOSPETTO D'HERODE | 337 | 46 | 109 | 216 |
| A MOST STRANGE BABE. WHO HERE CONCEAL'D BY THEM | SOSPETTO D'HERODE | 435 | 46 | 109 | 216 |
| O YOU, MY SOUL'S MOST CERTAIN WINGS. | TO THE NAME OF JESUS | 64 | 52 | 239 | 30 |
| OF A MOST WISE & WELL-ABUSED NIGHT | IN GLORIOUS EPIPHANIE | 210 | 52 | 253 | 39 |
| THE MOST FIRM FOOT NO MORE THEN STAND. | DIES IRAE | 24 | 52 | 298 | 186 |
| HAIL, MOST HIGH, MOST HUMBLE ONE. | O GLORIOSA DOMINA | 1 | 52 | 302 | 194 |
| HAIL, MOST HIGH, MOST HUMBLE ONE. | O GLORIOSA DOMINA | 1 | 52 | 302 | 194 |
| CROWN OF A MOST INCOMPARABLE LIGHT | IN GLORIOUS ASSUMPTION B. LADY | 61 | 52 | 304 | 114 |
| EVEN WHEN HE SHOW'D MUST POOR. | WEEPER | 117 | 52 | 307 | 120 |
| O MOST POOR-SPIRITED OF MEN. | FLAMING HEART | 19 | 52 | 324 | 61 |
| WHOSE LATEST & MOST LEADEN HOURES | TEMPERANCE | 45 | 52 | 342 | 510 |
| MOST TALL HYPERBOLE'S CANNOT DESCRY IT. | ON GUNPOWDER-TREASON | 47 | MS | 384 | 458 |

## MOTHER

| | | | | | |
|---|---|---|---|---|---|
| FROM THEIR HARD MOTHER EARTH, SPRANG HARDY MEN, | OUT OF VIRGIL | 30 | 46 | 155 | 529 |
| LOVE IS LOST, NOR CAN HIS MOTHER | OUT OF GREEKE CUPID'S CRYER | 1 | 46 | 159 | 519 |
| THE MOTHER THEN MUST SUCK THE SON. | BLESSED BE THE PAPS | 4 | 46 | 94 | 14 |
| THAT BREATHES AT ONCE BOTH MAID AND MOTHER. | A HYMNE OF THE NATIVITY | 63 | 46 | 106 | 76 |
| HOW SHE THAT IS A MAID SHOULD PROVE A MOTHER. | SOSPETTO D'HERODE | 163 | 46 | 109 | 216 |
| MARIA MOTHER OF OUR KING. | ON THE ASSUMPTION | 54 | 46 | 139 | 114 |
| O 'TWILL UNDOE OUR COMMON MOTHER. | UPON DEATH OF DESIRED HERRYS | 23 | 46 | 168 | 467 |
| FROM HIS MOTHER NATURES SIGHT. | UPON DEATH OF DESIRED HERRYS | 72 | 46 | 168 | 467 |
| HOW THY GREAT MOTHER NATURE DOATS ON THEE. | UPON YORKE HIS BIRTH | 26 | 46 | 176 | 500 |
| ARE TA'NE OUT AND TRANSCRIB'D BY THY GREAT MOTHER. | UPON YORKE HIS BIRTH | 41 | 46 | 176 | 500 |
| SEE'ST THOU THAT MARY THERE. O TEACH HER MOTHER | UPON YORKE HIS BIRTH | 53 | 46 | 176 | 500 |
| THOU ART THE MOTHER PHOENIX AND THY BREAST | UPON YORKE HIS BIRTH | 82 | 46 | 176 | 500 |
| AND SISTER PHOENIXES, AND STILL THE MOTHER. | UPON YORKE HIS BIRTH | 89 | 46 | 176 | 500 |
| AND SO IN EACH CHILD OFTEN PROVE A MOTHER. | UPON YORKE HIS BIRTH | 101 | 46 | 176 | 500 |
| ERST HATH MADE MY HEART A MOTHER. | LOVES HOROSCOPE | 2 | 46 | 185 | 483 |
| THAT BREATHES AT ONCE BOTH MAID & MOTHER. | IN HOLY NATIVITY | 89 | 52 | 246 | 76 |
| THE BLUSHES OF THY ALL-UNBLEMISH'T MOTHER. | IN GLORIOUS EPIPHANIE | 67 | 52 | 253 | 39 |
| NAME TO BE KNOWN, ALAS, BUT SORROW'S MOTHER. | SANCTA MARIA DOLORUM | 4 | 52 | 283 | 162 |
| DIVIDED LOVES, WHILE SON & MOTHER | SANCTA MARIA DOLORUM | 23 | 52 | 283 | 162 |
| O MOTHER TURTLE-DOVE. | SANCTA MARIA DOLORUM | 41 | 52 | 283 | 162 |
| COME YOUR WHOLE SELVES, SORROW'S GREAT SON & MOTHER. | SANCTA MARIA DOLORUM | 77 | 52 | 283 | 162 |
| THE FIRST EVE, MOTHER OF OUR FALL. | O GLORIOSA DOMINA | 11 | 52 | 302 | 194 |
| AND CALL THE MAIDEN EVE THEIR MOTHER. | O GLORIOSA DOMINA | 26 | 52 | 302 | 194 |
| MARIA, MOTHER OF OUR KING. | IN GLORIOUS ASSUMPTION B. LADY | 59 | 52 | 304 | 114 |
| SHOWES THIS THE MOTHER SERAPHIM. | FLAMING HEART | 16 | 52 | 324 | 61 |
| WAS MAIDEN WIFE & MAIDEN MOTHER TOO. | ALEXIAS THIRD ELEGIE | 30 | 52 | 336 | 209 |
| OH COME THEN. BRING THY MOTHER HER LOST JOY. | LUKE 2. QUAERIT JESUM | 15 | MS | 379 | 11 |
| WAS THY BLEST MOTHER. | LUKE 2. QUAERIT JESUM | 22 | MS | 379 | 11 |
| SHAME OF THY MOTHER SOYLE. ILL-NURTUR'D TREE. | HORATIJ ILLE & NEFASTO | 1 | MS | 382 | 530 |
| HEAVEN WAS ASHAM'D, TO SEE OUR MOTHER EARTH | UPON GUNPOWDER TREASON | 11 | MS | 386 | 460 |

## MOTHER-DIAMONDS

| | | | | | |
|---|---|---|---|---|---|
| SHEE 'GAINST THOSE MOTHER-DIAMONDS TRYES | A HYMNE OF THE NATIVITY | 69 | 46 | 106 | 76 |

## MOTHER-MAID

| | | | | | |
|---|---|---|---|---|---|
| GATHER NOW THY GREIF'S RIPE FRUIT. GREAT MOTHER-MAID. | OFFICE H. CROSS EVENSONG | 7 | 52 | 273 | 101 |

## MOTHER'S

| | | | | | |
|---|---|---|---|---|---|
| TWIXT'S MOTHER'S BRESTS IS GONE TO BED. | IN HOLY NATIVITY | 68 | 52 | 246 | 76 |
| SEEK FOR AMONGST HER MOTHER'S KISSES, | TERESA | 42 | 52 | 315 | 52 |
| MOTHER'S ARMES OR FATHER'S KNEE | TERESA | 62 | 52 | 315 | 52 |

## MOTHERS

| | | | | | |
|---|---|---|---|---|---|
| YOUR FERTILE MOTHERS. | THE WEEPER | 123 | 46 | 79 | 120 |
| THE MOTHERS MILKE, THE CHILDRENS BLOOD. | UPON INFANT MARTYRS | 2 | 46 | 95 | 10 |
| 'TWIXT MOTHERS BRESTS TO GOE TO BED. | A HYMNE OF THE NATIVITY | 50 | 46 | 106 | 76 |
| A THOUSAND SWEET BABES FROM THEIR MOTHERS BREST. | SOSPETTO D'HERODE | 4 | 46 | 109 | 216 |
| THAT FROM HIS MOTHERS BREST HEE MILKE SHOULD DRINKE, | SOSPETTO D'HERODE | 173 | 46 | 109 | 216 |
| SEEKE FOR, AMONGST HER MOTHERS KISSES. | IN MEMORY OF LADY MADRE TERESA | 42 | 46 | 131 | 52 |
| MOTHERS ARMES, OR FATHERS KNEE. | IN MEMORY OF LADY MADRE TERESA | 62 | 46 | 131 | 52 |
| FEATHERD WITH HIS MOTHERS SPARROWES. | OUT OF THE ITALIAN (1) | 18 | 46 | 188 | 545 |
| TORE NOT OFF HIS MOTHERS VEILE. | AN EPITAPH UPON ASHTON | 20 | 46 | 192 | 464 |
| YOUR FRUITFULL MOTHERS. | WEEPER | 165 | 52 | 307 | 120 |
| THE MOTHERS JOYES IN AN UNTIMELY CROP. | OUT OF GROTIUS | 26 | MS | 398 | 198 |

## MOTION

| | | | | | |
|---|---|---|---|---|---|
| INTO A WEEPING MOTION. | THE WEEPER | 92 | 46 | 79 | 120 |
| IMPATIENT NATURE HAD TAUGHT MOTION | UPON DEATH OF HERRYS | 6 | 46 | 167 | 466 |
| (WATCHING THEIR WATRY MOTION) | WEEPER | 146 | 52 | 307 | 120 |

## MOTIONS

| | | | | | |
|---|---|---|---|---|---|
| WHAT BUSY MOTIONS, WHAT WILD ENGINES STAND | SOSPETTO D'HERODE | 441 | 46 | 109 | 216 |
| THE OBSEQUIOUS MOTIONS OF LOVES FATE, | LOVES HOROSCOPE | 14 | 46 | 185 | 483 |
| TWO WALKING BATHS. TWO WEEPING MOTIONS. | WEEPER | 113 | 52 | 307 | 120 |

MOUNT

| | | | | |
|---|---|---|---|---|
| RAVISH THE DANCING ORBES, MAKE THEM MOUNT HIGHER | UPON KINGS CORONATION | 2 | MS 389 | 454 |

MOUNTED

| | | | | |
|---|---|---|---|---|
| HIGH MOUNTED ON AN ANT NANUS THE TALL | HIGH MOUNTED ON AN ANT | 1 | 46 161 | 523 |

MOUNTS

| | | | | |
|---|---|---|---|---|
| IN AZURE CHANNELLS WARME THROUGH MOUNTS OF SNOW. | UPON GUNPOWDER TREASON | 42 | MS 387 | 461 |

MOUNTAINE

| | | | | |
|---|---|---|---|---|
| AS EVER SILVER-TIPT, THE SIDE OF SHADY MOUNTAINE. | TO PONTIUS WASHING HANDS | 8 | 46 94 | 23 |
| AT MY FEET THE BLUBB'RING MOUNTAINE | PSALME 23 | 13 | 46 102 | 5 |
| OF FAITH, A MOUNTAINE WORD, MADE UP OF AIRE. | ON A TREATISE OF CHARITY | 53 | 46 137 | 69 |

MOUNTAINS

| | | | | |
|---|---|---|---|---|
| MOUNTAINS OF MYRRH, & BEDS OF SPICES. | TO THE NAME OF JESUS | 186 | 52 239 | 30 |
| JUSTLE DOWN MOUNTAINS, KINGS COURTS SHALL BE SENT, | ON GUNPOWDER-TREASON | 41 | MS 384 | 458 |
| THEY FORCE A LILLY PATH THROUGH ROSY MOUNTAINS. | AN ELEGIE ON DR PORTER | 42 | MS 395 | 476 |

MOUNTAINES

| | | | | |
|---|---|---|---|---|
| AND TIPT THE MOUNTAINES IN A TENDER RAY. | THE BEGINNING OF HELIODORUS | 2 | 46 158 | 517 |
| WITH MANNA, MILK, AND BALM, NEW BROACH THE MOUNTAINES. | SOSPETTO D'HERODE | 112 | 46 109 | 216 |
| AMONG THE GALILEAN MOUNTAINES, | WEEPER | 110 | 52 307 | 120 |
| MEN HAD NOT SPURN'D AT MOUNTAINES, NOR MADE WARRS | ALEXIAS THIRD ELEGIE | 9 | 52 336 | 209 |

MOURN

| | | | | |
|---|---|---|---|---|
| THINK MUCH THAT THOU SHOULDST MOURN ALONE. | SANCTA MARIA DOLORUM | 60 | 52 283 | 162 |

MOURN'D

| | | | | |
|---|---|---|---|---|
| INTO DIRE SABLE WEEDS, & SATE, & MOURN'D. | UPON GUNPOWDER TREASON | 48 | MS 386 | 460 |

MOURNE

| | | | | |
|---|---|---|---|---|
| IF HELL MUST MOURNE, HEAV'N SURE SHALL SYMPATHIZE | SOSPETTO D'HERODE | 247 | 46 109 | 216 |

MOURNFULL

| | | | | |
|---|---|---|---|---|
| A MOURNFULL DIRGE TO THEIR DECEASED KING. | UPON GUNPOWDER TREASON | 44 | MS 386 | 460 |
| THE SULLEN HEAVEN HAD VAIL'D ITS MOURNFULL BROW | UPON KINGS CORONATION | 2 | MS 390 | 453 |
| AMAZED SOL THROWES OF HIS MOURNFULL WEEDS, | UPON KINGS CORONATION | 15 | MS 390 | 453 |

MOUTH

| | | | | |
|---|---|---|---|---|
| THROUGH THE GREAT MOUTH THATS NAM'D FROM HERCULES) | THE BEGINNING OF HELIODORUS | 6 | 46 158 | 517 |
| STOPT THE MOUTH OF ELOQUENCE. | UPON THE DEATH OF A GENTLEMAN | 16 | 46 166 | 472 |
| LO, A MOUTH, WHOSE FULL-BLOOM'D LIPS | ON WOUNDS OF CRUCIFIED LORD | 5 | 46 99 | 24 |
| THIS FOOT HATH GOT A MOUTH AND LIPPES, | ON WOUNDS OF CRUCIFIED LORD | 13 | 46 99 | 24 |
| WHEN 'GAINST THE THUNDERS MOUTH WEE MARCHED FORTH. | SOSPETTO D'HERODE | 284 | 46 109 | 216 |
| HIS MOUTH WAS RHETORICKS BEST MOLD, | HIS EPITAPH (HERRYS) | 29 | 46 172 | 471 |
| AND MY MOUTH SHALL SHEW FORTH THY PRAYSE. | OFFICE H. CROSS MATINES | 4 | 52 265 | 86 |
| THE RECEIVING MOUTH HERE MAKES | LAUDA SION SALVATOREM | 43 | 52 294 | 178 |

FOULE-MOUTH'D

| | | | | |
|---|---|---|---|---|
| THAT FEARES THE FOULE-MOUTH'D AUSTER, OR THOSE STORMES OUT OF VIRGIL | | 19 | 46 155 | 529 |

FULL-MOUTH

| | | | | |
|---|---|---|---|---|
| A FULL-MOUTH DIAPASON SWALLOWES ALL. | MUSICKS DUELL | 156 | 46 149 | 535 |

MOUTHS

| | | | | |
|---|---|---|---|---|
| BOW'D TO THE LOWLY MOUTHS OF MEN. | LAUDA SION SALVATOREM | 62 | 52 294 | 178 |

MOUTHES

| | | | | |
|---|---|---|---|---|
| ARE THEY MOUTHES, OR ARE THEY EYES. | ON WOUNDS OF CRUCIFIED LORD | 2 | 46 99 | 24 |
| BE THEY MOUTHES, OR BE THEY EYNE, | ON WOUNDS OF CRUCIFIED LORD | 3 | 46 99 | 24 |
| KEPT THY MOUTHES GATE. | OUT OF MARTIALL | 2 | 46 188 | 527 |

MOVE

| | | | | |
|---|---|---|---|---|
| WHO SAW OUGHT IN THEE, THAT THEIR HATE COULD MOVE. | BUT NOW THEY HAVE SEEN | 4 | 46 96 | 21 |
| SO, EVEN SO STILL MAY I MOVE | PSALME 23 | 57 | 46 102 | 5 |
| THY BLOOD-REVOLVING BREST TO RAGE DOTH MOVE. | SOSPETTO D'HERODE | 514 | 46 109 | 216 |
| LEST FOR GRIEFE HIS LOSSE MAY MOVE, | UPON DEATH OF DESIRED HERRYS | 73 | 46 168 | 467 |
| BUT IF HER MILDER INFLUENCE MOVE. | LOVES HOROSCOPE | 33 | 46 185 | 483 |
| THEIR USE IS CHANG'D, NOT LOST, AND NOW THEY MOVE | VEXILLA REGIS | 17 | 52 277 | 156 |
| SO LUMPISH STEEL, UNTAUGHT TO MOVE, | AGAINST IRRESOLUTION AND DELAY | 51 | 52 347 | 146 |
| STUFT THEE SOE FULL WITH BLISSE, THOU CAN'ST NOT MOVE. | ON GUNPOWDER-TREASON | 6 | MS 384 | 458 |

MOV'D

| | | | | |
|---|---|---|---|---|
| OH CROWNE THESE PRAIE'RS (MOV'D IN A HAPPY HOWER) | EX EUPHORMIONE | 3 | MS 392 | 525 |

MOVES

    LOOKE IN WHAT POMPE THE MISTRESSE PLANET MOVES    SOSPETTO D'HERODE    237  46 109 216
    WHAT E'RE LOVE'S MATTER BE, HE MOVES    AGAINST IRRESOLUTION AND DELAY    53  52 347 146

MUCH

    SO MUCH AS TH' PICTURE OF A WELL-LIM'D VERSE.    WITH A PICTURE TO A FRIEND    4  46 156 494
    SAD REQUITALL, THUS MUCH DUST.    UPON THE DEATH OF A GENTLEMAN    14  46 166 472
    THUS MUCH, HEE'S DEAD, AND WEEPE THE REST.    UPON THE DEATH OF A GENTLEMAN    34  46 166 472
    ALL TORNE. WITH MUCH ADOE YET ERE HE DYES.    HIGH MOUNTED ON AN ANT    4  46 161 523
    MUCH RATHER WOULD IT TREMBLE HEERE,    THE WEEPER    41  46  79 120
    HIS HANDS WHOLE STRENGTH HERE, COULD NOT BE TOO MUCH.    THE DUMBE HEALED    4  46  87  16
    KNOW'ST THOU THIS, SOULDIER. 'TIS A MUCH CHANG'D    UPON THORNES FROM LORDS HEAD    1  46  96  23
            PLANT, WHICH YE
            T
    GOE NOW, MAKE MUCH OF THESE. WAGE STILL THEIR WARS    SOSPETTO D'HERODE    447  46 109 216
    SO MUCH. RUDE SHEPHEARDS. WHAT HIS STEEDS. ALAS    SOSPETTO D'HERODE    527  46 109 216
    MUCH LARGER IN IT SELFE THEN IN ITS LOOKE.    ON A PRAYER BOOKE    4  46 126 139
    HOW MUCH LESSE STRONG IS DEATH THEN LOVE.    IN MEMORY OF LADY MADRE TERESA    28  46 131  52
    AS MUCH AS SEES) SHALL WITH THESE SACRED LEAVES    ON A TREATISE OF CHARITY    24  46 137  69
    LEFT HIS YEARES SO MUCH BEHIND.    HIS EPITAPH (HERRYS)    8  46 172 471
    BUT MUCH MORE FRUITFULL IS. NOR DOES, AS SHEE,    UPON YORKE HIS BIRTH    84  46 176 500
    SO MUCH O'RE-MASTRING ALL HIS MIGHT.    OUT OF THE ITALIAN (3)    6  46 190 549
    HOW MUCH THEMSELVES MORE PRETIOUS ARE.    WISHES SUPPOSED MISTRESSE    48  46 195 479
    HOW MUCH MY SUMMER WAITES UPON THY SPRING.    UPON TWO GREENE APRICOCKES    34  46 220 494
    NOR MUST YOU THINK IT MUCH    TO THE NAME OF JESUS    51  52 239  30
    A DARKENES MADE OF TOO MUCH DAY,    IN GLORIOUS EPIPHANIE    18  52 253  39
    EMBOSOM'D IN A MUCH MORE ROSY MORN,    IN GLORIOUS EPIPHANIE    66  52 253  39
    NOR (MUCH LESSE) SHALL THEY LEAVE THESE EYES    IN GLORIOUS EPIPHANIE    87  52 253  39
    GUILTY OF BEING MUCH FOR THEM TOO GOOD.    IN GLORIOUS EPIPHANIE    108  52 253  39
    ALAS WITH HOW MUCH HEAVYER SHADE    IN GLORIOUS EPIPHANIE    117  52 253  39
    NOT SO MUCH THEIR SUN AS SHADE,    IN GLORIOUS EPIPHANIE    137  52 253  39
    THY CRIME IS TOO MUCH DUTY.    VEXILLA REGIS    27  52 277 156
    THY BURTHEN, TOO MUCH BEAUTY.    VEXILLA REGIS    28  52 277 156
    HOW MUCH DEATH WEIGH'D MORE LIGHT THEN LOVE.    VEXILLA REGIS    36  52 277 156
    SO MUCH A THING OF NOUGHT.    CHARITAS NIMIA    4  52 280  48
    LEAVING HER ONLY SO MUCH BREATH    SANCTA MARIA DOLORUM    39  52 283 162
    THINK MUCH THAT THOU SHOULDST MOURN ALONE.    SANCTA MARIA DOLORUM    60  52 283 162
    WHOM TOO MUCH LOVE HATH BOW'D MORE LOW FOR ME.    ADORO TE    4  52 291 172
    'TWAS PAY'D AT FIRST WITH TOO MUCH PAIN,    DIES IRAE    39  52 298 186
    THE RAIN IS GONE, EXCEPT SO MUCH AS WE    IN GLORIOUS ASSUMPTION B. LADY    21  52 304 114
    MUCH REATHER WOULD IT BE THY TEAR,    WEEPER    47  52 307 120
    SO MUCH MORE RICH WOULD HE ESTEEM    WEEPER    77  52 307 120
    MUCH LESSE MEAN WE TO TRACE    WEEPER    181  52 307 120
    HOW MUCH LESSE STRONG IS DEATH THEN LOVE.    TERESA    28  52 315  52
    MAKE NOT TOO MUCH HAST TO' ADMIRE    FLAMING HEART    3  52 324  61
    STARRS MUCH TOO FAIR & PURE TO WAIT UPON    TO SAME CONCERNING CHOISE    31  52 331  66
    AND PRIZE THEMSELVES. DOE MUCH, THAT MORE THEY MAY,    DESCRIPTION RELIGIOUS HOUSE    20  52 338 213
    TOO MUCH A GAINER BY'T, SHOULD WE    AGAINST IRRESOLUTION AND DELAY    64  52 347 146
    BUT AT THE LAST (HAVING NOT SOE MUCH POWE'R    UPON KINGS CORONATION    5  MS 390 453
    YOU TAKE UPON YOU TOO TOO MUCH.    UPON DEATH OF A FREIND    13  MS 393 477
    WAS NOT SO MUCH AS CLEANE. A STABLE KIND.    OUT OF GROTIUS    17  MS 396 198
    THE BROKEN MEATE WAS MUCH MORE THEN THE WHOLE.    OUT OF GROTIUS    64  MS 398 198

MUCH-CHANG'D

    KNOW'ST THOU THIS, SOULDIER. 'TIS A MUCH-CHANG'D    UPON CROWNE OF THORNS    1  52 290  23
            PLANT WHICH YET

MUCH-WRONG'D

    EXPOSTULATE MY WOES & MUCH-WRONG'D LOVES.    ALEXIAS SECONDE ELEGIE    14  52 335 207

MUDDY

    AND FOULE THE CLEARE TEXT WITH A MUDDY GLOSSE.    UPON BIRTH PRINCESSE E    54  MS 391 456

MUFLING

    BUT IN A VAILE OF CLOUDS MUFLING HER HEAD    UPON GUNPOWDER TREASON    17  MS 386 460

MULTIPLY

    WHILE OUR JOYES SO MULTIPLY,    OUT OF CATULLUS    19  46 194 523

MULTITUDE

    THE THRONGING CLOTTED MULTITUDE DOTH FEAST.    HORATIJ ILLE & NEFASTO    49  MS 382 530
    AND RUGGED TOUCH OF PLUTO'S MULTITUDE.    UPON GUNPOWDER TREASON    58  MS 387 461

MULTITUDES

    WAS LOSSE OF MULTITUDES. AND MISSING MEE    OUT OF GROTIUS    28  MS 398 198

MURTHER

    IS MURTHER NO SIN. OR A SIN SO CHEAPE,    TO PONTIUS WASHING HANDS    1  46  94  23

MURDRED

    WHICH SHORT-CUT LIVES OF MURDRED INFANTS LEAVE.    SOSPETTO D'HERODE    344  46 109 216
    MURDRED THE EARTH'S JUST PRIDE WITH A RUDE KISSE.    AN ELEGY MR STANNINOW    48  MS 394 473

MURD'RING

| | | | |
|---|---|---|---|
| AND THERE, AS MASTER OF THIS MURD'RING BROOD. | SOSPETTO D'HERODE | 318 | 46 109 216 |

MURMUR

| | | | |
|---|---|---|---|
| IN THE CLOSE MURMUR OF A SPARKLING NOYSE. | MUSICKS DUELL | 84 | 46 149 535 |
| AND MURMUR IN A BUZZING DINNE, THEN GINGLE | MUSICKS DUELL | 129 | 46 149 535 |
| OF SWEETS YOU HAVE. AND MURMUR THAT YOU HAVE NO MORE. | TO THE NAME OF JESUS | 67 | 52 239 30 |
| THE FOUNTAINS MURMUR. & EACH LOFTYEST TREE | IN GLORIOUS ASSUMPTION B. LADY | 29 | 52 304 114 |
| AND MURMUR FORTH THY WOES TO EVERY FLOWER. | AN ELEGIE ON DR PORTER | 21 | MS 395 476 |

MURMURE

| | | | |
|---|---|---|---|
| AND MURMURE IF THEY MEET A STAY. | AGAINST IRRESOLUTION AND DELAY | 40 | 52 347 146 |

MURMURS

| | | | |
|---|---|---|---|
| IN PANTING MURMURS, STILL'D OUT OF HER BREAST | MUSICKS DUELL | 65 | 46 149 535 |
| WHOSE TREMBLING MURMURS MELTING IN WILD AIRES | MUSICKS DUELL | 141 | 46 149 535 |
| GOLDEN TAGUS MURMURS THOUGH, | THE WEEPER | 80 | 46 79 120 |
| AND WITH SAD MURMURS, CHIDES THE HANDS THAT STAIN HER. | TO PONTIUS WASHING HANDS | 14 | 46 94 23 |
| OUR MURMURS HAVE THEIR MUSICK TOO. | TO THE NAME OF JESUS | 103 | 52 239 30 |
| NO QURRELLS, MURMURS, NO DELAY. | TEMPERANCE | 49 | 52 342 510 |

MURMURES

| | | | |
|---|---|---|---|
| IN HER OWNE MURMURES, THAT WHAT EVER MOOD | MUSICKS DUELL | 13 | 46 149 535 |
| AND IN THEIR MURMURES KEEPE THY MIGHTY NAME. | SOSPETTO D'HERODE | 32 | 46 109 216 |
| HE MURMURES, AND REBUKES THEIR BOLD DESIRE. | SOSPETTO D'HERODE | 465 | 46 109 216 |
| GOLDEN TAGUS MURMURES THO. | WEEPER | 74 | 52 307 120 |

MURMURING

| | | | |
|---|---|---|---|
| TO WOO THEM FROM THEIR BEDS, STILL MURMURING | MUSICKS DUELL | 79 | 46 149 535 |
| THAT IN THY EARES THUS KEEPS A MURMURING. | UPON YORKE HIS BIRTH | 107 | 46 176 500 |
| AND URGE THE MURMURING GRAVES TO BRING | DIES IRAE | 11 | 52 298 186 |
| RUNNES MURMURING ON THE STRINGS. ALCAEUS THERE | HORATIJ ILLE & NEFASTO | 41 | MS 382 530 |

MURMURINGS

| | | | |
|---|---|---|---|
| WITH CHATTING BIRDS DELICIOUS MURMURINGS. | OUT OF VIRGIL | 10 | 46 155 529 |

MUSE

| | | | |
|---|---|---|---|
| THEIR MUSE, THEIR SYREN. HARMLESSE SYREN SHEE) | MUSICKS DUELL | 10 | 46 149 535 |
| MUSE, NOW THE SERVANT OF SOFT LOVES NO MORE. | SOSPETTO D'HERODE | 1 | 46 109 216 |
| NOR NEEDS MY MUSE A BLUSH, OR THESE BRIGHT FLOWERS | SOSPETTO D'HERODE | 17 | 46 109 216 |
| FARRE MORE THEN MAITER FOR MY MUSE AND MEE. | SOSPETTO D'HERODE | 30 | 46 109 216 |
| WHAT SUCCOUR CAN I HOPE THE MUSE WILL SEND | TO THE MORNING | 1 | 46 183 497 |
| UNLESSE THE MUSE SING MY APOLOGY. | TO THE MORNING | 4 | 46 183 497 |
| IF MORPHEUS HAVE A MUSE TO WAIT ON MEE. | TO THE MORNING | 18 | 46 183 497 |
| DREST IN THE GLORIOUS MADNESSE OF A MUSE. | TO THE MORNING | 23 | 46 183 497 |
| NEW MATTER FOR OUR MUSE SUPPLIES, | TO THE QUEEN | 7 | 46 215 501 |
| AND THE DEARE MERITS OF YOUR MUSE, THEIR DUE, | UPON TWO GREENE APRICOCKES | 11 | 48 220 494 |
| BUT REST, AFFRIGHTED MUSE. THY SILVER WINGS | UPON GUNPOWDER TREASON | 27 | MS 387 461 |
| WHETHER THE MUSE THEY CLOTH SHALL LIVE OR DIE. | AT TH' IVORY TRIBUNALL | 4 | MS 397 492 |

MUSES

| | | | |
|---|---|---|---|
| THE MORNING MUSES PERCH LIKE BIRDS, AND SING | UPON DEATH OF HERRYS | 11 | 46 167 466 |
| HIM THE MUSES LOVE TO FOLLOW, | UPON DEATH OF DESIRED HERRYS | 11 | 46 168 467 |
| WHOSE BANKES THE MUSES DWELT UPON, | AN EPITAPH DOCTOR BROOKE | 3 | 46 175 465 |
| THE MUSES WITH THEIR TEARES SUPPLY. | AN EPITAPH DOCTOR BROOKE | 8 | 46 175 465 |
| O SPEAKE A LOWLY MUSES PARDON. SPEAKE | UPON YORKE HIS BIRTH | 108 | 46 176 500 |
| WHOSE DROWSINESSE HATH WRONG'D THE MUSES FRIEND. | TO THE MORNING | 2 | 46 183 497 |
| THE MUSES, & THE GRACES SUGRED NEASTS. | UPON GUNPOWDER TREASON | 38 | MS 387 461 |
| THE MUSES, & THE GRACES FRAGRANT POSIES. | AN ELEGY MR STANNINOW | 38 | MS 394 473 |
| A THOUSAND HELICONS THE MUSES SEND | AN ELEGIE ON DR PORTER | 39 | MS 395 476 |

MUSICALL

| | | | |
|---|---|---|---|
| ARE MUSICALL. | TO THE NAME OF JESUS | 58 | 52 239 30 |

MUSICALLY

| | | | |
|---|---|---|---|
| THE SWEET-LIP'T SISTERS MUSICALLY FRIGHTED, | MUSICKS DUELL | 113 | 46 149 535 |

MUSICK

| | | | |
|---|---|---|---|
| OUR MURMURS HAVE THEIR MUSICK TOO, | TO THE NAME OF JESUS | 103 | 52 239 30 |
| THEN TO HIS MUSICK. AND HIS SONG | WEEPER | 29 | 52 307 120 |
| HIS OWN MUSICK, HIS OWN HEALTH. | TEMPERANCE | 16 | 52 342 510 |
| TO THEIR OWNE MUSICK, NOR (UNTILL THEY SEE | UPON KINGS CORONATION | 23 | MS 390 453 |
| WHOSE WHOLE LIFE MUSICK WAS. WHEREIN | UPON DEATH OF A FREIND | 19 | MS 393 477 |
| AND THOUGH THAT MUSICK OF HIS LIFE BE STILL, | UPON DEATH OF A FREIND | 21 | MS 393 477 |
| THE MUSICK OF HIS NAME YETT SOUNDETH SHRILL. | UPON DEATH OF A FREIND | 22 | MS 393 477 |

MUSICK'S

| | | | |
|---|---|---|---|
| IN MUSICK'S RAVISH'T SOULE HEE DARE NOT TELL, | MUSICKS DUELL | 144 | 46 149 535 |

MUSICKE

| | | | | | |
|---|---|---|---|---|---|
| THEN TO HIS MUSICKE, AND HIS SONG | THE WEEPER | 29 | 46 | 79 | 120 |
| OUR HARPES THAT NOW NO MUSICKE UNDERSTOOD. | PSALME 137 | 3 | 46 | 104 | 7 |
| THE MUSICKE OF THY MEMORY. | PSALME 137 | 18 | 46 | 104 | 7 |
| HEDGE-QUIRISTERS WHOSE MUSICKE OWES | THOUGH NOW 'TIS NEITHER | 18 | MS | 397 | 492 |

MUSICKS

| | | | | | |
|---|---|---|---|---|---|
| THE MUSICKS SOFT REPORT. AND MOLD THE SAME | MUSICKS DUELL | 12 | 46 | 149 | 535 |
| MUSICKS BEST SEED-PLOT, WHENCE IN RIPEND AIRES | MUSICKS DUELL | 69 | 46 | 149 | 535 |
| ABOVE HER SELFE, MUSICKS ENTHUSIAST. | MUSICKS DUELL | 104 | 46 | 149 | 535 |
| FEELES MUSICKS PULSE IN ALL HER ARTERYES. | MUSICKS DUELL | 120 | 46 | 149 | 535 |
| OF MUSICKS HEAVEN. AND SEAT IT THERE ON HIGH | MUSICKS DUELL | 149 | 46 | 149 | 535 |
| OF MUSICKS DAINTY TOUCH, THEN I | PSALME 137 | 17 | 46 | 104 | 7 |
| HEE'S DEAD. OH WHAT HARSH MUSICKS THERE | UPON DEATH OF A FREIND | 1 | MS | 393 | 477 |

MUSITIANS

| | | | | | |
|---|---|---|---|---|---|
| IN THE MUSITIANS FACE. YET ONCE AGAINE | MUSICKS DUELL | 106 | 46 | 149 | 535 |

MUST

| | | | | | |
|---|---|---|---|---|---|
| THUS MUST WE DATE THY MEMORY. | THE WEEPER | 118 | 46 | 79 | 120 |
| 'CAUSE THOU STREIGHT MUST LAY THY HEAD | THE TEARE | 32 | 46 | 84 | 50 |
| (FOR TO HEAVEN THOU MUST GOE) | THE TEARE | 38 | 46 | 84 | 50 |
| THY SHADOW PETER, MUST SHEW ME THE SUN, | SICKE IMPLORE SHADOW | 3 | 46 | 87 | 28 |
| MUST HAVE ITS FOUNTAINE IN THINE EYES. | TO PONTIUS WASHING HANDS | 4 | 46 | 88 | 22 |
| WITH TH'PURPLE HE MUST WEARE IN HELL. | UPON LAZARUS HIS TEARES | 4 | 46 | 89 | 18 |
| THE MOTHER THEN MUST SUCK THE SON. | BLESSED BE THE PAPS | 4 | 46 | 94 | 14 |
| NO,NO,THY GOOD, SION, ALONE MUST CROWNE | PSALME 137 | 25 | 46 | 104 | 7 |
| TO THEE (DREAD LAMBE) WHOSE LOVE MUST KEEPE | A HYMNE OF THE NATIVITY | 81 | 46 | 106 | 76 |
| MUST THE BRIGHT ARMES OF HEAV'N. REBUKE THESE EYES. | SOSPETTO D'HERODE | 231 | 46 | 109 | 216 |
| IF HELL MUST MOURNE, HEAV'N SURE SHALL SYMPATHIZE | SOSPETTO D'HERODE | 247 | 46 | 109 | 216 |
| I THANKE YOU ALL, BUT ONE MUST SINGLE OUT, | SOSPETTO D'HERODE | 287 | 46 | 109 | 216 |
| BUT ALL HIS COUNSELLOURS MUST SUMMON'D BEE. | SOSPETTO D'HERODE | 507 | 46 | 109 | 216 |
| MUST BEE A SURE HOUSE KEEPER. | ON A PRAYER BOOKE | 31 | 46 | 126 | 139 |
| THAT DULL MORTALITY MUST NOT KNOW A NAME. | ON A PRAYER BOOKE | 80 | 46 | 126 | 139 |
| THOU ART LOVES VICTIM, AND MUST DYE | IN MEMORY OF LADY MADRE TERESA | 75 | 46 | 131 | 52 |
| HIS IS THE DART MUST MAKE THE DEATH | IN MEMORY OF LADY MADRE TERESA | 79 | 46 | 131 | 52 |
| MUST BE THE IMMORTALL INSTRUMENT. | IN MEMORY OF LADY MADRE TERESA | 89 | 46 | 131 | 52 |
| MUST LEARNE IN LIFE TO DYE LIKE THEE. | IN MEMORY OF LADY MADRE TERESA | 183 | 46 | 131 | 52 |
| TAKE THY FAREWEL POORE WORLD, HEAVEN MUST GO HOME. | ON THE ASSUMPTION | 2 | 46 | 139 | 114 |
| HEAV'N CALLS HER, AND SHE MUST AWAY, | ON THE ASSUMPTION | 21 | 46 | 139 | 114 |
| AND THOUGH THY DEAREST LOCKS MUST NOW BE LIGHT | ON THE ASSUMPTION | 31 | 46 | 139 | 114 |
| DEATH THOU MUST NOT HERE BE CRUELL. | UPON DEATH OF DESIRED HERRYS | 3 | 46 | 168 | 467 |
| THEREFORE IF HEE NEEDS MUST GO. | UPON DEATH OF DESIRED HERRYS | 65 | 46 | 168 | 467 |
| BEAUTY FROWNES, AND LOVE MUST DYE. | LOVES HOROSCOPE | 32 | 46 | 185 | 483 |
| TH' EGYPTIAN PYRAMIDS THEMSELVES MUST LIVE.) | ON FRONTISPIECE ISAACSONS | 20 | 46 | 191 | 491 |
| NEEDS MUST YOUR NOBLE PRAYSES STRENGTH | TO THE QUEEN | 13 | 48 | 215 | 501 |
| NOR NEED BE DOUBLE-GILT. HOW THEN MUST THESE. | UPON TWO GREENE APRICOCKES | 29 | 48 | 220 | 494 |
| IT MUST NOT FALL IN VAIN, IT MUST | TO COUNTESSE OF DENBIGH | 51 | 52 | 236 | 146 |
| IT MUST NOT FALL IN VAIN, IT MUST | TO COUNTESSE OF DENBIGH | 51 | 52 | 236 | 146 |
| WE MUST HAVE STORE. | TO THE NAME OF JESUS | 26 | 52 | 239 | 30 |
| NOR MUST YOU THINK IT MUCH | TO THE NAME OF JESUS | 51 | 52 | 239 | 30 |
| TO THEE, DREAD LAMB. WHOSE LOVE MUST KEEP | IN HOLY NATIVITY | 101 | 52 | 246 | 76 |
| CROWNES, & THE HEADS THEY KISSE, MUST COURT THESE FEET. | TO THE QUEEN'S MAJESTY | 20 | 52 | 261 | 47 |
| BEARES THAT HUGE TREE WHICH MUST BEAR HIM. | OFFICE H. CROSS SIXT | 4 | 52 | 270 | 97 |
| BUT MUST THY BED, LORD, BE A BOROW'D GRAVE | OFFICE H. CROSS COMPLINE | 9 | 52 | 274 | 105 |
| OF LOVE. HERE MUST SHE STAND | SANCTA MARIA DOLORUM | 36 | 52 | 283 | 162 |
| NOR TOUCH NOR TAST MUST LOOK FOR MORE | ADORO TE | 7 | 52 | 291 | 172 |
| MUST BE THE DAY OF THAT DREAD NIGHT. | DIES IRAE | 8 | 52 | 298 | 186 |
| TAKE THY FAREWELL, POOR WORLD. HEAVN MUST GOE HOME. | IN GLORIOUS ASSUMPTION B. LADY | 2 | 52 | 304 | 114 |
| HEAVN CALLS HER, AND SHE MUST AWAY. | IN GLORIOUS ASSUMPTION B. LADY | 35 | 52 | 304 | 114 |
| THUS MUST WE DATE THY MEMORY. | WEEPER | 154 | 52 | 307 | 120 |
| THOU ART LOVE'S VICTIME. & MUST DY | TERESA | 75 | 52 | 315 | 52 |
| HIS IS THE DART MUST MAKE THE DEATH | TERESA | 79 | 52 | 315 | 52 |
| MUST BE TH'IMMORTALL INSTRUMENT | TERESA | 89 | 52 | 315 | 52 |
| MUST LEARN IN LIFE TO DY LIKE THEE. | TERESA | 182 | 52 | 315 | 52 |
| YOU MUST TRANSPOSE THE PICTURE QUITE, | FLAMING HEART | 9 | 52 | 324 | 61 |
| MUST BE A SURE HOUSE-KEEPER. | PRAYER TO GENTLE-WOMAN | 37 | 52 | 328 | 139 |
| THAT DULL MORTALITY MUST NOT KNOW A NAME. | PRAYER TO GENTLE-WOMAN | 86 | 52 | 328 | 139 |
| NEEDS MUST MY MISERYES OWE THAT MAN A SPITE | ALEXIAS THIRD ELEGIE | 3 | 52 | 336 | 209 |
| ALONE MUST LY. | LUKE 2. QUAERIT JESUM | 12 | MS | 379 | 11 |
| HATH NOW PRAEPAR'D, & YOU MUST BE HIS GUEST. | UPON GUNPOWDER TREASON | 2 | MS | 387 | 461 |
| THY SCARLET ROBES. FOR HEERE YOU MUST NOT SHARE | UPON GUNPOWDER TREASON | 5 | MS | 387 | 461 |
| MUST HAVE A PASSAGE, OR 'TWILL FORCE A WAY. | UPON BIRTH PRINCESSE E | 14 | MS | 391 | 456 |
| WEE MUST THAT DISCORD SURELY CALL. | UPON DEATH OF A FREIND | 3 | MS | 393 | 477 |
| SINCE YOUTH MUST FALL, WHEN IT SHOULD RISE. | UPON DEATH OF A FREIND | 16 | MS | 393 | 477 |

MUSTER

| | | | | | |
|---|---|---|---|---|---|
| MUSTER FORTH INTO THE VALLEY. | PSALME 23 | 36 | 46 | 102 | 5 |

MUTE

| | | | | | |
|---|---|---|---|---|---|
| ABOVE HER MOCKE, OR BEE FOR EVER MUTE. | MUSICKS DUELL | 108 | 46 | 149 | 535 |
| FOR SEE APPOLLO ALL THIS WHILE STANDS MUTE. | UPON YORKE HIS BIRTH | 114 | 46 | 176 | 500 |
| LONG MADE TH'HARMONIOUS ORBES ALL MUTE TO US | IN GLORIOUS EPIPHANIE | 132 | 52 | 253 | 39 |

MUTUALL

| | | | | | |
|---|---|---|---|---|---|
| MUTUALL SWEETNESSE THEY EXPRESSE. | THE WEEPER | 88 | 46 | 79 | 120 |
| OF BROTHERS MUTUALL BLOOD, AND FATHERS BRAINES. | SOSPETTO D'HERODE | 328 | 46 | 109 | 216 |
| AND SO IN MUTUALL NAMES | OUT OF THE ITALIAN (2) | 13 | 46 | 190 | 547 |
| A MUTUALL TRADE | IN GLORIOUS EPIPHANIE | 215 | 52 | 253 | 39 |
| WHILE WITH A FAITHFULL, MUTUALL, FLOUD | SANCTA MARIA DOLORUM | 19 | 52 | 283 | 162 |
| MUTUALL SWEETNESSE THEY EXPRESSE. | WEEPER | 82 | 52 | 307 | 120 |
| HOW SWEET THE MUTUALL YOKE OF MAN & WIFE, | ALEXIAS THIRD ELEGIE | 51 | 52 | 336 | 209 |
| MIX THE MAD SONS OF MEN IN MUTUALL BLOOD. | DESCRIPTION RELIGIOUS HOUSE | 8 | 52 | 338 | 213 |

MYRRH

| | | | | | |
|---|---|---|---|---|---|
| MOUNTAINS OF MYRRH, & BEDS OF SPICES. | TO THE NAME OF JESUS | 186 | 52 | 239 | 30 |

MIRRH

| | | | | | |
|---|---|---|---|---|---|
| HIS GOLD, HIS MIRRH, HIS FRANKINCENCE. | IN GLORIOUS EPIPHANIE | 244 | 52 | 253 | 39 |

MYSTERIES

| | | | | | |
|---|---|---|---|---|---|
| BUT THESE VAST MYSTERIES HIS SENSES SMOTHER, | SOSPETTO D'HERODE | 161 | 46 | 109 | 216 |
| MOCKE ME, AND DAZLE MY DARKE MYSTERIES. | SOSPETTO D'HERODE | 232 | 46 | 109 | 216 |
| (BY ALL THY MYSTERIES THAT THERE LYE HID.) | AN APOLOGIE FOR HYMNE (TERESA) | 12 | 46 | 136 | 59 |

MYSTERIOUS

| | | | | | |
|---|---|---|---|---|---|
| O STRANGE MYSTERIOUS STRIFE | OFFICE H. CROSS NINTH | 9 | 52 | 271 | 99 |

MYSTERYES

| | | | | | |
|---|---|---|---|---|---|
| BECAUSE THOSE PRETIOUS MYSTERYES THAT DWELL, | MUSICKS DUELL | 143 | 46 | 149 | 535 |
| (BY ALL THY MYSTERYES THAT HERE LY HIDDE) | AN APOLOGIE FOR (TERESA) HYMNE | 12 | 52 | 322 | 59 |

MYSTICK

| | | | | | |
|---|---|---|---|---|---|
| WHAT MAGICK BOLTS, WHAT MYSTICK BARRES | TO COUNTESSE OF DENBIGH | 17 | 52 | 236 | 146 |
| COME FORTH GREAT MASTER OF THE MYSTICK DAY. | IN GLORIOUS EPIPHANIE | 207 | 52 | 253 | 39 |
| AND BY A MINDFULLL, MYSTICK BREATH | LAUDA SION SALVATOREM | 27 | 52 | 294 | 178 |
| LET MYSTICK DEATHS WAIT ON'T. & WISE SOULES BE | FLAMING HEART | 83 | 52 | 324 | 61 |
| AND MANY A MYSTICK THING | PRAYER TO GENTLE-WOMAN | 82 | 52 | 328 | 139 |
| TH'ORACULOUS DOCTOR'S MYSTICK BILLS. | TEMPERANCE | 7 | 52 | 342 | 510 |
| WHAT MAGICK-BOLTS, WHAT MYSTICK BARRS | AGAINST IRRESOLUTION AND DELAY | 11 | 52 | 347 | 146 |

MISTICK

| | | | | | |
|---|---|---|---|---|---|
| THE ORACULOUS DOCTORS MISTICK BILLS, | IN PRAISE OF LESSIUS | 7 | 46 | 156 | 510 |

MISTICKE

| | | | | | |
|---|---|---|---|---|---|
| AND MANY A MISTICKE THING, | ON A PRAYER BOOKE | 76 | 46 | 126 | 139 |

MYSTICALL

| | | | | | |
|---|---|---|---|---|---|
| A DEATH MORE MYSTICALL & HIGH. | TERESA | 76 | 52 | 315 | 52 |

MISTICALL

| | | | | | |
|---|---|---|---|---|---|
| A DEATH MORE MISTICALL AND HIGH. | IN MEMORY OF LADY MADRE TERESA | 76 | 46 | 131 | 52 |

NAILE

| | | | | | |
|---|---|---|---|---|---|
| OR NAILE, OR THORNE, OR SPEARE HAVE WRIT IN THEE, | ON MARKES OF SAVIOURS WOUNDS | 2 | 46 | 86 | 28 |

NAIL'D

| | | | | | |
|---|---|---|---|---|---|
| NAIL'D HANDS. & PEIRCED HEARTS. | SANCTA MARIA DOLORUM | 76 | 52 | 283 | 162 |

NAILES

| | | | | | |
|---|---|---|---|---|---|
| NAILES, HAMMERS, HATCHETS SHARPE, AND HALTERS STRONG, | SOSPETTO D'HERODE | 325 | 46 | 109 | 216 |
| ARE NAILES BLUNT PENS OF SUPERFICIALL SMART. | OFFICE H. CROSS SIXT | 11 | 52 | 270 | 97 |
| WHEN THE DEAR NAILES DID LOCK | OFFICE H. CROSS EVENSONG | 12 | 52 | 273 | 101 |
| AND FROM THE NAILES & SPEAR | VEXILLA REGIS | 15 | 52 | 277 | 156 |
| HIS NAILES WRITE SWORDS IN HER, WHICH SOON HER HEART | SANCTA MARIA DOLORUM | 27 | 52 | 283 | 162 |

NAKED

| | | | | | |
|---|---|---|---|---|---|
| MARS THOU HAST BEATEN NAKED, AND O THEN | UPON VENUS PUTTING ARMES | 3 | 46 | 161 | 523 |
| TH'HAVE LEFT THEE NAKED LORD, O THAT THEY HAD. | ON CRUCIFIED LORD BLOODY | 1 | 46 | 100 | 24 |
| WAS THE PRIDE OF NAKED TRUTH. | HIS EPITAPH (HERRYS) | 26 | 46 | 172 | 471 |
| THEY 'HAVE LEFT THEE NAKED, LORD, O THAT THEY HAD. | UPON BODY OF OUR LORD | 1 | 52 | 290 | 24 |

NAKED'ST

| | | | | | |
|---|---|---|---|---|---|
| EV'EN TO THE NAKED'ST VOWES. THOU ART MY FATE. | EX EUPHORMIONE | 9 | MS | 392 | 525 |

NAK'T

| | | | | | |
|---|---|---|---|---|---|
| THAT BEING NAK'T, THOU KNOW'ST COULD CONQUER THEE. | UPON THE SAME (VENUS ARMES) | 4 | 46 | 161 | 523 |
| HOW LOVE CAME NAK'T, A BOY, AND BLIND. | OUT OF THE ITALIAN (3) | 2 | 46 | 190 | 549 |

## NAKEDNESSE

| | | | | |
|---|---|---|---|---|
| AND CLOATH THEIR SIMPLEST NAKEDNESSE. | WISHES SUPPOSED MISTRESSE | 42 | 46 | 195 479 |

## NAME

| | | | | |
|---|---|---|---|---|
| FOUNDED TO TH' NAME OF GREAT APOLLO'S LYRE. | MUSICKS DUELL | 74 | 46 | 149 535 |
| THAT OW'ST A NAME TO MISERY. | UPON THE DEATH OF A GENTLEMAN | 26 | 46 | 166 472 |
| A NAME IN NOBLE DEEDES RIVALL TO THEE. | SOSPETTO D'HERODE | 28 | 46 | 109 216 |
| AND IN THEIR MURMURES KEEPE THY MIGHTY NAME. | SOSPETTO D'HERODE | 32 | 46 | 109 216 |
| IN ANSWER TO HER FORMIDABLE NAME. | SOSPETTO D'HERODE | 304 | 46 | 109 216 |
| THAT DULL MORTALITY MUST NOT KNOW A NAME. | ON A PRAYER BOOKE | 80 | 46 | 126 139 |
| AND THOUGH HERBERTS NAME DOE OWE | ON MR. G. HERBERTS BOOKE | 15 | 46 | 130 68 |
| THEIR GREAT LORDS GLORIOUS NAME, TO NONE | IN MEMORY OF LADY MADRE TERESA | 9 | 46 | 131 52 |
| SCARCE HAD SHEE LEARNT TO LISP A NAME | IN MEMORY OF LADY MADRE TERESA | 15 | 46 | 131 52 |
| WITH CHRISTS NAME INT IN CHANGE FOR DEATH. | IN MEMORY OF LADY MADRE TERESA | 50 | 46 | 131 52 |
| WHICH WRITES THY SPOWSES RADIANT NAME | IN MEMORY OF LADY MADRE TERESA | 82 | 46 | 131 52 |
| THUS HAVE I BACK AGAINE TO THY BRIGHT NAME | AN APOLOGIE FOR HYMNE (TERESA) | 1 | 46 | 136 59 |
| THAT KEEPS RELIGION WARME. NOT SWELL A NAME | ON A TREATISE OF CHARITY | 52 | 46 | 137 69 |
| THY GRACIOUS NAME, BUT TO THE LAST, | ON THE ASSUMPTION | 39 | 46 | 139 114 |
| THY SACRED NAME SHALL BEE | ON THE ASSUMPTION | 41 | 46 | 139 114 |
| NATURE LABOUR'D FOR A NAME, | UPON DEATH OF DESIRED HERRYS | 6 | 46 | 168 467 |
| OR CLOSE UNTO HIS NAME ANNEXT, | ANOTHER ON HERRYS | 51 | 46 | 170 469 |
| AND NAME DWELL SWEET IN SOME ETERNALL STORY. | UPON YORKE HIS BIRTH | 105 | 46 | 176 500 |
| HAVE NATURE ALL THE NAME. | WISHES SUPPOSED MISTRESSE | 98 | 46 | 195 479 |
| I SING THE NAME WHICH NONE CAN SAY | TO THE NAME OF JESUS | 1 | 52 | 239 30 |
| THE NAME OF OUR NEW PEACE. OUR GOOD. | TO THE NAME OF JESUS | 3 | 52 | 239 30 |
| THE NAME OF ALL OUR LIVES & LOVES. | TO THE NAME OF JESUS | 5 | 52 | 239 30 |
| OF THIS UNBOUNDED NAME BUILD YOUR WARM NEST. | TO THE NAME OF JESUS | 12 | 52 | 239 30 |
| ALL-SOVERAIGN NAME | TO THE NAME OF JESUS | 36 | 52 | 239 30 |
| NO OTHER NOTE FOR'T, BUT THE NAME WE SING | TO THE NAME OF JESUS | 45 | 52 | 239 30 |
| I HAVE AUTHORITY IN LOVE'S NAME TO TAKE YOU | TO THE NAME OF JESUS | 53 | 52 | 239 30 |
| WAKE. IN THE NAME | TO THE NAME OF JESUS | 55 | 52 | 239 30 |
| TO ALL THE DEAR-BOUGHT NATIONS THIS REDEEMING NAME, | TO THE NAME OF JESUS | 94 | 52 | 239 30 |
| THE NAME OF YOUR DELIGHTS & OUR DESIRES. | TO THE NAME OF JESUS | 101 | 52 | 239 30 |
| COME, LOVELY NAME. APPEARE FROM FORTH THE BRIGHT | TO THE NAME OF JESUS | 115 | 52 | 239 30 |
| COME, LOVELY NAME. LIFE OF OUR HOPE. | TO THE NAME OF JESUS | 125 | 52 | 239 30 |
| COME ROYALL NAME, & PAY THE EXPENCE | TO THE NAME OF JESUS | 139 | 52 | 239 30 |
| FAIR, FLOWRY NAME. IN NONE BUT THEE | TO THE NAME OF JESUS | 173 | 52 | 239 30 |
| CAN PROVE IT SELF SOME KIN (SWEET NAME) TO THEE. | TO THE NAME OF JESUS | 182 | 52 | 239 30 |
| SWEET NAME, IN THY EACH SYLLABLE | TO THE NAME OF JESUS | 183 | 52 | 239 30 |
| WELLCOME DEAR, ALL-ADORED NAME. | TO THE NAME OF JESUS | 225 | 52 | 239 30 |
| AND MITHRA NOW SHALL BE NO NAME. | IN GLORIOUS EPIPHANIE | 100 | 52 | 253 39 |
| WE NOW WILL OWN NO SHORTER WISH, NOR NAME A NARROWER WORD. | OFFICE H. CROSS COMPLINE | 18 | 52 | 274 105 |
| THY CROSSE, THY NATURE, & THY NAME | OFFICE H. CROSS COMPLINE | 22 | 52 | 274 105 |
| AND TEACH THY LOV'D NAME TO THEIR NOBLE LYRE. | CHARITAS NIMIA | 28 | 52 | 280 48 |
| THE PURPLE NAME | CHARITAS NIMIA | 59 | 52 | 280 48 |
| NAME TO BE KNOWN, ALAS, BUT SORROW'S MOTHER. | SANCTA MARIA DOLORUM | 4 | 52 | 283 162 |
| GROW, BUT IN NEW POWRES TO THY NAME & PRAISE. | ADORO TE | 36 | 52 | 291 172 |
| NATURE, & NAME, TO BE MADE GOOD | LAUDA SION SALVATOREM | 35 | 52 | 294 178 |
| THY PRETIOUS NAME SHALL BE | IN GLORIOUS ASSUMPTION B. LADY | 46 | 52 | 304 114 |
| THEIR GREAT LORD'S GLORIOUS NAME, TO NONE | TERESA | 9 | 52 | 315 52 |
| SCARSE HAS SHE LEARN'T TO LISP THE NAME | TERESA | 15 | 52 | 315 52 |
| WITH CHRIST'S NAME IN'T, IN CHANGE FOR DEATH. | TERESA | 50 | 52 | 315 52 |
| WHICH WRITES THY SPOUSE'S RADIANT NAME | TERESA | 82 | 52 | 315 52 |
| THUS HAVE I BACK AGAIN TO THY BRIGHT NAME | AN APOLOGIE FOR (TERESA) HYMNE | 1 | 52 | 322 59 |
| AND CATCH THE PRETIOUS NAME THIS PEICE PRETENDS. | FLAMING HEART | 2 | 52 | 324 61 |
| THAT DULL MORTALITY MUST NOT KNOW A NAME. | PRAYER TO GENTLE-WOMAN | 86 | 52 | 328 139 |
| THE NOTED SEA SHALL CHANGE HIS NAME WITH ME. | ALEXIAS FIRST ELEGIE | 23 | 52 | 334 204 |
| I, 'MONGST THE BLEST STARRES A NEW NAME SHALL BE. | ALEXIAS FIRST ELEGIE | 24 | 52 | 334 204 |
| CECILIA, GLORY OF HER NAME & BLOOD | ALEXIAS THIRD ELEGIE | 31 | 52 | 336 209 |
| I'D KNOW NO NAME OF LOVE ON EARTH BUT YOU. | ALEXIAS THIRD ELEGIE | 44 | 52 | 336 209 |
| THY TORCH, TERRESTRIALL LOVE, HAVE HERE NO NAME. | ALEXIAS THIRD ELEGIE | 50 | 52 | 336 209 |
| ROSE QUAKES AT NAME OF CINNAMON. | PETRONIJ ALES PHASIACIS PETITA | 19 | MS | 382 526 |
| THE PARTHIAN STARTS AT ROME'S IMPERIALL NAME, | HORATIJ ILLE & NEFASTO | 27 | MS | 382 530 |
| I SING IMPIETY BEYOND A NAME. | ON GUNPOWDER-TREASON | 1 | MS | 384 458 |
| I FEARE TO NAME IT, LEAST THAT HE, WHICH HEARES, | UPON GUNPOWDER TREASON | 9 | MS | 386 460 |
| THE MUSICK OF HIS NAME YETT SOUNDETH SHRILL. | UPON DEATH OF A FREIND | 22 | MS | 393 477 |

## NAME'S

| | | | | |
|---|---|---|---|---|
| OF SOULES WHICH IN THAT NAME'S SWEET GRACES | TERESA | 86 | 52 | 315 52 |

## NAMES

| | | | | |
|---|---|---|---|---|
| SWEETNESSE BY ALL HER NAMES. THUS, BRAVELY THUS | MUSICKS DUELL | 133 | 46 | 149 535 |
| PHALARIS, OCHUS, EZELINUS, NAMES | SOSPETTO D'HERODE | 363 | 46 | 109 216 |
| OF SOULES, WHICH IN THAT NAMES SWEET GRACES, | IN MEMORY OF LADY MADRE TERESA | 86 | 46 | 131 52 |
| OF THOUSAND SOULES WHOSE HAPPY NAMES, | IN MEMORY OF LADY MADRE TERESA | 175 | 46 | 131 52 |
| OF NAMES AND WORDS SO FARRE PREJUDICATE. | AN APOLOGIE FOR HYMNE (TERESA) | 14 | 46 | 136 59 |
| ARE MARS AND PHOEBUS UNDER DIVERS NAMES. | UPON YORKE HIS BIRTH | 34 | 46 | 176 500 |
| AND SEE SUCH NAMES OF JOY SIT WHITE UPON | UPON YORKE HIS BIRTH | 97 | 46 | 176 500 |
| AND SO IN MUTUALL NAMES | OUT OF THE ITALIAN (2) | 13 | 46 | 190 547 |
| THE HEIRS ELECT OF LOVE. WHOSE NAMES BELONG | TO THE NAME OF JESUS | 9 | 52 | 239 30 |
| FAIR KING OF NAMES, & COME. | TO THE NAME OF JESUS | 118 | 52 | 239 30 |
| IN DIFFERENT SPECIES, NAMES NOT THINGS. | LAUDA SION SALVATOREM | 39 | 52 | 294 178 |
| OF THOUSAND SOULES, WHOSE HAPPY NAMES | TERESA | 174 | 52 | 315 52 |
| OF NAMES & WORDES, SO FARR PRAEJUDICATE. | AN APOLOGIE FOR (TERESA) HYMNE | 14 | 52 | 322 59 |

NAMETH

ALL THE FLOWERS THAT NATURE NAMETH.                OUT OF THE ITALIAN (1)              6   46 166 545

NAM'D

THROUGH THE GREAT MOUTH THATS NAM'D FROM HERCULES)  THE BEGINNING OF HELIODORUS        6   46 158 517
ALL THE RIVERS NAM'D BEFORE.                        ON BLEEDING WOUNDS OF LORD        30   46 101 110
ALL THE RIVERS NAM'D BEFORE.                        UPON BLEEDING CRUCIFIX            26   52 288 110

BIG-NAM'D

SOME BIG-NAM'D COMPOSITION.                         TEMPERANCE                         6   52 342 510

BIGG-NAMED

SOME BIGG-NAMED COMPOSITION.                        IN PRAISE OF LESSIUS               6   46 156 510

NANUS

HIGH MOUNTED ON AN ANT NANUS THE TALL               HIGH MOUNTED ON AN ANT             1   46 161 523

NARCISSUS

NARCISSUS. FOOLISH PHAETON. .WHO FOR ALL            SOSPETTO D'HERODE                 79   46 109 216

NARROW

OF HEAVENS HIGH'ST ARCHES TO FALL NARROW.           OUT OF GREEKE CUPID'S CRYER       48   46 159 519
CALL HEAVEN TO LOOKE ON THEE WITH NARROW EYES.      UPON STANINOUGH'S DEATH           16   46 175 475
NARROW, & LOW, & INFINITELY LESSE                   TO THE NAME OF JESUS              22   52 239  30
TIME IS TOO NARROW FOR THY YEAR                     IN GLORIOUS EPIPHANIE             40   52 253  39
CALL HEAVN TO LOOK ON THEE WITH NARROW EYES.        DEATH'S LECTURE                   17   52 340 475
A POORE (YEA SCARCE A) ROOFE.  WHOSE NARROW PLACE   OUT OF GROTIUS                    16   MS 398 198

NARROWER

WE NOW WILL OWN NO SHORTER WISH, NOR NAME A NARROWER  OFFICE H. CROSS COMPLINE        18   52 274 105
                        WORD.

NATION

TO GLAD THE SPHEARE OF ANY NATION.                  UPON YORKE HIS BIRTH              14   46 176 500
THE AIERY NATION OF NEAT DOVES.                     AGAINST IRRESOLUTION AND DELAY    45   52 347 146

NATION'S

THE NATION'S TERROR NOW THEN ERST THEIR LOVE.       IN GLORIOUS EPIPHANIE            160   52 253  39

NATIONS

TO ALL THE DEAR-BOUGHT NATIONS THIS REDEEMING NAME,  TO THE NAME OF JESUS             94   52 239  30
THE DOATING NATIONS NOW NO MORE                      IN GLORIOUS EPIPHANIE           85   52 253  39
THE TOO-HARD-TEMPTED NATIONS.                        IN GLORIOUS EPIPHANIE           92   52 253  39
THE DAY-BREAK OF THE NATIONS.  THEIR FIRST RAY.      TO THE QUEEN'S MAJESTY           3   52 261  47
ALOFT, AND FILL THE NATIONS WITH THY NOBLE FRUIT.    VEXILLA REGIS                   36   52 277 156
YEE REDEEM'D NATIONS FARR & NEAR,                    O GLORIOSA DOMINA               27   52 302 194

NATIVE

HOW E'RE LOVES NATIVE HOURES WERE SET,              LOVES HOROSCOPE                   17   46 185 483
WHOSE NATIVE RAY,                                   WISHES SUPPOSED MISTRESSE         49   46 195 479
LEAVE ALL THY NATIVE GLORIES IN THEIR GORGEOUS NEST, TO THE NAME OF JESUS            119   52 239  30
WHOSE NATIVE FIRES DISDAINING                        PRAYER TO GENTLE-WOMAN            3   52 326 139

NATIVITY

LIFE, BY THIS LIGHT'S NATIVITY                      EASTER DAY                        13   46 100  26

NATIVITIE

AN ANTHEM AT THE DAYES NATIVITIE.                   TO THE MORNING                    44   46 183 497

NATIVITYE

LAY BLACKE ON LOVES NATIVITYE.                      LOVES HOROSCOPE                   36   46 185 483

NATURALL

POORE SIMPLE VOYCE, RAIS'D IN A NATURALL TONE.      MUSICKS DUELL                    164   46 149 535
THOSE, COURSE & NEGLIGENT, AS THE NATURALL LOCKES   DESCRIPTION RELIGIOUS HOUSE       13   52 338 213

NATURE

KINDLY SUPPLIES SICK NATURE, AND DOTH MOLD          OUT OF VIRGIL                     35   46 155 529
NATURE HER OWNE PHYSITIAN BEE.                      IN PRAISE OF LESSIUS              16   46 156 510
NATURE HATH LEARN'T T' EXTRACT A DEW,               THE WEEPER                        71   46  79 120
FROWNE I. AND CAN GREAT NATURE KEEP HER SEAT.       SOSPETTO D'HERODE                205   46 109 216
VILE HUMANE NATURE MEANS HE NOW T'INVEST            SOSPETTO D'HERODE                227   46 109 216
IS SHEE TO NATURE, THAT A GENERALL FRIGHT,          SOSPETTO D'HERODE                381   46 109 216
WHAT HE BY NATURE WAS, IS SHE BY ART.               SOSPETTO D'HERODE                420   46 109 216
THE GOD OF NATURE IN THE FIELD OF GRACE.            ON HOPE                           90   46 143  71
IMPATIENT NATURE HAD TAUGHT MOTION                  UPON DEATH OF HERRYS               6   46 167 466

```
                                                                                   PAGE 280


          NATURE LABOUR'D FOR A NAME,                UPON DEATH OF DESIRED HERRYS       6   46 168 467
          PUT POORE NATURE TO SUCH COST.             UPON DEATH OF DESIRED HERRYS      22   46 168 467
          WAS SO RICH IN GRACE AND NATURE,           ANOTHER ON HERRYS                 11   46 170 469
          OF ALL INTERPRETERS READ NATURE TRUE.      UPON STANINOUGH'S DEATH           30   46 175 475
          HOW THY GREAT MOTHER NATURE DOATS ON THEE. UPON YORKE HIS BIRTH              26   46 176 500
          JUSTLY, GREAT NATURE, MAY'ST THOU BRAG AND TELL  UPON YORKE HIS BIRTH        49   46 176 500
          ALL THE FLOWERS THAT NATURE NAMETH.        OUT OF THE ITALIAN (1)             6   46 188 545
          LET NATURE DIE, IF (PHOENIX-LIKE) FROM DEATH  ON FRONTISPIECE ISAACSONS       3   46 191 491
          REVIVED NATURE TAKE A SECOND BREATH.       ON FRONTISPIECE ISAACSONS          4   46 191 491
          HAVE NATURE ALL THE NAME,                  WISHES SUPPOSED MISTRESSE         98   46 195 479
          NATURE (METHINKS) MIGHT EASILY MEND HER GROWTH.  UPON TWO GREENE APRICOCKES  22   48 220 494
          GREAT NATURE FOR THE KEY OF HER HUGE CHEST TO THE NAME OF JESUS              29   52 239  30
          NATURE & ART.                              TO THE NAME OF JESUS              69   52 239  30
          NEW SIMILES TO NATURE.                     TO THE NAME OF JESUS              96   52 239  30
          THY CROSSE, THY NATURE, & THY NAME         OFFICE H. CROSS COMPLINE          22   52 274 105
          NATURE, & NAME, TO BE MADE GOOD            LAUDA SION SALVATOREM             35   52 294 178
          HORROR OF NATURE, HELL & DEATH.            DIES IRAE                         13   52 298 186
          NATURE HATH LEARN'T TO EXTRACT A DEAW      WEEPER                            53   52 307 120
          OF ALL INTERPRETERS READ NATURE TRUE.      DEATH'S LECTURE                   32   52 340 475
          NATURE HER OWN PHYSITIAN BE.               TEMPERANCE                        14   52 342 510
          THE GOD OF NATURE IN THE FEILDS OF GRACE.  (ON) HOPE                         50   52 345  71
          THE FEILD OF NATURE OR OF GRACE.           AGAINST IRRESOLUTION AND DELAY    30   52 347 146

NATURE'S

          HATH METT LOVE'S NOON IN NATURE'S NIGHT.   IN HOLY NATIVITY                   2   52 246  76
          WHERE NATURE'S LAWES NO LEAVE WILL GIVE,   LAUDA SION SALVATOREM             37   52 294 178
          IT LABOURS. STIF'LED NATURE'S IN A SWOUND. ON GUNPOWDER-TREASON              19   MS 384 458

NATUR'S

          AND NATUR'S WRONGS REJOICE TO DOE THEE RIGHT.  IN GLORIOUS EPIPHANIE        148   52 253  39

NATURES

          NATURES NEW WOMBE,                         EASTER DAY                         5   46 100  26
          RUINE, WHERE E'RE SHE SLEEPES AT NATURES FEET.  SOSPETTO D'HERODE           279   46 109 216
          THIS IS NATURES CHOYCEST JEWELL.           UPON DEATH OF DESIRED HERRYS       4   46 168 467
          FROM HIS MOTHER NATURES SIGHT.             UPON DEATH OF DESIRED HERRYS     72   46 168 467
          BUT IF NATURES                             OUT OF THE ITALIAN (1)            37   46 188 545
          THEN WHAT NATURES WHITE HAND SETS OPE.     WISHES SUPPOSED MISTRESSE         30   46 195 479
          NATURES VIRGINITY HAD NERE BEEN LOST.      ALEXIAS THIRD ELEGIE               6   52 336 209
          GREAT NATURES SELFE HATH SHRUNKE AND SPOKE MEE GOD.  OUT OF GROTIUS          50   MS 398 198

NAY

          WHERE NO CHURLISH RUB SAIES NAY            PSALME 23                         30   46 102   5
          WHAT DANGERS CAN THERE BE DARE SAY ME NAY. ALEXIAS FIRST ELEGIE              20   52 334 204
          NAY. STOPP THY CLOWDY EYES. IT IS NOT GOOD,  UPON GUNPOWDER TREASON          31   MS 387 461

NEAR

          YEE REDEEM'D NATIONS FARR & NEAR.          O GLORIOSA DOMINA                 27   52 302 194

NEARE

          SOE NEARE, IT PROV'D HIS VERY SIDE.        IN CICATRICES DOMINI JESU          8   MS 381  27

NEERER

          ONE NEERER TO GODS ALTAR TROD.             TWO WENT TO PRAY                   5   46  89  18
          MAY NOT ROW NEERER TO THESE DUSKY KINGS.   UPON GUNPOWDER TREASON            28   MS 387 461

NEAT

          THE AIERY NATION OF NEAT DOVES,            AGAINST IRRESOLUTION AND DELAY    45   52 347 146

NEATE

          FOR JOYE OF THIER NEATE COATES. BUT WOULD HAVE TORE  UPON GUNPOWDER TREASON  46   MS 386 460

NECK

          NUZZEL'D IN THE LILLY'S NECK.              WEEPER                            46   52 307 120
          UPON HER NECK THE WHITEST OF HIS SNOW.     UPON BIRTH PRINCESSE E            50   MS 391 456

NECK'D

          THE STIFFE NECK'D PHARISEES THAT USE TO MOCKE  OUT OF GROTIUS                42   MS 398 198

NECKE

          NUZZEL'D IN THE LILLIES NECKE.             THE WEEPER                        40   46  79 120

NECKS

          THE CROWNE, FOR WHICH UPON THEIR NECKS HE LAID  SOSPETTO D'HERODE           406   46 109 216

NECTAR

          THOSE PARTS OF SWEETNESSE WHICH WITH NECTAR DROP,  MUSICKS DUELL            125   46 149 535
          TO TAST THE NECTAR OF A KISSE              OUT OF GREEKE CUPID'S CRYER       12   46 159 519
          BALME AND NECTAR IN MY CUP,                PSALME 23                         70   46 102   5
          HEE SAW RICH NECTAR THAWES, RELEASE THE RIGOUR  SOSPETTO D'HERODE           105   46 109 216
```

## NECTAREALL

| | | | | | |
|---|---|---|---|---|---|
| WHO FEEDS WITH NECTAR HEAV'NS FAIRE FAMILY. | SOSPETTO D'HERODE | 174 | 46 | 109 | 216 |
| ITS TINCTURE FROM THE ROSIE NECTAR, WINE | AN APOLOGIE FOR HYMNE (TERESA) | 43 | 46 | 136 | 59 |
| IT'S TINCTURE FROM THE ROSY NECTAR. WINE | AN APOLOGIE FOR (TERESA) HYMNE | 43 | 52 | 322 | 59 |
| ONE DROPP OF THIS PURE NECTAR, WHICH DOTH FLOW | UPON GUNPOWDER TREASON | 41 | MS | 387 | 461 |
| LEAVING THOSE MINES OF NECTAR, THEIR SWEET FOUNTAINES, | AN ELEGIE ON DR PORTER | 41 | MS | 395 | 476 |

## NECTAREALL

| | | | | | |
|---|---|---|---|---|---|
| AND THY NECTAREALL FRAGRANCY. | TO THE NAME OF JESUS | 174 | 52 | 239 | 30 |

## NEED

| | | | | | |
|---|---|---|---|---|---|
| I PAINT SO ILL, MY PEECE HAD NEED TO BEE | WITH A PICTURE TO A FRIEND | 1 | 46 | 156 | 494 |
| BOTH WHICH AWAY, I SHOULD NOT NEED TO FEARE, | WITH A PICTURE TO A FRIEND | 7 | 46 | 156 | 494 |
| THAT WHICH MAKES US HAVE NO NEED | IN PRAISE OF LESSIUS | 13 | 46 | 156 | 510 |
| THERE IS NO NEED AT ALL | THE WEEPER | 67 | 46 | 79 | 120 |
| THE WIND HAD NEED BE ANGRY, AND THE WATER BLACK, | WHY ARE YEE AFRAID | 7 | 46 | 88 | 15 |
| WHAT NEED THY FAIRE HEAD BEARE A PART | ON BLEEDING WOUNDS OF LORD | 17 | 46 | 101 | 110 |
| WHAT NEED THEY HELPE TO DROWNE THINE HEART. | ON BLEEDING WOUNDS OF LORD | 19 | 46 | 101 | 110 |
| THEIR RANK MALICE NOT THEIR NEED. | PSALME 23 | 52 | 46 | 102 | 5 |
| THEY ROUSE HIM, WHEN HIS RANKE THOUGHTS NEED A STING. | SOSPETTO D'HERODE | 68 | 46 | 109 | 216 |
| WEE NEED TO GOE TO NONE OF ALL | IN MEMORY OF LADY MADRE TERESA | 3 | 46 | 131 | 52 |
| NOR NEED WEE KILL THY FRUIT TO SMELL THY FLOWER. | ON HOPE | 54 | 46 | 143 | 71 |
| TH'AST NEED O BRITTAINE TO BE TRULY GREAT. | UPON YORKE HIS BIRTH | 16 | 46 | 176 | 500 |
| DAYES, THAT NEED BORROW, | WISHES SUPPOSED MISTRESSE | 76 | 46 | 195 | 479 |
| NOR NEED BE DOUBLE-GILT. HOW THEN MUST THESE, | UPON TWO GREENE APRICOCKES | 29 | 48 | 220 | 494 |
| WHAT DID THE LAMB, THAT HE SHOULD NEED, | CHARITAS NIMIA | 53 | 52 | 280 | 48 |
| WHAT NEED THY FAIR HEAD BEAR A PART | UPON BLEEDING CRUCIFIX | 5 | 52 | 288 | 110 |
| WHAT NEED THEY HELP TO DROWN THY HEART. | UPON BLEEDING CRUCIFIX | 7 | 52 | 288 | 110 |
| THERE'S NO NEED AT ALL | WEEPER | 49 | 52 | 307 | 120 |
| FIRM HE, AS THOU ART FALSE, NOR NEED MY CRYES | ALEXIAS SECONDE ELEGIE | 9 | 52 | 335 | 207 |
| FOR HIM, ALAS, N'ERE SHALL I NEED TO BE | ALEXIAS SECONDE ELEGIE | 11 | 52 | 335 | 207 |
| THAT WHICH MAKES US HAVE NO NEED | TEMPERANCE | 11 | 52 | 342 | 510 |
| TILL NOW HELL WAS IMPERFECT. IT DID NEED | ON GUNPOWDER-TREASON | 61 | MS | 384 | 458 |
| NOR SHOULD WEE NEED THY CRISPED WAVES, FOR WEE | UPON GUNPOWDER TREASON | 35 | MS | 386 | 460 |
| THESE NEED NOE INVITATION. ONELY THOU, | UPON GUNPOWDER TREASON | 19 | MS | 387 | 461 |
| MY MINDS DEVOTION IN MY BODYES NEED. | OUT OF GROTIUS | 60 | MS | 398 | 198 |

## NEED'ST

| | | | | | |
|---|---|---|---|---|---|
| WHAT NEED'ST THOU PUT ON ARMES AGAINST POORE MEN. | UPON VENUS PUTTING ARMES | 4 | 46 | 161 | 523 |
| THAT THOU NEED'ST HEAPE | TO PONTIUS WASHING HANDS | 2 | 46 | 94 | 23 |

## NEEDS

| | | | | | |
|---|---|---|---|---|---|
| THAT UNDER HUNGERS TEETH WILL NEEDS BE SOUND. | ON MIRACLE OF LOAVES | 2 | 46 | 66 | 15 |
| HIS NEEDS A CLOUD | WHY ARE YEE AFRAID | 3 | 46 | 88 | 15 |
| WHICH TO BE SEENE NEEDS NOT HIS LIGHT. | A HYMNE OF THE NATIVITY | 14 | 46 | 106 | 76 |
| NOR NEEDS MY MUSE A BLUSH, OR THESE BRIGHT FLOWERS | SOSPETTO D'HERODE | 17 | 46 | 109 | 216 |
| DARKE, DUSTY MAN, HE NEEDS WOULD SINGLE FORTH, | SOSPETTO D'HERODE | 217 | 46 | 109 | 216 |
| THEREFORE IF HEE NEEDS MUST GO. | UPON DEATH OF DESIRED HERRYS | 65 | 46 | 168 | 467 |
| NEEDS MUST YOUR NOBLE PRAYSES STRENGTH | TO THE QUEEN | 13 | 48 | 215 | 501 |
| SINCE THOU WOULDST NEEDS BE THUS | OFFICE H. CROSS COMPLINE | 15 | 52 | 274 | 105 |
| WOULD NEEDS FALL IN | CHARITAS NIMIA | 50 | 52 | 280 | 48 |
| NEEDS MUST MY MISERYES OWE THAT MAN A SPITE | ALEXIAS THIRD ELEGIE | 3 | 52 | 336 | 209 |

## NEEDES

| | | | | | |
|---|---|---|---|---|---|
| WHICH TO BE SEEN NEEDES NOT HIS LIGHT. | IN HOLY NATIVITY | 14 | 52 | 246 | 76 |
| WHAT NEEDES MY VIRGIN LORD FLY THUS FROM ME, | ALEXIAS THIRD ELEGIE | 23 | 52 | 336 | 209 |
| HAVE FLOW'D TOGETHER. IF OUGHT FURTHER NEEDES | OUT OF GROTIUS | 6 | MS | 398 | 198 |

## NEEDFULL

| | | | | | |
|---|---|---|---|---|---|
| BY A NOBLER BREAD, MORE NEEDFULL BLOOD. | LAUDA SION SALVATOREM | 36 | 52 | 294 | 178 |
| DETAIN IN NEEDFULL TEARES TO WEEP THE WANT OF THEE. | IN GLORIOUS ASSUMPTION B. LADY | 22 | 52 | 304 | 114 |

## NEEDFULLY

| | | | | | |
|---|---|---|---|---|---|
| AND HE MORE NEEDFULLY & NOBLE PROVE | IN GLORIOUS EPIPHANIE | 159 | 52 | 253 | 39 |

## NEGATIVE

| | | | | | |
|---|---|---|---|---|---|
| BY THE FRUGALL NEGATIVE LIGHT | IN GLORIOUS EPIPHANIE | 209 | 52 | 253 | 39 |

## NEGLECT

| | | | | | |
|---|---|---|---|---|---|
| HEE SAW TH'OLD HEBREWES WOMBE, NEGLECT THE LAW | SOSPETTO D'HERODE | 101 | 46 | 109 | 216 |

## NEGLECTED

| | | | | | |
|---|---|---|---|---|---|
| IN A NEGLECTED STABLE LIES, AMONG | SOSPETTO D'HERODE | 436 | 46 | 109 | 216 |
| AND LEAVE HER OWN NEGLECTED SUN. | NEW YEAR'S DAY | 32 | 52 | 251 | 37 |

## NEGLIGENT

| | | | | | |
|---|---|---|---|---|---|
| THOSE, COURSE & NEGLIGENT, AS THE NATURALL LOCKES | DESCRIPTION RELIGIOUS HOUSE | 13 | 52 | 338 | 213 |

## NEGLIGENTLY

| | | | | | |
|---|---|---|---|---|---|
| TO THEIR OWNE DANCE. NOW NEGLIGENTLY RASH | MUSICKS DUELL | 29 | 46 | 149 | 535 |

## NEGOTIATE

| | | | | |
|---|---|---|---|---|
| TWINNE SUNNES,) & TAUGHT NOW TO NEGOTIATE YOU. | IN GLORIOUS EPIPHANIE | 204 | 52 253 | 39 |

## NEIGHBOUR

| | | | | |
|---|---|---|---|---|
| THE NEIGHBOUR DIAMOND, AND OUT FACES | WISHES SUPPOSED MISTRESSE | 44 | 46 195 | 479 |

## NEIGHBOURHOOD

| | | | | |
|---|---|---|---|---|
| THY NEIGHBOURHOOD TO NOTHING. | DEATH'S LECTURE | 20 | 52 340 | 475 |

## NEIGHBOUR-HOOD

| | | | | |
|---|---|---|---|---|
| THY NEIGHBOUR-HOOD TO NOTHING. HERE PUT ON | UPON STANINOUGH'S DEATH | 19 | 46 175 | 475 |

## NEIGHBOURING

| | | | | |
|---|---|---|---|---|
| A NIGHTINGALE, COME FROM THE NEIGHBOURING WOOD. | MUSICKS DUELL | 8 | 46 149 | 535 |

## NEITHER

| | | | | |
|---|---|---|---|---|
| THAT NEITHER ROME, NOR ATHENS CAN BRING FORTH | SOSPETTO D'HERODE | 27 | 46 109 | 216 |
| THAT TROUBLED NEITHER CHURCH NOR KING. | AN EPITAPH UPON ASHTON | 6 | 46 192 | 464 |
| THOUGH NOW 'TIS NEITHER MAY NOR JUNE | THOUGH NOW 'TIS NEITHER | 1 | MS 397 | 492 |
| BUT NEITHER ARE THERE THOSE IGNOBLE STINGS | DESCRIPTION RELIGIOUS HOUSE | 25 | 52 338 | 213 |

## NEPTUNE

| | | | | |
|---|---|---|---|---|
| IF SOE, OH NEPTUNE, MAY SHE FARRE BE THROUNE | ON GUNPOWDER-TREASON | 7 | MS 384 | 458 |
| BAD SPORTING NEPTUNE TO PLUCK IN HIS ARMES, | UPON GUNPOWDER TREASON | 32 | MS 386 | 460 |

## NEPTUNE'S

| | | | | |
|---|---|---|---|---|
| THAT TO THE MIGHTY NEPTUNE'S SELF DARE THREATEN WRACK. | WHY ARE YEE AFRAID | 8 | 46 88 | 15 |

## NEPTUNES

| | | | | |
|---|---|---|---|---|
| THY MAIDEN STREAMES SOE SOONE TO NEPTUNES BED. | AN ELEGIE ON DR PORTER | 2 | MS 395 | 476 |
| OF ALL PROUD NEPTUNES SILVER-SHEILDED GUARD. | AN ELEGIE ON DR PORTER | 34 | MS 395 | 476 |

## NERO

| | | | | |
|---|---|---|---|---|
| MIGHTY IN MISCHIEFE, WITH DREAD NERO TOO, | SOSPETTO D'HERODE | 364 | 46 109 | 216 |

## NERVE

| | | | | |
|---|---|---|---|---|
| WELL STRUNG WITH MANY A BROKEN NERVE. | IN CICATRICES DOMINI JESU | 14 | MS 381 | 27 |

## NEST

| | | | | |
|---|---|---|---|---|
| THAT EVER-BUBLING SPRING. THE SUGRED NEST | MUSICKS DUELL | 66 | 46 149 | 535 |
| TILL THE FLEDG'D NOTES AT LENGTH FORSAKE THEIR NEST. | MUSICKS DUELL | 90 | 46 149 | 535 |
| WOULDST SEE A NEST OF ROSES GROW | IN PRAISE OF LESSIUS | 41 | 46 156 | 510 |
| THY TOMBE, FAIRE IMMORTALITIES PERFUMED NEST. | EASTER DAY | 6 | 46 100 | 26 |
| WE SAW THEE IN THY BALMY NEST, | A HYMNE OF THE NATIVITY | 29 | 46 106 | 76 |
| A COMMING DEITY. HEE SAW THE NEST | SOSPETTO D'HERODE | 126 | 46 109 | 216 |
| WHO FINDS HIS WARME HEART, HATCHT INTO A NEST | AN APOLOGIE FOR HYMNE (TERESA) | 26 | 46 136 | 59 |
| OF WHATSOE'RE PERFUM'D THY EASTERN NEST. | ON A TREATISE OF CHARITY | 10 | 46 137 | 69 |
| THE PURE BIRTH OF EACH SPARKLING NEST, | AN HIMNE FOR CIRCUMCISION | 19 | 46 141 | 37 |
| ARABIA, THERE TO BUILD HER VIRGIN NEST, | UPON DEATH OF HERRYS | 14 | 46 167 | 466 |
| (SWEET AS IS THE PHAENIX NEST) | HIS EPITAPH (HERRYS) | 18 | 46 172 | 471 |
| THAT NEST OF HEROES, ALL OUR HOPES FINDE ROOME. | UPON YORKE HIS BIRTH | 81 | 46 176 | 500 |
| A FRAGRANT BREATH SUCKT FROM THE SPICY NEST | ON A FOULE MORNING | 21 | 46 181 | 495 |
| SHALL I BUILD HIS FUNERAL NEST. | LOVES HOROSCOPE | 50 | 46 185 | 483 |
| OF THIS UNBOUNDED NAME BUILD YOUR WARM NEST. | TO THE NAME OF JESUS | 12 | 52 239 | 30 |
| THEN ROUSE THE NEST | TO THE NAME OF JESUS | 32 | 52 239 | 30 |
| NOR YEILDS THE NOBLEST NEST | TO THE NAME OF JESUS | 105 | 52 239 | 30 |
| LEAVE ALL THY NATIVE GLORIES IN THEIR GORGEOUS NEST, | TO THE NAME OF JESUS | 119 | 52 239 | 30 |
| AND REINTHRON'D THEE IN THY ROSY NEST, | TO THE NAME OF JESUS | 221 | 52 239 | 30 |
| WE SAW THEE IN THY BAULMY NEST, | IN HOLY NATIVITY | 31 | 52 246 | 76 |
| THE PHAENIX BUILDS THE PHAENIX' NEST. | IN HOLY NATIVITY | 46 | 52 246 | 76 |
| WE SAW THEE IN THY BAULMY NEST, | IN HOLY NATIVITY | 72 | 52 246 | 76 |
| ROB THE RICH BIRTHS OF EACH BRIGHT NEST | NEW YEAR'S DAY | 19 | 52 251 | 37 |
| ARABIA, FOR THY ROYALL PHOENIX' NEST. | OFFICE H. CROSS COMPLINE | 6 | 52 274 | 105 |
| LO, HOW THE STREAMES OF LIFE, FROM THAT FULL NEST | VEXILLA REGIS | 7 | 52 277 | 156 |
| OF THINE (THE NOBLEST NEST | SANCTA MARIA DOLORUM | 46 | 52 283 | 162 |
| WHO FEELS HIS WARM HEART HATCH'D INTO A NEST | AN APOLOGIE FOR (TERESA) HYMNE | 26 | 52 322 | 59 |
| A NEST OF NEW-BORN SWEETS. | PRAYER TO GENTLE-WOMAN | 2 | 52 328 | 139 |
| THE BRIGHT AMBROSIALL NEST, | TO SAME CONCERNING CHOISE | 52 | 52 331 | 66 |
| 'TWAS NOT THE CHAST, & PURER SNOW, WHOSE NEST | AN ELEGY MR STANNINOW | 35 | MS 394 | 473 |

## NESTS

| | | | | |
|---|---|---|---|---|
| EYES, NESTS OF MILKY DOVES | WEEPER | 87 | 52 307 | 120 |
| YOU FROM THOSE NESTS OF NOBLE SORROW. | WEEPER | 168 | 52 307 | 120 |
| NESTS OF NEW SERAPHIMS HERE BELOW. | FLAMING HEART | 46 | 52 324 | 61 |
| WOULDST' SEE NESTS OF NEW ROSES GROW | TEMPERANCE | 39 | 52 342 | 510 |

## NEASTS

| | | | | |
|---|---|---|---|---|
| THE MUSES, & THE GRACES SUGRED NEASTS. | UPON GUNPOWDER TREASON | 38 | MS 387 | 461 |

## NET

| | | | | | |
|---|---|---|---|---|---|
| CAUGHT IN A NET WHICH THERE APPOLLO SPREADS, | MUSICKS DUELL | 121 | 46 | 149 | 535 |

## NETS

| | | | | | |
|---|---|---|---|---|---|
| THY GLORIOUS WISDOME BREAKES THE NETS. | NEITHER DURST MAN ASKE | 3 | 46 | 92 | 20 |
| TO CAST THY NETS ON ALL OCCASIONS WELL. | ON ST. PETER CASTING NETS | 2 | 46 | 98 | 13 |
| WHEN CHRIST CALLS, AND THY NETS WOULD HAVE THEE STAY. | ON ST. PETER CASTING NETS | 3 | 46 | 98 | 13 |

## NEVER

| | | | | | |
|---|---|---|---|---|---|
| STARRES IN THEIR HIGHER CHAMBERS. NEVER COU'D | OUT OF VIRGIL | 32 | 46 | 155 | 529 |
| FOR NEVER WERE HIS WORDS IN OUGHT | OUT OF GREEKE CUPID'S CRYER | 23 | 46 | 159 | 519 |
| STILL SPENDING, NEVER SPENT. I MEANE | THE WEEPER | 5 | 46 | 79 | 120 |
| THE DUST SHALL NEVER BEE THY BED. | THE TEARE | 34 | 46 | 84 | 50 |
| NOW LORD, OR NEVER, THEY'L BELEEVE ON THEE. | ON MIRACLE OF LOAVES | 1 | 46 | 88 | 16 |
| WAS NEVER MAN LORD SPAKE LIKE THEE. | THE BLIND CURED | 4 | 46 | 91 | 19 |
| O, NEVER COULD BEE FOUND GARMENTS TOO GOOD | ON CRUCIFIED LORD BLOODY | 5 | 46 | 100 | 24 |
| SINKE SION, DOWNE AND NEVER RISE. | PSALME 137 | 28 | 46 | 104 | 7 |
| WHERE NEVER WING OF ANGELL YET MADE WAY | SOSPETTO D'HERODE | 222 | 46 | 109 | 216 |
| FLOWERS OF NEVER FADING GRACES. | ON A PRAYER BOOKE | 36 | 46 | 126 | 139 |
| HAPPY SOULE WHO NEVER MISSES. | ON A PRAYER BOOKE | 98 | 46 | 126 | 139 |
| SHEE NEVER UNDERTOOKE TO KNOW. | IN MEMORY OF LADY MADRE TERESA | 19 | 46 | 131 | 52 |
| NEVER TILL NOW ESTEEMED TOYES. | IN MEMORY OF LADY MADRE TERESA | 60 | 46 | 131 | 52 |
| WISE HEAVEN WILL NEVER HAVE IT SO. | IN MEMORY OF LADY MADRE TERESA | 74 | 46 | 131 | 52 |
| YET SHALL OUR LIPS NEVER LET GOE | ON THE ASSUMPTION | 38 | 46 | 139 | 114 |
| THY GOLDEN HEAD NEVER HANGS DOWNE, | ON HOPE | 55 | 46 | 143 | 71 |
| HASTE HATH NEVER TIME TO HEARE. | UPON DEATH OF DESIRED HERRYS | 64 | 46 | 168 | 467 |
| ALL HOPE OF NEVER DYING, HERE LYES DEAD. | ANOTHER ON HERRYS | 62 | 46 | 170 | 469 |
| WHOSE DAY SHALL NEVER SLEEPE IN NIGHT. | AN EPITAPH HUSBAND AND WIFE | 16 | 46 | 174 | 478 |
| LET US LOVE AND NEVER FEARE, | OUT OF CATULLUS | 2 | 46 | 194 | 523 |
| (ALAS) WILL NEVER DOE. | TO THE NAME OF JESUS | 25 | 52 | 239 | 30 |
| OF HIM WHO NEVER SLEEPS, ALL THINGS THAT ARE, | TO THE NAME OF JESUS | 56 | 52 | 239 | 30 |
| NEVER MORE | IN GLORIOUS EPIPHANIE | 93 | 52 | 253 | 39 |
| MY DYING LIFE MAY DRAW A NEW, & NEVER FLEETING BREATH. | OFFICE H. CROSS RECOMMENDATION | 8 | 52 | 276 | 106 |
| O NEVER COULD THERE BE GARMENT TOO GOOD | UPON BODY OF OUR LORD | 5 | 52 | 290 | 24 |
| STILL SPENDING, NEVER SPENT. I MEAN | WEEPER | 5 | 52 | 307 | 120 |
| SHE NEVER UNDERTOOK TO KNOW | TERESA | 19 | 52 | 315 | 52 |
| (NEVER TILL NOW ESTEEMED TOYES) | TERESA | 60 | 52 | 315 | 52 |
| WISE HEAVN WILL NEVER HAVE IT SO | TERESA | 74 | 52 | 315 | 52 |
| TO LIVE, BUT THAT HE THUS MAY NEVER LEAVE TO DY. | TERESA | 104 | 52 | 315 | 52 |
| FOR IN LOVE'S FEILD WAS NEVER FOUND | FLAMING HEART | 71 | 52 | 324 | 61 |
| FLOWERS OF NEVER FADING GRACES | PRAYER TO GENTLE-WOMAN | 42 | 52 | 328 | 139 |
| HAPPY INDEED, WHO NEVER MISSES | PRAYER TO GENTLE-WOMAN | 104 | 52 | 328 | 139 |
| HIM WHO NEVER WILL DECEIVE YE. | TO SAME CONCERNING CHOISE | 40 | 52 | 331 | 66 |
| YOUR WISE SOUL, NEVER TO BE WONNE | TO SAME CONCERNING CHOISE | 56 | 52 | 331 | 66 |
| WHOSE DAY SHALL NEVER DY IN NIGHT. | AN EPITAPH UPON MARRIED COUPLE | 20 | 52 | 339 | 478 |
| THY GOLDEN, GROWING HEAD NEVER HANGS DOWN | (ON) HOPE | 25 | 52 | 345 | 71 |
| NEVER DURST HATCH BEFORE. EXTRACTED SEE | UPON GUNPOWDER TREASON | 7 | MS | 386 | 460 |
| SHOULD COOLE HIS FIERY WHEELS, & NEVER SINKE | UPON GUNPOWDER TREASON | 39 | MS | 386 | 460 |
| AND MAY SUCH PYTHONS NEVER LIVE TO SEE | UPON GUNPOWDER TREASON | 57 | MS | 386 | 460 |

## NEVER-DYING

| | | | | | |
|---|---|---|---|---|---|
| THE NEVER-DYING LIFE, OF A LONG DEATH. | SOSPETTO D'HERODE | 60 | 46 | 109 | 216 |

## NEVER-FADING

| | | | | | |
|---|---|---|---|---|---|
| AND FOR THE NEVER-FADING FIELDS OF LIGHT | SOSPETTO D'HERODE | 211 | 46 | 109 | 216 |

## NERE

| | | | | | |
|---|---|---|---|---|---|
| HAD NERE ANOTHER WORD TO SAY. | NEITHER DURST MAN ASKE | 16 | 46 | 92 | 20 |
| NERE WAS'T THOU IN A SENCE SO SADLY TRUE, | ON BLEEDING WOUNDS OF LORD | 41 | 46 | 101 | 110 |
| COME, NERE TO PART, | TO THE NAME OF JESUS | 68 | 52 | 239 | 30 |
| O HAD HE NERE BEEN AT THAT CRUELL COST | ALEXIAS THIRD ELEGIE | 5 | 52 | 336 | 209 |
| NATURES VIRGINITY HAD NERE BEEN LOST. | ALEXIAS THIRD ELEGIE | 6 | 52 | 336 | 209 |

## NE'RE

| | | | | | |
|---|---|---|---|---|---|
| BE NE'RE SO CURST, HIS TONGUE IS KIND. | OUT OF GREEKE CUPID'S CRYER | 22 | 46 | 159 | 519 |
| NE'RE SUFFRED, YET WITH LITTLE ARROW, | OUT OF GREEKE CUPID'S CRYER | 47 | 46 | 159 | 519 |
| SHE CAN SEE HEAVEN, AND NE'RE LIFT UP HER EYES. | ON VIRGINS BASHFULNESSE | 6 | 46 | 89 | 9 |
| AND THOU (HEAVEN-BURTHEN'D BEAST) HAST NE'RE A WORD | UPON ASSE THAT BORE SAVIOUR | 7 | 46 | 90 | 19 |
| HEE WAKES, AND WITH HIM (NE'RE TO SLEEPE) NEW FEARES. | SOSPETTO D'HERODE | 473 | 46 | 109 | 216 |
| WHICH ON FALSE TYRANTS HEAD NE'RE FIRMLY STOOD. | SOSPETTO D'HERODE | 492 | 46 | 109 | 216 |
| THE GLORYES OF THY YOUTH NE'RE KNEW, | UPON DEATH OF DESIRED HERRYS | 17 | 46 | 168 | 467 |
| NE'RE MAY A BIRTH OF THINE BE BOUGHT SO DEARE, | UPON YORKE HIS BIRTH | 94 | 46 | 176 | 500 |
| SICKNESSE, AND SORROW, WHOSE PALE LIDDS NE'RE KNOW | TO THE MORNING | 56 | 46 | 183 | 497 |
| NE'RE SO FARRE DISTANT, YET CHRONOLOGIE | ON FRONTISPIECE ISAACSONS | 8 | 46 | 191 | 491 |
| FOR LODG'D SO NE'RE YOUR SWEETEST THROTE | THOUGH NOW 'TIS NEITHER | 13 | MS | 397 | 492 |
| FOR THIS THE EVENING WEPT, AND WE NE'RE KNEW | IN GLORIOUS EPIPHANIE | 127 | 52 | 253 | 39 |
| FIX HERE, FAIR MAJESTY.  MAY YOUR HEART NE'RE MISSE | TO THE QUEEN'S MAJESTY | 21 | 52 | 261 | 47 |
| AND BIDDES THEE NE'RE FORGET | VEXILLA REGIS | 3 | 52 | 277 | 156 |
| WHAT WAS TILL NOW NE'RE UNDERSTOOD, | VEXILLA REGIS | 20 | 52 | 277 | 156 |
| HEAV'N NE'RE THE LESSE STILL HEAVN WOULD BE, | CHARITAS NIMIA | 11 | 52 | 260 | 48 |
| DEARE WIFE HATH NE'RE A HANDSOME LETTER, | PETRONIJ ALES PHASIACIS PETITA | 17 | MS | 362 | 526 |
| HEE THAT NE'RE HEARD NOW SPEAKES, AND FINDS A TONGUE | OUT OF GROTIUS | 73 | MS | 398 | 198 |

## N'ERE

| | | | | |
|---|---|---|---|---|
| N'ERE WAST THOU IN A SENSE SO SADLY TRUE, | UPON BLEEDING CRUCIFIX | 37 | 52 288 | 110 |
| FOR HIM, ALAS, N'ERE SHALL I NEED TO BE | ALEXIAS SECONDE ELEGIE | 11 | 52 335 | 207 |

## NEW

| | | | | |
|---|---|---|---|---|
| GIVES LIFE TO SOME NEW GRACE. THUS DOTH H'INVOKE | MUSICKS DUELL | 132 | 46 149 | 535 |
| IN THEIR OWNE BLOODS DEARE DELUGE, SOME NEW DEAD. | THE BEGINNING OF HELIODORUS | 17 | 46 158 | 517 |
| WHEN SOME NEW BRIGHT GUEST | THE WEEPER | 31 | 46 79 | 120 |
| GOE SMILING SOULES, YOUR NEW BUILT CAGES BREAKE. | TO INFANT MARTYRS | 1 | 46 88 | 10 |
| THIS NEW GUEST TO HER EYES NEW LAWES HATH GIVEN. | ON VIRGINS BASHFULNESSE | 7 | 46 89 | 9 |
| THIS NEW GUEST TO HER EYES NEW LAWES HATH GIVEN. | ON VIRGINS BASHFULNESSE | 7 | 46 89 | 9 |
| NATURES NEW WOMBE, | EASTER DAY | 5 | 46 100 | 26 |
| GRACE AND PEACE, TO MEET NEW LAIES | PSALME 23 | 33 | 46 102 | 5 |
| NEW MATTER, TO MAKE GOOD HIS GREAT SUSPECT. | SOSPETTO D'HERODE | 88 | 46 109 | 216 |
| WITH MANNA, MILK, AND BALM, NEW BROACH THE MOUNTAINES. | SOSPETTO D'HERODE | 112 | 46 109 | 216 |
| HOW BRIGHT A DAWNE OF ANGELS WITH NEW LIGHT | SOSPETTO D'HERODE | 115 | 46 109 | 216 |
| NOW WITH NEW RAGE, AND WAX TOO HOT FOR HELL. | SOSPETTO D'HERODE | 148 | 46 109 | 216 |
| WHILE NEW THOUGHTS BOYL'D IN HIS ENRAGED BREST, | SOSPETTO D'HERODE | 193 | 46 109 | 216 |
| RATHER MAKE UP TO THY NEW MISERIES, | SOSPETTO D'HERODE | 245 | 46 109 | 216 |
| THEIR NEW KING, AND THY SUCCESSOUR PROCLAIME. | SOSPETTO D'HERODE | 440 | 46 109 | 216 |
| HEE WAKES, AND WITH HIM (NE'RE TO SLEEPE) NEW FEARES. | SOSPETTO D'HERODE | 473 | 46 109 | 216 |
| BRINGING HIM NOTHING BUT NEW FEARES FROM TH'EAST, | SOSPETTO D'HERODE | 500 | 46 109 | 216 |
| EVEN THY DEATHS SHALL LIVE, AND NEW | IN MEMORY OF LADY MADRE TERESA | 152 | 46 131 | 52 |
| HEAV'N SET THEE DOWN NEW DREST. WHEN THY BRIGHT BIRTH | ON A TREATISE OF CHARITY | 5 | 46 137 | 69 |
| OR TO A NEW GOD DESOLATION. | ON A TREATISE OF CHARITY | 38 | 46 137 | 69 |
| NEW STRUCK BY LOVE, STILL TREMBLING ON HIS DART. | ON A TREATISE OF CHARITY | 46 | 46 137 | 69 |
| THEMSELVES NEW SWEETNESSE FROM IT. | ON THE ASSUMPTION | 52 | 46 139 | 114 |
| WITH A NEW MORNING MADE OF GEMS. | AN HIMNE FOR CIRCUMCISION | 22 | 46 141 | 37 |
| HAVE TAUGHT THEE NEW ASTROLOGY. | LOVES HOROSCOPE | 16 | 46 185 | 483 |
| NEW MATTER FOR OUR MUSE SUPPLIES, | TO THE QUEEN | 7 | 48 215 | 501 |
| THE NAME OF OUR NEW PEACE. OUR GOOD. | TO THE NAME OF JESUS | 3 | 52 239 | 30 |
| NEW SIMILES TO NATURE. | TO THE NAME OF JESUS | 96 | 52 239 | 30 |
| EACH WOUND OF THEIRS WAS THY NEW MORNING. | TO THE NAME OF JESUS | 220 | 52 239 | 30 |
| WITH A NEW MORNING MADE OF GEMMES. | NEW YEAR'S DAY | 22 | 52 251 | 37 |
| THAT SABLE JUDGMENT-SEAT SHALL BY NEW LAWES | IN GLORIOUS EPIPHANIE | 145 | 52 253 | 39 |
| HIS NEW PRODIGIOUS NIGHT, | IN GLORIOUS EPIPHANIE | 172 | 52 253 | 39 |
| THEIR NEW & ADMIRABLE LIGHT. | IN GLORIOUS EPIPHANIE | 173 | 52 253 | 39 |
| BY BEING SCHOLLER FIRST OF THAT NEW NIGHT, | IN GLORIOUS EPIPHANIE | 206 | 52 253 | 39 |
| TO REAP NEW CROWNES & KINGDOMS FROM THIS KISSE. | TO THE QUEEN'S MAJESTY | 22 | 52 261 | 47 |
| THE AGED HONORS OF THIS DAY STILL NEW. | TO THE QUEEN'S MAJESTY | 24 | 52 261 | 47 |
| PROV'D A NEW PATH OF PATIENT VICTORY. | OFFICE H. CROSS EVENSONG | 25 | 52 273 | 101 |
| MY DYING LIFE MAY DRAW A NEW, & NEVER FLEETING BREATH. | OFFICE H. CROSS RECOMMENDATION | 8 | 52 276 | 106 |
| AS FAST AS LOVE NEW LAWES CAN GIVE. | ADORO TE | 12 | 52 291 | 172 |
| GROW, BUT IN NEW POWRES TO THY NAME & PRAISE. | ADORO TE | 36 | 52 291 | 172 |
| LO THE NEW LAW OF A NEW LORD | LAUDA SION SALVATOREM | 19 | 52 294 | 178 |
| LO THE NEW LAW OF A NEW LORD | LAUDA SION SALVATOREM | 19 | 52 294 | 178 |
| WITH A NEW LAMB BLESSES THE BOARD. | LAUDA SION SALVATOREM | 20 | 52 294 | 178 |
| THE WORLD'S NEW EASTERN WINDOW BIN | O GLORIOSA DOMINA | 19 | 52 302 | 194 |
| THEMSELVES NEW SWEETNES FROM IT. | IN GLORIOUS ASSUMPTION B. LADY | 57 | 52 304 | 114 |
| WHEN SOME NEW BRIGHT GUEST | WEEPER | 67 | 52 307 | 120 |
| EV'N THY DEATHS SHALL LIVE. & NEW | TERESA | 151 | 52 315 | 52 |
| NESTS OF NEW SERAPHIMS HERE BELOW. | FLAMING HEART | 46 | 52 324 | 61 |
| NOR CAN I TELL (AND THIS NEW TEARES DOTH BREED) | ALEXIAS FIRST ELEGIE | 7 | 52 334 | 204 |
| I. 'MONGST THE BLEST STARRES A NEW NAME SHALL BE. | ALEXIAS FIRST ELEGIE | 24 | 52 334 | 204 |
| NEW DROPS, WASH OFF THE SWEAT OF THIS DAYE'S SORROWS. | DESCRIPTION RELIGIOUS HOUSE | 22 | 52 338 | 213 |
| WOULDST' SEE NESTS OF NEW ROSES GROW | TEMPERANCE | 39 | 52 342 | 510 |
| PAINT EACH FEATHER, AS IF NEW. | PETRONIJ ALES PHASIACIS PETITA | 8 | MS 382 | 526 |
| OR CALL HER CHEEKE A BED OF NEW BLOWNE ROSES. | UPON BIRTH PRINCESSE E | 45 | MS 391 | 456 |

## NEW-BLOOM'D

| | | | | |
|---|---|---|---|---|
| SEE SEE, HOW SOON HIS NEW-BLOOM'D CHEEK | IN HOLY NATIVITY | 67 | 52 246 | 76 |

## NEW-BORN

| | | | | |
|---|---|---|---|---|
| A NEST OF NEW-BORN SWEETS. | PRAYER TO GENTLE-WOMAN | 2 | 52 328 | 139 |

## NEW-BORNE

| | | | | |
|---|---|---|---|---|
| MY TEARES BUT TENDER AND MY DEATH NEW-BORNE. | OUR LORD IN HIS CIRCUMCISION | 12 | 46 98 | 9 |
| HE SAW HEAV'N BLOSSOME WITH A NEW-BORNE LIGHT. | SOSPETTO D'HERODE | 129 | 46 109 | 216 |
| HOVER O'RE THE NEW-BORNE DAY. | UPON DEATH OF DESIRED HERRYS | 48 | 46 168 | 467 |
| TWO EVER BLUSHING BEDS OF NEW-BORNE ROSES. | ON A FOULE MORNING | 18 | 46 181 | 495 |

## NEW-SALUTED

| | | | | |
|---|---|---|---|---|
| OF THE NEW-SALUTED DAY. | UPON DEATH OF DESIRED HERRYS | 34 | 46 168 | 467 |

## NEW-STRUNG

| | | | | |
|---|---|---|---|---|
| TO CHAUNT MY PRAYSES IN A NEW-STRUNG SONG. | OUT OF GROTIUS | 74 | MS 398 | 198 |

## NEWLY

| | | | | |
|---|---|---|---|---|
| THE SMILING MORNE HAD NEWLY WAK'T THE DAY, | THE BEGINNING OF HELIODORUS | 1 | 46 158 | 517 |
| SHEW'D, THAT STERNE WARRE HAD NEWLY BATH'D HIM THERE | THE BEGINNING OF HELIODORUS | 22 | 46 158 | 517 |
| TO BLOT THE NEWLY BLOSSOM'D LIGHT. | UPON DEATH OF DESIRED HERRYS | 54 | 46 168 | 467 |
| THEIR BASHFULL CHEEKES TOGETHER, NEWLY THEY | UPON YORKE HIS BIRTH | 61 | 46 176 | 500 |

## NEXT

| Line | Reference | | | |
|---|---|---|---|---|
| VERTUE WEARES HIM NEXT HER HEART. | UPON DEATH OF DESIRED HERRYS | 10 | 46 168 | 467 |
| HAVE MERCY THEN, AND WHEN HE NEXT SHALL RISE | TO THE MORNING | 35 | 46 183 | 497 |
| NEXT TO THEIR OWN LOW NOTHING THEY MAY LY, | TO THE NAME OF JESUS | 234 | 52 239 | 30 |
| THAT, AT THE NEXT REMOVE | TO SAME CONCERNING CHOISE | 48 | 52 331 | 66 |

## NIGH

| | | | | |
|---|---|---|---|---|
| ONE THAT GLADLY WILL BEE NIGH, | ON MR. G. HERBERTS BOOKE | 7 | 46 130 | 6d |
| MISCHEIFE, THAT SCORNES EXPRESSION SHOULD COME NIGH IT. | ON GUNPOWDER-TREASON | 48 | MS 384 | 458 |
| WHOSE PURER FLAMES TREMBLE TO BE SOE NIGH, | UPON GUNPOWDER TREASON | 15 | MS 387 | 461 |

## NIGHT

| | | | | |
|---|---|---|---|---|
| DOES THE NIGHT ARISE. | THE WEEPER | 109 | 46 79 | 120 |
| DOES NIGHT LOOSE HER EYES. | THE WEEPER | 111 | 46 79 | 120 |
| LET NIGHT OR DAY DOE WHAT THEY WILL | THE WEEPER | 113 | 46 79 | 120 |
| GLOOMY NIGHT EMBRAC'T THE PLACE | A HYMNE OF THE NATIVITY | 17 | 46 106 | 76 |
| SUMMER IN WINTER. DAY IN NIGHT. | A HYMNE OF THE NATIVITY | 55 | 46 106 | 76 |
| HIS EYES, THE SULLEN DENS OF DEATH AND NIGHT, | SOSPETTO D'HERODE | 49 | 46 109 | 216 |
| HEE SAW HOW IN THAT BLEST DAY-BEARING NIGHT, | SOSPETTO D'HERODE | 113 | 46 109 | 216 |
| THE GOLDEN EYES OF NIGHT, WHOSE BEAME MADE BRIGHT | SOSPETTO D'HERODE | 131 | 46 109 | 216 |
| (NOR ASKT LEAVE OF THE SUN) BY DAY AS NIGHT. | SOSPETTO D'HERODE | 133 | 46 109 | 216 |
| RAN TREMBLING THROUGH THE HOLLOW VAULTS OF NIGHT, | SOSPETTO D'HERODE | 151 | 46 109 | 216 |
| TO THIS DARKE HOUSE OF SHADES, HORROUR, AND NIGHT, | SOSPETTO D'HERODE | 213 | 46 109 | 216 |
| THRICE HOWL'D THE CAVES OF NIGHT, AND THRICE THE SOUND. | SOSPETTO D'HERODE | 297 | 46 109 | 216 |
| BUT SHUT THEIR FLOWRY LIDS FOR EVER. NIGHT, | SOSPETTO D'HERODE | 379 | 46 109 | 216 |
| HATE THE SWEET PEACE OF ALL-COMPOSING NIGHT. | SOSPETTO D'HERODE | 496 | 46 109 | 216 |
| (NIGHT HANGS YET HEAVY ON THE LIDS OF DAY) | SOSPETTO D'HERODE | 506 | 46 109 | 216 |
| OUR LIFE IN DEATH, OUR DAY IN NIGHT. | ON HOPE | 16 | 46 143 | 71 |
| AS IF HE SCORN'D TO THINKE OF NIGHT, | UPON DEATH OF DESIRED HERRYS | 50 | 46 168 | 467 |
| CALL'D FOR AN UNTIMELY NIGHT, | UPON DEATH OF DESIRED HERRYS | 53 | 46 168 | 467 |
| TILL THIS STORMY NIGHT BE GONE. | AN EPITAPH HUSBAND AND WIFE | 12 | 46 174 | 478 |
| WHOSE DAY SHALL NEVER SLEEPE IN NIGHT. | AN EPITAPH HUSBAND AND WIFE | 16 | 46 174 | 478 |
| MISTRESSE OF WONDERS. CYNTHIA'S IS THE NIGHT, | UPON YORKE HIS BIRTH | 77 | 46 176 | 500 |
| E'RE PROVE THE DISMALL MORNING OF THY NIGHT. | UPON YORKE HIS BIRTH | 93 | 46 176 | 500 |
| STUMBLING ON NIGHT. ROUZE THEE ILLUSTRIOUS YOUTH, | ON A FOULE MORNING | 3 | 46 181 | 495 |
| AND, THROUGH THE NIGHT OF ERROR AND DARK DOUBT, | ON FRONTISPIECE ISAACSONS | 12 | 46 191 | 491 |
| SET. O THEN, HOW LONG A NIGHT | OUT OF CATULLUS | 7 | 46 194 | 523 |
| AS THE COY BRIDES, WHEN NIGHT | WISHES SUPPOSED MISTRESSE | 71 | 46 195 | 479 |
| FROM A FORE SPENT NIGHT OF SORROW. | WISHES SUPPOSED MISTRESSE | 78 | 46 195 | 479 |
| OF A CLEERE MIND ARE DAY ALL NIGHT. | WISHES SUPPOSED MISTRESSE | 81 | 46 195 | 479 |
| OR GIVE DOWNE TO THE WINGS OF NIGHT. | WISHES SUPPOSED MISTRESSE | 96 | 46 195 | 479 |
| SAD SHADES AND SING DULL NIGHT ASLEEPE. | THOUGH NOW 'TIS NEITHER | 20 | MS 397 | 492 |
| OF DUST, WHERE IN THE BASHFULL SHADES OF NIGHT | TO THE NAME OF JESUS | 233 | 52 239 | 30 |
| HATH NIGHT LOVE'S NOON IN NATURE'S NIGHT. | IN HOLY NATIVITY | 2 | 52 246 | 76 |
| GLOOMY NIGHT EMBRAC'T THE PLACE | IN HOLY NATIVITY | 17 | 52 246 | 76 |
| SOMMER IN WINTER. DAY IN NIGHT. | IN HOLY NATIVITY | 81 | 52 246 | 76 |
| MERIDIAN NIGHT, | IN GLORIOUS EPIPHANIE | 17 | 52 253 | 39 |
| TO THEE, THOU DAY OF NIGHT. THOU EAST OF WEST. | IN GLORIOUS EPIPHANIE | 22 | 52 253 | 39 |
| SORDIDLY SHIFTING HANDS WITH SHADES & NIGHT. | IN GLORIOUS EPIPHANIE | 35 | 52 253 | 39 |
| THE DEEP HYPOCRISY OF DEATH & NIGHT | IN GLORIOUS EPIPHANIE | 58 | 52 253 | 39 |
| THE NIGHT & WINTER STILL OF DEATH & SIN. | IN GLORIOUS EPIPHANIE | 77 | 52 253 | 39 |
| THAT FORFEITURE OF NOON TO NIGHT SHALL PAY | IN GLORIOUS EPIPHANIE | 149 | 52 253 | 39 |
| ALL THE IDOLATROUS THEFTS DONE BY THIS NIGHT OF DAY. | IN GLORIOUS EPIPHANIE | 150 | 52 253 | 39 |
| OF AN UNSEASONABLE NIGHT, | IN GLORIOUS EPIPHANIE | 166 | 52 253 | 39 |
| HIS NEW PRODIGIOUS NIGHT, | IN GLORIOUS EPIPHANIE | 172 | 52 253 | 39 |
| AND MAKE THE NIGHT IT SELF THEIR TORCH TO THEE. | IN GLORIOUS EPIPHANIE | 188 | 52 253 | 39 |
| BY THE OBLIQUE AMBUSH OF THIS CLOSE NIGHT | IN GLORIOUS EPIPHANIE | 189 | 52 253 | 39 |
| BY BEING SCHOLLER FIRST OF THAT NEW NIGHT, | IN GLORIOUS EPIPHANIE | 206 | 52 253 | 39 |
| OF A MOST WISE & WELL-ABUSED NIGHT | IN GLORIOUS EPIPHANIE | 210 | 52 253 | 39 |
| BORROWING DAY & LENDING NIGHT. | IN GLORIOUS EPIPHANIE | 218 | 52 253 | 39 |
| LIFE OUT OF DEATH, DAY OUT OF NIGHT. | OFFICE H. CROSS MATINES | 23 | 52 265 | 86 |
| NOW IS THE NOON OF SORROW'S NIGHT. | OFFICE H. CROSS SIXT | 1 | 52 270 | 97 |
| AND THEIR NIGHT DYES INTO OUR DAY. | LAUDA SION SALVATOREM | 24 | 52 294 | 178 |
| MUST BE THE DAY OF THAT DREAD NIGHT, | DIES IRAE | 8 | 52 298 | 186 |
| THE CAVES OF NIGHT ANSWER ONE CALL. | DIES IRAE | 16 | 52 298 | 186 |
| LET NIGHT OR DAY DOE WHAT THEY WILL. | WEEPER | 137 | 52 307 | 120 |
| TILL THIS STORMY NIGHT BE GONE, | AN EPITAPH UPON MARRIED COUPLE | 16 | 52 339 | 478 |
| WHOSE DAY SHALL NEVER DY IN NIGHT. | AN EPITAPH UPON MARRIED COUPLE | 20 | 52 339 | 478 |
| BLENDS BOTH THE NOONES OF NIGHT & DAY. | (ON) HOPE | 6 | 52 345 | 71 |
| WHICH HAD THE HAPPINES TO WORKE I'TH' NIGHT. | ON GUNPOWDER-TREASON | 58 | MS 384 | 458 |
| SUCH AS THE SABLE PINIONS OF THE NIGHT | UPON GUNPOWDER TREASON | 6 | MS 386 | 460 |
| ENGENDER WITH THE NIGHT, & TEEME A BIRTH | UPON GUNPOWDER TREASON | 12 | MS 386 | 460 |
| THE QUEENE OF NIGHT GOTT THE GREENE SICKNES THEN, | UPON GUNPOWDER TREASON | 23 | MS 386 | 460 |
| WHEN NIGHT BEHELD THEM, SHAME DID ALMOST TURNE | UPON GUNPOWDER TREASON | 11 | MS 387 | 461 |
| SULPHUREOUS FLAMES, SNATCH'D FROM AETERNALL NIGHT, | UPON GUNPOWDER TREASON | 26 | MS 387 | 461 |
| WHOSE BLAZING BEAMES, MAUGRE THE BLACKEST NIGHT, | UPON KINGS CORONATION | 15 | MS 389 | 454 |
| TO WHOM HEAVENS LAMPES OFTEN IN SILENT NIGHT | UPON KINGS CORONATION | 27 | MS 389 | 454 |
| THEN WONDRING STARTS, & HAD THE CURTEOUS NIGHT | UPON KINGS CORONATION | 19 | MS 390 | 453 |

## NIGHT'S

| | | | | |
|---|---|---|---|---|
| NOW HAD THE NIGHT'S CAMPANION FROM HER DEN, | SOSPETTO D'HERODE | 385 | 46 109 | 216 |

## NIGHTS

| | | | | |
|---|---|---|---|---|
| DAYES KING DEPOSED BY NIGHTS QUEENE. | A HYMNE OF THE NATIVITY | 2 | 46 106 | 76 |
| TO SIT AND SCOULE UPON NIGHTS HEAVY BROW. | ON A FOULE MORNING | 34 | 46 181 | 495 |
| THAT SHUTS NIGHTS DYING EYES, SHALL OPEN MINE. | TO THE MORNING | 46 | 46 183 | 497 |

## NIGHTS, SWEET AS THEY,

| | | | | |
|---|---|---|---|---|
| NIGHTS, SWEET AS THEY, | WISHES SUPPOSED MISTRESSE | 82 | 46 | 195 479 |
| BOTH NIGHTS & DAYES. | CHARITAS NIMIA | 27 | 52 | 280 48 |

## NIGHTINGALE

| | | | | |
|---|---|---|---|---|
| A NIGHTINGALE, COME FROM THE NEIGHBOURING WOOD. | MUSICKS DUELL | 8 | 46 | 149 535 |
| A NIGHTINGALE, WHO MAY SHEE SPREAD | THOUGH NOW 'TIS NEITHER | 5 | MS | 397 492 |
| WHAT NIGHTINGALE CAN LOOSE HER NOATE. | THOUGH NOW 'TIS NEITHER | 14 | MS | 397 492 |

## NIGHTINGALES

| | | | | |
|---|---|---|---|---|
| AND NIGHTINGALES ARE OUT OF TUNE, | THOUGH NOW 'TIS NEITHER | 2 | MS | 397 492 |
| THERE ALL THE YEARE LOVES NIGHTINGALES | THOUGH NOW 'TIS NEITHER | 30 | MS | 397 492 |

## NILE

| | | | | |
|---|---|---|---|---|
| LOOKES DOWNE, AND SEES THE HUMBLE NILE BELOW | THE BEGINNING OF HELIODORUS | 4 | 46 | 158 517 |

## NILUS

| | | | | |
|---|---|---|---|---|
| THAT HATH A DOUBLE NILUS GOING, | ON BLEEDING WOUNDS OF LORD | 14 | 46 | 101 110 |
| THAT HATH A DOUBLE NILUS GOING. | UPON BLEEDING CRUCIFIX | 18 | 52 | 288 110 |

## NIMBLE

| | | | | |
|---|---|---|---|---|
| HIS NIMBLE HANDS INSTINCT THEN TAUGHT EACH STRING | MUSICKS DUELL | 27 | 46 | 149 535 |
| WITH NIMBLE FLAMES, AND THOUGH HIS MIND | OUT OF GREEKE CUPID'S CRYER | 21 | 46 | 159 519 |
| NO NIMBLE RAPTURE STARTS TO HEAVEN AND BRINGS | TO THE MORNING | 20 | 46 | 183 497 |
| OF NIMBLE ART, & TRAVERSE ROUND | TO THE NAME OF JESUS | 33 | 52 | 239 30 |
| WITH NIMBLE CAPERS, & FORCE ATLAS TREAD | UPON KINGS CORONATION | 3 | MS | 389 454 |
| DANCE, LIKE THE NIMBLE SPHAERES, A JOYFULL ROUND. | UPON BIRTH PRINCESSE E | 32 | MS | 391 456 |

## NIMBLEST

| | | | | |
|---|---|---|---|---|
| THE NIMBLEST OF THE LIGHTNING-WINGED LOVES. | SOSPETTO D'HERODE | 235 | 46 | 109 216 |

## NINTH

| | | | | |
|---|---|---|---|---|
| THE NINTH WITH AWFULL HORROR HEARKENED TO THOSE GROANES | OFFICE H. CROSS NINTH | 1 | 52 | 271 99 |

## NIOBE

| | | | | |
|---|---|---|---|---|
| EACH STONE HAD STREIGHT A NIOBE BECOME, | UPON GUNPOWDER TREASON | 49 | MS | 386 460 |

## NIP

| | | | | |
|---|---|---|---|---|
| THAT NIP THE BOSOME OF THE WORLDS BEST THINGS, | DESCRIPTION RELIGIOUS HOUSE | 26 | 52 | 338 213 |

## NIPPE

| | | | | |
|---|---|---|---|---|
| AND TOO UNGENTLE NIPPE OF FROSTY AGE. | AN ELEGY MR STANNINOW | 34 | MS | 394 473 |

## NOBLE

| | | | | |
|---|---|---|---|---|
| WHERE THE NOBLE INFANT LAY. | A HYMNE OF THE NATIVITY | 18 | 46 | 106 76 |
| A NAME IN NOBLE DEEDES RIVALL TO THEE. | SOSPETTO D'HERODE | 28 | 46 | 109 216 |
| BUT IF THE NOBLE BRIDEGROME WHEN HEE COMES | ON A PRAYER BOOKE | 41 | 46 | 126 139 |
| LOVES NOBLE HISTORY, WITH WITT | IN MEMORY OF LADY MADRE TERESA | 157 | 46 | 131 52 |
| A PLANT OF NOBLE STEMME, FORWARD AND FAIRE, | UPON DEATH OF HERRYS | 1 | 46 | 167 466 |
| FOR WHOSE MORE NOBLE SMART, | WISHES SUPPOSED MISTRESSE | 56 | 46 | 195 479 |
| NEEDS MUST YOUR NOBLE PRAYSES STRENGTH | TO THE QUEEN | 13 | 48 | 215 501 |
| OF NOBLE POWRES, I SEE. | TO THE NAME OF JESUS | 20 | 52 | 239 30 |
| OR YOU, MORE NOBLE ARCHITECTS OF INTELLECTUALL NOISE, | TO THE NAME OF JESUS | 77 | 52 | 239 30 |
| WHERE THE NOBLE INFANT LAY. | IN HOLY NATIVITY | 18 | 52 | 246 76 |
| AND HE MORE NEEDFULLY & NOBLE PROVE | IN GLORIOUS EPIPHANIE | 159 | 52 | 253 39 |
| THUS WE, WHO WHEN WITH ALL THE NOBLE POWRES | IN GLORIOUS EPIPHANIE | 219 | 52 | 253 39 |
| ALOFT, AND FILL THE NATIONS WITH THY NOBLE FRUIT. | VEXILLA REGIS | 38 | 52 | 277 136 |
| AND TEACH THY LOV'D NAME TO THEIR NOBLE LYRE. | CHARITAS NIMIA | 26 | 52 | 280 48 |
| NOR KEEP SUCH NOBLE SORROWES COMPANY. | SANCTA MARIA DOLORUM | 14 | 52 | 283 162 |
| YOU FROM THOSE NESTS OF NOBLE SORROW. | WEEPER | 168 | 52 | 307 120 |
| LOVE'S NOBLE HISTORY, WITH WITT | TERESA | 156 | 52 | 315 52 |
| BUT IF THE NOBLE BRIDEGROOM, WHEN HE COME. | PRAYER TO GENTLE-WOMAN | 47 | 52 | 328 139 |

## NOBLER

| | | | | |
|---|---|---|---|---|
| THY NOBLER BEAUTY SHALL BEREAVE HIM, | AN HIMNE FOR CIRCUMCISION | 33 | 46 | 141 37 |
| BY'A NOBLER BREAD, MORE NEEDFULL BLOOD. | LAUDA SION SALVATOREM | 36 | 52 | 294 178 |
| A NOBLER WEAPON THEN A WOUND. | FLAMING HEART | 72 | 52 | 324 61 |

## NOBLEST

| | | | | |
|---|---|---|---|---|
| NOR YEILDS THE NOBLEST NEST | TO THE NAME OF JESUS | 105 | 52 | 239 30 |
| POUR ON THY NOBLEST SWEETS, WHICH, WHEN THEY TOUCH | OFFICE H. CROSS COMPLINE | 7 | 52 | 274 105 |
| OF THINE (THE NOBLEST NEST | SANCTA MARIA DOLORUM | 46 | 52 | 283 162 |

## NOBLY

| | | | | |
|---|---|---|---|---|
| PROVE NOBLY, HERE, UNNATURAL. | O GLORIOSA DOMINA | 24 | 52 | 302 194 |

## NOD

| | | | | |
|---|---|---|---|---|
| WHAT WOULD THEY MORE. TH' AVE SEENE WHEN AT MY NOD | OUT OF GROTIUS | 49 | MS | 398 198 |

## NODS

| | | | | |
|---|---|---|---|---|
| WHICH NODS WITH MANY A HEAVY HEADED TREE. | SOSPETTO D'HERODE | 346 | 46 109 | 216 |

## NODDING

| | | | | |
|---|---|---|---|---|
| NODDING ON THE WILLOWES SLEPT, | PSALME 137 | 4 | 46 104 | 7 |

## NOISE

| | | | | |
|---|---|---|---|---|
| THY FAMES FULL NOISE, MAKES PROUD THE PATIENT EARTH, | SOSPETTO D'HERODE | 29 | 46 109 | 216 |
| AT LAST HER LISTING EARES THE NOISE O'RETAKES, | SOSPETTO D'HERODE | 300 | 46 109 | 216 |
| (THESE TUMULTUOUS SHOPS OF NOISE) | ON A PRAYER BOOKE | 60 | 46 126 | 139 |
| OR YOU, MORE NOBLE ARCHITECTS OF INTELLECTUALL NOISE, | TO THE NAME OF JESUS | 77 | 52 239 | 30 |
| LET LIPPES & HEARTS LIFT HIGH THE NOISE | LAUDA SION SALVATOREM | 15 | 52 294 | 178 |
| (THOSE TUMULTUOUS SHOPS OF NOISE) | PRAYER TO GENTLE-WOMAN | 66 | 52 328 | 139 |
| KIND LOVES KEEP HOUSE, LY CLOSE, AND MAKE NO NOISE, | DESCRIPTION RELIGIOUS HOUSE | 33 | 52 338 | 213 |

## NOYSE

| | | | | |
|---|---|---|---|---|
| IN THE CLOSE MURMUR OF A SPARKLING NOYSE. | MUSICKS DUELL | 84 | 46 149 | 535 |

## NONAGE

| | | | | |
|---|---|---|---|---|
| NOW'S BUT THE NONAGE OF MY PAINES, MY FEARES | OUR LORD IN HIS CIRCUMCISION | 9 | 46 98 | 9 |
| LOVE KNOWES NO NONAGE, NOR THE MIND. | IN MEMORY OF LADY MADRE TERESA | 32 | 46 131 | 52 |
| LOVE KNOWES NO NONAGE, NOR THE MIND. | TERESA | 32 | 52 315 | 52 |

## NONE

| | | | | |
|---|---|---|---|---|
| THE WINGED WAND'RER, AND THAT NONE | OUT OF GREEKE CUPID'S CRYER | 9 | 46 159 | 519 |
| LANGUAGE NONE MORE FLUENT IS. | UPON THE DEATH OF A GENTLEMAN | 22 | 46 166 | 472 |
| THEN IS SHEE DREST BY NONE BUT THEE. | THE WEEPER | 52 | 46 79 | 120 |
| THAT THOU FIND'ST NONE. | UPON ASSE THAT BORE SAVIOUR | 12 | 46 90 | 19 |
| SHE WAS A NIMPH, THE MEADOWES KNEW NONE SUCH, | TO PONTIUS WASHING HANDS | 5 | 46 94 | 23 |
| GIV'ST JOY, EVEN WHEN THOU GIVEST NONE. | VERILY YE SHALL WEEP | 6 | 46 95 | 22 |
| YET IS THE JOY I TAKE IN'T SMALL OR NONE. | UPON OUR LORDS LAST DISCOURSE | 3 | 46 95 | 21 |
| IN TEARS. AS IF THINE EYES HAD NONE. | ON BLEEDING WOUNDS OF LORD | 18 | 46 101 | 110 |
| TO HOLD THEM DOWN, AND LOOKE THAT NONE SEETHE O'RE. | SOSPETTO D'HERODE | 296 | 46 109 | 216 |
| WEE NEED TO GOE TO NONE OF ALL | IN MEMORY OF LADY MADRE TERESA | 3 | 46 131 | 52 |
| THEIR GREAT LORDS GLORIOUS NAME, TO NONE | IN MEMORY OF LADY MADRE TERESA | 9 | 46 131 | 52 |
| TAUGHT THEE BY NONE BUT HIM, WHILE HERE | IN MEMORY OF LADY MADRE TERESA | 158 | 46 131 | 52 |
| WHERE FLOWES SUCH WINE AS WE CAN HAVE OF NONE | AN APOLOGIE FOR HYMNE (TERESA) | 39 | 46 136 | 59 |
| NOW SEEM THEY TEMPLES CONSECRATE TO NONE, | ON A TREATISE OF CHARITY | 37 | 46 137 | 69 |
| TO NONE BUT THE BLEST HEAVENS, WHOSE BRIGHT | ON THE ASSUMPTION | 32 | 46 139 | 114 |
| NONE SO FAIRE THY BOSOME STROWES. | AN HIMNE FOR CIRCUMCISION | 10 | 46 141 | 37 |
| THE SECOND, NONE. | OUT OF MARTIALL | 4 | 46 168 | 527 |
| FOR LETT THEM KNOW SHEE'S NONE OF THOSE | THOUGH NOW 'TIS NEITHER | 17 | MS 397 | 492 |
| I SING THE NAME WHICH NONE CAN SAY | TO THE NAME OF JESUS | 1 | 52 239 | 30 |
| FAIR, FLOWRY NAME. IN NONE BUT THEE | TO THE NAME OF JESUS | 173 | 52 239 | 30 |
| NONE SO FAIR THY BOSOM STROWES. | NEW YEAR'S DAY | 10 | 52 251 | 37 |
| AH SHE. NOW BY NONE OTHER | SANCTA MARIA DOLORUM | 3 | 52 283 | 162 |
| IN SHOWRES, AS IF THINE EYES HAD NONE. | UPON BLEEDING CRUCIFIX | 6 | 52 288 | 110 |
| THOMAS MIGHT TOUCH. NONE BUT MIGHT SEE | ADORO TE | 23 | 52 291 | 172 |
| NONE CAN INDURE. YET NONE CAN FLY. | DIES IRAE | 20 | 52 298 | 186 |
| NONE CAN INDURE. YET NONE CAN FLY. | DIES IRAE | 20 | 52 298 | 186 |
| THEN IS SHE DREST BY NONE BUT THEE. | WEEPER | 40 | 52 307 | 120 |
| WEE'L NOW APPEAL TO NONE OF ALL | TERESA | 3 | 52 315 | 52 |
| THEIR GREAT LORD'S GLORIOUS NAME, TO NONE | TERESA | 9 | 52 315 | 52 |
| TAUGHT THEE BY NONE BUT HIM, WHILE HERE | TERESA | 157 | 52 315 | 52 |
| WHERE FLOWES SUCH WINE AS WE CAN HAVE OF NONE | AN APOLOGIE FOR (TERESA) HYMNE | 39 | 52 322 | 59 |
| WHOM LONG NONE COULD OBTAIN, THOUGH THOUSANDS TRY'D, | ALEXIAS FIRST ELEGIE | 2 | 52 334 | 204 |
| NO GAPING GORGON, THIS. NONE, LIKE THE REST | ALEXIAS THIRD ELEGIE | 41 | 52 336 | 209 |
| WHEN THOUSANDS SOUGHT MY LOVE, LOV'D NONE BUT THEE. | ALEXIAS THIRD ELEGIE | 54 | 52 336 | 209 |
| AND ROOM ENOUGH FOR MONARCHS, WHILE NONE SWELLS | DESCRIPTION RELIGIOUS HOUSE | 34 | 52 338 | 213 |
| NONE, BUT HIMSELFE, WHO FEELES IT, NONE CAN TELL. | IN AMOREM DIVINUM | 2 | MS 361 | 212 |
| NONE, BUT HIMSELFE, WHO FEELES IT, NONE CAN TELL. | IN AMOREM DIVINUM | 2 | MS 361 | 212 |
| NONE, NOT HIMSELFE, WHO FEELES IT, NONE CAN TELL. | IN AMOREM DIVINUM | 4 | MS 361 | 212 |
| NONE, NOT HIMSELFE, WHO FEELES IT, NONE CAN TELL. | IN AMOREM DIVINUM | 4 | MS 361 | 212 |
| THAT RUNNES IN VIOLETT PIPES, NONE OTHER FOOD | ON GUNPOWDER-TREASON | 64 | MS 384 | 458 |
| LETT NONE DARE SPEAKE OF THEE, BUT SUCH AS THENCE | UPON BIRTH PRINCESSE E | 9 | MS 391 | 456 |
| NOE. NONE OF THESE RAVISH'T THOSE VIRGIN ROSES, | AN ELEGY MR STANNINOW | 37 | MS 394 | 473 |

## NOOKE

| | | | | |
|---|---|---|---|---|
| WHAT FARTHEST NOOKE OF LOWEST HELL | OUT OF GREEKE CUPID'S CRYER | 35 | 46 159 | 519 |

## NOON

| | | | | |
|---|---|---|---|---|
| HATH METT LOVE'S NOON IN NATURE'S NIGHT. | IN HOLY NATIVITY | 2 | 52 246 | 76 |
| THAT FORFEITURE OF NOON TO NIGHT SHALL PAY | IN GLORIOUS EPIPHANIE | 149 | 52 253 | 39 |
| NOW IS THE NOON OF SORROW'S NIGHT. | OFFICE H. CROSS SIXT | 1 | 52 270 | 97 |

## NOONE

| | | | | |
|---|---|---|---|---|
| OF ALL THE GLORYES MAKE NOONE GAY | EASTER DAY | 7 | 46 100 | 26 |
| MAKE HIGH NOONE FORGET HIS BEAMES. | PSALME 23 | 16 | 46 102 | 5 |
| TILL IN THE LAP OF LOVES FULL NOONE | ON HOPE | 56 | 46 143 | 71 |
| OF NOONE WEARE THEIR OWNE SUNSHINE, O THOU BRIGHT | UPON YORKE HIS BIRTH | 76 | 46 176 | 500 |
| BUT THOU AT NOONE DOST SHINE, AND ART ALL DAY, | UPON YORKE HIS BIRTH | 78 | 46 176 | 500 |
| TILL IN THE LAPPE OF LOVES FULL NOONE | (ON) HOPE | 26 | 52 345 | 71 |
| THE GOLDEN HARVEST OF OUR JOYES, THE NOONE | AN ELEGY MR STANNINOW | 42 | MS 394 | 473 |

## NOONS

| | | | | | |
|---|---|---|---|---|---|
| OF NOONS HIGH GLORY, WHEN HARD BY THE STREAMS | MUSICKS DUELL | 2 | 46 | 149 | 535 |

## NOONES

| | | | | | |
|---|---|---|---|---|---|
| BLENDS BOTH THE NOONES OF NIGHT & DAY. | (ON) HOPE | 6 | 52 | 345 | 71 |

## NORTH

| | | | | | |
|---|---|---|---|---|---|
| THE ANGRY NORTH TO WAGE HIS WARRES. | A HYMNE OF THE NATIVITY | 24 | 46 | 106 | 76 |
| THE NORTH FORGOT HIS FIERCE INTENT, | A HYMNE OF THE NATIVITY | 25 | 46 | 106 | 76 |
| OF TH'ICY NORTH, FROM FROST-BOUNT ATLAS HANDS | SOSPETTO D'HERODE | 106 | 46 | 109 | 216 |
| IT SHALL NOT BE, SAID I, AND CLOMBE THE NORTH. | SOSPETTO D'HERODE | 221 | 46 | 109 | 216 |
| THE ANGRY NORTH TO WAGE HIS WARRES. | IN HOLY NATIVITY | 25 | 52 | 246 | 76 |
| THE NORTH FORGOTT HIS FEIRCE INTENT. | IN HOLY NATIVITY | 26 | 52 | 246 | 76 |

## NORTHERNE

| | | | | | |
|---|---|---|---|---|---|
| SUCH WAS THE BRIGHTNESSE OF THIS NORTHERNE STARRE, | UPON KINGS CORONATION | 29 | MS | 390 | 453 |

## NOSTRILLS

| | | | | | |
|---|---|---|---|---|---|
| FROM HIS BLACK NOSTRILLS, AND BLEW LIPS, IN SPIGHT | SOSPETTO D'HERODE | 53 | 46 | 109 | 216 |

## NOTE

| | | | | | |
|---|---|---|---|---|---|
| TRAYLES HER PLAYNE DITTY IN ONE LONG-SPUN NOTE, | MUSICKS DUELL | 37 | 46 | 149 | 535 |
| EACH STRING HIS NOTE, AS IF THEY MEANT TO CARRY | MUSICKS DUELL | 146 | 46 | 149 | 535 |
| NO OTHER NOTE FOR'T, BUT THE NAME WE SING | TO THE NAME OF JESUS | 45 | 52 | 239 | 30 |
| (WHEREOF THE BLUSHING WALLES TOOKE BLOODY NOTE) | HORATIJ ILLE & NEFASTO | 10 | MS | 382 | 530 |

## NOAT

| | | | | | |
|---|---|---|---|---|---|
| WITH THE COOLE EPODE OF A GRAVER NOAT, | MUSICKS DUELL | 99 | 46 | 149 | 535 |

## NOATE

| | | | | | |
|---|---|---|---|---|---|
| YET SUMMONS ALL HER SWEET POWERS FOR A NOATE | MUSICKS DUELL | 160 | 46 | 149 | 535 |
| WHAT NIGHTINGALE CAN LOOSE HER NOATE. | THOUGH NOW 'TIS NEITHER | 14 | MS | 397 | 492 |

## NOTED

| | | | | | |
|---|---|---|---|---|---|
| THE NOTED SEA SHALL CHANGE HIS NAME WITH ME. | ALEXIAS FIRST ELEGIE | 23 | 52 | 334 | 204 |

## NOTES

| | | | | | |
|---|---|---|---|---|---|
| QUICKE VOLUMES OF WILD NOTES, TO LET HIM KNOW | MUSICKS DUELL | 25 | 46 | 149 | 535 |
| AND FOLDS IN WAV'D NOTES WITH A TREMBLING BILL, | MUSICKS DUELL | 60 | 46 | 149 | 535 |
| WHOSE SYLVER-ROOFE RINGS WITH THE SPRIGHTLY NOTES | MUSICKS DUELL | 75 | 46 | 149 | 535 |
| TILL THE FLEDG'D NOTES AT LENGTH FORSAKE THEIR NEST. | MUSICKS DUELL | 90 | 46 | 149 | 535 |
| THAT NOTES THE TRAGICKE DOOMES OF MEN | ANOTHER ON HERRYS | 34 | 46 | 170 | 469 |

## NOTHING

| | | | | | |
|---|---|---|---|---|---|
| NOTHING SPEAKES OUR GRIEFE SO WELL | UPON THE DEATH OF A GENTLEMAN | 23 | 46 | 166 | 472 |
| AS TO SPEAKE NOTHING, COME THEN TELL | UPON THE DEATH OF A GENTLEMAN | 24 | 46 | 166 | 472 |
| O MIGHTY NOTHING, UNTO THEE, | AND HE ANSWERED NOTHING | 1 | 46 | 91 | 22 |
| NOTHING, WEE OWE ALL THINGS THAT BEE. | AND HE ANSWERED NOTHING | 2 | 46 | 91 | 22 |
| HEE SAV'D ALL WHEN HEE NOTHING SAID. | AND HE ANSWERED NOTHING | 4 | 46 | 91 | 22 |
| THE WORLD WAS MADE OF NOTHING THEN. | AND HE ANSWERED NOTHING | 5 | 46 | 91 | 22 |
| WHILE THEY SPEAKE NOTHING, THEY SPEAKE ALL | NEITHER DURST MAN ASKE | 21 | 46 | 92 | 20 |
| WHILE THEY SPEAKE NOTHING, THEY PROCLAIME | NEITHER DURST MAN ASKE | 23 | 46 | 92 | 20 |
| NOTHING BUT TEARES. | TO PONTIUS WASHING HANDS | 10 | 46 | 94 | 23 |
| BRINGING HIM NOTHING BUT NEW FEARES FROM TH'EAST, | SOSPETTO D'HERODE | 500 | 46 | 109 | 216 |
| OUR NOTHING HATH A DEFINITION. | ON HOPE | 14 | 46 | 143 | 71 |
| (HYPERBOLIZED NOTHING.) KNOW THY SPAN. | UPON STANINOUGH'S DEATH | 10 | 46 | 175 | 475 |
| THY NEIGHBOUR-HOOD TO NOTHING. HERE PUT ON | UPON STANINOUGH'S DEATH | 19 | 46 | 175 | 475 |
| YET CARRY NOTHING THENCE AWAY. | WISHES SUPPOSED MISTRESSE | 39 | 46 | 195 | 479 |
| BOVE ALL, NOTHING WITHIN THAT LOWRES. | WISHES SUPPOSED MISTRESSE | 93 | 46 | 195 | 479 |
| AND FULL OF NOTHING ELSE BUT EMPTY ME. | TO THE NAME OF JESUS | 21 | 52 | 239 | 30 |
| NEXT TO THEIR OWN LOW NOTHING THEY MAY LY, | TO THE NAME OF JESUS | 234 | 52 | 239 | 30 |
| AND NOTHING GAIN | IN GLORIOUS EPIPHANIE | 229 | 52 | 253 | 39 |
| LEAVE NOTHING OF MY SELF IN ME. | FLAMING HEART | 106 | 52 | 324 | 61 |
| HYPERBOLIZED NOTHING. KNOW THY SPAN. | DEATH'S LECTURE | 11 | 52 | 340 | 475 |
| THY NEIGHBOURHOOD TO NOTHING. | DEATH'S LECTURE | 20 | 52 | 340 | 475 |
| OUR NOTHING HAS A DEFINITION. | (ON) HOPE | 4 | 52 | 345 | 71 |
| THIS RISING SUNNE, THEIR FACES NOTHING WORE, | UPON KINGS CORONATION | 38 | MS | 390 | 453 |
| WAS NOTHING, THERE MY VOYCE WAS MED'CINALL. | OUT OF GROTIUS | 70 | MS | 398 | 198 |

## NOTHING'S

| | | | | | |
|---|---|---|---|---|---|
| SEE. NOTHING'S VULGAR, EVERY ATOME HEERE | UPON BIRTH PRINCESSE E | 39 | MS | 391 | 456 |

## NOTHYNG

| | | | | | |
|---|---|---|---|---|---|
| 'TIS MADE BY NOTHYNG NOW AGAINE. | AND HE ANSWERED NOTHING | 6 | 46 | 91 | 22 |

## NOUGHT

| | | | | | |
|---|---|---|---|---|---|
| CAN DOE NOUGHT BUT SMILE. | THE WEEPER | 63 | 46 | 79 | 120 |
| O SPEAKE THOU AND MY PIPE HATH NOUGHT TO SAY. | UPON YORKE HIS BIRTH | 113 | 46 | 176 | 500 |
| WHERE NOUGHT BUT SMILES, AND RUDDY JOYES ARE WORNE. | ON A FOULE MORNING | 36 | 46 | 181 | 495 |

| | | | | | |
|---|---|---|---|---|---|
| SO MUCH A THING OF NOUGHT. | CHARITAS NIMIA | 4 | 52 | 260 | 48 |

**NOWHERE**

| | | | | | |
|---|---|---|---|---|---|
| NOWHERE BUT HEERE DID EVER MEET | THE WEEPER | 59 | 46 | 79 | 120 |

**NUMBRED**

| | | | | | |
|---|---|---|---|---|---|
| THUS AT LAST WHEN WE HAVE NUMBRED | OUT OF CATULLUS | 15 | 46 | 194 | 523 |

**NUMBERS**

| | | | | | |
|---|---|---|---|---|---|
| IN HEBREW NUMBERS, THEN (O CRUELL JEST.) | PSALME 137 | 9 | 46 | 104 | 7 |
| NUMBERS, AND SWEETNESSE, AND AN INFLUENCE | UPON YORKE HIS BIRTH | 111 | 46 | 176 | 500 |
| IN HIGH-BUILT NUMBERS WAKES HIS GOLDEN LYRE, | HORATIJ ILLE & NEFASTO | 42 | MS | 382 | 530 |

**NUMBRING**

| | | | | | |
|---|---|---|---|---|---|
| THAT NUMBRING OF HIS VERTUES PRAISE. | HIS EPITAPH (HERRYS) | 9 | 46 | 172 | 471 |

**NUMEROUS**

| | | | | | |
|---|---|---|---|---|---|
| WHEN THESE THY DEATHS SO NUMEROUS, | IN MEMORY OF LADY MADRE TERESA | 111 | 46 | 131 | 52 |
| WHEN THESE THY DEATHS, SO NUMEROUS, | TERESA | 110 | 52 | 315 | 52 |

**NUMEROUSE**

| | | | | | |
|---|---|---|---|---|---|
| OF PEARLY DROPS, & SENT HER NUMEROUSE BIRTH | UPON KINGS CORONATION | 7 | MS | 390 | 453 |

**NUNNERY**

| | | | | | |
|---|---|---|---|---|---|
| WAS IN THE MODEST NUNNERY OF HIS BREST. | AN ELEGY MR STANNINOW | 36 | MS | 394 | 473 |

**NURSE**

| | | | | | |
|---|---|---|---|---|---|
| FAITH'S SISTER. NURSE OF FAIRE DESIRE. | ON HOPE | 81 | 46 | 143 | 71 |
| FAITH'S SISTER. NURSE OF FAIR DESIRE. | (ON) HOPE | 41 | 52 | 345 | 71 |
| THAT HAND, (WHAT E'RE IT WERE) THAT WAS THY NURSE | HORATIJ ILLE & NEFASTO | 3 | MS | 382 | 530 |
| HONESTIES NURSE, VERTUES BLEST GUARDIAN. | AN ELEGIE ON DR PORTER | 17 | MS | 395 | 476 |

**EARTH-NURST**

| | | | | | |
|---|---|---|---|---|---|
| OF POIS'NOUS AND UNNATURALL LOVES. EARTH-NURST. | SOSPETTO D'HERODE | 127 | 46 | 109 | 216 |

**HOPE-NURST**

| | | | | | |
|---|---|---|---|---|---|
| THE HEAD OF ALL MY HOPE-NURST JOYES. | PSALME 137 | 26 | 46 | 104 | 7 |

**ILL-NURTUR'D**

| | | | | | |
|---|---|---|---|---|---|
| SHAME OF THY MOTHER SOYLE. ILL-NURTUR'D TREE. | HORATIJ ILLE & NEFASTO | 1 | MS | 382 | 530 |

**NUZZEL'D**

| | | | | | |
|---|---|---|---|---|---|
| NUZZEL'D IN THE LILLIES NECKE. | THE WEEPER | 40 | 46 | 79 | 120 |
| NUZZEL'D IN THE LILLY'S NECK. | WEEPER | 46 | 52 | 307 | 120 |

**NYMPH**

| | | | | | |
|---|---|---|---|---|---|
| GREAT NYMPH, O'RELOOKE MY LOWNESSE. HEAV'N YOU KNOW, | EX EUPHORMIONE | 7 | MS | 392 | 525 |

**NIMPH**

| | | | | | |
|---|---|---|---|---|---|
| SHE WAS A NIMPH, THE MEADOWES KNEW NONE SUCH, | TO PONTIUS WASHING HANDS | 5 | 46 | 94 | 23 |

**NYMPHS**

| | | | | | |
|---|---|---|---|---|---|
| THE' ASTONISHT NYMPHS THEIR FLOOD'S STRANGE FATE DEPLORE. | TO COUNTESSE OF DENBIGH | 25 | 52 | 236 | 146 |
| TH'ASTONISH'D NYMPHS THEIR FLOUD'S STRANGE FATE DEPLORE. | AGAINST IRRESOLUTION AND DELAY | 25 | 52 | 347 | 146 |

**OAKE**

| | | | | | |
|---|---|---|---|---|---|
| UNDER PROTECTION OF AN OAKE. THERE SATE | MUSICKS DUELL | 4 | 46 | 149 | 535 |

**OAKES**

| | | | | | |
|---|---|---|---|---|---|
| AND HATEFULL SCHINIS HIS SO FEARED OAKES. | SOSPETTO D'HERODE | 360 | 46 | 109 | 216 |

**OARES**

| | | | | | |
|---|---|---|---|---|---|
| SEAS HAD NOT BIN REBUK'T BY SAWCY OARES | ALEXIAS THIRD ELEGIE | 7 | 52 | 336 | 209 |

**OATHES**

| | | | | | |
|---|---|---|---|---|---|
| OATHES OF WATER, WORDS OF WIND. | TO SAME CONCERNING CHOISE | 17 | 52 | 331 | 66 |

**OBEDIENCE**

| | | | | | |
|---|---|---|---|---|---|
| SHOULD BLEED IN HIS OWNE LAWES OBEDIENCE. | SOSPETTO D'HERODE | 186 | 46 | 109 | 216 |
| AND SOFT OBEDIENCE, FIND SWEET BIDING HERE. | DESCRIPTION RELIGIOUS HOUSE | 31 | 52 | 338 | 213 |

## OBEDIENT

| | | | | |
|---|---|---|---|---|
| OBEDIENT SLUMBERS, THAT CAN WAKE & WEEP, | DESCRIPTION RELIGIOUS HOUSE | 16 | 52 338 213 |
| BEFORE THE WORLD. OBEDIENT LO. I JOYNE | OUT OF GROTIUS | 4 | MS 398 198 |

## ALL-OBEDIENT

| | | | |
|---|---|---|---|
| THEN BOWES HIS ALL-OBEDIENT HEAD, & DYES | OFFICE H. CROSS NINTH | 5 | 52 271 99 |

## OBEY

| | | | |
|---|---|---|---|
| ON US THY DREAD COMMANDS, OURS TO OBEY. | SOSPETTO D'HERODE | 264 | 46 109 216 |

## T'OBEY

| | | | |
|---|---|---|---|
| T'OBEY MY BOLDER TOUCH. | TO THE NAME OF JESUS | 52 | 52 239 30 |

## OBJECT

| | | | |
|---|---|---|---|
| A WORTHIER OBJECT, OUR LORDS FEET. | THE WEEPER | 138 | 46 79 120 |
| AND SEEING THE LOATH'D OBJECT, HID FOR SHAME | TO THE MORNING | 12 | 46 183 497 |
| A WORTHY OBJECT, OUR LORD'S FEET. | WEEPER | 186 | 52 307 120 |

## OBJECTS

| | | | |
|---|---|---|---|
| THE OBJECTS OF HIS CRUELL SPORTS. | OUT OF GREEKE CUPID'S CRYER | 32 | 46 159 519 |
| ALL PLACES, TIMES, & OBJECTS BE | WEEPER | 131 | 52 307 120 |

## OBLIQUE

| | | | |
|---|---|---|---|
| BY THE OBLIQUE AMBUSH OF THIS CLOSE NIGHT | IN GLORIOUS EPIPHANIE | 189 | 52 253 39 |

## OBSCURE

| | | | |
|---|---|---|---|
| AND TEACH OBSCURE MANKIND A MORE CLOSE WAY | IN GLORIOUS EPIPHANIE | 208 | 52 253 39 |

## OBSCURED

| | | | |
|---|---|---|---|
| NOW ALL OBSCURED LYES | OUT OF THE ITALIAN (2) | 8 | 46 190 547 |

## OBSCURELY

| | | | |
|---|---|---|---|
| THROUGH THE THICK SHADES OBSCURELY MIGHT YOU SEE | SOSPETTO D'HERODE | 350 | 46 109 216 |

## OBSEQUIE

| | | | |
|---|---|---|---|
| OR TO THY SELFE, SING THINE OWNE OBSEQUIE. | MUSICKS DUELL | 110 | 46 149 535 |

## OBSEQUIOUS

| | | | |
|---|---|---|---|
| THE OBSEQUIOUS MOTIONS OF LOVES FATE. | LOVES HOROSCOPE | 14 | 46 185 483 |
| I SAW THE OBSEQUIOUS SERAPHIMS | IN HOLY NATIVITY | 58 | 52 246 76 |
| FROM THIS OBSEQUIOUS CLOUD. | IN GLORIOUS EPIPHANIE | 200 | 52 253 39 |

## TH'OBSEQUIOUS

| | | | |
|---|---|---|---|
| TH'OBSEQUIOUS HANDMAIDS OF THY HIGH COMMANDS. | SOSPETTO D'HERODE | 262 | 46 109 216 |

## OBTAIN

| | | | |
|---|---|---|---|
| WHOM LONG NONE COULD OBTAIN, THOUGH THOUSANDS TRY'D, | ALEXIAS FIRST ELEGIE | 2 | 52 334 204 |

## OBTAINS

| | | | |
|---|---|---|---|
| HE YEILDS, AND STRAIGHT BAPTIS'D, OBTAINS THE GRACE | ALEXIAS THIRD ELEGIE | 45 | 52 336 209 |

## OCCASIONS

| | | | |
|---|---|---|---|
| TO CAST THY NETS ON ALL OCCASIONS WELL. | ON ST. PETER CASTING NETS | 2 | 46 98 13 |

## OCEAN

| | | | |
|---|---|---|---|
| HEAVEN THE CHRISTALL OCEAN IS. | THE WEEPER | 24 | 46 79 120 |
| AN OCEAN COULD HAVE MADE T' HAVE DROWNED THEE. | UPON GUNPOWDER TREASON | 36 | MS 386 460 |
| THE WORLD WILL BE ONE OCEAN, ONE GREAT TEARE. | UPON KINGS CORONATION | 42 | MS 389 454 |

## OCEANS

| | | | |
|---|---|---|---|
| BRITTAINE, THE MIGHTY OCEANS LOVELY BRIDE. | UPON YORKE HIS BIRTH | 1 | 46 176 500 |
| PORTABLE, & COMPENDIOUS OCEANS. | WEEPER | 114 | 52 307 120 |
| WHISPER THY PLAINTS TO TH' OCEANS CURTEOUS EARES. | AN ELEGIE ON DR PORTER | 37 | MS 395 476 |

## OCHUS

| | | | |
|---|---|---|---|
| PHALARIS, OCHUS, EZELINUS, NAMES | SOSPETTO D'HERODE | 363 | 46 109 216 |

## ODORIFEROUS

| | | | |
|---|---|---|---|
| TO PASSE FOR ODORIFEROUS. | TO THE NAME OF JESUS | 180 | 52 239 30 |

ODS

| | | | | |
|---|---|---|---|---|
| ALL IS CAESAR'S, AND WHAT ODS | GIVE TO CAESAR AND TO GOD | 7 | 46 96 | 20 |
| COME FAST UPON THEE, AND THOSE GLORIOUS ODS, | UPON YORKE HIS BIRTH | 6 | 46 176 | 500 |
| ARE THEY NOT ODS, AND GLORIOUS, THAT TO THEE | UPON YORKE HIS BIRTH | 9 | 46 176 | 500 |

OFFENCE

| | | | | |
|---|---|---|---|---|
| HIMSELFE, THE FORFEIT OF HIS SLAVES OFFENCE. | SOSPETTO D'HERODE | 188 | 46 109 | 216 |

OFFEND

| | | | | |
|---|---|---|---|---|
| (NOR CAN THE CHANGE OFFEND) | ON WOUNDS OF CRUCIFIED LORD | 18 | 46 99 | 24 |

OFFER

| | | | | |
|---|---|---|---|---|
| IF HEE OFFER SUGRED KISSES, | OUT OF GREEKE CUPID'S CRYER | 65 | 46 159 | 519 |
| NOR WILL I OFFER ANY MORE TO THEE | TO THE MORNING | 50 | 46 163 | 497 |
| SHE'L OFFER THEM HER DEAREST BREATH, | TERESA | 49 | 52 315 | 52 |
| OFFER THY SELFE A VIRGIN SACRIFICE | UPON GUNPOWDER TREASON | 35 | MS 387 | 461 |
| OR THIRSTY TREASON OFFER ONCE TO SIPPE | UPON GUNPOWDER TREASON | 40 | MS 387 | 461 |

OFFERS

| | | | | |
|---|---|---|---|---|
| WHAT E'RE IT BE LOVE OFFERS, STILL PRESUME | OUT OF GREEKE CUPID'S CRYER | 73 | 46 159 | 519 |
| SHEE OFFERS THEM HER DEAREST BREATH, | IN MEMORY OF LADY MADRE TERESA | 49 | 46 131 | 52 |

OFFERINGS

| | | | | |
|---|---|---|---|---|
| PRETIOUS THEIR OFFERINGS THAT THEIR ALTARS TAKE. | UPON YORKE HIS BIRTH | 117 | 46 176 | 500 |

OFFRING

| | | | | |
|---|---|---|---|---|
| OFFRING THEIR WHITEST SHEETS OF SNOW, | A HYMNE OF THE NATIVITY | 37 | 46 106 | 76 |
| OFFRING THEIR WHITEST SHEETS OF SNOW | IN HOLY NATIVITY | 53 | 52 246 | 76 |

OFFRINGS

| | | | | |
|---|---|---|---|---|
| LO WHERE I SEE THY OFFRINGS WAKE, AND RISE | ON A TREATISE OF CHARITY | 17 | 46 137 | 69 |

OFFICERS

| | | | | |
|---|---|---|---|---|
| TO TH'HEADS AND OFFICERS OF EVERY BAND. | SOSPETTO D'HERODE | 511 | 46 109 | 216 |

OFFICIOUS

| | | | | |
|---|---|---|---|---|
| SO HIS OFFICIOUS BLINDNES NOW SHALL BE | IN GLORIOUS EPIPHANIE | 170 | 52 253 | 39 |

TH'OFFICIOUS

| | | | | |
|---|---|---|---|---|
| I SAW TH'OFFICIOUS ANGELS BRING, | A HYMNE OF THE NATIVITY | 41 | 46 106 | 76 |

THE'OFFICIOUS

| | | | | |
|---|---|---|---|---|
| FOR WHOM THE'OFFICIOUS HEAVNS DEVISE | IN GLORIOUS EPIPHANIE | 3 | 52 253 | 39 |

OFT

| | | | | |
|---|---|---|---|---|
| OFT IN HIS DEEPE THOUGHT HE REVOLVES THE DARKE | SOSPETTO D'HERODE | 91 | 46 109 | 216 |
| O HOW OFT SHALT THOU COMPLAINE | IN MEMORY OF LADY MADRE TERESA | 97 | 46 131 | 52 |
| THE SUNNE HIMSELFE OFT WISHT TO SIT, AND MADE | UPON DEATH OF HERRYS | 10 | 46 167 | 466 |
| OF THY SO OFT REPEATED RISING. | TO THE NAME OF JESUS | 219 | 52 239 | 30 |
| SO OFT WITH BLUBBER'D EYES. | IN GLORIOUS EPIPHANIE | 126 | 52 253 | 39 |
| O HOW OFT SHALT THOU COMPLAIN | TERESA | 97 | 52 315 | 52 |
| HOW OFT HAVE I WEPT OUT THE WEARY SUN. | ALEXIAS SECONDE ELEGIE | 19 | 52 335 | 207 |
| OFT HAVE THESE ARMES THY CRADLE ENVIED, | LUKE 2. QUAERIT JESUM | 27 | MS 379 | 11 |
| OFT TO THY EASY EARES HATH THIS SHRILL TONGUE | LUKE 2. QUAERIT JESUM | 29 | MS 379 | 11 |
| OFT HAVE I WRAPT THY SLUMBERS IN SOFT AIRES. | LUKE 2. QUAERIT JESUM | 31 | MS 379 | 11 |
| OFT HATH THIS HAND THOSE SILKEN CASEMENTS KEPT, | LUKE 2. QUAERIT JESUM | 33 | MS 379 | 11 |
| OFT HAVE MY HUNGRY KISSES MADE THINE EYES | LUKE 2. QUAERIT JESUM | 35 | MS 379 | 11 |
| OFT HAVE I SPOILD MY KISSES DAINTIEST DIET, | LUKE 2. QUAERIT JESUM | 37 | MS 379 | 11 |
| OFT FROM THIS BREAST TO THINE MY LOVE-TOST HEART | LUKE 2. QUAERIT JESUM | 39 | MS 379 | 11 |
| OFT MY SOULE HAVE I BIN GLAD TO SEEKE | LUKE 2. QUAERIT JESUM | 41 | MS 379 | 11 |
| OFT HAVE THESE ARMES (ALAS.) SHOW'D TO THESE EYES | LUKE 2. QUAERIT JESUM | 43 | MS 379 | 11 |
| AS IF THE OFT DEPARTING SUNNE HAD DY'D. | AN ELEGIE ON DR PORTER | 26 | MS 335 | 476 |

OFTEN

| | | | | |
|---|---|---|---|---|
| BY OFTEN KISSING THEM, AND NOW BEGUN | UPON DEATH OF HERRYS | 21 | 46 167 | 466 |
| AND SO IN EACH CHILD OFTEN PROVE A MOTHER. | UPON YORKE HIS BIRTH | 101 | 46 176 | 500 |
| THOSE SWEET AIRES THAT OFTEN SLEW MEE. | OUT OF THE ITALIAN (1) | 51 | 46 188 | 545 |
| TO WHOM HEAVENS LAMPES OFTEN IN SILENT NIGHT | UPON KINGS CORONATION | 27 | MS 389 | 454 |
| THEY OFTEN KIST, & IN THE SUGRED PLACE | AN ELEGY MR STANNINOW | 40 | MS 394 | 473 |

OINTMENT

| | | | | |
|---|---|---|---|---|
| HOW MY HEAD IN OINTMENT SWIMS. | PSALME 23 | 55 | 46 102 | 5 |

OLD

| | | | | |
|---|---|---|---|---|
| LIVE TO BEE OLD AND STILL A MAN. | IN PRAISE OF LESSIUS | 46 | 46 156 | 510 |
| MISCHIFES OLD MASTER, CLOSE ABOUT HIM CLINGS | SOSPETTO D'HERODE | 36 | 46 109 | 216 |
| AND FOR HIS OLD FAIRE ROABES OF LIGHT, HEE WEARES | SOSPETTO D'HERODE | 43 | 46 109 | 216 |

PAGE 292

| | | | | |
|---|---|---|---|---|
| THROUGH CLOUDS OF INFANT FLESH. THAT HEE THE OLD | SOSPETTO D'HERODE | 178 | 46 109 | 216 |
| THE SCEPTER, WHICH OF OLD GREAT DAVID SWAID. | SOSPETTO D'HERODE | 402 | 46 109 | 216 |
| (THAT OLD DRY STOCKE) A DESPAIR'D BRANCH IS SPRUNG | SOSPETTO D'HERODE | 434 | 46 109 | 216 |
| HAD SOWNE OF OLD THESE DOUBTS IN HIS DEEPE BREST. | SOSPETTO D'HERODE | 498 | 46 109 | 216 |
| THOSE THY OLD SOULDIERS, STOUT AND TALL | IN MEMORY OF LADY MADRE TERESA | 4 | 46 131 | 52 |
| ANGELLS THY OLD FRIENDS THERE SHALL GREET THEE, | IN MEMORY OF LADY MADRE TERESA | 138 | 46 131 | 52 |
| ALL THY OLD WOES SHALL NOW SMILE ON THEE. | IN MEMORY OF LADY MADRE TERESA | 146 | 46 131 | 52 |
| URNS. LIKE GODS SANCTUARIES THEY LOOKT OF OLD. | ON A TREATISE OF CHARITY | 36 | 46 137 | 69 |
| AND FRUITFULL CHARITIES FULL BREASTS (OF OLD) | ON A TREATISE OF CHARITY | 55 | 46 137 | 69 |
| IMAGIN'D HIM EXCEEDING OLD. | HIS EPITAPH (HERRYS) | 12 | 46 172 | 471 |
| UPON THE STOOPED SHOULDERS OF OLD TIME. | TO THE MORNING | 28 | 46 183 | 497 |
| CAN CROWNE OLD WINTERS HEAD WITH FLOWERS. | WISHES SUPPOSED MISTRESSE | 90 | 46 195 | 479 |
| PROGRESSIONS 'TWIXT WHOSE TERMES POOR TIME GROWS OLD. | UPON TWO GREENE APRICOCKES | 16 | 48 220 | 494 |
| BECAUSE SHEE BREAKES THE YEARES OLD RAIGNE | THOUGH NOW 'TIS NEITHER | 16 | MS 397 | 492 |
| WHEN THY OLD FREINDS OF FIRE, ALL FULL OF THEE, | TO THE NAME OF JESUS | 198 | 52 239 | 30 |
| IN THE AETERNITY OF THY OLD CARES. | CHARITAS NIMIA | 32 | 52 280 | 48 |
| THOSE THY OLD SOULDIERS, GREAT & TALL. | TERESA | 4 | 52 315 | 52 |
| ANGELS, THY OLD FREINDS, THERE SHALL GREET THEE | TERESA | 137 | 52 315 | 52 |
| ALL THY OLD WOES SHALL NOW SMILE ON THEE | TERESA | 145 | 52 315 | 52 |
| MY WATRY HOUR-GLASSE HATH OLD TIMES OUTRUNNE. | ALEXIAS SECONDE ELEGIE | 20 | 52 335 | 207 |
| LIVE TO BE OLD, AND STILL A MAN. | TEMPERANCE | 44 | 52 342 | 510 |
| FROM HIS OLD FATHER. THAT MANS BARBAROUS KNIFE | HORATIJ ILLE & NEFASTO | 8 | MS 382 | 530 |
| NOE. 'TWAS OLD DOTING DEATH, WHO, STEALING BY, | AN ELEGY MR STANNINOW | 45 | MS 394 | 473 |
| OF THY OLD GOODNESSE, KNOW THEE NOT FOR THEIRES, | OUT OF GROTIUS | 40 | MS 398 | 198 |
| OLD CLOUDS OF THICKEST BLINDNESSE FLED MY SIGHT | OUT OF GROTIUS | 71 | MS 398 | 198 |

TH'OLD

| | | | | |
|---|---|---|---|---|
| HE CALLS TO MIND TH'OLD QUARRELL, AND WHAT SPARKE | SOSPETTO D'HERODE | 89 | 46 109 | 216 |
| INTO TH'OLD PROPHESIES, TREMBLING TO MARKE | SOSPETTO D'HERODE | 93 | 46 109 | 216 |
| HEE SAW TH'OLD HEBREWES WOMBE, NEGLECT THE LAW | SOSPETTO D'HERODE | 101 | 46 109 | 216 |

OLIVE-CROWNES

| | | | | |
|---|---|---|---|---|
| THE CHOICEST OF HER OLIVE-CROWNES, & PRAISE | UPON KINGS CORONATION | 23 | MS 389 | 454 |

OLYMPIAN

| | | | | |
|---|---|---|---|---|
| OLYMPICK GAMES IN THE' OLYMPIAN PLAINES, | UPON GUNPOWDER TREASON | 21 | MS 386 | 460 |
| TRAVELD TH' OLYMPIAN PLAINES TO FIND RELEIFE. | UPON KINGS CORONATION | 4 | MS 390 | 453 |

OLYMPICK

| | | | | |
|---|---|---|---|---|
| OLYMPICK GAMES IN THE' OLYMPIAN PLAINES, | UPON GUNPOWDER TREASON | 21 | MS 386 | 460 |

OLYMPUS

| | | | | |
|---|---|---|---|---|
| UP TO OLYMPUS STATELY TOPP HE HIES, | UPON KINGS CORONATION | 17 | MS 390 | 453 |

OMEN

| | | | | |
|---|---|---|---|---|
| GAVE OMEN TO HIS INFANT HOWERS, | LOVES HOROSCOPE | 6 | 46 185 | 483 |

OMNIPOTENCE

| | | | | |
|---|---|---|---|---|
| HATH ONELY ANGER AN OMNIPOTENCE | UPON ASSE THAT BORE SAVIOUR | 1 | 46 90 | 19 |
| O THOU THE SPAN OF WHOSE OMNIPOTENCE | OUT OF GROTIUS | 1 | MS 398 | 198 |

ONCE

| | | | | |
|---|---|---|---|---|
| HORACE, SHRILL, AT ONCE, AS WHEN THE TRUMPETS CALL | MUSICKS DUELL | 54 | 46 149 | 535 |
| IN THE MUSITIANS FACE. YET ONCE AGAINE | MUSICKS DUELL | 106 | 46 149 | 535 |
| OF HIS TUN'D ACCENTS. BUT IF ONCE | OUT OF GREEKE CUPID'S CRYER | 28 | 46 159 | 519 |
| HERE, WHERE OUR LORD ONCE LAID HIS HEAD, | UPON SEPULCHRE OF OUR LORD | 1 | 46 86 | 26 |
| ONCE I DID SPELL | ON MARKES OF SAVIOURS WOUNDS | 6 | 46 86 | 28 |
| LOOKE, MARY, HERE SEE, WHERE THY LORD ONCE LAY, | COME SEE WHERE THE LORD LAY | 4 | 46 87 | 27 |
| LOOKE, MARY, HERE SEE, WHERE THY LORD ONCE LAY. | COME SEE WHERE THE LORD LAY | 6 | 46 87 | 27 |
| 'TWAS ONCE LOOKE UP, 'TIS NOW LOOKE DOWNE TO HEAVEN. | ON VIRGINS BASHFULNESSE | 8 | 46 89 | 9 |
| GOD SPAKE ONCE WHEN HEE ALL THINGS MADE, | AND HE ANSWERED NOTHING | 3 | 46 91 | 22 |
| THEY, BOTH AT ONCE THY CONQUESTS BEE. | NEITHER DURST MAN ASKE | 7 | 46 92 | 20 |
| COULD NOT ONCE BLINDING ME,CRUELL,SUFFICE. | SAMPSON TO HIS DALILAH | 1 | 46 102 | 8 |
| WHICH WHEN I LOSE, O MAY AT ONCE MY TONGUE | PSALME 137 | 19 | 46 104 | 7 |
| THAT BREATHES AT ONCE BOTH MAID AND MOTHER. | A HYMNE OF THE NATIVITY | 63 | 46 106 | 76 |
| THEE ALL THE BEAUTIES OF THY ONCE BRIGHT EYES. | SOSPETTO D'HERODE | 74 | 46 109 | 216 |
| HEAV'N SAW US STRUGGLE ONCE, AS BRAVE A FIGHT | SOSPETTO D'HERODE | 255 | 46 109 | 216 |
| AT ONCE, TEN THOUSAND PARADISES | ON A PRAYER BOOKE | 107 | 46 126 | 139 |
| HOW MANY HEAVENS AT ONCE IT IS. | ON A PRAYER BOOKE | 117 | 46 126 | 139 |
| MIGHT A WORD ONCE FLYE FROM OUT THEE. | OUT OF THE ITALIAN (1) | 33 | 46 188 | 545 |
| COME ONCE THE CONQUERING WAY. NOT TO CONFUTE | TO COUNTESSE OF DENBIGH | 39 | 52 236 | 146 |
| THAT BREATHES AT ONCE BOTH MAID & MOTHER. | IN HOLY NATIVITY | 89 | 52 246 | 76 |
| LOOSING IT ONCE AGAINE, STUMBLE'ON TRUE LIGHT | IN GLORIOUS EPIPHANIE | 167 | 52 253 | 39 |
| ONCE CALL'D A SUN. | IN GLORIOUS EPIPHANIE | 201 | 52 253 | 39 |
| THOU'HAST SAV'D AT ONCE THE WHOLE WORLD'S LOSSE. | OFFICE H. CROSS MATINES | 27 | 52 265 | 86 |
| THOU'HAST SAV'D AT ONCE THE WHOLE WORLD'S LOSSE. | OFFICE H. CROSS PRIME | 21 | 52 267 | 91 |
| THOU'HAST SAV'D AT ONCE THE WHOLE WORLD'S LOSSE. | OFFICE H. CROSS THIRD | 20 | 52 268 | 93 |
| THOU'HAST SAV'D AT ONCE THE WHOLE WORLD'S LOSSE. | OFFICE H. CROSS NINTH | 17 | 52 271 | 99 |
| HERE WHERE OUR LORD ONCE LAY'D HIS HEAD, | UPON THE H. SEPULCHER | 1 | 52 277 | 26 |
| EVER TO DOE WHAT HE ONCE DID. | LAUDA SION SALVATOREM | 26 | 52 294 | 178 |
| TO BE PAY'D TWICE, OR ONCE, IN VAIN. | DIES IRAE | 40 | 52 298 | 186 |
| OR QUICKLY WOULD, WERT THOU ONCE HERE. | IN GLORIOUS ASSUMPTION B. LADY | 16 | 52 304 | 114 |
| COMBIN'D AGAINST THIS BREST AT ONCE BREAK IN | FLAMING HEART | 89 | 52 324 | 61 |
| AT ONCE TEN THOUSAND PARADISES | PRAYER TO GENTLE-WOMAN | 113 | 52 328 | 139 |
| HOW MANY HEAV'NS AT ONCE IT IS | PRAYER TO GENTLE-WOMAN | 123 | 52 328 | 139 |
| WAS ONCE CALL'D THINE. | LUKE 2. QUAERIT JESUM | 26 | MS 379 | 11 |

## ONE

| | | | | | |
|---|---|---|---|---|---|
| LETT HER SURVIVE THIS DAY, ONCE MOCK HER FATE, | ON GUNPOWDER-TREASON | 9 | MS | 384 | 458 |
| OR THIRSTY TREASON OFFER ONCE TO SIPPE | UPON GUNPOWDER TREASON | 40 | MS | 387 | 461 |
| HE, THAT ONCE BORE THE BEST PART'S GONE. | UPON DEATH OF A FREIND | 16 | MS | 393 | 477 |
| TRAYLES HER PLAYNE DITTY IN ONE LONG-SPUN NOTE, | MUSICKS DUELL | 37 | 46 | 149 | 535 |
| OF CHATT'RING STRINGES, BY THE SMALL SIZE OF ONE | MUSICKS DUELL | 163 | 46 | 149 | 535 |
| YET SUCH A ONE AS (JOVE KNOWES HOW) | OUT OF GREEKE CUPID'S CRYER | 46 | 46 | 159 | 519 |
| ALL ONE GREAT EYE, ALL DROWN'D IN ONE GREAT TEARE. | UPON BISHOP ANDREWES PICTURE | 4 | 46 | 163 | 490 |
| ALL ONE GREAT EYE, ALL DROWN'D IN ONE GREAT TEARE. | UPON BISHOP ANDREWES PICTURE | 4 | 46 | 163 | 490 |
| AND ONE OF THEIR BRIGHT CHORUS MAKE THEE. | THE TEARE | 42 | 46 | 84 | 50 |
| AN EYE, BUT NOT A WEEPING ONE, | THE TEARE | 44 | 46 | 84 | 50 |
| ONE WENT TO BRAG, TH'OTHER TO PRAY. | TWO WENT TO PRAY | 2 | 46 | 89 | 18 |
| ONE STANDS UP CLOSE AND TREADS ON HIGH, | TWO WENT TO PRAY | 3 | 46 | 89 | 18 |
| ONE NEERER TO GODS ALTAR TROD, | TWO WENT TO PRAY | 5 | 46 | 89 | 18 |
| BUT O ME THINKES 'TIS A FARRE GREATER ONE | UPON ASSE THAT BORE SAVIOUR | 11 | 46 | 90 | 19 |
| ONE EYE, A THOUSAND RATHER, AND A THOUSAND MORE | IT IS BETTER TO GO WITH EYE | 1 | 46 | 93 | 16 |
| YET IF THOU'LT FILL ONE POORE EYE, WITH THY HEAVEN AND THEE, | IT IS BETTER TO GO WITH EYE | 4 | 46 | 93 | 16 |
| O GRANT (SWEET GOODNESSE) THAT ONE EYE MAY BE | IT IS BETTER TO GO WITH EYE | 5 | 46 | 93 | 16 |
| TWO DEVILLS AT ONE BLOW THOU HAST LAID FLAT, | UPON DUMBE DEVILL CAST OUT | 1 | 46 | 93 | 14 |
| A SPEAKING DIVELL THIS, A DUMBE ONE THAT. | UPON DUMBE DEVILL CAST OUT | 2 | 46 | 93 | 14 |
| UNMOV'D TO SEE ONE WRETCHED, IS TO MAKE HIM SO. | AND A CERTAINE PRIEST PASSED | 4 | 46 | 94 | 17 |
| HEE'L HAVE HIS TEAT E'RE LONG (A BLOODY ONE) | BLESSED BE THE PAPS | 3 | 46 | 94 | 14 |
| TO SEE BOTH BLENDED IN ONE FLOOD | UPON INFANT MARTYRS | 1 | 46 | 95 | 10 |
| IT IS TOO SWEET TO BE A LONG-LIV'D ONE. | UPON OUR LORDS LAST DISCOURSE | 4 | 46 | 95 | 21 |
| A DROP, ONE DROP, HOW SWEETLY ONE FAIRE DROP | DIVES ASKING A DROP | 1 | 46 | 96 | 18 |
| A DROP, ONE DROP, HOW SWEETLY ONE FAIRE DROP | DIVES ASKING A DROP | 1 | 46 | 96 | 18 |
| SPARE THIS ONE JEWELL. I'LE BE DIVES STILL. | DIVES ASKING A DROP | 4 | 46 | 96 | 18 |
| IS NOT THE SOILE A KIND ONE (THINKE YE) THAT RETURNS | UPON THORNES FROM LORDS HEAD | 7 | 46 | 96 | 23 |
| EACH BLEEDING PART SOME ONE SUPPLIES. | ON WOUNDS OF CRUCIFIED LORD | 4 | 46 | 99 | 24 |
| I COUNTED WRONG. THERE IS BUT ONE, | ON BLEEDING WOUNDS OF LORD | 31 | 46 | 101 | 110 |
| BUT O THAT ONE IS ONE ALL O'RE. | ON BLEEDING WOUNDS OF LORD | 32 | 46 | 101 | 110 |
| BUT O THAT ONE IS ONE ALL O'RE. | ON BLEEDING WOUNDS OF LORD | 32 | 46 | 101 | 110 |
| ONE OF SIONS SONGS TO DAY. | PSALME 137 | 12 | 46 | 104 | 7 |
| GREAT LITLE ONE, WHOSE GLORIOUS BIRTH, | A HYMNE OF THE NATIVITY | 57 | 46 | 106 | 76 |
| WARMES IN THE ONE, COOLES IN THE OTHER. | A HYMNE OF THE NATIVITY | 64 | 46 | 106 | 76 |
| THERE WHERE ONE CENTER RECONCILES ALL THINGS. | SOSPETTO D'HERODE | 34 | 46 | 109 | 216 |
| DISDAINEFULL WRETCH, HOW HATH ONE BOLD SINNE COST | SOSPETTO D'HERODE | 73 | 46 | 109 | 216 |
| HOW HATH ONE BLACKE ECLIPSE CANCELL'D, AND CROST | SOSPETTO D'HERODE | 75 | 46 | 109 | 216 |
| I THANKE YOU ALL, BUT ONE MUST SINGLE OUT, | SOSPETTO D'HERODE | 287 | 46 | 109 | 216 |
| OR RATHER ALL THE OTHER THREE IN ONE. | SOSPETTO D'HERODE | 290 | 46 | 109 | 216 |
| NO ONE SO MERCILESSE AS THIS OF HERS, | SOSPETTO D'HERODE | 306 | 46 | 109 | 216 |
| INHUMANE ERISI-CTHON TOO MAKES ONE. | SOSPETTO D'HERODE | 332 | 46 | 109 | 216 |
| WHAT ONE COMES TO REVEALE WHAT THEY CONSPIRE. | SOSPETTO D'HERODE | 446 | 46 | 109 | 216 |
| IT IS IN ONE RICH HANDFULL, HEAVEN AND ALL | ON A PRAYER BOOKE | 5 | 46 | 126 | 139 |
| A THOUSAND ANGELLS IN ONE POINT CAN DWELL. | ON A PRAYER BOOKE | 8 | 46 | 126 | 139 |
| ONE THAT GLADLY WILL BEE NIGH, | ON MR. G. HERBERTS BOOKE | 7 | 46 | 130 | 68 |
| A THOUSAND COLD DEATHS IN ONE CUP. | IN MEMORY OF LADY MADRE TERESA | 38 | 46 | 131 | 52 |
| SHALL ALL AT LAST DYE INTO ONE, | IN MEMORY OF LADY MADRE TERESA | 112 | 46 | 131 | 52 |
| SHALL OWNE THEE THERE. AND ALL IN ONE | IN MEMORY OF LADY MADRE TERESA | 142 | 46 | 131 | 52 |
| SOULES ARE NOT SPANIARDS TOO, ONE FRENDLY FLOOD | AN APOLOGIE FOR HYMNE (TERESA) | 15 | 46 | 136 | 59 |
| OF BAPTISME, BLENDS THEM ALL INTO ONE BLOOD. | AN APOLOGIE FOR HYMNE (TERESA) | 16 | 46 | 136 | 59 |
| CHRISTS FAITH MAKES BUT ONE BODY OF ALL SOULES, | AN APOLOGIE FOR HYMNE (TERESA) | 17 | 46 | 136 | 59 |
| OUR DUST, THAT IN ONE DRAUGHT, MORTALITY | AN APOLOGIE FOR HYMNE (TERESA) | 45 | 46 | 136 | 59 |
| WHICH THEY THEMSELVES WERE. EACH ONE PUTTING ON | ON A TREATISE OF CHARITY | 19 | 46 | 137 | 69 |
| RISE UP MY FAIRE, MY SPOTLESSE ONE, | ON THE ASSUMPTION | 9 | 46 | 139 | 114 |
| THAT BREAKES FROM ONE OF THESE FAIRE EYES. | AN HIMNE FOR CIRCUMCISION | 28 | 46 | 141 | 37 |
| BUT IN THY FAIREST EYES FIND TWO FOR ONE. | AN HIMNE FOR CIRCUMCISION | 38 | 46 | 141 | 37 |
| AND FATES WHOLE LOTTERY IS ONE BLANKE TO HER. | ON HOPE | 74 | 46 | 143 | 71 |
| ONE FACE MORE FUGITIVE THEN ALL THEY. | ON HOPE | 88 | 46 | 143 | 71 |
| O DOE THOU WATER IT WITH ONE KIND TEARE. | UPON DEATH OF HERRYS | 42 | 46 | 167 | 466 |
| AND WITH THE RUSH OF ONE RUDE BLAST, | UPON DEATH OF DESIRED HERRYS | 43 | 46 | 168 | 467 |
| IN BRIEFE, IF ANY ONE WERE FREE, | ANOTHER ON HERRYS | 53 | 46 | 170 | 469 |
| HEE WAS THAT ONE, AND ONELY HE. | ANOTHER ON HERRYS | 54 | 46 | 170 | 469 |
| BECAUSE THEY BOTH LIV'D BUT ONE LIFE. | AN EPITAPH HUSBAND AND WIFE | 6 | 46 | 174 | 478 |
| THIS POSTURE IS THE BRAVE ONE. THIS THAT LYES | UPON STANINOUGH'S DEATH | 27 | 46 | 175 | 475 |
| EACH ONE AN AGES LABOUR, THAT THY DAYES | UPON YORKE HIS BIRTH | 11 | 46 | 176 | 500 |
| BOTH LAWRELS LIVE INTO ONE WREATH, AND WOOE | UPON YORKE HIS BIRTH | 38 | 46 | 176 | 500 |
| THEIR ROSIE BEAMES, SO THAT THE MORNE FOR ONE | UPON YORKE HIS BIRTH | 57 | 46 | 176 | 500 |
| LIKE WERE THE PEARLES THEY WEPT, SO LIKE THAT ONE | UPON YORKE HIS BIRTH | 64 | 46 | 176 | 500 |
| OF ONE COY PHOENIX, WHILE WE HAVE A BROOD | UPON YORKE HIS BIRTH | 87 | 46 | 176 | 500 |
| THOU CHEAT'ST US FORD, MAK'ST ONE SEEME TWO BY ART. | UPON FORD'S TRAGEDYES | 1 | 46 | 181 | 495 |
| AND STROAKE HIS RADIANT CHEEKES. ONE TIMELY KISSE | TO THE MORNING | 37 | 46 | 183 | 497 |
| ONE BRIGHT SMILE TO CLEERE THE WEATHER. | OUT OF THE ITALIAN (1) | 27 | 46 | 188 | 545 |
| WOULD ANY ONE THE TRUE CAUSE FIND | OUT OF THE ITALIAN (3) | 1 | 46 | 190 | 549 |
| 'TIS THIS. LISTNING ONE DAY TOO LONG, | OUT OF THE ITALIAN (3) | 3 | 46 | 190 | 549 |
| TO THAT ONE SENSE, MADE ALL ELSE THRALL. | OUT OF THE ITALIAN (3) | 7 | 46 | 190 | 549 |
| ONE WHOSE CONSCIENCE WAS A THING, | AN EPITAPH UPON ASHTON | 5 | 46 | 192 | 464 |
| ONE OF THOSE FEW THAT IN THIS TOWNE. | AN EPITAPH UPON ASHTON | 7 | 46 | 192 | 464 |
| YETT IN THESE LEAVES (FAIRE ONE) THERE LYES | THOUGH NOW 'TIS NEITHER | 3 | MS | 397 | 492 |
| FAIR ONE, IT IS YOUR FATE. AND BRINGS | TO COUNTESSE OF DENBIGH | 53 | 52 | 236 | 146 |
| ONE LITTLE WORLD OR TWO | TO THE NAME OF JESUS | 24 | 52 | 239 | 30 |
| AND LOOSE THEM INTO ONE OF LOVE. | TO THE NAME OF JESUS | 87 | 52 | 239 | 30 |
| AND IN THE WEALTH OF ONE RICH WORD PROCLAIM | TO THE NAME OF JESUS | 95 | 52 | 239 | 30 |
| WELLCOME, ALL WONDERS IN ONE SIGHT. | IN HOLY NATIVITY | 79 | 52 | 246 | 76 |
| GREAT LITTLE ONE! WHOSE ALL-EMBRACING BIRTH | IN HOLY NATIVITY | 83 | 52 | 246 | 76 |
| WARMES IN THE ONE, COOLES IN THE OTHER. | IN HOLY NATIVITY | 90 | 52 | 246 | 76 |
| THAT BREAKES FROM ONE OF THESE BRIGHT EYES. | NEW YEAR'S DAY | 28 | 52 | 251 | 37 |
| THE WORLD'S ONE, ROUND, AETERNALL YEAR. | IN GLORIOUS EPIPHANIE | 27 | 52 | 253 | 39 |
| IS ONE CONSISTENT SOLID SMILE. | IN GLORIOUS EPIPHANIE | 31 | 52 | 253 | 39 |
| FOR THAT ONE ECLIPSE HE MADE | IN GLORIOUS EPIPHANIE | 119 | 52 | 253 | 39 |
| ALL WOES INTO ONE CRUCIFIX. | OFFICE H. CROSS SIXT | 8 | 52 | 270 | 97 |

| | | | | | |
|---|---|---|---|---|---|
| 'CAUSE, THOUGH A HARD & COLD ONE, YET IT IS THINE OWNE. | OFFICE H. CROSS COMPLINE | 12 | 52 | 274 | 105 |
| AND CRY WITH ONE ACCORD | OFFICE H. CROSS COMPLINE | 24 | 52 | 274 | 105 |
| THY LIFE IS ONE LONG DEBT | VEXILLA REGIS | 4 | 52 | 277 | 156 |
| SO FAST FOR ONE SOFT BREST. | SANCTA MARIA DOLORUM | 18 | 52 | 283 | 162 |
| DISCOURSE ALTERNATE WOUNDS TO ONE ANOTHER. | SANCTA MARIA DOLORUM | 24 | 52 | 283 | 162 |
| ONE SINGLE WOUND SHOULD NOT HAVE LEFT FOR YOU. | SANCTA MARIA DOLORUM | 80 | 52 | 283 | 162 |
| WOUNDS, AND BECOME ONE CRUCIFIX. | SANCTA MARIA DOLORUM | 100 | 52 | 283 | 162 |
| I COUNTED WRONG. THERE IS BUT ONE. | UPON BLEEDING CRUCIFIX | 27 | 52 | 288 | 110 |
| BUT O THAT ONE IS ONE ALL ORE. | UPON BLEEDING CRUCIFIX | 28 | 52 | 288 | 110 |
| BUT O THAT ONE IS ONE ALL ORE. | UPON BLEEDING CRUCIFIX | 28 | 52 | 288 | 110 |
| IS NOT THE SOILE A KIND ONE, WHICH RETURNES | UPON CROWNE OF THORNS | 5 | 52 | 290 | 23 |
| BUT STILL IN BOTH ONE CHRIST HE IS. | LAUDA SION SALVATOREM | 42 | 52 | 294 | 178 |
| LET ONE, OR ONE THOUSAND BE | LAUDA SION SALVATOREM | 45 | 52 | 294 | 178 |
| LET ONE, OR ONE THOUSAND BE | LAUDA SION SALVATOREM | 45 | 52 | 294 | 178 |
| THE CAVES OF NIGHT ANSWER ONE CALL. | DIES IRAE | 16 | 52 | 298 | 186 |
| HAIL, MOST HIGH, MOST HUMBLE ONE. | O GLORIOSA DOMINA | 1 | 52 | 302 | 194 |
| E'RE SHE BORE ANY ONE, SLEW ALL. | O GLORIOSA DOMINA | 12 | 52 | 302 | 194 |
| OF ONE FORBIDDEN BITT. | O GLORIOSA DOMINA | 16 | 52 | 302 | 194 |
| RISE UP, MY FAIR, MY SPOTTLESSE ONE. | IN GLORIOUS ASSUMPTION B. LADY | 9 | 52 | 304 | 114 |
| FOUNTAIN & GARDEN IN ONE FACE. | WEEPER | 90 | 52 | 307 | 120 |
| A THOUSAND COLD DEATHS IN ONE CUP. | TERESA | 38 | 52 | 315 | 52 |
| SHALL ALL AT LAST DY INTO ONE, | TERESA | 111 | 52 | 315 | 52 |
| SHALL OWN THEE THERE, AND ALL IN ONE | TERESA | 141 | 52 | 315 | 52 |
| SOULS ARE NOT SPANIARDS TOO, ONE FREINDLY FLOUD | AN APOLOGIE FOR (TERESA) HYMNE | 15 | 52 | 322 | 59 |
| CHRIST'S FAITH MAKES BUT ONE BODY OF ALL SOULES | AN APOLOGIE FOR (TERESA) HYMNE | 17 | 52 | 322 | 59 |
| OUR DUST, THAT AT ONE DRAUGHT, MORTALITY | AN APOLOGIE FOR (TERESA) HYMNE | 45 | 52 | 322 | 59 |
| ONE WOULD SUSPECT THOU MEANT'ST TO PAINT | FLAMING HEART | 25 | 52 | 324 | 61 |
| NOT ONE LOOSE SHAFT BUT LOVE'S WHOLE QUIVER. | FLAMING HEART | 70 | 52 | 324 | 61 |
| AND WALK THROUGH ALL TONGUES ONE TRIUMPHANT FLAME | FLAMING HEART | 78 | 52 | 324 | 61 |
| (FAIR ONE) FROM THY KIND HANDS | PRAYER TO GENTLE-WOMAN | 7 | 52 | 328 | 139 |
| IT IS, IN ONE CHOISE HANDFULL, HEAVENN, & ALL | PRAYER TO GENTLE-WOMAN | 11 | 52 | 328 | 139 |
| TEN THOUSAND ANGELS IN ONE POINT CAN DWELL. | PRAYER TO GENTLE-WOMAN | 14 | 52 | 328 | 139 |
| AND VENTURE TO SPEAK ONE GOOD WORD | TO SAME CONCERNING CHOISE | 6 | 52 | 331 | 66 |
| BOTH MIXT AT LAST THEIR BLOOD IN ONE RICH BED | ALEXIAS THIRD ELEGIE | 47 | 52 | 336 | 209 |
| 'CAUSE THEY BOTH LIVED BUT ONE LIFE. | AN EPITAPH UPON MARRIED COUPLE | 6 | 52 | 339 | 478 |
| THIS POSTURE IS THE BRAVE ONE THIS THAT LYES | DEATH'S LECTURE | 29 | 52 | 340 | 475 |
| THIS RARE ONE, READER, WOULDST THOU SEE. | TEMPERANCE | 51 | 52 | 342 | 510 |
| FORTUNE'S WHOLE LOTTERY IS ONE BLANK TO HER. | (ON) HOPE | 34 | 52 | 345 | 71 |
| ONE FACE MORE FUGITIVE THEN ALL THEY. | (ON) HOPE | 48 | 52 | 345 | 71 |
| (WHEN ONE POOR SIGH SENDS FOR HIM DOWN) | AGAINST IRRESOLUTION AND DELAY | 74 | 52 | 347 | 146 |
| DID EVER GREIFE, & JOY IN ONE POORE HEART | LUKE 2. QUAERIT JESUM | 3 | MS | 379 | 11 |
| ONE SMILE AT HOME. | LUKE 2. QUAERIT JESUM | 14 | MS | 379 | 11 |
| IN IT THERE SATE BUT ONE SOLE DART. | IN CICATRICES DOMINI JESU | 9 | MS | 381 | 27 |
| A PEIRCING ONE. HIS PEIRCED HEART. | IN CICATRICES DOMINI JESU | 10 | MS | 381 | 27 |
| SHALL WITH ONE FLASH OF LIGHTING BE STRUCK BLIND. | ON GUNPOWDER-TREASON | 32 | MS | 384 | 458 |
| SOE FOULE, ONE MINUTES LIGHT HAD IT BUT SEENE, | UPON GUNPOWDER TREASON | 13 | MS | 386 | 460 |
| DARES HUNGRY DEATH SNATCH OF ONE CHERRY LIPP. | UPON GUNPOWDER TREASON | 39 | MS | 387 | 461 |
| ONE DROPP OF THIS PURE NECTAR, WHICH DOTH FLOW | UPON GUNPOWDER TREASON | 41 | MS | 387 | 461 |
| AND SNATCH'D AWAY THE BANQUETT. EVERY ONE | UPON GUNPOWDER TREASON | 54 | MS | 387 | 461 |
| THE WORLD WILL BE ONE OCEAN, ONE GREAT TEARE. | UPON KINGS CORONATION | 42 | MS | 389 | 454 |
| THE WORLD WILL BE ONE OCEAN, ONE GREAT TEARE. | UPON KINGS CORONATION | 42 | MS | 389 | 454 |
| DROP DOWNE ONE SPARKE OF GLORY, & THEY'L PROVE | UPON BIRTH PRINCESSE E | 19 | MS | 391 | 456 |
| HAD YOU, LIKE OUR GREAT SUNNE, STAMPED BUT ONE | UPON BIRTH PRINCESSE E | 27 | MS | 391 | 456 |
| HAD YOU BUT DRAWNE ONE LIVELY COPPY FORTH, | UPON BIRTH PRINCESSE E | 29 | MS | 391 | 456 |
| BUT WITH ONE CORDIALL SMILE. FOR (LOE) THAT POWER | EX EUPHORMIONE | 4 | MS | 392 | 525 |
| KIND WINTER'S GUIFT, & IN A GREENE ONE DIGHT. | AN ELEGY MR STANNINOW | 6 | MS | 394 | 473 |
| 'TWAS NOT THE FROZEN ZONE, ONE SPARKE OF FIRE, | AN ELEGY MR STANNINOW | 31 | MS | 394 | 473 |
| (FAIRE ONE) THESE TENDER LEAVES DOE TREMBLING STAND. | AT TH' IVORY TRIBUNALL | 2 | MS | 397 | 492 |
| THE SEARCH OF ONE CHILD (CRUELL INDUSTRY.) | OUT OF GROTIUS | 27 | MS | 398 | 198 |

TH'ONE

| | | | | | |
|---|---|---|---|---|---|
| THAT TH'ONE SPAKE, OR THAT TH'OTHER HELD HIS PEACE. | UPON DUMBE DEVILL CAST OUT | 4 | 46 | 93 | 14 |

ONES

| | | | | | |
|---|---|---|---|---|---|
| WE (PRETIOUS ONES) IN YOU HAVE WON | IN GLORIOUS EPIPHANIE | 73 | 52 | 253 | 39 |

ONLY

| | | | | | |
|---|---|---|---|---|---|
| 'TWAS ONLY PARADICE, 'TIS ONELY THOU. | UPON TWO GREENE APRICOCKES | 19 | 48 | 220 | 494 |
| TO KISSE HIM ONLY AS THEIR ROD | IN GLORIOUS EPIPHANIE | 179 | 52 | 253 | 39 |
| LEAVING HER ONLY SO MUCH BREATH | SANCTA MARIA DOLORUM | 39 | 52 | 283 | 162 |
| THEN, & ONLY THEN, SHE WEARES | WEEPER | 41 | 52 | 307 | 120 |
| ONLY BE SURE | PRAYER TO GENTLE-WOMAN | 27 | 52 | 328 | 139 |
| WHO ONLY WISH HIS VIRGIN WIFE TO BE. | ALEXIAS THIRD ELEGIE | 24 | 52 | 336 | 209 |
| THE WORLD. ALL-DARING DUST & ASHES. ONLY YOU | DEATH'S LECTURE | 31 | 52 | 340 | 475 |
| ONLY A COSTLYER DISEASE. | TEMPERANCE | 10 | 52 | 342 | 510 |
| ONLY NOT SLOW TO BE UNDONE. | AGAINST IRRESOLUTION AND DELAY | 60 | 52 | 347 | 146 |
| ALL THIS IT ONLY THREATS. THE METEOR LY'D. | ON GUNPOWDER-TREASON | 49 | MS | 384 | 458 |
| FEARE IS AFRAID TO TAST OF. ONLY THIS, | UPON GUNPOWDER TREASON | 45 | MS | 387 | 461 |
| ONLY THE POPE A STOMACK STILL COULD FIND. | UPON GUNPOWDER TREASON | 51 | MS | 387 | 461 |

ONELY

| | | | | | |
|---|---|---|---|---|---|
| ONELY A COSTLYER DISEASE. | IN PRAISE OF LESSIUS | 10 | 46 | 156 | 510 |
| WEEPE THEN, ONELY BE EXPREST | UPON THE DEATH OF A GENTLEMAN | 33 | 46 | 166 | 472 |
| THEN, AND ONELY THEN SHEE WEARES | THE WEEPER | 53 | 46 | 79 | 120 |
| THE OTHER CAST AWAY, SHE ONELY GAVE. | WIDOWES MITES | 4 | 46 | 86 | 21 |
| HATH ONELY ANGER AN OMNIPOTENCE | UPON ASSE THAT BORE SAVIOUR | 1 | 46 | 90 | 19 |
| THY QUEL'D FOES ARE NOT ONELY NOW | NEITHER DURST MAN ASKE | 5 | 46 | 92 | 20 |
| AS IF THEY ONELY MEANT TO BREATH, | NEITHER DURST MAN ASKE | 13 | 46 | 92 | 20 |
| THE DIFFERENCE ONELY .THIS APPEARES, | ON WOUNDS OF CRUCIFIED LORD | 17 | 46 | 99 | 24 |

```
DEATH ONELY BY THIS DAYES JUST DOOME IS FORC'T TO DYE.  EASTER DAY                        15  46 100  26
AND SERVES MY PURER SIGHT, ONELY TO BEAT               SOSPETTO D'HERODE               203  46 109 216
ONELY BEE SURE.                                        ON A PRAYER BOOKE                 21  46 126 139
THEREFORE ONELY GIVE TO DAY,                           UPON DEATH OF DESIRED HERRYS      29  46 168 467
BURNING, ONELY IN HIS LOVE.                            ANOTHER ON HERRYS                 28  46 170 469
HEE WAS THAT ONE, AND ONELY HE.                        ANOTHER ON HERRYS                 54  46 170 469
THE WORLD--ALL DARING DUST AND ASHES.  ONELY YOU       UPON STANINOUGH'S DEATH           29  46 175 475
HER PARDON OR HER SENTENCE.  ONELY BREAKE              UPON YORKE HIS BIRTH             109  46 176 500
HER HOPES ARE CROWN'D, ONELY SHE FEARES THAT THAN,     UPON FAIRE ETHIOPIAN               5  46 183 493
NOT ONELY IN DESPIGHT OF ROME.                         AN EPITAPH UPON ASHTON            18  46 192 464
'TWAS ONLY PARADICE, 'TIS ONELY THOU,                  UPON TWO GREENE APRICOCKES        19  48 220 494
ONELY SUCH STRYNES AS SERVE TO KEEPE                   THOUGH NOW 'TIS NEITHER           19  MS 397 492
(DEAR WOUNDS) & ONELY NOW                              SANCTA MARIA DOLORUM              83  52 283 162
NOR DOE EMBRACES ONELY MAKE A BRIDE.                   ALEXIAS THIRD ELEGIE              28  52 336 209
THESE NEED NOE INVITATION. ONELY THOU,                 UPON GUNPOWDER TREASON            19  MS 367 461

OPEN

THROUGH THE SLEEKE PASSAGE OF HER OPEN THROAT.         MUSICKS DUELL                     38  46 149 535
OPEN THIS BOOKE, FAIRE QUEEN, AND TAKE THY CROWN.      ON A TREATISE OF CHARITY          12  46 137  69
THAT SHUTS NIGHTS DYING EYES, SHALL OPEN MINE.         TO THE MORNING                    46  46 183 497
OPEN SUNNES.  SHADY BOWERS.                            WISHES SUPPOSED MISTRESSE         92  46 195 479
FAIRLY TO OPEN IT, AND ENTER.                          TO COUNTESSE OF DENBIGH            4  52 236 146
THE SHUTTING OF HIS EYE SHALL OPEN THEIRS.             IN GLORIOUS EPIPHANIE            162  52 253  39
THOU SHALT OPEN MY LIPPES, O LORD.                     OFFICE H. CROSS MATINES            3  52 265  86
OF OPEN DEATH & HIDDEN LIFE.                           OFFICE H. CROSS NINTH             10  52 271  99
FAIRLY TO OPEN AND TO ENTER.                           AGAINST IRRESOLUTION AND DELAY     4  52 347 146

OPE

AND NOW TH'ART SET WIDE OPE, THE SPEARE'S SAD ART.    I AM THE DOORE                      1  46  90  17
THUS SET THEM OPE.                                     I AM THE DOORE                     6  46  90  17
THE FLOOD-GATE SHALL BE SET WIDE OPE FOR HIM.          OUR LORD IN HIS CIRCUMCISION       6  46  98   9
BEAUTY LAYES OPE LOVES FORTUNE-BOOKE.                  LOVES HOROSCOPE                   12  46 185 483
THEN WHAT NATURES WHITE HAND SETS OPE.                 WISHES SUPPOSED MISTRESSE         30  46 195 479
LO WE HOLD OUR HEARTS WIDE OPE.                        TO THE NAME OF JESUS             126  52 239  30
(LOVE'S EASTERN WINDOWES) ALL WIDE OPE                 TO THE NAME OF JESUS             146  52 239  30
AURORA SHALL SETT OPE                                  IN GLORIOUS EPIPHANIE             69  52 253  39

OPES

SHEE OPES THE FLOODGATE, AND LETS LOOSE A TIDE         MUSICKS DUELL                     93  46 149 535
AT MID-DAY OPES A PRESENCE WHICH HEAVENS EYE           UPON YORKE HIS BIRTH              70  46 176 500

OPENING

OPENING THE PURPLE WARDROBE OF THY SIDE.               ON CRUCIFIED LORD BLOODY           4  46 100  24
OPENING THE PURPLE WARDROBE IN THY SIDE.               UPON BODY OF OUR LORD              4  52 290  24

OPERATION

NOW ALL THEIR STEELY OPERATION,                        ANOTHER ON HERRYS                 23  46 170 469

OPPORTUNITY

THY TEARE'S SWEET OPPORTUNITY.                         WEEPER                           132  52 307 120

OPPRESSE

LOOKES THAT OPPRESSE                                   WISHES SUPPOSED MISTRESSE         40  46 195 479

SELF-OPPRESSED

AND SELF-OPPRESSED SPARK, THAT HAS SO LONG             IN GLORIOUS EPIPHANIE            135  52 253  39

OPPREST

A WELL CLOATHED SOULE THATS NOT OPPREST,               IN PRAISE OF LESSIUS              23  46 156 510
THOSE STINGS OF CARE THAT HIS STRONG HEART OPPREST,    SOSPETTO D'HERODE                199  46 109 216
THY BOSOME AND MAKE ROOME.  THOU ART OPPREST           UPON YORKE HIS BIRTH               3  46 176 500
THOSE BEAUTEOUS RAVISHERS OPPREST SO SORE              IN GLORIOUS EPIPHANIE             91  52 253  39
SO SIGH TORMENTED SWEETS, OPPREST                      WEEPER                           158  52 307 120
A WELL-CLOTH'D SOUL, THAT'S NOT OPPREST                TEMPERANCE                        21  52 342 510

OPREST

OPREST THE COMMON-PEOPLE OF THE SKYES.                 SOSPETTO D'HERODE                240  46 109 216

OPPRESSION

AND SWEET OPPRESSION, KINDLY CHEATING THEM             SOSPETTO D'HERODE                389  46 109 216

ORACULOUS

THE ORACULOUS DOCTORS MISTICK BILLS,                   IN PRAISE OF LESSIUS               7  46 156 510

TH'ORACULOUS

TH'ORACULOUS DOCTOR'S MYSTICK BILLS.                   TEMPERANCE                         7  52 342 510

ORBS

WHILE THROUGH THE CHRISTALL ORBS CLEARER THEN THEY     ON THE ASSUMPTION                  5  46 139 114
```

## ORBES

| | | | | | |
|---|---|---|---|---|---|
| TILL THE SINGING ORBES AWAKE THEE, | THE TEARE | 41 | 46 | 84 | 50 |
| YE MIGHTY ORBES, AS WELL AS YOU, | TO THE NAME OF JESUS | 104 | 52 | 239 | 30 |
| LONG MADE TH'HARMONIOUS ORBES ALL MUTE TO US | IN GLORIOUS EPIPHANIE | 132 | 52 | 253 | 39 |
| WHILE THROUGH THE CRYSTALL ORBES, CLEARER THEN THEY | IN GLORIOUS ASSUMPTION B. LADY | 5 | 52 | 304 | 114 |
| RAVISH THE DANCING ORBES, MAKE THEM MOUNT HIGHER | UPON KINGS CORONATION | 2 | MS | 389 | 454 |

## ORE

| | | | | | |
|---|---|---|---|---|---|
| OF DALLYING SWEETNESSE, HOVERS ORE HER SKILL, | MUSICKS DUELL | 59 | 46 | 149 | 535 |
| BUT O THAT ONE IS ONE ALL ORE. | UPON BLEEDING CRUCIFIX | 28 | 52 | 288 | 110 |
| I'AM WEDDED ORE AGAIN SINCE THOU ART GONE. | ALEXIAS SECONDE ELEGIE | 3 | 52 | 335 | 207 |

## ORGANS

| | | | | | |
|---|---|---|---|---|---|
| SOUND FORTH, CAELESTIALL ORGANS,LETT HEAVNS QUIRE | UPON KINGS CORONATION | 1 | MS | 389 | 454 |

## ORIENT

| | | | | | |
|---|---|---|---|---|---|
| WESTWARD TO FIND THE WORLDS TRUE ORIENT. | SOSPETTO D'HERODE | 136 | 46 | 109 | 216 |

## ORIENTALL

| | | | | | |
|---|---|---|---|---|---|
| AT TH' ORIENTALL GATES. AND DULY MOCKE | TO THE MORNING | 42 | 46 | 183 | 497 |

## ORIGINALL

| | | | | | |
|---|---|---|---|---|---|
| TO READ MORE LEGIBLE THINE ORIGINALL RAY. | IN GLORIOUS EPIPHANIE | 211 | 52 | 253 | 39 |
| HOME TO THE ORIGINALL SOURSE OF LIGHT & INTELLECTUALL | DESCRIPTION RELIGIOUS HOUSE | 39 | 52 | 338 | 213 |

## ORION

| | | | | | |
|---|---|---|---|---|---|
| ARE CHEATED OF THEIR PAINES. ORION THINKES | HORATIJ ILLE E NEFASTO | 55 | MS | 362 | 530 |

## ORNAMENT

| | | | | | |
|---|---|---|---|---|---|
| ART AND ORNAMENT THE SHAME. | WISHES SUPPOSED MISTRESSE | 99 | 46 | 195 | 479 |

## ORNAMENTS

| | | | | | |
|---|---|---|---|---|---|
| THEIR UGLY ORNAMENTS ARE THE BLOODY STAINES, | SOSPETTO D'HERODE | 311 | 46 | 109 | 216 |
| THE WALLS, (ABOMINABLE ORNAMENTS.) | SOSPETTO D'HERODE | 322 | 46 | 109 | 216 |

## ORPHAN

| | | | | | |
|---|---|---|---|---|---|
| PEACE IS AN ORPHAN NOW. HER FATHER'S DEAD. | AN ELEGIE ON DR PORTER | 16 | MS | 395 | 476 |

## OSYRIS

| | | | | | |
|---|---|---|---|---|---|
| THE ALTAR-STALL'D OX, FATT OSYRIS NOW | IN GLORIOUS EPIPHANIE | 96 | 52 | 253 | 39 |

## OTHER

| | | | | | |
|---|---|---|---|---|---|
| APPEAR'D WITH OTHER LADING, FOR HER BREST | THE BEGINNING OF HELIODORUS | 12 | 46 | 158 | 517 |
| AS HEAVENS OTHER SPANGLES DOE. | THE WEEPER | 16 | 46 | 79 | 120 |
| THE OTHER CAST AWAY, SHE ONELY GAVE. | WIDDOWES MITES | 4 | 46 | 86 | 21 |
| THE OTHER TO THE ALTARS GOD. | TWO WENT TO PRAY | 6 | 46 | 89 | 18 |
| SAVE THOSE OF FEARE, NO OTHER BANDS FEARE I. | I AM READY NOT ONELY BOUND | 3 | 46 | 98 | 29 |
| NOR OTHER DEATH THEN THIS. THE FEARE TO DYE. | I AM READY NOT ONELY BOUND | 4 | 46 | 98 | 29 |
| WARMES IN THE ONE, COOLES IN THE OTHER. | A HYMNE OF THE NATIVITY | 64 | 46 | 106 | 76 |
| OTHER THEN WHAT THEIR OWNE BLEST BEAUTIES BRING. | SOSPETTO D'HERODE | 18 | 46 | 109 | 216 |
| YET ON THE OTHER SIDE, FAINE WOULD HE START | SUSPETTO D'HERODE | 153 | 46 | 109 | 216 |
| OR RATHER ALL THE OTHER THREE IN ONE. | SOSPETTO D'HERODE | 290 | 46 | 109 | 216 |
| DOUBTLES SOME OTHER HEART | ON A PRAYER BOOKE | 54 | 46 | 126 | 139 |
| HIMSELFE SOME OTHER WHERE, | ON A PRAYER BOOKE | 86 | 46 | 126 | 139 |
| IF WHAT TO OTHER TONGUES IS TUN'D SO HIGH, | AN APOLOGIE FOR HYMNE (TERESA) | 10 | 46 | 136 | 59 |
| WHAT. THINKE WE TO NO OTHER END, | UPON DEATH OF DESIRED HERRYS | 25 | 46 | 168 | 467 |
| OUT OF NO OTHER SHOP, | WISHES SUPPOSED MISTRESSE | 29 | 46 | 195 | 479 |
| AND HAVE NO OTHER HEAD TO DRESSE. | WISHES SUPPOSED MISTRESSE | 69 | 46 | 195 | 479 |
| NO OTHER NOTE FOR'T, BUT THE NAME WE SING | TO THE NAME OF JESUS | 45 | 52 | 239 | 30 |
| WARMES IN THE ONE, COOLES IN THE OTHER. | IN HOLY NATIVITY | 90 | 52 | 246 | 76 |
| NO MORE THAT OTHER | IN GLORIOUS EPIPHANIE | 68 | 52 | 253 | 39 |
| AH SHE. NOW BY NONE OTHER | SANCTA MARIA DOLORUM | 3 | 52 | 283 | 162 |
| BUT HERE EV'N THAT'S HID TOO WHICH HIDES THE OTHER. | ADORO TE | 26 | 52 | 291 | 172 |
| 'TIS GRATITUDE TO FORGETT THAT OTHER | O GLORIOSA DOMINA | 25 | 52 | 302 | 194 |
| AS HEAVN'S OTHER SPANGLES DOE. | WEEPER | 16 | 52 | 307 | 120 |
| EACH OTHER KISSING & CONFUTING. | WEEPER | 94 | 52 | 307 | 120 |
| IF, WHAT TO OTHER TONGUES IS TUN'D SO HIGH, | AN APOLOGIE FOR (TERESA) HYMNE | 10 | 52 | 322 | 59 |
| DOUBTLESSE SOME OTHER HEART | PRAYER TO GENTLE-WOMAN | 60 | 52 | 328 | 139 |
| HIMSELF SOME OTHER WHERE, | PRAYER TO GENTLE-WOMAN | 92 | 52 | 328 | 139 |
| EACH BIGGE WITH BUSINESSE THRUSTS THE OTHER. | AGAINST IRRESOLUTION AND DELAY | 43 | 52 | 347 | 146 |
| I WAS MISTAKEN. SOME FAIRE SPHAERE, OR OTHER | LUKE 2. QUAERIT JESUM | 21 | MS | 379 | 11 |
| THAT RUNNES IN VIOLETT PIPES. NONE OTHER FOOD | ON GUNPOWDER-TREASON | 64 | MS | 364 | 458 |
| OTHER MENS HUNGER WITH STRANGE FEASTS I QUELL'D | OUT OF GROTIUS | 57 | MS | 398 | 198 |

## TH'OTHER

| | | | | | |
|---|---|---|---|---|---|
| ONE WENT TO BRAG, TH'OTHER TO PRAY. | TWO WENT TO PRAY | 2 | 46 | 89 | 18 |
| WHERE TH'OTHER DARES NOT SEND HIS EYE. | TWO WENT TO PRAY | 4 | 46 | 89 | 18 |
| THAT TH'ONE SPAKE, OR THAT TH'OTHER HELD HIS PEACE. | UPON DUMBE DEVILL CAST OUT | 4 | 46 | 93 | 14 |

OTHER'S

| | | | | | |
|---|---|---|---|---|---|
| FROM THIS WORLD'S EAST THE OTHER'S WEST. | IN GLORIOUS EPIPHANIE | 112 | 52 | 253 | 39 |

OTHERS

| | | | | | |
|---|---|---|---|---|---|
| THEY, THOUGH TO OTHERS NO RELEIFE | THE WEEPER | 77 | 46 | 79 | 120 |
| OTHERS BY DAYES, BY MONTHES, BY YEARES | THE WEEPER | 119 | 46 | 79 | 120 |
| THE OTHERS WANTON WEALTH FOAMS HIGH, AND BRAVE, | WIDOWES MITES | 3 | 46 | 86 | 21 |
| WITH THEE STRONG WINE OF LOVE, LET OTHERS SWIMME | AN APOLOGIE FOR HYMNE (TERESA) | 31 | 46 | 136 | 59 |
| WHILE OTHERS BEND THEIR KNEE, NO MORE SHALT THOU | ON A TREATISE OF CHARITY | 41 | 46 | 137 | 69 |
| SEEM'D BUT THE OTHERS KIND REFLECTION. | UPON YORKE HIS BIRTH | 65 | 46 | 176 | 500 |
| THEY, THOUGH TO OTHERS NO RELIEFE, | WEEPER | 59 | 52 | 307 | 120 |
| OTHERS BY MOMENTS, MONTHS, & YEARES | WEEPER | 155 | 52 | 307 | 120 |
| WITH THEE, STRONG WINE OF LOVE. LET OTHERS SWIMME | AN APOLOGIE FOR (TERESA) HYMNE | 31 | 52 | 322 | 59 |

OUGHT

| | | | | | |
|---|---|---|---|---|---|
| FOR NEVER WERE HIS WORDS IN OUGHT | OUT OF GREEKE CUPID'S CRYER | 23 | 46 | 159 | 519 |
| WHO SAW OUGHT IN THEE, THAT THEIR HATE COULD MOVE. | BUT NOW THEY HAVE SEEN | 4 | 46 | 96 | 21 |
| TO SHEW US OUGHT WORTH LOOKING AT. | A HYMNE OF THE NATIVITY | 10 | 46 | 106 | 76 |
| FOR IN THE LIFE OUGHT ELSE CAN GIVE, | LOVES HOROSCOPE | 45 | 46 | 185 | 483 |
| NOR FLAMES OF OUGHT TOO HOT WITHIN. | WISHES SUPPOSED MISTRESSE | 66 | 46 | 195 | 479 |
| TO THINK OUGHT SWEET BUT THAT WHICH SMELLS OF THEE. | TO THE NAME OF JESUS | 172 | 52 | 239 | 30 |
| TO SHOW US OUGHT WORTH LOOKING AT. | IN HOLY NATIVITY | 10 | 52 | 246 | 76 |
| HAVE FLOW'D TOGETHER. IF OUGHT FURTHER NEEDES | OUT OF GROTIUS | 6 | MS | 398 | 198 |

OUTRAGIOUS

| | | | | | |
|---|---|---|---|---|---|
| O TELL ME THEN, WHAT RUDE OUTRAGIOUS BLAST | AN ELEGY MR STANNINOW | 27 | MS | 394 | 473 |

OUTRUNNE

| | | | | | |
|---|---|---|---|---|---|
| MY WATRY HOUR-GLASSE HATH OLD TIMES OUTRUNNE. | ALEXIAS SECONDE ELEGIE | 20 | 52 | 335 | 207 |

OUT-STARE

| | | | | | |
|---|---|---|---|---|---|
| OUT-STARE THE BROAD-BEAM'D DAYES MERIDIAN) | ON FRONTISPIECE ISAACSONS | 10 | 46 | 191 | 491 |

OUT-STARES

| | | | | | |
|---|---|---|---|---|---|
| OUT-STARES THE LIDDES OF LARGE-LOOK'T TYRANNY. | UPON STANINOUGH'S DEATH | 26 | 46 | 175 | 475 |

OUTSTARES

| | | | | | |
|---|---|---|---|---|---|
| OUTSTARES THE LIDDES OF LARG-LOOK'T TYRANNY. | DEATH'S LECTURE | 28 | 52 | 340 | 475 |

OVERBOUGHT

| | | | | | |
|---|---|---|---|---|---|
| LORD WHAT IS MAN, THAT THOU HAST OVERBOUGHT | CHARITAS NIMIA | 3 | 52 | 280 | 48 |

OVERFLOW

| | | | | | |
|---|---|---|---|---|---|
| THREATNING ALL TO OVERFLOW, | ON BLEEDING WOUNDS OF LORD | 34 | 46 | 101 | 110 |
| BENT ALL TO DROWN & OVERFLOW. | UPON BLEEDING CRUCIFIX | 30 | 52 | 288 | 110 |

OVERFLOW'D

| | | | | | |
|---|---|---|---|---|---|
| BUT WHEN INDEED ALL'S OVERFLOW'D | ON BLEEDING WOUNDS OF LORD | 35 | 46 | 101 | 110 |
| BUT WHEN INDEED ALL'S OVERFLOW'D | UPON BLEEDING CRUCIFIX | 31 | 52 | 288 | 110 |

O'REFLOW'D

| | | | | | |
|---|---|---|---|---|---|
| SPRANG IN THE SPENDING FINGERS, AND O'REFLOW'D | OUT OF GROTIUS | 62 | MS | 398 | 198 |

O'REFLOWD

| | | | | | |
|---|---|---|---|---|---|
| IT WAS THE WITT OF LOVE O'REFLOWD THE BOUNDS | TO THE NAME OF JESUS | 223 | 52 | 239 | 30 |

O'REFLOWING

| | | | | | |
|---|---|---|---|---|---|
| TILL HIS O'REFLOWING PRIDE SUPPRESSE THE FLAME, | SOSPETTO D'HERODE | 487 | 46 | 109 | 216 |

O'RELOOK

| | | | | | |
|---|---|---|---|---|---|
| O'RELOOK ALL LIBANUS. THY LOFTY CROWN | OFFICE H. CROSS EVENSONG | 22 | 52 | 273 | 101 |

O'RELOOKE

| | | | | | |
|---|---|---|---|---|---|
| GREAT NYMPH, O'RELOOKE MY LOWNESSE. HEAV'N YOU KNOW, | EX EUPHORMIONE | 7 | MS | 392 | 525 |

ORELOOKS

| | | | | | |
|---|---|---|---|---|---|
| HOW MY CUP ORELOOKS HER BRIMS. | PSALME 23 | 56 | 46 | 102 | 5 |

OVERLAID

| | | | | | |
|---|---|---|---|---|---|
| E'RE HEBE'S HAND HAD OVERLAID | HIS EPITAPH (HERRYS) | 45 | 46 | 172 | 471 |

O'RE-MASTRING

| | | | | | |
|---|---|---|---|---|---|
| SO MUCH O'RE-MASTRING ALL HIS MIGHT. | OUT OF THE ITALIAN (3) | 6 | 46 | 190 | 549 |

OVERSEE

  HELLS SHOP OF SLAUGHTER SHEE DO'S OVERSEE.        SOSPETTO D'HERODE               291  46 109 216

OVERSHADOW

  OVERSHADOW EVEN THE SHADE.                      PSALME 23                         41  46 102   5

O'RETAKES

  AT LAST HER LISTING EARES THE NOISE O'RETAKES,      SOSPETTO D'HERODE               300  46 109 216

OWE

  MINE IS THE WAGGE. TIS I THAT OWE                  OUT OF GREEKE CUPID'S CRYER        8  46 159 519
  NOTHING. WEE OWE ALL THINGS OUGHT BEE.            AND HE ANSWERED NOTHING           2  46  91  22
  AND THOUGH HERBERTS NAME DOE OWE                   ON MR. G. HERBERTS BOOKE          15  46 130  68
  YET PAY LESSE ARROWES THEN THEY OWE.             WISHES SUPPOSED MISTRESSE       60  46 195 479
  NEEDS MUST MY MISERYES OWE THAT MAN A SPITE        ALEXIAS THIRD ELEGIE           3  52 336 209
  AND TO MY TOUCH DARKE EYES DID OWE THE LIGHT.       OUT OF GROTIUS                72  MS 398 198

OW'ST

  THAT OW'ST A NAME TO MISERY.                      UPON THE DEATH OF A GENTLEMAN   26  46 166 472

OW

  THE REDD, BUT OF THE BLUSH TO THEE THEY OW.        UPON TWO GREENE APRICOCKES       6  48 220 494

OWES

  OWES A DUTY.                                          OUT OF THE ITALIAN (1)         41  46 188 545
  THAT OWES NOT ALL HIS DUTY                       WISHES SUPPOSED MISTRESSE      17  46 195 479
  WHICH TO NO BOXE HIS BEING OWES.                 WISHES SUPPOSED MISTRESSE      36  46 195 479
  HEDGE-QUIRISTERS WHOSE MUSICKE OWES               THOUGH NOW 'TIS NEITHER          18  MS 397 492
  THE STORME OF FATE, TO WHICH HIS LIFE HE OWES.      HORATIJ ILLE & NEFASTO         24  MS 382 530

OWN

  MAY BALSAME BEE FOR THEIR OWN GRIEF.             THE WEEPER                      78  46  79 120
  EACH DROP'S A TEARE THAT WEEPS FOR HER OWN WAST.     TO PONTIUS WASHING HANDS       11  46  94  23
  THINE OWN DEARE BOOKS ARE GUILTY, FOR FROM THENCE    AN APOLOGIE FOR HYMNE (TERESA)  7  46 136  59
  PUT ON THY SELFE IN THINE OWN LOOKS, T' OUR EYES     ON A TREATISE OF CHARITY        2  46 137  69
  (THROUGH ALL YOUR PAINTING) SHOWES YOU YOUR OWN FACE.  UPON STANINOUGH'S DEATH        22  46 175 475
  KEEP THE FREE HEART FROM IT'S OWN HANDS.           TO COUNTESSE OF DENBIGH        20  52 236 146
  TO SEE THEMSELVES THEIR OWN SEVERER SHORE.         TO COUNTESSE OF DENBIGH        26  52 236 146
  LOOK FROM THINE OWN ILLUSTRIOUS HOME,             TO THE NAME OF JESUS          117  52 239  30
  TAKE THINE OWN WINGS, & COME AWAY.                TO THE NAME OF JESUS          150  52 239  30
  WITH BLUSH OF THINE OWN BLOOD THY DAY ADORNING,      TO THE NAME OF JESUS          222  52 239  30
  NEXT TO THEIR OWN LOW NOTHING THEY MAY LY,          TO THE NAME OF JESUS          234  52 239  30
  WE SAW THEE BY THINE OWN SWEET LIGHT.              IN HOLY NATIVITY              36  52 246  76
  LOVE'S ARCHITECTURE IS HIS OWN.                    IN HOLY NATIVITY              47  52 246  76
  MADE HIS OWN BED E'RE HE WAS BORN.                IN HOLY NATIVITY              49  52 246  76
  WE SAW THEE, BY THINE OWN SWEET LIGHT.             IN HOLY NATIVITY              77  52 246  76
  OUR SELVES BECOME OUR OWN BEST SACRIFICE.           IN HOLY NATIVITY             108  52 246  76
  WITH THINE OWN BLUSH THY CHEEKS ADORNING           NEW YEAR'S DAY                  3  52 251  37
  LET HIM EMBRACE HIS OWN BRIGHT TRESSES             NEW YEAR'S DAY                21  52 251  37
  AND LEAVE HER OWN NEGLECTED SUN.                   NEW YEAR'S DAY                32  52 251  37
  THY SELF OUR SUN, THOUGH THINE OWN SHADE.           IN GLORIOUS EPIPHANIE         47  52 253  39
  AND THE GREAT PENITENT PRESSE HIS OWN PALE LIPPS     IN GLORIOUS EPIPHANIE        151  52 253  39
  FROM OUR SINS & HIS OWN SORROWES.                  IN GLORIOUS EPIPHANIE        156  52 253  39
  FORFEIT OUR OWN                                     IN GLORIOUS EPIPHANIE        228  52 253  39
  POINTING US HOME TO OUR OWN SUN                   IN GLORIOUS EPIPHANIE        252  52 253  39
  HIS OWN LOVE'S, & OUR SIN'S GREAT SACRIFICE.        OFFICE H. CROSS NINTH          6  52 271  99
  LO, FOR THEIR OWN HEARTS, THEY REND HIS.           OFFICE H. CROSS EVENSONG       2  52 273 101
  US TO OUR OWN LIVE'S FUNERALL.                    OFFICE H. CROSS COMPLINE       2  52 274 105
  WE NOW WILL OWN NO SHORTER WISH, NOR NAME A NARROWER  OFFICE H. CROSS COMPLINE      18  52 274 105
                                      WORD.

  AND TOOK IT HOME TO HIS OWN HEART.                VEXILLA REGIS                 12  52 277 156
  THY COSTLY EXCELLENCE WITH THY KING'S OWN BLOOD.     VEXILLA REGIS                 30  52 277 156
  THE LAMB WHOM HIS OWN LOVE HATH SLAIN.             VEXILLA REGIS                 44  52 277 156
  O'RE HIS OWN WOUNDS.                                 CHARITAS NIMIA                16  52 280  48
  WHAT MINE OWN MADNESSES HAVE DONE WITH ME.          CHARITAS NIMIA                34  52 280  48
  MY BLUSHES WITH HIS OWN HEART-BLOOD.               CHARITAS NIMIA                62  52 280  48
  PAYES BACK, WITH MORE THEN THEIR OWN SMART          SANCTA MARIA DOLORUM         28  52 283 162
  O YOU, YOUR OWN BEST DARTS                        SANCTA MARIA DOLORUM         71  52 283 162
  THAT WOUNDED BOSOMES THEIR OWN WEAPONS BE.          SANCTA MARIA DOLORUM         74  52 283 162
  THAT STRIVES IN TORRENTS OF IT'S OWN.              UPON BLEEDING CRUCIFIX         8  52 268 110
  THEY SWIMME. ALAS, IN THEIR OWN FLOUD.             UPON BLEEDING CRUCIFIX       12  52 288 110
  FOR THEE TO WEAR, BUT THIS, OF THINE OWN BLOOD.      UPON BODY OF OUR LORD          6  52 290  24
  BUT EACH SITT STILL IN HIS OWN DORE.                ADORO TE                          8  52 291 172
  OF LOVE, WAS HIS OWN LEGACY.                         LAUDA SION SALVATOREM        12  52 294 178
  CONVICTORS OF THINE OWN FULL CUP,                  LAUDA SION SALVATOREM        76  52 294 178
  TO FEED OF THEE IN THINE OWN FACE.                LAUDA SION SALVATOREM        80  52 294 178
  AND WITH THE WINGS OF THINE OWN DOVE               DIES IRAE                      27  52 298 186
  O LET THINE OWN SOFT BOWELLS PAY                   DIES IRAE                      45  52 298 186
  BALSOM MAYBE, FOR THEIR OWN GREIFE.                WEEPER                          60  52 307 120
  THEIR MASTER'S WATER. THEIR OWN WINE.              WEEPER                          72  52 307 120
  BY YOUR OWN SHOWRES SEASONABLY DASH'T              WEEPER                          86  52 307 120
  IN YOUR OWN WELLS DECENTLY WASHT,                   WEEPER                          88  52 307 120
  HER LORD'S BLOOD,  OR AT LEST HER OWN.             TERESA                          56  52 315  52
  THY SELFE SHALL FEEL THINE OWN FULL JOYES           TERESA                         120  52 315  52
  GLAD AT THEIR OWN HOME NOW TO MEET THEE.            TERESA                         138  52 315  52

```
SHALL OWN THEE THERE. AND ALL IN ONE            TERESA                              141  52 315  52
THINE OWN DEAR BOOKES ARE GUILTY. FOR FROM THENCE AN APOLOGIE FOR (TERESA) HYMNE     7  52 322  59
AMONG HIS OWN FAIR SONNES OF FIRE.              TO SAME CONCERNING CHOISE            25  52 331  66
WHO KNOWES MY OWN HEART'S WOES SO WELL AS I.    ALEXIAS FIRST ELEGIE                 14  52 334 204
TAKE THINE OWN MEASURE HERE. DOWN, DOWN, & BOW  DEATH'S LECTURE                      12  52 340 475
NATURE HER OWN PHYSITIAN BE.                    TEMPERANCE                           14  52 342 510
WILT' SEE A MAN, ALL HIS OWN WEALTH,            TEMPERANCE                           15  52 342 510
HIS OWN MUSICK, HIS OWN HEALTH.                 TEMPERANCE                           16  52 342 510
HIS OWN MUSICK, HIS OWN HEALTH.                 TEMPERANCE                           16  52 342 510
KEEP THE FREE HEART FROM HIS OWN HANDS.         AGAINST IRRESOLUTION AND DELAY       14  52 347 146
POOR WATERS THEIR OWN PRISONERS BE.             AGAINST IRRESOLUTION AND DELAY       22  52 347 146
TO FIND THEMSELVES THEIR OWN SEVERER SHOAR.     AGAINST IRRESOLUTION AND DELAY       26  52 347 146
MAKE WINGS AT LEAST OF THEIR OWN WEIGHT,        AGAINST IRRESOLUTION AND DELAY       49  52 347 146
BY TH'EVEN WINGS OF HIS OWN DOVES.              AGAINST IRRESOLUTION AND DELAY       54  52 347 146
LIVES BY HIS OWN LAWS, AND DOES HOLD            AGAINST IRRESOLUTION AND DELAY       55  52 347 146
IN GROSSEST METALLS HIS OWN GOLD.               AGAINST IRRESOLUTION AND DELAY       56  52 347 146

OWNE

HEE LOST THE DAYES HEAT, AND HIS OWNE HOT CARES. MUSICKS DUELL                         6  46 149 535
IN HER OWNE MURMURES, THAT WHAT EVER MOOD        MUSICKS DUELL                        13  46 149 535
TO THEIR OWNE DANCE. NOW NEGLIGENTLY RASH        MUSICKS DUELL                        29  46 149 535
WING'D WITH THEIR OWNE WILD ECCHO'S PRATLING FLY. MUSICKS DUELL                       92  46 149 535
OR TO THY SELFE, SING THINE OWNE OBSEQUIE.       MUSICKS DUELL                       110  46 149 535
OF HIS OWNE BREATH. WHICH MARRYED TO HIS LYRE    MUSICKS DUELL                       117  46 149 535
NATURE HER OWNE PHYSITIAN BEE.                   IN PRAISE OF LESSIUS                 16  46 156 510
WOULDST SEE A MAN ALL, HIS OWNE WEALTH,          IN PRAISE OF LESSIUS                 17  46 156 510
HIS OWNE PHYSICK, HIS OWNE HEALTH.               IN PRAISE OF LESSIUS                 18  46 156 510
HIS OWNE PHYSICK, HIS OWNE HEALTH.               IN PRAISE OF LESSIUS                 18  46 156 510
IN THEIR OWNE BLOODS DEARE DELUGE, SOME NEW DEAD, THE BEGINNING OF HELIODORUS         17  46 158 517
WHO PROV'D THE FEAST TO THEIR OWNE FUNERALL.     THE BEGINNING OF HELIODORUS          28  46 158 517
THEIR MASTERS WATER, THEIR OWNE WINE.            THE WEEPER                           36  46  79 120
FOR HIS OWNE SANDS HEE'L USE THY SEAS.           THE WEEPER                          102  46  79 120
WEEPS FOR IT SELFE, IS ITS OWNE TEARE.           THE TEARE                            18  46  84  50
OF YOUR OWNE COWARDISE                           WHY ARE YEE AFRAID                   10  46  88  15
OF YOUR OWNE DOUBT.                              WHY ARE YEE AFRAID                   14  46  88  15
AND HIS OWNE HOPE                                I AM THE DOORE                        4  46  90  17
OF THY RENOUNE, AND THEIR OWNE SHAME.            NEITHER DURST MAN ASKE               12  46  92  20
TO BEE THE LIFE OF THEIR OWNE DEATH.             NEITHER DURST MAN ASKE               14  46  92  20
FOR THEE TO WEARE, BUT THESE, OF THINE OWNE BLOOD. ON CRUCIFIED LORD BLOODY            6  46 100  24
THEY SWIM, ALAS. IN THEIR OWNE FLOOD.            ON BLEEDING WOUNDS OF LORD            8  46 101 110
THAT STRIVES IN TORRENTS OF ITS OWNE.            ON BLEEDING WOUNDS OF LORD           20  46 101 110
WEE SAW THEE BY THINE OWNE SWEET LIGHT.          A HYMNE OF THE NATIVITY              34  46 106  76
WEE'L BURNE, OUR OWNE BEST SACRIFICE.            A HYMNE OF THE NATIVITY              88  46 106  76
OTHER THEN WHAT THEIR OWNE BLEST BEAUTIES BRING. SOSPETTO D'HERODE                    18  46 109 216
OF HELLS OWNE STINKE, A WORSER STENCH IS SPREAD. SOSPETTO D'HERODE                    54  46 109 216
SHOULD BLEED IN HIS OWNE LAWES OBEDIENCE.        SOSPETTO D'HERODE                   186  46 109 216
TO MAKE THE PARTNER OF HIS OWNE PURE RAY.        SOSPETTO D'HERODE                   218  46 109 216
BOUNDLESSE AND ABSOLUTE. HELL IS THINE OWNE.     SOSPETTO D'HERODE                   272  46 109 216
AND WHILE THE BLACK SOULES BOILE IN THEIR OWNE GORE, SOSPETTO D'HERODE               295  46 109 216
HIMSELFE A STRANGER TO, HIS OWNE HAD MADE.       SOSPETTO D'HERODE                   404  46 109 216
'GAINST THINE OWNE SONS AND BROTHERS THOU HAST STOOD SOSPETTO D'HERODE               453  46 109 216
HEE HIS OWNE FANCY-FRAMED FOES DEFIES.           SOSPETTO D'HERODE                   479  46 109 216
UPON THY CROWNE, WHO GIVES HIS OWNE AWAY.        SOSPETTO D'HERODE                   520  46 109 216
HER OWNES BLOOD, OR AT LEST HER OWNE.            IN MEMORY OF LADY MADRE TERESA       56  46 131  52
THY SELFE SHALT FEEL THINE OWNE FULL JOYES.      IN MEMORY OF LADY MADRE TERESA      121  46 131  52
GLAD AT THEIR OWNE HOME NOW TO MEET THEE.        IN MEMORY OF LADY MADRE TERESA      139  46 131  52
SHALL OWNE THEE THERE. AND ALL IN ONE            IN MEMORY OF LADY MADRE TERESA      142  46 131  52
AND THINE OWNE BEAMES ABOUT THEE. BRING THE BEST ON A TREATISE OF CHARITY              9  46 137  69
WITH THINE OWNE BLUSH THY CHEEKES ADORNING,      AN HIMNE FOR CIRCUMCISION             3  46 141  37
LET HIM EMBRACE HIS OWNE BRIGHT TRESSES,         AN HIMNE FOR CIRCUMCISION            21  46 141  37
HIS OWNE DELICIOUS PHOENIX FROM THE BLEST        UPON DEATH OF HERRYS                 13  46 167 466
WAS BUT THE GLOSSE OF HIS OWNE GOOD.             HIS EPITAPH (HERRYS)                 24  46 172 471
CIRCLED ROUND IN HIS OWNE RAYES.                 HIS EPITAPH (HERRYS)                 40  46 172 471
MORE THEN THEIR OWNE HELICON.                    AN EPITAPH DOCTOR BROOKE              4  46 175 465
TAKE THINE OWNE MEASURE HERE, DOWNE, DOWNE, AND BOW UPON STANINOUGH'S DEATH           11  46 175 475
WITH THINE OWNE GLORYES. AND ART STRANGELY BLEST UPON YORKE HIS BIRTH                  4  46 176 500
OF NOONE WEARE THEIR OWNE SUNSHINE. O THOU BRIGHT UPON YORKE HIS BIRTH                76  46 176 500
O MAYST THOU THUS MAKE ALL THE YEARE THINE OWNE, UPON YORKE HIS BIRTH                 96  46 176 500
FULL GLORY FLAMING IN HER OWNE FREE SPHEARE.     ON A FOULE MORNING                    8  46 181 495
TWICE DI'D IN THINE OWNE BLUSHES, AND DID'ST RUN TO THE MORNING                        9  46 183 497
MY OWNE APOLLO, TRY IF I CAN MAKE                TO THE MORNING                       16  46 183 497
HONOUR ALL PREACHERS. HEARE THEIR OWNE.          AN EPITAPH UPON ASHTON                8  46 192 464
BY ITS OWNE BEAUTY DREST,                        WISHES SUPPOSED MISTRESSE            26  46 195 479
THAT SUNSHINE BY THEIR OWNE SWEET GRACES.        WISHES SUPPOSED MISTRESSE            45  46 195 479
BEE ITS OWNE BLUSH, BEE ITS OWNE TEARE.          WISHES SUPPOSED MISTRESSE            54  46 195 479
BEE ITS OWNE BLUSH, BEE ITS OWNE TEARE.          WISHES SUPPOSED MISTRESSE            54  46 195 479
HER COUNSELL HER OWNE VERTUE BEE.                WISHES SUPPOSED MISTRESSE           102  46 195 479
DEFECTS I DRAW MINE OWNE DULL CHARACTER.         UPON TWO GREENE APRICOCKES           32  48 220 494
POOR WATERS THEIR OWNE PRISONERS BE.             TO COUNTESSE OF DENBIGH              22  52 236 146
'CAUSE, THOUGH A HARD & COLD ONE, YET IT IS THINE OFFICE H. CROSS COMPLINE            12  52 274 105
                                            OWNE.

ALL, MORE AT HOME IN HER OWNE HEART.             SANCTA MARIA DOLORUM                 10  52 283 162
WHAT, BUT THE FAIREST HEAVEN, COULD OWNE THE BIRTH LUKE 2. QUAERIT JESUM               23  MS 379  11
DAWNE THEN TO ME,THOU MORNE OF MINE OWNE DAY,    LUKE 2. QUAERIT JESUM                45  MS 379  11
THE FALL OF ALL THINGS IT PRAESAG'D, ITS OWNE    ON GUNPOWDER-TREASON                 52  MS 384 458
FULL GLORY FLAMING IN HER OWNE FREE SPHAERE.     UPON KINGS CORONATION                14  MS 390 453
TO THEIR OWNE MUSICK, NOR (UNTILL THEY SEE       UPON KINGS CORONATION                23  MS 390 453
AND BREAKE UPON MEE. MY OWNE VIRTUES HEIGHT      OUT OF GROTIUS                       33  MS 398 198
AND 'GAINST RELIGION HER OWNE COLOURS BEARE.     OUT OF GROTIUS                       44  MS 398 198
MINE OWNE WITH STRANGER FASTINGS, WHEN I HELD    OUT OF GROTIUS                       58  MS 398 198
HIMSELFE IN HIS OWNE HELL. AND NOW LETS LOOSE    OUT OF GROTIUS                       79  MS 398 198
```

## OX

| THE ALTAR-STALL'D OX, FATT OSYRIS NOW | IN GLORIOUS EPIPHANIE | 96 | 52 253 39 |

## OXE

| POORE BEASTS. A SLOW OXE, AND A SIMPLE ASSE. | SOSPETTO D'HERODE | 528 | 46 109 216 |

## OYL'D

| THAT USE NO VARNISH, NO OYL'D ARTS, | A HYMNE OF THE NATIVITY | 75 | 46 106 76 |

## PACE

| AND SOBER PACE MARCH ON TO MEET A GRAVE. | TO THE NAME OF JESUS | 202 | 52 239 30 |
| TO KEEP PACE WITH THOSE POWRFULL WORDS. | ADORO TE | 14 | 52 291 172 |
| OR PATTERN FOR THE PACE YOU USE. | AGAINST IRRESOLUTION AND DELAY | 32 | 52 347 146 |
| AN AEQUALL PACE THUS FARRE. THY WORD MY DEEDES | OUT OF GROTIUS | 5 | MS 398 198 |

## PADLED

| HIS HANDS HAVE PADLED IN. HIS HANDS, THAT FOUND | HORATIJ ILLE & NEFASTO | 13 | MS 362 530 |

## PAID

| THE DEBT IS PAID IN RUBY-TEARES, | ON WOUNDS OF CRUCIFIED LORD | 19 | 46 99 24 |
| PAID BACK THE FLESH HE TOOK FOR THEE. | VEXILLA REGIS | 6 | 52 277 156 |

## PAYD

| HOW DEARLY THOU HAST PAYD FOR ME | CHARITAS NIMIA | 64 | 52 280 48 |

## PAY'D

| 'TWAS PAY'D AT FIRST WITH TOO MUCH PAIN, | DIES IRAE | 39 | 52 298 186 |
| TO BE PAY'D TWICE. OR ONCE, IN VAIN. | DIES IRAE | 40 | 52 298 186 |

## PAYED'ST

| OUR PRICE FOR US THOU PAYED'ST. | VEXILLA REGIS | 34 | 52 277 156 |

## PAIN

| USURP'T THE PORTION OF THY PAIN, | VEXILLA REGIS | 14 | 52 277 156 |
| HER SWORDS, STILL GROWING WITH HIS PAIN. | SANCTA MARIA DOLORUM | 29 | 52 283 162 |
| 'TWAS PAY'D AT FIRST WITH TOO MUCH PAIN, | DIES IRAE | 39 | 52 298 186 |
| OF A SWEET & SUBTLE PAIN. | TERESA | 96 | 52 315 52 |
| TO THESE I TALK IN TEARES, & TELL MY PAIN. | ALEXIAS SECONDE ELEGIE | 17 | 52 335 207 |
| STILL ROWLING A ROUND SPHEAR OF STILL-RETURNING PAIN. | DESCRIPTION RELIGIOUS HOUSE | 18 | 52 338 213 |

## PAINE

| SHOULD TAKE THE MARKE OF SIN, AND PAINE OF SENCE. | SOSPETTO D'HERODE | 190 | 46 109 216 |
| OF A SWEET AND SUBTILE PAINE. | IN MEMORY OF LADY MADRE TERESA | 98 | 46 131 52 |
| THE REST POURTRAICTED ARE, THAT 'TIS NOE PAINE | UPON BIRTH PRINCESSE E | 35 | MS 391 456 |

## PAINS

| AND THY PAINS SET BRIGHT UPON THEE. | IN MEMORY OF LADY MADRE TERESA | 147 | 46 131 52 |

## PAINES

| NOW'S BUT THE NONAGE OF MY PAINES, MY FEARES | OUR LORD IN HIS CIRCUMCISION | 9 | 46 98 9 |
| OF SOME MORE PAINFULL THING THEN ALL HIS PAINES. | OFFICE H. CROSS NINTH | 4 | 52 271 99 |
| AND PAINES, HER PANGS & THROES. | SANCTA MARIA DOLORUM | 8 | 52 283 162 |
| AND THY PAINES SITT BRIGHT UPON THEE | TERESA | 146 | 52 315 52 |
| HANDS FULL OF HARTY LABOURS. PAINES THAT PAY | DESCRIPTION RELIGIOUS HOUSE | 19 | 52 338 213 |
| ARE CHEATED OF THEIR PAINES. ORION THINKES | HORATIJ ILLE & NEFASTO | 55 | MS 382 530 |

## PAINFULL

| OF SOME MORE PAINFULL THING THEN ALL HIS PAINES. | OFFICE H. CROSS NINTH | 4 | 52 271 99 |
| OF LOVE TO HIM, WHO ON THIS PAINFULL TREE | VEXILLA REGIS | 5 | 52 277 156 |

## PAINT

| I PAINT SO ILL, MY PEECE HAD NEED TO BEE | WITH A PICTURE TO A FRIEND | 1 | 46 156 494 |
| ONE WOULD SUSPECT THOU MEANT'ST TO PAINT | FLAMING HEART | 25 | 52 324 61 |
| PAINT EACH FEATHER, AS IF NEW. | PETRONIJ ALES PHASIACIS PETITA | 8 | MS 382 526 |
| TO PAINT ITS PERFUM'D FACE WITH COLOURS BRAVE. | AN ELEGIE ON DR PORTER | 24 | MS 395 476 |

## PAINTED

| PAINTED AGAINE BY SOME GOOD POESIE. | WITH A PICTURE TO A FRIEND | 2 | 46 156 494 |
| MY LOVE, OR FEIGN'D OR PAINTED SHOULD APPEARE. | WITH A PICTURE TO A FRIEND | 8 | 46 156 494 |
| BUT PAINTED SHAPES, | TO SAME CONCERNING CHOISE | 11 | 52 331 66 |
| (THOUGH YOU BE PAINTED) SHOWES YOU YOUR TRUE FACE. | DEATH'S LECTURE | 24 | 52 340 475 |
| THE PAINTED MEDDOWES WOULD HAVE LAUGHT NOE MORE | UPON GUNPOWDER TREASON | 45 | MS 386 460 |
| HER PAINTED INFANTS, FEDD WITH PLEASENT PAPPE, | AN ELEGY MR STANNINOW | 8 | MS 394 473 |

PAINTER

   PAINTER, WHAT DIDST THOU UNDERSTAND    FLAMING HEART    13  52 324  61

PAINTERS

   BOLD PAINTERS HAVE PUTT OUT HIS EYES.    CHARITAS NIMIA    8  52 280  46

PAINTING

   (THROUGH ALL YOUR PAINTING) SHOWES YOU YOUR OWN FACE.    UPON STANINOUGH'S DEATH    22  46 175 475

PAIR

   EACH HIS PAIR OF SYLVER DOVES.    IN HOLY NATIVITY    106  52 246  76
   SOME SLIPPERY PAIR    PRAYER TO GENTLE-WOMAN    57  52 328 139

PAIRE

   SOME SLIPPERY PAIRE,    ON A PRAYER BOOKE    51  46 126 139
   TO BRING A PAIRE OF MEEK AND HUMBLE EYES.    ON A TREATISE OF CHARITY    48  46 137  69

PAYRE

   EACH HIS PAYRE OF SILVER DOVES.    A HYMNE OF THE NATIVITY    86  46 106  76

PALACE

   SUCH TO THE FRIGHTED PALACE NOW SHEE COMES,    SOSPETTO D'HERODE    399  46 109 216
   AND STILL THY SPATIOUS PALACE RING.    CHARITAS NIMIA    20  52 280  46
   THAT WATCHES AT HIS PALACE DOORES    TO SAME CONCERNING CHOISE    28  52 331  66

PALACES

   MONGST ALL THE PALACES IN HELLS COMMAND,    SOSPETTO D'HERODE    305  46 109 216

PALATES

   THESE PLEASE OUR PALATES. & WHY THESE.    PETRONIJ ALES PHASIACIS PETITA    3  MS 352 526

PALE

   THE PRIMROSES PALE CHEEKE TO DECKE,    THE WEEPER    38  46  79 120
   PALE PROOFE OF HER FELL PRESENCE. TH'AIRE TOO WELL    SOSPETTO D'HERODE    374  46 109 216
   AND IN A PALE GHOST'S SHAPE TO SPARE HIS EYES.    SOSPETTO D'HERODE    416  46 109 216
   FROM THE PALE DUST OF THAT STRANGE SACRIFICE    ON A TREATISE OF CHARITY    18  46 137  69
   SICKNESSE, AND SORROW, WHOSE PALE LIDDS NE'RE KNOW    TO THE MORNING    56  46 183 497
   PALE SONS OF OUR POMONA. WHOSE WAN CHEEKES    UPON TWO GREENE APRICOCKES    3  48 220 494
   POORE FRUITES LOOKE PALE AT THY HESPERIDES.    UPON TWO GREENE APRICOCKES    30  48 220 494
   AND THE GREAT PENITENT PRESSE HIS OWN PALE LIPPS    IN GLORIOUS EPIPHANIE    151  52 253  39
   PALE MANKIND FORTH TO MEET HIS KING.    DIES IRAE    12  52 296 136
   ARE RED WITHOUT & PALE WITHIN.    DIES IRAE    44  52 296 136
   THE PRIMROSE'S PALE CHEEK TO DECK,    WEEPER    44  52 307 120

PALEFAC'T

   WHOM FAINT, & PALEFAC'T FEARE DOTH STILL ATTEND.    UPON GUNPOWDER TREASON    18  MS 387 461

PALE-FAC'T

   BUT HAD THY PALE-FAC'T PURPLE TOOK    FLAMING HEART    27  52 324  61

PALESTINE

   THE FIELDS OF PALESTINE, WITH SO PURE A FLOOD,    SOSPETTO D'HERODE    86  46 109 216

PALFREYS

   GIVING HIS WANTON PALFREYS LEAVE TO PLAY    UPON GUNPOWDER TREASON    20  MS 386 460

PALLACE

   UP, THROUGH THE SPATIOUS PALLACE PASSED SHE,    SOSPETTO D'HERODE    409  46 109 216

PALLAS

   PALLAS SAW VENUS ARM'D AND STREIGHT SHE CRY'D,    UPON THE SAME (VENUS ARMES)    1  46 161 523
   PALLAS BEARES ARMES, FORSOOTH, AND SHOULD THERE BE    ALEXIAS THIRD ELEGIE    39  52 336 209

PALLATS

   ON MY DRY PALLATS ROOFE TO REST    PSALME 137    23  46 104  7

PALSIE

   AN UNIVERSALL PALSIE SPREADING O'RE    SOSPETTO D'HERODE    382  46 109 216

PANEGYRIS

   THY WELL PRONOUNC'D PANEGYRIS.    NEITHER DURST MAN ASKE    20  46  92  20

PANGS

    AND PAINES, HER PANGS & THROES.                    SANCTA MARIA DOLORUM                    8    52  283  162

PANTING

    IN PANTING MURMURS, STILL'D OUT OF HER BREAST      MUSICKS DUELL                          65    46  149  535
    SOME PANTING IN THEIR YET WARME RUINES BLED.       THE BEGINNING OF HELIODORUS            18    46  158  517
    OF A POOR PANTING TURTLE-DOVE.                     TO THE NAME OF JESUS                  108    52  239   30

PANTS

    SOFTER THEN THAT WHICH PANTS IN HEBE'S CUP.        MUSICKS DUELL                         126    46  149  535
    THE WORLDS PROFOUND HEART PANTS. THERE PLACED IS   SOSPETTO D'HERODE                      35    46  109  216

PAPER

    MAKES MANY A MOURNING PAPER PUT ON BLACKE.         UPON STANINOUGH'S DEATH                 2    46  175  475
    MAKES MANY A MOURNING PAPER PUT ON BLACK.          DEATH'S LECTURE                         2    52  340  475

PAPERS

    WITH PEARLY PAPERS CARELESLY BESETT.               AN ELEGIE ON DR PORTER                  8    MS  395  476

PAPPE

    HER PAINTED INFANTS, FEDD WITH PLEASENT PAPPE.     AN ELEGY MR STANNINOW                   8    MS  394  473

PARADICE

    'TWAS ONLY PARADICE, 'TIS ONELY THOU.              UPON TWO GREENE APRICOCKES             19    48  220  494

PARADISES

    AT ONCE, TEN THOUSAND PARADISES                    ON A PRAYER BOOKE                     107    46  126  139
    AND TEN THOUSAND PARADISES                         TO THE NAME OF JESUS                  187    52  239   30
    AT ONCE TEN THOUSAND PARADISES.                    PRAYER TO GENTLE-WOMAN                113    52  328  139

PARAGON

    TO SHADDOW FORTH TH' ADMIRED PARAGON.              UPON BIRTH PRINCESSE E                 42    MS  391  456

PARALLEL

    WHICH POSETH MISCHEIFE'S SELFE TO PARALLEL.        AN ELEGIE ON DR PORTER                 14    MS  395  476

PARALELL

    HOW EVEN TH'AST DRAWNE THIS FAITHFULL PARALELL,    UPON YORKE HIS BIRTH                   50    46  176  500

PARAMOURS

    OF ALL HIS EASTERNE PARAMOURS.                     AN HIMNE FOR CIRCUMCISION              34    46  141   37
    OF ALL HIS EASTERN PARAMOURS.                      NEW YEAR'S DAY                         34    52  251   37

PARAPHRASE

    AND I'LE NOT BLURRE IT WITH MY PARAPHRASE.         UPON BIRTH PRINCESSE E                 60    MS  391  456

PARCAE

    BUT HER BEST HUSWIFES ARE THE PARCAE, WHICH        SOSPETTO D'HERODE                     340    46  109  216
    TO THEE THE PARCAE HAVE GIVEN UP OF LATE           EX EUPHORMIONE                         10    MS  392  525

PARDON

    SCARCE DAWNES, O PARDON, IF I DARE TO SAY          AN APOLOGIE FOR HYMNE (TERESA)          6    46  136   59
    PARDON (BRIGHT EXCELLENCE) AN UNTUN'D STRING,      UPON YORKE HIS BIRTH                  106    46  176  500
    O SPEAKE A LOWLY MUSES PARDON.  SPEAKE             UPON YORKE HIS BIRTH                  108    46  176  500
    HER PARDON OR HER SENTENCE.  ONELY BREAKE          UPON YORKE HIS BIRTH                  109    46  176  500
    THE SINNER'S PARDON & THE JUST MAN'S PEACE.        VEXILLA REGIS                          42    52  277  156
    SCARSE DAWNES.  O PARDON IF I DARE TO SAY          AN APOLOGIE FOR (TERESA) HYMNE          6    52  322   59

PARENT

    PEEPS FROM HER PARENT STEMME,                      THE TEARE                              27    46   84   50
    WHAT OF THY PARENT HEAVN YET SPEAKES IN THEE.      TO THE NAME OF JESUS                   18    52  239   30
    PEEPS FROM HER PARENT STEMME                       WEEPER                                 63    52  307  120

PARENTS

    PARENTS OF SILVER-FORDED RILLS.                    THE WEEPER                              2    46   79  120
    PARENTS OF SYLVER-FOOTED RILLS.                    WEEPER                                  2    52  307  120
    THY DEAREST PARENTS HAVE DESERV'D TO DY.           ALEXIAS THIRD ELEGIE                   18    52  336  209

PARENTAGE

    OF HONEST PARENTAGE OF UNSTAIN'D RACE,             TO PONTIUS WASHING HANDS                6    46   94   23

PARLOUR-SERMONS

    HIS PARLOUR-SERMONS RATHER WERE                    AN EPITAPH UPON ASHTON                 13    46  192  464

PART

| | | | | |
|---|---|---|---|---|
| THE TATLING STRINGS (EACH BREATHING IN HIS PART) | MUSICKS DUELL | 48 | 46 149 | 535 |
| EACH BLEEDING PART SOME ONE SUPPLIES. | ON WOUNDS OF CRUCIFIED LORD | 4 | 46 99 | 24 |
| WHAT NEED THY FAIRE HEAD BEARE A PART | ON BLEEDING WOUNDS OF LORD | 17 | 46 101 | 110 |
| BE IT THY PART, HELLS MIGHTY LORD, TO LAY | SOSPETTO D'HERODE | 263 | 46 109 | 216 |
| READY TO PERSONATE A MORTALL PART. | SOSPETTO D'HERODE | 416 | 46 109 | 216 |
| AGAINST THE GHOSTLY FOE TO TAKE YOUR PART. | ON A PRAYER BOOKE | 13 | 46 126 | 139 |
| LET PRAYER ALONE TO PLAY HIS PART. | ON A PRAYER BOOKE | 28 | 46 126 | 139 |
| NO PART OF THEIR GOOD MORROW. | WISHES SUPPOSED MISTRESSE | 77 | 46 195 | 479 |
| (INFINITE, SINCE PART OF YOU) | TO THE QUEEN | 6 | 48 215 | 501 |
| COME, NERE TO PART. | TO THE NAME OF JESUS | 68 | 52 239 | 30 |
| FOR THOU TOO HAST THY PART | TO THE NAME OF JESUS | 89 | 52 239 | 30 |
| EACH WOUND OF HIS, FROM EVERY PART, | SANCTA MARIA DOLORUM | 9 | 52 283 | 162 |
| WHAT NEED THY FAIR HEAD BEAR A PART | UPON BLEEDING CRUCIFIX | 5 | 52 288 | 110 |
| LOVE'S PASSIVES ARE HIS ACTIV'ST PART. | FLAMING HEART | 73 | 52 324 | 61 |
| AGAINST YOUR GHOSTLY FOES TO TAKE YOUR PART. | PRAYER TO GENTLE-WOMAN | 19 | 52 328 | 139 |
| LET PRAYER ALONE TO PLAY HIS PART, | PRAYER TO GENTLE-WOMAN | 34 | 52 328 | 139 |
| SOUL & BODY PART LIKE FREINDS. | TEMPERANCE | 46 | 52 342 | 510 |
| SOE SOONE CHANGE PART. | LUKE 2. QUAERIT JESUM | 4 | MS 379 | 11 |
| HATH LEAPT, TO PART. | LUKE 2. QUAERIT JESUM | 40 | MS 379 | 11 |
| WITTNESSE THIS MAPP OF BEAUTY. EVERY PART | UPON BIRTH PRINCESSE E | 37 | MS 391 | 456 |
| EACH VERTUE FOR A PART CAME IN. | UPON DEATH OF A FREIND | 20 | MS 393 | 477 |

PART'S

| | | | | |
|---|---|---|---|---|
| HE, THAT ONCE BORE THE BEST PART'S GONE. | UPON DEATH OF A FREIND | 16 | MS 393 | 477 |

PARTED

| | | | | |
|---|---|---|---|---|
| THOUGH, OUR POORE JOYES ARE PARTED SO, | ON THE ASSUMPTION | 37 | 46 139 | 114 |

PARTS

| | | | | |
|---|---|---|---|---|
| THOSE PARTS OF SWEETNESSE WHICH WITH NECTAR DROP, | MUSICKS DUELL | 125 | 46 149 | 535 |
| WEE IN THY PRAISE WILL HAVE OUR PARTS. | ON THE ASSUMPTION | 30 | 46 139 | 114 |
| WE IN THY PRAYSE WILL HAVE OUR PARTS. | IN GLORIOUS ASSUMPTION B. LADY | 45 | 52 304 | 114 |
| O HEART. THE AEQUALL POISE OF LOV'ES BOTH PARTS | FLAMING HEART | 75 | 52 324 | 61 |

PARTING

| | | | | |
|---|---|---|---|---|
| HARKE SHEE IS CALLED, THE PARTING HOURE IS COME. | ON THE ASSUMPTION | 1 | 46 139 | 114 |
| HARK. SHE IS CALL'D, THE PARTING HOURE IS COME. | IN GLORIOUS ASSUMPTION B. LADY | 1 | 52 304 | 114 |
| THAT SEIZ'D THY PARTING SOUL, & SEAL'D THEE HIS. | FLAMING HEART | 102 | 52 324 | 61 |

PARTAKE

| | | | | |
|---|---|---|---|---|
| OR ELSE PARTAKE MY FLAMES | OUT OF THE ITALIAN (2) | 11 | 46 170 | 547 |

PARTHENOPE

| | | | | |
|---|---|---|---|---|
| HOLDS HIGH THE REINE OF FAIRE PARTHENOPE, | SOSPETTO D'HERODE | 26 | 46 109 | 216 |

PARTHIAN

| | | | | |
|---|---|---|---|---|
| THE PARTHIAN STARTS AT ROME'S IMPERIALL NAME, | HORATIJ ILLE & NEFASTO | 27 | MS 382 | 530 |

PARTHIANS

| | | | | |
|---|---|---|---|---|
| BY PARTHIANS BOW THE SOLDJER LOOKES TO DIE. | HORATIJ ILLE & NEFASTO | 25 | MS 382 | 530 |

PARTICULARS

| | | | | |
|---|---|---|---|---|
| WHERE IN SAD PARTICULARS, | ANOTHER ON HERRYS | 43 | 46 170 | 469 |

PARTNER

| | | | | |
|---|---|---|---|---|
| TO MAKE THE PARTNER OF HIS OWNE PURE RAY. | SOSPETTO D'HERODE | 218 | 46 109 | 216 |

PASCHA

| | | | | |
|---|---|---|---|---|
| THE AGED PASCHA PLEADS NOT YEARES | LAUDA SION SALVATOREM | 21 | 52 294 | 178 |

PASCHAL

| | | | | |
|---|---|---|---|---|
| THE MANNA, & THE PASCHAL LAMB. | LAUDA SION SALVATOREM | 68 | 52 294 | 178 |

PASSAGE

| | | | | |
|---|---|---|---|---|
| THROUGH THE SLEEKE PASSAGE OF HER OPEN THROAT. | MUSICKS DUELL | 38 | 46 149 | 535 |
| A QUIET PASSAGE UNDER GROUND. | AN EPITAPH DOCTOR BROOKE | 6 | 46 175 | 465 |
| MUST HAVE A PASSAGE, OR 'TWILL FORCE A WAY. | UPON BIRTH PRINCESSE E | 14 | MS 391 | 456 |

PASSE

| | | | | |
|---|---|---|---|---|
| TO ASKE THE WINDOWES LEAVE, TO PASSE THAT WAY. | ON A PRAYER BOOKE | 70 | 46 126 | 139 |
| ENOUGH, NOW (IF THOU CANST) PASSE ON, | HIS EPITAPH (HERRYS) | 49 | 46 172 | 471 |
| TO PASSE FOR ODORIFEROUS, | TO THE NAME OF JESUS | 180 | 52 239 | 30 |
| YOUR DOWN SO WARM, WILL PASSE FOR PURE. | IN HOLY NATIVITY | 63 | 52 246 | 76 |
| TO ASK THE WINDOWS LEAVE TO PASSE THAT WAY. | PRAYER TO GENTLE-WOMAN | 76 | 52 328 | 139 |
| MAY PASSE ALONG | TO SAME CONCERNING CHOISE | 29 | 52 331 | 66 |

PASSED

| | | | | | |
|---|---|---|---|---|---|
| UP, THROUGH THE SPATIOUS PALLACE PASSED SHE, | SOSPETTO D'HERODE | 409 | 46 | 109 | 216 |

PASSEST

| | | | | | |
|---|---|---|---|---|---|
| MEANE WHILE WHO E'RE THOU ART THAT PASSEST HERE, | UPON DEATH OF HERRYS | 41 | 46 | 167 | 466 |
| BEFORE THOU PASSEST FURTHER ON. | HIS EPITAPH (HERRYS) | 4 | 46 | 172 | 471 |

THAT-PASSEST

| | | | | | |
|---|---|---|---|---|---|
| WHY DOST THOU WOUND MY WOUNDS, O THOU THAT-PASSEST BY | AND A CERTAINE PRIEST PASSED | 1 | 46 | 94 | 17 |

PASSES

| | | | | | |
|---|---|---|---|---|---|
| TIME AS BY THEE HE PASSES. | THE WEEPER | 97 | 46 | 79 | 120 |

PASSENGER

| | | | | | |
|---|---|---|---|---|---|
| PASSENGER WHO E'RE THOU ART, | HIS EPITAPH (HERRYS) | 1 | 46 | 172 | 471 |
| (PASSENGER WHO E'RE THOU ART) | HIS EPITAPH (HERRYS) | 51 | 46 | 172 | 471 |

PASSING

| | | | | | |
|---|---|---|---|---|---|
| FOR WHO SO HARD, BUT PASSING BY THAT WAY | ALEXIAS FIRST ELEGIE | 27 | 52 | 334 | 204 |

PASSIVE

| | | | | | |
|---|---|---|---|---|---|
| THESE THE PASSIVE WEAPONS ARE, | IN CICATRICES DOMINI JESU | 5 | MS | 381 | 27 |

PASSIVES

| | | | | | |
|---|---|---|---|---|---|
| LOVE'S PASSIVES ARE HIS ACTIV'ST PART. | FLAMING HEART | 73 | 52 | 324 | 61 |

PAST

| | | | | | |
|---|---|---|---|---|---|
| TO CROWNE THEIR PAST PREDICTIONS, BOTH HEE LAYES | SOSPETTO D'HERODE | 95 | 46 | 109 | 216 |
| INTANGLES HIS LOST THOUGHTS, PAST GETTING OUT. | SOSPETTO D'HERODE | 192 | 46 | 109 | 216 |
| THE WINTER'S PAST, THE RAINE IS GONE. | ON THE ASSUMPTION | 10 | 46 | 139 | 114 |
| THE WINTER'S PAST, THE RAIN IS GONE. | IN GLORIOUS ASSUMPTION B. LADY | 10 | 52 | 304 | 114 |
| THE WINTER'S PAST. | IN GLORIOUS ASSUMPTION B. LADY | 23 | 52 | 304 | 114 |

PASTURE

| | | | | | |
|---|---|---|---|---|---|
| NOR CHANGE THE PASTURE, BUT THE PLACE | LAUDA SION SALVATOREM | 79 | 52 | 294 | 178 |

PASTURES

| | | | | | |
|---|---|---|---|---|---|
| ON WHOSE PASTURES CHEEREFULL SPRING, | PSALME 23 | 5 | 46 | 102 | 5 |

PATH

| | | | | | |
|---|---|---|---|---|---|
| SPREADS A PATH CLEARE AS THE DAY, | PSALME 23 | 29 | 46 | 102 | 5 |
| PROV'D A NEW PATH OF PATIENT VICTORY. | OFFICE H. CROSS EVENSONG | 25 | 52 | 273 | 101 |
| IN WHAT STRANGE PATH MY LORD'S FOOTSTEPPES BLEED. | ALEXIAS FIRST ELEGIE | 8 | 52 | 334 | 204 |
| THEY FORCE A LILLY PATH THROUGH ROSY MOUNTAINS. | AN ELEGIE ON DR PORTER | 42 | MS | 395 | 476 |

PATHS

| | | | | | |
|---|---|---|---|---|---|
| ABOUT MY PATHS, SO SHALL I FIND | PSALME 23 | 61 | 46 | 102 | 5 |

PATHES

| | | | | | |
|---|---|---|---|---|---|
| TO PAVE HIS PATHES WITH ALL THE GOOD | LOVES HOROSCOPE | 29 | 46 | 185 | 483 |
| THOSE PURE UNTRODEN PATHES CAN SHOW, | THOUGH NOW 'TIS NEITHER | 8 | MS | 397 | 492 |

PATIENCE

| | | | | | |
|---|---|---|---|---|---|
| HAVE SPENT THE PATIENCE OF EXPECTING WEEKES, | UPON TWO GREENE APRICOCKES | 4 | 48 | 220 | 494 |
| OF ALL THIS PRETIOUS PATIENCE. | TO THE NAME OF JESUS | 140 | 52 | 239 | 30 |
| HIGH IN HIS PATIENCE, AS THEIR SPITE. | OFFICE H. CROSS SIXT | 2 | 52 | 270 | 97 |

PATIENT

| | | | | | |
|---|---|---|---|---|---|
| THY FAMES FULL NOISE, MAKES PROUD THE PATIENT EARTH, | SOSPETTO D'HERODE | 29 | 46 | 109 | 216 |
| PROV'D A NEW PATH OF PATIENT VICTORY. | OFFICE H. CROSS EVENSONG | 25 | 52 | 273 | 101 |

PATRON

| | | | | | |
|---|---|---|---|---|---|
| AND TO WHAT PATRON CHUSE TO PRAY. | DIES IRAE | 22 | 52 | 298 | 186 |

PATRONAGE

| | | | | | |
|---|---|---|---|---|---|
| MEE FROM HIS PATRONAGE. I PRAY, HE CHIDES. | TO THE MORNING | 14 | 46 | 183 | 497 |

PATTERN

| | | | | | |
|---|---|---|---|---|---|
| OR PATTERN FOR THE PACE YOU USE. | AGAINST IRRESOLUTION AND DELAY | 32 | 52 | 347 | 146 |

PATTERNE

| | | | | | |
|---|---|---|---|---|---|
| THE PATTERNE OF A PERFECT CREATURE. | UPON DEATH OF DESIRED HERRYS | 8 | 46 | 168 | 467 |
| PROUD IN THE PATTERNE OF THY PRETIOUS YOUTH, | UPON TWO GREENE APRICOCKES | 21 | 48 | 220 | 494 |

|   |   |   |   |   |   |
|---|---|---|---|---|---|
| THAT IN THE PRINCELY PATTERNE SHINES, FROM WHENCE | UPON BIRTH PRINCESSE E | 34 | MS | 391 | 456 |

**PAUSE**

|   |   |   |   |   |   |
|---|---|---|---|---|---|
| THUS SPOKE TH'IMPATIENT PRINCE, AND MADE A PAUSE, | SOSPETTO D'HERODE | 257 | 46 | 109 | 216 |

**PAUSES**

|   |   |   |   |   |   |
|---|---|---|---|---|---|
| AND SNATCHES THIS AGAINE, AND PAUSES THERE. | MUSICKS DUELL | 33 | 46 | 149 | 535 |

**PAVE**

|   |   |   |   |   |   |
|---|---|---|---|---|---|
| TO PAVE HIS PATHES WITH ALL THE GOOD | LOVES HOROSCOPE | 29 | 46 | 185 | 483 |

**STAR-PAV'D**

|   |   |   |   |   |   |
|---|---|---|---|---|---|
| I LEFT MY GLORIOUS FATHERS STAR-PAV'D COURT | OUT OF GROTIUS | 14 | MS | 398 | 198 |

**PAVEMENTS**

|   |   |   |   |   |   |
|---|---|---|---|---|---|
| NO SAILES OF TYRIAN SYLK PROUD PAVEMENTS SWEEPING. | DESCRIPTION RELIGIOUS HOUSE | 3 | 52 | 338 | 213 |

**PAY**

|   |   |   |   |   |   |
|---|---|---|---|---|---|
| TO PAY THE SWEET SUMME OF THY KISSES. | ON WOUNDS OF CRUCIFIED LORD | 14 | 46 | 99 | 24 |
| TO PAY THY TEARES, AN EYE THAT WEEPS | ON WOUNDS OF CRUCIFIED LORD | 15 | 46 | 99 | 24 |
| HEE MARKT HOW THE POORE SHEPHEARDS RAN TO PAY | SOSPETTO D'HERODE | 118 | 46 | 109 | 216 |
| THRICE WILL I PAY THREE TEARES, TO SHOW HOW TRUE | TO THE MORNING | 40 | 46 | 183 | 497 |
| YET PAY LESSE ARROWES THEN THEY OWE. | WISHES SUPPOSED MISTRESSE | 60 | 46 | 195 | 479 |
| OF BEAMES TO DAY, PAY BACK AGAINE TO MORROW, | UPON TWO GREENE APRICOCKES | 28 | 46 | 220 | 494 |
| COME ROYALL NAME, & PAY THE EXPENCE | TO THE NAME OF JESUS | 139 | 52 | 239 | 30 |
| THAT FORFEITURE OF NOON TO NIGHT SHALL PAY | IN GLORIOUS EPIPHANIE | 149 | 52 | 253 | 39 |
| DOES FIRST HIS SCEPTER, THEN HIMSELF IN SOLEMNE TRIBUTE PAY. | IN GLORIOUS EPIPHANIE | 237 | 52 | 253 | 39 |
| O LET THINE OWN SOFT BOWELLS PAY | DIES IRAE | 45 | 52 | 298 | 186 |
| HANDS FULL OF HARTY LABOURS. PAINES THAT PAY | DESCRIPTION RELIGIOUS HOUSE | 19 | 52 | 338 | 213 |
| MINE EYES A TRIBUTARY STREAME SHALL PAY. | ON GUNPOWDER-TREASON | 14 | MS | 384 | 458 |
| WITH TREMBLING LIPPES AN HUMBLE KISSE DO'ST PAY. | AN ELEGIE ON DR PORTER | 6 | MS | 395 | 476 |

**PAYES**

|   |   |   |   |   |   |
|---|---|---|---|---|---|
| NOT A HAIRE BUT PAYES HIS RIVER | ON BLEEDING WOUNDS OF LORD | 25 | 46 | 101 | 110 |
| PAYES BACK, WITH MORE THEN THEIR OWN SMART | SANCTA MARIA DOLORUM | 28 | 52 | 283 | 162 |
| NO HAIR SO SMALL, BUT PAYES HIS RIVER | UPON BLEEDING CRUCIFIX | 21 | 52 | 288 | 110 |

**PAYMENTS**

|   |   |   |   |   |   |
|---|---|---|---|---|---|
| WHAT EVER CAESAR'S PAYMENTS ARE. | GIVE TO CAESAR AND TO GOD | 4 | 46 | 96 | 20 |

**PEACE**

|   |   |   |   |   |   |
|---|---|---|---|---|---|
| 'TWAS TIME TO HOLD THEIR PEACE WHEN THEY, | NEITHER DURST MAN ASKE | 15 | 46 | 92 | 20 |
| TO HOLD THEIR PEACE IS ALL THE WAIES, | NEITHER DURST MAN ASKE | 25 | 46 | 92 | 20 |
| THAT TH'ONE SPAKE, OR THAT TH'OTHER HELD HIS PEACE. | UPON DUMBE DEVILL CAST OUT | 4 | 46 | 93 | 14 |
| GRACE AND PEACE, TO MEET NEW LAIES | PSALME 23 | 33 | 46 | 102 | 5 |
| HEE SAW THE TEMPLE SACRED TO SWEET PEACE, | SOSPETTO D'HERODE | 123 | 46 | 109 | 216 |
| HATE THE SWEET PEACE OF ALL-COMPOSING NIGHT. | SOSPETTO D'HERODE | 496 | 46 | 109 | 216 |
| PEACE SURE WITH PIETY, THOUGH IT DWELL IN SPAINE. | AN APOLOGIE FOR HYMNE (TERESA) | 20 | 46 | 136 | 59 |
| PEACE, GOOD READER, DOE NOT WEEPE. | AN EPITAPH HUSBAND AND WIFE | 7 | 46 | 174 | 478 |
| PEACE, THE LOVERS ARE ASLEEPE. | AN EPITAPH HUSBAND AND WIFE | 8 | 46 | 174 | 478 |
| OF PEACE AND WARRE. THOU FOR WHOSE MANLY BROW | UPON YORKE HIS BIRTH | 37 | 46 | 176 | 500 |
| PEACE, WHICH HEE LOV'D IN LIFE, DID LEND | AN EPITAPH UPON ASHTON | 23 | 46 | 192 | 464 |
| THE NAME OF OUR NEW PEACE. OUR GOOD. | TO THE NAME OF JESUS | 3 | 52 | 239 | 30 |
| THE SINNER'S PARDON & THE JUST MAN'S PEACE. | VEXILLA REGIS | 42 | 52 | 277 | 156 |
| AND FILL MY PORTION IN THY PEACE. | ADORO TE | 34 | 52 | 291 | 172 |
| PEACE, SURE, WITH PIETY, THOUGH IT COME FROM SPAIN. | AN APOLOGIE FOR (TERESA) HYMNE | 20 | 52 | 322 | 59 |
| SILENCE, & SACRED REST. PEACE, & PURE JOYES. | DESCRIPTION RELIGIOUS HOUSE | 32 | 52 | 338 | 213 |
| PEACE, GOOD READER, DOE NOT WEEP. | AN EPITAPH UPON MARRIED COUPLE | 7 | 52 | 339 | 478 |
| PEACE, THE LOVERS ARE ASLEEP. | AN EPITAPH UPON MARRIED COUPLE | 8 | 52 | 339 | 478 |
| PEACE, HEART. THE HEAVENS ARE ANGRY. ALL THEIR SPHAERES | LUKE 2. QUAERIT JESUM | 19 | MS | 379 | 11 |
| BROODETH THIS SACRED PLACE. HITHER PEACE BRINGS | UPON KINGS CORONATION | 22 | MS | 389 | 454 |
| PEACE IS AN ORPHAN NOW. HER FATHER'S DEAD. | AN ELEGIE ON DR PORTER | 16 | MS | 395 | 476 |

**PEACEFULL**

|   |   |   |   |   |   |
|---|---|---|---|---|---|
| HE'S WASHT, HIS GLOOMY SKIN A PEACEFULL SHADE | ON BAPTIZED AETHIOPIAN | 3 | 46 | 85 | 29 |
| REGIONS OF PEACEFULL LIGHT | TO THE NAME OF JESUS | 116 | 52 | 239 | 30 |
| MY POOR ALEXIS, THEN IN PEACEFULL LIFE, | ALEXIAS THIRD ELEGIE | 13 | 52 | 336 | 209 |

**PEACOCKS**

|   |   |   |   |   |   |
|---|---|---|---|---|---|
| PEACOCKS & APES, | TO SAME CONCERNING CHOISE | 12 | 52 | 331 | 66 |

**PEALE**

|   |   |   |   |   |   |
|---|---|---|---|---|---|
| AND WHILE SHEE THUS DISCHARGES A SHRILL PEALE | MUSICKS DUELL | 97 | 46 | 149 | 535 |

**PEARLE**

|   |   |   |   |   |   |
|---|---|---|---|---|---|
| SUCH A PEARLE AS THIS IS, | THE TEARE | 19 | 46 | 84 | 50 |
| OR PEARLE THAT DARE APPEARE, | WISHES SUPPOSED MISTRESSE | 53 | 46 | 195 | 479 |
| EVEN TO THE LAST PEARLE IN THY TREASURE. | WEEPER | 130 | 52 | 307 | 120 |

## PEARLES

| | | | | | |
|---|---|---|---|---|---|
| HER RICHEST PEARLES, I MEANE THY TEARES. | THE WEEPER | 54 | 46 | 79 | 120 |
| WHICH THOU IN PEARLES DID'ST LEND. | ON WOUNDS OF CRUCIFIED LORD | 20 | 46 | 99 | 24 |
| THE PUREST PEARLES, THAT WEPT HER EVENING DEATH, | UPON DEATH OF HERRYS | 19 | 46 | 167 | 466 |
| LIKE WERE THE PEARLES THEY WEPT, SO LIKE THAT ONE | UPON YORKE HIS BIRTH | 64 | 46 | 176 | 500 |
| BROTHER PEARLES, AND SISTER ROSES. | OUT OF THE ITALIAN (1) | 24 | 46 | 188 | 545 |
| HER PROUDEST PEARLES. I MEAN THY TEARES. | WEEPER | 42 | 52 | 307 | 120 |

## PEARLE-TIPT

| | | | | | |
|---|---|---|---|---|---|
| WOULD TREMBLE ON MY PEARLE-TIPT FINGERS TOP. | DIVES ASKING A DROP | 2 | 46 | 96 | 18 |

## PEARLY

| | | | | | |
|---|---|---|---|---|---|
| SO TO THE TREASURE OF THY PEARLY DEAW, | TO THE MORNING | 39 | 46 | 183 | 497 |
| TO DROUNE THY SELFE IN THIS PURE PEARLY FLOOD. | UPON GUNPOWDER TREASON | 32 | MS | 387 | 461 |
| OF PEARLY DROPS, & SENT HER NUMEROUSE BIRTH | UPON KINGS CORONATION | 7 | MS | 390 | 453 |
| WITH TH' RICHEST CLOWDS THEIR PEARLY TREASURIE. | AN ELEGY MR STANNINOW | 18 | MS | 394 | 473 |
| WITH PEARLY PAPERS CARELESLY BESETT. | AN ELEGIE ON DR PORTER | 8 | MS | 395 | 476 |

## PECULIAR

| | | | | | |
|---|---|---|---|---|---|
| BUT ISAACKS ISSUE THE PECULIAR HEYRES, | OUT OF GROTIUS | 39 | MS | 398 | 198 |

## PEDIGREE

| | | | | | |
|---|---|---|---|---|---|
| BUT SUCH ALONE WHOSE SACRED PEDIGREE | TO THE NAME OF JESUS | 181 | 52 | 239 | 30 |

## PEEP

| | | | | | |
|---|---|---|---|---|---|
| AND PEEP & PROFFER AT THY SPARKLING THRONE. | IN GLORIOUS EPIPHANIE | 225 | 52 | 253 | 39 |

## PEEPT

| | | | | | |
|---|---|---|---|---|---|
| PEEPT FORTH FROM THEIR FIRST BLUSHES. SO THAT NOW | UPON DEATH OF HERRYS | 24 | 46 | 167 | 466 |

## PEEP'T

| | | | | | |
|---|---|---|---|---|---|
| PEEP'T FROM THEIR BUDS, SHEW'D LIKE THE GARDENS EYES | UPON YORKE HIS BIRTH | 62 | 46 | 176 | 500 |

## PEEPE

| | | | | | |
|---|---|---|---|---|---|
| THAT HEE WHOM THE SUN SERVES, SHOULD FAINTLY PEEPE | SOSPETTO D'HERODE | 177 | 46 | 109 | 216 |
| NOT DARING TO PEEPE FORTH, LEAST THAT A STONE | UPON GUNPOWDER TREASON | 25 | MS | 386 | 460 |
| AND OUT OF THEIR GREENE MANTLETTS DARE TO PEEPE. | AN ELEGY MR STANNINOW | 26 | MS | 394 | 473 |

## PEEPS

| | | | | | |
|---|---|---|---|---|---|
| PEEPS FROM HER PARENT STEMME, | THE TEARE | 27 | 46 | 84 | 50 |
| PEEPS FROM HER PARENT STEMME | WEEPER | 63 | 52 | 307 | 120 |

## PEEPING

| | | | | | |
|---|---|---|---|---|---|
| AT EACH CORNER PEEPING FORTH, | HIS EPITAPH (HERRYS) | 38 | 46 | 172 | 471 |

## PEEVISH

| | | | | | |
|---|---|---|---|---|---|
| THAT SO, IN SPITE OF ALL THIS PEEVISH STRENGTH | TO COUNTESSE OF DENBIGH | 41 | 52 | 236 | 146 |
| WHY SHOULD A PIECE OF PEEVISH CLAY PLEAD SHARES | CHARITAS NIMIA | 31 | 52 | 280 | 48 |

## PEIRCE

| | | | | | |
|---|---|---|---|---|---|
| SPARE OUR EYES, BUT PEIRCE OUR HARTS. | IN GLORIOUS EPIPHANIE | 79 | 52 | 253 | 39 |

## PEIRCED

| | | | | | |
|---|---|---|---|---|---|
| NAIL'D HANDS, & PEIRCED HEARTS. | SANCTA MARIA DOLORUM | 76 | 52 | 283 | 162 |
| A PEIRCING ONE. HIS PEIRCED HEART. | IN CICATRICES DOMINI JESU | 10 | MS | 381 | 27 |

## WELL-PEIRC'T

| | | | | | |
|---|---|---|---|---|---|
| SAY, ALL YE WISE & WELL-PEIRC'T HEARTS | FLAMING HEART | 49 | 52 | 324 | 61 |

## PEIRCING

| | | | | | |
|---|---|---|---|---|---|
| SPIRITUALL AND SOULE PEIRCING GLANCES. | ON A PRAYER BOOKE | 65 | 46 | 126 | 139 |
| A PEIRCING ONE. HIS PEIRCED HEART. | IN CICATRICES DOMINI JESU | 10 | MS | 381 | 27 |

## SOUL-PEIRCING

| | | | | | |
|---|---|---|---|---|---|
| SPIRITUALL & SOUL-PEIRCING GLANCES | PRAYER TO GENTLE-WOMAN | 71 | 52 | 328 | 139 |

## PELICAN

| | | | | | |
|---|---|---|---|---|---|
| O SOFT SELF-WOUNDING PELICAN. | ADORO TE | 45 | 52 | 291 | 172 |

## PELOPS

| | | | | | |
|---|---|---|---|---|---|
| PROMETHEUS SELFE, & PELOPS STERVED SIRE | HORATIJ ILLE & NEFASTO | 54 | MS | 382 | 530 |

PEN

| | | | | | |
|---|---|---|---|---|---|
| BY THE FAIRE LAWES OF THY FIRM-POINTED PEN, | ON A TREATISE OF CHARITY | 28 | 46 | 137 | 69 |
| EVEN THE IRON-POINTED PEN, | ANOTHER ON HERRYS | 33 | 46 | 170 | 469 |
| AND BLOOD, WITH PEN OF TRUTH | WISHES SUPPOSED MISTRESSE | 32 | 46 | 195 | 479 |
| HAD THY COLD PENCIL KIST HER PEN | FLAMING HEART | 20 | 52 | 324 | 61 |
| THAT WITH EACH WORD, MY LOADEN PEN LETTS FALL, | UPON BIRTH PRINCESSE E | 3 | MS | 391 | 456 |
| THE WEEPING PEN WITH SABLE TEARES HATH DREST. | AN ELEGIE ON DR PORTER | 10 | MS | 395 | 476 |

PENS

| | | | | | |
|---|---|---|---|---|---|
| ARE NAILES BLUNT PENS OF SUPERFICIALL SMART. | OFFICE H. CROSS SIXT | 11 | 52 | 270 | 97 |

PENNES

| | | | | | |
|---|---|---|---|---|---|
| PULPITS AND PENNES SHALL SWEAT IN. TO REDEEM | ON A TREATISE OF CHARITY | 50 | 46 | 137 | 69 |

PENANCE

| | | | | | |
|---|---|---|---|---|---|
| HIS PENANCE, AS OUR FAULT, CONSPICUOUS. | IN GLORIOUS EPIPHANIE | 158 | 52 | 253 | 39 |

PENCIL

| | | | | | |
|---|---|---|---|---|---|
| HAD THY COLD PENCIL KIST HER PEN | FLAMING HEART | 20 | 52 | 324 | 61 |

PENITENT

| | | | | | |
|---|---|---|---|---|---|
| AND THE GREAT PENITENT PRESSE HIS OWN PALE LIPPS | IN GLORIOUS EPIPHANIE | 151 | 52 | 253 | 39 |

COMMON-PEOPLE

| | | | | | |
|---|---|---|---|---|---|
| OPREST THE COMMON-PEOPLE OF THE SKYES. | SOSPETTO D'HERODE | 240 | 46 | 109 | 216 |

PEOPLES

| | | | | | |
|---|---|---|---|---|---|
| THE PEOPLES HUNGER, AND WHEN ALL WERE FULL | OUT OF GROTIUS | 63 | MS | 398 | 198 |

PERCEIV'D

| | | | | | |
|---|---|---|---|---|---|
| THE MAN PERCEIV'D HIS RIVALL, AND HER ART, | MUSICKS DUELL | 15 | 46 | 149 | 535 |

PERCH

| | | | | | |
|---|---|---|---|---|---|
| THE MORNING MUSES PERCH LIKE BIRDS, AND SING | UPON DEATH OF HERRYS | 11 | 46 | 167 | 466 |

HIGH-PERCH'T

| | | | | | |
|---|---|---|---|---|---|
| THE HIGH-PERCH'T TREBLE CHIRPS AT THIS, AND CHIDES | MUSICKS DUELL | 51 | 46 | 149 | 535 |

PERTCH'T

| | | | | | |
|---|---|---|---|---|---|
| PERTCH'T IN THE MORNING'S WAY | IN GLORIOUS EPIPHANIE | 56 | 52 | 253 | 39 |
| OR PERTCH'T UPON FEAR'D DIADEMS. | WEEPER | 184 | 52 | 307 | 120 |

PERCHING

| | | | | | |
|---|---|---|---|---|---|
| TILL AT LENGTH HE PERCHING REST, | OUT OF GREEKE CUPID'S CRYER | 43 | 46 | 159 | 519 |

PERFECT

| | | | | | |
|---|---|---|---|---|---|
| NOT PERFECT YET, AND FEARING TO BEE OUT | MUSICKS DUELL | 36 | 46 | 149 | 535 |
| THE PATTERNE OF A PERFECT CREATURE. | UPON DEATH OF DESIRED HERRYS | 8 | 46 | 168 | 467 |
| I'AM PERFECT IN HEAVN'S STATE, WITH EVERY STARR | ALEXIAS SECONDE ELEGIE | 23 | 52 | 335 | 207 |
| BLACK DISMALL HORROR, COME, MAKE PERFECT NOW | UPON GUNPOWDER TREASON | 20 | MS | 387 | 461 |
| YEE PERFECT EMBLEMES OF DIVINITY. | UPON KINGS CORONATION | 38 | MS | 389 | 454 |

PERFECTION

| | | | | | |
|---|---|---|---|---|---|
| EARTH HER BEST PERFECTION. | UPON DEATH OF DESIRED HERRYS | 27 | 46 | 168 | 467 |
| IN HIM PERFECTION DID SET FORTH, | HIS EPITAPH (HERRYS) | 13 | 46 | 172 | 471 |
| POORE EARTH HATH NOT ENOUGH PERFECTION, | UPON BIRTH PRINCESSE E | 41 | MS | 391 | 456 |

PERFIDIOUS

| | | | | | |
|---|---|---|---|---|---|
| PERFIDIOUS TOTTERER, LONGING FOR THE STAINES | HORATIJ ILLE & NEFASTO | 15 | MS | 382 | 530 |

PERFUME

| | | | | | |
|---|---|---|---|---|---|
| THAT NO PERFUME | TO THE NAME OF JESUS | 176 | 52 | 239 | 30 |

PERFUMED

| | | | | | |
|---|---|---|---|---|---|
| THY TOMBE, FAIRE IMMORTALITIES PERFUMED NEST. | EASTER DAY | 6 | 46 | 100 | 26 |
| OF YOUR WELL PERFUMED PRAYER. | ON MR. G. HERBERTS BOOKE | 10 | 46 | 130 | 68 |

PERFUM'D

| | | | | | |
|---|---|---|---|---|---|
| OF WHATSOE'RE PERFUM'D THY EASTERN NEST. | ON A TREATISE OF CHARITY | 10 | 46 | 137 | 69 |
| THE FRAGRANT SPRING MAY BE PERFUM'D WITHALL. | UPON BIRTH PRINCESSE E | 4 | MS | 391 | 456 |
| AND PLANTS IT IN A PRECIOUS PERFUM'D BEDD. | AN ELEGY MR STANNINOW | 51 | MS | 394 | 473 |
| TO PAINT ITS PERFUM'D FACE WITH COLOURS BRAVE. | AN ELEGIE ON DR PORTER | 24 | MS | 395 | 476 |

## PERFUMES

| | | | | | |
|---|---|---|---|---|---|
| AND LEFT PERFUMES, IN STEAD OF SCARRES. | A HYMNE OF THE NATIVITY | 26 | 46 | 106 | 76 |
| AND LEFT PERFUMES IN STEAD OF SCARRES. | IN HOLY NATIVITY | 27 | 52 | 246 | 76 |
| SO DOE PERFUMES EXPIRE. | WEEPER | 157 | 52 | 307 | 120 |

## PERFUMING

| | | | | | |
|---|---|---|---|---|---|
| INTO PERFUMING CLOUDES. SO FAST | IN MEMORY OF LADY MADRE TERESA | 116 | 46 | 131 | 52 |
| INTO PERFUMING CLOUDS, SO FAST | TERESA | 115 | 52 | 315 | 52 |

## PERHAPS

| | | | | | |
|---|---|---|---|---|---|
| OF FALSE PERHAPS AS FAIRE | ON A PRAYER BOOKE | 52 | 46 | 126 | 139 |
| A LIFE PERHAPS UNTO HIS DEATH. | AN EPITAPH UPON ASHTON | 34 | 46 | 192 | 464 |
| YEILD QUICKLY, LEST PERHAPS YOU PROVE | TO COUNTESSE OF DENBIGH | 65 | 52 | 236 | 146 |
| OF FALSE, PERHAPS AS FAIR, | PRAYER TO GENTLE-WOMAN | 58 | 52 | 328 | 139 |
| YIELD QUICKLY, LEST PERHAPS YOU PROVE | AGAINST IRRESOLUTION AND DELAY | 87 | 52 | 347 | 146 |

## PERIOD

| | | | | | |
|---|---|---|---|---|---|
| BOUND IN THE PERIOD OF DEATH, | ANOTHER ON HERRYS | 46 | 46 | 170 | 469 |
| YETT O WHAT END. WHERE DOES THE PERIOD DWELL | OUT OF GROTIUS | 9 | MS | 398 | 198 |

## PERISH'T

| | | | | | |
|---|---|---|---|---|---|
| HERE PERISH'T SHE, POOR HEART, HEAVNS, BE MY VOWES | ALEXIAS FIRST ELEGIE | 31 | 52 | 334 | 204 |

## PERJURY

| | | | | | |
|---|---|---|---|---|---|
| NO WITNESSE PETER OF THY PERJURY. | ON ST. PETER CUTTING MALCHUS | 4 | 46 | 97 | 22 |

## PERSECUTIONS

| | | | | | |
|---|---|---|---|---|---|
| TO PERSECUTIONS. AND AGAINST THE FACE | TO THE NAME OF JESUS | 200 | 52 | 239 | 30 |

## PERSIAN

| | | | | | |
|---|---|---|---|---|---|
| HIS PERSIAN LOVERS ALL SHALL LEAVE HIM, | AN HIMNE FOR CIRCUMCISION | 35 | 46 | 141 | 37 |
| HIS PERSIAN LOVERS ALL SHALL LEAVE HIM. | NEW YEAR'S DAY | 35 | 52 | 251 | 37 |
| THEREFORE WITH HIS PROUD PERSIAN SPOILES | IN GLORIOUS EPIPHANIE | 80 | 52 | 253 | 39 |
| OF MY WEAKE FEET THE PERSIAN MAGI LAY | OUT OF GROTIUS | 37 | MS | 398 | 198 |

## PERSONATE

| | | | | | |
|---|---|---|---|---|---|
| READY TO PERSONATE A MORTALL PART. | SOSPETTO D'HERODE | 418 | 46 | 109 | 216 |

## PERSPICILL

| | | | | | |
|---|---|---|---|---|---|
| WILL HAVE A PERSPICILL TO FIND HER OUT, | ON FRONTISPIECE ISAACSONS | 11 | 46 | 191 | 491 |

## PERSUASIVE

| | | | | | |
|---|---|---|---|---|---|
| BY THOSE SWEET EYES PERSUASIVE POWERS, | A HYMNE OF THE NATIVITY | 27 | 46 | 106 | 76 |
| FOR ALL PERSUASIVE GRACES THENCE | HIS EPITAPH (HERRYS) | 33 | 46 | 172 | 471 |
| BY THOSE SWEET EYES' PERSUASIVE POWRS | IN HOLY NATIVITY | 28 | 52 | 246 | 76 |

## PERVERSE

| | | | | | |
|---|---|---|---|---|---|
| HOLD THE PERVERSE PRINCE IN ETERNALL TIES | SOSPETTO D'HERODE | 39 | 46 | 109 | 216 |
| PROUD MORNING OF A PERVERSE DAY. HOW LOST | SOSPETTO D'HERODE | 77 | 46 | 109 | 216 |
| NOR WITH PERVERSE LOVES & RELIGIOUS RAPES | IN GLORIOUS EPIPHANIE | 105 | 52 | 253 | 39 |

## PESTIFEROUSE

| | | | | | |
|---|---|---|---|---|---|
| A LIVING COMET, WHOSE PESTIFEROUSE BREATH | ON GUNPOWDER-TREASON | 17 | MS | 384 | 458 |

## PETER

| | | | | | |
|---|---|---|---|---|---|
| THY SHADOW PETER, MUST SHEW ME THE SUN, | SICKE IMPLORE SHADOW | 3 | 46 | 87 | 28 |
| WELL PETER DOST THOU WIELD THY ACTIVE SWORD. | ON ST. PETER CUTTING MALCHUS | 1 | 46 | 97 | 22 |
| NO WITNESSE PETER OF THY PERJURY. | ON ST. PETER CUTTING MALCHUS | 4 | 46 | 97 | 22 |
| THOU HAST THE ART ON'T PETER, AND CANST TELL | ON ST. PETER CASTING NETS | 1 | 46 | 98 | 13 |

## PHAETHON

| | | | | | |
|---|---|---|---|---|---|
| THUS DID I FALL, AND THUS FELL PHAETHON. | HIGH MOUNTED ON AN ANT | 6 | 46 | 161 | 523 |

## PHAETON

| | | | | | |
|---|---|---|---|---|---|
| NARCISSUS, FOOLISH PHAETON, WHO FOR ALL | SOSPETTO D'HERODE | 79 | 46 | 109 | 216 |

## PHALARIS

| | | | | | |
|---|---|---|---|---|---|
| PHALARIS, OCHUS, EZELINUS, NAMES | SOSPETTO D'HERODE | 363 | 46 | 109 | 216 |

## PHARIAN

| | | | | | |
|---|---|---|---|---|---|
| NOR EVER WAS THE PHARIAN TIDE | ON BLEEDING WOUNDS OF LORD | 15 | 46 | 101 | 110 |
| NOR EVER WAS THE PHARIAN TIDE | UPON BLEEDING CRUCIFIX | 19 | 52 | 288 | 110 |

PHARISEES

| | | | | |
|---|---|---|---|---|
| THE STIFFE NECK'D PHARISEES THAT USE TO MOCKE | OUT OF GROTIUS | 42 | MS 398 | 198 |

PHASIS

| | | | | |
|---|---|---|---|---|
| THE BIRD, THAT'S FETCH'T FROM PHASIS FLOUD, | PETRONIJ ALES PHASIACIS PETITA | 1 | MS 382 | 526 |

PHEREUS

| | | | | |
|---|---|---|---|---|
| HERE DIOMED'S HORSES, PHEREUS DOGS APPEARE, | SOSPETTO D'HERODE | 353 | 46 109 | 216 |

PHLEGETON

| | | | | |
|---|---|---|---|---|
| BELCH'D FROM THE SULPH'RY LUNGS OF PHLEGETON. | ON GUNPOWDER-TREASON | 16 | MS 384 | 458 |

PHOEBUS

| | | | | |
|---|---|---|---|---|
| HENRY AND JAMES, OR MARS AND PHOEBUS RATHER. | UPON YORKE HIS BIRTH | 31 | 46 176 | 500 |
| ARE MARS AND PHOEBUS UNDER DIVERS NAMES. | UPON YORKE HIS BIRTH | 34 | 46 176 | 500 |
| LOCKES, TO PHOEBUS FLAMING TRESSES. | OUT OF THE ITALIAN (1) | 12 | 46 188 | 545 |
| THAN ERE THE FRUITFULL PHOEBUS FLAMING KISSES | UPON TWO GREENE APRICOCKES | 9 | 48 220 | 494 |

PHAEBUS

| | | | | |
|---|---|---|---|---|
| AFFRIGHTED PHAEBUS WOULD HAVE LOST HIS WAY, | UPON GUNPOWDER TREASON | 19 | MS 386 | 460 |
| THIS GLORIOUS PHAEBUS SETT) WILL QUIET BEE. | UPON KINGS CORONATION | 24 | MS 390 | 453 |

PHOENIX

| | | | | |
|---|---|---|---|---|
| HIS OWNE DELICIOUS PHOENIX FROM THE BLEST | UPON DEATH OF HERRYS | 13 | 46 167 | 466 |
| THOU ART THE MOTHER PHOENIX AND THY BREAST | UPON YORKE HIS BIRTH | 82 | 46 176 | 500 |
| OF ONE COY PHOENIX, WHILE WE HAVE A BROOD | UPON YORKE HIS BIRTH | 87 | 46 176 | 500 |
| O'TH PRETIOUS PHOENIX, WARME UPON HER BREAST. | ON A FOULE MORNING | 22 | 46 181 | 495 |
| IT MADE THE VIRGIN PHOENIX COME FARRE | UPON KINGS CORONATION | 30 | MS 390 | 453 |

PHOENIX-LIKE

| | | | | |
|---|---|---|---|---|
| LET NATURE DIE, IF (PHOENIX-LIKE) FROM DEATH | ON FRONTISPIECE ISAACSONS | 3 | 46 191 | 491 |

PHOENIX'

| | | | | |
|---|---|---|---|---|
| ARABIA, FOR THY ROYALL PHOENIX' NEST. | OFFICE H. CROSS COMPLINE | 6 | 52 274 | 105 |

PHAENIX

| | | | | |
|---|---|---|---|---|
| (SWEET AS IS THE PHAENIX NEST) | HIS EPITAPH (HERRYS) | 18 | 46 172 | 471 |
| THE PHAENIX BUILDS THE PHAENIX' NEST. | IN HOLY NATIVITY | 46 | 52 246 | 76 |
| A PHAENIX, & IN CHASTEST FLAMES OF LOVE | UPON GUNPOWDER TREASON | 34 | MS 387 | 461 |
| WHO WOULD NOT BE A PHAENIX, & ASPIRE | UPON KINGS CORONATION | 35 | MS 389 | 454 |
| THE PHAENIX SELFE SHALL NOT MORE PROUDLY BURNE. | EX EUPHORMIONE | 15 | MS 392 | 525 |

PHAENIX'

| | | | | |
|---|---|---|---|---|
| THE PHAENIX BUILDS THE PHAENIX' NEST. | IN HOLY NATIVITY | 46 | 52 246 | 76 |

PHOENIXES

| | | | | |
|---|---|---|---|---|
| A BROOD OF PHOENIXES. WHILE WE HAVE BROTHER | UPON YORKE HIS BIRTH | 88 | 46 176 | 500 |
| AND SISTER PHOENIXES, AND STILL THE MOTHER. | UPON YORKE HIS BIRTH | 89 | 46 176 | 500 |
| THE HOUSE AND FAMILY OF PHOENIXES. | UPON YORKE HIS BIRTH | 91 | 46 176 | 500 |

PHYSICK

| | | | | |
|---|---|---|---|---|
| HIS OWNE PHYSICK, HIS OWNE HEALTH. | IN PRAISE OF LESSIUS | 18 | 46 156 | 510 |
| GOE, TAKE PHYSICK DOAT UPON | TEMPERANCE | 5 | 52 342 | 510 |
| OF PHYSICK, THAT'S PHYSICK INDEED. | TEMPERANCE | 12 | 52 342 | 510 |
| OF PHYSICK, THAT'S PHYSICK INDEED. | TEMPERANCE | 12 | 52 342 | 510 |

PHISICK

| | | | | |
|---|---|---|---|---|
| OF PHISICK THATS PHISICK INDEED. | IN PRAISE OF LESSIUS | 14 | 46 156 | 510 |
| OF PHISICK THATS PHISICK INDEED. | IN PRAISE OF LESSIUS | 14 | 46 156 | 510 |

PHISICKE

| | | | | |
|---|---|---|---|---|
| GOE TAKE PHISICKE, DOAT UPON | IN PRAISE OF LESSIUS | 5 | 46 156 | 510 |

PHYSITIAN

| | | | | |
|---|---|---|---|---|
| NATURE HER OWNE PHYSITIAN BEE. | IN PRAISE OF LESSIUS | 16 | 46 156 | 510 |
| NATURE HER OWN PHYSITIAN BE. | TEMPERANCE | 14 | 52 342 | 510 |

PICTURE

| | | | | |
|---|---|---|---|---|
| SO MUCH AS TH' PICTURE OF A WELL-LIM'D VERSE. | WITH A PICTURE TO A FRIEND | 4 | 46 156 | 494 |
| SEND NOR TRUE PICTURE, NOR TRUE POESIE. | WITH A PICTURE TO A FRIEND | 6 | 46 156 | 494 |
| PICTURE AND POESY. | WISHES SUPPOSED MISTRESSE | 101 | 46 195 | 479 |
| YOU MUST TRANSPOSE THE PICTURE QUITE. | FLAMING HEART | 9 | 52 324 | 61 |

PIECE

    WHY SHOULD A PIECE OF PEEVISH CLAY PLEAD SHARES        CHARITAS NIMIA                          31  52 280  48
    A PIECE OF HEAV'NLY EARTH, PURER & BRIGHTER            IN GLORIOUS ASSUMPTION B. LADY           3  52 304 114

PEECE

    I PAINT SO ILL, MY PEECE HAD NEED TO BEE               WITH A PICTURE TO A FRIEND               1  46 156 494
    AS WHEN A PEECE OF WANTON LAWNE,                       IN PRAISE OF LESSIUS                    27  46 156 510
    A PEECE OF HEAVENLY LIGHT PURER AND BRIGHTER           ON THE ASSUMPTION                        3  46 139 114

MASTER-PEECE

    AND MATCHT THY MASTER-PEECE. O THEN GO ON              UPON YORKE HIS BIRTH                    51  46 176 500

PEICE

    AND CATCH THE PRETIOUS NAME THIS PEICE PRETENDS.       FLAMING HEART                            2  52 324  61
    AS WHEN A PEICE OF WANTON LAWN                         TEMPERANCE                              25  52 342 510

PIETY

    PEACE SURE WITH PIETY, THOUGH IT DWELL IN SPAINE.      AN APOLOGIE FOR HYMNE (TERESA)          20  46 136  59
    PEACE, SURE, WITH PIETY, THOUGH IT COME FROM SPAIN.    AN APOLOGIE FOR (TERESA) HYMNE          20  52 322  59

PILE

    UNTO A DREADFULL PILE GIVES FIERY BREATH.              SOSPETTO D'HERODE                       58  46 109 216
    AS WHEN A PILE OF FOOD-PREPARING FIRE,                 SOSPETTO D'HERODE                      481  46 109 216

PILLOW

    A DURTY PILLOW IN DEATH'S BED.                         UPON THE DEATH OF A GENTLEMAN           12  46 166 472
    A PILLOW FOR THEE WILL I BRING,                        THE TEARE                               35  46  84  50
    NO MORE MY PILLOW SHALL THINE ALTAR BE,                TO THE MORNING                          49  46 183 497
    THEIR PILLOW STONE, THEIR SHEETES OF LEAD,             AN EPITAPH UPON MARRIED COUPLE          12  52 339 478
    (PILLOW HARD, & SHEETES NOT WARM)                      AN EPITAPH UPON MARRIED COUPLE          13  52 339 478

PILLS

    CERTAIN HARD WORDS MADE INTO PILLS.                    IN PRAISE OF LESSIUS                     8  46 156 510
    CERTAIN HARD WORDS MADE INTO PILLS,                    TEMPERANCE                               8  52 342 510

PILOT

    SO SLEEPS A PILOT, WHOSE POORE BARKE IS PREST          SOSPETTO D'HERODE                      425  46 109 216

PILAT

    CALL'D PILAT UP. TO TRY IF HE                          OFFICE H. CROSS PRIME                    3  52 267  91

PINIONS

    SUCH AS THE SABLE PINIONS OF THE NIGHT                 UPON GUNPOWDER TREASON                   6  MS 386 460
    TH' EPITOME OF HELL. OH LETT THY PINIONS               UPON GUNPOWDER TREASON                  21  MS 387 461

PINEONS

    WHEN THE ERINNYS HER BLACK PINEONS SPREAD,             SOSPETTO D'HERODE                      393  46 109 216

PIPE

    O SPEAKE THOU AND MY PIPE HATH NOUGHT TO SAY.          UPON YORKE HIS BIRTH                   113  46 176 500

PIPES

    COMPLAINING PIPES, & PRATTLING STRINGS,                TO THE NAME OF JESUS                    65  52 239  30
    THAT RUNNES IN VIOLETT PIPES. NONE OTHER FOOD          ON GUNPOWDER-TREASON                    64  MS 384 458

PITCH

    SWELL THY FULL GLORYES TO A PITCH SO HIGH,             UPON YORKE HIS BIRTH                     7  46 176 500
    THUS, O THUS FONDLY DOE WEE PITCH OUR FEARES           HORATIJ ILLE & NEFASTO                  30  MS 382 530

PITCHY

    HE STREIGHTWAY LIGHTED UPP HIS PITCHY TORCH.           ON GUNPOWDER-TREASON                    56  MS 384 458
    YOUR SELVES, YOU STYGIAN STATES. A PITCHY CLOWD        UPON GUNPOWDER TREASON                  24  MS 387 461

PITTY

    PITTY NOT HIM, BUT FEARE THY SELFE                     OUT OF GREEKE CUPID'S CRYER             59  46 159 519
    LET NOT PITTY WITH HER TEARES,                         UPON DEATH OF DESIRED HERRYS            61  46 168 467
    IF EVER PITTY WERE ACQUAINTED                          ANOTHER ON HERRYS                        1  46 170 469
    IN THE DUST. PITTY NOW SPEND                           ANOTHER ON HERRYS                       57  46 170 469
    BRIGHT LADY OF THE MORNE, PITTY DOTH LYE               TO THE MORNING                          33  46 183 497
    TO WRACK MY SUITE. OH KEEPE PITTY WARME                ON GUNPOWDER-TREASON                    12  MS 384 458

PITTY'S

    IN PITTY'S SOFT LAP LY A SLEEPING.                     TO THE NAME OF JESUS                   192  52 239  30

## PITTIES

| | | | | |
|---|---|---|---|---|
| FOR PITTIES SAKE O HIDE HIM QUITE, | UPON DEATH OF DESIRED HERRYS | 71 | 46 168 | 467 |

## PLACE

| | | | | |
|---|---|---|---|---|
| IS CROWN'D ABOUT. BUT O WHAT PLACE, | OUT OF GREEKE CUPID'S CRYER | 34 | 46 159 | 519 |
| SNATCH'T HER SELF HENCE, TO HEAVEN. FILL'D A BRIGHT PLACE, | UPON BISHOP ANDREWES PICTURE | 9 | 46 163 | 490 |
| EACH DROP LEAVING A PLACE SO DEARE, | THE TEARE | 17 | 46 84 | 50 |
| WERE IT ENOUGH TO SHOW THE PLACE, AND SAY, | COME SEE WHERE THE LORD LAY | 3 | 46 87 | 27 |
| THE PLACE THAT CALLS YOU HENCE, IS AT THE WORST | TO INFANT MARTYRS | 5 | 46 88 | 10 |
| GLOOMY NIGHT EMBRAC'T THE PLACE | A HYMNE OF THE NATIVITY | 17 | 46 106 | 76 |
| WOLVISH LYCAON HERE A PLACE HATH WON. | SOSPETTO D'HERODE | 334 | 46 109 | 216 |
| HAD THEIR GENERALL MEETING PLACE. | HIS EPITAPH (HERRYS) | 20 | 46 172 | 471 |
| BRING THEIR HEAVEN WITH THEM, THEIR GREAT FOOTSTEPS PLACE | UPON YORKE HIS BIRTH | 19 | 46 176 | 500 |
| AND PLACE IN THE GREAT THRONG | TO THE NAME OF JESUS | 90 | 52 239 | 30 |
| GLOOMY NIGHT EMBRAC'T THE PLACE | IN HOLY NATIVITY | 17 | 52 246 | 76 |
| NOR SINKS NOR SWELLS WITH TIME OR PLACE. | IN GLORIOUS EPIPHANIE | 29 | 52 253 | 39 |
| THE WORLD LYES WARM, & LIKES HIS PLACE. | IN GLORIOUS EPIPHANIE | 37 | 52 253 | 39 |
| WE GUILD THE HUMBLE CHEEK OF THIS CHAST PLACE. | IN GLORIOUS EPIPHANIE | 83 | 52 253 | 39 |
| THESE ROYALL SAGES SUE FOR DECENT PLACE. | TO THE QUEEN'S MAJESTY | 2 | 52 261 | 47 |
| THEMSELVES WITH REVERENCE LEAVE THEIR PLACE | LAUDA SION SALVATOREM | 34 | 52 294 | 178 |
| NOR CHANGE THE PASTURE, BUT THE PLACE | LAUDA SION SALVATOREM | 79 | 52 294 | 178 |
| HEAVN & EARTH SHALL FIND NO PLACE. | DIES IRAE | 6 | 52 298 | 186 |
| O WIT OF LOVE, THAT THUS COULD PLACE | WEEPER | 89 | 52 307 | 120 |
| SPURNS THE TAME LAWS OF TIME AND PLACE. | AGAINST IRRESOLUTION AND DELAY | 77 | 52 347 | 146 |
| BROODETH THIS SACRED PLACE. HITHER PEACE BRINGS | UPON KINGS CORONATION | 22 | MS 369 | 454 |
| AND SETT IT FORTH IN THE SAME HAPPY PLACE, | UPON BIRTH PRINCESSE E | 59 | MS 391 | 456 |
| THEY OFTEN KIST, & IN THE SUGRED PLACE | AN ELEGY MR STANNINOW | 40 | MS 394 | 473 |
| A POORE (YEA SCARCE A) ROOFE. WHOSE NARROW PLACE | OUT OF GROTIUS | 16 | MS 398 | 193 |

## PLACE'S

| | | | | |
|---|---|---|---|---|
| COME HOVERING O'RE THE PLACE'S HEAD. | IN HOLY NATIVITY | 52 | 52 246 | 76 |

## PLACED

| | | | | |
|---|---|---|---|---|
| THE WORLDS PROFOUND HEART PANTS. THERE PLACED IS | SOSPETTO D'HERODE | 35 | 46 109 | 216 |

## PLAC'T

| | | | | |
|---|---|---|---|---|
| INTO LOOSE EXTASIES, THAT SHEE IS PLAC'T | MUSICKS DUELL | 103 | 46 149 | 535 |
| OF A CRUELL STOP ILL PLAC'T. | ANOTHER ON HERRYS | 40 | 46 170 | 469 |

## WELL-PLAC'T

| | | | | |
|---|---|---|---|---|
| HERE A WELL-PLAC'T & WISE MISTAKE | FLAMING HEART | 8 | 52 324 | 61 |

## PLACES

| | | | | |
|---|---|---|---|---|
| COME HOVERING O'RE THE PLACES HEAD. | A HYMNE OF THE NATIVITY | 36 | 46 106 | 76 |
| IN THEIR PLACES, | OUT OF THE ITALIAN (1) | 23 | 46 188 | 545 |
| ALL PLACES, TIMES, & OBJECTS BE | WEEPER | 131 | 52 307 | 120 |

## PLAGUE

| | | | | |
|---|---|---|---|---|
| EACH HERBE A PLAGUE. THE WINDS SIGHES TIMED-BEE | SOSPETTO D'HERODE | 346 | 46 109 | 216 |

## PLAIN

| | | | | |
|---|---|---|---|---|
| HAD UNDER SOME LOW ROOFE LOV'D HIS PLAIN WIFE. | ALEXIAS THIRD ELEGIE | 14 | 52 336 | 209 |

## PLAYNE

| | | | | |
|---|---|---|---|---|
| TRAYLES HER PLAYNE DITTY IN ONE LONG-SPUN NOTE, | MUSICKS DUELL | 37 | 46 149 | 535 |

## PLAINES

| | | | | |
|---|---|---|---|---|
| THERE AMOROUSE SAPPHO PLAINES UPON HER LUTE | HORATIJ ILLE & NEFASTO | 39 | MS 382 | 530 |
| OLYMPICK GAMES IN TH' OLYMPIAN PLAINES, | UPON GUNPOWDER TREASON | 21 | MS 386 | 460 |
| TRAVELD TH' OLYMPIAN PLAINES TO FIND RELEIFE. | UPON KINGS CORONATION | 4 | MS 390 | 453 |

## PLAINTS

| | | | | |
|---|---|---|---|---|
| WHISPER THY PLAINTS TO TH' OCEANS CURTEOUS EARES, | AN ELEGIE ON DR PORTER | 37 | MS 395 | 476 |

## PLANET

| | | | | |
|---|---|---|---|---|
| LOOKE IN WHAT POMPE THE MISTRESSE PLANET MOVES | SOSPETTO D'HERODE | 237 | 46 109 | 216 |

## PLANT

| | | | | |
|---|---|---|---|---|
| KNOW'ST THOU THIS, SOULDIER. 'TIS A MUCH CHANG'D PLANT, WHICH YE T | UPON THORNES FROM LORDS HEAD | 1 | 46 96 | 23 |
| A PLANT OF NOBLE STEMME, FORWARD AND FAIRE. | UPON DEATH OF HERRYS | 1 | 46 167 | 466 |
| THUS GREW THIS GRATIOUS PLANT, IN WHOSE SWEET SHADE | UPON DEATH OF HERRYS | 9 | 46 167 | 466 |
| THE DAY, & PLANT IT FAIRER IN THY FACE. | IN GLORIOUS EPIPHANIE | 6 | 52 253 | 39 |
| THAT FATALL PLANT, SO GREAT OF FAME | OFFICE H. CROSS SIXT | 5 | 52 270 | 97 |
| KNOW'ST THOU THIS, SOULDIER. 'TIS A MUCH-CHANG'D PLANT WHICH YET | UPON CROWNE OF THORNS | 1 | 52 290 | 23 |
| EACH MINDFULL PLANT HASTS TO MAKE GOOD | AGAINST IRRESOLUTION AND DELAY | 35 | 52 347 | 146 |

PLANTS

| | | | | | |
|---|---|---|---|---|---|
| HERE STRONG PROCRUSTES PLANTS HIS BED OF BRASSE. | SOSPETTO D'HERODE | 358 | 46 | 109 | 216 |
| AND PLANTS IT IN A PRECIOUS PERFUM'D BEDD, | AN ELEGY MR STANNINOW | 51 | MS | 394 | 473 |

PLAT

| | | | | | |
|---|---|---|---|---|---|
| OF TIBER, ON THE SCEANE OF A GREENE PLAT, | MUSICKS DUELL | 3 | 46 | 149 | 535 |

PLAY

| | | | | | |
|---|---|---|---|---|---|
| COME, THEY CRY'D, COME SING AND PLAY | PSALME 137 | 11 | 46 | 104 | 7 |
| SING. PLAY. TO WHOM (AH) SHALL WE SING OR PLAY, | PSALME 137 | 13 | 46 | 104 | 7 |
| SING. PLAY. TO WHOM (AH) SHALL WE SING OR PLAY, | PSALME 137 | 13 | 46 | 104 | 7 |
| LET PRAYER ALONE TO PLAY HIS PART. | ON A PRAYER BOOKE | 28 | 46 | 126 | 139 |
| TO TAKE HER PLEASURES, AND TO PLAY | ON A PRAYER BOOKE | 46 | 46 | 126 | 139 |
| LIFE SHOULD SO LONG PLAY WITH THAT BREATH, | IN MEMORY OF LADY MADRE TERESA | 17 | 46 | 131 | 52 |
| FRESH FROM THE ROSIE EAST REJOYC'T TO PLAY. | UPON DEATH OF HERRYS | 16 | 46 | 167 | 466 |
| A LOVERS KISSE MAY PLAY, | WISHES SUPPOSED MISTRESSE | 38 | 46 | 195 | 479 |
| OF GEMS, THAT IN THEIR BRIGHT SHADES PLAY. | WISHES SUPPOSED MISTRESSE | 51 | 46 | 195 | 479 |
| MADE SHORT BY LOVERS PLAY, | WISHES SUPPOSED MISTRESSE | 83 | 46 | 195 | 479 |
| AT LEST TO PLAY | IN GLORIOUS EPIPHANIE | 223 | 52 | 253 | 39 |
| LIFE SHOULD SO LONG PLAY WITH THAT BREATH | TERESA | 17 | 52 | 315 | 52 |
| LET ALL THY SCATTER'D SHAFTS OF LIGHT, THAT PLAY | FLAMING HEART | 87 | 52 | 324 | 61 |
| LET PRAYER ALONE TO PLAY HIS PART, | PRAYER TO GENTLE-WOMAN | 34 | 52 | 328 | 139 |
| TO TAKE HER PLEASURE & TO PLAY | PRAYER TO GENTLE-WOMAN | 52 | 52 | 328 | 139 |
| GIVING HIS WANTON PALFREYS LEAVE TO PLAY | UPON GUNPOWDER TREASON | 20 | MS | 386 | 460 |

PLEA

| | | | | | |
|---|---|---|---|---|---|
| LOVE HA'S NO PLEA AGAINST HER EYE | LOVES HOROSCOPE | 31 | 46 | 185 | 483 |
| LO, HEART, THY HOPE'S WHOLE PLEA. HER PRETIOUS BREATH | SANCTA MARIA DOLORUM | 109 | 52 | 283 | 162 |

PLEAD

| | | | | | |
|---|---|---|---|---|---|
| PLEAD YOUR PRETENCES (O YOU STRONG | TO COUNTESSE OF DENBIGH | 9 | 52 | 236 | 146 |
| WHY SHOULD A PIECE OF PEEVISH CLAY PLEAD SHARES | CHARITAS NIMIA | 31 | 52 | 280 | 48 |
| PLEAD FOR ME, LOVE. ALLEAGE & SHOW | ADORO TE | 19 | 52 | 291 | 172 |
| PLEAD YOUR PRETENCES, (O YOU STRONG | AGAINST IRRESOLUTION AND DELAY | 17 | 52 | 347 | 146 |

PLEADS

| | | | | | |
|---|---|---|---|---|---|
| THE AGED PASCHA PLEADS NOT YEARES | LAUDA SION SALVATOREM | 21 | 52 | 294 | 178 |

PLEASANT

| | | | | | |
|---|---|---|---|---|---|
| LOWD & PLEASANT, SWEET & LONG. | LAUDA SION SALVATOREM | 14 | 52 | 294 | 178 |

PLEASENT

| | | | | | |
|---|---|---|---|---|---|
| HER PAINTED INFANTS, FEDD WITH PLEASENT PAPPE, | AN ELEGY MR STANNINOW | 8 | MS | 394 | 473 |

PLEASE

| | | | | | |
|---|---|---|---|---|---|
| THE SANDS HE US'D NO LONGER PLEASE, | THE WEEPER | 101 | 46 | 79 | 120 |
| THESE PLEASE OUR PALATES. & WHY THESE. | PETRONIJ ALES PHASIACIS PETITA | 3 | MS | 382 | 526 |
| 'CAUSE THEY CAN BUT SELDOME PLEASE. | PETRONIJ ALES PHASIACIS PETITA | 4 | MS | 382 | 526 |

PLEASING

| | | | | | |
|---|---|---|---|---|---|
| AND STRETCH THEIR COLD LIMBES IN A PLEASING FIRE. | HORATIJ ILLE & NEFASTO | 53 | MS | 382 | 530 |

PLEASURE

| | | | | | |
|---|---|---|---|---|---|
| PLEASURE SINGS MY SOULE TO REST, | PSALME 23 | 9 | 46 | 102 | 5 |
| TO TAKE HER PLEASURE & TO PLAY | PRAYER TO GENTLE-WOMAN | 52 | 52 | 328 | 139 |

PLEASURES

| | | | | | |
|---|---|---|---|---|---|
| TO TAKE HER PLEASURES, AND TO PLAY | ON A PRAYER BOOKE | 46 | 46 | 126 | 139 |
| OF PURE INEBRIATING PLEASURES, | ON A PRAYER BOOKE | 114 | 46 | 126 | 139 |
| FAREWELL ALL PLEASURES, SPORTS AND JOYES. | IN MEMORY OF LADY MADRE TERESA | 59 | 46 | 131 | 52 |
| OF RIPE PLEASURES | OUT OF THE ITALIAN (1) | 26 | 46 | 188 | 545 |
| FAREWELL, ALL PLEASURES, SPORTS, & JOYES, | TERESA | 59 | 52 | 315 | 52 |
| OF PURE INEBRIATING PLEASURES. | PRAYER TO GENTLE-WOMAN | 120 | 52 | 328 | 139 |

PLEDGE

| | | | | | |
|---|---|---|---|---|---|
| IN PUDDLES, WE WILL PLEDGE THIS SERAPHIM | AN APOLOGIE FOR HYMNE (TERESA) | 32 | 46 | 136 | 59 |
| IN PUDDLES, WE WILL PLEDGE THIS SERAPHIM | AN APOLOGIE FOR (TERESA) HYMNE | 32 | 52 | 322 | 59 |

PLENTY

| | | | | | |
|---|---|---|---|---|---|
| PLENTY WEARES ME AT HER BREAST, | PSALME 23 | 10 | 46 | 102 | 5 |

SEED-PLOT

| | | | | | |
|---|---|---|---|---|---|
| MUSICKS BEST SEED-PLOT, WHENCE IN RIPEND AIRES | MUSICKS DUELL | 69 | 46 | 149 | 535 |

PLOW'D

| | | | | | |
|---|---|---|---|---|---|
| HIS HONEY-DROPPING TOPS, PLOW'D BY HER BREATH | MUSICKS DUELL | 71 | 46 | 149 | 535 |

PLOUGH'D

 IS PLOUGH'D AS DEEPE, AS IS THE SEA WITH WIND,  HORATIJ ILLE & NEFASTO  20 MS 382 530

PLUCK

 BAD SPORTING NEPTUNE TO PLUCK IN HIS ARMES,  UPON GUNPOWDER TREASON  32 MS 386 460

PLUCKT

 REACH ME A QUILL, PLUCKT FROM THE FLAMING WING  UPON GUNPOWDER TREASON  1 MS 386 460

PLUME

 LETT TH' HALLOWED PLUME OF A SERAPHICK WING  UPON BIRTH PRINCESSE E  22 MS 391 456

PLUMES

 THESE WHITE PLUMES OF HIS HEELE LEND YOU,  ON MR. G. HERBERTS BOOKE  11 46 130 68
 TRICK THEIR TALL PLUMES, AND IN THAT GARB SHALL GO  ON A TREATISE OF CHARITY  25 46 137 69

PLUMP

 EACH BODY'S PLUMP AND JUCY, ALL THINGS FULL  OUT OF VIRGIL  15 46 155 529

PLUMPE

 MARROW TO MY PLUMPE GENIUS, MAKE IT LIVE  TO THE MORNING  22 46 183 497
 GROW PLUMPE, LEANE DEATH. HIS HOLINESSE A FEAST  UPON GUNPOWDER TREASON  1 MS 387 461
 THOSE PLUMPE SOFT RUBIES HAD BIN DREST SOE BRAVE.  UPON BIRTH PRINCESSE E  48 MS 391 456

PLUTO'S

 WHENCE THE FOURTH FURY, ANSWER'D PLUTO'S CALL.  SOSPETTO D'HERODE  368 46 109 216
 AT LAST IT STOPT AT PLUTO'S GLOOMY PORCH.  ON GUNPOWDER-TREASON  55 MS 384 458
 OF PLUTO'S MERCURY, THAT I MAY SING  UPON GUNPOWDER TREASON  2 MS 386 460
 BE' A GLOOMY CANOPY TO PLUTO'S MINIONS.  UPON GUNPOWDER TREASON  22 MS 387 461
 AND RUGGED TOUCH OF PLUTO'S MULTITUDE.  UPON GUNPOWDER TREASON  58 MS 387 461

PLYANT

 THE PLYANT SERIES OF HER SLIPPERY SONG.  MUSICKS DUELL  61 46 149 535

POASTING

 ARE SENT ABOUT, WHO POASTING EVERY WAY  SOSPETTO D'HERODE  510 46 109 216

POESY

 PICTURE AND POESY,  WISHES SUPPOSED MISTRESSE  101 46 195 479

POESIE

 PAINTED AGAINE BY SOME GOOD POESIE.  WITH A PICTURE TO A FRIEND  2 46 156 494
 SEND NOR TRUE PICTURE, NOR TRUE POESIE.  WITH A PICTURE TO A FRIEND  6 46 156 494

POINT

 A CLEARE UNWRINCKLED SONG, THEN DOTH SHEE POINT IT  MUSICKS DUELL  39 46 149 535
 A THOUSAND ANGELLS IN ONE POINT CAN DWELL,  ON A PRAYER BOOKE  8 46 126 139
 UPON WHOSE CHOICE POINT SHALL BE SPENT,  IN MEMORY OF LADY MADRE TERESA  90 46 131 52
 ALL THY WILD CIRCLE TO A POINT. O SINKE  UPON STANINOUGH'S DEATH  14 46 175 475
 POINT HERE THY BEAMES. O GLANCE ON YONDER FLOCKES,  ON A FOULE MORNING  5 46 181 495
 ALL-CIRCLING POINT. ALL CENTRING SPHEAR.  IN GLORIOUS EPIPHANIE  26 52 253 39
 TURN'D THE STEEL POINT OF FEAR,  VEXILLA REGIS  16 52 277 156
 WHEN LIFE, HIMSELF, AT POINT TO DY  LAUDA SION SALVATOREM  11 52 294 178
 UPON WHOSE CHOICE POINT SHALL BE SENT  TERESA  90 52 315 52
 TEN THOUSAND ANGELS IN ONE POINT CAN DWELL.  PRAYER TO GENTLE-WOMAN  14 52 328 139
 WHOSE ROSY BEAM SHALL POINT MY SUN TO ME.  ALEXIAS SECONDE ELEGIE  26 52 335 207
 ALL THY WILD CIRCLE TO A POINT. O SINK  DEATH'S LECTURE  15 52 340 475
 THE SUBTILE POINT OF HIS COY DESTINY,  HORATIJ ILLE & NEFASTO  16 MS 382 530

POINTED

 ALL POINTED IN HIS HEART SEEM'D TO INVADE HIM.  SOSPETTO D'HERODE  476 46 109 216
 POINTED HIM OUT IN ALL HIS WAYES.  HIS EPITAPH (HERRYS)  39 46 172 471

FIRM-POINTED

 BY THE FAIRE LAWES OF THY FIRM-POINTED PEN,  ON A TREATISE OF CHARITY  28 46 137 69

IRON-POINTED

 EVEN THE IRON-POINTED PEN,  ANOTHER ON HERRYS  33 46 170 469

WELL-POINTED

 TWAS HIS WELL-POINTED DART  WEEPER  103 52 307 120

POINTS

 THAT POINTS ME TO THESE WAYES OF BLISSE.  PSALME 23  4 46 102 5
 THE POINTS OF HER YOUNG EAGLES EYES.  A HYMNE OF THE NATIVITY  70 46 106 76

```
                                                                                  PAGE  314

         STANDS OFF AND POINTS AT.  IS'T SOME DEITY     UPON YORKE HIS BIRTH             71  46 176 500
         POINTS OF DEATH BID LOVE BE GONE               LOVES HOROSCOPE                  22  46 185 483

POYNTS

         GOOD WINE IN ALL POYNTS.  BUT THE EASY RATE.   OUT OF GROTIUS                   56  MS 398 198

POINTING

         AND POINTING TO DULL MORPHEUS, BIDS ME TAKE    TO THE MORNING                   15  46 183 497
         POINTING US HOME TO OUR OWN SUN                IN GLORIOUS EPIPHANIE           252  52 253  39

POISE

         TO POISE EACH PRETIOUS LIMB.                   OFFICE H. CROSS EVENSONG         18  52 273 101
         O HEART, THE AEQUALL POISE OF LOV'ES BOTH PARTS FLAMING HEART                   75  52 324  61

WELL-POIS'D

         A WELL-POIS'D SCEPTER.  DOES IT NOW SEEME GOOD SOSPETTO D'HERODE               451  46 109 216

POYSON

         EACH FLOWERS A PREGNANT POYSON, TRY'D AND GOOD, SOSPETTO D'HERODE              347  46 109 216

POYSONS

         POYSONS TO SPEED THEE.  YET THROUGH ALL THE LAND SOSPETTO D'HERODE             445  46 109 216
         AS ANTIDOTES & POYSONS ARE.                    OFFICE H. CROSS SIXT             16  52 270  97
         HUGE HIGH-FLOUNE POYSONS, EV'N OF COLCHOS BREED, HORATIJ ILLE & NEFASTO         11  MS 382 530

POIS'NOUS

         OF POIS'NOUS AND UNNATURALL LOVES, EARTH-NURST. SOSPETTO D'HERODE              127  46 109 216

POLES

         WHOSE VAST INTELLIGENCES TUN'D THE POLES       UPON YORKE HIS BIRTH             36  46 176 500

POMONA

         PALE SONS OF OUR POMONA, WHOSE WAN CHEEKES     UPON TWO GREENE APRICOCKES        3  48 220 494

POMPE

         LOOKE IN WHAT POMPE THE MISTRESSE PLANET MOVES SOSPETTO D'HERODE               237  46 109 216

POMPOUS

         RISING AND FALLING IN A POMPOUS TRAINE.        MUSICKS DUELL                    96  46 149 535
         AND COURTED IN THE POMPOUS MASK OF A MORE SPECIOUS IN GLORIOUS EPIPHANIE        53  52 253  39
                                               MIST.

PONDROUS

         TOGETHER, IN HIS PONDROUS MIND BOTH WEIGHES.   SOSPETTO D'HERODE                96  46 109 216

POOR

         TO THE PROUD HOPES OF POOR MORTALITY.          UPON STANINOUGH'S DEATH          24  46 175 475
         PROGRESSIONS 'TWIXT WHOSE TERMES POOR TIME GROWS OLD. UPON TWO GREENE APRICOCKES 16  48 220 494
         POOR WATERS THEIR OWNE PRISONERS BE.           TO COUNTESSE OF DENBIGH          22  52 236 146
         OF A POOR PANTING TURTLE-DOVE.                 TO THE NAME OF JESUS            108  52 239  30
         POOR WORLD (SAID I.) WHAT WILT THOU DOE        IN HOLY NATIVITY                 37  52 246  76
         BUT TO POOR SHEPHEARDS, HOME-SPUN THINGS.      IN HOLY NATIVITY                 94  52 246  76
         LET HIM MAKE POOR THE PURPLE EAST,             NEW YEAR'S DAY                   17  52 251  37
         THE POOR WORLD'S FAULT THAT HE IS FAIR.        IN GLORIOUS EPIPHANIE           104  52 253  39
         WHEN THIS SO PROUDLY POOR                      IN GLORIOUS EPIPHANIE           134  52 253  39
         WITH ALL THE POWRES MY POOR HEART HATH         ADORO TE                          1  52 291 172
         AH THEN, POOR SOUL, WHAT WILT THOU SAY.        DIES IRAE                        21  52 298 186
         TAKE THY FAREWELL, POOR WORLD. HEAVN MUST GOE HOME. IN GLORIOUS ASSUMPTION B. LADY 2 52 304 114
         EVEN WHEN HE SHOW'D MOST POOR,                 WEEPER                          117  52 307 120
         BE LOVE BUT THERE.  LET POOR SIX YEARES        TERESA                           29  52 315  52
         HERE PERISH'T SHE, POOR HEART, HEAVNS, BE MY VOWES ALEXIAS FIRST ELEGIE         31  52 334 204
         O I AM LEARNED GROWN, POOR LOVE & I            ALEXIAS SECONDE ELEGIE           21  52 335 207
         MY POOR ALEXIS, THEN IN PEACEFULL LIFE,        ALEXIAS THIRD ELEGIE             13  52 336 209
         HALF TRUE, ALAS, HALF FALSE, PROVES THAT POOR LINE. ALEXIAS THIRD ELEGIE        57  52 336 209
         TO THE LOWD BOASTS OF POOR MORTALITY           DEATH'S LECTURE                  26  52 340 475
         POOR WATERS THEIR OWN PRISONERS BE.            AGAINST IRRESOLUTION AND DELAY   22  52 347 146
         (WHEN ONE POOR SIGH SENDS FOR HIM DOWN)        AGAINST IRRESOLUTION AND DELAY   74  52 347 146

POOR-SPIRITED

         O MOST POOR-SPIRITED OF MEN.                   FLAMING HEART                    19  52 324  61

POORE

         POORE SIMPLE VOYCE, RAIS'D IN A NATURALL TONE. MUSICKS DUELL                   164  46 149 535
         GOE POORE MAN THINKE WHAT SHALL BEE,           IN PRAISE OF LESSIUS             11  46 156 510
         AND FRAUD. HEE MAKES POORE MORTALLS HURTS,     OUT OF GREEKE CUPID'S CRYER      31  46 159 519
         WHAT NEED'ST THOU PUT ON ARMES AGAINST POORE MEN. UPON VENUS PUTTING ARMES       4  46 161 523
         YET LET THE POORE DROPS WEEPE.                 THE WEEPER                       73  46  79 120
         WHICH WAY MY POORE TEARS TO HIMSELFE MAY GOE,  COME SEE WHERE THE LORD LAY       2  46  87  27
         TO FIX THOSE FULL-FAC'T GLORIES, O HE'S POORE  IT IS BETTER TO GO WITH EYE       2  46  93  16
```

| | | | | | |
|---|---|---|---|---|---|
| YET IF THOU'LT FILL ONE POORE EYE, WITH THY HEAVEN AND THEE. | IT IS BETTER TO GO WITH EYE | 4 | 46 | 93 | 16 |
| BUT TO POORE SHEPHEARDS, SIMPLE THINGS, | A HYMNE OF THE NATIVITY | 74 | 46 | 106 | 76 |
| TO A POORE GALILEAN VIRGIN SENT. | SOSPETTO D'HERODE | 98 | 46 | 109 | 216 |
| HEE MARKT HOW THE POORE SHEPHEARDS RAN TO PAY | SOSPETTO D'HERODE | 118 | 46 | 109 | 216 |
| HIS BLAZE, TO SHINE IN A POORE SHEPHEARDS EYE. | SOSPETTO D'HERODE | 170 | 46 | 109 | 216 |
| AS PRIS'NER IN A FEW POORE RAGS TO LYE. | SOSPETTO D'HERODE | 172 | 46 | 109 | 216 |
| AND POORE FOWLES INTERCEPTED IN THEIR FLIGHT. | SOSPETTO D'HERODE | 376 | 46 | 109 | 216 |
| SO SLEEPS A PILOT, WHOSE POORE BARKE IS PREST | SOSPETTO D'HERODE | 425 | 46 | 109 | 216 |
| POORE JEALOUSIE. WHY SHOULD HE WISH TO PREY | SOSPETTO D'HERODE | 519 | 46 | 109 | 216 |
| POORE BEASTS. A SLOW OXE, AND A SIMPLE ASSE. | SOSPETTO D'HERODE | 528 | 46 | 109 | 216 |
| BEE LOVE BUT THERE. LET POORE SIX YEARES, | IN MEMORY OF LADY MADRE TERESA | 29 | 46 | 131 | 52 |
| WHAT CAN THE POORE HOPE FROM US, WHEN WE BE | ON A TREATISE OF CHARITY | 57 | 46 | 137 | 69 |
| TAKE THY FAREWEL POORE WORLD, HEAVEN MUST GO HOME. | ON THE ASSUMPTION | 2 | 46 | 139 | 114 |
| THOUGH, OUR POORE JOYES ARE PARTED SO, | ON THE ASSUMPTION | 37 | 46 | 139 | 114 |
| LET HIM MAKE POORE THE PURPLE EAST, | AN HIMNE FOR CIRCUMCISION | 17 | 46 | 141 | 37 |
| PUT POORE NATURE TO SUCH COST. | UPON DEATH OF DESIRED HERRYS | 22 | 46 | 168 | 467 |
| IF POORE LOVE SHALL LIVE OR DY. | LOVES HOROSCOPE | 8 | 46 | 185 | 483 |
| IF POORE LOVE SHALL LIVE OR DYE. | LOVES HOROSCOPE | 20 | 46 | 185 | 483 |
| SHALL I HIDE POORE LOVE FROM DEATH. | LOVES HOROSCOPE | 44 | 46 | 185 | 483 |
| O. THAT POORE LOVE BE NOT FOR EVER SPOYLED. | OUT OF THE ITALIAN (2) | 5 | 46 | 190 | 547 |
| OF WORTH, MAY LEAVE HER POORE | WISHES SUPPOSED MISTRESSE | 104 | 46 | 195 | 479 |
| POORE FRUITES LOOKE PALE AT THY HESPERIDES. | UPON TWO GREENE APRICOCKES | 30 | 48 | 220 | 494 |
| POORE LAWES DIVIDE THE PUBLICKE YEARE, | THOUGH NOW 'TIS NEITHER | 24 | MS | 397 | 492 |
| O THOU ART POORE | TO THE NAME OF JESUS | 19 | 52 | 239 | 30 |
| YET LET THE POORE DROPS WEEP | WEEPER | 55 | 52 | 307 | 120 |
| DID EVER GREIFE, & JOY IN ONE POORE HEART | LUKE 2. QUAERIT JESUM | 3 | MS | 379 | 11 |
| TO TOSSE POORE MEN LIKE DUST INTO THE AIRE. | ON GUNPOWDER-TREASON | 40 | MS | 384 | 458 |
| POORE MEAGRE HORROR STREIGHTWAIS WAS AMAZ'D, | UPON GUNPOWDER TREASON | 47 | MS | 387 | 461 |
| POORE EARTH HATH NOT ENOUGH PERFECTION, | UPON BIRTH PRINCESSE E | 41 | MS | 391 | 456 |
| A POORE (YEA SCARCE A) ROOFE. WHOSE NARROW PLACE | OUT OF GROTIUS | 16 | MS | 398 | 198 |

POPE

| | | | | | |
|---|---|---|---|---|---|
| ONLY THE POPE A STOMACK STILL COULD FIND. | UPON GUNPOWDER TREASON | 51 | MS | 387 | 461 |

POPPY

| | | | | | |
|---|---|---|---|---|---|
| BESTOW THY POPPY UPON WAKEFULL WOE. | TO THE MORNING | 55 | 46 | 183 | 497 |

PORCH

| | | | | | |
|---|---|---|---|---|---|
| AT LAST IT STOPT AT PLUTO'S GLOOMY PORCH. | ON GUNPOWDER-TREASON | 55 | MS | 384 | 458 |

PORES

| | | | | | |
|---|---|---|---|---|---|
| WHAT DID THEIR WEAPONS BUT WITH WIDER PORES | TO THE NAME OF JESUS | 211 | 52 | 239 | 30 |

PORTABLE

| | | | | | |
|---|---|---|---|---|---|
| PORTABLE, & COMPENDIOUS OCEANS. | WEEPER | 114 | 52 | 307 | 120 |

PORTALLS

| | | | | | |
|---|---|---|---|---|---|
| MAKE PROUD THE RUBY PORTALLS OF THE EAST. | SOSPETTO D'HERODE | 122 | 46 | 109 | 216 |

PORTEND

| | | | | | |
|---|---|---|---|---|---|
| ABOUT HORROR'S DISPLAI'D. IT DOTH PORTEND, | ON GUNPOWDER-TREASON | 21 | MS | 384 | 458 |

PORTENTS

| | | | | | |
|---|---|---|---|---|---|
| PORTENTS BEFORE MINE EYES THEIR POWERS ADVANCE. | SOSPETTO D'HERODE | 202 | 46 | 109 | 216 |

PORTION

| | | | | | |
|---|---|---|---|---|---|
| A SEEMLY PORTION FOR THE SONS OF KINGS. | ON HOPE | 34 | 46 | 143 | 71 |
| USURP'T THE PORTION OF THY PAIN, | VEXILLA REGIS | 14 | 52 | 277 | 156 |
| OF GREIFES HIS PORTION, WHO (HAD ALL THEIR DUE) | SANCTA MARIA DOLORUM | 79 | 52 | 283 | 162 |
| AND FILL MY PORTION IN THY PEACE. | ADORO TE | 34 | 52 | 291 | 172 |
| A HASTY PORTION OF PRAESCRIBED SLEEP. | DESCRIPTION RELIGIOUS HOUSE | 15 | 52 | 338 | 213 |
| A SEEMLY PORTION FOR THE SONNES OF KINGS. | (ON) HOPE | 14 | 52 | 345 | 71 |
| FOR EARTH, 'T HAD BEENE AN AMPLE PORTION. | UPON BIRTH PRINCESSE E | 28 | MS | 391 | 456 |

PORTS

| | | | | | |
|---|---|---|---|---|---|
| YOUR PORTS ARE ALL SUPERFLUOUS HERE, | ADORO TE | 9 | 52 | 291 | 172 |

POSED

| | | | | | |
|---|---|---|---|---|---|
| BEE POSED WITH THE MATUREST FEARES | IN MEMORY OF LADY MADRE TERESA | 30 | 46 | 131 | 52 |

POS'D

| | | | | | |
|---|---|---|---|---|---|
| BE POS'D WITH THE MATUREST FEARES | TERESA | 30 | 52 | 315 | 52 |

POSETH

| | | | | | |
|---|---|---|---|---|---|
| POSETH HIS PROUDEST INTELLECTUALL POWER. | SOSPETTO D'HERODE | 166 | 46 | 109 | 216 |
| WHICH POSETH MISCHEIFE'S SELFE TO PARALLEL. | AN ELEGIE ON DR PORTER | 14 | MS | 395 | 476 |

POSIES

| | | | |
|---|---|---|---|
| THE MUSES, & THE GRACES FRAGRANT POSIES. | AN ELEGY MR STANNINOW | 38 | MS 394 473 |

POSSESSION

| | | | |
|---|---|---|---|
| WILL TAKE POSSESSION OF THE SACRED STORE | ON A PRAYER BOOKE | 57 | 46 126 139 |
| WILL TAKE POSSESSION OF THAT SACRED STORE | PRAYER TO GENTLE-WOMAN | 63 | 52 328 139 |

POSSEST

| | | | |
|---|---|---|---|
| SOFTLY MAY HE BE POSSEST. | UPON DEATH OF DESIRED HERRYS | 67 | 46 168 467 |

POSTERITIE

| | | | |
|---|---|---|---|
| SETT TO THE MISCHEIFE OF POSTERITIE. | HORATIJ ILLE & NEFASTO | 2 | MS 382 530 |

POSTURE

| | | | |
|---|---|---|---|
| THIS POSTURE IS THE BRAVE ONE. THIS THAT LYES | UPON STANINOUGH'S DEATH | 27 | 46 175 475 |
| THIS POSTURE IS THE BRAVE ONE THIS THAT LYES | DEATH'S LECTURE | 29 | 52 340 475 |

POUR

| | | | |
|---|---|---|---|
| POUR ON THY NOBLEST SWEETS, WHICH, WHEN THEY TOUCH | OFFICE H. CROSS COMPLINE | 7 | 52 274 105 |

POUR'D

| | | | |
|---|---|---|---|
| HER LITTLE SOULE IS RAVISHT. AND SO POUR'D | MUSICKS DUELL | 102 | 46 149 535 |
| STILL LIVES, WHICH WHEN WEAKE TIME SHALL BE POUR'D OUT | UPON DEATH OF HERRYS | 36 | 46 167 466 |

POURE

| | | | |
|---|---|---|---|
| AND POURE ABROAD | PRAYER TO GENTLE-WOMAN | 93 | 52 328 139 |
| FROM HEAVENS SWEET MILKY STREAME DOTH GENTLY POURE. | AN ELEGY MR STANNINOW | 10 | MS 394 473 |

POURING

| | | | |
|---|---|---|---|
| AND POURING ON HEAV'NS FACE THE SEAS HUGE FLOOD | SOSPETTO D'HERODE | 277 | 46 109 216 |

POURTRAICTED

| | | | |
|---|---|---|---|
| THE REST POURTRAICTED ARE, THAT 'TIS NOE PAINE | UPON BIRTH PRINCESSE E | 35 | MS 391 456 |

POWDER'D

| | | | |
|---|---|---|---|
| BUT YETT THEY WERE NOT POWDER'D TO HIS MIND. | UPON GUNPOWDER TREASON | 52 | MS 387 461 |

POWER

| | | | |
|---|---|---|---|
| POSETH HIS PROUDEST INTELLECTUALL POWER. | SOSPETTO D'HERODE | 166 | 46 109 216 |
| SHEE SHALL HAVE POWER, | ON A PRAYER BOOKE | 108 | 46 126 139 |
| OR SOME BASE HAND HAVE POWER TO RACE, | IN MEMORY OF LADY MADRE TERESA | 71 | 46 131 52 |
| OF ALL THE RANSOM'D WORLD, THOU HADST THE POWER | OFFICE H. CROSS EVENSONG | 16 | 52 273 101 |
| OR SOME BASE HAND HAVE POWER TO RACE | TERESA | 71 | 52 315 52 |
| SHE SHALL HAVE POWER | PRAYER TO GENTLE-WOMAN | 114 | 52 328 139 |
| BUT WITH ONE CORDIALL SMILE. FOR (LOE) THAT POWER | EX EUPHORMIONE | 4 | MS 392 525 |

POWE'R

| | | | |
|---|---|---|---|
| BUT AT THE LAST (HAVING NOT SOE MUCH POWE'R | UPON KINGS CORONATION | 5 | MS 390 453 |

POWR

| | | | |
|---|---|---|---|
| AND AT THY FEET POWR FORTH HIS FACE. | IN GLORIOUS EPIPHANIE | 84 | 52 253 39 |

POWR'D

| | | | |
|---|---|---|---|
| POWR'D OUT IN PRAYRS FOR THEE. THY LORD'S IN DEATH. | SANCTA MARIA DOLORUM | 110 | 52 283 162 |

POWRE

| | | | |
|---|---|---|---|
| AND POWRE ABROAD | ON A PRAYER BOOKE | 87 | 46 126 139 |
| RAISE THIS TALL TROPHEE OF THY POWRE. | TO COUNTESSE OF DENBIGH | 38 | 52 236 146 |

POWERS

| | | | |
|---|---|---|---|
| YET SUMMONS ALL HER SWEET POWERS FOR A NOATE | MUSICKS DUELL | 160 | 46 149 535 |
| BY THOSE SWEET EYES PERSUASIVE POWERS, | A HYMNE OF THE NATIVITY | 27 | 46 106 76 |
| PORTENTS BEFORE MINE EYES THEIR POWERS ADVANCE. | SOSPETTO D'HERODE | 202 | 46 109 216 |
| AND SHOULD WE POWERS OF HEAV'N, SPIRITS OF WORTH | SOSPETTO D'HERODE | 219 | 46 109 216 |
| AND ALL THE POWERS OF HELL IN FULL APPLAUSE | SOSPETTO D'HERODE | 259 | 46 109 216 |
| BLEST POWERS FORBID THY TENDER LIFE, | IN MEMORY OF LADY MADRE TERESA | 69 | 46 131 52 |
| AND SWEARE FAITH TO THY SWEETER POWERS. | AN HIMNE FOR CIRCUMCISION | 36 | 46 141 37 |
| COME THEN YOUTH, BEAUTY, AND BLOOD, ALL YE SOFT POWERS, | UPON STANINOUGH'S DEATH | 7 | 46 175 475 |
| SHEE ASKES IF SAD, OR SAVING POWERS. | LOVES HOROSCOPE | 5 | 46 185 483 |
| OF SWEET DISCOURSE, WHOSE POWERS | WISHES SUPPOSED MISTRESSE | 89 | 46 195 479 |
| UNTO WHOSE FEET IN REVERENCE OF THE POWERS, | AN ELEGIE ON DR PORTER | 4 | MS 395 476 |

## POWRES

| | | | | |
|---|---|---|---|---|
| MELTS ON THE BOSOME OF HIS LOVE. AND POWRES | OUT OF VIRGIL | 5 | 46 155 | 529 |
| OF NOBLE POWRES, I SEE. | TO THE NAME OF JESUS | 20 | 52 239 | 30 |
| BRING ALL THE POWRES OF PRAISE | TO THE NAME OF JESUS | 72 | 52 239 | 30 |
| POWRES OF MY SOUL, BE PROUD. | TO THE NAME OF JESUS | 92 | 52 239 | 30 |
| O DISSIPATE THY SPICY POWRES | TO THE NAME OF JESUS | 167 | 52 239 | 30 |
| CONTEND, YE POWRES OF HEAV'N & EARTH. | IN HOLY NATIVITY | 41 | 52 246 | 76 |
| AND SWEAR FAITH TO THY SWEETER POWRES. | NEW YEAR'S DAY | 36 | 52 251 | 37 |
| A COMMERCE OF CONTRARY POWRES, | IN GLORIOUS EPIPHANIE | 214 | 52 253 | 39 |
| THUS WE, WHO WHEN WITH ALL THE NOBLE POWRES | IN GLORIOUS EPIPHANIE | 219 | 52 253 | 39 |
| WITH ALL THE POWRES MY POOR HEART HATH | ADORO TE | 1 | 52 291 | 172 |
| GROW, BUT IN NEW POWRES TO THY NAME & PRAISE. | ADORO TE | 36 | 52 291 | 172 |
| STRETCH ALL THY POWRES. CALL IF YOU CAN | LAUDA SION SALVATOREM | 3 | 52 294 | 178 |
| MIXT.& MADE FRIENDS BY LOVE'S SWEET POWRES. | WEEPER | 102 | 52 307 | 120 |
| BLEST POWRES FORBID, THY TENDER LIFE | TERESA | 69 | 52 315 | 52 |
| ALL YE SOFT POWRES, | DEATH'S LECTURE | 8 | 52 340 | 475 |

## POWRS

| | | | | |
|---|---|---|---|---|
| BY THOSE SWEET EYES' PERSUASIVE POWRS | IN HOLY NATIVITY | 28 | 52 246 | 76 |

## POWERFULL

| | | | | |
|---|---|---|---|---|
| AS 'TIS POWERFULL THEREWITHALL. | OUT OF GREEKE CUPID'S CRYER | 38 | 46 159 | 519 |

## POWRFULL

| | | | | |
|---|---|---|---|---|
| TO KEEP PACE WITH THOSE POWRFULL WORDS. | ADORO TE | 14 | 52 291 | 172 |
| (WHO KNOWES HOW POWRFULL WELL-WRITT PRAIRES WOULD BE.) | ALEXIAS FIRST ELEGIE | 12 | 52 334 | 204 |

## PRACTICE

| | | | | |
|---|---|---|---|---|
| HIS PRACTICE PREACH'D THEM O'RE AGEN. | AN EPITAPH UPON ASHTON | 12 | 46 192 | 464 |

## PRACTISE

| | | | | |
|---|---|---|---|---|
| AS LEFT NO TIME TO PRACTISE ANY. | AN EPITAPH UPON ASHTON | 10 | 46 192 | 464 |

## PRAELUDIUM

| | | | | |
|---|---|---|---|---|
| INFORMES IT, IN A SWEET PRAELUDIUM | MUSICKS DUELL | 18 | 46 149 | 535 |
| THIS KNIFE MAY BE THE SPEARES PRAELUDIUM. | OUR LORD IN HIS CIRCUMCISION | 18 | 46 98 | 9 |

## PRAEPAR'D

| | | | | |
|---|---|---|---|---|
| HATH NOW PRAEPAR'D, & YOU MUST BE HIS GUEST. | UPON GUNPOWDER TREASON | 2 | MS 387 | 461 |

## PRAEROGATIVE

| | | | | |
|---|---|---|---|---|
| YEILD SOMTHING IN THY SAD PRAEROGATIVE | SANCTA MARIA DOLORUM | 57 | 52 283 | 162 |

## PRAESAGE

| | | | | |
|---|---|---|---|---|
| IT DOES PRAESAGE, THAT A GREAT PRINCE SHALL CLIMBE, | ON GUNPOWDER-TREASON | 35 | MS 384 | 458 |
| THE GOLD, IN WHICH HE FLAMES, DOES WELL PRAESAGE | UPON KINGS CORONATION | 17 | MS 389 | 454 |

## PRAESAG'D

| | | | | |
|---|---|---|---|---|
| THE FALL OF ALL THINGS IT PRAESAG'D, ITS OWNE | ON GUNPOWDER-TREASON | 52 | MS 384 | 458 |

## PRAESCRIBED

| | | | | |
|---|---|---|---|---|
| A HASTY PORTION OF PRAESCRIBED SLEEP. | DESCRIPTION RELIGIOUS HOUSE | 15 | 52 338 | 213 |

## PRAESCRIPTION

| | | | | |
|---|---|---|---|---|
| IF ALL'S PRAESCRIPTION, & PROUD WRONG | FLAMING HEART | 61 | 52 324 | 61 |

## PRAESUME

| | | | | |
|---|---|---|---|---|
| MY QUILL TO THEE MAY NOT PRAESUME TO SING. | UPON BIRTH PRINCESSE E | 21 | MS 391 | 456 |

## PRAISE

| | | | | |
|---|---|---|---|---|
| TO PRAISE THY LORD. | UPON ASSE THAT BORE SAVIOUR | 8 | 46 90 | 19 |
| THESE WRETCHES HAVE TO SPEAKE THY PRAISE. | NEITHER DURST MAN ASKE | 26 | 46 92 | 20 |
| TUN'D TO MY GREAT SHEPHEARDS PRAISE. | PSALME 23 | 34 | 46 102 | 5 |
| THY PRAISE MIGHT NOT SPEAK ENGLISH TOO, FORBID | AN APOLOGIE FOR HYMNE (TERESA) | 11 | 46 136 | 59 |
| WEE IN THY PRAISE WILL HAVE OUR PARTS. | ON THE ASSUMPTION | 30 | 46 139 | 114 |
| THAT NUMBRING OF HIS VERTUES PRAISE, | HIS EPITAPH (HERRYS) | 9 | 46 172 | 471 |
| A TROPHIE TO HER PRESENT PRAISE. | WISHES SUPPOSED MISTRESSE | 111 | 46 195 | 479 |
| BRING ALL THE POWRES OF PRAISE | TO THE NAME OF JESUS | 72 | 52 239 | 30 |
| THY SEEMLY PRAISE. | OFFICE H. CROSS MATINES | 21 | 52 265 | 86 |
| GROW, BUT IN NEW POWRES TO THY NAME & PRAISE. | ADORO TE | 36 | 52 291 | 172 |
| THY PRAISE MIGHT NOT SPEAK ENGLISH TOO. FORBID | AN APOLOGIE FOR (TERESA) HYMNE | 11 | 52 322 | 59 |
| THE CHOICEST OF HER OLIVE-CROWNES, & PRAISE | UPON KINGS CORONATION | 23 | MS 389 | 454 |

## PRAYSE

| | | | | |
|---|---|---|---|---|
| AND MY MOUTH SHALL SHEW FORTH THY PRAYSE. | OFFICE H. CROSS MATINES | 4 | 52 265 | 86 |
| KEEP WARM THY PRAYSE | CHARITAS NIMIA | 26 | 52 280 | 48 |
| TRIUMPHANT TEXT, PROVOKES THY PRAYSE. | LAUDA SION SALVATOREM | 8 | 52 294 | 178 |

```
                                                                    PAGE  318

      WE IN THY PRAYSE WILL HAVE OUR PARTS.           IN GLORIOUS ASSUMPTION B. LADY    45   52 304 114
      I LATE THE ROMAN YOUTH'S LOV'D PRAYSE & PRIDE,  ALEXIAS FIRST ELEGIE               1   52 334 204

PRAYSES

      NEEDS MUST YOUR NOBLE PRAYSES STRENGTH          TO THE QUEEN                      13   48 215 501
      TO CHAUNT MY PRAYSES IN A NEW-STRUNG SONG.      OUT OF GROTIUS                    74   MS 398 198

PRATLING

      WING'D WITH THEIR OWNE WILD ECCHO'S PRATLING FLY.   MUSICKS DUELL                 92   46 149 535

PRATTLING

      COMPLAINING PIPES, & PRATTLING STRINGS,         TO THE NAME OF JESUS              65   52 239  30

PRAY

      DRAW HIM, DRAG HIM, THOUGH HEE PRAY             OUT OF GREEKE CUPID'S CRYER       67   46 159 519
      TWO WENT TO PRAY. O RATHER SAY                  TWO WENT TO PRAY                   1   46  89  18
      ONE WENT TO BRAG, TH'OTHER TO PRAY.             TWO WENT TO PRAY                   2   46  89  18
      MEE FROM HIS PATRONAGE. I PRAY, HE CHIDES.      TO THE MORNING                    14   46 183 497
      AND TO WHAT PATRON CHUSE TO PRAY.               DIES IRAE                         22   52 298 186

PRAYER

      DOES THY SWEET BREATH'D PRAYER                  THE WEEPER                       105   46  79 120
      LET PRAYER ALONE TO PLAY HIS PART.              ON A PRAYER BOOKE                 28   46 126 139
      OF YOUR WELL PERFUMED PRAYER.                   ON MR. G. HERBERTS BOOKE          10   46 130  68
      LET PRAYER ALONE TO PLAY HIS PART,              PRAYER TO GENTLE-WOMAN            34   52 328 139

PRAIRE

      DOES THY SWEET-BREATH'D PRAIRE                  WEEPER                           141   52 307 120

PRAYERS

      HIS PRAYERS TOOKE THEIR PRICE AND STRENGTH      AN EPITAPH UPON ASHTON            15   46 192 464

PRAYRS

      POWR'D OUT IN PRAYRS FOR THEE. THY LORD'S IN DEATH.   SANCTA MARIA DOLORUM       110   52 283 162

PRAYRES

      THOUGH BOTH MY PRAYRES & TEARES COMBINE,        DIES IRAE                         53   52 298 186

PRAIRES

      (WHO KNOWES HOW POWRFULL WELL-WRITT PRAIRES WOULD BE.)   ALEXIAS FIRST ELEGIE     12   52 334 204

PRAIE'RS

      OH CROWNE THESE PRAIE'RS (MOV'D IN A HAPPY HOWER)   EX EUPHORMIONE                 3   MS 392 525

PRAI'RS

      IMPENETRABLE, BOTH TO PRAI'RS AND TEARS,        SOSPETTO D'HERODE                308   46 109 216

PREACHERS

      HONOUR ALL PREACHERS. HEARE THEIR OWNE.         AN EPITAPH UPON ASHTON             8   46 192 464

PREACH'D

      HIS PRACTICE PREACH'D THEM O'RE AGEN.           AN EPITAPH UPON ASHTON            12   46 192 464

PRECIOUS

      HIS PRECIOUS SWEETS,                            ON A PRAYER BOOKE                 88   46 126 139
      TO IMPROVE THAT PRECIOUS HOURE.                 ON A PRAYER BOOKE                 99   46 126 139
      SUCH WORDS, SOE PRECIOUS, AS THEY MAY NOT WEARE HORATIJ ILLE & NEFASTO             46   MS 382 530
      A PRECIOUS SEASON, & A GOLDEN AGE.              UPON KINGS CORONATION             18   MS 389 454
      A PRECIOUS INFLUENCE, AS SWEET AS THEE.         UPON BIRTH PRINCESSE E             2   MS 391 456
      AND PLANTS IT IN A PRECIOUS PERFUM'D BEDD,      AN ELEGY MR STANNINOW             51   MS 394 473

PREDICTIONS

      TO CROWNE THEIR PAST PREDICTIONS, BOTH HEE LAYES   SOSPETTO D'HERODE              95   46 109 216

PREFERRE

      PREFERRE SOFT ANTHEMS TO THE EARES OF MEN,      MUSICKS DUELL                     78   46 149 535

PREFERR'D

      PREFERR'D TO SOME PROUD FACE                    WEEPER                           183   52 307 120

PREGNANT

      THEIR PREGNANT BOSOMES IN A FRAGRANT BIRTH.     OUT OF VIRGIL                     14   46 155 529
      EACH FLOWERS A PREGNANT POYSON. TRY'D AND GOOD, SOSPETTO D'HERODE                347   46 109 216
      HIM HIS WISDOMES PREGNANT GROWTH                HIS EPITAPH (HERRYS)              15   46 172 471
```

PREJUDGE

| | | | | | |
|---|---|---|---|---|---|
| THEN SPOUSALL RITES PREJUDGE THE MARRIAGE-BED. | ON HOPE | 40 | 46 | 143 | 71 |
| THEN SPOUSALL RITES PREJUDGE THE MARRIAGE BED. | (ON) HOPE | 20 | 52 | 345 | 71 |

PREJUDICATE

| | | | | | |
|---|---|---|---|---|---|
| OF NAMES AND WORDS SO FARRE PREJUDICATE. | AN APOLOGIE FOR HYMNE (TERESA) | 14 | 46 | 136 | 59 |

PRAEJUDICATE

| | | | | | |
|---|---|---|---|---|---|
| OF NAMES & WORDES, SO FARR PRAEJUDICATE. | AN APOLOGIE FOR (TERESA) HYMNE | 14 | 52 | 322 | 59 |

FOOD-PREPARING

| | | | | | |
|---|---|---|---|---|---|
| AS WHEN A PILE OF FOOD-PREPARING FIRE, | SOSPETTO D'HERODE | 481 | 46 | 109 | 216 |

PRESENCE

| | | | | | |
|---|---|---|---|---|---|
| PALE PROOFE OF HER FELL PRESENCE. TH'AIRE TOO WELL | SOSPETTO D'HERODE | 374 | 46 | 109 | 216 |
| OUR ABSENT PRESENCE, AND OUR FUTURE NOW. | ON HOPE | 80 | 46 | 143 | 71 |
| AND SO THOU ART, THEIR PRESENCE MAKES THEE SO. | UPON YORKE HIS BIRTH | 17 | 46 | 176 | 500 |
| AT MID-DAY OPES A PRESENCE WHICH HEAVENS EYE | UPON YORKE HIS BIRTH | 70 | 46 | 176 | 500 |
| OUR ABSENT PRESENCE, AND OUR FUTURE NOW. | (ON) HOPE | 40 | 52 | 345 | 71 |

PRESENT

| | | | | | |
|---|---|---|---|---|---|
| HOW MANY PRESENT PRODIGIES CONSPIRE, | SOSPETTO D'HERODE | 94 | 46 | 109 | 216 |
| IMMORTALL FLOWERS TO HER FAIRE HAND PRESENT. | SOSPETTO D'HERODE | 100 | 46 | 109 | 216 |
| RENDERS THEE DOUBLE TO THY PRESENT WOES. | SOSPETTO D'HERODE | 244 | 46 | 109 | 216 |
| A TROPHIE TO HER PRESENT PRAISE. | WISHES SUPPOSED MISTRESSE | 111 | 46 | 195 | 479 |

PRAESENT

| | | | | | |
|---|---|---|---|---|---|
| A PRAESENT WORTHY OF APOLLO'S LOVE. | UPON BIRTH PRINCESSE E | 20 | MS | 391 | 456 |

PRESENTLY

| | | | | | |
|---|---|---|---|---|---|
| HIS ANGER KINDLE, PRESENTLY | OUT OF GREEKE CUPID'S CRYER | 29 | 46 | 159 | 519 |

PRESSE

| | | | | | |
|---|---|---|---|---|---|
| AND THE GREAT PENITENT PRESSE HIS OWN PALE LIPPS | IN GLORIOUS EPIPHANIE | 151 | 52 | 253 | 39 |
| UPWARDS, & PRESSE ON FOR THE PURE INTELLIGENTIALL PREY. | IN GLORIOUS EPIPHANIE | 222 | 52 | 253 | 39 |

WINE-PRESSE

| | | | | | |
|---|---|---|---|---|---|
| BUT HIM, WHO TROD THE WINE-PRESSE ALL ALONE. | AN APOLOGIE FOR HYMNE (TERESA) | 40 | 46 | 136 | 59 |
| BUT HIM WHO TROD THE WINE-PRESSE ALL ALONE | AN APOLOGIE FOR (TERESA) HYMNE | 40 | 52 | 322 | 59 |

PREST

| | | | | | |
|---|---|---|---|---|---|
| A SHIP THEY SAW, NO MEN SHEE HAD, YET PREST | THE BEGINNING OF HELIODORUS | 11 | 46 | 158 | 517 |
| SO SLEEPS A PILOT, WHOSE POORE BARKE IS PREST | SOSPETTO D'HERODE | 425 | 46 | 109 | 216 |

PRESUME

| | | | | | |
|---|---|---|---|---|---|
| WHAT E'RE IT BE LOVE OFFERS, STILL PRESUME | OUT OF GREEKE CUPID'S CRYER | 73 | 46 | 159 | 519 |
| FOR EVER SHALL PRESUME | TO THE NAME OF JESUS | 179 | 52 | 239 | 30 |

PRETENCE

| | | | | | |
|---|---|---|---|---|---|
| TO WHICH HE NOW HAS NO PRETENCE. | IN GLORIOUS EPIPHANIE | 245 | 52 | 253 | 39 |

PRETENCES

| | | | | | |
|---|---|---|---|---|---|
| PLEAD YOUR PRETENCES (O YOU STRONG | TO COUNTESSE OF DENBIGH | 9 | 52 | 236 | 146 |
| PLEAD YOUR PRETENCES, (O YOU STRONG | AGAINST IRRESOLUTION AND DELAY | 17 | 52 | 347 | 146 |

PRETENDS

| | | | | | |
|---|---|---|---|---|---|
| AND CATCH THE PRETIOUS NAME THIS PEICE PRETENDS. | FLAMING HEART | 2 | 52 | 324 | 61 |

PRETIOUS

| | | | | | |
|---|---|---|---|---|---|
| BECAUSE THOSE PRETIOUS MYSTERYES THAT DWELL, | MUSICKS DUELL | 143 | 46 | 149 | 535 |
| TO SHINE IN THINGS SO PRETIOUS. | THE WEEPER | 18 | 46 | 79 | 120 |
| TIME LAYES HIM UP. HE'S PRETIOUS. | THE WEEPER | 96 | 46 | 79 | 120 |
| WEEPE PRETIOUS TEARES UPON THE STONES. | PSALME 137 | 36 | 46 | 104 | 7 |
| BATHING THEIR HOT LIMBS IN LIFE'S PRETIOUS FLOOD. | SOSPETTO D'HERODE | 316 | 46 | 109 | 216 |
| THE TRUNKE. YET IN THIS GROUND HIS PRETIOUS ROOT | UPON DEATH OF HERRYS | 35 | 46 | 167 | 466 |
| AND MEANT TO LEAVE HIS PRETIOUS FEATURE, | UPON DEATH OF DESIRED HERRYS | 7 | 46 | 168 | 467 |
| FOR HEE WHOSE PRETIOUS MEMORY, | ANOTHER ON HERRYS | 7 | 46 | 170 | 469 |
| PRETIOUS THEIR OFFERINGS THAT THEIR ALTARS TAKE. | UPON YORKE HIS BIRTH | 117 | 46 | 176 | 500 |
| O'TH PRETIOUS PHOENIX, WARME UPON HER BREAST. | ON A FOULE MORNING | 22 | 46 | 181 | 495 |
| HOW MUCH THEMSELVES MORE PRETIOUS ARE. | WISHES SUPPOSED MISTRESSE | 48 | 46 | 195 | 479 |
| PROUD IN THE PATTERNE OF THY PRETIOUS YOUTH, | UPON TWO GREENE APRICOCKES | 21 | 46 | 220 | 494 |
| OF ALL THIS PRETIOUS PATIENCE. | TO THE NAME OF JESUS | 140 | 52 | 239 | 30 |
| WE (PRETIOUS ONES) IN YOU HAVE WON | IN GLORIOUS EPIPHANIE | 73 | 52 | 253 | 39 |
| PROUD TO HAVE GAIN'D THIS PRETIOUS LOSSE | IN GLORIOUS EPIPHANIE | 141 | 52 | 253 | 39 |
| TO POISE EACH PRETIOUS LIMB, | OFFICE H. CROSS EVENSONG | 16 | 52 | 273 | 101 |
| WHAT WAS IT TO THY PRETIOUS BLOOD | CHARITAS NIMIA | 47 | 52 | 280 | 48 |

```
                                                                        PAGE  320

   LO, HEART, THY HOPE'S WHOLE PLEA. HER PRETIOUS BREATH  SANCTA MARIA DOLORUM             109   52 283 162
   UNTOUCH'T HER PRETIOUS TOTALL HATH.                    LAUDA SION SALVATOREM             60   52 294 178
   THY PRETIOUS NAME SHALL BE                             IN GLORIOUS ASSUMPTION B. LADY    46   52 304 114
   TO SHINE IN THINGS SO PRETIOUS.                        WEEPER                            18   52 307 120
   O PRETIOUS PRODIGALL.                                  WEEPER                           127   52 307 120
   TIME LAYES HIM UP. HE'S PRETIOUS.                      WEEPER                           150   52 307 120
   AND CATCH THE PRETIOUS NAME THIS PEICE PRETENDS.       FLAMING HEART                      2   52 324  61
   HIS PRETIOUS SWEETS                                    PRAYER TO GENTLE-WOMAN            94   52 328 139
   TO IMPROVE THAT PRETIOUS HOUR.                         PRAYER TO GENTLE-WOMAN           105   52 328 139
   LAYES UP HIS PURER & MORE PRETIOUS VOWES,              TO SAME CONCERNING CHOISE         35   52 331  66
   THOU TO MAINTAIN THEIR PRETIOUS STRIFE                 TEMPERANCE                         3   52 342 510
   THE PRETIOUS BARBILL, NOW GROUNE RIFE,                 PETRONIJ ALES PHASIACIS PETITA    15   MS 382 526
   WHICH THEIR BRIGHT FATHER IN A PRETIOUS SHOWRE         AN ELEGY MR STANNINOW              9   MS 394 473

PRETTY

   AND MAKES A PRETTY EARTHQUAKE IN HER BREAST,          MUSICKS DUELL                      89   46 149 535

PREVENT

   OF AGE AND BARENNESSE, AND HER BABE PREVENT           SOSPETTO D'HERODE                 102   46 109 216

PREVENTS

   PREVENTS THE EYE-LIDDS OF THE BLUSHING DAY.           MUSICKS DUELL                      82   46 149 535

PREY

   HOPE OF A PREY. THERE TO THE MAINE LAND TY'D          THE BEGINNING OF HELIODORUS        10   46 158 517
   POORE JEALOUSIE. WHY SHOULD HE WISH TO PREY           SOSPETTO D'HERODE                 519   46 109 216
   SEIZE HER SWEET PREY.                                 ON A PRAYER BOOKE                 101   46 126 139
   DEATH'S PREY, BEFORE THE PRIZE OF LOVE.               TO COUNTESSE OF DENBIGH            66   52 236 146
   UPWARDS, & PRESSE ON FOR THE PURE INTELLIGENTIALL     IN GLORIOUS EPIPHANIE             222   52 253  39
      PREY.

   SEIZE HER SWEET PREY                                  PRAYER TO GENTLE-WOMAN            107   52 328 139
   DEATH'S PREY, BEFORE THE PRIZE OF LOVE.               AGAINST IRRESOLUTION AND DELAY     88   52 347 146
   A WINGED HERALD, GLADD OF SOE SWEET A PREY,           AN ELEGY MR STANNINOW              49   MS 394 473

PREYS

   WHOSE UNCONSUM'D CONSUMPTION PREYS UPON               SOSPETTO D'HERODE                  59   46 109 216

PRICE

   HIS PRAYERS TOOKE THEIR PRICE AND STRENGTH            AN EPITAPH UPON ASHTON             15   46 192 464
   THE WORLD'S PRICE SETT TO SALE, & BY THE BOLD         OFFICE H. CROSS MATINES            14   52 265  86
   US WITH OUR PRICE THOU WEIGHED'ST.                    VEXILLA REGIS                      33   52 277 156
   OUR PRICE FOR US THOU PAYED'ST.                       VEXILLA REGIS                      34   52 277 156
   WITH MY PRICE, & NOT WITH ME                          DIES IRAE                          38   52 298 186

PRICK

   THEY PRICK A BLEEDING HEART AT EVERY STITCH.          SOSPETTO D'HERODE                 342   46 109 216

PRIDE

   TO SWELL WITH FORWARD PRIDE, AND SEED DESIRE          OUT OF VIRGIL                       3   46 155 529
   'TIS THE SWEET PRIDE OF HER HUMILITY.                 ON VIRGINS BASHFULNESSE             2   46  89   9
   HIS MASTERS PRIDE.                                    UPON ASSE THAT BORE SAVIOUR         6   46  90  19
   GREAT ANTHONY. SPAINS WELL-BESEEMING PRIDE.           SOSPETTO D'HERODE                   9   46 109 216
   WHERE SEAV'N TALL HORNES (HIS EMPIRES PRIDE) ASPIRE.  SOSPETTO D'HERODE                  46   46 109 216
   NOR SHOULD'ST THOU BATE IN PRIDE, BECAUSE THAT NOW,   SOSPETTO D'HERODE                 267   46 109 216
   TILL HIS O'REFLOWING PRIDE SUPPRESSE THE FLAME,       SOSPETTO D'HERODE                 487   46 109 216
   OF HEAVEN, AND HUMBLE PRIDE OF EARTH.                 ON THE ASSUMPTION                  60   46 139 114
   ALL THE PURPLE PRIDE OF LACES,                        AN HIMNE FOR CIRCUMCISION           5   46 141  37
   THRIV'D IN THESE HAPPY GROUNDS, THE EARTH'S JUST      UPON DEATH OF HERRYS                3   46 167 466
      PRIDE.

   WITHIN HIMSELFE THE PURPLE PRIDE                      UPON DEATH OF DESIRED HERRYS       36   46 168 467
   IN HIS ASHES ALL HER PRIDE.                           ANOTHER ON HERRYS                  60   46 170 469
   WAS THE PRIDE OF NAKED TRUTH.                         HIS EPITAPH (HERRYS)               26   46 172 471
   ALL THE PURPLE PRIDE THAT LACES                       NEW YEAR'S DAY                      5   52 251  37
   OF HEAVN. THE HUMBLE PRIDE OF EARTH.                  IN GLORIOUS ASSUMPTION B. LADY     65   52 304 114
   WHAT PRINCE'S WANTON'ST PRIDE E'RE COULD              WEEPER                            119   52 307 120
   I LATE THE ROMAN YOUTH'S LOV'D PRAYSE & PRIDE,        ALEXIAS FIRST ELEGIE                1   52 334 204
   MY WOMBES CHAST PRIDE IS GONE, MY HEAV'NE-BORNE BOY.  LUKE 2. QUAERIT JESUM               7   MS 379  11
   OF BLISSE, DEBASE THEE. BUT WITH A JUST PRIDE         UPON KINGS CORONATION               8   MS 389 454
   MURDRED THE EARTH'S JUST PRIDE WITH A RUDE KISSE.     AN ELEGY MR STANNINOW              48   MS 394 473

PRIESTESSE

   NO SHEE'S A PRIESTESSE OF THAT GROVE                  THOUGH NOW 'TIS NEITHER            21   MS 397 492

PRIESTS

   THE BLOUD HOUND BROOD OF PRIESTS AGAINST MEE DRAW     OUT OF GROTIUS                     45   MS 398 198

PRIME

   THAT SELDOME LETT'ST A BLUSHING YOUTHFULL PRIME       UPON DEATH OF HERRYS               30   46 167 466
   CHERISHT IN HIS GOLDEN PRIME.                         HIS EPITAPH (HERRYS)               44   46 172 471
   THE EARLY PRIME BLUSHES TO SAY                        OFFICE H. CROSS PRIME               1   52 267  91
   FORC'T THIS PRIME FLOWRE OF YOUTH TO MAKE SUCH HAST   AN ELEGY MR STANNINOW              28   MS 394 473
```

## PRIMROSE'S

| | | | | | |
|---|---|---|---|---|---|
| THE PRIMROSE'S PALE CHEEK TO DECK, | WEEPER | 44 | 52 | 307 | 120 |

## PRIMROSES

| | | | | | |
|---|---|---|---|---|---|
| THE PRIMROSES PALE CHEEKE TO DECKE, | THE WEEPER | 38 | 46 | 79 | 120 |

## PRINCE

| | | | | | |
|---|---|---|---|---|---|
| HOLD THE PERVERSE PRINCE IN ETERNALL TIES | SOSPETTO D'HERODE | 39 | 46 | 109 | 216 |
| THUS SPOKE TH'IMPATIENT PRINCE, AND MADE A PAUSE, | SOSPETTO D'HERODE | 257 | 46 | 109 | 216 |
| TO BE THY GARLAND. SEE (SWEET PRINCE) O SEE | UPON YORKE HIS BIRTH | 39 | 46 | 176 | 500 |
| IT DOES PRAESAGE, THAT A GREAT PRINCE SHALL CLIMBE, | ON GUNPOWDER-TREASON | 35 | MS | 384 | 458 |

## PRINCE'S

| | | | | | |
|---|---|---|---|---|---|
| WHAT PRINCE'S WANTON'ST PRIDE E'RE COULD | WEEPER | 119 | 52 | 307 | 120 |

## PRINCES

| | | | | | |
|---|---|---|---|---|---|
| ADORE HER PRINCES BIRTH, FLAT ON HER BREST. | SOSPETTO D'HERODE | 124 | 46 | 109 | 216 |
| HE MIGHT PROVOKE THE WEALTH OF PRINCES. | WEEPER | 118 | 52 | 307 | 120 |
| THE EASTERN PRINCES TO THEIR INFANT KING. | ALEXIAS SECONDE ELEGIE | 28 | 52 | 335 | 207 |

## PRINCELY

| | | | | | |
|---|---|---|---|---|---|
| A COMMON BANQUETT. NOE, HEERE'S PRINCELY FARE | UPON GUNPOWDER TREASON | 6 | MS | 387 | 461 |
| THAT IN THE PRINCELY PATTERNE SHINES. FROM WHENCE | UPON BIRTH PRINCESSE E | 34 | MS | 391 | 456 |

## PRINCESSE

| | | | | | |
|---|---|---|---|---|---|
| LIVE RAREST PRINCESSE, AND MAY THE BRIGHT | ON THE ASSUMPTION | 55 | 46 | 139 | 114 |
| LIVE, ROSY PRINCESSE, LIVE. AND MAY THE BRIGHT | IN GLORIOUS ASSUMPTION B. LADY | 60 | 52 | 304 | 114 |

## PRINCIPALL

| | | | | | |
|---|---|---|---|---|---|
| THIS WELL-WROUGHT COPY THE FAIRE PRINCIPALL. | UPON YORKE HIS BIRTH | 48 | 46 | 176 | 500 |

## PRISON

| | | | | | |
|---|---|---|---|---|---|
| HERE SYLLA HIS SEVEREST PRISON HAS. | SOSPETTO D'HERODE | 356 | 46 | 109 | 216 |

## CALDRON-PRISON'D

| | | | | | |
|---|---|---|---|---|---|
| THE CALDRON-PRISON'D WATERS STREIGHT CONSPIRE, | SOSPETTO D'HERODE | 483 | 46 | 109 | 216 |

## SELFE-PRISON'D

| | | | | | |
|---|---|---|---|---|---|
| THESE CURTAIN'D WINDOWES, THIS SELFE-PRISON'D EYE, | UPON STANINOUGH'S DEATH | 25 | 46 | 175 | 475 |

## PRIS'NER

| | | | | | |
|---|---|---|---|---|---|
| AS PRIS'NER IN A FEW POORE RAGS TO LYE. | SOSPETTO D'HERODE | 172 | 46 | 109 | 216 |

## PRISONERS

| | | | | | |
|---|---|---|---|---|---|
| POOR WATERS THEIR OWNE PRISONERS BE. | TO COUNTESSE OF DENBIGH | 22 | 52 | 236 | 146 |
| THE PRISONERS LOOSE, THE JAYLOR BOUND. | OFFICE H. CROSS THIRD | 15 | 52 | 268 | 93 |
| POOR WATERS THEIR OWN PRISONERS BE. | AGAINST IRRESOLUTION AND DELAY | 22 | 52 | 347 | 146 |

## PRIVATE

| | | | | | |
|---|---|---|---|---|---|
| WEELL SEE HIM TAKE A PRIVATE SEAT, | IN MEMORY OF LADY MADRE TERESA | 12 | 46 | 131 | 52 |
| AND SEE HIM TAKE A PRIVATE SEAT, | TERESA | 12 | 52 | 315 | 52 |

## PRIZE

| | | | | | |
|---|---|---|---|---|---|
| DEATH'S PREY, BEFORE THE PRIZE OF LOVE. | TO COUNTESSE OF DENBIGH | 66 | 52 | 236 | 146 |
| O PRIZE OF THE RICH SPIRIT. WITH WHAT FEIRCE CHASE | IN GLORIOUS EPIPHANIE | 196 | 52 | 253 | 39 |
| IN STEAD OF BRINGING IN THE BLISSFULL PRIZE | IN GLORIOUS EPIPHANIE | 226 | 52 | 253 | 39 |
| AND PRIZE THEMSELVES. DOE MUCH, THAT MORE THEY MAY, | DESCRIPTION RELIGIOUS HOUSE | 20 | 52 | 338 | 213 |
| DEATH'S PREY, BEFORE THE PRIZE OF LOVE. | AGAINST IRRESOLUTION AND DELAY | 86 | 52 | 347 | 146 |

## PRISE

| | | | | | |
|---|---|---|---|---|---|
| SHEE DYES. AND LEAVES HER LIFE THE VICTORS PRISE, | MUSICKS DUELL | 166 | 46 | 149 | 535 |

## PRI'THEE

| | | | | | |
|---|---|---|---|---|---|
| THY LAZY CRAWLING STREAMES, PRI'THEE BE GONE, | AN ELEGIE ON DR PORTER | 20 | MS | 395 | 476 |

## PRETHEE

| | | | | | |
|---|---|---|---|---|---|
| PRETHEE, SWEET NOW LET ME GOE, | OUT OF GREEKE CUPID'S CRYER | 69 | 46 | 159 | 519 |

## PROCLAIM

| | | | | | |
|---|---|---|---|---|---|
| AND IN THE WEALTH OF ONE RICH WORD PROCLAIM | TO THE NAME OF JESUS | 95 | 52 | 239 | 30 |
| O WHEN THY LAST FROWN SHALL PROCLAIM | DIES IRAE | 57 | 52 | 298 | 186 |

PROCLAIME

| | | | |
|---|---|---|---|
| WHILE THEY SPEAKE NOTHING, THEY PROCLAIME | NEITHER DURST MAN ASKE | 23 | 46  92  20 |
| THEIR NEW KING, AND THY SUCCESSOUR PROCLAIME. | SOSPETTO D'HERODE | 440 | 46 109 216 |
| THEY SHALL PROCLAIME TO ALL, THAT THEY ARE THINE. | UPON BIRTH PRINCESSE E | 8 | MS 391 456 |

PROCLAYME

| | | | |
|---|---|---|---|
| AND WITH CLASP'T WINGES PROCLAYME A SPRING | THOUGH NOW 'TIS NEITHER | 11 | MS 397 492 |

PROCRUSTES

| | | | |
|---|---|---|---|
| HERE STRONG PROCRUSTES PLANTS HIS BED OF BRASSE. | SOSPETTO D'HERODE | 356 | 46 109 216 |

PRODIGAL

| | | | |
|---|---|---|---|
| STILL YOU ARE PRODIGAL OF YOUR LOVE'S EXPENCE | SOSPETTO D'HERODE | 265 | 46 109 216 |

PRODIGALL

| | | | |
|---|---|---|---|
| O PRETIOUS PRODIGALL. | WEEPER | 127 | 52 307 120 |

PRODIGIES

| | | | |
|---|---|---|---|
| HOW MANY PRESENT PRODIGIES CONSPIRE, | SOSPETTO D'HERODE | 94 | 46 109 216 |
| TO USHER IN THIS SHOALE OF PRODIGIES, | ON GUNPOWDER-TREASON | 37 | MS 384 458 |

PRODIGIOUS

| | | | |
|---|---|---|---|
| HIS NEW PRODIGIOUS NIGHT, | IN GLORIOUS EPIPHANIE | 172 | 52 253  39 |

PROFANE

| | | | |
|---|---|---|---|
| PROFANE SADOCUS TOO DOES FIERCELY LEAD | OUT OF GROTIUS | 47 | MS 398 198 |

PROPHANE

| | | | |
|---|---|---|---|
| FLY, FLY PROPHANE FOGS, FARRE HENCE FLY AWAY, | ON A FOULE MORNING | 31 | 46 181 495 |
| ALL FORCE OF SO PROPHANE A FALLACY | TO THE NAME OF JESUS | 171 | 52 239  30 |

PROFFER

| | | | |
|---|---|---|---|
| AND PEEP & PROFFER AT THY SPARKLING THRONE. | IN GLORIOUS EPIPHANIE | 225 | 52 253  39 |

PROFICIENCIE

| | | | |
|---|---|---|---|
| INTO THE PUBLICK YEARES PROFICIENCIE. | UPON TWO GREENE APRICOCKES | 24 | 48 220 494 |

PROFOUND

| | | | |
|---|---|---|---|
| THE WORLDS PROFOUND HEART PANTS. THERE PLACED IS | SOSPETTO D'HERODE | 35 | 46 109 216 |
| RUNG, THROUGH THE HOLLOW VAULTS OF HELL PROFOUND. | SOSPETTO D'HERODE | 299 | 46 109 216 |

PROGNE

| | | | |
|---|---|---|---|
| TANTALUS, ATREUS, PROGNE, HERE ARE GUESTS. | SOSPETTO D'HERODE | 333 | 46 109 216 |

PROGRESSIONS

| | | | |
|---|---|---|---|
| PROGRESSIONS 'TWIXT WHOSE TERMES POOR TIME GROWS OLD. | UPON TWO GREENE APRICOCKES | 16 | 48 220 494 |

PROJECTS

| | | | |
|---|---|---|---|
| IN OUR GREAT PROJECTS, BOTH 'GAINST HEAV'N AND EARTH. | SOSPETTO D'HERODE | 286 | 46 109 216 |

PROMETHEUS

| | | | |
|---|---|---|---|
| PROMETHEUS SELFE, & PELOPS STERVED SIRE | HORATIJ ILLE & NEFASTO | 54 | MS 382 530 |

PROMISE

| | | | |
|---|---|---|---|
| PROMISE THE EARTH, TO COUNTERSHINE | THE WEEPER | 11 | 46  79 120 |
| PROMISE THE EARTH TO COUNTER SHINE | WEEPER | 11 | 52 307 120 |
| THE HOPE AND PROMISE OF HIS BUD. | AGAINST IRRESOLUTION AND DELAY | 36 | 52 347 146 |

PRONOUNC'D

| | | | |
|---|---|---|---|
| THY WELL PRONOUNC'D PANEGYRIS. | NEITHER DURST MAN ASKE | 20 | 46  92  20 |

PROOF

| | | | |
|---|---|---|---|
| HAPPY PROOF, SHE SHAL DISCOVER | PRAYER TO GENTLE-WOMAN | 121 | 52 328 139 |

PROOFE

| | | | |
|---|---|---|---|
| THOU MAD'ST BOLD PROOFE UPON THE BROW OF HEAV'N, | SOSPETTO D'HERODE | 266 | 46 109 216 |
| PALE PROOFE OF HER FELL PRESENCE. TH'AIRE TOO WELL | SOSPETTO D'HERODE | 374 | 46 109 216 |

PROPHECY

| | | | |
|---|---|---|---|
| AND FEELE THE PULSE OF EVERY PROPHECY. | SOSPETTO D'HERODE | 156 | 46 109 216 |

## PROPHESY

| | | | | | |
|---|---|---|---|---|---|
| SWEET, LET ME PROPHESY THAT AT LAST T'WILL PROVE | TO SAME CONCERNING CHOISE | 33 | 52 | 331 | 66 |

## PROPHECIES

| | | | | | |
|---|---|---|---|---|---|
| A THOUSAND PROPHECIES THAT TALKE STRANGE THINGS, | SOSPETTO D'HERODE | 497 | 46 | 109 | 216 |

## PROPHESIES

| | | | | | |
|---|---|---|---|---|---|
| INTO TH'OLD PROPHESIES, TREMBLING TO MARKE | SOSPETTO D'HERODE | 93 | 46 | 109 | 216 |

## PROPHETICK

| | | | | | |
|---|---|---|---|---|---|
| THOUGH THE PROPHETICK KING | VEXILLA REGIS | 21 | 52 | 277 | 156 |

## PROPHETS

| | | | | | |
|---|---|---|---|---|---|
| THOU TRIM'ST A PROPHETS TOMBE, AND DOST BEQUEATH | YEE BUILD SEPULCHRES | 1 | 46 | 95 | 21 |

## PROPITIATE

| | | | | | |
|---|---|---|---|---|---|
| WHAT HOPE AURORA TO PROPITIATE THEE, | TO THE MORNING | 3 | 46 | 183 | 497 |

## PROPITIOUS

| | | | | | |
|---|---|---|---|---|---|
| (IN THAT PROPITIOUS HOUR) | OFFICE H. CROSS EVENSONG | 17 | 52 | 273 | 101 |

## PROSPECTIVE

| | | | | | |
|---|---|---|---|---|---|
| THEIR BLACK, BUT FAITHFULL PROSPECTIVE OF THEE. | IN GLORIOUS EPIPHANIE | 171 | 52 | 253 | 39 |

## PROSP'ROUS

| | | | | | |
|---|---|---|---|---|---|
| CAN HIS ATTEMPTS ABOVE STILL PROSP'ROUS BE, | SOSPETTO D'HERODE | 207 | 46 | 109 | 216 |

## PROTECTION

| | | | | | |
|---|---|---|---|---|---|
| UNDER PROTECTION OF AN OAKE, THERE SATE | MUSICKS DUELL | 4 | 46 | 149 | 535 |

## PROTESTANT

| | | | | | |
|---|---|---|---|---|---|
| HEE WAS A PROTESTANT AT HOME. | AN EPITAPH UPON ASHTON | 17 | 46 | 192 | 464 |

## PROUD

| | | | | | |
|---|---|---|---|---|---|
| LICKE HIS PROUD FEET, AND HAST INTO THE SEAS | THE BEGINNING OF HELIODORUS | 5 | 46 | 156 | 517 |
| UNDER TH' UNRULY BEASTS PROUD FEET HE LIES | HIGH MOUNTED ON AN ANT | 3 | 46 | 151 | 523 |
| PROUD WILL HIS SISTER BE TO WEARE | THE TEARE | 11 | 46 | 84 | 50 |
| OR WAVE SO PROUD. | WHY ARE YEE AFRAID | 6 | 46 | 88 | 15 |
| CONCEIVE PROUD HOPES OF PROVING ROSES. | ON BLEEDING WOUNDS OF LORD | 24 | 46 | 101 | 110 |
| RAINE-SWOLNE RIVERS MAY RISE PROUD | ON BLEEDING WOUNDS OF LORD | 33 | 46 | 101 | 110 |
| ON THE PROUD BANKES OF GREAT EUPHRATES FLOOD, | PSALME 137 | 1 | 46 | 104 | 7 |
| DOST LAUGH, PROUD BABELS DAUGHTER, DO, LAUGH ON, | PSALME 137 | 31 | 46 | 104 | 7 |
| THY FAMES FULL NOISE, MAKES PROUD THE PATIENT EARTH, | SOSPETTO D'HERODE | 29 | 46 | 109 | 216 |
| PROUD MORNING OF A PERVERSE DAY. HOW LUST | SOSPETTO D'HERODE | 77 | 46 | 109 | 216 |
| MAKE PROUD THE RUBY PORTALLS OF THE EAST. | SOSPETTO D'HERODE | 122 | 46 | 109 | 216 |
| DOWNE MY PROUD THOUGHT, AND LEAVE IT IN A TRANCE. | SOSPETTO D'HERODE | 204 | 46 | 109 | 216 |
| REPLY'D THE PROUD KING, O MY CROWNES DEFENCE. | SOSPETTO D'HERODE | 281 | 46 | 109 | 216 |
| THERE HAS THE PURPLE VENGEANCE A PROUD SEAT. | SOSPETTO D'HERODE | 313 | 46 | 109 | 216 |
| TO THE PROUD HOPES OF POOR MORTALITY. | UPON STANINOUGH'S DEATH | 24 | 46 | 175 | 475 |
| THEN LET THE EASTERNE WORLD BRAGGE AND BE PROUD | UPON YORKE HIS BIRTH | 86 | 46 | 176 | 500 |
| AND WILT COMMAND PROUD ZEPHYRUS TO SPORT HER | ON A FOULE MORNING | 12 | 46 | 181 | 495 |
| PROUD IN THE PATTERNE OF THY PRETIOUS YOUTH, | UPON TWO GREENE APRICOCKES | 21 | 48 | 220 | 494 |
| POWRES OF MY SOUL, BE PROUD. | TO THE NAME OF JESUS | 92 | 52 | 239 | 30 |
| PROUD WORLD, SAID I. CEASE YOUR CONTEST | IN HOLY NATIVITY | 44 | 52 | 246 | 76 |
| THE PROUD & MISPLAC'T GATES OF HELL, | IN GLORIOUS EPIPHANIE | 55 | 52 | 253 | 39 |
| THEREFORE WITH HIS PROUD PERSIAN SPOILES | IN GLORIOUS EPIPHANIE | 80 | 52 | 253 | 39 |
| PROUD SONS OF DEATH, THAT DURST COMPELL | IN GLORIOUS EPIPHANIE | 109 | 52 | 253 | 39 |
| PROUD TO HAVE GAIN'D THIS PRETIOUS LOSSE | IN GLORIOUS EPIPHANIE | 141 | 52 | 253 | 39 |
| AND GIVE IT SELF FOR SPORT TO THE PROUD WIND. | CHARITAS NIMIA | 30 | 52 | 280 | 48 |
| RAIN-SWOLN RIVERS MAY RISE PROUD, | UPON BLEEDING CRUCIFIX | 29 | 52 | 288 | 110 |
| DOWN DOWN, PROUD SENSE. DISCOURSES DY. | ADORO TE | 5 | 52 | 291 | 172 |
| WITH PROUD UNPITTYING FIRE. | WEEPER | 159 | 52 | 307 | 120 |
| PREFERR'D TO SOME PROUD FACE | WEEPER | 183 | 52 | 307 | 120 |
| IF ALL'S PRAESCRIPTION, & PROUD WRONG | FLAMING HEART | 61 | 52 | 324 | 61 |
| NO SAILES OF TYRIAN SYLK PROUD PAVEMENTS SWEEPING. | DESCRIPTION RELIGIOUS HOUSE | 3 | 52 | 338 | 213 |
| PROUD LOOKES, & LOFTY EYLIDDES, HERE PUTT ON | DEATH'S LECTURE | 21 | 52 | 340 | 475 |
| OF ALL PROUD NEPTUNES SILVER-SHEILDED GUARD. | AN ELEGIE ON DR PORTER | 34 | MS | 395 | 476 |

## PROUDEST

| | | | | | |
|---|---|---|---|---|---|
| POSETH HIS PROUDEST INTELLECTUALL POWER. | SOSPETTO D'HERODE | 166 | 46 | 109 | 216 |
| IF ALL FAILE WEE'L PUT ON OUR PROUDEST ARMES. | SOSPETTO D'HERODE | 276 | 46 | 109 | 216 |
| HER PROUDEST PEARLES, I MEAN THY TEARES. | WEEPER | 42 | 52 | 307 | 120 |

## PROUDLY

| | | | | | |
|---|---|---|---|---|---|
| THE LUTES LIGHT GENIUS NOW DOES PROUDLY RISE, | MUSICKS DUELL | 135 | 46 | 149 | 535 |
| WHEN THIS SO PROUDLY POOR | IN GLORIOUS EPIPHANIE | 134 | 52 | 253 | 39 |
| THE PHAENIX SELFE SHALL NOT MORE PROUDLY BURNE, | EX EUPHORMIONE | 15 | MS | 392 | 525 |

PROUDLY-REPOSED

    TO WHERE THE KINGS PROUDLY-REPOSED HEAD    SOSPETTO D'HERODE    410  46 109 216

PROVE

    HOW SHE THAT IS A MAID SHOULD PROVE A MOTHER,    SOSPETTO D'HERODE    163  46 109 216
    THAT A VILE MANGER HIS LOW BED SHOULD PROVE,    SOSPETTO D'HERODE    175  46 109 216
    TO PROVE THAT TRUE, SCHOOLES USE TO TELL,    ON A PRAYER BOOKE    7  46 126 139
    OF LIFE AND DEATH--TO PROVE THE WORD,    IN MEMORY OF LADY MADRE TERESA    2  46 131  52
    YET HAS SHEE A HEART DARES HOPE TO PROVE.    IN MEMORY OF LADY MADRE TERESA    27  46 131  52
    DRINKE WEE TILL WE PROVE MORE, NOT LESSE THEN MEN.    AN APOLOGIE FOR HYMNE (TERESA)    36  46 136  59
    WINE OF IMMORTALL MIXTURE, WHICH CAN PROVE    AN APOLOGIE FOR HYMNE (TERESA)    42  46 136  59
    ALL HER BIRTHS ABORTIVE PROVE.    UPON DEATH OF DESIRED HERRYS    74  46 168 467
    AND HIS FEAVER WISH'D TO PROVE    ANOTHER ON HERRYS    27  46 170 469
    E'RE PROVE THE DISMALL MORNING OF THY NIGHT.    UPON YORKE HIS BIRTH    93  46 176 500
    AND SO IN EACH CHILD OFTEN PROVE A MOTHER.    UPON YORKE HIS BIRTH    101  46 176 500
    YEILD QUICKLY, LEST PERHAPS YOU PROVE    TO COUNTESSE OF DENBIGH    65  52 236 146
    CAN PROVE IT SELF SOME KIN (SWEET NAME) TO THEE.    TO THE NAME OF JESUS    182  52 239  30
    AND HE MORE NEEDFULLY & NOBLE PROVE    IN GLORIOUS EPIPHANIE    159  52 253  39
    AND PROVE HOW LIGHT THE WORLD WAS, WHEN IT WEIGHD    OFFICE H. CROSS EVENSONG    19  52 273 101
        WITH HIM.

    SOON AS THE RIGHT-HAND SCALE REJOYC'T TO PROVE    VEXILLA REGIS    35  52 277 156
    THAT LOST AGAIN MY LIFE MAY PROVE    CHARITAS NIMIA    65  52 280  48
    THE CHILL LUMP WOULD RELENT, & PROVE    SANCTA MARIA DOLORUM    49  52 283 162
    COULD PROVE THE WHOLE SUMME (TOO SURE) DUE TO HIM.    SANCTA MARIA DOLORUM    94  52 283 162
    PROVE NOBLY, HERE, UNNATURAL.    O GLORIOSA DOMINA    24  52 302 194
    OF LIFE & DEATH. TO PROVE THE WORD,    TERESA    2  52 315  52
    YET HAS SHE'A HEART DARES HOPE TO PROVE    TERESA    27  52 315  52
    DRINK WE TILL WE PROVE MORE, NOT LESSE. THEN MEN,    AN APOLOGIE FOR (TERESA) HYMNE    36  52 322  59
    WINE OF IMMORTALL MIXTURE. WHICH CAN PROVE    AN APOLOGIE FOR (TERESA) HYMNE    42  52 322  59
    WHAT IS'T YOUR TASTFULL SPIRITS DOE PROVE    FLAMING HEART    51  52 324  61
    TO PROVE THAT TRUE, SCHOOLES USE TO TELL,    PRAYER TO GENTLE-WOMAN    13  52 328 139
    SWEET, LET ME PROPHESY THAT AT LAST T'WILL PROVE    TO SAME CONCERNING CHOISE    33  52 331  66
    YIELD QUICKLY, LEST PERHAPS YOU PROVE    AGAINST IRRESOLUTION AND DELAY    87  52 347 146
    BUT SINCE THEY ARE FIRE WORKES, RATHER PROVE    UPON GUNPOWDER TREASON    33  MS 387 461
    DROP DOWNE ONE SPARKE OF GLORY, & THEY'L PROVE    UPON BIRTH PRINCESSE E    19  MS 391 456

PROV'D

    WHO PROV'D THE FEAST TO THEIR OWNE FUNERALL.    THE BEGINNING OF HELIODORUS    28  46 158 517
    THOU TO THEIR TEETH HAST PROV'D THY DEITY.    ON MIRACLE OF LOAVES    2  46  88  16
    PROV'D A NEW PATH OF PATIENT VICTORY.    OFFICE H. CROSS EVENSONG    25  52 273 101
    SOE NEARE, IT PROV'D HIS VERY SIDE.    IN CICATRICES DOMINI JESU    8  MS 381  27

PROVES

    SUCK HIDDEN SWEETS, WHICH WELL DIGESTED PROVES    SOSPETTO D'HERODE    23  46 109 216
    HALF TRUE, ALAS, HALF FALSE, PROVES THAT POOR LINE.    ALEXIAS THIRD ELEGIE    57  52 336 209

PROVING

    CONCEIVE PROUD HOPES OF PROVING ROSES.    ON BLEEDING WOUNDS OF LORD    24  46 101 110

PROVINCES

    YOUR PROVINCES OF WELL-UNITED WORLDS CAN RAISE.    TO THE NAME OF JESUS    73  52 239  30

PROVOKE

    HE MIGHT PROVOKE THE WEALTH OF PRINCES.    WEEPER    118  52 307 120

PROVOK'ST

    WHY FOOLE, SAIES VENUS, THUS PROVOK'ST THOU MEE,    UPON THE SAME (VENUS ARMES)    3  46 161 523

PROVOKES

    TRIUMPHANT TEXT, PROVOKES THY PRAYSE.    LAUDA SION SALVATOREM    8  52 294 178

PSALM

    BOTH THE PSALM AND SYBYLL SINGS    DIES IRAE    2  52 298 186

PUBLICK

    INTO THE PUBLICK YEARES PROFICIENCIE,    UPON TWO GREENE APRICOCKES    24  48 220 494

PUBLICKE

    POORE LAWES DIVIDE THE PUBLICKE YEARE,    THOUGH NOW 'TIS NEITHER    24  MS 397 492

PUDDLES

    IN PUDDLES, WE WILL PLEDGE THIS SERAPHIM    AN APOLOGIE FOR HYMNE (TERESA)    32  46 136  59
    IN PUDDLES. WE WILL PLEDGE THIS SERAPHIM    AN APOLOGIE FOR (TERESA) HYMNE    32  52 322  59

PUFT

    HAD BEENE PUFT OUT, & FROM THEIR STATIONS HURL'D.    UPON GUNPOWDER TREASON    28  MS 386 460

## PULPITS

| | | | |
|---|---|---|---|
| PULPITS AND PENNES SHALL SWEAT IN. TO REDEEM | ON A TREATISE OF CHARITY | 50 | 46 137 69 |

## PULSE

| | | | |
|---|---|---|---|
| FEELES MUSICKS PULSE IN ALL HER ARTERYES, | MUSICKS DUELL | 120 | 46 149 535 |
| AND FEELE THE PULSE OF EVERY PROPHECY. | SOSPETTO D'HERODE | 156 | 46 109 216 |

## PUNISH

| | | | |
|---|---|---|---|
| AND PUNISH BEST THINGS WORST. BECAUSE THEY STOOD | IN GLORIOUS EPIPHANIE | 107 | 52 253 39 |

## PURCHAS'D

| | | | |
|---|---|---|---|
| OUR PURCHAS'D SELVES TOO SOON BESTOW | AGAINST IRRESOLUTION AND DELAY | 65 | 52 347 146 |

## PURE

| | | | |
|---|---|---|---|
| IN TH' EMPYRAEUM OF PURE HARMONY. | MUSICKS DUELL | 150 | 46 149 535 |
| FOUND THE PURE ISSUE OF HIS THOUGHT. | OUT OF GREEKE CUPID'S CRYER | 24 | 46 159 519 |
| THERE STILL TO READ TRUE PURE DIVINITY. | UPON BISHOP ANDREWES PICTURE | 12 | 46 163 490 |
| FRESH FROM THE PURE GLANCE OF THINE EYE, | PSALME 23 | 65 | 46 102 5 |
| THE FIELDS OF PALESTINE, WITH SO PURE A FLOOD, | SOSPETTO D'HERODE | 86 | 46 109 216 |
| A MIGHTY BABE, WHOSE PURE, UNSPOTTED BIRTH, | SOSPETTO D'HERODE | 159 | 46 109 216 |
| HOW A PURE SPIRIT SHOULD INCARNATE BEE. | SOSPETTO D'HERODE | 167 | 46 109 216 |
| TO MAKE THE PARTNER OF HIS OWNE PURE RAY. | SOSPETTO D'HERODE | 218 | 46 109 216 |
| THE HANDS BEE PURE, | ON A PRAYER BOOKE | 22 | 46 126 139 |
| WHOSE PURE AND SUBTLE LIGHTNING, FLIES | ON A PRAYER BOOKE | 66 | 46 126 139 |
| OF PURE INEBRIATING PLEASURES. | ON A PRAYER BOOKE | 114 | 46 126 139 |
| SO SPIRITUALL, PURE AND FAIRE, | IN MEMORY OF LADY MADRE TERESA | 88 | 46 131 52 |
| A SLUTTISHNESSE, FOR PURE RELIGION. | ON A TREATISE OF CHARITY | 30 | 46 137 69 |
| THE PURE BIRTH OF EACH SPARKLING NEST. | AN HIMNE FOR CIRCUMCISION | 19 | 46 141 37 |
| TAINT NOT THE PURE STREAMES OF THE SPRINGING DAY, | ON A FOULE MORNING | 32 | 46 181 495 |
| THOSE PURE UNTRODEN PATHES CAN SHOW, | THOUGH NOW 'TIS NEITHER | 8 | MS 397 492 |
| YOUR DOWN SO WARM, WILL PASSE FOR PURE. | IN HOLY NATIVITY | 63 | 52 246 76 |
| THE SUPERNATURALL DAWN OF THY PURE DAY. | IN GLORIOUS EPIPHANIE | 174 | 52 253 39 |
| UPWARDS, & PRESSE ON FOR THE PURE INTELLIGENTIALL PREY. | IN GLORIOUS EPIPHANIE | 222 | 52 253 39 |
| SO SPIRITUALL, PURE, & FAIR | TERESA | 88 | 52 315 52 |
| WHY MAN, THIS SPEAKES PURE MORTALL FRAME. | FLAMING HEART | 23 | 52 324 61 |
| THE HANDS BE PURE | PRAYER TO GENTLE-WOMAN | 26 | 52 328 139 |
| WHOSE PURE & SUBTIL LIGHTNING FLYES | PRAYER TO GENTLE-WOMAN | 72 | 52 328 139 |
| OF PURE INEBRIATING PLEASURES. | PRAYER TO GENTLE-WOMAN | 120 | 52 328 139 |
| STARRS MUCH TOO FAIR & PURE TO WAIT UPON | TO SAME CONCERNING CHOISE | 31 | 52 331 66 |
| O RISE, PURE LAMP, & LEND THY GOLDEN RAY | ALEXIAS SECONDE ELEGIE | 29 | 52 335 207 |
| SILENCE, & SACRED REST. PEACE, & PURE JOYES. | DESCRIPTION RELIGIOUS HOUSE | 32 | 52 338 213 |
| TO DROUNE THY SELFE IN THIS PURE PEARLY FLOOD. | UPON GUNPOWDER TREASON | 32 | MS 387 461 |
| ONE DROPP OF THIS PURE NECTAR, WHICH DOTH FLOW | UPON GUNPOWDER TREASON | 41 | MS 387 461 |
| CIRCLED WITH PURE REFINED GLORY. HEERE | UPON KINGS CORONATION | 13 | MS 389 454 |
| RICH DIAMONDS, SETT IN A PURE SILVER FOYLE. | UPON BIRTH PRINCESSE E | 44 | MS 391 456 |
| PURE, & UNMIXED CRUELTY THEY TELL, | AN ELEGIE ON DR PORTER | 13 | MS 395 476 |
| TWICE TWENTY DAYES PURE ABSTINENCE, TO FEED | OUT OF GROTIUS | 59 | MS 398 196 |

## PURER

| | | | |
|---|---|---|---|
| WILL I FIND A PURER AIRE | PSALME 23 | 68 | 46 102 5 |
| AND SERVES MY PURER SIGHT, ONELY TO BEAT | SOSPETTO D'HERODE | 203 | 46 109 216 |
| A PEECE OF HEAVENLY LIGHT PURER AND BRIGHTER | ON THE ASSUMPTION | 3 | 46 139 114 |
| A PIECE OF HEAV'NLY EARTH, PURER & BRIGHTER | IN GLORIOUS ASSUMPTION B. LADY | 3 | 52 304 114 |
| LAYES UP HIS PURER & MORE PRETIOUS VOWES. | TO SAME CONCERNING CHOISE | 35 | 52 331 66 |
| WHOSE PURER FLAMES TREMBLE TO BE SOE NIGH, | UPON GUNPOWDER TREASON | 15 | MS 387 461 |
| 'TWAS NOT THE CHAST, & PURER SNOW, WHOSE NEST | AN ELEGY MR STANNINOW | 35 | MS 394 473 |

## PUREST

| | | | |
|---|---|---|---|
| THE PUREST PEARLES, THAT WEPT HER EVENING DEATH, | UPON DEATH OF HERRYS | 19 | 46 167 466 |
| ABASH THE PUREST BEAUTIES OF THE DAY. | UPON KINGS CORONATION | 26 | MS 389 454 |

## PURPLE

| | | | |
|---|---|---|---|
| DEATH'S PURPLE TRIUMPH, ON THE BLUSHING GROUND | THE BEGINNING OF HELIODORUS | 15 | 46 158 517 |
| THESE PURPLE BUDS OF BLOOMING DEATH MAY BEE. | OUR LORD IN HIS CIRCUMCISION | 15 | 46 98 9 |
| OPENING THE PURPLE WARDROBE OF THY SIDE. | ON CRUCIFIED LORD BLOODY | 4 | 46 100 24 |
| ALL THY PURPLE RIVERS MEET. | ON BLEEDING WOUNDS OF LORD | 4 | 46 101 110 |
| THERE HAS THE PURPLE VENGEANCE A PROUD SEAT, | SOSPETTO D'HERODE | 313 | 46 109 216 |
| ALL THE PURPLE PRIDE OF LACES, | AN HIMNE FOR CIRCUMCISION | 5 | 46 141 37 |
| LET HIM MAKE POORE THE PURPLE EAST, | AN HIMNE FOR CIRCUMCISION | 17 | 46 141 37 |
| WITHIN HIMSELFE THE PURPLE PRIDE | UPON DEATH OF DESIRED HERRYS | 38 | 46 168 467 |
| FOR THEE, FAIR, PURPLE DOORES, OF LOVE'S DEVISING. | TO THE NAME OF JESUS | 217 | 52 239 30 |
| ALL THE PURPLE PRIDE THAT LACES | NEW YEAR'S DAY | 5 | 52 251 37 |
| LET HIM MAKE POOR THE PURPLE EAST, | NEW YEAR'S DAY | 17 | 52 251 37 |
| WITH PURPLE OF TOO RICH A RED. | VEXILLA REGIS | 26 | 52 277 156 |
| THE PURPLE NAME | CHARITAS NIMIA | 59 | 52 280 48 |
| ALL THE PURPLE RIVERS MEET. | UPON BLEEDING CRUCIFIX | 4 | 52 288 110 |
| OPENING THE PURPLE WARDROBE IN THY SIDE. | UPON BODY OF OUR LORD | 4 | 52 290 24 |
| BUT HAD THY PALE-FAC'T PURPLE TOOK | FLAMING HEART | 27 | 52 324 61 |
| ALONG THE SHORE IN A GRAVE PURPLE TIDE. | ON GUNPOWDER-TREASON | 34 | MS 384 458 |
| COME GRIMME DESTRUCTION, & IN PURPLE GORE | UPON GUNPOWDER TREASON | 3 | MS 387 461 |
| OR THAT THE PURPLE VIOLETS DID LACE | UPON BIRTH PRINCESSE E | 51 | MS 391 456 |
| THESE PURPLE CURRENTS HEDG'D WITH VIOLETS ROUND | AN ELEGY MR STANNINOW | 22 | MS 394 473 |

TH'PURPLE

| | | | | | |
|---|---|---|---|---|---|
| WITH TH'PURPLE HE MUST WEARE IN HELL. | UPON LAZARUS HIS TEARES | 4 | 46 | 89 | 18 |

PURPLING

| | | | | | |
|---|---|---|---|---|---|
| AND SMIL'D I'TH' BABE'S BRIGHT FACE, THE PURPLING BUD | TO THE QUEEN'S MAJESTY | 5 | 52 | 261 | 47 |
| BY THE PURPLING VINE PUT ON, | WEEPER | 62 | 52 | 307 | 120 |

PUT

| | | | | | |
|---|---|---|---|---|---|
| WHAT NEED'ST THOU PUT ON ARMES AGAINST POORE MEN. | UPON VENUS PUTTING ARMES | 4 | 46 | 161 | 523 |
| BY THE WANTON SPRING PUT ON, | THE TEARE | 26 | 46 | 84 | 50 |
| IF ALL FAILE WEE'L PUT ON OUR PROUDEST ARMES, | SOSPETTO D'HERODE | 276 | 46 | 109 | 216 |
| TO HIM, PUT ON (HEEL SAY) PUT ON | IN MEMORY OF LADY MADRE TERESA | 172 | 46 | 131 | 52 |
| TO HIM, PUT ON (HEEL SAY) PUT ON | IN MEMORY OF LADY MADRE TERESA | 172 | 46 | 131 | 52 |
| PUT ON THY SELFE IN THINE OWN LOOKS. T' OUR EYES | ON A TREATISE OF CHARITY | 2 | 46 | 137 | 69 |
| GODS SERVICES NO LONGER SHALL PUT ON | ON A TREATISE OF CHARITY | 29 | 46 | 137 | 69 |
| PUT ALL HIS RED EYED RUBIES ON. | AN HIMNE FOR CIRCUMCISION | 15 | 46 | 141 | 37 |
| THESE RUBIES SHALL PUT OUT HIS EYES. | AN HIMNE FOR CIRCUMCISION | 16 | 46 | 141 | 37 |
| PUT POORE NATURE TO SUCH COST. | UPON DEATH OF DESIRED HERRYS | 22 | 46 | 168 | 467 |
| MAKES MANY A MOURNING PAPER PUT ON BLACKE. | UPON STANINOUGH'S DEATH | 2 | 46 | 175 | 475 |
| THY NEIGHBOUR-HOOD TO NOTHING. HERE PUT ON | UPON STANINOUGH'S DEATH | 19 | 46 | 175 | 475 |
| BY THE COMPARRISON THEY SHALL PUT ON | UPON TWO GREENE APRICOCKES | 7 | 48 | 220 | 494 |
| PUT ALL HIS RED-EY'D RUBIES ON. | NEW YEAR'S DAY | 15 | 52 | 251 | 37 |
| BY THE PURPLING VINE PUT ON, | WEEPER | 62 | 52 | 307 | 120 |
| TO HIM, PUT ON (HEE'L SAY) PUT ON | TERESA | 171 | 52 | 315 | 52 |
| TO HIM, PUT ON (HEE'L SAY) PUT ON | TERESA | 171 | 52 | 315 | 52 |
| TO PUT HER DART INTO HIS HAND. | FLAMING HEART | 14 | 52 | 324 | 61 |
| MAKES MANY A MOURNING PAPER PUT ON BLACK. | DEATH'S LECTURE | 2 | 52 | 340 | 475 |

PUTT

| | | | | | |
|---|---|---|---|---|---|
| THESE RUBIES SHALL PUTT OUT THEIR EYES. | NEW YEAR'S DAY | 16 | 52 | 251 | 37 |
| BOLD PAINTERS HAVE PUTT OUT HIS EYES. | CHARITAS NIMIA | 8 | 52 | 280 | 48 |
| PROUD LOOKES, & LOFTY EYLIDDES, HERE PUTT ON | DEATH'S LECTURE | 21 | 52 | 340 | 475 |

PUTTING

| | | | | | |
|---|---|---|---|---|---|
| WHICH THEY THEMSELVES WERE. EACH ONE PUTTING ON | ON A TREATISE OF CHARITY | 19 | 46 | 137 | 69 |
| IF THOSE SHARPE RAYES PUTTING ON | LOVES HOROSCOPE | 21 | 46 | 185 | 483 |

PYRAMIDS

| | | | | | |
|---|---|---|---|---|---|
| HISTORY REARES HER PYRAMIDS MORE TALL | ON FRONTISPIECE ISAACSONS | 18 | 46 | 191 | 491 |
| TH' EGYPTIAN PYRAMIDS THEMSELVES MUST LIVE.) | ON FRONTISPIECE ISAACSONS | 20 | 46 | 191 | 491 |

PYTHONS

| | | | | | |
|---|---|---|---|---|---|
| AND MAY SUCH PYTHONS NEVER LIVE TO SEE | UPON GUNPOWDER TREASON | 57 | MS | 386 | 460 |

QUAFFE

| | | | | | |
|---|---|---|---|---|---|
| WHICH MIXT WITH GALL & BLOOD THEY QUAFFE BRIM FULL. | SOSPETTO D'HERODE | 336 | 46 | 109 | 216 |

QUAKES

| | | | | | |
|---|---|---|---|---|---|
| ROSE QUAKES AT NAME OF CINNAMON. | PETRONIJ ALES PHASIACIS PETITA | 19 | MS | 382 | 526 |

QUAK'ST

| | | | | | |
|---|---|---|---|---|---|
| FAIRE DROP, WHY QUAK'ST THOU SO. | THE TEARE | 31 | 46 | 84 | 50 |

QUALIFIES

| | | | | | |
|---|---|---|---|---|---|
| OF FLASHING AIRES. SHEE QUALIFIES THEIR ZEALE | MUSICKS DUELL | 98 | 46 | 149 | 535 |

QUARRELL

| | | | | | |
|---|---|---|---|---|---|
| AND CLOSES THE SWEET QUARRELL, ROWSING ALL | MUSICKS DUELL | 53 | 46 | 149 | 535 |
| HE CALLS TO MIND TH'OLD QUARRELL, AND WHAT SPARKE | SOSPETTO D'HERODE | 69 | 46 | 109 | 216 |

QURRELLS

| | | | | | |
|---|---|---|---|---|---|
| NO QURRELLS, MURMURS, NO DELAY. | TEMPERANCE | 49 | 52 | 342 | 510 |

QUARTERS

| | | | | | |
|---|---|---|---|---|---|
| MEE RANGING IN HIS QUARTERS. AND THE LAND | OUT OF GROTIUS | 83 | MS | 398 | 198 |

QUAVERING

| | | | | | |
|---|---|---|---|---|---|
| AND WITH A QUAVERING COYNESSE TASTS THE STRINGS. | MUSICKS DUELL | 112 | 46 | 149 | 535 |
| LONG TIME TO QUAVERING AGE YOU GIVE, | UPON DEATH OF A FREIND | 11 | MS | 393 | 477 |

QUEEN

| | | | | | |
|---|---|---|---|---|---|
| (FOR SHEE IS A QUEEN) | THE WEEPER | 51 | 46 | 79 | 120 |
| OPEN THIS BOOKE, FAIRE QUEEN, AND TAKE THY CROWN. | ON A TREATISE OF CHARITY | 12 | 46 | 137 | 69 |
| HAILE HOLY QUEEN OF HUMBLE HEARTS, | ON THE ASSUMPTION | 29 | 46 | 139 | 114 |
| LIVE CROWNE OF WOMEN, QUEEN OF MEN. | ON THE ASSUMPTION | 61 | 46 | 139 | 114 |
| QUEEN REGENT IN YOUNG LOVES MINORITIE. | ON HOPE | 84 | 46 | 143 | 71 |
| MIGHTY QUEEN, TO THINKE IT LONG, | TO THE QUEEN | 2 | 48 | 215 | 501 |

| | | | | |
|---|---|---|---|---|
| SAY THEN DREAD QUEEN, HOW MAY WE DOE | TO THE QUEEN | 9 | 48 215 | 501 |
| WE READ IN YOU (RARE QUEEN) RIPE & FULL-GROWN. | TO THE QUEEN'S MAJESTY | 10 | 52 261 | 47 |
| (GREAT QUEEN OF GREIFES) & GIVE | SANCTA MARIA DOLORUM | 58 | 52 283 | 162 |
| RICH QUEEN, LEND SOME RELEIFE. | SANCTA MARIA DOLORUM | 91 | 52 283 | 162 |
| HAIL, HOLY QUEEN OF HUMBLE HEARTS. | IN GLORIOUS ASSUMPTION B. LADY | 44 | 52 304 | 114 |
| LIVE, CROWN OF WOEMEN, QUEEN OF MEN. | IN GLORIOUS ASSUMPTION B. LADY | 66 | 52 304 | 114 |
| (FOR SHE IS A QUEEN) | WEEPER | 39 | 52 307 | 120 |
| THE QUEEN OF ANGELS, (AND MEN CHAST AS YOU) | ALEXIAS THIRD ELEGIE | 29 | 52 336 | 209 |
| QUEEN REGENT IN YONGE LOVE'S MINORITY. | (ON) HOPE | 44 | 52 345 | 71 |

QUEENE

| | | | | |
|---|---|---|---|---|
| DAYES KING DEPOSED BY NIGHTS QUEENE. | A HYMNE OF THE NATIVITY | 2 | 46 106 | 76 |
| IS IT SOME DEITY. OR IS'T OUR QUEENE. | UPON YORKE HIS BIRTH | 73 | 46 176 | 500 |
| THY GREISLY MAJESTY, HELL'S BLACKEST QUEENE. | HORATIJ ILLE & NEFASTO | 34 | MS 382 | 530 |
| THE QUEENE OF NIGHT GOTT THE GREENE SICKNES THEN. | UPON GUNPOWDER TREASON | 23 | MS 386 | 460 |

QUEENS

| | | | | |
|---|---|---|---|---|
| THE FOULE QUEENS MOST ABHORRED MAIDS OF HONOUR | SOSPETTO D'HERODE | 337 | 46 109 | 216 |

QUELL'D

| | | | | |
|---|---|---|---|---|
| OTHER MENS HUNGER WITH STRANGE FEASTS I QUELL'D | OUT OF GROTIUS | 57 | MS 398 | 198 |

QUEL'D

| | | | | |
|---|---|---|---|---|
| THY QUEL'D FOES ARE NOT ONELY NOW | NEITHER DURST MAN ASKE | 5 | 46 92 | 20 |

QUENCH

| | | | | |
|---|---|---|---|---|
| QUENCH HIS CURL'D FIRES, WEE'L WAKE WITH OUR ALARMES | SOSPETTO D'HERODE | 278 | 46 109 | 216 |
| TO QUENCH THE RAGE OF HELLISH DEITIES. | UPON GUNPOWDER TREASON | 36 | MS 387 | 461 |

QUENCH'T

| | | | | |
|---|---|---|---|---|
| THIS FLAME THUS QUENCH'T HATH BRIGHTER BEAMES. | SHE BEGAN TO WASH HIS FEET | 3 | 46 97 | 13 |

QUENCHLESSE

| | | | | |
|---|---|---|---|---|
| HEE FILLS A BURNISHT THRONE OF QUENCHLESSE FIRE. | SOSPETTO D'HERODE | 42 | 46 109 | 216 |

QUICK

| | | | | |
|---|---|---|---|---|
| (QUICK WITH WARME ZEPHIRES LIVELY BREATH) LAY FORTH | OUT OF VIRGIL | 13 | 46 155 | 529 |
| AND CATCHE THY QUICK REFLEX. AND SHARPLY SEE | IN GLORIOUS EPIPHANIE | 193 | 52 253 | 39 |
| QUICK DEATHS THAT GROW | SANCTA MARIA DOLORUM | 25 | 52 283 | 162 |
| QUICK BURYE'D IN THE WANTON TOMB | O GLORIOSA DOMINA | 15 | 52 302 | 194 |

QUICKE

| | | | | |
|---|---|---|---|---|
| QUICKE VOLUMES OF WILD NOTES. TO LET HIM KNOW | MUSICKS DUELL | 25 | 46 149 | 535 |
| FROM THIS TO THAT. THEN QUICKE RETURNING SKIPPS | MUSICKS DUELL | 32 | 46 149 | 535 |
| A SUBTLE INUNDATION OF QUICKE FOOD | OUT OF GROTIUS | 61 | MS 398 | 198 |

QUICKLY

| | | | | |
|---|---|---|---|---|
| TEARES, QUICKLY FLED, | WISHES SUPPOSED MISTRESSE | 73 | 46 195 | 479 |
| YEILD QUICKLY. LEST PERHAPS YOU PROVE | TO COUNTESSE OF DENBIGH | 65 | 52 236 | 146 |
| OR QUICKLY WOULD, WERT THOU ONCE HERE. | IN GLORIOUS ASSUMPTION B. LADY | 18 | 52 304 | 114 |
| YIELD QUICKLY, LEST PERHAPS YOU PROVE | AGAINST IRRESOLUTION AND DELAY | 87 | 52 347 | 146 |

QUICKSANDS

| | | | | |
|---|---|---|---|---|
| 'CAUSE THE QUICKSANDS HANSELLD IT. | PETRONIJ ALES PHASIACIS PETITA | 14 | MS 382 | 526 |

QUIET

| | | | | |
|---|---|---|---|---|
| CONTENT AND QUIET WOULD HE GOE. | THE WEEPER | 82 | 46 79 | 120 |
| HEE CHARGES TO BE QUIET, IT RUNS ROUND, | THE DUMBE HEALED | 2 | 46 87 | 16 |
| A QUIET PASSAGE UNDER GROUND. | AN EPITAPH DOCTOR BROOKE | 6 | 46 175 | 465 |
| CONTENT & QUIET HE WOULD GOE. | WEEPER | 76 | 52 307 | 120 |
| TO SPARE THY QUIET. | LUKE 2. QUAERIT JESUM | 38 | MS 379 | 11 |
| THIS GLORIOUS PHAEBUS SETT) WILL QUIET BEE. | UPON KINGS CORONATION | 24 | MS 390 | 453 |

QUILL

| | | | | |
|---|---|---|---|---|
| REACH ME A QUILL, PLUCKT FROM THE FLAMING WING | UPON GUNPOWDER TREASON | 1 | MS 386 | 460 |
| MY QUILL TO THEE MAY NOT PRAESUME TO SING. | UPON BIRTH PRINCESSE E | 21 | MS 391 | 456 |

QUINTESSENCE

| | | | | |
|---|---|---|---|---|
| THE VERY QUINTESSENCE OF VILLANIE. | UPON GUNPOWDER TREASON | 8 | MS 386 | 460 |
| OF WHICH DOTH SHOW THE QUINTESSENCE OF ART. | UPON BIRTH PRINCESSE E | 38 | MS 391 | 456 |

QUIRE

| | | | | |
|---|---|---|---|---|
| IN THAT SWEET SOYLE. IT SEEMES A HOLY QUIRE | MUSICKS DUELL | 73 | 46 149 | 535 |
| BLEST SERAPHIMS SHALL LEAVE THEIR QUIRE, | IN MEMORY OF LADY MADRE TERESA | 94 | 46 131 | 52 |
| BLEST SERAPHIM, SHALL LEAVE THEIR QUIRE | TERESA | 94 | 52 315 | 52 |
| SOUND FORTH, CAELESTIALL ORGANS,LETT HEAVNS QUIRE | UPON KINGS CORONATION | 1 | MS 389 | 454 |
| GOE LEARNE THAT FATALL QUIRE, SOE SPRUCELY DIGHT | AN ELEGIE ON DR PORTER | 27 | MS 395 | 476 |

## HEDGE-QUIRISTERS

| | | | | |
|---|---|---|---|---|
| HEDGE-QUIRISTERS WHOSE MUSICKE OWES | THOUGH NOW 'TIS NEITHER | 18 | MS 397 | 492 |

## QUITE

| | | | | |
|---|---|---|---|---|
| TO CAST THEM WELL'S TO CAST THEM QUITE AWAY. | ON ST. PETER CASTING NETS | 4 | 46 98 | 13 |
| AND FROM THE HEAD OF JUDAHS HOUSE QUITE TORNE | SOSPETTO D'HERODE | 405 | 46 109 | 216 |
| QUITE TURN'D. TH'INGRATEFULL REBELLS THIS THEIR YOUNG | SOSPETTO D'HERODE | 438 | 46 109 | 216 |
| FOR PITTIES SAKE O HIDE HIM QUITE, | UPON DEATH OF DESIRED HERRYS | 71 | 46 168 | 467 |
| WOULD QUITE HAVE LOST THE CRUELL FASHION. | ANOTHER ON HERRYS | 24 | 46 170 | 469 |
| WEE'L CONFOUND THE RECKONING QUITE, | OUT OF CATULLUS | 17 | 46 194 | 523 |
| NOR DARING QUITE TO LIVE NOR DY. | TO COUNTESSE OF DENBIGH | 12 | 52 236 | 146 |
| YOU MUST TRANSPOSE THE PICTURE QUITE. | FLAMING HEART | 9 | 52 324 | 61 |
| NOR COULDST THOU, CRUELL, LEAVE ME QUITE ALONE. | ALEXIAS SECONDE ELEGIE | 4 | 52 335 | 207 |
| NOT DARING QUITE TO LIVE NOR DIE. | AGAINST IRRESOLUTION AND DELAY | 20 | 52 347 | 146 |
| IT QUITE FORGOTT. THE FEARFULL EARTH GAVE WAY. | ON GUNPOWDER-TREASON | 53 | MS 384 | 458 |
| ALAS, THE EARTH, QUITE DRUNKE WITH TEARES, HAD REEL'D | UPON KINGS CORONATION | 9 | MS 390 | 453 |
| THAT ROME'S BOLD EAGLES NOW WERE BLINDED QUITE, | UPON KINGS CORONATION | 34 | MS 390 | 453 |

## QUIVER

| | | | | |
|---|---|---|---|---|
| THE GOLD THAT ON HIS QUIVER SMILES. | OUT OF GREEKE CUPID'S CRYER | 49 | 46 159 | 519 |
| HERE'S MY QUIVER SHAFTS AND BOW, | OUT OF GREEKE CUPID'S CRYER | 70 | 46 159 | 519 |
| LOVE HIS QUIVER, | OUT OF THE ITALIAN (1) | 14 | 46 188 | 545 |
| HATH IN LOVE'S QUIVER HID FOR YOU. | TO COUNTESSE OF DENBIGH | 48 | 52 236 | 146 |
| NOT ONE LOOSE SHAFT BUT LOVE'S WHOLE QUIVER. | FLAMING HEART | 70 | 52 324 | 61 |
| THERE SHINES HIS QUIVER, THERE HIS BOW. | IN CICATRICES DOMINI JESU | 4 | MS 381 | 27 |
| THE QUIVER, THAT HE BORE, DID BIDE | IN CICATRICES DOMINI JESU | 7 | MS 381 | 27 |
| STRANGE THE QUIVER, BOW, & DART. | IN CICATRICES DOMINI JESU | 15 | MS 381 | 27 |

## QUIVERS

| | | | | |
|---|---|---|---|---|
| FULL QUIVERS ON LOVES BOW. | WISHES SUPPOSED MISTRESSE | 59 | 46 195 | 479 |

## RABID

| | | | | |
|---|---|---|---|---|
| STROKES AND TAMES MY RABID GRIEFE, | PSALME 23 | 19 | 46 102 | 5 |

## RACE

| | | | | |
|---|---|---|---|---|
| OF HONEST PARENTAGE OF UNSTAIN'D RACE, | TO PONTIUS WASHING HANDS | 6 | 46 94 | 23 |
| OR SOME BASE HAND HAVE POWER TO RACE, | IN MEMORY OF LADY MADRE TERESA | 71 | 46 131 | 52 |
| SHEWES THE TWO TERMES AND LIMITS OF TIME'S RACE. | ON FRONTISPIECE ISAACSONS | 22 | 46 191 | 491 |
| 'MONGST THOSE LONG ROWES OF CROWNES THAT GUILD YOUR RACE, | TO THE QUEEN'S MAJESTY | 1 | 52 261 | 47 |
| OR SOME BASE HAND HAVE POWER TO RACE | TERESA | 71 | 52 315 | 52 |

## RACKES

| | | | | |
|---|---|---|---|---|
| WHERE RACKES & TORMENTS STRIV'D, IN VAIN, TO REACH THEE. | TO THE NAME OF JESUS | 206 | 52 239 | 30 |

## RADIANT

| | | | | |
|---|---|---|---|---|
| NO CLOUD SCOULE ON HIS RADIANT LIDS NO TEMPEST LOWRE. | EASTER DAY | 12 | 46 100 | 26 |
| AND RADIANT SCEPTER THIS BOLD HAND SHOULD BEARE. | SOSPETTO D'HERODE | 210 | 46 109 | 216 |
| WHICH WRITES THY SPOWSES RADIANT NAME | IN MEMORY OF LADY MADRE TERESA | 82 | 46 131 | 52 |
| EMBRACE THY RADIANT BROWES. O MAY THE BEST | ON THE ASSUMPTION | 57 | 46 139 | 114 |
| MADE HEAVENS RADIANT FACE LOOKE FOULE. | UPON DEATH OF DESIRED HERRYS | 52 | 46 168 | 467 |
| AND STROAKE HIS RADIANT CHEEKES. ONE TIMELY KISSE | TO THE MORNING | 37 | 46 183 | 497 |
| THAT HER WHOSE RADIANT BROWES. | WISHES SUPPOSED MISTRESSE | 107 | 46 195 | 479 |
| DOES RISE A RADIANT CROPPE OF ROYALLE STEMMS. | TO THE QUEEN'S MAJESTY | 12 | 52 261 | 47 |
| EMBRACE THY RADIANT BROWES. O MAY THE BEST | IN GLORIOUS ASSUMPTION B. LADY | 62 | 52 304 | 114 |
| WHICH WRITES THY SPOUSE'S RADIANT NAME | TERESA | 82 | 52 315 | 52 |
| ROSY FINGERS, RADIANT HAIR, | FLAMING HEART | 32 | 52 324 | 61 |
| THE ROSY HAND, THE RADIANT DART. | FLAMING HEART | 67 | 52 324 | 61 |
| THE RADIANT DARTS, SHOTT FROM HIS SPARKLING EYES, | UPON KINGS CORONATION | 35 | MS 390 | 453 |

## RAGE

| | | | | |
|---|---|---|---|---|
| NOW WITH NEW RAGE, AND WAX TOO HOT FOR HELL. | SOSPETTO D'HERODE | 148 | 46 109 | 216 |
| THERE RUDE IMPETUOUS RAGE DO'S STORME, AND FRET. | SOSPETTO D'HERODE | 317 | 46 109 | 216 |
| IN RAGE, MY ARMES, GIVE ME MY ARMES, HEE CRYES. | SOSPETTO D'HERODE | 480 | 46 109 | 216 |
| THY BLOOD-REVOLVING BREST TO RAGE DOTH MOVE. | SOSPETTO D'HERODE | 514 | 46 109 | 216 |
| SO RARE IS HOARY VERTUE) THE DIRE RAGE | UPON DEATH OF HERRYS | 32 | 46 167 | 466 |
| TO QUENCH THE RAGE OF HELLISH DEITIES. | UPON GUNPOWDER TREASON | 36 | MS 387 | 461 |
| THE ROSES FRESH, CONSERVED FROM THE RAGE, | UPON GUNPOWDER TREASON | 43 | MS 387 | 461 |
| AND MADE IT BURNE IN LOVE. 'TWAS NOT THE RAGE, | AN ELEGY MR STANNINOW | 33 | MS 394 | 473 |
| MADE LITLE, NOT A LITLE TO HIS RAGE) | OUT OF GROTIUS | 24 | MS 398 | 198 |

## RAGGED

| | | | | |
|---|---|---|---|---|
| OF RAGGED LIMBS, TORNE SCULLS, & DASHT OUT BRAINES. | SOSPETTO D'HERODE | 312 | 46 109 | 216 |

## RAGS

| | | | | |
|---|---|---|---|---|
| AS PRIS'NER IN A FEW POORE RAGS TO LYE. | SOSPETTO D'HERODE | 172 | 46 109 | 216 |

## RAIN

| | | | | |
|---|---|---|---|---|
| THE WINTER'S PAST, THE RAIN IS GONE. | IN GLORIOUS ASSUMPTION B. LADY | 10 | 52 304 | 114 |
| THE RAIN IS GONE, EXCEPT SO MUCH AS WE | IN GLORIOUS ASSUMPTION B. LADY | 21 | 52 304 | 114 |

| | | | | | |
|---|---|---|---|---|---|
| WHILE RAIN & SUNSHINE, CHEEKES & EYES | WEEPER | 95 | 52 | 307 | 120 |

**RAIN-SWOLN**

| | | | | | |
|---|---|---|---|---|---|
| RAIN-SWOLN RIVERS MAY RISE PROUD. | UPON BLEEDING CRUCIFIX | 29 | 52 | 288 | 110 |

**RAINE**

| | | | | | |
|---|---|---|---|---|---|
| RAINE SO TRUE A TEARE AS THINE. | THE TEARE | 16 | 46 | 84 | 50 |
| THE WINTER'S PAST, THE RAINE IS GONE. | ON THE ASSUMPTION | 10 | 46 | 139 | 114 |
| WHICH RARIFYED, AND IN A GENTLE RAINE | ON A FOULE MORNING | 15 | 46 | 181 | 495 |
| SHALL IN A SILVER RAINE RUNNE OUT, WHOSE CREAME | ON GUNPOWDER-TREASON | 24 | MS | 364 | 458 |
| HATH AGED WINTER, FLEDG'D WITH FEATHERED RAINE, | AN ELEGY MR STANNINOW | 1 | MS | 394 | 473 |

**RAINE-SWOLNE**

| | | | | | |
|---|---|---|---|---|---|
| RAINE-SWOLNE RIVERS MAY RISE PROUD | ON BLEEDING WOUNDS OF LORD | 33 | 46 | 101 | 110 |

**RAISE**

| | | | | | |
|---|---|---|---|---|---|
| CAN RAISE SO FAIRE AN HARVEST. LET HER BE | ON FRONTISPIECE ISAACSONS | 7 | 46 | 191 | 491 |
| MY FUTURE HOPES CAN RAISE, | WISHES SUPPOSED MISTRESSE | 110 | 46 | 195 | 479 |
| RAISE THIS TALL TROPHEE OF THY POWRE. | TO COUNTESSE OF DENBIGH | 38 | 52 | 236 | 146 |
| YOUR PROVINCES OF WELL-UNITED WORLDS CAN RAISE. | TO THE NAME OF JESUS | 73 | 52 | 239 | 30 |
| WHAT SONG SHALL RAISE | OFFICE H. CROSS MATINES | 20 | 52 | 265 | 86 |
| LETT NOT MY SUPPLIANT BREATH RAISE A RUDE STORME | ON GUNPOWDER-TREASON | 11 | MS | 364 | 458 |
| AND RAISE A DELUGE, WHERE THE FLAMING SUNNE | UPON GUNPOWDER TREASON | 38 | MS | 386 | 460 |

**RAIS'D**

| | | | | | |
|---|---|---|---|---|---|
| THAT FROM SO SMALL A CHANNELL SHOULD BE RAIS'D | MUSICKS DUELL | 44 | 46 | 149 | 535 |
| POORE SIMPLE VOYCE, RAIS'D IN A NATURALL TONE. | MUSICKS DUELL | 164 | 46 | 149 | 535 |
| BY WHOM (AS HEAV'NS ILLUSTRIOUS HAND-MAID) RAIS'D | SOSPETTO D'HERODE | 134 | 46 | 109 | 216 |
| HIS FOULE HAGS RAIS'D THEIR HEADS, & CLAPT THEIR HANDS. | SOSPETTO D'HERODE | 258 | 46 | 109 | 216 |

**RAM**

| | | | | | |
|---|---|---|---|---|---|
| OF RAM, HE-GOAT, OR REVEREND APE, | IN GLORIOUS EPIPHANIE | 90 | 52 | 253 | 39 |

**RAMME**

| | | | | | |
|---|---|---|---|---|---|
| THE RANSOM'D ISACK, & HIS RAMME. | LAUDA SION SALVATOREM | 67 | 52 | 294 | 178 |

**RAMPANT**

| | | | | | |
|---|---|---|---|---|---|
| OR RAMPANT FEATHER, OR RICH FAN. | WISHES SUPPOSED MISTRESSE | 21 | 46 | 195 | 479 |

**RAN**

| | | | | | |
|---|---|---|---|---|---|
| SO SMIL'D THE DAYES, AND SO THE TENOR RAN | OUT OF VIRGIL | 24 | 46 | 155 | 529 |
| HEE MARKT HOW THE POORE SHEPHEARDS RAN TO PAY | SOSPETTO D'HERODE | 118 | 46 | 109 | 216 |
| RAN TREMBLING THROUGH THE HOLLOW VAULTS OF NIGHT, | SOSPETTO D'HERODE | 151 | 46 | 109 | 216 |
| WHY RAN THE STARTED AIRE TREMBLING AWAY. | UPON YORKE HIS BIRTH | 67 | 46 | 176 | 500 |

**RANGING**

| | | | | | |
|---|---|---|---|---|---|
| MEE RANGING IN HIS QUARTERS. AND THE LAND | OUT OF GROTIUS | 83 | MS | 398 | 198 |

**RANK**

| | | | | | |
|---|---|---|---|---|---|
| THEIR RANK MALICE NOT THEIR NEED. | PSALME 23 | 52 | 46 | 102 | 5 |

**WELL-RANK'D**

| | | | | | |
|---|---|---|---|---|---|
| HOW FIT OUR WELL-RANK'D FEASTS DOE FOLLOW, | UPON POWDER DAY | 1 | 46 | 185 | 74 |

**RANKE**

| | | | | | |
|---|---|---|---|---|---|
| THEY ROUSE HIM, WHEN HIS RANKE THOUGHTS NEED A STING. | SOSPETTO D'HERODE | 68 | 46 | 109 | 216 |

**RANCK'D**

| | | | | | |
|---|---|---|---|---|---|
| FOURE TEETH THOU HAD'ST THAT RANCK'D IN GOODLY STATE | OUT OF MARTIALL | 1 | 46 | 188 | 527 |

**RANKES**

| | | | | | |
|---|---|---|---|---|---|
| AND IN HER FIRST RANKES MAKE THEE ROOME. | IN MEMORY OF LADY MADRE TERESA | 127 | 46 | 131 | 52 |
| AND IN HER FIRST RANKES MAKE THEE ROOM | TERESA | 126 | 52 | 315 | 52 |

**RANSOM'D**

| | | | | | |
|---|---|---|---|---|---|
| OF ALL THE RANSOM'D WORLD, THOU HADST THE POWER | OFFICE H. CROSS EVENSONG | 16 | 52 | 273 | 101 |
| THE RANSOM'D ISACK, & HIS RAMME. | LAUDA SION SALVATOREM | 67 | 52 | 294 | 178 |

**RAPE**

| | | | | | |
|---|---|---|---|---|---|
| A RAPE UPON'T. TILL THY ADULT'ROUS TOUCH | TO PONTIUS WASHING HANDS | 3 | 46 | 94 | 23 |

**RAPES**

| | | | | | |
|---|---|---|---|---|---|
| NOR WITH PERVERSE LOVES & RELIGIOUS RAPES | IN GLORIOUS EPIPHANIE | 105 | 52 | 253 | 39 |

```
RAPSODYES

   HEAV'D ON THE SURGES OF SWOLNE RAPSODYES.         MUSICKS DUELL                    136    46 149 535

RAPTURE

   NO NIMBLE RAPTURE STARTS TO HEAVEN AND BRINGS    TO THE MORNING                     20    46 183 497

RARE

   STRAINES HIGHER YET. THAT TICKLED WITH RARE ART  MUSICKS DUELL                      47    46 149 535
   THE RICH AND ROSEALL SPRING OF THOSE RARE SWEETS, ON A PRAYER BOOKE                110    46 126 139
   FIND EVERLASTING SMILES.  SO RARE.               IN MEMORY OF LADY MADRE TERESA     87    46 131  52
   THOSE RARE WORKES, WHERE THOU SHALT LEAVE WRIT.  IN MEMORY OF LADY MADRE TERESA    156    46 131  52
   THOSE RARE FRUITS DANGLED, WHENCE THE GOLDEN YEARE UPON DEATH OF HERRYS             28    46 167 466
   SO RARE IS HOARY VERTUE) THE DIRE RAGE           UPON DEATH OF HERRYS               32    46 167 466
   THIS IS HEE IN WHOSE RARE FRAME,                 UPON DEATH OF DESIRED HERRYS        5    46 168 467
   BUT WERE THE ROSES BLUSH SO RARE.                UPON DEATH OF DESIRED HERRYS       55    46 168 467
   WE READ IN YOU (RARE QUEEN) RIPE & FULL-GROWN.   TO THE QUEEN'S MAJESTY             10    52 261  47
   IN THY SO RICH & RARE EXPENSES,                  WEEPER                            116    52 307 120
   FIND EVERLASTING SMILES.  SO RARE.               TERESA                             87    52 315  52
   THOSE RARE WORKES WHERE THOU SHALT LEAVE WRITT,  TERESA                            155    52 315  52
   IN THAT RARE LIFE OF HER, AND LOVE.              FLAMING HEART                      52    52 324  61
   THE RICH & ROSEALL SPRING OF THOSE RARE SWEETS   PRAYER TO GENTLE-WOMAN            116    52 328 139
   O LIVE, SO RARE A LOVE. LIVE. & IN THEE          ALEXIAS FIRST ELEGIE               33    52 334 204
   THIS RARE ONE, READER, WOULDST THOU SEE.         TEMPERANCE                         51    52 342 510
   UNLESSE'T BE RARE, WHAT'S THOUGHT UPON.          PETRONIJ ALES PHASIACIS PETITA     20    MS 382 526
   THAT WONDERS MAY IN FASHION BE, NOT RARE.        ON GUNPOWDER-TREASON               27    MS 384 458
   SOME RARE CHOICE TORTURE. NOW 'TIS HELL INDEED.  ON GUNPOWDER-TREASON               62    MS 384 458

RAREFY'D

   OF JOYES & RAREFY'D DELIGHTS.                    PRAYER TO GENTLE-WOMAN             80    52 328 139

RARIFYED

   OF JOYES, AND RARIFYED DELIGHTS.                 ON A PRAYER BOOKE                  74    46 126 139
   WHICH RARIFYED, AND IN A GENTLE RAINE            ON A FOULE MORNING                 15    46 181 495

RARELY-TEMPER'D

   WITH MANY A RARELY-TEMPER'D KISSE,               A HYMNE OF THE NATIVITY            62    46 106  76
   WITH MANY A RARELY-TEMPER'D KISSE                IN HOLY NATIVITY                   88    52 246  76

RAREST

   A SET OF RAREST HARMONY.                         IN PRAISE OF LESSIUS               38    46 156 510
   LIVE RAREST PRINCESSE, AND MAY THE BRIGHT        ON THE ASSUMPTION                  55    46 139 114
   A SET OF RAREST HARMONY.                         TEMPERANCE                         36    52 342 510

RARITY

   AND RELLISH NOT OF RARITY.                       PETRONIJ ALES PHASIACIS PETITA     10    MS 382 526

RARITIE

   OF HEAVEN, & EARTH, & OF ALL RARITIE.            UPON BIRTH PRINCESSE E             58    MS 391 456

RASH

   TO THEIR OWNE DANCE. NOW NEGLIGENTLY RASH        MUSICKS DUELL                      29    46 149 535

RATE

   ARE HUSKS SO DEARE. TROTH 'TIS A MIGHTY RATE.    ON THE PRODIGALL                    4    46  86  17
   AT TOO DEARE A RATE ARE ROSES.                   ON WOUNDS OF CRUCIFIED LORD         6    46  99  24
   A SAVIOUR, & AT SUCH A RATE, FOR US.             OFFICE H. CROSS COMPLINE           16    52 274 105
   GOOD WINE IN ALL POYNTS.  BUT THE EASY RATE.     OUT OF GROTIUS                     56    MS 398 198

RATHER

   MUCH RATHER WOULD IT TREMBLE HEERE.              THE WEEPER                         41    46  79 120
   WHITHER TH'HADST RATHER THERE HAVE SHONE         THE TEARE                          46    46  84  50
   TWO WENT TO PRAY. O RATHER SAY                   TWO WENT TO PRAY                    1    46  89  18
   ONE EYE. A THOUSAND RATHER, AND A THOUSAND MORE  IT IS BETTER TO GO WITH EYE         1    46  93  16
   ROSES HENCE, OR LILLIES RATHER.                  UPON INFANT MARTYRS                 4    46  95  10
   RATHER MAKE UP TO THY NEW MISERIES,              SOSPETTO D'HERODE                 245    46 109 216
   OR RATHER ALL THE OTHER THREE IN ONE.            SOSPETTO D'HERODE                 290    46 109 216
   HENRY AND JAMES, OR MARS AND PHOEBUS RATHER.     UPON YORKE HIS BIRTH               31    46 176 500
   HIS PARLOUR-SERMONS RATHER WERE                  AN EPITAPH UPON ASHTON             13    46 192 464
   O RATHER USE THIS HEART, THUS FARR A FITTER STONE. OFFICE H. CROSS COMPLINE         11    52 274 105
   BUT SINCE THEY ARE FIRE WORKES, RATHER PROVE     UPON GUNPOWDER TREASON             33    MS 387 461

REATHER

   MUCH REATHER WOULD IT BE THY TEAR.               WEEPER                             47    52 307 120

RATLING

   WARRES RATLING TUMULTS, OR SOME TYRANTS FALL.    HORATIJ ILLE & NEFASTO             48    MS 382 530
```

RAVES

| | | | | | |
|---|---|---|---|---|---|
| TH'IMPATIENT LIQUOR, FRETS, AND FOAMES, AND RAVES. | SOSPETTO D'HERODE | 486 | 46 | 109 | 216 |

RAVISH

| | | | | | |
|---|---|---|---|---|---|
| RAVISH THE DANCING ORBES, MAKE THEM MOUNT HIGHER | UPON KINGS CORONATION | 2 | MS | 389 | 454 |
| TO RAVISH HEAVEN TO LIMBE THEM O'RE AGAINE. | UPON BIRTH PRINCESSE E | 36 | MS | 391 | 456 |

RAVISHT

| | | | | | |
|---|---|---|---|---|---|
| HER LITTLE SOULE IS RAVISHT, AND SO POUR'D | MUSICKS DUELL | 102 | 46 | 149 | 535 |
| RAVISHT THE MAIDEN BLOSSOMS, AND DOWNE BORE | UPON DEATH OF HERRYS | 34 | 46 | 167 | 466 |

RAVISH'T

| | | | | | |
|---|---|---|---|---|---|
| IN MUSICK'S RAVISH'T SOULE HEE DARE NOT TELL, | MUSICKS DUELL | 144 | 46 | 149 | 535 |
| NOE, NONE OF THESE RAVISH'T THOSE VIRGIN ROSES, | AN ELEGY MR STANNINOW | 37 | MS | 394 | 473 |

RAVISHERS

| | | | | | |
|---|---|---|---|---|---|
| THOSE BEAUTEOUS RAVISHERS OPPREST SO SORE | IN GLORIOUS EPIPHANIE | 91 | 52 | 253 | 39 |

RAVISHING

| | | | | | |
|---|---|---|---|---|---|
| AND CRUELL RAVISHING OF FROSTY AGE, | UPON GUNPOWDER TREASON | 44 | MS | 387 | 461 |

RAY

| | | | | | |
|---|---|---|---|---|---|
| AND TIPT THE MOUNTAINES IN A TENDER RAY. | THE BEGINNING OF HELIODORUS | 2 | 46 | 158 | 517 |
| TO MAKE THE PARTNER OF HIS OWNE PURE RAY. | SOSPETTO D'HERODE | 218 | 46 | 109 | 216 |
| IT SHINES, AND WITH A SOVERAIGNE RAY, | IN MEMORY OF LADY MADRE TERESA | 84 | 46 | 131 | 52 |
| BLUSHING, TO BEHOLD THE RAY | UPON DEATH OF DESIRED HERRYS | 33 | 46 | 168 | 467 |
| I'VE SEENE THE MORNINGS LOVELY RAY, | UPON DEATH OF DESIRED HERRYS | 47 | 46 | 168 | 467 |
| DISCERNE THE DAWNE OF TRUTH'S ETERNALL RAY, | ON FRONTISPIECE ISAACSONS | 13 | 46 | 191 | 491 |
| WHOSE NATIVE RAY, | WISHES SUPPOSED MISTRESSE | 49 | 46 | 195 | 479 |
| BUT TOUCH'T WITH AN INTERIOUR RAY. | TO THE NAME OF JESUS | 2 | 52 | 239 | 30 |
| HEAVN'S WHOLSOM RAY. | IN GLORIOUS EPIPHANIE | 61 | 52 | 253 | 39 |
| TO READ MORE LEGIBLE THINE ORIGINALL RAY. | IN GLORIOUS EPIPHANIE | 211 | 52 | 253 | 39 |
| THEREFORE TO THEE & THINE AUSPITIOUS RAY | IN GLORIOUS EPIPHANIE | 233 | 52 | 253 | 39 |
| THE DAY-BREAK OF THE NATIONS, THEIR FIRST RAY. | TO THE QUEEN'S MAJESTY | 3 | 52 | 261 | 47 |
| THE BLISSFULL SPRINGS OF JOY, FROM WHOSE ALL-CHEARING | OFFICE H. CROSS PRIME | 7 | 52 | 267 | 91 |
| OF A SURE JUDGE, FROM WHOSE SHARP RAY | DIES IRAE | 3 | 52 | 298 | 186 |
| IT SHINES, & WITH A SOVEREIGN RAY | TERESA | 84 | 52 | 315 | 52 |
| O RISE, PURE LAMP, & LEND THY GOLDEN RAY | ALEXIAS SECONDE ELEGIE | 29 | 52 | 335 | 207 |

RAIES

| | | | | | |
|---|---|---|---|---|---|
| TO HAVE THEM GUILDED WITH HIS COURTEOUS RAIES. | UPON KINGS CORONATION | 24 | MS | 389 | 454 |

RAYES

| | | | | | |
|---|---|---|---|---|---|
| HER MILD RAYES, THROUGH THY MELTING HEART. | IN MEMORY OF LADY MADRE TERESA | 137 | 46 | 131 | 52 |
| CIRCLED ROUND IN HIS OWNE RAYES. | HIS EPITAPH (HERRYS) | 40 | 46 | 172 | 471 |
| ARE GUILDED WITH THE UNION OF THOSE RAYES. | UPON YORKE HIS BIRTH | 12 | 46 | 176 | 500 |
| WHO'S THIS THAT COMES CIRCLED IN RAYES, THAT SCORNE | UPON YORKE HIS BIRTH | 68 | 46 | 176 | 500 |
| IF THOSE SHARPE RAYES PUTTING ON | LOVES HOROSCOPE | 21 | 46 | 185 | 483 |
| HER MILD RAYES THROUGH THY MELTING HEART. | TERESA | 136 | 52 | 315 | 52 |

REACH

| | | | | | |
|---|---|---|---|---|---|
| WOULD REACH THE BRASEN VOYCE OF WARR'S HOARCE BIRD. | MUSICKS DUELL | 101 | 46 | 149 | 535 |
| (MISTRESSE) I COME. NOW REACH A STRAINE MY LUTE | MUSICKS DUELL | 107 | 46 | 149 | 535 |
| RIPE AND FULL GROWNE, THAT COULD REACH DOWNE. | IN MEMORY OF LADY MADRE TERESA | 5 | 46 | 131 | 52 |
| WHERE THOU SHALT REACH ALL HEARTS, COMMAND EACH EYE. | ON A TREATISE OF CHARITY | 16 | 46 | 137 | 69 |
| WILL AS WEE MAY REACH AFTER THEE. | ON THE ASSUMPTION | 28 | 46 | 139 | 114 |
| WHERE RACKES & TORMENTS STRIV'D, IN VAIN, TO REACH THEE. | TO THE NAME OF JESUS | 206 | 52 | 239 | 30 |
| UPON THY WINGS, & REACH THE SKYES. | OFFICE H. CROSS PRIME | 16 | 52 | 267 | 91 |
| TO REACH AT THY LOV'D FACE. NOR CAN | ADORO TE | 29 | 52 | 291 | 172 |
| WILL, AS WE MAY, REACH AFTER THEE. | IN GLORIOUS ASSUMPTION B. LADY | 43 | 52 | 304 | 114 |
| RIPE MEN OF MARTYRDOM, THAT COULD REACH DOWN | TERESA | 5 | 52 | 315 | 52 |
| REACH ME A QUILL, PLUCKT FROM THE FLAMING WING | UPON GUNPOWDER TREASON | 1 | MS | 386 | 460 |

REACHES

| | | | | | |
|---|---|---|---|---|---|
| ALREADY REACHES AT A SWORD. THEY HIRE | SOSPETTO D'HERODE | 444 | 46 | 109 | 216 |

REACHING

| | | | | | |
|---|---|---|---|---|---|
| FEELES NOT THE STRENGTH, THE REACHING SPELL | OUT OF GREEKE CUPID'S CRYER | 36 | 46 | 159 | 519 |

READ

| | | | | | |
|---|---|---|---|---|---|
| THERE STILL TO READ TRUE PURE DIVINITY. | UPON BISHOP ANDREWES PICTURE | 12 | 46 | 163 | 490 |
| COULD HAVE BEEN FOUND 'TWOULD HAVE BEEN READ. | ANOTHER ON HERRYS | 49 | 46 | 170 | 469 |
| OF ALL INTERPRETERS READ NATURE TRUE. | UPON STANINOUGH'S DEATH | 30 | 46 | 175 | 475 |
| THY LITTLE SELFE IN LESSE, READ IN THESE EYNE | UPON YORKE HIS BIRTH | 43 | 46 | 176 | 500 |
| WELL READ IN THEIR SIMPLICITY. | IN HOLY NATIVITY | 96 | 52 | 246 | 76 |
| TO READ MORE LEGIBLE THINE ORIGINALL RAY. | IN GLORIOUS EPIPHANIE | 211 | 52 | 253 | 39 |
| WE READ IN YOU (RARE QUEEN) RIPE & FULL-GROWN. | TO THE QUEEN'S MAJESTY | 10 | 52 | 261 | 47 |
| IN ME, ME, SO TO READ | SANCTA MARIA DOLORUM | 52 | 52 | 283 | 162 |
| AND SPELL IT WRONG TO READ IT RIGHT. | FLAMING HEART | 10 | 52 | 324 | 61 |

|  |  |  |  |  |
|---|---|---|---|---|
| READ HIM FOR HER, & HER FOR HIM. | FLAMING HEART | 11 | 52 324 | 61 |
| LET ME SO READ THY LIFE, THAT I | FLAMING HEART | 107 | 52 324 | 61 |
| OF ALL INTERPRETERS READ NATURE TRUE. | DEATH'S LECTURE | 32 | 52 340 | 475 |

READE

| | | | | |
|---|---|---|---|---|
| LOOK ROUND AND READE THE WORLD'S WIDE FACE. | AGAINST IRRESOLUTION AND DELAY | 29 | 52 347 | 146 |

READER

| | | | | |
|---|---|---|---|---|
| HARKE HETHER, READER, WOULDST THOU SEE | IN PRAISE OF LESSIUS | 15 | 46 156 | 510 |
| PEACE, GOOD READER, DOE NOT WEEPE. | AN EPITAPH HUSBAND AND WIFE | 7 | 46 174 | 478 |
| BELEEVE MEE, READER CAN SAY MORE | AN EPITAPH UPON ASHTON | 2 | 46 192 | 464 |
| WRITE THESE LINES, READER, IN THY BROW. | AN EPITAPH UPON ASHTON | 30 | 46 192 | 464 |
| WRITE, WHAT THE READER SWEETLY RU'TH. | WISHES SUPPOSED MISTRESSE | 33 | 46 195 | 479 |
| PEACE, GOOD READER. DOE NOT WEEP. | AN EPITAPH UPON MARRIED COUPLE | 7 | 52 339 | 478 |
| HARK HITHER, READER. WILT THOU SEE | TEMPERANCE | 13 | 52 342 | 510 |
| THIS RARE ONE, READER, WOULDST THOU SEE. | TEMPERANCE | 51 | 52 342 | 510 |

READER'S

| | | | | |
|---|---|---|---|---|
| FROM THENCE INTO THE WONDRING READER'S BREST. | AN APOLOGIE FOR (TERESA) HYMNE | 25 | 52 322 | 59 |

READERS

| | | | | |
|---|---|---|---|---|
| FROM THENCE INTO THE WONDRING READERS BREAST. | AN APOLOGIE FOR HYMNE (TERESA) | 25 | 46 136 | 59 |
| WELL MEANING READERS. YOU THAT COME AS FREINDS | FLAMING HEART | 1 | 52 324 | 61 |
| READERS, BE RUL'D BY ME, & MAKE | FLAMING HEART | 7 | 52 324 | 61 |

READING

| | | | | |
|---|---|---|---|---|
| I TOOKE FROM READING THEE. 'TIS TO THY WRONG | AN APOLOGIE FOR HYMNE (TERESA) | 3 | 46 136 | 59 |
| I TOOK FROM READING THEE, TIS TO THY WRONG | AN APOLOGIE FOR (TERESA) HYMNE | 3 | 52 322 | 59 |

READILY

| | | | | |
|---|---|---|---|---|
| CARVES OUT HER DAINTY VOYCE AS READILY. | MUSICKS DUELL | 22 | 46 149 | 535 |

READY

| | | | | |
|---|---|---|---|---|
| READY TO PERSONATE A MORTALL PART. | SOSPETTO D'HERODE | 418 | 46 109 | 216 |
| READY TO DROPP INTO A CHAOS, ROUND | ON GUNPOWDER-TREASON | 20 | MS 384 | 458 |
| I SHRINKE NOT. BUT THUS READY STAND TO BEARE | OUT OF GROTIUS | 7 | MS 398 | 198 |

REALL

| | | | | |
|---|---|---|---|---|
| SEE, SEE THY REALL SHADOW. SEE THY BROTHER. | UPON YORKE HIS BIRTH | 42 | 46 176 | 500 |

REAP

| | | | | |
|---|---|---|---|---|
| TO REAP NEW CROWNES & KINGDOMS FROM THAT KISSE. | TO THE QUEEN'S MAJESTY | 22 | 52 261 | 47 |

REARE

| | | | | |
|---|---|---|---|---|
| THE LESTRIGONIANS HERE THEIR TABLE REARE. | SOSPETTO D'HERODE | 357 | 46 109 | 216 |

REAR'D

| | | | | |
|---|---|---|---|---|
| BY SHORT DIMINUTIVES, THAT BEING REAR'D | MUSICKS DUELL | 41 | 46 149 | 535 |
| AND WEPT AMAINE. THEN REAR'D A COSTLY TOMBE. | UPON GUNPOWDER TREASON | 50 | MS 386 | 460 |

REARES

| | | | | |
|---|---|---|---|---|
| A GOLDEN-HEADED HARVEST FAIRELY REARES | MUSICKS DUELL | 70 | 46 149 | 535 |
| HISTORY REARES HER PYRAMIDS MORE TALL | ON FRONTISPIECE ISAACSONS | 18 | 46 191 | 491 |

REASON

| | | | | |
|---|---|---|---|---|
| AND REASON (FOR WHAT'S FAITH TO HIM.) DEVOURE. | SOSPETTO D'HERODE | 162 | 46 109 | 216 |
| MAKE TO THY REASON MAN, AND MOCKE THY DOUBTS. | SOSPETTO D'HERODE | 521 | 46 109 | 216 |
| GOOD REASON FOR SHEE BREATHS ALL FIRE. | IN MEMORY OF LADY MADRE TERESA | 39 | 46 131 | 52 |
| GOOD REASON. FOR SHE BREATHES ALL FIRE. | TERESA | 39 | 52 315 | 52 |
| CRUELL RETURN. OR TELL THE REASON WHY | ALEXIAS THIRD ELEGIE | 17 | 52 336 | 209 |

REBELLIOUS

| | | | | |
|---|---|---|---|---|
| ETERNALLY BIND EACH REBELLIOUS LIMBE. | SOSPETTO D'HERODE | 140 | 46 109 | 216 |
| OF ALL THEIR CARES, TAM'D THE REBELLIOUS EYE | SOSPETTO D'HERODE | 390 | 46 109 | 216 |
| AND BEAT THE HOT BRASSE WITH REBELLIOUS WAVES. | SOSPETTO D'HERODE | 484 | 46 109 | 216 |

REBELLS

| | | | | |
|---|---|---|---|---|
| QUITE TURN'D. TH'INGRATEFULL REBELLS THIS THEIR YOUNG | SOSPETTO D'HERODE | 438 | 46 109 | 216 |

REBELL-WORD

| | | | | |
|---|---|---|---|---|
| BUT KILL THIS REBELL-WORD. IRRESOLUTE | TO COUNTESSE OF DENBIGH | 40 | 52 236 | 146 |

REBOUND

| | | | | |
|---|---|---|---|---|
| AND SEIZE THE SWIFT FLASH, IN REBOUND | IN GLORIOUS EPIPHANIE | 199 | 52 253 | 39 |

REBOUNDING

| REBOUNDING, THROUGH HELLS INMOST CAVERNES CAME, | SOSPETTO D'HERODE | 303 46 109 216 |

REBUKE

| MUST THE BRIGHT ARMES OF HEAV'N, REBUKE THESE EYES. | SOSPETTO D'HERODE | 231 46 109 216 |

HEAV'N-REBUKED

| THE HEAV'N-REBUKED SHADES MADE HAST AWAY. | SOSPETTO D'HERODE | 114 46 109 216 |

REBUK'T

| SEAS HAD NOT BIN REBUK'T BY SAWCY OARES | ALEXIAS THIRD ELEGIE | 7 52 336 209 |

REBUKES

| HE MURMURES, AND REBUKES THEIR BOLD DESIRE. | SOSPETTO D'HERODE | 485 46 109 216 |

RECEIVING

| THE RECEIVING MOUTH HERE MAKES | LAUDA SION SALVATOREM | 43 52 294 178 |

RECIPROCALLY

| WHICH THERE RECIPROCALLY LABOURETH | MUSICKS DUELL | 72 46 149 535 |

RECKON

| NO SURFETS WERE TO RECKON FOR. | AN EPITAPH UPON ASHTON | 26 46 192 464 |

RECKONS

| AND RECKONS UP IN SOFT DIVISIONS. | MUSICKS DUELL | 24 46 149 535 |

RECKONING

| WHAT A RECKONING HAST THOU MADE, | UPON THE DEATH OF A GENTLEMAN | 5 46 166 472 |
| DEATH LOST THE RECKONING OF HIS DAYES. | HIS EPITAPH (HERRYS) | 10 46 172 471 |
| WEE'L CONFOUND THE RECKONING QUITE. | OUT OF CATULLUS | 17 46 194 523 |

RECKNING

| JUST MERCY THEN, THY RECKNING BE | DIES IRAE | 37 52 298 186 |

RECLINE

| BOTH OF LOVE'S FIRES & FLOUDS) MIGHT I RECLINE | SANCTA MARIA DOLORUM | 47 52 283 162 |

RECONCILED

| EVERY RECONCILED GRACE, | HIS EPITAPH (HERRYS) | 19 46 172 471 |
| LET MY HEAT TO YOUR LIGHT BE RECONCILED. | OUT OF THE ITALIAN (2) | 6 46 190 547 |

RECONCILES

| THERE WHERE ONE CENTER RECONCILES ALL THINGS. | SOSPETTO D'HERODE | 34 46 109 216 |

RECOVERS

| THE SELF-REMEMBRING SOUL SWEETLY RECOVERS | DESCRIPTION RELIGIOUS HOUSE | 36 52 338 213 |

RECTIFIES

| BY THEM HIS STEPS HE RECTIFIES. | THE WEEPER | 100 46 79 120 |

RECTIFY

| RESUME & RECTIFY THY RUDE DESIGN. | FLAMING HEART | 39 52 324 61 |

RED

| WHEN THEY RED WITH WEEPING ARE, | THE WEEPER | 56 46 79 120 |
| EVERY RED LETTER | ON MARKES OF SAVIOURS WOUNDS | 7 46 86 28 |
| TO THIS RED SEA OF THY BLOOD. | ON BLEEDING WOUNDS OF LORD | 26 46 101 110 |
| SHEE SPREADS THE RED LEAVES OF THY LIPS. | A HYMNE OF THE NATIVITY | 67 46 106 76 |
| STARTLE THE DULL AYRE WITH A DISMALL RED. | SOSPETTO D'HERODE | 50 46 109 216 |
| ROSIE WITH A DOUBLE RED. | AN HIMNE FOR CIRCUMCISION | 2 46 141 37 |
| NOR SETS THEE IN SO RICH A RED. | AN HIMNE FOR CIRCUMCISION | 8 46 141 37 |
| PUT ALL HIS RED EYED RUBIES ON, | AN HIMNE FOR CIRCUMCISION | 15 46 141 37 |
| ROSY WITH A DOUBLE RED. | NEW YEAR'S DAY | 2 52 251 37 |
| NOR SETTS THEE IN SO RICH A RED. | NEW YEAR'S DAY | 8 52 251 37 |
| WITH A RED FACE CONFES'T THIS SCORN. | IN GLORIOUS EPIPHANIE | 122 52 253 39 |
| WITH PURPLE OF TOO RICH A RED. | VEXILLA REGIS | 26 52 277 156 |
| TO THIS RED SEA OF THY BLOOD | UPON BLEEDING CRUCIFIX | 22 52 288 110 |
| ARE RED WITHOUT & PALE WITHIN. | DIES IRAE | 44 52 298 186 |
| WHEN THEY RED WITH WEEPING ARE | WEEPER | 32 52 307 120 |
| THE RED CHEEKS OF A RIVALL'D LOVER. | FLAMING HEART | 44 52 324 61 |

RED-EY'D
    PUT ALL HIS RED-EY'D RUBIES ON.                         NEW YEAR'S DAY                          15   52 251  37
REDD
    THE REDD, BUT OF THE BLUSH TO THEE THEY OW.             UPON TWO GREENE APRICOCKES               6   48 220 494
REDEEM
    PULPITS AND PENNES SHALL SWEAT IN.  TO REDEEM           ON A TREATISE OF CHARITY                50   46 137  69
    REDEEM THIS INJURY OF THY ART.                          FLAMING HEART                           41   52 324  61
REDEEM'D
    YEE REDEEM'D NATIONS FARR & NEAR.                       O GLORIOSA DOMINA                       27   52 302 194
REDEEME
    REDEEME A WORTHY WRATH, ROUSE THEE, AND SHAKE           SOSPETTO D'HERODE                      461   46 109 216
REDEEMING
    TO ALL THE DEAR-BOUGHT NATIONS THIS REDEEMING NAME.     TO THE NAME OF JESUS                    94   52 239  30
REEL'D
    ALAS, THE EARTH, QUITE DRUNKE WITH TEARES, HAD REEL'D   UPON KINGS CORONATION                    9   MS 390 453
REFERR
    AND THAT FAIR WORD AT ALL REFERR TO THEE)               TO THE NAME OF JESUS                    14   52 239  30
REFINE
    THAT CAN EXALT WEAK EARTH, AND SO REFINE                AN APOLOGIE FOR HYMNE (TERESA)          44   46 136  59
    THAT CAN EXALT WEAK EARTH, & SO REFINE                  AN APOLOGIE FOR (TERESA) HYMNE          44   52 322  59
REFINED
    CIRCLED WITH PURE REFINED GLORY. HEERE                  UPON KINGS CORONATION                   13   MS 389 454
REFLECTION
    WHILE THE REFLECTION OF THY FOREPAST JOYES,             SOSPETTO D'HERODE                      243   46 109 216
    THY SELFE IN THIS UNFEIGN'D REFLECTION.                 UPON STANINOUGH'S DEATH                 20   46 175 475
    SEEM'D BUT THE OTHERS KIND REFLECTION.                  UPON YORKE HIS BIRTH                    65   46 176 500
    MORE SUMMER IN THEIR SHAMES REFLECTION.                 UPON TWO GREENE APRICOCKES               8   48 220 494
REFLEXION
    YOUR SELVES IN YOUR UNFAIGN'D REFLEXION.                DEATH'S LECTURE                         22   52 340 475
REFLEX
    AND CATCHE THY QUICK REFLEX. AND SHARPLY SEE            IN GLORIOUS EPIPHANIE                  193   52 253  39
REFRAINE
    AS TO REFRAINE) BROUGHT FORTH A COSTLY SHOWER           UPON KINGS CORONATION                    6   MS 390 453
REFT
    YOUR EYES THE LIGHT HATH REFT HIM.                      OUT OF THE ITALIAN (2)                   3   46 190 547
REFUS'D
    AM STILL REFUS'D.  BEFORE THE INFANT SHRINE             OUT OF GROTIUS                          36   MS 398 198
REGARDLES
    NOT MARK THE DRY REGARDLES DUST.                        TO COUNTESSE OF DENBIGH                 52   52 236 146
REGENT
    QUEEN REGENT IN YOUNG LOVES MINORITIE.                  ON HOPE                                 84   46 143  71
    QUEEN REGENT IN YONGE LOVE'S MINORITY.                  (ON) HOPE                               44   52 345  71
REGIONS
    REGIONS OF PEACEFULL LIGHT                              TO THE NAME OF JESUS                   116   52 239  30
REIGN
    LIVE, O FOR EVER LIVE & REIGN                           VEXILLA REGIS                           43   52 277 156
RAIGNE
    BECAUSE SHEE BREAKES THE YEARES OLD RAIGNE              THOUGH NOW 'TIS NEITHER                 16   MS 397 492

REIGNE

| | | | | | |
|---|---|---|---|---|---|
| THY FOE TO CROSSE THE SWEET ARTS OF THY REIGNE | TO LORD UPON WATER MADE WINE | 2 | 46 | 91 | 12 |

REIGNES

| | | | | | |
|---|---|---|---|---|---|
| THUS REIGNES THE WRATHFULL KING, AND WHILE HE REIGNES | SOSPETTO D'HERODE | 71 | 46 | 109 | 216 |
| THUS REIGNES THE WRATHFULL KING, AND WHILE HE REIGNES | SOSPETTO D'HERODE | 71 | 46 | 109 | 216 |

REINE

| | | | | | |
|---|---|---|---|---|---|
| HOLDS HIGH THE REINE OF FAIRE PARTHENOPE, | SOSPETTO D'HERODE | 26 | 46 | 109 | 216 |

RAINES

| | | | | | |
|---|---|---|---|---|---|
| HIS TREMBLING HANDS LOOSING THE GOLDEN RAINES. | UPON GUNPOWDER TREASON | 22 | MS | 386 | 460 |

REINTHRON'D

| | | | | | |
|---|---|---|---|---|---|
| AND REINTHRON'D THEE IN THY ROSY NEST, | TO THE NAME OF JESUS | 221 | 52 | 239 | 30 |

REJOICE

| | | | | | |
|---|---|---|---|---|---|
| AND NATUR'S WRONGS REJOICE TO DOE THEE RIGHT. | IN GLORIOUS EPIPHANIE | 148 | 52 | 253 | 39 |

REJOYC'T

| | | | | | |
|---|---|---|---|---|---|
| FRESH FROM THE ROSIE EAST REJOYC'T TO PLAY. | UPON DEATH OF HERRYS | 16 | 46 | 167 | 466 |
| SOON AS THE RIGHT-HAND SCALE REJOYC'T TO PROVE | VEXILLA REGIS | 35 | 52 | 277 | 156 |

REJOYCING

| | | | | | |
|---|---|---|---|---|---|
| AND REJOYCING SMILES TO SEE | PSALME 23 | 7 | 46 | 102 | 5 |

RELATING

| | | | | | |
|---|---|---|---|---|---|
| RELATING THIS SAD STORY. STREIGHTWAY HEE | UPON GUNPOWDER TREASON | 55 | MS | 386 | 460 |

RELEASE

| | | | | | |
|---|---|---|---|---|---|
| HEE SAW RICH NECTAR THAWES, RELEASE THE RIGOUR | SOSPETTO D'HERODE | 105 | 46 | 109 | 216 |

RELENT

| | | | | | |
|---|---|---|---|---|---|
| THAT COULD THE FATES KNOW TO RELENT. | ANOTHER ON HERRYS | 17 | 46 | 170 | 469 |
| BUT THERE WERE ROCKS WOULD NOT RELENT AT THIS. | OFFICE H. CROSS EVENSONG | 1 | 52 | 273 | 101 |
| THE CHILL LUMP WOULD RELENT, & PROVE | SANCTA MARIA DOLORUM | 49 | 52 | 283 | 162 |

RELENTLESSE

| | | | | | |
|---|---|---|---|---|---|
| HILLS & RELENTLESSE ROCKES, OR IF THERE BE | ALEXIAS SECONDE ELEGIE | 15 | 52 | 335 | 207 |

RELIEFE

| | | | | | |
|---|---|---|---|---|---|
| THEY, THOUGH TO OTHERS NO RELIEFE, | WEEPER | 59 | 52 | 307 | 120 |

RELEIFE

| | | | | | |
|---|---|---|---|---|---|
| THEY, THOUGH TO OTHERS NO RELEIFE | THE WEEPER | 77 | 46 | 79 | 120 |
| RICH QUEEN, LEND SOME RELEIFE. | SANCTA MARIA DOLORUM | 91 | 52 | 283 | 162 |
| O LET THY WRETCH FIND THAT RELEIFE | ADORO TE | 17 | 52 | 291 | 172 |
| TRAVEL'D TH' OLYMPIAN PLAINES TO FIND RELEIFE. | UPON KINGS CORONATION | 4 | MS | 390 | 453 |

RELIGION

| | | | | | |
|---|---|---|---|---|---|
| RISE THEN, IMMORTALL MAID. RELIGION RISE. | ON A TREATISE OF CHARITY | 1 | 46 | 137 | 69 |
| A SLUTTISHNESSE, FOR PURE RELIGION. | ON A TREATISE OF CHARITY | 30 | 46 | 137 | 69 |
| IN THEIR SAD RUINES . NOR RELIGION KEEP | ON A TREATISE OF CHARITY | 34 | 46 | 137 | 69 |
| THAT KEEPS RELIGION WARME. NOT SWELL A NAME | ON A TREATISE OF CHARITY | 52 | 46 | 137 | 69 |
| AND 'GAINST RELIGION HER OWNE COLOURS BEARE. | OUT OF GROTIUS | 44 | MS | 398 | 198 |

RELIGIOUS

| | | | | | |
|---|---|---|---|---|---|
| TO MEET RELIGIOUS WELCOMES AT HER RISE. | IN GLORIOUS EPIPHANIE | 72 | 52 | 253 | 39 |
| NOR WITH PERVERSE LOVES & RELIGIOUS RAPES | IN GLORIOUS EPIPHANIE | 105 | 52 | 253 | 39 |
| BUT REVERENT DISCIPLINE, & RELIGIOUS FEAR, | DESCRIPTION RELIGIOUS HOUSE | 30 | 52 | 338 | 213 |
| WITHOUT RELIGIOUS SILENCE. ABOVE ALL | HORATIJ ILLE & NEFASTO | 47 | MS | 382 | 530 |

RELIQUES

| | | | | | |
|---|---|---|---|---|---|
| DEARE RELIQUES OF A DISLODG'D SOULE, WHOSE LACKE | UPON STANINOUGH'S DEATH | 1 | 46 | 175 | 475 |
| DEAR RELIQUES OF A DISLODG'D SOUL, WHOSE LACK | DEATH'S LECTURE | 1 | 52 | 340 | 475 |

RELLISH

| | | | | | |
|---|---|---|---|---|---|
| AND RELLISH NOT OF RARITY. | PETRONIJ ALES PHASIACIS PETITA | 10 | MS | 382 | 526 |

REMAIN'D

| | | | | | |
|---|---|---|---|---|---|
| HEAV'N, EARTH, AND SEA, MY TRIUMPHS. WHAT REMAIN'D | OUT OF GROTIUS | 85 | MS | 398 | 198 |

REMAINES

   WHAT REMAINES THEN, BUT THAT THOU         AN EPITAPH UPON ASHTON         29  46  192  464

REMEDIE

   REMEDIE AGAINST THY REMEDIE.                IN PRAISE OF LESSIUS           12  46  156  510
   REMEDIE AGAINST THY REMEDIE.                IN PRAISE OF LESSIUS           12  46  156  510

REMEMBER

   DEAR, REMEMBER IN THAT DAY                  DIES IRAE                       29  52  298  186

SELF-REMEMBRING

   THE SELF-REMEMBRING SOUL SWEETLY RECOVERS    DESCRIPTION RELIGIOUS HOUSE    36  52  338  213

REMOVE

   THAT, AT THE NEXT REMOVE                    TO SAME CONCERNING CHOISE      48  52  331   66

REMOV'D

   THINKING HER FATHER HAD REMOV'D HIS COURT.   UPON KINGS CORONATION         32  MS  390  453

REND

   LO, FOR THEIR OWN HEARTS, THEY REND HIS.     OFFICE H. CROSS EVENSONG       2  52  273  101

RENDERS

   RENDERS THEE DOUBLE TO THY PRESENT WOES.     SOSPETTO D'HERODE            244  46  109  216
   WHICH RENDERS ALL THE STARRES SHE STOLE AWAY.  O GLORIOSA DOMINA             22  52  302  194

RENEW

   AND TO MANY DEATHS RENEW MEE.               OUT OF THE ITALIAN (1)        54  46  188  545

RENOUNE

   OF THY RENOUNE, AND THEIR OWNE SHAME.        NEITHER DURST MAN ASKE         12  46   92   20

REPAID

   NOW THOU SHAL'T HAVE ALL REPAID.            ON WOUNDS OF CRUCIFIED LORD    11  46   99   24

REPAIRD

   TO BE REPAIRD. HITHER SHE DID RESORT.       UPON KINGS CORONATION         31  MS  390  453

REPAIRE

   STEALE FROM THEIR STATIONS TO REPAIRE THEIR LIGHT.  UPON KINGS CORONATION      28  MS  389  454

REPEATED

   REPEATED, AND THAT SON STILL IN ANOTHER,     UPON YORKE HIS BIRTH         100  46  176  500
   OF THY SO OFT REPEATED RISING.              TO THE NAME OF JESUS         219  52  239   30

REPENT

   AND WRONGS REPENT TO DIADEMS.               IN MEMORY OF LADY MADRE TERESA 151  46  131   52
   AND WRONGS REPENT TO DIADEMMS.              TERESA                         150  52  315   52

REPLY'D

   REPLY'D THE PROUD KING, O MY CROWNES DEFENCE.  SOSPETTO D'HERODE          281  46  109  216

REPORT

   THE MUSICKS SOFT REPORT. AND MOLD THE SAME   MUSICKS DUELL              12  46  149  535
   WILL THY TOMBE REPORT OF THEE               THE WEEPER                   116  46   79  120
   SHALL THY TOMB REPORT OF THEE.              WEEPER                         152  52  307  120

REPOSE

   WHERE TO REPOSE HIS ROYALL HEAD              IN HOLY NATIVITY             66  52  246   76

PROUDLY-REPOSED

   TO WHERE THE KINGS PROUDLY-REPOSED HEAD     SOSPETTO D'HERODE          410  46  109  216

REPRIVE

   OR REPRIVE MEE,                              OUT OF THE ITALIAN (1)        53  46  188  545

REPULS'D

   HE IS REPULS'D INDEED, BUT YOU'R UNDONE.     AGAINST IRRESOLUTION AND DELAY  90  52  347  146

REPULST

| | | | | | |
|---|---|---|---|---|---|
| HE IS REPULST INDEED. BUT YOU ARE UNDONE. | TO COUNTESSE OF DENBIGH | 68 | 52 | 236 | 146 |

REQUEST

| | | | | | |
|---|---|---|---|---|---|
| GOE & REQUEST | TO THE NAME OF JESUS | 28 | 52 | 239 | 30 |

REQUIRES

| | | | | | |
|---|---|---|---|---|---|
| DOE THEN AS EQUALL RIGHT REQUIRES, | FLAMING HEART | 37 | 52 | 324 | 61 |

REQUITALL

| | | | | | |
|---|---|---|---|---|---|
| SAD REQUITALL, THUS MUCH DUST. | UPON THE DEATH OF A GENTLEMAN | 14 | 46 | 166 | 472 |

RESERVE

| | | | | | |
|---|---|---|---|---|---|
| A WILD RESERVE OF WANTON WRATH. | OFFICE H. CROSS EVENSONG | 4 | 52 | 273 | 101 |

RESOLVED

| | | | | | |
|---|---|---|---|---|---|
| WAY FOR A RESOLVED MIND. | PSALME 23 | 44 | 46 | 102 | 5 |

RESOLV'D

| | | | | | |
|---|---|---|---|---|---|
| OF WEAKNES, SHE MAY WRITE RESOLV'D AT LENGTH. | TO COUNTESSE OF DENBIGH | 42 | 52 | 236 | 146 |

RESOLVING

| | | | | | |
|---|---|---|---|---|---|
| IN A RESOLVING SIGH, AND THEN | TERESA | 117 | 52 | 315 | 52 |

RESORT

| | | | | | |
|---|---|---|---|---|---|
| TO BE REPAIRD. HITHER SHE DID RESORT. | UPON KINGS CORONATION | 31 | MS | 390 | 453 |

RESPIRATION

| | | | | | |
|---|---|---|---|---|---|
| A RESPIRATION OF REVIVING DEATHS. | DESCRIPTION RELIGIOUS HOUSE | 24 | 52 | 338 | 213 |

REST

| | | | | | |
|---|---|---|---|---|---|
| TILL AT LENGTH HE PERCHING REST, | OUT OF GREEKE CUPID'S CRYER | 43 | 46 | 159 | 519 |
| THUS MUCH, HEE'S DEAD, AND WEEPE THE REST. | UPON THE DEATH OF A GENTLEMAN | 34 | 46 | 166 | 472 |
| PLEASURE SINGS MY SOULE TO REST. | PSALME 23 | 9 | 46 | 102 | 5 |
| ON MY DRY PALLATS ROOFE TO REST | PSALME 137 | 23 | 46 | 104 | 7 |
| UNFILL'D FOR EVER. HERE AMONG THE REST. | SOSPETTO D'HERODE | 331 | 46 | 109 | 216 |
| SWEET ANGELS COME, AND SING THE REST. | ON THE ASSUMPTION | 64 | 46 | 139 | 114 |
| OF HIS MONUMENTALL REST. | UPON DEATH OF DESIRED HERRYS | 68 | 46 | 168 | 467 |
| THEE THEREFORE FROM THE REST APART SHE HURL'D. | UPON YORKE HIS BIRTH | 27 | 46 | 176 | 500 |
| AND CAN ALONE COMMEND THE REST. | WISHES SUPPOSED MISTRESSE | 27 | 46 | 195 | 479 |
| SWEET ANGELS COME, AND SING THE REST. | IN GLORIOUS ASSUMPTION B. LADY | 69 | 52 | 304 | 114 |
| TO FIND THE REST | PRAYER TO GENTLE-WOMAN | 9 | 52 | 328 | 139 |
| AMONGST THE REST | TO SAME CONCERNING CHOISE | 2 | 52 | 331 | 66 |
| OF LOVE, OF LIFE, & EVERLASTING REST. | TO SAME CONCERNING CHOISE | 53 | 52 | 331 | 66 |
| NO GAPING GORGON, THIS. NONE, LIKE THE REST | ALEXIAS THIRD ELEGIE | 41 | 52 | 336 | 209 |
| SILENCE, & SACRED REST. PEACE, & PURE JOYES. | DESCRIPTION RELIGIOUS HOUSE | 32 | 52 | 338 | 213 |
| MY SOULES SWEET REST. | LUKE 2. QUAERIT JESUM | 6 | MS | 379 | 11 |
| FARRE FROM DARKE HORRORS HOME APPEALE TO REST. | HORATIJ ILLE & NEFASTO | 38 | MS | 382 | 530 |
| BUT REST, AFFRIGHTED MUSE. THY SILVER WINGS | UPON GUNPOWDER TREASON | 27 | MS | 387 | 461 |
| THE REST POURTRAICTED ARE, THAT 'TIS NOE PAINE | UPON BIRTH PRINCESSE E | 35 | MS | 391 | 456 |

RESTLESSE

| | | | | | |
|---|---|---|---|---|---|
| THY RESTLESSE FEET THEY CANNOT GOE. | ON BLEEDING WOUNDS OF LORD | 5 | 46 | 101 | 110 |
| THY RESTLESSE FEET NOW CANNOT GOE | UPON BLEEDING CRUCIFIX | 9 | 52 | 288 | 110 |

RESUME

| | | | | | |
|---|---|---|---|---|---|
| RESUME & RECTIFY THY RUDE DESIGN. | FLAMING HEART | 39 | 52 | 324 | 61 |

RETIRED

| | | | | | |
|---|---|---|---|---|---|
| THESE CURTAIN'D WINDOWS, THIS RETIRED EYE | DEATH'S LECTURE | 27 | 52 | 340 | 475 |

RETYR'D

| | | | | | |
|---|---|---|---|---|---|
| HAD NOW RETYR'D HIMSELFE, AND BORROWED | SOSPETTO D'HERODE | 395 | 46 | 109 | 216 |

RETURN

| | | | | | |
|---|---|---|---|---|---|
| CRUELL RETURN. OR TELL THE REASON WHY | ALEXIAS THIRD ELEGIE | 17 | 52 | 336 | 209 |

RETURNED

| | | | | | |
|---|---|---|---|---|---|
| NOR MAY RETURNED FAIRER FLOWERS. | THE WEEPER | 90 | 46 | 79 | 120 |

RETURN'D

| | | | | | |
|---|---|---|---|---|---|
| NOR MAY RETURN'D MORE FAITHFULL FLOWRES. | WEEPER | 84 | 52 | 307 | 120 |

RETURNS
    IS NOT THE SOILE A KIND ONE (THINKE YE) THAT RETURNS    UPON THORNES FROM LORDS HEAD    7  46  96  23

RETURNES
    IS NOT THE SOILE A KIND ONE, WHICH RETURNES    UPON CROWNE OF THORNS    5  52  290  23

RETURNING
    FROM THIS TO THAT. THEN QUICKE RETURNING SKIPPS    MUSICKS DUELL    32  46  149  535

STILL-RETURNING
    STILL ROWLING A ROUND SPHEAR OF STILL-RETURNING PAIN.    DESCRIPTION RELIGIOUS HOUSE    18  52  338  213

REVEALE
    WHAT ONE COMES TO REVEALE WHAT THEY CONSPIRE.    SOSPETTO D'HERODE    446  46  109  216

REVEALD
    YET LIGHT WAS SEEN & LIFE REVEALD.    O GLORIOSA DOMINA    34  52  302  194

REVEAL'D
    O WHAT DELIGHT, WHEN REVEAL'D LIFE SHALL STAND    TERESA    129  52  315  52

REVELS
    DOE I NOT SEE JOY KEEPE HIS REVELS NOW,    UPON KINGS CORONATION    19  MS  389  454

REVENGE
    REVENGE THY BOUNTYES IN THEIR BEAUTEOUS SHAPES.    IN GLORIOUS EPIPHANIE    106  52  253  39

REVERENCE
    THEMSELVES WITH REVERENCE LEAVE THEIR PLACE    LAUDA SION SALVATOREM    34  52  294  178
    UNTO WHOSE FEET IN REVERENCE OF THE POWERS,    AN ELEGIE ON DR PORTER    4  MS  395  476

REVEREND
    IN A BED OF REVEREND SNOW.    IN PRAISE OF LESSIUS    42  46  156  510
    THIS REVEREND SHADOW CAST THAT SETTING SUN,    UPON BISHOP ANDREWES PICTURE    1  46  163  490
    MADE SO REVEREND, EVEN IN YOUTH,    HIS EPITAPH (HERRYS)    16  46  172  471
    OF RAM, HE-GOAT, OR REVEREND APE.    IN GLORIOUS EPIPHANIE    90  52  253  39
    THUS SHALL THAT REVEREND CHILD OF LIGHT,    IN GLORIOUS EPIPHANIE    205  52  253  39
    IN A BED OF REVEREND SNOW.    TEMPERANCE    40  52  342  510

REVERENT
    BUT REVERENT DISCIPLINE, & RELIGIOUS FEAR,    DESCRIPTION RELIGIOUS HOUSE    30  52  338  213

REVERENDLY
    HEE HEARD THEM REVERENDLY, AND THEN    AN EPITAPH UPON ASHTON    11  46  192  464

REV'RENTLY
    REV'RENTLY CIRCLED BY THE LESSER SEAVEN,    SOSPETTO D'HERODE    238  46  109  216

REVIVE
    WILL KILL HIS ANGER, AND REVIVE MY BLISSE.    TO THE MORNING    38  46  183  497
    SHALL REVIVE MEE,    OUT OF THE ITALIAN (1)    52  46  188  545
    THAT WE MAY LIVE, REVIVE HIS DEATH.    LAUDA SION SALVATOREM    28  52  294  178

REVIVED
    REVIVED NATURE TAKE A SECOND BREATH.    ON FRONTISPIECE ISAACSONS    4  46  191  491

REVIVING
    A RESPIRATION OF REVIVING DEATHS.    DESCRIPTION RELIGIOUS HOUSE    24  52  338  213

REVOLUTION
    HIS FINGERS FAIREST REVOLUTION    MUSICKS DUELL    154  46  149  535

REVOLUTIONS
    ON WHOSE FAIRE REVOLUTIONS WAIT    LOVES HOROSCOPE    13  46  185  483
    WHOSE REVOLUTIONS WAIT UPON    THOUGH NOW 'TIS NEITHER    25  MS  397  492

REVOLVES
    OFT IN HIS DEEPE THOUGHT HE REVOLVES THE DARKE    SOSPETTO D'HERODE    91  46  109  216

BLOOD-REVOLVING
    THY BLOOD-REVOLVING BREST TO RAGE DOTH MOVE.    SOSPETTO D'HERODE    514  46  109  216

## RHETORICALL

| | | | | |
|---|---|---|---|---|
| THEIR CADENCE IS RHETORICALL. | UPON THE DEATH OF A GENTLEMAN | 30 | 46 166 | 472 |

## RHETORICKS

| | | | | |
|---|---|---|---|---|
| HIS MOUTH WAS RHETORICKS BEST MOLD. | HIS EPITAPH (HERRYS) | 29 | 46 172 | 471 |

## RICH

| | | | | |
|---|---|---|---|---|
| MAKES SORROW HALFE SO RICH. | THE WEEPER | 45 | 46 79 | 120 |
| RICH LAZARUS. RICHER IN THOSE GEMS, THY TEARS. | UPON LAZARUS HIS TEARES | 1 | 46 89 | 18 |
| HEE SAW RICH NECTAR THAWES, RELEASE THE RIGOUR | SOSPETTO D'HERODE | 105 | 46 109 | 216 |
| HEE SAW A THREEFOLD SUN, WITH RICH ENCREASE, | SOSPETTO D'HERODE | 121 | 46 109 | 216 |
| AND RISING WITH RICH SPOILES UPON HIS BREST. | SOSPETTO D'HERODE | 229 | 46 109 | 216 |
| SUCH, AND SO RICH, THE FLAMES THAT FROM THINE EYES. | SOSPETTO D'HERODE | 239 | 46 109 | 216 |
| IT IS IN ONE RICH HANDFULL, HEAVEN AND ALL | ON A PRAYER BOOKE | 5 | 46 126 | 139 |
| O FAIRE, O FORTUNATE, O RICH, O DEARE. | ON A PRAYER BOOKE | 90 | 46 126 | 139 |
| THE RICH AND ROSEALL SPRING OF THOSE RARE SWEETS. | ON A PRAYER BOOKE | 110 | 46 126 | 139 |
| A DART THRICE DIPT IN THAT RICH FLAME. | IN MEMORY OF LADY MADRE TERESA | 81 | 46 131 | 52 |
| MY ROSY LOVE, THAT THY RICH ZONE. | IN MEMORY OF LADY MADRE TERESA | 173 | 46 131 | 52 |
| NOR SETS THEE IN SO RICH A RED. | AN HIMNE FOR CIRCUMCISION | 8 | 46 141 | 37 |
| ROB THE RICH STORE HER CABINETS KEEP, | AN HIMNE FOR CIRCUMCISION | 18 | 46 141 | 37 |
| TO MAKE HIMSELFE RICH IN HIS RISE. | AN HIMNE FOR CIRCUMCISION | 26 | 46 141 | 37 |
| WAS SO RICH IN GRACE AND NATURE, | ANOTHER ON HERRYS | 11 | 46 170 | 469 |
| OR RAMPANT FEATHER, OR RICH FAN. | WISHES SUPPOSED MISTRESSE | 21 | 46 195 | 479 |
| RIPE AS THOSE RICH COMPOSURES TIME COMPUTES | UPON TWO GREENE APRICOCKES | 13 | 48 220 | 494 |
| AND IN THE WEALTH OF ONE RICH WORD PROCLAIM | TO THE NAME OF JESUS | 95 | 52 239 | 30 |
| NOR SETTS THEE IN SO RICH A RED. | NEW YEAR'S DAY | 8 | 52 251 | 37 |
| ROB THE RICH BIRTHS OF EACH BRIGHT NEST | NEW YEAR'S DAY | 19 | 52 251 | 37 |
| TO MAKE HIMSELFE RICH IN HIS RISE. | NEW YEAR'S DAY | 26 | 52 251 | 37 |
| O PRIZE OF THE RICH SPIRIT. WITH WHAT FEIRCE CHASE | IN GLORIOUS EPIPHANIE | 196 | 52 253 | 39 |
| FOR FROM THIS DAY'S RICH SEED OF DIADEMS | TO THE QUEEN'S MAJESTY | 11 | 52 261 | 47 |
| WITH PURPLE OF TOO RICH A RED. | VEXILLA REGIS | 26 | 52 277 | 156 |
| RICH QUEEN, LEND SOME RELEIFE. | SANCTA MARIA DOLORUM | 91 | 52 263 | 162 |
| RICH, ROYALL FOOD. BOUNTYFULL BREAD. | ADORO TE | 39 | 52 291 | 172 |
| AND BOARD HIMSELF AT THY RICH BREST. | O GLORIOSA DOMINA | 8 | 52 302 | 194 |
| SO MUCH MORE RICH WOULD HE ESTEEM | WEEPER | 77 | 52 307 | 120 |
| IN THY SO RICH & RARE EXPENSES. | WEEPER | 116 | 52 307 | 120 |
| A DART THRICE DIP'T IN THAT RICH FLAME | TERESA | 81 | 52 315 | 52 |
| (MY ROSY LOVE) THAT THY RICH ZONE | TERESA | 172 | 52 315 | 52 |
| OF A RICH BINDING IN YOUR BREST. | PRAYER TO GENTLE-WOMAN | 10 | 52 328 | 139 |
| THE RICH & ROSEALL SPRING OF THOSE RARE SWEETS | PRAYER TO GENTLE-WOMAN | 116 | 52 328 | 139 |
| RICH, CHURLISH LAND. THAT HID'ST SO LONG IN THEE, | ALEXIAS THIRD ELEGIE | 1 | 52 336 | 209 |
| MY TREASURES, RICH, ALAS, BY ROBBING MEE. | ALEXIAS THIRD ELEGIE | 2 | 52 336 | 209 |
| BOTH MIXT AT LAST THEIR BLOOD IN ONE RICH BED | ALEXIAS THIRD ELEGIE | 47 | 52 336 | 209 |
| RICH HOPE. LOVE'S LEGACY, UNDER LOCK | (ON) HOPE | 11 | 52 345 | 71 |
| RICH, LIBERALL HEAVEN, WHAT, HATH YOUR TREASURE STORE | UPON BIRTH PRINCESSE E | 25 | MS 391 | 456 |
| RICH DIAMONDS, SETT IN A PURE SILVER FOYLE. | UPON BIRTH PRINCESSE E | 44 | MS 391 | 456 |

## RICHE

| | | | | |
|---|---|---|---|---|
| O FAIR, O FORTUNATE, O RICHE, O DEAR. | PRAYER TO GENTLE-WOMAN | 96 | 52 328 | 139 |

## RICHER

| | | | | |
|---|---|---|---|---|
| RICHER FAR DOES HE ESTEEME | THE WEEPER | 83 | 46 79 | 120 |
| RIPE, WILL MAKE THE RICHER WINE. | THE TEARE | 30 | 46 84 | 50 |
| RICH LAZARUS. RICHER IN THOSE GEMS, THY TEARS. | UPON LAZARUS HIS TEARES | 1 | 46 89 | 18 |
| BOWLES FULL OF RICHER BLOOD THEN BLUSH OF GRAPE | AN APOLOGIE FOR HYMNE (TERESA) | 33 | 46 136 | 59 |
| RIPE, WILL MAKE THE RICHER WINE. | WEEPER | 66 | 52 307 | 120 |
| BOWLES FULL OF RICHER BLOOD THEN BLUSH OF GRAPE | AN APOLOGIE FOR (TERESA) HYMNE | 33 | 52 322 | 59 |

## RICHEST

| | | | | |
|---|---|---|---|---|
| NOW WESTWARD SOL HAD SPENT THE RICHEST BEAMES | MUSICKS DUELL | 1 | 46 149 | 535 |
| HER RICHEST PEARLES. I MEANE THY TEARES. | THE WEEPER | 54 | 46 79 | 120 |
| SO SAID, HER RICHEST SNAKE, WHICH TO HER WRIST | SOSPETTO D'HERODE | 465 | 46 109 | 216 |
| THEIR RICHEST TIRES BUT DRESSE | WISHES SUPPOSED MISTRESSE | 41 | 46 195 | 479 |
| WITH TH' RICHEST CLOWDS THEIR PEARLY TREASURIE. | AN ELEGY MR STANNINOW | 18 | MS 394 | 473 |

## RICHLY

| | | | | |
|---|---|---|---|---|
| THEE WITH THY SELFE THEY HAVE TOO RICHLY CLAD. | ON CRUCIFIED LORD BLOODY | 3 | 46 100 | 24 |
| WITH ROSIE WINGS SO RICHLY BRIGHT. | UPON DEATH OF DESIRED MERRYS | 49 | 46 168 | 467 |
| THEE WITH THY SELF THEY HAVE TOO RICHLY CLAD. | UPON BODY OF OUR LORD | 3 | 52 290 | 24 |
| SNATCH'T UPP THE FALLING STARRE, SOE RICHLY GAY. | AN ELEGY MR STANNINOW | 50 | MS 394 | 473 |

## RIDDLE

| | | | | |
|---|---|---|---|---|
| A RIDDLE. (FATHER) STILL ACKNOWLEDG'D THINE | OUT OF GROTIUS | 35 | MS 398 | 198 |

## RIDDLES

| | | | | |
|---|---|---|---|---|
| THESE ARE THE KNOTTY RIDDLES, WHOSE DARKE DOUBT | SOSPETTO D'HERODE | 191 | 46 109 | 216 |

## RIDE

| | | | | |
|---|---|---|---|---|
| OF STREAMING SWEETNESSE, WHICH IN STATE DOTH RIDE | MUSICKS DUELL | 94 | 46 149 | 535 |

RIDES

    TO HEAVN RIDES IN A SUMMER'S DAY.  TEMPERANCE  32  52 342 510

RIFE

    THE PRETIOUS BARBILL, NOW GROUNE RIFE.  PETRONIJ ALES PHASIACIS PETITA  15  MS 382 526

RIFLE

    TO RIFLE AND DEFLOWER.  ON A PRAYER BOOKE  109  46 126 139
    TO RIFLE & DEFLOUR  PRAYER TO GENTLE-WOMAN  115  52 328 139

RIGHT

    WHOSE RIGHT BY DAVID'S LINAGE SO LONG WORNE.  SOSPETTO D'HERODE  403  46 109 216
    IF ON TIMES RIGHT HAND, SIT FAIRE HISTORIE.  ON FRONTISPIECE ISAACSONS  5  46 191 491
    FIRST DOES THE LONGING LOVER RIGHT.  WISHES SUPPOSED MISTRESSE  72  46 195 479
    O HAPPY YOU, IF IT HITT RIGHT.  TO COUNTESSE OF DENBIGH  50  52 236 146
    AND NATUR'S WRONGS REJOICE TO DOE THEE RIGHT.  IN GLORIOUS EPIPHANIE  148  52 253  39
    AND ROSY DAWN OF THE RIGHT ROYALL BLOOD.  TO THE QUEEN'S MAJESTY  6  52 261  47
    TO A HEART WHO BY SAD RIGHT OF SIN  SANCTA MARIA DOLORUM  93  52 283 162
    THAT I INHERITT THY RIGHT HAND.  DIES IRAE  64  52 298 186
    AND SPELL IT WRONG TO READ IT RIGHT.  FLAMING HEART  10  52 324  61
    DOE THEN AS EQUALL RIGHT REQUIRES.  FLAMING HEART  37  52 324  61

RIGHT-EY'D

    THE RIGHT-EY'D AREOPAGITE  IN GLORIOUS EPIPHANIE  191  52 253  39

RIGHT-HAND

    SOON AS THE RIGHT-HAND SCALE REJOYC'T TO PROVE  VEXILLA REGIS  35  52 277 156

RIGOUR

    HEE SAW RICH NECTAR THAWES, RELEASE THE RIGOUR  SOSPETTO D'HERODE  105  46 109 216
    OF AN ADAMANTINE RIGOUR.  ANOTHER ON HERRYS  4  46 170 469

RIGOUROUS

    THREE RIGOUROUS VIRGINS WAITING STILL BEHIND,  SOSPETTO D'HERODE  65  46 109 216

RILLS

    FOLLOWING THOSE LITTLE RILLS, HEE SINKES INTO  MUSICKS DUELL  123  46 149 535
    PARENTS OF SILVER-FORDED RILLS.  THE WEEPER  2  46  79 120
    PARENTS OF SYLVER-FOOTED RILLS.  WEEPER  2  52 307 120

RING

    UP TO THE THIRD RING, O'RE THE SHORE WAS SPREAD  THE BEGINNING OF HELIODORUS  14  46 158 517
    AND STILL THY SPATIOUS PALACE RING.  CHARITAS NIMIA  20  52 280  48

RINGS

    WHOSE SYLVER-ROOFE RINGS WITH THE SPRIGHTLY NOTES  MUSICKS DUELL  75  46 149 535
    HER WEAKE CONCEPTIONS. NO LOANE SHADE, BUT RINGS  OUT OF VIRGIL  9  46 155 529
    ABOUT THEIR SHADY BROWES IN WANTON RINGS.  SOSPETTO D'HERODE  70  46 109 216
    THE HOLY YOUTH OF HEAV'N, WHOSE GOLDEN RINGS  ON A TREATISE OF CHARITY  21  46 137  69
    OF HIS CAPTIVITY RINGS IN HIS EARES.  HORATIJ ILLE & NEFASTO  29  MS 382 530

RIOTOUS

    NO ROOFES OF GOLD O'RE RIOTOUS TABLES SHINING  DESCRIPTION RELIGIOUS HOUSE  1  52 338 213

RIPE

    RIPE, WILL MAKE THE RICHER WINE.  THE TEARE  30  46  84  50
    AND THENCE MY RIPE SOULE WILL I BREATH  PSALME 23  71  46 102   5
    THE FATES RIPE, IN THEIR GREAT CONSPIRACY.  SOSPETTO D'HERODE  432  46 109 216
    RIPE AND FULL GROWNE, THAT COULD REACH DOWNE.  IN MEMORY OF LADY MADRE TERESA  5  46 131  52
    THE RIPE ENDOWMENTS OF WHOSE MIND.  HIS EPITAPH (HERRYS)  7  46 172 471
    OF RIPE PLEASURES  OUT OF THE ITALIAN (1)  26  46 188 545
    TILL THAT RIPE BIRTH  WISHES SUPPOSED MISTRESSE  7  46 195 479
    YET ARE SCARCE RIPE ENOUGH AT BEST TO SHOW  UPON TWO GREENE APRICOCKES  5  48 220 494
    RIPE AS THOSE RICH COMPOSURES TIME COMPUTES  UPON TWO GREENE APRICOCKES  13  48 220 494
    WE READ IN YOU (RARE QUEEN) RIPE & FULL-GROWN.  TO THE QUEEN'S MAJESTY  10  52 261  47
    GATHER NOW THY GREIF'S RIPE FRUIT. GREAT MOTHER-MAID.  OFFICE H. CROSS EVENSONG  7  52 273 101
    RIPE, WILL MAKE THE RICHER WINE.  WEEPER  66  52 307 120
    RIPE MEN OF MARTYRDOM, THAT COULD REACH DOWN  TERESA  5  52 315  52

RIPEN

    GLAD TIME TO RIPEN EXPECTATION.  UPON DEATH OF HERRYS  22  46 167 466

RIPEND

    MUSICKS BEST SEED-PLOT, WHENCE IN RIPEND AIRES  MUSICKS DUELL  69  46 149 535

RIPER

| | | | | | |
|---|---|---|---|---|---|
| IN RIPER JOYES. MORE SHALL BEE HIS | OUT OF GREEKE CUPID'S CRYER | 15 | 46 | 159 | 519 |
| AND TILL MY RIPER WOES TO AGE ARE COME, | OUR LORD IN HIS CIRCUMCISION | 17 | 46 | 98 | 9 |

RISE

| | | | | | |
|---|---|---|---|---|---|
| THE LUTES LIGHT GENIUS NOW DOES PROUDLY RISE, | MUSICKS DUELL | 135 | 46 | 149 | 535 |
| IN MANY A SWEET RISE, MANY AS SWEET A FALL) | MUSICKS DUELL | 155 | 46 | 149 | 535 |
| RISE, HEIRE OF FRESH ETERNITY, | EASTER DAY | 1 | 46 | 100 | 26 |
| RISE MIGHTY MAN OF WONDERS, AND THY WORLD WITH THEE | EASTER DAY | 3 | 46 | 100 | 26 |
| RAINE-SWOLNE RIVERS MAY RISE PROUD | ON BLEEDING WOUNDS OF LORD | 33 | 46 | 101 | 110 |
| SINKE SION, DOWNE AND NEVER RISE, | PSALME 137 | 28 | 46 | 104 | 7 |
| IT WAS THY DAY, SWEET, AND DID RISE, | A HYMNE OF THE NATIVITY | 21 | 46 | 106 | 76 |
| THE GLORIES THAT DID GUILD THEE IN THY RISE. | SOSPETTO D'HERODE | 76 | 46 | 109 | 216 |
| HEAV'N SAW HER RISE, AND SAW HELL IN THE SIGHT. | SOSPETTO D'HERODE | 377 | 46 | 109 | 216 |
| RISE THEN, IMMORTALL MAID.  RELIGION RISE. | ON A TREATISE OF CHARITY | 1 | 46 | 137 | 69 |
| RISE THEN, IMMORTALL MAID.  RELIGION RISE. | ON A TREATISE OF CHARITY | 1 | 46 | 137 | 69 |
| LO WHERE I SEE THY OFFRINGS WAKE, AND RISE | ON A TREATISE OF CHARITY | 17 | 46 | 137 | 69 |
| SIGHS TO HIS SILVER MATE.  RISE UP MY LOVE, | ON THE ASSUMPTION | 8 | 46 | 139 | 114 |
| RISE UP MY FAIRE, MY SPOTLESSE ONE. | ON THE ASSUMPTION | 9 | 46 | 139 | 114 |
| RISE THOU FIRST AND FAIREST MORNING. | AN HIMNE FOR CIRCUMCISION | 1 | 46 | 141 | 37 |
| TO MAKE HIMSELFE RICH IN HIS RISE, | AN HIMNE FOR CIRCUMCISION | 26 | 46 | 141 | 37 |
| DANCE IN AN ENDLESSE ROUND, AGAINE SHALL RISE | UPON DEATH OF HERRYS | 38 | 46 | 167 | 466 |
| SHALL RISE IN A SWEET HARVEST.  WHICH DISCLOSES | ON A FOULE MORNING | 17 | 46 | 181 | 495 |
| RISE THEN (FAIRE BLEW-EY'D MAID) RISE AND DISCOVER | ON A FOULE MORNING | 27 | 46 | 181 | 495 |
| RISE THEN (FAIRE BLEW-EY'D MAID) RISE AND DISCOVER | ON A FOULE MORNING | 27 | 46 | 181 | 495 |
| INTO THY MODEST VEYLE.  HOW DID'ST THOU RISE | TO THE MORNING | 8 | 46 | 183 | 497 |
| HAVE MERCY THEN, AND WHEN HE NEXT SHALL RISE | TO THE MORNING | 35 | 46 | 183 | 497 |
| YOU STREIGHT SHALL SEE HER WAKE AND RISE | THOUGH NOW 'TIS NEITHER | 9 | MS | 397 | 492 |
| THE'ATTENDING WORLD, TO WAIT THY RISE. | TO THE NAME OF JESUS | 135 | 52 | 239 | 30 |
| IT WAS THY DAY, SWEET.  & DID RISE | IN HOLY NATIVITY | 21 | 52 | 246 | 76 |
| RISE, THOU BEST & BRIGHTEST MORNING. | NEW YEAR'S DAY | 1 | 52 | 251 | 37 |
| BURNISHT IN HIS BEST BEAMES RISE, | NEW YEAR'S DAY | 14 | 52 | 251 | 37 |
| TO MAKE HIMSELFE RICH IN HIS RISE, | NEW YEAR'S DAY | 26 | 52 | 251 | 37 |
| TO DISINHERITT THE SUN'S RISE, | IN GLORIOUS EPIPHANIE | 4 | 52 | 253 | 39 |
| TO MEET RELIGIOUS WELCOMES AT HER RISE. | IN GLORIOUS EPIPHANIE | 72 | 52 | 253 | 39 |
| IT WAS FOR THIS THE DAY DID RISE | IN GLORIOUS EPIPHANIE | 125 | 52 | 253 | 39 |
| DOES RISE A RADIANT CROPPE OF ROYALLE STEMMS, | TO THE QUEEN'S MAJESTY | 12 | 52 | 261 | 47 |
| SHE COULD NOT RISE SO SOON, AS THEY | OFFICE H. CROSS PRIME | 2 | 52 | 267 | 91 |
| THAT WE MAY RISE | OFFICE H. CROSS PRIME | 15 | 52 | 267 | 91 |
| RAIN-SWOLN RIVERS MAY RISE PROUD, | UPON BLEEDING CRUCIFIX | 29 | 52 | 288 | 110 |
| RISE, ROYALL SION.  RISE & SING | LAUDA SION SALVATOREM | 1 | 52 | 294 | 178 |
| RISE, ROYALL SION.  RISE & SING | LAUDA SION SALVATOREM | 1 | 52 | 294 | 178 |
| SIGHES TO HIS SYLVER MATE RISE UP, MY LOVE. | IN GLORIOUS ASSUMPTION B. LADY | 8 | 52 | 304 | 114 |
| RISE UP, MY FAIR, MY SPOTTLESSE ONE. | IN GLORIOUS ASSUMPTION B. LADY | 9 | 52 | 304 | 114 |
| DOES THE DAY-STARRE RISE. | WEEPER | 133 | 52 | 307 | 120 |
| RISE, FAIREST OF THOSE FIRES. WHATE'RE THOU BE | ALEXIAS SECONDE ELEGIE | 25 | 52 | 335 | 207 |
| O RISE, PURE LAMP, & LEND THY GOLDEN RAY | ALEXIAS SECONDE ELEGIE | 29 | 52 | 335 | 207 |
| TOO EARLY RISE. | LUKE 2.  QUAERIT JESUM | 36 | MS | 379 | 11 |
| SINCE SIGHS DOE RISE, AND TEARES DOE FALL. | UPON DEATH OF A FREIND | 4 | MS | 393 | 477 |
| TEARES FALL TOO LOW, SIGHES RISE TOO HIGH, | UPON DEATH OF A FREIND | 5 | MS | 393 | 477 |
| SINCE YOUTH MUST FALL, WHEN IT SHOULD RISE. | UPON DEATH OF A FREIND | 16 | MS | 393 | 477 |

RISES

| | | | | | |
|---|---|---|---|---|---|
| TELL HIM HEE RISES NOW TOO LATE, | A HYMNE OF THE NATIVITY | 9 | 46 | 106 | 76 |
| ALL FRESH AND FRAGRANT AS HEE RISES, | ON A PRAYER BOOKE | 102 | 46 | 126 | 139 |
| TELL HIM HE RISES NOW, TOO LATE | IN HOLY NATIVITY | 9 | 52 | 246 | 76 |
| ALL FRESH & FRAGRANT AS HE RISES | PRAYER TO GENTLE-WOMAN | 108 | 52 | 328 | 139 |

RISING

| | | | | | |
|---|---|---|---|---|---|
| RISING AND FALLING IN A POMPOUS TRAINE. | MUSICKS DUELL | 96 | 46 | 149 | 535 |
| AND RISING WITH RICH SPOILES UPON HIS BREST, | SOSPETTO D'HERODE | 229 | 46 | 109 | 216 |
| WHOSE RISING GLORIES MADE SUCH HASTE TO HIDE | UPON DEATH OF HERRYS | 4 | 46 | 167 | 466 |
| OF THY SO OFT REPEATED RISING. | TO THE NAME OF JESUS | 219 | 52 | 239 | 30 |
| THY RISING TOPP FIRST STAIND THE BASHFULL LIGHT. | HORATIJ ILLE & NEFASTO | 6 | MS | 382 | 530 |
| I VEIW A RISING SUNNE IN THIS OUR SPHAERE, | UPON KINGS CORONATION | 14 | MS | 369 | 454 |
| THIS RISING SUNNE.  THEIR FACES NOTHING WORE, | UPON KINGS CORONATION | 38 | MS | 390 | 453 |

RITES

| | | | | | |
|---|---|---|---|---|---|
| A THOUSAND UNKNOWNE RITES | ON A PRAYER BOOKE | 73 | 46 | 126 | 139 |
| THEN SPOUSALL RITES PREJUDGE THE MARRIAGE-BED. | ON HOPE | 40 | 46 | 143 | 71 |
| A THOUSAND UNKNOWN RITES | PRAYER TO GENTLE-WOMAN | 79 | 52 | 328 | 139 |
| THEN SPOUSALL RITES PREJUDGE THE MARRIAGE BED. | (ON) HOPE | 20 | 52 | 345 | 71 |

RIVALL

| | | | | | |
|---|---|---|---|---|---|
| THE MAN PERCEIV'D HIS RIVALL, AND HER ART, | MUSICKS DUELL | 15 | 46 | 149 | 535 |
| A NAME IN NOBLE DEEDES RIVALL TO THEE. | SOSPETTO D'HERODE | 28 | 46 | 109 | 216 |
| RIVALL THY TEARES. | LUKE 2.  QUAERIT JESUM | 20 | MS | 379 | 11 |
| FROM WHENCE HIS GLORIOUS RIVALL HEE ESPIES. | UPON KINGS CORONATION | 18 | MS | 390 | 453 |

RIVALL'D

| | | | | | |
|---|---|---|---|---|---|
| THE RED CHEEKS OF A RIVALL'D LOVER. | FLAMING HEART | 44 | 52 | 324 | 61 |

RIVER

| | | | | | |
|---|---|---|---|---|---|
| NOT A HAIRE BUT PAYES HIS RIVER | ON BLEEDING WOUNDS OF LORD | 25 | 46 | 101 | 110 |
| NO HAIR SO SMALL, BUT PAYES HIS RIVER | UPON BLEEDING CRUCIFIX | 21 | 52 | 288 | 110 |

RIVERS

| | | | | | |
|---|---|---|---|---|---|
| WHERE TH' MILKY RIVERS MEET, | THE WEEPER | 21 | 46 | 79 | 120 |
| ALL THY PURPLE RIVERS MEET. | ON BLEEDING WOUNDS OF LORD | 4 | 46 | 101 | 110 |
| ALL THE RIVERS NAM'D BEFORE. | ON BLEEDING WOUNDS OF LORD | 30 | 46 | 101 | 110 |
| RAINE-SWOLNE RIVERS MAY RISE PROUD | ON BLEEDING WOUNDS OF LORD | 33 | 46 | 101 | 110 |
| ALL THE PURPLE RIVERS MEET. | UPON BLEEDING CRUCIFIX | 4 | 52 | 288 | 110 |
| ALL THE RIVERS NAM'D BEFORE. | UPON BLEEDING CRUCIFIX | 26 | 52 | 288 | 110 |
| RAIN-SWOLN RIVERS MAY RISE PROUD, | UPON BLEEDING CRUCIFIX | 29 | 52 | 288 | 110 |
| WHERE TH'MILKY RIVERS CREEP, | WEEPER | 21 | 52 | 307 | 120 |

ROARING

| | | | | | |
|---|---|---|---|---|---|
| THE WIND IN ALL HIS ROARING BRAGS STOOD STILL | OUT OF GROTIUS | 65 | MS | 398 | 198 |

ROAVING

| | | | | | |
|---|---|---|---|---|---|
| THIS ROAVING WANTON SHALL DESCRY. | OUT OF GREEKE CUPID'S CRYER | 6 | 46 | 159 | 519 |

ROB

| | | | | | |
|---|---|---|---|---|---|
| ROB THE RICH STORE HER CABINETS KEEP, | AN HIMNE FOR CIRCUMCISION | 18 | 46 | 141 | 37 |
| ROB THE RICH BIRTHS OF EACH BRIGHT NEST | NEW YEAR'S DAY | 19 | 52 | 251 | 37 |

ROBBERY

| | | | | | |
|---|---|---|---|---|---|
| THIS GRATIOUS ROBBERY SHALL THY BOUNTY BE. | FLAMING HEART | 91 | 52 | 324 | 61 |

ROBBING

| | | | | | |
|---|---|---|---|---|---|
| MY TREASURES, RICH, ALAS, BY ROBBING MEE. | ALEXIAS THIRD ELEGIE | 2 | 52 | 336 | 209 |

ROBE

| | | | | | |
|---|---|---|---|---|---|
| HIS GLITTERING ROBE, HIS SPARKLING CROWN, | IN GLORIOUS EPIPHANIE | 243 | 52 | 253 | 39 |

ROBES

| | | | | | |
|---|---|---|---|---|---|
| THY SCARLET ROBES. FOR HEERE YOU MUST NOT SHARE | UPON GUNPOWDER TREASON | 5 | MS | 387 | 461 |

ROABES

| | | | | | |
|---|---|---|---|---|---|
| THEN DIVES IN THE ROABES HE WEARES. | UPON LAZARUS HIS TEARES | 2 | 46 | 89 | 18 |
| AND FOR HIS OLD FAIRE ROABES OF LIGHT, HEE WEARES | SOSPETTO D'HERODE | 43 | 46 | 109 | 216 |

ROCKE

| | | | | | |
|---|---|---|---|---|---|
| THIS ROCKE BUDS FORTH THE FOUNTAINE OF THE STREAMES OF DAY. | EASTER DAY | 9 | 46 | 100 | 26 |
| FROM THE SAME SNOWY ALABLASTER ROCKE | UPON YORKE HIS BIRTH | 45 | 46 | 176 | 500 |

ROCKS

| | | | | | |
|---|---|---|---|---|---|
| YOUR SELVES. YOU ARE THE ROCKS | WHY ARE YEE AFRAID | 13 | 46 | 88 | 15 |
| GLADDING THE SCYTHIAN ROCKS, AND LIBIAN SANDS. | SOSPETTO D'HERODE | 108 | 46 | 109 | 216 |
| WHEN STUBBORN ROCKS SHALL BOW | TO THE NAME OF JESUS | 230 | 52 | 239 | 30 |
| WHICH TAUGHT ATTENTION EV'N TO ROCKS & STONES. | OFFICE H. CROSS NINTH | 2 | 52 | 271 | 99 |
| BUT THERE WERE ROCKS WOULD NOT RELENT AT THIS. | OFFICE H. CROSS EVENSONG | 1 | 52 | 273 | 101 |
| WITH ROCKS. NOR BOLD HANDS STRUCK THE WORLD'S STRONG BARRES. | ALEXIAS THIRD ELEGIE | 10 | 52 | 336 | 209 |
| TO TH' CHURLISH ROCKS. & TEACH THE STUBBORNE STONES | AN ELEGIE ON DR PORTER | 32 | MS | 395 | 476 |

ROCKES

| | | | | | |
|---|---|---|---|---|---|
| HERE CRUELL SCYRON BOASTS HIS BLOODY ROCKES, | SOSPETTO D'HERODE | 359 | 46 | 109 | 216 |
| HILLS & RELENTLESSE ROCKES, OR IF THERE BE | ALEXIAS SECONDE ELEGIE | 15 | 52 | 335 | 207 |
| OF THESE LOOSE GROVES, ROUGH AS TH'UNPOLISH'T ROCKES. | DESCRIPTION RELIGIOUS HOUSE | 14 | 52 | 338 | 213 |

ROD

| | | | | | |
|---|---|---|---|---|---|
| THOU ART WITH ME. STILL THY ROD, | PSALME 23 | 46 | 46 | 102 | 5 |
| TO KISSE HIM ONLY AS THEIR ROD | IN GLORIOUS EPIPHANIE | 179 | 52 | 253 | 39 |

ROMAN

| | | | | | |
|---|---|---|---|---|---|
| I LATE THE ROMAN YOUTH'S LOV'D PRAYSE & PRIDE, | ALEXIAS FIRST ELEGIE | 1 | 52 | 334 | 204 |
| HERE'T WAS THE ROMAN MAID FOUND A HARD FATE | ALEXIAS FIRST ELEGIE | 29 | 52 | 334 | 204 |

ROME

| | | | | | |
|---|---|---|---|---|---|
| THAT NEITHER ROME, NOR ATHENS CAN BRING FORTH | SOSPETTO D'HERODE | 27 | 46 | 109 | 216 |
| NOT ONELY IN DESPIGHT OF ROME. | AN EPITAPH UPON ASHTON | 18 | 46 | 192 | 464 |
| NOR LOST IN TOO LARG BOUNDS, OUR LITTLE ROME | ALEXIAS THIRD ELEGIE | 11 | 52 | 336 | 209 |

ROME'S

| | | | | | |
|---|---|---|---|---|---|
| THE PARTHIAN STARTS AT ROME'S IMPERIALL NAME, | HORATIJ ILLE & NEFASTO | 27 | MS | 382 | 530 |
| THAT ROME'S BOLD EAGLES NOW WERE BLINDED QUITE, | UPON KINGS CORONATION | 34 | MS | 390 | 453 |

ROOF

| | | | | | |
|---|---|---|---|---|---|
| UPON THE ROOF OF HEAV'N. WHERE AY | TERESA | 83 | 52 | 315 | 52 |

ROOFE

| | | | | |
|---|---|---|---|---|
| THY GOD WAS MAKING HAST INTO THY ROOFE, | I AM NOT WORTHY | 1 | 46 90 | 13 |
| ON MY DRY PALLATS ROOFE TO REST | PSALME 137 | 23 | 46 104 | 7 |
| UPON THE ROOFE OF HEAVEN WHERE AY | IN MEMORY OF LADY MADRE TERESA | 83 | 46 131 | 52 |
| HAD UNDER SOME LOW ROOFE LOV'D HIS PLAIN WIFE. | ALEXIAS THIRD ELEGIE | 14 | 52 336 | 209 |
| A POORE (YEA SCARCE A) ROOFE. WHOSE NARROW PLACE | OUT OF GROTIUS | 16 | MS 398 | 198 |

SYLVER-ROOFE

| | | | | |
|---|---|---|---|---|
| WHOSE SYLVER-ROOFE RINGS WITH THE SPRIGHTLY NOTES | MUSICKS DUELL | 75 | 46 149 | 535 |

ROOFES

| | | | | |
|---|---|---|---|---|
| NO ROOFES OF GOLD O'RE RIOTOUS TABLES SHINING | DESCRIPTION RELIGIOUS HOUSE | 1 | 52 338 | 213 |

ROOM

| | | | | |
|---|---|---|---|---|
| TAKES UP AMONG THE STARRES A ROOM, | WEEPER | 66 | 52 307 | 120 |
| AND IN HER FIRST RANKES MAKE THEE ROOM | TERESA | 126 | 52 315 | 52 |
| AND ROOM ENOUGH FOR MONARCHS, WHILE NONE SWELLS | DESCRIPTION RELIGIOUS HOUSE | 34 | 52 338 | 213 |

ROOME

| | | | | |
|---|---|---|---|---|
| ROOME FOR HER SPATIOUS SELFE, UNTILL AT LENGTH | UPON BISHOP ANDREWES PICTURE | 7 | 46 163 | 490 |
| TAKES UP AMONG THE STARS A ROOME, | THE WEEPER | 32 | 46 79 | 120 |
| AND IN HER FIRST RANKES MAKE THEE ROOME. | IN MEMORY OF LADY MADRE TERESA | 127 | 46 131 | 52 |
| THY BOSOME AND MAKE ROOME. THOU ART OPPREST | UPON YORKE HIS BIRTH | 3 | 46 176 | 500 |
| THAT NEST OF HEROES, ALL OUR HOPES FINDE ROOME. | UPON YORKE HIS BIRTH | 81 | 46 176 | 500 |
| AND CHOOSE YOUR ROOME | TO SAME CONCERNING CHOISE | 24 | 52 331 | 66 |
| SHALL HANG THE ROOME, & FOR YOUR TAPERS BRIGHT, | UPON GUNPOWDER TREASON | 25 | MS 387 | 461 |

ROOMES

| | | | | |
|---|---|---|---|---|
| AND WITH SOFT FEET SEARCHES THE SILENT ROOMES. | SOSPETTO D'HERODE | 400 | 46 109 | 216 |

ROOT

| | | | | |
|---|---|---|---|---|
| THE TRUNKE. YET IN THIS GROUND HIS PRETIOUS ROOT | UPON DEATH OF HERRYS | 35 | 46 167 | 466 |
| HIS VERTUE THAT WITHIN HAD ROOT, | HIS EPITAPH (HERRYS) | 35 | 46 172 | 471 |
| OF THIS FAIR TREE TAKE OUR ETERNALL ROOT. | SANCTA MARIA DOLORUM | 64 | 52 283 | 162 |
| THY TRAITEROUS ROOT A DWELLING IN MY GROUND. | HORATIJ ILLE & NEFASTO | 14 | MS 382 | 530 |
| NOW THAT HIS ROOT SUCH FRUIT AGAINE MAY BEARE, | AN ELEGY MR STANNINOW | 55 | MS 394 | 473 |

ROOTES

| | | | | |
|---|---|---|---|---|
| OUR ROOTES WITH THINE, | OFFICE H. CROSS PRIME | 14 | 52 267 | 91 |

ROSE

| | | | | |
|---|---|---|---|---|
| THE ROSE BUDS SWEET LIP KISSES. | THE TEARE | 21 | 46 84 | 50 |
| AND SUCH THE ROSE ITS SELFE WHEN VEXT | THE TEARE | 22 | 46 84 | 50 |
| SHEE ROSE, AND WITH HER TO OUR WORLD DID BRING, | SOSPETTO D'HERODE | 373 | 46 109 | 216 |
| OUR SINNES HAVE SHAM'D INTO A ROSE. | AN HIMNE FOR CIRCUMCISION | 12 | 46 141 | 37 |
| OF A RUDDY ROSE THAT STOOD | UPON DEATH OF DESIRED HERRYS | 32 | 46 168 | 467 |
| MORE THEN A MORNING ROSE. | WISHES SUPPOSED MISTRESSE | 35 | 46 195 | 479 |
| OUR SINS HAVE SHAM'D INTO A ROSE. | NEW YEAR'S DAY | 12 | 52 251 | 37 |
| SUCH TEARES THE SUFFRING RUSE THAT'S VEXT | WEEPER | 160 | 52 307 | 120 |
| ROSE QUAKES AT NAME OF CINNAMON. | PETRONIJ ALES PHASIACIS PETITA | 19 | MS 382 | 526 |

ROSE'S

| | | | | |
|---|---|---|---|---|
| THE ROSE'S MODEST CHEEK | WEEPER | 177 | 52 307 | 120 |

ROSES

| | | | | |
|---|---|---|---|---|
| WOULDST SEE A NEST OF ROSES GROW | IN PRAISE OF LESSIUS | 41 | 46 156 | 510 |
| THE ROSES MODEST CHEEKE | THE WEEPER | 135 | 46 79 | 120 |
| ROSES HENCE, OR LILLIES RATHER. | UPON INFANT MARTYRS | 4 | 46 95 | 10 |
| ROSES FOR THORNES. | UPON THORNES FROM LORDS HEAD | 8 | 46 96 | 23 |
| AT TOO DEARE A RATE ARE ROSES. | ON WOUNDS OF CRUCIFIED LORD | 6 | 46 99 | 24 |
| CONCEIVE PROUD HOPES OF PROVING ROSES. | ON BLEEDING WOUNDS OF LORD | 24 | 46 101 | 110 |
| BUT WERE THE ROSES BLUSH SO RARE, | UPON DEATH OF DESIRED HERRYS | 55 | 46 168 | 467 |
| TWO EVER BLUSHING BEDS OF NEW-BORNE ROSES. | ON A FOULE MORNING | 18 | 46 181 | 495 |
| (WHEN THOSE ROSES | OUT OF THE ITALIAN (1) | 4 | 46 188 | 545 |
| BROTHER PEARLES, AND SISTER ROSES. | OUT OF THE ITALIAN (1) | 24 | 46 188 | 545 |
| ROSES FOR THORNES. | UPON CROWNE OF THORNS | 6 | 52 290 | 23 |
| WOULDST' SEE NESTS OF NEW ROSES GROW | TEMPERANCE | 39 | 52 342 | 510 |
| THE ROSES FRESH, CONSERVED FROM THE RAGE, | UPON GUNPOWDER TREASON | 43 | MS 387 | 461 |
| OR CALL HER CHEEKE A BED OF NEW BLOWNE ROSES. | UPON BIRTH PRINCESSE E | 45 | MS 391 | 456 |
| NOE. NONE OF THESE RAVISH'T THOSE VIRGIN ROSES, | AN ELEGY MR STANNINOW | 37 | MS 394 | 473 |

ROSEALL

| | | | | |
|---|---|---|---|---|
| THE RICH AND ROSEALL SPRING OF THOSE RARE SWEETS. | ON A PRAYER BOOKE | 110 | 46 126 | 139 |
| THE RICH & ROSEALL SPRING OF THOSE RARE SWEETS | PRAYER TO GENTLE-WOMAN | 116 | 52 328 | 139 |

ROSY

| | | | | |
|---|---|---|---|---|
| MY ROSY LOVE, THAT THY RICH ZONE, | IN MEMORY OF LADY MADRE TERESA | 173 | 46 131 | 52 |
| AND REINTHRON'D THEE IN THY ROSY NEST, | TO THE NAME OF JESUS | 221 | 52 239 | 30 |
| THEIR ROSY FLEECE OF FIRE BESTOW. | IN HOLY NATIVITY | 59 | 52 246 | 76 |
| ROSY WITH A DOUBLE RED. | NEW YEAR'S DAY | 2 | 52 251 | 37 |

EMBOSOM'D IN A MUCH MORE ROSY MORN,                          IN GLORIOUS EPIPHANIE              66   52 253   39
AND ROSY DAWN OF THE RIGHT ROYALL BLOOD.                     TO THE QUEEN'S MAJESTY              6   52 261   47
THINE WAS THE ROSY DAWN THAT SPRUNG THE DAY                  O GLORIOSA DOMINA                  21   52 302  194
LIVE, ROSY PRINCESSE, LIVE. AND MAY THE BRIGHT               IN GLORIOUS ASSUMPTION B. LADY     60   52 304  114
(MY ROSY LOVE) THAT THY RICH ZONE                            TERESA                            172   52 315   52
IT'S TINCTURE FROM THE ROSY NECTAR.  WINE                    AN APOLOGIE FOR (TERESA) HYMNE     43   52 322   59
ROSY FINGERS, RADIANT HAIR,                                  FLAMING HEART                      32   52 324   61
THE ROSY HAND, THE RADIANT DART.                             FLAMING HEART                      67   52 324   61
WHOSE ROSY BEAM SHALL POINT MY SUN TO ME.                    ALEXIAS SECONDE ELEGIE             26   52 335  207
OF ROSY MARTYRDOME, TWICE MARRIED.                           ALEXIAS THIRD ELEGIE               48   52 336  209
HER ROSY CHEEKES YOU SHOULD HAVE SEENE NOE MORE              UPON GUNPOWDER TREASON             15   MS 386  460
THEY FORCE A LILLY PATH THROUGH ROSY MOUNTAINS.              AN ELEGIE ON DR PORTER             42   MS 395  476

ROSIE

ITS TINCTURE FROM THE ROSIE NECTAR, WINE                     AN APOLOGIE FOR HYMNE (TERESA)     43   46 136   59
ROSIE WITH A DOUBLE RED.                                     AN HIMNE FOR CIRCUMCISION           2   46 141   37
FRESH FROM THE ROSIE EAST REJOYC'T TO PLAY.                  UPON DEATH OF HERRYS               16   46 167  466
WITH ROSIE WINGS SO RICHLY BRIGHT,                           UPON DEATH OF DESIRED HERRYS       49   46 168  467
THEIR ROSIE BEAMES, SO THAT THE MORNE FOR ONE                UPON YORKE HIS BIRTH               57   46 176  500
AS WHEN THE ROSIE MORNE BUDDS INTO DAY.                      ON FRONTISPIECE ISAACSONS          14   46 191  491

ROSIE-FINGERD

AND THE SAME ROSIE-FINGERD HAND OF THINE,                    TO THE MORNING                     45   46 183  497

ROUGH

A BAND OF MEN, ROUGH AS THE ARMES THEY WORE                  THE BEGINNING OF HELIODORUS        7    46 158  517
FAIRE YOUTH (SAID I) BE NOT TOO ROUGH,                       A HYMNE OF THE NATIVITY           45    46 106   76
OF THESE LOOSE GROVES, ROUGH AS TH'UNPOLISH'T ROCKES.        DESCRIPTION RELIGIOUS HOUSE       14    52 338  213

ROUGHLY

HAD DEALT TOO ROUGHLY WITH HER TENDER THROATE,               MUSICKS DUELL                    159    46 149  535

ROULE

AND ROULE THEMSELVES OVER HER LUBRICKE THROAT                MUSICKS DUELL                     64    46 149  535

ROWLING

STILL ROWLING A ROUND SPHEAR OF STILL-RETURNING PAIN.        DESCRIPTION RELIGIOUS HOUSE       18    52 338  213

ROUND

HEAVES HER SOFT BOSOME, WANDERS ROUND ABOUT,                 MUSICKS DUELL                     88    46 149  535
LED ROUND IN HIS GREAT CIRCLE. NO WINDS BREATH               OUT OF VIRGIL                     27    46 155  529
LOOK'T ROUND, FIRST TO THE SEA, THEN TO THE SHORE.           THE BEGINNING OF HELIODORUS        8    46 158  517
HEE CHARGES TO BE QUIET, IT RUNS ROUND,                      THE DUMBE HEALED                   2    46  87   16
SHEE LIFTS HER SOOTY LAMPES, AND LOOKING ROUND               SOSPETTO D'HERODE                301    46 109  216
THOU SHALT LOOKE ROUND ABOUT, AND SEE                        IN MEMORY OF LADY MADRE TERESA   166    46 131   52
GIRT ROUND THY AWFULL ALTARS, WITH BRIGHT WINGS              ON A TREATISE OF CHARITY          22    46 137   69
DANCE IN AN ENDLESSE ROUND, AGAINE SHALL RISE                UPON DEATH OF HERRYS              38    46 167  466
CIRCLED ROUND IN HIS OWNE RAYES.                             HIS EPITAPH (HERRYS)              40    46 172  471
AND KEEPE SILENCE ROUND ABOUT THEE.                          OUT OF THE ITALIAN (1)            36    46 188  545
OF NIMBLE ART, & TRAVERSE ROUND                              TO THE NAME OF JESUS              33    52 239   30
THE WORLD'S ONE, ROUND, AETERNALL YEAR.                      IN GLORIOUS EPIPHANIE             27    52 253   39
AN EVEN ROUND WITH THE CIRCLING SUN.                         DIES IRAE                         10    52 298  186
THOU SHALT LOOK ROUND ABOUT, & SEE                           TERESA                           165    52 315   52
STILL ROWLING A ROUND SPHEAR OF STILL-RETURNING PAIN.        DESCRIPTION RELIGIOUS HOUSE       18    52 338  213
LOOK ROUND AND READE THE WORLD'S WIDE FACE,                  AGAINST IRRESOLUTION AND DELAY    29    52 347  146
READY TO DROPP INTO A CHAOS, ROUND                           ON GUNPOWDER-TREASON              20    MS 384  458
AFFRIGHT TH' AMAZED AIRE, & DANCE A ROUND                    UPON KINGS CORONATION             22    MS 390  453
DANCE, LIKE THE NIMBLE SPHAERES, A JOYFULL ROUND.            UPON BIRTH PRINCESSE E            32    MS 391  456
 THESE PURPLE CURRENTS HEDG'D WITH VIOLETS ROUND             AN ELEGY MR STANNINOW             22    MS 394  473
WHERE ROUND ABOUT HOVERS WITH SILVER WING                    AN ELEGY MR STANNINOW             53    MS 394  473
HIS FEARE.  THE CIRCLE OF A YEARES ROUND GROWTH              OUT OF GROTIUS                    22    MS 398  198

ROUNDS

NOR SPHEARES LET FALL THEIR FAITHFULL ROUNDS.                CHARITAS NIMIA                    18    52 280   48

ROUSE

THEY ROUSE HIM, WHEN HIS RANKE THOUGHTS NEED A STING.        SOSPETTO D'HERODE                 68    46 109  216
REDEEME A WORTHY WRATH, ROUSE THEE, AND SHAKE                SOSPETTO D'HERODE                461    46 109  216
THEN ROUSE THE NEST                                          TO THE NAME OF JESUS              32    52 239   30

ROUZE

OF WOES, TOO LATE DOE ROUZE THY FEARES.                      PSALME 137                        34    46 104    7
STUMBLING ON NIGHT. ROUZE THEE ILLUSTRIOUS YOUTH,            ON A FOULE MORNING                 3    46 181  495
AND ROUZE THE SLEEPY ASHES OF THE DEAD.                      ON GUNPOWDER-TREASON              29    MS 384  458

ROWZ'D

(ROWZ'D IN AN ANGRY TEMPEST). OH THE SEA.                    HORATIJ ILLE & NEFASTO            21    MS 382  530

ROWSING

AND CLOSES THE SWEET QUARRELL, ROWSING ALL                   MUSICKS DUELL                     53    46 149  535

ROWZING

| | | | |
|---|---|---|---|
| WHO ROWZING HIS ILLUSTRIOUS TRESSES CAME, | TO THE MORNING | 11 | 46 183 497 |

ROW

| | | | |
|---|---|---|---|
| MAY NOT ROW NEERER TO THESE DUSKY KINGS. | UPON GUNPOWDER TREASON | 28 | MS 387 461 |

ROWES

| | | | |
|---|---|---|---|
| 'MONGST THOSE LONG ROWES OF CROWNES THAT GUILD YOUR RACE, | TO THE QUEEN'S MAJESTY | 1 | 52 261 47 |

ROYALL

| | | | |
|---|---|---|---|
| KNOW'ST THOU NOT HOW OF TH' HEBREWES ROYALL STEMME | SOSPETTO D'HERODE | 433 | 46 109 216 |
| HEAVENS ROYALL HOASTS INCAMPT, THUS SMALL. | ON A PRAYER BOOKE | 6 | 46 126 139 |
| UPON THY ROYALL ELME (FAIRE VINE) AND WHEN | UPON YORKE HIS BIRTH | 103 | 46 176 500 |
| COME ROYALL NAME, & PAY THE EXPENCE | TO THE NAME OF JESUS | 139 | 52 239 30 |
| WHERE TO REPOSE HIS ROYALL HEAD | IN HOLY NATIVITY | 66 | 52 246 76 |
| THESE ROYALL SAGES SUE FOR DECENT PLACE. | TO THE QUEEN'S MAJESTY | 2 | 52 261 47 |
| AND ROSY DAWN OF THE RIGHT ROYALL BLOOD. | TO THE QUEEN'S MAJESTY | 6 | 52 261 47 |
| ARABIA, FOR THY ROYALL PHOENIX' NEST. | OFFICE H. CROSS COMPLINE | 6 | 52 274 105 |
| RICH, ROYALL FOOD. BOUNTYFULL BREAD. | ADORO TE | 39 | 52 291 172 |
| RISE, ROYALL SION. RISE & SING | LAUDA SION SALVATOREM | 1 | 52 294 178 |
| HEAVN'S ROYALL HOST. INCAMP'T THUS SMALL | PRAYER TO GENTLE-WOMAN | 12 | 52 328 139 |

ROYALLE

| | | | |
|---|---|---|---|
| DOES RISE A RADIANT CROPPE OF ROYALLE STEMMS, | TO THE QUEEN'S MAJESTY | 12 | 52 261 47 |

ROYALLY

| | | | |
|---|---|---|---|
| LARG THRONE OF LOVE. ROYALLY SPRED | VEXILLA REGIS | 25 | 52 277 156 |

RUB

| | | | |
|---|---|---|---|
| WHERE NO CHURLISH RUB SAIES NAY | PSALME 23 | 30 | 46 102 5 |

RUBY

| | | | |
|---|---|---|---|
| MAKE PROUD THE RUBY PORTALLS OF THE EAST. | SOSPETTO D'HERODE | 122 | 46 109 216 |
| EACH RUBY THERE. | WISHES SUPPOSED MISTRESSE | 52 | 46 195 479 |
| THE RUBY WINDOWES WHICH INRICH'T THE EAST | TO THE NAME OF JESUS | 218 | 52 239 30 |
| HER RUBY CASEMENTS, OR HEREAFTER HOPE | IN GLORIOUS EPIPHANIE | 70 | 52 253 39 |

RUBY-TEARES

| | | | |
|---|---|---|---|
| THE DEBT IS PAID IN RUBY-TEARES, | ON WOUNDS OF CRUCIFIED LORD | 19 | 46 99 24 |

RUBIES

| | | | |
|---|---|---|---|
| PUT ALL HIS RED EYED RUBIES ON, | AN HIMNE FOR CIRCUMCISION | 15 | 46 141 37 |
| THESE RUBIES SHALL PUT OUT HIS EYES. | AN HIMNE FOR CIRCUMCISION | 16 | 46 141 37 |
| PUT ALL HIS RED-EY'D RUBIES ON. | NEW YEAR'S DAY | 15 | 52 251 37 |
| THESE RUBIES SHALL PUTT OUT THEIR EYES. | NEW YEAR'S DAY | 16 | 52 251 37 |
| THOSE PLUMPE SOFT RUBIES HAD BIN DREST SOE BRAVE. | UPON BIRTH PRINCESSE E | 48 | MS 391 456 |

RUDDY

| | | | |
|---|---|---|---|
| A THOUSAND RUDDY HOPES SMIL'D IN EACH BUD, | UPON DEATH OF HERRYS | 25 | 46 167 466 |
| OF A RUDDY ROSE THAT STOOD | UPON DEATH OF DESIRED HERRYS | 32 | 46 168 467 |
| WHEN A RUDDY STORME WHOSE SCOULE, | UPON DEATH OF DESIRED HERRYS | 51 | 46 168 467 |
| WHERE NOUGHT BUT SMILES, AND RUDDY JOYES ARE WORNE. | ON A FOULE MORNING | 36 | 46 181 495 |
| BUT SMILES, & RUDDY JOYES, & AT THIS DAY | UPON KINGS CORONATION | 39 | MS 390 453 |

RUDE

| | | | |
|---|---|---|---|
| THERE RUDE IMPETUOUS RAGE DO'S STORME, AND FRET. | SOSPETTO D'HERODE | 317 | 46 109 216 |
| SO MUCH. RUDE SHEPHEARDS. WHAT HIS STEEDS. ALAS | SOSPETTO D'HERODE | 527 | 46 109 216 |
| AND WITH THE RUSH OF ONE RUDE BLAST, | UPON DEATH OF DESIRED HERRYS | 43 | 46 168 467 |
| RESUME & RECTIFY THY RUDE DESIGN. | FLAMING HEART | 39 | 52 324 61 |
| LETT NOT MY SUPPLIANT BREATH RAISE A RUDE STORME | ON GUNPOWDER-TREASON | 11 | MS 384 458 |
| WHERE THEY WILL SAFELY KEEPE IT, FROM THE RUDE, | UPON GUNPOWDER TREASON | 57 | MS 387 461 |
| O TELL ME THEN, WHAT RUDE OUTRAGIOUS BLAST | AN ELEGY MR STANNINOW | 27 | MS 394 473 |
| MURDRED THE EARTH'S JUST PRIDE WITH A RUDE KISSE. | AN ELEGY MR STANNINOW | 48 | MS 394 473 |

RUDENES

| | | | |
|---|---|---|---|
| THE WEIGHTY RUDENES OF HIS BOYSTEROUS HEELE. | ON GUNPOWDER-TREASON | 44 | MS 384 458 |

RUGGED

| | | | |
|---|---|---|---|
| AND RUGGED TOUCH OF PLUTO'S MULTITUDE. | UPON GUNPOWDER TREASON | 58 | MS 387 461 |

RUIN

| | | | |
|---|---|---|---|
| SO DEAR. WHAT HAD HIS RUIN LOST THEE. | CHARITAS NIMIA | 2 | 52 280 48 |

RUINE

| | | | |
|---|---|---|---|
| TILL THY RUINE TEACH THEE TEARES, | PSALME 137 | 32 | 46 104 7 |
| RUINE, WHERE E'RE SHE SLEEPES AT NATURES FEET. | SOSPETTO D'HERODE | 279 | 46 109 216 |

|  |  |  |  |  |  |
|---|---|---|---|---|---|
| OF TIME, OR TEETH OF HUNGRY RUINE FEARES. | SOSPETTO D'HERODE | 310 | 46 | 109 | 216 |
| IF, FROM THE SEED OF EMPTY RUINE, SHE | ON FRONTISPIECE ISAACSONS | 6 | 46 | 191 | 491 |
| RUINE A TEMPLE. ON WHOSE FRUITFULL FALL | ON FRONTISPIECE ISAACSONS | 17 | 46 | 191 | 491 |

RUINES

|  |  |  |  |  |  |
|---|---|---|---|---|---|
| SOME PANTING IN THEIR YET WARME RUINES BLED. | THE BEGINNING OF HELIODORUS | 18 | 46 | 158 | 517 |
| IN THEIR SAD RUINES . NOR RELIGION KEEP | ON A TREATISE OF CHARITY | 34 | 46 | 137 | 69 |

RULE

|  |  |  |  |  |  |
|---|---|---|---|---|---|
| COMES NOT TO RULE IN WRATH, BUT SERVE IN LOVE. | SOSPETTO D'HERODE | 516 | 46 | 109 | 216 |
| ARE THESE THE BEAMES THAT RULE THY DAY. | LOVES HOROSCOPE | 10 | 46 | 185 | 483 |

RUL'D

|  |  |  |  |  |  |
|---|---|---|---|---|---|
| READERS, BE RUL'D BY ME, & MAKE | FLAMING HEART | 7 | 52 | 324 | 61 |

RUN

|  |  |  |  |  |  |
|---|---|---|---|---|---|
| WHOSE GLORIOUS COURSE THROUGH OUR HORRIZON RUN, | UPON BISHOP ANDREWES PICTURE | 2 | 46 | 163 | 490 |
| BUT WHILE I SPEAKE, WHITHER ARE RUN | ON BLEEDING WOUNDS OF LORD | 29 | 46 | 101 | 110 |
| THE FACE OF THINGS, FROM HER DIRE EYES HAD RUN, | SOSPETTO D'HERODE | 383 | 46 | 109 | 216 |
| TWICE DI'D IN THINE OWNE BLUSHES, AND DID'ST RUN | TO THE MORNING | 9 | 46 | 183 | 497 |
| FACE RUN SADLY DOWN. | OFFICE H. CROSS THIRD | 9 | 52 | 268 | 93 |
| RUN, MARY, RUN. BRING HITHER ALL THE BLEST | OFFICE H. CROSS COMPLINE | 5 | 52 | 274 | 105 |
| RUN, MARY, RUN. BRING HITHER ALL THE BLEST | OFFICE H. CROSS COMPLINE | 5 | 52 | 274 | 105 |
| E'RE THE LESSE GLORIOUS RUN. | CHARITAS NIMIA | 40 | 52 | 280 | 48 |
| BUT WHILE I SPEAK, WHITHER ARE RUN | UPON BLEEDING CRUCIFIX | 25 | 52 | 288 | 110 |
| O THAT TRUMP. WHOSE BLAST SHALL RUN | DIES IRAE | 9 | 52 | 298 | 186 |

RUNNE

|  |  |  |  |  |  |
|---|---|---|---|---|---|
| SHALL IN A SILVER RAINE RUNNE OUT, WHOSE CREAME | ON GUNPOWDER-TREASON | 24 | MS | 384 | 458 |
| TORRENTS OF SALT TEARES FROM OUR EYES SHOULD RUNNE, | UPON GUNPOWDER TREASON | 37 | MS | 386 | 460 |

RUNS

|  |  |  |  |  |  |
|---|---|---|---|---|---|
| RUNS TO AND FRO, COMPLAINING HIS SWEET CARES | MUSICKS DUELL | 142 | 46 | 149 | 535 |
| HEE CHARGES TO BE QUIET, IT RUNS ROUND. | THE DUMBE HEALED | 2 | 46 | 87 | 16 |
| SEE HOW HEE RUNS, WITH WHAT A HASTY FLIGHT | ON A FOULE MORNING | 29 | 46 | 181 | 495 |

RUNNES

|  |  |  |  |  |  |
|---|---|---|---|---|---|
| RUNNES MURMURING ON THE STRINGS. ALCAEUS THERE | HORATIJ ILLE & NEFASTO | 41 | MS | 382 | 530 |
| THAT RUNNES IN VIOLETT PIPES. NONE OTHER FOOD | ON GUNPOWDER-TREASON | 64 | MS | 384 | 458 |

RUNG

|  |  |  |  |  |  |
|---|---|---|---|---|---|
| RUNG, THROUGH THE HOLLOW VAULTS OF HELL PROFOUND. | SOSPETTO D'HERODE | 299 | 46 | 109 | 216 |

RURALL

|  |  |  |  |  |  |
|---|---|---|---|---|---|
| GIVE THEN THIS RURALL WREATH FIRE FROM THINE EYES. | UPON YORKE HIS BIRTH | 118 | 46 | 176 | 500 |
| THIS RURALL WREATH DARES BE THY SACRIFICE. | UPON YORKE HIS BIRTH | 119 | 46 | 176 | 500 |

RUSH

|  |  |  |  |  |  |
|---|---|---|---|---|---|
| AND WITH THE RUSH OF ONE RUDE BLAST, | UPON DEATH OF DESIRED HERRYS | 43 | 46 | 168 | 467 |
| THE RUSH OF DEATH'S UNRULY WAVE, | HIS EPITAPH (HERRYS) | 47 | 46 | 172 | 471 |

RUSTIC

|  |  |  |  |  |  |
|---|---|---|---|---|---|
| CHANT TO MY SELFE WITH RUSTIC MELODIE. | UPON BIRTH PRINCESSE E | 24 | MS | 391 | 456 |

RU'TH

|  |  |  |  |  |  |
|---|---|---|---|---|---|
| WRITE, WHAT THE READER SWEETLY RU'TH. | WISHES SUPPOSED MISTRESSE | 33 | 46 | 195 | 479 |

SABLE

|  |  |  |  |  |  |
|---|---|---|---|---|---|
| WITH A SABLE WING, THAT COVERS | PSALME 23 | 38 | 46 | 102 | 5 |
| THAT SABLE JUDGMENT-SEAT SHALL BY NEW LAWES | IN GLORIOUS EPIPHANIE | 145 | 52 | 253 | 39 |
| SUCH AS THE SABLE PINIONS OF THE NIGHT | UPON GUNPOWDER TREASON | 6 | MS | 386 | 460 |
| INTO DIRE SABLE WEEDS, & SATE, & MOURN'D. | UPON GUNPOWDER TREASON | 48 | MS | 386 | 460 |
| HER SABLE CHEEKES INTO A BLUSHING MORNE. | UPON GUNPOWDER TREASON | 12 | MS | 387 | 461 |
| THE WEEPING PEN WITH SABLE TEARES HATH DREST. | AN ELEGIE ON DR PORTER | 10 | MS | 395 | 476 |

SACK

|  |  |  |  |  |  |
|---|---|---|---|---|---|
| HELL FROM ME TOO, AND SACK MY TERRITORIES. | SOSPETTO D'HERODE | 226 | 46 | 109 | 216 |
| DRINKE UP ALL SPAINE IN SACK, LET MY SOULE SWELL | AN APOLOGIE FOR HYMNE (TERESA) | 30 | 46 | 136 | 59 |
| DRINK UP AL SPAIN IN SACK. LET MY SOUL SWELL | AN APOLOGIE FOR (TERESA) HYMNE | 30 | 52 | 322 | 59 |

SACKCLOTH

|  |  |  |  |  |  |
|---|---|---|---|---|---|
| THREE SAD HOUR'S SACKCLOTH THEN SHALL SHOW TO US | IN GLORIOUS EPIPHANIE | 157 | 52 | 253 | 39 |

SACRED

|  |  |  |  |  |  |
|---|---|---|---|---|---|
| TO BE THE SACRED HONOUR OF THY BROWES. | SOSPETTO D'HERODE | 16 | 46 | 109 | 216 |
| HEE SAW THE TEMPLE SACRED TO SWEET PEACE, | SOSPETTO D'HERODE | 123 | 46 | 109 | 216 |
| WILL TAKE POSSESSION OF THE SACRED STORE | ON A PRAYER BOOKE | 57 | 46 | 126 | 139 |
| SPARKLING WITH THE SACRED FLAMES. | IN MEMORY OF LADY MADRE TERESA | 174 | 46 | 131 | 52 |

| | | | | | |
|---|---|---|---|---|---|
| AS MUCH AS SEES) SHALL WITH THESE SACRED LEAVES | ON A TREATISE OF CHARITY | 24 | 46 | 137 | 69 |
| THY SACRED NAME SHALL BEE | ON THE ASSUMPTION | 41 | 46 | 139 | 114 |
| THE SACRED SWEETNESSE OF HIS MIND. | ANOTHER ON HERRYS | 16 | 46 | 170 | 469 |
| BUT SUCH ALONE WHOSE SACRED PEDIGREE | TO THE NAME OF JESUS | 181 | 52 | 239 | 30 |
| IN WHATSOE'RE MORE SACRED SHAPE | IN GLORIOUS EPIPHANIE | 89 | 52 | 253 | 39 |
| HIS SACRED UNSHORN TRESSES. | IN GLORIOUS EPIPHANIE | 239 | 52 | 253 | 39 |
| WHOSE SACRED INFLUENCE | WEEPER | 27 | 52 | 307 | 120 |
| SPARKLING WITH THE SACRED FLAMES | TERESA | 173 | 52 | 315 | 52 |
| WILL TAKE POSSESSION OF THAT SACRED STORE | PRAYER TO GENTLE-WOMAN | 63 | 52 | 328 | 139 |
| SUCH AS THE SACRED LIGHT THAT ERST DID BRING | ALEXIAS SECONDE ELEGIE | 27 | 52 | 335 | 207 |
| BUT LY'N LOCK'T UP SAFE IN THEIR SACRED SHORES. | ALEXIAS THIRD ELEGIE | 8 | 52 | 336 | 209 |
| MY CHASTITY IS SACRED. & MY SLEEP | ALEXIAS THIRD ELEGIE | 37 | 52 | 336 | 209 |
| SILENCE, & SACRED REST. PEACE, & PURE JOYES. | DESCRIPTION RELIGIOUS HOUSE | 32 | 52 | 338 | 213 |
| BROODETH THIS SACRED PLACE. HITHER PEACE BRINGS | UPON KINGS CORONATION | 22 | MS | 369 | 454 |

SACRIFICE

| | | | | | |
|---|---|---|---|---|---|
| WEE'L BURNE, OUR OWNE BEST SACRIFICE. | A HYMNE OF THE NATIVITY | 88 | 46 | 106 | 76 |
| TO KINDLE THIS HIS SACRIFICE. | ON MR. G. HERBERTS BOOKE | 4 | 46 | 130 | 68 |
| FROM THE PALE DUST OF THAT STRANGE SACRIFICE | ON A TREATISE OF CHARITY | 18 | 46 | 137 | 69 |
| BAK'T IN HOT SCORN, FOR A BURNT SACRIFICE. | ON A TREATISE OF CHARITY | 44 | 46 | 137 | 69 |
| WERE VOW'D LOVES FLAMING SACRIFICE. | HIS EPITAPH (HERRYS) | 42 | 46 | 172 | 471 |
| THIS RURALL WREATH DARES BE THY SACRIFICE. | UPON YORKE HIS BIRTH | 119 | 46 | 176 | 500 |
| WHAT IS LOVES SACRIFICE, BUT THE BROKEN HEART. | UPON FORD'S TRAGEDYES | 2 | 46 | 181 | 495 |
| MY SELFE A MELTING SACRIFICE. I'ME BORNE | TO THE MORNING | 51 | 46 | 183 | 497 |
| OUR SELVES BECOME OUR OWN BEST SACRIFICE. | IN HOLY NATIVITY | 108 | 52 | 246 | 76 |
| HIS OWN LOVE'S, & OUR SIN'S GREAT SACRIFICE. | OFFICE H. CROSS NINTH | 6 | 52 | 271 | 99 |
| LO, THE FULL, FINALL, SACRIFICE | LAUDA SION SALVATOREM | 65 | 52 | 294 | 178 |
| O LOVE, I AM THY SACRIFICE. | A SONG | 5 | 52 | 327 | 65 |
| OFFER THY SELFE A VIRGIN SACRIFICE | UPON GUNPOWDER TREASON | 35 | MS | 387 | 461 |
| TO SACRIFICE HIMSELFE IN SUCH SWEET FIRE. | UPON KINGS CORONATION | 36 | MS | 389 | 454 |
| MADE EVERY MORTALL GLADLY SACRIFICE | UPON KINGS CORONATION | 36 | MS | 390 | 453 |

SACRILEGIOUS

| | | | | | |
|---|---|---|---|---|---|
| WAS SACRILEGIOUS, (SURE) OR SOMEWHAT WORSE. | HORATIJ ILLE & NEFASTO | 4 | MS | 382 | 530 |

SAD

| | | | | | |
|---|---|---|---|---|---|
| SAD REQUITALL, THUS MUCH DUST. | UPON THE DEATH OF A GENTLEMAN | 14 | 46 | 166 | 472 |
| THE SAD LANGUAGE OF OUR EYES. | UPON THE DEATH OF A GENTLEMAN | 20 | 46 | 166 | 472 |
| SWEETNESSE SO SAD, SADNES SO SWEET. | THE WEEPER | 60 | 46 | 79 | 120 |
| TO BEE MADE SO SWEETLY SAD. | THE WEEPER | 66 | 46 | 79 | 120 |
| SAD THAT THEY ARE VANQUISH'T SO, | THE WEEPER | 76 | 46 | 79 | 120 |
| TOO TRUE A TEARE. FOR NO SAD EYNE, | THE TEARE | 14 | 46 | 84 | 50 |
| HOW SAD SO E'RE | THE TEARE | 15 | 46 | 84 | 50 |
| AND NOW TH'ART SET WIDE OPE, THE SPEARE'S SAD ART, | I AM THE DOORE | 1 | 46 | 90 | 17 |
| AND WITH SAD MURMURS, CHIDES THE HANDS THAT STAIN HER. | TO PONTIUS WASHING HANDS | 14 | 46 | 94 | 23 |
| IN THIS SAD HOUSE OF SLOW DESTRUCTION, | SOSPETTO D'HERODE | 61 | 46 | 109 | 216 |
| FROM DEATH'S SAD SHADES, TO THE LIFE-BREATHING AYRE, | SOSPETTO D'HERODE | 81 | 46 | 109 | 216 |
| WINTERS SAD FACE, AND THROUGH THE FLOWRY LANDS | SOSPETTO D'HERODE | 110 | 46 | 109 | 216 |
| A SAD YOAKE, UNDER WHICH THEY SIGH'D IN VAINE, | SOSPETTO D'HERODE | 407 | 46 | 109 | 216 |
| IN THEIR SAD RUINES . NOR RELIGION KEEP | ON A TREATISE OF CHARITY | 34 | 46 | 137 | 69 |
| WHERE IN SAD PARTICULARS, | ANOTHER ON HERRYS | 43 | 46 | 170 | 469 |
| SAD MORTALITY MAY HIDE, | ANOTHER ON HERRYS | 59 | 46 | 170 | 469 |
| SHEE ASKES IF SAD, OR SAVING POWERS, | LOVES HOROSCOPE | 5 | 46 | 185 | 483 |
| SAD SHADES AND SING DULL NIGHT ASLEEPE. | THOUGH NOW 'TIS NEITHER | 20 | MS | 397 | 492 |
| IN A SAD SELFE-CAPTIVITY. | TO COUNTESSE OF DENBIGH | 24 | 52 | 236 | 146 |
| COME, YE SOFT MINISTERS OF SWEET SAD MIRTH, | TO THE NAME OF JESUS | 62 | 52 | 239 | 30 |
| THREE SAD HOUR'S SACKCLOTH THEN SHALL SHOW TO US | IN GLORIOUS EPIPHANIE | 157 | 52 | 253 | 39 |
| THEN SITT THEE DOWN, & SING THINE EV'NSONG IN THE SAD | OFFICE H. CROSS EVENSONG | 8 | 52 | 273 | 101 |
| O SAD, SWEET TREE. | OFFICE H. CROSS EVENSONG | 9 | 52 | 273 | 101 |
| BUT THOUGH GREAT LOVE, GREEDY OF SUCH SAD GAIN | VEXILLA REGIS | 13 | 52 | 277 | 156 |
| IN SHADE OF DEATH'S SAD TREE | SANCTA MARIA DOLORUM | 1 | 52 | 283 | 162 |
| YEILD SOMTHING IN THY SAD PRAEROGATIVE | SANCTA MARIA DOLORUM | 57 | 52 | 283 | 162 |
| TO'A HEART WHO BY SAD RIGHT OF SIN | SANCTA MARIA DOLORUM | 93 | 52 | 283 | 162 |
| SWEETNESSE SO SAD, SADNESSE SO SWEET. | WEEPER | 36 | 52 | 307 | 120 |
| SAD THAT THEY ARE VANQUISH'T SO. | WEEPER | 58 | 52 | 307 | 120 |
| WELLCOME, MY SAD SWEET MATE. NOW HAVE I GOTT | ALEXIAS SECONDE ELEGIE | 7 | 52 | 335 | 207 |
| HER LOVES CROSSE FORTUNE, THAT THE SAD DISPUTE | HORATIJ ILLE & NEFASTO | 40 | MS | 382 | 530 |
| RELATING THIS SAD STORY. STREIGHTWAY HEE | UPON GUNPOWDER TREASON | 55 | MS | 386 | 460 |
| OF MY SAD LABOURS. NO DAY YETT COULD TELL | OUT OF GROTIUS | 10 | MS | 398 | 198 |

SADDEST

| | | | | | |
|---|---|---|---|---|---|
| TO SING THEIR SADDEST DIR'GES, SUCH AS MAY | AN ELEGIE ON DR PORTER | 29 | MS | 395 | 476 |

SADLY

| | | | | | |
|---|---|---|---|---|---|
| NERE WAS'T THOU IN A SENCE SO SADLY TRUE, | ON BLEEDING WOUNDS OF LORD | 41 | 46 | 101 | 110 |
| FACE RUN SADLY DOWN. | OFFICE H. CROSS THIRD | 9 | 52 | 268 | 93 |
| N'ERE WAST THOU IN A SENSE SO SADLY TRUE. | UPON BLEEDING CRUCIFIX | 37 | 52 | 288 | 110 |

SADNES

| | | | | | |
|---|---|---|---|---|---|
| SWEETNESSE SO SAD, SADNES SO SWEET. | THE WEEPER | 60 | 46 | 79 | 120 |

SADNESSE

| | | | | | |
|---|---|---|---|---|---|
| SADNESSE ALL THE WHILE | THE WEEPER | 61 | 46 | 79 | 120 |
| NOR BELEEVES SHEE SADNESSE IS. | THE WEEPER | 64 | 46 | 79 | 120 |
| SWEETNESSE SO SAD, SADNESSE SO SWEET. | WEEPER | 36 | 52 | 307 | 120 |

SADOCUS

    PROFANE SADOCUS TOO DOES FIERCELY LEAD           OUT OF GROTIUS                    47   MS 398 198

SAFE

    SAFE, THOU DARKE HOME OF THE DEAD,              UPON DEATH OF DESIRED HERRYS     69   46 168 467
    SAFE O HIDE HIS LOVED HEAD.                       UPON DEATH OF DESIRED HERRYS     70   46 168 467
    BUT LY'N LOCK'T UP SAFE IN THEIR SACRED SHORES.    ALEXIAS THIRD ELEGIE              8   52 336 209

SAFELY

    WHERE THEY WILL SAFELY KEEPE IT, FROM THE RUDE,    UPON GUNPOWDER TREASON            57   MS 387 461

SAGES

    THESE ROYALL SAGES SUE FOR DECENT PLACE.          TO THE QUEEN'S MAJESTY             2   52 261  47

SAID

    SO SAID, HIS HANDS SPRIGHTLY AS FIRE HEE FLINGS,   MUSICKS DUELL                    111   46 149 535
    HEE SAV'D ALL WHEN HEE NOTHING SAID.              AND HE ANSWERED NOTHING             4   46  91  22
    FORBEARE (SAID I) BE NOT TOO BOLD,                A HYMNE OF THE NATIVITY           39   46 106  76
    FAIRE YOUTH (SAID I) BE NOT TOO ROUGH,            A HYMNE OF THE NATIVITY           45   46 106  76
    SWEET CHOISE (SAID I) NO WAY BUT SO,              A HYMNE OF THE NATIVITY           51   46 106  76
    IT SHALL NOT BE, SAID I, AND CLOMBE THE NORTH,    SOSPETTO D'HERODE               221   46 109 216
    WEE (SAID THE HORRID SISTERS) WAIT THY LAWES,     SOSPETTO D'HERODE               261   46 109 216
    HER WORDS, SLEEP'ST THOU FOND MAN.   SLEEP'ST THOU.  SOSPETTO D'HERODE               424   46 109 216
                                     (SAID SHE)

    SO SAID, HER RICHEST SNAKE, WHICH TO HER WRIST    SOSPETTO D'HERODE               465   46 109 216
    'TIS BUT THE SAME IS SAID, HENRY AND JAMES        UPON YORKE HIS BIRTH              33   46 176 500
    POOR WORLD (SAID I.) WHAT WILT THOU DOE           IN HOLY NATIVITY                37   52 246  76
    PROUD WORLD, SAID I.  CEASE YOUR CONTEST         IN HOLY NATIVITY                44   52 246  76
    FORBEAR, SAID I.  BE NOT TOO BOLD.              IN HOLY NATIVITY                55   52 246  76
    WELL DONE, SAID I.  BUT ARE YOU SURE            IN HOLY NATIVITY                62   52 246  76
    SWEET CHOISE, SAID WE. NO WAY BUT SO              IN HOLY NATIVITY                69   52 246  76
    TAKE HEED (SAID SHE) TAKE HEED, VALERIAN.         ALEXIAS THIRD ELEGIE              34   52 336 209
    ALEXIS, HE ALONE IS MINE (SAID I)               ALEXIAS THIRD ELEGIE              56   52 336 209
    ENOUGH IS SAID. NOW, IF THOU CANST CROWD ON        AN ELEGIE ON DR PORTER             19   MS 395 476

SAILES

    WHICH LIKE TWO BOSOM'D SAILES EMBRACE THE DIMME    SOSPETTO D'HERODE               142   46 109 216
    NO SAILES OF TYRIAN SYLK PROUD PAVEMENTS SWEEPING.  DESCRIPTION RELIGIOUS HOUSE      3   52 338 213

SAINT

    BETIMES TO BE A SAINT, BEFORE A MAN.              SOSPETTO D'HERODE               104   46 109 216
    AND CALL THE SAINT THE SERAPHIM.                   FLAMING HEART                    12   52 324  61
    SOME WEAK, INFERIOUR, WOMAN SAINT.                 FLAMING HEART                    26   52 324  61

SAINTS

    COHEIRS OF SAINTS. THAT SO ALL MAY                LAUDA SION SALVATOREM              77   52 294 178

SAKE

    A GUILTY SWORD BLUSH FOR HER SAKE.                 IN MEMORY OF LADY MADRE TERESA   26   46 131  52
    FOR PITTIES SAKE O HIDE HIM QUITE,                 UPON DEATH OF DESIRED HERRYS     71   46 168 467
    A GUILTY SWORD BLUSH FOR HER SAKE.                 TERESA                           26   52 315  52

SALE

    THE WORLD'S PRICE SETT TO SALE, & BY THE BOLD     OFFICE H. CROSS MATINES            14   52 265  86

SALLY

    COME NOW ALL YEE TERRORS, SALLY                   PSALME 23                        35   46 102   5

SALOMON

    FOR A MORE THEN SALOMON.                           VEXILLA REGIS                    24   52 277 156

SALT

    TORRENTS OF SALT TEARES FROM OUR EYES SHOULD RUNNE. UPON GUNPOWDER TREASON            37   MS 386 460

HEAVN-SALUTING

    AND HILLS HANG DOWN THEIR HEAVN-SALUTING HEADS    TO THE NAME OF JESUS              231   52 239  30

NEW-SALUTED

    OF THE NEW-SALUTED DAY.                              UPON DEATH OF DESIRED HERRYS     34   46 168 467

SAME

    THE MUSICKS SOFT REPORT, AND MOLD THE SAME        MUSICKS DUELL                    12   46 149 535
    LOSE THIS SAME BUSIE SPEAKING ART                  PSALME 137                       20   46 104   7
    THE TYRRHENE SEAS, AND SHORES SOUND ALL THE SAME,  SOSPETTO D'HERODE                31   46 109 216
    OUR HARD HEARTS SHALL STRIKE FIRE, THE SAME       IN MEMORY OF LADY MADRE TERESA  161   46 131  52
    'TIS BUT THE SAME IS SAID, HENRY AND JAMES        UPON YORKE HIS BIRTH              33   46 176 500
    FROM THE SAME SNOWY ALABLASTER ROCKE              UPON YORKE HIS BIRTH              45   46 176 500

```
                                                                          PAGE 349

AND THE SAME ROSIE-FINGERD HAND OF THINE.       TO THE MORNING                   45  46 183 497
WHOSE FRUIT AND BLOSSOMS BOTH BLESSE THE SAME BOUGH.  UPON TWO GREENE APRICOCKES  20  48 220 494
AND BEAT A SUMMONS IN THE SAME                  TO THE NAME OF JESUS             35  52 239  30
OR, WHAT'S THE SAME.                            TO THE NAME OF JESUS             57  52 239  30
THE SAME BRIGHT BUSYNES (YE THIRD HEAVENS) WITH YOU.  TO THE NAME OF JESUS      110  52 239  30
THE SAME LEAVE BOTH TO EAT & LIVE.              ADORO TE                         42  52 291 172
BE ALL THE SAME TO EVERY GUEST,                 LAUDA SION SALVATOREM            50  52 294 178
YET ON THE SAME (LIFE-MEANING) BREAD            LAUDA SION SALVATOREM            51  52 294 178
DRINK THE SAME WINE.  AND THE SAME WAY.         LAUDA SION SALVATOREM            78  52 294 178
DRINK THE SAME WINE.  AND THE SAME WAY.         LAUDA SION SALVATOREM            78  52 294 178
HOPE TELLS MY HEART, THE SAME LOVES BE          DIES IRAE                        51  52 298 186
THE SAME TO THEE, SWEET SPIRIT BE DONE.         O GLORIOSA DOMINA                39  52 302 194
OUR HARD HEARTS SHALL STRIKE FIRE, THE SAME     TERESA                          160  52 315  52
LIVE IN THESE CONQUERING LEAVES. LIVE ALL THE SAME.  FLAMING HEART                77  52 324  61
WHO STILES IT ANY THINGE, KNOWES NOT THE SAME.  ON GUNPOWDER-TREASON              2  MS 384 458
AND SETT IT FORTH IN THE SAME HAPPY PLACE.      UPON BIRTH PRINCESSE E           59  MS 391 456

SELF-SAME

SO THAT WITH THE SELF-SAME BREAD                PSALME 23                        53  46 102   5

SANCTUARIES

URNS.  LIKE GODS SANCTUARIES THEY LOOKT OF OLD.  ON A TREATISE OF CHARITY        36  46 137  69

SANDS

THE SANDS HE US'D NO LONGER PLEASE,             THE WEEPER                      101  46  79 120
FOR HIS OWNE SANDS HEE'L USE THY SEAS.          THE WEEPER                      102  46  79 120
GLADDING THE SCYTHIAN ROCKS, AND LIBIAN SANDS.  SOSPETTO D'HERODE               108  46 109 216

SANS

DEATH TORE NOT (THEREFORE) BUT SANS STRIFE      AN EPITAPH UPON ASHTON           27  46 192 464

SAPPHO

THERE AMOROUSE SAPPHO PLAINES UPON HER LUTE     HORATIJ ILLE & NEFASTO           39  MS 382 530

SATE

UNDER PROTECTION OF AN OAKE, THERE SATE         MUSICKS DUELL                     4  46 149 535
THERE WE SATE, AND THERE WE WEPT.               PSALME 137                        2  46 104   7
(THOUGH THE HEAVENS IN COUNSELL SATE,           LOVES HOROSCOPE                  23  46 185 483
IN IT THERE SATE BUT ONE SOLE DART.             IN CICATRICES DOMINI JESU         9  MS 381  27
INTO DIRE SABLE WEEDS, & SATE, & MOURN'D.       UPON GUNPOWDER TREASON           48  MS 386 460
WHICH, WHILE THEY SMILING SATE UPON HIS FACE,   AN ELEGY MR STANNINOW            39  MS 394 473

SATISFIED

IS HEE NOT SATISFIED. MEANES HE TO WREST        SOSPETTO D'HERODE               225  46 109 216

SAUCY

AND LIKE A SAUCY BIRD HE HOVERS                 OUT OF GREEKE CUPID'S CRYER      40  46 159 519

SAWCY

SEAS HAD NOT BIN REBUK'T BY SAWCY OARES         ALEXIAS THIRD ELEGIE              7  52 336 209

SAUC'T

WITH BITTER SHAFTS 'TIS SAUC'T TOO WELL.        OUT OF GREEKE CUPID'S CRYER      52  46 159 519

SAVE

SAVE THOSE OF FEARE, NO OTHER BANDS FEARE I.    I AM READY NOT ONELY BOUND        3  46  98  29
TO SAVE YOUR LIFE, KILL YOUR DELAY              TO COUNTESSE OF DENBIGH          58  52 236 146
SAVE THOSE DOMESTICK WHICH HE BORROWES          IN GLORIOUS EPIPHANIE           155  52 253  39
O GOD MAKE SPEED TO SAVE ME.                    OFFICE H. CROSS MATINES           5  52 265  86
O SAVE US THEN                                  OFFICE H. CROSS COMPLINE         13  52 274 105
SAVE US, O SAVE US, LORD.                       OFFICE H. CROSS COMPLINE         17  52 274 105
SAVE US, O SAVE US, LORD.                       OFFICE H. CROSS COMPLINE         17  52 274 105
SAVE THEM, O SAVE THEM, LORD.                   OFFICE H. CROSS COMPLINE         25  52 274 105
SAVE THEM, O SAVE THEM, LORD.                   OFFICE H. CROSS COMPLINE         25  52 274 105
SAVE THAT WHICH LETS IN FAITH, THE EARE.        ADORO TE                         10  52 291 172
TO SAVE YOUR LIFE, KILL YOUR DELAY.             AGAINST IRRESOLUTION AND DELAY   82  52 347 146
BY THREE DAIES LOSSE AETERNALLY TO SAVE.        MATH. 16. 25.  WHOSOEVER SHALL    4  MS 381  16

SAV'D

HEE SAV'D ALL WHEN HEE NOTHING SAID.            AND HE ANSWERED NOTHING           4  46  91  22
SICK HIMSELFE TO HAVE SAV'D HIM.                ANOTHER ON HERRYS                26  46 170 469
THOU'HAST SAV'D AT ONCE THE WHOLE WORLD'S LOSSE.  OFFICE H. CROSS MATINES        27  52 265  86
THOU'HAST SAV'D AT ONCE THE WHOLE WORLD'S LOSSE.  OFFICE H. CROSS PRIME          21  52 267  91
THOU'HAST SAV'D AT ONCE THE WHOLE WORLD'S LOSSE.  OFFICE H. CROSS THIRD          20  52 268  93
THOU'HAST SAV'D THE WORLD FROM CERTAIN LOSSE.   OFFICE H. CROSS SIXT             24  52 270  97
THOU'HAST SAV'D AT ONCE THE WHOLE WORLD'S LOSSE.  OFFICE H. CROSS NINTH          17  52 271  99
THOU'HAST SAV'D THE WORLD FROM CERTAIN LOSSE.   OFFICE H. CROSS EVENSONG         31  52 273 101

SAVING

SHEE ASKES IF SAD, OR SAVING POWERS,            LOVES HOROSCOPE                   5  46 185 483
LORD, BY THY SWEET & SAVING SIGN,               OFFICE H. CROSS MATINES           1  52 265  86
```

| | | | | | |
|---|---|---|---|---|---|
| AND SHOW THOU ART, BY SAVING ME. | DIES IRAE | 56 | 52 | 298 | 186 |
| SAVIOUR | | | | | |
| A SAVIOUR, & AT SUCH A RATE, FOR US. | OFFICE H. CROSS COMPLINE | 16 | 52 | 274 | 105 |
| O MY SAVIOVR, MAKE ME SEE | CHARITAS NIMIA | 63 | 52 | 280 | 48 |
| HIMSELF TO ME MY SAVIOUR BRINGS, | LAUDA SION SALVATOREM | 40 | 52 | 294 | 178 |
| SAW | | | | | |
| A SHIP THEY SAW, NO MEN SHEE HAD. YET PREST | THE BEGINNING OF HELIODORUS | 11 | 46 | 158 | 517 |
| PALLAS SAW VENUS ARM'D AND STREIGHT SHE CRY'D. | UPON THE SAME (VENUS ARMES) | 1 | 46 | 161 | 523 |
| THOU SPAK'ST AND STREIGHT THE BLIND MAN SAW. | THE BLIND CURED | 2 | 46 | 91 | 19 |
| THEY SAW THEE NOT, THAT SAW AND HATED THEE. | BUT NOW THEY HAVE SEEN | 2 | 46 | 96 | 21 |
| THEY SAW THEE NOT, THAT SAW AND HATED THEE. | BUT NOW THEY HAVE SEEN | 2 | 46 | 96 | 21 |
| NO,NO, THEY SAW THE NOT, O LIFE, O LOVE, | BUT NOW THEY HAVE SEEN | 3 | 46 | 96 | 21 |
| WHO SAW OUGHT IN THEE, THAT THEIR HATE COULD MOVE. | BUT NOW THEY HAVE SEEN | 4 | 46 | 96 | 21 |
| THEN HEE HIMSELFE E'RE SAW BEFORE, | A HYMNE OF THE NATIVITY | 13 | 46 | 106 | 76 |
| WE SAW THEE IN THY BALMY NEST, | A HYMNE OF THE NATIVITY | 29 | 46 | 106 | 76 |
| WEE SAW THINE EYES BREAK FROM THE EAST, | A HYMNE OF THE NATIVITY | 31 | 46 | 106 | 76 |
| WEE SAW THEE (AND WEE BLEST THE SIGHT) | A HYMNE OF THE NATIVITY | 33 | 46 | 106 | 76 |
| WEE SAW THEE BY THINE OWNE SWEET LIGHT. | A HYMNE OF THE NATIVITY | 34 | 46 | 106 | 76 |
| I SAW THE CURL'D DROPS,SOFT AND SLOW | A HYMNE OF THE NATIVITY | 35 | 46 | 106 | 76 |
| I SAW TH'OFFICIOUS ANGELS BRING. | A HYMNE OF THE NATIVITY | 41 | 46 | 106 | 76 |
| HEAVENS GOLDEN-WINGED HERALD, LATE HEE SAW | SOSPETTO D'HERODE | 97 | 46 | 109 | 216 |
| HEE SAW TH'OLD HEBREWES WOMBE, NEGLECT THE LAW | SOSPETTO D'HERODE | 101 | 46 | 109 | 216 |
| HEE SAW RICH NECTAR THAWES, RELEASE THE RIGOUR | SOSPETTO D'HERODE | 105 | 46 | 109 | 216 |
| HEE SAW A VERNALL SMILE, SWEETLY DISFIGURE | SOSPETTO D'HERODE | 109 | 46 | 109 | 216 |
| HEE SAW HOW IN THAT BLEST DAY-BEARING NIGHT, | SOSPETTO D'HERODE | 113 | 46 | 109 | 216 |
| HEE SAW A THREEFOLD SUN, WITH RICH ENCREASE, | SOSPETTO D'HERODE | 121 | 46 | 109 | 216 |
| HEE SAW THE TEMPLE SACRED TO SWEET PEACE, | SOSPETTO D'HERODE | 123 | 46 | 109 | 216 |
| HEE SAW THE FALLING IDOLS, ALL CONFESSE | SOSPETTO D'HERODE | 125 | 46 | 109 | 216 |
| A COMMING DEITY. HEE SAW THE NEST | SOSPETTO D'HERODE | 126 | 46 | 109 | 216 |
| HE SAW HEAV'N BLOSSOME WITH A NEW-BORNE LIGHT, | SOSPETTO D'HERODE | 129 | 46 | 109 | 216 |
| HEAV'N SAW US STRUGGLE ONCE, AS BRAVE A FIGHT | SOSPETTO D'HERODE | 255 | 46 | 109 | 216 |
| HEAV'N SAW HER RISE, AND SAW HELL IN THE SIGHT. | SOSPETTO D'HERODE | 377 | 46 | 109 | 216 |
| HEAV'N SAW HER RISE, AND SAW HELL IN THE SIGHT. | SOSPETTO D'HERODE | 377 | 46 | 109 | 216 |
| THE FIELD'S FAIRE EYES SAW HER, AND SAW NO MORE, | SOSPETTO D'HERODE | 378 | 46 | 109 | 216 |
| THE FIELD'S FAIRE EYES SAW HER, AND SAW NO MORE, | SOSPETTO D'HERODE | 378 | 46 | 109 | 216 |
| THEN HEE HIMSELFE E'RE SAW BEFORE. | IN HOLY NATIVITY | 13 | 52 | 246 | 76 |
| WE SAW THEE IN THY BAULMY NEST. | IN HOLY NATIVITY | 31 | 52 | 246 | 76 |
| WE SAW THINE EYES BREAK FROM THEIR EASTE | IN HOLY NATIVITY | 33 | 52 | 246 | 76 |
| WE SAW THEE. & WE BLEST THE SIGHT | IN HOLY NATIVITY | 35 | 52 | 246 | 76 |
| WE SAW THEE BY THINE OWN SWEET LIGHT. | IN HOLY NATIVITY | 36 | 52 | 246 | 76 |
| I SAW THE CURL'D DROPS, SOFT & SLOW, | IN HOLY NATIVITY | 51 | 52 | 246 | 76 |
| I SAW THE OBSEQUIOUS SERAPHIMS | IN HOLY NATIVITY | 58 | 52 | 246 | 76 |
| WE SAW THEE IN THY BAULMY NEST. | IN HOLY NATIVITY | 72 | 52 | 246 | 76 |
| WE SAW THINE EYES BREAK FROM THEIR EAST | IN HOLY NATIVITY | 74 | 52 | 246 | 76 |
| WE SAW THEE. & WE BLEST THE SIGHT. | IN HOLY NATIVITY | 76 | 52 | 246 | 76 |
| WE SAW THEE, BY THINE OWN SWEET LIGHT. | IN HOLY NATIVITY | 77 | 52 | 246 | 76 |
| THE SUN SAW THAT. AND WOULD HAVE SEEN NO MORE. | OFFICE H. CROSS NINTH | 7 | 52 | 271 | 99 |
| SAY | | | | | |
| THIS DONE, HEE LISTS WHAT SHEE WOULD SAY TO THIS, | MUSICKS DUELL | 157 | 46 | 149 | 535 |
| START, AND SAY, THE SERPENT HISSES. | OUT OF GREEKE CUPID'S CRYER | 66 | 46 | 159 | 519 |
| WOOE, INTREAT, AND CRYING SAY | OUT OF GREEKE CUPID'S CRYER | 68 | 46 | 159 | 519 |
| WHAT. MARS HIS SWORD. FAIRE CYTHEREA SAY, | UPON VENUS PUTTING ARMES | 1 | 46 | 161 | 523 |
| SAY WATRY BROTHERS | THE WEEPER | 121 | 46 | 79 | 120 |
| WHITHER HAST YE THEN. O SAY | THE WEEPER | 131 | 46 | 79 | 120 |
| WERE IT ENOUGH TO SHOW THE PLACE. AND SAY, | COME SEE WHERE THE LORD LAY | 3 | 46 | 87 | 27 |
| THEN COULD I SHOW THESE ARMES OF MINE, AND SAY | COME SEE WHERE THE LORD LAY | 5 | 46 | 87 | 27 |
| TWO WENT TO PRAY. O RATHER SAY | TWO WENT TO PRAY | 1 | 46 | 89 | 18 |
| TO SPEAKE THUS, WAS TO SPEAKE (SAY I) | THE BLIND CURED | 5 | 46 | 91 | 19 |
| HAD NERE ANOTHER WORD TO SAY. | NEITHER DURST MAN ASKE | 16 | 46 | 92 | 20 |
| TO HIM, PUT ON (HEEL SAY) PUT ON | IN MEMORY OF LADY MADRE TERESA | 172 | 46 | 131 | 52 |
| SCARCE DAWNES, O PARDON, IF I DARE TO SAY | AN APOLOGIE FOR HYMNE (TERESA) | 6 | 46 | 136 | 59 |
| WHEN HEAVEN BIDS COME, WHO CAN SAY NO. | ON THE ASSUMPTION | 20 | 46 | 139 | 114 |
| CENTER OF THOSE THY GRANDSIRES, SHALL I SAY | UPON YORKE HIS BIRTH | 30 | 46 | 176 | 500 |
| O SPEAKE THOU AND MY PIPE HATH NOUGHT TO SAY. | UPON YORKE HIS BIRTH | 113 | 46 | 176 | 500 |
| SAY TO THE SULLEN MORNE, THOU COM'ST TO COURT HER. | ON A FOULE MORNING | 11 | 46 | 181 | 495 |
| BELEEVE MEE, READER CAN SAY MORE | AN EPITAPH UPON ASHTON | 2 | 46 | 192 | 464 |
| WHAT THE SOWREST FATHERS SAY. | OUT OF CATULLUS | 3 | 46 | 194 | 523 |
| AND WHEN IT COMES SAY WELCOME FRIEND. | WISHES SUPPOSED MISTRESSE | 87 | 46 | 195 | 479 |
| SAY THEN DREAD QUEEN, HOW MAY WE DOE | TO THE QUEEN | 9 | 48 | 215 | 501 |
| SAY, LINGRING FAIR. WHY COMES THE BIRTH | TO COUNTESSE OF DENBIGH | 7 | 52 | 236 | 146 |
| I SING THE NAME WHICH NONE CAN SAY | TO THE NAME OF JESUS | 1 | 52 | 239 | 30 |
| THE EARLY PRIME BLUSHES TO SAY | OFFICE H. CROSS PRIME | 1 | 52 | 267 | 91 |
| LOVE COULD NOT THINK, TRUTH COULD NOT SAY. | ADORO TE | 16 | 52 | 291 | 172 |
| AH THEN, POOR SOUL, WHAT WILT THOU SAY. | DIES IRAE | 21 | 52 | 298 | 186 |
| O SAY THE WORD MY SOUL SHALL LIVE. | DIES IRAE | 48 | 52 | 298 | 186 |
| LET HEARTS & LIPPES SPEAK LOWD. AND SAY | O GLORIOSA DOMINA | 31 | 52 | 302 | 194 |
| WHEN HEAVN BIDS COME, WHO CAN SAY NO. | IN GLORIOUS ASSUMPTION B. LADY | 34 | 52 | 304 | 114 |
| SAY, YE BRIGHT BROTHERS, | WEEPER | 163 | 52 | 307 | 120 |
| SWEET, WHITHER HAST YOU THEN. O SAY | WEEPER | 173 | 52 | 307 | 120 |
| TO HIM, PUT ON (HEE'L SAY) PUT ON | TERESA | 171 | 52 | 315 | 52 |
| SCARSE DAWNES. O PARDON IF I DARE TO SAY | AN APOLOGIE FOR (TERESA) HYMNE | 6 | 52 | 322 | 59 |
| THAT IS A SERAPHIM, THEY SAY | FLAMING HEART | 5 | 52 | 324 | 61 |
| SAY, ALL YE WISE & WELL-PEIRC'T HEARTS | FLAMING HEART | 49 | 52 | 324 | 61 |
| SAY & BEAR WITTNES. SENDS SHE NOT | FLAMING HEART | 53 | 52 | 324 | 61 |
| SAY, GENTLE SOUL, WHAT CAN YOU FIND | TO SAME CONCERNING CHOISE | 10 | 52 | 331 | 66 |

|  |  |  |
|---|---|---|
| TRUTH BIDDES ME SAY, 'TIS TIME YOU CEASE TO TRUST | TO SAME CONCERNING CHOISE | 18  52 331  66 |
| WHAT DANGERS CAN THERE BE DARE SAY ME NAY. | ALEXIAS FIRST ELEGIE | 20  52 334 204 |
| WILL TAKE ACQUAINTANCE OF MY WOES, & SAY | ALEXIAS FIRST ELEGIE | 28  52 334 204 |
| SAY, LINGRING FAIR, WHY COMES THE BIRTH | AGAINST IRRESOLUTION AND DELAY | 15  52 347 146 |
| AND SEEMS TO SAY, MAKE HASTE, MY BROTHER. | AGAINST IRRESOLUTION AND DELAY | 44  52 347 146 |
| AND SAY THAT IVORY HER FRONT COMPOSES. | UPON BIRTH PRINCESSE E | 46  MS 391 456 |
| OR SHOULD I SAY, THAT WITH A SCARLET WAVE | UPON BIRTH PRINCESSE E | 47  MS 391 456 |

## SAIES

|  |  |  |
|---|---|---|
| WHY FOOLE, SAIES VENUS, THUS PROVOK'ST THOU MEE, | UPON THE SAME (VENUS ARMES) | 3  46 161 523 |
| WHERE NO CHURLISH RUB SAIES NAY | PSALME 23 | 30  46 102   5 |

## SCALE

|  |  |  |
|---|---|---|
| SOON AS THE RIGHT-HAND SCALE REJOYC'T TO PROVE | VEXILLA REGIS | 35  52 277 156 |

## SCARCE

|  |  |  |
|---|---|---|
| I WRITE SO ILL, MY SLENDER LINE IS SCARCE | WITH A PICTURE TO A FRIEND | 3  46 156 494 |
| SCARCE TO THIS MONSTER COULD THE SHADY KING, | SOSPETTO D'HERODE | 369  46 109 216 |
| SCARCE HAD SHEE LEARNT TO LISP A NAME | IN MEMORY OF LADY MADRE TERESA | 15  46 131  52 |
| SCARCE HAD SHEE BLOOD ENOUGH, TO MAKE | IN MEMORY OF LADY MADRE TERESA | 25  46 131  52 |
| SCARCE DAWNES, O PARDON, IF I DARE TO SAY | AN APOLOGIE FOR HYMNE (TERESA) | 6  46 136  59 |
| SCARCE WAKT. LIKE WAS THE CRIMSON OF THEIR JOYES. | UPON YORKE HIS BIRTH | 63  46 176 500 |
| YET ARE SCARCE RIPE ENOUGH AT BEST TO SHOW | UPON TWO GREENE APRICOCKES | 5  48 220 494 |
| A POORE (YEA SCARCE A) ROOFE. WHOSE NARROW PLACE | OUT OF GROTIUS | 16  MS 398 198 |

## SCARSE

|  |  |  |
|---|---|---|
| BUT THE WORLD'S HOMAGE, SCARSE IN THESE WELL BLOWN, | TO THE QUEEN'S MAJESTY | 9  52 261  47 |
| SCARSE HAS SHE LEARN'T TO LISP THE NAME | TERESA | 15  52 315  52 |
| SCARSE HAS SHE BLOOD ENOUGH TO MAKE | TERESA | 25  52 315  52 |
| SCARSE DAWNES. O PARDON IF I DARE TO SAY | AN APOLOGIE FOR (TERESA) HYMNE | 6  52 322  59 |

## SCARE

|  |  |  |
|---|---|---|
| A WINTERS THUNDER WITH A GROANE SHALL SCARE, | ON GUNPOWDER-TREASON | 28  MS 384 458 |

## SCARLET

|  |  |  |
|---|---|---|
| THY SCARLET ROBES. FOR HEERE YOU MUST NOT SHARE | UPON GUNPOWDER TREASON | 5  MS 387 461 |
| OR SHOULD I SAY, THAT WITH A SCARLET WAVE | UPON BIRTH PRINCESSE E | 47  MS 391 456 |
| IN CRIMSON WAVELETTS, & IN SCARLET TIDE. | AN ELEGY MR STANNINOW | 24  MS 394 473 |

## SCAR'D

|  |  |  |
|---|---|---|
| MAKE THEIR SCAR'D SOULES TAKE WING, & FLY AWAY. | AN ELEGIE ON DR PORTER | 30  MS 395 476 |

## SCARRES

|  |  |  |
|---|---|---|
| AND LEFT PERFUMES, IN STEAD OF SCARRES. | A HYMNE OF THE NATIVITY | 26  46 106  76 |
| THY WOUNDS SHALL BLUSH TO SUCH BRIGHT SCARRES, | IN MEMORY OF LADY MADRE TERESA | 154  46 131  52 |
| AND LEFT PERFUMES IN STEAD OF SCARRES. | IN HOLY NATIVITY | 27  52 246  76 |
| THY WOUNDS SHALL BLUSH TO SUCH BRIGHT SCARRES | TERESA | 153  52 315  52 |

## SCARRS

|  |  |  |
|---|---|---|
| AND BRING HOME ON THY BREST MORE THANKLESSE SCARRS. | SOSPETTO D'HERODE | 448  46 109 216 |

## SCARUS

|  |  |  |
|---|---|---|
| BUT THE DAINTY SCARUS, SOUGHT | PETRONIJ ALES PHASIACIS PETITA | 11  MS 382 526 |

## SCATTERED

|  |  |  |
|---|---|---|
| WHERE HE MEANT FROSTS, HE SCATTERED FLOWERS. | A HYMNE OF THE NATIVITY | 28  46 106  76 |

## SCATTER'D

|  |  |  |
|---|---|---|
| LIE SCATTER'D LIKE THE BURNT AND MARTYR'D BONES | ON A TREATISE OF CHARITY | 32  46 137  69 |
| WHERE HE MEAN'T FROST, HE SCATTER'D FLOWRS. | IN HOLY NATIVITY | 29  52 246  76 |
| LET ALL THY SCATTER'D SHAFTS OF LIGHT, THAT PLAY | FLAMING HEART | 87  52 324  61 |

## SCEANE

|  |  |  |
|---|---|---|
| OF TIBER, ON THE SCEANE OF A GREENE PLAT, | MUSICKS DUELL | 3  46 149 535 |

## SCEPTER

|  |  |  |
|---|---|---|
| HIS SCEPTER AND HIMSELFE BOTH HE DISDAINES. | SOSPETTO D'HERODE | 72  46 109 216 |
| AND RADIANT SCEPTER THIS BOLD HAND SHOULD BEARE. | SOSPETTO D'HERODE | 210  46 109 216 |
| THE SCEPTER, WHICH OF OLD GREAT DAVID SWAID. | SOSPETTO D'HERODE | 402  46 109 216 |
| A WELL-POIS'D SCEPTER. DOES IT NOW SEEME GOOD | SOSPETTO D'HERODE | 451  46 109 216 |
| WHY DOST THOU SHAKE THY LEADEN SCEPTER. GOE | TO THE MORNING | 54  46 183 497 |
| DOES FIRST HIS SCEPTER, THEN HIMSELF IN SOLEMNE TRIBUTE PAY. | IN GLORIOUS EPIPHANIE | 237  52 253  39 |
| FLY TO THY SCEPTER OF SOFT LOVE. | DIES IRAE | 28  52 298 166 |

## IRON-SCEPTRED

|  |  |  |
|---|---|---|
| ASSIST THE THRONE OF TH' IRON-SCEPTRED KING. | SOSPETTO D'HERODE | 66  46 109 216 |

## SCEPTERS

| | | | | |
|---|---|---|---|---|
| WITH YOUR BRIGHT HEAD WHOLE GROVES OF SCEPTERS BEND | TO THE QUEEN'S MAJESTY | 17 | 52 261 | 47 |

## SCHEMES

| | | | | |
|---|---|---|---|---|
| WHAT EVER SCHEMES OF BLOOD, FANTASTICK FRAMES | SOSPETTO D'HERODE | 361 | 46 109 | 216 |

## SCHINIS

| | | | | |
|---|---|---|---|---|
| AND HATEFULL SCHINIS HIS SO FEARED OAKES. | SOSPETTO D'HERODE | 360 | 46 109 | 216 |

## SCHOLLER

| | | | | |
|---|---|---|---|---|
| BY BEING SCHOLLER FIRST OF THAT NEW NIGHT. | IN GLORIOUS EPIPHANIE | 206 | 52 253 | 39 |

## SCHOOLES

| | | | | |
|---|---|---|---|---|
| TO PROVE THAT TRUE, SCHOOLES USE TO TELL, | ON A PRAYER BOOKE | 7 | 46 126 | 139 |
| TO PROVE THAT TRUE, SCHOOLES USE TO TELL, | PRAYER TO GENTLE-WOMAN | 13 | 52 328 | 139 |

## SCORCHING

| | | | | |
|---|---|---|---|---|
| NOR ON GODS ALTAR CAST TWO SCORCHING EYES | ON A TREATISE OF CHARITY | 43 | 46 137 | 69 |

## SCORE

| | | | | |
|---|---|---|---|---|
| KEEPE BUT THE SCORE OF THEM THAT MADE HIM DYE. | YEE BUILD SEPULCHRES | 4 | 46 95 | 21 |
| HEAVEN KEEPS UPON THY SCORE (THY BRIGHT | IN MEMORY OF LADY MADRE TERESA | 176 | 46 131 | 52 |
| WHEN AGE AND DEATH CALL'D FOR THE SCORE. | AN EPITAPH UPON ASHTON | 25 | 46 192 | 464 |
| A THOUSAND, AND A HUNDRED, SCORE | OUT OF CATULLUS | 11 | 46 194 | 523 |
| HEAV'N KEEPS UPON THY SCORE. (THY BRIGHT | TERESA | 175 | 52 315 | 52 |

## SCORN

| | | | | |
|---|---|---|---|---|
| BAK'T IN HOT SCORN, FOR A BURNT SACRIFICE. | ON A TREATISE OF CHARITY | 44 | 46 137 | 69 |
| WITH A RED FACE CONFES'T THIS SCORN. | IN GLORIOUS EPIPHANIE | 122 | 52 253 | 39 |
| CONTEMPT & SCORN CAN SEND WOUNDS TO SEARCH THE INMOST | OFFICE H. CROSS SIXT | 12 | 52 270 | 97 |
| FLIGHTS SCORN THE LAZY DUST, & THINGS THAT DY. | AN APOLOGIE FOR (TERESA) HYMNE | 28 | 52 322 | 59 |

## SCORN'D

| | | | | |
|---|---|---|---|---|
| AS IF HE SCORN'D TO THINKE OF NIGHT, | UPON DEATH OF DESIRED HERRYS | 50 | 46 168 | 467 |

## SCORNE

| | | | | |
|---|---|---|---|---|
| FLIGHTS SCORNE THE LAZIE DUST, AND THINGS THAT DYE. | AN APOLOGIE FOR HYMNE (TERESA) | 28 | 46 136 | 59 |
| WHO'S THIS THAT COMES CIRCLED IN RAYES, THAT SCORNE | UPON YORKE HIS BIRTH | 68 | 46 176 | 500 |
| I MEANE THOSE THREE GREAT STARRES, WHO WELL MAY SCORNE | UPON KINGS CORONATION | 31 | MS 389 | 454 |
| MAKES ME CONFES'T. OH, DOE NOT THOU WITH SCORNE, | EX EUPHORMIONE | 6 | MS 392 | 525 |

## SCORNES

| | | | | |
|---|---|---|---|---|
| HE SCORNES THEM NOW, BUT O THEY'L SUTE FULL WELL | UPON LAZARUS HIS TEARES | 3 | 46 89 | 18 |
| MISCHEIFE, THAT SCORNES EXPRESSION SHOULD COME NIGH IT. | ON GUNPOWDER-TREASON | 48 | MS 384 | 458 |

## SCOULE

| | | | | |
|---|---|---|---|---|
| NO CLOUD SCOULE ON HIS RADIANT LIDS NO TEMPEST LOWRE. | EASTER DAY | 12 | 46 100 | 26 |
| WHEN A RUDDY STORME WHOSE SCOULE, | UPON DEATH OF DESIRED HERRYS | 51 | 46 168 | 467 |
| TO SIT AND SCOULE UPON NIGHTS HEAVY BROW. | ON A FOULE MORNING | 34 | 46 181 | 495 |

## SCOUTS

| | | | | |
|---|---|---|---|---|
| THOU ART A SOULDIER HEROD, SEND THY SCOUTS | SOSPETTO D'HERODE | 523 | 46 109 | 216 |

## SCRIPTURE

| | | | | |
|---|---|---|---|---|
| HEE STUDIES SCRIPTURE, STRIVES TO SOUND THE HEART, | SOSPETTO D'HERODE | 155 | 46 109 | 216 |

## SCULL

| | | | | |
|---|---|---|---|---|
| THE CUP THEY DRINKE IN IS MEDUSA'S SCULL. | SOSPETTO D'HERODE | 335 | 46 109 | 216 |

## SCULLS

| | | | | |
|---|---|---|---|---|
| OF RAGGED LIMBS, TORNE SCULLS, & DASHT OUT BRAINES. | SOSPETTO D'HERODE | 312 | 46 109 | 216 |

## SCYLLA

| | | | | |
|---|---|---|---|---|
| WITH CIRCE, SCYLLA, STAND TO WAIT UPON HER. | SOSPETTO D'HERODE | 339 | 46 109 | 216 |

## SCYRON

| | | | | |
|---|---|---|---|---|
| HERE CRUELL SCYRON BOASTS HIS BLOODY ROCKES, | SOSPETTO D'HERODE | 359 | 46 109 | 216 |

## SCYTHIAN

| | | | | |
|---|---|---|---|---|
| GLADDING THE SCYTHIAN ROCKS, AND LIBIAN SANDS. | SOSPETTO D'HERODE | 108 | 46 109 | 216 |

## SEA

| | | | | |
|---|---|---|---|---|
| A SEA OF HELICON. HIS HAND DOES GOE | MUSICKS DUELL | 124 | 46 149 | 535 |
| LOOK'T ROUND, FIRST TO THE SEA, THEN TO THE SHORE. | THE BEGINNING OF HELIODORUS | 8 | 46 158 | 517 |
| THE SHORE THAT SHEWED THEM WHAT THE SEA DENY'D. | THE BEGINNING OF HELIODORUS | 9 | 46 158 | 517 |
| EXPECT A SEA, MY HEART SHALL MAKE IT GOOD. | OUR LORD IN HIS CIRCUMCISION | 4 | 46 98 | 9 |
| TO THIS RED SEA OF THY BLOOD, | ON BLEEDING WOUNDS OF LORD | 26 | 46 101 | 110 |
| NOT TO BE SLAKT BUT BY A SEA OF BLOOD. | SOSPETTO D'HERODE | 490 | 46 109 | 216 |
| FAIRE SEA OF HOLY FIRES TRANSFUSED THE FLAME | AN APOLOGIE FOR HYMNE (TERESA) | 2 | 46 136 | 59 |
| NOW AFTER ALL HER TOYLES BY SEA AND LAND, | UPON FAIRE ETHIOPIAN | 3 | 46 183 | 493 |
| TO THIS RED SEA OF THY BLOOD | UPON BLEEDING CRUCIFIX | 22 | 52 288 | 110 |
| THE NOTED SEA SHALL CHANGE HIS NAME WITH ME. | ALEXIAS FIRST ELEGIE | 23 | 52 334 | 204 |
| IS PLOUGH'D AS DEEPE, AS IS THE SEA WITH WIND, | HORATIJ ILLE & NEFASTO | 20 | MS 382 | 530 |
| (ROWZ'D IN AN ANGRY TEMPEST). OH THE SEA. | HORATIJ ILLE & NEFASTO | 21 | MS 382 | 530 |
| HOW HARD BY SEA, BY WARRE, BY BANISHMENT. | HORATIJ ILLE & NEFASTO | 44 | MS 382 | 530 |
| THE SEA SHALL CHANGE HIS YOUTHFULL GREENE, & SLIDE | ON GUNPOWDER-TREASON | 33 | MS 384 | 458 |
| STREIGHT FROM THIS SEA OF TEARES THERE DOES APPEARE | UPON KINGS CORONATION | 13 | MS 390 | 453 |
| THEN WEEPE THYSELFE INTO A SEA OF TEARES. | AN ELEGIE ON DR PORTER | 38 | MS 395 | 476 |
| THE WILD WAVES COUCH'D. THE SEA FORGOTT TO SWEAT | OUT OF GROTIUS | 67 | MS 398 | 198 |
| HEAV'N, EARTH, AND SEA, MY TRIUMPHS. WHAT REMAIN'D | OUT OF GROTIUS | 85 | MS 398 | 198 |

## SEAS

| | | | | |
|---|---|---|---|---|
| LICKE HIS PROUD FEET, AND HAST INTO THE SEAS | THE BEGINNING OF HELIODORUS | 5 | 46 158 | 517 |
| FOR HIS OWNE SANDS HEE'L USE THY SEAS. | THE WEEPER | 102 | 46 79 | 120 |
| THE TYRRHENE SEAS, AND SHORES SOUND ALL THE SAME, | SOSPETTO D'HERODE | 31 | 46 109 | 216 |
| AND POURING ON HEAV'NS FACE THE SEAS HUGE FLOOD | SOSPETTO D'HERODE | 277 | 46 109 | 216 |
| MELTED & MEASUR'D OUT IN SEAS OF TEARES | TO THE NAME OF JESUS | 144 | 52 239 | 30 |
| SOMTHING FROM THY FULL SEAS OF SORROW. | SANCTA MARIA DOLORUM | 44 | 52 283 | 162 |
| SEAS HAD NOT BIN REBUK'T BY SAWCY OARES | ALEXIAS THIRD ELEGIE | 7 | 52 336 | 209 |
| THAT SWIM'ST AS DEEPE IN JOY, AS SEAS, NOW SMILE | UPON KINGS CORONATION | 6 | MS 389 | 454 |

## SISTER-SEAS

| | | | | |
|---|---|---|---|---|
| TWO SISTER-SEAS OF VIRGINS MILKE, | A HYMNE OF THE NATIVITY | 61 | 46 106 | 76 |
| TWO SISTER-SEAS OF VIRGIN-MILK, | IN HOLY NATIVITY | 87 | 52 246 | 76 |

## SEALD

| | | | | |
|---|---|---|---|---|
| THE FOUNTAIN SEALD, YET LIFE FOUND WAY. | O GLORIOSA DOMINA | 36 | 52 302 | 194 |

## SEAL'D

| | | | | |
|---|---|---|---|---|
| THE DOUR WAS SHUTT, THE FOUNTAIN SEAL'D. | O GLORIOSA DOMINA | 33 | 52 302 | 194 |
| THAT SEIZ'D THY PARTING SOUL, & SEAL'D THEE HIS. | FLAMING HEART | 102 | 52 324 | 61 |

## DEATH-SEAL'D

| | | | | |
|---|---|---|---|---|
| THESE DEATH-SEAL'D LIPPS ARE THEY DARE GIVE THE LYE, | UPON STANINOUGH'S DEATH | 23 | 46 175 | 475 |
| THESE DEATH-SEAL'D LIPPES ARE THEY DARE GIVE THE LY | DEATH'S LECTURE | 25 | 52 340 | 475 |

## SEALING

| | | | | |
|---|---|---|---|---|
| SEALING ALL BRESTS IN A LETHAEAN BAND. | SOSPETTO D'HERODE | 392 | 46 109 | 216 |

## SEARCH

| | | | | |
|---|---|---|---|---|
| DEATH'S BUSIE SEARCH I'LE EASILY BEGUILE. | SICKE IMPLORE SHADOW | 2 | 46 87 | 28 |
| SEARCH WHAT THE WORLD'S CLOSE CABINETS KEEP, | NEW YEAR'S DAY | 18 | 52 251 | 37 |
| CONTEMPT & SCORN CAN SEND WOUNDS TO SEARCH THE INMOST | OFFICE H. CROSS SIXT | 12 | 52 270 | 97 |
| THE SEARCH OF ONE CHILD (CRUELL INDUSTRY.) | OUT OF GROTIUS | 27 | MS 398 | 198 |

## SEARCHES

| | | | | |
|---|---|---|---|---|
| AND WITH SOFT FEET SEARCHES THE SILENT ROOMES. | SOSPETTO D'HERODE | 400 | 46 109 | 216 |

## SEASON

| | | | | |
|---|---|---|---|---|
| AND USE THE SEASON OF LOVE'S SHOWRE, | TO COUNTESSE OF DENBIGH | 44 | 52 236 | 146 |
| A PRECIOUS SEASON, & A GOLDEN AGE. | UPON KINGS CORONATION | 18 | MS 389 | 454 |

## SEASONABLE

| | | | | |
|---|---|---|---|---|
| SO SHALL THEY, BY THE SEASONABLE FRIGHT | IN GLORIOUS EPIPHANIE | 165 | 52 253 | 39 |

## SEASONABLY

| | | | | |
|---|---|---|---|---|
| BY YOUR OWN SHOWRES SEASONABLY DASH'T | WEEPER | 86 | 52 307 | 120 |

## SEAT

| | | | | |
|---|---|---|---|---|
| OF MUSICKS HEAVEN. AND SEAT IT THERE ON HIGH | MUSICKS DUELL | 149 | 46 149 | 535 |
| FROWNE I. AND CAN GREAT NATURE KEEP HER SEAT. | SOSPETTO D'HERODE | 205 | 46 109 | 216 |
| THERE HAS THE PURPLE VENGEANCE A PROUD SEAT, | SOSPETTO D'HERODE | 313 | 46 109 | 216 |
| WEELL SEE HIM TAKE A PRIVATE SEAT, | IN MEMORY OF LADY MADRE TERESA | 12 | 46 131 | 52 |
| O IF FOR THESE THOU MEAN'ST TO FIND A SEAT, | UPON YORKE HIS BIRTH | 15 | 46 176 | 500 |
| IT'S SEAT YOUR SOUL'S JUST CENTER BE. | TO COUNTESSE OF DENBIGH | 56 | 52 236 | 146 |
| AND SEE HIM TAKE A PRIVATE SEAT, | TERESA | 12 | 52 315 | 52 |

## JUDGMENT-SEAT

| | | | | |
|---|---|---|---|---|
| THAT SABLE JUDGMENT-SEAT SHALL BY NEW LAWES | IN GLORIOUS EPIPHANIE | 145 | 52 253 | 39 |

## SECOND

| | | | | |
|---|---|---|---|---|
| MEE YET A SECOND FALL. WEE'D TRY OUR STRENGTHS. | SOSPETTO D'HERODE | 254 | 46 109 | 216 |
| THOSE SECOND SMILES OF HEAVEN SHALL DART, | IN MEMORY OF LADY MADRE TERESA | 136 | 46 131 | 52 |
| THIS GRAVE'S THE SECOND MARRIAGE-BED. | AN EPITAPH HUSBAND AND WIFE | 2 | 46 174 | 478 |
| ACQUAINTANCE WITH THE SUNNE. WHAT SECOND MORNE | UPON YORKE HIS BIRTH | 69 | 46 176 | 500 |
| THE SECOND, NONE. | OUT OF MARTIALL | 4 | 46 188 | 527 |
| REVIVED NATURE TAKE A SECOND BREATH. | ON FRONTISPIECE ISAACSONS | 4 | 46 191 | 491 |
| THOUGH AS AT SECOND HAND, FROM EITHER HEART. | SANCTA MARIA DOLORUM | 70 | 52 283 | 162 |
| (THOSE SECOND SMILES OF HEAV'N) SHALL DART | TERESA | 135 | 52 315 | 52 |
| THIS GRAVE'S THEIR SECOND MARRIAGE-BED. | AN EPITAPH UPON MARRIED COUPLE | 2 | 52 339 | 478 |

## SECURE

| | | | | |
|---|---|---|---|---|
| MY SOULE SHEE WAS SECURE. STILL HAVE I BORNE | OUT OF GROTIUS | 11 | MS 398 | 198 |

## SEE

| | | | | |
|---|---|---|---|---|
| HARKE HETHER, READER, WOULDST THOU SEE | IN PRAISE OF LESSIUS | 15 | 46 156 | 510 |
| WOULDST SEE A MAN ALL, HIS OWNE WEALTH, | IN PRAISE OF LESSIUS | 17 | 46 156 | 510 |
| WOULD'ST THOU SEE A MAN WHOSE WELL WARMED BLOOD, | IN PRAISE OF LESSIUS | 35 | 46 156 | 510 |
| WOULDST SEE BLITH LOOKES, FRESH CHEEKS BEGUILE | IN PRAISE OF LESSIUS | 39 | 46 156 | 510 |
| AGE, WOULDST SEE DECEMBER SMILE. | IN PRAISE OF LESSIUS | 40 | 46 156 | 510 |
| WOULDST SEE A NEST OF ROSES GROW | IN PRAISE OF LESSIUS | 41 | 46 156 | 510 |
| IN SUMME, WOULDST SEE A MAN THAT CAN | IN PRAISE OF LESSIUS | 45 | 46 156 | 510 |
| THOUGH THOU SEE THE CRAFTY ELFE, | OUT OF GREEKE CUPID'S CRYER | 60 | 46 159 | 519 |
| LOOKE ON THE FOLLOWING LEAVES, AND SEE HIM BREATH. | UPON BISHOP ANDREWES PICTURE | 16 | 46 163 | 490 |
| SEE HERE AN EASIE FEAST THAT KNOWES NO WOUND, | ON MIRACLE OF LOAVES | 1 | 46 86 | 15 |
| LOOKE, MARY, HERE SEE, WHERE THY LORD ONCE LAY. | COME SEE WHERE THE LORD LAY | 4 | 46 87 | 27 |
| LOOKE, MARY, HERE SEE, WHERE THY LORD ONCE LAY. | COME SEE WHERE THE LORD LAY | 6 | 46 87 | 27 |
| SHE CAN SEE HEAVEN, AND NE'RE LIFT UP HER EYES. | ON VIRGINS BASHFULNESSE | 6 | 46 89 | 9 |
| TO SPEAKE AND MAKE THE BLIND MAN SEE, | THE BLIND CURED | 3 | 46 91 | 19 |
| UNMOV'D TO SEE ONE WRETCHED, IS TO MAKE HIM SO. | AND A CERTAINE PRIEST PASSED | 4 | 46 94 | 17 |
| SEE HOW SHE WEEPS, AND WEEPS, THAT SHE APPEARES | TO PONTIUS WASHING HANDS | 9 | 46 94 | 23 |
| TO SEE BOTH BLENDED IN ONE FLOOD | UPON INFANT MARTYRS | 1 | 46 95 | 10 |
| SEENE. AND YET HATED THEE. THEY DID NOT SEE. | BUT NOW THEY HAVE SEEN | 1 | 46 96 | 21 |
| AND REJOYCING SMILES TO SEE | PSALME 23 | 7 | 46 102 | 5 |
| THE HEAV'N EXPECTING AGES, HOPE TO SEE | SOSPETTO D'HERODE | 158 | 46 109 | 216 |
| EARTH NOW SHOULD SEE, AND TREMBLE AT THE SIGHT. | SOSPETTO D'HERODE | 256 | 46 109 | 216 |
| THROUGH THE THICK SHADES OBSCURELY MIGHT YOU SEE | SOSPETTO D'HERODE | 350 | 46 109 | 216 |
| SHE THINKES NOT FIT SUCH HE HER FACE SHOULD SEE, | SOSPETTO D'HERODE | 413 | 46 109 | 216 |
| A WAKING EYE AND HAND. LOOKE UP AND SEE | SOSPETTO D'HERODE | 431 | 46 109 | 216 |
| NO SOONER THEREFORE SHALL THE MORNING SEE | SOSPETTO D'HERODE | 505 | 46 109 | 216 |
| SEE HOW HEE'S FURNISH'T FOR SO FEAR'D A WARRE. | SOSPETTO D'HERODE | 524 | 46 109 | 216 |
| WEELL SEE HIM TAKE A PRIVATE SEAT, | IN MEMORY OF LADY MADRE TERESA | 12 | 46 131 | 52 |
| THOU SHALT LOOKE ROUND ABOUT, AND SEE | IN MEMORY OF LADY MADRE TERESA | 166 | 46 131 | 52 |
| WHICH WHO IN DEATH WOULD LIVE TO SEE, | IN MEMORY OF LADY MADRE TERESA | 182 | 46 131 | 52 |
| LO WHERE I SEE THY OFFRINGS WAKE, AND RISE | ON A TREATISE OF CHARITY | 17 | 46 137 | 69 |
| AND OUR DARKE WORLD NO MORE SHALL SEE. | ON THE ASSUMPTION | 36 | 46 139 | 114 |
| IN HIM GOODNESSE JOY'D TO SEE | HIS EPITAPH (HERRYS) | 21 | 46 172 | 471 |
| THOU BY THY SELFE MAIST SIT, (BLEST ISLE) AND SEE | UPON YORKE HIS BIRTH | 25 | 46 176 | 500 |
| TO BE THY GARLAND. SEE (SWEET PRINCE) O SEE | UPON YORKE HIS BIRTH | 39 | 46 176 | 500 |
| TO BE THY GARLAND. SEE (SWEET PRINCE) O SEE | UPON YORKE HIS BIRTH | 39 | 46 176 | 500 |
| SEE, SEE THY REALL SHADOW, SEE THY BROTHER, | UPON YORKE HIS BIRTH | 42 | 46 176 | 500 |
| SEE, SEE THY REALL SHADOW, SEE THY BROTHER, | UPON YORKE HIS BIRTH | 42 | 46 176 | 500 |
| SEE, SEE THY REALL SHADOW, SEE THY BROTHER, | UPON YORKE HIS BIRTH | 42 | 46 176 | 500 |
| AND SEE SUCH NAMES OF JOY SIT WHITE UPON | UPON YORKE HIS BIRTH | 97 | 46 176 | 500 |
| FOR SEE APPOLLO ALL THIS WHILE STANDS MUTE, | UPON YORKE HIS BIRTH | 114 | 46 176 | 500 |
| SEE HOW HEE RUNS, WITH WHAT A HASTY FLIGHT | ON A FOULE MORNING | 29 | 46 181 | 495 |
| HIS LETHE BE MY HELICON. AND SEE | TO THE MORNING | 17 | 46 183 | 497 |
| WHAT THESE LINES WISH TO SEE. | WISHES SUPPOSED MISTRESSE | 113 | 46 195 | 479 |
| YOU STREIGHT SHALL SEE HER WAKE AND RISE | THOUGH NOW 'TIS NEITHER | 9 | MS 397 | 492 |
| SO WHEN THE YEAR TAKES COLD, WE SEE | TO COUNTESSE OF DENBIGH | 21 | 52 236 | 146 |
| TO SEE THEMSELVES THEIR OWN SEVERER SHORE. | TO COUNTESSE OF DENBIGH | 26 | 52 236 | 146 |
| MEET IT WITH WIDE-SPREAD ARMES. & SEE | TO COUNTESSE OF DENBIGH | 55 | 52 236 | 146 |
| BRING HITHER THY WHOLE SELF. & LET ME SEE | TO THE NAME OF JESUS | 17 | 52 239 | 30 |
| OF NOBLE POWRES, I SEE, | TO THE NAME OF JESUS | 20 | 52 239 | 30 |
| O SEE, SO MANY WORLDS OF BARREN YEARES | TO THE NAME OF JESUS | 143 | 52 239 | 30 |
| O SEE, THE WEARY LIDDES OF WAKEFULL HOPE | TO THE NAME OF JESUS | 145 | 52 239 | 30 |
| SEE SEE, HOW SOON HIS NEW-BLOOM'D CHEEK | IN HOLY NATIVITY | 67 | 52 246 | 76 |
| SEE SEE, HOW SOON HIS NEW-BLOOM'D CHEEK | IN HOLY NATIVITY | 67 | 52 246 | 76 |
| LOOK UP, SWEET BABE, LOOK UP & SEE | IN GLORIOUS EPIPHANIE | 10 | 52 253 | 39 |
| SEE HIS HORN'D FACE, & DY FOR SHAME. | IN GLORIOUS EPIPHANIE | 99 | 52 253 | 39 |
| SHALL HENCEFORTH SEE | IN GLORIOUS EPIPHANIE | 178 | 52 253 | 39 |
| AND CATCHE THY QUICK REFLEX. AND SHARPLY SEE | IN GLORIOUS EPIPHANIE | 193 | 52 253 | 39 |
| EAGLES. AND SHUTT OUR EYES THAT WE MAY SEE. | IN GLORIOUS EPIPHANIE | 232 | 52 253 | 39 |
| LOVE IS TOO KIND, I SEE. & CAN | CHARITAS NIMIA | 5 | 52 280 | 48 |
| WHY SHOULD THOU BOW THY AWFULL BREST TO SEE | CHARITAS NIMIA | 33 | 52 280 | 48 |
| O MY SAVIOVR, MAKE ME SEE | CHARITAS NIMIA | 63 | 52 280 | 48 |
| WHO CAN LOOK ON & SEE, | SANCTA MARIA DOLORUM | 13 | 52 283 | 162 |
| TO SEE SO MANY UNKIND SWORDS CONTEST | SANCTA MARIA DOLORUM | 17 | 52 283 | 162 |
| SEE HER LIFE DY. | SANCTA MARIA DOLORUM | 38 | 52 283 | 162 |
| HAIL. & STRIKE HOME & MAKE ME SEE | SANCTA MARIA DOLORUM | 73 | 52 283 | 162 |
| THOMAS MIGHT TOUCH. NONE BUT MIGHT SEE | ADORO TE | 23 | 52 291 | 172 |
| WHEN THIS DRY SOUL THOSE EYES SHALL SEE, | ADORO TE | 53 | 52 291 | 172 |
| WHEN THE BLEST SIGNES THOU BROKE SHALL SEE. | LAUDA SION SALVATOREM | 55 | 52 294 | 178 |
| AND SEE HIM TAKE A PRIVATE SEAT, | TERESA | 12 | 52 315 | 52 |
| THOU SHALT LOOK ROUND ABOUT. & SEE | TERESA | 165 | 52 315 | 52 |
| WHICH WHO IN DEATH WOULD LIVE TO SEE, | TERESA | 181 | 52 315 | 52 |
| SEE, EVEN THE YEARES & SIZE OF HIM | FLAMING HEART | 15 | 52 324 | 61 |
| HER HAPPY FIRE-WORKS. HERE. COMES DOWN TO SEE. | FLAMING HEART | 18 | 52 324 | 61 |
| O KNEW I WHERE HE WANDER'D, I SHOULD SEE | ALEXIAS FIRST ELEGIE | 9 | 52 334 | 204 |
| BUT I. (SO HELP ME HEAVN MY HOPES TO SEE) | ALEXIAS THIRD ELEGIE | 53 | 52 336 | 209 |

| | | | |
|---|---|---|---|
| HARK HITHER, READER. WILT THOU SEE | TEMPERANCE | 13 | 52 342 510 |
| WILT' SEE A MAN, ALL HIS OWN WEALTH, | TEMPERANCE | 15 | 52 342 510 |
| WOULDST' SEE A MAN, WHOSE WELL-WARM'D BLOOD | TEMPERANCE | 33 | 52 342 510 |
| WOULDST' SEE BLITH LOOKES, FRESH CHEEKES BEGUIL | TEMPERANCE | 37 | 52 342 510 |
| AGE. WOULDST SEE DECEMBER SMILE. | TEMPERANCE | 38 | 52 342 510 |
| WOULDST' SEE NESTS OF NEW ROSES GROW | TEMPERANCE | 39 | 52 342 510 |
| IN SUMME, WOULDST SEE A MAN THAT CAN | TEMPERANCE | 43 | 52 342 510 |
| THIS RARE ONE, READER, WOULDST THOU SEE. | TEMPERANCE | 51 | 52 342 510 |
| SO WHEN THE YEAR TAKES COLD WE SEE | AGAINST IRRESOLUTION AND DELAY | 21 | 52 347 146 |
| WHEN LOVE OF US CALL'D HIM TO SEE | AGAINST IRRESOLUTION AND DELAY | 67 | 52 347 146 |
| YEILD TO HIS SIEGE, WISE SOUL, AND SEE | AGAINST IRRESOLUTION AND DELAY | 79 | 52 347 146 |
| COME, BRAVE SOLDIERS, COME, & SEE | IN CICATRICES DOMINI JESU | 1 | MS 381 27 |
| DO'ST THOU NOT SEE AN EXHALATION | ON GUNPOWDER-TREASON | 15 | MS 384 458 |
| NEVER DURST HATCH BEFORE. EXTRACTED SEE | UPON GUNPOWDER TREASON | 7 | MS 386 460 |
| HEAVEN WAS ASHAM'D, TO SEE OUR MOTHER EARTH | UPON GUNPOWDER TREASON | 11 | MS 386 460 |
| AND MAY SUCH PYTHONS NEVER LIVE TO SEE | UPON GUNPOWDER TREASON | 57 | MS 386 460 |
| TO SEE SOME FOWLER THAN HERSELFE) THESE STAND, | UPON GUNPOWDER TREASON | 13 | MS 387 461 |
| DOE NOT DECEIVE MEE, EYES. DOE I NOT SEE | UPON KINGS CORONATION | 11 | MS 389 454 |
| DOE I NOT SEE JOY KEEPE HIS REVELS NOW, | UPON KINGS CORONATION | 19 | MS 389 454 |
| DOE I NOT SEE A CYNTHIA, WHO MAY | UPON KINGS CORONATION | 25 | MS 389 454 |
| DOE I NOT SEE A CONSTELLATION. | UPON KINGS CORONATION | 29 | MS 389 454 |
| TO THEIR OWNE MUSICK, NOR (UNTILL THEY SEE | UPON KINGS CORONATION | 23 | MS 390 453 |
| SEE, NOTHING'S VULGAR, EVERY ATOME HEERE | UPON BIRTH PRINCESSE E | 39 | MS 391 456 |
| SEE ALL IN MOURNING NOW. THE WALLES ARE JETT. | AN ELEGIE ON DR PORTER | 7 | MS 395 476 |
| TO FREIND THE LIVING WORLD EVEN DEATH DID SEE | OUT OF GROTIUS | 82 | MS 398 198 |

SEE'ST

| | | | |
|---|---|---|---|
| SEE'ST THOU THAT MARY THERE. O TEACH HER MOTHER | UPON YORKE HIS BIRTH | 53 | 46 176 500 |

SEE'T

| | | | |
|---|---|---|---|
| SO SWORE THE LAMB'S DREAD SIRE. AND SO WE SEE'T. | TO THE QUEEN'S MAJESTY | 19 | 52 261 47 |

SEES

| | | | |
|---|---|---|---|
| LOOKES DOWNE, AND SEES THE HUMBLE NILE BELOW | THE BEGINNING OF HELIODORUS | 4 | 46 158 517 |
| 'TIS HEAV'N 'TIS HEAVEN SHE SEES, HEAVENS GOD THERE LYES | ON VIRGINS BASHFULNESSE | 5 | 46 89 9 |
| AS MUCH AS SEES) SHALL WITH THESE SACRED LEAVES | ON A TREATISE OF CHARITY | 24 | 46 137 69 |
| HANGING ALL TORN SHE SEES. AND IN HIS WOES | SANCTA MARIA DOLORUM | 7 | 52 283 162 |
| SHE SEES HER SON, HER GOD, | SANCTA MARIA DOLORUM | 31 | 52 283 162 |

SEEING

| | | | |
|---|---|---|---|
| AND SEEING THE LOATH'D OBJECT, HID FOR SHAME | TO THE MORNING | 12 | 46 183 497 |

SEED

| | | | |
|---|---|---|---|
| TO SWELL WITH FORWARD PRIDE, AND SEED DESIRE | OUT OF VIRGIL | 3 | 46 155 529 |
| IF, FROM THE SEED OF EMPTY RUINE, SHE | ON FRONTISPIECE ISAACSONS | 6 | 46 191 491 |
| FOR FROM THIS DAY'S RICH SEED OF DIADEMS | TO THE QUEEN'S MAJESTY | 11 | 52 261 47 |

SEED-PLOT

| | | | |
|---|---|---|---|
| MUSICKS BEST SEED-PLOT, WHENCE IN RIPEND AIRES | MUSICKS DUELL | 69 | 46 149 535 |

SEED-TIME

| | | | |
|---|---|---|---|
| TIS SEED-TIME STILL WITH THEE | THE WEEPER | 9 | 46 79 120 |
| 'TIS SEED-TIME STILL WITH THEE | WEEPER | 9 | 52 307 120 |

SEED-TIME'S

| | | | |
|---|---|---|---|
| SEED-TIME'S NOT ALL. THERE SHOULD BE HARVEST TOO. | AGAINST IRRESOLUTION AND DELAY | 37 | 52 347 146 |

SEEK

| | | | |
|---|---|---|---|
| GOE, SOUL, OUT OF THY SELF, & SEEK FOR MORE. | TO THE NAME OF JESUS | 27 | 52 239 30 |
| OF HUMBLE SOULES, THAT SEEK TO FIND | TO THE NAME OF JESUS | 121 | 52 239 30 |
| TO SEEK FOR HUMBLE BEDS | TO THE NAME OF JESUS | 232 | 52 239 30 |
| TO SEEK HER SELF IN THY SWEET EYES | IN GLORIOUS EPIPHANIE | 14 | 52 253 39 |
| OR E'RE THE SOONER SEEK HIS WESTERN BED. | CHARITAS NIMIA | 42 | 52 280 48 |
| WE GOE NOT TO SEEK, | WEEPER | 175 | 52 307 120 |
| SEEK FOR AMONGST HER MOTHER'S KISSES. | TERESA | 42 | 52 315 52 |
| SENDS UP MY SOUL TO SEEK THY FACE. | A SONG | 2 | 52 327 65 |

SEEKST

| | | | |
|---|---|---|---|
| WHOM THOU SEEKST WITH SO SWIFT VOWES, | TERESA | 66 | 52 315 52 |

SEEK'ST

| | | | |
|---|---|---|---|
| WHOM THOU SEEK'ST WITH SO SWIFT VOWES | IN MEMORY OF LADY MADRE TERESA | 66 | 46 131 52 |

SEEKE

| | | | |
|---|---|---|---|
| WE GOE NOT TO SEEKE | THE WEEPER | 133 | 46 79 120 |
| THE BABE NO SOONER 'GAN TO SEEKE, | A HYMNE OF THE NATIVITY | 47 | 46 106 76 |
| SEEKE FOR, AMONGST HER MOTHERS KISSES. | IN MEMORY OF LADY MADRE TERESA | 42 | 46 131 52 |
| I SEEKE NO FURTHER, IT IS SHEE. | WISHES SUPPOSED MISTRESSE | 114 | 46 195 479 |
| NO NO, YOUR KING'S NOT YET TO SEEKE | IN HOLY NATIVITY | 65 | 52 246 76 |
| OFT MY SOULE HAVE I BIN GLAD TO SEEKE | LUKE 2. QUAERIT JESUM | 41 | MS 379 11 |

SEEKES

SHEE SEEKES, SHEE SIGHS, BUT NO WHERE SPYES HIM.    OUT OF GREEKE CUPID'S CRYER           3   46 159 519

SEEKING

EVEN LOST THY SELF IN SEEKING ME.                   DIES IRAE                            32   52 298 186

SEEM

NOW SEEM THEY TEMPLES CONSECRATE TO NONE,           ON A TREATISE OF CHARITY             37   46 137  69
FOR THEY SEEM TO FALL,                              WEEPER                               15   52 307 120

SEEM'D

ALL POINTED IN HIS HEART SEEM'D TO INVADE HIM.      SOSPETTO D'HERODE                   476   46 109 216
AND SEEM'D TO MAKE AN ISLE, BUT MADE A WORLD.       UPON YORKE HIS BIRTH                 28   46 176 500
SEEM'D BUT THE OTHERS KIND REFLECTION.              UPON YORKE HIS BIRTH                 65   46 176 500
LIFE SEEM'D TO DY, DEATH DY'D INDEED.               OFFICE H. CROSS NINTH                12   52 271  99

SEEME

BY VARIOUS GLOSSES. NOW THEY SEEME TO GRUTCH,       MUSICKS DUELL                       128   46 149 535
FOR THEY BUT SEEME TO FALL                          THE WEEPER                           15   46  79 120
A WELL-POIS'D SCEPTER.  DOES IT NOW SEEME GOOD      SOSPETTO D'HERODE                   451   46 109 216
THOU CHEAT'ST US FORD, MAK'ST ONE SEEME TWO BY ART. UPON FORD'S TRAGEDYES                 1   46 181 495
NOR BE TO SHURT, NOR SEEME TO LONG.                 TO THE QUEEN                         12   48 215 501

SEEMS

AND SEEMS TO SAY, MAKE HASTE, MY BROTHER.           AGAINST IRRESOLUTION AND DELAY       44   52 347 146

SEEMES

IN THAT SWEET SOYLE. IT SEEMES A HOLY QUIRE         MUSICKS DUELL                        73   46 149 535

SEEMING

O'RE BEAUTIES FACE, SEEMING TO HIDE                 IN PRAISE OF LESSIUS                 29   46 156 510
OR'E BEAUTY'S FACE, SEEMING TO HIDE                 TEMPERANCE                           27   52 342 510

SEEMLY

A SEEMLY PORTION FOR THE SONS OF KINGS.             ON HOPE                              34   46 143  71
THY SEEMLY PRAISE.                                  OFFICE H. CROSS MATINES              21   52 265  86
A SEEMLY PORTION FOR THE SONNES OF KINGS.           (ON) HOPE                            14   52 345  71

SEEN

TELL HIM THYRSIS WHAT TH'HAST SEEN.                 A HYMNE OF THE NATIVITY              16   46 106  76
WAS IN HIS SHADY FOREHEAD SEEN EXPREST.             SOSPETTO D'HERODE                   195   46 109 216
SIGHTS WHICH ARE NOT SEEN WITH EYES,                ON A PRAYER BOOKE                    64   46 126 139
I'VE SEEN INDEED THE HOPEFULL BUD,                  UPON DEATH OF DESIRED HERRYS         31   46 168 467
WHICH TO BE SEEN NEEDES NOT HIS LIGHT.              IN HOLY NATIVITY                     14   52 246  76
TELL HIM, THYRSIS, WHAT TH'HAST SEEN.               IN HOLY NATIVITY                     16   52 246  76
THE SUN SAW THAT, AND WOULD HAVE SEEN NO MORE.      OFFICE H. CROSS NINTH                 7   52 271  99
YET LIGHT WAS SEEN & LIFE REVEALD.                  O GLORIOSA DOMINA                    34   52 302 194
WHEN SORROW WOULD BE SEEN                           WEEPER                               37   52 307 120
SIGHTS WHICH ARE NOT SEEN WITH EYES,                PRAYER TO GENTLE-WOMAN               70   52 328 139
YOU'AVE SEEN ALLREADY, IN THIS LOWER SPHEAR         TO SAME CONCERNING CHOISE             8   52 331  66

SEENE

WHEN SORROW WOULD BE SEENE                          THE WEEPER                           49   46  79 120
SEENE, AND YET HATED THEE, THEY DID NOT SEE,        BUT NOW THEY HAVE SEEN                1   46  96  21
COME WEE SHEPHEARDS WHO HAVE SEENE                  A HYMNE OF THE NATIVITY               1   46 106  76
WHICH TO BE SEENE NEEDS NOT HIS LIGHT.              A HYMNE OF THE NATIVITY              14   46 106  76
AS IT IS SEENE BY HELL.  AND SEENE WITH DREAD.      SOSPETTO D'HERODE                   414   46 109 216
AS IT IS SEENE BY HELL.   AND SEENE WITH DREAD.     SOSPETTO D'HERODE                   414   46 109 216
WHY THEN SHOULD IT E'RE BE SEENE,                   UPON DEATH OF DESIRED HERRYS         19   46 168 467
I'VE SEENE THE MORNINGS LOVELY RAY,                 UPON DEATH OF DESIRED HERRYS         47   46 168 467
HIM WHEN WRATH IT SELFE HAD SEENE,                  ANOTHER ON HERRYS                    29   46 170 469
SO HAVE I SEENE (TO DRESSE THEIR MISTRESSE MAY)     UPON YORKE HIS BIRTH                 59   46 176 500
STEPT FROM HER THRONE OF STARRES DEIGNES TO BE SEENE. UPON YORKE HIS BIRTH               72   46 176 500
A LITTLE MORE, & I HAD SURELY SEENE                 HORATIJ ILLE & NEFASTO               33   MS 382 530
SOE FOULE, ONE MINUTES LIGHT HAD IT BUT SEENE,      UPON GUNPOWDER TREASON               13   MS 386 460
HER ROSY CHEEKES YOU SHOULD HAVE SEENE NOE MORE     UPON GUNPOWDER TREASON               15   MS 386 460
WHAT WOULD THEY MORE.  TH' AVE SEENE WHEN AT MY NOD OUT OF GROTIUS                       49   MS 398 198

SEETHE

TO HOLD THEM DOWN, AND LOOKE THAT NONE SEETHE O'RE. SOSPETTO D'HERODE                   296   46 109 216

SEIGE

SOFT SUBJECT FOR THE SEIGE OF LOVE.                 SANCTA MARIA DOLORUM                 50   52 283 162

SEEGE

IT IS LOVE'S SEEGE.  AND SURE TO BE                 TO COUNTESSE OF DENBIGH              59   52 236 146

PAGE 356

SIEGE

| | | | | | |
|---|---|---|---|---|---|
| YEILD TO HIS SIEGE, WISE SOUL, AND SEE | AGAINST IRRESOLUTION AND DELAY | 79 | 52 | 347 | 146 |

SEIZE

| | | | | | |
|---|---|---|---|---|---|
| SEIZE HER SWEET PREY. | ON A PRAYER BOOKE | 101 | 46 | 126 | 139 |
| WHAT JOY SHALL SEIZE THY SOULE WHEN SHEE BEFORE, AND SEIZE UPON MATURITY. | IN MEMORY OF LADY MADRE TERESA | 134 | 46 | 131 | 52 |
| AND SEIZE THE SWIFT FLASH, IN REBOUND | UPON DEATH OF HERRYS | 8 | 46 | 167 | 466 |
| WHAT JOYES SHALL SEIZE THY SOUL, WHEN SHE | IN GLORIOUS EPIPHANIE | 199 | 52 | 253 | 39 |
| SEIZE HER SWEET PREY | TERESA | 133 | 52 | 315 | 52 |
| | PRAYER TO GENTLE-WOMAN | 107 | 52 | 328 | 139 |

SEIZ'D

| | | | | | |
|---|---|---|---|---|---|
| THAT SEIZ'D THY PARTING SOUL, & SEAL'D THEE HIS. | FLAMING HEART | 102 | 52 | 324 | 61 |

SELDOME

| | | | | | |
|---|---|---|---|---|---|
| THAT SELDOME LETT'ST A BLUSHING YOUTHFULL PRIME | UPON DEATH OF HERRYS | 30 | 46 | 167 | 466 |
| 'CAUSE THEY CAN BUT SELDOME PLEASE. | PETRONIJ ALES PHASIACIS PETITA | 4 | MS | 382 | 526 |

SELECTED

| | | | | | |
|---|---|---|---|---|---|
| SELECTED DOVE | PRAYER TO GENTLE-WOMAN | 96 | 52 | 328 | 139 |

SELF

| | | | | | |
|---|---|---|---|---|---|
| SNATCH'T HER SELF HENCE, TO HEAVEN. FILL'D A BRIGHT PLACE. | UPON BISHOP ANDREWES PICTURE | 9 | 46 | 163 | 490 |
| THAT TO THE MIGHTY NEPTUNE'S SELF DARE THREATEN WRACK. | WHY ARE YEE AFRAID | 8 | 46 | 88 | 15 |
| THY SELF DID'ST SET, | UPON THORNES FROM LORDS HEAD | 2 | 46 | 96 | 23 |
| NOW STRETCH THY SELF (FAIRE ILE) AND GROW, SPREAD WIDE | UPON YORKE HIS BIRTH | 2 | 46 | 176 | 500 |
| TO MEDIATE 'TWIXT YOUR SELF AND YOU. | TO THE QUEEN | 10 | 48 | 215 | 501 |
| BRING HITHER THY WHOLE SELF. & LET ME SEE | TO THE NAME OF JESUS | 17 | 52 | 239 | 30 |
| GOE, SOUL, OUT OF THY SELF, & SEEK FOR MORE. | TO THE NAME OF JESUS | 27 | 52 | 239 | 30 |
| OF HEAVNS, THE SELF INVOLVING SETT OF SPHEARS | TO THE NAME OF JESUS | 30 | 52 | 239 | 30 |
| AND GIVE THY SELF A WHILE THE GRACIOUS GUEST | TO THE NAME OF JESUS | 120 | 52 | 239 | 30 |
| CAN PROVE IT SELF SOME KIN (SWEET NAME) TO THEE. | TO THE NAME OF JESUS | 182 | 52 | 239 | 30 |
| TO SEEK HER SELF IN THY SWEET EYES | IN GLORIOUS EPIPHANIE | 14 | 52 | 253 | 39 |
| THY SELF OUR SUN, THOUGH THINE OWN SHADE. | IN GLORIOUS EPIPHANIE | 47 | 52 | 253 | 39 |
| HEAV'N IT SELF TO FIND THEM HELL. | IN GLORIOUS EPIPHANIE | 110 | 52 | 253 | 39 |
| AND MAKE THE NIGHT IT SELF THEIR TORCH TO THEE. | IN GLORIOUS EPIPHANIE | 188 | 52 | 253 | 39 |
| AND GIVE IT SELF FOR SPORT TO THE PROUD WIND. | CHARITAS NIMIA | 30 | 52 | 280 | 48 |
| THEE WITH THY SELF THEY HAVE TOO RICHLY CLAD. | UPON BODY OF OUR LORD | 3 | 52 | 290 | 24 |
| AND THAT TOO WAS THY SELF WHICH THEE DID COVER, | ADORO TE | 25 | 52 | 291 | 172 |
| THOUGH IN IT SELF THIS SOVERAIN FEAST | LAUDA SION SALVATOREM | 49 | 52 | 294 | 178 |
| O BY THY SELF VOUCHSAFE TO KEEP. | LAUDA SION SALVATOREM | 71 | 52 | 294 | 178 |
| TAKE SHELTER FROM THY SELF, IN THEE | DIES IRAE | 26 | 52 | 298 | 186 |
| EVEN LOST THY SELF IN SEEKING ME. | DIES IRAE | 32 | 52 | 298 | 186 |
| THY SELF. AND SO DISCHARGE THAT DAY. | DIES IRAE | 46 | 52 | 298 | 186 |
| BUT THOU THY BOUNTEOUS SELF STILL BE. | DIES IRAE | 55 | 52 | 298 | 186 |
| THY SELF TO US. & WE | IN GLORIOUS ASSUMPTION B. LADY | 47 | 52 | 304 | 114 |
| FAIR SPEND-THRIFT OF THY SELF. THY MEASURE | WEEPER | 128 | 52 | 307 | 120 |
| SOULES AS THY SHINING SELF, SHALL COME | TERESA | 125 | 52 | 315 | 52 |
| MAY DRINK IT SELF UP, AND FORGET TO DY. | AN APOLOGIE FOR (TERESA) HYMNE | 46 | 52 | 322 | 59 |
| AND TAKE AWAY FROM ME MY SELF & SIN, | FLAMING HEART | 90 | 52 | 324 | 61 |
| LEAVE NOTHING OF MY SELF IN ME. | FLAMING HEART | 106 | 52 | 324 | 61 |
| WHICH HERE CONTRACTS IT SELF, & COMES TO LY | PRAYER TO GENTLE-WOMAN | 16 | 52 | 328 | 139 |
| NOT FOR MY SELF ALAS, BUT FOR MY DEARER LORD. | TO SAME CONCERNING CHOISE | 7 | 52 | 331 | 66 |
| AH THOU THY SELF, ALAS, HAST TAUGHT ME HOW. | ALEXIAS FIRST ELEGIE | 16 | 52 | 334 | 204 |
| AND WIND THY SELF UP CLOSE IN THY COLD BED. | DEATH'S LECTURE | 4 | 52 | 340 | 475 |
| BEFORE THY SELF IN THINE IDAEA. THOU | DEATH'S LECTURE | 13 | 52 | 340 | 475 |
| HUGE EMPTYNES. CONTRACT THY SELF, & SHRINKE | DEATH'S LECTURE | 14 | 52 | 340 | 475 |
| HARK HITHER. AND THY SELF BE HE. | TEMPERANCE | 52 | 52 | 342 | 510 |
| IN LABOUR OF YOUR SELF TO LY, | AGAINST IRRESOLUTION AND DELAY | 19 | 52 | 347 | 146 |
| THIS FORT OF YOUR FAIR SELF IF'T BE NOT WONE, | AGAINST IRRESOLUTION AND DELAY | 89 | 52 | 347 | 146 |

SELF-CAPTIVITY

| | | | | | |
|---|---|---|---|---|---|
| IN A COLD SELF-CAPTIVITY. | AGAINST IRRESOLUTION AND DELAY | 24 | 52 | 347 | 146 |

SELF-OPPRESSED

| | | | | | |
|---|---|---|---|---|---|
| AND SELF-OPPRESSED SPARK, THAT HAS SO LONG | IN GLORIOUS EPIPHANIE | 135 | 52 | 253 | 39 |

SELF-REMEMBRING

| | | | | | |
|---|---|---|---|---|---|
| THE SELF-REMEMBRING SOUL SWEETLY RECOVERS | DESCRIPTION RELIGIOUS HOUSE | 36 | 52 | 338 | 213 |

SELF-SAME

| | | | | | |
|---|---|---|---|---|---|
| SO THAT WITH THE SELF-SAME BREAD | PSALME 23 | 53 | 46 | 102 | 5 |

SELF-SHUTT

| | | | | | |
|---|---|---|---|---|---|
| THE SELF-SHUTT CABINET OF AN UNSEARCHT SOUL. | TO COUNTESSE OF DENBIGH | 36 | 52 | 236 | 146 |

SELF-WOUNDING

| | | | | | |
|---|---|---|---|---|---|
| O SOFT SELF-WOUNDING PELICAN. | ADORO TE | 45 | 52 | 291 | 172 |

SELF'S

| | | | | | |
|---|---|---|---|---|---|
| IT GIVES, BUT O IT SELF'S THE GUIFT, | ON BLEEDING WOUNDS OF LORD | 11 | 46 | 101 | 110 |
| IT GIVES BUT O, IT SELF'S THE GIFT. | UPON BLEEDING CRUCIFIX | 15 | 52 | 268 | 110 |

SELFE

| | | | | | |
|---|---|---|---|---|---|
| WITH HER SWEET SELFE SHEE WRANGLES. HEE AMAZED | MUSICKS DUELL | 43 | 46 | 149 | 535 |
| ABOVE HER SELFE, MUSICKS ENTHUSIAST. | MUSICKS DUELL | 104 | 46 | 149 | 535 |
| OR TO THY SELFE, SING THINE OWNE OBSEQUIE. | MUSICKS DUELL | 110 | 46 | 149 | 535 |
| DOTH TUNE THE SPHAEARES, AND MAKE HEAVENS SELFE LOOKE | MUSICKS DUELL | 118 | 46 | 149 | 535 |
| WINTERS SELFE INTO A SPRING. | IN PRAISE OF LESSIUS | 44 | 46 | 156 | 510 |
| PITTY NOT HIM, BUT FEARE THY SELFE | OUT OF GREEKE CUPID'S CRYER | 59 | 46 | 159 | 519 |
| ROOME FOR HER SPATIOUS SELFE, UNTILL AT LENGTH | UPON BISHOP ANDREWES PICTURE | 7 | 46 | 163 | 490 |
| GLADNESSE IT SELFE WOULD BEE MORE GLAD | THE WEEPER | 65 | 46 | 79 | 120 |
| WEEPS FOR IT SELFE, IS ITS OWNE TEARE. | THE TEARE | 18 | 46 | 84 | 50 |
| AND SUCH THE ROSE ITS SELFE WHEN VEXT | THE TEARE | 22 | 46 | 84 | 50 |
| THERE THY SELFE SHALT BEE | THE TEARE | 43 | 46 | 84 | 50 |
| IS WASHT IT SELFE, IN WASHING HIM. | ON WATER OF LORDS BAPTISME | 2 | 46 | 65 | 12 |
| WHAT WOULD YE MORE. HERE FOOD IT SELFE IS FED. | ON MIRACLE OF LOAVES | 4 | 46 | 86 | 15 |
| SO LONG AS CAESAR'S SELFE IS GODS. | GIVE TO CAESAR AND TO GOD | 8 | 46 | 96 | 20 |
| WELL FOR THY SELFE (I MEANE) NOT FOR THY LORD. | ON ST. PETER CUTTING MALCHUS | 2 | 46 | 97 | 22 |
| THEE WITH THY SELFE THEY HAVE TOO RICHLY CLAD, | ON CRUCIFIED LORD BLOODY | 3 | 46 | 100 | 24 |
| AND MAKE DARKNESSE SELFE AFRAID. | PSALME 23 | 42 | 46 | 102 | 5 |
| WHEN HEAVEN IT SELFE LYES HERE BELOW. | A HYMNE OF THE NATIVITY | 44 | 46 | 106 | 76 |
| ART THOU UNTO THY SELFE, THOU TOO SELFE-WISE | SOSPETTO D'HERODE | 78 | 46 | 109 | 216 |
| AND LIFE SELFE IT WEARE DEATHS FRAILE LIVERY. | SOSPETTO D'HERODE | 168 | 46 | 109 | 216 |
| THAT GLORIES SELFE SHOULD SERVE OUR GRIEFS, & FEARES. | SOSPETTO D'HERODE | 183 | 46 | 109 | 216 |
| MY SELFE. MY STRENGTH TOO WITH MY INNOCENCE. | SOSPETTO D'HERODE | 250 | 46 | 109 | 216 |
| HER SELFE A WHILE SHE LAYES ASIDE, AND MAKES | SOSPETTO D'HERODE | 417 | 46 | 109 | 216 |
| OF THY GREAT SELFE, HATH STOLNE KING HEROD FROM THEE. | SOSPETTO D'HERODE | 458 | 46 | 109 | 216 |
| O CALL THY SELFE HOME TO THY SELFE, WAKE, WAKE, | SOSPETTO D'HERODE | 459 | 46 | 109 | 216 |
| O CALL THY SELFE HOME TO THY SELFE, WAKE, WAKE, | SOSPETTO D'HERODE | 459 | 46 | 109 | 216 |
| THY SELFE INTO A SHAPE THAT MAY BECOME THEE. | SOSPETTO D'HERODE | 462 | 46 | 109 | 216 |
| MUCH LARGER IN IT SELFE THEN IN ITS LOUKE. | ON A PRAYER BOOKE | 4 | 46 | 126 | 139 |
| WHICH HERE CONTRACTS IT SELFE AND COMES TO LYE | ON A PRAYER BOOKE | 10 | 46 | 126 | 139 |
| THE SOULE IT SELFE MORE FEELES THEN HEARES. | ON A PRAYER BOOKE | 62 | 46 | 126 | 139 |
| THY SELFE SHALT FEEL THINE OWNE FULL JOYES. | IN MEMORY OF LADY MADRE TERESA | 121 | 46 | 131 | 52 |
| SOULES AS THY SHINING SELFE, SHALL COME, | IN MEMORY OF LADY MADRE TERESA | 126 | 46 | 131 | 52 |
| MAY DRINKE IT SELFE UP, AND FORGET TO DY. | AN APOLOGIE FOR HYMNE (TERESA) | 46 | 46 | 136 | 59 |
| PUT ON THY SELFE IN THINE OWN LOOKS. T' OUR EYES | ON A TREATISE OF CHARITY | 2 | 46 | 137 | 69 |
| SH'L DRESSE THEE LIKE THY SELFE, SET THEE ON HIGH | ON A TREATISE OF CHARITY | 15 | 46 | 137 | 69 |
| THY SELFE TO US, AND WEE | ON THE ASSUMPTION | 42 | 46 | 139 | 114 |
| TO HATCH HER SELFE IN. 'MONGST HIS LEAVES THE DAY | UPON DEATH OF HERRYS | 15 | 46 | 167 | 466 |
| HIM WHEN WRATH IT SELFE HAD SEENE, | ANOTHER ON HERRYS | 29 | 46 | 170 | 469 |
| WRATH ITS SELFE HAD LOST HIS SPLEENE. | ANOTHER ON HERRYS | 30 | 46 | 170 | 469 |
| AND WIND THY SELFE UP CLOSE IN THY COLD BED. | UPON STANINOUGH'S DEATH | 4 | 46 | 175 | 475 |
| BEFORE THY SELFE IN THY IDAEA, THOU | UPON STANINOUGH'S DEATH | 12 | 46 | 175 | 475 |
| THY SELFE IN THIS UNFEIGN'D REFLECTION. | UPON STANINOUGH'S DEATH | 20 | 46 | 175 | 475 |
| BEYOND THY SELFE. FOR LO. THE GODS, THE GODS | UPON YORKE HIS BIRTH | 5 | 46 | 176 | 500 |
| THOU BY THY SELFE MAIST SIT, (BLEST ISLE) AND SEE | UPON YORKE HIS BIRTH | 25 | 46 | 176 | 500 |
| THY LITTLE SELFE IN LESSE, READ IN THESE EYNE | UPON YORKE HIS BIRTH | 43 | 46 | 176 | 500 |
| TO SHEW HER TO HER SELFE IN SUCH ANOTHER. | UPON YORKE HIS BIRTH | 54 | 46 | 176 | 500 |
| MY SELFE A MELTING SACRIFICE. I'ME BORNE | TO THE MORNING | 51 | 46 | 183 | 497 |
| IN LABOR OF YOUR SELFE TO LY. | TO COUNTESSE OF DENBIGH | 11 | 52 | 236 | 146 |
| THIS FORT OF YOUR FAIR SELFE, IF'T BE NOT WON, | TO COUNTESSE OF DENBIGH | 67 | 52 | 236 | 146 |
| IS TORTUR'D THIRST, IT SELFE, TOO SWEET A CUP. | OFFICE H. CROSS SIXT | 9 | 52 | 270 | 97 |
| THY SELFE DIDST SETT. | UPON CROWNE OF THORNS | 2 | 52 | 290 | 23 |
| MY LIFE, MY SOUL, MY SURER SELFE TO MEE. | ADORO TE | 44 | 52 | 291 | 172 |
| AS WITH THY SELFE THOU FEED'ST THY SHEEP. | LAUDA SION SALVATOREM | 72 | 52 | 294 | 178 |
| THY SELFE SHALL FEEL THINE OWN FULL JOYES | TERESA | 120 | 52 | 315 | 52 |
| DEAD TO MY SELFE, I LIVE IN THEE. | A SONG | 16 | 52 | 327 | 65 |
| THE SOUL IT SELFE MORE FEELS THEN HEARES. | PRAYER TO GENTLE-WOMAN | 68 | 52 | 328 | 139 |
| SENDING'S TOO SLOW A WORD, MY SELFE WOULD FLY. | ALEXIAS FIRST ELEGIE | 13 | 52 | 334 | 204 |
| FULL SWEETLY WITH IT SELFE HAD DWELL'T AT HOME. | ALEXIAS THIRD ELEGIE | 12 | 52 | 336 | 209 |
| WINTER'S SELFE INTO A SPRING. | TEMPERANCE | 42 | 52 | 342 | 510 |
| PROMETHEUS SELFE, & PELOPS STERVED SIRE | HORATIJ ILLE & NEFASTO | 54 | MS | 382 | 530 |
| TO DROUNE THY SELFE IN THIS PURE PEARLY FLOOD. | UPON GUNPOWDER TREASON | 32 | MS | 387 | 461 |
| OFFER THY SELFE A VIRGIN SACRIFICE | UPON GUNPOWDER TREASON | 35 | MS | 387 | 461 |
| CHANT TO MY SELFE WITH RUSTIC MELODIE. | UPON BIRTH PRINCESSE E | 24 | MS | 391 | 456 |
| THE PHAENIX SELFE SHALL NOT MORE PROUDLY BURNE, | EX EUPHORMIONE | 15 | MS | 392 | 525 |
| WHICH POSETH MISCHEIFE'S SELFE TO PARALLEL. | AN ELEGIE ON DR PORTER | 14 | MS | 395 | 476 |
| GREAT NATURES SELFE HATH SHRUNKE AND SPOKE MEE GOD. | OUT OF GROTIUS | 50 | MS | 398 | 198 |
| NOW BUT THE GRAVE. THE GRAVE IT SELFE I TAM'D. | OUT OF GROTIUS | 86 | MS | 398 | 198 |

SELFE-CAPTIVITY

| | | | | | |
|---|---|---|---|---|---|
| IN A SAD SELFE-CAPTIVITY. | TO COUNTESSE OF DENBIGH | 24 | 52 | 236 | 146 |

SELFE-PRISON'D

| | | | | | |
|---|---|---|---|---|---|
| THESE CURTAIN'D WINDOWES, THIS SELFE-PRISON'D EYE, | UPON STANINOUGH'S DEATH | 25 | 46 | 175 | 475 |

SELFE-TORMENTING

| | | | | | |
|---|---|---|---|---|---|
| AND SELFE-TORMENTING SIN) HAD A SOFT BED. | SOSPETTO D'HERODE | 412 | 46 | 109 | 216 |

SELFE-WISE

| | | | | | |
|---|---|---|---|---|---|
| ART THOU UNTO THY SELFE, THOU TOO SELFE-WISE | SOSPETTO D'HERODE | 78 | 46 | 109 | 216 |

## SELVES

| | | | | |
|---|---|---|---|---|
| YOUR SELVES, YOU ARE THE ROCKS | WHY ARE YEE AFRAID | 13 | 46 | 88 | 15 |
| AND LOSE OUR SELVES IN WILD DELIGHT. | OUT OF CATULLUS | 18 | 46 | 194 | 523 |
| YOUR SELVES INTO THE LONG | TO THE NAME OF JESUS | 84 | 52 | 239 | 30 |
| OUR SELVES BECOME OUR OWN BEST SACRIFICE. | IN HOLY NATIVITY | 108 | 52 | 246 | 76 |
| (SWEET) TO OUR SELVES, IN THEE. | IN GLORIOUS EPIPHANIE | 63 | 52 | 253 | 39 |
| THUS GRAFT OUR SELVES ON THEE. | VEXILLA REGIS | 40 | 52 | 277 | 156 |
| COME YOUR WHOLE SELVES, SORROW'S GREAT SON & MOTHER. | SANCTA MARIA DOLORUM | 77 | 52 | 283 | 162 |
| APPLAUD YOUR HAPPY SELVES IN HER, | O GLORIOSA DOMINA | 28 | 52 | 302 | 194 |
| YOUR SELVES IN YOUR UNFAIGN'D REFLEXION. | DEATH'S LECTURE | 22 | 52 | 340 | 475 |
| OUR PURCHAS'D SELVES TOO SOON BESTOW | AGAINST IRRESOLUTION AND DELAY | 65 | 52 | 347 | 146 |
| YOUR SELVES, YOU STYGIAN STATES, A PITCHY CLOWD | UPON GUNPOWDER TREASON | 24 | MS | 387 | 461 |

## SEND

| | | | | |
|---|---|---|---|---|
| YET MAY THE LOVE I SEND BE TRUE, THOUGH I | WITH A PICTURE TO A FRIEND | 5 | 46 | 156 | 494 |
| SEND NOT TRUE PICTURE, NOR TRUE POESIE. | WITH A PICTURE TO A FRIEND | 6 | 46 | 156 | 494 |
| WHERE TH'OTHER DARES NOT SEND HIS EYE. | TWO WENT TO PRAY | 4 | 46 | 89 | 18 |
| THOU ART A SOULDIER HEROD, SEND THY SCOUTS | SOSPETTO D'HERODE | 523 | 46 | 109 | 216 |
| WHICH EVERY DAY TO HEAVEN WILL SEND YOU. | ON MR. G. HERBERTS BOOKE | 12 | 46 | 130 | 68 |
| GRACIOUS HEAVENS DO USE TO SEND | UPON DEATH OF DESIRED HERRYS | 26 | 46 | 168 | 467 |
| WHAT SUCCOUR CAN I HOPE THE MUSE WILL SEND | TO THE MORNING | 1 | 46 | 183 | 497 |
| DEATH SHALL SEND MEE | OUT OF THE ITALIAN (1) | 44 | 46 | 188 | 545 |
| LIFE, THAT DARES SEND | WISHES SUPPOSED MISTRESSE | 85 | 46 | 195 | 479 |
| AND SEND IT BACK TO YOU AGAIN. | TO THE NAME OF JESUS | 114 | 52 | 239 | 30 |
| CONTEMPT & SCORN CAN SEND WOUNDS TO SEARCH THE INMOST | OFFICE H. CROSS SIXT | 12 | 52 | 270 | 97 |
| I'D SEND MY WOES IN WORDS SHOULD WEEP FOR ME. | ALEXIAS FIRST ELEGIE | 11 | 52 | 334 | 204 |
| THAT EARTH A SHOURE OF STONES TO HEAVEN SHALL SEND, | ON GUNPOWDER-TREASON | 22 | MS | 384 | 458 |
| A THOUSAND HELICONS THE MUSES SEND | AN ELEGIE ON DR PORTER | 39 | MS | 395 | 476 |

## SENDS

| | | | | |
|---|---|---|---|---|
| DECLARE WHO SENDS, AND WHAT IS HIS COMMAND. | SOSPETTO D'HERODE | 512 | 46 | 109 | 216 |
| SAY & BEAR WITTNES. SENDS SHE NOT | FLAMING HEART | 53 | 52 | 324 | 61 |
| SENDS UP MY SOUL TO SEEK THY FACE. | A SONG | 2 | 52 | 327 | 65 |
| (WHEN ONE POOR SIGH SENDS FOR HIM DOWN) | AGAINST IRRESOLUTION AND DELAY | 74 | 52 | 347 | 146 |

## SENDING'S

| | | | | |
|---|---|---|---|---|
| SENDING'S TOO SLOW A WORD, MY SELFE WOULD FLY. | ALEXIAS FIRST ELEGIE | 13 | 52 | 334 | 204 |

## SENSE

| | | | | |
|---|---|---|---|---|
| TO THAT ONE SENSE, MADE ALL ELSE THRALL, | OUT OF THE ITALIAN (3) | 7 | 46 | 190 | 549 |
| N'ERE WAST THOU IN A SENSE SO SADLY TRUE, | UPON BLEEDING CRUCIFIX | 37 | 52 | 288 | 110 |
| DOWN DOWN, PROUD SENSE. DISCOURSES DY. | ADORO TE | 5 | 52 | 291 | 172 |
| LORD, WHEN THE SENSE OF THY SWEET GRACE | A SONG | 1 | 52 | 327 | 65 |

## SENCE

| | | | | |
|---|---|---|---|---|
| THE TENDER GROWTH OF THINGS ENDURE THE SENCE | OUT OF VIRGIL | 33 | 46 | 155 | 529 |
| ARE IN ANOTHER SENCE | ON MARKES OF SAVIOURS WOUNDS | 3 | 46 | 86 | 26 |
| NERE WAS'T THOU IN A SENCE SO SADLY TRUE, | ON BLEEDING WOUNDS OF LORD. | 41 | 46 | 101 | 110 |
| SHOULD TAKE THE MARKE OF SIN, AND PAINE OF SENCE. | SOSPETTO D'HERODE | 190 | 46 | 109 | 216 |

## SENSES

| | | | | |
|---|---|---|---|---|
| BUT THESE VAST MYSTERIES HIS SENSES SMOTHER, | SOSPETTO D'HERODE | 161 | 46 | 109 | 216 |
| O FILL OUR SENSES, AND TAKE FROM US | TO THE NAME OF JESUS | 170 | 52 | 239 | 30 |

## SENT

| | | | | |
|---|---|---|---|---|
| WINTER CHID THE WORLD, AND SENT | A HYMNE OF THE NATIVITY | 23 | 46 | 106 | 76 |
| TO A POORE GALILEAN VIRGIN SENT. | SOSPETTO D'HERODE | 98 | 46 | 109 | 216 |
| ARE SENT ABOUT, WHO POASTING EVERY WAY | SOSPETTO D'HERODE | 510 | 46 | 109 | 216 |
| TAKE THESE, TIMES TARDY TRUANTS, SENT BY ME, | UPON TWO GREENE APRICOCKES | 1 | 48 | 220 | 494 |
| WINTER CHIDDE ALOUD, & SENT | IN HOLY NATIVITY | 24 | 52 | 246 | 76 |
| UPON WHOSE CHOICE POINT SHALL BE SENT | TERESA | 90 | 52 | 315 | 52 |
| JUSTLE DOWN MOUNTAINS, KINGS COURTS SHALL BE SENT, | ON GUNPOWDER-TREASON | 41 | MS | 384 | 458 |
| OF PEARLY DROPS, & SENT HER NUMEROUSE BIRTH | UPON KINGS CORONATION | 7 | MS | 390 | 453 |

## SENTENCE

| | | | | |
|---|---|---|---|---|
| HER PARDON OR HER SENTENCE. ONELY BREAKE | UPON YORKE HIS BIRTH | 109 | 46 | 176 | 500 |

## SENTENTIOUS

| | | | | |
|---|---|---|---|---|
| SENTENTIOUS SHOWERS, O LET THEM FALL, | UPON THE DEATH OF A GENTLEMAN | 29 | 46 | 166 | 472 |

## SERAPHICALL

| | | | | |
|---|---|---|---|---|
| THAT COULD BE FOUND SERAPHICALL. | FLAMING HEART | 30 | 52 | 324 | 61 |

## SERAPHICK

| | | | | |
|---|---|---|---|---|
| LETT TH' HALLOWED PLUME OF A SERAPHICK WING | UPON BIRTH PRINCESSE E | 22 | MS | 391 | 456 |
| THAT HEAVENLY MORTALL, THAT SERAPHICK MAN. | AN ELEGIE ON DR PORTER | 18 | MS | 395 | 476 |

## SERAPHIM

| | | | | |
|---|---|---|---|---|
| IN PUDDLES, WE WILL PLEDGE THIS SERAPHIM | AN APOLOGIE FOR HYMNE (TERESA) | 32 | 46 | 136 | 59 |
| OF WARBLING SERAPHIM TO THE EARES OF LOVE, | TO THE NAME OF JESUS | 106 | 52 | 239 | 30 |

```
BLEST SERAPHIM, SHALL LEAVE THEIR QUIRE             TERESA                              94   52 315   52
IN PUDDLES. WE WILL PLEDGE THIS SERAPHIM            AN APOLOGIE FOR (TERESA) HYMNE      32   52 322   59
THAT IS A SERAPHIM, THEY SAY                        FLAMING HEART                        5   52 324   61
AND CALL THE SAINT THE SERAPHIM.                    FLAMING HEART                       12   52 324   61
SHOWES THIS THE MOTHER SERAPHIM.                    FLAMING HEART                       16   52 324   61
UNDRESSE THY SERAPHIM INTO MINE.                    FLAMING HEART                       40   52 324   61
A SERAPHIM AT EVERY SHOTT.                          FLAMING HEART                       54   52 324   61
GIVE ME THE SUFFRING SERAPHIM.                      FLAMING HEART                       64   52 324   61
(FAIR SISTER OF THE SERAPHIM.)                      FLAMING HEART                      104   52 324   61

SERAPHIMS

BLEST SERAPHIMS SHALL LEAVE THEIR QUIRE,            IN MEMORY OF LADY MADRE TERESA      94   46 131   52
I SAW THE OBSEQUIOUS SERAPHIMS                      IN HOLY NATIVITY                    58   52 246   76
SERAPHIMS WILL NOT SLEEP                            CHARITAS NIMIA                      17   52 280   48
NESTS OF NEW SERAPHIMS HERE BELOW.                  FLAMING HEART                       46   52 324   61

SERIES

THE PLYANT SERIES OF HER SLIPPERY SONG.             MUSICKS DUELL                       61   46 149  535
AND EVERLASTING SERIES OF A DEATHLESSE SONG.        TO THE NAME OF JESUS                85   52 239   30

SERIOUS

THE SERIOUS SHOWRES ALONG HIS DECENT                OFFICE H. CROSS THIRD                8   52 268   93
HEARS'T THOU, MY SOUL, WHAT SERIOUS THINGS          DIES IRAE                            1   52 298  186

SERMONS

SERMONS HE HEARD, YET NOT SO MANY,                  AN EPITAPH UPON ASHTON               9   46 192  464

PARLOUR-SERMONS

HIS PARLOUR-SERMONS RATHER WERE                     AN EPITAPH UPON ASHTON              13   46 192  464

SERPENT

START, AND SAY, THE SERPENT HISSES.                 OUT OF GREEKE CUPID'S CRYER         66   46 159  519

SERVANT

MUSE, NOW THE SERVANT OF SOFT LOVES NO MORE,        SOSPETTO D'HERODE                    1   46 109  216
(SWORNE SERVANT TO YOUR SWEETEST EYES)              THOUGH NOW 'TIS NEITHER              4   MS 397  492

SERVE

THAT GLORIES SELFE SHOULD SERVE OUR GRIEFS, & FEARES. SOSPETTO D'HERODE                183   46 109  216
COMES NOT TO RULE IN WRATH, BUT SERVE IN LOVE.      SOSPETTO D'HERODE                  516   46 109  216
ONELY SUCH STRYNES AS SERVE TO KEEPE                THOUGH NOW 'TIS NEITHER             19   MS 397  492
AND MAKE OUR DARKNES SERVE THY DAY.                 IN GLORIOUS EPIPHANIE              212   52 253   39
FOR BOW HIS UNBENT HAND DID SERVE,                  IN CICATRICES DOMINI JESU           13   MS 381   27

SERV'D

FOR THEE. AND SERV'D THEREIN THY GLORIOUS ENDS.     TO THE NAME OF JESUS               210   52 239   30

SERVES

THAT HEE WHOM THE SUN SERVES, SHOULD FAINTLY PEEPE  SOSPETTO D'HERODE                  177   46 109  216
AND SERVES MY PURER SIGHT, ONELY TO BEAT            SOSPETTO D'HERODE                  203   46 109  216
AS SERVES TO KEEP ALIVE HER DEATH.                  SANCTA MARIA DOLORUM                40   52 283  162

SERVICE

(MOST DIVINE SERVICE) WHOSE SO EARLY LAY,           MUSICKS DUELL                       81   46 149  535

SERVICES

GODS SERVICES NO LONGER SHALL PUT ON                ON A TREATISE OF CHARITY            29   46 137   69

SET

THEN VENUS MILD INSTINCT (AT SET TIMES) YEILDS      OUT OF VIRGIL                       11   46 155  529
A SET OF RAREST HARMONY.                            IN PRAISE OF LESSIUS                38   46 156  510
AND NOW TH'ART SET WIDE OPE, THE SPEARE'S SAD ART,  I AM THE DOORE                       1   46  90   17
THUS SET THEM OPE.                                  I AM THE DOORE                       6   46  90   17
THY SELF DID'ST SET,                                UPON THORNES FROM LORDS HEAD         2   46  96   23
THE FLOOD-GATE SHALL BE SET WIDE OPE FOR HIM.       OUR LORD IN HIS CIRCUMCISION         6   46  98    9
SET THE CONTENDING SONS OF HEAV'N ON FIRE.          SOSPETTO D'HERODE                   90   46 109  216
WHERE HELLS CAPACIOUS CAULDRON IS SET ON.           SOSPETTO D'HERODE                  294   46 109  216
AND THY PAINS SET BRIGHT UPON THEE.                 IN MEMORY OF LADY MADRE TERESA     147   46 131   52
THOU HERE ART SET TO SHINE, WHERE THY FULL DAY      AN APOLOGIE FOR HYMNE (TERESA)       5   46 136   59
HEAV'N SET THEE DOWN NEW DREST. WHEN THY BRIGHT BIRTH ON A TREATISE OF CHARITY           5   46 137   69
SH'L DRESSE THEE LIKE THY SELFE, SET THEE ON HIGH   ON A TREATISE OF CHARITY            15   46 137   69
IN HIM PERFECTION DID SET FORTH,                    HIS EPITAPH (HERRYS)                13   46 172  471
HOW E'RE LOVES NATIVE HOURES WERE SET,              LOVES HOROSCOPE                     17   46 185  483
SET. O THEN, HOW LONG A NIGHT                       OUT OF CATULLUS                      7   46 194  523
OR A BOUGHT BLUSH, OR A SET SMILE.                  WISHES SUPPOSED MISTRESSE           24   46 195  479
A SET OF RAREST HARMONY.                            TEMPERANCE                          36   52 342  510

SETT

OF HEAVNS, THE SELF INVOLVING SETT OF SPHEARS       TO THE NAME OF JESUS                30   52 239   30
WHAT DID THEIR WEAPONS BUT SETT WIDE THE DOORES     TO THE NAME OF JESUS               216   52 239   30
```

## AURORA SHALL SETT OPE

| Phrase | Source | | | | |
|---|---|---|---|---|---|
| AURORA SHALL SETT OPE, | IN GLORIOUS EPIPHANIE | 69 | 52 | 253 | 39 |
| THE WORLD'S PRICE SETT TO SALE, & BY THE BOLD | OFFICE H. CROSS MATINES | 14 | 52 | 265 | 86 |
| SHALL I, SETT THERE | SANCTA MARIA DOLORUM | 81 | 52 | 283 | 162 |
| THY SELFE DIDST SETT. | UPON CROWNE OF THORNS | 2 | 52 | 290 | 23 |
| LIFT OUR LEAN SOULES, & SETT US UP | LAUDA SION SALVATOREM | 75 | 52 | 294 | 178 |
| WILL SETT THE WORLD IN SEVERE LIGHT. | DIES IRAE | 18 | 52 | 298 | 186 |
| THOU HERE ART SETT TO SHINE WHERE THY FULL DAY | AN APOLOGIE FOR (TERESA) HYMNE | 5 | 52 | 322 | 59 |
| SETT TO THE MISCHEIFE OF POSTERITIE. | HORATIJ ILLE & NEFASTO | 2 | MS | 382 | 530 |
| FOR IF YOU SETT, WHO MAY NOT JUSTLY FEARE, | UPON KINGS CORONATION | 41 | MS | 389 | 454 |
| THIS GLORIOUS PHAEBUS SETT) WILL QUIET BEE. | UPON KINGS CORONATION | 24 | MS | 390 | 453 |
| RICH DIAMONDS, SETT IN A PURE SILVER FOYLE. | UPON BIRTH PRINCESSE E | 44 | MS | 391 | 456 |
| AND SETT IT FORTH IN THE SAME HAPPY PLACE, | UPON BIRTH PRINCESSE E | 59 | MS | 391 | 456 |

## SETS

| Phrase | Source | | | | |
|---|---|---|---|---|---|
| NOR SETS THEE IN SO RICH A RED. | AN HIMNE FOR CIRCUMCISION | 8 | 46 | 141 | 37 |
| THEN WHAT NATURES WHITE HAND SETS OPE. | WISHES SUPPOSED MISTRESSE | 30 | 46 | 195 | 479 |

## SETTS

| Phrase | Source | | | | |
|---|---|---|---|---|---|
| HOME TO THE HEART, AND SETTS THE HOUSE ON FIRE. | ON A PRAYER BOOKE | 67 | 46 | 126 | 139 |
| NOR SETTS THEE IN SO RICH A RED. | NEW YEAR'S DAY | 8 | 52 | 251 | 37 |
| AND WHERESO'ERE HE SETTS HIS WHITE | TERESA | 179 | 52 | 315 | 52 |
| HOME TO THE HEART, & SETTS THE HOUSE ON FIRE | PRAYER TO GENTLE-WOMAN | 73 | 52 | 328 | 139 |

## SETTING

| Phrase | Source | | | | |
|---|---|---|---|---|---|
| THIS REVEREND SHADOW CAST THAT SETTING SUN, | UPON BISHOP ANDREWES PICTURE | 1 | 46 | 163 | 490 |

## SETTLE

| Phrase | Source | | | | |
|---|---|---|---|---|---|
| DECIDE & SETTLE THE GREAT CAUSE | IN GLORIOUS EPIPHANIE | 146 | 52 | 253 | 39 |

## SEVER

| Phrase | Source | | | | |
|---|---|---|---|---|---|
| IT COULD NOT SEVER MAN AND WIFE, | AN EPITAPH HUSBAND AND WIFE | 5 | 46 | 174 | 478 |

## SEVERALL

| Phrase | Source | | | | |
|---|---|---|---|---|---|
| TO WARN EACH SEVERALL KIND | TO THE NAME OF JESUS | 37 | 52 | 239 | 30 |

## SEVERE

| Phrase | Source | | | | |
|---|---|---|---|---|---|
| WILL SETT THE WORLD IN SEVERE LIGHT. | DIES IRAE | 18 | 52 | 298 | 186 |

## SEVERELY

| Phrase | Source | | | | |
|---|---|---|---|---|---|
| WITH TENDER ACCENTS, AND SEVERELY JOYNT IT | MUSICKS DUELL | 40 | 46 | 149 | 535 |

## SEVERER

| Phrase | Source | | | | |
|---|---|---|---|---|---|
| TO SEE THEMSELVES THEIR OWN SEVERER SHORE. | TO COUNTESSE OF DENBIGH | 26 | 52 | 236 | 146 |
| TO FIND THEMSELVES THEIR OWN SEVERER SHOAR. | AGAINST IRRESOLUTION AND DELAY | 26 | 52 | 347 | 146 |

## SEVEREST

| Phrase | Source | | | | |
|---|---|---|---|---|---|
| HERE SYLLA HIS SEVEREST PRISON HAS. | SOSPETTO D'HERODE | 356 | 46 | 109 | 216 |

## SEV'N

| Phrase | Source | | | | |
|---|---|---|---|---|---|
| DYE SEV'N TIMES DEEPER THAN THEY WERE BEFORE | UPON GUNPOWDER TREASON | 4 | MS | 387 | 461 |

## SEAVEN

| Phrase | Source | | | | |
|---|---|---|---|---|---|
| REV'RENTLY CIRCLED BY THE LESSER SEAVEN, | SOSPETTO D'HERODE | 238 | 46 | 109 | 216 |

## SEAV'N

| Phrase | Source | | | | |
|---|---|---|---|---|---|
| WHERE SEAV'N TALL HORNES (HIS EMPIRES PRIDE) ASPIRE. | SOSPETTO D'HERODE | 46 | 46 | 109 | 216 |
| SEAV'N CRESTED HYDRA'S HORRIBLY ADORNE. | SOSPETTO D'HERODE | 48 | 46 | 109 | 216 |

## SHACKLED

| Phrase | Source | | | | |
|---|---|---|---|---|---|
| THEIR SHACKLED TONGUES TO CHANT AN ELGIE. | AN ELEGIE ON DR PORTER | 36 | MS | 395 | 476 |

## SHADE

| Phrase | Source | | | | |
|---|---|---|---|---|---|
| HER WEAKE CONCEPTIONS. NO LOANE SHADE, BUT RINGS | OUT OF VIRGIL | 9 | 46 | 155 | 529 |
| HE'S WASHT, HIS GLOOMY SKIN A PEACEFULL SHADE | ON BAPTIZED AETHIOPIAN | 3 | 46 | 85 | 29 |
| OVERSHADOW EVEN THE SHADE, | PSALME 23 | 41 | 46 | 102 | 5 |
| AIRE, WITH A DISMALL SHADE, BUT ALL IN VAINE, | SOSPETTO D'HERODE | 143 | 46 | 109 | 216 |
| THE FOREHEAD'S SHADE IN GRIEFES EXPRESSION THERE, | SOSPETTO D'HERODE | 196 | 46 | 109 | 216 |
| FAIRE CLOUD OF FIRE, BOTH SHADE, AND LIGHT, | ON HOPE | 15 | 46 | 143 | 71 |
| THUS GREW THIS GRATIOUS PLANT, IN WHOSE SWEET SHADE | UPON DEATH OF HERRYS | 9 | 46 | 167 | 466 |
| HIDE HIS HOT BEAMES IN SHADE OF SILVER AGE. | UPON DEATH OF HERRYS | 31 | 46 | 167 | 466 |
| TO BE A SHADE FOR ANGELS WHILE THEY SING, | UPON DEATH OF HERRYS | 40 | 46 | 167 | 466 |
| HIS SMOOTH CHEEKES, WITH A DOWNY SHADE. | HIS EPITAPH (HERRYS) | 46 | 46 | 172 | 471 |
| THY SELF OUR SUN, THOUGH THINE OWN SHADE. | IN GLORIOUS EPIPHANIE | 47 | 52 | 253 | 39 |
| ALAS WITH HOW MUCH HEAVYER SHADE | IN GLORIOUS EPIPHANIE | 117 | 52 | 253 | 39 |
| NOT SO MUCH THEIR SUN AS SHADE, | IN GLORIOUS EPIPHANIE | 137 | 52 | 253 | 39 |
| COUCH'T IN THAT CONSCIOUS SHADE | IN GLORIOUS EPIPHANIE | 190 | 52 | 253 | 39 |
| 'TWIXT SUN & SHADE, | IN GLORIOUS EPIPHANIE | 216 | 52 | 253 | 39 |
| THEN SITT THEE DOWN, & SING THINE EV'NSONG IN THE SAD | OFFICE H. CROSS EVENSONG | 8 | 52 | 273 | 101 |
| BOTH WEEP & SING IN SHADE OF THEE. | OFFICE H. CROSS EVENSONG | 11 | 52 | 273 | 101 |

```
                                                                PAGE  362

    IN SHADE OF DEATH'S SAD TREE              SANCTA MARIA DOLORUM           1  52 283 162
    TO SHOW US THIS FAINT SHADE FOR HER       FLAMING HEART                 22  52 324  61
    SUBSTANTIALL SHADE, WHOSE SWEET ALLAY     (ON) HOPE                      5  52 345  71
    AND BE ECLIPSED WITH AN ENVIOUS SHADE.    AN ELEGY MR STANNINOW         44  MS 394 473

SHADES

    AND CHASE THE TREMBLING SHADES AWAY.      A HYMNE OF THE NATIVITY       32  46 106  76
    FROM DEATH'S SAD SHADES, TO THE LIFE-BREATHING AYRE,  SOSPETTO D'HERODE 81  46 109 216
    THE HEAV'N-REBUKED SHADES MADE HAST AWAY. SOSPETTO D'HERODE            114  46 109 216
    TO THIS DARKE HOUSE OF SHADES, HORROUR, AND NIGHT,  SOSPETTO D'HERODE  213  46 109 216
    THROUGH THE THICK SHADES OBSCURELY MIGHT YOU SEE   SOSPETTO D'HERODE   350  46 109 216
    OF GEMS, THAT IN THEIR BRIGHT SHADES PLAY. WISHES SUPPOSED MISTRESSE   51  46 195 479
    SAD SHADES AND SING DULL NIGHT ASLEEPE.   THOUGH NOW 'TIS NEITHER      20  MS 397 492
    OF DUST, WHERE IN THE BASHFULL SHADES OF NIGHT  TO THE NAME OF JESUS  233  52 239  30
    AND CHASE THE TREMBLING SHADES AWAY.      IN HOLY NATIVITY             34  52 246  76
    AND CHASE THE TREMBLING SHADES AWAY.      IN HOLY NATIVITY             75  52 246  76
    SORDIDLY SHIFTING HANDS WITH SHADES & NIGHT.  IN GLORIOUS EPIPHANIE    35  52 253  39
    WHEN GLORY'S SUN FAITH'S SHADES SHALL CHASE,  ADORO TE                 55  52 291 172
    TYPES YEILD TO TRUTHES. SHADES SHRINK AWAY. LAUDA SION SALVATOREM      23  52 294 178

SHADY

    AS EVER SILVER-TIPT, THE SIDE OF SHADY MOUNTAINE. TO PONTIUS WASHING HANDS  8  46  94  23
    A SHADY ARME ABOVE MY HEAD,               PSALME 23                    60  46 102   5
    ABOUT THEIR SHADY BROWES IN WANTON RINGS. SOSPETTO D'HERODE            70  46 109 216
    WAS IN HIS SHADY FOREHEAD SEEN EXPREST.   SOSPETTO D'HERODE           195  46 109 216
    SCARCE TO THIS MONSTER COULD THE SHADY KING.  SOSPETTO D'HERODE       369  46 109 216
    IN SHADY LEAVES OF DESTINY.               WISHES SUPPOSED MISTRESSE    6  46 195 479
    OPEN SUNNES, SHADY BOWERS,                WISHES SUPPOSED MISTRESSE   92  46 195 479
    UNFORC'T & GENUINE, BUT NOT SHADY THO.    DESCRIPTION RELIGIOUS HOUSE 10  52 338 213

SHADOW

    THIS REVEREND SHADOW CAST THAT SETTING SUN,  UPON BISHOP ANDREWES PICTURE  1  46 163 490
    UNDER THY SHADOW MAY I LURKE A WHILE,     SICKE IMPLORE SHADOW         1  46  87  28
    THY SHADOW PETER, MUST SHEW ME THE SUN,   SICKE IMPLORE SHADOW         3  46  87  28
    MY LIGHTS THY SHADOWES SHADOW, OR 'TIS DONE.  SICKE IMPLORE SHADOW     4  46  87  28
    SEE, SEE THY REALL SHADOW, SEE THY BROTHER,  UPON YORKE HIS BIRTH     42  46 176 500
    FOR SHELTER TO THE SHADOW OF THY TREE.    IN GLORIOUS EPIPHANIE      140  52 253  39
    SOMTHING A BRIGHTER SHADOW (SWEET) OF THEE.  IN GLORIOUS EPIPHANIE   249  52 253  39
    SOUND GOODNESSE WITH HER SHADOW WHICH THEY WEARE,  OUT OF GROTIUS     43  MS 398 198

SHADDOW

    TO SHADDOW FORTH TH' ADMIRED PARAGON.     UPON BIRTH PRINCESSE E      42  MS 391 456

SHADOWES

    MY LIGHTS THY SHADOWES SHADOW, OR 'TIS DONE.  SICKE IMPLORE SHADOW     4  46  87  28

SHAFT

    THAT HEALING SHAFT, WHICH HEAVN TILL NOW  TO COUNTESSE OF DENBIGH     47  52 236 146
    (FAIR YOUTH) SHOOTES BOTH THY SHAFT & THEE  FLAMING HEART             48  52 324  61
    NOT ONE LOOSE SHAFT BUT LOVE'S WHOLE QUIVER.  FLAMING HEART            70  52 324  61

SHAFTS

    WITH BITTER SHAFTS 'TIS SAUC'T TOO WELL.  OUT OF GREEKE CUPID'S CRYER 52  46 159 519
    HERE'S MY QUIVER SHAFTS AND BOW,          OUT OF GREEKE CUPID'S CRYER 70  46 159 519
    HER SHAFTS, AND SHEE FLY FARRE ABOVE,     ON HOPE                     75  46 143  71
    AND 'MONGST THY SHAFTS OF SOVERAIGN LIGHT TO COUNTESSE OF DENBIGH     32  52 236 146
    LET ALL THY SCATTER'D SHAFTS OF LIGHT, THAT PLAY  FLAMING HEART       87  52 324  61
    HER SHAFTS, AND SHEE FLY FARRE ABOVE,     (ON) HOPE                   35  52 345  71

SHAGGY

    THEIR SHAGGY LOCKS, THEIR FLOURY MANTLES TURN'D  UPON GUNPOWDER TREASON 47 MS 386 460

SHAKE

    REDEEME A WORTHY WRATH, ROUSE THEE, AND SHAKE  SOSPETTO D'HERODE     461  46 109 216
    WHY DOST THOU SHAKE THY LEADEN SCEPTER. GOE  TO THE MORNING           54  46 183 497

SHAME

    SHAME NOW AND ANGER MIXT A DOUBLE STAINE  MUSICKS DUELL              105  46 149 535
    OF THY RENOUNE, AND THEIR OWNE SHAME.     NEITHER DURST MAN ASKE      12  46  92  20
    LEAVE, LEAVE, FOR SHAME, OR ELSE (GOOD JUDGE) DECREE,  TO PONTIUS WASHING HANDS  15  46  94  23
    TO SHAME HIS SPRING.                      UPON THORNES FROM LORDS HEAD  4  46  96  23
    FOR WHICH IT IS NO SHAME,                 ON A PRAYER BOOKE           79  46 126 139
    OF MARTYR, YET SHEE THINKES IT SHAME      IN MEMORY OF LADY MADRE TERESA 16 46 131  52
    O IN THAT MORNING OF MY SHAME. WHEN I     TO THE MORNING               5  46 183 497
    AND SEEING THE LOATH'D OBJECT, HID FOR SHAME  TO THE MORNING          12  46 183 497
    ART AND ORNAMENT THE SHAME.               WISHES SUPPOSED MISTRESSE   99  46 195 479
    OR IF THERE BE SUCH SONNS OF SHAME,       TO THE NAME OF JESUS       228  52 239  30
    SEE HIS HORN'D FACE, & DY FOR SHAME.      IN GLORIOUS EPIPHANIE       99  52 253  39
    FOR FRUIT OF SORROW & OF SHAME,           OFFICE H. CROSS SIXT         6  52 270  97
    THY SORROWS CHIDE OUR SHAME.              OFFICE H. CROSS COMPLINE    21  52 274 105
    OF MY SIN'S SHAME.                        CHARITAS NIMIA              60  52 280  46
    OF MARTYR. YET SHE THINKS IT SHAME        TERESA                      16  52 315  52
    GIVE HIM THE VEIL, WHO KINDLY TAKES THE SHAME.  FLAMING HEART         58  52 324  61
    FOR WHICH IT IS NO SHAME                  PRAYER TO GENTLE-WOMAN      85  52 328 139
```

```
                                                                                         PAGE  363

SHAME OF THY MOTHER SOYLE. ILL-NURTUR'D TREE.         HORATIJ ILLE & NEFASTO             1    MS 382 530
WHEN NIGHT BEHELD THEM, SHAME DID ALMOST TURNE        UPON GUNPOWDER TREASON             11   MS 387 461

SHAM'D

OUR SINNES HAVE SHAM'D INTO A ROSE.                   AN HIMNE FOR CIRCUMCISION          12   46 141  37
SHAM'D NOT SPITEFULLY TO WAST                         UPON DEATH OF DESIRED HERRYS       44   46 168 467
OUR SINS HAVE SHAM'D INTO A ROSE.                     NEW YEAR'S DAY                     12   52 251  37

SHAMES

MORE SUMMER IN THEIR SHAMES REFLECTION,               UPON TWO GREENE APRICOCKES          8   48 220 494

SHAMETH

THAT SWEET BLUSH OF THINE THAT SHAMETH                OUT OF THE ITALIAN (1)              3   46 188 545

SHAMEFAC'T

THE SHAMEFAC'T LAMP HUNG DOWN HIS HEAD                IN GLORIOUS EPIPHANIE             118   52 253  39

SHAPE

AND IN A PALE GHOST'S SHAPE TO SPARE HIS EYES.        SOSPETTO D'HERODE                 416   46 109 216
JOSEPH THE KINGS DEAD BROTHERS SHAPE SHE TAKES,       SOSPETTO D'HERODE                 419   46 109 216
THY SELFE INTO A SHAPE THAT MAY BECOME THEE.          SOSPETTO D'HERODE                 462   46 109 216
WAS EVER GUILTY OF, CHANGE WEE OUR SHAPE,             AN APOLOGIE FOR HYMNE (TERESA)     34   46 136  59
AND SHAPE OF SWEETNES, BE THEY SUCH                   TO THE NAME OF JESUS               38   52 239  30
IN WHATSOE'RE MORE SACRED SHAPE                       IN GLORIOUS EPIPHANIE              89   52 253  39
WAS EVER GUILTY OF, CHANGE WE TOO 'OUR SHAPE          AN APOLOGIE FOR (TERESA) HYMNE     34   52 322  59

SHAPES

REVENGE THY BOUNTYES IN THEIR BEAUTEOUS SHAPES.       IN GLORIOUS EPIPHANIE             106   52 253  39
BUT PAINTED SHAPES,                                   TO SAME CONCERNING CHOISE          11   52 331  66

SHARE

THEIR SHARE, IN THY MEMORIALL.                        NEITHER DURST MAN ASKE             22   46  92  20
NOR HATH GOD A THINNER SHARE,                         GIVE TO CAESAR AND TO GOD           3   46  96  20
SO DEEP A SHARE                                       SANCTA MARIA DOLORUM               82   52 283 162
THY SCARLET ROBES, FOR HEERE YOU MUST NOT SHARE       UPON GUNPOWDER TREASON              5   MS 387 461
DOTH GRASPE THE FATE OF THINGES, AND SHARE TH' EVENTS OUT OF GROTIUS                      2   MS 398 198

SHAR'D

IN CONTROVERTING WARBLES EVENLY SHAR'D,               MUSICKS DUELL                      42   46 149 535

SHARES

WHY SHOULD A PIECE OF PEEVISH CLAY PLEAD SHARES       CHARITAS NIMIA                     31   52 280  48
O LET ME, HERE, CLAIM SHARES.                         SANCTA MARIA DOLORUM               56   52 283 162

SHARP

OF A SURE JUDGE, FROM WHOSE SHARP RAY                 DIES IRAE                           3   52 298 186

SHARPE

SHARPE AIRES, AND STAGGERS IN A WARBLING DOUBT        MUSICKS DUELL                      58   46 149 535
NAILES, HAMMERS, HATCHETS SHARPE, AND HALTERS STRONG, SOSPETTO D'HERODE                 325   46 109 216
IF THOSE SHARPE RAYES PUTTING ON                      LOVES HOROSCOPE                    21   46 165 483
(SHARPE SIGHTED AS THE EAGLES EYE, THAT CAN           ON FRONTISPIECE ISAACSONS           9   46 191 491

SHARPLY

AND CATCHE THY QUICK REFLEX. AND SHARPLY SEE          IN GLORIOUS EPIPHANIE             193   52 253  39

SHEATHED

A SOULE SHEATHED IN A CHRISTALL SHRINE,               IN PRAISE OF LESSIUS               25   46 156 510

SHEATH'D

WHOSE EVER-BRANDISHT SWORD IS SHEATH'D IN BLOOD.      SOSPETTO D'HERODE                 314   46 109 216
A SOUL SHEATH'D IN A CHRISTALL SHRINE.                TEMPERANCE                         23   52 342 510

SHED

WITH UNGENTLE FLAMES, DOES SHED,                      THE TEARE                          23   46  84  50
WHY TO SHOW LOVE SHEE SHOULD SHED BLOOD,              IN MEMORY OF LADY MADRE TERESA     22   46 131  52
AND THE DEARE DROPS THIS DAY WERE SHED.               AN HIMNE FOR CIRCUMCISION           4   46 141  37
AND VAINE, AS THOSE ARE SHED                          WISHES SUPPOSED MISTRESSE          74   46 195 479
AND THE DEAR DROPS THIS DAY WERE SHED.                NEW YEAR'S DAY                      4   52 251  37
WITH UNGENTLE FLAMES DOES SHED,                       WEEPER                            161   52 307 120
WHY TO SHOW LOVE, SHE SHOULD SHED BLOOD               TERESA                             22   52 315  52
FIXT IN YOUR SPHAERES OF GLORY, SHED FROM THENCE      UPON KINGS CORONATION              39   MS 389 454

SHEAD

THE SWEET DASH OF A SHOWER NOW SHEAD,                 UPON DEATH OF DESIRED HERRYS       36   46 168 467
```

SHEDD

| | | | | |
|---|---|---|---|---|
| BRIGHT STARRE OF MAJESTY, OH SHEDD ON MEE | UPON BIRTH PRINCESSE E | 1 | MS 391 | 456 |

SHEEP

| | | | | |
|---|---|---|---|---|
| THE SHEPHEARDS, MORE THEN THEY THE SHEEP. | IN HOLY NATIVITY | 102 | 52 246 | 76 |
| AND LET THY LOST SHEEP LIVE TO'INHERIT | VEXILLA REGIS | 45 | 52 277 | 156 |
| AS WITH THY SELFE THOU FEED'ST THY SHEEP. | LAUDA SION SALVATOREM | 72 | 52 294 | 178 |
| THY SHEEP WAS STRAY'D.  AND THOU WOULDST BE | DIES IRAE | 31 | 52 298 | 186 |
| AND ALL THY LOST SHEEP FOUND SHALL BE, | DIES IRAE | 59 | 52 298 | 186 |

SHEEPE

| | | | | |
|---|---|---|---|---|
| HAPPY ME. O HAPPY SHEEPE. | PSALME 23 | 1 | 46 102 | 5 |
| THE SHEPHEARDS, WHILE THEY FEED THEIR SHEEPE. | A HYMNE OF THE NATIVITY | 82 | 46 106 | 76 |

WINDING-SHEET

| | | | | |
|---|---|---|---|---|
| IS HER LIFES WING, OR HER DEATH'S WINDING-SHEET. | AT TH' IVORY TRIBUNALL | 6 | MS 397 | 492 |

SHEETS

| | | | | |
|---|---|---|---|---|
| OFFRING THEIR WHITEST SHEETS OF SNOW, | A HYMNE OF THE NATIVITY | 37 | 46 106 | 76 |
| OFFRING THEIR WHITEST SHEETS OF SNOW | IN HOLY NATIVITY | 53 | 52 246 | 76 |
| OF THESE IGNOBLE SHEETS, | PRAYER TO GENTLE-WOMAN | 5 | 52 328 | 139 |

SHEETES

| | | | | |
|---|---|---|---|---|
| THEIR PILLOW STONE, THEIR SHEETES OF LEAD, | AN EPITAPH UPON MARRIED COUPLE | 12 | 52 339 | 478 |
| (PILLOW HARD, & SHEETES NOT WARM) | AN EPITAPH UPON MARRIED COUPLE | 13 | 52 339 | 478 |

SHELTER

| | | | | |
|---|---|---|---|---|
| FOR SHELTER TO THE SHADOW OF THY TREE. | IN GLORIOUS EPIPHANIE | 140 | 52 253 | 39 |
| TAKE SHELTER FROM THY SELF, IN THEE | DIES IRAE | 26 | 52 298 | 186 |

SHEPHARD

| | | | | |
|---|---|---|---|---|
| OUR FOOD, & FAITHFULL SHEPHARD TOO. | LAUDA SION SALVATOREM | 70 | 52 294 | 178 |

SHEPHEARD

| | | | | |
|---|---|---|---|---|
| HEE (MY SHEPHEARD) IS MY GUIDE, | PSALME 23 | 23 | 46 102 | 5 |
| STILL MY SHEPHEARD, STILL MY GOD | PSALME 23 | 45 | 46 102 | 5 |
| THY SOUL'S KIND SHEPHEARD, THY HART'S KING. | LAUDA SION SALVATOREM | 2 | 52 294 | 178 |

SHEPHEARDS

| | | | | |
|---|---|---|---|---|
| TUN'D TO MY GREAT SHEPHEARDS PRAISE. | PSALME 23 | 34 | 46 102 | 5 |
| COME WEE SHEPHEARDS WHO HAVE SEENE | A HYMNE OF THE NATIVITY | 1 | 46 106 | 76 |
| BUT TO POORE SHEPHEARDS, SIMPLE THINGS, | A HYMNE OF THE NATIVITY | 74 | 46 106 | 76 |
| THE SHEPHEARDS, WHILE THEY FEED THEIR SHEEPE. | A HYMNE OF THE NATIVITY | 82 | 46 106 | 76 |
| HEE MARKT HOW THE POORE SHEPHEARDS RAN TO PAY | SOSPETTO D'HERODE | 118 | 46 109 | 216 |
| HIS BLAZE, TO SHINE IN A POORE SHEPHEARDS EYE. | SOSPETTO D'HERODE | 170 | 46 109 | 216 |
| SO MUCH.  RUDE SHEPHEARDS.  WHAT HIS STEEDS.  ALAS | SOSPETTO D'HERODE | 527 | 46 109 | 216 |
| COME WE SHEPHEARDS WHOSE BLEST SIGHT | IN HOLY NATIVITY | 1 | 52 246 | 76 |
| BUT TO POOR SHEPHEARDS, HOME-SPUN THINGS. | IN HOLY NATIVITY | 94 | 52 246 | 76 |
| THE SHEPHEARDS, MORE THEN THEY THE SHEEP. | IN HOLY NATIVITY | 102 | 52 246 | 76 |

SHEILD

| | | | | |
|---|---|---|---|---|
| STANDS ARM'D, TO SHEILD ME FROM ALL WANTON WRONG. | ALEXIAS THIRD ELEGIE | 36 | 52 336 | 209 |

SILVER-SHEILDED

| | | | | |
|---|---|---|---|---|
| OF ALL PROUD NEPTUNES SILVER-SHEILDED GUARD. | AN ELEGIE ON DR PORTER | 34 | MS 395 | 476 |

SHIELDS

| | | | | |
|---|---|---|---|---|
| MORE SWORDS AND SHIELDS | ON A PRAYER BOOKE | 19 | 46 126 | 139 |

SHEILDS

| | | | | |
|---|---|---|---|---|
| MORE SWORDS & SHEILDS | PRAYER TO GENTLE-WOMAN | 25 | 52 328 | 139 |

SHIFTING

| | | | | |
|---|---|---|---|---|
| SORDIDLY SHIFTING HANDS WITH SHADES & NIGHT. | IN GLORIOUS EPIPHANIE | 35 | 52 253 | 39 |

SHINE

| | | | | |
|---|---|---|---|---|
| THROUGH WHICH ALL HER BRIGHT FEATURES SHINE. | IN PRAISE OF LESSIUS | 26 | 46 156 | 510 |
| TO SHINE IN THINGS SO PRETIOUS. | THE WEEPER | 18 | 46 79 | 120 |
| AN EYE OF HEAVEN, OR STILL SHINE HERE | THE TEARE | 47 | 46 84 | 50 |
| THE WORLDS LIGHT SHINES, SHINE AS IT WILL. | BUT MEN LOVED DARKNESSE | 1 | 46 97 | 13 |
| HIS BLAZE, TO SHINE IN A POORE SHEPHEARDS EYE. | SOSPETTO D'HERODE | 170 | 46 109 | 216 |
| ALL THY SORROWS HERE SHALL SHINE, | IN MEMORY OF LADY MADRE TERESA | 148 | 46 131 | 52 |
| THOU HERE ART SET TO SHINE, WHERE THY FULL DAY | AN APOLOGIE FOR HYMNE (TERESA) | 5 | 46 136 | 59 |
| COULD NOT CHUSE BUT SHINE WITHOUT. | HIS EPITAPH (HERRYS) | 36 | 46 172 | 471 |
| FELLOW THIS WONDER TOO, NOR LET HER SHINE | UPON YORKE HIS BIRTH | 55 | 46 176 | 500 |
| BUT THOU AT NOONE DOST SHINE, AND ART ALL DAY, | UPON YORKE HIS BIRTH | 78 | 46 176 | 500 |
| OF CHRYSTALL FLESH, THROUGH WHICH TO SHINE. | WISHES SUPPOSED MISTRESSE | 12 | 46 195 | 479 |

| | | | | | |
|---|---|---|---|---|---|
| WHERE YOUR EYES SHINE HIS SUNS APPEARE. | THOUGH NOW 'TIS NEITHER | 28 | MS | 397 | 492 |
| WHOSE IS THE MASTER FIRE, WHICH SUN SHOULD SHINE. | IN GLORIOUS EPIPHANIE | 144 | 52 | 253 | 39 |
| THAT NOW DOST SHINE, | OFFICE H. CROSS PRIME | 10 | 52 | 267 | 91 |
| PROMISE THE EARTH TO COUNTER SHINE | WEEPER | 11 | 52 | 307 | 120 |
| TO SHINE IN THINGS SO PRETIOUS. | WEEPER | 18 | 52 | 307 | 120 |
| ALL THY SORROWS HERE SHALL SHINE, | TERESA | 147 | 52 | 315 | 52 |
| THOU HERE ART SETT TO SHINE WHERE THY FULL DAY | AN APOLOGIE FOR (TERESA) HYMNE | 5 | 52 | 322 | 59 |
| WHAT MAGAZINS OF IMMORTALL ARMES THERE SHINE. | FLAMING HEART | 55 | 52 | 324 | 61 |
| STILL SHINE ON ME, FAIR SUNS. THAT I | A SONG | 7 | 52 | 327 | 65 |
| FAREWELL. & SHINE, FAIR SOUL, SHINE THERE ABOVE | ALEXIAS FIRST ELEGIE | 35 | 52 | 334 | 204 |
| FAREWELL. & SHINE, FAIR SOUL, SHINE THERE ABOVE | ALEXIAS FIRST ELEGIE | 35 | 52 | 334 | 204 |
| THROUGH WHICH ALL HER BRIGHT FEATURES SHINE. | TEMPERANCE | 24 | 52 | 342 | 510 |
| SHINE FORTH,YE FLAMING SPARKES OF DEITY, | UPON KINGS CORONATION | 37 | MS | 389 | 454 |
| THE LUSTRE OF HIS FACE DID SHINE SOE BRIGHT, | UPON KINGS CORONATION | 33 | MS | 390 | 453 |
| DRINKE FAYLING THERE WHERE I A GUEST DID SHINE | OUT OF GROTIUS | 51 | MS | 398 | 198 |

COUNTERSHINE

| | | | | | |
|---|---|---|---|---|---|
| PROMISE THE EARTH, TO COUNTERSHINE | THE WEEPER | 11 | 46 | 79 | 120 |

SHIN'D

| | | | | | |
|---|---|---|---|---|---|
| THOSE TWINCKLING EYES OF HEAVEN, WHICH EV'N NOW SHIN'D, | ON GUNPOWDER-TREASON | 31 | MS | 384 | 458 |

SHINES

| | | | | | |
|---|---|---|---|---|---|
| THAT THOUGH IT SHINES, 'TIS FIRE AND WILL CONSUME. | OUT OF GREEKE CUPID'S CRYER | 74 | 46 | 159 | 519 |
| THE WORLDS LIGHT SHINES, SHINE AS IT WILL, | BUT MEN LOVED DARKNESSE | 1 | 46 | 97 | 13 |
| IT SHINES, AND WITH A SOVERAIGNE RAY, | IN MEMORY OF LADY MADRE TERESA | 84 | 46 | 131 | 52 |
| IT SHINES, & WITH A SOVERAIGN RAY | TERESA | 84 | 52 | 315 | 52 |
| THERE SHINES HIS QUIVER, THERE HIS BOW. | IN CICATRICES DOMINI JESU | 4 | MS | 381 | 27 |
| THAT IN THE PRINCELY PATTERNE SHINES, FROM WHENCE | UPON BIRTH PRINCESSE E | 34 | MS | 391 | 456 |

SHINING

| | | | | | |
|---|---|---|---|---|---|
| SOULES AS THY SHINING SELFE, SHALL COME, | IN MEMORY OF LADY MADRE TERESA | 126 | 46 | 131 | 52 |
| SOULES AS THY SHINING SELF, SHALL COME | TERESA | 125 | 52 | 315 | 52 |
| NO ROOFES OF GOLD O'RE RIOTOUS TABLES SHINING | DESCRIPTION RELIGIOUS HOUSE | 1 | 52 | 338 | 213 |

SHIP

| | | | | | |
|---|---|---|---|---|---|
| A SHIP THEY SAW, NO MEN SHEE HAD, YET PREST | THE BEGINNING OF HELIODORUS | 11 | 46 | 158 | 517 |

SHIPWRACK

| | | | | | |
|---|---|---|---|---|---|
| THE CALM THAT COOLS THINE EYE DOES SHIPWRACK MINE, FOR O. | AND A CERTAINE PRIEST PASSED | 3 | 46 | 94 | 17 |

SHIPWRACKS

| | | | | | |
|---|---|---|---|---|---|
| WITH SHIPWRACKS TOILE, OH, THAT IS SWEET, | PETRONIJ ALES PHASIACIS PETITA | 13 | MS | 382 | 526 |

SHIPWRACK'T

| | | | | | |
|---|---|---|---|---|---|
| IF I BE SHIPWRACK'T, LOVE SHALL TEACH TO SWIMME. | ALEXIAS FIRST ELEGIE | 21 | 52 | 334 | 204 |

SHOALE

| | | | | | |
|---|---|---|---|---|---|
| TO USHER IN THIS SHOALE OF PRODIGIES, | ON GUNPOWDER-TREASON | 37 | MS | 384 | 458 |

SHOALES

| | | | | | |
|---|---|---|---|---|---|
| FLUTTERING IN WANTON SHOALES, AND TO THE SKY | MUSICKS DUELL | 91 | 46 | 149 | 535 |

SHOCKE

| | | | | | |
|---|---|---|---|---|---|
| OUR GIDDY FEARES WITH AN UNLOOK'T FOR SHOCKE. | HORATIJ ILLE & NEFASTO | 32 | MS | 382 | 530 |

SHONE

| | | | | | |
|---|---|---|---|---|---|
| WHEN LIFES SWEET LIGHT FIRST SHONE ON BEASTS, AND WHEN | OUT OF VIRGIL | 29 | 46 | 155 | 529 |
| WHITHER TH'HADST RATHER THERE HAVE SHONE | THE TEARE | 46 | 46 | 84 | 50 |

SHOOK

| | | | | | |
|---|---|---|---|---|---|
| THE CENTER SHOOK. HER USELESSE VEIL TH'INGLORIOUS TEMPLE TORE. | OFFICE H. CROSS NINTH | 8 | 52 | 271 | 99 |

SHOOKE

| | | | | | |
|---|---|---|---|---|---|
| HEE SHOOKE HIMSELFE, AND SPREAD HIS SPATIOUS WINGS. | SOSPETTO D'HERODE | 141 | 46 | 109 | 216 |

SHOOT

| | | | | | |
|---|---|---|---|---|---|
| HAIL, OUR ALONE HOPE. LET THY FAIR HEAD SHOOT | VEXILLA REGIS | 37 | 52 | 277 | 156 |

SHOOTS

| | | | | | |
|---|---|---|---|---|---|
| FROM THY EYES HE SHOOTS HIS ARROWES, | OUT OF THE ITALIAN (1) | 15 | 46 | 188 | 545 |

SHOOTES

   (FAIR YOUTH) SHOUTES BOTH THY SHAFT & THEE　　　　　FLAMING HEART　　　　　　　　　　　48　52　324　61

SHOO-TY

   TO GAUDY TIRE, OR GLISTRING SHOO-TY.　　　　　　　WISHES SUPPOSED MISTRESSE　　　　　18　46　195　479

SHOP

   (HIS SHOP OF FLAMES) HEE FRYES HIMSELFE, BENEATH　SOSPETTO D'HERODE　　　　　　　　　62　46　109　216
   HELLS SHOP OF SLAUGHTER SHEE DO'S OVERSEE,　　　　SOSPETTO D'HERODE　　　　　　　　291　46　109　216
   OF SHOP, OR SILKEWORMES TOYLE　　　　　　　　　　　WISHES SUPPOSED MISTRESSE　　　　　23　46　195　479
   OUT OF NO OTHER SHOP,　　　　　　　　　　　　　　　WISHES SUPPOSED MISTRESSE　　　　　29　46　195　479
   THE AIERY SHOP OF SOUL-APPEASING SOUND.　　　　　　TO THE NAME OF JESUS　　　　　　　34　52　239　30

SHOPS

   (THESE TUMULTUOUS SHOPS OF NOISE)　　　　　　　　　ON A PRAYER BOOKE　　　　　　　　　60　46　126　139
   (THOSE TUMULTUOUSE SHOPS OF NOISE)　　　　　　　　 PRAYER TO GENTLE-WOMAN　　　　　　66　52　328　139

SHORE

   LOOK'T ROUND, FIRST TO THE SEA, THEN TO THE SHORE.　THE BEGINNING OF HELIODORUS　　　　8　46　158　517
   THE SHORE THAT SHEWED THEM WHAT THE SEA DENY'D,　　THE BEGINNING OF HELIODORUS　　　　9　46　158　517
   UP TO THE THIRD RING. O'RE THE SHORE WAS SPREAD　　THE BEGINNING OF HELIODORUS　　　 14　46　158　517
   TO SEE THEMSELVES THEIR OWN SEVERER SHORE.　　　　TO COUNTESSE OF DENBIGH　　　　　 26　52　236　146
   ALONG THE SHORE IN A GRAVE PURPLE TIDE.　　　　　　ON GUNPOWDER-TREASON　　　　　　　34　MS　384　458

SHOAR

   TO FIND THEMSELVES THEIR OWN SEVERER SHOAR.　　　　AGAINST IRRESOLUTION AND DELAY　26　52　347　146

SHOURE

   THAT EARTH A SHOURE OF STONES TO HEAVEN SHALL SEND,　ON GUNPOWDER-TREASON　　　　　　22　MS　384　458

SHOURES

   WARM SYLVER SHOURES WHERE'RE HE GOES.　　　　　　　WEEPER　　　　　　　　　　　　　126　52　307　120
   WHAT MEANE THESE SHOURES OF TEARES AMONGST US MEN.　AN ELEGY MR STANNINOW　　　　　16　MS　394　473

SHORES

   THE TYRRHENE SEAS, AND SHORES SOUND ALL THE SAME,　SOSPETTO D'HERODE　　　　　　　　31　46　109　216
   BUT LY'N LOCK'T UP SAFE IN THEIR SACRED SHORES.　　ALEXIAS THIRD ELEGIE　　　　　　　 8　52　336　209

SHORT

   BY SHORT DIMINUTIVES, THAT BEING REAR'D　　　　　　MUSICKS DUELL　　　　　　　　　　41　46　149　535
   OF SHORT THICKE SOBS, WHOSE THUNDRING VOLLEYES FLOAT,　MUSICKS DUELL　　　　　　　　63　46　149　535
   AND THE SHORT CLAUSE OF MORTALL BREATH,　　　　　　ANOTHER ON HERRYS　　　　　　　　 45　46　170　469
   SHUTS THE EYES OF OUR SHORT LIGHT.　　　　　　　　 OUT OF CATULLUS　　　　　　　　　　8　46　194　523
   MADE SHORT BY LOVERS PLAY.　　　　　　　　　　　　　WISHES SUPPOSED MISTRESSE　　　　83　46　195　479
   NOR BE TO SHORT, NOR SEEME TO LONG.　　　　　　　　TO THE QUEEN　　　　　　　　　　　12　48　215　501
   WHATE'RE FALSE SHOWES OF SHORT & SLIPPERY GOOD　　 DESCRIPTION RELIGIOUS HOUSE　　　 7　52　338　213
   BUT TO LARGE YOUTH SHORT TIME TO LIVE.　　　　　　　UPON DEATH OF A FREIND　　　　　　12　MS　393　477

SHORT-CUT

   WHICH SHORT-CUT LIVES OF MURDRED INFANTS LEAVE.　　SOSPETTO D'HERODE　　　　　　　　344　46　109　216

SHORTER

   WE NOW WILL OWN NO SHORTER WISH, NOR NAME A NARROWER　OFFICE H. CROSS COMPLINE　　　 18　52　274　105
            WORD.

SHOT

   SHOT THEE LIKE LIGHTNING, TO TH'ASTONISHT EARTH.　　ON A TREATISE OF CHARITY　　　　　 6　46　137　69

BLOOD-SHOT

   LO, A BLOOD-SHOT EYE, THAT WEEPES　　　　　　　　　ON WOUNDS OF CRUCIFIED LORD　　　　7　46　99　24

SHOTT

   A SERAPHIM AT EVERY SHOTT.　　　　　　　　　　　　　FLAMING HEART　　　　　　　　　　54　52　324　61
   THE RADIANT DARTS, SHOTT FROM HIS SPARKLING EYES,　UPON KINGS CORONATION　　　　　　　35　MS　390　453
   SHOTT FROM HIS FLAMING EYE, HAD THAW'D IT'S IRE,　 AN ELEGY MR STANNINOW　　　　　　　32　MS　394　473

BLOODSHOTT

   AND LEAST THY BLOODSHOTT EYES SHOULD LEAD ASIDE　　UPON GUNPOWDER TREASON　　　　　　 7　MS　387　461

SHOULDERS

   UPON THE STOOPED SHOULDERS OF OLD TIME.　　　　　　TO THE MORNING　　　　　　　　　　28　46　183　497

SHOW

   NOR DID THE FACE OF THIS DISASTER SHOW　　　　　　　THE BEGINNING OF HELIODORUS　　　23　46　158　517
   SHOW ME HIMSELFE, HIMSELFE (BRIGHT SIR) O SHOW　　　COME SEE WHERE THE LORD LAY　　　 1　46　87　27

PAGE 366

| | | | | | |
|---|---|---|---|---|---|
| SHOW ME HIMSELFE, HIMSELFE (BRIGHT SIR) O SHOW | COME SEE WHERE THE LORD LAY | 1 | 46 | 87 | 27 |
| WERE IT ENOUGH TO SHOW THE PLACE, AND SAY, | COME SEE WHERE THE LORD LAY | 3 | 46 | 87 | 27 |
| THEN COULD I SHOW THESE ARMES OF MINE, AND SAY | COME SEE WHERE THE LORD LAY | 5 | 46 | 87 | 27 |
| WHY TO SHOW LOVE SHEE SHOULD SHED BLOOD, | IN MEMORY OF LADY MADRE TERESA | 22 | 46 | 131 | 52 |
| WHILE HE SWEETLY 'GAN TO SHOW | UPON DEATH OF DESIRED HERRYS | 40 | 46 | 168 | 467 |
| TO SHOW A FACE, FIT TO CONFESSE THY KIN | UPON STANINOUGH'S DEATH | 18 | 46 | 175 | 475 |
| THRICE WILL I PAY THREE TEARES, TO SHOW HOW TRUE | TO THE MORNING | 40 | 46 | 183 | 497 |
| YET ARE SCARCE RIPE ENOUGH AT BEST TO SHOW | UPON TWO GREENE APRICOCKES | 5 | 48 | 220 | 494 |
| THOSE PURE UNTRODEN PATHES CAN SHOW, | THOUGH NOW 'TIS NEITHER | 8 | MS | 397 | 492 |
| TO SHOW US OUGHT WORTH LOOKING AT. | IN HOLY NATIVITY | 10 | 52 | 246 | 76 |
| TELL HIM WE NOW CAN SHOW HIM MORE | IN HOLY NATIVITY | 11 | 52 | 246 | 76 |
| THREE SAD HOUR'S SACKCLOTH THEN SHALL SHOW TO US | IN GLORIOUS EPIPHANIE | 157 | 52 | 253 | 39 |
| PLEAD FOR ME, LOVE. ALLEAGE & SHOW | ADORO TE | 19 | 52 | 291 | 172 |
| AND SHOW THOU ART, BY SAVING ME. | DIES IRAE | 56 | 52 | 298 | 186 |
| WHY TO SHOW LOVE, SHE SHOULD SHED BLOOD | TERESA | 22 | 52 | 315 | 52 |
| TO SHOW US THIS FAINT SHADE FOR HER | FLAMING HEART | 22 | 52 | 324 | 61 |
| ASHAM'D THAT OUR WORLD, NOW, CAN SHOW | FLAMING HEART | 45 | 52 | 324 | 61 |
| TO SHOW A FACE, FITT TO CONFESSE THY KIN, | DEATH'S LECTURE | 19 | 52 | 340 | 475 |
| OF WHICH DOTH SHOW THE QUINTESSENCE OF ART. | UPON BIRTH PRINCESSE E | 38 | MS | 391 | 456 |

SHOW'D

| | | | | | |
|---|---|---|---|---|---|
| THEN HE E'RE SHOW'D TO MORTALL SIGHT. | IN HOLY NATIVITY | 12 | 52 | 246 | 76 |
| FOR BEING SHOW'D BY THIS DAY'S LIGHT, HOW FARR | IN GLORIOUS EPIPHANIE | 246 | 52 | 253 | 39 |
| EVEN WHEN HE SHOW'D MOST POOR, | WEEPER | 117 | 52 | 307 | 120 |
| OFT HAVE THESE ARMES (ALAS.) SHOW'D TO THESE EYES | LUKE 2. QUAERIT JESUM | 43 | MS | 379 | 11 |

SHEW

| | | | | | |
|---|---|---|---|---|---|
| THY SHADOW PETER, MUST SHEW ME THE SUN, | SICKE IMPLORE SHADOW | 3 | 46 | 87 | 28 |
| TO SHEW US OUGHT WORTH LOOKING AT. | A HYMNE OF THE NATIVITY | 10 | 46 | 106 | 76 |
| TELL HIM WEE NOW CAN SHEW HIM MORE | A HYMNE OF THE NATIVITY | 11 | 46 | 106 | 76 |
| BRIGHTER HOPES THEN HE CAN SHEW. | UPON DEATH OF DESIRED HERRYS | 18 | 46 | 168 | 467 |
| TO SHEW HER TO HER SELFE IN SUCH ANOTHER. | UPON YORKE HIS BIRTH | 54 | 46 | 176 | 500 |
| AND MY MOUTH SHALL SHEW FORTH THY PRAYSE. | OFFICE H. CROSS MATINES | 4 | 52 | 265 | 86 |
| O SWEET INCENDIARY, SHEW HERE THY ART, | FLAMING HEART | 85 | 52 | 324 | 61 |

SHEW'D

| | | | | | |
|---|---|---|---|---|---|
| SHEW'D, THAT STERNE WARRE HAD NEWLY BATH'D HIM THERE | THE BEGINNING OF HELIODORUS | 22 | 46 | 158 | 517 |
| THE BABE LOOKT UP, AND SHEW'D HIS FACE. | A HYMNE OF THE NATIVITY | 19 | 46 | 106 | 76 |
| SUCH AS AT THEBES DIRE FEAST SHEE SHEW'D HER HEAD. | SOSPETTO D'HERODE | 397 | 46 | 109 | 216 |
| SHEW'D HIM HIS FEARES, AND KILL'D HIM WITH THE SIGHT. | SOSPETTO D'HERODE | 504 | 46 | 109 | 216 |
| PEEP'T FROM THEIR BUDS, SHEW'D LIKE THE GARDENS EYES | UPON YORKE HIS BIRTH | 62 | 46 | 176 | 500 |
| THE BABE LOOK'T UP & SHEW'D HIS FACE. | IN HOLY NATIVITY | 19 | 52 | 246 | 76 |

SHEWD

| | | | | | |
|---|---|---|---|---|---|
| THEN HEE E'RE SHEWD TO MORTALL SIGHT, | A HYMNE OF THE NATIVITY | 12 | 46 | 106 | 76 |

SHEWED

| | | | | | |
|---|---|---|---|---|---|
| THE SHORE THAT SHEWED THEM WHAT THE SEA DENY'D, | THE BEGINNING OF HELIODORUS | 9 | 46 | 158 | 517 |

SHEWES

| | | | | | |
|---|---|---|---|---|---|
| SHEWES THE TWO TERMES AND LIMITS OF TIME'S RACE. | ON FRONTISPIECE ISAACSONS | 22 | 46 | 191 | 491 |

SHOWES

| | | | | | |
|---|---|---|---|---|---|
| MORE SWEETLY SHOWES THE BLUSHING BRIDE. | IN PRAISE OF LESSIUS | 30 | 46 | 156 | 510 |
| WHERE DAWNING HOPE NO BEAME OF COMFORT SHOWES. | SOSPETTO D'HERODE | 242 | 46 | 109 | 216 |
| (THROUGH ALL YOUR PAINTING) SHOWES YOU YOUR OWN FACE. | UPON STANINOUGH'S DEATH | 22 | 46 | 175 | 475 |
| SHOWES THIS THE MOTHER SERAPHIM. | FLAMING HEART | 16 | 52 | 324 | 61 |
| WHATE'RE FALSE SHOWES OF SHORT & SLIPPERY GOOD | DESCRIPTION RELIGIOUS HOUSE | 7 | 52 | 338 | 213 |
| (THOUGH YOU BE PAINTED) SHOWES YOU YOUR TRUE FACE. | DEATH'S LECTURE | 24 | 52 | 340 | 475 |
| MORE SWEETLY SHOWES THE BLUSHING BRIDE. | TEMPERANCE | 28 | 52 | 342 | 510 |

SHOWNE

| | | | | | |
|---|---|---|---|---|---|
| HERE OR NO WHERE HEE'D HAVE SHOWNE IT. | ANOTHER ON HERRYS | 6 | 46 | 170 | 469 |

SHOWER

| | | | | | |
|---|---|---|---|---|---|
| THE SWEET DASH OF A SHOWER NOW SHEAD, | UPON DEATH OF DESIRED HERRYS | 36 | 46 | 168 | 467 |
| AS TO REFRAINE) BROUGHT FORTH A COSTLY SHOWER | UPON KINGS CORONATION | 6 | MS | 390 | 453 |
| THAT SOL FROM THEM MAY SUCK AN HONIED SHOWER, | UPON BIRTH PRINCESSE E | 5 | MS | 391 | 456 |

SHOWR

| | | | | | |
|---|---|---|---|---|---|
| DROPPING WITH A BAULMY SHOWR | PRAYER TO GENTLE-WOMAN | 109 | 52 | 328 | 139 |

SHOWRE

| | | | | | |
|---|---|---|---|---|---|
| DROPPING WITH A BALMY SHOWRE | ON A PRAYER BOOKE | 103 | 46 | 126 | 139 |
| AND USE THE SEASON OF LOVE'S SHOWRE. | TO COUNTESSE OF DENBIGH | 44 | 52 | 236 | 146 |
| WHICH THEIR BRIGHT FATHER IN A PRETIOUS SHOWRE | AN ELEGY MR STANNINOW | 9 | MS | 394 | 473 |

SHOWERS

| | | | | | |
|---|---|---|---|---|---|
| HIMSELFE INTO HER LAP IN FRUITFULL SHOWERS. | OUT OF VIRGIL | 6 | 46 | 155 | 529 |
| SENTENTIOUS SHOWERS, O LET THEM FALL, | UPON THE DEATH OF A GENTLEMAN | 29 | 46 | 166 | 472 |
| ALL THE SWEETEST SHOWERS, | ON THE ASSUMPTION | 47 | 46 | 139 | 114 |
| SYDNOEAN SHOWERS | WISHES SUPPOSED MISTRESSE | 88 | 46 | 195 | 479 |

|   |   |   |   |   |   |
|---|---|---|---|---|---|
| AND KNOW THE CALL OF HEAV'N'S KIND SHOWERS. | AGAINST IRRESOLUTION AND DELAY | 34 | 52 | 347 | 146 |

SHOWRES

|   |   |   |   |   |   |
|---|---|---|---|---|---|
| NO APRIL E'RE LENT SOFTER SHOWRES. | THE WEEPER | 89 | 46 | 79 | 120 |
| WATER'D BY THE SHOWRES THEY BRING. | ON BLEEDING WOUNDS OF LORD | 21 | 46 | 101 | 110 |
| YET WHEN YOUNG APRILS HUSBAND SHOWRES, | A HYMNE OF THE NATIVITY | 77 | 46 | 106 | 76 |
| GASP FOR THY GOLDEN SHOWRES.  WITH LONG STRETCH'T HANDS | TO THE NAME OF JESUS | 130 | 52 | 239 | 30 |
| THE SERIOUS SHOWRES ALONG HIS DECENT FLOW, TARDY FOUNTS. & INTO DECENT SHOWRES | OFFICE H. CROSS THIRD | 6 | 52 | 268 | 93 |
| IN SHOWRES, AS IF THINE EYES HAD NONE. | SANCTA MARIA DOLORUM | 87 | 52 | 283 | 162 |
| ALL THE SWEETEST SHOWRES | UPON BLEEDING CRUCIFIX | 6 | 52 | 288 | 110 |
| NO APRIL ERE LENT KINDER SHOWRES. | IN GLORIOUS ASSUMPTION B. LADY | 52 | 52 | 304 | 114 |
| BY YOUR OWN SHOWRES SEASONABLY DASH'T | WEEPER | 83 | 52 | 307 | 120 |
| O FLOUDS, O FIRES. O SUNS O SHOWRES. | WEEPER | 86 | 52 | 307 | 120 |
|   | WEEPER | 101 | 52 | 307 | 120 |

SHOWRS

|   |   |   |   |   |   |
|---|---|---|---|---|---|
| IN BALMY SHOWRS. | TO THE NAME OF JESUS | 169 | 52 | 239 | 30 |
| YET WHEN YOUNG APRIL'S HUSBAND SHOWRS | IN HOLY NATIVITY | 97 | 52 | 246 | 76 |

SHREDDS

|   |   |   |   |   |   |
|---|---|---|---|---|---|
| NOR BY ALTERNATE SHREDDS OF LIGHT | IN GLORIOUS EPIPHANIE | 34 | 52 | 253 | 39 |

SHREEKE

|   |   |   |   |   |   |
|---|---|---|---|---|---|
| AND GAVE A GASTLY SHREEKE, WHOSE HORRID YELL | SOSPETTO D'HERODE | 150 | 46 | 109 | 216 |

SHRILL

|   |   |   |   |   |   |
|---|---|---|---|---|---|
| BY THAT SHRILL TASTE, SHEE COULD DOE SOMETHING TOO. | MUSICKS DUELL | 26 | 46 | 149 | 535 |
| HORACE. SHRILL, AT ONCE. AS WHEN THE TRUMPETS CALL | MUSICKS DUELL | 54 | 46 | 149 | 535 |
| AND WHILE SHEE THUS DISCHARGES A SHRILL PEALE | MUSICKS DUELL | 97 | 46 | 149 | 535 |
| IN SHRILL TONGU'D ACCENTS. STRIVING TO BEE SINGLE. | MUSICKS DUELL | 130 | 46 | 149 | 535 |
| THE EARLY LARKES SHRILL ORIZONS TO BE | TO THE MORNING | 43 | 46 | 183 | 497 |
| THE SHRILL WINDS CHIDE, THE WATERS WEEP THY STAY. | IN GLORIOUS ASSUMPTION B. LADY | 28 | 52 | 304 | 114 |
| OFT TO THY EASY EARES HATH THIS SHRILL TONGUE | LUKE 2.  QUAERIT JESUM | 29 | MS | 379 | 11 |
| AMAZED TRITON WITH HIS SHRILL ALARMES | UPON GUNPOWDER TREASON | 31 | MS | 386 | 460 |
| THE MUSICK OF HIS NAME YETT SOUNDETH SHRILL. | UPON DEATH OF A FREIND | 22 | MS | 393 | 477 |

SHRILLEST

|   |   |   |   |   |   |
|---|---|---|---|---|---|
| THEE, WITH THE SHRILLEST TRUMPE OF FAME. | NEITHER DURST MAN ASKE | 24 | 46 | 92 | 20 |

SHRINE

|   |   |   |   |   |   |
|---|---|---|---|---|---|
| A SOULE SHEATHED IN A CHRISTALL SHRINE, | IN PRAISE OF LESSIUS | 25 | 46 | 156 | 510 |
| THAT WHILE I LAY THEM ON THE SHRINE | ON MR. G. HERBERTS BOOKE | 17 | 46 | 130 | 68 |
| IDAEA, TAKE A SHRINE | WISHES SUPPOSED MISTRESSE | 11 | 46 | 195 | 479 |
| A SOUL SHEATH'D IN A CHRISTALL SHRINE. | TEMPERANCE | 23 | 52 | 342 | 510 |
| AM STILL REFUS'D.  BEFORE THE INFANT SHRINE | OUT OF GROTIUS | 36 | MS | 398 | 198 |

SHRIN'D

|   |   |   |   |   |   |
|---|---|---|---|---|---|
| SO SWEET THE TEMPLE WAS, THAT SHRIN'D | ANOTHER ON HERRYS | 15 | 46 | 170 | 469 |

SHRINK

|   |   |   |   |   |   |
|---|---|---|---|---|---|
| COME DEATH, COME BANDS, NOR DO YOU SHRINK, MY EARS, | I AM READY NOT ONELY BOUND | 1 | 46 | 98 | 29 |
| TYPES YEILD TO TRUTHES.  SHADES SHRINK AWAY. | LAUDA SION SALVATOREM | 23 | 52 | 294 | 178 |

SHRINKE

|   |   |   |   |   |   |
|---|---|---|---|---|---|
| AND NOW THAT GRAVE ASPECT HATH DEIGN'D TO SHRINKE | UPON BISHOP ANDREWES PICTURE | 13 | 46 | 163 | 490 |
| THAT THE GREAT ANGELL-BLINDING LIGHT SHOULD SHRINK | SOSPETTO D'HERODE | 169 | 46 | 109 | 216 |
| HUGE EMPTINESSE CONTRACT THY BULKE, AND SHRINK | UPON STANINOUGH'S DEATH | 13 | 46 | 175 | 475 |
| HUGE EMPTYNES. CONTRACT THY SELF. & SHRINKE | DEATH'S LECTURE | 14 | 52 | 340 | 475 |
| I SHRINKE NOT.  BUT THUS READY STAND TO BEARE | OUT OF GROTIUS | 7 | MS | 398 | 198 |

SHRINKES

|   |   |   |   |   |   |
|---|---|---|---|---|---|
| SHRINKES, LIKE THE SICK MOONE AT THE WHOLSOME MORNE. | ON HOPE | 20 | 46 | 143 | 71 |
| SHRINKES, AS THE SICK MOON FROM THE WHOLSOME MORN. | (ON) HOPE | 10 | 52 | 345 | 71 |

SHROWD

|   |   |   |   |   |   |
|---|---|---|---|---|---|
| IN THIS INFERNALL MAJESTY CLOSE SHROWD | UPON GUNPOWDER TREASON | 23 | MS | 387 | 461 |
| DOTH HEE IN DOWNY SNOW THERE CLOSELY SHROWD | AN ELEGY MR STANNINOW | 3 | MS | 394 | 473 |

SHRUNKE

|   |   |   |   |   |   |
|---|---|---|---|---|---|
| GREAT NATURES SELFE HATH SHRUNKE AND SPOKE MEE GOD. | OUT OF GROTIUS | 50 | MS | 398 | 198 |

SHUT

|   |   |   |   |   |   |
|---|---|---|---|---|---|
| HATH SHUT THESE DOORES OF HEAVEN, THAT DURST | I AM THE DOORE | 5 | 46 | 90 | 17 |
| ETERNITY SHUT IN A SPAN. | A HYMNE OF THE NATIVITY | 54 | 46 | 106 | 76 |
| BUT SHUT THEIR FLOWRY LIDS FOR EVER. NIGHT, | SOSPETTO D'HERODE | 379 | 46 | 109 | 216 |
| SHUT IN THEIR TEARES.  SHUT OUT THEIR MISERYES. | TO THE MORNING | 58 | 46 | 183 | 497 |
| SHUT IN THEIR TEARES.  SHUT OUT THEIR MISERYES. | TO THE MORNING | 58 | 46 | 183 | 497 |

## SHUTT

| | | | | |
|---|---|---|---|---|
| AETERNITY SHUTT IN A SPAN. | IN HOLY NATIVITY | 80 | 52 246 | 76 |
| EAGLES, AND SHUTT OUR EYES THAT WE MAY SEE. | IN GLORIOUS EPIPHANIE | 232 | 52 253 | 39 |
| THE DOOR WAS SHUTT, THE FOUNTAIN SEAL'D. | O GLORIOSA DOMINA | 33 | 52 302 | 194 |
| THE DOOR WAS SHUTT, YET LET IN DAY, | O GLORIOSA DOMINA | 35 | 52 302 | 194 |

## SELF-SHUTT

| | | | | |
|---|---|---|---|---|
| THE SELF-SHUTT CABINET OF AN UNSEARCHT SOUL. | TO COUNTESSE OF DENBIGH | 36 | 52 236 | 146 |

## SHUTS

| | | | | |
|---|---|---|---|---|
| THAT SHUTS NIGHTS DYING EYES, SHALL OPEN MINE. | TO THE MORNING | 46 | 46 183 | 497 |
| SHUTS THE EYES OF OUR SHORT LIGHT. | OUT OF CATULLUS | 8 | 46 194 | 523 |

## SHUTTING

| | | | | |
|---|---|---|---|---|
| THE SHUTTING OF HIS EYE SHALL OPEN THEIRS. | IN GLORIOUS EPIPHANIE | 162 | 52 253 | 39 |

## SIBILLS

| | | | | |
|---|---|---|---|---|
| SIBILLS DIVINING LEAVES. HEE DOES ENQUIRE | SOSPETTO D'HERODE | 92 | 46 109 | 216 |

## SYBYLL

| | | | | |
|---|---|---|---|---|
| BOTH THE PSALM AND SYBYLL SINGS | DIES IRAE | 2 | 52 298 | 186 |

## SICK

| | | | | |
|---|---|---|---|---|
| KINDLY SUPPLIES SICK NATURE, AND DOTH MOLD | OUT OF VIRGIL | 35 | 46 155 | 529 |
| SHRINKES, LIKE THE SICK MOONE AT THE WHOLSOME MORNE. | ON HOPE | 20 | 46 143 | 71 |
| SICK HIMSELFE TO HAVE SAV'D HIM. | ANOTHER ON HERRYS | 26 | 46 170 | 469 |
| SHRINKES, AS THE SICK MOON FROM THE WHOLSOME MORN. | (ON) HOPE | 10 | 52 345 | 71 |

## LOVE-SICK

| | | | | |
|---|---|---|---|---|
| BY THE LOVE-SICK WORLD BIN MADE | IN GLORIOUS EPIPHANIE | 136 | 52 253 | 39 |

## SICKNES

| | | | | |
|---|---|---|---|---|
| THE QUEENE OF NIGHT GOTT THE GREENE SICKNES THEN, | UPON GUNPOWDER TREASON | 23 | MS 386 | 460 |

## SICKNESSE

| | | | | |
|---|---|---|---|---|
| SICKNESSE WOULD HAVE GLADLY BEEN, | ANOTHER ON HERRYS | 25 | 46 170 | 469 |
| SICKNESSE, AND SORROW, WHOSE PALE LIDDS NE'RE KNOW | TO THE MORNING | 56 | 46 183 | 497 |

## SIDE

| | | | | |
|---|---|---|---|---|
| AS EVER SILVER-TIPT, THE SIDE OF SHADY MOUNTAINE. | TO PONTIUS WASHING HANDS | 8 | 46 94 | 23 |
| OPENING THE PURPLE WARDROBE OF THY SIDE. | ON CRUCIFIED LORD BLOODY | 4 | 46 100 | 24 |
| FROM THY HEAD, AND FROM THY SIDE, | ON BLEEDING WOUNDS OF LORD | 3 | 46 101 | 110 |
| BUT O THY SIDE, THY DEEPE DIG'D SIDE | ON BLEEDING WOUNDS OF LORD | 13 | 46 101 | 110 |
| BUT O THY SIDE, THY DEEPE DIG'D SIDE | ON BLEEDING WOUNDS OF LORD | 13 | 46 101 | 110 |
| HEE'S BEFORE ME,ON MY SIDE, | PSALME 23 | 24 | 46 102 | 5 |
| YET ON THE OTHER SIDE, FAINE WOULD HE START | SOSPETTO D'HERODE | 153 | 46 109 | 216 |
| AND ON DEATH'S SIDE | OFFICE H. CROSS THIRD | 12 | 52 268 | 93 |
| FROM THY HANDS & FROM THY SIDE | UPON BLEEDING CRUCIFIX | 3 | 52 288 | 110 |
| BUT O THY SIDE, THEY DEEP-DIGG'D SIDE. | UPON BLEEDING CRUCIFIX | 17 | 52 288 | 110 |
| BUT O THY SIDE, THEY DEEP-DIGG'D SIDE. | UPON BLEEDING CRUCIFIX | 17 | 52 288 | 110 |
| OPENING THE PURPLE WARDROBE IN THY SIDE. | UPON BODY OF OUR LORD | 4 | 52 290 | 24 |
| AT LEAST THE SUFFRING SIDE OF THEE. | ADORO TE | 24 | 52 291 | 172 |
| THOSE LIMBS OF DEATH FROM THY LEFT SIDE, | DIES IRAE | 62 | 52 298 | 186 |
| SOE NEARE, IT PROV'D HIS VERY SIDE. | IN CICATRICES DOMINI JESU | 8 | MS 381 | 27 |
| A BLOODY SIDE, & HAND, & HEART. | IN CICATRICES DOMINI JESU | 16 | MS 381 | 27 |

## SIDES

| | | | | |
|---|---|---|---|---|
| WHILE HIS STEELE SIDES SOUND WITH HIS TAYLES STRONG LASH. | SOSPETTO D'HERODE | 64 | 46 109 | 216 |

## SIFTING

| | | | | |
|---|---|---|---|---|
| SIFTING THE SOULES OF GUILT, & YOU, (OH YOU,) | HORATIJ ILLE & NEFASTO | 36 | MS 382 | 530 |

## SIGH

| | | | | |
|---|---|---|---|---|
| STILL AT EACH SIGH, THAT IS EACH STOP. | THE WEEPER | 107 | 46 79 | 120 |
| TO WAIT UPON EACH MORNING SIGH. | ON MR. G. HERBERTS BOOKE | 8 | 46 130 | 68 |
| IN A DISOLVING SIGH, AND THEN | IN MEMORY OF LADY MADRE TERESA | 118 | 46 131 | 52 |
| AS SIGH WITH SUPPLE WIND | TO THE NAME OF JESUS | 39 | 52 239 | 30 |
| IF SIN CAN SIGH, LOVE CAN FORGIVE. | DIES IRAE | 47 | 52 298 | 186 |
| STILL AT EACH SIGH, THAT IS, EACH STOP, | WEEPER | 143 | 52 307 | 120 |
| SO SIGH TORMENTED SWEETS, OPPREST | WEEPER | 158 | 52 307 | 120 |
| IN A RESOLVING SIGH, AND THEN | TERESA | 117 | 52 315 | 52 |
| AND SING, & SIGH, & WORK, AND SLEEP AGAIN. | DESCRIPTION RELIGIOUS HOUSE | 17 | 52 338 | 213 |
| A KISSE, A SIGH, AND SO AWAY. | TEMPERANCE | 50 | 52 342 | 510 |
| (WHEN ONE POOR SIGH SENDS FOR HIM DOWN) | AGAINST IRRESOLUTION AND DELAY | 74 | 52 347 | 146 |

## SIGH'D

| | | | | |
|---|---|---|---|---|
| A SAD YOAKE, UNDER WHICH THEY SIGH'D IN VAINE, | SOSPETTO D'HERODE | 407 | 46 109 | 216 |
| AND LOOKING ON THEIR LOST STATE SIGH'D AGAINE. | SOSPETTO D'HERODE | 408 | 46 109 | 216 |

## SIGHS

| | | | | |
|---|---|---|---|---|
| SHEE SEEKES, SHEE SIGHS, BUT NO WHERE SPYES HIM. | OUT OF GREEKE CUPID'S CRYER | 3 | 46 159 | 519 |
| SIGHS TO HIS SILVER MATE. RISE UP MY LOVE, | ON THE ASSUMPTION | 8 | 46 139 | 114 |
| SINCE SIGHS DOE RISE, AND TEARES DOE FALL. | UPON DEATH OF A FREIND | 4 | MS 393 | 477 |

## SIGHES

| | | | | |
|---|---|---|---|---|
| EACH HERBE A PLAGUE. THE WINDS SIGHES TIMED-BEE | SOSPETTO D'HERODE | 348 | 46 109 | 216 |
| SIGHES TO HIS SYLVER MATE RISE UP, MY LOVE, | IN GLORIOUS ASSUMPTION B. LADY | 8 | 52 304 | 114 |
| EACH SOULE IN SIGHES HAD SPENT ITS DEAREST BREATH, | UPON GUNPOWDER TREASON | 41 | MS 386 | 460 |
| TEARES FALL TOO LOW, SIGHES RISE TOO HIGH, | UPON DEATH OF A FREIND | 5 | MS 393 | 477 |

## SIGHT

| | | | | |
|---|---|---|---|---|
| THEN HEE E'RE SHEWD TO MORTALL SIGHT, | A HYMNE OF THE NATIVITY | 12 | 46 106 | 76 |
| WEE SAW THEE (AND WEE BLEST THE SIGHT) | A HYMNE OF THE NATIVITY | 33 | 46 106 | 76 |
| WELCOME TO OUR WONDRING SIGHT | A HYMNE OF THE NATIVITY | 53 | 46 106 | 76 |
| AND SERVES MY PURER SIGHT, ONELY TO BEAT | SOSPETTO D'HERODE | 203 | 46 109 | 216 |
| EARTH NOW SHOULD SEE, AND TREMBLE AT THE SIGHT. | SOSPETTO D'HERODE | 256 | 46 109 | 216 |
| WITH A CHANG'D COUNTENANCE WITNEST THE SIGHT, | SOSPETTO D'HERODE | 375 | 46 109 | 216 |
| HEAV'N SAW HER RISE, AND SAW HELL IN THE SIGHT. | SOSPETTO D'HERODE | 377 | 46 109 | 216 |
| SHEW'D HIM HIS FEARES, AND KILL'D HIM WITH THE SIGHT. | SOSPETTO D'HERODE | 504 | 46 109 | 216 |
| FEED FOR EVER THEIR FAIRE SIGHT | ON THE ASSUMPTION | 34 | 46 139 | 114 |
| FROM HIS MOTHER NATURES SIGHT. | UPON DEATH OF DESIRED HERRYS | 72 | 46 168 | 467 |
| HOW AT THE SIGHT DID'ST THOU DRAW BACK THINE EYES, | TO THE MORNING | 7 | 46 183 | 497 |
| COME WE SHEPHEARDS WHOSE BLEST SIGHT | IN HOLY NATIVITY | 1 | 52 246 | 76 |
| THEN HE E'RE SHOW'D TO MORTALL SIGHT. | IN HOLY NATIVITY | 12 | 52 246 | 76 |
| WE SAW THEE. & WE BLEST THE SIGHT | IN HOLY NATIVITY | 35 | 52 246 | 76 |
| WE SAW THEE. & WE BLEST THE SIGHT. | IN HOLY NATIVITY | 76 | 52 246 | 76 |
| WELLCOME, ALL WONDERS IN ONE SIGHT. | IN HOLY NATIVITY | 79 | 52 246 | 76 |
| BLACK, AS THE DAY WAS DISMALL, IN WHOSE SIGHT | HORATIJ ILLE & NEFASTO | 5 | MS 382 | 530 |
| THEIR APPETITES WERE GONE AT TH' VERY SIGHT. | UPON GUNPOWDER TREASON | 49 | MS 387 | 461 |
| WITHHELD HER VAILE, H' HAD FORFEITED HIS SIGHT. | UPON KINGS CORONATION | 20 | MS 390 | 453 |
| OLD CLOUDS OF THICKEST BLINDNESSE FLED MY SIGHT | OUT OF GROTIUS | 71 | MS 398 | 198 |

## SIGHTED

| | | | | |
|---|---|---|---|---|
| (SHARPE SIGHTED AS THE EAGLES EYE, THAT CAN | ON FRONTISPIECE ISAACSONS | 9 | 46 191 | 491 |

## SIGHTS

| | | | | |
|---|---|---|---|---|
| SIGHTS WHICH ARE NOT SEEN WITH EYES, | ON A PRAYER BOOKE | 64 | 46 126 | 139 |
| SIGHTS WHICH ARE NOT SEEN WITH EYES. | PRAYER TO GENTLE-WOMAN | 70 | 52 328 | 139 |

## SIGN

| | | | | |
|---|---|---|---|---|
| LORD, BY THY SWEET & SAVING SIGN. | OFFICE H. CROSS MATINES | 1 | 52 265 | 86 |
| VICTORIOUS SIGN | OFFICE H. CROSS PRIME | 9 | 52 267 | 91 |

## SIGNE

| | | | | |
|---|---|---|---|---|
| IS WHAT IN SIGNE OF JOY AMONG THE BLEST | SOSPETTO D'HERODE | 197 | 46 109 | 216 |

## SIGNES

| | | | | |
|---|---|---|---|---|
| WHEN THE BLEST SIGNES THOU BROKE SHALL SEE, | LAUDA SION SALVATOREM | 55 | 52 294 | 178 |

## SILENCE

| | | | | |
|---|---|---|---|---|
| YET IS THEIR SILENCE UNTO THEE. | NEITHER DURST MAN ASKE | 17 | 46 92 | 20 |
| THEIR SILENCE SPEAKES ALOUD, AND IS | NEITHER DURST MAN ASKE | 19 | 46 92 | 20 |
| THY SILENCE. SPEAKE. AND SHE SHALL TAKE FROM THENCE | UPON YORKE HIS BIRTH | 110 | 46 176 | 500 |
| AND KEEPE SILENCE ROUND ABOUT THEE. | OUT OF THE ITALIAN (1) | 36 | 46 188 | 545 |
| SILENCE, & SACRED REST. PEACE, & PURE JOYES. | DESCRIPTION RELIGIOUS HOUSE | 32 | 52 338 | 213 |
| WITHOUT RELIGIOUS SILENCE. ABOVE ALL | HORATIJ ILLE & NEFASTO | 47 | MS 382 | 530 |
| OF DEEPEST SILENCE ANSWERED MY COMMAND. | OUT OF GROTIUS | 84 | MS 398 | 198 |

## SILENC'T

| | | | | |
|---|---|---|---|---|
| SILENC'T THE MORNING-SONS, & DAMP'T THEIR SONG | IN GLORIOUS EPIPHANIE | 130 | 52 253 | 39 |

## SILENT

| | | | | |
|---|---|---|---|---|
| AND WITH SOFT FEET SEARCHES THE SILENT ROOMES. | SOSPETTO D'HERODE | 400 | 46 109 | 216 |
| FOR THEE I TALK TO TREES. WITH SILENT GROVES | ALEXIAS SECONDE ELEGIE | 13 | 52 335 | 207 |
| TO WHOM HEAVENS LAMPES OFTEN IN SILENT NIGHT | UPON KINGS CORONATION | 27 | MS 389 | 454 |

## SILK

| | | | | |
|---|---|---|---|---|
| WELLCOME. THOUGH NOR TO GOLD NOR SILK. | IN HOLY NATIVITY | 85 | 52 246 | 76 |

## SILKE

| | | | | |
|---|---|---|---|---|
| WELCOME, THOUGH NOT TO GOLD, NOR SILKE. | A HYMNE OF THE NATIVITY | 59 | 46 106 | 76 |

SYLK

NO SAILES OF TYRIAN SYLK PROUD PAVEMENTS SWEEPING.    DESCRIPTION RELIGIOUS HOUSE         3   52 338 213

SILKEN

WHOSE SILKEN FLATTERYES SWELL A FEW FOND HOURES       UPON STANINOUGH'S DEATH             8   46 175 475
TWO SILKEN SISTER FLOWERS CONSULT, AND LAY            UPON YORKE HIS BIRTH               60   46 176 500
IN SILKEN VOLUMES. WHERESOE'RE SHEE'L TREAD,          ON A FOULE MORNING                 25   46 181 495
SOFT SILKEN HOURES,                                   WISHES SUPPOSED MISTRESSE          91   46 139 479
OFT HATH THIS HAND THOSE SILKEN CASEMENTS KEPT,       LUKE 2. QUAERIT JESUM              33   MS 379  11
IN VAILES OF DUST THEIR SILKEN HEADS THEY'LE HIDE.    AN ELEGIE ON DR PORTER             25   MS 395 476

SYLKEN

WHOSE SYLKEN FLATTERYES SWELL A FEW FOND HOWRES       DEATH'S LECTURE                     9   52 340 475

SILKEWORMES

OF SHOP, OR SILKEWORMES TOYLE                         WISHES SUPPOSED MISTRESSE          23   46 195 479

SILVER

THUS HIGH, THUS LOW, AS IF HER SILVER THROAT          MUSICKS DUELL                     100   46 149 535
THY SILVER, THEN HIS GOLDEN STREAME.                  THE WEEPER                         84   46  79 120
EACH HIS PAYRE OF SILVER DOVES.                       A HYMNE OF THE NATIVITY            86   46 106  76
DEARE SILVER BREASTED DOVE                            ON A PRAYER BOOKE                  92   46 126 139
SIGHS TO HIS SILVER MATE. RISE UP MY LOVE,            ON THE ASSUMPTION                   8   46 139 114
HIDE HIS HOT BEAMES IN SHADE OF SILVER AGE.           UPON DEATH OF HERRYS               31   46 167 466
THY SILVER BROW, AND MEET THY GOLDEN LOVER.           ON A FOULE MORNING                 28   46 181 495
SHALL IN A SILVER RAINE RUNNE OUT, WHOSE CREAME       ON GUNPOWDER-TREASON               24   MS 384 458
BUT REST, AFFRIGHTED MUSE. THY SILVER WINGS           UPON GUNPOWDER TREASON             27   MS 387 461
UPON HIS TIPTOES, E'RE HIS SILVER HEAD                UPON KINGS CORONATION               4   MS 389 454
UNMIXT FELICITY WITH SILVER WINGS                     UPON KINGS CORONATION              21   MS 389 454
RICH DIAMONDS, SETT IN A PURE SILVER FOYLE.           UPON BIRTH PRINCESSE E             44   MS 391 456
WHERE ROUND ABOUT HOVERS WITH SILVER WING             AN ELEGY MR STANNINOW              53   MS 394 473

SILVER-CROWNED

FOR A SILVER-CROWNED HEAD,                            UPON THE DEATH OF A GENTLEMAN      11   46 166 472

SILVER-DROPS

TELL DOWN HIS SILVER-DROPS UNTO THEE,                 OUT OF GREEKE CUPID'S CRYER        61   46 159 519

SILVER-FOOTED

STAY, SILVER-FOOTED CAME, STRIVE NOT TO WED           AN ELEGIE ON DR PORTER              1   MS 395 476

SILVER-FORDED

PARENTS OF SILVER-FORDED RILLS.                       THE WEEPER                          2   46  79 120

SILVER-SHEILDED

OF ALL PROUD NEPTUNES SILVER-SHEILDED GUARD.          AN ELEGIE ON DR PORTER             34   MS 395 476

SILVER-SWEATING

WHOSE SOFT SILVER-SWEATING STREAMES                   PSALME 23                          15   46 102   5

SILVER-TIPT

AS EVER SILVER-TIPT, THE SIDE OF SHADY MOUNTAINE.     TO PONTIUS WASHING HANDS            8   46  94  23

SYLVER

EACH HIS PAIR OF SYLVER DOVES.                        IN HOLY NATIVITY                  106   52 246  76
SIGHES TO HIS SYLVER MATE RISE UP, MY LOVE.           IN GLORIOUS ASSUMPTION B. LADY      8   52 304 114
THY SYLVER, THEN HIS GOLDEN STREAM.                   WEEPER                             78   52 307 120
WASH WITH SYLVER, WIPE WITH GOLD.                     WEEPER                            120   52 307 120
WARM SYLVER SHOURES WHERE'RE HE GOES.                 WEEPER                            126   52 307 120

SYLVER-FOOTED

PARENTS OF SYLVER-FOOTED RILLS.                       WEEPER                              2   52 307 120

SYLVER-ROOFE

WHOSE SYLVER-ROOFE RINGS WITH THE SPRIGHTLY NOTES     MUSICKS DUELL                      75   46 149 535

SIMILES

NEW SIMILES TO NATURE.                                TO THE NAME OF JESUS               96   52 239  30

SIMPERING

YEE SIMPERING SONS OF THOSE FAIRE EYES,               THE WEEPER                        122   46  79 120

SIMPLE

POORE SIMPLE VOYCE, RAIS'D IN A NATURALL TONE.        MUSICKS DUELL                     164   46 149 535
WHEN MY SIMPLE WEAKNESSE STRAYES.                     PSALME 23                          21   46 102   5

```
            BUT TO POORE SHEPHEARDS, SIMPLE THINGS,        A HYMNE OF THE NATIVITY         74  46 106  76
            OF SIMPLE GRACES, AND SWEET LOVES,             A HYMNE OF THE NATIVITY         84  46 106  76
            THEIR SIMPLE TRIBUTE TO THE BABE, WHOSE BIRTH  SOSPETTO D'HERODE              119  46 109 216
            POORE BEASTS.  A SLOW OXE, AND A SIMPLE ASSE.  SOSPETTO D'HERODE              528  46 109 216
            OF SIMPLE GRACES & SWEET LOVES.                IN HOLY NATIVITY               104  52 246  76
            MAKE BUT A SIMPLE MERCHANT MAN.                CHARITAS NIMIA                   6  52 280  48

      SIMPLEST

            AND CLOATH THEIR SIMPLEST NAKEDNESSE.          WISHES SUPPOSED MISTRESSE       42  46 195 479

      SIMPLICITY

            WELL READ IN THEIR SIMPLICITY.                 IN HOLY NATIVITY                96  52 246  76

      SIN

            IS MURTHER NO SIN, OR A SIN SO CHEAPE,         TO PONTIUS WASHING HANDS         1  46  94  23
            IS MURTHER NO SIN, OR A SIN SO CHEAPE,         TO PONTIUS WASHING HANDS         1  46  94  23
            SHOULD TAKE THE MARKE OF SIN, AND PAINE OF SENCE.  SOSPETTO D'HERODE          190  46 109 216
            OF SIN, AND DEATH, TWICE DIPT IN THE DIRE STAINES  SOSPETTO D'HERODE          327  46 109 216
            AND SELFE-TORMENTING SIN) HAD A SOFT BED.      SOSPETTO D'HERODE              412  46 109 216
            THE BURNISH OF NO SIN,                         WISHES SUPPOSED MISTRESSE       65  46 195 479
            THE NIGHT & WINTER STILL OF DEATH & SIN.       IN GLORIOUS EPIPHANIE           77  52 253  39
            WHOM THEY COMPELL'D BEFORE TO BE THEIR SIN)    IN GLORIOUS EPIPHANIE          177  52 253  39
            MERCHANTS OF DEATH & SIN, IS BOUGHT & SOLD.    OFFICE H. CROSS MATINES         15  52 265  86
            EVEN BALLANCE OF BOTH WORLDS. OUR WORLD OF SIN, VEXILLA REGIS                  31  52 277 156
            WITH GUILT & SIN,                              CHARITAS NIMIA                  51  52 280  48
            TO'A HEART WHO BY SAD RIGHT OF SIN             SANCTA MARIA DOLORUM            93  52 283 162
            THE CONSCIOUS COLORS OF MY SIN                 DIES IRAE                       43  52 298 186
            IF SIN CAN SIGH, LOVE CAN FORGIVE.             DIES IRAE                       47  52 298 186
            AND TAKE AWAY FROM ME MY SELF & SIN,           FLAMING HEART                   90  52 324  61
            THEN SIN HATH SNARES, OR HELL HATH DARTS.      PRAYER TO GENTLE-WOMAN          26  52 328 139
            OF THEIR MAD SIN, (HOW GREAT, AND YETT HOW VAYNE.)  OUT OF GROTIUS             30  MS 398 198

      SIN'S

            HIS OWN LOVE'S, & OUR SIN'S GREAT SACRIFICE.   OFFICE H. CROSS NINTH            6  52 271  99
            OF MY SIN'S SHAME.                             CHARITAS NIMIA                  60  52 280  48
            NOR IS'T LOVE'S FAULT, BUT SIN'S DIRE SKILL    LAUDA SION SALVATOREM           53  52 294 178

      SINNE

            DISDAINEFULL WRETCH. HOW HATH ONE BOLD SINNE COST  SOSPETTO D'HERODE           73  46 109 216
            THEN SINNE HATH SNARES, OR HELL HATH DARTS.    ON A PRAYER BOOKE               20  46 126 139

      SINS

            OUR SINS HAVE SHAM'D INTO A ROSE.              NEW YEAR'S DAY                  12  52 251  37
            NOR WAS'T OUR DEAFNES, BUT OUR SINS, THAT THUS IN GLORIOUS EPIPHANIE          131  52 253  39
            FROM OUR SINS & HIS OWN SORROWES.              IN GLORIOUS EPIPHANIE          156  52 253  39
            WHEN THE WOLF SINS, HIMSELF TO BLEED.          CHARITAS NIMIA                  54  52 280  48
            OF BORROWD SINS, AND SWIMME                    SANCTA MARIA DOLORUM            33  52 283 162
            TO WASH MY WORLDS OF SINS FROM ME.             ADORO TE                        50  52 291 172

      SINCE

            THOUGH SHEE BE DUMBE E'RE SINCE HIS DEATH,     UPON THE DEATH OF A GENTLEMAN   17  46 166 472
            FAST BOUND, SINCE FIRST HE FORFEITED THE SKIES. SOSPETTO D'HERODE              40  46 109 216
            SINCE TIS NOT TO BEE HAD AT HOME,              IN MEMORY OF LADY MADRE TERESA  43  46 131  52
            NO SWEETS SINCE THOU ART WANTING HERE.         ON THE ASSUMPTION               12  46 139 114
            SINCE THY GREAT SONNE WILL HAVE IT SO.         ON THE ASSUMPTION               26  46 139 114
            (INFINITE, SINCE PART OF YOU)                  TO THE QUEEN                     6  48 215 501
            SINCE HEAVN ITSELF LYES HERE BELOW.            IN HOLY NATIVITY                61  52 246  76
            SINCE THOU WOULDST NEEDS BE THUS               OFFICE H. CROSS COMPLINE        15  52 274 105
            SINCE THY DREAD SON WILL HAVE IT SO.           IN GLORIOUS ASSUMPTION B. LADY  41  52 304 114
            SINCE 'TIS NOT TO BE HAD AT HOME               TERESA                          43  52 315  52
            SINCE HIS THE BLUSHES BE, & HER'S THE FIRES,   FLAMING HEART                   38  52 324  61
            I'AM WEDDED ORE AGAIN SINCE THOU ART GONE.     ALEXIAS SECONDE ELEGIE           3  52 335 207
            BUT SINCE THEY ARE FIRE WORKES, RATHER PROVE   UPON GUNPOWDER TREASON          33  MS 387 461
            SINCE SIGHS DOE RISE, AND TEARES DOE FALL.     UPON DEATH OF A FREIND           4  MS 393 477
            SINCE YOUTH MUST FALL, WHEN IT SHOULD RISE.    UPON DEATH OF A FREIND          16  MS 393 477
            GONE BE ALL CONSORT, SINCE ALONE               UPON DEATH OF A FREIND          17  MS 393 477

      SING

            A CAPRING CHEEREFULLNESSE, AND MADE THEM SING  MUSICKS DUELL                   28  46 149 535
            THAT MEN CAN SLEEPE WHILE THEY THEIR MATTENS SING. MUSICKS DUELL               80  46 149 535
            OR TO THY SELFE, SING THINE OWNE OBSEQUIE.     MUSICKS DUELL                  110  46 149 535
            IN HEAV'N YOU'L LEARNE TO SING ERE HERE TO SPEAKE. TO INFANT MARTYRS            2  46  88  10
            ALL THE YEARE DOTH SIT AND SING,               PSALME 23                        6  46 102   5
            COME, THEY CRY'D, COME SING AND PLAY           PSALME 137                      11  46 104   7
            SING, PLAY, TO WHOM (AH) SHALL WE SING OR PLAY, PSALME 137                     13  46 104   7
            SING, PLAY, TO WHOM (AH) SHALL WE SING OR PLAY, PSALME 137                     13  46 104   7
            MARY, MEN AND ANGELS SING,                     ON THE ASSUMPTION               53  46 139 114
            SWEET ANGELS COME, AND SING THE REST.          ON THE ASSUMPTION               64  46 139 114
            THE MORNING MUSES PERCH LIKE BIRDS, AND SING   UPON DEATH OF HERRYS            11  46 167 466
            TO BE A SHADE FOR ANGELS WHILE THEY SING,      UPON DEATH OF HERRYS            40  46 167 466
            UNLESSE THE MUSE SING MY APOLOGY,              TO THE MORNING                   4  46 183 497
            WHERE LOVE AND SHEE SHALL SIT AND SING         THOUGH NOW 'TIS NEITHER         12  MS 397 492
            SAD SHADES AND SING DULL NIGHT ASLEEPE.        THOUGH NOW 'TIS NEITHER         20  MS 397 492
            SHALL SITT AND SING.                           THOUGH NOW 'TIS NEITHER         31  MS 397 492
            I SING THE NAME WHICH NONE CAN SAY             TO THE NAME OF JESUS             1  52 239  30
            AWAKE & SING                                   TO THE NAME OF JESUS            15  52 239  30
```

| | | | | | |
|---|---|---|---|---|---|
| NO OTHER NOTE FOR'T, BUT THE NAME WE SING | TO THE NAME OF JESUS | 45 | 52 | 239 | 30 |
| THE WAKEFULL MATINES HAST TO SING | OFFICE H. CROSS MATINES | 10 | 52 | 265 | 86 |
| THEN SITT THEE DOWN, & SING THINE EV'NSONG IN THE SAD | OFFICE H. CROSS EVENSONG | 8 | 52 | 273 | 101 |
| BOTH WEEP & SING IN SHADE OF THEE. | OFFICE H. CROSS EVENSONG | 11 | 52 | 273 | 101 |
| STILL WOULD THE YOUTHFULL SPIRITS SING. | CHARITAS NIMIA | 19 | 52 | 280 | 48 |
| RISE, ROYALL SION.  RISE & SING | LAUDA SION SALVATOREM | 1 | 52 | 294 | 178 |
| MARIA, MEN & ANGELS SING | IN GLORIOUS ASSUMPTION B. LADY | 58 | 52 | 304 | 114 |
| SWEET ANGELS COME, AND SING THE REST. | IN GLORIOUS ASSUMPTION B. LADY | 69 | 52 | 304 | 114 |
| AND SING, & SIGH, & WORK, AND SLEEP AGAIN. | DESCRIPTION RELIGIOUS HOUSE | 17 | 52 | 338 | 213 |
| I SING IMPIETY BEYOND A NAME. | ON GUNPOWDER-TREASON | 1 | MS | 384 | 458 |
| OF PLUTO'S MERCURY, THAT I MAY SING | UPON GUNPOWDER TREASON | 2 | MS | 386 | 458 |
| EACH WINGED CHORISTER WOULD SWAN-LIKE SING | UPON GUNPOWDER TREASON | 43 | MS | 386 | 460 |
| MY QUILL TO THEE MAY NOT PRAESUME TO SING. | UPON BIRTH PRINCESSE E | 21 | MS | 391 | 456 |
| TO SING THEIR SADDEST DIR'GES, SUCH AS MAY | AN ELEGIE ON DR PORTER | 29 | MS | 395 | 476 |

**SINGS**

| | | | | | |
|---|---|---|---|---|---|
| PLEASURE SINGS MY SOULE TO REST, | PSALME 23 | 9 | 46 | 102 | 5 |
| SHEE SINGS THY TEARES ASLEEPE, AND DIPS | A HYMNE OF THE NATIVITY | 65 | 46 | 106 | 76 |
| TO THE BELEEVING WORLD FAME BOLDLY SINGS. | SOSPETTO D'HERODE | 14 | 46 | 109 | 216 |
| OF THE BRIGHT YOUTH OF HEAVEN, THAT SINGS | ON THE ASSUMPTION | 24 | 46 | 139 | 114 |
| BOTH THE PSALM AND SYBYLL SINGS | DIES IRAE | 2 | 52 | 298 | 186 |
| OF THE BRIGHT YOUTH OF HEAVN, THAT SINGS | IN GLORIOUS ASSUMPTION B. LADY | 39 | 52 | 304 | 114 |

**SINGING**

| | | | | | |
|---|---|---|---|---|---|
| SINGING THEIR FEARES ARE FEARFULLY DELIGHTED. | MUSICKS DUELL | 114 | 46 | 149 | 535 |
| TILL THE SINGING ORBES AWAKE THEE, | THE TEARE | 41 | 46 | 64 | 50 |

**SINGLE**

| | | | | | |
|---|---|---|---|---|---|
| IN SHRILL TONGU'D ACCENTS, STRIVING TO BEE SINGLE. | MUSICKS DUELL | 130 | 46 | 149 | 535 |
| DARKE, DUSTY MAN, HE NEEDS WOULD SINGLE FORTH, | SOSPETTO D'HERODE | 217 | 46 | 109 | 216 |
| I THANKE YOU ALL, BUT ONE MUST SINGLE OUT, | SOSPETTO D'HERODE | 287 | 46 | 109 | 216 |
| I WOULD BE MARRIED TO A SINGLE LIFE. | ON MARRIAGE | 2 | 46 | 183 | 485 |
| ONE SINGLE WOUND SHOULD NOT HAVE LEFT FOR YOU. | SANCTA MARIA DOLORUM | 80 | 52 | 283 | 162 |
| HERE DIVIDERS, SINGLE HE | LAUDA SION SALVATOREM | 46 | 52 | 294 | 178 |

**SINK**

| | | | | | |
|---|---|---|---|---|---|
| ALL THY WILD CIRCLE TO A POINT. O SINK | DEATH'S LECTURE | 15 | 52 | 340 | 475 |

**SINKE**

| | | | | | |
|---|---|---|---|---|---|
| SINKE SION, DOWNE AND NEVER RISE, | PSALME 137 | 28 | 46 | 104 | 7 |
| THAT THE UNMEASUR'D GOD SO LOW SHOULD SINKE, | SOSPETTO D'HERODE | 171 | 46 | 109 | 216 |
| ALL THY WILD CIRCLE TO A POINT.  O SINKE | UPON STANINOUGH'S DEATH | 14 | 46 | 175 | 475 |
| SHOULD COOLE HIS FIERY WHEELS, & NEVER SINKE | UPON GUNPOWDER TREASON | 39 | MS | 386 | 460 |

**SINKS**

| | | | | | |
|---|---|---|---|---|---|
| NOR SINKS NOR SWELLS WITH TIME OR PLACE. | IN GLORIOUS EPIPHANIE | 29 | 52 | 253 | 39 |

**SINKES**

| | | | | | |
|---|---|---|---|---|---|
| FOLLOWING THOSE LITTLE RILLS, HEE SINKES INTO | MUSICKS DUELL | 123 | 46 | 149 | 535 |
| SINKES INTO HORROURS BOSOME, GLAD TO HIDE | OUT OF GROTIUS | 78 | MS | 398 | 198 |

**SINNER'S**

| | | | | | |
|---|---|---|---|---|---|
| THE SINNER'S PARDON & THE JUST MAN'S PEACE. | VEXILLA REGIS | 42 | 52 | 277 | 156 |

**SINNES**

| | | | | | |
|---|---|---|---|---|---|
| SUCH AS (E'RE OUR DARK SINNES TO DUST BETRAY'D THEE) | ON A TREATISE OF CHARITY | 4 | 46 | 137 | 69 |
| OUR SINNES HAVE SHAM'D INTO A ROSE. | AN HIMNE FOR CIRCUMCISION | 12 | 46 | 141 | 37 |
| AND WHATSOE'RE WILD SINNES BLACK THOUGHTS DOE FEED, | HORATIJ ILLE & NEFASTO | 12 | MS | 362 | 530 |

**SION**

| | | | | | |
|---|---|---|---|---|---|
| LOVELY SION THOUGHT ON THEE. | PSALME 137 | 6 | 46 | 104 | 7 |
| NO,NO,THY GOOD, SION, ALONE MUST CROWNE | PSALME 137 | 25 | 46 | 104 | 7 |
| SINKE SION, DOWNE AND NEVER RISE, | PSALME 137 | 28 | 46 | 104 | 7 |
| RISE, ROYALL SION.  RISE & SING | LAUDA SION SALVATOREM | 1 | 52 | 294 | 178 |

**SIONS**

| | | | | | |
|---|---|---|---|---|---|
| ONE OF SIONS SONGS TO DAY. | PSALME 137 | 12 | 46 | 104 | 7 |

**SIPPE**

| | | | | | |
|---|---|---|---|---|---|
| OR THIRSTY TREASON OFFER ONCE TO SIPPE | UPON GUNPOWDER TREASON | 40 | MS | 387 | 461 |

**SIPS**

| | | | | | |
|---|---|---|---|---|---|
| A BRISKE CHERUB SOMETHING SIPS | THE WEEPER | 26 | 46 | 79 | 120 |

**SIPPES**

| | | | | | |
|---|---|---|---|---|---|
| A BRISK CHERUB SOMTHING SIPPES | WEEPER | 26 | 52 | 307 | 120 |

SIR

| | | | | | |
|---|---|---|---|---|---|
| SHOW ME HIMSELFE, HIMSELFE (BRIGHT SIR) O SHOW | COME SEE WHERE THE LORD LAY | 1 | 46 | 87 | 27 |

SIRE

| | | | | | |
|---|---|---|---|---|---|
| TO GENERATION. HEAVENS ALMIGHTY SIRE | OUT OF VIRGIL | 4 | 46 | 155 | 529 |
| MAKES THE SUNNE (OF FLAMES THE SIRE) | OUT OF GREEKE CUPID'S CRYER | 55 | 46 | 159 | 519 |
| SO SWORE THE LAMB'S DREAD SIRE. AND SO WE SEE'T. | TO THE QUEEN'S MAJESTY | 19 | 52 | 261 | 47 |
| PROMETHEUS SELFE, & PELOPS STERVED SIRE | HORATIJ ILLE & NEFASTO | 54 | MS | 382 | 530 |
| OF FUTURE CHANCE. THE WORLD'S GRAND SIRE. AND MINE | OUT OF GROTIUS | 3 | MS | 398 | 198 |

SIREN

| | | | | | |
|---|---|---|---|---|---|
| EACH AERY SIREN NOW HATH GOTT HER SONG, | UPON KINGS CORONATION | 25 | MS | 390 | 453 |

SYREN

| | | | | | |
|---|---|---|---|---|---|
| THEIR MUSE, THEIR SYREN. HARMLESSE SYREN SHEE) | MUSICKS DUELL | 10 | 46 | 149 | 535 |
| THEIR MUSE, THEIR SYREN. HARMLESSE SYREN SHEE) | MUSICKS DUELL | 10 | 46 | 149 | 535 |

SYRENS

| | | | | | |
|---|---|---|---|---|---|
| TO TH' SYRENS IN MY MISTRESSE SONG, | OUT OF THE ITALIAN (3) | 4 | 46 | 190 | 549 |

SIRIAN

| | | | | | |
|---|---|---|---|---|---|
| NOR SIRIAN FLAME, NOR BOREAN FROST DEFLOWERS. | SOSPETTO D'HERODE | 21 | 46 | 109 | 216 |

SISTER

| | | | | | |
|---|---|---|---|---|---|
| HAILE SISTER SPRINGS, | THE WEEPER | 1 | 46 | 79 | 120 |
| PROUD WILL HIS SISTER BE TO WEARE | THE TEARE | 11 | 46 | 84 | 50 |
| FAITH'S SISTER. NURSE OF FAIRE DESIRE. | ON HOPE | 81 | 46 | 143 | 71 |
| TWO SILKEN SISTER FLOWERS CONSULT, AND LAY | UPON YORKE HIS BIRTH | 60 | 46 | 176 | 500 |
| AND SISTER PHOENIXES, AND STILL THE MOTHER. | UPON YORKE HIS BIRTH | 89 | 46 | 176 | 500 |
| BROTHER PEARLES, AND SISTER ROSES. | OUT OF THE ITALIAN (1) | 24 | 46 | 188 | 545 |
| WITH HIS FAIR SISTER COW, | IN GLORIOUS EPIPHANIE | 97 | 52 | 253 | 39 |
| HAIL, SISTER SPRINGS. | WEEPER | 1 | 52 | 307 | 120 |
| (FAIR SISTER OF THE SERAPHIM.) | FLAMING HEART | 104 | 52 | 324 | 61 |
| FAITH'S SISTER. NURSE OF FAIR DESIRE. | (ON) HOPE | 41 | 52 | 345 | 71 |
| DRAW TO THIS SISTER MIRACLE A BROTHER. | UPON BIRTH PRINCESSE E | 56 | MS | 391 | 456 |

SISTER-SEAS

| | | | | | |
|---|---|---|---|---|---|
| TWO SISTER-SEAS OF VIRGINS MILKE, | A HYMNE OF THE NATIVITY | 61 | 46 | 106 | 76 |
| TWO SISTER-SEAS OF VIRGIN-MILK, | IN HOLY NATIVITY | 87 | 52 | 246 | 76 |

SISTERS

| | | | | | |
|---|---|---|---|---|---|
| THE SWEET-LIP'T SISTERS MUSICALLY FRIGHTED, | MUSICKS DUELL | 113 | 46 | 149 | 535 |
| WEE (SAID THE HORRID SISTERS) WAIT THY LAWES. | SOSPETTO D'HERODE | 261 | 46 | 109 | 216 |
| THREE COLEBLACK SISTERS, (WHOSE LONG SUTTY HAIRE, | UPON GUNPOWDER TREASON | 9 | MS | 367 | 461 |

SIT

| | | | | | |
|---|---|---|---|---|---|
| HER GARMENTS THAT UPON HER SIT, | IN PRAISE OF LESSIUS | 21 | 46 | 156 | 510 |
| ALL THE YEARE DOTH SIT AND SING. | PSALME 23 | 6 | 46 | 102 | 5 |
| GIRT ALL THY GLORIES TO THEE. THEN SIT DOWN, | ON A TREATISE OF CHARITY | 11 | 46 | 137 | 69 |
| THE SUNNE HIMSELFE OFT WISHT TO SIT, AND MADE | UPON DEATH OF HERRYS | 10 | 46 | 167 | 466 |
| THOU BY THY SELFE MAIST SIT, (BLEST ISLE) AND SEE | UPON YORKE HIS BIRTH | 25 | 46 | 176 | 500 |
| AND SEE SUCH NAMES OF JOY SIT WHITE UPON | UPON YORKE HIS BIRTH | 97 | 46 | 176 | 500 |
| TO SIT AND SCOULE UPON NIGHTS HEAVY BROW. | ON A FOULE MORNING | 34 | 46 | 181 | 495 |
| WOULD SIT UNDER, | OUT OF THE ITALIAN (1) | 35 | 46 | 188 | 545 |
| THE HEAT COMMANDING IN MY HEART DOTH SIT. | OUT OF THE ITALIAN (2) | 4 | 46 | 190 | 547 |
| IF ON TIMES RIGHT HAND, SIT FAIRE HISTORIE. | ON FRONTISPIECE ISAACSONS | 5 | 46 | 191 | 491 |
| WHERE LOVE AND SHEE SHALL SIT AND SING | THOUGH NOW 'TIS NEITHER | 12 | MS | 397 | 492 |

SITH

| | | | | | |
|---|---|---|---|---|---|
| SWINGING A HUGE SITH STANDS IMPARTIALL DEATH, | SOSPETTO D'HERODE | 319 | 46 | 109 | 216 |

SITT

| | | | | | |
|---|---|---|---|---|---|
| SHALL SITT AND SING. | THOUGH NOW 'TIS NEITHER | 31 | MS | 397 | 492 |
| THEN SITT THEE DOWN, & SING THINE EV'NSONG IN THE SAD | OFFICE H. CROSS EVENSONG | 8 | 52 | 273 | 101 |
| BUT DOES SITT STILL IN HIS OWN DORE. | ADORO TE | 6 | 52 | 291 | 172 |
| AND THY PAINES SITT BRIGHT UPON THEE | TERESA | 146 | 52 | 315 | 52 |
| HER GARMENTS, THAT UPON HER SITT | TEMPERANCE | 19 | 52 | 342 | 510 |
| AND SITT TRIUMPHING IN EACH CHEERFULL BROW. | UPON KINGS CORONATION | 20 | MS | 389 | 454 |

SITS

| | | | | | |
|---|---|---|---|---|---|
| SITS SORROW WITH A FACE SO FAIRE. | THE WEEPER | 58 | 46 | 79 | 120 |
| SHEE SITS IN SUCH A THRONE AS THIS, | THE WEEPER | 62 | 46 | 79 | 120 |
| AS SITS ABOVE THY BEST CAPACITYE. | UPON YORKE HIS BIRTH | 8 | 46 | 176 | 500 |

SITTS

| | | | | | |
|---|---|---|---|---|---|
| AND WHERE SO E'RE HEE SITTS HIS WHITE | IN MEMORY OF LADY MADRE TERESA | 180 | 46 | 131 | 52 |
| THIS SOVERAIGN SUBJECT SITTS ABOVE | LAUDA SION SALVATOREM | 5 | 52 | 294 | 178 |
| SITTS SORROW WITH A FACE SO FAIR. | WEEPER | 34 | 52 | 307 | 120 |
| THAT ON THY BANKES SITTS IN A VERDANT BOWER, | AN ELEGIE ON DR PORTER | 22 | MS | 395 | 476 |

## SITTING

| | | | |
|---|---|---|---|
| SITTING SOE LONG AT EASE IN HER DARKE DENNE. | UPON GUNPOWDER TREASON | 24 | MS 386 460 |

## SIX

| | | | |
|---|---|---|---|
| BE LOVE BUT THERE.  LET POOR SIX YEARES | TERESA | 29 | 52 315 52 |

## SIXE

| | | | |
|---|---|---|---|
| BEE LOVE BUT THERE, LET POORE SIXE YEARES, | IN MEMORY OF LADY MADRE TERESA | 29 | 46 131 52 |

## SIZE

| | | | |
|---|---|---|---|
| OF CHATT'RING STRINGES, BY THE SMALL SIZE OF ONE | MUSICKS DUELL | 163 | 46 149 535 |
| LOWER, AND LOWER YET.  TILL THY SMALL SIZE, | UPON STANINOUGH'S DEATH | 15 | 46 175 475 |
| SEE, EVEN THE YEARES & SIZE OF HIM | FLAMING HEART | 15 | 52 324 61 |
| LOWER & LOWER YET. TILL THY LEANE SIZE | DEATH'S LECTURE | 16 | 52 340 475 |

## SKIES

| | | | |
|---|---|---|---|
| FAST BOUND, SINCE FIRST HE FORFEITED THE SKIES, | SOSPETTO D'HERODE | 40 | 46 109 216 |

## SKYES

| | | | |
|---|---|---|---|
| OPREST THE COMMON-PEOPLE OF THE SKYES. | SOSPETTO D'HERODE | 240 | 46 109 216 |
| UPON THY WINGS, & REACH THE SKYES. | OFFICE H. CROSS PRIME | 16 | 52 267 91 |
| THUS VEX THE EARTH & TEARE THE BEAUTEOUS SKYES. | ALEXIAS SECONDE ELEGIE | 10 | 52 335 207 |

## SKILL

| | | | |
|---|---|---|---|
| OF DALLYING SWEETNESSE, HOVERS ORE HER SKILL, | MUSICKS DUELL | 59 | 46 149 535 |
| FAITH IS MY SKILL.  FAITH CAN BELEIVE | ADORO TE | 11 | 52 291 172 |
| NOR IS'T LOVE'S FAULT, BUT SIN'S DIRE SKILL | LAUDA SION SALVATOREM | 53 | 52 294 178 |

## SKILLFULL

| | | | |
|---|---|---|---|
| MY SKILLFULL GREIFE IS GROWN FAMILIAR. | ALEXIAS SECONDE ELEGIE | 24 | 52 335 207 |

## SKIN

| | | | |
|---|---|---|---|
| HIS SKIN AS WITH A FIERY BLUSHING | OUT OF GREEKE CUPID'S CRYER | 19 | 46 159 519 |
| THOUGH BARE HIS SKIN, HIS MIND HEE COVERS, | OUT OF GREEKE CUPID'S CRYER | 39 | 46 159 519 |
| HE'S WASHT, HIS GLOOMY SKIN A PEACEFULL SHADE | ON BAPTIZED AETHIOPIAN | 3 | 46 85 29 |
| HIS SUPERFICIALL BEAMES SUN-BURN'T OUR SKIN. | IN GLORIOUS EPIPHANIE | 75 | 52 253 39 |

## SKIP

| | | | |
|---|---|---|---|
| MAKING THEM SKIP OUT OF THEIR DUSTY BED. | ON GUNPOWDER-TREASON | 30 | MS 384 458 |

## SKIPPS

| | | | |
|---|---|---|---|
| FROM THIS TO THAT. THEN QUICKE RETURNING SKIPPS | MUSICKS DUELL | 32 | 46 149 535 |

## SKIRMISHES

| | | | |
|---|---|---|---|
| HEE LIGHTLY SKIRMISHES ON EVERY STRING | MUSICKS DUELL | 20 | 46 149 535 |

## SKY

| | | | |
|---|---|---|---|
| FLUTTERING IN WANTON SHOALES, AND TO THE SKY | MUSICKS DUELL | 91 | 46 149 535 |

## SLAIN

| | | | |
|---|---|---|---|
| WERE SOLD AND SLAIN. | OFFICE H. CROSS SIXT | 19 | 52 270 97 |
| WHEN WONDERING DEATH BY DEATH WAS SLAIN. | OFFICE H. CROSS EVENSONG | 26 | 52 273 101 |
| THE LAMB WHOM HIS OWN LOVE HATH SLAIN. | VEXILLA REGIS | 44 | 52 277 156 |
| AND WOULD FOR EVER SO BE SLAIN. | TERESA | 102 | 52 315 52 |
| STILL LONGING SO TO BE STILL SLAIN, | A SONG | 10 | 52 327 65 |

## LOVE-SLAIN

| | | | |
|---|---|---|---|
| THE LOVE-SLAIN WITTNESSES OF THIS LIFE OF THEE. | FLAMING HEART | 84 | 52 324 61 |

## SLAINE

| | | | |
|---|---|---|---|
| AND WOULD FOR EVER SO BE SLAINE. | IN MEMORY OF LADY MADRE TERESA | 102 | 46 131 52 |

## SLAKT

| | | | |
|---|---|---|---|
| NOT TO BE SLAKT BUT BY A SEA OF BLOOD. | SOSPETTO D'HERODE | 490 | 46 109 216 |

## SLAKES

| | | | |
|---|---|---|---|
| SHE COMES TOTH' KING AND WITH HER COLD HAND SLAKES | SOSPETTO D'HERODE | 421 | 46 109 216 |

## SLAUGHTER

| | | | |
|---|---|---|---|
| HELLS SHOP OF SLAUGHTER SHEE DO'S OVERSEE, | SOSPETTO D'HERODE | 291 | 46 109 216 |
| ABOUT HER HATE, WRATH, WARRE, AND SLAUGHTER SWEAT. | SOSPETTO D'HERODE | 315 | 46 109 216 |

## SLAVES

| | | | | |
|---|---|---|---|---|
| HIMSELFE, THE FORFEIT OF HIS SLAVES OFFENCE. | SOSPETTO D'HERODE | 188 | 46 109 | 216 |

## SLAYEST

| | | | | |
|---|---|---|---|---|
| FOR WHILE THOU SWEETLY SLAYEST ME | A SONG | 15 | 52 327 | 65 |

## SLEEKE

| | | | | |
|---|---|---|---|---|
| THROUGH THE SLEEKE PASSAGE OF HER OPEN THROAT. | MUSICKS DUELL | 38 | 46 149 | 535 |

## SLEEP

| | | | | |
|---|---|---|---|---|
| CAN'ST THOU BE CARELESSE NOW. NOW CAN'ST THOU SLEEP. | SOSPETTO D'HERODE | 456 | 46 109 | 216 |
| THAT FLAMING IN THEIR FAIRE BED SLEEP. | AN HIMNE FOR CIRCUMCISION | 20 | 46 141 | 37 |
| NOT TO LY COLD, YET SLEEP IN SNOW. | IN HOLY NATIVITY | 70 | 52 246 | 76 |
| THAT FLAMING IN THEIR FAIR BEDS SLEEP, | NEW YEAR'S DAY | 20 | 52 251 | 37 |
| SERAPHIMS WILL NOT SLEEP | CHARITAS NIMIA | 17 | 52 280 | 48 |
| THE DEAW NO MORE WILL SLEEP | WEEPER | 45 | 52 307 | 120 |
| MY CHASTITY IS SACRED. & MY SLEEP | ALEXIAS THIRD ELEGIE | 37 | 52 336 | 209 |
| A HASTY PORTION OF PRAESCRIBED SLEEP. | DESCRIPTION RELIGIOUS HOUSE | 15 | 52 338 | 213 |
| AND SING, & SIGH, & WORK, AND SLEEP AGAIN. | DESCRIPTION RELIGIOUS HOUSE | 17 | 52 338 | 213 |
| CROWN'D WOES AWAKE. AS THINGS TOO WISE FOR SLEEP. | DESCRIPTION RELIGIOUS HOUSE | 29 | 52 338 | 213 |
| LET THEM SLEEP. LET THEM SLEEP ON. | AN EPITAPH UPON MARRIED COUPLE | 15 | 52 339 | 478 |
| LET THEM SLEEP. LET THEM SLEEP ON. | AN EPITAPH UPON MARRIED COUPLE | 15 | 52 339 | 478 |

## SLEEP'ST

| | | | | |
|---|---|---|---|---|
| HER WORDS. SLEEP'ST THOU FOND MAN. SLEEP'ST THOU. (SAID SHE) | SOSPETTO D'HERODE | 424 | 46 109 | 216 |
| HER WORDS. SLEEP'ST THOU FOND MAN. SLEEP'ST THOU. (SAID SHE) | SOSPETTO D'HERODE | 424 | 46 109 | 216 |

## SLEEPE

| | | | | |
|---|---|---|---|---|
| THAT MEN CAN SLEEPE WHILE THEY THEIR MATTENS SING. | MUSICKS DUELL | 80 | 46 149 | 535 |
| THE DEAW NO MORE WILL SLEEPE. | THE WEEPER | 39 | 46 79 | 120 |
| NUT TO LYE COLD, YET SLEEPE IN SNOW. | A HYMNE OF THE NATIVITY | 52 | 46 106 | 76 |
| HEE WAKES, AND WITH HIM (NE'RE TO SLEEPE) NEW FEARES. | SOSPETTO D'HERODE | 473 | 46 109 | 216 |
| LET THEM SLEEPE, LET THEM SLEEPE ON, | AN EPITAPH HUSBAND AND WIFE | 11 | 46 174 | 478 |
| LET THEM SLEEPE, LET THEM SLEEPE ON. | AN EPITAPH HUSBAND AND WIFE | 11 | 46 174 | 478 |
| WHOSE DAY SHALL NEVER SLEEPE IN NIGHT. | AN EPITAPH HUSBAND AND WIFE | 16 | 46 174 | 478 |
| BUT THOU, FAINT GOD OF SLEEPE. FORGET THAT I | TO THE MORNING | 47 | 46 183 | 497 |
| IF FLORA'S DARLINGS NOW AWAKE FROM SLEEPE, | AN ELEGY MR STANNINOW | 25 | MS 394 | 473 |

## SLEEPS

| | | | | |
|---|---|---|---|---|
| TO WAKE THE SUN THAT SLEEPS TOO LONG. | A HYMNE OF THE NATIVITY | 4 | 46 106 | 76 |
| SO SLEEPS A PILOT, WHOSE POORE BARKE IS PREST | SOSPETTO D'HERODE | 425 | 46 109 | 216 |
| OF HIM WHO NEVER SLEEPS, ALL THINGS THAT ARE, | TO THE NAME OF JESUS | 56 | 52 239 | 30 |

## SLEEPES

| | | | | |
|---|---|---|---|---|
| RUINE, WHERE E'RE SHE SLEEPES AT NATURES FEET. | SOSPETTO D'HERODE | 279 | 46 109 | 216 |
| LAY FOLDED UP IN SLEEPES CAPTIVITY. | TO THE MORNING | 6 | 46 183 | 497 |

## SLEEPER

| | | | | |
|---|---|---|---|---|
| AND YET NO SLEEPER. | ON A PRAYER BOOKE | 32 | 46 126 | 139 |
| AND YET NO SLEEPER. | PRAYER TO GENTLE-WOMAN | 38 | 52 328 | 139 |

## SLEEPING

| | | | | |
|---|---|---|---|---|
| IN PITTY'S SOFT LAP LY A SLEEPING. | TO THE NAME OF JESUS | 192 | 52 239 | 30 |

## SLEEPY

| | | | | |
|---|---|---|---|---|
| AND ROUZE THE SLEEPY ASHES OF THE DEAD, | ON GUNPOWDER-TREASON | 29 | MS 384 | 458 |

## SLEPT

| | | | | |
|---|---|---|---|---|
| NODDING ON THE WILLOWES SLEPT. | PSALME 137 | 4 | 46 104 | 7 |
| SLEPT, AND DREAMPT OF NO SUCH THING | A HYMNE OF THE NATIVITY | 6 | 46 106 | 76 |
| HE SLEPT. AND DREAM'T OF NO SUCH THING. | IN HOLY NATIVITY | 6 | 52 246 | 76 |
| WHILE THEIR SUNNES SLEPT. | LUKE 2. QUAERIT JESUM | 34 | MS 379 | 11 |

## SLENDER

| | | | | |
|---|---|---|---|---|
| I WRITE SO ILL, MY SLENDER LINE IS SCARCE | WITH A PICTURE TO A FRIEND | 3 | 46 156 | 494 |

## SLEW

| | | | | |
|---|---|---|---|---|
| DRESSE THE SOULE, WHICH LATE THEY SLEW. | IN MEMORY OF LADY MADRE TERESA | 153 | 46 131 | 52 |
| THOSE SWEET AIRES THAT OFTEN SLEW MEE. | OUT OF THE ITALIAN (1) | 51 | 46 188 | 545 |
| E'RE SHE BORE ANY ONE, SLEW ALL. | O GLORIOSA DOMINA | 12 | 52 302 | 194 |
| DRESSE THE SOUL THAT ERST THEY SLEW. | TERESA | 152 | 52 315 | 52 |

## SLIDE

| | | | | |
|---|---|---|---|---|
| BUT LEAST YOUR EYE DISCERNING SLIDE | OUT OF GREEKE CUPID'S CRYER | 17 | 46 159 | 519 |
| THE SEA SHALL CHANGE HIS YOUTHFULL GREENE, & SLIDE | ON GUNPOWDER-TREASON | 33 | MS 384 | 458 |
| TO CORRALLIZE, WHICH SOFTLY WONT TO SLIDE | AN ELEGY MR STANNINOW | 23 | MS 394 | 473 |

SLIPPERY

| | | | | | |
|---|---|---|---|---|---|
| THE PLYANT SERIES OF HER SLIPPERY SONG. | MUSICKS DUELL | 61 | 46 | 149 | 535 |
| SLIPPERY SOULES IN SMILING EYES) | A HYMNE OF THE NATIVITY | 73 | 46 | 106 | 76 |
| SOME SLIPPERY PAIRE, | ON A PRAYER BOOKE | 51 | 46 | 126 | 139 |
| SLIPPERY SOULES IN SMILING EYES. | IN HOLY NATIVITY | 93 | 52 | 246 | 76 |
| SOME SLIPPERY PAIR | PRAYER TO GENTLE-WOMAN | 57 | 52 | 328 | 139 |
| WHATE'RE FALSE SHOWES OF SHORT & SLIPPERY GOOD | DESCRIPTION RELIGIOUS HOUSE | 7 | 52 | 338 | 213 |

SLIPT

| | | | | | |
|---|---|---|---|---|---|
| (SLIPT FROM AURORA'S DEWY BREST) | THE TEARE | 20 | 46 | 84 | 50 |

SLOW

| | | | | | |
|---|---|---|---|---|---|
| I SAW THE CURL'D DROPS, SOFT AND SLOW | A HYMNE OF THE NATIVITY | 35 | 46 | 106 | 76 |
| IN THIS SAD HOUSE OF SLOW DESTRUCTION, | SOSPETTO D'HERODE | 61 | 46 | 109 | 216 |
| POORE BEASTS.  A SLOW OXE, AND A SIMPLE ASSE. | SOSPETTO D'HERODE | 528 | 46 | 109 | 216 |
| AH LINGER NOT, LOV'D SOUL. A SLOW | TO COUNTESSE OF DENBIGH | 13 | 52 | 236 | 146 |
| I SAW THE CURL'D DROPS, SOFT & SLOW. | IN HOLY NATIVITY | 51 | 52 | 246 | 76 |
| SENDING'S TOO SLOW A WORD, MY SELFE WOULD FLY. | ALEXIAS FIRST ELEGIE | 13 | 52 | 334 | 204 |
| AH. LINGER NOT, LOV'D SOUL, A SLOW | AGAINST IRRESOLUTION AND DELAY | 7 | 52 | 347 | 146 |
| ONLY NOT SLOW TO BE UNDONE. | AGAINST IRRESOLUTION AND DELAY | 60 | 52 | 347 | 146 |

SLOWLY

| | | | | | |
|---|---|---|---|---|---|
| OF YOUR BRAVE SOUL SO SLOWLY FORTH. | TO COUNTESSE OF DENBIGH | 8 | 52 | 236 | 146 |
| OF YOUR BRAVE SOUL SO SLOWLY FORTH. | AGAINST IRRESOLUTION AND DELAY | 16 | 52 | 347 | 146 |

SLOWNESSE

| | | | | | |
|---|---|---|---|---|---|
| FAINE WOULD I CHIDE THEIR SLOWNESSE, BUT IN THEIR | UPON TWO GREENE APRICOCKES | 31 | 48 | 220 | 494 |

SLUGGISH

| | | | | | |
|---|---|---|---|---|---|
| DULL SLUGGISH ILE. WHAT MORE THAN LETHARGY | ON GUNPOWDER-TREASON | 3 | MS | 384 | 458 |

SLUMBERS

| | | | | | |
|---|---|---|---|---|---|
| AND IN SOFT SLUMBERS BATH THY WOE. | THE TEARE | 40 | 46 | 84 | 50 |
| IN DEATH-LIKE SLUMBERS.  WHILE THY DANGERS CRAVE | SOSPETTO D'HERODE | 430 | 46 | 109 | 216 |
| NOR IVORY COUCHES COSTLYER SLUMBERS KEEPING. | DESCRIPTION RELIGIOUS HOUSE | 4 | 52 | 338 | 213 |
| OBEDIENT SLUMBERS. THAT CAN WAKE & WEEP, | DESCRIPTION RELIGIOUS HOUSE | 16 | 52 | 338 | 213 |
| OFT HAVE I WRAPT THY SLUMBERS IN SOFT AIRES. | LUKE 2. QUAERIT JESUM | 31 | MS | 379 | 11 |

SLUTTISH

| | | | | | |
|---|---|---|---|---|---|
| O WHITHER, FOR THE SLUTTISH EARTH | THE WEEPER | 126 | 46 | 79 | 120 |

SLUTTISHNESSE

| | | | | | |
|---|---|---|---|---|---|
| A SLUTTISHNESSE, FOR PURE RELIGION. | ON A TREATISE OF CHARITY | 30 | 46 | 137 | 69 |

SLY

| | | | | | |
|---|---|---|---|---|---|
| SLY, LURKING TREASON IS HIS BOSOME FREIND. | UPON GUNPOWDER TREASON | 17 | MS | 387 | 461 |

SMALL

| | | | | | |
|---|---|---|---|---|---|
| THAT FROM SO SMALL A CHANNELL SHOULD BE RAIS'D | MUSICKS DUELL | 44 | 46 | 149 | 535 |
| OF CHATT'RING STRINGES, BY THE SMALL SIZE OF ONE | MUSICKS DUELL | 163 | 46 | 149 | 535 |
| OF HIS SMALL HAND. YET NOT SO SMALL | OUT OF GREEKE CUPID'S CRYER | 37 | 46 | 159 | 519 |
| OF HIS SMALL HAND. YET NOT SO SMALL | OUT OF GREEKE CUPID'S CRYER | 37 | 46 | 159 | 519 |
| HIS TORCH IMPERIOUS THOUGH BUT SMALL | OUT OF GREEKE CUPID'S CRYER | 54 | 46 | 159 | 519 |
| YET IS THE JOY I TAKE IN'T SMALL OR NONE. | UPON OUR LORDS LAST DISCOURSE | 3 | 46 | 95 | 21 |
| HEAVENS ROYALL HOASTS INCAMPT, THUS SMALL. | ON A PRAYER BOOKE | 6 | 46 | 126 | 139 |
| LOWER, AND LOWER YET. TILL THY SMALL SIZE, | UPON STANINOUGH'S DEATH | 15 | 46 | 175 | 475 |
| THE MODEST FRONT OF THIS SMALL FLOORE | AN EPITAPH UPON ASHTON | 1 | 46 | 192 | 464 |
| NO HAIR SO SMALL, BUT PAYES HIS RIVER | UPON BLEEDING CRUCIFIX | 21 | 52 | 288 | 110 |
| HEAVN'S ROYALL HOST. INCAMP'T THUS SMALL | PRAYER TO GENTLE-WOMAN | 12 | 52 | 328 | 139 |

SMART

| | | | | | |
|---|---|---|---|---|---|
| FOR WHOSE MORE NOBLE SMART, | WISHES SUPPOSED MISTRESSE | 56 | 46 | 195 | 479 |
| ARE NAILES BLUNT PENS OF SUPERFICIALL SMART. | OFFICE H. CROSS SIXT | 11 | 52 | 270 | 97 |
| WITH THESE HE WASH'T THY STAIN, TRANSFER'D THY SMART, | VEXILLA REGIS | 11 | 52 | 277 | 156 |
| PAYES BACK, WITH MORE THEN THEIR OWN SMART | SANCTA MARIA DOLORUM | 28 | 52 | 283 | 162 |

SMELL

| | | | | | |
|---|---|---|---|---|---|
| AS THEN DID SMELL OF WINTER, OR OF DEATH. | OUT OF VIRGIL | 28 | 46 | 155 | 529 |
| NOR NEED WEE KILL THY FRUIT TO SMELL THY FLOWER. | ON HOPE | 54 | 46 | 143 | 71 |
| NOR DOES IT KILL THY FRUIT, TO SMELL THY FLOWRE. | (ON) HOPE | 24 | 52 | 345 | 71 |

SMELLS

| | | | | | |
|---|---|---|---|---|---|
| TO THINK OUGHT SWEET BUT THAT WHICH SMELLS OF THEE. | TO THE NAME OF JESUS | 172 | 52 | 239 | 30 |

SMILE

| | | | | | |
|---|---|---|---|---|---|
| AGE, WOULDST SEE DECEMBER SMILE. | IN PRAISE OF LESSIUS | 40 | 46 | 156 | 510 |
| CAN DOE NOUGHT BUT SMILE, | THE WEEPER | 63 | 46 | 79 | 120 |
| HEE SAW A VERNALL SMILE, SWEETLY DISFIGURE | SOSPETTO D'HERODE | 109 | 46 | 109 | 216 |

|   |   |   |   |   |
|---|---|---|---|---|
| THE FACES LIGHTNING, OR A SMILE IS HERE. | SOSPETTO D'HERODE | 198 | 46 109 | 216 |
| THE FAIREST, AND THE FIRST-BORNE SMILE OF HEAV'N. | SOSPETTO D'HERODE | 236 | 46 109 | 216 |
| ALL THY OLD WOES SHALL NOW SMILE ON THEE. | IN MEMORY OF LADY MADRE TERESA | 146 | 46 131 | 52 |
| WERE THE MORNINGS SMILE SO FAIRE | UPON DEATH OF DESIRED HERRYS | 56 | 46 168 | 467 |
| AN EVERLASTING SMILE UPON THE FACE, | UPON YORKE HIS BIRTH | 20 | 46 176 | 500 |
| THOU AND THE LOVELY HOPES THAT SMILE IN THEE | UPON YORKE HIS BIRTH | 40 | 46 176 | 500 |
| THE FACE OF THINGS, AN UNIVERSALL SMILE. | ON A FOULE MORNING | 10 | 46 181 | 495 |
| ONE BRIGHT SMILE TO CLEERE THE WEATHER. | OUT OF THE ITALIAN (1) | 27 | 46 188 | 545 |
| OR A BOUGHT BLUSH, OR A SET SMILE. | WISHES SUPPOSED MISTRESSE | 24 | 46 195 | 479 |
| NO FRUIT SHOULD HAVE THE FACE TO SMILE ON THEE | UPON TWO GREENE APRICOCKES | 25 | 48 220 | 494 |
| IS ONE CONSISTENT SOLID SMILE. | IN GLORIOUS EPIPHANIE | 31 | 52 253 | 39 |
| ALL THY OLD WOES SHALL NOW SMILE ON THEE | TERESA | 145 | 52 315 | 52 |
| AGE. WOULDST SEE DECEMBER SMILE. | TEMPERANCE | 38 | 52 342 | 510 |
| ONE SMILE AT HOME. | LUKE 2. QUAERIT JESUM | 14 | MS 379 | 11 |
| THAT SWIM'ST AS DEEPE IN JOY, AS SEAS, NOW SMILE | UPON KINGS CORONATION | 6 | MS 389 | 454 |
| BUT WITH ONE CORDIALL SMILE, FOR (LOE) THAT POWER | EX EUPHORMIONE | 4 | MS 392 | 525 |

SMIL'D

|   |   |   |   |   |
|---|---|---|---|---|
| SO SMIL'D THE DAYES, AND SO THE TENOR RAN | OUT OF VIRGIL | 24 | 46 155 | 529 |
| A THOUSAND RUDDY HOPES SMIL'D IN EACH BUD, | UPON DEATH OF HERRYS | 25 | 46 167 | 466 |
| AND SMIL'D I'TH' BABE'S BRIGHT FACE, THE PURPLING BUD | TO THE QUEEN'S MAJESTY | 5 | 52 261 | 47 |

SMILES

|   |   |   |   |   |
|---|---|---|---|---|
| THE GOLD THAT ON HIS QUIVER SMILES, | OUT OF GREEKE CUPID'S CRYER | 49 | 46 159 | 519 |
| WITH BAITED SMILES IF HE DISPLAY | OUT OF GREEKE CUPID'S CRYER | 63 | 46 159 | 519 |
| AND REJOYCING SMILES TO SEE | PSALME 23 | 7 | 46 102 | 5 |
| FIND EVERLASTING SMILES. SO RARE, | IN MEMORY OF LADY MADRE TERESA | 87 | 46 131 | 52 |
| THOSE SECOND SMILES OF HEAVEN SHALL DART, | IN MEMORY OF LADY MADRE TERESA | 136 | 46 131 | 52 |
| WHERE NOUGHT BUT SMILES, AND RUDDY JOYES ARE WORNE. | ON A FOULE MORNING | 36 | 46 181 | 495 |
| BEAUTY SMILES AND LOVE SHALL LIVE. | LOVES HOROSCOPE | 40 | 46 185 | 483 |
| SMILES, THAT CAN WARME | WISHES SUPPOSED MISTRESSE | 61 | 46 195 | 479 |
| FOUGHT AGAINST FROWNS WITH SMILES. GAVE GLORIOUS CHASE | TO THE NAME OF JESUS | 199 | 52 239 | 30 |
| WE COURT THY MORE CONCERNING SMILES. | IN GLORIOUS EPIPHANIE | 81 | 52 253 | 39 |
| WITH LOVES, OF TEARS WITH SMILES DISPUTING. | WEEPER | 92 | 52 307 | 120 |
| FIND EVERLASTING SMILES. SO RARE, | TERESA | 87 | 52 315 | 52 |
| (THOSE SECOND SMILES OF HEAV'N) SHALL DART | TERESA | 135 | 52 315 | 52 |
| THE FALSE SMILES OF A SUBLUNARY SUN. | TO SAME CONCERNING CHOISE | 32 | 52 331 | 66 |
| BUT SMILES, & RUDDY JOYES, & AT THIS DAY | UPON KINGS CORONATION | 39 | MS 390 | 453 |

SMILING

|   |   |   |   |   |
|---|---|---|---|---|
| THE SMILING MORNE HAD NEWLY WAK'T THE DAY, | THE BEGINNING OF HELIODORUS | 1 | 46 158 | 517 |
| SMILING IN THY CHEEKES, CONFESSE. | THE WEEPER | 86 | 46 79 | 120 |
| GOE SMILING SOULES, YOUR NEW BUILT CAGES BREAKE, | TO INFANT MARTYRS | 1 | 46 88 | 10 |
| SLIPPERY SOULES IN SMILING EYES) | A HYMNE OF THE NATIVITY | 73 | 46 106 | 76 |
| THEY WERE THE SMILING SONS OF THOSE SWEET BOWERS. | SOSPETTO D'HERODE | 19 | 46 109 | 216 |
| TO DANCE IN THE SUNNESHINE OF SOME SMILING | ON A PRAYER BOOKE | 48 | 46 126 | 139 |
| SLIPPERY SOULES IN SMILING EYES. | IN HOLY NATIVITY | 93 | 52 246 | 76 |
| SMILING IN THY CHEEKS, CONFESSE | WEEPER | 80 | 52 307 | 120 |
| TO DANCE ITH' SUNSHINE OF SOME SMILING | PRAYER TO GENTLE-WOMAN | 54 | 52 328 | 139 |
| WHICH, WHILE THEY SMILING SATE UPON HIS FACE. | AN ELEGY MR STANNINOW | 39 | MS 394 | 473 |

SMOOTH

|   |   |   |   |   |
|---|---|---|---|---|
| EVERY SMOOTH TURNE, EVERY DELICIOUS STROAKE | MUSICKS DUELL | 131 | 46 149 | 535 |
| AND ALL THE SMOOTH FACED KINDRED THERE. | ON MR. G. HERBERTS BOOKE | 14 | 46 130 | 68 |
| HIS SMOOTH CHEEKES, WITH A DOWNY SHADE. | HIS EPITAPH (HERRYS) | 46 | 46 172 | 471 |

SMOTHER

|   |   |   |   |   |
|---|---|---|---|---|
| BUT THESE VAST MYSTERIES HIS SENSES SMOTHER, | SOSPETTO D'HERODE | 161 | 46 109 | 216 |
| TILL ANOTHER THOUSAND SMOTHER | OUT OF CATULLUS | 13 | 46 194 | 523 |

SMUTCHES

|   |   |   |   |   |
|---|---|---|---|---|
| THOSE DURTY SMUTCHES, WHICH THEIR FAIRE FRONTS WORE. | AN ELEGY MR STANNINOW | 13 | MS 394 | 473 |

SNAKE

|   |   |   |   |   |
|---|---|---|---|---|
| SO SAID, HER RICHEST SNAKE, WHICH TO HER WRIST | SOSPETTO D'HERODE | 465 | 46 109 | 216 |
| TO THE KINGS HEART, THE SNAKE NO SOONER HIST, | SOSPETTO D'HERODE | 469 | 46 109 | 216 |

SNAKES

|   |   |   |   |   |
|---|---|---|---|---|
| A CURL'D KNOT OF EMBRACING SNAKES, THAT KISSE | SOSPETTO D'HERODE | 37 | 46 109 | 216 |
| THEIR LOCKES ARE BEDS OF UNCOMB'D SNAKES THAT WIND | SOSPETTO D'HERODE | 69 | 46 109 | 216 |
| FLOURISHT THEIR SNAKES, AND TOST THEIR FLAMING BRANDS. | SOSPETTO D'HERODE | 260 | 46 109 | 216 |
| A GEN'RALL HISSE, FROM THE WHOLE TIRE OF SNAKES | SOSPETTO D'HERODE | 302 | 46 109 | 216 |
| HAD NOT HER THICK SNAKES HID THEM FROM THE SUN. | SOSPETTO D'HERODE | 384 | 46 109 | 216 |
| THE FURIES CURL'D SNAKES MEET IN GENTLE TWINES. | HORATIJ ILLE & NEFASTO | 52 | MS 382 | 530 |

SNARES

|   |   |   |   |   |
|---|---|---|---|---|
| MIDST ALL THE DARKE AND KNOTTY SNARES, | NEITHER DURST MAN ASKE | 1 | 46 92 | 20 |
| THEN SINNE HATH SNARES, OR HELL HATH DARTS. | ON A PRAYER BOOKE | 20 | 46 126 | 139 |
| THEN SIN HATH SNARES, OR HELL HATH DARTS. | PRAYER TO GENTLE-WOMAN | 26 | 52 328 | 139 |

SNATCH

|   |   |   |   |   |
|---|---|---|---|---|
| DARES HUNGRY DEATH SNATCH OF ONE CHERRY LIPP. | UPON GUNPOWDER TREASON | 39 | MS 387 | 461 |

SNATCH'D

| | | | |
|---|---|---|---|
| SULPHUREOUS FLAMES, SNATCH'D FROM AETERNALL NIGHT. | UPON GUNPOWDER TREASON | 26 | MS 387 461 |
| AND SNATCH'D AWAY THE BANQUETT. EVERY ONE | UPON GUNPOWDER TREASON | 54 | MS 387 461 |

SNATCHT

| | | | |
|---|---|---|---|
| THEIR MASTERS BLEST SOULE (SNATCH OUT AT HIS EARES | MUSICKS DUELL | 147 | 46 149 535 |
| NOW THOUGH THE BLOW THAT SNATCH HIM HENCE, | UPON THE DEATH OF A GENTLEMAN | 15 | 46 166 472 |
| THEY, THEY THAT SNATCH US FROM OUR COUNTRIES BREST | PSALME 137 | 7 | 46 104   7 |
| TO MORROW TO BE SNATCH AWAY. | UPON DEATH OF DESIRED HERRYS | 30 | 46 168 467 |

SNATCH'T

| | | | |
|---|---|---|---|
| SNATCH'T HER SELF HENCE, TO HEAVEN. FILL'D A BRIGHT PLACE, | UPON BISHOP ANDREWES PICTURE | 9 | 46 163 490 |
| SNATCH'T UPP THE FALLING STARRE, SOE RICHLY GAY, | AN ELEGY MR STANNINOW | 50 | MS 394 473 |

SNATCHES

| | | | |
|---|---|---|---|
| AND SNATCHES THIS AGAINE, AND PAUSES THERE. | MUSICKS DUELL | 33 | 46 149 535 |

SNOW

| | | | |
|---|---|---|---|
| IN A BED OF REVEREND SNOW. | IN PRAISE OF LESSIUS | 42 | 46 156 510 |
| OFFRING THEIR WHITEST SHEETS OF SNOW, | A HYMNE OF THE NATIVITY | 37 | 46 106  76 |
| NOT TO LYE COLD, YET SLEEPE IN SNOW. | A HYMNE OF THE NATIVITY | 52 | 46 106  76 |
| SPITE OF ALL THE MAIDEN SNOW | THOUGH NOW 'TIS NEITHER | 7 | MS 397 492 |
| OFFRING THEIR WHITEST SHEETS OF SNOW | IN HOLY NATIVITY | 53 | 52 246  76 |
| NOT TO LY COLD, YET SLEEP IN SNOW. | IN HOLY NATIVITY | 70 | 52 246  76 |
| IN A BED OF REVEREND SNOW. | TEMPERANCE | 40 | 52 342 510 |
| IN AZURE CHANNELLS WARME THROUGH MOUNTS OF SNOW. | UPON GUNPOWDER TREASON | 42 | MS 387 461 |
| UPON HER NECK THE WHITEST OF HIS SNOW. | UPON BIRTH PRINCESSE E | 50 | MS 391 456 |
| DOTH HEE IN DOWNY SNOW THERE CLOSELY SHROWD | AN ELEGY MR STANNINOW | 3 | MS 394 473 |
| 'TWAS NOT THE CHAST, & PURER SNOW, WHOSE NEST | AN ELEGY MR STANNINOW | 35 | MS 394 473 |

SNOWY

| | | | |
|---|---|---|---|
| THAWING CHRISTALL. SNOWY HILLS. | THE WEEPER | 4 | 46  79 120 |
| AS FROM A SNOWY FORTRESSE OF DEFENCE | ON A PRAYER BOOKE | 12 | 46 126 139 |
| WHERE MONGST HER SNOWY FAMILY, | IN MEMORY OF LADY MADRE TERESA | 128 | 46 131  52 |
| FROM THE SAME SNOWY ALABLASTER ROCKE | UPON YORKE HIS BIRTH | 45 | 46 176 500 |
| LO WHERE IT COMES, UPON THE SNOWY DOVE'S | TO THE NAME OF JESUS | 159 | 52 239  30 |
| THAWING CRYSTALL. SNOWY HILLS, | WEEPER | 4 | 52 307 120 |
| WHERE 'MONGST HER SNOWY FAMILY | TERESA | 127 | 52 315  52 |
| AS FROM A SNOWY FORTRESSE OF DEFENCE. | PRAYER TO GENTLE-WOMAN | 18 | 52 328 139 |
| THAT ON THESE SNOWY LIMMES HATH LAID SUCH HOLD. | AN ELEGY MR STANNINOW | 20 | MS 394 473 |
| WHOSE SNOWY CHEEKES, LEAST JOY SHOULD BE EXPREST, | AN ELEGIE ON DR PORTER | 9 | MS 395 476 |

SOARE

| | | | |
|---|---|---|---|
| AND THOUGH THESE HUMBLE LINES SOARE NOT SOE HIGH, | UPON BIRTH PRINCESSE E | 17 | MS 391 456 |

SOBER

| | | | |
|---|---|---|---|
| A MAN WHOSE SOBER SOULE CAN TELL, | IN PRAISE OF LESSIUS | 19 | 46 156 510 |
| THE FLOURISH OF HIS SOBER YOUTH, | HIS EPITAPH (HERRYS) | 25 | 46 172 471 |
| AND SOBER PACE MARCH ON TO MEET A GRAVE. | TO THE NAME OF JESUS | 202 | 52 239  30 |
| A MAN WHOSE SOBER SOUL CAN TELL | TEMPERANCE | 17 | 52 342 510 |

SOBS

| | | | |
|---|---|---|---|
| OF SHORT THICKE SOBS, WHOSE THUNDRING VOLLEYES FLOAT, | MUSICKS DUELL | 63 | 46 149 535 |

SOFT

| | | | |
|---|---|---|---|
| THE MUSICKS SOFT REPORT. AND MOLD THE SAME | MUSICKS DUELL | 12 | 46 149 535 |
| AND RECKONS UP IN SOFT DIVISIONS. | MUSICKS DUELL | 24 | 46 149 535 |
| PREFERRE SOFT ANTHEMS TO THE EARES OF MEN, | MUSICKS DUELL | 78 | 46 149 535 |
| THERE MIGHT YOU HEARE HER KINDLE HER SOFT VOYCE, | MUSICKS DUELL | 83 | 46 149 535 |
| HEAVES HER SOFT BOSOME, WANDERS ROUND ABOUT, | MUSICKS DUELL | 88 | 46 149 535 |
| CREEPS IN THE SOFT TOUCH OF A TENDER TONE. | MUSICKS DUELL | 140 | 46 149 535 |
| AND BY A SOFT INSINUATION, MIXT | OUT OF VIRGIL | 7 | 46 155 529 |
| THE WORKING BEES SOFT MELTING GOLD, | OUT OF GREEKE CUPID'S CRYER | 25 | 46 159 519 |
| WHOSE SOFT INFLUENCE | THE WEEPER | 27 | 46  79 120 |
| NOT THE SOFT GOLD WHICH | THE WEEPER | 43 | 46  79 120 |
| WHAT BRIGHT SOFT THING IS THIS. | THE TEARE | 1 | 46  84  50 |
| AND IN SOFT SLUMBERS BATH THY WOE. | THE TEARE | 40 | 46  84  50 |
| WHOSE SOFT SILVER-SWEATING STREAMES | PSALME 23 | 15 | 46 102   5 |
| I SAW THE CURL'D DROPS,SOFT AND SLOW | A HYMNE OF THE NATIVITY | 35 | 46 106  76 |
| THE DOWNE THAT THEIR SOFT BRESTS DID STROW, | A HYMNE OF THE NATIVITY | 42 | 46 106  76 |
| THY DOWNE THOUGH SOFT'S NOT SOFT ENOUGH. | A HYMNE OF THE NATIVITY | 46 | 46 106  76 |
| TO THEE MEEKE MAJESTY, SOFT KING | A HYMNE OF THE NATIVITY | 83 | 46 106  76 |
| MUSE, NOW THE SERVANT OF SOFT LOVES NO MORE, | SOSPETTO D'HERODE | 1 | 46 109 216 |
| WITH HER SOFT WING, WIPT FROM THE BROWES OF MEN | SOSPETTO D'HERODE | 387 | 46 109 216 |
| OF SORROW, WITH A SOFT AND DOWNY HAND, | SOSPETTO D'HERODE | 391 | 46 109 216 |
| AND WITH SOFT FEET SEARCHES THE SILENT ROOMES. | SOSPETTO D'HERODE | 400 | 46 109 216 |
| (IF ANY CAN BE SOFT TO TYRANNY | SOSPETTO D'HERODE | 411 | 46 109 216 |
| AND SELFE-TORMENTING SIN) HAD A SOFT BED. | SOSPETTO D'HERODE | 412 | 46 109 216 |
| DELICIOUS DEATHS, SOFT EXHALATIONS | ON A PRAYER BOOKE | 71 | 46 126 139 |
| AND MILKY SOULE OF A SOFT CHILDE. | IN MEMORY OF LADY MADRE TERESA | 14 | 46 131  52 |
| LIKE A SOFT LUMPE OF INCENSE, HASTED | IN MEMORY OF LADY MADRE TERESA | 114 | 46 131  52 |
| THE SOFT TINCTURE OF A TEARE. | ANOTHER ON HERRYS | 20 | 46 170 469 |

|  |  |  |  |  |  |
|---|---|---|---|---|---|
| COME THEN YOUTH, BEAUTY, AND BLOOD, ALL YE SOFT POWERS. | UPON STANINOUGH'S DEATH | 7 | 46 | 175 | 475 |
| HEE WITH A DAINTY AND SOFT HAND, WILL TRIM | ON A FOULE MORNING | 23 | 46 | 181 | 495 |
| SO WARME IN THY SOFT BREST IT CANNOT DYE. | TO THE MORNING | 34 | 46 | 183 | 497 |
| SOFT SILKEN HOURES. | WISHES SUPPOSED MISTRESSE | 91 | 46 | 195 | 479 |
| COME, YE SOFT MINISTERS OF SWEET SAD MIRTH, | TO THE NAME OF JESUS | 62 | 52 | 239 | 30 |
| SOFT BACK. AND BRINGS A BOSOM BIG WITH LOVES. | TO THE NAME OF JESUS | 160 | 52 | 239 | 30 |
| IN PITTY'S SOFT LAP LY A SLEEPING. | TO THE NAME OF JESUS | 192 | 52 | 239 | 30 |
| I SAW THE CURL'D DROPS, SOFT & SLOW, | IN HOLY NATIVITY | 51 | 52 | 246 | 76 |
| TO THEE, MEEK MAJESTY. SOFT KING | IN HOLY NATIVITY | 103 | 52 | 246 | 76 |
| SO FAST FOR ONE SOFT BREST. | SANCTA MARIA DOLORUM | 18 | 52 | 283 | 162 |
| SOFT SOURSE OF LOVE | SANCTA MARIA DOLORUM | 42 | 52 | 283 | 162 |
| SOFT SUBJECT FOR THE SEIGE OF LOVE. | SANCTA MARIA DOLORUM | 50 | 52 | 283 | 162 |
| IF NOT MORE SOFT, MINE EYES. | SANCTA MARIA DOLORUM | 86 | 52 | 283 | 162 |
| O SOFT SELF-WOUNDING PELICAN. | ADORO TE | 45 | 52 | 291 | 172 |
| FLY TO THY SCEPTER OF SOFT LOVE. | DIES IRAE | 28 | 52 | 298 | 186 |
| O LET THINE OWN SOFT BOWELLS PAY | DIES IRAE | 45 | 52 | 298 | 186 |
| AND MILKY SOUL OF A SOFT CHILD. | TERESA | 14 | 52 | 315 | 52 |
| LIKE A SOFT LUMP OF INCENSE, HASTED | TERESA | 113 | 52 | 315 | 52 |
| DELICIOUS DEATHS. SOFT EXALATIONS | PRAYER TO GENTLE-WOMAN | 77 | 52 | 328 | 139 |
| AND SOFT OBEDIENCE, FIND SWEET BIDING HERE. | DESCRIPTION RELIGIOUS HOUSE | 31 | 52 | 338 | 213 |
| ALL YE SOFT POWRES, | DEATH'S LECTURE | 8 | 52 | 340 | 475 |
| FALL WITH SOFT WINGS, STUCK WITH SOFT FLOWRES. | TEMPERANCE | 46 | 52 | 342 | 510 |
| FALL WITH SOFT WINGS, STUCK WITH SOFT FLOWRES. | TEMPERANCE | 46 | 52 | 342 | 510 |
| OFT HAVE I WRAPT THY SLUMBERS IN SOFT AIRES. | LUKE 2. QUAERIT JESUM | 31 | MS | 379 | 11 |
| ON THY SOFT CHEEKE. | LUKE 2. QUAERIT JESUM | 42 | MS | 379 | 11 |
| THOSE PLUMPE SOFT RUBIES HAD BIN DREST SOE BRAVE. | UPON BIRTH PRINCESSE E | 48 | MS | 391 | 456 |

SOFT'S

|  |  |  |  |  |  |
|---|---|---|---|---|---|
| THY DOWNE THOUGH SOFT'S NOT SOFT ENOUGH. | A HYMNE OF THE NATIVITY | 46 | 46 | 106 | 76 |

SOFTER

|  |  |  |  |  |  |
|---|---|---|---|---|---|
| SOFTER THEN THAT WHICH PANTS IN HEBE'S CUP. | MUSICKS DUELL | 126 | 46 | 149 | 535 |
| NO APRIL E'RE LENT SOFTER SHOWRES, | THE WEEPER | 89 | 46 | 79 | 120 |
| WOULD HAVE LEARN'T A SOFTER STYLE, | ANOTHER ON HERRYS | 37 | 46 | 170 | 469 |
| THY SOFTER YET MORE CERTAINE DARTS | IN GLORIOUS EPIPHANIE | 78 | 52 | 253 | 39 |

SOFTLY

|  |  |  |  |  |  |
|---|---|---|---|---|---|
| SOFTLY LET THEM CREEPE | THE WEEPER | 75 | 46 | 79 | 120 |
| SOFTLY MAY HE BE POSSEST, | UPON DEATH OF DESIRED HERRYS | 67 | 46 | 168 | 467 |
| SOFTLY LET THEM CREEP, | WEEPER | 57 | 52 | 307 | 120 |
| TO CORRALLIZE, WHICH SOFTLY WONT TO SLIDE | AN ELEGY MR STANNINOW | 23 | MS | 394 | 473 |

SOILE

|  |  |  |  |  |  |
|---|---|---|---|---|---|
| IS NOT THE SOILE A KIND ONE (THINKE YE) THAT RETURNS | UPON THORNES FROM LORDS HEAD | 7 | 46 | 96 | 23 |
| A SOILE SO KIND. | UPON CROWNE OF THORNS | 4 | 52 | 290 | 23 |
| IS NOT THE SOILE A KIND ONE, WHICH RETURNES | UPON CROWNE OF THORNS | 5 | 52 | 290 | 23 |

SOYLE

|  |  |  |  |  |  |
|---|---|---|---|---|---|
| IN THAT SWEET SOYLE. IT SEEMES A HOLY QUIRE | MUSICKS DUELL | 73 | 46 | 149 | 535 |
| A SOYLE SO KIND. | UPON THORNES FROM LORDS HEAD | 6 | 46 | 96 | 23 |
| SHAME OF THY MOTHER SOYLE. ILL-NURTUR'D TREE. | HORATIJ ILLE & NEFASTO | 1 | MS | 382 | 530 |

SOL

|  |  |  |  |  |  |
|---|---|---|---|---|---|
| NOW WESTWARD SOL HAD SPENT THE RICHEST BEAMES | MUSICKS DUELL | 1 | 46 | 149 | 535 |
| WHERE ART THOU SOL, WHILE THUS THE BLIND-FOLD DAY | ON A FOULE MORNING | 1 | 46 | 181 | 495 |
| BRIGHTEST SOL THAT DYES TO DAY | OUT OF CATULLUS | 4 | 46 | 194 | 523 |
| AMAZED SOL THROWES OF HIS MOURNFULL WEEDS, | UPON KINGS CORONATION | 15 | MS | 390 | 453 |
| THAT SOL FROM THEM MAY SUCK AN HONIED SHOWER. | UPON BIRTH PRINCESSE E | 5 | MS | 391 | 456 |

SOLACE

|  |  |  |  |  |  |
|---|---|---|---|---|---|
| SOME SOLACE IN MY SORROW'S CERTAINTY | ALEXIAS FIRST ELEGIE | 10 | 52 | 334 | 204 |

SOLD

|  |  |  |  |  |  |
|---|---|---|---|---|---|
| MERCHANTS OF DEATH & SIN, IS BOUGHT & SOLD. | OFFICE H. CROSS MATINES | 15 | 52 | 265 | 86 |
| WERE SOLD AND SLAIN. | OFFICE H. CROSS SIXT | 19 | 52 | 270 | 97 |

SOLDJER

|  |  |  |  |  |  |
|---|---|---|---|---|---|
| BY PARTHIANS BOW THE SOLDJER LOOKES TO DIE. | HORATIJ ILLE & NEFASTO | 25 | MS | 382 | 530 |

SOULDIER

|  |  |  |  |  |  |
|---|---|---|---|---|---|
| KNOW'ST THOU THIS, SOULDIER. 'TIS A MUCH CHANG'D PLANT, WHICH YET | UPON THORNES FROM LORDS HEAD | 1 | 46 | 96 | 23 |
| THOU ART A SOULDIER HEROD, SEND THY SCOUTS | SOSPETTO D'HERODE | 523 | 46 | 109 | 216 |
| KNOW'ST THOU THIS, SOULDIER. 'TIS A MUCH-CHANG'D PLANT WHICH YET | UPON CROWNE OF THORNS | 1 | 52 | 290 | 23 |

SOULDIER'S

|  |  |  |  |  |  |
|---|---|---|---|---|---|
| TO GAZE ON THE FAIR SOULDIER'S GLORIOUS FACE. | ALEXIAS THIRD ELEGIE | 46 | 52 | 336 | 209 |

SOLDIERS

| | | | | |
|---|---|---|---|---|
| COME, BRAVE SOLDIERS, COME, & SEE | IN CICATRICES DOMINI JESU | 1 | MS 381 | 27 |

SOULDIERS

| | | | | |
|---|---|---|---|---|
| THOSE THY OLD SOULDIERS, STOUT AND TALL | IN MEMORY OF LADY MADRE TERESA | 4 | 46 131 | 52 |
| AND TURNE LOVES SOULDIERS, UPON THEE, | IN MEMORY OF LADY MADRE TERESA | 95 | 46 131 | 52 |
| THOSE THY OLD SOULDIERS, GREAT & TALL, | TERESA | 4 | 52 315 | 52 |
| AND TURN LOVE'S SOULDIERS, UPON THEE | TERESA | 95 | 52 315 | 52 |

SOLE

| | | | | |
|---|---|---|---|---|
| LOVE THOU ART ABSOLUTE, SOLE LORD | IN MEMORY OF LADY MADRE TERESA | 1 | 46 131 | 52 |
| LOVE, THOU ART ABSOLUTE SOLE LORD | TERESA | 1 | 52 315 | 52 |
| IN IT THERE SATE BUT ONE SOLE DART. | IN CICATRICES DOMINI JESU | 9 | MS 381 | 27 |

SOLEMN

| | | | | |
|---|---|---|---|---|
| OF SO JUST & SOLEMN JOYES, | LAUDA SION SALVATOREM | 16 | 52 294 | 178 |

SOLEMNE

| | | | | |
|---|---|---|---|---|
| DOES FIRST HIS SCEPTER, THEN HIMSELF IN SOLEMNE TRIBUTE PAY. | IN GLORIOUS EPIPHANIE | 237 | 52 253 | 39 |

SOLEMNITY

| | | | | |
|---|---|---|---|---|
| IS THE SOLEMNITY MY SORROW WEARES, | SOSPETTO D'HERODE | 215 | 46 109 | 216 |

SOLID

| | | | | |
|---|---|---|---|---|
| IS ONE CONSISTENT SOLID SMILE. | IN GLORIOUS EPIPHANIE | 31 | 52 253 | 39 |

SOLITARY

| | | | | |
|---|---|---|---|---|
| A SOLITARY LIFE SHE WOULD HAVE LED. | UPON GUNPOWDER TREASON | 18 | MS 386 | 460 |

SOLLICITERS

| | | | | |
|---|---|---|---|---|
| SOLLICITERS OF SOULES OR EARES. | TO THE NAME OF JESUS | 79 | 52 239 | 30 |

SOME

| | | | | |
|---|---|---|---|---|
| GIVES LIFE TO SOME NEW GRACE. THUS DOTH H'INVOKE | MUSICKS DUELL | 132 | 46 149 | 535 |
| PAINTED AGAINE BY SOME GOOD POESIE. | WITH A PICTURE TO A FRIEND | 2 | 46 156 | 494 |
| GOE NOW WITH SOME DAREING DRUGG, | IN PRAISE OF LESSIUS | 1 | 46 156 | 510 |
| SOME BIGG-NAMED COMPOSITION. | IN PRAISE OF LESSIUS | 6 | 46 156 | 510 |
| IN THEIR OWNE BLOODS DEARE DELUGE, SOME NEW DEAD, | THE BEGINNING OF HELIODORUS | 17 | 46 158 | 517 |
| SOME PANTING IN THEIR YET WARME RUINES BLED. | THE BEGINNING OF HELIODORUS | 18 | 46 158 | 517 |
| WHEN SOME NEW BRIGHT GUEST | THE WEEPER | 31 | 46 79 | 120 |
| YET MAY THESE UNFLEDG'D GRIEFES GIVE FATE SOME GUESSE, | OUR LORD IN HIS CIRCUMCISION | 13 | 46 98 | 9 |
| EACH BLEEDING PART SOME ONE SUPPLIES. | ON WOUNDS OF CRUCIFIED LORD | 4 | 46 99 | 24 |
| AND TO DARE SOMETHING, IS SOME VICTORY. | SOSPETTO D'HERODE | 224 | 46 109 | 216 |
| TO DANCE IN THE SUNNESHINE OF SOME SMILING | ON A PRAYER BOOKE | 48 | 46 126 | 139 |
| SOME SLIPPERY PAIRE, | ON A PRAYER BOOKE | 51 | 46 126 | 139 |
| DOUBTLES SOME OTHER HEART | ON A PRAYER BOOKE | 54 | 46 126 | 139 |
| HIMSELFE SOME OTHER WHERE, | ON A PRAYER BOOKE | 86 | 46 126 | 139 |
| OR SOME BASE HAND HAVE POWER TO RACE, | IN MEMORY OF LADY MADRE TERESA | 71 | 46 131 | 52 |
| MY SOULE, SOME DRINKE FROM MEN TO BEASTS. O THEN, | AN APOLOGIE FOR HYMNE (TERESA) | 35 | 46 136 | 59 |
| STANDS OFF AND POINTS AT. IS'T SOME DEITY | UPON YORKE HIS BIRTH | 71 | 46 176 | 500 |
| IS IT SOME DEITY, OR IS'T OUR QUEENE. | UPON YORKE HIS BIRTH | 73 | 46 176 | 500 |
| AND NAME DWELL SWEET IN SOME ETERNALL STORY. | UPON YORKE HIS BIRTH | 105 | 46 176 | 500 |
| THE YEARE HAD FOUND SOME FRUIT EARLY AS YOU. | UPON TWO GREENE APRICOCKES | 12 | 46 220 | 494 |
| CAN PROVE IT SELF SOME KIN (SWEET NAME) TO THEE. | TO THE NAME OF JESUS | 182 | 52 239 | 30 |
| OF SOME MORE PAINFULL THING THEN ALL HIS PAINES. | OFFICE H. CROSS NINTH | 4 | 52 271 | 99 |
| BECAUSE SOME DESPERATE FOOL'S UNDONE. | CHARITAS NIMIA | 36 | 52 280 | 48 |
| BECAUSE SOME FOOLISH FLY | CHARITAS NIMIA | 43 | 52 280 | 48 |
| (MY FLINTS) SOME DROPS ARE DUE | SANCTA MARIA DOLORUM | 16 | 52 283 | 162 |
| MY BREST MAY CATCH THE KISSE OF SOME KIND DART, | SANCTA MARIA DOLORUM | 69 | 52 283 | 162 |
| RICH QUEEN, LEND SOME RELEIFE. | SANCTA MARIA DOLORUM | 91 | 52 283 | 162 |
| WHEN SOME NEW BRIGHT GUEST | WEEPER | 67 | 52 307 | 120 |
| PREFERR'D TO SOME PROUD FACE | WEEPER | 183 | 52 307 | 120 |
| OR SOME BASE HAND HAVE POWER TO RACE | TERESA | 71 | 52 315 | 52 |
| (MY SOUL,) SOME DRINK FROM MEN TO BEASTS, O THEN | AN APOLOGIE FOR (TERESA) HYMNE | 35 | 52 322 | 59 |
| SOME WEAK, INFERIOUR, WOMAN SAINT. | FLAMING HEART | 26 | 52 324 | 61 |
| TO DANCE ITH' SUNSHINE OF SOME SMILING | PRAYER TO GENTLE-WOMAN | 54 | 52 328 | 139 |
| SOME SLIPPERY PAIR | PRAYER TO GENTLE-WOMAN | 57 | 52 328 | 139 |
| DOUBTLESSE SOME OTHER HEART | PRAYER TO GENTLE-WOMAN | 60 | 52 328 | 139 |
| HIMSELF SOME OTHER WHERE, | PRAYER TO GENTLE-WOMAN | 92 | 52 328 | 139 |
| SOME SOLACE IN MY SORROW'S CERTAINTY | ALEXIAS FIRST ELEGIE | 10 | 52 334 | 204 |
| HAD UNDER SOME LOW ROOFE LOV'D HIS PLAIN WIFE. | ALEXIAS THIRD ELEGIE | 14 | 52 336 | 209 |
| GOE NOW. AND WITH SOME DARING DRUGG | TEMPERANCE | 1 | 52 342 | 510 |
| SOME BIG-NAM'D COMPOSITION. | TEMPERANCE | 6 | 52 342 | 510 |
| I WAS MISTAKEN. SOME FAIRE SPHAERE, OR OTHER | LUKE 2. QUAERIT JESUM | 21 | MS 379 | 11 |
| WARRES RATLING TUMULTS, OR SOME TYRANTS FALL. | HORATIJ ILLE & NEFASTO | 48 | MS 382 | 530 |
| SOME RARE CHOICE TORTURE. NOW 'TIS HELL INDEED. | ON GUNPOWDER-TREASON | 62 | MS 384 | 458 |
| TO SEE SOME FOWLER THAN HERSELFE) THESE STAND, | UPON GUNPOWDER TREASON | 13 | MS 387 | 461 |
| CAST BACK SOME AMOROUSE GLANCES ON THE CATES, | UPON GUNPOWDER TREASON | 29 | MS 387 | 461 |

SOMETHING

| | | | | | |
|---|---|---|---|---|---|
| BY THAT SHRILL TASTE, SHEE COULD DOE SOMETHING TOO. | MUSICKS DUELL | 26 | 46 | 149 | 535 |
| A BRISKE CHERUB SOMETHING SIPS | THE WEEPER | 26 | 46 | 79 | 120 |
| SOMETHING TO THE GENERALL FLOOD. | ON BLEEDING WOUNDS OF LORD | 28 | 46 | 101 | 110 |
| AND TO DARE SOMETHING, IS SOME VICTORY. | SOSPETTO D'HERODE | 224 | 46 | 109 | 216 |
| SOMETHING MORE THAN | WISHES SUPPOSED MISTRESSE | 19 | 46 | 195 | 479 |

SOMTHING

| | | | | | |
|---|---|---|---|---|---|
| SOMTHING A BRIGHTER SHADOW (SWEET) OF THEE. | IN GLORIOUS EPIPHANIE | 249 | 52 | 253 | 39 |
| SOMTHING FROM THY FULL SEAS OF SORROW. | SANCTA MARIA DOLORUM | 44 | 52 | 283 | 162 |
| YEILD SOMTHING IN THY SAD PRAEROGATIVE | SANCTA MARIA DOLORUM | 57 | 52 | 283 | 162 |
| SOMTHING TO THE GENERALL FLOOD. | UPON BLEEDING CRUCIFIX | 24 | 52 | 288 | 110 |
| A BRISK CHERUB SOMTHING SIPPES | WEEPER | 26 | 52 | 307 | 120 |

SOMETIMES

| | | | | | |
|---|---|---|---|---|---|
| MEETS ART WITH ART, SOMETIMES AS IF IN DOUBT | MUSICKS DUELL | 35 | 46 | 149 | 535 |
| FORCING HIS SOMETIMES ECLIPS'D FACE TO BE | IN GLORIOUS EPIPHANIE | 115 | 52 | 253 | 39 |

SOMEWHAT

| | | | | | |
|---|---|---|---|---|---|
| WAS SACRILEGIOUS, (SURE) OR SOMEWHAT WORSE. | HORATIJ ILLE & NEFASTO | 4 | MS | 382 | 530 |
| SOMEWHAT MORE HORRID THAN AN ELEGY. | AN ELEGIE ON DR PORTER | 12 | MS | 395 | 476 |

SON

| | | | | | |
|---|---|---|---|---|---|
| THE MOTHER THEN MUST SUCK THE SON. | BLESSED BE THE PAPS | 4 | 46 | 94 | 14 |
| THE SPOUSE OF VIRGINS, AND THE VIRGINS SON. | ON A PRAYER BOOKE | 40 | 46 | 126 | 139 |
| THE FAIRE SON OF AN EVER-YOUTHFULL SPRING. | UPON DEATH OF HERRYS | 39 | 46 | 167 | 466 |
| MAYEST IN A SON OF HIS FIND EVERY SON | UPON YORKE HIS BIRTH | 99 | 46 | 176 | 500 |
| MAYEST IN A SON OF HIS FIND EVERY SON | UPON YORKE HIS BIRTH | 99 | 46 | 176 | 500 |
| REPEATED, AND THAT SON STILL IN ANOTHER. | UPON YORKE HIS BIRTH | 100 | 46 | 176 | 500 |
| AND TO THE SUN. | OFFICE H. CROSS MATINES | 8 | 52 | 265 | 86 |
| DIVIDED LOVES, WHILE SON & MOTHER | SANCTA MARIA DOLORUM | 23 | 52 | 283 | 162 |
| SHE SEES HER SON, HER GOD. | SANCTA MARIA DOLORUM | 31 | 52 | 283 | 162 |
| COME YOUR WHOLE SELVES, SORROW'S GREAT SON & MOTHER. | SANCTA MARIA DOLORUM | 77 | 52 | 283 | 162 |
| ABOVE THE WORLD, BELOW THY SON | O GLORIOSA DOMINA | 2 | 52 | 302 | 194 |
| TILL HE HAD MADE HIMSELF THY SON | O GLORIOSA DOMINA | 6 | 52 | 302 | 194 |
| GLORY TO THEE, GREAT VIRGIN'S SON | O GLORIOSA DOMINA | 37 | 52 | 302 | 194 |
| SINCE THY DREAD SON WILL HAVE IT SO. | IN GLORIOUS ASSUMPTION B. LADY | 41 | 52 | 304 | 114 |
| THE SPOUSE OF VIRGINS & THE VIRGIN'S SON. | PRAYER TO GENTLE-WOMAN | 46 | 52 | 328 | 139 |
| YOUR SOUL TO ANY SON OF DUST. | TO SAME CONCERNING CHOISE | 19 | 52 | 331 | 66 |

SONNE

| | | | | | |
|---|---|---|---|---|---|
| HOW GODS ETERNALL SONNE SHOULD BE MANS BROTHER. | SOSPETTO D'HERODE | 165 | 46 | 109 | 216 |
| SINCE THY GREAT SONNE WILL HAVE IT SO. | ON THE ASSUMPTION | 26 | 46 | 139 | 114 |

SONS

| | | | | | |
|---|---|---|---|---|---|
| YEE SIMPERING SONS OF THOSE FAIRE EYES. | THE WEEPER | 122 | 46 | 79 | 120 |
| THEY WERE THE SMILING SONS OF THOSE SWEET BOWERS, | SOSPETTO D'HERODE | 19 | 46 | 109 | 216 |
| SET THE CONTENDING SONS OF HEAV'N ON FIRE. | SOSPETTO D'HERODE | 90 | 46 | 109 | 216 |
| 'GAINST THY OWNE SONS AND BROTHERS THOU HAST STOOD | SOSPETTO D'HERODE | 453 | 46 | 109 | 216 |
| THE FAIREST, AND THE FIRST BORNE SONS OF FIRE. | IN MEMORY OF LADY MADRE TERESA | 93 | 46 | 131 | 52 |
| A SEEMLY PORTION FOR THE SONS OF KINGS. | ON HOPE | 34 | 46 | 143 | 71 |
| TO CALCULATE HER YOUNG SONS YEARES. | LOVES HOROSCOPE | 4 | 46 | 185 | 483 |
| BUT IF WE DARKE SONS OF SORROW | OUT OF CATULLUS | 6 | 46 | 194 | 523 |
| PALE SONS OF OUR POMONA, WHOSE WAN CHEEKES | UPON TWO GREENE APRICOCKES | 3 | 46 | 220 | 494 |
| THAT WE, DARK SONS OF DUST & SORROW, | TO THE NAME OF JESUS | 99 | 52 | 239 | 30 |
| PROUD SONS OF DEATH, THAT DURST COMPELL | IN GLORIOUS EPIPHANIE | 109 | 52 | 253 | 39 |
| STILL WOULD THOSE EVER-WAKEFULL SONS OF FIRE | CHARITAS NIMIA | 25 | 52 | 260 | 48 |
| THE FUGITIVE SONS OF THOSE FAIR EYES | WEEPER | 164 | 52 | 307 | 120 |
| THE FAIR'ST & FIRST-BORN SONS OF FIRE | TERESA | 93 | 52 | 315 | 52 |
| THEMSELVES THY CROWN, SONS OF THY VOWES | TERESA | 167 | 52 | 315 | 52 |
| MIX THE MAD SONS OF MEN IN MUTUALL BLOOD. | DESCRIPTION RELIGIOUS HOUSE | 8 | 52 | 338 | 213 |

MORNING-SONS

| | | | | | |
|---|---|---|---|---|---|
| SILENC'T THE MORNING-SONS, & DAMP'T THEIR SONG | IN GLORIOUS EPIPHANIE | 130 | 52 | 253 | 39 |

SONNES

| | | | | | |
|---|---|---|---|---|---|
| THEMSELVES THY CROWNE, SONNES OF THY VOWES. | IN MEMORY OF LADY MADRE TERESA | 168 | 46 | 131 | 52 |
| AMONG HIS OWN FAIR SONNES OF FIRE. | TO SAME CONCERNING CHOISE | 25 | 52 | 331 | 66 |
| MAY IT NOT BE AMONGST THE SONNES OF MEN. | TO SAME CONCERNING CHOISE | 59 | 52 | 331 | 66 |
| A SEEMLY PORTION FOR THE SONNES OF KINGS. | (ON) HOPE | 14 | 52 | 345 | 71 |
| AEOL KEPT IN HIS WRANGLING SONNES, LEAST THEY | UPON GUNPOWDER TREASON | 29 | MS | 386 | 460 |

SONNS

| | | | | | |
|---|---|---|---|---|---|
| OR IF THERE BE SUCH SONNS OF SHAME. | TO THE NAME OF JESUS | 228 | 52 | 239 | 30 |

SONG

| | | | | | |
|---|---|---|---|---|---|
| A CLEARE UNWRINCKLED SONG, THEN DOTH SHEE POINT IT | MUSICKS DUELL | 39 | 46 | 149 | 535 |
| THE PLYANT SERIES OF HER SLIPPERY SONG. | MUSICKS DUELL | 61 | 46 | 149 | 535 |
| AND LAY THE GROUND-WORKE OF HER HOPEFULL SONG, | MUSICKS DUELL | 85 | 46 | 149 | 535 |
| OR TUNE A SONG OF VICTORY TO MEE. | MUSICKS DUELL | 109 | 46 | 149 | 535 |
| THEN TO HIS MUSICKE, AND HIS SONG | THE WEEPER | 29 | 46 | 79 | 120 |
| DOES THY SONG LULL THE AYRE. | THE WEEPER | 103 | 46 | 79 | 120 |

| | | | | |
|---|---|---|---|---|
| FLOWES IN THY SONG (O FAIRE, O DYING SWAN.) | UPON OUR LORDS LAST DISCOURSE | 2 | 46 95 | 21 |
| WOULD HAVE A SONG CARV'D TO THEIR EARES | PSALME 137 | 8 | 46 104 | 7 |
| COME LIFT WE UP OUR LOFTY SONG, | A HYMNE OF THE NATIVITY | 3 | 46 106 | 76 |
| I KNOW THAT IN MY WEAK AND WORTHLESSE SONG | AN APOLOGIE FOR HYMNE (TERESA) | 4 | 46 136 | 59 |
| AND WHILE THOU GOEST, OUR SONG AND WEE, | ON THE ASSUMPTION | 27 | 46 139 | 114 |
| OUR LOVING SONG SHALL HOLD IT FAST. | ON THE ASSUMPTION | 40 | 46 139 | 114 |
| LIVE MISTRIS OF OUR SONG, AND WHEN | ON THE ASSUMPTION | 62 | 46 139 | 114 |
| TO TH' SYRENS IN MY MISTRESSE SONG, | OUT OF THE ITALIAN (3) | 4 | 46 190 | 549 |
| WHEN YOU ARE MISTRESSE OF THE SONG, | TO THE QUEEN | 1 | 48 215 | 501 |
| THAT SO OUR SWEETLY TEMPER'D SONG | TO THE QUEEN | 11 | 48 215 | 501 |
| UNTO THE EVERLASTING LIFE OF SONG. | TO THE NAME OF JESUS | 10 | 52 239 | 30 |
| HELP ME TO MEDITATE MINE IMMORTALL SONG. | TO THE NAME OF JESUS | 61 | 52 239 | 30 |
| TO THE CONSPIRACY OF OUR SPATIOUS SONG. | TO THE NAME OF JESUS | 71 | 52 239 | 30 |
| AND EVERLASTING SERIES OF A DEATHLESSE SONG. | TO THE NAME OF JESUS | 85 | 52 239 | 30 |
| OF THIS UNBOUNDED ALL-IMBRACING SONG. | TO THE NAME OF JESUS | 91 | 52 239 | 30 |
| BLEST HEAVNS, TO YOU, & YOUR SUPERIOUR SONG, | TO THE NAME OF JESUS | 98 | 52 239 | 30 |
| COME LIFT WE UP OUR LOFTYER SONG | IN HOLY NATIVITY | 3 | 52 246 | 76 |
| SILENC'T THE MORNING-SONS, & DAMP'T THEIR SONG | IN GLORIOUS EPIPHANIE | 130 | 52 253 | 39 |
| WHAT SONG SHALL RAISE | OFFICE H. CROSS MATINES | 20 | 52 265 | 86 |
| COME, LOVE, & LET US WORK A SONG | LAUDA SION SALVATOREM | 13 | 52 294 | 178 |
| AND WHILE THOU GOEST, OUR SONG & WE | IN GLORIOUS ASSUMPTION B. LADY | 42 | 52 304 | 114 |
| LIVE MISTRESE OF OUR SONG, AND WHEN | IN GLORIOUS ASSUMPTION B. LADY | 67 | 52 304 | 114 |
| THEN TO HIS MUSICK, AND HIS SONG | WEEPER | 29 | 52 307 | 120 |
| DOES THY SONG LULL THE AIR. | WEEPER | 139 | 52 307 | 120 |
| I KNOW, THAT IN MY WEAK & WORTHLESSE SONG | AN APOLOGIE FOR (TERESA) HYMNE | 4 | 52 322 | 59 |
| HEARKENS NOT TO AN HUMBLE SONG. | FLAMING HEART | 62 | 52 324 | 61 |
| EACH AERY SIREN NOW HATH GOTT HER SONG, | UPON KINGS CORONATION | 25 | MS 390 | 453 |
| TO CHAUNT MY PRAYSES IN A NEW-STRUNG SONG. | OUT OF GROTIUS | 74 | MS 398 | 198 |

SONGS

| | | | | |
|---|---|---|---|---|
| ONE OF SIONS SONGS TO DAY. | PSALME 137 | 12 | 46 104 | 7 |
| AND KEEP'T ALIVE WITH LASTING SONGS. | O GLORIOSA DOMINA | 30 | 52 302 | 194 |

SOON

| | | | | |
|---|---|---|---|---|
| SEE SEE, HOW SOON HIS NEW-BLOOM'D CHEEK | IN HOLY NATIVITY | 67 | 52 246 | 76 |
| AND SOON THIS SWEET TRUTH SHALL APPEAR | NEW YEAR'S DAY | 29 | 52 251 | 37 |
| SHE COULD NOT RISE SO SOON, AS THEY | OFFICE H. CROSS PRIME | 2 | 52 267 | 91 |
| SOON AS THE RIGHT-HAND SCALE REJOYC'T TO PROVE | VEXILLA REGIS | 35 | 52 277 | 156 |
| HIS NAILES WRITE SWORDS IN HER, WHICH SOON HER HEART | SANCTA MARIA DOLORUM | 27 | 52 283 | 162 |
| SO SOON AS THOU SHALT FIRST APPEAR, | TERESA | 122 | 52 315 | 52 |
| OUR PURCHAS'D SELVES TOO SOON BESTOW | AGAINST IRRESOLUTION AND DELAY | 65 | 52 347 | 146 |

SOONE

| | | | | |
|---|---|---|---|---|
| SO SOONE AS THOU SHALT FIRST APPEARE, | IN MEMORY OF LADY MADRE TERESA | 123 | 46 131 | 52 |
| AND SOONE THE SWEET TRUTH SHALL APPEARE, | AN HIMNE FOR CIRCUMCISION | 29 | 46 141 | 37 |
| SOE SOONE CHANGE PART. | LUKE 2. QUAERIT JESUM | 4 | MS 379 | 11 |
| LEFT MANY A STARRY TEARE, TO THINKE HOW SOONE | AN ELEGY MR STANNINOW | 41 | MS 394 | 473 |
| THY MAIDEN STREAMES SOE SOONE TO NEPTUNES BED. | AN ELEGIE ON DR PORTER | 2 | MS 395 | 476 |

SOONER

| | | | | |
|---|---|---|---|---|
| AH THEE JERUSALEM, AH SOONER MAY | PSALME 137 | 15 | 46 104 | 7 |
| THE BABE NO SOONER 'GAN TO SEEKE, | A HYMNE OF THE NATIVITY | 47 | 46 106 | 76 |
| TO THE KINGS HEART, THE SNAKE NO SOONER HIST, | SOSPETTO D'HERODE | 469 | 46 109 | 216 |
| NO SOONER THEREFORE SHALL THE MORNING SEE | SOSPETTO D'HERODE | 505 | 46 109 | 216 |
| OR E'RE THE SOONER SEEK HIS WESTERN BED, | CHARITAS NIMIA | 42 | 52 280 | 48 |

SOOTY

| | | | | |
|---|---|---|---|---|
| TO THESE THY SOOTY KINGDOMES THOU ART DRIVEN, | SOSPETTO D'HERODE | 268 | 46 109 | 216 |
| SHEE LIFTS HER SOOTY LAMPES, AND LOOKING ROUND | SOSPETTO D'HERODE | 301 | 46 109 | 216 |
| LEAST IT BREAKE FORTH, & BURNE THY SOOTY CELL. | ON GUNPOWDER-TREASON | 66 | MS 384 | 456 |

SUTTY

| | | | | |
|---|---|---|---|---|
| THREE COLEBLACK SISTERS, (WHOSE LONG SUTTY HAIRE, | UPON GUNPOWDER TREASON | 9 | MS 387 | 461 |

SORDID

| | | | | |
|---|---|---|---|---|
| FOR SURE THE SORDID EARTH | WEEPER | 170 | 52 307 | 120 |

SORDIDLY

| | | | | |
|---|---|---|---|---|
| SORDIDLY SHIFTING HANDS WITH SHADES & NIGHT. | IN GLORIOUS EPIPHANIE | 35 | 52 253 | 39 |

SORE

| | | | | |
|---|---|---|---|---|
| AND WINTER STROW HER WAY, YEA, SUCH A SORE | SOSPETTO D'HERODE | 380 | 46 109 | 216 |
| THOSE BEAUTEOUS RAVISHERS OPPREST SO SORE | IN GLORIOUS EPIPHANIE | 91 | 52 253 | 39 |

SORROW

| | | | | |
|---|---|---|---|---|
| MAKES SORROW HALFE SO RICH, | THE WEEPER | 45 | 46 79 | 120 |
| WHEN SORROW WOULD BE SEENE | THE WEEPER | 49 | 46 79 | 120 |
| SITS SORROW WITH A FACE SO FAIRE, | THE WEEPER | 58 | 46 79 | 120 |
| YOU FROM HER EYES SWOLNE WOMBES OF SORROW. | THE WEEPER | 126 | 46 79 | 120 |
| IS THE SOLEMNITY MY SORROW WEARES, | SOSPETTO D'HERODE | 215 | 46 109 | 216 |
| OF SORROW, WITH A SOFT AND DOWNY HAND, | SOSPETTO D'HERODE | 391 | 46 109 | 216 |
| HEE TO WHOM OUR SORROW BRINGS, | ANOTHER ON HERRYS | 9 | 46 170 | 469 |
| SICKNESSE, AND SORROW, WHOSE PALE LIDDS NE'RE KNOW | TO THE MORNING | 56 | 46 183 | 497 |
| TO MY LOVING, LINGRING SORROW. | OUT OF THE ITALIAN (1) | 42 | 46 188 | 545 |

| | | | | | |
|---|---|---|---|---|---|
| BUT IF WE DARKE SONS OF SORROW | OUT OF CATULLUS | 6 | 46 | 194 | 523 |
| FROM A FORE SPENT NIGHT OF SORROW. | WISHES SUPPOSED MISTRESSE | 78 | 46 | 195 | 479 |
| THAT WE, DARK SONS OF DUST & SORROW. | TO THE NAME OF JESUS | 99 | 52 | 239 | 30 |
| FOR FRUIT OF SORROW & OF SHAME. | OFFICE H. CROSS SIXT | 6 | 52 | 270 | 97 |
| SOMTHING FROM THY FULL SEAS OF SORROW. | SANCTA MARIA DOLORUM | 44 | 52 | 283 | 162 |
| SITTS SORROW WITH A FACE SO FAIR. | WEEPER | 34 | 52 | 307 | 120 |
| WHEN SORROW WOULD BE SEEN | WEEPER | 37 | 52 | 307 | 120 |
| YOU FROM THOSE NESTS OF NOBLE SORROW. | WEEPER | 168 | 52 | 307 | 120 |

SORROW'S

| | | | | | |
|---|---|---|---|---|---|
| NOW IS THE NOON OF SORROW'S NIGHT. | OFFICE H. CROSS SIXT | 1 | 52 | 270 | 97 |
| NAME TO BE KNOWN, ALAS, BUT SORROW'S MOTHER. | SANCTA MARIA DOLORUM | 4 | 52 | 283 | 162 |
| COME YOUR WHOLE SELVES, SORROW'S GREAT SON & MOTHER. | SANCTA MARIA DOLORUM | 77 | 52 | 283 | 162 |
| SOME SOLACE IN MY SORROW'S CERTAINTY | ALEXIAS FIRST ELEGIE | 10 | 52 | 334 | 204 |
| ALEXIS' WIDDOW NOW IS SORROW'S WIFE. | ALEXIAS SECONDE ELEGIE | 5 | 52 | 335 | 207 |

SORROWS

| | | | | | |
|---|---|---|---|---|---|
| ALL THY SORROWS HERE SHALL SHINE, | IN MEMORY OF LADY MADRE TERESA | 148 | 46 | 131 | 52 |
| THE UNKNOWN SORROWS OF OUR KING, | OFFICE H. CROSS MATINES | 11 | 52 | 265 | 86 |
| THY SORROWS CHIDE OUR SHAME. | OFFICE H. CROSS COMPLINE | 21 | 52 | 274 | 105 |
| IN SORROWS DRAW NO DIVIDEND WITH YOU. | SANCTA MARIA DOLORUM | 84 | 52 | 283 | 162 |
| ALL THY SORROWS HERE SHALL SHINE, | TERESA | 147 | 52 | 315 | 52 |
| NEW DROPS, WASH OFF THE SWEAT OF THIS DAYE'S SORROWS. | DESCRIPTION RELIGIOUS HOUSE | 22 | 52 | 338 | 213 |

SORROWES

| | | | | | |
|---|---|---|---|---|---|
| SORROWES BEST JEWELS LYE IN THESE | THE WEEPER | 47 | 46 | 79 | 120 |
| FROM OUR SINS & HIS OWN SORROWES. | IN GLORIOUS EPIPHANIE | 156 | 52 | 253 | 39 |
| NOR KEEP SUCH NOBLE SORROWES COMPANY. | SANCTA MARIA DOLORUM | 14 | 52 | 283 | 162 |

SORRY

| | | | | | |
|---|---|---|---|---|---|
| 'TWAS FOR SUCH SORRY MERCHANDISE | CHARITAS NIMIA | 7 | 52 | 280 | 48 |

SOUGHT

| | | | | | |
|---|---|---|---|---|---|
| THROUGH LEARNINGS UNIVERSE, AND (VAINELY) SOUGHT | UPON BISHOP ANDREWES PICTURE | 6 | 46 | 163 | 490 |
| WHILE THROUGH THE WORLD SHE SOUGHT HER WANDRING MATE. | ALEXIAS FIRST ELEGIE | 30 | 52 | 334 | 204 |
| WHEN THOUSANDS SOUGHT MY LOVE, LOV'D NONE BUT THEE. | ALEXIAS THIRD ELEGIE | 54 | 52 | 336 | 209 |
| BUT THE DAINTY SCARUS, SOUGHT | PETRONIJ ALES PHASIACIS PETITA | 11 | MS | 382 | 526 |

SOUL

| | | | | | |
|---|---|---|---|---|---|
| OF YOUR BRAVE SOUL SO SLOWLY FORTH. | TO COUNTESSE OF DENBIGH | 8 | 52 | 236 | 146 |
| AH LINGER NOT, LOV'D SOUL. A SLOW | TO COUNTESSE OF DENBIGH | 13 | 52 | 236 | 146 |
| THE SELF-SHUTT CABINET OF AN UNSEARCHT SOUL. | TO COUNTESSE OF DENBIGH | 36 | 52 | 236 | 146 |
| AWAKE, MY GLORY. SOUL, (IF SUCH THOU BE, | TO THE NAME OF JESUS | 13 | 52 | 239 | 30 |
| GOE, SOUL, OUT OF THY SELF, & SEEK FOR MORE. | TO THE NAME OF JESUS | 27 | 52 | 239 | 30 |
| SHALL WE DARE THIS, MY SOUL. WE'L DOE'T AND BRING | TO THE NAME OF JESUS | 44 | 52 | 239 | 30 |
| POWRES OF MY SOUL, BE PROUD. | TO THE NAME OF JESUS | 92 | 52 | 239 | 30 |
| THE SOUL THAT TASTS THEE TAKES FROM THENCE. | TO THE NAME OF JESUS | 188 | 52 | 239 | 30 |
| OF HIS STRONG SOUL, SHALL HE | IN GLORIOUS EPIPHANIE | 197 | 52 | 253 | 39 |
| LOOK UP, LANGUISHING SOUL. LO WHERE THE FAIR | VEXILLA REGIS | 1 | 52 | 277 | 156 |
| WHAT IF MY FAITHLESSE SOUL & I | CHARITAS NIMIA | 49 | 52 | 280 | 48 |
| AND IF THOU YET (FAINT SOUL.) DEFERR | SANCTA MARIA DOLORUM | 89 | 52 | 283 | 162 |
| MY LIFE, MY SOUL, MY SURER SELFE TO MEE. | ADORO TE | 44 | 52 | 291 | 172 |
| WHEN THIS DRY SOUL THOSE EYES SHALL SEE, | ADORO TE | 53 | 52 | 291 | 172 |
| HEARS'T THOU, MY SOUL, WHAT SERIOUS THINGS | DIES IRAE | 1 | 52 | 298 | 186 |
| AH THEN, POOR SOUL, WHAT WILT THOU SAY. | DIES IRAE | 21 | 52 | 298 | 186 |
| AND THIS LOV'D SOUL, JUDG'D WORTH NO LESSE | DIES IRAE | 35 | 52 | 298 | 186 |
| O SAY THE WORD MY SOUL SHALL LIVE. | DIES IRAE | 48 | 52 | 298 | 186 |
| AND MILKY SOUL OF A SOFT CHILD. | TERESA | 14 | 52 | 315 | 52 |
| A SOUL KEPT THERE SO SWEET, O NO. | TERESA | 73 | 52 | 315 | 52 |
| WHAT JOYES SHALL SEIZE THY SOUL, WHEN SHE | TERESA | 133 | 52 | 315 | 52 |
| DRESSE THE SOUL THAT ERST THEY SLEW. | TERESA | 152 | 52 | 315 | 52 |
| MADE FRUITFULL THY FAIR SOUL, GOE NOW | TERESA | 169 | 52 | 315 | 52 |
| AND LOVE'S THAT BODY'S SOUL, NO LAW CONTROWLLS | AN APOLOGIE FOR (TERESA) HYMNE | 18 | 52 | 322 | 59 |
| WHAT SOUL SO E'RE, IN ANY LANGUAGE, CAN | AN APOLOGIE FOR (TERESA) HYMNE | 21 | 52 | 322 | 59 |
| DRINK UP AL SPAIN IN SACK. LET MY SOUL SWELL | AN APOLOGIE FOR (TERESA) HYMNE | 30 | 52 | 322 | 59 |
| (MY SOUL,) SOME DRINK FROM MEN TO BEASTS, O THEN | AN APOLOGIE FOR (TERESA) HYMNE | 35 | 52 | 322 | 59 |
| THAT SEIZ'D THY PARTING SOUL, & SEAL'D THEE HIS. | FLAMING HEART | 102 | 52 | 324 | 61 |
| SENDS UP MY SOUL TO SEEK THY FACE. | A SONG | 2 | 52 | 327 | 65 |
| DEAR SOUL, BE STRONG. | PRAYER TO GENTLE-WOMAN | 39 | 52 | 328 | 139 |
| THE SOUL IT SELFE MORE FEELS THEN HEARES. | PRAYER TO GENTLE-WOMAN | 68 | 52 | 328 | 139 |
| OF SOUL, DEAR & DIVINE ANNIHILATIONS. | PRAYER TO GENTLE-WOMAN | 78 | 52 | 328 | 139 |
| ON THE FAIR SOUL WHOM FIRST HE MEETS. | PRAYER TO GENTLE-WOMAN | 95 | 52 | 328 | 139 |
| DEAR, HEAVN-DESIGNED SOUL. | TO SAME CONCERNING CHOISE | 1 | 52 | 331 | 66 |
| SAY, GENTLE SOUL, WHAT CAN YOU FIND | TO SAME CONCERNING CHOISE | 10 | 52 | 331 | 66 |
| YOUR SOUL TO ANY SON OF DUST. | TO SAME CONCERNING CHOISE | 19 | 52 | 331 | 66 |
| YOUR WISE SOUL, NEVER TO BE WONNE | TO SAME CONCERNING CHOISE | 56 | 52 | 331 | 66 |
| FAREWELL, & SHINE, FAIR SOUL, SHINE THERE ABOVE | ALEXIAS FIRST ELEGIE | 35 | 52 | 334 | 204 |
| THE SELF-REMEMBRING SOUL SWEETLY RECOVERS | DESCRIPTION RELIGIOUS HOUSE | 36 | 52 | 338 | 213 |
| 'TWIXT SOUL & BODY A DIVORCE. | AN EPITAPH UPON MARRIED COUPLE | 4 | 52 | 339 | 478 |
| DEAR RELIQUES OF A DISLODG'D SOUL, WHOSE LACK | DEATH'S LECTURE | 1 | 52 | 340 | 475 |
| A MAN WHOSE SOBER SOUL CAN TELL | TEMPERANCE | 17 | 52 | 342 | 510 |
| A WELL-CLOTH'D SOUL, THAT'S NOT OPPREST | TEMPERANCE | 21 | 52 | 342 | 510 |
| A SOUL SHEATH'D IN A CHRISTALL SHRINE. | TEMPERANCE | 23 | 52 | 342 | 510 |
| A SOUL, WHOSE INTELLECTUALL BEAMES | TEMPERANCE | 29 | 52 | 342 | 510 |
| A HAPPY SOUL, THAT ALL THE WAY | TEMPERANCE | 31 | 52 | 342 | 510 |
| SOUL & BODY PART LIKE FREINDS. | TEMPERANCE | 48 | 52 | 342 | 510 |
| THEIR SUPPLE ESSENCE WITH THE SOUL OF WINE. | (ON) HOPE | 30 | 52 | 345 | 71 |
| AH, LINGER NOT, LOV'D SOUL. A SLOW | AGAINST IRRESOLUTION AND DELAY | 7 | 52 | 347 | 146 |

| | | | | |
|---|---|---|---|---|
| OF YOUR BRAVE SOUL SO SLOWLY FORTH. | AGAINST IRRESOLUTION AND DELAY | 16 | 52 347 | 146 |
| YEILD TO HIS SIEGE, WISE SOUL, AND SEE | AGAINST IRRESOLUTION AND DELAY | 79 | 52 347 | 146 |

SOUL-APPEASING

| | | | | |
|---|---|---|---|---|
| THE AIERY SHOP OF SOUL-APPEASING SOUND. | TO THE NAME OF JESUS | 34 | 52 239 | 30 |

SOUL-PEIRCING

| | | | | |
|---|---|---|---|---|
| SPIRITUALL & SOUL-PEIRCING GLANCES | PRAYER TO GENTLE-WOMAN | 71 | 52 328 | 139 |

SOUL'S

| | | | | |
|---|---|---|---|---|
| IT'S SEAT YOUR SOUL'S JUST CENTER BE. | TO COUNTESSE OF DENBIGH | 56 | 52 236 | 146 |
| O YOU, MY SOUL'S MOST CERTAIN WINGS. | TO THE NAME OF JESUS | 64 | 52 239 | 30 |
| KEEP CLOSE, MY SOUL'S INQUIRING EY. | ADORO TE | 6 | 52 291 | 172 |
| THY SOUL'S KIND SHEPHEARD, THY HART'S KING. | LAUDA SION SALVATOREM | 2 | 52 294 | 178 |
| AND MELT THY SOUL'S SWEET MANSION. | TERESA | 112 | 52 315 | 52 |

SOULE

| | | | | |
|---|---|---|---|---|
| OF HER DELICIOUS SOULE, THAT THERE DOES LYE | MUSICKS DUELL | 67 | 46 149 | 535 |
| HER LITTLE SOULE IS RAVISHT. AND SO POUR'D | MUSICKS DUELL | 102 | 46 149 | 535 |
| IN MUSICK'S RAVISH'T SOULE HEE DARE NOT TELL, | MUSICKS DUELL | 144 | 46 149 | 535 |
| THEIR MASTERS BLEST SOULE (SNATCHT OUT AT HIS EARES | MUSICKS DUELL | 147 | 46 149 | 535 |
| ALAS. IN VAINE. FOR WHILE (SWEET SOULE) SHEE TRYES | MUSICKS DUELL | 161 | 46 149 | 535 |
| A MAN WHOSE SOBER SOULE CAN TELL, | IN PRAISE OF LESSIUS | 19 | 46 156 | 510 |
| A WELL CLOATHED SOULE THATS NOT OPPREST, | IN PRAISE OF LESSIUS | 23 | 46 156 | 510 |
| A SOULE SHEATHED IN A CHRISTALL SHRINE, | IN PRAISE OF LESSIUS | 25 | 46 156 | 510 |
| A SOULE WHOSE INTELECTUALL BEAMES | IN PRAISE OF LESSIUS | 31 | 46 156 | 510 |
| A HAPPY SOULE THAT ALL THE WAY, | IN PRAISE OF LESSIUS | 33 | 46 156 | 510 |
| WHOSE FAIRE ILLUSTRIOUS SOULE, LED HIS FREE THOUGHT | UPON BISHOP ANDREWES PICTURE | 5 | 46 163 | 490 |
| FOR HIS WHITE SOULE IS MADE. | ON BAPTIZED AETHIOPIAN | 4 | 46 85 | 29 |
| PLEASURE SINGS MY SOULE TO REST, | PSALME 23 | 9 | 46 102 | 5 |
| HEE CALLS HOME MY SOULE FROM DYING, | PSALME 23 | 18 | 46 102 | 5 |
| AND THENCE MY RIPE SOULE WILL I BREATH | PSALME 23 | 71 | 46 102 | 5 |
| WHY DOST THOU LET THY BRAVE SOULE LYE SUPPREST, | SOSPETTO D'HERODE | 429 | 46 109 | 216 |
| DEARE SOULE BEE STRONG, | ON A PRAYER BOOKE | 33 | 46 126 | 139 |
| THE SOULE IT SELFE MORE FEELES THEN HEARES. | ON A PRAYER BOOKE | 62 | 46 126 | 139 |
| SPIRITUALL AND SOULE PEIRCING GLANCES. | ON A PRAYER BOOKE | 65 | 46 126 | 139 |
| OF SOULE. DEARE, AND DIVINE ANNIHILATIONS. | ON A PRAYER BOOKE | 72 | 46 126 | 139 |
| ON THE FAIRE SOULE WHOM FIRST HEE MEETS. | ON A PRAYER BOOKE | 89 | 46 126 | 139 |
| HAPPY SOULE WHO NEVER MISSES, | ON A PRAYER BOOKE | 98 | 46 126 | 139 |
| O LET THAT HAPPY SOULE HOLD FAST | ON A PRAYER BOOKE | 105 | 46 126 | 139 |
| HAPPY SOULE SHEE SHALL DISCOVER, | ON A PRAYER BOOKE | 115 | 46 126 | 139 |
| AND MILKY SOULE OF A SOFT CHILDE. | IN MEMORY OF LADY MADRE TERESA | 14 | 46 131 | 52 |
| A SOULE KEPT THERE SO SWEET. O NO, | IN MEMORY OF LADY MADRE TERESA | 73 | 46 131 | 52 |
| WHAT JOY SHALL SEIZE THY SOULE WHEN SHEE | IN MEMORY OF LADY MADRE TERESA | 134 | 46 131 | 52 |
| DRESSE THE SOULE, WHICH LATE THEY SLEW. | IN MEMORY OF LADY MADRE TERESA | 153 | 46 131 | 52 |
| MADE FRUITFULL THY FAIRE SOULE. GOE NOW | IN MEMORY OF LADY MADRE TERESA | 170 | 46 131 | 52 |
| AND LOVES THAT BODIES SOULE. NO LAW CONTROULES | AN APOLOGIE FOR HYMNE (TERESA) | 18 | 46 136 | 59 |
| WHAT SOULE SOEVER IN ANY LANGUAGE CAN | AN APOLOGIE FOR HYMNE (TERESA) | 21 | 46 136 | 59 |
| DRINKE UP ALL SPAINE IN SACK, LET MY SOULE SWELL | AN APOLOGIE FOR HYMNE (TERESA) | 30 | 46 136 | 59 |
| MY SOULE, SOME DIVINE FROM MEN TO BEASTS. O THEN, | AN APOLOGIE FOR HYMNE (TERESA) | 35 | 46 136 | 59 |
| THEIR SUBTILE ESSENCE WITH THE SOULE OF WINE. | ON HOPE | 60 | 46 143 | 71 |
| 'TWIXT SOULE AND BODY A DIVORCE. | AN EPITAPH HUSBAND AND WIFE | 4 | 46 174 | 478 |
| DEARE RELIQUES OF A DISLODG'D SOULE, WHOSE LACKE | UPON STANINOUGH'S DEATH | 1 | 46 175 | 475 |
| OFT MY SOULE HAVE I BIN GLAD TO SEEKE | LUKE 2. QUAERIT JESUM | 41 | MS 379 | 11 |
| SHOULD HAVE HIS SOULE FRIGHTED BEYOND THE SPHAERES. | UPON GUNPOWDER TREASON | 10 | MS 386 | 460 |
| EACH SOULE IN SIGHES HAD SPENT ITS DEAREST BREATH, | UPON GUNPOWDER TREASON | 41 | MS 386 | 460 |
| MY SOULE SHEE WAS SECURE. STILL HAVE I BORNE | OUT OF GROTIUS | 11 | MS 398 | 198 |

SOULS

| | | | | |
|---|---|---|---|---|
| FOR WORTHY SOULS WHOSE WISE EMBRACES | ON A PRAYER BOOKE | 38 | 46 126 | 139 |
| SOULS ARE NOT SPANIARDS TOO, ONE FREINDLY FLOUD | AN APOLOGIE FOR (TERESA) HYMNE | 15 | 52 322 | 59 |
| SPEAK HEAV'N LIKE HER'S IS MY SOULS COUNTRY-MAN. | AN APOLOGIE FOR (TERESA) HYMNE | 22 | 52 322 | 59 |
| AND LASH EARTH-LABORING SOULS. | DESCRIPTION RELIGIOUS HOUSE | 27 | 52 338 | 213 |

SOULES

| | | | | |
|---|---|---|---|---|
| WHILE THEIR AFFRIGHTED SOULES, NOW WING'D FOR FLIGHT | THE BEGINNING OF HELIODORUS | 19 | 46 158 | 517 |
| GOE SMILING SOULES, YOUR NEW BUILT CAGES BREAKE, | TO INFANT MARTYRS | 1 | 46 88 | 10 |
| SLIPPERY SOULES IN SMILING EYES) | A HYMNE OF THE NATIVITY | 73 | 46 106 | 76 |
| GAVE FORTH YOUR BLOOD FOR BREATH, SPOKE SOULES FOR WORDS. | SOSPETTO D'HERODE | 8 | 46 109 | 216 |
| AND WHILE THE BLACK SOULES BOILE IN THEIR OWNE GORE, | SOSPETTO D'HERODE | 295 | 46 109 | 216 |
| OF SOULES, WHICH IN THAT NAMES SWEET GRACES, | IN MEMORY OF LADY MADRE TERESA | 86 | 46 131 | 52 |
| AND MELT THY SOULES SWEET MANSION. | IN MEMORY OF LADY MADRE TERESA | 113 | 46 131 | 52 |
| SOULES AS THY SHINING SELFE, SHALL COME, | IN MEMORY OF LADY MADRE TERESA | 126 | 46 131 | 52 |
| THEY FEED OUR SOULES, SHALL CLOATH THINE THERE. | IN MEMORY OF LADY MADRE TERESA | 159 | 46 131 | 52 |
| THOUSANDS OF CROWND SOULES, THRONG TO BEE | IN MEMORY OF LADY MADRE TERESA | 167 | 46 131 | 52 |
| OF THOUSAND SOULES WHOSE HAPPY NAMES, | IN MEMORY OF LADY MADRE TERESA | 175 | 46 131 | 52 |
| SOULES ARE NOT SPANIARDS TOO, ONE FRENDLY FLOOD | AN APOLOGIE FOR HYMNE (TERESA) | 15 | 46 136 | 59 |
| CHRISTS FAITH MAKES BUT ONE BODY OF ALL SOULES. | AN APOLOGIE FOR HYMNE (TERESA) | 17 | 46 136 | 59 |
| SPEAKE HEAVEN LIKE HERS, IS MY SOULES COUNTRY-MAN. | AN APOLOGIE FOR HYMNE (TERESA) | 22 | 46 136 | 59 |
| O THOU FULL MIXTURE OF THOSE MIGHTY SOULES, | UPON YORKE HIS BIRTH | 35 | 46 176 | 500 |
| ALL YE WISE SOULES, WHO IN THE WEALTHY BREST | TO THE NAME OF JESUS | 11 | 52 239 | 30 |
| SOLLICITERS OF SOULES OR EARES. | TO THE NAME OF JESUS | 79 | 52 239 | 30 |
| OF HUMBLE SOULES. THAT SEEK TO FIND | TO THE NAME OF JESUS | 121 | 52,239 | 30 |
| BODY OF BLESSINGS. SPIRIT OF SOULES EXTRACTED. | TO THE NAME OF JESUS | 166 | 52 239 | 30 |
| IN CENTER OF THEIR INMOST SOULES THEY WORE THEE, | TO THE NAME OF JESUS | 205 | 52 239 | 30 |
| SLIPPERY SOULES IN SMILING EYES. | IN HOLY NATIVITY | 93 | 52 246 | 76 |
| LIFT OUR LEAN SOULES, & SETT US UP | LAUDA SION SALVATOREM | 75 | 52 294 | 178 |

| | | | | | |
|---|---|---|---|---|---|
| OF SOULES WHICH IN THAT NAME'S SWEET GRACES | TERESA | 86 | 52 | 315 | 52 |
| SOULES AS THY SHINING SELF, SHALL COME | TERESA | 125 | 52 | 315 | 52 |
| THEY FEED OUR SOULES, SHALL CLOTH THINE THERE. | TERESA | 158 | 52 | 315 | 52 |
| THOUSANDS OF CROWN'D SOULES THRONG TO BE | TERESA | 166 | 52 | 315 | 52 |
| OF THOUSAND SOULES, WHOSE HAPPY NAMES | TERESA | 174 | 52 | 315 | 52 |
| CHRIST'S FAITH MAKES BUT ONE BODY OF ALL SOULES | AN APOLOGIE FOR (TERESA) HYMNE | 17 | 52 | 322 | 59 |
| LET MYSTICK DEATHS WAIT ON'T, & WISE SOULES BE | FLAMING HEART | 83 | 52 | 324 | 61 |
| FOR WORTHY SOULES, WHOSE WISE EMBRACES | PRAYER TO GENTLE-WOMAN | 44 | 52 | 328 | 139 |
| OF SOULES, DISDAIN THAT I DISCOVER | TO SAME CONCERNING CHOISE | 42 | 52 | 331 | 66 |
| BUT WALKES & UNSHORN WOODS. AND SOULES, JUST SO | DESCRIPTION RELIGIOUS HOUSE | 9 | 52 | 338 | 213 |
| MY SOULES SWEET REST. | LUKE 2. QUAERIT JESUM | 6 | MS | 379 | 11 |
| SIFTING THE SOULES OF GUILT. & YOU, (OH YOU.) | HORATIJ ILLE & NEFASTO | 36 | MS | 382 | 530 |
| THERE THESE BRAVE SOULES DEALE TO EACH WONDRING EARE | HORATIJ ILLE & NEFASTO | 45 | MS | 382 | 530 |
| NOW TO THOSE TOILING SOULES IT GIVES ITS LIGHT, | ON GUNPOWDER-TREASON | 57 | MS | 384 | 458 |
| MAKE THEIR SCAR'D SOULES TAKE WING, & FLY AWAY. | AN ELEGIE ON DR PORTER | 30 | MS | 395 | 476 |

SOUND

| | | | | | |
|---|---|---|---|---|---|
| THAT UNDER HUNGERS TEETH WILL NEEDS BE SOUND. | ON MIRACLE OF LOAVES | 2 | 46 | 86 | 15 |
| CHRIST BIDS THE DUMBE TONGUE SPEAKE, IT SPEAKES, THE SOUND | THE DUMBE HEALED | 1 | 46 | 87 | 16 |
| THE FULL SOUND OF THY VICTORY. | NEITHER DURST MAN ASKE | 18 | 46 | 92 | 20 |
| THE TYRRHENE SEAS, AND SHORES SOUND ALL THE SAME, | SOSPETTO D'HERODE | 31 | 46 | 109 | 216 |
| WHILE HIS STEELE SIDES SOUND WITH HIS TAYLES STRONG LASH. | SOSPETTO D'HERODE | 64 | 46 | 109 | 216 |
| HEE STUDIES SCRIPTURE, STRIVES TO SOUND THE HEART, | SOSPETTO D'HERODE | 155 | 46 | 109 | 216 |
| THRICE HOWL'D THE CAVES OF NIGHT, AND THRICE THE SOUND, | SOSPETTO D'HERODE | 297 | 46 | 109 | 216 |
| THE AIERY SHOP OF SOUL-APPEASING SOUND. | TO THE NAME OF JESUS | 34 | 52 | 239 | 30 |
| SOUND FORTH, CAELESTIALL ORGANS,LETT HEAVNS QUIRE | UPON KINGS CORONATION | 1 | MS | 389 | 454 |
| THE JOYFULL SPHAERES WITH A DELICIOUS SOUND | UPON KINGS CORONATION | 21 | MS | 390 | 453 |
| SOUND GOODNESSE WITH HER SHADOW WHICH THEY WEARE, | OUT OF GROTIUS | 43 | MS | 398 | 198 |

SOUNDS

| | | | | | |
|---|---|---|---|---|---|
| SWEET MISTRIS SOUNDS A GREAT DEALE BETTER. | PETRONIJ ALES PHASIACIS PETITA | 18 | MS | 382 | 526 |

SOUNDETH

| | | | | | |
|---|---|---|---|---|---|
| THE MUSICK OF HIS NAME YETT SOUNDETH SHRILL. | UPON DEATH OF A FREIND | 22 | MS | 393 | 477 |

SOURSE

| | | | | | |
|---|---|---|---|---|---|
| SOFT SOURSE OF LOVE | SANCTA MARIA DOLORUM | 42 | 52 | 283 | 162 |
| AND DRINK THE UNSEAL'D SOURSE OF THEE. | ADORO TE | 54 | 52 | 291 | 172 |
| HAIL, DOOR OF LIFE. & SOURSE OF DAY. | O GLORIOSA DOMINA | 32 | 52 | 302 | 194 |
| HOME TO THE ORIGINALL SOURSE OF LIGHT & INTELLECTUALL | DESCRIPTION RELIGIOUS HOUSE | 39 | 52 | 338 | 213 |

SOUTHWEST-WIND

| | | | | | |
|---|---|---|---|---|---|
| THAT THE SOUTHWEST-WIND HURRIES IN HIS ARMES, | OUT OF VIRGIL | 20 | 46 | 155 | 529 |

SOVERAIGN

| | | | | | |
|---|---|---|---|---|---|
| AND 'MONGST THY SHAFTS OF SOVERAIGN LIGHT | TO COUNTESSE OF DENBIGH | 32 | 52 | 236 | 146 |
| THAT BLOOD, WHOSE LEAST DROPS SOVERAIGN BE | ADORO TE | 49 | 52 | 291 | 172 |
| THIS SOVERAIGN SUBJECT SITTS ABOVE | LAUDA SION SALVATOREM | 5 | 52 | 294 | 178 |
| MORE SOVERAIGN & SWEET FROM YOU. | WEEPER | 54 | 52 | 307 | 120 |
| IT SHINES, & WITH A SOVERAIGN RAY | TERESA | 84 | 52 | 315 | 52 |
| THE VIRGIN-BIRTHS WITH WHICH THY SOVERAIGN SPOUSE | TERESA | 168 | 52 | 315 | 52 |

ALL-SOVERAIGN

| | | | | | |
|---|---|---|---|---|---|
| ALL-SOVERAIGN NAME | TO THE NAME OF JESUS | 36 | 52 | 239 | 30 |

SOVERAIGNE

| | | | | | |
|---|---|---|---|---|---|
| MORE SOVERAIGNE AND SWEET FROM YOU. | THE WEEPER | 72 | 46 | 79 | 120 |
| IT SHINES, AND WITH A SOVERAIGNE RAY, | IN MEMORY OF LADY MADRE TERESA | 84 | 46 | 131 | 52 |
| HIGH BEAUTIES SOVERAIGNE, THAT MY FUNERALL FLAMES | EX EUPHORMIONE | 13 | MS | 392 | 525 |

SOVERAIN

| | | | | | |
|---|---|---|---|---|---|
| THOUGH IN IT SELF THIS SOVERAIN FEAST | LAUDA SION SALVATOREM | 49 | 52 | 294 | 178 |

SOW'ST

| | | | | | |
|---|---|---|---|---|---|
| AND STARS THOU SOW'ST WHOSE HARVEST DARES | THE WEEPER | 10 | 46 | 79 | 120 |
| AND STARRES THOU SOW'ST, WHOSE HARVEST DARES | WEEPER | 10 | 52 | 307 | 120 |

SOWER

| | | | | | |
|---|---|---|---|---|---|
| THE GENEROUS WINE WITH AGE GROWES STRONG, NOT SOWER. | ON HOPE | 53 | 46 | 143 | 71 |
| THY GENEROUS WINE WITH AGE GROWES STRONG, NOT SOWER. | (ON) HOPE | 23 | 52 | 345 | 71 |

SOWN

| | | | | | |
|---|---|---|---|---|---|
| SO SHALL SHE LEAVE AMONGST THEM SOWN | TERESA | 55 | 52 | 315 | 52 |

SOWNE

| | | | | | |
|---|---|---|---|---|---|
| HAD SOWNE OF OLD THESE DOUBTS IN HIS DEEPE BREST. | SOSPETTO D'HERODE | 498 | 46 | 109 | 216 |
| SO SHALL SHEE LEAVE AMONGST THEM SOWNE, | IN MEMORY OF LADY MADRE TERESA | 55 | 46 | 131 | 52 |

## SOWREST

| | | | | | |
|---|---|---|---|---|---|
| WHAT THE SOWREST FATHERS SAY. | OUT OF CATULLUS | 3 | 46 | 194 | 523 |

## SPAIN

| | | | | | |
|---|---|---|---|---|---|
| PEACE, SURE, WITH PIETY, THOUGH IT COME FROM SPAIN. | AN APOLOGIE FOR (TERESA) HYMNE | 20 | 52 | 322 | 59 |
| DRINK UP AL SPAIN IN SACK. LET MY SOUL SWELL | AN APOLOGIE FOR (TERESA) HYMNE | 30 | 52 | 322 | 59 |

## SPAINS

| | | | | | |
|---|---|---|---|---|---|
| GREAT ANTHONY, SPAINS WELL-BESEEMING PRIDE, | SOSPETTO D'HERODE | 9 | 46 | 109 | 216 |

## SPAINE

| | | | | | |
|---|---|---|---|---|---|
| PEACE SURE WITH PIETY, THOUGH IT DWELL IN SPAINE. | AN APOLOGIE FOR HYMNE (TERESA) | 20 | 46 | 136 | 59 |
| DRINKE UP ALL SPAINE IN SACK, LET MY SOULE SWELL | AN APOLOGIE FOR HYMNE (TERESA) | 30 | 46 | 136 | 59 |

## SPAKE

| | | | | | |
|---|---|---|---|---|---|
| WAS NEVER MAN LORD SPAKE LIKE THEE. | THE BLIND CURED | 4 | 46 | 91 | 19 |
| GOD SPAKE ONCE WHEN HEE ALL THINGS MADE, | AND HE ANSWERED NOTHING | 3 | 46 | 91 | 22 |
| THAT TH'ONE SPAKE, OR THAT TH'OTHER HELD HIS PEACE. | UPON DUMBE DEVILL CAST OUT | 4 | 46 | 93 | 14 |

## SPAK'ST

| | | | | | |
|---|---|---|---|---|---|
| THOU SPAK'ST AND STREIGHT THE BLIND MAN SAW. | THE BLIND CURED | 2 | 46 | 91 | 19 |

## SPAN

| | | | | | |
|---|---|---|---|---|---|
| ETERNITY SHUT IN A SPAN. | A HYMNE OF THE NATIVITY | 54 | 46 | 106 | 76 |
| (HYPERBOLIZED NOTHING.) KNOW THY SPAN. | UPON STANINOUGH'S DEATH | 10 | 46 | 175 | 475 |
| AETERNITY SHUTT IN A SPAN. | IN HOLY NATIVITY | 80 | 52 | 246 | 76 |
| HYPERBOLIZED NOTHING. KNOW THY SPAN. | DEATH'S LECTURE | 11 | 46 | 340 | 475 |
| O THOU THE SPAN OF WHOSE OMNIPOTENCE | OUT OF GROTIUS | 1 | MS | 398 | 198 |

## SPANGLES

| | | | | | |
|---|---|---|---|---|---|
| AS HEAVENS OTHER SPANGLES DOE. | THE WEEPER | 16 | 46 | 79 | 120 |
| AS HEAVN'S OTHER SPANGLES DOE. | WEEPER | 16 | 52 | 307 | 120 |

## SPANIARDS

| | | | | | |
|---|---|---|---|---|---|
| SOULES ARE NOT SPANIARDS TOO, ONE FRENDLY FLOOD | AN APOLOGIE FOR HYMNE (TERESA) | 15 | 46 | 136 | 59 |
| SOULS ARE NOT SPANIARDS TOO, ONE FREINDLY FLOUD | AN APOLOGIE FOR (TERESA) HYMNE | 15 | 52 | 322 | 59 |

## SPANISH

| | | | | | |
|---|---|---|---|---|---|
| O 'TIS NOT SPANISH, BUT 'TIS HEAVEN SHE SPEAKES. | AN APOLOGIE FOR HYMNE (TERESA) | 23 | 46 | 136 | 59 |
| O 'TIS NOT SPANISH, BUT 'TIS HEAV'N SHE SPEAKS. | AN APOLOGIE FOR (TERESA) HYMNE | 23 | 52 | 322 | 59 |

## SPARE

| | | | | | |
|---|---|---|---|---|---|
| 'BOUT MEN AND WOMEN, NOR WILL SPARE | OUT OF GREEKE CUPID'S CRYER | 42 | 46 | 159 | 519 |
| SPARE THIS ONE JEWELL. I'LE BE DIVES STILL. | DIVES ASKING A DROP | 4 | 46 | 96 | 15 |
| FOR WELL THEY NOW CAN SPARE THEIR WINGS, | A HYMNE OF THE NATIVITY | 43 | 46 | 106 | 76 |
| AND IN A PALE GHOST'S SHAPE TO SPARE HIS EYES. | SOSPETTO D'HERODE | 416 | 46 | 109 | 216 |
| SPARE HIM DEATH, O SPARE HIM THEN, | UPON DEATH OF DESIRED HERRYS | 59 | 46 | 168 | 467 |
| SPARE HIM DEATH, O SPARE HIM THEN, | UPON DEATH OF DESIRED HERRYS | 59 | 46 | 168 | 467 |
| SPARE THE SWEETEST AMONG MEN. | UPON DEATH OF DESIRED HERRYS | 60 | 46 | 168 | 467 |
| BUT O THOU WILT NOT, CANST NOT SPARE. | UPON DEATH OF DESIRED HERRYS | 63 | 46 | 168 | 467 |
| SUCH A TEARME AS THIS, SPARE MEE. | ANOTHER ON HERRYS | 48 | 46 | 170 | 469 |
| FOR WELL THEY NOW CAN SPARE THEIR WINGS | IN HOLY NATIVITY | 60 | 52 | 246 | 76 |
| SPARE OUR EYES, BUT PEIRCE OUR HARTS. | IN GLORIOUS EPIPHANIE | 79 | 52 | 253 | 39 |
| FOR LOVE AT LARG TO FILL, SPARE BLOOD & SWEAT. | TERESA | 11 | 52 | 315 | 52 |
| TO SPARE THY QUIET. | LUKE 2. QUAERIT JESUM | 38 | MS | 379 | 11 |
| NOE, NOE, A GIANT WIND, THAT WILL NOT SPARE | ON GUNPOWDER-TREASON | 39 | MS | 364 | 458 |

## SPARK

| | | | | | |
|---|---|---|---|---|---|
| AND SELF-OPPRESSED SPARK, THAT HAS SO LONG | IN GLORIOUS EPIPHANIE | 135 | 52 | 253 | 39 |

## SPARKE

| | | | | | |
|---|---|---|---|---|---|
| A MOIST SPARKE IT IS, | THE TEARE | 3 | 46 | 84 | 50 |
| HE CALLS TO MIND TH'OLD QUARRELL, AND WHAT SPARKE | SOSPETTO D'HERODE | 89 | 46 | 109 | 216 |
| DROP DOWNE ONE SPARKE OF GLORY, & THEY'L PROVE | UPON BIRTH PRINCESSE E | 19 | MS | 391 | 456 |
| 'TWAS NOT THE FROZEN ZONE. ONE SPARKE OF FIRE, | AN ELEGY MR STANNINOW | 31 | MS | 394 | 473 |

## SPARKES

| | | | | | |
|---|---|---|---|---|---|
| HIS SPIRITS, THE SPARKES OF LIFE, AND CHILLS HIS HEART, | SOSPETTO D'HERODE | 422 | 46 | 109 | 216 |
| SHINE FORTH,YE FLAMING SPARKES OF DEITY, | UPON KINGS CORONATION | 37 | MS | 389 | 454 |

## SPARKLING

| | | | | | |
|---|---|---|---|---|---|
| IN THE CLOSE MURMUR OF A SPARKLING NOYSE. | MUSICKS DUELL | 84 | 46 | 149 | 535 |
| THE PURE BIRTH OF EACH SPARKLING NEST, | AN HIMNE FOR CIRCUMCISION | 19 | 46 | 141 | 37 |
| AND PEEP & PROFFER AT THY SPARKLING THRONE. | IN GLORIOUS EPIPHANIE | 225 | 52 | 253 | 39 |
| HIS GLITTERING ROBE, HIS SPARKLING CROWN, | IN GLORIOUS EPIPHANIE | 243 | 52 | 253 | 39 |
| SPARKLING WITH THE SACRED FLAMES | TERESA | 173 | 52 | 315 | 52 |
| THE RADIANT DARTS, SHOTT FROM HIS SPARKLING EYES. | UPON KINGS CORONATION | 35 | MS | 390 | 453 |

## SPARKLING

| | | | | | |
|---|---|---|---|---|---|
| THOSE SPARKLING TWINNES OF LIGHT SHOULD I NOW STILE | UPON BIRTH PRINCESSE E | 43 | MS | 391 | 456 |

## SPARKLING

| | | | | | |
|---|---|---|---|---|---|
| SPARKLING WITH THE SACRED FLAMES. | IN MEMORY OF LADY MADRE TERESA | 174 | 46 | 131 | 52 |
| FULL OF HIGH SPARKLING VIGOUR. TAUGHT BE MEE | OUT OF GROTIUS | 53 | MS | 398 | 198 |

## SPARROWES

| | | | | | |
|---|---|---|---|---|---|
| FEATHERD WITH HIS MOTHERS SPARROWES. | OUT OF THE ITALIAN (1) | 18 | 46 | 188 | 545 |

## SPATIOUS

| | | | | | |
|---|---|---|---|---|---|
| ROOME FOR HER SPATIOUS SELFE, UNTILL AT LENGTH | UPON BISHOP ANDREWES PICTURE | 7 | 46 | 163 | 490 |
| HEE SHOOKE HIMSELFE, AND SPREAD HIS SPATIOUS WINGS. | SOSPETTO D'HERODE | 141 | 46 | 109 | 216 |
| UP, THROUGH THE SPATIOUS PALLACE PASSED SHE, | SOSPETTO D'HERODE | 409 | 46 | 109 | 216 |
| TO THE CONSPIRACY OF OUR SPATIOUS SONG. | TO THE NAME OF JESUS | 71 | 52 | 239 | 30 |
| AND STILL THY SPATIOUS PALACE RING. | CHARITAS NIMIA | 20 | 52 | 280 | 48 |
| OF THOSE WHOSE SPATIOUS BOSOMES SPREAD A THRONE | TERESA | 10 | 52 | 315 | 52 |

## SPEAK

| | | | | | |
|---|---|---|---|---|---|
| THY PRAISE MIGHT NOT SPEAK ENGLISH TOO, FORBID | AN APOLOGIE FOR HYMNE (TERESA) | 11 | 46 | 136 | 59 |
| BUT WHILE I SPEAK, WHITHER ARE RUN | UPON BLEEDING CRUCIFIX | 25 | 52 | 288 | 110 |
| LET HEARTS & LIPPES SPEAK LOWD. AND SAY | O GLORIOSA DOMINA | 31 | 52 | 302 | 194 |
| SPEAK LOWD INTO THE FACE OF DEATH | TERESA | 8 | 52 | 315 | 52 |
| THY PRAISE MIGHT NOT SPEAK ENGLISH TOO. FORBID | AN APOLOGIE FOR (TERESA) HYMNE | 11 | 52 | 322 | 59 |
| SPEAK HEAV'N LIKE HER'S IS MY SOULS COUNTRY-MAN. | AN APOLOGIE FOR (TERESA) HYMNE | 22 | 52 | 322 | 59 |
| AND VENTURE TO SPEAK ONE GOOD WORD | TO SAME CONCERNING CHOISE | 6 | 52 | 331 | 66 |

## SPEAK'ST

| | | | | | |
|---|---|---|---|---|---|
| THOU SPEAK'ST THE WORD (THY WORD'S A LAW) | THE BLIND CURED | 1 | 46 | 91 | 19 |

## SPEAKE

| | | | | | |
|---|---|---|---|---|---|
| A LINE OR TWO, TO SPEAKE HIM DEAD. | UPON THE DEATH OF A GENTLEMAN | 8 | 46 | 166 | 472 |
| NOT US'D TO SPEAKE BUT IN HIS BREATH. | UPON THE DEATH OF A GENTLEMAN | 18 | 46 | 166 | 472 |
| AS TO SPEAKE NOTHING, COME THEN TELL | UPON THE DEATH OF A GENTLEMAN | 24 | 46 | 166 | 472 |
| CHRIST BIDS THE DUMBE TONGUE SPEAKE, IT SPEAKES, THE SOUND | THE DUMBE HEALED | 1 | 46 | 87 | 16 |
| IN HEAV'N YOU'L LEARNE TO SING ERE HERE TO SPEAKE, | TO INFANT MARTYRS | 2 | 46 | 88 | 10 |
| TO SPEAKE AND MAKE THE BLIND MAN SEE. | THE BLIND CURED | 3 | 46 | 91 | 19 |
| TO SPEAKE THUS, WAS TO SPEAKE (SAY I) | THE BLIND CURED | 5 | 46 | 91 | 19 |
| TO SPEAKE THUS, WAS TO SPEAKE (SAY I) | THE BLIND CURED | 5 | 46 | 91 | 19 |
| WHILE THEY SPEAKE NOTHING, THEY SPEAKE ALL | NEITHER DURST MAN ASKE | 21 | 46 | 92 | 20 |
| WHILE THEY SPEAKE NOTHING, THEY SPEAKE ALL | NEITHER DURST MAN ASKE | 21 | 46 | 92 | 20 |
| WHILE THEY SPEAKE NOTHING, THEY PROCLAIME | NEITHER DURST MAN ASKE | 23 | 46 | 92 | 20 |
| THESE WRETCHES HAVE TO SPEAKE THY PRAISE. | NEITHER DURST MAN ASKE | 26 | 46 | 92 | 20 |
| BUT WHILE I SPEAKE, WHITHER ARE RUN | ON BLEEDING WOUNDS OF LORD | 29 | 46 | 101 | 110 |
| SPEAKE LOWD UNTO THE FACE OF DEATH | IN MEMORY OF LADY MADRE TERESA | 8 | 46 | 131 | 52 |
| SPEAKE HEAVEN LIKE HERS. IS MY SOULES COUNTRY-MAN. | AN APOLOGIE FOR HYMNE (TERESA) | 22 | 46 | 136 | 59 |
| O SPEAKE A LOWLY MUSES PARDON. SPEAKE | UPON YORKE HIS BIRTH | 108 | 46 | 176 | 500 |
| O SPEAKE A LOWLY MUSES PARDON. SPEAKE | UPON YORKE HIS BIRTH | 108 | 46 | 176 | 500 |
| THY SILENCE. SPEAKE. AND SHE SHALL TAKE FROM THENCE | UPON YORKE HIS BIRTH | 110 | 46 | 176 | 500 |
| O SPEAKE THOU AND MY PIPE HATH NOUGHT TO SAY. | UPON YORKE HIS BIRTH | 113 | 46 | 176 | 500 |
| AND SPEAKE LOWD | TO THE NAME OF JESUS | 93 | 52 | 239 | 30 |
| LETT NONE DARE SPEAKE OF THEE, BUT SUCH AS THENCE | UPON BIRTH PRINCESSE E | 9 | MS | 391 | 456 |
| THEIR WRONGED BEAUTIES SPEAKE A TRAGAEDY. | AN ELEGIE ON DR PORTER | 11 | MS | 395 | 476 |

## SPEAKS

| | | | | | |
|---|---|---|---|---|---|
| O 'TIS NOT SPANISH, BUT 'TIS HEAV'N SHE SPEAKS. | AN APOLOGIE FOR (TERESA) HYMNE | 23 | 52 | 322 | 59 |

## SPEAKES

| | | | | | |
|---|---|---|---|---|---|
| NOTHING SPEAKES OUR GRIEFE SO WELL | UPON THE DEATH OF A GENTLEMAN | 23 | 46 | 166 | 472 |
| CHRIST BIDS THE DUMBE TONGUE SPEAKE, IT SPEAKES, THE SOUND | THE DUMBE HEALED | 1 | 46 | 87 | 16 |
| THEIR SILENCE SPEAKES ALOUD, AND IS | NEITHER DURST MAN ASKE | 19 | 46 | 92 | 20 |
| O 'TIS NOT SPANISH, BUT 'TIS HEAVEN SHE SPEAKES, | AN APOLOGIE FOR HYMNE (TERESA) | 23 | 46 | 136 | 59 |
| WHAT OF THY PARENT HEAVN YET SPEAKES IN THEE. | TO THE NAME OF JESUS | 16 | 52 | 239 | 30 |
| WHY MAN, THIS SPEAKES PURE MORTALL FRAME. | FLAMING HEART | 23 | 52 | 324 | 61 |
| SPEAKES THE GREAT WISDOME OF TH' ARTIFICER. | UPON BIRTH PRINCESSE E | 40 | MS | 391 | 456 |
| HEE THAT NE'RE HEARD NOW SPEAKES, AND FINDS A TONGUE | OUT OF GROTIUS | 73 | MS | 398 | 198 |

## SPEAKING

| | | | | | |
|---|---|---|---|---|---|
| A SPEAKING DIVELL THIS, A DUMBE ONE THAT. | UPON DUMBE DEVILL CAST OUT | 2 | 46 | 93 | 14 |
| LOSE THIS SAME BUSIE SPEAKING ART | PSALME 137 | 20 | 46 | 104 | 7 |

## LIFE-SPEAKING

| | | | | | |
|---|---|---|---|---|---|
| LET THOSE LIFE-SPEAKING LIPPS COMMAND | DIES IRAE | 63 | 52 | 298 | 186 |

## SPEAR

| | | | | | |
|---|---|---|---|---|---|
| SUPERFLUOUS SPEAR. BUT THERE'S A HEART STANDS BY | OFFICE H. CROSS EVENSONG | 5 | 52 | 273 | 101 |
| AND FROM THE NAILES & SPEAR | VEXILLA REGIS | 15 | 52 | 277 | 156 |

## SPEARE

| | | | | | |
|---|---|---|---|---|---|
| OR NAILE, OR THORNE, OR SPEARE HAVE WRIT IN THEE. | ON MARKES OF SAVIOURS WOUNDS | 2 | 46 | 86 | 28 |
| COULD SHE HAVE FIXT IT ON A FAIRER SPEARE. | ON VIRGINS BASHFULNESSE | 4 | 46 | 89 | 9 |

SPEARE'S

AND NOW TH'ART SET WIDE OPE, THE SPEARE'S SAD ART.    I AM THE DOORE                      1  46  90  17

SPEARS

SWORDS, SPEARS, WITH ALL THE FATALL INSTRUMENTS       SOSPETTO D'HERODE                 326  46 109 216

SPEARES

THIS KNIFE MAY BE THE SPEARES PRAELUDIUM.             OUR LORD IN HIS CIRCUMCISION       18  46  98   9
TO A VAST FIELD OF THORNES, TEN THOUSAND SPEARES      SOSPETTO D'HERODE                 475  46 109 216
TURN SPEARES, & STRAIGHT COME HOME AGAIN.             SANCTA MARIA DOLORUM               30  52 283 162

SPECIALL

(A SPECIALL WORME IT WAS AS EVER KIST                 SOSPETTO D'HERODE                 467  46 109 216

SPECIES

IN DIFFERENT SPECIES, NAMES NOT THINGS.               LAUDA SION SALVATOREM              39  52 294 178

SPECIOUS

AND COURTED IN THE POMPOUS MASK OF A MORE SPECIOUS    IN GLORIOUS EPIPHANIE              53  52 253  39
                                            MIST.

SPEED

POYSONS TO SPEED THEE.  YET THROUGH ALL THE LAND      SOSPETTO D'HERODE                 445  46 109 216
O GOD MAKE SPEED TO SAVE ME.                          OFFICE H. CROSS MATINES             5  52 265  86

SPEEDILY

SPEEDILY HARNESSING HIS FIERY STEEDS.                 UPON KINGS CORONATION              16  MS 390 453

SPELL

FEELES NOT THE STRENGTH, THE REACHING SPELL           OUT OF GREEKE CUPID'S CRYER        36  46 159 519
ONCE I DID SPELL                                      ON MARKES OF SAVIOURS WOUNDS        6  46  86  28
USE IT TO SPELL THY BEAUTYES BETTER.                  IN GLORIOUS EPIPHANIE             187  52 253  39
AND SPELL IT WRONG TO READ IT RIGHT.                  FLAMING HEART                      10  52 324  61

SPEND

SPEND THE DEARE TREASURE OF THY LIFE.                 IN PRAISE OF LESSIUS                4  46 156 510
WHY DID I SPEND MY LIFE, AND SPILL MY BLOOD.          SOSPETTO D'HERODE                 449  46 109 216
IN THE DUST.  PITTY NOW SPEND                         ANOTHER ON HERRYS                  57  46 170 469
SPEND THE DEAR TREASURES OF THY LIFE.                 TEMPERANCE                          4  52 342 510

SPENDING

STILL SPENDING, NEVER SPENT. I MEANE                  THE WEEPER                          5  46  79 120
STILL SPENDING, NEVER SPENT. I MEAN                   WEEPER                              5  52 307 120
OF FAITH. STILL SPENDING, & STILL GROWING STOCK.      (ON) HOPE                          12  52 345  71
SPRANG IN THE SPENDING FINGERS, AND O'REFLOW'D        OUT OF GROTIUS                     62  MS 398 198

SPEND-THRIFT

FAIR SPEND-THRIFT OF THY SELF. THY MEASURE            WEEPER                            128  52 307 120

SPENT

NOW WESTWARD SOL HAD SPENT THE RICHEST BEAMES         MUSICKS DUELL                       1  46 149 535
STILL SPENDING, NEVER SPENT. I MEANE                  THE WEEPER                          5  46  79 120
THY BROTHERS BLOOD BE-SPILT LIFE SPENT IN VAINE.      SOSPETTO D'HERODE                 452  46 109 216
WHICH SPENT CAN BUY SO BRAVE A DEATH.                 IN MEMORY OF LADY MADRE TERESA     18  46 131  52
UPON WHOSE CHOICE POINT SHALL BE SPENT.               IN MEMORY OF LADY MADRE TERESA     90  46 131  52
FROM A FORE SPENT NIGHT OF SORROW.                    WISHES SUPPOSED MISTRESSE          78  46 195 479
HAVE SPENT THE PATIENCE OF EXPECTING WEEKES.          UPON TWO GREENE APRICOCKES          4  48 220 494
TURN'D THEM TO TEARES, & SPENT THEM TOO.              TO THE NAME OF JESUS              138  52 239  30
STILL SPENDING, NEVER SPENT. I MEAN                   WEEPER                              5  52 307 120
WHICH SPENT CAN BUY SO BRAVE A DEATH.                 TERESA                             18  52 315  52
EACH SOULE IN SIGHES HAD SPENT ITS DEAREST BREATH.    UPON GUNPOWDER TREASON             41  MS 386 460
THE STAGGERING LUMPE. EACH EYE SPENT ALL ITS STORE.   UPON KINGS CORONATION              11  MS 390 453

SPHEAR

ALL-CIRCLING POINT.  ALL CENTRING SPHEAR.             IN GLORIOUS EPIPHANIE              26  52 253  39
YOU'AVE SEEN ALLREADY, IN THIS LOWER SPHEAR           TO SAME CONCERNING CHUISE           8  52 331  66
STILL ROWLING A ROUND SPHEAR OF STILL-RETURNING PAIN. DESCRIPTION RELIGIOUS HOUSE        18  52 338 213

HALF-SPHEAR

NOR MAKES THE WHOLE WORLD THY HALF-SPHEAR.            IN GLORIOUS EPIPHANIE              41  52 253  39

SPHEARE

FROM THINE EYE ITS SPHEARE.                           THE TEARE                           9  46  84  50
SPHEARE OF SWEET, AND SUGRED LIES.                    ON A PRAYER BOOKE                  50  46 126 139
TO TAKE ACQUAINTANCE OF THE SPHEARE.                  ON MR. G. HERBERTS BOOKE           13  46 130  68
TO GLAD THE SPHEARE OF ANY NATION.                    UPON YORKE HIS BIRTH               14  46 176 500
FULL GLORY, FLAMING IN HER OWNE FREE SPHEARE.         ON A FOULE MORNING                  8  46 181 495

SPHAERE

| | | | | |
|---|---|---|---|---|
| I WAS MISTAKEN. SOME FAIRE SPHAERE, OR OTHER | LUKE 2. QUAERIT JESUM | 21 | MS 379 | 11 |
| I VEIW A RISING SUNNE IN THIS OUR SPHAERE, | UPON KINGS CORONATION | 14 | MS 389 | 454 |
| FULL GLORY FLAMING IN HER OWNE FREE SPHAERE. | UPON KINGS CORONATION | 14 | MS 390 | 453 |

SPHEARS

| | | | | |
|---|---|---|---|---|
| OF HEAVNS, THE SELF INVOLVING SETT OF SPHEARS | TO THE NAME OF JESUS | 30 | 52 239 | 30 |
| CYMBALLS OF HEAV'N, OR HUMANE SPHEARS, | TO THE NAME OF JESUS | 78 | 52 239 | 30 |

SPHAEARES

| | | | | |
|---|---|---|---|---|
| DOTH TUNE THE SPHAEARES, AND MAKE HEAVENS SELFE LOOKE | MUSICKS DUELL | 118 | 46 149 | 535 |
| BY A STRONG EXTASY) THROUGH ALL THE SPHAEARES | MUSICKS DUELL | 148 | 46 149 | 535 |

SPHAERES

| | | | | |
|---|---|---|---|---|
| PEACE, HEART. THE HEAVENS ARE ANGRY. ALL THEIR SPHAERES | LUKE 2. QUAERIT JESUM | 19 | MS 379 | 11 |
| SHOULD HAVE HIS SOULE FRIGHTED BEYOND THE SPHAERES. | UPON GUNPOWDER TREASON | 10 | MS 386 | 460 |
| FIXT IN YOUR SPHAERES OF GLORY, SHED FROM THENCE | UPON KINGS CORONATION | 39 | MS 389 | 454 |
| THE JOYFULL SPHAERES WITH A DELICIOUS SOUND | UPON KINGS CORONATION | 21 | MS 390 | 453 |
| DANCE, LIKE THE NIMBLE SPHAERES, A JOYFULL ROUND. | UPON BIRTH PRINCESSE E | 32 | MS 391 | 456 |

SPHEARES

| | | | | |
|---|---|---|---|---|
| SHEE CONSULTS THE CONSCIOUS SPHEARES, | LOVES HOROSCOPE | 3 | 46 185 | 483 |
| NOR SPHEARES LET FALL THEIR FAITHFULL ROUNDS. | CHARITAS NIMIA | 18 | 52 280 | 48 |
| SPHEARES OF SWEET & SUGRED LYES, | PRAYER TO GENTLE-WOMAN | 56 | 52 328 | 139 |

SPHINXES

| | | | | |
|---|---|---|---|---|
| OF DRAGONS, HYDRAES, SPHINXES, FILL THE GROVE. | SOSPETTO D'HERODE | 352 | 46 109 | 216 |

SPICES

| | | | | |
|---|---|---|---|---|
| A DELICIOUS DEW OF SPICES. | ON A PRAYER BOOKE | 104 | 46 126 | 139 |
| MOUNTAINS OF MYRRH, & BEDS OF SPICES, | TO THE NAME OF JESUS | 186 | 52 239 | 30 |
| A DELICIOUS DEW OF SPICES. | PRAYER TO GENTLE-WOMAN | 110 | 52 328 | 139 |

SPICY

| | | | | |
|---|---|---|---|---|
| A FRAGRANT BREATH SUCKT FROM THE SPICY NEST | ON A FOULE MORNING | 21 | 46 181 | 495 |
| O DISSIPATE THY SPICY POWRES | TO THE NAME OF JESUS | 167 | 52 239 | 30 |

SPIDE

| | | | | |
|---|---|---|---|---|
| HIS SWELLING GLORYES, AUSTER SPIDE HIM, | UPON DEATH OF DESIRED HERRYS | 41 | 46 168 | 467 |

SPILL

| | | | | |
|---|---|---|---|---|
| WHY DID I SPEND MY LIFE, AND SPILL MY BLOOD, | SOSPETTO D'HERODE | 449 | 46 109 | 216 |

SPILT

| | | | | |
|---|---|---|---|---|
| THY HANDS ARE WASHT, BUT O THE WATERS SPILT, | TO PONTIUS WASHING HANDS | 1 | 46 88 | 22 |
| A BLOUD DRUNKE ERROUR SPILT THE COSTLY AYME | OUT OF GROTIUS | 29 | MS 398 | 198 |

BE-SPILT

| | | | | |
|---|---|---|---|---|
| THY BROTHERS BLOOD BE-SPILT LIFE SPENT IN VAINE. | SOSPETTO D'HERODE | 452 | 46 109 | 216 |

SPIRIT

| | | | | |
|---|---|---|---|---|
| HOW A PURE SPIRIT SHOULD INCARNATE BEE, | SOSPETTO D'HERODE | 167 | 46 109 | 216 |
| BODY OF BLESSINGS. SPIRIT OF SOULES EXTRACTED. | TO THE NAME OF JESUS | 166 | 52 239 | 30 |
| O PRIZE OF THE RICH SPIRIT. WITH WHAT FEIRCE CHASE | IN GLORIOUS EPIPHANIE | 196 | 52 253 | 39 |
| THE SAME TO THEE, SWEET SPIRIT BE DONE. | O GLORIOSA DOMINA | 39 | 52 302 | 194 |
| MY BOSOME'S GUARD, A SPIRIT GREAT & STRONG, | ALEXIAS THIRD ELEGIE | 35 | 52 336 | 209 |

POOR-SPIRITED

| | | | | |
|---|---|---|---|---|
| O MOST POOR-SPIRITED OF MEN. | FLAMING HEART | 19 | 52 324 | 61 |

SPIRITS

| | | | | |
|---|---|---|---|---|
| WARME THOUGHTS FREE SPIRITS, FLATTERING | IN PRAISE OF LESSIUS | 43 | 46 156 | 510 |
| AND SHOULD WE POWERS OF HEAV'N, SPIRITS OF WORTH | SOSPETTO D'HERODE | 219 | 46 109 | 216 |
| HIS SPIRITS, THE SPARKES OF LIFE, AND CHILLS HIS HEART, | SOSPETTO D'HERODE | 422 | 46 109 | 216 |
| WHENCE ALL HIS HIGH SPIRITS, AND HOT COURAGE CAME. | SOSPETTO D'HERODE | 488 | 46 109 | 216 |
| OF THE DEARE SPOWSE OF SPIRITS WITH THEM WILL BRING. | ON A PRAYER BOOKE | 78 | 46 126 | 139 |
| GENTLE SPIRITS, DOE NOT COMPLAIN. | TO THE NAME OF JESUS | 111 | 52 239 | 30 |
| THE CONDUCT OF ADORING SPIRITS, THAT THRONG | TO THE NAME OF JESUS | 152 | 52 239 | 30 |
| STILL WOULD THE YOUTHFULL SPIRITS SING. | CHARITAS NIMIA | 19 | 52 280 | 48 |
| WHAT IS'T YOUR TASTFULL SPIRITS DOE PROVE | FLAMING HEART | 51 | 52 324 | 61 |
| OF THE DEARE SPOUSE OF SPIRITS WITH THEM WILL BRING | PRAYER TO GENTLE-WOMAN | 84 | 52 328 | 139 |
| WARM THOUGHTS, FREE SPIRITS FLATTERING | TEMPERANCE | 41 | 52 342 | 510 |

## SPIRITUALL

| | | | | | |
|---|---|---|---|---|---|
| SPIRITUALL AND SOULE PEIRCING GLANCES. | ON A PRAYER BOOKE | 65 | 46 | 126 | 139 |
| SO SPIRITUALL, PURE AND FAIRE, | IN MEMORY OF LADY MADRE TERESA | 88 | 46 | 131 | 52 |
| SO SPIRITUALL, PURE, & FAIR | TERESA | 88 | 52 | 315 | 52 |
| SPIRITUALL & SOUL-PEIRCING GLANCES | PRAYER TO GENTLE-WOMAN | 71 | 52 | 328 | 139 |

## SPITE

| | | | | | |
|---|---|---|---|---|---|
| SPITE OF ALL THE MAIDEN SNOW | THOUGH NOW 'TIS NEITHER | 7 | MS | 397 | 492 |
| THAT SO, IN SPITE OF ALL THIS PEEVISH STRENGTH | TO COUNTESSE OF DENBIGH | 41 | 52 | 236 | 146 |
| IN SPITE OF DARKNES, IT WAS DAY. | IN HOLY NATIVITY | 20 | 52 | 246 | 76 |
| HIGH IN HIS PATIENCE, AS THEIR SPITE. | OFFICE H. CROSS SIXT | 2 | 52 | 270 | 97 |
| NEEDS MUST MY MISERYES OWE THAT MAN A SPITE | ALEXIAS THIRD ELEGIE | 3 | 52 | 336 | 209 |
| HURTES MEE FAR WORSE THEN HERODS HIGHEST SPITE. | OUT OF GROTIUS | 34 | MS | 398 | 198 |

## SPIGHT

| | | | | | |
|---|---|---|---|---|---|
| IN SPIGHT OF DARKNESSE IT WAS DAY. | A HYMNE OF THE NATIVITY | 20 | 46 | 106 | 76 |
| FROM HIS BLACK NOSTRILLS, AND BLEW LIPS, IN SPIGHT | SOSPETTO D'HERODE | 53 | 46 | 109 | 216 |
| OF WHICH THE MORNING KNEW NOT. MAD WITH SPIGHT | SOSPETTO D'HERODE | 117 | 46 | 109 | 216 |
| THE WHILE HIS TWISTED TAYLE HEE GNAW'D FOR SPIGHT. | SOSPETTO D'HERODE | 152 | 46 | 109 | 216 |
| AUSPICIOUS STILL, IN SPIGHT OF HELL AND ME. | SOSPETTO D'HERODE | 208 | 46 | 109 | 216 |
| DAYES, THAT IN SPIGHT | WISHES SUPPOSED MISTRESSE | 79 | 46 | 195 | 479 |

## SPITEFULL

| | | | | | |
|---|---|---|---|---|---|
| FOR WHILE IN SPORT HE WEARES A SPITEFULL CROWN, | OFFICE H. CROSS THIRD | 7 | 52 | 268 | 93 |

## SPITEFULLY

| | | | | | |
|---|---|---|---|---|---|
| SHAM'D NOT SPITEFULLY TO WAST | UPON DEATH OF DESIRED HERRYS | 44 | 46 | 168 | 467 |

## SPITTLE

| | | | | | |
|---|---|---|---|---|---|
| AND LAOTHSOM SPITTLE, BLOTT THOSE BEAUTEOUS EYES. | OFFICE H. CROSS PRIME | 6 | 52 | 267 | 91 |

## SPLEENE

| | | | | | |
|---|---|---|---|---|---|
| WRATH ITS SELFE HAD LOST HIS SPLEENE. | ANOTHER ON HERRYS | 30 | 46 | 170 | 469 |

## SPLENDOR

| | | | | | |
|---|---|---|---|---|---|
| THE SPLENDOR OF HIS BIRTH AND BLOOD. | HIS EPITAPH (HERRYS) | 23 | 46 | 172 | 471 |

## SPOILD

| | | | | | |
|---|---|---|---|---|---|
| OFT HAVE I SPOILD MY KISSES DAINTIEST DIET, | LUKE 2. QUAERIT JESUM | 37 | MS | 379 | 11 |

## SPOYLE

| | | | | | |
|---|---|---|---|---|---|
| AND HAVE BEEN ASHAM'D TO SPOYLE | ANOTHER ON HERRYS | 36 | 46 | 170 | 469 |
| MORE THEN THE SPOYLE | WISHES SUPPOSED MISTRESSE | 22 | 46 | 195 | 479 |

## SPOYLED

| | | | | | |
|---|---|---|---|---|---|
| O. THAT POORE LOVE BE NOT FOR EVER SPOYLED. | OUT OF THE ITALIAN (2) | 5 | 46 | 190 | 547 |

## SPOILES

| | | | | | |
|---|---|---|---|---|---|
| AND RISING WITH RICH SPOILES UPON HIS BREST, | SOSPETTO D'HERODE | 229 | 46 | 109 | 216 |
| WITH THOSE DEARE SPOILES THAT WONT TO DRESSE THE FAIRE | ON A TREATISE OF CHARITY | 54 | 46 | 137 | 69 |
| THEREFORE WITH HIS PROUD PERSIAN SPOILES | IN GLORIOUS EPIPHANIE | 80 | 52 | 253 | 39 |
| AND MY BEST FORTUNES SUCH FAIR SPOILES OF ME. | FLAMING HEART | 92 | 52 | 324 | 61 |
| THAT JARRES, AND SPOILES SWEET CONSORT SOE. | UPON DEATH OF A FREIND | 8 | MS | 393 | 477 |

## SPOKE

| | | | | | |
|---|---|---|---|---|---|
| GAVE FORTH YOUR BLOOD FOR BREATH, SPOKE SOULES FOR WORDS. | SOSPETTO D'HERODE | 8 | 46 | 109 | 216 |
| THUS SPOKE TH'IMPATIENT PRINCE, AND MADE A PAUSE, | SOSPETTO D'HERODE | 257 | 46 | 109 | 216 |
| OF LIGHTNING, OR THE WORDS HE SPOKE) LEFT HELL. | SOSPETTO D'HERODE | 372 | 46 | 109 | 216 |
| GREAT NATURES SELFE HATH SHRUNKE AND SPOKE MEE GOD. | OUT OF GROTIUS | 50 | MS | 398 | 198 |

## SPORT

| | | | | | |
|---|---|---|---|---|---|
| DISPOS'D TO GIVE THE LIGHT-FOOT LADY SPORT | MUSICKS DUELL | 16 | 46 | 149 | 535 |
| AND WILT COMMAND PROUD ZEPHIRUS TO SPORT HER | ON A FOULE MORNING | 12 | 46 | 181 | 495 |
| FOR WHILE IN SPORT HE WEARES A SPITEFULL CROWN, | OFFICE H. CROSS THIRD | 7 | 52 | 268 | 93 |
| AND GIVE IT SELF FOR SPORT TO THE PROUD WIND. | CHARITAS NIMIA | 30 | 52 | 260 | 48 |

## SPORTING

| | | | | | |
|---|---|---|---|---|---|
| BAD SPORTING NEPTUNE TO PLUCK IN HIS ARMES, | UPON GUNPOWDER TREASON | 32 | MS | 386 | 460 |

## SPORTS

| | | | | | |
|---|---|---|---|---|---|
| THE OBJECTS OF HIS CRUELL SPORTS. | OUT OF GREEKE CUPID'S CRYER | 32 | 46 | 159 | 519 |
| FAREWELL ALL PLEASURES, SPORTS AND JOYES. | IN MEMORY OF LADY MADRE TERESA | 59 | 46 | 131 | 52 |
| FAREWELL, ALL PLEASURES, SPORTS, & JOYES. | TERESA | 59 | 52 | 315 | 52 |

SPOTLESSE

RISE UP MY FAIRE, MY SPOTLESSE ONE,                    ON THE ASSUMPTION                              9   46  139  114

SPOTTLESSE

RISE UP, MY FAIR, MY SPOTTLESSE ONE.                   IN GLORIOUS ASSUMPTION B. LADY                 9   52  304  114

SPOTTED

OF LIONS NOW NOE MORE, OR SPOTTED LINX.                HORATIJ ILLE & NEFASTO                        56   MS  382  530

SPOUSALL

THEN SPOUSALL RITES PREJUDGE THE MARRIAGE-BED.         ON HOPE                                       40   46  143   71
THEN SPOUSALL RITES PREJUDGE THE MARRIAGE BED.         (ON) HOPE                                     20   52  345   71

SPOUSE

THE SPOUSE OF VIRGINS, AND THE VIRGINS SON.            ON A PRAYER BOOKE                             40   46  126  139
SWEET NOT SO FAST, LOE THY FAIRE SPOUSE,               IN MEMORY OF LADY MADRE TERESA                65   46  131   52
OF CROWNES, WITH WHICH THE KING THY SPOUSE,            IN MEMORY OF LADY MADRE TERESA               144   46  131   52
SWEET, NOT SO FAST.  LO THY FAIR SPOUSE                TERESA                                        65   52  315   52
OF CROWNS, WITH WHICH THE KING THY SPOUSE              TERESA                                       143   52  315   52
THE VIRGIN-BIRTHS WITH WHICH THY SOVERAIGN SPOUSE      TERESA                                       168   52  315   52
THE SPOUSE OF VIRGINS & THE VIRGIN'S SON.              PRAYER TO GENTLE-WOMAN                        46   52  328  139
OF THE DEARE SPOUSE OF SPIRITS WITH THEM WILL BRING    PRAYER TO GENTLE-WOMAN                        84   52  328  139
MAKES HAST TO MEET HER MORNING SPOUSE                  PRAYER TO GENTLE-WOMAN                       102   52  328  139
AND MEANES THEM FOR A FARRE MORE WORTHY SPOUSE         TO SAME CONCERNING CHOISE                     36   52  331   66
AS TRUE TO ME, AS SHE WAS TO HER SPOUSE.               ALEXIAS FIRST ELEGIE                          32   52  334  204

SPOUSE'S

WHICH WRITES THY SPOUSE'S RADIANT NAME                 TERESA                                        82   52  315   52

SPOWSE

OF THE DEARE SPOWSE OF SPIRITS WITH THEM WILL BRING.   ON A PRAYER BOOKE                             78   46  126  139
MAKES HASTE TO MEET HER MORNING SPOWSE.                ON A PRAYER BOOKE                             96   46  126  139
THE VIRGIN BIRTHS WITH WHICH THY SPOWSE                IN MEMORY OF LADY MADRE TERESA               169   46  131   52

SPOWSES

WHICH WRITES THY SPOWSES RADIANT NAME                  IN MEMORY OF LADY MADRE TERESA                82   46  131   52

SPRANG

BUT WHEN THE WORLD FIRST OUT OF CHAOS SPRANG           OUT OF VIRGIL                                 23   46  155  529
FROM THEIR HARD MOTHER EARTH, SPRANG HARDY MEN,        OUT OF VIRGIL                                 30   46  155  529
SPRANG IN THE SPENDING FINGERS, AND O'REFLOW'D         OUT OF GROTIUS                                62   MS  398  198

SPREAD

UP TO THE THIRD RING. O'RE THE SHORE WAS SPREAD        THE BEGINNING OF HELIODORUS                   14   46  158  517
STILL MAY THY SWEET MERCY SPREAD                       PSALME 23                                     59   46  102    5
OF HELLS OWNE STINKE, A WORSER STENCH IS SPREAD.       SOSPETTO D'HERODE                             54   46  109  216
HEE SHOOKE HIMSELFE, AND SPREAD HIS SPATIOUS WINGS.    SOSPETTO D'HERODE                            141   46  109  216
WHEN THE ERINNYS HER BLACK PINEONS SPREAD,             SOSPETTO D'HERODE                            393   46  109  216
(HIS TENDER TOPPE NOT FULLY SPREAD)                    UPON DEATH OF DESIRED HERRYS                  35   46  168  467
AND OUR HOPES FAIRE HARVEST SPREAD                     ANOTHER ON HERRYS                             56   46  170  469
NOW STRETCH THY SELF (FAIRE ILE) AND GROW, SPREAD WIDE UPON YORKE HIS BIRTH                           2   46  176  500
BRIGHT CLOUDS LIKE GOLDEN FLEECES SHALL BE SPREAD.     ON A FOULE MORNING                            26   46  181  495
A NIGHTINGALE, WHO MAY SHEE SPREAD                     THOUGH NOW 'TIS NEITHER                        5   MS  397  492
OF THOSE WHOSE SPATIOUS BOSOMES SPREAD A THRONE        TERESA                                        10   52  315   52

WIDE-SPREAD

MEET IT WITH WIDE-SPREAD ARMES.  & SEE                 TO COUNTESSE OF DENBIGH                       55   52  236  146

SPRED

WIDE MAIST THOU SPRED                                  OFFICE H. CROSS EVENSONG                      20   52  273  101
LARG THRONE OF LOVE. ROYALLY SPRED                     VEXILLA REGIS                                 25   52  277  156

SPREADS

CAUGHT IN A NET WHICH THERE APPOLLO SPREADS,           MUSICKS DUELL                                121   46  149  535
SPREADS A PATH CLEARE AS THE DAY,                      PSALME 23                                     29   46  102    5
CROWN'D ABUNDANCE SPREADS MY BORD.                     PSALME 23                                     50   46  102    5
SHEE SPREADS THE RED LEAVES OF THY LIPS.               A HYMNE OF THE NATIVITY                       67   46  106   76

SPREADING

AN UNIVERSALL PALSIE SPREADING O'RE                    SOSPETTO D'HERODE                            382   46  109  216

SPRIGHTLY

WHOSE SYLVER-ROOFE RINGS WITH THE SPRIGHTLY NOTES      MUSICKS DUELL                                 75   46  149  535
SO SAID, HIS HANDS SPRIGHTLY AS FIRE HEE FLINGS,       MUSICKS DUELL                                111   46  149  535

## SPRING

| | | | | |
|---|---|---|---|---|
| THAT EVER-BUBLING SPRING, THE SUGRED NEST | MUSICKS DUELL | 66 | 46 149 | 535 |
| ALL TREES, ALL LEAVY GROVES CONFESSE THE SPRING | OUT OF VIRGIL | 1 | 46 155 | 529 |
| OF THEIR FELICITY. A SPRING WAS THERE, | OUT OF VIRGIL | 25 | 46 155 | 529 |
| AN EVERLASTING SPRING, THE JOLLY YEARE | OUT OF VIRGIL | 26 | 46 155 | 529 |
| WINTERS SELFE INTO A SPRING. | IN PRAISE OF LESSIUS | 44 | 46 156 | 510 |
| BY THE WANTON SPRING PUT ON, | THE TEARE | 26 | 46 84 | 50 |
| TO SHAME HIS SPRING. | UPON THORNES FROM LORDS HEAD | 4 | 46 96 | 23 |
| (A CRUELL AND A COSTLY SPRING) | ON BLEEDING WOUNDS OF LORD | 23 | 46 101 | 110 |
| ON WHOSE PASTURES CHEEREFULL SPRING, | PSALME 23 | 5 | 46 102 | 5 |
| THAT DRINKE THE DEAW OF LIFE, WHOSE DEATHLESSE SPRING, | SOSPETTO D'HERODE | 20 | 46 109 | 216 |
| THE RICH AND ROSEALL SPRING OF THOSE RARE SWEETS, | ON A PRAYER BOOKE | 110 | 46 126 | 139 |
| THE SPRING IS COME, THE FLOWERS APPEARE, | ON THE ASSUMPTION | 11 | 46 139 | 114 |
| THE FAIRE SON OF AN EVER-YOUTHFULL SPRING, | UPON DEATH OF HERRYS | 39 | 46 167 | 466 |
| HOW MUCH MY SUMMER WAITES UPON THY SPRING. | UPON TWO GREENE APRICOCKES | 34 | 48 220 | 494 |
| AND WITH CLASP'T WINGES PROCLAYME A SPRING | THOUGH NOW 'TIS NEITHER | 11 | MS 397 | 492 |
| THERE ALL THE YEARE IS LOVES LONG SPRING. | THOUGH NOW 'TIS NEITHER | 29 | MS 397 | 492 |
| 'TWIXT SPRING & FROST, | IN GLORIOUS EPIPHANIE | 33 | 52 253 | 39 |
| THE SPRING IS COME, THE FLOWRS APPEAR | IN GLORIOUS ASSUMPTION B. LADY | 11 | 52 304 | 114 |
| THE SPRING IS COME, OR IF IT STAY, | IN GLORIOUS ASSUMPTION B. LADY | 19 | 52 304 | 114 |
| THE RICH & ROSEALL SPRING OF THOSE RARE SWEETS | PRAYER TO GENTLE-WOMAN | 116 | 52 328 | 139 |
| WINTER'S SELFE INTO A SPRING. | TEMPERANCE | 42 | 52 342 | 510 |
| ALAS, AND HAS THE YEAR NO SPRING FOR YOU. | AGAINST IRRESOLUTION AND DELAY | 38 | 52 347 | 146 |
| THE FRAGRANT SPRING MAY BE PERFUM'D WITHALL. | UPON BIRTH PRINCESSE E | 4 | MS 391 | 456 |
| I CANNOT HOLD, SUCH A SPRING TIDE OF JOY | UPON BIRTH PRINCESSE E | 13 | MS 391 | 456 |
| A GOLDEN SUMMER, AN AETERNALL SPRING. | AN ELEGY MR STANNINOW | 54 | MS 394 | 473 |

## SPRINGS

| | | | | |
|---|---|---|---|---|
| HAILE SISTER SPRINGS, | THE WEEPER | 1 | 46 79 | 120 |
| ALL THE STREAMES OF ALL HER SPRINGS. | ANOTHER ON HERRYS | 10 | 46 170 | 469 |
| THE BLISSFULL SPRINGS OF JOY, FROM WHOSE ALL-CHEARING | OFFICE H. CROSS PRIME | 7 | 52 267 | 91 |
| HAIL, SISTER SPRINGS. | WEEPER | 1 | 52 307 | 120 |

## SPRINGING

| | | | | |
|---|---|---|---|---|
| TAINT NOT THE PURE STREAMES OF THE SPRINGING DAY, | ON A FOULE MORNING | 32 | 46 181 | 495 |

## SPRUCELY

| | | | | |
|---|---|---|---|---|
| GOE LEARNE THAT FATALL QUIRE, SOE SPRUCELY DIGHT | AN ELEGIE ON DR PORTER | 27 | MS 395 | 476 |

## SPRUNG

| | | | | |
|---|---|---|---|---|
| (THAT OLD DRY STOCKE) A DESPAIR'D BRANCH IS SPRUNG | SOSPETTO D'HERODE | 434 | 46 109 | 216 |
| THINE WAS THE ROSY DAWN THAT SPRUNG THE DAY | O GLORIOSA DOMINA | 21 | 52 302 | 194 |

## HOME-SPUN

| | | | | |
|---|---|---|---|---|
| BUT TO POOR SHEPHEARDS, HOME-SPUN THINGS. | IN HOLY NATIVITY | 94 | 52 246 | 76 |

## LONG-SPUN

| | | | | |
|---|---|---|---|---|
| TRAYLES HER PLAYNE DITTY IN ONE LONG-SPUN NOTE, | MUSICKS DUELL | 37 | 46 149 | 535 |

## LOVE-SPUN

| | | | | |
|---|---|---|---|---|
| HEAVN'S GREAT ARTILLERY IN EACH LOVE-SPUN LINE. | FLAMING HEART | 56 | 52 324 | 61 |

## SPURN'D

| | | | | |
|---|---|---|---|---|
| MEN HAD NOT SPURN'D AT MOUNTAINES, NOR MADE WARRS | ALEXIAS THIRD ELEGIE | 9 | 52 336 | 209 |

## SPURNS

| | | | | |
|---|---|---|---|---|
| SPURNS THE TAME LAWS OF TIME AND PLACE, | AGAINST IRRESOLUTION AND DELAY | 77 | 52 347 | 146 |

## SPY

| | | | | |
|---|---|---|---|---|
| MANS DAINTIEST CARE, & CAUTION CANNOT SPY | HORATIJ ILLE & NEFASTO | 17 | MS 382 | 530 |

## SPYES

| | | | | |
|---|---|---|---|---|
| SHEE SEEKES, SHEE SIGHS, BUT NO WHERE SPYES HIM. | OUT OF GREEKE CUPID'S CRYER | 3 | 46 159 | 519 |
| THE AMOROUS SPYES | IN GLORIOUS EPIPHANIE | 224 | 52 253 | 39 |
| BUT SPYES LOVE'S DAWN, & DISAPPEARES. | LAUDA SION SALVATOREM | 22 | 52 294 | 178 |

## STABLE

| | | | | |
|---|---|---|---|---|
| IN A NEGLECTED STABLE LIES, AMONG | SOSPETTO D'HERODE | 436 | 46 109 | 216 |
| IN BROKEN FORMES A STABLE FAITH | LAUDA SION SALVATOREM | 59 | 52 294 | 178 |
| WAS NOT SO MUCH AS CLEANE. A STABLE KIND. | OUT OF GROTIUS | 17 | MS 398 | 198 |

## STAFFE

| | | | | |
|---|---|---|---|---|
| AND THY STAFFE, WHOSE INFLUENCE | PSALME 23 | 47 | 46 102 | 5 |

## STAGGER

| | | | | |
|---|---|---|---|---|
| WHEN STARRES THEMSELVES SHALL STAGGER, AND | DIES IRAE | 23 | 52 298 | 186 |

STAGGERS

| | | | | |
|---|---|---|---|---|
| SHARPE AIRES, AND STAGGERS IN A WARBLING DOUBT | MUSICKS DUELL | 58 | 46 149 | 535 |
| STAGGERS OUT OF THE EAST, LOOSES HER WAY | ON A FOULE MORNING | 2 | 46 181 | 495 |

STAGGERING

| | | | | |
|---|---|---|---|---|
| THE STAGGERING LUMPE. EACH EYE SPENT ALL ITS STORE, | UPON KINGS CORONATION | 11 | MS 390 | 453 |

STAIN

| | | | | |
|---|---|---|---|---|
| AND WITH SAD MURMURS, CHIDES THE HANDS THAT STAIN HER. | TO PONTIUS WASHING HANDS | 14 | 46 94 | 23 |
| WITH THESE HE WASH'T THY STAIN, TRANSFER'D THY SMART, | VEXILLA REGIS | 11 | 52 277 | 156 |

STAINE

| | | | | |
|---|---|---|---|---|
| SHAME NOW AND ANGER MIXT A DOUBLE STAINE | MUSICKS DUELL | 105 | 46 149 | 535 |
| HER EYES FLOOD LICKES HIS FEETS FAIRE STAINE, | SHE BEGAN TO WASH HIS FEET | 1 | 46 97 | 13 |

STAINED

| | | | | |
|---|---|---|---|---|
| THIS FLOOD THUS STAINED FAIRER STREAMES. | SHE BEGAN TO WASH HIS FEET | 4 | 46 97 | 13 |

STAIND

| | | | | |
|---|---|---|---|---|
| THY RISING TOPP FIRST STAIND THE BASHFULL LIGHT. | HORATIJ ILLE & NEFASTO | 6 | MS 382 | 530 |

STAINES

| | | | | |
|---|---|---|---|---|
| THEIR UGLY ORNAMENTS ARE THE BLOODY STAINES. | SOSPETTO D'HERODE | 311 | 46 109 | 216 |
| OF SIN, AND DEATH, TWICE DIPT IN THE DIRE STAINES | SOSPETTO D'HERODE | 327 | 46 109 | 216 |
| AND STAINES THE TIMEROUS LIGHT OF STARRES. | O GLORIOSA DOMINA | 4 | 52 302 | 194 |
| PERFIDIOUS TUTTERER. LONGING FOR THE STAINES | HORATIJ ILLE & NEFASTO | 15 | MS 382 | 530 |

STALE

| | | | | |
|---|---|---|---|---|
| IS CLOYING MEAT. HOW STALE IS WIFE. | PETRONIJ ALES PHASIACIS PETITA | 16 | MS 382 | 526 |

ALTAR-STALL'D

| | | | | |
|---|---|---|---|---|
| THE ALTAR-STALL'D OX, FATT OSYRIS NOW | IN GLORIOUS EPIPHANIE | 96 | 52 253 | 39 |

STALLIONS

| | | | | |
|---|---|---|---|---|
| SOE LOW TO GIVE HIS THIRSTY STALLIONS DRINKE. | UPON GUNPOWDER TREASON | 40 | MS 386 | 460 |

STAMPED

| | | | | |
|---|---|---|---|---|
| HAD YOU, LIKE OUR GREAT SUNNE, STAMPED BUT ONE | UPON BIRTH PRINCESSE E | 27 | MS 391 | 456 |

STAND

| | | | | |
|---|---|---|---|---|
| STONY AMAZEMENT MAKES THEM STAND | NEITHER DURST MAN ASKE | 9 | 46 92 | 20 |
| THE ADAMANTINE DOORS, FOR EVER STAND | SOSPETTO D'HERODE | 307 | 46 109 | 216 |
| WITH CIRCE, SCYLLA, STAND TO WAIT UPON HER. | SOSPETTO D'HERODE | 339 | 46 109 | 216 |
| WHAT BUSY MOTIONS, WHAT WILD ENGINES STAND | SOSPETTO D'HERODE | 441 | 46 109 | 216 |
| O WHAT DELIGHT WHEN SHEE SHALL STAND, | IN MEMORY OF LADY MADRE TERESA | 130 | 46 131 | 52 |
| OF STUDIED FATE STAND FORTH. | WISHES SUPPOSED MISTRESSE | 8 | 46 195 | 479 |
| OR ON HEAVN'S AZURE FOREHEAD HIGH TO STAND | IN GLORIOUS EPIPHANIE | 250 | 52 253 | 39 |
| OF LOVE. HERE MUST SHE STAND | SANCTA MARIA DOLORUM | 36 | 52 283 | 162 |
| THE MOST FIRM FOOT NO MORE THEN STAND. | DIES IRAE | 24 | 52 298 | 186 |
| O WHAT DELIGHT, WHEN REVEAL'D LIFE SHALL STAND | TERESA | 129 | 52 315 | 52 |
| TO SEE SOME FOWLER THAN HERSELFE) THESE STAND. | UPON GUNPOWDER TREASON | 13 | MS 387 | 461 |
| (FAIRE ONE) THESE TENDER LEAVES DOE TREMBLING STAND. | AT TH' IVORY TRIBUNALL | 2 | MS 397 | 492 |
| I SHRINKE NOT. BUT THUS READY STAND TO BEARE | OUT OF GROTIUS | 7 | MS 398 | 198 |

STANDS

| | | | | |
|---|---|---|---|---|
| ONE STANDS UP CLOSE AND TREADS ON HIGH, | TWO WENT TO PRAY | 3 | 46 89 | 18 |
| SWINGING A HUGE SITH STANDS IMPARTIALL DEATH, | SOSPETTO D'HERODE | 319 | 46 109 | 216 |
| THUS LOW STANDS UP (ME THINKES) THUS, AND DEFYES | UPON STANINOUGH'S DEATH | 28 | 46 175 | 475 |
| STANDS OFF AND POINTS AT. IS'T SOME DEITY | UPON YORKE HIS BIRTH | 71 | 46 176 | 500 |
| FOR SEE APPOLLO ALL THIS WHILE STANDS MUTE. | UPON YORKE HIS BIRTH | 114 | 46 176 | 500 |
| STANDS TREMBLING AT THE GATE OF BLISSE. | TO COUNTESSE OF DENBIGH | 2 | 52 236 | 146 |
| SUPERFLUOUS SPEAR. BUT THERE'S A HEART STANDS BY | OFFICE H. CROSS EVENSONG | 5 | 52 273 | 101 |
| STANDS ARM'D, TO SHEILD ME FROM ALL WANTON WRONG. | ALEXIAS THIRD ELEGIE | 36 | 52 336 | 209 |
| THUS LOW, STANDS UP (ME THINKES,) THUS & DEFIES | DEATH'S LECTURE | 30 | 52 340 | 475 |
| STANDS TREMBLING AT THE GATE OF BLISSE. | AGAINST IRRESOLUTION AND DELAY | 2 | 52 347 | 146 |

STAR

| | | | | |
|---|---|---|---|---|
| AND LEFT THEIR MITHRA FOR MY STAR. THIS THEY. | OUT OF GROTIUS | 38 | MS 398 | 198 |

STAR-PAV'D

| | | | | |
|---|---|---|---|---|
| I LEFT MY GLORIOUS FATHERS STAR-PAV'D COURT | OUT OF GROTIUS | 14 | MS 398 | 198 |

STARR

| | | | | |
|---|---|---|---|---|
| AND OF A METEOR MAKE A STARR. | TO COUNTESSE OF DENBIGH | 30 | 52 236 | 146 |
| BY THY FAIR STARR. | IN GLORIOUS EPIPHANIE | 20 | 52 253 | 39 |
| HE IS FROM SUN ENOUGH TO MAKE THY STARR, | IN GLORIOUS EPIPHANIE | 247 | 52 253 | 39 |
| I'AM PERFECT IN HEAVN'S STATE, WITH EVERY STARR | ALEXIAS SECONDE ELEGIE | 23 | 52 335 | 207 |

STARRE

| 'TIS A STARRE ABOUT TO DROP | THE TEARE | 8 | 46 | 84 | 50 |
| THE FAIRE STARRE IS WELL FIXT, FOR WHERE, O WHERE | ON VIRGINS BASHFULNESSE | 3 | 46 | 89 | 9 |
| ALONE, LIGHT SUCH ANOTHER STARRE, AND TWINE | UPON YORKE HIS BIRTH | 56 | 46 | 176 | 500 |
| SHEE ASKS EACH STARRE THAT THEN STOOD BY, | LOVES HOROSCOPE | 7 | 46 | 185 | 483 |
| SUCH WAS THE BRIGHTNESSE OF THIS NORTHERNE STARRE, | UPON KINGS CORONATION | 29 | MS | 390 | 453 |
| BRIGHT STARRE OF MAJESTY, OH SHEDD ON MEE | UPON BIRTH PRINCESSE E | 1 | MS | 391 | 456 |
| SNATCH'T UPP THE FALLING STARRE, SOE RICHLY GAY, | AN ELEGY MR STANNINOW | 50 | MS | 394 | 473 |

DAY-STARRE

| DOES THE DAY-STARRE RISE. | WEEPER | 133 | 52 | 307 | 120 |

OUT-STARE

| OUT-STARE THE BROAD-BEAM'D DAYES MERIDIAN) | ON FRONTISPIECE ISAACSONS | 10 | 46 | 191 | 491 |

STARS

| HEAVENS OF EVER-FALLING STARS, | THE WEEPER | 8 | 46 | 79 | 120 |
| AND STARS THOU SOW'ST WHOSE HARVEST DARES | THE WEEPER | 10 | 46 | 79 | 120 |
| STARS THEY ARE INDEED TOO TRUE. | THE WEEPER | 14 | 46 | 79 | 120 |
| TAKES UP AMONG THE STARS A ROOME, | THE WEEPER | 32 | 46 | 79 | 120 |
| WHO IN A THRONE OF STARS THUNDERS ABOVE. | SOSPETTO D'HERODE | 176 | 46 | 109 | 216 |
| OF STARS, THAT GUILD THE MORNE IN CHARGE WERE GIVEN. | SOSPETTO D'HERODE | 234 | 46 | 109 | 216 |
| THE FRIGHTED STARS TOOKE FAINT EXPERIENCE. | SOSPETTO D'HERODE | 283 | 46 | 109 | 216 |
| THEN THE CHAST STARS, WHOSE CHOICE LAMPS COME TO LIGHT HER. | ON THE ASSUMPTION | 4 | 46 | 139 | 114 |

STARRES

| STARRES IN THEIR HIGHER CHAMBERS. NEVER COU'D | OUT OF VIRGIL | 32 | 46 | 155 | 529 |
| THE MOONE OF MAIDEN STARRES. THY WHITE | IN MEMORY OF LADY MADRE TERESA | 124 | 46 | 131 | 52 |
| THAT KINDLED THEM TO STARRES,) AND SO | IN MEMORY OF LADY MADRE TERESA | 178 | 46 | 131 | 52 |
| HOPE KICKS THE CURL'D HEADS OF CONSPIRING STARRES. | ON HOPE | 72 | 46 | 143 | 71 |
| THE BEAMES THAT DANCE IN THOSE FULL STARRES OF THINE. | UPON YORKE HIS BIRTH | 44 | 46 | 176 | 500 |
| STEPT FROM HER THRONE OF STARRES DEIGNES TO BE SEENE. | UPON YORKE HIS BIRTH | 72 | 46 | 176 | 500 |
| WHEN STARRES THEMSELVES SHALL STAGGER. AND | DIES IRAE | 23 | 52 | 298 | 186 |
| AND STAINES THE TIMEROUS LIGHT OF STARRES. | O GLORIOSA DOMINA | 4 | 52 | 302 | 194 |
| WHICH RENDERS ALL THE STARRES SHE STOLE AWAY. | O GLORIOSA DOMINA | 22 | 52 | 302 | 194 |
| THEN THE CHAST STARRES, WHOSE CHOISE LAMPS COME TO LIGHT HER | IN GLORIOUS ASSUMPTION B. LADY | 4 | 52 | 304 | 114 |
| HEAVENS OF EVER-FALLING STARRES. | WEEPER | 8 | 52 | 307 | 120 |
| AND STARRES THOU SOW'ST, WHOSE HARVEST DARES | WEEPER | 10 | 52 | 307 | 120 |
| STARRES INDEED THEY ARE TOO TRUE. | WEEPER | 14 | 52 | 307 | 120 |
| TAKES UP AMONG THE STARRES A ROOM, | WEEPER | 68 | 52 | 307 | 120 |
| STILL THY STARRES DOE FALL & FALL | WEEPER | 134 | 52 | 307 | 120 |
| AND FOLLOW THOSE FAIR STARRES OF YOURS. | TO SAME CONCERNING CHOISE | 30 | 52 | 331 | 66 |
| SURE IN MY EARLY WOES STARRES WERE AT STRIFE, | ALEXIAS FIRST ELEGIE | 5 | 52 | 334 | 204 |
| I, 'MONGST THE BLEST STARRES A NEW NAME SHALL BE. | ALEXIAS FIRST ELEGIE | 24 | 52 | 334 | 204 |
| HOPE WALKS, & KICKES THE CURLD HEADS OF CONSPIRING STARRES. | (ON) HOPE | 32 | 52 | 345 | 71 |
| I MEANE THOSE THREE GREAT STARRES, WHO WELL MAY SCORNE | UPON KINGS CORONATION | 31 | MS | 389 | 454 |
| TO GAZE UPON SUCH STARRES EACH HUMBLE EYE | UPON KINGS CORONATION | 33 | MS | 389 | 454 |

OUTSTARES

| OUTSTARES THE LIDDES OF LARG-LOOK'T TYRANNY. | DEATH'S LECTURE | 28 | 52 | 340 | 475 |

OUT-STARES

| OUT-STARES THE LIDDES OF LARGE-LOOK'T TYRANNY. | UPON STANINOUGH'S DEATH | 26 | 46 | 175 | 475 |

STARRS

| AND THE GAY STARRS LEAD ON THEIR GOLDEN DANCE. | SOSPETTO D'HERODE | 206 | 46 | 109 | 216 |
| THE FAIR STARRS FILL THEIR WAKEFULL FIRES THE SUN HIMSELFE DRINKS DAY. | OFFICE H. CROSS PRIME | 8 | 52 | 267 | 91 |
| THE MOON OF MAIDEN STARRS, THY WHITE | TERESA | 123 | 52 | 315 | 52 |
| THAT KINDLED THEM TO STARRS,) AND SO | TERESA | 177 | 52 | 315 | 52 |
| STARRS MUCH TOO FAIR & PURE TO WAIT UPON | TO SAME CONCERNING CHOISE | 31 | 52 | 331 | 66 |
| HER KINDRED WITH THE STARRS. NOT BASELY HOVERS | DESCRIPTION RELIGIOUS HOUSE | 37 | 52 | 338 | 213 |

STARING

| OF STARING COMETS, THAT LOOKE KINGDOMES DEAD. | SOSPETTO D'HERODE | 52 | 46 | 109 | 216 |

STARRY

| HER STARRY THRONE. WHOSE HOLY HEATS CAN WARME | TO THE MORNING | 25 | 46 | 183 | 497 |
| WHAT EVER STARRY SYNOD MET, | LOVES HOROSCOPE | 18 | 46 | 185 | 483 |
| TO ENTERTAIN THIS STARRY STRANGER. | IN HOLY NATIVITY | 38 | 52 | 246 | 76 |
| AND GETT A STARRY THRONE BEFORE HIS TIME. | ON GUNPOWDER-TREASON | 36 | MS | 384 | 456 |
| FORTHWITH EACH GOD STEPT FROM HIS STARRY THRONE, | UPON GUNPOWDER TREASON | 53 | MS | 387 | 461 |
| MAY DRAW THEIR FIRST BREATH FROM THY STARRY BEAMES, | EX EUPHORMIONE | 14 | MS | 392 | 525 |
| LEFT MANY A STARRY TEARE, TO THINKE HOW SOONE | AN ELEGY MR STANNINOW | 41 | MS | 394 | 473 |

START

| START, AND SAY, THE SERPENT HISSES. | OUT OF GREEKE CUPID'S CRYER | 66 | 46 | 159 | 519 |
| YET ON THE OTHER SIDE, FAINE WOULD HE START | SOSPETTO D'HERODE | 153 | 46 | 109 | 216 |
| WILL GIT THE START, | ON A PRAYER BOOKE | 55 | 46 | 126 | 139 |

|     |     |     |     |     |     |
|---|---|---|---|---|---|
| TO START FROM TIME, AND CHEERFULLY TO FLY | UPON DEATH OF HERRYS | 7 | 46 | 167 | 466 |
| (DREST IN THOSE BEAMES) START FORTH | OUT OF THE ITALIAN (2) | 9 | 46 | 190 | 547 |
| START INTO LIFE, AND LEAP WITH ME | TO THE NAME OF JESUS | 49 | 52 | 239 | 30 |
| WILL GETT THE START | PRAYER TO GENTLE-WOMAN | 61 | 52 | 328 | 139 |
| AND START FROM OFF THY CENTER. HATH HEAVENS LOVE | ON GUNPOWDER-TREASON | 5 | MS | 384 | 458 |

STARTS

|     |     |     |     |     |     |
|---|---|---|---|---|---|
| THEN STARTS SHEE SUDDENLY INTO A THRONG | MUSICKS DUELL | 62 | 46 | 149 | 535 |
| NO NIMBLE RAPTURE STARTS TO HEAVEN AND BRINGS | TO THE MORNING | 20 | 46 | 183 | 497 |
| THE PARTHIAN STARTS AT ROME'S IMPERIALL NAME, | HORATIJ ILLE & NEFASTO | 27 | MS | 382 | 530 |
| THEN WONDRING STARTS, & HAD THE CURTEOUS NIGHT | UPON KINGS CORONATION | 19 | MS | 390 | 453 |

STARTED

|     |     |     |     |     |     |
|---|---|---|---|---|---|
| WHY RAN THE STARTED AIRE TREMBLING AWAY. | UPON YORKE HIS BIRTH | 67 | 46 | 176 | 500 |
| THE WATER BLUSH'D, AND STARTED INTO WINE. | OUT OF GROTIUS | 52 | MS | 398 | 198 |

STARTLE

|     |     |     |     |     |     |
|---|---|---|---|---|---|
| STARTLE THE DULL AYRE WITH A DISMALL RED. | SOSPETTO D'HERODE | 50 | 46 | 109 | 216 |

STARV'D

|     |     |     |     |     |     |
|---|---|---|---|---|---|
| THEY ARE STARV'D, AND I AM FED. | PSALME 23 | 54 | 46 | 102 | 5 |

STERVED

|     |     |     |     |     |     |
|---|---|---|---|---|---|
| PROMETHEUS SELFE, & PELOPS STERVED SIRE | HORATIJ ILLE & NEFASTO | 54 | MS | 382 | 530 |

STATE

|     |     |     |     |     |     |
|---|---|---|---|---|---|
| OF STREAMING SWEETNESSE, WHICH IN STATE DOTH RIDE | MUSICKS DUELL | 94 | 46 | 149 | 535 |
| WHAT ALL THY WEALTH IN COUNSAILE. ALL THY STATE. | ON THE PRODIGALL | 3 | 46 | 86 | 17 |
| AND LOOKING ON THEIR LOST STATE SIGH'D AGAINE. | SOSPETTO D'HERODE | 408 | 46 | 109 | 216 |
| FOURE TEETH THOU HAD'ST THAT RANCK'D IN GOODLY STATE | OUT OF MARTIALL | 1 | 46 | 188 | 527 |
| I'AM PERFECT IN HEAVN'S STATE, WITH EVERY STARR | ALEXIAS SECONDE ELEGIE | 23 | 52 | 335 | 207 |

STATES

|     |     |     |     |     |     |
|---|---|---|---|---|---|
| YOUR SELVES, YOU STYGIAN STATES. A PITCHY CLOWD | UPON GUNPOWDER TREASON | 24 | MS | 387 | 461 |

STATELY

|     |     |     |     |     |     |
|---|---|---|---|---|---|
| WITH HEAVEN ITSELF FOR STATELY MAJESTY. | UPON KINGS CORONATION | 10 | MS | 389 | 454 |
| UP TO OLYMPUS STATELY TOPP HE HIES. | UPON KINGS CORONATION | 17 | MS | 390 | 453 |

STATIONS

|     |     |     |     |     |     |
|---|---|---|---|---|---|
| HAD BEENE PUFT OUT, & FROM THEIR STATIONS HURL'D. | UPON GUNPOWDER TREASON | 28 | MS | 386 | 460 |
| STEALE FROM THEIR STATIONS TO REPAIRE THEIR LIGHT. | UPON KINGS CORONATION | 28 | MS | 389 | 454 |

STATUES

|     |     |     |     |     |     |
|---|---|---|---|---|---|
| LIKE STATUES FIXED TO THE FAME | NEITHER DURST MAN ASKE | 11 | 46 | 92 | 20 |

STATURE

|     |     |     |     |     |     |
|---|---|---|---|---|---|
| ERST THE FULL STATURE OF A FATALL TREE. | OUR LORD IN HIS CIRCUMCISION | 16 | 46 | 98 | 9 |

STAY

|     |     |     |     |     |     |
|---|---|---|---|---|---|
| WHEN CHRIST CALLS, AND THY NETS WOULD HAVE THEE STAY. | ON ST. PETER CASTING NETS | 3 | 46 | 98 | 13 |
| STAY OF MY STRONG HOPES, YOU OF WHOSE BRAVE WORTH, | SOSPETTO D'HERODE | 282 | 46 | 109 | 216 |
| YET DOTH NOT STAY | ON A PRAYER BOOKE | 69 | 46 | 126 | 139 |
| HEAVEN WILL NOT, AND SHE CANNOT STAY. | ON THE ASSUMPTION | 22 | 46 | 139 | 114 |
| STAY A WHILE, AND LET THY HEART | HIS EPITAPH (HERRYS) | 2 | 46 | 172 | 471 |
| O STAY A WHILE E'RE THOU DRAW IN THY HEAD, | UPON STANINOUGH'S DEATH | 3 | 46 | 175 | 475 |
| STAY BUT A LITTLE WHILE, UNTILL I CALL | UPON STANINOUGH'S DEATH | 5 | 46 | 175 | 475 |
| BUT STAY, WHAT GLIMPSE WAS THAT. WHY BLUSHT THE DAY. | UPON YORKE HIS BIRTH | 66 | 46 | 176 | 500 |
| THE HEAVENS WILL STAY NO LONGER, MAY THY GLORY | UPON YORKE HIS BIRTH | 104 | 46 | 176 | 500 |
| CONFESSING THEE. OR (IF TOO LONG I STAY) | UPON YORKE HIS BIRTH | 112 | 46 | 176 | 500 |
| FLY THEN, AND DOE NOT THINKE WITH HER TO STAY. | ON A FOULE MORNING | 37 | 46 | 181 | 495 |
| THE SPRING IS COME, OR IF IT STAY. | IN GLORIOUS ASSUMPTION B. LADY | 19 | 52 | 304 | 114 |
| THE SHRILL WINDS CHIDE, THE WATERS WEEP THY STAY. | IN GLORIOUS ASSUMPTION B. LADY | 28 | 52 | 304 | 114 |
| HEAVN WILL NOT, & SHE CANNOT STAY. | IN GLORIOUS ASSUMPTION B. LADY | 36 | 52 | 304 | 114 |
| YET DOES NOT STAY | PRAYER TO GENTLE-WOMAN | 75 | 52 | 328 | 139 |
| O STAY A WHILE, ERE THOU DRAW IN THY HEAD | DEATH'S LECTURE | 3 | 52 | 340 | 475 |
| STAY BUT A LITTLE WHILE, UNTILL I CALL | DEATH'S LECTURE | 5 | 52 | 340 | 475 |
| AND MURMURE IF THEY MEET A STAY. | AGAINST IRRESOLUTION AND DELAY | 40 | 52 | 347 | 146 |
| AND LETT HEAVEN STAY. | LUKE 2. QUAERIT JESUM | 46 | MS | 379 | 11 |
| AND DURST NOT TOUCH IT, HEERE IT MADE NOE STAY. | ON GUNPOWDER-TREASON | 54 | MS | 384 | 458 |
| STAY, SILVER-FOOTED CAME, STRIVE NOT TO WED | AN ELEGIE ON DR PORTER | 1 | MS | 395 | 476 |

STAY'D

|     |     |     |     |     |     |
|---|---|---|---|---|---|
| FEARES ANTIDOTE. A WISE, AND WELL STAY'D FIRE | ON HOPE | 82 | 46 | 143 | 71 |

WELL-STAY'D

|     |     |     |     |     |     |
|---|---|---|---|---|---|
| FEAR'S ANTIDOTE. A WISE & WELL-STAY'D FIRE. | (ON) HOPE | 42 | 52 | 345 | 71 |

## STAYES

| | | | | | |
|---|---|---|---|---|---|
| TIS A GEMME WHILE IT STAYES HERE, | ON WATER OF LORDS BAPTISME | 3 | 46 | 85 | 12 |

## STEAD

| | | | | | |
|---|---|---|---|---|---|
| IN STEAD OF TEARES SUCH GEMS AS THIS IS. | ON WOUNDS OF CRUCIFIED LORD | 16 | 46 | 99 | 24 |
| AND LEFT PERFUMES, IN STEAD OF SCARRES. | A HYMNE OF THE NATIVITY | 26 | 46 | 106 | 76 |
| IN STEAD OF STRIKING WOULD HAVE GAZ'D. | ANOTHER ON HERRYS | 32 | 46 | 170 | 469 |
| AND LEFT PERFUMES IN STEAD OF SCARRES. | IN HOLY NATIVITY | 27 | 52 | 246 | 76 |
| IN STEAD OF BRINGING IN THE BLISSFULL PRIZE | IN GLORIOUS EPIPHANIE | 226 | 52 | 253 | 39 |
| AND IN THE STEAD OF FEEDING STOOD, & GAZ'D. | UPON GUNPOWDER TREASON | 48 | MS | 387 | 461 |

## STEADY

| | | | | | |
|---|---|---|---|---|---|
| FALLS FROM A STEADY HEART, THOUGH TREMBLING HAND. | WIDOWES MITES | 2 | 46 | 86 | 21 |

## STEAL

| | | | | | |
|---|---|---|---|---|---|
| BUT HOW SHALL I STEAL HENCE, ALEXIS THOU | ALEXIAS FIRST ELEGIE | 15 | 52 | 334 | 204 |

## STEAL'ST

| | | | | | |
|---|---|---|---|---|---|
| THOU THUS STEAL'ST DOWNE A DISTANT KISSE, | ON HOPE | 38 | 46 | 143 | 71 |
| THOU STEAL'ST US DOWN A DISTANT KISSE. | (ON) HOPE | 18 | 52 | 345 | 71 |

## STEALE

| | | | | | |
|---|---|---|---|---|---|
| STEALE FROM THEIR STATIONS TO REPAIRE THEIR LIGHT. | UPON KINGS CORONATION | 28 | MS | 389 | 454 |

## STEALES

| | | | | | |
|---|---|---|---|---|---|
| STEALES FROM THE AMBER-WEEPING TREE, | THE WEEPER | 44 | 46 | 79 | 120 |

## STEALING

| | | | | | |
|---|---|---|---|---|---|
| NOE. 'TWAS OLD DOTING DEATH, WHO, STEALING BY, | AN ELEGY MR STANNINOW | 45 | MS | 394 | 473 |

## STEALTH

| | | | | | |
|---|---|---|---|---|---|
| HOPE'S CHAST STEALTH HARMES NO MORE JOYE'S MAIDENHEAD | (ON) HOPE | 19 | 52 | 345 | 71 |

## STEAMES

| | | | | | |
|---|---|---|---|---|---|
| NO MISTES DOE MASKE NO LAZY STEAMES. | IN PRAISE OF LESSIUS | 32 | 46 | 156 | 510 |
| NO MISTS DOE MASK, NO LAZY STEAMES. | TEMPERANCE | 30 | 52 | 342 | 510 |

## STEDFAST

| | | | | | |
|---|---|---|---|---|---|
| CHARG'D TO LOOK ON, & WITH A STEDFAST EY | SANCTA MARIA DOLORUM | 37 | 52 | 283 | 162 |

## STEEDS

| | | | | | |
|---|---|---|---|---|---|
| SO MUCH, RUDE SHEPHEARDS, WHAT HIS STEEDS, ALAS | SOSPETTO D'HERODE | 527 | 46 | 109 | 216 |
| SPEEDILY HARNESSING HIS FIERY STEEDS, | UPON KINGS CORONATION | 16 | MS | 390 | 453 |

## STEEL

| | | | | | |
|---|---|---|---|---|---|
| TURN'D THE STEEL POINT OF FEAR, | VEXILLA REGIS | 16 | 52 | 277 | 156 |
| SO LUMPISH STEEL, UNTAUGHT TO MOVE, | AGAINST IRRESOLUTION AND DELAY | 51 | 52 | 347 | 146 |

## STEELE

| | | | | | |
|---|---|---|---|---|---|
| WHILE HIS STEELE SIDES SOUND WITH HIS TAYLES STRONG LASH. | SOSPETTO D'HERODE | 64 | 46 | 109 | 216 |
| THE WALLS INEXORABLE STEELE, NO HAND | SOSPETTO D'HERODE | 309 | 46 | 109 | 216 |
| HIS WEAPONS WERE NOR STEELE, NOR BRASSE. | IN CICATRICES DOMINI JESU | 11 | MS | 381 | 27 |

## STEELY

| | | | | | |
|---|---|---|---|---|---|
| NOW ALL THEIR STEELY OPERATION, | ANOTHER ON HERRYS | 23 | 46 | 170 | 469 |

## STEMME

| | | | | | |
|---|---|---|---|---|---|
| PEEPS FROM HER PARENT STEMME, | THE TEARE | 27 | 46 | 84 | 50 |
| KNOW'ST THOU NOT HOW OF TH' HEBREWES ROYALL STEMME | SOSPETTO D'HERODE | 433 | 46 | 109 | 216 |
| A PLANT OF NOBLE STEMME, FORWARD AND FAIRE, | UPON DEATH OF HERRYS | 1 | 46 | 167 | 466 |
| PEEPS FROM HER PARENT STEMME | WEEPER | 63 | 52 | 307 | 120 |

## STEMMS

| | | | | | |
|---|---|---|---|---|---|
| DOES RISE A RADIANT CROPPE OF ROYALLE STEMMS, | TO THE QUEEN'S MAJESTY | 12 | 52 | 261 | 47 |

## STENCH

| | | | | | |
|---|---|---|---|---|---|
| OF HELLS OWNE STINKE, A WORSER STENCH IS SPREAD. | SOSPETTO D'HERODE | 54 | 46 | 109 | 216 |

## STEPS

| | | | | | |
|---|---|---|---|---|---|
| BY THEM HIS STEPS HE RECTIFIES. | THE WEEPER | 100 | 46 | 79 | 120 |
| AND TREADS WITH UNCONTROULED STEPS. | NEITHER DURST MAN ASKE | 4 | 46 | 92 | 20 |
| OF MY WEARY STEPS, AND UNDER | PSALME 23 | 28 | 46 | 102 | 5 |
| STEPS, WALKE WITH HIM THOSE WAYES OF LIGHT. | IN MEMORY OF LADY MADRE TERESA | 181 | 46 | 131 | 52 |

PAGE 398

| | | | | | |
|---|---|---|---|---|---|
| AND TEACH HER FAIRE STEPS TO OUR EARTH. | WISHES SUPPOSED MISTRESSE | 9 | 46 | 195 | 479 |

**STEPPS**

| | | | | | |
|---|---|---|---|---|---|
| STEPPS, WALK WITH HIM THOSE WAYES OF LIGHT | TERESA | 180 | 52 | 315 | 52 |

**STEPPES**

| | | | | | |
|---|---|---|---|---|---|
| HEE'S GONE. & HIS LOV'D STEPPES TO WAIT UPON. | LUKE 2. QUAERIT JESUM | 9 | MS | 379 | 11 |

**STEPPING**

| | | | | | |
|---|---|---|---|---|---|
| AND STEPPING IN BEFORE, | ON A PRAYER BOOKE | 56 | 46 | 126 | 139 |
| MEAN WHILE, & STEPPING IN BEFORE | PRAYER TO GENTLE-WOMAN | 62 | 52 | 328 | 139 |

**STEPT**

| | | | | | |
|---|---|---|---|---|---|
| STEPT FROM HER THRONE OF STARRES DEIGNES TO BE SEENE. | UPON YORKE HIS BIRTH | 72 | 46 | 176 | 500 |
| FORTHWITH EACH GOD STEPT FROM HIS STARRY THRONE. | UPON GUNPOWDER TREASON | 53 | MS | 387 | 461 |

**STERNE**

| | | | | | |
|---|---|---|---|---|---|
| SHEW'D, THAT STERNE WARRE HAD NEWLY BATH'D HIM THERE | THE BEGINNING OF HELIODORUS | 22 | 46 | 158 | 517 |
| WITH STERNE DEATH, IF E'RE HE FAINTED, | ANOTHER ON HERRYS | 2 | 46 | 170 | 469 |
| IF THIS WERE WISDOMES GOD, THAT WARS STERNE FATHER, | UPON YORKE HIS BIRTH | 32 | 46 | 176 | 500 |

**STEWARD**

| | | | | | |
|---|---|---|---|---|---|
| OF FAITH. THE STEWARD OF OUR GROWING STOCKE. | ON HOPE | 32 | 46 | 143 | 71 |

**STIFFE**

| | | | | | |
|---|---|---|---|---|---|
| BECAUSE HE'S STIFFE, AND WILL CONFESSE NO KNEE. | ON A TREATISE OF CHARITY | 40 | 46 | 137 | 69 |
| THE STIFFE NECK'D PHARISEES THAT USE TO MOCKE | OUT OF GROTIUS | 42 | MS | 398 | 198 |

**STIF'LED**

| | | | | | |
|---|---|---|---|---|---|
| IT LABOURS. STIF'LED NATURE'S IN A SWOUND. | ON GUNPOWDER-TREASON | 19 | MS | 384 | 458 |

**STILL**

| | | | | | |
|---|---|---|---|---|---|
| TO WOO THEM FROM THEIR BEDS. STILL MURMURING | MUSICKS DUELL | 79 | 46 | 149 | 535 |
| STILL KEEPING IN THE FORWARD STREAME. SO LONG | MUSICKS DUELL | 86 | 46 | 149 | 535 |
| OF ALL THE STRINGS, STILL BREATHING THE BEST LIFE | MUSICKS DUELL | 152 | 46 | 149 | 535 |
| LIVE TO BEE OLD AND STILL A MAN. | IN PRAISE OF LESSIUS | 46 | 46 | 156 | 510 |
| HIGH-COLOUR'D IS. HIS EYES STILL FLUSHING | OUT OF GREEKE CUPID'S CRYER | 20 | 46 | 159 | 519 |
| WHAT E'RE IT BE LOVE OFFERS. STILL PRESUME | OUT OF GREEKE CUPID'S CRYER | 73 | 46 | 159 | 519 |
| THERE STILL TO READ TRUE PURE DIVINITY. | UPON BISHOP ANDREWES PICTURE | 12 | 46 | 163 | 490 |
| STILL SPENDING, NEVER SPENT. I MEANE | THE WEEPER | 5 | 46 | 79 | 120 |
| TIS SEED-TIME STILL WITH THEE | THE WEEPER | 9 | 46 | 79 | 120 |
| THY TEARES JUST CADENCE STILL KEEPS TIME. | THE WEEPER | 104 | 46 | 79 | 120 |
| STILL AT EACH SIGH, THAT IS EACH STOP. | THE WEEPER | 107 | 46 | 79 | 120 |
| STILL THY TEARES DOE FALL, AND FALL. | THE WEEPER | 110 | 46 | 79 | 120 |
| STILL THE FOUNTAINE WEEPS FOR ALL. | THE WEEPER | 112 | 46 | 79 | 120 |
| THOU HAST THY TASKE, THOU WEEPEST STILL. | THE WEEPER | 114 | 46 | 79 | 120 |
| AN EYE OF HEAVEN. OR STILL SHINE HERE | THE TEARE | 47 | 46 | 84 | 50 |
| STILL LEGIBLE. | ON MARKES OF SAVIOURS WOUNDS | 4 | 46 | 86 | 28 |
| SPARE THIS ONE JEWELL. I'LE BE DIVES STILL. | DIVES ASKING A DROP | 4 | 46 | 96 | 18 |
| THE WORLD WILL LOVE ITS DARKNESSE STILL. | BUT MEN LOVED DARKNESSE | 2 | 46 | 97 | 13 |
| YET WILL THY HAND STILL GIVING BEE. | ON BLEEDING WOUNDS OF LORD | 10 | 46 | 101 | 110 |
| STILL MY SHEPHEARD, STILL MY GOD | PSALME 23 | 45 | 46 | 102 | 5 |
| STILL MY SHEPHEARD, STILL MY GOD | PSALME 23 | 45 | 46 | 102 | 5 |
| THOU ART WITH ME, STILL THY RUD, | PSALME 23 | 46 | 46 | 102 | 5 |
| SO, EVEN SO STILL MAY I MOVE | PSALME 23 | 57 | 46 | 102 | 5 |
| STILL MAY THY SWEET MERCY SPREAD | PSALME 23 | 59 | 46 | 102 | 5 |
| THREE RIGOUROUS VIRGINS WAITING STILL BEHIND, | SOSPETTO D'HERODE | 65 | 46 | 109 | 216 |
| CAN HIS ATTEMPTS ABOVE STILL PROSP'ROUS BE, | SOSPETTO D'HERODE | 207 | 46 | 109 | 216 |
| AUSPICIOUS STILL, IN SPIGHT OF HELL AND ME. | SOSPETTO D'HERODE | 208 | 46 | 109 | 216 |
| STILL YOU ARE PRODIGAL OF YOUR LOVE'S EXPENCE | SOSPETTO D'HERODE | 285 | 46 | 109 | 216 |
| AND STILL ASSIST THE EXECUTION. | SOSPETTO D'HERODE | 292 | 46 | 109 | 216 |
| STILL WORKE FOR HER, AND HAVE THEIR WAGES FROM HER. | SOSPETTO D'HERODE | 341 | 46 | 109 | 216 |
| GOE NOW, MAKE MUCH OF THESE. WAGE STILL THEIR WARS | SOSPETTO D'HERODE | 447 | 46 | 109 | 216 |
| EFFECTUALL WHISPERS WHOSE STILL VOYCE, | ON A PRAYER BOOKE | 61 | 46 | 126 | 139 |
| A STILL SURVIVING FUNERALL. | IN MEMORY OF LADY MADRE TERESA | 78 | 46 | 131 | 52 |
| TO LIVE, BUT THAT HE STILL MAY DY. | IN MEMORY OF LADY MADRE TERESA | 104 | 46 | 131 | 52 |
| NEW STRUCK BY LOVE, STILL TREMBLING ON HIS DART. | ON A TREATISE OF CHARITY | 46 | 46 | 137 | 69 |
| STILL LIVES, WHICH WHEN WEAKE TIME SHALL BE POUR'D OUT | UPON DEATH OF HERRYS | 36 | 46 | 167 | 466 |
| AND SISTER PHOENIXES, AND STILL THE MOTHER. | UPON YORKE HIS BIRTH | 89 | 46 | 176 | 500 |
| REPEATED, AND THAT SON STILL IN ANOTHER, | UPON YORKE HIS BIRTH | 100 | 46 | 176 | 500 |
| HIS HEAD IN THY FAIRE BOSOME, AND STILL HIDES | TO THE MORNING | 13 | 46 | 183 | 497 |
| HIS LIFE STILL KEPT ALIVE IN THEE. | AN EPITAPH UPON ASHTON | 36 | 46 | 192 | 464 |
| BUT MODESTY DARES STILL DENY IT. | WISHES SUPPOSED MISTRESSE | 120 | 46 | 195 | 479 |
| THE NIGHT & WINTER STILL OF DEATH & SIN. | IN GLORIOUS EPIPHANIE | 77 | 52 | 253 | 39 |
| THE AGED HONORS OF THIS DAY STILL NEW. | TO THE QUEEN'S MAJESTY | 24 | 52 | 261 | 47 |
| MAY THE GREAT TIME, IN YOU, STILL GREATER BE | TO THE QUEEN'S MAJESTY | 25 | 52 | 261 | 47 |
| THEIR DEADLY HATE LIVES STILL. & HATH | OFFICE H. CROSS EVENSONG | 3 | 52 | 273 | 101 |
| HEAV'N NE'RE THE LESSE STILL HEAVN WOULD BE. | CHARITAS NIMIA | 11 | 52 | 280 | 48 |
| STILL WOULD THE YOUTHFULL SPIRITS SING. | CHARITAS NIMIA | 19 | 52 | 280 | 48 |
| AND STILL THY SPATIOUS PALACE RING. | CHARITAS NIMIA | 20 | 52 | 280 | 48 |
| STILL WOULD THOSE BEAUTEOUS MINISTERS OF LIGHT | CHARITAS NIMIA | 21 | 52 | 280 | 48 |
| STILL THRONES & DOMINATIONS WOULD ADORE THEE | CHARITAS NIMIA | 24 | 52 | 280 | 48 |
| STILL WOULD THOSE EVER-WAKEFULL SONS OF FIRE | CHARITAS NIMIA | 25 | 52 | 280 | 48 |
| SHOULD NOT THE KING STILL KEEPE HIS THRONE | CHARITAS NIMIA | 35 | 52 | 280 | 48 |
| HER SWORDS, STILL GROWING WITH HIS PAIN. | SANCTA MARIA DOLORUM | 29 | 52 | 283 | 162 |

```
YET WILL THY HAND STILL GIVING BE.              UPON BLEEDING CRUCIFIX        14   52 288 110
BUT EACH SITT STILL IN HIS OWN DORE.            ADORO TE                       8   52 291 172
WHICH LIVES STILL, & ALLOWES US BREATH.         ADORO TE                      38   52 291 172
BUT STILL IN BOTH ONE CHRIST HE IS.             LAUDA SION SALVATOREM         42   52 294 178
STILL ALIVE.  AND STILL FOR ME.                 DIES IRAE                     52   52 298 186
STILL ALIVE.  AND STILL FOR ME.                 DIES IRAE                     52   52 298 186
BUT THOU THY BOUNTEOUS SELF STILL BE.           DIES IRAE                     55   52 298 186
STILL SPENDING, NEVER SPENT. I MEAN             WEEPER                         5   52 307 120
'TIS SEED-TIME STILL WITH THEE                  WEEPER                         9   52 307 120
STILL THY STARRES DOE FALL & FALL               WEEPER                       134   52 307 120
STILL THE FOUNTAIN WEEPS FOR ALL.               WEEPER                       136   52 307 120
THOU HAST THY TASK. THOU WEEPEST STILL.         WEEPER                       138   52 307 120
STILL AT EACH SIGH, THAT IS, EACH STOP,         WEEPER                       143   52 307 120
AND BLEED & WOUND, AND YEILD & CUNQUER STILL.   FLAMING HEART                 80   52 324  61
BE STILL TRIUMPHANT, BLESSED EYES.              A SONG                         6   52 327  65
STILL SHINE ON ME, FAIR SUNS. THAT I            A SONG                         7   52 327  65
STILL MAY BEHOLD, THOUGH STILL I DY.            A SONG                         8   52 327  65
STILL MAY BEHOLD, THOUGH STILL I DY.            A SONG                         8   52 327  65
THOUGH STILL I DY, I LIVE AGAIN.                A SONG                         9   52 327  65
STILL LONGING SO TO BE STILL SLAIN,             A SONG                        10   52 327  65
STILL LONGING SO TO BE STILL SLAIN,             A SONG                        10   52 327  65
STILL LIVE IN ME THIS LOVING STRIFE             A SONG                        13   52 327  65
EFFECTUALL WISPERS, WHOSE STILL VOICE           PRAYER TO GENTLE-WOMAN        67   52 328 139
UNKIND. YET ARE MY TEARES STILL TRUE TO ME      ALEXIAS SECONDE ELEGIE         2   52 335 207
STILL, AS THEIR VAIN TEARES MY VOWES DID TRY,   ALEXIAS THIRD ELEGIE          55   52 336 209
STILL ROWLING A ROUND SPEAR OF STILL-RETURNING PAIN.  DESCRIPTION RELIGIOUS HOUSE  18  52 338 213
LIVE TO BE OLD, AND STILL A MAN.                TEMPERANCE                    44   52 342 510
OF FAITH. STILL SPENDING, & STILL GROWING STOCK.  (ON) HOPE                   12   52 345  71
OF FAITH. STILL SPENDING, & STILL GROWING STOCK.  (ON) HOPE                   12   52 345  71
OH, WOULD'ST THOU HEERE STILL FIXE THY FAIRE ABODE,  LUKE 2. QUAERIT JESUM    47   MS 379  11
WHAT HINDERS, BUT MY BOSUME STILL MIGHT BE      LUKE 2. QUAERIT JESUM         49   MS 379  11
THE LIGHT'S FAIRE FACE, BUT STILL ABORTIVE BEE. UPON GUNPOWDER TREASON        58   MS 386 460
WHOM FAINT, & PALEFAC'T FEARE DOTH STILL ATTEND. UPON GUNPOWDER TREASON       18   MS 387 461
ONLY THE POPE A STOMACK STILL COULD FIND.       UPON GUNPOWDER TREASON        51   MS 387 461
AND THOUGH THAT MUSICK OF HIS LIFE BE STILL,    UPON DEATH OF A FREIND        21   MS 393 477
MY SOULE SHEE WAS SECURE.  STILL HAVE I BORNE   OUT OF GROTIUS                11   MS 398 198
A STILL INCREASING BURDEN.  WORSE HATH TORNE    OUT OF GROTIUS                12   MS 398 198
A RIDDLE.  (FATHER) STILL ACKNOWLEDG'D THINE    OUT OF GROTIUS                35   MS 398 198
AM STILL REFUS'D.  BEFORE THE INFANT SHRINE     OUT OF GROTIUS                36   MS 398 198
THE WIND IN ALL HIS ROARING BRAGS STOOD STILL   OUT OF GROTIUS                65   MS 398 198

STILL-RETURNING

STILL ROWLING A ROUND SPEAR OF STILL-RETURNING PAIN.  DESCRIPTION RELIGIOUS HOUSE  18  52 338 213

STILL-SURVIVING

A STILL-SURVIVING FUNERALL.                     TERESA                        78   52 315  52

STILL'D

IN PANTING MURMURS, STILL'D OUT OF HER BREAST   MUSICKS DUELL                 65   46 149 535
WET WITH TEARES STILL'D FROM THE EYES,          ANOTHER ON HERRYS             35   46 170 469

STIL

AND NOW HIS DREAM (HELS FIREBRAND) STIL MORE BRIGHT,  SOSPETTO D'HERODE      503   46 109 216

STING

THEY ROUSE HIM, WHEN HIS RANKE THOUGHTS NEED A STING.  SOSPETTO D'HERODE      68   46 109 216
HIS BREST A WHILE FROM CARE'S UNQUIET STING.    SOSPETTO D'HERODE            396   46 109 216

STINGS

THOSE STINGS OF CARE THAT HIS STRONG HEART OPPREST,  SOSPETTO D'HERODE       199   46 109 216
IMMORTALL STINGS TO THY GREAT THOUGHTS, AND THEE.  SOSPETTO D'HERODE         464   46 109 216
MORE DEEPE SUSPICIONS, AND MORE DEADLY STINGS.  SOSPETTO D'HERODE            501   46 109 216
NOT STINGS OF WRATH, BUT WOUNDS OF LOVE.        VEXILLA REGIS                 18   52 277 156
BY ALL THOSE STINGS                             SANCTA MARIA DOLORUM          95   52 283 162
BUT NEITHER ARE THERE THOSE IGNOBLE STINGS      DESCRIPTION RELIGIOUS HOUSE   25   52 338 213

STINKE

OF HELLS OWNE STINKE, A WORSER STENCH IS SPREAD.  SOSPETTO D'HERODE           54   46 109 216

STIRR

HER KEEL CUTTS NOT THE WAVES WHERE THESE WINDS STIRR  (UN) HOPE               33   52 345  71

STIRRE

HER KEELE CUTS NOT THE WAVES, WHERE OUR WINDS STIRRE,  ON HOPE                73   46 143  71

STITCH

THEY PRICK A BLEEDING HEART AT EVERY STITCH.    SOSPETTO D'HERODE            342   46 109 216

STOCK

AND GRAFT INTO THY GRACIOUS STOCK               OFFICE H. CROSS EVENSONG      13   52 273 101
OF FAITH. STILL SPENDING, & STILL GROWING STOCK.  (ON) HOPE                   12   52 345  71
```

## STOCKE

| | | | | | |
|---|---|---|---|---|---|
| (THAT OLD DRY STOCKE) A DESPAIR'D BRANCH IS SPRUNG OF FAITH. THE STEWARD OF OUR GROWING STOCKE. | SOSPETTO D'HERODE ON HOPE | 434 32 | 46 46 | 109 143 | 216 71 |

## STOLE

| | | | | | |
|---|---|---|---|---|---|
| WHICH RENDERS ALL THE STARRES SHE STOLE AWAY. | O GLORIOSA DOMINA | 22 | 52 | 302 | 194 |

## STOLNE

| | | | | | |
|---|---|---|---|---|---|
| OF THY GREAT SELFE, HATH STOLNE KING HEROD FROM THEE. | SOSPETTO D'HERODE | 458 | 46 | 109 | 216 |

## WELL-STOLN

| | | | | | |
|---|---|---|---|---|---|
| TO ALL OUR WORLD OF WELL-STOLN JOY | IN HOLY NATIVITY | 5 | 52 | 246 | 76 |

## STOMACK

| | | | | | |
|---|---|---|---|---|---|
| ONLY THE POPE A STOMACK STILL COULD FIND. TO GLUTT THE STOMACK OF HIS DARLING FLOWER. | UPON GUNPOWDER TREASON UPON BIRTH PRINCESSE E | 51 6 | MS MS | 387 391 | 461 456 |

## STOMACKS

| | | | | | |
|---|---|---|---|---|---|
| THESE FOR VULGAR STOMACKS BE. | PETRONIJ ALES PHASIACIS PETITA | 9 | MS | 382 | 526 |

## STONE

| | | | | | |
|---|---|---|---|---|---|
| TAKE ACQUAINTANCE OF THIS STONE. | HIS EPITAPH (HERRYS) | 3 | 46 | 172 | 471 |
| THIS STONE WILL TELL THEE THAT BENEATH, | HIS EPITAPH (HERRYS) | 5 | 46 | 172 | 471 |
| FOR NOW (ALAS) NOT IN THIS STONE | HIS EPITAPH (HERRYS) | 50 | 46 | 172 | 471 |
| O RATHER USE THIS HEART, THUS FARR A FITTER STONE, | OFFICE H. CROSS COMPLINE | 11 | 52 | 274 | 105 |
| ME TOO MY TEARES, WHO, THOUGH ALL STONE, | SANCTA MARIA DOLORUM | 59 | 52 | 283 | 162 |
| THEIR PILLOW STONE, THEIR SHEETES OF LEAD, | AN EPITAPH UPON MARRIED COUPLE | 12 | 52 | 339 | 478 |
| NOT DARING TO PEEPE FORTH, LEAST THAT A STONE | UPON GUNPOWDER TREASON | 25 | MS | 386 | 460 |
| EACH STONE HAD STREIGHT A NIOBE BECOME, | UPON GUNPOWDER TREASON | 49 | MS | 386 | 460 |

## STONES

| | | | | | |
|---|---|---|---|---|---|
| VAINE MAN, THE STONES THAT ON HIS TOMBE DOE LYE, | YEE BUILD SEPULCHRES | 3 | 46 | 95 | 21 |
| WEEPE PRETIOUS TEARES UPON THE STONES. | PSALME 137 | 36 | 46 | 104 | 7 |
| VERTUES OF STONES, NOR HERBES, USE STRONGER CHARMES, | SOSPETTO D'HERODE | 274 | 46 | 109 | 216 |
| NO LONGER SHALL OUR CHURCHES FRIGHTED STONES | ON A TREATISE OF CHARITY | 31 | 46 | 137 | 69 |
| WHICH TAUGHT ATTENTION EV'N TO ROCKS & STONES. | OFFICE H. CROSS NINTH | 2 | 52 | 271 | 99 |
| THAT EARTH A SHOURE OF STONES TO HEAVEN SHALL SEND, | ON GUNPOWDER-TREASON | 22 | MS | 384 | 458 |
| TO TH' CHURLISH ROCKS, & TEACH THE STUBBORNE STONES | AN ELEGIE ON DR PORTER | 32 | MS | 395 | 476 |

## STONY

| | | | | | |
|---|---|---|---|---|---|
| STONY AMAZEMENT MAKES THEM STAND | NEITHER DURST MAN ASKE | 9 | 46 | 92 | 20 |

## STOOD

| | | | | | |
|---|---|---|---|---|---|
| CLOSE IN THE COVERT OF THE LEAVES THERE STOOD | MUSICKS DUELL | 7 | 46 | 149 | 535 |
| THERE STOOD SHE LISTNING, AND DID ENTERTAINE | MUSICKS DUELL | 11 | 46 | 149 | 535 |
| 'GAINST THY OWNE SONS AND BROTHERS THOU HAST STOOD | SOSPETTO D'HERODE | 453 | 46 | 109 | 216 |
| WHICH ON FALSE TYRANTS HEAD NE'RE FIRMLY STOOD. | SOSPETTO D'HERODE | 492 | 46 | 109 | 216 |
| AND FLATTER'D EVERY GREEDY EYE THAT STOOD | UPON DEATH OF HERRYS | 26 | 46 | 167 | 466 |
| OF A RUDDY ROSE THAT STOOD | UPON DEATH OF DESIRED HERRYS | 32 | 46 | 168 | 467 |
| SHEE ASKS EACH STARRE THAT THEN STOOD BY, | LOVES HOROSCOPE | 7 | 46 | 165 | 483 |
| AND TO THE TEETH OF HELL STOOD UP TO TEACH THEE, | TO THE NAME OF JESUS | 204 | 52 | 239 | 30 |
| AND PUNISH BEST THINGS WORST. BECAUSE THEY STOOD | IN GLORIOUS EPIPHANIE | 107 | 52 | 253 | 39 |
| STOOD DOLEFULL SHEE. | SANCTA MARIA DOLORUM | 2 | 52 | 283 | 162 |
| AND IN THE STEAD OF FEEDING STOOD, & GAZ'D. | UPON GUNPOWDER TREASON | 48 | MS | 387 | 461 |
| THE WIND IN ALL HIS ROARING BRAGS STOOD STILL | OUT OF GROTIUS | 65 | MS | 398 | 198 |

## STOOPE

| | | | | | |
|---|---|---|---|---|---|
| THE SUNNE WILL STOOPE AND TAKE IT UP. | THE TEARE | 10 | 46 | 84 | 50 |

## STOOPED

| | | | | | |
|---|---|---|---|---|---|
| UPON THE STOOPED SHOULDERS OF OLD TIME. | TO THE MORNING | 28 | 46 | 183 | 497 |

## STOOPS

| | | | | | |
|---|---|---|---|---|---|
| LIFTS EARTH TO HEAVEN, STOOPS HEAVEN TO EARTH. | A HYMNE OF THE NATIVITY | 58 | 46 | 106 | 76 |

## STOOPES

| | | | | | |
|---|---|---|---|---|---|
| LIFTS EARTH TO HEAVEN, STOOPES HEAV'N TO EARTH. | IN HOLY NATIVITY | 84 | 52 | 246 | 76 |

## STOP

| | | | | | |
|---|---|---|---|---|---|
| STILL AT EACH SIGH, THAT IS EACH STOP. | THE WEEPER | 107 | 46 | 79 | 120 |
| OF A CRUELL STOP ILL PLAC'T. | ANOTHER ON HERRYS | 40 | 46 | 170 | 469 |
| STILL AT EACH SIGH, THAT IS, EACH STOP. | WEEPER | 143 | 52 | 307 | 120 |

## STOPP

| | | | | | |
|---|---|---|---|---|---|
| NAY, STOPP THY CLOWDY EYES. IT IS NOT GOOD, | UPON GUNPOWDER TREASON | 31 | MS | 387 | 461 |

## STOPT

| | | | | |
|---|---|---|---|---|
| STOPT THE MOUTH OF ELOQUENCE, | UPON THE DEATH OF A GENTLEMAN | 16 | 46 166 | 472 |
| AT LAST IT STOPT AT PLUTO'S GLOOMY PORCH. | ON GUNPOWDER-TREASON | 55 | MS 384 | 458 |

## STORE

| | | | | |
|---|---|---|---|---|
| OF EYES THAT HAS BUT ARGUS STORE, | IT IS BETTER TO GO WITH EYE | 3 | 46 93 | 16 |
| STORE UP THEMSELVES FOR HIM, WHO IS ALONE | ON A PRAYER BOOKE | 39 | 46 126 | 139 |
| WILL TAKE POSSESSION OF THE SACRED STORE | ON A PRAYER BOOKE | 57 | 46 126 | 139 |
| OF ALL THIS HIDDEN STORE | ON A PRAYER BOOKE | 81 | 46 126 | 139 |
| ROB THE RICH STORE HER CABINETS KEEP, | AN HIMNE FOR CIRCUMCISION | 18 | 46 141 | 37 |
| I WISH, HER STORE | WISHES SUPPOSED MISTRESSE | 103 | 46 195 | 479 |
| WE MUST HAVE STORE. | TO THE NAME OF JESUS | 26 | 52 239 | 30 |
| BRING ALL THE STORE | TO THE NAME OF JESUS | 66 | 52 239 | 30 |
| TIME HAS A DAY IN STORE | IN GLORIOUS EPIPHANIE | 133 | 52 253 | 39 |
| O THOU, THY LORD'S FAIR STORE. | WEEPER | 115 | 52 307 | 120 |
| STORE UP THEMSELVES FOR HIM, WHO IS ALONE | PRAYER TO GENTLE-WOMAN | 45 | 52 328 | 139 |
| WILL TAKE POSSESSION OF THAT SACRED STORE | PRAYER TO GENTLE-WOMAN | 63 | 52 328 | 139 |
| OF ALL THIS STORE | PRAYER TO GENTLE-WOMAN | 87 | 52 328 | 139 |
| THE STAGGERING LUMPE. EACH EYE SPENT ALL ITS STORE, | UPON KINGS CORONATION | 11 | MS 390 | 453 |
| RICH, LIBERALL HEAVEN, WHAT, HATH YOUR TREASURE STORE | UPON BIRTH PRINCESSE E | 25 | MS 391 | 456 |
| ARE TEEMING NOW WITH STORE OF FRESH SUPPLIES. | AN ELEGIE ON DR PORTER | 44 | MS 395 | 476 |

## STORIES

| | | | | |
|---|---|---|---|---|
| WITH HIS FAIRE TRIUMPHS FILL ALL FUTURE STORIES. | SOSPETTO D'HERODE | 230 | 46 109 | 216 |

## STORME

| | | | | |
|---|---|---|---|---|
| AS IF THE STORME MEANT HIM. | WHY ARE YEE AFRAID | 1 | 46 88 | 15 |
| THERE IS NO STORME BUT THIS | WHY ARE YEE AFRAID | 9 | 46 88 | 15 |
| YOU ARE THE STORME THAT MOCKS | WHY ARE YEE AFRAID | 12 | 46 88 | 15 |
| THERE RUDE IMPETUOUS RAGE DO'S STORME, AND FRET. | SOSPETTO D'HERODE | 317 | 46 109 | 216 |
| OF A MAD STORME THESE BLOOMY JOYES ALL TORE, | UPON DEATH OF HERRYS | 33 | 46 167 | 466 |
| WHEN A RUDDY STORME WHOSE SCOULE, | UPON DEATH OF DESIRED HERRYS | 51 | 46 168 | 467 |
| STORME AND THUNDER | OUT OF THE ITALIAN (1) | 34 | 46 188 | 545 |
| THE STORME OF FATE, TO WHICH HIS LIFE HE OWES. | HORATIJ ILLE & NEFASTO | 24 | MS 382 | 530 |
| LETT NOT MY SUPPLIANT BREATH RAISE A RUDE STORME | ON GUNPOWDER-TREASON | 11 | MS 384 | 458 |

## STORMES

| | | | | |
|---|---|---|---|---|
| THAT FEARES THE FOULE-MOUTH'D AUSTER, OR THOSE STORMES | OUT OF VIRGIL | 19 | 46 155 | 529 |

## STORMY

| | | | | |
|---|---|---|---|---|
| TILL THIS STORMY NIGHT BE GONE. | AN EPITAPH HUSBAND AND WIFE | 12 | 46 174 | 478 |
| TILL THIS STORMY NIGHT BE GONE. | AN EPITAPH UPON MARRIED COUPLE | 16 | 52 339 | 478 |

## STORY

| | | | | |
|---|---|---|---|---|
| WHAT EVER STORY OF THEIR CRUELTIE, | ON MARKES OF SAVIOURS WOUNDS | 1 | 46 86 | 28 |
| HIS LIVES SWEET STORY, BY THE HAST, | ANOTHER ON HERRYS | 39 | 46 170 | 469 |
| AND NAME DWELL SWEET IN SOME ETERNALL STORY. | UPON YORKE HIS BIRTH | 105 | 46 176 | 500 |
| BEE YE MY FICTIONS, BUT HER STORY. | WISHES SUPPOSED MISTRESSE | 126 | 46 195 | 479 |
| RELATING THIS SAD STORY. STREIGHTWAY HEE | UPON GUNPOWDER TREASON | 55 | MS 386 | 460 |

## STOUT

| | | | | |
|---|---|---|---|---|
| THOSE THY OLD SOULDIERS, STOUT AND TALL | IN MEMORY OF LADY MADRE TERESA | 4 | 46 131 | 52 |

## STRAIGHT

| | | | | |
|---|---|---|---|---|
| MAN TREMBLES AT, WEE STRAIGHT SHALL FIND | IN MEMORY OF LADY MADRE TERESA | 31 | 46 131 | 52 |
| TURN SPEARES, & STRAIGHT COME HOME AGAIN. | SANCTA MARIA DOLORUM | 30 | 52 283 | 162 |
| MAN TREMBLES AT, YOU STRAIGHT SHALL FIND | TERESA | 31 | 52 315 | 52 |
| HE YEILDS, AND STRAIGHT BAPTIS'D, OBTAINS THE GRACE | ALEXIAS THIRD ELEGIE | 45 | 52 336 | 209 |

## STREIGHT

| | | | | |
|---|---|---|---|---|
| PALLAS SAW VENUS ARM'D AND STREIGHT SHE CRY'D, | UPON THE SAME (VENUS ARMES) | 1 | 46 161 | 523 |
| 'CAUSE THOU STREIGHT MUST LAY THY HEAD | THE TEARE | 32 | 46 84 | 50 |
| THOU SPAK'ST AND STREIGHT THE BLIND MAN SAW. | THE BLIND CURED | 2 | 46 91 | 19 |
| BUT STREIGHT HIS EYES ADVIS'D HIS CHEEKE. | A HYMNE OF THE NATIVITY | 49 | 46 106 | 76 |
| THE CALDRON-PRISON'D WATERS STREIGHT CONSPIRE, | SOSPETTO D'HERODE | 483 | 46 109 | 216 |
| YOU STREIGHT SHALL SEE HER WAKE AND RISE | THOUGH NOW 'TIS NEITHER | 9 | MS 397 | 492 |
| EACH STONE HAD STREIGHT A NIOBE BECOME. | UPON GUNPOWDER TREASON | 49 | MS 386 | 460 |
| STREIGHT FROM THIS SEA OF TEARES THERE DOES APPEARE | UPON KINGS CORONATION | 13 | MS 390 | 453 |
| AND STREIGHT HIS AMOROUS SYTH (GREEDY OF BLISSE) | AN ELEGY MR STANNINOW | 47 | MS 394 | 473 |
| AND STREIGHT OF ALL THIS APPROBATION GATE | OUT OF GROTIUS | 55 | MS 398 | 198 |

## STREIGHTWAY

| | | | | |
|---|---|---|---|---|
| CHARG'D WITH A FLYING TOUCH, AND STREIGHTWAY SHEE | MUSICKS DUELL | 21 | 46 149 | 535 |
| HE STREIGHTWAY LIGHTED UPP HIS PITCHY TORCH. | ON GUNPOWDER-TREASON | 56 | MS 384 | 458 |
| RELATING THIS SAD STORY. STREIGHTWAY HEE | UPON GUNPOWDER TREASON | 55 | MS 386 | 460 |

## STREIGHTWAIS

| | | | | |
|---|---|---|---|---|
| POORE MEAGRE HORROR STREIGHTWAIS WAS AMAZ'D. | UPON GUNPOWDER TREASON | 47 | MS 387 | 461 |

STRAINE

| | | | |
|---|---|---|---|
| ON THE WAV'D BACKE OF EVERY SWELLING STRAINE. | MUSICKS DUELL | 95 | 46 149 535 |
| (MISTRESSE) I COME. NOW REACH A STRAINE MY LUTE | MUSICKS DUELL | 107 | 46 149 535 |

STRAINES

| | | | |
|---|---|---|---|
| OF CLOSER STRAINES, AND ERE THE WARRE BEGIN. | MUSICKS DUELL | 19 | 46 149 535 |
| STRAINES HIGHER YET. THAT TICKLED WITH RARE ART | MUSICKS DUELL | 47 | 46 149 535 |
| HEE STRAINES THESE WORDS. BASE ENVY, DOE, LAUGH ON. | HIGH MOUNTED ON AN ANT | 5 | 46 161 523 |

STRYNES

| | | | |
|---|---|---|---|
| ONELY SUCH STRYNES AS SERVE TO KEEPE | THOUGH NOW 'TIS NEITHER | 19 | MS 397 492 |

STRANGE

| | | | |
|---|---|---|---|
| A MOST STRANGE BABE. WHO HERE CONCEAL'D BY THEM | SOSPETTO D'HERODE | 435 | 46 109 216 |
| A THOUSAND PROPHECIES THAT TALKE STRANGE THINGS, | SOSPETTO D'HERODE | 497 | 46 109 216 |
| FROM THE PALE DUST OF THAT STRANGE SACRIFICE | ON A TREATISE OF CHARITY | 18 | 46 137 69 |
| MAINTAIN THE WILL IN THESE STRANGE WARRES. | TO COUNTESSE OF DENBIGH | 18 | 52 236 146 |
| TH' ASTONISHT NYMPHS THEIR FLOOD'S STRANGE FATE DEPLORE, | TO COUNTESSE OF DENBIGH | 25 | 52 236 146 |
| AND BY STRANGE WITT OF MADNES WREST | IN GLORIOUS EPIPHANIE | 111 | 52 253 39 |
| O STRANGE MYSTERIOUS STRIFE | OFFICE H. CROSS NINTH | 9 | 52 271 99 |
| IN WHAT STRANGE PATH MY LORD'S FOOTSTEPPES BLEED. | ALEXIAS FIRST ELEGIE | 8 | 52 334 204 |
| MAINTAIN THE WILL IN THESE STRANGE WARRS. | AGAINST IRRESOLUTION AND DELAY | 12 | 52 347 146 |
| TH'ASTONISH'D NYMPHS THEIR FLOUD'S STRANGE FATE DEPLORE, | AGAINST IRRESOLUTION AND DELAY | 25 | 52 347 146 |
| STRANGE THE QUIVER, BOW, & DART. | IN CICATRICES DOMINI JESU | 15 | MS 381 27 |
| STRANGE METAMORPHOSIS. IT WAS BUT NOW | UPON KINGS CORONATION | 1 | MS 390 453 |
| OTHER MENS HUNGER WITH STRANGE FEASTS I QUELL'D | OUT OF GROTIUS | 57 | MS 398 198 |

STRANGELY

| | | | |
|---|---|---|---|
| WITH THINE OWNE GLORYES. AND ART STRANGELY BLEST | UPON YORKE HIS BIRTH | 4 | 46 176 500 |
| WE, WHO STRANGELY WENT ASTRAY, | IN GLORIOUS EPIPHANIE | 15 | 52 253 39 |

STRANGER

| | | | |
|---|---|---|---|
| ON WHICH, AS ON A GLORIOUS STRANGER GAZ'D | SOSPETTO D'HERODE | 130 | 46 109 216 |
| HIMSELFE A STRANGER TO, HIS OWNE HAD MADE. | SOSPETTO D'HERODE | 404 | 46 109 216 |
| TO ENTERTAIN THIS STARRY STRANGER. | IN HOLY NATIVITY | 38 | 52 246 76 |
| MINE OWNE WITH STRANGER FASTINGS, WHEN I HELD | OUT OF GROTIUS | 58 | MS 398 198 |

STRANGERS

| | | | |
|---|---|---|---|
| CONSPIR'D WITH DARKNES 'GAINST THE STRANGERS THROATE. | HORATIJ ILLE & NEFASTO | 9 | MS 382 530 |

STRATAGEM

| | | | |
|---|---|---|---|
| OF HIS HIGH STRATAGEM TO WIN YOUR HEART. | TO SAME CONCERNING CHOISE | 44 | 52 331 66 |

STRAW

| | | | |
|---|---|---|---|
| BEASTS AND BASE STRAW. ALREADY IS THE STREAME | SOSPETTO D'HERODE | 437 | 46 109 216 |

STRAY'D

| | | | |
|---|---|---|---|
| THY SHEEP WAS STRAY'D. AND THOU WOULDST BE | DIES IRAE | 31 | 52 298 186 |

STRAYES

| | | | |
|---|---|---|---|
| WHEN MY SIMPLE WEAKNESSE STRAYES, | PSALME 23 | 21 | 46 102 5 |
| AND NOW WHERE'RE HE STRAYES. | WEEPER | 109 | 52 307 120 |

STREAM

| | | | |
|---|---|---|---|
| HEAVN'S BOSOME DRINKS THE GENTLE STREAM. | WEEPER | 20 | 52 307 120 |
| THY SYLVER, THEN HIS GOLDEN STREAM. | WEEPER | 78 | 52 307 120 |

STREAME

| | | | |
|---|---|---|---|
| STILL KEEPING IN THE FORWARD STREAME, SO LONG | MUSICKS DUELL | 66 | 46 149 535 |
| HEAVENS BOSOME DRINKS THE GENTLE STREAME. | THE WEEPER | 20 | 46 79 120 |
| THY SILVER, THEN HIS GOLDEN STREAME. | THE WEEPER | 84 | 46 79 120 |
| BEASTS AND BASE STRAW. ALREADY IS THE STREAME | SOSPETTO D'HERODE | 437 | 46 109 216 |
| A BROOKE WHOSE STREAME SO GREAT, SO GOOD, | AN EPITAPH DOCTOR BROOKE | 1 | 46 175 465 |
| MINE EYES A TRIBUTARY STREAME SHALL PAY. | ON GUNPOWDER-TREASON | 14 | MS 384 458 |
| AND CRACK THE CHRISTALL GLOBE. THE MILKY STREAME | ON GUNPOWDER-TREASON | 23 | MS 384 458 |
| FROM HEAVENS SWEET MILKY STREAME DOTH GENTLY POURE. | AN ELEGY MR STANNINOW | 10 | MS 394 473 |

STREAMS

| | | | |
|---|---|---|---|
| OF NOONS HIGH GLORY, WHEN HARD BY THE STREAMS | MUSICKS DUELL | 2 | 46 149 535 |

STREAMES

| | | | |
|---|---|---|---|
| BATHING IN STREAMES OF LIQUID MELODIE. | MUSICKS DUELL | 68 | 46 149 535 |
| THOSE YET FRESH STREAMES WHICH CRAWLED EVERY WHERE | THE BEGINNING OF HELIODORUS | 21 | 46 158 517 |
| THIS FLOOD THUS STAINED FAIRER STREAMES. | SHE BEGAN TO WASH HIS FEET | 4 | 46 97 13 |
| THIS ROCKE BUDS FORTH THE FOUNTAINE OF THE STREAMES OF DAY. | EASTER DAY | 9 | 46 100 26 |

|  |  |  |  |  |  |
|---|---|---|---|---|---|
| WHOSE SOFT SILVER-SWEATING STREAMES | PSALME 23 | 15 | 46 | 102 | 5 |
| ALL THE STREAMES OF ALL HER SPRINGS. | ANOTHER ON HERRYS | 10 | 46 | 170 | 469 |
| TAINT NOT THE PURE STREAMES OF THE SPRINGING DAY, | ON A FOULE MORNING | 32 | 46 | 181 | 495 |
| LO, HOW THE STREAMES OF LIFE, FROM THAT FULL NEST | VEXILLA REGIS | 7 | 52 | 277 | 156 |
| THY MAIDEN STREAMES SOE SOONE TO NEPTUNES BED. | AN ELEGIE ON DR PORTER | 2 | MS | 395 | 476 |
| THY LAZY CRAWLING STREAMES, PRI'THEE BE GONE. | AN ELEGIE ON DR PORTER | 20 | MS | 395 | 476 |

STREAMING

|  |  |  |  |  |  |
|---|---|---|---|---|---|
| OF STREAMING SWEETNESSE, WHICH IN STATE DOTH RIDE | MUSICKS DUELL | 94 | 46 | 149 | 535 |

STRENGTH

|  |  |  |  |  |  |
|---|---|---|---|---|---|
| FEELES NOT THE STRENGTH, THE REACHING SPELL | OUT OF GREEKE CUPID'S CRYER | 36 | 46 | 159 | 519 |
| SHEE FOUND THE WAY HOME, WITH AN HOLY STRENGTH | UPON BISHOP ANDREWES PICTURE | 8 | 46 | 163 | 490 |
| HIS HANDS WHOLE STRENGTH HERE, COULD NOT BE TOO MUCH. | THE DUMBE HEALED | 4 | 46 | 87 | 16 |
| MY SELFE, MY STRENGTH TOO WITH MY INNOCENCE. | SOSPETTO D'HERODE | 250 | 46 | 109 | 216 |
| IF USUALL WIT, AND STRENGTH WILL DOE NO GOOD, | SOSPETTO D'HERODE | 273 | 46 | 109 | 216 |
| THE STRENGTH OF HER UNITED WORTH. | HIS EPITAPH (HERRYS) | 14 | 46 | 172 | 471 |
| HIS PRAYERS TOOKE THEIR PRICE AND STRENGTH | AN EPITAPH UPON ASHTON | 15 | 46 | 192 | 464 |
| NEEDS MUST YOUR NOBLE PRAYSES STRENGTH | TO THE QUEEN | 13 | 48 | 215 | 501 |
| THAT SO, IN SPITE OF ALL THIS PEEVISH STRENGTH | TO COUNTESSE OF DENBIGH | 41 | 52 | 236 | 146 |
| FAITH IS MY FORCE. FAITH STRENGTH AFFORDS | ADORO TE | 13 | 52 | 291 | 172 |

STRENGTHS

|  |  |  |  |  |  |
|---|---|---|---|---|---|
| MEE YET A SECOND FALL. WEE'D TRY OUR STRENGTHS. | SOSPETTO D'HERODE | 254 | 46 | 109 | 216 |

STRETCH

|  |  |  |  |  |  |
|---|---|---|---|---|---|
| NOW STRETCH THY SELF (FAIRE ILE) AND GROW, SPREAD WIDE | UPON YORKE HIS BIRTH | 2 | 46 | 176 | 500 |
| STRETCH ALL THY POWRES. CALL IF YOU CAN | LAUDA SION SALVATOREM | 3 | 52 | 294 | 178 |
| AND STRETCH THEIR COLD LIMBES IN A PLEASING FIRE. | HORATIJ ILLE & NEFASTO | 53 | MS | 382 | 530 |

STRETCH'ST

|  |  |  |  |  |  |
|---|---|---|---|---|---|
| AND STRETCH'ST THY DISMALL VOICE TOO DEEPE. | UPON DEATH OF A FREIND | 10 | MS | 393 | 477 |

STRETCH'T

|  |  |  |  |  |  |
|---|---|---|---|---|---|
| GASP FOR THY GOLDEN SHOWRES. WITH LONG STRETCH'T HANDS | TO THE NAME OF JESUS | 130 | 52 | 239 | 30 |

STRIFE

|  |  |  |  |  |  |
|---|---|---|---|---|---|
| AT LENGTH (AFTER SO LONG, SO LOUD A STRIFE | MUSICKS DUELL | 151 | 46 | 149 | 535 |
| THOU TO MAINTAINE THEIR CRUELL STRIFE, | IN PRAISE OF LESSIUS | 3 | 46 | 156 | 510 |
| DISTILLS FROM THENCE THE TEARES OF WRATH AND STRIFE, | TO LORD UPON WATER MADE WINE | 3 | 46 | 91 | 12 |
| DEATH TORE NOT (THEREFORE) BUT SANS STRIFE | AN EPITAPH UPON ASHTON | 27 | 46 | 192 | 464 |
| O STRANGE MYSTERIOUS STRIFE | OFFICE H. CROSS NINTH | 9 | 52 | 271 | 99 |
| STILL LIVE IN ME THIS LOVING STRIFE | A SONG | 13 | 52 | 327 | 65 |
| SURE IN MY EARLY WOES STARRES WERE AT STRIFE, | ALEXIAS FIRST ELEGIE | 5 | 52 | 334 | 204 |
| THOU TO MAINTAIN THEIR PRETIOUS STRIFE | TEMPERANCE | 3 | 52 | 342 | 510 |

STRIKE

|  |  |  |  |  |  |
|---|---|---|---|---|---|
| TO STRIKE AT EARES, IS TO TAKE HEED THERE BEE | ON ST. PETER CUTTING MALCHUS | 3 | 46 | 97 | 22 |
| OUR HARD HEARTS SHALL STRIKE FIRE, THE SAME | IN MEMORY OF LADY MADRE TERESA | 161 | 46 | 131 | 52 |
| HAIL, & STRIKE HOME & MAKE ME SEE | SANCTA MARIA DOLORUM | 73 | 52 | 283 | 162 |
| OUR HARD HEARTS SHALL STRIKE FIRE, THE SAME | TERESA | 160 | 52 | 315 | 52 |
| AND STRIKE YOUR TROUBLED HEART | TO SAME CONCERNING CHOISE | 50 | 52 | 331 | 66 |

STRIKING

|  |  |  |  |  |  |
|---|---|---|---|---|---|
| IN STEAD OF STRIKING WOULD HAVE GAZ'D. | ANOTHER ON HERRYS | 32 | 46 | 170 | 469 |
| IN STRIKING WHERE YOU SHOULD NOT TOUCH. | UPON DEATH OF A FREIND | 14 | MS | 393 | 477 |

STRING

|  |  |  |  |  |  |
|---|---|---|---|---|---|
| HEE LIGHTLY SKIRMISHES ON EVERY STRING | MUSICKS DUELL | 20 | 46 | 149 | 535 |
| HIS NIMBLE HANDS INSTINCT THEN TAUGHT EACH STRING | MUSICKS DUELL | 27 | 46 | 149 | 535 |
| EACH STRING HIS NOTE, AS IF THEY MEANT TO CARRY | MUSICKS DUELL | 146 | 46 | 149 | 535 |
| PARDON (BRIGHT EXCELLENCE) AN UNTUN'D STRING, | UPON YORKE HIS BIRTH | 106 | 46 | 176 | 500 |
| THAT TALKES WITH TUNEFULL STRING. | TO THE NAME OF JESUS | 48 | 52 | 239 | 30 |
| STRUCK LOWD HIS FAITHFULL STRING. | VEXILLA REGIS | 22 | 52 | 277 | 156 |
| THAT GREIFE MAY CRACK THAT STRING, & NOW UNTIE | AN ELEGIE ON DR PORTER | 35 | MS | 395 | 476 |

STRINGS

|  |  |  |  |  |  |
|---|---|---|---|---|---|
| THE TATLING STRINGS (EACH BREATHING IN HIS PART) | MUSICKS DUELL | 48 | 46 | 149 | 535 |
| AND WITH A QUAVERING COYNESSE TASTS THE STRINGS. | MUSICKS DUELL | 112 | 46 | 149 | 535 |
| THE HUMOUROUS STRINGS EXPOUND HIS LEARNED TOUCH, | MUSICKS DUELL | 127 | 46 | 149 | 535 |
| OF ALL THE STRINGS, STILL BREATHING THE BEST LIFE | MUSICKS DUELL | 152 | 46 | 149 | 535 |
| HIS CORRESPONDENT CHEEKES. THESE LOATHSOME STRINGS | SOSPETTO D'HERODE | 38 | 46 | 109 | 216 |
| FAINE WOULD HEE HAVE FORGOT WHAT FATALL STRINGS, | SOSPETTO D'HERODE | 139 | 46 | 109 | 216 |
| WHEN YOUR HANDS UNTY THESE STRINGS, | ON MR. G. HERBERTS BOOKE | 5 | 46 | 130 | 68 |
| COMPLAINING PIPES, & PRATTLING STRINGS, | TO THE NAME OF JESUS | 65 | 52 | 239 | 30 |
| RUNNES MURMURING ON THE STRINGS. ALCAEUS THERE | HORATIJ ILLE & NEFASTO | 41 | MS | 382 | 530 |

STRINGES

|  |  |  |  |  |  |
|---|---|---|---|---|---|
| OF CHATT'RING STRINGES, BY THE SMALL SIZE OF ONE | MUSICKS DUELL | 163 | 46 | 149 | 535 |

## STRIVE

| | | | |
|---|---|---|---|
| BABELS BOLD ARTISTS STRIVE (BELOW) TO BUILD | ON FRONTISPIECE ISAACSONS | 16 | 46 191 491 |
| STAY, SILVER-FOOTED CAME, STRIVE NOT TO WED | AN ELEGIE ON DR PORTER | 1 | MS 395 476 |

## STRIV'D

| | | | |
|---|---|---|---|
| WHERE RACKES & TORMENTS STRIV'D, IN VAIN, TO REACH THEE. | TO THE NAME OF JESUS | 206 | 52 239 30 |

## STRIVES

| | | | |
|---|---|---|---|
| THAT STRIVES IN TORRENTS OF ITS OWNE. | ON BLEEDING WOUNDS OF LORD | 20 | 46 101 110 |
| HEE STUDIES SCRIPTURE, STRIVES TO SOUND THE HEART, | SOSPETTO D'HERODE | 155 | 46 109 216 |
| THAT STRIVES IN TORRENTS OF IT'S OWN. | UPON BLEEDING CRUCIFIX | 8 | 52 288 110 |

## STRIVING

| | | | |
|---|---|---|---|
| TILL A SWEET WHIRLE-WIND (STRIVING TO GETT OUT) | MUSICKS DUELL | 87 | 46 149 535 |
| IN SHRILL TONGU'D ACCENTS, STRIVING TO BEE SINGLE. | MUSICKS DUELL | 130 | 46 149 535 |

## STROKE

| | | | |
|---|---|---|---|
| WHOSE STROKE SHALL TAST THY HALLOW'D BREATH. | TERESA | 80 | 52 315 52 |

## STROAKE

| | | | |
|---|---|---|---|
| EVERY SMOOTH TURNE, EVERY DELICIOUS STROAKE | MUSICKS DUELL | 131 | 46 149 535 |
| WHOSE STROAKE SHALL TASTE THY HALLOWED BREATH. | IN MEMORY OF LADY MADRE TERESA | 80 | 46 131 52 |
| AND STROAKE HIS RADIANT CHEEKES. ONE TIMELY KISSE | TO THE MORNING | 37 | 46 183 497 |

## STROAKT

| | | | |
|---|---|---|---|
| HANGS HIS BLACK LUGGES, STROAKT WITH THOSE HEAVENLY LINES. | HORATIJ ILLE & NEFASTO | 51 | MS 382 530 |

## STROAK'T

| | | | |
|---|---|---|---|
| AND STROAK'T THY CARES. | LUKE 2. QUAERIT JESUM | 32 | MS 379 11 |

## STROKES

| | | | |
|---|---|---|---|
| STROKES AND TAMES MY RABID GRIEFE. | PSALME 23 | 19 | 46 102 5 |

## STRONG

| | | | |
|---|---|---|---|
| BY A STRONG EXTASY) THROUGH ALL THE SPHAEARES | MUSICKS DUELL | 148 | 46 149 535 |
| THOU, WHOSE STRONG HAND WITH SO TRANSCENDENT WORTH, | SOSPETTO D'HERODE | 25 | 46 109 216 |
| WHILE HIS STEELE SIDES SOUND WITH HIS TAYLES STRONG LASH. | SOSPETTO D'HERODE | 64 | 46 109 216 |
| OF STURDY ADAMANT IS HIS STRONG CHAINE. | SOSPETTO D'HERODE | 144 | 46 109 216 |
| THOSE STINGS OF CARE THAT HIS STRONG HEART OPPREST, | SOSPETTO D'HERODE | 199 | 46 109 216 |
| STAY OF MY STRONG HOPES, YOU OF WHOSE BRAVE WORTH, | SOSPETTO D'HERODE | 282 | 46 109 216 |
| NAILES, HAMMERS, HATCHETS SHARPE, AND HALTERS STRONG, | SOSPETTO D'HERODE | 325 | 46 109 216 |
| HERE STRONG PROCRUSTES PLANTS HIS BED OF BRASSE. | SOSPETTO D'HERODE | 358 | 46 109 216 |
| DEARE SCULE BEE STRONG, | ON A PRAYER BOOKE | 33 | 46 126 139 |
| WITH STRONG ARMES THEIR TRIUMPHANT CROWNE. | IN MEMORY OF LADY MADRE TERESA | 6 | 46 131 52 |
| HOW MUCH LESSE STRUNG IS DEATH THEN LOVE. | IN MEMORY OF LADY MADRE TERESA | 28 | 46 131 52 |
| HER WEAKE BREAST HEAVES WITH STRONG DESIRE, | IN MEMORY OF LADY MADRE TERESA | 40 | 46 131 52 |
| WITH THEE STRONG WINE OF LOVE, LET OTHERS SWIMME | AN APOLOGIE FOR HYMNE (TERESA) | 31 | 46 136 59 |
| THE GENEROUS WINE WITH AGE GROWES STRONG, NOT SOWER. | ON HOPE | 53 | 46 143 71 |
| HER EYE A STRONG APPEALE CAN GIVE, | LOVES HOROSCOPE | 39 | 46 185 483 |
| PLEAD YOUR PRETENCES (O YOU STRONG | TO COUNTESSE OF DENBIGH | 9 | 52 236 146 |
| AND FETCH HER FROM IT'S STRONG HOLD. | TO COUNTESSE OF DENBIGH | 28 | 52 236 146 |
| COME, & COME STRONG, | TO THE NAME OF JESUS | 70 | 52 239 30 |
| OF HIS STRONG SOUL, SHALL HE | IN GLORIOUS EPIPHANIE | 197 | 52 253 39 |
| WITH STRONG ARMES, THEIR TRIUMPHANT CROWN, | TERESA | 6 | 52 315 52 |
| HOW MUCH LESSE STRONG IS DEATH THEN LOVE. | TERESA | 28 | 52 315 52 |
| HER WEAKE BREST HEAVES WITH STRONG DESIRE | TERESA | 40 | 52 315 52 |
| WITH THEE, STRONG WINE OF LOVE, LET OTHERS SWIMME | AN APOLOGIE FOR (TERESA) HYMNE | 31 | 52 322 59 |
| DEAR SOUL, BE STRONG. | PRAYER TO GENTLE-WOMAN | 39 | 52 328 139 |
| WITH ROCKS, NOR BOLD HANDS STRUCK THE WORLD'S STRONG BARRES. | ALEXIAS THIRD ELEGIE | 10 | 52 336 209 |
| MY BOSOME'S GUARD, A SPIRIT GREAT & STRONG, | ALEXIAS THIRD ELEGIE | 35 | 52 336 209 |
| THY GENEROUS WINE WITH AGE GROWES STRONG, NOT SOWER. | (ON) HOPE | 23 | 52 345 71 |
| PLEAD YOUR PRETENCES, (O YOU STRONG | AGAINST IRRESOLUTION AND DELAY | 17 | 52 347 146 |

## STRONGER

| | | | |
|---|---|---|---|
| VERTUES OF STONES, NOR HERBES, USE STRONGER CHARMES, | SOSPETTO D'HERODE | 274 | 46 109 216 |

## STROVE

| | | | |
|---|---|---|---|
| LO HERE THE FAIRE CHARICLIA. IN WHOM STROVE | UPON FAIRE ETHIOPIAN | 1 | 46 183 493 |

## STROW

| | | | |
|---|---|---|---|
| THE DOWNE THAT THEIR SOFT BRESTS DID STROW, | A HYMNE OF THE NATIVITY | 42 | 46 106 76 |
| AND WINTER STROW HER WAY, YEA, SUCH A SORE | SOSPETTO D'HERODE | 380 | 46 109 216 |
| WILL WEE STROW UPON IT. | ON THE ASSUMPTION | 49 | 46 139 114 |
| WILL WE STROW UPON IT. | IN GLORIOUS ASSUMPTION B. LADY | 54 | 52 304 114 |

STROWES

| | | | | |
|---|---|---|---|---|
| NONE SO FAIRE THY BOSOME STROWES. | AN HIMNE FOR CIRCUMCISION | 10 | 46 141 | 37 |
| NONE SO FAIR THY BOSOM STROWES. | NEW YEAR'S DAY | 10 | 52 251 | 37 |
| A VOLUNTARY MINT, THAT STROWES | WEEPER | 125 | 52 307 | 120 |

STRUCK

| | | | | |
|---|---|---|---|---|
| NEW STRUCK BY LOVE, STILL TREMBLING ON HIS DART. | ON A TREATISE OF CHARITY | 46 | 46 137 | 69 |
| STRUCK LOWD HIS FAITHFULL STRING, | VEXILLA REGIS | 22 | 52 277 | 156 |
| WITH ROCKS. NOR BOLD HANDS STRUCK THE WORLD'S STRONG BARRES. | ALEXIAS THIRD ELEGIE | 10 | 52 336 | 209 |
| SHALL WITH ONE FLASH OF LIGHTING BE STRUCK BLIND. | ON GUNPOWDER-TREASON | 32 | MS 384 | 458 |

STROOKE

| | | | | |
|---|---|---|---|---|
| WHAT THOUGH I MIST MY BLOW. YET I STROOKE HIGH, | SOSPETTO D'HERODE | 223 | 46 109 | 216 |

STRUCKE

| | | | | |
|---|---|---|---|---|
| STRUCKE WITH THESE GREAT CONCURRENCES OF THINGS, | SOSPETTO D'HERODE | 137 | 46 109 | 216 |

STRUGGLE

| | | | | |
|---|---|---|---|---|
| HIS FINGERS STRUGGLE WITH THE VOCALL THREADS, | MUSICKS DUELL | 122 | 46 149 | 535 |
| HEAV'N SAW US STRUGGLE ONCE, AS BRAVE A FIGHT | SOSPETTO D'HERODE | 255 | 46 109 | 216 |

STRUGLING

| | | | | |
|---|---|---|---|---|
| LETT THY SWOLNE BREAST DISCHARGE THY STRUGLING GROANES | AN ELEGIE ON DR PORTER | 31 | MS 395 | 476 |

STRUNG

| | | | | |
|---|---|---|---|---|
| WELL STRUNG WITH MANY A BROKEN NERVE. | IN CICATRICES DOMINI JESU | 14 | MS 381 | 27 |

NEW-STRUNG

| | | | | |
|---|---|---|---|---|
| TO CHAUNT MY PRAYSES IN A NEW-STRUNG SONG. | OUT OF GROTIUS | 74 | MS 398 | 198 |

STUBBORN

| | | | | |
|---|---|---|---|---|
| WHEN STUBBORN ROCKS SHALL BOW | TO THE NAME OF JESUS | 230 | 52 239 | 30 |

STUBBORNE

| | | | | |
|---|---|---|---|---|
| TO TH' CHURLISH ROCKS, & TEACH THE STUBBORNE STONES | AN ELEGIE ON DR PORTER | 32 | MS 395 | 476 |

STUCK

| | | | | |
|---|---|---|---|---|
| FALL WITH SOFT WINGS, STUCK WITH SOFT FLOWRES. | TEMPERANCE | 46 | 52 342 | 510 |

STUDY

| | | | | |
|---|---|---|---|---|
| TO STUDY HIM SO, TILL WE MIX | SANCTA MARIA DOLORUM | 99 | 52 283 | 162 |

STUDIED

| | | | | |
|---|---|---|---|---|
| OF STUDIED FATE STAND FORTH, | WISHES SUPPOSED MISTRESSE | 8 | 46 195 | 479 |

STUDY'D

| | | | | |
|---|---|---|---|---|
| HAVE STUDY'D OVER ALL ASTROLOGY. | ALEXIAS SECONDE ELEGIE | 22 | 52 335 | 207 |

STUDIES

| | | | | |
|---|---|---|---|---|
| HEE STUDIES SCRIPTURE, STRIVES TO SOUND THE HEART, | SOSPETTO D'HERODE | 155 | 46 109 | 216 |

STUDYES

| | | | | |
|---|---|---|---|---|
| THAT STUDYES THIS HIGH ART, | ON A PRAYER BOOKE | 30 | 46 126 | 139 |
| THAT STUDYES THIS HIGH ART | PRAYER TO GENTLE-WOMAN | 36 | 52 328 | 139 |

STUFFE

| | | | | |
|---|---|---|---|---|
| BRING ALL YOUR HOUSHOLD STUFFE OF HEAVN ON EARTH, | TO THE NAME OF JESUS | 63 | 52 239 | 30 |

STUFT

| | | | | |
|---|---|---|---|---|
| STUFT WITH DOWNE OF ANGELS WING. | THE TEARE | 36 | 46 84 | 50 |
| STUFT THEE SOE FULL WITH BLISSE, THOU CAN'ST NOT MOVE. | ON GUNPOWDER-TREASON | 6 | MS 384 | 458 |

STUMBLE'ON

| | | | | |
|---|---|---|---|---|
| LOOSING IT ONCE AGAINE, STUMBLE'ON TRUE LIGHT | IN GLORIOUS EPIPHANIE | 167 | 52 253 | 39 |

STUMBLING

| | | | | |
|---|---|---|---|---|
| STUMBLING ON NIGHT. ROUZE THEE ILLUSTRIOUS YOUTH, | ON A FOULE MORNING | 3 | 46 181 | 495 |

STURDY

| | | | | |
|---|---|---|---|---|
| OF STURDY ADAMANT IS HIS STRONG CHAINE. | SOSPETTO D'HERODE | 144 | 46 109 | 216 |

STYGIAN

    YOUR SELVES, YOU STYGIAN STATES. A PITCHY CLOWD    UPON GUNPOWDER TREASON    24  MS 387 461

STYLE

    WOULD HAVE LEARN'T A SOFTER STYLE,    ANOTHER ON HERRYS    37  46 170 469

STILE

    TO CHANGE HER FACES STILE SHE DOTH DEVISE,    SOSPETTO D'HERODE    415  46 109 216
    THOSE SPARKLING TWINNES OF LIGHT SHOULD I NOW STILE    UPON BIRTH PRINCESSE E    43  MS 391 456

STILES

    WHO STILES IT ANY THINGE, KNOWES NOT THE SAME.    ON GUNPOWDER-TREASON    2  MS 384 458

SUBJECT

    SOFT SUBJECT FOR THE SEIGE OF LOVE.    SANCTA MARIA DOLORUM    50  52 283 162
    THIS SOVERAIGN SUBJECT SITTS ABOVE    LAUDA SION SALVATOREM    5  52 294 178

SUBLUNARY

    THE FALSE SMILES OF A SUBLUNARY SUN.    TO SAME CONCERNING CHOISE    32  52 331  66

SUBMIT

    AND FREE ETERNITY, SUBMIT TO YEARES.    SOSPETTO D'HERODE    184  46 109 216

SUBSTANTIALL

    SUBSTANTIALL SHADE. WHOSE SWEET ALLAY    (ON) HOPE    5  52 345  71

SUBTLE

    A SUBTLE HARVEST OF UNBOUNDED BREAD,    ON MIRACLE OF LOAVES    3  46  86  15
    WHOSE PURE AND SUBTLE LIGHTNING, FLIES    ON A PRAYER BOOKE    66  46 126 139
    OF A SWEET & SUBTLE PAIN.    TERESA    98  52 315  52
    A SUBTLE INUNDATION OF QUICKE FOOD    OUT OF GROTIUS    61  MS 398 198

SUBTILE

    OF A SWEET AND SUBTILE PAINE.    IN MEMORY OF LADY MADRE TERESA    98  46 131  52
    THEIR SUBTILE ESSENCE WITH THE SOULE OF WINE.    ON HOPE    60  46 143  71
    THE SUBTILE POINT OF HIS COY DESTINY,    HORATIJ ILLE & NEFASTO    18  MS 382 530

SUBTIL

    WHOSE PURE & SUBTIL LIGHTNING FLYES    PRAYER TO GENTLE-WOMAN    72  52 328 139

SUBTLEST

    SUBTLEST, BUT SUREST BEEING. THOU BY WHOM    (ON) HOPE    3  52 345  71

SUBT'LEST

    SUBT'LEST, BUT SUREST BEING. THOU BY WHOM    ON HOPE    13  46 143  71

SUCCESSIVE

    HIS WAY THROUGH BAD, TO MY SUCCESSIVE HURT.    OUT OF GROTIUS    13  MS 398 198

SUCCESSOUR

    THEIR NEW KING, AND THY SUCCESSOUR PROCLAIME.    SOSPETTO D'HERODE    440  46 109 216

SUCCOUR

    WHAT SUCCOUR CAN I HOPE THE MUSE WILL SEND    TO THE MORNING    1  46 183 497

SUCK

    THE MOTHER THEN MUST SUCK THE SON.    BLESSED BE THE PAPS    4  46  94  14
    SUCK HIDDEN SWEETS, WHICH WELL DIGESTED PROVES    SOSPETTO D'HERODE    23  46 109 216
    O LET ME SUCK THE WINE    SANCTA MARIA DOLORUM    101  52 283 162
    THAT SOL FROM THEM MAY SUCK AN HONIED SHOWER,    UPON BIRTH PRINCESSE E    5  MS 391 456

SUCKT

    A FRAGRANT BREATH SUCKT FROM THE SPICY NEST    ON A FOULE MORNING    21  46 181 495

SUCK'T

    SUCK'T THEIR SWEETEST INFLUENCE.    HIS EPITAPH (HERRYS)    34  46 172 471
    AND KNOW WHAT SWEETES ARE SUCK'T FROM OUT IT.    TO THE NAME OF JESUS    155  52 239  30

SUDDENLY

    THEN STARTS SHEE SUDDENLY INTO A THRONG    MUSICKS DUELL    62  46 149 535

## SUE

| | | | | | |
|---|---|---|---|---|---|
| THESE ROYALL SAGES SUE FOR DECENT PLACE. | TO THE QUEEN'S MAJESTY | 2 | 52 | 261 | 47 |

## SUFFERED

| | | | | | |
|---|---|---|---|---|---|
| THEN ALL THOSE HE SUFFERED. | IN GLORIOUS EPIPHANIE | 120 | 52 | 253 | 39 |

## SUFFRED

| | | | | | |
|---|---|---|---|---|---|
| NE'RE SUFFRED, YET HIS LITTLE ARROW. | OUT OF GREEKE CUPID'S CRYER | 47 | 46 | 159 | 519 |

## SUFFRING

| | | | | | |
|---|---|---|---|---|---|
| AT LEAST THE SUFFRING SIDE OF THEE. | ADORO TE | 24 | 52 | 291 | 172 |
| SUCH TEARES THE SUFFRING ROSE THAT'S VEXT | WEEPER | 160 | 52 | 307 | 120 |
| GIVE ME THE SUFFRING SERAPHIM. | FLAMING HEART | 64 | 52 | 324 | 61 |

## SUFFERINGS

| | | | | | |
|---|---|---|---|---|---|
| AND THY SUFFERINGS BEE DEVINE. | IN MEMORY OF LADY MADRE TERESA | 149 | 46 | 131 | 52 |

## SUFFRINGS

| | | | | | |
|---|---|---|---|---|---|
| ALL THY SUFFRINGS BE DIVINE. | TERESA | 148 | 52 | 315 | 52 |

## SUFFICE

| | | | | | |
|---|---|---|---|---|---|
| THE FLOOD, IF ANY CAN, THAT CAN SUFFICE. | TO PONTIUS WASHING HANDS | 3 | 46 | 88 | 22 |
| COULD NOT ONCE BLINDING ME,CRUELL,SUFFICE. | SAMPSON TO HIS DALILAH | 1 | 46 | 102 | 8 |
| ANGELLS CANNOT TELL, SUFFICE. | IN MEMORY OF LADY MADRE TERESA | 120 | 46 | 131 | 52 |
| OR (FOR TWO TURTLE DOVES) IT SHALL SUFFICE | ON A TREATISE OF CHARITY | 47 | 46 | 137 | 69 |
| LET IT SUFFICE, SHEE'L WEARE NO MASKE TO DAY. | ON A FOULE MORNING | 36 | 46 | 181 | 495 |
| ANGELLS CANNOT TELL, SUFFICE. | TERESA | 119 | 52 | 315 | 52 |
| THY INFANTS, AEOLUS, WILL NOT SUFFICE. | ON GUNPOWDER-TREASON | 38 | MS | 384 | 458 |

## SUGAR

| | | | | | |
|---|---|---|---|---|---|
| AS LUMPES OF SUGAR LOSE THEMSELVES, AND TWINE | ON HOPE | 59 | 46 | 143 | 71 |
| AS LUMPES OF SUGAR LOOSE THEMSELVES. AND TWINE | (ON) HOPE | 29 | 52 | 345 | 71 |

## SUGRED

| | | | | | |
|---|---|---|---|---|---|
| THAT EVER-BUBLING SPRING, THE SUGRED NEST | MUSICKS DUELL | 66 | 46 | 149 | 535 |
| IF HEE OFFER SUGRED KISSES, | OUT OF GREEKE CUPID'S CRYER | 65 | 46 | 159 | 519 |
| SPHEARE OF SWEET, AND SUGRED LIES. | ON A PRAYER BOOKE | 50 | 46 | 126 | 139 |
| SPHEARES OF SWEET & SUGRED LYES. | PRAYER TO GENTLE-WOMAN | 56 | 52 | 328 | 139 |
| THE MUSES, & THE GRACES SUGRED NEASTS. | UPON GUNPOWDER TREASON | 38 | MS | 387 | 461 |
| WITH SUCH A SUGRED LIVERY MADE FINE, | UPON BIRTH PRINCESSE E | 7 | MS | 391 | 456 |
| THEY OFTEN KIST, & IN THE SUGRED PLACE | AN ELEGY MR STANNINOW | 40 | MS | 394 | 473 |

## SUITE

| | | | | | |
|---|---|---|---|---|---|
| TO WRACK MY SUITE. OH KEEPE PITTY WARME | ON GUNPOWDER-TREASON | 12 | MS | 384 | 458 |

## SUTE

| | | | | | |
|---|---|---|---|---|---|
| HE SCORNES THEM NOW, BUT O THEY'L SUTE FULL WELL | UPON LAZARUS HIS TEARES | 3 | 46 | 89 | 18 |

## SUITOURS

| | | | | | |
|---|---|---|---|---|---|
| YEA SUITOURS. MAN ALONE IS WO'ED. | AGAINST IRRESOLUTION AND DELAY | 58 | 52 | 347 | 146 |

## SUTERS

| | | | | | |
|---|---|---|---|---|---|
| OF SUTERS THAT BESEIGE YOUR MAIDEN BREST, | TO SAME CONCERNING CHOISE | 3 | 52 | 331 | 66 |

## SULLEN

| | | | | | |
|---|---|---|---|---|---|
| THE SULLEN CYPRESSE O'RE HIS HERSE. | UPON THE DEATH OF A GENTLEMAN | 10 | 46 | 166 | 472 |
| HIS EYES, THE SULLEN DENS OF DEATH AND NIGHT, | SOSPETTO D'HERODE | 49 | 46 | 109 | 216 |
| SAY TO THE SULLEN MORNE, THOU COM'ST TO COURT HER. | ON A FOULE MORNING | 11 | 46 | 181 | 495 |
| THE SULLEN HEAVEN HAD VAIL'D ITS MOURNFULL BROW | UPON KINGS CORONATION | 2 | MS | 390 | 453 |

## SULLIED

| | | | | | |
|---|---|---|---|---|---|
| TAUGHT HER THESE SULLIED CHEEKS THIS BLUBBER'D FACE. | TO PONTIUS WASHING HANDS | 4 | 46 | 94 | 23 |

## SULPHUREOUS

| | | | | | |
|---|---|---|---|---|---|
| SULPHUREOUS FLAMES, SNATCH'D FROM AETERNALL NIGHT. | UPON GUNPOWDER TREASON | 26 | MS | 387 | 461 |

## SULPHUR-BREATHED

| | | | | | |
|---|---|---|---|---|---|
| HER SULPHUR-BREATHED TORCHES BRANDISHING. | SOSPETTO D'HERODE | 398 | 46 | 109 | 216 |

## SULPH'RY

| | | | | | |
|---|---|---|---|---|---|
| BELCH'D FROM THE SULPH'RY LUNGS OF PHLEGETON. | ON GUNPOWDER-TREASON | 16 | MS | 384 | 458 |

## SUMME

| | | | | |
|---|---|---|---|---|
| IN SUMME, WOULDST SEE A MAN THAT CAN | IN PRAISE OF LESSIUS | 45 | 46 156 | 510 |
| TO PAY THE SWEET SUMME OF THY KISSES. | ON WOUNDS OF CRUCIFIED LORD | 14 | 46 99 | 24 |
| THE HORRID SUMME OF HIS INTENTIONS TELL. | SOSPETTO D'HERODE | 370 | 46 109 | 216 |
| THE TOTALL SUMME OF MAN APPEARES, | ANOTHER ON HERRYS | 44 | 46 170 | 469 |
| COULD PROVE THE WHOLE SUMME (TOO SURE) DUE TO HIM. | SANCTA MARIA DOLORUM | 94 | 52 283 | 162 |
| IN SUMME, WOULDST SEE A MAN THAT CAN | TEMPERANCE | 43 | 52 342 | 510 |

## SUMMER

| | | | | |
|---|---|---|---|---|
| SUMMER IN WINTER. DAY IN NIGHT. | A HYMNE OF THE NATIVITY | 55 | 46 106 | 76 |
| MORE SUMMER IN THEIR SHAMES REFLECTION, | UPON TWO GREENE APRICOCKES | 8 | 48 220 | 494 |
| HOW MUCH MY SUMMER WAITES UPON THY SPRING. | UPON TWO GREENE APRICOCKES | 34 | 48 220 | 494 |
| A GOLDEN SUMMER, AN AETERNALL SPRING. | AN ELEGY MR STANNINOW | 54 | MS 394 | 473 |

## SUMMER'S

| | | | | |
|---|---|---|---|---|
| TO HEAVN RIDES IN A SUMMER'S DAY. | TEMPERANCE | 32 | 52 342 | 510 |

## SOMMER

| | | | | |
|---|---|---|---|---|
| SOMMER IN WINTER. DAY IN NIGHT. | IN HOLY NATIVITY | 81 | 52 246 | 76 |
| IF SOMMER COME NOT, HOW CAN WINTER GOE. | IN GLORIOUS ASSUMPTION B. LADY | 26 | 52 304 | 114 |

## SUMMERS

| | | | | |
|---|---|---|---|---|
| TO HEAVEN, HATH A SUMMERS DAY. | IN PRAISE OF LESSIUS | 34 | 46 156 | 510 |
| THAT NO MORE SUMMERS BEST DRESSES. | OUT OF THE ITALIAN (1) | 9 | 46 188 | 545 |

## SUMMON'D

| | | | | |
|---|---|---|---|---|
| BUT ALL HIS COUNSELLOURS MUST SUMMON'D BEE. | SOSPETTO D'HERODE | 507 | 46 109 | 216 |

## SUMMONS

| | | | | |
|---|---|---|---|---|
| YET SUMMONS ALL HER SWEET POWERS FOR A NOATE | MUSICKS DUELL | 160 | 46 149 | 535 |
| A SUMMONS, WORTHY OF THY FUNERALL. | UPON STANINOUGH'S DEATH | 6 | 46 175 | 475 |
| AND BEAT A SUMMONS IN THE SAME | TO THE NAME OF JESUS | 35 | 52 239 | 30 |
| A SUMMONS WORTHY OF THY FUNERALL. | DEATH'S LECTURE | 6 | 52 340 | 475 |

## SUN

| | | | | |
|---|---|---|---|---|
| TRUST HIS BELOVED BOSOME TO THE SUN | OUT OF VIRGIL | 17 | 46 155 | 529 |
| THIS REVEREND SHADOW CAST THAT SETTING SUN, | UPON BISHOP ANDREWES PICTURE | 1 | 46 163 | 490 |
| FOR THE SUN THAT DYES, | THE WEEPER | 57 | 46 79 | 120 |
| AND BLUSHES ON THE MANLY SUN. | THE TEARE | 28 | 46 84 | 50 |
| THY SHADOW PETER, MUST SHEW ME THE SUN, | SICKE IMPLORE SHADOW | 3 | 46 87 | 28 |
| TO WAKE THE SUN THAT SLEEPS TOO LONG. | A HYMNE OF THE NATIVITY | 4 | 46 106 | 76 |
| WHICH WITH THE SUN HIMSELFE WEIGH'S EQUALL WINGS. | SOSPETTO D'HERODE | 12 | 46 109 | 216 |
| HEE SAW A THREEFOLD SUN, WITH RICH ENCREASE. | SOSPETTO D'HERODE | 121 | 46 109 | 216 |
| (NOR ASKT LEAVE OF THE SUN) BY DAY AS NIGHT. | SOSPETTO D'HERODE | 133 | 46 109 | 216 |
| THAT HEE WHOM THE SUN SERVES, SHOULD FAINTLY PEEPE | SOSPETTO D'HERODE | 177 | 46 109 | 216 |
| HAD NOT HER THICK SNAKES HID THEM FROM THE SUN. | SOSPETTO D'HERODE | 384 | 46 109 | 216 |
| WHOSE EACH DIVIDED BEAME WOULD BE A SUN. | UPON YORKE HIS BIRTH | 13 | 46 176 | 500 |
| TO DRAW THE CURTAINES, AND AWAKE THE SUN. | TO THE MORNING | 10 | 46 183 | 497 |
| THE WILD TURNES OF THE WANTON SUN. | THOUGH NOW 'TIS NEITHER | 26 | MS 397 | 492 |
| AND WAKE THE SUN THAT LYES TOO LONG. | IN HOLY NATIVITY | 4 | 52 246 | 76 |
| BID THY GOLDEN GOD, THE SUN. | NEW YEAR'S DAY | 13 | 52 251 | 37 |
| AND LEAVE HER OWN NEGLECTED SUN. | NEW YEAR'S DAY | 32 | 52 251 | 37 |
| THY SELF OUR SUN, THOUGH THINE OWN SHADE. | IN GLORIOUS EPIPHANIE | 47 | 52 253 | 39 |
| A GENTLER MORN, A JUSTER SUN. | IN GLORIOUS EPIPHANIE | 74 | 52 253 | 39 |
| AND URGE THEIR SUN INTO THY CLOUD. | IN GLORIOUS EPIPHANIE | 114 | 52 253 | 39 |
| NOT SO MUCH THEIR SUN AS SHADE, | IN GLORIOUS EPIPHANIE | 137 | 52 253 | 39 |
| WHOSE IS THE MASTER FIRE, WHICH SUN SHOULD SHINE. | IN GLORIOUS EPIPHANIE | 144 | 52 253 | 39 |
| ONCE CALL'D A SUN. | IN GLORIOUS EPIPHANIE | 201 | 52 253 | 39 |
| 'TWIXT SUN & SHADE. | IN GLORIOUS EPIPHANIE | 216 | 52 253 | 39 |
| HE IS FROM SUN ENOUGH TO MAKE THY STARR. | IN GLORIOUS EPIPHANIE | 247 | 52 253 | 39 |
| POINTING US HOME TO OUR OWN SUN | IN GLORIOUS EPIPHANIE | 252 | 52 253 | 39 |
| THE FAIR STARRS FILL THEIR WAKEFULL FIRES THE SUN HIMSELFE DRINKS DAY. | OFFICE H. CROSS PRIME | 8 | 52 267 | 91 |
| THE SUN SAW THAT, AND WOULD HAVE SEEN NO MORE. | OFFICE H. CROSS NINTH | 7 | 52 271 | 99 |
| WILL THE GALLANT SUN | CHARITAS NIMIA | 39 | 52 280 | 48 |
| WHEN GLORY'S SUN FAITH'S SHADES SHALL CHASE, | ADORO TE | 55 | 52 291 | 172 |
| AN EVEN ROUND WITH THE CIRCLING SUN. | DIES IRAE | 10 | 52 298 | 186 |
| FOR THE SUN THAT DYES. | WEEPER | 33 | 52 307 | 120 |
| AND BLUSHES AT THE BRIDEGROOME SUN. | WEEPER | 64 | 52 307 | 120 |
| THE FALSE SMILES OF A SUBLUNARY SUN. | TO SAME CONCERNING CHOISE | 32 | 52 331 | 66 |
| NOW WITH A LOVE BELOW THE SUN. | TO SAME CONCERNING CHOISE | 57 | 52 331 | 66 |
| HOW OFT HAVE I WEPT OUT THE WEARY SUN. | ALEXIAS SECONDE ELEGIE | 19 | 52 335 | 207 |
| WHOSE ROSY BEAM SHALL POINT MY SUN TO ME. | ALEXIAS SECONDE ELEGIE | 26 | 52 335 | 207 |

## SUN-BORNE

| | | | | |
|---|---|---|---|---|
| BUT SUCH WHOSE SUN-BORNE BEAUTIES WHAT THEY BORROW | UPON TWO GREENE APRICOCKES | 27 | 48 220 | 494 |

## SUN-BURNT

| | | | | |
|---|---|---|---|---|
| WORSE THEN SUN-BURNT IN HIS FIRE. | OUT OF GREEKE CUPID'S CRYER | 56 | 46 159 | 519 |

## SUN-BURN'T

| | | | | |
|---|---|---|---|---|
| HIS SUPERFICIALL BEAMES SUN-BURN'T OUR SKIN. | IN GLORIOUS EPIPHANIE | 75 | 52 253 | 39 |

## SUN'S

| | | | | |
|---|---|---|---|---|
| TO DISINHERITT THE SUN'S RISE. | IN GLORIOUS EPIPHANIE | 4 | 52 253 | 39 |

## SUNNE

| | | | | |
|---|---|---|---|---|
| MAKES THE SUNNE (OF FLAMES THE SIRE) | OUT OF GREEKE CUPID'S CRYER | 55 | 46 159 | 519 |
| THE SUNNE WILL STOOPE AND TAKE IT UP. | THE TEARE | 10 | 46 84 | 50 |
| BID THE GOLDEN GOD THE SUNNE, | AN HIMNE FOR CIRCUMCISION | 13 | 46 141 | 37 |
| AND LEAVE THE LONG ADORED SUNNE. | AN HIMNE FOR CIRCUMCISION | 32 | 46 141 | 37 |
| NOR WHILE THEY LEAVE HIM SHALL THEY LOOSE THE SUNNE. | AN HIMNE FOR CIRCUMCISION | 37 | 46 141 | 37 |
| THE SUNNE HIMSELFE OFT WISHT TO SIT, AND MADE | UPON DEATH OF HERRYS | 10 | 46 167 | 466 |
| ACQUAINTANCE WITH THE SUNNE. WHAT SECOND MORNE | UPON YORKE HIS BIRTH | 69 | 46 176 | 500 |
| (NOR DOES THE SUNNE DENY'T) OUR CYNTHIA, | UPON YORKE HIS BIRTH | 79 | 46 176 | 500 |
| AND RAISE A DELUGE, WHERE THE FLAMING SUNNE | UPON GUNPOWDER TREASON | 38 | MS 366 | 460 |
| I`VEIW A RISING SUNNE IN THIS OUR SPHAERE, | UPON KINGS CORONATION | 14 | MS 389 | 454 |
| EACH LITTLE BEAME OF WHICH WOULD MAKE A SUNNE. | UPON KINGS CORONATION | 30 | MS 389 | 454 |
| THIS RISING SUNNE. THEIR FACES NOTHING WORE. | UPON KINGS CORONATION | 38 | MS 390 | 453 |
| HAD YOU, LIKE OUR GREAT SUNNE, STAMPED BUT ONE | UPON BIRTH PRINCESSE E | 27 | MS 391 | 456 |
| AS IF THE OFT DEPARTING SUNNE HAD DY'D. | AN ELEGIE ON DR PORTER | 26 | MS 395 | 476 |

## SUNS

| | | | | |
|---|---|---|---|---|
| HEIRE OF THE SUNS FIRST BEAMES. WHY THREAT'ST THOU SO. | TO THE MORNING | 53 | 46 183 | 497 |
| WHERE YOUR EYES SHINE HIS SUNS APPEARE. | THOUGH NOW 'TIS NEITHER | 28 | MS 397 | 492 |
| O FLOUDS, O FIRES. O SUNS O SHOWRES. | WEEPER | 101 | 52 307 | 120 |
| STILL SHINE ON ME, FAIR SUNS. THAT I | A SONG | 7 | 52 327 | 65 |
| WHOLE DAYES & SUNS DEVOUR'D WITH ENDLESSE DINING. | DESCRIPTION RELIGIOUS HOUSE | 2 | 52 338 | 213 |

## SUNNES

| | | | | |
|---|---|---|---|---|
| OPEN SUNNES. SHADY BOWERS, | WISHES SUPPOSED MISTRESSE | 92 | 46 195 | 479 |
| TWINNE SUNNES.) & TAUGHT NOW TO NEGOTIATE YOU. | IN GLORIOUS EPIPHANIE | 204 | 52 253 | 39 |
| WHILE THEIR SUNNES SLEPT. | LUKE 2. QUAERIT JESUM | 34 | MS 379 | 11 |

## SUNDER

| | | | | |
|---|---|---|---|---|
| IT COULD NOT SUNDER MAN & WIFE. | AN EPITAPH UPON MARRIED COUPLE | 5 | 52 339 | 478 |

## SUNG

| | | | | |
|---|---|---|---|---|
| TREMBLED, & SUNG. | LUKE 2. QUAERIT JESUM | 30 | MS 379 | 11 |

## SUNSHINE

| | | | | |
|---|---|---|---|---|
| OF NUONE WEARE THEIR OWNE SUNSHINE. O THOU BRIGHT | UPON YORKE HIS BIRTH | 76 | 46 176 | 500 |
| THAT SUNSHINE BY THEIR OWNE SWEET GRACES. | WISHES SUPPOSED MISTRESSE | 45 | 46 195 | 479 |
| WHILE RAIN & SUNSHINE, CHEEKES & EYES | WEEPER | 95 | 52 307 | 120 |
| TO DANCE ITH' SUNSHINE OF SOME SMILING | PRAYER TO GENTLE-WOMAN | 54 | 52 328 | 139 |

## SUNNESHINE

| | | | | |
|---|---|---|---|---|
| TO DANCE IN THE SUNNESHINE OF SOME SMILING | ON A PRAYER BOOKE | 48 | 46 126 | 139 |

## SUP

| | | | | |
|---|---|---|---|---|
| TO FEED MY LIFE WITH,THERE I'LE SUP | PSALME 23 | 69 | 46 102 | 5 |

## SUPERFICIALL

| | | | | |
|---|---|---|---|---|
| HIS SUPERFICIALL BEAMES SUN-BURN'T OUR SKIN. | IN GLORIOUS EPIPHANIE | 75 | 52 253 | 39 |
| ARE NAILES BLUNT PENS OF SUPERFICIALL SMART. | OFFICE H. CROSS SIXT | 11 | 52 270 | 97 |

## SUPERFLUOUS

| | | | | |
|---|---|---|---|---|
| SUPERFLUOUS SPEAR. BUT THERE'S A HEART STANDS BY | OFFICE H. CROSS EVENSONG | 5 | 52 273 | 101 |
| YOUR PURTS ARE ALL SUPERFLUOUS HERE. | ADORO TE | 9 | 52 291 | 172 |

## SUPERIOUR

| | | | | |
|---|---|---|---|---|
| BLEST HEAVNS, TO YOU, & YOUR SUPERIOUR SONG. | TO THE NAME OF JESUS | 98 | 52 239 | 30 |

## SUPERNATURALL

| | | | | |
|---|---|---|---|---|
| OUR BLISSE. & SUPERNATURALL BLOOD. | TO THE NAME OF JESUS | 4 | 52 239 | 30 |
| THE SUPERNATURALL DAWN OF THY PURE DAY. | IN GLORIOUS EPIPHANIE | 174 | 52 253 | 39 |

## SUPPLE

| | | | | |
|---|---|---|---|---|
| SHEE GIVES HIM BACKE. HER SUPPLE BREST THRILLS OUT | MUSICKS DUELL | 57 | 46 149 | 535 |
| OF SUPPLE MOISTURE. NO COY TWIG BUT WILL | OUT OF VIRGIL | 16 | 46 155 | 529 |
| AS SIGH WITH SUPPLE WIND | TO THE NAME OF JESUS | 39 | 52 239 | 30 |
| THEIR SUPPLE ESSENCE WITH THE SOUL OF WINE. | (ON) HOPE | 30 | 52 345 | 71 |

## SUPPLIANT

| | | | | |
|---|---|---|---|---|
| O HEAR A SUPPLIANT HEART. ALL CRUSH'T | DIES IRAE | 65 | 52 293 | 186 |
| LETT NOT MY SUPPLIANT BREATH RAISE A RUDE STORME | ON GUNPOWDER-TREASON | 11 | MS 384 | 458 |

## SUPPLIES

| | | | | | |
|---|---|---|---|---|---|
| KINDLY SUPPLIES SICK NATURE, AND DOTH MOLD | OUT OF VIRGIL | 35 | 46 | 155 | 529 |
| EACH BLEEDING PART SOME ONE SUPPLIES. | ON WOUNDS OF CRUCIFIED LORD | 4 | 46 | 99 | 24 |
| NEW MATTER FOR OUR MUSE SUPPLIES, | TO THE QUEEN | 7 | 48 | 215 | 501 |
| ARE TEEMING NOW WITH STORE OF FRESH SUPPLIES. | AN ELEGIE ON DR PORTER | 44 | MS | 395 | 476 |

## SUPPLY

| | | | | | |
|---|---|---|---|---|---|
| THE MUSES WITH THEIR TEARES SUPPLY. | AN EPITAPH DOCTOR BROOKE | 8 | 46 | 175 | 465 |
| THREE KINGDOMES TO SUPPLY THIS DAY'S THREE KINGS. | TO THE QUEEN'S MAJESTY | 28 | 52 | 261 | 47 |

## SUPPOSE

| | | | | | |
|---|---|---|---|---|---|
| SUPPOSE HE HAD BEEN TABLED AT THY TEATES, | BLESSED BE THE PAPS | 1 | 46 | 94 | 14 |

## SUPPRESSE

| | | | | | |
|---|---|---|---|---|---|
| TILL HIS O'REFLOWING PRIDE SUPPRESSE THE FLAME. | SOSPETTO D'HERODE | 487 | 46 | 109 | 216 |

## SUPPREST

| | | | | | |
|---|---|---|---|---|---|
| WHY DOST THOU LET THY BRAVE SOULE LYE SUPPREST, | SOSPETTO D'HERODE | 429 | 46 | 109 | 216 |

## SURE

| | | | | | |
|---|---|---|---|---|---|
| IF HELL MUST MOURNE, HEAV'N SURE SHALL SYMPATHIZE | SOSPETTO D'HERODE | 247 | 46 | 109 | 216 |
| ONELY BEE SURE. | ON A PRAYER BOOKE | 21 | 46 | 126 | 139 |
| MUST BEE A SURE HOUSE KEEPER, | ON A PRAYER BOOKE | 31 | 46 | 126 | 139 |
| PEACE SURE WITH PIETY, THOUGH IT DWELL IN SPAINE. | AN APOLOGIE FOR HYMNE (TERESA) | 20 | 46 | 136 | 59 |
| CHOOSE OUT THAT SURE DECISIVE DART | TO COUNTESSE OF DENBIGH | 33 | 52 | 236 | 146 |
| IT IS LOVE'S SEEGE. AND SURE TO BE | TO COUNTESSE OF DENBIGH | 59 | 52 | 236 | 146 |
| FOR SURE THERE IS NO KNEE | TO THE NAME OF JESUS | 226 | 52 | 239 | 30 |
| WELL DONE, SAID I. BUT ARE YOU SURE | IN HOLY NATIVITY | 62 | 52 | 246 | 76 |
| WELCOME, THE WORLD'S SURE WAY. | IN GLORIOUS EPIPHANIE | 60 | 52 | 253 | 39 |
| FAIR FIRST-FRUITS OF THE LAMB. SURE KINGS IN THIS. | TO THE QUEEN'S MAJESTY | 7 | 52 | 261 | 47 |
| SURE EV'EN FROM YOU | SANCTA MARIA DOLORUM | 15 | 52 | 283 | 162 |
| COULD PROVE THE WHOLE SUMME (TOO SURE) DUE TO HIM. | SANCTA MARIA DOLORUM | 94 | 52 | 283 | 162 |
| AND WORDS MORE SURE, MORE SWEET, THEN THEY | ADORO TE | 15 | 52 | 291 | 172 |
| OF A SURE JUDGE, FROM WHOSE SHARP RAY | DIES IRAE | 3 | 52 | 298 | 186 |
| FOR SURE THE SORDID EARTH | WEEPER | 170 | 52 | 307 | 120 |
| PEACE, SURE, WITH PIETY, THOUGH IT COME FROM SPAIN. | AN APOLOGIE FOR (TERESA) HYMNE | 20 | 52 | 322 | 59 |
| ONLY BE SURE | PRAYER TO GENTLE-WOMAN | 27 | 52 | 328 | 139 |
| MUST BE A SURE HOUSE-KEEPER, | PRAYER TO GENTLE-WOMAN | 37 | 52 | 328 | 139 |
| SURE IN MY EARLY WOES STARRES WERE AT STRIFE, | ALEXIAS FIRST ELEGIE | 5 | 52 | 334 | 204 |
| AND SURE WHERE LOVERS MAKE THEIR WATRY GRAVES | ALEXIAS FIRST ELEGIE | 25 | 52 | 334 | 204 |
| YET SURE THOU DID'ST LODGE HEERE. THIS WOMBE OF MINE | LUKE 2. QUAERIT JESUM | 25 | MS | 379 | 11 |
| WAS SACRILEGIOUS, (SURE) OR SOMEWHAT WORSE. | HORATIJ ILLE & NEFASTO | 4 | MS | 382 | 530 |

## SURELY

| | | | | | |
|---|---|---|---|---|---|
| LET THE FINDER SURELY KNOW | OUT OF GREEKE CUPID'S CRYER | 7 | 46 | 159 | 519 |
| A LITTLE MORE, & I HAD SURELY SEENE | HORATIJ ILLE & NEFASTO | 33 | MS | 382 | 530 |
| T' ENTOMBE THE LAB'RING EARTH. FOR SURELY SHEE | UPON GUNPOWDER TREASON | 51 | MS | 386 | 460 |
| WEE MUST THAT DISCORD SURELY CALL, | UPON DEATH OF A FREIND | 3 | MS | 393 | 477 |

## SURER

| | | | | | |
|---|---|---|---|---|---|
| MY LIFE, MY SOUL, MY SURER SELFE TO MEE. | ADORO TE | 44 | 52 | 291 | 172 |

## SUREST

| | | | | | |
|---|---|---|---|---|---|
| SUBT'LEST, BUT SUREST BEING. THOU BY WHOM | ON HOPE | 13 | 46 | 143 | 71 |
| SUBTLEST, BUT SUREST BEEING. THOU BY WHOM | (ON) HOPE | 3 | 52 | 345 | 71 |

## SURFETS

| | | | | | |
|---|---|---|---|---|---|
| NO SURFETS WERE TO RECKON FOR. | AN EPITAPH UPON ASHTON | 26 | 46 | 192 | 464 |

## SURFETT

| | | | | | |
|---|---|---|---|---|---|
| BUT YET THEIR EYES SURFETT WITH SWEET DELIGHT. | UPON GUNPOWDER TREASON | 50 | MS | 387 | 461 |

## SURGES

| | | | | | |
|---|---|---|---|---|---|
| HEAV'D ON THE SURGES OF SWOLNE RAPSODYES. | MUSICKS DUELL | 136 | 46 | 149 | 535 |

## SURLY

| | | | | | |
|---|---|---|---|---|---|
| IN SURLY GROANES DISDAINES THE TREBLES GRACE. | MUSICKS DUELL | 50 | 46 | 149 | 535 |

## SURMISES

| | | | | | |
|---|---|---|---|---|---|
| GOODLY SURMISES | TO SAME CONCERNING CHOISE | 15 | 52 | 331 | 66 |

## SURPLISSES

| | | | | | |
|---|---|---|---|---|---|
| IN DOWNY SURPLISSES, & VESTMENTS WHITE, | AN ELEGIE ON DR PORTER | 26 | MS | 395 | 476 |

## SURVIVE

| | | | | | |
|---|---|---|---|---|---|
| LETT HER SURVIVE THIS DAY, ONCE MOCK HER FATE, | ON GUNPOWDER-TREASON | 9 | MS | 384 | 458 |

## SURVIVING

| | | | | | |
|---|---|---|---|---|---|
| A STILL SURVIVING FUNERALL. | IN MEMORY OF LADY MADRE TERESA | 78 | 46 | 131 | 52 |

## STILL-SURVIVING

| | | | | | |
|---|---|---|---|---|---|
| A STILL-SURVIVING FUNERALL. | TERESA | 78 | 52 | 315 | 52 |

## SUSPECT

| | | | | | |
|---|---|---|---|---|---|
| NEW MATTER, TO MAKE GOOD HIS GREAT SUSPECT. | SOSPETTO D'HERODE | 88 | 46 | 109 | 216 |
| ONE WOULD SUSPECT THOU MEANT'ST TO PAINT | FLAMING HEART | 25 | 52 | 324 | 61 |

## SUSPICIONS

| | | | | | |
|---|---|---|---|---|---|
| MORE DEEPE SUSPICIONS, AND MORE DEADLY STINGS, | SOSPETTO D'HERODE | 501 | 46 | 109 | 216 |

## SUSTAINE

| | | | | | |
|---|---|---|---|---|---|
| THAT THY FIRME HAND FOR EVER MIGHT SUSTAINE | SOSPETTO D'HERODE | 450 | 46 | 109 | 216 |

## SWAID

| | | | | | |
|---|---|---|---|---|---|
| THE SCEPTER, WHICH OF OLD GREAT DAVID SWAID. | SOSPETTO D'HERODE | 402 | 46 | 109 | 216 |

## SWALLOWES

| | | | | | |
|---|---|---|---|---|---|
| A FULL-MOUTH DIAPASON SWALLOWES ALL. | MUSICKS DUELL | 156 | 46 | 149 | 535 |

## SWAN

| | | | | | |
|---|---|---|---|---|---|
| FLOWES IN THY SONG (O FAIRE, O DYING SWAN.) | UPON OUR LORDS LAST DISCOURSE | 2 | 46 | 95 | 21 |

## SWAN-LIKE

| | | | | | |
|---|---|---|---|---|---|
| EACH WINGED CHORISTER WOULD SWAN-LIKE SING | UPON GUNPOWDER TREASON | 43 | MS | 386 | 460 |

## SWARM

| | | | | | |
|---|---|---|---|---|---|
| LIKE DILIGENT BEES, AND SWARM ABOUT IT. | TO THE NAME OF JESUS | 153 | 52 | 239 | 30 |

## SWEAR

| | | | | | |
|---|---|---|---|---|---|
| AND SWEAR FAITH TO THY SWEETER POWRES. | NEW YEAR'S DAY | 36 | 52 | 251 | 37 |
| ALL THINGS SWEAR FRIENDS TO FAIR AND GOOD, | AGAINST IRRESOLUTION AND DELAY | 57 | 52 | 347 | 146 |

## SWEARE

| | | | | | |
|---|---|---|---|---|---|
| AND SWEARE FAITH TO THY SWEETER POWERS. | AN HIMNE FOR CIRCUMCISION | 36 | 46 | 141 | 37 |

## SWEAT

| | | | | | |
|---|---|---|---|---|---|
| ABOUT HER HATE, WRATH, WARRE, AND SLAUGHTER SWEAT. | SOSPETTO D'HERODE | 315 | 46 | 109 | 216 |
| DAY'S SWEAT. AND BY A GENTLE TYRANNY, | SOSPETTO D'HERODE | 388 | 46 | 109 | 216 |
| PULPITS AND PENNES SHALL SWEAT IN. TO REDEEM | ON A TREATISE OF CHARITY | 50 | 46 | 137 | 69 |
| FOR LOVE AT LARG TO FILL. SPARE BLOOD & SWEAT. | TERESA | 11 | 52 | 315 | 52 |
| NEW DROPS, WASH OFF THE SWEAT OF THIS DAYE'S SORROWS. | DESCRIPTION RELIGIOUS HOUSE | 22 | 52 | 338 | 213 |
| THE WILD WAVES COUCH'D. THE SEA FORGOTT TO SWEAT | OUT OF GROTIUS | 67 | MS | 398 | 196 |

## SWEAT-BEDEWED

| | | | | | |
|---|---|---|---|---|---|
| HIS SWEAT-BEDEWED BED HAD NOW BETRAI'D HIM. | SOSPETTO D'HERODE | 474 | 46 | 109 | 216 |

## SWEATING

| | | | | | |
|---|---|---|---|---|---|
| SWEATING IN TOO WARME A BED. | THE TEARE | 24 | 46 | 84 | 50 |
| SWEATING IN A TOO WARM BED. | WEEPER | 162 | 52 | 307 | 120 |

## BALSOM-SWEATING

| | | | | | |
|---|---|---|---|---|---|
| THAT THE BALSOM-SWEATING BOUGH | WEEPER | 50 | 52 | 307 | 120 |

## BALSAME-SWEATING

| | | | | | |
|---|---|---|---|---|---|
| THAT THE BALSAME-SWEATING BOUGH | THE WEEPER | 68 | 46 | 79 | 120 |

## HONY-SWEATING

| | | | | | |
|---|---|---|---|---|---|
| OF FAIRE ENGADDI HONY-SWEATING FOUNTAINES | SOSPETTO D'HERODE | 111 | 46 | 109 | 216 |

## SILVER-SWEATING

| | | | | | |
|---|---|---|---|---|---|
| WHOSE SOFT SILVER-SWEATING STREAMES | PSALME 23 | 15 | 46 | 102 | 5 |

## SWEEPING

| | | | | | |
|---|---|---|---|---|---|
| NO SAILES OF TYRIAN SYLK PROUD PAVEMENTS SWEEPING. | DESCRIPTION RELIGIOUS HOUSE | 3 | 52 | 338 | 213 |

## SWEET

| | | | | | |
|---|---|---|---|---|---|
| A SWEET LUTES-MASTER. IN WHOSE GENTLE AIRES | MUSICKS DUELL | 5 | 46 | 149 | 535 |
| (THE SWEET INHABITANT OF EACH GLAD TREE, | MUSICKS DUELL | 9 | 46 | 149 | 535 |
| INFORMES IT, IN A SWEET PRAELUDIUM | MUSICKS DUELL | 18 | 46 | 149 | 535 |

| | | | | | |
|---|---|---|---|---|---|
| INTO A THOUSAND SWEET DISTINGUISH'D TONES, | MUSICKS DUELL | 23 | 46 | 149 | 535 |
| WITH HER SWEET SELFE SHEE WRANGLES. HEE AMAZED | MUSICKS DUELL | 43 | 46 | 149 | 535 |
| COULD MELT INTO SUCH SWEET VARIETY | MUSICKS DUELL | 46 | 46 | 149 | 535 |
| AND CLOSES THE SWEET QUARRELL, ROWSING ALL | MUSICKS DUELL | 53 | 46 | 149 | 535 |
| IN THAT SWEET SOYLE. IT SEEMES A HOLY QUIRE | MUSICKS DUELL | 73 | 46 | 149 | 535 |
| TILL A SWEET WHIRLE-WIND (STRIVING TO GETT OUT) | MUSICKS DUELL | 87 | 46 | 149 | 535 |
| RUNS TO AND FRO, CUMPLAINING HIS SWEET CARES | MUSICKS DUELL | 142 | 46 | 149 | 535 |
| IN MANY A SWEET RISE, MANY AS SWEET A FALL) | MUSICKS DUELL | 155 | 46 | 149 | 535 |
| IN MANY A SWEET RISE, MANY AS SWEET A FALL) | MUSICKS DUELL | 155 | 46 | 149 | 535 |
| YET SUMMONS ALL HER SWEET POWERS FOR A NOATE | MUSICKS DUELL | 160 | 46 | 149 | 535 |
| ALAS. IN VAINE. FOR WHILE (SWEET SOULE) SHEE TRYES | MUSICKS DUELL | 161 | 46 | 149 | 535 |
| (THAT LIV'D SO SWEETLY) DEAD, SO SWEET A GRAVE. | MUSICKS DUELL | 168 | 46 | 149 | 535 |
| WHEN LIFES SWEET LIGHT FIRST SHONE ON BEASTS, AND WHEN | OUT OF VIRGIL | 29 | 46 | 155 | 529 |
| FLOW NOT SO SWEET AS DOE THE TONES | OUT OF GREEKE CUPID'S CRYER | 27 | 46 | 159 | 519 |
| PRETHEE, SWEET NOW LET ME GOE. | OUT OF GREEKE CUPID'S CRYER | 69 | 46 | 159 | 519 |
| THY FAIRE EYES SWEET MAGDALENE. | THE WEEPER | 6 | 46 | 79 | 120 |
| SWEETNESSE SO SAD, SADNES SO SWEET. | THE WEEPER | 60 | 46 | 79 | 120 |
| MORE SOVERAIGNE AND SWEET FROM YOU. | THE WEEPER | 72 | 46 | 79 | 120 |
| DOES THY SWEET BREATH'D PRAYER | THE WEEPER | 105 | 46 | 79 | 120 |
| SWEET MARY THY FAIRE EYES EXPENCE. | THE TEARE | 2 | 46 | 84 | 50 |
| THE ROSE BUDS SWEET LIP KISSES. | THE TEARE | 21 | 46 | 84 | 50 |
| SWEET IS THE DIFFERENCE. | ON MARKES OF SAVIOURS WOUNDS | 5 | 46 | 86 | 28 |
| 'TIS THE SWEET PRIDE OF HER HUMILITY. | ON VIRGINS BASHFULNESSE | 2 | 46 | 89 | 9 |
| THY FOE TO CROSSE THE SWEET ARTS OF THY REIGNE | TO LORD UPON WATER MADE WINE | 2 | 46 | 91 | 12 |
| O GRANT (SWEET GOODNESSE) THAT ONE EYE MAY BE | IT IS BETTER TO GO WITH EYE | 5 | 46 | 93 | 16 |
| IT IS TOO SWEET TO BE A LONG-LIV'D ONE. | UPON OUR LORDS LAST DISCOURSE | 4 | 46 | 95 | 21 |
| TO PAY THE SWEET SUMME OF THY KISSES. | ON WOUNDS OF CRUCIFIED LORD | 14 | 46 | 99 | 24 |
| WHOSE SWEET TEMPER TEACHES ME | PSALME 23 | 11 | 46 | 102 | 5 |
| STILL MAY THY SWEET MERCY SPREAD | PSALME 23 | 59 | 46 | 102 | 5 |
| IT WAS THY DAY, SWEET, AND DID RISE, | A HYMNE OF THE NATIVITY | 21 | 46 | 106 | 76 |
| BY THOSE SWEET EYES PERSUASIVE POWERS, | A HYMNE OF THE NATIVITY | 27 | 46 | 106 | 76 |
| WEE SAW THEE BY THINE OWNE SWEET LIGHT. | A HYMNE OF THE NATIVITY | 34 | 46 | 106 | 76 |
| SWEET CHOISE (SAID I) NO WAY BUT SO. | A HYMNE OF THE NATIVITY | 51 | 46 | 106 | 76 |
| OF SIMPLE GRACES, AND SWEET LOVES, | A HYMNE OF THE NATIVITY | 84 | 46 | 106 | 76 |
| A THOUSAND SWEET BABES FROM THEIR MOTHERS BREST. | SOSPETTO D'HERODE | 4 | 46 | 109 | 216 |
| THEY WERE THE SMILING SONS OF THOSE SWEET BOWERS. | SOSPETTO D'HERODE | 19 | 46 | 109 | 216 |
| HEE SAW THE TEMPLE SACRED TO SWEET PEACE, | SOSPETTO D'HERODE | 123 | 46 | 109 | 216 |
| AND SWEET OPPRESSION, KINDLY CHEATING THEM | SOSPETTO D'HERODE | 389 | 46 | 109 | 216 |
| HATE THE SWEET PEACE OF ALL-COMPOSING NIGHT. | SOSPETTO D'HERODE | 496 | 46 | 109 | 216 |
| (FEARE IT NOT, SWEET, | ON A PRAYER BOOKE | 2 | 46 | 126 | 139 |
| SPHEARE OF SWEET, AND SUGRED LIES, | ON A PRAYER BOOKE | 50 | 46 | 126 | 139 |
| AND MELTS IT DOWNE IN SWEET DESIRE. | ON A PRAYER BOOKE | 68 | 46 | 126 | 139 |
| SEIZE HER SWEET PREY. | ON A PRAYER BOOKE | 101 | 46 | 126 | 139 |
| SWEET NOT SO FAST, LOE THY FAIRE SPOUSE, | IN MEMORY OF LADY MADRE TERESA | 65 | 46 | 131 | 52 |
| A SOULE KEPT THERE SO SWEET. O NO, | IN MEMORY OF LADY MADRE TERESA | 73 | 46 | 131 | 52 |
| OF SOULES, WHICH IN THAT NAMES SWEET GRACES, | IN MEMORY OF LADY MADRE TERESA | 86 | 46 | 131 | 52 |
| OF A SWEET AND SUBTILE PAINE. | IN MEMORY OF LADY MADRE TERESA | 98 | 46 | 131 | 52 |
| AND MELT THY SOULES SWEET MANSION. | IN MEMORY OF LADY MADRE TERESA | 113 | 46 | 131 | 52 |
| WINE OF YOUTHS LIFE, AND THE SWEET DEATHS OF LOVE, | AN APOLOGIE FOR HYMNE (TERESA) | 41 | 46 | 136 | 59 |
| UNDER SO SWEET A BURDEN. GOE, | ON THE ASSUMPTION | 25 | 46 | 139 | 114 |
| BEHOLDERS LOST IN SWEET DELIGHT | ON THE ASSUMPTION | 33 | 46 | 139 | 114 |
| SWEET ANGELS COME, AND SING THE REST. | ON THE ASSUMPTION | 64 | 46 | 139 | 114 |
| GUILD THEE NOT WITH SO SWEET GRACES, | AN HIMNE FOR CIRCUMCISION | 7 | 46 | 141 | 37 |
| AND SOONE THE SWEET TRUTH SHALL APPEARE. | AN HIMNE FOR CIRCUMCISION | 29 | 46 | 141 | 37 |
| SWEET HOPE. KIND CHEAT. FAIRE FALLACY. BY THEE | ON HOPE | 77 | 46 | 143 | 71 |
| THUS GREW THIS GRATIOUS PLANT, IN WHOSE SWEET SHADE | UPON DEATH OF HERRYS | 9 | 46 | 167 | 466 |
| THE BALMY ZEPHYRUS GOT SO SWEET A BREATH | UPON DEATH OF HERRYS | 20 | 46 | 167 | 466 |
| THE SWEET DASH OF A SHOWER NOW SHEAD, | UPON DEATH OF DESIRED HERRYS | 36 | 46 | 168 | 467 |
| ALL HIS LEAVES, SO FRESH, SO SWEET, | UPON DEATH OF DESIRED HERRYS | 45 | 46 | 168 | 467 |
| SO SWEET THE TEMPLE WAS, THAT SHRIN'D | ANOTHER ON HERRYS | 15 | 46 | 170 | 469 |
| HIS LIVES SWEET STORY, BY THE HAST, | ANOTHER ON HERRYS | 39 | 46 | 170 | 469 |
| (SWEET AS IS THE PHAENIX NEST) | HIS EPITAPH (HERRYS) | 18 | 46 | 172 | 471 |
| THEY (SWEET TURTLES) FOLDED LYE, | AN EPITAPH HUSBAND AND WIFE | 9 | 46 | 174 | 478 |
| GREAT CHARLES. THOU SWEET DAWNE OF A GLORIOUS DAY, | UPON YORKE HIS BIRTH | 29 | 46 | 176 | 500 |
| TO BE THY GARLAND. SEE (SWEET PRINCE) O SEE | UPON YORKE HIS BIRTH | 39 | 46 | 176 | 500 |
| MAKE SUCH ANOTHER SWEET COMPARISON. | UPON YORKE HIS BIRTH | 52 | 46 | 176 | 500 |
| AND NAME DWELL SWEET IN SOME ETERNALL STORY. | UPON YORKE HIS BIRTH | 105 | 46 | 176 | 500 |
| SHALL RISE IN A SWEET HARVEST. WHICH DISCLOSES | ON A FOULE MORNING | 17 | 46 | 181 | 495 |
| THAT SWEET BLUSH OF THINE THAT SHAMETH | OUT OF THE ITALIAN (1) | 3 | 46 | 188 | 545 |
| THOSE SWEET AIRES THAT OFTEN SLEW MEE. | OUT OF THE ITALIAN (1) | 51 | 46 | 188 | 545 |
| THAT SUNSHINE BY THEIR OWNE SWEET GRACES. | WISHES SUPPOSED MISTRESSE | 45 | 46 | 195 | 479 |
| NIGHTS, SWEET AS THEY, | WISHES SUPPOSED MISTRESSE | 82 | 46 | 195 | 479 |
| OF SWEET DISCOURSE, WHOSE POWERS | WISHES SUPPOSED MISTRESSE | 89 | 46 | 195 | 479 |
| TO BE CHASTIS'D (SWEET FRIEND) AND CHIDD BY THEE. | UPON TWO GREENE APRICOCKES | 2 | 48 | 220 | 494 |
| COME, YE SOFT MINISTERS OF SWEET SAD MIRTH, | TO THE NAME OF JESUS | 62 | 52 | 239 | 30 |
| DEAREST SWEET, & COME AWAY. | TO THE NAME OF JESUS | 128 | 52 | 239 | 30 |
| TO THINK OUGHT SWEET BUT THAT WHICH SMELLS OF THEE. | TO THE NAME OF JESUS | 172 | 52 | 239 | 30 |
| CAN PROVE IT SELF SOME KIN (SWEET NAME) TO THEE. | TO THE NAME OF JESUS | 182 | 52 | 239 | 30 |
| SWEET NAME, IN THY EACH SYLLABLE | TO THE NAME OF JESUS | 183 | 52 | 239 | 30 |
| IT WAS THY DAY, SWEETY. & DID RISE | IN HOLY NATIVITY | 21 | 52 | 246 | 76 |
| BY THOSE SWEET EYES' PERSUASIVE POWRS | IN HOLY NATIVITY | 28 | 52 | 246 | 76 |
| WE SAW THEE BY THINE OWN SWEET LIGHT. | IN HOLY NATIVITY | 36 | 52 | 246 | 76 |
| SWEET CHOISE, SAID WE. NO WAY BUT SO | IN HOLY NATIVITY | 69 | 52 | 246 | 76 |
| WE SAW THEE, BY THINE OWN SWEET LIGHT. | IN HOLY NATIVITY | 77 | 52 | 246 | 76 |
| OF SIMPLE GRACES & SWEET LOVES. | IN HOLY NATIVITY | 104 | 52 | 246 | 76 |
| GUILDS THEE NOT WITH SO SWEET GRACES | NEW YEAR'S DAY | 7 | 52 | 251 | 37 |
| AND SOON THIS SWEET TRUTH SHALL APPEAR | NEW YEAR'S DAY | 29 | 52 | 251 | 37 |
| THE MORN INCURR A SWEET MISTAKE. | IN GLORIOUS EPIPHANIE | 2 | 52 | 253 | 39 |
| LOOK UP, SWEET BABE, LOOK UP & SEE | IN GLORIOUS EPIPHANIE | 10 | 52 | 253 | 39 |
| TO SEEK HER SELF IN THY SWEET EYES | IN GLORIOUS EPIPHANIE | 14 | 52 | 253 | 39 |
| (SWEET) TO OUR SELVES, IN THEE. | IN GLORIOUS EPIPHANIE | 63 | 52 | 253 | 39 |
| (DREAD SWEET.) LO THUS | IN GLORIOUS EPIPHANIE | 234 | 52 | 253 | 39 |
| SOMTHING A BRIGHTER SHADOW (SWEET) OF THEE. | IN GLORIOUS EPIPHANIE | 249 | 52 | 253 | 39 |
| LORD, BY THY SWEET & SAVING SIGN, | OFFICE H. CROSS MATINES | 1 | 52 | 265 | 86 |

| | | | | |
|---|---|---|---|---|
| IS TORTUR'D THIRST. IT SELFE, TOO SWEET A CUP. | OFFICE H. CROSS SIXT | 9 | 52 270 | 97 |
| O DEARE & SWEET DISPUTE | OFFICE H. CROSS SIXT | 13 | 52 270 | 97 |
| O SAD, SWEET TREE. | OFFICE H. CROSS EVENSONG | 9 | 52 273 | 101 |
| ALAS, SWEET LORD, WHAT WER'T TO THEE | CHARITAS NIMIA | 9 | 52 280 | 48 |
| OF LOVE, SWEET BITTER THINGS. | SANCTA MARIA DOLORUM | 96 | 52 283 | 162 |
| AND WORDS MORE SURE, MORE SWEET, THEN THEY | ADORO TE | 15 | 52 291 | 172 |
| SWEET, CONSIDER THEN, THAT I | ADORO TE | 27 | 52 291 | 172 |
| LOWD & PLEASANT, SWEET & LONG. | LAUDA SION SALVATOREM | 14 | 52 294 | 178 |
| THE SAME TO THEE, SWEET SPIRIT BE DONE. | O GLORIOSA DOMINA | 39 | 52 302 | 194 |
| UNDER SO SWEET A BURTHEN GOE. | IN GLORIOUS ASSUMPTION B. LADY | 40 | 52 304 | 114 |
| THOUGH OUR SWEET CANNOT MAKE | IN GLORIOUS ASSUMPTION B. LADY | 55 | 52 304 | 114 |
| SWEET ANGELS COME, AND SING THE REST. | IN GLORIOUS ASSUMPTION B. LADY | 69 | 52 304 | 114 |
| THY FAIR EYES, SWEET MAGDALENE. | WEEPER | 6 | 52 307 | 120 |
| SWEETNESSE SO SAD, SADNESSE SO SWEET. | WEEPER | 36 | 52 307 | 120 |
| MORE SOVERAIGN & SWEET FROM YOU. | WEEPER | 54 | 52 307 | 120 |
| O SWEET CONTEST. OF WOES | WEEPER | 91 | 52 307 | 120 |
| MIXT & MADE FRIENDS BY LOVE'S SWEET POWRES. | WEEPER | 102 | 52 307 | 120 |
| THY TEARE'S SWEET OPPORTUNITY. | WEEPER | 132 | 52 307 | 120 |
| SWEET, WHITHER HAST YOU THEN, O SAY | WEEPER | 173 | 52 307 | 120 |
| SWEET, NOT SO FAST. LO THY FAIR SPOUSE | TERESA | 65 | 52 315 | 52 |
| A SOUL KEPT THERE SO SWEET, O NO. | TERESA | 73 | 52 315 | 52 |
| OF SOULES WHICH IN THAT NAME'S SWEET GRACES | TERESA | 86 | 52 315 | 52 |
| OF A SWEET & SUBTLE PAIN. | TERESA | 98 | 52 315 | 52 |
| AND MELT THY SOUL'S SWEET MANSION. | TERESA | 112 | 52 315 | 52 |
| WINE OF YOUTH, LIFE, & THE SWEET DEATHS OF LOVE. | AN APOLOGIE FOR (TERESA) HYMNE | 41 | 52 322 | 59 |
| O SWEET INCENDIARY. SHEW HERE THY ART, | FLAMING HEART | 85 | 52 324 | 61 |
| LORD, WHEN THE SENSE OF THY SWEET GRACE | A SONG | 1 | 52 327 | 65 |
| SPHEARES OF SWEET & SUGRED LYES. | PRAYER TO GENTLE-WOMAN | 56 | 52 328 | 139 |
| AND MELTS IT DOWN IN SWEET DESIRE | PRAYER TO GENTLE-WOMAN | 74 | 52 328 | 139 |
| SEIZE HER SWEET PREY | PRAYER TO GENTLE-WOMAN | 107 | 52 328 | 139 |
| SWEET. LET ME PROPHESY THAT AT LAST T'WILL PROVE | TO SAME CONCERNING CHOISE | 33 | 52 331 | 66 |
| IF DROWN'D. SWEET IS THE DEATH INDUR'D FOR HIM, | ALEXIAS FIRST ELEGIE | 22 | 52 334 | 204 |
| WELLCOME, MY SEA SWEET MATE. NOW HAVE I GOTT | ALEXIAS SECONDE ELEGIE | 7 | 52 335 | 207 |
| HOW SWEET THE MUTUALL YOKE OF MAN & WIFE, | ALEXIAS THIRD ELEGIE | 51 | 52 336 | 209 |
| AND SOFT OBEDIENCE, FIND SWEET BIDING HERE. | DESCRIPTION RELIGIOUS HOUSE | 31 | 52 338 | 213 |
| THEY, SWEET TURTLES, FOLDED LY | AN EPITAPH UPON MARRIED COUPLE | 9 | 52 339 | 478 |
| AND WHEN LIFE'S SWEET FABLE ENDS. | TEMPERANCE | 47 | 52 342 | 510 |
| SUBSTANTIALL SHADE. WHOSE SWEET ALLAY | (ON) HOPE | 5 | 52 345 | 71 |
| SWEET HOPE. KIND CHEAT. FAIR FALLACY BY THEE | (ON) HOPE | 37 | 52 345 | 71 |
| MY SOULES SWEET REST. | LUKE 2. QUAERIT JESUM | 6 | MS 379 | 11 |
| OH COME, SWEET BOY. | LUKE 2. QUAERIT JESUM | 16 | MS 379 | 11 |
| WITH SHIPWRACKS TOILE, OH, THAT IS SWEET, | PETRONIJ ALES PHASIACIS PETITA | 13 | MS 382 | 526 |
| SWEET MISTRIS SOUNDS A GREAT DEALE BETTER. | PETRONIJ ALES PHASIACIS PETITA | 18 | MS 382 | 526 |
| BUT YET THEIR EYES SURFETT WITH SWEET DELIGHT. | UPON GUNPOWDER TREASON | 50 | MS 387 | 461 |
| CONVEY'D HIS SWEET DELICIOUS TRESURY | UPON GUNPOWDER TREASON | 55 | MS 387 | 461 |
| TO SACRIFICE HIMSELFE IN SUCH SWEET FIRE. | UPON KINGS CORONATION | 36 | MS 389 | 454 |
| A PRECIOUS INFLUENCE, AS SWEET AS THEE. | UPON BIRTH PRINCESSE E | 2 | MS 391 | 456 |
| THAT JARRES, AND SPOILES SWEET CONSORT SOE. | UPON DEATH OF A FREIND | 8 | MS 393 | 477 |
| FROM HEAVENS SWEET MILKY STREAME DOTH GENTLY POURE. | AN ELEGY MR STANNINOW | 10 | MS 394 | 473 |
| A WINGED HERALD, GLADD OF SOE SWEET A PREY, | AN ELEGY MR STANNINOW | 49 | MS 394 | 473 |
| LEAVING THOSE MINES OF NECTAR, THEIR SWEET FOUNTAINES, | AN ELEGIE ON DR PORTER | 41 | MS 395 | 476 |
| KNOWING 'TIS IN THE DOOME OF YOUR SWEET EYE | AT TH' IVORY TRIBUNALL | 3 | MS 397 | 492 |
| A SWEET INEBRIATED EXTASY. | OUT OF GROTIUS | 54 | MS 398 | 198 |

SWEET-BREATH'D

| | | | | |
|---|---|---|---|---|
| DOES THY SWEET-BREATH'D PRAIRE | WEEPER | 141 | 52 307 | 120 |

SWEET-LIPP'D

| | | | | |
|---|---|---|---|---|
| OF SWEET-LIPP'D ANGELL-IMPS, THAT SWILL THEIR THROATS | MUSICKS DUELL | 76 | 46 149 | 535 |

SWEET-LIPP'T

| | | | | |
|---|---|---|---|---|
| AND EVERY SWEET-LIPP'T THING | TO THE NAME OF JESUS | 47 | 52 239 | 30 |

SWEET-LIP'T

| | | | | |
|---|---|---|---|---|
| THE SWEET-LIP'T SISTERS MUSICALLY FRIGHTED, | MUSICKS DUELL | 113 | 46 149 | 535 |

SWEETS

| | | | | |
|---|---|---|---|---|
| SUCK HIDDEN SWEETS, WHICH WELL DIGESTED PROVES | SOSPETTO D'HERODE | 23 | 46 109 | 216 |
| OF HIDDEN SWEETS, AND HOLY JOYES, | ON A PRAYER BOOKE | 58 | 46 126 | 139 |
| HIS PRECIOUS SWEETS. | ON A PRAYER BOOKE | 88 | 46 126 | 139 |
| THE RICH AND ROSEALL SPRING OF THOSE RARE SWEETS, | ON A PRAYER BOOKE | 110 | 46 126 | 139 |
| NO SWEETS SINCE THOU ART WANTING HERE. | ON THE ASSUMPTION | 12 | 46 139 | 114 |
| OF SWEETS YOU HAVE. AND MURMUR THAT YOU HAVE NO MORE. | TO THE NAME OF JESUS | 67 | 52 239 | 30 |
| THE HIDDEN SWEETS | TO THE NAME OF JESUS | 122 | 52 239 | 30 |
| (CLOWD OF CONDENSED SWEETS) & BREAK UPON US | TO THE NAME OF JESUS | 168 | 52 239 | 30 |
| AN UNIVERSALL SYNOD OF ALL SWEETS. | TO THE NAME OF JESUS | 176 | 52 239 | 30 |
| POUR ON THY NOBLEST SWEETS, WHICH, WHEN THEY TOUCH | OFFICE H. CROSS COMPLINE | 7 | 52 274 | 105 |
| NO SWEETS, BUT THOU, ARE WANTING HERE. | IN GLORIOUS ASSUMPTION B. LADY | 12 | 52 304 | 114 |
| SO SIGH TORMENTED SWEETS, OPPREST | WEEPER | 158 | 52 307 | 120 |
| A NEST OF NEW-BORN SWEETS. | PRAYER TO GENTLE-WOMAN | 2 | 52 328 | 139 |
| OF HIDDEN SWEETS & HOLY JOYES. | PRAYER TO GENTLE-WOMAN | 64 | 52 328 | 139 |
| HIS PRETIOUS SWEETS | PRAYER TO GENTLE-WOMAN | 94 | 52 328 | 139 |
| THE RICH & ROSEALL SPRING OF THOSE RARE SWEETS | PRAYER TO GENTLE-WOMAN | 116 | 52 328 | 139 |

SWEETES

| | | | | |
|---|---|---|---|---|
| AND KNOW WHAT SWEETES ARE SUCK'T FROM OUT IT. | TO THE NAME OF JESUS | 155 | 52 239 | 30 |

## SWEETER

| | | | | | |
|---|---|---|---|---|---|
| IT SWEETER, THEY MAY TAKE | ON THE ASSUMPTION | 51 | 46 | 139 | 114 |
| AND SWEARE FAITH TO THY SWEETER POWERS. | AN HIMNE FOR CIRCUMCISION | 36 | 46 | 141 | 37 |
| AND SWEAR FAITH TO THY SWEETER POWRES. | NEW YEAR'S DAY | 36 | 52 | 251 | 37 |
| THIS SWEETER BODY, SHALL INDEED BE SUCH. | OFFICE H. CROSS COMPLINE | 8 | 52 | 274 | 105 |
| IT SWEETER, THEY CAN TAKE | IN GLORIOUS ASSUMPTION B. LADY | 56 | 52 | 304 | 114 |

## SWEETEST

| | | | | | |
|---|---|---|---|---|---|
| ADDS SWEETNESSE TO HIS SWEETEST LIPS. | THE WEEPER | 28 | 46 | 79 | 120 |
| ALL THE SWEETEST SHOWERS. | ON THE ASSUMPTION | 47 | 46 | 139 | 114 |
| SPARE THE SWEETEST AMONG MEN. | UPON DEATH OF DESIRED HERRYS | 60 | 46 | 168 | 467 |
| SUCK'T THEIR SWEETEST INFLUENCE. | HIS EPITAPH (HERRYS) | 34 | 46 | 172 | 471 |
| (SWORNE SERVANT TO YOUR SWEETEST EYES) | THOUGH NOW 'TIS NEITHER | 4 | MS | 397 | 492 |
| FOR LODG'D SO NE'RE YOUR SWEETEST THROTE | THOUGH NOW 'TIS NEITHER | 13 | MS | 397 | 492 |
| ALL THE SWEETEST SHOWRES | IN GLORIOUS ASSUMPTION B. LADY | 52 | 52 | 304 | 114 |
| ADDES SWEETNES TO HIS SWEETEST LIPPES. | WEEPER | 28 | 52 | 307 | 120 |

## SWEETLY

| | | | | | |
|---|---|---|---|---|---|
| (THAT LIV'D SO SWEETLY) DEAD, SO SWEET A GRAVE. | MUSICKS DUELL | 168 | 46 | 149 | 535 |
| A SWEETLY TEMPER'D MEANE, NOR HOT NOR COLD. | OUT OF VIRGIL | 36 | 46 | 155 | 529 |
| MORE SWEETLY SHOWES THE BLUSHING BRIDE. | IN PRAISE OF LESSIUS | 30 | 46 | 156 | 510 |
| TO BEE MADE SO SWEETLY SAD. | THE WEEPER | 66 | 46 | 79 | 120 |
| SWEETLY SHALT THOU LYE. | THE TEARE | 39 | 46 | 84 | 50 |
| A DROP, ONE DROP, HOW SWEETLY ONE FAIRE DROP | DIVES ASKING A DROP | 1 | 46 | 96 | 18 |
| HEE SAW A VERNALL SMILE, SWEETLY DISFIGURE | SOSPETTO D'HERODE | 109 | 46 | 109 | 216 |
| WHILE HE SWEETLY 'GAN TO SHOW | UPON DEATH OF DESIRED HERRYS | 40 | 46 | 168 | 467 |
| WRITE, WHAT THE READER SWEETLY RU'TH. | WISHES SUPPOSED MISTRESSE | 33 | 46 | 195 | 479 |
| THAT SO OUR SWEETLY TEMPER'D SONG | TO THE QUEEN | 11 | 48 | 215 | 501 |
| FOR WHILE THOU SWEETLY SLAYEST ME | A SONG | 15 | 52 | 327 | 65 |
| FULL SWEETLY WITH IT SELFE HAD DWELL'T AT HOME. | ALEXIAS THIRD ELEGIE | 12 | 52 | 336 | 209 |
| THE SELF-REMEMBRING SOUL SWEETLY RECOVERS | DESCRIPTION RELIGIOUS HOUSE | 36 | 52 | 338 | 213 |
| MORE SWEETLY SHOWES THE BLUSHING BRIDE. | TEMPERANCE | 28 | 52 | 342 | 510 |

## SWEETLY-KILLING

| | | | | | |
|---|---|---|---|---|---|
| KISSE THE SWEETLY-KILLING DART. | IN MEMORY OF LADY MADRE TERESA | 106 | 46 | 131 | 52 |
| KISSE THE SWEETLY-KILLING DART. | TERESA | 106 | 52 | 315 | 52 |

## SWEETNES

| | | | | | |
|---|---|---|---|---|---|
| AND SHAPE OF SWEETNES, BE THEY SUCH | TO THE NAME OF JESUS | 38 | 52 | 239 | 30 |
| THEMSELVES NEW SWEETNES FROM IT. | IN GLORIOUS ASSUMPTION B. LADY | 57 | 52 | 304 | 114 |
| ADDES SWEETNES TO HIS SWEETEST LIPPES. | WEEPER | 28 | 52 | 307 | 120 |
| YOUR SWEETNES CANNOT TAST | WEEPER | 171 | 52 | 307 | 120 |

## SWEETNESSE

| | | | | | |
|---|---|---|---|---|---|
| OF DALLYING SWEETNESSE, HOVERS ORE HER SKILL, | MUSICKS DUELL | 59 | 46 | 149 | 535 |
| OF STREAMING SWEETNESSE, WHICH IN STATE DOTH RIDE | MUSICKS DUELL | 94 | 46 | 149 | 535 |
| THOSE PARTS OF SWEETNESSE WHICH WITH NECTAR DROP, | MUSICKS DUELL | 125 | 46 | 149 | 535 |
| SWEETNESSE BY ALL HER NAMES. THUS, BRAVELY THUS | MUSICKS DUELL | 133 | 46 | 149 | 535 |
| ADDS SWEETNESSE TO HIS SWEETEST LIPS. | THE WEEPER | 28 | 46 | 79 | 120 |
| SWEETNESSE SO SAD, SADNES SO SWEET. | THE WEEPER | 60 | 46 | 79 | 120 |
| MUTUALL SWEETNESSE THEY EXPRESSE. | THE WEEPER | 88 | 46 | 79 | 120 |
| YOUR SWEETNESSE CANNOT TAST | THE WEEPER | 129 | 46 | 79 | 120 |
| ALL HYBLA'S HONEY, ALL THAT SWEETNESSE CAN | UPON OUR LORDS LAST DISCOURSE | 1 | 46 | 95 | 21 |
| THOUGH OUR SWEETNESSE CANNOT MAKE | ON THE ASSUMPTION | 50 | 46 | 139 | 114 |
| THEMSELVES NEW SWEETNESSE FROM IT. | ON THE ASSUMPTION | 52 | 46 | 139 | 114 |
| THE SACRED SWEETNESSE OF HIS MIND. | ANOTHER ON HERRYS | 16 | 46 | 170 | 469 |
| THAT TO HIS SWEETNESSE, ALL MENS EYES | HIS EPITAPH (HERRYS) | 41 | 46 | 172 | 471 |
| ILLUSTRIOUS SWEETNESSE. IN THY FAITHFULL WOMBE, | UPON YORKE HIS BIRTH | 80 | 46 | 176 | 500 |
| NUMBERS, AND SWEETNESSE, AND AN INFLUENCE | UPON YORKE HIS BIRTH | 111 | 46 | 176 | 500 |
| SWEETNESSE SO SAD, SADNESSE SO SWEET. | WEEPER | 36 | 52 | 307 | 120 |
| MUTUALL SWEETNESSE THEY EXPRESSE. | WEEPER | 82 | 52 | 307 | 120 |

## SWELL

| | | | | | |
|---|---|---|---|---|---|
| TO SWELL WITH FORWARD PRIDE, AND SEED DESIRE | OUT OF VIRGIL | 3 | 46 | 155 | 529 |
| DRINKE UP ALL SPAINE IN SACK. LET MY SOULE SWELL | AN APOLOGIE FOR HYMNE (TERESA) | 30 | 46 | 136 | 59 |
| THAT KEEPS RELIGION WARME. NOT SWELL A NAME | ON A TREATISE OF CHARITY | 52 | 46 | 137 | 69 |
| WHOSE SILKEN FLATTERYES SWELL A FEW FOND HOURES | UPON STANINOUGH'S DEATH | 8 | 46 | 175 | 475 |
| SWELL THY FULL GLORYES TO A PITCH SO HIGH, | UPON YORKE HIS BIRTH | 7 | 46 | 176 | 500 |
| AND TEACH IT TO EXPATIATE, AND SWELL | UPON YORKE HIS BIRTH | 23 | 46 | 176 | 500 |
| SHALL SWELL WITH BOTH FOR HIM. & MIX | OFFICE H. CROSS SIXT | 7 | 52 | 270 | 97 |
| DRINK UP AL SPAIN IN SACK. LET MY SOUL SWELL | AN APOLOGIE FOR (TERESA) HYMNE | 30 | 52 | 322 | 59 |
| WHOSE SYLKEN FLATTERYES SWELL A FEW FOND HOWRES | DEATH'S LECTURE | 9 | 52 | 340 | 475 |
| SWELL. SWELL TO SUCH AN HEIGHT, THAT THOU MAIST VYE | UPON KINGS CORONATION | 9 | MS | 389 | 454 |
| SWELL. SWELL TO SUCH AN HEIGHT, THAT THOU MAIST VYE | UPON KINGS CORONATION | 9 | MS | 389 | 454 |
| THE WORLD MY FATHER. THEN DOES ENVY SWELL | OUT OF GROTIUS | 32 | MS | 398 | 198 |

## SWELLS

| | | | | | |
|---|---|---|---|---|---|
| NOR SINKS NOR SWELLS WITH TIME OR PLACE. | IN GLORIOUS EPIPHANIE | 29 | 52 | 253 | 39 |
| SWELLS HIGH, FAIR CONFLUENCE OF ALL HIGHBORN BLOUD. | TO THE QUEEN'S MAJESTY | 16 | 52 | 261 | 47 |
| AND ROOM ENOUGH FOR MONARCHS, WHILE NONE SWELLS | DESCRIPTION RELIGIOUS HOUSE | 34 | 52 | 338 | 213 |

## SWELLING

| | | | | | |
|---|---|---|---|---|---|
| ON THE WAV'D BACKE OF EVERY SWELLING STRAINE, | MUSICKS DUELL | 95 | 46 | 149 | 535 |
| WHICH WITH A SWELLING BOSOME THERE SHEE MEETS, | ON A PRAYER BOOKE | 111 | 46 | 126 | 139 |

|  |  |  |  |  |  |
|---|---|---|---|---|---|
| HIS SWELLING GLORYES, AUSTER SPIDE HIM, | UPON DEATH OF DESIRED HERRYS | 41 | 46 | 168 | 467 |
| WHICH WITH A SWELLING BOSOME THERE SHE MEETS | PRAYER TO GENTLE-WOMAN | 117 | 52 | 328 | 139 |

SWEPT

|  |  |  |  |  |  |
|---|---|---|---|---|---|
| SWEPT HIM OFF INTO HIS GRAVE. | HIS EPITAPH (HERRYS) | 48 | 46 | 172 | 471 |

SWIFT

|  |  |  |  |  |  |
|---|---|---|---|---|---|
| BUT SHEE (SWIFT AS THE MOMENTARY WING | SOSPETTO D'HERODE | 371 | 46 | 109 | 216 |
| WHOM THOU SEEK'ST WITH SO SWIFT VOWES | IN MEMORY OF LADY MADRE TERESA | 66 | 46 | 131 | 52 |
| AND SEIZE THE SWIFT FLASH, IN REBOUND | IN GLORIOUS EPIPHANIE | 199 | 52 | 253 | 39 |
| WHOM THOU SEEKST WITH SO SWIFT VOWES, | TERESA | 66 | 52 | 315 | 52 |

SWILL

|  |  |  |  |  |  |
|---|---|---|---|---|---|
| OF SWEET-LIPP'D ANGELL-IMPS, THAT SWILL THEIR THROATS | MUSICKS DUELL | 76 | 46 | 149 | 535 |

SWIM

|  |  |  |  |  |  |
|---|---|---|---|---|---|
| THAT BRINGS HIM TO MEE, HEE SHALL SWIM | OUT OF GREEKE CUPID'S CRYER | 14 | 46 | 159 | 519 |
| THY WRATH THAT WADES HEERE NOW, E'RE LONG SHALL SWIM | OUR LORD IN HIS CIRCUMCISION | 5 | 46 | 98 | 9 |
| THEY SWIM, ALAS, IN THEIR OWNE FLOOD. | ON BLEEDING WOUNDS OF LORD | 8 | 46 | 101 | 110 |
| AND BRUSH HER AZURE MANTLE, WHICH SHALL SWIM | ON A FOULE MORNING | 24 | 46 | 181 | 495 |

SWIM'ST

|  |  |  |  |  |  |
|---|---|---|---|---|---|
| THAT SWIM'ST AS DEEPE IN JOY, AS SEAS, NOW SMILE | UPON KINGS CORONATION | 6 | MS | 389 | 454 |

SWIMME

|  |  |  |  |  |  |
|---|---|---|---|---|---|
| WITH THEE STRONG WINE OF LOVE, LET OTHERS SWIMME | AN APOLOGIE FOR HYMNE (TERESA) | 31 | 46 | 136 | 59 |
| OF BORROWD SINS, AND SWIMME | SANCTA MARIA DOLORUM | 33 | 52 | 283 | 162 |
| THEY SWIMME, ALAS, IN THEIR OWN FLOOD. | UPON BLEEDING CRUCIFIX | 12 | 52 | 288 | 110 |
| WITH THEE, STRONG WINE OF LOVE, LET OTHERS SWIMME | AN APOLOGIE FOR (TERESA) HYMNE | 31 | 46 | 322 | 59 |
| IF I BE SHIPWRACK'T, LOVE SHALL TEACH TO SWIMME. | ALEXIAS FIRST ELEGIE | 21 | 52 | 334 | 204 |

SWIMS

|  |  |  |  |  |  |
|---|---|---|---|---|---|
| HOW MY HEAD IN OINTMENT SWIMS. | PSALME 23 | 55 | 46 | 102 | 5 |

SWINE

|  |  |  |  |  |  |
|---|---|---|---|---|---|
| NOT TO BE CAST TO DOGGES, OR SWINE. | LAUDA SION SALVATOREM | 64 | 52 | 294 | 178 |

SWINGING

|  |  |  |  |  |  |
|---|---|---|---|---|---|
| SWINGING A HUGE SITH STANDS IMPARTIALL DEATH. | SOSPETTO D'HERODE | 319 | 46 | 109 | 216 |

SWOLNE

|  |  |  |  |  |  |
|---|---|---|---|---|---|
| HEAV'D ON THE SURGES OF SWOLNE RAPSODYES. | MUSICKS DUELL | 136 | 46 | 149 | 535 |
| YOU FROM HER EYES SWOLNE WOMBES OF SORROW. | THE WEEPER | 126 | 46 | 79 | 120 |
| LETT THY SWOLNE BREAST DISCHARGE THY STRUGLING GROANES | AN ELEGIE ON DR PORTER | 31 | MS | 395 | 476 |

BLOOD-SWOLNE

|  |  |  |  |  |  |
|---|---|---|---|---|---|
| SO BOYLES THE FIRED HERODS BLOOD-SWOLNE BREST, | SOSPETTO D'HERODE | 489 | 46 | 109 | 216 |

RAINE-SWOLNE

|  |  |  |  |  |  |
|---|---|---|---|---|---|
| RAINE-SWOLNE RIVERS MAY RISE PROUD | ON BLEEDING WOUNDS OF LORD | 33 | 46 | 101 | 110 |

RAIN-SWOLN

|  |  |  |  |  |  |
|---|---|---|---|---|---|
| RAIN-SWOLN RIVERS MAY RISE PROUD, | UPON BLEEDING CRUCIFIX | 29 | 52 | 288 | 110 |

SWORD

|  |  |  |  |  |  |
|---|---|---|---|---|---|
| WHAT. MARS HIS SWORD. FAIRE CYTHEREA SAY, | UPON VENUS PUTTING ARMES | 1 | 46 | 161 | 523 |
| WELL PETER DUST THOU WIELD THY ACTIVE SWORD. | ON ST. PETER CUTTING MALCHUS | 1 | 46 | 97 | 22 |
| WHOSE EVER-BRANDISHT SWORD IS SHEATH'D IN BLOOD. | SOSPETTO D'HERODE | 314 | 46 | 109 | 216 |
| ALREADY REACHES AT A SWORD. THEY HIRE | SOSPETTO D'HERODE | 444 | 46 | 109 | 216 |
| AND FENCE THE HANGING SWORD HEAV'N THROWS UPON THEE. | SOSPETTO D'HERODE | 460 | 46 | 109 | 216 |
| A GUILTY SWORD BLUSH FOR HER SAKE. | IN MEMORY OF LADY MADRE TERESA | 26 | 46 | 131 | 52 |
| A GUILTY SWORD BLUSH FOR HER SAKE. | TERESA | 26 | 52 | 315 | 52 |
| WHEN A WILD SWORD EV'N FROM THEIR BRESTS, DID LOP | OUT OF GROTIUS | 25 | MS | 398 | 198 |

SWORDS

|  |  |  |  |  |  |
|---|---|---|---|---|---|
| OF CONFESSOURS, WHOSE THROATES ANSWERING HIS SWORDS, | SOSPETTO D'HERODE | 7 | 46 | 109 | 216 |
| SWORDS, SPEARS, WITH ALL THE FATALL INSTRUMENTS | SOSPETTO D'HERODE | 326 | 46 | 109 | 216 |
| HERE ARE THEY ALL, HERE ALL THE SWORDS OR FLAMES | SOSPETTO D'HERODE | 365 | 46 | 109 | 216 |
| MORE SWORDS AND SHIELDS | ON A PRAYER BOOKE | 19 | 46 | 126 | 139 |
| TO SEE SO MANY UNKIND SWORDS CONTEST | SANCTA MARIA DOLORUM | 17 | 52 | 283 | 162 |
| HIS NAILES WRITE SWORDS IN HER, WHICH SOON HER HEART | SANCTA MARIA DOLORUM | 27 | 52 | 283 | 162 |
| HER SWORDS, STILL GROWING WITH HIS PAIN. | SANCTA MARIA DOLORUM | 29 | 52 | 283 | 162 |
| MORE SWORDS & SHEILDS | PRAYER TO GENTLE-WOMAN | 25 | 52 | 328 | 139 |

SWORE

|  |  |  |  |  |  |
|---|---|---|---|---|---|
| SO SWORE THE LAMB'S DREAD SIRE. AND SO WE SEE'T. | TO THE QUEEN'S MAJESTY | 19 | 52 | 261 | 47 |

SWORNE

   (SWORNE SERVANT TO YOUR SWEETEST EYES)          THOUGH NOW 'TIS NEITHER       4  MS 397 492

SWOUND

   IT LABOURS. STIF'LED NATURE'S IN A SWOUND.         ON GUNPOWDER-TREASON        19  MS 364 458

SYDNOEAN

   SYDNOEAN SHOWERS                                 WISHES SUPPOSED MISTRESSE      88  46 195 479

SYLLA

   HERE SYLLA HIS SEVEREST PRISON HAS.               SOSPETTO D'HERODE           356  46 109 216

SYLLABLE

   SWEET NAME, IN THY EACH SYLLABLE                  TO THE NAME OF JESUS         183  52 239  30

SYMPATHIZE

   IF HELL MUST MOURNE, HEAV'N SURE SHALL SYMPATHIZE  SOSPETTO D'HERODE           247  46 109 216

SYMPTOMES

   SYMPTOMES SO DEADLY, UNTO DEATH AND HIM.          SOSPETTO D'HERODE           138  46 109 216

SYNOD

   WHAT EVER STARRY SYNOD MET,                       LOVES HOROSCOPE             18  46 185 483
   AN UNIVERSALL SYNOD OF ALL SWEETS.                TO THE NAME OF JESUS         176  52 239  30

SYTH

   AND STREIGHT HIS AMOROUS SYTH (GREEDY OF BLISSE)   AN ELEGY MR STANNINOW       47  MS 394 473

TABLE

   THE LESTRIGONIANS HERE THEIR TABLE REARE.         SOSPETTO D'HERODE           357  46 109 216

TABLED

   SUPPOSE HE HAD BEEN TABLED AT THY TEATES,         BLESSED BE THE PAPS           1  46  94  14

TABLES

   THE TABLES FURNISHT WITH A CURSED FEAST,          SOSPETTO D'HERODE           329  46 109 216
   NO ROOFES OF GOLD O'RE RIOTOUS TABLES SHINING     DESCRIPTION RELIGIOUS HOUSE  1  52 338 213

TAFFATA

   TAFFATA OR TISSEW CAN.                              WISHES SUPPOSED MISTRESSE      20  46 195 479

TAGUS

   GOLDEN TAGUS MURMURS THOUGH,                      THE WEEPER                80  46  79 120
   GOLDEN TAGUS MURMURES THO.                        WEEPER                    74  52 307 120

TAINT

   TAINT NOT THE PURE STREAMES OF THE SPRINGING DAY,  ON A FOULE MORNING           32  46 181 495

TAKE

   GOE TAKE PHISICKE, DOAT UPON                     IN PRAISE OF LESSIUS           5  46 156 510
   I'LE GIVE THEE ALL, TAKE ALL, TAKE HEED           OUT OF GREEKE CUPID'S CRYER  71  46 159 519
   I'LE GIVE THEE ALL, TAKE ALL, TAKE HEED           OUT OF GREEKE CUPID'S CRYER  71  46 159 519
   THE SUNNE WILL STOOPE AND TAKE IT UP.             THE TEARE                 10  46  84  50
   YET IS THE JOY I TAKE IN'T SMALL OR NONE.         UPON OUR LORDS LAST DISCOURSE 3  46  95  21
   TO STRIKE AT EARES, IS TO TAKE HEED THERE BEE     ON ST. PETER CUTTING MALCHUS  3  46  97  22
   SHOULD TAKE THE MARKE OF SIN, AND PAINE OF SENCE.  SOSPETTO D'HERODE           190  46 109 216
   AGAINST THE GHOSTLY FOE TO TAKE YOUR PART.         ON A PRAYER BOOKE            13  46 126 139
   TO TAKE HER PLEASURES, AND TO PLAY                ON A PRAYER BOOKE            46  46 126 139
   WILL TAKE POSSESSION OF THE SACRED STORE         ON A PRAYER BOOKE            57  46 126 139
   TO TAKE ACQUAINTANCE OF THE SPHEARE,               ON MR. G. HERBERTS BOOKE     13  46 130  68
   WEELL SEE HIM TAKE A PRIVATE SEAT.                IN MEMORY OF LADY MADRE TERESA 12  46 131  52
   TEARES SHALL TAKE COMFORT, AND TURNE GEMS.         IN MEMORY OF LADY MADRE TERESA 150 46 131  52
   DULL MISTS AND MELANCHOLY CLOUDS. TAKE DAY         ON A TREATISE OF CHARITY     8  46 137  69
   OPEN THIS BOOKE, FAIRE QUEEN, AND TAKE THY CROWN.  ON A TREATISE OF CHARITY    12  46 137  69
   TAKE THY FAREWEL POORE WORLD. HEAVEN MUST GO HOME. ON THE ASSUMPTION            2  46 139 114
   IT SWEETER, THEY MAY TAKE                           ON THE ASSUMPTION            51  46 139 114
   TAKE ACQUAINTANCE OF THIS STONE,                   HIS EPITAPH (HERRYS)         3  46 172 471
   TAKE THINE OWNE MEASURE HERE, DOWNE, DOWNE, AND BOW UPON STANINOUGH'S DEATH      11  46 175 475
   THY SILENCE. SPEAKE. AND SHE SHALL TAKE FROM THENCE UPON YORKE HIS BIRTH       110  46 176 500
   PRETIOUS THEIR OFFERINGS THAT THEIR ALTARS TAKE.   UPON YORKE HIS BIRTH        117  46 176 500
   AND POINTING TO DULL MORPHEUS, BIDS ME TAKE      TO THE MORNING               15  46 183 497
   REVIVED NATURE TAKE A SECOND BREATH.               ON FRONTISPIECE ISAACSONS    4  46 191 491
   IDAEA, TAKE A SHRINE                                WISHES SUPPOSED MISTRESSE      11  46 195 479
   THAT CHASTITY SHALL TAKE NO HARME.                WISHES SUPPOSED MISTRESSE      63  46 195 479
   TAKE THESE, TIMES TARDY TRUANTS, SENT BY ME,      UPON TWO GREENE APRICOCKES   1  48 220 494
   TAKE THEM, AND ME IN THEM ACKNOWLEDGING,         UPON TWO GREENE APRICOCKES  33  48 220 494
   I HAVE AUTHORITY IN LOVE'S NAME TO TAKE YOU      TO THE NAME OF JESUS         53  52 239  30

| | | | | |
|---|---|---|---|---|
| TAKE THINE OWN WINGS, & COME AWAY. | TO THE NAME OF JESUS | 150 | 52 239 | 30 |
| O FILL OUR SENSES, AND TAKE FROM US | TO THE NAME OF JESUS | 170 | 52 239 | 30 |
| AND TO TAKE THEM | TO THE NAME OF JESUS | 195 | 52 239 | 30 |
| TAKE BOTH TO THINE ACCOUNT, THAT I & MINE | OFFICE H. CROSS RECOMMENDATION | 3 | 52 276 | 106 |
| OF THIS FAIR TREE TAKE OUR ETERNALL ROOT. | SANCTA MARIA DOLORUM | 64 | 52 283 | 162 |
| TAKE SHELTER FROM THY SELF, IN THEE | DIES IRAE | 26 | 52 298 | 186 |
| TAKE CHARGE OF ME, & OF MY END. | DIES IRAE | 68 | 52 298 | 186 |
| TAKE THY FAREWELL, POOR WORLD. HEAVN MUST GOE HOME. | IN GLORIOUS ASSUMPTION B. LADY | 2 | 52 304 | 114 |
| IT SWEETER, THEY CAN TAKE | IN GLORIOUS ASSUMPTION B. LADY | 56 | 52 304 | 114 |
| AND SEE HIM TAKE A PRIVATE SEAT, | TERESA | 12 | 52 315 | 52 |
| TEARES SHALL TAKE COMFORT, & TURN GEMMS | TERESA | 149 | 52 315 | 52 |
| AND TAKE AWAY FROM ME MY SELF & SIN, | FLAMING HEART | 90 | 52 324 | 61 |
| AGAINST YOUR GHOSTLY FOES TO TAKE YOUR PART, | PRAYER TO GENTLE-WOMAN | 19 | 52 328 | 139 |
| TO TAKE HER PLEASURE & TO PLAY | PRAYER TO GENTLE-WOMAN | 52 | 52 328 | 139 |
| WILL TAKE POSSESSION OF THAT SACRED STORE | PRAYER TO GENTLE-WOMAN | 63 | 52 328 | 139 |
| WILL TAKE ACQUAINTANCE OF MY WOES, & SAY | ALEXIAS FIRST ELEGIE | 28 | 52 334 | 204 |
| TAKE HEED (SAID SHE) TAKE HEED, VALERIAN. | ALEXIAS THIRD ELEGIE | 34 | 52 336 | 209 |
| TAKE HEED (SAID SHE) TAKE HEED, VALERIAN. | ALEXIAS THIRD ELEGIE | 34 | 52 336 | 209 |
| LOVE MADE THE BED. THEY'L TAKE NO HARM | AN EPITAPH UPON MARRIED COUPLE | 14 | 52 339 | 478 |
| TAKE THINE OWN MEASURE HERE. DOWN, DOWN, & BOW | DEATH'S LECTURE | 12 | 52 340 | 475 |
| GOE, TAKE PHYSICK DOAT UPON | TEMPERANCE | 5 | 52 342 | 510 |
| YOU TAKE UPON YOU TOO TOO MUCH, | UPON DEATH OF A FREIND | 13 | MS 393 | 477 |
| MAKE THEIR SCAR'D SOULES TAKE WING, & FLY AWAY. | AN ELEGIE ON DR PORTER | 30 | MS 395 | 476 |

TAKEN

| | | | | |
|---|---|---|---|---|
| BY HIS WORST FOES (BECAUSE HE WOULD) BESEIG'D & TAKEN. | OFFICE H. CROSS MATINES | 17 | 52 265 | 86 |

TANE

| | | | | |
|---|---|---|---|---|
| TO FROZEN CAUCASUS HIS FLIGHT NOW TANE. | AN ELEGY MR STANNINOW | 2 | MS 394 | 473 |

TA'NE

| | | | | |
|---|---|---|---|---|
| ARE TA'NE OUT AND TRANSCRIB'D BY THY GREAT MOTHER, | UPON YORKE HIS BIRTH | 41 | 46 176 | 500 |
| AND OUR CAPTIVITY HIS CAPTIVE TA'NE. | OFFICE H. CROSS EVENSONG | 27 | 52 273 | 101 |

TAKES

| | | | | |
|---|---|---|---|---|
| TAKES UP AMONG THE STARS A ROOME, | THE WEEPER | 32 | 46 79 | 120 |
| TAKES HIS TEARE AND GETS HIM GONE. | THE WEEPER | 94 | 46 79 | 120 |
| JOSEPH THE KINGS DEAD BROTHERS SHAPE SHE TAKES. | SOSPETTO D'HERODE | 419 | 46 109 | 216 |
| SO WHEN THE YEAR TAKES COLD, WE SEE | TO COUNTESSE OF DENBIGH | 21 | 52 236 | 146 |
| THE SOUL THAT TASTS THEE TAKES FROM THENCE. | TO THE NAME OF JESUS | 188 | 52 239 | 30 |
| AH HARTLESSE TASK. YET HOPE TAKES HEAD. | OFFICE H. CROSS COMPLINE | 3 | 52 274 | 105 |
| BOLD FAITH TAKES HEART, & DARES BELEIVE. | LAUDA SION SALVATOREM | 38 | 52 294 | 178 |
| NOR WOUND NOR BREACH IN WHAT HE TAKES. | LAUDA SION SALVATOREM | 44 | 52 294 | 178 |
| TAKES UP AMONG THE STARRES A ROOM, | WEEPER | 68 | 52 307 | 120 |
| TAKES HIS TEAR, & GETS HIM GONE. | WEEPER | 148 | 52 307 | 120 |
| GIVE HIM THE VEIL. WHO KINDLY TAKES THE SHAME. | FLAMING HEART | 58 | 52 324 | 61 |
| SO WHEN THE YEAR TAKES COLD WE SEE | AGAINST IRRESOLUTION AND DELAY | 21 | 52 347 | 146 |

TAKING

| | | | | |
|---|---|---|---|---|
| TAKING FRESH LIFE FROM YOUR FAYRE EYES. | THOUGH NOW 'TIS NEITHER | 10 | MS 397 | 492 |

TALK

| | | | | |
|---|---|---|---|---|
| FOR THEE I TALK TO TREES, WITH SILENT GROVES | ALEXIAS SECONDE ELEGIE | 13 | 52 335 | 207 |
| TO THESE I TALK IN TEARES, & TELL MY PAIN. | ALEXIAS SECONDE ELEGIE | 17 | 52 335 | 207 |

TALKE

| | | | | |
|---|---|---|---|---|
| A THOUSAND PROPHECIES THAT TALKE STRANGE THINGS, | SOSPETTO D'HERODE | 497 | 46 109 | 216 |

TALKES

| | | | | |
|---|---|---|---|---|
| THAT TALKES WITH TUNEFULL STRING. | TO THE NAME OF JESUS | 48 | 52 239 | 30 |

TALL

| | | | | |
|---|---|---|---|---|
| HIGH MOUNTED ON AN ANT NANUS THE TALL | HIGH MOUNTED ON AN ANT | 1 | 46 161 | 523 |
| WHERE SEAV'N TALL HORNES (HIS EMPIRES PRIDE) ASPIRE. | SOSPETTO D'HERODE | 46 | 46 109 | 216 |
| THOSE THY OLD SOULDIERS, STOUT AND TALL | IN MEMORY OF LADY MADRE TERESA | 4 | 46 131 | 52 |
| TRICK THEIR TALL PLUMES, AND IN THAT GARB SHALL GO | ON A TREATISE OF CHARITY | 25 | 46 137 | 69 |
| HISTORY REARES HER PYRAMIDS MORE TALL | ON FRONTISPIECE ISAACSONS | 18 | 46 191 | 491 |
| RAISE THIS TALL TROPHEE OF THY POWRE. | TO COUNTESSE OF DENBIGH | 36 | 52 236 | 146 |
| TALL TREE OF LIFE. THY TRUTH MAKES GOOD | VEXILLA REGIS | 19 | 52 277 | 156 |
| THOSE THY OLD SOULDIERS, GREAT & TALL, | TERESA | 4 | 52 315 | 52 |
| MOST TALL HYPERBOLE'S CANNOT DESCRY IT. | ON GUNPOWDER-TREASON | 47 | MS 384 | 458 |

TAME

| | | | | |
|---|---|---|---|---|
| BUT (FOR A LAMBE) THY TAME AND TENDER HEART | ON A TREATISE OF CHARITY | 45 | 46 137 | 69 |
| CAN TAME THE WANTON DAY | WISHES SUPPOSED MISTRESSE | 50 | 46 195 | 479 |
| SHALL KICK THE CLOUDS NO MORE. BUT LEAN & TAME, | IN GLORIOUS EPIPHANIE | 98 | 52 253 | 39 |
| SPURNS THE TAME LAWS OF TIME AND PLACE, | AGAINST IRRESOLUTION AND DELAY | 77 | 52 347 | 146 |

TAM'D

| | | | | |
|---|---|---|---|---|
| OF ALL THEIR CARES, TAM'D THE REBELLIOUS EYE | SOSPETTO D'HERODE | 390 | 46 109 | 216 |
| A WELL TAM'D HEART, | WISHES SUPPOSED MISTRESSE | 55 | 46 195 | 479 |
| TILL THUS TRIUMPHANTLY TAM'D (O YE TWO | IN GLORIOUS EPIPHANIE | 203 | 52 253 | 39 |
| NOW BUT THE GRAVE. THE GRAVE IT SELFE I TAM'D. | OUT OF GROTIUS | 86 | MS 398 | 198 |

TAMES

  STROKES AND TAMES MY RABID GRIEFE,               PSALME 23                         19  46 102    5

TANGLED

  (TANGLED IN FORBIDDEN WAYES)                       PSALME 23                         22  46 102    5

TANTALUS

  TANTALUS, ATREUS, PROGNE, HERE ARE GUESTS.        SOSPETTO D'HERODE                333  46 109 216

TAPERS

  JOVES TWINCKLING TAPERS, THAT DOE LIGHT THE WORLD,   UPON GUNPOWDER TREASON         27  MS 386 460
  SHALL HANG THE ROOME, & FOR YOUR TAPERS BRIGHT,     UPON GUNPOWDER TREASON         25  MS 387 461

TARDY

  TAKE THESE, TIMES TARDY TRUANTS, SENT BY ME,       UPON TWO GREENE APRICOCKES     1  48 220 494
  FLOW, TARDY FOUNTS, & INTO DECENT SHOWRES          SANCTA MARIA DOLORUM           87  52 283 162

TASK

  AH HARTLESSE TASK, YET HOPE TAKES HEAD.            OFFICE H. CROSS COMPLINE       3  52 274 105
  THOU HAST THY TASK, THOU WEEPEST STILL.            WEEPER                       138  52 307 120

TASKE

  THOU HAST THY TASKE, THOU WEEPEST STILL.           THE WEEPER                  114  46  79 120

TASTE

  BY THAT SHRILL TASTE, SHEE COULD DOE SOMETHING TOO.  MUSICKS DUELL               26  46 149 535
  WHOSE STROAKE SHALL TASTE THY HALLOWED BREATH.     IN MEMORY OF LADY MADRE TERESA  80  46 131  52

TAST

  TO TAST THE NECTAR OF A KISSE                     OUT OF GREEKE CUPID'S CRYER    12  46 159 519
  YOUR SWEETNESSE CANNOT TAST                      THE WEEPER                  129  46  79 120
  TAST THIS, AND AS THOU LIK'ST THIS LESSER FLOOD     OUR LORD IN HIS CIRCUMCISION   3  46  98   9
  HER HEAVENLY ARMEFULL, SHEE SHALL TAST           ON A PRAYER BOOKE            106  46 126 139
  BLOSSOMS, BUT OUR BLEST TAST CONFESSES FRUITS.     UPON TWO GREENE APRICOCKES    14  48 220 494
  NOR TOUCH NOR TAST MUST LOOK FOR MORE            ADORO TE                    7  52 291 172
  TAST THEE GOD, OR TOUCH THEE MAN                ADORO TE                   30  52 291 172
  YOUR SWEETNES CANNOT TAST                     WEEPER                       171  52 307 120
  WHOSE STROKE SHALL TAST THY HALLOW'D BREATH.       TERESA                       80  52 315  52
  HER HEAVNLY ARM-FULL, SHE SHALL TAST             PRAYER TO GENTLE-WOMAN     112  52 328 139
  FEARE IS AFRAID TO TAST OF, ONLY THIS,            UPON GUNPOWDER TREASON         45  MS 387 461

TASTES

  TASTES OF THIS BREAKFAST ALL DAY LONG.             THE WEEPER                  30  46  79 120

TASTS

  AND WITH A QUAVERING COYNESSE TASTS THE STRINGS.    MUSICKS DUELL              112  46 149 535
  THE SOUL THAT TASTS THEE TAKES FROM THENCE.        TO THE NAME OF JESUS        188  52 239  30
  TASTS OF THIS BREAKFAST ALL DAY LONG.              WEEPER                        30  52 307 120

TASTER

  YOUNG TIME IS TASTER TO ETERNITY.                ON HOPE                     52  46 143  71
  YOUNG TIME IS TASTER TO ETERNITY                 (ON) HOPE                   22  52 345  71

TASTFULL

  WHAT IS'T YOUR TASTFULL SPIRITS DOE PROVE          FLAMING HEART               51  52 324  61

TATLING

  THE TATLING STRINGS (EACH BREATHING IN HIS PART)    MUSICKS DUELL               48  46 149 535

TAUGHT

  HIS NIMBLE HANDS INSTINCT THEN TAUGHT EACH STRING   MUSICKS DUELL               27  46 149 535
  TAUGHT HER THESE SULLIED CHEEKS THIS BLUBBER'D FACE, TO PONTIUS WASHING HANDS      4  46  94  23
  TAUGHT THEE BY NONE BUT HIM, WHILE HERE           IN MEMORY OF LADY MADRE TERESA 158  46 131  52
  IMPATIENT NATURE HAD TAUGHT MOTION              UPON DEATH OF HERRYS         6  46 167 466
  AS MIGHT HAVE TAUGHT GRIEFE HOW TO WEEPE.         ANOTHER ON HERRYS            22  46 170 469
  HAVE TAUGHT THEE NEW ASTROLOGY.                 LOVES HOROSCOPE              16  46 185 483
  TWINNE SUNNES,) & TAUGHT NOW TO NEGOTIATE YOU.     IN GLORIOUS EPIPHANIE      204  52 253  39
  WHICH TAUGHT ATTENTION EV'N TO ROCKS & STONES.     OFFICE H. CROSS NINTH        2  52 271  99
  TRANSSUM'D, & TAUGHT TO TURN DIVINE.               LAUDA SION SALVATOREM       30  52 294 178
  WE' ARE TAUGHT BEST BY THY TEARES & THEE.          WEEPER                       24  52 307 120
  AND TAUGHT THE WOUNDED HEART                    WEEPER                       105  52 307 120
  TAUGHT THEE BY NONE BUT HIM, WHILE HERE           TERESA                       157  52 315  52
  AH THOU THY SELF, ALAS, HAST TAUGHT ME HOW.        ALEXIAS FIRST ELEGIE       16  52 334 204
  FULL OF HIGH SPARKELING VIGOUR. TAUGHT BE MEE      OUT OF GROTIUS               53  MS 398 198

PAGE 418

## TAYLE

| | | | | | |
|---|---|---|---|---|---|
| THE WHILE HIS TWISTED TAYLE HEE GNAW'D FOR SPIGHT. | SOSPETTO D'HERODE | 152 | 46 | 109 | 216 |

## TAYLES

| | | | | | |
|---|---|---|---|---|---|
| WHILE HIS STEELE SIDES SOUND WITH HIS TAYLES STRONG LASH. | SOSPETTO D'HERODE | 64 | 46 | 109 | 216 |

## TEACH

| | | | | | |
|---|---|---|---|---|---|
| TILL THY RUINE TEACH THEE TEARES. | PSALME 137 | 32 | 46 | 104 | 7 |
| THEM GOD, AND TEACH THEM HOW TO LIVE | IN MEMORY OF LADY MADRE TERESA | 52 | 46 | 131 | 52 |
| FOR HIM SHEEL TEACH THEM HOW TO DYE. | IN MEMORY OF LADY MADRE TERESA | 54 | 46 | 131 | 52 |
| AND TEACH THY LIPPS HEAVEN, WITH HER HAND, | IN MEMORY OF LADY MADRE TERESA | 131 | 46 | 131 | 52 |
| AND TEACH IT TO EXPATIATE, AND SWELL | UPON YORKE HIS BIRTH | 23 | 46 | 176 | 500 |
| SEE'ST THOU THAT MARY THERE. O TEACH HER MOTHER | UPON YORKE HIS BIRTH | 53 | 46 | 176 | 500 |
| AND TEACH HER FAIRE STEPS TO OUR EARTH. | WISHES SUPPOSED MISTRESSE | 9 | 46 | 195 | 479 |
| THE BLOOD, YET TEACH A CHARME, | WISHES SUPPOSED MISTRESSE | 62 | 46 | 195 | 479 |
| AND TO THE TEETH OF HELL STOOD UP TO TEACH THEE, | TO THE NAME OF JESUS | 204 | 52 | 239 | 30 |
| AND TEACH OBSCURE MANKIND A MORE CLOSE WAY | IN GLORIOUS EPIPHANIE | 208 | 52 | 253 | 39 |
| AND TEACH THY LOV'D NAME TO THEIR NOBLE LYRE. | CHARITAS NIMIA | 28 | 52 | 280 | 48 |
| O TEACH THOSE WOUNDS TO BLEED | SANCTA MARIA DOLORUM | 51 | 52 | 283 | 162 |
| O TEACH MINE TOO THE ART | SANCTA MARIA DOLORUM | 98 | 52 | 283 | 162 |
| THEM GOD, TEACH THEM HOW TO LIVE | TERESA | 52 | 52 | 315 | 52 |
| FOR HIM SHE'L TEACH THEM HOW TO DY. | TERESA | 54 | 52 | 315 | 52 |
| AND TEACH THY LIPPS HEAV'N WITH HIS HAND. | TERESA | 130 | 52 | 315 | 52 |
| IF I BE SHIPWRACK'T, LOVE SHALL TEACH TO SWIMME. | ALEXIAS FIRST ELEGIE | 21 | 52 | 334 | 204 |
| TO TH' CHURLISH ROCKS, & TEACH THE STUBBORNE STONES | AN ELEGIE ON DR PORTER | 32 | MS | 395 | 476 |

## TEACHES

| | | | | | |
|---|---|---|---|---|---|
| WHOSE SWEET TEMPER TEACHES ME | PSALME 23 | 11 | 46 | 102 | 5 |

## TEACHING

| | | | | | |
|---|---|---|---|---|---|
| HEE'L FAN HER BRIGHT LOCKS TEACHING THEM TO FLOW. | ON A FOULE MORNING | 19 | 46 | 161 | 495 |

## TEAR

| | | | | | |
|---|---|---|---|---|---|
| MUCH REATHER WOULD IT BE THY TEAR, | WEEPER | 47 | 52 | 307 | 120 |
| A BEAD, THAT IS, A TEAR, DOES DROP. | WEEPER | 144 | 52 | 307 | 120 |
| TAKES HIS TEAR, & GETS HIM GONE. | WEEPER | 148 | 52 | 307 | 120 |

## TEARE'S

| | | | | | |
|---|---|---|---|---|---|
| THY TEARE'S SWEET OPPORTUNITY. | WEEPER | 132 | 52 | 307 | 120 |

## TEARE

| | | | | | |
|---|---|---|---|---|---|
| ALL ONE GREAT EYE, ALL DROWN'D IN ONE GREAT TEARE. | UPON BISHOP ANDREWES PICTURE | 4 | 46 | 163 | 490 |
| AND LEAVE THEM BOTH TO BEE THY TEARE. | THE WEEPER | 42 | 46 | 79 | 120 |
| TAKES HIS TEARE AND GETS HIM GONE. | THE WEEPER | 94 | 46 | 79 | 120 |
| A BEAD, THAT IS A TEARE DOTH DROP. | THE WEEPER | 108 | 46 | 79 | 120 |
| O 'TIS NOT A TEARE, | THE TEARE | 7 | 46 | 84 | 50 |
| O 'TIS A TEARE, | THE TEARE | 13 | 46 | 84 | 50 |
| TOO TRUE A TEARE, FOR NO SAD EYNE, | THE TEARE | 14 | 46 | 84 | 50 |
| RAINE SO TRUE A TEARE AS THINE. | THE TEARE | 16 | 46 | 84 | 50 |
| WEEPS FOR IT SELFE, IS ITS OWNE TEARE. | THE TEARE | 18 | 46 | 84 | 50 |
| IN TH'HEAVEN OF MARY'S EYE, A TEARE. | THE TEARE | 48 | 46 | 84 | 50 |
| WHILE IT FALLS HENCE 'TIS A TEARE. | ON WATER OF LORDS BAPTISME | 4 | 46 | 85 | 12 |
| EACH DROP'S A TEARE THAT WEEPS FOR HER OWN WAST. | TO PONTIUS WASHING HANDS | 11 | 46 | 94 | 23 |
| AND MANY A CRUELL TEARE DISCLOSES. | ON WOUNDS OF CRUCIFIED LORD | 8 | 46 | 99 | 24 |
| MANY A KISSE, AND MANY A TEARE. | ON WOUNDS OF CRUCIFIED LORD | 10 | 46 | 99 | 24 |
| NOR WOULD HE THIS THY FEAR'D CROWN FROM THEE TEARE. | SOSPETTO D'HERODE | 517 | 46 | 109 | 216 |
| O DOE THOU WATER IT WITH ONE KIND TEARE. | UPON DEATH OF HERRYS | 42 | 46 | 167 | 466 |
| THE SOFT TINCTURE OF A TEARE. | ANOTHER ON HERRYS | 20 | 46 | 170 | 463 |
| BEE ITS OWNE BLUSH, BEE ITS OWNE TEARE. | WISHES SUPPOSED MISTRESSE | 54 | 46 | 195 | 479 |
| THUS VEX THE EARTH & TEARE THE BEAUTEOUS SKYES. | ALEXIAS SECONDE ELEGIE | 10 | 52 | 335 | 207 |
| THE WORLD WILL BE UNE OCEAN, ONE GREAT TEARE. | UPON KINGS CORONATION | 42 | MS | 389 | 454 |
| LEFT MANY A STARRY TEARE, TO THINKE HOW SOONE | AN ELEGY MR STANNINOW | 41 | MS | 394 | 473 |
| LET EACH EYE WATER'T WITH A COURTEOUS TEARE. | AN ELEGY MR STANNINOW | 56 | MS | 394 | 473 |

## TEARS

| | | | | | |
|---|---|---|---|---|---|
| WHICH WAY MY POORE TEARS TO HIMSELFE MAY GOE, | COME SEE WHERE THE LORD LAY | 2 | 46 | 87 | 27 |
| RICH LAZARUS, RICHER IN THOSE GEMS, THY TEARS, | UPON LAZARUS HIS TEARES | 1 | 46 | 89 | 18 |
| IN TEARS, AS IF THINE EYES HAD NONE. | ON BLEEDING WOUNDS OF LORD | 18 | 46 | 101 | 110 |
| THAT MANKINDS TORMENT WAITS UPON MY TEARS. | SOSPETTO D'HERODE | 216 | 46 | 109 | 216 |
| IMPENETRABLE, BOTH TO PRAI'RS AND TEARS, | SOSPETTO D'HERODE | 308 | 46 | 109 | 216 |
| WITH LOVES, OF TEARS WITH SMILES DISPUTING. | WEEPER | 92 | 52 | 307 | 120 |

## TEARES

| | | | | | |
|---|---|---|---|---|---|
| THY MIND IN TEARES WHO E'RE THOU BE, | UPON THE DEATH OF A GENTLEMAN | 25 | 46 | 166 | 472 |
| EYES ARE VOCALL, TEARES HAVE TONGUES, | UPON THE DEATH OF A GENTLEMAN | 27 | 46 | 166 | 472 |
| HER RICHEST PEARLES, I MEANE THY TEARES. | THE WEEPER | 54 | 46 | 79 | 120 |
| HIS MED'CINABLE TEARES. FOR NOW | THE WEEPER | 70 | 46 | 79 | 120 |
| THY TEARES JUST CADENCE STILL KEEPS TIME. | THE WEEPER | 104 | 46 | 79 | 120 |
| STILL THY TEARES DOE FALL, AND FALL. | THE WEEPER | 110 | 46 | 79 | 120 |
| MEASURE THEIR AGES, THOU BY TEARES. | THE WEEPER | 120 | 46 | 79 | 120 |
| DISTILLS FROM THENCE THE TEARES OF WRATH AND STRIFE, | TO LORD UPON WATER MADE WINE | 3 | 46 | 91 | 12 |
| NOTHING BUT TEARES. | TO PONTIUS WASHING HANDS | 10 | 46 | 94 | 23 |

| | | | | |
|---|---|---|---|---|
| TO ME MY LEGACY OF TEARES. | VERILY YE SHALL WEEP | 2 | 46 | 95 | 22 |
| MY TEARES BUT TENDER AND MY DEATH NEW-BORNE. | OUR LORD IN HIS CIRCUMCISION | 12 | 46 | 98 | 9 |
| TO PAY THY TEARES, AN EYE THAT WEEPS | ON WOUNDS OF CRUCIFIED LORD | 15 | 46 | 99 | 24 |
| IN STEAD OF TEARES SUCH GEMS AS THIS IS. | ON WOUNDS OF CRUCIFIED LORD | 16 | 46 | 99 | 24 |
| WHEN HARPES AND HEARTS WERE DROWN'D IN TEARES. | PSALME 137 | 10 | 46 | 104 | 7 |
| TILL THY RUINE TEACH THEE TEARES, | PSALME 137 | 32 | 46 | 104 | 7 |
| WEEPE PRETIOUS TEARES UPON THE STONES. | PSALME 137 | 36 | 46 | 104 | 7 |
| SHEE SINGS THY TEARES ASLEEPE, AND DIPS | A HYMNE OF THE NATIVITY | 65 | 46 | 106 | 76 |
| THE JUDGE OF TORMENTS, AND THE KING OF TEARES. | SOSPETTO D'HERODE | 41 | 46 | 109 | 216 |
| TEARES SHALL TAKE COMFORT, AND TURNE GEMS. | IN MEMORY OF LADY MADRE TERESA | 150 | 46 | 131 | 52 |
| LET NOT PITTY WITH HER TEARES. | UPON DEATH OF DESIRED HERRYS | 61 | 46 | 168 | 467 |
| BATHES IN TEARES OF EVERY EYE. | ANOTHER ON HERRYS | 8 | 46 | 170 | 469 |
| TEARES WOULD NOW HAVE FLOW'D SO DEEPE, | ANOTHER ON HERRYS | 21 | 46 | 170 | 469 |
| WET WITH TEARES STILL'D FROM THE EYES. | ANOTHER ON HERRYS | 35 | 46 | 170 | 469 |
| ALL THE TEARES THAT GRIEFE CAN LEND. | ANOTHER ON HERRYS | 58 | 46 | 170 | 469 |
| THE MUSES WITH THEIR TEARES SUPPLY. | AN EPITAPH DOCTOR BROOKE | 8 | 46 | 175 | 465 |
| THRICE WILL I PAY THREE TEARES, TO SHOW HOW TRUE | TO THE MORNING | 40 | 46 | 183 | 497 |
| SHUT IN THEIR TEARES.  SHUT OUT THEIR MISERYES. | TO THE MORNING | 58 | 46 | 183 | 497 |
| TEARES, QUICKLY FLED. | WISHES SUPPOSED MISTRESSE | 73 | 46 | 195 | 479 |
| TURN'D THEM TO TEARES, & SPENT THEM TOO. | TO THE NAME OF JESUS | 138 | 52 | 239 | 30 |
| MELTED & MEASUR'D OUT IN SEAS OF TEARES | TO THE NAME OF JESUS | 144 | 52 | 239 | 30 |
| HER EYES BLEED TEARES, HIS WOUNDS WEEP BLOOD. | SANCTA MARIA DOLORUM | 20 | 52 | 283 | 162 |
| ME TOO MY TEARES. WHO, THOUGH ALL STONE, | SANCTA MARIA DOLORUM | 59 | 52 | 283 | 162 |
| THOUGH BOTH MY PRAYRES & TEARES COMBINE, | DIES IRAE | 53 | 52 | 298 | 186 |
| DETAIN IN NEEDFULL TEARES TO WEEP THE WANT OF THEE. | IN GLORIOUS ASSUMPTION B. LADY | 22 | 52 | 304 | 114 |
| WE' ARE TAUGHT BEST BY THY TEARES & THEE. | WEEPER | 24 | 52 | 307 | 120 |
| HER PROUDEST PEARLES. I MEAN THY TEARES. | WEEPER | 42 | 52 | 307 | 120 |
| HIS MED'CINABLE TEARES. FOR NOW | WEEPER | 52 | 52 | 307 | 120 |
| AETERNALL TEARES SHOULD THUS DISTILL THEE. | WEEPER | 100 | 52 | 307 | 120 |
| THY FALLING TEARES KEEP FAITH FULL TIME. | WEEPER | 140 | 52 | 307 | 120 |
| MEASURE THEIR AGES. THOU, BY TEARES. | WEEPER | 156 | 52 | 307 | 120 |
| SUCH TEARES THE SUFFRING ROSE THAT'S VEXT | WEEPER | 160 | 52 | 307 | 120 |
| BECAUSE THEY WANT SUCH TEARES AS WE. | WEEPER | 180 | 52 | 307 | 120 |
| TEARES SHALL TAKE COMFORT, & TURN GEMMS | TERESA | 149 | 52 | 315 | 52 |
| T'EMBRACE MY TEARES, & KISSE AN UNKIND FATE. | ALEXIAS FIRST ELEGIE | 4 | 52 | 334 | 204 |
| NOR CAN I TELL (AND THIS NEW TEARES DOTH BREED) | ALEXIAS FIRST ELEGIE | 7 | 52 | 334 | 204 |
| UNKIND. YET ARE MY TEARES STILL TRUE TO ME | ALEXIAS SECONDE ELEGIE | 2 | 52 | 335 | 207 |
| TO THESE I TALK IN TEARES, & TELL MY PAIN. | ALEXIAS SECONDE ELEGIE | 17 | 52 | 335 | 207 |
| AND ANSWER TOO FOR THEM IN TEARES AGAIN. | ALEXIAS SECONDE ELEGIE | 18 | 52 | 335 | 207 |
| STILL, AS THEIR VAIN TEARES MY VOWES DID TRY, | ALEXIAS THIRD ELEGIE | 55 | 52 | 336 | 209 |
| RIVALL THY TEARES. | LUKE 2.  QUAERIT JESUM | 20 | MS | 379 | 11 |
| TORRENTS OF SALT TEARES FROM OUR EYES SHOULD RUNNE. | UPON GUNPOWDER TREASON | 37 | MS | 386 | 460 |
| ALAS, THE EARTH, QUITE DRUNKE WITH TEARES, HAD REEL'D | UPON KINGS CORONATION | 9 | MS | 390 | 453 |
| STREIGHT FROM THIS SEA OF TEARES THERE DOES APPEARE | UPON KINGS CORONATION | 13 | MS | 390 | 453 |
| SINCE SIGHS DOE RISE, AND TEARES DOE FALL. | UPON DEATH OF A FREIND | 4 | MS | 393 | 477 |
| TEARES FALL TOO LOW, SIGHES RISE TOO HIGH. | UPON DEATH OF A FREIND | 5 | MS | 393 | 477 |
| WHAT MEANE THESE SHOURES OF TEARES AMONGST US MEN. | AN ELEGY MR STANNINOW | 16 | MS | 394 | 473 |
| THE WEEPING PEN WITH SABLE TEARES HATH DREST. | AN ELEGIE ON DR PORTER | 10 | MS | 395 | 476 |
| THEN WEEPE THYSELFE INTO A SEA OF TEARES. | AN ELEGIE ON DR PORTER | 38 | MS | 395 | 476 |

RUBY-TEARES

| | | | | |
|---|---|---|---|---|
| THE DEBT IS PAID IN RUBY-TEARES. | ON WOUNDS OF CRUCIFIED LORD | 19 | 46 | 99 | 24 |

TEAT

| | | | | |
|---|---|---|---|---|
| HEE'L HAVE HIS TEAT E'RE LONG (A BLOODY ONE) | BLESSED BE THE PAPS | 3 | 46 | 94 | 14 |

TEATES

| | | | | |
|---|---|---|---|---|
| SUPPOSE HE HAD BEEN TABLED AT THY TEATES. | BLESSED BE THE PAPS | 1 | 46 | 94 | 14 |

TEDIOUSLY

| | | | | |
|---|---|---|---|---|
| TEDIOUSLY WO'ED, AND HARDLY WONE. | AGAINST IRRESOLUTION AND DELAY | 59 | 52 | 347 | 146 |

TEEME

| | | | | |
|---|---|---|---|---|
| ENGENDER WITH THE NIGHT, & TEEME A BIRTH | UPON GUNPOWDER TREASON | 12 | MS | 386 | 460 |

TEEMING

| | | | | |
|---|---|---|---|---|
| ARE TEEMING NOW WITH STORE OF FRESH SUPPLIES. | AN ELEGIE ON DR PORTER | 44 | MS | 395 | 476 |

TEETH

| | | | | |
|---|---|---|---|---|
| THAT UNDER HUNGERS TEETH WILL NEEDS BE SOUND. | ON MIRACLE OF LOAVES | 2 | 46 | 86 | 15 |
| THOU TO THEIR TEETH HAST PROV'D THY DEITY. | ON MIRACLE OF LOAVES | 2 | 46 | 88 | 16 |
| A MASSE OF WOES, HIS TEETH FOR TORMENT GNASH, | SOSPETTO D'HERODE | 63 | 46 | 109 | 216 |
| OF TIME, OR TEETH OF HUNGRY RUINE FEARES. | SOSPETTO D'HERODE | 310 | 46 | 109 | 216 |
| FOURE TEETH THOU HAD'ST THAT RANCK'D IN GOODLY STATE | OUT OF MARTIALL | 1 | 46 | 188 | 527 |
| AND TO THE TEETH OF HELL STOOD UP TO TEACH THEE, | TO THE NAME OF JESUS | 204 | 52 | 239 | 30 |

TELL

| | | | | |
|---|---|---|---|---|
| IN MUSICK'S RAVISH'T SOULE HEE DARE NOT TELL, | MUSICKS DUELL | 144 | 46 | 149 | 535 |
| A MAN WHOSE SOBER SOULE CAN TELL. | IN PRAISE OF LESSIUS | 19 | 46 | 156 | 510 |
| BUT O (TOO WELL MY WOUNDS CAN TELL) | OUT OF GREEKE CUPID'S CRYER | 51 | 46 | 159 | 519 |
| TELL DOWN HIS SILVER-DROPS UNTO THEE. | OUT OF GREEKE CUPID'S CRYER | 61 | 46 | 159 | 519 |
| AS TO SPEAKE NOTHING, COME THEN TELL | UPON THE DEATH OF A GENTLEMAN | 24 | 46 | 166 | 472 |
| TELL ME BRIGHT BOY, TELL ME MY GOLDEN LAD. | ON THE PRODIGALL | 1 | 46 | 86 | 17 |
| TELL ME BRIGHT BOY, TELL ME MY GOLDEN LAD. | ON THE PRODIGALL | 1 | 46 | 86 | 17 |
| THOU HAST THE ART ON'T PETER. AND CANST TELL | ON ST. PETER CASTING NETS | 1 | 46 | 98 | 13 |
| TELL HIM HEE RISES NOW TOO LATE. | A HYMNE OF THE NATIVITY | 9 | 46 | 106 | 76 |

| | | | | |
|---|---|---|---|---|
| TELL HIM WEE NOW CAN SHEW HIM MORE | A HYMNE OF THE NATIVITY | 11 | 46 106 | 76 |
| TELL HIM TITYRUS WHERE TH'HAST BEEN, | A HYMNE OF THE NATIVITY | 15 | 46 106 | 76 |
| TELL HIM THYRSIS WHAT TH'HAST SEEN. | A HYMNE OF THE NATIVITY | 16 | 46 106 | 76 |
| THE HORRID SUMME OF HIS INTENTIONS TELL. | SOSPETTO D'HERODE | 370 | 46 109 | 216 |
| TO PROVE THAT TRUE, SCHOOLES USE TO TELL, | ON A PRAYER BOOKE | 7 | 46 126 | 139 |
| YET THOUGH SHEE CANNOT TELL YOU WHY, | IN MEMORY OF LADY MADRE TERESA | 23 | 46 131 | 52 |
| ANGELLS CANNOT TELL, SUFFICE, | IN MEMORY OF LADY MADRE TERESA | 120 | 46 131 | 52 |
| THIS STONE WILL TELL THEE THAT BENEATH, | HIS EPITAPH (HERRYS) | 5 | 46 172 | 471 |
| JUSTLY, GREAT NATURE, MAY'ST THOU BRAG AND TELL | UPON YORKE HIS BIRTH | 49 | 46 176 | 500 |
| ON OUR LIPS, BEGIN AND TELL | OUT OF CATULLUS | 10 | 46 194 | 523 |
| TELL HIM HE RISES NOW, TOO LATE | IN HOLY NATIVITY | 9 | 52 246 | 76 |
| TELL HIM WE NOW CAN SHOW HIM MORE | IN HOLY NATIVITY | 11 | 52 246 | 76 |
| TELL HIM, TITYRUS, WHERE TH'HAST BEEN | IN HOLY NATIVITY | 15 | 52 246 | 76 |
| TELL HIM, THYRSIS, WHAT TH'HAST SEEN. | IN HOLY NATIVITY | 16 | 52 246 | 76 |
| YET THOUGH SHE CANNOT TELL YOU WHY, | TERESA | 23 | 52 315 | 52 |
| ANGELLS CANNOT TELL, SUFFICE, | TERESA | 119 | 52 315 | 52 |
| TO PROVE THAT TRUE, SCHOOLES USE TO TELL, | PRAYER TO GENTLE-WOMAN | 13 | 52 328 | 139 |
| NOR CAN I TELL (AND THIS NEW TEARES DOTH BREED) | ALEXIAS FIRST ELEGIE | 7 | 52 334 | 204 |
| TO THESE I TALK IN TEARES, & TELL MY PAIN. | ALEXIAS SECONDE ELEGIE | 17 | 52 335 | 207 |
| CRUELL RETURN. OR TELL THE REASON WHY | ALEXIAS THIRD ELEGIE | 17 | 52 336 | 209 |
| AND I, WHAT IS MY CRIME I CANNOT TELL. | ALEXIAS THIRD ELEGIE | 19 | 52 336 | 209 |
| A MAN WHOSE SOBER SOUL CAN TELL | TEMPERANCE | 17 | 52 342 | 510 |
| NONE, BUT HIMSELFE, WHO FEELES IT, NONE CAN TELL. | IN AMOREM DIVINUM | 2 | MS 381 | 212 |
| NONE, NOT HIMSELFE, WHO FEELES IT, NONE CAN TELL. | IN AMOREM DIVINUM | 4 | MS 381 | 212 |
| TO TELL THE WORLD, HOW HARD THE MATTER WENT, | HORATIJ ILLE & NEFASTO | 43 | MS 382 | 530 |
| O TELL ME THEN, WHAT RUDE OUTRAGIOUS BLAST | AN ELEGY MR STANNINOW | 27 | MS 394 | 473 |
| PURE, & UNMIXED CRUELTY THEY TELL, | AN ELEGIE ON DR PORTER | 13 | MS 395 | 476 |
| OF MY SAD LABOURS. NO DAY YETT COULD TELL | OUT OF GROTIUS | 10 | MS 398 | 198 |
| I CAL'D A HUNDRED MIRACLES TO TELL | OUT OF GROTIUS | 31 | MS 398 | 198 |

TELLS

| | | | | |
|---|---|---|---|---|
| HOPE TELLS MY HEART, THE SAME LOVES BE | DIES IRAE | 51 | 52 298 | 186 |

TEMPER

| | | | | |
|---|---|---|---|---|
| WHOSE SWEET TEMPER TEACHES ME | PSALME 23 | 11 | 46 102 | 5 |
| TEMPER TWIXT CHILL DESPAIR, & TORRID JOY. | (ON) HOPE | 43 | 52 345 | 71 |

TEMPER'D

| | | | | |
|---|---|---|---|---|
| A SWEETLY TEMPER'D MEANE, NOR HOT NOR COLD. | OUT OF VIRGIL | 36 | 46 155 | 529 |
| TEMPER'D 'TWIXT COLD DESPAIRE, AND TORRID JOY. | ON HOPE | 83 | 46 143 | 71 |
| THAT SO OUR SWEETLY TEMPER'D SONG | TO THE QUEEN | 11 | 48 215 | 501 |

RARELY-TEMPER'D

| | | | | |
|---|---|---|---|---|
| WITH MANY A RARELY-TEMPER'D KISSE, | A HYMNE OF THE NATIVITY | 62 | 46 106 | 76 |
| WITH MANY A RARELY-TEMPER'D KISSE | IN HOLY NATIVITY | 88 | 52 246 | 76 |

TEMPEST

| | | | | |
|---|---|---|---|---|
| NO CLOUD SCOULE ON HIS RADIANT LIDS NO TEMPEST LOWRE. | EASTER DAY | 12 | 46 100 | 26 |
| (ROWZ'D IN AN ANGRY TEMPEST). OH THE SEA. | HORATIJ ILLE & NEFASTO | 21 | MS 382 | 530 |

TEMPLE

| | | | | |
|---|---|---|---|---|
| THY TEMPLE, AND THOSE LOVELY WALLS | PSALME 23 | 63 | 46 102 | 5 |
| HEE SAW THE TEMPLE SACRED TO SWEET PEACE, | SOSPETTO D'HERODE | 123 | 46 109 | 216 |
| SO SWEET THE TEMPLE WAS, THAT SHRIN'D | ANOTHER ON HERRYS | 15 | 46 170 | 469 |
| RUINE A TEMPLE. ON WHOSE FRUITFULL FALL | ON FRONTISPIECE ISAACSONS | 17 | 46 191 | 471 |
| THE CENTER SHOOK. HER USELESSE VEIL TH'INGLORIOUS TEMPLE TORE. | OFFICE H. CROSS NINTH | 8 | 52 271 | 99 |

TEMPLES

| | | | | |
|---|---|---|---|---|
| NOW SEEM THEY TEMPLES CONSECRATE TO NONE, | ON A TREATISE OF CHARITY | 37 | 46 137 | 69 |

TOO-HARD-TEMPTED

| | | | | |
|---|---|---|---|---|
| THE TOO-HARD-TEMPTED NATIONS. | IN GLORIOUS EPIPHANIE | 92 | 52 253 | 39 |

TEN

| | | | | |
|---|---|---|---|---|
| TO A VAST FIELD OF THORNES, TEN THOUSAND SPEARES | SOSPETTO D'HERODE | 475 | 46 109 | 216 |
| OF BLESSINGS, AND TEN THOUSAND MORE. | ON A PRAYER BOOKE | 82 | 46 126 | 139 |
| AT ONCE, TEN THOUSAND PARADISES | ON A PRAYER BOOKE | 107 | 46 126 | 139 |
| AND TEN THOUSAND PARADISES | TO THE NAME OF JESUS | 187 | 52 239 | 30 |
| TEN THOUSAND ANGELS IN ONE POINT CAN DWELL. | PRAYER TO GENTLE-WOMAN | 14 | 52 328 | 139 |
| OF BLESSINGS & TEN THOUSAND MORE | PRAYER TO GENTLE-WOMAN | 88 | 52 328 | 139 |
| AT ONCE TEN THOUSAND PARADISES. | PRAYER TO GENTLE-WOMAN | 113 | 52 328 | 139 |
| AND BREAKES THROUGH ALL TEN HEAV'NS TO OUR EMBRACE. | AGAINST IRRESOLUTION AND DELAY | 78 | 52 347 | 146 |

TEND

| | | | | |
|---|---|---|---|---|
| IN A BRIGHT CHRISTALL TIDE, TO THEE THEY TEND. | AN ELEGIE ON DR PORTER | 40 | MS 395 | 476 |

TENDER

| | | | | |
|---|---|---|---|---|
| WITH TENDER ACCENTS, AND SEVERELY JOYNT IT | MUSICKS DUELL | 40 | 46 149 | 535 |
| CREEPS ON THE SOFT TOUCH OF A TENDER TONE. | MUSICKS DUELL | 140 | 46 149 | 535 |
| HAD DEALT TOO ROUGHLY WITH HER TENDER THROATE. | MUSICKS DUELL | 159 | 46 149 | 535 |
| THE TENDER GROWTH OF THINGS ENDURE THE SENCE | OUT OF VIRGIL | 33 | 46 155 | 529 |
| AND TIPT THE MOUNTAINES IN A TENDER RAY. | THE BEGINNING OF HELIODORUS | 2 | 46 158 | 517 |

|  |  |  |  |  |  |
|---|---|---|---|---|---|
| MY TEARES BUT TENDER AND MY DEATH NEW-BORNE. | OUR LORD IN HIS CIRCUMCISION | 12 | 46 | 98 | 9 |
| HIS TRUMPETS. TENDER CRYES, HIS MEN TO DARE | SOSPETTO D'HERODE | 526 | 46 | 109 | 216 |
| BLEST POWERS FORBID THY TENDER LIFE, | IN MEMORY OF LADY MADRE TERESA | 69 | 46 | 131 | 52 |
| BUT (FOR A LAMBE) THY TAME AND TENDER HEART | ON A TREATISE OF CHARITY | 45 | 46 | 137 | 69 |
| (HIS TENDER TOPPE NOT FULLY SPREAD) | UPON DEATH OF DESIRED HERRYS | 35 | 46 | 168 | 467 |
| THE TENDER DROPS WHICH TREMBLE ON HER CHEEKE. | ON A FOULE MORNING | 14 | 46 | 181 | 495 |
| BLEST POWRES FORBID, THY TENDER LIFE | TERESA | 69 | 52 | 315 | 52 |
| (FAIRE ONE) THESE TENDER LEAVES DOE TREMBLING STAND. | AT TH' IVORY TRIBUNALL | 2 | MS | 397 | 492 |

TENEMENT

|  |  |  |  |  |  |
|---|---|---|---|---|---|
| MANS BREST (HIS TENEMENT) AND BREAKES UP HOUSE. | OUT OF GROTIUS | 80 | MS | 398 | 198 |

TENOR

|  |  |  |  |  |  |
|---|---|---|---|---|---|
| SO SMIL'D THE DAYES, AND SO THE TENOR RAN | OUT OF VIRGIL | 24 | 46 | 155 | 529 |

TERESA

|  |  |  |  |  |  |
|---|---|---|---|---|---|
| TERESA IS NO MORE FOR YOU. | IN MEMORY OF LADY MADRE TERESA | 58 | 46 | 131 | 52 |
| TERESA IS NO MORE FOR YOU. | TERESA | 58 | 52 | 315 | 52 |

TERESIA

|  |  |  |  |  |  |
|---|---|---|---|---|---|
| AND THIS THE GREAT TERESIA. | FLAMING HEART | 6 | 52 | 324 | 61 |

TERME

|  |  |  |  |  |  |
|---|---|---|---|---|---|
| THE VERY TERME, I THINK, WAS FOUND | THE TEARE | 5 | 46 | 84 | 50 |

TEARME

|  |  |  |  |  |  |
|---|---|---|---|---|---|
| SUCH A TEARME AS THIS, SPARE HERE | ANOTHER ON HERRYS | 48 | 46 | 170 | 469 |

TERMES

|  |  |  |  |  |  |
|---|---|---|---|---|---|
| SHEWES THE TWO TERMES AND LIMITS OF TIME'S RACE. | ON FRONTISPIECE ISAACSONS | 22 | 46 | 191 | 491 |
| PROGRESSIONS 'TWIXT WHOSE TERMES POOR TIME GROWS OLD. | UPON TWO GREENE APRICOCKES | 16 | 48 | 220 | 494 |

TERRESTRIALL

|  |  |  |  |  |  |
|---|---|---|---|---|---|
| THY TORCH, TERRESTRIALL LOVE, HAVE HERE NO NAME. | ALEXIAS THIRD ELEGIE | 50 | 52 | 336 | 209 |

TERRITORIES

|  |  |  |  |  |  |
|---|---|---|---|---|---|
| HELL FROM ME TOO, AND SACK MY TERRITORIES. | SOSPETTO D'HERODE | 226 | 46 | 109 | 216 |

TERROR

|  |  |  |  |  |  |
|---|---|---|---|---|---|
| THE NATION'S TERROR NOW THEN ERST THEIR LOVE. | IN GLORIOUS EPIPHANIE | 160 | 52 | 253 | 39 |

TERRORS

|  |  |  |  |  |  |
|---|---|---|---|---|---|
| COME NOW ALL YEE TERRORS, SALLY | PSALME 23 | 35 | 46 | 102 | 5 |
| ALL HIS TERRORS TO AFFRIGHT MEE. | OUT OF THE ITALIAN (1) | 45 | 46 | 188 | 545 |
| AND THOSE TERRORS SHALL DELIGHT MEE. | OUT OF THE ITALIAN (1) | 48 | 46 | 188 | 545 |

TEXT

|  |  |  |  |  |  |
|---|---|---|---|---|---|
| THE FAIRE GLOSSE OF A FAIRER TEXT. | ANOTHER ON HERRYS | 52 | 46 | 170 | 469 |
| TRIUMPHANT TEXT, PROVOKES THY PRAYSE. | LAUDA SION SALVATOREM | 8 | 52 | 294 | 178 |
| AND FOULE THE CLEARE TEXT WITH A MUDDY GLOSSE. | UPON BIRTH PRINCESSE E | 54 | MS | 391 | 456 |

THAN

|  |  |  |  |  |  |
|---|---|---|---|---|---|
| HER HOPES ARE CROWN'D, ONELY SHE FEARES THAT THAN, | UPON FAIRE ETHIOPIAN | 5 | 46 | 183 | 493 |
| SOMETHING MORE THAN | WISHES SUPPOSED MISTRESSE | 19 | 46 | 195 | 479 |
| THAN ERE THE FRUITFULL PHOEBUS FLAMING KISSES | UPON TWO GREENE APRICOCKES | 9 | 48 | 220 | 494 |
| WHAT KIND OF MARBLE THAN | SANCTA MARIA DOLORUM | 11 | 52 | 283 | 162 |
| AND LESSE TO LEAN ON. BECAUSE THAN | ADORO TE | 21 | 52 | 291 | 172 |
| DULL SLUGGISH ILE. WHAT MORE THAN LETHARGY | ON GUNPOWDER-TREASON | 3 | MS | 384 | 458 |
| DYE SEV'N TIMES DEEPER THAN THEY WERE BEFORE | UPON GUNPOWDER TREASON | 4 | MS | 387 | 461 |
| TO SEE SOME FOWLER THAN HERSELFE) THESE STAND. | UPON GUNPOWDER TREASON | 13 | MS | 387 | 461 |
| WHAT MORE THAN WINTER HATH THAT DIRE ART FOUND, | AN ELEGY MR STANNINOW | 21 | MS | 394 | 473 |
| SOMEWHAT MORE HORRID THAN AN ELEGY. | AN ELEGIE ON DR PORTER | 12 | MS | 395 | 476 |

THANKE

|  |  |  |  |  |  |
|---|---|---|---|---|---|
| I THANKE YOU ALL, BUT ONE MUST SINGLE OUT, | SOSPETTO D'HERODE | 287 | 46 | 109 | 216 |

THANKLESSE

|  |  |  |  |  |  |
|---|---|---|---|---|---|
| AND BRING HOME ON THY BREST MORE THANKLESSE SCARRS. | SOSPETTO D'HERODE | 448 | 46 | 109 | 216 |

THAW

|  |  |  |  |  |  |
|---|---|---|---|---|---|
| THOU THAT ALONE CANST THAW THIS COLD. | TO COUNTESSE OF DENBIGH | 27 | 52 | 236 | 146 |

THAW'D

|  |  |  |  |  |  |
|---|---|---|---|---|---|
| SHOTT FROM HIS FLAMING EYE, HAD THAW'D IT'S IRE, | AN ELEGY MR STANNINOW | 32 | MS | 394 | 473 |

THAWES

HEE SAW RICH NECTAR THAWES, RELEASE THE RIGOUR     SOSPETTO D'HERODE           105  46 109 216

THAWING

THAWING CHRISTALL. SNOWY HILLS.                    THE WEEPER                    4  46  79 120
THAWING CRYSTALL. SNOWY HILLS,                     WEEPER                        4  52 307 120

THEBES

SUCH AS AT THEBES DIRE FEAST SHEE SHEW'D HER HEAD. SOSPETTO D'HERODE           397  46 109 216

THEFTS

ALL THE IDOLATROUS THEFTS DONE BY THIS NIGHT OF DAY. IN GLORIOUS EPIPHANIE     150  52 253  39

THEIFE

THOU DIDST AFFORD THE FAITHFULL THEIFE.            ADORO TE                     18  52 291 172

THEME

THIS SHALL FROM HENCE-FORTH BE THE MASCULINE THEME ON A TREATISE OF CHARITY    49  46 137  69

THEAME

HERE'S A THEAME WILL DRINKE TH'EXPENCE,            UPON THE DEATH OF A GENTLEMAN 31  46 166 472
HATE IS THY THEAME, AND HEROD, WHOSE UNBLEST       SOSPETTO D'HERODE             2  46 109 216

THENCE

DISTILLS FROM THENCE THE TEARES OF WRATH AND STRIFE. TO LORD UPON WATER MADE WINE   3  46  91  12
AND THENCE MY RIPE SOULE WILL I BREATH             PSALME 23                    71  46 102   5
CLOSE COUCHT IN YOUR WHITE BOSOME, AND FROM THENCE ON A PRAYER BOOKE            11  46 126 139
THINE OWN DEARE BOOKS ARE GUILTY, FOR FROM THENCE  AN APOLOGIE FOR HYMNE (TERESA)  7  46 136  59
FROM THENCE INTO THE WONDRING READERS BREAST,      AN APOLOGIE FOR HYMNE (TERESA) 25  46 136  59
FOR ALL PERSUASIVE GRACES THENCE                   HIS EPITAPH (HERRYS)         33  46 172 471
THY SILENCE.  SPEAKE. AND SHE SHALL TAKE FROM THENCE UPON YORKE HIS BIRTH      110  46 176 500
YET CARRY NOTHING THENCE AWAY.                     WISHES SUPPOSED MISTRESSE    39  46 195 479
THE SOUL THAT TASTS THEE TAKES FROM THENCE.        TO THE NAME OF JESUS        188  52 239  30
THINE OWN DEAR BOOKES ARE GUILTY.  FOR FROM THENCE AN APOLOGIE FOR (TERESA) HYMNE  7  52 322  59
FROM THENCE INTO THE WONDRING READER'S BREST.      AN APOLOGIE FOR (TERESA) HYMNE 25  52 322  59
CLOSE COUCH'T IN YOUR WHITE BOSOM, & FROM THENCE   PRAYER TO GENTLE-WOMAN       17  52 328 139
THENCE HE MIGHT TOSSE YOU                          TO SAME CONCERNING CHOISE    49  52 331  66
FIXT IN YOUR SPHAERES OF GLORY, SHED FROM THENCE   UPON KINGS CORONATION        39  MS 389 454
LETT NONE DARE SPEAKE OF THEE, BUT SUCH AS THENCE  UPON BIRTH PRINCESSE E        9  MS 391 456

THEREWITHALL

AS 'TIS POWERFULL THEREWITHALL.                    OUT OF GREEKE CUPID'S CRYER  38  46 159 519

THERODAMAS

WITH THE FIERCE LYONS OF THERODAMAS.               SOSPETTO D'HERODE           354  46 109 216

THICK

THROUGH THE THICK SHADES OBSCURELY MIGHT YOU SEE   SOSPETTO D'HERODE           350  46 109 216
HAD NOT HER THICK SNAKES HID THEM FROM THE SUN.    SOSPETTO D'HERODE           384  46 109 216

THICKE

OF SHORT THICKE SOBS, WHOSE THUNDRING VOLLEYES FLOAT, MUSICKS DUELL             63  46 149 535

THICKEST

OLD CLOUDS OF THICKEST BLINDNESSE FLED MY SIGHT    OUT OF GROTIUS               71  MS 398 198

THIN

WHAT ARMOUR DOES HE WEARE.  A FEW THIN CLOUTS.     SOSPETTO D'HERODE           525  46 109 216

THINNE

A THINNE AIEREALL VAILE IS DRAWNE                  IN PRAISE OF LESSIUS         28  46 156 510
FROM THEE THEIR THINNE DILEMMA WITH BLUNT HORNE    ON HOPE                      19  46 143  71
A THINNE, AERIALL VEIL, IS DRAWN                   TEMPERANCE                   26  52 342 510

THINNER

NOR HATH GOD A THINNER SHARE,                      GIVE TO CAESAR AND TO GOD     3  46  96  20

THINE

OR TO THY SELFE, SING THINE OWNE OBSEQUIE.         MUSICKS DUELL               110  46 149 535
THINE CRAWLES ABOVE AND IS THE CREAME.             THE WEEPER                   22  46  79 120
AND DRAW FROM THESE FULL EYES OF THINE.            THE WEEPER                   35  46  79 120
THE APRIL IN THINE EYES,                           THE WEEPER                   87  46  79 120
BY THINE EYES TINCT ENOBLED THUS                   THE WEEPER                   95  46  79 120
FROM THINE EYE ITS SPHEARE.                        THE TEARE                     9  46  84  50
THIS THINE EYES JEWELL IN HER EARE.                THE TEARE                    12  46  84  50
RAINE SO TRUE A TEARE AS THINE.                    THE TEARE                    16  46  84  50

| | | | | | |
|---|---|---|---|---|---|
| A WOUND OF THINE. | ON MARKES OF SAVIOURS WOUNDS | 8 | 46 | 86 | 28 |
| MUST HAVE ITS FOUNTAINE IN THINE EYES. | TO PONTIUS WASHING HANDS | 4 | 46 | 88 | 22 |
| THE CALM THAT COOLS THINE EYE DOES SHIPWRACK MINE, FOR O. | AND A CERTAINE PRIEST PASSED | 3 | 46 | 94 | 17 |
| O THESE WAKEFULL WOUNDS OF THINE. | ON WOUNDS OF CRUCIFIED LORD | 1 | 46 | 99 | 24 |
| FOR THEE TO WEARE, BUT THESE, OF THINE OWNE BLOOD. | ON CRUCIFIED LORD BLOODY | 6 | 46 | 100 | 24 |
| IN TEARS, AS IF THINE EYES HAD NONE. | ON BLEEDING WOUNDS OF LORD | 18 | 46 | 101 | 110 |
| WHAT NEED THEY HELPE TO DROWNE THINE HEART, | ON BLEEDING WOUNDS OF LORD | 19 | 46 | 101 | 110 |
| FRESH FROM THE PURE GLANCE OF THINE EYE. | PSALME 23 | 65 | 46 | 102 | 5 |
| WEE SAW THINE EYES BREAK FROM THE EAST. | A HYMNE OF THE NATIVITY | 31 | 46 | 106 | 76 |
| WEE SAW THEE BY THINE OWNE SWEET LIGHT. | A HYMNE OF THE NATIVITY | 34 | 46 | 106 | 76 |
| SUCH, AND SO RICH, THE FLAMES THAT FROM THINE EYES, | SOSPETTO D'HERODE | 239 | 46 | 109 | 216 |
| BOUNDLESSE AND ABSOLUTE. HELL IS THINE OWNE. | SOSPETTO D'HERODE | 272 | 46 | 109 | 216 |
| THY SELFE SHALT FEEL THINE OWNE FULL JOYES. | IN MEMORY OF LADY MADRE TERESA | 121 | 46 | 131 | 52 |
| THEY FEED OUR SOULES, SHALL CLOATH THINE THERE. | IN MEMORY OF LADY MADRE TERESA | 159 | 46 | 131 | 52 |
| THINE OWN DEARE BOOKS ARE GUILTY, FOR FROM THENCE | AN APOLOGIE FOR HYMNE (TERESA) | 7 | 46 | 136 | 59 |
| PUT ON THY SELFE IN THINE OWN LOOKS. T' OUR EYES | ON A TREATISE OF CHARITY | 2 | 46 | 137 | 69 |
| AND THINE OWNE BEAMES ABOUT THEE. BRING THE BEST | ON A TREATISE OF CHARITY | 9 | 46 | 137 | 69 |
| WITH THINE OWN BLUSH THY CHEEKES ADORNING, | AN HIMNE FOR CIRCUMCISION | 3 | 46 | 141 | 37 |
| BLUSHING FROM THINE EASTERNE BED. | UPON DEATH OF DESIRED HERRYS | 16 | 46 | 168 | 467 |
| THAT HIS SHOULD FADE, WHILE THINE IS GREENE. | UPON DEATH OF DESIRED HERRYS | 20 | 46 | 168 | 467 |
| KEEPE SUCH DISTANCE FROM THINE OWNE. | UPON DEATH OF DESIRED HERRYS | 62 | 46 | 168 | 467 |
| TAKE THINE OWNE MEASURE HERE. DOWNE, DOWNE, AND BOW | UPON STANINOUGH'S DEATH | 11 | 46 | 175 | 475 |
| WITH THINE OWNE GLORYES. AND ART STRANGELY BLEST | UPON YORKE HIS BIRTH | 4 | 46 | 176 | 500 |
| THE BEAMES THAT DANCE IN THOSE FULL STARRES OF THINE. | UPON YORKE HIS BIRTH | 44 | 46 | 176 | 500 |
| THESE HANDS AND THINE WERE HEW'N, THESE CHERRYES MOCKE | UPON YORKE HIS BIRTH | 46 | 46 | 176 | 500 |
| NE'RE MAY A BIRTH OF THINE BE BOUGHT SO DEARE. | UPON YORKE HIS BIRTH | 94 | 46 | 176 | 500 |
| O MAYST THOU THUS MAKE ALL THE YEARE THINE OWNE, | UPON YORKE HIS BIRTH | 96 | 46 | 176 | 500 |
| GIVE THEN THIS RURALL WREATH FIRE FROM THINE EYES. | UPON YORKE HIS BIRTH | 118 | 46 | 176 | 500 |
| HOW AT THE SIGHT DID'ST THOU DRAW BACK THINE EYES, | TO THE MORNING | 7 | 46 | 183 | 497 |
| TWICE DI'D IN THINE OWNE BLUSHES, AND DID'ST RUN | TO THE MORNING | 9 | 46 | 183 | 497 |
| AND THE SAME ROSIE-FINGERD HAND OF THINE, | TO THE MORNING | 45 | 46 | 183 | 497 |
| NO MORE MY PILLOW SHALL THINE ALTAR BE, | TO THE MORNING | 49 | 46 | 183 | 497 |
| THAT SWEET BLUSH OF THINE THAT SHAMETH | OUT OF THE ITALIAN (1) | 3 | 46 | 188 | 545 |
| THINE EYES GRACES, | OUT OF THE ITALIAN (1) | 46 | 46 | 188 | 545 |
| LOOK FROM THINE OWN ILLUSTRIOUS HOME, | TO THE NAME OF JESUS | 117 | 52 | 239 | 30 |
| TAKE THINE OWN WINGS, & COME AWAY. | TO THE NAME OF JESUS | 150 | 52 | 239 | 30 |
| WITH BLUSH OF THINE OWN BLOOD THY DAY ADORNING, | TO THE NAME OF JESUS | 222 | 52 | 239 | 30 |
| NOT FROM THE EAST, BUT FROM THINE EYES. | IN HOLY NATIVITY | 22 | 52 | 246 | 76 |
| WE SAW THINE EYES BREAK FROM THEIR EASTE | IN HOLY NATIVITY | 33 | 52 | 246 | 76 |
| WE SAW THEE BY THINE OWN SWEET LIGHT. | IN HOLY NATIVITY | 36 | 52 | 246 | 76 |
| WE SAW THINE EYES BREAK FROM THEIR EAST | IN HOLY NATIVITY | 74 | 52 | 246 | 76 |
| WE SAW THEE, BY THINE OWN SWEET LIGHT. | IN HOLY NATIVITY | 77 | 52 | 246 | 76 |
| WITH THINE OWN BLUSH THY CHEEKS ADORNING | NEW YEAR'S DAY | 3 | 52 | 251 | 37 |
| THY SELF OUR SUN, THOUGH THINE OWN SHADE. | IN GLORIOUS EPIPHANIE | 47 | 52 | 253 | 39 |
| SHALL ANY DAY BUT THINE ADORE. | IN GLORIOUS EPIPHANIE | 86 | 52 | 253 | 39 |
| TO READ MORE LEGIBLE THINE ORIGINALL RAY. | IN GLORIOUS EPIPHANIE | 211 | 52 | 253 | 39 |
| AND FASTENING ON THINE EYES, | IN GLORIOUS EPIPHANIE | 227 | 52 | 253 | 39 |
| THEREFORE TO THEE & THINE AUSPITIOUS RAY | IN GLORIOUS EPIPHANIE | 233 | 52 | 253 | 39 |
| DEFEND US FROM OUR FOES & THINE. | OFFICE H. CROSS MATINES | 2 | 52 | 265 | 86 |
| OUR ROOTES WITH THINE, | OFFICE H. CROSS PRIME | 14 | 52 | 267 | 91 |
| THEN SITT THEE DOWN, & SING THINE EV'NSONG IN THE SAD | OFFICE H. CROSS EVENSONG | 8 | 52 | 273 | 101 |
| THINE ARMES. AND WITH THY BRIGHT & BLISFULL HEAD | OFFICE H. CROSS EVENSONG | 21 | 52 | 273 | 101 |
| 'CAUSE, THOUGH A HARD & COLD ONE, YET IT IS THINE OWNE. | OFFICE H. CROSS COMPLINE | 12 | 52 | 274 | 105 |
| TAKE BOTH TO THINE ACCOUNT, THAT I & MINE | OFFICE H. CROSS RECOMMENDATION | 3 | 52 | 276 | 106 |
| IN THAT HOUR, & IN THESE, MAY BE ALL THINE. | OFFICE H. CROSS RECOMMENDATION | 4 | 52 | 276 | 106 |
| OF THINE (THE NOBLEST NEST | SANCTA MARIA DOLORUM | 46 | 52 | 283 | 162 |
| IN SHOWRES, AS IF THINE EYES HAD NONE. | UPON BLEEDING CRUCIFIX | 6 | 52 | 288 | 110 |
| FOR THEE TO WEAR, BUT THIS, OF THINE OWN BLOOD. | UPON BODY OF OUR LORD | 6 | 52 | 290 | 24 |
| CONVICTORS OF THINE OWN FULL CUP. | LAUDA SION SALVATOREM | 76 | 52 | 294 | 178 |
| TO FEED OF THEE IN THINE OWN FACE. | LAUDA SION SALVATOREM | 80 | 52 | 294 | 178 |
| AND WITH THE WINGS OF THINE OWN DOVE | DIES IRAE | 27 | 52 | 298 | 186 |
| O LET THINE OWN SOFT BOWELLS PAY | DIES IRAE | 45 | 52 | 298 | 186 |
| THINE WAS THE ROSY DAWN THAT SPRUNG THE DAY | O GLORIOSA DOMINA | 21 | 52 | 302 | 194 |
| THINE FLOATES ABOVE, & IS THE CREAM. | WEEPER | 22 | 52 | 307 | 120 |
| AND DRAW FROM THESE FULL EYES OF THINE | WEEPER | 71 | 52 | 307 | 120 |
| THE APRIL IN THINE EYES. | WEEPER | 81 | 52 | 307 | 120 |
| WHO CALLS'T HIS CROWN TO BE CALL'D THINE, | WEEPER | 122 | 52 | 307 | 120 |
| BY THINE EY'S TINCT ENOBLED THUS | WEEPER | 149 | 52 | 307 | 120 |
| THY SELFE SHALL FEEL THINE OWN FULL JOYES | TERESA | 120 | 52 | 315 | 52 |
| THEY FEED OUR SOULES, SHALL CLOTH THINE THERE. | TERESA | 158 | 52 | 315 | 52 |
| THINE OWN DEAR BOOKES ARE GUILTY. FOR FROM THENCE | AN APOLOGIE FOR (TERESA) HYMNE | 7 | 52 | 322 | 59 |
| TAKE THINE OWN MEASURE HERE. DOWN, DOWN, & BOW | DEATH'S LECTURE | 12 | 52 | 340 | 475 |
| BEFORE THY SELF IN THINE IDAEA. THOU | DEATH'S LECTURE | 13 | 52 | 340 | 475 |
| WAS ONCE CALL'D THINE. | LUKE 2. QUAERIT JESUM | 26 | MS | 379 | 11 |
| OFT HAVE MY HUNGRY KISSES MADE THINE EYES | LUKE 2. QUAERIT JESUM | 35 | MS | 379 | 11 |
| OFT FROM THIS BREAST TO THINE MY LOVE-TOST HEART | LUKE 2. QUAERIT JESUM | 39 | MS | 379 | 11 |
| THEY SHALL PROCLAIME TO ALL, THAT THEY ARE THINE. | UPON BIRTH PRINCESSE E | 8 | MS | 391 | 456 |
| A RIDDLE. (FATHER) STILL ACKNOWLEDG'D THINE | OUT OF GROTIUS | 35 | MS | 398 | 198 |

THING

| | | | | | |
|---|---|---|---|---|---|
| FOND AND FAITHLESSE THING. THAT THUS, | UPON THE DEATH OF A GENTLEMAN | 3 | 46 | 166 | 472 |
| NO SUCH THING. WE GOE TO MEET | THE WEEPER | 137 | 46 | 79 | 120 |
| WHAT BRIGHT SOFT THING IS THIS. | THE TEARE | 1 | 46 | 84 | 50 |
| SLEPT, AND DREAMPT OF NO SUCH THING | A HYMNE OF THE NATIVITY | 6 | 46 | 106 | 76 |
| AND MANY A MISTICKE THING, | ON A PRAYER BOOKE | 76 | 46 | 126 | 139 |
| ONE WHOSE CONSCIENCE WAS A THING, | AN EPITAPH UPON ASHTON | 5 | 46 | 192 | 464 |
| AND EVERY SWEET-LIPP'T THING | TO THE NAME OF JESUS | 47 | 52 | 239 | 30 |
| HE SLEPT. AND DREAM'T OF NO SUCH THING. | IN HOLY NATIVITY | 6 | 52 | 246 | 76 |
| OF SOME MORE PAINFULL THING THEN ALL HIS PAINES. | OFFICE H. CROSS NINTH | 4 | 52 | 271 | 99 |
| SO MUCH A THING OF NOUGHT. | CHARITAS NIMIA | 4 | 52 | 280 | 48 |
| A LOST THING TO THE WORLD, AS IT TO ME. | SANCTA MARIA DOLORUM | 104 | 52 | 283 | 162 |

| | | | | | |
|---|---|---|---|---|---|
| AND MANY A MYSTICK THING | PRAYER TO GENTLE-WOMAN | 82 | 52 | 328 | 139 |

**THINGE**

| | | | | | |
|---|---|---|---|---|---|
| WHO STILES IT ANY THINGE, KNOWES NOT THE SAME. | ON GUNPOWDER-TREASON | 2 | MS | 384 | 458 |

**THINGS**

| | | | | | |
|---|---|---|---|---|---|
| EACH BODY'S PLUMP AND JUCY, ALL THINGS FULL | OUT OF VIRGIL | 15 | 46 | 155 | 529 |
| THE TENDER GROWTH OF THINGS ENDURE THE SENCE | OUT OF VIRGIL | 33 | 46 | 155 | 529 |
| EVER BUBLING THINGS. | THE WEEPER | 3 | 46 | 79 | 120 |
| TO SHINE IN THINGS SO PRETIOUS. | THE WEEPER | 18 | 46 | 79 | 120 |
| NOTHING, WEE OWE ALL THINGS THAT BEE. | AND HE ANSWERED NOTHING | 2 | 46 | 91 | 22 |
| GOD SPAKE ONCE WHEN HEE ALL THINGS MADE, | AND HE ANSWERED NOTHING | 3 | 46 | 91 | 22 |
| BUT TO POORE SHEPHEARDS, SIMPLE THINGS, | A HYMNE OF THE NATIVITY | 74 | 46 | 106 | 76 |
| THERE WHERE ONE CENTER RECONCILES ALL THINGS. | SOSPETTO D'HERODE | 34 | 46 | 109 | 216 |
| STRUCKE WITH THESE GREAT CONCURRENCES OF THINGS, | SOSPETTO D'HERODE | 137 | 46 | 109 | 216 |
| THE FACE OF THINGS, FROM HER DIRE EYES HAD RUN, | SOSPETTO D'HERODE | 383 | 46 | 109 | 216 |
| A THOUSAND PROPHECIES THAT TALKE STRANGE THINGS, | SOSPETTO D'HERODE | 497 | 46 | 109 | 216 |
| FLIGHTS SCORNE THE LAZIE DUST, AND THINGS THAT DYE. | AN APOLOGIE FOR HYMNE (TERESA) | 28 | 46 | 136 | 59 |
| THE ENTITY OF THINGS THAT ARE NOT YET. | ON HOPE | 12 | 46 | 143 | 71 |
| THE FACE OF THINGS, AN UNIVERSALL SMILE. | ON A FOULE MORNING | 10 | 46 | 181 | 495 |
| OF HIM WHO NEVER SLEEPS, ALL THINGS THAT ARE, | TO THE NAME OF JESUS | 56 | 52 | 239 | 30 |
| BUT TO POOR SHEPHEARDS, HOME-SPUN THINGS. | IN HOLY NATIVITY | 94 | 52 | 246 | 76 |
| AND PUNISH BEST THINGS WORST. BECAUSE THEY STOOD | IN GLORIOUS EPIPHANIE | 107 | 52 | 253 | 39 |
| WHO LEND'ST TO ALL THINGS ALL THE LIFE THEY HAVE. | OFFICE H. CROSS COMPLINE | 10 | 52 | 274 | 105 |
| OF LOVE, SWEET BITTER THINGS. | SANCTA MARIA DOLORUM | 96 | 52 | 283 | 162 |
| IN DIFFERENT SPECIES, NAMES NOT THINGS. | LAUDA SION SALVATOREM | 39 | 52 | 294 | 178 |
| HEARS'T THOU, MY SOUL, WHAT SERIOUS THINGS | DIES IRAE | 1 | 52 | 298 | 186 |
| HE THAT MADE ALL THINGS, HAD NOT DONE | O GLORIOSA DOMINA | 5 | 52 | 302 | 194 |
| THE FEAST OF ALL THINGS FEEDS ON THEE. | O GLORIOSA DOMINA | 10 | 52 | 302 | 194 |
| EVER BUBLING THINGS. | WEEPER | 3 | 52 | 307 | 120 |
| TO SHINE IN THINGS SO PRETIOUS. | WEEPER | 18 | 52 | 307 | 120 |
| FLIGHTS SCORN THE LAZY DUST, & THINGS THAT DY. | AN APOLOGIE FOR (TERESA) HYMNE | 28 | 52 | 322 | 59 |
| ALL THOSE FAIR & FLAGRANT THINGS, | FLAMING HEART | 34 | 52 | 324 | 61 |
| HIS BE THE BRAVERY OF ALL THOSE BRIGHT THINGS, | FLAMING HEART | 65 | 52 | 324 | 61 |
| TO BEAR ME HARMLESSE THROUGH THE HARDEST THINGS. | ALEXIAS FIRST ELEGIE | 18 | 52 | 334 | 204 |
| THINGS THAT IN HARDNESSE MORE ALLUDE TO THEE. | ALEXIAS SECONDE ELEGIE | 16 | 52 | 335 | 207 |
| THAT NIP THE BOSOME OF THE WORLDS BEST THINGS, | DESCRIPTION RELIGIOUS HOUSE | 26 | 52 | 338 | 213 |
| CROWN'D WOES AWAKE. AS THINGS TOO WISE FOR SLEEP. | DESCRIPTION RELIGIOUS HOUSE | 29 | 52 | 338 | 213 |
| LOVE, THAT LENDS HASTE TO HEAVIEST THINGS, | AGAINST IRRESOLUTION AND DELAY | 27 | 52 | 347 | 146 |
| CHIDE YOUR DELAY. YEA THOSE DULL THINGS, | AGAINST IRRESOLUTION AND DELAY | 47 | 52 | 347 | 146 |
| ALL THINGS SWEAR FRIENDS TO FAIR AND GOOD. | AGAINST IRRESOLUTION AND DELAY | 57 | 52 | 347 | 146 |
| THE FALL OF ALL THINGS IT PRAESAG'D, ITS OWNE | ON GUNPOWDER-TREASON | 52 | MS | 384 | 458 |
| HER GLORIES I SHOULD DIMME WITH THINGS SOE GROSSE, | UPON BIRTH PRINCESSE E | 53 | MS | 391 | 456 |

**THINGES**

| | | | | | |
|---|---|---|---|---|---|
| DOTH GRASPE THE FATE OF THINGES, AND SHARE TH' EVENTS | OUT OF GROTIUS | 2 | MS | 398 | 198 |

**THINK**

| | | | | | |
|---|---|---|---|---|---|
| THE VERY TERME, I THINK, WAS FOUND | THE TEARE | 5 | 46 | 84 | 50 |
| NOR MUST YOU THINK IT MUCH | TO THE NAME OF JESUS | 51 | 52 | 239 | 30 |
| TO THINK OUGHT SWEET BUT THAT WHICH SMELLS OF THEE. | TO THE NAME OF JESUS | 172 | 52 | 239 | 30 |
| THINK MUCH THAT THOU SHOULDST MOURN ALONE. | SANCTA MARIA DOLORUM | 60 | 52 | 283 | 162 |
| LOVE COULD NOT THINK, TRUTH COULD NOT SAY. | ADORO TE | 16 | 52 | 291 | 172 |

**THINKE**

| | | | | | |
|---|---|---|---|---|---|
| GOE POORE MAN THINKE WHAT SHALL BEE. | IN PRAISE OF LESSIUS | 11 | 46 | 156 | 510 |
| MAY THINKE HIS LABOUR VAINELY GONE, | OUT OF GREEKE CUPID'S CRYER | 10 | 46 | 159 | 519 |
| INTO THIS LESSE APPEARANCE. IF YOU THINKE, | UPON BISHOP ANDREWES PICTURE | 14 | 46 | 163 | 490 |
| IS NOT THE SOILE A KIND ONE (THINKE YE) THAT RETURNS | UPON THORNES FROM LORDS HEAD | 7 | 46 | 96 | 23 |
| DISDAINES TO THINKE THAT HEAV'N THUNDERS ALONE. | SOSPETTO D'HERODE | 56 | 46 | 109 | 216 |
| ABOVE HIS FEARES, AND THINKE IT CANNOT BE. | SOSPETTO D'HERODE | 154 | 46 | 109 | 216 |
| THINKE YOU HAVE AN ANGELL BY TH' WINGS. | ON MR. G. HERBERTS BOOKE | 6 | 46 | 130 | 68 |
| WHAT. THINKE WE TO NO OTHER END, | UPON DEATH OF DESIRED HERRYS | 25 | 46 | 168 | 467 |
| AS IF HE SCORN'D TO THINKE OF NIGHT, | UPON DEATH OF DESIRED HERRYS | 50 | 46 | 168 | 467 |
| FLY THEN, AND DOE NOT THINKE WITH HER TO STAY. | ON A FOULE MORNING | 37 | 46 | 181 | 495 |
| MIGHTY QUEEN, TO THINKE IT LONG, | TO THE QUEEN | 2 | 48 | 215 | 501 |
| THAT MAN (I THINKE) WRESTED THE FEEBLE LIFE | HORATIJ ILLE & NEFASTO | 7 | MS | 382 | 530 |
| LEFT MANY A STARRY TEARE, TO THINKE HOW SOONE | AN ELEGY MR STANNINOW | 41 | MS | 394 | 473 |

**THINKS**

| | | | | | |
|---|---|---|---|---|---|
| YET THINKS IT SO. BUT EV'N THAT TOO | TO THE QUEEN | 5 | 48 | 215 | 501 |
| OF MARTYR. YET SHE THINKS IT SHAME | TERESA | 16 | 52 | 315 | 52 |

**THINKES**

| | | | | | |
|---|---|---|---|---|---|
| BUT O ME THINKES 'TIS A FARRE GREATER ONE | UPON ASSE THAT BORE SAVIOUR | 11 | 46 | 90 | 19 |
| SHE THINKES NOT FIT SUCH HE HER FACE SHOULD SEE, | SOSPETTO D'HERODE | 413 | 46 | 109 | 216 |
| OF MARTYR, YET SHEE THINKES IT SHAME | IN MEMORY OF LADY MADRE TERESA | 16 | 46 | 131 | 52 |
| THUS LOW STANDS UP (ME THINKES) THUS, AND DEFYES | UPON STANINOUGH'S DEATH | 28 | 46 | 175 | 475 |
| THUS LOW, STANDS UP (ME THINKES,) THUS & DEFIES | DEATH'S LECTURE | 30 | 52 | 340 | 475 |
| ARE CHEATED OF THEIR PAINES. ORION THINKES | HORATIJ ILLE & NEFASTO | 55 | MS | 382 | 530 |

**THINKING**

| | | | | | |
|---|---|---|---|---|---|
| THINKING HER FATHER HAD REMOV'D HIS COURT. | UPON KINGS CORONATION | 32 | MS | 390 | 453 |

THIRD

| | | | | | |
|---|---|---|---|---|---|
| UP TO THE THIRD RING. O'RE THE SHORE WAS SPREAD | THE BEGINNING OF HELIODORUS | 14 | 46 | 156 | 517 |
| TH'HAST LEFT THE THIRD COUGH NOW NO BUSINESSE HERE. | OUT OF MARTIALL | 6 | 46 | 188 | 527 |
| THE SAME BRIGHT BUSYNES (YE THIRD HEAVENS) WITH YOU. | TO THE NAME OF JESUS | 110 | 52 | 239 | 30 |
| THE THIRD HOUR'S DEAFEN'D WITH THE CRY | OFFICE H. CROSS THIRD | 1 | 52 | 268 | 93 |

THIRST

| | | | | | |
|---|---|---|---|---|---|
| NOR LET THE MILKY FONTS THAT BATH YOUR THIRST, | TO INFANT MARTYRS | 3 | 46 | 88 | 10 |
| TO DROWNE THE WANTONNESSE OF HIS WILD THIRST. | OUR LORD IN HIS CIRCUMCISION | 8 | 46 | 98 | 9 |
| SUCH THIRST TO DYE, AS DARE DRINKE UP, | IN MEMORY OF LADY MADRE TERESA | 37 | 46 | 131 | 52 |
| IS TORTUR'D THIRST, IT SELFE, TOO SWEET A CUP. | OFFICE H. CROSS SIXT | 9 | 52 | 270 | 97 |

THIRSTS

| | | | | | |
|---|---|---|---|---|---|
| SUCH THIRSTS TO DY, AS DARES DRINK UP, | TERESA | 37 | 52 | 315 | 52 |
| AND BY THY THIRSTS OF LOVE MORE LARGE THEN THEY. | FLAMING HEART | 98 | 52 | 324 | 61 |

THIRSTY

| | | | | | |
|---|---|---|---|---|---|
| LO HOW THE THIRSTY LANDS | TO THE NAME OF JESUS | 129 | 52 | 239 | 30 |
| SOE LOW TO GIVE HIS THIRSTY STALLIONS DRINKE. | UPON GUNPOWDER TREASON | 40 | MS | 386 | 460 |
| OR THIRSTY TREASON OFFER ONCE TO SIPPE | UPON GUNPOWDER TREASON | 40 | MS | 387 | 461 |

THOMAS

| | | | | | |
|---|---|---|---|---|---|
| THOMAS MIGHT TOUCH. NONE BUT MIGHT SEE | ADORO TE | 23 | 52 | 291 | 172 |

THORNE

| | | | | | |
|---|---|---|---|---|---|
| OR NAILE, OR THORNE, OR SPEARE HAVE WRIT IN THEE. | ON MARKES OF SAVIOURS WOUNDS | 2 | 46 | 86 | 28 |

THORNES

| | | | | | |
|---|---|---|---|---|---|
| ROSES FOR THORNES. | UPON THORNES FROM LORDS HEAD | 8 | 46 | 96 | 23 |
| THE THORNES THAT THY BLEST BROWES ENCLOSES | ON BLEEDING WOUNDS OF LORD | 22 | 46 | 101 | 110 |
| TO A VAST FIELD OF THORNES, TEN THOUSAND SPEARES | SOSPETTO D'HERODE | 475 | 46 | 109 | 216 |
| ROSES FOR THORNES. | UPON CROWNE OF THORNS | 6 | 52 | 290 | 23 |
| WITH WHIPS OF THORNES AND KNOTTY VIPERS TWIN'D | SOSPETTO D'HERODE | 67 | 46 | 109 | 216 |

THRONES

| | | | | | |
|---|---|---|---|---|---|
| STILL THRONES & DOMINATIONS WOULD ADORE THEE | CHARITAS NIMIA | 24 | 52 | 280 | 48 |

THOUGHT

| | | | | | |
|---|---|---|---|---|---|
| FOUND THE PURE ISSUE OF HIS THOUGHT. | OUT OF GREEKE CUPID'S CRYER | 24 | 46 | 159 | 519 |
| WHOSE FAIRE ILLUSTRIOUS SOULE, LED HIS FREE THOUGHT | UPON BISHOP ANDREWES PICTURE | 5 | 46 | 163 | 490 |
| LOVELY SION THOUGHT ON THEE. | PSALME 137 | 6 | 46 | 104 | 7 |
| OFT IN HIS DEEPE THOUGHT HE REVOLVES THE DARKE | SOSPETTO D'HERODE | 91 | 46 | 109 | 216 |
| DOWNE MY PROUD THOUGHT, AND LEAVE IT IN A TRANCE. | SOSPETTO D'HERODE | 204 | 46 | 109 | 216 |
| LITTLE, ALAS, THOUGHT THEY | TO THE NAME OF JESUS | 207 | 52 | 239 | 30 |
| UNLESSE'T BE RARE, WHAT'S THOUGHT UPON. | PETRONIJ ALES PHASIACIS PETITA | 20 | MS | 382 | 526 |

THOUGHTS

| | | | | | |
|---|---|---|---|---|---|
| WARME THOUGHTS FREE SPIRITS, FLATTERING | IN PRAISE OF LESSIUS | 43 | 46 | 156 | 510 |
| THEY ROUSE HIM, WHEN HIS RANKE THOUGHTS NEED A STING. | SOSPETTO D'HERODE | 68 | 46 | 109 | 216 |
| INTANGLES HIS LOST THOUGHTS, PAST GETTING OUT. | SOSPETTO D'HERODE | 192 | 46 | 109 | 216 |
| WHILE NEW THOUGHTS BOYL'D IN HIS ENRAGED BREST, | SOSPETTO D'HERODE | 193 | 46 | 109 | 216 |
| IMMORTALL STINGS TO THY GREAT THOUGHTS, AND THEE. | SOSPETTO D'HERODE | 464 | 46 | 109 | 216 |
| WARM THOUGHTS, FREE SPIRITS FLATTERING | TEMPERANCE | 41 | 52 | 342 | 510 |
| AND WHATSOE'RE WILD SINNES BLACK THOUGHTS DOE FEED. | HORATIJ ILLE & NEFASTO | 12 | MS | 382 | 530 |

THOUSAND

| | | | | | |
|---|---|---|---|---|---|
| INTO A THOUSAND SWEET DISTINGUISH'D TONES, | MUSICKS DUELL | 23 | 46 | 149 | 535 |
| ONE EYE. A THOUSAND RATHER, AND A THOUSAND MORE | IT IS BETTER TO GO WITH EYE | 1 | 46 | 93 | 16 |
| ONE EYE. A THOUSAND RATHER, AND A THOUSAND MORE | IT IS BETTER TO GO WITH EYE | 1 | 46 | 93 | 16 |
| A THOUSAND SWEET BABES FROM THEIR MOTHERS BREST. | SOSPETTO D'HERODE | 4 | 46 | 109 | 216 |
| TO A VAST FIELD OF THORNES, TEN THOUSAND SPEARES | SOSPETTO D'HERODE | 475 | 46 | 109 | 216 |
| A THOUSAND PROPHECIES THAT TALKE STRANGE THINGS, | SOSPETTO D'HERODE | 497 | 46 | 109 | 216 |
| A THOUSAND ANGELLS IN ONE POINT CAN DWELL. | ON A PRAYER BOOKE | 8 | 46 | 126 | 139 |
| A THOUSAND UNKNOWNE RITES | ON A PRAYER BOOKE | 73 | 46 | 126 | 139 |
| AN HUNDRED THOUSAND LOVES AND GRACES, | ON A PRAYER BOOKE | 75 | 46 | 126 | 139 |
| OF BLESSINGS, AND TEN THOUSAND MORE. | ON A PRAYER BOOKE | 82 | 46 | 126 | 139 |
| AT ONCE, TEN THOUSAND PARADISES | ON A PRAYER BOOKE | 107 | 46 | 126 | 139 |
| A THOUSAND COLD DEATHS IN ONE CUP. | IN MEMORY OF LADY MADRE TERESA | 38 | 46 | 131 | 52 |
| OF THOUSAND SOULES WHOSE HAPPY NAMES, | IN MEMORY OF LADY MADRE TERESA | 175 | 46 | 131 | 52 |
| A THOUSAND RUDDY HOPES SMIL'D IN EACH BUD, | UPON DEATH OF HERRYS | 25 | 46 | 167 | 466 |
| A THOUSAND, AND A HUNDRED, SCORE | OUT OF CATULLUS | 11 | 46 | 194 | 523 |
| AN HUNDRED, AND A THOUSAND MORE, | OUT OF CATULLUS | 12 | 46 | 194 | 523 |
| TILL ANOTHER THOUSAND SMOTHER | OUT OF CATULLUS | 13 | 46 | 194 | 523 |
| MANY A THOUSAND, MANY A HUNDRED. | OUT OF CATULLUS | 16 | 46 | 194 | 523 |
| A THOUSAND BLEST ARABIAS DWELL. | TO THE NAME OF JESUS | 184 | 52 | 239 | 30 |
| A THOUSAND HILLS OF FRANKINCENSE. | TO THE NAME OF JESUS | 185 | 52 | 239 | 30 |
| AND TEN THOUSAND PARADISES | TO THE NAME OF JESUS | 187 | 52 | 239 | 30 |
| HOW MANY THOUSAND MERCYES THERE | TO THE NAME OF JESUS | 191 | 52 | 239 | 30 |
| LET ONE, OR ONE THOUSAND BE | LAUDA SION SALVATOREM | 45 | 52 | 294 | 178 |
| A THOUSAND COLD DEATHS IN ONE CUP. | TERESA | 38 | 52 | 315 | 52 |
| OF THOUSAND SOULES, WHOSE HAPPY NAMES | TERESA | 174 | 52 | 315 | 52 |
| TEN THOUSAND ANGELS IN ONE POINT CAN DWELL. | PRAYER TO GENTLE-WOMAN | 14 | 52 | 328 | 139 |

|  |  |  |  |  |  |
|---|---|---|---|---|---|
| A THOUSAND UNKNOWN RITES | PRAYER TO GENTLE-WOMAN | 79 | 52 | 328 | 139 |
| A HUNDRED THOUSAND GOODS, GLORIES, & GRACES, | PRAYER TO GENTLE-WOMAN | 81 | 52 | 328 | 139 |
| OF BLESSINGS & TEN THOUSAND MORE | PRAYER TO GENTLE-WOMAN | 88 | 52 | 328 | 139 |
| AT ONCE TEN THOUSAND PARADISES. | PRAYER TO GENTLE-WOMAN | 113 | 52 | 328 | 139 |
| A THOUSAND HELICONS THE MUSES SEND | AN ELEGIE ON DR PORTER | 39 | MS | 395 | 476 |

THOUSANDS

|  |  |  |  |  |  |
|---|---|---|---|---|---|
| THOUSANDS OF CROWND SOULES, THRONG TO BEE | IN MEMORY OF LADY MADRE TERESA | 167 | 46 | 131 | 52 |
| THOUSANDS OF CROWN'D SOULES THRONG TO BE | TERESA | 166 | 52 | 315 | 52 |
| WHOM LONG NONE COULD OBTAIN, THOUGH THOUSANDS TRY'D, | ALEXIAS FIRST ELEGIE | 2 | 52 | 334 | 204 |
| WHEN THOUSANDS SOUGHT MY LOVE, LOV'D NONE BUT THEE. | ALEXIAS THIRD ELEGIE | 54 | 52 | 336 | 209 |

THRALL

|  |  |  |  |  |  |
|---|---|---|---|---|---|
| TO THAT ONE SENSE, MADE ALL ELSE THRALL. | OUT OF THE ITALIAN (3) | 7 | 46 | 190 | 549 |

THREAD

|  |  |  |  |  |  |
|---|---|---|---|---|---|
| GENTLY UNTWIN'D HIS THREAD OF LIFE. | AN EPITAPH UPON ASHTON | 26 | 46 | 192 | 464 |

THREADS

|  |  |  |  |  |  |
|---|---|---|---|---|---|
| HIS FINGERS STRUGGLE WITH THE VOCALL THREADS. | MUSICKS DUELL | 122 | 46 | 149 | 535 |

THREDS

|  |  |  |  |  |  |
|---|---|---|---|---|---|
| HER CRUELL CLOATHES OF COSTLY THREDS THEY WEAVE, | SOSPETTO D'HERODE | 343 | 46 | 109 | 216 |
| MY THREDS OF LIFE, IF THEN I SHALL NOT LIVE | EX EUPHORMIONE | 11 | MS | 392 | 525 |

THREATS

|  |  |  |  |  |  |
|---|---|---|---|---|---|
| WHICH WAY IT THREATS, WITH FEARE THE MERCHANTS MIND | HORATIJ ILLE & NEFASTO | 19 | MS | 382 | 530 |
| ALL THIS IT THREATS, & MORE HORROR, THAT FLIES | ON GUNPOWDER-TREASON | 45 | MS | 384 | 458 |
| ALL THIS IT ONLY THREATS. THE METEOR LY'D. | ON GUNPOWDER-TREASON | 49 | MS | 384 | 458 |

THREAT'ST

|  |  |  |  |  |  |
|---|---|---|---|---|---|
| HEIRE OF THE SUNS FIRST BEAMES, WHY THREAT'ST THOU SO. | TO THE MORNING | 53 | 46 | 183 | 497 |

THREATEN

|  |  |  |  |  |  |
|---|---|---|---|---|---|
| THAT TO THE MIGHTY NEPTUNE'S SELF DARE THREATEN WRACK. | WHY ARE YEE AFRAID | 8 | 46 | 88 | 15 |

THREATNING

|  |  |  |  |  |  |
|---|---|---|---|---|---|
| THREATNING ALL TO OVERFLOW, | ON BLEEDING WOUNDS OF LORD | 34 | 46 | 101 | 110 |

THREE

|  |  |  |  |  |  |
|---|---|---|---|---|---|
| THREE RIGOUROUS VIRGINS WAITING STILL BEHIND, | SOSPETTO D'HERODE | 65 | 46 | 109 | 216 |
| THREE KINGS (OR WHAT IS MORE) THREE WISE MEN WENT | SOSPETTO D'HERODE | 135 | 46 | 109 | 216 |
| THREE KINGS (OR WHAT IS MORE) THREE WISE MEN WENT | SOSPETTO D'HERODE | 135 | 46 | 109 | 216 |
| OR RATHER ALL THE OTHER THREE IN ONE. | SOSPETTO D'HERODE | 290 | 46 | 109 | 216 |
| THRICE WILL I PAY THREE TEARES, TO SHOW HOW TRUE | TO THE MORNING | 40 | 46 | 183 | 497 |
| THREE SAD HOUR'S SACKCLOTH THEN SHALL SHOW TO US | IN GLORIOUS EPIPHANIE | 157 | 52 | 253 | 39 |
| THREE KINGDOMES TO SUPPLY THIS DAY'S THREE KINGS. | TO THE QUEEN'S MAJESTY | 28 | 52 | 261 | 47 |
| THREE KINGDOMES TO SUPPLY THIS DAY'S THREE KINGS. | TO THE QUEEN'S MAJESTY | 28 | 52 | 261 | 47 |
| BY THREE DAIES LOSSE AETERNALLY TO SAVE. | MATH. 16. 25. WHOSOEVER SHALL | 4 | MS | 381 | 16 |
| THREE COLEBLACK SISTERS, (WHOSE LONG SUTTY HAIRE, | UPON GUNPOWDER TREASON | 9 | MS | 387 | 461 |
| I MEANE THOSE THREE GREAT STARRES, WHO WELL MAY SCORNE | UPON KINGS CORONATION | 31 | MS | 389 | 454 |

THREEFOLD

|  |  |  |  |  |  |
|---|---|---|---|---|---|
| HEE SAW A THREEFOLD SUN, WITH RICH ENCREASE, | SOSPETTO D'HERODE | 121 | 46 | 109 | 216 |

THREW

|  |  |  |  |  |  |
|---|---|---|---|---|---|
| THREW ALL THE LOSSE. | OFFICE H. CROSS THIRD | 13 | 52 | 268 | 93 |

THRICE

|  |  |  |  |  |  |
|---|---|---|---|---|---|
| THRICE HOWL'D THE CAVES OF NIGHT, AND THRICE THE SOUND, | SOSPETTO D'HERODE | 297 | 46 | 109 | 216 |
| THRICE HOWL'D THE CAVES OF NIGHT, AND THRICE THE SOUND, | SOSPETTO D'HERODE | 297 | 46 | 109 | 216 |
| O HAPPY AND THRICE HAPPY SHEE | ON A PRAYER BOOKE | 91 | 46 | 126 | 139 |
| A DART THRICE DIPT IN THAT RICH FLAME, | IN MEMORY OF LADY MADRE TERESA | 81 | 46 | 131 | 52 |
| THRICE WILL I PAY THREE TEARES, TO SHOW HOW TRUE | TO THE MORNING | 40 | 46 | 183 | 497 |
| A DART THRICE DIP'T IN THAT RICH FLAME | TERESA | 81 | 52 | 315 | 52 |
| O HAPPY & THRICE HAPPY SHE | PRAYER TO GENTLE-WOMAN | 97 | 52 | 328 | 139 |

SPEND-THRIFT

|  |  |  |  |  |  |
|---|---|---|---|---|---|
| FAIR SPEND-THRIFT OF THY SELF, THY MEASURE | WEEPER | 128 | 52 | 307 | 120 |

THRILLS

|  |  |  |  |  |  |
|---|---|---|---|---|---|
| SHEE GIVES HIM BACKE, HER SUPPLE BREST THRILLS OUT | MUSICKS DUELL | 57 | 46 | 149 | 535 |

## THRIVE

| | | | | |
|---|---|---|---|---|
| BY WHICH THEY THRIVE, | TO THE NAME OF JESUS | 157 | 52 239 | 30 |
| OUR GOD WOULD THRIVE TOO FAST, AND BE | AGAINST IRRESOLUTION AND DELAY | 63 | 52 347 | 146 |

## THRIV'D

| | | | | |
|---|---|---|---|---|
| THRIV'D IN THESE HAPPY GROUNDS, THE EARTH'S JUST PRIDE, | UPON DEATH OF HERRYS | 3 | 46 167 | 466 |

## THROAT

| | | | | |
|---|---|---|---|---|
| THROUGH THE SLEEKE PASSAGE OF HER OPEN THROAT. | MUSICKS DUELL | 38 | 46 149 | 535 |
| AND ROULE THEMSELVES OVER HER LUBRICKE THROAT | MUSICKS DUELL | 64 | 46 149 | 535 |
| THUS HIGH, THUS LOW, AS IF HER SILVER THROAT | MUSICKS DUELL | 100 | 46 149 | 535 |

## THROTE

| | | | | |
|---|---|---|---|---|
| FOR LODG'D SO NE'RE YOUR SWEETEST THROTE | THOUGH NOW 'TIS NEITHER | 13 | MS 397 | 492 |

## THROATE

| | | | | |
|---|---|---|---|---|
| HAD DEALT TOO ROUGHLY WITH HER TENDER THROATE, | MUSICKS DUELL | 159 | 46 149 | 535 |
| CONSPIR'D WITH DARKNES 'GAINST THE STRANGERS THROATE. | HORATIJ ILLE & NEFASTO | 9 | MS 382 | 530 |

## THROATS

| | | | | |
|---|---|---|---|---|
| OF SWEET-LIPP'D ANGELL-IMPS, THAT SWILL THEIR THROATS | MUSICKS DUELL | 76 | 46 149 | 535 |

## THROATES

| | | | | |
|---|---|---|---|---|
| OF CONFESSOURS, WHOSE THROATES ANSWERING HIS SWORDS, | SOSPETTO D'HERODE | 7 | 46 109 | 216 |

## THROES

| | | | | |
|---|---|---|---|---|
| AND PAINES, HER PANGS & THROES. | SANCTA MARIA DOLORUM | 8 | 52 283 | 162 |

## THRONE

| | | | | |
|---|---|---|---|---|
| SHEE SITS IN SUCH A THRONE AS THIS, | THE WEEPER | 62 | 46 79 | 120 |
| HEE FILLS A BURNISHT THRONE OF QUENCHLESSE FIRE. | SOSPETTO D'HERODE | 42 | 46 109 | 216 |
| ASSIST THE THRONE OF TH' IRON-SCEPTRED KING. | SOSPETTO D'HERODE | 66 | 46 109 | 216 |
| WHO IN A THRONE OF STARS THUNDERS ABOVE. | SOSPETTO D'HERODE | 176 | 46 109 | 216 |
| OF THOSE WHOSE LARGE BREASTS BUILT A THRONE | IN MEMORY OF LADY MADRE TERESA | 10 | 46 131 | 52 |
| A MAJESTIE THAT MAY BESEEM THY THRONE. | ON A TREATISE OF CHARITY | 20 | 46 137 | 69 |
| STEPT FROM HER THRONE OF STARRES DEIGNES TO BE SEENE. | UPON YORKE HIS BIRTH | 72 | 46 176 | 500 |
| HER STARRY THRONE. WHOSE HOLY HEATS CAN WARME | TO THE MORNING | 25 | 46 183 | 497 |
| AND PEEP & PROFFER AT THY SPARKLING THRONE. | IN GLORIOUS EPIPHANIE | 225 | 52 253 | 39 |
| THE KING HIMSELF IS. THOU HIS HUMBLE THRONE. | OFFICE H. CROSS EVENSONG | 23 | 52 273 | 101 |
| IT WAS THY WOOD HE MEANT SHOULD MAKE THE THRONE | VEXILLA REGIS | 23 | 52 277 | 156 |
| LARG THRONE OF LOVE. ROYALLY SPRED | VEXILLA REGIS | 25 | 52 277 | 156 |
| SHOULD NOT THE KING STILL KEEPE HIS THRONE | CHARITAS NIMIA | 35 | 52 280 | 48 |
| OF THOSE WHOSE SPATIOUS BOSOMES SPREAD A THRONE | TERESA | 10 | 52 315 | 52 |
| AND GETT A STARRY THRONE BEFORE HIS TIME. | ON GUNPOWDER-TREASON | 36 | MS 364 | 458 |
| SHOULD BEATE HER HEADLONG FROM HER JETTY THRONE. | UPON GUNPOWDER TREASON | 26 | MS 386 | 460 |
| FORTHWITH EACH GOD STEPT FROM HIS STARRY THRONE. | UPON GUNPOWDER TREASON | 53 | MS 387 | 461 |

## THRON'D

| | | | | |
|---|---|---|---|---|
| THRON'D IN THY GRAVE. | EASTER DAY | 17 | 46 100 | 26 |

## THRONG

| | | | | |
|---|---|---|---|---|
| THEN STARTS SHEE SUDDENLY INTO A THRONG | MUSICKS DUELL | 62 | 46 149 | 535 |
| EVEN SUCH AS THESE, LAUGH, TILL A VENGING THRONG | PSALME 137 | 33 | 46 104 | 7 |
| THOUSANDS OF CROWND SOULES, THRONG TO BEE | IN MEMORY OF LADY MADRE TERESA | 167 | 46 131 | 52 |
| THOSE MIGHTY GENII THRONG, WHICH WELL MIGHT BEE | UPON YORKE HIS BIRTH | 10 | 46 176 | 500 |
| AND PLACE IN THE GREAT THRONG | TO THE NAME OF JESUS | 90 | 52 239 | 30 |
| THE CONDUCT OF ADORING SPIRITS, THAT THRONG | TO THE NAME OF JESUS | 152 | 52 239 | 30 |
| IN THIS ILLUSTRIOUS THRONG, YOUR LOFTY FLOUD | TO THE QUEEN'S MAJESTY | 15 | 52 261 | 47 |
| THOUSANDS OF CROWN'D SOULES THRONG TO BE | TERESA | 166 | 52 315 | 52 |
| THE GOLDEN THRONG | TO SAME CONCERNING CHOISE | 27 | 52 331 | 66 |

## THRONGING

| | | | | |
|---|---|---|---|---|
| THE THRONGING CLOTTED MULTITUDE DOTH FEAST. | HORATIJ ILLE & NEFASTO | 49 | MS 382 | 530 |

## THRUW

| | | | | |
|---|---|---|---|---|
| AND FRISKE IN CURL'D MAEANDERS. HEE WILL THROW | ON A FOULE MORNING | 20 | 46 181 | 495 |

## THROWS

| | | | | |
|---|---|---|---|---|
| AND FENCE THE HANGING SWORD HEAV'N THROWS UPON THEE. | SOSPETTO D'HERODE | 460 | 46 109 | 216 |

## THROWES

| | | | | |
|---|---|---|---|---|
| HEE THROWES HIS ARME, AND WITH A LONG DRAWNE DASH | MUSICKS DUELL | 30 | 46 149 | 535 |
| AMAZED SOL THROWES OF HIS MOURNFULL WEEDS, | UPON KINGS CORONATION | 15 | MS 390 | 453 |

## THROWNE

| | | | |
|---|---|---|---|
| WAS THROWNE ALAS, AND GOT A DEADLY FALL. | HIGH MOUNTED ON AN ANT | 2 | 46 161 523 |

## THROUNE

| | | | |
|---|---|---|---|
| IF SOE, OH NEPTUNE, MAY SHE FARRE BE THROUNE | ON GUNPOWDER-TREASON | 7 | MS 384 458 |
| HEAVEN KICKT THE MONSTER DOUNE. DOUNE IT WAS THROUNE, | ON GUNPOWDER-TREASON | 51 | MS 384 458 |

## THRUST

| | | | |
|---|---|---|---|
| HER FALLING THOU DID'ST URGE AND THRUST, | PSALME 137 | 29 | 46 104 7 |

## THRUSTS

| | | | |
|---|---|---|---|
| EACH BIGGE WITH BUSINESSE THRUSTS THE OTHER, | AGAINST IRRESOLUTION AND DELAY | 43 | 52 347 146 |

## THUNDER

| | | | |
|---|---|---|---|
| THAT HE SHOULD FIND A TONGUE AND VOCALL THUNDER, | UPON ASSE THAT BORE SAVIOUR | 9 | 46 90 19 |
| IN LANGUAGE OF HIS THUNDER, THOU ART EVEN | SOSPETTO D'HERODE | 270 | 46 109 216 |
| STORME AND THUNDER | OUT OF THE ITALIAN (1) | 34 | 46 166 545 |
| A WINTERS THUNDER WITH A GROANE SHALL SCARE, | ON GUNPOWDER-TREASON | 28 | MS 384 458 |

## THUNDERS

| | | | |
|---|---|---|---|
| DISDAINES TO THINKE THAT HEAV'N THUNDERS ALONE. | SOSPETTO D'HERODE | 56 | 46 109 216 |
| WHO IN A THRONE OF STARS THUNDERS ABOVE. | SOSPETTO D'HERODE | 176 | 46 109 216 |
| WHEN 'GAINST THE THUNDERS MOUTH WEE MARCHED FORTH. | SOSPETTO D'HERODE | 284 | 46 109 216 |

## THUNDRING

| | | | |
|---|---|---|---|
| OF SHORT THICKE SOBS, WHOSE THUNDRING VOLLEYES FLOAT, | MUSICKS DUELL | 63 | 46 149 535 |
| THUNDRING UPON THE BANKES OF THOSE BLACK LAKES | SOSPETTO D'HERODE | 298 | 46 109 216 |

## THUNDERER

| | | | |
|---|---|---|---|
| UPP TO TH' ALMIGHTY THUNDERER THEY HIED, | UPON GUNPOWDER TREASON | 54 | MS 386 460 |

## THYRSIS

| | | | |
|---|---|---|---|
| TELL HIM THYRSIS WHAT TH'HAST SEEN. | A HYMNE OF THE NATIVITY | 16 | 46 106 76 |
| TELL HIM, THYRSIS, WHAT TH'HAST SEEN. | IN HOLY NATIVITY | 16 | 52 246 76 |

## THYSELFE

| | | | |
|---|---|---|---|
| THEN WEEPE THYSELFE INTO A SEA OF TEARES. | AN ELEGIE ON DR PORTER | 38 | MS 395 476 |

## TIBER

| | | | |
|---|---|---|---|
| OF TIBER, ON THE SCEANE OF A GREENE PLAT, | MUSICKS DUELL | 3 | 46 149 535 |

## TICKLED

| | | | |
|---|---|---|---|
| STRAINES HIGHER YET, THAT TICKLED WITH RARE ART | MUSICKS DUELL | 47 | 46 149 535 |

## TIDE

| | | | |
|---|---|---|---|
| SHEE OPES THE FLOODGATE, AND LETS LOOSE A TIDE | MUSICKS DUELL | 93 | 46 149 535 |
| JESU, NO MORE, IT IS FULL TIDE | ON BLEEDING WOUNDS OF LORD | 1 | 46 101 110 |
| NOR EVER WAS THE PHARIAN TIDE | ON BLEEDING WOUNDS OF LORD | 15 | 46 101 110 |
| JESU, NO MORE. IT IS FULL TIDE. | UPON BLEEDING CRUCIFIX | 1 | 52 288 110 |
| NOR EVER WAS THE PHARIAN TIDE | UPON BLEEDING CRUCIFIX | 19 | 52 288 110 |
| ALONG THE SHORE IN A GRAVE PURPLE TIDE. | ON GUNPOWDER-TREASON | 34 | MS 384 458 |
| LETT NOT THY WEIGHTY GLORIES, THIS FULL TIDE | UPON KINGS CORONATION | 7 | MS 349 454 |
| I CANNOT HOLD, SUCH A SPRING TIDE OF JOY | UPON BIRTH PRINCESSE E | 13 | MS 391 456 |
| IN CRIMSON WAVELETTS, & IN SCARLET TIDE. | AN ELEGY MR STANNINOW | 24 | MS 394 473 |
| IN A BRIGHT CHRISTALL TIDE, TO THEE THEY TEND, | AN ELEGIE ON DR PORTER | 40 | MS 395 476 |

## TIES

| | | | |
|---|---|---|---|
| HOLD THE PERVERSE PRINCE IN ETERNALL TIES | SOSPETTO D'HERODE | 39 | 46 109 216 |

## TY

| | | | |
|---|---|---|---|
| IN THE LAST KNOTT LOVE COULD TY. | AN EPITAPH UPON MARRIED COUPLE | 10 | 52 339 478 |

## TYE

| | | | |
|---|---|---|---|
| IN THE LAST KNOT THAT LOVE COULD TYE. | AN EPITAPH HUSBAND AND WIFE | 10 | 46 174 478 |

## TY'D

| | | | |
|---|---|---|---|
| HOPE OF A PREY, THERE TO THE MAINE LAND TY'D | THE BEGINNING OF HELIODORUS | 10 | 46 158 517 |
| FOR A BESEEMING BRACELET SHEE HAD TY'D. | SOSPETTO D'HERODE | 466 | 46 109 216 |
| LOVE'S TRUEST KNOTT BY VENUS IS NOT TY'D. | ALEXIAS THIRD ELEGIE | 27 | 52 336 209 |

## TILL

| | | | |
|---|---|---|---|
| TILL A SWEET WHIRLE-WIND (STRIVING TO GETT OUT) | MUSICKS DUELL | 87 | 46 149 535 |
| TILL THE FLEDG'D NOTES AT LENGTH FORSAKE THEIR NEST. | MUSICKS DUELL | 90 | 46 149 535 |
| TILL AT LENGTH HE PERCHING REST, | OUT OF GREEKE CUPID'S CRYER | 43 | 46 159 519 |
| TILL THE SINGING ORBES AWAKE THEE, | THE TEARE | 41 | 46 84 50 |

| | | | | | |
|---|---|---|---|---|---|
| A RAPE UPON'T. TILL THY ADULT'ROUS TOUCH | TO PONTIUS WASHING HANDS | 3 | 46 | 94 | 23 |
| AND TILL MY RIPER WOES TO AGE ARE COME, | OUR LORD IN HIS CIRCUMCISION | 17 | 46 | 98 | 9 |
| THE WELL OF LIVING WATERS, LORD, TILL NOW. | ON BLEEDING WOUNDS OF LORD | 42 | 46 | 101 | 110 |
| TILL THY RUINE TEACH THEE TEARES, | PSALME 137 | 32 | 46 | 104 | 7 |
| EVEN SUCH AS THESE, LAUGH, TILL A VENGING THRONG | PSALME 137 | 33 | 46 | 104 | 7 |
| LAUGH, TILL THY CHILDRENS BLEEDING BONES | PSALME 137 | 35 | 46 | 104 | 7 |
| AND CRUSH THE WORLD TILL HIS WIDE CORNERS MEET. | SOSPETTO D'HERODE | 280 | 46 | 109 | 216 |
| TILL HIS O'REFLOWING PRIDE SUPPRESSE THE FLAME, | SOSPETTO D'HERODE | 487 | 46 | 109 | 216 |
| NEVER TILL NOW ESTEEMED TOYES. | IN MEMORY OF LADY MADRE TERESA | 60 | 46 | 131 | 52 |
| DRINKE WEE TILL WE PROVE MORE, NOT LESSE THEN MEN. | AN APOLOGIE FOR HYMNE (TERESA) | 36 | 46 | 136 | 59 |
| TILL IN THE LAP OF LOVES FULL NOONE | ON HOPE | 56 | 46 | 143 | 71 |
| TILL THIS STORMY NIGHT BE GONE. | AN EPITAPH HUSBAND AND WIFE | 12 | 46 | 174 | 478 |
| LOWER, AND LOWER YET. TILL THY SMALL SIZE, | UPON STANINOUGH'S DEATH | 15 | 46 | 175 | 475 |
| LESSER AND LESSER YET, TILL THOU BEGIN | UPON STANINOUGH'S DEATH | 17 | 46 | 175 | 475 |
| TILL ANOTHER THOUSAND SMOTHER | OUT OF CATULLUS | 13 | 46 | 194 | 523 |
| TILL THAT RIPE BIRTH | WISHES SUPPOSED MISTRESSE | 7 | 46 | 195 | 479 |
| TILL THAT DIVINE | WISHES SUPPOSED MISTRESSE | 10 | 46 | 195 | 479 |
| THAT HEALING SHAFT, WHICH HEAVN TILL NOW | TO COUNTESSE OF DENBIGH | 47 | 52 | 236 | 146 |
| TILL BURNT AT LAST IN FIRE OF THY FAIR EYES. | IN HOLY NATIVITY | 107 | 52 | 246 | 76 |
| TILL DEARLY THUS UNDONE, | IN GLORIOUS EPIPHANIE | 202 | 52 | 253 | 39 |
| TILL THUS TRIUMPHANTLY TAM'D (O YE TWO | IN GLORIOUS EPIPHANIE | 203 | 52 | 253 | 39 |
| WHAT WAS TILL NOW NE'RE UNDERSTOOD. | VEXILLA REGIS | 20 | 52 | 277 | 156 |
| TO STUDY HIM SO, TILL WE MIX | SANCTA MARIA DOLORUM | 99 | 52 | 283 | 162 |
| TILL DRUNK OF THE DEAR WOUNDS, I BE | SANCTA MARIA DOLORUM | 103 | 52 | 283 | 162 |
| THE WELL OF LIVING WATERS, LORD, TILL NOW. | UPON BLEEDING CRUCIFIX | 38 | 52 | 288 | 110 |
| TILL HE HAD MADE HIMSELF THY SON | O GLORIOSA DOMINA | 6 | 52 | 302 | 194 |
| (NEVER TILL NOW ESTEEMED TOYES) | TERESA | 60 | 52 | 315 | 52 |
| DRINK WE TILL WE PROVE MORE, NOT LESSE, THEN MEN, | AN APOLOGIE FOR (TERESA) HYMNE | 36 | 52 | 322 | 59 |
| TILL THIS STORMY NIGHT BE GONE, | AN EPITAPH UPON MARRIED COUPLE | 16 | 52 | 339 | 478 |
| TILL THE' AETERNALL MORROW DAWN | AN EPITAPH UPON MARRIED COUPLE | 17 | 52 | 339 | 478 |
| LOWER & LOWER YET. TILL THY LEANE SIZE | DEATH'S LECTURE | 16 | 52 | 340 | 475 |
| LESSER & LESSER YET. TILL THOU BEGIN | DEATH'S LECTURE | 18 | 52 | 340 | 475 |
| TILL IN THE LAPPE OF LOVES FULL NOONE | (ON) HOPE | 26 | 52 | 345 | 71 |
| HEE'S GONE. NOT LEAVING WITH ME, TILL HE COME, | LUKE 2. QUAERIT JESUM | 13 | MS | 379 | 11 |
| TILL NOW HELL WAS IMPERFECT. IT DID NEED | ON GUNPOWDER-TREASON | 61 | MS | 384 | 458 |

TIME

| | | | | | |
|---|---|---|---|---|---|
| TIME LAYES HIM UP. HE'S PRETIOUS. | THE WEEPER | 96 | 46 | 79 | 120 |
| TIME AS BY THEE HE PASSES, | THE WEEPER | 97 | 46 | 79 | 120 |
| THY TEARES JUST CADENCE STILL KEEPS TIME. | THE WEEPER | 104 | 46 | 79 | 120 |
| 'TWAS TIME TO HOLD THEIR PEACE WHEN THEY. | NEITHER DURST MAN ASKE | 15 | 46 | 92 | 20 |
| OF TIME, OR TEETH OF HUNGRY RUINE FEARES. | SOSPETTO D'HERODE | 310 | 46 | 109 | 216 |
| YOUNG TIME IS TASTER TO ETERNITY. | ON HOPE | 52 | 46 | 143 | 71 |
| TO START FROM TIME, AND CHEERFULLY TO FLY | UPON DEATH OF HERRYS | 7 | 46 | 167 | 466 |
| GLAD TIME TO RIPEN EXPECTATION. | UPON DEATH OF HERRYS | 22 | 46 | 167 | 466 |
| HIS CROWNE EXPECTED, WHEN (O FATE, O TIME | UPON DEATH OF HERRYS | 29 | 46 | 167 | 466 |
| STILL LIVES, WHICH WHEN WEAKE TIME SHALL BE POUR'D OUT | UPON DEATH OF HERRYS | 36 | 46 | 167 | 466 |
| HASTE HATH NEVER TIME TO HEARE. | UPON DEATH OF DESIRED HERRYS | 64 | 46 | 168 | 467 |
| HIM WHILE FRESH AND FRAGRANT TIME | HIS EPITAPH (HERRYS) | 43 | 46 | 172 | 471 |
| UPON THE STOOPED SHOULDERS OF OLD TIME. | TO THE MORNING | 28 | 46 | 183 | 497 |
| AS LEFT NO TIME TO PRACTISE ANY. | AN EPITAPH UPON ASHTON | 10 | 46 | 192 | 464 |
| NOW IF TIME KNOWES | WISHES SUPPOSED MISTRESSE | 106 | 46 | 195 | 479 |
| RIPE AS THOSE RICH COMPOSURES TIME COMPUTES | UPON TWO GREENE APRICOCKES | 13 | 48 | 220 | 494 |
| PROGRESSIONS 'TWIXT WHOSE TERMES POOR TIME GROWS OLD. | UPON TWO GREENE APRICOCKES | 16 | 48 | 220 | 494 |
| WHO GRANTS AT LAST, LONG TIME TRYD | TO COUNTESSE OF DENBIGH | 15 | 52 | 236 | 146 |
| NOR SINKS NOR SWELLS WITH TIME OR PLACE. | IN GLORIOUS EPIPHANIE | 29 | 52 | 253 | 39 |
| TIME IS TOO NARROW FOR THY YEAR | IN GLORIOUS EPIPHANIE | 40 | 52 | 253 | 39 |
| TIME HAS A DAY IN STORE | IN GLORIOUS EPIPHANIE | 133 | 52 | 253 | 39 |
| MAY THE GREAT TIME, IN YOU, STILL GREATER BE | TO THE QUEEN'S MAJESTY | 25 | 52 | 261 | 47 |
| 'TIS TO KEEP TIME WITH THY DELAY. | IN GLORIOUS ASSUMPTION B. LADY | 20 | 52 | 304 | 114 |
| THY FALLING TEARES KEEP FAITH FULL TIME. | WEEPER | 140 | 52 | 307 | 120 |
| TIME LAYES HIM UP. HE'S PRETIOUS. | WEEPER | 150 | 52 | 307 | 120 |
| TRUTH BIDDES ME SAY, 'TIS TIME YOU CEASE TO TRUST | TO SAME CONCERNING CHOISE | 18 | 52 | 331 | 66 |
| 'TIS TIME YOU LISTEN TO A BRAVER LOVE. | TO SAME CONCERNING CHOISE | 20 | 52 | 331 | 66 |
| YOUNG TIME IS TASTER TO ETERNITY | (ON) HOPE | 22 | 52 | 345 | 71 |
| SPURNS THE TAME LAWS OF TIME AND PLACE, | AGAINST IRRESOLUTION AND DELAY | 77 | 52 | 347 | 146 |
| AND GETT A STARRY THRONE BEFORE HIS TIME. | ON GUNPOWDER-TREASON | 36 | MS | 384 | 458 |
| O DEATH, 'TIS THOU, YOU FALSE TIME KEEPE. | UPON DEATH OF A FREIND | 9 | MS | 393 | 477 |
| LONG TIME TO QUAVERING AGE YOU GIVE, | UPON DEATH OF A FREIND | 11 | MS | 393 | 477 |
| BUT TO LARGE YOUTH SHORT TIME TO LIVE. | UPON DEATH OF A FREIND | 12 | MS | 393 | 477 |
| WAS NOT YETT FULL, (A TIME THAT TO MY AGE | OUT OF GROTIUS | 23 | MS | 398 | 198 |

SEED-TIME

| | | | | | |
|---|---|---|---|---|---|
| TIS SEED-TIME STILL WITH THEE | THE WEEPER | 9 | 46 | 79 | 120 |
| 'TIS SEED-TIME STILL WITH THEE | WEEPER | 9 | 52 | 307 | 120 |

TIME'S

| | | | | | |
|---|---|---|---|---|---|
| LET HOARY TIME'S VAST BOWELS BE THE GRAVE | ON FRONTISPIECE ISAACSONS | 1 | 46 | 191 | 491 |
| NOW THAT TIME'S EMPIRE MIGHT BE AMPLY FILL'D, | ON FRONTISPIECE ISAACSONS | 15 | 46 | 191 | 491 |
| SHEWES THE TWO TERMES AND LIMITS OF TIME'S RACE. | ON FRONTISPIECE ISAACSONS | 22 | 46 | 191 | 491 |

SEED-TIME'S

| | | | | | |
|---|---|---|---|---|---|
| SEED-TIME'S NOT ALL. THERE SHOULD BE HARVEST TOO. | AGAINST IRRESOLUTION AND DELAY | 37 | 52 | 347 | 146 |

TIMED-BEE

| | | | | | |
|---|---|---|---|---|---|
| EACH HERBE A PLAGUE. THE WINDS SIGHES TIMED-BEE | SOSPETTO D'HERODE | 348 | 46 | 109 | 216 |

## TIMES

| | | | | |
|---|---|---|---|---|
| THEN VENUS MILD INSTINCT (AT SET TIMES) YEILDS | OUT OF VIRGIL | 11 | 46 155 | 529 |
| IF ON TIMES RIGHT HAND, SIT FAIRE HISTORIE. | ON FRONTISPIECE ISAACSONS | 5 | 46 191 | 491 |
| TAKE THESE, TIMES TARDY TRUANTS, SENT BY ME, | UPON TWO GREENE APRICOCKES | 1 | 48 220 | 494 |
| ALL PLACES, TIMES, & OBJECTS BE | WEEPER | 131 | 52 307 | 120 |
| MY WATRY HOUR-GLASSE HATH OLD TIMES OUTRUNNE. | ALEXIAS SECONDE ELEGIE | 20 | 52 335 | 207 |
| DYE SEV'N TIMES DEEPER THAN THEY WERE BEFORE | UPON GUNPOWDER TREASON | 4 | MS 387 | 461 |

## TIMELY

| | | | | |
|---|---|---|---|---|
| AND STROAKE HIS RADIANT CHEEKES. ONE TIMELY KISSE | TO THE MORNING | 37 | 46 183 | 497 |

## TIMEROUS

| | | | | |
|---|---|---|---|---|
| AND STAINES THE TIMEROUS LIGHT OF STARRES. | O GLORIOSA DOMINA | 4 | 52 302 | 194 |

## TIMOUROUS

| | | | | |
|---|---|---|---|---|
| THE TIMOUROUS MAIDEN-BLOSSOMES ON EACH BOUGH, | UPON DEATH OF HERRYS | 23 | 46 167 | 466 |

## TINCT

| | | | | |
|---|---|---|---|---|
| BY THINE EYES TINCT ENOBLED THUS | THE WEEPER | 95 | 46 79 | 120 |
| BY THINE EY'S TINCT ENOBLED THUS | WEEPER | 149 | 52 307 | 120 |

## TINCTURE

| | | | | |
|---|---|---|---|---|
| ITS TINCTURE FROM THE ROSIE NECTAR, WINE | AN APOLOGIE FOR HYMNE (TERESA) | 43 | 46 136 | 59 |
| THE SOFT TINCTURE OF A TEARE. | ANOTHER ON HERRYS | 20 | 46 170 | 469 |
| IT'S TINCTURE FROM THE ROSY NECTAR. WINE | AN APOLOGIE FOR (TERESA) HYMNE | 43 | 52 322 | 59 |

## TIPT

| | | | | |
|---|---|---|---|---|
| AND TIPT THE MOUNTAINES IN A TENDER RAY. | THE BEGINNING OF HELIODORUS | 2 | 46 158 | 517 |

## PEARLE-TIPT

| | | | | |
|---|---|---|---|---|
| WOULD TREMBLE ON MY PEARLE-TIPT FINGERS TOP. | DIVES ASKING A DROP | 2 | 46 96 | 16 |

## SILVER-TIPT

| | | | | |
|---|---|---|---|---|
| AS EVER SILVER-TIPT, THE SIDE OF SHADY MOUNTAINE. | TO PONTIUS WASHING HANDS | 8 | 46 94 | 23 |

## TIPTOE

| | | | | |
|---|---|---|---|---|
| ON TIPTOE IN THEIR GIDDY BRAYNES. TH' HAVE FIRE | SOSPETTO D'HERODE | 442 | 46 109 | 216 |

## TIPTOES

| | | | | |
|---|---|---|---|---|
| UPON HIS TIPTOES, E'RE HIS SILVER HEAD | UPON KINGS CORONATION | 4 | MS 389 | 454 |

## TIRE

| | | | | |
|---|---|---|---|---|
| A GLOOMY MANTLE OF DARKE FLAMES, THE TIRE | SOSPETTO D'HERODE | 44 | 46 109 | 216 |
| A GEN'RALL HISSE, FROM THE WHOLE TIRE OF SNAKES | SOSPETTO D'HERODE | 302 | 46 109 | 216 |
| TO GAUDY TIRE, OR GLISTRING SHOO-TY. | WISHES SUPPOSED MISTRESSE | 18 | 46 195 | 479 |
| HIS GORGEOUS TIRE | IN GLORIOUS EPIPHANIE | 241 | 52 253 | 39 |

## TIRES

| | | | | |
|---|---|---|---|---|
| THEIR RICHEST TIRES BUT DRESSE | WISHES SUPPOSED MISTRESSE | 41 | 46 195 | 479 |

## TISSEW

| | | | | |
|---|---|---|---|---|
| TAFFATA OR TISSEW CAN, | WISHES SUPPOSED MISTRESSE | 20 | 46 195 | 479 |

## TITYRUS

| | | | | |
|---|---|---|---|---|
| TELL HIM TITYRUS WHERE TH'HAST BEEN, | A HYMNE OF THE NATIVITY | 15 | 46 106 | 76 |
| TELL HIM, TITYRUS, WHERE TH'HAST BEEN | IN HOLY NATIVITY | 15 | 52 246 | 76 |

## TOGETHER

| | | | | |
|---|---|---|---|---|
| BLENDS ALL TOGETHER. THEN DISTINCTLY TRIPPS | MUSICKS DUELL | 31 | 46 149 | 535 |
| TOGETHER, IN HIS PONDROUS MIND BOTH WEIGHES. | SOSPETTO D'HERODE | 96 | 46 109 | 216 |
| THEIR BASHFULL CHEEKES TOGETHER, NEWLY THEY | UPON YORKE HIS BIRTH | 61 | 46 176 | 500 |
| BOTH WILL BE GOOD FRIENDS TOGETHER. | OUT OF THE ITALIAN (1) | 30 | 46 188 | 545 |
| OF LOVE, BURNE BOTH TOGETHER. | OUT OF THE ITALIAN (2) | 14 | 46 190 | 547 |
| HAVE FLOW'D TOGETHER. IF OUGHT FURTHER NEEDES | OUT OF GROTIUS | 6 | MS 398 | 198 |

## TOILE

| | | | | |
|---|---|---|---|---|
| WITH SHIPWRACKS TOILE, OH, THAT IS SWEET, | PETRONIJ ALES PHASIACIS PETITA | 13 | MS 382 | 526 |

## TOYLE

| | | | | |
|---|---|---|---|---|
| OF SHOP, OR SILKEWORMES TOYLE | WISHES SUPPOSED MISTRESSE | 23 | 46 195 | 479 |

## TOYLES

| | | | | |
|---|---|---|---|---|
| NOW AFTER ALL HER TOYLES BY SEA AND LAND, | UPON FAIRE ETHIOPIAN | 3 | 46 183 | 493 |

TOILING

NOW TO THOSE TOILING SOULES IT GIVES ITS LIGHT.             ON GUNPOWDER-TREASON                    57   MS 384 458

TOKENS

(AS TOKENS OF HER GREIFE) UNTO THE EARTH.                   UPON KINGS CORONATION                    8   MS 390 453

TOLD

AND BELIEVING WHAT THEY TOLD.                               HIS EPITAPH (HERRYS)                    11   46 172 471

TOMB

AND TOMB.                                                   TO OUR B. LORD                           4   52 279  25
QUICK BURYE'D IN THE WANTON TOMB                            O GLORIOSA DOMINA                       15   52 302 194
SHALL THY TOMB REPORT OF THEE.                              WEEPER                                 152   52 307 120

TOMBE

WILL THY TOMBE REPORT OF THEE                               THE WEEPER                             116   46  79 120
AND TOMBE.                                                  UPON OUR SAVIOURS TOMBE                  4   46  93  25
THOU TRIM'ST A PROPHETS TOMBE, AND DOST BEQUEATH            YEE BUILD SEPULCHRES                     1   46  95  21
VAINE MAN, THE STONES THAT ON HIS TOMBE DOE LYE,            YEE BUILD SEPULCHRES                     3   46  95  21
FROM THY VIRGIN TOMBE.                                      EASTER DAY                               2   46 100  26
THY TOMBE, THE UNIVERSALL EAST.                             EASTER DAY                               4   46 100  26
THY TOMBE, FAIRE IMMORTALITIES PERFUMED NEST.               EASTER DAY                               6   46 100  26
AND WEPT AMAINE. THEN REAR'D A COSTLY TOMBE.                UPON GUNPOWDER TREASON                  50   MS 386 460

TONE

CREEPS ON THE SOFT TOUCH OF A TENDER TONE.                  MUSICKS DUELL                          140   46 149 535
POORE SIMPLE VOYCE, RAIS'D IN A NATURALL TONE.              MUSICKS DUELL                          164   46 149 535

TONES

INTO A THOUSAND SWEET DISTINGUISH'D TONES.                  MUSICKS DUELL                           23   46 149 535
FLOW NOT SO SWEET AS DOE THE TONES                          OUT OF GREEKE CUPID'S CRYER             27   46 159 519

TONGUE

BE NE'RE SO CURST, HIS TONGUE IS KIND.                      OUT OF GREEKE CUPID'S CRYER             22   46 159 519
CHRIST BIDS THE DUMBE TONGUE SPEAKE. IT SPEAKES, THE        THE DUMBE HEALED                         1   46  87  16
                                                SOUND
WHY ELSE HAD BAALAMS ASSE A TONGUE TO CHIDE                 UPON ASSE THAT BORE SAVIOUR             5    46  90  19
THAT HE SHOULD FIND A TONGUE AND VOCALL THUNDER.            UPON ASSE THAT BORE SAVIOUR             9    46  90  19
WHICH WHEN I LOSE, O MAY AT ONCE MY TONGUE                  PSALME 137                             19    46 104   7
HIS TONGUE THE TOUCHSTONE OF HER GOLD.                      HIS EPITAPH (HERRYS)                   30    46 172 471
OFT TO THY EASY EARES HATH THIS SHRILL TONGUE               LUKE 2. QUAERIT JESUM                  29    MS 379  11
YET SHALL MY LOYALL TONGUE KEEPE THIS COMMAND.              UPON BIRTH PRINCESSE E                 15    MS 391 456
HEE THAT NE'RE HEARD NOW SPEAKES, AND FINDS A TONGUE        OUT OF GROTIUS                         73    MS 398 198

TONGU'D

IN SHRILL TONGU'D ACCENTS. STRIVING TO BEE SINGLE.          MUSICKS DUELL                         130    46 149 535

TONGUES

EYES ARE VOCALL, TEARES HAVE TONGUES.                       UPON THE DEATH OF A GENTLEMAN          27    46 166 472
O WHAT. ASKE NOT THE TONGUES OF MEN,                        IN MEMORY OF LADY MADRE TERESA        119    46 131  52
IF WHAT TO OTHER TONGUES IS TUN'D SO HIGH,                  AN APOLOGIE FOR HYMNE (TERESA)         10    46 136  59
O WHAT. ASK NOT THE TONGUES OF MEN.                         TERESA                                118    52 315  52
IF, WHAT TO OTHER TONGUES IS TUN'D SO HIGH,                 AN APOLOGIE FOR (TERESA) HYMNE         10    52 322  59
AND WALK THROUGH ALL TONGUES ONE TRIUMPHANT FLAME           FLAMING HEART                          78    52 324  61
THEIR SHACKLED TONGUES TO CHANT AN ELGIE.                   AN ELEGIE ON DR PORTER                 36    MS 395 476

TOUNGS

THEIR HANDS WITH LASHES ARM'D, THEIR TOUNGS WITH LYES.      OFFICE H. CROSS PRIME                   5    52 267  91

TOOK

THEY TOOK A KINGDOM WHILE THEY GAVE A KISSE.                TO THE QUEEN'S MAJESTY                  8    52 261  47
PAID BACK THE FLESH HE TOOK FOR THEE.                       VEXILLA REGIS                           6    52 277 156
AND TOOK IT HOME TO HIS OWN HEART.                          VEXILLA REGIS                          12    52 277 156
I TOOK FROM READING THEE, TIS TO THY WRONG                  AN APOLOGIE FOR (TERESA) HYMNE          3    52 322  59
BUT HAD THY PALE-FAC'T PURPLE TOOK                          FLAMING HEART                          27    52 324  61

TOOK'ST

THE LIFE THOU TOOK'ST FROM HIM UNTO HIS DEATH.              YEE BUILD SEPULCHRES                     2   46  95  21

TOOKE

WHEN BEASTS TOOKE UP THEIR LODGING IN THE WOOD.             OUT OF VIRGIL                           31   46 155 529
THE FRIGHTED STARS TOOKE FAINT EXPERIENCE,                  SOSPETTO D'HERODE                      283   46 109 216
I TOOKE FROM READING THEE. 'TIS TO THY WRONG                AN APOLOGIE FOR HYMNE (TERESA)           3   46 136  59
HIS PRAYERS TOOKE THEIR PRICE AND STRENGTH                  AN EPITAPH UPON ASHTON                  15   46 192 464
(WHEREOF THE BLUSHING WALLES TOOKE BLOODY NOTE)             HORATIJ ILLE & NEFASTO                  10   MS 382 530

```
TOOLES

ARE TOOLES OF WRATH, ANVILLS OF TORMENTS HUNG.        SOSPETTO D'HERODE                      323   46 109 216

TOP

WOULD TREMBLE ON MY PEARLE-TIPT FINGERS TOP.          DIVES ASKING A DROP                      2   46  96  18
BOWES LOW'ST HIS HEAVY TOP, TO LOOK FOR THEE.         IN GLORIOUS ASSUMPTION B. LADY          30   52 304 114

TOPP

THY RISING TOPP FIRST STAIND THE BASHFULL LIGHT.      HORATIJ ILLE & NEFASTO                   6   MS 382 530
UP TO OLYMPUS STATELY TOPP HE HIES.                   UPON KINGS CORONATION                   17   MS 390 453

TOPPE

(HIS TENDER TOPPE NOT FULLY SPREAD)                   UPON DEATH OF DESIRED HERRYS            35   46 168 467

TOPS

HIS HONEY-DROPPING TOPS, PLOW'D BY HER BREATH         MUSICKS DUELL                           71   46 149 535
THEIR WEALTHY TOPS, & FOR THESE FEET CONTEND.         TO THE QUEEN'S MAJESTY                  18   52 261  47

TORCH

HIS TORCH IMPERIOUS THOUGH BUT SMALL                  OUT OF GREEKE CUPID'S CRYER             54   46 159 519
AND MAKE THE NIGHT IT SELF THEIR TORCH TO THEE.       IN GLORIOUS EPIPHANIE                  188   52 253  39
THY TORCH, TERRESTRIALL LOVE, HAVE HERE NO NAME.      ALEXIAS THIRD ELEGIE                    50   52 336 209
HE STREIGHTWAY LIGHTED UPP HIS PITCHY TORCH.          ON GUNPOWDER-TREASON                    56   MS 384 458

TORCHES

HER SULPHUR-BREATHED TORCHES BRANDISHING,             SOSPETTO D'HERODE                      398   46 109 216

TORE

HAND (O WHAT DARES NOT JEALOUS GREATNESSE.) TORE      SOSPETTO D'HERODE                        3   46 109 216
OF A MAD STORME THESE BLOOMY JOYES ALL TORE,          UPON DEATH OF HERRYS                    33   46 167 466
TORE NOT OFF HIS MOTHERS VEILE.                       AN EPITAPH UPON ASHTON                  20   46 192 464
DEATH TORE NOT (THEREFORE) BUT SANS STRIFE            AN EPITAPH UPON ASHTON                  27   46 192 464
WHO TORE THE FAIR BRESTS OF THY FREINDS.              TO THE NAME OF JESUS                   208   52 239  30
THE CENTER SHOOK. HER USELESSE VEIL TH'INGLORIOUS     OFFICE H. CROSS NINTH                    8   52 271  99
                                   TEMPLE TORE.

FOR JOYE OF THIER NEATE COATES. BUT WOULD HAVE TORE   UPON GUNPOWDER TREASON                  46   MS 386 460

TORMENT

A MASSE OF WOES, HIS TEETH FOR TORMENT GNASH,         SOSPETTO D'HERODE                       63   46 109 216
THAT MANKINDS TORMENT WAITS UPON MY TEARS.            SOSPETTO D'HERODE                      216   46 109 216

TORMENTED

SO SIGH TORMENTED SWEETS, OPPREST                     WEEPER                                 158   52 307 120

TORMENTS

THE JUDGE OF TORMENTS, AND THE KING OF TEARES.        SOSPETTO D'HERODE                       41   46 109 216
ARE TOOLES OF WRATH, ANVILLS OF TORMENTS HUNG.        SOSPETTO D'HERODE                      323   46 109 216
WHERE RACKES & TORMENTS STRIV'D, IN VAIN, TO REACH    TO THE NAME OF JESUS                   206   52 239  30
                                   THEE.

CRADLE-TORMENTS

THESE CRADLE-TORMENTS HAVE THEIR TOWARDNESSE.         OUR LORD IN HIS CIRCUMCISION            14   46  98   9

SELFE-TORMENTING

AND SELFE-TORMENTING SIN) HAD A SOFT BED.             SOSPETTO D'HERODE                      412   46 109 216

TORN

HANGING ALL TORN SHE SEES. AND IN HIS WOES            SANCTA MARIA DOLORUM                     7   52 283 162
WHICH THESE TORN HANDS TRANSCRIB'D ON THY TRUE HEART  SANCTA MARIA DOLORUM                    97   52 283 162

TORNE

ALL TORNE. WITH MUCH ADOE YET ERE HE DYES.            HIGH MOUNTED ON AN ANT                   4   46 161 523
OF RAGGED LIMBS, TORNE SCULLS, & DASHT OUT BRAINES.   SOSPETTO D'HERODE                      312   46 109 216
AND FROM THE HEAD OF JUDAHS HOUSE QUITE TORNE         SOSPETTO D'HERODE                      405   46 109 216
A STILL INCREASING BURDEN. WORSE HATH TORNE           OUT OF GROTIUS                          12   MS 398 198

TORRENT

THE TORRENT OF A VOYCE, WHOSE MELODY                  MUSICKS DUELL                           45   46 149 535

TORRENTS

THAT STRIVES IN TORRENTS OF ITS OWNE.                 ON BLEEDING WOUNDS OF LORD              20   46 101 110
THAT STRIVES IN TORRENTS OF IT'S OWN.                 UPON BLEEDING CRUCIFIX                   8   52 288 110
TORRENTS OF SALT TEARES FROM OUR EYES SHOULD RUNNE.   UPON GUNPOWDER TREASON                  37   MS 386 460
```

TORRID

| | | | | | |
|---|---|---|---|---|---|
| TEMPER'D 'TWIXT COLD DESPAIRE, AND TORRID JOY. | ON HOPE | 83 | 46 | 143 | 71 |
| TEMPER TWIXT CHILL DESPAIR, & TORRID JOY. | (ON) HOPE | 43 | 52 | 345 | 71 |

TORTURE

| | | | | | |
|---|---|---|---|---|---|
| SOME RARE CHOICE TORTURE. NOW 'TIS HELL INDEED. | ON GUNPOWDER-TREASON | 62 | MS | 384 | 458 |

TORTUR'D

| | | | | | |
|---|---|---|---|---|---|
| IS TORTUR'D THIRST, IT SELFE, TOO SWEET A CUP. | OFFICE H. CROSS SIXT | 9 | 52 | 270 | 97 |

TOSSE

| | | | | | |
|---|---|---|---|---|---|
| THENCE HE MIGHT TOSSE YOU | TO SAME CONCERNING CHOISE | 49 | 52 | 331 | 66 |
| TO TOSSE POORE MEN LIKE DUST INTO THE AIRE. | ON GUNPOWDER-TREASON | 40 | MS | 384 | 458 |

TOST

| | | | | | |
|---|---|---|---|---|---|
| HEE TOST HIS TROUBLED EYES, EMBERS THAT GLOW | SOSPETTO D'HERODE | 147 | 46 | 109 | 216 |
| FLOURISHT THEIR SNAKES, AND TOST THEIR FLAMING BRANDS. | SOSPETTO D'HERODE | 260 | 46 | 109 | 216 |
| NOT VEXT & TOST | IN GLORIOUS EPIPHANIE | 32 | 52 | 253 | 39 |

LOVE-TOST

| | | | | | |
|---|---|---|---|---|---|
| OFT FROM THIS BREAST TO THINE MY LOVE-TOST HEART | LUKE 2. QUAERIT JESUM | 39 | MS | 379 | 11 |

TOTALL

| | | | | | |
|---|---|---|---|---|---|
| THE TOTALL SUMME OF MAN APPEARES, | ANOTHER ON HERRYS | 44 | 46 | 170 | 469 |
| UNTOUCH'T HER PRETIOUS TOTALL HATH. | LAUDA SION SALVATOREM | 60 | 52 | 294 | 178 |

TOTTERER

| | | | | | |
|---|---|---|---|---|---|
| PERFIDIOUS TOTTERER. LONGING FOR THE STAINES | HORATIJ ILLE & NEFASTO | 15 | MS | 382 | 530 |

TOUCH

| | | | | | |
|---|---|---|---|---|---|
| CHARG'D WITH A FLYING TOUCH. AND STREIGHTWAY SHEE | MUSICKS DUELL | 21 | 46 | 149 | 535 |
| THE HUMOUROUS STRINGS EXPOUND HIS LEARNED TOUCH, | MUSICKS DUELL | 127 | 46 | 149 | 535 |
| CREEPS ON THE SOFT TOUCH OF A TENDER TONE. | MUSICKS DUELL | 140 | 46 | 149 | 535 |
| IF IN THE FIRST HE US'D HIS FINGERS TOUCH. | THE DUMBE HEALED | 3 | 46 | 87 | 16 |
| A RAPE UPON'T. TILL THY ADULT'ROUS TOUCH | TO PONTIUS WASHING HANDS | 3 | 46 | 94 | 23 |
| HARKE HOW AT EVERY TOUCH SHE DOES COMPLAINE HER. | TO PONTIUS WASHING HANDS | 12 | 46 | 94 | 23 |
| OF MUSICKS DAINTY TOUCH, THEN I | PSALME 137 | 17 | 46 | 104 | 7 |
| OR ANSWER ARTFULL TOUCH, | TO THE NAME OF JESUS | 40 | 52 | 239 | 30 |
| T'OBEY MY BOLDER TOUCH. | TO THE NAME OF JESUS | 52 | 52 | 239 | 30 |
| POUR ON THY NOBLEST SWEETS, WHICH, WHEN THEY TOUCH | OFFICE H. CROSS COMPLINE | 7 | 52 | 274 | 105 |
| NOR TOUCH NOR TAST MUST LOOK FOR MORE | ADORO TE | 7 | 52 | 291 | 172 |
| THOMAS MIGHT TOUCH. NONE BUT MIGHT SEE | ADORO TE | 23 | 52 | 291 | 172 |
| TAST THEE GOD, OR TOUCH THEE MAN | ADORO TE | 30 | 52 | 291 | 172 |
| AND DURST NOT TOUCH IT, HEERE IT MADE NOE STAY. | ON GUNPOWDER-TREASON | 54 | MS | 384 | 458 |
| AND RUGGED TOUCH OF PLUTO'S MULTITUDE. | UPON GUNPOWDER TREASON | 58 | MS | 387 | 461 |
| IN STRIKING WHERE YOU SHOULD NOT TOUCH. | UPON DEATH OF A FREIND | 14 | MS | 393 | 477 |
| AND TO MY TOUCH DARKE EYES DID OWE THE LIGHT. | OUT OF GROTIUS | 72 | MS | 398 | 198 |

TOUCHT

| | | | | | |
|---|---|---|---|---|---|
| TOUCHT WITH THE WORLDS TRUE ANTIDOTE TO BURST. | SOSPETTO D'HERODE | 128 | 46 | 109 | 216 |
| LOVE TOUCHT HER HEART, AND LOE IT BEATS | IN MEMORY OF LADY MADRE TERESA | 35 | 46 | 131 | 52 |

TOUCH'T

| | | | | | |
|---|---|---|---|---|---|
| BUT TOUCH'T WITH AN INTERIOUR RAY. | TO THE NAME OF JESUS | 2 | 52 | 239 | 30 |
| LOVE TOUCH'T HER HEART, & LO IT BEATES | TERESA | 35 | 52 | 315 | 52 |

TOUCHSTONE

| | | | | | |
|---|---|---|---|---|---|
| HIS TONGUE THE TOUCHSTONE OF HER GOLD. | HIS EPITAPH (HERRYS) | 30 | 46 | 172 | 471 |

TOWARDNESSE

| | | | | | |
|---|---|---|---|---|---|
| THESE CRADLE-TORMENTS HAVE THEIR TOWARDNESSE. | OUR LORD IN HIS CIRCUMCISION | 14 | 46 | 98 | 9 |

TOWERS

| | | | | | |
|---|---|---|---|---|---|
| FIXE HEERE THY WAT'RY EYES UPON THESE TOWERS, | AN ELEGIE ON DR PORTER | 3 | MS | 395 | 476 |

TOWNE

| | | | | | |
|---|---|---|---|---|---|
| ONE OF THOSE FEW THAT IN THIS TOWNE, | AN EPITAPH UPON ASHTON | 7 | 46 | 192 | 464 |

TOYES

| | | | | | |
|---|---|---|---|---|---|
| NEVER TILL NOW ESTEEMED TOYES. | IN MEMORY OF LADY MADRE TERESA | 60 | 46 | 131 | 52 |
| CROWN'D HEADS ARE TOYES. WE GOE TO MEET | WEEPER | 185 | 52 | 307 | 120 |
| (NEVER TILL NOW ESTEEMED TOYES) | TERESA | 60 | 52 | 315 | 52 |

TRACE

| | | | | | |
|---|---|---|---|---|---|
| AND TRACE ETERNITY--BUT ALL IS DEAD, | TO THE MORNING | 29 | 46 | 183 | 497 |
| MUCH LESSE MEAN WE TO TRACE | WEEPER | 181 | 52 | 307 | 120 |

TRAC'D

FOOTSTEPS OF THEIR EFFECTS, HEE TRAC'D TOO WELL.      SOSPETTO D'HERODE                    146    46 109 216

TRADE

SHEEL TO THE MOORES, AND TRADE WITH THEM,             IN MEMORY OF LADY MADRE TERESA        47   46 131  52
A MUTUALL TRADE                                       IN GLORIOUS EPIPHANIE                215   52 253  39
SH'EL TO THE MOORES.  AND TRADE WITH THEM,            TERESA                                47   52 315  52

TRAFFIQUE

OUR FREE TRAFFIQUE FOR HEAV'N, WE MAY MAINTAINE       AN APOLOGIE FOR (TERESA) HYMNE        19   52 322  59

TRAFICK

OUR FREE TRAFICK FOR HEAVEN, WE MAY MAINTAINE,        AN APOLOGIE FOR HYMNE (TERESA)        19   46 136  59

TRAGAEDY

MIGHT BE AN ACTOR IN THIS TRAGAEDY.                   UPON GUNPOWDER TREASON                34   MS 386 460
THEIR WRONGED BEAUTIES SPEAKE A TRAGAEDY,             AN ELEGIE ON DR PORTER                11   MS 395 476

TRAGICKE

THAT NOTES THE TRAGICKE DOOMES OF MEN                 ANOTHER ON HERRYS                     34   46 170 469

TRAINE

RISING AND FALLING IN A POMPOUS TRAINE.               MUSICKS DUELL                         96   46 149 535

TRAITEROUS

THY TRAITEROUS ROOT A DWELLING IN MY GROUND.          HORATIJ ILLE & NEFASTO                14   MS 382 530

TRANCE

DOWNE MY PROUD THOUGHT, AND LEAVE IT IN A TRANCE.     SOSPETTO D'HERODE                    204   46 109 216

TRANCES

AMOROUS LANGUISHMENTS, LUMINOUS TRANCES,              ON A PRAYER BOOKE                     63   46 126 139
AMOROUSE LANGUISHMENTS. LUMINOUS TRANCES.             PRAYER TO GENTLE-WOMAN                69   52 328 139

TRANSCENDENT

THOU, WHOSE STRONG HAND WITH SO TRANSCENDENT WORTH,   SOSPETTO D'HERODE                     25   46 109 216

TRANSCRIB'D

ARE TA'NE OUT AND TRANSCRIB'D BY THY GREAT MOTHER,    UPON YORKE HIS BIRTH                  41   46 176 500
TRANSCRIB'D ABOVE                                     OFFICE H. CROSS PRIME                 11   52 267  91
WHICH THESE TORN HANDS TRANSCRIB'D ON THY TRUE HEART  SANCTA MARIA DOLORUM                  97   52 283 162

TRANSFER'D

WITH THESE HE WASH'T THY STAIN, TRANSFER'D THY SMART, VEXILLA REGIS                         11   52 277 156

TRANSFUSED

FAIRE SEA OF HOLY FIRES TRANSFUSED THE FLAME          AN APOLOGIE FOR HYMNE (TERESA)         2   46 136  59

TRANSFUS'D

(FAIR FLOOD OF HOLY FIRES.) TRANSFUS'D THE FLAME      AN APOLOGIE FOR (TERESA) HYMNE         2   52 322  59

TRANSPIRE

MORE FREELY TO TRANSPIRE                              TO THE NAME OF JESUS                 213   52 239  30

TRANSPOSE

YOU MUST TRANSPOSE THE PICTURE QUITE.                 FLAMING HEART                          9   52 324  61

TRANSSUM'D

TRANSSUM'D, & TAUGHT TO TURN DIVINE.                  LAUDA SION SALVATOREM                 30   52 294 178

TRAVAIL

SHE'L TRAVAIL TO A MARTYRDOM.                         TERESA                                44   52 315  52

TRAVELD

TRAVELD TH' OLYMPIAN PLAINES TO FIND RELEIFE.         UPON KINGS CORONATION                  4   MS 390 453

TRAVELL

SHEEL TRAVELL TO A MARTYRDOME.                        IN MEMORY OF LADY MADRE TERESA        44   46 131  52

TRAVERSE

OF NIMBLE ART, & TRAVERSE ROUND                         TO THE NAME OF JESUS              33   52 239  30

TRAYLES

TRAYLES HER PLAYNE DITTY IN ONE LONG-SPUN NOTE,         MUSICKS DUELL                     37   46 149 535

TREAD

OF THE GLAD EARTH THEY TREAD ON.  WHILE WITH THEE       UPON YORKE HIS BIRTH              21   46 176 500
IN SILKEN VOLUMES, WHERESOE'RE SHEE'L TREAD,            ON A FOULE MORNING                25   46 181 495
WITH NIMBLE CAPERS, & FORCE ATLAS TREAD                 UPON KINGS CORONATION              3   MS 389 454

TREADS

ONE STANDS UP CLOSE AND TREADS ON HIGH,                 TWO WENT TO PRAY                   3   46  89  18
AND TREADS WITH UNCONTROULED STEPS.                     NEITHER DURST MAN ASKE             4   46  92  20

TREASON

WERE TREASON 'GAINST THAT MAJESTY                       TO THE QUEEN                       3   48 215 501
SLY, LURKING TREASON IS HIS BOSOME FREIND.              UPON GUNPOWDER TREASON            17   MS 387 461
OR THIRSTY TREASON OFFER ONCE TO SIPPE                  UPON GUNPOWDER TREASON            40   MS 387 461

TREASURE

SPEND THE DEARE TREASURE OF THY LIFE.                   IN PRAISE OF LESSIUS               4   46 156 510
SO TO THE TREASURE OF THY PEARLY DEAW,                  TO THE MORNING                    39   46 183 497
EVEN TO THE LAST PEARLE IN THY TREASURE.                WEEPER                           130   52 307 120
RICH, LIBERALL HEAVEN, WHAT, HATH YOUR TREASURE STORE   UPON BIRTH PRINCESSE E            25   MS 391 456

TREASURES

BOTTOMLESSE TREASURES,                                  ON A PRAYER BOOKE                113   46 126 139
FROM THESE TREASURES                                    OUT OF THE ITALIAN (1)            25   46 188 545
BOTTOMLES TREASURES                                     PRAYER TO GENTLE-WOMAN           119   52 328 139
MY TREASURES, RICH, ALAS, BY ROBBING MEE.               ALEXIAS THIRD ELEGIE               2   52 336 209
SPEND THE DEAR TREASURES OF THY LIFE.                   TEMPERANCE                         4   52 342 510
THE TREASURES OF OUR LIVES, YOUR INFLUENCE.             UPON KINGS CORONATION             40   MS 389 454
HIS BALMY TREASURES TO THE BEDD OF DEATH.               AN ELEGY MR STANNINOW             30   MS 394 473

TREASURIE

WITH TH' RICHEST CLOWDS THEIR PEARLY TREASURIE.         AN ELEGY MR STANNINOW             18   MS 394 473

TRESURY

CONVEY'D HIS SWEET DELICIOUS TRESURY                    UPON GUNPOWDER TREASON            55   MS 387 461

TREBLE

THE HIGH-PERCH'T TREBLE CHIRPS AT THIS, AND CHIDES      MUSICKS DUELL                     51   46 149 535

TREBLES

IN SURLY GROANES DISDAINES THE TREBLES GRACE.           MUSICKS DUELL                     50   46 149 535

TREE

(THE SWEET INHABITANT OF EACH GLAD TREE,                MUSICKS DUELL                      9   46 149 535
STEALES FROM THE AMBER-WEEPING TREE,                    THE WEEPER                        44   46  79 120
ERST THE FULL STATURE OF A FATALL TREE.                 OUR LORD IN HIS CIRCUMCISION      16   46  98   9
WHICH NODS WITH MANY A HEAVY HEADED TREE.               SOSPETTO D'HERODE                346   46 109 216
FOR SHELTER TO THE SHADOW OF THY TREE.                  IN GLORIOUS EPIPHANIE            140   52 253  39
ALL HAIL, FAIR TREE.                                    OFFICE H. CROSS MATINES           18   52 265  86
BEARES THAT HUGE TREE WHICH MUST BEAR HIM.              OFFICE H. CROSS SIXT               4   52 270  97
BY THAT FIRST FATALL TREE                               OFFICE H. CROSS SIXT              17   52 270  97
O SAD, SWEET TREE.                                      OFFICE H. CROSS EVENSONG           9   52 273 101
OF LOVE TO HIM, WHO ON THIS PAINFULL TREE               VEXILLA REGIS                      5   52 277 156
TALL TREE OF LIFE. THY TRUTH MAKES GOOD                 VEXILLA REGIS                     19   52 277 156
IN SHADE OF DEATH'S SAD TREE                            SANCTA MARIA DOLORUM               1   52 283 162
OF THIS FAIR TREE TAKE OUR ETERNALL ROOT.               SANCTA MARIA DOLORUM              64   52 283 162
THE FOUNTAINS MURMUR, & EACH LOFTYEST TREE              IN GLORIOUS ASSUMPTION B. LADY    29   52 304 114
SHAME OF THY MOTHER SOYLE, ILL-NURTUR'D TREE.           HORATIJ ILLE & NEFASTO             1   MS 382 530

TREE'S

THEN SITT THEE DOWN, & SING THINE EV'NSONG IN THE SAD   OFFICE H. CROSS EVENSONG           8   52 273 101

TREES

ALL TREES, ALL LEAVY GROVES CONFESSE THE SPRING         OUT OF VIRGIL                      1   46 155 529
FOR THEE I TALK TO TREES, WITH SILENT GROVES            ALEXIAS SECONDE ELEGIE            13   52 335 207

TREMBLE

MUCH RATHER WOULD IT TREMBLE HEERE.                     THE WEEPER                        41   46  79 120
WOULD TREMBLE ON MY PEARLE-TIPT FINGERS TOP.            DIVES ASKING A DROP                2   46  96  18
EARTH NOW SHOULD SEE, AND TREMBLE AT THE SIGHT.         SOSPETTO D'HERODE                256   46 109 216
TURNING HER OUT TO TREMBLE IN THE COLD.                 ON A TREATISE OF CHARITY          56   46 137  69
THE TENDER DROPS WHICH TREMBLE ON HER CHEEKE.           ON A FOULE MORNING                14   46 181 495
AND LEAVE THEM BOTH TO TREMBLE HERE.                    WEEPER                            48   52 307 120

```
WHOSE PURER FLAMES TREMBLE TO BE SOE NIGH,     UPON GUNPOWDER TREASON             15   MS 387 461

TREMBLED

  TREMBLED, & SUNG.                            LUKE 2. QUAERIT JESUM              30   MS 379  11

TREMBLES

  MAN TREMBLES AT, WEE STRAIGHT SHALL FIND     IN MEMORY OF LADY MADRE TERESA     31   46 131  52
  MAN TREMBLES AT, YOU STRAIGHT SHALL FIND     TERESA                             31   52 315  52

TREMBLING

  AND FOLDS IN WAV'D NOTES WITH A TREMBLING BILL,   MUSICKS DUELL                  60   46 149 535
  TREMBLING AS WHEN APPOLLO'S GOLDEN HAIRES         MUSICKS DUELL                 115   46 149 535
  WHOSE TREMBLING MURMURS MELTING IN WILD AIRES     MUSICKS DUELL                 141   46 149 535
  FALLS FROM A STEADY HEART, THOUGH TREMBLING HAND. WIDOWES MITES                   2   46  86  21
  AND CHASE THE TREMBLING SHADES AWAY.              A HYMNE OF THE NATIVITY        32   46 106  76
  INTO TH'OLD PROPHESIES, TREMBLING TO MARKE        SOSPETTO D'HERODE              93   46 109 216
  RAN TREMBLING THROUGH THE HOLLOW VAULTS OF NIGHT, SOSPETTO D'HERODE             151   46 109 216
  NEW STRUCK BY LOVE, STILL TREMBLING ON HIS DART.  ON A TREATISE OF CHARITY       46   46 137  69
  AND LAY THEM TREMBLING AT HIS FEET.               UPON DEATH OF DESIRED HERRYS   46   46 158 467
  WHY RAN THE STARTED AIRE TREMBLING AWAY.          UPON YORKE HIS BIRTH           67   46 176 500
  STANDS TREMBLING AT THE GATE OF BLISSE.           TO COUNTESSE OF DENBIGH         2   52 236 146
  AND CHASE THE TREMBLING SHADES AWAY.              IN HOLY NATIVITY               34   52 246  76
  AND CHASE THE TREMBLING SHADES AWAY.              IN HOLY NATIVITY               75   52 246  76
  STANDS TREMBLING AT THE GATE OF BLISSE.           AGAINST IRRESOLUTION AND DELAY  2   52 347 146
  HIS TREMBLING HANDS LOOSING THE GOLDEN RAINES.    UPON GUNPOWDER TREASON         22   MS 386 460
  WITH TREMBLING LIPPES AN HUMBLE KISSE DO'ST PAY.  AN ELEGIE ON DR PORTER          6   MS 395 476
  (FAIRE ONE) THESE TENDER LEAVES DOE TREMBLING STAND.  AT TH' IVORY TRIBUNALL      2   MS 397 492

TRESSES

  LET HIM EMBRACE HIS OWNE BRIGHT TRESSES.     AN HIMNE FOR CIRCUMCISION          21   46 141  37
  WHO ROWZING HIS ILLUSTRIOUS TRESSES CAME,    TO THE MORNING                     11   46 183 497
  LOCKES, TO PHOEBUS FLAMING TRESSES.          OUT OF THE ITALIAN (1)             12   46 188 545
  TRESSES, THAT WEARE                          WISHES SUPPOSED MISTRESSE          46   46 195 479
  LET HIM EMBRACE HIS OWN BRIGHT TRESSES       NEW YEAR'S DAY                     21   52 251  37
  HIS SACRED UNSHORN TRESSES.                  IN GLORIOUS EPIPHANIE             239   52 253  39

TRIBUNALL

  AND AEACUS ON HIS TRIBUNALL TOO,             HORATIJ ILLE & NEFASTO             35   MS 362 530
  AT TH' IVORY TRIBUNALL OF YOUR HAND          AT TH' IVORY TRIBUNALL              1   MS 397 492

TRIBUTARY

  AND NOW OF LATE CAME TRIBUTARY KINGS,        SOSPETTO D'HERODE                 499   46 109 216
  MINE EYES A TRIBUTARY STREAME SHALL PAY.     ON GUNPOWDER-TREASON               14   MS 384 458

TRIBUTE

  THEIR SIMPLE TRIBUTE TO THE BABE, WHOSE BIRTH     SOSPETTO D'HERODE            119   46 109 216
  DOES FIRST HIS SCEPTER, THEN HIMSELF IN SOLEMNE   IN GLORIOUS EPIPHANIE        237   52 253  39
     TRIBUTE PAY.

TRICK

  TRICK THEIR TALL PLUMES, AND IN THAT GARB SHALL GO   ON A TREATISE OF CHARITY  25   46 137  69

TRIM

  HEE WITH A DAINTY AND SOFT HAND, WILL TRIM   ON A FOULE MORNING                 23   46 181 495

TRIM'ST

  THOU TRIM'ST A PROPHETS TOMBE, AND DOST BEQUEATH   YEE BUILD SEPULCHRES          1   46  95  21

TRIP

  WHY YEE TRIP SO FAST AWAY.                   THE WEEPER                        132   46  79 120
  WHY YOU TRIP SO FAST AWAY.                   WEEPER                            174   52 307 120

TRIPP

  TO WHOM THE MERRY LAMBES DOE TRIPP ALONG     UPON KINGS CORONATION              26   MS 390 453

TRIPPS

  BLENDS ALL TOGETHER, THEN DISTINCTLY TRIPPS  MUSICKS DUELL                      31   46 149 535

TRIPT

  ATLAS SHALL BE TRIPT UPP, JOVE'S GATE SHALL FEELE   ON GUNPOWDER-TREASON        43   MS 384 458

TRITON

  AMAZED TRITON WITH HIS SHRILL ALARMES        UPON GUNPOWDER TREASON             31   MS 386 460

TRIUMPH

  DEATH'S PURPLE TRIUMPH, ON THE BLUSHING GROUND    THE BEGINNING OF HELIODORUS   15   46 158 517
  YOUR TRIUMPH, THOUGH HIS VICTORY.                 TO COUNTESSE OF DENBIGH       60   52 236 146
  YOUR TRIUMPH IN HIS VICTORY.                      AGAINST IRRESOLUTION AND DELAY 80  52 347 146
```

PAGE 438

```
         THE WEAPONS NOW OF TRIUMPH BE,                    IN CICATRICES DOMINI JESU          19   MS 381  27

TRIUMPHS

         WITH HIS FAIRE TRIUMPHS FILL ALL FUTURE STORIES.  SOSPETTO D'HERODE                 230   46 109 216
         HEAV'N, EARTH, AND SEA, MY TRIUMPHS.  WHAT REMAIN'D  OUT OF GROTIUS                  85   MS 398 198

TRIUMPHES

         THY TRIUMPHES, BUT THY TROPHIES TOO.              NEITHER DURST MAN ASKE              6   46  92  20

TRIUMPHING

         AND SITT TRIUMPHING IN EACH CHEERFULL BROW.       UPON KINGS CORONATION              20   MS 369 454

TRIUMPHANT

         WHERE TRIUMPHANT DARKNESSE HOVERS                 PSALME 23                          37   46 102   5
         WITH STRONG ARMES THEIR TRIUMPHANT CROWNE.        IN MEMORY OF LADY MADRE TERESA      6   46 131  52
         SHALL BUILD UP THY TRIUMPHANT BROWES.             IN MEMORY OF LADY MADRE TERESA    145   46 131  52
         TRIUMPHANT TEXT, PROVOKES THY PRAYSE.             LAUDA SION SALVATOREM               8   52 294 178
         WITH STRONG ARMES, THEIR TRIUMPHANT CROWN,        TERESA                              6   52 315  52
         SHALL BUILD UP THY TRIUMPHANT BROWES.             TERESA                            144   52 315  52
         AND WALK THROUGH ALL TONGUES ONE TRIUMPHANT FLAME FLAMING HEART                      78   52 324  61
         BE STILL TRIUMPHANT, BLESSED EYES.                A SONG                              6   52 327  65

TRIUMPHANTLY

         TILL THUS TRIUMPHANTLY TAM'D (O YE TWO            IN GLORIOUS EPIPHANIE             203   52 253  39

TROD

         ONE NEERER TO GODS ALTAR TROD,                    TWO WENT TO PRAY                    5   46  89  18
         BUT HIM, WHO TROD THE WINE-PRESSE ALL ALONE.      AN APOLOGIE FOR HYMNE (TERESA)     40   46 136  59
         BUT HIM WHO TROD THE WINE-PRESSE ALL ALONE        AN APOLOGIE FOR (TERESA) HYMNE     40   52 322  59

TROPHIE

         A TROPHIE TO HER PRESENT PRAISE.                  WISHES SUPPOSED MISTRESSE         111   46 195 479

TROPHEE

         RAISE THIS TALL TROPHEE OF THY POWRE.             TO COUNTESSE OF DENBIGH            38   52 236 146

TROPHIES

         THY TRIUMPHES, BUT THY TROPHIES TOO.              NEITHER DURST MAN ASKE              6   46  92  20

TROTH

         ARE HUSKS SO DEARE.  TROTH 'TIS A MIGHTY RATE.    ON THE PRODIGALL                    4   46  86  17

TROUBLED

         HEE TOST HIS TROUBLED EYES, EMBERS THAT GLOW      SOSPETTO D'HERODE                 147   46 109 216
         TO MEET THEIR TROUBLED LORD WITHOUT DELAY.        SOSPETTO D'HERODE                 508   46 109 216
         WHY ART THOU TROUBLED HEROD.  WHAT VAINE FEARE    SOSPETTO D'HERODE                 513   46 109 216
         THAT TROUBLED NEITHER CHURCH NOR KING.            AN EPITAPH UPON ASHTON              6   46 192 464
         AND STRIKE YOUR TROUBLED HEART                    TO SAME CONCERNING CHOISE          50   52 331  66

TROUBLESOM

         TROUBLESOM TO THE WORLD, THUS, AS FOR THEE.       ALEXIAS SECONDE ELEGIE             12   52 335 207

TRUANTS

         TAKE THESE, TIMES TARDY TRUANTS, SENT BY ME.      UPON TWO GREENE APRICOCKES          1   48 220 494

TRUE

         YET MAY THE LOVE I SEND BE TRUE, THOUGH I         WITH A PICTURE TO A FRIEND          5   46 156 494
         SEND NOR TRUE PICTURE, NOR TRUE POESIE.           WITH A PICTURE TO A FRIEND          6   46 156 494
         SEND NOR TRUE PICTURE, NOR TRUE POESIE.           WITH A PICTURE TO A FRIEND          6   46 156 494
         THERE STILL TO READ TRUE PURE DIVINITY.           UPON BISHOP ANDREWES PICTURE       12   46 163 490
         STARS THEY ARE INDEED TOO TRUE,                   THE WEEPER                         14   46  79 120
         TOO TRUE A TEARE. FOR NO SAD EYNE,                THE TEARE                          14   46  84  50
         RAINE SO TRUE A TEARE AS THINE.                   THE TEARE                          16   46  84  50
         ALL IS GOD'S, AND YET 'TIS TRUE                   GIVE TO CAESAR AND TO GOD           5   46  96  20
         NERE WAS'T THOU IN A SENCE SO SADLY TRUE,         ON BLEEDING WOUNDS OF LORD         41   46 101 110
         TOUCHT WITH THE WORLDS TRUE ANTIDOTE TO BURST.    SOSPETTO D'HERODE                 128   46 109 216
         WESTWARD TO FIND THE WORLDS TRUE ORIENT.          SOSPETTO D'HERODE                 136   46 109 216
         TO PROVE THAT TRUE, SCHOOLES USE TO TELL,         ON A PRAYER BOOKE                   7   46 126 139
         THOSE OF TURTLES, CHAST, AND TRUE,                ON A PRAYER BOOKE                  24   46 126 139
         TRUE HOPE'S A GLORIOUS HUNTRESSE, AND HER CHASE   ON HOPE                            89   46 143  71
         OF ALL INTERPRETERS READ NATURE TRUE.             UPON STANINOUGH'S DEATH            30   46 175 475
         SO FALSE A FORTUNE, AND SO TRUE A LOVE.           UPON FAIRE ETHIOPIAN                2   46 183 493
         SHEE SHALL APPEARE TRUE ETHIOPIAN.                UPON FAIRE ETHIOPIAN                6   46 183 493
         THRICE WILL I PAY THREE TEARES, TO SHOW HOW TRUE  TO THE MORNING                     40   46 183 497
         WOULD ANY ONE THE TRUE CAUSE FIND                 OUT OF THE ITALIAN (3)              1   46 190 549
         TRUE BEAUTY, TO TRUE HOLINESSE.                   AN EPITAPH UPON ASHTON             22   46 192 464
         TRUE BEAUTY, TO TRUE HOLINESSE.                   AN EPITAPH UPON ASHTON             22   46 192 464
         LOOSING IT ONCE AGAINE, STUMBLE ON TRUE LIGHT     IN GLORIOUS EPIPHANIE             167   52 253  39
         WHICH THESE TORN HANDS TRANSCRIB'D ON THY TRUE HEART  SANCTA MARIA DOLORUM           97   52 283 162
         N'ERE WAST THOU IN A SENSE SO SADLY TRUE.         UPON BLEEDING CRUCIFIX             37   52 288 110
```

| | | | |
|---|---|---|---|
| JESU MASTER, JUST & TRUE. | LAUDA SION SALVATOREM | 69 | 52 294 178 |
| STARRES INDEED THEY ARE TOO TRUE. | WEEPER | 14 | 52 307 120 |
| TO PROVE THAT TRUE, SCHOOLES USE TO TELL, | PRAYER TO GENTLE-WOMAN | 13 | 52 328 139 |
| THOSE OF TURTLES, CHAST & TRUE. | PRAYER TO GENTLE-WOMAN | 30 | 52 328 139 |
| AS TRUE TO ME, AS SHE WAS TO HER SPOUSE. | ALEXIAS FIRST ELEGIE | 32 | 52 334 204 |
| UNKIND. YET ARE MY TEARES STILL TRUE TO ME | ALEXIAS SECONDE ELEGIE | 2 | 52 335 207 |
| NO FORTRESSE BUILT FOR TRUE VIRGINITY. | ALEXIAS THIRD ELEGIE | 40 | 52 336 209 |
| HALF TRUE, ALAS, HALF FALSE, PROVES THAT POOR LINE. | ALEXIAS THIRD ELEGIE | 57 | 52 336 209 |
| (THOUGH YOU BE PAINTED) SHOWES YOU YOUR TRUE FACE. | DEATH'S LECTURE | 24 | 52 340 475 |
| OF ALL INTERPRETERS READ NATURE TRUE. | DEATH'S LECTURE | 32 | 52 340 475 |
| TRUE HOPE'S A GLORIOUS HUNTER & HER CHASE, | (ON) HOPE | 49 | 52 345 71 |

TRULY

| | | | |
|---|---|---|---|
| TH'AST NEED O BRITTAINE TO BE TRULY GREAT. | UPON YORKE HIS BIRTH | 16 | 46 176 500 |
| HERE LYES A TRULY HONEST MAN. | AN EPITAPH UPON ASHTON | 4 | 46 192 464 |

TRUELY

| | | | |
|---|---|---|---|
| AND SHEE'S AN ISLAND TRUELY FORTUNATE. | ON GUNPOWDER-TREASON | 10 | MS 384 458 |

TRUEST

| | | | |
|---|---|---|---|
| LOVE'S TRUEST KNOTT BY VENUS IS NOT TY'D. | ALEXIAS THIRD ELEGIE | 27 | 52 336 209 |

TRUMP

| | | | |
|---|---|---|---|
| O THAT TRUMP, WHOSE BLAST SHALL RUN | DIES IRAE | 9 | 52 298 186 |

TRUMPE

| | | | |
|---|---|---|---|
| THEE, WITH THE SHRILLEST TRUMPE OF FAME. | NEITHER DURST MAN ASKE | 24 | 46 92 20 |
| MASTER (WITH VOYCE FREE AS THE TRUMPE OF FAME) | SOSPETTO D'HERODE | 439 | 46 109 216 |

TRUMPETS

| | | | |
|---|---|---|---|
| HORACE, SHRILL, AT ONCE, AS WHEN THE TRUMPETS CALL | MUSICKS DUELL | 54 | 46 149 535 |
| HIS TRUMPETS. TENDER CRYES, HIS MEN TO DARE | SOSPETTO D'HERODE | 526 | 46 109 216 |

TRUNKE

| | | | |
|---|---|---|---|
| THE TRUNKE. YET IN THIS GROUND HIS PRETIOUS ROOT | UPON DEATH OF HERRYS | 35 | 46 167 466 |

TRUST

| | | | |
|---|---|---|---|
| TRUST HIS BELOVED BOSOME TO THE SUN | OUT OF VIRGIL | 17 | 46 155 529 |
| FOR SO DEARE, SO DEEP A TRUST, | UPON THE DEATH OF A GENTLEMAN | 13 | 46 166 472 |
| TRUTH BIDDES ME SAY, 'TIS TIME YOU CEASE TO TRUST | TO SAME CONCERNING CHOISE | 18 | 52 331 66 |

TRUTH

| | | | |
|---|---|---|---|
| AND SOONE THE SWEET TRUTH SHALL APPEARE, | AN HIMNE FOR CIRCUMCISION | 29 | 46 141 37 |
| WAS THE PRIDE OF NAKED TRUTH. | HIS EPITAPH (HERRYS) | 26 | 46 172 471 |
| AND BLOOD, WITH PEN OF TRUTH | WISHES SUPPOSED MISTRESSE | 32 | 46 135 479 |
| AND SOON THIS SWEET TRUTH SHALL APPEAR | NEW YEAR'S DAY | 29 | 52 251 37 |
| TALL TREE OF LIFE, THY TRUTH MAKES GOOD | VEXILLA REGIS | 19 | 52 277 156 |
| LOVE COULD NOT THINK, TRUTH COULD NOT SAY. | ADORO TE | 16 | 52 291 172 |
| TRUTH BIDDES ME SAY, 'TIS TIME YOU CEASE TO TRUST | TO SAME CONCERNING CHOISE | 18 | 52 331 66 |

TRUTH'S

| | | | |
|---|---|---|---|
| DISCERNE THE DAWNE OF TRUTH'S ETERNALL RAY, | ON FRONTISPIECE ISAACSONS | 13 | 46 191 491 |

TRUTHES

| | | | |
|---|---|---|---|
| TYPES YEILD TO TRUTHES. SHADES SHRINK AWAY. | LAUDA SION SALVATOREM | 23 | 52 294 178 |

TRY

| | | | |
|---|---|---|---|
| COME TRY WHO DARES, HEAV'N, EARTH, WHAT ERE DOST BOAST, | SOSPETTO D'HERODE | 251 | 46 109 216 |
| MEE YET A SECOND FALL. WEE'D TRY OUR STRENGTHS. | SOSPETTO D'HERODE | 254 | 46 109 216 |
| THAT HEAVENLY MAXIM GAVE ME HEART TO TRY | AN APOLOGIE FOR HYMNE (TERESA) | 9 | 46 136 59 |
| MY OWNE APOLLO, TRY IF I CAN MAKE | TO THE MORNING | 16 | 46 183 497 |
| CALL'D PILAT UP. TO TRY IF HE | OFFICE H. CROSS PRIME | 3 | 52 267 91 |
| BUT THERE IS WITT IN WRATH, AND THEY WILL TRY | OFFICE H. CROSS THIRD | 5 | 52 268 93 |
| THAT HOPEFULL MAXIME GAVE ME HART TO TRY | AN APOLOGIE FOR (TERESA) HYMNE | 9 | 52 322 59 |
| MY FORTUNE TRY | TO SAME CONCERNING CHOISE | 5 | 52 331 66 |
| STILL, AS THEIR VAIN TEARES MY VOWES DID TRY, | ALEXIAS THIRD ELEGIE | 55 | 52 336 209 |

TRYD

| | | | |
|---|---|---|---|
| WHO GRANTS AT LAST, LONG TIME TRYD | TO COUNTESSE OF DENBIGH | 15 | 52 236 146 |

TRY'D

| | | | |
|---|---|---|---|
| COME IF THOU DAR'ST, THUS, THUS LET US BE TRY'D. | UPON THE SAME (VENUS ARMES) | 2 | 46 161 523 |
| EACH FLOWERS A PREGNANT POYSON, TRY'D AND GOOD, | SOSPETTO D'HERODE | 347 | 46 109 216 |
| WHOM LONG NONE COULD OBTAIN, THOUGH THOUSANDS TRY'D, | ALEXIAS FIRST ELEGIE | 2 | 52 334 204 |
| AND TRY'D TO MAKE A WIDOW ERE A WIFE. | ALEXIAS FIRST ELEGIE | 6 | 52 334 204 |

TRY'DE

    WHO GRANTS AT LAST, A GREAT TRY'DE,                      AGAINST IRRESOLUTION AND DELAY     9   52 347 146

TRYES

    ALAS. IN VAINE. FOR WHILE (SWEET SOULE) SHEE TRYES    MUSICKS DUELL                    161  46 149 535
    SHEE 'GAINST THOSE MOTHER-DIAMONDS TRYES              A HYMNE OF THE NATIVITY          69  46 106  76

TUGG

    BAITE THY DISEASE, AND WHILE THEY TUGG                IN PRAISE OF LESSIUS           2  46 156 510

TUGGE

    BAIT THY DISEASE, AND WHILST THEY TUGGE,              TEMPERANCE                        2  52 342 510

TUMULTS

    WARRES RATLING TUMULTS, OR SOME TYRANTS FALL.        HORATIJ ILLE & NEFASTO         48  MS 382 530

TUMULTUOUS

    (THESE TUMULTUOUS SHOPS OF NOISE)                    ON A PRAYER BOOKE            60  46 126 139
    FALSE LIGHTS OF FLAIRING GEMMES, TUMULTUOUS JOYES.    DESCRIPTION RELIGIOUS HOUSE    5  52 338 213

TUMULTUOUSE

    (THOSE TUMULTUOUSE SHOPS OF NOISE)                 PRAYER TO GENTLE-WOMAN        66  52 328 139

TUNE

    OR TUNE A SONG OF VICTORY TO MEE.                   MUSICKS DUELL                109  46 149 535
    DOTH TUNE THE SPHAEARES, AND MAKE HEAVENS SELFE LOOKE  MUSICKS DUELL                118  46 149 535
    EXPECTING BY THY VOYCE TO TUNE HIS LUTE.              UPON YORKE HIS BIRTH        115  46 176 500
    AND NIGHTINGALES ARE OUT OF TUNE.                   THOUGH NOW 'TIS NEITHER       2  MS 397 492
    HOW OUT OF TUNE THE WORLD NOW LIES.                 UPON DEATH OF A FREIND       15  MS 393 477

TUNED

    A MAN WHOSE TUNED HUMOURS BEE,                     IN PRAISE OF LESSIUS        37  46 156 510
    A MAN, WHOSE TUNED HUMORS BE                      TEMPERANCE                      35  52 342 510

TUN'D

    OF HIS TUN'D ACCENTS. BUT IF ONCE                   OUT OF GREEKE CUPID'S CRYER   28  46 159 519
    TUN'D TO MY GREAT SHEPHEARDS PRAISE.                PSALME 23                     34  46 102   5
    IF WHAT TO OTHER TONGUES IS TUN'D SO HIGH,           AN APOLOGIE FOR HYMNE (TERESA) 10  46 136  59
    WHOSE VAST INTELLIGENCES TUN'D THE POLES             UPON YORKE HIS BIRTH        36  46 176 500
    IF, WHAT TO OTHER TONGUES IS TUN'D SO HIGH,          AN APOLOGIE FOR (TERESA) HYMNE 10  52 322  59

FITT-TUN'D

    INTO A HASTY FITT-TUN'D HARMONY.                   TO THE NAME OF JESUS        50  52 239  30

TUNEFULL

    THAT TALKES WITH TUNEFULL STRING.                  TO THE NAME OF JESUS        48  52 239  30

TURN

    TURN SPEARES, & STRAIGHT COME HOME AGAIN.             SANCTA MARIA DOLORUM        30  52 283 162
    TRANSSUM'D, & TAUGHT TO TURN DIVINE.                LAUDA SION SALVATOREM       30  52 294 178
    AND TURN LOVE'S SOULDIERS, UPON THEE               TERESA                        95  52 315  52
    TEARES SHALL TAKE COMFORT, & TURN GEMMS              TERESA                     149  52 315  52
    AND TURN NOT BEASTS, BUT ANGELS.  LET THE KING       AN APOLOGIE FOR (TERESA) HYMNE 37  52 322  59

TURN'D

    QUITE TURN'D. TH'INGRATEFULL REBELLS THIS THEIR YOUNG  SOSPETTO D'HERODE           43b  46 109 216
    FIRST TURN'D TO EYES.                                      TO THE NAME OF JESUS       136  52 239  30
    TURN'D THEM TO TEARES, & SPENT THEM TOO.              TO THE NAME OF JESUS       138  52 239  30
    TURN'D THE STEEL POINT OF FEAR,                    VEXILLA REGIS                16  52 277 156
    THEIR SHAGGY LOCKS, THEIR FLOURY MANTLES TURN'D      UPON GUNPOWDER TREASON       47  MS 386 460

TURN'ST

    THOU WATER TURN'ST TO WINE (FAIRE FRIEND OF LIFE)    TO LORD UPON WATER MADE WINE   1  46  91  12

TURNE

    EVERY SMOOTH TURNE, EVERY DELICIOUS STROAKE           MUSICKS DUELL                131  46 149 535
    AND TURNE LOVES SOULDIERS, UPON THEE.               IN MEMORY OF LADY MADRE TERESA 95  46 131  52
    TEARES SHALL TAKE COMFORT, AND TURNE GEMS.           IN MEMORY OF LADY MADRE TERESA 150  46 131  52
    AND TURNE NOT BEASTS, BUT ANGELS.  LET THE KING,     AN APOLOGIE FOR HYMNE (TERESA) 37  46 136  59
    WHEN NIGHT BEHELD THEM, SHAME DID ALMOST TURNE       UPON GUNPOWDER TREASON       11  MS 387 461

TURNES

    AND SO TURNES WINE TO WATER BACKE AGAINE.            TO LORD UPON WATER MADE WINE   4  46  91  12
    THE WILD TURNES OF THE WANTON SUN.                  THOUGH NOW 'TIS NEITHER      26  MS 397 492

## TURNING

| | | | | | |
|---|---|---|---|---|---|
| HANDLING & TURNING THEM WITH AN UNWOUNDED EYE. | AND A CERTAINE PRIEST PASSED | 2 | 46 | 94 | 17 |
| TURNING HER OUT TO TREMBLE IN THE COLD. | ON A TREATISE OF CHARITY | 56 | 46 | 137 | 69 |

## TURTLE

| | | | | | |
|---|---|---|---|---|---|
| OR (FOR TWO TURTLE DOVES) IT SHALL SUFFICE | ON A TREATISE OF CHARITY | 47 | 46 | 137 | 69 |

## TURTLE-DOVE

| | | | | | |
|---|---|---|---|---|---|
| OF A POOR PANTING TURTLE-DOVE. | TO THE NAME OF JESUS | 108 | 52 | 239 | 30 |
| O MOTHER TURTLE-DOVE. | SANCTA MARIA DOLORUM | 41 | 52 | 283 | 162 |

## TURTLES

| | | | | | |
|---|---|---|---|---|---|
| THOSE OF TURTLES, CHAST, AND TRUE, | ON A PRAYER BOOKE | 24 | 46 | 126 | 139 |
| THEY (SWEET TURTLES) FOLDED LYE, | AN EPITAPH HUSBAND AND WIFE | 9 | 46 | 174 | 478 |
| THOSE OF TURTLES, CHAST & TRUE. | PRAYER TO GENTLE-WOMAN | 30 | 52 | 328 | 139 |
| THEY, SWEET TURTLES, FOLDED LY | AN EPITAPH UPON MARRIED COUPLE | 9 | 52 | 339 | 478 |

## TWELVE

| | | | | | |
|---|---|---|---|---|---|
| TO THE GREAT TWELVE DISTRIBUTED | LAUDA SION SALVATOREM | 10 | 52 | 294 | 178 |

## TWENTY

| | | | | | |
|---|---|---|---|---|---|
| TWICE TWENTY DAYES PURE ABSTINENCE, TO FEED | OUT OF GROTIUS | 59 | MS | 398 | 198 |

## TWICE

| | | | | | |
|---|---|---|---|---|---|
| OF SIN, AND DEATH, TWICE DIPT IN THE DIRE STAINES | SOSPETTO D'HERODE | 327 | 46 | 109 | 216 |
| TWICE DI'D IN THINE OWNE BLUSHES, AND DID'ST RUN | TO THE MORNING | 9 | 46 | 183 | 497 |
| TO BE PAY'D TWICE. OR ONCE, IN VAIN. | DIES IRAE | 40 | 52 | 298 | 186 |
| OF ROSY MARTYRDOME, TWICE MARRIED. | ALEXIAS THIRD ELEGIE | 48 | 52 | 336 | 209 |
| TWICE TWENTY DAYES PURE ABSTINENCE, TO FEED | OUT OF GROTIUS | 59 | MS | 398 | 198 |

## TWIG

| | | | | | |
|---|---|---|---|---|---|
| OF SUPPLE MOISTURE. NO COY TWIG BUT WILL | OUT OF VIRGIL | 16 | 46 | 155 | 529 |

## TWINCKLING

| | | | | | |
|---|---|---|---|---|---|
| THOSE TWINCKLING EYES OF HEAVEN, WHICH EV'N NOW SHIN'D, | ON GUNPOWDER-TREASON | 31 | MS | 384 | 458 |
| JOVES TWINCKLING TAPERS, THAT DOE LIGHT THE WORLD, | UPON GUNPOWDER TREASON | 27 | MS | 386 | 460 |

## TWINE

| | | | | | |
|---|---|---|---|---|---|
| AS LUMPES OF SUGAR LOSE THEMSELVES, AND TWINE | ON HOPE | 59 | 46 | 143 | 71 |
| BOTH LAWRELS TWINE INTO ONE WREATH, AND WOOE | UPON YORKE HIS BIRTH | 38 | 46 | 176 | 500 |
| ALONE, LIGHT SUCH ANOTHER STARRE, AND TWINE | UPON YORKE HIS BIRTH | 56 | 46 | 176 | 500 |
| O LET US TWINE | OFFICE H. CROSS PRIME | 13 | 52 | 267 | 91 |
| AS LUMPES OF SUGAR LOOSE THEMSELVES. AND TWINE | (ON) HOPE | 29 | 52 | 345 | 71 |

## TWIN'D

| | | | | | |
|---|---|---|---|---|---|
| WITH WHIPS OF THRONES AND KNOTTY VIPERS TWIN'D | SOSPETTO D'HERODE | 67 | 46 | 109 | 216 |
| THOUGH THEIR BEST ASPECTS TWIN'D UPON | LOVES HOROSCOPE | 25 | 46 | 185 | 483 |

## TWINES

| | | | | | |
|---|---|---|---|---|---|
| THE FURIES CURL'D SNAKES MEET IN GENTLE TWINES, | HORATIJ ILLE & NEFASTO | 52 | MS | 382 | 530 |

## TWINNE

| | | | | | |
|---|---|---|---|---|---|
| TWINNE SUNNES.) & TAUGHT NOW TO NEGOTIATE YOU. | IN GLORIOUS EPIPHANIE | 204 | 52 | 253 | 39 |

## TWINNES

| | | | | | |
|---|---|---|---|---|---|
| THOSE SPARKLING TWINNES OF LIGHT SHOULD I NOW STILE | UPON BIRTH PRINCESSE E | 43 | MS | 391 | 456 |

## TWISTED

| | | | | | |
|---|---|---|---|---|---|
| THE WHILE HIS TWISTED TAYLE HEE GNAW'D FOR SPIGHT. | SOSPETTO D'HERODE | 152 | 46 | 109 | 216 |

## TWO

| | | | | | |
|---|---|---|---|---|---|
| A LINE OR TWO, TO SPEAKE HIM DEAD. | UPON THE DEATH OF A GENTLEMAN | 8 | 46 | 166 | 472 |
| TWO MITES, TWO DROPS, (YET ALL HER HOUSE AND LAND) | WIDOWES MITES | 1 | 46 | 86 | 21 |
| TWO MITES, TWO DROPS, (YET ALL HER HOUSE AND LAND) | WIDOWES MITES | 1 | 46 | 86 | 21 |
| TWO WENT TO PRAY. O RATHER SAY | TWO WENT TO PRAY | 1 | 46 | 89 | 16 |
| TWO DEVILLS AT ONE BLOW THOU HAST LAID FLAT, | UPON DUMBE DEVILL CAST OUT | 1 | 46 | 93 | 14 |
| TWO SISTER-SEAS OF VIRGINS MILKE, | A HYMNE OF THE NATIVITY | 61 | 46 | 106 | 76 |
| WHICH LIKE TWO BOSOM'D SAILES EMBRACE THE DIMME | SOSPETTO D'HERODE | 142 | 46 | 109 | 216 |
| NOR ON GODS ALTAR CAST TWO SCORCHING EYES | ON A TREATISE OF CHARITY | 43 | 46 | 137 | 69 |
| OR (FOR TWO TURTLE DOVES) IT SHALL SUFFICE | ON A TREATISE OF CHARITY | 47 | 46 | 137 | 69 |
| BUT IN THY FAIREST EYES FIND TWO FOR ONE. | AN HIMNE FOR CIRCUMCISION | 38 | 46 | 141 | 37 |
| TWO SILKEN SISTER FLOWERS CONSULT, AND LAY | UPON YORKE HIS BIRTH | 60 | 46 | 176 | 500 |
| THOU CHEAT'ST US FORD, MAK'ST ONE SEEME TWO BY ART. | UPON FORD'S TRAGEDYES | 1 | 46 | 181 | 495 |
| TWO EVER BLUSHING BEDS OF NEW-BORNE ROSES. | ON A FOULE MORNING | 18 | 46 | 176 | 495 |
| THE FIRST BLAST OF THY COUGH LEFT TWO ALONE, | OUT OF MARTIALL | 3 | 46 | 188 | 527 |
| WE TWO BETWIXT US HAVE DIVIDED IT. | OUT OF THE ITALIAN (2) | 2 | 46 | 190 | 547 |

|   |   |   |   |   |   |
|---|---|---|---|---|---|
| SHEWES THE TWO TERMES AND LIMITS OF TIME'S RACE. | ON FRONTISPIECE ISAACSONS | 22 | 46 | 191 | 491 |
| ONE LITTLE WORLD OR TWO | TO THE NAME OF JESUS | 24 | 52 | 239 | 30 |
| TWO SISTER-SEAS OF VIRGIN-MILK, | IN HOLY NATIVITY | 87 | 52 | 246 | 76 |
| TILL THUS TRIUMPHANTLY TAM'D (O YE TWO | IN GLORIOUS EPIPHANIE | 203 | 52 | 253 | 39 |
| HE'S FOLLOW'D BY TWO FAITHFULL FOUNTAINES. | WEEPER | 112 | 52 | 307 | 120 |
| TWO WALKING BATHS. TWO WEEPING MOTIONS. | WEEPER | 113 | 52 | 307 | 120 |
| TWO WALKING BATHS. TWO WEEPING MOTIONS. | WEEPER | 113 | 52 | 307 | 120 |

TYMPANIE

|   |   |   |   |   |   |
|---|---|---|---|---|---|
| CURE THEE OF THY DELIGHTFULL TYMPANIE. | UPON BIRTH PRINCESSE E | 12 | MS | 391 | 456 |

TYPES

|   |   |   |   |   |   |
|---|---|---|---|---|---|
| TYPES YEILD TO TRUTHES. SHADES SHRINK AWAY. | LAUDA SION SALVATOREM | 23 | 52 | 294 | 178 |

TYRANNY

|   |   |   |   |   |   |
|---|---|---|---|---|---|
| DAY'S SWEAT, AND BY A GENTLE TYRANNY, | SOSPETTO D'HERODE | 388 | 46 | 109 | 216 |
| (IF ANY CAN BE SOFT TO TYRANNY | SOSPETTO D'HERODE | 411 | 46 | 109 | 216 |
| OUT-STARES THE LIDDES OF LARGE-LOOK'T TYRANNY. | UPON STANINOUGH'S DEATH | 26 | 46 | 175 | 475 |
| OUTSTARES THE LIDDES OF LARG-LOOK'T TYRANNY. | DEATH'S LECTURE | 28 | 52 | 340 | 475 |

TYRANT

|   |   |   |   |   |   |
|---|---|---|---|---|---|
| THOSE LAWLESSE TYRANT MASTERS OF THE LAW. | OUT OF GROTIUS | 46 | MS | 398 | 198 |

TYRANTS

|   |   |   |   |   |   |
|---|---|---|---|---|---|
| ASSYRIAN TYRANTS, OR EGYPTIAN KNEW. | SOSPETTO D'HERODE | 366 | 46 | 109 | 216 |
| WHICH ON FALSE TYRANTS HEAD NE'RE FIRMLY STOOD. | SOSPETTO D'HERODE | 492 | 46 | 109 | 216 |
| WARRES RATLING TUMULTS, OR SOME TYRANTS FALL. | HORATIJ ILLE & NEFASTO | 48 | MS | 382 | 530 |

TYRIAN

|   |   |   |   |   |   |
|---|---|---|---|---|---|
| NO SAILES OF TYRIAN SYLK PROUD PAVEMENTS SWEEPING. | DESCRIPTION RELIGIOUS HOUSE | 3 | 52 | 338 | 213 |

TYRRHENE

|   |   |   |   |   |   |
|---|---|---|---|---|---|
| THE TYRRHENE SEAS, AND SHORES SOUND ALL THE SAME. | SOSPETTO D'HERODE | 31 | 46 | 109 | 216 |

UGLY

|   |   |   |   |   |   |
|---|---|---|---|---|---|
| THEIR UGLY ORNAMENTS ARE THE BLOODY STAINES. | SOSPETTO D'HERODE | 311 | 46 | 109 | 216 |

UNBENT

|   |   |   |   |   |   |
|---|---|---|---|---|---|
| FOR BOW HIS UNBENT HAND DID SERVE. | IN CICATRICES DOMINI JESU | 13 | MS | 381 | 27 |

UNBLEMISHT

|   |   |   |   |   |   |
|---|---|---|---|---|---|
| THAT THE UNBLEMISHT LAMBE, BLESSED FOR EVER, | SOSPETTO D'HERODE | 189 | 46 | 109 | 216 |

ALL-UNBLEMISH'T

|   |   |   |   |   |   |
|---|---|---|---|---|---|
| THE BLUSHES OF THY ALL-UNBLEMISH'T MOTHER. | IN GLORIOUS EPIPHANIE | 67 | 52 | 253 | 39 |

UNBLEST

|   |   |   |   |   |   |
|---|---|---|---|---|---|
| HATE IS THY THEAME, AND HEROD, WHOSE UNBLEST | SOSPETTO D'HERODE | 2 | 46 | 109 | 216 |

UNBOUNDED

|   |   |   |   |   |   |
|---|---|---|---|---|---|
| A SUBTLE HARVEST OF UNBOUNDED BREAD, | ON MIRACLE OF LOAVES | 3 | 46 | 86 | 15 |
| OF THIS UNBOUNDED NAME BUILD YOUR WARM NEST. | TO THE NAME OF JESUS | 12 | 52 | 239 | 30 |
| OF THIS UNBOUNDED ALL-IMBRACING SONG. | TO THE NAME OF JESUS | 91 | 52 | 239 | 30 |

UNBROKEN

|   |   |   |   |   |   |
|---|---|---|---|---|---|
| COME LESSE UNBROKEN TO OUR BED, | ON HOPE | 36 | 46 | 143 | 71 |
| COME LESSE UNBROKEN TO OUR BED, | (ON) HOPE | 16 | 52 | 345 | 71 |

UNCASE

|   |   |   |   |   |   |
|---|---|---|---|---|---|
| THY BREASTS CHAST CABINET, AND UNCASE | IN MEMORY OF LADY MADRE TERESA | 72 | 46 | 131 | 52 |
| THY BREST'S CHAST CABINET, & UNCASE | TERESA | 72 | 52 | 315 | 52 |

UNCHARITABLE

|   |   |   |   |   |   |
|---|---|---|---|---|---|
| UNCHARITABLE EV'N TO CHARITIE. | ON A TREATISE OF CHARITY | 58 | 46 | 137 | 69 |

UNCLOATH

|   |   |   |   |   |   |
|---|---|---|---|---|---|
| LO I UNCLOATH AND CLEARE, | WISHES SUPPOSED MISTRESSE | 116 | 46 | 195 | 479 |

UNCOMB'D

|   |   |   |   |   |   |
|---|---|---|---|---|---|
| THEIR LOCKES ARE BEDS OF UNCOMB'D SNAKES THAT WIND | SOSPETTO D'HERODE | 69 | 46 | 109 | 216 |

UNCONSUM'D

|   |   |   |   |   |   |
|---|---|---|---|---|---|
| WHOSE UNCONSUM'D CONSUMPTION PREYS UPON | SOSPETTO D'HERODE | 59 | 46 | 109 | 216 |

UNCONTROULED

| AND TREADS WITH UNCONTROULED STEPS. | NEITHER DURST MAN ASKE | 4 | 46 | 92 | 20 |
| TO CROWNE AN UNCONTROULED FATE, | LOVES HOROSCOPE | 24 | 46 | 185 | 483 |

UNDANTED

| O THOU UNDANTED DAUGHTER OF DESIRES. | FLAMING HEART | 93 | 52 | 324 | 61 |

UNDEFIL'D

| WAKEFULL, HER DEAR VOWES UNDEFIL'D TO KEEP. | ALEXIAS THIRD ELEGIE | 38 | 52 | 336 | 209 |

UNDERSTAND

| PAINTER, WHAT DIDST THOU UNDERSTAND | FLAMING HEART | 13 | 52 | 324 | 61 |

UNDERSTOOD

| OUR HARPES THAT NOW NO MUSICKE UNDERSTOOD, | PSALME 137 | 3 | 46 | 104 | 7 |
| NOR HATH SHEE ERE YET UNDERSTOOD | IN MEMORY OF LADY MADRE TERESA | 21 | 46 | 131 | 52 |
| WHAT WAS TILL NOW NE'RE UNDERSTOOD, | VEXILLA REGIS | 20 | 52 | 277 | 136 |
| NOR HAS SHE E'RE YET UNDERSTOOD | TERESA | 21 | 52 | 315 | 52 |

UNDERTOOK

| SHE NEVER UNDERTOOK TO KNOW | TERESA | 19 | 52 | 315 | 52 |

UNDERTOOKE

| SHEE NEVER UNDERTOOKE TO KNOW, | IN MEMORY OF LADY MADRE TERESA | 19 | 46 | 131 | 52 |

UNDOE

| THEY'R COUNTERFEIT, AND WILL UNDOE THEE. | OUT OF GREEKE CUPID'S CRYER | 62 | 46 | 159 | 519 |
| O 'TWILL UNDOE OUR COMMON MOTHER, | UPON DEATH OF DESIRED HERRYS | 23 | 46 | 168 | 467 |

UNDONE

| HE IS REPULST INDEED. BUT YOU'ARE UNDONE. | TO COUNTESSE OF DENBIGH | 68 | 52 | 236 | 146 |
| TILL DEARLY THUS UNDONE, | IN GLORIOUS EPIPHANIE | 202 | 52 | 253 | 39 |
| BECAUSE SOME DESPERATE FOOL'S UNDONE. | CHARITAS NIMIA | 36 | 52 | 260 | 48 |
| ONLY NOT SLOW TO BE UNDONE. | AGAINST IRRESOLUTION AND DELAY | 60 | 52 | 347 | 146 |
| HE IS REPULS'D INDEED, BUT YOU'R UNDONE. | AGAINST IRRESOLUTION AND DELAY | 90 | 52 | 347 | 146 |

UNDRESSE

| UNDRESSE THY SERAPHIM INTO MINE. | FLAMING HEART | 40 | 52 | 324 | 61 |

UNDRESSES

| THUS HE UNDRESSES | IN GLORIOUS EPIPHANIE | 238 | 52 | 253 | 39 |

UNFEIGN'D

| THY SELFE IN THIS UNFEIGN'D REFLECTION. | UPON STANINOUGH'S DEATH | 20 | 46 | 175 | 475 |

UNFAIGN'D

| YOUR SELVES IN YOUR UNFAIGN'D REFLEXION, | DEATH'S LECTURE | 22 | 52 | 340 | 475 |

UNFILL'D

| UNFILL'D FOR EVER. HERE AMONG THE REST, | SOSPETTO D'HERODE | 331 | 46 | 109 | 216 |

UNFLEDG'D

| YET MAY THESE UNFLEDG'D GRIEFES GIVE FATE SOME GUESSE, | OUR LORD IN HIS CIRCUMCISION | 13 | 46 | 98 | 9 |

UNFOLD

| UNFOLD THY FAIRE FRONT, AND THERE SHALL APPEARE | ON A FOULE MORNING | 7 | 46 | 181 | 495 |
| UNFOLD AT LENGTH, UNFOLD FAIR FLOWRE | TO COUNTESSE OF DENBIGH | 43 | 52 | 236 | 146 |
| UNFOLD AT LENGTH, UNFOLD FAIR FLOWRE | TO COUNTESSE OF DENBIGH | 43 | 52 | 236 | 146 |
| UNFOLD THY FAIR CONCEPTIONS. AND DISPLAY | TO THE NAME OF JESUS | 163 | 52 | 239 | 30 |

UNFORC'T

| UNFORC'T & GENUINE. BUT NOT SHADY THO. | DESCRIPTION RELIGIOUS HOUSE | 10 | 52 | 338 | 213 |

UNGENTLE

| WITH UNGENTLE FLAMES, DOES SHED, | THE TEARE | 23 | 46 | 84 | 50 |
| WITH UNGENTLE FLAMES DOES SHED, | WEEPER | 161 | 52 | 307 | 120 |
| AND TOO UNGENTLE NIPPE OF FROSTY AGE. | AN ELEGY MR STANNINOW | 34 | MS | 394 | 473 |

TH'INGRATEFULL

| QUITE TURN'D. TH'INGRATEFULL REBELLS THIS THEIR YOUNG | SOSPETTO D'HERODE | 438 | 46 | 109 | 216 |

UNHAPPY

  WHILE UNHAPPY CAPTIV'D WEE                PSALME 137                          5   46 104    7

UNION

  ARE GUILDED WITH THE UNION OF THOSE RAYES.      UPON YORKE HIS BIRTH            12   46 176 500

UNITED

  THE STRENGTH OF HER UNITED WORTH.             HIS EPITAPH (HERRYS)             14   46 172 471

WELL-UNITED

  YOUR PROVINCES OF WELL-UNITED WORLDS CAN RAISE.   TO THE NAME OF JESUS             73   52 239   30

UNIVERSAL

  TO THEE, THE WORLD'S GREAT UNIVERSAL EAST.       IN GLORIOUS EPIPHANIE            24   52 253   39

UNIVERSALL

  THY TOMBE, THE UNIVERSALL EAST,               EASTER DAY                          4   46 100   26
  AN UNIVERSALL PALSIE SPREADING O'RE           SOSPETTO D'HERODE               382   46 109 216
  THE FACE OF THINGS, AN UNIVERSALL SMILE.        ON A FOULE MORNING              10   46 181 495
  AN UNIVERSALL SYNOD OF ALL SWEETS.            TO THE NAME OF JESUS            176   52 239   30

UNIVERSE

  THROUGH LEARNINGS UNIVERSE, AND (VAINELY) SOUGHT   UPON BISHOP ANDREWES PICTURE     6   46 163 490

UNKIND

  THAT COULD BE SO UNKIND.                      WHY ARE YEE AFRAID              5   46   88   15
  TO SEE SO MANY UNKIND SWORDS CONTEST          SANCTA MARIA DOLORUM           17   52 283 162
  OF HER UNKIND GIFT MIGHT WE HAVE             O GLORIOSA DOMINA               13   52 302 194
  T'EMBRACE MY TEARES, & KISSE AN UNKIND FATE.     ALEXIAS FIRST ELEGIE             4   52 334 204
  UNKIND. YET ARE MY TEARES STILL TRUE TO ME       ALEXIAS SECONDE ELEGIE           2   52 335 207

UNKINDLY

  KEPT THEM FROM BEING SO UNKINDLY KIS'T.         IN GLORIOUS EPIPHANIE           124   52 253   39
  THOU COULDST NOT SO UNKINDLY ERR              FLAMING HEART                  21   52 324   61

UNKNOWN

  HOW MANY UNKNOWN WORLDS THERE ARE             TO THE NAME OF JESUS            189   52 239   30
  THE UNKNOWN SORROWS OF OUR KING,             OFFICE H. CROSS MATINES          11   52 265   86
  A THOUSAND UNKNOWN RITES                     PRAYER TO GENTLE-WOMAN           79   52 328 139

UNKNOWNE

  A THOUSAND UNKNOWNE RITES                    ON A PRAYER BOOKE               73   46 126 139
  BY THY KIND ARMES TO A KIND WORLD UNKNOWNE.     ON GUNPOWDER-TREASON             8   MS 384 458

UNLESSE

  UNLESSE THE MUSE SING MY APOLOGY.             TO THE MORNING                  4   46 183 497
  UNLESSE IT BE A CRIME TO'HAVE LOV'D TOO WELL.    ALEXIAS THIRD ELEGIE             20   52 336 209

UNLESSE'T

  UNLESSE'T BE RARE, WHAT'S THOUGHT UPON.         PETRONIJ ALES PHASIACIS PETITA   20   MS 382 526

UNLOAD

  DOUBTLES HEE WILL UNLOAD                     ON A PRAYER BOOKE               85   46 126 139
  DOUBTLESSE HE WILL UNLOAD                    PRAYER TO GENTLE-WOMAN           91   52 328 139

UNLOCK

  UNLOCK THY CABINET OF DAY                    TO THE NAME OF JESUS            127   52 239   30

UNLOCKT

  LO, HATH UNLOCKT THEE AT THE VERY HEART.        I AM THE DOORE                   2   46   90   17

UNLOOK'T

  OUR GIDDY FEARES WITH AN UNLOOK'T FOR SHOCKE.   HORATIJ ILLE & NEFASTO          32   MS 382 530

UNLUCKILY

  THEN WAS I KNOWNE,   AND KNOWNE UNLUCKILY       OUT OF GROTIUS                  19   MS 398 198

UNMATED

  UNMATED MALICE. OH UNPEER'D DESPIGHT.          UPON GUNPOWDER TREASON           5   MS 386 460

UNMEASUR'D

  THAT THE UNMEASUR'D GOD SO LOW SHOULD SINKE.   SOSPETTO D'HERODE               171   46 109 216

| | | | |
|---|---|---|---|
| UNMIXED | | | |
| PURE, & UNMIXED CRUELTY THEY TELL, | AN ELEGIE ON DR PORTER | 13 | MS 395 476 |
| UNMIXT | | | |
| UNMIXT FELICITY WITH SILVER WINGS | UPON KINGS CORONATION | 21 | MS 389 454 |
| UNMOV'D | | | |
| UNMOV'D TO SEE ONE WRETCHED, IS TO MAKE HIM SO. | AND A CERTAINE PRIEST PASSED | 4 | 46 94 17 |
| UNNATURAL | | | |
| PROVE NOBLY, HERE, UNNATURAL. | O GLORIOSA DOMINA | 24 | 52 302 194 |
| UNNATURALL | | | |
| OF POIS'NOUS AND UNNATURALL LOVES. EARTH-NURST. | SOSPETTO D'HERODE | 127 | 46 109 216 |
| UNPARTIALL | | | |
| HERE GALLANT LADYES, THIS UNPARTIALL GLASSE | UPON STANINOUGH'S DEATH | 21 | 46 175 475 |
| HERE, GALLANT LADYES. THIS UNPARTIALL GLASSE | DEATH'S LECTURE | 23 | 52 340 475 |
| UNPEARCHT | | | |
| UNPEARCHT, HER VOCALL ARTERIES UNSTRUNG, | PSALME 137 | 21 | 46 104 7 |
| UNPEER'D | | | |
| UNMATED MALICE. OH UNPEER'D DESPIGHT. | UPON GUNPOWDER TREASON | 5 | MS 386 460 |
| UNPITTYING | | | |
| WITH PROUD UNPITTYING FIRE. | WEEPER | 159 | 52 307 120 |
| TH'UNPOLISH'T | | | |
| OF THESE LOOSE GROVES, ROUGH AS TH'UNPOLISH'T ROCKES. | DESCRIPTION RELIGIOUS HOUSE | 14 | 52 338 213 |
| UNQUIET | | | |
| HIS BREST A WHILE FROM CARE'S UNQUIET STING. | SOSPETTO D'HERODE | 396 | 46 109 216 |
| UNREST | | | |
| THE WORME OF JEALOUS ENVY AND UNREST. | SOSPETTO D'HERODE | 493 | 46 109 216 |
| UNRULY | | | |
| UNDER TH' UNRULY BEASTS PROUD FEET HE LIES | HIGH MOUNTED ON AN ANT | 3 | 46 161 523 |
| THE RUSH OF DEATH'S UNRULY WAVE, | HIS EPITAPH (HERRYS) | 47 | 46 172 471 |
| UNSEAL'D | | | |
| AND DRINK THE UNSEAL'D SOURSE OF THEE. | ADORO TE | 54 | 52 291 172 |
| UNSEARCHT | | | |
| THE SELF-SHUTT CABINET OF AN UNSEARCHT SOUL. | TO COUNTESSE OF DENBIGH | 36 | 52 236 146 |
| UNSEASONABLE | | | |
| OF AN UNSEASONABLE NIGHT, | IN GLORIOUS EPIPHANIE | 166 | 52 253 39 |
| UNSEENE | | | |
| WHILE FROM ANOTHER (UNSEENE) CORNER BLOWES | HORATIJ ILLE & NEFASTO | 23 | MS 382 530 |
| UNSHORN | | | |
| HIS SACRED UNSHORN TRESSES. | IN GLORIOUS EPIPHANIE | 239 | 52 253 39 |
| BUT WALKES & UNSHORN WOODS. AND SOULES, JUST SO | DESCRIPTION RELIGIOUS HOUSE | 9 | 52 338 213 |
| UNSPOTTED | | | |
| A MIGHTY BABE, WHOSE PURE, UNSPOTTED BIRTH, | SOSPETTO D'HERODE | 159 | 46 109 216 |
| UNSTAINED | | | |
| WHY SHOULD HIS UNSTAINED BREST MAKE GOOD | CHARITAS NIMIA | 61 | 52 280 48 |
| UNSTAIN'D | | | |
| OF HONEST PARENTAGE OF UNSTAIN'D RACE. | TO PONTIUS WASHING HANDS | 6 | 46 94 23 |
| UNSTRUNG | | | |
| UNPEARCHT, HER VOCALL ARTERIES UNSTRUNG. | PSALME 137 | 21 | 46 104 7 |

UNTAUGHT

   SO LUMPISH STEEL, UNTAUGHT TO MOVE,　　　　　　　　AGAINST IRRESOLUTION AND DELAY　　51　52 347 146

UNTIE

   THAT GREIFE MAY CRACK THAT STRING, & NOW UNTIE　AN ELEGIE ON DR PORTER　　　　　　　35　MS 395 476

UNTIMELY

   CALL'D FOR AN UNTIMELY NIGHT,　　　　　　　　　　UPON DEATH OF DESIRED HERRYS　　53　46 168 467
   IF WINTER'S GONE, WHENCE THIS UNTIMELY COLD,　　AN ELEGY MR STANNINOW　　　　　　19　MS 394 473
   THE MOTHERS JOYES IN AN UNTIMELY CROP.　　　　　OUT OF GROTIUS　　　　　　　　　　26　MS 398 198

UNTOUCH'T

   UNTOUCH'T HER PRETIOUS TOTALL HATH.　　　　　　　LAUDA SION SALVATOREM　　　　　　60　52 294 178
   THEN TO A VIRGIN GRAVE UNTOUCH'T TO GOE.　　　　ALEXIAS THIRD ELEGIE　　　　　　 26　52 336 209

UNTRODEN

   THOSE PURE UNTRODEN PATHES CAN SHOW,　　　　　　THOUGH NOW 'TIS NEITHER　　　　　 8　MS 397 492

UNTUN'D

   PARDON (BRIGHT EXCELLENCE) AN UNTUN'D STRING,　UPON YORKE HIS BIRTH　　　　　　 106　46 176 500

UNTWIN'D

   GENTLY UNTWIN'D HIS THREAD OF LIFE.　　　　　　　AN EPITAPH UPON ASHTON　　　　　 28　46 192 464

UNTY

   WHEN YOUR HANDS UNTY THESE STRINGS,　　　　　　　ON MR. G. HERBERTS BOOKE　　　　　5　46 130　68

UNVALUED

   FOR THIS UNVALUED DIADEM,　　　　　　　　　　　　IN MEMORY OF LADY MADRE TERESA　46　46 131　52
   FOR THIS UNVALUED DIADEM.　　　　　　　　　　　　TERESA　　　　　　　　　　　　　 46　52 315　52

UNWELLCOME

   OR MORE UNWELLCOME WAYES.　　　　　　　　　　　　WEEPER　　　　　　　　　　　　 111　52 307 120

UNWOUNDED

   HANDLING & TURNING THEM WITH AN UNWOUNDED EYE.　AND A CERTAINE PRIEST PASSED　　 2　46　94　17

UNWRINCKLED

   A CLEARE UNWRINCKLED SONG, THEN DOTH SHEE POINT IT　MUSICKS DUELL　　　　　　　 39　46 149 535

ALL-UNWRINKLED

   WHOSE FULL & ALL-UNWRINKLED FACE　　　　　　　　IN GLORIOUS EPIPHANIE　　　　　　28　52 253　39

UPHELD

   FROM OF HER CENTER, HAD NOT JOVE UPHELD　　　　UPON KINGS CORONATION　　　　　　10　MS 390 453

TH'UPRIGHT

   NO MORE THE HYPOCRITE SHALL TH'UPRIGHT BE　　　ON A TREATISE OF CHARITY　　　　39　46 137　69

UPWARDS

   UPWARDS THOU DOST WEEPE,　　　　　　　　　　　　THE WEEPER　　　　　　　　　　　19　46　79 120
   UPWARDS, & PRESSE ON FOR THE PURE INTELLIGENTIALL　IN GLORIOUS EPIPHANIE　　　 222　52 253　39
                    PREY.

   UPWARDS THOU DOST WEEP.　　　　　　　　　　　　　WEEPER　　　　　　　　　　　　　19　52 307 120

URGE

   HER FALLING THOU DID'ST URGE AND THRUST,　　　 PSALME 137　　　　　　　　　　　29　46 104　 7
   AND URGE THEIR SUN INTO THY CLOUD.　　　　　　　IN GLORIOUS EPIPHANIE　　　　　114　52 253　39
   AND URGE THE MURMURING GRAVES TO BRING　　　　 DIES IRAE　　　　　　　　　　　　11　52 298 186
   BOTH WINDS AND WATERS URGE THEIR WAY,　　　　　AGAINST IRRESOLUTION AND DELAY　39　52 347 146

URNE

   TO LIFT ME FROM MY LAZY URNE, TO CLIMBE　　　　TO THE MORNING　　　　　　　　　27　46 183 497
   THAT FETCHETH FRESH LIFE FROM HER FRUITFULL URNE.　EX EUPHORMIONE　　　　　　　 16　MS 392 525

URNS

   URNS, LIKE GODS SANCTUARIES THEY LOOKT OF OLD.　ON A TREATISE OF CHARITY　　　 36　46 137　69

USE

   FOR HIS OWNE SANDS HEE'L USE THY SEAS.　　　　 THE WEEPER　　　　　　　　　　 102　46　79 120
   THAT USE NO VARNISH, NO OYL'D ARTS,　　　　　　A HYMNE OF THE NATIVITY　　　　 75　46 106　76
   VERTUES OF STONES, NOR HERBES. USE STRONGER CHARMES,　SOSPETTO D'HERODE　　　274　46 109 216
   TO PROVE THAT TRUE, SCHOOLES USE TO TELL.　　　ON A PRAYER BOOKE　　　　　　　　 7　46 126 139

| | | | | |
|---|---|---|---|---|
| LET CONSTANT USE BUT KEEP IT BRIGHT, | ON A PRAYER BOOKE | 16 | 46 126 | 139 |
| GRACIOUS HEAVENS DO USE TO SEND | UPON DEATH OF DESIRED HERRYS | 26 | 46 166 | 467 |
| AND USE THE SEASON OF LOVE'S SHOWRE, | TO COUNTESSE OF DENBIGH | 44 | 52 236 | 146 |
| AND THEIR BEST USE OF HIM THEY WORSHIP'T BE | IN GLORIOUS EPIPHANIE | 181 | 52 253 | 39 |
| USE IT TO SPELL THY BEAUTYES BETTER. | IN GLORIOUS EPIPHANIE | 187 | 52 253 | 39 |
| O RATHER USE THIS HEART, THUS FARR A FITTER STONE, | OFFICE H. CROSS COMPLINE | 11 | 52 274 | 105 |
| THEIR USE IS CHANG'D, NOT LOST, AND NOW THEY MOVE | VEXILLA REGIS | 17 | 52 277 | 156 |
| WHOSE USE DENYES US TO THE DEAD. | ADORO TE | 40 | 52 291 | 172 |
| TO PROVE THAT TRUE, SCHOOLES USE TO TELL, | PRAYER TO GENTLE-WOMAN | 13 | 52 328 | 139 |
| LET CONSTANT USE BUT KEEP IT BRIGHT, | PRAYER TO GENTLE-WOMAN | 22 | 52 328 | 139 |
| OR PATTERN FOR THE PACE YOU USE. | AGAINST IRRESOLUTION AND DELAY | 32 | 52 347 | 146 |
| THE STIFFE NECK'D PHARISEES THAT USE TO MOCKE | OUT OF GROTIUS | 42 | MS 398 | 198 |

US'D

| | | | | |
|---|---|---|---|---|
| NOT US'D TO SPEAKE BUT IN HIS BREATH, | UPON THE DEATH OF A GENTLEMAN | 16 | 46 166 | 472 |
| THE SANDS HE US'D NO LONGER PLEASE, | THE WEEPER | 101 | 46 79 | 120 |
| IF IN THE FIRST HE US'D HIS FINGERS TOUCH. | THE DUMBE HEALED | 3 | 46 87 | 16 |

USELESSE

| | | | | |
|---|---|---|---|---|
| THE CENTER SHOOK. HER USELESSE VEIL TH'INGLORIOUS TEMPLE TORE. | OFFICE H. CROSS NINTH | 8 | 52 271 | 99 |

USHER

| | | | | |
|---|---|---|---|---|
| TO USHER IN THIS SHOALE OF PRODIGIES, | ON GUNPOWDER-TREASON | 37 | MS 384 | 458 |
| ACQUAINTANCE WITH THE USHER OF THE MORNE. | UPON KINGS CORONATION | 32 | MS 369 | 454 |

USUALL

| | | | | |
|---|---|---|---|---|
| IF USUALL WIT, AND STRENGTH WILL DOE NO GOOD. | SOSPETTO D'HERODE | 273 | 46 109 | 216 |

USURP'T

| | | | | |
|---|---|---|---|---|
| USURP'T THE PORTION OF THY PAIN, | VEXILLA REGIS | 14 | 52 277 | 156 |

VAIN

| | | | | |
|---|---|---|---|---|
| IT MUST NOT FALL IN VAIN, IT MUST | TO COUNTESSE OF DENBIGH | 51 | 52 236 | 146 |
| WHERE RACKES & TORMENTS STRIV'D, IN VAIN, TO REACH THEE. | TO THE NAME OF JESUS | 206 | 52 239 | 30 |
| TO BE PAY'D TWICE. OR ONCE, IN VAIN. | DIES IRAE | 40 | 52 298 | 186 |
| VAIN LOVES AVANT. BOLD HANDS FORBEAR. | WEEPER | 107 | 52 307 | 120 |
| STILL, AS THEIR VAIN TEARES MY VOWES DID TRY, | ALEXIAS THIRD ELEGIE | 55 | 52 336 | 209 |

VAINE

| | | | | |
|---|---|---|---|---|
| ALAS. IN VAINE. FOR WHILE (SWEET SOULE) SHEE TRYES | MUSICKS DUELL | 161 | 46 149 | 535 |
| VAINE MAN. THE STONES THAT ON HIS TOMBE DOE LYE, | YEE BUILD SEPULCHRES | 3 | 46 95 | 21 |
| AIRE, WITH A DISMALL SHADE, BUT ALL IN VAINE, | SOSPETTO D'HERODE | 143 | 46 109 | 216 |
| A SAD YOAKE, UNDER WHICH THEY SIGH'D IN VAINE, | SOSPETTO D'HERODE | 407 | 46 109 | 216 |
| THY BROTHERS BLOOD BE-SPILT LIFE SPENT IN VAINE. | SOSPETTO D'HERODE | 452 | 46 109 | 216 |
| WHY ART THOU TROUBLED HEROD. WHAT VAINE FEARE | SOSPETTO D'HERODE | 513 | 46 109 | 216 |
| AND VAINE, AS THOSE ARE SHED | WISHES SUPPOSED MISTRESSE | 74 | 46 195 | 479 |

VAYNE

| | | | | |
|---|---|---|---|---|
| OF THEIR MAD SIN. (HOW GREAT, AND YETT HOW VAYNE.) | OUT OF GROTIUS | 30 | MS 398 | 198 |

VAINLY

| | | | | |
|---|---|---|---|---|
| THOUGH THE VEXT CHYMICK VAINLY CHASES | ON HOPE | 85 | 46 143 | 71 |
| THAT (AT THY COST) ARE CALL'D, NOT VAINLY, OURS | IN GLORIOUS EPIPHANIE | 220 | 52 253 | 39 |
| THOUGH THE VEXT CHYMICK VAINLY CHASES | (ON) HOPE | 45 | 52 345 | 71 |

VAINELY

| | | | | |
|---|---|---|---|---|
| MAY THINKE HIS LABOUR VAINELY GONE, | OUT OF GREEKE CUPID'S CRYER | 10 | 46 159 | 519 |
| THROUGH LEARNINGS UNIVERSE, AND (VAINELY) SOUGHT | UPON BISHOP ANDREWES PICTURE | 6 | 46 163 | 490 |

VALERIAN

| | | | | |
|---|---|---|---|---|
| TAKE HEED (SAID SHE) TAKE HEED, VALERIAN. | ALEXIAS THIRD ELEGIE | 34 | 52 336 | 209 |

VALLEY

| | | | | |
|---|---|---|---|---|
| MUSTER FORTH INTO THE VALLEY, | PSALME 23 | 36 | 46 102 | 5 |

VANISH

| | | | | |
|---|---|---|---|---|
| BUT TO VANISH AND BE GONE. | UPON DEATH OF DESIRED HERRYS | 28 | 46 168 | 467 |

VANISHT

| | | | | |
|---|---|---|---|---|
| ALL MELANCHOLY CLOWDS VANISHT AWAY. | UPON KINGS CORONATION | 40 | MS 390 | 453 |

VANQUISH'T

| | | | | |
|---|---|---|---|---|
| SAD THAT THEY ARE VANQUISH'T SO, | THE WEEPER | 76 | 46 79 | 120 |
| SAD THAT THEY ARE VANQUISH'T SO. | WEEPER | 58 | 52 307 | 120 |

## VARIETY

| | | | | |
|---|---|---|---|---|
| COULD MELT INTO SUCH SWEET VARIETY | MUSICKS DUELL | 46 | 46 149 | 535 |
| OF BLEST VARIETY ATTENDING ON | MUSICKS DUELL | 153 | 46 149 | 535 |

## VARIOUS

| | | | | |
|---|---|---|---|---|
| BY VARIOUS GLOSSES. NOW THEY SEEME TO GRUTCH, | MUSICKS DUELL | 128 | 46 149 | 535 |

## VARNISH

| | | | | |
|---|---|---|---|---|
| THAT USE NO VARNISH, NO OYL'D ARTS, | A HYMNE OF THE NATIVITY | 75 | 46 106 | 76 |

## VARY

| | | | | |
|---|---|---|---|---|
| BUT WHISPER TO THE WORLD. THUS DOE THEY VARY | MUSICKS DUELL | 145 | 46 149 | 535 |

## VAST

| | | | | |
|---|---|---|---|---|
| BUT THESE VAST MYSTERIES HIS SENSES SMOTHER, | SOSPETTO D'HERODE | 161 | 46 109 | 216 |
| TO A VAST FIELD OF THORNES, TEN THOUSAND SPEARES | SOSPETTO D'HERODE | 475 | 46 109 | 216 |
| WHOSE VAST INTELLIGENCES TUN'D THE POLES | UPON YORKE HIS BIRTH | 36 | 46 176 | 500 |
| LET HOARY TIME'S VAST BOWELS BE THE GRAVE | ON FRONTISPIECE ISAACSONS | 1 | 46 191 | 491 |

## VAULTS

| | | | | |
|---|---|---|---|---|
| RAN TREMBLING THROUGH THE HOLLOW VAULTS OF NIGHT, | SOSPETTO D'HERODE | 151 | 46 109 | 216 |
| RUNG, THROUGH THE HOLLOW VAULTS OF HELL PROFOUND. | SOSPETTO D'HERODE | 299 | 46 109 | 216 |

## VEIL

| | | | | |
|---|---|---|---|---|
| THE CENTER SHOOK. HER USELESSE VEIL TH'INGLORIOUS TEMPLE TORE. | OFFICE H. CROSS NINTH | 8 | 52 271 | 99 |
| AND FOR THY VEIL GIVE MY THY FACE. | ADORO TE | 56 | 52 291 | 172 |
| GIVE HIM THE VEIL, WHO KINDLY TAKES THE SHAME. | FLAMING HEART | 58 | 52 324 | 61 |
| A THINNE, AERIALL VEIL, IS DRAWN | TEMPERANCE | 26 | 52 342 | 510 |

## VEILE

| | | | | |
|---|---|---|---|---|
| TORE NOT OFF HIS MOTHERS VEILE. | AN EPITAPH UPON ASHTON | 20 | 46 192 | 464 |

## VAIL

| | | | | |
|---|---|---|---|---|
| GIVE HIM THE VAIL, GIVE HER THE DART. | FLAMING HEART | 42 | 52 324 | 61 |
| GIVE HIM THE VAIL. THAT HE MAY COVER | FLAMING HEART | 43 | 52 324 | 61 |

## VAIL'D

| | | | | |
|---|---|---|---|---|
| THE SULLEN HEAVEN HAD VAIL'D ITS MOURNFULL BROW | UPON KINGS CORONATION | 2 | MS 390 | 453 |

## VAILE

| | | | | |
|---|---|---|---|---|
| A THINNE AIEREALL VAILE IS DRAWNE | IN PRAISE OF LESSIUS | 28 | 46 156 | 510 |
| BUT IN A VAILE OF CLOUDS MUFLING HER HEAD | UPON GUNPOWDER TREASON | 17 | MS 386 | 460 |
| WITHHELD HER VAILE, H' HAD FORFEITED HIS SIGHT. | UPON KINGS CORONATION | 20 | MS 390 | 453 |

## VEYLE

| | | | | |
|---|---|---|---|---|
| INTO THY MODEST VEYLE. HOW DID'ST THOU RISE | TO THE MORNING | 8 | 46 183 | 497 |

## VAILES

| | | | | |
|---|---|---|---|---|
| IN VAILES OF DUST THEIR SILKEN HEADS THEY'LE HIDE, | AN ELEGIE ON DR PORTER | 25 | MS 395 | 476 |

## VEINE

| | | | | |
|---|---|---|---|---|
| DIRE FLAMES DIFFUSE THEMSELVES THROUGH EVERY VEINE, | SOSPETTO D'HERODE | 471 | 46 109 | 216 |

## VEIW

| | | | | |
|---|---|---|---|---|
| I VEIW A RISING SUNNE IN THIS OUR SPHAERE, | UPON KINGS CORONATION | 14 | MS 389 | 454 |

## VENGEANCE

| | | | | |
|---|---|---|---|---|
| THERE HAS THE PURPLE VENGEANCE A PROUD SEAT. | SOSPETTO D'HERODE | 313 | 46 109 | 216 |

## VENGING

| | | | | |
|---|---|---|---|---|
| EVEN SUCH AS THESE, LAUGH, TILL A VENGING THRONG | PSALME 137 | 33 | 46 104 | 7 |

## VENTURE

| | | | | |
|---|---|---|---|---|
| HOLDS FAST THE DOOR, YET DARES NOT VENTURE | TO COUNTESSE OF DENBIGH | 3 | 52 236 | 146 |
| AND VENTURE TO SPEAK ONE GOOD WORD | TO SAME CONCERNING CHOISE | 6 | 52 331 | 66 |
| HOLDS FAST THE DOOR, YET DARES NOT VENTURE | AGAINST IRRESOLUTION AND DELAY | 3 | 52 347 | 146 |

## VENUS

| | | | | |
|---|---|---|---|---|
| THEN VENUS MILD INSTINCT (AT SET TIMES) YEILDS | OUT OF VIRGIL | 11 | 46 155 | 529 |
| FROM VENUS LIPPS. BUT AS FOR HIM | OUT OF GREEKE CUPID'S CRYER | 13 | 46 159 | 519 |
| (VENUS ASSURES HIM) THEN A KISSE. | OUT OF GREEKE CUPID'S CRYER | 16 | 46 159 | 519 |
| PALLAS SAW VENUS ARM'D AND STREIGHT SHE CRY'D, | UPON THE SAME (VENUS ARMES) | 1 | 46 161 | 523 |
| WHY FOOLE. SAIES VENUS, THUS PROVOK'ST THOU MEE, | UPON THE SAME (VENUS ARMES) | 3 | 46 161 | 523 |

|  |  |  |  |  |
|---|---|---|---|---|
| VENUS, MAY HAVE A CONSTELLATION. | UPON YORKE HIS BIRTH | 58 | 46 176 | 500 |
| LOVE'S TRUEST KNOTT BY VENUS IS NOT TY'D. | ALEXIAS THIRD ELEGIE | 27 | 52 336 | 209 |

**VERDANT**

|  |  |  |  |  |
|---|---|---|---|---|
| THAT ON THY BANKES SITTS IN A VERDANT BOWER, | AN ELEGIE ON DR PORTER | 22 | MS 395 | 476 |

**VERMILLION**

|  |  |  |  |  |
|---|---|---|---|---|
| DY'D IN VERMILLION BLUSHES, AS BEFORE. | UPON GUNPOWDER TREASON | 16 | MS 386 | 460 |

**VERNALL**

|  |  |  |  |  |
|---|---|---|---|---|
| HEE SAW A VERNALL SMILE, SWEETLY DISFIGURE | SOSPETTO D'HERODE | 109 | 46 109 | 216 |

**VERSE**

|  |  |  |  |  |
|---|---|---|---|---|
| SO MUCH AS TH' PICTURE OF A WELL-LIM'D VERSE. | WITH A PICTURE TO A FRIEND | 4 | 46 156 | 494 |
| FOR THE LAURELL IN HIS VERSE. | UPON THE DEATH OF A GENTLEMAN | 9 | 46 166 | 472 |

**VERTUE**

|  |  |  |  |  |
|---|---|---|---|---|
| BUT VERTUE HEARD IT, AND AWAY SHEE HY'D, | SOSPETTO D'HERODE | 470 | 46 109 | 216 |
| VERTUE TO ACTION, THAT LIFE-FEEDING FLAME | ON A TREATISE OF CHARITY | 51 | 46 137 | 69 |
| SO RARE IS HOARY VERTUE) THE DIRE RAGE | UPON DEATH OF HERRYS | 32 | 46 167 | 466 |
| VERTUE WEARES HIM NEXT HER HEART. | UPON DEATH OF DESIRED HERRYS | 10 | 46 168 | 467 |
| HIS VERTUE THAT WITHIN HAD ROOT, | HIS EPITAPH (HERRYS) | 35 | 46 172 | 471 |
| VERTUE THEIR MISTRESSE, | WISHES SUPPOSED MISTRESSE | 68 | 46 195 | 479 |
| HER COUNSELL HER OWNE VERTUE BEE. | WISHES SUPPOSED MISTRESSE | 102 | 46 195 | 479 |
| YOUR VERTUE WEARS.  YOUR MODESTY | TO THE QUEEN | 4 | 48 215 | 501 |
| EACH VERTUE FOR A PART CAME IN. | UPON DEATH OF A FREIND | 20 | MS 393 | 477 |

**VERTUES**

|  |  |  |  |  |
|---|---|---|---|---|
| VERTUES OF STONES, NOR HERBES, USE STRONGER CHARMES, | SOSPETTO D'HERODE | 274 | 46 109 | 216 |
| THAT NUMBRING OF HIS VERTUES PRAISE. | HIS EPITAPH (HERRYS) | 9 | 46 172 | 471 |
| LOVE, BRAVE VERTUES YOUNGER BROTHER, | LOVES HOROSCOPE | 1 | 46 185 | 483 |
| HONESTIES NURSE, VERTUES BLEST GUARDIAN, | AN ELEGIE ON DR PORTER | 17 | MS 395 | 476 |

**VERY**

|  |  |  |  |  |
|---|---|---|---|---|
| THE VERY TERME, I THINK, WAS FOUND | THE TEARE | 5 | 46 84 | 50 |
| LO, HATH UNLOCKT THEE AT THE VERY HEART. | I AM THE DOORE | 2 | 46 90 | 17 |
| SOE NEARE, IT PROV'D HIS VERY SIDE. | IN CICATRICES DOMINI JESU | 8 | MS 381 | 27 |
| FLEDG'D WITH HER EAGLES WING, THE VERY CHAINE | HORATIJ ILLE & NEFASTO | 28 | MS 332 | 530 |
| THE VERY QUINTESSENCE OF VILLANIE. | UPON GUNPOWDER TREASON | 8 | MS 386 | 460 |
| THEIR APPETITES WERE GONE AT TH' VERY SIGHT. | UPON GUNPOWDER TREASON | 49 | MS 387 | 461 |

**VESSELLS**

|  |  |  |  |  |
|---|---|---|---|---|
| VESSELLS OF VOCALL JOYES, | TO THE NAME OF JESUS | 76 | 52 239 | 30 |

**VESTMENTS**

|  |  |  |  |  |
|---|---|---|---|---|
| IN DOWNY SURPLISSES, & VESTMENTS WHITE, | AN ELEGIE ON DR PORTER | 28 | MS 395 | 476 |

**VEX**

|  |  |  |  |  |
|---|---|---|---|---|
| THUS VEX THE EARTH & TEARE THE BEAUTEOUS SKYES. | ALEXIAS SECONDE ELEGIE | 10 | 52 335 | 207 |

**VEXT**

|  |  |  |  |  |
|---|---|---|---|---|
| AND SUCH THE ROSE ITS SELFE WHEN VEXT | THE TEARE | 22 | 46 84 | 50 |
| THOUGH THE VEXT CHYMICK VAINLY CHASES | ON HOPE | 85 | 46 143 | 71 |
| NOT VEXT & TOST | IN GLORIOUS EPIPHANIE | 32 | 52 253 | 39 |
| SUCH TEARES THE SUFFRING ROSE THAT'S VEXT | WEEPER | 160 | 52 307 | 120 |
| THOUGH THE VEXT CHYMICK VAINLY CHASES | (ON) HOPE | 45 | 52 345 | 71 |

**VEX'T**

|  |  |  |  |  |
|---|---|---|---|---|
| OR HIDING HIS VEX'T CHEEKS IN A HIR'D MIST | IN GLORIOUS EPIPHANIE | 123 | 52 253 | 39 |

**VICE-APOLLO**

|  |  |  |  |  |
|---|---|---|---|---|
| HIM THEY CALL THEIR VICE-APOLLO. | UPON DEATH OF DESIRED HERRYS | 12 | 46 168 | 467 |

**VICTIM**

|  |  |  |  |  |
|---|---|---|---|---|
| THOU ART LOVES VICTIM, AND MUST DYE | IN MEMORY OF LADY MADRE TERESA | 75 | 46 131 | 52 |

**VICTIME**

|  |  |  |  |  |
|---|---|---|---|---|
| THOU ART LOVE'S VICTIME, & MUST DY | TERESA | 75 | 52 315 | 52 |

**VICTORY**

|  |  |  |  |  |
|---|---|---|---|---|
| OR TUNE A SONG OF VICTORY TO MEE. | MUSICKS DUELL | 109 | 46 149 | 535 |
| THE FULL SOUND OF THY VICTORY. | NEITHER DURST MAN ASKE | 18 | 46 92 | 20 |
| AND TO DARE SOMETHING, IS SOME VICTORY. | SOSPETTO D'HERODE | 224 | 46 109 | 216 |
| YOUR TRIUMPH, THOUGH HIS VICTORY. | TO COUNTESSE OF DENBIGH | 60 | 52 236 | 146 |
| PROV'D A NEW PATH OF PATIENT VICTORY. | OFFICE H. CROSS EVENSONG | 25 | 52 273 | 101 |
| YOUR TRIUMPH IN HIS VICTORY. | AGAINST IRRESOLUTION AND DELAY | 80 | 52 347 | 146 |

VICTORIE

THAT WERE BEFORE OF VICTORIE.					IN CICATRICES DOMINI JESU			20	MS 381  27

VICTORIES

WA'ST THY FULL VICTORIES FAIRER INCREASE.			UPON DUMBE DEVILL CAST OUT		 3	46  93  14

VICTORIOUS

WAITING ON THY VICTORIOUS HAND.				NEITHER DURST MAN ASKE			10	46  92  20
VICTORIOUS SIGN						OFFICE H. CROSS PRIME			 9	52 267  91

VICTORS

SHEE DYES. AND LEAVES HER LIFE THE VICTORS PRISE.		MUSICKS DUELL				166	46 149 535

VIE

THESE CATARACTS OF GREIFE, THAT DARE EV'N VIE		AN ELEGY MR STANNINOW			17	MS 394 473

VYE

SWELL. SWELL TO SUCH AN HEIGHT, THAT THOU MAIST VYE		UPON KINGS CORONATION			 9	MS 389 454

VIGOROUS

SHALL WITH A VIGOROUS GUESSE INVADE				IN GLORIOUS EPIPHANIE			192	52 253  39

VIGOUR

HIS ADAMANTINE FETTERS FALL. GREENE VIGOUR			SOSPETTO D'HERODE			107	46 109 216
OR FORGOT THE CRUELL VIGOUR.				ANOTHER ON HERRYS			  3	46 170 469
FULL OF HIGH SPARKELING VIGOUR. TAUGHT BE MEE		OUT OF GROTIUS				 53	MS 398 198

VILE

THAT A VILE MANGER HIS LOW BED SHOULD PROVE.		SOSPETTO D'HERODE			175	46 109 216
VILE HUMANE NATURE MEANS HE NOW T'INVEST			SOSPETTO D'HERODE			227	46 109 216

VILLANIE

THE VERY QUINTESSENCE OF VILLANIE.				UPON GUNPOWDER TREASON			  8	MS 386 460

VINDICATE

THESE LEARNED LEAVES SHALL VINDICATE TO THEE		ON A TREATISE OF CHARITY		 13	46 137  69

VINE

(GROWNE LUSTY NOW.) NO VINE SO WEAKE AND YOUNG		OUT OF VIRGIL				 18	46 155 529
UPON THY ROYALL ELME (FAIRE VINE) AND WHEN			UPON YORKE HIS BIRTH			103	46 176 500
SO LONG OF THIS CHAST VINE					SANCTA MARIA DOLORUM			102	52 283 162
BY THE PURPLING VINE PUT ON.				WEEPER					 62	52 307 120
THAT DIGG'D THESE WELLS, & DREST THIS VINE.			WEEPER					104	52 307 120

VIOLET'S

NOR THE VIOLET'S HUMBLE HEAD.				WEEPER					178	52 307 120

VIOLETT

THAT RUNNES IN VIOLETT PIPES. NONE OTHER FOOD		ON GUNPOWDER-TREASON			 64	MS 384 458

VIOLETS

NOR THE VIOLETS HUMBLE HEAD.				THE WEEPER				136	46  79 120
OR THAT THE PURPLE VIOLETS DID LACE				UPON BIRTH PRINCESSE E			 51	MS 391 456
 THESE PURPLE CURRENTS HEDG'D WITH VIOLETS ROUND		AN ELEGY MR STANNINOW			 22	MS 394 473

VIOLLS

ANGELS WITH CRYSTALL VIOLLS COME				WEEPER					 70	52 307 120

VIPEROUS

OF CERBERUS, OR ALECTO'S VIPEROUS BROOD.			UPON GUNPOWDER TREASON			  4	MS 386 460

VIPERS

WITH WHIPS OF THRONES AND KNOTTY VIPERS TWIN'D		SOSPETTO D'HERODE			 67	46 109 216

VIRGIN

THOU HAD'ST A VIRGIN WOMBE					UPON OUR SAVIOURS TOMBE			  3	46  93  25
FROM THY VIRGIN TOMBE.					EASTER DAY				  2	46 100  26
TO A POORE GALILEAN VIRGIN SENT.				SOSPETTO D'HERODE			 98	46 109 216
FROM A CHAST VIRGIN WOMBE, SHOULD BLESSE THE EARTH.		SOSPETTO D'HERODE			160	46 109 216
YET KEEPE INVIOLATE HER VIRGIN FLOWER.			SOSPETTO D'HERODE			164	46 109 216
THE VIRGIN BIRTHS WITH WHICH THY SPOWSE			IN MEMORY OF LADY MADRE TERESA	169	46 131  52
ARABIA, THERE TO BUILD HER VIRGIN NEST,			UPON DEATH OF HERRYS			 14	46 167 466
CHAST AS THAT VIRGIN HONOUR OF THE EAST,			UPON YORKE HIS BIRTH			 83	46 176 500
NOT ON THE FRESH CHEEKES OF THE VIRGIN MORNE,		ON A FOULE MORNING			 35	46 181 495

|  |  |  |  |  |
|---|---|---|---|---|
| YOUR VIRGIN BOSOME.  THEN WHAT E'RE | THOUGH NOW 'TIS NEITHER | 23 | MS | 397 492 |
| THOU HADST A VIRGIN WOMB, | TO OUR B. LORD | 3 | 52 | 279  25 |
| WHAT NEEDES MY VIRGIN LORD FLY THUS FROM ME. | ALEXIAS THIRD ELEGIE | 23 | 52 | 336 209 |
| WHO ONLY WISH HIS VIRGIN WIFE TO BE. | ALEXIAS THIRD ELEGIE | 24 | 52 | 336 209 |
| THEN TO A VIRGIN GRAVE UNTOUCH'T TO GOE. | ALEXIAS THIRD ELEGIE | 26 | 52 | 336 209 |
| NOR WILL THE VIRGIN JOYES WE WED | (ON) HOPE | 15 | 52 | 345  71 |
| ADULTERATES THE VIRGIN AIRE. WITH DEATH | ON GUNPOWDER-TREASON | 18 | MS | 384 458 |
| OFFER THY SELFE A VIRGIN SACRIFICE | UPON GUNPOWDER TREASON | 35 | MS | 387 461 |
| IT MADE THE VIRGIN PHOENIX COME FARRE | UPON KINGS CORONATION | 30 | MS | 390 453 |
| NOE. NONE OF THESE RAVISH'T THOSE VIRGIN ROSES, | AN ELEGY MR STANNINOW | 37 | MS | 394 473 |

VIRGIN-BIRTHS

|  |  |  |  |  |
|---|---|---|---|---|
| THE VIRGIN-BIRTHS WITH WHICH THY SOVERAIGN SPOUSE | TERESA | 168 | 52 | 315  52 |

VIRGIN-JOYES

|  |  |  |  |  |
|---|---|---|---|---|
| NOR WILL THE VIRGIN-JOYES WEE WED | ON HOPE | 35 | 46 | 143  71 |

VIRGIN-MILK

|  |  |  |  |  |
|---|---|---|---|---|
| TWO SISTER-SEAS OF VIRGIN-MILK. | IN HOLY NATIVITY | 87 | 52 | 246  76 |

VIRGIN'S

|  |  |  |  |  |
|---|---|---|---|---|
| GLORY TO THEE, GREAT VIRGIN'S SON | O GLORIOSA DOMINA | 37 | 52 | 302 194 |
| THE SPOUSE OF VIRGINS & THE VIRGIN'S SON. | PRAYER TO GENTLE-WOMAN | 46 | 52 | 328 139 |

VIRGINS

|  |  |  |  |  |
|---|---|---|---|---|
| TWO SISTER-SEAS OF VIRGINS MILKE. | A HYMNE OF THE NATIVITY | 61 | 46 | 106  76 |
| THREE RIGOUROUS VIRGINS WAITING STILL BEHIND. | SOSPETTO D'HERODE | 65 | 46 | 109 216 |
| THE SPOUSE OF VIRGINS, AND THE VIRGINS SON. | ON A PRAYER BOOKE | 40 | 46 | 126 139 |
| THE SPOUSE OF VIRGINS, AND THE VIRGINS SON. | ON A PRAYER BOOKE | 40 | 46 | 126 139 |
| THE SPOUSE OF VIRGINS & THE VIRGIN'S SON. | PRAYER TO GENTLE-WOMAN | 46 | 52 | 328 139 |

VIRGINITY

|  |  |  |  |  |
|---|---|---|---|---|
| NATURES VIRGINITY HAD NERE BEEN LOST. | ALEXIAS THIRD ELEGIE | 6 | 52 | 336 209 |
| NO FORTRESSE BUILT FOR TRUE VIRGINITY. | ALEXIAS THIRD ELEGIE | 40 | 52 | 336 209 |

VIRTUES

|  |  |  |  |  |
|---|---|---|---|---|
| AND BREAKE UPON MEE.  MY OWNE VIRTUES HEIGHT | OUT OF GROTIUS | 33 | MS | 398 198 |

VISAGES

|  |  |  |  |  |
|---|---|---|---|---|
| AND GREISLY VISAGES DOE FRIGHT THE AIRE. | UPON GUNPOWDER TREASON | 10 | MS | 387 461 |

VITALL

|  |  |  |  |  |
|---|---|---|---|---|
| MY DEAR LORD'S VITALL DEATH. | SANCTA MARIA DOLORUM | 108 | 52 | 283 162 |
| WHOSE VITALL GUST ALONE CAN GIVE | ADORO TE | 41 | 52 | 291 172 |

VOCALL

|  |  |  |  |  |
|---|---|---|---|---|
| HIS FINGERS STRUGGLE WITH THE VOCALL THREADS. | MUSICKS DUELL | 122 | 46 | 149 535 |
| EYES ARE VOCALL, TEARES HAVE TONGUES, | UPON THE DEATH OF A GENTLEMAN | 27 | 46 | 166 472 |
| THAT HE SHOULD FIND A TONGUE AND VOCALL THUNDER, | UPON ASSE THAT BORE SAVIOUR | 9 | 46 |  90  19 |
| UNPEARCHT, HER VOCALL ARTERIES UNSTRUNG, | PSALME 137 | 21 | 46 | 104   7 |
| VESSELLS OF VOCALL JOYES, | TO THE NAME OF JESUS | 76 | 52 | 239  30 |

VOICE

|  |  |  |  |  |
|---|---|---|---|---|
| LIFES FORGE. FAIN'D IS HER VOICE, AND FALSE TOO, BE | SOSPETTO D'HERODE | 423 | 46 | 109 216 |
| EFFECTUALL WISPERS, WHOSE STILL VOICE | PRAYER TO GENTLE-WOMAN | 67 | 52 | 328 139 |
| AND STRETCH'ST THY DISMALL VOICE TOO DEEPE. | UPON DEATH OF A FREIND | 10 | MS | 393 477 |

VOYCE

|  |  |  |  |  |
|---|---|---|---|---|
| HIS CURIOUS FINGERS LENT, HER VOYCE MADE GOOD. | MUSICKS DUELL | 14 | 46 | 149 535 |
| CARVES OUT HER DAINTY VOYCE AS READILY. | MUSICKS DUELL | 22 | 46 | 149 535 |
| THE TORRENT OF A VOYCE, WHOSE MELODY | MUSICKS DUELL | 45 | 46 | 149 535 |
| THERE MIGHT YOU HEARE HER KINDLE HER SOFT VOYCE. | MUSICKS DUELL | 63 | 46 | 149 535 |
| WOULD REACH THE BRASEN VOYCE OF WARR'S HOARCE BIRD. | MUSICKS DUELL | 101 | 46 | 149 535 |
| POORE SIMPLE VOYCE, RAIS'D IN A NATURALL TONE. | MUSICKS DUELL | 164 | 46 | 149 535 |
| MASTER (WITH VOYCE FREE AS THE TRUMPE OF FAME) | SOSPETTO D'HERODE | 439 | 46 | 109 216 |
| EFFECTUALL WHISPERS WHOSE STILL VOYCE, | ON A PRAYER BOOKE | 61 | 46 | 126 139 |
| EXPECTING BY THY VOYCE TO TUNE HIS LUTE. | UPON YORKE HIS BIRTH | 115 | 46 | 176 500 |
| WAS NOTHING, THERE MY VOYCE WAS MED'CINALL. | OUT OF GROTIUS | 70 | MS | 398 198 |

VOLLEYES

|  |  |  |  |  |
|---|---|---|---|---|
| OF SHORT THICKE SOBS, WHOSE THUNDRING VOLLEYES FLOAT, | MUSICKS DUELL | 63 | 46 | 149 535 |

VOLUME

|  |  |  |  |  |
|---|---|---|---|---|
| LOE HERE A LITTLE VOLUME, BUT LARGE BOOKE, | ON A PRAYER BOOKE | 1 | 46 | 126 139 |
| IN THE DARKE VOLUME OF OUR FATE, | ANOTHER ON HERRYS | 41 | 46 | 170 469 |
| LO HERE A LITTLE VOLUME, BUT GREAT BOOK. | PRAYER TO GENTLE-WOMAN | 1 | 52 | 328 139 |

VOLUMES

| | | | | | |
|---|---|---|---|---|---|
| QUICKE VOLUMES OF WILD NOTES, TO LET HIM KNOW | MUSICKS DUELL | 25 | 46 | 149 | 535 |
| FOR LIFE BY VOLUMES LENGTHENED, | UPON THE DEATH OF A GENTLEMAN | 7 | 46 | 166 | 472 |
| IN SILKEN VOLUMES, WHERESOE'RE SHEE'L TREAD, | ON A FOULE MORNING | 25 | 46 | 181 | 495 |

VOLUNTARY

| | | | | | |
|---|---|---|---|---|---|
| A VOLUNTARY MINT, THAT STROWES | WEEPER | 125 | 52 | 307 | 120 |

VOTE

| | | | | | |
|---|---|---|---|---|---|
| SO GOES THE VOTE (NOR ASK THEM, WHY.) | OFFICE H. CROSS THIRD | 3 | 52 | 268 | 93 |

VOTERY

| | | | | | |
|---|---|---|---|---|---|
| WAS EVER KNOWNE TO BE THY VOTERY. | TO THE MORNING | 48 | 46 | 183 | 497 |

VOUCHSAFE

| | | | | | |
|---|---|---|---|---|---|
| O BY THY SELF VOUCHSAFE TO KEEP, | LAUDA SION SALVATOREM | 71 | 52 | 294 | 178 |
| IF WEE'D VOUCHSAFE HIS COMPANY, | AGAINST IRRESOLUTION AND DELAY | 68 | 52 | 347 | 146 |

VOUCHSAFES

| | | | | | |
|---|---|---|---|---|---|
| WHOM MY GOD VOUCHSAFES TO KEEPE | PSALME 23 | 2 | 46 | 102 | 5 |

VOW

| | | | | | |
|---|---|---|---|---|---|
| WE VOW TO MAKE BRAVE WAY | IN GLORIOUS EPIPHANIE | 221 | 52 | 253 | 39 |
| THEIR HOPE, THEIR VOW. | LUKE 2. QUAERIT JESUM | 2 | MS | 379 | 11 |

VOW'D

| | | | | | |
|---|---|---|---|---|---|
| AMONG HIS BRANCHES. YEA, AND VOW'D TO BRING | UPON DEATH OF HERRYS | 12 | 46 | 167 | 466 |
| WERE VOW'D LOVES FLAMING SACRIFICE. | HIS EPITAPH (HERRYS) | 42 | 46 | 172 | 471 |

VOWES

| | | | | | |
|---|---|---|---|---|---|
| WITH WINGED VOWES, | ON A PRAYER BOOKE | 95 | 46 | 126 | 139 |
| WHOM THOU SEEK'ST WITH SO SWIFT VOWES | IN MEMORY OF LADY MADRE TERESA | 66 | 46 | 131 | 52 |
| THEMSELVES THY CROWNE, SONNES OF THY VOWES. | IN MEMORY OF LADY MADRE TERESA | 168 | 46 | 131 | 52 |
| WEAVE THEM A GARLAND OF MY VOWES. | WISHES SUPPOSED MISTRESSE | 108 | 46 | 195 | 479 |
| WHOM THOU SEEKST WITH SO SWIFT VOWES, | TERESA | 66 | 52 | 315 | 52 |
| THEMSELVES THY CROWN. SONS OF THY VOWES | TERESA | 167 | 52 | 315 | 52 |
| WITH WINGED VOWES | PRAYER TO GENTLE-WOMAN | 101 | 52 | 328 | 139 |
| LAYES UP HIS PURER & MORE PRETIOUS VOWES. | TO SAME CONCERNING CHOISE | 35 | 52 | 331 | 66 |
| HERE PERISH'T SHE, POOR HEART, HEAVNS, BE MY VOWES | ALEXIAS FIRST ELEGIE | 31 | 52 | 334 | 204 |
| WITTNESSE, CHAST HEAVNS. NO HAPPYER VOWES I KNOW | ALEXIAS THIRD ELEGIE | 25 | 52 | 336 | 209 |
| WITH HAPPY GAIN HER MAIDEN VOWES MADE GOOD. | ALEXIAS THIRD ELEGIE | 32 | 52 | 336 | 209 |
| WAKEFULL, HER DEAR VOWES UNDEFIL'D TO KEEP. | ALEXIAS THIRD ELEGIE | 38 | 52 | 336 | 209 |
| STILL, AS THEIR VAIN TEARES MY VOWES DID TRY, | ALEXIAS THIRD ELEGIE | 55 | 52 | 336 | 209 |
| EV'EN TO THE NAKED'ST VOWES. THOU ART MY FATE. | EX EUPHORMIONE | 9 | MS | 392 | 525 |

VULGAR

| | | | | | |
|---|---|---|---|---|---|
| THESE FOR VULGAR STOMACKS BE, | PETRONIJ ALES PHASIACIS PETITA | 9 | MS | 382 | 526 |
| SEE, NOTHING'S VULGAR, EVERY ATOME HEERE | UPON BIRTH PRINCESSE E | 39 | MS | 391 | 456 |

WADES

| | | | | | |
|---|---|---|---|---|---|
| THY WRATH THAT WADES HEERE NOW, E'RE LONG SHALL SWIM | OUR LORD IN HIS CIRCUMCISION | 5 | 46 | 98 | 9 |

WAGE

| | | | | | |
|---|---|---|---|---|---|
| THE ANGRY NORTH TO WAGE HIS WARRES. | A HYMNE OF THE NATIVITY | 24 | 46 | 106 | 76 |
| GOE NOW, MAKE MUCH OF THESE. WAGE STILL THEIR WARS | SOSPETTO D'HERODE | 447 | 46 | 109 | 216 |
| THE ANGRY NORTH TO WAGE HIS WARRES. | IN HOLY NATIVITY | 25 | 52 | 246 | 76 |

WAGES

| | | | | | |
|---|---|---|---|---|---|
| STILL WORKE FOR HER, AND HAVE THEIR WAGES FROM HER. | SOSPETTO D'HERODE | 341 | 46 | 109 | 216 |
| AND WORK FOR WORK, NOT WAGES. LET TO MORROW'S | DESCRIPTION RELIGIOUS HOUSE | 21 | 52 | 338 | 213 |

WAGGE

| | | | | | |
|---|---|---|---|---|---|
| MINE IS THE WAGGE. TIS I THAT OWE | OUT OF GREEKE CUPID'S CRYER | 8 | 46 | 159 | 519 |

WAIT

| | | | | | |
|---|---|---|---|---|---|
| WEE (SAID THE HORRID SISTERS) WAIT THY LAWES, | SOSPETTO D'HERODE | 261 | 46 | 109 | 216 |
| WITH CIRCE, SCYLLA, STAND TO WAIT UPON HER. | SOSPETTO D'HERODE | 339 | 46 | 109 | 216 |
| TO WAIT UPON EACH MORNING SIGH. | ON MR. G. HERBERTS BOOKE | 8 | 46 | 130 | 68 |
| IMMORTALL WELLCOMES WAIT ON THEE. | IN MEMORY OF LADY MADRE TERESA | 129 | 46 | 131 | 52 |
| TO WAIT UPON THEE HOME. | ON THE ASSUMPTION | 17 | 46 | 139 | 114 |
| IF MORPHEUS HAVE A MUSE TO WAIT ON MEE. | TO THE MORNING | 18 | 46 | 183 | 497 |
| ON WHOSE FAIRE REVOLUTIONS WAIT | LOVES HOROSCOPE | 13 | 46 | 185 | 483 |
| WHOSE REVOLUTIONS WAIT UPON | THOUGH NOW 'TIS NEITHER | 25 | MS | 397 | 492 |
| TO WAIT AT THE LOVE-CROWNED DOORES OF | TO THE NAME OF JESUS | 42 | 52 | 239 | 30 |
| THE'ATTENDING WORLD, TO WAIT THY RISE, | TO THE NAME OF JESUS | 135 | 52 | 239 | 30 |
| TO WAIT UPON THEE HOME. COME COME AWAY. | IN GLORIOUS ASSUMPTION B. LADY | 16 | 52 | 304 | 114 |
| IMMORTALL WELLCOMES WAIT FOR THEE. | TERESA | 128 | 52 | 315 | 52 |
| LET MYSTICK DEATHS WAIT ON'T. & WISE SOULES BE | FLAMING HEART | 83 | 52 | 324 | 61 |

## WAIT

| | | | | | |
|---|---|---|---|---|---|
| STARRS MUCH TOO FAIR & PURE TO WAIT UPON | TO SAME CONCERNING CHOISE | 31 | 52 | 331 | 66 |
| HEE'S GONE. & HIS LOV'D STEPPES TO WAIT UPON, | LUKE 2. QUAERIT JESUM | 9 | MS | 379 | 11 |

## WAITE

| | | | | | |
|---|---|---|---|---|---|
| AS GLAD TO WAITE UPON THEIR KING IN DEATH. | UPON GUNPOWDER TREASON | 42 | MS | 356 | 460 |

## WAITED

| | | | | | |
|---|---|---|---|---|---|
| AND WAITED FOR THEE AT THE DOORE. | IN MEMORY OF LADY MADRE TERESA | 141 | 46 | 131 | 52 |
| THAT WAITED ON HER BIRTH. SHE GAVE TO THEM | UPON DEATH OF HERRYS | 18 | 46 | 167 | 466 |
| WAITED ON BY A WANDRING MINE, | WEEPER | 124 | 52 | 307 | 120 |
| AND WAITED FOR THEE, AT THE DOOR, | TERESA | 140 | 52 | 315 | 52 |

## WAITETH

| | | | | | |
|---|---|---|---|---|---|
| EACH MINUTE WAITETH HEERE. | THE WEEPER | 93 | 46 | 79 | 120 |

## WAITS

| | | | | | |
|---|---|---|---|---|---|
| THAT MANKINDS TORMENT WAITS UPON MY TEARS. | SOSPETTO D'HERODE | 216 | 46 | 109 | 216 |
| EACH WINGED MOMENT WAITS, | WEEPER | 147 | 52 | 307 | 120 |

## WAITES

| | | | | | |
|---|---|---|---|---|---|
| HOW MUCH MY SUMMER WAITES UPON THY SPRING. | UPON TWO GREENE APRICOCKES | 34 | 48 | 220 | 494 |

## WAITING

| | | | | | |
|---|---|---|---|---|---|
| WAITING ON THY VICTORIOUS HAND, | NEITHER DURST MAN ASKE | 10 | 46 | 92 | 20 |
| THREE RIGOUROUS VIRGINS WAITING STILL BEHIND, | SOSPETTO D'HERODE | 65 | 46 | 109 | 216 |

## WAIWARD

| | | | | | |
|---|---|---|---|---|---|
| WHEN MY WAIWARD BREATH IS FLYING. | PSALME 23 | 17 | 46 | 102 | 5 |

## WAKE

| | | | | | |
|---|---|---|---|---|---|
| TO WAKE THE SUN THAT SLEEPS TOO LONG. | A HYMNE OF THE NATIVITY | 4 | 46 | 106 | 76 |
| QUENCH HIS CURL'D FIRES, WEE'L WAKE WITH OUR ALARMES | SOSPETTO D'HERODE | 278 | 46 | 109 | 216 |
| O CALL THY SELFE HOME TO THY SELFE, WAKE, WAKE, | SOSPETTO D'HERODE | 459 | 46 | 109 | 216 |
| O CALL THY SELFE HOME TO THY SELFE, WAKE, WAKE, | SOSPETTO D'HERODE | 459 | 46 | 109 | 216 |
| LO WHERE I SEE THY OFFRINGS WAKE, AND RISE | ON A TREATISE OF CHARITY | 17 | 46 | 137 | 69 |
| YOU STREIGHT SHALL SEE HER WAKE AND RISE | THOUGH NOW 'TIS NEITHER | 9 | MS | 397 | 492 |
| WAKE LUTE & HARP | TO THE NAME OF JESUS | 46 | 52 | 239 | 30 |
| AND TO THE WORKE OF LOVE THIS MORNING WAKE YOU | TO THE NAME OF JESUS | 54 | 52 | 239 | 30 |
| WAKE. IN THE NAME | TO THE NAME OF JESUS | 55 | 52 | 239 | 30 |
| AND WAKE THE SUN THAT LYES TOO LONG. | IN HOLY NATIVITY | 4 | 52 | 246 | 76 |
| THAT THUS SHALL WAKE | TO SAME CONCERNING CHOISE | 55 | 52 | 331 | 66 |
| OBEDIENT SLUMBERS. THAT CAN WAKE & WEEP, | DESCRIPTION RELIGIOUS HOUSE | 16 | 52 | 336 | 213 |
| AND THEY WAKE INTO A LIGHT, | AN EPITAPH UPON MARRIED COUPLE | 19 | 52 | 339 | 478 |

## WAKT

| | | | | | |
|---|---|---|---|---|---|
| SCARCE WAKT. LIKE WAS THE CRIMSON OF THEIR JOYES, | UPON YORKE HIS BIRTH | 63 | 46 | 176 | 500 |

## WAK'T

| | | | | | |
|---|---|---|---|---|---|
| THE SMILING MORNE HAD NEWLY WAK'T THE DAY, | THE BEGINNING OF HELIODORUS | 1 | 46 | 158 | 517 |

## WAKEN

| | | | | | |
|---|---|---|---|---|---|
| AND THEY WAKEN WITH THAT LIGHT, | AN EPITAPH HUSBAND AND WIFE | 15 | 46 | 174 | 478 |

## WAKES

| | | | | | |
|---|---|---|---|---|---|
| HEE WAKES, AND WITH HIM (NE'RE TO SLEEPE) NEW FEARES. | SOSPETTO D'HERODE | 473 | 46 | 109 | 216 |
| IN HIGH-BUILT NUMBERS WAKES HIS GOLDEN LYRE, | HORATIJ ILLE & NEFASTO | 42 | MS | 382 | 530 |

## WAKING

| | | | | | |
|---|---|---|---|---|---|
| A WAKING EYE AND HAND. LOOKE UP AND SEE | SOSPETTO D'HERODE | 431 | 46 | 109 | 216 |

## WAKEFULL

| | | | | | |
|---|---|---|---|---|---|
| O THESE WAKEFULL WOUNDS OF THINE. | ON WOUNDS OF CRUCIFIED LORD | 1 | 46 | 99 | 24 |
| WAKEFULL, AND WISE | ON A PRAYER BOOKE | 25 | 46 | 126 | 139 |
| MY GRIEFE IS. SO MY WAKEFULL LAY SHALL KNOCKE | TO THE MORNING | 41 | 46 | 183 | 497 |
| BESTOW THY POPPY UPON WAKEFULL WOE, | TO THE MORNING | 55 | 46 | 183 | 497 |
| O SEE, THE WEARY LIDDES OF WAKEFULL HOPE | TO THE NAME OF JESUS | 145 | 52 | 239 | 30 |
| THE WAKEFULL MATINES HAST TO SING | OFFICE H. CROSS MATINES | 10 | 52 | 265 | 86 |
| THE FAIR STARRS FILL THEIR WAKEFULL FIRES THE SUN HIMSELFE DRINKS DAY. | OFFICE H. CROSS PRIME | 8 | 52 | 267 | 91 |
| WAKEFULL & WISE. | PRAYER TO GENTLE-WOMAN | 31 | 52 | 328 | 139 |
| WAKEFULL, HER DEAR VOWES UNDEFIL'D TO KEEP. | ALEXIAS THIRD ELEGIE | 38 | 52 | 336 | 209 |

## EVER-WAKEFULL

| | | | | | |
|---|---|---|---|---|---|
| STILL WOULD THOSE EVER-WAKEFULL SONS OF FIRE | CHARITAS NIMIA | 25 | 52 | 280 | 46 |

## WALK

| | | | | | |
|---|---|---|---|---|---|
| STEPPS, WALK WITH HIM THOSE WAYES OF LIGHT | TERESA | 180 | 52 | 315 | 52 |
| AND WALK THROUGH ALL TONGUES ONE TRIUMPHANT FLAME | FLAMING HEART | 78 | 52 | 324 | 61 |

|   |   |   |   |   |   |
|---|---|---|---|---|---|
| WALK IN A CROWD OF LOVES & MARTYRDOMES. | FLAMING HEART | 82 | 52 | 324 | 61 |

WALKE

|   |   |   |   |   |   |
|---|---|---|---|---|---|
| STEPS, WALKE WITH HIM THOSE WAYES OF LIGHT. | IN MEMORY OF LADY MADRE TERESA | 181 | 46 | 131 | 52 |
| WHOSE FEET CAN WALKE THE MILKY WAY, AND CHUSE | TO THE MORNING | 24 | 46 | 183 | 497 |

WALKS

|   |   |   |   |   |   |
|---|---|---|---|---|---|
| HOPE WALKS. & KICKES THE CURLD HEADS OF CONSPIRING STARRES. | (ON) HOPE | 32 | 52 | 345 | 71 |

WALKES

|   |   |   |   |   |   |
|---|---|---|---|---|---|
| BUT WALKES & UNSHORN WOODS. AND SOULES, JUST SO | DESCRIPTION RELIGIOUS HOUSE | 9 | 52 | 338 | 213 |

WALKING

|   |   |   |   |   |   |
|---|---|---|---|---|---|
| TWO WALKING BATHS. TWO WEEPING MOTIONS. | WEEPER | 113 | 52 | 307 | 120 |

WALLS

|   |   |   |   |   |   |
|---|---|---|---|---|---|
| THY TEMPLE, AND THOSE LOVELY WALLS | PSALME 23 | 63 | 46 | 102 | 5 |
| THE WALLS INEXORABLE STEELE. NO HAND | SOSPETTO D'HERODE | 309 | 46 | 109 | 216 |
| THE WALLS, (ABOMINABLE ORNAMENTS.) | SOSPETTO D'HERODE | 322 | 46 | 109 | 216 |

WALLES

|   |   |   |   |   |   |
|---|---|---|---|---|---|
| (WHEREOF THE BLUSHING WALLES TOOKE BLOODY NOTE) | HORATIJ ILLE & NEFASTO | 10 | MS | 382 | 530 |
| SEE ALL IN MOURNING NOW. THE WALLES ARE JETT. | AN ELEGIE ON DR PORTER | 7 | MS | 395 | 476 |

WALLOWED

|   |   |   |   |   |   |
|---|---|---|---|---|---|
| DEEP IN THE GROANING WATERS WALLOWED | THE BEGINNING OF HELIODORUS | 13 | 46 | 158 | 517 |

WAN

|   |   |   |   |   |   |
|---|---|---|---|---|---|
| PALE SONS OF OUR POMONA. WHOSE WAN CHEEKES | UPON TWO GREENE APRICOCKES | 3 | 48 | 220 | 494 |

WANDER'D

|   |   |   |   |   |   |
|---|---|---|---|---|---|
| O KNEW I WHERE HE WANDER'D, I SHOULD SEE | ALEXIAS FIRST ELEGIE | 9 | 52 | 334 | 204 |

WANDERS

|   |   |   |   |   |   |
|---|---|---|---|---|---|
| HEAVES HER SOFT BOSOME, WANDERS ROUND ABOUT. | MUSICKS DUELL | 88 | 46 | 149 | 535 |

WANDRING

|   |   |   |   |   |   |
|---|---|---|---|---|---|
| SHALL FIND THE WANDRING HEART FROM HOME. | ON A PRAYER BOOKE | 42 | 46 | 126 | 139 |
| WAITED ON BY A WANDRING MINE. | WEEPER | 124 | 52 | 307 | 120 |
| WHILE THROUGH THE WORLD SHE SOUGHT HER WANDRING MATE. | ALEXIAS FIRST ELEGIE | 30 | 52 | 334 | 204 |
| WHO E'RE HE BE WAS THE FIRST WANDRING KNIGHT. | ALEXIAS THIRD ELEGIE | 4 | 52 | 336 | 209 |

WAND'RER

|   |   |   |   |   |   |
|---|---|---|---|---|---|
| THE WINGED WAND'RER, AND THAT NONE | OUT OF GREEKE CUPID'S CRYER | 9 | 46 | 159 | 519 |

WANT

|   |   |   |   |   |   |
|---|---|---|---|---|---|
| NOR WANTON, NOR IN WANT TO BE. | PSALME 23 | 12 | 46 | 102 | 5 |
| AND WANT OF COURAGE NOT TO YEILD. | TO COUNTESSE OF DENBIGH | 62 | 52 | 236 | 146 |
| DETAIN IN NEEDFULL TEARES TO WEEP THE WANT OF THEE. | IN GLORIOUS ASSUMPTION B. LADY | 22 | 52 | 304 | 114 |
| BECAUSE THEY WANT SUCH TEARES AS WE. | WEEPER | 180 | 52 | 307 | 120 |
| AND WANT OF COURAGE NOT TO YEILD. | AGAINST IRRESOLUTION AND DELAY | 84 | 52 | 347 | 146 |

WANTING

|   |   |   |   |   |   |
|---|---|---|---|---|---|
| NO SWEETS SINCE THOU ART WANTING HERE. | ON THE ASSUMPTION | 12 | 46 | 139 | 114 |
| NO SWEETS, BUT THOU, ARE WANTING HERE. | IN GLORIOUS ASSUMPTION B. LADY | 12 | 52 | 304 | 114 |

WANTON

|   |   |   |   |   |   |
|---|---|---|---|---|---|
| FLUTTERING IN WANTON SHOALES, AND TO THE SKY | MUSICKS DUELL | 91 | 46 | 149 | 535 |
| ARE FAN'D AND FRIZLED, IN THE WANTON AYRES | MUSICKS DUELL | 116 | 46 | 149 | 535 |
| AS WHEN A PEECE OF WANTON LAWNE. | IN PRAISE OF LESSIUS | 27 | 46 | 156 | 510 |
| THIS ROAVING WANTON SHALL DESCRY. | OUT OF GREEKE CUPID'S CRYER | 6 | 46 | 159 | 519 |
| WITH WANTON WING, NOW HERE, NOW THERE. | OUT OF GREEKE CUPID'S CRYER | 41 | 46 | 159 | 519 |
| BY THE WANTON SPRING PUT ON, | THE TEARE | 26 | 46 | 84 | 50 |
| THE OTHERS WANTON WEALTH FOAMS HIGH, AND BRAVE, | WIDOWES MITES | 3 | 46 | 86 | 21 |
| NOR WANTON, NOR IN WANT TO BE. | PSALME 23 | 12 | 46 | 102 | 5 |
| ABOUT THEIR SHADY BROWES IN WANTON RINGS. | SOSPETTO D'HERODE | 70 | 46 | 109 | 216 |
| WITH WANTON GALES. HIS BALMY BREATH SHALL LICKE | ON A FOULE MORNING | 13 | 46 | 181 | 495 |
| CAN TAME THE WANTON DAY | WISHES SUPPOSED MISTRESSE | 50 | 46 | 195 | 479 |
| THE WILD TURNES OF THE WANTON SUN. | THOUGH NOW 'TIS NEITHER | 26 | MS | 397 | 492 |
| BY WANTON HEYFER SHALL BE WORN | IN GLORIOUS EPIPHANIE | 94 | 52 | 253 | 39 |
| A WILD RESERVE OF WANTON WRATH. | OFFICE H. CROSS EVENSONG | 4 | 52 | 273 | 101 |
| GROWES WANTON, & WILL DY. | CHARITAS NIMIA | 44 | 52 | 280 | 48 |
| QUICK BURYE'D IN THE WANTON TOMB | O GLORIOSA DOMINA | 15 | 52 | 302 | 194 |
| STANDS ARM'D. TO SHEILD ME FROM ALL WANTON WRONG. | ALEXIAS THIRD ELEGIE | 36 | 52 | 336 | 209 |
| AS WHEN A PEICE OF WANTON LAWN | TEMPERANCE | 25 | 52 | 342 | 510 |
| GIVING HIS WANTON PALFREYS LEAVE TO PLAY | UPON GUNPOWDER TREASON | 20 | MS | 386 | 460 |

## WANTON'ST

| | | | | | |
|---|---|---|---|---|---|
| WHAT PRINCE'S WANTON'ST PRIDE E'RE COULD | WEEPER | 119 | 52 | 307 | 120 |

## WANTONNESSE

| | | | | | |
|---|---|---|---|---|---|
| TO DROWNE THE WANTONNESSE OF HIS WILD THIRST. | OUR LORD IN HIS CIRCUMCISION | 8 | 46 | 98 | 9 |

## WARBLES

| | | | | | |
|---|---|---|---|---|---|
| IN CONTROVERTING WARBLES EVENLY SHAR'D. | MUSICKS DUELL | 42 | 46 | 149 | 535 |

## WARBLING

| | | | | | |
|---|---|---|---|---|---|
| SHARPE AIRES, AND STAGGERS IN A WARBLING DOUBT | MUSICKS DUELL | 58 | 46 | 149 | 535 |
| OF WARBLING SERAPHIM TO THE EARES OF LOVE, | TO THE NAME OF JESUS | 106 | 52 | 239 | 30 |

## WARDROBE

| | | | | | |
|---|---|---|---|---|---|
| OPENING THE PURPLE WARDROBE OF THY SIDE. | ON CRUCIFIED LORD BLOODY | 4 | 46 | 100 | 24 |
| OPENING THE PURPLE WARDROBE IN THY SIDE. | UPON BODY OF OUR LORD | 4 | 52 | 290 | 24 |

## WARM

| | | | | | |
|---|---|---|---|---|---|
| OF THIS UNBOUNDED NAME BUILD YOUR WARM NEST. | TO THE NAME OF JESUS | 12 | 52 | 239 | 30 |
| YOUR DOWN SO WARM, WILL PASSE FOR PURE. | IN HOLY NATIVITY | 63 | 52 | 246 | 76 |
| THE WORLD LYES WARM, & LIKES HIS PLACE. | IN GLORIOUS EPIPHANIE | 37 | 52 | 253 | 39 |
| KEEP WARM THY PRAYSE | CHARITAS NIMIA | 26 | 52 | 280 | 48 |
| WARM SYLVER SHOURES WHERE'RE HE GOES. | WEEPER | 126 | 52 | 307 | 120 |
| SWEATING IN A TOO WARM BED. | WEEPER | 162 | 52 | 307 | 120 |
| WHO FEELS HIS WARM HEART HATCH'D INTO A NEST | AN APOLOGIE FOR (TERESA) HYMNE | 26 | 52 | 322 | 59 |
| (PILLOW HARD, & SHEETES NOT WARM) | AN EPITAPH UPON MARRIED COUPLE | 13 | 52 | 339 | 478 |
| WARM THOUGHTS, FREE SPIRITS FLATTERING | TEMPERANCE | 41 | 52 | 342 | 510 |

## WARME

| | | | | | |
|---|---|---|---|---|---|
| (QUICK WITH WARME ZEPHIRES LIVELY BREATH) LAY FORTH | OUT OF VIRGIL | 13 | 46 | 155 | 529 |
| WARME THOUGHTS FREE SPIRITS, FLATTERING | IN PRAISE OF LESSIUS | 43 | 46 | 156 | 510 |
| SOME PANTING IN THEIR YET WARME RUINES BLED. | THE BEGINNING OF HELIODORUS | 18 | 46 | 158 | 517 |
| SWEATING IN TOO WARME A BED. | THE TEARE | 24 | 46 | 84 | 50 |
| WARME INTO THE ARMES OF DEATH. | PSALME 23 | 72 | 46 | 102 | 5 |
| WHO FINDS HIS WARME HEART, HATCHT INTO A NEST | AN APOLOGIE FOR HYMNE (TERESA) | 26 | 46 | 136 | 59 |
| THAT KEEPS RELIGION WARME. NOT SWELL A NAME | ON A TREATISE OF CHARITY | 52 | 46 | 137 | 69 |
| WHAT WORD SO E'RE HIS BREATH KEPT WARME, | HIS EPITAPH (HERRYS) | 31 | 46 | 172 | 471 |
| O'TH PRETIOUS PHOENIX, WARME UPON HER BREAST. | ON A FOULE MORNING | 22 | 46 | 181 | 495 |
| HER STARRY THRONE. WHOSE HOLY HEATS CAN WARME | TO THE MORNING | 25 | 46 | 183 | 497 |
| SO WARME IN THY SOFT BREST IT CANNOT DYE. | TO THE MORNING | 34 | 46 | 183 | 497 |
| SMILES, THAT CAN WARME | WISHES SUPPOSED MISTRESSE | 61 | 46 | 195 | 479 |
| TO WRACK MY SUITE. OH KEEPE PITTY WARME | ON GUNPOWDER-TREASON | 12 | MS | 384 | 458 |
| IN AZURE CHANNELLS WARME THROUGH MOUNTS OF SNOW. | UPON GUNPOWDER TREASON | 42 | MS | 387 | 461 |

## WARMED

| | | | | | |
|---|---|---|---|---|---|
| WOULD'ST THOU SEE A MAN WHOSE WELL WARMED BLOOD, | IN PRAISE OF LESSIUS | 35 | 46 | 156 | 510 |

## WELL-WARM'D

| | | | | | |
|---|---|---|---|---|---|
| WOULDST' SEE A MAN, WHOSE WELL-WARM'D BLOOD | TEMPERANCE | 33 | 52 | 342 | 510 |

## WARMES

| | | | | | |
|---|---|---|---|---|---|
| WARMES IN THE ONE, COOLES IN THE OTHER. | A HYMNE OF THE NATIVITY | 64 | 46 | 106 | 76 |
| THAT WARMES THE BED OF YOUTH AND BLOOD) | LOVES HOROSCOPE | 30 | 46 | 185 | 483 |
| WARMES IN THE ONE, COOLES IN THE OTHER. | IN HOLY NATIVITY | 90 | 52 | 246 | 76 |

## WARMEST

| | | | | | |
|---|---|---|---|---|---|
| THEN GLUTT THY DIRE LAMPE WITH THE WARMEST BLOOD, | ON GUNPOWDER-TREASON | 63 | MS | 384 | 458 |

## WARN

| | | | | | |
|---|---|---|---|---|---|
| TO WARN EACH SEVERALL KIND | TO THE NAME OF JESUS | 37 | 52 | 239 | 30 |

## WARR

| | | | | | |
|---|---|---|---|---|---|
| ALLMIGHTY LOVE. END THIS LONG WARR, | TO COUNTESSE OF DENBIGH | 29 | 52 | 236 | 146 |

## WARR'S

| | | | | | |
|---|---|---|---|---|---|
| WOULD REACH THE BRASEN VOYCE OF WARR'S HOARCE BIRD. | MUSICKS DUELL | 101 | 46 | 149 | 535 |

## WARRE

| | | | | | |
|---|---|---|---|---|---|
| OF CLOSER STRAINES, AND ERE THE WARRE BEGIN, | MUSICKS DUELL | 19 | 46 | 149 | 535 |
| SHEW'D, THAT STERNE WARRE HAD NEWLY BATH'D HIM THERE | THE BEGINNING OF HELIODORUS | 22 | 46 | 158 | 517 |
| WHERE HUNGRY WARRE HAD MADE HIMSELF A GUEST. | THE BEGINNING OF HELIODORUS | 26 | 46 | 158 | 517 |
| ABOUT HER HATE, WRATH, WARRE, AND SLAUGHTER SWEAT. | SOSPETTO D'HERODE | 315 | 46 | 109 | 216 |
| SEE HOW HEE'S FURNISH'T FOR SO FEAR'D A WARRE. | SOSPETTO D'HERODE | 524 | 46 | 109 | 216 |
| OF PEACE AND WARRE. THOU FOR WHOSE MANLY BROW | UPON YORKE' HIS BIRTH | 37 | 46 | 176 | 500 |
| THAT MADE GREAT LOVE A MAN OF WARRE. | IN CICATRICES DOMINI JESU | 6 | MS | 381 | 27 |
| (THE DUST OF WARRE CLEANE WIP'D AWAY) | IN CICATRICES DOMINI JESU | 18 | MS | 381 | 27 |
| HOW HARD BY SEA, BY WARRE, BY BANISHMENT. | HORATIJ ILLE & NEFASTO | 44 | MS | 382 | 530 |

## WARS

| | | | | |
|---|---|---|---|---|
| GOE NOW, MAKE MUCH OF THESE.  WAGE STILL THEIR WARS | SOSPETTO D'HERODE | 447 | 46 109 | 216 |
| IF THIS WERE WISDOMES GOD, THAT WARS STERNE FATHER, | UPON YORKE HIS BIRTH | 32 | 46 176 | 500 |

## WARRES

| | | | | |
|---|---|---|---|---|
| THE ANGRY NORTH TO WAGE HIS WARRES. | A HYMNE OF THE NATIVITY | 24 | 46 106 | 76 |
| AS KEEP ACCOUNT OF THE LAMBES WARRES | IN MEMORY OF LADY MADRE TERESA | 155 | 46 131 | 52 |
| FORTUNE ALAS ABOVE THE WORLDS LAW WARRES. | ON HOPE | 71 | 46 143 | 71 |
| MAINTAIN THE WILL IN THESE STRANGE WARRES. | TO COUNTESSE OF DENBIGH | 18 | 52 236 | 146 |
| THE ANGRY NORTH TO WAGE HIS WARRES. | IN HOLY NATIVITY | 25 | 52 246 | 76 |
| AND IN THESE CHAST WARRES WHILE THE WING'D WOUNDS FLEE | SANCTA MARIA DOLORUM | 67 | 52 283 | 162 |
| AS KEEP ACCOUNT OF THE LAMB'S WARRES. | TERESA | 154 | 52 315 | 52 |
| FORTUNE. ALAS, ABOVE THE WORLD'S LOW WARRES | (ON) HOPE | 31 | 52 345 | 71 |
| WARRES RATLING TUMULTS, OR SOME TYRANTS FALL. | HORATIJ ILLE & NEFASTO | 48 | MS 382 | 530 |

## WARRS

| | | | | |
|---|---|---|---|---|
| MEN HAD NOT SPURN'D AT MOUNTAINES. NOR MADE WARRS | ALEXIAS THIRD ELEGIE | 9 | 52 336 | 209 |
| MAINTAIN THE WILL IN THESE STRANGE WARRS. | AGAINST IRRESOLUTION AND DELAY | 12 | 52 347 | 146 |

## WARY

| | | | | |
|---|---|---|---|---|
| YOUR WARY LOVE | TO SAME CONCERNING CHOISE | 34 | 52 331 | 66 |

## WASH

| | | | | |
|---|---|---|---|---|
| TO WASH AN AETHIOPE. | ON BAPTIZED AETHIOPIAN | 2 | 46 85 | 29 |
| WHAT WATER SHAL WASH THIS, WHEN THIS HATH WASHED THEE. | TO PONTIUS WASHING HANDS | 16 | 46 94 | 23 |
| TO WASH MY WORLDS OF SINS FROM ME. | ADORO TE | 50 | 52 291 | 172 |
| WASH WITH SYLVER, WIPE WITH GOLD. | WEEPER | 120 | 52 307 | 120 |
| NEW DROPS, WASH OFF THE SWEAT OF THIS DAYE'S SORROWS. | DESCRIPTION RELIGIOUS HOUSE | 22 | 52 338 | 213 |
| AND WITH A GOLDEN WAVE WASH CLEANE AWAY | AN ELEGY MR STANNINOW | 12 | MS 394 | 473 |

## WASHED

| | | | | |
|---|---|---|---|---|
| WHAT WATER SHAL WASH THIS, WHEN THIS HATH WASHED THEE. | TO PONTIUS WASHING HANDS | 16 | 46 94 | 23 |

## WASHT

| | | | | |
|---|---|---|---|---|
| IS WASHT IT SELFE, IN WASHING HIM. | ON WATER OF LORDS BAPTISME | 2 | 46 85 | 12 |
| HE'S WASHT, HIS GLOOMY SKIN A PEACEFULL SHADE | ON BAPTIZED AETHIOPIAN | 3 | 46 85 | 29 |
| THY HANDS ARE WASHT, BUT O THE WATERS SPILT, | TO PONTIUS WASHING HANDS | 1 | 46 88 | 22 |
| THAT LABOUR'D TO HAVE WASHT THY GUILT. | TO PONTIUS WASHING HANDS | 2 | 46 88 | 22 |
| IN YOUR OWN WELLS DECENTLY WASHT, | WEEPER | 88 | 52 307 | 120 |

## WASH'T

| | | | | |
|---|---|---|---|---|
| WITH THESE HE WASH'T THY STAIN, TRANSFER'D THY SMART, | VEXILLA REGIS | 11 | 52 277 | 156 |

## WASHING

| | | | | |
|---|---|---|---|---|
| IS WASHT IT SELFE, IN WASHING HIM. | ON WATER OF LORDS BAPTISME | 2 | 46 85 | 12 |

## WASTED

| | | | | |
|---|---|---|---|---|
| LIFTS HIS MALIGNANT EYES, WASTED WITH CARE, | SOSPETTO D'HERODE | 83 | 46 109 | 216 |
| BY TOO HOT A FIRE, AND WASTED, | IN MEMORY OF LADY MADRE TERESA | 115 | 46 131 | 52 |
| BY TOO HOTT A FIRE, & WASTED | TERESA | 114 | 52 315 | 52 |

## WATCH

| | | | | |
|---|---|---|---|---|
| AND NOW CROSSE FATES A WATCH ABOUT THEE KEEPE. | SOSPETTO D'HERODE | 455 | 46 109 | 216 |
| IT CAN DIGEST. THEN WATCH THE WILDFIRE WELL. | ON GUNPOWDER-TREASON | 65 | MS 384 | 458 |

## WATCHES

| | | | | |
|---|---|---|---|---|
| THAT WATCHES AT HIS PALACE DOORES | TO SAME CONCERNING CHOISE | 28 | 52 331 | 66 |

## WATCHING

| | | | | |
|---|---|---|---|---|
| (WATCHING THEIR WATRY MOTION) | WEEPER | 146 | 52 307 | 120 |

## WATER

| | | | | |
|---|---|---|---|---|
| THEIR MASTERS WATER, THEIR OWNE WINE. | THE WEEPER | 36 | 46 79 | 120 |
| THE WATER OF A DIAMOND. | THE TEARE | 6 | 46 84 | 50 |
| THE WIND HAD NEED BE ANGRY, AND THE WATER BLACK, | WHY ARE YEE AFRAID | 7 | 46 88 | 15 |
| THOU WATER TURN'ST TO WINE (FAIRE FRIEND OF LIFE) | TO LORD UPON WATER MADE WINE | 1 | 46 91 | 12 |
| AND SO TURNES WINE TO WATER BACKE AGAINE. | TO LORD UPON WATER MADE WINE | 4 | 46 91 | 12 |
| WHAT WATER SHAL WASH THIS, WHEN THIS HATH WASHED THEE. | TO PONTIUS WASHING HANDS | 16 | 46 94 | 23 |
| O DOE THOU WATER IT WITH ONE KIND TEARE. | UPON DEATH OF HERRYS | 42 | 46 167 | 466 |
| OF WATER WEDDING BLOOD. | VEXILLA REGIS | 10 | 52 277 | 156 |
| THEIR MASTER'S WATER. THEIR OWN WINE. | WEEPER | 72 | 52 307 | 120 |
| OATHES OF WATER, WORDS OF WIND. | TO SAME CONCERNING CHOISE | 17 | 52 331 | 66 |
| THE WATER BLUSH'D, AND STARTED INTO WINE. | OUT OF GROTIUS | 52 | MS 398 | 198 |

## WATER'D

| | | | | |
|---|---|---|---|---|
| WATER'D BY THE SHOWRES THEY BRING, | ON BLEEDING WOUNDS OF LORD | 21 | 46 101 | 110 |

## WATER'T

| | | | | |
|---|---|---|---|---|
| LET EACH EYE WATER'T WITH A COURTEOUS TEARE. | AN ELEGY MR STANNINOW | 56 | MS 394 | 473 |

## WATERS

| | | | | |
|---|---|---|---|---|
| DEEP IN THE GROANING WATERS WALLOWED | THE BEGINNING OF HELIODORUS | 13 | 46 158 | 517 |
| THY HANDS ARE WASHT, BUT O THE WATERS SPILT, | TO PONTIUS WASHING HANDS | 1 | 46 88 | 22 |
| THE WELL OF LIVING WATERS, LORD, TILL NOW. | ON BLEEDING WOUNDS OF LORD | 42 | 46 101 | 110 |
| THE CALDRON-PRISON'D WATERS STREIGHT CONSPIRE, | SOSPETTO D'HERODE | 483 | 46 109 | 216 |
| POOR WATERS THEIR OWNE PRISONERS BE. | TO COUNTESSE OF DENBIGH | 22 | 52 236 | 146 |
| THE WELL OF LIVING WATERS, LORD, TILL NOW. | UPON BLEEDING CRUCIFIX | 38 | 52 288 | 110 |
| THE SHRILL WINDS CHIDE, THE WATERS WEEP THY STAY. | IN GLORIOUS ASSUMPTION B. LADY | 28 | 52 304 | 114 |
| WATERS ABOVE TH' HEAVNS, WHAT THEY BE | WEEPER | 23 | 52 307 | 120 |
| POOR WATERS THEIR OWN PRISONERS BE. | AGAINST IRRESOLUTION AND DELAY | 22 | 52 347 | 146 |
| BOTH WINDS AND WATERS URGE THEIR WAY, | AGAINST IRRESOLUTION AND DELAY | 39 | 52 347 | 146 |
| UNDER MY FEET, THE WATERS TO BEE WETT. | OUT OF GROTIUS | 68 | MS 398 | 198 |

## WATRY

| | | | | |
|---|---|---|---|---|
| OF ALL THY WATRY ELOQUENCE, | UPON THE DEATH OF A GENTLEMAN | 32 | 46 166 | 472 |
| SAY WATRY BROTHERS | THE WEEPER | 121 | 46 79 | 120 |
| A WATRY DIAMOND. FROM WHENCE | THE TEARE | 4 | 46 84 | 50 |
| THIS WATRY BLOSSOME OF THY EYNE | THE TEARE | 29 | 46 84 | 50 |
| WHICH OF THEM DEEP'ST SHALL DIGGE HER WATRY GRAVE. | SOSPETTO D'HERODE | 428 | 46 109 | 216 |
| THIS WATRY BLOSSOM OF THY EYN, | WEEPER | 65 | 52 307 | 120 |
| (WATCHING THEIR WATRY MOTION) | WEEPER | 146 | 52 307 | 120 |
| AND SURE WHERE LOVERS MAKE THEIR WATRY GRAVES | ALEXIAS FIRST ELEGIE | 25 | 52 334 | 204 |
| MY WATRY HOUR-GLASSE HATH OLD TIMES OUTRUNNE. | ALEXIAS SECONDE ELEGIE | 20 | 52 335 | 207 |

## EVER-WATRY

| | | | | |
|---|---|---|---|---|
| MAKES THY EVER-WATRY EYES | THE WEEPER | 98 | 46 79 | 120 |

## WAT'RY

| | | | | |
|---|---|---|---|---|
| FIXE HEERE THY WAT'RY EYES UPON THESE TOWERS, | AN ELEGIE ON DR PORTER | 3 | MS 395 | 476 |

## WAVE

| | | | | |
|---|---|---|---|---|
| OR WAVE SO PROUD. | WHY ARE YEE AFRAID | 6 | 46 88 | 15 |
| WITH MANY A MERCYLESSE O'RE MASTRING WAVE. | SOSPETTO D'HERODE | 426 | 46 109 | 216 |
| THE RUSH OF DEATH'S UNRULY WAVE. | HIS EPITAPH (HERRYS) | 47 | 46 172 | 471 |
| OR SHOULD I SAY, THAT WITH A SCARLET WAVE | UPON BIRTH PRINCESSE E | 47 | MS 391 | 456 |
| AND WITH A GOLDEN WAVE WASH CLEANE AWAY | AN ELEGY MR STANNINOW | 12 | MS 394 | 473 |
| AND IS INSTRUCTED BY THY GLASSY WAVE | AN ELEGIE ON DR PORTER | 23 | MS 395 | 476 |

## WAV'D

| | | | | |
|---|---|---|---|---|
| AND FOLDS IN WAV'D NOTES WITH A TREMBLING BILL, | MUSICKS DUELL | 60 | 46 149 | 535 |
| ON THE WAV'D BACKE OF EVERY SWELLING STRAINE, | MUSICKS DUELL | 95 | 46 149 | 535 |

## WAVES

| | | | | |
|---|---|---|---|---|
| AND BEAT THE HOT BRASSE WITH REBELLIOUS WAVES. | SOSPETTO D'HERODE | 484 | 46 109 | 216 |
| HER KEELE CUTS NOT THE WAVES, WHERE OUR WINDS STIRRE, | ON HOPE | 73 | 46 143 | 71 |
| THE WEEPING MARINER WILL AUGMENT THE WAVES. | ALEXIAS FIRST ELEGIE | 26 | 52 334 | 204 |
| HER KEEL CUTTS NOT THE WAVES WHERE THESE WINDS STIRR | (ON) HOPE | 33 | 52 345 | 71 |
| MARK HOW THE CURL'D WAVES WORK AND WIND, | AGAINST IRRESOLUTION AND DELAY | 41 | 52 347 | 146 |
| NOR SHOULD WEE NEED THY CRISPED WAVES, FOR WEE | UPON GUNPOWDER TREASON | 35 | MS 386 | 460 |
| THE WILD WAVES COUCH'D. THE SEA FORGOTT TO SWEAT | OUT OF GROTIUS | 67 | MS 398 | 198 |

## WAVELETTS

| | | | | |
|---|---|---|---|---|
| IN CRIMSON WAVELETTS, & IN SCARLET TIDE. | AN ELEGY MR STANNINOW | 24 | MS 394 | 473 |

## WAX

| | | | | |
|---|---|---|---|---|
| NOW WITH NEW RAGE, AND WAX TOO HOT FOR HELL. | SOSPETTO D'HERODE | 148 | 46 109 | 216 |

## WAXEN

| | | | | |
|---|---|---|---|---|
| THAT WHICH THEIR WAXEN MINES ENFOLD, | OUT OF GREEKE CUPID'S CRYER | 26 | 46 159 | 519 |

## WAY

| | | | | |
|---|---|---|---|---|
| A HAPPY SOULE THAT ALL THE WAY, | IN PRAISE OF LESSIUS | 33 | 46 156 | 510 |
| HIS FAWNING CHEEKS, LOOKE NOT THAT WAY | OUT OF GREEKE CUPID'S CRYER | 64 | 46 159 | 519 |
| SHEE FOUND THE WAY HOME, WITH HOLY STRENGTH | UPON BISHOP ANDREWES PICTURE | 8 | 46 163 | 490 |
| WHICH WAY MY POORE TEARS TO HIMSELFE MAY GOE, | COME SEE WHERE THE LORD LAY | 2 | 46 87 | 27 |
| MILKE ALL THE WAY. | TO INFANT MARTYRS | 6 | 46 88 | 10 |
| WAY FOR A RESOLVED MIND. | PSALME 23 | 44 | 46 102 | 5 |
| SWEET CHOISE (SAID I) NO WAY BUT SO, | A HYMNE OF THE NATIVITY | 51 | 46 106 | 76 |
| THE WAY TO BETH'LEM, AND AS BOLDLY BLAZ'D. | SOSPETTO D'HERODE | 132 | 46 109 | 216 |
| WHERE NEVER WING OF ANGELL YET MADE WAY | SOSPETTO D'HERODE | 222 | 46 109 | 216 |
| AND WINTER STROW HER WAY, YEA, SUCH A SORE | SOSPETTO D'HERODE | 380 | 46 109 | 216 |
| ARE SENT ABOUT, WHO POASTING EVERY WAY | SOSPETTO D'HERODE | 510 | 46 109 | 216 |
| TO ASKE THE WINDOWES LEAVE, TO PASSE THAT WAY. | ON A PRAYER BOOKE | 70 | 46 126 | 139 |
| SHEE CLIMBES, AND MAKES A FARRE MORE MILKY WAY. | ON THE ASSUMPTION | 6 | 46 139 | 114 |
| STAGGERS OUT OF THE EAST, LOOSES HER WAY | ON A FOULE MORNING | 2 | 46 181 | 495 |
| WHOSE FEET CAN WALKE THE MILKY WAY, AND CHUSE | TO THE MORNING | 24 | 46 183 | 497 |
| AH MY HEART, IS THAT THE WAY. | LOVES HOROSCOPE | 9 | 46 185 | 483 |
| COME ONCE THE CONQUERING WAY. NOT TO CONFUTE | TO COUNTESSE OF DENBIGH | 39 | 52 236 | 146 |

```
                                                                        PAGE  458

    THEIR FURY BUT MADE WAY                     TO THE NAME OF JESUS          209  52 239  30
    OF WRATH, & MADE THEE WAY THROUGH ALL THOSE WOUNDS.  TO THE NAME OF JESUS 224  52 239  30
    SWEET CHOISE, SAID WE. NO WAY BUT SO        IN HOLY NATIVITY               69  52 246  76
    LO AT LAST HAVE FOUND OUR WAY.              IN GLORIOUS EPIPHANIE          21  52 253  39
    LO WE AT LAST HAVE FOUND THE WAY.           IN GLORIOUS EPIPHANIE          23  52 253  39
    PERTCH'T IN THE MORNING'S WAY               IN GLORIOUS EPIPHANIE          56  52 253  39
    WELCOME, THE WORLD'S SURE WAY.              IN GLORIOUS EPIPHANIE          60  52 253  39
    MISS-LEDDE BEFORE THEY LOST THEIR WAY.      IN GLORIOUS EPIPHANIE         164  52 253  39
    AND TEACH OBSCURE MANKIND A MORE CLOSE WAY  IN GLORIOUS EPIPHANIE         208  52 253  39
    WE VOW TO MAKE BRAVE WAY                    IN GLORIOUS EPIPHANIE         221  52 253  39
    AT LEAST BE IN LOVES WAY.                   SANCTA MARIA DOLORUM           66  52 283 162
    AH THIS WAY BEND THY BENIGN FLOUD           ADORO TE                       47  52 291 172
    DRINK THE SAME WINE. AND THE SAME WAY.      LAUDA SION SALVATOREM          78  52 294 178
    WHO WAS THE CAUSE THOU CAMS'T THIS WAY.     DIES IRAE                      30  52 298 186
    THEN ALL THAT WAY, AND WEARYNESSE.          DIES IRAE                      36  52 298 186
    THE FOUNTAIN SEALD, YET LIFE FOUND WAY.     O GLORIOSA DOMINA              36  52 302 194
    SHE CLIMBS. AND MAKES A FARRE MORE MILKEY WAY.  IN GLORIOUS ASSUMPTION B. LADY  6  52 304 114
    WERE HIS WAY BY THEE,                       WEEPER                         75  52 307 120
    THE WAY INTO THESE WEEPING EYN.             WEEPER                        106  52 307 120
    TO ASK THE WINDOWS LEAVE TO PASSE THAT WAY. PRAYER TO GENTLE-WOMAN         76  52 328 139
    LOVE TOO. THAT LEADS THE WAY, WOULD LEND THE WINGS  ALEXIAS FIRST ELEGIE  17  52 334 204
    AND WHERE LOVE LENDS THE WING, & LEADS THE WAY,  ALEXIAS FIRST ELEGIE     19  52 334 204
    FOR WHO SO HARD, BUT PASSING BY THAT WAY    ALEXIAS FIRST ELEGIE           27  52 334 204
    THAT WEARY LOVE AT LAST MAY FIND HIS WAY.   ALEXIAS SECONDE ELEGIE         30  52 335 207
    BELOW. BUT MEDITATES HER IMMORTALL WAY      DESCRIPTION RELIGIOUS HOUSE    38  52 338 213
    A HAPPY SOUL, THAT ALL THE WAY              TEMPERANCE                     31  52 342 510
    BOTH WINDS AND WATERS URGE THEIR WAY.       AGAINST IRRESOLUTION AND DELAY 39  52 347 146
    WHICH WAY IT THREATS. WITH FEARE THE MERCHANTS MIND  HORATIJ ILLE & NEFASTO 19 MS 382 530
    IT QUITE FORGOTT. THE FEARFULL EARTH GAVE WAY,  ON GUNPOWDER-TREASON       53 MS 384 458
    AFFRIGHTED PHAEBUS WOULD HAVE LOST HIS WAY. UPON GUNPOWDER TREASON         19 MS 386 460
    MUST HAVE A PASSAGE, OR 'TWILL FORCE A WAY. UPON BIRTH PRINCESSE E         14 MS 391 456
    HIS WAY THROUGH BAD, TO MY SUCCESSIVE HURT. OUT OF GROTIUS                 13 MS 398 198

WAYES

    THAT POINTS ME TO THESE WAYES OF BLISSE.    PSALME 23                       4  46 102   5
    (TANGLED IN FORBIDDEN WAYES)                PSALME 23                      22  46 102   5
    STEPS, WALKE WITH HIM THOSE WAYES OF LIGHT. IN MEMORY OF LADY MADRE TERESA 181 46 131  52
    POINTED HIM OUT IN ALL HIS WAYES.           HIS EPITAPH (HERRYS)           39  46 172 471
    OR MORE UNWELLCOME WAYES.                   WEEPER                        111  52 307 120
    STEPPS. WALK WITH HIM THOSE WAYES OF LIGHT  TERESA                        180  52 315  52
    WHOSE WAYES HAVE LEAST TO DOE WITH WINGS,   AGAINST IRRESOLUTION AND DELAY 48  52 347 146

WAIES

    TO HOLD THEIR PEACE IS ALL THE WAIES,       NEITHER DURST MAN ASKE         25  46  92  20

WEAK

    I KNOW THAT IN MY WEAK AND WORTHLESSE SONG  AN APOLOGIE FOR HYMNE (TERESA)  4  46 136  59
    THAT CAN EXALT WEAK EARTH, AND SO REFINE    AN APOLOGIE FOR HYMNE (TERESA) 44  46 136  59
    OUR WEAK DESIRES HAVE DONE THEIR BEST.      ON THE ASSUMPTION              63  46 139 114
    OUR WEAK DESIRES HAVE DONE THEIR BEST,      IN GLORIOUS ASSUMPTION B. LADY 68  52 304 114
    I KNOW, THAT IN MY WEAK & WORTHLESSE SONG   AN APOLOGIE FOR (TERESA) HYMNE  4  52 322  59
    THAT CAN EXALT WEAK EARTH. & SO REFINE      AN APOLOGIE FOR (TERESA) HYMNE 44  52 322  59
    SOME WEAK, INFERIOUR, WOMAN SAINT.          FLAMING HEART                  26  52 324  61

WEAKE

    HER WEAKE CONCEPTIONS. NO LOANE SHADE, BUT RINGS  OUT OF VIRGIL             9  46 155 529
    (GROWNE LUSTY NOW.) NO VINE SO WEAKE AND YOUNG  OUT OF VIRGIL              18  46 155 529
    HEAVENS KING, WHO DOFFS HIMSELFE WEAKE FLESH TO WEARE,  SOSPETTO D'HERODE 515 46 109 216
    HER WEAKE BREAST HEAVES WITH STRONG DESIRE. IN MEMORY OF LADY MADRE TERESA 40 46 131  52
    STILL LIVES, WHICH WHEN WEAKE TIME SHALL BE POUR'D OUT  UPON DEATH OF HERRYS 36 46 167 466
    HER WEAKE BREST HEAVES WITH STRONG DESIRE   TERESA                         40  52 315  52
    A WEAKE A WRETCHED CHILD. EV'N THEN WAS I   OUT OF GROTIUS                 20 MS 398 198
    OF MY WEAKE FEET THE PERSIAN MAGI LAY       OUT OF GROTIUS                 37 MS 398 198

WEAKNES

    IN WEAKNES. WHY YOU CHOOSE SO LONG          TO COUNTESSE OF DENBIGH        10  52 236 146
    OF WEAKNES, SHE MAY WRITE RESOLV'D AT LENGTH,  TO COUNTESSE OF DENBIGH     42  52 236 146
    IT WAS THEIR WEAKNES WOO'D HIS BEAUTY.      IN GLORIOUS EPIPHANIE         183  52 253  39

WEAKNESSE

    WHEN MY SIMPLE WEAKNESSE STRAYES,           PSALME 23                      21  46 102   5
    IN WEAKNESSE) WHY YOU CHUSE SO LONG         AGAINST IRRESOLUTION AND DELAY 18  52 347 146

WEALTH

    WOULDST SEE A MAN ALL, HIS OWNE WEALTH,     IN PRAISE OF LESSIUS           17  46 156 510
    THE OTHERS WANTON WEALTH FOAMS HIGH, AND BRAVE,  WIDOWES MITES              3  46  86  21
    WHAT ALL THY WEALTH IN COUNSAILE.  ALL THY STATE.  ON THE PRODIGALL         3  46  86  17
    MY WEALTH IS GONE, O GOE IT WHERE IT WILL,  DIVES ASKING A DROP             3  46  96  18
    AND IN THE WEALTH OF ONE RICH WORD PROCLAIM TO THE NAME OF JESUS           95  52 239  30
    THE WORTH, THE WEALTH                       OFFICE H. CROSS EVENSONG       15  52 273 101
    HE MIGHT PROVOKE THE WEALTH OF PRINCES.     WEEPER                        118  52 307 120
    WILT' SEE A MAN, ALL HIS OWN WEALTH,        TEMPERANCE                     15  52 342 510

WEALTH'S

    WHOSE WEALTH'S THEIR FLOCK. WHOSE WITT, TO BE  IN HOLY NATIVITY            95  52 246  76
```

## WEALTHY

| | | | | |
|---|---|---|---|---|
| AND WEARE IN THEM HIS WEALTHY DRESSES, | AN HIMNE FOR CIRCUMCISION | 23 | 46 141 | 37 |
| ALL YE WISE SOULES, WHO IN THE WEALTHY BREST | TO THE NAME OF JESUS | 11 | 52 239 | 30 |
| AND WEAR, IN THOSE HIS WEALTHY DRESSES, | NEW YEAR'S DAY | 23 | 52 251 | 37 |
| THEIR WEALTHY TOPS, & FOR THESE FEET CONTEND. | TO THE QUEEN'S MAJESTY | 18 | 52 261 | 47 |

## WEAPON

| | | | | |
|---|---|---|---|---|
| HIS WEAPON IS A LITTLE BOW, | OUT OF GREEKE CUPID'S CRYER | 45 | 46 159 | 519 |
| A NOBLER WEAPON THEN A WOUND. | FLAMING HEART | 72 | 52 324 | 61 |
| THE WEAPON, THAT HE WORE, HE WAS. | IN CICATRICES DOMINI JESU | 12 | MS 381 | 27 |

## WEAPONS

| | | | | |
|---|---|---|---|---|
| THAT HOLD THESE WEAPONS AND THE EYES | ON A PRAYER BOOKE | 23 | 46 126 | 139 |
| WHAT DID THEIR WEAPONS BUT WITH WIDER PORES | TO THE NAME OF JESUS | 211 | 52 239 | 30 |
| WHAT DID THEIR WEAPONS BUT SETT WIDE THE DOORES | TO THE NAME OF JESUS | 216 | 52 239 | 30 |
| THAT WOUNDED BOSOMES THEIR OWN WEAPONS BE. | SANCTA MARIA DOLORUM | 74 | 52 283 | 162 |
| 'THAT HOLD THESE WEAPONS, & THE EYES | PRAYER TO GENTLE-WOMAN | 29 | 52 328 | 139 |
| THESE THE PASSIVE WEAPONS ARE, | IN CICATRICES DOMINI JESU | 5 | MS 381 | 27 |
| HIS WEAPONS WERE NOR STEELE, NOR BRASSE. | IN CICATRICES DOMINI JESU | 11 | MS 381 | 27 |
| THE WEAPONS NOW OF TRIUMPH BE, | IN CICATRICES DOMINI JESU | 19 | MS 381 | 27 |

## WEAR

| | | | | |
|---|---|---|---|---|
| AND WEAR, IN THOSE HIS WEALTHY DRESSES. | NEW YEAR'S DAY | 23 | 52 251 | 37 |
| FOR THEE TO WEAR, BUT THIS, OF THINE OWN BLOOD. | UPON BODY OF OUR LORD | 6 | 52 290 | 24 |
| HOW TO WEAR HER GARMENTS WELL. | TEMPERANCE | 18 | 52 342 | 510 |

## WEARE

| | | | | |
|---|---|---|---|---|
| HOW TO WEARE HER GARMENTS WELL. | IN PRAISE OF LESSIUS | 20 | 46 156 | 510 |
| PROUD WILL HIS SISTER BE TO WEARE | THE TEARE | 11 | 46 84 | 50 |
| WITH TH'PURPLE HE MUST WEARE IN HELL. | UPON LAZARUS HIS TEARES | 4 | 46 89 | 18 |
| FOR THEE TO WEARE, BUT THESE, OF THINE OWNE BLOOD. | ON CRUCIFIED LORD BLOODY | 6 | 46 100 | 24 |
| DEIGNE THOU TO WEARE THIS HUMBLE WREATH THAT BOWES, | SOSPETTO D'HERODE | 15 | 46 109 | 216 |
| AND LIFE SELFE IT WEARE DEATHS FRAILE LIVERY. | SOSPETTO D'HERODE | 168 | 46 109 | 216 |
| HEAVENS KING, WHO DOFFS HIMSELFE WEAKE FLESH TO WEARE, | SOSPETTO D'HERODE | 515 | 46 109 | 216 |
| WHAT ARMOUR DOES HE WEARE. A FEW THIN CLOUTS. | SOSPETTO D'HERODE | 525 | 46 109 | 216 |
| AND WEARE IN THEM HIS WEALTHY DRESSES, | AN HIMNE FOR CIRCUMCISION | 23 | 46 141 | 37 |
| OF NOONE WEARE THEIR OWNE SUNSHINE, O THOU BRIGHT | UPON YORKE HIS BIRTH | 76 | 46 176 | 500 |
| LET IT SUFFICE, SHEE'L WEARE NO MASKE TO DAY. | ON A FOULE MORNING | 38 | 46 181 | 495 |
| TRESSES, THAT WEARE | WISHES SUPPOSED MISTRESSE | 46 | 46 195 | 479 |
| THAT CHAST & CHEAP, AS THE FEW CLOTHES WE WEARE. | DESCRIPTION RELIGIOUS HOUSE | 12 | 52 338 | 213 |
| SUCH WORDS, SOE PRECIOUS, AS THEY MAY NOT WEARE | HORATIJ ILLE & NEFASTO | 46 | MS 382 | 530 |
| SOUND GOODNESSE WITH HER SHADOW WHICH THEY WEARE, | OUT OF GROTIUS | 43 | MS 398 | 198 |

## WEARS

| | | | | |
|---|---|---|---|---|
| YOUR VERTUE WEARS, YOUR MODESTY | TO THE QUEEN | 4 | 48 215 | 501 |

## WEARES

| | | | | |
|---|---|---|---|---|
| THEN, AND ONELY THEN SHEE WEARES | THE WEEPER | 53 | 46 79 | 120 |
| THEN DIVES IN THE ROABES HE WEARES. | UPON LAZARUS HIS TEARES | 2 | 46 89 | 18 |
| PLENTY WEARES ME AT HER BREAST, | PSALME 23 | 10 | 46 102 | 5 |
| AND FOR HIS OLD FAIRE ROABES OF LIGHT, HEE WEARES | SOSPETTO D'HERODE | 43 | 46 109 | 216 |
| IS THE SOLEMNITY MY SORROW WEARES, | SOSPETTO D'HERODE | 215 | 46 109 | 216 |
| VERTUE WEARES HIM NEXT HER HEART. | UPON DEATH OF DESIRED HERRYS | 10 | 46 158 | 467 |
| WITH THEE ALONE HE WEARES NO BEARD, THY BRAINE | UPON TWO GREENE APRICOCKES | 17 | 48 220 | 494 |
| FOR WHILE IN SPORT HE WEARES A SPITEFULL CROWN, | OFFICE H. CROSS THIRD | 7 | 52 268 | 93 |
| THEN, & ONLY THEN, SHE WEARES | WEEPER | 41 | 52 307 | 120 |
| WHAT E'RE THIS YOUTH OF FIRE WEARES FAIR, | FLAMING HEART | 31 | 52 324 | 61 |

## WEARY

| | | | | |
|---|---|---|---|---|
| OF MY WEARY STEPS, AND UNDER | PSALME 23 | 28 | 46 102 | 5 |
| O SEE, THE WEARY LIDDES OF WAKEFULL HOPE | TO THE NAME OF JESUS | 145 | 52 239 | 30 |
| WEARY OF THIS GLORIOUS WRONG | IN GLORIOUS EPIPHANIE | 138 | 52 253 | 39 |
| LO THE FAINT LAMB, WITH WEARY LIMB | OFFICE H. CROSS SIXT | 3 | 52 270 | 97 |
| WITH HIM SHALL I WEEP OUT MY WEARY LIFE. | ALEXIAS SECONDE ELEGIE | 6 | 52 335 | 207 |
| HOW OFT HAVE I WEPT OUT THE WEARY SUN. | ALEXIAS SECONDE ELEGIE | 19 | 52 335 | 207 |
| THAT WEARY LOVE AT LAST MAY FIND HIS WAY. | ALEXIAS SECONDE ELEGIE | 30 | 52 335 | 207 |

## WEARYNESSE

| | | | | |
|---|---|---|---|---|
| THEN ALL THAT WAY, AND WEARYNESSE. | DIES IRAE | 36 | 52 298 | 186 |

## WEATHER

| | | | | |
|---|---|---|---|---|
| ONE BRIGHT SMILE TO CLEERE THE WEATHER. | OUT OF THE ITALIAN (1) | 27 | 46 188 | 545 |

## WEAVE

| | | | | |
|---|---|---|---|---|
| HER CRUELL CLOATHES OF COSTLY THREDS THEY WEAVE, | SOSPETTO D'HERODE | 343 | 46 109 | 216 |
| WEAVE A CONSTELLATION | IN MEMORY OF LADY MADRE TERESA | 143 | 46 131 | 52 |
| WEAVE THEM A GARLAND OF MY VOWES. | WISHES SUPPOSED MISTRESSE | 108 | 46 195 | 479 |
| WEAVE A CONSTELLATION | TERESA | 142 | 52 315 | 52 |

WED

NOR WILL THE VIRGIN-JOYES WEE WED                    ON HOPE                              35   46 143  71
TO THESE, WHOM DEATH AGAIN DID WED,                  AN EPITAPH HUSBAND AND WIFE           1   46 174 478
TO THESE, WHOM DEATH AGAIN DID WED,                  AN EPITAPH UPON MARRIED COUPLE        1   52 339 478
NOR WILL THE VIRGIN JOYES WE WED                     (ON) HOPE                            15   52 345  71
STAY, SILVER-FOOTED CAME, STRIVE NOT TO WED          AN ELEGIE ON DR PORTER                1   MS 395 476

WEDDED

I'AM WEDDED ORE AGAIN SINCE THOU ART GONE.           ALEXIAS SECONDE ELEGIE                3   52 335 207

WEDDING

OF WATER WEDDING BLOOD.                              VEXILLA REGIS                        10   52 277 156

WEEDS

INTO DIRE SABLE WEEDS, & SATE, & MOURN'D.            UPON GUNPOWDER TREASON               48   MS 386 460
AMAZED SOL THROWES OF HIS MOURNFULL WEEDS,           UPON KINGS CORONATION                15   MS 390 453

WEEKES

HAVE SPENT THE PATIENCE OF EXPECTING WEEKES,         UPON TWO GREENE APRICOCKES            4   48 220 494

WEEP

THOSE DELICIOUS WOUNDS THAT WEEP                     IN MEMORY OF LADY MADRE TERESA      108   46 131  52
OF DEAD DEVOTION. NOR FAINT MARBLES WEEP             ON A TREATISE OF CHARITY             33   46 137  69
BOTH WEEP & SING IN SHADE OF THEE.                   OFFICE H. CROSS EVENSONG             11   52 273 101
LET HIM GOE WEEP                                     CHARITAS NIMIA                       15   52 280  48
WEEP FOR EVERY WORM THAT DYES.                       CHARITAS NIMIA                       38   52 280  48
HER EYES BLEED TEARES, HIS WOUNDS WEEP BLOOD.        SANCTA MARIA DOLORUM                 20   52 283 162
TO BLEED WITH HIM, FAIL NOT TO WEEP WITH HER.        SANCTA MARIA DOLORUM                 90   52 283 162
DETAIN IN NEEDFULL TEARES TO WEEP THE WANT OF THEE.  IN GLORIOUS ASSUMPTION B. LADY       22   52 304 114
THE SHRILL WINDS CHIDE, THE WATERS WEEP THY STAY.    IN GLORIOUS ASSUMPTION B. LADY       28   52 304 114
UPWARDS THOU DOST WEEP.                              WEEPER                               19   52 307 120
THE DEAW NO MORE WILL WEEP                           WEEPER                               43   52 307 120
YET LET THE POORE DROPS WEEP                         WEEPER                               55   52 307 120
THOSE DELICIOUS WOUNDS, THAT WEEP                    TERESA                              108   52 315  52
I'D SEND MY WOES IN WORDS SHOULD WEEP FOR ME.        ALEXIAS FIRST ELEGIE                 11   52 334 204
WITH HIM SHALL I WEEP OUT MY WEARY LIFE.             ALEXIAS SECONDE ELEGIE                6   52 335 207
OBEDIENT SLUMBERS, THAT CAN WAKE & WEEP,             DESCRIPTION RELIGIOUS HOUSE          16   52 338 213
PEACE, GOOD READER. DOE NOT WEEP.                    AN EPITAPH UPON MARRIED COUPLE        7   52 339 478

WEEPEST

THOU HAST THY TASKE, THOU WEEPEST STILL.             THE WEEPER                          114   46  79 120
THOU HAST THY TASK, THOU WEEPEST STILL.              WEEPER                              138   52 307 120

WEEPE

WEEPE THEN, ONELY BE EXPREST                         UPON THE DEATH OF A GENTLEMAN        33   46 166 472
THUS MUCH, HEE'S DEAD, AND WEEPE THE REST.           UPON THE DEATH OF A GENTLEMAN        34   46 166 472
UPWARDS THOU DOST WEEPE,                             THE WEEPER                           19   46  79 120
THE DEW NO MORE WILL WEEPE,                          THE WEEPER                           37   46  79 120
YET LET THE POORE DROPS WEEPE,                       THE WEEPER                           73   46  79 120
I'LE WEEPE, AND WEEPE, AND WILL THEREFORE            VERILY YE SHALL WEEP                  3   46  95  22
I'LE WEEPE, AND WEEPE, AND WILL THEREFORE            VERILY YE SHALL WEEP                  3   46  95  22
WEEPE, 'CAUSE I CAN WEEPE NO MORE.                   VERILY YE SHALL WEEP                  4   46  95  22
WEEPE, 'CAUSE I CAN WEEPE NO MORE.                   VERILY YE SHALL WEEP                  4   46  95  22
WEEPE PRETIOUS TEARES UPON THE STONES.               PSALME 137                           36   46 104   7
ETERNALL WORD SHOULD BEE A CHILD, AND WEEPE.         SOSPETTO D'HERODE                   179   46 109 216
AS MIGHT HAVE TAUGHT GRIEFE HOW TO WEEPE.            ANOTHER ON HERRYS                    22   46 170 469
PEACE, GOOD READER, DOE NOT WEEPE.                   AN EPITAPH HUSBAND AND WIFE           7   46 174 478
AS IF HEEREAFTER THEY WOULD WEEPE NOE MORE.          UPON KINGS CORONATION                12   MS 390 453
IF HEAVEN HATH NOW FORGOT TO WEEPE, O THEN           AN ELEGY MR STANNINGW                15   MS 394 473
THEN WEEPE THYSELFE INTO A SEA OF TEARES.            AN ELEGIE ON DR PORTER               38   MS 395 476

WEEPS

STILL THE FOUNTAINE WEEPS FOR ALL.                   THE WEEPER                          112   46  79 120
WEEPS FOR IT SELFE, IS ITS OWNE TEARE.               THE TEARE                            18   46  84  50
SEE HOW SHE WEEPS, AND WEEPS, THAT SHE APPEARES      TO PONTIUS WASHING HANDS              9   46  94  23
SEE HOW SHE WEEPS, AND WEEPS, THAT SHE APPEARES      TO PONTIUS WASHING HANDS              9   46  94  23
EACH DROP'S A TEARE THAT WEEPS FOR HER OWN WAST.     TO PONTIUS WASHING HANDS             11   46  94  23
TO PAY THY TEARES, AN EYE THAT WEEPS                 ON WOUNDS OF CRUCIFIED LORD          15   46  99  24
BY A BLACK FOUNT, WHICH WEEPS INTO A FLOOD.          SOSPETTO D'HERODE                   349   46 109 216
STILL THE FOUNTAIN WEEPS FOR ALL.                    WEEPER                              136   52 307 120

WEEPES

LO, A BLOOD-SHOT EYE, THAT WEEPES                    ON WOUNDS OF CRUCIFIED LORD           7   46  99  24
WHOSE BREST WEEPES BALM FOR WOUNDED MAN.             ADORO TE                             46   52 291 172

WEEPING

WHEN THEY RED WITH WEEPING ARE,                      THE WEEPER                           56   46  79 120
WEEPING IS THE EASE OF WOE,                          THE WEEPER                           74   46  79 120
INTO A WEEPING MOTION,                               THE WEEPER                           92   46  79 120
AN EYE, BUT NOT A WEEPING ONE,                       THE TEARE                            44   46  84  50
WEEPING, MELTS INTO A FOUNTAINE,                     PSALME 23                            14   46 102   5
HER KISSES IN THY WEEPING EYE,                       A HYMNE OF THE NATIVITY              66   46 106  76

|   |   |   |   |   |   |
|---|---|---|---|---|---|
| WHEN THEY RED WITH WEEPING ARE | WEEPER | 32 | 52 | 307 | 120 |
| (WEEPING IS THE EASE OF WOE) | WEEPER | 56 | 52 | 307 | 120 |
| THE WAY INTO THESE WEEPING EYN. | WEEPER | 106 | 52 | 307 | 120 |
| TWO WALKING BATHS. TWO WEEPING MOTIONS. | WEEPER | 113 | 52 | 307 | 120 |
| AT THESE THY WEEPING GATES. | WEEPER | 145 | 52 | 307 | 120 |
| THE WEEPING MARINER WILL AUGMENT THE WAVES. | ALEXIAS FIRST ELEGIE | 26 | 52 | 334 | 204 |
| THE WEEPING PEN WITH SABLE TEARES HATH DREST. | AN ELEGIE ON DR PORTER | 10 | MS | 395 | 476 |

AMBER-WEEPING

|   |   |   |   |   |   |
|---|---|---|---|---|---|
| STEALES FROM THE AMBER-WEEPING TREE. | THE WEEPER | 44 | 46 | 79 | 120 |

WEEPERS

|   |   |   |   |   |   |
|---|---|---|---|---|---|
| THOUGH THE FEILD'S EYES TOO WEEPERS BE | WEEPER | 179 | 52 | 307 | 120 |

WEIGHED'ST

|   |   |   |   |   |   |
|---|---|---|---|---|---|
| US WITH OUR PRICE THOU WEIGHED'ST. | VEXILLA REGIS | 33 | 52 | 277 | 156 |

WEIGHD

|   |   |   |   |   |   |
|---|---|---|---|---|---|
| AND PROVE HOW LIGHT THE WORLD WAS, WHEN IT WEIGHD WITH HIM. | OFFICE H. CROSS EVENSONG | 19 | 52 | 273 | 101 |

WEIGH'D

|   |   |   |   |   |   |
|---|---|---|---|---|---|
| HOW MUCH DEATH WEIGH'D MORE LIGHT THEN LOVE. | VEXILLA REGIS | 36 | 52 | 277 | 156 |

WAY'D

|   |   |   |   |   |   |
|---|---|---|---|---|---|
| AND THAT OF GRACE HEAVN WAY'D IN HIM, | VEXILLA REGIS | 32 | 52 | 277 | 156 |

WEIGHES

|   |   |   |   |   |   |
|---|---|---|---|---|---|
| TOGETHER, IN HIS PONDROUS MIND BOTH WEIGHES. | SOSPETTO D'HERODE | 96 | 46 | 109 | 216 |

WEIGH'S

|   |   |   |   |   |   |
|---|---|---|---|---|---|
| WHICH WITH THE SUN HIMSELFE WEIGH'S EQUALL WINGS. | SOSPETTO D'HERODE | 12 | 46 | 109 | 216 |

WEIGHT

|   |   |   |   |   |   |
|---|---|---|---|---|---|
| MAKE WINGS AT LEAST OF THEIR OWN WEIGHT, | AGAINST IRRESOLUTION AND DELAY | 49 | 52 | 347 | 146 |

WEIGHTY

|   |   |   |   |   |   |
|---|---|---|---|---|---|
| THE WEIGHTY RUDENES OF HIS BOYSTEROUS HEELE. | ON GUNPOWDER-TREASON | 44 | MS | 384 | 458 |
| LETT NOT THY WEIGHTY GLORIES, THIS FULL TIDE | UPON KINGS CORONATION | 7 | MS | 389 | 454 |

WELCOME

|   |   |   |   |   |   |
|---|---|---|---|---|---|
| WELCOME MY GRIEFE, MY JOY. HOW DEARE'S | VERILY YE SHALL WEEP | 1 | 46 | 95 | 22 |
| WELCOME TO OUR WONDRING SIGHT | A HYMNE OF THE NATIVITY | 53 | 46 | 106 | 76 |
| WELCOME, THOUGH NOT TO GOLD, NOR SILKE. | A HYMNE OF THE NATIVITY | 59 | 46 | 106 | 76 |
| WELCOME, (THOUGH NOT TO THOSE GAY FLYES | A HYMNE OF THE NATIVITY | 71 | 46 | 106 | 76 |
| AND WHEN IT COMES SAY WELCOME FRIEND. | WISHES SUPPOSED MISTRESSE | 87 | 46 | 195 | 479 |
| WELCOME TO OUR DARK WORLD, THOU | TO THE NAME OF JESUS | 161 | 52 | 239 | 30 |
| WELCOME, THOUGH NOT TO THOSE GAY FLYES. | IN HOLY NATIVITY | 91 | 52 | 246 | 76 |
| WELCOME, THE WORLD'S SURE WAY. | IN GLORIOUS EPIPHANIE | 60 | 52 | 253 | 39 |

WELLCOME

|   |   |   |   |   |   |
|---|---|---|---|---|---|
| WELLCOME DEAR, ALL-ADORED NAME. | TO THE NAME OF JESUS | 225 | 52 | 239 | 30 |
| WELLCOME, ALL WONDERS IN ONE SIGHT. | IN HOLY NATIVITY | 79 | 52 | 246 | 76 |
| WELLCOME. THOUGH NOR TO GOLD NOR SILK. | IN HOLY NATIVITY | 85 | 52 | 246 | 76 |
| WELLCOME TO US. AND WE | IN GLORIOUS EPIPHANIE | 62 | 52 | 253 | 39 |
| WELLCOME, MY SAD SWEET MATE. NOW HAVE I GOTT | ALEXIAS SECONDE ELEGIE | 7 | 52 | 335 | 207 |

WELCOMES

|   |   |   |   |   |   |
|---|---|---|---|---|---|
| TO MEET RELIGIOUS WELCOMES AT HER RISE. | IN GLORIOUS EPIPHANIE | 72 | 52 | 253 | 39 |

WELLCOMES

|   |   |   |   |   |   |
|---|---|---|---|---|---|
| IMMORTALL WELLCOMES WAIT ON THEE. | IN MEMORY OF LADY MADRE TERESA | 129 | 46 | 131 | 52 |
| IMMORTALL WELLCOMES WAIT FOR THEE. | TERESA | 128 | 52 | 315 | 52 |

WELLS

|   |   |   |   |   |   |
|---|---|---|---|---|---|
| IN YOUR OWN WELLS DECENTLY WASHT, | WEEPER | 88 | 52 | 307 | 120 |
| THAT DIGG'D THESE WELLS, & DREST THIS VINE. | WEEPER | 104 | 52 | 307 | 120 |

WENT

|   |   |   |   |   |   |
|---|---|---|---|---|---|
| TWO WENT TO PRAY. O RATHER SAY | TWO WENT TO PRAY | 1 | 46 | 89 | 18 |
| ONE WENT TO BRAG, TH'OTHER TO PRAY. | TWO WENT TO PRAY | 2 | 46 | 89 | 18 |
| THREE KINGS (OR WHAT IS MORE) THREE WISE MEN WENT | SOSPETTO D'HERODE | 135 | 46 | 109 | 216 |
| ALL THY GOOD WORKES WHICH WENT BEFORE, | IN MEMORY OF LADY MADRE TERESA | 140 | 46 | 131 | 52 |
| WE, WHO STRANGELY WENT ASTRAY, | IN GLORIOUS EPIPHANIE | 15 | 52 | 253 | 39 |
| ALL THY GOOD WORKES WHICH WENT BEFORE | TERESA | 139 | 52 | 315 | 52 |
| TO TELL THE WORLD, HOW HARD THE MATTER WENT, | HORATIJ ILLE & NEFASTO | 43 | MS | 382 | 530 |

## WEPT

| | | | | |
|---|---|---|---|---|
| THERE WE SATE, AND THERE WE WEPT. | PSALME 137 | 2 | 46 104 | 7 |
| THE PUREST PEARLES, THAT WEPT HER EVENING DEATH, | UPON DEATH OF HERRYS | 19 | 46 167 | 466 |
| LIKE WERE THE PEARLES THEY WEPT, SO LIKE THAT ONE | UPON YORKE HIS BIRTH | 64 | 46 176 | 500 |
| FOR THIS THE EVENING WEPT. AND WE NE'RE KNEW | IN GLORIOUS EPIPHANIE | 127 | 52 253 | 39 |
| HOW OFT HAVE I WEPT OUT THE WEARY SUN. | ALEXIAS SECONDE ELEGIE | 19 | 52 335 | 207 |
| AND WEPT AMAINE. THEN REAR'D A COSTLY TOMBE, | UPON GUNPOWDER TREASON | 50 | MS 386 | 460 |
| AND MAKE THEM LAUGH, WHICH FROWN'D, & WEPT BEFORE. | AN ELEGY MR STANNINOW | 14 | MS 394 | 473 |

## WEST

| | | | | |
|---|---|---|---|---|
| TO THEE, THOU DAY OF NIGHT. THOU EAST OF WEST. | IN GLORIOUS EPIPHANIE | 22 | 52 253 | 39 |
| FROM THIS WORLD'S EAST THE OTHER'S WEST. | IN GLORIOUS EPIPHANIE | 112 | 52 253 | 39 |

## WESTERN

| | | | | |
|---|---|---|---|---|
| OR E'RE THE SOONER SEEK HIS WESTERN BED, | CHARITAS NIMIA | 42 | 52 280 | 48 |

## WESTWARD

| | | | | |
|---|---|---|---|---|
| NOW WESTWARD SOL HAD SPENT THE RICHEST BEAMES | MUSICKS DUELL | 1 | 46 149 | 535 |
| WESTWARD TO FIND THE WORLDS TRUE ORIENT. | SOSPETTO D'HERODE | 136 | 46 109 | 216 |

## WET

| | | | | |
|---|---|---|---|---|
| WET WITH TEARES STILL'D FROM THE EYES, | ANOTHER ON HERRYS | 35 | 46 170 | 469 |

## WETT

| | | | | |
|---|---|---|---|---|
| UNDER MY FEET, THE WATERS TO BEE WETT. | OUT OF GROTIUS | 66 | MS 398 | 198 |

## WHEELS

| | | | | |
|---|---|---|---|---|
| SHOULD COOLE HIS FIERY WHEELS, & NEVER SINKE | UPON GUNPOWDER TREASON | 39 | MS 386 | 460 |

## WHETHER

| | | | | |
|---|---|---|---|---|
| BRIGHT GODDESSE, (WHETHER JOVE THY FATHER BE. | EX EUPHORMIONE | 1 | MS 392 | 525 |
| WHETHER THE MUSE THEY CLOTH SHALL LIVE OR DIE. | AT TH' IVORY TRIBUNALL | 4 | MS 397 | 492 |

## WHIPS

| | | | | |
|---|---|---|---|---|
| WITH WHIPS OF THRONGS AND KNOTTY VIPERS TWIN'D | SOSPETTO D'HERODE | 67 | 46 109 | 216 |

## WHIRLE-WIND

| | | | | |
|---|---|---|---|---|
| TILL A SWEET WHIRLE-WIND (STRIVING TO GETT OUT) | MUSICKS DUELL | 87 | 46 149 | 535 |

## WHISPER

| | | | | |
|---|---|---|---|---|
| BUT WHISPER TO THE WORLD. THUS DOE THEY VARY | MUSICKS DUELL | 145 | 46 149 | 535 |
| AT THE WHISPER OF THY WORD | PSALME 23 | 49 | 46 102 | 5 |
| WHISPER THY PLAINTS TO TH' OCEANS CURTEOUS EARES. | AN ELEGIE ON DR PORTER | 37 | MS 395 | 476 |
| AND LISTNED TO THE WHISPER OF MY WILL. | OUT OF GROTIUS | 66 | MS 398 | 198 |

## WHISPER'D

| | | | | |
|---|---|---|---|---|
| AS EVER WHISPER'D TO THE MORNING AIRE | UPON DEATH OF HERRYS | 2 | 46 167 | 466 |
| AND WHISPER'D THE CONFEDERATE EARTH | LOVES HOROSCOPE | 26 | 46 185 | 483 |

## WHISPERS

| | | | | |
|---|---|---|---|---|
| EFFECTUALL WHISPERS WHOSE STILL VOYCE, | ON A PRAYER BOOKE | 61 | 46 126 | 139 |

## WISPERS

| | | | | |
|---|---|---|---|---|
| EFFECTUALL WISPERS, WHOSE STILL VOICE | PRAYER TO GENTLE-WOMAN | 67 | 52 328 | 139 |

## WHIT

| | | | | |
|---|---|---|---|---|
| ALL, AND EVERY WHIT OF ME. | IT IS BETTER TO GO WITH EYE | 6 | 46 93 | 16 |

## WHITE

| | | | | |
|---|---|---|---|---|
| FOR HIS WHITE SOULE IS MADE. | ON BAPTIZED AETHIOPIAN | 4 | 46 85 | 29 |
| IN JOYES WHITE ANNALS LIVE THIS HOURE, | EASTER DAY | 10 | 46 100 | 26 |
| YOUR FLEECE IS WHITE, BUT 'TIS TOO COLD. | A HYMNE OF THE NATIVITY | 40 | 46 106 | 76 |
| CLOSE COUCHT IN YOUR WHITE BOSOME. AND FROM THENCE | ON A PRAYER BOOKE | 11 | 46 126 | 139 |
| THESE WHITE PLUMES OF HIS HEELE LEND YOU, | ON MR. G. HERBERTS BOOKE | 11 | 46 130 | 68 |
| OF YOUR WHITE HAND, THEY ARE MINE. | ON MR. G. HERBERTS BOOKE | 18 | 46 130 | 68 |
| THE MOONE OF MAIDEN STARRES. THY WHITE | IN MEMORY OF LADY MADRE TERESA | 124 | 46 131 | 52 |
| AND WHERE SO E'RE HEE SITTS HIS WHITE | IN MEMORY OF LADY MADRE TERESA | 180 | 46 131 | 52 |
| OF EVERLASTING JOYES BATH THY WHITE BREST. | ON THE ASSUMPTION | 58 | 46 139 | 114 |
| WRIT IN WHITE LETTERS O'RE HIS HEAD. | ANOTHER ON HERRYS | 50 | 46 170 | 469 |
| AND SEE SUCH NAMES OF JOY SIT WHITE UPON | UPON YORKE HIS BIRTH | 97 | 46 176 | 500 |
| O MAY SHE BUT ARRIVE AT YOUR WHITE HAND, | UPON FAIRE ETHIOPIAN | 4 | 46 183 | 493 |
| THEN WHAT NATURES WHITE HAND SETS UPE. | WISHES SUPPOSED MISTRESSE | 30 | 46 195 | 479 |
| IN YOUR WHITE BOSOME HER CHAST BED, | THOUGH NOW 'TIS NEITHER | 6 | MS 397 | 492 |
| YOUR FLEECE IS WHITE BUT T'IS TOO COLD. | IN HOLY NATIVITY | 56 | 52 246 | 76 |
| FAREWELL, THE WHITE | IN GLORIOUS EPIPHANIE | 49 | 52 253 | 39 |
| BY CONFEDERAT BLACK & WHITE | IN GLORIOUS EPIPHANIE | 217 | 52 253 | 39 |
| AND CROWD FOR KISSES FROM THE LAMB'S WHITE FEET. | TO THE QUEEN'S MAJESTY | 14 | 52 261 | 47 |

```
                                                                                            PAGE  463

      WHY SHOULD THE WHITE                          CHARITAS NIMIA                   57  52 280  48
      WHICH ON HIS WHITE BROWES THIS BRIGHT DAY     LAUDA SION SALVATOREM            17  52 294 178
      OF EVERLASTING JOYES BATH THY WHITE BREST.    IN GLORIOUS ASSUMPTION B. LADY   63  52 304 114
      THE LAMB HATH DIPP'T HIS WHITE FOOT HERE.     WEEPER                          108  52 307 120
      THE MOON OF MAIDEN STARRS, THY WHITE          TERESA                          123  52 315  52
      AND WHERESO'ERE HE SETTS HIS WHITE            TERESA                          179  52 315  52
      CLOSE COUCH'T IN YOUR WHITE BOSOM. & FROM THENCE  PRAYER TO GENTLE-WOMAN       17  52 328 139
      WHIL'ST THE GOOSE SOE GOODLY WHITE,           PETRONIJ ALES PHASIACIS PETITA    5  MS 382 526
      IS TH' EARTH DISROBED OF HER APRON WHITE,     AN ELEGY MR STANNINOW             5  MS 394 473
      IN DOWNY SURPLISSES, & VESTMENTS WHITE,       AN ELEGIE ON DR PORTER           28  MS 395 476

WHITEST

      OFFRING THEIR WHITEST SHEETS OF SNOW.         A HYMNE OF THE NATIVITY          37  46 106  76
      OFFRING THEIR WHITEST SHEETS OF SNOW          IN HOLY NATIVITY                 53  52 246  76
      UPON HER NECK THE WHITEST OF HIS SNOW.        UPON BIRTH PRINCESSE E           50  MS 391 456

WHOLE

      HIS HANDS WHOLE STRENGTH HERE, COULD NOT BE TOO MUCH.  THE DUMBE HEALED         4  46  87  16
      A GEN'RALL HISSE, FROM THE WHOLE TIRE OF SNAKES  SOSPETTO D'HERODE            302  46 109 216
      AND FATES WHOLE LOTTERY IS ONE BLANKE TO HER.  ON HOPE                         74  46 143  71
      IN HER WHOLE FRAME,                           WISHES SUPPOSED MISTRESSE        97  46 195 479
      BRING HITHER THY WHOLE SELF. & LET ME SEE     TO THE NAME OF JESUS             17  52 239  30
      NOR MAKES THE WHOLE WORLD THY HALF-SPHEAR.    IN GLORIOUS EPIPHANIE            41  52 253  39
      WITH YOUR BRIGHT HEAD WHOLE GROVES OF SCEPTERS BEND  TO THE QUEEN'S MAJESTY    17  52 261  47
      THOU'HAST SAV'D AT ONCE THE WHOLE WORLD'S LOSSE.  OFFICE H. CROSS MATINES      27  52 265  86
      THOU'HAST SAV'D AT ONCE THE WHOLE WORLD'S LOSSE.  OFFICE H. CROSS PRIME        21  52 267  91
      THOU'HAST SAV'D AT ONCE THE WHOLE WORLD'S LOSSE.  OFFICE H. CROSS THIRD        20  52 268  93
      THOU'HAST SAV'D AT ONCE THE WHOLE WORLD'S LOSSE.  OFFICE H. CROSS NINTH        17  52 271  99
      HER'S, & THE WHOLE WORLD'S JOYES,             SANCTA MARIA DOLORUM              6  52 283 162
      COME YOUR WHOLE SELVES, SORROW'S GREAT SON & MOTHER.  SANCTA MARIA DOLORUM     77  52 283 162
      COULD PROVE THE WHOLE SUMME (TOO SURE) DUE TO HIM.  SANCTA MARIA DOLORUM       94  52 283 162
      LO, HEART, THY HOPE'S WHOLE PLEA. HER PRETIOUS BREATH  SANCTA MARIA DOLORUM   109  52 283 162
      LESSE THEN WHOLE CHRIST IN EVERY CRUMME.      LAUDA SION SALVATOREM            58  52 294 178
      THE WHOLE WORLD'S HOST WOULD BE THY GUEST     O GLORIOSA DOMINA                 7  52 302 194
      NOT ONE LOOSE SHAFT BUT LOVE'S WHOLE QUIVER.  FLAMING HEART                    70  52 324  61
      WHOLE DAYES & SUNS DEVOUR'D WITH ENDLESSE DINING.  DESCRIPTION RELIGIOUS HOUSE  2  52 338 213
      FORTUNE'S WHOLE LOTTERY IS ONE BLANK TO HER.  (ON) HOPE                        34  52 345  71
      NOR CAN THE CARES OF HIS WHOLE CROWN          AGAINST IRRESOLUTION AND DELAY   73  52 347 146
      WHOSE WHOLE LIFE MUSICK WAS. WHEREIN          UPON DEATH OF A FREIND           19  MS 393 477
      THE BROKEN MEATE WAS MUCH MORE THEN THE WHOLE.  OUT OF GROTIUS                 64  MS 398 198

WHOLSOME

      SHRINKES, LIKE THE SICK MOONE AT THE WHOLSOME MORNE.  ON HOPE                  20  46 143  71
      AND HAST TO DRINK THE WHOLSOME DART.          TO COUNTESSE OF DENBIGH          46  52 236 146
      SHRINKES, AS THE SICK MOON FROM THE WHOLSOME MORN.  (ON) HOPE                  10  52 345  71

WHOLSOM

      HEAVN'S WHOLSOM RAY.                          IN GLORIOUS EPIPHANIE            61  52 253  39
      THEIR HATED LOVES CHANGD INTO WHOLSOM FEARES. IN GLORIOUS EPIPHANIE           161  52 253  39

WIDE

      AND NOW TH'ART SET WIDE OPE. THE SPEARE'S SAD ART,  I AM THE DOORE              1  46  90  17
      THE FLOOD-GATE SHALL BE SET WIDE OPE FOR HIM. OUR LORD IN HIS CIRCUMCISION      6  46  98   9
      MAPPE OF HEROICK WORTH, WHOM FARRE AND WIDE   SOSPETTO D'HERODE                13  46 109 216
      AND CRUSH THE WORLD TILL HIS WIDE CORNERS MEET.  SOSPETTO D'HERODE            280  46 109 216
      NOW STRETCH THY SELF (FAIRE ILE) AND GROW, SPREAD WIDE  UPON YORKE HIS BIRTH    2  46 176 500
      LO WE HOLD OUR HEARTS WIDE OPE.               TO THE NAME OF JESUS            126  52 239  30
      (LOVE'S EASTERN WINDOWES) ALL WIDE OPE        TO THE NAME OF JESUS            146  52 239  30
      WHAT DID THEIR WEAPONS BUT SETT WIDE THE DOORES  TO THE NAME OF JESUS         216  52 239  30
      WIDE MAIST THOU SPRED                         OFFICE H. CROSS EVENSONG         20  52 273 101
      LOOK ROUND AND READE THE WORLD'S WIDE FACE.   AGAINST IRRESOLUTION AND DELAY   29  52 347 146

WIDE-SPREAD

      MEET IT WITH WIDE-SPREAD ARMES. & SEE         TO COUNTESSE OF DENBIGH          55  52 236 146

WIDER

      WHAT DID THEIR WEAPONS BUT WITH WIDER PORES   TO THE NAME OF JESUS            211  52 239  30

WIDOW

      AND TRY'D TO MAKE A WIDOW ERE A WIFE.         ALEXIAS FIRST ELEGIE              6  52 334 204

WIDDOW

      ALEXIS' WIDDOW NOW IS SORROW'S WIFE.          ALEXIAS SECONDE ELEGIE            5  52 335 207

WIELD

      WELL PETER DOST THOU WIELD THY ACTIVE SWORD.  ON ST. PETER CUTTING MALCHUS      1  46  97  22

WIFE

      IT COULD NOT SEVER MAN AND WIFE,              AN EPITAPH HUSBAND AND WIFE       5  46 174 478
      I WOULD BE MARRIED, BUT I'DE HAVE NO WIFE,    ON MARRIAGE                       1  46 183 485
      AND TRY'D TO MAKE A WIDOW ERE A WIFE.         ALEXIAS FIRST ELEGIE              6  52 334 204
      ALEXIS' WIDDOW NOW IS SORROW'S WIFE.          ALEXIAS SECONDE ELEGIE            5  52 335 207
      HAD UNDER SOME LOW ROOFE LOV'D HIS PLAIN WIFE.  ALEXIAS THIRD ELEGIE           14  52 336 209
```

```
                                                                 PAGE  464

     WHO ONLY WISH HIS VIRGIN WIFE TO BE.          ALEXIAS THIRD ELEGIE              24    52 336 209
     WAS MAIDEN WIFE & MAIDEN MOTHER TOO.          ALEXIAS THIRD ELEGIE              30    52 336 209
     HOW SWEET THE MUTUALL YOKE OF MAN & WIFE,     ALEXIAS THIRD ELEGIE              51    52 336 209
     IT COULD NOT SUNDER MAN & WIFE.               AN EPITAPH UPON MARRIED COUPLE     5    52 339 478
     IS CLOYING MEAT. HOW STALE IS WIFE.           PETRONIJ ALES PHASIACIS PETITA    16    MS 362 526
     DEARE WIFE HATH NE'RE A HANDSOME LETTER,      PETRONIJ ALES PHASIACIS PETITA    17    MS 382 526

WILD

     QUICKE VOLUMES OF WILD NOTES. TO LET HIM KNOW MUSICKS DUELL                     25    46 149 535
     WING'D WITH THEIR OWNE WILD ECCHO'S PRATLING FLY. MUSICKS DUELL                 92    46 149 535
     WHOSE TREMBLING MURMURS MELTING IN WILD AIRES MUSICKS DUELL                    141    46 149 535
     TO MEASURE ALL THOSE WILD DIVERSITIES         MUSICKS DUELL                    162    46 149 535
     TO DROWNE THE WANTONNESSE OF HIS WILD THIRST. OUR LORD IN HIS CIRCUMCISION       8    46  98   9
     WHAT BUSY MOTIONS, WHAT WILD ENGINES STAND    SOSPETTO D'HERODE                441    46 109 216
     ALL THY WILD CIRCLE TO A POINT. O SINKE       UPON STANINOUGH'S DEATH           14    46 175 475
     AND LOSE OUR SELVES IN WILD DELIGHT.          OUT OF CATULLUS                   18    46 194 523
     THE WILD TURNES OF THE WANTON SUN.            THOUGH NOW 'TIS NEITHER           26    MS 397 492
     A WILD RESERVE OF WANTON WRATH.               OFFICE H. CROSS EVENSONG           4    52 273 101
     ALL THY WILD CIRCLE TO A POINT. O SINK        DEATH'S LECTURE                   15    52 340 475
     AND WHATSOE'RE WILD SINNES BLACK THOUGHTS DOE FEED, HORATIJ ILLE & NEFASTO      12    MS 382 530
     WHEN A WILD SWORD EV'N FROM THEIR BRESTS, DID LOP OUT OF GROTIUS                25    MS 398 198
     THE WILD WAVES COUCH'D. THE SEA FORGOTT TO SWEAT OUT OF GROTIUS                 67    MS 398 198

WILDFIRE

     IT CAN DIGEST. THEN WATCH THE WILDFIRE WELL,  ON GUNPOWDER-TREASON              65    MS 384 458

WILES

     DECEIVES MENS FEARES WITH FLATTERING WILES.   OUT OF GREEKE CUPID'S CRYER       50    46 159 519
     CRAFT IN ALL HER KNOTTY WILES.                PSALME 23                         26    46 102   5

WIN

     YEILD THEN, O YEILD, THAT LOVE MAY WIN        TO COUNTESSE OF DENBIGH           63    52 236 146
     OF HIS HIGH STRATAGEM TO WIN YOUR HEART,      TO SAME CONCERNING CHOISE         44    52 331  66
     YIELD THEN, O YIELD, THAT LOVE MAY WIN        AGAINST IRRESOLUTION AND DELAY    85    52 347 146

WILLFULL

     HE FLYES. & INTO WILLFULL EXILE GOES.         ALEXIAS THIRD ELEGIE              16    52 336 209

WILLOWES

     NODDING ON THE WILLOWES SLEPT,                PSALME 137                         4    46 104   7

WILL

     MAINTAIN THE WILL IN THESE STRANGE WARRES.    TO COUNTESSE OF DENBIGH           18    52 236 146
     MAINTAIN THE WILL IN THESE STRANGE WARRS.     AGAINST IRRESOLUTION AND DELAY    12    52 347 146
     AND LISTNED TO THE WHISPER OF MY WILL.        OUT OF GROTIUS                    66    MS 398 198

WIND

     WAS EVER FROWARD WIND                         WHY ARE YEE AFRAID                 4    46  88  15
     THE WIND HAD NEED BE ANGRY, AND THE WATER BLACK, WHY ARE YEE AFRAID              7    46  88  15
     THEIR LOCKES ARE BEDS OF UNCOMB'D SNAKES THAT WIND SOSPETTO D'HERODE            69    46 109 216
     AS IS HE, NOR CLOUD, NOR WIND                 UPON DEATH OF DESIRED HERRYS      57    46 168 467
     AND WIND THY SELFE UP CLOSE IN THY COLD BED.  UPON STANINOUGH'S DEATH            4    46 175 475
     AS SIGH WITH SUPPLE WIND                      TO THE NAME OF JESUS              39    52 239  30
     AND GIVE IT SELF FOR SPORT TO THE PROUD WIND. CHARITAS NIMIA                    30    52 280  48
     OATHES OF WATER, WORDS OF WIND.               TO SAME CONCERNING CHOISE         17    52 331  66
     AND WIND THY SELF UP CLOSE IN THY COLD BED.   DEATH'S LECTURE                    4    52 340 475
     MARK HOW THE CURL'D WAVES WORK AND WIND,      AGAINST IRRESOLUTION AND DELAY    41    52 347 146
     THE LATE WINGS OF THE LAZY WIND,              AGAINST IRRESOLUTION AND DELAY    76    52 347 146
     IS PLOUGH'D AS DEEPE, AS IS THE SEA WITH WIND, HORATIJ ILLE & NEFASTO           20    MS 382 530
     NOE, NOE, A GIANT WIND, THAT WILL NOT SPARE   ON GUNPOWDER-TREASON              39    MS 384 458
     THE WIND IN ALL HIS ROARING BRAGS STOOD STILL OUT OF GROTIUS                    65    MS 398 198

SOUTHWEST-WIND

     THAT THE SOUTHWEST-WIND HURRIES IN HIS ARMES, OUT OF VIRGIL                     20    46 155 529

WHIRLE-WIND

     TILL A SWEET WHIRLE-WIND (STRIVING TO GETT OUT) MUSICKS DUELL                   87    46 149 535

WINDS

     LED ROUND IN HIS GREAT CIRCLE. NO WINDS BREATH OUT OF VIRGIL                    27    46 155 529
     EACH HERBE A PLAGUE. THE WINDS SIGHES TIMED-BEE SOSPETTO D'HERODE              348    46 109 216
     FOR WHOM (AS DEAD) THE WRATHFULL WINDS CONTEST, SOSPETTO D'HERODE              427    46 109 216
     HER KEELE CUTS NOT THE WAVES, WHERE OUR WINDS STIRRE, ON HOPE                   73    46 143  71
     WINDS CLING TO THEE,                          OUT OF THE ITALIAN (1)            32    46 188 545
     THE SHRILL WINDS CHIDE, THE WATERS WEEP THY STAY. IN GLORIOUS ASSUMPTION B. LADY 28   52 304 114
     HER KEEL CUTTS NOT THE WAVES WHERE THESE WINDS STIRR (ON) HOPE                  33    52 345  71
     BOTH WINDS AND WATERS URGE THEIR WAY,         AGAINST IRRESOLUTION AND DELAY    39    52 347 146

WINDING-SHEET

     IS HER LIFES WING, OR HER DEATH'S WINDING-SHEET. AT TH' IVORY TRIBUNALL          6    MS 397 492
```

## WINDOW

| | | | | |
|---|---|---|---|---|
| THE WORLD'S NEW EASTERN WINDOW BIN | O GLORIOSA DOMINA | 19 | 52 302 | 194 |

## WINDOWS

| | | | | |
|---|---|---|---|---|
| TO ASK THE WINDOWS LEAVE TO PASSE THAT WAY. | PRAYER TO GENTLE-WOMAN | 76 | 52 328 | 139 |
| THESE CURTAIN'D WINDOWS, THIS RETIRED EYE | DEATH'S LECTURE | 27 | 52 340 | 475 |

## WINDOWES

| | | | | |
|---|---|---|---|---|
| TO ASKE THE WINDOWES LEAVE, TO PASSE THAT WAY. | ON A PRAYER BOOKE | 70 | 46 126 | 139 |
| THESE CURTAIN'D WINDOWES, THIS SELFE-PRISON'D EYE, | UPON STANINOUGH'S DEATH | 25 | 46 175 | 475 |
| (LOVE'S EASTERN WINDOWES) ALL WIDE OPE | TO THE NAME OF JESUS | 146 | 52 239 | 30 |
| THE RUBY WINDOWES WHICH INRICH'T THE EAST | TO THE NAME OF JESUS | 218 | 52 239 | 30 |

## WINE

| | | | | |
|---|---|---|---|---|
| THEIR MASTERS WATER, THEIR OWNE WINE. | THE WEEPER | 36 | 46 79 | 120 |
| RIPE, WILL MAKE THE RICHER WINE. | THE TEARE | 30 | 46 84 | 50 |
| THOU WATER TURN'ST TO WINE (FAIRE FRIEND OF LIFE) | TO LORD UPON WATER MADE WINE | 1 | 46 91 | 12 |
| AND SO TURNES WINE TO WATER BACKE AGAINE. | TO LORD UPON WATER MADE WINE | 4 | 46 91 | 12 |
| WITH THEE STRONG WINE OF LOVE, LET OTHERS SWIMME | AN APOLOGIE FOR HYMNE (TERESA) | 31 | 46 136 | 59 |
| WHERE FLOWES SUCH WINE AS WE CAN HAVE OF NONE | AN APOLOGIE FOR HYMNE (TERESA) | 39 | 46 136 | 59 |
| WINE OF YOUTHS LIFE, AND THE SWEET DEATHS OF LOVE, | AN APOLOGIE FOR HYMNE (TERESA) | 41 | 46 136 | 59 |
| WINE OF IMMORTALL MIXTURE, WHICH CAN PROVE | AN APOLOGIE FOR HYMNE (TERESA) | 42 | 46 136 | 59 |
| ITS TINCTURE FROM THE ROSIE NECTAR, WINE | AN APOLOGIE FOR HYMNE (TERESA) | 43 | 46 136 | 59 |
| THE GENEROUS WINE WITH AGE GROWES STRONG, NOT SOWER. | ON HOPE | 53 | 46 143 | 71 |
| THEIR SUBTILE ESSENCE WITH THE SOULE OF WINE. | ON HOPE | 60 | 46 143 | 71 |
| O LET ME SUCK THE WINE | SANCTA MARIA DOLORUM | 101 | 52 283 | 162 |
| WITH A WELL-BLES'T BREAD & WINE | LAUDA SION SALVATOREM | 29 | 52 294 | 178 |
| THE CHILDREN'S BREAD. THE BRIDEGROOM'S WINE. | LAUDA SION SALVATOREM | 63 | 52 294 | 178 |
| DRINK THE SAME WINE. AND THE SAME WAY. | LAUDA SION SALVATOREM | 78 | 52 294 | 178 |
| RIPE, WILL MAKE THE RICHER WINE. | WEEPER | 66 | 52 307 | 120 |
| THEIR MASTER'S WATER. THEIR OWN WINE. | WEEPER | 72 | 52 307 | 120 |
| WITH THEE, STRONG WINE OF LOVE. LET OTHERS SWIMME | AN APOLOGIE FOR (TERESA) HYMNE | 31 | 52 322 | 59 |
| WHERE FLOWES SUCH WINE AS WE CAN HAVE OF NONE | AN APOLOGIE FOR (TERESA) HYMNE | 39 | 52 322 | 59 |
| WINE OF YOUTH, LIFE, & THE SWEET DEATHS OF LOVE. | AN APOLOGIE FOR (TERESA) HYMNE | 41 | 52 322 | 59 |
| WINE OF IMMORTALL MIXTURE. WHICH CAN PROVE | AN APOLOGIE FOR (TERESA) HYMNE | 42 | 52 322 | 59 |
| IT'S TINCTURE FROM THE ROSY NECTAR. WINE | AN APOLOGIE FOR (TERESA) HYMNE | 43 | 52 322 | 59 |
| THY GENEROUS WINE WITH AGE GROWES STRONG, NOT SOWER. | (ON) HOPE | 23 | 52 345 | 71 |
| THEIR SUPPLE ESSENCE WITH THE SOUL OF WINE. | (ON) HOPE | 30 | 52 345 | 71 |
| THE WATER BLUSH'D, AND STARTED INTO WINE. | OUT OF GROTIUS | 52 | MS 398 | 198 |
| GOOD WINE IN ALL POYNTS. BUT THE EASY RATE. | OUT OF GROTIUS | 56 | MS 398 | 198 |

## WINE-PRESSE

| | | | | |
|---|---|---|---|---|
| BUT HIM, WHO TROD THE WINE-PRESSE ALL ALONE. | AN APOLOGIE FOR HYMNE (TERESA) | 40 | 46 136 | 59 |
| BUT HIM WHO TROD THE WINE-PRESSE ALL ALONE | AN APOLOGIE FOR (TERESA) HYMNE | 40 | 52 322 | 59 |

## WING

| | | | | |
|---|---|---|---|---|
| WITH WANTON WING, NOW HERE, NOW THERE, | OUT OF GREEKE CUPID'S CRYER | 41 | 46 159 | 519 |
| STUFT WITH DOWNE OF ANGELS WING. | THE TEARE | 36 | 46 84 | 50 |
| WITH A SABLE WING, THAT COVERS | PSALME 23 | 38 | 46 102 | 5 |
| FROM WHENCE HEAV'N-LABOURING BEES WITH BUSIE WING, | SOSPETTO D'HERODE | 22 | 46 109 | 216 |
| WHERE NEVER WING OF ANGELL YET MADE WAY | SOSPETTO D'HERODE | 222 | 46 109 | 216 |
| BUT SHEE (SWIFT AS THE MOMENTARY WING | SOSPETTO D'HERODE | 371 | 46 109 | 216 |
| WITH HER SOFT WING, WIPT FROM THE BROWES OF MEN | SOSPETTO D'HERODE | 387 | 46 109 | 216 |
| AND BE ALL WING. | TO THE NAME OF JESUS | 16 | 52 239 | 30 |
| AND WHERE LOVE LENDS THE WING, & LEADS THE WAY, | ALEXIAS FIRST ELEGIE | 19 | 52 334 | 204 |
| FLEDG'D WITH HER EAGLES WING. THE VERY CHAINE | HORATIJ ILLE & NEFASTO | 28 | MS 382 | 530 |
| REACH ME A QUILL, PLUCKT FROM THE FLAMING WING | UPON GUNPOWDER TREASON | 1 | MS 386 | 460 |
| LETT TH' HALLOWED PLUME OF A SERAPHICK WING | UPON BIRTH PRINCESSE E | 22 | MS 391 | 456 |
| WHERE ROUND ABOUT HOVERS WITH SILVER WING | AN ELEGY MR STANNINOW | 53 | MS 394 | 473 |
| MAKE THEIR SCAR'D SOULES TAKE WING, & FLY AWAY. | AN ELEGIE ON DR PORTER | 30 | MS 395 | 476 |
| IS HER LIFES WING, OR HER DEATH'S WINDING-SHEET. | AT TH' IVORY TRIBUNALL | 6 | MS 397 | 492 |

## WINGED

| | | | | |
|---|---|---|---|---|
| THE WINGED WAND'RER, AND THAT NONE | OUT OF GREEKE CUPID'S CRYER | 9 | 46 159 | 519 |
| WITH WINGED VOWES, | ON A PRAYER BOOKE | 95 | 46 126 | 139 |
| EACH WINGED MOMENT WAITS, | WEEPER | 147 | 52 307 | 120 |
| WITH WINGED VOWES | PRAYER TO GENTLE-WOMAN | 101 | 52 328 | 139 |
| EACH WINGED CHORISTER WOULD SWAN-LIKE SING | UPON GUNPOWDER TREASON | 43 | MS 386 | 460 |
| BUT WHEN JOVES WINGED HERALDS THIS ESPIED, | UPON GUNPOWDER TREASON | 53 | MS 386 | 460 |
| A WINGED HERALD, GLADD OF SOE SWEET A PREY, | AN ELEGY MR STANNINOW | 49 | MS 394 | 473 |

## GOLDEN-WINGED

| | | | | |
|---|---|---|---|---|
| HEAVENS GOLDEN-WINGED HERALD, LATE HEE SAW | SOSPETTO D'HERODE | 97 | 46 109 | 216 |

## LIGHTNING-WINGED

| | | | | |
|---|---|---|---|---|
| THE NIMBLEST OF THE LIGHTNING-WINGED LOVES. | SOSPETTO D'HERODE | 235 | 46 109 | 216 |

## WING'D

| | | | | |
|---|---|---|---|---|
| WING'D WITH THEIR OWNE WILD ECCHO'S PRATLING FLY. | MUSICKS DUELL | 92 | 46 149 | 535 |
| WHILE THEIR AFFRIGHTED SOULES, NOW WING'D FOR FLIGHT | THE BEGINNING OF HELIODORUS | 19 | 46 158 | 517 |
| AND IN THESE CHAST WARRES WHILE THE WING'D WOUNDS FLEE | SANCTA MARIA DOLORUM | 67 | 52 283 | 162 |

WINGS

| | | | | |
|---|---|---|---|---|
| FOR WELL THEY NOW CAN SPARE THEIR WINGS, | A HYMNE OF THE NATIVITY | 43 | 46 106 | 76 |
| WHICH WITH THE SUN HIMSELFE WEIGH'S EQUALL WINGS. | SOSPETTO D'HERODE | 12 | 46 109 | 216 |
| HEE SHOOKE HIMSELFE, AND SPREAD HIS SPATIOUS WINGS. | SOSPETTO D'HERODE | 141 | 46 109 | 216 |
| THINKE YOU HAVE AN ANGELL BY TH' WINGS. | ON MR. G. HERBERTS BOOKE | 6 | 46 130 | 68 |
| GIRT ROUND THY AWFULL ALTARS, WITH BRIGHT WINGS | ON A TREATISE OF CHARITY | 22 | 46 137 | 69 |
| GOE THEN, GOE (GLORIOUS) ON THE GOLDEN WINGS | ON THE ASSUMPTION | 23 | 46 139 | 114 |
| WITH ROSIE WINGS SO RICHLY BRIGHT, | UPON DEATH OF DESIRED HERRYS | 49 | 46 168 | 467 |
| HENCE 'TIS MY HUMBLE FANCY FINDS NO WINGS. | TO THE MORNING | 19 | 46 183 | 497 |
| OR GIVE DOWNE TO THE WINGS OF NIGHT. | WISHES SUPPOSED MISTRESSE | 96 | 46 195 | 479 |
| AETERNALL WORLDS UPON IT'S WINGS. | TO COUNTESSE OF DENBIGH | 54 | 52 236 | 146 |
| O YOU, MY SOUL'S MOST CERTAIN WINGS. | TO THE NAME OF JESUS | 64 | 52 239 | 30 |
| TAKE THINE OWN WINGS, & COME AWAY. | TO THE NAME OF JESUS | 150 | 52 239 | 30 |
| FOR WELL THEY NOW CAN SPARE THEIR WINGS | IN HOLY NATIVITY | 60 | 52 246 | 76 |
| UPON THY WINGS, & REACH THE SKYES. | OFFICE H. CROSS PRIME | 16 | 52 267 | 91 |
| AND WITH THE WINGS OF THINE OWN DOVE | DIES IRAE | 27 | 52 298 | 186 |
| ON THE GOLDEN WINGS | IN GLORIOUS ASSUMPTION B. LADY | 38 | 52 304 | 114 |
| GLOWING CHEEK, & GLISTERING WINGS, | FLAMING HEART | 33 | 52 324 | 61 |
| THE GLOWING CHEEKES, THE GLISTERING WINGS. | FLAMING HEART | 66 | 52 324 | 61 |
| LOVE TOO, THAT LEADS THE WAY, WOULD LEND THE WINGS | ALEXIAS FIRST ELEGIE | 17 | 52 334 | 204 |
| FALL WITH SOFT WINGS, STUCK WITH SOFT FLOWRES. | TEMPERANCE | 46 | 52 342 | 510 |
| IN YOU ALONE HATH LOST HIS WINGS. | AGAINST IRRESOLUTION AND DELAY | 28 | 52 347 | 146 |
| WHOSE WAYES HAVE LEAST TO DOE WITH WINGS, | AGAINST IRRESOLUTION AND DELAY | 48 | 52 347 | 146 |
| MAKE WINGS AT LEAST OF THEIR OWN WEIGHT. | AGAINST IRRESOLUTION AND DELAY | 49 | 52 347 | 146 |
| BY TH'EVEN WINGS OF HIS OWN DOVES. | AGAINST IRRESOLUTION AND DELAY | 54 | 52 347 | 146 |
| THE LATE WINGS OF THE LAZY WIND. | AGAINST IRRESOLUTION AND DELAY | 76 | 52 347 | 146 |
| THOUGH HIS WINGS CONCEITED HEWE | PETRONIJ ALES PHASIACIS PETITA | 7 | MS 382 | 526 |
| BUT REST, AFFRIGHTED MUSE. THY SILVER WINGS | UPON GUNPOWDER TREASON | 27 | MS 387 | 461 |
| UNMIXT FELICITY WITH SILVER WINGS | UPON KINGS CORONATION | 21 | MS 389 | 454 |

WINGES

| | | | | |
|---|---|---|---|---|
| AND WITH CLASP'T WINGES PROCLAYME A SPRING | THOUGH NOW 'TIS NEITHER | 11 | MS 397 | 492 |

WINTER

| | | | | |
|---|---|---|---|---|
| AS THEN DID SMELL OF WINTER, OR OF DEATH. | OUT OF VIRGIL | 28 | 46 155 | 529 |
| WINTER CHID THE WORLD, AND SENT | A HYMNE OF THE NATIVITY | 23 | 46 106 | 76 |
| SUMMER IN WINTER. DAY IN NIGHT. | A HYMNE OF THE NATIVITY | 55 | 46 106 | 76 |
| AND WINTER STROW HER WAY, YEA, SUCH A SORE | SOSPETTO D'HERODE | 380 | 46 109 | 216 |
| WINTER CHIDDE ALOUD. & SENT | IN HOLY NATIVITY | 24 | 52 246 | 76 |
| SOMMER IN WINTER. DAY IN NIGHT. | IN HOLY NATIVITY | 81 | 52 246 | 76 |
| THE NIGHT & WINTER STILL OF DEATH & SIN. | IN GLORIOUS EPIPHANIE | 77 | 52 253 | 39 |
| IF SOMMER COME NOT, HOW CAN WINTER GOE. | IN GLORIOUS ASSUMPTION B. LADY | 26 | 52 304 | 114 |
| THEIR WINTER COATES COVER'D WITH FLAMING GOLD. | UPON KINGS CORONATION | 28 | MS 390 | 453 |
| HATH AGED WINTER, FLEDG'D WITH FEATHERED RAINE, | AN ELEGY MR STANNINOW | 1 | MS 394 | 473 |
| WHAT MORE THAN WINTER HATH THAT DIRE ART FOUND, | AN ELEGY MR STANNINOW | 21 | MS 394 | 473 |

WINTER'S

| | | | | |
|---|---|---|---|---|
| THE WINTER'S PAST, THE RAINE IS GONE. | ON THE ASSUMPTION | 10 | 46 139 | 114 |
| THE WINTER'S PAST, THE RAIN IS GONE. | IN GLORIOUS ASSUMPTION B. LADY | 10 | 52 304 | 114 |
| THE WINTER'S PAST. | IN GLORIOUS ASSUMPTION B. LADY | 23 | 52 304 | 114 |
| WINTER'S SELFE INTO A SPRING. | TEMPERANCE | 42 | 52 342 | 510 |
| KIND WINTER'S GUIFT, & IN A GREENE ONE DIGHT. | AN ELEGY MR STANNINOW | 6 | MS 394 | 473 |
| IF WINTER'S GONE, WHENCE THIS UNTIMELY COLD. | AN ELEGY MR STANNINOW | 19 | MS 394 | 473 |

WINTERS

| | | | | |
|---|---|---|---|---|
| WINTERS SELFE INTO A SPRING. | IN PRAISE OF LESSIUS | 44 | 46 156 | 510 |
| WINTERS SAD FACE, AND THROUGH THE FLOWRY LANDS | SOSPETTO D'HERODE | 110 | 46 109 | 216 |
| CAN CROWNE OLD WINTERS HEAD WITH FLOWERS, | WISHES SUPPOSED MISTRESSE | 90 | 46 195 | 479 |
| A WINTERS THUNDER WITH A GROANE SHALL SCARE, | ON GUNPOWDER-TREASON | 28 | MS 384 | 458 |

WIPE

| | | | | |
|---|---|---|---|---|
| FROM TH' DAWN OF THY FAIRE EYE-LIDS WIPE AWAY | ON A TREATISE OF CHARITY | 7 | 46 137 | 69 |
| THAT, AND THAT WIPE OF ANOTHER. | OUT OF CATULLUS | 14 | 46 194 | 523 |
| WASH WITH SYLVER, WIPE WITH GOLD. | WEEPER | 120 | 52 307 | 120 |

WIP'D

| | | | | |
|---|---|---|---|---|
| (THE DUST OF WARRE CLEANE WIP'D AWAY) | IN CICATRICES DOMINI JESU | 18 | MS 381 | 27 |

WIPT

| | | | | |
|---|---|---|---|---|
| WITH HER SOFT WING, WIPT FROM THE BROWES OF MEN | SOSPETTO D'HERODE | 387 | 46 109 | 216 |

WISDOM

| | | | | |
|---|---|---|---|---|
| THE FATHER'S WORD & WISDOM, MADE | OFFICE H. CROSS MATINES | 12 | 52 265 | 86 |

WISDOME

| | | | | |
|---|---|---|---|---|
| THY GLORIOUS WISDOME BREAKES THE NETS, | NEITHER DURST MAN ASKE | 3 | 46 92 | 20 |
| THEIR WISDOME NOW, AS WELL AS DUTY. | IN GLORIOUS EPIPHANIE | 185 | 52 253 | 39 |
| SPEAKES THE GREAT WISDOME OF TH' ARTIFICER. | UPON BIRTH PRINCESSE E | 40 | MS 391 | 456 |

WISDOMES

| | | | | |
|---|---|---|---|---|
| HIM HIS WISDOMES PREGNANT GROWTH | HIS EPITAPH (HERRYS) | 15 | 46 172 | 471 |
| IF THIS WERE WISDOMES GOD, THAT WARS STERNE FATHER, | UPON YORKE HIS BIRTH | 32 | 46 176 | 500 |

## WISE

| | | | | |
|---|---|---|---|---|
| THREE KINGS (OR WHAT IS MORE) THREE WISE MEN WENT | SOSPETTO D'HERODE | 135 | 46 109 | 216 |
| WAKEFULL, AND WISE | ON A PRAYER BOOKE | 25 | 46 126 | 139 |
| FOR WORTHY SOULS WHOSE WISE EMBRACES | ON A PRAYER BOOKE | 38 | 46 126 | 139 |
| WISE HEAVEN WILL NEVER HAVE IT SO. | IN MEMORY OF LADY MADRE TERESA | 74 | 46 131 | 52 |
| FEARES ANTIDOTE. A WISE, AND WELL STAY'D FIRE | ON· HOPE | 82 | 46 143 | 71 |
| MEET HIS WELL-MEANING WOUNDS, WISE HEART. | TO COUNTESSE OF DENBIGH | 45 | 52 236 | 146 |
| ALL YE WISE SOULES, WHO IN THE WEALTHY BREST | TO THE NAME OF JESUS | 11 | 52 239 | 30 |
| O THEY ARE WISE. | TO THE NAME OF JESUS | 154 | 52 239 | 30 |
| OF A MOST WISE & WELL-ABUSED NIGHT | IN GLORIOUS EPIPHANIE | 210 | 52 253 | 39 |
| O BE MORE WISE | SANCTA MARIA DOLORUM | 85 | 52 283 | 162 |
| LET THEN THE AGED WORLD BE WISE, & ALL | O GLORIOSA DOMINA | 23 | 52 302 | 194 |
| WISE HEAVN WILL NEVER HAVE IT SO | TERESA | 74 | 52 315 | 52 |
| HERE A WELL-PLAC'T & WISE MISTAKE | FLAMING HEART | 8 | 52 324 | 61 |
| SAY, ALL YE WISE & WELL-PEIRC'T HEARTS | FLAMING HEART | 49 | 52 324 | 61 |
| LET MYSTICK DEATHS WAIT ON'T, & WISE SOULES BE | FLAMING HEART | 83 | 52 324 | 61 |
| WAKEFULL & WISE. | PRAYER TO GENTLE-WOMAN | 31 | 52 328 | 139 |
| FOR WORTHY SOULES, WHOSE WISE EMBRACES | PRAYER TO GENTLE-WOMAN | 44 | 52 328 | 139 |
| YOUR WISE SOUL, NEVER TO BE WONNE | TO SAME CONCERNING CHOISE | 56 | 52 331 | 66 |
| CROWN'D WOES AWAKE, AS THINGS TOO WISE FOR SLEEP. | DESCRIPTION RELIGIOUS HOUSE | 29 | 52 338 | 213 |
| FEAR'S ANTIDOTE. A WISE & WELL-STAY'D FIRE. | (ON) HOPE | 42 | 52 345 | 71 |
| YEILD TO HIS SIEGE, WISE SOUL, AND SEE | AGAINST IRRESOLUTION AND DELAY | 79 | 52 347 | 146 |

## SELFE-WISE

| | | | | |
|---|---|---|---|---|
| ART THOU UNTO THY SELFE, THOU TOO SELFE-WISE | SOSPETTO D'HERODE | 78 | 46 109 | 216 |

## WISH

| | | | | |
|---|---|---|---|---|
| POORE JEALOUSIE, WHY SHOULD HE WISH TO PREY | SOSPETTO D'HERODE | 519 | 46 109 | 216 |
| I WISH HER BEAUTY, | WISHES SUPPOSED MISTRESSE | 16 | 46 195 | 479 |
| I WISH, HER STORE | WISHES SUPPOSED MISTRESSE | 103 | 46 195 | 479 |
| WHAT THESE LINES WISH TO SEE. | WISHES SUPPOSED MISTRESSE | 113 | 46 195 | 479 |
| WE NOW WILL OWN NO SHORTER WISH, NOR NAME A NARROWER WORD. | OFFICE H. CROSS COMPLINE | 18 | 52 274 | 105 |
| WHO ONLY WISH HIS VIRGIN WIFE TO BE. | ALEXIAS THIRD ELEGIE | 24 | 52 336 | 209 |

## WISH--NO

| | | | | |
|---|---|---|---|---|
| OF WISHES. AND I WISH--NO MORE. | WISHES SUPPOSED MISTRESSE | 105 | 46 195 | 479 |

## WISH'D

| | | | | |
|---|---|---|---|---|
| AND HIS FEAVER WISH'D TO PROVE | ANOTHER ON HERRYS | 27 | 46 170 | 469 |

## WISHT

| | | | | |
|---|---|---|---|---|
| THE SUNNE HIMSELFE OFT WISHT TO SIT, AND MADE | UPON DEATH OF HERRYS | 10 | 46 167 | 466 |

## WISHES

| | | | | |
|---|---|---|---|---|
| OF WHAT SHEE MAY WITH FRUITLESSE WISHES | IN MEMORY OF LADY MADRE TERESA | 41 | 46 131 | 52 |
| ON WHICH THOU NOW MAIST TO THY WISHES, | IN MEMORY OF LADY MADRE TERESA | 132 | 46 131 | 52 |
| MEET YOU HER MY WISHES, | WISHES SUPPOSED MISTRESSE | 13 | 46 195 | 479 |
| OF WISHES. AND I WISH--NO MORE. | WISHES SUPPOSED MISTRESSE | 105 | 46 195 | 479 |
| MY WISHES CLOUDY CHARACTER, | WISHES SUPPOSED MISTRESSE | 117 | 46 195 | 479 |
| SHALL FIXE MY FLYING WISHES. | WISHES SUPPOSED MISTRESSE | 122 | 46 195 | 479 |
| KINDLED ON THEIR COLD LIPS. O HAD MY WISHES | UPON TWO GREENE APRICOCKES | 10 | 48 220 | 494 |
| OF WHAT SHE MAY WITH FRUITLES WISHES | TERESA | 41 | 52 315 | 52 |
| ON WHICH THOU NOW MAIST TO THY WISHES | TERESA | 131 | 52 315 | 52 |

## WIT

| | | | | |
|---|---|---|---|---|
| BLACKE WIT OR MALICE CAN OR DARES, | NEITHER DURST MAN ASKE | 2 | 46 92 | 20 |
| IF USUALL WIT, AND STRENGTH WILL DOE NO GOOD, | SOSPETTO D'HERODE | 273 | 46 109 | 216 |
| O WIT OF LOVE, THAT THUS COULD PLACE | WEEPER | 89 | 52 307 | 120 |

## WITT

| | | | | |
|---|---|---|---|---|
| LOVES NOBLE HISTORY, WITH WITT | IN MEMORY OF LADY MADRE TERESA | 157 | 46 131 | 52 |
| IT WAS THE WITT OF LOVE O'REFLOWD THE BOUNDS | TO THE NAME OF JESUS | 223 | 52 239 | 30 |
| WHOSE WEALTH'S THEIR FLOCK, WHOSE WITT, TO BE | IN HOLY NATIVITY | 95 | 52 246 | 76 |
| AND BY STRANGE WITT OF MADNES WREST | IN GLORIOUS EPIPHANIE | 111 | 52 253 | 39 |
| BUT THERE IS WITT IN WRATH, AND THEY WILL TRY | OFFICE H. CROSS THIRD | 5 | 52 268 | 93 |
| LOVE'S NOBLE HISTORY, WITH WITT | TERESA | 156 | 52 315 | 52 |

## WITCH

| | | | | |
|---|---|---|---|---|
| MEDAEA, JEZABELL, MANY A MEAGER WITCH | SOSPETTO D'HERODE | 338 | 46 109 | 216 |

## WITHER'D

| | | | | |
|---|---|---|---|---|
| A WITHER'D LEAFE, AN IDLE GUEST. | PSALME 137 | 24 | 46 104 | 7 |

## WITHHELD

| | | | | |
|---|---|---|---|---|
| WITHHELD HER VAILE, H' HAD FORFEITED HIS SIGHT. | UPON KINGS CORONATION | 20 | MS 390 | 453 |

## WITHIN

| | | | | |
|---|---|---|---|---|
| WITHIN THE LIPS OF LOVE AND JOY DOTH DWELL | UPON ASSE THAT BORE SAVIOUR | 3 | 46 90 | 19 |
| WITHIN HIMSELFE THE PURPLE PRIDE | UPON DEATH OF DESIRED HERRYS | 38 | 46 168 | 467 |

|   |   |   |   |   |
|---|---|---|---|---|
| HIS VERTUE THAT WITHIN HAD ROOT, | HIS EPITAPH (HERRYS) | 35 | 46 172 471 |
| NOR FLAMES OF OUGHT TOO HOT WITHIN. | WISHES SUPPOSED MISTRESSE | 66 | 46 195 479 |
| BOVE ALL. NOTHING WITHIN THAT LOWRES. | WISHES SUPPOSED MISTRESSE | 93 | 46 195 479 |
| BUT LEFT WITHIN | IN GLORIOUS EPIPHANIE | 76 | 52 253 39 |
| ARE RED WITHOUT & PALE WITHIN. | DIES IRAE | 44 | 52 298 186 |

WITHOUT

|   |   |   |   |
|---|---|---|---|
| TO MEET THEIR TROUBLED LORD WITHOUT DELAY. | SOSPETTO D'HERODE | 508 | 46 109 216 |
| COULD NOT CHUSE BUT SHINE WITHOUT. | HIS EPITAPH (HERRYS) | 36 | 46 172 471 |
| ARE RED WITHOUT & PALE WITHIN. | DIES IRAE | 44 | 52 298 186 |
| WITHOUT RELIGIOUS SILENCE. ABOVE ALL | HORATIJ ILLE & NEFASTO | 47 | MS 382 530 |

WITNESSE

|   |   |   |   |
|---|---|---|---|
| NO WITNESSE PETER OF THY PERJURY. | ON ST. PETER CUTTING MALCHUS | 4 | 46 97 22 |

WITNEST

|   |   |   |   |
|---|---|---|---|
| WITH A CHANG'D COUNTENANCE WITNEST THE SIGHT. | SOSPETTO D'HERODE | 375 | 46 109 216 |

WITTNES

|   |   |   |   |
|---|---|---|---|
| SAY & BEAR WITTNES. SENDS SHE NOT | FLAMING HEART | 53 | 52 324 61 |

WITTNESSE

|   |   |   |   |
|---|---|---|---|
| BOTH YET BELEIVE. AND WITTNESSE THEE | ADORO TE | 31 | 52 291 172 |
| WITTNESSE. CHAST HEAVNS. NO HAPPYER VOWES I KNOW | ALEXIAS THIRD ELEGIE | 25 | 52 336 209 |
| WITTNESSE THIS MAPP OF BEAUTY. EVERY PART | UPON BIRTH PRINCESSE E | 37 | MS 391 456 |

WITTNESSES

|   |   |   |   |
|---|---|---|---|
| THE LOVE-SLAIN WITTNESSES OF THIS LIFE OF THEE. | FLAMING HEART | 84 | 52 324 61 |

WOE

|   |   |   |   |
|---|---|---|---|
| WEEPING IS THE EASE OF WOE, | THE WEEPER | 74 | 46 79 120 |
| AND IN SOFT SLUMBERS BATH THY WOE. | THE TEARE | 40 | 46 84 50 |
| AND DOES WOE ME INTO LIFE. | PSALME 23 | 20 | 46 102 5 |
| BESTOW THY POPPY UPON WAKEFULL WOE, | TO THE MORNING | 55 | 46 183 497 |
| (WEEPING IS THE EASE OF WOE) | WEEPER | 56 | 52 307 120 |

WOES

|   |   |   |   |
|---|---|---|---|
| THE DAY OF MY DARKE WOES IS YET BUT MORNE. | OUR LORD IN HIS CIRCUMCISION | 11 | 46 98 9 |
| AND TILL MY RIPER WOES TO AGE ARE COME. | OUR LORD IN HIS CIRCUMCISION | 17 | 46 98 9 |
| OF WOES, TOO LATE DOE ROUZE THY FEARES. | PSALME 137 | 34 | 46 104 7 |
| A MASSE OF WOES, HIS TEETH FOR TORMENT GNASH, | SOSPETTO D'HERODE | 63 | 46 109 216 |
| RENDERS THEE DOUBLE TO THY PRESENT WOES. | SOSPETTO D'HERODE | 244 | 46 109 216 |
| ALL THY OLD WOES SHALL NOW SMILE ON THEE. | IN MEMORY OF LADY MADRE TERESA | 146 | 46 131 52 |
| ALL WOES INTO ONE CRUCIFIX. | OFFICE H. CROSS SIXT | 8 | 52 270 97 |
| WHAT HAVE HIS WOES TO DOE WITH THEE. | CHARITAS NIMIA | 14 | 52 280 48 |
| HANGING ALL TORN SHE SEES. AND IN HIS WOES | SANCTA MARIA DOLORUM | 7 | 52 283 162 |
| IN WOES THAT WERE NOT MADE FOR HIM. | SANCTA MARIA DOLORUM | 34 | 52 283 162 |
| O SWEET CONTEST. OF WOES | WEEPER | 91 | 52 307 120 |
| ALL THY OLD WOES SHALL NOW SMILE ON THEE | TERESA | 145 | 52 315 52 |
| SURE IN MY EARLY WOES STARRES WERE AT STRIFE, | ALEXIAS FIRST ELEGIE | 5 | 52 334 204 |
| I'D SEND MY WOES IN WORDS SHOULD WEEP FOR ME. | ALEXIAS FIRST ELEGIE | 11 | 52 334 204 |
| WHO KNOWES MY OWN HEART'S WOES SO WELL AS I. | ALEXIAS FIRST ELEGIE | 14 | 52 334 204 |
| WILL TAKE ACQUAINTANCE OF MY WOES, & SAY | ALEXIAS FIRST ELEGIE | 28 | 52 334 204 |
| EXPOSTULATE MY WOES & MUCH-WRONG'D LOVES. | ALEXIAS SECONDE ELEGIE | 14 | 52 335 207 |
| CROWN'D WOES AWAKE. AS THINGS TOO WISE FOR SLEEP. | DESCRIPTION RELIGIOUS HOUSE | 29 | 52 338 213 |
| AND MURMUR FORTH THY WOES TO EVERY FLOWER, | AN ELEGIE ON DR PORTER | 21 | MS 395 476 |

WOFULL

|   |   |   |   |
|---|---|---|---|
| WOFULL & JOYFULL WE | OFFICE H. CROSS EVENSONG | 10 | 52 273 101 |

WOLF

|   |   |   |   |
|---|---|---|---|
| WHEN THE WOLF SINS, HIMSELF TO BLEED. | CHARITAS NIMIA | 54 | 52 280 48 |

WOLVISH

|   |   |   |   |
|---|---|---|---|
| WOLVISH LYCAON HERE A PLACE HATH WON. | SOSPETTO D'HERODE | 334 | 46 109 216 |

WOMAN

|   |   |   |   |
|---|---|---|---|
| SOME WEAK, INFERIOUR, WOMAN SAINT. | FLAMING HEART | 26 | 52 324 61 |

WOMB

|   |   |   |   |
|---|---|---|---|
| WOMB OF DAY. | TO THE NAME OF JESUS | 162 | 52 239 30 |
| THOU HADST A VIRGIN WOMB, | TO OUR B. LORD | 3 | 52 279 25 |
| HAD NOT THY HEALTHFULL WOMB | O GLORIOSA DOMINA | 18 | 52 302 194 |

WOMBE

|   |   |   |   |
|---|---|---|---|
| THOU HAD'ST A VIRGIN WOMBE | UPON OUR SAVIOURS TOMBE | 3 | 46 93 25 |
| NATURES NEW WOMBE, | EASTER DAY | 5 | 46 100 26 |
| HEE SAW TH'OLD HEBREWES WOMBE, NEGLECT THE LAW | SOSPETTO D'HERODE | 101 | 46 109 216 |
| FROM A CHAST VIRGIN WOMBE, SHOULD BLESSE THE EARTH. | SOSPETTO D'HERODE | 160 | 46 109 216 |
| ILLUSTRIOUS SWEETNESSE. IN THY FAITHFULL WOMBE, | UPON YORKE HIS BIRTH | 80 | 46 176 500 |

PAGE 469

| | | | | | |
|---|---|---|---|---|---|
| YET SURE THOU DID'ST LODGE HEERE. THIS WOMBE OF MINE | LUKE 2. QUAERIT JESUM | 25 | MS | 379 | 11 |

WOMBES

| | | | | | |
|---|---|---|---|---|---|
| YOU FROM HER EYES SWOLNE WOMBES OF SORROW. | THE WEEPER | 126 | 46 | 79 | 120 |
| MY WOMBES CHAST PRIDE IS GONE, MY HEAV'NE-BORNE BOY. | LUKE 2. QUAERIT JESUM | 7 | MS | 379 | 11 |

WOMEN

| | | | | | |
|---|---|---|---|---|---|
| 'BOUT MEN AND WOMEN, NOR WILL SPARE | OUT OF GREEKE CUPID'S CRYER | 42 | 46 | 159 | 519 |
| LIVE CROWNE OF WOMEN, QUEEN OF MEN. | ON THE ASSUMPTION | 61 | 46 | 139 | 114 |

WOEMEN

| | | | | | |
|---|---|---|---|---|---|
| LIVE, CROWN OF WOEMEN. QUEEN OF MEN. | IN GLORIOUS ASSUMPTION B. LADY | 66 | 52 | 304 | 114 |

WON

| | | | | | |
|---|---|---|---|---|---|
| WOLVISH LYCAON HERE A PLACE HATH WON. | SOSPETTO D'HERODE | 334 | 46 | 109 | 216 |
| THIS FORT OF YOUR FAIR SELFE, IF'T BE NOT WON, | TO COUNTESSE OF DENBIGH | 67 | 52 | 236 | 146 |
| WE (PRETIOUS ONES) IN YOU HAVE WON | IN GLORIOUS EPIPHANIE | 73 | 52 | 253 | 39 |

WONE

| | | | | | |
|---|---|---|---|---|---|
| TEDIOUSLY WO'ED, AND HARDLY WONE. | AGAINST IRRESOLUTION AND DELAY | 59 | 52 | 347 | 146 |
| THIS FORT OF YOUR FAIR SELF IF'T BE NOT WONE, | AGAINST IRRESOLUTION AND DELAY | 89 | 52 | 347 | 146 |

WONNE

| | | | | | |
|---|---|---|---|---|---|
| YOUR WISE SOUL, NEVER TO BE WONNE | TO SAME CONCERNING CHOISE | 56 | 52 | 331 | 66 |
| BUT NOW THE FEILD IS WONNE. & THEY | IN CICATRICES DOMINI JESU | 17 | MS | 381 | 27 |

WONDER

| | | | | | |
|---|---|---|---|---|---|
| WAS A GREAT WONDER. | UPON ASSE THAT BORE SAVIOUR | 10 | 46 | 90 | 19 |
| HEE EXPOUNDS THE GIDDY WONDER | PSALME 23 | 27 | 46 | 102 | 5 |
| FELLOW THIS WONDER TOO, NOR LET HER SHINE | UPON YORKE HIS BIRTH | 55 | 46 | 176 | 500 |
| WHAT WONDER, WHEN THE HUNDRED-HEADED BEAST | HORATIJ ILLE & NEFASTO | 50 | MS | 382 | 530 |

WONDERS

| | | | | | |
|---|---|---|---|---|---|
| RISE MIGHTY MAN OF WONDERS, AND THY WORLD WITH THEE | EASTER DAY | 3 | 46 | 100 | 26 |
| MISTRESSE OF WONDERS. CYNTHIA'S IS THE NIGHT, | UPON YORKE HIS BIRTH | 77 | 46 | 176 | 500 |
| WELLCOME, ALL WONDERS IN ONE SIGHT. | IN HOLY NATIVITY | 79 | 52 | 246 | 76 |
| THAT WONDERS MAY IN FASHION BE, NOT RARE. | ON GUNPOWDER-TREASON | 27 | MS | 384 | 458 |

WONDERING

| | | | | | |
|---|---|---|---|---|---|
| WHEN WONDERING DEATH BY DEATH WAS SLAIN. | OFFICE H. CROSS EVENSONG | 26 | 52 | 273 | 101 |

WONDRING

| | | | | | |
|---|---|---|---|---|---|
| WELCOME TO OUR WONDRING SIGHT | A HYMNE OF THE NATIVITY | 53 | 46 | 106 | 76 |
| FROM THENCE INTO THE WONDRING READERS BREAST, | AN APOLOGIE FOR HYMNE (TERESA) | 25 | 46 | 136 | 59 |
| WHILE WONDRING THEY | IN GLORIOUS EPIPHANIE | 175 | 52 | 253 | 39 |
| FROM THENCE INTO THE WONDRING READER'S BREST. | AN APOLOGIE FOR (TERESA) HYMNE | 25 | 52 | 322 | 59 |
| THERE THESE BRAVE SOULES DEALE TO EACH WONDRING EARE | HORATIJ ILLE & NEFASTO | 45 | MS | 382 | 530 |
| THEN WONDRING STARTS, & HAD THE CURTEOUS NIGHT | UPON KINGS CORONATION | 19 | MS | 390 | 453 |

WONT

| | | | | | |
|---|---|---|---|---|---|
| AS THEY ARE WONT. WHAT THOUGH. | ON BLEEDING WOUNDS OF LORD | 7 | 46 | 101 | 110 |
| WITH THOSE DEARE SPOILES THAT WONT TO DRESSE THE FAIRE | ON A TREATISE OF CHARITY | 54 | 46 | 137 | 69 |
| O THAT IT WERE AS IT WAS WONT TO BE. | TO THE NAME OF JESUS | 197 | 52 | 239 | 30 |
| AS THEY WERE EVER WONT. WHAT THOUGH. | UPON BLEEDING CRUCIFIX | 11 | 52 | 288 | 110 |
| TO CORRALLIZE, WHICH SOFTLY WONT TO SLIDE | AN ELEGY MR STANNINOW | 23 | MS | 394 | 473 |

WOO

| | | | | | |
|---|---|---|---|---|---|
| HOT MARS TO TH' HARVEST OF DEATHS FIELD, AND WOO | MUSICKS DUELL | 55 | 46 | 149 | 535 |
| TO WOO THEM FROM THEIR BEDS, STILL MURMURING | MUSICKS DUELL | 79 | 46 | 149 | 535 |

WOO'D

| | | | | | |
|---|---|---|---|---|---|
| IT WAS THEIR WEAKNES WOO'D HIS BEAUTY. | IN GLORIOUS EPIPHANIE | 183 | 52 | 253 | 39 |

WO'ED

| | | | | | |
|---|---|---|---|---|---|
| YEA SUITOURS. MAN ALONE IS WO'ED. | AGAINST IRRESOLUTION AND DELAY | 58 | 52 | 347 | 146 |
| TEDIOUSLY WO'ED, AND HARDLY WONE. | AGAINST IRRESOLUTION AND DELAY | 59 | 52 | 347 | 146 |

WOOE

| | | | | | |
|---|---|---|---|---|---|
| WOOE, INTREAT, AND CRYING SAY | OUT OF GREEKE CUPID'S CRYER | 68 | 46 | 159 | 519 |
| BOTH LAWRELS TWINE INTO ONE WREATH, AND WOOE | UPON YORKE HIS BIRTH | 38 | 46 | 176 | 500 |
| THE AIRE DOES WOOE THEE, | OUT OF THE ITALIAN (1) | 31 | 46 | 188 | 545 |

WOOD

| | | | | | |
|---|---|---|---|---|---|
| A NIGHTINGALE, COME FROM THE NEIGHBOURING WOOD. | MUSICKS DUELL | 8 | 46 | 149 | 535 |
| WHEN BEASTS TOOKE UP THEIR LODGING IN THE WOOD, | OUT OF VIRGIL | 31 | 46 | 155 | 529 |
| THE HOUSE IS HERS'D ABOUT WITH A BLACK WOOD, | SOSPETTO D'HERODE | 345 | 46 | 109 | 216 |
| IT WAS THY WOOD HE MEANT SHOULD MAKE THE THRONE | VEXILLA REGIS | 23 | 52 | 277 | 156 |

WOODS

| | | | | |
|---|---|---|---|---|
| BUT WALKES & UNSHORN WOODS. AND SOULES, JUST SO | DESCRIPTION RELIGIOUS HOUSE | 9 | 52 338 | 213 |

WORD

| | | | | |
|---|---|---|---|---|
| AND THOU (HEAVEN-BURTHEN'D BEAST) HAST NE'RE A WORD | UPON ASSE THAT BORE SAVIOUR | 7 | 46 90 | 19 |
| THOU SPEAK'ST THE WORD (THY WORD'S A LAW) | THE BLIND CURED | 1 | 46 91 | 19 |
| HAD NERE ANOTHER WORD TO SAY. | NEITHER DURST MAN ASKE | 16 | 46 92 | 20 |
| AT THE WHISPER OF THY WORD | PSALME 23 | 49 | 46 102 | 5 |
| ETERNALL WORD SHOULD BEE A CHILD, AND WEEPE. | SOSPETTO D'HERODE | 179 | 46 109 | 216 |
| OF LIFE AND DEATH--TO PROVE THE WORD. | IN MEMORY OF LADY MADRE TERESA | 2 | 46 131 | 52 |
| EACH HEAVENLY WORD, BY WHOSE HID FLAME | IN MEMORY OF LADY MADRE TERESA | 160 | 46 131 | 52 |
| OF FAITH, A MOUNTAINE WORD, MADE UP OF AIRE. | ON A TREATISE OF CHARITY | 53 | 46 137 | 69 |
| WHAT WORD SO E'RE HIS BREATH KEPT WARME, | HIS EPITAPH (HERRYS) | 31 | 46 172 | 471 |
| WAS NO WORD NOW BUT A CHARME. | HIS EPITAPH (HERRYS) | 32 | 46 172 | 471 |
| MIGHT A WORD ONCE FLYE FROM OUT THEE. | OUT OF THE ITALIAN (1) | 33 | 46 188 | 545 |
| AND THAT FAIR WORD AT ALL REFERR TO THEE) | TO THE NAME OF JESUS | 14 | 52 239 | 30 |
| AND IN THE WEALTH OF ONE RICH WORD PROCLAIM | TO THE NAME OF JESUS | 95 | 52 239 | 30 |
| THE FATHER'S WORD & WISDOM, MADE | OFFICE H. CROSS MATINES | 12 | 52 265 | 86 |
| WE NOW WILL OWN NO SHORTER WISH, NOR NAME A NARROWER WORD. | OFFICE H. CROSS COMPLINE | 18 | 52 274 | 105 |
| O SAY THE WORD MY SOUL SHALL LIVE. | DIES IRAE | 48 | 52 298 | 166 |
| OF LIFE & DEATH. TO PROVE THE WORD, | TERESA | 2 | 52 315 | 52 |
| EACH HEAVNLY WORD BY WHOSE HID FLAME | TERESA | 159 | 52 315 | 52 |
| AND VENTURE TO SPEAK ONE GOOD WORD | TO SAME CONCERNING CHOISE | 6 | 52 331 | 66 |
| SENDING'S TOO SLOW A WORD, MY SELFE WOULD FLY. | ALEXIAS FIRST ELEGIE | 13 | 52 334 | 204 |
| THAT WITH EACH WORD, MY LOADEN PEN LETTS FALL, | UPON BIRTH PRINCESSE E | 3 | MS 391 | 456 |
| AN AEQUALL PACE THUS FARRE. THY WORD MY DEEDES | OUT OF GROTIUS | 5 | MS 398 | 198 |

REBELL-WORD

| | | | | |
|---|---|---|---|---|
| BUT KILL THIS REBELL-WORD, IRRESOLUTE | TO COUNTESSE OF DENBIGH | 40 | 52 236 | 146 |

WORD'S

| | | | | |
|---|---|---|---|---|
| THOU SPEAK'ST THE WORD (THY WORD'S A LAW) | THE BLIND CURED | 1 | 46 91 | 19 |

WORDS

| | | | | |
|---|---|---|---|---|
| CERTAIN HARD WORDS MADE INTO PILLS. | IN PRAISE OF LESSIUS | 8 | 46 156 | 510 |
| FOR NEVER WERE HIS WORDS IN OUGHT | OUT OF GREEKE CUPID'S CRYER | 23 | 46 159 | 519 |
| AND THERE BE WORDS NOT MADE WITH LUNGS. | UPON THE DEATH OF A GENTLEMAN | 28 | 46 166 | 472 |
| HEE STRAINES THESE WORDS. BASE ENVY, DOE, LAUGH ON. | HIGH MOUNTED ON AN ANT | 5 | 46 161 | 523 |
| AT THOSE HARD WORDS MANS COWARDISE CALLS FEARES. | I AM READY NOT ONELY BOUND | 2 | 46 98 | 29 |
| GAVE FORTH YOUR BLOOD FOR BREATH, SPOKE SOULES FOR WORDS. | SOSPETTO D'HERODE | 8 | 46 109 | 216 |
| OF LIGHTNING, OR THE WORDS HE SPOKE) LEFT HELL. | SOSPETTO D'HERODE | 372 | 46 109 | 216 |
| HER WORDS. SLEEP'ST THOU FOND MAN. SLEEP'ST THOU. (SAID SHE) | SOSPETTO D'HERODE | 424 | 46 109 | 216 |
| WORDS WHICH ARE NOT HEARD WITH EARES, | ON A PRAYER BOOKE | 59 | 46 126 | 139 |
| OF NAMES AND WORDS SO FARRE PREJUDICATE. | AN APOLOGIE FOR HYMNE (TERESA) | 14 | 46 136 | 59 |
| TO KEEP PACE WITH THOSE POWRFULL WORDS. | ADORO TE | 14 | 52 291 | 172 |
| AND WORDS MORE SURE, MORE SWEET, THEN THEY | ADORO TE | 15 | 52 291 | 172 |
| WORDS WHICH ARE NOT HEARD WITH EARES | PRAYER TO GENTLE-WOMAN | 65 | 52 328 | 139 |
| OATHES OF WATER, WORDS OF WIND. | TO SAME CONCERNING CHOISE | 17 | 52 331 | 66 |
| I'D SEND MY WOES IN WORDS SHOULD WEEP FOR ME. | ALEXIAS FIRST ELEGIE | 11 | 52 334 | 204 |
| CERTAIN HARD WORDS MADE INTO PILLS. | TEMPERANCE | 8 | 52 342 | 510 |
| SUCH WORDS, SOE PRECIOUS, AS THEY MAY NOT WEARE | HORATIJ ILLE & NEFASTO | 46 | MS 382 | 530 |

WORDES

| | | | | |
|---|---|---|---|---|
| OF NAMES & WORDES, SO FARR PRAEJUDICATE. | AN APOLOGIE FOR (TERESA) HYMNE | 14 | 52 322 | 59 |

WORE

| | | | | |
|---|---|---|---|---|
| A BAND OF MEN, ROUGH AS THE ARMES THEY WORE | THE BEGINNING OF HELIODORUS | 7 | 46 158 | 517 |
| IN CENTER OF THEIR INMOST SOULES THEY WORE THEE, | TO THE NAME OF JESUS | 205 | 52 239 | 30 |
| THE WEAPON, THAT HE WORE, HE WAS. | IN CICATRICES DOMINI JESU | 12 | MS 381 | 27 |
| THIS RISING SUNNE. THEIR FACES NOTHING WORE, | UPON KINGS CORONATION | 38 | MS 390 | 453 |
| THOSE DURTY SMUTCHES, WHICH THEIR FAIRE FRONTS WORE, | AN ELEGY MR STANNINOW | 13 | MS 394 | 473 |

WORK

| | | | | |
|---|---|---|---|---|
| COME, LOVE. & LET US WORK A SONG | LAUDA SION SALVATOREM | 13 | 52 294 | 178 |
| AND SING, & SIGH, & WORK, AND SLEEP AGAIN. | DESCRIPTION RELIGIOUS HOUSE | 17 | 52 338 | 213 |
| AND WORK FOR WORK, NOT WAGES. LET TO MORROW'S | DESCRIPTION RELIGIOUS HOUSE | 21 | 52 338 | 213 |
| AND WORK FOR WORK, NOT WAGES. LET TO MORROW'S | DESCRIPTION RELIGIOUS HOUSE | 21 | 52 338 | 213 |
| MARK HOW THE CURL'D WAVES WORK AND WIND, | AGAINST IRRESOLUTION AND DELAY | 41 | 52 347 | 146 |

WORKE

| | | | | |
|---|---|---|---|---|
| STILL WORKE FOR HER, AND HAVE THEIR WAGES FROM HER. | SOSPETTO D'HERODE | 341 | 46 109 | 216 |
| AND TO THE WORKE OF LOVE THIS MORNING WAKE YOU | TO THE NAME OF JESUS | 54 | 52 239 | 30 |
| WHICH HAD THE HAPPINES TO WORKE I'TH' NIGHT. | ON GUNPOWDER-TREASON | 58 | MS 384 | 458 |
| BEE CONSECRATED TO THIS WORKE, WHILE I | UPON BIRTH PRINCESSE E | 23 | MS 391 | 456 |

GROUND-WORKE

| | | | | |
|---|---|---|---|---|
| AND LAY THE GROUND-WORKE OF HER HOPEFULL SONG, | MUSICKS DUELL | 85 | 46 149 | 535 |

FIRE-WORKS

| | | | | | |
|---|---|---|---|---|---|
| HER HAPPY FIRE-WORKS, HERE, COMES DOWN TO SEE. | FLAMING HEART | 18 | 52 | 324 | 61 |

WORKES

| | | | | | |
|---|---|---|---|---|---|
| ALL THY GOOD WORKES WHICH WENT BEFORE, | IN MEMORY OF LADY MADRE TERESA | 140 | 46 | 131 | 52 |
| THOSE RARE WORKES, WHERE THOU SHALT LEAVE WRIT, | IN MEMORY OF LADY MADRE TERESA | 156 | 46 | 131 | 52 |
| ALL THY GOOD WORKES WHICH WENT BEFORE | TERESA | 139 | 52 | 315 | 52 |
| THOSE RARE WORKES WHERE THOU SHALT LEAVE WRITT, | TERESA | 155 | 52 | 315 | 52 |
| BUT SINCE THEY ARE FIRE WORKES, RATHER PROVE | UPON GUNPOWDER TREASON | 33 | MS | 367 | 461 |

WORKING

| | | | | | |
|---|---|---|---|---|---|
| THE WORKING BEES SOFT MELTING GOLD, | OUT OF GREEKE CUPID'S CRYER | 25 | 46 | 159 | 519 |

WORLD

| | | | | | |
|---|---|---|---|---|---|
| BUT WHISPER TO THE WORLD. THUS DOE THEY VARY | MUSICKS DUELL | 145 | 46 | 149 | 535 |
| BUT WHEN THE WORLD FIRST OUT OF CHAOS SPRANG | OUT OF VIRGIL | 23 | 46 | 155 | 529 |
| WHAT HATH OUR WORLD THAT CAN ENTICE | THE WEEPER | 124 | 46 | 79 | 120 |
| THE WORLD WAS MADE OF NOTHING THEN, | AND HE ANSWERED NOTHING | 5 | 46 | 91 | 22 |
| THE WORLD WILL LOVE ITS DARKNESSE STILL. | BUT MEN LOVED DARKNESSE | 2 | 46 | 97 | 13 |
| RISE MIGHTY MAN OF WONDERS, AND THY WORLD WITH THEE | EASTER DAY | 3 | 46 | 100 | 26 |
| WINTER CHID THE WORLD, AND SENT | A HYMNE OF THE NATIVITY | 23 | 46 | 106 | 76 |
| TO THE BELEEVING WORLD FAME BOLDLY SINGS. | SOSPETTO D'HERODE | 14 | 46 | 109 | 216 |
| AMAZ'D THE MIDNIGHT WORLD, AND MADE A DAY | SOSPETTO D'HERODE | 116 | 46 | 109 | 216 |
| AND CRUSH THE WORLD TILL HIS WIDE CORNERS MEET. | SOSPETTO D'HERODE | 280 | 46 | 109 | 216 |
| SHEE ROSE, AND WITH HER TO OUR WORLD DID BRING. | SOSPETTO D'HERODE | 373 | 46 | 109 | 216 |
| FAREWELL THEN ALL THE WORLD, ADEIU, | IN MEMORY OF LADY MADRE TERESA | 57 | 46 | 131 | 52 |
| FANNING THY FAIRE LOCKS (WHICH THE WORLD BELEEVES | ON A TREATISE OF CHARITY | 23 | 46 | 137 | 69 |
| TAKE THY FAREWELL POORE WORLD, HEAVEN MUST GO HOME. | ON THE ASSUMPTION | 2 | 46 | 139 | 114 |
| AND OUR DARKE WORLD NO MORE SHALL SEE. | ON THE ASSUMPTION | 36 | 46 | 139 | 114 |
| AND SEEM'D TO MAKE AN ISLE, BUT MADE A WORLD. | UPON YORKE HIS BIRTH | 28 | 46 | 176 | 500 |
| THEN LET THE EASTERNE WORLD BRAGGE AND BE PROUD | UPON YORKE HIS BIRTH | 86 | 46 | 176 | 500 |
| ON THESE SHE LIFTS THE WORLD. AND ON THEIR BASE | ON FRONTISPIECE ISAACSONS | 21 | 46 | 191 | 491 |
| ONE LITTLE WORLD OR TWO | TO THE NAME OF JESUS | 24 | 52 | 239 | 30 |
| THE ATTENDING WORLD, TO WAIT THY RISE, | TO THE NAME OF JESUS | 135 | 52 | 239 | 30 |
| WELCOME TO OUR DARK WORLD, THOU | TO THE NAME OF JESUS | 161 | 52 | 239 | 30 |
| ON THEIR BOLD BRESTS ABOUT THE WORLD THEY BORE THEE | TO THE NAME OF JESUS | 203 | 52 | 239 | 30 |
| TO ALL OUR WORLD OF WELL-STOLN JOY | IN HOLY NATIVITY | 5 | 52 | 246 | 76 |
| POOR WORLD (SAID I.) WHAT WILT THOU DOE | IN HOLY NATIVITY | 37 | 52 | 246 | 76 |
| PROUD WORLD, SAID I. CEASE YOUR CONTEST | IN HOLY NATIVITY | 44 | 52 | 246 | 76 |
| THE WORLD LYES WARM, & LIKES HIS PLACE. | IN GLORIOUS EPIPHANIE | 37 | 52 | 253 | 39 |
| NOR MAKES THE WHOLE WORLD THY HALF-SPHEAR. | IN GLORIOUS EPIPHANIE | 41 | 52 | 253 | 39 |
| THE BLINDNES OF THE WORLD DID CALL THE EYE. | IN GLORIOUS EPIPHANIE | 45 | 52 | 253 | 39 |
| BY THE LOVE-SICK WORLD BIN MADE | IN GLORIOUS EPIPHANIE | 136 | 52 | 253 | 39 |
| MAINTAINING T'WIXT THY WORLD & OURS | IN GLORIOUS EPIPHANIE | 213 | 52 | 253 | 39 |
| WHEN THE DARK WORLD DAWN'D INTO CHRISTIAN DAY | TO THE QUEENE'S MAJESTY | 4 | 52 | 261 | 47 |
| THE CAPTIVE WORLD AWAK'T, & FOUND | OFFICE H. CROSS THIRD | 14 | 52 | 266 | 93 |
| THOU'HAST SAV'D THE WORLD FROM CERTAIN LOSSE. | OFFICE H. CROSS SIXT | 24 | 52 | 270 | 97 |
| OF ALL THE RANSOM'D WORLD, THOU HADST THE POWER | OFFICE H. CROSS EVENSONG | 16 | 52 | 273 | 101 |
| AND PROVE HOW LIGHT THE WORLD WAS, WHEN IT WEIGHD WITH HIM. | OFFICE H. CROSS EVENSONG | 19 | 52 | 273 | 101 |
| THOU'HAST SAV'D THE WORLD FROM CERTAIN LOSSE. | OFFICE H. CROSS EVENSONG | 31 | 52 | 273 | 101 |
| EVEN BALANCE OF BOTH WORLDS. OUR WORLD OF SIN, | VEXILLA REGIS | 31 | 52 | 277 | 156 |
| A LOST THING TO THE WORLD, AS IT TO ME. | SANCTA MARIA DOLORUM | 104 | 52 | 283 | 162 |
| THE WORLD IN FLAMES SHALL FLY AWAY. | DIES IRAE | 4 | 52 | 290 | 186 |
| WILL SETT THE WORLD IN SEVERE LIGHT. | DIES IRAE | 18 | 52 | 298 | 186 |
| ABOVE THE WORLD. BELOW THY SON | O GLORIOSA DOMINA | 2 | 52 | 302 | 194 |
| LET THEN THE AGED WORLD BE WISE, & ALL | O GLORIOSA DOMINA | 23 | 52 | 302 | 194 |
| TAKE THY FAREWELL, POOR WORLD. HEAVN MUST GOE HOME. | IN GLORIOUS ASSUMPTION B. LADY | 2 | 52 | 304 | 114 |
| FAREWEL THEN, ALL THE WORLD. ADIEU, | TERESA | 57 | 52 | 315 | 52 |
| ASHAM'D THAT OUR WORLD, NOW, CAN SHOW | FLAMING HEART | 45 | 52 | 324 | 61 |
| THEN THIS WORLD OF LYES CAN GIVE YE | TO SAME CONCERNING CHOISE | 37 | 52 | 331 | 66 |
| WHILE THROUGH THE WORLD SHE SOUGHT HER WANDRING MATE. | ALEXIAS FIRST ELEGIE | 30 | 52 | 334 | 204 |
| TROUBLESOM TO THE WORLD, THUS, AS FOR THEE, | ALEXIAS SECONDE ELEGIE | 12 | 52 | 335 | 207 |
| THE WORLD, ALL-DARING DUST & ASHES. ONLY YOU | DEATH'S LECTURE | 31 | 52 | 340 | 475 |
| TO TELL THE WORLD, HOW HARD THE MATTER WENT, | HORATIJ ILLE & NEFASTO | 43 | MS | 382 | 530 |
| BY THY KIND ARMES TO A KIND WORLD UNKNOWNE. | ON GUNPOWDER-TREASON | 8 | MS | 384 | 458 |
| JOVES TWINCKLING TAPERS, THAT DOE LIGHT THE WORLD, | UPON GUNPOWDER TREASON | 27 | MS | 386 | 460 |
| THE WORLD WILL BE ONE OCEAN, ONE GREAT TEARE. | UPON KINGS CORONATION | 42 | MS | 389 | 454 |
| HOW OUT OF TUNE THE WORLD NOW LIES, | UPON DEATH OF A FREIND | 15 | MS | 393 | 477 |
| BEFORE THE WORLD. OBEDIENT LO. I JOYNE | OUT OF GROTIUS | 4 | MS | 398 | 198 |
| THE WORLD MY FATHER. THEN DOES ENVY SWELL | OUT OF GROTIUS | 32 | MS | 398 | 198 |
| TO FREIND THE LIVING WORLD EVEN DEATH DID SEE | OUT OF GROTIUS | 82 | MS | 398 | 198 |

WORLD--ALL

| | | | | | |
|---|---|---|---|---|---|
| THE WORLD--ALL DARING DUST AND ASHES. ONELY YOU | UPON STANINOUGH'S DEATH | 29 | 46 | 175 | 475 |

WORLD'S

| | | | | | |
|---|---|---|---|---|---|
| I DOUBT THOUGH WHEN THE WORLD'S IN HELL, | BUT MEN LOVED DARKNESSE | 3 | 46 | 97 | 13 |
| THAT, THE WORLD'S MORNING, THIS HER MIDNIGHT IS. | ON FRONTISPIECE ISAACSONS | 24 | 46 | 191 | 491 |
| SEARCH WHAT THE WORLD'S CLOSE CABINETS KEEP, | NEW YEAR'S DAY | 18 | 52 | 251 | 37 |
| TO THEE, THE WORLD'S GREAT UNIVERSAL EAST. | IN GLORIOUS EPIPHANIE | 24 | 52 | 253 | 39 |
| THE WORLD'S ONE, ROUND, AETERNALL YEAR. | IN GLORIOUS EPIPHANIE | 27 | 52 | 253 | 39 |
| FAREWELL, THE WORLD'S FALSE LIGHT. | IN GLORIOUS EPIPHANIE | 48 | 52 | 253 | 39 |
| WELCOME, THE WORLD'S SURE WAY. | IN GLORIOUS EPIPHANIE | 60 | 52 | 253 | 39 |
| THE POOR WORLD'S FAULT THAT HE IS FAIR. | IN GLORIOUS EPIPHANIE | 104 | 52 | 253 | 39 |
| FROM THIS WORLD'S EAST THE OTHER'S WEST. | IN GLORIOUS EPIPHANIE | 112 | 52 | 253 | 39 |
| TO WHICH THE LOW WORLD'S LAWES | IN GLORIOUS EPIPHANIE | 153 | 52 | 253 | 39 |

```
THE WORLD'S & HIS HYPERION.                              IN GLORIOUS EPIPHANIE            253   52 253   39
BUT THE WORLD'S HOMAGE, SCARSE IN THESE WELL BLOWN,      TO THE QUEEN'S MAJESTY             9   52 261   47
THE WORLD'S PRICE SETT TO SALE, & BY THE BOLD            OFFICE H. CROSS MATINES           14   52 265   86
THOU'HAST SAV'D AT ONCE THE WHOLE WORLD'S LOSSE.         OFFICE H. CROSS MATINES           27   52 265   86
THOU'HAST SAV'D AT ONCE THE WHOLE WORLD'S LOSSE.         OFFICE H. CROSS PRIME             21   52 267   91
THOU'HAST SAV'D AT ONCE THE WHOLE WORLD'S LOSSE.         OFFICE H. CROSS THIRD             20   52 268   93
THOU'HAST SAV'D AT ONCE THE WHOLE WORLD'S LOSSE.         OFFICE H. CROSS NINTH             17   52 271   99
OR WILL THE WORLD'S ILLUSTRIOUS EYES.                    CHARITAS NIMIA                    37   52 280   48
HER'S, & THE WHOLE WORLD'S JOYES,                        SANCTA MARIA DOLORUM               6   52 283  162
THE WHOLE WORLD'S HOST WOULD BE THY GUEST                O GLORIOSA DOMINA                  7   52 302  194
THE WORLD'S NEW EASTERN WINDOW BIN                       O GLORIOSA DOMINA                 19   52 302  194
WITH ROCKS. NOR BOLD HANDS STRUCK THE WORLD'S STRONG     ALEXIAS THIRD ELEGIE              10   52 336  209
    BARRES.

FORTUNE. ALAS, ABOVE THE WORLD'S LOW WARRES              (ON) HOPE                         31   52 345   71
LOOK ROUND AND READE THE WORLD'S WIDE FACE,              AGAINST IRRESOLUTION AND DELAY    29   52 347  146
OF FUTURE CHANCE.  THE WORLD'S GRAND SIRE.  AND MINE     OUT OF GROTIUS                     3   MS 398  198

WORLDS

THE WORLDS LIGHT SHINES, SHINE AS IT WILL,               BUT MEN LOVED DARKNESSE            1   46  97   13
THE WORLDS PROFOUND HEART PANTS. THERE PLACED IS         SOSPETTO D'HERODE                 35   46 109  216
TOUCHT WITH THE WORLDS TRUE ANTIDOTE TO BURST.           SOSPETTO D'HERODE                128   46 109  216
WESTWARD TO FIND THE WORLDS TRUE ORIENT.                 SOSPETTO D'HERODE                136   46 109  216
FORTUNE ALAS ABOVE THE WORLDS LAW WARRES.                ON HOPE                           71   46 143   71
GIVES HIM THE MORNING WORLDS FRESH GOLD AGAINE.          UPON TWO GREENE APRICOCKES        18   48 220  494
(YOUNG MASTER OF THE WORLDS MATURITIE)                   UPON TWO GREENE APRICOCKES        26   48 220  494
AETERNALL WORLDS UPON IT'S WINGS.                        TO COUNTESSE OF DENBIGH           54   52 236  146
YOUR PROVINCES OF WELL-UNITED WORLDS CAN RAISE.          TO THE NAME OF JESUS              73   52 239   30
MIX ALL YOUR MANY WORLDS, ABOVE,                         TO THE NAME OF JESUS              86   52 239   30
O SEE, SO MANY WORLDS OF BARREN YEARES                   TO THE NAME OF JESUS             143   52 239   30
HOW MANY UNKNOWN WORLDS THERE ARE                        TO THE NAME OF JESUS             189   52 239   30
EVEN BALLANCE OF BOTH WORLDS. OUR WORLD OF SIN,          VEXILLA REGIS                     31   52 277  136
TO WASH MY WORLDS OF SINS FROM ME.                       ADORO·TE                          50   52 291  172
THAT NIP THE BOSOME OF THE WORLDS BEST THINGS,           DESCRIPTION RELIGIOUS HOUSE       26   52 338  213

WORM

WEEP FOR EVERY WORM THAT DYES.                           CHARITAS NIMIA                    38   52 280   48

WORME

(A SPECIALL WORME IT WAS AS EVER KIST                    SOSPETTO D'HERODE                467   46 109  216
THE WORME OF JEALOUS ENVY AND UNREST.                    SOSPETTO D'HERODE                493   46 109  216

WORMES

AND WE, LOW WORMES HAVE LEAVE TO DOE                     TO THE NAME OF JESUS             109   52 239   30
ALL-IDOLIZING WORMES. THAT THUS COULD CROWD              IN GLORIOUS EPIPHANIE            113   52 253   39
IF THERE WERE NO SUCH WORMES AS WE.                      CHARITAS NIMIA                    10   52 280   48

WORN

BY WANTON HEYFER SHALL BE WORN                           IN GLORIOUS EPIPHANIE             94   52 253   39

WORNE

WHOSE RIGHT BY DAVID'S LINAGE SO LONG WORNE,             SOSPETTO D'HERODE                403   46 109  216
WHERE NOUGHT BUT SMILES, AND RUDDY JOYES ARE WORNE.      ON A FOULE MORNING                36   46 181  495

WORSE

WORSE THEN SUN-BURNT IN HIS FIRE.                        OUT OF GREEKE CUPID'S CRYER       56   46 159  519
OF DEATHS, & WORSE.                                      SANCTA MARIA DOLORUM              22   52 283  162
WAS SACRILEGIOUS, (SURE) OR SOMEWHAT WORSE.              HORATIJ ILLE & NEFASTO             4   MS 382  530
A STILL INCREASING BURDEN. WORSE HATH TORNE              OUT OF GROTIUS                    12   MS 398  198
HURTES MEE FAR WORSE THEN HERODS HIGHEST SPITE.          OUT OF GROTIUS                    34   MS 398  198

WORSER

OF HELLS OWNE STINKE, A WORSER STENCH IS SPREAD.         SOSPETTO D'HERODE                 54   46 109  216

WORSHIP

TO LEARN OF HIM AT LEST, TO WORSHIP THEE.                IN GLORIOUS EPIPHANIE            182   52 253   39

WORSHIP'T

AND THEIR BEST USE OF HIM THEY WORSHIP'T BE              IN GLORIOUS EPIPHANIE            181   52 253   39

WORST

THE PLACE THAT CALLS YOU HENCE, IS AT THE WORST          TO INFANT MARTYRS                  5   46  88   10
HEE TO HIMSELFE (I FEARE THE WORST)                      I AM THE DOORE                     3   46  90   17
THEN LET HIM DRINKE, AND DRINKE, AND DOE HIS WORST,      OUR LORD IN HIS CIRCUMCISION       7   46  98    9
AND PUNISH BEST THINGS WORST. BECAUSE THEY STOOD         IN GLORIOUS EPIPHANIE            107   52 253   39
BY HIS WORST FOES (BECAUSE HE WOULD) BESEIG'D & TAKEN.   OFFICE H. CROSS MATINES           17   52 265   86
OF WORST FAULTS TO BE FORTUNATE.                         FLAMING HEART                     60   52 324   61

WORTH

TO SHEW US OUGHT WORTH LOOKING AT.                       A HYMNE OF THE NATIVITY           10   46 106   76
MAPPE OF HEROICK WORTH, WHOM FARRE AND WIDE              SOSPETTO D'HERODE                 13   46 109  216
THOU, WHOSE STRONG HAND WITH SO TRANSCENDENT WORTH,      SOSPETTO D'HERODE                 25   46 109  216
AND SHOULD WE POWERS OF HEAV'N, SPIRITS OF WORTH         SOSPETTO D'HERODE                219   46 109  216
```

```
                                                                      PAGE  473

    STAY OF MY STRONG HOPES, YOU OF WHOSE BRAVE WORTH,    SOSPETTO D'HERODE                282  46 109 216
    THE STRENGTH OF HER UNITED WORTH.                     HIS EPITAPH (HERRYS)              14  46 172 471
    AND TH'HEART-BRED LUSTRE OF HIS WORTH,                HIS EPITAPH (HERRYS)              37  46 172 471
    SO SHALL THESE FLAMES, WHOSE WORTH                    OUT OF THE ITALIAN (2)             7  46 190 547
    OF WORTH, MAY LEAVE HER POORE                         WISHES SUPPOSED MISTRESSE        104  46 195 479
    SUCH WORTH AS THIS IS,                                WISHES SUPPOSED MISTRESSE        121  46 195 479
    TO SHOW US OUGHT WORTH LOOKING AT.                    IN HOLY NATIVITY                  10  52 246  76
    THE WORTH, THE WEALTH                                 OFFICE H. CROSS EVENSONG          15  52 273 101
    AND THIS LOV'D SOUL, JUDG'D WORTH NO LESSE            DIES IRAE                         35  52 298 186
    THAT MIGHT INTERPRET OUR FAIRE CYNTHIA'S WORTH.       UPON BIRTH PRINCESSE E            30  MS 391 456
    FOR JURYES KING AN ENEMY, EVEN WORTH                  OUT OF GROTIUS                    21  MS 398 198

WORTHIER

    A WORTHIER OBJECT, OUR LORDS FEET.                    THE WEEPER                       138  46  79 120

WORTHLESSE

    I KNOW THAT IN MY WEAK AND WORTHLESSE SONG            AN APOLOGIE FOR HYMNE (TERESA)     4  46 136  59
    BOTH WORTHLESSE ARE.  FOR THEY ARE MINE,              DIES IRAE                         54  52 298 186
    I KNOW, THAT IN MY WEAK & WORTHLESSE SONG             AN APOLOGIE FOR (TERESA) HYMNE     4  52 322  59

WORTHY

    REDEEME A WORTHY WRATH, ROUSE THEE, AND SHAKE         SOSPETTO D'HERODE                461  46 109 216
    FOR WORTHY SOULS WHOSE WISE EMBRACES                  ON A PRAYER BOOKE                 38  46 126 139
    A SUMMONS, WORTHY OF THY FUNERALL.                    UPON STANINOUGH'S DEATH            6  46 175 475
    A WORTHY OBJECT, OUR LORD'S FEET.                     WEEPER                           186  52 307 120
    FOR WORTHY SOULES, WHOSE WISE EMBRACES                PRAYER TO GENTLE-WOMAN            44  52 328 139
    AND MEANES THEM FOR A FARRE MORE WORTHY SPOUSE        TO SAME CONCERNING CHOISE         36  52 331  66
    A SUMMONS WORTHY OF THY FUNERALL.                     DEATH'S LECTURE                    6  52 340 475
    A PRAESENT WORTHY OF APOLLO'S LOVE.                   UPON BIRTH PRINCESSE E            20  MS 391 456

WOUND

    SEE HERE AN EASIE FEAST THAT KNOWES NO WOUND,         ON MIRACLE OF LOAVES               1  46  86  15
    A WOUND OF THINE,                                     ON MARKES OF SAVIOURS WOUNDS       8  46  86  28
    WHY DOST THOU WOUND MY WOUNDS, O THOU THAT-PASSEST BY AND A CERTAINE PRIEST PASSED       1  46  94  17
    EACH WOUND OF THEIRS WAS THY NEW MORNING.             TO THE NAME OF JESUS             220  52 239  30
    EACH WOUND OF HIS, FROM EVERY PART,                   SANCTA MARIA DOLORUM               9  52 283 162
    ONE SINGLE WOUND SHOULD NOT HAVE LEFT FOR YOU.        SANCTA MARIA DOLORUM              80  52 283 162
    NOR WOUND NOR BREACH IN WHAT HE TAKES.                LAUDA SION SALVATOREM             44  52 294 178
    A NOBLER WEAPON THEN A WOUND.                         FLAMING HEART                     72  52 324  61
    AND BLEED & WOUND, AND YEILD & CONQUER STILL.         FLAMING HEART                     80  52 324  61

WOUNDED

    THAT WOUNDED BOSOMES THEIR OWN WEAPONS BE.            SANCTA MARIA DOLORUM              74  52 283 162
    WHOSE BREST WEEPES BALM FOR WOUNDED MAN.              ADORO TE                          46  52 291 172
    AND TAUGHT THE WOUNDED HEART                          WEEPER                           105  52 307 120
    THE WOUNDED IS THE WOUNDING HEART.                    FLAMING HEART                     74  52 324  61

WOUNDS

    BUT O (TOO WELL MY WOUNDS CAN TELL)                   OUT OF GREEKE CUPID'S CRYER       51  46 159 519
    WHY DOST THOU WOUND MY WOUNDS, O THOU THAT-PASSEST BY AND A CERTAINE PRIEST PASSED       1  46  94  17
    O THESE WAKEFULL WOUNDS OF THINE.                     ON WOUNDS OF CRUCIFIED LORD        1  46  99  24
    THOSE DELICIOUS WOUNDS THAT WEEP                      IN MEMORY OF LADY MADRE TERESA   108  46 131  52
    THY WOUNDS SHALL BLUSH TO SUCH BRIGHT SCARRES,        IN MEMORY OF LADY MADRE TERESA   154  46 131  52
    MEET HIS WELL-MEANING WOUNDS, WISE HEART.             TO COUNTESSE OF DENBIGH           45  52 236 146
    OF WRATH, & MADE THEE WAY THROUGH ALL THOSE WOUNDS.   TO THE NAME OF JESUS             224  52 239  30
    CONTEMPT & SCORN CAN SEND WOUNDS TO SEARCH THE INMOST OFFICE H. CROSS SIXT              12  52 270  97
    WILL LOOK NO WOUNDS BE LOST, NO DEATHS SHALL DY.      OFFICE H. CROSS EVENSONG           6  52 273 101
    THY WOUNDS GIVE US FAIR HOLD.                         OFFICE H. CROSS COMPLINE          20  52 274 105
    NOT STINGS OF WRATH, BUT WOUNDS OF LOVE.              VEXILLA REGIS                     18  52 277 156
    O'RE HIS OWN WOUNDS.                                  CHARITAS NIMIA                    16  52 280  48
    HER EYES BLEED TEARES, HIS WOUNDS WEEP BLOOD.         SANCTA MARIA DOLORUM              20  52 283 162
    DISCOURSE ALTERNATE WOUNDS TO ONE ANOTHER.            SANCTA MARIA DOLORUM              24  52 283 162
    O TEACH THOSE WOUNDS TO BLEED                         SANCTA MARIA DOLORUM              51  52 283 162
    AND IN THESE CHAST WARRES WHILE THE WING'D WOUNDS FLEE SANCTA MARIA DOLORUM             67  52 283 162
    COME WOUNDS, COME DARTS.                              SANCTA MARIA DOLORUM              75  52 283 162
    (DEAR WOUNDS) & ONELY NOW                             SANCTA MARIA DOLORUM              83  52 283 162
    WOUNDS, AND BECOME ONE CRUCIFIX.                      SANCTA MARIA DOLORUM             100  52 283 162
    TILL DRUNK OF THE DEAR WOUNDS, I BE                   SANCTA MARIA DOLORUM             103  52 283 162
    THOUGH HIDD AS GOD, WOUNDS WRITT THEE MAN,            ADORO TE                          22  52 291 172
    THOSE DELICIOUS WOUNDS, THAT WEEP                     TERESA                           108  52 315  52
    THY WOUNDS SHALL BLUSH TO SUCH BRIGHT SCARRES         TERESA                           153  52 315  52
    BIGGE ALIKE WITH WOUNDS & DARTS.                      FLAMING HEART                     76  52 324  61

WOUNDING

    THE WOUNDED IS THE WOUNDING HEART.                    FLAMING HEART                     74  52 324  61

SELF-WOUNDING

    O SOFT SELF-WOUNDING PELICAN.                         ADORO TE                          45  52 291 172

WRACK

    THAT TO THE MIGHTY NEPTUNE'S SELF DARE THREATEN WRACK. WHY ARE YEE AFRAID                8  46  88  15
    TO WRACK MY SUITE. OH KEEPE PITTY WARME               ON GUNPOWDER-TREASON              12  MS 384 458
```

## WRANGLES

| | | | | |
|---|---|---|---|---|
| WITH HER SWEET SELFE SHEE WRANGLES. HEE AMAZED | MUSICKS DUELL | 43 | 46 149 | 535 |

## WRANGLING

| | | | | |
|---|---|---|---|---|
| AEOL KEPT IN HIS WRANGLING SONNES, LEAST THEY | UPON GUNPOWDER TREASON | 29 | MS 386 | 460 |

## WRAPT

| | | | | |
|---|---|---|---|---|
| OFT HAVE I WRAPT THY SLUMBERS IN SOFT AIRES, | LUKE 2. QUAERIT JESUM | 31 | MS 379 | 11 |
| HIS BEDRID LIMMES, WRAPT IN A FLEECY CLOWD. | AN ELEGY MR STANNINOW | 4 | MS 394 | 473 |

## WRATH

| | | | | |
|---|---|---|---|---|
| DISTILLS FROM THENCE THE TEARES OF WRATH AND STRIFE, | TO LORD UPON WATER MADE WINE | 3 | 46 91 | 12 |
| THY WRATH THAT WADES HEERE NOW, E'RE LONG SHALL SWIM | OUR LORD IN HIS CIRCUMCISION | 5 | 46 98 | 9 |
| ABOUT HER HATE, WRATH, WARRE, AND SLAUGHTER SWEAT. | SOSPETTO D'HERODE | 315 | 46 109 | 216 |
| ARE TOOLES OF WRATH, ANVILLS OF TORMENTS HUNG. | SOSPETTO D'HERODE | 323 | 46 109 | 216 |
| REDEEME A WORTHY WRATH, ROUSE THEE, AND SHAKE | SOSPETTO D'HERODE | 461 | 46 109 | 216 |
| COMES NOT TO RULE IN WRATH, BUT SERVE IN LOVE. | SOSPETTO D'HERODE | 516 | 46 109 | 216 |
| HIM WHEN WRATH IT SELFE HAD SEENE, | ANOTHER ON HERRYS | 29 | 46 170 | 469 |
| WRATH ITS SELFE HAD LOST HIS SPLEENE. | ANOTHER ON HERRYS | 30 | 46 170 | 469 |
| OF WRATH, & MADE THEE WAY THROUGH ALL THOSE WOUNDS. | TO THE NAME OF JESUS | 224 | 52 239 | 30 |
| BUT THERE IS WITT IN WRATH, AND THEY WILL TRY | OFFICE H. CROSS THIRD | 5 | 52 268 | 93 |
| A WILD RESERVE OF WANTON WRATH. | OFFICE H. CROSS EVENSONG | 4 | 52 273 | 101 |
| NOT STINGS OF WRATH, BUT WOUNDS OF LOVE. | VEXILLA REGIS | 18 | 52 277 | 156 |

## WRATHFULL

| | | | | |
|---|---|---|---|---|
| THUS REIGNES THE WRATHFULL KING, AND WHILE HE REIGNES | SOSPETTO D'HERODE | 71 | 46 109 | 216 |
| FOR WHOM (AS DEAD) THE WRATHFULL WINDS CONTEST, | SOSPETTO D'HERODE | 427 | 46 109 | 216 |

## WREATH

| | | | | |
|---|---|---|---|---|
| DEIGNE THOU TO WEARE THIS HUMBLE WREATH THAT BOWES, | SOSPETTO D'HERODE | 15 | 46 109 | 216 |
| BOTH LAWRELS TWINE INTO ONE WREATH, AND WOOE | UPON YORKE HIS BIRTH | 38 | 46 176 | 500 |
| GIVE THEN THIS RURALL WREATH FIRE FROM THINE EYES. | UPON YORKE HIS BIRTH | 118 | 46 176 | 500 |
| THIS RURALL WREATH DARES BE THY SACRIFICE. | UPON YORKE HIS BIRTH | 119 | 46 176 | 500 |

## WREST

| | | | | |
|---|---|---|---|---|
| IS HEE NOT SATISFIED. MEANES HE TO WREST | SOSPETTO D'HERODE | 225 | 46 109 | 216 |
| AND BY STRANGE WITT OF MADNES WREST | IN GLORIOUS EPIPHANIE | 111 | 52 253 | 39 |

## WRESTED

| | | | | |
|---|---|---|---|---|
| THAT MAN (I THINKE) WRESTED THE FEEBLE LIFE | HORATIJ ILLE & NEFASTO | 7 | MS 382 | 530 |

## WRETCH

| | | | | |
|---|---|---|---|---|
| DISDAINEFULL WRETCH. HOW HATH ONE BOLD SINNE COST | SOSPETTO D'HERODE | 73 | 46 109 | 216 |
| AH WRETCH. WHAT BOOTES THEE TO CAST BACK THY EYES, | SOSPETTO D'HERODE | 241 | 46 109 | 216 |
| O LET THY WRETCH FIND THAT RELEIFE | ADORO TE | 17 | 52 291 | 172 |

## WRETCHED

| | | | | |
|---|---|---|---|---|
| UNMOV'D TO SEE ONE WRETCHED, IS TO MAKE HIM SO. | AND A CERTAINE PRIEST PASSED | 4 | 46 94 | 17 |
| A WEAKE A WRETCHED CHILD. EV'N THEN WAS I | OUT OF GROTIUS | 20 | MS 398 | 198 |

## WRETCHES

| | | | | |
|---|---|---|---|---|
| THESE WRETCHES HAVE TO SPEAKE THY PRAISE. | NEITHER DURST MAN ASKE | 26 | 46 92 | 20 |

## WRINCKLES

| | | | | |
|---|---|---|---|---|
| IN THE DEEPE WRINCKLES OF HIS ANGRY BROW, | TO THE MORNING | 31 | 46 183 | 497 |

## WRIST

| | | | | |
|---|---|---|---|---|
| SO SAID, HER RICHEST SNAKE, WHICH TO HER WRIST | SOSPETTO D'HERODE | 465 | 46 109 | 216 |

## WRITE

| | | | | |
|---|---|---|---|---|
| I WRITE SO ILL, MY SLENDER LINE IS SCARCE | WITH A PICTURE TO A FRIEND | 3 | 46 156 | 494 |
| WRITE THESE LINES, READER, IN THY BROW. | AN EPITAPH UPON ASHTON | 30 | 46 192 | 464 |
| WRITE, WHAT THE READER SWEETLY RU'TH. | WISHES SUPPOSED MISTRESSE | 33 | 46 195 | 479 |
| OF WEAKNES, SHE MAY WRITE RESOLV'D AT LENGTH, | TO COUNTESSE OF DENBIGH | 42 | 52 236 | 146 |
| LAMB'S BOSOM WRITE | CHARITAS NIMIA | 58 | 52 280 | 48 |
| HIS NAILES WRITE SWORDS IN HER, WHICH SOON HER HEART | SANCTA MARIA DOLORUM | 27 | 52 283 | 162 |

## WRIT

| | | | | |
|---|---|---|---|---|
| OR NAILE, OR THORNE, OR SPEARE HAVE WRIT IN THEE. | ON MARKES OF SAVIOURS WOUNDS | 2 | 46 86 | 28 |
| THOSE RARE WORKES, WHERE THOU SHALT LEAVE WRIT, | IN MEMORY OF LADY MADRE TERESA | 156 | 46 131 | 52 |
| WRIT IN WHITE LETTERS O'RE HIS HEAD. | ANOTHER ON HERRYS | 50 | 46 170 | 469 |
| THIS BOOK OF LOVES, THUS WRIT | SANCTA MARIA DOLORUM | 53 | 52 283 | 162 |

## WRITT

| | | | | |
|---|---|---|---|---|
| THOUGH HIDD AS GOD, WOUNDS WRITT THEE MAN. | ADORO TE | 22 | 52 291 | 172 |
| THOSE RARE WORKES WHERE THOU SHALT LEAVE WRITT, | TERESA | 155 | 52 315 | 52 |

## WELL-WRITT

| | | | | | |
|---|---|---|---|---|---|
| (WHO KNOWES HOW POWRFULL WELL-WRITT PRAIRES WOULD BE.) | ALEXIAS FIRST ELEGIE | 12 | 52 | 334 | 204 |

## WRITES

| | | | | | |
|---|---|---|---|---|---|
| WHICH WRITES THY SPOWSES RADIANT NAME | IN MEMORY OF LADY MADRE TERESA | 82 | 46 | 131 | 52 |
| WHICH WRITES THY SPOUSE'S RADIANT NAME | TERESA | 82 | 52 | 315 | 52 |

## WRONG

| | | | | | |
|---|---|---|---|---|---|
| I COUNTED WRONG. THERE IS BUT ONE. | ON BLEEDING WOUNDS OF LORD | 31 | 46 | 101 | 110 |
| I TOOKE FROM READING THEE. 'TIS TO THY WRONG | AN APOLOGIE FOR HYMNE (TERESA) | 3 | 46 | 136 | 59 |
| MAY IT BE NO WRONG | TO THE NAME OF JESUS | 97 | 52 | 239 | 30 |
| THIS DAYLY WRONG | IN GLORIOUS EPIPHANIE | 129 | 52 | 253 | 39 |
| WEARY OF THIS GLORIOUS WRONG | IN GLORIOUS EPIPHANIE | 138 | 52 | 253 | 39 |
| I COUNTED WRONG. THERE IS BUT ONE. | UPON BLEEDING CRUCIFIX | 27 | 52 | 288 | 110 |
| I TOOK FROM READING THEE, TIS TO THY WRONG | AN APOLOGIE FOR (TERESA) HYMNE | 3 | 52 | 322 | 59 |
| AND SPELL IT WRONG TO READ IT RIGHT. | FLAMING HEART | 10 | 52 | 324 | 61 |
| IF ALL'S PRAESCRIPTION, & PROUD WRONG | FLAMING HEART | 61 | 52 | 324 | 61 |
| STANDS ARM'D, TO SHEILD ME FROM ALL WANTON WRONG. | ALEXIAS THIRD ELEGIE | 36 | 52 | 336 | 209 |

## WRONGED

| | | | | | |
|---|---|---|---|---|---|
| THEIR WRONGED BEAUTIES SPEAKE A TRAGAEDY. | AN ELEGIE ON DR PORTER | 11 | MS | 395 | 476 |

## WRONG'D

| | | | | | |
|---|---|---|---|---|---|
| WHOSE DROWSINESSE HATH WRONG'D THE MUSES FRIEND. | TO THE MORNING | 2 | 46 | 183 | 497 |

## MUCH-WRONG'D

| | | | | | |
|---|---|---|---|---|---|
| EXPOSTULATE MY WOES & MUCH-WRONG'D LOVES. | ALEXIAS SECONDE ELEGIE | 14 | 52 | 335 | 207 |

## WRONGS

| | | | | | |
|---|---|---|---|---|---|
| AND WRONGS REPENT TO DIADEMS. | IN MEMORY OF LADY MADRE TERESA | 151 | 46 | 131 | 52 |
| HOPES CHASTE KISSE WRUNGS NO MORE JOYES MAIDENHEAD. | ON HOPE | 39 | 46 | 143 | 71 |
| AND NATUR'S WRONGS REJOICE TO DOE THEE RIGHT. | IN GLORIOUS EPIPHANIE | 148 | 52 | 253 | 39 |
| AND WRONGS REPENT TO DIADEMMS. | TERESA | 150 | 52 | 315 | 52 |

## WELL-WROUGHT

| | | | | | |
|---|---|---|---|---|---|
| THIS WELL-WROUGHT COPY THE FAIRE PRINCIPALL. | UPON YORKE HIS BIRTH | 48 | 46 | 176 | 500 |

## YEA

| | | | | | |
|---|---|---|---|---|---|
| AND WINTER STROW HER WAY, YEA, SUCH A SORE | SOSPETTO D'HERODE | 380 | 46 | 109 | 216 |
| AMONG HIS BRANCHES. YEA, AND VOW'D TO BRING | UPON DEATH OF HERRYS | 12 | 46 | 167 | 466 |
| OF HIS BEST FRIENDS (YEA OF HIMSELF) FORSAKEN, | OFFICE H. CROSS MATINES | 16 | 52 | 265 | 86 |
| YEA LET MY LIFE & ME | SANCTA MARIA DOLORUM | 61 | 52 | 283 | 162 |
| CHIDE YOUR DELAY. YEA THOSE DULL THINGS, | AGAINST IRRESOLUTION AND DELAY | 47 | 52 | 347 | 146 |
| YEA SUITOURS. MAN ALONE IS WO'ED, | AGAINST IRRESOLUTION AND DELAY | 58 | 52 | 347 | 146 |
| A POORE (YEA SCARCE A) ROOFE. WHOSE NARROW PLACE | OUT OF GROTIUS | 16 | MS | 398 | 198 |

## YEAR

| | | | | | |
|---|---|---|---|---|---|
| SO WHEN THE YEAR TAKES COLD, WE SEE | TO COUNTESSE OF DENBIGH | 21 | 52 | 236 | 146 |
| THE WORLD'S ONE, ROUND, AETERNALL YEAR. | IN GLORIOUS EPIPHANIE | 27 | 52 | 253 | 39 |
| TIME IS TOO NARROW FOR THY YEAR | IN GLORIOUS EPIPHANIE | 40 | 52 | 253 | 39 |
| WHILE ALL THE YEAR IS YOUR EPIPHANY. | TO THE QUEEN'S MAJESTY | 26 | 52 | 261 | 47 |
| SO WHEN THE YEAR TAKES COLD WE SEE | AGAINST IRRESOLUTION AND DELAY | 21 | 52 | 347 | 146 |
| ALAS. AND HAS THE YEAR NO SPRING FOR YOU. | AGAINST IRRESOLUTION AND DELAY | 38 | 52 | 347 | 146 |

## YEARE

| | | | | | |
|---|---|---|---|---|---|
| AN EVERLASTING SPRING, THE JOLLY YEARE | OUT OF VIRGIL | 26 | 46 | 155 | 529 |
| THUS DOST THOU MELT THE YEARE | THE WEEPER | 91 | 46 | 79 | 120 |
| ALL THE YEARE DOTH SIT AND SING. | PSALME 23 | 6 | 46 | 102 | 5 |
| THOSE RARE FRUITS DANGLED, WHENCE THE GOLDEN YEARE | UPON DEATH OF HERRYS | 28 | 46 | 167 | 466 |
| O MAYST THOU THUS MAKE ALL THE YEARE THINE OWNE, | UPON YORKE HIS BIRTH | 96 | 46 | 176 | 500 |
| THE YEARE HAD FOUND SOME FRUIT EARLY AS YOU. | UPON TWO GREENE APRICOCKES | 12 | 48 | 220 | 494 |
| POORE LAWES DIVIDE THE PUBLICKE YEARE. | THOUGH NOW 'TIS NEITHER | 24 | MS | 397 | 492 |
| THERE ALL THE YEARE IS LOVES LONG SPRING. | THOUGH NOW 'TIS NEITHER | 29 | MS | 397 | 492 |
| THERE ALL THE YEARE LOVES NIGHTINGALES | THOUGH NOW 'TIS NEITHER | 30 | MS | 397 | 492 |

## YEERE

| | | | | | |
|---|---|---|---|---|---|
| BEE YOU THE LADY OF LOVES YEERE. | THOUGH NOW 'TIS NEITHER | 27 | MS | 397 | 492 |

## YEARES

| | | | | | |
|---|---|---|---|---|---|
| OTHERS BY DAYES, BY MONTHES, BY YEARES | THE WEEPER | 119 | 46 | 79 | 120 |
| ARE YET BUT IN THEIR HOPES, NOT COME TO YEARES. | OUR LORD IN HIS CIRCUMCISION | 10 | 46 | 98 | 9 |
| AND FREE ETERNITY, SUBMIT TO YEARES. | SOSPETTO D'HERODE | 184 | 46 | 109 | 216 |
| BEE LOVE BUT THERE, LET POORE SIXE YEARES. | IN MEMORY OF LADY MADRE TERESA | 29 | 46 | 131 | 52 |
| TIS LOVE, NOT YEARES, OR LIMBES, THAT CAN | IN MEMORY OF LADY MADRE TERESA | 33 | 46 | 131 | 52 |
| LEFT HIS YEARES SO MUCH BEHIND, | HIS EPITAPH (HERRYS) | 8 | 46 | 172 | 471 |
| TO CALCULATE HER YOUNG SUNS YEARES. | LOVES HOROSCOPE | 4 | 46 | 165 | 483 |
| INTO THE PUBLICK YEARES PROFICIENCIE, | UPON TWO GREENE APRICOCKES | 24 | 46 | 220 | 494 |
| BECAUSE SHEE BREAKES THE YEARES OLD RAIGNE | THOUGH NOW 'TIS NEITHER | 16 | MS | 397 | 492 |
| O SEE, SO MANY WORLDS OF BARREN YEARES | TO THE NAME OF JESUS | 143 | 52 | 239 | 30 |
| THE AGED PASCHA PLEADS NOT YEARES | LAUDA SION SALVATOREM | 21 | 52 | 294 | 178 |

```
OTHERS BY MOMENTS, MONTHS, & YEARES              WEEPER                            155   52 307 120
BE LOVE BUT THERE.  LET POOR SIX YEARES          TERESA                             29   52 315  52
'TIS LOVE, NOT YEARES OR LIMBS THAT CAN          TERESA                             33   52 315  52
SEE, EVEN THE YEARES & SIZE OF HIM               FLAMING HEART                      15   52 324  61
HIS FEARE.  THE CIRCLE OF A YEARES ROUND GROWTH  OUT OF GROTIUS                     22   MS 398 198
```

YEARLY

```
IN THY COLD BREAST, & YEARLY ON THIS DAY         ON GUNPOWDER-TREASON               13   MS 384 458
```

YEE

```
YEE SIMPERING SONS OF THOSE FAIRE EYES,          THE WEEPER                        122   46  79 120
WHY YEE TRIP SO FAST AWAY,                       THE WEEPER                        132   46  79 120
COME NOW ALL YEE TERRORS, SALLY                  PSALME 23                          35   46 102   5
OF LANGUAGE TO MY INFANT LIPS, YEE BEST          SOSPETTO D'HERODE                   6   46 109 216
AND BEE YEE CALL'D MY ABSENT KISSES.             WISHES SUPPOSED MISTRESSE          15   46 195 479
MY FANCYES, FLY BEFORE YEE,                      WISHES SUPPOSED MISTRESSE         125   46 195 479
YEE REDEEM'D NATIONS FARR & NEAR,                O GLORIOSA DOMINA                  27   52 302 194
YEE PERFECT EMBLEMES OF DIVINITY.                UPON KINGS CORONATION              38   MS 389 454
```

YELL

```
AND GAVE A GASTLY SHREEKE, WHOSE HORRID YELL     SOSPETTO D'HERODE                 150   46 109 216
```

YES

```
O YES. IF ANY HAPPY EYE,                         OUT OF GREEKE CUPID'S CRYER         5   46 159 519
```

YIELD

```
YIELD THEN, O YIELD, THAT LOVE MAY WIN           AGAINST IRRESOLUTION AND DELAY     85   52 347 146
YIELD THEN, O YIELD, THAT LOVE MAY WIN           AGAINST IRRESOLUTION AND DELAY     85   52 347 146
YIELD QUICKLY, LEST PERHAPS YOU PROVE            AGAINST IRRESOLUTION AND DELAY     87   52 347 146
```

YEELD

```
AND THE DRAKE YEELD NOE DELIGHT,                 PETRONIJ ALES PHASIACIS PETITA      6   MS 382 526
```

YEILD

```
AND WANT OF COURAGE NOT TO YEILD.                TO COUNTESSE OF DENBIGH            62   52 236 146
YEILD THEN, O YEILD, THAT LOVE MAY WIN           TO COUNTESSE OF DENBIGH            63   52 236 146
YEILD THEN, O YEILD, THAT LOVE MAY WIN           TO COUNTESSE OF DENBIGH            63   52 236 146
YEILD QUICKLY.  LEST PERHAPS YOU PROVE           TO COUNTESSE OF DENBIGH            65   52 236 146
YEILD SOMTHING IN THY SAD PRAEROGATIVE           SANCTA MARIA DOLORUM               57   52 283 162
TYPES YEILD TO TRUTHES.  SHADES SHRINK AWAY.     LAUDA SION SALVATOREM              23   52 294 178
AND BLEED & WOUND. AND YEILD & CONQUER STILL.    FLAMING HEART                      80   52 324  61
YEILD TO HIS SIEGE, WISE SOUL, AND SEE           AGAINST IRRESOLUTION AND DELAY     79   52 347 146
AND WANT OF COURAGE NOT TO YEILD.                AGAINST IRRESOLUTION AND DELAY     84   52 347 146
```

YEELDS

```
YOUL FIND IT YEELDS                              ON A PRAYER BOOKE                  17   46 126 139
```

YEILDS

```
THEN VENUS MILD INSTINCT (AT SET TIMES) YEILDS   OUT OF VIRGIL                      11   46 155 529
NOR YEILDS THE NOBLEST NEST                      TO THE NAME OF JESUS              105   52 239  30
YOU'L FIND IT YEILDS                             PRAYER TO GENTLE-WOMAN             23   52 328 139
HE YEILDS, AND STRAIGHT BAPTIS'D, OBTAINS THE GRACE  ALEXIAS THIRD ELEGIE           45   52 336 209
```

YEILDING

```
WHERE YEILDING & YET CONQUERING HE               OFFICE H. CROSS EVENSONG           24   52 273 101
```

YOKE

```
HOW SWEET THE MUTUALL YOKE OF MAN & WIFE,        ALEXIAS THIRD ELEGIE               51   52 336 209
```

YOAKE

```
A SAD YOAKE, UNDER WHICH THEY SIGH'D IN VAINE,   SOSPETTO D'HERODE                 407   46 109 216
```

YONDER

```
POINT HERE THY BEAMES.  O GLANCE ON YONDER FLOCKES,  ON A FOULE MORNING              5   46 181 495
```

YOUNG

```
(GROWNE LUSTY NOW.) NO VINE SO WEAKE AND YOUNG   OUT OF VIRGIL                      18   46 155 529
THE POINTS OF HER YOUNG EAGLES EYES.             A HYMNE OF THE NATIVITY            70   46 106  76
YET WHEN YOUNG APRILS HUSBAND SHOWRES,           A HYMNE OF THE NATIVITY            77   46 106  76
QUITE TURN'D. TH'INGRATEFULL REBELLS THIS THEIR YOUNG  SOSPETTO D'HERODE           438   46 109 216
OF LITTLE EAGLES, AND YOUNG LOVES, WHOSE HIGH    AN APOLOGIE FOR HYMNE (TERESA)     27   46 136  59
YOUNG TIME IS TASTER TO ETERNITY.                ON HOPE                            52   46 143  71
QUEEN REGENT IN YOUNG LOVES MINORITIE.           ON HOPE                            84   46 143  71
TO CALCULATE HER YOUNG SONS YEARES.              LOVES HOROSCOPE                     4   46 185 483
(YOUNG MASTER OF THE WORLDS MATURITIE)           UPON TWO GREENE APRICOCKES         26   48 220 494
YOUNG DAWN OF OUR AETERNALL DAY,                 IN HOLY NATIVITY                   32   52 246  76
YET WHEN YOUNG APRIL'S HUSBAND SHOWRS            IN HOLY NATIVITY                   97   52 246  76
OF LITTLE EAGLES & YOUNG LOVES, WHOSE HIGH       AN APOLOGIE FOR (TERESA) HYMNE     27   52 322  59
THE LUSTY BRIDEGROOM MADE APPROACH. YOUNG MAN,   ALEXIAS THIRD ELEGIE               33   52 336 209
YOUNG TIME IS TASTER TO ETERNITY                 (ON) HOPE                          22   52 345  71
```

PAGE 476

YONGE

  QUEEN REGENT IN YONGE LOVE'S MINORITY.                (ON) HOPE                                  44  52 345  71

YOUNGER

  LOVE, BRAVE VERTUES YOUNGER BROTHER.                  LOVES HOROSCOPE                           1  46 185 483

YONGER-BROTHER

  NOR GRUDGE A YONGER-BROTHER                             SANCTA MARIA DOLORUM                    78  52 283 162

YOUTH

```
  FAIRE YOUTH (SAID I) BE NOT TOO ROUGH.            A HYMNE OF THE NATIVITY          45  46 106  76
  HOW LOW THE BRIGHT YOUTH BOW'D, AND WITH WHAT AWE SOSPETTO D'HERODE                99  46 109 216
  THE HOLY YOUTH OF HEAV'N, WHOSE GOLDEN RINGS      ON A TREATISE OF CHARITY         21  46 137  69
  OF THE BRIGHT YOUTH OF HEAVEN, THAT SINGS         ON THE ASSUMPTION                24  46 139 114
  THE GLORYES OF THY YOUTH NE'RE KNEW,              UPON DEATH OF DESIRED HERRYS     17  46 168 467
  THE FRESH HOPES OF HIS LOVELY YOUTH,              ANOTHER ON HERRYS                13  46 170 469
  MADE SO REVEREND, EVEN IN YOUTH,                  HIS EPITAPH (HERRYS)             16  46 172 471
  THE FLOURISH OF HIS SOBER YOUTH,                  HIS EPITAPH (HERRYS)             25  46 172 471
  COME THEN YOUTH, BEAUTY, AND BLOOD, ALL YE SOFT   UPON STANINOUGH'S DEATH           7  46 175 475
                                         POWERS,

  STUMBLING ON NIGHT. ROUZE THEE ILLUSTRIOUS YOUTH, ON A FOULE MORNING                3  46 181 495
  THAT WARMES THE BED OF YOUTH AND BLOOD)           LOVES HOROSCOPE                  30  46 185 483
  A CHEEKE WHERE YOUTH,                             WISHES SUPPOSED MISTRESSE        31  46 195 479
  PROUD IN THE PATTERNE OF THY PRETIOUS YOUTH,      UPON TWO GREENE APRICOCKES       21  48 220 494
  OF THE BRIGHT YOUTH OF HEAVN, THAT SINGS          IN GLORIOUS ASSUMPTION B. LADY   39  52 304 114
  WINE OF YOUTH, LIFE, & THE SWEET DEATHS OF LOVE.  AN APOLOGIE FOR (TERESA) HYMNE   41  52 322  59
  WHAT E'RE THIS YOUTH OF FIRE WEARES FAIR,         FLAMING HEART                    31  52 324  61
  (FAIR YOUTH) SHOOTES BOTH THY SHAFT & THEE        FLAMING HEART                    48  52 324  61
  COME THEN, YOUTH, BEAUTY, & BLOOD.                DEATH'S LECTURE                   7  52 340 475
  BUT TO LARGE YOUTH SHORT TIME TO LIVE.            UPON DEATH OF A FREIND           12  MS 393 477
  SINCE YOUTH MUST FALL, WHEN IT SHOULD RISE.       UPON DEATH OF A FREIND           16  MS 393 477
  FORC'T THIS PRIME FLOWRE OF YOUTH TO MAKE SUCH HAST AN ELEGY MR STANNINOW          28  MS 394 473
```

YOUTH'S

  I LATE THE ROMAN YOUTH'S LOV'D PRAYSE & PRIDE,       ALEXIAS FIRST ELEGIE                   1  52 334 204

YOUTHS

  WINE OF YOUTHS LIFE, AND THE SWEET DEATHS OF LOVE,   AN APOLOGIE FOR HYMNE (TERESA)  41  46 136  59

YOUTHFULL

```
  THAT SELDOME LETT'ST A BLUSHING YOUTHFULL PRIME   UPON DEATH OF HERRYS             30  46 167 466
  STILL WOULD THE YOUTHFULL SPIRITS SING.           CHARITAS NIMIA                   19  52 280  48
  THE SEA SHALL CHANGE HIS YOUTHFULL GREENE, & SLIDE ON GUNPOWDER-TREASON            33  MS 384 458
```

EVER-YOUTHFULL

  THE FAIRE SON OF AN EVER-YOUTHFULL SPRING,           UPON DEATH OF HERRYS                  39  46 167 466

ZEALE

```
  OF FLASHING AIRES. SHEE QUALIFIES THEIR ZEALE     MUSICKS DUELL                    98  46 149 535
  HEE LOV'D HIS FATHER. YET HIS ZEALE               AN EPITAPH UPON ASHTON           19  46 192 464
```

ZEPHIRES

  (QUICK WITH WARME ZEPHIRES LIVELY BREATH) LAY FORTH  OUT OF VIRGIL                         13  46 155 529

ZEPHIRUS

```
  THE BALMY ZEPHIRUS GOT SO SWEET A BREATH          UPON DEATH OF HERRYS             20  46 167 466
  AND WILT COMMAND PROUD ZEPHIRUS TO SPORT HER      ON A FOULE MORNING               12  46 181 495
```

ZONE

```
  MY ROSY LOVE, THAT THY RICH ZONE.                 IN MEMORY OF LADY MADRE TERESA  173  46 131  52
  (MY ROSY LOVE) THAT THY RICH ZONE                 TERESA                          172  52 315  52
  'TWAS NOT THE FROZEN ZONE, ONE SPARKE OF FIRE,    AN ELEGY MR STANNINOW            31  MS 394 473
```

**OHIO UNIVERSITY LIBRARY**

Please return this book as soon as you
'e finished with it. In order to avoid a